POPULAR CYCLOPÆDIA

OF

BIBLICAL LITERATURE

THE

POPULAR CYCLOPÆDIA

OF

BIBLICAL LITERATURE

BY

JOHN KITTO, D. D., F. S. A.,

AUTHOR OF 'THE PICTORIAL BIBLE,' 'THE HISTORY AND PHYSICAL GEOGRAPHY OF PALESTINE,' ETC.,
AND EDITOR OF THE JOURNAL OF SACRED LITERATURE.

ASSISTED BY

REV. JAMES TAYLOR, D. D.,

OF GLASGOW.

ILLUSTRATED BY NUMEROUS ENGRAVINGS.

Fredonia Books
Amsterdam, The Netherlands

The Popular Cyc...

by
John Kitto

ISBN: 1-4101-0876-7

Reprinted from the 1852 edition

Fredonia Books
Amsterdam, The Netherlands
http://www.fredoniabooks.com

In order to make original editions of historical works available to scholars at an economical price, this facsimile of the original edition of 1852 is reproduced from the best available copy and has been digitally enhanced to improve legibility, but the text remains unaltered to retain historical authenticity.

PREFACE.

THE CYCLOPÆDIA OF BIBLICAL LITERATURE was designed to furnish a Dictionary of the Bible, not framed, as others had been, out of old materials, but embodying the products of the best and most recent researches in Biblical Literature, in which the scholars of this country and of the continent had been engaged. That work — the result of an immense labour and research, and enriched by the contributions of writers of distinguished eminence in the various departments of Sacred Literature — has been, by universal consent, pronounced to be the first work of its class, and the one best suited to the advanced knowledge of the present day, in all the studies connected with Theological Science. But although that Cyclopædia is regarded as indispensable to the libraries of all Ministers and Theological Students, it has been concluded that a Compendious Abridgment of its contents, embracing all the matter suited to popular and general use, might be acceptable to very many whose studies have not created a need for the larger work, or whose means do not enable them to secure the possession of it. In the present volume an attempt has, therefore, been made to supply this want, by providing such a popular Abridgment of the Cyclopædia of Biblical Literature as may be suited to the use of the great body of the religious public, and which may be expected to be of essential service to parents and teachers in the important business of Biblical Education, while to many young persons it may serve as an introduction to the more extensive work.

The original publication is above twice the size of the present. The Epitome now offered for popular use has been prepared with much care and solicitude, by the condensation of most of the matter in the original work, and by the entire omission of some articles which were supposed to be of less interest to the general reader than to the Clergyman and the Theological

Student. In the work, as it here stands, is offered such an exhibition of the results of large research, without the details and authorities, as could not, it is believed, have been produced, had not the larger Cyclopædia previously existed, and its valuable materials been made available for this service. Drawn from such a source, it is believed that this Abridgment will possess the same superiority over POPULAR Cyclopædias of this class, as the original work confessedly does over those which aspire to higher erudition.

In the Cyclopædia of Biblical Literature the initials of the writers are annexed to their respective contributions. This has not been deemed necessary in the present Abridgment; but a list is given of all the writers who coöperated with the editor in the production of the original work, from which the present Compendium has been formed.

Many articles in the larger Cyclopædia, more especially in the department of Natural History, are treated under the Hebrew or Greek form of word; but, in the present popular Compendium, it has been judged better that these articles should appear under the names by which they are represented in the authorized version of the Scriptures, and take their place in the alphabetical position they hold under these names.

It remains only to be added, that although the editor has taken some part of the labour, and has supervised the whole operation, the substantial work of the Abridgment has been executed by the careful hands of the Reverend JAMES TAYLOR, D. D., of Glasgow.

JOHN KITTO.

LIST OF CONTRIBUTORS.

REV. W. L. ALEXANDER, D. D., Author of 'The Connexion and Harmony of the Old and New Testaments,' &c.

REV. G. BAUR, Ph. D., Extraordinary Professor of Evangelical Theology in the University of Giessen.

REV. J. R. BEARD, D. D., Member of the Historico-Theological Society of Leipzig.

G. M. BELL, Author of 'Universal Mechanism,' &c.

REV. C. H. F. BIALLOBLOTZKY, Ph. D., Göttingen, Author of 'De Abrogatione Legis.'

REV. JOHN BROWN, D. D., Professor of Exegetical Theology to the United Presbyterian Church.

REV. GEORGE BUSH, Professor of Hebrew and Oriental Literature in the University of New York.

REV. JAMES D. BUTLER, Abbot Resident, Theological Seminary, Andover, United States.

K. A. CREDNER, D. D., Professor of Theology in the University of Giessen.

REV. S. DAVIDSON, LL. D., Professor of Biblical Literature and Oriental Languages in the Lancashire Independent College.

REV. BENJAMIN DAVIES, D. D.

REV. J. F. DENHAM, M. A., St. John's College, Cambridge, F. R. S.

REV. J. W. DORAN, LL. D., Association Secretary of the Church Missionary Society

REV. JOHN EADIE, LL. D., Professor of Biblical Literature to the United Presbyterian Church.

G. H. A. VON EWALD, D. D., Professor of Theology in the University of Göttingen.

REV. F. W. GOTCH, M. A., Trinity College, Dublin.

H. A. C. HAVERNICK, D. D., Professor of Theology in the University of Königsberg.

E. W. HENGSTENBERG, D. D., Professor of Theology in the University of Berlin.

REV. J. JACOBI, of the University of Berlin.

Rev. R. Jamieson, M. A., Editor of 'Paxton's Illustrations of Scripture.'

Rev. E. A. Lawrence, Haverhill, United States.

Rev. Robert Lee, D. D., Edinburgh.

Frederick R. Lees, Ph. D., F. S. S. A.; Editor of 'The Truth-Seeker,' &c.

E. Michelson, Ph. D. of the University of Heidelberg.

Rev. Peter Mearns, Author of 'Tirosh,' &c.

Rev. N. Morren, M. A., Author of 'Biblical Theology,' and Translator of 'Rosenmüller's Biblical Geography.'

F. W. Newman, late Fellow of Balliol College, Oxford, Professor of Latin Language and Literature in the University of London.

John Nicholson, B. A., Oxford, Ph. D., Tübingen; Author of 'An Account of the Establishment of the Fatemite Dynasty,' Translator of 'Ewald's Hebrew Grammar.'

W. A. Nicholson, M. D.

Rev. John Phillips Potter, M. A., Oriel College, Oxford.

Rev. Baden Powell, M. A., F. R. S., F. G. S., Savillian Professor of Geometry in the University of Oxford.

J. F. Royle, M. D., F. R. S., F. L. S., F. G. S., Member of the Royal Asiatic Societies of Calcutta and London; Professor of Materia Medica and Therapeutics in King's College, London.

J. E. Ryland, Translator of 'Neander's Church History,' and of 'Semisch's Justin Martyr.'

Lieut.-Colonel C. Hamilton Smith, K. H. and K. W., F. R. and L. S., President of the Devon and Cornwall Natural History Society, &c. &c.

Rev. J. Pye Smith, D. D., F. R. S., F. G. S.

Rev. H. Stebbing, D. D., of St. John's College, Cambridge, Author of 'A History of the Church,' &c.

Rev. A. Tholuck, D. D., Professor of Theology in the University of Halle.

Rev. David Welsh, D. D., Professor of Divinity and Church History, New College, Edinburgh.

Rev. Leonard Woods, D. D., Professor of Theology in the Andover Theological Seminary, United States.

Rev. William Wright, LL. D. of Trinity College, Dublin, Translator of 'Seiler's Biblical Hermeneutics.'

LIST OF ILLUSTRATIONS.

LIST OF ILLUSTRATIONS.

LIST OF ILLUSTRATIONS.

LIST OF ILLUSTRATIONS.

CYCLOPÆDIA

OF

BIBLICAL LITERATURE

AA'RON, the eldest son of Amram and Jochebad, of the tribe of Levi, and brother of Moses. He was born B.C. 1574 (Hales, B.C. 1730), three years before Moses, and one year before Pharaoh's edict to destroy the male children of the Israelites (Exod. vi. 20; vii. 7). His name first occurs in the mysterious interview which Moses had with the Lord, who appeared to him in the burning bush, while he kept Jethro's flock in Horeb. Among other excuses by which Moses sought to evade the great commission of delivering Israel, one was that he lacked that persuasive readiness of speech (literally was 'not a man of words') which appeared to him essential to such an undertaking. But he was reminded that his brother Aaron possessed in a high degree the endowment which he deemed so needful, and could therefore speak in his name and on his behalf (Exod. iv. 14). During the forty years' absence of Moses in the land of Midian, Aaron had married a woman of the tribe of Judah, named Elisheba (or Elizabeth), who had born to him four sons, Nadab, Abihu, Eleazer, and Ithamar; and Eleazer had, before the return of Moses, become the father of Phinehas (Exod. vi. 23-25).

In obedience to an intimation from God, Aaron went into the wilderness to meet his brother, and conduct him back to Egypt. After forty years of separation they met and embraced each other at the mount of Horeb. When they arrived in Goshen, Aaron introduced his brother to the chiefs of Israel, and assisted him in opening and enforcing the great commission which had been confided to him (Exod. iv. 27-31). In the subsequent transactions, from the first interview with Pharaoh till after the delivered nation had passed the Red Sea, Aaron appears to have been almost always present with Moses, assisting and supporting him; and no separate act of his own is recorded. This co-operation was ever afterwards maintained. Aaron and Hur were present on the hill from which Moses surveyed the battle which Joshua fought with the Amalekites; and these two long sustained the weary hands upon whose uplifting the fate of the battle was found to depend (Exod. xvii. 10-12).

While Moses was absent in the mountain to receive the tables of the law, the people seem to have looked upon Aaron as their head, and growing impatient at the protracted absence of their great leader, they gathered around Aaron, and clamorously demanded that he should provide them with a visible symbolic image of their God, that they might worship him as other gods were worshipped. Aaron ventured not to stem the torrent, but weakly complied with their demand; and with the ornaments of gold which they freely offered, cast the figure of a calf or young bull, being doubtless that of the bull-god Apis at Memphis, whose worship extended throughout Egypt. However, to fix the meaning of this image as a symbol of the true God, Aaron was careful to proclaim a feast to Jehovah for the ensuing day. On that day the people met to celebrate the feast, after the fashion of the Egyptian festivals of the calf-idol, with dancing, with shouting, and with sports.

Meanwhile Moses had been dismissed from the mountain, provided with the decalogue, written 'by the finger of God,' on two tablets of stone. These, as soon as he came sufficiently near to observe the proceedings in the camp, he cast from him with such force that they brake in pieces. His re-appearance confounded the multitude, who quailed under his stern rebuke, and quietly submitted to see their new-made idol destroyed. For this sin the population was decimated by sword and plague (Exod. xxxii.).

During his long absence in the mountain, Moses had received instructions regarding the ecclesiastical establishment, the tabernacle [TABERNACLE], and the priesthood [PRIESTS], which he soon afterwards proceeded to execute. Under the new institution Aaron was to be high-priest, and his sons and descendants priests; and the whole tribe to which he belonged, that of Levi, was set apart as the sacerdotal or learned caste [LEVITES]. Accordingly, after the tabernacle had been completed, and every preparation made for the commencement of actual service, Aaron and his sons were consecrated by Moses, who anointed them with the holy oil and invested them with the sacred garments. The high-priest applied himself assiduously to the duties of his exalted office, and during the

B

period of nearly forty years that it was filled by him, the incidents which bring him historically before us are very few. It is recorded to his honour that 'he held his peace' when his two eldest sons were, for their great offence, struck dead before the sanctuary (Lev. x. 1-11) [ABIHU]. Aaron would seem to have been liable to some fits of jealousy at the superior influence and authority of his brother; for he at least sanctioned the invidious conduct of his sister Miriam [MIRIAM], who, after the wife of Moses had been brought to the camp by Jethro, became apprehensive for her own position, and cast reflections upon Moses, much calculated to damage his influence, on account of his marriage with a foreigner—always an odious thing among the Hebrews. For this, Miriam was struck with temporary leprosy, which brought the high-priest to a sense of his sinful conduct, and he sought and obtained forgiveness (Num. xii.).

Some twenty years after (B.C. 1471), when the camp was in the wilderness of Paran, a formidable conspiracy was organized against the sacerdotal authority exercised by Aaron and his sons, and the civil authority exercised by Moses. This conspiracy was headed by chiefs of influence and station—Korah, of the tribe of Levi, and Dathan and Abiram, of the tribe of Reuben [KORAH]. But the Divine appointment was confirmed by the signal destruction of the conspirators: and the next day, when the people assembled tumultuously and murmured loudly at the destruction which had overtaken their leaders and friends, a fierce pestilence broke out among them, and they fell by thousands on the spot. When this was seen, Aaron, at the command of Moses, filled a censer with fire from the altar, and, rushing forward, 'he stood between the dead and the living,' and the plague was stayed (Num. xvi.). This was in fact another attestation of the Divine appointment; and, for its further confirmation, the chiefs of the several tribes were required to lay up their staves overnight in the tabernacle, together with the rod of Aaron for the tribe of Levi; and in the morning it was found that, while the other rods remained as they were, that of Aaron had budded, blossomed, and yielded the fruit of almonds. The rod was preserved in the tabernacle in evidence of the Divine appointment of the Aaronic family to the priesthood (Num. xvii. 1).

Aaron was not allowed to enter the Promised Land, on account of the distrust which he, as well as his brother, manifested when the rock was stricken at Meribah (Num. xx. 8-13). His death indeed occurred very soon after that event. For when the host arrived at Mount Hor, the Divine mandate came, that Aaron, accompanied by his brother Moses and by his son Eleazer, should ascend to the top of that mountain in the view of all the people; and that he should there transfer his pontifical robes to Eleazer, and then die. He was 123 years old when his career thus terminated; and his son and his brother buried him in a cavern of the mountain [HOR, MOUNT]. The Israelites mourned for him thirty days; and on the first day of the month Ab the Jews still hold a fast in commemoration of his death.

AARONITES, the descendants of Aaron, who served as priests at the sanctuary (Num. iv. 5, seq.; 1 Chron. xii. 27; xxvii. 17).

AB (*father*) is found as the first member of several compound Hebrew proper names—such as Abner, *father of light*; Abiezer, *father of help*; &c. By a process which it is not difficult to conceive, the idea of a natural father became modified into that of *author, cause, source* (as when it is said, 'has the rain a father?'—Job xxxviii. 28). So that, in course of time, the original meaning was so far modified that the word sometimes applied to a woman, as in Abigail, *father of joy*.

AB is the Chaldee name of that month which is the fifth of the ecclesiastical and eleventh of the civil year of the Jews. It commenced with the new moon of our *August* (the reasons for this statement will be given in the article MONTHS), and always had 30 days. This month is preeminent in the Jewish calendar as the period of the most signal national calamities. The 1st is memorable for the death of Aaron (Num. xxxiii. 38). The 9th is the date assigned to the following events:—the declaration that no one then adult, except Joshua and Caleb, should enter into the Promised Land (Num. xiv. 30); the destruction of the first Temple by Nebuchadnezzar (to these first two 'the fast of the fifth month,' in Zech. vii. 5, viii. 19, is supposed to refer); the destruction of the second Temple by Titus; the devastation of the city Bettar, and the slaughter of Ben Cozibah (Bar Cocâb), and of several thousand Jews there; and the ploughing up of the foundations of the Temple by Turnus Rufus —the two last of which happened in the time of Hadrian.

The 9th of the month is observed by the Jews as a fast, in commemoration of the destruction of the first Temple: the 15th is the day appointed for the festival of the wood-offering, in which the wood for the burnt-offering was stored up in the court of the Temple: to which Nehemiah alludes in x. 34, and xiii. 31. Lastly, the 18th is a fast in the memory of the western lamp going out in the Temple in the time of Ahaz (2 Chron. xxix. 7, where the extinction of the lamps is mentioned as a part of Ahaz's attempts to suppress the Temple service). For an inquiry into what is meant by the *western* or *evening* lamp, see the article CANDLESTICK.

ABAD'DON, or APOLLYON (*destruction*). The former is the Hebrew name, and the latter the Greek, for the angel of death, described (Rev. ix. 11) as the king and chief of the Apocalyptic locusts under the fifth trumpet, and as the angel of the abyss or 'bottomless pit' [HADES].

AB'ANA, or, as it is given in the marginal reading, AMANA, the name of one of the rivers which are mentioned by Naaman (2 Kings v. 12), 'Abana and Pharpar,' as 'rivers of Damascus.' Amana signifies 'perennial,' and is probably the true name. At the present day it is scarcely possible to discover with certainty the stream to which this name was applied. The most recent conjecture seeks the Abana in the small river Fidgi, which rises in a pleasant valley fifteen or twenty miles to the north-west of Damascus and falls into the Barrada, the main stream by which Damascus is irrigated.

AB'ARIM, a mountain, or rather chain of mountains, which form or belong to the mountainous district east of the Dead Sea and the lower Jordan. It presents many distinct masses and elevations, commanding extensive views of the country west of the river. From one of the highest of these, called Mount Nebo, Moses surveyed the Promised Land before he died. From the manner in which the names Abarim, Nebo, and Pisgah are connected (Deut. xxxii. 49, 'Get thee up into this mountain Abarim, unto Mount Nebo;' and xxxiv. 1, 'Unto the mountain of Nebo, to the top of Pisgah'), it would seem that Nebo was a mountain of the Abarim chain, and that Pisgah was the highest and most commanding peak of that mountain. The loftiest mountain of the neighbourhood is Mount Attarus, about ten miles north of the Arnon; and travellers have been disposed to identify it with Mount Nebo. It is represented as barren, its summit being marked by a wild pistachio-tree overshadowing a heap of stones.

ABBA is the Hebrew word Ab, *father*, under a form peculiar to the Chaldee idiom (Mark xiv. 36; Rom. viii. 15; Gal. iv. 6).

1. ABDON (*a servant*), the son of Hillel, of the tribe of Ephraim, and tenth judge of Israel. He succeeded Elon, and judged Israel eight years. Nothing is recorded of him but that he had forty sons and thirty nephews, who rode on young asses—a mark of their consequence (Judg. xii. 13-15). Abdon died B.C. 1112.

There were three other persons of this name, which appears to have been rather common. They are mentioned in 1 Chron. viii. 23; ix. 36; and 2 Chron. xxxiv. 20.

2. ABDON, a city of the tribe of Asher, which was given to the Levites of Gershom's family (Josh. xxi. 30; 1 Chron. vi. 74).

ABED'NEGO (*servant of Nego*, i. e. *Nebo*), the Chaldee name imposed by the king of Babylon's officer upon Azariah, one of the three companions of Daniel. With his two friends, Shadrach and Meshach, he was miraculously delivered from the burning furnace, into which they were cast for refusing to worship the golden statue which Nebuchadnezzar had caused to be set up (Dan. iii.).

A'BEL, properly Hebel, the second son of Adam, who was slain by Cain, his elder brother (Gen. iv. 1-16). The circumstances of that mysterious transaction are considered elsewhere [CAIN]. To the name *Abel* a twofold interpretation has been given. Its primary signification is *weakness* or *vanity*. By another rendering it signifies *grief* or *lamentation*, both meanings being justified by the Scripture narrative. CAIN (*a possession*) was so named to indicate both the joy of his mother and his right to the inheritance of the first-born: Abel received a name indicative of his weakness and poverty when compared with the supposed glory of his brother's destiny, and *prophetically* of the pain and sorrow which were to be inflicted on him and his parents.

ABEL, a name of several villages in Israel, with additions in the case of the more important, to distinguish them from one another. It appears to mean *fresh grass;* and the places so named may be conceived to have been in peculiarly verdant situations.

ABEL, ABEL-BETH-MAACAH, or ABEL-MAIM, a city in the north of Palestine, which seems to have been of considerable strength from its history, and of importance from its being called 'a

mother in Israel' (2 Sam. xx. 19). The identity of the city under these different names will be seen by a comparison of 2 Sam. xx. 14, 15, 18; 1 Kings xv. 20; 2 Chron. xvi. 4. The addition of 'Maacah' marks it as belonging to, or being near to, the region Maacah, which lay eastward of the Jordan under Mount Lebanon. This is the town in which Sheba posted himself when he rebelled against David. Eighty years afterwards it was taken and sacked by Benhadad, king of Syria; and 200 years subsequently by Tiglath-pileser, who sent away the inhabitants captives into Assyria (2 Kings xv. 29).

A'BEL-BETH-MAA'CAH, that is, Abel near the house or city of Maacah: the same as Abel.

A'BEL-CARMA'IM (*place of the vineyards*), a village of the Ammonites, about six miles from Philadelphia, or Rabbath Ammon, according to Eusebius, in whose time the place was still rich in vineyards (Judg. xi. 33).

A'BEL-MA'IM. The same as ABEL.

A'BEL-MEHO'LAH, or ABEL-MEA (*place of the dance*), a town supposed to have stood near the Jordan, and some miles (Eusebius says ten) to the south of Bethshan or Scythopolis (1 Kings iv. 12). It is remarkable in connection with Gideon's victory over the Midianites (Judg. vii. 22), and as the birth-place of Elisha (1 Kings xix. 16).

A'BEL-MIZRA'IM (*the mourning of the Egyptians*), the name of a threshing-floor, so called on account of the 'great mourning' made there for Jacob by the funeral party from Egypt (Gen. L. 11). Jerome places it between Jericho and the Jordan, where Bethagla afterwards stood.

A'BEL-SHIT'TIM (*place of acacias*), a town in the plains of Moab, on the east of the Jordan, between which and Beth-Jesimoth was the last encampment of the Israelites on that side the river (Num. xxxiii. 49). It is more frequently called Shittim merely (Num. xxv. 1; Josh. ii. 1; Mic. vi. 5). The place is noted for the punishment which was there inflicted upon the Israelites for their worship of Baal-Peor.

ABELA. [ABILA.]

A'BI, the mother of King Hezekiah (2 Kings xviii. 2), called also Abijah (2 Chron. xxix. 1). Her father's name was Zachariah, perhaps the same who was taken by Isaiah (viii. 2) for a witness.

ABI'A. [ABIJAH, 3.]

ABI'AH, or ABIJAH, one of the sons of Samuel who were intrusted with the administration of justice, and whose misconduct afforded the ostensible ground on which the Israelites demanded that their government should be changed into a monarchy (1 Sam. viii. 1-5).

ABI-AL'BON. [ABIEL, 2.]

ABI'ATHAR (*father of abundance*), the tenth high-priest of the Jews, and fourth in descent from Eli. When his father, the high-priest Abimelech, was slain with the priests at Nob, for suspected partiality to the fugitive David, Abiathar escaped the massacre; and bearing with him the most essential part of the priestly raiment, the ephod [PRIESTS], repaired to the son of Jesse, who was then in the cave of Adullam (1 Sam. xxii. 20-23; xxiii. 6). He was well received by David, and became the priest of the party during its wanderings. As such he

B 2

sought and received for David responses from God. When David became king of Judah, he made Abiathar high-priest. Meanwhile Zadok had been appointed high-priest by Saul, and continued to act in this capacity while Abiathar was high-priest in Judah. The appointment of Zadok was not only unexceptionable in itself, but was in accordance with the divine sentence of deposition which had been passed upon the house of Eli (1 Sam. ii. 30-36). When, therefore, David acquired the kingdom of Israel, he had no just ground on which Zadok could be removed, and Abiathar set in his place; and the attempt to do so would probably have been offensive to his new subjects. The king got over this difficulty by allowing both appointments to stand; and until the end of David's reign Zadok and Abiathar were joint high-priests. As high-priest Abiathar must have been perfectly aware of the divine intention that Solomon should be the successor of David: he was therefore the least excusable, in some respects, of all those who were parties in the attempt to raise Adonijah to the throne. So his conduct seems to have been viewed by Solomon, who, in deposing him from the high-priesthood, plainly told him that only his sacerdotal character, and his former services to David, preserved him from death. This deposition of Abiathar completed the doom long before denounced upon the house of Eli, who was of the line of Ithamar, the younger son of Aaron. Zadok, who remained the high-priest, was of the elder line of Eleazer (1 Kings i. 7, 19; ii. 26, 27).

A'BIB. [NISAN.]

1. AB'IEL (*father of strength*, i. e. *strong*), the father of Kish, whose son Saul was the first king of Israel, and of Ner, whose son Abner was captain of the host to his cousin Saul (1 Sam. ix. 1: xiv. 51).

2. ABIEL, one of the thirty most distinguished men of David's army (1 Chron. xi. 32). He is called Abi-albon in 2 Sam. xxiii. 31; a name which has precisely the same signification (*father of strength*) as the other.

ABIE'ZER (*father of help*, Josh. xvii. 2), a son of Gilead, the grandson of Manasseh (Num. xxvi. 30), and founder of the family to which Gideon belonged, and which bore his name as a patronymic—Abiezrites (Judg. vi. 34; viii. 2).

AB'IGAIL (*father of joy*), the wife of a prosperous sheep-master, called Nabal, who dwelt in the district of Carmel, west of the Dead Sea. She is known chiefly for the promptitude and discretion of her conduct in taking measures to avert the wrath of David, which had been violently excited by the insulting treatment which his messengers had received from her husband [NABAL]. She hastily prepared a liberal supply of provisions, of which David's troop stood in much need, and went forth to meet him. Her beauty and prudence made such an impression upon David on this occasion, that when, not long after, he heard of Nabal's death, he sent for her, and she became his wife (1 Sam. xxv. 14-42). It is usually stated that he had by her two sons, Chileab and Daniel; but it is more likely that the Chileab of 2 Sam. iii. 3, is the same as the Daniel of 1 Chron. iii. 1; the son of Abigail being known by both these names.

1. ABIHA'IL (*father of light* or *splendour*), the wife of Rehoboam, king of Judah. She is called the daughter of Eliab, David's elder brother (2 Chron. xi. 18); but was doubtless only his descendant.

2. ABIHAIL (*father of might*, i. e. *mighty*). This name should be written ABICHAIL. It was borne by several persons: 1. ABICHAIL, the son of Huri, one of the family-chiefs of the tribe of Gad, who settled in Bashan (1 Chron. v. 14). 2. ABICHAIL, the father of Zuriel, who was the father of the Levitical tribes of Merari (Num. iii. 35). 3. ABICHAIL, the father of Queen Esther, and brother of Mordecai (Esth. ii. 15).

ABI'HU (*father of him*), the second of the sons of Aaron, who, with his brothers Nadab, Eleazer, and Ithamar, was set apart and consecrated for the priesthood (Exod. xxviii. 1). He and his brother Nadab having presumed to offer incense in censers filled with 'strange' or common fire, they were instantly struck dead by lightning, and were taken away and buried in their clothes without the camp. As immediately after the record of this transaction comes a prohibition of wine or strong drink to the priests on duty at the tabernacle, it is not unfairly surmised that they were intoxicated when they committed this serious error in their ministrations (Lev. x. 1-11).

1. ABI'JAH (see signif. in ABIAH, 2 Chron. xiii. 1). He is also called Abijam (1 Kings xv.). Abijah was the second king of the separate kingdom of Judah, being the son of Rehoboam, and grandson of Solomon. He began to reign B.C. 957, in the eighteenth year of Jeroboam, king of Israel; and he reigned three years. At the commencement of his reign Abijah made a vigorous attempt to bring back the ten tribes to their allegiance. In this he failed; although a signal victory over Jeroboam, who had double his force and much greater experience, enabled him to take several cities which had been held by Israel. The numbers reputed to have been present in this action are 800,000 on the side of Jeroboam, 400,000 on the side of Abijah, and 500,000 left dead on the field. The book of Chronicles mentions nothing concerning Abijah adverse to the favourable impressions which we receive from his conduct on this occasion; but in Kings we are told that 'he walked in all the sins of his father' (1 Kings xv. 3). He had fourteen wives, by whom he left twenty-two sons and sixteen daughters. Asa succeeded him.

2. ABIJAH, son of Jeroboam I., king of Israel. His severe and threatening illness induced Jeroboam to send his wife with a present, suited to the disguise in which she went, to consult the prophet Ahijah respecting his recovery. This prophet was the same who had, in the days of Solomon, foretold to Jeroboam his elevation to the throne of Israel. Though blind with age, he knew the disguised wife of Jeroboam, and was authorized, by the prophetic impulse that came upon him, to reveal to her that, because there was found in Abijah only, of all the house of Jeroboam, 'some good thing towards the Lord,' he only, of all that house, should come to his grave in peace, and be mourned in Israel. Accordingly, when the mother returned home, the youth died as she crossed the threshold of

the door. ' And they buried him, and all Israel mourned for him' (1 Kings xiv. 1-18).

3. ABIJAH, one of the descendants of Eleazer, the son of Aaron, and chief of one of the twenty-four courses or orders into which the whole body of the priesthood was divided by David (1 Chron. xxiv. 10; Luke i. 5). Of these the course of Abijah was the eighth.

ABI'JAM. [ABIJAH, 1.]

ABI'LA, capital of the Abilene of Lysanias (Luke iii. 1); and distinguished from other places of the same name as the Abila of Lysanias, and (by Josephus) as ' the Abila of Lebanon.' Abila has been supposed to be the same as Abel-beth-Maacah, but without foundation, for that was a city of Naphtali, which Abila was not. About eighteen miles north-west of Damascus is Souk Wady Barrada, where an inscription was found by Mr. Bankes, which, beyond doubt, identifies that place with the Abila of Lysanias. Burckhardt states that there are here two villages, built on the opposite sides of the Barrada.

ABILE'NE (Luke iii. 1), the small district or territory which took its name from the chief town, Abila. Its situation is in some degree determined by that of the town; but its precise limits and extent remain unknown. Northward it must have reached beyond the Upper Barrada, in order to include Abila; and it is probable that its southern border may have extended to Mount Hermon (Jebel es-Sheikh). It seems to have included the eastern declivities of Anti-Libanus, and the fine valleys between its base and the hills which front the eastern plains. This territory had been governed as a tetrarchate by Lysanias, son of Ptolemy and grandson of Mennæus, but he was put to death, B.C. 33, through the intrigues of Cleopatra, who then took possession of the province. After her death it fell to Augustus, who rented it out to one Zenodorus; but as he did not keep it clear of robbers, it was taken from him, and given to Herod the Great. At his death a part (the southern, doubtless) of the territory was added to Trachonitis and Ituræa to form a tetrarchy for his son Philip; but by far the larger portion, including the city of Abila, was then, or shortly afterwards, bestowed on another Lysanias, mentioned by Luke (iii. 1), who is supposed to have been a descendant of the former Lysanias, but who is nowhere mentioned by Josephus. About ten years after the time referred to by Luke, the emperor Caligula gave Abilene to Agrippa I. as ' the tetrarchy of Lysanias,' to whom it was afterwards confirmed by Claudius. At his death, it was included in that part of his possessions which went to his son Agrippa II.

1. ABIM'ELECH (*father of the king*. or perhaps *royal father*), the name of the Philistine king of Gerar in the time of Abraham (Gen. xx. 1, *sqq.*: B.C. 1898; Hales, B.C. 2054); but, from its recurrence, it was probably less a proper name than a titular distinction, like PHARAOH for the kings of Egypt, or AUGUSTUS for the emperors of Rome. Abraham removed into his territory after the destruction of Sodom; and fearing that the beauty of Sarah might bring him into difficulties, he declared her to be his sister. The conduct of Abimelech in taking Sarah into his harem shows that kings even then

claimed the right of taking to themselves the unmarried females not only of their natural subjects, but of those who sojourned in their dominions. But Abimelech, obedient to a divine warning, restored her to her husband. As a mark of his respect he added valuable gifts, and offered the patriarch a settlement in any part of the country; but he nevertheless did not forbear to visit with a gentle rebuke the deception which had been practised upon him (Gen. xx.). Nothing further is recorded of King Abimelech, except that a few years after he repaired to the camp of Abraham, who had removed southward beyond his borders, accompanied by Phichol, ' the chief captain of his host,' to invite the patriarch to contract with him a league of peace and friendship. Abraham consented; and this first league on record [ALLIANCE] was confirmed by a mutual oath, made at a well which had been digged by Abraham, but which the herdsmen of Abimelech had seized without their lord's knowledge. It was restored to the rightful owner, on which Abraham named it BEERSHEBA (*the Well of the Oath*), and consecrated the spot to the worship of Jehovah (Gen. xxi. 22-34).

2. ABIMELECH, another king of Gerar, in the time of Isaac (about B.C. 1804; Hales, 1960), who is supposed to have been the son of the preceding. Isaac sought refuge in his territory during a famine; and having the same fear respecting his fair Mesopotamian wife, Rebekah, as his father had entertained respecting Sarah, he reported her to be his sister. This brought upon him the rebuke of Abimelech, when he accidentally discovered the truth. In those times, as now, wells of water were of so much importance for agricultural as well as pastoral purposes, that they gave a proprietary right to the soil, not previously appropriated, in which they were dug. Abraham had digged wells during his sojourn in the country; and, to bar the claim which resulted from them, the Philistines had afterwards filled them up; but they were now cleared out by Isaac, who proceeded to cultivate the ground to which they gave him a right. The virgin soil yielded him a hundredfold; and his other possessions, his flocks and herds, also received such prodigious increase that the jealousy of the Philistines could not be suppressed; and Abimelech desired him to seek more distant quarters, in language which gives a high notion of the wealth of the patriarchal chiefs, and the extent of their establishments:— ' Depart from us: *for thou art more and mightier than we.*' Isaac complied, and went out into the open country, and digged wells for his cattle. But the shepherds of the Philistines were not inclined to allow the claim to exclusive pasturage in these districts to be thus established; and their opposition induced the quiet patriarch to make successive removals, until he reached such a distance that his operations were no longer disputed. Afterwards, when he was at Beersheba, he received a visit from Abimelech, who was attended by Ahuzzath, his friend, and Phichol, the chief captain of his army. The king having explained that it was his wish to renew, with one so manifestly blessed of God, the covenant of peace which had been contracted between their fathers, Isaac willingly consented, and the desired covenant was, with due cere-

mony, contracted accordingly (Gen. xxvi.) [PHI-
LISTINES].

3. ABIMELECH, a son of Gideon, by a concubine-wife, a native of Shechem, where her
family had considerable influence. Through
that influence Abimelech was proclaimed king
after the death of his father, who had himself
refused that honour, when tendered to him, both
for himself and his children (Judg. viii. 22-24).
In a short time, a considerable part of Israel
seems to have recognised his rule. One of the
first acts of his reign was to destroy his brothers,
seventy in number, being the first example of a
system of barbarous state policy of which there
have been frequent instances in the East. Only
one, the youngest, named Jotham, escaped; and
he had the boldness to make his appearance on
Mount Gerizim, where the Shechemites were assembled for some public purpose, and rebuke
them in his famous parable of the trees choosing
a king [JOTHAM; PARABLE]. In three years
the Shechemites found ample cause to repent of
what they had done. They eventually revolted
during Abimelech's absence, and caused an
ambuscade to be laid in the mountains, with the
design of destroying him on his return. But
Zebul, his governor in Shechem, contrived to
apprise him of these circumstances, so that he
was enabled to avoid the snare laid for him;
and, having hastily assembled some troops, appeared unexpectedly before Shechem. The
people of that place had meanwhile secured the
assistance of one Gaal and his followers [GAAL],
who marched out to give Abimelech battle. He
was defeated, and returned into the town; and
his inefficiency and misconduct in the action had
been so manifest, that the people were induced
by Zebul to expel him and his followers. The
people still ventured out to the labours of the
field; which being told Abimelech, who was
at Arumah, he laid an ambuscade in four bodies
in the neighbourhood; and when the men came
forth in the morning, two of the ambushed
parties rose against them, while the other two
seized the city gates to prevent their return.
Afterwards the whole force united against the
city, which, being now deprived of its most
efficient inhabitants, was easily taken, and completely destroyed by the exasperated victor.
The fortress, however, still remained; but the
occupants, deeming it untenable, withdrew to
the temple of Baal-Berith, which stood in a
more commanding situation. This building
Abimelech set on fire and destroyed, with the
thousand men who were in it. Afterwards
Abimelech went to reduce Thebez, which had
also revolted. The town was taken with little
difficulty, and the people withdrew into the
citadel. Here Abimelech resorted to his favourite operation, and while heading a party to
burn down the gate, he was struck on the head
by a large stone cast down by a woman from
the wall above. Perceiving that he had received
a death-blow, he directed his armour-bearer to
thrust him through with his sword, lest it
should be said that he fell by a woman's hand
(Judg. ix.). Vainly did Abimelech seek to avoid
this disgrace; for the fact of his death by the
hand of a woman was long after associated with
his memory (2 Sam. xi. 21).

ABIN'ADAB (*father of nobleness*, or *noble*

father). There are several persons of this name,
all of whom are also called AMINADAB—the
letters *b* and *m* being very frequently inter-
changed in Hebrew.

1. ABINADAB, one of the eight sons of
Jesse, and one of the three who followed Saul to
the war with the Philistines (1 Sam. xvi. 8).

2. ABINADAB, one of Saul's sons, who was
slain at the battle of Gilboa (1 Sam. xxxi. 2).

3. ABINADAB, the Levite of Kirjath-jearim,
in whose house, which was on a hill, the Ark of
the Covenant was deposited, after being brought
back from the land of the Philistines. It was
committed to the special charge of his son Eleazer; and remained there seventy years, until it
was removed by David (1 Sam. vii. 1, 2; 1 Chron.
xiii. 7) [ARK].

1. ABI'RAM (*father of altitude*, i. e. *high*),
one of the family-chiefs of the tribe of Reuben,
who, with Dathan and On of the same tribe,
joined Korah, of the tribe of Levi, in a conspiracy against Aaron and Moses (Num. xvi.)
[AARON].

2. ABIRAM, eldest son of Hiel the Bethelite
(1 Kings xvi. 34) [HIEL; JERICHO].

AB'ISHAG (*father of error*), a beautiful young
woman of Shunam, in the tribe of Issachar, who
was chosen by the servants of David to be introduced into the royal harem, for the special
purpose of ministering to him, and cherishing
him in his old age. She became his wife; but
the marriage was never consummated. Some
time after the death of David, Adonijah, his
eldest son, persuaded Bathsheba, the mother of
Solomon, to entreat the king that Abishag might
be given to him in marriage. But as rights and
privileges peculiarly regal were associated with
the control and possession of the harem of the
deceased kings, Solomon detected in this application a fresh aspiration to the throne, which he
visited with death (1 Kings i. 1-4; ii. 13-25)
[ADONIJAH].

ABISHA'I (*father of gifts*), a nephew of
David by his sister Zeruiah, and brother of Joab
and Asahel. The three brothers devoted themselves zealously to the interests of their uncle
during his wanderings. Though David had
more reliance upon the talents of Joab, he
appears to have given more of his private confidence to Abishai, whom we find near his person
on several critical occasions. He alone accompanied David to the camp of Saul (1 Sam. xxvi.
5-9). He fled with him beyond the Jordan
from Absalom, and commanded one of three
divisions of the army which crushed that rebellion (2 Sam. xviii. 2). He rescued David
when in imminent peril of his life from a giant
named Ishbi-benob (2 Sam. xxi. 15-17), and was
also the chief of the three 'mighties,' who
performed the chivalrous exploit of breaking
through the host of the Philistines to procure
David a draught of water from the well of his
native Bethlehem (2 Sam. xxiii. 14-17). Among
the exploits of this hero it is mentioned that he
withstood 300 men and slew them with his
spear: but the occasion of this adventure, and
the time and manner of his death, are equally
unknown.

ABISHU'A (*father of safety*), the son of Phinehas, and fourth high-priest of the Jews
(1 Chron. vi. 50). The commencement and

duration of his pontificate are uncertain, but the latter is inferred, from circumstances, to have included the period in which Ehud was judge, and probably the preceding period of servitude to Eglon of Moab. He is called Abiezer by Josephus (*Antiq.* v. 11. 5).

ABLUTION, the ceremonial washing, whereby, as a symbol of purification from uncleanness, a person was considered—1. to be cleansed from the taint of an inferior and less pure condition, and initiated into a higher and purer state (Lev. viii. 6); 2. to be cleansed from the soil of common life, and fitted for special acts of religious service (Exod. xxx. 17-21); 3. to be cleansed from defilements contracted by particular acts or circumstances, and restored to the privileges of ordinary life (Lev. xii.-xv.); 4. as absolving or purifying himself, or declaring himself absolved and purified, from the guilt of a particular act (Deut. xxi. 1-9). We do not meet with any such ablutions in patriarchal times: but under the Mosaical dispensation they all occur.

After the rise of the sect of the Pharisees, the practice of ablution was carried to such excess, from the affectation of excessive purity, that it is repeatedly brought under our notice in the New Testament through the severe animadversions of our Saviour on the consummate hypocrisy involved in this fastidious attention to the external types of moral purity, while the heart was left unclean. All the practices there exposed come under the head of purification from uncleanness;—the acts involving which were made so numerous that persons of the stricter sect could scarcely move without contracting some involuntary pollution. For this reason they never entered their houses without ablution, from the strong probability that they had unknowingly contracted some defilement in the streets; and they were especially careful never to eat without washing the hands (Mark vii. 1-5), because they were peculiarly liable to be defiled; and as unclean hands were held to communicate uncleanness to all food (excepting fruit) which they touched, it was deemed that there was no security against eating unclean food but by always washing the hands ceremonially before touching any meat. The Israelites, who, like other Orientals, fed with their fingers, washed their hands before meals, for the sake of cleanliness [WASHING]. But these customary washings were distinct from the ceremonial ablutions. It was the latter which the Pharisees judged to be so necessary. When therefore some of that sect remarked that our Lord's disciples ate 'with unwashen hands' (Mark vii. 2), it is not to be understood literally that they did not at all wash their hands, but that they did not *plunge* them ceremonially according to their own practice. In at least an equal degree the Pharisees multiplied the ceremonial pollutions which required the ablution of inanimate objects—'cups and pots, brazen vessels and tables;' the rules given in the law (Lev. vi. 28; xi. 32-36; xv. 23) being extended to these multiplied contaminations. Articles of earthenware which were of little value were to be broken; and those of metal and wood were to be scoured and rinsed with water.

ABNER (*father of light*), the cousin of Saul (being the son of his uncle Ner), and the commander-in-chief of his army. After the death of Saul (B.C. 1056), Abner's experience and character for ability and decision enabled him to uphold the interests of his family for seven years; and while David reigned in Hebron over Judah, Ishbosheth, a surviving son of Saul, was, by Abner's influence, made king over the ten tribes, and reigned in Mahanaim, beyond Jordan. A sort of desultory warfare arose between the rival monarchs, in which the advantage appears to have been always on the side of David. In an engagement fought at Gibeon, the forces of Ishbosheth were beaten. Abner, their general, fled for his life, but was closely pursued by Asahel, the brother of Joab and Abishai. Abner, dreading a blood-feud with Joab, entreated Asahel, but in vain, to desist from the pursuit; and finding that his life was in danger, he at length ran his pursuer through the body (2 Sam. ii. 8-32). This, according to the law of honour which still prevails in the East, put a strife of blood between Joab and Abner [BLOOD-REVENGE].

As time went on, Abner, probably rendered arrogant and presumptuous by the conviction that he was the only remaining prop of the house of Saul, took to his own harem a woman who had been a concubine-wife of Saul. This act, from the ideas connected with the harem of a deceased king, was not only a great impropriety, but was open to the suspicion of a political design, which Abner may very possibly have entertained. A mild rebuke from Ishbosheth, however, enraged him so much, that he immediately declared his intention henceforth to abandon his cause and to devote himself to the interests of David. Accordingly after explaining his views to the elders of the tribes which still adhered to the house of Saul, he repaired to Hebron with authority to make certain overtures to David on their behalf. He was received with great attention and respect; and David even thought it prudent to promise that he should still have the chief command of the armies, when the desired union of the two kingdoms took place. Joab, David's general, happened to be absent at the time, but he returned to Hebron just as Abner had left it. He speedily understood what had passed; and his dread of the superior influence which such a man as Abner might establish with David, quickened his remembrance of the vengeance which his brother's blood required. Unknown to the king, but apparently in his name, he sent a message after Abner to call him back; and as he returned, Joab met him at the gate, and, leading him aside, as if to confer privately with him, suddenly thrust his sword into his body (B.C. 1048). The lamentations of David, and the public mourning which he ordered, and the funeral honours which were paid to the remains of Abner, the king himself following the bier as chief mourner, exonerated him in public opinion from having been privy to this assassination. As for Joab, his privilege as a blood-avenger must to a great extent have justified his treacherous act in the opinion of the people; and that, together with his influence with the army, screened him from punishment (2 Sam. iii. 6-39).

ABOMINATION. This word describes generally any object of detestation or disgust (Lev. xviii. 22; Deut. vii. 25); and is applied to an impure or detestable action (Ezek. xxii. 11; xxxiii. 26; Mal. ii. 11, &c.); to any thing causing a ceremonial pollution (Gen. xliii. 32; xlvi. 34; Deut. xiv. 3); but more especially to idols (Lev. xviii. 22; xx. 13; Deut. vii. 26; 1 Kings xi. 5, 7; 2 Kings xxiii. 13); and also to food offered to idols (Zech. ix. 7); and to filth of every kind (Nahum iii. 6). Especial attention has been drawn to two or three of the texts in which the word occurs, on account of their peculiar interest or difficulty. The *first* is Gen. xliii. 32: 'The Egyptians might not eat bread with the Hebrews; for that is an abomination unto the Egyptians.' The primary reason of this seems to have been that the cow, which was a sacred animal in Egypt, was eaten by the Jews and most other nations, and therefore the Egyptians considered themselves ceremonially defiled if they ate with any strangers.

The *second* passage is Gen. xlvi. 34. Joseph is telling his brethren how to conduct themselves when introduced to the king of Egypt; and he instructs them that when asked concerning their occupation they should answer: 'Thy servants' trade hath been about cattle from our youth even until now, *both we and also our fathers.*' And the reason is added: 'That ye may dwell in the land of Goshen,—*for every shepherd is an abomination* unto the Egyptians.' In the former instance they were 'an abomination' *as strangers*, with whom the Egyptians could not eat; here they are a further abomination as *nomade shepherds*, whom the Egyptians held in peculiar abhorrence. For this aversion two reasons are given: one is the grievous oppression which the inhabitants of Lower and Middle Egypt had suffered from a tribe of nomade shepherds, to whom they had for many years been subject, who had only of late been expelled. The other reason, not necessarily superseding the former, but rather strengthening it, is, that the Egyptians, as a settled and civilized people, detested the lawless and predatory habits of the wandering shepherd tribes, which then, as now, bounded the valley of the Nile, and occupied the Arabias.

The *third* marked use of this word again occurs in Egypt. The king tells the Israelites to offer to their god the sacrifices which they desired, without going to the desert for that purpose. To which Moses objects, that they should have to sacrifice to the Lord '*the abomination of the Egyptians*,' who would thereby be highly exasperated against them (Exod. viii. 25, 26). A reference back to the first explanation shows that this 'abomination' was the cow, the only animal which *all* the Egyptians agreed in holding sacred; whereas, in the great sacrifice which the Hebrews proposed to hold, not only would heifers be offered, but the people would feast upon their flesh.

THE ABOMINATION OF DESOLATION. In Dan. ix. 27, literally, '*the abomination of the desolater*,' which, without doubt, means the idol or idolatrous apparatus which the desolater of Jerusalem should establish in the holy place. This appears to have been a prediction of the pollution of the temple by Antiochus Epiphanes, who caused an idolatrous altar to be built on the altar of burnt-offerings, whereon unclean things were offered

to Jupiter Olympius, to whom the temple itself was dedicated. The phrase is quoted by Jesus (Matt. xxiv. 15), and is applied by him to what was to take place at the advance of the Romans against Jerusalem. They who saw 'the abomination of desolation standing in the holy place' were enjoined to 'flee to the mountains.' And this may with probability be referred to the advance of the Roman army against the city with their image-crowned standards, to which idolatrous honours were paid, and which the Jews regarded as idols. The unexpected retreat and discomfiture of the Roman forces afforded such as were mindful of our Saviour's prophecy an opportunity of obeying the injunction which it contained. Those however who suppose that 'the holy place' of the text must be the temple itself, may find the accomplishment of the prediction in the fact that, when the city had been taken by the Romans, and the holy house destroyed, the soldiers brought their standards in due form to the temple, set them up over the eastern gate, and *offered sacrifice to them*, for almost the entire religion of the Roman camp consisted in worshipping the ensigns, swearing by the ensigns, and in preferring the ensigns before all the other gods.

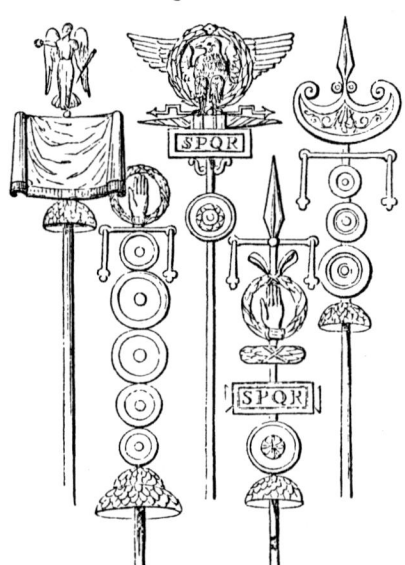

1. Roman Standards.

Nor was this the last appearance of 'the abomination of desolation, in the holy place:' for, not only did Hadrian, with studied insult to the Jews, set up the figure of a boar over the Bethlehem gate of the city which rose upon the site and ruins of Jerusalem; but he erected a temple to Jupiter upon the very site of the Jewish temple, and caused an image of himself to be set up in the part which answered to the sanctuary. This was a consummation of all the abominations which the iniquities of the Jews brought upon their holy place.

AB'RAHAM (*father of a multitude*), the

founder of the Hebrew nation. Up to Gen. xvii. 4, 5, he is uniformly called ABRAM (*father of elevation*, or *high father*); and this was his original name; but the extended form, which it always afterwards bears, was given to make it significant of the promise of a numerous posterity which was at the same time made to him.

Abraham was a native of Chaldea, and descended, through Heber, in the ninth generation, from Shem the son of Noah. His father was Terah, who had two other sons, Nahor and Haran. Haran died prematurely 'before his father,' leaving a son Lot, and two daughters, Milcah and Iscah. Lot attached himself to his uncle Abraham; Milcah became the wife of her uncle Nahor; and Iscah, who was also called Sarai, became the wife of Abraham (Gen. ix. 26-29) [SARAH].

Abraham was born A.M. 2008, B.C. 1996 (Hales, A.M. 3258, B.C. 2153), in 'Ur of the Chaldees' (Gen. xi. 28).

Although he is, by way of eminence, named first, it appears probable that he was the youngest of Terah's sons, and born by a second wife, when his father was 130 years old. Terah was seventy years old when the eldest son was born (Gen. xi. 32; xii. 4; xx. 12); and that eldest son appears to have been Haran, from the fact that his brothers married his daughters, and that his daughter Sarai was only ten years younger than his brother Abraham (Gen. xvii. 17). Abraham was 60 years old when the family quitted their native city of Ur, and went and abode in Charran. The reason for this movement does not appear in the Old Testament; but it is mentioned in Acts vii. 2-4: 'The God of glory appeared to our father Abraham while he was (at Ur of the Chaldees) in Mesopotamia, *before he dwelt in Charran*, and said unto him, Depart from *thy land*, and from thy kindred, and come hither to *a land* which *I will* shew thee. Then departing from the land of the Chaldees, he dwelt in Charran.' This *first* call is not recorded, but only implied in Gen. xii.: and it is distinguished by several pointed circumstances from the *second*, which alone is there mentioned. Accordingly Abraham departed, and his family, including his aged father, removed with him. They proceeded not at once to the land of Canaan, but they came to Charran, and tarried at that convenient station for fifteen years, until Terah died, at the age of 205 years. Being free from his filial duties, Abraham, now 75 years of age, received a second and more pointed call to pursue his destination: 'Depart from thy land, and from thy kindred, and *from thy father's house*, unto the *land* which I will shew thee' (Gen. xii. 1). This second call required the patriarch to isolate himself, not only from his country, but from his family. He however took with him his nephew Lot, whom, having no children of his own, he appears to have regarded as his heir, and then went forth 'not knowing whither he went' (Heb. xi. 8), but trusting implicitly to the Divine guidance.

When Abraham arrived in the land of Canaan, he found it occupied by the Canaanites in a large number of small independent communities, which cultivated the districts around their several towns. The country was however but thinly peopled; and, as in the more recent times

of its depopulation, it afforded ample pasture-ground for the wandering pastors. In their eyes Abraham must have appeared one of that class. In Mesopotamia, though the family had been pastoral, they had dwelt in towns and houses, and had sent out their flocks and herds under the care of shepherds. But the migratory life to which Abraham had now been called, compelled him to take to the tent-dwelling form of pastoral life. The rich pastures in that part of the country tempted Abraham to form his first encampment in the vale of Moreh, which lies between the mountains of Ebal and Gerizim. Here the strong faith which had brought the childless man thus far from his home was rewarded by the grand promise from God:—' I will make of thee a great nation, and I will bless thee and make thy name great, and thou shalt be a blessing; and I will bless them that bless thee, and curse them that curse thee: and in thee shall all the families of the earth be blessed' (Gen. xii. 2, 3). It was further promised that to his posterity should be given the rich heritage of that beautiful country into which he had come (v. 7). The implied condition on his part was, that he should publicly profess the worship of the true God, and accordingly ' he built there an altar unto the Lord, who appeared unto him.' He soon after removed to the district between Bethel and Ai, where he also built an altar to that 'JEHOVAH' whom the world was then hastening to forget. His farther removals tended southward, until at length a famine in Palestine compelled him to withdraw into Egypt, where corn abounded. Here his apprehension that the beauty of his wife Sarai might bring him into danger with the dusky Egyptians, overcame his faith and rectitude, and he gave out that she was his sister. As he had feared, the beauty of the fair stranger excited the admiration of the Egyptians, and at length reached the ears of the king, who forthwith exercised his regal right of calling her to his harem, and to this Abraham, appearing as only her brother, could offer no resistance. As, however, the king had no intention to act harshly in the exercise of his privilege, he loaded Abraham with valuable gifts, suited to his condition, consisting chiefly of slaves and cattle. These presents could not have been refused by him without an insult which, under all the circumstances, the king did not deserve. A grievous disease inflicted on Pharaoh and his household relieved Sarai from her danger, by revealing to the king that she was a married woman; on which he sent for Abraham, and, after rebuking him for his conduct, restored his wife to him, and recommended him to withdraw from the country. He accordingly returned to the land of Canaan, much richer than when he left it ' in cattle, in silver, and in gold' (Gen. xii. 8; xiii. 2).

Lot also had much increased his possessions: and soon after their return to their previous station near Bethel, the disputes between their respective shepherds about water and pasturage soon taught them that they had better separate. The recent promise of posterity to Abraham himself, although his wife had been accounted barren, probably tended also in some degree to weaken the tie by which the uncle and nephew had hitherto been united. The subject was broached by Abraham, who generously conceded to Lot the choice of pasture-grounds. Lot chose the well-watered plain in which Sodom and other towns were situated, and removed thither [Lot]. Immediately afterwards the patriarch was cheered and encouraged by a more distinct and formal reiteration of the promises which had been previously made to him, of the occupation of the land in which he lived by a posterity numerous as the dust. Not long after, he removed to the pleasant valley of Mamre, in the neighbourhood of Hebron (then called Arba), and pitched his tent under a terebinth tree (Gen. xiii.).

It appears that fourteen years before this time the south and east of Palestine had been invaded by a king called Chedorlaomer, from beyond the Euphrates, who brought several of the small disunited states of those quarters under tribute. Among them were the five cities of the Plain of Sodom, to which Lot had withdrawn. This burden was borne impatiently by these states, and they at length withheld their tribute. This brought upon them a ravaging visitation from Chedorlaomer and four other (perhaps tributary) kings, who scoured the whole country east of the Jordan, and ended by defeating the kings of the plain, plundering their towns, and carrying the people away as slaves. Lot was among the sufferers. When this came to the ears of Abraham, he immediately armed such of his slaves as were fit for war, in number 318, and being joined by the friendly Amoritish chiefs, Aner, Eshcol, and Mamre, pursued the retiring invaders. They were overtaken near the springs of the Jordan; and their camp being attacked on opposite sides by night, they were thrown into disorder, and fled. Abraham and his men pursued them as far as the neighbourhood of Damascus, and then returned with all the men and goods which had been taken away. When the victors had reached 'the king's dale' on their return, they were met by several of the native princes, among whom was Melchizedek, king of Salem, which is generally supposed to have been Jerusalem. He was one of the few native princes, if not the only one, who retained the knowledge and worship of 'the Most High God,' whom Abraham served. This circumstance created a peculiar relation between the king and the patriarch, which the former recognised by bringing forth 'bread and wine,' and probably other refreshments to Abraham, and which the latter acknowledged by presenting to Melchizedek a tenth of the spoils. By strict right, founded on the war usages which still subsist in Arabia, the recovered goods became the property of Abraham, and not of those to whom they originally belonged. This was acknowledged by the king of Sodom, who met the victors in the valley near Salem. He said, 'Give me the persons, and keep the goods to thyself.' But with becoming pride and disinterestedness Abraham answered, 'I have lifted up mine hand [i. e. I have sworn] unto Jehovah, the most high God, that I will not take from a thread even to a sandal-thong, and that I will not take any thing that is thine, *lest thou shouldest say. I have made Abram rich*' (Gen. xiv.).

Soon after his return to Mamre the faith of Abraham was rewarded and encouraged, not only by a more distinct and detailed repetition of the promises formerly made to him, but by the confirmation of a solemn covenant contracted, as nearly as might be, 'after the manner of men' [Covenant] between him and God. It was now that he first understood that his promised posterity were to grow up into a nation under foreign bondage; and that, in 400 years after (or, strictly, 405 years, counting from the birth of Isaac to the Exode), they should come forth from that bondage as a nation, to take possession of the land in which he sojourned (Gen. xv.).

After ten years' residence in Canaan (B.C. 1913), Sarai, being then 75 years old, and having long been accounted barren, chose to put her own interpretation upon the promised blessing of a progeny to Abraham, and persuaded him to take her woman slave Hagar, an Egyptian, as a secondary or concubine wife, with the view that whatever child might proceed from this union should be accounted her own [Hagar]. The son who was born to Abraham by Hagar, and who received the name of Ishmael [Ishmael], was accordingly brought up as the heir of his father and of the promises (Gen. xvi.). Thirteen years after (B.C. 1900), when Abraham was 99 years old, he was favoured with still more explicit declarations of the Divine purposes. He was reminded that the promise to him was that he should be the father of *many* nations; and to indicate this intention his name was now changed (as before described) from *Abram* to *Abraham*. The Divine Being then solemnly renewed the covenant to be a God to him and to the race that should spring from him; and in token of that covenant directed that he and his should receive in their flesh the sign of circumcision [Circumcision]. Abundant blessings were promised to Ishmael; but it was then first announced, in distinct terms, that the heir of the special promises was not yet born, and that the barren Sarai, then 90 years old, should twelve months thence be his mother. Then also her name was changed from Sarai to Sarah (*the princess*); and to commemorate the laughter with which the prostrate patriarch received such strange tidings, it was directed that the name of Isaac (*laughing*) should be given to the future child. The very same day, in obedience to the Divine ordinance, Abraham himself, his son Ishmael, and his house-born and purchased slaves were all circumcised (Gen. xvii.).

Three months after this, as Abraham sat in his tent door during the heat of the day, he saw three travellers approaching, and hastened to meet them, and hospitably pressed upon them refreshment and rest. They assented, and under the shade of a terebinth tree partook of the abundant fare which the patriarch and his wife provided. From the manner in which one of the strangers spoke, Abraham soon gathered that his visitants were no other than the Lord himself and two attendant angels in human form. The promise of a son by Sarah was renewed; and when Sarah herself, who overheard this within the tent, laughed inwardly at the tidings, which, on account of her great age, she at first disbelieved, she incurred the striking rebuke, 'Is any thing too hard for Jehovah?' The strangers then addressed themselves to their journey, and Abraham walked some way with them. The two angels went forward in the direction of Sodom, while the Lord made known to him that, for their enormous iniquities, Sodom and the other ' cities of the plain ' were about to be made signal monuments of his wrath and of his moral government. Moved by compassion and by remembrance of Lot, the patriarch ventured, reverently but perseveringly, to intercede for the doomed Sodom; and at length obtained a promise that, if but ten righteous men were found therein, the whole city should be saved for their sake. Early the next morning Abraham arose to ascertain the result of this concession: and when he looked towards Sodom, the smoke of its destruction, rising ' like the smoke of a furnace,' made known to him its terrible overthrow [Sodom]. Almost immediately after, Abraham removed into the territories of Abimelech, king of Gerar, where, by a most extraordinary infatuation and lapse of faith, he allowed himself to stoop to the same prevarication in denying his wife, which, twenty-three years before, had occasioned him so much trouble in Egypt [Abimelech].

The same year Sarah gave birth to the long-promised son; and, according to previous direction, the name of Isaac was given to him [Isaac]. This greatly altered the position of Ishmael, and appears to have created much ill-feeling both on his part and that of his mother towards the child; which was in some way manifested so pointedly, on occasion of the festivities which attended the weaning, that the wrath of Sarah was awakened, and she insisted that both Hagar and her son should be sent away. This was a very hard matter to a loving father; and Abraham was greatly distressed; but being apprised in a dream that this demand was in accordance with the Divine intentions respecting both Ishmael and Isaac, he, with his habitual uncompromising obedience, hastened them away early in the morning, with provision for the journey. Their adventures belong to the article Hagar.

When Isaac was about 25 years old (B.C. 1872) it pleased God to subject the faith of Abraham to a severer trial than it had yet sustained, or than has ever fallen to the lot of any other mortal man. He was commanded to go into the mountainous country of Moriah (probably where the temple afterwards stood), and there offer up in sacrifice the son of his affection, and the heir of so many hopes and promises, which his death must nullify. But Abraham's ' faith shrunk not, assured that what God had promised he would certainly perform, and that he was able to restore Isaac to him even from the dead ' (Heb. xi. 17-19), and he rendered a ready, however painful, obedience. Assisted by two of his servants, he prepared wood suitable for the purpose, and without delay set out upon his melancholy journey. On the third day he descried the appointed place; and informing his attendants that he and his son would go some distance farther to worship, and then return, he proceeded to the spot. To the touching question of his son respecting the victim to be offered, the patriarch replied by expressing his faith that God himself would provide the sacrifice; and probably he availed himself of this opportunity of acquainting him with the Divine command. Isaac submitted patiently to be bound and laid out as a victim on the wood of the altar, and would most

certainly have been slain by his father's uplifted hand, had not the angel of Jehovah interposed at the critical moment to arrest the fatal stroke. A ram which had become entangled in a thicket was seized and offered; and a name was given to the place (*Jehovah-Jir h* — ' the Lord will provide ') alluding to the believing answer which Abraham had given to his son's inquiry respecting the victim. The promises before made to Abraham were again confirmed in the most solemn manner (comp. Heb. vi. 13, 17). The father and son then rejoiced their servants, and returned rejoicing to Beersheba (Gen. xxiii. 19).

Eight years after (B.C. 1860) Sarah died at the age of 120 years, being then at or near Hebron. This loss first taught Abraham the necessity of acquiring possession of a family sepulchre in the land of his sojourning. His choice fell on the cave of Machpelah [Machpelah], and after a striking negotiation with the owner in the gate of Hebron, he purchased it, and had it legally secured to him. This was the only possession he ever had in the Land of Promise (Gen. xxiii.). The next care of Abraham was to provide a suitable wife for his son Isaac. It has always been the practice among pastoral tribes to keep up the family ties by intermarriages of blood-relations: and now Abraham had a further inducement in the desire to maintain the purity of the separated race from foreign and idolatrous connections. He therefore sent his aged and confidential steward Eliezer, under the bond of a solemn oath to discharge his mission faithfully, to renew the intercourse between his family and that of his brother Nahor, whom he had left behind in Charran. He prospered in his important mission [Isaac], and in due time returned, bringing with him Rebekah, the daughter of Nahor's son Bethuel, who became the wife of Isaac, and was installed as chief lady of the camp, in the separate tent which Sarah had occupied (Gen. xxiv.). Some time after Abraham himself took a wife named Keturah, by whom he had several children. These, together with Ishmael, seem to have been portioned off by their father in his lifetime, and sent into the east and south-east, that there might be no danger of their interference with Isaac, the divinely appointed heir. There was time for this: for Abraham lived to the age of 175 years, 100 of which he had spent in the land of Canaan. He died in B.C. 1822 (Hales, 1978), and was buried by his two eldest sons in the family sepulchre which he had purchased of the Hittites (Gen. xxv. 1-10).

ABRAHAM'S BOSOM. There was no name which conveyed to the Jews the same associations as that of Abraham. As undoubtedly he was in the highest state of felicity of which departed spirits are capable, ' to be with Abraham' implied the enjoyment of the same felicity; and ' to be in Abraham's bosom ' meant to be in repose and happiness with him. The latter phrase is obviously derived from the custom of sitting or reclining at table which prevailed among the Jews in and before the time of Christ [Accubation]. It was quite usual to describe a just person as being with Abraham, or as lying on Abraham's bosom; and as such images were unobjectionable, Jesus accommodated his speech to them, to render himself the more intelligible by familiar notions, when, in the beautiful parable of the rich man and Lazarus, he describes the state of the latter after death under these conditions (Luke xvi. 22, 23).

AB'SALOM (*father of peace*), the third son of David, and his only son by Maachah, daughter of Talmai, king of Geshur (2 Sam. iii. 3). He was deemed the handsomest man in the kingdom; and was particularly noted for the profusion of his beautiful hair, which appears to have been regarded with great admiration. David's other child by Maachah was a daughter named Tamar, who was also very beautiful. She became the object of lustful regard to her half-brother Amnon, David's eldest son; and was violated by him. In all cases where polygamy is allowed, we find that the honour of a sister is in the guardianship of her full brother, more even than in that of her father, whose interest in her is considered less peculiar and intimate. We trace this notion even in the time of Jacob (Gen. xxxiv. 6, 13, 25, sqq.). So in this case the wrong of Tamar was taken up by Absalom, who kept her secluded in his own house, and said nothing for the present, but brooded silently over the wrong he had sustained and the vengeance which devolved upon him. It was not until two years had passed that Absalom found opportunity for the bloody revenge he had meditated. He then held a great sheep-shearing feast at Baal-hazor near Ephraim, to which he invited all the king's sons. Amnon attended among the other princes; and, when they were warm with wine, he was slain by the servants of Absalom, according to the previous directions of their master. Absalom then hastened to Geshur, and remained there three years with his father-in-law, king Talmai.

Now Absalom, with all his faults, was eminently dear to the heart of his father, who mourned every day after the banished fratricide. His secret wishes to have home his beloved though guilty son were however discerned by Joab, who employed a clever woman of Tekoah to lay a supposed case before him for judgment; and she applied the anticipated decision so adroitly to the case of Absalom, that the king discovered the object, and detected the interposition of Joab. Regarding this as in some degree expressing the sanction of public opinion, David gladly commissioned Joab to 'call home his banished.' Absalom returned; but David, still mindful of his duties as a king and father, controlled the impulse of his feelings, and declined to admit him to his presence. After two years, however, Absalom, impatient of his disgrace, found means to compel the attention of Joab to his case; and through his means a complete reconciliation with the king was effected (2 Sam. xiii. xiv.).

Absalom was now, by the death of his elder brothers, Amnon and Chileab, become the eldest surviving son of David, and heir apparent to the throne. But under the peculiar theocratic institutions of the Hebrews, the Divine king reserved the power of bestowing the crown on any person whom he might prefer. The house of David was now established as the reigning dynasty, and out of his family Solomon had been selected by God as the successor of his father. In this fact, which was probably well known to the mass of the nation, we have a clear motive for the rebellion of Absalom, who wished to secure the throne, which he deemed to be his by the laws of primogeniture, during the lifetime of his father, while the destined successor was yet a child.

The fine person of Absalom, his superior birth, and his natural claim, pre-disposed the people to regard his pretensions with favour: and this pre-disposition was strengthened by the condescending sympathy with which he accosted the suitors who repaired for justice or favour to the royal audience, combined with the state and attendance with which, as the heir apparent, he appeared in public. By these influences 'he stole the hearts of the men of Israel;' and when at length, four years after his return from Geshur, he repaired to Hebron, and there proclaimed himself king, the great body of the people declared for him. So strong ran the tide of opinion in his favour, that David found it expedient to quit Jerusalem and retire to Mahanaim, beyond the Jordan.

When Absalom heard of this, he proceeded to Jerusalem and took possession of the throne without opposition. Among those who had joined him was Ahithophel, who had been David's counsellor, and whose profound sagacity caused his counsels to be regarded like oracles in Israel. This defection alarmed David more than any other circumstance, and he persuaded his friend Hushai to go and join Absalom, in the hope that he might be made instrumental in turning the sagacious counsels of Ahithophel to foolishness. The first piece of advice which Ahithophel gave Absalom was, that he should publicly take possession of that portion of his father's harem which had been left behind in Jerusalem. This was not only a mode by which the succession of the throne might be confirmed [ABISHAG], but in the present case this villanous measure would dispose the people to throw themselves the more unreservedly into his cause, from the assurance that no possibility of reconciliation between him and his father remained. Hushai had not then arrived. Soon after he came, when a council of war was held to consider the course of operations to be taken against David. Ahithophel counselled that the king should be pursued that very night, and smitten, while he was 'weary and weak handed, and before he had time to recover strength.' Hushai, however, whose object was to gain time for David, speciously urged, from the known valour of the king, the possibility and fatal consequences of a defeat, and advised that all Israel should be assembled against him in such force as it would be impossible for him to withstand. Fatally for Absalom, the counsel of Hushai was preferred to that of Ahithophel; and time was thus given to enable the king to collect his resources. A large force was soon raised, which he properly organized and separated into three divisions, commanded severally by Joab, Abishai, and Ittai of Gath. The king himself intended to take the chief command; but the people refused to allow him to risk his valued life, and the command then devolved upon Joab. The battle took place in the borders of the forest of Ephraim; and the tactics of Joab, in drawing the enemy into the wood, and there hemming them in, so that they were destroyed with ease, eventually, under the providence of God, decided the action against Absalom. Twenty thousand of his troops were slain, and the rest fled to their homes. Absalom himself fled on a swift mule; but as he went. the boughs of a terebinth tree caught the long hair in which he gloried, and he was left suspended there. The charge which David had given to the troops to respect the life of Absalom prevented any one from slaying him: but when Joab heard of it, he hastened to the spot, and pierced him through with three darts. His body was then taken down and cast into a pit there in the forest, and a heap of stones was raised upon it.

David's fondness for Absalom was unextinguished by all that had passed; and no sooner did he hear that his son was dead, than he retired to his chamber and gave vent to his paternal anguish in the most bitter wailings—' O my son Absalom! my son, my son Absalom! would God I had died for thee, O Absalom, my son, my son!' The consequences might have been most dangerous, had not Joab gone up to him, and, after sharply rebuking him for thus discouraging those who had risked their lives in his cause, induced him to go down and cheer the returning warriors by his presence (2 Sam. xiii.-xix. 8).

ABSALOM'S TOMB. A remarkable monument bearing this name makes a conspicuous figure in the Valley of Jehoshaphat, outside Jerusalem; and it has been noticed and described by almost all travellers. It is close by the lower bridge over the Kidron, and is a square isolated block hewn out from the rocky ledge so as to leave an area or niche around it. The body of this monument is about 24 feet square.

2. Absalom's Tomb.

The elevation is about 18 or 20 feet to the top of the architrave, and thus far it is wholly cut from the rock. The upper part of the tomb, which is about 20 feet high (the whole has therefore an elevation of about 40 feet), has been

carried up with mason-work of large stones. There is a small excavated chamber in the body of the tomb, into which a hole had been broken through one of the sides several centuries ago.

The old travellers who refer to this tomb, as well as Calmet after them, are satisfied that they find the history of it in 2 Sam. xviii. 18, which states that Absalom, having no son, built a monument to keep his name in remembrance, and that this monument was called 'Absalom's Hand '—that is, *index, memorial,* or *monument.* With our later knowledge, a glance at this and the other monolithic tomb bearing the name of Zecharias, is quite enough to show that they had no connection with the times of the persons whose names have been given to them. But tradition seems never to have become fully settled as to the individuals whose names they should bear, and to the present day the accounts of travellers have been varying and inconsistent.

ABSTINENCE is a refraining from the use of certain articles of food usually eaten; or from all food during a certain time for some particular object. It is distinguished from TEMPERANCE, which is moderation in ordinary food; and from FASTING, which is abstinence from a religious motive. The first example of abstinence which occurs in Scripture is that in which the use of blood is forbidden to Noah (Gen. ix. 4) [BLOOD]. The next is that mentioned in Gen. xxxii. 32: ' The children of Israel eat not of the sinew which shrank, which is upon the hollow of the thigh, *unto this day,* because he (the angel) touched the hollow of Jacob's thigh in the sinew that shrank.' By the law, abstinence from blood was confirmed, and the use of the flesh of even lawful animals was forbidden, if the manner of their death rendered it impossible that they should be, or uncertain that they were, duly exsanguinated (Exod. xxii. 31; Deut. xiv. 21). A broad rule was also laid down by the law, defining whole classes of animals that might not be eaten (Lev. xi.) [FOOD]. Certain parts of lawful animals, as being sacred to the altar, were also interdicted. These were the large lobe of the liver, the kidneys and the fat upon them, as well as the tail of the ' fat-tailed ' sheep (Lev. iii. 9-11). Everything consecrated to idols was also forbidden (Exod. xxxiv. 15). Instances of abstinence from allowed food are not frequent, except in commemorative or afflictive fasts. The forty days' abstinence of Moses, Elijah, and Jesus are peculiar cases requiring to be separately considered [FASTING]. The priests were commanded to abstain from wine previous to their actual ministrations (Lev. x. 9), and the same abstinence was enjoined to the Nazarites during the whole period of their separation (Num. vi. 3). A constant abstinence of this kind was, at a later period, voluntarily undertaken by the Rechabites (Jer. xxxv. 14-18). Among the early Christian converts there were some who deemed themselves bound to adhere to the Mosaical limitations regarding food, and they accordingly abstained from flesh sacrificed to idols, as well as from animals which the law accounted unclean; while others contemned this as a weakness, and exulted in the liberty wherewith Christ had made his followers free (Rom. xiv.

1-3; 1 Cor. viii.). Mention is made by the apostle Paul of certain sectaries who should arise, forbidding marriage and enjoining abstinence from meats which God had created to be received with thanksgiving (1 Tim iv. 3, 4) The council of the apostles at Jerusalem decided that no other abstinence regarding food should be imposed upon the converts than 'from meats offered to idols, from blood, and from things strangled' (Acts xv. 29).

ABYSS. The Greek word means literally *without bottom*, but actually *deep, profound.* In the New Testament it is used as a noun to describe Hades, or the place of the dead generally (Rom. x. 7); but more especially that part of Hades in which the souls of the wicked were supposed to be confined (Luke viii. 31; Rev. ix. 1, 2, 11; xx. 1, 3; comp. 2 Pet. ii. 4). In the Revelation the authorized version invariably renders it 'bottomless pit,' elsewhere 'deep.'

Most of these uses of the word are explained by reference to some of the cosmological notions which the Hebrews entertained in common with other Eastern nations. It was believed that the abyss, or sea of fathomless waters, encompassed the whole earth. The earth floated on the abyss, of which it covered only a small part. According to the same notion, the earth was founded upon the waters, or, at least, had its foundations in the abyss beneath (Ps. xxiv. 2; cxxxvi. 6). Under these waters, and at the bottom of the abyss, the wicked were represented as groaning, and undergoing the punishment of their sins. There were confined the Rephaim—those old giants who, while living, caused surrounding nations to tremble (Prov. ix. 18; xxx. 16). In those dark regions the sovereigns of Tyre, Babylon, and Egypt are described by the prophets as undergoing the punishment of their cruelty and pride (Jer. xxv. 34; Ezek. xxviii. 10, &c.). This was 'the deep' into which the evil spirits in Luke, viii. 31, besought that they might not be cast, and which was evidently dreaded by them [COSMOGONY; HADES].

AC'CAD, one of the five cities in 'the land of Shinar,' or Babylonia, which are said to have been built by Nimrod, or rather, to have been 'the beginning of his kingdom' (Gen. x. 10). It seems that several of the ancient translators found in their Hebrew MSS. Achar instead of Achad, and it is probable that this was really the name of the city. Its situation has been much disputed, but in all probability it may be identified with a remarkable pile of ancient buildings called *Akker-kúf*, in the district of Siticene, where there was a river named *Argades.* These buildings are called by the Turks *Akker-i-Nimrúd* and *Akker-i-Babil.*

Akker-kúf is about nine miles west of the Tigris, at the spot where that river makes its nearest approach to the Euphrates. The heap of ruins to which the name of Nimrod's Hill— *Tel-i-Nimrúd*, is more especially appropriated, consists of a mound surmounted by a mass of brickwork, which looks like either a tower or an irregular pyramid, according to the point from which it is viewed. It is about 400 feet in circumference at the bottom, and rises to the height of 125 feet above the sloping elevation on which it stands. The mound, which seems to form the foundation of the pile, is a mass of

rubbish accumulated by the decay of the superstructure. In the ruin itself, the layers of sundried bricks, of which it is composed, can be traced very distinctly. They are cemented together by line or bitumen, and are divided into courses varying from 12 to 20 feet in height, and are separated by layers of reeds, as is usual in the more ancient remains of this primitive

3. Akker-kuf.

region. Travellers have been perplexed to make out the use of this remarkable monument, and various strange conjectures have been hazarded. The embankments of canals and reservoirs, and the remnants of brickwork and pottery occupying the place all around, evince that the Tel stood in an important city; and, as its construction announces it to be a Babylonian relic, the greater probability is that it was one of those pyramidal structures erected upon high places, which were consecrated to the heavenly bodies, and served at once as the temples and the observatories of those remote times. Such buildings were common to all Babylonian towns; and those which remain appear to have been constructed more or less on the model of that in the metropolitan city of Babylon.

AC'CHO, a town and haven within the nominal territory of the tribe of Asher, which however never acquired possession of it (Judg. i. 31). The Greek and Roman writers call it ACE, but it was eventually better known as PTOLEMAIS, which name it received from the first Ptolemy, king of Egypt, by whom it was much improved. By this name it is mentioned in the New Testament (Acts xxi. 7). It was also called *Colonia Claudii Cæsaris*, in consequence of its receiving the privileges of a Roman city from the emperor Claudius. But the names thus imposed or altered by foreigners never took with the natives, and the place is still known in the country by the name of AKKA. During the Crusades the place was usually known to Europeans by the name of ACON: afterwards, from the occupation of the Knights of St. John of Jerusalem, as St. JEAN D'ACRE, or simply ACRE.

This famous city and haven is situated in N. lat. 32° 55', and E. long. 35° 5', and occupies the north-western point of a commodious bay, called the Bay of Acre, the opposite or southwestern point of which is formed by the promontory of Mount Carmel. The city lies on the plain to which it gives its name. Its western side is washed by the waves of the Mediterranean, and on the south lies the bay, beyond which may be seen the town of Caipha, on the site of the ancient Calamos, and, rising high above both, the shrubby heights of Carmel. The mountains belonging to the chain of Anti-Libanus are seen at the distance of about four leagues to the north, while to the east the view is bounded by the fruitful hills of the Lower Galilee. The bay, from the town of Acre to the promontory of Mount Carmel, is three leagues wide and two in depth. The port, on account of its shallowness, can only be entered by vessels of small burden; but there is excellent anchorage on the other side of the bay, before Caipha, which is, in fact, the roadstead of Acre. In the time of Strabo Accho was a great city, and it has continued to be a place of importance down to the present time. But after the Turks gained possession of it, Acre so rapidly declined, that the travellers of the sixteenth and seventeenth centuries concur in describing it as much fallen from its former glory. Traces of its ancient magnificence, however, still remained in the fragments of spacious buildings, sacred and secular, and in portions of old walls of extraordinary height and thickness. An impulse was given to the prosperity of the place by the measures of Sheikh Daher, and afterwards of Djezzar Pasha, and the town greatly increased in actual importance. The population in 1819 was computed at 10,000, of whom 3000 were Turks, the rest Christians of various denominations. Approached from Tyre the city presented a beautiful appearance, from the trees in the inside, which rise above the wall, and from the ground immediately around it on the outside being planted with orange, lemon, and palm trees. Inside, the streets had the usual narrowness and filth of Turkish towns; the houses solidly built with stone, with flat roofs; the bazaars mean, but tolerably well supplied. The principal objects were the mosque built by Djezzar Pasha, the pasha's seraglio, the granary, and the arsenal. The trade was not considerable; the exports consisted chiefly of grain and cotton, the produce of the neighbouring plain; and the imports chiefly of rice, coffee, and sugar from Damietta. As thus described, the city was all but demolished in 1832 by the hands of Ibrahim Pasha; and although considerable pains were taken to restore it, yet, as lately as 1837, it still exhibited a most wretched appearance, with ruined houses and broken arches in every direction.

As the fame of Acre is rather modern than biblical, its history must in this place be briefly told. It belonged to the Phœnicians, until they, in common with the Jews, were subjugated by the Babylonians. By the latter it was doubtless maintained as a military station against Egypt, as it was afterwards by the Persians. In the distribution of Alexander's dominions Accho fell to the lot of Ptolemy Soter, who valued the acquisition, and gave it his own name. Afterwards it fell into the hands of the kings of Syria; and is repeatedly mentioned in the wars of the Maccabees. It was at one time the headquarters of their heathen enemies. In the endeavour of Demetrius Soter and Alexander

Balas to bid highest for the support of Jonathan, the latter gave Ptolemais and the lands around to the temple at Jerusalem. Jonathan was afterwards invited to meet Alexander and the king of Egypt at that place, and was treated with great distinction by them, but there he at length (B.C. 144) met his death through the treachery of Tryphon. Alexander Jannæus took advantage of the civil war between Antiochus Philometor and Antiochus Cyzicenus to besiege Ptolemais, as the only maritime city in those parts, except Gaza, which he had not subdued; but the siege was raised by Ptolemy Lathyrus (then king of Cyprus), who got possession of the city, of which he was soon deprived by his mother Cleopatra. She probably gave it, along with her daughter Selene, to Antiochus Grypus, king of Syria. At least, after his death, Selene held possession of that and some other Phœnician towns, after Tigranes, king of Armenia, had acquired the rest of the kingdom. But an injudicious attempt to extend her dominions drew upon her the vengeance of that conqueror, who, in B.C. 70, reduced Ptolemais, and, while thus employed, received with favour the Jewish embassy which was sent by Queen Alexandra, with valuable presents, to seek his friendship. A few years after, Ptolemais was absorbed, with all the country, into the Roman empire; and the rest of its *ancient* history is obscure and of little note. It is only mentioned in the New Testament from St. Paul having spent a day there on his voyage to Cæsarea (Acts xxi. 7). It continued a place of importance, and was the seat of a bishopric in the first ages of the Christian Church. The see was filled sometimes by orthodox and sometimes by Arian bishops; and it has the equivocal distinction of having been the birth-place of the Sabellian heresy. Accho, as we may now again call it, was an imperial garrison town when the Saracens invaded Syria, and was one of those that held out until Cæsarea was taken by Amru in A.D. 638.

The Franks first became masters of it in A.D. 1110, when it was taken by Baldwin, king of Jerusalem. But in A.D. 1187 it was recovered by Salahed-din, who retained it till A.D. 1191, when it was retaken by the Christians. This was the famous siege in which Richard Cœur-de-Lion made so distinguished a figure. The Christians kept it exactly one hundred years, or till A.D. 1291; and it was the very last place of which they were dispossessed. It had been assigned to the Knights Hospitallers of Jerusalem, who fortified it strongly, and defended it valiantly, till it was at length wrested from them by Khalil ben Kelaoun, or Melek Seruf, Sultan of Egypt. Under this dominion it remained till A.D. 1517, when the Mamluke dynasty was overthrown by Selim I., and all its territories passed to the Turks. After this Acre remained in quiet obscurity till the middle of the last century, when the Arab Sheikh Daher took it by surprise. Under him the place recovered some of its trade and importance. He was succeeded by the barbarous but able tyrant Djezzar Pasha, who strengthened the fortifications and improved the town. Under him it rose once more into fame, through the gallant and successful resistance which, under the direction of Sir Sidney Smith, it offered to the arms of Buonaparte. After that famous siege the fortifications were further strengthened, till it became the strongest place in all Syria. In 1832 the town was besieged for nearly six months by Ibrahim Pasha, during which 35,000 shells were thrown into it, and the buildings were literally beaten to pieces. It had by no means recovered from this calamity, when it was subjected to the operations of the English fleet under Admiral Stopford, in pursuance of the plan for restoring Syria to the Porte. On the 3rd of November, 1840, it was bombarded for several hours, when the explosion of the powder-magazine destroyed the garrison and laid the town in ruins.

ACCOMMODATION (exegetical or special) is principally employed in the application of certain passages of the Old Testament to events in the New, to which they had no actual historical or typical reference. Citations of this description are apparently very frequent throughout the whole New Testament, but especially in the Epistle to the Hebrews.

It cannot be denied that many such passages, although apparently introduced as referring to, or predictive of, certain events recorded in the New Testament, seem to have, in their original connection, an exclusive reference to quite other objects. The difficulty of reconciling such *seeming* misapplications, or deflections from their original design, has been felt in all ages, although it has been chiefly reserved to recent times to give a solution of the difficulty by the theory of *accommodation*. By this it is meant that the prophecy or citation from the Old Testament was not designed literally to apply to the event in question, but that the New Testament writer merely adopted it for the sake of ornament, or in order to produce a strong impression, by showing a remarkable parallelism between two analogous events, which had in themselves no mutual relation.

There is a catalogue of more than seventy of these accommodated passages adduced by the Rev. T. H. Horne, in support of this theory, in his *Introduction* (ii. 343, 7th ed. 1834), but it will suffice for our purpose to select the following specimens:—

Matt. xiii. 35, cited from Psalm lxxviii. 2.
  „   viii. 17   „   Isaiah liii. 4.
  „   ii. 15   „   Hosea xi. 1.
  „   ii. 17, 18 ,   Jeremiah xxxi. 15.
  „   iii. 3   „   Isaiah xl. 3.

It will be necessary, for the complete elucidation of the subject, to bear in mind the distinction not only between accommodated passages and such as must be properly explained (as those which are absolutely adduced as proofs), but also between such passages and those which are merely borrowed, and applied by the sacred writers, sometimes in a higher sense than they were used by the original authors. Passages which do not strictly and literally predict future events, but which can be applied to an event recorded in the New Testament by an accidental parity of circumstances, can alone be thus designated. Such accommodated passages therefore, if they exist, can only be considered as descriptive, and not predictive.

It will here be necessary to consider the various modes in which the prophecies of the Old Testament are supposed to be fulfilled in the New. For instance, the opinion has been maintained by several divines, that there is sometimes a literal, sometimes only a mediate, typical, or spiritual fulfilment. Sometimes a prophecy is cited merely by way of illustration (accommodation), while at other times nothing more exists than a mere allusion. Some prophecies are supposed to have an immediate literal fulfilment, and to have been afterwards accomplished in a larger and more extensive sense; but as the full development of this part of the subject appertains more properly to the much controverted question of the single and double sense of prophecy, we shall here dwell no further on it than to observe, that not only are commentators who support the theory of a double sense divided on the very important question, what are literal prophecies and what are only prophecies in a secondary sense, but they who are agreed on this question are at variance as to what appellation shall be given to those passages which are applied by the New Testament writers to the ministry of our Saviour, and yet historically belong to an antecedent period. In order to lessen the difficulty, a distinction has been attempted to be drawn from the formula with which the quotation is ushered in. Passages, for instance, introduced by the formula 'that it might be fulfilled,' are considered, on this account, as direct predictions by some, who are willing to consider citations introduced with the expression 'then was fulfilled' as nothing more than accommodations. The use of the former phrase, as applied to a mere accommodation, they maintain is not warranted by Jewish writers: such passages, therefore, they hold to be prophecies, at least in a secondary sense. Bishop Kidder appositely observes, in regard to this subject, that 'a scripture may be said to be fulfilled several ways, viz., properly and in the letter, as when that which was foretold comes to pass; or again, when what was fulfilled in the type is fulfilled again in the antitype; or else a scripture may be fulfilled more improperly, viz., by way of *accommodation*, as when an event happens to any place or people like to that which fell out some time before.' He instances the citation, Matt. ii. 17, 'In Ramah was a voice heard,' &c. 'These words,' he adds, 'are made use of by way of allusion to express this sorrow by. The evangelist doth not say "that it might be fulfilled," but "then was fulfilled," *q. d.*, such another scene took place.'

It must at the same time be admitted that this distinction in regard to the formula of quotation is not acknowledged by the majority of commentators, either of those who admit or of those who deny the theory of accommodation. Among the former it will suffice to name Calmet, Doddridge, Rosenmüller, and Jahn, who look upon passages introduced by the formula 'that it might be fulfilled,' as equally accommodations with those which are prefaced by the words 'then was fulfilled;' while those who deny the accommodative theory altogether, consider both as formulas of direct prophecies, at least in a secondary or typical sense. This, for instance, is the case especially in regard to the two citations of this description which first present themselves in the New Testament, viz., Matt. ii. 15, and Matt. ii. 17, the former of which is introduced by the first, and the latter by the second of these formulas. But inasmuch as the commentators above referred to cannot perceive how the citation from Hosea xi. 1, 'Out of Egypt have I called my son,' although prefaced by the formula 'that it might be fulfilled,' and which literally relates to the calling of the children of Israel out of Egypt, can be prophetically diverted from its historical meaning, they look upon it as a simple accommodation, or applicable quotation. Mr. Horne observes, that 'it was a familiar idiom of the Jews, when quoting the writings of the Old Testament, to say, *that it might be fulfilled which was spoken by such and such a prophet*, not intending it to be understood that such a particular passage in one of the sacred books was ever designed to be a *real prediction* of what they were then relating, but signifying only that the words of the Old Testament might be properly adopted to express their meaning and illustrate their ideas.' 'The apostles,' he adds, 'who were Jews by birth, and wrote and spoke in the Jewish idiom, frequently thus cite the Old Testament, intending no more by this mode of speaking, than that the words of such an ancient writer might with equal propriety be adopted to characterize any similar occurrence which happened in their times. The formula "that it might be fulfilled," does not therefore differ in signification from the phrase "then was fulfilled," applied in the following citation in Matt. ii. 17, 18, from Jer. xxxi. 15-17, to the massacre of the infants at Bethlehem. They are a beautiful quotation, and not a prediction of what then happened, and are therefore applied to the massacre of the infants according not to their original and historical meaning, but according to Jewish phraseology.' Dr. Adam Clarke, also, in his Commentary on Jeremiah (xxxi. 15-17), takes the same view:—'St. Matthew, who is ever fond of accommodation, applied these words to the massacre of the children of Bethlehem; that is, they were suitable to that occasion, and therefore he applied them, but they are not a prediction of that event.'

D. J. G. Rosenmüller gives as examples, which he conceives clearly show the use of these formulas, the passages Matt. i. 22, 23; ii. 15, 17, 23; xv. 7; Luke iv. 21; James ii. 23; alleging that they were designed only to denote that something took place which resembled the literal and historical sense. The sentiments of a distinguished English divine are to the same effect: 'I doubt not that this phrase, "that it might be fulfilled," and the like were used first in quoting real prophecies, but that this, by long use, sunk in its value, and was more vulgarly applied, so that at last it was given to Scripture only accommodated.' And again, 'If prophecy could at last come to signify singing (Titus i. 12; 1 Sam. x. 10; 1 Cor. xiv. 1), why might not the phrase *fulfilling of Scripture* and *prophecy* signify only quotation' (Nicholl's *Conference with a Theist*, 1698, part iii. p. 13).

The accommodation theory in exegetics has been equally combated by two classes of opponents. Those of the more ancient school consider such mode of application of the Old Testament passages not only as totally irreconcilable with the plain grammatical construction and obvious meaning of the controverted passages which are said to be so applied, but as an unjustifiable artifice, altogether unworthy of a divine teacher; while the other class of expositors, who are to be found chiefly among the most modern of the German Rationalists, maintain that the sacred writers, having been themselves trained in this erroneous mode of teaching, had mistakenly, but *bonâ fide*, interpreted the passages which they had cited from the Old Testament in a sense altogether different from their historical meaning, and thus applied them to the history of the Christian dispensation. Some of these have maintained that the accommodation theory was a mere shift resorted to by commentators who could not otherwise explain the application of Old Testament prophecies in the New consistently with the inspiration of the sacred writers: while the advocates of the system consider that the apostles, in adapting themselves to the mode of interpretation which was customary in their days, and in further adopting what may be considered an argument *e concessis*, were employing the most persuasive mode of oratory, and the one most likely to prove effectual; and that it was therefore lawful to adopt a method so calculated to attract attention to their divine mission, which they were at all times prepared to give evidence of by other and irrefragable proofs.

ACCUBATION, the posture of reclining on couches at table, which prevailed among the Jews in and before the time of Christ. We see no reason to think that, as commonly alleged, they borrowed this custom from the Romans after Judea had been subjugated by Pompey. But it is best known to us as a Roman custom, and as such must be described. The dinner-bed, or *triclinium*, stood in the middle of the dining-room, clear of the walls, and formed three sides of a square which enclosed the table. The open end of the square, with the central hollow, allowed the servants to attend and serve the table. In all the existing representations of the dinner-bed it is shown to have been higher than the enclosed table. Among the Romans the

4.

usual number of guests on each couch was three, making nine for the three couches, but sometimes there were four to each couch. The Greeks went beyond this number; the Jews appear to have had no particular fancy in the matter, and we know that at our Lord's last supper *thirteen* persons were present. As each guest leaned, during the greater part of the entertainment, on his left elbow, so as to leave the right arm at liberty, and as two or more lay on the same couch, the head of one man was near the breast of the man who lay behind him, and he was, therefore, said ' to lie in the bosom' of the other. This phrase was in use among the Jews (Luke xvi. 22, 23; John i. 18; xiii. 23), and occurs in such a manner as to show that to lie next below, or ' in the bosom' of the master of the feast, was considered the most favoured place, and was usually assigned to near and dear connections. Thus it was ' the disciple whom Jesus loved' who ' reclined upon his breast' at the last supper. The frame of the dinner-bed was laid with mattresses variously stuffed, and, latterly, was furnished with rich coverings and hangings. Each person was usually provided with a cushion or bolster on which to support the upper part of his person in a somewhat raised position ; as the left arm alone could not long without weariness sustain the weight. The lower part of the body being extended diagonally on the bed, with the feet outward, it is at once perceived how easy it was for ' the woman that was a sinner' to come behind between the dinner-bed and the wall, and anoint the feet of Jesus (Luke vii. 37, 38; John xii. 3).

The dinner-beds were so various at different times, in different places, and under different circumstances, that no one description can apply to them all. Even among the Romans they were at first (after the Punic war) of rude form and materials, and covered with mattresses stuffed with rushes or straw; mattresses of hair and wool were introduced at a later period. At first the wooden frames were small, low, and *round ;* and it was not until the time of Augustus that square and ornamented couches came into fashion. In the time of Tiberius the most splendid sort were veneered with costly woods or tortoiseshell, and were covered with valuable embroideries, the richest of which came from Babylon, and cost large sums. The Jews perhaps had all these varieties, though it is not likely that the usage was ever carried to such a pitch of luxury as among the Romans; and it is probable that the mass of the people fed in the ancient manner—seated on stools or on the ground. It appears that couches were often so low, that the feet rested on the ground; and that cushions or bolsters were in general use. It would also seem, from the mention of two and of three couches, that the arrangement was more usually square than semi-circular or round.

It is utterly improbable that the Jews derived this custom from the Romans, as is constantly alleged. They certainly knew it as existing among the Persians long before it had been adopted by the Romans themselves (Esth. i. 6; vii. 8); and the presumption is that they adopted it while subject to that people. The Greeks also had the usage (from the Persians) before the Romans; and with the Greeks of Syria the Jews had very much intercourse. Besides, the Romans adopted the custom from the Carthaginians, and, that *they* had it, implies that it previously existed in Phœnicia, in the neighbourhood of the Jews. Thus, that in the time of Christ the custom had been lately adopted from the Romans, is very improbable. It is also unlikely that in so short a time it should have become usual and even (as the Talmud asserts) obli-

gatory to eat the Passover in that posture of indulgent repose, and in no other.

ACCURSED. [ANATHEMA.]

ACCUSER. The original word, which bears this leading signification, means—1. One who has a cause or matter of contention ; the accuser, opponent, or plaintiff in any suit (Judg. xii. 2; Matt. v. 25; Luke xii. 58). We have little information respecting the manner in which causes were conducted in the Hebrew courts of justice, except from the Rabbinical authorities, who, in matters of this description, may be supposed well informed as to the later customs of the nation. Even from these we learn little more than that great care was taken that, the accused being deemed innocent until convicted, he and the accuser should appear under equal circumstances before the court, that no prejudicial impression might be created to the disadvantage of the defendant, whose interests, we are told, were so anxiously guarded, that any one was allowed to speak whatever he knew or had to say in his favour, which privilege was withheld from the accuser. The word is also applied in Scripture, in the general sense, to any adversary or enemy (Luke xviii. 3; 1 Pet. v. 8). In the latter passage there is an allusion to the old Jewish opinion that Satan was the accuser or calumniator of men before God (Job i. 6, *sq.*; Rev. xii. 10, *sq.*; comp. Zech. iii. 1). In this application the forensic sense was still retained, Satan being represented as laying to man's charge a breach of the law, as in a court of justice, and demanding his punishment [SATAN].

ACELDAMA (*field of blood*), the field purchased with the money for which Judas betrayed Christ, and which was appropriated as a place of burial for strangers (Matt. xxvii. 8; Acts i. 19). It was previously ' a potter's field.' The field now shown as Aceldama lies on the slope of the hills beyond the valley of Hinnom, south of Mount Zion. Sandys thus writes of it: ' On the south side of this valley, neere where it meeteth with the valley of Jehoshaphat, mounted a good height on the side of the mountain, is *Aceldama*, or the field of blood, purchased with the restored reward of treason, for a buriall place for strangers. In the midst whereof a large square roome was made by the mother of Constantine; the south side, walled with the naturall rocke ; flat at the top, and equall with the vpper level; out of which ariseth certaine little cupoloes, open in the midst to let doune the dead bodies. Thorow these we might see the bottome, all couered with bones, and certaine corses but newly let doune, it being now the sepulchre of the Armenians. A greedy graue, and great enough to deuoure the dead of a whole nation. For they say (and I believe it) that the earth thereof within the space of eight and forty houres will consume the flesh that is laid thereon.' He then relates the common story, that the empress referred to, caused 270 ship-loads of this flesh-consuming mould to be taken to Rome, to form the soil of the Campo Santo, to which the same virtue is ascribed. Castela affirms that great quantities of the wondrous mould were removed by divers Christian princes in the time of the Crusades, and to this source assigns the similar sarcophagic properties claimed not only by the Campo Santo at Rome, but by the cemetery of St. Innocents at Paris, by the cemetery at Naples, and, we may add, that of the Campo Santo at Pisa.

The plot of ground originally bought ' to bury strangers in,' seems to have been early set apart by the Latins, as well as by the Crusaders, as a place of burial for pilgrims. In the fourteenth century it belonged to the Knights-Hospitallers. Early in the seventeenth century it was in the possession of the Armenians, who bought it for the burial of their own pilgrims. The erection of the charnel-house is ascribed to them. In the time of Maundrell they rented it at a sequin a day from the Turks. Corpses were still deposited there; and the traveller observes that they were in various stages of decay, from which he conjectures that the grave did not make that quick despatch with the bodies committed to it which had been reported. ' The earth, hereabouts,' he observes, ' is of a chalky substance; the plot of ground was not above thirty yards long by fifteen wide; and a moiety of it was occupied by the charnel-house, which was twelve yards high.' Richardson affirms that bodies were thrown in as late as 1818; but Dr. Robinson alleges that it has the appearance of having been for a much longer time abandoned : ' The field or plat is not now marked by any boundary to distinguish it from the rest of the hill-side; and the former charnel-house, now a ruin, is all that remains to point out the site.... An opening at each end enabled us to look in ; but the bottom was empty and dry, excepting a few bones much decayed.'

ACHA'IA, a region of Greece, which in the restricted sense occupied the north-western portion of the Peloponnesus, including Corinth and its isthmus. By the poets it was often put for the whole of Greece, whence Achaioi, *the Greeks.* Under the Romans, Greece was divided into two provinces, Macedonia and Achaia, the former of which included Macedonia proper, with Illyricum, Epirus, and Thessaly ; and the latter, all that lay southward of the former. It is in this latter acceptation that the name of Achaia is always employed in the New Testament (Acts xviii. 12, 27; xix. 21; Rom. xv. 26; xvi. 5; 1 Cor. xvi. 15; 2 Cor. i. 1; ix. 2; xi. 10; 1 Thess. i. 7, 8). Achaia was at first a senatorial province, and, as such, was governed by proconsuls. Tiberius changed the two into one imperial province under procurators; but Claudius restored them to the senate and to the proconsular form of government. Hence the exact and minute propriety with which St. Luke expresses himself in giving the title of proconsul to Gallio, who was appointed to the province in the time of Claudius (Acts xviii. 12).

ACHA'ICUS, a native of Achaia, and a follower of the apostle Paul. He, with Stephanus and Fortunatus, was the bearer of the 1st Epistle to the Corinthians, and was recommended by the apostle to their special respect (1 Cor. xvi. 17).

A'CHAN (*troubler*); in 1 Chron. ii. 7 written ACHAR. From the peculiarly appropriate significance of the name, it is supposed to have been imposed *after* the occurrence of the facts which rendered it notorious. The city of Jericho, before it was taken, was put under that awful ban, whereby all the inhabitants (except-

ing Rahab and her family) were devoted to destruction, all the combustible goods to be consumed by fire, and all the metals to be consecrated to God. This vow of devotement was rigidly observed by all the troops when Jericho was taken, save by one man, Achan, a Judahite, who could not resist the temptation of secreting an ingot of gold, a quantity of silver, and a costly Babylonish garment, which he buried in his tent. But God made known this infraction, which (the vow having been made by the nation as one body) had involved the whole nation in his guilt. The Israelites were defeated, with serious loss, in their first attack upon Ai; and as Joshua was well assured that this humiliation was designed as the punishment of a crime which had inculpated the entire people, he took immediate measures to discover the criminal. As in other cases, the matter was referred to the Lord by the lot, and the lot ultimately indicated the actual criminal. The conscience-stricken offender then confessed his crime to Joshua; and his confession being verified by the production of his ill-gotten treasure, the people, actuated by the strong impulse with which men tear up, root and branch, a polluted thing, hurried away not only Achan, but his tent, his goods, his spoil, his cattle, his children, to the valley (afterwards called) of Achor, north of Jericho, where they stoned him, and all that belonged to him; after which the whole was consumed with fire, and a cairn of stones raised over the ashes. The severity of this act, as regards the *family* of Achan, has provoked some remark. Instead of vindicating it, as is generally done, by the allegation that the members of Achan's family were probably accessories to his crime after the fact, we prefer the supposition that they were included in the doom by one of those sudden impulses of indiscriminate popular vengeance to which the Jewish people were exceedingly prone, and which, in this case, it would not have been in the power of Joshua to control by any authority which he could under such circumstances exercise.

A'CHAR. [ACHAN.]

A'CHISH (called Abimelech in the title of Ps. xxxiv.), the Philistine king of Gath, with whom David twice sought refuge when he fled from Saul (1 Sam. xxi. 10-15; xxvii. 1-3). The first time David was in imminent danger; for he was recognised and spoken of by the officers of the court as one whose glory had been won at the cost of the Philistines. This talk filled David with such alarm that he feigned himself mad when introduced to the notice of Achish, who, seeing him ' scrabbling upon the doors of the gate, and letting his spittle fall down upon his beard,' rebuked his people sharply for bringing him to his presence, asking, ' Have I need of madmen, that ye have brought this fellow to play the madman in my presence? Shall this fellow come into my house?' After this David lost no time in quitting the territories of Gath. About four years after, when the character and position of David became better known, and when he was at the head of not less than 600 resolute adherents, he again repaired with his troop to King Achish, who received him in a truly royal spirit, and treated him with a generous confidence, of which David took perhaps

c 2

rather more advantage than was creditable to him [DAVID].

ACHMETHA (Ezra vi. 2; in the Apocrypha 2 Macc. ix. 3; Judith i. 1, 2; Tob. iii. 7; Joseph. *Antiq.* x. 11, 7; xi. 4, 6; also, in Greek authors, Ecbatana), a city in Media. The name seems to have been applied exclusively to cities having a fortress for the protection of the royal treasures. In Ezra we learn that in the reign of Darius Hystaspes the Jews petitioned that search might be made in the king's treasure-house at Babylon, for the decree which Cyrus had made in favour of the Jews (Ezra v. 17). Search was accordingly made in the record-office ('house of the rolls'), where the treasures were kept at Babylon (vi. 1): but it appears not to have been found there, as it was eventually discovered 'at Achmetha, in the palace of the province of the Medes' (vi. 2). In Judith i. 2-4, there is a brief account of Ecbatana, in which we are told that it was built by Arphaxad, king of the Medes, who made it his capital. It was built of hewn stones, and surrounded by a high and thick wall, furnished with wide gates and strong and lofty towers. Herodotus speaks of it in similar terms, and ascribes its foundation to Dejoces, who was probably the same with the Arphaxad of Judith.

Ecbatana has been usually identified with the present Hamadan, which is still an important town, and the seat of one of the governments into which the Persian kingdom is divided. It is situated in north lat. 34° 53', east long. 40°, at the extremity of a rich and fertile plain, on a gradual ascent, at the base of the Elwund Mountains, whose higher summits are covered with perpetual snow. Some remnants of ruined walls of great thickness, and also of towers of sun-dried bricks, present the only positive evidence of a more ancient city than the present on the same spot. Heaps of comparatively recent ruins, and a wall fallen to decay, attest that Hamadan has declined from even its modern importance. The population is said by Southgate to be about 30,000, which, from what the present writer has seen of the place, he should judge to exceed the truth very considerably. It is little distinguished, inside, from other Persian towns of the same rank, save by its excellent and well-supplied bazaars, and the unusually large number of khans of rather a superior description. This is the result of the extensive transit trade of which it is the seat, it being the great centre where the routes of traffic between Persia, Mesopotamia, and Persia converge and meet. Its own manufactures are chiefly in leather. Many Jews reside here, claiming to be descended from those of the Captivity who remained in Media. Benjamin of Tudela says that in his time the number was 50,000. Modern travellers assign them 500 houses; but the Rabbi David de Beth Hillel, who was not likely to understate the fact, and who had the best means of information, gives them but 200 families. He says they are mostly in good circumstances, having fine houses and gardens, and are chiefly traders and goldsmiths. In the midst of the city is a tomb, which is said to be that of Mordecai and Esther. As Ecbatana was then the summer residence of the Persian court, it is probable enough that Mordecai and Esther died and were buried there; and traditional tes-

timony, taken in connection with this fact, and with such a monument in a place where Jews have been permanently resident, is better evidence than is usually obtained for the allocation of ancient sepulchres. The tomb is in charge of the Jews, and is one of their places in pilgrimage.

History notices another Ecbatana, in Palestine, at the foot of Mount Carmel, towards Ptolemais, where Cambyses died. It is not mentioned by this or any similar name in the Hebrew writings.

A'CHOR, a valley between Jericho and Ai, which received this name (signifying *trouble*) from the trouble brought upon the Israelites by the sin of Achan (Josh. vii. 24) [ACHAN].

AC'HSAH (*an anklet*), the daughter of Caleb, whose hand her father offered in marriage to him who should lead the attack on the city of Debir, and take it. The prize was won by his nephew Othniel; and as the bride was conducted with the usual ceremony to her future home, she alighted from her ass, and sued her father for an addition of springs of water to her dower in lands. It is probable that custom rendered it unusual, or at least ungracious, for a request tendered under such circumstances by a daughter to be refused; and Caleb, in accordance with her wish, bestowed upon her 'the upper and the nether springs' (Josh. xv. 16-19; Judg. i. 9-15).

AC'HSHAPH, a royal city of the Canaanites (Josh. xi. 1), has been supposed by many to be the same as ACHZIB, both being in the tribe of Asher. But a careful consideration of Josh. xix. 25 and 29, will make it probable that the places were different. There is more reason in the conjecture that Achshaph was another name for Accho or Acre, seeing that Accho otherwise does not occur in the list of towns in the lot of Asher, although it is certain, from Judg. i. 31, that Accho was in the portion of that tribe.

AC'HZIB. There were two places of this name, not usually distinguished.

1. ACHZIB, in the tribe of Asher nominally, but almost always in the possession of the Phœnicians; being, indeed, one of the places from which the Israelites were unable to expel the former inhabitants (Judg. i. 31). In the Talmud it is called CHEZIB. The Greeks called it ECDIPPA; and it still survives under the name of ZIB. It is upon the Mediterranean coast, about ten miles north of Acre. It stands on an ascent close by the sea-side, and is described as a small place, with a few palm-trees rising above the dwellings.

2. ACHZIB, in the tribe of Judah (Josh. xv. 44; Mic. i. 14), of which there is no historical mention, but, from its place in the catalogue, it appears to have been in the middle part of the western border-land of the tribe, towards the Philistines. This is very possibly the Chezib of Gen. xxxviii. 5.

ACRABATE'NE, a district in that portion of Judæa which lies towards the south end of the Dead Sea, occupied by the Edomites during the Captivity, and afterwards known as Idumæa. It is mentioned in 1 Macc. v. 3; Joseph. *Antiq.* xii. 8. 1. It is assumed to have taken its name from the Maaleh Akrabbim, or *Steep of the Scorpions*, mentioned in Num. xxxiv. 4, and Josh.

xv. 3, as the southern extremity of the tribe of Judah [ARRABBIM]. Another district of the same name is mentioned by Josephus as extending between Shechem and Jericho, but it is not mentioned in Scripture.

ACRE. [Accho.]

ACTS OF THE APOSTLES. This is the title of one of the canonical books of the New Testament, the fifth in order in the common arrangement, and the last of those properly of an historical character. Commencing with a reference to an account given in a former work of the sayings and doings of Jesus Christ before his ascension, its author proceeds to conduct us to an acquaintance with the circumstances attending that event, the conduct of the disciples on their return from witnessing it, the outpouring on them of the Holy Spirit according to Christ's promise to them before his crucifixion, and the amazing success which, as a consequence of this, attended the first announcement by them of the doctrine concerning Jesus as the promised Messiah and the Saviour of the World. After giving the history of the mother-church at Jerusalem up to the period when the violent persecution of its members by the rulers of the Jews had broken up their society and scattered them, with the exception of the apostles, throughout the whole of the surrounding region; and after introducing to the notice of the reader the case of a remarkable conversion of one of the most zealous persecutors of the church, who afterwards became one of its most devoted and successful advocates, the narrative takes a wider scope and opens to our view the gradual expansion of the church by the free admission within its pale of persons directly converted from heathenism and who had not passed through the preliminary stage of Judaism. The first step towards this more liberal and cosmopolitan order of things having been effected by Peter, to whom the honour of laying the foundation of the Christian church, both within and without the confines of Judaism, seems, in accordance with our Lord's declaration concerning him (Matt. xvi. 18), to have been reserved, Paul, the recent convert and the destined apostle of the Gentiles, is brought forward as the main actor on the scene. On his course of missionary activity, his successes and his sufferings, the chief interest of the narrative is thenceforward concentrated, until, having followed him to Rome, whither he had been sent as a prisoner to abide his trial, on his own appeal, at the bar of the emperor himself, the book abruptly closes, leaving us to gather further information concerning him and the fortunes of the church from other sources.

Respecting the *authorship* of this book there can be no ground for doubt or hesitation. It is, unquestionably, the production of the same writer by whom the third of the four Gospels was composed, as is evident from the introductory sentences of both (comp. Luke i. 1-4, with Acts i. 1). That this writer was Luke has not in either case been called in question, and is uniformly asserted by tradition. From the book itself, also, it appears that the author accompanied Paul to Rome when he went to that city as a prisoner (xxviii.). Now, we know from two epistles written by Paul at that time, that *Luke* was with him at Rome (Col. iv. 14; 2 Tim.

iv. 11), which favours the supposition that he was the writer of the narrative of the apostle's journey to that city. It was rejected by certain heretics in the primitive times, such as the Marcionites, the Severians, and the Manicheans, or we should rather say, it was cast aside by them because it did not favour their peculiar views. A complaint made by Chrysostom would lead us to infer that in his day, though received as genuine, the Acts was generally omitted from the number of books publicly read in the churches, and had consequently become little known among the people attending those churches.

Many critics are inclined to regard the Gospel by Luke and the Acts of the Apostles as having formed originally only one work, consisting of two parts. But this opinion is at variance with Luke's own description of the relation of these two writings to each other (being called by him, the one the former and the other the latter treatise); and also with the fact that the two works have invariably, and from the earliest times, appeared with *distinct titles*.

Of the greater part of the events recorded in the Acts the writer himself appears to have been witness. He is for the first time introduced into the narrative in ch. xvi. 11, where he speaks of accompanying Paul to Philippi. He then disappears from the narrative until Paul's return to Philippi, more than two years afterwards, when it is stated that they left that place in company (xx. 6); from which it may be justly inferred that Luke spent the interval in that town. From this time to the close of the period embraced by his narrative he appears as the companion of the apostle. For the materials, therefore, of all he has recorded from ch. xvi. 11, to xxviii. 31, he may be regarded as having drawn upon his own recollection or on that of the apostle. To the latter source, also, may be confidently traced all he has recorded concerning the earlier events of the apostle's career; and as respects the circumstances recorded in the first twelve chapters of the Acts, and which relate chiefly to the church at Jerusalem and the labours of the apostle Peter, we may readily suppose that they were so much the matter of general notoriety among the Christians with whom Luke associated, that he needed no assistance from any other merely human source in recording them.

With regard to the *design* of the evangelist in writing this book, a prevalent popular opinion is, that Luke, having in his Gospel given a history of the life of Christ, intended to follow that up by giving in the Acts a narrative of the establishment and early progress of his religion in the world. That this, however, could not have been his design is obvious from the very partial and limited view which his narrative gives of the state of things in the church generally during the period through which it extends. As little can we regard this book as designed to record the official history of the apostles Peter and Paul, for we find many particulars concerning both these apostles mentioned incidentally elsewhere, of which Luke takes no notice (comp. 2 Cor. xi.; Gal. i. 17; ii. 11; 1 Pet. v. 13). Some are of opinion that no particular design should be ascribed to the evangelist in composing this book beyond that of furnishing his friend Theophilus with a pleasing and instructive narrative of such events as had come under his own notice; but such a view savours too much of the lax opinions which these writers unhappily entertained regarding the sacred writers, to be adopted by those who regard all the sacred books as designed for the permanent instruction and benefit of the church universal. Much more deserving of attention is the opinion that 'the general design of the author of this book was, by means of his narratives, to set forth the co-operation of God in the diffusion of Christianity, and along with that, to prove, by remarkable facts, the dignity of the apostles and the perfectly equal right of the Gentiles with the Jews to a participation in the blessings of that religion.' Perhaps we should come still closer to the truth if we were to say that the design of Luke in writing the Acts was to supply, by select and suitable instances, an illustration of the power and working of that religion which Jesus had died to establish. In his Gospel he had presented to his readers an exhibition of Christianity as embodied in the person, character, and works of its great founder; and having followed him in his narration until he was taken up out of the sight of his disciples into heaven, this second work was written to show how his religion operated when committed to the hands of those by whom it was to be announced 'to all nations, beginning at Jerusalem' (Luke xxiv. 47).

Respecting the *time* when this book was composed it is impossible to speak with certainty. As the history is continued up to the close of the second year of Paul's imprisonment at Rome, it could not have been written before A.D. 63; it was probably, however, composed very soon after, so that we shall not err far if we assign the interval between the year 63 and the year 65 as the period of its completion. Still greater uncertainty hangs over the *place* where Luke composed it, but as he accompanied Paul to Rome, perhaps it was at that city and under the auspices of the apostle that it was prepared.

The *style* of Luke in the Acts is, like his style in his Gospel, much purer than that of most other books in the New Testament. The Hebraisms which occasionally occur are almost exclusively to be found in the speeches of others which he has reported. His mode of narrating events is clear, dignified, and lively; and, as Michaelis observes, 'he has well supported the character of each person whom he has introduced as delivering a public harangue, and has very faithfully and happily preserved the manner of speaking which was peculiar to each of his orators.'

Whilst, as Lardner and others have very satisfactorily shown, the *credibility* of the events recorded by Luke is fully authenticated both by internal and external evidence, very great obscurity attaches to the *chronology* of these events. Our space will not permit us to enter at large into this point, we shall therefore content ourselves with merely presenting, in a tabular form, the dates affixed to the leading events by those writers whose authority is most deserving of consideration in such an inquiry.

	Usher.	Pearson.	Michaelis.	Hug.	Haenlein.	Greswell.	Ager.
The Ascension of Christ	33	33	33	31	33	30	31
Stoning of Stephen	34	34	—	—	36	37	37
Conversion of Paul	35	35	37?	35	36-38	37	38
Paul's first journey to Jerusalem (Acts ix. 26)	38	38	—	38	39	41	41
James's Martyrdom, &c.	44	44	44	44	44	43	43
Paul's second journey to Jerusalem (Acts xi. 30)	44	44	44	44	44	43	44
Paul's first missionary tour	45-46	44-47	—	44	—	44	44
Paul's third journey to Jerusalem (Acts xv.)	53	49	—	52	49?	48	48
Paul arrives at Corinth	54	52	54?	53	54	50	52
Paul's fourth journey to Jerusalem (Acts xviii. 22)	56	54	—	55	54	52	54
Paul's abode at Ephesus	56-59	54-57	—	56-58	—	53-55	55-59
Paul's fifth journey to Jerusalem (Acts xxi. 17)	59	58	60	59	60	56	58
Paul arrives in Rome	63	61	63	62	63	59	61

ACTS, SPURIOUS [APOCRYPHA]. This term has been applied to several ancient writings pretended to have been composed by, or to supply historical facts respecting our Blessed Saviour and his disciples, or other individuals whose actions are recorded in the holy Scriptures. Some of these writings are still extant; others are only known to have existed, by the accounts of them which are to be met with in ancient authors.

Such, for example, is the beautiful sentiment cited by St. Paul (Acts xx. 35), *It is more blessed to give than to receive,* which some have supposed to be taken from some lost apocryphal book But the probability is that St. Paul received the passage by tradition from the other apostles. Various other sayings, ascribed to Christ by early writers, which are alleged to be derived from apocryphal gospels, are in all probability nothing more than loose quotations from the Scriptures, which were very common among the apostolical fathers.

The most remarkable of the apocrypha. Acts ascribed to our Lord is the letter which he is said to have written to Agbarus, king of Edessa, in answer to a request from that monarch that he would come to heal a disease under which he laboured. Some few historians have maintained the genuineness of these letters, but most writers, including the great majority of Roman Catholic divines, reject them as spurious; and there is good reason to believe that the whole chapter of Eusebius which contains these documents is tself an interpolation.

ACTS OF THE APOSTLES, SPURIOUS.

Of these several are extant, others are lost, or only fragments of them are come down to us.

The following is a catalogue of the principal spurious Acts still extant: — *The Creed of the Apostles.*—*The Epistles of Barnabas, Clement, Ignatius, and Polycarp.*—*The Recognitions of Clement,* or the *Travels of Peter.*—*The Shepherd of Hermas.*—*The Acts of Pilate* (spurious), or the *Gospel of Nicodemus.*—*The Acts of Paul,* or the *Martyrdom of Thecla.*—Abdias's *History of the Twelve Apostles.*—*The Constitutions of the Apostles.*—*The Canons of the Apostles.*—*The Liturgies of the Apostles.*—*St. Paul's Epistle to the Laodiceans.*—*St. Paul's Letters to Seneca.*

AD'AD is the name of the chief deity of the Syrians, the *sun.* The name of this Syrian deity is most probably an element in the names of the Syrian kings Benhadad and Hadadezer.

ADAD-RIM'MON, properly HADAD-RIMMON (*a garden of pomegranates*), a city in the valley of Jezreel, where was fought the famous battle between King Josiah and Pharaoh-Necho (2 Kings xxiii. 29; Zech. xii. 11). Adad-rimmon was afterwards called Maximianopolis, in honour of the emperor Maximian. It was seventeen Roman miles from Cæsarea, and ten miles from Jezreel.

A'DAH (*adornment, comeliness*): 1. one of the wives of Lamech (Gen. iv. 19); 2. one of the wives of Esau, daughter of Elon the Hittite (Gen. xxxvi. 4). She is called Judith in Gen. xxvi. 34.

AD'AM, the word by which the Bible designates the first human being.

It is evident that, in the earliest use of language, the vocal sound employed to designate the first perceived object, of any kind, would be an appellative, and would be formed from something known or apprehended to be a characteristic property of that object. The word would, therefore, be at once the appellative and the proper name. But when other objects of the same kind were discovered, or subsequently came into existence, difficulty would be felt; it would become necessary to guard against confusion, and the inventive faculty would be called upon to obtain a discriminative term for each and singular individual, while some equally appropriate term would be fixed upon for the whole kind. Different methods of effecting these two purposes might be resorted to, but the most natural would be to retain the original term in its simple state, for the first individual: and to make some modification of it by prefixing another sound, or by subjoining one, or by altering the vowel or vowels in the body of the word, in order to have a term for the kind, and for the separate individuals of the kind.

This reasoning is exemplified in the first applications of the word before us: (Gen. i. 26),

'Let us make man [Adam] in our image;' (i. 27), 'And God created the man [the Adam] in his own image.' The next instance (ii. 7) expresses the source of derivation, a character or property; namely, the material of which the human body was formed: 'And the Lord God [Jehovah Elohim] formed the man [the Adam] dust from the ground [the adamah]'. The meaning of the primary word is, most probably, any kind of *reddish tint,* as a beautiful human complexion (Lam. iv. 7); but its various derivatives are applied to different objects of a red or brown hue, or approaching to such. The word *Adam,* therefore, is an appellative noun made into a proper one. It is further remarkable that, in all the other instances in the second and third chapters of Genesis, which are nineteen, it is put with the article, *the man,* or *the Adam.*

The question arises, Was the uttered sound, originally employed for this purpose, the very vocable *Adam,* or was it some other sound of correspondent signification? This is equivalent to asking, what was the primitive language of men?

That language originated in the instinctive cries of human beings herding together in a condition like that of common animals, is an hypothesis which, apart from all testimony of revelation, must appear unreasonable to a man of serious reflection. There are other animals, besides man, whose organs are capable of producing articulate sounds, through a considerable range of variety, and distinctly pronounced. How, then, is it that parrots, jays, and starlings have not among themselves developed an articulate language, transmitted it to their successive generations, and improved it, both in the life-time of the individual and in the series of many generations? Those birds never attempt to speak till they are compelled by a difficult process on the part of their trainers, and they never train each other.

Upon the mere ground of reasoning from the necessity of the case, it seems an inevitable conclusion that not the capacity merely, but the actual use of speech, with the corresponding faculty of promptly understanding it, was given to the first human beings by a superior power: and it would be a gratuitous absurdity to suppose that power to be any other than the Almighty Creator. In what manner such communication or infusion of what would be equivalent to a habit took place, it is in vain to inquire; the subject lies beyond the range of human investigation: but, from the evident exigency, it must have been instantaneous, or nearly so. It is not necessary to suppose that a copious language was thus bestowed upon the human creatures in the first stage of their existence. We need to suppose only so much as would be requisite for the notation of the ideas of natural wants and the most important mental conceptions; and from these, as germs, the powers of the mind and the faculty of vocal designation would educe new words and combinations as occasion demanded.

That the language thus formed continued to be the universal speech of mankind till after the deluge, and till the great cause of diversity took place, is in itself the most probable supposition [TONGUES, CONFUSION OF]. If there were any families of men which were not involved in the crime of the Babel-builders, they would almost certainly retain the primeval language. The longevity of the men of that period would be a powerful conservative of that language against the slow changes of time. That there were such exceptions seems to be almost an indubitable inference from the fact that Noah long survived the unholy attempt. His faithful piety would not have suffered him to fall into the snare; and it is difficult to suppose that none of his children and descendants would listen to his admonitions, and hold fast their integrity by adhering to him: on the contrary, it is reasonable to suppose that the habit and character of piety were established in many of them.

The confusion of tongues, therefore, whatever was the nature of that judicial visitation, would not fall upon that portion of men which was the most orderly, thoughtful, and pious, among whom the second father of mankind dwelt as their acknowledged and revered head.

If this supposition be admitted, we can have no difficulty in regarding as the mother of languages, not indeed the Hebrew, absolutely speaking, but that which was the stock whence branched the Hebrew, and its sister tongues, usually called the Shemitic, but more properly, by Dr. Prichard, the Syro-Arabian. It may then be maintained that the actually spoken names of Adam and all the others mentioned in the antediluvian history were those which we have in the Hebrew Bible, very slightly and not at all essentially varied.

It is among the clearest deductions of reason, that men and all dependent beings have been *created*, that is, produced or brought into their first existence by an intelligent and adequately powerful being. A question, however, arises of great interest and importance. Did the Almighty Creator produce only one man and one woman, from whom all other human beings have descended?—or did he create several parental pairs, from whom distinct stocks of men have been derived? The affirmative of the latter position has been maintained by some, and, it must be confessed, not without apparent reason. The manifest and great differences in complexion and figure, which distinguish several races of mankind, are supposed to be such as entirely to forbid the conclusion that they have all descended from one father and one mother. The question is usually regarded as equivalent to this: whether there is only one species of men, or there are several. But we cannot, in strict fairness, admit that the questions are identical. It is hypothetically *conceivable* that the Adorable God might give existence to any number of creatures, which should all possess the properties that characterize identity of species, even without such differences as constitute varieties, or with any degree of those differences.

But the admission of the possibility is not a concession of the reality. So great is the evidence in favour of the derivation of the entire mass of human beings from one pair of ancestors, that it has obtained the suffrage of the men most competent to judge upon a question of comparative anatomy and physiology.

The animals which render eminent services to man, and peculiarly depend upon his protection, are widely diffused—the horse, the dog, the hog, the domestic fowl. Now of these, the varieties in each species are numerous and different, to a degree so great, that an observer ignorant of physiological history would scarcely believe them to be of the same species. But man is the most widely diffused of any animal. In the progress of ages and generations, he has naturalized himself to every climate, and to modes of life which would prove fatal to an individual man suddenly transferred from a remote point of the field. The alterations produced affect every part of the body, internal and external, without extinguishing the marks of the specific identity. A further and striking evidence is, that when persons of different varieties are conjugally united, the offspring, especially in two or three generations, becomes more prolific, and acquires a higher perfection in physical and mental qualities than was found in either of the parental races. From the deepest African black to the finest Caucasian white, the change runs through imperceptible gradations; and, if a middle hue be assumed, suppose some tint of brown, all the varieties of complexion may be explained upon the principle of divergence influenced by outward circumstances. The conclusion may be fairly drawn, in the words of the able translators and illustrators of Baron Cuvier's great work:—' We are fully warranted in concluding, both from the comparison of man with inferior animals, so far as the inferiority will allow of such comparison, and, beyond that, by comparing him with himself, that the great family of mankind loudly proclaim a descent, at some period or other, from one common origin.'

Thus, by an investigation totally independent of historical authority, we are brought to the conclusion of the inspired writings, that the Creator ' hath made of one blood all nations of men, for to dwell on all the face of the earth' (Acts xvii. 26).

We shall now follow the course of those sacred documents in tracing the history of the first man, persuaded that their right interpretation is a sure basis of truth. At the same time we shall not reject illustrations from natural history and the reason of particular facts.

It is evident upon a little reflection, and the closest investigation confirms the conclusion, that the first human pair must have been created in a state equivalent to that which all subsequent human beings have had to reach by slow degrees, in growth, experience, observation, imitation, and the instruction of others: that is, a state of prime maturity, and with an infusion, concreation, or whatever we may call it, of knowledge and habits, both physical and intellectual, suitable to the place which man had to occupy in the system of creation, and adequate to his necessities in that place. Had it been otherwise, the new beings could not have preserved their animal existence, nor have held rational converse with each other, nor have paid to their Creator the homage of knowledge and love, adoration, and obedience; and reason clearly tells us that the last was the noblest end of existence. Those whom unhappy prejudices lead to reject revelation must either admit this, or must resort to suppositions of palpable absurdity and impossibility. If they will not admit a direct action of Divine power in creation and adaptation to the designed mode of existence, they must admit something far beyond the miraculous, an infinite succession of finite beings, or a spontaneous production of order, organization, and systematic action, from some unintelligent origin. The Bible coincides with this dictate of honest reason, expressing these facts in simple and artless language, suited to the circumstances of the men to whom revelation was first granted. That this production in a mature state was the fact with regard to the vegetable part of the creation, is declared in Gen. ii. 4, 5: 'In the day of Jehovah God's making the earth and the heavens, and every shrub of the field before it should be in the earth, and every herb of the field before it should bud.' The two terms, shrubs and herbage, are put to designate the whole vegetable kingdom. The reason of the case comprehends the other division of organized nature; and this is applied to man and all other animals, in the words, ' Out of the ground—dust out of the ground—Jehovah God formed them.'

It is to be observed that there are two narratives at the beginning of the Mosaic records, different in style and manner, distinct and independent; at first sight somewhat discrepant, but when strictly examined, perfectly compatible, and each one illustrating and completing the other. The first is contained in Gen. i. 1, to ii. 3; and the other, ii. 4, to iv. 26. As is the case with the Scripture history generally, they consist of a few principal facts, detached anecdotes, leaving much of necessary implication which the good sense of the reader is called upon to supply; and passing over large spaces of the history of life, upon which all conjecture would be fruitless.

In the second of these narratives we read, ' And Jehovah God formed the man [*Heb.* the Adam], dust from the ground [*ha-adamah*], and blew into his nostrils the breath of life; and the man became a living animal' (Gen. ii. 7). Here are two objects of attention, the organic mechanism of the human body, and the vitality with which it was endowed.

The mechanical material, formed (moulded, or arranged, as an artificer models clay or wax) into the human and all other animal bodies, is called ' dust from the ground.' This would be a natural and easy expression to men in the early ages, before chemistry was known or minute philosophical distinctions were thought of, to convey, in a general form, the idea of *earthy matter*, the constituent substance of the ground on which we tread. To say, that of this the human and every other animal body was formed, is a position which would be at once the most easily apprehensible to an uncultivated mind, and which yet is the most exactly true upon the highest philosophical grounds. We now know, from chemical analysis, that the animal body is composed, in the inscrutable manner called *organization*, of carbon, hydrogen, oxygen, nitrogen, lime, iron, sulphur, and phosphorus. Now all these are mineral substances, which in their various combinations form a very large part of the solid ground.

The expression which we have rendered

' living animal' sets before us the ORGANIC LIFE of the animal frame, that mysterious something which man cannot create nor restore, which baffles the most acute philosophers to search out its nature, and which reason combines with Scripture to refer to the immediate agency of the Almighty—' in him we live, and move, and have our being.'

The other narrative is contained in these words, ' God created man in his own image: in the image of God created he him; male and female created he them' (Gen. i. 27). *The image* (resemblance, such as a shadow bears to the object which casts it) *of God* is an expression which breathes at once archaic simplicity and the most recondite wisdom; for what term could the most cultivated and copious language bring forth more suitable to the purpose? It presents to us man as made in a resemblance to the author of his being, a true resemblance, but faint and shadowy; an outline, faithful according to its capacity, yet infinitely remote from the reality: a distant form of the *intelligence, wisdom, power, rectitude, goodness*, and *dominion* of the Adorable Supreme. To the inferior sentient beings with which he is connected man stands in the place of God. We have every reason to think that none of them are capable of conceiving a being higher than man. All, in their different ways, look up to him as their superior; the ferocious generally flee before him, afraid to encounter his power, and the gentle court his protection and show their highest joy to consist in serving and pleasing him. Even in our degenerate state it is manifest that if we treat the domesticated animals with wisdom and kindness, their attachment is most ardent and faithful.

Thus had man the shadow of the divine *dominion* and *authority* over the inferior creation. The attribute of *power* was also given to him, in his being made able to convert the inanimate objects and those possessing only the vegetable life, into the instruments and the materials for supplying his wants, and continually enlarging his sphere of command.

In such a state of things *knowledge* and *wisdom* are implied: the one quality, an acquaintance with those substances and their changeful actions which were necessary for a creature like man to understand, in order to his safety and comfort; the other, such sagacity as would direct him in selecting the best objects of desire and pursuit, and the right means for attaining them.

Above all, *moral excellence* must have been comprised in this ' image of God;' and not only forming a part of it, but being its crown of beauty and glory. The Christian inspiration, than which no more perfect disclosure of God is to take place on this side eternity, casts its light upon this subject: for this apostle Paul, in urging the obligations of Christians to perfect holiness, evidently alludes to the endowments of the first man in two parallel and mutually illustrative epistles; '— the new man, renewed in knowledge after the image of HIM that created him; the new man which, after [according to] GOD, is created in righteousness and true holiness' (Col. iii. 10; Eph. iv. 24).

In this perfection of faculties, and with these

high prerogatives of moral existence, did human nature, in its first subject, rise up from the creating hand. The whole Scripture-narrative implies that this STATE of existence was one of correspondent *activity* and *enjoyment*. It plainly represents the DEITY himself as condescending *to assume a human form and to employ human speech*, in order to instruct and exercise the happy creatures whom (to borrow the just and beautiful language of the Apocryphal ‘Wisdom’) ‘God created for incorruptibility, and made him an image of his own nature’ (Wisd. Sol. ii. 23).

The noble and sublime idea that man thus had his Maker for his teacher and guide, precludes a thousand difficulties. It shows us the simple, direct, and effectual method by which the newly formed creature would have communicated to him all the intellectual knowledge, and all the practical arts and manipulations, which were needful and beneficial for him.

Religious knowledge and its appropriate habits also required an immediate infusion: and these are pre-eminently comprehended in the ‘image of God.’ On the one hand, it is not to be supposed that the newly created man and his female companion were inspired with a very ample share of the doctrinal knowledge which was communicated to their posterity by the successive and accumulating revolutions of more than four thousand years: and, on the other, we cannot imagine that they were left in gross ignorance upon the existence and excellencies of the Being who had made them, their obligations to him, and the way in which they might continue to receive the greatest blessings from him. It is self-evident that, to have attained such a kind and degree of knowledge, by spontaneous effort, under even the favourable circumstances of a state of negative innocence, would have been a long and arduous work. But the sacred narrative leaves no room for doubt upon this head. In the primitive style it tells of God as speaking to them, commanding, instructing, assigning their work, pointing out their danger, and showing how to avoid it. All this, reduced to the dry simplicity of detail, is equivalent to saying that the Creator, infinitely kind and condescending, by the use of forms and modes adapted to their capacity, fed their minds with truth, gave them a ready understanding of it and that delight in it which constituted holiness, taught them to hold intercourse with himself by direct addresses in both praise and prayer, and gave some disclosures of a future state of blessedness when they should have fulfilled the condition of their probation.

An especial instance of this instruction and infusion of practical habits is given to us in the narrative: ‘Out of the ground Jehovah God formed every beast of the field and every fowl of the air; and brought them unto the man, to see what he would call them’ (Gen. ii. 19). This, taken out of the style of condescending anthropomorphism, amounts to such a statement as the following: the Creator had not only formed man with organs of speech, but he taught him the use of them, by an immediate communication of the practical faculty and its accompanying intelligence; and he guided the man, as yet the solitary one of his species, to this among the first applications of speech, the

designating of the animals with which he was connected, by appellative words which would both be the help of his memory and assist his mental operations, and thus would be introductory and facilitating to more enlarged applications of thought and language. We are further warranted, by the recognised fact of the anecdotal and fragmentary structure of the Scripture history, to regard this as the selected instance for exhibiting a whole kind or class of operations or processes; implying that, in the same or similar manner, the first man was led to understand something of the qualities and relations of vegetables, earthy matters, the visible heavens, and the other external objects to which he had a relation.

The next important article in this primeval history is the creation of the human female. The narrative is given in the more summary manner in the former of the two documents:— ‘Male and female created he them’ (Gen. i. 27). It stands a little more at length in a *third* document, which begins the fifth chapter, and has the characteristic heading or title by which the Hebrews designated a separate work. ‘This, the book of the generations of Adam. In the day God created Adam; he made him in the likeness of God, male and female he created them; and he blessed them, and he called their name Adam, in the day of their being created’ (ver. 1, 2).

The second of the narratives is more circumstantial: ‘And Jehovah God said, it is not good the man’s being alone: I will make for him a help suitable for him.’ Then follows the passage concerning the review and the naming of the inferior animals; and it continues—‘ but for Adam he found not a help suitable for him. And Jehovah God caused a deep sleep to fall upon the man [the Adam], and he slept: and he took one out of his ribs, and closed up the flesh in its place: and Jehovah God built up the rib which he had taken from the man into a woman, and he brought her to the man.’

The next particular into which the sacred history leads us, is one which we cannot approach without a painful sense of its difficulty and delicacy. It stands thus in the authorized version: ‘And they were both naked, the man and his wife; and were not ashamed’ (ii. 25). The common interpretation is, that, in this respect, the two human beings, the first and only existing ones, were precisely in the condition of the youngest infants, incapable of perceiving any incongruity in the total destitution of artificial clothing. But a little reflection will tell us, and the more carefully that reflection is pursued the more it will appear just, that this supposition is inconsistent with what we have established on solid grounds, the supernatural infusion into the minds of our first parents and into their nervous and muscular faculties, of the knowledge and practical habits which their descendants have had to acquire by the long process of instruction and example. We have seen the necessity that there must have been communicated to them, directly by the Creator, no inconsiderable measure of natural knowledge and the methods of applying it, or their lives could not have been secured; and of moral and spiritual ‘knowledge, righteousness, and true holiness,’ such a measure as would belong to the sinless state, and would enable them to render an intelligent and perfect worship to the Glorious Deity. It seems impossible for that state of mind and habits to exist without a correct sensibility to proprieties and decencies which infant children cannot understand or feel; and the capacities and duties of their conjugal state are implied in the narrative. Further, it cannot be overlooked that, though we are entitled to ascribe to the locality of Eden the most bland atmosphere and delightful soil, yet the action of the sun's rays upon the naked skin, the range of temperature through the day and the night, the alternations of dryness and moisture, the various labour among trees and bushes, and exposure to insects, would render some protective clothing quite indispensable.

From these considerations we feel ourselves obliged to understand the word *arom* in that which is its *most usual* signification in the Hebrew language, as importing *not an absolute*, but a *partial* or *comparative* nudity, a stripping off of the upper garment, or of some other usual article of dress, when all the habiliments were not laid aside; and this is a more frequent signification than that of entire destitution. If it be asked, Whence did Adam and Eve derive this clothing? we reply, that, as a part of the divine instruction which we have established, they were taught to take off the inner bark of some trees, which would answer extremely well for this purpose. If an objection be drawn from Gen. iii. 7, 10, 11, we reply, that, in consequence of the transgression, the clothing was disgracefully injured.

Another inquiry presents itself. How long did the state of paradisiac innocence and happiness continue? Some have regarded the period as very brief, not more even than a single day; but this manifestly falls very short of the time which a reasonable probability requires. The first man was brought into existence in the region called Eden; then he was introduced into a particular part of it, the garden, replenished with the richest productions of the Creator's bounty for the delight of the eye and the other senses; the most agreeable labour was required 'to dress and to keep it,' implying some arts of culture, preservation from injury, training flowers and fruits, and knowing the various uses and enjoyments of the produce: making observation upon the works of God, of which an investigation and designating of animals is expressly specified; nor can we suppose that there was no contemplation of the magnificent sky and the heavenly bodies: above all, the wondrous communion with the condescending Deity, and probably with created spirits of superior orders, by which the mind would be excited, its capacity enlarged, and its holy felicity continually increased. It is also to be remarked, that the narrative (Gen. ii. 19, 20) conveys the implication that some time was allowed to elapse, that Adam might discover and feel his want of a companion of his own species, 'a help correspondent to him.'

These considerations impress us with a sense of probability, amounting to a conviction, that a period not very short was requisite for the exercise of man's faculties, the disclosures of his happiness, and the service of adoration which he could pay to his Creator. But all these considerations are strengthened by the recollection that they attach to man's solitary state; and that they all require new and enlarged application when the addition of conjugal life is brought into the account. The conclusion appears irresistible that a duration of many days, or rather weeks or months, would be requisite for so many and important purposes.

Thus divinely honoured and happy were the progenitors of mankind in the state of their creation.

The next scene which the sacred history brings before us is a dark reverse. Another agent comes into the field and successfully employs his arts for seducing Eve, and by her means Adam, from their original state of rectitude, dignity, and happiness.

Among the provisions of divine wisdom and goodness were two vegetable productions of wondrous qualities and mysterious significancy, ' the tree of life in the midst of the garden, and the tree of knowledge of good and evil' (Gen. ii. 9). It would add to the precision of the terms, and perhaps aid our understanding of them, if we were to adhere strictly to the Hebrew by retaining the definite prefix: and then we have ' the tree of the life' and ' the tree of the knowledge.' Thus would be indicated THE particular *life* of which the one was a symbol and instrument, and THE fatal *knowledge* springing from the abuse of the other. At the same time, we do not maintain that these appellations were given to them at the beginning. We rather suppose that they were applied afterwards, suggested by the events and connection, and so became the historical names.

We see no sufficient reason to understand, as some do, ' the tree of life,' collectively, as implying a species, and that there were many trees of that species. The figurative use of the expression in Rev. xxii. 2, where a plurality is plainly intended, involves no evidence of such a design in this literal narrative. The phraseology of the text best agrees with the idea of a single tree, designed for a special purpose, and not intended to perpetuate its kind. Though in the state of innocence, Adam and Eve might be liable to some corporal suffering from the changes of the season and the weather, or accidental circumstances; in any case of which occurring, this tree had been endowed by the bountiful Creator with a medicinal and restorative property, probably in the way of instantaneous miracle. We think also that it was designed for a sacramental or symbolical purpose, a representation and pledge of ' the life,' emphatically so called, heavenly immortality when the term of probation should be happily completed. Yet we by no means suppose that this ' tree of the life' possessed any intrinsic property of communicating immortality. In the latter view, it was a sign and seal of the divine promise. But, with regard to the former intention, we see nothing to forbid the idea that it had most efficacious medicinal properties in its fruit, leaves, and other parts. Such were called *trees of life* by the Hebrews (Prov. iii. 18; xi. 30; xiii. 12; xv. 4).

The ' tree of the knowledge of good and evil' might be any tree whatever; it might be of any species even yet remaining, though, if it were so, we could not determine its species, for the plain reason, that no name, description, or information whatever is given that could possibly lead to the ascertainment. Yet we cannot but think the more reasonable probability to be, that it was a tree having poisonous properties, stimulating, and intoxicating, such as are found in some existing species, especially in hot climates. On this ground, the prohibition to eat or even touch the tree was a beneficent provision against the danger of pain and death. But the revealed object of this 'tree of the knowledge of good and evil' was that which would require no particular properties beyond some degree of external beauty and fruit of an immediately pleasant taste. That object was to be a *test of obedience*. For such a purpose, it is evident that to select an indifferent act, to be the object prohibited, was necessary; as the obligation to refrain should be only that which arises simply, so far as the subject of the law can know, from the sacred will of the lawgiver. This does not, however, nullify what we have said upon the possibility, or even probability, that the tree in question had noxious qualities: for upon either the affirmative or the negative of the supposition, the subjects of this positive law, having upon all antecedent grounds the fullest conviction of the perfect rectitude and benevolence of their Creator, would see in it the simple character of a test, a means of proof, whether they would or would not implicitly confide in him. For so doing they had every possible reason; and against any thought or mental feeling tending to the violation of the precept, they were in possession of the most powerful motives. There was no difficulty in the observance. They were surrounded with a paradise of delights, and they had no reason to imagine that any good whatever would accrue to them from their seizing upon anything prohibited. If perplexity or doubt arose, they had ready access to their divine benefactor for obtaining information and direction. But they allowed the thought of disobedience to form itself into a disposition, and then a purpose.

Thus was the seal broken, the integrity of the heart was gone, the sin was generated, and the outward act was the consummation of the dire process. Eve, less informed, less cautious, less endowed with strength of mind, became the more ready victim. 'The woman, being deceived, was in the transgression;' but 'Adam was not deceived' (1 Tim. ii. 14). He rushed knowingly and deliberately to ruin. The offence had grievous aggravations. It was the preference of a trifling gratification to the approbation of the Supreme Lord of the universe; it implied a denial of the wisdom, holiness, goodness, veracity, and power of God; it was marked with extreme ingratitude; it involved a contemptuous disregard of consequences, awfully impious as it referred to their immediate connection with the moral government of God, and cruelly selfish as it respected their posterity.

The instrument of the temptation was a serpent; whether any one of the existing kinds it is evidently impossible for us to know. Of that numerous order many species are of brilliant colours and playful in their attitudes and manners, so that one may well conceive of such an object attracting and fascinating the first woman. Whether it spoke in an articulate voice, like the human, or expressed the sentiments attributed to it by a succession of remarkable and significant actions, may be a subject of reasonable question. The latter is possible, and it seems the preferable hypothesis, as, without a miraculous intervention, the mouth and throat of no serpent could form a vocal utterance of words; and we cannot attribute to any wicked spirit the power of working miracles.

This part of the narrative begins with the words, 'And the serpent was crafty above every animal of the field' (Gen. iii. 1). It is to be observed that this is not said of the order of serpents, as if it were a general property of them, but of *that* particular serpent. Indeed, this 'cunning craftiness, lying in wait to deceive' (Eph. iv. 14), is the very character of that malignant creature of whose wily stratagems the reptile was a mere instrument. The existence of spirits, superior to man, and of whom some have become depraved, and are labouring to spread wickedness and misery to the utmost of their power, has been found to be the belief of all nations, ancient and modern, of whom we possess information. It has also been the general doctrine of both Jews and Christians, that one of those fallen spirits was the real agent in this first and successful temptation; and this doctrine receives strong confirmation from the declarations of our Lord and his apostles. See 2 Cor. ii. 11; xi. 3, 14; Rev. xii. 9; xx. 2; John viii. 44. The summary of these passages presents almost a history of the Fall—the tempter, his manifold arts, his serpentine disguises, his falsehood, his restless activity, his bloodthirsty cruelty, and his early success in that career of deception and destruction.

The condescending Deity, who had held gracious and instructive communion with the parents of mankind, assuming a human form and adapting all his proceedings to their capacity, visibly stood before them; by a searching interrogatory drew from them the confession of their guilt, which yet they aggravated by evasions and insinuations against God himself; and pronounced on them and their seducer the sentence due. On the woman he inflicted the pains of child-bearing, and a deeper and more humiliating dependence upon her husband. He doomed the man to hard and often fruitless toil, instead of easy and pleasant labour. On both, or rather on human nature universally, he pronounced the awful sentence of death. The denunciation of the serpent partakes more of a symbolical character, and so seems to carry a strong implication of the nature and the wickedness of the concealed agent. The human sufferings threatened are all, excepting the last, which will require a separate consideration, of a remedial and corrective kind.

Of a quite different character are the penal denunciations upon the serpent. If they be understood literally, and of course applied to the whole order of Ophidia, they will be found to be so flagrantly at variance with the most demonstrated facts in their physiology and economy, as to lead to inferences unfavourable to belief in revelation. Let us examine the particulars:—

'Because thou hast done this cursed art thou

above all cattle;' literally, 'above every *behe-mah.*' But *the serpent tribe cannot be classed* with that of the *behemoth.* The word is of very frequent occurrence in the Old Testament; and though, in a few instances, it seems to be put for brevity so as to be inclusive of the flocks as well as the herds, and in poetical diction it sometimes stands metonymically for *animals* generally (as Job xviii. 3; Ps. lxxiii. 22; Eccles. iii. 18, 19, 21); yet its proper and universal application is to the large animals (pachyderms and ruminants), such as the elephant, camel, deer, horse, ox, rhinoceros, hippopotamus, &c. [BEHEMOTH].

As little will the declaration, 'cursed —,' agree with natural truth. It may, indeed, be supposed to be verified in the shuddering which persons generally feel at the aspect of any one of the order of serpents; but this takes place also in many other cases. It springs from fear of the formidable weapons with which some species are armed, as few persons know beforehand which are venomous and which are harmless; and, after all, this is rather an advantage than a curse to the animal. It is an effectual defence without effort. Indeed, we may say that no tribe of animals is so secure from danger, or is so able to obtain its sustenance and all the enjoyments which its capacity and habits require, as the whole order of serpents. If, then, we decline to urge the objection from the word *behemah*, it is difficult to conceive that serpents have more causes of suffering than any other great division of animals, or even so much.

Further, 'going upon the belly' is to none of them a punishment. With some differences of mode, their progression is produced by the pushing of scales, shields, or rings against the ground, by muscular contractions and dilatations, by elastic springings, by vertical undulations, or by horizontal wrigglings; but, in every variety, the *entire organization*—skeleton, muscles, nerves, integuments—is *adapted* to the mode of progression belonging to each species. That mode, in every variety of it, is sufficiently easy and rapid (often very rapid) for all the purposes of the animal's life and the amplitude of its enjoyments. To imagine this mode of motion to be, in any sense, a change from a prior attitude and habit of the erect kind, or being furnished with wings, indicates a perfect ignorance of the anatomy of serpents. Yet it has been said by learned and eminent theological interpreters, that, before this crime was committed, the serpent probably did 'not go upon his belly, but moved upon the hinder part of his body, with his head, breast, and belly upright' (Clarke's *Bible,* p. 1690). This notion may have obtained credence from the fact that some of the numerous serpent species, when excited, raise the neck pretty high; but the posture is to strike, and they cannot maintain it in creeping except for a very short distance.

Neither do they 'eat dust.' All serpents are carnivorous; their food, according to the size and power of the species, is taken from the tribes of insects, worms, frogs, and toads, and newts, birds, mice, and other small quadrupeds, till the scale ascends to the pythons and boas, which can master and swallow very large animals. The excellent writer just cited, in his anxiety to do honour, as he deemed it, to the accuracy of Scripture allusions, has said of the serpent, 'Now that he creeps with his very mouth upon the earth, he must necessarily take his food out of the dust, and so lick in some of the dust with it.' But this is not the fact. Serpents habitually obtain their food among herbage or in water; they seize their prey with the mouth, often elevate the head, and are no more exposed to the necessity of swallowing adherent earth than are carnivorous birds or quadrupeds. At the same time, it may be understood figuratively. '*Eating the dust* is but another term for grovelling in the dust; and this is equivalent to being reduced to a condition of meanness, shame, and contempt.— See Micah vii. 17.'

But these and other inconsistencies and difficulties (insuperable they do indeed appear to us) are swept away when we consider the fact before stated, that the Hebrew, literally rendered, is THE *serpent was*, &c., and that it refers specifically and personally to a rational and accountable being, *the spirit of lying and cruelty, the devil, the Satan, the old serpent.* That God, the infinitely holy, good, and wise, should have permitted any one or more celestial spirits to apostatize from purity, and to be the successful seducers of mankind, is indeed an awful and overwhelming mystery. But it is not more so than the permitted existence of many among mankind, whose rare talents and extraordinary command of power and opportunity, combined with extreme depravity, have rendered them the plague and curse of the earth; and the whole merges into the awful and insolvable problem, Why has the All-perfect Deity permitted evil at all? We are firmly assured that He will bring forth, at last, the most triumphant evidence that 'He is righteous in all his ways, and holy in all his works.' In the mean time, our happiness lies in the implicit confidence which we cannot but feel to be due to the Being of Infinite Perfection.

The remaining part of the denunciation upon the false and cruel seducer sent a beam of light into the agonized hearts of our guilty first parents: 'And enmity will I put between thee and the woman, and between thy seed and her seed: he will attack thee [on] the head, and thou wilt attack him [at] the heel.' Christian interpreters generally regard this as the first gospel-promise, and we think with good reason. It was a manifestation of mercy: it revealed a Deliverer, who 'should be a human being, in a peculiar sense the offspring of the female, who should also, in some way not yet made known, counteract and remedy the injury inflicted, and who, though partially suffering from the malignant power, should, in the end, completely conquer it, and convert its very success into its own punishment' (J. Pye Smith, *Scripture Testimony to the Messiah*, vol. i. p. 226).

The awful threatening to man was, 'In the day that thou eatest of it, thou wilt die the death.' The infliction is *Death* in the most comprehensive sense, that which stands opposed to *Life*, the life of not only animal enjoyment, but holy happiness, the life which comported with the image of God. This was lost by the fall; and the sentence of physical death was pronounced, to be executed in due time. Divine mercy gave a long respite.

The same mercy was displayed in still more tempering the terrors of justice. The garden of delights was not to be the abode of rebellious creatures. But before they were turned out into a bleak and dreary wilderness, God was pleased to direct them to make clothing suitable to their new and degraded condition, of the skins of animals. That those animals had been offered in sacrifice is a conjecture supported by so much probable evidence, that we may regard it as a well-established truth. Any attempt to force back the way, to gain anew the tree of life, and take violent or fraudulent possession, would have been equally impious and nugatory. The sacrifice (which all approximative argument obliges us to admit), united with the promise of a deliverer, and the promise of substantial clothing, contained much hope of pardon and grace. The terrible debarring by lightning flashes and their consequent thunder, and by visible supernatural agency (Gen. iii. 22-24), from a return to the bowers of bliss, are expressed in the characteristic patriarchal style of anthropopathy; but the meaning evidently is, that the fallen creature is unable by any efforts of his own to reinstate himself in the favour of God, and that whatever hope of restoration he may be allowed to cherish must spring solely from free benevolence. Thus, in laying the first stone of the temple, which shall be an immortal habitation of the Divine glory, it was manifested that ' Salvation is of the Lord,' and that ' grace reigneth through righteousness unto eternal life.'

From this time we have little recorded of the lives of Adam and Eve. Their three sons are mentioned with important circumstances in connection with each of them. See the articles CAIN, ABEL, and SETH. Cain was probably born in the year after the fall; Abel, possibly some years later; Seth, certainly one hundred and thirty years from the creation of his parents. After that, Adam lived eight hundred years, and had sons and daughters, doubtless by Eve, and then he died, nine hundred and thirty years old. In that prodigious period many events, and those of great importance, must have occurred; but the wise providence of God has not seen fit to preserve to us any memorial of them, and scarcely any vestiges or hints are afforded of the occupations and mode of life of men through the antediluvian period [ANTEDILUVIANS].

2. ADAM, a city at some distance east from the Jordan, to which, or beyond which, the overflow of the waters of that river extended when the course of the stream to the Dead Sea was stayed to afford the Israelites a passage across its channel.

AD'AMAH. [ADMAH.]

ADAMANT. The word thus rendered is, in Hebrew, SHAMIR. It occurs in Jer. xvii. 1; Ezek. iii. 9; Zech. vii. 12. The Sept. in Jer. xvii. 1, and the Vulgate in all these passages, take it for the diamond. The signification of the word, ' a sharp point,' countenances this interpretation, the diamond being for its hardness used in perforating and cutting other minerals. Indeed, this use of the *shamir* is distinctly alluded to in Jer. xvii. 1, where the *stylus* pointed with it is distinguished from one of iron. The two other passages also favour this view by using it figuratively to express the hardness and

obduracy of the Israelites. Our Authorized Version has ' diamond ' in Jer. xvii. 1, and ' adamant ' in the other texts: but in the original the word is the same in all. Bochart, however, rejects the usual explanation, and conceives it to mean ' emery.' This is a calcined iron mixed with siliceous earth, occurring in livid scales of such hardness that in ancient times, as at present, it was used for polishing and engraving precious stones, diamonds excepted. Rosenmüller urges in favour of this notion that if the Hebrews had been acquainted with the diamond, and with the manner of working it, we should doubtless have found it among the stones of the high-priest's breastplate; and that, as the *shamir* was not one of the stones thus employed, therefore it was not the diamond. But to this it may be answered, that it was perhaps not used because it could not be engraved on, or was possibly not introduced until a later period.

A'DAR (Esth. iii. 7) is the sixth month of the civil and the twelfth of the ecclesiastical year of the Jews. The name was first introduced after the Captivity. The following are the chief days in it which are set apart for commemoration:—The 7th is a fast for the death of Moses (Deut. xxxiv. 5, 6). On the 9th there was a fast in memory of the contention or open rupture of the celebrated schools of Hillel and Shammai, which happened but a few years before the birth of Christ. The 13th is the so-called ' Fast of Esther.' Iken observes (*Antiq. Hebr.* p. 150) that this was not an actual fast, but merely a commemoration of Esther's fast of three days (Esth. iv. 16), and a preparation for the ensuing festival. Nevertheless, as Esther appears, from the date of Haman's edict, and from the course of the narrative, to have fasted in Nisan, Buxtorf adduces from the Rabbins the following account of the name of this fast, and of the foundation of its observance in Adar, that the Jews assembled together on the 13th, in the time of Esther, and that, after the example of Moses, who fasted when the Israelites were about to engage in battle with the Amalekites, they devoted that day to fasting and prayer, in preparation for the perilous trial which awaited them on the morrow. In this sense, this fast would stand in the most direct relation to the feast of Purim. The 13th was also, ' by a common decree,' appointed as a festival in memory of the death of Nicanor (2 Macc. xv. 36). The 14th and 15th were devoted to the feast of Purim (Esth. ix. 21). In case the year was an intercalary one, when the month of Adar occurred twice, this feast was first moderately observed in the intercalary Adar, and then celebrated with full splendour in the ensuing Adar. The former of these two celebrations was then called the *lesser*, and the latter the *great Purim*.

ADA'SA, or ADARSA, called also by Josephus ADAZER, ADACO, and ACODACO, a city in the tribe of Ephraim, said to have been four miles from Beth-horon, and not far from Gophna. It was the scene of some important transactions in the history of the Maccabees (1 Mac. vii. 40, 45; Joseph. *Antiq.* xii. 10. 5; *Bell. Jud.* i. 1).

ADB'EEL, one of the twelve sons of Ishmael, and founder of an Arabian tribe (Gen. xxv. 13, 16).

ADDER, the English name of a kind of serpent. It occurs several times in the English version of the Bible, and is there used not for a particular species, but generally for several of this dangerous class of reptiles. We have before us a list, far from complete, of the erpetology of Palestine, Arabia, and Egypt, in which there are, among forty-three species indicated, about eight whose bite is accompanied with a venomous effusion, and therefore almost all very dangerous. In our present state of knowledge we deem it best to discuss, under the words SERPENT and VIPER, all the Hebrew names not noticed in this article, and to refer to them those occurring in our version under the appellations of ' asp,' ' cockatrice,' &c.; and likewise to review the allusions to colossal boas and pythons, and, finally, to notice water-snakes and mumræne, which translators and biblical naturalists have totally overlooked, although they must exist in the lakes of the Delta, are abundant on the north coast of Africa, and often exceed eight feet in length.

In this place we shall retain that genus alone which Laurenti and Cuvier have established upon characters distinguished from the innocuous coluber, and the venomous vipera, and denominated *naja*.

The genus Naja—Haridi (?) of Savary—is distinguished by a plaited head, large, very venomous fangs, a neck dilatable under excitement, which raises the ribs of the anterior part of the body into the form of a disk or hood, when the scales, usually not imbricated, but lying in juxta-position, are separated, and expose the skin, which at that time displays bright iridescent gleams, contrasting highly with their brown, yellow, and bluish colours. The species attain at least an equal, if not a superior, size to the generality of the genus viper; are more massive in their structure; and some possess the faculty of self-inflation to triple their diameter, gradually forcing the body upwards into an erect position, until, by a convulsive crisis, they are said suddenly to strike backwards at an enemy or a pursuer. With such powers of destroying animal life, and with an aspect at once terrible and resplendent, it may be easily imagined how soon fear and superstition would

5.
Naja Haje; and the form of Cneph from the Egyptian Monuments.

6.
Naja Tripudians and Cobra di Capello; or, Hooded and Spectacled Snakes.

combine, at periods anterior to historical data, to raise these monsters into divinities, and endeavour to deprecate their wrath by the blandishments of worship; and how design and cupidity would teach these very votaries the manner of subduing their ferocity, of extracting their instruments of mischief, and making them subservient to the wonder and amusement of the vulgar, by using certain cadences of sound which affect their hearing, and exciting in them a desire to perform a kind of pleasurable movements that may be compared to dancing. Hence the *naças* of the East, the *hag-worms* of the West, and the *haje*, have all been deified, styled agathodæmon or good spirit; and figures of them occur wherever the superstition of Pagan antiquitiy has been accompanied by the arts of civilization.

The most prominent species of the genus at present is the *naja tripudians, cobra di capello*, hooded or spectacled snake of India, venerated by the natives; even by the serpent-charmers styled the good serpent to this day, and yet so ferocious that it is one of the very few that will attack a man when surprised in its haunt, although it may be gorged with prey. This species is usually marked on the nape with two round spots, transversely connected in the form of a pair of spectacles; but among several varieties, one, perhaps distinct, is without the marks, and has a glossy golden hood, which may make it identical with the *naja haje* of Egypt, the undoubted Ihh-nuphi, ceneph, or agathodæmon of Ancient Egypt, and accurately represented on the walls of its temples, in almost innumerable instances, both in form and colour. This serpent also inflates the skin on the neck, not in the expanded form of a hood, but rather into an intumefaction of the neck. As in the former, there is no marked difference of appearance between the sexes; but the psilli, or charmers, by a particular pressure on the neck have the power of rendering the inflation of the animal, already noticed as a character of the genus, so intense, that the serpent becomes rigid, and can be held out horizontally as if it were a rod.

This practice explains what the soothsayers of Pharaoh could perform when they were opposing Moses. That the rods of the magicians of Pharaoh were of the same external character with the rod of Aaron, is evident from no different denomination being given to them: therefore we may infer that they used a real serpent as a rod—namely the species now called *haje*—for their imposture; since they no doubt did what the present serpent-charmers perform with the same species, by means of the temporary *asphyxiation*, or suspension of vitality, before noticed, and producing restoration to active life by liberating or throwing down. Thus we have the miraculous character of the prophet's mission shown by his real rod becoming a serpent, and the magicians' real serpents merely assuming the form of rods; and when both were opposed in a state of animated existence, by the rod devouring the living animals, conquering the great typical personification of the protecting divinity of Egypt.

This species of serpent may be regarded as extending to India and Ceylon; and probably the *naja tripudians* is likewise an inhabitant of Arabia, if not of Egypt, although the assertion of the fact (common in authors) does not exclude a supposition that they take the two species to be only one. We are disposed to refer the 'winged' or 'flying' serpent to the *naja tripudians*, in one of its varieties, because—with its hood dilated into a kind of shining wings on each side of the neck, standing, in undulating motion, one-half or more erect, rigid, and fierce in attack, and deadly poisonous, yet still denominated 'good spirit,' and in Egypt ever figured in combination with the winged globe—it well may have received the name of *saraph, swallowing* or *devouring*, and may thus meet all the valid objections, and conciliate seemingly opposite comments (see Num. xxi. 6, 8; Deut. viii. 15; Isa. xiv. 29; xxx. 6).

ACHSUB is another name of a serpent which may be considered as specifically different from the former, though it is most probably one more of this group of terrible creatures. The root of the name implies bending back, recurving, but not coiling up, for all snakes have that faculty. The syllable *ach*, however, shows a connection with the former denominations; and both are perfectly reconcilable with a serpent very common at the Cape of Good Hope, not unfrequent in Western Africa, and probably extending over that whole continent, excepting perhaps Morocco. It is the 'poff-adder' of the Dutch colonists, about three feet in length, and about six inches in circumference at the middle of the body; the head is larger than is usual in serpents; the eyes are large, and very brilliant; the back beautifully marked in half circles, and the colours black, bright yellow, and dark brown; the belly yellow; the appearance at all times, but chiefly when excited, extremely brilliant; the upper jaw greatly protruding, somewhat like what occurs in the shark, places the mouth back towards the throat, and this structure is said to be connected with the practice of the animal when intending to bite, to swell its skin till it suddenly rises up, and strikes backwards as if it fell over. It is this faculty which appears to be indicated by the Hebrew name *achsub*, and therefore we

believe it to refer to that species, or to one nearly allied to it. The Dutch name (poff-adder, or spooch-adder) shows that, in the act of swelling, remarkable eructations and spittings take place, all which no doubt are so many warnings, the bite being fatal. The poff-adder usually resides among brushwood in stony places and rocks, is fond of basking in the sun, rather slow in moving, and is by nature timid [SERPENT; VIPER].

AD'DON, one of several places mentioned in Neh. vii. 61, being towns in the land of captivity, from which those who returned to Palestine were unable to 'shew their father's house, or their seed, whether they were of Israel.' This, probably, means that they were unable to furnish such undeniable legal proof as was required in such cases. And this is in some degree explained by the subsequent (v. 63) mention of priests who were expelled the priesthood because their descent was not found to be genealogically registered. These instances show the importance which was attached to their genealogies by the Jews [GENEALOGY].

ADIABE'NE, the principal of the six provinces into which Assyria was divided. Pliny and Ammianus comprehend the whole of Assyria under this name, which, however, properly denoted only the province which was watered by the rivers Diab and Adiab, or the Great and Little Zab (Dhab), which flow into the Tigris below Nineveh (Mosul), from the north-east. This region is not mentioned in Scripture; but in Josephus, its queen Helena and her son Izates, who became converts to Judaism, are very often named (Joseph. *Antiq.* xx. 2, 4; *Bell. Jud.* ii. 16, 19; v. 4, 6, 11).

AD'IDA, a fortified town in the tribe of Judah. In 1 Macc. xii. 38, we read that Simon Maccabæus set up 'Adida in Saphela, and made it strong with bolts and bars.' Eusebius says that Sephela was the name given in his time to the open country about Eleutheropolis. And this Adida in Sephela is probably the same which is mentioned in the next chapter (xiii. 13) as 'Adida over against the plain,' where Simon Maccabæus encamped to dispute the entrance into Judæa of Tryphon, who had treacherously seized on Jonathan at Ptolemais. In the parallel passage Josephus (*Antiq.* xiii. 6, 5) adds that this Adida was upon a hill, before which lay the plains of Judæa. One of the places which Josephus calls Adida (*Bell. Jud.* iv. 9, 1) appears to have been near the Jordan, and was probably the Hadid of Ezra ii. 33.

ADJURATION. This is a solemn act or appeal, whereby one man, usually a person vested with natural or official authority, imposes upon another the obligation of speaking or acting as if under the solemnity of an oath. We have an example of this in the New Testament, when the high-priest thus calls upon Christ, 'I adjure thee by the living God, tell us' &c.—(Matt. xxvi. 63; see also Mark v. 7; Acts xix. 13; 1 Thes. v. 27). An oath, although thus imposed upon one without his consent, was not only binding, but solemn in the highest degree; and when connected with a question, an answer was compulsory, which answer being as upon oath, any falsehood in it would be perjury. Thus our Saviour, who had previously disdained to reply to the charges brought against him, now felt himself bound to answer the question put to him.

AD'MAH, one of the cities in the vale of Siddim (Gen. x. 19), which had a king of its own (Gen. xiv. 2). It was destroyed along with Sodom and Gomorrah (Gen. xix. 24; Hos. xi. 8).

ADONIBE'ZEK (*lord of Bezek*), king or lord of Bezek, a town which Eusebius places 17 miles east of Neapolis or Shechem. The small extent of the kingdoms in and around Palestine at the time of its invasion by the Hebrews is shown by the fact that this petty king had subdued no less than seventy of them; and the barbarity of the war-usages in those early times is painfully shown by his cutting off all the thumbs and great toes of his prisoners, and allowing them no food but that which they gathered under his table. These conquests made Adonibezek ' a triton among the minnows;' and we find him at the head of the confederated Canaanites and Perizzites, against whom the tribes of Judah and Simeon marched after the death of Joshua. His army was routed and himself taken prisoner. The victors failed not to express their indignation at the mode in which he had treated his captives, by dealing with him in the same manner.

ADONI'JAH (*Jehovah* [*is*] *my Lord*), the fourth son of David, by Haggith. He was born after his father became king, but when he reigned over Judah only (2 Sam. iii. 4). According to the Oriental notion developed in the article ABSALOM, Adonijah might have considered his claim superior to that of his eldest brother Amnon, who is supposed to have been born while his father was in a private station; but not to that of Absalom, who was not only his elder brother, and born while his father was a king, but was of royal descent on the side of his mother. When, however, Amnon and Absalom were both dead, he became, by order of birth, the heir-apparent to the throne. But this order had been set aside in favour of Solomon, who was born while his father was king of all Israel. Absalom perished in attempting to assert his claim of primogeniture, in opposition to this arrangement. Unawed by this example, Adonijah assumed the state of an heir-apparent, who, from the advanced age of David, must soon be king. But it does not appear to have been his wish to trouble his father as Absalom had done; for he waited till David appeared at the point of death, when he called around him a number of influential men, whom he had previously gained over, and caused himself to be proclaimed king. This was a formidable attempt to subvert the appointment made by the Divine king of Israel; for Adonijah was supported by such men as Joab, the general-in-chief, and Abiathar, the high-priest; both of whom had followed David in all his fortunes. But his plot was, notwithstanding, defeated by the prompt measure taken by David, who directed Solomon to be at once proclaimed, and crowned, and admitted to the real exercise of the sovereign power. Adonijah then saw that all was lost, and fled to the altar, which he refused to leave without a promise of pardon from King Solomon. This he received, but was warned that any further attempt of the same kind would be fatal to him. Accordingly, when, some time

after the death of David, Adonijah covertly endeavoured to reproduce his claim through a marriage with Abishag, the virgin widow of his father [ABISHAG], his design was at once penetrated by the king, by whose order he was instantly put to death (1 Kings i.-ii. 13-25).

ADONI'RAM (*lord of height*, that is, *high lord*) (1 Kings iv. 6). This name is exhibited in the contracted form of ADORAM in 2 Sam. xx. 24; 1 Kings xii. 18; and of Hadoram in 2 Chron. x. 18.

1. ADONIRAM, or HADORAM, son of Toi, king of Hamath, who was sent by his father to congratulate David on his victory over their common enemy Hadarezer, king of Syria (1 Chron. xviii. 10). This prince is called Joram in 2 Sam. viii. 10.

2. ADONIRAM. A person of this name is mentioned as receiver-general of the imposts in the reigns of David, Solomon, and Rehoboam. Only one incident is recorded in connection with this person. When the ten tribes seceded from the house of David, and made Jeroboam king, Rehoboam sent Adoniram among them, for the purpose, we may presume, of collecting the usual imposts, which had become very heavy. Perhaps he had been rigid in his invidious office under Solomon: at all events the collector of the imposts which had occasioned the revolt was not the person whose presence was the most likely to soothe the exasperated passions of the people. They rose upon him, and stoned him till he died (1 Kings xii. 18).

ADONIZE'DEK. The name denotes *lord of justice*, i. e. *just lord*, but some would rather have it to mean *king of Zedek*. He was the Canaanitish king of Jerusalem when the Israelites invaded Palestine; and the similarity of the name to that of a more ancient king of (as is supposed) the same place, Melchi-zedek (*king of justice*, or *king of Zedek*), has suggested that Zedek was one of the ancient names of Jerusalem. Be that as it may, this Adonizedek was the first of the native princes that attempted to make head against the invaders. After Jericho and Ai were taken, and the Gibeonites had succeeded in forming a treaty with the Israelites, Adonizedek was the first to rouse himself from the stupor which had fallen on the Canaanites (Josh. x. 1, 3), and he induced the other Amoritish kings of Hebron, Jarmuth, Lachish, and Eglon, to join him in a confederacy against the enemy. They did not, however, march directly against the invaders, but went and besieged the Gibeonites, to punish them for the discouraging example which their secession from the common cause had afforded. Joshua no sooner heard of this than he marched all night from Gilgal to the relief of his allies; and falling unexpectedly upon the besiegers, soon put them to utter rout. The pursuit was long, and was signalized by Joshua's famous command to the sun and moon, as well as by a tremendous hail-storm, which greatly distressed the fugitive Amorites [JOSHUA]. The five kings took refuge in a cave; but were observed, and by Joshua's order the mouth of it was closed with large stones, and a guard set over it, until the pursuit was over. When the pursuers returned, the cave was opened, and the five kings brought out. The Hebrew chiefs then set their feet upon the necks of the prostrate

D

monarchs—an ancient mark of triumph, of which the monuments of Persia and Egypt still afford illustrations. They were then slain, and their bodies hanged on trees until the evening, when, as the law forbade a longer exposure of the dead (Deut. xxi. 23), they were taken down, and cast into the cave, the mouth of which was filled up with large stones, which remained long after (Josh. x. 1-27). The severe treatment of these kings by Joshua has been censured and defended with equal disregard of the real circumstances, which are, that the war was avowedly one of extermination, no quarter being given or expected on either side: and that the war-usages of the Jews were neither worse nor better than those of the people with whom they fought, who would most certainly have treated Joshua and the other Hebrew chiefs in the same manner, had they fallen into their hands.

ADOPTION. The Old Testament does not contain any word equivalent to this; but the act occurs in various forms. The New Testament has the word often (Rom. viii. 15, 23; ix. 4; Gal. iv. 5; Eph. i. 5); but no example of the act occurs. The term signifies the *placing as a son* of one who is not so by birth.

The practice of adoption had its origin in the desire for male offspring among those who have, in the ordinary course, been denied that blessing, or have been deprived of it by circumstances. This feeling is common to our nature; but its operation is less marked in those countries where the equalizing influences of high civilization lessen the peculiar privileges of the paternal character, and where the security and the well-observed laws by which estates descend and property is transmitted, withdraw one of the principal inducements to the practice. And thus most of the instances in the Bible occur in the patriarchal period. The law of Moses, by settling the relations of families and the rules of descent, and by formally establishing the Levirate law, which in some sort secured a representative posterity even to a man who died without children, appears to have put some check upon this custom. The allusions in the New Testament are mostly to practices of adoption which then existed among the Greeks and Romans, and rather to the latter than to the former; for among the more highly civilized Greeks adoption was less frequent than among the Romans. In the East the practice has always been common, especially among the Semitic races, in whom the love of offspring has at all times been strongly manifested.

It is scarcely necessary to say that adoption was confined to sons. The whole Bible history affords no example of the adoption of a female.

The first instances of adoption which occur in Scripture are less the acts of men than of women, who, being themselves barren, gave their female slaves to their husbands, with the view of adopting the children they might bear. Thus Sarah gave her handmaid Hagar to Abraham; and the son that was born, Ishmael, appears to have been considered as her son as well as Abraham's, until Isaac was born. In like manner Rachel, having no children, gave her handmaid Bilhah to her husband, who had by her Dan and Naphtali (Gen. xxx. 5-9); on which his other wife, Leah, although she had sons of her own, yet fearing that she had left off bearing, claimed the right of giving her handmaid Zilpah to Jacob, that she might thus increase their number; and by this means she had Gad and Asher (Gen. xxx. 9-13). In this way the greatest possible approximation to a natural relation was produced. The child was the son of the husband, and, the mother being the property of the wife, the progeny must be her property also; and the act of more particular appropriation seems to have been that, at the time of birth, the handmaid brought forth her child 'upon the knees of the adoptive mother' (Gen. xxx. 3). A curious fact is elicited by the peculiar circumstances in Sarah's case, which were almost the only circumstances that could have arisen to try the question, whether a mistress retained her power, as such, over a female slave whom she had thus vicariously employed, and over the progeny of that slave, even though by her own husband. The answer is given, rather startlingly, in the affirmative in the words of Sarah, who, when the birth of Isaac had wholly changed her feelings and position, and when she was exasperated by the offensive conduct of Hagar and her son, addressed her husband thus, 'Cast forth *this bondwoman* and her son; for *the son of this bondwoman* shall not be heir with *my son*, even with Isaac' (Gen. xxi. 10).

A previous instance of adoption in the history of Abraham, when as yet he had no children, appears to be discoverable in his saying, 'One born in my house is mine heir.' This unquestionably denotes a house-born slave, as distinguished from one bought with money. Abraham had several such; and the one to whom he is supposed here to refer is his faithful and devoted steward Eliezer. This, therefore, is a case in which a slave was adopted as a son—a practice still very common in the East. A boy is often purchased young, adopted by his master, brought up in his faith, and educated as his son; or if the owner has a daughter, he adopts him through a marriage with that daughter, and the family which springs from this union is counted as descended from him. But house-born slaves are usually preferred, as these have never had any home but their master's house, are considered members of his family, and are generally the most faithful of his adherents. This practice of slave adoption was very common among the Romans; and, as such, is more than once referred to by St. Paul (Rom. viii. 15; Gal. iv. 5-6), the transition from the condition of a slave to that of a son, and the privilege of applying the tender name of 'Father' to the former 'Master,' affording a beautiful illustration of the change which takes place from the bondage of the law to the freedom and privileges of the Christian state.

As in most cases the adopted son was to be considered dead to the family from which he sprung, the separation of natural ties and connections was avoided by this preference of slaves, who were mostly foreigners or of foreign descent. For the same reason the Chinese make their adoptions from children in the hospitals, who have been abandoned by their parents. The Tartars are the only people we know who prefer to adopt their near relatives—nephews or cousins, or, failing them, a Tartar of their own banner. The only Scriptural example of this kind is that in which Jacob adopted his own grandsons Ephraim and Manasseh to be counted as his sons (Gen. xlviii. 6). The object of this remarkable adoption was, that whereas Joseph himself could only have one share of his father's heritage along with his brothers, the adoption of his two sons enabled Jacob, through them, to bestow two portions upon his favourite son. The adoption of Moses by Pharaoh's daughter (Exod. ii. 1-10) is an incident rather than a practice; but it recalls what has just been stated respecting the adoption of outcast children by the Chinese. In 1 Chron. ii. 34, &c., there is an instance recorded of a daughter being married to a free slave, and the children being counted as those of the woman's father. The same chapter gives another instance. Machir (grandson of Joseph) gives his daughter in marriage to Hezron, of the tribe of Judah. She gave birth to Segub, who was the father of Jair. Jair possessed twenty-three cities in the land of Gilead, which came to him in right of his grandmother, the daughter of Machir; and he acquired other towns in the same quarter, which made up his possessions to three-score towns or villages (1 Chron. ii. 21-24; Josh. xiii. 30; 1 Kings iv. 13). Now this Jair, though of the tribe of Judah by his grandfather, is, in Num. xxxii. 41, counted as of Manasseh, for the obvious reason which the comparison of these texts suggests, that, through his grandmother, he inherited the property, and was the lineal representative of Machir, the son of Manasseh.

ADORA′IM, a town in the south of Judah, enumerated along with Hebron and Mareshah, as one of the cities fortified by Rehoboam (2 Chron. xi. 9). This town does not occur in any writer after Josephus, until the recent researches of Dr. Robinson, who discovered it under the name of Dura, the first feeble letter having been dropped. It is situated five miles W. by S. from Hebron, and is a large village, seated on the eastern slope of a cultivated hill, with olive-groves and fields of grain all around. There are no ruins.

ADORATION. This word is compounded of *ad* 'to,' and *os, oris,* 'the mouth,' and literally signifies to apply the hand to the mouth,' that is, 'to kiss the hand.' The *act* is described in Scripture as one of worship (Job xxxi. 26, 27). And this very clearly intimates that kissing the hand was considered an overt act of worship in the East.

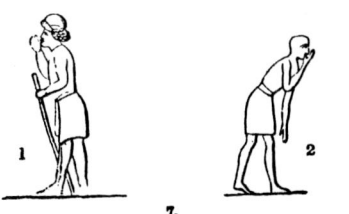

7.

The same act was used as a mark of respect in the presence of kings and persons high in office or station. Or rather, perhaps, the hand was not merely kissed and then withdrawn from the mouth, but held continuously before or upon the mouth, to which allusion is made in such texts as Judg. xviii. 19; Job xxi. 5; xxix. 9; xl. 4; Ps. xxxix. 9. In one of the sculptures at Persepolis a king is seated on his throne, and before him a person standing in a bent posture, with his hand laid upon his mouth as he addresses the sovereign (fig. 1). Exactly the same attitude is observed in the sculptures at Thebes, where one person, among several (in various postures of respect) who appear before the scribes to be registered, has his hand placed thus submissively upon his mouth (fig. 2).

ADRAM′MELECH is mentioned, together with Anammelech, in 2 Kings xvii. 31, as one of the idols whose worship the inhabitants of Sepharvaim established in Samaria, when they were transferred thither by the king of Assyria, and whom they worshipped by the sacrifice of their children by fire. This constitutes the whole of our certain knowledge of this idol.

2. ADRAMMELECH, one of the sons and murderers of Sennacherib, king of Assyria (2 Kings xix. 37; Isa. xxxvii. 38).

ADRAMYT′TIUM, a sea-port town in the province of Mysia in Asia Minor, opposite the isle of Lesbos, and an Athenian colony. It is mentioned in Scripture only, from the fact that the ship in which Paul embarked at Cæsarea as a prisoner on his way to Italy, belonged to Adra-myttium (Acts xxvii. 2). It was rare to find a vessel going direct from Palestine to Italy. The usual course, therefore, was to embark in some ship bound to one of the ports of Asia Minor, and there go on board a vessel sailing for Italy. This was the course taken by the centurion who had charge of Paul. The ship of Adramyttium took them to Myra in Lycia, and here they embarked in an Alexandrian vessel bound for Italy. Adramyttium is still called Adramyt. It is built on a hill, contains about 1000 houses, and is still a place of some commerce.

ADRIATIC SEA (Acts xxvii. 27). This name is now confined to the gulf lying between Italy on one side, and the coasts of Dalmatia and Albania on the other. But in St. Paul's time it extended to all that part of the Mediterranean between Crete and Sicily. This fact is of importance, as relieving us from the necessity of finding the island of Melita on which Paul was shipwrecked, in the *present* Adriatic gulf; and consequently removing the chief difficulty in the way of the identification of that island with the present Malta.

A′DRIEL (*the flock of God*), the person to whom Saul gave in marriage his daughter Merab, who had been originally promised to David (1 Sam. xviii. 19). Five sons sprung from this union, who were taken to make up the number of Saul's descendants, whose lives, on the principle of blood-revenge, were required by the Gibeonites to avenge the cruelties which Saul had exercised towards their race [GIBEONITES].

ADUL′LAM, an old city (Gen. xxxviii. 1, 12, 20) in the plain country of the tribe of Judah (Josh. xv. 35), and one of the royal cities of the Canaanites (Josh. xii. 15). It was one of the towns which Rehoboam fortified (2 Chron. xi. 7; Micah i. 15), and is mentioned after the Captivity (Neh. xi. 30; 2 Macc. 12, 38). It is evident that Adullam was one of the cities of 'the valley,' or plain between the hill country of Judah and the sea; and from its place in the lists of names (especially 2 Chron. xi. 7), it appears not to have been far from the Philistine city of Gath. It is probable, however, that the 'cave of Adullam' (1 Sam. xxii. 1) was not in the vicinity of the city, where no such cave has been found, but in the mountainous wilderness in the west of Judah towards the Dead Sea. This conjecture is favoured by the fact that the usual haunts of David were in this quarter; whence he moved into the land of Moab, which was quite contiguous, whereas he must have crossed the whole breadth of the land, if the cave of Adullam had been near the city of that name. The particular cave, usually pointed out as 'the cave of Adullam,' is about six miles south-west of Bethlehem, in the side of a deep ravine which passes below the Frank's mountain on the south. It is an immense natural cavern, with numerous passages, the mouth of which can be approached only on foot along the side of the cliff. It seems probable that David, as a native of Bethlehem, must have been well acquainted with this remarkable spot, and had probably often availed himself of its shelter when out with his father's flocks. It would therefore naturally occur to him as a place of refuge when he fled from Gath; and his purpose of forming a band of followers was much more likely to be realized here, in the neighbourhood of his native place, than in the westward plain, where the *city* of Adullam lay.

ADULTERY. In the common acceptation of the word, adultery denotes the sexual intercourse of a married woman with any other man than her husband, or of a married man with any other woman than his wife. But the crime is not understood in this extent among Eastern nations, nor was it so understood by the Jews. With them, adultery was the act whereby any married man was exposed to the risk of having a spurious offspring imposed upon him. An adulterer was, therefore, any man who had illicit intercourse with a married or betrothed woman; and an adulteress was a betrothed or married woman who had intercourse with any other man than her husband. An intercourse between a married man and an unmarried woman was not, as with us, deemed adultery, but fornication; a great sin, but not, like adultery, involving the contingency of polluting a descent, of turning aside an inheritance, or of imposing upon a man a charge which did not belong to him. Adultery was thus considered a great social wrong, against which society protected itself by much severer penalties than attended an unchaste act not involving the same contingencies.

It will be seen that this Oriental limitation of adultery is intimately connected with the existence of polygamy. If adultery be defined as a breach of the marriage covenant, then, where the contract is between one man and one woman, as in Christian countries, the man as much as the woman infringes the covenant, or commits adultery, by *every* act of intercourse with any other woman: but where polygamy is allowed, where the husband may marry other wives, and take to himself concubines and slaves, the marriage contract cannot and does not convey to the woman a legal title that the man should belong to her alone. If, therefore, a Jew associated

with a woman who was not his wife, his concubine, or his slave, he was guilty of unchastity, but committed no offence which gave a wife reason to complain that her legal rights had been infringed. If, however, the woman with whom he associated was the wife of another, he was guilty of adultery, not by infringing his own marriage covenant, but by causing a breach of that which existed between that woman and her husband. By thus excluding from the name and punishment of adultery the offence which did *not* involve the enormous wrong of imposing upon a man a supposititious offspring, in a nation where the succession to landed property went entirely by birth, so that a father could not by his testament alienate it from any one who was regarded as his son—the law was enabled, with less severity than if the inferior offence had been included, to punish the crime with death. It is still so punished wherever the practice of polygamy has similarly operated in limiting the crime—not, perhaps, that the law expressly assigns that punishment, but it recognises the right of the injured party to inflict it, and, in fact, leaves it, in a great degree, in his hands. Now death was the punishment of adultery before the time of Moses; and if he had assigned a less punishment, his law would have been inoperative, for private vengeance, sanctioned by usage, would still have inflicted death. But by adopting it into the law, those restrictions were imposed upon its operation which necessarily arise when the calm inquiry of public justice is substituted for the impulsive action of excited hands. Thus, death would be less frequently inflicted; and that this effect followed seems to be implied in the fact that the whole biblical history offers no example of capital punishment for the crime. Eventually, divorce superseded all other punishment.

It seems that the Roman law made the same important distinction with the Hebrew, between the infidelity of the husband and of the wife. 'Adultery' was defined by the civilians to be the violation of another man's bed, so that the infidelity of the husband to his own wife could not alone constitute the offence.

It is understood that the crime was punished among the Assyrians and Chaldeans by cutting off the nose and the ears; and this brings to mind the passage in which the prophet Ezekiel (xxiii. 25), after, in the name of the Lord, reproving Israel and Judah for their adulteries (*i.e.* idolatries) with the Assyrians and Chaldeans, threatens the punishment, ' they shall take away thy nose and thy ears.' One or both of these mutilations, most generally that of the nose, were also inflicted by other nations, as the Persians and Egyptians, and even the Romans; but we suspect that among the former, as with the latter, it was less a judicial punishment than a summary infliction by the aggrieved party. It would also seem that these mutilations were more usually inflicted on the male than the female adulterer. In Egypt, however, cutting off the nose was the female punishment, and the man was beaten terribly with rods. The respect with which the conjugal union was treated in that country in the earliest times is manifested in the history of Abraham (Gen. xii. 19).

ADULTERY, TRIAL OF. It would be

unjust to the spirit of the Mosaical legislation to suppose that the trial of the suspected wife by the bitter water, called the *Water of Jealousy*, was by it first produced. It is to be regarded as an attempt to mitigate the evils of, and to bring under legal control, an old custom which could not be entirely abrogated.

The original usage, which it was designed to mitigate, was probably of the kind which we still find in Western Africa, where, when a party is accused of murder, adultery, or witchcraft, if he denies the crime, he is required to drink the red water, and on refusing is deemed guilty of the offence. But in Africa the drink is highly poisonous in itself, and, if rightly prepared, the only chance of escape is the rejection of it by the stomach, whereas, among the Hebrews, the 'water of jealousy,' however unpleasant, was prepared in a prescribed manner with ingredients known to all to be perfectly innocent. It could not therefore injure the innocent, and its action upon the guilty must have resulted, not from the effects of the drink itself, but from the consciousness of having committed a horrible perjury. As regulated, then, by the law of Moses, the trial for suspected adultery by the bitter water amounted to this, that a woman suspected of adultery by her husband was allowed to repel the charge by a public oath of purgation, which oath was designedly made so solemn in itself, and was attended by such awful circumstances, that it was in the highest degree unlikely that it would be dared by any woman not supported by the consciousness of innocence. And the fact that no instance of the actual application of the ordeal occurs in Scripture, affords some countenance to the assertion of the Jewish writers, that the trial was so much dreaded by the women, that those who were really guilty generally avoided it by confession; and that thus the trial itself early fell into disuse. And if, as we have supposed, this mode of trial was only *tolerated* by Moses, the ultimate neglect of it must have been desired and intended by him. In later times, indeed, it was disputed in the Jewish schools, whether the husband was bound to prosecute his wife to this extremity, or whether it was not lawful for him to connive at and pardon her act, if he were so inclined. There were some who held that he was bound by his duty to prosecute, while others maintained that it was left to his pleasure.

From the same source we learn that this form of trial was finally abrogated about forty years before the destruction of Jerusalem. The reason assigned is, that the men themselves were at that time generally adulterous; and that God would not fulfil the imprecations of the ordeal oath upon the wife while the husband was guilty of the same crime (John viii. 1-8).

ADULTERY, in the symbolical language of the Old Testament, means idolatry and apostacy from the worship of the true God (Jer. iii. 8, 9; Ezek. xvi. 32; xxiii. 37; also Rev. ii. 22). Hence an *Adulteress* meant an apostate church or city, particularly 'the daughter of Jerusalem,' or the Jewish church and people (Isa. i. 21; Jer. iii. 6, 8, 9; Ezek. xvi. 22; xxiii. 7). This figure resulted from the primary one, which describes the connection between God and his separated people as a marriage between him and them.

By an application of the same figure, 'An adulterous generation' (Matt. xii. 39; xvi. 4; Mark vii. 38) means a faithless and impious generation.

ADUM'MIM, a place which is only twice named in Scripture. Once (Josh. xv. 7), where, from the context, it seems to indicate the border between Judah and Benjamin, and that it was an ascending road between Gilgal (and also Jericho) and Jerusalem. The second notice (Josh. xviii. 17) adds no further information, but repeats ' *the ascent to* Adummim.' Most commentators take the name to mean *the place of blood*, and follow Jerome, who finds the place in the dangerous or mountainous part of the road between Jerusalem and Jericho, and supposes that it was so called from the frequent effusion of blood by the robbers, by whom it was much infested. These are curious interpretations of the original word, which merely denotes the *redness* of the soil or rock. However, as a difficult pass in a desolate rocky region, between important cities, the part of the road indicated by Jerome, and all after him, was as likely to be infested by robbers in earlier times as in those of Jerome and at the present day. Indeed, the character of the road was so notorious, that Christ lays the scene of the parable of the good Samaritan (Luke x.) upon it; and Jerome informs us that Adummim or Adommim was believed to be the place where the traveller (taken as a real person) 'fell among thieves.' He adds that a fort and garrison was maintained here for the safeguard of travellers. The travellers of the present century mention the spot and neighbourhood nearly in the same terms as those of older date. They all represent the road as still infested by robbers, from whom some of them have not escaped without danger. The place thus indicated is about eight miles from Jerusalem, and four from Jericho.

ADVOCATE, one who pleads the cause of another; also one who exhorts, defends, comforts, prays for another. It is an appellation given to the Holy Spirit by Christ (John xiv. 16; xv. 26; xvi. 7), and to Christ himself by an apostle (1 John ii. 1; see also Rom. viii. 34; Heb. vii. 25).

In the forensic sense, advocates or pleaders were not known to the Jews until they came under the dominion of the Romans, and were obliged to transact their law affairs after the Roman manner. Being then little conversant with the Roman laws, and with the forms of the jurists, it was necessary for them, in pleading a cause before the Roman magistrates, to obtain the assistance of a Roman lawyer or *advocate*, who was well versed in the Greek and Latin languages. In all the Roman provinces such men were found, who devoted their time and labour to the pleading of causes and the transacting of other legal business in the provincial courts. It also appears that many Roman youths who had devoted themselves to forensic business used to repair to the provinces with the consuls and prætors, in order, by managing the causes of the provincials, to fit themselves for more important ones at Rome. Such an advocate was Tertullus, whom the Jews employed to accuse Paul before Felix (Acts xxiv. 1) [ACCUSER].

ÆGYPT. [EGYPT.]

Æ'NON, *fountain;* the name of a place near Salem, where John baptized (John iii. 23); the reason given, 'because there was much water there,' would suggest that he baptized at the springs from which the place took its name.

ÆTHIO'PIA. [ETHIOPIA.]

AFFINITY is relationship by marriage, as distinguished from *consanguinity,* which is relationship by blood. Marriages between persons thus related, in various degrees, were forbidden by the law of Moses, which previous usage, in different conditions of society, had allowed. These degrees are enumerated in Lev. xviii. 7, *sq.* The examples before the law are those of Cain and Abel, who, as the necessity of the case required, married their own sisters. Abraham married Sarah, the daughter of his father by another wife, or else, as some suppose, the daughter of his elder brother by a former wife of his father. Jacob also married the two sisters Leah and Rachel. In the first instance, and even in the second, there was an obvious consanguinity, and only the last offered a previous relationship of affinity merely. So also, in the prohibition of the law, a consanguinity can be traced in what are usually set down as degrees of affinity merely. The degrees of real affinity interdicted are, that a man shall not (nor a woman in the corresponding relations) marry his—1. Father's widow (not his own mother); 2. The daughter of his father's wife by another husband; 3. The widow of his paternal uncle; 4. Nor his brother's widow if he has left children by her; but, if not, he was bound to marry her to raise up children to his deceased brother. The other prohibitions are connected with the condition of polygamy, and they prohibited a man from having—1. a mother and her daughter for wives at the same time; 2. or two sisters for wives at the same time. These prohibitions, although founded in Oriental notions, adapted to a *particular* condition of society, and connected with the peculiarities of the Levitical marriage law, have been imported wholesale into our canon law. The fitness of this is doubted by many: but as, apart from any moral questions, the prohibited marriages are such as few would, in the present condition of European society, desire to contract, and such as would be deemed repugnant to good taste and correct manners, there is little real matter of regret in this adoption of the Levitical law. Indeed, the objections to this adoption have rested chiefly upon one point; and that happens to be a point in which the law itself appears to have been egregiously misunderstood. This is in the injunction which, under permitted polygamy, forbade a man to have two sisters at once; an injunction which has been construed, under the Christian law, which allows but one wife, to apply equally to the case of a man marrying the sister of a deceased wife. The law itself is, however, so plain, that it is difficult to conceive how its true object—concerning which nearly all commentators are agreed—could have been thus interpreted. It is rendered in our version, 'Neither shalt thou take a wife to her sister, to vex her (or rather, perhaps, to rival her), to uncover her nakedness, *beside the other in her lifetime.*' And the design seems evidently to be to prevent the occurrence of such unseemly jealousies and contentions between sister-wives as embittered the life of Jacob—the father of the twelve tribes. The more recondite sense has been extracted, with rather ungentle violence to the principles of Hebrew construction, by making 'vex her' the antecedent of 'in her lifetime,' instead of 'take her sister to her, in her lifetime.' And it is explained, under this view, that the married sister should not be 'vexed' in her lifetime by the prospect that her sister might succeed her. It may be safely said that such an idea would never have occurred in the East, where unmarried sisters are far more rarely than in Europe brought into such acquaintance with the husband of the married sister as to give occasion for such 'vexation' or 'rivalry' as this. This view of the matter, though completely exploded among real biblical critics, is perhaps not calculated to do much harm, except under peculiar circumstances, and except as it may prove a snare to some sincere but weak consciences.

AFFIRMATIVES. Among the Jews the formula of assent or affirmation was *thou hast said,* or *thou hast rightly said.* It is stated by Aryda and others that this is the prevailing mode in which a person expresses his assent, at this day, in Lebanon, especially when he does not wish to assert anything in express terms. This explains the answer of our Saviour to the high-priest Caiaphas (Matt. xxvi. 64), when he was asked whether he was the Christ, the son of God, and replied, *thou hast said* (see also Matt. xxvi. 25). All readers of even translations are familiar with a frequent elegancy of the Scriptures, or rather of the Hebrew language, in using an affirmative and negative together, by which the sense is rendered more emphatic: sometimes the negative first, as Ps. cxviii. 17, 'I shall not die, but live,' &c.; sometimes the negative first, as Isa. xxxviii. 1, 'Thou shalt die, and not live.' In John i. 20, there is a remarkable instance of emphasis produced by a negative being placed between two affirmatives—'And he confessed, and denied not, but confessed, I am not the Christ.'

AFRICA. This 'quarter of the world' is not mentioned as such by any general name in Scripture, although some of its regions are indicated. It is thought by some, however, that Africa, or as much of it as was then known, is denoted by 'the land of Ham,' in several of the Psalms. But we are inclined to think that the context rather restricts this designation of Egypt. Whether Africa was really 'the land of Ham,' that is, was peopled by the descendants of Ham, is quite another question [HAM].

AG'ABUS, the name of 'a prophet,' supposed to have been one of the seventy disciples of Christ. He, with others, came from Judæa to Antioch, while Paul and Barnabas (A.D. 43) were there, and announced an approaching famine, which actually occurred the following year. Some writers suppose that the famine was general; but most modern commentators unite in understanding that the terms of the original apply not *to the whole world,* nor even to all the Roman empire, but, as in Luke ii. 1, to Judæa only, and that the reference is to that famine which, in the fourth year of Claudius, overspread Palestine. The poor Jews, *in general,* were then relieved by the Queen of Adiabene, who sent to purchase corn in Egypt for them; and for the relief of the Christians in that country contributions were raised by the brethren at Antioch, and conveyed to Jerusalem by Paul and Barnabas (Acts xi. 27-30). Many years after, this same Agabus met Paul at Cæsarea, and warned him of the sufferings which awaited him if he prosecuted his journey to Jerusalem.

A'GAG, the name of two kings of the Amalekites, and perhaps a common name of all their kings, like Pharaoh in Egypt (comp. Num. xxiv. 7; 1 Sam. xv. 8, 9, 20, 32). The first of these passages would imply that the king of the Amalekites was, then at least, a greater monarch, and his people a greater people, than is commonly imagined [AMALEKITES]. The latter references are to that king of the Amalekites who was spared by Saul, contrary to that solemn vow of devotement to destruction, whereby the nation, as such, had of old precluded itself from giving any quarter to that people (Exod. xvii. 14; Deut. xxv. 17-19). Hence, when Samuel arrived in the camp of Saul, he ordered Agag to be brought forth. He came 'pleasantly,' deeming secure the life which the king had spared. But the prophet ordered him to be cut in pieces; and the expression which he employed—'As thy sword hath made women childless, so shall thy mother be childless among women'—indicates that, apart from the obligations of the vow, some such example of retributive justice was intended as had been exercised in the case of Adonibezek; or, in other words, that Agag had made himself infamous by the same treatment of some prisoners of distinction (probably Israelites) as he now received from Samuel. The unusual mode in which his death was inflicted strongly supports this conclusion.

AGAGITE, used as a Gentile name for Amalekite in Est. iii. 1, 10; viii. 3, 5.

AGATE, a precious or rather ornamental stone, which was one of those in the breast-plate of the high-priest (Exod. xxviii. 19, xxxix. 12). This stone is popularly known in this country under the name of Scotch pebble. There are few countries in which agates of some quality or other are not produced. The finest are those of India; they are plentiful, and sometimes fine, in Italy, Spain, and Germany; but those found in this country are seldom good.

Agate is one of the numerous modifications of form under which silica presents itself, almost in a state of purity, forming 98 per cent. of the entire mineral. The siliceous particles are not so arranged as to produce the transparency of rock crystal, but a semi-pellucid, sometimes almost opaque substance, with a resinous or waxy fracture; and various shades of colour are produced by minute quantities of iron. The same stone sometimes contains parts of different degrees of translucency, and of various shades of colour; and the endless combinations of these produce the beautiful and singular internal forms, for which, together with the high polish they are capable of receiving, agates obtain their value as precious stones. The Scripture text shows the early use of this stone for engraving; and several antique agates, engraved with exquisite beauty, are still preserved in the cabinets of the curious.

AGE. [CHRONOLOGY; GENERATION; LONGEVITY.]

AGE, OLD. The strong desire of a protracted life, and the marked respect with which aged persons were treated among the Jews, are very often indicated in the Scriptures. The most striking instance which Job can give of the respect in which he was once held, is that *even* old men stood up as he passed them in the streets (Job xxix. 8), the force of which is illustrated by the injunction in the law, 'Before the hoary head thou shalt stand up, and shalt reverence the aged' (Lev. xix. 32). Similar injunctions are repeated in the Apocrypha, so as to show the deportment expected from young men towards their seniors in company. Thus, in describing a feast, the author of Ecclesiasticus (xxxii. 3, 7) says, 'Speak thou that art the elder, for it becometh thee. Speak, young man, if there be need of thee, and yet scarcely, when thou art twice asked.'

Thus the attainment of old age is constantly promised or described as a blessing (Gen. xv. 15; Job v. 26), and communities as highly favoured in which old people abound (Isa. lxv. 20; Zech. viii. 4), while premature death is the greatest of calamities upon individuals, and to the families to which they belong (1 Sam. ii. 32); the aged are constantly supposed to excel in understanding and judgment (Job. xii. 20; xv. 10; xxxii. 9; 1 Kings xii. 6, 8), and the mercilessness of the Chaldeans is expressed by their having ' no compassion' upon the 'old man, or him who stooped for age' (2 Chron. xxxvi. 17).

The strong desire to attain old age was necessarily in some degree connected with or resembled the respect paid to aged persons; for people would scarcely desire to be old, were the aged neglected or regarded with mere sufferance.

Attention to age was very general in ancient times; and is still observed in all such conditions of society as those through which the Israelites passed. Among the Egyptians, the young men rose before the aged, and always yielded to them the first place. The youth of Sparta did the same, and were silent—or, as the Hebrews would say, laid their hand upon their mouth—whenever their elders spoke. At Athens, and in other Greek states, old men were treated with corresponding respect. In China the deference for the aged, and the honours and distinctions awarded to them, form a capital point in the government, and among the Moslems of Western Asia, whose usages offer so many analogies to those of the Hebrews, the same regard for seniority is strongly shown. Among the Arabs it is very seldom that a youth can be permitted to eat with men. With the Turks, age, even between brothers, is the object of marked deference.

AGONY, a word directly meaning *contest*, and especially the contests by wrestling, &c. in the public games; whence it is applied metaphorically to a severe *struggle* or *conflict* with pain and suffering. *Agony* is the actual struggle with present evil, and is thus distinguished from *anguish*, which arises from the reflection on evil that is past. In the New Testament the word is only used by Luke (xx. 44), and is employed by him with terrible significance to describe the fearful struggle which our Lord sustained in the garden of Gethsemane. The circumstances of this mysterious transaction are recorded in Matt. xxvi. 36-46; Mark xiv. 32-42; Luke xx. 39-48; Heb. v. 7, 8. None of these passages, taken separately, contains a full history of our Saviour's agony. Each of the three Evangelists has omitted some things which the others have recorded, and all are very brief. The passage in Hebrews is only an incidental notice. The three Evangelists appear to have had the same design, namely, to convey to their readers an idea of the intensity of the Lord's distress; but they compass it in different ways. Luke alone notices the agony, the bloody sweat, and the appearance of an angel from heaven strengthening him. Matthew and Mark alone record the change which appeared in his countenance and manner, the complaint which he uttered of the overpowering sorrows of his soul, and the repetition of the same prayer. All agree that he prayed for the removal of what he called ' this cup,' and are careful to note that he qualified this earnest petition by a preference of his Father's will to his own.

With regard to the cause of his overwhelming distress, Jesus himself points it out in the prayer, ' If it be possible, *let this cup pass from me ;*' the cup which his Father had appointed for him; and the question is, what does he mean by ' this cup.' Doddridge and others think that he means the instant agony, the trouble that he then actually endured. But this is satisfactorily answered by Dr. Mayer, who shows by reference to John xviii. 18, that the cup respecting which he prayed was one that was then before him, which he had not yet taken up to drink, and which he desired, if possible, that the Father should remove. It could, therefore, be no other than the scene of suffering upon which he was about to enter. It was the death which the Father had appointed for him—the death of the cross—with all the attending circumstances which aggravated its horror; that scene of woe which began with his arrest in the garden, and was consummated by his death on Calvary. Jesus had long been familiar with this prospect, and had looked to it as the appointed termination of his ministry (Matt. xvi. 21; xvii. 9-12; xx. 17, 19, 28; Mark x. 32-34; John x. 18; xii. 32, 33). But when he looked forward to this destination, as the hour approached, a chill of horror sometimes came over him, and found expression in external signs of distress (John xii. 27; comp. Luke xii. 49, 50). It is manifest, therefore, that something more than the cross was now before him, and that he was now placed in a new and hitherto untried situation. Dr. Mayer says: ' I have no hesitation in believing that he was here put upon the trial of his obedience. It was the purpose of God to subject the obedience of Jesus to a severe ordeal, in order that, like gold tried in the furnace, it might be an act of more perfect and illustrious virtue; and for this end he permitted him to be assailed by the fiercest temptation to disobey his will and to refuse the appointed cup. In pursuance of this purpose, the mind of Jesus was left to pass under a dark cloud, his views lost their clearness, the Father's will was shrouded in obscurity, the cross appeared in ten-fold horror, and nature was left to indulge her feelings, and to put forth her reluctance.'

Under another head [BLOODY SWEAT] will be found the considerations suggested by one of the remarkable circumstances of this event.

AGRARIAN LAW. To this, or some such heading, belongs the consideration of the peculiar laws by which the distribution and tenure of land were regulated among the Hebrew people; while the modes and forms in which the land was cultivated belong to AGRICULTURE.

The Hebrews were for the most part a pastoral people until they were settled in Palestine, and their pastoral habits were mainly instrumental in keeping them distinct and separate from the Egyptians, who were agriculturists, and had a strong dislike to a shepherd life (Gen. xlvi. 34). But when they became an independent and sovereign nation, the same result of separation from other nations was to be aided by inducing them to devote their chief attention to the culture of the soil.

It was, doubtless, in subservience to this object, and to facilitate the change, that the Israelites were put in possession of a country already in a state of high cultivation (Deut. vi. 11). And it was in order to retain them in this condition, to give them a vital interest in it, and to make it a source of happiness to them, that a very peculiar agrarian law was given to them. An equal distribution of the soil (Num. xxvi. 53-54) was the basis of the agrarian law. By it provision was made for the support of 600,000 yeomanry, with (according to different calculations) from sixteen to twenty-five acres of land each. This land they held independent of all temporal superiors, by direct tenure from Jehovah their sovereign, by whose power they were to acquire the territory, and under whose protection they were to enjoy and retain it. But this law was guarded by other provisions equally wise and salutary. The accumulation of debt was prevented, first, by prohibiting every Hebrew from accepting of interest (Lev. xxv. 35, 36) from any of his fellow-citizens; next, by establishing a regular release of debts every seventh year; and, finally, by ordering that no lands could be alienated for ever, but must, on each year of Jubilee, or every seventh Sabbatic year, revert to the families which originally possessed them. Thus, without absolutely depriving individuals of all temporary dominion over their landed property, it re-established, every fiftieth year, that original and equal distribution of it, which was the foundation of the national polity; and as the period of such reversion was fixed and regular, all parties had due notice of the terms on which they negotiated; so that there was no ground for public commotion or private complaint.

This law, by which landed property was released in the year of Jubilee from all previous obligations, did not extend to houses in towns, which, if not redeemed within one year after being sold, were alienated for ever (Lev. xxv. 29, 30). This must have given to property in the country a decided preference over property in cities, and must have greatly contributed to the essential object of all those regulations, by affording an inducement to every Hebrew to reside on and cultivate his land. Further, the original distribution of the land was to the several tribes according to their families, so that each tribe was, so to speak, settled in the same county, and each family in the same barony or hundred. Nor was the estate of any family in one tribe permitted to pass into another, even by the marriage of an heiress (Num. xxvii.); so that not only was the original balance of property preserved, but the closest and dearest connections of affinity attached to each other the inhabitants of every vicinage.

For this land a kind of quit-rent was payable to the sovereign proprietor, in the form of a tenth or tithe of the produce, which was assigned to the priesthood [TITHES]. The condition of military service was also attached to the land: as it appears that every freeholder (Deut. xx. 5) was obliged to attend at the general muster of the national army, and to serve in it, at his own expense (often more than repaid by the plunder), as long as the occasion required. In this direction, therefore, the agrarian law operated in securing a body of 600,000 men, inured to labour and industry, always assumed to be ready, as they were bound, to come forward at their country's call. This great body of national yeomanry, every one of whom had an important stake in the national independence, was officered by its own hereditary chiefs, heads of tribes and families (comp. Exod. xviii. and Num. xxxi. 14); and must have presented an insuperable obstacle to treacherous ambition and political intrigue, and to every attempt to overthrow the Hebrew commonwealth and establish despotic power. Nor were these institutions less wisely adapted to secure the state against foreign violence, and at the same time prevent offensive wars and remote conquests. For while this vast body of hardy yeomanry were always ready to defend their country, when assailed by foreign foes, yet, being constantly employed in agriculture, attached to domestic life, and enjoying at home the society of the numerous relatives who peopled their neighbourhood, war must have been in a high degree averse to their tastes and habits. Religion also took part in preventing them from being captivated by the splendour of military glory. On returning from battle, even if victorious, in order to bring them back to more peaceful feelings after the rage of war, the law required them to consider themselves as polluted by the slaughter, and unworthy of appearing in the camp of Jehovah until they had employed an entire day in the rites of purification (Num. xix. 13-16; xxxi. 19). Besides, the force was entirely infantry; the law forbidding even the kings to multiply horses in their train (Deut. xvii. 16); and this, with the ordinance requiring the attendance of all the males three times every year at Jerusalem, proved the intention of the legislator to confine the natives within the limits of the Promised Land, and rendered long and distant wars and conquests impossible without the virtual renunciation of that religion which was incorporated with their whole civil polity, and which was, in fact, the charter by which they held their property and enjoyed all their rights.

AGRICULTURE. The antiquity of agriculture is intimated in the brief history of Cain and Abel (Gen. iv. 2, 3). But of the actual state of agriculture before the deluge we know nothing. Whatever knowledge was possessed by the old world was doubtless transmitted to the new by Noah and his sons; and that this knowledge was considerable is implied in the fact that one of the operations of Noah, when he ' began to be a husbandman,' was to plant a vineyard, and to make wine with the fruit (Gen. ix. 20). There are few agricultural notices belonging to the patriarchal period, but they suffice to show that the land of Canaan was in a state of cultivation, and that the inhabitants possessed what were at a later date the principal products of the soil in the same country. In giving to the Israelites possession of a country already under cultivation, it was the Divine intention that they should keep up that cultivation, and become themselves an agricultural people; and in doing this they doubtless adopted the practices of agriculture which they found already established in the country.

As the condition of the seasons lies at the root of all agricultural operations, it should be noticed that the variations of sunshine and rain, which with us extend throughout the year, are in Palestine confined chiefly to the latter part of autumn and the winter. During all the rest of the year the sky is almost uninterruptedly cloudless, and rain very rarely falls. The autumnal rains usually commence at the latter end of October or the beginning of November, not suddenly, but by degrees, which gives opportunity to the husbandman to sow his wheat and barley. The rains continue during November and December, but afterwards they occur at longer intervals; and rain is rare after March, and almost never occurs as late as May. The cold of winter is not severe; and as the ground is never frozen, the labours of the husbandman are not entirely interrupted. Snow falls in different parts of the country, but never lies long on the ground. In the plains and valleys the heat of summer is oppressive, but not in the more elevated tracts. In such high grounds the nights are cool, often with heavy dew. The total absence of rain in summer soon destroys the verdure of the fields, and gives to the general landscape, even in the high country, an aspect of drought and barrenness. No green thing remains but the foliage of the scattered fruit-trees, and occasional vineyards and fields of millet. In autumn the whole land becomes dry and parched; the cisterns are nearly empty; and all nature, animate and inanimate, looks forward with longing for the return of the rainy season. In the hill country the time of harvest is later than in the plains of the Jordan and of the sea-coast. The barley harvest is about a fortnight earlier than that of wheat. In the plain of the Jordan the wheat harvest is early in May; in the plains of the coast and of Esdraelon it is towards the latter end of that month; and in the hills, not until June. The general vintage is in September, but the first grapes ripen in July; and from that time the towns are well supplied with this fruit.

SOIL, &c.—The geological characters of the soil in Palestine have never been satisfactorily stated; but the different epithets of description which travellers employ enable us to know tha it differs considerably, both in its appearance and character, in different parts of the land; but wherever soil of any kind exists, even to a very slight depth, it is found to be highly fertile. As parts of Palestine are hilly, and hills have seldom much depth of soil, the mode of cultivating them in terraces was anciently, and is now, much employed. A series of low stone walls, one above another, across the face of the hill, arrested the soil brought down by the rains, and afforded a series of levels for the operations of the husbandman. This mode of cultivation is usual in Lebanon, and is not unfrequent in Palestine, where the remains of terraces across the hills, in various parts of the country, attest the extent to which it was anciently carried.

In such a climate as that of Palestine, water is the great fertilizing agent. The rains of autumn and winter, and the dews of spring, suffice for the ordinary objects of agriculture; but the ancient inhabitants were able, in some parts, to avert even the aridity which the summer droughts occasioned, and to keep up a garden-like verdure, by means of aqueducts communicating with the brooks and rivers (Ps. i. 3; lxv. 10; Prov. xxi. 1; Isa. xxx. 25; xxxii. 2, 20; Hos. xii. 11). Hence springs, fountains, and rivulets were as much esteemed by husbandmen as by shepherds (Josh. xv. 19; Judg. i. 15). The soil was also cleared of stones, and carefully cultivated; and its fertility was increased by the ashes to which the dry stubble and herbage were occasionally reduced by burning over the surface of the ground (Prov. xxiv. 31; Isa. vii. 23; x. 17; xxxii. 13; xlvii. 14; Matt. iii. 12; Luke iii. 17). The dung, and, in the neighbourhood of Jerusalem, the blood of animals, were also used to enrich the soil (2 Kings ix. 37; Ps. lxxxiii. 10; Isa. xxv. 10; Jer. ix. 22; Luke xiv. 34, 35).

That the soil might not be exhausted, it was ordered that every seventh year should be a sabbath of rest to the land. There was to be no sowing or reaping, no pruning of vines or olives, no vintage or gathering of fruits; and whatever grew of itself was to be left to the poor, the stranger, and the beast of the field (Lev. xxv. 1-7). But such an observance required more faith than the Israelites were prepared to exercise. It was for a long time utterly neglected (Lev. xxvi. 34, 35; 2 Chron. xxxvi. 21), but after the Captivity it was more observed. By this remarkable institution the Hebrews were also trained to habits of economy and foresight, and invited to exercise a large degree of trust in the bountiful providence of their Divine King.

FIELDS.—Syria, including Palestine, was regarded by the ancients as one of the first countries for corn. Wheat was abundant and excellent; and there is still one bearded sort, the ear of which is three times as heavy, and contains twice as many grains, as our common English wheat. Barley was also much cultivated, not only for bread, but because it was the only kind of corn which was given to beasts; for oats and rye do not grow in warm climates. Hay was not in use; and therefore the barley was mixed with chopped straw to form the food of cattle (Gen. xxiv. 25, 32; Judg. xix. 19, &c.). Other objects of field culture were millet, spelt, various kinds of beans and peas, pepperwort, cummin, cucumbers, melons, flax, and, perhaps, cotton. Many other articles might be mentioned as being now cultivated in Palestine; but, as their names do not occur in Scripture, we cannot with certainty know which of them were grown there in the ancient times.

Anciently, as now, in Palestine and the East the arable lands were not divided by hedges into fields, as in this country. The ripening products therefore presented an expanse of culture unbroken, although perhaps variegated, in a large view, by the difference of the products grown. The boundaries of lands were therefore marked by stones as landmarks, which, even in patriarchal times, it was deemed a heinous wrong to remove (Job. xxiv. 2); and the law pronounced a curse upon those who, without authority, displaced them (Deut. xix. 14; xxvii. 17). The walls and hedges which are occasionally mentioned in Scripture belonged to orchards, gardens, and vineyards.

8. Modern Syrian Plough.

AGRICULTURAL OPERATIONS.—Of late years much light has been thrown upon the agricultural operations and implements of ancient times, by the discovery of various representations on the sculptured monuments and painted tombs of Egypt. As these agree surprisingly with the notices in the Bible, and, indeed, differ little from what is still employed in Syria and Egypt, it is very safe to receive the instruction which they offer.

Ploughing.—This has always been a light and superficial operation in the East. At first, the ground was opened with pointed sticks; then, a kind of hoe was employed; and this, in many parts of the world, is still the substitute for a plough. But the plough was known in Egypt and Syria before the Hebrews became cultivators (Job i. 14). In the East, however, it has always been a light and inartificial implement. At first, it was little more than a stout branch of a tree, from which projected another limb, shortened and pointed. This, being turned into the ground, made the furrows; while at the farther end of the larger branch was fastened a transverse yoke, to which the oxen were harnessed. Afterwards a handle to guide the plough was added. Thus the plough consisted of—1. the pole; 2. the point or share; 3. the handle; 4. the yoke. The Syrian plough is, and doubtless was, light enough for a man to carry in his hand. We annex a figure of the ancient Egyptian plough, which

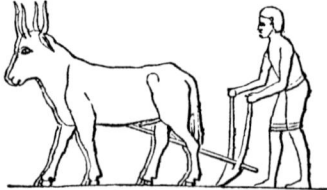

9. Ancient Egyptian Plough.

had the most resemblance to the one now used (as figured in No. 8), and the comparison between them will probably suggest a fair idea of the plough which was in use among the Hebrews.

The following cut (from Sir Charles Fellows' work on Asia Minor) shows the parts of a still lighter plough used in Asia Minor and Syria, with but a single handle, and with different shares according to the work it has to execute.

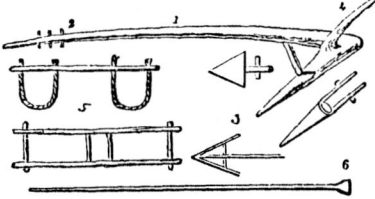

10.

1. The plough. 2. The pole. 3. Shares (various).
4. Handle. 5. Yokes. 6. Ox-goad.

The plough was drawn by oxen, which were sometimes impelled by a scourge (Isa. x. 26; Nahum iii. 2); but oftener by a long staff, furnished at one end with a flat piece of metal for clearing the plough, and at the other with a spike for goading the oxen. This ox-goad might be easily used as a spear (Judg. iii. 31; 1 Sam. xiii. 21). Sometimes men followed the plough with hoes to break the clods (Isa. xxviii. 24); but in later times a kind of hammer was employed, which appears to have been then, as now, merely a thick block of wood, pressed down by a weight, or by a man sitting on it, and drawn over the ploughed field.

Sowing.--The ground, having been ploughed as soon as the autumnal rains had mollified the soil, was fit, by the end of October, to receive the seed; and the sowing of wheat continued, in different situations, through November into December. Barley was not generally sown till January and February. The seed appears to have been sown and harrowed at the same time; although sometimes it was ploughed in by a cross furrow.

11. Sowing. Ancient Egyptian.

Ploughing in the Seed.--The Egyptian paintings illustrate the Scriptures by showing that in those soils which needed no previous preparation

12. Ploughing and Sowing. Ancient Egyptian.

by the hoe (for breaking the clods) the sower followed the plough, holding in the left hand a basket of seed, which he scattered with the right hand, while another person filled a fresh basket. We also see that the mode of sowing was what we call 'broad-cast,' in which the seed is thrown loosely over the field (Matt. xiii. 3-8). In Egypt, when the levels were low, and the water had continued long upon the land, they often dispensed with the plough altogether; and probably, like the present inhabitants, broke up the ground with hoes, or simply dragged the moist mud with bushes after the seed had been thrown upon the surface. To this cultivation without ploughing Moses probably alludes (Deut. xi. 10), when he tells the Hebrews that the land to which they were going was *not* like the land of Egypt, where they 'sowed their seed and watered it with their foot *as a garden of herbs.*' It does not seem that any instrument resembling our *harrow* was known; the word rendered *to harrow,* in Job xxxix. 10, means literally *to break the clods,* and is so rendered in Isa. xxviii. 24; Hos. x. 11: and for this purpose the means used have been already indicated. The passage in Job is, however, important. It shows that this breaking of clods was not always by hand, but that some

kind of instrument was drawn by an animal over the ploughed field, most probably the rough log which is still in use.

Harvest.--It has been already indicated that the time of the wheat harvest in Palestine varies, in different situations, from early in May to late in June; and that the barley harvest is about a fortnight earlier than that of wheat. Among the Israelites, as with all other people, the harvest was a season of joy, and as such is more than once alluded to in Scripture (Ps. xxvi. 5; Isa. ix. 3).

Reaping.--Different modes of reaping are indicated in Scripture, and illustrated by the Egyp-

13. Reaping.

tian monuments. In the most ancient times, the

corn was plucked up by the roots, which continued to be the practice with particular kinds of grain after the sickle was known. In Egypt, at this day, barley and dhurah (maize) are pulled up by the roots. 'Wheat, as well as barley in general,' says Russell, 'does not grow half as high as in Britain; and is therefore, like other grain, not reaped with the sickle, but plucked up by the roots with the hand. In other parts of the country, where the corn grows ranker, the sickle is used.' When the sickle was used, the wheat was either cropped off under the ear or cut close to the ground. In the former case, the straw was afterwards plucked up for use; in the latter, the stubble was left and burnt on the ground for manure. As the Egyptians needed not such manure, and were economical of straw, they generally followed the former method; while the Israelites, whose lands derived benefit from the burnt stubble, used the latter; although the practice of cutting off the ears was also

14. Binding Sheaves.

known to them (Job xxiv. 24). Cropping the ears short, the Egyptians did not generally bind them into sheaves, but removed them in baskets. Sometimes, however, they bound them into *double* sheaves; and such as they plucked up were bound into single long sheaves. The Israelites appear generally to have made up their corn into sheaves (Gen. xxxvii. 7; Lev. xxiii. 10-15; Ruth ii. 7, 15; Job xxiv. 10; Jer. ix. 22; Mich. iv. 12), which were collected into a heap, or removed in a cart (Amos ii. 13) to the threshing-floor. The carts were probably similar to those which are still employed for the same purpose.

With regard to the sickles, there appear to have been two kinds in use as among the Egyptians. The figures of these Egyptian sickles probably mark the difference between them. One

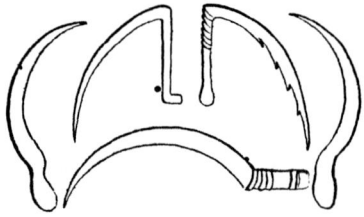

15. Sickles.

was very much like our common reaping-*hook*, while the other had more resemblance in its shape to a scythe, and in the Egyptian examples appears to have been toothed. The reapers were the owners and their children, men-servants and women-servants, and day-labourers (Ruth ii. 4,

6, 21, 23; John iv. 36; James v. 4). Refreshments were provided for them, especially drink, of which the gleaners were allowed to partake (Ruth ii. 9). So in the Egyptian harvest-scenes, we perceive a provision of water in skins, hung against trees, or in jars upon stands, with the reapers drinking, and gleaners applying to share the draught. Among the Israelites, gleaning

16. Egyptian Harvest Scene.

was one of the stated provisions for the poor: and for their benefit the corners of the field were left unreaped, and the reapers might not return for a forgotten sheaf. The gleaners were however to obtain in the first place the express permission of the proprietor or his steward (Lev. xix. 9, 10; Deut. xxiv. 19; Ruth ii. 2, 7).

17. Threshing by Cattle.

Threshing.—The ancient mode of threshing, as described in Scripture and figured on the Egyptian monuments, is still preserved in Palestine. Formerly the sheaves were conveyed from the field to the threshing-floor in carts; but now they are borne, generally, on the backs of camels and asses. The threshing-floor is a level plot of ground, of a circular shape, generally about fifty feet in diameter, prepared for use by beating down the earth till a hard floor is formed (Gen. l. 10; Judg. vi. 37; 2 Sam. xxiv. 16, 24). Sometimes several of these floors are contiguous to each other. The sheaves are spread out upon them; and the grain is trodden out by oxen, cows, and young cattle, arranged five abreast, and driven in a circle, or rather in all directions, over the floor. This was the common mode in the Bible times; and Moses forbade that the oxen thus employed should be muzzled to prevent them from tasting the corn (Deut. xxv. 4; Isa. xxviii. 28). *Flails*, or sticks, were only used in threshing small quantities, or for the lighter kinds of grain (Ruth ii. 17; Isa. xxviii. 27). There were, however, some kinds of threshing-machines, which are still used in Palestine and Egypt. One of them, represented in the annexed figure, is very much used in Palestine. It is composed of two thick planks, fastened together side by side, and bent upwards in front. Sharp fragments of stone are fixed into holes bored in the bottom. This machine is drawn over the corn by oxen, a man or boy sometimes sitting on it to increase the weight. It not only separates the grain, but cuts the straw and makes it fit for fodder (2 Kings xiii. 7). This is, most probably, the

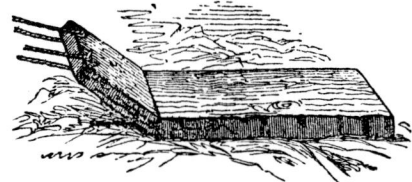

18. Syrian Corn-Drag.

'corn-drag,' which is mentioned in Scripture (Isa. xxviii. 27; xli. 15; Amos i. 3, rendered 'threshing instrument'), and would seem to have been sometimes furnished with iron points instead of stones. The Bible also notices a machine called a *Moreg* (2 Sam. xxiv. 22; 1 Chron. xxi. 23; Isa. xli. 15), which is unquestionably the same which bears in Arabic the name of *Noreg.* This machine is not now often seen in Palestine; but is more used in some parts of Syria, and is common in Egypt. It is a sort of

19. Threshing by the Noreg.

frame of wood, in which are inserted three wooden rollers, armed with iron teeth, &c. It bears a sort of seat or chair, in which the driver sits to give the benefit of his weight. It is generally drawn over the corn by two oxen, and separates the grain, and breaks up the straw even more effectually than the drag. In all these processes, the corn is occasionally turned by a fork; and, when sufficiently threshed, is thrown up by the same fork against the wind to separate the grain, which is then gathered up and winnowed.

Winnowing. — This was generally accomplished by repeating the process of tossing up the grain against the wind with a fork (Jer. iv. 11, 12), by which the broken straw and chaff were dispersed, and the grain fell to the ground.

20. Winnowing.

The grain afterwards passed through a sieve to separate the bits of earth and other impurities. After this, it underwent a still further purification, by being tossed up with wooden scoops or short-handled shovels, such as we see in Egyptian paintings.

AGRIP′PA [HERODIAN FAMILY]. Although of the two Herods, father and son, who also bore the name of Agrippa, the latter is best known by his Roman name, it seems best to include him with the other members of the Herodian dynasty, under the name which he bore among his own people.

A′GUR, the author of the sayings contained in Prov. xxx., which the inscription describes as composed of the precepts delivered by 'Agur, the son of Jakeh,' to his friends 'Ithiel and Ucal.' Beyond this everything that has been stated of him, and of the time in which he lived, is pure conjecture.

A′HAB (*father's brother*), son of Omri, and the sixth king of Israel, who reigned twenty-two years, beginning in B.C. 918 and ending in 897. Ahab was, upon the whole, the weakest of all the Israelitish monarchs; and although there are occasional traits of character which show that he was not without good feelings and dispositions, the history of his reign shows that weakness of character in a king may sometimes be as injurious in its effects as wickedness. Many of the evils of his reign may be ascribed to the close connection which he formed with the Phœnicians. The wife of Ahab was Jezebel, the daughter of Ethbaal, or Ithobaal, king of Tyre. She was a woman of a decided and energetic character, and, as such, soon established that influence over her husband which such women always acquire over weak, and not unfrequently also over strong, men. Ahab, being entirely under the control of Jezebel, sanctioned the introduction, and eventually established the worship of the Phœnician idols, and especially of the sun-god Baal. Hitherto the golden calves in Dan and Bethel had been the only objects of idolatrous worship in Israel, and they were intended as symbols of JEHOVAH. But all reserve and limitation were now abandoned. The king built a temple at Samaria, and erected an image, and consecrated a grove to Baal. A multitude of the priests and prophets of Baal were maintained. Idolatry became the predominant religion; and Jehovah, with the golden calves as symbolical representations of him, were viewed with no more reverence than Baal and his image. At length the judgment of God on Ahab and on his house was pronounced by Elijah, that, during the reign of his son, his whole race should be exterminated. Ahab died of the wounds which he received in a battle with the Syrians, according to a prediction of Micaiah, which the king disbelieved, but yet endeavoured to avert by disguising himself in the action (1 Kings xvi. 29; xxii. 40).

2. AHAB and ZEDEKIAH. The names of two false prophets, who deceived the Israelites at Babylon. For this they were threatened by Jeremiah, who foretold that they should be put to death by the king of Babylon in the presence of those whom they had beguiled; and that in following times it should become a common malediction to say, 'The Lord make thee like Ahab

and Zedekiah, whom the king of Babylon roasted in the fire' (Jer. xxix. 21, 22).

AHASUE'RUS, or ACHASHVEROSH, is the name, or rather the *title*, of four Median and Persian monarchs mentioned in the Bible.

The first Ahasuerus is incidentally mentioned, in Dan. ix. 1, as the father of Darius the Mede. It is generally agreed that the person here referred to is the Astyages of profane history. See the article DARIUS.

The second Ahasuerus occurs in Ezra iv. 6, where it is said that in the beginning of his reign the enemies of the Jews wrote an accusation against them, the result of which is not mentioned. The Persian king here meant seems to be the immediate successor of Cyrus, the frantic tyrant Cambyses, who came to the throne B.C. 529, and died after a reign of seven years and five months.

The third Ahasuerus is the Persian king of the book of Esther. The chief facts recorded of him there, and the *dates* of their occurrence, which are important in the subsequent inquiry, are these: In the *third* year of his reign he made a sumptuous banquet for all his nobility, and prolonged the feast for 180 days. Being on one occasion merry with wine, he ordered his queen Vashti to be brought out, to show the people her beauty. On her refusal to violate the decorum of her sex, he not only indignantly divorced her, but published an edict concerning her disobedience, in order to insure to every husband in his dominions the rule in his own house. In the *seventh* year of his reign he married Esther, a Jewess, who, however, concealed her parentage. In the *twelfth* year of his reign, his minister Haman, who had received some slights from Mordecai the Jew, offered him 10,000 talents of silver for the privilege of ordering a massacre of the Jews in all parts of the empire on an appointed day. The king refused this immense sum, but acceded to his request; and couriers were despatched to the most distant provinces to enjoin the execution of this decree. Before it was accomplished, however, Mordecai and Esther obtained such an influence over him, that he so far annulled his recent enactment as to despatch other couriers to empower the Jews to defend themselves manfully against their enemies on that day; the result of which was, that they slew 800 of his native subjects in Shushan, and 75,000 of them in the provinces.

Although almost every Medo-Persian king, from Cyaxares I. down to Artaxerxes III. (Ochus), has in his turn found some champion to assert his title to be the Ahasuerus of Esther, some have contended on very plausible grounds that Darius Hystaspes is the monarch referred to. But in the first place, it is impossible to find the name of Darius in Achashverosh; and, in the second, the moral evidence is against him. The mild and just character ascribed to Darius renders it highly improbable that, after favouring the Jews from the second to the sixth year of his reign, he should become a senseless tool in the hands of Haman, and consent to their extirpation. Lastly, we read of his marrying two daughters and a grand-daughter of Cyrus, and a daughter of Otanes—and these only; would Darius have repudiated one of these for such a trifle, when his peculiar position, as the first king of his race, must have rendered such alliances indispensable?

The whole question, therefore, lies between Xerxes and his successor, Artaxerxes Longimanus. As Artaxerxes allowed Ezra to go to Jerusalem with a colony of exiles in the seventh year of his reign (Ezra vii. 1-7); and as he issued a decree in terms so exceedingly favourable to the religious as well as civil interests of the Jews (Ezra vii. 11-26), how could Haman, *five years afterwards*, venture to describe the Jews to him as a people whom, on the very account of their law, it was not for the king's profit to suffer? And how could Haman so directly propose their extermination, in the face of a decree so signally in their favour, and so recently issued by the same king? especially as the laws of the Medes and Persians might not be altered! Again, as Artaxerxes (assuming always that *he* is the Artachshast of Ezra vii. 1, and not *Xerxes*) was capable of such liberality to the Jews in the seventh year of his reign, let us not forget that, if he is the Ahasuerus of the book of Esther, it was in that same year that he married the Jewess. Now, if—by taking the first and tenth months in the seventh year of the king (the dates of the departure of Ezra, and of the marriage of Esther) to be the first and tenth months of the *Hebrew year* (as is the usual mode of notation), and not the first and tenth from the period of his *accession*—we assume that the departure of Ezra took place *after* his marriage with her, his clemency might be the effect of her influence on his mind. Then we have to explain how he could be induced to consent to the extirpation of the Jews in the twelfth year of his reign, notwithstanding that her influence still continued, for we find it evidently at work in the twelfth year. But if, on the other hand, his indulgence to Ezra was *before* his marriage, then we have even a greater difficulty to encounter. For then Artaxerxes must have acted from his own unbiassed lenity, and his purposed cruelty in the twelfth year would place him in an incongruous opposition with himself. As we, moreover, find Artaxerxes again propitious to their interests, in the twentieth year of his reign —when he allowed Nehemiah to return to Jerusalem—it is much easier to believe that he was also favourably disposed to them in the twelfth. At any rate, it would be allowing Esther a long time to exercise an influence on his disposition, if his clemency in the twentieth year was due to her, and not to his own inclination. Besides, the fact that neither Ezra nor Nehemiah gives the least hint that the liberal policy of Artaxerxes towards them was owing to the influence of their countrywoman, is an important negative point in the scale of probabilities. In this case also there is a serious difficulty in the name. As Artaxerxes is called *Artachshast* in Ezra and Nehemiah, we certainly might expect the author of the book of Esther to agree with them in the name of a king whom they all had had such occasion to know. Nor is it perhaps unimportant to add, that Norberg asserts, on the authority of native Persian historians, that the *mother* of Bahman, *i. e.* Artaxerxes Longimanus, was a *Jewess*. This statement would agree excellently with the theory that *Xerxes* was Ahasuerus. Lastly, the joint testimony borne to his clemency and magnanimity by the acts recorded of him in Ezra and Nehemiah, and by the accordant voice of profane writers, prevents us from recognising Artaxerxes in the debauched, imbecile, and cruel tyrant of the book of Esther.

On the ground of moral resemblance to that tyrant, however, every trait leads us to Xerxes. The king who scourged and fettered the sea; who beheaded his engineers because the elements destroyed their bridge over the Hellespont; who so ruthlessly slew the eldest son of Pythius because his father besought him to leave him one sole support of his declining years; who dishonoured the remains of the valiant Leonidas; and who beguiled the shame of his defeat by such a course of sensuality, that he publicly offered a reward for the inventor of a new pleasure—is just the despot to divorce his queen because she would not expose herself to the gaze of drunken revellers; is just the despot to devote a whole people, his subjects, to an indiscriminate massacre; and, by way of preventing that evil, to restore them the right of self-defence (which it is hard to conceive how the first edict ever could have taken away), and thus to sanction their slaughtering thousands of his other subjects.

There are also remarkable coincidences of date between the history of Xerxes and that of Ahasuerus. In the third year of his reign the latter gave a grand feast to his nobles, which lasted 180 days (Esth. i. 3); the former, in *his* third year, also assembled his chief officers to deliberate on the invasion of Greece. Again, Ahasuerus married Esther at Shushan, in the seventh year of his reign: in the same year of *his* reign, Xerxes returned to Susa with the mortification of his defeat, and sought to forget himself in pleasure;—not an unlikely occasion for *that* quest for fair virgins for the harem (Esth. ii. 2). Lastly, the tribute imposed on the land and isles of the sea also accords with the state of his revenue exhausted by his insane attempt against Greece. In fine, these arguments, negative and affirmative, render it so highly probable that Xerxes is the Ahasuerus of the book of Esther, that to demand more conclusive evidence, would be to mistake the very nature of the question.

The fourth Ahasuerus is mentioned in Tobit xiv. 15, in connection with the destruction of Nineveh. That circumstance points out Cyaxares I. as the person intended.

AHA'VA, Ezra viii. 21, 31, the river by which the Jewish exiles assembled their second caravan under Ezra, when returning to Jerusalem. It would seem from ch. viii. 15, that it was designated from a town of the same name: ' I assembled them at the river that flows towards Ahava.' In that case, it could not have been of much importance in itself; and probably it was no other than one of the numerous streams or canals of Mesopotamia communicating with the Euphrates, somewhere in the north-west of Babylonia.

A'HAZ (*possessor*), son of Jotham, and eleventh king of Judah, who reigned sixteen years, beginning in B.C. 741, and ending in 726. Ahaz was the most corrupt monarch that had hitherto appeared in Judah. He respected neither Jehovah, the law, nor the prophets; he broke through all the restraints which law and custom had imposed upon the Hebrew kings, and had regard only to his own depraved inclinations. He introduced the religion of the Syrians into Jerusalem, erected altars to the Syrian gods, altered the temple in many respects after the Syrian model, and at length ventured to shut it up altogether. Such a man could not exercise that *faith* in Jehovah, as the political head of the nation, which formed the *courage* of a Hebrew king. Hence, after he had sustained a few repulses from Pekah and Rezin, his allied foes, when the Edomites had revolted from him, and the Philistines were making incursions into his country, notwithstanding a sure promise of divine deliverance, he called Pul, the king of Assyria, to his aid [ASSYRIA]. He even became tributary to that monarch, on condition of his obliging Syria and Israel to abandon their design of destroying the kingdom of Judah; and thus afforded to Tiglath-pilezer, the successor of Pul, an opportunity of conquering Syria, Israel beyond Jordan, and Galilee. The Assyrians afforded Ahaz no real assistance; on the contrary, they drove him to such extremities that he was scarcely able, with all the riches of the temple, of the nobility, and of the royal treasury, to purchase release from his troublesome protectors. He died at the age of thirty-six (2 Kings xvi.; 2 Chron. xxviii.; Isa. vii.).

1. AHAZI'AH (*whom Jehovah sustains*); son and successor of Ahab, and seventh king of Israel. He reigned two years, B.C. 897, 896. It seems that Jezebel exercised over her son the same influence which had guided her husband; and Ahaziah pursued the evil courses of his father. The most signal public event of his reign was the revolt of the Moabites, who took the opportunity of the defeat and death of Ahab to discontinue the tribute which they had paid to the Israelites. Ahaziah became a party in the attempt of Jehoshaphat, king of Judah, to revive the maritime traffic by the Red Sea; in consequence of which the enterprise was blasted, and came to nothing (2 Chron. xx. 35-37). Soon after, Ahaziah, having been much injured by a fall from the roof-gallery of his palace, had the infatuation to send to consult the oracle of Baalzebub, the god of Ekron, respecting his recovery. But the messengers were met and sent back by Elijah, who himself announced to the king that he should rise no more from the bed on which he lay (1 Kings xxii. 51, to 2 Kings i. 18).

2. AHAZIAH, otherwise JEHOAHAZ, son of Jehoram by Athaliah, daughter of Ahab and Jezebel, and sixth king of Judah. He reigned but one year (B.C. 885), and that wickedly, suffering himself in all things to be guided by the wicked counsels of his idolatrous mother, Athaliah. He cultivated the connections which had unhappily grown up between the two dynasties, and which had now been cemented by marriage. Hence he joined his uncle Jehoram of Israel in an expedition against Hazael, king of Damacene-Syria, for the recovery of Ramoth-Gilead; and afterwards paid him a visit while he lay wounded in his summer palace of Jezreel. The two kings rode out in their several chariots to meet Jehu; and when Jehoram was shot through the heart, Ahaziah attempted to escape, but was pursued, and being mortally wounded, had only strength to reach Megiddo, where he died. His body was

conveyed by his servants in a chariot to Jerusalem for interment (2 Kings ix. 28).

1. AHI'AH (*friend of Jehovah*); (1 Sam. xiv. 3), son of Ahitub, and high-priest in the reign of Saul, and brother and predecessor of the Abimelech whom Saul slew for assisting David. Seeing that Abimelech was also high-priest in the same reign, and was also the son of Ahitub (1 Sam. xxii. 11), some have thought that both names belonged to the same person; but this seems less likely than the explanation which has just been given.

2. AHIAH, one of the two secretaries of Solomon (1 Kings iv. 3). Two other persons of this name occur in 1 Sam. xiv. 3; 1 Chron. viii. 7.

AHI'AM, one of David's thirty heroes (2 Sam. xxiii. 33).

AHIE'ZER (*brother of help*), the hereditary chief or prince of the tribe of Dan at the time that the Israelites quitted Egypt (Num. i. 12).

AHI'HUD (*brother*, i. e. *friend of the Jews*), the prince of the tribe of Asher, who, with the other chiefs of tribes, acted with Joshua and Eleazer in dividing the Promised Land (Num. xxxiv. 27).

AHI'JAH (same name as AHIAH), a prophet residing in Shiloh in the times of Solomon and Jeroboam. He appears to have put on record some of the transactions of the former reign (2 Chron. ix. 29). It devolved on him to announce and sanction the separation of the ten tribes from the house of David, as well as the foundation (1 Kings xi. 29-39), and, after many years, the subversion of the dynasty of Jeroboam (1 Kings xiv. 7-11) [JEROBOAM].

AHI'KAM (*brother of the enemy*), one of the four persons of distinction whom Josiah sent to consult Huldah, the prophetess (2 Kings xxii. 12-14). Ahikam and his family are honourably distinguished for their protection of the prophet Jeremiah (Jer. xxvi. 24; xxxix. 14).

AHIMA'AZ (*brother of anger*, i. e. *irascible*), son and successor of Zadok, who was joint high-priest in the reign of David, and sole high-priest in that of Solomon. His history belongs to the time of David, to whom he rendered an important service during the revolt of Absalom. David having refused to allow the ark of God to be taken from Jerusalem when he fled thence, the high-priests, Zadok and Abiathar, necessarily remained in attendance upon it; but their sons, Ahimaaz and Jonathan, concealed themselves outside the city, to be in readiness to bear off to David any important information, respecting the movements and designs of Absalom, which they might receive from within. Accordingly, Hushai having communicated to the priests the result of the council of war, in which his own advice was preferred to that of Ahithophel [ABSALOM], they instantly sent a girl (probably to avoid suspicion) to direct Ahimaaz and Jonathan to speed away with the intelligence. The transaction was, however, witnessed and betrayed by a lad, and the messengers were so hotly pursued that they took refuge in a dry cistern, over which the woman of the house placed a covering, and spread thereon parched corn. She told the pursuers that the messengers had passed on in haste; and when all was safe, she released them, on which they made their way to David (2 Sam.

xv. 24-37; xvii. 15-21). As may be inferred from his being chosen for this service, Ahimaaz was swift of foot. Of this we have a notable example soon after, when, on the defeat and death of Absalom, he prevailed on Joab to allow him to carry the tidings to David. Another messenger, Cushi, had previously been despatched, but Ahimaaz outstripped him, and first came in with the news. He was known afar off by the manner of his running, and the king said, 'He is a good man, and cometh with good tidings;' and this favourable character is justified by the delicacy with which he waived that part of his intelligence concerning the death of Absalom, which he knew would greatly distress so fond a father as David (2 Sam. xviii. 19-33).

AHIM'AN (*brother of a gift*), one of three famous giants, of the race of Anak, who dwelt at Hebron when the Hebrew spies explored the land (Num. xiii. 22).

AHIM'ELECH (*brother of the king*, i. e. *the king's friend*); he was son of Ahitub, and brother of Ahiah, who was most probably his predecessor in the high-priesthood [AHIAH]. When David fled from Saul, he went to Nob, a city of the priests in Benjamin, where the tabernacle then was; and by representing himself as on pressing business from the king, he obtained from Ahimelech, who had no other, some of the sacred bread which had been removed from the presence-table. He was also furnished with the sword which he had himself taken from Goliah, and which had been laid up as a trophy in the tabernacle (1 Sam. xxi. 1-9). These circumstances were witnessed by Doeg, an Edomite in the service of Saul, and were so reported by him to the jealous king as to appear acts of connivance at, and support to, David's imagined disloyal designs. Saul immediately sent for Ahimelech and the other priests then at Nob, and laid this crime to their charge, which they repelled by declaring their ignorance of any hostile designs on the part of David towards Saul and his kingdom. This, however, availed them not; for the king commanded his guard to slay them. Their refusal to fall upon persons invested with so sacred a character might have brought even Saul to reason; but he repeated the order to Doeg himself, and was too readily obeyed by that malignant person, who, with the men under his orders, not only slew the priests then present, eighty-six in number, but marched to Nob, and put to the sword every living creature it contained. The only one of the priests that escaped was Abiathar, son of Ahimelech, who fled to David, and afterwards became high priest (1 Sam. xxii.) [ABIATHAR].

AHIN'ADAB (*liberal*, or, *noble brother*), one of the twelve officers who, in as many districts into which the country was divided, raised supplies of provisions in monthly rotation for the royal household. Ahinadab's district was the southern half of the region beyond the Jordan (1 Kings iv. 14).

AHIN'OAM (*brother of pleasantness*), a woman of Jezreel, one of the wives of David, and mother of Amnon. She was taken captive by the Amalekites when they plundered Ziklag, but was recovered by David (1 Sam. xxv. 43; xxvii. 3; xxx. 5; 2 Sam. ii. 2; iii. 2).

AHI'O (*brotherly*), one of the sons of Abinadab, who, with his brother Uzzah, drove the new cart on which the ark was placed when David first attempted to remove it to Jerusalem. Ahio went before to guide the oxen, while Uzzah walked by the cart (2 Sam. vi. 3, 4) [UZZAH].

AHI'RA (*brother of evil*), chief of the tribe of Naphtali when the Israelites quitted Egypt (Num. i. 15).

AHI'SHAR (*brother of the dawn*), the officer who was 'over the household' of King Solomon (1 Kings iv. 6). This has always been a place of high importance and great influence in the East.

AHITH'OPHEL (*brother of foolishness*), the very singular name of a man who, in the time of David, was renowned throughout all Israel for his worldly wisdom. He is, in fact, the only man mentioned in the Scriptures as having acquired a reputation for political sagacity among the Jews; and they regarded his counsels as oracles (2 Sam. xvi. 23). He was of the council of David; but was at Giloh, his native place, at the time of Absalom's revolt, whence he was summoned to Jerusalem; and it shows the strength of Absalom's cause in Israel that a man so capable of foreseeing results, and of estimating the probabilities of success, took his side in so daring an attempt (2 Sam. xv. 12). The news of this defection appears to have occasioned David more alarm than any other single incident in the rebellion. He earnestly prayed God to turn the sage counsel of Ahithophel ' to foolishness' (probably alluding to his name); and being immediately after joined by his old friend Hushai, he induced him to go over to Absalom with the express view that he might be instrumental in defeating the counsels of this dangerous person (xv. 31-37). Psalm lv. is supposed to contain (12-14) a further expression of David's feelings at this treachery of one whom he had so completely trusted, and whom he calls, ' My companion, my guide, and my familiar friend.' The detestable advice which Ahithophel gave Absalom to appropriate his father's harem, committed him absolutely to the cause of the young prince, since after that he could hope for no reconcilement with David (2 Sam. xvi. 20-23). His proposal as to the conduct of the war undoubtedly indicated the best course that could have been taken under the circumstances; and so it seemed to the council, until Hushai interposed with his plausible advice, the object of which was to gain time to enable David to collect his resources [ABSALOM]. When Ahithophel saw that his counsel was rejected for that of Hushai, the far-seeing man gave up the cause of Absalom for lost; and he forthwith saddled his ass, returned to his home at Giloh, deliberately settled his affairs, and then hanged himself, and was buried in the sepulchre of his fathers, B.C. 1023 (ch. xvii.). This is the only case of suicide which the Old Testament records, unless the last acts of Samson and Saul may be regarded as such.

1. AHI'TUB (*brother of goodness*), son of Phinehas, and grandson of the high-priest Eli. His father Phinehas having been slain when the ark of God was taken by the Philistines, he succeeded his grandfather Eli B.C. 1141, and was himself succeeded by his son Ahiab about B.C. 1093.

2. AHITUB was also the name of the father of Zadok, who was made high-priest by Saul after the death of Ahimelech (2 Sam. viii. 17; 1 Chron. vi. 8). There is not the slightest ground for the notion that this Ahitub was ever high-priest himself—indeed, it is historically impossible.

AHO'LAH (*her tent*) and AHOLIBAH (*my tent* is *in her*), two fictitious or symbolical names adopted by Ezekiel (xxiii. 4) to denote the two kingdoms of Samaria (Israel) and Judah. They are both symbolically described as lewd women, adulteresses, prostituting themselves to the Egyptians and the Assyrians, in imitating their abominations and idolatries; wherefore Jehovah abandoned them to those very people for whom they showed such inordinate and impure affection. They were carried into captivity, and reduced to the severest servitude. The allegory is an epitome of the history of the Jewish church.

AHO'LIAB (*tent of his father*), of the tribe of Dan, a skilful artificer appointed along with Bezaleel to construct the Tabernacle (Exod. xxxv. 34).

AHUZ'ZATH (*possession*), the ' friend' of Abimelech II., king of Gerar, who attended him on his visit to Isaac (Gen. xxvi. 26). In him occurs the first instance of that unofficial but important personage in ancient Oriental courts, called ' the king's friend,' or favourite.

AI (Josh. vii. 2; Gen. xii. 8; Neh. xi. 31; Isa. x. 28), a royal city of the Canaanites, which lay east of Bethel. It existed in the time of Abraham, who pitched his tent between the two cities (Gen. xii. 8; xiii. 3); but it is chiefly noted for its capture and destruction by Joshua (vii. 2-5; viii. 1-29). This, as a military transaction, is noticed elsewhere [AMBUSCADE]. At a later period Ai was rebuilt, and is mentioned by Isaiah (x. 28), and also after the Captivity. The site was known, and some scanty ruins still existed in the time of Eusebius and Jerome, but Dr. Robinson was unable to discover any certain traces of either.

AIR, the atmosphere, as opposed to the ether, or higher and purer region (Acts xxii. 24; 1 Thess. iv. 17; Rev. ii. 2; xvi. 17). The phrase *to speak into the air* (1 Cor. xiv. 9) is a proverbial expression to denote speaking in vain, and *to beat the air* (1 Cor. ix. 26), denotes *acting in vain*, and is a proverbial allusion to an abortive stroke into the air in pugilistic contests. The later Jews, in common with the Gentiles, especially the Pythagoreans, believed the air to be peopled with spirits, under the government of a chief, who there held his seat of empire. These spirits were supposed to be powerful, but malignant, and to incite men to evil. The early Christian fathers entertained the same belief, which has indeed come down to our own times.

AJ'ALON, a town and valley in the tribe of Dan (Josh. xix. 42), which was given to the Levites (Josh. xxi. 24; 1 Chron. vi. 69). It was not far from Bethshemesh (2 Chron. xxviii. 18); it was one of the places which Rehoboam fortified (2 Chron. xi. 10), and among the strongholds which the Philistines took from Ahaz (2 Chron. xxviii. 18). But the town, or rather the valley to which the town gave name, derives its chief renown from the circumstance that

E

when Joshua, in pursuit of the five kings, arrived at some point near Upper Beth-horon, looking back upon Gibeon and down upon the noble valley before him, he uttered the celebrated command: ' Sun, stand thou still on Gibeon, and thou moon, in the valley of Ajalon ' (Josh. x. 12). The site of the town has been identified with the small village of Yàlo near Beit Ur (Beth-horon), and a broad wady to the north of it appears to be the valley of the same name.

AKRAB'BIM (*Scorpion-height*), an ascent, hill, or chain of hills, which, from the name, would appear to have been much infested by scorpions and serpents, as some districts in that quarter certainly were (Deut. viii. 15). It was one of the points which are only mentioned in describing the frontier-line of the Promised Land southward (Judg. i. 36), and has been conjectured to be the same with the mountains of Akabah, which bound the great valley of Arabah on the east.

ALABASTER. This word occurs in the New Testament only in the notice of the ' alabaster *box*,' or rather *vessel*, of ' ointment of spikenard, very precious,' which a woman broke, and with its valuable contents anointed the head of Jesus, as he sat at supper in Bethany in the house of Simon the leper (Matt. xxvi. 7 ; Mark xiv. 3). At Alabastron, in Egypt, there was a manufactory of small pots and vessels for holding perfumes, which were made from a stone found in the neighbouring mountains. The Greeks gave to these vessels the name of the

21.

city from which they came. This name was eventually extended to the stone of which they were formed ; and at length it was applied without distinction to all perfume vessels, of whatever materials they consisted. It does not, therefore, by any means follow that the alabastron which the woman used at Bethany was really of alabaster: but a probability that it was such arises from the fact, that vessels made of this stone were deemed peculiarly suitable for the most costly and powerful perfumes.

ALEXAN'DER THE GREAT. This mighty king is named in the opening of the first book of Maccabees, and is alluded to in the prophecies of

Daniel. These, however, are not the best reasons for giving his name a place in this work : he is chiefly entitled to notice here because his military career permanently affected the political state of the Jewish people, as well as their philosophy and literature. It is not our part, therefore, to detail even the outlines of his history, but to point out the causes and nature of this great revolution, and the influence which, formally through Alexander, Greece has exerted over the religious history of the West.

The conquest of Western Asia by Greeks was so thoroughly provided for by predisposing causes, as to be no mere accident ascribable to Alexander as an individual. The personal genius

22.

of the Macedonian hero, however, determined the form and the suddenness of the conquest ; and, in spite of his premature death, the policy which he pursued seems to have left some permanent effects.

His respectful behaviour to the Jewish highpriest has been much dwelt on by Josephus (*Antiq*. xi. 8. 4-6), a writer whose trustworthiness has been much overrated. The story has been questioned on several grounds. Some of the results, however, can hardly be erroneous, such as, that Alexander guaranteed to the Jews, not in Judæa only, but in Babylonia and Media, the free observance of their hereditary laws, and on this ground exempted them from tribute every seventh (or sabbatical) year. It is then far from improbable that the politic invader affected to have seen and heard the high-priest in a dream (as Josephus relates), and showed him great reverence, as to one who had declared ' that he would go before him and give the empire of Persia into his hand.'

Immediately after, Alexander invaded and conquered Egypt, and showed to its gods the same respect as to those of Greece. Almost without a pause he founded the celebrated city of Alexandria (B.C. 332), an event which, perhaps more than any other cause, permanently altered the state of the East, and brought about a direct interchange of mind between Greece, Egypt, and Judæa [ALEXANDRIA].

The great founder of Alexandria died in his thirty-second year, B.C. 323. The empire which he then left to be quarrelled for by his generals comprised the whole dominions of Persia, with the homage and obedience of Greece superadded. But on the final settlement which took place after the battle of Ipsus (B.C. 301), Seleucus, the

Greek representative of Persian majesty, reigned over a less extended district than the last Darius. Not only were Egypt and Cyprus severed from the Eastern empire, but Palestine and Cœlosyria also fell to their ruler, placing Jerusalem for nearly a century beneath an Egyptian monarch. On this subject, see further under ANTIOCHUS.

23.

2. ALEXANDER, surnamed BALAS, from his mother Bala, a personage who figures in the history of the Maccabees and in Josephus. His extraction is doubtful; but he professed to be the natural son of Antiochus Epiphanes, and in that capacity, out of opposition to Demetrius Soter, he was recognised as king of Syria by the king of Egypt, by the Romans, and eventually by Jonathan Maccabæus, on the part of the Jews (1 Macc. x. 18). Demetrius was not long after slain in battle, and Balas obtained possession of the kingdom. He then sought to strengthen himself by a marriage with the king of Egypt's daughter. Prosperity ruined Alexander; his voluptuousness, debauchery, and misgovernment rendered his reign odious, and encouraged Demetrius Nicator, the eldest son of the late Demetrius Soter, to appear in arms, and claim his father's crown. Alexander took the field against him; but the defection of his father-in-law Ptolemy proved fatal to his cause; he was defeated in a pitched battle, and fled with 500 cavalry to Abæ in Arabia, and sought refuge with the emir Zabdiel. This Arabian murdered his confiding guest in the fifth year of his reign over Syria, and sent his head to Ptolemy, who himself died the same year, B.C. 145. Balas left a young son, who was eventually made king of Syria by Tryphon, under the name of Antiochus Theos.

3. ALEXANDER JANNÆUS, the first prince of the Maccabæan dynasty who assumed the name of king [MACCABEES].

4. ALEXANDER, son of Herod the Great and Mariamne [HERODIAN FAMILY].

5. ALEXANDER, a Jew of Ephesus, known only from the part he took in the uproar about Diana, which was raised there by the preaching of Paul. As the inhabitants confounded the Jews and Jewish Christians, the former put forward Alexander to speak on their behalf, but he was unable in the tumult to obtain a hearing (Acts xix. 33).

6. ALEXANDER, a coppersmith or brazier (mentioned in 1 Tim. i. 20; 2 Tim. iv. 14), who with Hymenæus and others broached certain heresies touching the resurrection, for which they were excommunicated by St. Paul. These persons, and especially Alexander, appear to have maligned the faith they had forsaken, as well as the character of the apostle.

ALEXAN′DRIA (Acts vi. 9; xviii. 24; xxvii. 6), the chief maritime city and long the metropolis of Lower Egypt. It is situated on the Mediterranean, twelve miles west of the Canopic mouth of the Nile, in 31° 13′ N. lat. and 25° 53′ E. long. It owes its origin to the comprehensive policy of Alexander, who perceived that the usual channels of commerce might be advantageously altered; and that a city occupying this site could not fail to become the common emporium for the traffic of the eastern and western worlds, by means of the river Nile, and the two adjacent seas, the Red Sea and the Mediterranean: and the high prosperity which, as such, Alexandria very rapidly attained, proved the soundness of his judgment, and exceeded any expectations which even he could have entertained. For a long period Alexandria was the greatest of known cities; for Nineveh and Babylon had fallen, and Rome had not yet risen to pre-eminence: and even when Rome became the mistress of the world, and Alexandria only the metropolis of a province, the latter was second only to the former in wealth, extent, and importance; and was honoured with the magnificent titles of the second metropolis of the world, the city of cities, the queen of the East, a second Rome.

The city was founded in B.C. 332, and was built under the superintendence of the same architect (Dinocrates) who had rebuilt the Temple of Diana at Ephesus. The ancient city appears to have been of seven times the extent of the modern. If we may judge from the length of the two main streets (crossing each other at right angles) by which it was intersected, the city was about four miles long by one and a half wide: and in the time of Diodorus it contained a free population of 300,000 persons, or probably 600,000, if we double the former number, as Mannert suggests, in order to include the slaves. The port of Alexandria was secure, but difficult of access; in consequence of which, a magnificent pharos, or lighthouse, was erected upon an islet at the entrance, which was connected with the mainland by a dyke. This pharos was accounted one of the 'seven' wonders of the world. It was begun by Ptolemy Soter, and completed under Ptolemy Philadelphus, by Sostratus of Cnidus, B.C. 283. It was a square structure of white marble, on the top of which fires were kept constantly burning for the direction of mariners. It was erected at a cost of 800 talents, which, if Attic, would amount to 165,000*l.*, if Alexandrian, to twice that sum. It was a wonder in those times, when such erections were almost unknown; but, in itself, the Eddystone lighthouse is, in all probability, ten times more wonderful.

The business of working out the great design of Alexander could not have devolved on a more fitting person than Ptolemy Soter. From his first arrival in Egypt, he made Alexandria his residence: and no sooner had he some respite from war, then he bent all the resources of his mind to draw to his kingdom the whole trade of the East, which the Tyrians had, up to his time, carried on by sea to Elath, and from thence, by the way of Rhinocorura, to Tyre. He built a

24.

city on the west side of the Red Sea, whence he sent out fleets to all those countries to which the Phœnicians traded from Elath. But, observing that the Red Sea, by reason of rocks and shoals, was very dangerous towards its northern extremity, he transferred the trade to another city, which he founded at the greatest practicable distance southward. This port, which was almost on the borders of Ethiopia, he called, from his mother, Berenice; but the harbour being found inconvenient, the neighbouring city of Myos Hormos was preferred. Thither the products of the East and South were conveyed by sea; and were from thence taken on camels to Coptus, on the Nile, where they were again shipped for Alexandria, and from that city were dispersed to all the nations of the west, in exchange for merchandise which was afterwards exported to the East. By these means, the whole trade was fixed at Alexandria, which thus became the chief mart of all the traffic between the East and West, and which continued to be the greatest emporium in the world for above seventeen centuries, until the discovery of the passage by the Cape of Good Hope opened another channel for the commerce of the East.

Alexandria became not only the seat of commerce, but of learning and the liberal sciences. This distinction also it owed to Ptolemy Soter, himself a man of education, who founded an academy, or society of learned men, who devoted themselves to the study of philosophy, literature, and science. For their use he made a collection of choice books, which, by degrees, increased under his successors until it became the finest library in the world, and numbered 700,000 volumes. It sustained repeated losses, by fire and otherwise, but these losses were as repeatedly repaired; and it continued to be of great fame

and use in those parts, until it was at length burnt by the Saracens when they made themselves masters of Alexandria in A.D. 642. Undoubtedly the Jews at Alexandria shared in the benefit of these institutions, as the Christians did afterwards; for the city was not only a seat of heathen, but of Jewish, and subsequently of Christian learning. It will be remembered that the celebrated translation of the Hebrew Scriptures into Greek [SEPTUAGINT] was made, under every encouragement from Ptolemy Philadelphus, principally for the use of the Jews in Alexandria, who knew only the Greek language.

At its foundation Alexandria was peopled less by Egyptians than by colonies of Greeks, Jews, and other foreigners. The Jews, however much their religion was disliked, were valued as citizens; and every encouragement was held out by Alexander himself and by his successors in Egypt, to induce them to settle in the new city. The same privileges as those of the first class of inhabitants (the Greeks) were accorded to them, as well as the free exercise of their religion and peculiar usages: and this, with the protection and peace which a powerful state afforded against the perpetual conflicts and troubles of Palestine, and with the inclination to traffic, which had been acquired during the Captivity, gradually drew such immense numbers of Jews to Alexandria, that they eventually formed a very large portion of its vast population, and at the same time constituted a most thriving and important section of the Jewish nation. The Jewish inhabitants of Alexandria are therefore often mentioned in the later history of the nation; and their importance as a section of that nation would doubtless have been more frequently indicated, had not the Jews of Egypt thrown off their ecclesiastical dependence upon Jerusalem and its temple, and formed a separate establishment of their own, in imitation of it, at a place about twelve miles north of Heliopolis, and called Onion, from Onias, the expelled highpriest, by whom it was founded.

The inhabitants of Alexandria were divided into three classes: 1. The Macedonians, the original founders of the city; 2. the mercenaries who had served under Alexander; 3. the native Egyptians. Through the favour of Alexander and Ptolemy Soter, the Jews were admitted into the first of these classes, and this privilege was so important that it had great effect in drawing them to the new city.

The dreadful persecution which the Jews of Alexandria underwent in A.D. 39, shows that, notwithstanding their long establishment there, no relations of friendliness had arisen between them and the other inhabitants, by whom in fact they were intensely hated. This feeling was so well known, that at the date indicated, the Roman governor Avillius Flaccus, who was anxious to ingratiate himself with the citizens, was persuaded that the surest way of winning their affections was to withdraw his protection from the Jews, against whom the emperor was already exasperated by their refusal to acknowledge his right to divine honours, which he insanely claimed, or to admit his images into their synagogues. In consequence of the connivance of Flaccus, the unfortunate Jews were treated with every species of outrage and insult. Their synagogues were levelled with the ground, consumed by fire, or profaned by the emperor's statues. They were deprived of the rights of citizenship, and declared aliens. Their houses, shops, and warehouses were plundered of their effects, and they themselves were pent up in one narrow corner of the city, where the greater part were obliged to lie in the open air, and where the supplies of food being cut off, many of them died of hardship and hunger; and whoever was found beyond the boundary, whether he had escaped from the assigned limits, or had come in from the country, was seized and put to death with horrid tortures.

At length king Herod Agrippa, who stayed long enough in Alexandria to see the beginning of these atrocities, transmitted to the emperor such a report of the real state of affairs as induced him to send a centurion to arrest Flaccus, and bring him a prisoner to Rome. This put the rioters in a false position, and brought some relief to the Jews; but the tumult still continued, and as the magistrates refused to acknowledge the citizenship of the Jews, it was at length agreed that both parties should send delegates, five on each side, to Rome, and refer the decision of the controversy to the emperor. At the head of the Jewish delegation was the celebrated Philo, to whom we owe the account of these transactions; and at the head of the Alexandrians was the noted Apion. The latter chiefly rested their case upon the fact that the Jews were the only people who refused to consecrate images to the emperor, or to swear by his name. But on this point the Jewish delegates defended themselves so well, that Caligula himself said, 'These men are not so wicked as ignorant and unhappy, in not believing me to be a god!' The

ultimate result of this appeal is not known, but the Jews of Alexandria continued to be harassed during the remainder of Caligula's reign; and their alabarch Alexander Lysimachus (brother of Philo) was thrown into prison, where he remained till he was discharged by Claudius, upon whose accession to the empire the Alexandrian Jews betook themselves to arms. This occasioned such disturbances that they attracted the attention of the emperor, who, at the joint entreaty of Herod and Agrippa, issued an edict conferring on the Jews of Egypt all their ancient privileges. The state of feeling in Alexandria which these facts indicate, was very far from being allayed when the revolt of the Jews in Palestine caused even those of the nation who dwelt in foreign parts to be regarded as enemies, both by the populace and the government. In Alexandria, on a public occasion, they were attacked, and those who could not save themselves by flight were put to the sword. Only three were taken alive, and they were dragged through the city to be consigned to the flames. The indignation of the Jews rose beyond all bounds at this spectacle. They first assailed the Greek citizens with stones, and then rushed with lighted torches to the amphitheatre, to set it on fire and burn all the people who were there assembled. The Roman prefect Tiberius Alexander, finding that milder measures were of no avail, sent out a body of 17,000 soldiers, who slew about 50,000 of the Jews, and plundered and burned their dwellings.

After the close of the war in Palestine, new disturbances were excited in Egypt by the Sicarii, many of whom had fled thither. They endeavoured to persuade the Jews to acknowledge no king but God, and to throw off the Roman yoke. Such persons as opposed their designs and tendered wiser counsels to their brethren, they secretly assassinated, according to their custom. But the principal Jews in Alexandria having in a general assembly earnestly warned the people against these fanatics, who had been the authors of all the troubles in Palestine, about 600 of them were delivered up to the Romans. Several fled into the Thebaïd, but were apprehended and brought back. The most cruel tortures which could be devised had no effect in compelling them to acknowledge the emperor for their sovereign; and even their children seemed endowed with souls fearless of death, and bodies incapable of pain. Vespasian, when informed of these transactions, sent orders that the Jewish temple in Egypt should be destroyed. Lupus the prefect, however, only shut it up, after having taken out the consecrated gifts: but his successor Paulinus stripped it completely, and excluded the Jews entirely from it. This was in A.D. 75, being the 343rd year from the building of the temple by Onias.

St. Mark is said to have introduced the Christian religion into Alexandria, which early became one of the strongholds of the true faith. The Jews continued to form a principal portion of the inhabitants, and remained in the enjoyment of their civil rights till A.D. 415, when they incurred the hatred of Cyril the patriarch, at whose instance they were expelled, to the number of 40,000, and their synagogues destroyed. However, when Amrou, in A.D. 640, took the place for the caliph Omar, he wrote to his master in these terms: 'I have taken the great city of the west, which contains 4000 palaces, 4000 baths, 400 theatres, 12,000 shops for the sale of vegetable food, *and* 40,000 *tributary Jews*.' From that time the prosperity of Alexandria very rapidly declined; and when, in 969, the Fatemite caliphs seized on Egypt and built New Cairo, it was speedily reduced to the rank of a secondary Egyptian city. The discovery of the passage to the East by the Cape, in 1497, almost annihilated its remaining commercial importance; and although the commercial and maritime enterprises of Mehemet Ali have again raised it to some distinction, Alexandria must still be accounted as one of those great ancient cities whose glory has departed. The number of Jews does not now exceed 500. The whole population at the present time (1843) is between 36,000 and 40,000, of whom 4876 are foreigners.

AL'GUM, or AL'MUG TREES (1 Kings x. 11; 2 Chron. ix. 10, 11). With regard to Ophir, the place from which these trees were brought to us, there appears no doubt that it was to the southward of the Red Sea, and was most probably in some part of India. Various trees have been attempted to be identified with the almug, but the balance of evidence seems to be in favour of the sandal-wood, which is known and highly esteemed in India. The tree which produces it is a native of the mountainous parts of the coast of Malabar, where large quantities are cut for export to China, to different parts of India, and to the Persian and Arabian gulfs. The outer parts of this tree are white and without odour; the parts near the root are most fragrant, especially of such trees as grow in hilly situations and stony ground. The trees vary in diameter from 9 inches to a foot, and are about 25 or 30 feet in height, but the stems soon begin to branch. This wood is white, fine-grained, and agreeably fragrant, and is much employed for making rosaries, fans, elegant boxes, and cabinets.

25   [Santalum album.]

As sandal-wood has been famed in the East from very early times, it is more likely than any other to have attracted the notice of, and been desired by, more northern nations.

That it, therefore, might have attained celebrity, even in very early ages, is not at all unlikely; that it should have attracted the notice of Phœnician merchants visiting the west coast of India is highly probable; and also that they should have thought it worthy of being taken as a part of their cargo on their return from Ophir. That it is well calculated for musical instruments is confirmed by the authority of Professor Wheatstone, who says, 'I know no reason why sandal-wood should not have been employed in ancient days for constructing musical instruments. It is not so employed at present, because there are many much cheaper woods which present a far handsomer appearance. Musical instruments would appear very unfinished to modern taste unless varnished or French-polished, and it would be worse than useless to treat fragrant woods in this way. Formerly perhaps it might have been more the fashion to delight the senses of smell and hearing simultaneously than it is with us, in which case odoriferous woods would be preferred for things so much handled as musical instruments are.'

ALLEGORY. This word is found in the Authorized Version of Gal. iv. 24, but it does not actually exist as a noun in the Greek Testament, nor even in the Septuagint. In the passage in question Saint Paul cites the history of the free-born Isaac and the slave-born Ishmael, and in proceeding to apply it spiritually, he says, not as in our version, 'which things are *an allegory*,' but 'which things are *allegorized*.' This is of some importance; for in the one case the Apostle is made to declare a portion of Old Testament history an allegory, whereas in truth he only speaks of it as allegorically applied. *Allegories* themselves are, however, of frequent occurrence in Scripture, although that name is not then applied to them.

An ALLEGORY has been sometimes considered as only a lengthened *metaphor*; at other times, as *a continuation of metaphors*. But the nature of allegory itself, and the character of allegorical interpretation, will be best understood by attending to the origin of the term which denotes it. Now the term 'Allegory,' according to its original and proper meaning, denotes a representation of one thing which is intended to excite the representation of another thing. Every allegory must therefore be subjected to a *twofold* examination: we must first examine the *immediate representation*, and then consider what *other representation* it is intended to excite. In most allegories the immediate representation is made in the form of a narrative; and, since it is the object of the allegory itself to convey a moral, not an historic truth, the narrative is commonly fictitious. The *immediate* representation is of no further value than as it leads to the *ultimate* representation. It is the application or the moral of the allegory which constitutes its worth.

Every parable is a kind of allegory; and as an example, especially clear and correct, we may refer to the parable of the sower (Luke viii. 5-15). In this we have a plain narrative, a statement of a few simple and intelligible facts, such, probably, as had fallen within the observation of the persons to whom our Saviour addressed himself. When he had finished the narrative, or the immediate representation of the allegory, he then gave the explanation or ultimate representation of it; that is, he gave the allegorical interpretation of it. And that the interpretation was an interpretation, not of the words, but of the things signified by the words, is evident from the explanation itself: ' The seed is the word of God; those by the wayside are they that hear,' &c. (ver. 11, &c.). The impressive and pathetic allegory addressed by Nathan to David affords a similar instance of an allegorical narrative accompanied with its explanation (2 Sam. xii. 1-14).

But allegorical narratives are frequently left to explain themselves, especially when the resemblance between the immediate and ultimate representation is sufficiently apparent to make an explanation unnecessary. Of this kind we cannot have a more striking example than that beautiful one contained in the 80th Psalm: ' Thou broughtest a vine out of Egypt,' &c.

The use of allegorical interpretation is not, however, confined to mere allegory, or fictitious narratives, but is extended also to history, or real narratives. And in this case the grammatical meaning of a passage is called its *historical* meaning, in contradistinction to its *allegorical* meaning. There are two different modes in which Scripture history has been thus allegorized. According to one mode, facts and circumstances, especially those recorded in the Old Testament, have been applied to other facts and circumstances, of which they have been described as *representative*. According to the other mode, these facts and circumstances have been described as mere *emblems*. The former mode is warranted by the practice of the sacred writers themselves; for when facts and circumstances are so applied, they are applied as *types* of those things to which the application is made: but no such authority in favour of the latter mode of allegorical interpretation can be produced.

ALLELU'IA. [Hallelujah.]

ALLIANCES. From a dread lest the example of foreign nations should draw the Israelites into the worship of idols, they were made a peculiar and separate people, and intercourse and alliance with such nations were strongly interdicted (Lev. xviii. 3, 4; xx. 22, 23). The tendency to idolatry was in those times so strong, that the safety of the Israelites lay in the most complete isolation that could be realized; and it was to assist this object that a country more than usually separated from others by its natural boundaries was assigned to them. It was shut in by the sea on the west, by deserts on the south and east, and by mountains and forests on the north. Among a people so situated we should not expect to hear much of alliances with other nations.

By far the most remarkable alliance in the political history of the Hebrews is that between Solomon and Hiram king of Tyre, which may primarily be referred to the affection which the latter entertained for David (1 Kings v. 2). He ' sent carpenters and masons ' to build David an house (2 Sam. v. 11), and wishing to cultivate the friendly intercourse thus opened with the Hebrew nation, on the death of David he sent an embassy to condole with Solomon on the death of his father, and to congratulate him on his ac-

cession (1 Kings v. 1). The plans of the young king rendered the friendship of Hiram a matter of importance, and accordingly ' a league' was formed (1 Kings v. 12) between them : and that this league had a reference not merely to the special matter then in view, but was a general league of amity, is evinced by the fact that more than 250 years after, a prophet denounces the Lord's vengeance upon Tyre, because she ' remembered not the brotherly covenant ' (Amos i. 9). Under this league large bodies of Jews and Phœnicians were associated, first in preparing the materials for the Temple (1 Kings v. 6-18), and afterwards in navigating the Red Sea and the Indian Ocean (1 Kings ix. 26-28). The disastrous consequences of even the seemingly least objectionable alliances may be seen in the long train of evils, both to the kingdom of Israel and of Judah, which ensued from the marriage of Ahab with Jezebel, the king of Tyre's daughter [Ahab; Jezebel]. These consequences had been manifested even in the time of Solomon; for he formed matrimonial alliances with most of the neighbouring kingdoms, and to the influence of his idolatrous wives are ascribed the abominations which darkened the latter days of the wise king (1 Kings xi. 1-8).

The prophets, who were alive to these consequences, often raised their voices against such dangerous connections (1 Kings xi. 11 ; 2 Chron. xvi. 7; xix. 2; xxv. 7, &c.; Isa. vii. 17), without effect. The Jewish history, after Solomon, affords examples of several treaties with different kings of Syria, and with the kings of Assyria and Babylon (see 1 Kings xv. 16-20; 2 Kings xvi. 5, &c.; 2 Chron. xviii. 16, &c.). In later times, the Maccabees appear to have considered themselves unrestrained by any but the ordinary prudential considerations in contracting alliances. The most remarkable alliance of this kind was the treaty made with the Romans by Judas Maccabæus, which, having been concluded at Rome, was graven upon brass and deposited in the Capitol (1 Macc. viii. 22-28; Josephus, *Antiq.* xii. 10).

Anterior to the Mosaical institutions, such alliances with foreigners were permitted. or at least tolerated. Abraham was in alliance with some of the Canaanitish princes (Gen. xiv. 13); he also entered into a regular treaty of alliance, being the first on record, with the Philistine king Abimelech (xxi. 22, *sq.*), which was renewed by their sons (xxvi. 26-30). Even after the law, it appears, from some of the instances already adduced, that such alliances with distant nations as could not be supposed to have any dangerous effect upon the religion or morals of the people, were not deemed to be interdicted. The treaty with the Gibeonites is a remarkable proof of this. Believing that the ambassadors came from a great distance, Joshua and the elders readily entered into an alliance with them; and are condemned for it only on the ground that the Gibeonites were in fact their near neighbours (Josh. ix. 3-27).

From the time of the patriarchs, a covenant of alliance was sealed by the blood of some victim. A heifer, a goat, a ram, a turtle dove, and a young pigeon, were immolated in confirmation of the covenant between the Lord and Abraham (Gen. xv. 9). The animal or animals sacrificed were cut in two (except birds, ver. 10), to typify the doom of perjurers. For allusions to this usage see Jer. xxxiv. 18; Sus. 55, 59; Matt. xxiv. 51; Luke xii. 46. The perpetuity of covenants of alliance thus contracted is expressed by calling them 'covenants of salt' (Num. xviii. 19; 2 Chron. xiii. 5), salt being the symbol of incorruption. The case of the Gibeonites affords an exemplary instance, scarcely equalled in the annals of any nation, of scrupulous adherence to such engagements. The Israelites had been absolutely cheated into the alliance; but, having been confirmed by oaths, it was deemed to be inviolable (Josh. ix. 19). The prophet Ezekiel (xvii. 13-16) pours terrible denunciations upon king Zedekiah, for acting contrary to his sworn covenant with the king of Babylon. In this respect the Jews were certainly most favourably distinguished among the ancient nations; and, from numerous intimations in Josephus, it appears that their character for fidelity to their engagements was so generally recognised after the Captivity, as often to procure for them highly favourable consideration from the rulers of Western Asia and of Egypt.

AL'LON-BAC'HUTH (*the oak of weeping*), a place in Bethel, where Rebekah's nurse was buried (Gen. xxxv. 8).

AL'MON, one of the three cities which belonged to the priests in the tribe of Benjamin (Josh. xxi. 18). It is supposed to be the same as the Alemeth of 1 Chron. vi. 60.

AL'MON-DIB'LATHAIM, one of the stations of the Israelites on their way from Mount Hor to the plains of Moab, round by Mount Seir (Num. xxxiii. 46).

ALMOND TREE (Gen. xliii. 11; Num. xvii. 8; Eccles. xii. 5; Jer. i. 11). This tree is a native of Syria and Palestine, and is highly ornamental from the beauty of its blossoms.

26. [Almond Tree.]

The form of the almond would lead to its selection for ornamental carved work (Exod. xxv. 33, 34; xxxvii. 19), independently of its form-

ing an esteemed esculent, as well as probably yielding a useful oil. In Eccles. xii. 5, it is said, 'The almond tree shall flourish, and the fruit of the caper droop, because man goeth to his long home.' This evidently refers to the profuse flowering and white appearance of the almond tree when in full bloom, and before its leaves appear. It is hence adduced as illustrative of the hoary hairs of age, in the same way as the drooping of the fruit of the caper seems to refer to the hanging down of the head. Dr. Kitto mentions the almond among the first trees that flower in January. 'There are two species of Amygdalus in Palestine: the common *almond* tree, and the *peach* tree, and both are this month in blossom in every part of Palestine, on both sides of the Jordan. It was doubtless from this winter blossoming of the almond tree, not less than from the snowy whiteness of the blossoms, that the hoary head of the aged man is, by a beautiful metaphor, said in Scripture to flourish like the almond tree' (*Physic. Hist. of Palestine*).

ALMS. The regulations of the Mosaic law respecting property, and its benign spirit towards the poor, went far to prevent the existence of penury as a permanent condition in society, and, consequently, by precluding beggary, to render the need of almsgiving unnecessary. Poverty, however, considered as a state of comparative want, Moses seems to have contemplated as a probable event in the social frame which he had established; and accordingly, by the appointment of specific regulations, and the enjoining of a general spirit of tender-heartedness, he sought to prevent destitution and its evil consequences (Lev. xxv. 35; Deut. xv. 7, &c.). The great antiquity of the practice of benevolence towards the poor is shown in the very beautiful passage which is found in Job xxix. 13 *et seq.* How high the esteem in which this virtue continued to be held in the time of the Hebrew monarchy may be learnt from Ps. xli. 1; see also Ps. cxii. 9; Prov. xiv. 31. The progress of social corruption, however, led to the oppression of the poor, which the prophets, after their manner, faithfully reprobated (Isa. lviii. 7); where, among other neglected duties, the Israelites are required to deal their bread to the hungry, and to bring the outcast poor to their house. See also Isa. x. 2; Amos ii. 7; Jer. v. 28; Ezek. xxii. 29.

However favourable to the poor the Mosaic institutions were, they do not appear to have wholly prevented beggary; for the imprecation found in Psalm cix. 10, 'Let his children be vagabonds and beg,' implies the existence of beggary as a known social condition. Begging naturally led to almsgiving, though the language of the Bible does not present us with a term for 'alms' till the period of the Babylonish captivity, during the calamities attendant on which the need probably introduced the practice. From Dan. iv. 27 it would appear that almsgiving had come to be regarded as a means of conciliating God's favour and of warding off evil. At a still later period this idea took a firm seat in the national mind, and alms-deeds were regarded as a mark of distinguished virtue. That begging was customary in the time of the Saviour is clear from Mark x. 46. And that it was usual for the worshippers, as they entered the temple, to give relief, appears from the context, and particularly from the fine answer to the lame man's entreaty, made by the apostle Peter. The general spirit of Christianity, in regard to succouring the needy, is nowhere better seen than in 1 John iii. 17: 'Whoso hath this world's good, and seeth his brother have need, and shutteth up his bowels from him, how dwelleth the love of God in him?' With the faithful and conscientious observance of the 'royal law' of love, particular manifestations of mercy to the poor seem to be left by Christianity to be determined by time, place, and circumstances; and it cannot be supposed that a religion, one of whose principles is 'that, if any would not work, neither should he eat' (2 Thess. iii. 10), can give any sanction to indiscriminate almsgiving, or intend to encourage the crowd of wandering, idle beggars with which some parts of the world are still infested. The emphatic language employed by the Lord Jesus Christ and others (Luke iii. 11; vi. 30; xi. 41; xii. 33; Matt. vi. 1; Acts ix. 36; x. 2, 4) is designed to enforce the general duty of a merciful and practical regard to the distresses of the indigent; while the absence of ostentation, and even secrecy, which the Saviour enjoined in connection with almsgiving, was intended to correct actual abuses, and bring the practice into harmony with the spirit of the Gospel. In the remarkable reflections of Jesus on the widow's mite (Mark xii. 42) is found a principle of great value, to the effect that the magnitude of men's offerings to God is to be measured by the disposition of mind whence they proceed; a principle which cuts up by the very roots the idea that merit attaches itself to almsgiving as such, and increases in proportion to the number and costliness of our alms-deeds.

One of the earliest effects of the working of Christianity in the hearts of its professors was the care which it led them to take of the poor and indigent in the 'household of faith.' Neglected and despised by the world, cut off from its sympathies, and denied any succour it might have given, the members of the early churches were careful not only to make provision in each case for its own poor, but to contribute to the necessities of other though distant communities (Acts xi. 29; xxiv. 17; 2 Cor. ix. 12). This commendable practice seems to have had its Christian origin in the deeply interesting fact (which appears from John xiii. 29) that the Saviour and his attendants were wont, notwithstanding their own comparative poverty, to contribute out of their small resources something for the relief of the needy.

ALOES, the two words which are so rendered occur in several passages of the Old Testament, as in Psalm xlv. 8; Prov. vii. 17; Canticles iv. 14, and evidently mean some odoriferous substance which ought not to be confounded with the bitter and nauseous aloes famed only as a medicine, and which is usually disagreeable in odour and nauseous in taste, and could never have been employed as a perfume. The words referred to seem to indicate a kind of fragrant wood called *Agallochum*, which was brought from India and Arabia. There can be little or no doubt that the same odoriferous wood is intended in John xix. 39, where we are told

that when the body of our Saviour was taken down from the cross, Nicodemus brought myrrh and aloes for the purpose of winding up the body in linen clothes with these spices.

AL'PHA (A), the first letter of the Greek alphabet, corresponding to the Hebrew *Aleph*. Both the Hebrews and the Greeks employed the letters of their alphabets as numerals, and A (*Alpha* or *Aleph*) therefore denoted *one* or *the first*. Hence our Lord says of himself, that he is *Alpha and Omega, i. e.* the first and the last, the beginning and the ending, as he himself explains it (Rev. i. 8, 11; xxi. 6; xxii 13).

1. ALPHÆ'US, father of James the Less (Matt. x. 3; Luke vi. 15), and husband of Mary, the sister of our Lord's mother (John xix. 25); for which reason James is called 'the Lord's brother' [BROTHER]. By comparing John xix. 25, with Luke xxiv. 10, and Matt. x. 3, it appears that Alphæus is the same person as Cleophas; Alphæus being his Greek, and Cleophas his Hebrew or Syriac name [NAMES].

2. ALPHÆUS, the father of the evangelist Levi or Matthew (Mark ii. 14).

ALTAR. The first altar we read of in the Bible was that erected by Noah on leaving the ark. Mention is made of altars erected by Abraham (Gen. xii. 7; xiii. 4; xxii. 9); by Isaac (xxvi. 25); by Jacob (xxxiii. 20; xxxv. 1, 3); by Moses (Exod. xvii. 15). After the giving of the law, the Israelites were commanded to make an altar of earth; they were also permitted to employ stones, but no iron tool was to be applied to them. This has been generally understood as an interdiction of sculpture, in order to guard against a violation of the second commandment. Altars were frequently built on high places. Thus Solomon *built* an high place for Chemosh (1 Kings xi. 7), and Josiah brake down and burnt the high place, and stamped it small to powder (2 Kings xxiii. 15). This practice, however, was forbidden by the Mosaic law (Deut. xii. 13; xvi. 5), except in particular instances. such as those of Gideon (Judg. vi. 26) and David (2 Sam. xxiv. 18). It is said of Solomon 'that he loved the Lord, walking in the statutes of David, his father, only he sacrificed the burnt incense on the high places' (1 Kings iii. 3). Altars were sometimes built on the roofs of houses: in 2 Kings xxiii. 12, we read of the altars that were on the top of the upper chamber of Ahaz. In the tabernacle, and afterwards in the temple, two altars were erected, one for sacrifices, the other for incense: the table for the shew-bread is also sometimes called an altar.

1. The altar of burnt-offering belonging to the tabernacle was a hollow square, five cubits in length and breadth, and three cubits in height; it was made of Shittim-wood [SHITTIM], and overlaid with plates of brass. In the middle there was a ledge or projection, on which the priest stood while officiating; immediately below this, a brass grating was let down into the altar to support the fire, with four rings attached, through which poles were passed, when the altar was removed. As the priests were forbidden to go up by steps to the altar (Exod. xx. 26), a slope of earth was probably made rising to a level with the ledge.

In Exod. xxvii. 3, the following utensils are

mentioned as belonging to the altar, all of which were to be made of brass. (1) pans or dishes to receive the ashes that fell through the grating. (2) shovels for cleaning the altar. (3) vessels for receiving the blood and sprinkling it on the altar. (4) large forks to turn the pieces of flesh or to take them off the fire (see 1 Sam. ii. 13). (5) '*fire-pans;*' the same word is elsewhere translated *censers*, Num. xvi. 17; but in Exod. xxv. 38, ' *snuff-dishes.*'

2. The altar of burnt-offering in Solomon's temple was of much larger dimensions, ' twenty cubits in length and breadth, and ten in height' (2 Chron. iv. 1), and was made entirely of brass. It is said of Asa that he renewed, that is, either *repaired* (in which sense the word is evidently used in 2 Chron. xxiv. 4) or *reconsecrated* the altar of the Lord that was before the porch of the Lord (2 Chron. xv. 8). This altar was removed by king Ahaz (2 Kings xvi. 14); it was 'cleansed' by Hezekiah; and in the latter part of Manasseh's reign was rebuilt.

3. Of the altar of burnt-offering in the second temple, the canonical scriptures give us no information excepting that it was erected before the foundations of the temple were laid (Ezra iii. 3, 6) on the same place where it had formerly been built. From the Apocrypha, however, we may infer that it was made, not of brass, but of unhewn stone.

4. The altar of burnt-offering erected by Herod is thus described by Josephus : ' Before this temple stood the altar, fifteen cubits high, and equal both in length and breadth, each of which dimensions was fifty cubits. The figure it was built in was a square, and it had corners like horns, and the passage up to it was by an insensible acclivity from the south. It was formed without any iron tool, nor did any iron tool so much as touch it at any time.' The dimensions of this altar, however, are differently stated in the Mishna. On the south side was an inclined plane, 32 cubits long and 16 cubits broad, made likewise of unhewn stones. A pipe was connected with the south-west horn, through which the blood of the victims was discharged by a subterraneous passage into the brook Kedron Under the altar was a cavity to receive the drink- offerings, which was covered with a marble slab, and cleansed from time to time. On the north side of the altar several iron rings were fixed to fasten the victims. Lastly, a red line was drawn round the middle of the altar to distinguish between the blood that was to be sprinkled above and below it.

II. The second altar belonging to the Jewish worship was *the altar of incense*, called also the golden altar (Num. iv. 11). It was placed between the table of shew-bread and the golden candlestick, in the most holy place.

1. This altar in the tabernacle was made of Shittim-wood overlaid with gold plates, one cubit in length and breadth, and two cubits in height. It had horns (Lev. iv. 7) of the same materials; and round the flat surface was a border of gold, underneath which were the rings to receive ' the staves made of Shittim-wood, overlaid with gold to bear it withal' (Exod. xxx. 1-5).

2. The altar in Solomon's Temple was similar, but made of cedar (1 Kings vi. 20; vii. 48; 1 Chron. xxviii. 18) overlaid with gold.

3. The altar in the second temple was taken away by Antiochus Epiphanes (1 Macc. i. 21), and restored by Judas Maccabæus (1 Macc. iv. 49). On the arch of Titus there appears no altar of incense.

ALTARS, FORMS OF. In the preceding article the reader is furnished with all the positive information which we possess respecting the altars mentioned in Scripture; but as, with regard to material objects so frequently named as altars, we feel a desire to have distinct images in the mind, some further remarks respecting the forms which they probably bore, may not be unacceptable.

The direction to the Israelites, at the time of their leaving Egypt, to construct their altars of unhewn stones or of earth, is doubtless to be understood as an injunction to follow the usage of their patriarchal ancestors; and not to adopt the customs, full of idolatrous associations, which they had seen in Egypt, or might see in the land of Canaan. As they were also strictly enjoined to destroy the altars of the Canaanites, it is more than probable that the direction was levelled against such usages as those into which that people had fallen. The conclusion deducible from this, that the patriarchal altars were of unhewn stones or of earth, is confirmed by the circumstances under which they were erected, and by the fact that they are always described as being ' built.' The provision that they *might* be made of earth, applies doubtless to situations in which stones could not be easily obtained, as in the open plains and wildernesses. Familiar analogies lead to the inference that the largest stones that could be found in the neighbourhood would be employed to form the altar; but where no large stones could be had, that heaps of smaller ones might be made to serve.

As these altars were erected in the open air, and were very carefully preserved, there is at least a strong probability that some of those ancient monuments of unhewn stone, usually called Druidical remains, which are found in all parts of the world, were derived from the altars of primitive times. These are diversified in their forms; and their peculiar uses have been very much disputed. It is admitted, however, that some of them must have been altars; but the difficulty is, to determine whether these altars are to be sought in the Cromlechs or the Kistvaens. It seems to us that the arguments preponderate in favour of the opinion that the Cromlechs are the representatives of the primitive altars, and that the Kistvaens (stones disposed in a chest-like form) are analogous to the arks of the Jewish ritual and of some of the pagan religions [ARK].

Cromlechs, as is well known, are somewhat in the form of a table, one large stone being supported, in a horizontal or slightly inclined position, upon three or more, but usually three stones, set upright. That they were used as altars is almost instinctively suggested to every one that views them; and this conclusion is strengthened when, as is often the case, we observe a small circular hole through which probably the rope was run by which the victims, when slaughtered, were bound to the altar, as they were to the angular projections or ' horns' of the Jewish altar (Ps. cxviii. 27). It was

27.

natural that where a sufficiency of large stones could not be found, heaps of smaller ones should be employed; and that, when practicable, a large flat stone would be placed on the top, to give a proper level for the fire and the sacrifice. Such are the cairn-altars, of which many still remain; but as they are sometimes found in places where stones of large size might have been obtained, it seems that in later times *such* altars had a special appropriation; and that the sacred fires were burned on them, and sacrifices offered to Bel, Baal, or the Sun.

28.

The injunction that there should be no ascent by steps to the *altar* appears to have been imperfectly understood. There are no accounts or figures of altars so elevated in their fabric as to require such steps for the officiating priests; but when altars are found on rocks or hills, the ascent to them is sometimes facilitated by steps *cut in the rock*. This, therefore, may have been an indirect way of preventing that erection of altars in high places which the Scriptures so often reprobate.

It is usually supposed, however, that the effect of this prohibition was, that the tabernacle altar, like most ancient altars, was so low as to need no ascent; or else that some other kind of ascent was provided. The former is probably right, for the altar was but three cubits high, and was designed to be portable. There is one error in these and other figures of the Jewish altars composed from the descriptions; namely, with regard to the ' horns,' which were placed at the corners, called ' the horns of the altar ' (Exod. xxvii. 2; xxix. 12; 1 Kings ii. 28), and to which the victims were tied at the time of sacrifice. The word horn was applied by the Jews as an epithet descriptive of any point projecting in any direction after the manner of a horn (not necessarily like a horn in shape); and there is no reason to doubt that the horns of the successive altars of burnt-offerings resembled those corners projecting upwards which are seen in many ancient altars. These are shown in the view depicting the probable form of the Jewish altar of burnt-offerings.

By the time of Solomon it appears to have

been understood that the interdiction of steps of ascent did not imply that the altar was to be low, but rather that it was to be high, and that only a particular mode of ascent was forbidden. The altar of the temple was not less than ten cubits high, and some means of ascent must have been provided. The usual representations of Solomon's altar are formed chiefly from the descriptions of that in Herod's temple given by Josephus and the Rabbins; and although this last was almost one-third higher and larger than the other, it was doubtless upon the same model. The altar of the first temple had been seen, and could be described, by many of those who were present when that of the second temple was erected; and the latter was known to those by whom Herod's altar was built. Very different figures, however, have been formed from these descriptions, and that which we here introduce is perhaps the best and most probable of them.

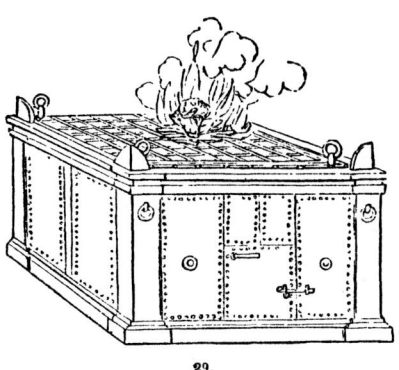

29.

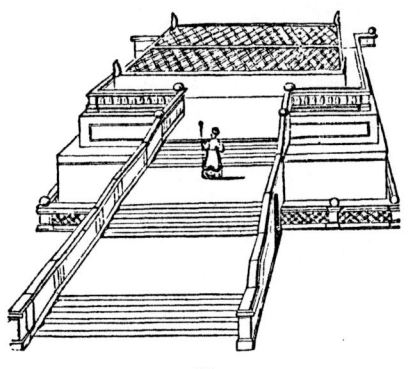

30.

THE ALTAR OF INCENSE, being very simple in its parts and uses, has been represented with so little difference, except in some ornamental details, that one of the figures designed from the descriptions may suffice.

It is not our object to describe the altars of other nations; but, to supply materials for comparison and illustration, a group of the altars of the principal nations of Oriental and classical antiquity is here introduced. One obvious remark occurs, namely, that all the Oriental altars are square or oblong, whereas those of Greece

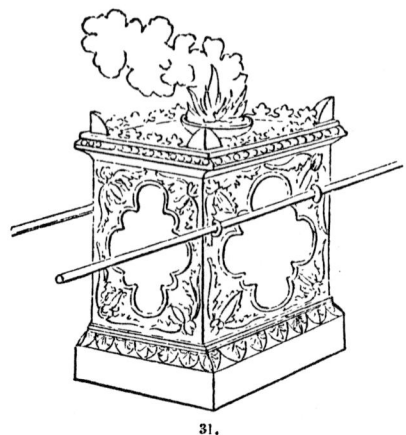

31.

and Rome are more usually round; and that, upon the whole, the Hebrew altars were in accordance with the general Oriental type. In all of them we observe bases with corresponding projections at the top; and in some we find the true model of the 'horns,' or prominent and pointed angles.

32. [1, 2, 3. Greek. 4. Egyptian. 5. Babylonian. 6. Roman. 7, 8. Persian.]

ALTAR AT ATHENS. St. Paul, in his admired address before the judges of the Areopagus at Athens, declares that he perceived that the Athenians were in all things too superstitious, for that, as he was passing by and beholding their devotions, he found an altar, inscribed, 'TO THE UNKNOWN GOD;' and adds, with unexpected force, '*Him* whom ye worship without knowing, I set forth unto you' (Acts xvii. 22, 23). The questions suggested by the mention of an altar at Athens, thus inscribed 'to the unknown God,' have engaged much attention. Different opinions have been entertained on the subject, and various conjectures made regarding it. No certain information, however, can now be obtained respecting the precise reference of the apostle,

and we are content to rest in the conclusion of Professor Robinson: 'So much at least is certain, that altars to an unknown god or gods existed at Athens. But the attempt to ascertain definitively whom the Athenians worshipped under this appellation must ever remain fruitless for want of sufficient data. The inscription afforded to Paul a happy occasion of proclaiming the Gospel; and those who embraced it found indeed that the being whom they had thus "ignorantly worshipped," was the one only living and true God.'

A'LUSH, one of the places at which the Hebrews rested on their way to Mount Sinai (Num. xxxiii. 13). It was between Dophkah and Rephidim. The Jewish Chronology makes it twelve miles from the former and eight from the latter station.

AM'ALEK, a son of Eliphaz (the first-born of Esau) by his concubine Timna: he was the chieftain, or Emir, of an Idumæan tribe (Gen. xxxvi. 16).

AM'ALEKITES, the name of a nation inhabiting the country to the south of Palestine between Idumæa and Egypt, and to the east of the Dead Sea and Mount Seir. 'The Amalekites dwell in the land of the south' (Num. xiii. 29). 'Saul smote the Amalekites from Havilah until thou comest to Shur, that is over against Egypt' (1 Sam. xv. 7). 'David went up and invaded the Geshurites, and Gezrites, and the Amalekites, for those nations were of old the inhabitants of the land as thou goest to Shur, even unto the land of Egypt' (1 Sam. xxvii. 8). In 1 Chron. iv. 42, it is said that the sons of Simeon went to Mount Seir and smote the rest of the Amalekites that were escaped. According to Josephus the Amalekites inhabited Gobolitis and Petra, and were the most warlike of the nations in those parts: and elsewhere he speaks of them as 'reaching from Pelusium of Egypt to the Red Sea.' We find, also, that they had a settlement in that part of Palestine which was allotted to the tribe of Ephraim. The first mention of the Amalekites in the Bible is Gen. xiv. 7; Chedorlaomer and his confederates returned and came to En-Mishpat, which is Kadesh, and smote all the country of the Amalekites, and also the Amorites that dwelt in Hazezon-tamar. The Amalekites were the first assailants of the Israelites after their passage through the Red Sea (Exod. xvii.). It has been thought improbable that in so short a period the descendants of Esau's grandson could have been sufficiently numerous and powerful to attack the host of Israel; but within nearly the same period the tribe of Ephraim had increased so that it could muster 40,500 men able to bear arms, and Manasseh 32,200: and admitting in the case of the Israelites an extraordinary rate of increase (Exod. i. 12, 20), still, if we consider the prostrating influence of slavery on the national character, and the absence of warlike habits, it is easy to conceive that a comparatively small band of marauders would be a very formidable foe to an undisciplined multitude, circumstanced as the Israelites were, in a locality so adapted to irregular warfare. It appears too that the attack was made on the most defenceless portion of the host. 'Remember (said Moses) what Amalek did unto thee by the way when ye were come forth out of Egypt; how he met thee by the way and smote the hindmost of thee, even all *that were feeble behind thee*, when thou wast faint and weary ' (Deut. xxv. 17, 18). In the Pentateuch the Amalekites are frequently mentioned in connection with the Canaanites (Num. xiv. 25, 43, 45), and, in the book of Judges, with the Moabites and Ammonites (Judg. iii. 13); with the Midianites (Judg. vi. 3; vii. 12: 'The Midianites, and the Amalekites, and all the children of the East lay along in the valley like grasshoppers for multitude; and their camels were without number, as the sand by the sea-side for multitude'); with the Kenites (1 Sam. xv. 6). By divine command, as a retribution for their hostility to the Israelites on leaving Egypt (1 Sam. xv. 2), Saul invaded their country with an army of 210,000 men, and '*utterly destroyed* all the people with the edge of the sword,' but he preserved their king Agag alive, and the best of the cattle, and by this act of disobedience forfeited the regal authority over Israel. About twenty years later they were attacked by David during his residence among the Philistines (1 Sam. xxvii.). It is said 'that he smote the land and left neither man nor woman alive:' this language must be taken with some limitation, for shortly after the Amalekites were sufficiently recovered from their defeat to make reprisals, and burnt Ziklag with fire (1 Sam. xxx.). David, on his return from the camp of Achish, surprised them while celebrating their success, 'eating, and drinking, and dancing,' and 'smote them from twilight even unto the evening of the next day, and there escaped not a man of them save 400 young men which rode upon camels, and fled' (1 Sam. xxx. 17). At a later period, we find that David dedicated to the Lord the silver and gold of Amalek and other conquered nations (2 Sam. viii. 12). The last notice of the Amalekites as a nation is in 1 Chron. iv. 43, from which we learn that in the days of Hezekiah, king of Judah, 500 men of the sons of Simeon ' went to Mount Seir, and smote the rest of the Amalekites that were escaped.'

In the book of Esther, Haman is called the Agagite, and was probably a descendant of the royal line (Num. xxiv. 7; 1 Sam. xv. 8). Josephus says that he was by birth an Amalekite.

AMA'NA, a mountain mentioned in Cant. iv. 8. Some have supposed it to be Mount Amanus in Cilicia, to which the dominion of Solomon is alleged to have extended northward. But the context, with other circumstances, leaves little doubt that this Mount Amana was rather the southern part or summit of Anti-Libanus, and was so called perhaps from containing the sources of the river Amana [ABANA].

1. AMARI'AH (*whom Jehovah said*, i. e. *promised*, equivalent to the Greek name Theophrastus), mentioned in 1 Chron. vi. 7, in the list of the descendants of Aaron by his eldest son Eleazer. He was the son of Meraioth and the father of Ahitub, who was (not the grandson and successor of Eli of the same name, but) the father of that Zadok in whose person Saul restored the high-priesthood to the line of Eleazer. The years during which the younger line of Ithamar enjoyed the pontificate in the persons of Eli, Ahitub, and Abimelech (who was slain by king Saul at Nob) doubtless more than cover the time

of Amariah and his son Ahitub; and it is therefore sufficiently certain that they never were high-priests in fact, although their names are given so to carry on the direct line of succession to Zadok.

2. AMARIAH, high-priest at a later period, the son of Azariah, and also father of a second Ahitub (1 Chron. vi. 11). In like manner, in the same list, there are three high-priests bearing the name of Azariah.

3. AMARIAH, great-grandfather of the prophet Zephaniah (Zeph. i. 1).

1. AMA'SA (*burden*), son of Abigail, a sister of king David. As his name does not occur prior to Absalom's rebellion (2 Sam. xvii. 25), he must have been neglected by David in comparison with Joab and Abishai, the sons of his other sister Zeruiah, who had before then been raised to great power and influence. This apparent estrangement may perhaps be connected with the fact that Abigail had married an Ishmaelite called Jether, who was the father of Amasa. This is the more likely, as the fact is pointedly mentioned (1 Chron. ii. 17), or covertly indicated (2 Sam. xvii. 25) whenever the name of Abigail occurs, whereas we are quite ignorant who was the husband of the other sister, Zeruiah, and father of her distinguished sons. We may thus form a conjecture of the grounds on which Amasa joined Absalom, and obtained the command of the rebel army. He was defeated by his cousin Joab, who commanded the army of David. This transaction appears to have made David sensible of the neglect with which Amasa had been treated; and he eventually offered him not only pardon, but the command of the army in the room of Joab (2 Sam. xix. 13), whose overbearing conduct had become intolerable to him, and to whom he could not entirely forgive the death of Absalom. David, however, was too good a soldier himself to have made this offer, had not Amasa, notwithstanding his defeat, displayed high military qualities during his command of Absalom's army. But on the breaking out of Sheba's rebellion, Amasa was so tardy in his movements (probably from the reluctance of the troops to follow him), that David despatched Abishai with the household troops in pursuit of Sheba, and Joab joined his brother as a volunteer. When they reached 'the great stone of Gibeon,' they were overtaken by Amasa with the force he had been able to collect. Joab thought this a favourable opportunity of getting rid of so dangerous a rival, and immediately executed the treacherous purpose he had formed. He saluted Amasa, asked him of his health, and took his beard in his *right* hand to kiss him, while with the unheeded *left* hand he smote him dead with his sword. Joab then put himself at the head of the troops, and continued the pursuit of Sheba; and such was his popularity with the army, that David was unable to remove him from the command, or to call him to account for this bloody deed: B.C. 1022 [ABNER; ABSALOM; JOAB].

2. AMASA, a chief of Ephraim, who, with others, vehemently resisted the retention as prisoners of the persons whom Pekah, king of Israel, had taken captive in a successful campaign against Ahaz, king of Judah (2 Chron. xxviii. 12).

AMASA'I, the principal leader of a considerable body of men from the tribes of Judah and Benjamin, who joined David at Ziklag. The words with which David received them indicate some apprehension, which was instantly dissipated by a fervent declaration of attachment from Amasai (1 Chron. xii. 16-18).

1. AMAZI'AH (*whom Jehovah strengthens*, i. e. *God-strengthened*), son of Joash, and eighth king of Judah. He was 25 years old when he began to reign, and he reigned 29 years—from B.C. 838 to B.C. 809. He commenced his sovereignty by punishing the murderers of his father; and it is mentioned that he respected the law of Moses, by not including the children in the doom of their parents, which seems to show that a contrary practice had previously existed. In the twelfth year of his reign Amaziah attempted to re-impose upon the Edomites the yoke of Judah, which they had cast off in the time of Jehoram. The strength of Edom is evinced by the fact that Amaziah considered the unaided strength of his own kingdom unequal to this undertaking, and therefore hired an auxiliary force of 100,000 men from the king of Israel for 100,000 talents of silver. This is the first example of a mercenary army that occurs in the history of the Jews. It did not, however, render any other service than that of giving Amaziah an opportunity of manifesting that he knew his true place in the Hebrew constitution, as the viceroy and vassal of the king JEHOVAH [KING]. A prophet commanded him, in the name of the Lord, to send back the auxiliaries, on the ground that the state of alienation from God in which the kingdom of Israel lay, rendered such assistance not only useless but dangerous. The king obeyed this seemingly hard command, and sent the men home, although by doing so he lost not only their services and the 100,000 talents, which had been already paid, but incurred the resentment of the Israelites, who were naturally exasperated at the indignity shown to them.

But the obedience of Amaziah was rewarded by a great victory over the Edomites, ten thousand of whom were slain in battle, and ten thousand more were savagely destroyed by being hurled down from the high cliffs of their native mountains. But the Edomites afterwards were avenged; for among the goods which fell to the conqueror were some of their idols, which, although impotent to deliver their own worshippers, Amaziah betook himself to worship. This proved his ruin. Puffed up by his late victories, he thought also of reducing the ten tribes under his dominion. In this attempt he was defeated by king Joash of Israel, who carried him a prisoner to Jerusalem. Joash broke down great part of the city wall, plundered the city, and even laid his hands upon the sacred things of the temple. He, however, left Amaziah on the throne, but not without taking hostages for his good behaviour. The disasters which Amaziah's infatuation had brought upon Judah probably occasioned the conspiracy in which he lost his life. On receiving intelligence of this conspiracy he hastened to throw himself into the fortress of Lachish; but he was pursued and slain by the conspirators, who brought back his body 'upon horses' to Jerusalem for interment in the royal sepulchre (2 Kings xiv.; 2 Chron. xxv.).

2. AMAZIAH, the priest of the golden calves at Bethel, in the time of Jeroboam II. He complained to the king of Amos's prophecies of coming evil, and urged the prophet himself to withdraw into the kingdom of Judah and prophesy there (Amos vii. 10-17).

AMBER. The substance thus designated in the Authorized Version is in Hebrew called CHASMIL, and was probably a composition of several sorts of metal, since even the term by which the word is rendered by the Greeks frequently signifies a composition of gold and silver. The ancients were acquainted with the art of amalgamating various species of metal; and the Latin *aurichalcum* is said to have possessed the *brightness of gold* and the *hardness of copper*, and might not improbably have been our present *platina*, which has been re-discovered in the Ural mountains, after having long been known as an American fossil. It is not improbable that this was the metal termed 'fine copper' (Ezra viii. 27).

AMBIDEXTER, one who can use the left hand as well as the right, or, more literally, one whose hands are both right hands. It was long supposed that both hands are naturally equal, and that the preference of the right hand, and comparative incapacity of the left, are the result of education and habit. But it is now known that the difference is really physical, and that the ambidexterous condition of the hands is *not* a natural development.

The capacity of equal action with both hands was highly prized in ancient times, especially in war. Among the Hebrews this quality seems to have been most common in the tribe of Benjamin, as all the persons noticed as being endued with it were of that tribe. By comparing Judg. iii. 15, xx. 16, with 1 Chron. xii. 2, we may gather that the persons mentioned in the two former texts as 'left-handed,' were really ambidexters. In the latter text we learn that the Benjamites who joined David at Ziklag were 'mighty men, helpers of the war. They were armed with bows, and could use both the right hand and the left in hurling [slinging] and shooting arrows out of a bow.' There were thirty of them; and as they appear to have been all of one family, it might almost seem as if the greater commonness of this power among the Benjamites arose from its being an hereditary peculiarity of certain families in that tribe. It may also partly have been the result of cultivation; for although the left hand is not naturally an equally strong and ready instrument as the right hand, it may doubtless be often rendered such by early and suitable training.

AMEN. This word is strictly an adjective, signifying '*firm*,' and, metaphorically, '*faithful*.' Thus in Rev. iii. 14, our Lord is called 'the *amen*, the *faithful* and *true* witness.' In Isa. lxv. 16, the Heb. has 'the God of amen,' which our version renders 'the God of *truth*,' i. e. of *fidelity*. In its adverbial sense Amen means *certainly*, *truly*, *surely*. It is used in the beginning of a sentence by way of emphasis—rarely in the Old Test. (Jer. xxviii. 6), but often by our Saviour in the New, where it is commonly translated '*Verily*.' In John's gospel alone it is often used by him in this way double, *i. e.* 'verily, verily.' In the end of a sentence it often occurs singly or repeated, especially at the end of hymns or prayers, as 'amen and amen' (Ps. **xli.** 13; lxxii. 19; lxxxix. 52). The proper signification of it in this position is to confirm the words which have preceded, and invoke the fulfilment of them: 'so be it.' Hence in oaths, after the priest has repeated the words of the covenant or imprecation, all those who pronounced the *amen* bound themselves by the oath (Num. v. 22; Deut. xxvii. 15, 26; Neh. v. 13; viii. 6; 1 Chron. xvi. 36; comp. Ps cvi. 48).

AMETHYST. The word thus translated in the common version is in Hebrew ACHLAMAH, and is the name of the precious stone mentioned in Scripture as the ninth in the breastplate of the high-priest (Exod. xxviii. 19; xxxix. 12): in the New Testament the precise word *amethyst* (which is Greek) designates the twelfth stone in the foundations of the New Jerusalem (Rev. xxi. 20).

The transparent gems called amethysts are of a colour which seems composed of a strong blue and deep red; and according as either of these prevails, exhibit different tinges of purple, sometimes approaching to violet, and sometimes declining even to a rose colour. All the varieties of it are comprehended under two species, the *Oriental Amethyst* and the *Occidental Amethyst*. The Oriental amethyst is very scarce, and of great hardness, lustre, and beauty. It is in fact a rare variety of the adamantine spar, or corundum. Next to the diamond, it is the hardest substance known. It contains about 90 per cent. of alumine, a little iron, and a little silica. Of this species, emery, used in cutting and polishing glass, &c., is a granular variety. To this species also belongs the sapphire, the most valuable of gems next to the diamond; and of which the Oriental amethyst is merely a violet variety. Like other sapphires, it loses its colour in the fire, and comes out with so much of the lustre and colour of the diamond, that the most experienced jeweller may be deceived by it.

The more common, or Occidental amethyst, is a variety of quartz, or rock crystal, and is found in various forms in many parts of the world, as India, Siberia, Sweden, Germany, Spain; and even in England very beautiful specimens of tolerable hardness have been discovered. This also loses its colour in the fire.

Amethysts were much used by the ancients for rings and cameos; and the reason given by Pliny — because they were easily cut — shows that the Occidental species is to be understood. The ancients believed that the amethyst possessed the power of dispelling drunkenness in those who wore or touched it, and hence its Greek name. In like manner, the Rabbins derive its Jewish name from its supposed power of procuring dreams to the wearer.

1. AMIN'ADAB (*kindred of the prince*), one of the ancestors of David and of Christ (Matt. i. 4). He was the son of Aram, and the father of Naasson, and of Elisheba, who became the wife of Aaron (Exod. vi. 23).

2. AMINADAB, in Cant. vi. 12. The chariots of this Aminadab are mentioned as proverbial for their swiftness. Of himself we know nothing more than what is here glanced at, from which he appears to have been, like Jehu, one of the most celebrated charioteers of his day.

AM'MAN. [RABBAH.]

AM'MON. [No AMMON.]

AM'MONITES, the descendants of the younger son of Lot (Gen. xix. 38). They originally occupied a tract of country east of the Amorites, and separated from the Moabites by the river Arnon. It was previously in the possession of a gigantic race called Zamzummims (Deut. ii. 20), 'but the Lord destroyed them before the Ammonites, and they succeeded them and dwelt in their stead.' The Israelites on reaching the borders of the Promised Land, were commanded not to molest the children of Ammon, for the sake of their progenitor Lot. But, though thus preserved from the annoyance which the passage of such an immense host through their country might have occasioned, they showed them no hospitality or kindness; they were therefore prohibited from 'entering the congregation of the Lord' (*i. e.* from being admitted into the civil community of the Israelites) 'to the tenth generation for ever' (Deut. xxiii. 3). This is evidently intended to be a perpetual prohibition, and was so understood by Nehemiah (Neh. xiii. 1). The first mention of their active hostility against Israel occurs in Judges iii. 13. About 140 years later we are informed that the children of Israel forsook Jehovah and served the gods of various nations, including those of the children of Ammon, and the anger of Jehovah was kindled against them, and he sold them into the hands of the Philistines and of the children of Ammon. The Ammonites crossed over the Jordan, and fought with Judah, Benjamin, and Ephraim, so that 'Israel was sore distressed.' In answer to Jephthah's messengers (Judg. xi. 12), the king of Ammon charged the Israelites with having taken away that part of his territories which lay between the rivers Arnon and Jabbok, which, in Joshua xiii. 25, is called 'half the land of the children of Ammon,' but was in the possession of the Amorites when the Israelites invaded it; and this fact was urged by Jephthah, in order to prove that the charge was ill-founded. Jephthah 'smote them from Aroer to Minnith, even twenty cities, with a very great slaughter' (Judg. xi. 33). The Ammonites were again signally defeated by Saul (B.C. 1095) (1 Sam. xi. 11), and, according to Josephus, their king Nahash was slain. His successor, who bore the same name, was a friend of David, and died some years after his accession to the throne. In consequence of the gross insult offered to David's ambassadors by his son Hanun (2 Sam. x. 4), a war ensued, in which the Ammonites were defeated, and their allies the Syrians were so daunted 'that they feared to help the children of Ammon any more' (2 Sam. x. 19). In the following year David took their metropolis, Rabbah, and great abundance of spoil, which is probably mentioned by anticipation in 2 Sam. viii. 12 (2 Sam. x. 14; xii. 26-31). In the reign of Jehoshaphat (B.C. 896) the Ammonites joined with the Moabites and other tribes belonging to Mount Seir, to invade Judah; but, by the divine intervention, were led to destroy one another. Jehoshaphat and his people were three days in gathering the spoil (2 Chron. xx. 25). The Ammonites gave gifts' to Uzziah (2 Chron. xxvi. 8), and paid a tribute to his son Jotham for three successive years, consisting of 100 talents of silver, 1000 measures of wheat, and as many of barley. When the two and a half tribes were carried away captive, the Ammonites took possession of the towns belonging to the tribe of Gad (Jerem. xlix. 1). 'Bands of the children of Ammon' and of other nations came up with Nebuchadnezzar against Jerusalem (B.C. 607), and joined in exulting over its fall (Ezek. xxv. 3, 6). Yet they allowed some of the fugitive Jews to take refuge among them, and even to intermarry (Jer. xl. 11; Neh. xiii. 23). On the return of the Jews from Babylon the Ammonites manifested their ancient hostility by deriding and opposing the rebuilding of Jerusalem (Neh. iv. 3, 7, 8). Both Ezra and Nehemiah expressed vehement indignation against those Jews who had intermarried with the heathen, and thus transgressed the divine command (Deut. vii. 3; Ezra x.; Neh. xiii. 25). Judas Maccabæus (B.C. 164) fought many battles with the Ammonites, and took Jazer with the towns belonging to it. Justin Martyr affirms that in his time the Ammonites were still numerous.

The national idol of the Ammonites was Molech or Milcom, whose worship was introduced among the Israelites by the Ammonitish wives of Solomon (1 Kings xi. 5, 7); and the high places built by that sovereign for this 'abomination' were not destroyed till the reign of Josiah (B.C. 610) (2 Kings xxiii. 13).

Besides Nahash and Hanun, an Ammonitish king Baalis is mentioned by Jeremiah (xl. 14).

In the writings of the prophets terrible denunciations are uttered against the Ammonites on account of their rancorous hostility to the people of Israel; and the destruction of their metropolis, Rabbah, is distinctly foretold (Zeph. ii. 8; Jer. xlix. 1-6; Ezek. xxv. 1-5, 10; Amos i. 13-15).

AM'NON (*faithful*), the eldest son of David, by Ahinoam of Jezreel. He was born at Hebron, about B.C. 1056. He is only known for his atrocious conduct towards his half-sister Tamar, which her full-brother Absalom revenged two years after, by causing him to be assassinated while a guest at his table, in B.C. 1032 (2 Sam. xiii.) [Absalom].

A'MON (Jer. xlvi. 25) is the name of an Egyptian god, in whom the classical writers unanimously recognise their own Zeus and Jupiter. His chief temple and oracle in Egypt were at Thebes, a city peculiarly consecrated to him, and which is probably meant by the No and No Amon of the prophets. He is generally represented on Egyptian monuments by the seated figure of a man with a ram's head, or by that of an entire ram, and of a blue colour. In honour of him, the inhabitants of the Thebaid abstained from the flesh of sheep, but they annually sacrificed a ram to him and dressed his image in the hide.

As for the power which was worshipped under the form of Amon, it has been asserted that the Libyans adored the setting sun under that of their Ammon; others have endeavoured to prove that Amon represented the sun at the vernal equinox. But nothing very definite is known upon the subject, though the fact seems placed beyond a doubt that Amon bears some relation to the sun.

AMON (*artificer*), son of Manasseh, and fourteenth king of Judah, who began to reign B.C. 641, and reigned two years. He appears to have derived little benefit from the instructive example which the sin, punishment, and repentance of his father offered; for he restored idolatry, and again set up the images which Manasseh had cast down. He was assassinated in a court conspiracy: but the people put the regicides to death, and raised to the throne his son Josiah, then but eight years old (2 Kings xxi. 19-26; 2 Chron. xxxiii. 21-25).

AM'ORITES, the descendants of one of the sons of Canaan. They were the most powerful and distinguished of the Canaanitish nations. We find them first noticed in Gen. xiv. 7. In the promise to Abraham (Gen. xv. 21), the Amorites are specified as one of the nations whose country would be given to his posterity. But at that time three confederates of the patriarch belonged to this tribe; Mamre, Aner, and Eshcol (Gen. xiv. 13, 24). When the Israelites were about to enter the promised land, the Amorites occupied a tract on both sides of the Jordan. That part of their territories which lay to the east of the Jordan was allotted to the tribes of Reuben, Gad, and half the tribe of Manasseh. They were under two kings—Sihon, king of Heshbon, and Og, king of Bashan (Deut. i. 4; Josh. xii. 4; xiii. 12). Before hostilities commenced messengers were sent to Sihon, requesting permission to pass through his land; but Sihon refused, and came to Jahaz and fought with Israel; and Israel smote him with the edge of the sword, and possessed his land from Arnon (Modjeb) unto Jabbok (Zerka) (Num. xxi. 24). Og also gave battle to the Israelites at Edrei, and was totally defeated. After the capture of Ai, five kings of the Amorites, whose dominions lay within the allotment of the tribe of Judah, leagued together to wreak vengeance on the Gibeonites for having made a separate peace with the invaders. Joshua, on being apprised of their design, marched to Gibeon and defeated them with great slaughter (Josh. x. 10). Another confederacy was shortly after formed on a still larger scale; the associated forces are described as 'much people, even as the sand upon the sea-shore in multitude, with horses and chariots very many' (Josh. xi. 4). Joshua came suddenly upon them by the waters of Merom (the modern lake Huleh), and Israel

23.

smote them until they left none remaining (Josh. xi. 8). Still, after their severe defeats, the Amorites, by means of their war-chariots and cavalry, confined the Danites to the hills, and would not suffer them to settle in the plains: they even succeeded in retaining possession of some of the mountainous parts (Judg. i. 34-36). It is mentioned as an extraordinary circumstance that in the days of Samuel there was peace between Israel and the Amorites (1 Sam. vii. 14). In Solomon's reign a tribute of bond-service was levied on the remnant of the Amorites and other Canaanitish nations (1 Kings ix. 21 ; 2 Chron. viii. 8).

A'MOS (*borne*), one of the twelve minor prophets, and a contemporary of Isaiah and Hosea. He was a native of Tekoah, about six miles south of Bethlehem, inhabited chiefly by shepherds, to which class he belonged, being also a dresser of sycamore-trees. The period during which he filled the prophetic office was of short duration, unless we suppose that he uttered other predictions which are not recorded. It is stated expressly that he prophesied in the days of Uzziah, king of Judah, and in the days of Jeroboam, the son of Joash, king of Israel, two years before the earthquake (Amos i. 1). As Uzziah and Jeroboam were contemporaries for about fourteen years, from B C. 798 to 784, the latter of these dates will mark the period when Amos prophesied.

When Amos received his commission, the kingdom of Israel, which had been ' cut short' by Hazael (2 Kings x. 32) towards the close of Jehu's reign, was restored to its ancient limits and splendour by Jeroboam the Second (2 Kings xiv. 25). But the restoration of national prosperity was followed by the prevalence of luxury, licentiousness, and oppression, to an extent that again provoked the divine displeasure, and Amos was called from the sheep-folds to be the harbinger of the coming judgments. Not that his commission was limited entirely to Israel. The thunder-storm (as Ruckert poetically expresses it) rolls over all the surrounding kingdoms, touches Judah in its progress, and at length settles upon Israel. Chap. i.; ii. 1-5, form a solemn prelude to the main subject; nation after nation is summoned to judgment. Israel is then addressed in the same style, and in chap. iii. (after a brief rebuke of the twelve tribes collectively) its degenerate state is strikingly portrayed, and the denunciations of divine justice are intermingled, like repeated thunder-claps, to the end of chap. vi. The seventh and eighth chapters contain various symbolical visions, with a brief historical episode (vii. 10-17). In the ninth chapter the majesty of Jehovah and the terrors of his justice are set forth with a sublimity of diction which rivals and partly copies that of the royal Psalmist (comp. vers. 2, 3, with Ps. cix., and ver. 6 with Ps. civ.). Towards the close the scene brightens, and from the eleventh verse to the end the promises of the divine mercy and returning favour to the chosen race are exhibited in imagery of great beauty taken from rural life.

The writings of this prophet afford clear evidence that the existing religious institutions both of Judah and Israel (with the exception of the corruptions introduced by Jeroboam) were framed according to the rules prescribed in the Pentateuch, a fact which furnishes a conclusive argument for the genuineness of the Mosaic records.

The canonicity of the book of Amos is amply supported both by Jewish and Christian authorities. Philo, Josephus, and the Talmud include it among the minor prophets. It is also in the catalogues of Melito, Jerome, and the 60th canon of the Council of Laodicea. Justin Martyr, quotes a considerable part of the 5th and 6th chapters, which he introduces by saying,— ' Hear how he speaks concerning these by Amos, one of the twelve.' There are two quotations from it in the New Testament : the first (v. 25, 26) by the proto-martyr Stephen, Acts vii. 42 ; the second (ix. 11) by the apostle James, Acts xv. 16.

A'MOSIS, an Egyptian monarch, the founder of the eighteenth dynasty, who ascended the throne in B.C. 1575. The period of his accession, and the change which then took place in the reigning family, strongly confirm the opinion of his being the 'new king who knew not Joseph' (Exod. i. 8) ; and if it be considered that he was from the distant province of Thebes, it is reasonable to expect that the Hebrews would be strangers to him, and that he would be likely to look upon them with the same distrust and contempt with which the Egyptians usually regarded foreigners.

AMPHIP'OLIS, a city of Greece, through which Paul and Silas passed on their way from Philippi to Thessalonica (Acts xvii. 1). It was situated on the left bank of the river Strymon just below its egress from the lake Kerkine (now Takino), and about three miles above its influx into the sea. This situation upon the banks of a navigable river, a short distance from the sea, with the vicinity of the woods of Kerkine, and the gold-mines of Mount Pangæus, rendered Amphipolis a place of much importance, and an object of contest between the Thracians, Athenians, Lacedæmonians, and Macedonians, to whom it successively belonged. It has long been in ruins ; and a village of about one hundred houses, called Jeni-keui, now occupies part of its site.

AM'RAM, son of Kohath, of the tribe of Levi. He married his father's sister Jochebed, by whom he had Aaron, Miriam, and Moses. He died in Egypt, at the age of 137 years (Exod. vi.).

AM'RAPHEL, king of Shinar, one of the four kings who invaded Palestine in the time of Abraham (Gen. xiv. 1, 2, *sq.*) [ABRAHAM ; CHEDORLAOMER].

AMULET (Isa. iii. 20). From the earliest ages the Orientals have believed in the influences of the stars, in spells, witchcraft, and the malign power of the evil eye ; and to protect themselves against the maladies and other evils which such influences were supposed to occasion, almost all the ancient nations wore amulets. These amulets consisted, and still consist, chiefly of tickets inscribed with sacred sentences, and of certain stones or pieces of metal. Not only were persons thus protected, but even houses were, as they still are, guarded from supposed malign influences by certain holy inscriptions upon the doors.

The previous existence of these customs is

implied in the attempt of Moses to turn them to becoming uses, by directing that certain passages extracted from the law should be employed (Exod. xiii. 9, 16; Deut. vi. 8; xi. 18). The door-schedules being noticed elsewhere, we here limit our attention to personal amulets. By this religious appropriation the then all-pervading tendency to idolatry was in this matter obviated, although in later times, when the tendency to idolatry had passed away, such written scrolls degenerated into instruments of superstition.

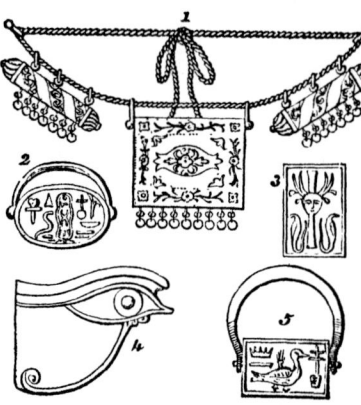

34. [1. Modern Oriental. 2, 3, 4, 5. Ancient Egyptian.]

The *ear-rings* (Auth. Vers.) of Isa. iii. 20, it is now allowed, denote *amulets*, although they served also the purpose of ornament. They were probably precious stones, or small plates of gold or silver, with sentences of the law or magic formulæ inscribed on them, and worn in the ears, or suspended by a chain round the neck. It is certain that earrings were sometimes used in this way as instruments of superstition, and that at a very early period (Gen. xxxv. 4), and they are still used as charms in the East. Augustin speaks strongly against ear-rings that were worn as amulets in his time.

Some have supposed that these amulets were charms inscribed on silver and gold similar to those ornamental little cases for written charms which are still used by Arab women. This is represented in the first figure of the cut No. 34. The writing is covered with waxed cloth, and enclosed in a case of thin embossed gold or silver, which is attached to a silk string, or a chain, and generally hung on the right side, above the girdle, the string or chain being passed over the left shoulder. Amulets of this shape, or of a triangular form, are worn by women and children; and those of the latter shape are often attached to children's head-dress.

The superstitions connected with amulets grew to a great height in the later periods of the Jewish history. 'There was hardly any people in the whole world,' says Lightfoot, 'that more used or were more fond of amulets, charms, mutterings, exorcisms, and all kinds of enchantments. . . . The amulets were either little roots hung about the neck of sick persons, or, what was more common, bits of paper (and parchment), with words written on them, whereby it was supposed that diseases were either driven away or cured. They wore such amulets all the week, but were forbidden to go abroad with them on the Sabbath, unless they were "approved amulets," that is, were prescribed by a person who knew that at least three persons had been

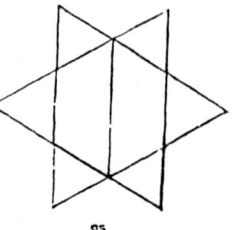

35.

cured by the same means. In these amulets mysterious names and characters were occasionally employed, in lieu of extracts from the law. One of the most usual of these was the cabalistic hexagonal figure known as the " shield of David " and " the seal of Solomon." '

A'NAB, one of the cities in the mountains of Judah, from which Joshua expelled the Anakim (Josh. xi. 21; xv. 50).

A'NAH (*responder*), son of Zibeon the Hivite, and father of Esau's wife Aholibamah (Gen. xxxvi. 24). While feeding asses in the desert he discovered 'warm springs,' as the original is rendered by Jerome. Gesenius and most modern critics think this interpretation correct, supported as it is by this fact that warm springs are still found in the region east of the Dead Sea.

AN'AKIM, or BENE-ANAK and BENE-ANAKIM, a wandering nation of southern Canaan, descended from Anak, whose name it bore (Josh. xi. 21). It was composed of three tribes, descended from and named after the three sons of Anak—Ahiman, Sesai, and Talmai. When the Israelites invaded Canaan, the Anakim were in possession of Hebron, Debir, Anak, and other towns in the country of the south. Their formidable stature and appearance alarmed the Hebrew spies; but they were eventually overcome and expelled by Caleb, when the remnant of the race took refuge among the Philistines (Num. xiii. 33; Deut. ix. 2; Josh. xi. 21; xiv. 12; Judg. i. 20).

ANAM'MELECH (2 Kings xvii. 31) is mentioned, together with Adrammelech, as a god of the people of Sepharvaim, who colonized Samaria. He was also worshipped by the sacrifice of children by fire. No satisfactory etymology of the name has been discovered. The same obscurity prevails as to the form under which the god was worshipped.

1. ANANI'AS (same name as Hananiah, *whom Jehovah hath graciously given*), son of Nebedæus, was made high-priest in the time of the procurator Tiberius Alexander, about A.D. 47, by Herod, king of Chalcis, who for this purpose removed Joseph, son of Camydus, from the high-priesthood. He held the office with credit, until Agrippa gave it to Ismael, the son of Tabi, who succeeded a short time before the departure of

the procurator Felix, and occupied the station also under his successor Festus. Ananias, after retiring from his high-priesthood, 'increased in glory every day,' and obtained favour with the citizens, and with Albinus, the Roman procurator, by a lavish use of the great wealth he had hoarded. His prosperity met with a dark and painful termination. The assassins, who played so fearful a part in the Jewish war, set fire to his house in the commencement of it, and compelled him to seek refuge by concealment; but being discovered in an aqueduct, he was captured and slain.

It was this Ananias before whom Paul was brought, by the procuratorship of Felix (Acts xxiii.). After this hearing Paul was sent to Cæsarea, whither Ananias repaired, in order to lay a formal charge against him before Felix, who postponed the matter, detaining the apostle meanwhile, and placing him under the supervision of a Roman centurion (Acts xxiv.).

2. ANANIAS, a Christian belonging to the infant church at Jerusalem, who, conspiring with his wife Sapphira to deceive and defraud the brethren, was overtaken by sudden death, and immediately buried. The Christian community at Jerusalem appear to have entered into a solemn agreement, that each and all should devote their property to the great work of furthering the Gospel and giving succour to the needy. Accordingly they proceeded to sell their possessions, and brought the proceeds into the common stock of the church. Thus Barnabas (Acts iv. 36, 37) 'having land, sold it, and brought the money, and laid it at the apostles' feet.' The apostles then had the general disposal, if they had not also the immediate distribution, of the common funds. The contributions, therefore, were designed for the sacred purposes of religion (Acts v. 1-11).

As all the members of the Jerusalem church had thus agreed to hold their property in common, for the furtherance of the holy work in which they were engaged, if any one of them withheld a part, and offered the remainder as a whole, he committed two offences—he defrauded the church, and was guilty of falsehood: and as his act related not to secular but to religious affairs, and had an injurious bearing, both as an example, and as a positive transgression against the Gospel while it was yet struggling into existence, Ananias lied not unto man, but unto God, and was guilty of a sin of the deepest dye. Had Ananias chosen to keep his property for his own worldly purposes, he was at liberty, as Peter intimates, so to do; but he had in fact alienated it to pious purposes, and it was therefore no longer his own. Yet he wished to deal with it in part as if it were so, showing at the same time that he was conscious of his misdeed, by presenting the residue to the common treasury as if it had been his entire property. He wished to satisfy his selfish cravings, and at the same time to enjoy the reputation of being purely disinterested, like the rest of the church. He attempted to serve God and Mammon.

With strange inconsistency on the part of those who deny miracles altogether, unbelievers have accused Peter of cruelly smiting Ananias and his wife with instant death. The sacred narrative, however, ascribes to Peter nothing more than a spirited exposure of their aggravated offence. Their death, the reader is left to infer, was by the hand of God; nor is any ground afforded in the narrative (Acts v. 1-11) for holding that Peter was in any way employed as an immediate instrument of the miracle.

3. ANANIAS, a Christian of Damascus (Acts ix. 10; xxii. 12), held in high repute, to whom the Lord appeared in a vision, and bade him proceed to 'the street which is called Straight, and inquire in the house of Judas for one called Saul of Tarsus: for, behold, he prayeth.' Ananias had difficulty in giving credence to the message, remembering how much evil Paul had done to the saints at Jerusalem, and knowing that he had come to Damascus with authority to lay waste the church of Christ there. Receiving, however, an assurance that the persecutor had been converted, and called to the work of preaching the Gospel to the Gentiles, Ananias went to Paul, and, putting his hands on him, bade him receive his sight, when immediately there fell from his eyes as it had been scales; and, recovering the sight which he had lost when the Lord appeared to him on his way to Damascus, Paul, the new convert, arose, and was baptized, and preached Jesus Christ.

Tradition represents Ananias as the first that published the Gospel in Damascus, over which place he was subsequently made bishop; but having roused, by his zeal, the hatred of the Jews, he was seized by them, scourged, and finally stoned to death in his own church.

ANATH'EMA, literally anything laid up or suspended, and hence anything laid up in a temple, set apart as sacred.

The corresponding Hebrew word means a person or thing consecrated or devoted irrevocably to God (Lev. xxvii. 21, 28): hence, in reference to living creatures, the devoted thing, whether man or beast, must be put to death (Lev. xxvii. 29). The prominent idea, therefore, which the word conveyed was that of a person or thing *devoted to destruction*, or *accursed*. Thus the cities of the Canaanites were anathematized (Num. xxi. 2, 3). Thus, again, the city of Jericho was made an anathema to the Lord (Josh. vi. 17), that is, every living thing in it (except Rahab and her family) was devoted to death; that which could be destroyed by fire was burnt, and all that could not be thus consumed (as gold and silver) was for ever alienated from man and devoted to the use of the sanctuary (Josh. vi. 24). The prominence thus given to the idea of a *thing accursed* led naturally to the use of the word in cases where there was no reference whatever to consecration to the service of God, as in Deut. vii. 26; it is sometimes used to designate the curse itself (*e. g.* Deut. xx. 17).

In this sense, also, the Jews of later times use the Hebrew term, though with a somewhat different meaning as to the curse intended, employing it to signify excommunication or exclusion from the Jewish church. The more recent Rabbinical writers reckon three kinds or degrees of excommunication. The first of these is merely a temporary separation or suspension from ecclesiastical privileges, involving, however, various civil inconveniences, particularly seclusion from society to the distance of four cubits. The person thus excommunicated was not debarred entering the temple, but instead of going in on the right hand, as was customary, he was obliged to enter on the left, the usual way of departure; if he died whilst in this condition there was no mourning for him, but a stone was thrown on his coffin to indicate that he was separated from the people and had deserved stoning. This kind of excommunication lasted thirty days, and was pronounced without a curse. If the individual did not repent at the expiration of the term, the second kind of excommunication was resorted to. This could only be pronounced by an assembly of at least ten persons, and was always accompanied with curses. A person thus excommunicated was cut off from all religious and social privileges: and it was unlawful either to eat or drink with him (compare 1 Cor. v. 11). If the excommunicated person still continued impenitent, a yet more severe sentence was pronounced against him, which is described as a complete excision from the church and the giving up of the individual to the judgment of God and to final perdition. There is, however, reason to believe that these three grades are of comparatively recent origin.

As it is on all hands admitted that the Hebrew term which is the equivalent of *anathema* properly denotes, in its Rabbinical use, an excommunication accompanied with the most severe curses and denunciations of evil, we are prepared to find that the *anathema* of the New Testament always implies execration; but it is very doubtful whether it is ever used to designate a judicial act of excommunication. The phrase 'to call Jesus anathema' (1 Cor. xii. 3) refers not to a judicial sentence pronounced by the Jewish authorities, but to the act of any private individual who execrated him and pronounced him accursed. The term, as it is used in reference to any who should preach another gospel, 'Let him be anathema' (Gal. i. 8, 9), has the same meaning as, let him be accounted execrable and accursed. There is very great diversity of opinion respecting the meaning of the word in Rom. ix. 3; some understand it to signify excommunication from the Christian church, whilst most of the fathers, together with a great number of modern interpreters, explain the term as referring to the Jewish practice of excommunication. On the other hand, many adopt the more general meaning of accursed. The great difficulty is to ascertain the extent of the evil which Paul expresses his willingness to undergo; Chrysostom, Calvin, and many others understand it to include final separation, not indeed from the love, but from the presence of Christ; others limit it to a violent death; and others, again, explain it as meaning the same kind of curse as that under which the Jews then were, from which they might be delivered by repentance and the reception of the Gospel. There seems, however, little reason to suppose that a judicial act of the Christian Church is intended, and we may remark that much of the difficulty which commentators have felt seems to have arisen from their not keeping in mind that the Apostle does not speak of his wish as a possible thing, and their consequently pursuing to all its results what should be regarded simply as an expression of the most intense desire.

The phrase 'let him be anathema maran-atha,'

seems to be intended as simply an expression of detestation. Though, however, we find little or no evidence of the use of the word anathema in the New Testament as the technical term for excommunication, it is certain that it obtained this meaning in the early ages of the church.

AN'ATHOTH, one of the towns belonging to the priests in the tribe of Benjamin, and as such a city of refuge (Josh. xxi. 18; Jer. i. 1). It occurs also in 2 Sam. xxiii. 27; Ezra ii. 23; Neh. vii. 27; but is chiefly memorable as the birthplace and usual residence of the prophet Jeremiah (Jer. i. 1; xi. 21-23; xxix. 27). Dr. Robinson appears to have discovered this place in the present village of *Anata*, at the distance of an hour and a quarter from Jerusalem. It is seated on a broad ridge of hills, and commands an extensive view of the eastern slope of the mountainous tract of Benjamin; including also the valley of the Jordan, and the northern part of the Dead Sea. It seems to have been once a walled town and a place of strength. Portions of the wall still remain, built of large hewn stones, and apparently ancient, as are also the foundations of some of the houses. It is now a small and very poor village. From the vicinity a favourite kind of building-stone is carried to Jerusalem.

ANCHOR. [SHIP.]

AN'DREW, one of the twelve apostles. He was a native of the city of Bethsaida in Galilee, and brother of Simon Peter. He was at first a disciple of John the Baptist, and was led to receive Jesus as the Messiah in consequence of John's expressly pointing him out as 'the Lamb of God' (John i. 36). His first care, after he had satisfied himself as to the validity of the claims of Jesus, was to bring to him his brother Simon. Neither of them, however, became at that time stated attendants on our Lord; for we find that they were still pursuing their occupation of fishermen on the sea of Galilee when Jesus, after John's imprisonment, called them to follow him (Mark i. 14, 18). Very little is related of Andrew by any of the evangelists: the principal incidents in which his name occurs during the life of Christ are, the feeding of the five thousand (John vi. 8); his introducing to our Lord certain Greeks who desired to see him (John xii. 22); and his asking, along with his brother Simon and the two sons of Zebedee, for a further explanation of what our Lord had said in reference to the destruction of the temple (Mark xiii. 3). Of his subsequent history and labours we have no authentic record. Tradition assigns Scythia, Greece, and Thrace as the scenes of his ministry: and he is said to have suffered crucifixion at Patræ in Achaia, on a cross of the form (✕), commonly known as 'St. Andrew's cross.'

1. ANDRON'ICUS, the regent-governor of Antioch in the absence of Antiochus Epiphanes, who, at the instigation of Menelaus, put to death the deposed high-priest Onias; for which deed he was himself ignominiously slain on the return of Antiochus (2 Macc. iv.) B.C. 169 [ONIAS].

2. ANDRONICUS, a Jewish Christian, the kinsman and fellow-prisoner of Paul (Rom. xvi. 7).

1. A'NER, ESH'COL, and MAM'RE, three Canaanitish chiefs in the neighbourhood of He-

bron, who joined their forces with those of Abraham in pursuit of Chedorlaomer and his allies, who had pillaged Sodom and carried Lot away captive (Gen. xiv 24). These chiefs did not, however, imitate the disinterested conduct of the patriarch, but retained their portion of the spoil [ABRAHAM].

2. ANER, a city of Manasseh, given to the Levites of Kohath's family (1 Chron. vi. 70).

ANGELS, a word signifying, both in Hebrew and Greek, *messengers*, and therefore used to denote whatever God employs to execute his purposes, or to manifest his presence or his power. In some passages it occurs in the sense of an ordinary messenger (Job. i. 14; 1 Sam. xi. 3; Luke vii. 24; ix. 52): in others it is applied to prophets (Isa. xlii. 19; Hag. i. 13; Mal. iii.): to priests (Eccl. v. 6; Mal. ii. 7): to ministers of the New Testament (Rev. i. 20). It is also applied to impersonal agents; as to the pillar of cloud (Exod. xiv. 19): to the pestilence (2 Sam. xxiv. 16, 17; 2 Kings xix. 35): to the winds (' who maketh the winds his angels,' Ps. civ. 4): so likewise, plagues generally, are called 'evil angels' (Ps. lxxviii. 49), and Paul calls his thorn in the flesh an 'angel of Satan' (2 Cor. xii. 7).

But this name is more eminently and distinctively applied to certain spiritual beings or heavenly intelligences, employed by God as the ministers of His will, and usually distinguished as *angels of God* or *angels of Jehovah*. In this case the name has respect to their official capacity as 'messengers,' and not to their nature or condition. In the Scriptures we have frequent notices of spiritual intelligences, existing in another state of being, and constituting a celestial family, or hierarchy, over which Jehovah presides. The practice of the Jews, of referring to the agency of angels every manifestation of the greatness and power of God, has led some to contend that angels have no real existence, but are mere personifications of unknown powers of nature: but there are numerous passages in the Scriptures which are wholly inconsistent with this notion, and if Matt. xxii. 30. stood alone in its testimony, it ought to settle the question. So likewise, the passage in which the high dignity of Christ is established, by arguing that he is superior to the angels (Heb. i. 4. *sqq.*), would be without force or meaning if angels had no real existence.

That these superior beings are very numerous is evident from the following expressions, Dan. vii. 10, 'thousands of thousands,' and 'ten thousand times ten thousand;' Matt. xxvi. 53, 'more than twelve legions of angels;' Luke ii. 13, 'multitude of the heavenly host;' Heb. xii. 22, 23, 'myriads of angels.' It is probable, from the nature of the case, that among so great a multitude there may be different grades and classes, and even natures—ascending from man towards God, and forming a chain of being to fill up the vast space between the Creator and man—the lowest of his intellectual creatures. This may be inferred from the analogies which pervade the chain of being on the earth whereon we live, which is as much the divine creation as the world of spirits. Accordingly the Scriptures describe angels as existing in a society composed of members of unequal dignity, power,

and excellence, and as having chiefs and rulers (Zech. i. 11; iii. 7; Dan. x. 13; Jude 9; 1 Thess. iv. 16).

In the Scriptures angels appear with bodies, and in the human form; and no intimation is anywhere given that these bodies are not real, or that they are only assumed for the time and then laid aside. The fact that angels always appeared in the human form, does not, indeed, prove that this form naturally belongs to them. But that which is not pure spirit must have some form or other: and angels *may* have the human form; but other forms are possible. The question as to the food of angels has been very much discussed. If they do eat, we can know nothing of their actual food; for the manna is manifestly called 'angels' food' (Ps. lxxviii. 25), merely by way of expressing its excellence. The only real question, therefore, is whether they feed at all or not. We sometimes find angels, in their terrene manifestations, eating and drinking (Gen. xviii. 8; xix. 3); but in Judg. xiii. 15, 16, the angel who appeared to Manoah declined, in a very pointed manner, to accept his hospitality.

The passage already referred to in Matt. xxii. 30, teaches by implication that there is no distinction of sex among the angels. In the Scriptures indeed the angels are all males: but they appear to be so represented, not to mark any distinction of sex, but because the masculine is the more honourable gender. Angels are never described with marks of age, but sometimes with those of youth (Mark xvi. 5). The constant absence of the features of age indicates the continual vigour and freshness of immortality. The angels never die (Luke xx. 36). But no being besides God himself has essential immortality (1 Tim. vi. 16): every other being therefore is mortal in itself, and can be immortal only by the will of God. Angels, consequently, are not eternal, but had a beginning, although there is no record of their creation.

The preceding considerations apply chiefly to the *existence* and *nature* of angels. Some of their *attributes* may be collected from other passages of Scripture. That they are of superhuman intelligence is implied in Mark xiii. 32: 'But of that day and hour knoweth no man, not *even* the angels in heaven.' That their power is great, may be gathered from such expressions as 'mighty angels' (2 Thess. i. 7); 'angels, powerful in strength' (Ps. ciii. 20); 'angels who are greater [than man] in power and might.' The moral perfection of angels is shown by such phrases as 'holy angels' (Luke ix. 26): 'the elect angels' (1 Tim. v. 21). Their felicity is beyond question in itself, but is evinced by the passage (Luke xx. 36) in which the blessed in the future world are said to be 'like unto the angels, and sons of God.'

The *ministry* of angels, or that they are employed by God as the instruments of His will, is very clearly taught in the Scriptures. The very name, as already explained, shows that God employs their agency in the dispensations of His Providence. And it is further evident, from certain actions which are ascribed wholly to them (Matt. xiii. 41, 49; xxiv. 31; Luke xvi. 22); and from the Scriptural narratives of other events, in the accomplishment of which they acted a visible part (Luke i. 11, 26; ii. 9, *sq.*; Acts, v. 19, 20; x 3, 19; xii. 7; xxvii. 23), that their agency is employed principally in the guidance of the destinies of man. In those cases also in which the agency is concealed from our view, we may admit the probability of its existence; because we are told that God sends them forth ' to minister to those who shall be heirs of salvation' (Heb. i. 14; also Ps. xxxiv. 7; xci. 11; Matt. xviii. 10. But the angels, when employed for our welfare, do not act independently, but as the instruments of God, and by His command (Ps. ciii. 20; civ. 4; Heb. i. 13, 14): not unto them, therefore, are our confidence and adoration due, but only unto him (Rev. xix. 10; xxii. 9) whom the angels themselves reverently worship.

It was a favourite opinion of the Christian fathers that every individual is under the care of a particular angel, who is assigned to him as a guardian. They spoke also of two angels, the one good, the other evil, whom they conceived to be attendant on each individual; the good angel prompting to all good, and averting ill; and the evil angel prompting to all ill, and averting good. The Jews (excepting the Sadducees) entertained this belief. There is, however, nothing to authorise this notion in the Bible. The passages (Ps. xxxiv. 7; Matt. xviii. 10) usually referred to in support of it, have assuredly no such meaning. The former, divested of its poetical shape, simply denotes that God employs the ministry of angels to deliver his people from affliction and danger; and the celebrated passage in Matthew cannot well mean anything more than that the infant children of believers, or, if preferable, the least among the disciples of Christ, whom the ministers of the church might be disposed to neglect from their apparent insignificance, are in such estimation elsewhere, that the angels do not think it below their dignity to minister to them [SATAN].

ANGLING. The Scripture contains several allusions to this mode of taking fish. The first of these occurs as early as the time of Job:— ' Canst thou draw out leviathan with an hook; or his tongue [*palate*, which is usually pierced by the hook] with a cord [line], which thou lettest down? Canst thou put a hook into his

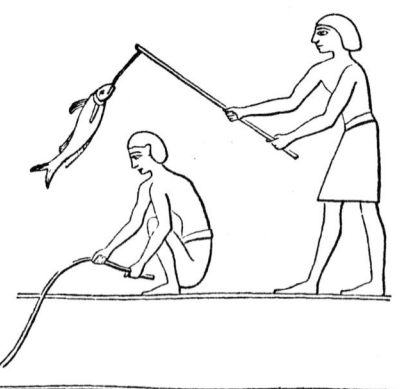

37.

nose, or bore his jaw through with a thorn? (Job xli. 1, 2). This last phrase obviously refers to the thorns which were sometimes used as hooks, and which are long after mentioned (Amos iv. 2), in the Auth. Vers. ' fish-hooks,' literally, the thorns of fishing.

Of the various passages relating to this subject the most remarkable is that which records, as an important part of the ' burden of Egypt, that ' the fishers also shall mourn; and all they that cast angle [the hook] into the brooks shall lament, and they that spread nets upon the waters shall languish' (Isa. xix. 8). In this poetical description of a part of the calamities which were to befal Egypt, we are furnished with an account of the various modes of fishing practised in that country, which is in exact conformity with the scenes depicted in the old tomb of Egypt. Angling appears to have been regarded chiefly as an amusement, in which the Egyptians of all ranks found much enjoyment Not content with the abundance afforded by the Nile, they constructed within their ground spacious sluices or ponds for fish (Isa. xix. 10), where they fed them for the table, where they amused themselves by angling, and by the dexterous use of the *bident*. These favourite occupations were not confined to young persons, nor thought unworthy of men of serious habits; and an Egyptian of consequence is frequently represented in the sculptures catching fish in a canal or lake, with the line, or spearing them as they glided past the bank. Sometimes the angler posted himself in a shady spot at the water's edge, and having ordered his servant to spread a mat upon the ground, he sat upon it as he threw the line; and some, with higher notion, of comfort, used a chair for the same purpose The rod was short, and apparently of one pieces the line usually single, though instances occur of a double line, each furnished with its own hook, The fishermen generally used the net in preference to the line, but on some occasions they used the latter, seated or standing on the bank. It is, however, probable that there were people who could not afford the expense of nets; and the use of the line is generally confined in like manner at the present day to the poorer classes, who depend upon skill or good fortune for their subsistence.

This last was doubtless the state of many in ancient Palestine, and probably furnished the only case in which angling was there practised, as we find no instance of it for mere amusement The fish caught in the lake of Tiberias were. some time since, taken exclusively with the rod and line, in the absence of boats upon that water; and probably this is the case still. The Egyptian hooks were of bronze, as appears from the specimens that have been found. Insects, natural or artificial, were not used in angling, ground bait being exclusively employed: and the float does not appear to have been known.

ANISE. The original Greek word ANETHON, which occurs in Matt. xxiii. 23, was commonly employed by the Greek and Roman writers to designate a plant used both medicinally and as an article of diet. In Europe the word has always been used to denote a similar plant, which is familiarly known by the name of Dill, and there is no doubt that in the above passage it should have been so rendered. The common dill is an annual plant, growing wild among the corn in Spain and Portugal; and on the coast of Italy, in Egypt, and about Astracan. It resembles *fennel*, but is smaller, has more glaucous leaves, and a less pleasant smell: the fruit or seeds, which are finely divided by capillary segments, are elliptical, broader, flatter, and surrounded with a membraneous disk. They have a warm and aromatic taste, owing to the presence of a pale yellow volatile oil, which itself has a hot taste and a peculiar penetrating odour.

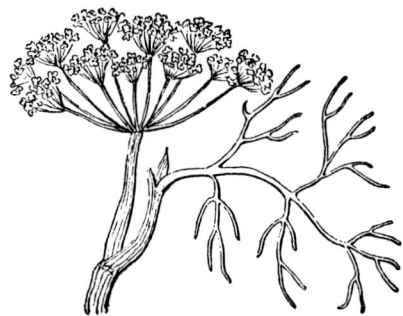

36. [Anethum graveolens.]

The error in translation here pointed out is not of very great consequence, as both the *anise* and the *dill* are umbelliferous plants, which are found cultivated in the south of Europe. The seeds of both are employed as condiments and carminatives, and have been so from very early times; but the *anethon* is more especially a genus of Eastern cultivation, since either the *dill* or another species is reared in all the countries from Syria to India. Jewish authorities state that the seed, the leaves, and the stem of *dill* were 'subject to tithe,' which indicates that the herb was eaten, as is indeed the case with the Eastern species in the present day.

ANKLETS. This word does not occur in Scripture, but the ornament which it denotes is clearly indicated by 'the tinkling (or *jingling*) ornaments about the feet,' mentioned in the curious description of female attire which we find in Isa. iii. Even in the absence of special notice, we might very safely conclude that an ornament to which the Oriental women have always been so partial was not unknown to the Jewish ladies. In Egypt anklets of gold have been found, which are generally in the shape of simple rings, often however in that of snakes, and sometimes inlaid with enamel or even precious stones. The sculptures show that they were worn by men as well as women. Their present use among the women of Arabia and Egypt sufficiently illustrates the Scriptural allusion. The Koran (xxiv. 31) forbids women 'to make a noise with their feet,' which, says Mr. Lane, 'alludes to the practice of knocking together the anklets, which the Arab women in the time of the prophet used to wear, and which are still worn by many women in Egypt.' The same writer states that 'Anklets of solid gold and silver, and of the form here sketched (like fig. 3), are worn by some ladies, but are more

uncommon than they formerly were. They are of course very heavy, and, knocking together as the woman walks, make a ringing noise.' He thinks that in the text referred to (Isa. iii. 16) the prophet alludes to this kind of anklet, but admits that the description may apply to another kind, which he describes as 'Anklets of solid silver, worn by the wives of some of the richer peasants, and of the sheykhs of villages. Small ones of iron are worn by many children. It was also a common custom among the Arabs for girls or young women to wear a string of bells on their feet. I have seen many little girls in Cairo with small round bells attached to their anklets. Perhaps it is to the sound of ornaments of this kind, rather than of the more common anklet, that Isaiah alludes.' The anklets in use

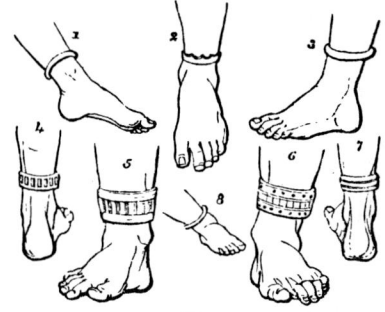

38.
[1, 2, 5, 6, 7. Ancient Oriental. 3, 4, 8. Modern Oriental.]

among the Arab women in the country of the Tigris and Euphrates are not usually solid, but hollow, so that, in striking against each other, they emit a much more sharp and sonorous sound than solid ones.

1. AN'NA, wife of Tobit, whose history is contained in the apocryphal book named after him (Tob. i. 9, &c.).

2. ANNA, an aged widow, daughter of Phanuel, of the tribe of Asher. She had married early, but after seven years her husband died, and during her long widowhood she daily attended the morning and evening services of the Temple. Anna was eighty-four years old when the infant Jesus was brought to the Temple by his mother, and entering as Simeon pronounced his thanksgiving, she also broke forth in praise to God for the fulfilment of his ancient promises (Luke ii. 36, 37).

ANOINTING. The practice of anointing with perfumed oils or ointments appears to have been very common among the Hebrews, as it was among the ancient Egyptians. The practice, as to its essential meaning, still remains in the East; but perfumed waters are now far more commonly employed than oils or ointments.

In the Scriptures three kinds of anointing are distinguishable:—1. For consecration and inauguration; 2. For guests and strangers; 3. For health and cleanliness. Of these in order.

1. *Consecration and Inauguration.*—The act of anointing appears to have been viewed as emblematical of a particular sanctification; of a designation to the service of God; or to a holy and sacred use. Hence the anointing of the high-

priests (Exod. xxix. 29; Lev. iv. 3), and even of the sacred vessels of the tabernacle (Exod. xxx. 26, &c.); and hence also, probably, the anointing of the king, who, as 'the Lord's anointed,' and, under the Hebrew constitution, the viceroy of Jehovah, was undoubtedly invested with a sacred character.

The first instance of anointing which the Scriptures record is that of Aaron, when he was solemnly set apart to the high-priesthood. Being first invested with the rich robes of his high office, the sacred oil was poured in much profusion upon his head. It is from this that the high-priest, as well as the king, is called 'the Anointed' (Lev. iv. 3, 5, 16; vi. 20; Ps. cxxxiii. 2). In fact, anointing being the principal ceremony of regal inauguration among the Jews, as crowning is with us, 'anointed,' as applied to a king, has much the same signification as 'crowned.'

As the custom of inaugural anointing first occurs among the Israelites immediately after they left Egypt, and no example of the same kind is met with previously, it is fair to conclude that the practice and the notions connected with it were acquired in that country. With the Egyptians, as with the Jews, the investiture to any sacred office, as that of king or priest, was confirmed by this external sign; and as the Jewish lawgiver mentions the ceremony of pouring oil upon the head of the high-priest *after* he had put on his entire dress, with the mitre and crown, the Egyptians represent the anointing of their priests and kings *after* they were attired in their full robes, with the cap and crown upon their heads. Some of the sculptures introduce a priest pouring oil over the monarch.

39.

2. The anointing of our Saviour's feet by 'the woman who was a sinner' (Luke vii. 38), led to the remark that the host himself had neglected to anoint his head (vii. 46); whence we learn that this was a mark of attention which those who gave entertainments paid to their guests. Among the Egyptians anointing was the ordinary token of welcome to guests in every party at the house of a friend; and in Egypt, no less than in Judæa, the metaphorical expression 'anointed with the oil of gladness' was fully understood, and applied to the ordinary occurrences of life. It was customary for a servant

to attend every guest as he seated himself, and to anoint his head.

3. It is probable, however, that the Egyptians, as well as the Greeks and Jews, anointed themselves at home, before going abroad, although they expected the observance of this etiquette on the part of their entertainer. That the Jews thus anointed themselves, not only when paying a visit, but on ordinary occasions, is shown by many passages, especially those which describe the omission of it as a sign of mourning (Deut. xxviii. 40; Ruth iii. 3; 2 Sam. xiv. 2; Dan. x. 3; Amos vi. 6; Mic. vi. 15; Esth. ii. 12; Ps. civ. 15; Isa. lxi. 3; Eccles. ix. 8; Cant. i. 3; iv. 10; also Judith x. 3; Sus. 17; Ecclus. xxxix. 26; Wisd. ii. 7). One of these passages (Ps. civ. 15, 'oil that maketh the face to shine') shows very clearly that not only the hair but the skin was anointed.

Anointing the Sick.—The Orientals are indeed strongly persuaded of the sanative properties of oil; and it was under this impression that the Jews anointed the sick, and applied oil to wounds (Ps. cix. 18; Isa. i. 6; Mark vi. 13; Luke x. 34; James v. 14). Anointing was used in sundry disorders, as well as to promote the general health of the body. It was hence, as a salutary and approved medicament, that the seventy disciples were directed to 'anoint the sick' (Mark vi. 13); and hence also the sick man is directed by St. James to send for the elders of the church, who were 'to pray for him, anointing him with oil in the name of the Lord.'

Anointing the Dead.—The practice of anointing the bodies of the dead is intimated in Mark xiv. 8, and Luke xxiii. 56. This ceremony was performed after the body was washed, and was designed to check the progress of corruption. Although, from the mode of application, it is called anointing, the substance employed appears to have been a solution of odoriferous drugs. This (together with the laying of the body in spices) was the only kind of embalment in use among the Jews [BURIAL].

ANT, fifth order of insects, occurs Prov. vi. 6; xxx. 25. Ants have only latterly become the subjects of accurate observation, and the result has dissipated many erroneous notions respecting them, and revealed much interesting information concerning their domestic polity, language, migrations, affections, passions, virtues, wars, diversions, &c. The following facts are selected as relevant to Scriptural illustration. Ants dwell together in societies; and although they have 'no guide, overseer, or ruler,' yet they have all one soul, and are animated by one object—their own welfare and the welfare of each other. Each individual strenuously pursues his own peculiar duties; and regards (except in the case of females), and is regarded by, every other member of the republic with equal respect and affection. They devote the utmost attention to their young. The egg is cleaned and licked, and gradually expands under this treatment, till the worm is hatched, which is then tended and fed with the most affectionate care. They continue their assiduity to the pupa, or chrysalis, which is the third transformation. They heap up the pupæ, which *greatly resemble so many grains of wheat*, or *rather rice*, by hundreds in their spacious lodges, watch them in an attitude of defence, carry them out to enjoy the radiance of the sun, and remove them to different situations in the nest, according to the required degree of temperature; open the pupa, and at the precise moment of the transformation, disenthral the new-born insect of its habiliments.

The most prevalent and inexcusable error, however, respecting ants, has been the belief that they hoard up grains of corn, chiefly wheat, for their supply during winter, having first bitten out the germ to prevent it from growing in their nests. This notion, however, is now completely exploded with regard to European ants. The mistake has no doubt arisen from the great similarity, both in shape, size, and colour, before mentioned, of the pupa or chrysalis of the ant to a grain of corn, and from the ants being observed to carry them about, and to open the cuticle to let out the enclosed insect. It is now also ascertained beyond a doubt that no European ants, hitherto properly examined, feed on *corn*, or *any other* kind of grain. Nor has any species of ant been yet found of *any kind* laid up in its nest. The truth is, that ants are chiefly carnivorous, preying indiscriminately on all the soft parts of other insects, and especially the viscera; also upon worms, whether dead or alive, and small birds or animals. If unable to drag their booty to the nest, they make an abundant meal upon it, and, like the bee, disgorge it, upon their return home, for the use of their companions; and they appear able to retain at pleasure the nutritious juices unchanged for a considerable time. Ants are also extremely fond of saccharine matter, which they obtain from the exudation of trees, or from ripe fruits, &c.; but their favourite food is the saccharine exudation from the body of the aphides, or plant-lice. These insects insert their tube or sucker between the fibres of vegetables, where they find a most substantial nutriment. This nutriment they retain a considerable time, if no ant approaches them. The ant has the talent of procuring it from the aphides at pleasure. It approaches the aphis, strikes it gently and repeatedly with its antennæ, when it instantly discharges the juice by two tubes, easily discerned to be standing out from its body. These creatures are the *milch kine* of the ants. By a remarkable coincidence, which M. Huber justly considers too much to be ascribed to chance, the aphides and the ants become torpid at the same degree of cold (27° Fahr.), and revive together at the same degree of warmth. He says, 'I am not acquainted with any ants to whom the art of obtaining from the pucerons (aphides) their subsistence is unknown. We might even venture to affirm that these insects are made for their use' (Huber, *Natural History of Ants*, p. 210, &c.).

It is highly probable that the exotic ants subsist by similar means. The accounts given us of the termites, or ants, inhabiting the hottest climates, clearly show that they are carnivorous. Bosman, in his description of Guinea, says that they will devour a sheep in one night, and that a fowl is amusement to them only for an hour. In these situations living animals often become their victims. An Italian missionary at Congo relates that a cow in a stall had been known to be devoured by these devastators. We have therefore every reason to conclude that the ants of Palestine, like those of Europe, are carnivorous, become torpid in winter, and need no magazine of provisions. The words of Solomon (Prov. vi. 6, &c.), properly considered, give no countenance to the ancient error respecting ants. He does not affirm that the ant, which he proposes to the sluggard as an example, laid up in her magazine stores of grain against winter, but that, with considerable prudence and foresight, she makes use of *proper seasons* to collect a supply of provisions sufficient for her purposes. There is not a word in them implying that she stores up grain or other provisions. She prepares her bread and gathers her food (namely, such food as is suited to her) in summer and harvest (that is, when it is most plentiful), and thus shows her wisdom and prudence by using the advantages offered to her. The sense is thus ably given by Dr. Hammond: '*As in the matter just mentioned* the least *delay* is pernicious, so *in all things else sluggishness*, or *negligence* of those things *which concern us most nearly*, should ever be avoided; and if we need any instructor on this head, we may go to one of the least and meanest of creatures.' The *moral*, then, intended in Solomon's allusion to the ant, is simply to avail one's self of the *favourable time without delay*.

ANTEDILUVIANS, the name given collectively to the people who lived before the Deluge. The interval from the Creation to that event is not less, even according to the Hebrew text, than 1657 years, being not more than 691 years shorter than that between the Deluge and the birth of Christ, and only 167 years less than from the birth of Christ to the present time, and equal to about two-sevenths of the whole period from the Creation. By the Samaritan and Septuagint texts (as adjusted by Hales) a much greater duration is assigned to the antediluvian period—namely, 2256 years, which nearly equals the Hebrew interval from the Deluge to the birth of Christ, and much exceeds the interval from the birth of Christ to the present time.

In the article 'ADAM' it has been shown that the father of men was something more than 'the noble savage,' or rather the grown-up infant, which some have represented him. He was an instructed man;—and the immediate descendants of a man so instructed could not be an ignorant or uncultivated people. Their pursuits from the first were agricultural and pastoral; for it is remarkable that of the strictly savage or hunting condition of life there is not the slightest trace before the Deluge. In fact, savageism is not discoverable before the Confusion of Tongues, and was in all likelihood a degeneracy from a state of cultivation, eventually produced in particular communities by that great social convulsion. All that was peculiar in the circumstances of the antediluvian period was eminently favourable to civilization.

By reason of their length of life, the antediluvians had ample opportunities of acquiring the highest skill in the mechanical arts. They had also more encouragement in protracted undertakings, and stronger inducements to the erection of superior, more costly, more durable, and more capacious edifices and monuments, public and private, than exist at present. They might reasonably calculate on reaping the benefit of their labour and expenditure. The earth itself was probably more equally fertile, and its climate more uniformly healthful, and more auspicious to longevity, and consequently to every kind of mental and corporeal exertion and enterprise, than has been the case since the great convulsion which took place at the Deluge.

But probably the greatest advantage enjoyed by the antediluvians, and which must have been in the highest degree favourable to their advancement in the arts of life, was the uniformity of language. Nothing could have tended more powerfully to maintain, equalize, and promote whatever advantages were enjoyed, and to prevent any portion of the human race from degenerating into savage life.

The opinion that the old world was acquainted with *astronomy*, is chiefly founded on the ages of Seth and his descendants being particularly set down (Gen. v. 6, *sqq.*), and the precise year, mouth, and day being stated in which Noah and his family, &c. entered the ark, and made their egress from it (Gen. vii. 11; viii. 13). The knowledge of *zoology*, which Adam possessed, was doubtless imparted to his children; and we find that Noah was so minutely informed on the subject as to distinguish between clean and unclean beasts, and that his instructions extended to birds of every kind (Gen. vii. 2-4). A knowledge of some essential principles in *botany* is shown by the fact that Adam knew how to distinguish 'seed-bearing herb' and 'tree in which is a seed-bearing fruit,' with 'every green herb' (Gen. i. 29, 30). With *mineralogy* the antediluvians were at least so far acquainted as to distinguish metals; and in the description of the garden of Eden gold and precious stones are noticed (Gen. ii. 12). That the antediluvians were acquainted with *music* is certain; for it is expressly said that Jubal (while Adam was still alive) became 'the father of those who handle the *kinnur* and *hugab*' (Gen. iv. 21). The *hinnur* was evidently a stringed instrument resembling a lyre; and the *hugab* was without doubt the pandæan pipe, composed of reeds of different lengths joined together. This clearly intimates considerable progress in the science.

Our materials are too scanty to allow us to affirm that the antediluvians possessed the means of communicating their ideas by writing or by hieroglyphics, although tradition, and a hint or two in the Scriptures, might support the assertion. With regard to *architecture*, it is a singular and important fact that Cain, when he was driven from his first abode, built a city in the land to which he went, and called it Enoch, after his son. This shows that the descendants of Adam lived in houses and towns from the first, and consequently affords another confirmation of the argument for the original cultivation of the human family. The *metallurgy* of the antediluvians has been noticed in 'ADAM;' and to what is there said of *agriculture* we shall only add a reference to the case of Noah, who, immediately after the Flood, became a husbandman, and planted a vineyard. He also knew the method of fermenting the juice of the grape; for it is said he drank of the wine, which produced inebriation (Gen. ix. 20, 21). This knowledge he doubtless obtained from his progenitors anterior to the destruction of the old world.

Pasturage appears to have been coeval with husbandry. Abel was a keeper of sheep, while his brother was a tiller of the ground (Gen. iv. 2); but there is no necessity for supposing that Cain's husbandry excluded the care of cattle. The class of tent-dwelling pastors – that is, of those who live in tents that they may move with their flocks and herds from one pasture-ground to another—did not originate till comparatively late after the Fall; for Jabal, the seventh from Adam in the line of Cain, is said to have been the 'father' or founder of that mode of life (Gen. iv. 20).

It is impossible to speak with any decision respecting the form or forms of government which prevailed before the Deluge. The slight intimations to be found on the subject seem to favour the notion that the particular governments were patriarchal, subject to a general theocratical control. The right of property was recognised, for Abel and Jabal possessed flocks, and Cain built a city. From Noah's familiarity with the distinction of clean and unclean beasts (Gen. vii. 2), it would seem that the Levitical rules on this subject were by no means new when laid down in the code of Moses.

Marriage, and all the relations springing from it, existed from the beginning (Gen. ii. 23-25); and although polygamy was known among the antediluvians (Gen. iv. 19), it was most probably unlawful; for it must have been obvious that, if more than one wife had been necessary for a man, the Lord would not have confined the first man to one woman. The marriage of the sons of Seth with the daughters of Cain appears to have been prohibited, since the consequence of it was that universal depravity in the family of Seth so forcibly expressed in this short passage, '*All* flesh had corrupted its way upon the earth' (Gen. vi. 12).

It is probable that even the longevity of the antediluvians may have contributed to the general corruption of manners. As there was probably a good deal of time upon their hands, the temptations to idleness were likely to be very strong; and the next step would be to licentious habits and selfish violence. The ample leisure possessed by the children of Adam might have been employed for many excellent purposes of social life and religious obedience, and undoubtedly it was so employed by many; but to the larger part it became a snare and the occasion of temptations, so that 'the wickedness of man became great, the earth was corrupt before God, and was filled with violence.'

ANTICHRIST. The meaning attached to this word has been greatly modified by the controversies of various churches and sects. In Scripture, however, and the early Christian writers, it has an application sufficiently distinct from partial interpretations. Antichrist, according to St. John, is the ruling spirit of error, the enemy of the truth of the Gospel as it is displayed in the divinity and holiness of Christ. This is the primary meaning of the term, and we are led at once to consider it as the proper title of Satan. But the same apostle speaks of the existence of many antichrists; whence we learn that it is applicable to any being who opposes Christ in the high places of spiritual wickedness.

ANTI-LIB'ANUS. [LEBANON.]

AN'TIOCH. Two places of this name are mentioned in the New Testament. 1. A city on the banks of the Orontes, 300 miles north of Jerusalem, and about 30 from the Mediterranean. It was situated in the province of Seleucis, called Tetrapolis. It was the metropolis of Syria, the

40.

residence of the Syrian kings, and afterwards became the capital of the Roman provinces in Asia. It ranked third, after Rome and Alexandria, among the cities of the empire, and was little inferior in size and splendour to the latter. Its suburb Daphne was celebrated for its grove and fountains, its asylum and temple were dedicated to Apollo and Diana. It was very populous; within 150 years after its erection the Jews slew 100,000 persons in it in one day. In the time of Chrysostom the population was computed at 200,000, of whom one-half, or even a greater proportion, were professors of Christianity. Cicero speaks of the city as distinguished by men of learning and the cultivation of the arts. A multitude of Jews resided in it. Seleucus Nicator granted them the rights of citizenship, and placed them on a perfect equality with the other inhabitants. These privileges were continued to them by Vespasian and Titus. Antioch is called *libera* by Pliny, having obtained from Pompey the privilege of being governed by its own laws.

The Christian faith was introduced at an early period into Antioch, and with great success (Acts xi. 19. 21, 24). The name ' *Christians*' was here first applied to its professors (Acts xi. 26) Antioch soon became a central point for the diffusion of Christianity among the Gentiles, and maintained for several centuries a high rank in the Christian world. A controversy which arose between certain Jewish believers from Jerusalem and the Gentile converts at Antioch respecting the permanent obligation of the right of circumcision was the occasion of the first apostolic council or convention (Acts xv.). Antioch was the scene of the early labours of the apostle Paul, and the place whence he set forth on his first missionary labours (Acts xi. 26; xiii. 2). Ignatius

was the second bishop or overseer of the church, for about forty years, till his martyrdom in A.D. 107.

As the ecclesiastical system became gradually assimilated to the political, the churches in those cities which held the highest civil rank assumed a corresponding superiority in relation to other Christian communities. Such was the case at Rome, Alexandria, and Antioch, and. in the course of time. at Constantinople and Jerusalem, where the term Exarch was applied to the resident bishop, but shortly exchanged for that of Patriarch. At the present time there are three prelates in Syria who claim the title of patriarchs of Antioch. namely: (1) the patriarch of the Greek church; (2) of the Syrian Monophysites; (3) of the Maronites.

Few cities have undergone and survived greater vicissitudes and disasters than Antioch. In A.D. 260 Sapor, the Persian king, surprised and pillaged it, and multitudes of the inhabitants were slain or sold as slaves. It has been frequently brought to the verge of utter ruin by earthquakes; by that of A.D. 526 no less than 250,000 persons were destroyed, the population being swelled by an influx of strangers to the festival of the Ascension. The emperor Justinian gave forty-five centenaries of gold (180,000*l.*) to restore the city. Scarcely had it resumed its ancient splendour (A.D. 540) when it was again taken and delivered to the flames by Chosroes. In A.D. 658 it was captured by the Saracens. In A.D. 975 it was retaken by Nicephoras Phocas. In A.D. 1080 the son of the governor Philaretus betrayed it into the hands of Soliman. Seventeen years after the Duke of Normandy entered it at the head of 300,000 Crusaders; but as the citadel still held out, the victors were in their turn besieged by a fresh host under Kerboga and twenty-eight emirs, which at last gave way to their desperate valour. In A.D. 1268 Antioch was occupied and ruined by Boadocbar or Bibars, sultan of Egypt and Syria; this first seat of the Christian name being dispeopled by the slaughter of 17,000 persons, and the captivity of 100,000. About the middle of the fifteenth century the three patriarchs of Alexandria, Antioch, and Jerusalem convoked a synod, and renounced all connection with the Latin church.

Antioch at present belongs to the Pashalic of Haleb (Aleppo), and bears the name of *Antakia*. The inhabitants are said to have amounted to twenty thousand before the earthquake of 1822, which destroyed four or five thousand. The present town stands on scarcely one-third of the area enclosed by the ancient wall, of which the line may be easily traced.

2. ANTIOCH *in* (or *near*) *Pisidia*, being a border city, was considered at different times as belonging to different provinces. It was founded by Seleucus Nicator, and its first inhabitants were from Magnesia on the Mæander. After the defeat of Antiochus (III.) the Great by the Romans, it came into the possession of Eumenes, king of Pergamus, and was afterwards transferred to Amyntas. On his death the Romans made it the seat of a proconsular government, and invested it with the privileges of immunity from taxes and a municipal constitution similar to that of the Italian towns. When Paul and Barnabas visited this city (Acts xiii. 14), they

found a Jewish synagogue and a considerable number of proselytes, and met with great success among the Gentiles (v. 48), but, through the violent opposition of the Jews, were obliged to leave the place, which they did in strict accordance with their Lord's injunction (v. 51, compared with Matt. x. 14; Luke ix. 5).

Till within a very recent period Antioch was supposed to have been situated where the town of *Ak-Sheker* now stands; but later investigations have determined its site to be adjoining the town of Yalobatch; and Mr. Arundell observed there the remains of several temples and churches, besides a theatre and a magnificent aqueduct; of the latter twenty-one arches still remained in a perfect state.

ANTI'OCHUS, a name which may be interpreted *he who withstands*, or *lasts out ;* and denotes military prowess, as do many other of the Greek names. It was borne by one of the generals of Philip, whose son, Seleucus, by the help of the first Ptolemy, established himself (B.C. 312) as ruler of Babylon. For eleven years more the contest in Asia continued, while Antigonus was grasping at universal supremacy. At length, in 301, he was defeated and slain in the decisive battle of Ipsus, in Phrygia. Ptolemy, son of Lagos, had meanwhile become master of southern Syria; and Seleucus was too much indebted to him to be disposed to eject him by force from this possession. In fact, the three first Ptolemies (B.C. 323-222) looked on their extra-Egyptian possessions as their sole guarantee for the safety of Egypt itself against their formidable neighbour, and succeeded in keeping the mastery, not only of Palestine and Cœle-Syria, and of many towns on that coast, but of Cyrene and other parts of Libya, of Cyprus, and other islands, with numerous maritime posts all round Asia Minor. A permanent fleet was probably kept up at Samos, so that their arms reached to the Hellespont; and for some time they ruled over Thrace. Thus Syria was divided between two great powers, the *northern* half falling to Seleucus and his successors, the *southern* to the Ptolemies; and this explains the titles 'king of the north' and 'king of the south,' in the 11th chapter of Daniel. The line dividing them was drawn somewhat to the north of Damascus, the capital of Cœle-Syria.

The first Seleucus built a prodigious number of cities with Greek institutions, not, like Alexander, from military or commercial policy, but to gratify ostentation, or his love for Greece. To people his new cities was often a difficult matter; and this led to the bestowal of premiums on those who were willing to become citizens. Hence we may account for the extraordinary privileges which the Jews enjoyed in them all, having equal rights with Macedonians. But there was still another cause which recommended the Jews to the Syrian kings. A nation thus diffused through their ill-compacted empire, formed a band most useful to gird its parts together. To win the hearts of the Jews, was to win the allegiance of a brave brotherhood, who would be devoted to their protector, and who could never make common cause with any spirit of local independence. For this reason Antiochus the Great, and doubtless his predecessors also, put peculiar trust in Jewish garrisons.

41. [Antiochus the Great.]

Again: through the great revolution of Asia, the Hebrews of Palestine were now placed nearly on the frontier of two mighty monarchies; and it would seem that the rival powers *bid* against one another for their good will—so great were the benefits showered upon them by the second Ptolemy. Even when a war broke out for the possession of Cœle-Syria, under Antiochus the Great, and the fourth Ptolemy (B.C. 218, 217), though the people of Judæa, as part of the battle-field and contested possession, were exposed to severe suffering, it was not the worse for their ultimate prospects. Antiochus at least, when at a later period (B.C. 198) left master of southern Syria, did but take occasion to heap on the Jews and Jerusalem new honours and exemptions.

The Syrian empire, as left by Antiochus the Great to his son, was greatly weaker than that which the first Seleucus founded. Scarcely, indeed, had the second of the line begun to reign (B.C. 280) when four sovereigns in Asia Minor established their complete independence:—the kings of Pontus, Bithynia, Cappadocia, and Pergamus. In the next reign—that of Antiochus Theos—the revolt of the Parthians under Arsaces (B.C. 250) was followed speedily by that of the distant province of Bactriana. For thirty years together the Parthians continued to grow at the expense of the Syrian monarchy. The great Antiochus passed a life of war (B.C. 223-187). In his youth he had to contend against his revolted satrap of Media, and afterwards against his kinsman Achæus, in Asia Minor. Besides this, he was seven years engaged in successful campaigns against the Parthians and the king of Bactriana; and, finally, met unexpected and staggering reverses in war with the Romans, so that his last days were inglorious and his resources thoroughly broken. Respecting the reign of his son, Seleucus Philopator (B.C. 187-176), we know little, except that he left his kingdom tributary to the Romans [see also SELEUCUS PHILOPATOR]. In Daniel, xi. 20, he is named *a raiser of taxes*, which shows what was the chief direction of policy in his reign. Seleucus having been assassinated by one of his courtiers, his brother Antiochus Epiphanes hastened to occupy the vacant throne, although the natural heir, Demetrius, son of Seleucus, was alive, but a hostage at Rome. In Daniel xi. 21 it is indicated that he gained the kingdom *by flatteries ;* and there can be no doubt that a most lavish bribery was his chief instrument. According to the description in Livy (xli. 20), the magnificence of his largesses had almost the appearance of insanity.

A prince of such a temper and in such a position, whose nominal empire was still extensive, though its real strength and wealth were departing, may naturally have conceived, the first moment that he felt pecuniary need, the design of plundering the Jewish temple. At such a crisis, the advantage of the deed might seem to overbalance the odium incurred: yet, as he would convert every Jew in his empire into a deadly enemy, a second step would become necessary—

42. [Antiochus Epiphanes.]

to crush the power of the Jews, and destroy their national organization. The design, therefore, of prohibiting circumcision and their whole ceremonial, would naturally ally itself to the plan of spoliation, without supposing any previous enmity against the nation on his part. We have written enough to show how surprising to the Jews must have been the sudden and almost incredible change of policy on the part of the rulers of Syria; and how peculiarly aggravated the enmity Antiochus Epiphanes must in any case have drawn on himself. Instead of crushing his apparently puny foes, he raised up heroes against himself [Maccabees], who, helped by the civil wars of his successors, at length achieved the deliverance of their people; so that in the 170th year of the Seleucidæ (b.c. 143) their independence was formally acknowledged, and they began to date from this period as a new birth of their nation.

The change of policy, from conciliation to cruel persecution, which makes the reign of Epiphanes an era in the relation of the Jews to the Syrian monarchy, has perhaps had great permanent moral results. It is not impossible that perseverance in the conciliating plan might have sapped the energy of Jewish national faith: while it is certain that persecution kindled their zeal and cemented their unity. Jerusalem, by its sufferings, became only the more sacred in the eyes of its absent citizens; who vied in replacing the wealth which the sacrilegious Epiphanes had ravished. According to 1 Maccab. vi. 1-16, this king died shortly after an attempt to plunder a temple at Elymais; and Josephus follows that account.

An outline of the deeds of the kings of Syria in war and peace, down to Antiochus Epiphanes, is presented in the 11th chapter of Daniel; in which Epiphanes and his father are the two principal figures. The wars and treaties of the kings of Syria and Egypt ffom b.c. 280 to b.c. 165 are described so minutely and so truly, in vv. 6-36, as to force all reasonable and well-informed men to choose between the alternatives,— either that it is a most signal and luminous prediction, or that it was written after the event.

Besides Antiochus Epiphanes, the book of Maccabees mentions his son, called Antiochus Eupator, and another young Antiochus, son of Alexander Balas, the usurper; both of whom were murdered at a tender age. In the two last chapters of the book a fourth Antiochus appears, called by the Greeks *Sidetes*, from the town of Sida, in Pamphylia. This is the last king of that house, whose reputation and power were not unworthy of the great name of Seleucus. In the year b.c. 134 he besieged Jerusalem, and having taken it next year, after a severe siege, he pulled down the walls, and reduced the nation once more to subjection, after only ten years' independence.

AN'TIPAS, a person named as 'a faithful witness,' or martyr, in Rev. ii. 13.

2. ANTIPAS, or Herod-Antipas. [Herodian Family.]

ANTIPA'TER. [Herodian Family.]

ANTIPA'TRIS, a city built by Herod the Great, on the site of a former place called Caphar-saba. The spot was well watered, and fertile; a stream flowed round the city, and in its neighbourhood were groves of large trees. Caphar-saba was 120 stadia from Joppa; and between the two places Alexander Balas drew a trench, with a wall and wooden towers, as a defence against the approach of Antiochus. Antipatris also lay between Cæsarea and Lydia, its distance from the former place being twenty-six Roman miles. On the road from Ramlah to Nazareth, north of Ras-el Ain, there is a village called Kaffr Saba; and as its position is almost in exact agreement with the position assigned to Antipatris, it is supposed to be the same place, this Kaffr Saba being no other than the reproduced name of Caphar-saba, which, as in many other instances, has again supplanted the foreign, arbitrary, and later name of Antipatris. St. Paul was brought from Jerusalem to Antipatris by night, on his route to Cæsarea (Acts xxiii. 31).

ANTO'NIA, a fortress in Jerusalem, on the north side of the area of the temple, often mentioned by Josephus in his account of the later wars of the Jews. It was originally built by the Maccabees, under the name of Baris, and was afterwards rebuilt with great strength and splendour by the first Herod. This fortress is the 'castle' into which Paul was carried from the temple by the soldiers: from the stairs of which he addressed the people collected in the adjacent court (Acts xxi. 31-40).

APE. The word is in the Hebrew Koph, and it occurs only in 1 Kings x. 22 and 2 Chron. ix. 21, as among the curiosities in natural history brought back by Solomon's ships from their distant voyages to Ophir. The name seems to have been introduced along with the animals, for in Sanscrit and Malabaric *hapi* is the name for an ape. We cannot of course attempt to determine the species brought into Palestine on the occasion indicated; and the probability indeed is, that the name is a general one for all or any of the quadrumana of which the Hebrews had any knowledge. When we consider the mode in which these animals were introduced, it is curious to compare this with the scene in the tomb of Thothmes III. at Thebes, where the presents and tributes of various distant nations are represented as being brought to the king. Among these are several living animals, includ-

43. [Apes from Egyptian Monuments.]

ing six quadrumanous animals. The smallest and most effaced may be apes; but the others, and in particular the three here copied, are undoubtedly Macaci or Cynocephali, that is, a species of the genus baboon, or baboon-like apes. The association renders these figures interesting; but it is impossible to say that the animals brought to Solomon were of these kinds, or indeed to say to what species they should be referred [SATYR].

APEL'LES, a Christian at Rome, whom Paul salutes in his Epistle to the Church there (Rom. xvi. 10), and calls 'approved in Christ,' *i. e.* an approved Christian. According to the old church traditions Apelles was one of the seventy disciples, and bishop either of Smyrna or Heracleia.

APHAR'SACHITES or APHARSATHCHITES, the name of the nation to which belonged one portion of the colonists whom the Assyrian king planted in Samaria (Ezra iv. 9; v. 6).

A'PHEK: the name signifies *strength* ; hence a citadel or fortified town. There were at least three places so called, viz. :—

1. APHEK, a city in the tribe of Asher (Josh. xiii. 4; xix. 30), called Aphik in Judg. i. 31, where we also learn that the tribe was unable to gain possession of it. A village called Afka is still found in Lebanon, situated at the bottom of a valley, and may possibly mark the site of this Aphek.

2. APHEK, a town near which Benhadad was defeated by the Israelites (1 Kings xx. 26. *sq*), which seems to correspond to the Aphaca of Eusebius, situated to the east of the Sea of Galilee, and which is mentioned by Burckhardt, Seetzen, and others under the name of Feik.

3. APHEK, a city in the tribe of Issachar, not far from Jezreel, where the Philistines twice encamped before battles with the Israelites (1 Sam. iv. 1; xxix. 1; comp. xxviii. 4). Either

this or the first Aphek, but most probably this, was the *Aphek* mentioned in Josh. xii. 18, as a royal city of the Canaanites.

APHE'KAH, a town in the mountains of Judah (Josh. xv. 23).

APHER'EMA, one of the three toparchies added to Judæa by the kings of Syria (1 Macc. xi. 34). This is perhaps the Ephræm or Ephraim mentioned in John xi. 54.

APH'SES, head of the eighteenth sacerdotal family of the twenty-four into which the priests were divided by David for the service of the temple (1 Chron. xxiv. 15).

APOC'RYPHA (*hidden, secreted, mysterious*), a term in theology, applied in various senses to denote certain books claiming a sacred character.

In the *Bibliothèque Sacrée*, by the Rev. Dominican Fathers Richard and Giraud (Paris, 1822), the term is defined to signify—(1) anonymous or pseudepigraphal books; (2) those which are not publicly read, although they may be read with edification in private; (3) those which do not pass for authentic and of divine authority, although they pass for being composed by a sacred author or an apostle, as the *Epistle of Barnabas ;* and (4) dangerous books composed by ancient heretics to favour their opinions. They also apply the name 'to books which, after having been contested, are put into the canon by consent of the churches, as Tobit,' &c. And Jahn applies it in its most strict sense, and that which it has borne since the fourth century, to books which, from their inscription or the author's name, or the subject, might easily be taken for inspired books, but are not so in reality.

The apocryphal books, such as the 3d and 4th books of Esdras, the Book of Enoch, &c., which were all known to the ancient Fathers, have descended to our times ; and, although incontestably spurious, are of considerable value from their antiquity, as throwing light upon the religious and theological opinions of the first centuries. The most curious are the 3rd and 4th books of Esdras, and the Book of Enoch, which has been but recently discovered, and has acquired peculiar interest from its containing the passage cited by the apostle Jude [ENOCH]. Nor are the apocryphal books of the New Testament destitute of interest. Although the spurious Acts extant have no longer any defenders of their genuineness, they are not without their value to the Biblical student, and have been applied with success to illustrate the style and language of the genuine books, to which they bear a close analogy. Some of the apocryphal books have not been without their defenders in modern times. They are, however, regarded by most as originally not of an earlier date than the second century, and as containing interpolations which betray the fourth or fifth : they can, therefore, only be considered as evidence of the practice of the Church at the period when they were written.

Most of the apocryphal Gospels and Acts noticed by the fathers. and which are generally thought to have been the fictions of heretics in the second century, have long since fallen into oblivion. Of those which remain, although some have been considered by learned men as genuine works of the apostolic age, yet the greater part are universally rejected as spurious, and as written in the second and third centuries. Whatever authority is to be ascribed to these documents, it cannot be denied that the early Church evinced a high degree of discrimination in the difficult task of distinguishing the genuine from the spurious books. 'It is not so easy a matter,' says Jones, 'as is commonly imagined, rightly to settle the canon of the New Testament. For my own part, I declare, with many learned men, that in the whole compass of learning I know no question involved with more intricacies and perplexing difficulties than this' (*New and Full Method*, i. 15). This writer conceives that testimony and tradition are the principal means of ascertaining whether a book be canonical or apocryphal. Inquiries of this kind, however, must of necessity be confined to the few. The mass of Christians, who have neither time nor other means of satisfying themselves, must confide, in questions of this kind, either in the judgment of the learned, or the testimony at least, if not the authority, of the Church; and it ought to be a matter of much thankfulness to the private Christian, that the researches of the most learned and diligent inquirers have conspired, in respect to the chief books of Scripture, in adding the weight of their evidence to the testimony of the Church Universal.

APOLLO'NIA, a city of Macedonia, in the province of Mygdonia, situated between Amphipolis and Thessalonica, thirty Roman miles from the former, and thirty-six from the latter. St. Paul passed through Amphipolis and Apollonia in his way to Thessalonica (Acts xvii. 1).

APOL'LOS, a Jew of Alexandria, is described as a *learned*, or, as some understand it, an *eloquent man*, well versed in the Scriptures and the Jewish religion (Acts xviii. 24). About A.D. 56 he came to Ephesus, where, in the synagogues, 'he spake boldly the things of the Lord, knowing only the baptism of John' (ver. 25); by which we are probably to understand that he knew and taught the doctrine of *a* Messiah, whose coming John had announced, but knew not that *Jesus* was the Christ. His fervour, however, attracted the notice of Aquila and Priscilla, whom Paul had left at Ephesus; and they instructed him in this higher doctrine, which he thenceforth taught openly, with great zeal and power (ver. 26). Having heard from his new friends, who were much attached to Paul, of that apostle's proceedings in Achaia, and especially at Corinth, he resolved to go thither, and was encouraged in this design by the brethren at Ephesus, who furnished him with letters of introduction. On his arrival there he was very useful in watering the seed which Paul had sown, and was instrumental in gaining many new converts from Judaism. There was perhaps no apostle or apostolical man who so much resembled Paul in attainments and character as Apollos. His immediate disciples became so much attached to him, as well nigh to have produced a schism in the Church, some saying, 'I am of Paul;' others, 'I am of Apollos;' others, 'I am of Cephas' (1 Cor. iii. 4-7, 22). There must, probably, have been some difference in their mode of teaching to occasion this; and from the first Epistle to the Corinthians it would appear that Apollos was not prepared to go so far

as Paul in abandoning the figments of Judaism, and insisted less on the (to the Jews) obnoxious position that the Gospel was open to the Gentiles. There was nothing, however, to prevent these two eminent men from being perfectly united in the bonds of Christian affection and brotherhood. When Apollos heard that Paul was again at Ephesus, he went thither to see him; and as he was there when the first Epistle to the Corinthians was written (A.D. 59), there can be no doubt that the apostle received from him his information concerning the divisions in that church, which he so forcibly reproves. It strongly illustrates the character of Apollos and Paul, that the former, doubtless in disgust at those divisions with which his name had been associated, declined to return to Corinth; while the latter, with generous confidence, urged him to do so (1 Cor. xvi. 12). Paul again mentions Apollos kindly in Tit. iii. 13, and recommends him and Zenas the lawyer to the attention of Titus, knowing that they designed to visit Crete, where Titus then was.

APOSTLE, *a person sent by another; a messenger.*

The term is generally employed in the New Testament as the descriptive appellation of a comparatively small class of men, to whom Jesus Christ entrusted the organization of his church and the dissemination of his religion among mankind. At an early period of his ministry 'he ordained twelve' of his disciples 'that they should be with him.' 'These he named apostles.' Some time afterwards 'he gave to them power against unclean spirits to cast them out, and to heal all manner of disease;' 'and he sent them to preach the kingdom of God' (Mark iii. 14; Matt. x. 1-5; Mark vi. 7; Luke vi. 13; ix. 1). To them he gave 'the keys of the kingdom of God,' and constituted them princes over the spiritual Israel, that 'people whom God was to take from among the Gentiles, for his name' (Matt. xvi. 19; xviii. 18; xix. 28; Luke xxii. 30). Previously to his death he promised to them the Holy Spirit, to fit them to be the founders and governors of the Christian church (John xiv. 16, 17, 26; xv. 26, 27; xvi. 7-15). After his resurrection he solemnly confirmed their call, saying, 'As the Father hath sent me, so send I you;' and gave them a commission to 'preach the Gospel to every creature' (John xx. 21-23; Matt. xviii. 18-20). After his ascension he, on the day of Pentecost, communicated to them those supernatural gifts which were necessary to the performance of the high functions he had commissioned them to exercise; and in the exercise of these gifts, they, in the Gospel history and in their epistles, with the Apocalypse, gave a complete view of the will of their Master in reference to that new order of things of which he was the author. They 'had the mind of Christ.' They spoke 'the wisdom of God in a mystery.' That mystery 'God revealed to them by his Spirit,' and they spoke it 'not in words which man's wisdom teacheth. but which the Holy Ghost teacheth.' They were 'ambassadors for Christ,' and besought men, 'in Christ's stead, to be reconciled to God.' They authoritatively taught the doctrine and the law of their Lord; they organized churches, and required them to 'keep the traditions,' *i. e.* the doctrines and 'ordinances *delivered* to them' (Acts ii.

1 Cor. ii. 16; ii. 7, 10, 13; 2 Cor. v. 20; 1 Cor. xi. 2). Of the twelve originally ordained to the apostleship, one, Judas Iscariot, 'fell from it by transgression,' and Matthias, 'who had companied' with the other Apostles 'all the time that the Lord Jesus went out and in among them,' was by lot substituted in his place (Acts i. 17-26). Saul of Tarsus, afterwards termed Paul, was also miraculously added to the number of these permanent rulers of the Christian society (Acts ix.; xxii.; xxvi. 15-18; 1 Tim. i. 12; ii. 7; 2 Tim. j. 11).

The characteristic features of this highest office in the Christian church have been very accurately delineated by M'Lean, in his *Apostolic Commission.* 'It was essential to their office—1. That they should have seen the Lord, and been eye and ear witnesses of what they testified to the world (John xv. 27). This is laid down as an essential requisite in the choice of one to succeed Judas (Acts i. 21, 22) Paul is no exception here; for, speaking of those who saw Christ after his resurrection, he adds, 'and last of all he was seen of me' (1 Cor. xv. 8). And this he elsewhere mentions as one of his apostolic qualifications: 'Am I not an apostle? have I not seen the Lord?' (1 Cor. ix. 1). So that his 'seeing that Just One and hearing the word of his mouth' was necessary to his being 'a witness of what he thus saw and heard' (Acts xxii. 14, 15). 2. They must have been immediately called and chosen to that office by Christ himself. This was the case with every one of them (Luke vi. 13; Gal. i. 1), Matthias not excepted; for, as he had been a chosen disciple of Christ before, so the Lord, by determining the lot, declared his choice, and immediately called him to the office of an apostle (Acts i. 24-26). 3. Infallible inspiration was also essentially necessary to that office (John xvi. 13; 1 Cor. ii. 10; Gal. i. 11, 12). They had not only to explain the true sense and spirit of the Old Testament (Luke xxiv. 27; Acts xxvi. 22, 23; xxviii. 23), which were hid from the Jewish doctors, but also to give forth the New Testament revelation to the world, which was to be the unalterable standard of faith and practice in all succeeding generations (1 Pet. i. 25; 1 John iv. 6). 4. Another apostolic qualification was the power of working miracles (Mark xvi. 20; Acts ii. 43), such as speaking with divers tongues, curing the lame, healing the sick, raising the dead, discerning of spirits, conferring these gifts upon others, &c. (1 Cor. xii. 8-11). These were the credentials of their divine mission (2 Cor. xii. 12). Miracles were necessary to confirm their doctrine at its first publication, and to gain credit to it in the world as a revelation from God, and by these 'God bare them witness' (Heb. ii. 4). 5. To these characteristics may be added the *universality* of their mission. Their charge was not confined to any particular visible church, like that of ordinary pastors, but, being the oracles of God to men, they had 'the care of all the churches' (2 Cor. xi. 28). They had a power to settle their faith and order as a model to future ages, to determine all controversies (Acts xvi. 4), and to exercise the rod of discipline upon all offenders, whether pastors or flock (1 Cor. v. 3-6; 2 Cor. x. 8; xiii. 10).

It must be obvious, from this scriptural account of the apostolical office, that the Apostles had, in the strict sense of the term, no successors. Their qualifications were supernatural, and their work, once performed, remains in the infallible record of the New Testament, for the advantage of the Church and the world in all future ages. They are the only authoritative teachers of Christian doctrine and law. All official men in Christian churches can legitimately claim no higher place than expounders of the doctrines and administrators of the laws found in their writings.

The word 'apostle' occurs once in the New Testament (Heb. iii. 1) as a descriptive designation of Jesus Christ: 'The apostle of our profession,' *i. e.* the apostle whom we profess or acknowledge. The Jews were in the habit of applying the corresponding Hebrew term to the person who presided over the synagogue, and directed all its officers and affairs. The Church is represented as 'the house or family of God,' over which he had placed, during the Jewish economy, Moses, as the superintendent, —over which he has placed, under the Christian economy, Christ Jesus. The import of the term *apostle,* is—divinely-commissioned superintendent; and of the whole phrase, '*the apostle of our profession,*' the divinely-commissioned superintendent, whom WE Christians acknowledge, in contradistinction to the divinely-appointed superintendent Moses, whom the Jews acknowledged.

It is scarcely worth while to remark that the Creed, commonly called The Apostles', though very ancient, has no claim to the name, except as it contains apostolical doctrine.

APPEAL. The right of appeal to superior tribunals has generally been considered an essential concomitant of inferior judicatories. When, from the paucity of the population or any other cause, the subjects of litigation are few, justice is usually administered by the first authority in the state, from whose award no appeal can lie. But when the multiplication of causes precludes the continuance of this practice, and one or more inferior courts take cognizance of the less important matters, the right of appeal to the superior tribunal is allowed, with increasing restrictions as, in the course of time, subjects of litigation multiply, and as the people become weaned from the notion that the administration of justice is the proper function of the chief civil magistrate.

In the desert Moses at first judged all causes himself; and when, finding his time and strength unequal to his duty, he, at the suggestion of Jethro, established a series of judicatories in a numerically ascending scale (Exod. xviii. 13-26), he arranged that cases of difficulty should be referred from the inferior to the superior tribunals, aud in the last instance to himself. Although not distinctly stated, it appears from various circumstances that the clients had a right of appeal, similar to that which the courts had of reference. When the prospective distribution into towns, of the population which had hitherto remained in one compact body, made other arrangements necessary, it was directed that there should be a similar reference of difficult cases to the metropolitan court or chief magistrate ('the judge that shall be in those days') for the time being (Deut. xvi. 18; xvii. 8-12). That there was a concurrent right of appeal, appears from the use Absalom made of the delay of justice, which arose from the great number of cases that came before the king his father (2 Sam. xv. 2-4). These were doubtless appeal cases according to the above direction.

Of the later practice, before and after the time of Christ, we have some clearer knowledge from Josephus and the Talmudists. It seems that a man could carry his case by appeal through all the inferior courts to the Grand Sanhedrim at Jerusalem, whose decision was in the highest degree absolute and final. The Jews themselves trace the origin of these later usages up to the time of Moses : they were at all events based on early principles, and therefore reflect back some light upon the intimations respecting the right of appeal which we find in the sacred books.

The most remarkable case of appeal in the New Testament belongs to another class. It is the celebrated appeal of St. Paul from the tribunal of the Roman procurator Festus to that of the emperor ; in consequence of which he was sent as a prisoner to Rome (Acts xxv. 10, 11). Such an appeal having been once lodged, the governor had nothing more to do with the case : he could not even dismiss it, although he might be satisfied that the matter was frivolous, and not worth forwarding to Rome. Accordingly, when Paul was again heard by Festus and king Agrippa (merely to obtain materials for a report to the emperor), it was admitted that the apostle might have been liberated if he had not appealed to Cæsar (Acts xxvi. 32).

It may easily be seen that a right of appeal which, like this, involved a long and expensive journey, was by no means frequently resorted to. In lodging his appeal Paul exercised one of the high privileges of Roman citizenship which belonged to him by birth (Acts xxii. 28). [CITIZENSHIP.] The right of appeal connected with that privilege originated in the Valerian, Porcian, and Sempronian laws, by which it was enacted that if any magistrate should order flagellation or death to be inflicted upon a Roman citizen, the accused person might appeal to *the judgment of the people*. But what was originally the prerogative of the people had in Paul's time become that of the emperor, and appeal therefore was made to *him*. Hence Pliny mentions that he had sent to Rome some Christians, who were Roman citizens, and had appealed unto Cæsar. This privilege could not be disallowed by any magistrate to any person whom the law entitled to it. Indeed, very heavy penalties were attached to any refusal to grant it, or to furnish the party with facilities for going to Rome.

APPHIA, the name of a woman (Philemon 2) who is supposed by Chrysostom and Theodoret to have been the wife of Philemon.

APPII-FO'RUM, a market town in Italy, 43 Roman miles from Rome, on the great road from Rome to Brundusium, constructed by Appius Claudius. The remains of an ancient town, supposed to be Appii-Forum, are still observed at a place called Casarillo di Santa Maria, on the border of the Pontine marshes. When Saint Paul was taken to Italy, some of the Christians of Rome, being apprised of his approach, journeyed to meet him as far as ' Appii-Forum and

the Three Taverns' (Acts xxviii. 15), a town eight or ten miles nearer to Rome than Appii-Forum. The ' Three Taverns' was certainly a place of rest and refreshment, probably on account of the badness of the water at Appii-Forum, and the probability is that some of the Christians remained at the ' Three Taverns,' where it was known the advancing party would rest, while some others went on as far as Appii-Forum to meet Paul on the road.

APPLE. The word *Tappuach* is thus rendered in the Authorized Version. Most authors on Biblical Botany admit that *apple* is not the correct translation, for that fruit is indifferent in Palestine, being produced of good quality only on Mount Lebanon, and in Damascus. Many contend that ' quince' is the correct translation of Tappuach. Though somewhat more suitable than the apple, we think that neither the quince tree nor fruit is so superior to others as to be selected for notice in the passages of Scripture where *tappuach* occurs. The citron, we think, has the best claim to be considered the *Tappuach* of Scripture, as it was esteemed by the ancients, and known to the Hebrews, and conspicuously different, both as a fruit and a tree, from the ordinary vegetation of Syria, and the only one of the orange tribe which was known to the ancients. The orange, lemon, and lime, were introduced to the knowledge of Europeans at a much later period, probably by the Arabs from India. That the citron was well known to the Hebrews we have the assurance in the fact mentioned by Josephus, that at the Feast of Tabernacles king Alexander Jannæus was pelted with *citrons*, which the Jews had in their hands ; for, as he says, ' the law required that at that feast every one should have branches of the palm-tree and *citron*-tree. There is nothing improbable in the Hebrews having made use of boughs of the citron, as it was a native of Media, and well known to the Greeks at a very early period ; and indeed on some old coins of Samaria, the citron may be seen, as well as the palm-tree ; and it is not an unimportant confirmation that the Jews still continue to make offerings of citrons at the Feast of Tabernacles. Citrons, accordingly, are imported in considerable quantities for this purpose, and are afterwards sold, being more highly esteemed after having been so offered.

The *tappuach*, or citron-tree, is mentioned chiefly in the Canticles, ch. ii. 3, ' as the citron tree among the trees of the wood ;' ver. 5, ' Comfort me with citrons, for I am sick of love ;' vii. 8, ' The smell of thy nose like citrons ;' so in viii. 5. Again, in Prov. xxv. 11, ' A word fitly spoken is like apples of gold (or rather golden citrons) in baskets of silver.' In Joel i. 12, it is enumerated with the vine, the fig-tree, the palm, and pomegranate, as among the most valuable trees of Palestine. The rich colour, fragrant odour, and handsome appearance of the tree, whether in flower or in fruit, are particularly suited to all the above passages of Scripture.

AQUILA, a Jew with whom Paul became acquainted on his first visit to Corinth ; a native of Pontus, and by occupation a tent-maker. He and his wife Priscilla had been obliged to leave Rome in consequence of an edict issued by the

Emperor Claudius, by which all Jews were banished from Rome. Whether Aquila and Priscilla were at that time converts to the Christian faith cannot be positively determined; but at all events, they had embraced Christianity before Paul left Corinth; for we are informed that they accompanied him to Ephesus, and meeting there with Apollos, who 'knew only the baptism of John,' they 'instructed him in the way of God more perfectly' (Acts xviii. 25, 26). From that time they appear to have been zealous promoters of the Christian cause. Paul styles them his 'helpers in Christ Jesus,' and intimates that they had exposed themselves to imminent danger on his account (Rom. xvi. 3, 4). When Paul wrote his epistle to the Romans they were at Rome; but some years after they returned to Ephesus, for Paul sends salutations to them in his Second Epistle to Timothy (2 Tim. iv. 19). Their occupation as tent-makers probably rendered it necessary for them to keep a number of workmen constantly resident in their family, and to these (to such of them at least as had embraced the Christian faith) may refer the remarkable expression, '*the Church that is in their house.*'

AR, the capital city of the Moabites (Num. xxi. 28; Deut. ii. 9, 18, 29), near the river Arnon (Deut. ii. 18, 24; Num. xxi. 13-15). It appears to have been burnt by King Sihon (Num. xxi. 28), and Isaiah, in describing the future calamities of the Moabites, says, 'In the night, Ar of Moab is laid waste and brought to silence' (Isa. xv. 1). In his comment on this passage, Jerome states that in his youth there was a great earthquake, by which Ar was destroyed in the night-time.

This city was also called Rabbah or Rabbath, and, to distinguish it from Rabbath of Ammon, Rabbath-Moab. The site still bears the name of Rabbah. It is about 17 miles east of the Dead Sea, 10 miles south of the Arnon (Modjeb), and about the same distance north of Kerek. The ruins of Rabbah are situated on a low hill, which commands the whole plain. They present nothing of interest except two old Roman temples and some tanks.

ARA'BIA, an extensive region occupying the south-western extremity of Asia, between 12° 45' and 34½° N. lat., and 32½° and 60° E. long. from Greenwich; having on the W. the Isthmus of Suez and the Red Sea (called from it the *Arabian* Gulf), which separate it from Africa; on the S. the Indian Ocean; and on the E. the Persian Gulf and the Euphrates. The boundary to the north has never been well defined. It is one of the few countries of the south where the descendants of the aboriginal inhabitants have neither been extirpated nor expelled by northern invaders. They have not only retained possession of their ancestral homes, but have sent forth colonies to all the adjacent regions, and even to more distant lands, both in Africa and Asia.

With the history of no country save that of Palestine are there connected so many hallowed and impressive associations as with that of Arabia. Here lived and suffered the holy patriarch Job; here Moses, when 'a stranger and a shepherd,' saw the burning, unconsuming bush; here Elijah found shelter from the rage

of persecution; here was the scene of all the marvellous displays of divine power and mercy that followed the deliverance of Israel from the Egyptian yoke, and accompanied their journeyings to the Promised Land; and here Jehovah manifested himself in visible glory to his people. From the influence of these associations, combined with its proximity to Palestine, and the close affinity in blood, manners, and customs between the northern portion of its inhabitants and the Jews, Arabia is a region of peculiar interest to the student of the Bible; and it is chiefly in its relation to subjects of Bible study that we are now to consider it.

In early times the Hebrews included a part of what we call Arabia among the countries they vaguely designated as 'the East,' the inhabitants being numbered among the 'Sons of the East,' *i. e.* Orientals. But there is no evidence to show that these phrases are ever applied to the *whole* of the country known to us as Arabia. They appear to have been commonly used in speaking of those parts which lay due *east* of Palestine, or on the north-east and south-east; though occasionally they do seem to point to tracts which lay indeed to the south and south-west of that country, but to the east and southeast of Egypt.

44. [Bedouin Arabs.]

We find the name *Arab* first beginning to occur about the time of Solomon. It designated a portion of the country, an inhabitant being called Arabi, an Arabian (Isa. xiii. 20), or in later Hebrew, Arbi (Neh. ii. 19), the plural of which was Arbim (2 Chr. xxi. 16), or Arbiim (*Arabians*) (2 Chr. xvii. 11). In some places these names seem to be given to the Nomadic tribes generally (Isa. xiii. 20; Jer. iii. 2) and their country (Isa. xxi. 13). The kings of

Arabia from whom Solomon (2 Chr. ix. 14) and Jehosaphat (2 Chr. xvii. 11) received gifts were, probably, Bedouin chiefs; though in the place parallel to the former text (1 Kings x. 15), instead of *Arab* we find *Ereb*, rendered in Jer. xxv. 20, 24, 'mingled people,' but which Gesenius, following the Chaldee, understands to mean 'foreign allies.' It is to be remarked, however, that in all the passages where the word *Arab* occurs it designates only a small portion of the territory known to us as Arabia. Thus in the account given by Ezekiel (xxvii. 21) of the Arabian tribes that traded with Tyre, mention is specially made of *Arab* (comp. Jer. xxv. 24). In 2 Chr. xxi. 16; xxii. 1; xxvi. 7; Neh. iv. 7, we find the Arabians classed with the Philistines, the Ethiopians (*i. e.* the Asiatic Cushites, of whom they are said to have been neighbours), the Mehunims, the Ammonites, and Ashdodites. At what period this name *Arab* was extended to the whole region it is impossible to ascertain. From it the Greeks formed the word Arabia, which occurs twice in the New Testament; in Gal. i. 17, in reference probably to the tract adjacent to Damascene Syria, and in Gal. iv. 25, in reference to the peninsula of Mount Sinai. Arabs are mentioned among the strangers assembled at Jerusalem at the Pentecost (Acts ii. 11).

The early Greek geographers mention only two divisions of this vast region, *Happy* and *Desert* Arabia. But after the city of Petra, in Idumæa, had become celebrated as the metropolis of a commercial people, the Nabathæans, it gave name to a third division, viz. Arabia *Petræa* (improperly translated *Stony* Arabia); and this threefold division has obtained throughout Europe ever since.

1. ARABIA FELIX, i. e. *Happy Arabia.* This part of Arabia lies between the Red Sea on the west and the Persian Gulf on the east, the boundary to the north being an imaginary line drawn between their respective northern extremities, Akaba and Basra or Bussora. It thus embraces by far the greater portion of the country known to us as Arabia.

Arabia may be described generally as an elevated table-land, the mountain ranges of which are by some regarded as a continuation of those of Syria. In Arabia Felix the ridges, which are very high in the interior, slope gently on the east towards the Persian Gulf, and on the northeast towards the vast plains of the desert. On the west the declivities are steeper, and on the north-west the chains are connected with those of Arabia Petræa. Commencing our survey at the north end of the Red Sea, the first province which lies along its shore is the *Hedjaz.* This was the cradle of Mohammedan superstition, containing both Mecca, where the prophet was born, and Medina, where he was buried; and hence it became the Holy Land of the Moslem, whither they resort in pilgrimage from all parts of the East. It is on the whole a barren tract, consisting chiefly of rugged mountains and sandy plains. Still more unproductive, however, is the long, flat, dreary belt, of varying width, called *Tehâma,* which runs along the coast to the south of Hedjaz, and was at no distant period covered by the sea. But next to this comes *Yemen,* the true Arabia Felix of the ancients,

'Araby the Blest' of modern poets, and doubtless the finest portion of the peninsula. Yet if it be distinguished for fertility and beauty, it is chiefly in the way of contrast, for it is far from coming up to the expectations which travellers had formed of it. Turning from the west to the south coast of the peninsula, we next come to the extensive province of *Hhadramaut* (the Hazarmaveth of the Bible), a region not unlike Yemen in its general features, with the exception of the tracts called Mahrah and Sahar, which are dreary deserts. The south-east corner of the peninsula, between Hhadramaut and the Persian Gulf, is occupied by the important district of *Oman,* which has been in all ages famous for its trade, which has been greatly extended by the present imaum of Muscat. Along the Persian Gulf northward stretches the province of *Lahsa,* or rather *El Hassa,* to which belong the Bahrein Islands, famous for their pearls. The districts we have enumerated all lie along the coasts, but beyond them in the south stretches the vast desert of Akhaf, or Roba-el-Khali, *i.e.* 'the empty abode,' a desolate and dreary unexplored waste of sand. To the north of this extends the great central province of *Nedched* or *Nejd.* It may be described as having been the great *officina gentium* of the south, as were Scandinavia and Tartary of the north; for it is the region whence there issued at different periods those countless hordes of Arabs which overran a great part of Asia and Africa. Here too was the origin and the seat of the Wahabees (so formidable until subdued in 1818 by Mehemet Ali, pasha of Egypt), their chief town being Dereyeh.

The *geological* structure and *mineralogical* productions of this part of Arabia are in a great measure unknown. In the mountains about Mecca and Medina the predominant rocks are of grey and red granite, porphyry, and limestone. This is also the case in the great chain that runs southward towards Maskat; only that in the ridge that rises behind the Tehama there is found schistus and basalt instead of granite. Traces of volcanic action may be perceived around Medina, as also at Aden and in many other parts of the peninsula. Hot-springs are of frequent occurrence on the Hadjee or pilgrim road to Mecca. The ancients believed that Arabia yielded both gold and precious stones, but Niebuhr doubts if this ever was the case. The most valuable ore found now is the lead of Oman: what is called the Mocha stone is a species of agate that comes from India. The native iron is coarse and brittle; at Loheia and elsewhere there are hills of fossil salt. Arabia Felix has always been famous for frankincense, myrrh, aloes, balsam, gums, cassia, &c.; but it is doubtful whether the last-mentioned and other articles supposed to be indigenous were not imported from India. Here are found all the fruits of temperate and warm climates, among which the *date,* the fruit of the palm tree, is the most common, and is, along with the species of grain called *dhourra,* the staple article of food. But the most valuable vegetable production is coffee; for Yemen, if not its native country, is the *habitat* where it has reached the greatest state of perfection. In the *animal* kingdom Arabia possesses, in common with the adjacent regions, the camel, panthers, lynxes, hyænas, jackals, gazelles, asses (wild and tame), monkeys, &c. But the glory of Arabia is its *horse*. As in no other country is that animal so much esteemed, so in no other are its noble qualities of swiftness, endurance, temper, attachment to man, so finely developed. Of the insect tribes, the locust, both from its numbers and its destructiveness, is the most formidable scourge to vegetation. The Arabian seas swarm with fish, seafowl, and shells; coral abounds in the Red Sea, and pearls in the Persian Gulf.

2. ARABIA DESERTA. This takes in that portion of the country which lies north of Arabia Felix, and is bounded on the north-east by the Euphrates, on the north-west by Syria, and on the west by Palestine and Arabia Petræa. So far as it has yet been explored, Desert Arabia appears to be one continuous, elevated, interminable *steppe*, occasionally intersected by ranges of hills. Sand and salt are the chief elements of the soil, which in many places is entirely bare, but elsewhere yields stunted and thorny shrubs or thinly-scattered saline plants. That part of the wilderness called *El Hhammad* lies on the Syrian frontier, extending from the Hauran to the Euphrates, and is one immense dead and dreary level, very scantily supplied with water, except near the banks of the river, where the fields are irrigated by wheels and other artificial contrivances.

The sky in these deserts is generally cloudless, but the burning heat of the sun is moderated by cooling winds, which, however, raise fearful tempests of sand and dust. Here, too, as in other regions of the East, occasionally prevails the burning, suffocating south-east wind, called by the Arabs *El Hharūr* (the Hot), but more commonly *Samūm*, and by the Turks *Samyeli* (both words meaning 'the Poisonous'), the effects of which, however, have by some travellers been greatly exaggerated. This is probably 'the east wind' and the 'wind from the desert' spoken of in Scripture. Another phenomenon, which is not peculiar, indeed, to Desert Arabia, but is seen there in greatest frequency and perfection, is what the French call the *mirage*, the delusive appearance of an expanse of water, created by the tremulous, undulatory movement of the vapours raised by the excessive heat of a meridian sun. It is called in Arabic *serab*, and is no doubt the Hebrew *sarab* of Isa. xxxv. 7, which our translators have rendered 'the parched ground.'

3. ARABIA PETRÆA appears to have derived its name from its chief town *Petra* (i. e. a rock), although (as is remarked by Burckhardt) the epithet is also appropriate on account of the rocky mountains and stony plains which compose its surface. It embraces all the north-western portion of the country; being bounded on the east by Desert and Happy Arabia, on the north by Palestine and the Mediterranean, on the west by Egypt, and on the south by the Red Sea. This division of Arabia has been of late years visited by a great many travellers from Europe, and is consequently much better known than the other portions of the country. Confining ourselves at present to a general outline, we refer for details to the articles SINAI, EXODUS, EDOM, MOAB, &c. Beginning at the northern frontier, there meets the elevated plain of Belka, to the east of the Dead Sea, the district of Kerak (Kir), the ancient territory of the Moabites, their kinsmen of Ammon having settled to the north of this, in Arabia Deserta. The north border of Moab was the brook Arnon, now the Wady-el-Modjeb; to the south of Moab, separated from it by the Wady-el-Ahsy, lay Mount Seir, the dominion of the Edomites, or *Idumæa*, reaching as far as to Elath on the Red Sea. The great valley which runs from the Dead Sea to that point consists, first, of el-Ghor, which is comparatively low, but gradually rises by a succession of limestone cliffs into the more elevated plain of *el Arabah*, formerly mentioned. 'We were now,' says Professor Robinson (*Biblical Researches*, vol. ii. p. 502), 'upon the plain or rather the rolling desert, of the *Arabah*; the surface was in general loose gravel and stones, everywhere furrowed and torn with the beds of torrents. A more frightful desert it had hardly been our lot to behold. The mountains beyond presented a most uninviting and hideous aspect; precipices and naked conical peaks of chalky and gravelly formation rising one above another without a sign of life or vegetation.' The character of the mountains on the east of Arabah is quite different from those on the west. The latter, which seemed to be not more than two-thirds as high, are wholly desert and sterile; while these on the east appear to enjoy a sufficiency of rain, and are covered with tufts of herbs and occasional trees. This mountainous region is divided into two districts: that to the north is called *Jebál* (i. e. mountains, the Gebal of Ps. lxxxiii. 7); that to the south *Esh-Sherah*. To the district of Esh-Sherah belongs Mount Hor, the burial-place of Aaron, towering above the Wady Mousa (valley of Moses), where are the celebrated ruins of Petra (the ancient capital of the Nabathæo-Idumæans), the mountainous tract immediately west of the Arabah, is a desert limestone region, full of precipitous ridges, through which no travelled road has ever passed.

To the west of Idumæa extends the 'great and terrible wilderness' of *et-Tih*, i. e. 'the Wandering.' so called from being the scene of the wanderings of the children of Israel. It consists of vast interminable plains, a hard gravelly soil, and irregular ridges of limestone hills. It appears that the middle of this desert is occupied by a long central basin, extending from Jebel-et-Tih (i. e. the mountain of the wandering, a chain pretty far south) to the shores of the Mediterranean. This basin descends towards the north with a rapid slope, and is drained through all its length by Wady-el-Arish, which enters the sea near the place of the same name, on the borders of Egypt.

This description of the formation of the northern desert will enable us to form a more distinct conception of the general features of the peninsula of Sinai, which lies south of it, being formed by the two arms of the Red Sea, the Gulfs of Akaba and Suez. If the parallel of the north coast of Egypt be extended eastward to the great Wady-el-Arabah, it appears that the desert, south of this parallel, rises gradually towards the south, until on the summit of the ridge Et-Tîh, between the two gulfs, it attains the elevation of 4322 feet. The waters of all this great tract flow off northward either to the Mediterranean or the Dead Sea. The Tih forms a sort of offset, and along its southern base the surface sinks at once to the height of only about 3000 feet, forming the sandy plain which extends nearly across the peninsula. After this the mountains of the peninsula proper commence, and rise rapidly through the formations of sandstone, grünstein, porphyry, and granite, into the lofty masses of St. Catherine and Um Shaumer, the former of which has an elevation of 8168 Paris feet, or nearly double that of the Tih. Here the waters all run eastward or westward to the Gulfs of Akaba and Suez.

The soil of the Sinaitic peninsula is in general very unproductive, yielding only palm-trees, acacias, tamarisks, coloquintida, and dwarfish, thorny shrubs. Among the animals may be mentioned the mountain-goat, gazelles, leopards, a kind of marmot called *wabber* [CONEY], the *sheeb*, supposed by Col. C. Hamilton Smith to be a species of wild wolf-dog, &c.: of birds there are eagles, partridges, pigeons, the *katta*, a species of quail, &c. There are serpents, as in ancient times (Num. xxi. 4, 6), and travellers speak of a large lizard called *dhob*, common in the desert, but of unusually frequent occurrence here. The peninsula is inhabited by Bedouin Arabs, and its entire population was estimated by Burckhardt at not more than 4000 souls.

Though this part of Arabia must ever be memorable as the scene of the journeying of the Israelites from Egypt to the Promised Land, yet very few of the spots mentioned in Scripture can now be identified; nor, after the lapse of so many centuries, ought that to be occasion of surprise. According to Niebuhr, Robinson, &c. they crossed the Red Sea near Suez, but the tradition of the country fixes the point of transit eight or ten miles south of Suez, opposite the place called Ayoun Mousa, *i. e.* the Fountains of Moses, where Robinson recently found seven wells, some of which, however, were mere excavations in the sand. About 15½ hours (33 geographical miles) south-east of that is the Well of Hawârah, the *Marah* of Scripture, whose bitter water is pronounced by the Arabs to be the worst in these regions. Two or three hours south of Hawârah the traveller comes to the Wady Ghurundel, supposed to be the *Elim* of Moses. From the plain of El-kaa, which Robinson takes to be the desert of Sin (not to be confounded with that of *Zin*, which belonged to the great desert of Kadesh), they would enter the Sinaitic range, probably along the upper part of Wady Feiran and through the Wady-esh-Sheikh, one of the principal valleys of the peninsula. The Arabs call this whole cluster of mountains *Jebel-et-Tûr*; the Christians generally designate it as ' *Sinai,*' and give the name of *Horeb* to a particular mountain, whereas in Scripture the names are used interchangeably. [SINAI.]

Having now taken a rapid survey of this extensive region in its three divisions, let us advert to the people by whom it was at first settled, and by whose descendants it is still inhabited. There is a prevalent notion that the Arabs, both of the south and north, are descended from Ishmael; but the idea of the southern Arabs being of the posterity of Ishmael is entirely without foundation, and seems to have originated in the tradition invented by Arab vanity, that they, as well as the Jews, are of the seed of Abraham— a vanity which, besides disfiguring and falsifying the whole history of the patriarch and his son Ishmael, has transferred the scene of it from Palestine to Mecca. If we go to the most authentic source of ancient ethnography, the book of Genesis, we there find that the vast tracts of country known to us under the name of Arabia gradually became peopled by a variety of tribes of different lineage, though it is now impossible to determine the precise limits within which they fixed their permanent or nomadic abode. We shall here exhibit a tabular view of these races in chronological order, *i. e.* according to the successive æras of their respective progenitors:—

I. HAMITES, *i. e.* the posterity of *Cush*, Ham's eldest son, whose descendants appear to have settled in the south of Arabia, and to have sent colonies across the Red Sea to the opposite coast of Africa; and hence *Cush* became a general name for ' the south,' and specially for Arabian and African Ethiopia. The sons of Cush (Gen. x. 7) were Seba, Havilah, Sabtah, Raamah or Ragma (his sons, Sheba and Dedan), and Sabtheca.

II. SHEMITES, including the following:

A. *Joktanites*, *i. e.* the descendants of Joktan, the second son of Eber, Shem's great-grandson (Gen. x. 25, 26). According to Arab tradition Joktan, after the confusion of tongues and dispersion at Babel, settled in Yemen, where he reigned as king. Joktan had thirteen sons, some of whose names may be obscurely traced in the designations of certain districts in Arabia Felix. Their names were Almodad, Shaleph, Hhazarmaveth (preserved in the name of the province of Hhadramaut), Jarach, Hadoram, Uzal (believed by the Arabs to have been the founder of Sanaa in Yemen), Dikla, Obal, Abimael, Sheba, Ophir, Havilah, and Jobab.

B. *Abrahamites*, divided into—

(*a*) *Hagarenes* or *Hagarites*, so called from Hagar the mother; otherwise termed *Ishmaelites* from her son. The twelve sons of Ishmael (Gen. xxv. 13-15), who gave names to separate tribes, were Nebaioth (the Nabathæans in Arabia Petræa), Kedar, Abdeel, Mibsam, Mishma, Dumah, Massa, Hadad or Hadar, Thema, Jetur, Naphish (the Ituræans and Naphishæans near the tribe of Gad: 1 Chron. v. 19, 20), and Kedmah. They appear to have been for the most part located near to Palestine on the east and south-east.

(*b*) *Keturahites*, *i. e.* the descendants of Abraham and his second wife Keturah, by whom he had six sons (Gen. xxv. 2): Simram, Jokshan (who, like Raamah, son of Cush, was also the father of two sons, Sheba and Dedan), Medan, Midian, Jishbak, and Shuach. Among these, the posterity of *Midian* became the best known.

(*c*) *Edomites*, *i. e.* the descendants of Esau, who possessed Mount Seir and the adjacent region, called from them Idumæa. They and the Nabathæans formed in later times a flourishing commercial state, the capital of which was the remarkable city called Petra.

C. *Nahorites*, the descendants of Nahor, Abraham's brother, who seem to have peopled the land of *Uz*, the country of Job, and of *Buz*, the country of his friend Elihu the Buzite, these being the names of Nahor's sons (**Gen. xxii.** 21).

D. *Lotites,* viz.:

(*a*) *Moabites,* who occupied the northern portion of Arabia Petræa, as above described; and their kinsmen, the—

(*b*) *Ammonites,* who lived north of them, in Arabia Deserta.

Besides these, the Bible mentions various other tribes who resided within the bounds of Arabia, but whose descent is unknown, *e. g.* the Amalekites, the Kenites, the Horites, the inhabitants of Maon, Hazor, Vedan, and Javan-Meusal (Ezek. xxvii. 19).

In process of time some of these tribes were perhaps wholly extirpated (as seems to have been the case with the Amalekites), but the rest were more or less mingled together by inter-marriages, by military conquests, political revolutions, and other causes of which history has preserved no record; and thus amalgamated, they became known to the rest of the world as the ' ARABS,' a people whose physical and mental characteristics are very strongly and distinctly marked. In both respects they rank very high among the nations; so much so, that some have regarded them as furnishing the *prototype*—the primitive model form—the standard figure of the human species.

The inhabitants of Arabia have, from remote antiquity, been divided into two great classes, viz. the *townsmen* (including villagers), and the *men of the desert,* such being the meaning of the word ' *Bedawees* ' or Bedouins, the designation given to the ' dwellers in the wilderness.' From the nature of their country, the latter are necessitated to lead the life of *nomades,* or wandering shepherds; and since the days of the patriarchs (who were themselves of that occupation) the extensive *steppes* which form so large a portion of Arabia, have been traversed by a pastoral but warlike people, who, in their mode of life, their food, their dress, their dwellings, their manners, customs, and government, have always continued, and still continue, almost unalterably the same. They consist of a great many separate tribes, who are collected into different encampments dispersed through the territory which they claim as their own; and they move from one spot to another (commonly in the neighbourhood of pools or wells) as soon as the stinted pasture is exhausted by their cattle. It is only here and there that the ground is susceptible of cultivation, and the tillage of it is commonly left to peasants, who are often the vassals of the Bedawees, and whom (as well as all ' townsmen ') they regard with contempt as an inferior race. Having constantly to shift their residence, they live in movable tents (comp. Isa. xiii. 20; Jer. xlix. 29), from which circumstance they received from the Greeks the name of *Scenites,* dwellers in tents [TENTS]. The heads of tribes are called *sheikhs,* a word of various import, but used in this case as a title of honour; the government is hereditary in the family of each sheikh, but elective as to the particular individual appointed. Their allegiance, however, consists more in following his example as a leader than in obeying his commands; and, if dissatisfied with his government, they will depose or abandon him. As the independent lords of their own

deserts, the Bedawees have from time immemorial demanded tribute or presents from all travellers or caravans (Isa. xxi. 13) passing through their country; the transition from which to robbery is so natural, that they attach to the latter no disgrace, plundering without mercy all who are unable to resist them, or who have not secured the protection of their tribe. Their watching for travellers ' in the ways,' *i. e.* the frequented routes through the desert, is alluded to Jer. iii. 2; Ezra viii. 31; and the fleetness of their horses in carrying them into the ' depths of the wilderness,' beyond the reach of their pursuers, seems what is referred to in Isa. lxiii. 13, 14. Their warlike incursions into more settled districts are often noticed (*e. g.* Job i. 15; 2 Chron. xxi. 16; xxvi. 7). The acuteness of their bodily senses is very remarkable, and is exemplified in their astonishing sagacity in tracing and distinguishing the footsteps of men and cattle. The law of blood-revenge sows the seeds of perpetual feuds; and what was predicted (Gen. xvi. 12) of the posterity of Ishmael, the ' wild-ass man ' (a term most graphically descriptive of a Bedawee), holds true of the whole people [BLOOD-REVENGE]. They show bravery in repelling a public enemy, but when they fight for plunder, they behave like cowards. Their bodily frame is spare, but athletic and active, inured to fatigue and capable of undergoing great privations: their minds are acute and inquisitive; and though their manners are somewhat grave and formal, they are of a lively and social disposition. Of their moral virtues it is necessary to speak with caution. They were long held up as models of good faith, incorruptible integrity, and the most generous hospitality to strangers; but many recent travellers deny them the possession of these qualities; and it is certain that whatever they may have been once, the Bedawees, like all the unsophisticated ' children of nature,' have been much corrupted by the influx of foreigners, and the national character is in every point of view lowest where they are most exposed to the continual passage of strangers.

In the language of the Arabians we find the full and adult development of the genius of that group of languages of Western Asia which is now usually distinguished as the Syro-Arabian. In the abundance of its roots, in the manifold variety of its formations, in the syntactical delicacies of its construction, it stands pre-eminent as a language among all its sisters. Every class of composition also: the wild and yet noble lyrics of the son of the desert, who had ' nothing to glory in but his sword, his guest, and his fervid tongue;' the impassioned and often sublime appeals of the Koran; the sentimental poetry of a Mutanabbi; the artless simplicity of their usual narrative style, and the philosophic disquisition of an Ibn Chaldûn; the subtleties of the grammarian and scholiast; medicine, natural history, and the metaphysical speculations of the Aristotelian school—all have found the Arabic language a fitting exponent of their feeling and thought. And, although confined within the bounds of the Peninsula by circumstances to which we owe the preservation of its pure antique form, yet Islam made it the written and spoken language of the whole of Western Asia, of Eastern and Northern Africa, of Spain, and of some of the islands of the Mediterranean; and the ecclesiastical language of Persia, Turkey, and all other lands which receive the Mohammedan faith; in all which places it has left sensible traces of its *former* occupancy, and in many of which it is still the living or the learned idiom. The close affinity, and consequently the incalculable philological use, of the Arabic with regard to the Hebrew language and its other sisters, may be considered partly as a question of theory, and partly as one of fact. The former would regard the concurrent records which the Old Testament and their own traditions have preserved of the several links by which the Arabs were connected with different generations of the Hebrew line, and the evidences which Scripture offers of persons speaking Arabic being intelligible to the Hebrews; the latter would observe the demonstrable identity between them in the main features of a language, and the more subtle, but no less convincing traces of resemblance even in the points in which their diversity is most apparent. Thus springing from the same root as the Hebrew, and possessing such traces of affinity to a late period of Scripture history, this dialect was further enabled, by several circumstances in the social state of the nation, to retain its native resemblance of type until the date of the earliest extant written documents. These circumstances were, the almost insular position of the country, which prevented conquest or commerce from debasing the language of its inhabitants; the fact that so large a portion of the nation adhered to a mode of life in which every impression was, as it were, stereotyped, and knew no variation for ages; and the great and just pride which they felt in the purity of their language, which is still a characteristic of the Bedouins.

The principal source of the wealth of ancient Arabia was its *commerce*. So early as the days or Jacob (Gen. xxxvii. 28) we read of a mixed caravan of Arab merchants (Ishmaelites and Midianites) who were engaged in the conveyance of various foreign articles to Egypt, and made no scruple to add Joseph, 'a slave,' to their other purchases. The Arabs were, doubtless, the first navigators of their own seas, and the great carriers of the produce of India, Abyssinia, and other remote countries to Western Asia and Egypt. Various Indian productions thus obtained were common among the Hebrews at an early period of their history (Exod. xxx. 23, 25). The traffic of the Red Sea was to Solomon a source of great profit; and the extensive commerce of *Sabæa* (Sheba, now Yemen) is mentioned by profane writers as well as alluded to in Scripture (1 Kings x. 10-15). In the description of the foreign trade of Tyre (Ezek. xxvii. 19-24) various Arab tribes are introduced (comp. Isa. lx. 6; Jer. vi. 20; 2 Chron. ix. 14). The Nabathæo-Idumæans became a great trading people, their capital being Petra. The transit-trade from India continued to enrich Arabia until the discovery of the passage to India by the Cape of Good Hope; but the invention of steam-navigation has now restored the ancient route for travellers by the Red Sea.

Arabia, in ancient times, generally preserved its independence, unaffected by those great events which changed the destiny of the surrounding nations; and in the sixth century of our æra, the decline of the Roman empire and the corruptions and distractions of the Eastern church favoured the impulse given by a wild and warlike fanaticism. Mahomet arose, and succeeded in gathering around his standard the nomadic tribes of central Arabia; and in less than fifty years that standard waved triumphant 'from the straits of Gibraltar to the hitherto unconquered regions beyond the Oxus.' The khalifs transferred the seat of government successively to Damascus, Kufa, and Bagdad; but amid the distractions of their foreign wars, the chiefs of the interior of Arabia gradually shook off their feeble allegiance, and resumed their ancient habits of independence, which, notwithstanding the revolutions that have since occurred, they for the most part retain. At present, indeed, the authority of Mehemet Ali, the Pasha of Egypt, is acknowledged over a great portion of the northern part of Arabia, while in the south the Imam of Maskat exercises dominion over a much greater extent of country than did any of his predecessors.

ARAD, an ancient city on the southernmost borders of Palestine, whose inhabitants drove back the Israelites as they attempted to penetrate from Kadesh into Canaan (Num. xxi. 1), but were eventually subdued by Joshua, along with the other southern Canaanites (Josh. xii. 14, comp. x. 41; also Judg. i. 16). Eusebius and Jerome place Arad twenty Roman miles from Hebron. This accords well with the situation of a hill called Tell 'Arad, which Dr. Robinson observed on the road from Petra to Hebron. He describes it as 'a barren-looking eminence rising above the country around.' He did not examine the spot, but the Arabs said there were no ruins upon or near it, but only a cavern. The name alone is, however, too decisive to admit a doubt that the hill marks the site of the ancient Arad.

A'RAM, the name given by the Hebrews to the tract of country lying between Phœnicia on the west, Palestine on the south, Arabia Deserta and the river Tigris on the east, and the mountain range of Taurus on the north. Many parts of this extensive territory have a much lower level than Palestine, but it might receive the designation of 'the highlands,' because it does rise to a greater elevation than that country at most points of immediate contact, and especially on the side of Lebanon. Aram, or Aramæa, seems to have corresponded generally to the *Syria* and *Mesopotamia* of the Greeks and Romans (see those articles). We find the following divisions expressly noticed in Scripture:—1. ARAM-DAMMESEK, the 'Syria of Damascus' conquered by David, 2 Sam. viii. 5, 6, where it denotes only the territory around Damascus; but elsewhere 'Aram,' in connection with its capital 'Damascus,' appears to be used in a wider sense for Syria Proper (Isa. vii. 1, 8; xvii. 3; Amos i. 5). To this part of Aram the 'land of Hadrach' seems to have belonged (Zech. ix. 1). 2. ARAM-MAACHAH (1 Chron. xix. 6), or simply *Maachah* (2 Sam. x. 6, 8), was not far from the northern border of the Israelites on the east of the Jordan (comp. Deut. iii. 14, with Josh. xiii. 11, 13). 3. ARAM-BETH-RECHOB, the precise locality of which cannot with certainty be determined. 4. ARAM-ZOBAH (2 Sam. x. 6). Jewish tradition has placed Zobah at Aleppo, whereas Syrian tradition identifies it with Nisibis, a city in the north-east of Mesopotamia. The former seems a much nearer approximation to the truth. We may gather from 2 Sam. viii. 3, x. 16, that the eastern boundary of Aram-Zobah was the Euphrates, but Nisibis was far beyond that river. The people of Zobah are uniformly spoken of as near neighbours of the Israelites, the Damascenes, and other Syrians; and in one place (2 Chron. viii. 3) Hamath is called Hamath-Zobah, as pertaining to that district. We, therefore, conclude that Aram-Zobah extended from the Euphrates westward, perhaps as far north as to Aleppo. It was long the most powerful of the petty kingdoms of Aramæa, its princes commonly bearing the name of Hadadezer or Hadarezer. 5. ARAM-NAHARAIM, i. e. *Aram of the Two Rivers*, or Mesopotamia. The rivers which enclose Mesopotamia are the Euphrates on the west and the Tigris on the east; but it is doubtful whether the Aram-Naharaim of Scripture embraces the whole of that tract or only the northern portion of it (comp. Gen. xxiv. 10; Deut. xxiii. 4; Judg. iii. 8). A part of this region of Aram is also called *Padan-Aram*, the plain of Aram (Gen. xxv. 20; xxviii. 2, 6, 7; xxxi. 18; xxxiii. 18), and once simply *Padan* (Gen. xlviii. 7), also *Sedeh-Aram*, the field of Aram (Hos. xii. 13).

But though the districts now enumerated be the only ones *expressly named* in the Bible as belonging to Aram, there is no doubt that many more territories were included in that extensive region, e. g. Geshur, Hul, Arpad, Riblah, Tadmor, Hauran, Abilene, &c., though some of them may have formed part of the divisions already specified. It appears from the ethnographic table in the tenth chapter of Genesis (vers. 22, 23) that Aram was a son of Shem, and that his own sons were Uz, Hul, Gether, and Mash. Another Aram is mentioned (Gen. xxii. 21) as the grandson of Nahor and son of Kemuel, but he is not to be thought of here. The descent of the Aramæans from a son of Shem is confirmed by their language, which was one of the branches of the Semitic family, and nearly allied to the Hebrew.

The Aramaic language—that whole, of which the Chaldee and Syriac dialects form the parts—constitutes the northern and least developed branch of the Syro-Arabian family of tongues. Its cradle was probably on the banks of the Cyrus, according to the best interpretation of Amos ix. 7; but Mesopotamia, Babylonia, and Syria form what may be considered its home and proper domain. Political events, however, subsequently caused it to supplant Hebrew in Palestine; and then it became the prevailing form of speech from the Tigris to the shore of the Mediterranean, and, in a contrary direction, from Armenia down to the confines of Arabia. After obtaining such a wide dominion, it was forced, from the ninth century onwards, to give way before the encroaching ascendency of Arabic; and it now only survives, as a living tongue, among the Syrian Christians in the neighbourhood of Mosul. According to historical records, and also according to the comparatively ruder form of the Aramaic language itself, we might suppose that it represents, even

in the state in which we have it, some image of that aboriginal type which the Hebrews and Arabians, under more favourable social and climatical influences, subsequently developed into fulness of sound and structure. But it is difficult for us now to discern the particular vestiges of this archaic form; for, not only did the Aramaic not work out its own development of the original elements common to the whole Syro-Arabian sisterhood of languages, but it was pre-eminently exposed, both by neighbourhood and by conquest, to harsh collision with languages of an utterly different family. Moreover, it is the only one of the three great Syro-Arabian branches which has no fruits of a purely national literature to boast of. We possess no monument whatever of its own genius; not any work which may be considered the product of the political and religious culture of the nation, and characteristic of it—as is so emphatically the case both with the Hebrews and the Arabs. The first time we see the language, it is used by Jews as the vehicle of Jewish thought; and although, when we next meet it, it is employed by native authors, yet they write under the literary impulses of Christianity, and under the Greek influence on thought and language which necessarily accompanied that religion. These two modifications, which constitute and define the so-called Chaldee and Syriac dialects, are the only forms in which the normal and standard Aramaic has been preserved to us.

AR'ARAT occurs nowhere in Scripture as the name of a mountain, but only as the name of a country, upon the 'mountains' of which the ark rested during the subsidence of the flood (Gen. viii. 4).

The only other passages where 'Ararat' occurs are 2 Kings xix. 37 (Isa. xxxvii. 38) and Jer. li. 27. In the former it is spoken of as the country whither the sons of Sennacherib, king of Assyria, fled, after they had murdered their father. This points to a territory which did not form part of the immediate dominion of Assyria, and yet might not be far off from it. The description is quite applicable to Armenia, and is supported by the tradition of that country. The other Scripture text (Jer. li. 27) mentions Ararat, along with Minni and Ashkenaz, as kingdoms summoned to arm themselves against Babylon. In the parallel place in Isa. xiii. 2-4, the invaders of Babylonia are described as 'issuing from the mountains;' and if by *Minni* we understand the *Minyas* in Armenia, and by *Ashkenaz* some country on the *Euxine* Sea, which may have had its original name, *Axenos*, from Ashkenaz, a son of Gomer, the progenitor of the Cimmerians (Gen. x. 2, 3)—then we arrive at the same conclusion, viz., that Ararat was a mountainous region north of Assyria, and in all probability in Armenia. In Ezek. xxxviii. 6, we find Togarmah, another part of Armenia, connected with Gomer, and in Ezek. xxvii. 14, with Meshech and Tubal, all tribes of the north. With this agree the traditions of the Jewish and Christian churches, and likewise the accounts of the native Armenian writers.

But though it may be concluded with tolerable certainty that the land of Ararat is to be identified with a portion of Armenia, we possess no historical data for fixing on any one mountain

In that country as the resting-place of the ark.

The earliest tradition fixed on one of the chain of mountains which separate Armenia on the south from Mesopotamia, and which, as they also inclose Kurdistan, the land of the Kurds, obtained the name of the Kardu, or Carduchian range, corrupted into Gordiæan and Cordyræan. This was at one time the prevalent opinion among the Eastern churches, but it has now declined in credit and given place (at least among the Christians of the West) to that which now obtains, and according to which the ark rested on a great mountain in the north of Armenia— to which (so strongly did the idea take hold of the popular belief) was, in course of time, given the very name of Ararat, as if no doubt could be entertained that it was the Ararat of Scripture. We have seen, however, that in the Bible Ararat is nowhere the name of a mountain, and by the native Armenians the mountain in question was never so designated. Still there is no doubt of the antiquity of the tradition of this being (as it is sometimes termed) the 'Mother of the World.' The Persians call it Kuhi Nuch, 'Noah's Mountain.'

The mountain thus known to Europeans as Ararat consists of two immense conical elevations (one peak considerably lower than the other), towering in massive and majestic grandeur from the valley of the Aras, the ancient Araxes. Smith and Dwight give its position N. 57° W. of Nakhchevan, and S. 25° W. of Erivan; and remark, in describing it before the recent earthquake, that in no part of the world had they seen any mountain whose imposing appearance could plead half so powerfully as this a claim to the honour of having once been the

45.

stepping-stone between the old world and the new. 'It appeared,' says Ker Porter, 'as if the hugest mountains of the world had been piled upon each other to form this one sublime immensity of earth and rocks and snow. The icy peaks of its double heads rose majestically into the clear and cloudless heavens; the sun blazed bright upon them, and the reflection sent forth a dazzling radiance equal to other suns. My eye, not able to rest for any length of time upon the blinding glory of its summits, wandered down the apparently interminable sides, till I could no longer trace their vast lines in the mists of the horizon; when an irrepressible impulse immediately carrying my eye upwards, again refixed my gaze upon the awful glare of Ararat.' To the same effect Morier writes:—' Nothing can be more beautiful than its shape, more awful than its height. All the surrounding mountains sink into insignificance when compared to it. It is perfect in all its parts; no hard rugged feature, no unnatural prominences, everything is in harmony, and all combines to render it one of the sublimest objects in nature.'

Several attempts had been made to reach the top of Ararat, but few persons had got beyond the limit of perpetual snow. The honour was reserved to a German, Dr. Parrot, in the employment of Russia, who, in his Journey to Ararat, gives the following particulars:—' The summit of the Great Ararat is in 39° 42′ N. lat., and 61° 55′ E. long. from Ferro. Its perpendicular height is 16,254 Paris feet above the level of the sea, and 13,350 above the plain of the Araxes. The Little Ararat is 12,284 Paris feet above the sea, and 9561 above the plain of the Araxes.' After he and his party had failed in two attempts to ascend, the third was successful, and on the 27th September (o. s.), 1829, they stood on the summit of Mount Ararat. It was a slightly convex, almost circular platform, about 200 Paris feet in diameter, composed of eternal ice, unbroken by a rock or stone: on account of the immense distances, nothing could be seen distinctly.

Since the memorable ascent of Dr. Parrot, Ararat has been the scene of a fearful calamity. An earthquake, which in a few moments changed the entire aspect of the country, commenced on the 20th of June (o. s.), 1840, and continued, at intervals, until the 1st of September. The destruction of houses and other property in a wide tract of country around was very great; fortunately, the earthquake having happened during the day, the loss of lives did not exceed fifty. The scene of greatest devastation was in the narrow valley of Akorhi, where the masses of rock, ice, and snow, detached from the summit of Ararat and its lateral points, were thrown at one single bound from a height of 6000 feet to the bottom of the valley; where they lay scattered over an extent of several miles.

ARAU'NAH, or ORNAN, a man of the Jebusite nation, which possessed Jerusalem before it was taken by the Israelites. His threshing-floor was on Mount Moriah; and when he understood that it was required for the site of the Temple, he liberally offered the ground to David as a free gift; but the king insisted on paying the full value for it (2 Sam. xxiv. 18; 1 Chron. xxi. 18).

AR'BA. [HEBRON.]

ARCHELA'US, son of Herod the Great, and his successor in Idumæa, Judæa, and Samaria (Matt. ii. 22) [HERODIAN FAMILY].

ARCHERY. [ARMS.]

ARCHIP'PUS, a Christian minister, whom St. Paul calls his 'fellow-soldier,' in Philem. 2, and whom he exhorts to renewed activity in Col. iv. 17. From the latter reference it would seem that Archippus had exercised the office of Evangelista sometimes at Ephesus, sometimes elsewhere; and that he finally resided at Colosse, and there discharged the office of presiding presbyter or bishop when St. Paul wrote to the Colossian church.

ARCHITECTURE. It was formerly common to claim for the Hebrews the invention of scientific architecture, and to allege that classic antiquity was indebted to the Temple of Solomon for the principles and many of the details of the art. This statement, however, is totally without foundation.

There has never in fact been any people for whom a peculiar style of architecture could with less probability be claimed than for the Israelites. On leaving Egypt they could only be acquainted with Egyptian art. On entering Canaan they necessarily occupied the buildings of which they had dispossessed the previous inhabitants; and the succeeding generations would naturally erect such buildings as the country previously contained. The architecture of Palestine, and, as such, eventually that of the Jews, had doubtless its own characteristics, by which it was suited to the climate and condition of the country; and in the course of time many improvements would no doubt arise from the causes which usually operate in producing change in any practical art.

From the want of historical data and from the total absence of architectural remains, the degree in which these causes operated in imparting a peculiar character to the Jewish architecture cannot now be determined; for the oldest ruins in the country do not ascend beyond the period of the Roman domination. It does, however, seem probable that among the Hebrews architecture was always kept within the limits of a mechanical craft, and never rose to the rank of a fine art. Their usual dwelling-houses differed little from those of other Eastern nations, and we nowhere find anything indicative of exterior embellishment. Splendid edifices, such as the palace of David and the temple of Solomon, were completed by the assistance of Phœnician artists (2 Sam. v. 11; 1 Kings v. 6, 18; 1 Chron. xiv. 1). After the Babylonish exile, the assistance of such foreigners was likewise resorted to for the restoration of the Temple (Ezra iii. 7). From the time of the Maccabæan dynasty, the Greek taste began to gain ground, especially under the Herodian princes, and was shown in the structure and embellishment of many towns, baths, colonnades, theatres and castles. The Phœnician style, which seems to have had some affinity with the Egyptian, was not, however, superseded by the Grecian; and even as late as the Mishna, we read of Tyrian windows, Tyrian porches, &c. [HOUSE].

With regard to the instruments used by builders—besides the more common, such as the axe, saw, &c., we find incidental mention of the compass, the plumb-line (Amos vii. 7), and the measuring-line.

AREOP'AGUS, an Anglicized form of the original words, signifying in reference to place, Mars Hill, but in reference to persons, the Council, which was held on the hill. The Council was also termed the Council on Mars Hill; sometimes the Upper Council, from the elevated position where it was held; and sometimes simply, but emphatically, the Council; but it retained, till a late period, the original designation of Mars Hill. The place and the Council are topics of interest to the Biblical student, chiefly from their being the scene of the interesting narrative and sublime discourse found in Acts xvii., where it appears that the apostle Paul, feeling himself moved, by the evidences of idolatry with which the city of Athens was crowded, to preach Jesus and the resurrection, both in the Jewish synagogues and in the market-place, was set upon by certain Epicurean and Stoic philosophers, and led to the Areopagus, in order that they might learn from him the meaning and design of his new doctrine. Whether or not the Apostle was criminally arraigned, as a setter forth of strange gods, before the tribunal which held its sittings on the hill, may be considered as undetermined, though the balance of evidence seems to incline to the affirmative. Whichever view on this point is adopted, the dignified, temperate, and high-minded bearing of Paul under the peculiar circumstances in which he was placed are worthy of high admiration, and will appear the more striking the more the associations are known and weighed which covered and surrounded the spot where he stood. Nor does his eloquent discourse appear to have been without good effect; for though some mocked, and some procrastinated, yet others believed, among whom was a member of the Council, 'Dionysius, the Areopagite.'

The court of Areopagus was one of the oldest and most honoured, not only in Athens, but in the whole of Greece, and, indeed, in the ancient world. Through a long succession of centuries, it preserved its existence amid changes corresponding with those which the state underwent, till at least the age of the Cæsars.

Its origin ascends back into the darkest mythical period. From the first its constitution was essentially aristocratic; a character which to some extent it retained even after the democratic reforms which Solon introduced into the Athenian constitution. Following the political tendencies of the state, the Areopagus became in process of time less and less aristocratical, and parted piecemeal with most of its important functions. First its political power was taken away, then its jurisdiction in cases of murder, and even its moral influence gradually departed. During the sway of the Thirty Tyrants its power, or rather its political existence, was destroyed. On their overthrow it recovered some consideration, and the oversight of the execution of the laws was restored to it by an express decree. The precise time when it ceased to exist cannot be determined; but evidence is not wanting to show that in later periods its members ceased to be uniformly characterized by blameless morals.

It is not easy to give a correct summary of its several functions, as the classic writers are not agreed in their statements, and the jurisdiction of the court varied, as has been seen, with times and circumstances. They have, however, been divided into six general classes: – I. Its judicial function; II. Its political; III. Its police function; IV. Its religious; V. Its educational; and VI. (only partially) Its financial.

Passing by certain functions, such as acting as a court of appeal, and of general supervision, which under special circumstances, and when empowered by the people, the Areopagus from time to time discharged, we will say a few words in explanation of the points already named, giving a less restricted space to those which concern its moral and religious influence. Its judicial function embraced trials for murder and manslaughter, and was the oldest and most peculiar sphere of its activity. The indictment was brought by the second or king-archon, whose duties were for the most part of a religious nature. Then followed the oath of both parties, accompanied by solemn appeals to the gods. After this the accuser and the accused had the option of making a speech, which, however, they were obliged to keep free from all extraneous matter, as well as from mere rhetorical ornaments. After the first speech, the accused was permitted to go into voluntary banishment, if he had no reason to expect a favourable issue. Theft, poisoning, wounding, incendiarism, and treason, belonged also to this department of jurisdiction in the court of the Areopagus.

Its political function consisted in the constant watch which it kept over the legal condition of the state, acting as overseer and guardian of the laws.

Its police function also made it a protector and upholder of the institutions and laws. In this character the Areopagus had jurisdiction over novelties in religion, in worship, in customs, in everything that departed from the traditionary and established usages and modes of thought, which a regard to their ancestors endeared to the nation. The members of the court had a right to take oversight of festive meetings in private houses. In ancient times they fixed the number of the guests, and determined the style of the entertainment. If a person had no obvious means of subsisting, or was known to live in idleness, he was liable to an action before the Areopagus; if condemned three times, he was punished with the loss of his civil rights. In later times the court possessed the right of giving permission to teachers (philosophers and rhetoricians) to establish themselves and pursue their profession in the city.

Its strictly religious jurisdiction extended itself over the public creed, worship, and sacrifices, embracing generally everything which could come under the denomination of sacred things. It was its special duty to see that the religion of the state was kept pure from all foreign elements. The accusation of impiety— the vagueness of which admitted almost any charge connected with religious innovations— belonged in a special manner to this tribunal. The freethinking poet Euripides stood in fear of, and was restrained by, the Areopagus. Its proceeding in such cases was sometimes rather of an admonitory than punitive character.

Not less influential was its moral and educational power. Isocrates speaks of the care which it took of good manners and good order. Quintilian relates that the Areopagus condemned a boy for plucking out the eyes of a quail—a proceeding which has been both misunderstood and misrepresented, but which its original narrator approved, assigning no insufficient reason, namely, that the act was a sign of a cruel disposition, likely in advanced life to lead to baneful actions. The court exercised a salutary influence in general over the Athenian youth, their educators and their education.

Its financial position is not well understood; most probably it varied more than any other part of its administration with the changes which the constitution of the city underwent. It may suffice to mention, that in the Persian war the Areopagus had the merit of completing the number of men required for the fleet, by paying eight drachmæ to each.

ARETAS, the common name of several Arabian kings. 1. The first of whom we have any notice was a contemporary of the Jewish high-priest Jason and of Antiochus Epiphanes about B.C. 170 (2 Macc. v. 8). 2. Josephus mentions an Aretas, king of the Arabians contemporary with Alexander Jannæus (died B.C. 79) and his sons. After defeating Antiochus Dionysus, he reigned over Cœle-Syria, 'being called to the government by those that held Damascus by reason of the hatred they bore to Ptolemy Mennæus.' He took part with Hyrcanus in his contest for the sovereignty with his brother Aristobulus, and laid siege to Jerusalem, but, on the approach of the Roman general Scaurus, he retreated to Philadelphia. Hyrcanus and Aretas were pursued and defeated by Aristobulus, at a place called Papyron, and lost above 6000 men. Three or four years after, Scaurus, to whom Pompey had committed the government of Cœle-Syria, invaded Petræa, but finding it difficult to obtain provisions for his army, he consented to withdraw on the offer of 300 talents from Aretas. 3. Aretas, whose name was originally Æneas, succeeded Obodas. He was the father-in-law of Herod Antipas. The latter made proposals of marriage to the wife of his half-brother Herod-Philip, Herodias, the daughter of Aristobulus their brother, and the sister of Agrippa the Great. In consequence of this, the daughter of Aretas returned to her father, and a war (which had been fomented by previous disputes about the limits of their respective countries) ensued between Aretas and Herod. The army

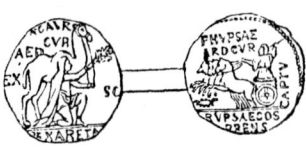

46.

of the latter was totally destroyed, and on his sending an account of his disaster to Rome, the emperor immediately ordered Vitellius to bring Aretas prisoner alive, or, if dead, to send his head. But while Vitellius was on his march to Petra, news arrived of the death of Tiberius, upon which, after administering the oath of allegiance to his troops, he dismissed them to winter-quarters and returned to Rome. It must have been at this juncture that Aretas took possession of Damascus, and placed a governor in it with a garrison. For a knowledge of this fact we are indebted to the apostle Paul.

AR'GOB, a district in Bashan, east of the Lake of Gennesareth, which was given to the half-tribe of Manasseh (Deut. iii. 4, 13; 1 Kings iv. 13.)

1. A'RIEL, a word meaning 'lion of God,' and correctly enough rendered by 'lion-like,' in 2 Sam. xxiii. 20; 1 Chron. xi. 22. It was applied as an epithet of distinction to bold and warlike persons, as among the Arabians, who surnamed Ali 'The Lion of God.'

2. ARIEL. The same word is used as a local proper name in Isa. xxix. 1, 2, applied to Jerusalem—'as victorious under God'—says Dr. Lee; and in Ezek. xliii. 15, 16, to the altar of burnt-offerings.

ARIMATHE'A, the birth-place of the wealthy Joseph, in whose sepulchre our Lord was laid (Matt. xxvii. 57; John xix. 38). The Arimathea of Joseph is generally regarded as the same place as the Ramathaim of Samuel, which stood near Lydda or Diospolis. Hence it has by some been identified with the existing Ramleh.

Ramleh is in N. lat. 31° 59', and E. long 35° 28', 8 miles S.E. from Joppa, and 24 miles N.W. by W. from Jerusalem. It lies in the fine undulating plain of Sharon, upon the eastern side of a broad low swell rising from a fertile though sandy plain. Like Gaza and Jaffa, this town is surrounded by olive-groves and gardens of vegetables and delicious fruits. Occasional

palm-trees are also seen, as well as the kharob and the sycamore. The streets are few; the houses are of stone, and many of them large and well built. There are five mosques, two or more of which are said to have once been Christian churches; and there is here one of the largest Latin convents in Palestine. The place is supposed to contain about 3000 inhabitants, of whom two-thirds are Moslems, and the rest Christians, chiefly of the Greek church, with a

47.

few Armenians. The inhabitants carry on some trade in cotton and soap. The great caravan-road between Egypt and Damascus, Smyrna, and Constantinople passes through Ramleh, as well as the most frequented road for European pilgrims and travellers between Joppa and Jerusalem. The isolated tower, of which a figure is here given, is the most conspicuous object in or about the city. It is about 120 feet in height, of Saracenic architecture, square, and built with well-hewn stone. According to the Moslem account it belonged to a ruined mosque. It bears the date 718 A.H. (A.D. 1310), and an Arabian author reports the completion at Ramleh, in that year, of a minaret unique for its loftiness and grandeur, by the sultan of Egypt, Nazir Mohammed ibn Kelawan. Among the plantations which surround the town occur, at every step, dry wells, cisterns fallen in, and vast vaulted reservoirs, which show that the city must in former times have been upwards of a league and a half in extent.

ARISTAR'CHUS, a faithful adherent of St. Paul, whose name repeatedly occurs in the Acts and Epistles (Acts xix. 29; xx. 4; xxvii. 2; Col. iv. 10; Philem. 24). He was a native of Thessalonica, and became the companion of St. Paul, whom he accompanied to Ephesus, where he was seized and nearly killed in the tumult raised by the silversmiths. He left that city with the Apostle, and accompanied him in his subsequent journeys, even when taken as a prisoner to Rome: indeed, Aristarchus was himself sent thither as a prisoner, or became such while there, for Paul calls him his 'fellow-prisoner' (Col. iv. 10). The traditions of the Greek church represent Aristarchus as bishop of Apamea in Phrygia.

ARISTOBU'LUS, a person named by Paul in Rom. xvi. 10, where he sends salutations to his household. He is not himself saluted; hence he may not have been a believer, or he may have been absent or dead. Nothing certain is known respecting him.

Aristobulus is a Greek name, adopted by the Romans, and in very common use among them. It was also adopted by the Jews, and was borne by several persons in the Maccabæan and Herodian families mentioned by Josephus and in the books of Maccabees.

ARITHMETIC, the science of numbers or reckoning, was unquestionably practised as an art in the dawn of civilization. In the absence of positive information we seem authorized in referring the first knowledge of arithmetic to the East. From India, Chaldæa, Phœnicia, and Egypt, the science passed to the Greeks, who extended its laws, improved its processes, and widened its sphere. To what extent the Orientals carried their acquaintance with arithmetic cannot be determined. The greatest discovery in this department of the mathematics, namely, the establishment of our system of ciphers, belongs undoubtedly not to Arabia, as is generally supposed, but to the remote East, probably India. Our numerals were made known to these western parts by the Arabians, who, though they were nothing more than the medium of transmission, have enjoyed the honour of giving them their name.

The Hebrews were not a scientific, but a religious and practical nation. What they borrowed from others of the arts of life they used without surrounding it with theory or expanding and framing it into a system. Of their knowledge of arithmetic little is known beyond what may be fairly inferred from the pursuits and trades which they carried on, for the successful prosecution of which some skill at least in its simpler processes must have been absolutely necessary;

and the large amounts which appear here and there in the sacred books serve to show that their acquaintance with the art of reckoning was considerable. Even in fractions they were not inexperienced. For figures, the Jews, after the Babylonish exile, made use of the letters of the alphabet; and it is not unlikely that the ancient Hebrews did the same.

ARK, NOAH'S (Gen. vi. 14). Vast labour and much ingenuity have been employed by various writers, in the attempt to determine the form of Noah's ark and the arrangement of its parts. The success has not been equal to the exertion; for, on comparing the few simple facts in the Scripture narrative, every one feels how slight positive data there are for the minute descriptions and elaborate representations which such writers have given. That form of the ark which repeated pictorial representations have rendered familiar—a kind of house in a kind of boat—has not only no foundation in Scripture, but is contrary to reason. The form thus given to it is fitted for progression and for cutting the waves; whereas the ark of Noah was really destined to float idly upon the waters, without any other motion than that which it received from them. If we examine the passage in Gen. vi. 14-16, we can only draw from it the conclusion that the ark was not a boat or ship, but a building in the form of a parallelogram, 300 cubits long, 50 cubits broad, and 30 cubits high. So far as the *name* affords any evidence, it also goes to show that the ark of Noah was not a regularly-built vessel, but merely intended to float at large upon the waters. We may, therefore, probably with justice, regard it as a large, oblong, floating house, with a roof either flat or only slightly inclined. It was constructed with three stories, and had a door in the side. There is no mention of windows *in the side*, but *above, i. e.* probably in the flat roof, where Noah was commanded to make them of a cubit in size (Gen. vi. 16).

The purpose of this ark was, to preserve certain persons and animals from the Deluge with which God intended to overwhelm the land, in punishment for man's iniquities. The persons were eight—Noah and his wife, with his three sons and their wives (Gen. vii. 7; 2 Pet. ii. 5). The animals were, one pair of every 'unclean' animal, and seven pairs of all that were 'clean.' By 'clean,' we understand fit, and by 'unclean,' unfit for food or for sacrifice. Of birds there were seven pairs (Gen. vii. 2, 3). Those who have written professedly and largely on the subject, have at great pains to provide for all the existing species of animals in the ark of Noah, showing how they might be distributed, fed, and otherwise provided for. But they are very far from having cleared the matter of all its difficulties; which are much greater than they, in their general ignorance of natural history, were aware of. These difficulties, however, chiefly arise from the assumption that the species of *all the earth* were collected in the ark. The number of such species has been vastly under-rated by these writers—partly from ignorance, and partly from the desire to limit the number for which they imagined they required to provide. They have usually satisfied themselves with a provision for three or four hundred species at most. 'But of the existing mammalia,' says Dr. J. Pye Smith, 'considerably more than one thousand species are known; of birds, fully five thousand; of reptiles, very few kinds of which can live in water, two thousand; and the researches of travellers and naturalists are making frequent and most interesting additions to the number of these and all other classes. Of insects (using the word in the popular sense) the number of species is immense; to say one hundred thousand would be moderate: each has its appropriate habitation and food, and these are necessary to its life; and the larger number could not live in water. Also the innumerable millions upon millions of animalcules must be provided for; for they have all their appropriate and diversified places and circumstances of existence.' Nor do these numbers form the only difficulty; for, as the same writer observes:— 'All land animals have their geographical regions, to which their constitutional natures are congenial, and many could not live in any other situation. We cannot represent to ourselves the idea of their being brought into one small spot, from the polar regions, the torrid zone, and all the other climates of Asia, Africa, Europe, America, Australia, and the thousands of islands, their preservation and provision, and the final disposal of them, without bringing up the idea of miracles more stupendous than any which are recorded in Scripture.'

The difficulty of assembling in one spot, and of providing for in the ark, the various mammalia and birds alone, even without including the otherwise essential provision for reptiles, insects, and fishes, is quite sufficient to suggest some error in the current belief. We are to consider the different kinds of accommodation and food which would be required for animals of such different habits and climates, and the necessary provision for ventilation and for cleansing the stables or dens. And if so much ingenuity has been required in devising arrangements for the comparatively small number of species which the writers on the ark have been willing to admit into it; what provision can be made for the immensely larger number which, under the supposed conditions, would really have required its shelter?

There seems no way of meeting these difficulties but by adopting the suggestion of Bishop Stillingfleet, approved by Matthew Poole, Dr. J. Pye Smith, Le Clerc, Rosenmüller, and others, namely, that, as the object of the Deluge was to sweep man from the earth, it did not extend beyond that region of the earth which man then inhabited, and that only the animals of that region were preserved in the ark. The bishop expresses his belief that the Flood was universal as to mankind, and that all men, except those preserved in the ark, were destroyed; but he sees no evidence from Scripture that the whole earth was then inhabited; he does not think that it can ever be proved to have been so; and he asks, what reason there can be to extend the Flood beyond the occasion of it? [DELUGE.]

As Noah was the progenitor of all the nations of the earth, and as the ark was the second cradle of the human race, we might expect to find in all nations traditions and reports more or less distinct respecting him, the ark in which he was saved, and the Deluge in general. Accordingly no nation is known in which such traditions have not been found. Our present concern, however, is only with the ark. And as it appears that an ark, that is, a boat or chest, was carried about with great ceremony in most of the ancient mysteries, and occupied an eminent station in the holy places, it has with much reason been concluded that this was originally intended to represent the ark of Noah, which eventually came to be regarded with superstitious reverence. On this point the historical and mythological testimonies are very clear and conclusive. The tradition of a deluge, by which the race of man was swept from the face of the earth, has been traced among the Chaldæans, Egyptians, Phœnicians, Assyrians, Persians, Greeks, Romans, Goths, Druids, Chinese, Hindoos, Burmese.

48.

Mexicans, Peruvians, Brazilians, Nicaraguans, the inhabitants of Western Caledonia, and the islanders of the Pacific; and among most of them also the belief has prevailed that certain individuals were preserved in an ark, ship, boat, or raft, to replenish the desolated earth with inhabitants. These traditions, moreover, are corroborated by coins and monuments of stone. Of the latter there are the sculptures of Egypt and of India; and it is not unlikely that those of the monuments called Druidical, which bear the name of kist-vaens, and in which the stones are disposed in the form of a chest or house, were intended as memorials of the ark.

49.

50.

With regard to the evidence furnished by coins, we shall confine our illustrations to the two famous medals of Apamea. These medals belong, the one to the elder Philip, and the other to Pertinax. In the former it is extremely interesting to observe that on the front of the ark is the name of Noah, in Greek characters. The designs on these medals correspond remarkably, although the legends somewhat vary. In both we perceive the ark floating on the water, containing the patriarch and his wife, the dove on wing, the olive-branch, and the raven perched on the ark. These medals also represent Noah and his wife on *terra firma*, in the attitude of rendering thanks for their safety. The genuineness of these medals has been established beyond all question, and the coincidences which they offer are at least exceedingly curious.

ARK OF THE COVENANT. The word here used for ark is, as already explained, different from that which is applied to the ark of Noah. It is the common name for a chest or coffer, whether applied to the ark in the tabernacle, to a coffin, to a mummy-chest (Gen. l. 26), or to a chest for money (2 Kings xii. 9, 10). Our word *ark* has the same meaning, being derived from the Latin *arca*, a chest. The distinction between *aron* and the present word has already been suggested. The sacred chest is distinguished from others as the 'ark of God' (1 Sam. iii. 3); 'ark of the covenant' (Josh. iii. 6); and 'ark of the law' (Exod. xxv. 22). This ark was a kind of chest, of an oblong shape, made of shittim (acacia) wood, a cubit and a half broad and high, two cubits long, and covered on all sides with the purest gold. It was ornamented on its upper surface with a border or rim of gold; and on each of the two sides, at equal distances from the top, were two gold rings, in which were placed (to remain there perpetually) the gold-covered poles by which the ark was carried, and which continued with it after it was deposited in the tabernacle. The lid or cover of the ark was of the same length and breadth, and made of the purest gold. Over it, at the two extremities, were two cherubim, with their faces turned towards each other, and inclined a little towards the lid (otherwise called the *mercy-seat*). Their wings, which were spread out over the top of the ark, formed the throne of God, the King of Israel, while the ark itself was his footstool (Exod. xxv. 10-22; xxxvii. 1-9).

This ark was the most sacred object among the Israelites: it was deposited in the innermost and holiest part of the tabernacle, called 'the holy of holies' (and afterwards in the corresponding apartment of the Temple), where it stood so that one end of each of the poles by which it was carried (which were drawn out so far as to allow the ark to be placed against the back wall), touched the veil which separated the two apartments of the tabernacle (1 Kings viii. 8). In the ark were deposited the tables of the law (Exod. xxv. 16). A quantity of manna was laid up beside the ark in a vase of gold (Exod. xvi. 32, 36; 1 Kings viii. 9); as were also the rod of Aaron (Num. xvii. 10), and a copy of the book of the law (Deut. xxxi. 26).

Nothing is more apparent throughout the historical Scriptures than the extreme sanctity which attached to the ark, as the material symbol of the Divine presence. During the marches of the Israelites it was covered with a purple pall, and borne by the priests, with great reverence and care, in advance of the host (Num. iv. 5, 6; x. 33). It was before the ark, thus in advance, that the waters of the Jordan separated; and it remained in the bed of the river, with the attendant priests, until the whole host had passed over; and no sooner was it also brought up than the waters resumed their course (Josh. iii.; iv. 7, 10, 11, 17, 18). The ark was similarly conspicuous in the grand procession round Jericho (Josh. vi. 4, 6, 8, 11, 12). It is not wonderful therefore that the neighbouring nations, who had no notion of spiritual worship, looked upon it as the God of the Israelites (1 Sam. iv. 6, 7), a delusion which may have been strengthened by the figures of the cherubim on it. After the settlement of the Jews in Palestine, the ark remained in the tabernacle at Shiloh, until, in the time of Eli, it was carried along with the army in the war against the Philistines, under the superstitious notion that it would secure the victory for the Hebrews. They were, however, not only beaten, but the ark itself was taken by the Philistines (1 Sam. iv. 3-11), whose triumph was, however, very short lived, as they were so oppressed by the hand of God, that, after seven months, they were glad to send it back again (1 Sam. v. 7). After that it remained apart from the tabernacle, at Kirjath-jearim (vii. 1, 2), where it continued until the time of David, who purposed to remove it to Jerusalem; but the old prescribed mode of removing it from place to place was so much neglected as to cause the death of Uzzah, in consequence of which it was left in the house of Obededom (2 Sam. vi. 1-11); but after three months David took courage, and succeeded in effecting its safe removal, in grand procession, to Mount Zion (ver. 12-19). When the Temple of Solomon was completed, the ark was deposited in the sanctuary (1 Kings viii. 6-9). The passage in 2 Chron. xxxv. 3, in which Josiah directs the Levites to restore the ark to the holy place, is understood by some to imply that it had either been removed by Amon, who put an idol in its place, which is assumed to have been the 'trespass' of which he is said to have been guilty (2 Chron. xxxiii. 23); or that the priests themselves had withdrawn it during idolatrous times, and preserved it in some secret place, or had removed it from one place to another. But it seems more likely that it had been taken from the holy of holies during the purification and repairs of the temple by this same Josiah, and that he, in this passage, merely directs it to be again set in its place. What became of the ark when the Temple was plundered and destroyed by the Babylonians is not known, and all conjecture is useless. It is certain, however, from the consent of all the Jewish writers, that the old ark was not contained in the second temple, and there is no evidence that any new one was made. Indeed the absence of the ark is one of the important particulars in which this temple was held to be inferior to that of Solomon. The most holy place is therefore generally considered to have been empty in the second temple.

ARK'ITES, the inhabitants of Arka, mentioned in Gen. x. 17; 1 Chron. i. 15, as descended from the Phœnician or Sidonian branch of the great family of Canaan. This, in fact, as well as the other small northern states of Phœnicia, was a colony from the great parent state of Sidon. Arka, or Acra, their chief town, lay between Tripolis and Antaradus, at the western base of Lebanon, 32 R. miles from Antaradus, and 18 miles from Tripoli. Burckhardt, in travelling from the north-east of Lebanon to Tripoli, at the distance of about four miles south of the Nahr-el-keber (Eleutherus), came to a hill called Tel-Arka, which, from its regularly flattened conical form and smooth sides, appeared to be artificial. Upon an elevation on its east and south sides, which commands a beautiful view over the plain, the sea, and the Anzeyry mountains, are large and extensive heaps of rubbish, traces of ancient dwellings, blocks of hewn stone, remains of walls, and fragments of granite columns. These are no doubt the remains of Arka; and the hill was probably the acropolis or citadel, or the site of a temple.

ARM. This word is frequently used in Scripture in a metaphorical sense to denote power. Hence, to ' break the arm' is to diminish or destroy the power (Ps. x. 15; Ezek. xxx. 21; Jer. xlviii. 25). It is also employed to denote the infinite power of God (Ps. lxxxix. 13; xlviii. 2; Isa. liii. 1; John xii. 38). In a few places the metaphor is, with great force, extended to the action of the arm, as :—' I will redeem you with a stretched out arm' (Exod. vi. 5), that is, with a power fully exerted. The figure is here taken from the attitude of ancient warriors baring and outstretching the arm for fight. Thus in Isa. lii. 10, ' Jehovah hath made bare his holy arm in the sight of all the nations.'

ARMAGED'DON, properly ' the mountain of Megiddo,' a city on the west of the river Jordan, rebuilt by Solomon (1 Kings ix. 15). Both Ahaziah and Josias died there. In the mystical language of prophecy, the word mountain represents the Church, and the events which took place at Megiddo are supposed to have had a typical reference to the sorrows and triumphs of the people of God under the Gospel. ' In that day,' says Zechariah, xii. 11, 'shall there be a great mourning in Jerusalem, as the mourning of Hadadrimmon in the valley of Megiddon;' referring to the death of Josias. But the same spot witnessed, at an earlier period, the greatest triumph of Israel, when ' fought the kings of Canaan in Taanach by the waters of Megiddo' (Judg. v. 19). ' He gathered them together into a place called in the Hebrew tongue Armageddon,' is the language of the Apocalypse; and the word has been translated by some as ' the mountain of destruction,' by others as ' the mountain of the gospel;' many ingenious speculations having been employed on the passage in which it occurs, but with little satisfaction to the more sober readers of divine revelation.

ARME'NIA, a country of Western Asia, is not mentioned in Scripture under that name, but is supposed to be alluded to in the three following Hebrew designations, which seem to refer either to the country as a whole, or to particular districts. I. Ararat, the land upon (or over) the mountains of which the ark rested at the Deluge (Gen. viii. 4); whither the sons of Sennacherib fled after murdering their father (2 Kings xix. 37; Isa. xxxvii. 38); and one of the ' kingdoms'

summoned, along with Minni and Ashkenaz, to arm against Babylon (Jer. li. 27). II. Minni is mentioned in Jer. li. 27, along with Ararat and Ashkenaz, as a kingdom called to arm itself against Babylon. The name is by some taken for a contraction of ' Armenia.' III. Thogarmah, mentioned by the prophet Ezekiel xxvii. 14: xxxviii. 6.

The boundaries of Armenia may be described generally as the southern range of the Caucasus on the north, and a branch of the Taurus on the south. It forms an elevated table-land, whence rise mountains which (with the exception of the gigantic Ararat) are of moderate height. The climate is generally cold, but salubrious. The country abounds in romantic forest and mountain scenery, and rich pasture-land, especially in the districts which border upon Persia. Ancient writers notice the wealth of Armenia in metals and precious stones. The great rivers Euphrates and Tigris both take their rise in this region, as also the Araxes, and the Kur or Cyrus. Armenia is commonly divided into Greater and Lesser, the line of separation being the Euphrates; but the former constitutes by far the larger portion, and indeed the other is often regarded as pertaining rather to Asia Minor. There was anciently a kingdom of Armenia, with its metropolis Artaxata: it was sometimes an independent state, but most commonly tributary to some more powerful neighbour. Indeed at no period was the whole of this region ever comprised under one government, but Assyria, Media, Syria, and Cappadocia shared the dominion or allegiance of some portion of it, just as it is now divided among the Persians, Russians, Turks, and Kurds. In later times Armenia was the border-country where the Romans and Parthians fruitlessly strove for the mastery; and since then it has been the frequent battle-field of the neighbouring states. Towards the end of the last war between Russia and Turkey, large bodies of native Armenians emigrated into the Russian dominions, so that their number in what is termed Turkish Armenia is now considerably reduced. By the treaty of Turkomanshee (21st Feb. 1828) Persia ceded to Russia the Khanats of Erivan and Nakhshivan. The boundary-line (drawn from the Turkish dominions) passes over the Little Ararat; the line of separation between Persian and Turkish Armenia also begins at Ararat: so that this famous mountain is now the central boundary-stone of these three empires.

Christianity was first established in Armenia in the fourth century; the Armenian church has a close affinity to the Greek church in its forms and polity; it is described by the American missionaries who are settled in the country as in a state of great corruption and debasement. The total number of the Armenian nation throughout the world is supposed not to exceed 2,000,000. Their favourite pursuit is commerce, and their merchants are found in all parts of the East.

The Armenian or Haikan language, notwithstanding the great antiquity of the nation to which it belongs, possesses no literary documents prior to the fifth century of the Christian era. The translation of the Bible, begun by Miesrob in the year 410, is the earliest monument of the language that has come down to us. The dialect in which this version is written, and in which it is still publicly read in their churches, is called the old Armenian. The dialect now in use—the modern Armenian—in which they preach and carry on the intercourse of daily life, not only departs from the elder form by dialectual changes in the native elements of the language itself, but also by the great intermixture of Persian and Turkish words which has resulted from the conquest and subjection of the country. It is, perhaps, this diversity of the ancient and modern idioms which has given rise to the many conflicting opinions that exist as to the relation in which the Armenian stands to other languages. As to form, it is said to be rough and full of consonants; to possess *ten* cases in the noun—a number which is only exceeded by the Finnish; to have no dual; to have no mode of denoting gender in the noun by change of form; to bear a remarkable resemblance to Greek in the use of the participle, and in the whole syntactical structure; and to have adopted the Arabian system of metre.

ARMLET. Although this word has the same meaning as *bracelet*, yet the latter is practically so exclusively used to denote the ornament of the wrist, that it seems proper to distinguish by *armlet* the similar ornament which is worn on the upper arm. There is also this difference between them, that in the East bracelets are generally worn by women, and armlets only by

51.

men. The armlet, however, is in use among men only as one of the insignia of sovereign power. The Egyptian kings are represented with armlets, which were also worn by the Egyptian women. These, however, are not jewelled, but of plain or enamelled metal, as was in all likelihood the case among the Hebrews.

ARMS, ARMOUR. In order to give a clear view of this subject, we shall endeavour to show succinctly, and from the best authorities now available, what were the weapons, both offensive and defensive, used by the ancient Asiatics.

The instruments at first employed in the chace, or to repel wild beasts, but converted by the wicked to the destruction of their fellow-men, or used by the peaceable to oppose aggression, were naturally the most simple. Among these were the club and the throwing-bat. The first consisted originally of a heavy piece of wood, variously shaped, made to strike with, and, according to its form, denominated a mace, a bar, a hammer, or a maul. This weapon was in use among the Hebrews; for, in the time of the kings, wood had already been superseded by metal; and the rod of iron (Ps. ii. 9) is supposed to mean a mace, or gavelock, or crowbar. It is an instrument of great power when used by a

strong arm. The throwstick, made of thorn-wood, is the same instrument which we see

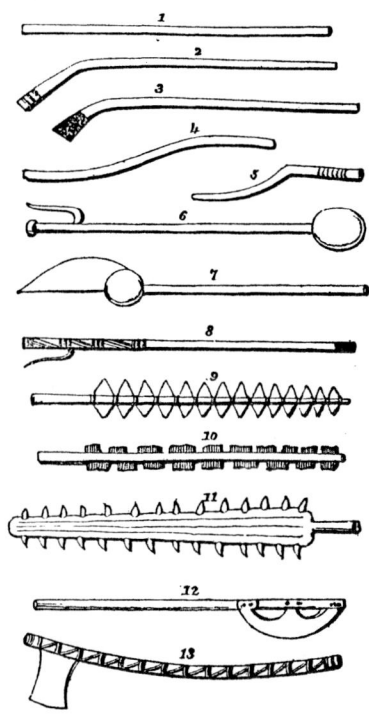

52.

1, 2, 3. Clubs.
4, 5. Crooked Billets, or throwing-bats.
6. Mace.
7. Battle axe.
8. Hardwood Sword.
9. Sharks-teeth Sword.
10. Flint Sword.
11. Saw-fish Sword.
12, 13. Egyptian Battle-axes.

figured on Egyptian monuments. By the native Arabs it is still called *lissan*, and was anciently known among us by the name of crooked billet. These instruments, supplied with a sharp edge, would naturally constitute a battle-axe, and a kind of sword; and such in the rudest ages we find them, made with flints set into a groove, or with sharks' teeth firmly secured to the staff with twisted sinews. On the earliest monuments of Egypt, for these ruder instruments is already seen substituted a piece of metal with a steel or bronze blade fastened into a globe, thus forming a falchion-axe; and also a lunate-blade, riveted in three places to the handle, forming a true battle-axe; and there were, besides, true bills or axes in form like our own.

Next came the dirk or poniard, the Hebrew name of which may possibly retain some allusion to the original instrument made of the antelope's horn, merely sharpened, which is still used in every part of the East where the material can be procured. From existing figures, the dirk appears to have been early made of metal in Egypt, and worn stuck in a girdle; but, from several texts (1 Sam xvii. 39; 2 Sam. xx. 8; and 1 Kings xx. 11), it is evident that the real

H

sword was slung in a belt, and that 'girding' and 'loosing the sword' were synonymous terms

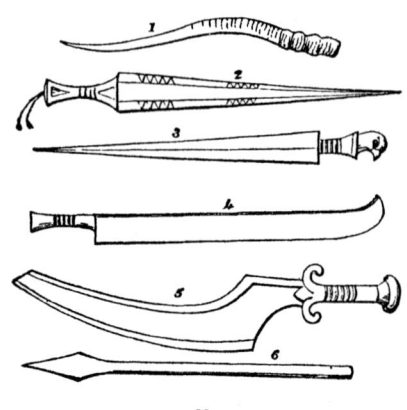

53.

1. Horn Dagger.   4, 5. Tulwar Swords.
2, 3. Swords.   6. Quarter-pike.

for commencing and ending a war. The blades were, it seems, always short; and the dirk-sword, at least, was always double-edged. The sheath was ornamented and polished. In Egypt there were larger and heavier swords, more nearly like modern tulwars, and of the form of an English round-pointed table-knife. But while metal was scarce, there were also swords which might be called quarter-pikes, being composed of a very short wooden handle, surmounted by a spear-head. In Nubia, swords of heavy wood are still in use.

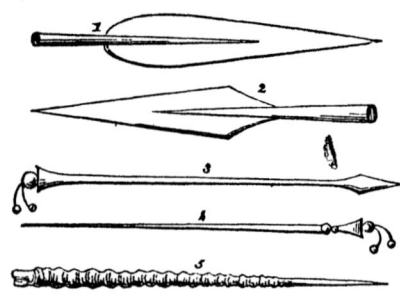

54.

1, 2. Spear-heads.   3, 4. Darts.
5. Oryx horn spear-head.

The spear was another offensive weapon common to all the nations of antiquity, and was of various size, weight, and length. Probably the shepherd Hebrews, like nations similarly situated in northern Africa, anciently made use of the horn of an oryx, or a leucoryx, above three feet long, straightened in water, and sheathed upon a thorn-wood staff. When sharp-ened, this instrument would penetrate the hide of a bull, and, according to Strabo, even of an elephant: it was light, very difficult to break, resisted the blow of a battle-axe, and the animals which furnished it were abundant in Arabia and

in the desert east of Palestine. At a later period, the head was of brass, and afterwards of iron. Very ponderous weapons of this kind were often used in Egypt by the heavy infantry; and, from various circumstances, it may be inferred that among the Hebrews and their immediate neigh-bours, commanders in particular were distin-guished by heavy spears. Among these were generally ranked the most valiant in fight and the largest in stature; such as Goliath, 'whose spear was like a weaver's beam' (1 Sam. xvii. 7), and whose spear's head weighed six hundred shekels of iron; which by some is asserted to be equal to twenty-five pounds weight. The spear had a point of metal at the but-end to fix it in the ground, perhaps with the same massy globe above it, which is still in use, intended to counter-balance the point. It was with this ferrel that Abner slew Asahel (2 Sam. ii. 22, 23).

The javelins appear to have had different forms. In most nations of antiquity the infantry, not bearing a spear, carried two darts, those lightly armed using both for long casts, and the heavy-armed only one for that purpose; the second, more ponderous than the other, being re-served for throwing when close to the enemy, or for handling in the manner of a spear. While on the subject of the javelin, it may be remarked that, by the act of casting one at David (1 Sam. xix. 9, 10), Saul virtually absolved him from his allegiance; for by the customs of ancient Asia, preserved in the usages of the Teutonic and other nations, the custom of the East Franks, &c., to throw a dart at a freedman, who escaped from it by flight, was the demonstrative token of manumission given by his lord or master; he was thereby sent out of hand, manumissus, well expressed in the old English phrase 'scot-free.' But for this act of Saul, David might have been viewed as a rebel.

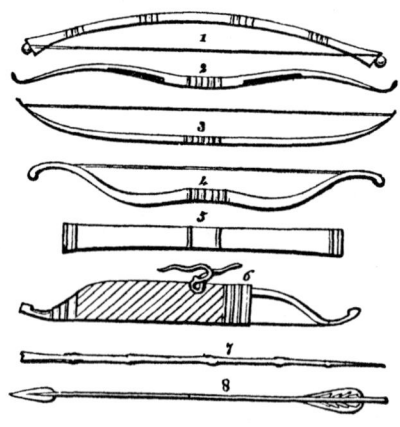

55.

1, 2, 3, 4. Bows.   5, 6. Quivers.   7, 8. Arrows.

But the chief offensive weapon in Egypt, and, from the nature of the country, it may be in-ferred, in Palestine also, was the war-bow. From the simple implements used by the first hunters, consisting merely of an elastic reed, a branch of a tree, or rib of palm, the bow became in the course of time very strong and tall, was made of brass, of wood backed with horn, or of horn entirely, and even of ivory; some being shaped like the common English bow, and others, particularly those used by riding nations, like the buffalo horn. There were various modes of bending this instrument, by pressure of the knee, or by the foot treading the bow, or by setting one end against the foot, drawing the middle with the hand of the same side towards the hip, and pushing the upper point forward with the second hand, till the thumb passed the loop of the string beyond the nock. The horned bows of the cavalry, shaped like those of the Chinese, occur on monuments of antiquity. This was the Parthian bow, as is proved by several Persian bas-reliefs, and may have been in use in the time of the Elamites, who were a mounted people. These bows were carried in cases to protect the string, which was composed of deer sinews, from injury, and were slung on the right hip of the rider, except when on the point of engaging. Then the string was often cast over the head, and the bow hung upon the breast, with the two nocks above each shoulder, like a pair of horns. The arrows were likewise enclosed in a case or quiver, hung sometimes on the shoulder, and at other times on the left side; and six or eight flight-arrows were commonly stuck in the edge of the cap, ready to be pulled out and put to the string. The infantry always carried the arrows in a quiver on the right shoulder, and the bow was kept unbent until the moment of action. On a march it was carried on the shield arm, where there was frequently also a horn bracer secured below the elbow to receive the shock from the string when an arrow was discharged. The flight or long-range arrows were commonly of reed, not always feathered, and mostly tipped with flint points; but the shot or aimed arrows, used for nearer purposes, were of wood tipped with metal, about 30 inches long, and winged with three lines of feathers, like those in modern use: they varied in length at different periods, and according to the substance of the bows.

The last missile instrument to be mentioned is the sling (Job xli. 28), an improvement upon

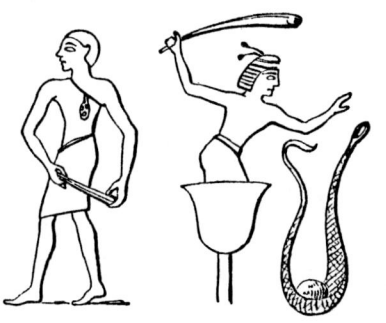

56.

[Egyptian Slingers and Sling.]

the simple act of throwing stones. It was the favourite weapon of the Benjamites, a small tribe, not making a great mass in an order of battle, but well composed for light troops. They could also boast of using the sling equally well with the left hand as with the right. The sling was made of plaited thongs, somewhat broad in the middle, to lodge the stone or leaden missile, and was twirled two or three times round before the stone was allowed to take flight. Stones could not be cast above 400 feet, but leaden bullets could be thrown as far as 600 feet. The force as well as precision of aim which might be attained in the use of this instrument was remarkably shown in the case of David; and several nations of antiquity boasted of great skill in the practice of the sling.

All these hand-weapons were in use at different periods, not only among the Hebrews and Egyptians, but likewise in Assyria, Persia, Greece, and Macedonia. The Roman pilum was a kind of dart, distinguished from those of other nations chiefly by its weight, and the great proportional length of the metal or iron part, which constituted one half of the whole, or from two and a half to three feet. Much of this length was hollow, and received nearly twenty inches of the shaft within it: the point was never hooked like that of common darts.

DEFENSIVE ARMS.—The most ancient defensive piece was the shield, buckler, roundel, or target, composed of a great variety of materials,

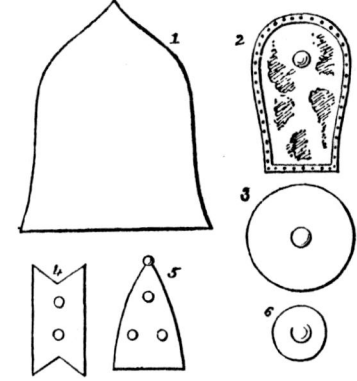

57.

1. The Tzenna, or Great Shield. 2. Common Egyptian Shield. 3. Target. 4, 5. Ancient Shields of unknown tribes. 6. Roundel.

very different in form and size. The Hebrews had the word tsenna, a great shield for defence and protection (Gen. xv. 1; Ps. xlvii. 9; Prov. xxx. 5), which is commonly found in connection with spear, and was the shelter of heavily-armed infantry; and the magin, a buckler, or smaller shield, which, from a similar juxtaposition with sword, bow, and arrows, appears to have been the defence of other-armed infantry and of chiefs: a third called sohairah or roundel, may have been appropriated to archers and slingers; and there were others called shelatim, apparently similar to the magin, and only differing from it in ornament. In the more advanced eras of civilization shields were made of light wood not liable to split, covered with bull-hide of two or more thicknesses and bordered with metal: the lighter kinds were made of wicker-work or osier, similarly, but less solidly covered; of double ox-hide cut into a round form. There were others of a single hide, extremely thick from having been boiled; their surface presented an appearance of many folds, like round waves up and down, which yielded, but could rarely be penetrated. We may infer that at first the Hebrews borrowed the forms in use in Egypt, and had their common shields, a kind of parallelogram, broadest and arched at the top, and cut square beneath, bordered with metal, the surface being covered with raw hide with the hair on. The lighter shields may have been soaked in oil and dried in the shade to make them hard. During the Assyrian and Persian supremacy the Hebrews may have used the square, oblong, and round shields of these nations, and may have subsequently copied those of Greece and Rome. The princes of Israel had shields of precious metals: all were managed by a wooden or leathern handle, and often slung by a thong over the neck. The tsenna was most likely what in the feudal ages would have been called a *pavise*, for such occurs on the Egyptian monuments. This was about five feet high, with a pointed arch above and square below, resembling the feudal knight's shield, but that the point was reversed. Shields were hung upon the battlements of walls, and, as still occurs, chiefly above gates of cities by the watch and ward. In time of peace they were covered to preserve them from the sun, and in war uncovered; this sign was poetically used to denote coming hostilities, as in Isa. xxii. 6, &c.

The Helmet was next in consideration, and in the earliest ages was made of osier, or rushes, in the form of a beehive, or of a skull-cap. The skins of the heads of animals—of lions, bears, wild boars, bulls, and horses—were likewise adopted,

which the turban is usually wound; but these were almost invariably supplied with long lappets to cover the ears and the back of the head, and princes usually wore a radiated crown on the summit. This was the form of the Syrian, probably of the Assyrian helmets, excepting that the last mentioned were of brass, though they still retained the low cylindrical shape. Some helmet of this kind was worn by the trained infantry, who were spearmen among the Hebrews; but archers and slingers had round skull-caps of skins, felts, or quilted stuffs, such as are still in use among the Arabs.

Body Armour.—The most ancient Persian idols are clad in shagged skins. In Egypt cuirasses were manufactured of leather, of brass, and of a succession of iron hoops, chiefly covering the abdomen and the shoulders; but a more ancient national form was a kind of thorax, tippet, or square, with an opening for the head in it, the four points covering the breast, back, and both upper arms. This was affected in particular by the royal band of relatives who surrounded the Pharaoh, were his subordinate commanders, messengers, and body-guards, bearing his standards, ensign-fans, and sun-screens, his portable throne, his bow and arrows. Beneath this square was another piece, protecting the trunk of the body, and both were in general covered with a red-coloured cloth or stuff. On the oldest fictile vases a shoulder-piece likewise occurs, worn by Greek and Etruscan warriors. It covers the upper edge of the body armour, is perforated in the middle for the head to pass, but hangs equal on the breast and back, square on the shoulders, and is evidently of leather. By the use of metal for defensive armour, the Carians appear to have created astonishment among the Egyptians, and therefore to have been the first nation so pro-

58.

1. Of Rushes.
2. Egyptian.
3, 4. Western Asia.
5. Carian.
6, 7. Egyptian.
8. Assyrian.
9. Greek.
10. Ionian.
11. Parthian.
12, 13. Other Asiatic tribes.

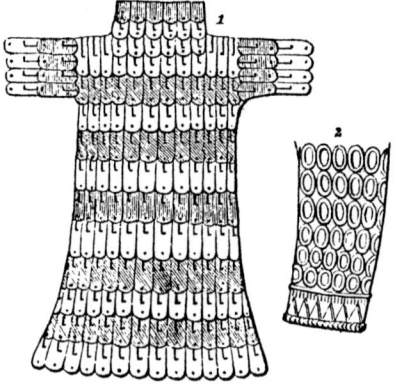

59.

1. Egyptian tigulated.   2. Sleeve of ring-mail, Ionian.

and were adorned with rows of teeth, manes, and bristles. Wood, linen cloth in many folds, and a kind of felt, were also in early use, and some of them may be observed worn by the nations of Asia at war with the conqueror kings of Egypt, even before the departure of Israel. At that time also these kings had helmets of metal, of rounded or pointed forms. The nations of farther Asia used the woollen or braided caps, still retained, and now called kaouk and fez, around

tected in Western Asia; nevertheless, in the tombs of the kings near Thebes, a tigulated hauberk is represented, composed of small three-coloured pieces of metal; one golden, the others reddish and green. It is this kind of armour which may be meant by the Hebrew word *techera*, the closest interpretation of which appears to be a tiling. In 2 Chron. xviii. 33, Ahab may have been struck in one of the grooves or slits in the squares of his techera, or between two of them where they do not overlap; or perhaps, with more probability, between the metal hoops of the trunk of the tippet before mentioned, where the thorax overlaps the abdomen. The term 'scales,' in the case of Goliath's armour, denotes squamous armour, most likely where the pieces were sewed upon a cloth, and not hinged to each other, as in the techera. The techera could not well be worn without an under-garment of some density to resist the friction of metal; and this was probably the dress which Saul put upon David before he assumed the breastplate and girdle.

The Cuirass and *Corslet* were, strictly speaking, of prepared leather, but often composed of quilted cloths: the former in general denotes, in antiquity, a suit with leathern appendages at the bottom and at the shoulder, as used by the Romans; the latter, one in which the barrel did not come down below the hips. In later ages it

60.

1, 2. Early Greek.   4, 5. Roman.
3. Greek.   6. Barbarian.

always designates a breast and back piece of steel. It is, however, requisite to observe, that in estimating the meaning of Hebrew names for armour of all kinds, they are liable to the same laxity of use which all other languages have manifested.

The *Girdle*, or more properly the baldric or belt, was of leather, studded with metal plates or bullæ; broad when the armour was slight, and then might be girt upon the hips; otherwise it supported the sword scarf-wise from the shoulder.

Greaves were likewise known, even so early as the time of David, for Goliath wore them. They consisted of a pair of shin-covers of brass or strong leather, bound by thongs round the calves and above the ankles. They reached only to the knees, excepting among the Greeks, whose greaves, elastic behind, caught nearly the

whole leg, and were raised in front above the knees.

AR'NON, a river forming the southern boundary of trans-Jordanic Palestine, and separating it from the land of Moab (Num. xxi. 13, 26; Deut. ii. 24; iii. 8, 16; Josh. xii. 1; Isa. xvi. 2; Jer. xlviii. 20). It now bears the name of Wady Modjeb, and rises in the mountains of Gilead. near Katrane, whence it pursues a circuitous course of about eighty miles to the Dead Sea. It flows in a rocky bed, and, at the part visited by Burckhardt, in a channel so deep and precipitous as to appear inaccessible; yet along this, winding among huge fragments of rock, lies the most frequented road, and, not being far from Dibon, probably that taken by the Israelites. The stream is almost dried up in summer; but huge masses of rock, torn from the banks, and deposited high above the usual channel, evince its fulness and impetuosity in the rainy season.

ARO'ER, a town on the north side of the river Arnon, and therefore on the southern border of the territory conquered from the Amorites, which was assigned to the tribes of Reuben and Gad (Deut. ii. 36; Josh. xii. 2; xiii. 9). The Amorites had previously dispossessed the Ammonites of this territory; and although in the texts cited the town seems to be given to Reuben, it is mentioned as a Moabitish city by Jeremiah (xlviii. 19). Burckhardt found the ruins of this town under the name of Araayr, on the edge of a precipice overlooking the river. Aroer is always named in conjunction with 'the city that is in the midst of the river;' whence it has been conjectured that, like Rabbath Ammon [which see], it consisted of two parts, or distinct cities; the one on the bank of the river, and the other in the valley beneath, surrounded, either naturally or artificially, by the waters of the river.

2. AROER, one of the towns 'built,' or probably rebuilt, by the tribe of Gad (Num. xxxii. 34). Burckhardt, in journeying from Szalt towards Rabbath Ammon, notices a ruined site, called Ayra, as 'one of the towns built by the tribe of Gad.' It is about seven miles south-west from Szalt. Aroer of Gad is also mentioned in Judg. xi. 33, and 2 Sam. xxiv. 5.

3. AROER, a city in the tribe of Judah (1 Sam. xxx. 28).

4. AROER, a city in the south of Judah, to which David sent presents after recovering the spoil of Ziklag (1 Sam. xxx. 26, 28). At the distance of twenty geographical miles S. by W. from Hebron, there is a broad valley called Ararah, in which are evident traces of an ancient village or town. The identity of name shows that this was the Aroer of Judah.

AR'PHAD, or ARPAD, a Syrian city, having its own king, and always associated in Scripture with Hamath, the Epiphania of the Greeks (2 Kings xviii. 34; xix. 34; Isa. x. 9; xxxvi. 19). But all the explanations given respecting it are purely conjectural, and Arphad must still be numbered among unascertained Scriptural sites.

ARPHAX'AD, the son of Shem, and father of Salah; born one year after the Deluge, and died B. C. 1904, aged 438 years (Gen. xi. 12, &c.).

ARROW. This word is frequently used as the symbol of calamities or diseases inflicted by God (Job vi. 4; xxxiv. 6; Ps. xxxviii. 2; Deut. xxxii. 23; comp. Ezek. v. 16; Zech. ix. 14).

Lightnings are, by a very fine figure, described as the arrows of God (Ps. xviii. 14; cxliv. 6; Habak. iii. 11; comp. Wisd. v. 21; 2 Sam. xxii. 15). 'Arrow' is occasionally used to denote some sudden or inevitable danger; as in Ps. xci. 5:—'The arrow that flieth by day.' It is also figurative of anything injurious, as a deceitful tongue (Ps. cxxix. 4; Jer. ix. 7); a bitter word (Ps. lxiv. 3): a false testimony (Prov. xxv. 18). The arrow is, however, not always symbolical of evil. In Ps. cxxvii. 4, 5, well-conditioned children are compared to 'arrows in the hands of a mighty man;' *i. e.* instruments of power and action. The arrow is also used in a good sense to denote the efficient and irresistible energy of the word of God in the hands of the Messiah (Ps. xlv. 6; Isa. xliv. 2).

ARROWS. [ARMS.]

ARROWS, DIVINATION BY. [DIVINATION.]

ARTAXERX'ES, ARTACHSHAST. The word, which is supposed to mean *great king*, is the title under which more than one Persian king is mentioned in the Old Testament.

The first ARTACHSHAST is mentioned in Ezra iv. 7-24, as the Persian king who, at the instigation of the adversaries of the Jews, obstructed the rebuilding of the Temple, from his time to that of Darius, king of Persia. According to the arguments adduced in the article AHASUERUS, this king is the immediate predecessor of Darius Hystaspis, and can be no other than the Magian impostor, Smerdis, who seized on the throne B.C. 521, and was murdered after a usurpation of less than eight months (Herod. iii. 61-78).

As to the second ARTACHSHAST, in the seventh year of whose reign Ezra led a second colony of the Jewish exiles back to Jerusalem (Ezra vii. 1, *sq.*), the opinions are divided between Xerxes and his son Artaxerxes Longimanus, and it is difficult, if not impossible, to arrive at any certain conclusion on the subject.

The third ARTACHSHAST is the Persian king who, in the twentieth year of his reign, considerately allowed Nehemiah to go to Jerusalem for the furtherance of purely national objects, invested him with the government of his own people, and allowed him to remain there for twelve years (Neh. ii. 1, *sq.*; v. 14). It is almost unanimously agreed that the king here intended is Artaxerxes Longimanus, who reigned from the year 464 to 425 B.C.

AR'TEMAS. This name (which is a contraction for Artemidorus) occurs only once (Tit. iii. 12), as that of an esteemed disciple whom St. Paul designed to send into Crete to supply the place of Titus, whom he invited to visit him at Nicopolis. When the Epistle was written, the Apostle seems not to have decided whether he should send Artemas or Tychicus for this purpose.

AR'VAD, or, as it might be spelt, ARUAD, whence the present name Ruad, a small island and city on the coast of Syria, called by the Greeks Aradus, by which name it is mentioned in 1 Macc. xv. 23. It is a small rocky island, opposite the mouth of the river Eleutherus, to the north of Tripolis, about one mile in circumference and two miles from the shore. Strabo describes it as a rock rising in the midst of the waves, and modern travellers state that it is steep on every side. Strabo also describes the houses as exceedingly lofty, and were doubtless so built, on account of the scantiness of the site: hence, for its size, it was exceedingly populous.

AR'VADITES (Gen. x. 18; 1 Chron. i. 16), the inhabitants of the island Aradus [ARVAD], and doubtless also of the neighbouring coast. The Arvadites were descended from Arvad, one of the sons of Canaan (Gen. x. 18). Strabo describes the Arvadites as a colony from Sidon. They were noted mariners (Ezek. xxvii. 8, 11), and formed a distinct state, with a king of their own; yet they appear to have been in some dependence upon Tyre, for the prophet represents them as furnishing their contingent of mariners to that city (Ezek. xxvii. 8, 11). The Arvadites took their full share in the maritime traffic for which the Phœnician nation was celebrated, particularly after Tyre and Sidon had fallen under the dominion of the Græco-Syrian kings.

ARU'MAH, otherwise RUMAH, a city near Shechem, where Abimelech encamped (Judg. ix. 41).

A'SA (*healing* or *physician*), son of Abijah, grandson of Rehoboam, and third king of Judah. He began to reign two years before the death of Jeroboam, in Israel, and he reigned forty-one years, from B.C. 955 to 914. As Asa was very young at his accession, the affairs of the government were administered by his mother, or, according to some (comp. 1 Kings xv. 1, 10), his grandmother Maachah, who is understood to have been a granddaughter of Absolom [MAACHAH]. She gave much encouragement to idolatry; but the young king, on assuming the reins of government, zealously rooted out the idolatrous practices which had grown up during his minority and under the preceding reigns; and only the altars in the 'high places' were suffered to remain (1 Kings xv. 11-13; 2 Chron. xiv. 2-5). He neglected no human means of putting his kingdom in the best possible military condition, for which ample opportunity was afforded by the peace which he enjoyed in the ten first years of his reign. And his resources were so well organized, and the population had so increased, that he was eventually in a condition to count on the military services of 580,000 men (2 Chron. xiv. 6-8). In the eleventh year of his reign, relying upon the Divine aid, Asa attacked and defeated the numerous host of the Cushite king Zerah, who had penetrated through Arabia Petræa into the vale of Zephathah, with an immense host (2 Chron. xiv. 9-15.) As the triumphant Judahites were returning, laden with spoil, to Jerusalem, they were met by the prophet Azariah, who declared this splendid victory to be a consequence of Asa's confidence in Jehovah, and exhorted him to perseverance. Thus encouraged, the king exerted himself to extirpate the remnants of idolatry, and caused the people to renew their covenant with Jehovah (2 Chron. xv. 1-15). It was this clear knowledge of his dependent political position, as the vice-gerent of Jehovah, which won for Asa the highest praise that could be given to a Jewish king—that he walked in the steps of his ancestor David (1 Kings xv. 11).

Nevertheless, the king failed towards the latter end of his reign to maintain the character he had thus acquired. When Baasha, king of Israel, had renewed the war between the two kingdoms, and had taken Ramah, which he was proceeding to fortify as a frontier barrier, Asa, the conqueror of Zerah, was so far wanting to his kingdom and his God as to employ the wealth of the Temple and of the royal treasures to induce the king of Syria (Damascus) to make a diversion in his favour by invading the dominions of Baasha. By this means he recovered Ramah, indeed ; but his treasures were squandered, and he incurred the rebuke of the prophet Hanani, whom he cast into prison, being, as it seems, both alarmed and enraged at the effect his address was calculated to produce upon the people. Other persons (who had probably manifested their disapprobation) also suffered from his anger (1 Kings xv. 16-22 ; 2 Chron. xvi. 1-10). In the three last years of his life Asa was afflicted with a grievous ' disease in his feet ;' and it is mentioned to his reproach that he placed too much confidence in his physicians. At his death, however, it appeared that his popularity had not been substantially impaired ; for he was honoured with a funeral of unusual cost and magnificence (2 Chron. xvi. 11-14).

AS'AHEL (*God-created*), son of David's sister Zeruiah, and brother of Joab and Abishai. He was noted for his swiftness of foot ; and after the battle at Gibeon he pursued and overtook Abner, who, with great reluctance, and to preserve his own life, slew him with a backthrust of his spear, B.C. 1055 [ABNER] (2 Sam. ii. 18-23).

A'SAPH (*assembler*), a Levite, son of Barachias (1 Chron. vi. 39 ; xv. 17), eminent as a musician, and appointed by David to preside over the sacred choral services which he organized. The ' sons of Asaph' are afterwards mentioned as choristers of the temple (1 Chron. xxv. 1, 2 ; 2 Chron. xx. 14 ; xxix. 13 ; Ezra ii. 41 ; iii. 10 ; Neh. vii. 44 ; xi. 22) : and this office appears to have been made hereditary in his family (1 Chron. xxv. 1, 2). Asaph was celebrated in after times as a prophet and poet (2 Chron. xxix. 30 ; Neh. xii. 16), and the titles of twelve of the Psalms (lxxiii. to lxxxiii.) bear his name. The merits of this appropriation are elsewhere examined [PSALMS]. —There were two other persons named Asaph : one who occupied the distinguished post of ' recorder' to king Hezekiah (2 Kings xviii. 18 ; Isa. xxxvi. 3) ; another who was keeper of the royal forests under Artaxerxes (Neh. ii. 8).

ASCENSION. The event spoken of under this title is among those which Christians of every age have contemplated with the most profound satisfaction. It was in his ascension that Christ exhibited the perfect triumph of humanity over every antagonist, whether in itself, or in the circumstances under which it may be supposed to exist. The contemplation of this, the entrance of the Redeemer into glory, inspired the prophets of old with the noblest views of his kingdom. ' Thou hast ascended on high ; thou hast led captivity captive ; thou hast received gifts for men ; yea, for the rebellious also, that the Lord God might dwell among them' (Ps. lxviii. 18) ; and ' Lift up your heads, O ye gates ; and be ye lift up, ye everlasting doors, and the king of glory shall come in' (Ps. xxiv. 9). That something of vast importance, in respect to the completion of the great scheme of salvation, was involved in this event, appears

from the words of our Lord himself, ' Touch me not, for I am not yet ascended to my Father : but go to my brethren, and say unto them, I ascend unto my Father, and your Father ; and to my God and your God' (John xx. 17). Nor was it till this had taken place that he poured out the grace of the Spirit upon his church, or began the higher exercises of his office as a mediating priest. In the primitive church, the feast of the Ascension, called also by St. Chrysostom the Assumption of Christ, was considered, like the solemn days of the Nativity and the Passion, as of apostolic origin. St. Chrysostom, in his homily on the subject, calls it an illustrious and refulgent day, and describes the exaltation of Christ as the grand proof of God's reconciliation to mankind.

AS'ENATH, the daughter of Potipherah, priest of On, whom the king of Egypt bestowed in marriage upon Joseph, with the view probably of strengthening his position in Egypt by this high connection. The considerations suggested by this marriage belong to another place [JOSEPH] ; and attention is here only required to *the name*, which, in common with other words of foreign origin, has attracted considerable notice. The most probable interpretation is that it means *worshipper of Neith*—the titular goddess of Sais, the Athene of the Greeks.

ASH. The word thus translated occurs only once in Scripture (Isa. xliv. 14), and is variously translated. Some consider *pine-tree* to be the correct translation, others the *rubus* or *bramble*. Celsius quotes from the Arab author, 'Abu l Fadli, the description of a tree called *aran*, which appears well suited to the passage, though it has not yet been ascertained what tree is intended. The *aran* is said to be a tree of Arabia Petræa, of a thorny nature, inhabiting the valleys, but found also in the mountains, where it is however less thorny. The wood is said to be much valued for cleaning the teeth. The fruit is in bunches like small grapes. The berry is noxious while green, and bitter like galls ; as it ripens it becomes red, then black and somewhat sweetish, and when eaten is grateful to the stomach, &c., and seems to act as a stimulant medicine. Sprengel supposes this to be the caper plant. To us it appears to agree in some respects with *Salvadora persica*, but not in all points, and therefore it is preferable to leave it as one of those still requiring investigation by some traveller in Syria conversant both with plants and their Oriental names and uses.

ASH'DOD, the AZOTUS of the Greeks and Romans, and so called in 1 Macc. iv. 15 ; Acts viii. 40 ; a city on the summit of a grassy hill, near the Mediterranean coast, nearly mid-way between Gaza and Joppa, being 18 geog. miles N. by E. from the former, and 21 S. from the latter ; and it is more exactly mid-way between Askelon and Ekron, being 10 geog. miles N. by E. from the former, and S. by W. from the latter. Ashdod was a city of the Philistines, and the chief town of one of their five states (Josh. xiii. 3 ; 1 Sam. vi. 17). It was the seat of the worship of Dagon (1 Sam. v. 5 ; 1 Macc. xi. 4) ; and it was before its shrine in this city that the captured ark was deposited and triumphed over the idol (1 Sam. v. 1-9). Ashdod was assigned to Judah ; but many centuries passed before this and the other Philistine towns were subdued [PHILISTINES]; and it appears never to have been permanently in possession of the Judahites, although it was dismantled by Uzziah, who built towns in the territory of Ashdod (1 Chron. xxvi. 6). It is mentioned to the reproach of the Jews returned from captivity, that they married wives of Ashdod, with the result that the children of these marriages spoke a mongrel dialect, half Hebrew and half in the speech of Ashdod (Neh. xiii. 23, 24). These facts indicate the ancient importance of Ashdod. It was indeed a place of great strength; and being on the usual military route between Syria and Egypt, the possession of it became an object of importance in the wars between Egypt and the great northern powers. Hence it was secured by the Assyrians before invading Egypt (Isa. i. 1, *sq.*); and at a later date it was taken by Psammetichus, after a siege of twenty-nine years, being the longest siege on record. The destruction of Ashdod was foretold by the prophets (Jer. xxv. 20; Amos i. 8; iii. 9; Zeph. ii. 4; Zach. ix. 5); and was accomplished by the Maccabees (1 Macc. v. 68: x. 77-84; xi. 4). It was, however, rebuilt, and was included in the dominion of Herod the Great, who bequeathed it, with two other towns, to his sister Salome. The evangelist Philip was found at Ashdod after he had baptized the Ethiopian eunuch (Acts viii. 40). Azotus early became the seat of a bishopric; and we find a bishop of Azotus present at the councils of Nice, of Chalcedon, A.D. 359, of Seleucia, and of Jerusalem, A.D. 536.

Ashdod exists at present as an inconsiderable village. The site is marked by ancient ruins, such as broken arches, and partly buried fragments of marble columns; there is also what has the appearance of a very ancient khan, the principal chamber of which had obviously, at some former period, been used as a Christian chapel. The place is still called *Esdud.*

ASH'ER (*happy*), one of the sons of Jacob by Zilpah, the handmaid of Leah (Gen. xxx. 13; xxxv. 26), and founder of one of the twelve tribes (Num. xxvi. 44-47). Asher had four sons and one daughter (Gen. xlix. 20; Deut. xxxiii. 24). On quitting Egypt the number of adult males in the tribe of Asher was 41,500, which made it the ninth of the tribes (excluding Levi) in numbers—Ephraim, Manasseh, and Benjamin only being below it. But before entering Canaan an increase of 11,900—an increase exceeded only by Manasseh—raised the number to 53,400, and made it the fifth of the tribes in population (comp. Num. i. 40, 41; xxvi. 47). The inheritance of this tribe lay in a very fruitful country, on the sea-coast, with Lebanon north, Carmel and the tribe of Issachar south, and Zebulon and Naphtali east. It is usually stated that the whole of the Phœnician territories, including Sidon, were assigned to this tribe. But there are various considerations which militate against this conclusion. The Asherites were unable to gain possession for a long time of the territories actually assigned them, but 'dwelt among the Canaanites, the inhabitants of the land' (Judg. i. 32); and, 'as it is not usual to say of a larger number that it dwells among the smaller, the inference is, that they expelled but comparatively few of the Canaanites, leaving them, in fact, a majority of the population.'

ASHES, in the symbolical language of Scripture, denote human frailty (Gen. xviii. 27), deep humiliation (Esth. iv. 1; Jonah iii. 6; Matt. xi. 21; Luke x. 13; Job xlii. 6; Dan. ix. 3). To sit in ashes was a token of grief and mourning (Job ii. 8; Lam. iii. 16; Ezek. xxvii. 30), as was also strewing them upon the head (2 Sam. xiii. 10; Isa. xli. 3) [MOURNING]. 'Feeding on ashes,' in Ps. cii. 9, appears to express grief, as of one with whose food the ashes with which he is covered mingle. But in Isa. xliv. 20, 'feeding on ashes,' which afford no nourishment, is judged to denote ineffectual means, labour to no purpose. Compare Hos. xii. 1.

ASH'IMA (2 Kings xvii. 30), only once mentioned in the Old Testament as the god of the people of Hamath. The Babylonian Talmud, and the majority of Jewish writers, assert that Ashima was worshipped under the form of a *goat without wool;* the Talmud of Jerusalem says, under that of a *lamb.* Elias Levita, a learned Rabbi of the sixteenth century, assigns the word the sense of *ape.* Jurieu and Calmet have proposed other fanciful conjectures. The opinion that this idol had the form of a goat, however, appears to be the one best supported by arguments as well as by authorities.

ASH'KENAZ (Gen. x. 3), and ASHCHENAZ (Jer. li. 27), the name of a son of Gomer, son of Japhet, and of a tribe of his descendants. In Jeremiah it is placed with Ararat and Minni, provinces of Armenia; whence it is probable that Ashkenaz was a province of Armenia; or at least that it lay not far from it, near the Caucasus, or towards the Black Sea.

ASH'PENAZ, chief of the eunuchs of king Nebuchadnezzar, to whose care Daniel and his companions were consigned, and who changed their names (Dan. i. 3, 7).

ASH'TAROTH and ASHTAROTH-CARNAIM, a town of Bashan (Deut. i. 4; Josh. ix. 10) which was included in the territory of the half-tribe of Manasseh (Josh. xiii. 31), and was assigned to the Levites (1 Chron. vi. 71). It is placed by Eusebius 6 miles from Edrei, the other principal town of Bashan, and 25 miles from Bostra. The town existed in the time of Abraham (Gen. xiv. 5); and as its name of Ashtaroth appears to be derived from the worship of the moon under that name [see the following article], there is little room to look farther than the crescent of that luminary and its symbolical image for an explanation of the addition CARNAIM, or rather KARNAIM, 'horned.' Astaroth-Carnaim is now usually identified with Mezareib, the situation of which corresponds accurately enough with the distances given by Eusebius. Here is the first castle on the great pilgrim road from Damascus to Mecca, which was built about 340 years ago by the Sultan Selim. There are no dwellings beyond the castle, and within it only a few mud huts upon the flat roofs of the warehouses, occupied by the peasants who cultivate the neighbouring grounds.

ASH'TORETH (1 Kings xi. 5) is the name of a goddess of the Sidonians (1 Kings xi. 5, 33), but also of the Philistines (1 Sam. xxxi. 10), whose worship was introduced among the Israelites during the period of the judges (Jud. ii. 13; 1 Sam. vii. 4), was celebrated by Solomon himself (1 Kings xi. 5), and was finally put down by Josiah (2 Kings xxiii. 13). She is frequently mentioned in connection with Baal, as the corresponding female divinity (Jud. ii. 13); and, from the addition of the words, 'and all the host of heaven,' in 2 Kings xxiii. 4, it is probable that she represented one of the celestial bodies. There is also reason to believe that she is meant by the 'queen of heaven,' in Jer. vii. 18; xliv. 17; whose worship is there said to have been solemnised by burning incense, pouring libations, and offering cakes.

According to the testimonies of profane writers, the worship of this goddess, under different names, existed in all countries and colonies of the Syro-Arabian nations. She was especially the chief female divinity of the Phœnicians and Syrians, and there can be no doubt was worshipped also at ancient Carthage. The classical writers, who usually endeavoured to identify the gods of other nations with their own, rather than to discriminate between them, have recognised several of their own divinities in Ashtoreth. Thus she was considered to be *Juno* or *Venus,* especially Venus Urania.

As for the power of nature, which was worshipped under the name of Ashtoreth, Creuzer and Münter assert that it was the principle of conception and parturition—that subordinate power which is fecundated by a superior influence, but which is the agent of all births throughout the universe. As such, Münter maintains that the *original* form under which Ashtoreth was worshipped was the *moon;* and that the transition from that to the *planet* Venus was unquestionably an innovation of a later date. It is evident that the moon alone can be properly called the queen of heaven; as also that the dependent relation of the moon to the sun makes it a more appropriate symbol of that sex, whose functions as female and mother, throughout the whole extent of animated nature, were embodied in Ashtoreth [Baal].

The rites of her worship, if we may assume their resembling those which profane authors describe as paid to the cognate goddesses, in part agree with the few indications in the Old Test., in part complete the brief notices there into an accordant picture. The *cakes* mentioned in Jer. vii. 18, were also known to the Greeks, and were by them made in the shape of a sickle, in reference to the new moon. Among animals, the dove, the crab, and, in later times, the lion, were sacred to her; and among fruits, the pomegranate. No blood was shed *on* her altar; but male animals, and chiefly *kids,* were sacrificed to her. The most prominent part of her worship, however, consisted of those libidinous orgies, which Augustine, who was an eye-witness of their horrors in Carthage, describes with such indignation. Her priests were eunuchs in women's attire (1 Kings xiv. 24), and women (Hos. iv. 14), who, like the Bayadéres of India, prostituted themselves to enrich the temple of this goddess. The prohibition in Deut. xxiii. 18 appears to allude to the dedication of such funds to such a purpose. As for the places consecrated to her worship, although the numerous passages in which the authorized version erroneously speaks of *groves,* are to be deducted (as is explained below), there are yet several occasions on which *gardens* and *shady trees* are mentioned

as peculiar seats of (probably, *her*) lascivious rites (Isa. i. 29; lxv. 3; 1 Kings xiv. 23; Hos. iv. 13; Jer. ii. 20; iii. 13). She also had celebrated temples (1 Sam. xxxi. 10).

As to the form and attributes with which Ashtoreth was represented, the oldest known image, that in Paphos, was a white conical stone. In Canaan she was probably represented as a *cow.* In Phœnicia, she had the head of a cow or bull, as she is seen on coins. Sanchoniathon states that 'Astarte adopted the head of a bull as a symbol of her sovereignty;' he also accounts for the *star* which is her most usual emblem, by saying that 'when she passed through the earth, she found a fallen star, which she consecrated in Tyre. At length, she was figured with the human form, as Lucian expressly testifies of the Syrian goddess—which is substantially the same

61.

as Ashtoreth; and she is so found on coins of Severus, with her head surrounded with rays, sitting on a lion, and holding a thunderbolt and a sceptre in either hand.

To come now to Asherah (Judg. vi. 25). Selden was the first who endeavoured to show that this word—which in the LXX. and Vulgate is generally rendered *grove,* in which our authorized version has followed them—must in *some* places, for the sake of the sense, be taken to mean a *wooden image* of Ashtoreth; and it may now be regarded as a settled point that Asherah is a *name,* and also denotes an image of this goddess.

Some of the arguments which support this opinion are briefly as follows. It is argued that Asherah almost always occurs with words which denote *idols* and *statues of idols;* that the verbs which are employed to express the making an Asherah, are incompatible with the idea of a grove, as they are such as *to build, to shape, to erect;* that the words used to denote the destruction of an Asherah are those of *breaking to pieces, subverting;* that the *image* of Asherah is placed in the Temple (2 Kings xxi. 7); and that Asherah is coupled with Baal in precisely the same way as Ashtoreth is: comp. Judg. ii. 13; x. 6; 1 Kings xviii. 19; 2 Kings xxiii. 4; and particularly Judges iii. 7, and ii. 13, where the plural form of both words is explained as of itself denoting *images* of this goddess. Besides, Selden objects that the signification *grove* is even incongruous in 2 Kings xvii. 10, where we read of 'setting up groves *under every green tree.*' On the strength of these arguments most modern scholars assume that Asherah is a *name* for Ashtoreth, and that it denotes more especially the relation of that goddess to the *planet* Venus, as the lesser star of good fortune. It appears, namely, to be an indisputable fact that both Baal and Ashtoreth, although their primary relation was to the sun and moon, came in process of time to be connected, in the religious conceptions of the Syro-Arabians, with the planets Jupiter and Venus, as the two stars of good fortune [See the article MENI].

ASIA. The ancients had no divisions of the world into parts or quarters; and hence the word Asia, in the modern large sense, does not occur in Scripture. Indeed it does not at all occur, in any sense, in the Hebrew Scriptures, but is found in the books of the Maccabees and in the New Testament. It there applies, in the *largest* sense, to that peninsular portion of Asia which, since the fifth century, has been known by the name of Asia Minor; and, in a narrower sense, to a certain portion thereof which was known as Asia Proper. Thus, it is now generally agreed,—1. That ' Asia' denotes the whole of ASIA MINOR, in the texts Acts xix. 26, 27; xx. 4, 16, 18; xxvii. 2. &c.: but, 2. That only ASIA PROPER, the Roman or Proconsular Asia, is denoted in Acts ii. 9; vi. 9; xix. 10, 22; 2 Tim. i. 15; 1 Pet. i. 6; Rev. i. 4, 11. ASIA MINOR comprehended Bithynia, Pontus, Galatia, Cappadocia, Cicilia, Pamphylia, Pisidia, Lycaonia, Phrygia, Mysia, Troas (all of which are mentioned in the New Testament), Lydia, Ionia, Æolis (which are sometimes included under Lydia), Caria, Doris, and Lycia. ASIA PROPER, or Proconsular Asia, comprehended the provinces of Phrygia, Mysia, Caria, and Lydia. But it is evident that St. Luke uses the term Asia in a sense still more restricted, for in one place he counts Phrygia (Acts ii. 9, 10), and in another Mysia (xvi. 6, 7), as provinces distinct from Asia. Hence it is probable that in many, if not all, of the second set of references the word Asia denotes only Ionia, or the entire western coast, of which Ephesus was the capital, and in which the seven churches were situated. This is called Asia also by Strabo.

ASIAR'CHÆ (Acts xix. 31; Auth. Vers. ' certain of the chief of Asia'). These asiarchæ, who derived their appellation from the name of the province over which they presided (as Syriarchæ, 2 Macc. xii. 2. Lyciarch, Cariarch, &c.), were in Proconsular Asia the chief presidents of the religious rites, whose office it was to exhibit every year, in honour of the gods and of the Roman emperor, solemn games in the theatre. This they did at their own expense, whence none but the most opulent persons could bear the office, although only of one year's continuance. The appointment was much as follows: at the beginning of every year (*i. e.* about the autumnal equinox) each of the cities of Asia held a public assembly, in order to nominate one of their citizens as asiarch. A person was then sent to the general council of the province, at some one of the principal cities, as Ephesus, Smyrna, Sardis, &c., to announce the name of the individual who had been selected. Of the persons thus nominated by the cities the council designated ten, and it is probable that one chosen by the proconsul was pre-eminently the asiarch, but that the other nine acted as his assessors and also bore that title.

AS'KELON, a city of the Philistines, and seat of one of their five states (Judg. xiv. 19 ; 1 Sam. vi. 17; 2 Sam. i. 20). It was situated on the Mediterranean coast, between Gaza and Ashdod, twelve geog. miles north of the former, and ten S. by W. from the latter, and thirty-seven S.W.W. from Jerusalem. It was the only one of the five great Philistine towns that was a maritime port, and stood out close to the shore. Askelon was assigned to the tribe of Judah (Josh. xiii. 13; comp. Judg. i. 18); but it was never for any length of time in possession of the Israelites. The part of the country in which it stood abounded in aromatic plants, onions, and vines. It was well fortified, and early became the seat of the worship of Decerto. After the time of Alexander it shared the lot of Phœnicia, and also of Judæa, being tributary sometimes to Egypt, and at other times to Syria. The magnificent Herod was born at Askelon, and although the city did not belong to his dominion, he adorned it with fountains, baths, and colonnades; and after his death Salome, his sister, resided there in a palace which Cæsar bestowed upon her. It suffered much in the Jewish war with the Romans, but afterwards it again revived, and in the middle ages was noted not only as a stronghold, but as a wealthy and important town. The town bears a prominent part in the history of the Crusades. After being several times dismantled and re-fortified in the times of Saladin and Richard, its fortifications were at length totally destroyed by the Sultan Bibars in A.D. 1270, and the port filled up with stones, for fear of future attempts on the part of the Crusaders. Its desolation has long been complete, and little now remains of it but the walls, with numerous fragments of granite pillars. The situation is described as strong; the thick walls, flanked with towers, were built on the top of a ridge of rock that encircles the town, and terminates at each end in the sea. The place still bears the name of Askulan.

ASMODE'US (Tob. iii. 8), a demon or evil spirit, mentioned in the Apocryphal book of Tobit as having beset Sarah, the daughter of Raguel, and killed the seven husbands whom she had married before Tobit. The Rabbins call Asmodeus, as well as Beelzebub, ' the prince of devils,' whence the two names have been supposed to refer to the same demon. But this title they also give to ' the angel of death,' as the destroyer of all mankind. Thus the story in Tobit means no more than that the seven husbands died successively on their marriage with Sarah.

ASMONE'ANS. [MACCABEES.]

ASNAP'PER, the name of the king, or possibly Assyrian satrap, who sent the Cuthean colonies into Palestine (Ezra iv. 10). Taking him for king of Assyria, he is generally identified with Esar-haddon, although some believe the name to denote Salmanezer. The title (' most noble') which is given to him belonged to the satraps.

ASPA'LATHUS, a name which occurs only in the Apocrypha (Ecclus. xxiv. 15), where the substance which it indicates is enumerated with the other spices and perfumes to which wisdom is compared. Though this drug is not mentioned in the canonical Scriptures, it is probable that it may have been one of the substances comprehended under the general name of spices. It was no doubt one of the substances employed by the ancients as a perfume and incense, as it forms one of the ingredients of the cyphi, or compound incense made use of by the Egyptian priests. The substance which was called aspalathus has not been very clearly ascertained.

ASPHAL'TUM (Auth. Vers. ' pitch') doubtless derives its name from the Lake Asphaltites (Dead Sea), whence it was abundantly obtained. Usually asphaltum is of a shining black colour; it is solid and brittle, with a conchoidal fracture, altogether not unlike common pitch. Its specific gravity is from 1 to 1 6, and it consists chiefly of bituminous oil, hydrogen gas, and charcoal. It is found partly as a solid dry fossil, intermixed in layers of plaster, marl, or slate, and partly as liquid tar flowing from cavities in rocks or in the earth, or swimming upon the surface of lakes or natural wells. To judge from Gen. xiv. 10, mines of asphaltum must have existed formerly on the spot where subsequently the Dead Sea, or Lake Asphaltites, was formed. The Palestine earth-pitch seems, however, to have had the preference over all the other sorts. It was used among the ancients partly for covering boats, paying the bottoms of vessels (Gen. vi. 14: Exod. ii. 3), and partly as a substitute for mortar in buildings; and it is thought that the bricks of which the walls of Babylon were built (Gen. xi. 3) had been cemented with hot bitumen, which imparted to them great solidity. In ancient Babylon asphaltum was made use of also as fuel, as the environs have from the earliest times been renowned for the abundance of asphalt-mines. Neither were the ancient Jews unacquainted with the medicinal properties of that mineral.

The asphaltum was also used among the ancient Egyptians for embalming the dead. This operation was performed in three different ways: the first with slaggy mineral pitch alone; the second with a mixture of this bitumen and a liquor extracted from the cedar; and the third with a similar mixture, to which resinous and aromatic substances were added.

Asphaltum is found in masses on the shore of the Dead Sea, or floating on the surface of its waters. The local Arabs affirm that the bitumen only appears after earthquakes. They allege that after the earthquake of 1834 huge quantities of it were cast upon the shore, of which the Jehalin Arabs alone took about 60 kuntars (each of 98 lbs.) to market. There was another earthquake on January 1, 1837, and soon after a large mass of asphaltum (compared by one person to an island, and by another to a house) was discovered floating on the sea, and was driven aground on the western side, near Usdum. The neighbouring Arabs assembled, cut it up with axes. removed it by camels' loads, and sold it at the rate of four piastres the *rutl*, or pound; the product is said to have been about 3000 dollars. Except during these two years, the Sheik of the Jehalin, a man fifty years old, had never known bitumen appear in the sea, nor heard of it from his fathers.

ASS. 1. The common working ass of Western Asia (called in the Hebrew *Chamor*), is an animal of small stature, frequently represented on Egyptian monuments with panniers on the back, usually of a reddish colour. It appears to be a domesticated race of the wild ass of Arabia, Mesopotamia, and Southern Persia.

In its natural state it never seeks woody, but upland pasture, mountainous and rocky retreats; and it is habituated to stand on the brink of precipices (a practice not entirely obliterated in our own domestic races), whence, with protruded ears, it surveys the scene below, blowing and at length braying in extreme excitement. This habit is beautifully depicted by Jeremiah (xvii. 6; xlviii. 6).

The Auth. Vers. translates the Hebrew words *Oir, Oirim*, ' young ass,' ' colt;' but this rendering does not appear on all occasions to be correct, the word being sometimes used where the Oirim or Ourim carry loads and till the ground, which seems to afford evidence of, at least, full growth (Isa. xxx. 6, 24). The word *Aton, Atunuth*, is unsatisfactorily rendered ' she-ass,' unless we suppose it to refer to a breed of greater beauty and importance than the common, namely, the silver grey of Africa; which being large and indocile, the females were anciently selected in preference for riding, and on that account formed

62. [Domestic Ass of Western Asia.]

a valuable kind of property. It is now the fashion, as it was during the Parthian empire, and probably in the time of the Judges, to dapple this breed with spots of orange or crimson, or of both colours together; and although the taste may be puerile, we conceive that it is the record of remote conquest achieved by a nation of Central Asia mounted on spotted or clouded horses, and revived by the Parthians, who were similarly equipped.

As this animal was most serviceable to man, its name was held in respect rather than contempt. It is alleged, indeed, that the ass was held in contempt in Egypt; but among the Arabs and Jews we have ' the voice of one crying in the wilderness,' a solemn allusion derived from the wild ass, almost the only voice in the desert; and in the distinguishing epithet of Mirvan II., last Ommiad caliph, who was called the wild ass of Mesopotamia—proofs that no idea of contempt was associated with the prophet's metaphor, and that, by such a designation, no insult was intended to the person or dignity of the prince.

2. WILD ASS. By this term the Scripture seems

to intend the horse-ass, or wild mule. The species is first noticed by Aristotle, who mentions nine of these animals as being brought to Phrygia by Pharnaces the satrap, whereof three were living in the time of his son Pharnabazus. The allusion of Jeremiah, in speaking of the wild ass (xiv. 6), most forcibly depicts the scarcity of food when this species, inured to the desert and to want of water, are made the prominent example of suffering. They were most likely used in traces to draw chariots (Isa. xxi. 7). The wild ass is little inferior to the wild horse; in shape it resembles a mule, in gracefulness a horse, and in colour it is silvery, with broad spaces of flaxen or bright bay on the thigh, flank, shoulder, neck, and head; the ears are wide like the zebra's, and the neck is clothed with a vertical dark mane prolonged in a stripe to the tuft of the tail. The company of this animal is liked by horses, and, when domesticated, it is gentle: it is now found wild from the deserts of

63. [Wild Ass.]

the Oxus and Jaxartes to China and Central India. In Cutch it is never known to drink, and in whole districts which it frequents water is not to be found. Though the natives talk of the fine flavour of the flesh, and the Gour in Persia is the food of heroes, to an European its smell is abominable.

MULE occurs in 2 Sam. xiii. 29; 1 Kings i. 33; x. 25; and in other places. This animal is sufficiently well known to require no particular description. Where, or at what period, breeding mules was first commenced is totally unknown, although, from several circumstances, Western Asia may be regarded as the locality; and the era as coinciding with that of the first kings of Israel. In the time of David, to be allowed to ride on the king's own mule was an understood concession of great, if not sovereign authority, and several years before the mention of this event all the king's sons already rode upon mules. It does not appear that the Hebrew people, at this early period at least, bred mules; they received them from Armenia; but the most beautiful were no doubt brought from the vicinity of Bassora.

ASSH'UR, a son of Shem, who gave his name to Assyria (Gen. x. 11-22) [ASSYRIA].

ASSIDÆ'ANS (the *pious* or *righteous*; 1 Macc. vii. 13). As a description of a particular body of men this word does not occur in the canonical Scriptures, nor in Josephus; but in the First Book of Maccabees it is applied to the body of zealous and devoted men who rose at the signal for armed resistance given by Mattathias, the father of the Maccabees, and who, under him and his successors, upheld with the sword the great doctrine of the unity of God, and stemmed the advancing tide of Grecian manners and idolatries.

In the entire absence of collateral information, it seems the safest course to conclude that the Assidæans were a body of eminently zealous men, devoted to the Law, who joined Mattathias very early, and remained the constant adherents of him and his son Judas—not, like the mass of their supporters, rising occasionally and then relapsing into the ordinary pursuits of life. It is possible that, as Jennings conjectures, the name came to be applied to them by their enemies as a term of reproach, like 'Puritans' formerly in this country, and 'saints' very often in the present day.

AS'SOS, a town of Lesser Mysia, or of Adramyttium, opposite the island of Lesbos, or Mitylene. Paul came hither on foot from Troas, to meet with his friends, in order to take shipping for Mitylene (Acts xx. 13, 14). It is now a miserable village, called Beiram, built high upon the rocks on the side towards the land.

ASSYR'IA. We must here distinguish between the *country* of Assyria, and the Assyrian *empire*. They are both designated in Hebrew by Asshur. The Asshurim of Gen. xxv. 3, were, however, an Arab tribe; and in Ezek. xxvii. 6, the word *ashurim* (in our version 'Ashurites') is only an abbreviated form of *teashur*, box-wood.

1. ASSYRIA PROPER was a region east of the Tigris, the capital of which was Nineveh. It derived its name from the progenitor of the aboriginal inhabitants—*Asshur*, the second son of Shem (Gen. x. 22; 1 Chron. i. 17). Its limits in early times are unknown; but when its monarchs enlarged their dominions by conquest, the name of this metropolitan province was extended to the whole empire.

According to Ptolemy, Assyria was in his day bounded on the north by Armenia, the Gordiæan or Carduchian mountains, especially by Mount Niphates; on the west by the river Tigris and Mesopotamia; on the south by Susiana, or Chuzistan, in Persia, and by Babylonia; and on the east by a part of Media, and mounts Choathras and Zagros. It corresponded to the modern Kurdistan, or country of the Kurds (at least to its larger and western portion), with a part of the pashalik of Mosul. 'Assyria,' says Mr. Ainsworth (*Researches in Assyria, Babylonia, and Chaldæa*, Lond. 1838), 'including Taurus, is distinguished into *three* districts: by its *structure*, into a district of plutonic and metamorphic rocks, a district of sedentary formations, and a district of alluvial deposits; by *configuration*, into a district of mountains, a district of stony or sandy plains, and a district of low watery plains: by *natural productions*, into a country of forests and fruit-trees, of olives, wine, corn, and pasturage, or of barren rocks; a country of mulberry, cotton, maize, tobacco, or of barren clay, sand, pebbly or rocky plains; and into a country of date-trees, rice, and pasturage, or a land of saline plants.' The northern part is little else then a mass of mountains, which, near Julamerk, rise to a very great height, Mount Jewar being supposed to have an elevation of 15,000 feet; in the south it is more level, but the plains are often burnt up with scorching heat, while the traveller, looking northward, sees a snowy alpine ridge hanging like a cloud in mid air. On the west this country is skirted by the great river Tigris, the Hiddekel of the Hebrews (Gen. ii. 14; Dan. x. 4), noted for the impetuosity of its current [TIGRIS].

The most remarkable feature, says Ainsworth, in the vegetation of Taurus, is the abundance of trees, shrubs, and plants in the northern, and their comparative absence in the southern district. Besides the productions above enumerated, Kurdistan yields gall-nuts, gum-arabic, mastich, manna (used as sugar), madder, castor-oil, and various kinds of grain, pulse, and fruit. Rich informs us that a great quantity of honey, of the finest quality, is produced; the bees (comp. Isa. vii. 18, 'the bee in the land of Assyria') are kept in hives of mud. The naphtha springs, on the east of the Tigris, are less productive than those in Mesopotamia, but they are much more numerous. The zoology of the mountain district includes bears (black and brown), panthers, lynxes, wolves, foxes, marmots, dormice, fallow and red deer, roebucks, antelopes, &c., and likewise goats, but not (as was once supposed) of the Angora breed. In the plains are found lions, tigers, hyænas, beavers, jerboas, wild boars, camels, &c.

Ptolemy divides Assyria into *six* provinces. Farthest north lay *Arrapachitis*, south of it was *Calakine*, perhaps the Chalach of 2 Kings xvii. 6; xviii. 11. Next came *Adiabene*, so called from the above-mentioned rivers Dhab or Diab; it was so important a district of Assyria, as sometimes to give name to the whole country [ADIABENE]. North-east of it lay *Arbelitis*, in which was Arbela, famous for the battle in which Alexander triumphed over Darius. South of this lay the two provinces of *Apolloniatis* and *Sittakene*. The capital of the whole country was Nineveh, the Ninos of the Greeks, the Hebrew name being supposed to denote 'the abode of Ninos,' the founder of the empire. Its site is believed to have been on the east bank of the Tigris, opposite the modern town of Mosul, where there is now a small town called Nebbi Yunus (*i. e.* the prophet Jonah) [NINEVEH]. At the town of Al Kosh, N. of Mosul, tradition places the birth and burial of the prophet Nahum, and the Jews resort thither in pilgrimage to his tomb.

The greater part of the country which formed Assyria Proper is under the nominal sway of the Turks, who compose a considerable proportion of the population of the towns and larger villages, filling nearly all public offices, and differing in nothing from other Osmanlis. But the aboriginal inhabitants of the country, and of the whole mountain-tract that here divides Turkey from Persia, are the *Kurds*, from whom the country is now designated Kurdistan. They are still, as of old, a barbarous and warlike race, occasionally yielding a formal allegiance, on the west, to the Turks, and, on the east, to the Persians, but never wholly subdued; indeed, some of the more powerful tribes, such as the Hakkary, have maintained an entire independence. Some of them are stationary in villages, while others roam far and wide, beyond the limits of their own country, as nomadic shepherds; but they are all, more or less, addicted to predatory habits, and are regarded with great dread by their more peaceful neighbours. They profess the faith of Islam, and are of the Soonee sect. All travellers have remarked many points of resemblance between them and the ancient Highlanders of Scotland.

The Christian population is scattered over the whole region, but is found chiefly in the north. It includes Chaldæans, who form that branch of the Nestorians that adheres to the church of Rome, a few Jacobites, or monophysite Syrians, Armenians, &c. But the most interesting portion is the ancient church of the primitive *Nestorians*, a lively interest in which has lately been excited in the religious world by the publications of the American missionaries, especially by a work entitled *The Nestorians*, by Asahel Grant, M.D. Lond. 1841. Besides the settlements of this people in the plain of Ooroomiah to the east, and in various parts of Kurdistan, where they are in a state of vassalage, there has been for ages an independent community of Nestorians in the wildest and most inaccessible part of the country. It lies at nearly equal distances from the lakes of Van and Ooroomiah, and the Tigris, and is hemmed in on every side by tribes of ferocious Kurds; but, entrenched in their fastnesses, the Nestorians have defied the storms of revolution and desolation that have so often swept over the adjacent regions; and in their character of bold and intrepid, though rude and fierce mountaineers, have so entirely maintained their independence unto the present day, as to bear among the neighbours the proud title of *Ashiret*, 'the tributeless.' The attempts lately made by Dr. Grant and others to prove that this interesting people are the descendants of the ten 'lost' tribes of Israel, cannot be regarded as successful, and will not bear the test of rigid examination. Another peculiar race that is met with in this and the neighbouring countries is that of the Yezidees, whom Grant and Ainsworth would likewise connect with the ten tribes; but it seems much more probable that they are an offshoot from the ancient Manichees, their alleged worship of the Evil Principle amounting to no more than a reverence which keeps them from speaking of him with disrespect. Besides the dwellers in towns, and the agricultural population, there are a vast number of wandering tribes, not only of Kurds, but of Arabs, Turkomans, and other classes of robbers, who, by keeping the settled inhabitants in constant dread of property and life, check every effort at improvement; and, in consequence of this, and the influence of bad government, many of the finest portions of the country are little better than unproductive wastes.

2. THE ASSYRIAN EMPIRE. No portion of ancient history is involved in greater obscurity than that of the empire of Assyria. In attempting to arrange even the facts deducible from Scripture, a difficulty presents itself at the outset, arising from the ambiguity of the account given of the origin of the earliest Assyrian state in Gen. x. 11. After describing Nimrod, son of

Cush, ' as a mighty one in the earth,' the historian adds (ver. 10), ' And the beginning of his kingdom (or rather, the first theatre of his dominion) was Babel, and Erech, and Accad, and Calneh, in the land of Shinar,' i. e. *Babylonia.* Then follow the words :— ' Out of that land went forth Asshur and builded Nineveh,' or (as it is in the margin) ' out of that land he (i. e. Nimrod) went out into Assyria and builded Nineveh.' Looking at the entire context, and following the natural current of the writer's thoughts, we shall find that the *second* translation yields the most congruous sense. It likewise agrees with the native tradition, that the founder of the Assyrian monarchy and the builder of Nineveh was one and the same person, viz. Ninus, from whom it derived its name, and in that case the designation of Nimrod (the Rebel) was not his proper name, but an opprobrious appellation imposed on him by his enemies. Modern local tradition likewise connects Nimrod with Assyria.

But though Nimrod's ' kingdom ' embraced the lands both of Shinar and Asshur, we are left in the dark as to whether Babylon or Nineveh became the permanent seat of government, and consequently, whether his empire should be designated that of Babylonia or that of Assyria. No certain traces of it, indeed, are to be found in Scripture for ages after its erection. In the days of Abraham, we hear of a king of Elam (i. e. Elymais, in the south of Persia) named Chedorlaomer, who had held in subjection for twelve years five petty princes of Palestine (Gen. xiv. 4), and who, in consequence of their rebellion, invaded that country along with three other kings, one of whom was ' Amraphel, king of *Shinar.'* It is possible that Chedorlaomer was an Assyrian viceroy, and the others his deputies; for at a later period the Assyrian boasted, ' Are not my princes altogether kings ? ' (Isa. x. 8). Yet some have rather concluded from the narrative, that by this time the monarchy of Nimrod had been broken up, or that at least the seat of government had been transferred to Elam. Be this as it may, the name of Assyria as an independent state does not again appear in Scripture till the closing period of the age of Moses. Balaam, a seer from the northern part of Mesopotamia, in the neighbourhood of Assyria, addressing the Kenites, a mountain tribe on the east side of the Jordan, ' took up his parable,' i. e. raised his oracular, prophetic chant, and said, ' Durable is thy dwelling-place ! Yea in a rock puttest thou thy nest : nevertheless, wasted shall be the Kenite, until Asshur shall lead them captive.' The prediction found its fulfilment in the Kenites being gradually reduced in strength (comp. 1 Sam. xv. 6), till they finally shared the fate of the trans-Jordanite tribes, and were swept away into captivity by the Assyrians (1 Chron. v. 26 ; 2 Kings xvi. 9 ; xix. 12, 13 ; 1 Chron. ii. 55). But as a counterpart to this, Balaam next sees a vision of retaliatory vengeance on their oppressors, and the awful prospect of the threatened devastations, though beheld in far distant times, extorts from him the exclamation, ' Ah ! who shall live when God doeth this ? For ships shall come from the coast of Chittim, and shall afflict Asshur, and shall afflict Eber, but he also [the invader] shall perish for ever.' This is not without obscurity ; but it has commonly been sup-

posed to point to the conquest of the regions that once formed the Assyrian empire, first by the Macedonians from Greece, and then by the Romans, both of whose empires were in their turn overthrown.

In the time of the Judges, the people of Israel became subject to a king of Mesopotamia, Chushanrishathaim (Judg. iii. 8), who is by Josephus styled King of the Assyrians ; but we are left in the same ignorance as in the case of Chedorlaomer, as to whether he was an independent sovereign or only a vicegerent for another. The first king of Assyria alluded to in the Bible, is he who reigned at Nineveh when the prophet Jonah was sent thither (Jon. iii. 6). Hales supposes him to have been the father of Pul, the first Assyrian monarch *named* in Scripture, and dates the commencement of his reign B.C. 821. By that time the metropolis of the empire had become ' an exceeding great ' and populous city, but one pre-eminent in wickedness (Jon. i. 2 : iii. 3 ; iv. 11).

The first expressly recorded appearance of the Assyrian power in the countries west of the Euphrates is in the reign of Menahem, king of Israel, against whom ' the God of Israel stirred up the spirit of *Pul* (or *Phul*), king of Assyria ' (1 Chron. v. 26), who invaded the country, and exacted a tribute of a thousand talents of silver ' that his hand ' i. e. his favour, ' might be with him to confirm the kingdom in his hand ' (2 Kings xv. 19, 20). Newton places this event in the year B.C. 770, in the twentieth year of Pul's reign, the commencement of which he fixes in the year B.C. 790. About this period we find the prophet Hosea making frequent allusions to the practice both of Israel and Judæa, to throw themselves for support on the kings of Assyria. The supposition of Newton is adopted by Hales, that at Pul's death his dominions were divided between his two sons, Tiglath-pileser and Nabonassar, the latter being made ruler at Babylon, from the date of whose government or reign the celebrated *era of Nabonassar* took its rise, corresponding to B.C. 747. When Ahaz, king of Judah, was hard pressed by the combined forces of Pekah, king of Israel, and Rezin, king of Damascene-Syria, he purchased Tiglath-pileser's assistance with a large sum, taken out of his own and the Temple treasury. The Assyrian king accordingly invaded the territories of both the confederated kings, and annexed a portion of them to his own dominions, carrying captive a number of their subjects (2 Kings xv. 29 ; xvi. 5-10 ; 1 Chron. v. 26 ; 2 Chron. xxviii. 16 ; Isa. vii. 1-11 ; comp. Amos i. 5 ; ix. 7). His successor was *Shalman* (Hos. x. 4), *Shalmaneser* or *Salmanasser*, the Enemessar of the apocryphal book Tobit (ch. i. 2). He made Hoshea, king of Israel, his tributary vassal (2 Kings xvii. 3) ; but finding him secretly negotiating with So or Sobaco (the Sabakoph of the monuments), king of Egypt, he laid siege to the Israelitish capital, Samaria, took it after an investment of three years (B.C. 719), and then reduced the country of the ten tribes to a province of his empire, carrying into captivity the king and his people, and settling Cuthæans from Babylonia in their room (2 Kings xvii. 3-6 ; xviii. 9-11). Hezekiah, king of Judah, seems to have been for a time his vassal (2 Kings xviii. 7). The empire of Assyria seems now to have reached its greatest extent, having had the Mediterranean for its boundary on the west, and including within its limits Media and Kir on the north, as well as Elam on the south (2 Kings xvi. 9; xvii. 6; Isa. xx. 6). In the twentieth chapter of Isaiah (ver. 1), there is mention of a king of Assyria, *Sargon*, in whose reign Tartan besieged and took Ashdod in Philistia. He is supposed to have been the successor of Shalmaneser, and to have had a short reign of two or three years. His attack on Egypt may have arisen from the jealousy which the Assyrians entertained of that nation's influence over Palestine ever since the negotiation between its king So, and Hoshea, king of Israel. From many incidental expressions in the book of Isaiah we can infer that there was at this time a strong Egyptian party among the Jews, for that people are often warned against relying for help on Egypt, instead of simply confiding in Jehovah (Isa. xxx. 2; xxxi. 1; comp. xx. 5, 6). The result of Tartan's expedition against Egypt and Ethiopia was predicted by Isaiah while that general was yet on the Egyptian frontier at Ashdod (Isa. xx. 1-4); and it is not improbable that it is to this Assyrian invasion that the prophet Nahum refers when he speaks (iii. 8-10) of the subjugation of No, *i. e.* No-Ammun, or Thebes, the capital of Upper Egypt, and the captivity of its inhabitants. The occupation of the country by the Assyrians, however, must have been very transient, for in the reign of Sargon's successor, *Sennacherib*, or *Sancherib*, we find Hezekiah, king of Judah, throwing off the Assyrian yoke, and allying himself with Egypt (2 Kings xviii. 7, 21). This brought against him Sennacherib with a mighty host, which, without difficulty, subdued the fenced cities of Judah, and compelled him to purchase peace by the payment of a large tribute. But 'the treacherous dealer dealt very treacherously' (Isa. xxxiii. 1); and, notwithstanding the agreement, proceeded to invest Jerusalem. In answer, however, to the prayers of the 'good king' of Judah, the Assyrian was diverted from his purpose, partly by the 'rumour' (Isa. xxxvii. 6) of the approach of Tirhakah, king of Ethiopia, and partly by the sudden and miraculous destruction of a great part of his army (2 Kings xviii. 13-37; xix.; Isa. xxxvi. and xxxvii.). He himself fled to Nineveh, where, in course of time, when worshipping in the temple of his god Nisroch, he was slain by his sons Adrammelech and Sharezer, the parricides escaping into the land of Armenia —a fact which is preserved in that country's traditional history [ARARAT].

Sennacherib was succeeded by his son Esarhaddon, or Assarhaddon, who had been his father's viceroy at Babylon (2 Kings xix. 37; Isa. xxxvii. 38). Hales regards him as the first Sardanapalus. The only notice taken of him in Scripture is that he settled some colonists in Samaria (Ezra iv. 2), and as (at ver. 10) that colonization is ascribed to the 'great and noble Asnapper,' it is supposed that that was another name for Esarhaddon, but it may have been one of the great officers of his empire. It seems to have been in his reign that the captains of the Assyrian host invaded and ravaged Judah, carrying Manasseh, the king, captive to Babylon.

The subsequent history of the empire is involved in almost as much obscurity as that of its origin and rise. The Medes had already shaken off the yoke, and the Chaldæans soon appear on the scene as the dominant nation of Western Asia; yet Assyria, though much reduced in extent, existed as an independent state for a considerable period after Esarhaddon. The *last* monarch was Sarac, or Sardanapalus II. (B.C. 636), in whose reign Cyaxares, king of Media, and Nabopolassar, viceroy of Babylon, combined against Assyria, took Nineveh, and, dividing what remained of the empire between them, reduced Assyria Proper to a province of Media (B.C. 606).

In this brief sketch of the history of the Assyrian empire, we have mainly followed the writers of the Old Testament, from whom alone any consistent account can be derived.

The political constitution of the Assyrian empire was no doubt similar to that of other ancient states of the East, such as Chaldæa and Persia. The monarch, called 'the great king' (2 Kings xviii. 19; Isa. xxxvi. 4), ruled as a despot, surrounded with his guards, and only accessible to those who were near his person. Under him there were provincial satraps, called in Isa. x. 8, 'princes' of the rank and power of ordinary kings. The great officers of the household were commonly eunuchs. The religion of the Assyrians was, in its leading features, the same as that of the Chaldæans, *viz.* the symbolical worship of the heavenly bodies, especially the planets. In Scripture there is mention of Nisroch, Adrammelech, Anammelech, Nebchaz, Tartak, &c., as the names of idols worshipped by the natives either of Assyria Proper or of the adjacent countries which they had subdued.

ASTRONOMY, that science which treats of the laws of the stars, or heavenly bodies, considered in reference to their magnitude, movements, and respective influence upon one another. Astronomy may be divided into empirical and scientific; the first being founded on the apparent phenomena and movements of the heavenly bodies, the second upon their real phenomena and movements. The knowledge of the ancients was limited to the first; or if they possessed any truths connected with the second, they were nothing more than bold or fortunate guesses, which were not followed out to their legitimate consequences, nor formed into a systematic whole.

The cradle of astronomy is to be found in Asia. The few and imperfect notices which have come down to these times give a concurrent testimony in favour of this statement, and therewith agrees the fact that the climate, the mode of life, and the occupations of the Oriental nations that were first civilized, prompted them to watch and observe the starry heavens. The Chaldæans are accounted to have excelled in astronomical knowledge.

Pliny, in his celebrated enumeration of the inventors of the arts, sciences, and conveniences of life, ascribes the discovery of astronomy to Phœnician mariners; and in the same chapter he speaks of astronomical observations found on burnt bricks among the Babylonians, which ascend to above 2200 years B.C. Alexander sent to Aristotle from Babylon a series of astronomical observations, extending through 1900 years. The astronomical knowledge of the Chinese and Indians goes up to a still earlier period. From the remote East astronomy travelled in a westerly direction. The Egyptians at a very early period had some acquaintance with it. To them is to be ascribed a pretty near determination of the length of the year, as consisting of 365 days 6 hours. The Egyptians were the teachers of the Greeks.

Some portion of the knowledge which prevailed on the subject would no doubt penetrate to and become the inheritance of the Hebrews, who do not, however, appear to have possessed any views of astronomy which raised their knowledge to the rank of a science, or made it approach to a more correct theory of the mechanism of the heavens than that which was generally held. Nor, if the Bible is taken as the witness, do the ancient Israelites appear to have had extensive knowledge in the matter. They possessed such an acquaintance with it as tillers of the ground and herdsmen might be expected to form while pursuing their business, having, as was natural, their minds directed to those regions of the heavens which night after night brought before their eyes: accordingly, the peculiar Oriental names of the constellations are derived from circumstances connected with a nomade people. A peculiarity of the greatest importance belongs to the knowledge which the Israelites display of the heavens, namely, that it is thoroughly imbued with a religious character; nor is it possible to find in any other writings, even at this day, so much pure and elevated piety, in connection with observations on the starry firmament, as may be gathered even in single books of the Bible (Amos v. 8; Psalm xix.).

As early as the days of the patriarchs the minds of pious men were attracted and enraptured by the splendour of the skies (Gen. xxxvii. 9); and imagery borrowed from the starry world soon fixed itself firmly in human speech. The sun and moon were distinguished from other heavenly bodies, in consequence of their magnitude and their brilliancy, as being the lights of heaven and earth (Gen. i. 16); and from the course of the moon time was divided into parts, or months, of which the oldest form of the year, the lunar, was made up. Every new moon was greeted with religious festivities. While, however, the sun in his power, the moon walking in brightness, and all the stars of light conspired to excite devotion, their influence on the hearts of the ancient Israelites, who were happily instructed in a knowledge of the true God, the one Jehovah, the sole Creator of the world, stopped short of that idolatrous feeling, and was free from those idolatrous practices to which, among nations of less religious knowledge—and especially among their own neighbours, the Babylonians, for instance—it is unhappily known to have led.

As early as the time of the composition of perhaps the oldest book in the Bible, namely, that of Job, the constellations were distinguished one from another, and designated by peculiar and appropriate names (Job ix. 9; xxxviii. 31). In the Bible are found—1. the morning star, the planet Venus (Isa. xiv. 12; Rev. ii. 28); 2. (Job ix. 9; xxxviii. 35; Amos v. 8), the Pleiades; 3. Orion, a large and brilliant constellation,

which stands in a line with the Pleiades. The Orientals seemed to have conceived of Orion as a huge giant who had warred against God, and as bound in chains to the firmament of heaven (Job xxxviii. 31); and it has been conjectured that this notion is the foundation of the history of Nimrod; 4. Arcturus (Job ix. 9), the Great Bear; 5. (Job xxvi. 13, 'the crooked serpent'), Draco, between the Great and the Little Bear; a constellation which spreads itself in windings across the heavens; 6. Castor and Pollux (Acts xxviii. 11), Gemini, or the Twins, on the belt of the Zodiac, which is mentioned in 2 Kings xxiii. 5, under the general name of 'the planets.' The entire body of the stars was called 'the host of heaven' (Isa. xl. 26; Jer. xxxiii. 22).

No trace is found in the Old Testament of a division of the heavenly bodies into planets, fixed stars, and comets; but in Jude 13, the phrase 'wandering stars' is employed figuratively.

After the Babylonish exile the Jews were compelled, even for the sake of their calendar, to attend at least to the course of the moon, which became an object of study, and delineations were made of the shapes that she assumes.

At an early period of the world the worship of the stars arose from that contemplation of them which in every part of the globe, and particularly in the East, has been found a source of deep and tranquil pleasure. 'Men by nature' 'deemed either fire or wind, or the swift air, or the circle of the stars, or the violent water, or the lights of heaven, to be the gods which govern the world;' 'with whose beauty being delighted, they took them to be gods' (Wisdom xiii. 2). Accordingly, the religion of the Egyptians, of the Chaldees, Assyrians, and the ancient Arabians, was nothing else than star-worship, although in the case of the first its origin is more thickly veiled. The sun, moon, and seven planets excited most attention, and won the greatest observance. We thus find among the Babylonians Jupiter (Belus, Isa. lxv. 11), Venus (Isa. lxv. 11, where the first is rendered in the common version 'that troop,' the second 'that number'). Both these were considered good principles. Mercury, honoured as the secretary of heaven, is also found in Isa. xlvi. 1, 'Nebo stoopeth;' Saturn (Amos, v. 26); Mars (2 Kings, xvii. 30): the two last were worshipped as principles of evil. The character of this worship was formed from the notions which were entertained of the good or ill which certain stars occasioned. Astrology found its sphere principally in stars connected with the birth of individuals. It concerned itself also with the determination of lucky and unlucky days: so in Job. iii. 3, 'Let the day perish wherein I was born;' and Gal. iv. 10, 'Ye observe days, and months, and times, and years.' The Chaldæans, who studied the stars at a very early period, were much given to astrology, and were celebrated for their skill in that pretended science (Isa. xlvii. 13). In Daniel ii. 27; v. 11, the calculators of nativities are named. Comets were for the most part considered heralds of evil tidings. The Orientals of the present day hold astrology in honour, and stipendiary astrologers form a part of their court.

AT'AD, the person on whose threshing-floor the sons of Jacob and the Egyptians who accompanied them performed their final act of solemn mourning for Jacob (Gen. l. 11); on which account the place was afterwards called Abel-Mizraim, 'the mourning of the Egyptians.'

AT'AROTH. Several places of this name (which means *crowns*) occur in the Scriptures. 1. *Ataroth-beth-Joab*, in the tribe of Judah (1 Chron. ii. 54). 2. *Ataroth*, on the borders of Ephraim (Josh. xvi. 2, 7), which some identify with, and others distinguish from, the *Ataroth-Addar* of the same tribe mentioned in Josh. xvi. 5; xviii. 13. 3. *Ataroth*, in the tribe of Gad, beyond the Jordan (Num. xxxii. 3, 34). 4. *Ataroth-Shophan*, in the same tribe (Num. xxxii. 35), which some identify with the preceding; but it appears more likely that the addition was used to distinguish the one from the other.

ATERGA'TIS is the name of a Syrian goddess, whose temple is mentioned in 2 Macc. xii. 26. That temple appears, by comparing 1 Macc. v. 43, to have been situated at Ashteroth-Karnaim. Her worship also flourished at Mabûg (*i. e.* Bambyce), afterwards called Hierapolis according to Pliny.

There is little doubt that Atergatis is the same divinity as Derketo, which was worshipped in Phœnicia and at Ascalon under the form of a woman with a fish's tail, or with a woman's face only and the entire body of a fish; that fishes were sacred to her, and that the inhabitants abstained from eating them in honour of her.

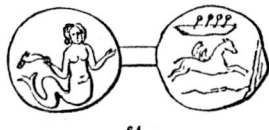

64.

Atergatis is thus a name under which the ancients worshipped some modification of the same power which was adored under that of Ashtoreth. The fish-form shows that Atergatis bears some relation, perhaps that of a female counterpart, to DAGON.

ATHALI'AH (*whom Jehovah afflicts*), daughter of Ahab, king of Israel, doubtless by his idolatrous wife Jezebel. She is also called the daughter of Omri (2 Chron. xxii. 2), who was the father of Ahab; but by a comparison of texts it would appear that she is so called only as being his grand-daughter. Athaliah became the wife of Jehoram, the son of Jehoshaphat, king of Judah. This marriage may fairly be considered the act of the parents; and it is one of the few stains upon the character of the good Jehoshaphat that he was so ready, if not anxious, to connect himself with the idolatrous house of Ahab. Had he not married the heir of his crown to Athaliah, many evils and much bloodshed might have been spared to the royal family and to the kingdom. When Jehoram came to the crown, he, as might be expected, 'walked in the ways of the house of Ahab,' which the sacred writer obviously attributes to this marriage, by adding, 'for he had the daughter of Ahab to wife' (2 Chron. xxi. 6). This king died B.C. 885, and was succeeded by his youngest son Ahaziah, who reigned but one year, and whose death arose from his being, by blood and by circumstances, involved in the doom of Ahab's house [AHAZIAH]. Before

this Athaliah had acquired much influence in public affairs, and had used that influence for evil; and when the tidings of her son's untimely death reached Jerusalem, she resolved to seat herself upon the throne of David, at whatever cost. To this end she caused all the male branches of the royal family to be massacred (2 Kings xi. 1); and by thus shedding the blood of her own grand-children, she undesignedly became the instrument of giving completion to the doom on her father's house. which Jehu had partially accomplished, B.C. 884. One infant son of Ahaziah, however, was saved by his aunt Jehosheba, wife of the high-priest Jehoiada, and was concealed within the walls of the temple, and there brought up so secretly that his existence was unsuspected by Athaliah. But in the seventh year (B.C. 878) of her blood-stained and evil reign, the sounds of unwonted commotion and exulting shouts within the temple courts drew her thither, where she beheld the young Joash standing as a crowned king by the pillar of inauguration, and acknowledged as sovereign by the acclamations of the assembled multitude. Her cries of 'Treason!' failed to excite any movement in her favour, and Jehoiada, the high-priest, who had organized this bold and successful attempt, without allowing time for pause, ordered the Levitical guards to remove her from the sacred precincts to instant death (2 Kings xi.; 2 Chron. xxi. 6; xxii. 10-12; xxiii.).

A'THENS. This celebrated city, as the birthplace of Plato, and through him so widely influential on Judaism and Christianity, deserves something else than a geographical notice here. We shall briefly allude to the stages of her history, and remark on some of the causes of her pre-eminent greatness in arms, arts, and intellectual subtlety.

The earlier and more obscure period of the Grecian province named Attica reaches down nearly to the final establishment of democracy in it. Yet we know enough to see that the foundations of her greatness were then already laid. To a king named Theseus (whose deeds are too much mixed with fable to be narrated as history) is ascribed the credit of uniting all the country-towns of Attica into a single state, the capital of which was Athens. This is the first political event that we can trust as historical, although its date and circumstances are by no means free from obscurity.

The population of this province was variously called Pelasgian, Achaian, and Ionian, and probably corresponds most nearly to what was afterwards called Æolian. The first name carries the mind back to an extremely primitive period. When the Dorians, another tribe of Greeks of very different temperament, invaded and occupied the southern peninsula, great numbers of its Achaian inhabitants took refuge in Attica. Shortly after, the Dorians were repulsed in an inroad against Athens, an event which has transmitted to legendary renown the name of King Codrus; and thenceforward Athens was looked upon as the bulwark of the Ionian tribes against the barbarous Dorians. Overloaded with population, Attica now poured forth colonies into Asia; some of which, as Miletus, soon rose to great eminence, and sent out numerous colonies themselves; so that Athens was reverenced as a

I

mother of nations, by powerful children scattered along the western and northern coasts of Anatolia.

Dim tradition shows us isolated priesthoods and elective kings in the earliest times of Attica; these however gradually gave way to an aristocracy, which in a series of years established themselves as a hereditary ruling caste. But a country 'ever unravaged' (and such was their boast) could not fail to increase in wealth and numbers; and after two or three centuries, while the highest commoners pressed on the nobles, the lowest became overwhelmed with debt. The disorders caused by the strife of the former were vainly sought to be stayed by the institutions of Draco; the sufferings of the latter were ended, and the sources of violence dried up, by the enactments of Solon. Henceforth the Athenians revered *the laws of Solon* as the groundwork of their whole civil polity; yet they retained by the side of them *the ordinances of Draco* in many matters pertaining to religion. The date of Solon's reforms was probably B.C. 594.

The usurpation of Pisistratus and his sons made a partial breach in the constitution; but upon their expulsion, a more serious change was effected by Cleisthenes, head of the noble house of the Alcmæonidæ (B.C. 508), almost in the same year in which Tarquin was expelled from Rome. An entirely new organization of the Attic tribes was framed, which destroyed whatever remained of the power of the nobles as an order, and established among the freemen a democracy, in fact, as well as in form. Out of this proceeded all the good and all the evil with which the name of Athens is associated; and though greatness which shot up so suddenly could not be permanent, there can be no diffi-

J. JACKSON.

culty in deciding that the good greatly preponderated.

Very soon after this commenced hostilities with Persia; and the self-denying, romantic, successful bravery of Athens, with the generous affability and great talents of her statesmen, soon raised her to the head of the whole Ionian confederacy. As long as Persia was to be feared, Athens was loved; but after tasting the sweets of power, her sway degenerated into a despotism, and created at length, in the war called the Peloponnesian, a coalition of all Dorian and Æolian Greece against her (B.C. 431). In spite of a fatal pestilence and the revolt of her Ionian subjects, the naval skill of Athenian seamen and the enterprise of Athenian commanders proved more than a match for the hostile confederacy; and when Athens at last fell (B.C. 404), she fell by the effects of internal sedition more truly than by Spartan lances or Persian gold, or even by her own rash and overgrasping ambition. The demoralizing effects of this war on all Greece were infinitely the worst result of it, and they were transmitted to succeeding generations. It was substantially a *civil* war in every province; and, as all the inhabitants of Attica were every summer forced to take refuge in the few fortresses they possessed, or in Athens itself, the simple countrymen became transformed into a hungry and profligate town rabble.

From the earliest times the Ionians loved the lyre and the song, and the hymns of poets formed the staple of Athenian education. The constitution of Solon admitted and demanded in the people a great knowledge of law, with a large share in its daily administration. Thus the acuteness of the lawyer was grafted on the imagination of the poet. These are the two intellectual elements out of which Athenian wisdom was developed; but it was stimulated and enriched by extended political action and political experience. History and Philosophy, as the words are understood in modern Europe, had their birth in Athens about the time of the Peloponnesian war. Then first, also, the Oratory of the bar and of the popular assembly was systematically cultivated, and the elements of mathematical science were admitted into the education of an accomplished man.

In the imitative arts of Sculpture and Painting, as well as in Architecture, it need hardly be said that Athens carried off the palm in Greece : yet, in all these, the Asiatic colonies vied with her. Miletus took the start of her in literary composition ; and, under slight conceivable changes, might have become the Athens of the world. But all details on these subjects would be here out of place.

That Athens after the Peloponnesian war never recovered the political place which she previously held, can excite no surprise—that she rose so high towards it was truly wonderful. Sparta and Thebes, which successively aspired to the ' leadership ' of Greece, abused their power as flagrantly as Athens had done, and, at the same time, more coarse'y. The never-ending cabals, the treaties made and violated, the coalitions and breaches, the alliances and wars, recurring every few years, destroyed all mutual confidence, and all possibility of again uniting Greece in any permanent form of independence ; and, in consequence, the whole country was soon swallowed up in the kingdom of Macedonia. With the loss of civil liberty, Athens lost her genius, her manly mind, and whatever remained of her virtue : she long continued to produce talents, which were too often made tools of iniquity, panders to power, and petty artificers of false philosophy.

A Christian church existed in Athens soon after the apostolic times ; but as the city had no political importance, the church never assumed any eminent position.

ATONEMENT (See Rom. xi. 15 ; 2 Cor. v. 18, 19). In ecclesiastical writers, and in the canons of Councils, the word rendered *atonement* is employed to signify the reconciliation of offenders to the Church after a due course of penitence. Of this there are said to have been two kinds : the one consisting merely in the remission of punishment ; the other, in the restoration of the penitent to all the rights and privileges of communion. For the doctrine of Atonement, see articles SACRIFICE, REDEMPTION.

ATONEMENT, DAY OF (*day of pardon*, Lev. xxiii. 27 ; xxv. 9). Though perhaps originally meant as a temporary day of expiation for the sin of the golden calf (as some would infer from Exod. xxxiii.), yet it was permanently instituted by Moses as a day of atonement for sins in general ; and this day—the 10th of Tishri (our September)—is indeed the only fast ordained by Moses. This great fast commenced at sunset of the previous day, and lasted twenty-four hours, that is, from sunset to sunset. The ceremonies observed on this occasion are minutely described in Leviticus xvi., and were of a very laborious character, especially for the high-priest, who had to prepare himself during the previous seven days in nearly solitary confinement for the peculiar services that awaited him, and abstain during that period from all that could render him unclean, or disturb his devotions. The most remarkable ceremony of the day was the entrance of the high-priest into the Sanctuary, a thing not allowed on any other day, and to which Paul alludes, Heb. ix. 7.

The other duties of the high-priest on that day consisted in frequent washings, changing his clothes, lighting the lamps, burning incense, &c. ; which operations commenced soon after midnight of the 10th of the seventh month (Tishri). The ceremonies of worship peculiar to this day alone (besides those which were common to it with all other days) were : 1. That the high-priest, in his pontifical dress, confessed his own sins and those of his family, for the expiation of which he offered a bullock, on which he laid them ; 2. That two goats were set aside, one of which was by lot sacrificed to Jehovah, while the other (Azazel), which was determined by lot to be set at liberty, was sent to the desert burdened with the sins of the people (Lev. xvi.).

On this day also the high-priest gave his blessing to the whole nation ; and the remainder of the day was spent in prayers and other works of penance.

Among the present orthodox Jews, for the scape-goat of old, a cock seems to have been substituted, which they call pardon, and which, on the eve of the day of Atonement, they turn three times round their head, each time saying (in Hebrew) that the cock is to be sacrificed instead of them, after which it is slaughtered and eaten. Towards evening of the 9th of Tishri, and before they take the last meal for the next twenty-four hours, they repair to the synagogue, and each inflicts upon his neighbour thirty-nine blows with a piece of leather. Most of the Jews on that day (of atonement) wear a white gown—the same shrouds in which they are buried ; while *all* of them are obliged to stand the whole day without shoes, or even slippers.

ATTALI'A, a maritime city of Pamphylia, in Asia Minor, near the mouth of the river Catarrhactes. It derived its name from its founder, Attalus Philadelphus, king of Pergamos. It was visited by Paul and Barnabas, A.D. 45 (Acts xiv. 25). It still exists under the name of Adalia, and extensive and important ruins attest the former consequence of the city.

ATTITUDES. The allusions in Scripture to attitudes and postures expressive of adoration, supplication, and respect, are very numerous. From these we learn enough to perceive that the usages of the Hebrews in this respect were very nearly, if not altogether, the same as those which are still practised in the East, and which the paintings and sculptures of Egypt show to have been of old employed in that country. These sources supply ample materials for illustration, which it may be well to arrange under those heads into which such acts naturally divide themselves.

ADORATION AND HOMAGE.—The Moslems in their prayers throw themselves successively, and according to an established routine, into the various postures (nine in number) which they deem the most appropriate to the several parts of the service. For the sake of reference and comparison, we have introduced them all at the head of this article ; as we have no doubt that the Hebrews employed on one occasion or another nearly all the various postures which the Moslems exhibit on one occasion. This is the chief difference. In public and common worship the Hebrews prayed *standing* ; but in their sepa-

66.

rate and private acts of worship they assumed the position which, according to their modes of doing homage or showing respect, seemed to them the most suitable to their present feelings or objects. It would appear, however, that some form of kneeling was most usual in private devotions (1 Kings viii. 54; Ezra ix. 5; Dan. vi. 10; 2 Chron. vi. 13).

STANDING in public prayer is still the practice of the Jews. This posture was adopted from the synagogue by the primitive Christians; and is still maintained by the Oriental Churches. This appears, from their monuments, to have been the custom also among the ancient Persians

67.

and Egyptians, although the latter certainly sometimes kneeled before their gods. In the Moslem worship, four of the nine positions (cut 66, figs. 1, 2, 4, 8) are standing ones; and that posture which is repeated in three out of these four (2, 4, 8), may be pointed out as the proper Oriental posture of reverential standing, with folded hands. It is the posture in which people stand before kings and great men.

While in this attitude of worship, the hands were sometimes stretched forth towards heaven in supplication or invocation (1 Kings viii. 22; 2 Chron. vi. 12, 29; Isa. i. 15). This was per-

68.

haps not so much the conventional posture (1 in the Moslem series), as the more natural posture of standing adoration with outspread hands, which we observe on the Egyptian monuments. The uplifting of one hand (the right) only in taking an oath was so common, that to say, 'I have lifted up my hand,' was equivalent to 'I

have sworn' (Gen. xiv. 22; comp. xli. 44; Deut. xxxii. 40). This posture was also common among other ancient nations; and we find examples of it in the sculptures of Persia (fig. 1) and Rome (fig. 2).

KNEELING is very often described as a posture of worship (1 Kings viii. 54; Ezra ix. 5; Dan. vi. 10; 2 Chron. vi. 13; comp. 1 Kings xix. 18; Luke xxii. 41; Acts vii. 60). This is still an Oriental custom, and three forms of it occur (5, 6, 9) in the Moslem devotions. It was also in use, although not very frequent, among the ancient Egyptians; who likewise, as well as the Hebrews (Exod. xxxiv. 8; 2 Chron. xxix. 29; Isa. i. 15), sometimes prostrated themselves upon the ground. The usual mode of prostration among the Hebrews by which they expressed the most intense humiliation, was by bringing not only the body but the head to the ground.

69.

The ordinary mode of prostration at the present time, and probably anciently, is that shown in one of the postures of Moslem worship (5), in which the body is not thrown flat upon the ground, but rests upon the knees, arms, and head. In order to express devotion, sorrow, compunction, or humiliation, the Israelites threw dust upon their heads (Josh. vii. 6; Job ii. 12; Lam. ii. 10; Ezek. xxiv. 7; Rev. xviii. 19), as was done also by the ancient Egyptians, and is still done by the modern Orientals. Under similar circumstances it was usual to smite the breast (Luke xviii. 13). This was also a prac-

70.

tice among the Egyptians, and the monuments at Thebes exhibit persons engaged in this act while they kneel upon one knee.

In 1 Chron. xvii. 16 we are told that 'David the king came and *sat* before the Lord,' and in that posture gave utterance to eloquent prayer, or rather thanksgiving, which the sequel of the chapter contains. Those unacquainted with Eastern manners are surprised at this. But there is a mode of sitting in the East which is highly respectful and even reverential. It is that which occurs in the Moslem forms of worship (9). The person first kneels, and then sits back upon his heels. Attention is also paid to the position of the hands, which they cross, fold, or hide in the opposite sleeves. The variety of this formal sitting, which the following figure

71.

represents, is highly respectful. The prophet Elijah must have been in this or some other similar posture when he inclined himself so much forward in prayer that his head almost touched his knees (1 Kings xviii. 42).

SUPPLICATION, when addressed externally to man, cannot possibly be exhibited in any other forms than those which are used in supplication to God. Uplifted hands, kneeling, prostration, are common to both. On the Egyptian monuments, suppliant captives, of different nations, are represented as kneeling or standing with outspread hands. *Prostration*, or *falling at the feet* of a person, is often mentioned in Scripture as

72.

an act of supplication or of reverence, or of both (1 Sam. xxv. 24; 2 Kings iv. 37; Esth. viii. 3; Matt. xviii. 29; xxviii. 9; Mark v. 22; Luke viii. 41; John xi. 32; Acts x. 25). Sometimes in this posture, or with the knees bent as before indicated, the Orientals bring their forehead to the ground, and before resuming an erect position either kiss the earth, or the feet, or border of the garment of the king or prince before whom they are allowed to appear. There is no doubt that a similar practice existed among the Jews (Matt. ix. 20; Luke vii. 38, 45). *Kissing the hand* of another as a mark of affectionate respect, we do not remember as distinctly mentioned in Scripture. But as the Jews had the other forms of Oriental salutation, we may conclude that they had this also, although it does not happen to have been specially noticed. Kissing one's own hand is mentioned as early as the time of Job (xxxi. 27), as an act of homage to the heavenly bodies. It was properly a salutation, and as such an act of adoration to them. The Romans in like manner kissed their hands

as they passed the temples or statues of their gods [ADORATION].

It appears from 1 Sam. x. 1; 1 Kings xix. 18; Ps. ii. 12; that there was a peculiar kiss of homage, the character of which is not indicated. It was probably that kiss upon the forehead expressive of high respect which was formerly, if not now, in use among the Bedouins.

BOWING.—In the Scriptures there are different words descriptive of various postures of respectful bowing; as *to incline or bow down the head, to bend down the body very low, to bend the knee, also to bless*. These terms indicate a conformity with the existing usages of the East, in which the modes of bowing are equally diversified, and, in all likelihood, the same. These are—1. touching the lips and the forehead with

73.

the right hand, with or without an inclination of the head or of the body, and with or without previously touching the ground; 2. placing the right hand upon the breast, with or without an inclination of the head or of the body; 3. bending the body very low, with folded arms; 4. bending the body and resting the hands on the knees: this is one of the postures of prayer, and is indicative of the highest respect in the presence of kings and princes.

It appears to have been usual for a person to receive a blessing in a kneeling posture. We know also that the person who gave the blessing laid his hands upon the head of the person blessed (Gen. xlviii. 14). This is exactly the case at the present day in the East, and a picture of the existing custom would furnish a perfect illustration of the patriarchal form of blessing. This may be perceived from the annexed engraving.

74.

AVA (2 Kings xvii. 24), also IVAH (2 Kings xviii. 34; xix. 13; Isa. xxxvii. 13), the capital of a small monarchical state conquered by the Assyrians, and from which king Shalmaneser sent colonies into Samaria. It is most probable that Ava was a Syrian or Mesopotamian town, of which no trace can now be found either in ancient writers or in the Oriental topographers.

AVEN, a plain, ' the plain of the sun,' of Damascene Syria (Amos i. 5). It is usually supposed to be the same as the plain of Baalbec, or valley of Baal, where there was a magnificent temple dedicated to the sun.

AUGUSTUS (*venerable*), the title assumed by Octavius, who, after his adoption by Julius Cæsar, took the name of Octavianus (*i. e. Ex-*Octavius, according to the Roman fashion; and was the first peacefully acknowledged emperor of Rome. He was emperor at the birth and during half the lifetime of our Lord; but his name has no connection with Scriptural events, and occurs only once (Luke ii. 1) in the New Testament.

A'VIM, called also AVITES and HIVITES, a people descended from Canaan (Gen. x. 17), who originally occupied the southernmost portion of that territory in Palestine along the Mediterranean coast, which the Caphtorim or Philistines afterwards possessed (Deut. ii. 23). As the territory of the Avim is mentioned in Josh. xiii. 3, in addition to the five Philistine states, it would appear that it was not included in theirs, and that the expulsion of the Avim was by a Philistine invasion prior to that by which the five principalities were founded. The territory began at Gaza, and extended southward to 'the river of Egypt' (Deut. ii. 23), forming what was the sole Philistine kingdom of Gerar in the time of Abraham, when we do not hear of any other Philistine states. There were then Avim, or Hivites, at Shechem (Gen. xxxiv. 2), and we afterwards find them also at Gibeon (Josh. ix. 7), and beyond the Jordan, at the foot of Mount Hermon (Josh. xi. 3); but we have no means of knowing whether these were original settlements of the Avim, or were formed out of the fragments of the nation which the Philistines expelled from southern Palestine. The original country of the Avim is called Hazerim in Deut. ii. 23 [GERAR; PHILISTINES].

AWL. The Hebrew word which denotes an awl or other instrument for boring a small hole, occurs in Exod. xxi. 6; Deut. xv. 17. Considering that the Israelites had at that time recently withdrawn from their long sojourn in Egypt,

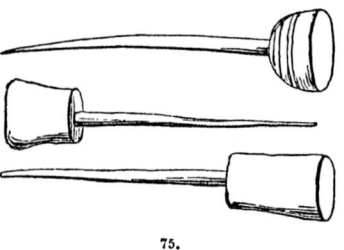

75.

there can be no doubt that the instruments were the same as those of that country, the forms of which, from actual specimens in the British Museum, are shown in the annexed cut. They are such as were used by the sandal-makers and other workers in leather.

AXE. Several instruments of this description are so discriminated in Scripture as to show that the Hebrews had them of different forms and for various uses. 1. *garzen*, which occurs in Deut. xix. 5; xx. 19; 1 Kings vi. 7; Isa. x. 15. From these passages it appears that this kind was employed in felling trees, and in hewing large timber for building. The conjecture of Gesenius,

that in 1 Kings v. 7 it denotes the axe of a stone-mason, is by no means conclusive. The first text supposes a case of the head slipping from the helve in felling a tree. This would suggest that it was shaped like fig. 3, which is just the same instrument as our common hatchet, and appears to have been applied by the ancient Egyptians to the same general use as with us. 2. *maatzad*, which occur only in Isa. xliv. 12; and Jer. x. 3. From these passages it appears to have been a lighter implement than the former, or a kind of adze, used for fashioning or carving wood into shape; it was probably, therefore, like figs. 4 to 7, which the Egyptians employed for this purpose. The differences of form and size, as indicated in the figures, appear to have been determined with reference to light or heavy work: fig. 3 is a finer carving-tool. 3. *qardom;* this is the commonest name for an axe or hatchet. It is of this which we read in Judg. ix. 48; Ps. lxxiv. 5; 1 Sam. xiii. 20, 21; Jer. xlvi. 22. It appears to have been more exclusively employed than the *garzen* for felling trees, and had therefore probably a heavier head. In one of the

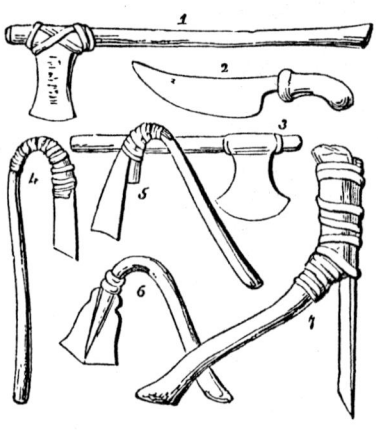

76.

Egyptian sculptures the inhabitants of Lebanon are represented as felling pine-trees with axes like fig. 1. As the one used by the Egyptians for the same purpose was also of this shape, there is little doubt that it was also in use among the Hebrews.

The word rendered 'axe' in 2 Kings vi. 5 is literally 'iron;' but as an axe is certainly intended, the passage is valuable as showing that the axe-heads among the Hebrews were of iron. Those which have been found in Egypt are of bronze, which was very anciently and generally used for the purpose.

AZARI'AH (*whom Jehovah aids*), a very common name among the Hebrews, and hence borne by a considerable number of persons mentioned in Scripture.

1. AZARIAH, a high-priest (1 Chron. vi. 9), perhaps the same with Amariah, who lived under Jehoshaphat king of Judah (2 Chron. xix. 11), about B.C. 896.

2. AZARIAH, son of Johanan, a high-priest (1 Chron. vi. 10), whom some suppose the same

as Zechariah, son of Jehoiada, who was killed B.C. 840 (2 Chron. xxiv. 20-22).

3. AZARIAH, the high-priest who opposed king Uzziah in offering incense to Jehovah (2 Chron. xxvi. 17).

4. AZARIAH, a high-priest in the time of Hezekiah (2 Chron. xxxi. 10).

5. AZARIAH, the father of Seraiah, who was the last high-priest before the Captivity (1 Chron. vi. 14).

6. AZARIAH, son of the high-priest Zadok; but it is uncertain if he succeeded his father (1 Kings iv. 2).

7. AZARIAH, captain of King Solomon's guards (1 Kings iv. 5).

8. AZARIAH, otherwise called Uzziah, king of Judah [UZZIAH].

9. AZARIAH, a prophet who met king Asa on his return from a great victory over the Cushite king Zerah (2 Chron. xxiii. 1) [ASA].

10. AZARIAH, a person to whom the high-priest Jehoiada made known the secret of the existence of the young prince Joash, and who assisted in placing him on the throne (2 Chron. xv. 1).

11. AZARIAH, one of the two sons of king Jehoshaphat (2 Chron. xxi. 2).

12. AZARIAH, one of the 'proud men' who rebuked Jeremiah for advising the people that remained in Palestine, after the expatriation to Babylon, not to retire into Egypt; and who took the prophet himself and Baruch along with them to that country (Jer. xliii. 2-7).

13. AZARIAH, the Chaldæan name of Abed-nego, one of Daniel's three friends who were cast into the fiery furnace (Dan. i. 7; iii. 9).

AZ'ZAH, a mode of spelling the Hebrew name which is elsewhere rendered Gaza. The name occurs in this form in Deut. ii. 23; Jer. xxv. 20; which last clearly shows that Gaza is intended.

B.

BA'AL (lord, master). As the idolatrous nations of the Syro-Arabian race had several gods, this word, by means of some accessory distinction, became applicable as a name to many different deities.

1. BAAL (with the definite article, Judg. ii. 13; Jer. xix. 5; xxxix. 35; Rom. xi. 4) is appropriated to the chief male divinity of the Phœnicians, the principal seat of whose worship was at Tyre. The idolatrous Israelites adopted the worship of this god (almost always in conjunction with that of Ashtoreth) in the period of the Judges (Judg. ii. 13); they continued it in the reigns of Ahaz and Manasseh, kings of Judah (2 Chron. xxviii. 2; 2 Kings xxi. 3); and, among the kings of Israel, especially in the reign of Ahab, who, partly through the influence of his wife, the daughter of the Sidonian king Ethbaal, appears to have made a systematic attempt to suppress the worship of God altogether, and to substitute that of Baal in its stead (1 Kings xvi. 31); and in that of Hosea (2 Kings xvii. 16), although Jehu and Jehoiada once severally destroyed the temples and priesthood of the idol (2 Kings x. 18, sq.; xi. 18).

We read of altars, images, and temples erected to Baal (1 Kings xvi. 32; 2 Kings iii. 2). The altars were generally on heights, as the summits of hills or the roofs of houses (Jer. xix. 5; xxxii. 29). His priesthood were a very numerous body (1 Kings xviii. 19), and were divided into the two classes of prophets and of priests (2 Kings x. 19). As to the rites by which he was worshipped, there is most frequent mention of incense being offered to him (2 Kings xxiii. 5), but also of bullocks being sacrificed (1 Kings xviii. 26), and even of children, as to Moloch (Jer. xix. 5). According to the description in 1 Kings xviii., the priests, during the sacrifice, danced about the altar, and, when their prayers were not answered, cut themselves with knives until the blood flowed. We also read of homage paid to him by bowing the knee, and by kissing his image (1 Kings xix. 18), and that his worshippers used to swear by his name (Jer. xii. 16).

As to the power of nature which was adored under the form of the Tyrian Baal, many of the passages above cited show evidently that it was one of the heavenly bodies; or, if we admit that resemblance between the Babylonian and Persian religions which Munter assumes, not one of the heavenly bodies really, but the astral spirit residing in one of them; and the same line of induction as that which is pursued in the case of Ashtoreth, his female counterpart, leads to the conclusion that it was the sun.

2. BA'AL BE'RITH, covenant-lord (Judg. ix. 4), is the name of a god worshipped by the people of Shechem (Judg. viii. 33; ix. 4, 46).

3. BAA'L PE'OR appears to have been properly the idol of the Moabites (Num. xxv. 1-9; Deut. iv. 3; Jos. xxii. 17; Ps. cvi. 28; Hos. ix. 10); but also of the Midianites (Num. xxxi. 15, 16).

It is the common opinion that this god was worshipped by obscene rites. The utmost, however, that the passages in which this god is named express, is the fact that the Israelites received this idolatry from the women of Moab, and were led away to eat of their sacrifices (cf. Ps. cvi. 28); but it is very possible for that sex to have been the means of seducing them into the adoption of their worship, without the idolatry itself being of an obscene kind. It is also remarkable that so few authors are agreed even as to the general character of these rites. Most Jewish authorities represent his worship to have consisted of rites which are filthy in the extreme, but not lascivious. With regard to the origin of the term Peor, it is supposed to have been the original name of the mountain; and Baal Peor to be the designation of the god worshipped there. Some identify this god with CHEMOSH.

4. BA'ALZE'BUB (fly-lord) occurs in 2 Kings i. 2-16, as the god of the Philistines at Ekron, whose oracle Ahaziah sent to consult. There is much diversity of opinion as to the signification of this name, according as authors consider the title to be one of honour, as used by his worshippers, or one of contempt.

The analogy of classical idolatry would lead us to conclude that all these Baals are only the same god under various modifications of attributes and emblems: but the scanty notices to which we owe all our knowledge of Syro-Arabian idolatry do not furnish data for any decided opinion on this subject.

BAAL is often found as the first element of compound names of places. In this case, Gesenius thinks that it seldom, if ever, has any reference to the god of that name; but that it denotes the place which *possesses*, which is the *abode* of the thing signified by the latter half of the compound.

BA'ALAH, BAALE-JUDAH, KIRJATH-BAAL [KIRJATH JEARIM].

BAALAH (Josh. xv. 29), BALAH (Josh. xix. 3), BILHAH (1 Chron. iv. 29), a town in the tribe of Simeon, usually confounded with Baalath; but, as the latter was in Dan and this in Simeon, they would appear to have been distinct.

BA'ALATH, a town in the tribe of Dan (Josh. xix. 44), apparently the same that was afterwards rebuilt by Solomon (1 Kings ix. 18).

BA'ALATH-BE'ER, probably the same as the Baal of 1 Chron. iv. 33—a city of Simeon; called also Ramath-Negeb, or Southern Ramath (Josh. xix. 8; comp. 1 Sam. xxx. 27).

BA'AL-GAD, a city ' in the valley of Lebanon under Mount Hermon '(Josh. xi. 17; xii. 7). We are also informed that among those parts of Palestine which were unsubdued by the Hebrews at the death of Joshua, was ' all Lebanon towards the sun-rising, from Baal-gad, under Mount Hermon, unto the entering into Hamath' (Josh. xiii 5). This position of Baal-Gad is not unfavourable to the conclusion which some have reached, that it is no other than the place which, from a temple consecrated to the sun, that stood there, was called by the Greeks *Heliopolis, i. e.* city of the sun; and which the natives called and still call Baalbek, a word apparently of the same meaning.

Baalbek is pleasantly situated on the lowest declivity of Anti-Libanus, at the opening of a small valley into the plain El-Bekaa. Through

this valley runs a small stream, divided into numberless rills for irrigation. The place is in N. lat. 34° 1' 30", and E. long. 36° 11", distant 109 geogr. miles from Palmyra, and 38¾ from Tripoli.

Its origin appears to be lost in the most remote antiquity, and the historical notices of it are very scanty. In the absence of more positive information we can only conjecture that its situation on the high-road of commerce between Tyre, Palmyra, and the farther East, must have contributed largely to the wealth and magnificence which it manifestly attained. It is mentioned under the name of Heliopolis by Josephus, and also by Pliny. From the reverses of Roman coins we learn that Heliopolis was constituted a colony by Julius Cæsar; that it was the seat of a Roman garrison in the time of Augustus. Some of the coins of later date contain curious representations of the temple.

After the age of Constantine the splendid temples of Baalbek were probably consigned to neglect and decay, unless indeed, as some appearances indicate, they were then consecrated to Christian worship. From the accounts of Oriental writers Baalbek seems to have continued a place of importance down to the time of the Moslem invasion of Syria. They describe it as one of the most splendid of Syrian cities, enriched with stately palaces, adorned with monuments of ancient times, and abounding with trees, fountains, and whatever contributes to luxurious enjoyment. On the advance of the Moslems, it was reported to the emperor Heraclius as protected by a citadel of great strength, and well able to sustain a siege. After the capture of Damascus it was regularly invested by the Moslems, and—containing an overflowing population, amply supplied with provisions and military stores—it made a courageous defence, but at length capitulated. Its importance at that period is attested by the ransom exacted by the conquerors, consisting of 2000 ounces of gold, 4000 ounces of silver, 2000 silk vests, and 1000 swords, together with the arms of the garrison. It afterwards became the mart for the rich pillage of Syria: but its prosperity soon received a fatal blow from the khalif of Damascus, by whom it was sacked and dismantled, and the principal inhabitants put to the sword (A.D. 748). During the Crusades, being incapable of making any resistance, it seems to have quietly submitted to the strongest. In the year 1400 it was pillaged by Timour Beg, in his progress to Damascus, after he had taken Aleppo. Afterwards it fell into the hands of the Metaweli—a barbarous predatory tribe, who were nearly exterminated when Djezzar Pasha permanently subjected the whole district to Turkish supremacy.

The ruins of Heliopolis lie on an eastern branch of the mountain, and are called, by way of eminence, the Castle. The most prominent objects visible from the plain are a lofty portico of six columns, part of the great temple, and the walls and columns of another smaller temple a little below, surrounded by green trees. There is also a singular and unique circular temple, if it may be so called, of which we give a figure. These, with a curious column on the highest point within the walls, form the chief erect portions of the ruins. The ruins at Baalbek in the mass are apparently of three successive eras: first, the gigantic hewn stones, in the face of the platform or basement on which the temple stands, and which appear to be remains of older buildings, perhaps of the more ancient temple which occupied the site. These celebrated blocks, which in fact form the great wonder of the place, vary from 30 to 40 feet in length; but there are three, forming an upper course 20 feet from the ground, which together measure 190 feet, being severally of the enormous dimensions of 63 and 64 feet in length, by 12 in breadth and thickness. 'They are,' says Richter, 'the largest stones I have ever seen, and might of themselves have easily given rise to the popular opinion that Baalbek was built by angels at the command of Solomon. The whole wall, indeed, is composed of immense stones, and its resemblance to the remains of the Temple of Solomon, which are still shown in the foundations of the mosque Es-Sakkara on Mount Moriah, cannot f il to be observed.' In the neighbouring quarries, from which they were cut, one stone, hewn out but not carried away, is of much larger dimensions than any of those which have been mentioned. To the second and third eras belong the Roman temples, which, being of and about the time of Antoninus Pius, present some of the finest specimens of Corinthian architecture in existence, and possess a wonderful grandeur and majesty from their lofty and imposing situation (Addison, ii. 57).

The present Baalbek is a small village to the east of the ruins, in a sad state of wretchedness and decay. It is little more than a heap of rubbish, the houses being built of mud and sundried bricks. The population of 5000, which the place is said to have contained in 1751, is now reduced to barely 2000 persons; the two handsome mosques and fine serai of the Emir,

mentioned by Burckhardt, are no longer distinguishable; and travellers may now inquire in vain for the grapes, the pomegranates, and the fruits which were formerly so abundant.

BA'AL-GUR, or GUR-BAAL. We read in 2 Chron. xxvi. 7, that 'the Lord assisted Uzziah against the Philistines, and against the Arabians that dwelt in Gur-Baal.' It was doubtless some town of Arabia-Petræa.

BA'AL-HAM'ON, a place where Solomon is said to have had a vineyard (Cant. viii. 11). There was a place called Hamon, in the tribe of Asher (Josh. xix. 28), which Ewald thinks was the same as Baal-Hamon. The book of Judith (viii. 3) places a Balamon or Belamon in central Palestine, which suggests another alternative.

BA'AL-HA'ZOR, the place where Absalom kept his flocks, and held his sheep-shearing feast (2 Sam. xiii. 23). It is said to have been 'beside Ephraim,' not in the tribe of that name, but near the city called Ephraim which was in the tribe of Judah, and is mentioned in 2 Chron. xiii. 19, John xi. 54. This Ephraim is placed by Eusebius eight miles from Jerusalem on the road to Jericho; and is supposed by Reland to have been between Bethel and Jericho.

BA'AL-HER'MON (1 Chron. v. 23; Judg. iii. 3). It seems to have been a place in or near Mount Hermon, and not far from Baal-gad, if it was not, as some suppose, the same place.

BA'AL-ME'ON (Num. xxxii. 38; 1 Chron. v. 8; otherwise BETH-MEON, Jer. xlviii. 23, and BETH-BAAL-MEON, Josh. xiii. 17), a town in the tribe of Reuben beyond the Jordan, but which was in the possession of the Moabites in the time of Ezekiel (xxv. 9). At the distance of two miles south-east of Heshbon, Burckhardt found the ruins of a place called Myoun, or (as Dr. Robinson corrects it) Mäïn, which is doubtless the same.

BA'AL-PER'AZIM. This name, meaning 'place of breaches,' was imposed by David upon a place in or near the valley of Rephaim, where he defeated the Philistines (2 Sam. v. 20; comp. 1 Chron. xiv. 11; Isa. xxviii. 21).

BA'AL-SHAL'ISHA (2 Kings iv. 42), a place in the district of Shalisha (1 Sam. ix. 4). Eusebius and Jerome describe it as a city fifteen Roman miles north from Diospolis, near Mount Ephraim.

BA'AL-TA'MAR, a place near Gibeah, in the tribe of Benjamin, where the other tribes fought with the Benjamites (Judg. xx. 33).

BA'AL-ZE'PHON, a town belonging to Egypt, on the border of the Red Sea (Exod. xiv. 2; Num. xxxiii. 7). Nothing is known of its situation.

BA'BEL, TOWER OF. From the account given in Genesis xi. 1-9, it appears that the primitive fathers of mankind having, from the time of the Deluge, wandered without fixed abode, settled at length in the land of Shinar, where they took up a permanent residence. As yet they had remained together without experiencing those vicissitudes and changes in their outward lot which encourage the formation of different modes of speech, and were, therefore, of one language. Arrived however in the land of Shinar, and finding materials suitable for the construction of edifices, they proceeded to make and burn bricks, and using the bitumen, in which parts of the country abound, for cement, they built a city and a tower of great elevation. A divine interference, however, is related to have taken place. In consequence, the language of the builders was confounded, so that they were no longer able to understand each other. They therefore 'left off to build the city,' and were scattered 'abroad upon the face of all the earth.' The narrative adds that the place took its name of Babel (confusion) from this confusion of tongues. That the work was subsequently resumed, and in process of time completed, is known on the best historical vouchers.

The sacred narrative (Gen. xi. 4) assigns as the reason which prompted men to the undertaking, a desire to possess a building so large and high as might be a mark and rallying point in the vast plains where they had settled, in order to prevent their being scattered abroad, and thus the ties of kindred be rudely sundered, individuals be involved in peril, and their numbers be prematurely thinned at a time when population was weak and insufficient. Such an attempt agrees with the circumstances in which the sons of Noah were placed, and is in itself of a commendable nature. But that some ambitious and unworthy motives were blended with these feelings is clearly implied in the sacred record.

After the lapse of so many centuries, and the occurrence in 'the land of Shinar' of so many revolutions, it is not to be expected that the identification of the Tower of Babel with any actual ruin should be easy, or lead to any very certain result. The majority of opinions, however, among the learned, make it the same as the temple of Belus described by Herodotus, which is found in the dilapidated remains of the Birs Nimrud.

FS.

From the Holy Scriptures it appears that when Nebuchadnezzar conquered Jerusalem and levelled most of the city with the ground, 'he brought away the treasures of the temple, and the treasures of the king's house, and put them all into the temple of Bel at Babylon.' The brazen and other vessels which Solomon had caused to be made for the service of Jehovah are said to have been broken up by order of the Assyrian monarch, and formed into the famous gates of brass which so long adorned the superb entrances into the great area of the temple of Belus. The purposes to which this splendid edifice was appropriated varied in some degree with the changes in opinions and manners which successive ages brought. Consecrated at the first, as it probably was, to the immoderate ambition of the monotheistic children of the Deluge, it passed to the Sabian religion, and thus falling one degree from purity of worship, became a temple of the sun and the rest of the host of heaven, till, in the natural progress of corruption, it sank into gross idolatry; and was polluted by the vices which generally accompanied the observances of heathen superstition. In one purpose it undoubtedly proved of service to mankind. The Babylonians were given to the study of astronomy. This ennobling pursuit was one of the peculiar functions of the learned men, denominated by Herodotus, Chaldæans, the priests of Belus; and the temple was crowned by an astronomical observatory, from the elevation of which the starry heavens could be most advantageously studied over plains so open and wide, and in an atmosphere so clear and bright, as those of Babylonia.

The present appearance of the tower as preserved in the Birs Nimrud is deeply impressive, rising suddenly as it does out of a wide desert plain, with its rent, fragmentary, and fire-blasted pile, masses of vitrified matter lying around, and the whole hill itself on which it stands caked and hardened out of the materials with which the temple had been built. A very considerable space round the tower, forming a vast court or area, is covered with ruins, affording abundant vestiges of former buildings; exhibiting uneven heaps of various sizes, covered with masses of broken brick, tiles, and vitrified fragments—all bespeaking some signal overthrow in former days. The towerlike ruin on the summit is a solid mass 28 feet broad, constructed of the most beautiful brick masonry. It is rent from the top nearly halfway to the bottom. It is perforated in ranges of square openings. At its base lie several immense unshapen masses of fine brickwork—some changed to a state of the hardest vitrification, affording evidence of the action of fire which seems to have been the lightning of heaven. The base of the tower, at present, measures 2082 feet in circumference. Hardly half of its former altitude remains. From its summit, the view in the distance presents to the south an arid desert plain; to the west the same trackless waste; towards the north-east marks of buried ruins are visible to a vast distance.

BAB'YLON; the name in Hebrew is Babel, from the confusion of tongues (Gen. xi. 1-9). In Daniel iv. 27 the place is appropriately termed 'Babylon the Great.' This famous city was the metropolis of the province of Babylon and of the Babylonio-Chaldæan empire. It was situated in a wide plain on the Euphrates, which divided it into two nearly equal parts. According to the book of Genesis, its foundations were laid at the same time with those of the tower of Babel. In the revolutions of centuries it underwent many changes, and received successive reparations and additions. Semiramis and Nebuchadnezzar are those to whom the city was indebted for its greatest augmentations and its chief splendour.

Its site has been ascertained to be near Hillah, about forty miles from Bagdad.

According to Herodotus, the walls of Babylon were sixty miles in circumference, built of large bricks cemented together with bitumen, and raised round the city in the form of an exact square; hence they measured fifteen miles along each face. They were 87 feet thick and 350 feet high protected on the outside by a vast ditch lined with the same material, and proportioned in depth and width to the elevation of the walls. The city was entered by twenty-five gates on each side, made of solid brass, and additionally strengthened by 250 towers, so placed that between every two gates were four towers, and four additional ones at the four corners. The whole city contained 676 squares, each two miles and a quarter in circumference. The river ran through the city from north to south; and on each side was a quay of the same thickness as the walls of the city, and 100 stadia in length. In these quays were gates of brass, and from each of them steps descending into the river. A bridge was thrown across the river, of great beauty and admirable contrivance, a furlong in length and 30 feet in breadth. The greatest circumference ascribed by the ancients to the city walls is 480 stadia, the most moderate 360. The smallest computation supposes an area for the city of which we can now scarcely form an idea. Its population however may not have been in proportion to its extent. The place was probably what in these days would be considered an enclosed district rather than a compact city.

One or two additional facts may aid in conveying a full idea of this great and magnificent city. When Cyrus took Babylon by turning the Euphrates into a neighbouring lake, the dwellers in the middle of the place were not for some time aware that their fellow-townsmen who were near the walls had been captured. From the fallen towers of Babylon have arisen not only all the present cities in its vicinity, but others which, like itself, have long since gone down into the dust. Since the days of Alexander four capitals, at least, have been built out of its remains—Seleucia by the Greeks, Ctesiphon by the Parthians, Al Maidan by the Persians, and Kufa by the Caliphs; with towns, villages, and caravansaries without number. The necessary fragments and materials were transported along the rivers and the canals. The new palace built by Nebuchadnezzar was prodigious in size and superb in embellishments. Its outer wall embraced six miles; within that circumference were two other embattled walls, besides a great tower. Three brazen gates led into the grand area, and every gate of consequence throughout the city was of brass.

The palace was splendidly decorated with statues of men and animals, with vessels of gold and silver, and furnished with luxuries of all kinds brought thither from conquests in Egypt, Palestine, and Tyre. Its greatest boast were the hanging gardens. They are attributed to the gallantry of Nebuchadnezzar, who constructed them in compliance with a wish of his queen Amytis to possess elevated groves such as she had enjoyed on the hills around her native Ecbatana. Babylon was all flat; and to accomplish so extravagant a desire an artificial mountain

was reared, 400 feet on each side, while terraces one above another rose to a height that overtopped the walls of the city, that is, above 300 feet in elevation. The ascent from terrace to terrace was made by corresponding flights of steps. The level of each terrace or garden was then formed in the following manner: the top of the piers was first laid over with flat stones, 16 feet in length and 4 feet in width; on these stones were spread beds of matting, then a thick layer of bitumen; after which came two courses of bricks, which were covered with sheets of solid lead. The earth was heaped on this platform; and in order to admit the roots of large trees, prodigious hollow piers were built and filled with mould. From the Euphrates, which flowed close to the foundation, water was drawn up by machinery. The whole had, to those who saw it from a distance, the appearance of woods overhanging mountains. Such was the completion of Nebuchadnezzar's work, when he found himself at rest in his house, and flourished in his palace. The king spoke and said, 'Is not this great Babylon that I have built for the house of the kingdom by the might of my power, and the honour of my majesty' (Dan. iv.). Nowhere could the king have taken so comprehensive a view of the city he had so magnificently constructed and adorned as when walking on the highest terrace of the gardens of his palace.

The remains of this palace are supposed to be found in the vast mound or hill called by the natives Kasr. It is of irregular form, 800 yards in length and 600 yards in breadth. Its appear-

79.

ance is constantly undergoing change from the continual digging which takes place in its inexhaustible quarries for brick of the strongest and finest material. Hence the mass is furrowed into deep ravines, crossing and recrossing each other in every direction. On the north side of the Kasr, amongst the mouldering fragments, and elevated on a sort of ridge, stands the famous solitary tree, called by the Arabs Atheleh; it bears every mark of antiquity in appearance, situation, and tradition. Its trunk was originally enormous; but, worn away by the lapse of ages, it is now but a ruin amid ruins: nevertheless it bears spreading and ever-green branches. This tree is revered by the Arabs as holy, from a tradition current among them, that the Almighty himself preserved it here from the earliest time, to form a refuge for the Caliph Ali, who, fainting with fatigue from the battle of Hillah, found secure repose under its shade.

In digging in the extensive mounds which constitute the ruins of Babylon, an endless succession of curious objects is found from time to time.

Babylon, as the centre of a great kingdom, was the seat of boundless luxury, and its inhabitants were notorious for their addiction to self-indulgence and effeminacy. On the ground of their awful wickedness the Babylonians were threatened with condign punishment, through the mouths of the prophets; and the tyranny with which the rulers of the city exercised their sway was not without a decided effect in bringing on them the terrific consequences of the Divine vengeance. Nor in the whole range of literature is there anything to be found approaching to the sublimity, force, and terror with which Isaiah and others speak on this painful subject (Isa. xiv. 11; xlvii. 1; Jer. li. 39; Dan. v. 1).

Under Nabonnidus, the last king, B.C. 538 or 539, Babylon was taken by Cyrus, after a siege of two years. An insurrection, under Darius Hystaspis (B.C. 500), the object of which was to gain emancipation from Persian bondage, led that prince to punish the Babylonians by throwing down the walls and gates which had been left by Cyrus, and by expelling them from their homes. Xerxes plundered and destroyed the temple of Belus, which Alexander the Great would probably, but for his death, have restored. Under Seleucus Nicator the city began to sink speedily, after that monarch built Seleucia on the Tigris, and made it his place of abode. In the time of Strabo and Diodorus Siculus the place lay in ruins. Jerome, in the fourth century of the Christian era, learnt that the site of Babylon had been converted into a park or hunting-ground for the recreation of the Persian monarchs, and that, in order to preserve the game, the walls had been from time to time repaired.

More thorough destruction than that which has overtaken Babylon cannot well be conceived. Rich was unable to discover any traces of its vast walls, and even its site has been a subject of dispute. 'On its ruins,' says he, 'there is not a single tree growing, except the old one,' which only serves to make the desolation more apparent. Ruins like those of Babylon, composed of rubbish impregnated with nitre, cannot be cultivated. The ruins of Babylon and its vicinity consist in general of mounds of earth formed by the decomposition of buildings, channelled and furrowed by the weather, and having the surface strewed with pieces of brick, bitumen, and pottery.

Neither the ancient nor the modern authorities are in exact agreement respecting particular places and localities, and any attempt to fix them now can be nothing more than an approach to the reality.

BABYLO'NIA (so called from the name of its chief city, termed also Chaldæa, from those who at a later period inhabited it), a province of Middle Asia, bordered on the north by Mesopotamia, on the east by the Tigris, on the south by the Persian Gulf, and on the west by the Arabian Desert. On the north it begins at the point where the Euphrates and Tigris approach each other, and extends to their common outlet in the Persian Gulf, pretty nearly comprising the country now designated Irak Arabi. The climate is temperate and salubrious. The country in ancient times was very prolific, especially in corn and palms. Timber-trees it did not produce. Many parts had springs of naphtha. As rain is infrequent, even in the winter months, the country owes its fruitfulness to the annual overflow of the Euphrates and the Tigris, whose waters are conveyed over the land by means of canals.

The alluvial plains of Babylonia, Chaldæa, and Susiana, including all the river, lake, and newer marine deposits at the head of the Persian Gulf, occupy an extent of about 32,400 square geographic miles. The rivers are the Euphrates and its tributaries, the Tigris and its tributaries, the Kerah, the Karun and its tributaries, the Jerahi, and the Idiyan; constituting, altogether, a vast hydrographical basin of 189,200 geographic square miles; containing, within itself, a central deposit of 32,400 miles of alluvium, almost entirely brought down by the waters of the various rivers, and which have been accumulating from periods long antecedent to all historical records. The modern accumulation of soil in Babylonia from annual inundations is still very great. Several canals convey water at certain seasons of the year from one river and part of the country to another. In general, the alluvium that is brought down by canals and rivulets, and deposited at their mouths, is a fine clay. The great extent of the plain of Babylonia is everywhere altered by artificial works. There is still some cultivation and some irrigation. Flocks pasture in meadows of coarse grasses; the Arabs' dusky encampments are met with here and there; but, except on the banks of the Euphrates, there are few remains of the date-groves, the vineyards, and the gardens which adorned the same land in the days of Artaxerxes; and still less of the population and labour which must have made a garden of such soil in the time of Nebuchadnezzar. The vegetation of these tracts is characterized by the usual saline plants, the river banks being fringed by shrubberies of tamarisk and acacia, and occasional groves of a poplar which has been mistaken for a willow.

The Euphrates is still a majestic stream, but wanders through a dreary solitude. Its banks are hoary with reeds, and the grey osier-willows are yet there on which the captives of Israel hung up their harps, and, while Jerusalem was not, refused to be comforted. According to Rennel its breadth at Babylon is about 491 English feet. Rich ascertained its depth to be 2½ fathoms, and that the current runs gently at the medium rate of about two knots an hour. The Euphrates is far less rapid than the Tigris, and rises at an earlier period. When at its height—from the latter end of April to the latter end of June—it overflows the surrounding country. The ruins of Babylon are then so inundated as to render many parts of them inaccessible. The course of the river through the site of Babylon is north and south. During the three great empires of the East, no tract of the whole appears to have been so reputed for fertility and riches as the district of Babylonia, which arose in the main from the proper management of the mighty river which flowed through it. But the abundance of the country has vanished as clean away as if 'the besom of desolation' had swept it from north to south; the whole land, from the outskirts of Bagdad to the farthest reach of sight, lying a melancholy waste.

In order to defend the country against hostile attacks from its neighbours, northward from Babylon, between the two rivers, a wall was built, which is known under the name of the Median Wall. The Babylonians were famous for the manufacture of cloth and carpets: they also excelled in making perfumes, in carving in wood, and in working in precious stones. They were a commercial as well as a manufacturing people, and carried on a very extensive trade alike by land and by sea. Babylon was indeed a commercial depôt between the Eastern and the Western worlds (Ezek. xvii. 4; Isa. xliii. 14). Thus favoured by nature and aided by art, Babylonia became the first abode of social order and the cradle of civilization.

The original inhabitants were without doubt of the Shemitic family; and their language belonged to the class of tongues spoken by that race, particularly to the Aramaic branch, and was indeed a dialect similar to that which is now called Chaldee.

From the account which is found in Gen. x. 8, *Nimrod*, the son of Cush, appears to have founded the kingdom of Babylon, and to have been its first sovereign. In the 14th chap. of the same book, *Amraphel* is cursorily mentioned as king of Shinar. In the reign of Hezekiah (A.C. 713)— 2 Kings xx. 12—'Berodach-baladan, the son of Baladan,' was 'king of Babylon,' and 'sent letters and a present unto Hezekiah, for he had heard that Hezekiah had been sick.' About a hundred years later, Jeremiah and Habakkuk speak of the invasion of the Babylonians under the name of the Chaldæans; and now *Nebuchadnezzar* appears in the historical books (2 Kings xxiv. 1, *sq.*; Jer. xxxvi. 9, 27) as head of the all-subduing empire of Babylon. *Evilmerodach* (2 Kings xxv. 27; Jer. lii. 31), son of the preceding, is also mentioned as 'king of Babylon;' and with *Belshazzar* (Dan. v. 1, 30) the line of the Chaldæan kings was closed: he perished in the conquest of Babylon by the Medo-Persians (Dan. v. 31), 'and Darius, the Median, took the kingdom.'

The domination of the Chaldæans in Babylon has given historians some trouble to explain. The Chaldæans appear to have originally been a nomadic tribe in the mountains of Armenia, numbers of whom are thought to have settled in Babylon as subjects, where, having been civilized and grown powerful, they seized the supreme power and founded a Chaldæo-Babylonian empire.

There can be little doubt that the Chaldæans were a distinct nation. In connection with Babylonia they are to be regarded as a conquering nation as well as a learned people: they introduced a correct method of reckoning time, and began their reign with Nabonassar, B.C. 747. The brilliant period of the Chaldæo-Babylonian empire extended to B.C. 538, when the great city, in accordance with the prophecy of Daniel, was sacked and destroyed. Babylonia, during this period, was 'the land of the Chaldæans,' the same as that into which the children of Judah were carried away captive (Jer. xxiv. 5); which contained Babylon (Jer. l. 1; Ezek. xii. 13); was the seat of the king of Babylon (Jer. xxv. 12), and contained the house of the god of Nebuchadnezzar (Dan. i. 1, 2).

BA'CA and BECAIM occur, the first in Ps. lxxxiv. 6, 'Who passing through the valley of Baca make it a well; the rain also filleth the pools;' the second in 2 Sam. v. 23, 24, and in 1 Chron. xiv. 14, 15, 'And let it be, when thou hearest the sound of a going in the tops of the mulberry trees, that thou shalt bestir thyself.' Neither the *mulberry* nor the *pear-tree*, considered by some to be the baca of the Scriptures, satisfies translators and commentators, because they do not possess any characters particularly suitable to the above passages.

It is evident that the tree alluded to, whatever it is, must be common in Palestine, must grow in the neighbourhood of water, have its leaves easily moved, and have a name in some of the cognate languages similar to the Hebrew Baca. The only one with which we are acquainted answering to these conditions is that called *bak* by the Arabs, or rather *shajrat al-bak*—that is, the *fly* or *gnat* tree.

As it appears to us sufficiently clear that the bak-tree is a kind of poplar, and as the Arabic 'bak' is very similar to the Hebrew 'Baca,' so it is probable that one of the kinds of poplar may be intended in the above passages of Scripture. And it must be noted that the poplar is as appropriate as any tree can be for the elucidation of the passages in which baca occurs. For the poplar is well known to delight in moist situations, and Bishop Horne, in his *Comm.* on Psalm lxxxiv., has inferred that in the valley of Baca the Israelites, on their way to Jerusalem, were refreshed by plenty of water. It is not less appropriate in the passages in 2 Samuel and 1 Chronicles, as no tree is more remarkable than the poplar for the ease with which its leaves are rustled by the slightest movement of the air; an effect which might be caused in a still night even by the movement of a body of men on the ground, when attacked in flank or when unprepared. That poplars are common in Palestine may be proved from Kitto's *Palestine*, i. 114: 'Of poplars we only know, with certainty, that the black poplar, the aspen, and the Lombardy poplar grow in Palestine. The aspen, whose long leaf-stalks cause the leaves to tremble with every breath of wind, unites with the willow and the oak to overshadow the watercourses of the Lower Lebanon, and, with the oleander and the acacia, to adorn the ravines of southern Palestine: we do not know that the Lombardy poplar has been noticed but by Lord Lindsay, who describes it as growing with the walnut-tree and weeping-willow under the deep torrents of the Upper Lebanon.'

BADGER. This is unquestionably a wrong interpretation of the word *tachash*, since the badger is not found in Southern Asia, and has not as yet been noticed out of Europe. The word occurs in the plural form in Exod. xxv. 5; xxvi. 14; xxxv. 7, 23; xxxvi. 19; xxxix. 34; Num. iv. 6, 8, 10, 11, 12, 14, 25; and Ezek. xvi. 10; and in connection with *oroth*, skins, is used to

denote the covering of the Tabernacle. Negro-
land and Central and Eastern Africa contain a
number of ruminating animals of the great antelope family; which are known to the natives
under various names, such as pacasse, empacasse,
thacasse, facasse, and tachaitze, all more or less
varieties of the word tachash: they are of considerable size; often of slaty and purple grey
colours, and might be termed stag-goats and ox-
goats. Of these one or more occur in the hunt-
ing-scenes on Egyptian monuments, and therefore we may conclude that the skins were accessible in abundance, and may have been dressed
with the hair on for coverings of baggage, and
for boots, such as we see worn by the human
figures in the same processions. Thus we have
the greater number of the conditions of the question sufficiently realized to enable us to draw the
inference that tachash refers to a ruminant of
the Aigocerine or Damaline groups, most likely
of an iron-grey or slaty-coloured species.

BAG, a purse or pouch (Deut. xxv. 13; Job
xiv. 17; 1 Sam. xvii. 40; Luke xii. 33). The
money deposited in the treasuries of Eastern
princes, or intended for large payments, or to be
sent to a government as taxes or tribute, is collected in long narrow bags or purses, each containing a certain amount of money, and sealed
with the official seal. As the money is counted
for this purpose, and sealed with great care by
officers properly appointed, the bag, or purse,
passes current, as long as the seal remains unbroken, for the amount marked thereon. In the
receipt and payment of large sums, this is a great
and important convenience in countries where
the management of large transactions by paper
is unknown, or where a currency is chiefly or
wholly of silver: it saves the great trouble of
counting or weighing loose money. This usage
is so well established, that, at this day, in the
Levant, 'a purse' is the very name for a certain
amount of money (now five pounds sterling), and
all large payments are stated in 'purses.' The
antiquity of this custom is attested by the monu-

80.

ments of Egypt, in which the ambassadors of
distant nations are represented as bringing their
tributes in sealed bags of money to Thothmes
III.: and we see the same bags deposited intact
in the royal treasury. When coined money was
not used, the seal must have been considered a
voucher not only for the amount, but for the
purity of the metal. The money collected in
the Temple, in the time of Joash, seems to have
been made up into bags of equal value after this
fashion; which were probably delivered, sealed,
to those who paid the workmen (2 Kings xii. 10;
comp. also 2 Kings v. 23; Tobit ix. 5; xi. 16).

BAHU'RIM, a place not far from Jerusalem,
beyond the Mount of Olives, on the road to the

Jordan, where Shimei cursed and threw stones at
David (2 Sam. xvi. 5).

BA'LAAM is supposed by some to mean *lord
of the people*; but by others *destruction of the
people*—an allusion to his supposed supernatural
powers. The first mention of this remarkable
person is in Numbers xxii. 5, where we are informed that Balak 'sent messengers unto Balaam
the son of Beor to Pethor, which is by the river
of the land of the children of his people. Of
the numerous paradoxes which we find in 'this
strange mixture of a man,' as Bishop Newton
terms him, not the least striking is that with the
practice of an art expressly forbidden to the
Israelites (Deut. xviii. 10), he united the knowledge and worship of Jehovah, and was in the
habit of receiving intimations of his will (Num.
xxii. 8). The inquiry naturally arises, by what
means did he become acquainted with the true
religion? Dr. Hengstenberg suggests that he
was led to renounce idolatry by the reports that
reached him of the miracles attending the
Exodus; and that having experienced the deceptive nature of the soothsaying art, he hoped by
becoming a worshipper of the God of the Hebrews, to acquire fresh power over nature, and a
clearer insight into futurity. Yet the sacred
narrative gives us no reason to suppose that he
had any previous knowledge of the Israelites.
In Num. xxii. 11, he merely repeats Balak's
message, 'Behold there is a people come out of
Egypt,' &c., without intimating that he had
heard of the miracles wrought on their behalf.
The allusion in Num. xxiii. 22 might be
prompted by the Divine afflatus which he then
felt. And had he been actuated, in the first
instance, by motives of personal aggrandizement,
it seems hardly probable that he would have
been favoured with those divine communications
with which his language in Num. xxii. 8 implies a
familiarity. Since, in the case of Simon Magus,
the offer to 'purchase the gift of God with money'
(Acts viii. 20) called forth an immediate and
awful rebuke from the Apostles, would not
Balaam's attempt to obtain a similar gift with a
direct view to personal emolument and fame have
met with a similar repulse? In the absence of
more copious and precise information, may we
not reasonably conjecture that Jacob's residence
for twenty years in Mesopotamia contributed to
maintain some just ideas of religion, though mingled with much superstition? To this source
and the existing remains of Patriarchal religion,
Balaam was probably indebted for that truth
which he unhappily 'held in unrighteousness'
(Rom. i. 18).

On the narrative contained in Numbers xxii.
22-35 a difference of opinion has long existed,
even among those who fully admit its authenticity. The advocates for a literal interpretation
urge, that in a historical work and a narrative
bearing the same character, it would be unnatural
to regard any of the occurrences as taking place
in vision, unless expressly so stated;—that it
would be difficult to determine where the vision
begins, and where it ends;—that Jehovah's
'opening the mouth of the ass' (Num. xxii. 28)
must have been an external act; and, finally, that
Peter's language is decidedly in favour of the
literal sense:—'The dumb ass, speaking with a
man's voice, reproved the madness of the Pro-

phet' (2 Peter ii. 16). Those who conceive that the speaking of the ass and the appearance of the Angel occurred in vision to Balaam insist upon the fact that dreams and visions were the ordinary methods by which God made himself known to the Prophets (Num. xii. 6); they remark that Balaam, in the introduction to his third and fourth prophecies (xxiv. 3, 4, 15), speaks of himself as 'the man who had his eyes shut' (v. Lam. iii. 8), and who, on falling down in prophetic exstasy, had his eyes opened;—that he expressed no surprise on hearing the ass speak; and that neither his servants nor the Moabitish princes who accompanied him appear to have been cognizant of any supernatural appearance.

BAL'ADAN. [Merodach-Baladan.]

BA'LAK (emptier, spoiler), son of Zippor, and king of the Moabites (Num. xxii. 2, 4), who was so terrified at the approach of the victorious army of the Israelites, who in their passage through the desert had encamped near the confines of his territory, that he applied to Balaam, who was then reputed to possess great influence with the higher spirits, to curse them. From Judg. xiv. 25, it is clear that Balak was so certain of the fulfilment of Balaam's blessing, 'blessed is he that blesseth thee, and cursed is he that curseth thee' (Num. xxiv. 9), that he never afterwards made the least military attempt to oppose the Israelites (comp. Mic. vi. 5; Rev. ii. 14).

BALANCE. [Weighing.]

BALDNESS may be artificial or natural. Artificial baldness, caused by cutting or shaving off the hair of the head, a custom among all the ancient and Eastern nations, in token of mourning for the death of a near relative (Jer. xvi. 6; Amos viii. 10; Micah i. 16), Moses forbade to the Israelites (Deut. xiv. 1), probably for the very reason of its being a heathen custom; for a leading object of his policy was to remove the Jews as far as possible from the ways and customs of the surrounding nations. Natural baldness was always treated among the Israelites with contempt (Lev. xiii. 40, &c.), and a bald man was not unfrequently exposed to the ridicule of the mob (2 Kings ii. 23; Isa. iii. 17)· perhaps from the suspicion of being under some leprous taint. The public prejudice thus entertained against a bald-headed man was perhaps the main reason why he was declared unfit for the priestly office (Lev. xxi. 20).

BALM. This substance is mentioned in Gen. xxxviii. 25; xliii. 11; Jer. viii. 22; xli. 8; xlvi. 11; Ezek. xxvii. 17, as a medicinal aromatic. It is shown in the following article that this 'balm' could not have been the product of the so called balsam-tree, or balm of Gilead tree; and the product actually denoted by the word is in fact unknown.

BALSAM-TREE. The balsam-tree was one of the most celebrated and highly esteemed among the ancients. It is supposed to be referred to under the Hebrew names Basam and Baal-shemen, translated 'spices,' in Exod. xxxv. 28; 1 Kings x. 10; Sol. Song, v. 1, 13. It would appear, however, from ancient authors that the plant yielding balsam was never very common in Palestine—in fact, that it was confined to one locality. where it was found only as a plant in cultivation, though it may have been, and pro-

bably was, introduced at a very early period. That it has long disappeared from thence is evident from the testimony of all travellers in Palestine. That it was a southern plant we may believe from its being cultivated in the warm southern valley of Jericho, and that it was introduced into that locality we have the testimony of Josephus, who says that it was brought thither by the Queen of Sheba.

The balsam-tree, or balm of Gilead tree, as it is also very generally called, is not a native of that region, nor indeed does it appear ever to have been cultivated there. The true balsam, we have seen, was cultivated near Jericho, and at a later age in Egypt. From that country it has been traced to Arabia.

The balsam-tree, having been described by various travellers, is now pretty well known. It forms a middle-sized tree, with spreading branches and a smooth ash-coloured bark, but which is no doubt rough in the older parts. The ultimate branches are short, and thorn-like, with small very short abortive branchlets, bearing at their extremities the leaves and flowers. The fruit is pointed, fleshy, with a viscid pulp.

This species is now considered to be identical with the Amyris opobalsamum of Forskal, found by him in Arabia, in the neighbourhood of the caravanserai of Oude, not far from Has, and the wounded bark of which yields opobalsamum, or balsam of Mecca. It is as highly esteemed by all Orientals in the present day as it was by the civilized nations of antiquity. Another species was discovered by Forskal, and called by him Amyris Kafal. It is a tree with reddish-coloured wood, and with branches rather spinous. The younger leaflets are described as being villous and acute, the old ones smooth, often obtuse; the berry compressed, with an elevated ridge on each side, the apex forming a black prominent point. The wood he describes as forming an article

81.

of considerable commerce, especially to Egypt, where water-vessels are impregnated with its smoke. It is probably the twigs of this species which are taken to India, and there sold under the name of aod-i balessan; that is, the wood of the balsam-tree. Carpobalsamum was probably only the fruit of one of these species. Opobalsamum, or juice of the balsam, is generally described as the finest kind, of a greenish colour, and found in the kernel of the fruit. Carpobalsamum is said to have been made by the expression of the fruit when in maturity, and xylobalsamum, by the expression or decoction of the small new twigs, which are of a reddish colour. But the ancients probably employed both the fruit and the wood for macerating in oil, which would extract the odour. The greatest quantity of balsam, and the best in quality, must in all times have been produced by an incision into the bark when the juice is in its strongest circulation, in July, August, and the beginning of September. It is then received into a small earthen bottle, and every day's produce is poured into a larger, which is kept closely corked. The whole quantity collected is but small. When Sultan Selim conquered Egypt and Arabia in 1516, three pounds were ordered to be sent yearly as a tribute to Constantinople.

BANQUETS. Festive meetings among the Jews were held only towards the close of the day, as it was not till business was over that the Jews freely indulged in the pleasures of the table; and although in the days of Christ these meals were, after the Roman fashion, called *suppers*, they corresponded exactly to the dinners of modern times, the hour fixed for them varying from five to six o'clock P.M., or sometimes later.

On occasions of ceremony the company were invited a considerable time previous to the celebration of the feast; and on the day and at the hour appointed, an express by one or more servants, according to the number and distance of the expected guests, was despatched to announce that the preparations were completed, and that their presence was looked for immediately (Matt. xxii. 8; Luke xiv. 17). This custom obtains in the East at the present day; and the second invitation, which is sent to none but such as have been already invited, and have declared their acceptance, is always verbal, and is delivered by the messenger in his master's name, and frequently in the very language of Scripture.

At the small entrance door a servant was stationed to receive the tablets or cards of those who were expected; and as curiosity usually collected a crowd of troublesome spectators, anxious to press forward into the scene of gaiety, the gate was opened only so far as was necessary for the admission of a single person at a time, who, on presenting his invitation ticket, was conducted through a long and narrow passage into the receiving-room; and then, after the whole company were assembled, the master of the house shut the door with his own hands—a signal for the servant to allow himself to be prevailed on neither by noise nor by importunities, however loud and long continued, to admit the bystanders. To this custom there is a manifest reference in Luke xiii. 24, and Matt. xxv. 10.

One of the first marks of courtesy shown to the guests, after saluting the host, was the refreshment of water and fragrant oil or perfumes; and hence we find our Lord complaining of Simon's omission of these customary civilities (Luke vii. 44; see also Mark vii. 4) [ANOINTING]. But a far higher, though necessarily less frequent attention paid to their friends by the great, was the custom of furnishing each of the company with a magnificent habit of a light and showy colour, and richly embroidered, to be worn during the festivity (Eccles. ix. 8; Rev. iii. 4, 5). The loose and flowing style of this gorgeous mantle made it equally suitable for all; and it is almost incredible what a variety of such sumptuous garments the wardrobes of some great men could supply to equip a numerous party. In a large company, even of respectable persons, some might appear in a plainer and humbler garb than accorded with the taste of the entertainer; and where this arose from necessity or limited means, it would have been harsh and unreasonable in the extreme to attach blame, or to command the instant and ignominious expulsion of the guest from the banquet-room. But where a well-appointed and sumptuous wardrobe was opened for the use of every guest,—to refuse the gay and splendid costume which the munificence of the host provided, and to persist in appearing in one's own habiliments, implied a contempt both for the master of the house and his entertainment, which could not fail to provoke resentment—and our Lord therefore spoke in accordance with a well-known custom of his country, when, in the parable of the marriage of the king's son, he describes the stern displeasure of the king on discovering one of the guests without a wedding-garment, and his instant command to thrust him out (Matt. xxii. 11). At private banquets the master of the house of course presided, and did the honours of the occasion; but in large and mixed companies it was anciently customary to elect a governor of the feast (John ii. 8; see also Ecclus. xxxii. 1), who should not merely perform the office of chairman, in preserving order and decorum, but take upon himself the general management of the festivities. As this office was considered a post of great responsibility and delicacy, as well as honour, the choice which among the Greeks and Romans was left to the decision of dice, was more wisely made by the Jews to fall upon him who was known to be possessed of the requisite qualities—a ready wit and convivial turn, and at the same time firmness of character and habits of temperance. The guests were scrupulously arranged according to their respective ranks. This was done either by the host or governor, who, in the case of a family, placed them according to seniority (Gen. xliii. 33), and in the case of others, assigned the most honourable a place near his own person; or it was done by the party themselves, on their successive arrivals, and after surveying the company, taking up the position which it appeared fittest for each according to their respective claims to occupy. It might be expected that among the Orientals, by whom the laws of etiquette in these matters are strictly observed, many absurd and ludicrous contests for precedence must take place, from the arrogance of some and the determined perseverance of others to wedge themselves into the seat they deem themselves entitled to. Accordingly Morier informs us, that, in Persia, 'it is easy to observe by the countenances of those present, when any one has taken a higher place than he ought.' 'On one occasion,' he adds, 'when an assembly was nearly full, the governor of Kashan, a man of humble mien, came in, and had seated himself at the lowest place, when the host, after having testified his particular attentions to him by numerous expressions of welcome, pointed with his hand to an upper seat, which he desired him to take' (*Second Journey*). As a counterpart to this, Dr. Clarke states that ' at a wedding feast he attended in the house of a rich merchant at St. Jean d'Acre, two persons who had seated themselves at the top were noticed by the master of ceremonies, and obliged to move lower down.' The knowledge of these peculiarities serves to illustrate several passages of Scripture (Prov. xxv. 6, 7; Matt. xxiii. 6; and especially Luke xiv. 7, where we find Jesus making the unseemly ambition of the Pharisees the subject of severe and merited animadversion).

It would be difficult within a short compass to describe the form and arrangements of the table, as the entertainments spoken of in Scripture were not all conducted in a uniform style. In ancient Egypt, as in Persia, the tables were ranged along the sides of the room, and the guests were placed with their faces towards the walls. Persons of high official station were honoured with a table apart for themselves at the head of the room; and in these particulars every reader of the Bible will trace an exact correspondence to the arrangements of Joseph's entertainment to his brethren. According to Lightfoot, the tables of the Jews were either wholly uncovered, or two-thirds were spread with a cloth, the remaining third was left bare for the dishes and vegetables. In the days of our Lord the prevailing form was the triclinium, the mode of reclining at which is described elsewhere [ACCUBATION]. This effeminate practice was not introduced until near the close of the Old Testament history, for the ancient Israelites sat round a low table, crosslegged, like the Orientals of the present day.

The convenience of knives and forks being unknown in the East, or, where known, being a modern innovation, the hand is the only instrument used in conveying food to the mouth, and the common practice, their food being chiefly prepared in a liquid form, is to dip their thin wafer-like bread into the dish, and folding it between their thumb and two fingers, enclose a portion of the contents. It is not uncommon to see several hands plunged into one dish at the same time. But where the party is numerous, the two persons near or opposite are commonly joined in one dish; and accordingly, at the last Passover, Judas, being close to his master, was pointed out as the traitor by being designated as the person ' dipping his hand with Jesus in the dish.' The Apostle John, whose advantageous situation enabled him to hear the minutest parts of the conversation, has recorded the fact of our Lord, in reply to the question ' Who is it?' answering it by ' giving a sop to Judas when he had dipped' (John xiii. 26); and this leads us to mention it as not the least among the peculiarities of Oriental manners, that a host often dips his hand into a dish, and lifting a handful of what he considers a dainty, offers the sop to one of his friends. In earlier ages, a double or a more liberal portion, or a choice piece of cookery, was the form in which a landlord showed his respect for the individual he delighted to honour (Gen. xliii. 34; 1 Sam. i. 4; ix. 23; Prov. xxxi. 15).

In the course of the entertainment servants are frequently employed in sprinkling the head and person of the guests with odoriferous perfumes, which, probably to counteract the effects of too copious perspiration, they use in great profusion, and the fragrance of which, though generally too strong for Europeans, is deemed an agreeable refreshment (see Ps. xlv. 8; xxiii. 5; cxxxiii. 2).

The various items of which an Oriental entertainment consists, bread, flesh, fish, fowls, melted butter, honey, and fruits, are in many places set on the table at once, in defiance of all taste. They are brought in upor trays—one, containing several dishes, being assigned to a group of two or at most three persons, and the number and quality of the dishes being regulated according to the rank and consideration of the party seated before it. In ordinary cases four or five dishes constitute the portion allotted to a guest; but if he be a person of consequence, or one to whom the host is desirous of showing more than ordinary marks of attention, other viands are successively brought in, until, if every vacant corner of the tray is occupied, the bowls are piled one above another. The object of this rude but liberal hospitality is, not that the individual thus honoured is expected to surfeit himself by an excess of indulgence in order to testify his sense of the entertainer's kindness, but that he may enjoy the means of gratifying his palate with greater variety; and hence we read of Joseph's displaying his partiality for Benjamin by making his ' mess five times so much as any of theirs' (Gen. xliii. 34). The shoulder of a lamb, roasted, and plentifully besmeared with butter and milk, is regarded as a great delicacy still, as it was also in the days of Samuel. But according to the favourite cookery of the Orientals, their animal food is for the most part cut into small pieces, stewed, or prepared in a liquid state, such as seems to have been the 'broth' presented by Gideon to the angel (Judg. vi. 19). The made-up dishes are 'savoury meat,' being highly seasoned, and bring to remembrance the marrow and fatness which were esteemed as the most choice morsels in ancient times. As to drink, when particular attention was intended to be shown to a guest, his cup was filled with wine till it ran over (Ps. xxiii. 5), and it is said that the ancient Persians began their feasts with wine, whence it was called 'a banquet of wine' (Esther v. 6).

The hands, for occasionally both were required, besmeared with grease during the process of eating, were anciently cleaned by rubbing them with the soft part of the bread, the crumbs of which, being allowed to fall, became the portion of dogs (Matt. xv. 27; Luke xvi. 21). But the most common way now at the conclusion of a feast is for a servant to go round to each guest with water to wash, a service which is performed by the menial pouring a stream over their hands, which is received into a strainer at the bottom of the basin. This humble office Elisha performed to his master (2 Kings iii. 11).

People of rank and opulence in the East frequently give public entertainments to the poor. The rich man in the parable, whose guests disappointed him, despatched his servants on the instant to invite those that might be found sitting by the hedges and the highways—a measure which, in the circumstances, was absolutely necessary, as the heat of the climate would spoil the meats long before they could be consumed by the members of his own household. But many of the great, from benevolence or ostentation, are in the habit of proclaiming set days for giving feasts to the poor; and then, at the time appointed, may be seen crowds of the blind, the halt, and the mairied bending their steps to the scene of entertainment. This species of charity claims a venerable antiquity. Our Lord recommended his wealthy hearers to practise it rather than spend their fortunes, as they did, on luxurious living (Luke xiv. 12); and as such invitations to the poor are of necessity given by public proclamation, and female messengers are employed to publish them, it is probably to the same venerable practice that Solomon alludes in Prov. ix. 3.

BAPTISM. A conviction of the holiness of God excites in man the notion that he cannot possibly come into any amicable relation with him before he is cleansed of sin, which separates him from God. This sentiment found a very widely extended symbolic expression in the lustrations which formed an essential part of the ceremonial creeds of the ancient nations. In the language of the prophets, cleansing with water is used as an emblem of the purification of the heart, which in the Messianic age is to glorify the soul in her innermost recesses, and to embrace the whole of the theocratic nat'on (Ezek. xxxvi. 25, sq.; Zech. xiii. 1). Such declarations gave rise to or nourished the expectation that the advent of the Messiah would manifest itself by a preparatory lustration, by which Elijah or some other great prophet would pave the way for him. This supposition lies evidently at the bottom of the questions which the Jews put to John the Baptist (John i. 25: comp. Matt. and Luke, iii. 7), whether he was the Messiah, or Elijah, or some other prophet? and if not, why he undertook to baptize? Thus we can completely clear up the historical derivation of the rite, as used by John and Christ, from the general and natural symbol of baptism, from the Jewish custom in particular, and from the expectation of a Messianic consecration. Dans, Ziegler, and others have, nevertheless, supposed it to be derived from the Jewish ceremonial of baptizing *proselytes*; and Wetstein has traced that rite up to a date earlier than Christianity. But this opinion is not at all tenable: for, as an act which strictly gives *validity* to the admission of a proselyte, and is no mere *accompaniment* to his admission, baptism certainly is not alluded to in the New Testament; while, as to the passages quoted in proof from the classical (profane) writers of that period, they are all open to the most fundamental objections. Nor is the utter silence of Josephus and Philo on the subject, notwithstanding their various opportunities of touching on it, a less weighty argument against this view. It is true that mention is made in the Talmud of that regulation as already existing in the first century A.D.; but such statements belong only to the traditions of the Gemara, and require careful investigation before they can serve as proper authority. This Jewish rite was probably originally only a purifying ceremony; and it was raised to the character of an initiating and indispensable rite coordinate with that of sacrifice and circumcision,

only *after* the destruction of the Temple, when sacrifices had ceased, and the circumcision of proselytes had, by reason of public edicts, become more and more impracticable.

BAPTISM OF JOHN. - It was the principal object of John the Baptist to combat the prevailing opinion, that the performance of external ceremonies was sufficient to secure participation in the kingdom of God and his promises; he required repentance, therefore, as a preparation for the approaching kingdom of the Messiah. That he may possibly have baptized *heathens* also, seems to follow from his censuring the Pharisees for confiding in their descent from Abraham, while they had no share in his spirit: yet it should not be overlooked that this remark was drawn from him by the course of the argument (Matt. iii. 8, 9; Luke iii. 7, 8). We must, on the whole, assume that John considered the existing Judaism as a stepping-stone by which the Gentiles were to arrive at the kingdom of God in its Messianic form. The general point of view from which John contemplated the Messiah and his kingdom was that of the Old Testament, though closely bordering on Christianity. He regards, it is true, an alteration in the mind and spirit as an indispensable condition for partaking in the kingdom of the Messiah; still he looked for its establishment by means of conflict and external force, with which the Messiah was to be endowed; and he expected in him a Judge and Avenger, who was to set up outward and visible distinctions. It is, therefore, by no means a matter of indifference whether baptism be administered in the name of that Christ who floated before the mind of John, or of the suffering and glorified One, such as the apostles knew him; and whether it was considered a preparation for a political, or a consecration into a spiritual theocracy. John was so far from this latter view, so far from contemplating a purely spiritual development of the kingdom of God, that he even began subsequently to entertain doubts concerning Christ (Matt. xi. 2). John's baptism had not the character of an immediate, but merely of a preparatory consecration for the glorified theocracy (John i. 31). The Apostles, therefore, found it necessary to re-baptize the disciples of John, who had still adhered to the notions of their master on that head (Acts xix.). To this apostolic judgment Tertullian appeals, and in his opinion coincide the most eminent teachers of the ancient church, both of the East and the West.

THE BAPTISM OF JESUS BY JOHN (Matt. iii. 13, *sq.*; Mark i. 9, *sq.*; Luke iii. 21, *sq.*; comp. John i. 19, *sq.*; the latter passage refers to a time *after* the baptism, and describes, ver. 32, the incidental facts attending it).—The baptism of Jesus, as the first act of his public career, is one of the most important events recorded in evangelical history: great difficulty is also involved in reconciling the various accounts given by the Evangelists of that transaction, and the several points connected with it. To question the fact itself, not even the *negative criticism* of Dr. Strauss has dared. This is, however, all that has been conceded by that criticism, viz., the mere and bare fact 'that Christ was baptized by John,' while all the circumstances of the event are placed in the region of mythology or fiction.

Critical inquiry suggests the following questions :—

1. In what relation did Jesus stand to John before the baptism ?

2. What object did Jesus intend to obtain by that baptism ?

3. In what sense are we to take the miraculous incidents attending that act ?

With regard to the first point, we might be apt to infer, from Luke and Matthew, that there had been an acquaintance between Christ and John even prior to the baptism ; and that hence John declines (Matt. iii. 14) to baptize Jesus, arguing that he needed to be baptized by him. This, however, seems to be at variance with John i. 31, 33. Lücke (*Comment.* i. p. 416, *sq.* 3rd edit.) takes the words ' I knew him not' in their strict and exclusive sense. John, he says, could not have spoken in this manner if he had at all known Jesus; and had he known him, he could not, as a prophet, have failed to discover, even at an earlier period, the but too evident ' glory' of the Messiah. In fact, the narrative of the first three Gospels presupposes the same, since, as the herald of the Messiah, he could give that refusal (Matt. iii. 14) to the Messiah alone.

With regard to the second point at issue, *as to the object of Christ in undergoing baptism,* we find, in the first instance, that he ranked this action among those of his Messianic calling. This object is still more defined by John the Baptist (John i. 31), which Lücke interprets in the following words : ' Only by entering into that community which was to be introductory to the Messianic, by attaching himself to the Baptist like any other man, was it possible for Christ to reveal himself to the Baptist, and through him to others.' Christ, with his never-failing reliance on God, never for a moment could doubt of his own mission, or of the right period when his character was to be made manifest by God ; but John needed to receive that assurance, in order to be the herald of the Messiah who was actually come. For all others whom John baptized, either before or after Christ, this act was a mere preparatory consecration to the kingdom of the Messiah; while for Jesus it was a direct and immediate consecration, by means of which he manifested the commencem_nt of his career as the founder of the new theocracy, which began at the very moment of his baptism, the initiatory character of which constituted its general principle and tendency.

With respect to the *miraculous incidents which accompanied the baptism of Jesus,* if we take for our starting-point the narration of the three first Gospels, that the Holy Spirit really and visibly descended in the form of a dove, and proclaimed Jesus, in an audible voice, to be the Son of God, there can be ro difficulty in bringing it to harmonize with the statement in the Gospel of John. This literal sense of the text has, indeed, for a long time been the prevailing interpretation, though many doubts respecting it had very early forced themselves on the minds of sober inquirers, traces of which are to be found in Origen, and which Strauss has more elaborately renewed. To the natural explanations belong that of Paulus, that the dove was a *real* one, which had by chance flown near the spot at that moment; that of Meyer, that it was the figure of a meteor which was just then visible in the sky ; and that of Kuincel (*ad Matth.* iii.), who considers the dove as a figure for lightning, and the voice for that of thunder, which the eyewitnesses, in their extatic feelings, considered as a divine voice, such as the Jews called a *Bath-kol* (Meyer). Such interpretations are not only irreconcilable with the evangelical text, but even presuppose a violation of the common order of nature, in favour of adherence to which these interpretations are advanced.

A more close investigation of the subject, however, induces us to take as a starting-point the account of the Apostle St. John. It is John the Baptist himself who speaks. He was an eyewitness, nay, to judge from Matthew and John, the only one present with Jesus, and is consequently the only source—with or without Christ —of information. Indeed, if there were more people present, as we are almost inclined to infer from Luke, they cannot have perceived the miracles attending the baptism of Jesus, or John and Christ would no doubt have appealed to their testimony in verification of them.

In thus taking the statement in St. John for the authentic basis of the whole history, a few slight hints in it may afford us the means of solving the difficulties attending the *literal* conception of the text. John the Baptist knows nothing of an external and audible voice, and when he assures us (i. 33) that he had in the Spirit received the promise, that the Messiah would be made manifest by the Spirit descending upon him, and *remaining*—be it *upon* or *in* him— there ; this very *remaining* assuredly precludes any material appearance in the shape of a bird. The internal probability of the text, therefore, speaks in favour of a spiritual vision in the mind of the Baptist; this view is still more strengthened by the fact, that Luke supposes there were many more present, who notwithstanding perceived nothing at all of the miraculous incidents. The reason that the Spirit in the vision assumed the figure of a dove, we would rather seek in the peculiar flight and movement of that bird, than in its form and shape. This interpretation moreover has the advantage of exhibiting the philosophic connection of the incidents, since the Baptist appears more conspicuously as the immediate end of the divine dispensation. Christ had thus the intention of being introduced by him into the Messianic sphere of operation, while the Baptist recognises this to be his own peculiar calling : the signs by which he was to know the Messiah had been intimated to him, and now that they had come to pass, the prophecy and his mission were fulfilled.

None of the Evangelists give any authority for the common tradition that the descent of the Spirit upon Christ was sensibly witnessed by *the multitude.* Matthew simply states that the vision appeared to Christ; Mark adds that the Spirit appeared to him ' as a dove descending upon him;' Luke, more generally, states only the fact of the Spirit's descent in a sensible form; and John informs us that besides Christ this vision was witnessed also by the Baptist.

CHRISTIAN BAPTISM.—Jesus, having undergone baptism as the founder of the new kingdom, ordained it as a legal act by which individuals were to obtain the rights of citizens therein.

K 2

Though he caused many to be baptized by his disciples (John iv. 1, 2), yet *all* we're not baptized who were converted to him; neither was it even necessary after they had obtained participation in him by his personal choice and forgiving of sin. But when he could no longer personally and immediately choose and receive members of his kingdom, when at the same time all had been accomplished which the founder thought necessary for its completion, he gave power to the spiritual community to receive, in his stead, members by *baptism* (Matt. xxviii. 19 ; Mark xvi. 16). Baptism essentially denotes the regenerating of him who receives it, his participation both in the divine life of Christ and the promises rested on it, as well as his reception as a member of the Christian community.

Each of these momentous points implies all the rest; and the germ of all is contained in the words of Christ (Matt. xxviii. 19). The details are variously digested by the Apostles according to their peculiar modes of thinking. John dwells—in like manner as he does on the holy communion—almost exclusively on the internal nature of baptism, the immediate mystical union of the Spirit with Christ; baptism is with him equivalent to ' being born again' (John iii. 5, 7). Paul gives more explicitly and completely the other points also. He understands by it not only the union of the individual with the Head, by the giving one's self up to the Redeemer and the receiving of his life (Gal. iii. 27), but also the union with the other members (*ib.* 28; 1 Cor. xii. 13 ; Ephes. iv. 5; v. 26). He expresses a spiritual purport by saying that it intimates on the part of those who have received it, their being joined with Christ in his death and raised with him in his resurrection.

As regards the *design* of Christian Baptism, different views have been adopted by different parties. The principal are the following :—

1. *That it is a direct instrument of grace ;* the application of water to the person by a properly qualified functionary being regarded as the appointed vehicle by which God bestows regenerating grace upon men. This is the Romanist and Anglo-Catholic view.

2. *That though not an instrument it is a seal of grace ;* divine blessings being thereby confirmed and obsignated to the individual. This is the doctrine of the Confessions of the majority of the Reformed Churches.

3. *That it is neither an instrument nor a seal of grace, but simply a ceremony of initiation into Church membership.* This is the Socinian view of the ordinance.

4. *That it is a token of regeneration ;* to be received only by those who give evidence of being really regenerated. This is the view adopted by the Baptists.

5. *That it is a symbol of purification ;* the use of which simply announces that the religion of Christ is a purifying religion, and intimates that the party receiving the rite assumes the profession, and is to be instructed in the principles, of that religion. This opinion is extensively entertained amongst the Congregationalists of England.

Differences of opinion have also been introduced respecting the proper *mode* of baptism. Some contend that it should be by *immersion* alone; others, that it should be only by *affusion* or *sprinkling ;* and others, that it matters not in which way it be done, the only thing required being the ritual application of water to the person. The first class appeal to the use of *baptizo* by the classical authors, with whom they affirm it is always used in the sense of *dipping* or *immersing ;* and to such expressions as ' being buried with Christ in baptism,' &c., where they understand an allusion to a typical burial, by submersion in water. The second class rely upon the usage of *baptizo* by the sacred writers, who, they allege, employ it frequently where immersion is not to be supposed, as when they speak of ' baptism with fire,' and ' baptism with the Spirit;' upon the alleged impossibility of immersing such multitudes as we learn were baptized at once in Jerusalem on the day of Pentecost; upon the supposed improbability of an Eastern female like Lydia allowing herself to be publicly immersed by a man whom she had never seen before ; upon the language used by Paul at Philippi, when he commanded water to be *brought* into the room, that he might baptize the jailor and his family, language which, it is said, cannot be understood of such a quantity of water as would be required to immerse in succession a whole household ; and upon the use of the term *baptism,* to designate what is elsewhere spoken of as the *outpouring* of the Spirit. The third class maintain, that according to universal usage *baptizo* signifies simply *to wet,* and that the following preposition determines whether it is to be taken in the sense of wetting by immersion or not; they urge especially that the word *rs* used in the New Testament possesses so much of a *technical* character, that it is not possible from it to deduce any correct inference as to the *mode* of baptizing; and they adduce historical evidence to show that baptism was performed indifferently by immersion or affusion as convenience dictated.

In fine, differences of opinion have arisen respecting the proper *subjects* of baptism. Here also we have three classes.

1. Those who maintain that baptism is to be administered only to those who believe and give evidence of being regenerated. This opinion is grounded chiefly upon the positions that, Repentance and Faith are distinctly prescribed in the New Testament as conditions of baptism, and the alleged fact that the Apostles did not baptize any, until satisfied that they sincerely believed It is urged also by the advocates of this opinion, against the practice of infant baptism, that not only are infants excluded from baptism by their inability to comply with the required terms, but that they are virtually excluded by their baptism not being expressly *enjoined* in the New Testament. It is also alleged that infant baptism was unknown to the Early Church, and was a corrupt invention of the patristic age.

2. Those who contend that baptism is to be administered not only to believers who have not been before baptized, but to the infant offspring of believers. This opinion is chiefly based on the covenant established by God with Abraham. This covenant it is maintained was the everlasting covenant, the covenant of grace; under it a connection of a spiritual kind was recognised as existing between parents and their children; in

virtue of this the latter received the sign of the covenanted blessings; no evidence can be adduced that this divinely-appointed connection has been abrogated, though the sign of the covenant has been changed; on the contrary, there is abundant evidence to show that the Apostles administered to the children of converts to Christianity the same rite, that of baptism, which they administered to the converts themselves. It is also affirmed by this party that the requiring of faith and repentance as a condition of baptism in the case of adults cannot be fairly held as including children, inasmuch as by the same reasoning children dying in infancy would be excluded from salvation. It is denied that the absence of any express injunction to baptize children virtually prohibits their baptism; and the assertion that infant baptism was unknown in the primitive age is rebutted by historical evidence.

3. Those who assert that baptism is to be administered to all who either will place themselves under Christian instruction, such as adults who have grown up as heathens, Jews, or infidels; or who may be thus placed by their parents or guardians, such as infants. In support of this view, stress is laid upon our Lord's words when he commanded his Apostles to go and teach and baptize *all nations*; the 'baptizing' being regarded as associated with the 'teaching' and commensurate with it, whilst what is said about 'believing' is regarded as relating to something which may or may not follow the teaching and baptizing, but which is declared to be essential to salvation. It is argued that the Apostolic practice was altogether in accordance with this view of our Lord's commission, inasmuch as the multitudes frequently baptized by the Apostles were such, that to obtain satisfactory evidence of the knowledge and piety of each individual was impossible in the time which elapsed between the Apostles' preaching and the baptizing to which it led; whilst such cases as those of Simon Magus and the Philippian Jailor show that even very ignorant men, and men who could not possibly give what any person would receive as credible evidence of piety, were at once baptized. The practice of the Apostles also in baptizing whole households, including children and servants, without asking any questions as to their knowledge and belief, is urged in favour of this opinion, as well as the corresponding practice of the Church.

BAPTISM FOR THE DEAD.—Paul (1 Cor. xv. 29) uses this phrase. Few passages have undergone more numerous and arbitrary emendations than this text. We shall examine first—

A. *Those interpretations which take it to be some particular application of baptism.*

1. Some imagine that Paul speaks of a baptism which a living man receives in the place of a dead one.

Various passages have been quoted from the fathers in support of this opinion; but all we can infer from their statements is, that baptism by substitution had taken place among the Marcionites, and perhaps also among the Cerinthians and other smaller sects towards the end of the fourth century; but that it existed between that period and the time when Paul wrote the above passage is wholly unsubstantiated.

The idea, then, that such a superstitious custom existed in the Corinthian community is devoid of all historical evidence.

The difficulties will still more increase, if we were to admit, with Olhausen, Rückert, and De Wette, that the Apostle approved of the absurd practice in question, since he would thus be brought into contradiction with his own principles on the importance of faith and external works, which he developes in his Epistle to the Galatians. In the words of Paul we discover no opinion of his own concerning the justice or injustice of the rite; it is merely brought in as an *argumentum ex concesso* in favour of the object which he pursues through the whole chapter (comp. 1 Cor. ii. 5). However much may be objected against this interpretation, it is by far more reasonable than the explanations given by other critics. The Corinthian community was certainly of a mixed character, consisting of individuals of various views, ways of thinking, and different stages of education: so that there might still have existed a small number among them capable of such absurdities. We are not sufficiently acquainted with all the particulars of the case to maintain the contrary, while the simple grammatical sense of the passage is decidedly in favour of the proposed interpretation.

2. Origen, Luther, Chemnitz, and Joh. Gerhard, interpret the words as relating to baptism over the graves of the members of the community, a favourite *rendezvous* of the early Christians. Luther says that in order to strengthen their faith in the resurrection, the Christians baptized over the tombs of the dead. But the custom alluded to dates from a much later period.

3. Epiphanius mentions also a view, according to which the word rendered '*dead*' is to be translated *mortally ill* persons whose baptism was expedited by sprinkling water upon them on their death-bed, instead of immersing them in the usual way; the rite is known under the name of *baptismus clinicus, lectualis.* But few of the modern theologians (among whom, however, are Calvin and Estius) advocate this view, which transgresses not less against the words of the text than against all historical knowledge of the subject.

B. *The interpretations which suppose that the text speaks of general church baptism.* To these belongs the oldest opinion we know of, given in Tertullian, according to which the Greek word rendered '*for*' is here taken in the sense of *on account of*, and the word rendered '*the dead*' in that of *dead bodies*, they themselves, the baptized, as dead persons. The notion which lies at the bottom of this version is, that the body possesses a guarantee for resurrection in the act of baptism, in which it also shares. The sinking under and rising up is with them a symbol of burying and resurrection.

2. A later view, expressed by Chrysostom, adopts the same meaning as regards 'the dead,' but construes the whole clause 'in behalf of the dead,' to signify 'in the belief of the resurrection of the dead.' This ungrammatical version is adopted by Theophylact: 'Why are men baptized at all in behalf of resurrection, that is, in expectation of resurrection, if the dead rise not?'

3. Pelagius, Olearius, Fabricius, are of opinion that the phrase 'on account of the dead,' or 'of those who are dead,' although strictly plural,

here alludes to an individual, namely, to Christ, 'on account of whom' we are baptized, alluding to Rom. vi. 3.

4. Among the best interpretations is that of Spanheim and Joh. Christ. Wolf. They consider 'the dead' to be martyrs and other believers, who, by firmness and cheerful hope of resurrection, have given in death a worthy example, *by which* others were also animated to receive baptism. Still this meaning would be almost too briefly and enigmatically expressed, when no particular reason for it is known, while also the allusion to the exemplary death of many Christians could chiefly apply to the martyrs alone, of whom there were as yet none at Corinth.

5. Olhausen's interpretation is of a rather doubtful character. The meaning of the passage he takes to be, that 'all who are converted to the church are baptized—*for the good* of the dead, as it requires a certain number (Rom. xi. 12-25), a "fullness" of believers, before the resurrection can take place. Every one therefore who is baptized is so for the good of believers collectively, and of those who have already died in the Lord.' Olhausen is himself aware that the Apostle could not have expected that such a difficult and remote idea, which he himself calls 'a mystery,' would be understood by his readers without a further explanation and development of his doctrine. He therefore proposes an explanation, in which it is argued that the miseries and hardships Christians have to struggle against in this life can only be compensated by resurrection. Death causes, as it were, vacancies in the full ranks of the believers, which are again filled up by other individuals. 'What would it profit those who are baptized *in the place* of the dead (to fill up their place in the community) if there be no resurrection?'

BAR, a Hebrew word meaning *son*, but used only poetically in that language (Ps. ii. 12; Prov. xxxi. 2). In Syriac, however, *Bar* answered to the more common Hebrew word for son, i. e. *ben;* and hence in later times, in the New Testament, it takes the same place in the formation of proper names which *Ben* had formerly occupied in the Old Testament.

BARAB'BAS, a person who had forfeited his life for sedition and murder (Mark xv. 7; Luke xxiii. 25). As a rebel, he was subject to the punishment laid down by the Roman law for such political offences; while, as a murderer, he could not escape death even by the civil code of the Jews. But the latter were so bent on the death of Jesus, that, of the two, they preferred pardoning this double criminal (Matt. xxvii. 16-26; Mark xv. 7-15; Luke xxiii. 18-25; John xviii. 40).

BARACHI'AS, father of the Zechariah (Zecharias) mentioned in Matt. xxiii. 35 [ZECHARIAH].

BARAK, *lightning;* son of Abinoam of Kedesh-Naphtali, a Galilean city of refuge in the tribe of Naphthali (Judg. iv. 6; comp. Josh. xix. 37; xxi. 32). He was summoned by the prophetess Deborah to take the field against the hostile army of the Canaanitish king Jabin, commanded by Sisera, with 10,000 men from the tribes of Naphthali and Zebulon, and to encamp on Mount Tabor, probably because the 900 chariots of iron (Judg. iv. 3), in which the main force of Sisera consisted, could not so easily manœuvre on uneven ground. After some hesi-

tation, he resolved to do her bidding, on condition that she would go with him, which she readily promised. Confiding, therefore, in the God of Israel, he attacked the hostile army by surprise, put them to flight, and routed them to the last man. In conjunction with Deborah, he afterwards composed a song of victory in commemoration of that event (Judg. v. 14, 15, 16).

BARBARIAN. This term is used in the New Testament, as in classical writers, to denote other nations of the earth in distinction from the Greeks. 'I am debtor both to the Greeks and Barbarians.' In Coloss. iii. 11, 'Greek nor Jew—Barbarian, Scythian'—*Barbarian* seems to refer to those nations of the Roman empire who did not speak Greek, and *Scythian* to nations not under the Roman dominion. In 1 Cor. xiv. 11 the term is applied to a difference of language: 'If I know not the meaning of the voice, I shall be unto him that speaketh a barbarian ('as of another language,' *Geneva Vers.*), and he that speaketh shall be a barbarian ('as of another language,' *Geneva Vers.*) unto me.' Strabo (xiv. 2) suggests that the word *Bar-bar-os* was originally an imitative sound, designed to express a harsh dissonant language, or sometimes the indistinct articulation of the Greek by foreigners.

BAR-JE'SUS. [ELYMAS.]

BAR-JO'NA (*son of Jonas*), the patronymic appellation of the Apostle Peter (Matt. xvi. 17).

BARLEY. This grain is mentioned in Scripture as cultivated and used in Egypt (Exod. ix. 31), and in Palestine (Lev. xxvii. 16; Deut. viii. 8; 2 Chron. ii. 10; Ruth ii. 17; 2 Sam. xiv. 30; Isa. xxviii. 25; Jer. xli. 8; Joel i. 11). Barley was given to cattle, especially horses (1 Kings iv. 28), and was indeed the only corn grain given to them, as oats and rye were unknown to the Hebrews, and are not now grown in Palestine. This is the chief use of barley in Western Asia. Bread made of barley was, however, used by the poorer classes (Judg. vii. 13; 2 Kings iv. 42; John vi. 9, 13; comp. Ezek. iv. 9). In Palestine barley was for the most part sown at the time of the autumnal rains, October—November, and again in early spring, or rather as soon as the *depth* of winter had passed. The barley of the first crop was ready by the time of the Passover, in the month Abib, March—April (Ruth i. 22; 2 Sam. xxi. 9; Judith viii. 2); April is the month in which the barley-harvest is chiefly gathered in, although it begins earlier in some parts and later in others.

In Exod. ix. 31, we are told that the plague of hail, some time *before* the Passover, destroyed the barley, which was then in the green ear; but not the wheat or the rye, which were only in the blade. This is minutely corroborated by the fact that the barley sown after the inundation is reaped, some after ninety days, some in the fourth month, and that it there ripens a month earlier than the wheat.

BARNABAS. His name was originally *Joses*, or *Joseph* (Acts iv. 36), but he received from the Apostles the surname of Barnabas, which signifies *the Son of Prophecy*. Luke interprets it by *Son of Exhortation*. It can hardly be doubted that this name was given to Joses to denote his eminence as a Christian teacher. He is described by Luke as 'a good man, full of the Holy Ghost and of faith' (Acts xi. 24). He was a native of

Cyprus, but the son of Jewish parents of the tribe of Levi. From Acts iv. 36, 37, it appears that he was possessed of land, but whether in Judæa or Cyprus is not stated. He generously disposed of the whole for the benefit of the Christian community, and 'laid the money at the Apostles' feet.' As this transaction occurred soon after the day of Pentecost, he must have been an early convert to the Christian faith.

When Paul made his first appearance in Jerusalem after his conversion, Barnabas introduced him to the Apostles, and attested his sincerity (Acts ix. 27). Though the conversion of Cornelius and his household, with its attendant circumstances, had given the Jewish Christians clearer views of the comprehensive character of the new dispensation, yet the accession of a large number of Gentiles to the church at Antioch was an event so extraordinary, that the Apostles and brethren at Jerusalem resolved on deputing one of their number to investigate it. Their choice was fixed on Barnabas. After witnessing the flourishing condition of the church, and adding fresh converts by his personal exertions, he visited Tarsus to obtain the assistance of Saul, who returned with him to Antioch, where they laboured for a whole year (Acts xi. 23-26). In anticipation of the famine predicted by Agabus, the Antiochian Christians made a contribution for their poorer brethren at Jerusalem, and sent it by the hands of Barnabas and Saul (Acts xi. 28-30), who speedily returned, bringing with them John Mark, a nephew of the former. By divine direction (Acts xiii. 2) they were separated to the office of missionaries, and as such visited Cyprus and some of the principal cities in Asia Minor (Acts xiii. 14). Soon after their return to Antioch, the peace of the church was disturbed by certain zealots from Judæa, who insisted on the observance of the rite of circumcision by the Gentile converts. To settle the controversy, Paul and Barnabas were deputed to consult the Apostles and elders at Jerusalem (Acts xv. 1, 2); they returned to communicate the result of their conference (ver. 22), accompanied by Judas Barsabas and Silas, or Silvanus. On preparing for a second missionary tour, a dispute arose between them on account of John Mark, which ended in their taking different routes; Paul and Silas went through Syria and Cilicia, while Barnabas and his nephew revisited his native island (Acts xv. 36-41). At this point Barnabas disappears from Luke's narrative, which to its close is occupied solely with the labours and sufferings of Paul. From the Epistles of the latter a few hints (the only authentic sources of information) may be gleaned relative to his early friend and associate. From 1 Cor. ix. 5, 6, it would appear that Barnabas was unmarried, and supported himself, like Paul, by some manual occupation. In Gal. ii. 1, we have an account of the reception given to Paul and Barnabas by the Apostles at Jerusalem, probably on the occasion mentioned in Acts xv. In the same chapter (ver. 13) we are informed that Barnabas so far yielded to the Judaizing zealots at Antioch, as to separate himself for a time from communion with the Gentile converts. Respecting the later years of Barnabas we have no authentic information. The year when he died cannot be determined with certainty; if his nephew, as some have supposed, joined Paul

after that event, it must have taken place not later than A.D. 63 or 64.

BARRENNESS is, in the East, the hardest lot that can befal a woman, and was considered among the Israelites as the heaviest punishment with which the Lord could visit a female (Gen. xvi. 2; xxx. 1-23; 1 Sam. i. 6, 29; Isa. xlvii. 9; xlix. 21; Luke i. 25). This general notion of the disgrace of barrenness in a woman may early have given rise, in the patriarchal age, to the custom among barren wives of introducing to their husbands their maid-servants, and of regarding the children born in that concubinage as their own, by which they thought to cover their own disgrace of barrenness (Gen. xvi. 2; xxx. 3).

BAR'SABAS. [JOSEPH BARSABAS; JUDAS BARSABAS.]

BARTHOL'OMEW (the son of Talmai, 2 Sam. xiii. 37) was one of the twelve Apostles, and is generally supposed to have been the same individual who in John's Gospel is called Nathanael. The reason of this opinion is, that in the three first Gospels Philip and Bartholomew are constantly named together, while Nathanael is nowhere mentioned; on the contrary, in the fourth Gospel the names of Philip and Nathanael are similarly combined, but nothing is said of Bartholomew. Nathanael therefore must be considered as his real name, while Bartholomew merely expresses his filial relation. He was a native of Cana in Galilee (John xxi. 2). He was introduced by Philip to Jesus, who, on seeing him approach, at once pronounced that eulogy on his character which has made his name almost synonymous with sincerity: 'Behold an Israelite indeed, in whom there is no guile' (John i. 47). He was one of the disciples to whom our Lord appeared after his resurrection, at the Sea of Tiberias (John xxi. 2); he was also a witness of the Ascension, and returned with the other Apostles to Jerusalem (Acts i. 4, 12, 13). Of his subsequent history we have little more than vague traditions.

BARTIME'US, son of Timeus, the blind beggar of Jericho whom Christ restored to sight (Mark x. 46).

BA'RUCH, blessed; the faithful friend and amanuensis of the prophet Jeremiah, was of a noble family of the tribe of Judah, and generally considered to be the brother of the prophet Seraiah, both being represented as sons of Neriah; and to Baruch the prophet Jeremiah dictated all his oracles. During the siege of Jerusalem, Baruch was selected as the depositary of the deed of purchase which Jeremiah had made of the territory of Hanameel, to which deed he had been a witness. In the fourth year of the reign of Jehoiachim, king of Judah (B.C. 605), Baruch was directed to write all the prophecies delivered by Jeremiah up to that period, and to read them to the people, which he did from a window in the Temple upon two solemn occasions. He afterwards read them before the counsellors of the king at a private interview, when Baruch being asked to give an account of the manner in which the prophecy had been composed, gave an exact description of the mode in which he had taken it down from the prophet's dictation. Upon this they ordered him to leave the roll, advising that he and Jeremiah should conceal themselves. They then informed the king of what had taken place, upon which he had the roll read to him; but, after hearing a part of it, he cut it with a penknife, and, notwithstanding the remonstrances of his counsellors, threw it into the fire of his winter parlour, where he was sitting. He then ordered Jeremiah and Baruch to be seized. but they could not be found. The Jews to this day commemorate the burning of this roll by an annual fast. Another roll was now written by Baruch from the prophet's dictation, containing all that was in the former, with some additions, the most remarkable of which is the prophecy respecting the ruin of Jehoiachim and his house, as the punishment of his impious act. This roll is the prophecy of Jeremiah which we now possess. Baruch, being himself terrified at the threats contained in the prophetic roll, received the comforting assurance that he would himself be delivered from the calamities which should befal Judah and Jerusalem. After the capture of Jerusalem, in the eleventh year of the reign of king Zedekiah, when the Jews, after their return from Babylon, obstinately persisted in their determination to migrate to Egypt, against the remonstrances of the prophet, both Baruch and Jeremiah accompanied them to that country, where they remained until the death of Jeremiah. There is no account in Scripture of Baruch's return from Egypt, but the Rabbins allege that he died in Babylon, in the twelfth year of the exile. Josephus asserts that he was well skilled in the Hebrew language; and that, after the taking of Jerusalem, Nebuzaradan treated Baruch with consideration, from respect to Jeremiah, whose misfortunes he had shared, and whom he had accompanied to prison and exile (*Antiq.* x. 11).

BARUCH, BOOK OF (APOCRYPHA), follows next after the book of Jeremiah in the Septuagint Version. Several learned writers strongly contend for its canonicity; but the weight of evidence is generally believed to preponderate against it.

The subject of the book is (1) an exhortation to wisdom and a due observance of the law. (2) It then introduces Jerusalem as a widow, comforting her children with the hope of a return. (3) An answer follows in confirmation of this hope. A prologue is prefixed, stating that Baruch had read his book to Jeremiah and the people in Babylon by the river Sud (Euphrates), by which the people were brought to repentance, and sent the book with a letter and presents to Jerusalem.

BARZIL'LAI, a wealthy old Gileadite of Rogelim, who distinguished himself by his loyalty when David fled beyond the Jordan from his son Absalom. He sent in a liberal supply of provisions, beds, and other conveniences for the use of the king's followers (2 Sam. xvii. 27; xix. 32). On the king's triumphant return, Barzillai attended him as far as the Jordan, but declined, by reason of his advanced age, to proceed to Jerusalem and receive the favours to which he had entitled himself.

BA'SHAN. a name which probably denotes the peculiar fertility of the soil. The sacred writers include in Bashan that part of the country eastward of the Jordan which was given to half the tribe of Manasseh, situated to the north of Gilead. The first notice of this country is in Gen. xiv. 5; compare with Josh. xii. 4. When the Israelites invaded the Promised Land, Argob, a province of

Bashan, contained 'sixty fenced cities, with walls and gates and brazen bars, besides unwalled towns a great many' (Deut. iii. 4, 5; 1 Kings iv. 13). These were all taken by the Israelites, and Og and his people utterly destroyed. Golan, one of the cities of refuge, was situated in this country (Deut. iv. 43; Josh. xx. 8; xxi. 27). Solomon appointed twelve officers to furnish the monthly supplies for the royal household, and allotted the region of Argob to the son of Geber (1 Kings iv. 13). Towards the close of Jehu's reign Hazael invaded the land of Israel, and smote the whole eastern territory, 'even Gilead and Bashan' (2 Kings x. 33); but after his death the cities he had taken were recovered by Jehoash (Joash) (2 Kings xiii. 25), who defeated the Syrians in three battles, as Elisha had predicted (2 Kings xiii. 19). After the captivity the name Batanæa was applied to only a part of the ancient Bashan; the rest being called Trachonitis, Auranitis, and Gaulanitis. All these provinces were granted by Augustus to Herod the Great, and on his death Batanæa formed a part of Philip's tetrarchy At his decease, A.D. 34, it was annexed, by Tiberius. to the province of Syria; but in A.D. 37 it was given by Caligula to Herod Agrippa, the son of Aristobulus, with the title of king (Acts xii. 1). From the time of Agrippa's death, in A.D. 44, to A.D. 53, the government again reverted to the Romans, but it was then restored by Claudius to Agrippa II. (Acts xxv. 13). The richness of the pasture-land of Bashan, and the consequent superiority of its breed of cattle, are frequently alluded to in the Scriptures. We read in Deut. xxxii. 14, of 'rams of the breed of Bashan' (Ezek. xxxix. 18). ' Rams, lambs, bulls, goats, all of them fatlings of Bashan.' The oaks of Bashan are mentioned in connection with the cedars of Lebanon (Isa. ii. 13; Zech. xi. 2). In Ezekiel's description of the wealth and magnificence of Tyre it is said, ' Of the oaks of Bashan have they made their oars' (xxvii. 6). The ancient commentators on Amos iv. 1, 'the kine of Bashan,' Jerome, Theodoret, and Cyril, speak in the strongest terms of the exuberant fertility of Bashan, and modern travellers corroborate their assertions.

BASKET. There are several words in the Hebrew Scriptures by which different kinds of baskets appear to be indicated:—

1. DUD, which occurs in 2 Kings x. 7, where the heads of Ahab's sons are sent from Samaria to Jezreel in baskets; Jer. xxiv. 2, as containing figs; and Ps. lxxxi. 6 (rendered *pots*), also as containing figs; where, therefore, deliverance from the baskets means deliverance from the

82.

bondage of carrying burdens in baskets. In fact, very heavy burdens were thus carried in Egypt, as corn in very large baskets from the field to the threshing-floor, and from the threshing-floor to the granaries. They were carried between two men by a pole resting on their *shoulders;* which agrees with the previous clause of the cited text, 'I removed his shoulder from the burden.' This labour and form of the basket are often shown in the Egyptian sculptures.

2. TEBA, which occurs in connection with agricultural objects, 'the *basket* and the store' (Deut. xxvi. 2-4; xxviii. 5-17), and would therefore appear to have been somewhat similar to the above; and, in fact, the Egyptian sculptures show different baskets applied to this use.

3. KELUB. From the etymology, this appears to have been an interwoven basket, made of leaves or rushes. In Lev v. 27, however, it is used for a bird-cage, which must have been of open work, and probably not unlike our own wicker bird-cages. The name is also applied to fruit-baskets (Amos viii. 1, 2), Egyptian examples of which are presented in figs. 2 and 4 (which contain pomegranates) of the annexed cut.

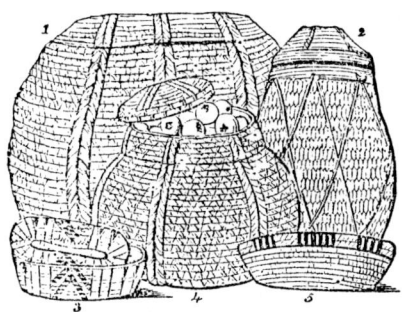

63. [Ancient Egyptian.]

4. SALSILLOTH, occurs only in Jer. vi. 9, where it obviously denotes baskets in which grapes were deposited as they were gathered. The form of the baskets used for this purpose is often shown on the Egyptian monuments, and is similar to that represented in fig. 4, cut 83.

5. In all the other places where the word basket occurs, we are doubtless to understand a basket made of rushes, similar both in form and material to those used by carpenters for carrying their tools. This is still the common kind of basket throughout Western Asia; and its use in ancient Egypt is shown by an actual specimen which was found in a tomb at Thebes, and which is now in the British Museum. It was, in fact, a carpenter's basket, and contained his tools (fig. 1, cut 83).

The specimens of Egyptian baskets in the British Museum, represented in our cut, convey a favourable idea of the basket-work of ancient times. Some of these are worked ornamentally with colours (figs. 3, 5, cut 83). And besides these the monuments exhibit a large variety of hand-baskets, of different shapes, and so extensively employed as to show the numerous applications of basket-work in the remote times to which these representations extend. They are mostly manufactured, the stronger and larger sorts of the fibres, and the finer of the leaves of the palm-tree, and not unfrequently of rushes, but more seldom of reeds.

BASTARD (Deut. xxiii. 2, and Zech. ix. 6). Some understand by this word the offspring of prostitutes, but they forget that prostitutes were expressly forbidden to be tolerated by the law of Moses (Lev. xix. 29; Deut. xxiii. 17). The most probable conjecture is that which applies the term to the offspring of heathen prostitutes in the neighbourhood of Palestine; since no provision was made by Moses against their toleration, and who were a sort of priestesses to the Syrian goddess Astarte (comp. Num. xxv. 1, *sq* ; Hos iv. 14; 1 Kings xiv. 24; xv. 12; xxii. 47; 2 Kings xxiii. 7).

That there existed such bastard offspring among the Jews, is proved by the history of Jephthah (Judg. xi. 1-7), who on this account was expelled, and deprived of his patrimony.

BAT occurs in Lev. xi. 19; Deut. xiv. 18; Isa. ii. 20; and Baruch vi. 22. In Hebrew the word implies flying in the dark; which, taken in connection with the sentence 'moreover the othelaph and every *creeping thing that flieth* is unclean unto you; they shall not be eaten,' is so clear, that there cannot be a mistake respecting the order of animals meant. At first sight, animals so diminutive, lean, and repugnant to the senses, must appear scarcely to have required the legislator's attention; but the fact evidently shows that there were at the time men or tribes who ate animals classed with bats, a practice still in vogue in the great Australasian islands, where the frugivorous Pteropi of the harpi or goblin family, by our seamen denominated flying-dogs, and erroneously vampyres, are caught and eaten; but where the insectivorous true bats, such as the genera common in Europe, are rejected. Some of the species of harpies are of the bulk of a rat, with from three to four feet of expanse between the tips of the wings; they have a fierce dog-like head, and are nearly all marked with a space of rufous hair from the forehead over the neck and along part of the back. They reside in the most dense foliage of large trees, whence they fly out at night and do considerable damage to the plantations of fruit-trees. It was to one or more species of this section of Cheiroptera that the Mosaic prohibition was perhaps directed; and it is likewise to them that may be referred the foundation of the ancient legends concerning harpies, which, however much they may be distorted, have a basis of truth. Indeed, when we consider their voice, the faculty they have of feeding with their thumbs, their formidable teeth, their habit of flying in the day during dark weather, and their willingness, though they are frugivorous, to devour not only insects, but also the blood and flesh of small animals, we may admit that originally they were more daring in the presence of man; that their true characters are but moderately amplified by poetical fancy; and that the Mosaic injunction was strikingly appropriate.

In the text of Scripture where allusion is made to caverns and dark places, true Vespertilionidæ, or insect-eating bats, similar to the European, are clearly designated.

BATH-SHE'BA, also BATH-SHUA, daughter of Eliam, grand-daughter of Ahitophel, and wife of Uriah; she was seduced and became pregnant by King David during the absence of her husband, who was then engaged at the siege of Rabbah (2 Sam. xi. 4, 5 ; Ps. li. 2). The child thus born in adultery became ill and died (2 Sam. xii. 15-18). After the lapse of the period of mourning for her husband. who was slain by the contrivance of David (xi. 15), she was legally married to the king (xi. 27), and bore him Solomon (xii. 24; 1 Kings i. 11; ii. 13). In 1 Chron. iii. 5, she is called Bath-shua instead of Bath-sheba; and her father Ammiel, instead of Eliam (comp. Matt. i. 6). The other children of Bath-sheba are named in 2 Sam. v. 14; 1 Chron. iii. 5. She is afterwards mentioned only in consequence of her good-natured intercession for Adonijah, which incidentally displays the respect with which she was treated by king Solomon, her son (1 Kings ii. 19). [DAVID ; ADONIJAH.]

BATTLE, SYSTEM OF. Though the Hebrews in their mode of conducting warlike operations varied somewhat in the course of ages, and are elsewhere shown to have been swayed by the practice of greater and more military nations, still, from the period when the institution of royalty gave rise to an organized system, it was a maxim to spare the soldiers all unnecessary fatigue before an engagement, and to supply them liberally with food. Their arms were enjoined to be in the best order, and when drawn up for battle they formed a line of solid squares of a hundred men, each square being ten deep, and with sufficient interval between them to allow of facility in movements, and for the slingers to pass through. The archers may have occupied the two flanks, or formed in the rear, according to the intentions of the commander on the occasion; but the slingers were always stationed in the rear until they were ordered forward to impede a hostile approach, or to commence an engagement somewhat in the manner of modern skirmishers. Meantime, while the trumpets waited to sound the last signal, the king, or his representative, appeared in his sacred dress, except when he wished to remain unknown, as at Megiddo (2 Chron. xxxv. 22), and proceeded to make the final dispositions, in the middle of his chosen braves, attended by priests who, by their exhortations, animated the ranks within hearing. It was now, we may suppose, when the enemy was at hand, that the slingers would be ordered to pass between the intervals of the line of solid squares, open their order, and with shouts, let fly their stone or leaden missiles, until by the gradual approach of the opposing fronts they would be hemmed in, and be recalled to the rear, or to cover a flank. Then would come the signal to charge, and the great shout of battle ; the heavy infantry, receiving the order to attack, would press direct upon the front of the enemy, under cover of their shields and levelled spears ; the rear ranks might then, if so armed, cast their second darts, and archers from their rear shoot high, so as to pitch the arrows over their own main line of spearmen into the dense masses beyond them. If the enemy broke through the intervals, we may imagine that a line of charioteers in reserve, breaking from their position, might in part charge among the disordered ranks of the foe, drive them back, and facilitate the restoration of the oppressed masses,

or wheeling round a flank, fall upon the enemy, or be encountered by a similar manœuvre, and perhaps repulsed. The king, meanwhile, surrounded by his princes, posted close to the rear of his line of battle, and in the middle of the showered missiles, would watch the enemy and remedy every disorder. Thus it was that several of the sovereigns of Judah were slain (2 Chron. xviii. 33, and xxxv. 23), and that such an enormous waste of human life took place : for the shock of two hostile lines of masses at least ten in depth, advancing under the confidence of breastplate and shield, when once engaged hand to hand, had difficulties of no ordinary nature to retreat ; because the hindermost ranks not feeling personally the first slaughter, would not, and the foremost could not, fall back : neither could the commanders disengage the line without a certainty of being defeated. The fate of the day was therefore no longer within the control of the chief, and nothing but obstinate valour was left to decide the victory. Under such circumstances defeat led to irretrievable confusion ; and where either party possessed superiority in cavalry and chariots of war, it would be materially increased : but where the infantry alone had principally to pursue a broken enemy, that force, laden with shields, and preserving order, could overtake very few who chose to abandon their defensive armour, unless they were hemmed in by the locality. Sometimes a part of the army was posted in ambush, but this manœuvre was most commonly practised against the garrisons of cities (Josh. viii. 12 ; Judg. xx. 38). In the case of Abraham (Gen. xiv. 16), when he led a small body of his own people suddenly collected, and fell upon the guard of the captives, released them, and recovered the booty, it was a surprise, not an ambush ; nor is it necessary that he should have fallen in with the main army of the enemy. At a later period, there is no doubt the Hebrew armies, in imitation of the Romans, formed into more than one line of masses ; but, it may be added, there is ample evidence that they always possessed more stubborn valour than discipline.

BATTLEMENT. [House.]

BAY-TREE. or LAUREL. This word occurs only once in Scripture, namely in Ps. xxxvii. 35 : ' I have seen the wicked in great power, spreading himself like a green bay-tree.' Commentators and translators have differed respecting the meaning of this word, some supposing it to indicate a specific tree, as the laurel ; and others, supported by the Septuagint and Vulgate, the cedar of Lebanon. It is by some considered to mean an evergreen tree, and by others, a green tree that grows in its native soil, or that has not suffered by transplanting, as such a tree spreads itself luxuriantly. It appears to us that the Hebrew word would indicate some tree resembling the bay-tree, rather than the bay-tree itself ; but until that can be discovered, the latter is, upon the whole, well suited to stand as its representative

The laurel, or bay-tree, *laurus nobilis* of botanists, is well known to the Asiatics by its Arabic name of *ghar*, under which it is mentioned by Serapion and Avicenna, who quote chiefly Dioscorides and Galen, thus indicating that they had not much original information of their own respecting a tree which is probably not indigenous in the countries in which they wrote. The leaves and berries of the laurel, as well as the bark and the root, were employed in medicine: the berries continue, even in the present day, to be exported to India, where we found them in the bazaars, under the name of

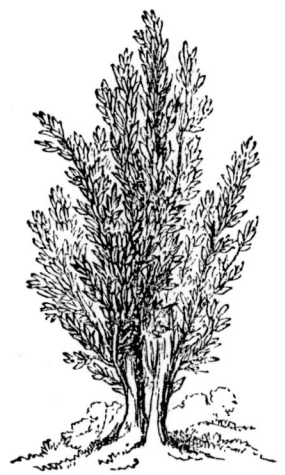

84. [Bay-tree. Laurus nobilis.]

hubal-ghar, being still esteemed as a stimulant medicinal, though not possessed of any properties superior to those of the laurels of more southern latitudes. The bay-tree is well known to be common in the south of Europe, as in Spain, Italy, Greece, and the Levant. It is usually from 20 to 30 feet in height, often having a bushy appearance, from throwing up so many suckers; but in England it has attained a height of 60 feet, which is not unusual in warmer climates. It is unnecessary to allude further to the celebrity which it attained among the ancients—a celebrity which has not yet passed away, the laurel-wreath being still the symbolical crown as well of warriors as of poets. Its ever green grateful appearance, its thick shade, and the agreeable spicy odour of its leaves, point it out as that which was most likely in the eye of the Psalmist.

BDEL'LIUM. This word occurs but twice in the Scriptures: in Gen. ii. 12, as a product of the land of Havilah; and Num. xi. 7, where the manna is likened to it. It has been much disputed among critics, both ancient and modern. Some consider it as a precious stone, and the Jewish Rabbins, together with some modern commentators, translate it by *pearl.* But it is more than probable that the pearl was as yet unknown in the time of Moses; and it is nowhere mentioned in the Old Testament under its proper name except in Esth. i. 6.

It is, therefore, most probable that the Hebrew *bedolach* is the aromatic gum *bdellium,* which issues from a tree growing in Arabia, Media, and the Indies. Pliny's description of the tree from which the bdellium is taken makes Kæmpfer's assertion highly probable, that it is the sort of palm-tree so frequently met with on the Persian

coast and in Arabia Felix. The term bdellium, however, is applied to two gummy resinous substances. One of them is the *Indian bdellium,* or *false myrrh* (perhaps the bdellium of the Scriptures), which is obtained from *Amyris* (balsamodendron?) *Commiphora.* The trunk of the tree is covered with a light-coloured pellicle, as in the common birch, which peels off from time to time, exposing to view a smooth green coat, which in succession supplies other similar exfoliations. This tree diffuses a grateful fragrance, like that of the finest myrrh, to a considerable distance around. Dr. Royle was informed that this species yielded bdellium; and in confirmation of this statement, we may add that many of the specimens of this bdellium in the British Museum have a yellow pellicle adhering to them, precisely like that of the common birch, and that some of the pieces are perforated by spiny branches—another character serving to recognise the origin of the bdellium. Indian bdellium has considerable resemblance to myrrh. Many of the pieces have hairs adhering to them.

The other kind of bdellium is called *African bdellium.* It is a natural production of Senegal, and is called by the natives, who make toothpicks of its spines, *niottout.* It consists of rounded or oval tears, from one to two inches in diameter, of a dull and waxy fracture, which in the course of time become opaque, and are covered externally by a white or yellowish dust. It has a feeble but peculiar odour, and a bitter taste.

BEANS. This word occurs twice in Scripture. The first occasion is in 2 Sam. xvii. 28, where beans are described as being brought to David, as well as wheat, barley, lentils, &c., as is the custom at the present day in many parts of the East when a traveller arrives at a village. So in Ezekiel iv. 9, the prophet is directed to take wheat, barley, *beans,* lentils, &c., and make bread thereof. The common beans, or at least one of its varieties, has been employed as an article of diet from the most ancient times. Beans were employed as articles of diet by the ancients, as they are by the moderns; and are considered to give rise to flatulence, but otherwise to be wholesome and nutritious. They are cultivated over a great part of the old world, from the north of Europe to the south of India; in the latter, however, forming the cold weather cultivation, with wheat, peas, &c. They are extensively cultivated in Egypt and Arabia. Dr. Kitto states that the extent of their cultivation in Palestine he had no means of knowing. In Egypt they are sown in November, and reaped in the middle of February (three and a half months in the ground); but in Syria they may be had throughout the spring. The stalks are cut down with the scythe, and these are afterwards cut and crushed, to fit them for the food of camels, oxen, and goats. The beans themselves, when sent to a market, are often deprived of their skins. Basnage reports it as the sentiment of some of the Rabbins, that beans were not lawful to the priests, on account of their being considered the appropriate food of mourning and affliction: but he does not refer to the authority; and neither in the sacred books nor in the Mishna can be found any traces of the notion to which he alludes. So far from attaching any sort of impurity to this legume, it is described as among the first-fruit offerings; and several other articles in the latter collection prove that the Hebrews had beans largely in use, after they had passed them through the mill.

BEAR is noticed in 1 Sam. xvii. 34, 36, 37; 2 Sam. xvii. 8; 2 Kings ii. 24; Prov. xvii. 12; xxviii. 15; Isa. xi. 7; Lam. iii. 10; Hos. xiii. 8; Amos v. 19, &c. The genus Ursus is the largest of all the plantigrade carnassiers, and with the faculty of subsisting on fruit or honey unites a greater or less propensity, according to the species, to slaughter and animal food. To a sullen and ferocious disposition it joins immense strength, little vulnerability, considerable sagacity, and the power of climbing trees. The brown bear, Ursus arctos, is the most sanguinary of the species of the Old Continent, and Ursus Syriacus, or the

85. [Syrian Bear.]

bear of Palestine, is one very nearly allied to it, differing only in the stature being proportionably lower and longer, the head and tail more prolonged, and the colour a dull buff or light bay, often clouded, like the Pyrenæan variety, with darker brown. On the back there is a ridge of long semi-erect hairs running from the neck to the tail. It is still found in the elevated woody parts of Lebanon.

BEARD (THE). Ancient nations in general agreed with the modern inhabitants of the East in attaching a great value to the possession of a beard. The total absence of it, or a spare and stinted sprinkling of hair upon the ·chin, is thought by the Orientals to be as great a deformity to the features as the want of a nose would appear to us.; while, on the contrary, a long and bushy beard, flowing down in luxuriant profusion to the breast, is considered not only a most graceful ornament to the person, but as contributing in no small degree to respectability and dignity of character. With this knowledge of the extraordinary respect and value which have in all ages been attached to the beard in the East, we are prepared to expect that a corresponding care would be taken to preserve and improve its appearance; and, accordingly, to dress and anoint it with oil and perfume was, with the better classes at least, an indispensable part of their daily toilet (Ps. cxxxiii. 2). In many cases it was dyed with variegated colours, by a tedious and troublesome operation. On the other hand, the allowing the beard to remain in a foul and dishevelled state, or to cut it off, was one of the most striking outward indications of

deep and overwhelming sorrow (2 Sam. xix. 24 · Ezra ix. 13; Isa. xv. 2; Jer. xli. 5.

Nor was less jealousy shown in guarding the honour of, than in setting off to advantage, this attribute of manhood. The slightest exhibition of contempt, by sneering, spitting at, pulling, or even pressing against it in a rude and careless manner, was resented as an insult, such as would now, among men of the world, be deemed expiable only by a duel. No one was permitted to touch it except in the way of respectful and affectionate salutation, which was done by gently taking hold of its extremity with the right hand and kissing it; but even in that case it was only wives in approaching their husbands, children their parents, or the nearest and most attached friends, to whom this unusual liberty was granted. The act itself being an expression of kind and cordial familiarity, its performance by Joab shows in a flagrant light the base and unprincipled conduct of that ruthless veteran, when he took Amasa by the beard with his right hand to kiss him (rather it), and then having assumed this attitude under the mask of the most friendly feelings, smote his unsuspecting victim under the fifth rib (2 Sam. xx. 9).

To be deprived of a beard was, and still is, in some places of the East, the badge of servitude —a mark of infamy, that degraded a person from the ranks of men to those of slaves and women. Among people influenced by such ideas, we can easily conceive how deep and intolerable was the affront which the king of the Ammonites put upon the ambassadors of David, when, among other acts of insolence, he shaved off one-half of their beards, and sent them home in that grotesque condition, exposed to the derision of their countrymen (2 Sam. x.). Persons of their high rank, who, in all probability, were fastidious about the orderly state and graceful appearance of their beards, would be even more sensitive as to this ignominious treatment than those of an humbler condition; and, as the shaving off one-half of the beard was among some ancient nations the punishment of cowardice, these circumstances united will help to account for the spirit of determined revenge which the king and the whole nation of Israel breathed, on intelligence of the national outrage.

From the above facts it is clear that the Israelites maintained their beard and the ideas connected with it, during their abode among the Egyptians, who were a shaven people. This is not unimportant among the indications which evince that, whatever they learned of good or evil in that country, they preserved the appearance and habits of a separate people. As the Egyptians shaved their beards off entirely, the injunction in Lev. xix. 27 against shaving ' the corners of the beard' must have been levelled against the practice of some other and bearded nation. The prohibition is usually understood to apply against rounding the corners of the beard where it joins the hair; and the reason is supposed to have been to preclude a superstition of certain Arabian tribes, who, by shaving off or rounding away the beard where it joined the hair of the head, devoted themselves to a certain deity who held among them the place which Bacchus did among the Greeks (comp. Jer. ix. 26; xxv. 23; xlix. 32). The ultimate effect seems to have been altogether to prevent the Jews from shaving off the edges of their beards. The effect of this prohibition in establishing a distinction of the Jews from other nations cannot be understood, unless we contemplate the extravagant diversity in which the beard was and is treated by the nations of the East. The cut is very interesting, being a collection of bearded heads of foreigners obtained from the

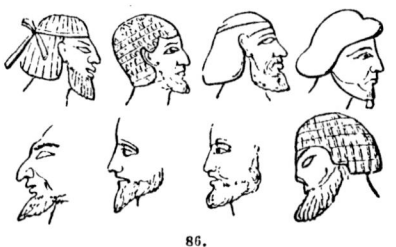

86.

Egyptian monuments, and, without doubt, including the beards, head-dresses, and physiognomies of most of the nations bordering on Egypt and Palestine. In nearly all of them we see that the upper edges of the beard were shaven off, and apparently the hair of the upper lip.

The ancient Egyptians, although they shaved their beards, had the singular custom of tying a false beard upon the chin. This was probably in the way of a compromise between their love of cleanliness and their desire to preserve some trace of the distinguishing sign of manhood. They were made of plaited hair, and had a peculiar form according to the rank of the persons by whom they were worn. Private individuals had a small beard, scarcely two inches long; that of a king was of considerable length, and square at the bottom; and the figures of gods were distinguished by its turning up at the end.

87. [2, 3, 5, 11. Gods.   1, 4, 6, 9, 10. Kings.
7, 8. Private persons.]

BEASTS. In the Bible, this word, when used in contradistinction to *man* (Ps. xxxvi. 6), denotes a brute creature generally; when in contradistinction to *creeping things* (Rev. xi. 2-7; xxvii. 26), it has reference to four-footed animals; and when to *wild mammalia*, as in Gen. i. 25, means domesticated cattle.

The zoology of Scripture may, in a general sense, be said to embrace the whole range of ani-

mated nature; but after the first brief notice of the creation of animals recorded in Genesis, it is limited more particularly to the animals found in Egypt, Arabia, Palestine, Syria, and the countries eastward, in some cases, to beyond the Euphrates. It comprehends mammalia, birds, reptiles, fishes, and invertebrate animals: but in a work like the Bible, written for a far different purpose, we might naturally expect that only a small part of these would be found described, and that generical indications would more frequently occur than specific characteristics. As the intention of Scripture, in its allusions to animate or inanimate objects, was not scientific description, but the illustration of arguments and precepts by images drawn from objects familiar to those to whom it was addressed, it is not to be expected that zoology or botany should be treated systematically, or in terms such as modern science has adopted; yet where we can now fully ascertain the true meaning of the text, the imagery drawn from natural history is always forcible, correct, and effective, even where it treats the subject under the conditions of the contemporary popular belief; for, had the inspired writers entered into explanations on matters of science not then commonly understood, the poetical force of the imagery, and consequently its intended effect, must necessarily have been greatly diminished; yet, where system is appropriate, we find a classified general distribution of the creation, simple indeed, but sufficiently applicable to all the purposes for which it was introduced. It resembles other parts of the philosophy of the earliest nations, in which the physical distribution of matter, excepting so far as man is concerned, proceeds by triads. Botany is treated under the heads of grass, shrubs, and trees: in animated nature, beginning with the lowest organized in the watery element, we have first 'the moving creature that hath life,' animalcula, crustacea, insecta, &c.; second, fishes and amphibia, including the huge tenants of the waters, whether or not they also frequent the land, crocodiles, python serpents, and perhaps even those which are now considered as of a more ancient zoology than the present system, the great Saurians of geology; and third, it appears, birds, 'flying creatures' (Gen. i. 20); and still advancing (cetaceans, pinnatipeds, whales and seals being excluded), we have quadrupeds, forming three other divisions or orders: 1st, cattle, embracing the ruminant herbivora, generally gregarious, and capable of domesticity; 2nd, wild beasts, carnivora, including all beasts of prey; and 3rd, reptiles, minor quadrupeds, such as creep by means of many feet, or glide along the surface of the soil, serpents, annelides, &c.; finally, we have man, standing alone in intellectual supremacy. The classification of Moses, as it may be drawn from Deuteronomy, appears to be confined to *Vertebrata* alone, or animals having a spine and ribs, although the fourth class might include others: taking man as one, it forms five classes—1st, Man; 2nd, Beasts; 3rd, Birds; 4th, Reptiles; 5th, Fishes. It is the same as that in Leviticus xi., where beasts are further distinguished into those with solid hoofs and those with cloven feet. But the passage specially refers to animals that might be lawfully eaten because they were clean, and others prohibited because they were declared unclean, although some of them, according to the common belief of the time, might ruminate; for it may be repeated that the Scriptures were not intended to embrace anatomical disquisitions aiming at the advancement of human science, but to convey moral and religious truth, without disturbing the received opinions of the time on questions having little or no relation to their main object. In like manner, fishes and birds are divided into clean and unclean; and, taken altogether, the classification now described forms an excellent series of distinctions, which, even at the present day, and in countries far distant from the scene where it was ordained, still remains applicable, with little exception, and from its intrinsic propriety will remain in force, notwithstanding our present knowledge of the manners and opinions of the East and of Egypt has rendered many of the earlier comments upon it in a great measure useless.

BEDS. The manner of sleeping in warm Eastern climates was, and is, very different from that which is followed in our colder regions. The present usages appear to be the same as those of the ancient Jews, and sufficiently explain the passages of Scripture which bear on the subject. Beds of feathers are altogether unknown, and the Orientals lie exceedingly hard. Poor people who have no certain home, or when on a journey, or employed distant from their homes, sleep on mats or wrapped in their outer garment, which from its importance in this respect was forbidden to be retained in pledge over night from the owner (Gen. ix. 21, 23; Exod. xxii. 27; Deut. xxv. 13). Under such circumstances a stone covered with some folded cloth or piece of dress is often used for a pillow (Gen. xxviii. 11). The more wealthy classes sleep on mattresses stuffed with wool or cotton, and which are often no other than a quilt thickly padded, either used singly or one or more placed upon each other. A similar quilt of finer materials forms the coverlet in winter, and in summer a thin blanket suffices; but sometimes the convenient outer garment is used for the latter purpose, and was so among the Jews, as we see from 1 Sam. xix. 3. The difference of use here is, that the poor *wrap themselves up* in it, and it forms all their bed; whereas when used by the rich it is as *a covering* only. A pillow is placed upon the mattress, and over both, in good houses, is laid a sheet. The bolsters are more valuable than the mattresses, both for their coverings and material: they are usually stuffed with cotton or other soft substance (Ezek. xviii. 20); but instead of these, skins of goats or sheep appear to have been formerly used by the poorer classes and in the hardier ages. These skins were probably sewed up in the natural shape, like water-skins, and stuffed with chaff or wool (1 Sam. xix. 13).

It has been doubted whether different Hebrew words translated ' couch,' and ' bed,' and ' bedstead ' in the authorized version were actually bedsteads of different sorts, or simply the standing and fixed divans, such as those on which the Western Asiatics commonly make their beds at night. It has been usually thought that the choice lay between these alternatives, because it has not been understood that in the East there

is, in fact, a varied arrangement in this matter: and there is reason to think that the different Hebrew words answer to and describe similarly different arrangements, although we may be unable now to give to the several Hebrew words the distinctive applications to still subsisting *things.*

The divan, or daïs, is a slightly elevated platform at the upper end, and often along the sides of the room. On this are laid the mattresses on which the Western Asiatics sit cross-legged in the day-time, with large cushions against the wall to support the back. At night the light bedding is usually laid out upon this divan, and beds for many persons are easily formed. The bedding is removed in the morning, and deposited in recesses in the room, made for the purpose. This is, however, a sort of general sleeping-room for the males of the family and for guests, none but the master having access to the inner parts of the house, where alone there are proper and distinct bed-chambers, where the bedding is either laid on the carpeted floor or placed on a low frame or bedstead.

The most common bedstead in Egypt and Arabia is of this shape, framed rudely of palm-

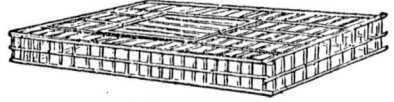

88.

sticks. It was used in ancient Egypt, and is figured in the mural paintings. In Palestine, Syria, Persia, where the palm-tree is not common, and where timber is more plentiful, a bed-frame of similar shape is made of boards. This kind of bedstead is also used upon the house-tops during the season in which people sleep there. It is more than likely that Og's bedstead was of this description (Deut. iii. 11). In the times in which he lived the palm-tree was more common in Palestine than at present, and those in ordinary use were probably formed of palm-sticks. Thus formed, they are incapable of sustaining any undue weight without being disjointed and bent awry; and this would dictate the necessity of making the bedstead destined to sustain the vast bulk of Og rather with rods of iron than with the mid-ribs of the palm-fronds. These bedsteads are also of a length seldom more than a few inches beyond the average human stature (commonly 6 feet 3 inches), and hence the propriety with which the length of Og's bedstead is stated to convey an idea of his stature.

It is not necessary to suppose that the bedsteads were all of this sort. There are traces of a sort of portable couch (1 Sam. xix. 15), which appears to have served as a sofa for sitting on in the day-time (1 Sam. xxviii. 23; Ezek. xxiii. 41; Amos vi. 4); and there is now the less reason to doubt that the ancient Hebrews had a convenience of this sort, as we find such couches in use among the neighbouring nations, and figured on their monuments. The subjoined example is from ancient Egypt.

A bed with a tester is mentioned in Judith xvi. 23, which, with other indications and the frequent mention of rich tapestries hung upon and about a bed for luxuriousness and ornament, proves that such beds as are still used by royal and distin-

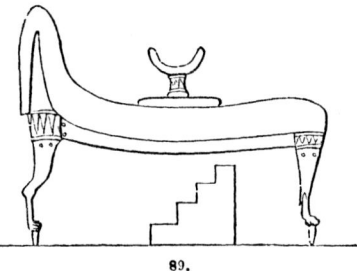

89.

guished personages were not unknown under the Hebrew monarchies (comp. Esth. i. 6 ; Prov. vii. 16, *sq.* ; Ezek. xxiii. 41).

It is evident that the ancient Jews, like the modern inhabitants of their land, seldom or never changed their dress on going to bed. Most people only divest themselves of their outer garment, and loosen the ligature of the waist, excepting during the hottest part of the summer, when they sleep almost entirely unclad.

BEE (occurs in Deut. i. 44 ; Judg. xiv. 8 ; Ps. cxviii. 12 ; Isa. vii. 18). This insect belongs to the family *apidæ*, order *hymenoptera*, species *apis mellifica*, commonly called the honey-bee, because this species has often yielded honey to man.

In proceeding to notice the principal passages of Scripture in which the bee is mentioned, we first pause at Deut. i. 44, where Moses alludes to the irresistible vengeance with which bees pursue their enemies : ' The Amorites came out against you and chased you as bees do, and destroyed you in Seir unto Hormah.' The powerlessness of man under the united attacks of these insects is well attested. Pliny relates that bees were so troublesome in some parts of Crete, that the inhabitants were compelled to forsake their homes ; and Ælian records that some places in Scythia were formerly inaccessible on account of the swarms of bees with which they were infested. Park relates that at Doofroo, some of the people being in search of honey, unfortunately disturbed a swarm of bees, which came out in great numbers, attacked both men and beasts, obliged them to fly in all directions, so that he feared an end had been put to his journey, and that one ass died the same night, and another the next morning. Even in this country the stings of two exasperated hives have been known to kill a horse in a few minutes.

The reference to the bee contained in Judg. xiv. 8, has attracted the notice of most readers. It is related in the 5th and 6th verses that Samson, aided by supernatural strength, rent a young lion, that warred against him, as he would have rent a kid, and that ' after a time,' as he returned to *take his wife*, he turned aside to see the carcass of the lion, and, behold, there was a swarm of bees and honey in the carcass of the lion. It has been hastily concluded that this narrative favours the mistaken notion of the ancients, possibly derived from misunderstanding this very account, that bees might be engendered in the dead bodies of animals, and ancient authors are quoted to testify to the aversion of bees to flesh, unpleasant smells,

and filthy places. But it may readily be perceived that it is not said that the bees were *bred* in the body of the lion. Again, the frequently recurring phrase, ' after a time,' literally ' after days,' introduced into the text, proves that at least sufficient time had elapsed for all the flesh of the animal to have been removed by birds and beasts of prey, the ants. &c. The Syriac version translates ' the bony carcass.' The learned Bochart remarks that the Hebrew phrase sometimes signifies *a whole year*, and in this passage it would seem likely to have this meaning. because such was the length of time which usually elapsed between espousal and marriage (see ver. 7). The circumstance that ' *honey* ' was found in the carcass as well as bees, shows that sufficient time had elapsed since their possession of it, for all the flesh to be removed. Nor is such an abode for bees, probably in the skull or thorax, more unsuitable than a hollow in a rock, or in a tree, or in the ground, in which we know they often reside, or those clay nests which they build for themselves in Brazil. Nor is the fact without parallel. Herodotus relates that a swarm of bees took up their abode in the skull of one Silius, an ancient invader of Cyprus, which they filled with honeycombs, after the inhabitants had suspended it over the gate of their city. A similar story is told by Aldrovandus of some bees that inhabited and built their combs in a human skeleton in a tomb in a church at Verona.

The phrase in Ps. cxviii. 12, ' They compassed me about like bees,' is easily understood by all who know the manner in which bees attack the object of their fury.

The only remaining passage has been strangely misunderstood (Isa. vii. 18) : ' The Lord shall *hiss* for the fly that is in the uttermost parts of the river of Egypt, and for the bee that is in the land of Assyria.' Here the fly and the bee are no doubt personifications of those inveterate enemies of Israel, the Egyptians and Assyrians, whom the Lord threatened to excite against his disobedient people. But the *hissing* for them has been interpreted, even by modern writers of eminence, as involving ' an allusion to the practice of calling out the bees from their hives, by a hissing or whistling sound, to their labour in the fields, and summoning them to return when the heavens begin to lower, or the shadows of evening to fall.' No one has offered any proof of the existence of such a custom, and the idea will itself seem sufficiently strange to all who are acquainted with the habits of bees. The true reference is, no doubt, to the custom of the people of the East, and even of many parts of Europe, of calling the attention of any one in the street, &c. by a significant *hiss* or rather *hist*, as Bishop Lowth translates the word both here and in Isa. v. 26. Hissing, or rather histing, is in use among us for setting a dog on any object. Hence the sense of the threatening is, I will direct the hostile attention of the Egyptians and Assyrians against you.

BEEL'ZEBUL, the name assigned (Matt. xii. 24) to the prince of the dæmons. There is no doubt that the reading *Beelzebul* is the one which has the support of almost every critical authority ; and the *Beelzebub* of the Peshito (if indeed it is not a corruption, as Michaelis thinks), and of the Vulgate, and of some modern versions, has probably been accommodated to the name of the

Philistine god *Baalzebub*. Some of those who consider the latter to have been a reverential title for that god, believe that Beelzebul is a wilful corruption of it, in order to make it contemptible. [BAAL.]

BEER, *a well* : a local proper name, denoting, whether by itself or in composition, the presence of a well of water. There were two places so called.—1. A place in the land of Moab, which was one of the encampments of the Israelites (Num. xxi. 16).—2. A town in the tribe of Judah. It is mentioned only once in Scripture (Judg. ix. 21), as the place to which Jotham fled. It is supposed to be the same with the modern Bireh, a large village situated on the ridge, running from east to west, which bounds the northern prospect, as beheld from Jerusalem and its vicinity, and may be seen from a great distance north and south. It contains a population of 700 Moslems. The houses are low, and many of them half underground. Many large stones and various substructions evince the antiquity of the site; and there are remains of a fine old church of the time of the Crusades.

BEE'ROTH, the plural of Beer, and by many taken for the same place. It is mentioned as a city of the Gibeonites (Josh. ix. 17), and was reckoned in the tribe of Benjamin (2 Sam. iv. 2; Ezra ii. 25).

BE'ER-SHE'BA, *well of the oath* ; a place in the southernmost part of Canaan, celebrated for the sojourn of the patriarchs. It took its name from the *well* which was dug there by Abraham, and the oath which confirmed his treaty with Abimelech (Gen. xxi. 31). It seems to have been a favourite station of that patriarch, and here he planted one of those 'groves' which formed the temples of those remote times (Gen. xxi. 33). A town of some consequence afterwards arose on the spot, and retained the same name. It was first assigned to the tribe of Judah (Josh. xv. 28), and afterwards transferred to Simeon (Josh. xix. 2), but was still popularly ascribed to Judah (2 Sam. xxiv. 7). Being the southernmost city of the land, its name is of frequent occurrence as being proverbially used in describing the extent of the land, in the phrase 'from Dan (in the north) to Beersheba' (in the south), and reversely, 'from Beersheba unto Dan' (Judg. xx. 1; 2 Sam. xvii. 11; 1 Chron. xxi. 2; 2 Chron. xxx. 5). It was at Beersheba that Samuel established his sons as judges for the southernmost districts (1 Sam. viii. 2): it was from thence that Elijah wandered out into the southern desert (1 Kings xix. 3): here was one of the chief seats of idolatrous worship in the time of Uzziah (Amos v. 5; viii. 14); and to this place, among others, the Jews returned after the Captivity (Neh. xi. 27, 30). This is the last time its name occurs in the Old Testament. In the New Testament it is not once mentioned; and for many centuries it seems to have been in a great measure forgotten. Its site was recently visited by Dr. Robinson, who, on converging from the desert and entering the borders of Palestine, came upon two deep wells still called Bir-es-Leba, situate on the northern side of a wide watercourse called Wady ir-Leba. These wells are 55 rods apart. They are circular, and stoned up very neatly with masonry, apparently very ancient. The water in both was pure and sweet, and in great abundance; the finest, indeed,

the travellers had found since leaving Sinai. Both wells were surrounded with drinking-troughs of stone for camels and flocks, such as were doubtless used of old by the flocks which were fed on the adjacent hills. No ruins were at first visible; but, on examination, foundations of former dwellings were traced, dispersed loosely over the low hills to the north of the wells, and in the hollows between. They seem to have been built chiefly of round stones, although some of the stones are squared and some hewn; suggesting the idea of a small straggling city. The site of the wells is nearly midway between the southern end of the Dead Sea and the Mediterranean at Raphæa, or twenty-seven miles south-east from Gaza, and about the same distance south-by-west from Hebron.

BEEVES. The rearing of horned cattle was encouraged by the people of Israel. These animals were protected in some cases by express provisions of the law; they were held clean, being the usual sacrifice of consideration, and the chief article of flesh diet of the population. Judging from Egyptian remains, there were two great breeds of straight-backed cattle, the long-horned and the short-horned; and in Upper Egypt at least, there was one without horns. Another hunched species existed, which served to draw chariots, yoked in the same manner as the Brahminee bulls of India are at present.

In Egypt the straight-backed or common cattle appear to have formed a very handsome breed with lunate horns. They were generally spotted black or red upon a white ground, and there were, besides, others white, red, or black. They all served for common use, but those without red were selected when new sacred bulls were to be supplied; for they alone had the colours which could show the marks made by chance or by art, and required to fit the animal for the purpose intended. There was, besides, a sacred cow; and a black bull was worshipped at Hermonthis.

In Palestine the breed of cattle was most likely in ancient times, as it still is, inferior in size to the Egyptian.

Unless the name be taken synonymously with that of other species, there is not in the Bible any indication of the buffalo. The Asiatic species was not known in Greece till the time of Aristotle. The indigenous buffaloes of Africa, amounting at least to two very distinct species, appear to have belonged to the south and west of that continent, and only at a later period to have approached Egypt as far as the present Bornou; for none are figured on any known monument in either Upper or Lower Egypt. With regard, however, to wild oxen of the true Taurine genus, some may, at a very remote period, have been found in Bashan, evidently the origin of the name,—a region where mountain, wood, and water, all connecting the Syrian Libanus with Taurus, were favourable to their existence; but the wild bulls of the district, mentioned in Ps. xxii. 12, and in various other passages, appear, nevertheless, to refer to domestic species, probably left to propagate without much human superintendence, except annually marking the increase, and selecting a portion for consumption, in the same manner as is still practised in some parts of Europe.

BEGGARS. [ALMS.]

BE'HEMOTH (Job xl. 15) is regarded as the plural of *behemah*, but commentators are by no means agreed as to its true meaning. A number of learned men, with Bochart and Calmet at their head, understand the word in the singular number as a specific name, denoting the hippopotamus, seeking to prove, by somewhat forced

90. [Hippopotamus.]

interpretations of the beautiful poetical allusions in Job xl. 15-24, the exactness of the description when compared with the species, which, however, in some respects is more applicable to the elephant, while in others it is equally so to both animals. Hence the term behemoth, taken intensely (for in some places it is admitted to designate cattle in general), may be assumed to be a poetical personification of the great Pachydermata, or even Herbivora, wherein the idea of hippopotamus is predominant. This view accounts for the ascription to it of characters not truly applicable to one species; for instance, the tail is likened to a cedar, which is only admissible in the case of the elephant; again, 'the mountains bring him forth food;' 'he trusteth that he can draw up Jordan,' a river which elephants alone could reach; 'his nose pierceth through snares,' certainly more indicative of that animal's proboscis with its extraordinary delicacy of scent and touch, ever cautiously applied, than of the obtuse perceptions of the river-horse. Finally, the elephant is far more dangerous as an enemy than the hippopotamus, which numerous pictorial sculptures on the monuments of Egypt represent as fearlessly speared by a single hunter standing on his float of log and reeds. Yet although the elephant is scarcely less fond of water, the description referring to manners, such as lying under the shade of willows among reeds, in fens, &c., is more directly characteristic of the hippopotamus. The book of Job appears, from many internal indications, to have been written in Asia, and is full of knowledge, although that knowledge is not expressed according to the precise technicalities of modern science; it offers pictures in magnificent outline, without condescending to minute and laboured details. Considered in this light, the expression in Ps. l. 10, 'For every beast of the forest is mine, and the cattle (behemoth) upon a thousand hills,' acquires a grandeur and force far surpassing the mere idea of cattle of various kinds. If, therefore, we take this plural noun to bear the meaning here briefly indicated, we may likewise consider the leviathan, its counterpart, a similarly generalized term with the idea of the crocodile most prominent; but from the very name indicating a twisting animal, and which from various texts

evidently include the great pythons, cetacea, and sharks of the surrounding seas and deserts, it conveys a more sublime allusion than if limited to the crocodile, an animal familiar to every Egyptian, and well known even in Palestine.

BE'KAH, half a shekel. [WEIGHTS.]

BEL is the name under which the national god of the Babylonians is cursorily mentioned in Isa. xlvi. 1; Jer. l. 2; li. 44. This deity is also noticed in Bar. vi. 40, and the apocryphal addition to the book of Daniel, where we read of meat and drink being daily offered to him, according to a usage occurring in classical idolatry. A particular account of the pyramidal temple of Bel, at Babylon, is given by Herodotus, who also states that the sacrifices of this god consisted of adult cattle, of their young, when sucking, and of incense.

The question whether the sun or the planet Jupiter was the power of nature adored under the name of Bel, is discussed under the article BAAL.

BEL and DRAGON. [DANIEL, APOCRYPHAL ADDITIONS TO.]

BE'LA. [ZOAR.]

BELL. The first bells known in history are those small golden bells which were attached to the lower part of the blue robe (the robe of the ephod) which formed part of the dress of the high-priest in his sacerdotal ministrations (Exod. xxviii. 33, 34; comp. Ecclus. xlv. 11). They were there placed alternately with the pomegranate-shaped knobs, one of these being between every two of the bells. The number of these bells is not mentioned in Scripture; but tradition states that there were sixty-six. We need not seek any other reason for this rather singular use of bells than that which is assigned: 'His sound shall be heard when he goeth into the holy place before the Lord, and when he cometh out, that he die not' (Exod. xxviii. 35); by which we may understand that the sound of the bells manifested that he was properly arrayed in the robes of ceremony which he was required to wear when he entered the presence-chamber of the Great King; and that as no minister can enter the presence of an earthly potentate abruptly and unannounced, so he (whom no human being *could* introduce) was to have his entrance harbingered by the sound of the bells he wore. This sound, heard outside, also notified to the people the time in which he was engaged in his sacred ministrations, and during which they remained in prayer (Luke i. 9, 10).

'BELLS OF THE HORSES' are mentioned in Zech. xiv. 20, which were probably such as were hung to the bridles or foreheads, or to belts around the necks, of horses trained for war, that they might thereby be accustomed to noise and tumult, and not by their alarm expose the riders to danger in actual warfare. We incline to think, however, that the use of horse-bells with which the Jews were most familiar, and which the prophet had in view, was that which at present exists in the East, and in other countries where carriage by pack-horses and mules is common. The laden animals, being without riders, have bells hung from their necks, that they may be kept together, in traversing by night the open plains and deserts, by paths and roads unconfined by fences or boundaries; **that** they may be cheered by the sound of the bells; and that if any horse strays, its place may be known by the sound of its bell, while the general sound from the caravan enables the traveller who has strayed or lingered, to find and regain his party, even in the night.

That the same motto, HOLINESS TO THE LORD, which was upon the mitre of the high-priest, should, in the happy days foretold by the prophet, be inscribed even upon the bells of the horses, manifestly signifies that all things, from the highest to the lowest, should in those days be sanctified to God.

It is remarkable that there is no appearance of bells of any kind in the Egyptian monuments.

BELLOWS. This word only occurs in Jer. vi. 29, and is there used with reference to the casting of metal. As fires in the East are always of wood or charcoal, a sufficient heat for ordinary purposes is soon raised by the help of fans, and the use of bellows is confined to the workers in metal. Such was the case anciently; and in the mural paintings of Egypt we observe no bellows but such as are used for the forge or furnace. They thus occur as early as the time of Moses, being represented in a tomb at Thebes which bears the name of Thothmes III. They

91.

consisted of a leathern bag, secured and fitted into a frame, from which a long pipe extended for carrying the wind to the fire. They were worked by the feet, the operator standing upon them with one under each foot and pressing them alternately, while he pulled up each exhausted skin with a string he held in his hand. In one instance it is observed from the painting, that when the man left the bellows they were raised as if filled with air, and this would imply a knowledge of the valve.

BELLY. Among the Hebrews, and with most ancient nations, the belly was regarded as the seat of the carnal affections, as being, according to the notions of antiquity, that which first partakes of sensual pleasures (Tit. i. 12; Phil. iii. 19; Rom. xvi. 18). It is used likewise symbolically for the heart, the innermost recesses of the soul (Prov. xviii. 8; xx. 27; xxii. 18). The *embittering* of the belly signifies all the train of evils which may come upon a man (Jer. iv. 19; ix, 15; comp. Numb. v. 27).

BELSHAZ'ZAR is the name given in the book of Daniel to the last king of the Chaldees, under whom Babylon was taken by the Medes and Persians. Nothing is really known of this king except from the book of Daniel.

BELTESHAZ'ZAR. [DANIEL.]

BEN (*son*), is often found as the first element of proper names; in which case the word which follows it is always to be considered dependent on it, in the relation of our genitive. The word which follows *Ben* may either be of itself a proper name, or be an appellative or abstract, the principle of the connection being essentially the same in both cases. [BAR.]

BENAI'AH, son of Jehoiada, and commander of David's guard (the Cherethites and Pelethites, 2 Sam. viii. 18). His exploits were celebrated in Israel. He overcame two Moabitish champions ('lions of God'), slew an Egyptian giant with his own spear, and went down into an exhausted cistern and destroyed a lion which had fallen into it when covered with snow (2 Sam. xxiii. 21). Benaiah (doubtless with the guard he commanded) adhered to Solomon when Joab and others attempted to set up Adonijah; and when that attempt failed, he, as belonged to his office, was sent to put Joab to death, after which he was appointed commander in chief in his place (1 Kings i. 36; ii. 29). Some persons named Benaiah returned from the exile with Ezra (x. 25, 30, 35, 43).

BENHA'DAD (*son of Hadad*), the name of three kings of Damascene-Syria. As to the latter part of this name, Hadad, there is little doubt that it is the name of the Syrian god ADAD.

1. BENHADAD, the king of Syria who was subsidised by Asa king of Judah to invade Israel, and thereby compel Baasha (who had invaded Judah) to return to defend his own kingdom (1 Kings xv. 18). [ASA.] This Benhadad has, with some reason, been supposed to be Hadad the Edomite who rebelled against Solomon (1 Kings xi. 25).

2. BENHADAD, king of Syria, son of the preceding. His earlier history is much involved in that of Ahab, with whom he was constantly at war [AHAB]. He owed the signal defeat in which that war terminated to the vain notion that assimilated JEHOVAH to the local deities which the nations of Syria worshipped, deeming Him 'a God of the hills,' but impotent to defend his votaries in 'the plains' (1 Kings xx. 1-30). Instead of pursuing his victory, Ahab concluded a peace with the defeated Benhadad, which was observed for about twelve years, when the Syrian king declared war against Jehoram the son of Ahab, and invaded Israel: but all his plans and operations were frustrated by being made known to Jehoram by the prophet Elisha (2 Kings vi. 8, *ad fin.*). After some years he however renewed the war, and besieged Jehoram in his capital, Samaria, until the inhabitants were reduced to the last extremities and most revolting resources by famine. The siege was then unexpectedly raised, according to a prediction of Elisha, through a panic infused into the besiegers, who concluding that a noise which they seemed to hear portended the advance upon them of a foreign host procured by Jehoram, thought only of saving themselves by flight. The next year Benhadad, learning that Elisha, through whom so many of his designs had been brought to nought, had arrived at Damascus, sent an officer of distinction named Hazael with presents, to consult him as to his recovery from an illness under which he then suffered. The prophet answered, that his disease was not mortal, but that he would nevertheless

die. This was accomplished a few days after by this very Hazael, who smothered the sick monarch in his bed, and mounted the throne in his stead, B.C. 884 (2 Kings viii. 7-15). [ELISHA; HAZAEL: JEHORAM.]

3. BENHADAD, king of Syria, son of the Hazael just mentioned. He was thrice defeated by Jehoash, king of Israel, who recovered from him all the territories beyond Jordan which Hazael had rent from the dominion of Israel (2 Kings xiii. 3, 24, 25).

BEN'JAMIN, youngest son of Jacob, by Rachel (Gen. xxxv. 18). His mother died immediately after he was born, and with her last breath named him Ben-Oni, ' Son of my pain,' which the father changed into Benjamin, a word of nearly the same sound, but portending comfort and consolation, ' Son of my right hand,' probably alluding to the support and protection he promised himself from this, his last child, in his old age.

The tribe of Benjamin, though the least numerous of Israel, became nevertheless a considerable race in process of time. In the desert it counted 35,400 warriors, all above twenty years of age (Num. i. 36; ii. 22); and, at the entrance of Israel into Canaan, even as many as 45,600. The portion allotted to this tribe was in proportion to its small number, and was encompassed by the districts of Ephraim, Dan, and Judah, in central Palestine. The territory, though rather small, was highly-cultivated and naturally fertile, and contained thirty-six towns (with the villages appertaining to them), which are named in Josh. xviii. 21-28; and the principal of which were Jericho, Bethagla, Bethel, Gibeon, Ramah, and Jebus or Jerusalem. This latter place subsequently became the capital of the whole Jewish empire; but was, after the division of the land, still in possession of the Jebusites. The lower or less fortified part had been taken by Judah (Judg. i. 8), who in this matter had almost a common interest with *Benjamin;* but Zion, the upper part, was not finally wrested from the Jebusites till the time of David (2 Sam. v. 6, *sq.*). In the time of the Judges, the tribe of Benjamin became involved in a civil war with the other eleven tribes, for having refused to give up to justice the miscreants of Gibeon who had publicly violated and caused the death of a concubine of a man of Ephraim, who had passed with her through Gibeon. This war terminated in the almost utter extinction of the tribe; leaving no hope for its regeneration from the circumstance, that, not only had nearly all the women of that tribe been previously slain by their foes, but the eleven other tribes had engaged themselves by a solemn oath not to marry their daughters to any man belonging to Benjamin. When the thirst of revenge, however, had abated, they found means to evade the letter of the oath, and to revive the tribe again by an alliance with them (Judg. xxi. 20, 21). This revival was so rapid, that in the time of David it already numbered 59,434 able warriors (1 Chron. vii. 6-12); in that of Asa, 280,000 (2 Chron. xiv. 8); and in that of Jehoshaphat, 200,000 (2 Chron. xvii. 17).

This tribe had also the honour of giving the first king to the Jews, Saul being a Benjamite (1 Sam. ix. 1, 2). After his death, the Benjamites, as might have been expected, declared themselves for his son Ishbosheth (2 Sam. ii. 8, *sq.*); until, after the assassination of that prince, David became king of all Israel. David having at last expelled the Jebusites from Zion, and made it his own residence, the close alliance that seems previously to have existed between the tribes of Benjamin and Judah (Judg. i. 8) was cemented by the circumstance that, while Jerusalem actually belonged to the district of Benjamin, that of Judah was immediately contiguous to it. Thus it happened, that, at the division of the kingdom after the death of Solomon, Benjamin espoused the cause of Judah, and formed, together with it, a kingdom by themselves. Indeed, the two tribes stood always in such a close connection, as often to be included under the single term Judah (1 Kings xi. 13; xii. 20). After the exile, also, these two tribes constituted the flower of the new Jewish colony in Palestine (comp. Ezr. xi. 1; x. 9).

BERE'A (Acts xvii. 10), a city of Macedonia, situate on the river Astræus, not far from Pella, towards the south-west, and near Mount Bermius. It was afterwards called Irenopolis, and is now known by the name of Boor. Paul and Silas withdrew to this place from Thessalonica; and the Jewish residents are described as more ingenuous, and of a better disposition (not ' more noble,' as in the Authorized Version) ' than those of Thessalonica,' in that they diligently searched the Scriptures to ascertain the truth of the doctrines taught by the Apostles.

BERNI'CE, eldest daughter of Herod Agrippa I., and sister of the younger Agrippa (Acts xxv. 13, 23; xxvi. 30). She was married to her uncle Herod, king of Chalcis; and after his death, in order to avoid the merited suspicion of incest with her brother Agrippa, she became the wife of Polemon, king of Cilicia. This connection being soon dissolved, she returned to her brother, and afterwards became the mistress of Vespasian and Titus.

BER'YL. This is supposed by some to be the precious stone intended by the word *shoham,* which occurs in Gen. ii. 12; Exod. xxviii. 9; xxxv. 9-27; Job xxviii. 16; Ezek. xxviii. 13. Whether the beryl be the *shoham* or not, it is a Scriptural stone by virtue of the mention of it in Rev. xxi. 20. There is no doubt that the stone which we call beryl is the substance to which the ancients gave the same name. It is of a pale sea-green colour, inclining sometimes to water blue, and sometimes to yellow. In its crystallized form it exhibits sexagonal columns striped longitudinally. The *shoham* furnished the shoulder-pieces in the breastplate of the high-priest, on each of which six names were engraven, and for this purpose the stalky beryl, consisting of long, stout, hexagonal pieces, was peculiarly suited. Beryls are found, but not often, in collections of ancient gems. In Gen. ii. 12, the *shoham* is named as the product of Havilah; in Job xxviii. 16, it is mentioned as a stone of great value, being classed with the sapphire and the gold of Ophir; in Ezek. xxviii. 13, it appears as a valuable article of commerce.

Luther, relying upon the authority of some ancient versions, makes the *shoham* to have been the onyx. This indeed is the stone usually given for the *shoham* in Hebrew lexicons, and

L 2

is the one which the Authorized Version has also adopted.

BE'SOR, a brook mentioned in 1 Sam. xxx. 9. It is without doubt the same that Richardson crossed on approaching Gaza from the south, and which he calls Oa di Gaza (Wady Gaza). The bed was thirty yards wide, and its stream was, early in April, already exhausted, although some stagnant water remained.

BETH (*house*) is often found as the first element of proper names of places in the Bible. It is only necessary to observe that, in all such compounds, as Bethel, &c., the latter part of the word must be considered, according to our Occidental languages, to depend on the former in the relation of the *genitive;* so that Bethel can only mean 'house of God.' The notion of *house* is, of course, capable of a wide application, and is used to mean temple, habitation, place, according to the sense of the word with which it is combined.

BETHAB'ARA or BETHBARAH. This name means *place of the ford, i. e.* of or over the Jordan; and is mentioned in John i. 28, as the place where John baptized. The best manuscripts and recent editions, however, have Bethany : the reading Bethabara appears to have arisen from the conjecture of Origen, who in his day found no such place on the Jordan as Bethany, but knew a town called Bethabara, where John was said to have baptized, and therefore took the unwarrantable liberty of changing the reading.

BETH'ANY (*place of dates*). 1. The place near the Jordan where John baptized, the exact situation of which is unknown. Some copies here read Bethabara, as stated in the preceding article. 2. BETHANY, a town or village about fifteen furlongs east-south-east from Jerusalem, beyond the Mount of Olives (John xi. 18), so called, probably, from the number of palm-trees that grew around. It was the residence of Lazarus and his sisters Mary and Martha, and Jesus often went out from Jerusalem to lodge there (Matt. xxi. 17; xxvi. 6; Mark xi. 1, 11, 12; xiv. 3; Luke xix. 29; xxiv. 50; John xi. 1, 18; xii. 1). The place still subsists in a shallow wady on the eastern slope of the Mount of Olives. Dr. Robinson reached Bethany in three-quarters of an hour from the Damascus gate of Jerusalem; which gives a distance corresponding to the fifteen furlongs (stadia) of the Evangelist. It is a poor village of about twenty families. The only marks of antiquity are some hewn stones from more ancient buildings, found in the walls of some of the houses. The monks, indeed, show the house of Mary and Martha, and of Simon the leper, and also the sepulchre of Lazarus, all of which are constantly mentioned in the narratives of pilgrims and travellers. The sepulchre is a deep vault, like a cellar, excavated in the limestone rock in the middle of the village, to which there is a descent by twenty-six steps. Dr. Robinson alleges that there is not the slightest probability of its ever having been the tomb of Lazarus. The form is not that of the ancient sepulchres, nor does its situation accord with the narrative of the New Testament, which implies that the tomb was not in the town (John xvi. 31, 38).

BETH-AR'BEL, a place mentioned only in Hos. x. 14; and as it there seems to be implied that it was an impregnable fortress, the probability is strengthened of its being the same as the Arbela of Josephus. This was a village in Galilee, near which were certain fortified caverns. They are first mentioned in connection with the march of Bacchides into Judæa, at which time they were occupied by many fugitives, and the Syrian general encamped there long enough to subdue them. At a later period these caverns formed the retreats of banded robbers, who greatly distressed the inhabitants throughout that quarter, and were at length extirpated by Herod These same caverns were afterwards fortified by Josephus himself against the Romans during his command in Galilee. There is little doubt that Arbela of Galilee, with its fortified caverns, may be identified with the present Kulat ibn Maan and the adjacent ruins now known as Irbid.

BETH-A'VEN (*house of idols*), a nickname for the town of Bethel, applied to it after it became the seat of the worship of the golden calves [BETHEL]. There was, however, a town of this name not far from Bethel eastward (Josh. vii. 2; 1 Sam. xiii. 5), the existence of which, perhaps, occasioned the transfer of the name to Bethel. There was also a desert of the same name (Josh. xviii. 12).

BETH'EL, originally Luz, an ancient town which Eusebius places 12 R. miles north of Jerusalem, on the right hand of the road to Shechem. Jacob rested here one night on his way to Padan-Aram, and commemorated the vision with which he was favoured by erecting and pouring oil upon the stone which had served him for a pillow, and giving to the place the name of Bethel (*place* or *house of God*), which eventually superseded the more ancient designation of Luz (Gen. xxviii. 11-19). Under that name it is mentioned proleptically with reference to the earlier *time* of Abraham (Gen. xii. 8; xiii. 3). After his prosperous return, Bethel became a favourite station with Jacob: here he built an altar, buried Deborah, received the name of Israel (for the second time), and promises of blessing; and here also he accomplished the vow which he had made on his going forth (Gen. xxxv. 1-15; comp. xxxii. 28, and xxviii. 20-22). It seems not to have been a town in those early times; but at the conquest of the land, Bethel is mentioned as the royal city of the Canaanites (Josh. xii. 16). It became a boundary town of Benjamin towards Ephraim (Josh. xviii. 22), and was actually conquered by the latter tribe from the Canaanites (Judg. i. 22-26). At this place, already consecrated in the time of the patriarchs, the ark of the covenant was apparently for a long while deposited [ARK], and probably the tabernacle also (Judg. xx. 26; comp. 1 Sam. x. 3). It was also one of the places at which Samuel held in rotation his court of justice (1 Sam. vii. 16). After the separation of the kingdoms Bethel was included in that of Israel, which seems to show, that although originally in the formal distribution assigned to Benjamin, it had been actually possessed by Ephraim in right of conquest from the Canaanites—which might have been held by that somewhat unscrupulous tribe to determine the right of possession to a place of importance close on their own frontier. Jeroboam made it the southern seat (Dan being the northern) of the worship of the golden calves; and it seems to have been the chief seat of that worship (1 Kings xii. 28-33; xiii. 1). This appropriation, however, completely desecrated

Bethel in the estimation of the orthodox Jews; and the prophets name it with abhorrence and contempt—even applying to it the name of Beth-aven (*house of idols*) instead Bethel (house of God) (Amos i. 5; Hos. iv. 15; v. 8; x. 5, 8). The town was taken from Jeroboam by Abijah, king of Judah (2 Chron. xiii. 19); but it again reverted to Israel (2 Kings x. 28). After the Israelites were carried away captive by the Assyrians, all traces of this illegal worship were extirpated by Josiah, king of Judah, who thus fulfilled a prophecy made to Jeroboam 350 years before (2 Kings xiii. 1, 2; xxiii. 15-18). The place was still in existence after the Captivity, and was in the possession of the Benjamites (Ezra ii. 28; Neh. vii. 32). In the time of the Maccabees Bethel was fortified by Bacchides for the king of Syria. It is not named in the New Testament; but it still existed, and was taken by Vespasian. It is described by Eusebius and Jerome as a small village; and this is the last notice of it as an inhabited place. Bethel and its name were believed to have perished until within these few years; when it has been identified with Beitin, the situation of which corresponds very exactly with the position assigned to the ancient Bethel. The ruins, which are considerable, lie upon the point of a low hill, between the heads of two shallow wadys which unite below, and run off into a deep and rugged valley. The spot is shut in by higher land on every side.

BE'THER. The Mountains of Bether are only mentioned in Cant. ii. 17; viii. 14; and no place called Bether occurs elsewhere. The word means, properly, *dissection*. The mountains of Bether may therefore be *mountains of disjunction*, of *separation*, etc , that is, mountains cut up, divided by ravines, etc.

BETHE'SDA (*house* or *place of mercy*), a pool at the Sheep-gate of Jerusalem, built round with porches for the accommodation of the sick who sought benefit from the healing virtues of the water, and upon one of whom Christ performed the healing miracle recorded by St. John (v. 2-9). That which is now, and has long been pointed out as the Pool of Bethesda, is a dry basin or reservoir outside the northern wall of the enclosure around the Temple Mount, of which wall its southern side may be said to form a part. The east end of it is close to the present gate of St. Stephen. The pool measures 360 feet in length,

92. [Pool of Bethesda.]

130 feet in breadth, and 75 in depth from the bottom, besides the rubbish which has been accumulated in it for ages. Dr. Robinson is of opinion that this excavation is not entitled to the designation it bears; but his arguments have been so forcibly met by more recent and not less useful inquirers, that until some better alternative is offered, it will be well to acquiesce in the local conclusion.

BETH-HO'RON: two places of this name are distinguished in Scripture as the Upper and Nether Beth-horon (Josh. xvi. 3, 5; xviii. 13; 1 Chron. vii. 24). The Nether Beth-horon lay in the N.W. corner of Benjamin; and between the two places was a pass called both the ascent and descent of Beth-horon, leading from the region of Gibeon (el-Jib) down to the western plain (Josh. xviii. 13, 14; x. 10, 11). Down this pass the five kings of the Amorites were driven by Joshua (Josh. x. 11). The upper and lower towns were both fortified by Solomon (1 Kings ix. 17; 2 Chron. viii. 5). Cestius Gallus, the Roman pro-consul of Syria, in his march from Cæsarea to Jerusalem, after having burned Lydda, ascended the mountain by Beth-horon and encamped near Gibeon. From these intimations it would appear that in ancient times, as at the present day, the great road of communication and of heavy transport between Jerusalem and the sea-coast was by the pass of Beth-horon.

The two Beth-horons still exist under the name of Beit-Ur. The Lower Beit-Ur is upon the top of a low ridge, which is separated by a wady, or narrow valley, from the foot of the mountain upon which the Upper Beit-Ur stands. Both are now inhabited villages. The lower is very small, but foundations of large stones indicate an ancient site—doubtless that of the Nether Beth-horon. The Upper Beit-Ur is likewise small, but also exhibits traces of ancient walls and foundations. In the steep ascent to it the rock is in some parts cut away, and the path formed into steps, indicating an ancient road. On the first offset or step of the ascent are foundations of huge stones, the remains perhaps of a castle that once guarded the pass.

It is remarkable that the places are still distinguished as Beit-Ur el-Foka (the Upper), and Beit-Ur el-Tahta (the Lower).

BETH'LEHEM, (*house* or *place of bread*, i. q. *Bread-town*;) a city of Judah (Judg. xvii. 7), six miles southward from Jerusalem, on the road to Hebron. It was generally called Bethlehem-Judah, to distinguish it from another Bethlehem in Zebulun (Josh. xix. 15; Judg. xii. 10). It is also called Ephratah (the fruitful), and its inhabitants Ephratites (Gen. xlviii. 7; Mic. v. 2). Bethlehem is chiefly celebrated as the birth place of David and of Christ, and as the scene of the Book of Ruth. It was fortified by Reho boam (2 Chron. xi. 6); but it does not appear to have been a place of much importance; for Micah, extolling the moral pre-eminence of Bethlehem, says, 'Thou Bethlehem Ephratah, *though thou be little among the thousands of Judah*,' &c (Mic. v. 2). There never has been any dispute or doubt about the site of Bethlehem, which has always been an inhabited place, and, from its sacred associations, has been visited by an unbroken series of pilgrims and travellers. It is now a large straggling village, beautifully situated on the brow of a high hill, and consisting chiefly of one broad and principal street. The houses are built for the most part of clay and bricks; and every house is provided with an apiary, the beehives of which are constructed of a series of earthen pots, ranged on the house-tops. The inhabitants are said to be 3000, and were all native Christians at the time of the most recent visits; for Ibrahim Pasha, finding that the Moslem and Christian inhabitants were always at strife, caused the former to withdraw, and left the village in quiet possession of the latter, whose numbers had always greatly pre-dominated. The chief trade and manufacture of the inhabitants consist of beads, crosses, and other relics, which are sold at a great profit. Some of the articles, wrought in mother-of-pearl, are carved with more skill than one would expect to find in that remote quarter; and the workmanship in some instances would not dis-credit the artists of Britain. The people are said to be remarkable for their ferocity and rude-ness, which is indeed the common character of the inhabitants of most of the places accounted holy in the East.

At the farthest extremity of the town is the Latin convent, connected with which is the Church of the Nativity, said to have been built by the empress Helena. It has suffered much from time, but still bears manifest traces of its Grecian origin; and is alleged to be the most chaste architectural building now remaining in Palestine. Two spiral staircases lead to the cave called the 'Grotto of the Nativity,' which is about 20 feet below the level of the church. This cave is lined with Italian marbles, and lighted by numerous lamps. Here the pilgrim is conducted with due solemnity to a star inlaid in the marble, marking the exact spot where the Saviour was born, and corresponding to that in the firmament occupied by the meteor which intimated that great event; he is then led to one of the sides, where, in a kind of recess, a little below the level of the rest of the floor, is a block of white marble, hollowed out in the form of a manger, and said to mark the place of the one in which the infant Jesus was laid. His attention is afterwards directed to the 'Sepulchre of the Innocents;' to the grotto in which St. Jerome passed the greater portion of his life; and to the chapels dedicated to Joseph and other saints. There has been much controversy respecting the claims of this grotto to be regarded as the place in which our Lord was born. Tradition is in its favour, but facts and probabilities are against it. It is useless to deny that there is much force in a tradition regarding a locality, which can be traced up to a period not remote from that of the event commemorated; and this event was so important as to make the scene of it a point of such unremitting attention, that the knowledge of the spot was not likely to be lost. This view would be greatly strengthened if it could be satisfactorily proved that Hadrian, to cast odium upon the mysteries of the Christian religion, not only erected statues of Jupiter and Venus over the holy Sepulchre and on Calvary, but placed one of Adonis over the spot of the Nativity at Bethlehem. This part of the evidence is exa-mined under another head [GOLGOTHA]. Against tradition, whatever may be its value in the pre-

sent case, we have to place the utter improbability that a *subterranean* cavern like this, with a steep descent, should ever have been used as a stable for cattle, and, what is more, for the stable of a khan or caravanserai, which doubtless the 'inn' of Luke ii. 7 was. Although therefore it is true that cattle are, and always have been, stabled in caverns in the East; yet certainly not in such caverns as this, which appears to have been ori-ginally a tomb. Old empty tombs often, it is argued, afford shelter to man and cattle; but such was not the case among the Jews, who held themselves ceremonially defiled by contact with sepulchres. Besides, the circumstance of Christ's having been born in a cave would not have been less remarkable than his being laid in a manger, and was more likely to have been noticed by the Evangelist, if it had occurred: and it is also to be observed that the present grotto is at some distance from the town, whereas Christ appears to have been born *in* the town, and whatever may be the case in the open country, it has never been usual in towns to employ caverns as stables for cattle.

On the north-east side of the town is a deep valley, alleged to be that in which the angels appeared to the shepherds announcing the birth of the Saviour (Luke ii. 8). In the same valley is a fountain of delicious water, said with reasonable probability to be that for which David longed, and which three of his mighty men procured for him at the hazard of their lives (2 Sam. xxiii. 15-18).

BETH-NIM'RA, or simply NIMRA, a town in the tribe of Gad (Num. xxxii. 3, 36; Josh. xiii. 27), which Eusebius places five Roman miles north of Livias. This leaves no doubt of its being the same ruined city called Nimrin, south of Szalt, which Burckhardt mentions as situated near the point where the Wady Shoeb joins the Jordan.

BETHPHA'GE (*house of figs*),—comp. Cant. ii. 13), a small village, which our Lord, coming from Jericho, appears to have entered before reaching Bethany (Matt. xxi. 1; Luke xix. 29); it probably, therefore, lay near the latter place, a little below it to the east. No trace of it now exists.

BETH-RE'HOB. [REHOB.]

BETHSA'IDA (*fishing-town*), a town (John i. 45; Mark viii. 23) in Galilee (John xii. 21), on the western side of the sea of Tiberias, towards the middle, and not far from Capernaum (Mark vi. 45; viii. 22). It was the native place of Peter, Andrew, and Philip, and the frequent residence of Jesus. This gives some notion of the neighbourhood in which it lay; but the pre-cise site is utterly unknown, and the very name has long eluded the search of travellers.

2. BETHSAIDA. Christ fed the 5000 'near to a city called Bethsaida' (Luke ix. 10); but it is evident from the parallel passages (Matt. xiv. 13; Mark vi. 32-45), that this event took place, not in Galilee, but on the eastern side of the lake. This was held to be one of the greatest difficulties in sacred geography, till the ingenious Reland afforded materials for a satisfactory solu-tion of it, by distinguishing *two* Bethsaidas; one on the western, and the other on the north-eastern border of the lake. The former was undoubt-edly 'the city of Andrew and Peter;' and, it is in perfect agreement with the sacred text to

conclude that it was the Bethsaida near which Christ fed the five thousand, and also, probably, where the blind man was restored to sight. It was originally only a village, called Bethsaida, but was rebuilt and enlarged by Philip the Tetrarch not long after the birth of Christ, and received the name of Julias in honour of Julia the daughter of Augustus (Luke iii. 1). Philip seems to have made it his occasional residence; and here he died, and was buried in a costly tomb.

BETH-SHA'N (*house of rest*, or *Rest-town*), a city belonging to the half-tribe of Manasseh, west of the Jordan, and situated in a valley of that river, where it is bounded westward by a low chain of the Gilboa mountains. It is on the road from Jerusalem to Damascus, and is about two miles from the Jordan, eighteen from the southern end of Lake Gennesareth, and twenty-three from Nazareth. It also bore the name of Scythopolis, perhaps because Scythians had settled there in the time of Josiah (B.C. 631), in their passage through Palestine towards Egypt. Although Bethshan was assigned to Manasseh (Josh. xvii. 11), it was not conquered by that tribe (Judg. i. 17). The body of Saul was fastened to the wall of Bethshan by the Philistines (1 Sam. xxxi. 10). The ancient native name, as well as the town itself, still exists in the Beisan of the present day. It stands on a rising ground somewhat above the valley of the Jordan, or in the valley of Jezreel, where it opens into the Jordan valley. It is a poor place, containing not more than sixty or seventy houses, inhabited by Moslems. The ruins of the ancient city are of considerable extent. It was built along the banks of the rivulet which waters the town and in the valleys formed by its several branches, and must have been nearly three miles in circumference. The chief remains are large heaps of black hewn stones, with many foundations of houses and fragments of a few columns.

BETH-SHE'MESH (*house of the sun*, i. q. *Sun-town;*) a sacerdotal city (Josh. xxi. 16; 1 Sam. vi. 15; 1 Chron. vi. 59) in the tribe of Judah, on the south-east border of Dan (Josh. xv. 10), and the land of the Philistines (1 Sam. vi. 12), probably in a lowland plain (2 Kings xiv. 1); and placed by Eusebius ten Roman miles from Eleutheropolis, in the direction of the road to Nicopolis. It belonged at an early date to the Philistines, and they had again obtained possession of it in the time of Ahaz (1 Kings iv. 9; 2 Chron. xxviii. 18). It was to this place that the ark was taken by the milch kine from the land of the Philistines, and it was here that, according to the present text, 'fifty thousand and threescore and ten men' were miraculously slain for irreverently exploring the sacred shrine (1 Sam. vi. 19). This number has occasioned much discussion. It appears likely that the text has been corrupted in transcription by an erroneous solution of an arithmetical sign. The Syriac and Arabic have 5070 instead of 50070. At the distance, and in the vicinity indicated by Eusebius and Jerome, a place called Ain Shems was found by Dr. Robinson, and, with great probability, identified with Beth-Shemesh. The name is applied to the ruins of an Arab village constructed of ancient materials. To the west of the village,

upon and around the plateau of a low swell or mound, are the vestiges of a former extensive city, consisting of many foundations and the remains of ancient walls of hewn stone.

BETHU'EL, son of Abraham's brother Nahor, and father of Laban and of Rebecca, whom Isaac married (Gen. xxii. 22, 23).

BETHULI'A, a place mentioned only in the Apocryphal book of Judith (iv. 5: vii. 1, 3), and which appears to have lain near the plain of Esdraelon on the south, not far from Dothaim, and to have guarded one of the passes towards Jerusalem. Its site is still undetermined.

BETH'-ZUR, a town in the tribe of Judah (Josh. xv. 58), twenty Roman miles from Jerusalem, on the road to Hebron, and consequently two miles from the latter city. It was fortified by Rehoboam (2 Chron. xi. 7). The inhabitants assisted in building the walls of Jerusalem (Neh. iii. 16). Lysias was defeated in the neighbourhood by Judas Maccabæus, who fortified the place as a stronghold against Idumæa. It was besieged and taken by Antiochus Eupator, and fortified by Bacchides, whose garrison defended themselves against Jonathan Maccabæus; but it was taken and fortified by his brother Simon. Josephus calls Beth-zur the strongest fortress in Judæa. Its site has not been ascertained.

BETROTHING. [MARRIAGE.]

BE'ZEK, a city over which Adoni-bezek was king (Judg. i. 4, sq.), and where Saul mustered his army to march to the relief of Jabesh-Gilead (1 Sam. xi. 8). Eusebius and Jerome mention two towns of this name close together, seventeen miles from Neapolis in Shechem, on the road to Bethshan.

BE'ZER, a city beyond the Jordan, in the tribe of Reuben, and one of the six cities of refuge (Deut. iv. 43; Josh. xx. 8). The site is unknown.

BIBLE, a name supposed to have been first applied in the fifth century to denote the collective volume of the sacred writings. The word occurs in the Prologue to Ecclesiasticus, 'the Law, the Prophets, and the rest of the books,' and 2 Tim. iv. 13, 'and the books.' Before the adoption of this name the more usual terms in the Christian Church by which the sacred books were denominated were, the Scripture or Writing, the *Scriptures*, the Sacred Writings, and the *Sacred Letters*. The term in question was first applied to the entire collection of sacred writings by St. Chrysostom. In the course of time it superseded all others both in the Eastern and Western Church, and is now everywhere the popular appellation.

The Bible is divided into the Old and New Testaments. The name Old Testament is applied to the books of Moses by St. Paul (2 Cor. iii. 14), inasmuch as the former covenant comprised the whole scheme of the Mosaic revelation, and the history of this is contained in them. The names given to the Old Testament were, the Scriptures (Matt. xxi. 42); Scripture (2 Pet. i. 20); the Holy Scriptures (Rom. i. 2); the sacred letters (2 Tim. iii. 15); the holy books, the law (John xii. 34); the law, the prophets, and the psalms (Luke xxiv. 44); the law and the prophets (Matt. v. 17); the law, the prophets, and the other books (Prol. Ecclus.); the books of the old covenant (Neh. viii. 8); the book of the covenant (1 Macc. i. 57; 2 Kings xxiii. 2).

The other books (not in the canon) were called apocryphal, ecclesiastical, and deuterocanonical. The term New Testament has been in common use since the third century, and is employed by Eusebius in the same sense in which it is now commonly applied. Tertullian employs the same phrase, and also that of 'the Divine Instrument' in the same signification. For detailed information on subjects connected with BIBLE, see SCRIPTURE, HOLY.

BIER. [BURIAL.]

BIG'THAN, an eunuch in the court of king Ahasuerus, whose conspiracy against that monarch was frustrated through the disclosures of Mordecai (Esth. ii. 21).

BIL'DAD the Shuhite, one of the friends of Job, and the second of his opponents in the disputation (Job ii. 11; viii. 1; xviii. 1; xxv. 1). The Shuah of which the Septuagint makes Bildad the prince, or patriarch, was probably the district assigned to Shuah, the sixth son of Abraham by Keturah, and called by his name. This was doubtless in Arabia Petræa, if Shuah settled in the same quarter as his brothers, of which there can be little doubt; and to this region we are to refer the town and district to which he gave his name, and in which Bildad was doubtless a person of consequence, if not the chief [SHUAH].

BIL'HAH, the handmaid whom the childless Rachel bestowed upon her husband Jacob, that through her she might have children. Bilhah became the mother of Dan and Naphtali (Gen. xxx. 1-8).

BIRD-CAGES are named in Jer. v. 27; Rev. xviii. 2; and are perhaps implied in Job xli. 5, where 'playing with a bird' is mentioned. This just suffices to show that the ancient Israelites kept birds in cages; but we have no further information on the subject, nor any allusions to the singing of birds so kept. The cages were

93.

probably of the some forms which we still observe in the East, and which are shown in the annexed engraving. It is remarkable that there is no appearance of bird-cages in any of the domestic scenes which are portrayed on the mural tablets of the Egyptians.

BIRDS may be defined oviparous vertebrated animals, organized for flight.

In the Mosaic law, birds were distinguished as clean and unclean: the first being allowed for the table, because they fed on grain, seeds, and vegetables; and the second forbidden, because they subsisted on flesh and carrion. The birds most anciently used in sacrifice were, it seems, turtle-doves and pigeons. In Kitto's *Physical History of Palestine* there is a more complete notice than exists elsewhere of the actual ornithology of the Holy Land.

BIRDS'-NESTS. The law in Deut. xxii. 6, 7, directs that if one falls in with a bird's-nest with eggs or young, he shall allow the dam to escape, and not take her as well as the nest. The reason Maimonides gives for this is, 'The eggs on which the dam is sitting, or the young ones which have need of her, are not, in general, permitted to be eaten; and when the dam is allowed to escape, she is not distressed by seeing her young ones carried off. It thus frequently happens that all are untouched, because that which might be taken may not be lawfully eaten.'

BIRTH. In Eastern countries child-birth is usually attended with much less pain and difficulty than in our northern regions; although Oriental females are not to be regarded as exempt from the common doom of woman, 'in sorrow shalt thou bring forth children' (Gen. iii. 16). It is however uncertain whether the difference arise from the effect of climate or from the circumstances attending advanced civilization; perhaps both causes operate, to a certain degree, in producing the effect. Climate must have *some* effect; but it is observed that the difficulty of childbirth, under any climate, increases with the advance of civilization, and that in any climate the class on which the advanced condition of society most operates finds the pangs of childbirth the most severe. Such consideration may probably account for the fact that the Hebrew women, after they had long been under the influence of the Egyptian climate, passed through the childbirth pangs with much more facility than the women of Egypt, whose habits of life were more refined and self-indulgent (Exod. i. 19). The child was no sooner born than it was washed in a bath and rubbed with salt (Ezek. xvi. 4); it was then tightly swathed o. bandaged to prevent those distortions to which the tender frame of an infant is so much exposed during the first days of life (Job xxxviii. 9; Ezek. xvi. 4; Luke ii. 7, 11).

It was the custom at a very ancient period for the father, while music celebrated the event, to clasp the new-born child to his bosom, and by this ceremony he was understood to declare it to be his own (Gen. l. 23; Job iii. 3; Ps. xxii. 10). This practice was imitated by those wives who adopted the children of their handmaids (Gen. xvi. 2; xxx. 3-5). The messenger who brought to the father the first news that a son was born unto him was received with pleasure and rewarded with presents (Job iii. 3; Jer. xx. 15), as is still the custom in Persia and other Eastern countries. The birth of a daughter was less noticed, the disappointment at its not being a son subduing for the time the satisfaction which the birth of any child naturally occasions. Among the Israelites, the mother, after the birth of a son, continued unclean seven days: and she remained at home during the thirty-three days succeeding the seven of uncleanness, forming altogether forty days of seclusion. After the birth of a daughter the number of the days of uncleanness and seclusion at home was doubled. At the expiration of this period she went into the tabernacle or temple, and presented a yearling lamb, or, if she was poor, two turtle-doves and two young pigeons, as a sacrifice of purification (Lev. xii. 1-8; Luke ii. 22) [CHILDREN].

BIRTH-DAYS. The observance of birthdays may be traced to a very ancient date; and the birth-day of the first-born son seems in particular to have been celebrated with a degree of festivity proportioned to the joy which the event of his actual birth occasioned (Job i. 4, 13, 18). The birth-days of the Egyptian kings were celebrated with great pomp as early as the time of Joseph (Gen. xl. 20). These days were in Egypt looked upon as holy; no business was done upon them, and all parties indulged in festivities suitable to the occasion. Every Egyptian attached much importance to the day, and even to the hour of his birth; and it is probable that, as in Persia, each individual kept his birth-day with great rejoicings, welcoming his friends with all the amusements of society, and a more than usual profusion of delicacies of the table. In the Bible there is no instance of birth-day celebrations among the Jews themselves. The example of Herod the tetrarch (Matt. xiv. 6), the celebration of whose birth-day cost John the Baptist his life, can scarcely be regarded as such, the family to which he belonged being notorious for its adoption of heathen customs. In fact, the later Jews at least regarded birth-day celebrations as parts of idolatrous worship; and this probably on account of the idolatrous rites with which they were observed in honour of those who were regarded as the patron gods of the day on which the party was born.

BIRTH-RIGHT. This term denotes the rights or privileges belonging to the first-born among the Hebrews. The particular advantages which these conferred were the following:—

1. A right to the priesthood. The first-born became the priest in virtue of his priority of descent, provided no blemish or defect attached to him. Reuben was the first-born of the twelve patriarchs, and therefore the honour of the priesthood belonged to his tribe. God, however, transferred it from the tribe of Reuben to that of Levi (Num. iii. 12, 13; viii. 18). Hence the first-born of the other tribes were redeemed from serving God as priests, by a sum not exceeding five shekels. Being presented before the Lord in the temple, they were redeemed immediately after the thirtieth day from their birth (Num. xviii. 15, 16; Luke ii. 22). It is to be observed, that only the first-born who were *fit for the priesthood* (i. e. such as had no defect, spot, or blemish) were thus presented to the priest.

2. The first-born received a double portion of his father's property. There is some difficulty in determining precisely what is meant by a double portion. Some suppose that half the inheritance was received by the elder brother, and that the other half was equally divided among the remaining brethren. This is not probable. The Rabbins believe that the elder brother received twice as much as any of the rest; and there is no reason to doubt the correctness of this opinion. When the first-born died before his father's property was divided, and left children, the right of the father descended to the children, and not to the brother next of age.

3. He succeeded to the official authority possessed by his father. If the latter was a king, the former was regarded as his legitimate successor, unless some unusual event or arrangement interfered.

After the law was given through Moses, the right of primogeniture could not be transferred from the first-born to a younger child at the father's option. In the patriarchal age, however, it was in the power of the parent thus to convey it from the eldest to another child (Deut. xxi. 15-17; Gen. xxv. 31, 32).

It is not difficult to perceive the reason why the first-born enjoyed greater privileges than the rest of the children. The peculiar honour attaching to them is easily accounted for. They are to be viewed as having reference to the Redeemer, the first-born of the Virgin. Hence in the Epistle to the Romans (viii. 29), it is written concerning the Son, 'that he might be the *first-born* among many brethren;' and in Col. i 18, 'who is the beginning, the *first-born* from the dead; that in all things he might have the pre-eminence.' (see also Heb. i. 4, 5, 6) As the first-born had a double portion, so the Lord Jesus, as Mediator, has an inheritance superior to his brethren; he is exalted to the right hand of the Majesty on high, where he reigns until all his enemies shall be subdued. The universe is his rightful dominion in his mediatorial character. Again, he alone is a true priest: he fulfilled all the functions of the sacerdotal office; and the Levites, to whom, under the law, the priesthood was transferred from all the first-born of Israel, derived the efficacy of their ministrations from their connection with the great high-priest.

BISHOP. The active controversy in which the subject of episcopacy has been involved, although it has not reconciled conflicting opinions, has brought out the historical facts in their fullest clearness. The able and candid on opposite sides can scarcely be said to differ as to the facts themselves; but they differ in their estimate of them.

The Apostles originally appointed men to superintend the spiritual, and occasionally even the secular wants of the churches (Acts xiv. 23; xi. 30; see also 2 Tim. ii. 2), who were ordinarily called *elders*, from their age, sometimes *overseers* (bishops), from their office. They were also said to *preside* (1 Thess. v. 12; 1 Tim. v. 17), never to *rule*, which has far too despotic a sound. In the Epistle to the Hebrews (xiii 7, 17, 24) they are named *leading men* (comp. Acts xv. 22); and figuratively, *shepherds* (Ephes. iv. 11). But that they did not always teach is clear from 1 Tim. v 17; and the name Elders proves that originally age, experience, and character were their most necessary qualifications. They were to be married men with families (1 Tim. iii. 4), and with converted children (Tit. i. 6) In the beginning there had been no time to train teachers, and teaching was regarded far more in the light of a gift than an office; yet St. Paul places 'ability to teach' among episcopal qualifications (1 Tim. iii. 2; Titus i. 9; the latter of which passages should be translated, 'that he may be able both to exhort men by sound teaching, and also to refute opposers'). That teachers had obtained in St. Paul's day a fixed official position, is manifest from Gal. vi. 6, and 1 Cor. ix. 14, where he claims for them a right to worldly maintenance: in fact, that the *shepherds* ordered to 'feed the flock,' and be its 'overseers' (1 Pet. v. 2), were to feed them with knowledge and instruction, will never be disputed, except to support a hypothesis. The *leaders* also, in Heb. xiii. 7, are described as 'speaking unto you the word of God.' Ecclesiastical history joins in proving that the two offices of teaching and superintending were, with few exceptions, combined in the same persons, as, indeed, the nature of things dictated.

That during St. Paul's lifetime no difference between elders and bishops yet existed in the consciousness of the church, is manifest from the entire absence of distinctive names (Acts xx. 17-28; 1 Pet. v. 1, 2). The mention of bishops and deacons in Phil. i. 1, and 1 Tim. iii., without any notice of elders, proves that at that time no difference of *order* subsisted between bishops and elders. A formal ceremony, it is generally believed, was employed in appointing elders, although it does not appear that as yet any fixed name was appropriated to the idea of ordination. In 1 Cor. xvi. 15 we find the house of Stephanas to have volunteered the task of 'ministering to the saints;' and that this was a ministry 'of the word,' is evident from the Apostle's urging the church 'to submit themselves to such.' It would appear then that a formal investiture into the office was not as yet regarded *essential*. Be this as it may, no one doubts that an ordination by laying on of hands soon became general or universal. Hands were first laid on not to bestow an office, but to solicit a spiritual gift (1 Tim. iv. 14; 2 Tim. i. 6; Acts xiii. 3; xiv. 26; xv. 40). To the same effect Acts viii. 17; xix. 6;—passages which explain Heb. vi. 2. On the other hand, the absolute silence of the Scriptures, even if it were not confirmed, as it is, by positive testimony, would prove that no idea of consecration, as distinct from ordination, at that time existed at all; and, consequently, although individual elders may have really discharged functions which would afterwards have been called episcopal, it was not by virtue of a second ordination, nor, therefore, of episcopal rank.

The Apostles themselves, it is held by some, were the real *bishops* of that day, and it is quite evident that they performed many episcopal functions. It may well be true, that the only reason why no bishops (in the modern sense) were then wanting was, because the Apostles were living; but it cannot be inferred that in any strict sense prelates are co-ordinate in rank with the Apostles, and can claim to exercise their powers. The later 'bishop' did not come forward as a successor to the Apostles, but was developed out of the presbyter; much less can it be proved, or alleged with plausibility, that the Apostles took any measures for securing substitutes for themselves (in the high character of Apostles) after their decease. It has been with many a favourite notion that Timothy and Titus exhibit the episcopal type even during the life of Paul; but this is an obvious misconception. They were attached to the person of the Apostle, and not to any one church. In the last Epistle written by him (2 Tim. iv. 9) he calls Timothy suddenly to Rome, in words which prove that the latter was not, at least as yet, bishop, either of Ephesus or of any other church. That Timothy was an *evangelist* is distinctly stated (2 Tim. iv. 5), and that he had received spiritual gifts (i. 6, &c.); there is then no difficulty in accounting for the authority vested in him (1 Tim. v. 1; xix. 22), without imagining him to have been a bishop; which is in fact disproved even by the same Epistle (i. 3). That Titus, moreover, had no local attachment to Crete, is plain from Titus iii. 13, to say nothing of the earlier Epistle, 2 Cor. *passim*. Nor is it true that the episcopal

power developed itself out of wandering Evangelists any more than out of the Apostles.

On the other hand it would seem that the bishop began to elevate himself above the presbyter while the Apostle John was yet alive, and in churches to which he is believed to have peculiarly devoted himself. The meaning of the title *angel*, in the opening chapters of the Apocalypse, has been mystically explained by some; but its true meaning is clear from the nomenclature of the Jewish synagogues. In them, we are told, the minister who ordinarily read the prayers of the congregation, besides acting as their chief functionary in matters of business, was entitled *messenger of the church*. The term 'angel of the church' appears therefore to be nothing but a harsh Hebraism for 'minister of the church.' We therefore here see a single officer, in these rather large Christian communities, elevated into a peculiar prominence, which has been justly regarded as episcopal.

Episcopalians, Presbyterians, and Congregationalists agree in one point, viz. that (because of its utility and general convenience) it is lawful for Christians to take a step for which they have no clear precedent in the Scripture, that of breaking up a church, when it becomes of unwieldy magnitude, into fixed divisions, whether parishes, or congregations. The question then arises, whether the organic union is to be still retained at all. To this (1) Congregationalists reply in the negative, saying that the congregations in different parts of a great city no more need to be in organic union, than those of two different cities; (2) Presbyterians would keep up the union by means of a synod of the elders; (3) Episcopalians desire to unite the separate churches by retaining them under the supervision of a single head — the bishop. It seems impossible to refer to the practice of the Apostles as deciding in favour of *any one* of these methods; for the case had not yet arisen which could have led to the discussion. The city churches had not yet become so large as to make subdivision positively necessary; and, as a fact, it did not take place. To organize distant churches into a fixed and formal connection by synods of their bishops, was, of course, quite a later process; but such unions are by no means rejected, even by Congregationalists, as long as they are used for deliberation and advice, not as assemblies for ruling and commanding. The *spirit* of Episcopacy depends far less on the episcopal form itself, than on the size and wealth of dioceses, and on the union of bishops into synods, whose decisions are to be authorative on the whole church: to say nothing of territorial establishment and the support of the civil government. If, under any ecclesiastical form, either oppression or disorder should arise, it cannot be defended; but no form is a security against such evils. Our experience may, in these later times, possibly show us which of these systems is on the whole preferable; but the discussion must belong to ecclesiastical history, and would be quite out of place here.

BITH'RON (2 Sam. ii. 29). This name has the same meaning as Bether. It probably denotes a region of hills and valleys, and not any definite place.

BITHYN'IA, a province of Asia Minor, on the Euxine Sea and the Propontis; bounded on the west by Mysia, on the south and east by Phrygia and Galatia, and on the east by Paphlagonia. The Bithynians were a rude and uncivilized people, Thracians who had colonized this part of Asia, and occupied no towns, but lived in *villages*. That Christian congregations were formed at an early period in Bithynia, is evident from the Apostle Peter having addressed the first of his Epistles to them (1 Pet. i. 1). The Apostle Paul was at one time inclined to go into Bithynia with his assistants Silas and Timothy, ' but the Spirit suffered him not' (Acts xvi. 7).

BITTER, BITTERNESS. Bitterness (Exod. i. 14; Ruth i. 20; Jer. ix. 15) is symbolical of affliction, misery, and servitude. It was for this reason that, in the celebration of the Passover, the servitude of the Israelites in Egypt was typically represented by *bitter herbs*.

The gall of bitterness (Acts viii. 23) describes a state of extreme wickedness, highly offensive to God, and hurtful to others.

A root of bitterness (Heb. xiii. 15) expresses a wicked or scandalous person, or any dangerous sin leading to apostacy.

BITTER HERBS, literally *bitters*. There has been much difference of opinion respecting the kind of herbs denoted by this word.

It however seems very doubtful whether any particular herbs were intended by so general a term as *bitters;* it is far more probable that it denotes whatever bitter herbs, obtainable in the place where the Passover was eaten, might be fitly used with meat.

BITTERN. The word thus rendered occurs but three times in Scripture (Isa. xiv. 23; xxxiv. 11; and Zeph. ii. 14), and has been variously interpreted—owl, osprey, tortoise, porcupine, otter, and in the Arabic, bustard. Bochart, Shaw, Lowth. and other great authorities, have supported the opinion that it refers to the porcupine; but this is in the highest degree improbable, for the texts above quoted make it clear that the animal referred to must from its habits be not a hedgehog, nor even a mammal, but a bird. We think the term most applicable to the heron tribes, whose beaks are formidable spikes that often kill hawks; a fact well known to Eastern hunters. Of these, the common night-heron, with its pencil of white feathers in the crest, is a species not uncommon in the marshes of Western Asia ; and of several species of bittern, *Ardea* (*botaurus*) *stellaris* has pointed long feathers on the neck and breast, freckled with black, and a strong pointed bill. After the breeding-season it migrates and passes the winter in the south, frequenting the marshes and rivers of Asia and Europe, where it then roosts high above ground, uttering a curious note before and after its evening flight, very distinct from the booming sound produced by it in the breeding-season, and while it remains in the marshes. Though not building, like the stork, on the tops of houses, it resorts, like the heron, to ruined structures, and we have been informed that it has been seen on the summit of Tauk Kesra at Ctesiphon.

BITUMEN. [ASPHALTUM.]

BLACK. Although the Orientals do not wear black in mourning, they, as did the ancient Jews, regard the colour as a symbol of affliction, disaster, and privation. In fact, the custom of wearing black in mourning is a sort of visible expression of what is in the East a figure of speech. In Scripture blackness is used as symbolical of afflictions occasioned by drought and famine (Job xxx. 30; Jer. xiv. 2; Lam. iv. 8; v. 10).

In connection with this subject it may be remarked that black is studiously avoided in dress by all Orientals, except in certain garments of hair or wool, which are naturally of that colour. Black is also sometimes imposed as a mark of humiliating distinction by dominant nations upon subject or tributary tribes, the most familiar instance of which is the obligation laid upon the Jews in Turkey of wearing black turbans.

BLASPHEMY signifies a false, irreverent, injurious use of God's names, attributes, words, and works. Whenever men *intentionally* and *directly* attack the perfections of Jehovah, and thus lessen the reverence which others entertain for him, they are *blasphemers*.

By the Mosaic law *blasphemy* was punished with death (Lev. xxiv. 10–16); and the laws of some countries still visit it with the same punishment. Fines, imprisonment, and various corporal inflictions are annexed to the crime by the laws of Great Britain. It is matter, however, of sincere satisfaction, that there are very few instances in which these enactments require to be enforced.

Much has been said and written respecting *the blasphemy* against the Holy Ghost. usually but improperly denominated *the unpardonable sin* against the Holy Ghost. Some refer it to continued opposition to the Gospel, *i. e.* obstinate impenitence or final unbelief.

But we object to this opinion, because it generalizes the nature of the sin in question. On the contrary, the Scripture account narrows it to a particular sin of a special kind, discountenancing the idea that it is of frequent occurrence, and marked by no circumstances of unwonted aggravation. Besides, all the notices which we have refer it not so much to a state of mind. as to the outward manifestation of a singularly malignant disposition *by the utterance of the lips*.

The occasion on which Christ introduced his mention of it (Matt. xii. 31, &c.; Mark iii. 28, &c.), the subsequent context, and, above all, the words of Mark iii. 30 (' because they said, He hath an unclean spirit') indicate, with tolerable plainness, that the sin in question consisted in attributing the miracles wrought by Christ, or his Apostles in His name, to the agency of Satan. It was by the power of the Holy Ghost, given to the Redeemer without measure, that he cast out devils : and whoever maligned the Saviour by affirming that an unclean spirit actuated and enabled him to expel other spirits, maligned the Holy Ghost.

It is difficult to discover the ' sin unto death,' noticed by the Apostle John (1 John v. 16), although it has been generally thought to coincide with the blasphemy against the Holy Spirit; but the language of John does not afford data for pronouncing them one and the same. The first three Gospels alone describe the *blasphemy* which shall not be forgiven: from it the 'sin unto death' stands apart.

BLASTUS, a man who was *cubicularius* to king Herod Agrippa, or who had the charge of his bedchamber (Acts xii. 20). Such persons had usually great influence with their masters, and hence the importance attached to Blastus's favouring the peace with Tyre and Sidon.

BLESSING. The terms 'blessing' and 'to bless' occur very often in the Scriptures, and in applications too obvious to require explanation or comment. The patriarchal blessings of sons form the exception, these being, in fact, prophecies rather than blessings, or blessings only in so far as they for the most part involved the invocation and the promise of good things to come upon the parties concerned. The most remarkable instances are those of Isaac 'blessing' Jacob and Esau (Gen. xxvii.); of Jacob 'blessing' his twelve sons (Gen. xlix.); and of Moses 'blessing the twelve tribes (Deut. xxxii.).

BLESSING, VALLEY OF, a translation of the name Valley of Berachah (benediction), which was borne by the valley in which Jehoshaphat celebrated the miraculous overthrow of the Moabites and Ammonites. It was from this circumstance it derived its name; and from the indications in the text, it must have been in the tribe of Judah, near the Dead Sea and Engedi, and in the neighbourhood of Tekoa (2 Chron. xx. 23-26).

BLINDING. [PUNISHMENTS.]

BLINDNESS. The frequent occurrence of blindness in the East has always excited the astonishment of travellers. Volney says that, out of a hundred persons in Cairo, he has met twenty quite blind, ten wanting one eye, and twenty others having their eyes red, purulent, or blemished. This is principally owing to the Egyptian ophthalmia, which is endemic in that country and on the coast of Syria. This disease is contagious; but it is not often communicated from one individual to another. It is not confined to the East, but appears here and there throughout Europe. The French and English suffered greatly from it while they were in Egypt, and subsequently.

Small pox is another great cause of blindness in the East.

In the New Testament, blind mendicants are frequently mentioned (Matt. ix. 27; xii. 22; xx. 30; xxi. 14; John v. 3). The blindness of Bar Jesus (Acts xiii. 6) was miraculously produced, and of its nature we know nothing. Examples of blindness from old age occur in Gen. xxvii. 1; 1 Kings xiv. 4; 1 Sam. iv. 15. The Syrian army that came to apprehend Elisha was suddenly smitten with blindness in a miraculous manner (2 Kings vi. 18); and so also was St. Paul (Acts ix. 9). The Mosaic law has not neglected to inculcate humane feelings towards the blind (Lev. xix. 14; Deut. xxvii. 18). Blindness is sometimes threatened in the Old Testament as a punishment for disobedience (Deut. xxviii. 28; Lev. xxvi. 16; Zeph. i. 17).

BLOOD. There are two respects in which the ordinances of the Old and New Testaments concerning blood deserve notice here—the prohibition of its use as an article of food, and the appointment and significance of its use in the ritual of sacrifice; both of which appear to rest on a common ground.

In Gen. ix. 4, where the use of animal food is allowed, it is first absolutely forbidden to eat 'flesh with its soul, its blood;' which expression, were it otherwise obscure, is explained by the mode in which the same terms are employed in Deut. xii. 23. In the Mosaic law the prohibition is repeated with frequency and emphasis; although it is generally introduced in connection with sacrifices, as in Lev. iii. 17; vii. 26; xvii. 10-14; xix. 26; Deut. xii. 16-23; xv. 23. In cases where the prohibition is introduced in connection with the lawful and unlawful articles of diet, the reason which is generally assigned in the text is, that 'the blood is the soul;' and it is ordered that it be poured on the ground like water. But where it is introduced in reference to the portions of the victim which were to be offered to the Lord, then the text, in addition to the former reason, insists that 'the blood expiates by the soul' (Lev. xvii. 11, 12). This strict injunction not only applied to the Israelites, but even to the strangers residing among them. The penalty assigned to its transgression was the being 'cut off from the people;' by which the punishment of death appears to be intended (cf. Heb. x. 28), although it is difficult to ascertain whether it was inflicted by the sword or by stoning. To this is to be added, that the Apostles and elders, assembled in council at Jerusalem, when desirous of settling the extent to which the ceremonial observances were binding upon the converts to Christianity, renewed the injunction to abstain from blood, and coupled it with things offered to idols (Acts xv. 29).

In direct opposition to this emphatic prohibition of blood in the Mosaic law, the customs of uncivilized heathens sanctioned the cutting of slices from the living animal, and the eating of the flesh while quivering with life and dripping with blood. Even Saul's army committed this barbarity, as we read in 1 Sam. xiv. 32; and the prophet also lays it to the charge of the Jews in Ezek. xxxiii. 25. This practice, according to Bruce's testimony, exists at present among the Abyssinians. Moreover, pagan religions, and that of the Phœnicians among the rest, appointed the eating and drinking of blood, mixed with wine, as a rite of idolatrous worship, and especially in the ceremonial of swearing. To this the passage in Ps. xvi. 4, appears to allude.

The appointment and significance of the use of blood in the ritual of sacrifice belongs indeed to this head; but their further notice will be more appropriately pursued in the art. SACRIFICE.

BLOOD-REVENGE, or revenge for bloodshed, was regarded among the Jews, as among all the ancient and Asiatic nations, not only as a right, but even as a duty, which devolved upon the nearest relative of the murdered person.

The Mosaical law (Num. xxxv. 31) expressly forbids the acceptance of a ransom for the forfeited life of the murderer, although it might be saved by his seeking an asylum at the altar of the Tabernacle, in case the homicide was accidentally committed (Exod. xxi. 13; 1 Kings i. 50; ii. 28). If, however, after Judaism had been fully developed, no other sanctuary had been tolerated but that of the Temple at Jerusalem, the chances of escape of such an homicide from the hands of the avenger, ere he reached the gates of the Temple, must have become less in proportion to the distance of the spot where the murder was committed from Jerusalem: six *cities of refuge* were therefore appointed for the momentary safety of the murderer, in various parts of the kingdom, the roads to which were kept in good order to facilitate his escape (Deut. xix. 3). Thither the avenger durst not follow him, and there he lived in safety until a proper examination had taken place before the authorities of the place (Jos. xx. 6, 9), in order to ascertain whether the murder was a wilful act or not. In the former case he was instantly delivered up to the *Goël*, or avenger of blood, against whom not even the altar could protect him (Exod. xxi. 14; 1 Kings ii. 29); in the latter case, though he was not actually delivered into the hands of the *Goël*, he was notwithstanding not allowed to quit the precincts of the town, but was obliged to remain there all his lifetime, or until the death of the high-priest (Num. xxxv. 6; Deut. xix. 3; Josh. xx. 1-6), if he would not run the risk of falling into the hands of the avenger, and be slain by him with impunity (Num. xxxv. 26; Deut. xix. 6). That such a voluntary exile was considered more in the light of a punishment for manslaughter than a provision for the safe retreat of the homicide is evident from Num. xxxv. 32, where it is expressly forbidden to release him from his confinement on any condition whatever. That the decease of the high-priest should have been the means of restoring him to liberty was probably owing to the general custom among the ancients, of granting free pardon to certain prisoners at the demise of their legitimate prince or sovereign, whom the high-priest represented, in a spiritual sense, among the Jews. These wise regulations of the Mosaical law, as far as the spirit of the age allowed it, prevented all family hatred, persecution, and war from ever taking place, as was inevitably the case among the other nations, where any bloodshed whatever, whether wilful or accidental, laid the homicide open to the *duteous* revenge of the relatives and family of the slain person, who again in their turn were then similarly watched and hunted by the opposite party, until a family-war of extermination had *legally* settled itself from generation to generation, without the least prospect of ever being brought to a peaceful termination. Nor do we indeed find in the Scriptures the least trace of any abuse or mischief ever having arisen from these regulations (comp. 2 Sam. ii. 19, *sq.*; iii. 21, *sq.*).

That such institutions are altogether at variance with the spirit of Christianity may be judged from the fact that revenge, so far from being counted a right or duty, was condemned by Christ and his apostles as a vice and passion to be shunned (Acts vii. 60; Matt. v. 44; Luke vi. 28; Rom. xii. 14, *sq.;* comp. Rom. xiii., where the power of executing revenge is vested in the authorities alone).

BLOODY SWEAT. According to Luke xxii. 44, our Lord's sweat was 'as great drops of blood falling to the ground.' Michaelis takes the passage to mean nothing more than that the drops were as *large* as falling drops of blood. This, which also appears to be a common explanation, is liable to some objection. For, if an ordinary observer compares a fluid which he is accustomed to see colourless, to blood, which is so well known and so well characterised by its colour, and does not specify any particular point of resemblance, he would more naturally be understood to allude to the colour, since it is the most prominent and characteristic quality.

There are several cases recorded by the older medical writers, under the title of bloody sweat. With the exception of one or two instances, not above suspicion of fraud, they have, however, all been cases of general hæmorrhagic disease, in which blood has flowed from different parts of the body, such as the nose, eyes, ears, lungs, stomach, and bowels, and, lastly, from various parts of the skin. When blood oozes from the skin, it must reach the external surface through orifices in the epidermis, which have been produced by rupture, or we must suppose that it has been extravasated into the sweat-ducts. But, even in this latter case, we must no more consider hæmorrhage of the skin to be a modification of the function of sweating, than bleeding from the nose to be a modification of the secretion of mucus. The blood is simply mixed with the sweat, precisely in the same way as, when spit up from the lungs. it is mixed with mucus and saliva in passing through the air-tubes and mouth. It is, therefore, incorrect to suppose that hæmorrhage from the skin indicates a state of body at all analogous to that which occasions sweating.

But while experience teaches that cutaneous hæmorrhage, when it does occur, is the result of disease, or, at any rate, of a very peculiar idiosyncrasy, and is in no way indicative of the state of the mind, daily experience and the accumulated testimony of ages prove that intense mental emotion and pain produce on the body effects even severer in degree, but of a very different nature. It is familiar to all that terror will blanch the hair, occasion momentary paralysis, fainting, convulsions, melancholy, imbecility, and even sudden death. Excessive grief and joy will produce some of the worst of these. Sweat is caused by fear, and by bodily pain; but not by sorrow, which excites no secretion except tears.

It is very evident, then, that medical experience does not bear at all upon the words of St. Luke. The circumstances connected with our Lord's sufferings in the garden must be considered by themselves, without any reference to actual observation; otherwise, we shall be in danger of rendering a statement, which may be easily received on its own grounds, obscure and contradictory.

BOANERGES (*sons of thunder*, Mark iii. 17), a surname given by Christ to James and John, probably on account of their fervid, impetuous spirit.

BOAR occurs in Lev. xi. 7; Deut. xiv. 8; Ps. lxxx. 13; Prov. xi. 22; Isa. lxv. 4; lxvi. 3, 17.

The Hebrew, Egyptian, Arabian, Phœnician, and other neighbouring nations abstained from hog's flesh, and consequently, excepting in Egypt, and (at a later period) beyond the Sea of Galilee, no domesticated swine were reared. Although in Palestine, Syria, and Phœnicia hogs were rarely domesticated, wild boars are often mentioned in the Scriptures, and they were frequent in the time of the Crusades. At present wild boars frequent the marshes of the Delta, and are not uncommon on Mount Carmel and in the valley of Ajalah. They are abundant about the sources of the Jordan, and lower down where the river enters the Dead Sea. The wild boar of the East, though commonly smaller than the old breeds of domestic swine, grows occasionally to a very large size. It is passive while unmolested, but vindictive and fierce when roused. It is doubtful whether the species is the same as that of Europe, for the farrow are not striped: most likely it is identical with the wild hog of India.

1. BO'AZ, a wealthy Bethlehemite, and near kinsman of the first husband of Ruth, whom he eventually espoused under the obligations of the Levirate law, which he willingly incurred. The conduct of Boaz—his fine spirit, just feeling, piety, and amenity of manners—appears to great advantage in the book of Ruth, and forms an interesting portraiture of the condition and deportment of what was in his time the upper class of Israelites. By his marriage with Ruth he became the father of Obed, from whom came Jesse, the father of David. He was thus one of the direct ancestors of Christ, and as such his name occurs in Matt. i. 5 [RUTH; GENEALOGY].

2. BOAZ, the name given to one of the two brazen pillars which Solomon erected in the court of the Temple [JACHIN AND BOAZ].

BO'CHIM (weepings), the name given to a place (probably near Shiloh, where the tabernacle then was), where an 'angel of the Lord' reproved the assembled Israelites for their disobedience in making leagues with the inhabitants of the land, and for their remissness in taking possession of their heritage. This caused the bitter weeping among the people for which the place took its name (Judg. iii. 1).

BO'HAN (a thumb), a Reubenite, in whose honour a stone was erected which afterwards served as a boundary-mark on the frontier between Judah and Benjamin (Josh. xv. 6: xviii. 17). It does not appear from the text whether this stone was a sepulchral monument, or set up to commemorate some great exploit performed by this Bohan in the conquest of Canaan.

BOND, BONDAGE. [SLAVERY.]

BOOK. [WRITING.]

BOOK OF LIFE. In Phil. iv. 3, Paul speaks of Clement and other of his fellow-labourers, 'whose names are written in the book of life.' On this Heinrichs observes that as the future life is represented under the image of a citizenship, community, political society, just before (iii. 20), it is in agreement with this to suppose (as usual) a catalogue of the citizens' names, both natural and adopted (Luke x. 20; Rev. xx. 15; xxi. 27), and from which the unworthy are erased (Rev. iii. 5). Thus the names of the good are often represented as registered in heaven (Luke x. 20). But this by no means implies a certainty of salvation, but only that at that time the persons were on the list, from which (as in Rev. iii. 5) the names of unworthy members might be erased. This explanation is sufficient and satisfactory for the other important passage in Rev. iii. 5, where the glorified Christ promises to 'him that overcometh,' that he will not blot his name out of the book of life. When God threatened to destroy the Israelites altogether, and make of Moses a great nation—the legislator im-

plored forgiveness for them, and added—'if not, blot me, I pray thee, out of the book which thou hast written' (Exod. xxxii. 34). By this he meant nothing so foolish or absurd as to offer to forfeit eternal life in the world to come—but only that he, and not they, should be cut off from the world and brought to an untimely end.

A sealed book (Isa. xxix. 11; Rev. v. 1-3) is a book whose contents are secret, and have for a very long time been so, and are not to be published till the seal is removed.

A book or roll written within and without, i. e. on the back side (Rev. v. 1), may be a book containing a long series of events; it not being the custom of the ancients to write on the back side of the roll, unless when the inside would not contain the whole of the writing.

To eat a book signifies to consider it carefully, and digest it well in the mind (Jer. xv. 16; Rev. x. 9).

BOOTH, a hut made of branches of trees, and thus distinguished from a tent properly so called. Such were the booths in which Jacob sojourned for a while on his return to the borders of Canaan, whence the place obtained the name of Succoth (Gen. xxxiii. 17); and such were the temporary green sheds in which the Israelites were directed to celebrate the Feast of Tabernacles (Lev. xxiii. 42, 43). As this observance was to commemorate the abode of the Israelites in the wilderness, it has been rather unwisely concluded by some that they there lived in such booths. But it is evident from the narrative, that, during their wanderings, they dwelt in tents; and, indeed, where, in that treeless region, could they have found branches with which to construct their booths? Such structures are only available in well-wooded regions; and it is obvious that the direction to celebrate the feast in booths, rather than in tents, was given because, when the Israelites became a settled people in Palestine, and ceased to have a general use of tents, it was easier for them to erect a temporary shed of green branches than to provide a tent for the occasion.

BORROWING. On the general subject, as a matter of law or precept, see LOAN.

In Exod. xii 35, we are told that the Israelites, when on the point of their departure from Egypt, 'borrowed of the Egyptians jewels of silver, and jewels of gold, and raiment;' and it is added, that 'the Lord gave the people favour in the sight of the Egyptians, so that they lent unto them such things as they required. And they spoiled the Egyptians.' This was in pursuance of a Divine command which had been given to them through Moses (Exod. iii. 22; xi. 2). This has suggested a difficulty, seeing that the Israelites had certainly no intention to return to Egypt, or to restore the valuables which they thus obtained from their Egyptian 'neighbours.' The general acceptation of the word rendered borrow is to request or demand, and some have affirmed that it should be so rendered here—that the Israelites did not borrow the valuables, but demanded them of their Egyptian neighbours, as an indemnity for their services, and for the hard and bitter bondage which they had endured. To this it has been objected, that the Israelites had been public servants, rendering certain onerous services to the state, but not in personal bondage to individual Egyptians, whom, nevertheless, they, according to this account, mulcted of much valuable property in compensation for wrongs committed by the state. And that this mode of extorting private and partial compensation for public wrong will not stand the test of our rules of public morality, any more than that of borrowing without the intention to restore. Others are inclined to adhere to the old interpretation, that the Israelites actually did *borrow* the valuables of the Egyptians, with the understanding, on the part of the latter, that they were to be restored. Turn which way we will in this matter, there is but a choice of difficulties; and this leads us to suspect that we are not acquainted with all the facts bearing on the case, in the absence of which we spend our strength for nought in labouring to explain it. One of the difficulties is somewhat softened by the conjecture of Professor Bush, who, in his Note on Exod. xi. 2, observes, ' We are by no means satisfied that Moses was required to *command* the people to practise the device here mentioned. We regard it rather, as far as *they* were concerned, as the mere *prediction* of a fact that should occur.'

BOSOM. It is usual with the Western Asiatics to carry various sorts of things in the bosom of their dress, which forms a somewhat spacious depository, being wide above the girdle, which confines it so tightly around the waist as to prevent anything from slipping through.

To have one in our bosom implies kindness, secrecy, intimacy (Gen. xvi. 5; 2 Sam. xii. 8). Christ is *in the bosom of the Father*; that is, possesses the closest intimacy with, and most perfect knowledge of, the Father (John i. 18). Our Saviour is said *to carry his lambs in his bosom*, which touchingly represents his tender care and watchfulness over them.

BOSSES, the thickest and strongest parts, the prominent points of a buckler [ARMS, ARMOUR].

BOTTLE. Natural objects, it is obvious, would be the earliest things employed for holding and preserving liquids; and of natural objects those would be preferred which either

94.

presented themselves nearly or quite ready for use, or such as could speedily be wrought into the requisite shape. The skins of animals afford in themselves more conveniences for the purpose

than any other natural product. The first bottles therefore were probably made of the skins of animals. Accordingly we learn from Herodotus that it was customary among the ancient Egyptians to use bottles made of skins; and this is confirmed by the monuments, on which such various forms as the above occur. Fig. 1 is curious as showing the mode in which they were carried by a yoke; and as it balances a large bottle in a case, this skin may be presumed to have contained wine. Fig. 7 is such a skin of water as in the agricultural scenes is suspended from the bough of a tree, and from which the labourers occasionally drink. Figs. 2 and 3 represent two men with skins at their backs, belonging to a party of nomades entering Egypt. This party has been with some plausibility supposed to represent the sons of Jacob.

Skin-bottles doubtless existed among the Hebrews even in patriarchal times; but the first clear notice of them does not occur till Joshua ix. 4, where it is said that the Gibeonites, wishing to impose upon Joshua as if they had come from a long distance, took ' old sacks upon their asses, and wine-bottles *old and rent and bound up*.' Age, then, had the effect of wearing and tearing the bottles in question, which must consequently have been of skin. Our Saviour's language (Matt. ix. 17; Luke v. 37, 38; Mark ii. 22) is thus clearly

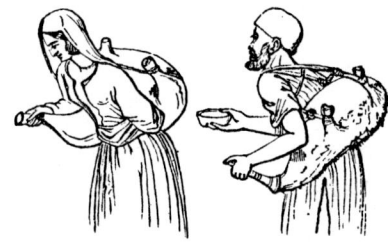

95.

explained: ' Men do not put new wine into old bottles, else the bottles break and the wine runneth out, and the bottles perish;' ' New wine must be put in new bottles, and both are preserved.' To the conception of an English reader who knows of no bottles but such as are made of clay or glass, the idea of bottles breaking through age presents an insuperable difficulty; but skins may become ' old, rent, and bound up;' they also prove, in time, hard and inelastic, and would in such a condition be very unfit to hold new wine, probably in a state of active fermentation. Even new skins might be unable to resist the internal pressure caused by fermentation.

As the drinking of wine is illegal among the Moslems who are now in possession of Western Asia, little is seen of the ancient use of skin-bottles for wine, unless among the Christians of Georgia, Armenia, and Lebanon, where they are still thus employed. In Georgia the wine is stowed in large ox-skins, and is moved or kept at hand for use in smaller skins of goats or kids. But skins are still most extensively used throughout Western Asia for water. Their most usual forms are shown in the above cut (95), which also displays the manner in which they are carried. The water-carriers bear water in such skins and in this manner.

It is an error to represent bottles as being made exclusively of dressed or undressed skins among the ancient Hebrews. Among the Egyptians ornamental vases were of hard stone, alabaster, glass, ivory, bone, porcelain, bronze, silver, or gold; and also for the use of the people generally, of glazed pottery or common earthenware. As early as Thothmes III., assumed to be the Pharaoh of the Exodus, B.C. 1490, vases are known to have existed of a shape so elegant and of workmanship so superior, as to show that the art was not, even then, in its infancy.

Many of the bronze vases found at Thebes and in other parts of Egypt are of a quality which cannot fail to excite admiration, and which proves the skill possessed by the Egyptians in the art of working and compounding metals. Their shapes are most various—some neat, some plain, some grotesque; some in form not unlike our cream-jugs, others as devoid of taste as the wine-bottles of our cellars or the flower-pots of our conservatories. They had also bottles, small vases, and pots, used for holding ointment or for other purposes connected with the toilet, which were made of alabaster, glass, porcelain, and hard stone.

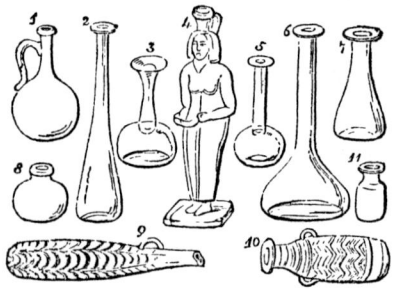

1, 3, Earthenware; 2, 5, 6 7, Green glass; 4, Blue glass; 8, 11, Alabaster; 9, 10, Porcelain.

96.

The perishable nature of skin-bottles led, at an early period, to the employment of instruments of a more durable kind; and it is to be presumed that the children of Israel would, during their sojourn in Egypt, learn, among other arts practised by their masters, that of working in pottery ware. Thus, as early as the days of the Judges (iv. 19; v. 25), bottles or vases composed of some earthy material, and apparently of a superior make, were in use; for what in the fourth chapter is termed ' a bottle,' is in the fifth designated ' a lordly dish.' Isaiah (xxx. 14) expressly mentions 'the bottle of the potters,' as the reading in the margin gives it, being a literal translation from the Hebrew, while the terms which the prophet employs show that he could not have intended any thing made of skin—' he shall *break it* as the *breaking* of the potter's vessel that is *broken* in pieces, so that there shall not be found in the bursting of it *a sherd* to take fire from the hearth, or to take water out of the pit.' (See also Jerem. xix. 1-10, 11, and chap. xiii. 12-14.) Metaphorically the word bottle is used, especially in poetry, for the clouds considered as pouring out and pouring down water (Iob xxxviii. 37).

BOW. [ARMS.] The bow is frequently men-

tioned symbolically in Scripture. In Ps. vii. 12, it implies victory, signifying judgments laid up in store against offenders. It is sometimes used to denote lying and falsehood (Ps. lxiv. 4; cxx. 4; Jer. ix. 3), probably from the many circumstances which tend to render a bow inoperative, especially in unskilful hands. Hence also ' a deceitful bow' (Ps. lxxviii. 57; Hos. vii. 16). The bow also signifies *any kind* of arms. The bow and spear are the most frequently mentioned, because the ancients used these most (Ps. xliv. 6; xlvi. 9; Zech. x. 4; Josh. xxiv. 12). In Habakk. iii. 9 ' thy bow was *made bare,*' means that it was drawn out of its case. The Orientals used to carry their bows in a case hung on their girdles.

BOWELS are often put by the Hebrew writers for the internal parts generally, the inner man, and so also for *heart,* as we use that term. Hence the bowels are made the seat of tenderness, mercy, and compassion; and thus the Scriptural expressions of the bowels being moved, bowels of mercy, straitened in the bowels, &c. By a similar association of ideas, the bowels are also sometimes made the seat of wisdom and understanding (Job xxxviii. 36; Ps. li. 10; Isa. xvi. 11).

BOWING. [ATTITUDES.]

BOX-TREE (Isa. lx. 13; xli. 19). It is not very certain that the box-tree is really denoted by the Hebrew and so translated: but nothing more probable has been suggested, and it agrees well enough with the indications afforded by the texts in which the name occurs.

The box is a native of most parts of Europe. It grows well in England, as at Boxhill, &c., while that from the Levant is most valued in commerce, in consequence of its being highly esteemed by wood-engravers. Turkey box is yielded by *Buxus Balearica,* a species which is found in Minorca, Sardinia, and Corsica, and also in both European and Asiatic Turkey, and is imported from Constantinople, Smyrna, and the Black Sea. Box is also found on Mount Caucasus, and a species extends even to the Himalaya mountains. It is much employed in the present day by the wood-engraver, the turner, carver, mathematical instrument maker, and the comb and flute maker.

The box-tree, being a native of mountainous regions, was peculiarly adapted to the calcareous formations of Mount Lebanon, and therefore likely to be brought from thence with the coniferous woods for the building of the temple, and was as well suited as the fir and the pine trees for changing the face of the desert.

BOZ'RAH, an ancient city, known also to the Greeks and Romans by the name of BOSTRA. In most of the passages of the Old Testament where it is mentioned, it appears as a chief city of the Edomites (Isa. xxxiv. 6; lxiii. 1; Amos i. 12; Jer. xlix. 13, 22); but it appears to have been afterwards taken from them by the Moabites, who for a time retained it in their possession.

Bozrah lay southward from Edrei, one of the capitals of Bashan, and, according to Eusebius, 24 Roman miles distant from it. Alexander Severus made it the seat of a Roman colony. In the acts of the Nicene, Ephesian, and Chalcedonian councils mention is made of bishops of Bozrah, and at a later period it became an important seat of the Nestorians. Abulfeda makes

It the capital of the Hauran, in which, according to Burckhardt, it is still one of the most important towns. It has recently been visited by various travellers, who give a very ample description of its ruins, the extent and importance of which are alone sufficient to evince the ancient consequence of the place. They are of various kinds, Greek, Roman, and Saracenic, with traces of the native works in the private dwellings.

These monuments of ancient grandeur serve but to heighten the impression which is created by the present desolation and decay. 'Bozrah,' says Lord Lindsay, 'is now for the most part a heap of ruins, a most dreary spectacle: here and there the direction of a street or alley is discernible, but that is all. The modern inhabitants—a mere handful—are almost lost in the maze of ruins. Olive-trees grew here within a few years, they told us—all extinct now, like the vines tor

97. [Bozrah.]

which the Bostra of the Romans was famous. And such, in the nineteenth century, and under Moslem rule, is the condition of a city which even in the seventh century, at the time of its capture by the Saracens, was called by Caled "the market-place of Syria, Irak, and the Hedjaz." " I have sworn by myself, saith the Lord of Hosts, that Bozrah shall become a desolation and reproach, a waste and a curse; and all the cities thereof shall be perpetual wastes!" (Jer. xlix. 13.) And it is so.'

BRACELET. This name, in strict propriety, is as applicable to circlets worn on the upper part of the arm as to those worn on the wrist; but as it has been found convenient to distinguish the former as ARMLETS, the term bracelet must be restricted to the latter. These are, and always have been, much in use among Eastern females. Many of them are of the same shapes and patterns as the armlets, and are often of such considerable weight and bulk as to appear more like manacles than ornaments. Many are often worn one above another on the same arm, so as to occupy the greater part of the space between the wrist and the elbow. The materials vary according to the condition of the wearer. Among the higher classes they are of mother-of-pearl, of fine flexible gold, and of silver, the last being the most common. The poorer women use plated steel, horn, brass, copper, beads, and other materials of a cheap description. Some notion of

the size and value of the bracelets used both now and in ancient times may be formed from the fact that those which were presented by Eleazer to Rebecca weighed ten shekels (Gen. xxiv. 22). The bracelets are sometimes flat, but more frequently round or semicircular, except at the point where they open to admit the hand, where they are flattened. They are frequently hollow, giving the show of bulk (which is much desired) without the inconvenience. Bracelets of gold twisted rope-wise are those now most used in Western Asia: but we cannot determine to what extent this fashion may have existed in ancient times.

BRAMBLE. [THORN.]

BRANCH. As trees, in Scripture, denote great men and princes, so branches, boughs, sprouts, or plants denote their offspring. In conformity with this way of speaking, Christ, in respect of his human nature, is styled a rod from the stem of Jesse, and a branch out of his roots (Isa. xi. 1), that is, a prince arising from the family of David.

A branch is the symbol of kings descended from royal ancestors, as branches from the root (Ezek. xvii. 3, 10; Dan. xi. 7). As only a vigorous tree can send forth vigorous branches, a branch is used as a general symbol of prosperity (Job viii. 16). From these explanations it is easy to see how a *branch* becomes the symbol of the Messiah (Isa. xi. 1: iv. 2; Jer. xxiii 15; Zech. iii. 8: vi. 12; and elsewhere). *Branch* is also used as the symbol of idolatrous worship (Ezek. viii. 17), probably in allusion to the general custom of carrying branches as a sign of honour. An *abominable branch* (Isa. xiv. 19) means a tree on which a malefactor has been hanged. In Ezek. xvii. 3 Jehoiachim is called the *highest branch* of the cedar, as being a king.

BRASS. This word occurs in the Authorized Version. But brass is a factitious metal, not known to the early Hebrews, and wherever it occurs, *copper* is to be understood [COPPER]. That copper is meant is shown by the text, 'Out of whose hills thou mayest dig brass' (Deut. viii. 9), it being of course impossible to dig a factitious metal, whether brass or bronze, out of mines.

Brass (to retain the word) is in Scripture the symbol of insensibility, baseness, and presumption or obstinacy in sin (Isa. xlviii. 4; Jer. vi. 28; Ezek. xxii. 18). Brass is also a symbol of strength (Ps. cvii. 16; Isa. xlviii. 4; Mic. iv. 13). So in Jer. i. 18 and xv. 20, brazen walls signify a strong and lasting adversary or opponent.

BREAD. The word 'bread' was of far more extensive meaning among the Hebrews than with us. There are passages in which it appears to be applied to all kinds of victuals (Luke xi. 3); but it more generally denotes all kinds of baked and pastry articles of food. It is also used, however, in the more limited sense of bread made from wheat or barley, for rye is little cultivated in the East. Barley being used chiefly by the poor, and for feeding horses [BARLEY], *bread*, in the more limited sense, chiefly denotes the various kinds of cake-like bread prepared from *wheaten* flour.

Corn is ground daily in the East. After the wheaten flour is taken from the hand-mill, it is

M

made into a dough or paste in a small wooden trough. It is next leavened; after which it is made into thin cakes or flaps, round or oval, and then baked.

The *kneading*-troughs, in which the dough is prepared, have no resemblance to ours in size or shape, but are small wooden bowls in which only a comparatively small quantity of dough is prepared. The Bedouin Arabs, indeed, use for this purpose a leather, which can be drawn up into a bag by a running cord along the border. and in which they prepare and often carry their dough. It is clear, from the history of the departure from Egypt, that the flour had first been made into a dough by water only, in which state it had been kept some little time before it was leavened; for when the Israelites were unexpectedly (as to the moment) compelled in all haste to withdraw, it was found that, although the dough had been prepared in the kneading-trough, it was still unleavened (Exod. xii. 34; comp. Hos. vii. 4); and it was in commemoration of this circumstance that they and their descendants in all ages were enjoined to eat only unleavened bread at the feast of the Passover. The dough thus prepared is not always baked at home In towns there are public ovens and bakers by trade; and although the general rule in large and respectable families is to bake the bread at home, much bread is bought of the bakers by unsettled individuals and poor persons; and many small households send their dough to be baked at the public oven, the baker receiving for his trouble a portion of the baked bread, which he adds to his day's stock of bread for sale. Such public ovens and bakers by trade must have existed anciently in Palestine, and in the East generally, as is evident from Hos. vii. 4 and Jer. xxxvii. 21.

For their larger operations the bakers have ovens of brick, not altogether unlike our own; and in large houses there are similar ovens. The ovens used in domestic baking are, however, usually of a portable description, and are large vessels of stone, earthenware, or copper, inside of which, when properly heated, small loaves and cakes are baked, and on the outer surface of which thin flaps of bread, or else a large wafer-like biscuit, may be prepared.

Another mode of baking bread is much used, especially in the villages A pit is sunk in the middle of the floor of the principal room, about four or five feet deep by three in diameter, well lined with compost or cement. When sufficiently heated by a fire kindled at the bottom, the bread is made by the thin pancake-like flaps of dough being, by a peculiar knack of hand in the women, struck against the oven, to which they adhere for a few moments, till they are sufficiently dressed.

Another sort of oven, or rather mode of baking, is much in use among the pastoral tribes. A shallow hole, about six inches deep by three or four feet in diameter, is made in the ground: this is filled up with dry brushwood, upon which, when kindled, pebbles are thrown to concentrate and retain the heat. Meanwhile the dough is prepared; and when the oven is sufficiently heated, the ashes and pebbles are removed, and the spot well cleaned out. The dough is then deposited in the hollow, and is left there over

night. The cakes thus baked are about two fingers thick, and are very palatable. There can be little doubt that this kind of oven and mode of baking bread were common among the Jews.

There is a baking utensil called in Arabic *tajen*, which appears to have been in use among the ancient Hebrews. It is a sort of pan of earthenware or iron (usually the latter), flat, or slightly convex, which is put over a slow fire, and on which the thin flaps of dough are laid and baked with considerable expedition, although only one cake can be baked in this way at a time. This is not a household mode of preparing bread, but is one of the simple and primitive processes employed by the wandering and semi-wandering tribes, shepherds, husbandmen and others, who have occasion to prepare a small quantity of daily bread in an easy off-hand manner. Bread is also baked in a manner which, although apparently very different, is but a modification of the principle of the *tajen*, and is used chiefly in the houses of the peasantry. There is a cavity in the fire-hearth, in which, when required for baking, a fire is kindled and burnt down to hot embers. A plate of iron, or sometimes copper, is placed over the hole, and on this the bread is baked.

Another mode of baking is in use chiefly among the pastoral tribes, and by travellers in the open country, but is not unknown in the villages. A smooth clear spot is chosen in the loose ground, a sandy soil—so common in the Eastern deserts and harder lands—being preferred. On this a fire is kindled, and, when the ground is sufficiently heated, the embers and ashes are raked aside, and the dough is laid on the heated spot, and then covered over with the glowing embers and ashes which had just been removed. The bread is several times turned, and in less than half an hour is sufficiently baked. Bread thus baked is referred to in Gen. xviii. 6; 1 Kings xviii. 13; xix. 6; Ezek. iv. 12. This is the kind of *ash*-bread which Sarah, on the arrival of the three strangers, was required to bake 'quickly' for the hospitable entertainment of the unknown travellers.

BREASTPLATE, a piece of defensive armour. [ARMS, ARMOUR.]

BREASTPLATE OF THE HIGH-PRIEST, a splendid ornament covering the breast of the high-priest. It was composed of richly embroidered cloth, in which were set, in four rows, twelve precious stones, on each of which was engraven the name of one of the twelve tribes of Israel (Exod. xxviii. 15-29; xxxix. 8-21). [PRIESTS.]

BRICKS. Bricks compacted with straw and dried in the sun, are those which are chiefly mentioned in the Scriptures. Of such bricks the tower of Babel was doubtless composed [BABEL, BABYLON], and the making of such formed the chief labour of the Israelites when bondsmen in Egypt (Exod. i. 13, 14).

The use of crude brick, baked in the sun, was universal in Upper and Lower Egypt, both for public and private buildings; and the brick-field gave abundant occupation to numerous labourers throughout the country. We find that, independent of native labourers, a great many foreigners were constantly engaged in the brickfields at Thebes and other parts of Egypt. The Jews, of course, were not excluded from this drudgery; and, like the captives detained in the Thebaïd, they were condemned to the same labour in Lower Egypt. They erected granaries, treasure-cities, and other public buildings for the Egyptian monarch. It has been supposed by some that the captive foreigners represented on the monuments as engaged in brick-making were Jews, and that the scenes represented were those of their actual operations in Egypt. Whether this supposition is correct or not, it is curious to discover other foreign captives occupied in the same manner, and overlooked by similar 'taskmasters,' and performing the very same labours as the Israelites described in the Bible; and it is worthy of remark, as noticed by Wilkinson, that *more bricks bearing the name of Thothmes III. (who is supposed to have been the king at the time of the Exode) have been discovered than at any other period.*

[98. Egyptian Brickmaking.]

The process of manufacture indicated by the representations in cut 98, does not materially differ from that which is still followed in the same country. The clay was brought in baskets from the Nile, thrown into a heap, thoroughly saturated with water, and worked up to a proper temper by the feet of the labourers. This part of the labour in such a climate must have been very fatiguing and unwholesome, and it consequently appears to have been shunned by the native Egyptians. There is an allusion to the severity of this labour in Nahum iii. 14, 15. The clay, when tempered, was cut by an instrument somewhat resembling the agricultural hoe, and moulded in an oblong trough; the bricks were then dried in the sun, and some from their colour appear to have been baked or burned, but no trace of this operation has yet been discovered in the monuments.

BRIDE, BRIDEGROOM. [Marriage.]

BRIERS. [Thorns.]

BROOK. The original word (Nahal) thus translated might better be rendered by *torrent.* It is applied, 1. to small streams arising from a subterraneous spring, and flowing through a deep valley, such as the Arnon, Jabbok, Kidron, Sorek, &c.; and also the brook of the willows, mentioned in Isa. xv. 7; 2. to winter-torrents, arising from rains, and which are soon dried up in the warm season (Job vi. 15, 19). Such is the noted river (brook) of Egypt, so often mentioned as at the southernmost border of Canaan (Num. xxxiv. 5; Josh. xv. 4, 47). and, in fact, such are most of the brooks and streams of Pales-

tine, which are numerous in winter and early spring. but of which very few survive the beginning of the summer.

BROTHER. This term is so variously and extensively applied in Scripture, that it becomes important carefully to distinguish the different acceptations in which it is used.

1. It denotes a brother in the natural sense, whether the offspring of the same father only (Matt. i. 2; Luke iii. 1, 19), or of the same father and mother (Luke vi. 14, &c.).—2. A near relative or kinsman by blood, cousin (Gen. xiii. 8; xiv. 16; Matt. xii 46; John vii. 3; Acts i. 14; Gal. i. 19).—3. One who is connected with another by any tie of intimacy or fellowship: hence—4. One born in the same country, descended from the same stock, a fellow countryman (Matt. v. 47; Acts iii. 22; Heb. vii. 5: Exod. ii. 11; iv. 18).—5. One of equal rank and dignity (Job xxx. 29; Prov. xviii. 9; Matt. xxiii. 8).—6. Disciples, followers, &c. (Matt. xxv. 40; Heb. ii. 11, 12). – 7. One of the same faith (Amos i. 9; Acts ix. 30; xi. 29; 1 Cor. v. xi.); from which and other texts it appears that the first converts to the faith of Jesus were known to each other by the title of Brethren, till the name of Christians was given to them at Antioch (Acts xi. 26).—8. An associate, colleague in office or dignity, &c. (Ezra iii. 2; 1 Cor. i. 1; 2 Cor. i. 1; &c.)—9. One of the same nature, a fellow man (Gen. xiii. 8; xxvi. 31; Matt. v. 22, 23, 24; vii. 5; Heb. ii. 17; viii. 11).—10. One beloved, *i. e.* as a brother, in a direct address (Acts ii. 29; vi. 3; 1 Thess. v. 1).

BURIAL and SEPULCHRES. Throughout the whole of their national history the Israelites observed the practice of burial. Amongst them, it was deemed not only an act of humanity, but a sacred duty of religion to pay the last honours to the departed; while, to be deprived of these, as was frequently the fate of enemies at the hands of ruthless conquerors (2 Sam. xxi. 9-14; 2 Kings ix. 28, 34; Ps. lxxix. 2; Eccles. vi. 3), was considered the greatest calamity and disgrace which a person could suffer.

On the death of any member of a family, preparations were forthwith made for the burial, which among the Jews, were in many respects similar to those which are common in the East at the present day, and were more or less expensive according to circumstances. After the solemn ceremony of the last kiss and closing the eyes, the corpse, which was perfumed by the nearest relative, having been laid out and the head covered with a napkin, was subjected to entire ablution in warm water (Acts ix. 37), a precaution probably adopted to guard against premature interment. But, besides this first and indispensable attention, other cares of a more elaborate and costly description were amongst certain classes bestowed on the remains of deceased friends, and all of which may be included under the general head of embalming. Nowhere was this operation performed with such religious care and in so scientific a manner as in ancient Egypt, which could boast of a class of professional men trained to the business; and such adepts had these 'physicians' become in the art of preserving dead bodies, that there are *mummies* still found, which must have existed for many thousand years. The bodies of Jacob and

Joseph underwent this eminently Egyptian pre-paration for burial, which on both occasions was doubtless executed in a style of the greatest mag-nificence (Gen. l. 2, 26). Whether this expen-sive method of embalming was imitated by the earlier Hebrews, we have no distinct accounts; but we learn from their practice in later ages that they had some observance of the kind, only

they substituted a simpler and more expeditious though it must have been a less efficient process, which consisted in merely swathing the corpse round with numerous folds of linen, and some-times a variety of stuffs, and anointing it with a mixture of aromatic substances, of which aloes and myrrh were the chief ingredients (John xix. 39-40).

99. [Ancient Jewish Funeral : Costume, Modern Syrian.]

The corpse, after receiving the preliminary attentions, was enveloped in the grave-clothes, which were sometimes nothing more than the ordinary dress, or folds of linen cloth wrapped round the body, and a napkin about the head;

100. [Grave-clothes.]

though in other cases a shroud was used. The body thus dressed was deposited in an upper chamber in solemn state, open to the view of all visitors (Acts ix. 37). From the moment the vital spark was extinguished, the members of the family, especially the females, in the violent style of Oriental grief, burst out into shrill, loud, and doleful lamentations, and were soon joined by their friends and neighbours, who, on hearing of the event, crowded to the house in great numbers (Mark v. 38). By the better classes, this duty of sympathizing with the bereaved family was, and still is, performed by a class of females who engaged themselves as professional mourners, and who, seated amid the mourning circle, studied, by vehement sobs and gesticulations, and by singing dirges in which they eulogized the personal qualities or virtuous and benevolent actions of the deceased (Acts ix. 39), to stir the source of tears, and give fresh impulse to the grief of the afflicted relatives. Numbers of these singing men and women lamented the death of Josiah (2 Chron. xxxv. 25). The period between the death and the burial was much shorter than custom sanctions in our country; for a long delay in the removal of a corpse would have been attended with much inconvenience, from the heat of the climate generally, and, among the Jews in particular, from the circumstance that every one that came near the chamber was unclean for a week. Interment, therefore, where there was no embalming, was never postponed beyond twenty-four hours after death, and generally it took place much earlier. There are two instances in sacred history where consignment to the grave followed immediately after decease (Acts v. 6, 10).

Persons of distinction were deposited in coffins.

But the most common mode of carrying a corpse to the grave was on a bier or *bed* (2 Sam. iii. 31), which in some cases must have been furnished in a costly and elegant style. The bier, however, in use among the common and meaner sort of people was nothing but a plain wooden board, on which, supported by two poles, the body lay concealed only by a slight coverlet from the view of the attendants. On such a humble vehicle was the widow's son of Nain carried (Luke vii. 14), and 'this mode of per-forming funeral obsequies,' says an intelligent

101. [Ancient Sarcophagi in Palestine.]

traveller, 'obtains equally in the present day among the Jews, Mohammedans, and Christians of the East.' The nearest relatives kept close by the bier, and performed the office of bearers, in which, however, they were assisted by the com-pany in succession. In cases where the expense could be afforded, hired mourners accompanied the procession, and, by every now and then lift-ing the covering and exposing the corpse, gave the signal to the company to renew their shouts of lamentation.

Sepulchres were, as they still are in the East, —by a prudent arrangement sadly neglected in our country—situated without the precincts of cities. Among the Jews, in the case of Levitical cities, the distance required to be 2000 cubits, and in all it was considerable. Nobody was allowed to be buried within the walls, Jerusalem forming the only exception, and even there the privilege was reserved for the royal family of David and a few persons of exalted character (1 Kings ii. 10; 2 Kings xiv. 20). In the vicinity of this capital were public cemeteries for the general accommodation of the inhabitants, besides a field appropriated to the *burial of strangers.*

The style of the public cemeteries around the cities of ancient Palestine in all probability resembled that of the present burying-places of the East, of which Dr. Shaw gives the following description:—'They occupy a large space, a great extent of ground being allotted for the purpose. Each family has a portion of it walled in like a garden, where the bones of its ancestors have remained undisturbed for many generations. For in these inclosures the graves are all distinct and separate; each of them having a stone placed upright, both at the head and feet, inscribed with the name or title of the deceased; whilst the intermediate space is either planted with flowers, bordered round with stone, or paved with tiles.'

There were other sepulchres which were private property, erected at the expense and for the use of several families in a neighbourhood, or provided by individuals as a separate burying-place for themselves. These were situated either in some conspicuous place, as Rachel's on the highway to Bethlehem (Gen. xxxv. 19), or in some lonely and sequestered spot, under a wide-spreading tree (Gen. xxxv. 8) in a field or a garden. In common cases, sepulchres were formed by digging a small depth into the ground. Over these, which were considered an humble kind of tomb, the wealthy and great

102. [Sepulchral Cupola.]

often erected small stone buildings, in the form of a house or cupola, to serve as their family sepulchre. 'This custom,' says Carne, 'which is of great antiquity, and particularly prevails in the lonely parts of Lebanon, may serve to explain some passages of Scripture. The prophet Samuel was buried in his own house at Ramah, and Joab was buried in his house in the wilderness. These, it is evident, were not their dwelling-houses, but mansions for the dead, or family vaults which they had built within

their own policies.' Not unfrequently, however, the richer classes purchased, like Abraham, some of the natural caverns with which Palestine abounded, and converted them by some suitable alterations into family sepulchres; while others with vast pains and expense made excavations in the solid rock (Matt. xxvii. 60). Many sepulchres of this description are still found in Palestine. Along the sides of those vast caverns niches were cut, or sometimes shelves ranged one above another, on which were deposited the bodies of the dead, while in others the ground-floor of the tomb was raised so as to make different compartments, the lowest place in the family vaults being reserved for the servants. These interior arrangements may be the better understood by the help of the annexed engravings. No. 103 is the interior of the celebrated Tomb of the Kings (so

103. [Interior of Tomb of the Kings.]

called), near Jerusalem. In it are some further specimens of the stone sarcophagi already noticed.

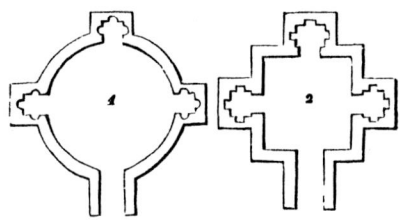

104. [Ground-plans of Sepulchres.]

No. 104 contains two ground-plans showing the general character of the interior arrangements of the more extensive crypts. Some of those found near Tyre, and at Alexandria, are of the round form shown in fig. 1, but these seem exceptions; for the tombs at Jerusalem, in Asia Minor, and generally in Egypt and the East, offer the arrangement shown in fig. 2.

The mouth of the sepulchre was secured by a huge stone (Matt. xxvii. 60; John xi. 38). But the entrance-porch, to which the removal of this rude door gave admittance, was so large that several persons could stand in it and view the interior; and hence we read that the women who visited the sepulchre of our Lord, 'entering in saw a young man sitting, clothed in a long white garment' (Mark xvi. 5); and in like manner, in reference to the flight of steps, that Peter 'stooping down, and looking in, saw the linen clothes lying' (John xx. 5). Some of the more splendid of these tombs, however, instead of the block of stone, have the porches surmounted with tasteful mason-work, and supported by well-finished colonnades; and as they stand open and exposed, do now, as they did formerly, afford retreats to numbers of vagrants and lawless characters. The rocky valleys around Jerusalem exhibit numberless specimens of these sepulchral excavations. Monuments of this elegant description were erected to many of the prophets and other holy men who figured as prominent characters in the early history of Israel, and it seems to have been considered, in the degenerate age of our Lord, an act of great piety to repair and ornament with

|05. [Exterior of Sepulchre: Jerusalem.]

fresh devices the sepulchres of those ancient worthies (Matt. xxiii. 29). All the tombs, however, in the neighbourhood of Jerusalem were at certain seasons whitewashed (Matt. xxiii. 27). The origin of this prevailing custom is to be traced to a desire of making the sepulchres easily discernible, and so preventing the risk of contracting ceremonial defilement through accident or ignorance. To paint them with white was obviously the best preservative against the apprehended danger; and the season chosen for this garniture of the sepulchres was on the return of spring, a little before the Passover, when, the winter rains being over, a long unbroken tract of dry weather usually ensued. The words of Christ referred to were spoken but a few days before the Passover, when the fresh coating of white paint would be conspicuous on all the adjoining hills and valleys; and when we consider the striking contrast that must have been presented between the graceful architecture and carefully dressed appearance of these tombs without, and the disgusting relics of mortality that were mouldering within, we cannot fail to perceive the emphatic energy of the language in which our Lord rebuked the *hypocrisy* of the Pharisees.

It remains only to notice that, during the first few weeks after a burial, members of a family, especially the females, paid frequent visits to the tomb (John xi 31). This affecting custom still continues in the East.

BURNT-OFFERINGS, sacrifices which owed their Hebrew name (*olah*, literally, 'what goes up,' from *alah*, 'to ascend'), to the circumstance that the whole of the offering was to be consumed by fire upon the altar, and to *rise*, as it were, in smoke towards heaven.

Such burnt-offerings are among the most ancient, if not the earliest, on Scriptural record. We find them already in use in the patriarchal times; hence the opinion of some, that *Abel's* offering (Gen. iv. 4) was a burnt-offering as regarded the firstlings of his flock, while the pieces of fat which he offered was a thank-offering, just in the manner that Moses afterwards ordained, or rather confirmed from ancient custom (Lev. i. *sq.*). It was a burnt-offering that Noah offered to the Lord after the Deluge (Gen. viii. 20).

Only oxen, male sheep or goats, or turtle-doves and young pigeons, all without blemish, were fit for burnt-offerings. The offerer, in person, was obliged to carry this sacrifice first of all into the fore-court, as far as the gate of the tabernacle or temple, where the animal was examined by the officiating priest to ascertain that it was without blemish. The offerer then laid his hand upon the victim, confessing his sins, and dedicated it as his sacrifice to propitiate the Almighty. The animal was then killed (which might be done by the offerer himself) towards the north of the altar (Lev. i. 11), in allusion, as the Talmud alleges, to the coming of inclement weather (typical of the Divine wrath) from the northern quarter of the heavens. After this began the ceremony of taking up the blood and sprinkling it *around* the altar, that is, upon the lower part of the altar, not immediately upon it, lest it should extinguish the fire thereon (Lev. iii. 2; Deut. xii. 27; 2 Chron. xxix. 22).

The next act was the skinning or flaying of the animal, and the cutting of it into pieces, actions which the offerer himself was allowed to perform (Lev. i. 6). The skin alone belonged to the officiating priest (Lev. vii. 8). The dissection of the animal began with the head, legs, &c., and it was divided into twelve pieces. The priest then took the right shoulder, breast, and entrails, and placing them in the hands of the offerer, he put his own hands beneath those of the former, and thus waved the sacrifice up and down several times in acknowledgment of the all-powerful presence of God. The officiating priest then retraced his steps to the altar, placed the wood upon it in the form of a cross, and lighted the fire. The entrails and legs being cleansed with water, the separated pieces were placed together upon the altar in the form of a slain animal. Poor people were allowed to bring a turtle-dove or a young pigeon as a burnt offering, these birds being very common and cheap in Palestine. The mode of killing them was by nipping off the head with the nails of the hand.

Standing public burnt-offerings were those used daily morning and evening (Num. xxviii. 3; Exod. xxix. 38), and on the three great festivals (Lev. xxiii. 37; Num. xxviii. 11-27; xxix. 2-22; Lev. xvi. 3; comp. 2 Chron. xxxv. 12-16).

Private and occasional burnt-offerings were those brought by women rising from childbed (Lev. xii. 6); those brought by persons cured of leprosy (*ib.* xiv. 19-22); those brought by persons cleansed from issue (*ib.* xv. 14, *sq*); and those brought by the Nazarites when rendered unclean by having come in contact with a dead body (Num. vi. 9), or after the days of their separation were fulfilled (*ib.* vi. 14).

Nor were the burnt-offerings confined to these cases alone; we find them in use almost on all important occasions, events, and solemnities, whether private or public, and often in very large numbers (comp. Judg. xx. 26 ; 1 Sam. vii. 9 ; 2 Chron. xxxi. 2 ; 1 Kings iii. 4 ; 1 Chron. xxix. 21 ; 2 Chron. xxix. 21 ; Ezra vi. 17 ; viii. 35). Heathens also were allowed to offer burnt-offerings in the temple, and Augustus gave orders to sacrifice for him every day in the temple at Jerusalem a burnt-offering, consisting of two lambs and one ox.

BUSHEL is used in the Auth. Vers. to express a measure of about a peck.

BUTTER. [MILK.]

BUZ, son of Nahor and Milcah, and brother of Huz (Gen xxii. 21). Elihu. one of Job's friends, who is distinguished as an Aramæan or Syrian (Job xxxii. 2), was doubtless descended from this Buz. Judgments are denounced upon the tribe of Buz by Jeremiah (xxv. 23 ; and from the context this tribe appears to have been located in Arabia Deserta.

C.

CAB, a measure mentioned in 2 Kings vi. 25. The Rabbins make it the sixth part of a *seah* or *satum*, and the eighteenth part of an ephah. In that case a cab contained 3½ pints of our wine measure. or 2⅝ pints of our corn measure.

CA'BUL, a district given to Hiram, king of Tyre, by Solomon, in acknowledgment of the important services which he had rendered towards the building of the Temple (1 Kings ix. 13). Hiram was by no means pleased with the gift, and the district received the name of Cabul (*unpleasing*) from this circumstance. The situation of Cabul has been disputed ; but we are content to accept the information of Josephus, who seems to place it in the north-west part of Galilee, adjacent to Tyre.

CÆ'SAR, a name assumed by, or conferred upon, all the Roman emperors after Julius Cæsar. In this way it became a sort of title like Pharaoh, and, as such, is usually applied to the emperors in the New Testament, without their distinctive proper names (AUGUSTUS). The Cæsars mentioned in the New Testament are Augustus (Luke ii. 1) ; Tiberius (Luke iii. 1 ; xx. 22). Claudius (Acts xi. 28) ; Nero (Acts xxv. 8) ; Caligula, who succeeded Tiberius, is not mentioned.

CÆSARE'A. There were two important towns in Palestine thus named in compliment to Roman emperors.

1. CÆSAREA PALESTINA, or Cæsarea of Palestine, so called to distinguish it from the other Cæsarea, from its eminence as the Roman metropolis of Palestine, and the residence of the procurator. It was built by Herod the Great, with much of beauty and convenience, twenty-two years before the birth of Christ. Here he erected one of the most stupendous works of antiquity—a semicircular mole, which protected the port of Cæsarea on the south and west, leaving only a sufficient opening for vessels to enter from the north ; so that, within the enclosed space, a fleet might ride at all weathers in perfect security. The mole was constructed of immense blocks of stone brought from a great distance, and sunk to the depth of 20 fathoms in the sea. Besides this, Herod added many splendid buildings to the city : and when the whole was finished, which was within twelve years from the commencement of the undertaking, he fixed his residence there, and thus elevated the city to the rank of the civil and military capital of Judæa, which rank it continued to enjoy as long as the country remained a province of the Roman empire. Vespasian raised Cæsarea to the rank of a Roman colony, granting it first, exemption from the capitation tax, and afterwards, from the ground taxes. The place was, however, inhabited chiefly by Gentiles, though some thousands of Jews lived in it.

Cæsarea is the scene of several interesting circumstances described in the New Testament, such as the conversion of Cornelius, the first-fruits of the Gentiles (Acts x.) ; the residence of Philip the Evangelist (Acts xxi. 8) ; the journey thither of St. Paul ; his pleading there before Felix ; his imprisonment for two years ; and his final pleading before Festus and King Agrippa (Acts xxiv.). It was here also, in the amphitheatre built by his father, that Herod Agrippa was smitten of God and died (Acts xii. 21-23).

On the commencement of the war with the Romans, all the Jewish inhabitants of Cæsarea, to the number of 20,000, were massacred by the Gentiles, who had long held them at feud.

In later times, Cæsarea is chiefly noted as the birth-place and episcopate of Eusebius, the celebrated Church historian, in the beginning of the 4th century.

Cæsarea is almost thirty-five miles north of Joppa or Jaffa, and fifty-five miles from Jerusalem. It still retains the ancient name in the form of Kaiseraih ; but has long been desolate. The most conspicuous ruin is that of an old castle, at the extremity of the ancient mole. A great extent of ground is covered by the remains of the city. The water is abundant and of excellent quality ; and the small vessels of the country often put in here to take in their supplies. Cæsarea is, apparently, never frequented for any other purpose ; even the high-road leaves it wide ; and it has been visited by very few of the numerous travellers in Palestine. The present tenants of the ruins are snakes, scorpions, lizards, wild boars, and jackals.

2. CÆSAREA PHILIPPI. Towards the springs of the Jordan, and near the foot of Isbel Shrik, or the Prince's Mount, a lofty branch of Lebanon, forming in that direction the boundary between Palestine and Syria Proper. stands a city originally called Banias, which was in later times much enlarged and beautified by Philip the tetrarch, who called it Cæsarea in honour of Tiberius the emperor, adding the cognomen of Philippi to distinguish it from Cæsarea of Palestine. It lay about 120 miles north from Jerusalem, and a day and a half's journey from Damascus (Matt. xvi. 13 ; Mark viii. 27). Herod Agrippa also still further extended and embellished it. In compliment to the emperor Nero, its name was afterwards changed to Neronias ; and Titus, after the overthrow of Jerusalem, exhibited some public games here, in which the Jewish prisoners were compelled to fight like

gladiators. Under the Christians it was erected into a bishopric of Phœnicia. It has now resumed its original name of Bâuiâs, and has dwindled into a paltry and insignificant village, whose mean and destitute condition contrasts strikingly with the rich and luxuriant character of the surrounding country. It is said that many remains of ancient architecture are found in the neighbourhood. The ruins of the castle of Bâniâs, which appears to have been a work of the Saracens, crown the summit of the adjoining mountain, and display a wall 10 feet in thickness, by which the fortress was defended. The ruins of another fortified castle are visible on the south of the village, and a substantial bridge which conducts to it, inscribed with an Arabic legend, its date being of the age of the Crusades.

CAIAPHAS, whom Josephus calls Joseph Caiaphas, was high-priest of the Jews in the reign of Tiberius Cæsar (Luke iii. 2). We learn from Josephus that he succeeded Simon the son of Camith (about A.D. 27 or 28), and held the office nine years, when he was deposed. His wife was the daughter of Annas, or Ananus, who had formerly been high-priest, and who still possessed great influence and control in sacerdotal matters, several of his family successively holding the high-priesthood. The names of Annas and Caiaphas are coupled by Luke—'Annas and Caiaphas being the high-priests;' and this has given occasion to no small amount of discussion. The most probable opinion is that Caiaphas was the high-priest, and that Annas was his vicar or deputy. Caiaphas is the high-priest who rent his clothes, and declared Jesus to be worthy of death. When Judas had betrayed him, our Lord was first taken to Annas, who sent him to Caiaphas (John xviii. 13), who perhaps abode in another part of the same palace. What became of Caiaphas after his deposition in A.D. 38, is not known.

CAIN. The derivation of this word is disputed; but it probably signifies *an acquisition* or *possession*. Some degree of mystery attends the immediate origin of the horrible crime of Cain. Abel, it appears, brought two offerings, the one an oblation, the other a sacrifice. Cain brought but the former—a mere acknowledgment, it is supposed, of the sovereignty of God; neglecting to offer the sacrifice which would have been a confession of fallen nature, and, typically, an atonement for sin. It was not, therefore, the mere difference of feeling with which the two offerings were brought which constituted the virtue of the one, or the guilt of the other brother. God's righteous indignation against sin had been plainly revealed; and there can be no doubt that the means of safety, of reconciliation and atonement, were as plainly made known to Adam and his offspring. The refusal, therefore, of the sacrifice was a virtual denial of God's right to condemn the sinner, and at the same time a proud rejection of the proffered means of grace.

The punishment which attended the crime was such as could only be inflicted by an Almighty avenger. It admitted of no escape, scarcely of any conceivable alleviation. Cursed from the earth himself, the earth was doomed to a double barrenness wherever the offender should set his foot. Physical want and hardship, therefore, were among the first of the miseries heaped upon his

head. Next came those of mind and conscience: ' The voice of thy brother's blood crieth unto me from the ground,' was the announcement of his discovered guilt. He could now hear that same voice himself; nor did any retreat remain to him from the terrors of his own soul or those of Divine vengeance. By the statement that ' Cain went out from the presence of the Lord,' probability is given to the conjecture which represents him as abiding, till thus exiled, in some favoured spot where the Almighty still, by visible signs, manifested himself to his fallen creatures. The expression of dread lest, as he wandered over the face of the earth, he might be recognised and slain, has an awful sound when falling from the mouth of a murderer. But he was to be protected against the wrath of his fellow-men; and of this God gave him assurance, not by setting a mark upon him, which is a false translation, but by appointing a sign or token which he himself might understand as a proof that he should not perish by the hand of another, as Abel had perished by his.

It may be worthy of observation, that especial mention is made of the fact, that Cain having travelled into the land of Nod there built a city; and further, that his descendants were chiefly celebrated for their skill in the arts of social life. In both accounts may probably be discovered the powerful struggles with which Cain strove to overcome the difficulties which attended his position as one to whom the tillage of the ground was virtually prohibited.

CAINAN (*possessor*). 1. Son of Enos, and father of Mahaleel (Gen. v. 9; 1 Chron. i. 2). 2. Son of Arphaxad, the son of Shem, and father of Salah. His name is wanting in the present copies of the Hebrew Scriptures; but is found in the Septuagint version of Gen. x. 24; xi. 12; and in Luke iii. 36. It is supposed, however, on good grounds, that his name was not originally in the Hebrew text and the Septuagint versions derived from it, and that it was inserted in the text of Luke by some inadvertent transcribers, who, remarking it in some copies of the Septuagint, added it.

CAKES. [BREAD].

CALAH, or rather CALACH, a city of Assyria, built by Ashur or Nimrod. It was at some distance from Nineveh, the city of Resen lying between them. Most writers concur in placing it on the Great Zab (the ancient Lycus) not far from its junction with the Tigris.

CALEB (*dog*), son of Jephunneh, of the tribe of Judah. He was sent with Joshua and others to explore the land of Canaan, and in consequence of his joining with Joshua in opposing the discouraging accounts brought back by the other spies, they were both specially exempted from the decree of death which was pronounced on the generation to which they belonged (Num. xiii. 6; xiv. 6, 24, 38). When the land of Canaan had been invaded and partly conquered, Caleb was privileged to choose Kirjatharba, or Hebron, and its neighbourhood, for his possession (Josh. xiv. 6-15). He accordingly went and wrested it from the native inhabitants, and thence proceeded to Debir, which was taken for him by his nephew Othniel, who, as his reward, received in marriage the hand of Caleb's daughter [ACHSAH], with a valuable dower (Josh. xv.

13-19). Caleb is usually supposed to have outlived Joshua.

CALF is mentioned in several places, but not requiring a zoological explanation, it may be sufficient to make a few remarks on the worship of calves and other superstitious practices connected with them. The most ancient and remarkable notice in the Scriptures on this head, is that of the golden calf which was cast by Aaron from the earrings of the people, while the Israelites were encamped at the foot of Sinai and Moses was absent on the Mount. The next notice refers to an event which occurred ages after, when Jeroboam, king of Israel, set up two idols in the form of a calf, the one in Dan and the other in Bethel. This almost incomprehensible degradation of human reason was, more particularly in the first instance, no doubt the result of the debasing influences which operated on the minds of the Israelites during their sojourn in Egypt, where, amid the daily practice of the most degrading and revolting religious ceremonies, they were accustomed to see the image of a sacred calf, surrounded by other symbols, carried in solemn pomp at the head of marching armies; such as may be still seen depicted in the processions of Rameses the Great or Sesostris.

106. [Egyptian Calf-Idol.]

A similar divinity belonged to the earliest Indian, Greek, and even Scandinavian mythologies; and therefore it may be conceived that the symbol, enduring even to this day, was at that period generally understood by the multitude. and consequently that it was afterwards revived by Jeroboam without popular opposition. With regard to Jer. xxxiv. 18, 19, it may be sufficient to mention that many nations of antiquity had a practice of binding themselves to certain resolutions by the ceremony of cutting a calf or other victim into two halves or sides, laying them on the ground, and passing between the severed parts. This was considered as constituting a peculiarly binding obligation (comp. Gen. xv. 10, 17).

CAL'NEH, or rather CHALNEH, the fourth of Nimrod's cities (Gen. x. 10), and probably not different from the Calno of Isa. x. 9, or the Canneh of Ezek. xxvii. 23. According to the Chaldee translation, with which Eusebius and Jerome agree, this is the same place that was subsequently called Ctesiphon. It lay on the Tigris, opposite Celeucia, and was for a time the capital of the Parthians. In the time of the prophet Amos, Calneh appears to have constituted an independent principality (Amos vi. 1, 2): but not long after it became, with the rest of

Western Asia, a prey to the Assyrians (Isa. x. 9). About 150 years later, Calneh was still a considerable town, as may be inferred from its being mentioned by Ezekiel (xxvii. 23) among the places which traded with Tyre. The site of Ctesiphon, or Calneh, was afterwards occupied by El-Madain, i. e. the two cities, of which the only remains are the ruins of a remarkable palace called Teuk-kesra, some mounds of rubbish, and a considerable extent of massive wall towards the river.

CAL'VARY, the place where Christ was crucified See GOLGOTHA.

CAMBY'SES. [AHASUERUS.]

CAMEL. The genus Camelus, as constituted by modern naturalists, comprises two species positively distinct, but still possessing the common characters of being ruminants without horns, without muzzle, with nostrils forming oblique slits, the upper lid divided, and separately movable and extensile, the soles of the feet horny, with two toes covered by unguiculated claws, the limbs long, the abdomen drawn up, and the neck, long and slender, is bent down and up, the reverse of that of a horse, which is arched. Camels have thirty-six teeth in all. They have callosities on the breast-bone and on the flexures of the joints. Of the four stomachs, which they have in common with other animals chewing the cud, the paunch is provided with membranous cells to contain an extra provision of water, enabling the species to subsist for four or more days without drinking. But when in the desert, the camel has the faculty of smelling it afar off, and then, breaking through all control, he rushes onwards to drink, stirring the element previously with a fore foot until quite muddy. Camels are temperate animals, being fed on a march only once in twenty-four hours, with about a pound weight of dates, beans, or barley, and are enabled in the wilderness, by means of their long flexible necks and strong cuspidate teeth, to snap as they pass at thistles and thorny plants. They are emphatically called the ships of the desert; having to cross regions where no vegetation whatever is met with, and where they could not be enabled to continue their march but for the aid of the double or single hunch on the back, which, being composed of muscular fibre, and cellular substance highly adapted for the accumulation of fat, swells in proportion as the animal is healthy and well fed, or sinks by absorption as it supplies the want of sustenance under fatigue and scarcity. Now, when to these endowments are added a lofty stature and great agility; eyes that discover minute objects at a distance; a sense of smelling of prodigious acuteness—ever kept in a state of sensibility by the animal's power of closing the nostrils to exclude the acrid particles of the sandy deserts; a spirit, moreover, of patience, not the result of fear, but of forbearance, carried to the length of self-sacrifice in the practice of obedience, so often exemplified by the camel's bones in great numbers strewing the surface of the desert; when we perceive it furnished with a dense wool, to avert the solar heat and nightly cold, while on the animal, and to clothe and lodge his master when manufactured, and know that the female carries milk to feed him,—we have one of the most incontrovertible examples of Almighty power and beneficence in the adaptation of means to a direct purpose, that can well be submitted to the apprehension of man; for, without the existence of the camel, immense portions of the surface of the earth would be uninhabitable. and even impassable. Surely the Arabs are right, ' Job's beast is a monument of God's mercy!' The two species are—1. The Bactrian camel, which is large and robust; naturally but one hunch, and originally a native of the highest table-lands of Central Asia, where even now, wild individuals may be found. The species extends through China, Tartary, and Russia, and is principally impo·ted across the mountains into Asia Minor, Syria, and Persia.

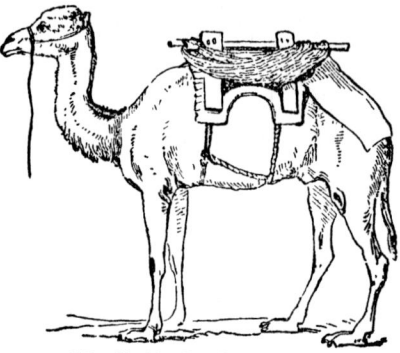

107.   [Arabian Camel: baggage.]

2. The Arabian camel or dromedary, which has naturally but one hunch, and may be considered as of Western-Asiatic or of African origin, although no kind of camel is figured on any monument of Egypt. We find, however, camels mentioned in Genesis xii.; but being placed last among the cattle given by Pharaoh to Abraham, the fact seems to show that they were not considered as the most important part of his donation. This can be true only upon the supposition that only a few of these animals were delivered to him, and therefore that they were still rare in the valley of the Nile; though soon after there is abundant evidence of the nations of Syria and Palestine having whole herds of them fully domesticated.

108.   [Arabian Camel: saddle.]

Of the Arabian species two very distinct races are noticed; those of stronger frame but slower pace used to carry burdens, varying from 500 to 700 weight, and travelling little more than twenty-four miles per day; and those of lighter form bred for the saddle with single riders, whereof the fleetest serve to convey intelligence, &c., and travel at the rate of 200 miles in twenty-four hours.

All camels, from their very birth, are taught to bend their limbs and lie down to receive a load or a rider They are often placed circularly in a recumbent posture, and together with their loads form a sufficient rampart of defence against robbers on horseback. The milk of she-camels is still considered a very nutritive cooling drink, and when turned it becomes intoxicating. Their dung supplies fuel in the desert, and in sandy regions where wood is scarce; and occasionally it is a kind of resource for horses when other food is wanting in the wilderness. Their flesh, particularly the hunch, is in request among the Arabs, but was forbidden to the Hebrews, more perhaps from motives of economy, and to keep the people from again becoming wanderers, than from any real uncleanness. Camels were early a source of riches to the patriarchs, and from that period became an increasing object of rural importance to the several tribes of Israel, who inhabited the grazing and border districts, but still they never equalled the numbers possessed by the Arabs of the desert. On swift dromedaries the trotting motion is so hard that to endure it the rider requires a severe apprenticeship; but riding upon slow camels is not disagreeable, on account of the measured step of their walk; ladies and women in general are conveyed upon them in a kind of wickerwork sedan.

With regard to the passage in Matt. xix. 24, ' It is easier for a camel to go through the eye of a needle,' &c., and that in Matt. xxiii. 24, ' Ye strain at a gnat, and swallow a camel,' it may be sufficient to observe, that both are proverbial expressions, similarly applied in the kindred languages of Asia.

CAM'PHIRE occurs twice in the Song of Solomon (i. 14; iv. 13). The Hebrew word is *Kopher*, and has been supposed by some to denote in these places a bunch of grapes, and by others camphor. The word *camphire* is the old mode of spelling *camphor;* but this substance does not appear to have been known to ancient commerce. The word *Kopher* is certainly very like *Kafoor*, the Eastern name for *camphor*, but it also closely resembles the Greek *Kupros*, usually written *Cypros*. Indeed, as has been observed, it is the same word, with the Greek pronunciation and termination. The *Kupros* of the Greeks is, no doubt, the *Lawsonia inermis* of botanists. If we examine the works of Oriental travellers and naturalists, we shall find that this plant is universally esteemed in Eastern countries, and appears to have been so from the earliest times, both on account of the fragrance of its flowers, and the colouring properties of its leaves.

Thus Rauwolff, when at Tripoli, 'found there another tree, not unlike unto our privet, by the Arabians called *Alcana*, or *Henna*, and by the Grecians, in their vulgar tongue, *Schenna*, which they have from Egypt, where, but above all in Cayre, they grow in abundance. The Turks and Moors nurse these up with great care and diligence, because of their sweet-smelling flowers. They also, as I am informed, keep their leaves all winter, which leaves they powder and mix with the juice of citrons, and stain therewith against great holidays the hair and nails of their children of a red colour, which colour may perhaps be seen with us on the manes and tails of Turkish horses.' This custom of dyeing the nails and the palms of the hands and soles of the feet, of an iron-rust colour, with *henna*, exists throughout the East, from the Mediterranean to the Ganges, as well as in Northern Africa. In some parts the practice is not confined to women and children, but is also followed by men, especially in Persia. In dyeing the beard, the hair is turned to red by this application, which is

109. [Lawsonia inermis.]

then changed to black by a preparation of indigo. In dyeing the hair of children, and the tails and manes of horses and asses, the process is allowed to stop at the red colour which the *henna* produces. In reference to this universal practice of the East, Dr. Harris observes that 'the expression in Deut. xxi. 12, "pare her nails," may perhaps rather mean "adorn her nails," and imply the antiquity of this practice. This is a universal custom in Egypt, and not to conform to it would be considered indecent. It seems to have been practised by the ancient Egyptians, for the nails of the mummies are most commonly of a reddish hue.'

CA'NA, a town in Galilee, not far from Capernaum, where Christ performed his first miracle by turning water into wine (John iv. 46). *This* Cana is not named in the Old Testament, but is mentioned by Josephus as a village of Galilee. The site has long been identified with the present Kefr Kenna, a small place about four miles north-east from Nazareth, on one of the roads to Tiberias.

There is a ruined place called Kâna el-Jelil, about eight miles N. ½ E. from Nazareth, which Dr. Robinson is inclined to regard as the more probable site of Cana. His reasons are certainly of considerable weight.

CA'NAAN, son of Ham and grandson of Noah. The transgression of his father Ham (Gen. ix. 22-27), to which some suppose Canaan to have been in some way a party, gave occasion to Noah to pronounce that doom on the descendants of Canaan which was, perhaps, at that moment made known to him by one of those extemporaneous inspirations with which the patriarchal fathers appear in other instances to have been favoured.

CA'NAAN, LAND OF, the ancient name of that portion of Palestine which lay to the west of the Jordan (Gen. xiii. 12; Num. xxxiii. 51; Deut. xi. 30; Judg. xxi. 12), the part beyond the Jordan eastward being distinguished by the general name of Gilead (comp. Judg. xxi. 12). The denomination Canaan included Philistia and Phœnicia (comp. Isa. xxiii. 11; Ezek. xvi. 29; Zeph ii. 5). The name occurs on Phœnician coins, and was not even unknown to the Carthaginians. For an account of the geography, &c of the country, see PALESTINE.

CA'NAANITES, the descendants of Canaan, the son of Ham and grandson of Noah, inhabitants of the land of Canaan and the adjoining districts. A general account of the different nations included in the term is given in the present article, and a more detailed account of each will be found under their respective names.

The Israelites were delivered from Egypt by Moses, in order that they might take possession of the land which God had promised to their fathers. This country was then inhabited by the descendants of Canaan, who were divided into seven distinct nations, viz., the Hittites, Girgashites, Amorites, Canaanites, Perizzites, Hivites, and Jebusites. All these tribes are included in the most general acceptation of the term Canaanites; but the word, in its more restricted sense, as applied to one tribe, designated those ' who dwelt by the sea, and by the coasts of Jordan' (Num. xiii. 29). Besides these ' seven nations,' there were several tribes of the Canaanites who lived beyond the borders of the Promised Land, northward. These were the Arkites, Sinites, Arvadites, Zemarites, and Hamathites (Gen. x. 17, 18), with whom, of course, the Israelites had no concern. There were also other tribes of Canaanitish origin (or possibly other names given to some of those already mentioned), who were dispossessed by the Israelites. The chief of these were the Amalekites, the Anakites, and the Rephaim (or ' giants,' as they are frequently called in our translation). These nations, and especially the six or seven so frequently mentioned by name, the Israelites were commanded to dispossess and utterly to destroy (Exod. xxiii. 23; Num. xxxiii. 53; Deut. xx. 16, 17). The destruction, however, was not to be accomplished at once. The promise on the part of God was that he would ' put out those nations by little and little,' and the command to the Israelites corresponded with it; the reason given being, ' lest the beasts of the field increase upon thee' (Exod. xxiii. 29; Deut. vii. 22).

The destructive war commenced with an

attack on the Israelites, by Arad, king of the Canaanites, which issued in the destruction of several cities in the extreme south of Palestine, to which the name of Hormah was given (Num. xxi. 1-3). The Israelites, however, did not follow up this victory, which was simply the consequence of an unprovoked assault on them; but turning back, and compassing the land of Edom, they attempted to pass through the country on the other side of the Jordan, inhabited by a tribe of the Amorites. Their passage being refused, and an attack made on them by Sihon, king of the Amorites, they not only forced their way through his land, but destroyed its inhabitants, and proceeding onwards towards the adjoining kingdom of Bashan, they in like manner destroyed the inhabitants of that district, and slew Og. their king, who was the last of the Rephaim, or giants (Deut. iii. 11). The tract of which they thus became possessed was subsequently allotted to the tribes of Reuben and Gad, and the half tribe of Manasseh.

After the death of Moses the Israelites crossed the Jordan, and, under the conduct of Joshua, took possession of the greater part of the Promised Land, and destroyed its inhabitants. Several cities, however, still held out, particularly Jebus, afterwards Jerusalem, which was not taken till the time of David (2 Sam. v. 6), and Sidon, which seems never to have yielded to the tribe of Asher, to whom it was allotted (Judg. i. 31). Scattered portions also of the Canaanitish nations escaped, and were frequently strong enough to harass, though not to dispossess, the Israelites. The inhabitants of Gibeon, a tribe of the Hivites, made peace by stratagem, and thus escaped the destruction of their fellow-countrymen. Individuals from amongst the Canaanites seem, in later times, to have united themselves, in some way, to the Israelites, and not only to have lived in peace, but to have been capable of holding places of honour and power; thus Uriah, one of David's captains, was a Hittite (1 Chron. xi. 41). In the time of Solomon, when the kingdom had attained its highest glory and greatest power, all the remnants of these nations were made tributary, and bond-service was exacted from them (1 Kings ix. 20). The Girgashites seem to have been either wholly destroyed or absorbed in other tribes. We find no mention of them subsequent to the book of Joshua. The Anakites were completely destroyed by Joshua, except in three cities, Gaza, Gath, and Ashdod (Josh. xi. 21-23); and the powerful nation of the Amalekites, many times defeated and continually harassing the Israelites, were at last totally destroyed by the tribe of Simeon (1 Chron. iv. 43). Even after the return of the Jews from the Babylonish captivity, there were survivors of five of the Canaanitish nations, with whom alliances had been made by the Jews, contrary to the commands which had been given them. Some of the Canaanites, according to ancient tradition, left the land of Canaan on the approach of Joshua, and emigrated to the coast of Africa. Procopius relates that there were in Numidia, at Tigisis (*Tingis*), two columns on which were inscribed, in Phœnician characters, 'We are those who fled from the face of Joshua, the robber, the son of Naue.'

The manner in which the Israelites became possessed of the Promised Land has been so frequently brought as an objection to the inspired character of the Old Testament, and indeed is so far removed from the ordinary providential government of God, that it will be proper, in closing this account, to notice the difficulty which has been felt, and to advert to some of the hypotheses by which it is sought to be removed. Many have asserted, in order to alleviate the difficulty, that an allotment of the world was made by Noah to his three sons, and that by this allotment the Land of Promise fell to the share of Shem—that the descendants of Ham were therefore usurpers and interlopers, and that on this ground the Israelites, as the descendants of Shem, had the right to dispossess them. Others justify the war on the ground that the Canaanites were the first aggressors—a justification which applies only to the territory on the other side of the Jordan. Michaelis asserts that the Israelites had a right to the land of Canaan, as the common pasture land of their herdsmen, in consequence of the undisturbed possession and appropriation of it from the time of Abraham till the departure of Jacob into Egypt—that this claim had never been relinquished, and was well known to the Canaanites, and that therefore the Israelites only took possession of that which belonged to them. The same hypothesis is maintained by Jahn. Another ground of justification has been sought in the supposed identity of race of the Egyptian dynasty under which the Israelites were oppressed, with the tribes that overran Canaan—so that the destruction of the latter was merely an act of retributive justice for the injuries which their compatriots in Egypt had inflicted on the Israelites. To all these and similar attempts to justify, on the ground of *legal right*, the forcible occupation of the land by the Israelites, and the extermination (at least to a great extent) of the existing occupants, it is to be objected, that no such reason as any of these is hinted at in the sacred record. The right to carry on a war of extermination is there rested simply on the divine command to do so. That the Israelites were instruments in God's hand is a lesson not only continually impressed on their minds by the teaching of Moses, but enforced by their defeat whenever they relied on their own strength.

It may be said that this is only shifting the difficulty, and that just in proportion as we exculpate the Israelites from the charges of robbery and murder, in their making war without *legal* ground, we lower the character of the Being whose commands they obeyed, and throw doubt on those commands being really given by God. This has indeed been a favourite objection of infidels to the divine authority of the Old Testament. Such objectors would do well to consider whether God has not an absolute right to dispose of men as he sees fit, and whether an exterminating war, from which there was at least the opportunity of escape by flight, is at all more opposed to our notions of justice than a destroying flood, or earthquake, or pestilence. Again, whether the fact of making a chosen nation of *His* worshippers the instruments of punishing those whose wickedness was notoriously great, did not much more impressively vindicate his character as the only God, who 'will not give his glory to another, nor his praise to graven images,' than if the punishment had been brought about by natural causes. Such considerations as these must, we apprehend, silence those who complain of injustice done to the Canaanites. But then it is objected further, that such an arrangement is fraught with evil to those who are made the instruments of punishment, and, as an example, is peculiarly liable to be abused by all who have the power to persecute. As to the first of these objections, it must be remembered, that the conduct of the war was never put into the hands of the Israelites—that they were continually reminded that it was for the wickedness of those nations that they were driven out, and, above all, that they themselves would be exposed to similar punishment if they were seduced into idolatry—an evil to which they were especially prone. As to the example, it can apply to no case where there is not an equally clear expression of God's will.

CANDA'CE, or, more correctly, KANDAKE, was the name of that queen of the Ethiopians whose high treasurer was converted to Christianity under the preaching of Philip the Evangelist (Acts viii. 27). The country over which she ruled was not, as some writers allege, what is known to us as Abyssinia; it was that region in Upper Nubia which was called by the Greeks *Meroë*, and is supposed to correspond to the present province of Atbara, lying between 13° and 18° north latitude. The city of Meroë stood near the present Assour, about twenty miles north of Shendy; and the extensive and magnificent ruins found not only there, but along the upper valley of the Nile, attest the art and civilization of the ancient Ethiopians. Meroë, from being long the centre of commercial intercourse between Africa and the south of Asia, became one of the richest countries upon earth; the 'merchandise' and wealth of Ethiopia (Isa. xlv. 14) was the theme of the poets both of Palestine and Greece; and since much of that affluence would find its way into the royal coffers, the circumstance gives emphasis to the phrase—'*all* the treasure' of Queen Candace. It is further interesting to know, from the testimonies of various profane authors, that for some time both before and after the Christian era, Ethiopia Proper was under the rule of female sovereigns, who all bore the appellation of 'Candace,' which was not so much a proper name as a distinctive title, common to every successive queen, like 'Pharaoh' and 'Ptolemy' to the kings of Egypt, and 'Cæsar' to the emperors of Rome.

A curious confirmation of the fact of female sovereignty having prevailed in Ethiopia has been remarked on the existing monuments of the country. Thus, on the largest sepulchral pyramid near Assour, the ancient Meroë, a female warrior, with the royal ensigns on her head, drags forward a number of captives as offerings to the gods; on another compartment she is in a warlike habit, about to destroy the same group. Heeren, after describing the monuments at Naga, or Naka, south-east of Shendy, says, 'It is evident that these representations possess many peculiarities, and that they are not pure Egyptian. The most remarkable difference appears in the persons offering. The queens appear with the kings; and not merely as presenting offerings, but as heroines and conquerors. Nothing of this

kind has yet been discovered on the Egyptian reliefs, either in Egypt or Nubia. It may therefore with certainty be concluded, that they are subjects peculiar to Ethiopia. It is singular enough, that when Bruce was at Shendy, the government of the district was in the hands of a female called *Sittina*, i. e. the lady or mistress. Irenæus and Eusebius ascribe to Candace's minister her own conversion to Christianity, and the promulgation of the Gospel throughout her kingdom: and with this agrees the Abyssinian tradition, that he was likewise the apostle of Tagré, that part of Abyssinia which lay nearest to Meroë; it is added that he afterwards preached the Gospel in Arabia Felix, and also in the island of Ceylon, where he suffered martyrdom.

CANDLESTICK. The candelabrum which Moses was commanded to make for the tabernacle, after the model shown him in the Mount, is chiefly known to us by the passages in Exod. xxv. 31-40; xxxvii. 17-24; on which some additional light is thrown by the Jewish writers, and by the representation of the spoils of the Temple on the arch of Titus.

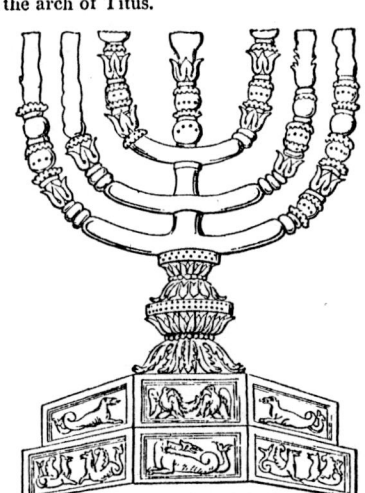

110.

The material of which it was made was fine gold, of which an entire talent was expended on the candelabrum itself and its appendages. The mode in which the metal was to be worked is described by a term which appears to mean *wrought* with the hammer, as opposed to *cast* by fusion. The structure of the candelabrum, as far as it is defined in the passages referred to, consisted of a base; of a shaft rising out of it; of six arms, which came out by threes from two opposite sides of the shaft; of seven lamps, which were supported on the summits of the central shaft and the six arms; and of three different kinds of ornaments belonging to the shaft and arms. These ornaments are called by names which mean *cups*, *globes*, and *blossoms*.

This candelabrum was placed in the Holy Place, on the *south* side (i. e. to the *left* of a person entering the tabernacle), opposite the table of shew-bread (Exod. xxvi. 35). Its lamps, which were supplied with pure olive oil only, were lighted every evening, and extinguished (as it seems) every morning (Exod. xxvii. 21; xxx. 7, 8; Lev. xxiv. 3; 1 Sam. iii. 3; 2 Chron. xiii. 11). Although the tabernacle had no windows, there is no good ground for believing that the lamps burnt by day in it, whatever may have been the usage of the second temple.

In the first temple, instead of this single candelabrum, there were ten candelabra of pure gold, one half of which stood on the north and the other on the south side of the Holy Place. These were carried away to Babylon (Jer. lii. 19). In the temple of Zerubbabel there appears to have been only one candelabrum again (1 Mac. i. 21; iv. 49, 50). It is probable that it also had only seven lamps. At least, that was the case in the candelabrum of the Herodian temple. This candelabrum is the one which, after the destruction of Jerusalem, was carried with other spoils to Rome; then, A.D. 455, became part of the plunder which Genseric transported to Africa; was again, about A.D. 533, recaptured from the Vandals by Belisarius, and carried to Constantinople, and was thence sent off to Jerusalem, and from that time has disappeared altogether. It is to this candelabrum that the representation on the arch of Titus at Rome was intended to apply; and there is reason to believe that, on the whole, it may be relied upon as a reasonably correct representation of the Herodian candelabrum.

CANE (or CALAMUS), SWEET, an aromatic reed, mentioned among the drugs with which sacred perfumes were compounded (Ezek. xxvii. 19). [REED.]

CANKER-WORM. [LOCUST.]

CAN′NEH (Ezek. xxvii. 23), probably the same as CALNEH (Gen. x. 10), which see.

CA′NON. This word was frequently employed to denote a *rule* or *standard*, by a reference to which the rectitude of opinions or actions may be determined; and as the great standard in all matters of faith and duty was the revealed will of God contained in the Scriptures of the Old and New Testaments, the term came insensibly to be applied to the collective body of those writings which were designated THE CANON or RULE.

The Canon then may be defined to be 'The Authoritative Standard of Religion and Morals, composed of those writings which have been given for this purpose by God to men.'

According to this definition, in order to establish the Canon of Scripture, it is necessary to show that all the books of which it is composed are of divine authority; that they are entire and incorrupt; that, having them, it is complete without any addition from any other source; and that it comprises the whole of those books for which divine authority can be proved. It is obvious that, if any of these four particulars be not true, Scripture cannot be the *sole and supreme* standard of religious truth and duty.

Respecting the *evidence* by which the Canon is thus to be established, there exists considerable difference of opinion amongst Christians. Some contend, with the Catholics, that the authoritative decision of the Church is alone competent to determine the Canon; others appeal to the concurrent testimony of the Jewish and early Christian writers; and others rest their strongest reliance on the internal evidence furnished by the books of Scripture themselves. We cannot say that we are satisfied with any of these sources of evidence exclusively. As Michaelis remarks, the first is one to which no consistent Protestant can appeal, for the matter to be determined is of such a kind, that, unless we grant the Church to be infallible, it is quite possible that she may at any given period of her existence determine erroneously; and one sees not why the question may not be as successfully investigated by a private individual as by the Church. The concurrent testimony of the ancient witnesses is invaluable so far as it goes; but it may be doubted if it be sufficient of itself to *settle* this question, for the question is not *entirely* one of facts, and testimony is good proof only for *facts*. As for the internal evidence, one needs only look at the havoc which Semler and his school have made of the Canon, to be satisfied that where doctrinal considerations are allowed to determine exclusively such questions, each man will extend or extruncate the Canon so as to adjust it to the Procrustean couch of his own preconceived notions. As the question is one partly of fact and partly of opinion, the appropriate grounds of decision will be best secured by a combination of authentic testimony with the evidence supplied by the books themselves. We want to know that these books were really written by the persons whose names they bear; we want to be satisfied that these persons were commonly reputed and held by their contemporaries to be assisted by the divine spirit in what they wrote; and we want to be sure that care was taken by those to whom their writings were first addressed, that these should be preserved entire and uncorrupt. For all this we must appeal to the testimony of competent witnesses, as the only suitable evidence for such matters. But after we have ascertained these points affirmatively, we still require to be satisfied that the books themselves contain nothing obviously incompatible with the ascription to their authors of the divine assistance, but, on the contrary, are in all respects favourable to this supposition. We want to see that they are in harmony with each other; that the statements they contain are credible; that the doctrines they teach are not foolish, immoral, or self-contradictory; that their authors really assumed to be under the divine direction in what they wrote, and afforded competent proofs of this to those around them; and that all the circumstances of the case, such as the style of the writers, the allusions made by them to places and events, &c., are in keeping with the conclusion to which the external evidence has already led. In this way we advance to a complete moral proof of the divine authority and canonical claims of the sacred writings.

The books specified as canonical in the 6th Article of the Church of England, and the 1st of the Confession of the Church of Scotland, are received as such by the majority of Protestants. To these the Church of Rome adds, as part of the Old Testament, ten other books, or parts of books, which Protestants reject as Apocryphal [APOCRYPHA]. For the evidence in support of the genuineness and divine authority of those books universally regarded by Christians as canonical, taken individually, we may refer to the articles in this work under the titles of these books respectively.

CANTICLES, SOLOMON'S SONG, or Song of Songs as it is designated in the inscription, is generally believed to have been so denominated to denote the superior beauty and excellence of this poem.

In favour of the canonical authority of this book (which has been questioned in ancient and modern times) we may observe, that it is found in all the copies of the Hebrew Bible which have descended to our times, as well as in the version of the Seventy, which was finished some time in the second century before the Christian era. It is also found in all the ancient catalogues which have come down to us from the early Christian church. It has consequently all the external marks of canonicity possessed by any other book of the Old Testament not expressly cited in the New. Those who have questioned its right to a place in the sacred volume have proceeded more on dogmatical than on historico-critical grounds.

The subject of this book is confessedly LOVE. But it has been a matter of much controversy, especially in modern times, what kind of love is here celebrated. It is equally a matter of dispute among divines whether the interpretation of the poem is limited to its obvious and primary meaning, or whether it does not also include a latent mystical and allegorical sense. We shall speak of these subjects in order. And, first, as to the literal and primary meaning, the earliest information which we have is contained in the preface of Origen to his commentary on this book. This eminent scholar holds it to be an epithalamium, or marriage-song, in the form of a drama. This idea has been, in modern times, improved by Lowth, Bossuet, Michaelis, and other commentators. 'The Song of Songs,' says Bishop Lowth, 'for so it is entitled, either on account of the excellence of the subject or of the composition, is an epithalamium, or nuptial dialogue, or rather, if we may be allowed to give it a title more agreeable to the genius of the Hebrews, a Song of Loves. Such is the title of Psalm xlv. It is expressive of the utmost fervour as well as delicacy of passion: it is instinct with all the spirit and sweetness of affection. The principal characters are Solomon himself and his bride, who are represented speaking both in dialogue, and in soliloquy, when accidentally separated. Virgins, also the companions of the bride, are introduced, who seem to be constantly on the stage, and bear a part of the dialogue. Mention is also made of young men, friends of the bridegroom, but they are mute persons. This is exactly conformable to the manners of the Hebrews, who had always a number of companions to the bridegroom, thirty of whom were present in honour of Samson at his nuptial feast (Judg. xiv. 11). In the New Testament, according to the Hebrew idiom, they are called children, or sons of the bridechamber, and friends of the bridegroom. There, too, we find mention of ten virgins who went forth to meet the bridegroom and conduct him home; which circumstances indicate that this poem is founded on the nuptial rites of the Hebrews, and is expressive of the forms or ceremonial of their marriage.'

Bossuet's idea of this poem was, that it is a regular drama, or pastoral eclogue, consisting of seven acts, each act filling a day, concluding with the Sabbath, inasmuch as the bridegroom on this day does not, as usual, go forth to his rural employments, but proceeds from the marriage chamber into public with his bride. Lowth so far differs from Bossuet as to deny the existence of a regular drama, inasmuch as there is no termination to the plot. Michaelis, in his notes to his German translation of Lowth's *Prelections*, endeavours to overturn the views of Bossuet and Lowth, and to show that this poem can have no relation to the celebration of a marriage, inasmuch as the bridegroom is compelled in his nuptial week to quit his spouse and friends for whole days, in order to attend to his cattle in the pastures. His opinion is, that this poem has no reference to a future marriage, but that the chaste loves of conjugal and domestic life are described. This state, he conceives, in the East, admits of more of the perplexities, jealousies, plots, and artifices of love than it does with us; the scene is more varied, and there is consequently greater scope for invention.

But the idea that the conjugal state, or the loves of married persons, are here referred to, has been strongly opposed by some of the ablest modern writers, who maintain that the chaste mutual loves of two young persons antecedent to marriage are here celebrated.

Here it may be necessary to state, that the learned are divided on the point whether the Canticles consist of one continued and connected poem, or of a number of detached songs or amorets. The first person who maintained the latter opinion was Father Simon, who was on this account unjustly accused of denying the canonicity of the book. This opinion has been subsequently defended by Eichhorn, Jahn, Pareau, and many others. A very general opinion is, that it is an idyl, or rather, a number of idyls, all forming a collective whole. Such is the opinion held, among others, by Sir William Jones and Dr. J. Mason Good, in his beautiful translation of the Song of Songs. Ewald considers the poem to consist of a drama in four parts. The heroine of the poem, according to this writer, is a country maiden, a native of Engedi, who, while rambling in the plains, fell in with the chariots of Solomon, and was carried by him into his palace.

It has been in all ages a matter of dispute, whether we are to seek for any hidden or occult meaning under the envelope of the literal and obvious sense. While several eminent men have maintained that the object of these poems is confined to the celebration of the mutual love of the sexes, or that its main design, in so far as its sacred character is considered, is the inculcation of marriage, and especially of monogamy, the majority of Christian interpreters, at least since the days of Origen (who wrote ten books of commentaries on this poem), have believed that a divine allegory is contained under the garb of an epithalamium, founded on the historical fact of the marriage of Solomon with the daughter of Pharaoh: others have held it to be a simple allegory, having no historical truth for its basis.

As, however, the Scriptures give no intimation that this book contains a mystical or allegorical sense, recourse has been had to the analogy of some of the Messianic Psalms, whose application to spiritual objects is recognised in the New Testament. Especially a great resemblance has been observed between the character of the Canticles and the 45th Psalm; and it will suffice for our present purpose to cite the opinion of Rosenmüller, one of the ablest commentators on the Messianic Psalms, in reference to this subject. Professing to follow the opinion of the ancient Hebrews, communicated by the Chaldee paraphrast, and the writer of the Epistle to the Hebrews—namely, that the 45th Psalm celebrated the excellences and praises of the great Messiah; he observes, 'Throughout the latter part of the psalm this allegory, in which the Hebrew poets particularly delighted, is maintained. They were accustomed to represent God as entertaining towards his chosen people, feelings which they compared to conjugal affections, and which they deduced, under this figure, into all the various and even minute expressions. In the illustrating and beautifying of this allegory, the whole of the Song of Songs is occupied: that the subject of that poem, and that of the psalm before us, is the same, there is no doubt among sound interpreters.' The reader may also refer, in illustration of this subject, to the many passages of the Old and New Testament in which this figure is retained by the sacred writers: such as Isaiah liv. 5; lxii. 5; Jerem. iii. 1, &c.; Ezek. xvi. and xxiii.; Matt. ix. 15; John iii. 29; 2 Cor. xi. 2; Ephes. v. 23, &c.; Rev. xix. 7; xxi. 2; xxii. 17. The tradition of the Jews as preserved by the ancient Chaldee paraphrast is that the poem embodies a figurative description of the gracious conduct of Jehovah towards his people, in delivering them from the Egyptian bondage, conferring great benefits on them during their progress through the wilderness, and conveying them in safety to the promised land. Aben Ezra considered that the Canticles represented the history of the Jews from Abraham to the Messiah. Others have conceived the bride to be Wisdom, with whom Solomon was acquainted from his childhood, and with whose beauty he was captivated. Luther, in his *Commentary on Canticles*, maintained the allegorical interpretation, conceiving Jehovah to be the bridegroom, the bride the Jewish nation, and the poem itself a figurative description of Solomon's civil government. In his *Commentary* on 1 Peter, however, he explains the bride to be the New Testament church.

The modern writers of the Roman church have, in general, followed Origen and Jerome in their allegorical interpretations.

The opinion of those who have acknowledged no other than the literal interpretation of the Canticles has had a considerable influence in the question of the canonicity of the book. Nor is it at all surprising that those who were in the habit of attaching a spiritual meaning to it should find it difficult to believe that a book treating of human love should have a place in the inspired volume.

The author and age of Canticles have been also much disputed. The inscription ascribes it to Solomon; and this is confirmed by the universal voice of antiquity, although some of the Jews have attributed it to Hezekiah.

CAPER'NAUM, a city on the north western side of the Lake of Gennesareth, and on the border of the tribes of Zebulun and Naphtali. The infidelity and impenitence of the inhabitants of this place, after the evidence given to them by our Saviour himself of the truth of his mission, brought upon them this heavy denunciation:— 'And thou, Capernaum, which art exalted unto heaven, shalt be brought down to hell: for if the mighty works which have been done in thee had been done in Sodom, it would have remained unto this day,' &c. (Matt. xi 23) This seems to have been more than any other place the residence of Christ after he commenced his great mission; and hence the force of the denunciation, which has been so completely accomplished, that even the site of Capernaum is quite uncertain. Dr. Robinson is inclined to look for the site in a place marked only by a mound of ruins, called by the Arabs, Khan Minyeh. This is situated in the fertile plain on the western border of the Lake of Gennesareth, to which the name of 'the land of Gennesareth' is given by Josephus. This plain is a sort of triangular hollow, formed by the retreat of the mountains about the middle of the western shore. In this plain there are now two fountains, one called 'Ain el Madauwarah, the 'Round Fountain'—another called 'Ain et-Tin, near the northern extremity of the plain, and not far from the lake. This is the fountain which Dr. Robinson inclines to regard as that which Josephus mentions under the name of Capharnaum; and which we may conclude was not far from the town, and took its name from it. Near this fountain is a low mound of ruins, occupying a considerable circumference, which certainly offer the best probability that has yet been produced of being the remains of the doomed city: and if these be all its remains, it has, according to that doom, been brought low indeed.

CAPH'TOR (Deut. ii. 23; Jer. xlvii. 4; Amos ix. 7) was the real and proper country of the Philistines. There has been a great diversity of opinion with regard to the exact situation of that country. The general opinion that Caphtor was Cappadocia is not founded on any sound argument. Others, again, have tried to prove that the Philistines derived their origin from the island of *Crete*. By far more probable is the opinion, that Caphtor is the island of *Cyprus*. From the geographical situation of that island, it may have been known to the Egyptians at a very early period, and they may have sent colonies thither, who afterwards removed, from some reason or other, to the southern coast of Palestine bordering on Egypt.

CAPPADO'CIA, an ancient province of Asia Minor, bounded on the north by Pontus, on the east by the Euphrates and Armenia Minor, on the south by Mount Taurus (beyond which are Cilicia and Syria), and on the east by Phrygia and Galatia. The country is mountainous and abounds in water, and was celebrated for the production of wheat, for its fine pastures, and for its excellent breed of horses, asses, and sheep. The inhabitants were notorious for their dulness and vice. Cappadocia was subjugated by the Persians under Cyrus; but after the time of Alexander the Great it had kings of its own, who bore the common name of Ariarathes. It continued to be governed by tributary kings under the Romans till A.D. 17, when Tiberius made it a Roman province. Christianity was very early propagated in Cappadocia, for St. Peter names it in addressing the Christian churches in Asia Minor (1 Pet. i. 1). Cappadocians were present at Jerusalem on the day of Pentecost (Acts ii. 9).

CAPTIVITIES. The word *Captivity*, as applied to the people of Israel, has been appropriated, contrary to the analogy of our language, to mean Expatriation. The violent removal of the entire population of a city, or sometimes even of a district, is not an uncommon event in ancient history. As a measure of policy, no objection to it on the ground of humanity was felt by any one; since, in fact, it was a very mild proceeding, in comparison with that of selling a tribe or nation into slavery. Every such destruction of national existence, even in modern times, is apt to be embittered by the simultaneous disruption of religious bonds; but in the ancient world, the positive sanctity attributed to special places, and the local attachment of Deity, made expatriation doubly severe. The Hebrew people, for instance, in many most vital points, could no longer obey their sacred law at all, when personally removed from Jerusalem; and in many others they were forced to modify it by reason of their change of circumstances.

Two principal motives impelled conquering powers thus to transport families in the mass; first, the desire of rapidly filling with a valuable population new cities, built for pride or for policy; next, the determination to break up hostile organizations, or dangerous reminiscences of past greatness. Both might sometimes be combined in the same act. To attain the former object, the skilled artisans would in particular be carried off; while the latter was better effected by transporting all the families of the highest birth, and all the well-trained soldiery.

The expatriation of the Jewish people belongs to two great eras, commonly called the first and second Captivity; yet differing exceedingly in character. It is to the former that the above remarks chiefly apply. In it, the prime of the nation were carried eastward by the monarchs of Assyria and Babylon, and were treated with no unnecessary harshness, even under the dynasty that captured them. That which we name the first Captivity, was by no means brought about by a single removal of the population. In fact, from beginning to end, the period of deportation occupied full 150 years; as the period of return reaches probably through 100. The first blow fell upon the more distant tribes of Israel, about 741 B.C.; when Tiglath-pileser, king of Assyria (2 Kings xv. 29), carried off the pastoral population which lived beyond the Jordan, with Zebulon and Naphtali. (To this event allusion is made in Isaiah ix. 1; a passage very ill translated in our received version.) In the time of this conquering monarch, Assyria was rapidly rising into power, and to aggrandize Nineveh was probably a great object of policy. It is therefore credible, as he had received no particular provocation from the Israelites, that he carried off these masses of population to stock his huge city with. His successor Shalmanezer made the Israelitish king Hoshea, tributary. When the

tribute was withheld, he attacked and reduced Samaria (B.C. 721), and, by way of punishment and of prevention, transported into Assyria and Media its king and all the most valuable population remaining to the ten tribes (2 Kings xvii. 6). The families thus removed were, in great measure, settled in very distant cities; many of them probably not far from the Caspian Sea; and their place was supplied by colonies from Babylon and Susis (2 Kings xvii. 24). Such was the end of Israel as a kingdom.—An interval of more than a century followed before Judah was to suffer a similar fate. Two separate deportations are narrated in the book of Kings, three in that of Jeremiah, while a fourth and earlier one appears in the book of Daniel i. 1–3. But it is pretty clear that the people of Judah, as of Israel, were carried out of their land by TWO principal removals. The former, B.C. 598, was directed to swell the armies and strengthen the towns of the conqueror; for of the 18,000 then carried away, 1000 were 'craftsmen and smiths, all strong and apt for war,' and the rest are called 'mighty men of valour.' It was not until the rebellion of Zedekiah that Nebuchadnezzar proceeded to the extremity of breaking up the national existence, B.C. 588. As the temple was then burnt, with all the palaces and the city walls, and no government was left but that of the Babylonian satrap, this latter date is evidently the true era of the captivity. Previously Zedekiah was tributary; but so were Josiah and Ahaz long before; the national existence was still saved.

Details concerning the *Return* from the captivity are preserved in the books denominated after Ezra and Nehemiah; and in the prophecies of two contemporaries, Haggai and Zechariah. The first great event is the decree of Cyrus, B.C. 536, in consequence of which 42,360 Jews of Babylon returned under Sheshbazzar, with 7337 slaves, besides cattle. This ended in their building the altar, and laying the foundation of the second temple, 53 years after the destruction of the first. The progress of the work was, however, almost immediately stopped: for Zerubbabel, Jeshua, and the rest abruptly refused all help from the half-heathen inhabitants of Samaria, and soon felt the effects of the enmity thus induced. That the mind of Cyrus was changed by their intrigues, we are not informed; but he was probably absent in distant parts, through continual war. When Darius (Hystaspis), an able and generous monarch, ascended the throne, the Jews soon obtained his favour. At this crisis, Zerubbabel was in chief authority (Sheshbazzar perhaps being dead), and under him the temple was begun in the second and ended in the sixth year of Darius, B.C. 520–516. Although this must be reckoned an era in the history, it is not said to have been accompanied with any new immigration of Jews. We pass on to 'the seventh year of king Artaxerxes' (Longimanus), Ezra vii. 7, that is, B.C. 458, when Ezra comes up from Babylon to Jerusalem, with the king's commendatory letters, accompanied by a large body of his nation. The enumeration in Ezra viii. makes them under 1800 males, with their families; perhaps amounting to 5000 persons, young and old: of whom 113 are recounted as having heathen wives (Ezra **x.** 18 43). In the twentieth year of the same king, or B.C. 445,

N

Nehemiah, his cupbearer, gains his permission to restore 'his fathers' sepulchres,' and the walls of his native city ; and is sent to Jerusalem with large powers. This is the crisis which decided the national restoration of the Jewish people : for before their city was fortified, they had no defence against the now confirmed enmity of their Samaritan neighbours ; and, in fact, before the walls could be built, several princes around were able to offer great opposition [SANBALLAT]. The Jewish population was overwhelmed with debt, and had generally mortgaged their little estates to the rich ; but Nehemiah's influence succeeded in bringing about a general forfeiture of debts, or at least of the interest: after which we may regard the new order of things to have been finally established in Judæa [NEHEMIAH]. From this time forth it is probable that numerous families returned in small parties, as to a secure home, until all the waste land in the neighbourhood was re-occupied.

There has been great difference of opinion as to how the 70 years of captivity spoken of by Jeremiah (xxv. 12 ; xxix. 10) are to be estimated. A plausible opinion would make them last from the destruction of the first temple, B.C. 588, to the finishing of the second, B.C. 516 : but the words of the text so specify ' the punishing of the king of Babylon' as the end of the 70 years—which gives us the date B.C. 538—that many still cling to the belief that a first captivity took place in the third year of Jehoiakim, B.C. 605. But, in fact, if we read Jeremiah himself, it may appear that in ch. xxv. he intends to compute the 70 years from the time *at which he speaks* (ver. 1, 'in the fourth year of Jehoiakim,' *i. e.* B.C. 604); and that in xxix. 10, the number ' seventy years ' is still kept up, in remembrance of the former prophecy, although the language there used is very lax.

The great mass of the Israelitish race nevertheless remained in dispersion. Previous to the captivity, many Israelites had settled in Egypt (Zech. x. 11 ; Isa. xix. 18), and many Jews afterwards fled thither from Nebuzaradan (Jer. xli. 17). Others appear to have established themselves in Sheba, where Jewish influence became very powerful [SHEBA].

It is maintained by some that the ten tribes intermarried so freely with the surrounding population as to have become completely absorbed ; and it appears to be a universal opinion that no one now knows where their descendants are. But it is a harsh assumption that such intermarriages were commoner with the ten tribes than with the two ; and certainly, in the apostolic days, the *twelve* tribes are referred to as a well-known people, sharply defined from the heathen (James i. 1 ; Acts xxiv. 7). Not a trace appears that any repulsive principle existed at that time between the Ten and the Two. ' Ephraim no longer envied Judah, nor Judah vexed Ephraim ;' but they had become ' one nation ;' though only partially ' on the mountains of Israel ' (Isa. xi. 13 ; Ezek. xxxvii. 22). It would seem, therefore, that one result of the captivity was to blend all the tribes together, and produce a national union which had never been effected in their own land. If ever there was a difference between them as to the books counted sacred, that difference entirely vanished ; at least no evidence appears of the contrary fact. When, moreover, the laws of landed inheritance no longer enforced the maintenance of separate tribes and put a difficulty in the way of their intermarriage, an almost inevitable result in course of time was the entire obliteration of this distinction ; and as a fact, no modern Jews know to what tribe they belong, although vanity always makes them choose to say that they are of the two or three, and not of the ten tribes. That all Jews now living have in them the blood of all the ten tribes, ought (it seems) to be believed, until some better reason than mere assertion is advanced against it.

When Cyrus gave permission to the Israelites to return to their own country, and restored their sacred vessels, it is not wonderful that few persons of the ten tribes were eager to take advantage of it. In two centuries they had become thoroughly naturalized in their eastern settlements ; nor had Jerusalem ever been the centre of proud aspirations to them. It was therefore to be expected that only those would return to Jerusalem whose expatriation was very recent ; and principally those whose parents had dwelt in the Holy City or its immediate neighbourhood. The century which followed their return was, on the whole, one of great religious activity and important permanent results on the moral character of the nation. Even the prophetic spirit by no means disappeared for a century and a half ; although at length both the true and the false prophet were supplanted among them by the learned and diligent scribe, the anxious commentator, and the over-literal or over-figurative critic. In place of a people prone to go astray after sensible objects of adoration, and readily admitting heathen customs ; attached to monarchical power, but inattentive to a hierarchy ; careless of a written law, and movable by alternate impulses of apostasy and repentance ; we henceforth find in them a deep and permanent reverence for Moses and the prophets, an aversion to foreigners and foreign customs, and a profound hatred of idolatry. Now first, as far as can be ascertained, were the synagogues and houses of prayer instituted, and the law periodically read aloud. Now began the close observance of the Passover, the Sabbath, and the Sabbatical year. From this era the civil power was absorbed in that of the priesthood, and the Jewish people affords the singular spectacle of a nation in which the priestly rule came later in time than that of hereditary kings.

In their habits of life also, the Jewish nation was permanently affected by the first captivity. The love of agriculture, which the institutions of Moses had so vigorously inspired, had necessarily declined in a foreign land ; and they returned with a taste for commerce, banking, and retail trade, which was probably kept up by constant intercourse with their brethren who remained in dispersion. The same intercourse in turn propagated towards the rest the moral spirit which reigned at Jerusalem. The Egyptian Jews, it would seem, had gained little good from the contact of idolatry (Jer. xliv. 8) ; but those who had fallen in with the Persian religion, probably about the time of its great reform by Zoroaster, had been preserved from such temptations, and returned purer than they went. Thenceforward it was the honourable function of Jerusalem to act as a religious metropolis to the whole dispersed nation ; and it cannot be doubted that the ten tribes, as well as the two, learned to be proud of the Holy City, as the great and free centre of their name and their faith. The same religious influences thus diffused themselves through all the twelve tribes of Israel.

Thus in Egypt and Arabia, in Babylonia, Assyria, Media, masses of the nation were planted, who, living by traffic and by banking, were necessitated to spread in all directions as their numbers increased. By this natural progress they moved westward as well as eastward, and, in the time of St. Paul, were abundant in Asia Minor, Greece, and the chief cities of Italy.

The extermination suffered by the Jewish inhabitants of Palestine, under the Romans, far better deserves the name of captivity : for after the massacre of countless thousands, the captives were reduced to a real bondage. According to Josephus, 1,100,000 men fell in the siege of Jerusalem by Titus, and 97,000 were captured in the whole war. Of the latter number the greatest part was distributed among the provinces, to be butchered in the amphitheatres or cast there to wild beasts ; others were doomed to work as public slaves in Egypt: only those under the age of seventeen were sold into private bondage. An equally dreadful destruction fell upon the remains of the nation, which had once more assembled in Judæa, under the reign of Hadrian (A.D. 133) ; and by these two savage wars the Jewish population must have been effectually extirpated from the Holy Land itself, a result which did not follow from the Babylonian captivity. Afterwards, a dreary period of fifteen hundred years' oppression crushed in Europe all who bore the name of Israel, and Christian nations have visited on *their* head a crime perpetrated by a few thousand inhabitants of Jerusalem, who were not the real forefathers of the European Jews. Nor in the East has their lot been much more cheering. With few and partial exceptions, they have ever since been a despised, an oppressed, and naturally a degraded people ; though from them have spread light and truth to the distant nations of the earth.

CARAVAN is the name given to a body of merchants or pilgrims as they travel in the East. A multitude of people, of all ages and conditions, assembling to undertake a journey, and prosecuting it *en masse* for days and weeks together, is a thing unknown in Europe, where, from the many facilities for travelling, and a well organized system of police, travellers can go alone and unprotected along the highways to any distance with the most perfect security. But in Eastern countries the dangers arising from the vast deserts that intersect these regions, as well as from wild beasts and bands of marauding Arabs, are too numerous and imminent for single traders or solitary travellers to encounter ; and hence merchants and pilgrims are accustomed to unite for mutual protection in traversing these wild and inhospitable parts, as well as for offering a more effectual resistance to the attacks of robbers. Through this kind of intercourse, which principally obtains in Turkey, Persia, and Arabia, most of the inland commerce of the East is carried on. Any person can, under certain regulations, form a caravan at any time. But generally there are stated periods, which are well known as the regular starting-times for the mercantile journeys ; and the merchants belonging to the company, or those travellers who are de-

sirous of accompanying it for the benefit of a safe conduct, repair to the place of rendezvous where the caravan is to be formed, exhibiting, as their goods and camels successively arrive, a motley group—a busy and tumultuous scene of preparation, which can be more easily conceived than described. As in the hot season the travelling is performed under night, the previous part of the day on which the caravan leaves is consumed in the preparatory labours of packing—an indispensable arrangement, which has been observed with unbroken uniformity since the days of Ezekiel (xii. 3) ; and then, about eight o'clock, the usual starting-time, the whole party put themselves in motion, and continue their journey without interruption till midnight (Luke xi. 5, 6) or later. At other seasons they travel all day, only halting for rest and refreshment during the heat of noon. The average rate of travel is from 17 to 20 miles per day.

The earliest caravan of merchants we read of is the itinerant company to whom Joseph was sold by his brethren (Gen. xxxvii.). The date of this transaction is more than seventeen centuries before the Christian era, and notwithstanding its antiquity, it has all the genuine features of a caravan crossing the desert at the present hour. This caravan was a mixed one, consisting of three classes, Ishmaelites (ver. 25). Midianites (ver. 28), and Medanites, as the Hebrew calls the last (ver. 36), who, belonging to the mountainous region of Gilead, would seem, like the nomade tribes of Africa in the present day, to have engaged themselves as commercial travellers, and were then, in passing over the plain of Dothan, on the high caravan-road for the market of Egypt.

Besides these communities of travelling merchants in the East, there are caravans of pilgrims, *i. e.* of those who go for religious purposes to Mecca, comprising vastly greater multitudes of people. Four of these start regularly every year : one from Cairo, consisting of Mahommedans from Barbary ; a second from Damascus, conveying the Turks ; a third from Babylon, for the accommodation of the Persians ; and a fourth from Zibith, at the mouth of the Red Sea, which is the rendezvous for those coming from Arabia and India. The organization of the immense hordes which, on such occasions, assemble to undertake a distant expedition, strangers to each other, and unaccustomed to the strict discipline which is indispensable for their comfort and security during the march, though, as might be expected, a work of no small difficulty, is accomplished in the East by a few simple arrangements which are the result of long experience. One obvious bond of union to the main body, when travelling by night and through extensive deserts, is the music of the Arab servants, who by alternate songs in their national manner beguile the tedium of the way : while the incessant jingling of innumerable bells fastened to the necks of the camels enlivens the patient beasts, frightens animals of prey, and keeps the party together. To meet all the exigencies of the journey, however, the caravan is placed under the charge of a *caravan bashè*, the chief who presides over all, and under whom there are five leading officers appointed to different departments :—one who regulates the march ; a second, whose duties only commence at halting time ; a third who superintends the servants and cattle ; a fourth who takes charge of the baggage; a fifth who acts as paymaster, &c.; and besides these, there are the officers of the military escort that always accompanies it. Another functionary of the highest importance is the *hybeer*, or guide, whose services are indispensable in crossing the great deserts, such as that along the coast of the Red Sea or on the western extremities of Africa. He is commonly a person of influence, belonging to some powerful tribe, whose personal qualifications must embrace an extensive and accurate acquaintance with the whole features of the land. It is absolutely necessary that he understand the prognostics of the weather, the time and places where the terrible simoom or hot wind blows, and the tracts occupied by shifting sands; and that he know the exact locality and qualities of the wells, the oases that afford the refreshments of shade for the men and grass for the cattle, the situation of hostile or treacherous tribes, and the means of escaping those threatened dangers.

There is a close and very striking resemblance between the arrangements of these caravans and the order adopted by the Israelites during their journey through almost the same extensive deserts. The arrangement of those vast travelling bodies seems to have undergone no material alteration for nearly four thousand years, and therefore affords the best possible commentary illustrative of the Mosaic narrative of the Exodus. Like them, the immense body of Israelitish emigrants, while the chief burden devolved on Moses, was divided into companies, each company being under the charge of a subordinate officer, called a prince (Num vii.). Like them, the Hebrews made their first stage in a hurried manner and in tumultuous disorder (Exod. xii. 11); and, like them, each tribe had its respective standard [STANDARDS]; which was pitched at the different stages, or thrust perpendicularly into the ground, and thus formed a central point, around which the straggling party spread themselves during their hours of rest and leisure (Num. ii. 2). Like them, the signal for starting was given by the blast of a trumpet, or rather trumpets (Num. x. 2, 5); and the time of march and halting was regulated by the same rules that have been observed by all travellers from time immemorial during the hot season. Like theirs, too, the elevation of the standard, as it was borne forward in the van of each company, formed a prominent object to prevent dispersion, or enable wanderers to recover their place within the line or division to which they belonged. Nor was there any difference here, except that, while the Israelites in like manner prosecuted their journey occasionally by night as well as by day, they did not, like the caravans of pilgrims, require the aid of fires in their standards, as the friendly presence of the fiery pillar superseded the necessity of any artificial lights. One other point of analogy remains to be traced in the circumstance of Hobab being enlisted in the service of the Hebrew caravan as its guide through the great Arabian desert. The extreme solicitude of Moses to secure the services of his brother-in-law in that capacity will be accounted for if it is borne in mind, that although the pillar of cloud by day and of fire by night sufficed to regulate the main stages of the Hebrews, foraging parties would at short intervals require to be sent out, and scouts to reconnoitre the country for fuel, or

to negotiate with the native tribes for provender and water. And who so well qualified to assist in these important services as Hobab, from his intimate acquaintance with the localities, his influence as a Sheikh, and his family connection with the leader of Israel?

The nature and economy of the modern Hadj caravans might be applied also to illustrate the return of the Hebrew exiles under Ezra from the land of their captivity.

The bands of Jewish pilgrims that annually repaired from every corner of Judæa to attend the three great festivals in Jerusalem, wanted this government and distribution into distinct companies, and seem to have resembled less the character of the great Mecca caravans than the irregular processions of the Hindoos to and from the scene of some of their religious pageants. On such occasions multitudes of men, women, and children, amounting to ten or twenty thousand, may be seen bending their way to the place of ceremonial, with their beds, cooking implements, and other luggage on their heads, prosecuting their journey in this manner from day to day, by longer or shorter stages, as custom or physical strength may dictate. As in a crowd of this motley description not the slightest regard is paid to regularity or order, and every one of course takes the place or mingles with the group that pleases him, the separation of the nearest friends for a whole day must, in such circumstances, be a common and unavoidable occurrence; and yet anxiety is never felt, unless the missing one fail to appear at the appointed rendezvous of the family. In like manner among the ancient Jews, the inhabitants of the same village or district would naturally form themselves into travelling parties, for mutual security as well as for enjoying the society of acquaintance. The poorer sort would have to travel on foot, while females and those of the better class might ride on asses and camels. But as their country was divided into tribes, and those who lived in the same hamlet or canton would be more or less connected by family ties, the young, the volatile, and active among the Jewish pilgrims had far more inducements to disperse themselves amongst the crowd than those of the modern processions, numbers of whom are necessarily strangers to each other. In these circumstances it is easy to understand how the young Jesus might mingle successively with groups of his kindred and acquaintance, who, captivated with his precocious wisdom and piety, might be fond to detain him in their circle, while his mother, together with Joseph, felt no anxiety at his absence, knowing the grave and sober character of their companions in travel; and the incident is the more natural that his parents are said to have gone 'one day's journey from Jerusalem before they missed him;' since, according to the present, and probably the ancient, practice of the East, the first stage is always a short one, seldom exceeding two or three hours. Beer—the modern el-Bireh, where Mary's discovery is reputed to have been made—is scarcely three miles from Jerusalem, where the caravan of Galilæan pilgrims halted.

CARAVANSERAI. [INN]

CAR'BUNCLE. There are two Hebrew words rendered by 'Carbuncle' in the Authorized Version. One of them, NOPHECH, which occurs in

Exod. xxviii. 18; xxxix. 11; Ezek. xxviii. 13, appears to have been a kind of ruby or garnet, perhaps the noble Oriental garnet, which is a transparent red stone, with a violet shade, and strong glossy lustre. The other word is EK-DACH, which occurs in Isa. liv. 12, where the gates of the new Jerusalem are described as being composed of it. It seems to denote some stone of a fiery lustre, but the particular kind cannot well be determined.

CAR'CHEMISH is mentioned in Isa. x. 9 among other places in Syria which had been subdued by an Assyrian king, probably Tiglath-pileser. It appears to have been a frontier town and a stronghold on the Euphrates (Jer. xlvi. 2; 2 Chron. xxxv. 20), and is probably therefore the city which the Greeks called Kirkesion, the Latins Cercusium, and the Arabs, Kerkesiyeh; for this too lay on the western bank of the Euphrates, where it is joined by the Chaboras. It was a large city, and surrounded by strong walls, which, in the time of the Romans, were occasionally renewed, as this was the remotest outpost of their empire, towards the Euphrates, in the direction of Persia. It is unknown whether any traces of it still exist; for, as it lies off the usual route of caravans, it has not been noticed by modern travellers.

CAR'IA, a country lying at the south-western extremity of Asia Minor, to which, among others, the Romans wrote in favour of the Jews (1 Macc. xv. 22, 33). Its principal towns were Halicarnassus, Cnidus, and Myndus. which are all mentioned in the rescript of the Roman senate, to which we refer. Halicarnassus was the birthplace of Herodotus; Cnidus is mentioned in Acts xxvii. 7, as having been passed by St. Paul on his voyage to Rome.

CAR'MEL, a range of hills extending northwest from the plain of Esdraelon, and ending in a promontory, or cape, which forms the Bay of Acre. The extent of this range of hills is about six miles, not in a direct line; but the two extremities (on the western side towards the sea) jut

111.

out, and stand over against each other, forming a bow in the middle. The height is about 1500 feet: and at the foot of the mountain. on the north east, runs the brook Kishon, and a little further north, the river Belus. Mount Carmel

consists rather of several connected hills than of one ridge; the north and eastern parts being somewhat higher than the southern and western. The foot of the northern portion approaches the water very closely, but further south it retires more inland, so as to leave between the mountain and the sea an extensive and very fertile plain.

Mount Carmel forms the only great promontory upon the coast of Palestine. According to the reports of most travellers, the mountain well deserves its Hebrew name (Carmel – *country of vineyards and gardens*). It is entirely covered with verdure. On its summit are pines and oaks, and further down olives and laurel trees. everywhere plentifully watered. It gives rise to a multitude of crystal brooks, the largest of which issues from the so-called Fountain of Elijah; and they all hurry along, between banks thickly overgrown with bushes, to the Kishon. Every species of tillage succeeds here admirably, under this mild and cheerful sky. The prospect from the summit of the mountain over the gulf of Acre and its fertile shores, and over the blue heights of Lebanon and the White Cape, is enchanting.

The mountain is of compact limestone, and, as often happens where that is the case [CAVES], there are in it very many caverns—it is said, more than a thousand. In one tract, called the Monk's Cavern, there are as many as four hundred adjacent to each other, furnished with windows and with places for sleeping hewn in the rock. That the grottoes and caves of Mount Carmel were already, in very ancient times, the abode of prophets and other religious persons is well known. The prophets Elijah and Elisha often resorted thither (1 Kings xviii. 19, *sq.* 42; 2 Kings ii. 25; iv. 25; and comp. perhaps 1 Kings xviii. 4, 13). At the present day is shown a cavern called the cave of Elijah, a little below the Monks' Cavern already mentioned, and which is now a Moslem sanctuary. Upon the summit is an ancient establishment of Carmelite monks, which order, indeed, derived its name from this mountain. The old convent was destroyed by Abdallah Pasha, who converted the materials to his own use; but it has of late years been rebuilt on a somewhat imposing scale by the aid of contributions from Europe.

2. CARMEL. Another Carmel, among the mountains of Judah, is named in Josh. xv. 55. It was here that Saul set up the trophy of his victory over Amalek (1 Sam. xv. 12). and where Nabal was shearing his sheep when the affair took place between him and David in which Abigail bore so conspicuous a part (1 Sam. xxv. 2, *sq.*). This Carmel is described by Eusebius and Jerome as, in their day, a village, with a Roman garrison, ten miles from Hebron, verging towards the east. From the time of the Crusades till the present century its name seems to have been forgotten. But it has been recently recognised by travellers under the name of Kurmul. The place is now utterly desolate, but the ruins indicate a town of considerable extent and importance. The most remarkable ruin is that of a castle. quadrangular, standing on a swell of ground in the midst of the town. The distance of this place from Hebron is nearer eight Roman miles than ten, as assigned by Eusebius and Jerome.

CARPENTER. [HANDICRAFT.]

CAR'PUS, a disciple of Paul, who dwelt at Troas (2 Tim. iv. 13).

CART. The Hebrew word rendered by our translators in some places by 'waggon,' and in others by 'cart,' denotes any vehicle moving on wheels and usually drawn by oxen; and their particular character must be determined by the context indicating the purpose for which they were employed. First, we have the carts which the king of Egypt sent to assist in transporting Jacob's family from Canaan (Gen. xlv. 19, 27). From their being so sent it is manifest that they were not used in the latter country; and that they were known there as being peculiar to Egypt is shown by the confirmation which they afforded to Jacob of the truth of the strange story told by his sons. The carts or wains represented

112.

in the Egyptian sculptures are the following, which, however, appear to belong to a foreign people. But that the Egyptians had something like them of their own appears from figs. 1, 2, in cut 113.

Elsewhere (Num vii. 3, 6; 1 Sam. vi. 7) we read of carts used for the removal of the sacred arks and utensils. These also were drawn by two oxen. In Rosellini we have found a very

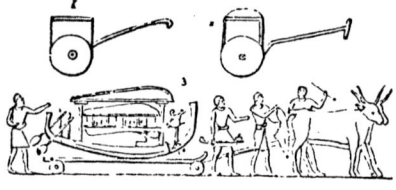

113.

curious representation of the vehicle used for such purposes by the Egyptians (No. 113, fig. 3). It is little more than a platform on wheels; and the apprehension which induced Uzzah to put forth his hand to stay the ark when shaken by the oxen (2 Sam. vi. 6), may suggest that the cart employed on that occasion was not unlike this, as it would be easy for a jerk to displace whatever might be upon it.

CASLU'HIM, properly Casluchim, a people whose progenitor was a son of Mizraim (Gen. x. 14; 1 Chron. i. 12). He, or they, for the word applies rather to a people than to an individual, are supposed by Bochart and others to have carried a colony from Egypt, which settled in the district between Pelusium and Gaza, or, in other words, between the Egyptians and the Philistines. There are some grounds for this conjecture; but it is impossible to obtain any certainty on so obscure a subject.

CASSIA. Our translators have rendered two distinct Hebrew words by this term. One of these (Ketzioth) is mentioned in three places

(Exod. xxx. 24: Ezek. xxvii. 19; and in Ps. xlv. 8), in conjunction with myrrh, cinnamon, sweet calamus, and ahalim, or eagle-wood. All these are aromatic substances, and, with the exception of myrrh, which is obtained from Africa, are products of India and its islands. It is probable, therefore, that ketzioth is of a similar nature, and obtained from the same countries. It is supposed, however, that the substance referred to is not cassia; but it will be preferable to treat of the whole subject in connection with cinnamon. [KINNAMON.]

The other word rendered cassia in our Authorized Version is kiddah. It occurs first in Exod. xxx. 24, where cassia (kiddah) is mentioned in connection with olive oil, pure myrrh, sweet cinnamon, and sweet calamus; secondly, in Ezek. xxviii. 19, where Dan and Javan are described as bringing bright iron, cassia (kiddah), and calamus to the markets of Tyre. There is no reason why the substance now called cassia might not have been imported from the shores of India into Egypt and Palestine. The Arabian Koost (Aucklandia Costus), known in Calcutta by the name of Puchuk, an aromatic substance exported in large quantities from Cashmere into the Punjab, whence it finds its way to Bombay and Calcutta, for export to China, where it is highly valued as one of the ingredients in the incense which the Chinese burn in their temples and private houses.

CASTLE. [FORTIFICATIONS.]

CAS'TOR AND POL'LUX, in heathen mythology, the twin sons of Jupiter by Leda. They had the special province of assisting persons in danger of shipwreck; and hence their figures were often adopted for 'the sign,' from which a ship derived its name, as was the case with that 'ship of Alexandria' in which St. Paul sailed on his journey for Rome (Acts xxviii. 11).

CAT. It might be assumed that the cat was an useful, if not a necessary, domestic animal to the Hebrew people in Palestine, where corn was grown for exportation, as well as for consumption of the resident population, twenty or thirty-fold more than at present, and where, moreover, the conditions of the climate required the precaution of a plentiful store being kept in reserve to meet the chances of scarcity. The animal could not be unknown to the people, for their ancestors had witnessed the Egyptians treating it

114.

as a divinity. Yet we find the cat nowhere mentioned in the canonical books as a domestic animal. And in Baruch it is noticed only as a tenant of Pagan temples, where no doubt the fragments of sacrificed animals and vegetables attracted vermin, and rendered the presence of cats necessary. This singular circumstance, perhaps, resulted from the animal being deemed unclean, and being thereby excluded domestic familiarity, though the Hebrews may still have encouraged it, in common with other vermin-hunters, about the outhouses and farms, and corn-stores, at the risk of some loss among the broods of pigeons which, in Palestine, were a substitute for poultry.

With regard to the neighbouring nations just named, they all had domestic cats, it is presumed, derived from a wild species found in Nubia, and first described by Ruppel under the name of Felis Maniculata. The typical animal is smaller, more slender, and more delicately limbed than the European. The fur is pale yellowish grey, with some dark streaks across the paws, and at the tip of the tail. In the domesticated state it varies in colours and markings, for the ancient monuments of Egypt contain many painted figures, which show them cross-barred like our wild species in Europe. Two specimens are here given from these paintings; one clearly a cat; the other, which is not apparently a cat but a species of gennet or paradoxurus, is, in the original, figured as catching birds, acting like a retriever for his master, who is fowling in a boat.

CATERPILLAR occurs in the Auth. Vers. 1 Kings viii. 37; 2 Chron. vi. 28; Ps. lxxviii. 46; cv. 34; Isa. xxxiii. 4; Jer. li. 14. 27; Joel i. 4; ii. 25. But it is more than doubtful whether any species of caterpillar is here intended. The name in the original indicates a creature whose chief characteristic is voracity, and which also attaches to all the species of *locusts*. The ancients, indeed, concur in referring the word to the locust tribe of insects, but are not agreed whether it signifies any particular *species* of locust, or is the name for any of those *states* or *transformations* through which the locust passes from the egg to the perfect insect. The Latin Fathers take it to mean the *larva* of the locust, and the *Greek* understand it as the name of an *adult* locust. On the whole it seems probable that the Hebrew word means a locust, but of which species it is impossible to determine.

CATTLE. [BEASTS; BULL.]

CAVES. The geological formation of Syria is highly favourable to the production of caves. It consists chiefly of limestone, in different degrees of density, and abounds with subterranean rivulets. The springs issuing from limestone generally contain carbonate of lime, and most of them yield a large quantity of free carbonic acid upon exposure to the air. To the erosive effect upon limestone rocks, of water charged with this acid, the formation of caves is chiefly to be ascribed. The subordinate strata of Syria, sandstone, chalk, basalt, natron, &c. favour the formation of caves. Consequently the whole region abounds with subterranean hollows of different dimensions. Some of them are of immense extent, such as those noticed by Strabo, who speaks of a cavern near Damascus capable of holding 4000 men. The first mention of a cave in Scripture relates to that into which Lot and his two daughters retired from Zoar, after the destruction of Sodom and Gomorrah (Gen. xix. 30). The next is the *Cave of Machpelah*, in the field of Ephron, which Abraham purchased of the sons of Heth (Gen. xxv. 3, 10). There Abraham buried Sarah, and was himself afterwards buried; there also Isaac, Rebecca, Leah, and Jacob, were buried (Gen. xlix. 31;

l. 13). The cave of Machpelah is said to be under a Mahometan mosque, surrounded by a high wall called the Haram; but even the Moslems are not allowed to descend into the cavern. The tradition that this is the burial-place of the patriarchs is supported by an immense array of evidence.

The situation of the *Cave at Makkedah*, into which the five kings of the Amorites retired upon their defeat by Joshua, and into which their carcases were ultimately cast, is not known (Josh. x. 16, 27). Some of the caves mentioned in the Scriptures were artificial, or consisted of natural fissures enlarged or modified for the purposes intended. It is recorded (Judg. vi. 2) that ' because of the Midianites, the children of Israel *made* them the dens which are in the mountains, and caves, and strongholds.' Caves made by art are met with in various quarters. An innumerable multitude of excavations are found in the rocks and valleys round Wady Musa, which were probably formed at first as sepulchres, but afterwards inhabited, like the tombs of Thebes. Caves were used as dwelling-places by the early inhabitants of Syria. The Horites, the ancient inhabitants of Idumæa Proper, were Troglodytes or dwellers in caves, as their name imports. Jerome records that in his time Idumæa was full of habitations in caves, the inhabitants using subterranean dwellings on account of the great heat. The Scriptures abound with references to habitations in rocks; among others, see Num. xxiv. 21; Cant. ii. 14; Jer. xlix. 16; Obad. 3. Even at the present time many persons live in caves. Caves afford excellent refuge in the time of war. Thus the Israelites (1 Sam. xiii. 6) are said to have hid themselves in caves, and in thickets, and in rocks, and in high places, and in pits. See also Jer. xli. 9. Hence, then, to ' enter into the rock, to go into the holes of the rocks, and into the caves of the earth' (Isa. ii. 19), would, to the Israelites, be a very proper and familiar way to express terror and consternation. The pits spoken of seem to have consisted of large wells, in ' the sides' of which excavations were made, leading into various chambers. Such pits were sometimes used as prisons (Isa. xxiv. 22; li. 14; Zech. ix. 11); and with *niches* in the sides, for burying-places (Ezek. xxxii. 23). Many of these vaulted pits remain to this day. The *strongholds of Engedi*, which afforded a retreat to David and his followers (1 Sam. xxiii. 29; xxiv. 1), can be clearly identified. They are now called Ain Tidy by the Arabs, which means the same as the Hebrew, namely, ' The Fountain of the Kid.' ' On all sides the country is full of caverns, which might serve as lurking-places for David and his men, as they do for outlaws at the present day. The whole scene is drawn to the life.' *The Cave of Adullam*, to which David retired to avoid the persecutions of Saul (1 Sam. xxii. 1, 2), and in which he cut off the skirt of Saul's robe (1 Sam. xxiv. 4), is an immense natural cavern at the Wady Khureitun, which passes below the Frank mountain. Such is the extent of the cavern, that it is quite conceivable how David and his men might ' remain in the sides of the cave,' and not be noticed by Saul (*Travels*, vol. ii. p. 41) Caverns were also frequently fortified and occupied by soldiers. Josephus relates also that Herod sent horsemen and footmen to destroy the robbers that dwelt in caves, and did much mischief in the country They were very near to a village called Arbela (now called Kûlat Ibn Ma'an). The occupants were not subdued without great difficulty. Herod then laid siege to certain other caverns containing robbers, but found operations against them very difficult. These were situated on the middle of abrupt and precipitous mountains, and could not be come at from any side, since they had only some winding pathways, very narrow, by which they got up to them. The rock that lay on their front overhung valleys of immense depth, and of an almost perpendicular declivity. To meet these difficulties Herod caused large boxes filled with armed men to be lowered from the top of the mountain. These men had long hooks in their hands with which they might pull out those who resisted them, and tumble them down the mountains. From these boxes they at length slipped into the caverns, destroyed the robbers, and set fire to their goods. Certain caves were afterwards fortified by Josephus himself during his command in Galilee under the Romans. A fortified cavern existed in the time of the Crusades. It is mentioned by William of Tyre, as situate in the country beyond the Jordan, sixteen Roman miles from Tiberias. The cave of Elijah is pretended to be shown, at the foot of Mount Sinai, in a chapel dedicated to him; and a hole near the altar is pointed out as the place where he lay.

CEDAR. There is a difference of opinion among authors whether the original term thus translated in the numerous passages of Scripture where it occurs is always used in the same signification; that is, whether it is always intended to specify only one particular kind of the pine tribe, or whether it is not sometimes used generically. In this latter opinion we are disposed

115. [Cedar of Lebanon.]

to concur, for if we proceed to compare the several passages of Scripture in which the word occurs, we shall equally find that one plant is not strictly applicable to them all. The earliest notice of the cedar is in Lev. xiv 4. 6, where we are told that Moses commanded the leper that

was to be cleansed to make an offering of two sparrows, cedar-wood, wool dyed in scarlet, and hyssop; and in ver. 49, 51, 52, the houses in which the lepers dwell are directed to be purified with the same materials. Again, in Num. xix. 6, Moses and Aaron are commanded to sacrifice a red heifer: 'And the priest shall take cedar-wood and hyssop and scarlet.' As remarked by Lady Callcott (Script. Herbal, p. 92), 'The cedar was not a native of Egypt, nor could it have been procured in the desert without great d fficulty; but the juniper is most plentiful there, and takes deep root in the crevices of the rocks of Mount Sinai.' That some, at least, of the cedars of the ancients were a species of juniper is evident from the passages we have quoted; the wood of most of them is more or less aromatic. The ancients, it may be remarked, threw the berries of the juniper on funeral piles, to protect the departing spirit from evil influences, and offered its wood in sacrifice to the infernal gods, because they believed its presence was acceptable to them. They also burned it in their dwelling-houses to keep away demons. It is curious that, in the remote parts of the Himalayan Mountains, another species of this genus is similarly employed.

At a later period we have notices of the various uses to which the wood of the cedar was applied, as 2 Sam. v. 11; vii. 2-7; 1 Kings v. 6, 8, 10; vi. 9, 10, 15, 16, 18, 20; vii. 2, 3, 7, 11. 12; ix. 11; x. 27; 1 Chron. xvii. 6; 2 Chron. ii. 8; ix. 27; xxv. 18. In these passages we are informed of the negotiations with Hiram, King of Tyre, for the supply of cedar-trees out of Lebanon, and of the uses to which the timber was applied in the construction of the Temple, and of the king's palace: he 'covered the house with beams and boards of cedar;' 'the walls of the house within were covered with boards of cedar;' there were 'cedar pillars,' and 'beams of cedar;' and the altar was of cedar. In all these passages there is nothing distinctive stated respecting the character of the wood, from which we might draw any certain conclusion, further than that, from the selection made and the constant mention of the material used, it may be fairly inferred that it must have been considered as well fitted, or rather of a superior quality, for the purpose of building the Temple and palace. From this, however, proceeds the difficulty in admitting that what we call the cedar of Lebanon was the only tree intended. For modern experience has ascertained that its wood is not of a superior quality. To determine this point, we must not refer to the statements of those who take their descriptions from writers who, indeed, describe cedar-wood, but do not prove that it was derived from the cedar of Lebanon. The term 'cedar' seems to have been as indefinite in ancient as in modern times, when we find it applied to the wood of the red or pencil cedar, to that of the Bermuda cedar, and to many other woods, as to white cedar, and Indian cedar.

Mr. Loudon, in his Arboretum (p. 2417), describes it thus: 'The wood of the cedar is of a reddish white, light and spongy, easily worked, but very apt to shrink and warp, and by no means durable.' But when the tree is grown on mountains, the annual layers of wood are much narrower and the fibre much finer than when it is grown on plains; so much so that a piece of cedar-wood brought from Mount Lebanon by Dr. Parisel, in 1829, and which he had made into a small piece of furniture. presented a surface compact, agreeably veined, and variously shaded, and which, on the whole. may be considered handsome. But Dr. Pococke, who brought away a piece of one of the large cedars which had been blown down by the wind, says that the wood does not differ in appearance from white deal, and that it does not appear to be harder. Mr. Loudon says that a table which Sir J. Banks had made out of the Hillingdon cedar was soft, without scent (except that of common deal), and possessed little variety of veining. Though we have seen both temples and palaces built entirely with one kind of cedar, we think it more probable that, as the timber had to be brought from a distance, where all the kinds of cedar grew, the common pine-tree and the cedar of Lebanon would both furnish some of the timber required for the building of the Temple, together with juniper cedar. Celsius was of opinion that the cedar indicated the Pinus sylvestris or Scotch pine, which yields the red and yellow deals of Norway, and which is likewise found on Mount Lebanon. This opinion seems to be confirmed by Ezekiel xxvii. 5, 'They have made all thy ship boards of fir-trees of Senir, they have taken cedar from Lebanon to make masts for thee.' For it is not probable that any other tree than the common pine would be taken for masts.

Though Celsius appears to us to be quite right in concluding that the cedar, in some of the passages of Scripture, refers to the pine-tree, yet it seems equally clear that there are other passages to which this tree will not answer, and if we consider some of the remaining passages of Scripture, we cannot fail to perceive that they forcibly apply to the cedar of Lebanon and to the cedar of Lebanon only. Thus. in Ps. xcii. 12, it is said. 'The righteous shall flourish like a palm-tree, and spread abroad like a cedar of Lebanon.' It has been well remarked, 'that the flourishing head of the palm and the spreading abroad of the cedar are equally characteristic.' But the prophet Ezekiel (ch. xxxi.) is justly adduced as giving the most magnificent, and at the same time the most graphic, description of this celebrated tree: (ver. 3) 'Behold, the Assyrian was a cedar in Lebanon with fair branches, and with a shadowy shroud, and of an high stature; and his top was among the thick boughs:' (ver. 5) 'Therefore his height was exalted above all the trees of the field, and his boughs were multiplied, and his branches became long because of the multitude of waters:' (ver. 6) 'All the fowls of heaven made their nests in his boughs, and under his branches did all the beasts of the field bring forth their young.' In this description, Mr. Gilpin has well observed, 'the principal characteristics of the cedar are marked: first, the multiplicity and length of its branches. Few trees divide so many fair branches from the main stem. or spread over so large a compass of ground. 'His boughs are multiplied,' as Ezekiel says, 'and his branches become long,' which David calls spreading abroad. His very boughs are equal to the stem of a fir or a chestnut. The second characteristic is what Ezekiel, with great beauty and aptness, calls his shadowy shroud.

No tree in the forest is more remarkable than the cedar for its close-woven leafy canopy. Ezekiel's cedar is marked as a tree of full and perfect growth, from the circumstance of its top being among the thick boughs. The other principal passages in which the cedar is mentioned are 1 Kings iv. 33; 2 Kings xix. 23; Job xl. 17; Ps. xxix. 5; lxxx. 10; xcii. 12; civ. 16; cxlviii. 9; Cant. i. 17; v. 15; viii. 9; Isa. ii. 13; ix. 8, 10; xiv. 8; xxxvii. 24; xli. 19; xliv. 14; Jer. xxii. 7, 14, 23; Ezek. xvii. 3, 22, 23; Amos ii. 9; Zeph. ii. 14: Zech. xi. 1, 2; and in the Apocrypha, 1 Esdras iv. 48; v. 55; Ecclus. xxiv. 13; l. 12; but it would occupy too much space to adduce further illustrations from them of what indeed is the usually admitted opinion.

It is, however, necessary before concluding to give some account of this celebrated tree, as noticed by travellers in the East, all of whom make a pilgrimage to its native sites. The cedar of Lebanon is well known to be a widely-spreading tree, generally from 50 to 80 feet high, and when standing singly, often covering a space with its branches, the diameter of which is much greater than its height. The horizontal branches, when the tree is exposed on all sides, are very large in proportion to the trunk, being disposed in distinct layers or stages, and the distance to which they extend diminishes as they approach the top, where they form a pyramidal head. broad in proportion to its height. The branchlets are disposed in a flat fan-like manner on the branches. The leaves, produced in tufts, are straight, about one inch long, slender, nearly cylindrical, tapering to a point, and are on short footstalks. The cones, when they approach maturity, become from 2½ inches to 5 inches long. Every part of the cone abounds with resin, which sometimes exudes from between the scales. Speaking of the cedars of Lebanon, M. Lamartine, in 1832, says, 'These trees diminish in every succeeding age. Travellers formerly counted 30 or 40; more recently, 17; more recently still, only 12. There are now but 7. These, however, from their size and general appearance, may be fairly presumed to have existed in biblical times. Around these ancient witnesses of ages long since past, there still remains a little grove of yellow cedars, appearing to me to form a group of from 400 to 500 trees or shrubs. Every year, in the month of June, the inhabitants of Beschierai, of Eden, of Kandbin, and the other neighbouring valleys and villages, climb up to these cedars, and celebrate mass at their feet. How many prayers have resounded under these branches, and what more beautiful canopy for worship can exist?'

CEILING. The Orientals bestow much attention upon the ceilings of their principal rooms. Where wood is not scarce, they are usually composed of one curious piece of joinery, framed entire, and then raised and nailed to the joists. These ceilings are often divided into small square compartments; but are sometimes of more complicated patterns. Wood of a naturally dark colour is commonly chosen, and it is never painted. In places where wood is scarce, and sometimes where it is not particularly so, the ceilings are formed of fine plaster. with tasteful mouldings and ornaments, coloured and relieved with gilding, and with pieces of mirror inserted in the hollows formed by the involutions of the raised mouldings of the arabesques. which enclose them as in a frame. The antiquity of this taste can be clearly traced by actual examples up to the times of the Old Testament, through the Egyptian monuments, which display ceilings painted with rich colours in such patterns as are shown in the annexed cut. The explanation thus

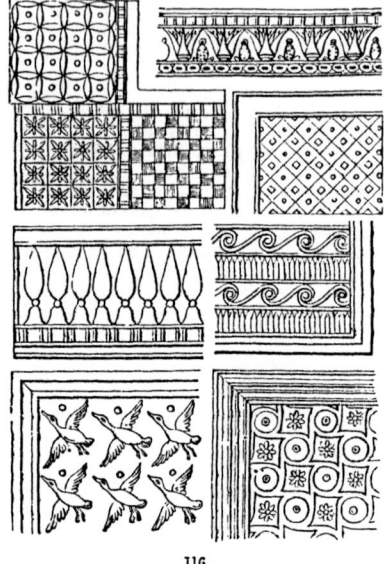

116.

obtained satisfactorily illustrates the peculiar emphasis with which 'ceiled houses' and 'ceiled chambers' are mentioned by Jeremiah (xxii. 14) and Haggai (i. 4).

CENCHRE'A, one of the ports of Corinth, whence Paul sailed for Ephesus (Acts xviii. 18). It was situated on the eastern side of the isthmus, about seventy stadia from the city: the other port on the western side of the isthmus was called Lechæum. [CORINTH.]

CENSER, the vessel in which incense was presented in the temple (2 Chron. xxvi. 19 ; Ezek. viii. 11 : Ecclus. l. 9). Censers were used in the daily offering of incense, and yearly on the day of atonement, when the high-priest entered the Holy of Holies. On the latter occasion the priest filled the censer with live coals from the sacred fire on the altar of burnt-offering, and bore it into the sanctuary, where he threw upon the burning coals the 'sweet incense beaten small' which he had brought in his hand (Lev. xvi. 12, 13). In this case the incense was burnt while the high-priest held the censer in his hand; but in the daily offering the censer in which the live coals were brought from the altar of burnt-offering was set down upon the altar of incense. This alone would suggest the probability of some difference of shape between the censers used on these occasions. The daily censers must have had a base or stand to admit of their being placed on the golden altar, while those employed on the day of atonement were probably furnished with a handle. In fact, there are different names

for these vessels. We learn also that the daily censers were of brass (Num xvi. 39), whereas the yearly one was of gold. The form of the daily censer we have no means of determining beyond the fact that it was a pan or vase, with a stand whereon it might rest on the golden altar. The numerous figures of Egyptian cen-

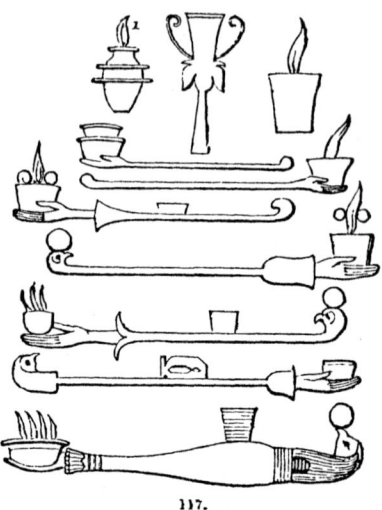

117.

sers, consisting of a small cup at the end of a long shaft or handle (often in the shape of a hand), probably offer adequate illustration of those employed by the Jews on the day of atonement. There was, however, another kind of censer (Fig. 1), less frequently seen on the Egyptian monuments, and likewise furnished with a handle, which will probably be regarded by many as offering a more probable resemblance.

CENSUS. [POPULATION.]

CENTU'RION, a Roman military officer in command of a hundred men, as the title implies. Cornelius, the first Gentile convert to Christianity, held this rank (Acts x. 1, 22). Other Centurions are mentioned in Matt. viii. 5, 8, 13 ; xxvii. 54 ; Luke vii. 2, 6 ; Acts xxi. 32 ; xxii. 25, 26 ; xxiii. 17, 23 ; xxiv. 23 ; xxvii. 1, 6, 11, 31, 43 ; xxviii. 16.

CE'PHAS, a surname which Christ bestowed upon Simon (John i. 42), and which corresponds with Peter, both words meaning a 'rock,' which is the signification of the original [PETER].

CHAFF, the refuse of winnowed corn. It is used as a symbol for unprofitable and worthless characters (Ps. i. 4 ; Matt. iii. 12).

CHAIN. Chains of gold appear to have been as much used among the Hebrews, for ornament or official distinction, as they are among ourselves at the present day. The earliest mention of them occurs in Gen. xli. 42, where we are told that a chain of gold formed a part of the investiture of Joseph in the high office to which he was raised in Egypt; a later instance occurs in Dan. v. 29, from which we learn that a golden chain was part of a dress of honour at Babylon. In Egypt the judges wore chains of gold, to which was attached a jewelled figure of Thmei, or Truth ; and in that country similar chains were also worn as ornaments by the women. It is not, however, necessary to suppose that the Hebrews derived this custom from the Egyptians; for the fact that chains are mentioned among the spoil of the Midianites shows that they were in use among people whose condition of life more nearly resembled that of the Israelites before they obtained possession of Canaan. It would seem that chains were worn both by men and women (Prov. i. 9; Ezek. xvi. 11), and we find them enumerated among the ornaments of brides (Cant. i. 10; iv. 9).

It was a custom among the Romans to fasten a prisoner with a light chain to the soldier who was appointed to guard him. One end of it was attached to the right hand of the prisoner, and the other to the left hand of the soldier. This is the *chain* by which Paul was so often bound, and to which he repeatedly alludes (Acts xxviii. 20; Eph. vi. 20; 2 Tim. i. 16). When the utmost security was desired, the prisoner was attached by two chains to two soldiers, as was the case with Peter (Acts xii. 6).

CHAL'CEDONY (Rev. xxi. 19), a precious stone, forming a variety of amorphous quartz. It is harder than flint (specific gravity 2·04), commonly semi-transparent, and is generally of one uniform colour throughout, usually a light brown and often nearly white; but other shades of colour are not infrequent, such as grey, yellow, green, and blue. Chalcedony occurs in irregular masses, commonly forming grotesque cavities, in trap rocks and even granite. It is found in most parts of the world; and in the East is employed in the fabrication of cups and plates, and articles of taste, which are wrought with great skill and labour, and treasured among precious things. In Europe it is made into snuff-boxes, buttons, knife-handles, and other minor articles.

CHALDÆ'ANS is the name which is found appropriated in parts of the Old Testament to inhabitants of Babylon and subjects of the Babylonian kingdom. In 2 Kings xxv., where an account is given of the siege of Jerusalem in the reign of Zedekiah, by Nebuchadnezzar, the latter monarch is expressly designated 'King of Babylon,' while his troops in general are spoken of as 'Chaldees,' 'the army of the Chaldees.' In Isaiah xiii. 19, Babylon is called 'the glory of kingdoms, the beauty of the Chaldees' excellency;' and in xxiii. 13 of the same book, the country is termed 'the land of the Chaldæans.' So in Daniel ix. 1, 'In the first year of Darius, of the seed of the Medes, which was made king over the realm of the Chaldæans.' The origin and condition of the people who gave this name to the Babylonians, have been subjects of dispute among the learned. Probably, however, they were the same people that are described in Greek writers as having originally been an uncultivated tribe of mountaineers, placed on the Carduchian mountains, in the neighbourhood of Armenia, whom Xenophon describes as brave and fond of freedom. In Habakkuk i. 6-10 the Chaldæans are spoken of in corresponding terms: ' Lo, I raise up the Chaldæans, that bitter and hasty nation, which shall march through the breadth of the land to possess the dwelling-places that are not theirs; they are terrible and dreadful; their horses are swifter than leopards and more fierce than evening wolves; their horsemen shall spread themselves; they shall fly as the eagle that

hasteth to eat.' They are also mentioned in Job i. 17: 'Chaldæans fell upon the camels (of Job) and carried them away.' These passages show not only their warlike and predatory habits, but, especially that in Job, the early period in history at which they were known.

As in all periods of history hardy and brave tribes of mountaineers have come down into the plains and conquered their comparatively civilized and effeminate inhabitants, so these Armenian Chaldæans appear to have descended on Babylon, made themselves masters of the city and the government, and eventually founded a dominion, to which they gave their name, as well as to the inhabitants of the city and the country tributary to it, infusing at the same time young blood and fresh vigour into all the veins and members of the social frame. What length of time the changes herein implied may have taken cannot now be ascertained.

Of the kingdom of Babylon, Nimrod (Gen. x. 8, sqq.) was the founder and first sovereign. The next name of a Babylonian monarch is found in Gen. xiv. 1, where 'Amraphel, king of Shinar,' is cursorily mentioned. A long interval occurs, till at last, in 2 Kings xx. 12, 13, the name of another is given: ' Berodach-baladan, the son of Baladan, king of Babylon,' it appears 'sent letters and a present unto Hezekiah; for he had heard that Hezekiah had been sick. And Hezekiah hearkened unto them, and showed them all the house of his precious things: there was nothing in his house, nor in his dominion, that Hezekiah showed them not.' On becoming acquainted with this fact, the prophet Isaiah announced that the treasures of the kingdom would be plundered and taken to Babylon along with the descendants of Hezekiah, who were to become eunuchs in the palace of the king of Babylon. The friendly act which passed between these two kings took place in the year B.C. 713. About a hundred years later, the prophets Jeremiah and Habakkuk speak of the invasion of the Chaldæan army. Nebuchadnezzar now appears in the historical books, and, in Ezra v. 12, is described as ' the king of Babylon, the Chaldæan, who destroyed this house (the temple), and carried the people away into Babylon.' How extensive and powerful his empire was, may be gathered from the words of Jeremiah xxxiv. 1—' Nebuchadnezzar, king of Babylon, and all his army, and all the kingdoms of the earth of his dominion, and all the people, fought against Jerusalem.' The result was, that the city was surrendered, and the men of war fled, together with king Zedekiah, but were overtaken in the plains of Jericho and completely routed. The Israelitish monarch was carried before Nebuchadnezzar, who ordered his eyes to be put out, after he had been compelled to witness the slaughter of his sons: he was then bound in fetters of brass and conveyed a captive to Babylon. The next Chaldee-Babylonian monarch given in the Scriptures is the son of the preceding, Evil-merodach, who (2 Kings xxv. 27) began his reign (B.C. 562) by delivering Jehoiachin, king of Judah, after the unfortunate sovereign had endured captivity, if not incarceration, for a period of more than six and thirty years. Circumstances incidentally recorded in connection with this event serve to display the magnitude and grandeur of the empire; for it appears (ver.

28) that there were other captive kings in Babylon besides Jehoiachin, and that each one of them was indulged with the distinction of having his own throne. With Belshazzar (B.C. 538), the son of Nebuchadnezzar, closes the line of Chaldæan monarchs. In the seventeenth year of his reign, this sovereign was put to death, while engaged with all his court in high revelry, by Cyrus, when he took the city of Babylon in the night season (Dan. v. 3:), and established in the city and its dependencies the rule of the Medo-Persians [BELSHAZZAR].

It has been seen, from the foregoing statements, that the history of Babylon supplied by the Scriptures is brief, imperfect, and fragmentary. Little additional light can be borrowed from other quarters, in relation to the period comprised within the Biblical accounts.

Authentic history affords no information as to the time when the Chaldæan immigration took place.

The kingdom of the Chaldees is found among the four 'thrones' spoken of by Daniel (vii. 3, sqq.), and is set forth under the symbol of a lion having eagles' wings. The government was despotic, and the will of the monarch, who bore the title of 'King of Kings' (Dan. ii. 37), was supreme law. as may be seen in Dan. iii. 12; v. 19. The kings lived inaccessible to their subjects in a well-guarded palace. The number of court and state servants was not small; in Dan. vi. 1, Darius is said to have set over the whole kingdom no fewer than 'an hundred and twenty princes.' The chief officers appear to have been a sort of 'mayor of the palace,' or prime minister, to which high office Daniel was appointed (Dan. ii 49), 'a master of the eunuchs' (Dan. i. 3), 'a captain of the king's guard' (Dan. ii. 14), and 'a master of the magicians,' or president of the Magi (Dan. iv. 9). Distinct probably from the foregoing was the class termed (Dan. iii. 24, 27) 'the king's counsellors,' who seem to have formed a kind of 'privy council' or even 'cabinet' for advising the monarch and governing the kingdom. The entire empire was divided into several provinces (Dan. ii. 48; iii. 1), presided over by officers of various ranks. An enumeration of several kinds may be found in Dan. iii. 2, 3. The head officers, who united in themselves the highest civil and military power, were denominated 'presidents (Dan. vi 2); those who presided over single provinces or districts bore the title of 'governor.' The administration of criminal justice was rigorous and cruel, will being substituted for law, and human life and human suffering being totally disregarded. Nebuchadnezzar (Dan ii. 5) declares to the college of the Magi—'If ye will not make known unto me the dream with the interpretation thereof, ye shall be cut in pieces, and your houses shall be made a dunghill' (see also Dan. iii. 19; vi. 8; Jer. xxix. 22). The religion of the Chaldees was, as with the ancient Arabians and Syrians, the worship of the heavenly bodies; the planets Jupiter, Mercury, and Venus were honoured as Bel, Nebo, and Meni, besides Saturn and Mars. Astrology was naturally connected with this worship of the stars, and the astronomical observations which have made the Chaldæan name famous were thereby guided and advanced. The language spoken in Babylon was what is designated Chaldee, which is Shemitic in its origin, belong-

ing to the Aramaic branch. The immigrating Chaldæans spoke probably a quite different tongue, which the geographical position of their native country shows to have belonged to the Medo-Persian stock.

The term Chaldæans represents also a branch of the order of Babylonian Magi. In Dan. ii. 2 they appear among 'the magicians, and the astrologers, and the sorcerers,' who were 'called for to shew the king his dream.' In the 10th verse of the same chapter they are represented as speaking in the name of the rest; or otherwise theirs was a general designation which comprised the entire class (Dan. iv. 7; v. 7): a general description of these different orders is found in Dan. v. 8, as 'the king's wise men.'

CHAMBERS OF IMAGERY. These are mentioned in Ezek. viii. 12, as among the abominations within the precincts of the holy place at Jerusalem, which were disclosed to the prophet in vision where he was among the captives on the banks of the Chebar, with the design of justifying and explaining the judgments which had been brought and were still to be brought upon the chosen people. A heavenly guide conducts the prophet to view in succession the various idolatries of alienated Judah. After having shown him enough to excite his horror and indignation, the angel bade him turn another way, and he would see greater abominations. Leading him to that side of the court along which were ranged the houses of the priests, his conductor pointed to a mud-wall (ver. 7), which, to screen themselves from observation, the apostate servants of the true God had raised; and in that wall was a small chink, by widening which he discovered a passage into a secret chamber, which was completely impervious to the rays of the sun, but which he found, on entering it, lighted up by a profusion of brilliant lamps. The sides of it were covered with numerous paintings of beasts and reptiles—the favourite deities of Egypt; and, with their eyes intently fixed on these decorations, was a conclave of seventy persons, in the garb of priests—the exact number, and, in all probability, the individual members of the Sanhedrim, who stood in the attitude of adoration, holding in their hands each a golden censer, containing all the costly and odoriferous materials which the pomp and magnificence of the Egyptian ritual required. 'There was every form of creeping things and abominable beasts, and all the idols of the house of Israel portrayed round about.' The scene described was wholly formed on the model of Egyptian worship; and every one who has read the works of Wilkinson, Belzoni, Richardson, and others, will perceive the close resemblance that it bears to the outer walls, the sanctuaries, and the hieroglyphical figures that distinguished the ancient mythology of Egypt.

In order to show the reader still further how exactly this inner chamber that Ezekiel saw was constructed after the Egyptian fashion, we subjoin an extract from the work of Mr. Madden, descriptive of the great Temple of Edfou, one of the admired relics of antiquity; from which it will be seen that the degenerate priests of Jerusalem had borrowed the whole style of the edifice, in which they were celebrating their hidden rites—its form, its entrance, as well as its pictorial ornaments on the walls—from their idolatrous neighbours of Egypt:—'Considerably below the surface of the adjoining building.' says he, 'my conductor pointed out to me a *chink in an old wall*, which, he told me, I should creep through on my hands and feet; the aperture was not two feet and a half high, and scarcely three feet and a half broad. My companion had the courage to go first, thrusting in a lamp before him: I followed. The passage was so narrow that my mouth and nose were almost buried in the dust, and I was nearly suffocated. After proceeding about ten yards in utter darkness, the heat became excessive, the breathing was laborious, the perspiration poured down my face, and I would have given the world to have got out; but my companion, whose person I could not distinguish, though his voice was audible, called out to me to crawl a few feet farther, and that I should find plenty of room. I joined him at length, and had the inexpressible satisfaction of standing once more upon my feet. We found ourselves in a *splendid apartment of great magnitude*, adorned with an incredible profusion of sacred *paintings and hieroglyphics*.'

CHAMELEON, a small species of lizard, celebrated for the faculty it has of changing the colour of its skin. This property, however, has no reference to the substance it may be placed on, as generally asserted, but is solely derived from the bulk of its respiratory organs acting upon a transparent skin, and on the blood of the animal. The chameleons form a small genus of Saurians, easily distinguished by the shagreened character of the skin, and the five toes on the feet, divided differently from those of most other animals, there being, if the expression may be allowed, two thumbs opposed to three fingers. Their eyes are telescopic, move separately, and can be directed backwards or forwards. Chameleons are slow, inoffensive, and capable of considerable abstinence from food; which consists solely of flies, caught by the rapid protrusion of a long and viscous tongue. Among themselves they are

118. [Chameleon Africanus.]

irascible, and are then liable to change their colours rapidly; dark yellow or grey is predominant when they are in a quiescent state, but, while the emotions are in activity, it passes into green, purple, and even ashy black. The species found in Palestine and all Northern Africa, is the common African chameleon, and is that referred to in Lev. xi. 30, where unclean animals are mentioned.

CHAMOIS (Deut. xiv. 5). Some suppose that the animal meant is the Camelopard, others the Elk. But it is plain that the Mosaical enumeration of clean animals would not include such as were totally out of the reach of the Hebrew people, and at best only known to them from specimens seen in Egypt, consisting of presents sent from Nubia, or in pictures on the walls of temples. The Camelopard or Giraffe is exclusively an inhabitant of Southern Africa, and therefore could not come in the way of the people of Israel. The same objection applies to the Elk, because that species of deer never appears further to the south than Northern Germany and Poland; and with regard to the Chamois, which has been adopted in our version, though it did exist in the mountains of Greece, and is still found in Central Asia, there is no vestige of its having at any time frequented Libanus or any other part of Syria. We may, therefore, with more propriety refer to the ruminants indigenous in the regions which were in the contemplation of the sacred legislator, and the only species that seems to answer to the conditions required is a wild sheep, still not uncommon in the Mokattam rocks near Cairo, found in Sinai, and eastward in the broken ridges of Stony Arabia, where it is known under the name of Kebsch.

119. [Kebsch. Ovis Tragelaphus.]

CHAOS, a term taken from the Greek mythology, and employed to denote the unformed condition of the world. Our present object is to inquire what the Chaos was of which Moses speaks (Gen. i. 2). Was it the first form in which matter was created? and do the succeeding operations described relate to the very beginning of material order and animal life? Or was it merely a condition preparatory to the reorganization of the world, which had already been the abode of living beings?—in other words, is the first verse of the inspired record to be dissociated from the succeeding, and to be understood only as a declaration of the important truth, that the visible universe was not made from anything already existing (Heb. xi. 3); whilst the confusion and darkness which are described in the succeeding verse, relate to a state long subsequent to the 'beginning,' and were introductory to a new order of material existence, of which man is the chief and lord? The first of these opinions is not only in accordance with the ancient notions of chaos to which we have referred, but is that which would be naturally maintained, unless cause be shown to the contrary. No one would gratuitously assume a long interval, where it must be admitted there is no intimation of such an interval having occurred. Accordingly, most interpreters, who have been ignorant of geological phenomena, have at once decided that the chaos of which Moses speaks was the form in which matter was first created. Some have even declared that there cannot have been any such interval as we have spoken of. But, on the other hand, the world gives intimations, in the rocks which compose its crust, of various and long-continued changes both of condition and of inhabitants. Those who have carefully examined these different forms of being, and have attentively studied the circumstances in which their remains are now found, have been forced to the conviction, that in many cases the rocks have been gradually formed by deposition at the bottom of an ocean, which has been successively the habitation of races differing alike from each other and from those now existing; that the coeval land likewise has had its distinct races of inhabitants, and that the land and water have changed places many times in the history of the world. It is impossible to do more than barely glance at these geological facts; but it will be seen that they lead to these three conclusions—(1) That the world has existed during some long period *before* the Mosaic record of creation in six days—(2) That, during that period, it was the abode of animals differing in organization and structure from those now found on its surface—and (3) That it has been exposed to various convulsions and reorganizations, more or less general. In the face of these facts it appears impossible to hold the ordinarily received opinion that the universe was created only just before the creation of man; and the question then is, how are these facts to be reconciled with the Mosaic narrative? Not by denying the evidence of our senses, nor, on the other hand, by treating the Mosaic account as an allegorical representation, but surely by re-examining the interpretation *we* have put on the words of Scripture, and by seeking to ascertain whether the discrepancy does not arise from *our view* of the narrative. A favourite mode of explaining the Mosaic account, a few years back, was to take the six days of creation for unlimited periods, during which the changes we are speaking of took place. This ground has, however, been almost completely abandoned, both because the account so understood does not agree with the physical phenomena, and because such an interpretation is, to say the least, hardly admissible on exegetical principles. If we keep in mind that the revelation of God to man is not intended to teach physical science—that it never speaks the language of philosophy, but of appearances—and that it tells of these only so far as they relate to the human race, we obtain a clue by which we may be safely guided through these difficulties. We shall not then wonder that no notice should be taken of previous conditions and inhabitants of this earth, supposing such to have existed. The first sentence of the inspired record will then be regarded as the majestic declaration of a fact, which the world had lost sight of, but which it deeply concerned men to know. What occurred subsequently, until the earth was to be furnished for the abode of man, is to be gathered not from the written word, but from the memorials engraven on the tablets of the world itself. The succeeding verse of the Mosaic account then relates to a state of chaos, or confusion, into which the world was thrown immediately before the last reorganization of it. Geologists are not indeed at present (if ever they may be) in a condition to identify the disruption and confusion of which we suppose Moses to speak with any one of these violent convulsions, of which geological phenomena plainly tell; but that events which might be described in his language have taken place in the world's history, over considerable portions of its surface, seems to be fully established. Whether the chaos of which we are now speaking was universal, or was confined to those regions which formed the cradle of the human race, is a question on which we do not feel it needful to enter. We do not regard the evidence which geology furnishes as complete enough to decide such a point.

CHARIOTS. The Scriptures employ different words to denote carriages of different sorts, but it is not in every case easy to distinguish the kind of vehicle which these words severally denote. We are now, however, through the discovery of ancient sculptures and paintings, in possession of such information respecting the chariots of Egypt, Assyria, Babylon, and Persia, as gives advantages in the discussion of this subject which were not possessed by earlier writers. The chariots of these nations are, in fact, mentioned in the Scriptures; and by connecting the known with the unknown, we may arrive at more determinate conclusions than have hitherto been attainable.

The first chariots mentioned in Scripture are those of the Egyptians; and by close attention to the various notices which occur respecting them, we may be able to discriminate the different kinds which were in use among that people.

The earliest notice of chariots in Scripture occurs in Gen. xli. 43, where the king of Egypt honours Joseph by commanding that he should ride in the second of the royal chariots. This was doubtless a state-chariot, and the state-chariots of the Egyptians do not appear to have been different from their war-chariots, the splendid military appointments of which rendered them fit for purposes of royal pomp. We also observe

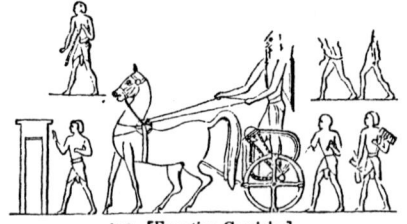

120. [Egyptian Curricle.]

that where private carriages were known, as in Egypt, they were of the same shape as those used in war, and only differed from them by having less complete military accoutrements, although even in these the case for arrows is not wanting. One of the most interesting of the Egyptian paintings represents a person of quality arriving late at an entertainment in his curricle, drawn (like all the Egyptian chariots) by two horses. He is attended by a number of running footmen, one of whom hastens forward to knock at the door of the house, another advances to take the reins, a third bears a stool to assist his master in alighting, and most of them carry their sandals in their hands that they may run with the more ease. This conveys a lively illustration of such passages as 1 Sam. viii. 11; 2 Sam. xv. 1. The principal distinction between these private chariots and those actually used in war was, as appears from the monuments, that in the former the party drove himself, whereas in war the chariot, as among the Greeks, often contained a second person to drive it, that the warrior might be at liberty to employ his weapons with the more effect. But this was not always the case: for in the Egyptian monuments we often see even royal personages alone in their chariots, warring furiously, with the reins lashed round their waist (No. 121). So it appears that Jehu (who certainly rode in a war-chariot) drove himself; for his peculiar style of driving was recognised at a considerable distance (2 Kings ix. 20).

In the prophecy of Nahum, who was of the first captivity, and resident (if not born) at Elkosh in Assyria, there is much allusion to chariots, suggested doubtless by their frequency before his eyes in the streets of Nineveh and throughout the Assyrian empire. In fact, when prophesying the downfal of Nineveh, he gives a particular and animated description of their action in the streets of the great city:—

' The shield of his mighties is made red:
The valiant men are clothed in scarlet:
The chariots are as the fire of lamps, in the
     day when he prepareth them.
And the horsemen spread fear
In the streets, the chariots madden:
They run to and fro in the broad places:
Their appearance is as lamps, they run
   as lightning.'   Nahum ii. 3, 4.

These allusions to the horsemen and chariots of Nineveh give much interest to some recent discoveries on the site of that very ancient city, of various inscriptions and sculptures, which seem to show that the work was earlier than the age of Cyrus, and may be referred to the times of the Assyrian empire. Some of the sculptures represent horsemen completely armed and at full gallop. But the matter of greatest interest is the discovery of a curious bas-relief, representing a chariot drawn by two horses, and containing three persons. The principal of these appears to be a bearded man, lifting his right arm, and holding in his left hand a bow. He wears a tiara painted red (' the valiant men are clothed in scarlet'); behind him is a beardless slave, carrying a fringed parasol, and at his left is the charioteer holding the reins and the whip. The principal person and the charioteer wear earrings. The chariot-wheels have eight spokes: the chariot itself has been covered with carving, now impossible to be made out. The horses are admirably drawn, and afford indications of pure Arabian blood. Their harness is very rich, and still bears evident traces of colouring, among which blue and red only can be distinguished, the rest having turned black. Behind the chariot

rides a cavalier, bearing a lance, with a sword at his belt, and a quiver over his shoulder.

CHARIOTS OF WAR. The Egyptians used horses in the equipment of an armed force before Jacob and his sons had settled in Goshen; they had chariots of war, and mounted asses and mules, and therefore could not be ignorant of the art of riding; but for ages after that period Arab nations rode on the bare back, and guided the animals with a wand. Others, and probably the shepherd invaders, noosed a single rope in a slipknot round the lower jaw, forming an imperfect bridle, with only one rein; a practice still in vogue among the Bedouins. Thus cavalry were but little formidable compared with chariots, until a complete command over the horse was obtained by the discovery of a true bridle. This seems to have been first introduced by chariot-drivers, and there are figures of well-constructed harness, reins, and mouth pieces, in very early Egyptian monuments, representing both native and foreign chariots of war. These differed little from each other, both consisting of a light pole, suspended between and on the withers of a pair of horses, the after-end resting on a light axle-tree, with two low wheels. Upon the axle stood a light frame, open behind and floored for the warrior and his charioteer, who both stood within: on the sides of the frame hung the war-bow, in its case: a large quiver with arrows, and darts had commonly a particular sheath. In Persia, the chariots, elevated upon wheels of considerable diameter, had four horses abreast; and, in early ages, there were occasionally hooks or scythes attached to the axles. In fighting from chariots great dexterity was shown by the warrior, not only in handling his weapons, but also in stepping out upon the pole to the horses' shoulders, in order the better to reach his enemies, and the charioteer was an important person, sometimes equal in rank to the warrior himself. Both the kingdoms of Judah and Israel had war-chariots, and, from the case of king Josiah at the battle of

121. [Egyptian War Chariot.]

Megiddo, it is clear they had also travelling-vehicles, for being wounded he quitted his fighting-chariot, and in a second, evidently more commodious, he was brought to Jerusalem (2 Chron. xxxv. 24) Chariots of war continued to be used in Syria in the time of the Maccabees (2 Mac. xiii. 5), and in Britain when Cæsar invaded the island.

CHARITY. The Greek word *agape* frequently thus rendered in the Authorized Version of the

New Testament (*e. g.* 1 Cor. xiii. throughout), is that which is more usually translated 'love' in the same version (*e. g.* John xv. throughout). The translation of the word by 'love' is the more proper, seeing that 'charity' has acquired a signification in our language which limits it to overt acts of beneficence. The Greek word denotes that kindly state of mind or feeling which renders a person full of such goodwill or affectionate regard towards others as is always ready to evince itself in word or action. In short, it describes that state of feeling which the apostle enjoined the Romans (xii. 10) to entertain : ' Be ye *kindly affectioned* one to another.' This extended meaning of the word explains the pre-eminence which the Apostle assigns to the virtue which it implies over every other Christian grace (1 Cor. xiii.).

CHARMING OF SERPENTS. [ADDER.]

CHE'BAR, a river of Mesopotamia, upon the banks of which king Nebuchadnezzar planted a colony of Jews, among whom was the prophet Ezekiel (2 Kings xxiv. 15; Ezek. i. 1, 3; iii. 15, 23; x. 15, 22). This is without doubt the same river that was known among the Greeks as the Chabo·as, and which now bears the name of Khabour. It fows to the Euphrates through Mesopotamia, and is the only considerable stream which enters that river. It is formed by the junction of a number of small brooks, which rise in the neighbourhood of a ruined town called Ras-el-Ain, 13 furlongs south-west of Merdin. It takes a southerly direction till it receives the waters of another stream equal to itself, when it bends westward to the Euphrates, which it enters at Kerkesia, the Carchemish of Scripture. [CARCHEMISH.]

CHEDORLAO'MER, King of Elam, and leader of the five kings who invaded Canaan in the time of Abraham (Gen. xiv.). [ABRAHAM; ASSYRIA; ELAM]

CHEESE. There is much reason to conclude that the cheese used by the Jews differed in no respect from that still common in the East; which is usually exhibited in small cakes about the size of a tea saucer, white in colour, and excessively salt. It has no rind, and soon becomes exceedingly hard and dry—being, indeed, not made for long keeping. It is best when new and comparatively soft; and, in this state, large quantities are consumed in lumps or crumbs not made up into cakes. All cheese in the East is of very indifferent quality; and it is within the writer's own knowledge that the natives infinitely prefer English or Dutch cheese when they can obtain it. In making cheese, the common rennet is either butter-milk or a decoction of the great-headed thistle, or wild artichoke. The curds are afterwards put into small baskets made of rushes or palm leaves, which are then tied up close, and the necessary pressure applied.

CHE'MOSH is the name of a national god of the Moabites (1 Kings xi. 7; 2 Kings xxiii. 13; Jer. xlviii. 7; who are for this reason called the 'people of Chemosh,' in Num. xxi. 29), and of the Ammonites (Judg. xi. 24), whose worship was introduced among the Israelites by Solomon (1 Kings xi. 7). No attempt which has been made to identify this god with others whose attributes are better known, are sufficiently plausible to deserve particular notice. The only

theory which rests on any probability is that which assumes a resemblance between Chemosh and Arabian idolatry. Jewish tradition affirms that he was worshipped under the symbol of a black star; and Maimonides states that his worshippers went bare-headed, and abstained from the use of garments sewn together by the needle. The black star, the connection with Arabian idolatry, and the fact that Chemosh is coupled with Moloch, favour the theory that he had some analogy with the planet Saturn.

CHENANI'AH, *God's goodness;* a master of the temple music, who conducted the grand musical services when the ark was removed from the house of Obed-edom to Jerusalem (1 Chron. xv. 22).

CHER'ETHITES and PEL'ETHITES, names borne by the royal life-guards in the time of David (2 Sam. viii. 18; 1 Chron. xviii. 17). Prevailing opinion translates their names, ' Headsmen and Foot-runners.' In the later years of David, their captain, Benaiah, rose to a more commanding importance than the generals of the regular troops; just as in imperial Rome the præfect of the prætorian guards became the second person in the empire. It is evident that. to perpetrate any summary deed, Benaiah and the guards were chiefly relied on. That they were strictly a body-guard is distinctly stated in 2 Sam. xxiii. 23. In 1 Sam. xxx. 14, the Cherethites are named as a nation of the south, and in 2 Sam. xv. 15, the Cherethites and Pelethites are mentioned along with the Gittites, who were undoubtedly foreigners. It has therefore been supposed, with some probability, that David entrusted the care of his person to foreign guards.

CHE'RITH, a river in Palestine, on the banks of which the prophet Elijah found refuge (1 Kings xvii. 3-7). Local traditions have uniformly placed the Cherith on this side the Jordan; and this agrees with the history and with Josephus. Dr. Robinson drops a suggestion that it may be the Wady Kelt, which is formed by the union of many streams in the mountains west of Jericho, issuing from a deep gorge, in which it passes by that village and then across the plain to the Jordan. It is dry in summer.

CHER'UBIM (*Cherub,* pl. *Cherubim*) is the name of certain symbolical figures frequently mentioned in Scripture. The derivation and meaning of the term cannot now be known with certainty.

Figures of the cherubim were conspicuous implements in the Levitical tabernacle. Two of them were placed at each end of the mercy-seat, standing in a stooping attitude, as if looking down towards it, while they overshadowed it with their expanded wings--and, indeed, they were component parts of it, formed out of the same mass of pure gold as the mercy-seat itself (Exod. xxv. 19).

These figures were afterwards transferred to the most holy place in Solomon's temple, and it has been supposed from 1 Chron. xxviii. 18, that that prince constructed two additional ones after the same pattern, and of the same solid and costly material; but whether it was with a view to increase their number in accordance with the more spacious and magnificent edifice to which they were removed, or merely to supply the place of those made by Moses, which in the many vicissitudes that befel the ark might have been mutilated or entirely separated from the mercy-seat to which they were attached—is not ascertained. This much, however, is known, that Solomon erected two of colossal dimensions, in an erect posture with their faces towards the walls (2 Chron. iii. 13), covering with their outstretched wings the entire breadth of the most holy place. These sacred hieroglyphics were profusely embroidered on the tapestry of the tabernacle, on the curtains and the great vail that separated the holy from the most holy place (Exod. xxvi. 1, 31), as well as carved in several places (1 Kings viii. 6-8) on the walls, doors, and sacred utensils of the temple. The position occupied by these singular images at each extremity of the mercy-seat—while the Shechinah, or sacred flame that symbolized the divine presence, and the awful name of Jehovah in written characters were in the intervening space—gave rise to the well-known phraseology of the sacred writers, which represents the Deity dwelling between or inhabiting the cherubim; and, in fact, so intimately associated were they with the manifestation of the divine glory, that whether the Lord is described as at rest or in motion, as seated on a throne, or riding in a triumphal chariot, these symbolic figures were essential elements in the description (Numb. vii. 89; Ps. xviii. 10; lxxx. 1; xcix. 1-9; Isa. vi. 2; xxxvii. 16).

The first occasion on which the Cherubim are mentioned in Scripture is on the expulsion of our first parents from Eden, when the Lord placed cherubim on the east of the garden; or as it may be rendered, ' before or on the edge of the garden.' The word in the original translated ' on the east,' may signify as well · before or on the edge of;' and the historian does not say that the Lord placed there ' cherubim,' but ' the cherubim.' The word rendered by our translators ' placed,' signifies properly ' to place in a tabernacle,' an expression which, viewed in connection with some incidents in the after history of the primæval family (Gen. iv. 14-16), seems a conclusive establishment of the opinion that this was a local tabernacle, in which the symbols of the Divine presence were manifested, suitably to the altered circumstances in which man after the Fall came before God, and to the acceptable mode of worship he was taught to observe. That consecrated place, with its striking symbols, called ' the presence of the Lord,' there is reason to believe, continued till the time of the Deluge, otherwise there would have been nothing to guard the way to the tree of life: and thus the knowledge of their form, from the longevity of the antediluvians, could have been easily transmitted to the time of Abraham. Moreover, it is an approved opinion that, when those emblems were removed at the close of the patriarchal dispensation from the place of public worship, the ancestors of that patriarch formed small models of them for domestic use, under the name of Seraphim or Teraphim. The next occasion in the course of the sacred history on which the cherubim are noticed is when Moses was commanded to provide the furniture of the tabernacle; and, although he received instructions to make all things according to the pattern shown

him in the Mount, and although it is natural to suppose that he saw a figure of the cherubim, yet we find no minute and special description of them, as is given of everything else, for the direction of the artificers (Exod. xxvi. 31). The simple mention which the sacred historian makes, in both these passages, of the cherubim, conveys the impression that the symbolic figures which had been introduced into the Levitical tabernacle were substantially the same with those established in the primæval place of worship on the outskirts of Eden, and that by traditional information, or some other means, their form was so well known, both to Bezaleel and the whole congregation of Israel, as to render superfluous all further description of them. On no other ground can we account for the total silence as to their configuration, unless we embrace the groundless and unworthy opinion of those who impute to the author of the Pentateuch a studied concealment of some parts of his ritual, after the manner of the Mystics. But there was no mystery as to those remarkable figures, for Ezekiel knew at once (x. 20) the living creatures which appeared in his vision supporting the throne of God, and bearing it in majesty from place to place, to be cherubim, from having frequently seen them, in common with all other worshippers, in the carved work of the outer sanctuary. Moreover, as is the opinion of many eminent divines, the visionary scene with which this prophet was favoured, exhibited a transcript of the Temple, which was shown in pattern to David, and afterwards erected by his son and successor: and, as the chief design of that later vision was to inspire the Hebrew exiles in Babylon with the hope of seeing, on their return to Judæa, another temple, more glorious than the

122. [Babylonian.]

one then in ruins, it is reasonable to believe that, as the whole style and apparatus of this mystic temple bore an exact resemblance (1 Kings vi. 20) to that of Solomon's magnificent edifice, so the cherubs also that appeared to his fancy portrayed on the walls would be fac-similes of those that belonged to its ancient prototype. Taking then his description of them to be the proper appearance that belonged in common to all his cherubic creatures (chaps. i. x. xli.), we are led to conclude that they were compound figures, unlike any living animals or real object in nature, but rather a combination, in one nondescript artificial image, of the distinguishing features and properties of several. The ox, as chief among

o

the tame and useful animals, the lion among the wild ones, the eagle among the feathery tribes, and man, as head over all—were the animals which, or rather parts of which, composed the symbolical figures. Each cherub had four distinct faces on one neck—that of a man in front, that of a lion on the right side, and of an ox on the left; while behind was the face of an eagle. Each had four wings, the two under ones covering the lower extremities (Heb. the feet), in token of decency and humility, while the upper ones, spread out on a level with the head and shoulders, were so joined together, to the edge of his neighbours', as to form a canopy; and in this manner they soared rather than flew, without any vibratory motion with their wings, through the air. Each had straight feet. The Hebrew version renders it 'a straight foot;' and the probability is, that the legs were destitute of any flexible joint at the knee, and so joined together that its locomotions must have been performed in some other way than by the ordinary process of walking, or lifting one foot after another. The ideal picture, then, which Ezekiel's description would lead us to form of the cherub, is that of a winged man, or winged ox, according to the particular phase it exhibited or the particular direction from which

123. [Persian.]

it was seen. To use the words of Dr. Watts, ' That figure which would have had all four faces visible if it had stood forth as a real animal or a statue, could have had but two faces, or at most three, visible when figured on a wall or curtain, the other being hid behind; and thus the cherubs may be in all places of Scripture the same four-faced animals, and yet only two or three of their faces appear, according to their designed situation and the art of perspective.

124. [Egyptian.]

Whether the golden calf constructed by Aaron might be—not the Apis of Egypt—but a representation of the antediluvian Cherubim—as some suppose, from its being made on ' a feast to the Lord,' and called ' the gods of Israel ' (Exod.

xxxii. 5), and whether Jeroboam, in the erection of his two calves, intended a schismatic imitation of the sacred symbols in the Temple of Jerusalem rather than the introduction of a new species of idolatry (1 Kings xii. 28), we shall not stop to inquire. But, as paganism is a corruption of patriarchal worship—each nation having added something according to its own taste and fancy—perhaps we may find a confirmation of the views given above of the compound form of the cherubim in the strangely compounded figures under which some of the heathen deities are represented, or which symbolised their attributes, as shown in the preceding engravings. Many of these have outspread or lowering wings, after the manner of the Hebrew cherubim; and there are perhaps few subjects which admit of more ample illustration from ancient monuments.

The opinions concerning the design of the cherubim are as diversified as those relative to their form. All are agreed that they had a symbolical meaning, although it is not easy to ascertain it. The ancients, as well as the fathers, considered that they had both a physical and a metaphysical object. The opinions of the moderns may be reduced to three systems. Hutchinson and his followers consider the cherubim as emblems of the Trinity, with man incorporated into the divine essence. But the grand objection to this theory, where it is at all intelligible. is, that not only are the cherubim, in all the places of Scripture where they are introduced, described as distinct from God, and no more than his attendants, but that it represents the divine Being. who is a pure spirit, without parts, passions, or anything material, making a visible picture of himself, when in the beginning of time, he has expressly prohibited ' the likeness of anything in heaven above' Another system regards the cherubim as symbolical of the chief ruling powers by which God carries on the operations of nature. As the heaven of heavens was typified by the holy of holies in the Levitical tabernacle (Heb. ix. 3-12, 24-28), this system considers that the visible heavens may be typified by the holy place or the outer sanctuary, and accordingly finding, as its supporters imagine they do, the cherubim identified with the aërial firmament and its elements in such passages as the following: Ps. xviii. 10; Deut. xxxiii. 26; Ps. lxviii. 4 ; he is said to descend in fire (Exod. xix. 18), and between which he dwelt in light (1 Tim. vi. 16), and it was in this very manner he manifested his divine glory in the tabernacle and temple—they interpret the cherubim, on which the Lord is described as riding, to be symbolical of the wind, the clouds, the fire, the light; in short, the heavens, the atmosphere, the great physical powers by which the Creator and preserver of the universe carries on the operations of nature.

A third system considers the cherubim, from their being instituted immediately after the Fall, as having particular reference to the redemption of man, and as symbolical of the great and active rulers or ministers of the church. Those who adopt this theory as the true explanation of their emblematical meaning, are accustomed to refer to the living creatures, or cherubim, mentioned in the Apocalyptic vision (Rev. iv. 6). improperly rendered in our English translation 'beasts,' and which, it is clear, were not angels, but redeemed men connected with the church, and deeply interested in the blessings and glory procured by the Lamb. The same character may be ascribed to the living creatures in Ezekiel's visions, and to the cherubim, which stood over and looked into the mercy-seat, sprinkled with the blood of the atonement, and on the Shechinah, or divine glory arising from it, as well as the cherubic figures which were placed on the edge of Eden ; and thus the cherubim, which are prominently introduced in all the three successive dispensations of the covenant of grace, appear to be symbols of those who, in every age, should officially study and proclaim the glory and manifold wisdom of God.

CHESTNUT-TREE, a tree which is named thrice in the Scriptures. It occurs among the 'speckled rods' which Jacob placed in the watering-troughs before the sheep (Gen. xxx. 37): its grandeur is indicated in Ezek. xxxi. 8, as well as in Ecclus. xxiv. 19 : it is noted for its magnificence, shooting its high boughs aloft. This

125. [Plane-tree—Platanus Orientalis.]

description agrees well with the plane-tree, which is adopted by all the ancient translators, and scarcely any one now doubts that this is the tree which is meant.

The Oriental plane-tree is a native of Westernmost Asia, although, according to Professor Royle, it extends as far eastward as Cashmere. The stem is tall, erect, and covered with a smooth bark which annually falls off. The flowers are small and scarcely distinguishable : they come out a little before the leaves. The wood of the plane-tree is fine-grained, hard, and rather brittle than tough; when old, it is said to acquire dark veins, and to take the appearance of walnut wood.

In those situations which are favourable to its growth, huge branches spread out in all directions from the massive trunk, invested with broad, deeply-divided, and glossy green leaves. This body of rich foliage, joined to the smoothness of the stem, and the symmetry of the general growth, renders the plane-tree one of the noblest objects in the vegetable kingdom. It has now, and had also of old, the reputation of being the tree which most effectually excludes the sun's beams in summer, and most readily admits them in winter—thus affording the best shelter from the extremes of both seasons.

For this reason it was planted near public buildings and palaces, a practice which the Greeks and Romans adopted ; and the former delighted to adorn with it their academic walks and places of public exercise. In the East, the plane seems to have been considered sacred, as the oak was formerly in Britain. This distinction is in most countries awarded to the most magnificent species of tree which it produces. In Palestine, for instance, where the plane does not appear to have been very common, the terebinth seems to have possessed pre-eminence. No one is ignorant of the celebrated story of Xerxes arresting the march of his grand army before a noble plane-tree in Lydia, that he might render honour to it, and adorn its boughs with golden chains, bracelets, and other rich ornaments.

The Oriental plane endures our own climate well, and grows to a fine tree ; but not to the enormous size which it sometimes attains in the East. Evelyn (in his *Sylva*) seems to ascribe the introduction of the plane-tree into England to the great Lord Bacon, who planted some which were still flourishing at Verulam in 1706. This was, perhaps, the first plantation of any note; but it appears from Turner's *Herbal* (published in 1551), that the tree was known and cultivated in this country before the chancellor was born.

CHILDREN. The more children—especially male children—a person had among the Hebrews, the more was he honoured, it being considered as a mark of divine favour, while sterile people were, on the contrary, held in contempt (comp. Gen. xi. 30 ; xxx. 1 ; 1 Sam. ii. 5 ; 2 Sam. vi. 23 ; Ps. cxxvii. 3, *sq.*; cxxviii. 3 ; Luke i. 7 ; ii. 5). That children were often taken as bondsmen by a creditor for debts contracted by the father, is evident from 2 Kings iv. 1 ; Isa. l. 1 ; Neh. v. 5. Among the Hebrews, a father had almost unlimited power over his children, nor do we find any law in the Pentateuch restricting that power to a certain age; it was indeed the parents who even selected wives for their sons (Gen. xxi. 21 ; Exod. xxi. 9, 10, 11 ; Judg. xiv. 2, 5). It would appear, however, that a father's power over his daughters was still greater than that over his sons, since he might even annul a sacred vow made by a daughter, but not one made by a son (Num. xxx 4, 16). Children cursing or assaulting their parents were punished by the Mosaical Law with death (Exod. xxi. 15, 17 ; Lev. xx. 9). Before the time of Moses a father had the right to choose among his male children, and declare one of them (usually the child of his favourite wife) as his first-born, though he was perhaps only the youngest. Properly speaking, the 'first-born' was he who was first begotten by the father, since polygamy excluded all regard in that respect to the mother. Thus Jacob had sons by all his four wives, while only one of them was called the first-born (Gen. xlix. 3); we find, however, instances where that name is applied also to the first-born on the mother's side (1 Chron. ii. 50; comp. v. 42; Gen. xxii.

o 2

21). The privileges of the first-born were considerable, as shown in BIRTHRIGHT.

The first-born son, if not expressly deprived by the father of his peculiar rights, as was the case with Reuben (Gen. xlix.), was at liberty to sell them to a younger brother, as happened in the case of Esau and Jacob (Gen. xxv. 31, *sq.*). Considering the many privileges attached to first-birth, we do not wonder that the Apostle called Esau a *thoughtless person* (Heb. xii. 16). There are some allusions in Scripture to the modes in which children were carried. These appear to be adequately represented by the existing usages, as represented in the following cut (No. 126), in which fig. 1 represents a Nestorian woman bearing her child bundled at her back, and fig. 2, an Egyptian female bearing her child on her shoulder. The former mode appears to be alluded to

126.

in several places, and the latter in Isa. xlix. 22. For other matters regarding children, see ADOPTION, BIRTH, BIRTHRIGHT, EDUCATION.

CHI'OS, one of the principal islands of the Ionian Archipelago, mentioned in Acts xx. 15. It belonged to Ionia, and lay between the islands Lesbos and Samos, and distant eight miles from the nearest promontory of Asia Minor. It is thirty miles long from N. to S., and its greatest breadth ten miles. It is very fertile in cotton, silk, and fruit, and was anciently celebrated for its wine. The principal town was also called Chios, and had the advantage of a good harbour. The island is now called by the Greeks Khio, and by the Italians Scio. The wholesale massacre and enslavement of the inhabitants by the Turks in 1822 forms one of the most shocking incidents of the Greek war.

CHIS'LEV (1 Macc. i. 54) is the name of that month which is the third of the civil, and the ninth of the ecclesiastical year of the Jews, and which commences with the new moon of our December.

The memorable days which were observed in this month were:—The feast of the dedication of the Temple, in commemoration of its being purified from the heathen abominations of the Syrians, which was celebrated by illuminations and great demonstrations of joy for eight days, beginning from the 25th of this month (1 Macc. iv. 59): and a fast on account of Jehoiakim having, in this month, burnt the roll containing Jeremiah's prophecy (Jer. xxxvi. 22, 23). There is some dispute whether this fast was observed on the 6th or on the 28th of the month. It is an argument in favour of the earlier day that the other would fall in the middle of the eight days' festival of the dedication.

CHIT'TIM, or KITTIM, a branch of the de-

scendants of Javan, the son of Japheth (Gen. x. 4). On the authority of Josephus, who is followed by Epiphanius and Jerome, it has been generally admitted that the Chittim migrated from Phœnicia to Cyprus, and founded there the town of Citium, the modern Chitti. 'Chethimus possessed the island of Chethima, which is now called Cyprus, and from this, all islands and maritime places are called Chethim by the Hebrews.' Cicero, it may be remarked, speaks of the Citians as a Phœnician colony. Some passages in the prophets (Ezek. xxvii. 6; Isa. xxiii. 1, 12) imply an intimate connection between Chittim and Tyre. At a later period the name was applied to the Macedonians. Hengstenberg has lately endeavoured to prove that in every passage in the Old Testament where the word occurs, it means Cyprus, or the Cyprians.

After a careful examination of the works in which this point is discussed, the writer is disposed to acquiesce in the opinion expressed by the editor of the *Pictorial Bible:* 'Chittim seems to be a name of large signification (such as our Levant), applied to the islands and coasts of the Mediterranean, in a loose sense, without fixing the particular part, though particular and different parts of the whole are probably in most cases to be understood' (v. notes on Ezek. xxvii. 6).

CHI'UN. [REMPHAN.]

CHLO'E, a Christian woman at Corinth, some members of whose family afforded Paul intelligence concerning the divisions which reigned in the church at that place (1 Cor. i. 11).

CHORA'ZIN, a town mentioned in Matt. xi. 21; Luke x. 13, in connection with Bethsaida and Capernaum, not far from which, in Galilee, it appears to have been situated. Jerome makes it a village of Galilee, on the shore of the lake Tiberias, two miles from Capernaum. But no place of the name has been historically noticed since his days; and not only the town, but its very name appears to have long since perished. [BETHESDA; CAPERNAUM.]

CHRIST. [JESUS.]

CHRON'ICLES. This name seems to have been first given to two historical books of the Old Testament by Jerome. The Hebrews call them *words of days, diaries, or journals,* and reckon them but one book.

In 1 Chron. i.-ix. is given a series of genealogical tables interspersed with historical notices. These genealogies are not complete.

1 Chron. x.-xxix. contains the history of David, partly agreeing with the account given of him in the books of Samuel, though with several important additions relating to the Levites.

2 Chron. i.-ix. contains the history of Solomon.

2 Chron. x.-xxviii. furnishes a succinct account of the kingdom of *Judah* while *Israel* still remained, but separate from the history of the latter.

2 Chron. xxix.-xxxvi. describes the kingdom of Judah after the downfall of Israel, especially with reference to the worship of God.

From this analysis it appears that the Chronicles contain an epitome of sacred history, particularly from the origin of the Jewish nation to the end of the first captivity.

The diction of the Chronicles is such as suits the time *immediately* subsequent to the captivity

It is substantially the same with that of Ezra, Nehemiah, and Esther, which were all written shortly after the Babylonish exile. It is mixed with *Aramœisms*, marking at once the decline of the Jews in power, and the corruption of their native tongue. The pure Hebrew had been then laid aside. It was lost during their sojourn in Babylon.

Internal evidence sufficiently demonstrates that the Chronicles were written after the captivity. Thus the history is brought down to the end of the exile, and mention is made of the restoration by Cyrus (2 Chron. xxxvi. 21. 22). It is certain that they were compiled after the time of Jeremiah (2 Chron. xxxv. 25), who lived to see the destruction of Jerusalem by the Chaldæans. The genealogy of Zerubbabel is even continued to the time of Alexander (1 Chron. iii. 19-24). The same opinion is supported by the character of the *orthography* and the nature of the *language* employed, as we have already seen, both which are Aramæan in complexion, and harmonize with the books confessedly written after the exile. The Jews generally ascribe the Chronicles to Ezra, and it is extremely probable that they were really written by him.

The principal design of the writer seems to have been to maintain the proper distinctions between the tribes and families of the returning Hebrews, that the Messiah's descent out of the tribe and family whence he was to spring according to prophecy, might be made manifest. Accordingly, the family of David is specially noticed and prominently portrayed. The author also shows how the lands had been distributed before the captivity, that the people might obtain the ancient inheritance of their fathers. In doing so he goes back to the most ancient times, and presents to his countrymen their earliest history, lest, during their exile, they might have forgotten their original and lost the traces of their real ancestry. In addition to this object it was also intended to show how the worship of God should be properly resumed and orderly re-established. In accordance with such a purpose he gives the genealogy of the priests and Levites more fully than any other writer, records their functions and rank, and enters with particularity into the arrangements established among them by David and Solomon. These two purposes, which are closely allied, will serve to demonstrate the perfect congruity of all that is peculiar in the Chronicles. They account for the genealogical tables, the specifications of tribes and families with their situation, as also for a variety of references to the priests and Levites, to the preparations made by David for building the temple, the reformations which took place at different periods, the prosperity of such kings as feared Jehovah and walked in his ways, to the marvellous interpositions of Heaven on behalf of those who trusted in Him alone, to the idolatry of Israel and their consequent misfortunes.

The books of Chronicles as compared with those of Kings are more *didactic* than *historical*. The *historical* tendency is subordinated to the *didactic*. Indeed, the purely historic form appears to be preserved only in so far as it presented an appropriate medium for those religious and moral observations which the author was directed to adduce. Samuel and Kings are more occupied with the relation of *political* occurrences; while the Chronicles furnish detailed accounts of *ecclesiastical* institutions.

A thorough examination of these books as compared with those of Samuel and Kings will satisfy the inquirer that the latter were known to Ezra and extensively used by him in the composition of Chronicles.

But these books are not the only source from which the Chronicles have been taken. Public documents formed the common groundwork of the three histories. The Pentateuch has also been used in their compilation. A comparison of the first nine chapters of 1 Chron. with the Mosaic books will show the parallelism existing between them; and it should be especially noticed that 1 Chron. i. 43-54 agrees *verbatim* with Genesis xxxvi. 31-43. Perhaps, however, this passage in both has been drawn from the same source.

As the Almighty does nothing superfluously, and puts forth no exertion of his power where his infinite wisdom does not perceive a fitting necessity, it would have been unnecessary, as far as we can perceive, to suggest anew to the mind of the writer facts with which he must have been partially acquainted by tradition, and which he had an opportunity of knowing from the sacred records. It is evident that the Chronicles were compiled not only from former inspired writings, but, for the most part, from public records, registers, and genealogies belonging to the Jews. That national annals existed there can be no doubt. They are expressly mentioned, as in 1 Chron. xxvii. 24. They contained an account of the most important events in the history of the Hebrews, and were generally lodged in the tabernacle or temple, where they could be most conveniently consulted.

The histories of kings appear to have been usually written by *prophets* (1 Chron. xxix. 29; 2 Chron. ix. 29; xii. 15; xiii. 22). Hence they constantly refer to the divine rewards and punishments characterizing the theocracy. These historical writings of the prophets were, for the most part, inserted in the public annals, as is evident from 2 Chron. xx. 34; xxxii. 32; xii. 15; xxiv. 27. Whether they were *always* so inserted is questionable, for they seem to be distinguished from the annals of the kingdom in 2 Chron. xxxiii. 19. From such sources Ezra extracted the accounts which he was prompted to write for the use of mankind in all ages. We cannot believe that his selection was indiscriminate or careless. His inspiration effectually secured him against everything that was inaccurate or unsuitable to the purposes for which he was supernaturally enlightened. That he committed mistakes cannot for a moment be admitted, else his history is impugned and its position in the canon inexplicable. His veracity, integrity, and scrupulous exactness must be held fast by every right-minded believer.

From an inspection of 1 Chron. xvi. 4-41; 1 Chron. xxii.-xxvi. 28; xxviii. xxix.; 2 Chron. xv. 1-15; 2 Chron. xvii. 7, &c.; xxvi. 16-21; xxx.; xxxi., it will be manifest, that it was one design of Ezra to notice with particularity the order of the divine worship as established by David and Solomon, with various reformations in the theocracy that took place at different times. The Levitical priesthood, and the public service of God, are specially noticed and prominently brought into view. From. 2 Chron. xiii.; xx. 21, &c.; xix. 2, &c.; xxv. 7, &c., it is evident that God's miraculous interference on behalf of Judah, and his displeasure with idolatrous Israel, were also intended to be depicted. In accordance with the same object, pious kings evincing appropriate zeal for the glory of Jehovah are commended, and their efforts marked with approval (comp. 2 Chron. xiv. 6-15; xvii. 10, &c.; xx.; xxvi. 5, &c.; xxvii. 4-6, &c.), while the ruin of idolatrous practices is forcibly adduced (2 Chron. xxi. 11, &c.; xxviii. 5, &c.; xxxiii. 11, &c.; xxv. 14, &c.; xxxvi. 6).

Such are the characteristic peculiarities of these books; and we now ask the impartial reader to consider if they be not worthy of the Holy Spirit under whose guidance the Chronicles were written. Are they not admirably in unison with the character of Ezra the high-priest and reformer? What more natural, or more accordant with the solicitudes of this holy man, than to dwell upon such matters as relate to the worship of Jehovah, to the priests, and Levites? Surely he was appropriately directed to record the reformations effected by godly kings, and the disastrous consequences of forsaking the true God, whose zeal was abundantly manifested in reform, and to whom idolatry was peculiarly offensive. And yet upon these very chapters and paragraphs charges the most flagrant have been founded. The author of them has been accused of hatred to Israel, predilection for the Levites, love of the marvellous, design to magnify pious kings and to heighten the mistakes of the kingdom of Israel. It is unnecessary to enter into any refutation of these monstrous accusations. They bear with them their own condemnation. They are the offspring of that Rationalism which resolves to see nothing but what it relishes. On every page of these historical books are impressed *genuineness* and *honesty*. The writer candidly refers to the sources whence his information was derived; and contemporary readers, placing implicit reliance on his statements, allowed the original documents to perish. He relates many things disgraceful to Judah and its kings, while he evinces no desire to palliate or conceal sin. He even retains, as we have seen before, expressions incongruous with his own age, and therefore exactly copied from the ancient records. Surely a writer guilty of falsification would have been careful to alter these into exact correspondence with his own times. Transparent simplicity of character needs not such minutiæ.

CHRYS'OLITE. This word occurs only in Rev xxi. 20 in the enumeration of the stones which formed the foundation of the heavenly Jerusalem. This stone is found solid, and in grains, or in angular pieces. The prevailing colour is yellowish green, and pistachio green of every variety and degree of shade, but always with a yellow and gold lustre. Although this stone is not mentioned in the Authorized Version of the Old Testament, it is supposed to be intended by the Hebrew word *Tharshish*, which occurs in Exod. xxviii. 20; xxxix. 13; Ezek. i. 6; x. 9; xxviii. 13; Cant. v. 4; Dan. x. 6, and is in all these places translated 'beryl.' The name *Tharshish stone* seems to intimate that it was known to the Hebrews as brought from the part so called. [THARSHISH.]

CHRYSOP'RASUS. This occurs only in Rev. xxi. 20. The name literally signifies 'leek-green stone,' and it is, as that name imports, of a greenish golden colour like a leek, that is usually apple-green passing into grass green.

CHURCH. The original Greek word which is thus rendered, in its larger signification denotes a number of persons called together for *any* purpose, an assembly of any kind, civil or religious. As, however, it is usually applied in the New Testament to religious assemblages, it is very properly translated by 'assembly,' in the few instances in which it occurs in the civil sense (Acts xix. 32, 39, 41). It is, however, well to note that the word rendered 'assembly' in these verses is the same which is rendered 'church' everywhere else.

In a few places the word occurs in the Jewish sense of a congregation, an assembly of the people for worship, either in a synagogue (Matt. xviii. 17) or generally of the Jews regarded as a religious body (Acts vii. 38; Heb. ii. 12).

But the word most frequently occurs in the Christian sense of an assemblage (of Christians) generally (1 Cor. xi. 18). Hence it denotes a church, the Christian church; in which, however, we distinguish certain shades of meaning, viz.—1. A particular church, a church in a certain place, as in Jerusalem (Acts viii. 1; xi. 22, &c.), in Antioch (Acts xi. 26; xiii. 1, &c.), in Corinth (1 Cor. i. 2; 2 Cor. i. 1), &c. &c. 2. Churches of (Gentile) Christians, without distinguishing place (Rom. xvi. 4). 3. An assembly of Christians which meets anywhere, as in the house of any one (Rom. xvi. 5; 1 Cor. xvi. 19: Philem. 2). The Church universal—the whole body of Christian believers (Matt. xvi. 18; 1 Cor. xii. 28; Gal. i. 13; Eph. i. 22; iii. 10; Heb. xii. 23, &c.).

CHU'SHAN-RISHATHA'IM, a king of Mesopotamia, by whom the Israelites were oppressed for eight years (B.C. 1394 to B.C. 1402), until delivered by Othniel (Judg. iii. 8-10).

CHU'ZA, steward of Herod Antipas, whose wife Joanna was one of those who employed their means in contributing to the wants of Christ and his apostles (Luke viii. 3).

CILIC'IA, the south-eastern part of Asia Minor, bounded on the W. by Pamphylia; separated on the N. from Cappadocia by the Taurus range, and on the E. by Amanus from Syria; and having the gulf of Issus (Iskenderoon) and the Cilician Sea (Acts xxvii. 5) on the South. By the ancients the eastern part was called Cilicia Proper, or the level Cilicia; and the western, the rough, or mountainous. The former was well-watered, and abounded in various kinds of grain and fruits. The chief towns in this division were *Issus*, at the south-eastern extremity, celebrated for the victory of Alexander over Darius Codomanus (B.C. 333), and not far from the passes of Amanus; *Solæ*, originally a colony of Argives and Rhodians; and *Tarsus*, the birth-place of the Apostle Paul [TARSUS]. Cilicia Trachea furnished an inexhaustible supply of cedars and firs for ship-building; it was also noted for a species of goat, of whose skins cloaks and tents were manufactured. Its breed of horses was so superior, that 360 (one for each day of the year) formed part of the annual tribute to the king of Persia. The neighbourhood of

Corycus produced large quantities of saffron. Though partially subjected to the Assyrians, Medes, Persians, Syrians, and Romans, the Eleuthero- (or free) Cilicians, as the inhabitants of the mountainous districts were called, were governed by their own kings, till the time of Vespasian. The sea-coast was for a long time occupied by pirates, who carried on the appropriate vocation of slave-merchants, and found ample encouragement for that nefarious traffic among the opulent Romans; but at last their depredations became so formidable, that Pompey was invested with extraordinary powers for their suppression, which he accomplished in forty days. He settled the surviving freebooters at Solæ, which he rebuilt and named Pompeiopolis. Cicero was proconsul of Cilicia (A.U.C. 702), and gained some successes over the mountaineers of Amanus, for which he was rewarded with a triumph. Many Jews were settled in Cilicia (Acts vi. 9).

According to the modern Turkish divisions of Asia Minor, Cilicia Proper belongs to the Pashalic of Adana; and Cilicia Trachea to the Liwah of Itchil in the Mousselimlik of Cyprus.

CIN'NAMON occurs in three places of Scripture; first, about 1600 years before the Christian era, in Exod. xxx. 23, where it is enumerated as one of the ingredients employed in the preparation of the holy anointing oil: 'Take thou also unto thee powerful spices, myrrh, and of sweet cinnamon (*kinnamon besem*) half as much (*i. e.* 250 shekels), together with sweet calamus and cassia.' It is next mentioned in Prov. vii. 17, and again in Cant. iv. 14; while in Rev. xxiii. 13, among the merchandise of Babylon, we have 'cinnamon, and odours, and ointments, and frankincense.'

Many writers have doubted whether the *kinnamon* of the Hebrews is the same article that we now call cinnamon. Others have doubted whether our cinnamon was at all known to the ancients. But the same thing has been said of almost every other drug which is noticed by them. If we were to put faith in all these doubts, we should be left without any substances possessed of sufficiently remarkable properties to have been articles of ancient commerce.

Cinnamon of the best quality is imported in the present day from Ceylon, and also from the Malabar coast, in consequence of the cinnamon plant having been introduced there from Ceylon. An inferior kind is also exported from the peninsula of India. From these countries the cinnamon and cassia of the ancients must most likely have been obtained, though both are also produced in the islands of Sumatra and Borneo, in China, and in Cochinchina. Cinnamon is imported in bales and chests—the bundles weighing about one pound each. The pieces consist of compound quills, are about three feet long, slender, and inclose within them several smaller quills. These are thin, smooth, of a brownish colour, of a warm, sweetish, and agreeable taste, and fragrant odour; but several kinds are known in modern markets, as they were in ancient times.

In Ceylon cinnamon is carefully cultivated, the best cinnamon gardens being on the south-western coast, where the soil is light and sandy, and the atmosphere moist from the prevalent southern winds. The plants begin to yield cinnamon when about six or seven years old, after which the shoots may be cut every three or four years. The best kinds of cinnamon are obtained from twigs and shoots; less than half, or more than two or three inches in diameter, are not peeled. 'The peeling is effected by making two opposite, or when the branch is thick, three or four longitudinal incisions, and then elevating the bark by introducing the peeling knife beneath it. In twenty-four hours the epidermis and greenish pulpy matter are carefully scraped off. In a few hours the smaller quills are introduced into the larger ones, and in this way congeries of quills are formed, often measuring forty inches in length. The bark is then dried in the sun, and afterwards made into bundles, with pieces of split bamboo twigs.' Besides cinnamon, an oil of cinnamon is obtained in Ceylon, by macerating the coarser pieces of the bark, after being reduced to a coarse powder, in sea-water, for two days, when both are submitted to distillation. A fatty substance is also obtained by bruising and boiling the riper fruit, when an oily body floats on the surface, which on cooling concretes into a dirty whitish, rather hard, fatty matter. Some camphor may be procured from the roots.

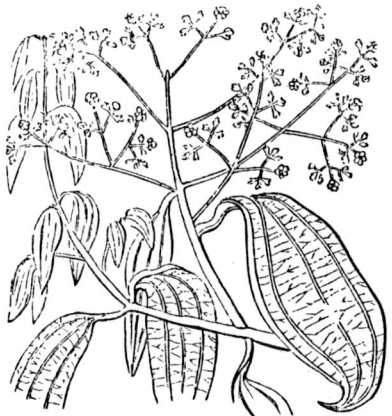

127. [Kinnamomum cassia.]

Cassia bark was distinguished with difficulty from cinnamon by the ancients. In the present day it is often sold for cinnamon; indeed, unless a purchaser specify *true* cinnamon, he will probably be supplied with nothing but cassia. It is made up into similar bundles with cinnamon, has the same general appearance, smell, and taste; but its substance is thicker and coarser, its colour darker, its flavour much less sweet and fine than that of Ceylon cinnamon, while it is more pungent, and is followed by a bitter taste; it is also less closely quilled, and breaks shorter than genuine cinnamon. Dr. Pereira, whose description we have adopted, has ascertained that cassia is imported into the London market from Bombay (the produce of the Malabar coast), and also from the Mauritius, Calcutta, Batavia, Singapore, the Philippine Islands, and Canton. Mr. Reeves says, 'Vast quantities both of cassia seeds (buds) and cassia lignea are annually brought to

Canton from the province of **Kwangse**, whose principal city (*Kweihin*, literally 'cassia forest') derives its name from the forests of cassia around it. The Chinese themselves use a much thicker bark, unfit for the European market.' The Malabar cassia lignea is thicker and coarser than that of China. From the various sources, independently of the different qualities, it is evident, as in the case of cinnamon, that the ancients might have been, as no doubt they were, acquainted with several varieties of cassia. These, we have no doubt, are yielded by more than one species. Mr. Marshall, from information obtained while he was staff-surgeon in Ceylon, maintained that cassia, or at least a part of it, was the coarser bark of the true cinnamon. Dr. Wight has ascertained that more than one species yields the cassia of Malabar, often called cinnamon. Besides cassia bark, there is also a cassia oil, and cassia buds, supposed to be produced by the same tree. There can be no reasonable doubt, as cinnamon and cassia were known to the Greeks, that they must have been known to the Hebrews also, as the commerce with India can be proved to have been much more ancient than is generally supposed.

CIN'NERETH, or CINNEROTH, one of the 'fenced cities' of the tribe of Naphtali (Josh. xix. 35; Deut. iii. 17; Josh. xi. 2). In the last of the texts cited it seems to indicate a district. It is also the earlier name of the lake Gennesareth (which is supposed to be a corruption of Cinnereth), from which we may collect that the town lay on the western border of the lake, and was of sufficient consequence to give its own name to it. It is even supposed that Cinnereth, afterwards Gennesareth, was the earlier name of the town of Tiberias, and under the latter change still extended its own denomination to the lake; nor is there anything improbable in this conjecture.

CIRCUMCI'SION. The history of Jewish Circumcision lies on the surface of the Old Testament. Abraham received the rite from Jehovah, Moses established it as a national ordinance, and Joshua carried it into effect before the Israelites entered the land of Canaan. Males only were subjected to the operation, and it was to be performed on the eighth day of the child's life: foreign slaves also were forced to submit to it, on entering an Israelite's family. Those who are unacquainted with other sources of information on the subject besides the Scriptures might easily suppose that the rite was original with Abraham, characteristic of his seed, and practised among those nations only who had learned it from them. This, however, appears not to have been the case.

First of all, *the Egyptians* were a circumcised people. It has been alleged by some writers that this was not true of the whole nation, but of the priests only. A great preponderance of argument, however, appears to us to prove that the rite was universal among the old Egyptians, as long as their native institutions flourished; although there is no question that, under Persian and Greek rule, it gradually fell into disuse, and was retained chiefly by the priests and by those who desired to cultivate ancient wisdom.

The Colchians, who, according to Herodotus, were a colony from Egypt, learnt the practice from the Egyptians, as also did the savage Troglodytes of Africa. Herodotus, moreover, tells us that the Ethiopians were also circumcised; and he was in doubt whether they had learned the rite from the Egyptians, or the Egyptians from them. By the Ethiopians we must understand him to mean the inhabitants of Meroë or Sennaar. In the present day the Coptic Church continues to practise it; the Abyssinian Christians do the same; and that it was *not* introduced among the latter with a Judaical Christianity appears from their performing it upon both sexes. Oldendorp describes the rite as widely spread through Western Africa—16° on each side of the Line—even among natives that are not Mohammedan. In later times it has been ascertained that it is practised by the Kafir nations in South Africa, whom Prichard supposes to form 'a great part of the native population of Africa to the southward of the Equator.'

How far the rite was extended through the Syro-Arabian races is uncertain, but there can be no doubt that it was widely diffused among them. The Philistines, in the days of Saul, were however uncircumcised; so also, says Herodotus, were all the Phœnicians who had intercourse with the Greeks. That the Canaanites, in the days of Jacob, were not all circumcised, is plain from the affair of Dinah and Shechem. The story of Zipporah (Exod. iv. 25), who did not circumcise her son until fear came over her, that Jehovah would slay her husband Moses, proves that the family of Jethro, the Midianite, had no fixed rule about it, although the Midianites are generally regarded as children of Abraham by Keturah. On the other hand, we have the distinct testimony of Josephus, that the Ishmaelite Arabs, inhabiting the district of Nabathæa, were circumcised after their thirteenth year. The fact that the books of Moses, of Joshua, and of Judges, never bestow the epithet *uncircumcised* as a reproach on any of the seven nations of Canaan, any more than on the Moabites or Ammonites, the Amalekites, the Midianites, or other inland tribes with whom they came into conflict, taken in connection with the circumstance, that as soon as the Philistines became prominent in the narrative, after the birth of Samson, this epithet is of rather common occurrence, and that the bringing back, as a trophy, the foreskins of slain enemies, never occurs except against the Philistines (1 Sam. xviii.), would lead us to conclude, that while the Philistines, like the Sidonians and the other maritime Syrian nations known to the Greeks, were wholly strangers to the practice, it was common among the Canaanites and all the more inland tribes.

How far the rite of circumcision spread over the south-west of Arabia no definite record subsists. The silence of the Koran confirms the statement of Abulfedà, that the custom is older than Mohammed, who, it would appear, in no respect regarded it as a religious rite. Nevertheless it has extended itself with the Mohammedan faith, as though it were a positive ordinance. Pocock cites a tradition, which ascribes to Mohammed the words—'Circumcision is an ordinance for men, and honourable in women.' This extension of the rite to the other sex might, in itself, satisfy us that it did not come to those nations from Abraham and Ishmael. We have already seen that Abyssinian circumcision has the same peculiarity: so that it is every way probable that Southern Arabia had the rite from the same source or influence as Ethiopia. In fact, the very closest relations are known to have subsisted between the nations on the opposite coasts of the Red Sea.

The moral meaning of the word 'uncircumcised' was a natural result of its having been made legally essential to Hebrew faith. 'Uncircumcised in heart and ears' was a metaphor to which a prophet would be carried, as necessarily as a Christian teacher to such phrases as 'unbaptized in soul,' or 'washed by regeneration.' If, however, we try to take a step farther back still, and ask *why* this ordinance in particular was selected, as so eminently essential to the seed of Abraham, we probably find that we have reached a point at which we must be satisfied with knowing the fact without the reason. *Every* external ordinance, as for instance baptism, must have more or less that is arbitrary in it. It is, however, abundantly plain that circumcision was *not* intended to separate the Jews from other nations generally, for it could not do so: and, least of all, from the Egyptians, as the words in Joshua (v. 9) show. Rather, it was a well known and already understood *symbol of purity*.

CISTERN. In a country which has scarcely more than one perennial stream, where fountains are not abundant, and where the months of summer pass without rain, the preservation of the rain-water in cisterns must always have been a matter of vast importance, not only in the pasture-grounds, but in gardens, and, above all, in towns. Hence the frequent mention of cisterns in Scripture, and more especially of those which are found in the open country. These were, it seems, the property of those by whom they were formed (Num. xxi. 22). They are usually little more than large pits, but sometimes take the character of extensive subterraneous vaults, open only by a small mouth, like that of a well. They are filled with rain-water, and (where the climate allows) with snow during winter, and are then closed at the mouth with large flat stones, over which sand is spread in such a way as to prevent their being easily discovered. If by any chance the waters which the shepherd has thus treasured up are lost by means of an earthquake or some other casualty, or are stolen, both he and his flocks are exposed to great and imminent danger; as are also travellers who hasten to a cistern and find its waters gone. For this reason a failure of water is used as the image of any great calamity (Isa. xli. 17, 18; xliv. 3). There is usually a large deposit of mud at the bottom of these cisterns, so that he who falls into them, even when they are without water, is liable to perish miserably (Gen. xxxvii. 22, *sq.*; Jer. xxxviii. 6; Lam. iii. 53; Ps. xl. 2; lxix. 15). Cisterns were sometimes used, when empty, as prisons, and indeed prisons which were constructed under ground received the same name (Gen. xxxix. 20; xl. 15).

In cities the cisterns were works of much labour, for they were either hewn in the rocks or surrounded with subterraneous walls, and lined with a fine incrustation. The system which in this respect formerly prevailed in Palestine is, doubtless, the same that exists at present; and

indeed there is every probability that most of the cisterns now in use were constructed in very ancient times. Professor Robinson assures us, that 'the main dependence of Jerusalem at the present day is on its cisterns; and this has probably always been the case.' He then mentions the immense cisterns now and anciently existing within the area of the Temple: supplied partly by rain water, and partly by an aqueduct from Solomon's Pools, and which, of themselves, would furnish a tolerable supply in case of a siege. But, in addition to these, almost every private house in Jerusalem, of any size, is understood to have at least one or more cisterns, excavated in the soft limestone rock on which the city is built. The cisterns have usually merely a round opening at the top, sometimes built up with stonework above, and furnished with a curb and a wheel for the bucket; so that they have externally much the appearance of an ordinary well. The water is conducted into them from the roofs of the houses during the rainy season; and, with proper care, remains pure and sweet during the whole summer and autumn. In this manner most of the larger houses and the public buildings are supplied. The Latin convent, in particular, is said to be amply furnished; and in seasons of drought is able to deal out a sufficiency for all the Christian inhabitants of the city.

Most of these cisterns have undoubtedly come down from ancient times; and their immense extent furnishes a full solution of the question as to the supply of water for the city. Under the disadvantages of its position in this respect, Jerusalem must necessarily have always been dependent on its cisterns; and a city which thus annually laid in its supply for seven or eight months could never be overtaken by a want of water during a siege. Nor is this a trait peculiar to the Holy City; for the case is the same throughout all the hill country of Judah and Benjamin. Fountains and streams are few, as compared with Europe and America; and the inhabitants, therefore, collect water during the rainy season in tanks and cisterns in the cities, in the fields, and along the high roads, for the sustenance of themselves and of their flocks and herds, and for the comfort of the passing traveller. Many, if not the most, of these are obviously antique; and they exist not unfrequently along the ancient roads which are now deserted. Thus, on the long-forgotten way from Jericho to Bethel, 'broken cisterns' of high antiquity are found at regular intervals. That Jerusalem was thus actually supplied of old with water is apparent also from the numerous remains of ancient cisterns still existing in the tract north of the city, which was once enclosed within the walls.

CITIES OF REFUGE. Places of refuge where, under the cover of religion, the guilty and the unfortunate might find shelter and protection were not unknown among the ancient heathen. The right of shelter and impunity was enjoyed by certain places reputed sacred, such as groves, temples, and altars. This protective power commonly spread itself over a considerable district round the holy spot, and was watched over and preserved by severe penalties. Among the Greeks and Romans the number of these places of asylum became in process of time very great, and led, by abuse, to a fresh increase of criminals. Tiberius, in consequence, caused a solemn inquiry into their effects to be made, which resulted in a diminution of their number and a limitation of their privileges.

This pagan custom passed into Christianity. As early as Constantine the Great, Christian churches were asylums for the unfortunate persons whom an outraged law or powerful enemies pursued. Theodosius, in 431, extended this privilege to the houses, gardens, and other places which were under the jurisdiction of the churches, and the synod of Toledo, in 681, widened the right of asylum to thirty paces from every church. Since then this ecclesiastical privilege prevailed in the whole of Catholic Christendom, and was preserved undiminished, at least in Italy, so long as the papal independence remained. The right acted beneficially in ages when violence and revenge predominated, and fixed habitations were less common than now; but its tendency to transfer power from the magistrate to the priesthood was injurious to the inviolability of law and the steady administration of justice. It has accordingly in recent times been abrogated by most governments.

Among the Jews the 'cities of refuge' bore some resemblance to the asylum of the classic nations, but were happily exempt from the evil consequences to which reference has been made, and afford, even to the present day, no mean proof of the superior wisdom and benignant spirit of the Jewish laws.

The institution was framed with a view to abate the evils which ensued from the old established rights of the blood-avenger [BLOOD-REVENGE], and thereby to further the prevalence in the nation of a mild, gentle, and forgiving spirit.

From the laws on this point (Exod. xxi. 13; Num. xxxv. 9-34; Deut. xix. 1-13) it appears that Moses set apart out of the sacerdotal cities six as 'cities of refuge.' There were, on the eastern side of the Jordan, three, namely, 'Bezer in the wilderness, in the plain country of the Reubenites, and Ramoth in Gilead of the Gadites, and Golan in Bashan of the Manassites' (Deut. iv. 43); on the western side three, namely, 'Kedesh in Galilee in Mount Naphtali, and Shechem in Mount Ephraim, and Kirjath-arba, which is Hebron, in the mountain of Judah' (Josh. xx. 7). If found desirable, then other cities might be added. An inspection of the map will show how wisely these places were chosen so as to make a city of refuge easy of access from all parts of the land. To any one of these cities a person who had unawares and unintentionally slain any one might flee, and if he reached it before he was overtaken by the avenger of blood, he was safe within its shelter, provided he did not remove more than a thousand yards from its circuit, nor quit the refuge till the decease of the high-priest under whom the homicide had taken place. If, however, he transgressed these provisions, the avenger might lawfully put him to death. The roads leading to the cities of refuge were to be kept in good repair. Before, however, the fugitive could avail himself of the shelter conceded by the laws, he was to undergo a solemn trial, and make it appear to the satisfaction of the magistrates of the place where the homicide was committed that it was purely accidental. Should he, however, be found to have been guilty of murder, he was delivered 'into the hand of the avenger of blood, that he might die.' And the Israelites were strictly forbidden to spare him either from considerations of pity or in consequence of any pecuniary ransom. This disallowal of a compensation by money in the case of murder shows a just regard for human life, and appears much to the advantage of the Hebrew legislation when compared with the practice of other countries (Athens, for instance, and Islam), in which pecuniary atonements were allowed, if not encouraged, and where, in consequence, the life of the poor must have been in as great jeopardy as the character of the wealthy.

The asylum afforded by Moses displays the same benign regard to human life in respect of the homicide himself. Had no obstacle been put in the way of the Goel, instant death would have awaited any one who had the misfortune to occasion the death of another. By his wise arrangements, however, Moses interposed a seasonable delay, and enabled the manslayer to appeal to the laws and justice of his country. Momentary wrath could hardly execute its fell purposes, and a suitable refuge was provided for the guiltless and unfortunate.

Yet as there is a wide space between the innocence of mere homicide and the guilt of actual murder, in which various degrees of blame might easily exist, so the legislator took means to make the condition of the manslayer less happy than it was before the act or the mischance, lest entire impunity might lead to the neglect of necessary precaution and care. With great propriety, therefore, was the homicide made to feel some legal inconvenience. Accordingly he was removed from his patrimony, restricted in his sphere of locomotion, affected indirectly in his pecuniary interests, and probably reduced from an affluent or an easy station to one of service and labour. The benefit of the protection afforded was common to strangers and sojourners with native Israelites.

What ensues rests on the authority of the Rabbins. In order to give the fugitive all possible advantage in his flight, it was the business of the Sanhedrim to make the roads that led to the cities of refuge convenient by enlarging them and removing every obstruction that might hurt his foot or hinder his speed. No hillock was left, no river was allowed over which there was not a bridge, and the road was at least two and thirty cubits broad. At every turning there were posts erected bearing the words *Refuge, Refuge,* to guide the unhappy man in his flight; and two students in the law were appointed to accompany him, that, if the avenger should overtake him before he reached the city, they might attempt to pacify him till the legal investigation could take place.

When once settled in the city of refuge, the manslayer had a convenient habitation assigned him gratuitously, and the citizens were to teach him some trade whereby he might support himself. To render his confinement more easy, the mothers of the high-priests used to feed and clothe these unfortunate fugitives, that they might not be impatient and pray for the death of their sons, on whose decease they were restored to their liberty and their property. If the slayer died in the city of refuge before he was released, his bones were delivered to his relations, after the death of the high-priest, to be buried in the sepulchre of his fathers.

In addition to this right of asylum, a custom appears to have prevailed from very early times, both among the chosen people and the nations of the world, of fleeing, in case of personal danger, to the altar. With the Jews it was customary for the fugitive to lay hold of the horns of the altar, whether in the tabernacle or temple; by which, however, shelter and security were obtained only for those who had committed sins of ignorance or inadvertence (Exod. xxi. 14; 1 Kings i. 50; ii. 28). From the two last passages it seems that state-criminals also sought the protection of the altar, probably more from the force of custom than any express law. Their safety, however, depended on the will of the king; for in the passages referred to it appears that in one case (that of Adonijah) life was spared, but in the other (that of Joab) it was taken away even 'by the altar.' Compare Matt. xxiii. 35.

CITIZENSHIP. Strict isolation did by no means, as some suppose, form the leading principle in the system of theocracy as laid down by Moses, since even non-Israelites not only were allowed to reside in Palestine, but had the fullest protection of the law, equally with the descendants of Abraham (Exod. xii. 19; Lev. xxiv. 22; Num. xv. 15; xxxv. 15; Deut. i. 16; xxiv. 17: the law of usury, Deut. xxiii. 20, made, however, an exception), and were besides recommended in general terms by Moses to humanity and charity (Exod. xxii. 21; xxiii. 9; Lev. xix. 33, 34; Deut. x. 18; comp. Jer. vii. 6; Mal. iii. 5), as well as to a participation in certain prerogatives granted to the poor of the land, such as a share in the tithe and feast-offering, and the harvest in the Jubilee-year (Deut. xiv. 29; xvi. 10, 14; xxvi. 11; Lev. xxv. 6). In return, it was required on the part of non-Israelites not to commit acts by which the religious feelings of the people might be hurt (Exod. xx. 10; Lev. xvii. 10; xviii. 26; xx. 2; xxiv. 16; Deut. v. 14. The eating of an animal which had died a natural death, Deut xiv. 21, seems to have been the sole exception). The advantage the Jew had over the Gentile was thus strictly spiritual, in his being a citizen, a member of the theocracy, of the community of God, on whom positive laws were enjoined. But even to this spiritual privilege Gentiles were admitted under certain restrictions (Deut. xxiii. 1-9). The only nations that were altogether excluded from the citizenship of the theocracy by especial command of the Lord, were the Ammonites and Moabites, from a feeling of vengeance against them: and in the same situation were all castrated persons, and bastards, from a feeling of disgrace and shame (Deut. xxiii. 1-6). In the time of Solomon, no less than 153,600 strangers were resident in Palestine (2 Chron. ii. 17).

Roman citizenship (Acts xxii. 28), was granted in the times of the Emperors to whole provinces and cities, as also to single individuals, for some service rendered to the state or the imperial family, or even for a certain sum of money (Acts

xxii. 28). The Apostle Paul was a Roman citizen by family (Acts, l c), and hence his protesting against corporal or capital punishment.

CLAU'DA, a small island off the S.W. coast of Crete, mentioned in Acts xxvii. 16. It now bears the name of Gozzo.

CLAU'DIA, a Christian female of Rome, mentioned in 2 Tim iv 21.

CLAU'DIUS, the fifth Roman emperor, and successor of Caligula, A.D. 41-54 (Acts xi. 28; xviii. 2). His full name was Tiberius Claudius Nero Germanicus. Previously to his accession he led rather a dissolute life, and the throne was in a great measure secured to him through the address and solicitations of Herod Agrippa. This obligation he returned by great and peculiar favours to that personage: and the Jews were generally treated with indulgence till the ninth year of his reign, when those who abode at Rome were all banished thence (Acts xviii. 2). Several famines occurred under Claudius, one of which, in the fourth year of his reign, extended to Palestine and Syria, and appears to be that which was foretold by Agabus (Acts xi. 28).

CLAUDIUS LYSIAS. [LYSIAS.]

CLAUDIUS FELIX. [FELIX.]

CLAY, a substance frequently mentioned in Scripture, chiefly with reference to its employment by the potter, the elegant and useful forms assumed by the rude material under his hands supplying a significant emblem of the Divine power over the destinies of man (Isa. lxiv. 8; Rom. ix. 21). A remarkable allusion to the use of clay in sealing occurs in Job xxxviii. 14, ' He turneth it as clay to the seal.' This may be explained by reference to the ancient practice of impressing unburnt bricks with certain marks and inscriptions which were obviously made by means of a large seal or stamp. We trace this in the bricks of Egypt and Babylon [BRICKS]. Modern Oriental usages supply another illustration. Travellers, when entering the khans in towns, often observe the rooms in which goods have been left in charge of the *khanjee* sealed on the outside with clay. A piece of clay is placed over the lock, and impressed by a large wooden stamp or seal.

CLE'MENT, a person mentioned by Paul (Phil. iv. 3), as one whose name was in the book of life. For the meaning of this phrase, see BOOK OF LIFE. This Clement was, by the ancient church, identified with the bishop of Rome of the same name; and that opinion has naturally been followed by Roman Catholic expositors. It cannot now be proved incorrect; but the suspicion exists that the case here may be as with many other names in the New Testament, which have been assigned to celebrated persons of a later period. Clement is said to have lived to the third year of the emperor Trajan (A.D. 100), when he suffered martyrdom.

1. CLEOPAS, one of the two disciples to whom Jesus appeared in the way to Emmaus (Luke xxiv. 18). He is not to be confounded with the other Cleophas, who was also called Alphæus.

2. CLEOPHAS, or rather Clopas, who was also called Alphæus, which see.

CLIMATE. [PALESTINE.]

CLOUD. The allusions to clouds in Scripture, as well as their use in symbolical language, must be understood with reference to the nature of the climate, where the sky scarcely exhibits the trace of a cloud from the beginning of May to the end of September, during which period clouds so rarely appear, and rains so seldom fall, as to be considered phenomena—as was the case with the harvest rain which Samuel invoked (1 Sam. xii. 17, 18), and with the little cloud, not larger than a man's hand, the appearance of which in the west was immediately noticed as something remarkable not only in itself, but as a sure harbinger of rain (1 Kings xviii. 44).

As in such climates clouds refreshingly veil the oppressive glories of the sun, clouds often symbolize the Divine presence, as indicating the splendour, insupportable to man, of that glory which they wholly or partially conceal (Exod. xvi. 10; xxxiii. 9: xxxiv. 5; xl. 34, 35; Num. xi 25; xxi. 5; Job xxii. 14; Ps. xviii. 11, 12; xcvii. 2; civ. 3; Isa. xix. 1; Matt. xvii. 5; xxiv. 30, &c.; Acts i. 9; Rev. i. 7: xiv. 14, 16). Somewhat allied to this use is that which makes clouds the symbols of the Divine power (2 Sam. xxii. 12; Ps. lxviii. 34; lxxxix. 6; civ. 3; Nahum i. 3).

Clouds are also the symbol of armies and multitudes of people (Jer. iv. 13; Isa. lx. 8; Heb. xii. 1).

There are many other dispersed symbolical allusions to clouds in Scripture not coming under these descriptions; but their purport is in every case too obvious to need explanation (see particularly Prov. xvi. 16; Eccles. xii. 2; Isa. iv. 5; xliv. 22; 2 Pet. ii. 17: Jude 12).

CNI'DUS, otherwise GNIDUS, a town and peninsula of Doris in Caria, jutting out from the south-west part of Asia Minor, between the islands of Rhodes and Cos. It was celebrated for the worship of Venus. The Romans wrote to this city in favour of the Jews (1 Macc. xv. 23), and St. Paul passed it in his way to Rome (Acts xxvii. 7).

COAL. It is generally assumed that, in those numerous passages of our version in which the word coal occurs, *charcoal*, or some other kind of *artificial* fuel, is to be understood; at all events, that the word has not its English meaning. The idea is founded upon the supposition that fossil coal was not known to the ancients as an article of fuel, and especially to the ancient inhabitants of Syria, whose country it is generally imagined did not produce it. But the existence of coal in *Syria* is now placed beyond a doubt. Many indications of coal occur in the Lebanon mountains; the seams of this mineral even protrude through the superincumbent strata in various directions. At Cornale, eight hours from Beirout, at 2500 feet above the level of the sea, where the coal seams are three feet in thickness, a mine is actually being worked by order of Mohammed Ali, in which more than 100 men are employed. The coal is of good quality, and mixed with iron pyrites. In 1837 the quantity of coal extracted was 14,700 cantars of 217 okes, each making about 4000 tons. A furnace for smelting the ore and a railroad to convey the coals to Beirout were then in contemplation.

It appears from the testimony of Theophrastus that pit-coal was used by artificers in *Greece*, nearly 300 years B.C., and the well-ascertained existence of coal in *Syria*, emerging to the very surface, may, in conjunction with some particulars respecting the mention of coal in the Scriptures, tend to show the possibility that coal, in the proper sense, was not wholly unknown or unemployed by the ancient Hebrews, &c.

COCK. It is somewhat singular that this bird and poultry in general should not be distinctly noticed in the Hebrew Scriptures. They were, it may be surmised, unknown in Egypt when the Mosaic law was promulgated, and, though imported soon after, they always remained in an undetermined condition, neither clean nor unclean, but liable to be declared either, by decisions swayed by prejudice, or by fanciful analogies; perhaps chiefly the latter; because poultry are devourers of unclean animals, scorpions, sculopendra, small lizards, and young serpents of every kind.

But although rearing of common fowls was not encouraged by the Hebrew population, it is evidently drawing inferences beyond their proper bounds, when it is asserted that they were unknown in Jerusalem, where civil wars, and Greek and Roman dominion, had greatly affected the national manners. In the denials of Peter, described in the four Gospels, where the cock-crowing is mentioned by our Lord, the words are plain and direct, not we think admitting of cavil, or of being taken to signify anything but the real voice of the bird, in its literal acceptation, and not as denoting the sound of a trumpet, so called, because it proclaimed a watch in the night; for, to what else than a real hen and her brood does our Saviour allude in Luke xiii. 34, where the text is proof that the image of poultry was familiar to the disciples, and consequently that they were not rare in Judea? To the present time in the East, and on the Continent of Europe, this bird is still often kept, as amongst the Celtæ, not so much for food as for the purpose of announcing the approach and dawn of day.

COCKATRICE. [SERPENT.]

COCKCROWING. The cock usually crows several times about midnight, and again about break of day. The latter time, because he then crows loudest, and his 'shrill clarion' is most useful by summoning man to his labours, obtained the appellation of *the* cockcrowing emphatically, and by way of eminence; though sometimes the distinctions of the *first* and *second* cockcrowing are met with in Jewish and heathen writers. These times, and these names for them, were, no doubt, some of the most ancient divisions of the night adopted in the East, where 'the bird of dawning' is most probably indigenous. In our Lord's time the Jews had evidently adopted the Greek and Roman division of the night into four periods, or watches; each consisting of three hours; the first beginning at six in the evening (Luke xii. 38; Matt. xiv. 25; Mark vi. 48; viii. 35).

It has been considered a contradiction that Matthew (xxvi. 34) records our Lord to have said to Peter, 'Before the cock crow thou shalt deny me thrice;' whereas St. Mark (xiv. 30) says, 'Before the cock crow thrice.' But Matthew, giving only the *general sense* of the admonition (as also Luke xxii. 34; John xiii. 38), evidently alludes to that only which was *customarily* called *the* cockcrowing, but Mark, who wrote under Peter's inspection, more accurately recording *the very words*, mentions the *two* cockcrowings.

COCKLE. This word occurs in the singular

form in Job xxxi. 40, and in the plural form in Isaiah v. 2 and 4, where, however, it is rendered 'wild grapes.' It is probable that the same plant is referred to in these two passages; but difficulties have here, as elsewhere, been experienced in ascertaining the precise plant intended. All, however, are agreed that some useless, if not noxious, herb must be understood in both cases. The probability is in favour of its being the ox's grape or wolf-grape, either of which somewhat resembles the grape in the form of its berried fruit, but is very different in its properties, being narcotic and poisonous. Hasselquist, in reference to the passage of Isaiah, says, 'I am inclined to believe that the prophet here means the hoary nightshade, because it is common in Egypt and Palestine, and the Arabian name agrees well with it. The Arabs call it *anib-el-dib, i. e.* wolf-grape. The prophet could not have found a plant more opposite to the vine than this, for it grows much in the vineyards, and is very pernicious to them, wherefore they root it out: it likewise resembles a vine by its shrubby stalk.'

CŒLESY'RIA, the *hollow* Syria. This name, which is evidently of Grecian origin in the times of the Seleucidæ, was originally applied to the valley lying between the mountain-ranges of Libanus and Anti-Libanus. It was also used to denote the whole tract of country (with the exception of Judæa and Phœnicia) reaching from Seleucis to Arabia and the confines of Egypt. In the time of David, Cœlesyria was probably included in 'Syria of Damascus,' which was conquered by that monarch (2 Sam. viii. 6), but recovered from Solomon by Rezon the son of Eliadah (1 Kings xi. 24). The possession of it was an object of many struggles between the Seleucidæ and the kings of Egypt. Bochart supposes that Syrophœnicia is the same as Cœlesyria. Scythopolis and Gadara are mentioned by Josephus as cities of Cœlesyria. Under the Emperor Dioclesian, Phœnice and Cœlesyria formed one province, called Phœnicia Libanica. Under the present Turkish government the western part of Cœlesyria is in the Pashalic of Saide, and the eastern in the Pashalic of Damascus.

COFFER. The name given in the Authorized Version to the receptacle (1 Sam. vi. 8, 11, 15) which the Philistines placed beside the ark when they sent it home, and in which they deposited the golden mice and emerods that formed their trespass-offering. It is supposed to be the same, or nearly the same thing, as the Arabian *rijaza*, which is a kind of wallet, into which stones are put: it is hung to one of the two sides of the haudaj [a litter borne by a camel or mule] when it inclines towards the other.

COFFIN. [BURIAL.]

COLONY. This distinction is applied to Philippi in Macedonia (Acts xvi. 12). Augustus Cæsar had deported to Macedonia most of the Italian communities which had espoused the cause of Antony; by which means the towns of Philippi, Dyrrachium, &c., acquired the rank of Roman colonies, which possessed the privilege of a free municipal constitution, such as was customary in Italy, in exemption from personal and land taxes, and in the commerce of the soil, or the right of selling the land.

COLOS'SÆ, a city of Phrygia, on the river Lycus (now Gorduk), not far from its confluence with the Mæander, and near the towns of Laodicea, Apamea, and Hieropolis (Col. ii. 1; iv. 13, 15). A Christian church was formed here very early, probably by Epaphras (Col. i. 7; iv. 12, *sq.*), consisting of Jews and Gentiles, to whom Paul, who does not appear to have ever visited Colossæ in person (Col. ii. 1), addressed an Epistle from Rome. Not long after, the town was, together with Laodicea and Hierapolis, destroyed by an earthquake. This, according to Eusebius, was in the ninth year of Nero; but the town must have been immediately rebuilt, for in his twelfth year it continued to be named as a flourishing place. It still subsists as a village named

Khonas. The huge range of Mount Cadmus rises immediately behind the village, close to which there is in the mountain an immense perpendicular chasm, affording an outlet for a wide mountain torrent. The ruins of an old castle stand on the summit of the rock forming the left side of this chasm. There are some traces of ruins and fragments of stone in the neighbourhood, but barely more than sufficient to attest the existence of an ancient site; and that this site was that of Colossæ is satisfactorily established by the Rev. F. V. J. Arundell, whose book (*Discoveries in Asia Minor*) contains an ample description of the place.

COLOS'SIANS, EPISTLE TO THE. That this Epistle is the genuine production of the Apostle Paul is proved by the most satisfactory evidence, and has never indeed been seriously called in question. It is less certain, however, *when* and *where* it was composed by him. The common opinion is that he wrote it at Rome during his imprisonment in that city (Acts xxviii. 16, 30), and although it has been controverted, the balance of evidence is decidedly in its favour. The Epistle to the Ephesians and to Philemon are supposed to have been written about the same time.

In what *order* these three epistles were written, it is not possible clearly to determine. Between that to the Colossians and that to the Ephesians the coincidences are so close and numerous that the one must have been written immediately after the other, whilst the mind of the Apostle was occupied with the same leading train of thought. By the greater part the priority is assigned to the Epistle to the Colossians. The Epistle to Philemon being a mere friendly letter, intended chiefly to facilitate the reconciliation of Onesimus to his master, was probably written immediately before the departure of the party by whom it was to be carried.

The Epistle to the Colossians was written, apparently, in consequence of information received by Paul through Epaphras concerning the internal state of their church (i. 6, 8). Whether the Apostle had ever himself before this time visited Colossæ is matter of uncertainty and dispute. From ch. ii. 1, where he says, ' I would that ye knew what great conflict I have for you and for them at Laodicea, and for as many as have not seen my face in the flesh,' &c., it has by some been very confidently concluded that he had not. To this it is replied by Theodoret, Lardner, and others, that Paul does not intend to *include* the Colossians and Laodiceans among those who had not seen his face, but specifies the latter as a distinct class; as is evident, they think, from his using the *third* person in ver. 2. This latter consideration, however, is of no weight, for the use of the third person here is easily accounted for on the principle that the pronoun takes the person of the nearer noun rather than that of the more remote (cf. Gal. i. 8); and it certainly would be absurd to maintain that all contained in the second verse has no relation to the Colossians and Laodiceans, notwithstanding the reference to them in ver. 1, and again in ver. 4. As respects the words in ver. 1, they will, in a mere philological point of view, bear to be understood in either way. It has been urged, however, that when, in ver. 5, the Apostle says, ' though I am absent in the flesh, yet am I with you in the spirit,' &c., his language is strongly indicative of his having formerly been amongst the Colossians, for the verb rendered ' I am absent ' is used properly only of such absence as arises from the person's *having gone away from* the place of which his absence is predicted. In support of the same view have been adduced Paul's having twice visited and gone through Phrygia (Acts xvi. 6; xviii. 23), in which Colossæ was a chief city; his familiar acquaintance with so many of the Colossian Christians, Epaphras, Archippus, Philemon (who was one of his own converts, Phil. 13, 19), and Apphia, probably the wife of Philemon [APPHIA]: his apparent acquaintance with Onesimus, the servant of Philemon, so that he recognised him again at Rome; the cordiality of friendship and interest subsisting between the Apostle and the Colossians as a body (Col. i. 24, 25; ii. 1; iv. 7, &c.); the Apostle's familiar acquaintance with their state and relations (i. 6; ii. 6, 7, &c.); and their knowledge of so many of his companions, and especially of Timothy, whose name the Apostle associates with his own at the commencement of the Epistle, a circumstance which is worthy of consideration from this, that Timothy was the companion of Paul during his first tour through Phrygia, when probably the Gospel was first preached at Colossæ. Of these considerations it must be allowed that the cumulative force is very strong in favour of

the opinion that the Christians at Colossæ had been privileged to enjoy the personal ministrations of Paul. At the same time, if the Colossians and Laodiceans are not to be included among those of whom Paul says they had not seen his face, it seems unaccountable that, in writing to the Colossians, he should have referred to this class at all. If, moreover, he had visited the Colossians, was it not strange that he should have no deeper feeling towards them than he had for the multitudes of Christians scattered over the world whose faces he had never seen? In fine, as it is quite *possible* that Paul may have been twice in Phrygia without being once in Colossæ, is it not easy also to account for his interest in the church at Colossæ, his knowledge of their affairs, and his acquaintance with individuals among them, by supposing that members of that church had frequently visited him in different places, though he had never visited Colossæ?

A great part of this Epistle is directed against certain false teachers who had crept into the church at Colossæ. To what class these teachers belonged has not been fully determined. Some contend that they were disciples of John the Baptist; others, with more show of reason, conclude that they were Essenes. The most probable opinion is that they were a party of speculatists who endeavoured to combine the doctrines of Oriental theosophy and asceticism with Christianity, and promised thereby to their disciples a deeper insight into the spiritual world, and a fuller approximation to heavenly purity and intelligence, than simple Christianity could yield. Against this party the Apostle argues by reminding the Colossians that in Jesus Christ, as set before them in the Gospel, they had all that they required—that he was the image of the invisible God, that he was before all things, that by him all things consist, that they were complete in him, and that he would present them to God holy, unblamable, and unreprovable, provided they continued stedfast in the faith. He then shows that the prescriptions of a mere carnal asceticism are not worthy of being submitted to by Christians; and concludes by directing their attention to the elevated principles which should regulate the conscience and conduct of such, and the duties of social and domestic life to which these would prompt.

In the conclusion of the Epistle, the Apostle, after sending to the Colossians the salutations of himself and others who were with him, enjoins the Colossians to send this Epistle to the Laodiceans, and that they likewise should read ' *that from Laodicea.*' It is disputed whether by these concluding words Paul intends an Epistle from him to the Laodiceans or one from the Laodiceans to him. The former seems the more probable interpretation of the Apostle's words; for supposing him to refer to a letter from the Laodiceans to him, the questions arise, How were the Colossians to procure this unless he himself sent it to them? And of what use would such a document be to them? To this latter question it has been replied that probably the letter from the Laodiceans contained some statements which influenced the Apostle in writing to the Colossians, and which required to be known before his letter in reply could be perfectly un derstood. But this is said without the slightest shadow of reason from the Epistle before us; and it is opposed by the fact that the Laodicean epistle was to be used by the Colossians *after* they had read that to themselves. It seems, upon the whole, most likely that Paul in this passage refers to an epistle sent by him to the church in Laodicea at the same time with that to the church at Colossæ. It is probable also that this Epistle is now lost, though the suggestion of Grotius that it was the same with the Canonical Epistle to the Ephesians has found some advocates [EPHESI-ANS, EPISTLE TO THE]. The extant Epistle to the Laodiceans is on all hands allowed to be a clumsy forgery.

COMFORTER (*Paracletus*). The word thus rendered is applied to Christ in 1 John ii 1. Indeed, in that famous passage in which Christ promises the Holy Spirit as a paraclete to his sorrowing disciples, he takes the title himself: 'I will send you *another* paraclete' (John xiv. 16), implying that he was himself one, and that on his departure he would send another. The question then is, In what sense does Christ denominate himself and the Spirit sent from him and the Father, *paraclete?* Origen explains the term where it is applied to the Holy Spirit by 'Consolator,' while in 1 John ii. 1, he adopts the signification of 'Deprecator.' Others would translate it 'teacher.' But as both of these renderings are open to serious objections, the balance is in favour of a third sense, which is that of 'assistant,' 'helper,' 'advocate' (intercessor). This view is supported by Rom. viii. 26, and, which is still more to the purpose, is appropriate to all the passages in the New Testament where the word occurs. The Authorized Version renders the word by 'advocate' in 1 John ii. 1, but in other places (John xiv. 16, 26; xv 26; xvi. 7) by 'comforter.' How much better, however, the more extensive term 'helper' (including teacher, monitor, advocate) agrees with these passages than the narrow term 'comforter, may be shown by a single instance. Jesus says to his disciples, 'I will send you *another* paraclete' (John xiv 16), implying that he himself had been such to them. But he had not been in any distinguishing sense a 'comforter' or 'consoler,' because, having Him present with them, they had not mourned (Matt. ix. 15). But he had been eminently a helper, in the extensive sense which has been indicated; and such as he had been to them—to teach, to guide, and to uphold—the Holy Spirit would become to them after his removal

COMMERCE. The idea conveyed by this word is represented in the Sacred Writings by the word trade.

Commerce, in its usual acceptation, means the exchange of one thing for another—the exchange of what we have to spare for what we want, in whatever country it is produced. The origin of commerce must have been nearly coeval with the world. As pasturage and agriculture were the only employments of the first inhabitants, so cattle, flocks, and the fruits of the earth were the only objects of the first commerce, or that species of it called barter. It would appear that some progress had been made in manufactures in the ages before the flood. The building of a city or village by Cain, however insignificant the houses may have been, sup-

poses the existence of some mechanical knowledge. The musical instruments, such as harps and organs, the works in brass and in iron exhibited by the succeeding generations, confirm the belief that the arts were considerably advanced. The construction of Noah's ark, a ship of three decks, covered over with pitch, and much larger than any modern effort of architecture, proves that many separate trades were at that period carried on. There must have been parties who supplied Noah and his three sons with the great quantity and variety of materials which they required, and this they would do in exchange for other commodities and perhaps money. That enormous pile of building, the tower of Babel, was constructed of bricks, the process of making which, appears to have been well understood.

Such of the descendants of Noah as lived near the water may be presumed to have made use of vessels built in imitation of the ark—if, as some think, that was the first floating vessel ever seen in the world—but on a smaller scale, for the purpose of crossing rivers. In the course of time the descendants of his son Japhet settled in 'the isles of the Gentiles,' by which are understood the islands at the east end of the Mediterranean sea, and those between Asia Minor and Greece, whence their colonies spread into Greece, Italy, and other western lands.

Sidon, which afterwards became so celebrated for the wonderful mercantile exertions of its inhabitants, was founded about 2200 years before the Christian era. The neighbouring mountains, being covered with excellent cedar-trees, furnished the best and most durable timber for ship-building. The inhabitants of Sidon accordingly built numerous ships, and exported the produce of the adjoining country, and the various articles of their own manufacture, such as fine linen, embroidery, tapestry, metals, glass, both coloured and figured, cut, or carved, and even mirrors. They were unrivalled by the inhabitants of the Mediterranean coasts in works of taste, elegance, and luxury. Their great and universally acknowledged pre-eminence in the arts procured for the Phœnicians, whose principal seaport was Sidon, the honour of being esteemed, among the Greeks and other nations, as the inventors of commerce, ship-building, navigation, the application of astronomy to nautical purposes, and particularly as the discoverers of several stars nearer to the north pole than and that were known to other nations; of naval war, writing, arithmetic, book-keeping, measures and weights; to which it is probable they might have added money.

Egypt appears to have excelled all the neighbouring countries in agriculture, and particularly in its abundant crops of corn The fame of its fertility induced Abraham to remove thither with his numerous family (Gen. xii. 10).

The earliest accounts of bargain and sale reach no higher than the time of Abraham, and his transaction with Ephron. He is said to have weighed unto him '400 shekels of silver, current money with the merchant' (Gen. xxiii. 16). The word merchant implies that the standard of money was fixed by usage among merchants, who comprised a numerous and respectable class of the community. Manufactures were by this time so far advanced, that not only those more immediately connected with agriculture, such as flour ground from corn, wine, oil, butter, and also the most necessary articles of clothing and furniture, but even those of luxury and magnificence, were much in use, as appears by the ear-rings, bracelets of gold and of silver, and other precious things presented by Abraham's steward to Rebekah (Gen. xxiv. 22, 53).

In the book of Job, whose author, in the opinion of the most learned commentators, resided in Arabia, and was contemporary with the earlier portion of Biblical history, much light is thrown upon the commerce, manufactures, and science of the age and country in which he lived. There is mention of gold, iron, brass, lead, crystal, jewels, the art of weaving, merchants, gold brought from Ophir, which implies commerce with a remote country, and topazes from Ethiopia; ship-building, so far improved that some ships were distinguished for the velocity of their motion; writing in a book, and engraving letters or writing on plates of lead and on stone with iron pens, and also seal-engraving; fishing with hooks, and nets, and spears; musical instruments, the harp, and organ; astronomy, and names given to particular stars. These notices tend to prove that, although the patriarchal system of making pasturage the chief object of attention was still maintained by many of the greatest inhabitants where the author of the book of Job resided, the sciences were actively cultivated, the useful and ornamental arts in an advanced state, and commerce prosecuted with diligence and success.

The inhabitants of Arabia appear to have availed themselves, at a very early period, of their advantageous situation between the two fertile and opulent countries of India and Egypt, and to have obtained the exclusive monopoly of a very profitable carrying trade between those countries. They were a class of people who gave their whole attention to merchandise as a regular and established profession, and travelled with caravans through Arabia and Egypt, carrying upon the backs of camels the spiceries of India, the balm of Canaan, and the myrrh produced in their own country, or of a superior quality from the opposite coast of Abyssinia—all of which were in great demand among the Egyptians for embalming the dead, in their religious ceremonies, and for ministering to the pleasures of that superstitious and luxurious people. The merchants of one of these caravans bought Joseph from his brothers for twenty pieces of silver, and carried him into Egypt. The southern Arabs were eminent traders, and enjoyed a large proportion, and in general the entire monopoly, of the trade between India and the western world, from the earliest ages, until the system of that important commerce was totally overturned when the inhabitants of Europe discovered a direct route to India by the Cape of Good Hope.

At the period when Joseph's brethren visited Egypt, 'inns' or caravanserais were established for the accommodation of travellers in that country and in the northern parts of Arabia. The more civilized southern parts of the peninsula would no doubt be furnished with caravanserais still more commodious.

During the residence of the Israelites in Egypt manufactures of almost every description were carried to great perfection. Flax, fine linen, gar-ments of cotton, rings and jewels of gold and silver, works in all kinds of materials, chariots for pleasure and chariots for war, are all mentioned by Moses. They had extensive manufactories of bricks. Literature was in a flourishing state; and, in order to give an enlarged idea of the accomplishments of Moses, it is said he was 'learned in all the wisdom of the Egyptians' (Acts xii. 22).

The expulsion of the Canaanites from a great part of their territories by the Israelites under Joshua, led to the gradual establishment of colonies in Cyprus, Rhodes, and several islands in the Ægean Sea; they penetrated into the Euxine or Black Sea, and spreading along the shores of Sicily, Sardinia, Gaul, Spain, and Africa, established numerous trading places, which gradually rose into more or less importance. At this period mention is first made of Tyre as a strong or fortified city, whilst Sidon is dignified with the title of Great.

During the reign of David, king of Israel, that powerful monarch disposed of a part of the wealth obtained by his conquests in purchasing cedar-timber from Hiram, king of Tyre, with whom he kept up a friendly correspondence while he lived He also hired Tyrian masons and carpenters for carrying on his works. Solomon, the son of David, cultivated the arts of peace, and indulged his taste for magnificence and luxury to a great extent. He employed the wealth collected by his father in works of architecture, and in strengthening and improving his kingdom. He built the famous Temple and fortifications of Jerusalem, and many cities, among which was the celebrated Tadmor or Palmyra. From the king of Tyre he obtained cedar and fir, or cypress-timbers, and large stones cut and prepared for building, which the Tyrians conveyed by water to the most convenient landing-place in Solomon's dominions. Hiram also sent a vast number of workmen to assist and instruct Solomon's people, none of whom had skill ' to hew timber like the Sidonians.' Solomon, in exchange, furnished the Tyrians with corn, wine, and oil, and received a balance in gold. Solomon and Hiram appear to have subsequently entered into a trading speculation or adventure upon a large scale. Tyrian shipwrights were accordingly sent to build vessels for both kings at Eziongeber, Solomon's port on the Red Sea, whither he himself went to animate them with his presence (2 Chron. viii. 17). These ships, conducted by Tyrian navigators, sailed in company to some rich countries called Ophir and Tarshish. The voyage occupied three years, yet the returns in this new found trade were very great and profitable. This fleet took in apes, ebony, and parrots on the coasts of Ethiopia, gold at Ophir, or the place of traffic whither the people of Ophir resorted; it traded on both sides of the Red Sea, on the coasts of Arabia and Ethiopia, in all parts of Ethiopia beyond the straits when it had entered the ocean: thence it passed up the Persian Gulf, and might visit the places of trade upon both its shores, and run up the Tigris or the Euphrates as far as these rivers were navigable.

After the reign of Solomon the commerce of the Israelites seems to have very materially declined. An attempt was made by Jehoshaphat, king of Judah, and Ahaziah, king of Israel, to effect its revival; but the ships which they built at Ezion-geber having been wrecked in the harbour, the undertaking was abandoned. It does not appear that they had any assistance from the Phœnicians in fitting out this fleet. Great efforts were made by the Egyptians to extend the commerce of their country, among which not the least considerable was the unsuccessful attempt to construct a canal from the Nile to the Arabian Gulf.

The rising prosperity of Tyre soon eclipsed the ancient and long-flourishing commercial city of Sidon. About 600 years before Christ her commercial splendour appears to have been at its height, and is graphically described by Ezekiel xxvii). The imports into Tyre were fine linen from Egypt; blue and purple from the isles of Elisha; silver, iron, tin, and lead from Tarshish —the south part of Spain; slaves and brazen vessels from Javan or Greece, Tubal and Meshech; horses, slaves bred to horsemanship, and mules from Togarmah; emeralds, purple, embroidery, fine linen, corals, and agates from Syria; corn, balm, honey, oil, and gums from the Israelites; wine and wool from Damascus, polished ironware, precious oils, and cinnamon from Dan, Javan, and Mezo; magnificent carpets from Dedan; sheep and goats from the pastoral tribes of Arabia; costly spices, some the produce of India, precious stones, and gold from the merchants of Sheba or Sabæa, and Ramah or Regma. countries in the south part of Arabia; blue cloths, embroidered works, rich apparel in corded cedarchests, supposed to be original India packages, and other goods from Sheba, Ashur, and Chilmad, and from Haran, Canneh, and Eden, trading ports on the south coast of Arabia. The vast wealth that thus flowed into Tyre from all quarters brought with it its too general concomitants — extravagance, dissipation, and relaxation of morals.

The subjection of Tyre, 'the renowned city which was strong in the sea, whose merchants were princes, whose traffickers were the honourable of the earth,' by Cyrus. and its subsequent overthrow by Alexander, after a determined and most formidable resistance, terminated alike the grandeur of that city and the history of ancient commerce, as far as they are alluded to in Scripture.

COMMON. The Greek term properly signifies *what belongs to all* (as in Wisd. vii. 3), but the Hellenists applied it to what was profane, *i. e. not holy*, and therefore of common or promiscuous use (Acts x. 14). They also applied the term to what was *impure*, whether naturally or legally (as in Mark vii. 2, compared with Macc. i. 47, 62). And, finally, it was used of meats forbidden, or such as had been partaken of by idolaters, and which, as they rendered the partakers thereof impure, were themselves called common and unclean.

COMMUNION, a fellowship or agreement, when several persons join and partake together of one thing (2 Cor. vi. 14; 1 John i. 3); hence its application to the celebration of the Lord's supper as an act of fellowship among Christians (1 Cor. x. 16); and it is to this act of participation or fellowship that the word ' communion ' is now restricted in the English language, the more familiar application of it having fallen into disuse.

CONCORDANCE, the name assigned to a book which gives the words contained in the Holy Scriptures in alphabetical order, with a reference to the place where each may be found.

CONCUBINAGE, in a Scriptural sense, means the state of cohabiting lawfully with a wife of second rank, who enjoyed no other conjugal right but that of cohabitation, and whom the husband could repudiate, and send away with a small present (Gen. xxi. 14). In like manner, he could, by means of presents, exclude his children by her from the heritage (Gen. xxv. 6). Such concubines had Nahor (Gen. xxii. 24), Abraham (xxv. 6), Jacob (xxxv. 22), Eliphas (xxxvi. 12), Gideon (Judg. viii. 3), Saul (2 Sam. iii. 7), David (1 Sam. v. 13; xv. 16; xvi. 21), Solomon (1 Kings xi. 3), Caleb (1 Chron. ii. 46), Manasseh (*ib.* vii. 14), Rehoboam (2 Chron. xi. 21), Abiah (2 Chr. xiii. 21), and Belshazzar (Dan. v. 2). To judge from the conjugal histories of Abraham and Jacob (Gen. xvi. and xxx.), the immediate cause of concubinage was the barrenness of the lawful wife, who in that case introduced her maid-servant, of her own accord, to her husband, for the sake of having children. Accordingly we do not read that Isaac, son of Abraham, had any concubine, Rebekah, his wife, not being barren. In process of time, however, concubinage appears to have degenerated into a regular custom among the Jews, and the institutions of Moses were directed to prevent excess and abuse in that respect, by wholesome laws and regulations (Exod. xxi. 7-9; Deut. xxi. 10-14). It would seem that the unfaithfulness of a concubine was not regarded as an act of real adultery (Lev. xix. 20). When a son had intercourse with the concubine of his father, a sort of family punishment, we are informed, was inflicted on him (Gen. xxxv. 22; 1 Chron. v. 1).

In the Talmud, the Rabbins differ as to what constitutes concubinage; some regarding as its distinguishing feature the absence of the betrothing ceremonies, and of the portion of property allotted to a woman by special engagement, and to which she was entitled on the marriage day, after the decease of the husband, or in case of repudiation; others, again, the absence of the latter alone.

The Roman law calls concubinage an allowed custom. When this expression occurs in the constitutions of the Christian emperors, it signifies what we now sometimes call a *marriage of conscience*. The concubinage tolerated among the Romans, in the time of the Republic and of the heathen emperors, was that between persons not capable of contracting legal marriage. Inheritances might descend to children that sprung from such a tolerated cohabitance. Concubinage between such persons they looked on as a kind of marriage, and even allowed it several privileges; but then it was confined to a single person, and was of perpetual obligation, as much as marriage itself. Concubinage is also used to signify a marriage with a woman of inferior condition, to whom the husband does not convey his rank. Dajos (Paratilla) observes, that the ancient laws allowed a man to espouse, under the title of concubine, certain persons who were esteemed unequal to him, on account of the want of some qualities requisite to sustain the full honour of marriage: and he adds, that though such concubinage was beneath marriage both as to dignity

P

and civil rights, yet was concubine a reputable title, and very different from that of 'mistress' among us. The connection was considered so lawful that the concubine might be accused of adultery in the same manner as a wife.

This kind of concubinage is still in use in some countries, particularly in Germany, under the title of halb-ehe (half-marriage), or left-hand marriage, in allusion to the manner of its being contracted, namely, by the man giving the woman his left hand instead of the right. This is a real marriage, though without the usual solemnity, and the parties are both bound to each other for ever, though the female cannot bear the husband's name and title.

CONY, in the original *Shaphan*, occurs in Lev. xl. 5; Deut. xiv. 7; Ps. civ. 18; Prov. xxx. 26. Commentators in general now conclude, on the most satisfactory grounds, that those versions which give Cony for the Hebrew Shaphan are incorrect. The Shaphan in scientific zoology is one of the small genus Hyrax, distinguished by the specific name of Syrian. Externally it is somewhat of the size, form, and brownish colour of a rabbit, and, though it has short round ears, sufficiently like for inexact observers to mistake the one for the other. Navigators and colonists often carry the local names of their native land to other countries, and bestow them upon new objects with little propriety : this seems to have been done in the instance before us, there being reason to believe that the Phœnicians on visiting the western shores of the European side of the Mediterranean, found the country, as other authorities likewise assert, infested with rabbits or conies, and that without attending to the difference they bestowed upon them the Hebrew or Phœnician name of Shaphan.

129. [Hyrax Syriacus.]

The hyrax is of clumsier structure than the rabbit, without tail, having long, bristly hairs scattered through the general fur ; the feet are naked below, and all the nails are flat and rounded, save those on each inner toe of the hind feet, which are long and awl-shaped ; therefore the species cannot dig, and is by nature intended to reside, not, like rabbits, in burrows, but in the clefts of rocks. This character is correctly applied to the Shaphan by David.

Their timid gregarious habits, and the tenderness of their paws, make them truly ' the wise and feeble folk ' of Solomon ; for the genus lives in colonies in the crevices of stony places in Syria, Palestine, Arabia, Eastern Egypt, Abyssinia, and even at the Cape of Good Hope, where one or two additional species exist. In every locality they are quiet, gentle creatures, loving to bask in the sun, never stirring far from their retreats, moving with caution, and shrinking from the shadow of a passing bird, for they are often the prey of eagles and hawks ; their habits are strictly diurnal, and they feed on vegetables and seeds.

CONFLAGRATION, GENERAL. The opinion that the end of the world is to be effected by the agency of fire is very ancient, and was common amongst heathen philosophers. It is not easy to discover the origin of this opinion ; it can scarcely be traced to tradition derived from revelation, since there is no distinct reference to such a catastrophe in the Old Testament. It is, moreover, remarkable, considering how universal and definite is the ordinary belief on the subject, that there is only one passage in the New Testament, viz. 2 Pet. iii. 7-10, which can be adduced as speaking distinctly of this event. This passage is, indeed, very explicit, but it should not be forgotten that some learned and able expositors have referred it altogether to the destruction of Jerusalem and of the Jewish polity. If, however, with the majority of interpreters, we refer the prediction to the end of the world, to which it seems most naturally to apply, we could not have a more distinct statement of the fact that the present order of things is to be terminated and the world we inhabit and all the works of man it contains being ' burnt up.' There is no reason for assuming that the whole material universe is to be involved in this catastrophe ; the mention of the heavens leads our thoughts no further than the atmosphere and vapours surrounding this planet. Nor should we regard this conflagration as involving the absolute *destruction* or annihilation of the world ; it is more consistent with the narrative itself, as well as with physical science, to consider it as introductory to a new and better state of things— ' new heavens and a new earth wherein dwelleth righteousness' (v. 11). By what means the conflagration is to be effected we are not informed, and all attempts to explain how this is to be accomplished must be mere speculation, into which we do not think it necessary or advantageous to enter. We have only at present to remark that such an event is not inconsistent with physical facts. We know that the temperature of the earth increases gradually and with considerable regularity as we descend below the surface, and have every reason to believe that the central mass is intensely hot. We know, moreover, that there are subterranean fires of great extent, if not forming part of this heated central mass. The means, therefore, of combustion are near at hand. But even if there were no such central heat, chemistry points out very easy means by which the conflagration may be effected through the agency of various elementary substances. We find evidence also in the pyrogenous rocks which form so large a part of the crust of the earth, that the world has already been subjected, if not to conflagration, yet to a more intense and general action of heat than any which is now observed on the surface of the earth ; and it is clearly not impossible that the action may be yet more intense and more general.

CONI'AH. [JECONIAH.]

CO'OS, Cos or Co (now Stan-Co or Stanchio), a small and fertile island in the Ægean Sea, near the coast of Caria, in Asia Minor, almost between the promontories on which the cities Cnidus and Halicarnassus were situated. It was celebrated

for its wine, silks, and cotton of a beautiful texture. The island is mentioned in 1 Macc. xv. 23;
Acts xxi. 1.

COPPER. Tubal-cain is recorded as the first
artificer in brass and iron (Gen. iv. 22). In the
time of Solomon, Hiram of Tyre was celebrated
as a worker in brass (1 Kings vii. 14; comp.
2 Chron. ii. 14). To judge from Hesiod and
Lucretius, the art of working in copper was even
prior to that in iron, probably from its being
found in larger masses, and from its requiring
less labour in the process of manufacture. Palestine abounded in copper (Deut. viii. 9), and David
left behind him an immense quantity of it to be
employed in building the Temple (1 Chron. xxii.
3-14). Of copper were made all sorts of vessels
in the Tabernacle and Temple (Lev. vi. 28;
Num. xvi. 39; 2 Chron. iv. 16; Ezra viii. 27),
weapons, and more especially helmets, armour,
shields, spears (1 Sam. xvii. 5, 6, 38; 2 Sam.
xxi. 16), also chains (Judg. xvi. 21), and mirrors
(Exod. xxxviii. 8). The larger vessels were
moulded in founderies, as also the pillars for
architectural ornaments (1 Kings vii.). It would
however appear (1 Kings vii. 14) that the art of
copper-founding was, even in the time of Solomon, but little known among the Jews, and was
peculiar to foreigners, particularly the Phœnicians. Michaelis observes, that Moses seems to
have given to copper vessels the preference
over earthen, and on that ground endeavours to
remove the common prejudice against their use
for culinary purposes. From copper, also, money
was coined (Matt. x. 9).

CORAL (Job xxviii. 18; Ezek. xxvii. 16), a
hard, cretaceous marine production arising from
the deposit of calcareous matter by a minute po-
lypous animal, in order to form the cell or poly-
pidom into whose hollows the tenant can wholly
or partially retire. The corals thus produced are
of various shapes, most usually branched like a
tree. The masses are often enormous in the
tropical seas, where they top the reefs and cap the
submarine mountains, frequently rising to or near
the surface so as to form what are called coral
islands and coral reefs. These abound in the
Red Sea; from which, most probably, was derived
the coral with which the Hebrews were acquainted; but coral is also found in the Mediterranean. It is of different colours, white, black,
red. The red kind was anciently, as at present,
the most valued, and was worked into various
ornaments.

COR'BAN, a Hebrew word employed in the
Hellenistic Greek, to designate an oblation of any
kind to God. It occurs only once in the New
Testament (Mark vii. 11). There is some difficulty in the exact meaning of this passage and
the corresponding one, Matt. xv. 5. Many interpreters, at the head of whom stands Beza, suppose
that a gift of the property of the son had actually
been made to the service of God. The sense is
then, 'Whatever of mine might benefit thee is
corban, is already dedicated to God, and I have
therefore no power over it.' Others, more correctly as we think, translate the sentence, 'Be it
corban (that is, devoted) whatever of mine shall
profit thee.' Lightfoot notices a formula of frequent occurrence in the Talmud which seems to
be exactly that quoted by our Lord, '[Be it] corban, [as to] which I may be profitable to thee.'

He, as well as Grotius, shows that this and similar
formulæ were not used to signify that the thing
was actually devoted, but was simply intended
to prohibit the use of it from the party to whom it
was thus made corban, as though it were said, If
I give you anything or do anything for you, may
it be as though I gave you that which is devoted
to God, and may I be accounted perjured and sacrilegious. This view of the passage certainly
gives much greater force to the charge made by
our Lord that the command 'Whoso curseth
father or mother let him die the death' was nul-
lified by the tradition. It would, indeed, seem
surprising that such a vow as this (closely analogous to the modern profanity of imprecating
curses on one's self if certain conditions be not
fulfilled) should be considered to involve a religious obligation from which the party could not
be freed even if afterwards he repented of his
rashness and sin. It appears, however, from
Rabbinical authority that anything thus devoted
was irreclaimable, and that even the hasty utterance of a word implying a vow was equivalent to
a vow formally made. This, indeed, seems to be
the force of the expression used in Mark, ' ye
suffer him no more to do aught for his father or
his mother.' A more striking instance of the
subversion of a command of God by the tradition
of men can hardly be conceived.

CORIANDER occurs in two places in Scripture, viz. Exod. xvi. 31, 'And it (manna) was
like coriander seed, white; and the taste of it was
like wafers made of honey;' Num. xi. 7, 'And
the manna was as coriander seed, and the colour
thereof as the colour of bdellium.' The coriander
is known throughout Arabia, Persia, and India,

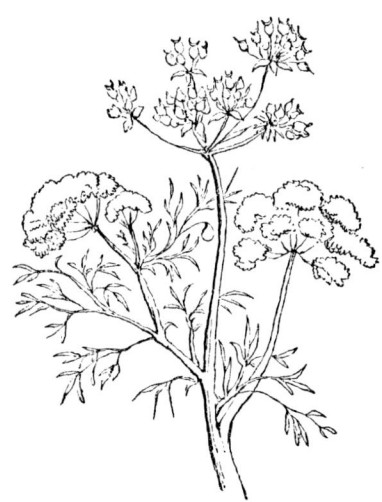

130. [Coriandrum sativum.

in all of which it is cultivated, being universally
employed as a grateful spice, and as one of the
ingredients of currie-powder. It is also common
in Egypt. It is now very common in the south
of Europe, and also in this country, being cultivated, especially in Essex, on account of its seeds,

which are required by confectioners, druggists, and distillers, in large quantities : in gardens it is reared on account of its leaves, which are used in soups and salads. The coriander is an umbelliferous plant, the *Coriandrum sativum* of botanists. The fruit, commonly called seeds, is globular, greyish-coloured, about the size of peppercorn, having its surface marked with fine striæ. Both its taste and smell are agreeable, depending on the presence of a volatile oil, which is separated by distillation.

CO'RINTH, a Grecian city, placed on the isthmus which joins Peloponnesus (now called the Morea) to the continent of Greece. A lofty rock rises above it, on which was the citadel, or the Acrocorinthus. It had two harbours : Cenchreæ, on the eastern side, about 70 stadia distant; and Lechæum, on the modern Gulf of Lepanto, only 12 stadia from the city. Its earliest name, as given by Homer, is *Ephyre*. Owing to the great difficulty of weathering Malea, the southern promontory of Greece, merchandise passed through Corinth from sea to sea; the city becoming an *entrepôt* for the goods of Asia and Italy (Strabo, viii. 6). At the same time it commanded the traffic by land from north to south. An attempt made to dig through the isthmus was frustrated by the rocky nature of the soil; at one period, however, they had an invention for drawing galleys across from sea to sea on trucks. With such advantages of position, Corinth was very early renowned for riches, and seems to have been made by nature for the capital of Greece. The numerous colonies which she sent forth, chiefly to the west and to Sicily, gave her points of attachment in many parts ; and the good will, which, as a mercantile state, she carefully maintained, made her a valuable link between the various Greek tribes. The public and foreign policy of Corinth appears to have been generally remarkable for honour and justice ; and the Isthmian games, which were celebrated there every other year, might have been converted into a national congress, if the Corinthians had been less peaceful and more ambitious.

When the Achæan league was rallying the chief powers of southern Greece, Corinth became its military centre ; and as the spirit of freedom was active in that confederacy, they were certain, sooner or later, to give the Romans a pretence for attacking them. The fatal blow fell on Corinth (B.C. 146), when L. Mummius, by order of the Roman Senate, barbarously destroyed that beautiful town, eminent even in Greece for painting, sculpture, and all working in metal and pottery ; and as the territory was given over to the Sicyonians, we must infer that the whole population was sold into slavery.

The Corinth of which we read in the New Testament was quite a new city, having been rebuilt and established as a Roman colony, and *peopled with freedmen from Rome* by the dictator Cæsar, a little before his assassination. Although the soil was too rocky to be fertile, and the territory very limited, Corinth again became a great and wealthy city in a short time, especially as the Roman proconsuls made it the seat of government (Acts xviii.) for *southern* Greece, which was now called the province of Achaia. In earlier times Corinth had been celebrated for the great wealth of its Temple of Venus, which had a gainful traffic of a most dishonourable kind with the numerous merchants resident there. The same phenomena, no doubt, reappeared in the later and Christian age. The little which is said in the New Testament seems to indicate a wealthy and luxurious community, prone to impurity of morals; nevertheless, all Greece was so contaminated, that we may easily overcharge the accusation against Corinth.

The Corinthian Church is remarkable in the Epistles of the Apostle Paul by the variety of its spiritual gifts, which seem for the time to have eclipsed or superseded the office of the elder or bishop, which in most churches became from the beginning so prominent. Very soon, however, this peculiarity was lost, and the bishops of Corinth take a place co-ordinate to those of other capital cities One of them, Dionysius, appears to have exercised a great influence over many and distant churches, in the latter part of the second century.

CORINTHIANS, EPISTLES TO THE.—
FIRST EPISTLE. The testimony of Christian antiquity is unanimous in ascribing this inspired production to the pen of the Apostle Paul, and with this the internal evidence arising from allusions, undesigned coincidences, style, and tone of thought, fully accords. The epistle seems to have been occasioned partly by some intelligence received by the Apostle concerning the Corinthian church from the domestics of Chloe, a pious female connected with that church (i. 11), and, probably, also from common report ; and partly by an epistle which the Corinthians themselves had addressed to the Apostle, asking advice and instruction on several points (vii. 1), and which probably was conveyed to him by Stephanas, Fortunatus, and Achaicus (xvi. 17). Apollos, also, who succeeded the Apostle at Corinth, but who seems to have been with him at the time this epistle was written (xvi. 12), may have given him information of the state of things among the Christians in that city. From these sources the Apostle had become acquainted with the painful fact that since he had left Corinth (Acts xviii. 18) the church in that place had sunk into a state of great corruption and error. One prime source of this evil state of things, and in itself an evil of no inferior magnitude, was the existence of schisms or party divisions in the church. 'Every one of you,' Paul tells them, 'saith I am of Paul, and I of Apollos, and I of Cephas, and I of Christ' (i. 12). This has led to the conclusion that four great parties had arisen in the church, which boasted of Paul, Apollos, Peter, and Christ, as their respective heads, and various conjectures have been made respecting the peculiarities of sentiment by which these parties may be supposed to have been distinguished from each other. But serious doubts may be entertained whether there really were in the Corinthian church sects or parties specifically distinguished from each other by peculiarities of doctrinal sentiment. That erroneous doctrines were entertained by individuals in the church, and that a schismatical spirit pervaded it, cannot be questioned ; but that these two stood formally connected with each other may fairly admit of doubt. Schisms often arise in churches from causes which have little or nothing to do with diversities of doctrinal sentiment among the members; and that such were

the schisms which disturbed the church at Corinth appears to us probable, from the circumstance that the existence of these is condemned by the Apostle, without reference to any doctrinal errors out of which they might arise: whilst, on the other hand, the doctrinal errors condemned by him are denounced without reference to their having led to party strifes. From this we are inclined to the opinion that the schisms arose merely from quarrels among the Corinthians as to the comparative excellence of their respective teachers—those who had learned of Paul boasting that he excelled all others, and the converts of Apollos and Peter advancing a similar claim for them, whilst a fourth party haughtily repudiated all subordinate teaching, and pretended that they derived all their religious knowledge from the direct teaching of Christ. The language of the Apostle in the first four chapters, where alone he speaks directly of these schisms, and where he resolves their criminality not into their relation to false doctrine, but into their having their source in a disposition to glory in men, must be regarded as greatly favouring this view. Comp. also 2 Cor. v. 16.

Besides the schisms and the erroneous opinions which had invaded the church at Corinth, the Apostle had learned that many immoral and disorderly practices were tolerated among them, and were in some cases defended by them. A connection of a grossly incestuous character had been formed by one of the members, and gloried in by his brethren (v. 1, 2); law-suits before heathen judges were instituted by one Christian against another (vi. 1); licentious indulgence was not so firmly denounced and so carefully avoided as the purity of Christianity required (vi. 9-20); the public meetings of the brethren were brought into disrepute by the women appearing in them unveiled (xi. 3-10), and were disturbed by the confused and disorderly manner in which the persons possessing spiritual gifts chose to exercise them (xii.-xiv.); and in fine the 'love feasts,' which were designed to be scenes of love and union, became occasions for greater contention through the selfishness of the wealthier members, who, instead of sharing in a common meal with the poorer, brought each his own repast, and partook of it by himself, often to excess, while his needy brother was left to fast (xi. 20-34). The judgment of the Apostle had also been solicited by the Corinthians concerning the comparative advantages of the married and the celibate state (vii. 1-40), as well as, apparently, the duty of Christians in relation to the use for food of meat which had been offered to idols (viii. 1-13). For the correction of these errors, the remedying of these disorders, and the solution of these doubts, this epistle was written by the Apostle. It consists of four parts. The first (i.-iv.) is designed to reclaim the Corinthians from schismatic contentions; the second (v.-vi.) is directed against the immoralities of the Corinthians; the third (vii.-xiv.) contains replies to the queries addressed to Paul by the Corinthians, and strictures upon the disorders which prevailed in their worship; and the fourth (xv.-xvi.) contains an elaborate defence of the Christian doctrine of the resurrection, followed in the close of the epistle by some general instructions, intimations, and greetings.

From 2 Cor. xii. 14, and xiii. 1, compared with 2 Cor. ii. 1, and xiii. 2, it appears that before the writing of that epistle Paul had *twice* visited Corinth, and that one of these visits had been after the Church had fallen into an evil state. Did this second visit to Corinth precede also the writing of the first epistle? On this point the Acts give us no help, as the writer is totally silent concerning this second visit of Paul to Corinth. But we may safely infer from 2 Cor. i. 15, 16, 23, that Paul had not been at Corinth between the writing of the first and second epistles, so that we must place his second visit before the writing of the first epistle. When this second visit took place we can only conjecture; but Billroth's suggestion that it was made some time during the period of Paul's residence of three years at Ephesus (Acts xx. 31), perhaps on the first reception of unpleasant news from Corinth, is extremely probable. Supposing the Apostle to have made this short visit and to have returned to Ephesus, this first epistle may have been written either in that city or in Macedonia, through which Paul probably journeyed on his way from Corinth to Ephesus. This latter is the traditional opinion, and is greatly favoured by the way in which Paul speaks of Ephesus (1 Cor. xv. 32) as a place in which he *had been* rather than one in which he *was* when writing this epistle. From the allusion to the Passover in ch. v. 7, 8, most have inferred that the epistle was written at the time of Easter; but this does not necessarily follow from the Apostle's allusion. As to the year, great diversity of opinion prevails, but most are agreed that it was not earlier than 56 nor later than 59.

The subscription above referred to intimates that this epistle was conveyed to Corinth by Stephanas, Fortunatus, Achaicus, and Timothy. As respects the last named there is evidently a mistake, for from ch. xvi. 10 it appears that Timothy's visiting Corinth was a thing not certain when this letter was finished, and from 2 Cor. viii. 17, 18, it appears that Timothy did not visit Corinth till afterwards. Comp. also Acts xix. 22. As respects the others, this tradition is probably correct.

SECOND EPISTLE. Not long after the transmission of the first epistle, the Apostle left Ephesus in consequence of the uproar excited against him by Demetrius the silversmith, and betook himself to Troas (Acts xix. 23, sq.). Here he expected to meet Titus with intelligence from Corinth of the state of things in that church. In this expectation, Paul was disappointed. He accordingly went into Macedonia, where, at length, his desire was gratified, and the wished-for information obtained (2 Cor. ii. 13; vii. 15, sq.).

The intelligence brought by Titus concerning the church at Corinth was on the whole favourable. The censures of the former epistle had produced in their minds a godly sorrow, had awakened in them a regard to the proper discipline of the church, and had led to the exclusion from their fellowship of the incestuous person. This had so wrought on the mind of the latter that he had repented of his evil courses, and showed such contrition that the Apostle now pities him, and exhorts the church to restore him to their communion (2 Cor. ii. 6-11; vii. 8, sq.) A cordial response had also been given to the appeal that had been made on behalf of the saints in Palestine (ix. 2). But with all these pleasing symptoms there were some of a painful kind. The anti-Pauline influence in the church had increased, or at least had become more active; and those who were actuated by it had been seeking by all means to overturn the authority of the Apostle, and discredit his claims as an ambassador of Christ.

This intelligence led the Apostle to compose his second epistle, in which the language of commendation and love is mingled with that of censure. and even of threatening. This epistle may be divided into three sections. In the first (i.-iii.) the Apostle chiefly dwells on the effects produced by his first epistle and the matters therewith connected. In the second (iv.-ix.) he discourses on the substance and effects of the religion which he proclaimed, and turns from this to an appeal on behalf of the claims of the poor saints on their liberality And in the third (x.-xiii.) he vindicates his own dignity and authority as an apostle against the parties by whom these were opposed.

CORMORANT (Hebrew *Salach*) occurs Lev. xi. 17; Deut. xiv. 17. The name is considered to have reference to darting, rushing, or stooping like a falcon. Nothing is known of it but that it was an unclean bird. Cuvier considers Gesner to be right in considering it to denote a gull, and it might certainly be applied with propriety to the black-backed gull; but although birds of such powerful wing and marine *habitat* are spread over a great part of the world, it does not appear that, if known at the extremity of the Mediterranean, they were sufficiently common to have been clearly indicated by either the Hebrew or Greek names, or to have merited being noticed in the Mosaic prohibition. Both the above are in general northern residents, being rarely seen even so low as the Bay of Biscay. With regard

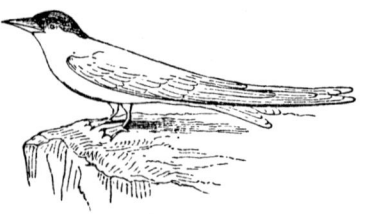

131. [Caspian Tern.]

to the cormorant, birds of that genus are no doubt found on the coasts of Palestine, where high cliffs extend to the sea-shore; but all the species dive, and none of them rush flying upon their prey. We therefore conclude the *salach* to have been a species of 'tern,' considered to be identical with the 'Sterna Caspica,' so called because it is found about the Caspian Sea; but it is equally common to the Polar, Baltic, and Black Seas, and if truly the same, is not only abundant for several months in the year on the coast of Palestine, but frequents the lakes and pools far inland; flying across the deserts to the Euphrates, and to the Persian and Red Seas, and proceeding up the Nile. It is the largest of the tern or sea-swallow genus, being about the weight of a pigeon, and near two feet in length, having a large black

naped head; powerful, pointed crimson bill; a white and grey body, with forked tail, and wings greatly exceeding the tips of the tail: the feet are very small, weak, and but slightly webbed, so that it swims perhaps only accidentally, but with sufficient power on land to spring up and to rise from level ground. It flies with immense velocity, darting along the surface of the sea to snap at mollusca or small fishes, or wheeling through the air in pursuit of insects; and in calm weather, after rising to a great height, it drops perpendicularly down to near the surface of the water, but never alights except on land; and it is at all times disposed to utter a kind of laughing scream. This tern nestles in high cliffs, sometimes at a very considerable distance from the sea. We figure one that was shot among a flight of these birds, some distance up the river Orontes.

CORN. The word *dagan*, which is rendered 'grain,' 'corn,' and sometimes 'wheat' in the Authorized Version, is the most general of the Hebrew terms representing 'corn,' and is more comprehensive than any word in our language, seeing that it probably includes not only all the proper corn-grains, but also various kinds of pulse and seeds of plants, which we never comprehend under the name of 'corn' or even of 'grain.' It may, therefore, be taken to represent all the commodities which we describe by the different words corn, grain, seeds, peas, beans. Among other places in which this word occurs, see Gen. xxvii. 28-37; Num. xviii. 27; Deut. xxviii. 51; Lam. ii. 12, &c.

The different products coming under the denomination of corn, are noticed under the usual heads, as BARLEY, WHEAT, &c.; their culture, under AGRICULTURE; their preparation, under BREAD, FOOD, MILL, &c.

CORNELIUS. The centurion of this name, whose history occurs in Acts x., most probably belonged to the Cornelii, a noble and distinguished family at Rome. He is reckoned by Julian the Apostate as one of the few persons of *distinction* who embraced Christianity. His station in society will appear upon considering that the Roman soldiers were divided into legions, each legion into ten cohorts, each cohort into three bands, and each band into two centuries or hundreds; and that Cornelius was a commander of one of these centuries, belonging to the *Italic* band; so called from its consisting chiefly of Italian soldiers, formed out of one of the six cohorts granted to the procurators of Judæa, five of which cohorts were stationed at Cæsarea, the usual residence of the procurators. The *religious position* of Cornelius, before his interview with Peter, has been the subject of much debate. It is contended by some that he was what is called a *proselyte of the gate*, or a Gentile, who, having renounced idolatry and worshipping the true God, frequented the synagogue, and offered sacrifices by the hands of the priests; but, not having received circumcision, was not reckoned among the Jews. But, on the whole, it is more probable that he belonged to the class of pious Gentiles who had so far benefited by their contact with the Jewish people as to have become convinced that theirs was the true religion, who consequently worshipped the true God, were acquainted with the Scriptures of the Old Testament, most probably in the Greek translation, and observed several Jewish customs, as, for instance, their hours of prayer, or anything else that did not involve an act of special profession. This class of persons seems referred to in Acts xiii. 16, where they are plainly distinguished from the Jews, though certainly mingled with them. To the same class is to be referred Candace's treasurer (Acts viii. 27, &c.): and in earlier times, the midwives of Egypt (Exod. i. 17), Rahab (Josh. vi. 25), Ruth, Araunah the Jebusite (2 Sam. xxiv. 18, &c.), the persons mentioned 1 Kings viii. 41, 42, 43, Naaman (2 Kings v. 16, 17). We regard Cornelius, therefore, as having been selected of God to become *the firstfruits of the Gentiles.* His character appears suited, as much as possible, to abate the prejudices of the Jewish converts against what appeared to them so great an innovation. It is well observed by Theophylact, that Cornelius, though neither a Jew nor a Christian, lived the *life* of a good Christian. He was influenced by spontaneous reverence to God. He practically obeyed the restraints of religion, for he feared God, and this latter part of the description is extended to all his family or household (ver. 2). He was liberal in alms to the Jewish people, which showed his respect for them; and he 'prayed to God always,' at all the hours of prayer observed by the Jewish nation. Such piety, obedience, faith, and charity, prepared him for superior attainments and benefits, and secured to him their bestowment (Ps. xxv. 9; l. 23; Matt. xiii. 12; Luke viii. 15; John vii. 17).

The remarkable circumstances under which these benefits were conferred upon him are too plainly and forcibly related in Acts x. to require much comment. While in prayer, at the ninth hour of the day, he beheld, in waking vision, an angel of God, who declared that 'his prayers and alms had come up for a memorial before God,' and directed him to send to Joppa for Peter, who was then abiding 'at the house of one Simon, a tanner.' Cornelius sent accordingly; and when his messenger had nearly reached that place, Peter was prepared by the symbolical revelations of a noonday ecstacy, or trance, to understand that nothing which God had cleansed was to be regarded as common or unclean.

It is well remarked by Paley, that the circumstances of the two visions are such as to take them entirely out of the case of momentary miracles, or of such as may be accounted for by a *false perception.* 'The vision might be a dream; the message could not. Either communication taken separately might be a delusion; the concurrence of the two was impossible to happen without a supernatural cause.' (*Evidences,* prop. i. chap. 2). The inquiries of the messengers from Cornelius suggested to Peter the application of his vision, and he readily accompanied them to Joppa, attended by six Jewish brethren, and hesitated not to enter the house of one whom he, as a Jew, would regard as unclean. The Apostle waived the too fervent reverence of Cornelius, which, although usual in the East, was rendered by Romans only to their gods; and mutual explanations then took place between him and the centurion. After this the Apostle proceeded to address Cornelius and his assembled friends, and expressed his conviction that the Gentiles were

no longer to be called unclean, and stated the leading evidence and chief doctrines of the Gospel. While he was discoursing, the miraculous gifts of the Holy Spirit, contrary to the order hitherto observed of being preceded by baptism and imposition of hands, fell on his Gentile auditors. Of this fact Peter and his companions were convinced, for they heard them speak with tongues, foreign and before unknown to them, and which Peter and his companions knew to be such by the aid of their own miraculous gifts, and, under divine impulse, glorify God as the author of the Gospel. The Jewish brethren who accompanied Peter were astonished upon perceiving, by these indubitable indications, that the Holy Spirit was poured out upon the Gentiles, as upon themselves at the beginning (x. 45). Peter, already prepared by his vision for the event, and remembering that baptism was by the command of Jesus, *associated* with these miraculous endowments, said, 'Can any man forbid water that these should be baptized, who have received the Holy Ghost as well as we?' and yet, agreeably to the apostolic rule of committing the administration of baptism to others, and, considering that the consent of the Jewish brethren would be more explicit if they performed the duty, he ordered *them* to baptize Cornelius and his friends, his household, whose acceptance as members of the Christian church had been so abundantly testified.

CORNER-STONE. The symbolical title of 'chief corner stone' is applied to Christ in Eph. ii. 20, and 1 Pet. ii. 8, 16, which last passage is a quotation from Isa. xxviii. 16. There seems no valid reason for distinguishing this from the stone called 'the head of the corner' (Matt. xxi. 42), although some contend that the latter is the top-stone or coping. The 'corner-stone' was a large and massive stone so formed as, when placed at a corner, to bind together two outer walls of an edifice. This properly makes no part of the *foundation,* from which it is distinguished in Jer. li. 56; though, as the edifice rests thereon, it may be so called. Sometimes it denotes those massive slabs which, being placed towards the bottom of any wall, serve to bind the work together, as in Isa. xxviii. 16. Of these there were often two layers, without cement or mortar. This explanation will sufficiently indicate the sense in which the title of 'chief corner-stone' is applied to Christ.

COTTON. Cotton is well known to be a wool-like substance which envelopes the seeds, and is contained within the roundish-pointed capsule or fruit of the cotton-shrub. Every one also knows that cotton has, from the earliest ages, been characteristic of India. But in the present day cotton, by the aid of machinery, has been manufactured in this country on so extensive a scale, and sold at so cheap a rate, as to have driven the manufacture of India almost entirely out of the market. Still, however, until a very recent period, the calicoes and chintzes of India formed very extensive articles of commerce from that country to Europe. India possesses two very distinct species of plants from which cotton is obtained: 1. *K. Gossipium herbaceum* of botanists, of which there are several varieties, some of which have spread north, and also into the south of Europe, and into Africa. 2. *Gossi-*

pium arboreum, or cotton-tree, which is little cultivated on account of its small produce, but which yields a fine kind of cotton. This must not be confounded, as it often is, with the silk-cotton tree, or *Bombyx heptaphyllum*, which does not yield a cotton fit for spinning. Cotton is now chiefly cultivated in Central India, from whence it is carried to and exported from Broach. It is also largely cultivated in the districts of the Bombay Presidency, as also in that of Madras, but less in Bengal, except for home manufacture, which of course requires a large supply, where so large a population are all clothed in cotton. The supplies of cotton which we derive from America are obtained from two entirely distinct species—*Gossipium Barbadense*, of which different varieties yield the Sea Island, Upland, Georgian, and the New Orleans cottons; while *G. Peruvianum* yields the Brazil, Pernambuco, and other South American cottons. These species are original natives of America. It is probable that cotton was imported into Egypt and known to the Hebrews, but it is extremely difficult to prove the fact: the subject has been extensively investigated, but the point is still undetermined.

COUCH. [BED.]

COVENANTS. Among other instances of anthropomorphic forms of speech employed in Scripture is the use of the term *covenant*, to designate the divine dealings with mankind, or with individuals of the race. In all such cases, the *proper* idea of a covenant or mutual contract between parties, each of which is bound to render certain benefits to the other, is obviously excluded, and one of a merely *analogical* nature substituted in its place. Where God is one of the parties, and man the other, in a covenant, all the benefits conferred must be on the part of the former, and all the obligations sustained on the part of the latter. Such a definition, therefore, of a divine covenant as would imply that both parties are under conditions to each other is obviously incorrect, and incompatible with the relative position of the parties. We should prefer defining God's covenant with man as a gracious engagement on the part of God to communicate certain unmerited favours to men, in connection with a particular constitution or system, through means of which these favours are to be enjoyed. Hence in Scripture the covenant of God is called his 'counsel,' his 'oath,' his 'promise' (Ps. lxxxix. 3, 4; cv. 8-11; Heb. vi. 13-20; Luke i. 68-75; Gal. iii. 15-18, &c.); and it is described as consisting wholly in the gracious bestowal of blessing on men (Isa. lix. 21; Jer. xxxi. 33, 34). Hence also the application of the term covenant to designate such fixed arrangements, or laws of nature, as the regular succession of day and night (Jer. xxxiii. 20), and such religious institutions as the Sabbath (Exod. xxxi. 16); circumcision (Gen. xvii. 9, 10); the Levitical institute (Lev. xxvi. 15); and in general any precept or ordinance of God (Jer. xxxiv. 13, 14); all such appointments forming part of that system or arrangement in connection with which the blessings of God's grace were to be enjoyed.

The divine covenants were ratified with the sacrifice of a piacular victim, the design of which was to show that without an atonement there could be no communication of blessing from God to man. Thus when God made a covenant with Abraham certain victims were slain and divided into halves, between which a smoking furnace and a burning lamp, the symbols of the divine presence, passed, to indicate the ratification of the promises conveyed in that covenant to Abraham; and here it is deserving of notice, as illustrating the definition of a divine covenant above given, that the divine glory *alone* passed between the pieces ; whereas had the covenant been one of mutual stipulation, Abraham also would have performed the same ceremony (Gen. xv. 1-18). In like manner, the Levitical covenant was ratified by sacrifice (Exod. xxiv. 6-8); and the Apostle expressly affirms, on this ground, the necessity of the death of Christ, as the mediator of the new covenant; declaring that where a covenant is, there also of necessity must be the death of the appointed victim (Heb. ix. 16).

Of the divine covenants mentioned in Scripture the first place is due to that which is emphatically styled by Jehovah ' *My* covenant.' This is God's gracious engagement to confer salvation and eternal glory on all who come to him through Jesus Christ. It is called sometimes 'the everlasting covenant' (Isa. lv. 3; Heb. xiii. 20), to distinguish it from those more temporary arrangements which were confined to particular individuals or classes; and the *second*, or *new*, or *better covenant*, to distinguish it from the Levitical covenant, which was *first* in order of time, because first ratified by sacrifice, and became *old*, and was shown to be *inferior*, because on the appearance of the Christian dispensation it was superseded, and passed away (Jer. xxxi. 31; Gal. iv. 24; Heb. vii. 22; viii. 6-13; ix. 15-23; xii. 24). Though this covenant was not, strictly speaking, ratified before the death of Christ, the great sacrificial victim (Heb. xiii. 20), yet it was revealed to the saints who lived before his advent, and who enjoyed salvation through the retrospective power of his death (Rom. iii. 25; Heb. ix. 15). To the more highly favoured of these, God gave specific assurances of his gracious purpose, and on such occasions he was said to establish or make his covenant with them. Thus he established his covenant with Noah (Gen. ix. 8, 9); with Abraham (Gen. xvii. 4, 5); and with David (Ps. lxxxix. 3, 4). These were not distinct covenants, so much as renewals of the promises of the everlasting covenant, coupled with certain temporal favours, as types and pledges of the fulfilment of these promises.

The old or Sinaitic covenant was that given by God to the Israelites through Moses. It respected especially the inheritance of the land of Canaan, and the temporal blessings therewith connected; but it stood related to the new covenant, as embodying a typical representation of those great truths and blessings which the Christian dispensation unfolds and conveys.

In the system of a certain class of theologians great importance is attached to what they have technically called 'the covenant of works.' By this they intend the constitution established by God with Adam, during the period of his innocence. So far as this phraseology is not understood to imply that man, even in his sinless state, was competent to bind Jehovah by any conditions, it cannot be objected to. It seems also to have the sanction of one passage of Scripture, viz. Hos. vi. 7, which almost all the best interpreters agree in rendering thus: 'But they *like Adam* have transgressed the covenant.'

Theologians have also spoken of 'the covenant of redemption,' by which they mean an engagement entered into between God the Father and God the Son from all eternity, whereby the former secured to the latter a certain number of ransomed sinners, as his church or elect body, and the latter engaged to become their surety and substitute. By many the propriety of this doctrine has been doubted; but the references to it in Scripture are of such a kind that it seems unreasonable to refuse to admit it. With it stand connected the subjects of election, predestination, the special love of Christ to his people, and the certain salvation of all that the Father hath given him.

Sometimes a mere human contract is called God's covenant, in the sense of involving an appeal to the Almighty, who, as the Judge of the whole earth, will hold both parties bound to fulfil their engagment. Compare 1 Sam. xx. 8; Jer. xxxiv. 18, 19; Ezek. xvii. 18, 19.

CRANE (Isa. xxxviii. 14; Jer. viii. 7). The correctness of the translation in these passages has however been called in question, for if the 'crane' of Europe had been meant by either denomination, the clamorous habits of the species would not have been expressed as 'chattering;' and it is most probable that the striking characteristics of that bird, which are so elegantly and forcibly displayed in Hesiod and Aristophanes, would have supplied the lofty diction of prophetical inspiration with associations of a character still more exalted. It is supposed, therefore, that the 'Ardea virgo' of Linn. the 'Grus virgo' of later writers, and 'Anthropoides virgo'

132. [Numidian Crane: Grus Virgo.]

of some, is the bird really meant, though not coming from the north, but from Central Afreia, down the Nile, and in the spring arriving in Palestine, while troops of them proceed to Asia Minor, and some as far north as the Caspian. They are frequently found portrayed on Egyptian monuments, and Hasselquist, who saw them on the Nile, afterwards shot one near Smyrna: they visit the swamp above that city, and the lake of Tiberias, and depart in the fall, but do not utter the *clangor* of the crane, nor adopt its flight in two columns, forming an acute angle, the better to cleave the air. This bird is not more than three feet in length; it is of a beautiful bluish grey, with the cheeks, throat, breast, and tips of the long hinder feathers and quills black, and a tuft of delicate white plumes behind

each eye. It has a peculiar dancing walk, which gave rise to its French denomination of 'demoiselle.'

CRES'CENS, an assistant of St. Paul, and generally supposed to have been one of the seventy disciples of Christ. It is alleged in the *Apostolical Constitutions* (vii. 46), and by the fathers of the church, that he preached the Gospel in Galatia, a fact probably deduced conjecturally from the only text (2 Tim. iv. 10) in which his name occurs.

CRETE, one of the largest islands in the Mediterranean, now called Candia, and by the Turks, Kirid. It is 160 miles long, but of very unequal width—varying from thirty-five to six miles. It is situated at the entrance of the Archipelago, having the coast of the Morea to the south-west, that of Asia Minor to the north-east, and that of Libya to the south. Great antiquity was affected by the inhabitants, and it has been supposed by some that the island was originally peopled from Egypt; but this is founded on the conclusion that Crete was the Caphtor of Deut. ii. 23, &c., and the country of the Philistines, which seems more than doubtful. Surrounded on all sides by the sea, the Cretans were excellent sailors, and their vessels visited all the neighbouring coasts. The island was highly prosperous and full of people in very ancient times. The chief glory of the island, however, lay in its having produced the legislator Minos, whose institutions had such important influence in softening the manners of a barbarous age, not in Crete only, but also in Greece, where these institutions were imitated. The natives were celebrated as archers. Their character was not of the most favourable description; the Cretans or Kretans being, in fact, one of the three K's against whose unfaithfulness the Greek proverb was intended as a caution—Kappadokia, Krete, and Kilikia. In short, the ancient notices of their character fully agree with the quotation which St. Paul produces from 'one of their own poets,' in his Epistle to Titus (i. 12), who had been left in charge of the Christian church in the island:—'The Cretans are always liars (eternal liars), evil beasts (literally "brutes"), slow bellies' (gorbellies, bellies which take long to fill).

Crete is named in 1 Macc. x. 67. But it derives its strongest Scriptural interest from the circumstances connected with St. Paul's voyage to Italy. The vessel in which he sailed, being forced out of her course by contrary winds, was driven round the island, instead of keeping the direct course to the north of it. In doing this, the ship first made the promontory of Salmone on the eastern side of the island, which they passed with difficulty, and took shelter at a place called Fair-Havens, near to which was the city Lasea. But after spending some time at this place, and not finding it, as they supposed, sufficiently secure to winter in, they resolved, contrary to the advice of St. Paul (the season being far advanced), to make for Phœnice, a more commodious harbour on the western part of the island; in attempting which they were driven far out of their course by a furious east wind called Euroclydon, and wrecked on the island of Melita (Acts xxvii.).

CRIMSON. [PURPLE.]

CRIS'PUS, chief of the Jewish Synagogue at

Corinth (Acts xviii. 8), converted by St. Paul (1 Cor. i. 14). According to tradition he was afterwards bishop of Ægina.

CROCODILE. We shall in this place confine ourselves to some notice of crocodiles strictly so called, and shall point out some leading characters in the animal coinciding with allusions to it in the Scriptures, which could not be properly noticed elsewhere.

133.

The crocodiles which we have to notice at present consist of three varieties, or perhaps species, all natives of the Nile, distinguishable by the different arrangement of the scutæ or bony studs on the neck, and the number of rows of the same processes along the back. Their general lizard form is too well known to need particular description; but it may be remarked that of the whole family of crocodiles, comprehending the sharp-beaked gavials of India, the alligators of the west, and the crocodiles properly so called, the last are supplied with the most vigorous instruments for swimming, both from the strength and vertical breadth of their tails, and from the fingers of their paws having deeper webs. Although all have from thirty to forty teeth in each jaw, shaped like spikes, without breadth so as to cut, or surface so as to admit of grinding, the true crocodile alone has one or more teeth on each side in both jaws, exserted, that is, not closing within but outside the jaw. They have no external ear beyond a follicle of skin, and the eyes have a position above the plane of the head, the pupils being contractile, like those of a cat, and in some having a luminous greenish tinge, which may have suggested the allusion to 'the lids of the morning' (Job xli. 18). The upper jaw is not movable, but, as well as the forehead, is extremely dense and bony; the rest of the upper surface being covered with several rows of bosses, or plated ridges, which on the tail are at last reduced from two to one, each scale having a high horny crest, which acts as part of a great fin. Although destitute of a real voice, crocodiles when angry produce a snorting sound, something like a deep growl; and occasionally they open the mouth very wide, remain for a time thus exposed facing the breeze, and, closing the jaws with a sudden snap, cause a report like the fall of a trap-door. The gullet of the crocodile is very wide, the tongue being completely tied to the lower jaw; and beneath it are

glands exuding a musky substance. On land the crocodile, next to the gavial, is the most active, and in the water it is also the species that most readily frequents the open sea. Of the immense number of genera which we have seen or examined, none reached to 25 feet in length, and we believe the specimen in the vaults of the British Museum to be one of the largest. Sheep are observed to be unmolested by these animals; but where they abound, no pigs can be kept, perhaps from their frequenting the muddy shores; for we have known only one instance of crocodiles being encountered in woods not immediately close to the water's side : usually they bask on sandy islands. As their teeth are long, but not fitted for cutting, they seize their prey, which they cannot masticate, and swallow it nearly entire, or bury it beneath the waves to macerate. Having very small excretory organs, their digestion requires, and accordingly they are found to possess, an immense apparatus. They are oviparous, burying their eggs in the sand; and the female remains in the vicinity to dig them out on the day the young have broken the shell. Crocodiles are caught with hooks, and they seldom succeed in cutting the rope when properly prepared. Though a ball fired point blank will penetrate between the scales which cover the body, they may be regarded as furnishing an all but unfailing protection against such injuries and wounds as occasion death to other animals.

That crocodiles and alligators take the sea, and are found on islands many leagues distant from other land, we have ourselves witnessed; and the fact is particularly notorious at the Grand Caymanas in the sea of Mexico, which is almost destitute of fresh water. It is indeed owing to this circumstance that the same species may frequent all the rivers of a great extent of coast, as is the case with some found in Africa, whence they spread to India and the Malayan islands.

CROSS. In its simplest form, consisting of two pieces of wood, one standing erect, the other *crossing* it at right angles, the cross was known at an early age in the history of the world. Its use as an instrument of punishment was probably suggested by the shape so often taken by branches of trees, which seem to have been the first crosses that were employed. Trees are known to have been used as crosses, and to every kind of hanging which bore a resemblance to crucifixion, such as that of Prometheus, Andromeda, &c., the name was commonly applied. Among the Scythians, Persians, Carthaginians, Greeks, Romans, and the ancient Germans, traces are found of the cross as an instrument of punishment. The sign of the cross is found as a holy symbol among several ancient nations. Among the Indians and Egyptians the cross often appears in their ceremonies, sometimes in the shape of the letter T, at others in this shape ☩. At Susa, Ker Porter saw a stone cut with hieroglyphics and cuneiform inscriptions, on which in one corner was a figure of a cross, thus ⊞. The cross, he says, is generally understood to be symbolical of the divinity or eternal life; and certainly a cross was to be seen in the temple of Serapis as the Egyptian emblem of the future state. Porter also states that the Egyptian priests urged its being found on the walls of their temple of Serapis, as an argument with the victorious army of Theodosius to save it from destruction.

According to Lipsius, there were in general two kinds of crosses;—1, the simple cross; 2, the compound cross. The first consisted of a stake on which the criminal was fastened or by which he was impaled. For the first kind of punishment a tree or a specially prepared stake was used, on which the criminal was bound, and either left to perish, or immediately put to death. For *impaling* a long and sharpened piece of wood (*pale*) was employed, on which the criminal was put as on a spit. This cruel mode of execution was formerly very customary in Russia, China, Turkey, and other countries, and is not yet universally abolished by law.

Of the compound cross there were three sorts: 1, one shaped like the letter X, also called Andrew's cross, because tradition reports that on a cross of this kind the Apostle Andrew suffered death. 2. Another sort was formed by putting a cross piece of wood on a perpendicular one, so that no part of the latter may stand above the former. This form is found in the figure T. 3. The third sort is described as 'a cross in which the longer piece of wood or pale stands above the shorter piece which runs across it near the top.' It is distinguished from the preceding by the part of the longer beam which is above the shorter or transverse, thus ✝. This form is found in paintings more frequently than any other, and on a cross of this kind our Saviour is believed to have suffered death.

According to the statement of certain ecclesiastical historians, the cross on which our Lord was crucified was found in the year 326 by the Empress Helena, mother of Constantine the Great. Having built a church over the sacred spot where it was discovered, Helena deposited within it the chief part of the real cross. The remainder she conveyed to Constantinople, a part of which Constantine inserted in the head of a statue of himself, and the other part was sent to Rome, and placed in the church of Sta. Croce in Gerusalemme, which was built expressly to receive the precious relic. When subsequently a festival to commemorate the discovery had been established, the Bishop of Jerusalem, on Easter Sunday, exhibited to the grateful eyes of eager pilgrims the object to see which they had travelled so far and endured so much. Those who were persons of substance were further gratified by obtaining, at their full price, small pieces of the cross set in gold and gems; and that wonder might not pass into incredulity, the proper authorities gave the world an assurance that the holy wood possessed the power of self-multiplication, and, notwithstanding the innumerable pieces which had been taken from it for the pleasure and service of the faithful, remained intact and entire as at the first.

The capture of Jerusalem by the Persians, A.D. 614, placed the remains of the cross in the hands of Chosroes II., who mockingly conveyed them to his capital. Fourteen years afterwards, Heraclius recovered them, and had them carried first to Constantinople, and then to Jerusalem, in such pomp, that on his arrival before the latter city, he found the gate barred, and entrance forbidden. Instructed as to the cause of this hinderance, the Emperor laid aside the trappings of his greatness, and, barefooted, bore on his own shoulders the sacred relic up to the gate, which then opened of itself, and allowed him to enter, and thus place his charge beneath the dome of the sepulchre.

From this time no more is heard of the true cross, which may have been destroyed by the Saracens on their conquest of Jerusalem, A.D. 637.

CROWNS are often mentioned in Scripture, and in such a manner as in most cases to indicate the circumstances under which, and the persons by whom, they were worn; for crowns were less exclusively worn by sovereigns than among modern nations. Perhaps it would be better to say that the term 'crowns' was applied to other ornaments for the head than those exclusively worn by royal personages, and to which modern usage would give such distinctive names as coronet, band, mitre, tiara, garland, &c.

The royal crown originated in the diadem, which was a simple fillet fastened round the head, and tied behind. This obviously took its rise among a people who wore long hair, and used a band to prevent it from falling over the face. The idea occurred of distinguishing kings by a fillet of different colour from that usually worn; and being thus established as a regal distinction, it continued to be used as such even among nations who did not wear the hair long, or was employed to confine the head-dress. We some-

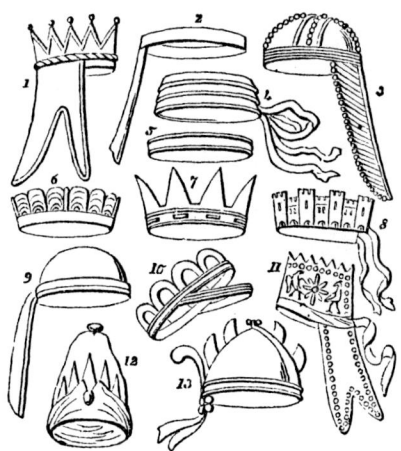

134. [Ancient Asiatic Crowns.]

times see this diadem as a simple fillet, about two inches broad, fastened round the otherwise bare head; we then find it as a band of gold (No. 134, figs. 2, 5). In this shape it sometimes forms the basis of raised ornamental work (figs. 6, 7, 8, 10), in which case it becomes what we should consider a crown; and indeed the original diadem may be traced in most ancient crowns. Fig. 10 is curious, not only from the simplicity of its form, but on account of the metallic loop to be passed under the chin—a mode of securing the crown probably adopted in war or in the chace. Then we find the diadem surrounding the head-dress or cap (figs. 3, 9, 13), and when this also is ornamented, the diadem may be considered as having become a crown. The word *nezer* is supposed to denote a diadem. It is applied to the inscribed plate of gold in front of the high-priest's mitre, which was tied behind by a ribbon (Exod. xxix. 6; xxxix. 30), and which was doubtless something of the same kind that we see in figs. 8, 11. This word is also employed to denote the diadem which Saul wore in battle, and which was brought to David (2 Sam. i. 10), and also that which was used at the coronation of the young Joash (2 Kings xi. 12): and, as another word is applied elsewhere to the crown used in this ceremonial, the probability is that the Hebrew kings wore sometimes a diadem and sometimes a crown, and that the diadem only was accessible to the high-priest, by whom Joash was crowned, the crown itself being most likely in the possession of Athaliah. As Psalm lxxxix. was certainly composed by David, the regal use of the diadem is further indicated in verse 39.

The more general word for a crown is *atarah*; and it is applied to crowns and head ornaments of different sorts, including those used by the kings. When applied to their crowns, it appears to denote the state crown as distinguished from the diadem. This, the Rabbins allege, was of gold set with jewels; such was the crown which David took from the king of the Amorites (2 Sam. xii. 30), and afterwards wore himself, as did probably his successors. Of its shape it is impossible to form any notion, unless by reference to the examples of ancient crowns contained in the preceding cut. These figures, however, being taken mostly from coins, are not of that very remote antiquity which we should desire to illustrate matters pertaining to the period of the Hebrew monarchies. In Egypt and Persia there are sculptures of earlier date, representing royal crowns in the shape of a distinguishing tiara, cap, or helmet, of metal, and of cloth, or partly cloth and partly metal. Such are the Egyptian

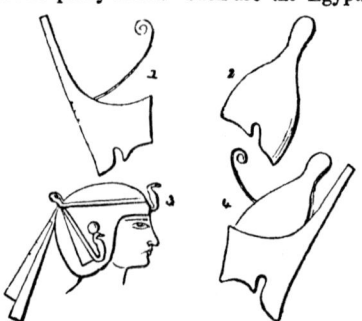

135. [Ancient Egyptian Crowns.]

crowns as represented in the above engraving (No. 135). Fig. 1 is the crown of Lower, and fig. 2 that of Upper Egypt; and when both kingdoms were under one sovereign, the two crowns were united, as in fig. 3. Such union of the crowns of different countries upon one head is matter of historical record. Thus when Ptolemy Philometer entered Antioch as a conqueror, he placed on his head the crowns of Egypt and of Asia. This would, in fact, form *three* crowns, as his previous one was doubtless the double crown of Upper and Lower Egypt. The diadem of

two or three fillets (figs. 3, 4, No. 134) may have been similarly significant of dominion over two or three countries. There are allusions to this custom in Scripture (Rev. xii. 3; xix. 12). These Egyptian tiaras were worn in war, and on occasions of state; but on ordinary occasions a fillet or diadem was used, affording corroboration of a previous remark.

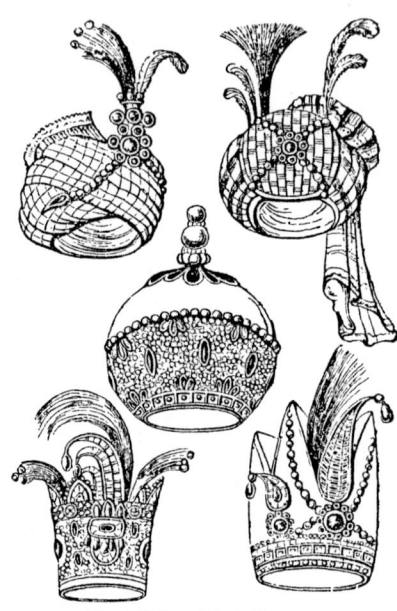

136. [Modern Asiatic Crowns.]

It is important to observe that the mitre of the high-priest, which is also called a crown (Exod. xxxix. 30), was of similar construction, if not shape, with the addition of the golden fillet or diadem. Similar also in construction and material, though not in form, was the ancient Persian crown. From the descriptions given of it, this seems to have been a somewhat conical cap, surrounded by a wreath or fold; and this would suggest a resemblance to fig. 12, No. 134; which is in fact copied from a Parthian or later Persian coin. This one is worthy of very particular attention, because it forms a connecting link between the ancient and modern Oriental crowns, the latter consisting either of a cap, with a fold or turban, variously enriched with aigrettes, as this is; or of a stiff cap of cloth, studded with precious stones. It must often occur to the student of Biblical antiquities that the modern usages of the East have more resemblance to the most ancient, than have those which prevailed during that intermediate or classical period in which its peculiar manners and institutions were subject to much extraneous influence from the domination of the Greeks and Romans. So, in the present instance, we are strongly of opinion that such head tires and caps as those represented in Nos. 135 and 136, more correctly represent the regal 'crowns' of the Old Testament, than those figured in No. 134 (with the exception of fig. 12, and the simple diadems); which however may be taken to represent the style of the crowns which prevailed in and before the time of the New Testament.

Crowns were so often used symbolically to express honour and power, that it is not always safe to infer national usages from the passages in which they occur. Hence we would scarcely conclude from Ezek. xxiii. 42, that crowns were worn by Jewish females, although that they wore some ornament which might be so called is probable from other sources. Mr. Lane (*Arabian Nights*, i. 424) mentions that, until about two centuries ago, a kind of crown was worn by Arabian females of wealth and distinction. It was generally a circle of jewelled gold (the lower edge of which was straight, and the upper fancifully heightened to a mere point), surmounting the lower part of a dome-shaped cap, with a jewel or some other ornament at the summit.

It is certain that 'crowns' of this or some similar kind were worn at marriages (Cant. iii. 11; Isa. lxi. 10); and it would appear that at feasts and public festivals 'crowns of rejoicing' were customary. These were probably garlands (Wisd. ii. 8; iv. 2; Ecclus. i. 11). The 'crowns' or garlands which were given to the victors in the public games are more than once alluded to in the Epistles (1 Cor. ix. 25; 2 Tim. ii. 5; iv. 8; 1 Pet. v. 4).

CROWN OF THORNS. [THORNS.]

CRUCIFIXION. Crucifixion was a most cruel and disgraceful punishment; the terms applied to it by ancient writers are, 'the most cruel and disgraceful,' 'the worst possible punishment,' 'the worst punishment in the world.' It was the punishment chiefly of slaves; accordingly the word 'cross-bearer' was a term of reproach for slaves, and the punishment is termed 'a slave's punishment.' Free-born persons also suffered crucifixion, but only those of low condition and provincials. Citizens could not be crucified. This punishment was reserved for the greatest crimes, as robbery, piracy, assassination, perjury, sedition, treason, and (in the case of soldiers) desertion. Its origin is ancient. In Thucydides we read of Inarus, an African king, who was crucified by the Egyptians. The similar fate of Polycrates, who suffered under the Persians, is detailed by Herodotus, who adds, in the same book, that no less than 300 persons were condemned to the cross by Darius, after his successful siege of Babylon. Valerius Maximus makes crucifixion the common military punishment of the Carthaginians. That the Greeks adopted it is plain from the cruel executions which Alexander ordered after the capture of Tyre, when 2000 captives were nailed to crosses along the sea-shore. With the Romans it was used under their early monarchical government, and was the death to which Horatius was adjudged for the stern and savage murder of his sister, where the terms employed show that the punishment was not at that time limited to any rank or condition. It appears also from the passage that scourging then preceded crucifixion, as undoubtedly was customary in later times. The column to which Jesus was fastened during this cruel infliction is stated by Jerome to have existed in his time in the portico of the holy sepulchre, and to have retained marks of his

blood. The Jews received the punishment of crucifixion from the Romans. Though it has been a matter of debate, yet it appears clear that crucifixion, properly so called, was not originally a Hebrew punishment. The condemned, after having been scourged, had to bear their cross, or at least the transverse beam, to the place of execution, which was generally in some frequented place without the city. The cross itself, or the upright beam, was fixed in the ground. Arrived at the spot the delinquent was supplied with an intoxicating drink, made of myrrh and other bitter herbs, and having been stripped of his clothing, was raised and affixed to the cross, by nails driven into his hands, and more rarely into his feet; sometimes the feet were fastened by one nail driven through both. The feet were occasionally bound to the cross by cords, and Xenophon asserts that it was usual among the Egyptians to bind in this manner not only the feet but the hands. A small tablet, declaring the crime, was placed on the top of the cross. The body of the crucified person rested on a sort of seat. The criminal died under the most frightful sufferings—so great that even amid the raging passions of war, pity was sometimes excited. Sometimes the suffering was shortened and abated by breaking the legs of the criminal. After death, among the heathens, the bodies commonly remained on the cross till they wasted away, or were devoured by birds of prey. A military guard was set near the cross, to prevent the corpse from being taken away for burial; but among the Jews the dead body was customarily taken down and buried. The execution took place at the hands of the hangman, attended by a band of soldiers, and in Rome, under the supervision of the Triumviri Capitales. The accounts given in the Gospels of the execution of Jesus Christ are in entire agreement with the customs and practices of the Romans in this particular. The punishment continued in the Roman empire till the time of Constantine, when it was abolished through the influence of the Christian religion. Examples of it are found in the early part of the emperor's reign, but the reverence which, at a later period, he was led to feel for the cross, induced him to put an end to the inhuman practice.

Death by crucifixion (physically considered) is to be attributed to the sympathetic fever which is excited by the wounds, and aggravated by exposure to the weather, privation of water, and the painfully constrained position of the body. Traumatic fever corresponds, in intensity and in character, to the local inflammation of the wound. In the first stage, while the inflammation of the wound is characterized by heat, swelling, and great pain, the fever is highly inflammatory; and the sufferer complains of heat, throbbing headache, intense thirst, restlessness, and anxiety. As soon as suppuration sets in, the fever somewhat abates, and gradually ceases as suppuration diminishes and the stage of cicatrisation approaches. But if the wound be prevented from healing, and suppuration continue, the fever assumes a hectic character, and will sooner or later exhaust the powers of life. When, however, the inflammation of the wound is so intense as to produce mortification, nervous depression is the immediate consequence; and if the cause of this excessive inflammation of the wound still continues, as is the case in crucifixion, the sufferer rapidly sinks. He is no longer sensible of pain, but his anxiety and sense of prostration are excessive; hiccup supervenes, his skin is moistened with a cold clammy sweat, and death ensues. It is in this manner that death on the cross must have taken place, in an ordinarily healthy constitution. The wounds in themselves were not fatal; but, as long as the nails remained in them, the inflammation must have increased in intensity until it produced gangrene. De la Condamine witnessed the crucifixion of two women of those fanatic Jansenists called Convulsionnaires. One of them, who had been crucified thrice before, remained on the cross for three hours. They suffered most pain from the operation of extracting the nails; and it was not until then that they lost more than a few drops of blood from their wounds. After they were taken down, they seemed to suffer little, and speedily recovered. The probabilities of recovery after crucifixion would of course depend on the degree of constitutional irritation that had been already excited. Josephus relates that of three of his friends, for whom he had obtained a release from the cross, only one survived. The period at which death occurred was very variable, as it depended on the constitution of the sufferer, as well as on the degree of exposure and the state of the weather. It may, however, be asserted that death would not take place until the local inflammation had run its course; and though this process may be much hastened by fatigue and the alternate exposure to the rays of the sun and the cold night air, it is not completed before forty-eight hours, under ordinary circumstances, and in healthy constitutions; so that we may consider thirty-six hours to be the earliest period at which crucifixion would occasion death in a healthy adult. Many of the wounded at Waterloo were brought into the hospitals after having lain three days on the field, and even then sometimes recovered from severe operations. It cannot be objected that the heat of an Eastern climate may not have been duly considered in the above estimate; for many cases are recorded of persons having survived a much longer time than is here mentioned, even as long as eight or nine days. Eusebius says that many of the martyrs in Egypt, who were crucified with their heads downwards, perished by hunger. This assertion, however, must not be misunderstood. It was very natural to suppose that hunger was the cause of death, when it was known that no food had been taken, and when, as must have happened in lingering cases of crucifixion, the body was seen to be emaciated. But it has been shown above that the nails in the hands and feet must inevitably have given rise to such a degree of inflammation as to produce mortification, and ultimately death; and it is equally certain that food would not, under such circumstances, have contributed to support life. Moreover, it may be added that after the first few hours, as soon as fever had been fully excited, the sufferer would lose all desire for food. The want of water was a much more important privation. It must have caused the sufferer inexpressible anguish, and have contributed in no slight degree to hasten death. As-Sujuti,

a celebrated Arabic writer, gives an interesting account of a young Turk who was crucified at Damascus A.D. 1247. It is particularly mentioned that his hands and feet were nailed, and even his arms (but not as if it was in any way remarkable). He complained of intense thirst on the first day, and his sufferings were greatly increased by his continually seeing before him the waters of the Barada, on the banks of which he was crucified. He survived two days, from the noon of Friday to the noon of Sunday.

CRUSE (1 Sam. xxvi. 11; 1 Kings xiv. 3; 2 Kings ii. 20). This now obsolete English word denotes a small vessel for holding water or other liquids. Such are noticed under BOTTLE, DISH, PITCHER.

CRYSTAL. There seems to be no doubt that crystal is intended by the Greek word in Rev. xxi. 11, as indeed the phrase of comparison 'clear as crystal' would seem naturally to suggest. In Ezek. i. 22 the Hebrew word *kerach*, which literally denotes ice, is employed with a similar signification. This is the more apparent when we recollect that crystal was anciently held to be only pure water, congealed by great length of time into ice harder than the common, and hence the Greek word for it, in its more proper signification, also signifies ice. From this it necessarily followed that crystal could only be produced in the regions of perpetual ice; and this was accordingly the ancient belief; but we now know that it is found in the warmest regions. Theophrastus (54) reckons crystal among the pellucid stones used for engraved seals. In common parlance we apply the term *crystal* (as the ancients apparently did) to a glass-like transparent stone, commonly of a hexagonal form, which, from being found in rocks, is called by mineralogists rock-crystal. It is a stone of the flint family, the most refined kind of quartz.

CUBIT is a word derived immediately from the Latin *cubitus*, the lower arm. The length of the cubit has varied in different nations, and at different times. Derived as the measure is from a part of the human body, and as the human stature has been of very dissimilar length, the cubit must of necessity have been various. That the cubit among the Hebrews was derived as a measure from the human body is clear from Deut. iii. 11—'after the cubit of a man.' But it is difficult to determine whether this cubit was understood as extending to the wrist or the end of the third finger. As, however, the latter seems most natural, since men, when ignorant of anatomy, and seeking in their own frames standards of measure, were likely to take both the entire foot and the entire fore-arm, the probability is that the longer was the original cubit, namely, the length from the elbow to the extremity of the longest finger.

The hand-breadth is found as a measure in 1 Kings vii. 26, comp. Jer. lii. 21. In the latter passage the finger-breadth is another measure. The span also occurs Exod. xxviii. 16. So that, it appears, measures of length were, for the most part, borrowed by the Hebrews from members of the human body. Still no absolute and invariable standard presents itself. If the question, What is a hand or a finger-breadth? be asked, the answer can be only an approximation to fact. If, however, the palm or hand-breadth is taken at 3½ inches, then the cubit will amount to 21 inches.

In addition to the common cubit, the Egyptians had a longer one of 6 palms 4 inches. The Hebrews also have been thought to have had a longer cubit; for, in Ezek. xl. 5, we read of a cubit which seems to be an ordinary 'cubit and an hand-breadth;' see also Ezek. xliii. 13, where it is expressly said 'the cubit is a cubit and an hand-breadth.' The prophet has been supposed to refer here to the then current Babylonian cubit —a measure which it is thought the Jews borrowed during the period of their captivity. In the New Testament our Lord characteristically employs the term cubit (Matt. xxvii. 6; Luke xii. 25) for the enforcement of a moral and spiritual lesson. The term also occurs in John xxi. 8, and in Rev. xxi. 17. In Lev. xix. 35 justice in measures, as well as in weights, is strictly enjoined.

CUCKOW occurs only in Lev. xi. 16, among birds of prey not clearly identified, but declared to be unclean. The accuracy of the translation has been called in question, but great obscurity hangs over the subject, and in the present state of our knowledge it is impossible to ascertain what kind of bird was really meant.

CUCUMBER first occurs in Num. xi. 5, in the verse where the Israelites, when in the desert, express their longings for the melons and the cucumbers of Egypt. All travellers in the East notice the extensive cultivation and consumption of cucumbers and other herbs of the same tribe, especially where there is any moisture of soil, or the possibility of irrigation. Thus even in the driest parts, the neighbourhood of a well is often occupied by a field of cucurbitaceous plants, generally with a man or boy set to guard it from plunder, perched up on a temporary scaffolding, with a slight protection from the sun, where he may himself be safe from the attacks of the more powerful wild animals. That such plants appear to have been similarly cultivated among the Hebrews is evident from Isa. i. 8, 'The daughter of Zion is left like a cottage in a vineyard, like a lodge in a garden of cucumbers;' as well as from Baruch vi. 70, 'As a scarecrow in a garden of cucumbers keepeth nothing, so are their gods of wood.'

CUMMIN, or KAMMON, is an umbelliferous plant, mentioned both in the Old and New Testaments, and which, like the dill and the coriander, continues to be cultivated in modern, as it was in ancient times, in Eastern countries. These are similar to, and used for many of the same purposes as the anise and caraway, which supply their place, and are more common in Europe. All these plants produce fruits, commonly called seeds, which abound in essential oil of a more or less grateful flavour, and warm stimulating nature: hence they were employed in ancient as in modern times, both as condiments and as medicines.

Cummin is first mentioned in Isaiah (xxviii 25): 'When he (the ploughman) hath made plain the face thereof, doth he not cast abroad the fitches, and scatter the cummin?' showing that it was extensively cultivated, as it is in the present day, in Eastern countries, as far even as India. In the south of Europe it is also cultivated to some extent. England is chiefly supplied from Malta

and Sicily; 53 cwt. having been imported in the year 1839 from these islands. In the above chapter of Isaiah (ver. 27) cummin is again mentioned: 'For the fitches are not threshed with a threshing instrument, neither is a cart-wheel turned about upon the cummin; but the fitches are beaten out with a staff, and the cummin with a rod.' This is most applicable to the fruit of the common cummin, which, when ripe, may be separated from the stalk with the slightest stroke, and would be completely destroyed by the turning round of a wheel, which, bruising the seed, would press out the oil on which its virtues depend.

137.

In the New Testament cummin is mentioned in Matt. xxiii. 23, where our Saviour denounces the scribes and Pharisees, who paid their 'tithe of mint, and anise, and cummin,' but neglected the weightier matters of the law.

CUSH, the eldest son of Ham (Gen. x. 6; 1 Chron. i. 8), from whom seems to have been derived the name of the *land* of Cush.

The locality of the land of Cush is a question upon which eminent authorities have been divided; for while Bochart maintained that it was exclusively in Arabia, Gesenius held with no less pertinacity that it is to be sought for nowhere but in Africa. Others again, such as Michaelis and Rosenmüller, have supposed that the name Cush was applied to tracts of country both in Arabia and Africa—a circumstance which would easily be accounted for, on the very probable supposition that the descendants of the primitive Cushite tribes, who had settled in the former country, emigrated across the Red Sea to the latter region of the earth, carrying with them the name of Cush, their remote progenitor.

The existence of an *African* Cush cannot reasonably be questioned, though the term is employed in Scripture with great latitude, sometimes denoting an extensive but undefined country (Ethiopia), and at other times one particular kingdom (Meroë). It is expressly described by Ezekiel as lying to the south of Egypt beyond Syene (xxix. 10; comp. xxx. 4-6). Hence we find Mizraim and Cush (i. e. Egypt and Ethiopia) so often classed together by the prophets, e. g. Ps. lxviii. 31; Isa. xi. 11; xx. 4; xliii. 3; xlv. 14;

Nahum iii. 9. The inhabitants are elsewhere spoken of in connection with the Lubim and Sukkiim (2 Chron. xii. 3; xvi. 8; Jer. xlvi. 7; Dan. xi. 43), supposed to be the Libyans and Ethiopic Troglodytes, and certainly nations of Africa, for they belonged to the vast army with which Shishak, king of Egypt, 'came out' of that country, against Rehoboam, king of Judah. In these, and indeed in most other passages where 'Cush' occurs, Arabia is not to be thought of; the Ethiopia of Africa is beyond all doubt exclusively intended, and to the article ETHIOPIA we refer the reader for the Scriptural notices regarding it.

Though there is a great lack of evidence to show that the name of Cush was ever applied to any part of Arabia, there seems no reason to doubt that a portion of the Cushite race did early settle there. By referring to the relative geographical positions of the south-west coast of Arabia and the east coast of Africa, it will be seen that nothing separates them but the Red Sea, and it is not unlikely that while a part of the Cushite population immigrated to Africa, others remained behind, and were occasionally called by the same name. Thus in 2 Chron. xxi. 16, among those who were stirred up against the Hebrews are mentioned the Philistines, and 'the Arabs that were near the Cushites,' and the expression 'near' in this connection can scarcely apply to any but dwellers in the Arabian peninsula.

CUTH'AH, a district in Asia, whence Shalmaneser transplanted certain colonists into the land of Israel, which he had desolated (2 Kings xvii. 24-30). From the intermixture of these colonists with the remaining natives sprung the Samaritans. The situation of the Cuthah from which these colonists came is altogether unknown. Josephus places it in central Persia, and finds there a river of the same name. Rosenmüller and others incline to seek it in the Arabian Irak, where Abulfeda and other Arabic and Persian writers place a town of this name, in the tract near the Nahr-Malca, or royal canal, which connected the Euphrates and Tigris to the south of the present Bagdad. Winer seems to prefer the conjecture of Stephen Morin and Le Clerc, which identifies the Cuthites with the Cossæi in Susiana. All these conjectures refer essentially to the same quarter, and any of them is preferable to the one suggested by Michaelis, that the Cuthites were Phœnicians from the neighbourhood of Sidon.

CUTTINGS IN THE FLESH. Amongst the prohibitory laws which God gave the Israelites there was one that expressly forbad the practice embraced in those words, viz. 'Ye shall not make any cuttings in your flesh for the dead' (Lev. xix. 28). It is evident from this law that such a species of self-inflicted torture obtained amongst the nations of Canaan; and it was, doubtless, to guard His people against the adoption of so barbarous a habit, in its idolatrous form, that God led Moses to reiterate the prohibition: 'They shall not make baldness upon their heads, neither shall they shave off the corner of their beards, nor make any cuttings in their flesh' (Lev. xxi. 5; Deut. xiv. 1).

Investing his imaginary deities with the attributes of cruelty, man has, at all times and in all countries, instituted a form of religion consisting in cruel rites and bloody ceremonies. If then we look to the practices of the heathen world, whether of ancient or modern times, we shall find that almost the entire of their religion consisted of rites of deprecation. Fear of the Divine displeasure would seem to have been the leading feature in their religious impressions. The universal prevalence of human sacrifices throughout the Gentile world is, in itself, a decisive proof of the light in which the human mind, unaided by revelation, is disposed to view the Divinity.

It was doubtless such mistaken views of the character of God that led the prophets of Baal (1 Kings xviii. 28) to cut their bodies with lancets, supposing that, by mingling their own blood with that of the offered sacrifice, their god must become more attentive to the voice of entreaty. In fact it was a current opinion amongst the ancient heathen that the gods were jealous of human happiness; and in no part of the heathen world did this opinion more prevail, according to Sanchoniathon's account, than amongst the inhabitants of those very countries which surrounded that land where God designed to place his people Israel. Hence we see why God would lay them under the wholesome influence of such a prohibitory law as that under consideration: 'Ye shall not make any cutting in your flesh for the dead.' The ancients were very violent in their expression of sorrow. Virgil represents the sister of Dido as tearing her face with her nails, and beating her breasts with her fists.

The present writer has seen in India the same wild exhibition of grief for the departed relative or friend. Some of the learned think that that law of Solon's, which was transferred by the Romans into the Twelve Tables, that women in mourning should not scratch their cheeks, derived its origin from this law of Moses (Lev. xix. 28). But, however this opinion may be questioned, it would appear that the simple tearing of their flesh out of grief and anguish of spirit is taken, in other parts of Scripture, as a mark of affection: thus (Jer. xlviii. 37), 'Every head shall be bald, every beard clipped, and upon all cuttings.' Again (ch. xvi. 6): 'Both the great and the small shall die in the land: they shall not be buried, neither shall men lament for them, nor cut themselves.' So (ch. xli. 5): 'There came from Samaria fourscore men having their heads shaven and their clothes rent, and having cut themselves, with offerings to the house of the Lord.'

The spirit of Islam is less favourable than that of heathenism to displays of this kind: yet examples of them are not of rare occurrence even in the Moslem countries of Western Asia, including Palestine itself. The annexed figure is copied

138.

from one which is represented in many of the books of travel in Egypt and Palestine which were printed in the seventeenth century. It is described by the missionary Eugene Roger as representing ' one of those calenders or devotees whom the Arabs name Balhoaua,' and whom the simple people honour as holy martyrs. He appears in public with a scimitar stuck through the fleshy part of his side, with three heavy iron spikes thrust through the muscles of his arm, and with a feather inserted into a cut in his forehead. He moves about with great composure, and endures all these sufferings, hoping for recompense in the Paradise of Mohammed.

From the examples which have been produced, we may very safely conclude that the expression ' cuttings in the flesh,' in these passages of Scripture, was designed, as already intimated, to declare the feeling of *strong* affection; as though the living would say, ' See how little we regard the pleasures of life, since now the object of our affection is removed from us!' We must therefore come back to our former position, that it was against those self-inflicted tortures, by which the unhappy devotees vainly thought to deprecate the wrath of their angry gods towards their deceased relatives and friends, this law of Moses *was especially aimed.'*

CYMBALS. [MUSIC.]

CYPRUS, the modern *Kebris*, one of the largest islands in the Mediterranean, and next to Sicily in importance. It is about 140 miles in length, and varies in breadth from 50 to 5 miles. From its numerous headlands and promontories, it was called *Kerastis*, or *the Horned;* and from its exuberant fertility, *Macaria*, or *the blessed*. Its proximity to Asia Minor, Phœnicia, and Egypt, and its numerous havens, made it a general rendezvous for merchants. ' Corn, wine, and oil.' which are so often mentioned in the Old Testament as the choicest productions of Palestine (Deut. xii. 17; 1 Chron. ix. 29; Neh. x. 39; Jer. xxxi. 12), were found here in the highest perfection. The forests also furnished large supplies of timber for ship-building, which rendered the conquest of the island a favourite project of the Egyptian kings. It was the boast of the Cyprians that they could build and complete their vessels without any aid from foreign countries. Among the mineral products were diamonds, emeralds, and other precious stones, alum, and asbestos; besides iron, lead, zinc, with a portion of silver, and, above all, copper.

Cyprus was originally peopled from Phœnicia [CHITTIM]. Amasis I., king of Egypt, subdued the whole island. In the time of Herodotus the population consisted of Athenians, Arcadians, Phœnicians, and Ethiopians. Under the Persians and Macedonians the whole island was divided into nine petty sovereignties After the death of Alexander the Great it fell to the share of Ptolemy, the son of Lagus. It was brought under the Roman dominion by Cato. Under the Emperor Augustus it was at first an imperial province, and afterwards, with Gallia Narbonensis, made over to the senate. When the empire was divided it fell to the share of the Byzantine emperors. Richard I. of England conquered it in 1191, and gave it to Guy Lusignan, by whose family it was retained for nearly three centuries. In 1473 the republic of Venice obtained possession

of it; but in 1571 it was taken by Selim II., and ever since has been under the dominion of the Turks. The majority of the population belong to the Greek church; the archbishop resides at Leikosia. Cyprus was one of the first places out of Palestine in which Christianity was promulgated, though at first to Jews only (Acts xi. 19), by ' those who were scattered abroad' after Stephen's martyrdom. It was visited by Barnabas and Paul on their first missionary tour (Acts xiii. 4), and subsequently by Barnabas and John Mark (Acts xv. 39). Paul sailed to the south of the island on his voyage to Rome (Acts xxvii. 4). [ELYMAS; PAPHOS; SERGIUS PAULUS; SALAMIS.]

CYRENE, a city in Upper Libya, founded about the year B.C. 632, by a colony of Greeks from Thera (Santorini), a small island in the Ægean sea. Its name is generally supposed to be derived from a fountain called Cyre, near its site. It was built on a table-land, 1800 feet above the level of the sea, in a region of extraordinary fertility and beauty. It was the capital of a district, called from it Cyrenaica (Barca), which extended from the Gulf of Platea (Bomba) to the Great Syrtis (Gulf of Sidra). With its port Apollonia (Musa Soosa), about 10 miles distant, and the cities Barca, Teuchira, and Hesperis, which at a later period were named Ptolemais, Arsinoe, and Berenice, it formed the Cyrenaic Pentapolis. For above 180 years the form of government was monarchical; it then became republican; and at last, the country became tributary to Egypt, under Ptolemy Soter. It was bequeathed to the Romans by Apion, the natural son of Ptolemy Physcon, about 97 B.C., and was then formed into a province with Crete. Strabo says, that in Cyrene there were four classes of persons, namely—citizens, husbandmen, foreigners, and Jews, and that the latter enjoyed their own customs and laws. At the commencement of the Christian era, the Jews of Cyrene were so numerous in Jerusalem that they had a synagogue of their own (Acts ii. 10; vi. 9). Some of the first Christian teachers were natives of Cyrene (Acts xi. 20; xiii. 1). Simeon, who was compelled to assist in bearing the cross of the Saviour, was a Cyrenian (Matt. xxvii. 32; Mark xv. 21; Luke xxiii. 26).

CYRENIUS, or, according to his Latin appellation, P. SULPITIUS QUIRINUS, governor of Syria (Luke ii. 1, 2). The mention of his name in connection with the census which was in progress at the time of our Lord's birth, presents very serious difficulties, of which, from the want of adequate data, historical and critical inquiry has not yet attained a satisfactory solution. The passage is thus translated in the Authorized Version: ' Now this taxing was first made when Cyrenius was governor of Syria.' Instead of ' taxing' it is now agreed that the rendering should be ' enrolment,' or ' registration,' as it is clear from Josephus that no taxing did take place till many years after this period. The whole passage, as it now stands, may be properly read, ' This enrolment was the first while Cyrenius was governor of Syria.'

This appears very plain, and would suggest no difficulty, were it not for the knowledge which we obtain from other quarters, which is to the effect, 1. that there is no historical notice of any enrolment at or near the time of our Lord's birth; and, 2. that the enrolment which actually did take place under Cyrenius was not until ten years after that event.

With regard to the extent of the enrolment, there can be little doubt that the words ' the whole world ' in our common version should be rendered ' the whole land,' as it is clear Judæa only is meant.

As for the difficulties just mentioned, various attempts have been made to remove them, but perhaps the most satisfactory solution is that which is sanctioned by the names of Calvin, Valesius, Wetstein, Hales, and others, who render the passage thus: In those days there went forth a decree from Augustus, that the whole land should be enrolled; but the *enrolment itself* was first made when Cyrenius was governor of Syria.' The supposition here is, that the census was commenced under Saturninus, but was not com pleted till two years after, under Quirinus.

In support of this view Hales reminds us that a little before the birth of Christ, Herod had marched an army into Arabia to redress certain wrongs which he had received; and this proceeding had been so misrepresented to Augustus that he wrote a very harsh letter to Herod, the substance of which was, that ' *having hitherto treated him as a friend, he would now treat him as a subject.*' And when Herod sent an embassy to clear himself, the emperor repeatedly refused to hear them, and so Herod was forced to submit to all the *injuries* offered to him. Now it may be collected that the chief of these injuries was the performance of his threat of treating him as a subject, by the degradation of his kingdom to a Roman province. For soon after Josephus incidentally mentions that ' the whole nation of the Jews took an oath of fidelity to Cæsar and the king jointly, except 6000 of the Pharisees, who, through their hostility to the regal government, refused to take it.' The date of this transaction is determined by its having been shortly before the death of Pheroras, and coincides with the time of this decree of enrolment and of the birth of Christ. The oath which Josephus mentions would be administered at the same time, according to the usage of the Roman census, in which a return of persons, ages, and properties, was required to be made upon oath, under penalty of confiscation of goods, as we learn from Ulpian. That Cyrenius, a Roman senator and procurator, was employed to make this enrolment, we learn not only from St. Luke, but by the joint testimony of Justin Martyr, Julian the Apostate, and Eusebius; and it was made while Saturninus was president of Syria (to whom it was attributed by Tertullian) in the thirty-third year of Herod's reign, corresponding to the date of Christ's birth. Cyrenius, who is described by Tacitus as ' an active soldier and rigid commissioner,' was well qualified for an employment so odious to Herod and his subjects; and probably came to execute the decree with an armed force. The enrolment of the inhabitants, ' each in his own city,' was in conformity with the wary policy of the Roman jurisprudence, to prevent insurrections and to expedite the business; and if this precaution was judged prudent even in Italy, much more must it have appeared necessary in turbulent provinces like Judæa and Galilee.

At the present juncture, however, it appears that the census proceeded no further than the first act, namely, of the enrolment of persons in the Roman register. For Herod sent his trusty minister, Nicolas of Damascus, to Rome; who, by his address and presents, found means to mollify and undeceive the emperor, so that he proceeded no further in the design which he had entertained. The census was consequently at this time suspended; but it was afterwards carried into effect upon the deposal and banishment of Archelaus, and the settlement of Judæa as a Roman province. On this occasion the trusty Cyrenius was sent again, as president of Syria, with an armed force, to confiscate the property of Archelaus, and to complete the census for the purposes of taxation. This taxation was a poll-tax of two drachmæ a-head upon males from fourteen, and females from twelve to sixty-five years of age — equal to about fifteen pence of our money. This was the ' tribute-money ' mentioned in Matt. xvii. 24-27. The payment of it became very obnoxious to the Jews, and the imposition of it occasioned the insurrection under Judas of Galilee, which Luke himself describes as having occurred ' in the days of the taxing ' (Acts v. 37).

By this statement Hales considers that ' the Evangelist is critically reconciled with the varying accounts of Josephus, Justin Martyr, and Tertullian; and an historical difficulty satisfactorily solved, which has hitherto set criticism at defiance.' This is perhaps saying too much; but the explanation is undoubtedly one of the best that has yet been given.

CY′RUS, the celebrated Persian conqueror of Babylon, who promulgated the first edict for the restoration of the Jews to their own land (Ezra i. 1, &c.). We are informed by Strabo that his original name was Agradates; but he assumed that of Kouros, or Khouresh (which means *the Sun*), doubtless on ascending the throne.

Herodotus and Xenophon agree that Cyrus was son of Cambyses prince of Persia, and of Mandane daughter of Astyages, king of the Median empire. Ctesias denies that there was any relationship at all between Cyrus and Astyages. According to him, when Cyrus had defeated and captured Astyages, he *adopted* him as a grandfather, and invested Amytis, or Amyntis, the daughter of Astyages (whose name is in all probability only another form of Mandane), with all the honours of queen dowager. His object in so doing was to facilitate the submission of the more distant parts of the empire, which were not yet conquered; and he reaped excellent fruit of his policy in winning the homage of the ancient, rich, and remote province of Bactria. Ctesias adds, that Cyrus afterwards married Amytis. It is easy to see that the latter account is by far the more historical, and that the story followed by Herodotus and Xenophon is that which the courtiers published in aid of the Persian prince's designs. Yet there is no reason for doubting that, on the father's side, Cyrus belonged to the Achæmenidæ, the royal clan of the military tribe of the Persians.

It was the frequent practice of the Persian monarchs, and probably therefore of the Medes before them, to choose the provincial viceroys from the royal families of the subject nations, and thereby to leave to the vanquished much both of the semblance and of the reality of freedom. This will be sufficient to account for the first steps of Cyrus towards eminence. But as the Persian armies were at that time composed of ruder and braver men than the Medes—(indeed, to this day, the men of Shiráz are proverbially braver than those of Isfahán)—the account of Xenophon is credible, that in the general wars of the empire, Cyrus won the attachment of the whole army by his bravery; while, as Herodotus tells, the atrocious cruelties of Astyages may have revolted the hearts of the Median nobility.

Xenophon's romance omits the fact that the transference of the empire was effected by a civil war; nevertheless, the same writer in his *Anabasis* confesses it. Herodotus, Ctesias, Isocrates, Strabo, and, in fact, all who allude to the matter at all, agree that it was so. In Xenophon we find the Upper Tigris to have been the seat of one campaign, where the cities of Larissa and Mespila were besieged and taken by Cyrus. From Strabo we learn that the decisive battle was fought on the spot where Cyrus afterwards built Pasargadæ, in Persis, for his native capital. Yet Ctesias represents Astyages as finally captured in the palace of Ecbatana. Cyrus (says Herodotus) did Astyages no harm, but kept him by his side to the end of his life. This is like the generosity of the Persian kings to vanquished foreigners, but very unlike the conduct of fortunate usurpers, east or west, towards a fallen superior. The tale in Ctesias is more like the current imperial craft. There we read that Cyrus at first made Astyages ruler of the Barcanians, and afterwards sent for him by the eunuch Petisacas to visit his daughter and son-in-law, who were longing to see him. The eunuch, however, put him to death on the road ; and Cyrus, indignant at the deed, gave up the murderer to the cruel vengeance of the queen. Astyages had certainly lived long enough for the policy of Cyrus; who, by the Roman Cassius's test of ' Who gained by it ? ' cannot be accounted innocent.

The Medes were by no means made subject to the Persians at first. It is highly probable that, as Herodotus and Xenophon represent, many of the noblest Medes sided with Cyrus, and during his reign the most trusted generals of the armies were Medes. Yet even this hardly explains the phenomenon of a Darius the Mede, who, in the book of Daniel, for two years holds the government in Babylon, after the capture of the city by the Medes and Persians. Indeed, the language used concerning the kingdom of Darius might be explained as Oriental hyperbole, and Darius be supposed a mere satrap of Babylon, only that Cyrus is clearly put forward as a *successor* to Darius the Mede. Many have been the attempts to reconcile this with the current Grecian accounts; but there is one only that has the least plausibility, viz., that which, with Xenophon, teaches that Astyages had a son still living (whom Xenophon calls Cyaxares). and that this son is no other than Darius the Mede ; to whom Cyrus, by a sort of nephew's piety, conceded a nominal supremacy at Babylon. Objections to this likewise are evident, but they must be discussed under Darius the Mede, or the book of Daniel.

In the reign of the son of Cyrus the depression of the Medes probably commenced. At his death

the Magian conspiracy took place, after the defeat of which the Medes doubtless sunk lower still. At a later time they made a general insurrection against the Persian power, and its suppression seems to have brought them to a level with Hyrcanians, Bactrians, and other vassal nations, which spoke the tongue of Persia.

The descriptions given us in Ctesias, and in Plutarch's Artaxerxes, concerning the Persian mode of fighting, are quite *Homeric* in their character. No skill seems to be needed by the general ; no tactics are thought of : he does his duty best by behaving as the bravest of common soldiers, and by acting the part of champion, like a knight in the days of chivalry. We cannot suppose that there was any *greater* advance of the military art in the days of Cyrus. It is agreed by all that he subdued the Lydians, the Greeks of Asia Minor, and the Babylonians : we may doubtless add Susiana, which must have been incorporated with his empire before he commenced his war with Babylon ; where also he fixed his military capital (Susa, or Shushan), as more central for the necessities of his administration than Pasargadæ. Yet the latter city continued to be the more sacred and beloved home of the Persian court, the place of coronation and of sepulture. All Syria and Phœnicia appear to have come over to Cyrus peaceably.

In regard to the Persian wars, the few facts from Ctesias, which the epitomator has extracted as differing from Herodotus, carry with them high probability. He states that, after receiving the submission of the Bactrians, Cyrus made war on the Sacians, a Scythian (*i. e.* a Sclavonic) people, who seem to have dwelt, or perhaps rather roved, along the Oxus, from Bokhara to Khiva ; and, that, after alternate successes in battle, he attached the whole nation to himself in faithful allegiance. Their king is called Amorges by Ctesias. They are undoubtedly the same people that Herodotus calls *Amyrgian Sacians*; and it is highly probable that they gave to the district of Margiana its name. Their women fought in ranks, as systematically as the men. Strabo has cursorily told us of a tradition that Cyrus escaped with but seven men through the deserts of Getrosia, fleeing from the ' Indians'—which might denote an unsuccessful war against Candahar, &c., a country which certainly was not reduced to the Persian empire until the reign of Darius Hystaspis.

The closing scene of the career of Cyrus was in battle with a people living on one or both banks of the river Iaxartes, now the Syr-deria. Two battles were fought on successive days, in the former of which Cyrus was mortally wounded, but was carried off by his people. In the next, the Sacian cavalry and the faithful Amorges came to support him, and the enemy sustained a total and bloody defeat. Cyrus died the third day after his wound : his body was conveyed to Pasargadæ, and buried in the celebrated monument, which was broken open by the Macedonians two centuries afterwards. The inscription, reported by Aristobulus, an eye-witness, is this :— ' O man, I am Cyrus, who acquired the empire for the Persians, and was king of Asia. Grudge me not then this monument.'

The kings of Assyria and Babylon had carried the Jews into captivity, both to remove a disaffected nation from the frontier, and to people their new cities. By *undoing* this work, Cyrus attached the Jews to himself as a garrison at an important post. But we may believe that a nobler motive conspired with this. The Persian religion was primitively monotheistic, and strikingly free from idolatry; so little *Pagan* in its spirit, that, whatever of the mystical and obscure it may contain, not a single impure, cruel, or otherwise immoral practice was united to any of its ceremonies. It is credible, therefore, that a sincere admiration of the Jewish faith actuated the noble Persian when he exclaimed, in the words of the book of Ezra, 'Go ye up, and build in Jerusalem the house of Jehovah, God of Israel; *He is God!'*—and forced the Babylonian temples to disgorge their ill-gotten spoil. It is the more remarkable, since the Persians disapproved the confinement of temples. Nevertheless, impediments to the fortification of Jerusalem afterwards arose, even during the reign of Cyrus (Ezra iv. 5).

Perhaps no great conqueror ever left behind him a fairer fame than Cyrus the Great. His mighty achievements have been borne down to us on the voice of the nation which he elevated; his evil deeds had no historian to record them. What is more, it was his singular honour and privilege to be the first Gentile friend to the people of Jehovah in the time of their sorest trouble, and to restore them to the land whence light was to break forth for the illumination of all nations. To this high duty he is called by the prophet (Isa. xliv. 28; xlv. 1), and for performing it he seems to be entitled 'The righteous man' (xli. 2; xlv. 13).

D.

DAB'ERATH, a town in the tribe of Issachar, assigned to the Levites (Josh. xix. 12; xxi. 28; 1 Chron. vi. 72). It is recognised in the present Debûrieh, a small village lying on the side of a ledge of rocks, just at the base of Taboon on the north-west.

DA'GON is the name of a national god of the Philistines at Gaza and Ashdod (Judg. xvi. 21, 23; 1 Sam. v. 1 sq.; 1 Chron. x. 10). As to the meaning of the name, it is probably derived from a word signifying *fish*, and there is every reason to believe that it had the body of a fish with the head and hands of a man. That such was the figure of the idol is asserted by Kimchi, and is admitted by most modern scholars. It is also supported by the analogies of other fish deities among the Syro-Arabians. Besides the ATERGATIS of the Syrians, the Babylonians had a tradition, according to Berosus, that at the very beginning of their history an extraordinary being, called Oannes, having the entire body of a fish, but the head, hands, feet, and voice of a man, emerged from the Erythræan sea, appeared in Babylonia, and taught the rude inhabitants the use of letters, arts, religion, law, and agiculture; that, after long intervals between. other similar beings appeared and communicated the same precious lore in detail, and that the last of these was

called Odakon. Selden is persuaded that this Odakon is the Philistine god Dagon. The temple of Dagon at Ashdod was destroyed by Jonathan the brother of Judas the Maccabee, about the year B.C. 148 (1 Mac. x. 84).

DALMANU'THA, a village near Magdala (Mark viii. 10; comp. Matt. xv. 39); probably on the western shore of the lake of Gennesareth, a little to the north of Tiberias.

DALMA'TIA, a province of Europe on the east of the Adriatic Sea, forming part of Illyricum, and contiguous to Macedonia. Titus was sent into this region by Paul to spread the knowledge of the Gospel.

DAM'ARIS, a woman of Athens, who was led to embrace Christianity by the preaching of St Paul (Acts xvii. 34). Some suppose she was the wife of Dionysius the Areopagite, who is mentioned before her; but the construction in the Greek will not sanction this conclusion.

DAMAS'CUS, called by the natives Es-Sham, a city of Syria, capital of an important pashalic of the same name, and indeed the chief or capital city of Syria, lies in a plain at the eastern foot of Anti-Libanus. The plain is about 400 stadia from the Mediterranean, and from six to eight days' journey from Jerusalem.

Damascus—by some held to be the most ancient city in the world—is called by the Orientals ' a pearl surrounded by emeralds.' Nothing can be more beautiful than its position, whether approached from the side of Mount Lebanon, from the Desert to the east, or by the high-road from the north from Aleppo and Hamah. For many miles the city is girdled by fertile fields, or gardens, as they are called, which, being watered by rivers and sparkling streams, give to the vegetation, consisting principally of olive-trees, a remarkable freshness and beauty. The plain of Damascus owes its fertility and loveliness to the river Barrada, which is supposed to be either the Abana or Pharpar of 2 Kings v. [ABANA].

The view of Damascus, when the traveller emerges from Anti-Libanus, is of the most enchanting kind, and the surrounding country presents the appearance of a vast superficies of rich luxuriant foliage. But the interior of the city does not correspond with the exquisite beauty of its environs. In the Armenian quarter the houses are built with mud, and pierced towards the street by a very few small grated windows with red painted shutters. They are low, and the flat arched doors resemble those of stables. A filthy dunghill and a pool of stinking water are almost invariably before the doors. In some of these dwellings, belonging to the principal Armenian merchants, there is great internal richness and elegance. There is a fine wide street, formed by the palaces of the agas of Damascus, who are the nobility of the land. The fronts of these palaces, however, towards the street, are like long prison or hospital walls, mere grey mud walls, with few or no windows, whilst at intervals is a great gate opening on a court. But the interior is magnificent; the saloons being ornamented in the costliest style of Eastern art. The great bazaar is about half a league long. They are long streets covered in with high wood-work, and lined with shops, stalls, magazines, and cafés. The shops, as in other Eastern towns, are narrow, and go only a short way back. The magazines are stored with merchandise of all sorts, and particularly with Indian manufactures, which are brought in great profusion by the caravans from Bagdad. In the midst of the bazaars stands the finest khan in the East, that of Hassan Pasha, built about fifty years since. It is an immense cupola, whose bold springing arch recalls that of St. Peter at Rome; it is in like manner borne on granite pillars. Not far distant is the principal mosque, formerly a church consecrated to St. John, whose skull and sepulchre, found in this holy place, give it such a sanctity that it is death for even a Mohammedan to enter the room where the relics are kept.

Situated at the edge of the desert, at the mouth of the plains of Cœle-Syria and the valleys of Galilee, of Idumæa, and of the coasts of the Sea of Syria, Damascus was needed as a resting-place for the caravans to India. It is essentially a commercial town. Two hundred merchants are permanently settled in it. Foreign trade is carried on by the Great Mecca caravan, the Bagdad caravan, the Aleppo, and by several small ones to Beirout (its sea-port), Tripoli, Acre, &c. Lamartine makes its population to be some 300,000, of whom 30,000 are Christians. Another estimate gives only from 120,000 to 150,000 inhabitants, comprising 12,000 Christians, and as many Jews; and our own information leads us to suspect that even this estimate is too high.

Political changes and social influences have lessened and mitigated the proverbial bigotry of the Damascenes. The lower classes, indeed, are still fanatical, but a better feeling on religion prevails in the higher.

Mr. Addison was conducted to the spot where, according to tradition among the Christians, Saul saw the light from heaven. Winding round the walls on the outskirts of the city, he and his companions came to a point where they were broken

139. [Damascus.]

at the top, at which Paul is said to have been let down in a basket, to escape the indignation of the Jews, when (Acts ix.) ' the disciples took him by night, and let him down by the wall in a basket.' From hence, passing on through some pretty lanes, they came to an open green spot, surrounded by trees, over the tops of which were seen the distant summits of Mount Hermon. At this place they were ' informed Saul had arrived when (Acts ix. 3) as he journeyed he came near Damascus, and suddenly there shined round about him a great light from heaven.' These localities are pointed out with the greatest confidence by the Damascene Christians of all sects, and are held in great veneration; nor is it difficult to suppose that the true spots have been handed down by tradition among the followers of the cross. ' The street which is called Straight' (Acts ix. 11) is still found in Damascus, or at any rate a street bearing that name. Addison says it is 'a mile in length,' and ' so called because it leads direct from the gate to the castle or palace of the Pasha.' The house of Judas, also, to which Ananias went, is still pointed out, as well as that of Ananias himself. How much credulity may have had to do in fixing on and perpetuating the recollection of these localities, it is probably easier to suspect than to ascertain.

Of the origin of Damascus nothing certain is known. That the city existed as early as the days of Abraham is clear from Gen. xiv. 15; xv. 2; but the way in which it is spoken of in these passages shows that even at the time to which they refer it was not a new nor an unknown place; for Abraham's steward is characterized as being of Damascus, and the locality of another town (Hobah) is fixed by stating that it lay ' on the left hand of Damascus.' How long it may have retained its independence cannot be determined; but it appears (2 Sam. viii. 5, 6:

1 Chron. xix 4) that its monarch having unadvisedly attacked the victorious David, the Hebrew sovereign defeated the Syrians, making a great slaughter of them, and, in his turn, subdued Damascus, and exacted tribute from its inhabitants. This subjection was not of long duration, for under his successor (1 Kings xi. 24) one Rezon, a servant of Hadadezer, king of Zobah, made himself master of Damascus, and, ruling over Syria, 'was an adversary to Israel all the days of Solomon.' After Rezon, Hezion occupied the throne; he was succeeded by his son Tabrimon (1 Kings xv. 18, 19), who was in alliance with Asa, king of Judah. Preserving the same direct line, the crown then fell to Benhadad, who, having been in a league with Baasha, king of Israel, was bribed by Asa to desert his ally, and join himself in attacking Baasha, on whom the united forces inflicted great injury (1 Kings xv. 19, 20). In the time of Benhadad, son of the preceding monarch, Damascus was the head of a very powerful empire, since it appears (1 Kings xx. 1) that 'thirty and two kings' (doubtless petty princes or pashas, governors of provinces) accompanied him in a campaign which he undertook against Samaria. The insolent demands of the Syrian king having roused the spirit of Ahab, who was at first disposed to succumb to the great power which he saw arrayed against him, a battle took place, in which the Syrians were defeated, and their king effected his retreat with difficulty. The subsequent operations of the Damascenes, under their king, have already been stated [BENHADAD]. Hazael, the successor of Benhadad, unwilling to give up hope of being master of Ramoth-Gilead, was attacked by the united forces of Judah and Israel, whom he vanquished, wounding Joram (2 Kings viii. 28); and, at a later period, under Jehu (2 Kings x, 32), laid waste a large portion of the Israelitish kingdom, and 'threshed Gilead with threshing instruments of iron' (Amos i. 3). Determined on revenge (2 Kings xii. 17), Hazael marched to Jerusalem, and was bought off by king Jehoash by a most costly sacrifice. He, however, took the kingdom of Israel (2 Kings xiii. 3), and, though he treated the people oppressively, he was able to hand them over in subjection to his son, Benhadad III., who was thrice beaten (2 Kings xiii. 24) by the Israelitish king Jehoash, and deprived of all his conquests. Jeroboam II. (2 Kings xiv. 28) pursued these advantages, and captured Damascus itself. Subsequently a junction took place between Israel and Damascus, when (2 Kings xv. 37) Rezin, king of the latter, and Pekah, king of the former, entered into a confederacy, and undertook an expedition against Ahaz, king of Judah (Isa. vii. 1). They succeeded in 'recovering Elath to Syria,' but could not prevail against Jerusalem (2 Kings xvi. 6). Ahaz, however, urged by necessity, applied for aid to Tiglath-pileser, king of Assyria, who, being bribed by a munificent present, fell on Damascus, took it, carried the people of it captive to Kir (on the river Kur), slew Rezin, and united the Damascene territory with his own kingdom (2 Kings xvi. 9; Isa. viii. 4; x. 9; xvii. 1). Damascus after this fell under the power of the Babylonians and Persians, from whom it was taken by Alexander the Great, as one consequence of his victory at Issus. Then it made a part of the kingdom of the Seleucidæ,

from whom it passed into the hands of the Romans. In the time of the Apostle Paul it belonged to the dependent kingdom of the Arabian prince Aretas. At a later period it was reckoned among the cities of Decapolis; then it was added to the province of Phœnice; and at last made a part of the province of Phœnicia Libanesia. From the time of Hadrian it bore the honorary title of Metropolis, without enjoying the rights of a metropolis. Under the Greek emperors of Constantinople Damascus was the most celebrated city of the East, remarkable for its wealth, luxury, magnificence, and its numerous Christian population. A great era in its history is its conquest by the Saracens. The war was begun about A.D. 633, by the celebrated Abubekr, the successor of Mohammed; and ended in the capture of the city, and the substitution of Islamism for Christianity. It then became the capital of the whole Mussulman world, till the Caliphate was removed from it to Bagdad. The city continued under the sway of the caliphs of Bagdad, till it came into the hands of the Turks, and was held and rendered famous by Noureddin and Saladin. In 1301 Timour the Tartar captured the city and barbarously treated its inhabitants. From Josephus it appears that its population contained great numbers of Jews.

Damascus is famous in the first age of Christianity for the conversion and first preaching of the Apostle Paul (Acts ix. 3, 20; Gal. i. 12). The consequences might have been fatal to the Apostle, for his life was endangered in this fanatical city. 'In Damascus the governor under Aretas the king, kept the city of the Damascenes with a garrison, desirous to apprehend me; and through a window in a basket was I let down by the wall, and escaped his hands' (2 Cor. xi. 32-3).

DAN, son of Jacob by the concubine Bilhah (Gen. xxx. 3; xxxv. 25), and founder of one of the tribes of Israel. Dan had but one son, called Hushim (Gen. xlvi. 23): notwithstanding which, when the Israelites came out of Egypt, this tribe contained 62,700 adult males (Num. i. 39), which made it the second of the tribes in number, Judah only being above it. Its numbers were less affected in the desert than those of many other tribes; for at the census, before entering Canaan, it mustered 64,400 (Num. xxvi. 43), being an increase of 1700, which gave it still the second rank in population. But there is nothing in the history of the tribe corresponding to this eminence in population: the most remarkable circumstance in its history, however, is connected with this fact. The original settlement assigned to the tribe in south-western Palestine being too small for its large population, a body of them went forth to seek a settlement in the remote north, and seized and remained in permanent occupation of the town and district of Laish, the inhabitants of which dwelt in greater security and were more easily conquered than the neighbours of the tribe in its own proper territory (Josh. xix. 47; Judg. i. 34; xviii.). The district regularly allotted to the tribe, although contracted, was very fertile. It had the country of the Philistines on the west, part of Judah with Benjamin on the east, Ephraim on the north, and Simeon on the south. The territory proved inadequate chiefly from the inability of the Danites to expel the Philistines and Amorites, who occupied parts of the land assigned to them. There is no doubt that the territory as allotted, but not possessed, extended to the Mediterranean through the country of the Philistines. Samson was of this tribe, and its proximity to the Philistines explains many circumstances in the history of that hero. It appears from that history that there was an under-current of private and social intercourse between the Philistines and the Danites, notwithstanding the public enmity between Israel and the former (Judg. xiii.—xvi.).

DAN, the town, anciently called LAISH, or LESHEM, mentioned in the preceding article as having been conquered by a warlike colony of Danites, who named it after their tribe. The terms in which the condition of Laish is described, previously to the conquest, indicate that the place belonged to the Sidonians, and that the inhabitants lived quiet and secure, 'after the manner of the Sidonians,' enjoying abundance of all things (Judg. xviii. 7). They seem to have derived their security from the absence of any adverse powers in their neighbourhood, and from confidence in the protection of Sidon, which was, however, too far off to render aid in the case of such a sudden assault as that by which they were overpowered. This distance of Sidon was carefully noted by the Danite spies as a circumstance favourable to the enterprise; and it does not appear that Sidon ever made any effort to dispossess the intruders. Dan afterwards became a chief seat of Jeroboam's idolatry, and one of the golden calves was set up there (1 Kings xii. 28, 29). It was conquered, along with other towns, by the Syrians (1 Kings xv. 20); and the name is familiar from the recurrence of the proverbial expression, 'from Dan to Beersheba,' to denote the extent of the Promised Land (Judg. xx. 1; 1 Sam. iii. 20; xvii. 11). [BEERSHEBA.] In the days of Eusebius, Dan was still a small village, which is placed by him four miles from Paneas, towards Tyre. As this distance corresponds to the position of the fountain at Tel el-Kadi, which forms one of the sources of the Jordan, and is doubtless that which is called Dan by Josephus (Antiq. i. 10. 2), the situation of the city of Dan could not therefore have been that of Paneas itself, with which it has been in later times confounded. [CÆSAREA PHILIPPI.] There are no longer any ruins near the spring at Tel el-Kadi, but at about a quarter of an hour north, Burckhardt noticed ruins of ancient habitations; and the hill which overhangs the fountains appears to have been built upon, though nothing is now visible.

DANCE. The character of the ancient dance was very different from that of ours, as appears from the conduct of Miriam, who 'took a timbrel in her hand, and all the women went out after her with timbrels and with dances.' Precisely similar is the Oriental dance of the present day, which, accompanied of course with music, is led by the principal person of the company, the rest imitating the steps. The evolutions, as well as the songs, are extemporaneous—not confined to a fixed rule, but varied at the pleasure of the leading dancer; and yet they are generally executed with so much grace, and the time so well kept with the simple notes of the music, that the group of attendants show wonderful address and propriety in following the variations of the leader's feet.

At a very early period dancing was enlisted into the service of religion among the heathen; the dance, enlivened by vocal and instrumental music, was a usual accompaniment in all the processions and festivals of the gods; and, indeed, so indispensable was this species of violent merriment, that no ceremonial was considered duly accomplished—no triumph rightly celebrated, without the aid of dancing. The Hebrews, in common with other nations, had their sacred dances, which were performed on their solemn anniversaries, and other occasions of commemorating some special token of the divine goodness and favour, as means of drawing forth, in the liveliest manner, their expressions of joy and thanksgiving. The performers were usually a band of females, who, in cases of public rejoicing, volunteered their services (Exod. xv. 20; Sam. xviii. 6), and who, in the case of religious observances, composed the regular chorus of the temple (Ps. cxlix. 3; cl. 4), although there are not wanting instances of men also joining in the dance on these seasons of religious festivity. Thus David deemed it no way derogatory to his royal dignity to dance on the auspicious occasion of the ark being brought up to Jerusalem. His conduct was imitated by the later Jews, and the dance incorporated among their favourite usages as an appropriate close of the joyous occasion of the Feast of Tabernacles.

From being exclusively, or at least principally, reserved for occasions of religious worship and festivity, dancing came gradually to be practised in common life on any remarkable seasons of mirth and rejoicing (Jer. xxxi. 4; Ps. xxx. 11). In early times, indeed, those who perverted the exercise from a sacred use to purposes of amusement were considered profane and infamous; and hence Job introduces it as a distinguishing feature in the character of the ungodly rich, that they encouraged a taste for dancing in their families (Job xxi. 11). During the classic ages of Greece and Rome society underwent a complete revolution of sentiment on this subject; insomuch that not only at Rome, but through all the provinces of the empire, it was a favourite pastime, resorted to not only to enliven feasts, but in the celebration of domestic joy (Luke xv. 25; Matt. xiv. 6). Notwithstanding, however, the strong partiality cherished for this inspiriting amusement, it was considered beneath the dignity of persons of rank and character to practise it. The well-known words of Cicero, that 'no one dances unless he is either drunk or mad,' express the prevailing sense as to the impropriety of respectable individuals taking part in it; and hence the gay circles of Rome and its provinces derived all their entertainment, as is done in the East to this day, from the exhibitions of professional dancers.

Amateur dancing in high life was by no means uncommon in the voluptuous times of the later emperors. But in the age of Herod it was exceedingly rare and almost unheard of; and therefore the condescension of Salome, who volunteered, in honour of the anniversary of that monarch's birthday, to exhibit her handsome person as she led the mazy dance in the saloons of Machærus—for though she was a child at this time, as some suppose, she was still a princess—was felt to be a compliment that merited the highest reward. The folly and rashness of Herod in giving her an unlimited promise, great as they were, have been equalled and even surpassed by the munificence which many other Eastern monarchs have lavished upon favourite dancers.

It remains to notice further that the Jewish dance was performed by the sexes separately. There is no evidence from sacred history that the diversion was promiscuously enjoyed, except it might be at the erection of the deified calf, when, in imitation of the Egyptian festival of Apis, all classes of the Hebrews intermingled in the frantic revelry. In the sacred dances, although both sexes seem to have frequently borne a part in the procession or chorus, they remained in distinct and separate companies (Ps. lxviii. 25; Jerem. xxxi. 13).

DAN'IEL (*judge of God*), a celebrated prophet in the Chaldæan and Persian period. There are in the Bible two other persons of the same name: a son of David (1 Chron. iii. 1), and a Levite of the race of Ithamar (Ezra viii. 2; Neh. x. 6).

Daniel was descended from one of the highest families in Judah, if not even of royal blood (Dan. i. 3). Jerusalem was thus probably his birth-place.

We find him at the age of twelve or sixteen years, already in Babylon, whither he had been carried together with three other Hebrew youths of rank, Ananiah, Mishael, and Azariah, at the first deportation of the people of Judah in the fourth year of Jehoiakim. He and his companions were obliged to enter the service of the royal court of Babylon, on which occasion he received the Chaldæan name of *Belshatzar*, according to Eastern custom when a change takes place in one's condition of life, and more especially if his personal liberty is thereby affected (comp. 2 Kings xxiii. 34; xxiv. 17; Esth. ii. 7; Ezra v. 14).

In this his new career, Daniel received that thorough polish of education which Oriental etiquette renders indispensable in a courtier, and was more especially instructed 'in the writing and speaking Chaldæan' (Dan. i. 4). Already at an early period he had acquired renown for high wisdom, piety, and strict observance of the Mosaic law (comp. Ezek. xiv. 14, 20; xxviii. 3; Dan. i. 8-16). A proper opportunity of evincing both the acuteness of his mind, and his religious notions, soon presented itself in the custom of the Eastern courts to entertain the officers attached to them from the royal table. Daniel was thus exposed to the temptation of partaking of unclean food, and of participating in the idolatrous ceremonies attendant on heathen banquets. His prudent proceedings, wise bearing, and absolute refusal to comply with such customs, were crowned with the Divine blessing, and had the most splendid results.

After the lapse of the three years fixed for his education, Daniel was attached to the court of Nebuchadnezzar, where, by the Divine aid, he succeeded in interpreting a dream of that prince to his satisfaction, by which means—as Joseph of old in Egypt—he rose into high favour with the king, and was entrusted with two important offices—the governorship of the province of Babylon, and the head-inspectorship of the sacerdotal caste (Dan. ii.).

Considerably later, in the reign of Nebuchadnezzar, we find Daniel interpreting another dream of the king's, to the effect that, in punishment of his pride, he was to lose, for a time, his throne, but to be again restored to it after his humiliation had been completed (Dan. iv.). Here he displays not only the most touching anxiety, love, loyalty, and concern for his princely benefactor, but also the energy and solemnity becoming his position, pointing out with vigour and power the only course left for the monarch to pursue for his peace and welfare.

Under the unworthy successors of Nebuchadnezzar, Daniel and his deservings seem to have been forgotten, and he was removed from his high posts. His situation at court appears to have been confined to a very inferior office (comp. Dan. viii. 27); neither is it likely that he should have retained his rank as head inspector of the *order of the Magians* in a country where these were the principal actors in effecting changes in the administration whenever a new succession to the throne took place.

We thus lose sight of Daniel until the first and third year of king Belshazzar (Dan. v. 7, 8), generally understood to have been the last king of Babylon (called by profane writers Nebonnedus), but who—to judge from Dan. v. 11, 13, 18, 22—was, more probably, the son and successor of Nebuchadnezzar, usually called Evil-Merodach, though passing in Daniel by his Chaldæan title and rank. After a reign of two years, this monarch was assassinated by his brother-in-law Neriglissar. Shortly before this event Daniel was again restored to the royal favour, and became moral preacher to the king, who overwhelmed him with honours and titles in consequence of his being able to read and solve the meaning of a sentence miraculously displayed, which tended to rouse the conscience of the wicked prince.

Under the same king we see Daniel both alarmed and comforted by two remarkable visions (Dan. vii. viii.), which disclosed to him the future course of events, and the ultimate fate of the most powerful empires of the world, but in particular their relations to the kingdom of God, and its development to the great consummation.

After the conquest of Babylon by the united powers of Media and Persia, Daniel seriously busied himself under the short reign (two years) of Darius the Mede or Cyaxares II. with the affairs of his people and their possible return from exile, the term of which was fast approaching, according to the prophecies of Jeremiah. In deep humility and prostration of spirit, he then prayed to the Almighty, in the name of his people, for forgiveness of their sins, and for the Divine mercy in their behalf: and the answering promises he received far exceeded the tenor of his prayer, for the visions of the Seer were extended to the end of time (Dan. ix.).

In a practical point of view also Daniel appeared at that time a highly-favoured instrument of Jehovah. Occupying, as he did, one of the highest posts of honour in the state, the strictness and scrupulousness with which he fulfilled his official duties could not fail to rouse envy and jealousy in the breasts of his colleagues, who well knew how to win the weak monarch, whom they at last induced to issue a decree imposing certain acts, the performance of which, they well knew, was altogether at variance with the creed of which Daniel was a zealous professor. For his disobedience the prophet suffered the penalty specified in the decree: he was thrown into a den of lions, but was miraculously saved by the mercy of God—a circumstance which enhanced his reputation, and again raised him to the highest posts of honour under Darius and Cyrus (Dan. vi.).

He had at last, the happiness to see his most ardent wishes accomplished—to behold his people restored to their own land. Though his advanced age would not allow him to be among those who returned to Palestine, yet did he never for a moment cease to occupy his mind and heart with his people and their concerns (Dan. x. 12).

In the third year of Cyrus, he had a series of visions, in which he was informed of the minutest details respecting the future history and sufferings of his nation, to the period of their true redemption through Christ, as also a consolatory notice to himself to proceed calmly and peaceably to the end of his days, and then await patiently the resurrection of the dead at the end of time.

From that period the accounts respecting him are vague, sometimes confused, and even strange; and we hardly need mention the various fables which report his death to have taken place in Palestine, Babylon, or Susa.

DANIEL, BOOK OF. This important and in many respects remarkable book takes its name not only from the principal person in it, but also and chiefly from him as its real author: there being no doubt whatever that, as the book itself testifies, it was composed by Daniel (comp. vii. 1, 28; viii. 2; ix. 2).

The book of Daniel divides itself into two parts, *historical* (ch. i.-vi.) and *prophetic* (ch. vii.-xii.), arranged respectively in chronological order. Its object is by no means to give a summary historical account of the period of the exile, or of the life of Daniel himself, since it contains only a few isolated points both as to historical facts and prophetic revelations. But the plan or tendency which so consistently runs through the whole book, is of a far different character; it is to show the extraordinary and wonderful means which the Lord made use of, in a period of the deepest misery, when the theocracy *seemed* dissolved and fast approaching its extinction, to afford assistance to his people, proving to them that he had not entirely forsaken them, and making them sensible of the fact, that His merciful presence still continued to dwell with them, even without the Temple and beyond the Land of Promise.

The wonders related in Daniel (ch. i.-vi.) are thus mostly of a peculiar, prominent, and striking character, and resemble in many respects those performed of old time in Egypt. Their divine tendency was, on the one hand, to lead the heathen power, which proudly fancied itself to be the conqueror of the theocracy, to the acknowledgment that there was an essential difference between the *world* and the *kingdom of God;* and, on the other, to impress degenerate and callous Israel with the full conviction, that the power of God was still the same as it was of old in Egypt.

The following are the essential features of the prophetic tenor of the book of Daniel, while the visions in ch. ii and vii., together with their different symbols, may be considered as embodying the leading notion of the whole. The development of the whole of the heathen power, until the completion and glorification of the kingdom of God, appeared to the prophet in the shape of four powers of the world, each successive power always surpassing the preceding in might and strength, namely, the Babylonian, Medo-Persian, Greek, and Roman. The kingdom of God proves itself conqueror of them all: a power which alone is everlasting, and showing itself in its utmost glorification in the appearance of the Messiah, as Judge and Lord of the world. Until the coming of the Messiah, the people of God have yet to go through a period of heavy trials. That period is particularly described, ch. viii. and xi., in the struggles of the Maccabæan time, illustrative of the last and heaviest combats which the kingdom of God would have to endure. The period until the appearance of the Messiah is a fixed and sacred number: seventy weeks of years (ch. ix.). After the lapse of that period ensues the death of the Messiah; the expiation of the people is realised; true justice is revealed, but Jerusalem and the Temple are in punishment given up to destruction. The true rise from this fall and corruption ensues only at the end of time, in the general resurrection (ch. xii.).

The authenticity of the book has frequently been called in question. The oldest known opponent of it is the heathen philosopher Porphyry, in the third century of the Christian era. He found no successor in his views until the time of the English Deists, when Collins attempted to attack the authenticity of Daniel, as was done by Semler in Germany. In later times its authenticity has been disputed by a number of German critics, who have made the most elaborate attacks against it.

The objections of these writers have been fully met and confuted. They rest, to a great extent, partly on historical errors, partly on the want of a sound exegesis, and, lastly, on the perversion of a few passages in the text. Thus it has turned out that several of the arguments have led to a far different and even opposite result from what was originally meant, namely, to the *defence* of the authenticity of the book. The existence, *ex. gr.,* of a king Darius of the Medians, mentioned in ch. vi., is a thorough historical fact; and the very circumstance that such an insignificant prince, eclipsed as his name was by the splendour of Cyrus, and therefore unnoticed in the fabulous and historical chronicles of Persia, should be known and mentioned in this book, is in itself a proof of the high historical authority of Daniel.

The following are the more important of the arguments which evidence the genuineness of the book.

1. The existence and authority of the book are most decidedly testified by the New Testament. Christ himself refers to it (Matt. xxiv. 15), and gives himself (in virtue of the expression in Dan. vii. 13) the name of *Son of Man;* while the Apostles repeatedly appeal to it as an authority (*ex. gr.,* 1 Cor. vi. 2; 2 Thess. ii. 3; Heb. xi. 33, sq.).

2. The period of the exile would be altogether incomprehensible without the existence of a man like Daniel, exercising great influence upon his own people, and whose return to Palestine was effected by means of his high station in the state, as well as through the peculiar assistance of God with which he was favoured. Without this assumption, it is impossible to explain the continued state of independence of the people of God during that period, or to account for the interest which Cyrus took in their affairs. The exile and its termination are indicative of uncommon acts of God towards highly-gifted and favoured men; and the appearance of such a man as Daniel is described in that book to have been, is an indispensable requisite for the right understanding of this portion of the Jewish history.

3. An important hint of the existence of the book in the time of Alexander is found in Josephus, *Antiq.*, xi. 8, 4, according to which the prophecies of Daniel had been pointed out to that king on his entrance into Jerusalem.

4. The first book of the Maccabees, which is almost contemporary with the events related in it, not only pre-supposes the existence of the book of Daniel, but actually betrays acquaintance with the Alexandrian version of the same (1 Macc. i. 54; comp. Dan. ix. 27; ii. 59; comp. Dan. iii.) —a proof that the book must have been written long before that period.

5. The reception of the book into the canon is also an evidence of its authenticity. In the Maccabæan age the canon had long been completed and closed; but even doubting that point, it is not likely that, at a time when so much scrupulous adherence was shown towards all that was hallowed by time and old usage, and when Scriptural literature was already flourishing—it is not probable, we say, that a production then recent should have been raised to the rank of a canonical book.

6. We have an important testimony for the authenticity of the book in Ezekiel xiv. 14, 20; xxviii. 3. Daniel is there represented as an unusual character, as a model of justice and wisdom, to whom had been allotted superior divine insight and revelation. This sketch perfectly agrees with that contained in our book.

7. The book betrays such an intimate acquaintance with Chaldæan manners, customs, history, and religion, as none but a contemporary writer could fairly be supposed to possess. Thus, *ex. gr.*, the description of the Chaldæan Magians and their regulations perfectly agrees with the accounts of the classics respecting them. The account of the illness and insanity of Nebuchadnezzar is confirmed by Berosus. The edict of Darius the Mede (Dan. v.) may be satisfactorily explained from the notions peculiar to the Medo-Persian religion, and the importance attached in it to the king, who was considered as a sort of incarnate deity.

8. The religious views, the ardent belief in the Messiah, the purity of that belief, the absence of all the notions and ceremonial practices of later Judaism, &c., the agreement of the book in these respects with the genuine prophetic books, and more especially with the prophets in and after the exile,—all this testifies to the genuineness of Daniel.

DANIEL, Apocryphal Addenda to. In the version of the Seventy, and that of Theodotion are found some considerable additions to the book of Daniel which are wanting in the Hebrew canon. These are,

1. The Prayer of Azarias, &c. (Dan. iii. 24-51).

2. The Song of the Three Children (Dan. iii. 52-90).

3. The History of Susanna (Dan. xiii.).

4. The Narrative of Bel and the Dragon (Dan. xiv.).

St. Jerome, who translated these together with the canonical parts of the book of Daniel from the Greek version of Theodotion, observes: 'Daniel, as received among the Hebrews, contains neither the History of Susanna, nor the Hymn of the Three Children, nor the Fables of Bel and the Dragon, all of which, as they are dispersed throughout the world, we have added, lest to the ignorant we should seem to have cut off a considerable part of the book, transfixing them at the same time with a dagger.'

Jerome further observes that the history of Susanna is considered by nearly all the Hebrews as a fable; and that it is not read in the synagogues: for who, say they, could believe that captives had the power of starving their princes and judges?

The subject of the Prayer of Azarias, and of the Song of the three youths, Azarias, Ananias, and Misael (the Hebrew names of Shadrach, Meshach, and Abed-nego), consists in a petition for deliverance from the furnace, and a hymn of thanksgiving, on the part of the young men, for their preservation in the midst of the flames. De Wette conceives that the Prayer and the Hymn betray marks of two different authors, and that the latter has the appearance of being written with a liturgical object. Certain it is that, from a very early period, it formed part of the church service, and it is one of the canticles still sung on all festivals in the Roman, and retained in the daily service of the Anglican church.

The *History of Susanna* is probably a moral parable, founded perhaps on some fact, and affording a beautiful lesson of chastity.

The object of the Jewish author of the history of the destruction of *Bel and the Dragon* was, according to Jahn, 'to warn against the sin of idolatry some of his brethren, who had embraced Egyptian superstitions. The book was, therefore, well adapted to the time, and shows that philosophy was not sufficient to keep men from apostatising into the most absurd and degrading superstitions.' The time of the writing Jahn ascribes to the age of the Ptolemies, when serpents were still worshipped at Thebes.

Bel and the Dragon is read in the Roman office on Ash-Wednesday, and in the church of England on the 23rd of November. Susanna is read in the Anglican Church on the 22nd of November, and in the Roman on the vigil of the fourth Sunday in Lent.

We shall conclude with the following observation of Erasmus. 'It is astonishing that what Jerome stabbed with his dagger is now everywhere read and sung in the churches; nay, we read, without any mark of distinction, what Jerome did not fear to call a fable, the history of Bel and the Dragon, and which he would not have added, had he not been apprehensive of seeming to have cut off a considerable portion of the sacred volume. But to whom did he fear to seem to do so? To *the ignorant*, as he himself observes. Of so much more weight to the ignorant multitude is custom, than the judgment of the learned!'

DARIUS, or rather DARJAVESH, is the name under which three Medo-Persian kings are mentioned in the Old Testament.

The first Darius is ' Darjavesh, the son of Achashverosh, of the seed of the Medes,' in the book of Daniel (ix. 1). Much difference of opinion has prevailed as to the person here intended; but there is good reason to believe that it is Cyaxares the Second, the son and successor of Astyages [AHASUERUS], and the immediate predecessor of Cyrus.

The second ' Darjavesh king of Persia' is mentioned in the book of Ezra (iv.-vii.), in Haggai, and in Zechariah, as the king who, in the second year of his reign, effected the execution of those decrees of Cyrus which granted the Jews the liberty to rebuild the temple, the fulfilment of which had been obstructed by the malicious representations which their enemies had made to the immediate successors of Cyrus. It is agreed that this prince was Darius Hystaspis, who succeeded the usurper Smerdis B.C. 521, and reigned thirty-six years.

The third ' Darjavesh the Persian,' occurs in Neh. xii. 22, in a passage which merely states that the succession of priests was registered up to his reign. It is commonly believed that this king was Darius Nothus, who came to the throne (B C 423), and reigned nineteen years.

Darius Codomannus is evidently the Persian king alluded to in 1 Macc. i. 1.

DARKNESS. In the Gospels of Matthew (xxvii. 45) and Luke (xxii. 44) we read that, while Jesus hung upon the cross, ' from the sixth hour there was darkness over all the land unto the ninth hour.' That this darkness could not have proceeded from an eclipse of the sun is placed beyond all doubt by the fact that, it being then the time of the Passover, the moon was at the full. This darkness may therefore be ascribed to an extraordinary and preternatural obscuration of the solar light, which might precede and accompany the earthquake which took place on the same occasion. For it has been noticed that often before an earthquake such a mist arises from sulphureous vapours as to occasion a darkness almost nocturnal. Such a darkness might extend over Judæa, or that division of Palestine in which Jerusalem stood, to which the best authorities agree that here, as in some other places, it is necessary to limit the phrase rendered ' all the land.'

Darkness is often used symbolically in the Scriptures as opposed to light, which is the symbol of joy and safety, to express misery and adversity (Job xviii. 6; Ps. cvii. 10; cxliii. 3; Isa. viii. 22; ix. 1; lix. 9, 10; Ezek. xxx. 18; xxxii. 7, 8; xxxiv. 12). Darkness of the sun, moon, and stars is used figuratively to denote a general darkness or deficiency in the government or body politic (Isa. xiii. 10; Ezek. xxxii. 7; Joel ii. 10-31). In Eph. v. 1!, the expression ' works of darkness' is applied to the heathen mysteries, on account of the impure actions which the initiated performed in them. ' Outer

darkness' in Matt. viii. 12, and elsewhere, refers to the darkness outside, in the streets or open country, as contrasted with the blaze of cheerful light in the house, especially when a convivial party is held in the night time. And it may be observed that the streets in the East are utterly dark after nightfall, there being no shops with lighted windows, nor even public or private lamps to impart to them the light and cheerfulness to which we are accustomed. This gives the more force to the contrast of the ' outer darkness' with the inner light.

Darkness is used to represent the state of the dead (Job x. 21; xvii. 13). It is also employed as the proper and significant emblem of ignorance (Isa. ix. 2; lx. 2; Matt. vi. 23; John iii. 9; 2 Cor. iv. 1-6).

DATES. [PALM TREE.]

DA'THAN, one of the chiefs of Reuben who joined Korah in the revolt against the authority of Moses and Aaron (Num. xvi. 1) [AARON].

DAUGHTER. In the Scriptures the word daughter is used in a variety of senses, some of which are unknown to our own language, or have only become known through familiarity with Scriptural forms of speech. Besides its usual and proper sense of—1. A daughter sent or adopted, we find it used to designate—2. A uterine sister, niece, or *any* female descendant (Gen. xx. 12; xxiv. 48; xxxviii. 6; xxxvi. 2; Num. xxv. 1; Deut. xxiii. 17).—3. Women, as natives, residents, or professing the religion of certain places, as ' the daughter of Zion' (Isa. iii. 16); ' daughters of the Philistines' (2 Sam. i. 20); ' daughter of a strange God' (Mal. ii. 11).— 4. Metaphorically, small towns are called daughters of neighbouring large cities, to which they belonged, or from which they were derived, as ' Heshbon and all the daughters [Auth. Vers. *villages*] thereof' (Num. xxi. 25); so Tyre is called the daughter of Sidon (Isa. xxii. 12), as having been originally a colony from thence; and hence also the town of Abel is called ' a mother in Israel' (2 Sam. xx. 19); and Gath is in one place (comp. 2 Sam. vii. 1; 1 Chron. xviii. 1) called Gath-Ammah, or Gath the *mother* town, to distinguish it from its own dependencies, or from another place called Gath. See other instances in Num. xxi. 32; Judg. xi. 26; Josh. xv. 45, &c.—5. The people collectively of any place, the name of which is given; as ' the daughter (*i. e.* the people) of Jerusalem hath shaken her head at thee' (Isa. xxxvii. 22; see also Ps. xlv. 13; cxxxvii. 8; Isa. x. 30; Jer. xlvi. 19; Lam. iv. 22; Zech. ix. 9).

Respecting the condition of daughters in families, see art. WOMEN and MARRIAGE.

DA'VID. The word probably means *beloved*. The reign of David is the great critical era in the history of the Hebrews. It decided that they were to have for nearly five centuries a national monarchy, a fixed line of priesthood, and a solemn religious worship by music and psalms of exquisite beauty; it finally separated Israel from the surrounding heathen, and gave room for producing those noble monuments of sacred writ, to the influence of which over the whole world no end can be seen. His predecessor, Saul, had many successes against the Philistines, but it is clear that he made little impression on their real power; for he died fighting against them, not on their own border, but on the opposite side of his kingdom, in Mount Gilboa. As for all the other ' enemies on every side '—Moabites, Ammonites, Edomites, and the kings of Zobah,—however much he may have ' vexed them ' (1 Sam. xiv. 47), they, as well as the Amalekites, remained unsubdued, if weakened. The real work of establishing Israel as lord over the whole soil of Canaan was left for David.

The life of David naturally divides itself into three portions :—I The time which he lived under Saul. II. His reign over Judah in Hebron. III. His reign over all Israel.

I. In the first period we may trace the origin of all his greatness. His susceptible temperament, joined to his devotional tendencies, must, at a very early age, have made him a favourite pupil of the prophets, whose peculiar mark was the harp and the psalm (1 Sam. x. 1-12 and xix. 20-24; see also 2 Kings iii. 15). His hospitable reception, when in distress, by Ahimelech the priest, and the atrocious massacre innocently brought by him on Nob, the city of the priests (1 Sam. xxi. and xxii. 9-19), must have deeply affected his generous nature, and laid the foundation of his cordial affection for the whole priestly order, whose ministrations he himself helped to elevate by his devotional melodies. At an early period he attracted the notice of Samuel; and if we are to arrange events according to their probable connection, we may believe that *after* David had been driven away from Saul and his life several times attempted, Samuel ventured on the solemn step of anointing him king. Whenever this took place, it must have produced on David a profound impression, and prepared him to do that in which Saul had so eminently failed, viz. to reconcile his own military government with a filial respect for the prophets and an honourable patronage of the priesthood. Besides this, he became knit into a bond of brotherhood with his heroic comrades, to whom he was eminently endeared by his personal self-denial and liberality (1 Sam. xxx. 21-31; 1 Chron. xi. 18). This, indeed, drew after it one most painful result, viz. the necessity of enduring the turbulence of his violent but able nephew Joab; nor could we expect that of a band of freebooters many should be like David. Again, during his outlawry David became acquainted in turn not only with all the wild country in the land, but with the strongholds of the enemy all round. By his residence among the Philistines he must have learned all their arts and weapons of war, in which it is reasonable to believe the Israelites previously inferior (1 Sam. xiii. 19-23). With Nahash the Ammonite he was in intimate friendship (2 Sam. x. 2); to the king of Moab he entrusted the care of his parents (1 Sam. xxii. 3); from Achish of Gath he received the important present of the town of Ziklag (1 Sam. xxvii. 6). That Ziklag was a strong place may be inferred from 1 Chron. xii. 1, 20. The celebrity acquired in successful guerilla warfare, even in modern days, turns the eyes of whole nations on a chieftain; and in an age which regarded personal heroism as the first qualification of a general (1 Chron. xi. 6) and of a king, to triumph over the persecutions of Saul gave David the fairest prospects of a kingdom.

The account transmitted to us of David's dangers and escapes in the first period is too fragmentary to work up into a history: nevertheless, it seems to be divisible into two parts, differing in character. During the former he is a fugitive and outlaw in the land of Saul, hiding in caves, pitching in the wilderness, and occasionally with great risk entering walled cities (1 Sam. xxiii. 7): in the latter he abandons his native soil entirely, and lives among the Philistines as one of their chieftains (xxvii. 1). While a rover in the land of Judah, his position (to our eyes) is anything but honourable; being a focus to which ' all who were in distress, in debt, or discontented, gathered themselves ' (xxii. 2). Yet as the number of his followers became large (six hundred, we read, xxiii 13), and David knew how to conciliate the neighbouring sheep-masters by his urbanity and kind services, he gradually felt himself to be their protector and to have a right of maintenance and tribute for them. Hence he resents the refusal of Nabal to supply his demands, as a clear injustice; and, after David's anger has been turned away by the prudent policy of Abigail. in blessing her for saving him from slaying Nabal and every male of his family, the thought seems not to have entered his mind that the intention of such a massacre was more guilty than Nabal's refusal to pay him tribute (xxv 34). This whole narrative is characteristic and instructive. By his marriage with Abigail he afterwards probably became rich (for she seems to have been a widow at her own disposal), and on passing immediately after into the land of the Philistines, he was enabled to assume a more dignified place. Becoming possessed of the stronghold of Ziklag, he now appeared like a legitimate chieftain with fixed possessions, and no longer a mere vagabond and freebooter. This was accordingly a transition-state in which David was prepared for assuming the kingdom over Judah. In Ziklag he was joined, not, as before, by mere outcasts from Israelitish life, but by men of consideration and tried warriors (1 Chron. xii. 1-22), not only of the tribe of Judah, but from Gad. Manasseh, and even ' from Saul's brethren of Benjamin.'

II. Immediately upon the death of Saul the tribe of Judah invited David to become their prince.

His first step, after his election, was to fix on Hebron as the centre of his administration—an ancient city, honourable by its association with the name of Abraham, and in the middle of his own tribe. He then strengthened himself by a marriage with Maacah, daughter of Talmai, king of Geshur (2 Sam. iii. 3); a petty monarch whose dominions were near the sources of the Jordan, and whose influence at the opposite end of the land must have added a great weight into David's scale. From Abigail, widow of the churlish Nabal, David, as we have already observed. seems to have received a large private fortune. Concerning his other wives we know nothing in particular; only it is mentioned that he had six sons by six different mothers in Hebron. The chief jealousy was between the two tribes of Benjamin and Judah, as Saul had belonged to the former; and a tournament was turned by mutual ill-will into a battle, in which Abner unwillingly slew young Asahel, brother of Joab. ' Long war,' after this, was carried on between ' the house of Saul and the house of David.' We may infer that the rest of Israel took little part in the contest; and although the nominal possession of the kingdom enabled the little tribe of Benjamin to struggle for some time against Judah, the skill and age of Abner could not prevail against the vigour and popular fame of David. A quarrel between Abner and Ishbosheth decided the former to bring the kingdom over to David. The latter refused to treat unless, as a preliminary proof of Abner's sincerity, Michal, daughter of Saul, was restored to David. The possession of such a wife was valuable to one who was aspiring to the kingdom. His demand was immediately complied with. After giving her back, Abner proceeded to win the elders of Israel over to David; but Joab discerned that if this should be so brought about, Abner of necessity would displace him from his post of chief captain. He, therefore, seized the opportunity of murdering him when he was come on a peaceful embassy, and covered the atrocity by pleading the duty of revenging his brother's blood. This deed was perhaps David's first taste of the miseries of royal power. He dared not proceed actively against his ruthless nephew, but he vented his abhorrence in a solemn curse on Joab and his posterity, and followed Abner to the grave with weeping. Anxious to purge himself of the guilt, he ordered a public wearing of sackcloth, and refused to touch food all the day. The feeble Ishbosheth, left alone, was unequal to the government, and shortly suffered the same fate of assassination. David, following the universal policy of sovereigns, and his own profound sense of the sacredness of royalty, took vengeance on the murderers, and buried Ishbosheth in Abner's tomb at Hebron.

III. The death of Ishbosheth gave to David supremacy over all Israel. The kingdom was not at first a despotic, but a constitutional one; for it is stated, ' David made *a league* with the elders of Israel in Hebron before Jehovah ; and they anointed David king over Israel ' (2 Sam. v. 3). This is marked out as the era which determined the Philistines to hostility (ver. 17), and may confirm our idea, that their policy was to hinder Israel from becoming united under a single king. Two victories of David over them follow, both near the valley of Rephaim ; and these were probably the first battles fought by David after becoming king of all Israel.

Perceiving that Hebron was no longer a suitable capital, he resolved to fix his residence farther to the north. On the very border of the tribes of Judah and Benjamin lay the town of Jebus, which with its neighbourhood was occupied by Jebusites, a remnant of the old Canaanitish nation so called. In spite of the great strength of the fort of Zion, it was captured, and the Jebusites were entirely expelled or subdued; after which David adopted the city as his new capital, greatly enlarged the fortifications, and gave or restored the name of Jerusalem [JERUSALEM]. After becoming master of Jerusalem, David made a league with Hiram, king of Tyre, who supplied him with skilful artificers to build a splendid palace at the new capital. That the mechanical arts should have been in a very low state among the Israelites, was to be expected; since, before the reign of Saul even smiths' forges were not allowed among them by the Philistines. Nothing, however, could have been more profitable for the

Phœnicians than the security of cultivation enjoyed by the Israelites in the reigns of David and Solomon. The trade between Tyre and Israel became at once extremely lucrative to both, and the league between the two states was quickly very intimate.

Once settled in Jerusalem, David proceeded to increase the number of his wives, perhaps in part from the same political motive that actuates other Oriental monarchs, viz. in order to take *hostages* from the chieftains round in the least offensive mode. We know nothing further concerning his family relations, than the names of eleven sons born in Jerusalem (2 Sam. v. 14, 15), of whom four were children of Bathsheba (1 Chron. iii. 5), and therefore much younger than the elder sons.

Jerusalem, now become the civil metropolis of the nation, was next to be made its religious centre ; and the king applied himself to elevate the priestly order, to swell the ranks of attending Levites and singers, and to bring the ark to Jerusalem. The bringing of the ark from Kirjathjearim to Jerusalem established the line of highpriests in direct service before it ; and from this time we may presume that the ceremonies of the great day of Atonement began to be observed.

When the ark entered Jerusalem in triumph, David put on a priest's ephod and danced before it. This proved the occasion of the rupture between him and his royal spouse, Michal (2 Sam. vi. 21). After this event, the king, contrasting his cedar palace with the curtains of the tabernacle, was desirous of building a temple for the ark ; such a step, moreover, was likely to prevent any future change of its abode. The prophet Nathan, however, forbade it, on pious and intelligible grounds.

David's further victories are narrated in the following order — Philistines, Moab, Zobah, Edom, Northern League stirred up by the Ammonites, Ammon. 1. The short notice concerning the Philistines just gives us to understand that this is the era of their decisive, though not final, subjugation. Their towns were despoiled of their wealth (2 Sam. viii. 12), and doubtless all their arms and munitions of war passed over into the service of the conqueror. 2. The Moabites were a pastoral people, whose general relations with Israel appear to have been peaceful. The slight notice of Saul's hostilities with them (1 Sam. xiv. 47) is the only breach recorded since the time of Eglon and Ehud. In the book of Ruth we see them as friendly neighbours, and much more recently (1 Sam. xxii. 3, 4) David committed his parents to the care of the king of Moab. We know no cause, except David's strength, which now drew his arms upon them. A people long accustomed to peace, in conflict with a veteran army, was struck down at once, but the fierceness of his triumph may surprise us. Two-thirds of the population (if we rightly interpret the words, 2 Sam. viii. 2) were put to the sword: the rest became tributary. 3. Who are meant by the Syrians of Zobah, is still a problem [ZOBAH]. We here follow the belief that it was a power of northern Syria, then aiming at extensive empire, which had not only defeated and humbled the king of Hamath, but had obtained homage beyond the Euphrates. The trans-Jordanic tribes in the time of Saul had founded a little empire for themselves by conquering their eastern neighbours, the Hagarenes; and, perhaps, occasionally overran the district on the side of the Euphrates, which Hadadezer, king of Zobah, considered as his own. His efforts 'to recover his border at the river Euphrates' first brought him into collision with David, perhaps by an attack which he made on the roaming Eastern tribes. David defeated not merely his army, but that of Damascus too, which came, too late, with succour; and put Israelite garrisons into the towns of the Damascenes. 4. Another victory, gained 'in the valley of salt,' ought, perhaps, to be read, as in 1 Chron. xviii. 12, and in the superscription of Ps. lx., 'over the *Edomites*,' not 'over the *Syrians.*' 5. After David had become master of all Israel, of the Philistine towns, of Edom, and of Moab, while the Eastern tribes, having conquered the Hagarenes, threatened the Ammonites on the north, as did Moab on the south, the Ammonites were naturally alarmed, and called in the powers of Syria to their help against a foe who was growing dangerous even to them. The coalition against David is described as consisting of the Syrians of Bethrehob and of Maacah, of Zobah and of Tob. The last country appears to have been in the district of Trachonitis, the two first immediately on the north of Israel. In this war, we may believe that David enjoyed the important alliance of Toi, king of Hamath, who, having suffered from Hadadezer's hostility, courted the friendship of the Israelitish monarch (2 Sam. viii. 9, 10). We are barely informed that one division of the Israelites under Abishai was posted against the Ammonites; a second under Joab met the confederates from the north, 30,000 strong, and prevented their junction with the Ammonites. In both places the enemy was repelled, though, it would seem, with no decisive result. A second campaign took place. The king of Zobah brought in an army of Mesopotamians, in addition to his former troops, and David found it necessary to make a levy of all Israel to meet the pressing danger. A pitched battle on a great scale was then fought at Helam—far beyond the limits of the twelve tribes—in which David was victorious. The Syrians henceforth left the Ammonites to their fate, and the petty chiefs who had been in allegiance to Hadadezer hastened to do homage to David. 6. Early in the next season Joab was sent to take vengeance on the Ammonites in their own home, by attacking their chief city, or Rabbah of Ammon. The natural strength of their border could not keep out veteran troops and an experienced leader; and though the siege of the city occupied many months (if, indeed, it was not prolonged into the next year), it was at last taken. It is characteristic of Oriental despotism, that Joab, when the city was nearly reduced, sent to invite David to command the final assault in person. David gathered a large force, easily captured the royal town, and despoiled it of all its wealth. His vengeance was as much more dreadful on the unfortunate inhabitants than formerly on the Moabites, as the danger in which the Ammonites had involved Israel had been more imminent (2 Sam. xii. 31; 1 Chron. xx. 3). During the campaign against Rabbah of Ammon the painful and never-to-be-forgotten outrage of David against Bathsheba and her husband Uriah the Hittite took place. It is principally through this narrative that we know the tedious-

ness of that siege; since the adultery with Bathsheba and the birth of at least one child took place during the course of it.

The latter years of David's reign were afflicted by the inevitable results of polygamy and despotism. viz. the quarrels of the sons of different mothers, and their eagerness to seize the kingdom before their father's death. Of all his sons, Absalom had naturally the greatest pretensions, being, by his mother's side, grandson of Talmai, king of Geshur; while through his personal beauty and winning manners he was high in popular favour. It is evident, moreover, that he was the darling son of his father. When his own sister Tamar had been dishonoured by her half-brother Amnon, the eldest son of David, Absalom slew him in vengeance, but, in fear of his father, then fled to his grandfather at Geshur. Joab, discerning David's longings for his son, effected his return after three years; but the conflict in the king's mind is strikingly shown by his allowing Absalom to dwell two full years in Jerusalem before he would see his face.

The insurrection of Absalom against the king was the next important event; in the course of which there was shown the general tendency of men to look favourably on young and untried princes, rather than on those whom they know for better and for worse. Absalom erected his royal standard at Hebron first, and was fully prepared to slay his father outright, which might probably have been done, if the energetic advice of Ahithophel had been followed. While they delayed, David escaped beyond the Jordan, and with all his troop met a most friendly reception, not only from Barzillai and Machir, wealthy chiefs of pastoral Gilead, but from Shobi, the son of the Ammonite king Nahash, whose power he had destroyed, and whose people he had hewed in pieces. We likewise learn on this occasion that the fortunes of David had been all along attended by 600 men of Gath, who now, under the command of Ittai the Gittite, crossed the Jordan with all their households, in spite of David's generous advice that they would return to their own country. Strengthened by the warlike eastern tribes, and surrounded by his experienced captains, the king no longer hesitated to meet Absalom in the field. A decisive victory was won at the wood of Ephraim, and Absalom was slain by Joab in the retreat. The old king was heart-stricken at this result, and, ignorant of his own weakness, superseded Joab in the command of the host by Amasa, Absalom's captain. Perhaps Joab on the former occasion, when he murdered Abner, had blinded the king by pleading revenge for the blood of Asahel; but no such pretence could here avail. The king was now probably brought to his determination, partly by his disgust at Joab, partly by his desire to give the insurgents confidence in his amnesty. If Amasa is the same as Amasai, David may likewise have retained a grateful remembrance of the cordial greeting with which he had led a strong band to his assistance at the critical period of his abode in Ziklag (1 Chron. xii. 18); moreover, Amasa, equally with Joab, was David's nephew, their two mothers, Abigail and Zeruiah, being sisters to David by at least one parent (2 Sam. xvii. 25; 1 Chron. ii. 13, 16). The unscrupulous Joab, however, was not so to be set aside. Before long, catching an opportunity, he assassinated his unsuspecting cousin with his own hand; and David, who had used the instrumentality of Joab to murder Uriah, did not dare to resent the deed.

A quarrel which took place between the men of Judah and those of the other tribes in bringing the king back, had encouraged a Benjamite named Sheba to raise a new insurrection, which spread with wonderful rapidity. Amasa was collecting troops as David's general at the time when he was treacherously assassinated by his cousin, who then, with his usual energy, pursued Sheba, and blockaded him in Bethmaachah before he could collect his partisans. Sheba's head was cut off, and thrown over the wall; and so ended the new rising. Yet this was not the end of trouble; for the intestine war seems to have inspired the Philistines with the hope of throwing off the yoke. Four successive battles are recorded (2 Sam. xxi. 15-22), in the first of which the aged David was nigh to being slain. His faithful officers kept him away from all future risks, and Philistia was once more, and finally, subdued.

The last commotion recorded took place when David's end seemed nigh, and Adonijah, one of his elder sons, feared that the influence of Bathsheba might gain the kingdom for her own son Solomon. Adonijah's conspiracy was joined by Abiathar, one of the two chief priests, and by the redoubted Joab; upon which David took the decisive measure of raising Solomon at once to the throne. Of two young monarchs, the younger and the less known was easily preferred, when the sanction of the existing government was thrown into his scale; and the cause of Adonijah immediately fell to the ground. Amnesty was promised to the conspirators, yet it was not very faithfully observed [Solomon].

Numerous indications remain to us that, however eminently David was embued with faith in Jehovah as the national God of Israel, and however he strove to unite all Israel in common worship, he still had no sympathy with the later spirit which repelled all foreigners from co-operation with Jews. In his early years necessity made him intimate with Philistines, Moabites, and Ammonites: policy led him into league with the Tyrians. He himself took in marriage a daughter of the king of Geshur: it is the less wonderful that we find Uriah the Hittite (2 Sam. xi.), Gether the Ishmaelite (1 Chron. ii. 17), and others, married to Israelitish wives. The fidelity of Ittai the Gittite, and his six hundred men, has been already alluded to. It would appear, on the whole, that in tolerating foreigners Solomon did not go beyond the principles established by his father, though circumstances gave them a fuller development.

No attempt seems to have been made in David's reign to maintain horses or chariots for military purposes. Even chieftains in battle, as Absalom on his fatal day, appear mounted only on mules. Yet horses were already used in state equipages, apparently as a symbol of royalty (2 Sam. xv. 1). That in the opening of Saul's reign the Philistines had deprived the Israelites of all the most formidable arms, is well known. It is probable that this may have led to a more careful practice of the sling and of the bow, especially among the southern tribes, who were more immediately pressed by the power of the Philistines. Such

weapons cannot be kept out of the hands of the rustics, and must have been essential against wild beasts. But, from causes unknown, the Benjamites were peculiarly celebrated as archers and slingers (Judg. xx. 16; 1 Chron. viii. 40; xii. 2; 2 Chron. xiv. 8; xvii. 17), while the pastoral tribes beyond the Jordan were naturally able to escape all attempts of the Philistines to deprive them of shield, spear, and sword. Hence the Gadites, who came to David at Ziklag, are described as formidable and full-armed warriors, 'with faces like lions, and swift as mountain roes' (1 Chron. xii. 8).

The standing army which Saul had begun to maintain was greatly enlarged by David. An account of this is given in 1 Chron. xxvii; from which it would seem that 24,000 men were constantly maintained on service, though there was a relieving of guard every month. Hence, twelve times this number, or 288,000, were under a permanent military organization, with a general for each division in his month. Besides this host, the register proceeds to recount twelve princes over the tribes of Israel, who may perhaps be compared to the lord-lieutenants of English counties.

The *cabinet* of David (if we may use a modern name) is thus given (1 Chron. xxvii. 32-34) with reference to a time which preceded Absalom's revolt:—1, Jonathan, David's uncle, a counsellor, wise man, and scribe; 2, Jehiel, son of Hachmoni, tutor (?) to the king's sons; 3, Ahithophel, the king's counsellor; 4, Hushai, the king's companion; 5, after Ahithopel, Jehoiada, the son of Benaiah; 6, Abiathar the priest. It is added, 'and the general of the king's army was Joab.'

Twelve royal bailiffs are recited as a part of David's establishment (1 Chron. xxvii. 25, 31), having the following departments under their charge: 1, The treasures of gold, silver, &c.; 2, the magazines; 3, the tillage (wheat, &c.?); 4, the vineyards; 5, the wine-cellars; 6, the olive and sycamore trees; 7, the oil-cellars; 8, the herds in Sharon; 9, the herds in the valleys; 10, the camels; 11, the asses; 12, the flocks. The eminently prosperous state in which David left his kingdom to Solomon appears to prove that he was on the whole faithfully served, and that his own excellent intentions, patriotic spirit, and devout piety (measured, as it must be measured, by the standard of those ages), made his reign beneficial to his subjects.

DAY. The earliest measure of time on record is the day:—'The *evening* and the *morning* were the first *day*' (Gen. i. 5). Here the word 'day' denotes the civil or calendar day of twenty-four hours, including 'the evening,' or natural night, and the 'morning,' or natural day. It is remarkable that in this account 'the evening,' or natural night, precedes 'the morning,' or natural day. Hence the Hebrew compound 'evening-morning,' which is used by Daniel (viii. 14) to denote a civil day. In fact, the Jewish civil day began, as it still does, not with the morning, but the evening—thus the Sabbath commences with the sunset of Friday, and ends with the sunset of Saturday.

The inconveniences resulting from a variable commencement of the civil day, earlier or later, according to the different seasons of the year, as well as the equally varying duration of the natural day and night, must have been very considerable, and are sensibly felt by Europeans when travelling in the East, where the ancient custom in this matter is still observed. These inconveniences must be less obvious to the people themselves, who know no better system; yet they were apparent to several ancient nations—the Egyptians, the Ausonians, and others—and induced them to reckon their civil day from midnight to midnight, as from a fixed invariable point; and this usage has been adopted by most of the modern nations of Europe. We thus realize the advantage of having our divisions of the day, the hours, of equal duration, day and night, at all times of the year; whereas among the Orientals the hours, and all other divisions of the natural day and night, are of constantly varying duration, and the divisions of the day vary from those of the night, excepting at the equinoxes.

The natural day was at first divided into three parts, morning, noon, and evening, which are mentioned by David as hours or times of prayer (Ps. lv. 17).

The natural night was also originally divided into three parts, or watches (Ps. lxiii. 6; xc. 4). The *first*, or *beginning of the watches*, is mentioned in Lam. ii. 19; the *middle watch*, in Judg. vii. 19; and the *morning watch*, in Exod. xiv. 24. Afterwards the strictness of military discipline among the Greeks and Romans introduced an additional night-watch. The *second and third watches of the night* are mentioned in Luke xii. 38, and the *fourth* in Matt. xiv. 25. The four are mentioned together by our Lord, in Mark xiii. 35, and described by the terms ' the late watch;' ' the midnight;' ' the cock-crowing;' and ' the morning.' The precise beginning and ending of each of the four watches is thus determined:

1. ' *The late*' began at sunset and ended with the third hour of the night, including the evening dawn, or twilight. It was also called ' eventide ' (Mark xi. 11), or simply ' evening ' (John xx. 19).

2. ' *The midnight*' lasted from the third hour till midnight.

3. ' *The cock-crowing*' lasted from midnight till the third hour after, or to the ninth hour of the night. It included the two cock-crowings, with the second of which it ended.

4. ' *Early*' lasted from the ninth to the twelfth hour of the night, or sunrise, including the morning dawn, or twilight. It was also called ' morning,' or ' morning-tide' (John xviii. 28).

The division of the day into twelve hours was common among the Jews after the captivity in Babylon. The word hour first occurs in the book of Daniel (iv. 19); and it is admitted by the Jewish writers that this division of the day was borrowed by them from the Babylonians. Our Lord appeals to this ancient, and then long-established, division, as a matter of public notoriety : ' Are there not twelve hours in the day ?' (John xi. 9).

This, however, was the division of the natural day into twelve hours, which were therefore variable according to the seasons of the year, at all places except the equator; and equal, or of the mean length, only at the vernal and autumnal equinoxes; being longer in the summer half-year, and shorter in the winter. The inconvenience of this has already been intimated.

The *first hour* of the day began at sunrise; the *sixth hour* ended at mid-day, or noon; the *seventh hour* began at noon; and the *twelfth hour* ended at sunset.

The days of the week had no proper names among the Hebrews, but were distinguished only by their numeral order [WEEK].

DEACON. This word in its more extended sense is used, both in Scripture and in ecclesiastical writers, to designate *any person who ministers in God's service*. In 2 Cor. vi. 4, the Apostle says, ' But in all things approving ourselves as the ministers (*deacons*) of God.' Again, Eph. iii. 7, ' Whereof I was made a minister' (*deacon*); and in Col. i. 23, he employs the same epithet to express the character of his office. In Rom. xv. 8, St. Paul calls our Lord ' minister of the circumcision,' literally *deacon of the circumcision;* and, in his Epistle to the Philippians, he addresses himself to the *bishops* and *deacons* (Phil. i. 1).

But it is in its more confined sense, as it expresses the *third* order of the ministry of the primitive Church, that we are to examine the meaning of the word *Deacon*.

In Acts vi. we have an account of the election of seven persons to the office of deaconship for the purpose of superintending the distribution of the church's bounty. That their duties, however, were not of an exclusively secular character is clear from the fact that both Philip and Stephen preached, and that one of them also *baptized*. Ignatius, a martyr-disciple of St. John, and bishop of Antioch, A.D. 68, styles them at once ' ministers of the mysteries of Christ;' adding, that they are not ministers of meats and drinks, but of the Church of God.

Cyprian, bishop of Carthage, A.D. 250 (whilst referring their origin to Acts vi.), styles them ministers of episcopacy and of the church : at the same time he asserts that they were called to the ministry of the altar.

Tertullian, a celebrated Father of the second century, classes them with bishops and presbyters as guides and leaders to the laity.

The fourth Council of Carthage expressly forbids the deacon to assume any one function peculiar to the priesthood, by declaring the deacon as consecrated not to the priesthood but to the ministry.

His ordination, moreover, differed from that of presbyter both in its form and in the powers which it conferred. For in the ordination of a presbyter, the presbyters who were present were required to join in the imposition of hands with the bishop : but the ordination of a deacon might be performed by the bishop alone, because, as the 4th Can. of the 4th Council of Carthage declares, he was ordained not to the priesthood, but to the inferior services of the Church. We now proceed to notice what these services specifically were.

1. The deacon's more ordinary duty was to assist the bishop and presbyter in the service of the sanctuary ; especially was he charged with the care of the utensils and ornaments appertaining to the holy table.

2. In the administration of the Eucharist, it was theirs to hand the consecrated elements to the people.

3. Deacons had power to administer the sacrament of baptism.

4. The office of the deacon was not to preach, so much as to instruct and catechise the catechumens. His part was, when the bishop or presbyter did not preach, to read a homily from one of the Fathers. St. Ambrose, Bishop of Milan, A.D. 380, says expressly that deacons, in his time, did not preach, though he thinks that they were all originally Evangelists, as were Philip and Stephen.

5. It was the deacon's business to receive the offerings of the people; and having presented them to the bishop or presbyter, to give expression in a *loud voice* to the names of the offerers.

6. Deacons were sometimes authorised, as the bishops' special delegates, to give to penitents the solemn imposition of hands, which was the sign of reconciliation.

7. Deacons had power to suspend the inferior clergy; this, however, was done only when the bishop and presbyter were absent, and the case urgent.

8. The ordinary duty of deacons, with regard to general Councils, was to act as scribes and disputants according as they were directed by their bishops. In some instances they voted as proxies for bishops who could not attend in person; but in no instance do we find them voting in a general Council by virtue of their office. But in provincial synods the deacons were sometimes allowed to give their voice, as well as the presbyters, in their own name.

9. But, besides the above, there were some other offices which the deacon was called upon to fill abroad. One of these was to take care of the necessitous, orphans, widows, martyrs in prison, and all the poor and sick who had any claim upon the public resources of the church. It was also his especial duty to notice the spiritual, as well as the bodily, wants of the people; and wherever he detected evils which he could not by his own power and authority cure, it was for him to refer them for redress to the bishop.

In general the number of deacons varied with the wants of a particular church. Sozomen (vii. 19, p. 100) informs us that the church of Rome, after the apostolic model, never had more than seven deacons.

It was not till the close of the third century that deacons were forbidden to marry. The Council of Ancyra, A.D. 344, in its 10th Can., ordains that if a deacon declared at the time of his ordination that he would marry, he should not be deprived of his function if he did marry; but that if he married without having made such a declaration, 'he must fall into the rank of laicks!'

The *qualifications* required in deacons by the primitive church were the same that were required in bishops and presbyters; and the characteristics of a deacon, given by St. Paul in his Second Epistle to Timothy, were the rule by which a candidate was judged fit for such an office. The second Council of Carthage, 4th Can., forbids the ordination of a deacon before the age of twenty-five; and both the Civil and Canon Law fixed his age to the same period.

The primitive church had its archdeacon, though when the office was first instituted is a matter of dispute with learned men. He was not in priests' orders; but was selected from the deacons by the bishop, and had considerable authority over the other deacons and inferior orders.

DEACONESS. That the order of Deaconess existed in the Christian church, *even in apostolic days*, is evident from Rom. xvi. 1 : ' I commend unto you Phebe, our sister, which is a servant (a deaconess) of the church which is at Cenchrea.' The *earliest* Fathers of the church, moreover, speak of the same order of persons.

Certain qualifications were necessary in those who were taken into this order.

1. It was necessary that she should be a *widow*.

2. No widow, unless she had borne children, could become a *deaconess*. This rule arose out of a belief that no person but a mother can possess those sympathizing and tender feelings which ought to animate the deaconess in the discharge of her *peculiar* duties.

3. The early church was very strict in exacting the rule which prohibits the election of any to be deaconesses who had been twice married, though lawfully, and successively to two husbands, one after the other.

It is a disputed point with some learned men whether deaconesses were ordained by imposition of hands. However, the fifteenth Can. of the Council of Chalcedon expressly declares that deaconesses were so ordained, and this is fully confirmed by the author of the *Apost. Constitutions*, viii. 19. Still, deaconesses were not consecrated to any *priestly* function. Some heretics, indeed, allowed women to teach, exorcise, and to administer baptism; but all this he sharply rebukes as being contrary to the apostolic rule.

5. One of the peculiar duties of the deaconesses was to assist at the baptism of *women*.

6. Another duty the deaconesses had to perform was to instruct and prepare the catechumens for baptism.

7. In times of danger and persecution it was the duty of the deaconesses to visit the martyrs in prison, because they could more easily gain access to them, and with less suspicion and hazard than the deacons.

8. The deaconesses stood at the entrance of the church in order to direct the women as to the place each one should occupy during divine service.

How long this order continued in the Christian church is not quite certain. It was not however discontinued everywhere at once, and it was not till the tenth century that it was wholly abrogated.

DEAD SEA. [SEA.]

DEATH. Since death can be regarded in various points of view, the descriptions of it must necessarily vary. If we consider the state of a dead man, as it strikes the senses, death is the cessation of natural life. If we consider the cause of death, we may place it in that permanent and entire cessation of the feeling and motion of the body which results from the destruction of the body. Among theologians, death is commonly said to consist in the separation of soul and body, implying that the soul still exists when the body perishes. Death does not consist in this separation, but this separation is the consequence of death. As soon as the body loses feeling and motion, it is henceforth useless to the soul, which is therefore separated from it.

R

Scriptural representations, names, and modes of speech respecting death :—

(*a.*) One of the most common in the Old Testament is, *to return to the dust,* or *to the earth.* Hence the phrase, *the dust of death.* It is founded on the description Gen. ii. 7, and iii. 19, and denotes the dissolution and destruction of the *body.* Hence the sentiment in Eccles. xii. 7,— ' The dust shall return to the earth as it was, the spirit unto God who gave it.'

(*b.*) A withdrawing, exhalation, or removal of the breath of life (Ps. civ. 29).

(*c.*) A removal from the body, a being absent from the body, a departure from it, &c. This description is founded on the comparison of the body with a tent or lodgment in which the soul dwells during this life. Death destroys this tent or house, and commands us to travel on (Job iv. 21; Isa. xxxviii. 12; Ps. liii. 7; 2 Cor. v. 1; 2 Peter i. 13, 14).

(*d.*) Paul likewise uses the term to be *unclothed,* in reference to death (2 Cor. v. 3, 4); because the body is represented as the garment of the soul, as Plato calls it. The soul, therefore, as long as it is in the body, is clothed; and as soon as it is disembodied, is naked.

(*e.*) The terms which denote *sleep* are applied frequently in the Bible, as everywhere else, to death (Ps. lxxvi. 5; Jer. li. 39; John xi. 13, sqq.).

(*f.*) Death is frequently compared with and named from *a departure, a going away* (Job x. 21; Ps. xxxix. 4; Matt. xxvi. 24; Phil. i. 23; 2 Tim. iv. 6).

Death, when personified, is described as a ruler and tyrant, having vast power and a great kingdom, over which he reigns. But the ancients also represented it under some figures which are not common among us. We represent it as a man with a scythe, or as a skeleton, &c.; but the Jews, before the exile, frequently represented death as a hunter, who lays *snares* for men (Ps. xviii. 5, 6; xci. 3). After the exile, they represented him as a man, or sometimes as an angel (the angel of Death), with a cup of poison, which he reaches to men. From this representation appears to have arisen the phrase, which occurs in the New Testament, *to taste death* (Matt. xvi. 28; Heb. ii. 9), which, however, in common speech. signifies merely to *die,* without reminding one of the origin of the phrase. The case is the same with the phrase to *see death* (Ps. lxxxix. 48; Luke ii. 26).

DE'BIR, a city in the tribe of Judah, about thirty miles south-west from Jerusalem, and ten miles west of Hebron. It was also called Kirjath-sepher (Josh. xv. 15), and Kirjath-sannah (xv. 49). The name Debir means 'a word' or 'oracle,' and is applied to that most secret and separated part of the Temple, or of the most holy place, in which the ark of the covenant was placed, and in which responses were given from above the cherubim. From this, coupled with the fact that Kirjath-sepher means 'book-city,' it has been conjectured that Debir was some particularly sacred place or seat of learning among the Canaanites, and a repository of their records. 'It is not indeed probable,' as Professor Bush remarks, 'that writing and books, in our sense of the words, were very common among the Canaanites; but some method of recording events, and a sort of

learning, was doubtless cultivated in those regions.' Debir was taken by Joshua (xi. 38); but it being afterwards retaken by the Canaanites, Caleb, to whom it was assigned, gave his daughter Achsah in marriage to his nephew Othniel for his bravery in carrying it by storm (Josh. xv. 16). The town was afterwards given to the priests (xxi. 15). No trace of it is to be found at the present time.

There were two other places called Debir: one belonging to Gad, beyond Jordan (Josh. xiii. 26); the other to Benjamin, though originally in Judah.

DEB'ORAH (*a bee*), a prophetess, wife of Lapidoth. She dwelt, probably, in a tent, under a well-known palm-tree between Ramah and Bethel, where she judged Israel (Judg. iv. 4, 5). This in all likelihood means that she was the organ of communication between God and his people, and probably, on account of the influence and authority of her character, was accounted in some sort as the head of the nation, to whom questions of doubt and difficulty were referred for decision. In her triumphal song she says—
' In the days of Shamgar, son of Anath,
   In the days of Jael, the ways lay desert,
   And high-way travellers went in winding by-paths.
Leaders failed in Israel, they failed,
Until that I Deborah arose,
That I arose, a mother in Israel.'
From the further intimations which that song contains, and from other circumstances, the people would appear to have sunk into a state of total discouragement under the oppression of the Canaanites; so that it was difficult to rouse them from their despondency and to induce them to make any exertion to burst the fetters of their bondage. From the gratitude which Deborah expresses towards the people for the effort which they finally made, we are warranted in drawing the conclusion that she had long endeavoured to instigate them to this step in vain. At length she summoned Barak, the son of Abinoam, from Kedesh, a city of Naphtali, on a mountain not far from Hazor, and made known to him the will of God that he should undertake an enterprise for the deliverance of his country. But such was his disheartened state of feeling, and at the same time such his confidence in the superior character and authority of Deborah, that he assented to go only on the condition that she would accompany him. To this she at length consented. They then repaired together to Kedesh, and collected there—in the immediate vicinity of Hazor, the capital of the dominant power—ten thousand men, with whom they marched southward, and encamped on Mount Tabor. Sisera, the general of Jabin, king of Hazor, who was at the head of the Canaanitish confederacy, immediately collected an army, pursued them, and encamped in face of them in the great plain of Esdraelon. Encouraged by Deborah, Barak boldly descended from Tabor into the plain with his ten thousand men to give battle to the far superior host of Sisera, which was rendered the more formidable to the Israelites by nine hundred chariots of iron. The Canaanites were beaten; and Barak pursued them northward to Harosheth. Sisera himself, being hotly pursued, alighted from his chariot and escaped on foot to the tent of Heber the Kenite,

by whose wife he was slain. This great victory (dated about B.C. 1296), which seems to have been followed up, broke the power of the native princes, and secured to the Israelites a repose of forty years' duration. During part of this time Deborah probably continued to exercise her former authority; but nothing more of her history is known.

The song of triumph, which was composed in consequence of the great victory over Sisera, is said to have been 'sung by Deborah and Barak.' It is usually regarded as the composition of Deborah; and was probably indited by her to be sung on the return of Barak and his warriors from the pursuit. It is a peculiarly fine specimen of the earlier poetry of the Hebrews.

2. DEBORAH. The nurse of Rebekah, whom she accompanied to the land of Canaan; she died near Beth-el, and was buried under an oak, which for that reason was thenceforth called Allon-bachuth—' the oak of weeping' (Gen. xxxv. 8).

DECALOGUE, the *ten words* (Exod. xxxiv. 28; Deut. iv. 13; x. 4). This is the name most usually given by the Greek Fathers to the law of the two tables, given by God to Moses on Mount Sinai. The Decalogue was written on two stone slabs (Exod. xxxi. 18), which, having been broken by Moses (xxxii. 19), were renewed by God (xxxiv. 1, &c.). They are said (Deut. ix. 10) to have been written by the finger of God, an expression which always implies an immediate act of the Deity. The decalogue is five times alluded to in the New Testament, there called *commandments*, but only the latter precepts are specifically cited, which refer to our duties to each other (Matt. xvii. 18, 19, &c.; Mark x. 19; Luke xviii. 20; Rom. xiii. 9; vii. 7, 8; Matt. v.; 1 Tim. i. 9, 10). [LAW.]

The circumstance of these precepts being called *the ten words* has doubtless led to the belief that the two tables contained ten distinct precepts, five in each table; while some have supposed that they were called by this name to denote their perfection, *ten* being considered the most perfect of numbers. Philo-Judæus divides them into two pentads, the first pentad ending with Exod. xx. 12, 'Honour thy father and thy mother,' &c., or the *fifth* commandment of the Greek, Reformed, and Anglican churches; while the more general opinion among Christians is that the first table contained our duty to God, ending with the law to keep the sabbath holy, and the second, our duty to our neighbour. As they are not numerically divided in the Scriptures, so that we cannot positively say which is the first, which the second, &c., it may not prove uninteresting to the student in Biblical literature, if we here give a brief account of the different modes of dividing them which have prevailed among Jews and Christians. These may be classed as the Talmudical, the Origenian, and the two Masoretic divisions.

According to the division contained in the Talmud, the first commandment consists of the words ' I am the Lord thy God, who brought thee out of the land of Egypt, out of the house of bondage' (Exod. xx. 2; Deut. v. 6); the second (Exod. iii. 4), 'Thou shalt have none other gods beside me; thou shalt not make to thyself any graven image,' &c. to ver. 6; the third, 'Thou shalt not take

God's name in vain,' &c.; the fourth, 'Remember to keep holy the sabbath day,' &c.; the fifth, ' Honour thy father and thy mother,' &c.; the sixth, 'Thou shalt not kill;' the seventh, 'Thou shalt not commit adultery ;' the eighth, 'Thou shalt not steal ;' the ninth, 'Thou shalt not bear false witness,' &c.; and the tenth, 'Thou shalt not covet,' &c. to the end.

The next division is that approved by Origen, and is the one in use in the Greek and in all the Reformed Churches, except the Lutheran.

Although Origen was acquainted with the differing opinions which existed in his time in regard to this subject, it is evident from his own words that he knew nothing of that division by which the number *ten* is completed by making the prohibition against coveting either the house or the wife a distinct commandment. In his eighth *Homily on Genesis*, after citing the words, 'I am the Lord thy God, who brought thee out of the land of Egypt,' he adds, ' this is not a part of the commandment.' The first commandment is, 'Thou shalt have no other gods but me,' and then follows, 'Thou shalt not make an idol.' These together are thought by some to make one commandment; but in this case the number ten will not be complete—where then will be the truth of the decalogue? But if it be divided as we have done in the last sentence, the full number will be evident. The first commandment therefore is, ' Thou shalt have no other gods but me,' and the second, 'Thou shalt not make to thyself an idol, nor a likeness,' &c. Gregory Nazianzen and Jerome take the same view with Origen. It is also supported by the learned Jews Philo and Josephus, who speak of it as the received division of the Jewish Church.

It appears to have been forgotten in the Western Church, but was revived by Calvin in 1536, and is also received by that section of the Lutherans who followed Bucer, called the Tetrapolitans. It is adopted by Calmet, and is that followed in the present Russian Church, as well as by the Greeks in general. It appeared in the Bishops Book in 1537, and was adopted by the Anglican Church at the Reformation (1548), substituting *seventh* for sabbath-day in her formularies. The same division was published with approbation by Bonner in his *Homilies* in 1555.

We shall next proceed to describe the two Masoretic divisions. The first is that in Exodus. According to this arrangement, the two first commandments (according to the Origenian or Greek division), that is, the commandment concerning the worship of one God, and that concerning images, make but one; the second is, ' Thou shalt not take the name of the Lord thy God in vain,' and so on until we arrive at the two last, the former of which is, ' Thou shalt not covet thy neighbour's house,' and the last or tenth, ' Thou shalt not covet thy neighbour's wife. nor his servant,' &c., to the end. This was the division approved by Luther, and it has been ever since his time received by the Lutheran Church. This division is also followed in the Trent catechism, and may therefore be called the Roman Catholic division.

Those who follow this division have been accustomed to give the decalogue very-generally in an abridged form: thus the first commandment in the Lutheran shorter catechism is simply, 'Thou shalt have no other gods but me;' the second, 'Thou shalt not take the name of thy God in vain;' the third, 'Thou shalt sanctify the sabbath-day.' A similar practice is followed by the Roman Catholics, although they, as well as the Lutherans, in their larger catechisms (as the Douay) give them at full length. This practice has given rise to the charge made against those denominations of leaving out the second commandment, whereas it would have been more correct to say that they had mutilated the first, or at least that the form in which they give it has the effect of concealing a most important part of it from such as had only access to their shorter catechisms.

The last division is the *second Masoretic*, or that of Deuteronomy, sometimes called the Augustinian. This division differs from the former simply in placing the precept 'Thou shalt not covet thy neighbour's wife' before 'Thou shalt not covet thy neighbour's house,' &c.; and for this transposition it has the authority of Deut. v. 21. The authority of the Masoretes cannot, however, be of sufficient force to supersede the earlier traditions of Philo and Josephus.

DECAP'OLIS. This appears to denote not, as is frequently stated, a particular province or district, but certain *Ten Cities*, including the adjacent villages, which resembled each other in being inhabited mostly by Gentiles, and in their civic institutions and privileges. In Matt. iv. 25, it is said, 'Multitudes followed Jesus from Galilee, and from Decapolis, and from Jerusalem, and from Judæa, and from beyond Jordan.' This must be considered as a popular mode of expression, just as, in describing a public meeting in this country, it might be said 'numbers attended it from Kent and Sussex, and from the Cinque Ports.' We, therefore, cannot agree with Dr. Lightfoot in thinking it 'absurd to reckon the most famed cities of Galilee for cities of Decapolis, when, both in sacred and profane authors, Galilee is plainly distinguished from Decapolis.' One at least of the Decapolitan towns (Scythopolis, formerly Bethshan) was in Galilee, and several, if not all the rest, were in the country beyond Jordan. Pliny gives the following list, but allows that a difference of opinion existed as to its correctness. 1. Damascus; 2. Philadelphia; 3. Raphana; 4. Scythopolis; 5. Gadara; 6. Hippos; 7. Dion; 8. Pella; 9. Galasa; 10. Canatha. Josephus speaks of Gadara and Hippos as Grecian cities, and calls Scythopolis the greatest city of the Decapolis, from which it may be inferred that he excluded Damascus from the number. For Damascus and Raphana, Cellarius substitutes Cæsarea Philippi and Gergesa, and Ptolemy Capitolias. The name Decapolis was in course of time applied to more than *ten* towns, a circumstance which may in part account for the discrepancies in the lists given by various writers. The Decapolitan towns referred to in the Gospels were evidently situated not far from the sea of Galilee (Mark v. 20; vii. 31).

DE'DAN. Two persons of this name are mentioned in Scripture; one the son of Cush (Gen. x. 7), and the other the second son of Jokshan, Abraham's son by Keturah (Gen. xxv. 3). Both were founders of tribes, afterwards repeatedly named in Scripture.

Of the descendants of the Cushite Dedan, very little is known. It is supposed that they settled in southern Arabia, near the Persian Gulf; but the existence in this quarter of a place called Dadan or Dadena, is the chief ground for this conclusion.

The descendants of the Abrahamite Jokshan seem to have lived in the neighbourhood of Idumæa; for the prophet Jeremiah (xlix. 8) calls on them to consult their safety, because the calamity of the sons of Esau, *i. e.* the Idumæans, was at hand. The same prophet (xxv. 23) connects them with Thema and Buz, two other tribes of Arabia Petræa, or Arabia Deserta, as does Ezekiel (xxv. 13) with Theman, a district of Edom. It is not always clear when the name occurs which of the two Dedans is intended; but it is probably the Cushite tribe, which is described as addicted to commerce, or rather, perhaps, engaged in the carrying-trade. Its 'travelling companies,' or caravans, are mentioned by Isaiah (xxi. 13); in Ezekiel (xxvii. 20), the Dedanites are described as supplying the markets of Tyre with flowing riding-cloths: and elsewhere (xxxviii. 13) the same prophet names them along with the merchants of Tarshish.

DEDICATION, a religious ceremony, whereby anything is dedicated or consecrated to the service of God; and it appears to have originated in the desire *to commence*, with peculiar solemnity, the practical use and application of whatever had been set apart to the divine service. Thus Moses dedicated the Tabernacle in the Wilderness (Exod. xl.; Num. vii.); Solomon his temple (1 Kings viii.); the returned exiles theirs (Ezra vi. 16, 17); Herod his. The Maccabees, having cleansed the temple from its pollutions under Antiochus Epiphanes, again dedicated the altar (1 Macc. iv. 52-9), and an annual festival was established in commemoration of the event. This feast was celebrated not only at Jerusalem, but everywhere throughout the country; in which respect it differed from the feasts of the Passover, Pentecost, and Tabernacles, which could only be observed at Jerusalem.

In John x. 22, 23, we are told that Jesus was at Jerusalem, walking in Solomon's porch at the time of 'the feast of the dedication, and it was winter.' This is usually supposed to have been the feast commemorating the dedication by Judas Maccabæus, which was celebrated in the month Cislev, about the winter solstice (answering to the 15th of December). There seems no reason to disturb this conclusion; for the dedication of Solomon's temple was in the seventh month, or autumn; that of Zerubbabel's temple in the month Adar, in the spring; and, although that of Herod's temple was in the winter, we know not that it was celebrated by an annual feast, while the Maccabæan dedication was a festival much observed in the time of Christ.

Not only were sacred places thus dedicated; but some kind of dedicatory solemnity was observed with respect to cities, walls, gates, and even private houses (Deut. xx. 5; Ps. xxx. title; Neh. xii. 27). We may trace the continuance of these usages in the custom of consecrating or dedicating churches and chapels; and in the ceremonies connected with the 'opening' of roads, markets, bridges, &c., and with the launching of ships.

DEGREES, PSALMS OF. [PSALMS.]

DEL'ILAH, the woman whom Samson loved, and who betrayed him to his enemies (Judg. xvi.) [Samson].

DELUGE. The narrative of a flood, given in the book of Genesis (vii. and viii.), by which, according to the literal sense of the description, the whole world was overwhelmed and every terrestrial creature destroyed, with the exception of one human family and the representatives of each species of animal, supernaturally preserved in an ark, constructed by divine appointment for the purpose, need not here be followed in detail. The account furnished by the sacred historian is circumstantially distinct; and the whole is expressly ascribed to divine agency: but, in several of the lesser particulars, secondary causes, as rain, 'the opening of the windows of Heaven' (vii. 11), and the 'breaking up of the fountains of the great deep,' are mentioned, and again the effect of wind in drying up the waters (viii. 1). It is chiefly to be remarked that the whole event is represented as both commencing and terminating in the most gradual and quiet manner, without anything at all resembling the catastrophes and convulsions often pictured in vulgar imagination as accompanying it. When the waters subsided, so little was the surface of the earth changed that the *vegetation* continued *uninjured*; the olive-trees remained from which the dove brought its token.

We allude particularly to these circumstances in the narrative as being those which bear most upon the probable *nature* and extent of the event, which it is our main object in the present article to examine, according to the tenor of what little evidence can be collected on the subject, whether from the terms of the narrative or from other sources of information which may be opened to us by the researches of science.

Much, indeed, might be said on the subject in other points of view; and especially in a more properly theological sense, it may be dwelt upon as a part of the great series of divine interpositions and dispensations which the sacred history discloses. But our present object, as well as limits, will restrict us from enlarging on these topics; or, again, upon the various ideas which have prevailed on the subject apart from Scripture on the one hand, or science on the other. Thus, we need merely allude to the fact that in almost all nations, from the remotest periods, there have prevailed certain mythological narratives and legendary tales of similar catastrophes. Such narratives have formed a part of the rude belief of the Egyptians, Chaldæans, Greeks, Scythians, and Celtic tribes. They have also been discovered among the Peruvians and Mexicans, and the South Sea Islanders. For details on these points we refer our readers to the work of Bryant (*Ancient Mythology*), and more especially to the treatise of the Rev. L. V. Harcourt on the Deluge, who appears to have collected everything of this kind bearing on the subject.

With reference to our present design the most material question is that of the existence of those traces which it might be supposed would be discovered of the action of such a deluge on the existing surface of the globe; and the consequent views which we must adopt according to the degree of accordance or discordance which such evidences may offer, as compared with the written narrative.

The evidence which geology may disclose and which can in any degree bear on our present subject must, from the nature of the case, be confined to indications of superficial action attributable to the agency of water, subsequent to the latest period of the regular geological formations, and, corresponding in character to a temporary inundation of a *quiet* and tranquil nature, of a depth sufficient to cover the highest mountains, and, lastly (as indeed this condition implies), extending over the whole globe; or, if these conditions should not be fulfilled, then, indications of at least something approaching to this, or with which the terms of the description may be fairly understood and interpreted to correspond.

The general result of the geological researches into this subject is briefly this: the traces of currents, and the like, which the surface of the earth does exhibit, and which *might* be ascribed to diluvial action of some kind, are certainly not the results of *one universal* simultaneous submergence, but of *many distinct*, local, aqueous forces, for the most part continued in action for long periods, and of a kind precisely analogous to such agency as is now at work. While, further, many parts of the existing surface show no traces of such operations; and the phenomena of the volcanic districts prove distinctly that during the enormous periods which have elapsed since the craters were active, no deluge could possibly have passed over them without removing all those lighter portions of their exuviæ which have evidently remained wholly untouched since they were ejected.

Upon the whole it is thus apparent, that we have no evidence whatever of any great aqueous revolution at any comparatively recent period having affected the earth's surface over any considerable tract: changes, doubtless, may have been produced on a small scale in isolated districts. The phenomena presented by caves containing bones, as at Kirkdale and other localities, are not of a kind forming any breach in the continuity of the analogies by which all the changes in the surface are more and more seen to have been carried on. But a recent simultaneous influx of water covering the globe, and ascending above the level of the mountains, must have left indisputable traces of its influence, which not only is *not* the case, but *against* which we have *positive* facts standing out. Apart from the testimonies of geology there are other sciences which must be interrogated on such a subject. These are, chiefly, terrestrial physics, to assign the possibility of a supply of water to stand all over the globe five miles in depth *above* the level of the ordinary sea;—natural history, to count the myriads of species of living creatures to be preserved and continued in the ark;—mechanics, to construct such a vessel;—with some others not less necessary to the case. But we have no disposition to enter more minutely on such points: the reader will find them most clearly and candidly stated in Dr. Pye Smith's *Geology and Scripture*, &c. p. 130, 2nd edit.

Let us now glance at the nature and possible solutions of the difficulty thus presented. We believe only two main solutions have been attempted. One is that proposed by Dr. Pye Smith (ib. p. 294), who expressly contends that there is no real contradiction between these facts and the description in the Mosaic record, *when the latter is correctly interpreted.* This more correct interpretation then refers, in the first instance, to the proper import of the Scripture terms commonly taken to imply the *universality* of the deluge. These the author shows, by a large comparison of similar passages, are only to be understood as expressing *a great extent;* often, indeed, the very same phrase is applied to a very limited region or country, as in Gen. xli. 56 ; Deut. ii. 25 ; Acts ii. 5, &c. Thus, so far as these expressions are concerned, the description may apply to a local deluge.

Next, the destruction of the whole existing human race does not by any means imply this universality, since, by ingenious considerations as to the multiplication of mankind at the alleged era of the deluge, the author has shown that they probably had not extended beyond a comparatively limited district of the East. A local destruction of animal life would also allow of such a reduction of the numbers to be included in the ark, as might obviate objections on that score ; and here again the Oriental idiom may save the necessity of the *literal* supposition of every actual species being included.

Again, certain peculiar difficulties connected with the resting of the ark on Mount Ararat are combated by supposing the name incorrectly applied to the mountain now so designated, and really to belong to one of much lower elevation.

Lastly, this author suggests considerations tending to fix the region which may have been the scene of the actual inundation described by Moses, in about that part of Western Asia where there is a large district now considerably depressed below the level of the sea : this might have been submerged by the joint action of rain, and an elevation of the bed of the Persian and Indian Seas. And, finally, he quotes the opinions of several approved divines in confirmation of such a view, especially as bearing upon all the essential religious instruction which the narrative is calculated to convey.

Other attempts have been made with more or less probability to assign particular localities as the scene of the Mosaic deluge, if understood to have been partial. Some diluvial beds posterior to the tertiary formations have been occasionally pointed out as offering some probability of such an origin. Thus, *e. g.* Mr. W. J. Hamilton, secretary to the Geological Society, in his *Tour in Asia Minor* (vol. ii. p. 386), found in the plains of Armenia, especially in some localities near Khorassan and on the banks of the Arpachai or Araxes, a remarkable thin bed of marl containing shells of tertiary (*qu.* recent?) species : these he attributes to a local deluge occurring (as the position of the bed indicates) after the cessation of the volcanic action which has taken place in that district. He expressly adds that he regards this deluge as probably coincident with the Mosaic ; understanding the latter in a restricted or partial sense, and imagining it explained by physical causes which might have followed the volcanic action.

The only other mode of viewing the subject is that which, accepting the letter of the Scriptural narrative, makes the deluge strictly universal ; and allowing (as they *must* be allowed) all the difficulties, not to say contradictions, in a natural sense, involved in it, accounts for them all by *supernatural* agency. In fact, the terms of the narrative, strictly taken, may perhaps be understood throughout as representing the whole event, from beginning to end, as entirely of a miraculous nature. If so, it may be said, there is an end to all difficulties or question, since there are no limits to omnipotence ; and one miracle is not greater than another. Thus, Mr. Lyell (*Principles of Geol.* iv. 219. 4th ed.), after ably recapitulating the main points of evidence, as far as physical causes are concerned, remarks, ' If we believe the flood to have been a temporary suspension of the ordinary laws of the natural world, requiring a miraculous intervention of the divine power, then it is evident that the credibility of such an event cannot be enhanced by any series of inundations. however analogous, of which the geologist may imagine he has discovered the proofs. For my own part, I have always considered the flood, when its universality, in the strictest sense of the term, is insisted on. as a preternatural event far beyond the reach of philosophical inquiry, whether as to the causes employed to produce it, or the effects most likely to result from it.'

In a word, if we suppose the flood to have been miraculously produced, and all the difficulties thus overcome, we must also suppose that it was not only miraculously terminated also, but every trace and mark of it supernaturally effaced and destroyed.

Now, considering the immense amount of supernatural agency thus rendered necessary, this hypothesis has appeared to some quite untenable. Dr. Pye Smith, in particular (whom no one will suspect of any leaning to scepticism), enlarges on the difficulty (p. 157, and note), and offers some excellent remarks on the general question of miracles (p. 84-89); and there can be no doubt that, however plausible may be the assertion that all miracles are alike, yet the idea of supernatural agency to so enormous an amount as in the present instance is, to many minds at least, very staggering, if not wholly inadmissible. In fact, in stretching the argument to such an extent, it must be borne in mind, that we may be trenching upon difficulties in another quarter, and not sufficiently regarding the force of the evidence on which *any* miracles are supported [MIRACLE].

In any point of view, it must be admitted that the subject involves difficulties of no inconsiderable amount ; and if, after due consideration of the suggestions offered for their solution, we should still feel it necessary to retain a cautious suspense of judgment on the subject, it may be also borne in mind that such hesitation will not involve the dereliction of any material religious doctrine.

DE′MAS, a Thessalonian Christian who was for a time associated with St. Paul, but who afterwards abandoned him at Rome, either from being discouraged by the hardships and perils of the service, or in pursuit of temporal advantages (Col. iv. 14 ; Philem. 24 ; 2 Tim. iv. 10).

DEME′TRIUS, a man's name, denoting *a votary of Ceres,* and very common among the Greeks The persons of this name mentioned in the history of the Maccabees, and in the New Testament, are—

1. DEME′TRIUS SOTER, king of Syria. He was son of Seleucus IV., surnamed Philopa-

tor; but, being an hostage at Rome at the time of his father's death, his uncle, the notorious Antiochus Epiphanes, assumed the crown of Syria, and retained it eleven years. After him it was held two years by his son Antiochus Eupator, who was put to death in B.C. 162 by Demetrius, who then arrived in Syria and secured the royal heritage from which he had so long been excluded. He reigned twelve years, B.C. 162–150. The points in which his history connects him with the Jews are alone of interest in this work, and these points belong to the history of the Maccabees [see art. MACCABEES]. To his time belong the latter end of the government of Judas in Israel and the beginning of that of Jonathan. He acted oppressively and unjustly towards them; but, when a rival arose in the person of Alexander Balas, he bade so high for the support of Jonathan as to create a doubt of his sincerity; for which cause, as well as from resentment at the injuries he had inflicted on them, the Jews espoused the cause of Balas, to whose success they in no slight degree contributed [ALEXANDER BALAS].

2. DEMETRIUS NICATOR, or NICANOR, son of the preceding, but who was excluded from the throne till B.C. 146, by the success of Alexander Balas, and then recovered it chiefly by the assistance of his father-in-law Ptolemy Philometor. He at first treated the Jews well, but eventually gave them so much cause for dissatisfaction that they readily espoused the cause of Antiochus Theos, son of Alexander Balas. Demetrius underwent many vicissitudes. and passed several years (B.C. 141–135) in captivity among the Parthians, from which he eventually returned and recovered his throne, which he continued to occupy till B.C. 126, when he was defeated in battle by the pretender Alexander Zebina, and afterwards slain at Tyre, whither he had fled [MACCABEES].

3. DEMETRIUS, a silversmith at Ephesus, who, being alarmed at the progress of the Gospel under the preaching of Paul, assembled his fellow-craftsmen, and excited a tumult by haranguing them on the danger that threatened the worship of the great goddess Diana, and consequently their own craft as silversmiths. Their employment was to make 'silver shrines for Diana' (Acts xix. 24); and it is now generally agreed that these 'shrines' were silver models of the temple, or of its adytum or chapel, in which perhaps a little image of the goddess was placed. These, it seems, were purchased by foreigners, who either could not perform their devotions at the temple itself, or who, after having done so, carried them away as memorials or for purposes of worship. The continual resort of foreigners to Ephesus from all parts, on account of the singular veneration in which the image of the goddess was held, must have rendered this manufacture very profitable, and sufficiently explains the anxiety of Demetrius and his fellow-craftsmen.

4. DEMETRIUS, a Christian, mentioned with commendation in 3 John 12. From the connexion of St. John with Ephesus at the time the Epistle was written, some have supposed that this Demetrius is the same as the preceding, and that he had been converted to Christianity. But this is a mere conjecture, rendered the more uncertain by the commonness of the name.

DEMON. This word is used by heathen writers with great latitude, being applied by them, 1. to every order of beings superior to man, including even the Highest; 2. it is applied to any particular divinity; 3. to the inferior divinities; 4. to a class of beings between gods and men. Of these latter some were habitually benevolent, and others malignant. To the former class belong the tutelary genii of cities, and the guardian spirits of individuals, as the demon of Socrates. By an easy metonymy it is used to denote fortune, chance, fate. Since no distinct ideas of the ancient Jewish doctrines concerning demons can be obtained from the Septuagint, we next have recourse to the heathens, and from their writings, owing to the universal prevalence of belief in demons, ample information may be obtained. The following is offered as a summary of their opinions.

1. Demons, in the theology of the Gentiles, are middle beings, between gods and mortals. This is the judgment of Plato, which will be considered decisive:—' Every demon is a middle being between God and mortal.'

2 Demons were of two kinds; the one were the souls of good men, which upon their departure from the body were called heroes, were afterwards raised to the dignity of demons, and subsequently to that of gods. It was also believed that the souls of bad men became evil demons. The other kind of demons were of more noble origin than the human race, having never inhabited human bodies.

3. Those demons who had once been souls of men were the objects of immediate worship among the heathens (Deut. xxvi. 14; Ps. cvi. 28; Isa. viii. 19), and it is in contradistinction to these that Jehovah is so frequently called 'the living God' (Deut. v. 6, &c. &c.).

4. The heathens held that some demons were malignant by nature, and not merely so when provoked and offended. Plutarch says, 'It is a very ancient opinion that there are certain wicked and malignant demons, who envy good men, and endeavour to hinder them in the pursuit of virtue, lest they should be partakers of greater happiness than they enjoy.' Pythagoras held that certain demons sent diseases to men and cattle.

In later times Josephus uses the word demon always in a bad sense, as do the writers of the New Testament, when using it as from themselves, and in their own sense of it. 'Demons are no other than the spirits of the wicked, that enter into men and kill them, unless they can obtain some help against them.'

It is frequently supposed that the demons of the New Testament are fallen angels; on the contrary it is maintained by Farmer, that the word is never applied to the Devil and his angels, and that there is no sufficient reason for restricting the term to spirits of a higher order than mankind. They who uphold the former opinion urge that our Lord, when accused of casting out demons by Beelzebub, the prince of demons, replies, How can Satan cast out Satan (Mark iii. 23, &c.)? It is further urged, that it is but fair and natural to suppose that the writers of the New Testament use the word demons in the same sense in which it was understood by their contemporaries, which, as it appears from Josephus and other authorities, was, that of the spirits of the wicked; and that if these writers had meant anything else they would have given notice of so wide a deviation from popular usage.

DEMONIACS, demonized persons, in the New Testament, are those who were supposed to have a demon or demons occupying them, suspending the faculties of their minds, and governing the members of their bodies, so that what was said and done by the demoniacs was ascribed to the in-dwelling demon.

The correctness of the opinion respecting those who are called demoniacs in the New Testament which prevailed among the Jews and other nations in the time of our Lord and his Apostles, has been called in question. On the one hand it is urged that the details of the evangelical history afford decisive evidence of the truth and reality of demoniacal possessions in the sense already explained, at least during the commencement of Christianity; on the other hand it is contended that the accounts in question may all be understood as the phenomena of certain diseases, particularly hypochondria, insanity, and epilepsy; that the sacred writers used the *popular language* in reference to the subject, but that they themselves understood no more than that the persons were the subjects of ordinary diseases. Here issue is joined—and it is to the evidence in this cause that our attention will now be directed.

Those who contend that the demoniacs were really possessed by an evil spirit, urge the following considerations :—

1. The demoniacs express themselves in a way unusual for hypochondriacal, insane, or epileptic persons (Matt. viii. 29; Mark i. 24); they possessed supernatural strength (Mark v. 4); they adjure Jesus not to torment them; they answer the questions proposed to them in a rational manner; they are distinctly said to have 'come out of' men and to have 'entered into swine,' and that consequently the whole herd, amounting to about two thousand, ran violently down a precipice into the sea (Matt. viii. 32: Mark v. 13). The supposition which has been maintained by Lardner among others, that the swine were *driven into* the sea by the *demoniacs*, is irreconcilable with the language of the narrative, being also highly improbable in itself: madmen do not act in concert, and rarely pursue the same train of maniacal reasoning.

2. No mental diseases are predicated of the dumb (Matt. ix. 32), or of the blind and dumb (Matt. xii. 22). Do such diseases ever produce blindness?

3. It is admitted that the symptoms of the youth described Matt. xvii. 15; Mark ix. 17; Luke ix. 39, coincide precisely with those of epilepsy, but they are attributed to the agency of the demon in that very account.

4. The damsel at Philippi is said to have been possessed with a spirit of *divination*, which was the means of obtaining much gain to her masters, and to have understood the divine commission of Paul and his companions (Acts xvi. 17). Is this to be ascribed merely to an aberration of mind?

5. The demoniacs themselves confess that they were possessed with demons (Mark. v. 9): the same is asserted of them by their relatives (Matt. xv. 22). The Apostles and Evangelists assert that persons possessed with demons were brought

unto Jesus (Matt. iv. 24; Mark i. 32), or met him (Luke viii. 27). Jesus commands them not to make him known as the Messiah (Mark i. 34, margin); rebuked them (Matt. xvii. 18). The Evangelists declare that the demons departed from their victims at his command (Matt. xvii. 18; Mark ix. 25, 26; Luke iv. 35; xi. 14); and Jesus himself asserts it (Luke xiii. 32).

6. The writers of the New Testament make distinctions between the diseased and the demoniacs (Mark i. 32; Luke vi. 17, 18); and Jesus himself does so (Matt. x. 8, &c.).

7. The demoniacs knew Jesus to be the son of God (Matt. viii. 29; Mark i. 24; v. 7), and the Christ (Luke iv. 41).

8. Jesus addresses the demons (Matt. viii. 32; Mark v. 18; ix. 25; Luke iv. 35): so does Paul (Acts xvi. 18). Jesus bids them be silent (Mark i. 25); to depart, and enter no more into the person (Mark ix. 25).

9. In Luke x. the seventy are related to have returned to Jesus, saying, 'Lord, even the demons are subject to us through thy name;' and Jesus replies, ver. 18, 'I beheld Satan, as lightning, fall from heaven.'

10. When Jesus was accused by the Pharisees of casting out demons by Beelzebub, the prince of the demons, he argued that there could be no discord among demoniacal beings (Matt. xii. 25, &c.).

11. Jesus makes certain *gratuitous* observations respecting demons (see Matt. xii. 43, 44); which seem like facts in their natural history. In regard to the demon cast out of the youth, which the disciples could not cast out, he says, 'this *kind* (i. e. demons) goeth not out but by prayer and fasting.' Can these words be understood otherwise than as revealing a real and particular fact respecting the nature of demons (Matt. xvii. 21)?

12. The woman which had a spirit of infirmity, and was bowed together (Luke xiii. 11), is, by our Lord himself, said to have been bound by Satan (v. 16). In the same way St. Peter speaks of all the persons who were healed by Jesus, as being 'oppressed of the devil' (Acts x. 38).

13. It is further pleaded, that it sinks the importance and dignity of our Saviour's miracles, to suppose that when he is said to have cast out devils, all that is meant is, that he healed diseases.

To these arguments the opponents of the theory of real demoniacal possessions reply, generally, that there can be no doubt that it was the *general belief* of the Jewish nation, with the exception of the Sadducees, and of most other nations, that the spirits of dead men, especially of those who had lived evil lives, and died by violent deaths, were permitted to enter the bodies of men, and to produce the effects ascribed to them in the *popular* creed; but the *fact* and real state of the case was, that those who were considered to be *possessed* were afflicted with some peculiar diseases of mind or body, which, their true *causes* not being generally understood, were, as is usual in such cases, ascribed to supernatural powers; and that Jesus and his apostles, wishing of course to be understood by their contemporaries, and owing to other reasons which can be pointed out, were under the *necessity* of expressing themselves in popular language, and of seeming to admit, or at least of not denying, its correctness. They further plead that the fact, admitted on all hands, that the demon so actuated the possessed, as that whatever *they* did, was not to be distinguished from *his* agency, reduces the question, so far as *phenomena* are concerned, to one simple inquiry, namely, whether these phenomena are such as can be accounted for without resorting to supernatural agency. They assert that the symptoms predicated of demoniacs correspond with the ordinary symptoms of disease, and especially of hypochondria, insanity, and epilepsy; that the sacred writers themselves give intimations, as plain as could be expected under their circumstances, that they employed popular language; that consequently they are not to be considered as teaching doctrines or asserting facts when they use such language; and that the doctrine of the agency of departed spirits on the bodies of men is inconsistent with certain peculiar and express doctrines of Christ and his apostles.

With regard to the *symptoms* related of the demoniacs, it is urged that such persons as were called demoniacs in other countries, and who seem to have laboured under precisely the same symptoms, are recorded to have been cured by the use of *medicines*. Josephus and the Jewish physicians speak of medicines composed of stones, roots, and herbs, being useful to demoniacs. The cure of *diseases* by such methods is intelligible; but is it rational to believe that the spirits of dead men were dislodged from human bodies by medical prescriptions?

1. With regard to the two demoniacs at Gadara (or *one*, according to Mark and Luke), it is concluded that they were madmen, who fancied that there were within them innumerable spirits of dead men. Accordingly they dwelt among the *tombs*, about which the souls of the dead were believed to hover, went naked, were ungovernable, cried aloud, attacked passengers, beat themselves, and had in their phrensy broken every chain by which they had been bound. Strength almost superhuman is a common attendant on insanity. Their question, 'Art thou come to torment us?' refers to the cruel treatment of the insane in those times, and which they had no doubt shared, in the endeavours of men to 'tame' them. Both Mark and Luke the *physician* describe the demoniac as in 'his *right mind*,' when healed, which implies previous *insanity* (see also Matt. xii. 22; xv. 28; xvii. 18; Luke vii. 21; viii. 2; ix. 42). It is true that these demoniacs address Jesus as the Son of God, but they might have heard in their lucid intervals that Jesus, whose fame was already diffused throughout Syria, was regarded by the people as the Messiah. They show their insanity, 'their *shaping* fancies,' by imagining they were demons without number, and by requesting permission to enter the swine. Would actual demons choose such an habitation? They speak and answer, indeed, in a rational manner, but agreeably to Locke's definition of madmen, they reason right on false principles, and, taking fancies for realities, make right deductions from them. Thus you shall find a distracted man fancying himself a king, and with a right inference require suitable attendance. Others, who have thought themselves glass, take the needful care to preserve such brittle bodies. It is true

that Jesus commands the *unclean* spirit (so called because believed to be the spirit of a *dead* man), but he does this merely to excite the attention of the people, and to give them full opportunity to observe the miracle. It is not necessary to suppose that the madmen drove the swine, but merely that, *in keeping with all the circumstances*, the *insanity* of the demoniacs was transferred to them, as the leprosy of Naaman was transferred to Gehazi, for the purpose of illustrating the miraculous power of Christ; and though this was a *punitive* miracle, it might serve the good purpose of discouraging the expectation of temporal benefits from him. If the demoniac is represented as worshipping Jesus, it should be remembered that the insane often show great respect to particular persons.

2. The men who were dumb, and both blind and dumb, are not said to have been disordered in their intellects, any more than the blind man in John v. The disease in their organs was *popularly ascribed* to the influence of demons. It is observable that in the parallel passage (Matt. ix. 32), the evangelist says the *man* was dumb.

3. The symptoms of epilepsy in the youth described Matt. xvii. 15, are too evident not to be acknowledged. If the opinion of relatives is to be pressed, it should be noticed that in this case the father says his 'son is lunatic.' It was most probably a case of combined epilepsy and lunacy, which has been common in all ages. Epilepsy was ascribed to the influence of the moon in those times. The literal interpretation of popular language would therefore require us to believe that he was 'moonstruck,' as well as a demoniac.

4. The damsel at Philippi is said by Luke to have been possessed with a spirit of *Apollo*. It was *her* fixed idea. The gift of divination is said by Cicero to have been ascribed to Apollo. Insane persons, pretending to prophesy under the influence of Apollo, would be likely to gain money from the *credulous*. A belief among the common people that the ravings of insanity were sacred, was not confined to Egypt. The apostle, who taught that an 'idol is nothing in the world,' did not believe in the reality of her soothsaying. Many demoniacs are mentioned, the peculiar symptoms of whose diseases are not stated, as Mary Magdalene (Mark xvi. 9), out of whom Jesus cast seven demons, *i. e.* restored from an inveterate insanity (seven being the Jewish number of perfection), supposed to be caused by the united agency of seven spirits of the dead. Yet she is said to have been *healed* (Luke viii. 2).

5. If Jesus forbade the demoniacs to say he was the Christ, it was because the declaration of such persons on the subject would do more harm than good. If he *rebuked* them he also rebuked the wind (Matt. viii. 26), and the fever (Luke iv. 39). If it be said of them, they departed, so it is also said of the leprosy (Mark i. 42).

6. It may be questioned whether the writers of the New Testament make a distinction between the diseased and those possessed of demons, or whether they specify the demoniacs by themselves, as they specify the lunatics (Matt. iv. 24), merely as a distinct and *peculiar class* of the sick. It is, however, most important to observe that St. Peter includes 'all' who were healed by Jesus, under the phrase *them that were oppressed of the*

devil, many of whom were not described by the Evangelists as subjects of demoniacal possession. Sometimes the specification of the demoniacs is omitted in the general recitals of miraculous cures (Matt. xi. 5), and this, too, on the important occasion of our Lord sending to John the Baptist an account of the miraculous evidence attending his preaching (Matt. xi. 5). Does not this look as if they were considered as included under the sick?

7. It cannot be proved that *all* the demoniacs knew Jesus to be the Messiah.

8. It is admitted that Jesus addresses the demons, but then it may be said that his doing so has reference partly to the *persons themselves* in whom demons were supposed to be, and partly to the bystanders; for the same reason that he rebuked the winds in an audible voice, as also the fever.

9. With regard to our Lord's reply to the seventy, it will not be urged that it was intended of a local fall of Satan from heaven, unless it may be supposed to allude to his primeval expulsion; but this sense is scarcely relevant to the occasion. If, then, the literal sense be necessarily departed from, a choice must be made out of the various figurative interpretations of which the words admit; and taking the word Satan here in its generic sense, of *whatever* is inimical or opposed to the Gospel, Jesus may be understood to say, I foresaw the glorious results of your mission in the triumphs which would attend it over the most formidable obstacles. Heaven is often used in the sense of political horizon (Isa. xiv. 12, 13; Matt. xxiv. 29). To be cast from heaven to hell is a phrase for total downfall (Luke x. 15; Rev. xii. 7-9). Cicero says to Mark Antony, You have hurled your colleagues down from heaven. Satan is here used tropically. Our Lord does not, therefore, assert the real operation of demons.

10. In the refutation of the charge that he cast out demons by Beelzebub, the prince of the demons, he simply argues with the Pharisees upon their *own principles*, and 'judges them out of their own mouth,' without assuming the *truth* of those principles.

11. The facts he seems to assert respecting the wandering of demons through dry places (Matt. xii. 45), were already admitted in the popular creed of the Jews. They believed that demons wandered in desolate places (Baruch iv. 35). Upon these ideas he founds a parable or similitude, without involving an opinion of their accuracy, to describe 'the end of this generation.' The observations respecting prayer and fasting seem to have relation to that faith in God which he exhorts his apostles to obtain. Prayer and fasting would serve to enable them to perceive the divine suggestion which accompanied every miracle, and which the apostles had not *perceived* upon this occasion, though given them, because their animal nature had not been sufficiently subdued.

12. The application of the term Satan to the case of the woman who had a spirit of infirmity, is plainly an arguing with the Jews on their own principles. It is intended to heighten the antithesis between the *loosing* of an ox from his stall, and *loosing* the daughter of Abraham whom *Satan*, as *they believed*, had bound eighteen years.

13. The objection taken from the supposed consequence of explaining the casting out of demons to signify no more than the cure of diseases, that it tends to lower the dignity of the Saviour's miracles, depends upon the reader's complexion of mind, our prior knowledge of the relative dignity of miracles, and some other things, perhaps, of which we are not competent judges.

It has further been observed, that the theory of demoniacal possessions is opposed to the known and express doctrines of Christ and his Apostles. They teach us that the spirits of the dead enter a state corresponding to their character, no more to return to this world (Luke xvi. 22. &c.; xxiii. 43; 2 Cor. v. 1; Phil. i. 21). With regard to the fallen angels, the representations of their *confinement* are totally opposed to the notion of their wandering about the world and tormenting its inhabitants (2 Pet. ii. 4; Jude, ver. 6). If it be said that Jesus did not correct the popular opinion, still he nowhere denies that the phenomena in question arose from diseases only. He took no side; it was not his province. It was not necessary to attack the misconception in a formal manner; it would be supplanted whenever his doctrine respecting the state of the dead was embraced. To have done so would have engaged our Lord in prolix arguments with a people in whom the notion was so deeply rooted, and have led him away too much from the purposes of his ministry. 'It was one of the many things he had to say, but they could not then bear them.' It is finally urged that the antidemoniacal theory does not detract from the divine authority of the Saviour, the reality of his miracles, or the integrity of the historians.

DENA'RIUS, the principal silver coin of the Romans, which took its name from having been originally equal to *ten* ases. It was in later times (after B.C. 217) current also among the Jews, and is the coin which is called 'a penny' in the Auth. Vers. The denarii were first coined in B.C. 269, or four years after the first Punic war, and the more ancient specimens are much heavier than those of later date. Those coined in the early period of the commonwealth have the average weight of 60 grains, and those coined under the empire of 52·5 grains. With some allowance for alloy, the former would be worth 8½d., and the latter 7½d. It has been supposed, how-

140.

ever, that the reduction of weight did not take place till the time of Nero; and in that case the denarii mentioned in the Gospels must have been of the former weight and value, although 7½d. is the usual computation. A denarius was the day-wages of a labourer in Palestine (Matt. xx. 2, 9, 13); and the daily pay of a Roman soldier was less. In the time of Christ the denarius bore the image of the emperor (Matt. xxii. 19; Mark xii.

16), but formerly it was impressed with the symbols of the republic.

DER'BE, a small town of Lycaonia, in Asia Minor, at the foot of the Taurian mountains, 60 miles south by east from Iconium, and 18 miles east of Lystra. It was the birthplace of Gaius, the friend and f.llow-traveller of Paul (Acts xx. 4); and it was to this place that Paul and Barabas fled when expelled from Iconium, A.D. 41 (Acts xiv. 6).

DESERTS. In the East, wide, extended plains are usually liable to drought, and consequently to barrenness. Hence the Hebrew language describes *a plain*, *a desert*, and *an unfruitful waste*, by the same word. The term which is in general rendered ' wilderness,' means, properly, *a grazing tract*, uncultivated and destitute of wood, but fit for pasture—a heath or steppe. The *pastures of the wilderness* are mentioned in Ps. lxv. 13: Joel i. 19; Luke xv. 4; and may be very well explained by reference to the fact, that even the Desert of Arabia, which is utterly burnt up with excessive drought in summer, is in winter and spring covered with rich and tender herbage. Whence it is that the Arabian tribes retreat into their deserts on the approach of the autumnal rains, and when spring has ended and the droughts commence, return to the lands of rivers and mountains, in search of the pastures which the deserts no longer afford. The same word may therefore denote a region which is desert, and also one which, at stated seasons, contains rich and abundant pastures. But in fact the word translated in our Bibles by 'desert' or ' wilderness' often means no more than the common, uncultivated grounds in the neighbourhood of towns on which the inhabitants grazed their domestic cattle.

The term a great desert or wilderness is especially applied to that desert of Stony Arabia in which the Israelites sojourned under Moses (Num. xxi. 20; xxiii. 28; Ps. lxviii. 7; lxxviii. 40, &c.). This was the most terrible of the deserts with which the Israelites were acquainted, and the only *real* desert in their immediate neighbourhood. It is described under ARABIA; as is also that Eastern desert extending from the eastern border of the country beyond Judæa to the Euphrates. It is emphatically called ' the Desert,' without any proper name, in Exod. xxiii. 31; Deut. xi. 24.

The several deserts or wildernesses mentioned in Scripture are the following, which will be found under their respective names: the deserts of Edom, Etham, Judah, Kadesh, Maon, Paran, Shur. Sin, Sinai.

DEVIL. [DEMON; SATAN.]

DEUTERON'OMY, the Greek name given by the Alexandrian Jews to the fifth book of Moses. It comprises that series of addresses which the Lawgiver delivered (orally and by writing, i. 5; xxviii. 58, &c.) to assembled Israel in the second month of the fortieth year of their wandering through the desert, when the second generation was about to cross the Jordan, and when the parting hour of Moses had nearly arrived.

The speeches begin with the enumeration of the wonderful dealings of God with the chosen people in the early period of their existence. Moses clearly proves to them the punishment of unbelief, the obduracy of Israel, and the faithfulness of Jehovah with regard to his promises, which were now on the point of being accomplished. Fully aware of the tendencies of the people, and foreseeing their alienations, Moses conjures them most impressively to hold fast the commands of the Lord, and not to forget his revelations, lest curses should befall them instead of blessings (ch. i.-iv.). The Lawgiver then expatiates on the spirit of the law, and its reception into the hearts of men, both in a positive and negative way. *Fear*, he says, is the primary *effect* of the law, as also its *aim*. As Israel had once listened to the announcement of the fundamental laws of the theocracy with a sacred *fear*, in like manner should man also receive, through the whole system of the law, a lively and awful impression of the holiness and majesty of God (ch. v.). But as the essence and sum of the law is *love* to Jehovah, the only and true God, man shall by the law be reminded of the Divine mercy, so variously manifested in deeds; and this reflection is calculated to rouse in man's heart *love* for God. This love is the only and true source from which proper respect and obedience to the law can proceed (ch. vi.).

There were, however, two tempting deviations, in following which the people were sure to be led astray. The law, in its strict rigour, was but too apt to tempt them to desert Jehovah, and to yield to idolatry (the very approval of which even in thought polluted the heart), by discontinuing to bear the heavy yoke of the law. Hence the most impressive warnings against Canaan's inhabitants and idols; and hence the declarations that Israel, in placing themselves on a par with the heathens, should have to endure an equal fate with them, and be repulsed from the presence of Jehovah (ch. vii. viii.).

The other, not less dangerous, deviation is that of self-righteousness—the proud fancy that all the favours Jehovah had shown to his people were merely in consequence of their own deservings. Therefore Jehovah tells them that it was not through their own worthiness and purity of heart that they inherited the land of the heathens. It was only through his free favour; for their sins bore too strong and constant testimony how little they ought to take credit to themselves for it (ch. ix.).

The history of the people, before and after the exile, shows these two deviations in their fullest bearings. Idolatry we find to have been the besetting sin *before* that period, and presumptuous pride of heart *after* it: a proof how intimately acquainted the Lawgiver was with the character and disposition of his people, and how necessary therefore those warnings had been.

Therefore, adds Moses, turn to that which Jehovah, in giving you the tables of the law, and establishing the Tabernacle and priesthood, has intimated as a significant symbol, ' to circumcise the foreskin of your heart,' and to cherish love in your inward soul. Think of Jehovah, the just and merciful, whose blessings and curses shall be set before your eyes as a lasting monument upon the mounts Ebal and Gerizim (ch. x. xi.).

The mention of that fact leads the Lawgiver to the domestic and practical life of the people when domesticated in their true home, the Land of Promise: which he further regulates by a fixed and solid rule, by new laws, which for this, their new design and purport, form a sort of complement to the laws already given. There, in the land of their forefathers, Jehovah will appoint *one* fixed place for his lasting sanctuary, when every other place dedicated to the worship of idols is to be destroyed. At that chosen spot alone are the sacrifices to be killed, while cattle in general, which are not destined for sacred purposes, but merely for food, may be slaughtered at all places according to convenience—a regulation which still leaves in full force the previous laws concerning the eating of blood, and the share of Jehovah in slaughtered cattle. This sanctuary was to be considered as the central point for all sacred objects. The whole land was, by means of the sanctuary established in the midst of it, consecrated and dedicated to Jehovah. This consecration was incompatible with any defilement whatsoever. On that account the Canaanites must be exterminated, and all idolatrous abominations destroyed, since nothing ought to be added to or taken from the laws of God (ch. xii.). For the same reason (*i. e.* for the sake of the holiness of the land, diffused from the sacred centre), no false prophets or soothsayers are to be tolerated, as they may turn the minds of the people from *the* law, by establishing a different one, and therefore even a whole town given to the worship of idols must be demolished by force of arms (ch. xiii.). Neither, in like manner, must the heathen customs of mourning be imitated, or unclean beasts eaten; but the people must always remain true to the *previous* laws concerning food, &c., and show their real attachment to Jehovah and his religion by willingly paying the *tithe* as ordained by the law (ch. xiv.). To the same end likewise shall the regulations concerning the years of release and the festivals of Jehovah (to be solemnized in the place of the new-chosen Sanctuary) be most scrupulously observed (ch. xv. xvi.). Only *unblemished* sacrifices shall be offered, for all idol-worshippers must irrevocably be put to death by stoning. For the execution of due punishment, honest judges must govern the nation, while the highest tribunal shall exist in the place chosen for the Sanctuary, consisting of the priests and judges of the land. If a king be given by God to the people, he shall first of all accommodate himself to the laws of God, and not lead a heathen life. Next to the regal and judicial dignities, the ecclesiastical power shall exist in its full right; and again, next to it, the prophetic order (ch. xvii. xviii.). Of all these institutions, the duties of the judicial power are most clearly defined; for Jehovah does as little suffer that in his land the right of the innocent shall be turned aside, as that indulgence shall be shown to the evil-doer (ch. xix.). The exposition of the civil law is followed by that of the martial law, which has some bearing upon the then impending war with Canaan, as the most important war and representing that with the heathen nations in general (ch. xx.). These are again followed by a series of laws in reference to the preceding, and referring chiefly to hard cases in the judicial courts, by which Moses obviously designed to exhibit the whole of the civil life of his people in its strict application to the theocratic system of law and right. Therefore the form of prayer to be spoken at the offering up of the firstlings and

tithe—the theocratic *confession of faith*—**by which** every Israelite acknowledges in person that he is what God has enjoined and called him to be, forms a beautiful conclusion of the whole legislation (ch. xxi.–xxvi.).

The blessings and curses of Jehovah, the two opposite extremes which were to be impressed upon the minds of the people at their entrance into Canaan, and which have hitherto been spoken of only in general terms, are now set forth in their fullest detail, picturing in the most lively colours the delightful abundance of rich blessings on the one hand, and the awful visitations of Heaven's wrath on the other. The prophetic speeches visibly and gradually increase in energy and enthusiasm, until the perspective of the remotest future of the people of God lies open to the eye of the inspired Lawgiver in all its chequered details, when his words resolve themselves into a flight of poetical extacy, into the strains of a splendid triumphal song in which the tone of grief and lamentation is as heart-rending as the announcement of divine salvation therein is jubilant (ch. xxvii. xxviii.). The history of the law concludes with a supplement concerning him who was deemed worthy by the Lord to transmit his law to Israel (ch. xxxiv.).

Thus much regarding the contents and connection of the book of Deuteronomy.

The *date*, however, of the composition of the book, as well as its *authenticity*, has given rise to a great variety of opinion, more especially among those who are opposed to the authorship of Moses. The older critics considered Deuteronomy as the *latest* production of all the books of the Pentateuch; while the more recent critics have come to just the contrary opinion, and declare it to be the *earliest* of the Mosaic writings.

A very strong proof of the genuineness of the book lies in its relation to the later writings of the prophets. Of all the books of the Pentateuch, Deuteronomy has been made most use of by the prophets, simply because it is best calculated to serve as a model for prophetic declarations, as also because of the inward harmony that exists between the *prophecies* and the *laws* upon which they are based.

Among the arguments advanced against the authenticity of Deuteronomy, are:

1. The *contradictions* said to exist between this and the other books of Moses;

2. Certain *anachronisms* committed by the author.

These contradictions are more especially alleged to exist in the festival laws, where but arbitrary and unwarranted views are mostly entertained by such critics with regard to the nature and original meaning of the festivals, which they identify altogether with *natural* or *season* festivals, and without lending to them a more spiritual character and signification.

3. That the *Sinai* of the other books is always called *Horeb* in Deuteronomy.—They forget, however, that *Horeb* is the general name of the whole mountain, while *Sinai* is the special name of a particular part of it. This distinction is, indeed, most scrupulously observed everywhere in the Pentateuch.

4. That in Deuteronomy i. 44 are mentioned the *Amorites*, instead of the *Amalekites*, as in Num. xiv. 45.—Here also they have forgotten to notice

that, in the sequel of the very passage alluded to in Deuteronomy, both the *Amorites* and *Amalekites* are mentioned.

5. That the cause of the punishment of Moses is differently stated in Num. xxvii. 14, and Deuteronomy iii. 26.—To this objection we reply, that both the guilt and punishment of Moses are described in both books as originating with the people ; comp. also Deut. xxxii. 51, etc.

Among the anachronisms in Deuteronomy are reckoned the allusions made in it to the Temple (xii. xvi. 1, sqq.), to the royal and prophetic powers (xiii. xvii. xviii.), to the different modes of idol-worship (iv. 19 ; xvii. 3), and to the exile (xxviii. sq.). In suggesting these critical points, however, they do not consider that all these subjects are most closely and intimately connected with the spirit and principles of the law itself, and that all these regulations and prophecies appear here in Deuteronomy, as necessary finishing-points to the Law, so indispensable for the better consolidation of the subsequent and later relations of the theocracy.

More *anachronisms* are said to be,

1. The sixty dwelling-places of Jair mentioned Deut. iii. 14, sq. (comp. Judg. x. 3, sq.). We consider, however, that the men mentioned in the two passages are evidently different persons, though of the same name. Nor is it difficult to prove from other sources, that there really existed at the time of Moses a man by name Jair.

2. The notice (iii. 11) concerning king Og, which looks more like a note of a subsequent writer in corroboration of the story told in the chapter. But this hypothesis falls to the ground when we consider that Moses did not write for his contemporaries merely, but also for late posterity.

The book contains, moreover, not a small number of plain, though indirect traces, indicative of its Mosaic origin. We thus find in it:

1. Numerous notices concerning nations with whom the Israelites had then come in contact, but who, after the Mosaic period, entirely disappeared from the pages of history : such are the accounts of the residences of the kings of Bashan (i. 4).

2. The appellation of 'mountain of the Amorites,' used throughout the whole book (i. 7, 19, 20, 44), while even in the book of Joshua, soon after the conquest of the land, the name is already exchanged for ' mountains of Judah' (Josh. xi. 16, 21).

3. The observation (ii. 10), that the *Emim* had formerly dwelt in the plain of Moab: they were a great people, equal to the *Anakim*. This observation quite accords with Genesis xiv. 5.

4. A detailed account (ii. 11) concerning the Horim and their relations to the Edomites.

5. An account of the Zamzummim (ii. 20, 21), one of the earliest races of Canaan, though mentioned nowhere else.

6. A very circumstantial account of the Rephaim (iii. 3, sq.), with whose concerns the author seems to have been well acquainted.

The standing-point also of the author of Deuteronomy is altogether in the Mosaic time, and had it been assumed and fictitious, there must necessarily have been moments when the spurious author would have been off his guard, and unmindful of the part he had to play. But no discrepancies of this kind can be traced ; and this is in itself an evidence of the genuineness of the book.

A great number of other passages force us likewise to the conclusion, that the whole of Deuteronomy originated in the time of Moses. Such are the passages where

1. A comparison is drawn between Canaan and Egypt (xi. 10, sq.), with the latter of which the author seems thoroughly acquainted.

2. Detailed descriptions are given of the fertility and productions of Egypt (viii. 7, sq.).

3. Regulations are given relating to the conquest of Canaan (xii. 1, sq.; xx. 1, sq.), which cannot be understood otherwise than by assuming that they had been framed in the Mosaic time, since they could be of no use after that period.

Besides, whole pieces and chapters in Deuteronomy, such as xxxii., xxxiii., betray in form, language, and tenor, a very early period in Hebrew literature. Nor are the laws and regulations in Deuteronomy less decisive of the authenticity of the book. We are struck with the most remarkable phenomenon, that many laws from the previous books are here partly repeated and impressed with more energy, partly modified, and partly altogether abolished, according to the contingencies of the time, or as the new aspect of circumstances among the Jews rendered such steps necessary (comp. *e. g.* Deut. xv. 17 with Exod. xxi. 7 ; Deut. xii. with Lev. xvii.). Such pretensions to raise, or even to oppose his own private opinions to the authority of divine law, are found in no author of the subsequent periods, since the whole of the sacred literature of the later times is, on the contrary, rather the echo than otherwise of the Pentateuch, and is altogether founded on it. Add to this the fact, that the law itself forbids most impressively to add to, or take anything from it, a prohibition which is repeated even in Deuteronomy (comp. iv. 2 ; xiii. 1); and it is but too evident, that, if the opinion of the critics be correct, that this book contains nothing more than a gradual development of the law—it clashes too often with its own principles, and pronounces thus its own sentence of condemnation.

The part of Deuteronomy (xxxiv.) respecting the death of Moses requires a particular explanation. That the whole of this section is to be regarded as a piece altogether apart from what precedes it, or as a supplement from another writer, has already been maintained by the elder theologians; and this opinion is confirmed not only by the contents of the chapter, but also by the express declaration of the book itself on that event and its relations; for chapter xxxi. contains the conclusion of the work, where Moses describes himself as the author of the previous contents, as also of the Song (ch. xxxii.), and the blessings (ch. xxxiii.) belonging to it. All that follows is, consequently, not from Moses, the work being completed and concluded with chapter xxxiii. There is another circumstance which favours this opinion, namely, the close connection that exists between the last section of Deuteronomy and the beginning of Joshua (comp. Deut. xxxiv. 9 with Josh. i. 1), plainly shows that chapter xxxiv. of Deuteronomy is intended to serve as a *point of transition* to the book of Joshua, and that it was written by the same author as the latter. The correct view of this chapter, therefore, is to consider it as a *real supplement*, but by no means as an *interpolation*.

On the literature of Deuteronomy, compare the article PENTATEUCH.

DEW. The various passages of Scripture in which dew is mentioned, as well as the statements of travellers, might, unless carefully considered, convey the impression that in Palestine the dews fall copiously at night during the height of summer, and supply in some degree the lack of rain. But we find that those who mention dews travelled in spring and autumn, while those who travelled in summer make no mention of them. In fact, scarcely any dew does fall during the summer months—from the middle of May to the middle of August; but as it continues to fall for some time after the rains of spring have ceased, and begins to fall before the rains of autumn commence, we may from this gather the sense in which the Scriptural references to dew are to be understood. Without the dews continuing to fall after the rains have ceased, and commencing before the rains return, the season of actual drought, and the parched appearance of the country, would be of much longer duration than they really are. The partial refreshment thus afforded to the ground at the end of a summer without dews or rains, is of great value in Western Asia, and would alone explain all the Oriental references to the effects of dew. This explanation is of further interest as indicating the times of the year to which the Scriptural notices of dew refer; for as it does not, in any perceptible degree, fall in summer, and as few would think of mentioning it in the season of rain, we may take all such notices to refer to the months of April, May, part of August, and September.

DIADEM. [CROWN.]

DIAL. The invention of the sun-dial belongs most probably to the Babylonians. The first mention in Scripture of the 'hour,' is made by Daniel, at Babylon (ch. iii. 6). The circumstances connected with the dial of Ahaz (2 Kings xx. 11; Isa. xxxviii. 8), which is perhaps the earliest of which we have any clear mention, entirely concur with the derivation of gnomonics from the Babylonians. Ahaz had formed an alliance with Tiglath-pileser, king of Assyria (2 Kings xvi. 7, 9), and that he was ready to adopt foreign improvements, appears from his admiration of the altar at Damascus, and his introduction of a copy of it into Jerusalem (2 Kings xvi. 10). 'The princes of Babylon sent unto him to inquire of the wonder that was done in the land' (2 Chron. xxxii. 31). Hence the dial also, which was called after his name, was probably an importation from Babylon. Different conjectures have been formed respecting the construction of this instrument. On the whole it seems to have been a distinct contrivance, rather than any part of a house. It would also seem probable, from the circumstances, that it was of such a size, and so placed, that Hezekiah, now convalescent (Isa. xxxviii. 21, 22), but not perfectly recovered, could witness the miracle from his chamber or pavilion. May it not have been situate ' in the middle court' mentioned 2 Kings xx. 4? The cut given below (No. 141) presents a dial discovered in Hindostan, near Delhi, the ancient capital of the Mogul empire, whose construction would well suit the circumstances recorded of the dial of Ahaz. It seems to have answered the double purpose of an observatory and a dial—a rectangled hexangle, whose hypothenuse is a staircase, apparently parallel to the axis of the earth, and bisects a zone or coping of a wall, which wall connects the two terminating towers

141.

right and left. The coping itself is of a circular form, and accurately graduated to mark, by the shadow of the gnomon above, the sun's progress before and after noon; for when the sun is in the zenith, he shines directly on the staircase, and the shadow falls beyond the coping. A *flat surface* on *the top of the staircase*, and a gnomon. fitted the building for the purpose of an observatory. According to *the known laws of refraction*, a cloud or body of air of different density from the common atmosphere, interposed between the gnomon and the coping of the dial plate below, would, if the cloud were denser than the atmosphere, cause the shadow to recede from the perpendicular height of the staircase, and of course to re-ascend the steps on the coping. by which it had before noon gone down; and if the cloud were rarer, a contrary effect would take place. The phenomenon on the dial of Ahaz, however, was doubtless of a miraculous nature, even should such a *medium* of the miracle be admitted: nothing less than a divine communication could have enabled Isaiah to predict its occurrence at that time and place: besides, he gave the king his own choice whether the shadow should advance or retire ten degrees. There seems, however, to be no necessity for seeking *any* medium for this miracle, and certainly no necessity for supposing any actual interference with the revolution of the earth, or the position of the sun. The miracle, from all the accounts of it, might consist only of the retrogression of the shadow ten degrees, by a simple act of Almighty power, without any medium, or, at most, by that of refracting those rays only which fell upon the dial. It is not said that any time was lost to the inhabitants of the world at large: it was not even observed by the astronomers of Babylon, for the deputation came to inquire concerning the wonder that was done in the *land* It was temporary, local, and confined to the observation of Hezekiah and his court, being designed chiefly for the satisfaction of that monarch. It is remarkable that no instrument for keeping time is mentioned in the Scripture before the dial of Ahaz, B.C. 700; nor does it appear that the Jews generally, even after this period, divided their day into hours. The dial of Ahaz was probably an object only of curious recreation, or served at most to regulate the occupations of the palace.

DIAMOND. The diamond is named in the Authorized Version as one of the stones in the breastplate of the high priest (Exod. xxviii. 18; xxxix. 11). But as these stones were engraved, it is by no means likely that the original word (*yahalom*) really denotes the diamond; and it is generally understood that the onyx is intended. The diamond again occurs in the Authorized Version of Jer. xvii .1; Ezek. iii. 9; Zech. vii. 12; and in these places the word (*shamir*) is different from the above, and its signification, 'a sharp point,' countenances this interpretation, the diamond being for its hardness used in perforating and cutting other minerals. Indeed, this use of the *shamir* is distinctly alluded to in Jer. xvii. 1, where the *stylus* pointed with it is distinguished from one of iron (comp. Plin. *Hist. Nat.* xxxvii. 15). The two other passages also favour this view by using it figuratively to express the hardness and obduracy of the Israelites. Our Authorized Version has 'diamond' in Jer. xvii. 1, and 'adamant' in the other texts: but in the original the word is the same in all.

DIANA (Acts xix. 24). Artemis, the Diana of the Romans, is a goddess known under various

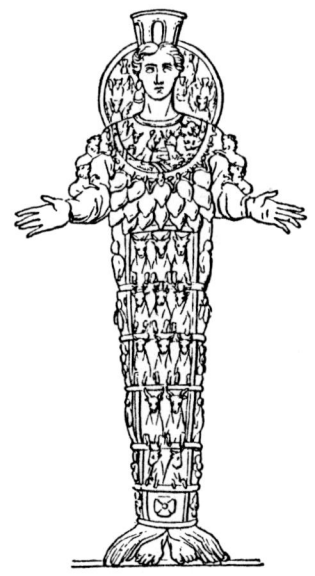

142.

modifications, and with almost incompatible attributes. As the tutelary divinity of Ephesus, in which character alone she concerns us here, she was undoubtedly a representative of the same power presiding over conception and birth which was adored in Palestine under the name of ASHTORETH.

Her earliest image, which was said to have fallen from heaven, was probably very rude, and, to judge from its representation on ancient coins, little more than a head with a shapeless trunk,

supported by a staff on each side. There is some dispute as to the material of which her image

143.

was made. Most authorities say it was of ebony. The later image with the full development of attributes, of which we give a representation, is a Pantheon of Asiatic and Egyptian deities. Even in it, however, we see how little influence Greek art had in modifying its antique rudeness. It is still more like a mummy than a Greek statue. Her priests were called Megabyzi, and were eunuchs.

DI'BON, or DIMON (Isa. xv. 9), called also Dibon-Gad, from its having been rebuilt by the tribe of that name (Num. xxxii. 34), a city on the northern bank of the Arnon, at the point where the Israelites crossed that river on their journey to the Jordan, and where their first encampment was made after having passed it. In later times we find it, with other towns in this quarter, in the hands of the Moabites (Jer. xlviii. 22). The site has been recognised by Seetzen, Burckhardt, and Irby and Mangles, at a place which bears the name of Diban, in a low tract of the district called the Koura, about three miles north of the Arnon (Modjeb). The ruins are here extensive, but offer nothing of interest. There was another place called Dibon in the tribe of Judah (Neh. xi. 25), perhaps the same that is called Dimonah in Josh. xiii. 26.

DI'DRACHMON (*a double drachma*), a silver coin equal to two Attic drachmæ, and also to the Jewish half shekel (Joseph. *Antiq.* iii. 8. 2). It was therefore equivalent to about 1s. 4d. of our money. By the law every Jew was required to pay half a shekel to the Temple (Exod. xxx. 13, sq.), and this amount is represented by the didrachma in Matt. xvii. 24, where it is used for the 'tribute-money' demanded of Christ.

DID'YMUS (*a twin*), a surname of the Apostle Thomas, denoting that he was a twin; and if translated, he would be called ' Thomas the Twin ' (John xi. 16). [THOMAS.]

DI'KE, the heathen Goddess of Justice; described as the daughter of Zeus and Themis. The punishment of murderers is particularly ascribed to her; and therefore, besides being the goddess of punishment in a general sense, she is often to be considered the same as Nemesis or Vengeance. The word occurs in Acts xxviii. 4, and is there rendered 'vengeance,' appellatively.

DIKLAH, a tribe descended from Joktan (Gen. x. 27). As the name in Aramaic and Arabic means a *palm-tree*, it has been judged necessary to seek the seat of the tribe in some territory rich in palm-trees. Bochart finds it in Southern Arabia, Michaelis in the region of the Tigris (from the analogy of the name Diglath); but where the ground of search is so uncertain, it is impossible to obtain any satisfactory result.

DI'NAH, a daughter of Jacob by Leah (Gen. xxx. 21), and therefore full sister of Simeon and Levi. While Jacob's camp was in the neighbourhood of Shechem, Dinah was seduced by Shechem, the son of Hamor, the Hivite chief or head-man of the town. Partly from dread of the consequences of his misconduct, and partly, it would seem, out of love for the damsel, he solicited a marriage with her, leaving the 'marriage price' (see MARRIAGE) to be fixed by her family. To this Dinah's brothers would only consent on the further condition that all the inhabitants of the place should be circumcised. Even this was yielded; and Simeon and Levi took a most barbarous advantage of the compliance by falling upon the town on the third day, when the people were disabled by the effects of the operation, and slew them all (Gen. xxxiv.). For this act of truly Oriental vindictiveness no excuse can be offered, and Jacob himself repeatedly alludes to it with abhorrence and regret (Gen. xxxiv. 30; xlix. 5-7). To understand the act at all, however, it is necessary to remember, that any stain upon the honour of a sister, and especially of an only sister, is even at this day considered as an insupportable disgrace and inexpiable offence among all the nomade tribes of Western Asia. If the woman be single, her brothers more than her father, if she be married, her brothers more than her husband, are aggrieved, and are considered bound to avenge the wrong. Hence the active vengeance of Dinah's full brothers, and the comparative passiveness of her father in these transactions. Of Dinah's subsequent lot nothing is known.

DIONYS'IUS THE AREOPAGITE. The name of 'Dionysius the Areopagite' enlivens the scanty account of success which attended the visit of Paul to Athens (Acts xvii. 34). Nothing further is related of him in the New Testament; but ecclesiastical historians record some particulars concerning his career, both before and after his conversion. Suidas recounts that he was an Athenian by birth, and eminent for his literary attainments; that he studied first at Athens and afterwards at Heliopolis in Egypt; and that, while in the latter city, he beheld that remarkable eclipse of the sun, as he terms it, which took place at the death of Christ, and exclaimed to his friend Apollophanes, 'Either the Divinity suffers, or sympathises with some sufferer.' He futher details, that after Dionysius returned to Athens, he was admitted into the Areopagus; and, having embraced Christianity about A.D. 50, was constituted Bishop of Athens by the Apostle Paul himself. Syncellus and Nicephorus both record the last particular. Aristides, an Athenian philosopher, asserts that he suffered martyrdom—a fact generally admitted by historians; but the precise period of his death, whether under Trajan or Adrian, or, which is most likely, under Domitian, they do not determine. It is impossible now to determine what credit is to be given to these traditions.

DIOT'REPHES (*Jove-nourished*), a person who seems to have been one of the false teachers condemned by St. John in his third epistle. He appears to have been a presbyter or deacon—probably the former. He refused to receive the letter sent by John, thereby declining to submit to his directions or acknowledge his authority (3 John 9).

DISCERNING OF SPIRITS. This is now usually understood to mean a high faculty, enjoyed by certain persons in the apostolic age, of diving into the heart and discerning the secret dispositions of men. It appears to have been one of the gifts peculiar to that age, and was especially necessary at a time when the standards of doctrine were not well established or generally understood, and when many deceivers were abroad (2 John ii. 7). This faculty seems to have been exercised chiefly upon those who came forward as teachers of others, and with whose real character and designs it was important that the infant churches should be acquainted.

DISCIPLE, a scholar or follower of any teacher, in the general sense. It is hence applied in the Gospels not only to the followers of Christ, but to those of John the Baptist (Matt. ix. 14, &c.), and of the Pharisees (Matt. xxii. 16). Although used of the followers of Christ generally, it is applied in a special manner to the twelve apostles (Matt. x. 1; xi. 1; xx. 17; Luke ix. 1). After the death of Christ the word took the wider sense of a believer, or Christian; *i. e.* a follower of Jesus Christ.

DISEASES OF THE JEWS. The most prevalent diseases of the East are cutaneous diseases, malignant fevers, dysentery, and ophthalmia. Of the first of these the most remarkable are leprosy and elephantiasis [LEPROSY]. To the same class also belongs the singular disease called the mal d'Aleppo, which is confined to Aleppo, Bagdad, Aintab, and the villages on the Segour and Kowick. It consists in an eruption of one or more small red tubercles, which give no uneasiness at first, but, after a few weeks, become prurient, discharge a little moisture, and sometimes ulcerate. Its duration is from a few months to a year. It does not affect the general health at all, and is only dreaded on account of the scars it leaves. Foreigners who have visited Aleppo have sometimes been affected by it several years after their return to their own country. It is a remarkable fact that dogs and cats are likewise attacked by it. The Egyptians are subject to an eruption of red spots and pimples, which cause a troublesome smarting. The eruption returns every year towards the end of June or beginning of July, and is on that account attributed to the rising of the Nile. Malignant fevers are very frequent, and of this class is the great scourge of the East, the plague, which surpasses all others in virulence and contagiousness [PESTILENCE]. The Egyptian ophthalmia is prevalent throughout Egypt and Syria, and is the cause of blindness being so frequent in those countries [BLINDNESS]. Of inflammatory diseases in general, Dr. Russell says that at Aleppo he has not found them more frequent, nor more rapid in their course, than in Great Britain. Epilepsy and diseases of the mind are commonly met with. Melancholy monomaniacs are regarded as sacred persons in Egypt, and are held in the highest veneration by all Mahometans.

Diseases are not unfrequently alluded to in the

Old Testament; but, as no description is given of them, except in one or two instances, it is for the most part impossible even to hazard a conjecture concerning their nature.

Hezekiah suffered, according to our version, from a *boil*. The term here used means literally *inflammation*; but we have no means of identifying it with what we call boil. The same may be said of the plague of boils and blains [BLAINS], and of the names of diseases mentioned in the 28th chapter of Deuteronomy, such as pestilence, consumption, fever, botch of Egypt, itch, scab. The case of Job, in which the term translated *boil* also occurs, demands a separate notice [JOB]. Nebuchadnezzar's disease was a species of melancholy monomania, called by authors zoanthropia, or more commonly lycanthropia, because the transformation into a wolf was the most ordinary illusion. Esquirol considers it to have originated in the ancient custom of sacrificing animals. But, whatever effect this practice might have had at the time, the cases recorded are independent of any such influence; and it really does not seem necessary to trace this particular hallucination to a remote historical cause, when we remember that the imaginary transformations into inanimate objects, such as glass, butter, &c., which are of every-day occurrence, are equally irreconcilable with the natural instincts of the mind. The same author relates that a nobleman of the court of Louis XIV. was in the habit of frequently putting his head out of a window, in order to satisfy the urgent desire he had to bark. Calmet informs us that the nuns of a German convent were transformed into cats, and went mewing over the whole house at a fixed hour of the day. Antiochus and Herod died, like Sylla, from phthiriasis, a disease which was well known to the ancients. Nothing is known respecting the immediate causes of this malady; but there is no doubt that it depends on the general state of the constitution, and must not be attributed to uncleanliness. Alibert mentions the case of a person who, as soon as these animals had been destroyed, fell into a typhoid state, and shortly after died. The question of alleged demoniacal possession, so often mentioned in the New Testament, has been considered under another head [DEMONIACS], and need not be re-opened in this place.

DISH. Various kinds of dishes are mentioned in Scripture; but it is impossible to form any other idea of their particular forms than may be suggested by those of ancient Egypt and of the

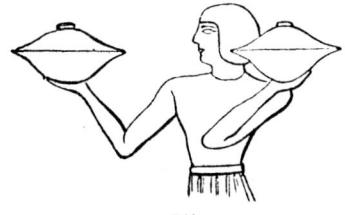

144.

modern East, which have much resemblance to each other. The sites of such ancient towns as were built of sun-dried bricks are usually covered with broken potsherds, some of them large enough to indicate the form of the entire vessel. These are remarkably similar to those in modern use, and are for the most part made of a rather coarse earthenware, covered with a compact and strong glaze, with bright colours, mostly green, blue, or yellow. Dishes and other vessels of copper, coarsely but thickly tinned, are now much used in the East; but how far this may have been anciently the case we have not the means of knowing. The cut (No. 144) represents a slave bringing dishes to table; the dishes have covers, and the manner in which they are carried on the reverted hand is the mode still used by Eastern servants.

DIVINATION is a general term descriptive of the various illusory arts anciently practised for the discovery of things secret or future. The human mind has always shown a strong curiosity to ascertain the course of fortune, and the issue of present or contemplated schemes; and in those countries and ages where ignorance of physical laws has combined with superstition to debase it, it has sought to gratify this innate disposition to pry into futurity, by looking for presages in things between which and the object of its anxiety no connection existed but in the diviner's imagination. Scarcely a single department of nature but was appealed to, as furnishing, on certain conditions, good or bad omens of human destiny; and the aspect of things, which, perhaps by the most casual coincidence, marked some event or crisis in the life of one or two individuals, came to be regarded, by blind credulity, as the fixed and invariable precursor of a similar result in the affairs of mankind in general. By such childish and irrational notions was the conduct of the heathen guided in the most important, no less than in the most ordinary occurrences of life; and hence arose the profession of augurs, soothsayers, *et hoc genus omne* of impostors, who, ingrafting vulgar traditions on a small stock of natural knowledge, established their claims to the possession of an occult science, the importance and influence of which they dexterously increased by associating it with all that was pompous and imposing in the ceremonies of their religion.

This science, if that can be called science which was the product of ignorance and fraud united, was divided into various branches, each of which had its separate professors. In a general view, divination may be considered as either natural or artificial: the first being founded on the notion that the soul possesses, from its spiritual nature, some prescience of futurity, which it exemplifies particularly in dreams, and at the approach of death: the second, resting on a peculiar interpretation of the course of nature, as well as on such arbitrary observations and experiments as superstition introduced. The different systems and methods that were anciently in vogue are almost incredible: as, for instance, Aëromancy, divining by the air; Arithmomancy, by means of numbers; Capnomancy, by the smoke of sacrifices; Chiromancy, by the lines on the palms of the hands; Hydromancy, by water; Pyromancy, by fire, &c. But without attempting an enumeration and explanation of all the arts of divination that were anciently practised, let us confine ourselves to the mention of those which occur in sacred history. 1. Wise men (Exod. vii. 11; Isa. xliv. 25; Jer. l. 35; Dan. ii. 12, &c.), a term

s

applied generally to magicians, or men who were skilled in natural science. 2. 'Wizards' or wise men, and 'a witch,' from an Arabic verb signifying 'to reveal,' both practising divination by the same arts, *i. e.* pretending to reveal secrets, to discover things lost, find hidden treasure, and interpret dreams. 3. One who foretold what was to happen by the flight of birds, or the use of lots [LOTS]. 4. One who, though rendered by our translators 'an observer of times,' foretold political or physical changes by the motion of the clouds, along with whom Isaiah conjoins those who made the same predictions from eclipses, and the conjunction of the stars (xlvii. 13). 5. 'An enchanter' was probably one who practised Ophiomancy, or the art of charming serpents, which was, and still is, a favourite trick of jugglery in the East. 6. 'A charmer,' one who placed words and things in a certain arrangement, or muttered them, as a kind of spell. 7. 'A consulter with familiar spirits,' or 'a ventriloquist,' was a wizard who asked counsel of his familiar, and gave the responses received from him to others—the name being applied in reference to the spirit or demon that animated the person, and inflated the belly, so that it protuberated like the side of a *bottle* (see Levit. xx. 27; 1 Sam. xxviii. 8; also Acts xvi. 16). 8. 'A necromancer,' one who, by frequenting tombs, by inspecting corpses, &c., like the witch of Endor, pretended to evoke the dead, and bring secrets from the invisible world (Gen. xli. 8; Exod. vii. 11; Lev. xix. 26; Deut. xviii. 10-12). 9. Belomancy, as it is called, a form of divination by means of arrows (Ezek. xxi. 21; see also 2 Kings xiii. 14-19), a notable example of which occurs in the history of Nebuchadnezzar, who, being undecided whether to march first against Jerusalem or Rabbah, allowed neither his policy nor resentment to decide the course of his expedition, but was determined wholly by the result of superstitious rites. The way of divining by arrows was, having first made them bright 'in order the better to follow them with the eye,' to shoot them, and to prosecute the march according to the direction in which the greatest number of arrows fell; or, having 'mixed together' some arrows with the names of the devoted cities marked on them, to attack that first which was first drawn out; or to put in a bag three arrows, as is the practice of the Arabs, one of which is inscribed with the words 'Command me, Lord,' the second with 'Forbid me, Lord,' while the third is left blank; so that if the first is taken out, he was to go; if the second, he was to desist; if the third is drawn, no decision being given, the experiment is to be repeated. 10. Rhabdomancy, or divination by rods (Hos. iv. 12). This has been confounded with the preceding. But the instruments of divination which Hosea alludes to are entirely different from those described by Ezekiel, arrows being used by the latter, whereas the former speaks of 'staff.' The form of divination by the staff was, after placing it upright, to let it fall, and decide by the direction in which it fell, or, according to others, by measuring the staff with the finger, saying at each span, 'I will go,' or 'I will not go,' and determining the course, according as it happened to be the one or the other at the last measurement. Both of these, as Jerome informs us, were frequently practised by the

Assyrians and Babylonians. Herodotus (vi.) describes the Alani women as gathering and searching anxiously for very smooth and straight wands to be used in this superstitious manner. 11. Another way of divining was by 'images' (Ezek. xxi. 21), which are generally considered talismans, but which the Persian and other versions render astrological instruments or tables. 12. Another form of divination was, 'by looking into the liver' of a newly killed sacrifice, and by observing its state and colour according to certain rules, to draw a favourable or unfavourable omen. The last form which it is of consequence to notice as alluded to in Scripture was by 'the cup.' But in what manner it was practised; whether it was by observing the appearance of some magical ingredients that were infused into the vessel; or whether allusion is made to a famous cup which the immemorial tradition of the East says has been in the possession of some great personages, and represents the whole world; or, finally, whether the original word rendered 'divineth,' should be rendered by 'searching' or 'inquiring earnestly,' as many learned writers, anxious to save the character of Joseph from the imputation of sorcery (Gen. xliv. 5), have laboured to prove, it is absolutely impossible, and we shall not attempt, to determine.

Egypt, the cradle of arts and sciences, if she did not give it birth, seem to have encouraged the practice of divination at an early age, and whether any of its forms had become objects of popular superstition, or were resorted to for the purposes of gain in the days of Joseph, it is well known that at the time of the Hebrew Exodus there were magicians in that country whose knowledge of the arcana of nature, and whose dexterity in the practice of their art, enabled them, to a certain extent, to equal the miracles of Moses. By what extraordinary powers they achieved those feats, how they changed their rods into serpents, the river water into blood, and introduced frogs in unprecedented numbers, is an inquiry that has occasioned great perplexity to many men of learning and piety. Some have imagined that the only way of accounting for the phenomena is to ascribe them to jugglery and legerdemain; the serpents, the frogs, and the other materials requisite having been secretly provided and dexterously produced at the moment their performances were to be exhibited. Others contend that these conjurors were aided by familiar spirits or infernal agents, with the Divine permission, in the performance of their wonderful feats. 'Earth, air, and ocean,' says a sensible writer, 'may contain many things of which our philosophy has never dreamt. If this consideration tend to humble the pride of learning, it may remind the Christian that secret things belong not to him, but to a higher power.'

It is reasonable to suppose that as Moses never had been in any other civilized country, all the allusions contained in his writings to the various forms of divination were those which were practised in Egypt; and, indeed, so strong a taste had his countrymen imbibed there for this species of superstition, that throughout the whole course of their history it seems to have infected the national character and habits. The diviners, who abounded both amongst the aborigines of Canaan and their Philistine neighbours (Isa. ii. 6), proved a great snare to the Israelites after their settlement in the promised land; and yet, notwithstanding the stern prohibitions of the law, no vigorous efforts were made to put an end to the crime by extirpating the practitioners of the unhallowed art, until the days of Saul, who himself, however, violated the statute on the night previous to his disastrous fall (1 Sam. xxviii.). But it was Chaldæa to which the distinction belongs of being the mother country of diviners. Such a degree of power and influence had they attained in that country, that they formed the highest caste and enjoyed a place at court; nay, so indispensable were they in Chaldæan society that no step could be taken, not a relation could be formed, a house built, a journey undertaken, a campaign begun, until the diviners had ascertained the lucky day and promised a happy issue. A great influx of these impostors had, at various times, poured from Chaldæa and Arabia into the land of Israel to pursue their gainful occupation, more especially during the reign of the later kings (Isa. viii. 19), and we find Manasseh not only their liberal patron, but zealous to appear as one of their most expert accomplices (2 Kings xxi. 6; 2 Chron. xxxiii. 6). The long captivities in Babylon spread more widely than ever among the Jews a devoted attachment to this superstition; for after their return to their own country, having entirely renounced idolatry, and, at the same time, no longer enjoying the gift of prophecy or access to the sacred oracles, they gradually abandoned themselves, as Lightfoot has satisfactorily shown, before the advent of Christ, to all the prevailing forms of divination (*Comment. on Matt.*).

Against every species and degree of this superstition the sternest denunciations of the Mosaic law were directed (Exod. xxii. 18; Lev. xix. 26, 31; xx. 27; Deut. xviii. 10, 11), as fostering a love for unlawful knowledge and withdrawing the mind from God only wise; while, at the same time, repeated and distinct promises were given that, in place of diviners and all who used enchantments, God would send them prophets, messengers of truth, who would declare the divine will, reveal futurity, and afford them all the useful knowledge which was vainly sought for from those pretended oracles of wisdom. Much discussion, however, has been carried on by learned men to determine the question whether the ancient tribe of diviners merely pretended to the powers they exercised, or were actually assisted by demoniacal agency. The latter opinion is embraced by almost all the fathers of the primitive church. On the other hand, it has been, with great ability and erudition, maintained that the whole arts of divination were a system of imposture, and that Scripture itself frequently ridicules those who practised them as utterly helpless and incapable of accomplishing anything beyond the ordinary powers of nature (Isa. xliv. 25; xlvii. 11-13; Jer. xiv. 14; Jonah ii. 8).

DIVORCE. [MARRIAGE.]

DOD'ANIM, the descendants of the fourth son of Javan (Gen. x. 4). Bochart and other commentators on the ethnographical sketch in Gen. x. suppose that the first settlements of the Dodanim were in the south-west part of Asia Minor; and that settlers of this family may be traced in Thessaly and Epirus, where the name is traced

in the city of Dodona and in the country of Doris. But there seems much of uncertainty in all these speculations.

DO'EG, an Edomite, and chief overseer of king Saul's flocks, which is an important trust in Oriental courts. At Nob he was witness of the assistance which the high-priest Ahimelech seemed to afford to the fugitive David, by furnishing him with the sword of Goliath, and by supplying him with bread even from the sacred table (1 Sam. xxi. 7). Of this he failed not to inform the king, who, regardless of the explanation offered by Ahimelech, and finding that the chiefs censured him, and hesitated to lay their hands upon a person so sacred, commanded Doeg to slay him and his priests—a task which was executed with equal readiness and cruelty by the Edomite (1 Sam. xxii. 18, sqq.).

DOG occurs in many places of Scripture (Exod. xxii. 31; 1 Sam. xvii. 43; xxiv. 14; 2 Sam. ix. 8; 2 Kings viii. 13; Ps. lix. 6, 14, 15; Prov. xxvi. 11, 17, &c.). An animal so well known, whose numerous varieties come under daily observation, requires no detailed description. There is, however, in Asia still extant one, perhaps more than one, species, that never have been the companions of man, and there are races of uncertain origin, that may have been formerly domesticated, but which are now feral, and as fierce as wolves; while, from the particular opinions of Oriental nations, there are others, exceedingly numerous, neither wild nor domesticated, but existing in all the cities and towns of the Levant, without owners; feeding on carrion and offals, and still having the true instinct of protecting property, guarding the inhabitants of the district or quarter where they are tolerated; and so far cherished, that water and some food are not unusually placed within their reach.

145.

The true wild species of Upper and Eastern Asia is a low, sharp-nosed, reddish cur-dog, not unlike a fox, but with less tail. In Persia and Turkey there exists a larger dog resembling a wolf, exceedingly savage. Both are gregarious, hunt in packs, but are occasionally seen alone. They are readily distinguished from a wolf by their shorter unfurnished tails. In the time of the sojourning of Israel in Egypt, there were already in existence domestic dogs of the principal races now extant—the cur-dog or fox-dog, the hound, the greyhound, and even a kind of low-legged turnspit. All the above, both wild and reclaimed, there is every reason to believe, were known to the Hebrews, and, notwithstanding the presumed Mosaic prohibition, anterior habits, and, in some measure, the necessity of their condition, must have caused cattle-dogs to be retained as property (Deut. xxiii. 18); for we find one of that race, or a house-dog, actually attending on travellers (Tobit v. 16; xi. 4). It is to be presumed that practically the street-dogs alone were considered as absolutely unclean; though all, as is the case among Mohammedans, were excluded from familiarity.

Beside the cattle-dog, the Egyptian hound and one or two varieties of greyhound were most likely used for hunting—a pastime, however, which the Hebrews mostly pursued on foot.

The street-dog, without master, apparently derived from the rufous cur, and in Egypt partaking of the mongrel greyhound, often more or less bare, with a mangy unctuous skin, frequently with several teeth wanting, was, as it now is, considered a defiling animal. It is to animals of this class, which no doubt followed the camp of Israel, and hung on its skirts, that allusion is more particularly made in Exod. xxii. 31; for the same custom exists at this day, and the race of street-dogs still retains their ancient habits. But with regard to the dogs that devoured Jezebel, and licked up Ahab's blood (1 Kings xxi. 23), they may have been of the wild races, a species of which is reported to have particularly infested the banks of the Kishon and the district of Jezreel.

The cities of the East are still greatly disturbed in the night by the howlings of street-dogs, who, it seems, were similarly noisy in ancient times, the fact being noticed in Ps. lix. 6, 14; and dumb or silent dogs not unfrequently seen, such as Isaiah alludes to (lvi. 10).

DOORS. [GATES.]

DOPH'KAH, an encampment of the Israelites in the Wilderness [WANDERING, THE].

DOR, a town on the border of the Mediterranean, which Jerome places nine Roman miles north of Cæsarea. It was one of the royal towns of the Canaanites (Josh. xi. 2; xii. 23), and was included in the heritage of Manasseh (Josh. xvii. 11). The place, or rather the region to which it gave name, occurs again in 1 Kings iv. 11. A place still exists, at the distance indicated by Jerome, under the name of Tortura, which Buckingham describes as a small village with about forty or fifty houses and five hundred inhabitants. It has a small port, formed by a narrow range of rocky islets, at a short distance from the sandy beach.

DO'THAN or DOTHAIM, the place where Joseph found his brethren, who had wandered thither with their flocks from Shechem, and where he was treacherously sold by them to the Ishmaelites (Gen. xxxvii. 17). It was here also that the Syrians were smitten with blindness at the word of Elisha (2 Kings vi. 13). Dothan is placed by Eusebius and Jerome twelve Roman miles north of Sebaste or Samaria, and it was obviously on the caravan track from Syria to Egypt. The well into which Joseph was cast by his brothers, and consequently the site of Dothan, has, however, been placed by tradition in a very distant quarter, namely, about three miles southeast from Safed, where there is a khan called Khan Jubb Yusuf, the Khan of Joseph's Pit, because the well connected with it has long passed among Christians and Moslems for the well in question.

DOVE. There are probably several species of

doves or pigeons included in the Hebrew name *joneh*. It may contain all those that inhabit Palestine, exclusive of the turtle-doves properly so called. Thus generalized, the dove is, figuratively, next to man, the most exalted of animals, symbolizing the Holy Spirit, the meekness, purity, and splendour of righteousness. By the Hebrew law doves and turtle-doves were the only birds that could be offered in sacrifice, and they were usually selected for that purpose by the less wealthy (Gen. xv. 9; Lev. v. 7; xii. 6; Luke ii. 24); and to supply the demand for them, dealers in these birds sat about the precincts of the Temple (Matt. xxi. 12, &c.).

146.

All pigeons in their true wild plumage have iridescent colours about the neck, and often reflected flashes of the same colours on the shoulders, which are the source of the silver and gold feathers ascribed to them in poetical diction; and thence the epithet of purple bestowed upon them all, though most applicable to the vinous and slaty-coloured species. The coasts and territory of Syria are noted for the great number of doves frequenting them, though they are not so abundant there as in the Coh-i Suleiman chain near the Indus. Syria possesses several species of pigeon; the stock-dove, ring-dove, the common pigeon in several varieties, such as the Barbary, Turkish or Persian carrier, crisp, and shaker. These are still watched in their flight in the same manner as anciently their number, gyrations, and other manœuvres were observed by soothsayers. The wild species, as well as the turtle-doves, migrate from Palestine to the south; but stock and ring doves are not long absent.

The figure we give is that of the more rare species of white and pink carrier, and the Phœnician sacred ensign of the dove.

DOVES' DUNG. This expression is by many considered to signify literally the dung of pigeons, as in the passage of 2 Kings vi. 25. Different opinions, however, have been entertained respecting the meaning of the words which are the subject of this article, namely, whether they should be taken literally, or as a figurative name of some vegetable substance. The strongest point in favour of the former view is that all ancient Jewish writers have understood the term literally. Taking it, however, in this sense, various explanations have been given of the use to which the doves' dung was applied. Some of the rabbins were of opinion, that the doves' dung was used for fuel, and Josephus, that it was purchased for its salt. Mr. Harmer has suggested that it might have been a valuable article, as being of great use for quickening the growth of esculent plants, particularly melons. Mr. Edwards is disposed to understand it as meaning the offals or refuse of all sorts of grain, which was wont to be given to pigeons, &c. Dr. Harris, however, observes that the stress of the famine might have been so great as to have compelled the poor among the besieged in Samaria to devour either the intestines of the doves, after the more wealthy had eaten the bodies, or, as it might perhaps be rendered, the *crops*.

Bochart, however, has shown that the term 'pigeons' dung' was applied by the Arabs to different vegetable substances, and supposes that it was one of the pulses used in ancient times, as at the present day, as an article of diet. With reference to this grain it has been observed that 'large quantities of it are parched and dried, and stored in magazines at Cairo and Damascus. It is much used during journeys, and particularly by the great pilgrim-caravan to Mecca ; and if this conjecture be correct it may be supposed to have been among the provisions stored up in the besieged city, and sold at the extravagant price mentioned in the text' (*Pict. Bible*). The late Lady Callcott, in her *Scripture Herbal*, 1842, adduces the common Star of Bethlehem as the 'doves' dung' of Scripture, and assigns this, as well as 'birds' milk,' as two of its vernacular names. It is a native of this country, and also of Taurus, Caucasus, and Northern Africa. Dioscorides states that its bulbs were sometimes cooked with bread, in the same way as the *melanthium*, and also that it was eaten both raw and roasted. The roots were also commonly eaten in Italy and other southern countries at an early period.

DRACH'MA, a coin of silver, the most common among the Greeks, and which after the Exile became also current among the Jews (2 Macc. iv. 19 ; x. 20 ; xii. 43 ; Luke xv. 8, 9). The earlier Attic drachmæ were of the average weight of 66·5 grains, and in a comparison with the shilling would be equal to 9¾*d*. But the specimens of later times are of the average weight of only 61 grains, and some of less. In this state the drachma was counted equal to the denarius, which was at first worth 8½*d*., and afterwards only 7½*d*. The value of the drachma of the New Testament may therefore have been about 8*d*. The woman's 'ten pieces of silver' (*drachmæ*) in Luke xv. 8, would hence be equal to 6*s*. 8*d*. of our money—that is, in nominal value, for the real value of money was far greater in the time of Christ than at present.

DRAGON occurs principally in the plural form (Job xxx. 29 ; Ps. xliv. 19, 20 ; Isa. xiii. 22 ; xxxiv. 13 ; xxxv. 7 ; Jer. ix. 11 : xiv. 6 : xlix. 33 ; and Micah i. 8). These texts, in general, present pictures of ruined cities and of desolation in the wilderness. Where dragons are associated with birds of the desert, they clearly indicate serpents of various species, both small and large, as already noticed in the article ADDER. In Jer. xiv. 6, where wild asses snuffing up the wind are compared to dragons, the image will appear in its full strength, if we understand by dragons, great boas and python-serpents, such as are figured in the Prænestine mosaics. They were common in ancient times,

and are still far from rare in the tropics of both continents. Several of the species grow to an enormous size, and, during their periods of activity, are in the habit of raising a considerable portion of their length into a vertical position, like pillars, 10 or 12 feet high, in order to survey the vicinity above the surrounding bushes, while with open jaws they drink in a quantity of the current air. The same character exists in smaller serpents ; but it is not obvious, unless when, threatening to strike, they stand on end nearly three-fourths of their length. Most, if not all, of these species are mute, or can utter only a hissing sound ; and although the mallipambu, the great rock-snake of Southern Asia, is said to wail in the night, we have never witnessed such a phenomenon, nor heard it asserted that any other boa, python, or erpeton had a real voice ; but they hiss, and, like crocodiles, may utter sounds somewhat akin to howling.

DRAM. Gesenius and most others are of opinion that the word which occurs in 1 Chron. xxix. 7 ; Ezra viii. 27 ; ii. 69 ; Neh. vii. 70-72 ; denotes the *Persian Daric*, a gold coin, which must have been in circulation among the Jews during their subjection to the Persians. This coin is of interest, not only as the most ancient gold coin of which any specimens have been preserved to the present day, but as the earliest coined money which, we can be sure, was known to and used by the Jews. The distinguishing mark of the coin was a crowned archer, who appears with some slight variations on different

147.

specimens. His garb is the same which is seen in the sculptures at Persepolis, and the figure on the coin is called, in numismatics, Sagittarius. The specimens weighed by Dr. Bernard were fifteen grains heavier than an English guinea, and their intrinsic value may, therefore, be reckoned at twenty-five shillings.

DREAMS. Of all the subjects upon which the mind of man has speculated, there is perhaps none which has more perplexed than that of dreaming.

Whatever may be the difficulties attending the subject, still we know that it has formed a channel through which Jehovah was pleased in former times to reveal his character and dispensations to his people.

In regard to the immediate cause of dreaming, the opinions of the ancients were very various.

We believe that dreams are ordinarily the re-embodiment of thoughts which have before, in some shape or other, occupied our minds. They are broken fragments of our former conceptions revived, and heterogeneously brought together. If they break off from their connecting chain, and become loosely associated, they exhibit ofttimes absurd combinations, but the *elements still sub-*

sist. If, for instance, any irritation, such as pain, fever, &c., should excite the *perceptive* organs, while the reflective ones are under the influence of sleep, we have a consciousness of objects, colours, or sounds being presented to us, just as if the former organs were actually stimulated by having such impressions communicated to them by the external senses; whilst, in consequence of the repose of the reflecting power, we are unable to rectify the illusion, and conceive that the scenes passing before us, or the sounds that we hear, have a real existence. This want of mutual co-operation between the different faculties of the mind may account for the *disjointed* character of dreams. This position might be fully substantiated by an appeal to the evidence of fact. Dr. Beattie speaks of a man who could be made to dream anything by whispering in his ear. Dr. Gregory relates of himself that, having once had occasion to apply a bottle of hot water to his own feet when he retired to bed, he dreamed that he was ascending the side of Mount Ætna, and that he found the heat of the ground almost insufferable. Persons who have had a blister applied to their head have been known to dream of being scalped by a party of North American Indians. Sleeping in a smoky room, we may dream of a house or city being in flames. The smell of a flower applied to the nostrils may call forth the idea of walking in a garden; and the sound of a flute may excite in us the most pleasurable associations.

The only one of our mental powers which is not suspended while dreaming is fancy, or imagination. We often find *memory* and *judgment* alternately suspended and exercised. Sometimes we fancy ourselves contemporaneous with persons who have lived ages before: here memory is at work, but judgment is set aside. We dream of carrying on a very connected discourse with a deceased friend, and are not conscious that he is no more: here judgment is awake, but memory suspended. These *irregularities*, or want of mutual co-operation in the different faculties of the mind may form, for aught we know, the plan by which God gives health and vigour to the whole soul.

How God revealed himself by dreams, and raised up persons to interpret them, the Scriptures abundantly testify. Under the three successive dispensations we find this channel of communication with man adopted. It was doubtless in this way that God appeared to the father of the faithful, ordering him to forsake country, kindred, and his father's house, and to go into the land that he would show him. To this divine command, Abraham paid a ready obedience. It was by a similar prompt obedience to the admonition conveyed to him in a dream, that Abimelech (Gen. xx. 3) himself and Abraham, too, were saved from the evil consequences of his meditated act. To Jacob, also, God appeared frequently in a dream (Gen. xxviii. 19; xxxi. 10); and his son Joseph, while yet a child, had dreams *predictive* of his future advancement (Gen. xxxvii. 6-11).

Such were some of the dreams by which God revealed himself under the patriarchal dispensation, and that the same divine mode of communicating with man was continued under that of Moses is evident from an express word of pro-mise (Num. xii. 6). That dreams were one of the ways whereby God was wont to signify his pleasure, and from the complaint of Saul to the spirit of Samuel (whom the witch pretended to raise up), when he asked him, 'Why hast thou disquieted me to bring me up?' Saul answered, 'I am sore distressed; for the Philistines make war against me, and God is departed from me, and answers me no more; neither by prophets, nor by *dreams:* therefore I have called thee that thou mayest make known to me what I shall do.' And, in order to guard against imposition, Moses pronounced a penalty against dreams which were invented and wickedly made use of, for the promotion of idolatry (Deut. xiii. 1-5). Thus Zechariah (x. 2) complains: 'The idols have spoken vanity, and the diviners have spoken a lie, and have told *false dreams;* they comfort in vain.' And so Jeremiah (xxiii. 25), 'I have heard what the prophets said that prophesy lies in my name, saying, I have dreamed, I have dreamed,' &c. Yet this abuse did not alter God's plan in the right use of them; for in the 28th verse of the same chapter, it is said, 'the prophet that hath a *dream*, and he that hath my word, let him speak my word faithfully. What is the chaff to the wheat? saith the Lord.'

When Gideon warred with the Amalekites, and was alarmed at their vast multitudes, he was encouraged to do God's will by overhearing one of them relate his dream, and another giving the interpretation (Judg. vii.). Again, it was in a dream that God was pleased to grant Solomon a promise of wisdom and understanding (1 Kings iii. 5, &c.). Here we may perceive what converse the Lord was pleased to hold with Solomon in a dream; and the sacred record informs us how punctually everything herein promised was fulfilled.

The knowledge of visions and dreams is reckoned amongst the principal gifts and graces sometimes bestowed by God upon them that fear him; so it is said of Daniel and his companion, that 'God gave them knowledge and skill in all learning and wisdom: and Daniel had understanding in all visions and dreams (Dan. i. 17). And the God who had imparted this spirit unto his servant Daniel soon, in the arrangement of his providence, gave the signal occasion for its exercise recorded in the second chapter of his book. In the dream of Nebuchadnezzar a great variety of ends were attained in reference to *Babylon*, Israel, and indeed the world—all of which were worthy of God's miraculous interference.

That this method of God's revealing himself was not confined to the legal dispensation, but was to be extended to the Christian, is evident from Joel (ii. 28), 'And afterwards (saith the Lord) I will pour out my spirit upon all flesh; and your sons and your daughters shall prophesy; your young men shall see visions, and your old men shall *dream dreams.*' In Acts ii. 17, we find the Apostle Peter applying this to the illumination of the Holy Ghost. Accordingly, we read that when Joseph designed to put Mary away, because he perceived her to be with child, he was turned from his purpose by a dream, in which an angel made the truth of the matter known to him (Matt. i. 20). And in the following chapter it is stated, that God, in a dream, warned the wise men not to return to Herod. Moreover, in verses 13 and 19, Joseph is instructed to flee into and return from Egypt with the child Jesus.

We inquire not *how* far God may have revealed himself to man beyond what Holy Scripture records. Some of the dreams both of ancient and modern times, which lay claim to a divine character, are certainly striking, and may, for aught we know, have had, and may still have, a collateral bearing on the development of God's purposes.

DRESS. The subject of the costume of the ancient Hebrews is involved in much obscurity and doubt. The allusions to dress in the Scriptures form the only source of our positive information. They are often, indeed, obscure, and of uncertain interpretation; but they are invaluable in so far as they enable us to compare and verify the information derivable from other sources. These sources are—

1. The costume of neighbouring ancient nations, as represented in their monuments.

2. The alleged costume of Jews as represented in the same monuments.

3. The present costumes (which are known to be ancient) of Syria and Arabia.

4. Tradition.

1. The range of inquiry into monumental costume is very limited. Syria, Arabia, and Egypt, are the only countries where monuments would be likely to afford any useful information: but Arabia has left no monumental figures, and Syria none of sufficiently ancient date; and it is left for Egypt to supply all the information likely to be of use. The extent and value of this information, for the particular purpose, we believe to be far less than is usually represented. That we are not disposed to undervalue the information derivable from the Egyptian monuments for the purpose of illustrating Biblical history and antiquities, the pages of the present work will sufficiently evince; and its editor may indeed claim to have been the first in this country to work this mine of materials for Biblical illustration. But the rage for this kind of illustration has been carried to such preposterous lengths, that it may not be an unwholesome caution to remind our readers that the Egyptians and the Hebrews were an exceedingly different people—as different in *every* respect as can well be conceived; and that the climates which they inhabited were so very different as to *necessitate* a greater difference of food and *dress* than might be pre-supposed of countries so near to each other. It is true that the Jewish nation was cradled in Egypt: and this circumstance may have had some influence on ceremonial dresses, and the ornaments of women; but we do not find that nations circumstanced as the Jews were ready to adopt the costumes of other nations, especially when their residence in Egypt was always regarded by them as temporary, and when their raiment was of home manufacture—spun and woven by the women from the produce of their flocks (Exod. xxxv. 25). We find also that, immediately after leaving Egypt, the principal article of dress among the Hebrews was some ample woollen garment, fit to sleep in (Exod. xxii. 27), to which nothing similar is to be seen among the costumes of Egypt.

2. With respect to the supposed representation of Jews in ancient monuments, if any authentic examples could be found, even of a single figure, in the ancient costume, it would afford much satisfaction as tending to elucidate many passages of Scripture which cannot at present be with certainty explained. The sculptures and paintings supposed to represent ancient Hebrews are contained in—

(*a*) A painting at Beni Hassan, representing the arrival of some foreigners in Egypt, and supposed to figure the arrival of Joseph's brethren in that country. The accessories of the scene, the physiognomies of the persons, and the time to which the picture relates, are certainly in unison with that event; and, though we must speak with hesitation on the subject, the conjecture is probably correct. The annexed cut shows the

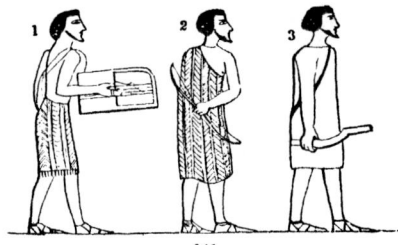

148.

variety of costume which this scene displays. All the men wear sandals. Some of them are clad only in a short tunic or shirt, with close sleeves (fig. 3); others wear over this a kind of sleeveless plaid or mantle, thrown over the left shoulder, and passing under the right arm (fig. 2). It is of a striped and curiously figured pattern, and looks exceedingly like the fine grass woven cloth of the South Sea. Others have, instead of this, a *fringed* skirt of the same material (fig. 1). All the figures are bare-headed, and wear beards, which are circumstances favourable to the identification. The fringed skirt of fig. 1 is certainly a remarkable circumstance. Moses directed that the people should wear a fringe at the hem of their garments (Num. xv. 38); and the probability is that this command merely perpetuated a more ancient usage.

(*b*) This fringe re-appears, much enlarged, in the other Egyptian sculpture in which Jews are supposed to be represented. These are in a tomb discovered by Belzoni, in the valley of Bab-el Melook, near Thebes. There are captives of

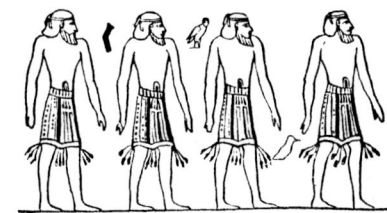

149.

different nations, and among them four figures, supposed to represent Jews. The scene is imagined to commemorate the triumphs of Pharaoh-Necho in that war in which the Jews were defeated at Megiddo, and their king Josiah slain (2 Chron. xxxv. xxxvi.). It will be seen that the dress of these figures differs little, excepting in the length of the fringe, from that of the skirted figure in the earlier painting; and so far this is a corroborative circumstance in favour of both.

There is no reason to think that the dress of the Jews was in any important respect different from that of the other inhabitants of the same and immediately bordering countries. It is therefore fortunate that the Egyptian monuments offer such representations of the Canaanitish and neighbouring nations, as enable us to see that the prevailing style of dress was a close tunic under a loose outer robe, the place of the latter being sometimes supplied by a large cape, as shown in the annexed engraving (No. 150), which appears to represent inhabitants of

150.

Syria and Lebanon. The evidence for the latter (fig. 2) is as conclusive as can be obtained, for not only is there the name Lemanon, but the persons thus attired are represented as inhabiting a mountainous country, and felling *fir*-trees to impede the chariots of the Egyptian invaders. The dresses are similar to each other, and this similarity strengthens the probability that the dress of the Jews was not very different. The figures are bearded, and the cap, or head-dress, is bound round with a fillet. The figures are arrayed in a long gown reaching to the ankles, and confined around the waist by a girdle, and the shoulders are covered by the cape which appears to have been common to several nations,

151.

perhaps as an occasional or a summer substitute for the loose mantle which some other figures exhibit. The dresses are often of brilliant colours, sometimes in variegated patterns; and the outer mantle is seen to be sometimes lined, by the inside and outside being of different colours, such as yellow lined with blue, etc. The military dress was more compact than that in civil use; and among the accoutrements we readily recognise the helmet, and the military girdle so often mentioned in the Sacred Book.

Such is the amount of the information to be derived from ancient monuments.

152.

That to be obtained from tradition is embodied —1. In the dresses of monks and pilgrims, which may be traced to an ancient date, and which are an intended imitation of the dresses supposed to have been worn by the first disciples and apostles of Christ. 2. The garb conventionally assigned by painters to Scriptural characters, which were equally intended to embody the dress of the apostolical period, and is corrected in some degree by the notions of Oriental costume which were collected during the Crusades.

Let us now consider the modern sources of illustration. With the exceptions of the foreign Turkish costume, and the modifications thereof, and with certain local exceptions, chiefly in mountainous regions, it may be said that there is one prevailing costume in all the countries of Asia between the Tigris and Mediterranean, and throughout Northern Africa, from the Nile to Morocco and the banks of the Senegal. This costume is substantially Arabian, and owes its extension to the wide conquests of the Arabians under the first caliphs; and it is through the Arabians—the least changed of ancient nations, and almost the only one which has remained as a nation from ancient times—that the antiquity of this costume may be proved. This is undoubtedly the most ancient costume of Western Asia, and while one set of proofs would carry it up to Scriptural times, another set of strong probabilities and satisfactory analogies will take it back to the most remote periods of Scriptural history, and will suggest that the dress of the Jews themselves was very similar, without being strictly identical.

It is to be observed, however, that there are two very different sorts of dresses among the Arabians. One is that of the Bedouin tribes, and the other that of the inhabitants of towns. The distinction between these is seldom clearly understood, or correctly stated; but it is of the utmost importance for the purpose of the present notice. Instead therefore of speaking of the Arabian costume as one thing, we must regard it as two things—the desert costume, and the town costume.

If, then, our views of Hebrew costume were based on the actual costume of the Arabians, we should be led to conclude that the desert costume represented that which was worn during the patriarchal period, and until the Israelites had been some time settled in Canaan; and the town costume that which was adopted from their neighbours when they became a settled people.

This is a subject which, more than any other, requires the aid of pictorial illustration to render the details intelligible. Having provided ourselves with these, our further observations will most advantageously take the form of explanations of them, and of comments upon them.

Under the notion that the desert costume belongs to the patriarchal period, the precedence is here given to it. Only the outer articles of dress are *distinctive*, those which are worn underneath being similar to other articles worn by the town and peasant classes, and which as such will be hereafter noticed.

The annexed cut (No. 153) represents, in fig. 2, a Bedouin, or desert Arab, in the dress usually

153.

worn in Asia; and in fig. 1 represents a townsman in a cloak of the same kind, adopted from the Arabs, and worn very extensively as an outermost covering in all the countries from the Oxus (for even the Persians use it) to the Mediterranean. The distinctive head-dress of the Bedouin, and which has not been adopted by any other nation, or even by the Arabian townsmen, is a kerchief folded triangularly, and thrown over the head so as to fall down over the neck and shoulders, and bound to the head by a band of twisted wool or camel's hair. We forbear at the moment from inquiring whether this was or was not in use among the ancient Hebrews. The cloak is called an *abba*. It is made of wool and hair, and of various degrees of fineness. It is sometimes entirely black, or entirely white, but is more usually marked with broad stripes, the colours of which (never more than two, one of which is always white) are distinctive of the tribe by which

it is worn. The cloak is altogether shapeless, being like a square sack, with an opening in front, and with slits at the sides to let out the arms. The Arab who wears it by day, sleeps in it by night, as does often the peasant by whom it has been adopted; and in all probability this was the garment similarly used by the ancient Hebrews, and which a benevolent law, delivered while Israel was still in the desert, forbade to be kept in pledge beyond the day, that the poor might not be without a covering at night (Exod. xxii. 27). This article of dress appears to have been little known to Biblical illustrators, although it is the principal and most common outermost garment in Western Asia. This singular neglect has arisen from their information being chiefly derived from Shaw and others, who describe the costume of the Arab tribes or Moors of Northern Africa, where the outer garment is more generally the *bournoos* (No. 153, fig. 3), a woollen cloak, not unlike the *abba*, but furnished with a hood, and which is sometimes strangely confounded even by well-informed persons with a totally different outer garment worn in the same regions, usually called the *hyke*, but which is also, according to its materials, quality, or colour, distinguished by various other names. Regardless of these minute distinctions, this part of dress may be described as a large woollen blanket, either white or brown, and in summer a cotton sheet (usually blue or white, or both colours together). Putting one corner before over the left shoulder, the wearer brings it behind, and then under the right arm, and so over the body, throwing it behind over the left shoulder, and leaving the right arm free for action. This very picturesque mode of wearing the *hyke* is shown in fig. 2 (No. 154).

154.

Another mode of wearing it is shown in fig. 3. It is sometimes thrown over the head as a protection from the sun or wind (fig. 1), and calls to mind the various passages of Scripture in which persons are described as covering their heads with their mantles (2 Sam. xv. 30; 1 Kings xix. 13; Esther vi. 12). This article of dress, originally borrowed from the nomades, is known in Arabia, and extends westward to the shores of the Atlantic, being most extensively used by all classes of the population. The seat of this dress, and of the abba respectively, is indicated by the direction of their importation into Egypt. The hykes are imported from the west (*i. e.* from

North Africa), and the abbas from Syria. The close resemblance of the above group of real costume to those in which the traditionary ecclesiastical and traditionary artistical costumes are displayed, must be obvious to the most cursory observer. It may also be noticed that the hyke is not without some resemblance, as to the manner in which it was worn, to the outer garment of one of the figures in the Egyptian family, supposed to represent the arrival of Joseph's brethren in Egypt (No. 148, fig. 1).

We now turn to the costumes which are seen in the towns and villages of south-western Asia.

In the Scriptures *drawers* are only mentioned in the injunction that the high-priest should wear them (Exod. xxviii. 42), which seems to show that they were not generally in use; nor have we any evidence that they ever became common. Drawers descending to the middle of the thighs were worn by the ancient Egyptians, and workmen often laid aside all the rest of their dress when occupied in their labours. As far as this part of dress was used at all by the Hebrews, it was doubtless either like this, or similar to those which are now worn in Western Asia by all, except some among the poorer peasantry, and by many of the Bedouin Arabs. They are of linen or cotton, of ample breadth, tied around the body by a running string, or band, and always worn next the skin, not over the shirt as in Europe.

It will be asked, when the poor Israelite had pawned his outer garment 'wherein he slept,' what dress was left to him? The answer is probably supplied by the annexed engraving (No. 155), which represents slightly different garments of cotton, or woollen frocks or shirts, which often, in warm weather, form the sole dress of the Bedouin peasants, and the lower class of townspeople. To this the abba or hyke is the proper outer robe (as in fig. 1, No. 154), but is usually, in summer, dispensed with in the day-time, and in the ordinary pursuits and occupations of life. It is sometimes (as in No. 155, fig. 2) worn with-

155.

out, but more usually with, a girdle; and it will be seen that the shorter specimens are not unlike the dress of one of the figures (fig. 3, No. 148) in the earliest of the Egyptian subjects which have been produced. The shirt worn by the superior classes is of the same shape, but of finer materials. This is shown in the following figure

156.

(No. 156), which represents a gentleman as just risen from bed. If we call this a shirt, the Hebrews doubtless had it—the sole dress (excepting the cloak) of the poor, and the inner robe of the rich. Such, probably, were the 'sheets' (translated 'shirts' in some versions), of which Samson despoiled thirty Philistines to pay the forfeit of his riddle (Judg. iv. 13, 19). It is shown from the Talmud, indeed, that the Hebrews of later days had a shirt called *chaluk*, which it would appear was often of wool, and which is described as the ordinary inner garment, the outer being the cloak or mantle. This shows that the shirt or frock was, as in modern usage, the ordinary dress of the Jews, to which a mantle (abba, hyke, or bournoos) was the outer covering.

In all the annexed figures (No. 157), representing persons of the superior class, we observe the

157.

shirt covered by a striped (sometimes figured) gown or caftan, of mingled silk and cotton. It descends to the ankles, with long sleeves, extending a few inches beyond the fingers' ends, but divided from a point a little above the wrist, so that the hand is generally exposed, though it may be concealed by the sleeve when necessary; for it is customary to cover the hands in the presence of a person of high rank. It is very common, especially in winter, for persons to sleep without removing this gown, but only unloosing the girdle by which it is bound.' It is not unusual within doors to see persons without any article of dress outside this; but it is considered decidedly as an undress, and no respectable person is beheld out of doors, or receives or pays visits, without an outer covering. Hence persons clad in this alone are said to be 'naked' in Scripture—that is, not in the usual complete dress; for there can be no manner of doubt that this, or something like this, is referred to in Exod. xxviii. 40; Job xxx. 18; Isa. xxii. 21, &c. A similar robe is worn by the women, as was also the case among the Israelites (2 Sam. xiii. 18, 19 , Cant. v. 3). It is in the bosom of this robe that various articles are carried, and hence the Scriptural expression of giving things 'into the bosom.'

The girdle worn over this, around the waist, is usually a coloured shawl, or long piece of figured white muslin. The girdle of the poorer classes is of coarse stuff, and often of leather, with clasps. This leathern girdle is also much used by the Arabs, and by persons of condition when equipped for a journey. It is sometimes ornamented with workings in coloured worsted, or silk, or with metal studs, shells, beads, &c. Both kinds of girdles were certainly in use among the Hebrews (2 Kings i. 8; Matt. iii. 4; Mark i. 6; comp. Jer. xiii. 1). It is known to all readers of Scripture how often the 'girdle' and the act of 'girding the loins' is mentioned. It seems from 2 Sam. xx. 8 (comp. also the Syrian figure, No. 151, fig. 1), that it was usual to wear a knife or poniard in the girdle. This custom is still general, and denotes not any deadly disposition, but the want of clasp-knives. Men of literary vocations replace it by an inkhorn, as was also the case among the Israelites (Ezek. ix. 2).

Over the gown is worn either the short-sleeved *gibbeh* (fig. 3), which is a long coat of woollen cloth; or the long-sleeved *benish* (fig. 2), which is also of woollen cloth, and may be worn either over or instead of the other. The benish is, by reason of its long sleeves (with which the hands may be covered), the robe of ceremony, and is worn in the presence of superiors and persons of ranks. Over one or both of these robes may be worn the abba, bournoos, or hyke, in any of the modes already indicated. Aged persons often wrap up the head and shoulders with the latter, in the manner shown in fig. 4.

This hyke or wrapper is usually taken by persons going on a journey, for the purpose of being used in the same manner as a protection from the sun or wind. This is shown in the annexed cut, representing a group of persons equipped for travel. The robe is here more succinct and compact, and the firm manner in which the whole dress is girded up about the loins calls to mind the passages of Scripture in which the action of 'girding up the loins' for a journey is mentioned.

From this it is also seen that travellers usually wear a sword, and the manner in which it is worn is correctly shown. It would also appear that the Jews had swords for such occasional uses (Matt. xxvi. 51; Luke xxii. 36).

The necessity of baring the arm for any kind of exertion, must be evident from the manner in which it is encumbered in all the dresses we have produced. This action is often mentioned in Scripture, which alone proves that the arm was in ordinary circumstances similarly encumbered

158.

by the dress. For ordinary purposes a hasty tucking up of the sleeve of the right arm suffices; but for a continued action special contrivances are necessary. These are curious, as will be seen by the cut (No. 159). The full sleeves of the shirt are sometimes drawn up by means of cords, which pass round each shoulder, and cross behind, where they are tied in a knot. This custom is particularly affected by servants and workmen, who have constant occasion for baring the arm; but others, whose occasions are more incidental, and who are, therefore, unprovided with the necessary cords, draw up the sleeves and tie them together behind between the shoulders (fig. 2).

159.

For the dress of females we must refer to the article WOMEN. See also the article SANDAL.

DRINK, STRONG. The Hebrew thus rendered seems to demand a more particular elucidation than it has yet received, inasmuch as it had in all probability a much wider signification than is now conveyed by the phrase 'strong drink.' We shall class the various senses of the word under three heads, in the order in which we conceive them to have been developed.

1. *Shechar*, luscious, *saccharine* drink, or SWEET SYRUP, especially sugar or *honey of dates*, or of the

palm-tree ; also, by accommodation, occasionally the sweet fruit itself. By sugar or honey the Jews understood not only honey of bees, but also syrups made from the fruit or juice of the palm and other trees. 'In Solomon's time, and afterwards,' says Dr. Harris, 'the wine and sweet cordials seem generally to have been used *separately.*' It seems more probable, however, that the *palm syrup* or honey was used both as a sweetmeat or article of food, and *cs* a *drink,* diluted with water, as with the modern grape and honey syrups or sherbets (Prov. ix. 2, 5). The derivatives of *shechar,* expressive of its first signification, are numerous. Eastward and southward, following the Arabian channel and the Saracenic conquests, we meet with the most obvious forms of the Hebrew words still expressive of sugar. Thus we have the Arabic *sakar;* Persic and Bengálí, *shukkur* (whence our word for sugar-candy, *shukur-kund,* 'rock-sugar'); common Indian, *jaggree* or *zhaggery;* Moresque, *sekkour;* Spanish, *azncar;* and Portuguese, *assucar* (molasses being *mel-de-assucar,* 'honey of sugar,' abbreviated). The wave of population has also carried the original sense and form northwards, embodying the word in the Grecian and Teutonic languages. Hence Greek, *sakhar;* Latin, *saccharum;* Italian, *zucchero;* German, *sucher* and *juderiq;* Dutch, *suiker;* Russian, *sachar;* Danish, *sukker;* Swedish, *socker;* Welsh, *siwgwr;* French, *sucre;* and our own common words *sukhar* (sweetmeat), *sugar,* and *saccharine.*

2. Date or PALM WINE in its fresh and unfermented state. Bishop Lowth translates Isa. xxiv. 9 thus:—

'With songs they shall no more drink wine
    [*i. e.* of grapes];
The *palm wine* shall be *bitter* to them that
    drink it.'—

Herodotus, in his account of Assyria, remarks that 'the palm is very common in this country,' and that 'it produces them bread, *wine,* and honey.'

The Mohammedan traveller (A.D. 850) says that 'palm wine, *if drunk fresh,* is *sweet like honey;* but if kept, it turns to *vinegar.*'

Mandelslo (1640), speaking of the village of Damre near Surat, records thus: — '*Terry or Palm Wine.* In this village we found some *terry,* which is a liquor drawn out of the palm-trees, and drank of it in cups made of the leaves of the same tree. To get out the juice, they go up to the top of the tree, where they make an incision in the bark, and fasten under it an earthen pot, which they leave there all night, in which time it is fill'd with a certain *sweet liquor* very pleasant to the taste. They get out some also in the day-time, but that [owing to the great heat] *corrupts immediately,* and is good only for vinegar, which is *all the use they make of it.*'

Adam Fabroni, an Italian writer of celebrity, informs us that 'the palm-trees, which particularly abounded in the vicinity of Jericho and Engaddi, also served to make a *very sweet wine,* which is made all over the East, being called palm wine by the Latins, and *syra* in India, from the Persian *shir,* which means luscious liquor or drink.'

Dr. Shaw thus describes the unfermented palm wine :—'This liquor, which has a more luscious sweetness than honey, is of the consistence of a thin syrup, but *quickly grows tart and ropy,* ac-

quiring an intoxicating quality.' Sir G. T. Temple says, 'We were daily supplied with the sap of the date-tree, which is a delicious and wholesome beverage *when drunk quite fresh;* but if allowed to remain for some hours, it acquires a sharp taste not unlike cider. The Landers inform us that '*Palm wine* is the common and favourite drink of the natives' of Africa—that 'the *juice* is called wine,' and that 'it is either used in this state, or preserved till it acquires rather a BITTER flavour.' With these facts before us, the language employed by the prophet in the sublime chapter from which we quoted above, becomes beautifully apposite. His prediction is that 'the land shall be utterly spoiled,' that the light of joy shall be turned into the gloom of sorrow, even as the *sweet drink* which corrupts, grows *sour* and *bitter* to those who drink it. The passage clearly indicates the nature of the drink to have been *sweet* in what the Jews esteemed its most valuable condition, but *bitter* in its fermented state. Hence the drunkard is represented in ch. v. 20-22, as one who 'puts bitter for sweet, and sweet for bitter.' This palm wine, like the honey of dates and sugar, was much valued as a medicine and cordial.

3. SAKAR, in its third sense as a noun, denotes both in the Hebrew and the Arabic, fermented or INTOXICATING PALM WINE. Various forms of the noun in process of time became applied to *other* kinds of intoxicating drink, whether made from fruit or from grain. Arrack has been commonly, but erroneously, derived from *sakar,* and some have confounded the *arrack* with the palm wine, forgetting that the original wine existed long prior to the discovery of arrack distillation. The true palm wine, also, is exclusively the juice of the palm-tree or fruit, whereas *arrack* is applied to the spirit obtained from fermented rice and other things, and is, as Dr. Shaw remarks, 'the general name for all hot liquors extracted by the alembick.'

The palm wine of the East, as we have explained, is made intoxicating either by allowing it to corrupt and ferment, thereby losing the sweet luscious character for which the Orientals esteem it, and becoming ropy, tart, and bitter; or, in its fresh or boiled state, by an admixture of stimulating or stupefying ingredients, of which there is an abundance. Such a practice seems to have existed amongst the ancient Jews, and to have called down severe reprobation (comp. Prov. xxiii. 30; Isa. i. 22; v. 11, 22).

DROMEDARY. [CAMEL.]

DRUSIL'LA, youngest daughter of Herod Agrippa I. She was much celebrated for her beauty, and was betrothed to Epiphanes, prince of Commagene; but was afterwards married to Azizas, king of Emesa, whom the procurator Felix induced her to abandon, in order to live with him. She is mentioned in Acts xxiv. 24.

DULCIMER. [MUSIC.]

DU'MAH, a tribe and country of the Ishmaelites in Arabia (Gen. xxv. 14; Isa. xxi. 11). It is doubtless the same that is still called by the Arabs *Duma the Stony,* and *the Syrian Duma,* situated on the confines of the Arabian and Syrian deserts, with a fortress.

DUMAH was also the name of a town in the tribe of Judah (Josh. xv. 52), which Eusebius and Jerome place seventeen R. miles from Eleutheropolis, in Daroma.

DUNG. Among the Israelites, as with the modern Orientals, dung was used both for manure and for fuel. In a district where wood is scarce, dung is so valuable for the latter purpose, that little of it is spared for the former.

The use of dung for manure is indicated in Isa. xxv. 10, from which we also learn that its bulk was increased by the addition of straw, which was of course, as with us, left to rot in the dunghill. Some of the regulations connected with this use of dung we learn from the Talmud. The heaping up of a dunghill in a public place exposed the owner to the repair of any damage it might occasion, and any one was at liberty to take it away. Another regulation forbade the accumulation of the dunghill to be removed, in the seventh or sabbatic year, to the vicinity of any ground under culture, which was equivalent to an interdiction of the use of manure in that year; and this must have occasioned some increase of labour in the year ensuing.

The use of cow-dung for fuel is known to our own villagers, who, at least in the west of England, prefer it in baking their bread ' under the crock,' on account of the long-continued and equable heat which it maintains. It is there also not unusual in a summer evening to see aged people traversing the green lanes with baskets to collect the cakes of cow-dung which have dried upon the road. This helps out the ordinary fire of wood, and makes it burn longer. In many thinly-wooded parts of south-western Asia the dung of cows, camels, horses, asses, whichever may happen to be the most common, is collected with great zeal and diligence from the streets and ·highways, chiefly by young girls. They also hover on the skirts of the encampments of travellers, and there are often amusing scrambles among them for the droppings of the cattle. The dung is mixed up with chopped straw, and made into cakes, which are stuck up by their own adhesiveness against the walls of the cottages, or are laid upon the declivity of a hill, until sufficiently dried. It is not unusual to see a whole village with its walls thus garnished, which has a singular and not very agreeable appearance to a European traveller. Towards the end of autumn, the result of the summer collection of fuel for winter is shown in large conical heaps or stacks of dried dung upon the top of every cottage. The usages of the Jews in this matter were probably similar in *kind,* although the *extent* to which they prevailed cannot now be estimated.

DU'RA, the plain in which Nebuchadnezzar set up his golden image (Dan. iii. 1). It is clear from the context that ' the plain of Dura ' could be no other than that plain (or some part of it) in which Babylon itself was situated.

DUST. For storms of dust, &c., see STORM; for throwing dust on the head, see MOURNING.

E.

EAGLE (Exod. xix. 4; Lev. xi. 13, &c). The Eagle, in zoology, forms a family of several genera of birds of prey, mostly distinguished for their size, courage, powers of flight, and arms for attack. The bill is strong and bent into a plain pointed hook, without the notch in the inner curve which characterizes falcons; the nostrils are covered with a naked cere or skin, of a yellow or a blue colour; the eyes are lateral, sunken, or placed beneath an overhanging brow; the head and neck covered with abundance of longish, narrow-pointed feathers; the chest broad, the legs and thighs exceedingly stout and sinewy, and feathered down to the toes; the feathers in general are brownish and rust-coloured, and the tail is black, grey, or deep brown. Sea-eagles have the legs half bare and covered with horny scales; not unusually the head, back, and tail more or less white. The larger species of both measure, from head to tip of tail, 3 feet 6 inches or more. and spread their wings above 7 feet 6 inches. The claws of the fore and hind toe are particularly strong and sharp; in the sea-eagles they form more than half a circle, and in length measure from 1½ to 1¾ of an inch. These majestic birds have their abode in Europe, on the shores of the Mediterranean, in Syria and Arabia, wherever there are vast woody mountains and lofty cliffs: they occupy each a single district, always by pairs, excepting on the coasts, where the sea-eagle and the osprey may be found not remote from the region possessed by the rough-legged eagles. It is in this last genus, most generally represented by the golden eagle, that the most powerful and largest birds are found. That species in its more juvenile plumage, known as the ring-tailed eagle, the Imperial eagle, and the booted eagle, is found in Syria; and at least one species of the sea-eagles frequents the coasts, and is even of stronger wing

160. [Aquila heliaca.]

than the others. These build usually in the cliffs of Phœnicia, while the others are more commonly domiciliated within the mountains. According to their strength and habits the former subsist on antelopes, hares, hyrax, bustard, stork, tortoises, and serpents; and the latter usually on fish; both pursue the catta, partridge, and lizard. The osprey alone being migratory retires to Southern Arabia in winter. None, excepting the last-mentioned, are so exclusively averse to carrion as is commonly asserted: from choice or necessity they all, but in particular the sea-eagles, occasionally feed upon carcases of horses, &c.; and it is well known in the East that they follow armies for that purpose. Hence the allusions in Job and Matt. xxiv. 28, though vultures may be included, are perfectly correct. So again are those which refer to the eagle's eyrie, fixed in the most elevated cliffs. The swiftness of this bird, stooping among a flock of wild geese, with the rushing sound of a whirlwind, we have witnessed; and all know its towering flight, suspended on its broad wings among the clouds with little motion or effort. Thus the predictions, in which terrible nations coming from afar are assimilated to eagles, have a poetical and absolute truth, since there are species like the golden, which really inhabit the whole circumference of the earth, and the nations alluded to bore eagles' wings for standards, and for ornaments on their shields, helmets, and shoulders. The species here figured is the one most common in Syria, and is distinguished from the others by a spot of white feathers on each shoulder.

EARING. This word, which occurs in the Authorized Version (Gen. xlv. 6), is very often supposed to mean 'collecting the *ears* of corn,' which would confound it with harvest, from which it is distinguished in this very passage. But the word is radically the same with *harrow*, and denotes *ploughing*, from the Anglo-Saxon *erian*, 'to plough.'

EARNEST, a pledge, given and received, to assure the fulfilment of an engagement. Hesychius explains it as somewhat given beforehand. This idea attaches to all the *particular* applications of the word, as anything given by way of warrant or security for the performance of a promise; part of a debt paid as an assurance of paying the remainder; part of the price of anything paid beforehand to confirm the bargain between buyer and seller; part of a servant's wages paid at the time of hiring, for the purpose of ratifying the engagement on both sides. The idea that the earnest is either to be returned upon the fulfilment of the engagement, or to be considered as part of the stipulation, is also included. The word is used three times in the New Testament, but always in a figurative sense: in the first (2 Cor. i. 22), it is applied to the *gifts* of the Holy Spirit, which God bestowed upon the *apostles*, and by which he might be said to have hired them to be the servants of his son; and which were the earnest, assurance, and commencement of those far superior blessings which He would bestow on them in the life to come, as the wages of their *faithful* services:—in the two latter (2 Cor. v. 5; Eph. i. 13, 14), it is applied to the gifts bestowed on *Christians generally* upon whom, after baptism, the Apostles had laid their hands, and which were to them an *earnest* of obtaining an heavenly habitation and inheritance, upon the supposition of their fidelity. This use of the term finely illustrates the augmented powers and additional capacities promised in a future state.

EAR-RINGS. No custom is more ancient or universal than that of wearing ear-rings, from which it would appear to be a very natural idea to attach such an ornament to the pendulous lobe of the ear. Of the two words in Hebrew denoting ear-rings, one (Num. **xxxi.** 50; Ezek. xvi.

12) implies *roundness*, and it is a fact that nearly all the ancient ear-rings exhibited in the sculptures of Egypt and Persepolis are of a circular shape. The other word is also applied to a nose-jewel, from which we may suppose that it was a kind of ear-ring, different from the other and more similar to the nose-jewel. Ear-rings of certain kinds were anciently, and are still, in the East, instruments or appendages of idolatry and superstition, being regarded as talismans and amulets. Such probably were the ear-rings of Jacob's family, which he buried with the strange gods at Beth-el (Gen. xxxv. 4).

No conclusion can be formed as to the shape of the Hebrew ear-rings except from the signification of the words employed, and from the analogy of similar ornaments in ancient sculpture. Those worn by the Egyptian ladies were large, round, single hoops of gold, from one inch and a half to two inches and one-third in diameter, and frequently of still greater size, or made of six single rings soldered together. Such probably was the round 'agil' of the Hebrews. Among persons of high or royal rank the ornament was sometimes in the shape of an asp, whose body was of gold set with precious stones [AMULETS]. Silver ear-rings have also been found at Thebes, either plain hoops like the ear-rings of gold, or simple studs. The modern Oriental ear-rings are more usually jewelled drops or pendants than circlets of gold. But the writer has seen a small round plate of silver or gold suspended from a small ring inserted into the ear. This circular plate (about the size of a halfpenny) is either marked with fanciful figures or set with small stones. It is the same kind of thing which, in that country (Mesopotamia), is worn as a nose-jewel, and in it we perhaps find the Hebrew ear-ring which is denoted by the same word that describes a nose-jewel.

The use of ear-rings appears to have been confined to the women among the Hebrews. That they were not worn by men is implied in Judg. xiv. 24, where gold ear-rings are mentioned as distinctive of the Ishmaelite tribes.

EARTH. Besides the ordinary senses of the word or words rendered 'earth' in our translation —namely, as denoting mould, the surface of the earth, and the terrestrial globe—there are others in Scripture which require to be discriminated. 1. 'The earth' denotes '*the inhabitants of the earth*' (Gen. vi. 11; xi. 1). 2. *Heathen countries*, as distinguished from the land of Israel, especially during the theocracy, *i.e.* all the rest of the world excepting Israel (2 Kings xviii. 25; 2 Chron. xiii. 9, &c.). 3. In the New Testament especially, 'the earth' appears in our translation as applied to the land of Judæa. As in many of these passages it might seem as if the habitable globe were intended, the use of so ambiguous a term as 'the earth' should have been avoided, and the original rendered by 'the land,' as in Lev. xxv. 23; Isa. x. 23; and elsewhere. This is the sense which the original bears in Matt. xxiii. 35; xxvii. 45; Mark xv. 33; Luke iv. 25; xxi. 23; Rom. ix. 28; James v. 17. For the cosmological uses of the term, see GEOGRAPHY.

EARTHENWARE. [POTTER.]

EARTHQUAKE. The proximate cause of earthquakes, though by no means accurately defined, seems referable to the action of internal heat or fire. That the earth was once subject to the action of a vast internal power springing probably from the development of subterranean or central heat, the elevations and depressions, and the generally scarred and torn character of its exterior, make sufficiently evident. A power similar in kind, but more restricted in degree, is still at work in the bowels of the earth, and occasionally breaks down all barriers and devastates certain parts of the world.

The manifestation of these awful phenomena is restricted in its range. Accordingly geologists have laid down certain volcanic regions or bands within which this manifestation takes place. Over these regions various traces of volcanic agency are found, such as either gaseous vapours or hot springs, or bituminous substances, and in some instances (occasionally) active volcanoes. Several sources of bitumen are found on the Tigris, in the Persian mountains, near the Kharoon, and at Bushire, as well as along the Euphrates. At Hit, especially, on the last-mentioned river, it exists on a very large scale, and, having been much used from the earliest times, seems inexhaustible. Abundant traces of it are also to be seen amid the ruins and over the entire vicinity of Hillah—the ancient Babylon. Syria and Palestine abound in volcanic appearances. Between the river Jordan and Damascus lies a volcanic tract. The entire country about the Dead Sea presents indubitable tokens of volcanic agency.

Accordingly these places come within one of the volcanic regions. The chief of these are—1. that which extends from the Caspian Sea to the Azores; 2. from the Aleutian Isles to the Moluccas; 3. that of the Andes; 4. the African; 5. the Icelandic. Syria and Palestine are embraced within the first band; and these countries have not unfrequently been subject to earthquakes. The first visitation of the kind, recorded to have happened to Palestine, was in the reign of Ahab (B.C. 918-897; 1 Kings xix. 11, 12). A terrible earthquake took place 'in the days of Uzziah, king of Judah' (B.C. 811-759). Its awful character may be learnt from the fact that Zechariah (xiv. 5) thus speaks respecting it—'Ye shall flee as ye fled from before the earthquake in the days of Uzziah, king of Judah:' and also that it appears from Amos (i. 1) that the event was so striking, and left such deep impressions on men's minds, that it became a sort of epoch from which to date and reckon; the prophet's words are, 'two years before the earthquake.'

That earthquakes were among the extraordinary phenomena of Palestine in ancient times is shown in their being an element in the poetical imagery of the Hebrews, and a source of religious admonition and devout emotion (see Ps. xviii. 7; Hab. iii. 6; Nah. i. 5; Isa. v. 25). The only earthquake mentioned in the New Testament is that which happened at the crucifixion of the Saviour of mankind (Matt. xxvii. 50-1; Luke xxiii. 44-5; Mark xv. 33). This darkness has been misunderstood, and then turned to the prejudice of Christianity [DARKNESS]. The obscuration was obviously an attendant on the earthquake. Earthquakes are not seldom attended by accompaniments which obscure the light of day during (as in this case, from the sixth to the ninth hour, that is, from 12 o'clock at noon to 3

o'clock P.M.) several hours. If this is the fact, then the record is consistent with natural phenomena, and the darkness which sceptics have pleaded against speaks actually in favour of the credibility of the Gospel. Now it is well known to naturalists that such obscurations are by no means uncommon.

An earthquake devastated Judæa some years (31) before the birth of our Lord, at the time of the battle of Actium, which Josephus reports was such ' as had not happened at any other time, which brought great destruction upon the cattle in that country. About ten thousand men also perished by the fall of houses.' Jerome writes of an earthquake which, in the time of his childhood (about A.D. 315), destroyed Rabbath Moab. The writers of the middle ages also speak of earthquakes in Palestine, stating that they were not only formidable, but frequent. In 1834 an earthquake shook Jerusalem, and injured the chapel of the nativity at Bethlehem. As late as the year 1836 (Jan. 1) Jerusalem and its vicinity were visited by severe shocks of earthquake, yet the city remains without serious injury from these subterranean causes.

EAST. This word, which is used by English writers in only two senses, viz. to denote either the quarter of the heavens where the sun rises, or the regions in the eastern part of the world, has frequently *three* senses in the Authorized Version of the Bible. Thus, it is sometimes used to mean the *sun-rising* (Ps. ciii. 12), ' as far as the east is from the west;' and *very frequently* it corresponds to *kedem*, the name given by the ancient Hebrews to a certain region, without any regard to its relation to the eastern part of the heavens, comprehending not only Arabia Deserta and the lands of Moab and Ammon, which really lay to the east of Palestine, but also Armenia, Assyria, Mesopotamia, Babylonia, and Chaldæa, which were situated rather to the north than the east of Judæa. Its geographical boundaries include Syria, the countries beyond the Tigris and Euphrates, the shores of the Indian ocean and of the Arabian gulf. The name given to this entire region by the Hebrews was the land of Kedem or East, and its miscellaneous population were called by them Sons of the East, or Orientals. It seems that the inhabitants of this region were distinguished for their proficiency in the arts and sciences (comp. 1 Kings i. 4, 30), and were addicted in the time of Isaiah to superstition (Isa. xxvi.). The wise men, who came from the East to Jerusalem at the birth of the Saviour, no doubt belonged to this tract of country, ' saying, We have seen his star in the East.' Campbell remarks that ' to see either star or meteor in the east,' means, in English, to see it in the East-quarter of the heavens, or looking eastward. But this cannot be the Evangelist's meaning. The meaning manifestly is, that when the magians themselves were in the East, they saw the star. So far were they from seeing the star in the East, according to the English acceptation of the phrase, that they must have seen it in the West, as they were by its guidance brought out of the East country westwards to Jerusalem.

EAST WIND. [WIND.]

E'BAL and GER'IZIM, two mountains of Samaria, forming the opposite sides of the valley which contained the ancient town of Shechem, the present Nabulus. From this connection it is best to notice them together. The valley which these mountains enclose is about 200 or 300 paces wide, by above 3 miles in length; and Mount Ebal rises on the right hand and Gerizim on the left hand of the valley (which extends west-north-west) as a person approaches Shechem from Jerusalem. It was on Mount Ebal that God commanded to be reared up an altar, and a pillar inscribed with the law; and the tribes were to be assembled, half on Ebal and half on Gerizim, to hear the fearful maledictions pronounced by the Levites upon all who should violate the obligations of the sacred code, and the blessings promised to those who should observe them. The tribes which responded with simultaneous 'Amens' to the curses were to be stationed on Mount Ebal, and those who answered to the blessings, on Mount Gerizim. This grand ceremony—perhaps the most grand in the history of nations—could not have found a more fitting scene; and it was duly performed by Joshua as soon as he gained possession of the Promised Land (Deut. xxvii.; Josh. viii. 30-35). Dr. Robinson (*Bib. Researches*, iii. 96) says—' Mounts Gerizim and Ebal rise in steep, rocky precipices, immediately from the valley on each side, apparently some 800 feet in height. The sides of both these mountains as here seen (*i. e.* from Nabulus) were, to our eyes, equally naked and sterile, although some travellers have chosen to describe Gerizim as fertile, and confine the sterility to Ebal. The only exception in favour of the former, as far as we could perceive, is a small ravine coming down opposite to the west end of the town, which indeed is full of fountains and trees; in other respects both mountains, as here seen, are desolate, except that a few olive-trees are scattered upon them. The side of the northern mountain, Ebal, along the foot, is full of ancient excavated sepulchres. The southern mountain is now called by the inhabitants Jebel-et-Tûr, though the name Gerizim is known, at least, to the Samaritans. The modern appellation of Ebal we did not learn.'

EBEN-E'ZEL (*stone of departure*), an old stone of testimonial, mentioned in 1 Sam. xx. 19. The circumstance which it commemorated is not known.

EBEN-E'ZER (*stone of help*), the name given to a stone which Samuel set up between Mizpeh and Shen, in witness of the divine assistance obtained against the Philistines (1 Sam. vii. 12).

EBONY occurs only in one passage of Scripture, where the prophet Ezekiel (xxvii. 15), referring to the commerce of Tyre, says, 'The men of Dedan were thy merchants; many isles were the merchandise of thine hand: they brought thee for a present horns of ivory and *ebony*.'

Ebony wood was highly esteemed by the ancients, and employed by them for a variety of purposes. It is very appropriately placed in juxtaposition with ivory, because both were obtained from the same countries—Ethiopia and India; and, among the comparatively few articles of ancient commerce, must, from this cause, always have been associated together, while their contrast of colour and joint employment in inlaid work, would contribute as additional reasons for their being adduced as articles characteristic of a distinct commerce.

161. [Diospyros Ebenum.]

But it is not in Ezekiel only that ebony and ivory are mentioned together. For Diodorus, as quoted by Bochart, tells us that an ancient king of Egypt imposed on the Ethiopians the payment of a tribute of ebony, gold, and elephants' teeth. So Herodotus (iii. 97), as translated by Bochart, says, 'Æthiopes Persis pro triennali tributo vehunt duos chœnices auri apyri (*id est, ignem nondum experti*), et ducentas *ebeni* phalangas, et magnos elephanti dentes viginti.' Pliny, referring to this passage, remarks, ' But Herodotus assigneth it rather to Ethiopia, and saith, that every three years the Ethiopians were wont to pay, by way of tribute, unto the kings of Persia, 100 billets of the timber of that tree (that is Ebene), together with gold and yvorie;' and, again, ' From Syene (which confineth and boundeth the lands of our empire and dominion) as farre as to the island Meroë, for the space of 996 miles, there is little ebene found: and that in all those parts betweene there be few other trees to be found but date-trees, which peradventure may be a cause that Ebene was counted a rich tribute, and deserved the third place, after gold and ivorie' (Holland's *Pliny*, xii. 4). This however is a mistake, for several of the ancients mention both Indian and Ethiopian ebony.

If we look to the modern history of ebony, we shall find that it is still derived from more than one source. Thus, Mr. Holtzappfel, in his recent work on Turning, describes three kinds of ebony. 1. One from the Mauritius, in round sticks like scaffold poles, seldom exceeding fourteen inches in diameter, the blackest and finest in the grain, the hardest and most beautiful. 2. The East Indian, which is grown in Ceylon and the Peninsula of India, and exported from Madras and Bombay in logs from six to twenty, and sometimes even twenty-eight inches in diameter, and also in planks. This is less wasteful, but of an inferior grain and colour to the above. 3. The African, shipped from the Cape of Good Hope in billets, the general size of which is from three to six feet long, three to six inches broad, and two to four inches thick. This is the least wasteful, as all the refuse is left behind; but it is the most porous, and the worst in point of colour. No Abyssinian ebony is at present imported: this, however, is more likely to be owing to the different routes which commerce has taken, but which is again returning to its ancient channels, than to the want of ebony in the ancient Ethiopia. From the nature of the climate, and the existence of forests in which the elephant abounds, there can be no doubt of its being well suited to the group of plants which have been found to yield the ebony of Mauritius, Ceylon, and India, namely, the genus Diospyros of botanists.

E'BER. [HEBER.]

ECBAT'ANA. [ACHMETHA.]

ECCLESIASTES. This book has obtained its Hebrew name *Koheleth* from the designation of the principal person mentioned in it, who is thus styled in several passages. Some have supposed that Koheleth means a body or academy of sages, whose dicta are contained in this book; but this opinion is contradicted by the heading of the book itself, which thus commences: *Words of Koheleth, the son of David, the king in Jerusalem.* Hence it appears that Koheleth is intended for an epithet of Solomon. Various interpretations have been given of its meaning, but in all probability it means *assembler, preacher,* or *teacher.*

The circumstance that Solomon is introduced as the speaker in this book has induced most of the ancient interpreters to consider him as its author. Others, however, are of opinion that words are used in it which show that it must have been written at a later period than the time of Solomon.

The diversity of sentiment as to the authorship has of course led also to a difference of opinion as to the date of the book. But one thing is clear,— that whoever may have been the author, the book cannot have been written after the times of Ezra and Nehemiah, under whom the canon was completed.

Those who maintain that Ecclesiastes was not written by Solomon are of opinion that it was not composed during the latter period of the first, but rather during the time of the second temple, since idolatry does not occur amongst the deviations combated by the author. The whole book seems to presuppose that the people were externally devoted to the Lord. The admonitions of the author to a serene enjoyment of life, and against murmuring; exhortations to be contented with Divine Providence, and the attacks upon a selfish righteousness of works, may best be explained by supposing the author to have lived in a period like that of Malachi, in which there prevailed a Pharisaical self-righteousness, and melancholy murmurings because God would not recognise the alleged *rights* which they produced before him, and refused to acknowledge the *claims* they made upon him.

The author places the fundamental idea of the nothingness of all earthly things both at the beginning and at the end of his book, and during its course repeatedly returns to the same. This has induced many interpreters to suppose that the purpose of the author was to demonstrate this one idea; an opinion which, down to the most recent times, has been unfavourable to the true interpretation of the book, because every thing,

however reluctant, has been forced into an imaginary connection. The following is the correct view. The object of the author is not to teach an especial tendency of wisdom, but wisdom in general. Consequently it is not at all surprising if the connection suddenly ceases, and a new subject commences. That the idea of the nothingness of earthly matters should strongly predominate may easily be explained, since according to our author it forms a very important part of wisdom. He never, however, intended to confine himself to this one idea, although he likes frequently to point it out in passing, even when he is considering a matter from another point of view. 'The plan of this book,' says Herder, 'has been the subject of much investigation. It is best to consider this plan as free as possible, and to employ its separate parts for its support. The commencement and the conclusion show the unity of the whole. The greater part consists of isolated observations concerning the course of the world, and the experience of his life. These are connected with general sentences; and, finally, a very simple conclusion is deduced from the whole. It seems to me that a more artificial texture ought not to be sought for.'

With regard to the contents and objects of the book, we have to consider only the fundamental idea, omitting isolated sentences of wisdom, and rules for the conduct of life. Nobody can entertain any doubt concerning this fundamental idea. It is contained in the sentence: 'Vanity of vanities; all is vanity.' It is, however, very important that this should be rightly understood. The question is, What is that ALL which is vanity? The author does not mean ALL in general, but only ALL of a certain genus. He himself explains this, by defining this ALL in numerous passages; as, 'all that is under the sun;' that is, earthly things in their separation from the heavenly. To this leads also the enumeration of the ALL, in which occur only those things which belong to the earth—riches, sensual pleasure, honour, sphere of activity, human wisdom apart from God, self-righteousness. From many passages it appears that the author was far from comprehending the fear of God and active obedience to his laws among that ALL which was vanity. This appears most strikingly from the conclusion, which, as such, is of the highest importance, and furnishes the undoubted measure for the correctness of the whole interpretation. 'Let us hear the conclusion of the whole matter: Fear God and keep his commandments: for this is the whole duty of man [*i. e.* in this consists all that is incumbent upon him; and his whole salvation depends upon it]. For God shall bring every work into judgment, with every secret thing, whether good, or whether evil.' (Compare ch. xii. 1: 'Remember now thy Creator in the days of thy youth;' ch. v. 5-7, 'Fear thou God;' ch. vii. 18, and many other passages.) A deep religious sense pervades the whole book. In reference to the prevailing idea, Ewald strikingly remarks, p. 182, 'There blows throughout this book a piercing chill against every earthly aim, and every vain endeavour; a contempt which changes into a bitter sneer against every thing which in the usual proceedings of men is onesided and perverse; an indefatigable penetration in the discovery of all human vanities and fooleries. In

T

no earlier writing has all cause of pride and vain imagination so decidedly and so comprehensively been taken from man; and no book is pervaded by such an outcry of noble indignation against all that is vain in this world.'

From the contents of the book results its object. The author had received the mission to treat professedly and in a concentrated manner the highly important sentence, 'Vanity of vanities; all is vanity,' which pervades the whole of Holy Writ; but he is not content with the mere theoretical demonstration, so as to leave to another teacher its practical application, but places before us these practical results themselves: What is incumbent upon man, since every thing else is nought? What real good remains for us, after the appearance in every seeming good has been destroyed? The answer is, Man shall not gain by cunning and grasping; shall not consume himself in vain meditations, nor in a hurried activity; he shall not murmur about the loss of that which is naught, he shall not by means of a self-made righteousness constrain God to grant him salvation; but he shall instead fear God (ch. xii. 13; v. 6, 7), and be mindful of his Creator (ch. xii. 1); he shall do good as much as he is able (ch. iii. 12); and in other passages. And all this, as it is constantly inculcated by the author, with a contented and grateful heart, freed from care and avarice; living for the present moment, joyfully taking from the hand of the Lord what he offers in a friendly manner. Man shall not be of a sorrowful countenance, but in quiet serenity enjoy the gifts of God. What would avail him all his cares and all his avarice? By them he cannot turn any thing aside from him, or obtain any thing, since every thing happens as it shall happen.

ECCLESIAS'TICUS. [WISDOM OF SIRACH.]

ECDIP'PA. [ACHZIB.]

E'DEN. [PARADISE.]

E'DOM. [ESAU.]

E'DOMITES. [IDUMÆA.]

ED'REI, one of the metropolitan towns (Ashtaroth being the other) of the kingdom of Bashan, beyond the Jordan. It was here that Og, the gigantic king of Bashan, was defeated by the Israelites, and lost his kingdom (Num. xxi. 33-35: Deut. i. 4; iii. 1-3). Edrei afterwards belonged 'o eastern Manasseh (Josh. xiii. 81). It was the seat of a bishop in the early ages of Christianity. The place now bears the name of Draa, and has been visited in the present century by most of the travellers who have explored the country beyond the Jordan. It is situated in a deep valley, two hours south-east from Mezareib; and the ruins cover an extent of about two miles in circumference, the principal being an immense rectangular building, with a double covered colonnade all around, and a cistern in the middle. This seems to have been originally a Christian church, and afterwards a mosque. Near the town, in the hollow of the mountains, is a large reservoir cased with stone, near which are the ruins of a large building, with a cupola of light materials.

EG'LON, a king of Moab, who, assisted by the Ammonites and Amalekites, subdued the Israelites beyond the Jordan, and the southern tribes on this side the river, and made Jericho the seat, or one of the seats, of his government. This subjection to a power always present must have been more galling to the Israelites than any they

had previously suffered. It lasted eighteen years, when (B.C. 1428) they were delivered, through the instrumentality of Ehud, who slew the Moabitish king (Judg. iii. 12-33).

E'GYPT, the land of Ham, a son of Noah, from whom was derived the ancient native appellation of the country, Chemi. From Mizraim, the second son of Ham, comes the ordinary Biblical name, Mizraim, a word which properly denotes Lower Egypt, as being that part of the country with which the Israelites were nearest and best, if not (in the earlier periods of their history) solely, acquainted. This designation, however, is sometimes used for Egypt indiscriminately, and was by the later Arabs extended to the entire country.

Egypt is the land of the Nile, the country through which that river flows from the Island of Philæ, situated just above the Cataracts of Syene, in lat. 24° 1′ 36″, to Damietta, in 31° 35′ N., where its principal stream pours itself into the Mediterranean Sea. On the east it is bounded by Palestine, Idumæa, Arabia Petræa, and the Arabian Gulf. On the west, the moving sands of the wide Libyan desert obliterate the traces of all political or physical limits. Inhabited Egypt, however, is restricted to the valley of the Nile, which, having a breadth of from two to three miles, is enclosed on both sides by a range of hills: the chain on the eastern side disappears at Mocattam; that on the west extends to the sea. In lat. 30° 1′, the Nile divides into two principal streams, which, in conjunction with a third that springs somewhat higher up, forms the Delta, so called from its resemblance to the Greek letter Δ. These mountains are interesting, if for no other reason than that they served as the bed whence the materials were obtained out of which were constructed the wonderful buildings for which Egypt is justly distinguished. The superficial extent of Egypt has been estimated at about 11,000 square miles. The soil, which is productive, consists almost exclusively of mud brought down and deposited by the river, whose waters are indispensable every year for the purposes of agriculture to such an extent that the limits of their flow are the limits of vegetation. The Delta owes its very existence to the deposits of the Nile, and but for the waters of this stream, carried over its surface by natural or artificial means, would soon be a desert: it was therefore with propriety, as indeed was the entire country, termed 'the gift of the Nile.' The agency of the stream is the more necessary because rain very seldom falls in Lower Egypt. The land, placed as it is on the confines of Africa and Asia, yet so adjacent and accessible to Europe, in itself a garden and a store-house, may well have held an important position in the ancient world, and can hardly fail, unless political influences are very adverse, to rise to a commanding attitude in modern times. As to the number of its inhabitants, nothing very definite is known. Its fertility would doubtless give birth to, and support, a teeming population. In very remote times as many as 8,000,000 of souls are said to have lived on its soil. In the days of Diodorus Siculus they were estimated at 3,000,000. Volney made the number 2,300,000. The present government estimate is 3,200,000, which seems to be somewhat beyond the fact.

Egypt naturally divides itself into two great sections at the apex of the Delta, the country lying south of that point being designated Upper Egypt, that north of it Lower Egypt. Under the Ptolemies, and probably at a very early period, the whole country was divided into thirty-six cantons or provinces, which division was maintained till the invasion of the Saracens. It is now composed of 24 departments, which, according to the French system of geographical arrangement, are subdivided into arrondissements and cantons.

The Nile is never mentioned by name in our translation of the Old Testament; it is always called the river of Egypt, although the word Nile occurs in the original (Isa. xxvii. 12; Josh. xv. 4; 2 Kings xxiv. 7).

Till within a few years the sources of the Nile and the termination of the Niger were hid in alike mysterious obscurity. The latter has been discovered, but the former, notwithstanding many strenuous efforts and some pretence, remain to reward the enterprise of some more fortunate traveller. The various branches of the Nile have their rise in the highlands north of the equator. The three principal branches of the Nile are—1, the Bahr el Abiad, or White River, to the west, which is now known to be the largest and longest; 2, the Bahr el Azrek, or Blue River, in the centre; 3, the Tacazzé, or Abara, which is the eastern branch. The Nile, from its confluence with the Tacazzé (17° 45' north lat.) down to its entrance into the Mediterranean (1200 geographical miles), receives no permanent streams: but in the rainy season it receives wadys, or torrents, from the mountains. The annual overflow of the river, on which the ancients wrote so obscurely, is known to arise from the periodical rains which fall within the tropics. The rich alluvial deposits which the Nile spreads over Nubia and Egypt are mainly derived through the Blue River; the White River, or longest stream, bringing nothing of the kind. Owing to the yearly deposit of alluvial matter, both the bed of the Nile and the land of Egypt are being gradually raised. The river proceeds in its current uniformly and quietly at the rate of two and a half or three miles an hour, always deep enough for navigation. Its water is usually blue, but it becomes of a deep brick-red during the period of its overflow. It is salubrious when drunk, meriting the encomiums which it has so abundantly received. On the river the land is wholly dependent. If the Nile does not rise a sufficient height, sterility and dearth, if not famine, ensue. An elevation of sixteen cubits is essential to secure the prosperity of the country. Such, however, is the regularity of nature, and such the faithfulness of God, that for thousands of years, with but few and partial exceptions, these inundations have in essential particulars been the same. The waters of the stream are conveyed over the surface of the country by canals when natural channels fail. During the overflow the land is naturally inundated, and has the appearance of a sea dotted with islands. Wherever the waters reach, abundance springs forth. The cultivator has scarcely more to do than to scatter the seed. No wonder that a river whose waters are so grateful, salubrious, and beneficial, should in days of ignorance have been regarded as an object of worship, and that it is still revered and beloved.

Well may Egypt have been visited as a granary by the needy in ancient times (Gen. xii. 10; Exod. xvi. 3). Besides corn, the country produced onions, garlic, beans, pumpkins, cucumbers, melons, flax, cotton, and wine. The acacia, sycamore, palm, and fig-tree adorned the land; but there was a want of timber. The Nile produced the useful papyrus, and abounded in fish. On its banks lurked the crocodile and hippopotamus. The Egyptian oxen were celebrated in the ancient world. Horses abounded (1 Kings x. 28); hence the use of war-chariots in fight (Isa. xxxi. 1; Diod. Sic. i. 45), and the celebrity of Egyptian charioteers (Jer. xlvi. 4; Ezek. xvii. 15). The land was not destitute of mineral treasures. Gold mines were wrought in Upper Egypt.

The climate is very regular and exceedingly hot; the atmosphere clear and shining: a shade is not easily found. Though rain falls even in the winter months very rarely, it is not altogether wanting, as was once believed. Thunder and lightning are still more unfrequent, and are so completely divested of their terrific qualities that the Egyptians never associate with them the idea of destructive force. Showers of hail descending from the hills of Syria are sometimes known to reach the confines of Egypt: the formation of ice is very uncommon. Dew is produced in great abundance. The wind blows from the north from May to September, when it veers round to the east, assumes a southerly direction, and fluctuates till the close of April. The southerly vernal winds, traversing the arid sands of Africa, are most changeable as well as most unhealthy: they form the simoom or samiel, and have proved fatal to caravans and even to armies. Musquitos, locusts, frogs, together with the plague, the small pox, and leprosy, are the great evils of the country.

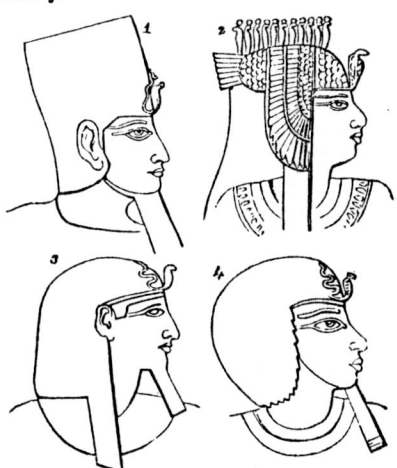

162. 1. Egypto-Ethiopian (the Tirhakah of Scripture);
      2. 4. Ethiopian; 3. Egyptian.

The most recent inquiries have shown that the extreme limit at Philæ was only of a political nature; for the natives of the country below it were of the same race as those who lived above that spot—a tribe which passed down into the fertile valley of the Nile from its original abode in the south. These Ethiopians and the Egyptians were not negroes, but a branch of the great Caucasian family. Their colour—at least the colour of the higher castes—was brown; their frame slender, but of great strength. The women were very fruitful.

The mode of life of the Egyptians was influenced by their locality: those who dwelt on high lands on the east, as well as those who dwelt on the marshy flat country in the Delta, were shepherds, as their land did not admit cultivation. The people who lived along the Nile became fishermen and sailors. The cultivated part of the natives who lived on the plains and over the surface of the country diligently and most successfully practised all the arts of life, and have left ever-during memorials of their proficiency and skill.

On this natural diversity of pursuits, as well as on a diversity of blood, was founded the institution of castes, which Egypt had in common with India, and which pervaded the entire life of the nation. These, according to Herodotus, were seven in number: the priestly caste was the most honoured and influential: it had in every large city a temple dedicated to the deity of the place, together with a high-priest, who stood next to the king and restricted his power. The priesthood possessed the finest portions of the country: they were the judges, physicians, astrologers, architects,—in a word, they united in themselves all the highest culture and most distinguished offices of the land, while with them alone lay tradition, literature, and the sacred writings. This class exerted the most decided and extensive influence on the culture not only of their own country, but of the world; for during the brightest periods of Grecian history the love of knowledge carried into Egypt men who have done much to form the character of after-ages, such as Solon, Pythagoras, Archytas, Thales, Herodotus, Plato, and others (comp. Gen. xli. 8; Exod. vii. 11; viii. 11; xiii. 7).

The peculiarities of the ancient Egyptians of the lower castes seem to have survived best, and to be represented, at least in some particulars, by the Fellahs of the present day. These Fellahs discharge all the duties of tilling the country and gathering its rich abundance: their attachment to it is very strong, and their love to the Nile almost a passion. They are a quiet, contented, submissive race, always living, through an unjust government, on the edge of starvation, yet always happy, with no thought for the morrow, no care for, no interest in, political change.

The only other tribe we have room to notice is that of the Copts, equally with the preceding, indigenous. They are Christians by hereditary transmission, and have suffered centuries of cruel persecutions and humiliations, though now they seem to be rising in importance, and promise to fill an important page in the future history of Egypt. In character they are amiable, pacific, and intelligent, having of course the faults and vices of dissimulation, falsehood, and meanness, which slavery never fails to engender. In office they are the scribes, the arithmeticians, the measurers, the clerks—in a word, the learned men of the country. The Copts have been under-estimated at 150,000 souls, divided into twelve episcopal districts, the bishops of which unite to elect a patriarch.

'The wisdom of Egypt' was a phrase which, at an early period, passed into a proverb, so high was the opinion entertained by antiquity of the knowledge and skill of the ancient Egyptians (1 Kings iv. 30; Herod. ii. 160; Joseph. Antiq. viii. 25: Acts vii. 22). It was long thought that the hieroglyphical inscriptions on the monumental remains of Egypt contained treasures of wisdom no less boundless than hidden; and, indeed, hieroglyphics were, in the opinion of some, invented by the priests of the land, if not expressly to conceal their knowledge from the profane vulgar, yet as a safe receptacle and convenient storehouse for their mysterious but invaluable doctrines. Great, consequently, was the expectation of the public when it was announced that a key had been discovered which opened the portal to these long-concealed treasures. Men of profound learning, great acuteness of mind, and distinguished reputation, have engaged and persevered in the inquiry; but, after all, the conclusions and positions which have been drawn and set forth are only in a few cases (comparatively) definite and unimpeachable.

The difficulties that oppose the formation of a satisfactory Egyptian chronology are great and numerous. The most distinguished writers differ egregiously in their statements.

Various efforts, however, have been made to remove difficulties, reconcile contradictions, and harmonize dissonances; but the success has been far from distinguished.

What, however, we know to be definite, and believe to be accurate in its disclosures, and what we judge to be far more important in an historical relation, is to be found in the paintings and sculptures with which the Egyptians left the walls of their tombs and temples decorated in forms and colours which have not yet faded from the sight. It is true that these instances of real picture-writing may do little for fixing the epoch of the accession of a king or the termination of a dynasty. Yet in this they are not entirely mute.

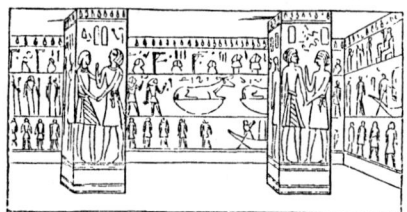

163. Interior of Pictured Tomb.

Among the innumerable mural sculptures in the temple at Karnak, Champollion discovered one in which a king, Sheshonk (Shishak), is presenting captives of various nations to his God as trophies of victory. One of these, distinguished by a long beard and Jewish physiognomy, bears the hieroglyphical title Youdah Malck, king of Judah. But for any practical purpose, the determination of a date, or the identification of an event, is of small comparative moment; and far too much importance has been attached to mere chronological details. To learn when an Egyptian or Chinese king ascended the throne, or departed this life, may gratify the antiquary, or even reward much learned toil, but the world at large has an interest in history in the main, if not exclusively, so far as it discloses what men thought, felt, did; what they hoped, feared, and achieved in the days of old; thereby affording to posterity warnings, encouragement, light, and impulse. Now for these highly important purposes the most abundant materials are presented in Egypt, and may be found described in the works of Champollion, Wilkinson, and others. Let any one visit the Egyptian gallery in the British Museum, and he will be surprised and delighted to find Egypt almost resuscitated. The tombs have given up their dead. Buried treasures, over whose silence centuries had rolled before our era began, crowd on the sight and gratify the mind. And paintings, too, strike the eye, which may not indeed conform very exactly to the laws of perspective, but which lay open, and set before the spectator, the Egyptian, as he was in the days of his glory and pride Indeed, from the paintings and sculptures which have been discovered and described, we are enabled to follow this most singular and deeply interesting people through all the classes of society, through all the operations of science and husbandry, into the transactions of public life, the details of house-keeping, the achievements of war, the amusements of hunting, fishing, feasting, and the solemn rites of a most august and imposing religious ceremonial.

Amid the various profane authors who have written more or less in detail on Egypt, the Bible remains our best and fullest authority for the early history of the country. This history, it is true, is not presented in a chronological series of events, nor supplied respecting any period with nice exactitude and minute details. The disclosures made by inscriptions on public buildings, of kings, wars, and conquests, may, when verified as to age, and placed in their probable order by the aid of learning and criticism, reveal more as to the dynasties and individual sovereigns; but on such information, even when free from doubt, and most accurate, little real value can be set; while the Bible supplies, either by express statement or obvious implication, facts and principles which constitute genuine history, and go far to give the past all the value which it can possess for the men of these times. And what makes these disclosures the more valuable is not only that they wear the character of genuine and uncorrupted history—free from the false, deep, and unnatural colourings of mythology; but that they relate to the earliest forms of civilized life, and to ages over which profane historians have left the thickest darkness. Narrations and implications, such as the Bible affords in regard to the early history of Egypt, want no corroboration; they wear in their naturalness, simplicity, and correspondence with what would be expected in the ages to which they refer, evidence that they represent actual realities, which none can resist who has studied either human nature or human society. Still it may not be supererogatory to remark that the little which learning and industry have succeeded in extracting from the monumental inscriptions, and the very great deal which funereal and religious paintings have of late made known; and indeed all, from whatever source gathered, that we now known of the country and its institutions and usages, are in entire harmony with what the

Scriptures directly or indirectly teach respecting Egypt. And it is certainly a very great point to have ascertained beyond doubt that the Egypt of the Bible is Egypt indeed, not a fiction, nor an imposture, nor a blunder—as writers of the Voltaire school would persuade the world—but a reality, so far as it goes, a picture copied from actual life.

We learn from the Old Testament that while the Jews, the earliest nation that has handed down to us the history of its rise and civilization, were yet a tribe of wandering shepherds, under Abraham, depending solely upon the unbought gifts of nature, who, when they had exhausted one district, instead of cultivating it, drove off their flocks in search of a new pasture-ground, after the manner of the American Indians; the Egyptians were acquainted with agriculture and all those arts of civilization and government which indicate a social existence, extending backwards for at least several ages. This is confirmed in a striking manner by architectural remains that have survived the ravages of above thirty centuries; for while the Israelites, under the immediate successors of Joshua, were still warring with the Canaanites for the possession of the land of promise, or yet earlier, while they were yet slaves in Egypt, that most interesting land was distinguished for palaces, temples, porticos, obelisks, statues, and canals, which declare that they had been preceded by a long period of civilization, and which still remain the admiration of the world. The pyramids of Lower Egypt, requiring for their erection the least quantity of architectural knowledge. no elegance of design, no taste in detail, might possibly have been the work of men driven by task-masters to their daily labour; but that the palaces, tombs, and temples of Upper Egypt, which present to us the earliest known instances of architecture, sculpture, and painting; the colossal statues of Amenoph and Rameses, requiring considerable anatomical knowledge for the original design, and a mechanical skill in the execution, exceeding perhaps even that of the Greeks themselves; the vast works for irrigation; and the correct division of the calendar, implying great knowledge of mathematics—that these should have been the works of a people suffering under political disadvantages, and not far advanced in all the arts and refinements of social life, would contradict all that observation or history has made known. Some considerable degree therefore of political freedom, as well as a high cultivation, must at an early period have been enjoyed by the Egyptians.

In Gen. x. we find the colonization of Egypt traced up to the immediate children of Noah, for it is there stated that Mizraim was the second son of Ham, who was himself the second son of Noah. Immediately after these genealogical statements the sacred narrative (Gen. xii) informs us that the patriarch Abraham, pressed by famine, went down (about B.C. 1920) into Egypt, where it appears he found a monarch, a court, princes and servants, and where he found also those supplies of food which the well-known fertility of the country had led him to seek there; for it is expressly stated that the favour which his wife had won in the reigning Pharaoh's eyes procured him sheep and oxen, as well as he-asses, and men-servants, and maid-servants, and she-asses and camels. In Gen. xxi. 9, mention is made in the case of Ishmael, the son of Hagar the Egyptian, whose mother took him a wife out of the land of Egypt, of a mixed race between the Egyptians and the Chaldæans, a race which in after times became a great nation. In Gen. xxxix. begins the interesting story of Joseph's being carried down to Egypt, with all its important consequences for the great-grandchildren of Abraham. The productiveness of the country is the allurement, famine the impulse. Attendant circumstances show that Egypt was then famous also for its commercial pursuits; and the entire narrative gives the idea of a complex system of society (about B.C. 1720), and a well-constituted yet arbitrary form of government. As in eastern courts at later periods of history, elevation to high offices was marked and sudden. The slave Joseph is taken from prison and from impending death, and raised to the dignity of prime vizier, and is entrusted with making provision for an approaching dearth of food, which he had himself foretold, during which he effects in favour of the ruling sovereign one of the greatest revolutions of property which history has recorded. The high consideration in which the priestly caste was held is apparent. Joseph himself marries a daughter of the priest of On. Out of respect towards, as well as by the direct influence of, Joseph, the Hebrews were well treated. The Scriptural record, however, distinctly states (xlvi. 34) that before the descent of Israel and his sons 'every shepherd' was 'an abomination unto the Egyptians.' The Hebrews, whose 'trade had been about cattle,' must have been odious in the eyes of the Egyptians, yet are they expressly permitted to dwell 'in the best of the land' (xlvii. 6), which is identified with the land of Goshen, the place which the Israelites had prayed might be assigned to them, and which they obviously desired on account of the adaptation of its soil to their way of life as herdsmen. Having settled his father and family satisfactorily in the land, Joseph proceeded to supply the urgent wants of a hungry nation, and at the same time converted the tenure of all property from freehold into tenancy-at-will, with a rent-charge of one-fifth of the produce, leaving their lands, however, in the hands of the priests; and thus he gave another evidence of the greatness of their power.

The richness of Goshen was favourable, and the Israelites 'grew and multiplied exceedingly,' so that the land was filled with them. But Joseph was now dead; time had passed on, and there rose up a new king (probably one of a new dynasty) which *knew* (Exod. i. 8) not Joseph, having no personal knowledge, and it may be no definite information of his services: who, becoming jealous of the increase of the Hebrews, set about persecuting them with the avowed intention of diminishing their numbers and crippling their power. Severe task-masters are therefore set over them; heavy tasks are imposed: the Hebrews are compelled to build 'treasure cities, Pithom and Raamses.' It is found, however, that they only increase the more. In consequence, their burdens are doubled and their lives made bitter with hard bondage (Exod. i. 14), 'in mortar and in brick, and in all manner of service in the field.' Their first-born males,

moreover, are doomed to destruction the moment they come into being. The deepest heart-burnings ensue; hatred arises between the oppressor and the oppressed; the Israelites seek revenge in private and by stealth (Exod. ii. 12). At last a higher power interferes, and the afflicted race is permitted to quit Egypt. At this time Egypt appears to have been a well-peopled and well-cultivated country, with numerous cities, under a despotic monarch, surrounded by officers of his court and a life-guard. There was a ceremonial at audience, a distinction of ranks, a state-prison, and a prime minister. Great buildings were carried on. There was set apart from the rest of the people an order of priests who probably filled offices in the civil government; the priest of Midian and the priest of On seem to have ruled over the cities so named. There was in the general class of priests an order—wise men, sorcerers, and magicians—who had charge of a certain secret knowledge: there were physicians or embalmers of the dead; the royal army contained chosen captains and horsemen and chariots. The attention which the people at large paid to agriculture, and the fixed notions of property which they in consequence had, made them hold the shepherd or nomade tribes in abhorrence, as freebooters only less dangerous than hunting tribes.

The ill feelings which the peculiar circumstances connected with the exode from Egypt had occasioned served to keep the Israelites and the Egyptians strangers, if not enemies, one to another during the lapse of centuries, till the days of David and Solomon, when (1 Kings iii., vii., ix., xi.) friendly relations again spring up between the two countries. Solomon marries the daughter of a Pharaoh, who burns the city of Gezer, and who in consequence must have been master of Lower Egypt. 'And Solomon had horses brought out of Egypt, and linen yarn:' six hundred shekels of silver was the price of a chariot, and one hundred and fifty the price of a horse. Jeroboam, however, who 'had lifted up his hand against the king,' and become subsequently monarch of the revolted ten tribes, found refuge and protection in Egypt, which was then (about B.C. 975) governed by *Shishak*. From 2 Chron. xii. it appears that in the fifth year of Solomon's successor, Rehoboam, this same Shishak 'came against Jerusalem' with a very large army, consisting of chariots, horse and foot soldiers, besides auxiliary foreigners; and having captured the fortified cities which lay on his march, he entered and plundered the metropolis. The language which is employed in Joel (iii. 19) shows that, in the ninth century before Christ, Egypt had, in conjunction with Edom, displayed both its power and its cruelty towards the kingdom of Judah. The rise and oppressiveness of the Assyrian power soon, however, inclined the Egyptians and the Israelites, from a sense of common danger, to cultivate friendly relations with one another. In 2 Kings xvii. we find that in the twelfth year of Ahaz king of Judah (B.C. 730) Hoshea king of Israel desisted from paying his usual tribute to the king of Assyria, and courted the alliance of So, king of Egypt, who must have been a very powerful monarch to have been thought able to give assistance in opposition to Assyria. Against this mere human resource the prophet Isaiah (xxxi.) warmly protested, declaring its utter inefficiency, and striving to lead his countrymen to the practice of that righteousness and piety by neglecting which they had been forsaken of God. Upon this act of king Hoshea, however, the Assyrians overran Samaria and carried (2 Kings xvii. 6) Israel away into Assyria. In the reign of Hezekiah (B.C. 726) it appears (2 Kings xviii. 21) that the kingdom of Judah still ' trusted upon the staff of this bruised reed, even Egypt, on which if a man lean, it will go into his hand and pierce it: so is Pharaoh king of Egypt unto all that trust on him.' In the last year of the reign of Josiah (B.C. 609) Egypt seems to have attempted to increase its influence in Palestine, when Pharaoh Nechoh (2 Kings xxiii. 29) ' went up against the king of Assyria to the river Euphrates,' and Josiah going against him was slain in battle. His successor, Jehoahaz, was dethroned after a brief reign of three months, and imprisoned at Riblah by the Egyptian monarch, who imposed on the country a heavy tribute. Pharaoh-Nechoh then made his elder brother Eliakim king, having changed his name to Jehoiakim. Jehoahaz afterwards died in Egypt. But the Egyptian influence over Judah soon ended; for in the fourth year of Jehoiakim (B.C. 604) Nebuchadnezzar king of Babylon marched against (Jer. xlvi.; 2 Kings xxiv.) Judæa and its allies, defeated Pharaoh-Nechoh, and retook from the Egyptians Arabia Petræa and all that belonged to them between the Euphrates and the Nile. Zedekiah, the next king of Judah, rebelling against Nebuchadnezzar, made an alliance with Pharaoh-Hophra (Jer. xliv.): and when Nebuchadnezzar besieged Jerusalem, on the march of the Egyptian army, the Chaldees raised the siege (Jer. xxxvii. 5) and withdrew the army. But this was the last time that the Egyptian power was able to serve the Jews. The Assyrian party in the state, indeed, was in the minority; though assisted by the influence of Jeremiah and Ezekiel (Ezek. xxix.; Jer. xxv.); yet it predominated: the Jews were carried captive to Babylon, and in less than a century afterwards Egypt was made a province of the same empire.

After the time of the exile the Egyptian Ptolemies were for a long while (from B.C. 301 to about 180) masters of Palestine, and during this period Egypt became as of old a place of refuge to the Jews, to whom many favours and privileges were conceded. This shelter seems not to have been for ages withdrawn (Matt. ii. 13). Yet it cannot be said that the Jews were held in esteem by the Egyptians. Indeed it was from an Egyptian, Manetho (B.C. 300), that the most defamatory misrepresentations of Jewish history were given to the world; and, in the days of Augustus, Chæremon took special pains to make the Jewish people appear despicable.

In the reign of Ptolemy Philometor, Onias, whose father, the third high-priest of that name, had been murdered, fled into Egypt, and rose into high favour with the king and Cleopatra his queen. The high-priesthood of the temple of Jerusalem, which belonged of right to his family, having passed from it to the family of the Maccabees, by the nomination of Jonathan to this office (B.C. 153), Onias used his influence with the court to procure the establishment of a temple

and ritual in Egypt which should detach the Jews who lived there from their connection with the temple at Jerusalem. The king complied with the request. To reconcile the Egyptian Jews to a second temple, Onias alleged Isa. xix. 18, 19. He chose for the purpose a ruined temple of Bubastis, at Leontopolis, in the Heliopolitan nome, one hundred and fifty stadia from Memphis, which place he converted into a sort of miniature Jerusalem, erecting an altar in imitation of that in the temple, and constituting himself high-priest. The king granted a tract of land around the temple for the maintenance of the worship, and it remained in existence till destroyed by Vespasian. The district in which this temple stood appears to have been, after Alexandria, the chief seat of the Jews in Egypt.

The most brilliant periods of Egyptian art were the reigns of the second and third Rameses. Most of the obelisks and colossal statues were wrought before or during the reign of Rameses II., the Sesostris of the Greek writers. Under this enterprising monarch, the ancient Theban empire attained its highest pinnacle of prosperity and power. Rameses III. undertook distant military expeditions, roused the energies of the country, encouraged art, and erected the splendid temple of Medinet Abu. At a later age the sceptre of Egypt was swayed by powerful monarchs, who built on a grand scale; but the seat of the government was then in the Delta, and there remain only a few obelisks.

The valley of the Nile is all along at intervals strewed with wrecks of ancient monumental grandeur; at Thebes, however, they are found on both sides of the river in greatest profusion. Next to the pyramids, the most wonderful relic of Egyptian art is the great hall of the temple of Karnak, on the east bank of the Nile. Its superficial area is 314 feet by 164. The massive stone roof is supported by 134 columns ranged in sixteen rows, most of which are 9 feet in diameter, and nearly 43 feet high: those of the central avenue are not less than 11 feet 6 inches in diameter, and 72 feet high; the diameter of their capitals at their widest spread is 22 feet. The walls, columns, architraves, ceilings, every surface exposed to the eye, is overspread with intaglio sculptures—gods, heroes, and hieroglyphics, painted in once vivid colours. But the hall of columns was but a part of this wonderful fabric. Immense pylons, half-buried quadrangles and halls, granite obelisks, and tremendous piles of fallen masonry, once formed a range of buildings upwards of 1200 feet in length. An avenue of colossal sphinxes led from the temple to Luxor, forming a vista which extended nearly a mile and a half, and was admirably adapted for the pageantry of religious processions. All these buildings formed parts of one magnificent whole; all were constructed of gigantic blocks, and most were covered with sculpture. ' Such was the imperial palace of the Pharaohs when Europe was yet in primæval barbarism, ages before Romulus took his omen on the Palatine hill.' Now the ruins are strewn in chaotic confusion over a sandy plain, broken into shapeless mounds.

Among the most remarkable works of the Egyptians must be ranked the vast sepulchres excavated in the seclusion of the Theban mountains to receive their dead monarchs. ' It was,' says Wathen, 'about an hour before sunset one evening that I set out to visit this Necropolis, intending to pass the night in one of the royal sepulchres. On approaching the gorge, the first thing that struck me was the quantity of bones, fragments of mummies, rolls of mummy cloth, and other relics of rifled (Egyptian) tombs that strewed the ground. Princes, priests, and warriors, after reposing thousands of years, are now dragged forth by poor peasants, and their bones lie scattered before the doors of their sepulchres. Candles were lighted: I passed the threshold, and looked round with silent wonder on the scene within. A large corridor or gallery ran back hundreds of feet into the heart of the mountain, divided by lateral projections into lengthening vistas of apartments. The walls were elegantly adorned with columns of blue hieroglyphics on a white ground, 3000 years old, yet retaining almost the freshness of yesterday. In a large chamber at the end of the gallery was a massive sarcophagus. Here once lay the royal mummy, but it had long been open, and was empty. There are eight or nine of these large painted tombs in a group, besides others of less interest. They vary in length from 100 to upwards of 400 feet. In most, you find on entering a long descending corridor or gallery, running off in a straight line into the heart of the mountain. At its farther end the corridor expands into one or more large apartments, whose roofs are supported by massive piers of the living rock. The walls and piers throughout are generally decorated with paintings still wonderfully retaining their freshness: the subjects are chiefly processions, religious rites, and allegoric and enigmatical devices.' The object seems to have been to enshrine the corpse deep within the earth in a mass of masonry, far from the stir of the living world. For these royal sepulchres of Thebes they first selected the loneliest ravine; for each tomb they carried a gallery deep into the hill, and then placed the corpse in the remotest part. But the tombs of the kings form only a part of this great city of the dead. The sides of the hills overlooking the plain and the ravines intersecting them, contain innumerable sepulchral excavations. One valley was appropriated to the queens, and in a remote corner the apes had a cemetery. The priests seized the best spots.

The purpose for which the pyramids were erected was once as little known as were most other things connected with Egypt. It now appears satisfactorily ascertained that they were designed to be mausoleums; and what an idea does it give us of the grandeur of conception, the splendour in every respect of the monarchs to whom they owe their origin, that they should have devised and executed tombs so stupendous! 'On leaving the village of Gizeh, on the river bank opposite old Cairo (Memphis), the pyramids rise before you glittering white against the blue sky; but the flatness of the plain and the purity of the atmosphere effectually deceive the eye as to their distance and consequently their size: you almost appear at their base while several miles really intervene. As you advance gradually they unfold their gigantic dimensions; but you must have been some time on the spot, your eye must have repeatedly travelled along the great pyramid's 740 feet of base, and up its steep towering

angles, before you can fully understand its immensity, and the actual amount of labour involved in its erection' (Wathen). According to Pliny

164. [Pyramid of Cheops.]

366,000 men were employed for 20 years in erecting the great pyramid, and Herodotus reports from an inscription which it bore, that the expense of providing the workmen with onions and other roots amounted to 1600 talents. Whole mosques have probably been built out of spoils from it alone. Yet the integrity of its form remains substantially unimpaired, and from a distance scarcely a trace of violence or decay can be seen. The existing masonry has been estimated at above six millions of tons, which was raised over an area of thirteen English acres and a half; and, supposing the cost of the structure to have been one shilling a cubic foot, including carriage, materials, and workmanship, the erection required an outlay of nearly five millions sterling. The original perpendicular height was 480 feet, exceeding that of St. Peter's by 43 feet, and that of St. Paul's by 110.

The relation in which the religion of Egypt stands to that of Moses is one of very considerable interest and importance, and one which has not yet received the kind and degree of attention which it merits. Michaelis, and others of the same school, have given valuable aid, but they wrote with, compared with what is now known, insufficient knowledge, if not with somewhat too much of a foregone conclusion. Other learned men, influenced by their philosophical notions, or prejudiced against the Hebrew religion, have made Moses a mere copyist of institutions and retailer of ideas which he found in Egypt. As a basis for such a view it was necessarily assumed that a purer system of religion was found in Egypt in the days of Moses than existed in any other part of the world. In particular, the Egyptian mysteries were set forth as the depositories of high and valuable religious doctrines Scripture and history (the Acts of the Apostles; Josephus, Philo) were adduced to show that Moses had been instructed in this priceless lore, and initiated into these mysteries; whence he was declared to have drawn his system of Monotheism. These views, however, rest on no solid foundation whatever, if, indeed, they may not be to some extent considered as the illusory and almost posthumous offspring of the old and exploded notion which ascribed boundless knowledge to the ancient Egyptians. Nor can they for a moment be held in these days after the light thrown on early Egypt by the monumental disclosures. The brief notion given above of the general characteristics of the earliest religion of the country, shows how utterly baseless such a theory is. In truth, the inhabitants of Palestine, so far back as we have been able to learn anything of them, seem to have possessed far better and purer religious opinions than those of the valley of the Nile, and in all probability did something to improve and elevate the religious system of the latter.

E'HUD, of the tribe of Benjamin, one of the 'Judges' of Israel, or rather of that part of Israel which he delivered from the dominion of the Moabites by the assasination of their king Eglon. These were the tribes beyond the Jordan, and the southern tribes on this side the river. Ehud obtained access to Eglon as the bearer of tribute from the subjugated tribes, and being left-handed, or rather ambidextrous, he was enabled to have with a sure and fatal aim a dagger concealed under a part of his dress, where it was unsuspected, because it would there have been useless to a person employing his right hand. The Israelites continued to enjoy for eighty years the independence obtained through this deed of Ehud (Judg. iii. 15-30).

EK'RON, the chief of the five Philistine states (Josh. xiii. 3), and the northernmost of the five. In the general distribution of territory (unconquered as well as conquered) Ekron was assigned to Judah, as being upon its border (Josh xiii. 3; xv. 11, 45): but was afterwards apparently given to Dan, although conquered by Judah (Josh. xv. 11, 45; xix. 43; Judg. i. 18). In Scripture Ekron is chiefly remarkable from the ark having been sent home from thence, upon a new cart drawn by two milch kine (1 Sam. v. 10; vi. 1-8). In later days it is named with the other cities of the Philistines in the denunciations of the prophets against that people (Jer. xxv 20; Amos i. 8; Zeph. ii. 4; Zech. ix. 5). The name of Ekron, or rather Accaron, occurs incidentally in the histories of the Crusades; and it has lately been recognised by Dr. Robinson in that of Akri, in a situation corresponding to all we know of Ekron. Akri is a small Moslem village, five miles south of Ramleh. It is built of unburnt bricks, and, as there are no apparent ruins, the ancient town was probably of the same materials. It is alleged, however, that cisterns and the stones of hand-mills are often found at Akri and in the adjacent fields.

E'LAH, son of Baasha king of Israel. After a reign of two years (B.C. 930-929) he was assassinated while drunk, and all his kinsfolk and friends cut off, by Zimri, 'the captain of half his chariots.' He was the last king of Baasha's line, and by this catastrophe the predictions of the prophet Jehu were accomplished (1 Kings xvi. 6-14).

E'LAH, a valley in which the Israelites were encamped when David fought Goliath (1 Sam. xvii. 19). It doubtless received this name from the terebinth trees, or from some remarkable terebinth tree, growing in it. Ecclesiastical traditions identify it with the present valley of Beit Hanina, about eight miles north-west from Jerusalem. In this valley olive trees and carob trees now prevail, and terebinth trees are few: but the brook is still indicated whence the youthful champion selected the 'smooth stones' where-

with he smote the Philistine. The brook is dry in summer, but in winter it becomes a mighty torrent, which inundates the vale. Dr Robinson, however, disputes this ancient tradition, and finds that the conditions of the history require him to identify the valley of Elah with the Wady es-Sumt (acacia valley), which he crossed on the road from Jerusalem to Gaza, about eleven miles south-west from the former city. His reasons are given in *Biblical Researches*, iii. 350; and he remarks that the largest specimen of the terebinth tree which he saw in Palestine still stands in the vicinity.

E'LAM, which is mentioned in Gen. x. 22, as a tribe descended from Shem, is, in ch. xiv. 1, introduced along with the kingdom of Shinar in Babylon, and in Isa. xxi. 2, and Jer. xxv. 25, is connected with Media. In Ezra iv. 9. the Elamites are described among the nations of the Persian empire; and in Dan. viii. 2, Susa is said to lie on the river Ulai (Eulæus or Choaspes) in the province of Elam. These accounts lead to the conclusion that Elam was the same land which was designated by the Greeks and Romans by the name of Elymais, and which formed a part of the ancient Susiana, the modern Khusistan. Elam was inhabited by various tribes of people. The Elymæi or Elamæi, together with the Kissi, seem to have been the oldest inhabitants not only of Susiana Proper but also of Persia; whence the sacred writers, under the name of Elam, comprehended the country of the Persians in general. They were celebrated for their skill in archery; hence the historical propriety of the Scriptural allusion to the quiver and the bow of the Elamites (Isa. xxii. 6; Jer. xlix. 34).

It would seem that Elam was very early a separate state with its own kings: for in the time of Abraham we find that Chedorlaomer king of Elam extended his conquests west of the Euphrates as far as the Jordan and the Dead Sea (Gen. xiv.); but whether he acted for himself, or only as the viceroy or general of the Assyrians, must remain a matter of doubt. Ezekiel (xxxii. 24) mentions Elam among the mighty uncircumcised nations which had been the terror of the world; and about the same period (B.C. 590) Jeremiah threatened it with conquest and destruction by the Chaldæans (Jer. xlix. 30, 34, sqq.). This was accomplished probably by Nebuchadnezzar, who subjected Western Asia to his dominion; for we find his successor Belshazzar residing at Susa, the capital of Elam, a province then subject to that monarch (Dan. viii. 1, 2). With this the Scriptural notices of Elam end, unless we add that Elamites are found among those who were at Jerusalem at the feast of Pentecost (Acts ii. 9); which implies that Jews descended from the exiles were settled in that country.

E'LATH, now called AILAH. It was a city of Idumæa, having a port on the eastern arm or gulf of the Red Sea, which thence received the name of Sinus Elaniticus (Gulf of Akaba). According to Eusebius, it was ten miles east from Petra. It lies at the extremity of the valley of Elghor, which runs at the bottom of two parallel ranges of hills, north and south, through Arabia Petræa, from the Dead Sea to the northern parts of the Elanitic Gulf.

The first time that it is mentioned in the Scriptures is in Deut. ii. 8, where, in speaking of the journey of the Israelites towards the Promised Land, these words occur—'When we passed by from our brethren the children of Esau, which dwelt in Seir, through the way of the plain from Elath, and from Eziongeber.' These two places are mentioned together again in 1 Kings ix. 26, in such a manner as to show that Elath was more ancient than Eziongeber, and was of so much repute as to be used for indicating the locality of other places: the passage also fixes the spot where Elath itself was to be found: 'and King Solomon made a navy of ships in Eziongeber, which is beside Elath, on the shore (Num. xxxiii. 35) of the Red Sea, in the land of Edom.' The use which David made of the vicinity of Elath shows that the country was at that time in his possession. Accordingly, in 2 Sam. viii. 14, we learn that he had previously made himself master of Idumæa, and garrisoned its strong-holds with his own troops. Under his successor, Joram (2 Kings viii. 20), the Idumæans revolted from Judah, and elected a king over themselves. Joram thereupon assembled his forces, 'and all the chariots with him,' and, falling on the Idumæans by night, succeeded in defeating and scattering their army. The Hebrews, however, could not prevail, but 'Edom revolted from under the hand of Judah unto this day;' thus exemplifying the striking language employed (Gen. xxvii. 40) by Isaac—'by thy sword shalt thou live, and shalt serve thy brother: and it shall come to pass, when thou shalt have the dominion, that thou shalt break his yoke from off thy neck.' From 2 Kings xiv. 22, however, it appears that Uzziah recovered Elath, and, having so repaired and adorned the city as to be said to have built, that is rebuilt, it, he made it a part of his dominions. This connection was not of long continuance; for in ch. xvi. ver. 6 of the same book, we find the Syrian king Rezin interposing, who captured Elath, drove out the Jews, and annexed the place to his Syrian kingdom, and 'the Syrians came to Elath, and dwelt there unto this day.' At a later period it fell under the power of the Romans, and was for a time guarded by the tenth legion, forming part of Palæstina Tertia. It subsequently became the residence of a Christian bishop. In the days of its prosperity it was much distinguished for commerce, which continued to flourish under the auspices of Christianity. In the sixth century it is spoken of by Procopius as being inhabited by Jews subject to the Roman dominion. In A.D. 630, the Christian communities of Arabia Petræa found it expedient to submit to Mohammed, when John, the Christian governor of Ailah, became bound to pay an annual tribute of 300 gold-pieces. Henceforward, till the present century, Ailah lay in the darkness of Islamism. Mounds of rubbish alone mark the site of the town, while a fortress, occupied by a governor and a small garrison under the Pasha of Egypt, serves to keep the neighbouring tribes of the desert in awe, and to minister to the wants and protection of the annual Egyptian Haj, or pilgrim caravan. This place has always been an important station upon the route of the Egyptian Haj. Such is the importance of this caravan of pilgrims from Cairo to Mecca, both in a religious and political point of view, that the rulers of Egypt from the earliest period have given it convoy and protection. For this purpose a line of fortresses similar to that of Akaba has been established at intervals along the route, with wells of water and supplies of provisions.

EL'DAD and ME'DAD, two of the seventy elders appointed by Moses to assist him in the government of the people. Although not present with the others at the door of the tabernacle, they were equally filled with the divine spirit, and began to 'prophesy' in the camp. Joshua, thinking this irregular, requested Moses to forbid them, and received an answer eminently characteristic of the great lawgiver:—'Enviest thou for my sake? Would to God that all the Lord's people were prophets, and that the Lord would put his spirit upon them' (Num. xi. 24-29).

ELDER, literally, one of the older men, and because, in ancient times, older persons would naturally be selected to hold public offices, out of regard to their presumed superiority in knowledge and experience, the term came to be used as the designation for the office itself, borne by an individual, of whatever age. But the term 'elder' appears to be also expressive of respect and reverence in general. The word occurs in this sense in Gen. l. 7, 'Joseph went up to bury his father, and with him went up all the servants of Pharaoh, the elders of his house, and all the elders of the land of Egypt.' These elders of Egypt were, probably, the various state-officers. The elders of Israel, of whom such frequent mention is made, may have been, in early times, the lineal descendants of the patriarchs (Exod. xii. 21). To the elders Moses was directed to open his commission (Exod. iii. 16). They accompanied Moses in his first interview with Pharaoh, as the representatives of the Hebrew nation (ver. 18); through them Moses issued his communications and commands to the whole people (Exod. xix. 7; Deut. xxxi. 9); they were his immediate attendants in all the great transactions in the wilderness (Exod. xvii. 5); seventy of their number were selected to attend Moses, Aaron, Nadab, and Abihu, at the giving of the law (Exod. xxiv. 1), on which occasion they are called the *nobles* of the children of Israel, who did eat and drink before God, in ratification of the covenant, as representatives of the nation. In Num. xi. 16, 17, we meet with the appointment of seventy elders to bear the burden of the people along with Moses; these were selected by Moses out of the whole number of the elders, and are described as being, already, officers over the children of Israel. It is the opinion of Michaelis, that this council, chosen to assist Moses, should not be confounded with the Sanhedrim, which, he thinks, was not instituted till after the return from the Babylonish captivity [SANHEDRIM]. After the settlement in Canaan the elders seem to have been the administrators of the laws in all the cities (Deut. xix. 12; xxi. 3, 6, 19; xxii. 15, 25). The continuance of the office may be traced during the time of the judges (Judg. ii. 7); during that of Samuel (1 Sam. xvi. 4); under Saul (1 Sam. xxx. 26); and David (1 Chron. xxi. 16). The elders of Israel are mentioned during the captivity (Ezra x. 14), consisting either of those who had sustained that office in their own land, or were permitted by the Baby-

Ionians to exercise it still among their country-men. We meet with them again at the restoration (Ezra v. 5), and by them the temple was rebuilt (vi. 14). After the restoration and during the time of the Maccabees, the Sanhedrim, according to Michaelis, was instituted, being first mentioned under Hyrcanus II.; but elders are still referred to in 1 Macc. vii. 33. Among the members of the Sanhedrim were the 'elders.' Like the scribes, they obtained their seat in the Sanhedrim by election, or nomination from the executive authority. The word elder, with many other Jewish terms, was introduced into the Christian church. In the latter it is the title of inferior ministers, who were appointed overseers *among* not *over* the flock (Acts xx. 17, 28; Tit. i. 5, 7; 1 Pet. v. 1-5). The term is applied even to the apostles (2 John; 3 John). So also 'the Presbytery' certainly includes even St. Paul himself (comp. 1 Tim. iv. 14 and 2 Tim. i. 6). Still the apostles are distinguished from the elders elsewhere (Acts xv. 6). The elder was constituted by an apostle or some one invested with apostolic authority (Acts xiv. 23; see also the epistles to Timothy and John). The elders preached, confuted gainsayers (Tit. i. 9), and visited the sick (James v. 14). The word elders is sometimes used in the sense of ancients, ancestors, predecessors (Matt. v. 21; Heb. xi. 2).

ELEA'LEH, a town of the Reubenites east of the Jordan (Num. xxxii. 3, 37); but which is named by the prophets as a city of the Moabites (Isa. xv. 4; xvi. 9; Jer. xlviii. 34). It is usually mentioned along with Heshbon; and accordingly travellers find in the neighbourhood of that city a ruined place, bearing the name of El Aal, which doubtless represents Elealeh. It stands upon the summit of a hill, and takes its name from its situation, Aal meaning 'high.' It commands the whole plain, and the view from it is very extensive. It is about a mile and a quarter north-east of Heshbon.

ELEA'ZAR (*God-helped*). This was an exceedingly common name among the Hebrews, being borne by a considerable number of persons in Scripture (as well as in the Apocrypha and Josephus), of whom the principal are the following.

1. ELEAZAR, eldest son of Aaron (Exod. vi. 23, 25), who acted in his father's lifetime as chief of the tribe of Levi (Num. iii. 32), and at his death succeeded him in the high-priesthood (Num. xx. 35, sq.). His pontificate was contemporary with the military government of Joshua, whom he appears to have survived. A perfectly good understanding seems at all times to have subsisted between Eleazar and Joshua, as we constantly trace that co-operation and mutual support which the circumstances of the time and of the nation rendered so necessary. Eleazar is supposed to have lived twenty-five years after the passage of the Jordan, and the book of Joshua concludes with a notice of his death and burial.

2. ELEAZAR, who was set apart to attend upon the ark while it remained under the roof of his father Abinadab (1 Sam. vii. 1).

3. ELEAZAR, one of the three most eminent of David's heroes, who 'fought till his hand was weary' in maintaining with David and the other two a daring stand against the Philistines after 'the men of Israel had gone away.' He was also one of the same three when they broke through the Philistine host, to gratify David's longing for a drink of water from the well of his native Bethlehem (2 Sam. xxiii. 9, 10, 13).

4. ELEAZAR, the fourth of the Maccabæan brothers, sons of the priest Mattathias (1 Macc. ii. 5). He was crushed to death by the fall of an elephant which he stabbed under the belly in the belief that it bore the king, Antiochus Eupator (1 Macc. vi. 43-46).

5. ELEAZAR, an aged and venerable scribe who, 'as became his age, and the excellency of his ancient years, and the honour of his grey head,' chose rather to submit to the most cruel torments than conform to the polluting enactments of Antiochus Epiphanes (2 Macc. vii. 18-31).

ELEPHANT occurs only in 1 Macc. vi. 34. The animals of this genus consist at present of two very distinct species, one a native of Southern

165. [Asiatic Elephant.]

Asia, once spread considerably to the westward of the Upper Indus, and the other occupying southern and middle Africa to the edge of the great Sahara. In a fossil state there are besides six more species clearly distinguished. The elephant is the largest of all terrestrial animals, sometimes reaching to above eleven feet of vertical height at the shoulders, and weighing from five to seven thousand pounds: he is of a black or slaty-ash colour, and almost destitute of hair. The head, which is proportionably large, is provided with two broad pendulous ears, particularly in those of the African species, which are occasionally six feet in length. The eyes are comparatively small, with a malevolent expression, and on the temples are pores which exude a viscous humour; the tail is long, hanging nearly to the heels, and distichous at the end. But the most remarkable organ of the elephant, that which equally enables the animal to reach the ground and to grasp branches of trees at a considerable height, is the proboscis or trunk; a cylindrical elastic instrument, in ordinary condition reaching nearly down to the ground, but contractile to two-thirds of its usual length, and extensile to one-third beyond it; provided with nearly 4000 muscles crossing each other in such a manner that the proboscis is flexible in every direction, and so abundantly supplied with nerves as to render the organ one of the most delicate in nature. Within is the double canal of the nostrils, and at the terminal opening a finger-like process, with which the animal can take up very minute objects and grasp others, even to a writing pen, and mark paper with it. By means of the proboscis the elephant has a power of suction capable of raising nearly 200 pounds weight; and with this instrument he gathers food from trees and from the earth, draws up drink to squirt it down his throat, draws corks, unties small knots, and performs numberless other minute operations; and, if necessary, tears down branches of trees more than five inches in diameter with no less dexterity than strength. The gait of an elephant is an enormous stride, performed with his high and ponderous legs, and sufficiently rapid to require smart galloping on horseback to outstrip him.

Elephants are peaceable towards all inoffensive animals; sociable among themselves, and ready to help each other; gregarious in grassy plains, but more inclined to frequent densely-wooded mountain glens: at times not unwilling to visit the more arid wastes, but fond of rivers and pools, where they wallow in mud and water among reeds and under the shade of trees.

The Asiatic species, carrying the head higher, has more dignity of appearance, and is believed to have more sagacity and courage than the African; which, however, is not inferior in weight or bulk, and has never been in the hands of such experienced managers as the Indian mohauts are, who have acquired such deep knowledge of the character of these beasts that they make them submit to almost incredible operations; such, for example, as suffering patiently the extraction of a decayed part of a tooth, a kind of chisel and mallet being the instruments used for the purpose. Elephants walk under water as long as the end of the proboscis can remain above the surface; but when in greater depth, they float with the head and back only about a foot beneath it. They are steady, assiduous workmen in many laborious tasks, often using discretion when they require some dexterity and attention in the performance. Good will is all man can trust to in directing them, for correction cannot be enforced beyond their patience; but flattery, good treatment, kind words, promises and rewards, even to the wear of finery, have the desired effect. In history they appear most conspicuous as formidable elements of battle. From the remotest ages they were trained for war by the nations of India, and by their aid they no doubt acquired and long held possession of several regions of High Asia westward of the Indus.

ELEUTHEROP'OLIS, a place not named in Scripture, but which was an episcopal city of such importance in the time of Eusebius and Jerome, that they assumed it as the point whence to estimate the distances and positions of other cities in Southern Palestine. It continued to be a great city until the sixth century: but after that all traces of it were lost. In recent times, however, Professor Robinson has identified it with Beit-Jibrin, a village of moderate size, the capital of a district in the province of Gaza. In and around this village are ruins of different ages,

more extensive and massy than any which had been seen in Palestine, excepting the substructions of the ancient temple at Jerusalem and the Haram at Hebron. These ruins consist principally of the remains of a fortress of immense strength, in the midst of an irregular rounded enclosure, encompassed by a very ancient and strong wall. This outer wall is built of large squared stones, uncemented. Along this wall on the inside, towards the west and north-west, is a row of ancient massive vaults with fine round arches, apparently of the same age as the wall itself, and both undoubtedly of Roman origin. In the midst of the area stands an irregular castle, the lower parts of which seem to be as ancient as the exterior wall, but it has obviously been built up again in modern times. An inscription over the gate shows that it was last repaired by the Turks A.H. 958 (A.D. 1551), nearly two years after the present walls of Jerusalem were built. Remains of ancient walls and dwellings extend up the valley; and at the distance of twenty minutes from the present village are the ruins of an ancient church, bearing the name of Santa Hanneh (St. Anne). Only the eastern end is now standing, including the niche of the great altar and that of a side chapel, built of large hewn stones of strong and beautiful masonry. Beit-Jibrin is twenty miles east of Askelon, and thirteen miles east-north-east from Hebron.

E'LI (*the highest*), high-priest of the Jews when the ark was in Shiloh (1 Sam. i. 3, 9). He was the first high-priest of the line of Ithamar, Aaron's youngest son. This is deduced from 1 Chron. xxiv. 3, 6. It also appears from the omission of the names of Eli and his immediate successors in the enumeration of the high-priests of Eleazar's line in 1 Chron. vi. 4-6. What occasioned this remarkable transfer is not known —most probably the incapacity or minority of the then sole representative of the elder line; for it is very evident that it was no unauthorized usurpation on the part of Eli (1 Sam. ii. 27, 28). Eli also acted as regent or civil judge of Israel after the death of Samson. This function, indeed, seems to have been intended, by the theocratical constitution, to devolve upon the high-priest, by virtue of his office, in the absence of any person specially appointed by the Divine King, to deliver and govern Israel. He is said to have judged Israel forty years (1 Sam. iv. 18). As Eli died at the age of ninety-eight (1 Sam. iv. 15), the forty years must have commenced when he was fifty-eight years old.

Eli seems to have been a religious man; and the only fault recorded of him was an excessive easiness of temper, most unbefitting the high responsibilities of his official character. His sons, Hophni and Phinehas, whom he invested with authority, misconducted themselves so outrageously as to excite deep disgust among the people, and render the services of the tabernacle odious in their eyes. Of this misconduct Eli was aware, but contented himself with mild and ineffectual remonstrances, where his station required severe and vigorous action. For this neglect the judgment of God was at length denounced upon his house, through the young Samuel, who, under peculiar circumstances [SAMUEL], had been attached from childhood to his person (1 Sam. ii. 29; iii. 18). Some years passed without any apparent fulfilment of this denunciation—but it came at length in one terrible crash, by which the old man's heart was broken. The Philistines had gained the upper hand over Israel, and the ark of God was taken to the field, in the confidence of victory and safety from its presence. But in the battle which followed, the ark itself was taken by the Philistines, and the two sons of Eli, who were in attendance upon it, were slain. The high-priest, then blind with age, sat by the way-side at Shiloh, awaiting tidings from the war, 'for his heart trembled for the ark of God.' A man of Benjamin, with his clothes rent, and with earth upon his head, brought the fatal news: and Eli heard that Israel was defeated—that his sons were slain—that the ark of God was taken—at which last word he fell heavily from his seat, and died (1 Sam. iv).

The ultimate doom upon Eli's house was accomplished when Solomon removed Abiathar (the last high-priest of this line) from his office, and restored the line of Eleazar in the person of Zadok [ABIATHAR].

ELI'AKIM. [JEHOIAKIM.]

ELI'AS. [ELIJAH.]

ELIE'ZER. This is the same name as Eleazar—whence came the abbreviated Lazar or Lazarus of the New Testament. Mention is made (Gen. xv. 2, 3) of Eliezer, whom before the birth of Ishmael and Isaac Abraham regarded as his heir. Abraham, being promised a son, says:—'I go childless, and the steward of my house is this Eliezer of Damascus. . . . . Behold, to me thou hast given no seed: and, lo, one born in mine house is mine heir' (Gen. xv. 2, 3). The common notion is that Eliezer was Abraham's house-born slave, adopted as his heir, and meanwhile his chief and confidential servant, and the same who was afterwards sent into Mesopotamia to seek a wife for Isaac. This last point we may dismiss with the remark, that there is not the least evidence that 'the elder servant of his house' (Gen. xxiv. 2), whom Abraham charged with this mission, was the same as Eliezer: and our attention may therefore be confined to the verses which have been quoted.

It is obvious that the third verse is not properly a sequel to the second, but a repetition of the statement contained in the second; and, being thus regarded as parallel passages, the two may be used to explain each other.

'Eliezer of Damascus,' or 'Damascene-Eliezer,' is the subject of both verses. The obvious meaning is, that Eliezer was born in Damascus: and how is this compatible with the notion of his being Abraham's house-born slave, seeing that Abraham's household never was at Damascus?

The expression, 'the steward of my house,' in ver. 2, will explain the sense of 'one born in mine house is mine heir,' in ver. 3. The first phrase, literally translated, is 'the son of possession of my house,' *i. e.* one who shall possess my house, my property, after my death; and is therefore exactly the same as the phrase in the next verse, 'the son of my house (paraphrased by 'one born in mine house') is mine heir.' This removes the whole difficulty; for it is no longer necessary to suppose that Eliezer was a house-born slave, or a servant at all; and leaves it more probable that he was some near relative whom Abraham regarded as his heir-at-law. In this

case Abraham obviously means to say, 'Behold, to me thou hast given no children, and not the son of my loins. but the son of my house (*i. e.* of my family—the son whom my house gives me—the heir at law) is mine heir.' It is by no means certain that 'this Eliezer' was present in Abraham's camp at all: and we, of course, cannot know in what degree he stood related to Abraham, or under what circumstances he was born at, or belonged to Damascus. It is possible that he lived there at the very time when Abraham thus spoke of him, and that he is hence called 'Eliezer of Damascus.'

2. ELIEZER. The second of the two sons born to Moses while an exile in the land of Midian (Exod. xviii. 4). Eliezer had a son called Rebadiah (1 Chron. viii. 17).

ELI'HU (*Jehovah is God*). One of Job's friends, described as 'the son of Barachel, a Buzite, of the kindred of Ram' (Job xxxii. 2). This is usually understood to imply that he was descended from Buz, the son of Abraham's brother Nahor, from whose family the city called Buz (Jer. xxv. 23) also took its name. Elihu's name does not appear among those of the friends who came in the first instance to condole with Job, nor is his presence indicated till the debate between the afflicted man and his three friends had been brought to a conclusion. Then, finding there was no answer to Job's last speech, he comes forward with considerable modesty, which he loses as he proceeds, to remark on the debate, and to deliver his own opinion on the points at issue. The character and scope of his orations are described elsewhere [JOB, BOOK OF]. It appears, from the manner in which Elihu introduces himself, that he was by much the youngest of the party; and it is evident that he had been present from the commencement of the discussion, to which he had paid very close attention. This would suggest that the debate between Job and his friends was carried on in the presence of a deeply-interested auditory, among which was this Elihu, who could not forbear from interfering when the controversy appeared to have reached an unsatisfactory conclusion.

ELI'JAH (*Jehovah is God*). This wonder-working prophet is introduced to our notice like another Melchizedek (Gen. xiv. 18; Heb. vii. 3), without any mention of his father or mother, or of the beginning of his days. From this silence of Scripture as to his parentage and birth, much vain speculation has arisen. Some suppose that Elijah is called a Tishbite from Tishbeh, a city beyond the Jordan. The very first sentence that the prophet utters is a direful denunciation against Ahab; and this he supports by a solemn oath: 'As the Lord God of Israel liveth, before whom I stand, there shall not be dew or rain these years (*i. e.* three and a half years, Luke iv. 25; James v. 17), but according to my word' (1 Kings xvii. 1). Before, however, he spoke thus, it would seem that he had been warning this most wicked king as to the fatal consequences which must result both to himself and his people, from the iniquitous course he was then pursuing: and this may account for the apparent abruptness with which he opens his commission.

We can imagine Ahab and Jezebel being greatly incensed against Elijah for having foretold and prayed that such calamities might befall them.

For some time they might attribute the drought under which the nation suffered to natural causes, and not to the interposition of the prophet. When, however, they saw the denunciation of Elijah taking effect far more extensively than had been anticipated, they would naturally seek to wreak their vengeance upon him as the cause of their sufferings. But we do not find him taking one step for his own preservation, till the God whom he served said, ' Get thee hence, and turn thee eastward, and hide thyself by the brook Cherith, that is before Jordan: and it shall be that thou shalt drink of the brook; and I have commanded the ravens to feed thee there' (1 Kings xvii. 3, 4). Other and better means of protection from the impending danger might seem open to him; but, regardless of these, he hastened to obey the divine mandate, and ' went and dwelt by the brook Cherith that is before Jordan' (1 Kings xvii. 5).

A fresh trial now awaits this servant of God (B.C. 909), and in the manner in which he bears it, we see the strength of his faith. For one year, as some suppose, God had miraculously provided for his bodily wants at Cherith; but the brook which, heretofore, had afforded him the needful refreshment there, became dried up. Encouraged by past experience of his heavenly Father's care of him, the prophet still waited patiently till He said, ' Arise (1 Kings xvii. 9), get thee to Zarephath, which belongeth to Zidon, and dwell there: behold, I have commanded a widow woman there to sustain thee.' He then, at once, set out on the journey, and now arrived at Zarephath, he, in the arrangement of God's providence, met, as he entered its gate, the very woman who was deputed to give him immediate support. But his faith is again put to a sore test, for he found her engaged in a way which was well calculated to discourage all his hopes; she was gathering sticks for the purpose, as she assured him, of cooking her last meal, and now that the famine prevailed there, as it did in Israel, she saw nothing before her and her only son but starvation and death. How then could the prophet ask for, and how could she think of giving, a part of her last morsel? The same Divine Spirit inspired him to assure her that she and her child should be even miraculously provided for during the continuance of the famine: and also influenced her heart to receive, without doubting, the assurance! The kindness of this widow in baking the first cake for Elijah was well requited with a prophet's reward (Matt. x. 41, 42); she afforded one meal to him, and God afforded many to her (see 1 Kings xv. 16). While residing here God accordingly saw fit to visit the family with a temporary calamity. ' And it came to pass that the son of the woman, the mistress of the house, fell sick: and his sickness was so sore that there was no life left in him' (1 Kings xvii. 17). Verse 18 contains the expostulation with the prophet of this bereaved widow; she rashly imputes the death to his presence. Elijah retaliates not, but calmly takes the dead child out of the mother's bosom, and lays it on his own bed (verse 19), that there he may, in private, pray the more fervently for its restoration. His prayer was heard, and answered by the restoration of life to the child, and of gladness to the widow's heart.

Since now, however, the long-protracted famine, with all its attendant horrors, failed to detach Ahab and his guilty people from their abominable idolatries, God mercifully gave them another opportunity of repenting and turning to Himself. For three years and six months (James v. 17) the destructive famine had spread its deadly influence over the whole nation of Israel. The prophet was then called by the word of the Lord to return to Israel. Wishing not to tempt God by going unnecessarily into danger, he first presented himself to good Obadiah (1 Kings xviii. 7). This principal servant of Ahab was also a true servant of God ; and on recognising the prophet he treated him with honour and respect. Elijah requested him to announce to Ahab that he had returned. Obadiah, apparently stung by the unkindness of this request, replied, ' What have I sinned, that thou shouldest thus expose me to Ahab's rage, who will certainly slay me for not apprehending thee, for whom he has so long and so anxiously sought in all lands and in confederate countries, that they should not harbour a traitor whom he looks upon as the author of the famine,' &c. Moreover, he would delicately intimate to Elijah how he had actually jeoparded his own life in securing that of one hundred of the Lord's prophets, and whom he had fed at his own expense. Satisfied with Elijah's reply to this touching appeal, wherein he removed all his fears about the Spirit's carrying himself away (as 2 Kings ii. 11-16 ; Ezek. viii. 3 ; Acts viii. 39), he resolves to be the prophet's messenger to Ahab. Intending to be revenged on him, or to inquire when rain might be expected, Ahab now came forth to meet Elijah. He at once charged him with being the main cause of all the calamities which he and the nation had suffered. But Elijah flung back the charge upon himself, assigning the real cause to be his own sin of idolatry. Regarding, however, his magisterial position, while he reproved his sin, he requests him to exercise his authority in summoning an assembly to Mount Carmel, that the controversy between them might be decided, whether the king or the prophet was the troubler of Israel. Whatever were the secret motives which induced Ahab to comply with this proposal, God directed the result. Elijah offered to decide this controversy between God and Baal by a miracle from Heaven. As fire was the element over which Baal was supposed to preside, the prophet proposes (wishing to give them every advantage) that, two bullocks being slain, and laid each upon a distinct altar, the one for Baal, the other for Jehovah, whichever should be consumed by fire must proclaim whose the people of Israel were, and whom it was their duty to serve. The people consent to this proposal. Elijah will have summoned not only all the elders of Israel, but also the four hundred priests of Baal belonging to Jezebel's court, and the four hundred and fifty who were dispersed over the kingdom. Confident of success, because doubtless God had revealed the whole matter to him, he enters the lists of contest with the four hundred and fifty priests of Baal. Having reconstructed an altar which had once belonged to God, with twelve stones—as if to declare that the twelve tribes of Israel should again be united in the service of Jehovah—and having laid thereon his bullock, and filled the trench by which it was surrounded with large quantities of water, lest any suspicion of deceit might occur to any mind, the prophet gives place to the Baalites—allows them to make trial first. In vain did these deceived and deceiving men call, from morning till evening, upon Baal—in vain did they now mingle their own blood with that of the sacrifice: no answer was given—no fire descended.

Elijah having rebuked their folly and wickedness with the sharpest irony, and it being at last evident to all that their efforts to obtain the wished-for fire were vain, now, at the time of the evening sacrifice, offered up his prayer. The prayer of the Baalites was long, that of the prophet was short—charging God with the care of His covenant, of His truth, and of His glory—when, behold, 'the fire came down. licked up the water, and consumed not only the bullock, but the very stones of the altar also.' The effect of this on the mind of the people was what the prophet desired: acknowledging the awful presence of the Godhead, they exclaim, as with one voice, 'Jehovah He is the God! Jehovah He is the God!' Seizing the opportunity whilst the people's hearts were- warm with the fresh conviction of this miracle, he bade them take those juggling priests and destroy them; and this he might lawfully do at God's direction, and under the sanction of His law (Deut. xiii. 5 ; xviii. 20). Ahab having now publicly vindicated God's violated law by giving his royal sanction to the execution of Baal's priests, Elijah informed him that he may go up to his tent on Carmel to take refreshment, for God will send the desired rain. In the meantime he prayed earnestly (James v. 17, 18) for this blessing: God heard and answered: a little cloud arose out of the Mediterranean sea, in sight of which the prophet now was, diffused itself gradually over the entire face of the heavens, and then emptied its refreshing waters upon the whole land of Israel. Here was another proof of the Divine mission of the prophet, from which, we should imagine, the whole nation must have profited; but subsequent events would seem to prove that the impression produced by these dealings of God was of a very partial and temporary character. Impressed with the hope that the report of God's miraculous actings at Carmel might not only reach the ear, but also penetrate and soften the hard heart of Jezebel; and anxious that the reformation of his country should spread in and about Jezreel also, Elijah, strengthened, as we are told, from on high, now accompanies Ahab thither on foot. How ill-founded the prophet's expectation was, subsequent events too painfully proved. Jezebel, instead of receiving Elijah obviously as the messenger of God for good to her nation, now secretly conceived and openly declared her fixed purpose to put him to death. Dreading the vile woman's design, and probably thinking that there was no hope of producing any reformation among the people, he fled into the wilderness, and there longed for death. But God is still gracious to him, and at once touches his heart and corrects his petulancy by the ministration of His angel, and by an awful exhibition of His Divine power. And having done this, revealing Himself in the gentle accents of a still voice, He announces to him that he must go and anoint Hazael king over Syria, Jehu king over Israel, and Elisha prophet in his own place, ere death can put a period to

his labours. When God had comforted His prophet by telling him of these three instruments he had in store to vindicate his own insulted honour, then he convinced him of his mistake in saying 'I only am left alone,' &c., by the assurance that there were seven thousand in Israel who had not bowed the knee to Baal.

Leaving the cave of Horeb (B C. 906), Elijah now proceeded to the field where he found Elisha in the act of ploughing, and he cast his prophet's mantle over him, as a symbol of his being clothed with God's spirit. The Divine impression produced upon the mind of Elisha by this act of Elijah made him willing to leave all things and follow him.

For about six years from this calling of Elisha we find no notice in the sacred history of Elijah, till God sent him once again to pronounce sore judgments upon Ahab and Jezebel for the murder of unoffending Naboth (1 Kings xxi. 17, &c.). How he and his associate in the prophetic office employed themselves during this time we are not told. We need not dwell upon the complicated character of Ahab's wickedness (1 Kings xxi.), in winking at the murderous means whereby Jezebel procured for him the inalienable property of Naboth [AHAB; NABOTH]. When he seemed to be triumphing in the possession of his ill-obtained gain, Elijah stood before him, and threatened him, in the name of the Lord (2 Kings ix. 21-26 inclusive), that God would retaliate blood for blood, and that not on himself only—' his seventy sons shall die, and (2 Kings x. 6) Jezebel shall become meat for dogs.' Fearing that these predictions would prove true, as those about the rain and fire had done, Ahab now assumed the manner of a penitent; and, though subsequent acts proved that his repentance was not permanent, yet God rewards his temporary abasement by a temporary arrest of judgment. We see, however, in after parts of this sacred history, how the judgments denounced against him, his abandoned consort, and children, took effect to the very letter.

Elijah again retired from the history till an act of blasphemy on the part of Ahaziah, the son and successor of Ahab, causes God to call him forth. Ahaziah met with an injury, and, fearing that it might be unto death, he, as if to prove himself worthy of being the son of idolatrous Ahab and Jezebel, sent to consult Baalzebub, the idol-god of Ekron; but the angel of the Lord told Elijah to go forth and meet the messengers of the king (2 Kings i. 3, 4), and assure them that he should not recover. Suddenly reappearing before their master, he said unto them, 'Why are ye now turned back?' when they answered, 'There came a man up to meet us, and said unto us, Go, turn again unto the king that sent you, and say unto him, Thus saith the Lord: Is it not because there is no God in Israel that thou sendest to inquire of Baalzebub, the god of Ekron? Wherefore thou shalt not come down from that bed on which thou art gone up, but shalt surely die.' Conscience seems to have at once whispered to him that the man who dared to arrest his messengers with such a communication must be Elijah, the bold but unsuccessful reprover of his parents. Determined to chastise him for such an insult, he sent a captain and fifty armed men to bring him into his presence; but at Elijah's word fire descended from Heaven and consumed the whole band. Attributing this destruction of his men to some natural cause, he sent forth another company, on whom though the same judgment fell, this impious king is not satisfied till another and a similar effort is made to capture the prophet. The captain of the third band implored and found mercy at the hands of the prophet, who at once descended from Carmel and accompanied him to Ahaziah. Fearless of his wrath, Elijah now repeats to the king himself what he had before said to his messengers, and agreeably thereto, the sacred narrative informs us that Ahaziah died.

The above was the last more public effort which the prophet made to reform Israel. His warfare being now accomplished on earth, God, whom he had so long and so faithfully served, will translate him in a chariot of fire to Heaven. Conscious of this, he determines to spend his last moments in imparting divine instruction to, and pronouncing his last benediction upon, the students in the colleges of Beth-el and Jericho; accordingly, he made a circuit from Gilgal, near the Jordan, to Beth-el, and from thence to Jericho. Wishing either to be alone at the moment of being caught up to Heaven; or, what is more probable, anxious to test the affection of Elisha (as Christ did that of Peter), he delicately intimates to him not to accompany him in this tour. But the faithful Elisha, to whom, as also to the schools of the prophets, God had revealed his purpose to remove Elijah, declares his fixed determination not to forsake his master now at the close of his earthly pilgrimage. Ere yet, however, the chariot of God descended for him, he asks what he should do for Elisha. The latter, conscious of the complicated and difficult duties which now awaited him, asks for a double portion of Elijah's spirit. Elijah, acknowledging the magnitude of the request, yet promises to grant it on the contingency of Elisha seeing him at the moment of his rapture. Possibly this contingency was placed before him in order to make him more on the watch, that the glorious departure of Elijah should not take place without his actually seeing it. Whilst standing on the other side of the Jordan, whose waters were miraculously parted for them to pass over on dry ground, angels descended, as in a fiery chariot, and, in the sight of fifty of the sons of the prophets and Elisha, carried Elijah into Heaven. Elisha, at this wonderful sight, cried out, like a bereaved child, 'My Father, my Father, the chariot of Israel and the horsemen thereof;' as if he had said, Alas! the strength and saviour of Israel is now departed! But it was not so; for God designed that the mantle which fell from Elijah as he ascended should now remain with Elisha as a pledge that the office and spirit of the former had now fallen upon himself.

E'LIM, one of the stations of the Israelites in the route to Mount Sinai [SINAI].

ELIM'ELECH (*God the king*), a native of Bethlehem, husband of Naomi, and father by her of two sons, Mahlon and Chilion. In a time of scarcity he withdrew with his family into the land of Moab, where he died (Ruth i. 1-3). [NAOMI; RUTH.]

1. ELI'PHAZ (*God the strong*), a son of Esau and Adah (Gen. xxxvi. 10).

2. ELI'PHAZ, one of the three friends who came to condole with Job in his affliction, and who took part in that remarkable discussion which occupies the book of Job. He was of Temân in Idumæa; and as Eliphaz the son of Esau had a son called Teman, from whom the place took its name, there is reason to conclude that this Eliphaz was a descendant of the former Eliphaz. Some, indeed, even go so far as to suppose that the Eliphaz of Job was no other than the son of Esau. This view is of course confined to those who refer the age of Job to the time of the patriarchs.

Eliphaz is the first of the friends to take up the debate, in reply to Job's passionate complaints. The scope of his argument and the character of his oratory are described under another head [JOB, BOOK OF]. He appears to have been the oldest of the speakers, from which circumstance, or from natural disposition, his language is more mild and sedate than that of any of the other speakers. He begins his orations with delicacy, and conducts his part of the argument with considerable address. His share in the controversy occupies chapters iv. v. xv. xxii.

ELIS'ABETH, wife of Zacharias, and mother of John the Baptist (Luke i. 5). The name in this precise shape does not occur in the Old Testament, where the names of few females are given. But it is a Hebrew name, the same in fact as Elisheba, which see.

ELI'SHA (*God the deliverer*). The manner, and the circumstances in which Elisha was called to the prophetic office have been noticed in the article ELIJAH.

Anxious to enter at once upon the duties of his sacred office, Elisha determined to visit the schools of the prophets which were on the other side of the Jordan. Accordingly, returning to this river, and wishing that sensible evidence should be afforded, both to himself and others, of the spirit and power of his departed master resting upon him, he struck its waters with Elijah's mantle, when they parted asunder and opened a way for him to pass over on dry land. Witnessing this miraculous transaction, the fifty sons of the prophets, who had seen from the opposite side Elijah's ascension, and who were awaiting Elisha's return, now, with becoming reverence, acknowledged him their spiritual head.

The divine authority by which Elisha became the successor of Elijah received further confirmation from the miracle whereby the bitter waters of Jericho were made sweet, and the place thereby rendered fit for the habitation of man (2 Kings ii. 19-22).

As general visitor of the schools of the prophets, Elisha now passes on from Jericho to the college which was at Beth-el. Ere, however, he entered Beth-el, there met him from thence (2 Kings ii. 23, 24) little children, who, no doubt instigated by their idolatrous parents, tauntingly told him to ascend into heaven, as did his master, Elijah. There was in their expressions an admixture of rudeness, infidelity, and impiety. But the inhabitants of Beth-el were to know, from bitter experience, that to dishonour God's prophets was to dishonour Himself; for Elisha was at the moment inspired to pronounce the judgment which at once took effect: God, who never wants for instruments to accomplish his purposes, caused two she-bears to emerge from a neighbouring wood, and destroy the young delinquents.

Jehoram, who reigned over Israel at this time, though not a *Baalite*, was yet addicted to the sin of Jeroboam : still he inherits the friendship of Jehoshaphat, the good King of Judæa, whose counsel, possibly, under God, had detached him from the more gross idolatry of his father Ahab. Wishing to see the now (B.C. 895) revolted king of Moab reduced to his wonted allegiance to Israel, Jehoshaphat determined to go up to battle against him, together with Jehoram, and his own tributary the king of Edom. These combined armies met together on the plains of Edom. Confident in their own powers they press onward against the enemy ; but, not meeting him, another of a more formidable character started up before them. In the midst of the arid plains of Arabia Petræa they could find no water. Jehoram deplored the calamity into which they had fallen, but Jehoshaphat inquired for a prophet. On this, one of his courtiers said to Jehoram, ' Here is Elisha, the son of Shaphat, who poured water on the hands of Elijah.' No sooner were they made acquainted with the fact that Elisha was at hand than the three kings waited upon him. Elisha, feeling that it was nought but superstitious fear, joined to the influence of Jehoshaphat, which led Jehoram thus to consult him, now indignantly and tauntingly advised him to go for succour to the gods of his father Ahab and of his mother Jezebel. The reproved monarch was then led to acknowledge the impotency of those gods in whom he had trusted, and the power of that God whom he had neglected. Still the man of God, seeing the hollowness of Jehoram's humiliation, continues : ' As the Lord liveth, before whom I stand, surely were it not that I regard the presence of Jehoshaphat, the king of Judah, I would not look toward thee.' Having thus addressed Jehoram, Elisha desired a minstrel to be brought before him; and now when his spirit was calmed by, perhaps, one of the songs of Zion, ' The hand of the Lord came upon him.' The minstrel ceased, and Elisha made known the joyful intelligence that not only should water be miraculously supplied, but also that Moab should be overcome. Accordingly the next morning they realized the truth of this prediction. But the same water which preserves their lives becomes the source of destruction to their enemies. The Moabites, who had received intelligence of the advance of the allied army, were now assembled upon their frontiers. When the sun was up, and its rosy light first fell upon the water, their van-guard, beholding it at a distance, supposed it to be blood. Thus the notion was rapidly spread from one end to another that the kings were surely slain, having fallen out amongst themselves. Hence there was a universal shout, ' Moab, to the spoil !' and they went forward confident of victory. But beholding the Israelitish squadrons advancing to meet them, they fled in the utmost panic and confusion (2 Kings iii. 20, &c.).

The war having terminated in the signal overthrow of the revolters, Elisha, who had returned home, is again employed in ministering blessings. The widow of a pious prophet presented herself before him (2 Kings iv.), informed him that her husband having died in debt, his creditors were about to sell her two only sons, which, by an ex-

tension of the law (Exod. xxi. 7, and Lev. xxv. 39), and by virtue of another (Exod. xxii. 3), they had the power to do ; and against this hard-hearted act she implores the prophet's assistance. Elisha then inquired how far she herself had the power to avert the threatened calamity. She replied that the only thing of which she was possessed was one pot of oil. By multiplying this, as did his predecessor Elijah in the case of the widow of Zarephath, he enabled her at once to pay off her debts and thereby to preserve the liberty of her children (2 Kings iv. 1-7).

It is next related that in his visitations to the schools of the prophets his journey lay through the city of Shunem, where lived a rich and godly woman. Wishing that he should take up, more than occasionally, his abode under her roof, she proposed to her husband to construct a chamber for his reception. The husband at once consented, and, the apartment being completed and fitted up in a way that showed their proper conception of his feeling, the prophet becomes its occupant. The woman was childless; and the gratitude of the prophet for her disinterested kindness was evinced by the gift of a son, which the Lord, at his prayer, bestowed upon her. This new pledge of their affection grows up till he is able to visit his fond father in the harvest-field, when all the hopes they had built up in him were overthrown by his being suddenly laid prostrate in death. The bereaved mother, out of tenderness towards the feelings of the father, concealed the fact that the child was no more till she should see if it might please God, through Elisha, to restore him to life. She therefore hastened to Carmel, where she found the prophet, and informed him what had taken place. Conceiving probably that it was a case of mere suspended animation or a swoon, the prophet sent Gehazi, his servant, to place his staff on the face of the child, in the hope that it might act as a stimulus to excite the animal motions. But the mother, conscious that he was actually departed, continued to entreat that he himself would come to the chamber of the dead. He did so, and found that the soul of the child had indeed fled from the earthly tenement. Natural means belong to man; those that are supernatural belong to God : we should do our part, and beg of God to do his. On this principle the prophet on this occasion acted. God blessed the means used, and answered the prayer presented by Elisha. The child is raised up and restored to the fond embrace of its grateful and rejoicing parents.

The next remarkable event in the history of Elisha was the miraculous healing of the incurable leprosy of the Syrian general, Naaman, whereby the neighbouring nation had the opportunity of learning the beneficence of that God of Israel, whose judgments had often brought them very low. The particulars are given under another head [NAAMAN].

Soon after this transaction we find this man of God in Gilgal, miraculously neutralizing the poison which had, by mistake, been mixed with the food of the prophets, and also feeding one hundred of them with twenty small loaves which had been sent for his own consumption (2 Kings iv. 38, &c.).

Notwithstanding the general profligacy of Israel, the schools of the prophets increased, B.C.

U

890. This was, doubtless, owing to the influence of Elisha. Accompanied by their master, a party of these young prophets, or theological students, came to the Jordan, and whilst one of them was 'felling a beam (for the purpose of constructing there a house) the axe-head fell into the water.' This accident was the more distressing because the axe was borrowed property. Elisha, however, soon relieved him by causing it miraculously to rise to the surface of the river.

The sacred record again leads us to contemplate the prophet's usefulness, in reference to his country at large. Does the king of Syria devise well-concerted schemes for the destruction of Israel? God inspires Elisha to detect and lay them open to Jehoram. Benhadad, on hearing that it was he that thus caused his hostile movements to be frustrated, sent an armed band to Dothan in order to bring him bound to Damascus. The prophet's servant, on seeing the host of the enemy which invested Dothan, was much alarmed, but by the prayer of Elisha, God reveals to him the mighty company of angels which were set for their defence. Regardless of consequences, the prophet went forth to meet the hostile band : and having again prayed, God so blinded them that they could not recognize the object of their search. The prophet then promised to lead them to where they might see him with the natural eye. Trusting to his guidance, they followed on till they reached the centre of Samaria, when, the optical illusion being removed, Elisha stood in his recognized form before them. The king was for putting them all to death ; but, through the interposition of him whom they had just before sought to destroy, they were honourably dismissed to their own country (B.C. 892). But a year had scarcely elapsed from this time when Benhadad, unmindful of Israel's kindness and forbearance, invested Samaria and reduced its inhabitants to a state of the most cruel famine. Yet the king of Israel plunged still deeper into sin, for he ordered Elisha to be put to death, conceiving that it was his prayer which brought these sufferings upon himself and nation. But God forewarned the prophet of his danger, and inspired him to predict to the wicked king that by to-morrow 'a measure of fine flour should be sold for a shekel, and two measures of barley for a shekel, in the gate of Samaria.' This assurance was not more comfortable than *incredible;* but when the lord on whose hand the king leaned expressed his disbelief, he was awfully rebuked by the assurance that he should see but not enjoy the benefit. The next night God caused the Syrians to hear the noise of chariots and horses; and conceiving that Jehoram had hired against them the kings of the Hittites and the king of Egypt, they fled from before the walls of Samaria—leaving their tents filled with gold and provisions—in the utmost panic and confusion. In this way did God, according to the word of Elisha, miraculously deliver the inhabitants of Samaria from a deadly enemy without, and from sore famine within, its walls : another prediction, moreover, was accomplished; for the distrustful lord was trampled to death by the famished people in rushing through the gate of the city to the forsaken tents of the Syrians (2 Kings vii.).

We next find the prophet in Damascus, but are not told what led him thither (B.C. 885).

Benhadad, the king, whose counsels he had so often frustrated, rejoiced to hear of his presence ; and now, as if he had forgotten the attempt he once made upon his life, dispatches a noble messenger with a costly present, to consult him concerning his sickness and recovery. The prophet replied that he should then die, though his indisposition was not of a deadly character. Seeing moreover, in prophetic vision, that the man Hazael, who now stood before him, should be king in Benhadad's stead ; and that, as such, he would commit unheard-of cruelties upon his country, the prophet was moved to tears. How these painful anticipations of Elisha were realized the subsequent history of this man proved.

For a considerable time after Elisha had sent to anoint Jehu king over Israel we find no mention of him in the sacred record. We have reason to suppose that he was utterly neglected by Jehu, Jehoahaz, and Joash, who reigned in succession. Neither the sanctity of his life nor the stupendous miracles he wrought had the effect of reforming the nation at large : much of the time of his latter years was, doubtless, spent in the schools of the prophets. At length, worn out by his public and private labours, and at the age of 90—during 60 of which he is supposed to have prophesied—he is called into eternity. Nor was the manner of his death inglorious; though he did not enter into rest as did Elijah (2 Kings xiii. 14, &c.). Amongst his weeping attendants was Joash, the king of Israel. He was probably stung with remorse for having so neglected to acknowledge his national worth ; yet, though late, God does not suffer this public recognition of his aged and faithful servant to go unrequited. The spirit of prophecy again entering the dying Elisha, he informed Joash that he should prevail against the Syrians. Even after death God would put honour upon Elisha : a dead body having touched his bones came to life again. (2 Kings xiii. 21.)

Elisha was not less eminent than his predecessor Elijah. His miracles are various and stupendous, and, like those which were wrought by Christ, were on the whole of a *merciful* character. In this they were remarkably distinguished, in many instances, from the miracles of Elijah.

ELIS'HAH, a son of Javan (Gen. x. 4), who seems to have given name to 'the isles of Elishah,' which are described as exporting fabrics of purple and scarlet to the markets of Tyre (Ezek. xxvii. 7). If the descendants of Javan peopled Greece, we may expect to find Elishah in some province of that country ; but no certainty can be arrived at on the subject.

ELISH'EBA, *covenant-God :* wife of Aaron, and hence the mother of the priestly family (Exod. vi. 23).

EL'KANAH, *God the Creator.* Several persons of this name are mentioned in Scripture, as a son of Korah (Exod. vi. 24 ; 1 Chron. vi. 23); the father of Samuel (1 Sam. i. 1, seq. ; ii. 11-20 ; 1 Chron. vi. 27); a friend of king Ahab (2 Chron. xxviii. 7); one of David's heroes (1 Chron. xii. 6); Levites (1 Chron. vi. 23, 25, 26, 27 ; xv. 23).

EL'KOSH. The prophet Nahum is called an Elkoshite, that is a native of some place called Elkosh (Nahum i. 1). There was a village of this name in Galilee in the time of Jerome ; but the prophet was more probably born of Jewish exiles at Elkosh or Alkush in Assyria, near

Mosul. The Jews themselves believe that he was born and buried there; and Jewish pilgrims from all parts still visit his alleged tomb. Alkosh is thirty-four miles north of Mosul (Nineveh), and is situated a little way up the side of a mountain, in the range to which it gives its name. It is entirely inhabited by Chaldee Christians, who have a convent higher up the mountains.

ELLA'SAR, a territory in Asia, whose king, Arioch, was one of the four who invaded Canaan in the time of Abraham (Gen. xiv. 1). The association of this king with those of Elam and Shinar, indicates the region in which the kingdom should be sought; but nothing further is known of it, unless it be the same as Thelassar mentioned in 2 Kings xix. 12 [THELASSAR].

E'LON, of the tribe of Zebulon, who judged Israel ten years. He was preceded by Ibzan of Bethlehem, and succeeded by Abdon of Ephraim. The whole period covered by their administration was twenty-five years (from B.C. 1190 to 1174); but it is probable that they were for a part of this time contemporary, each exercising authority over a few of the tribes. They appear to have overawed the enemies of Israel by their judicious administration; for no war is mentioned in their time (Judg. xii. 8-15).

E'LUL, Neh. vi. 15, is the name of that month which was the sixth of the ecclesiastical, and twelfth of the civil, year of the Jews, and which began with the new moon of our September. According to the Megillat Taanith, the 17th day of this month was a public fast for the death of the spies who brought back a bad report of the land (Num. xiv. 37).

EL'YMAS, an appellative supposed to mean *a wise man*, applied to a Jew named Bar-Jesus, mentioned in Acts xiii. 6-11. Chrysostom observes, in reference to the blindness inflicted by the Apostle on Bar-Jesus, that the limiting clause '*for a season*,' shows that it was not intended so much for the punishment of the sorcerer as for the conversion of the deputy.

EMBALMING. [BURIAL.]

EMERALD, *Nophech*, a precious stone, named in Exod. xxviii. 18; xxxix. 11; Ezek. xxviii. 16; xxviii. 13; in all of which places it is rendered Emerald in the Authorized Version. The Sept. and Josephus render it by Carbuncle. This name, denoting a live coal, the ancients gave to several glowing red stones resembling live coals, particularly rubies and garnets. The most valued of the carbuncles seems, however, to have been the Oriental garnet, a transparent red stone, with a violet shade, and strong vitreous lustre.· It was engraved upon and was probably not so hard as the ruby, which, indeed, is the most beautiful and costly of the precious stones of a red colour, but is so hard that it cannot easily be subjected to the graving-tool. The Hebrew *nophech*, in the breastplate of the high-priest, was certainly an engraved stone; and there is no evidence that the ancients could engrave the ruby, although this has in modern times been accomplished. Upon the whole, the particular kind of stone denoted by the Hebrew word must be regarded as uncertain.

EMERODS, a painful disease with which the Philistines were afflicted (1 Sam. v. 6).

E'MIM, a numerous and gigantic race of people who, in the time of Abraham, occupied the country beyond the Jordan, afterwards possessed by the Moabites (Gen. xiv. 5; Deut. ii. 10).

EMMA'US (*hot baths*), a village 60 stadia, or 7½ miles, from Jerusalem, noted for our Lord's interview with two disciples on the day of his resurrection (Luke xxiv. 13). The same place is mentioned by Josephus (*De Bell. Jud* vii. 6. 6), and placed at the same distance from Jerusalem, in stating that Vespasian left 800 soldiers in Judæa, to whom he gave the village of Emmaus. The site is not now known. The other Emmaus, also called Nicopolis, is identified with Luisun, about midway between Jerusalem and Ramleh. There was another Emmaus, near Tiberias, on the lake of the same name, where the hot baths which gave name to it are still frequented, and have a temperature of 130° Fahrenheit. Neither of these places is named in Scripture.

EN, properly AIN, a word signifying 'fountain;' and hence entering into the composition of sundry local names, which are explained under AIN.

ENCAMPMENTS. Of the Jewish system of encampment the Mosaic books have left a detailed description. From the period of the sojourn in the wilderness to the crossing of the Jordan the twelve tribes were formed into four great armies. encamping in as many fronts, or forming a square, with a great space in the rear, where the tabernacle of the Lord was placed, surrounded by the tribe of Levi and the bodies of carriers, &c., by the stalls of the cattle and the baggage : the four fronts faced the cardinal points while the march was eastward, but as Judah continued to lead the van, it follows that when the Jordan was to be crossed the direction became westward, and therefore the general arrangement, so far as the cardinal points were concerned, was reversed. It does not appear that, during this time, Israel ever had lines of defence thrown up; but in after ages, when only single armies came into the field, it is probable that the castral disposition was not invariably quadrangular; and, from the many positions indicated on the crests of steep mountains, the fronts were clearly adapted to the ground and to the space which it was necessary to occupy. The rear of such positions, or the square camps in the plain, appear from the marginal reading of 1 Sam. xvii. 20, and xxvi. 5, to have been enclosed with a line of carts or chariots, which, from the remotest period, was a practice among all the nomade nations of the north. The book of Numbers is so explicit on the subject of encampment, and the march of the Israelites, that no particular explanation seems to be necessary.

ENCHANTMENTS. [DIVINATION.]

EN'DOR (*house-fountain*); a town of Galilee, assigned to Manasseh, although lying beyond the limits of that tribe (Josh. xvii. 11). It is mentioned in connection with the victory of Deborah and Barak (Ps. lxxxiii. 10); but is chiefly memorable as the abode of the sorceress whom Saul consulted on the eve of the battle in which he perished (1 Sam. xxviii. 7, sq.). The name is not found in the New Testament; but in the time of Eusebius and Jerome the place still existed as a large village, four miles south of Mount Tabor. At this distance, on the northern slope of the lower ridge of Hermon, a village with this name still exists.

EN-EGLA'IM (*calves' fountain*); a town of Moab (Ezek. xlvii. 10), which Jerome places at the northern end of the Dead Sea, at the influx of the Jordan.

EN-GAN'NIM (*gardens' fountain*). 1. A town of Judah (Josh. xv. 34), which Jerome places near Beth-el. 2. A Levitical city in Issachar (Josh. xix. 21; xxi. 29), probably the same as the Ginaen of Josephus (*Antiq.* xx. 6, 1), and which Biddulph (in *Purchas*, vol. ii. p. 135) identifies with the present Jenin, a town 15 miles south of Mount Tabor, and which he and others describe as still a place of gardens and abundant water. 3. Jerome mentions another place, called En-gannim, beyond the Jordan, near Geraza; and the name seems, indeed, to have been very common for places where water, and consequently gardens, abounded.

EN-GE'DI (*kids' fountain*), a city of Judah, which gave its name to a part of the desert to which David withdrew for fear of Saul (Josh. xv. 62; 1 Sam. xxiv. 1-4). Its more ancient Hebrew name was Hazezon-tamar; and by that name it is mentioned before the destruction of Sodom, as being inhabited by the Amorites, and near the cities of the plain (Gen. xiv. 7). In 2 Chron. xx. 1, 2, bands of the Moabites and Ammonites are described as coming up against king Jehoshaphat, apparently round the south end of the Dead Sea, as far as En-gedi. And this, as we learn from Dr. Robinson, is the route taken by the Arabs in their marauding expeditions at the present day. It has been identified with the Ain-jidy of the Arabs, situated at a point of the western shore, nearly equidistant from both extremities of the lake. The site lies among the mountains which here confine the lake, a considerable way down the descent to its shore. Here is the beautiful fountain of Ain-jidy, bursting forth at once in a fine stream upon a sort of narrow terrace or shelf of the mountain, above 400 feet above the level of the lake. The whole of the descent below appears to have been once terraced for tillage and gardens; and near the foot are the ruins of a town, exhibiting nothing of particular interest, and built mostly of unhewn stones. This we may conclude to have been the town which took its name from the fountain.

THE WILDERNESS OF EN-GEDI is doubtless the immediately neighbouring part of the wild region, west of the Dead Sea, which must be traversed to reach its shores. It was here that David and his men lived among the ' rocks of the wild goats,' and where the former cut off the skirts of Saul's robe in a cave (1 Sam. xxi. 1-4). · On all sides,' says Dr. Robinson, ' the country is full of caverns, which might then serve as lurking-places for David and his men, as they do for outlaws at the present day.'

ENGINES OF WAR were certainly known much earlier than the Greek writers appear to admit, since figures of them occur in Egyptian monuments, where two kinds of the testudo, or pent-house, used as shelters for the besiegers, are represented, and a colossal lance, worked by men who, under the cover of a testudo, drive the point between the stones of a city wall. The chief projectiles were the catapulta for throwing darts, and the balista for throwing stones. Both these kinds of instruments were prepared by

Uzziah for the defence of Jerusalem (2 Chron. xxvi. 15), and battering the wall is mentioned in the reign of king David (2 Sam. xx. 15); but the instrument itself for throwing it down may have been that above-noticed, and not the battering-ram. The ram was, however, a simple machine, and capable of demolishing the strongest walls, provided access to the foot was practicable; for the mass of cast metal which formed the head could be fixed to a beam lengthened sufficiently to require between one and two hundred men to lift and impel it; and when it was still heavier, and hung in the lower floor of a moveable tower, it became a most formidable engine of war—one

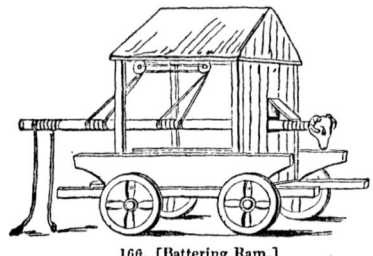

166. [Battering Ram.]

used in all great sieges from the time of Demetrius, about B.C. 306, till long after the invention of gunpowder. Towers of this kind were largely used at the destruction of Jerusalem by the Romans. Of the balistæ and catapultæ it may be proper to add that they were of various powers. For battering walls there were some that threw stones of fifty, others of one hundred, and some of three hundred weight; in the field of battle they were of much inferior strength. Darts varied similarly from small beams to large arrows, and the range they had, exceeded a quarter of a mile, or about 450 yards. All these engines were constructed upon the principle of the sling, the bow, or the spring, the last being an elastic bar, bent back by a screw or a cable of

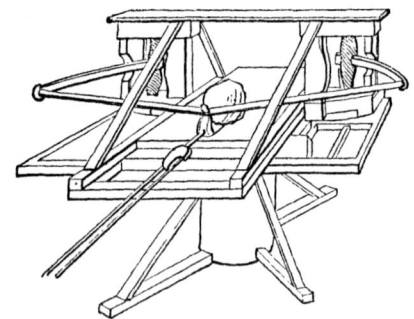

167. [Balista.]

sinews, with a trigger to set it free, and contrived either to impel darts by its stroke, or to throw stones from a kind of spoon formed towards the summit of the spring.

E'NOCH (*initiated*). Four persons bearing this name are mentioned in the Old Testament, the most distinguished of whom was the son of Jared and father of Methuselah. According to the Old Testament, *he walked with God;* and, after 365 years, *he was not, for God took him* (Gen. v. 24). The inspired writer of the Epistle to the Hebrews says, ' By faith Enoch was translated that he should not see death, and was not found, because God had translated him ' (xi. 5). *Walking with God* implies the closest fellowship with Jehovah which it is possible for a human being to enjoy on earth. As a reward, therefore, of his extraordinary sanctity, he was transported into heaven without the experience of death. Elijah was in like manner translated; and thus was the doctrine of immortality *palpably* taught under the ancient dispensation.

ENOCH, BOOK OF. The interest that once attached to the apocryphal book of Enoch has now partly subsided. Yet a document quoted, as is generally believed, by an inspired apostle, can never be wholly devoid of importance or utility in sacred literature.

With regard to the author of the book and the time when it was written, various conflicting opinions have been promulgated. Without entering into the controversy, we may state that it seems to us to have been composed a little before Christ's appearance, by a Jew who had studied well the book of Daniel. Several circumstances render it apparent that it was originally composed in the Hebrew or Chaldee language.

The Greek translation, in which it was known to the fathers, appears to be irrecoverably lost. There is no trace of it after the eighth century.

The leading object of the writer, who was manifestly imbued with deep piety, was to comfort and strengthen his contemporaries. He lived in times of distress and persecution, when the enemies of religion oppressed the righteous. The outward circumstances of the godly were such as to excite doubts of the divine equity in their minds, or at least to prevent it from having that hold on their faith which was necessary to sustain them in the hour of trial. In accordance with this, the writer exhibits the reward of the righteous and the punishment of the wicked. To give greater authority to his affirmations, he puts them into the mouth of Enoch. Thus they have all the weight belonging to the character of an eminent prophet and saint. Various digressions are not without their bearing on the author's main purpose. The narrative of the fallen angels and their punishment, as also of the flood, exemplifies the retributive justice of Jehovah; while the Jewish history, continued down to the Maccabees, exhibits the final triumph of His people, notwithstanding all their vicissitudes. Doubtless the author lived amid fiery trial; and, looking abroad over the desolation, sought to cheer the sufferers by the consideration that they should be recompensed in another life. As for their wicked oppressors, they were to experience terrible judgments. The writer seems to delight in uttering dire anathemas against the wicked. It is plain that the book grew out of the time when the author lived, and the circumstances by which he was surrounded. It gives us a glimpse not only of the religious opinions, but also of the general features that characterized the period.

The question, Did Jude really quote the book of Enoch? has given rise to a good deal of discussion. Some are most unwilling to believe that an inspired writer could cite an Apocryphal production. Such an opinion destroys, in their view, the character of the writing said to be inspired. and reduces it to the level of an ordinary composition. But this is preposterous. The Apostle Paul quotes several of the heathen poets; yet who ever supposed that by such references he sanctions the productions from which his citations are made, or renders them of greater value? All that can be reasonably inferred from such a fact is, that if the inspired writer cites a particular sentiment with approbation, it must be regarded as just and right, irrespective of the remainder of the book in which it is found. The Apostle's sanction extends no farther than the passage to which he alludes. Other portions of the original document may exhibit the most absurd and superstitious notions.

Others suppose that Jude quoted a *traditional* prophecy or saying of Enoch, and we see no improbability in the assumption. Others, again, believe that the words apparently cited by Jude were suggested to him by the Holy Spirit. But surely this hypothesis is unnecessary. Until it can be shown that the book of Enoch did not exist in the time of Jude, or that his quoting it is unworthy of an Apostle, or that such knowledge was not handed down traditionally within the Apostle's reach, we abide by the opinion that Jude really quoted the book of Enoch. While there are probable grounds for believing that Jude might have become acquainted with the circumstance independently of inspiration, we ought not to have recourse to the hypothesis of *immediate suggestion.* On the whole, it is most likely that the book of Enoch existed before the time of Jude, and that the latter really quoted it in accordance with the current tradition. If so, the prophecy ascribed to Enoch was *truly* ascribed to him, because it is scarcely credible that Jude writing by inspiration would have sanctioned a false statement.

Presuming that it was written by a Jew, the book before us is an important document in the history of Jewish opinions. It indicates an essential portion of the Jewish creed before the appearance of Christ; and assists us in comparing the theological views of the later with those of the earlier Jews. It also serves to establish the fact that some doctrines of great importance in the eyes of evangelical Christians ought not to be regarded as the growth of an age in which Christianity had been corrupted by the inventions of men. We would not appeal to it as possessing *authority.* The place of *authority* can be assigned to the Bible alone. But apart from all ideas of *authority,* it may be fairly regarded as an index of the state of opinion at the time when it was written. Hence it subserves the confirmation of certain opinions, provided they can be shown to have a good foundation in the word of God. If it be conceded that certain doctrines are contained by express declaration or fair inference in the volume of inspiration, it is surely some attestation of their truth that they lie on the surface of this ancient book. Let us briefly allude to several representations which occur in its pages:—

1. Respecting the nature of the Deity.—There are distinct allusions to a plurality in the God-

head. The doctrine of the Trinity seems to have been received by the writer and his contemporaries.

In accordance with this view Christ is represented as *existing from eternity*: as the object of invocation and worship; and as the supreme Judge of men and angels.

2. The doctrine of a future state of retribution is implied in many passages, and the *eternity* of future punishment is also distinctly contained in it.

Whatever value may be attached to the theological opinions expressed in the book of Enoch, it is apparent from these statements that certain sentiments to which evangelical Christians assign a high importance, because, in their view, they are contained in Scripture, appear to have prevailed at the commencement of the Christian era. To the serious inquirer they can never be of trifling interest.

E'NON. [Ænon.]

EN-RO'GEL. The name means *Foot-fountain*, and is construed by the Targum into 'Fuller's Fountain,' because the fullers trod the clothes there with their feet. It was near Jerusalem, on the boundary-line between the tribes of Judah and Benjamin (Josh. xv. 7; xviii. 6; 2 Sam. xvii. 17; 1 Kings i. 9). It has been usually supposed the same as the Fountain of Siloam. But Dr. Robinson is more inclined to find it in what is called by Frank Christians the Well of Nehemiah, but by the native inhabitants the Well of Job. There are only three sources, or rather receptacles of living water, now accessible at Jerusalem, and this is one of them. It is situated just below the junction of the Valley of Hinnom with that of Jehoshaphat. It is a very deep well, measuring 125 feet in depth; 50 feet of which were, at the time of Dr. Robinson's visit (in the middle of April), nearly full of water. The water is sweet, but not very cold, and at the present day is drawn up by the hand.

ENSIGNS. [Standards.]

EPENE'TUS, a Christian resident at Rome when Paul wrote his Epistle to the Church in that city, and one of the persons to whom he sent special salutations (Rom. xvi. 5). In the received text he is spoken of as being '*the first fruits of Achaia;*' but 'the first fruits of *Asia*' is the reading of the best MSS.

EP'APHRAS, an eminent teacher in the church at Colossæ, denominated by Paul 'his dear fellow-servant,' and 'a faithful minister of Christ' (Coloss. i. 7; iv. 12). From Paul's Epistle to Philemon it appears that he suffered imprisonment with the Apostle at Rome. It has been inferred from Coloss. i. 7, that he was the founder of the Colossian Church, and most probably he was one of its earliest and most zealous instructors.

EPAPHRODI'TUS, a messenger of the church at Philippi to the Apostle Paul during his imprisonment at Rome, who was entrusted with their contributions for his support (Phil. ii. 25; iv. 18). Paul's high estimate of his character is shown by an accumulation of honourable epithets, and by fervent expressions of gratitude for his recovery from a dangerous illness brought on in part by a generous disregard of his personal welfare in ministering to the Apostle (Phil. ii. 30). Epaphroditus, on his return to Philippi,

was the bearer of the epistle which forms part of the canon.

EPHAH, a dry measure of capacity, equivalent to the bath for liquids. It contained three pecks and three pints. [Weights and Measures.]

EPHE'SIANS, EPISTLE TO THE. This Epistle expressly claims to be the production of the Apostle Paul (i. 1; iii. 1); and this claim the writer in the latter of these passages follows up by speaking of himself in language such as that Apostle is accustomed to use in describing his own position as an ambassador of Christ (iii. 1, 3, 8, 9). The justice of this claim seems to have been universally admitted by the early Christians, and it is expressly sanctioned by several of the fathers of the second and third centuries.

The question to whom was this Epistle addressed has received different answers. Grotius, reviving the opinion of the ancient heretic Marcion, maintains that the party addressed in this Epistle was the church at Laodicea, and that we have in this the Epistle to that church which is commonly supposed to have been lost; whilst others contend that this was addressed to no church in particular, but was a sort of circular letter, intended for the use of several churches, of which Ephesus may have been the first or centre.

Without entering into a minute consideration of these theories, which our limits will not permit, we may remark that both are unsupported by satisfactory evidence, and that we fully concur in the common opinion that the party to whom this Epistle was sent was the church at Ephesus.

The Epistle is so much the utterance of a mind overflowing with thought and feeling that it does not present any precisely marked divisions under which its different parts may be ranked. After the usual apostolic salutation Paul breaks forth into an expression of thanksgiving to God and Christ for the scheme of redemption (i. 3-10), from which he passes to speak of the privileges actually enjoyed by himself and those to whom he was writing, through Christ (i. 11-23). He then reminds the Ephesians of their former condition when they were without Christ, and of the great change which, through divine grace, they had experienced (ii. 1-22). An allusion to himself as enjoying by divine revelation the knowledge of the mystery of Christ leads the Apostle to enlarge upon the dignity of his office and the blessed results that were destined to flow from the exercise of it to others (iii. 1-12). On this he grounds an exhortation to his brethren not to faint on account of his sufferings for the Gospel, and affectionately invokes on their behalf the divine blessing, concluding this, which may be called the more doctrinal part of his Epistle, with a doxology to God (iii. 13-21). What follows is chiefly hortatory, and is directed partly to the inculcation of general consistency, stedfastness in the faith, and propriety of deportment (iv. 1; v. 21), and partly to the enforcement of relative duties (v. 22; vi. 9). The Epistle concludes with an animated exhortation to fortitude, watchfulness and prayer, followed by a reference to Tychicus as the bearer of the Epistle, and by the usual apostolic benediction (vi. 10-24).

This Epistle was written during the earlier part of the Apostle's imprisonment at Rome, at the same time with that to the Colossians [COLOSSIANS, EPISTLE TO THE].

EPH'ESUS, an old and celebrated city, capital of Ionia, one of the twelve Ionian cities in Asia Minor in the Mythic times. It lay on the river Cayster, not far from the coast of the Icarian sea, between Smyrna and Miletus. It was also one of the most considerable of the Greek cities in Asia Minor; but while, about the epoch of the introduction of Christianity, the other cities declined, Ephesus rose more and more. It owed its prosperity in part to the favour of its governors, for Lysimachus named the city Arsinoe, in honour of his second wife, and Attalus Philadelphus furnished it with splendid wharfs and docks; iu part to the favourable position of the place, which naturally made it the emporium of Asia on this side the Taurus. Under the Romans Ephesus was the capital not only of Ionia, but of the entire province of Asia, and bore the honourable title of the first and greatest metropolis of Asia. In the days of Paul Jews were found settled in the city in no inconsiderable number, and from them the Apostle collected a Christian community (Acts xviii. 19; xix. 1; xx. 16), which, being fostered and extended by the hand of Paul himself, became the centre of Christianity in Asia Minor. On leaving the city the Apostle left Timothy there (1 Tim. i. 3): at a later period, according to a tradition which prevailed extensively in ancient times, we find the Apostle John in Ephesus, where he employed himself most diligently for the spread of the Gospel, and where he not only died, at a very old age, but was buried, with Mary the mother of the Lord. In the book of Revelations (ii. 1) a favourable testimony is borne to the Christian churches at Ephesus.

The classic celebrity of this city is chiefly owing to its famous temple, and the goddess in whose honour it was built, namely, 'Diana of the Ephesians.' This goddess has been already noticed, and a figure given of her famous image at Ephesus [DIANA].

Around the image of the goddess was afterwards erected, according to Callimachus, a large and splendid temple. This temple was burnt down on the night in which Alexander was born, by an obscure person of the name of Eratostratus, who thus sought to transmit his name to posterity; and, as it seemed somewhat unaccountable that the goddess should permit a place which redounded so much to her honour to be thus recklessly destroyed, it was given out that Diana was so engaged with Olympias, in aiding to bring Alexander into the world, that she had no time nor thought for any other concern. At a subsequent period, Alexander made an offer to rebuild the temple, provided he was allowed to inscribe his name on the front, which the Ephesians refused. Aided, however, by the whole of Asia Minor, they succeeded in erecting a still more magnificent temple, which the ancients have lavishly praised and placed among the seven wonders of the world. It took two hundred and twenty years to complete. It was built of cedar, cypress, white marble, and even gold, with which it glittered. Costly and magnificent offerings of various kinds were made to the

goddess, and treasured in the temple; such as paintings, statues, &c., the value of which almost exceeded computation. The fame of the temple, of the goddess, and of the city itself, was spread not only through Asia but the world, a celebrity which was enhanced and diffused the more readily because sacred games were practised there, which called competitors and spectators from every country. Among his other enormities Nero is said to have despoiled the temple of Diana of much of its treasure. It continued to conciliate no small portion of respect, till it was finally burnt by the Goths in the reign of Gallienus. The 'silver shrines' of the Ephesian Artemis, mentioned in Acts xix. 24, have been already noticed [DEMETRIUS, 3].

Ephesus was celebrated for the constant use of those arts which pretend to lay open the secrets of nature, and arm the hand of man with supernatural powers, no less than for the refinements of a voluptuous and artificial civilization. Indeed, in the age of Jesus and his Apostles, adepts in the occult sciences were numerous: they travelled from country to country, and were found in great numbers in Asia, deceiving the credulous multitude and profiting by their expectations. They were sometimes Jews, who referred their skill and even their forms of proceeding to Solomon, who is still regarded in the East as head or prince of magicians (Acts viii. 9; xiii. 6, 8). In Asia Minor Ephesus had a high reputation for magical arts.

The books mentioned Acts xix. 19, were doubtless books of magic. How extensively they were in use may be learnt from the fact that 'the price of them' was 'fifty thousand pieces of silver.' Very celebrated were the Ephesian letters, which appear to have been a sort of magical formulæ written on paper or parchment, designed to be fixed as amulets on different parts of the body, such as the hands and the head. Erasmus says that they were certain signs or marks which rendered their possessor victorious in everything.

The ruins of Ephesus lie two short days' journey from Smyrna, in proceeding from which towards the south-east the traveller passes the pretty village of Sedekuy; and two hours and a half onwards he comes to the ruined village of Danizzi, on a wide, solitary, uncultivated plain, beyond which several burial-grounds may be observed; near one of these, on an eminence, are the supposed ruins of Ephesus, consisting of shattered walls, in which some pillars, architraves, and fragments of marble have been built. The soil of the plain appears rich. It is covered with a rank, burnt-up vegetation, and is everywhere deserted and solitary, though bordered by picturesque mountains. A few corn-fields are scattered along the site of the ancient city, which is marked by some large masses of shapeless ruins and stone walls. Towards the sea extends the ancient port, a pestilential marsh. Along the slope of the mountain and over the plain are scattered fragments of masonry and detached ruins, but nothing can now be fixed upon as the great temple of Diana. There are some broken columns and capitals of the Corinthian order of white marble: there are also ruins of a theatre, consisting of some circular seats and numerous arches, supposed to be the one in which Paul was

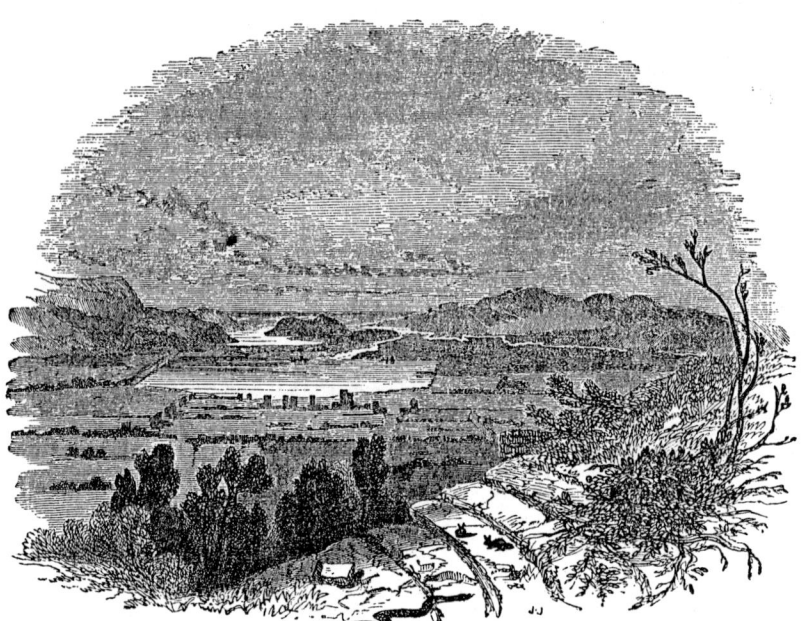

168. [Ephesus.]

preaching when interrupted by shouts of, 'Great is Diana of the Ephesians.' A splendid circus or stadium remains tolerably entire, and there are numerous piles of buildings seen alike at Pergamus and Troy as well as here, by some called gymnasia, by others temples; by others again, with more propriety, palaces. They all came with the Roman conquest. No one but a Roman emperor could have conceived such structures. In Italy they have parallels in Adrian's villa near Tivoli, and perhaps in the pile upon the Palatine. Many other walls remain to show the extent of the buildings of the city, but no inscription or ornament is to be found, cities having been built out of this quarry of worked marble. The ruins of the adjoining town, which rose about four hundred years ago, are entirely composed of materials from Ephesus. There are a few huts within these ruins (about a mile and a half from Ephesus), which still retain the name of the parent city, *Asalook*—a Turkish word, which is associated with the same idea as Ephesus, meaning the City of the Moon. A church dedicated to St. John is thought to have stood near, if not on the site of, the present mosque. The tomb of St. John was in or under his church.

Though Ephesus presents few traces of human life, and little but scattered and mutilated remains of its ancient grandeur, yet the environs, diversified as they are with hill and dale, and not scantily supplied with wood and water, present many features of great beauty.

When Dr. Chandler visited Ephesus in 1764, 'Its population consisted of a few Greek peasants, living in extreme wretchedness, dependence, and insensibility, the representatives of an illustrious people, and inhabiting the wreck of their greatness—some the substructure of the glorious edifices which they raised; some beneath the vaults of the stadium, once the crowded scene of their diversions; and some in the abrupt precipice, in the sepulchres which received their ashes. Such are the present citizens of Ephesus, and such is the condition to which that renowned city has been reduced. However much the Church at Ephesus may (Rev. ii. 2), in its earliest days, have merited praise for its 'works, labour, and patience,' yet it appears soon to have 'left its first love,' and to have received in vain the admonition — 'Remember, therefore, from whence thou art fallen, and repent and do the first works; or else I will come unto thee quickly, and will remove thy candlestick out of his place, except thou repent.' If any repentance was produced by this solemn warning, its effects were not durable, and the place has long since afforded an evidence of the truth of prophecy, and the certainty of the divine threatenings, as well as a melancholy subject for thought to the contemplative Christian. Its fate is that of the once-flourishing seven churches of Asia: its fate is that of the entire country—a garden has become a desert. Busy centres of civilization, spots where the refinements and delights of the age were collected, are now a prey to silence, destruction, and death. Consecrated first of all to the purposes of idolatry, Ephesus next had Christian temples almost rivalling the pagan in splendour, wherein the image of the great Diana lay prostrate before the cross; and, after the lapse of some centuries, Jesus gives place to Mahomed, and the crescent glittered on the dome of the recently Christian church. A few more scores of years, and Ephesus has neither temple, cross, crescent, nor city, but is 'a desolation, a dry land, and a wilderness.' Even the sea has retired from the scene of devastation, and a pestilential morass, covered with mud and rushes, has succeeded to the waters which brought up ships laden with merchandise from every part of the known world.

E'PHOD, an article of dress worn by the Hebrew priests. [PRIESTS.]

E'PHRAIM (*fruitfulness*), the younger son of Joseph, but who received precedence over the elder in and from the blessing of Jacob (Gen. xli. 52; xlviii. 1). That blessing was an adoptive act, whereby Ephraim and his brother Manasseh were counted as sons of Jacob in the place of their father; the object being to give to Joseph, through his sons, a double portion in the brilliant prospects of his house. Thus the descendants of Joseph formed *two* of the tribes of Israel, whereas every other of Jacob's sons counted but as one. There were thus, in fact, thirteen tribes of Israel; but the number twelve is usually preserved, either by excluding that of Levi (which had no territory), when Ephraim and Manasseh are separately named, or by counting these two together as the tribe of Joseph, when Levi is included in the account. The intentions of Jacob were fulfilled, and Ephraim and Manasseh were counted as tribes of Israel at the departure from Egypt, and as such shared in the territorial distribution of the Promised Land (Num. i. 33; Josh. xvii. 14; 1 Chron. vii. 20).

At the departure from Egypt the population of the two tribes of Ephraim and Manasseh together amounted to 72,700 men capable of bearing arms, greatly exceeding that of any single tribe, except Judah, which had somewhat more. During the wandering their number increased to 95,200, which placed the two tribes much higher than even Judah. At the Exode, Ephraim singly had 40,500, and Manasseh only 32,200; but a great change took place in their relative numbers during the wandering. Ephraim lost 8000, and Manasseh gained 20,500; so that just before entering Canaan, Ephraim stood at 32,500, and Manasseh at 52,700.

One of the finest and most fruitful parts of Palestine, occupying the very centre of the land, was assigned to this tribe. It extended from the borders of the Mediterranean on the west to the Jordan on the east: on the north it had the half-tribe of Manasseh, and on the south Benjamin and Dan (Josh. xvi. 5, sq.; xvii. 7, sq.). This fine country included most of what was afterwards called Samaria, as distinguished from Judæa on the one hand, and from Galilee on the other. The tabernacle and the ark were deposited within its limits, at Shiloh; and the possession of the sacerdotal establishment, which was a central object of attraction to all the other tribes, must in no small degree have enhanced its importance, and increased its wealth and population. The domineering and haughty spirit of the Ephraimites is more than once indicated (Josh. xvii. 14; Judg. viii. 1-3; xii. 1) before the establishment of the regal government; but the particular enmity of Ephraim against the other great tribe of Judah, and the rivalry between them, do not come out distinctly until the establishment of the monarchy. In the election of Saul from the least considerable tribe in Israel, there was nothing to excite the jealousy of

Ephraim; and, after his heroic qualities had conciliated respect, it rendered the new king true allegiance and support. But when the great tribe of Judah produced a king in the person of David, the pride and jealousy of Ephraim were thoroughly awakened, and it was doubtless chiefly through their means that Abner was enabled to uphold for a time the house of Saul; for there are manifest indications that by this time Ephraim influenced the views and feelings of all the other tribes. They were at length driven by the force of circumstances to acknowledge David upon conditions; and were probably not without hope that, as the king of the nation at large, he would establish his capital in their central portion of the land. But when he not only established his court at Jerusalem, but proceeded to remove the ark thither, making his native Judah the seat both of the theocratical and civil government, the Ephraimites became thoroughly alienated, and longed to establish their own ascendancy. The building of the temple at Jerusalem, and other measures of Solomon, strengthened this desire; and although the minute organization and vigour of his government prevented any overt acts of rebellion, the train was then laid, which, upon his death, rent the ten tribes from the house of David, and gave to them a king, a capital, and a religion suitable to the separate views and interests of the tribe. Thenceforth the rivalry of Ephraim and Judah was merged in that between the two kingdoms; although still the predominance of Ephraim in the kingdom of Israel was so conspicuous as to occasion the whole realm to be called by its name, especially when that rivalry is mentioned.

2. EPHRAIM, a city in the wilderness of Judæa, to which Jesus withdrew from the persecution which followed the miracle of raising Lazarus from the dead (John xi. 54). It is placed by Eusebius eight Roman miles north of Jerusalem. This indication would seem to make it the same with the Ephrain which is mentioned in 2 Chron. xiii. 19, along with Bethel and Jeshanah, as towns taken from Jeroboam by Abijah.

3. EPHRAIM, a mountain or group of mountains in central Palestine, in the tribe of the same name, on or towards the borders of Benjamin (Josh. xvii. 15; xix. 50; xx. 7; Judg. vii. 24; xvii. 1; 1 Sam. ix. 4; 1 Kings iv. 8). From a comparison of these passages it may be collected that the name of 'Mount Ephraim' was applied to the whole of the ranges and groups of hills which occupy the central part of the southernmost border of this tribe, and which are prolonged southward into the tribe of Benjamin. In the time of Joshua these hills were densely covered with trees (Josh. xvii. 18), which is by no means the case at present.

4. EPHRAIM, THE FOREST OF, in which Absalom lost his life (2 Sam. xviii. 6-8), was in the country east of the Jordan, not far from Mahanaim. How it came to bear the name of a tribe on the other side the river is not known.

EPH'RATAH, otherwise BETHLEHEM, which see.

E'PHRON, a Hittite residing in Hebron, who sold to Abraham the cave and field of Machpelah as a family sepulchre (Gen. xxiii. 6).

EPISTLES. In directing our inquiry first of

all towards the relation in which the Epistles stand to the other component parts of the New Testament, we find that both the Old and New Testament have been arranged by divine wisdom after one and the same plan. All the revelations of God to mankind rest upon history. Therefore in the Old, as well as in the New Testament, the history of the deeds of God stands FIRST, as being the basis of Holy Writ; thereupon follow the books which exhibit the doctrines and internal life of the men of God—in the Old Testament the Psalms, the writings of Solomon, &c., and in the New Testament the Epistles of the Apostles; finally, there follow in the Old Testament the writings of the prophets, whose vision extends into the times of the New Testament; and at the conclusion of the New Testament stands its only prophetic book, the Revelation of John.

In this also we must thankfully adore divine wisdom, that the Epistles, which lay down the doctrines of the Christian religion, originate, not from one Apostle alone, but from all the four principal Apostles; so that one and the same divine truth is presented to our eyes in various forms as it were in various mirrors, by which its richness and manifold character are the better displayed.

The Epistles of the New Testament divide themselves into two parts—the PAULINE and the so-called CATHOLIC.

The PAULINE Epistles are thirteen in number; or fourteen, if we add to them the Epistle to the Hebrews. The very peculiar character of the Pauline Epistles is so striking as to leave not the least doubt of their genuineness. Depth of thought, fire of speech, firmness of character—these manly features, joined withal to the indulgence of feelings of the most devoted love and affection, characterize these Epistles. The amiable personal character of the Apostle may be most beautifully traced in his Epistles to the Philippians and to Philemon.

All the Epistles, except the one to the Romans, were called forth by circumstances and particular occasions in the affairs of the communities to which they were addressed. Not all, however, were preserved; it is, at least, evident, from 1 Cor. v. 9, that a letter to the Corinthians has been lost; from Col. iv. 16, it has also been concluded —though probably erroneously, since there perhaps the letter to the Ephesians is referred to— that another letter to the community of Laodicea has likewise been lost. Press of business usually compelled Paul—what was, besides, not uncommon in those times—to use his companions as amanuenses. He mentions (Gal. vi. 11), as something peculiar, that he had written this letter with his own hand. Paul himself exhorted the communities mutually to impart to each other his letters to them, and read them aloud in their assemblies (Col. iv. 16). It is therefore probable that copies of these letters had been early made by the several communities, and deposited in the form of collections.

The letters of Paul may be chronologically arranged into those written before his Roman imprisonment, and those written during and after it; thus beginning with his first letter to the Thessalonians, and concluding with his second to Timothy, embracing an interval of about ten years (A.D. 54-64). In our Bibles, however, the letters are arranged according to the pre-eminent parts and stations of the communities to whom they were addressed, and conclude with the Epistles to the two bishops and a private letter to Philemon.

THE CATHOLIC EPISTLES.—There is, in the first instance, a diversity of opinion respecting their name: some refer it to their WRITERS (letters from all the other Apostles who had entered the stage of authorship along with Paul); some, again, to their CONTENTS (letters of no special but general Christian tenor); others, again, to the RECEIVERS (letters addressed to no community in particular). This last opinion is most decidedly justified by passages from the ancient writers. The Pauline Epistles had all their particular directions, while the letters of Peter, James, 1 John, and Jude were circular epistles. The Epistles 2 and 3 John were subsequently added, and included on account of their shortness, and to this collection was given the name CATHOLIC LETTERS, in contradistinction to the PAULINE.

ERAS'TUS, a Corinthian, and one of Paul's disciples, whose salutations he sends from Corinth to the Church at Rome as those of 'the chamberlain of the city' (Rom. xvi. 23). The words so rendered denote the city treasurer or steward, an officer of great dignity in ancient times. We find this Erastus with Paul at Ephesus, whence he was sent along with Timothy into Macedonia (Acts xix. 22). They were both with the Apostle at Corinth when he wrote, as above, from that city to the Romans: at a subsequent period Erastus was still at Corinth (2 Tim. iv. 20), which would seem to have been the usual place of his abode.

E'RECH, one of the cities which formed the beginning of Nimrod's kingdom in the plain of Shinar (Gen. x. 10). It is not said that he built these cities, but that he established his power over them; from which we may conclude that they previously existed. Bochart seeks the name in the Aracca or Aracha of the old geographers, which was on the Tigris, upon the borders of Babylonia and Susiana. Rosenmüller happily conjectures that Erech probably lay nearer to Babylon than Aracca; and this has been lately confirmed by Col. Taylor, the British resident at Bagdad, who is disposed to find the site of the ancient Erech in the great mounds of primitive ruins, indifferently called Irak, Irka, and Senkerah, by the nomade Arabs: and sometimes El Asayiah, 'the place of pebbles.' These mounds, which are now surrounded by the almost perpetual marshes and inundations of the lower Euphrates, lie some miles east of that stream, about midway between the site of Babylon and its junction with the Tigris.

E'SAR-HADDON. [ASSYRIA.]

E'SAU (*hairy, rough*). The origin and meaning of the name are not quite free from ambiguity; Simon deriving it from a word signifying covered with hair; and some such reason as this implies, seems involved in the passage Gen. xxv. 25. Cruden, however, explains the name as meaning *one who does*, an actor or agent. His surname of Edom (red) was given him, it appears (Gen. xxv. 30), from the red pottage which he asked of Jacob. Esau was the eldest son of 'Isaac, Abraham's son' (Gen. xxv. 19) by Rebekah, 'the daughter of Bethuel the Syrian of Padan-aram, the sister to Laban the Syrian.'

The marriage remaining for some time (about 19 years: compare xxv. 20, 26) unproductive, Isaac entreated Jehovah, and she became pregnant. Led by peculiar feelings 'to inquire of Jehovah,' Rebekah was informed that she should give birth to twins, whose fate would be as diverse as their character, and, what in those days was stranger still, that the elder should serve the younger. On occasion of her delivery the child that was born first was 'red, all over like an hairy garment; and they called his name Esau.' Immediately afterwards Jacob was born.

In process of time the different natural endowments of the two boys began to display their effects in dissimilar aptitudes and pursuits. While Jacob was led by his less robust make and quiet disposition to fulfil the duties of a shepherd's life, and pass his days in and around his tent, Esau was impelled by the ardour and lofty spirit which agitated his bosom, to seek in the toils, adventures, and perils of the chace, his occupation and sustenance: and, as is generally the case in natures like his, he gained high repute by his skill and daring.

A hunter's life is of necessity one of uncertainty as well as hardship; days pass in which the greatest vigilance and the most strenuous exertions may fail even to find, much less capture, game. Esau had on one occasion experienced such a disappointment, and, wearied with his unproductive efforts, exhausted for want of sustenance, and despairing of capturing any prey, he was fain to turn his steps to his father's house for succour in his extremity. On reaching home he found his brother enjoying a carefully prepared dish of pottage: attracted by the odour of which he besought Jacob to allow him to share in the meal. His brother saw the exigency in which Esau was, and determined not to let it pass unimproved. Accordingly he puts a price on the required food. Esau was the elder, and had in consequence immunities and privileges which were of high value. The surrender of these to himself Jacob makes the condition of his complying with Esau's petition. Urged by the cravings of hunger, alarmed even by the fear of instant death, Esau sold his birth-right to his younger brother, confirming the contract by the sanction of an oath. Jacob having thus got his price, supplied the famishing Esau with needful refreshments.

Arrived now at years of maturity, Esau, when 40 years of age, married two wives, Judith and Bashemath. Some unhappy feelings appear to have previously existed in the family; for while Esau was a favourite with his father, in consequence, it appears, of the presents of venison which the youth gave him, Jacob was regarded with special affection by the mother. These partialities, and their natural consequences in unamiable feelings, were increased and exaggerated by Esau's marriage. Even his father's preference of him may have been injuriously affected. The way was thus in some measure smoothed for the transference of the coveted birthright to the younger son.

The time for the fulfilment of the compact between the brothers at length arrived. Isaac is 'sick unto death.' His appetite, as well as his strength, having failed, is only to be gratified by provocatives. He desires some savoury venison,

and gives the requisite instructions to Esau, who accordingly proceeds in quest of it. On this Rebekah begins to feel that the critical time has come. If the hated Hittites are not to enter with her less favoured son into possession of the family property, the sale of the birthright must now in some way be confirmed and consummated. One essential particular remained—the father's blessing. If this should be given to Esau, all hope was gone; for this, like our modern wills, would hand the inheritance and the accompanying headship of the tribe to Esau and his wives.

Isaac, however, had lost his sight—indeed, all his senses were dull and feeble. It was therefore not very difficult to pass off Jacob upon him as Esau. Rebekah takes her measures, and, notwithstanding Jacob's fears, succeeds. Isaac, indeed, is not without suspicion, but a falsehood comes to aid Jacob in his otherwise discreditable personation of Esau. The blessing is pronounced, and thus the coveted property and ascendancy are secured. The affectionate endearments which pass between the deceiver and the abused old blind father, stand in painful contrast with the base trickery by which mother and son had accomplished their end.

Esau, however, returns from the field, approaches his decrepid and sightless father, declaring who he is. 'And Isaac trembled very exceedingly, and said, Who? where is he that hath taken venison and brought it me, and I have eaten of all before thou camest, and have blessed him?—yea, and he shall be blessed.' On this Esau becomes agitated, and entreats a blessing for himself—'Bless me, even me also, O my father.' Urging this entreaty again and again, even with tears, Isaac at length said unto him, 'Behold, thy dwelling shall be the fatness of the earth, and of the dew of heaven from above; and by thy sword shalt thou live, and shalt serve thy brother; and it shall come to pass when thou shalt have the dominion that thou shalt break his yoke from off thy neck' (Gen. xxvii.).

Thus, deprived for ever of his birthright, in virtue of the irrevocable blessing, Esau but too naturally conceived and entertained a hatred of Jacob, and even formed a resolution to seize the opportunity for slaying him, which the days of mourning consequent on the approaching decease of their father would be likely to afford. Words to this effect, which Esau let drop, were repeated to his mother, who thereupon prevailed on her younger son to flee to his uncle Laban, who lived in Haran, there to remain until time, with its usual effect, might have mitigated Esau's wrath. Meanwhile Esau had grown powerful in Idumæa, and when, after many years, Jacob intended to return within the borders of the Jordan, he feared lest his elder brother might intercept him on his way, to take revenge for former injuries. He accordingly sent messengers to Esau, in order, if possible, to disarm his wrath. Esau appears to have announced in reply, that he would proceed to meet his returning brother. When, therefore, Jacob was informed that Esau was on his way for this purpose with a band of four hundred men, he was greatly distressed, in fear of that hostility which his conscience told him he had done something to deserve. What then must have been his surprise when he saw Esau running with extended arms to greet and embrace him? and Esau 'fell on his neck, and kissed him, and they wept.' Jacob had prepared a present for Esau, hoping thus to conciliate his favour; but Esau at first courteously refused the gift—' I have enough, my brother, keep that thou hast unto thyself' (Gen. xxxiii.).

The whole of this rencontre serves to show that if Jacob had acquired riches, Esau had gained power and influence as well as property; and the homage which is paid to him indirectly, and by implication, on the part of Jacob, and directly, and in the most marked and respectful manner, by the females and children of Jacob's family, leads to the supposition that he had made himself supreme in the surrounding country of Idumæa.

Esau from this time appears but very little in the sacred narrative. He was ready to accompany Jacob, or to send with him an escort, probably for protection, but Jacob's fears and suspicions induced him to decline these friendly offers; and they separated on the same day that they met, after an interview in which Jacob's bearing is rather that of an inferior to his lord than that of a brother, and Esau's has all the generousness which a high nature feels in forgiving an injury and aiming to do good to the injurer. The latter, we are merely told, ' returned on his way to Seir' (Gen. xxxiii. 16).

Jacob and Esau appear together again at the funeral rites which were paid to their deceased father; but the book of Genesis furnishes no particulars of what took place.

Esau is once more presented to us (Gen. xxxvi.) in a genealogical table, in which a long line of illustrious descendants is referred to 'Esau, the father of the Edomites' (Gen. xxxvi. 43).

ESDRAE'LON, PLAIN OF. [PALESTINE.]

ES'DRAS, BOOKS OF (APOCRYPHA). In several manuscripts of the Latin Vulgate, as well as in all the printed editions anterior to the decree of the Council of Trent, and in many since that period, there will be found four books following each other, entitled the 1st, 2nd, 3rd, and 4th books of Ezra. The two first are the canonical books of Ezra and Nehemiah, the 3rd and 4th form the subject of the present article. They are the same which are called 1st and 2nd Esdras in the English Authorized Version.

The THIRD BOOK OF EZRA is little more than a recapitulation of the history contained in the canonical Ezra, interspersed with some remarkable interpolations, the chief of which are chap. i., taken from 2 Chron. xxxv. xxxvi., part of the last chapter, from Nehem. viii., and the narration of the themes or sentences of Zorobabel and the two other young men of Darius's body-guard (3 Esd. iii. 4). The book is more properly a version than an original work. It was made use of by Josephus, who cites it largely in his *Antiquities*, but nothing further has been ascertained respecting the age either of the original or the translation.

This book was regarded as apocryphal by Jerome, Augustine, and others of the Fathers. It does not appear to have been included in the catalogue of any council, nor has any portion of it been read in the offices of the church. It was also rejected as apocryphal by the Council of Trent.

The FOURTH BOOK OF EZRA is quite of a different character from the former, and it has been even doubted whether it more properly belongs to the Apocrypha of the Old or the New Testament; but the circumstance of the author's personating the celebrated scribe of that name has been supposed to have led to its obtaining a place in the former. It consists of a number of similitudes or visions, resembling in some passages the Apocalypse. The descriptions are acknowledged to be sometimes most spirited and striking, occasionally rising to great sublimity of thought, energy of conception, and elegance of expression.

With regard to its author and age, Jahn supposes the author to have been a Jew, educated in Chaldea, who borrowed his style from Daniel, and who, having become a Christian, still retained his reverence for Cabalistic traditions. He places him in the first or early in the second century. Archbishop Laurence, on the other hand, conceives that the author was a Jew who never changed his creed.

Dr. Lee is strongly of opinion that the author of this book was contemporary with the author of the book of Enoch, or rather that both these books were written by one and the same author. It does not appear that Josephus was aware of its existence.

ESH'BAAL. [ISHBOSHETH.]

1. ESH'COL (*a cluster*), one of the Amoritish chiefs with whom Abraham was in alliance when his camp was near Hebron, and who joined with him in the pursuit of Chedorlaomer and his allies, for the rescue of Lot (Gen. xiv. 13, 24).

2. ESHCOL. The name of the valley in which the Hebrew spies obtained the fine cluster of grapes which they took back with them, borne ' on a staff between two,' as a specimen of the fruits of the Promised Land (Num. xiii. 24). The cluster was doubtless large; but the fact that it was carried in this manner does not, as usually understood, imply that the bunch was as much as two men could carry, seeing that it was probably so carried to prevent its being bruised in the journey. The valley of Eshcol probably took its name from the distinguished Amorite already mentioned, and is hence to be sought in the neighbourhood of Hebron. Accordingly the valley through which lies the commencement of the road from Hebron to Jerusalem is indicated as that of Eshcol. This valley is now full of vineyards and olive-yards; the former chiefly in the valley itself, the latter up the sides of the enclosing hills. 'These vineyards are still very fine, and produce the finest and largest grapes in all the country.'

ES'THER (*a star*), a damsel of the tribe of Benjamin, born during the Exile, and whose family did not avail itself of the permission to return to Palestine, under the edict of Cyrus. Her parents being dead, Esther was brought up by her uncle Mordecai. The reigning king of Persia, Ahasuerus, having divorced his queen, Vashti, on account of the becoming spirit with which she refused to submit to the indignity which a compliance with his drunken commands involved, search was made throughout the empire for the most beautiful maiden to be her successor. Those whom the officers of the harem deemed the most beautiful were removed thither, the eventual choice among them remaining with the king him self. That choice fell on Esther, who found favour in the eyes of Ahasuerus, and was advanced to a station enviable only by comparison with that of the less favoured inmates of the royal harem. Her Jewish origin was at the time unknown; and hence, when she avowed it to the king, she seemed to be included in the doom of extirpation which a royal edict had pronounced against all the Jews in the empire. This circumstance enabled her to turn the royal indignation upon Haman, the chief minister of the king, whose resentment against Mordecai had led him to obtain from the king this monstrous edict. The laws of the empire would not allow the king to recal a decree once uttered; but the Jews were authorized to stand on their defence; and this, with the known change in the intentions of the court, averted the worst consequences of the decree. The Jews established a yearly feast in memory of this deliverance, which is observed among them to this day [Purim]. Such is the substance of the history of Esther, as related in the book which bears her name.

It should be observed that Esther is the name which the damsel received upon her introduction into the royal harem, her Hebrew name having been HADASSAH, *myrtle* (Esth. ii. 7). Esther is most probably a Persian word. According to the second Targum on Esther, 'She was called Esther from the name of the star Venus, which in Greek is *Aster*.'

The difficulties of the history of the book of Esther, especially as regards the identity of the king, have been examined under AHASUERUS, and are also noticed in the following article.

ESTHER, BOOK OF, historical books of Scripture, called by the Jews *Megillah Esther*. In the Christian Church it has been also called *Ahasuerus*.

The Jews hold this book in veneration next to the books of Moses, and there appears to be no authentic foundation for the statement of Richard Baxter (*Saint's Rest*, part iv.), that the book of Esther was treated so ignominiously by the Jews that they were in the habit of throwing it on the ground before reading it.

As the subject of this book has been treated of under the article AHASUERUS, it will be sufficient to refer to that head; only we may here observe that the book of Esther has this peculiarity among the historical books, that although the author, a Persian Jew, records a remarkable preservation from destruction of that portion of his countrymen which remained in Persia after the exile, he does not refer their deliverance to the act of God, whose name is not even once mentioned. This has been explained by supposing that the author wished to avoid giving offence to the Persians, or that the whole was taken from the Persian annals, which are appealed to, ch. x. 2.

The age and authorship of Esther is a question involved in much difficulty. Of the author nothing is known, nor have we any data on which to form a reasonable conjecture.

Some doubts have been thrown on the canonical authority of this book, but whatever hesitation may have been felt by some of the Christian fathers as to its authenticity, it does not appear that it was ever doubted by the Jews or by the Christian Church in its collective capacity.

E'TAM, a town in the tribe of Judah, which was decorated by Solomon with gardens and streams of water, and fortified by Rehoboam along with Bethlehem and Tekoa (1 Chron. iv. 3, 32; 2 Chron. xi. 6). From this place, according to the Rabbins, water was carried by an aqueduct to Jerusalem. Dr. Robinson inclines to find Etam at a place about a mile and a half south of Bethlehem, where there is a ruined village called Urtas, at the bottom of a pleasant valley of the same name. Here there are traces of ancient ruins, and also a fountain, sending forth a copious supply of fine water, which forms a beautiful purling rill along the bottom of the valley. It is usually supposed that 'the rock Etam,' to which Samson withdrew (Judg. xv. 8, 11), was near the town of the same name. Urtas seems too far inland for this; there is, however, a little to the east, the Frank mountain, which (this consideration apart) would have furnished just such a retreat as the hero seems to have found.

E'THAM, the third station of the Israelites when they quitted Egypt [Exodus].

1. E'THAN (*firm*), one of four persons ('Ethan the Ezrahite, and Heman, and Chalcol, and Darda, the sons of Mahol') who were so renowned for their sagacity that it is mentioned to the honour of Solomon that his wisdom excelled theirs. In 1 Kings iv. 31, Ethan is distinguished as 'the Ezrahite,' from the others, who are called 'sons of Mahol'—unless, indeed, this word *Mahol* be taken not as a proper name, but appellatively, for 'sons of music, dancing,' &c., in which case it would apply to Ethan as well as to the others. This interpretation is strengthened by our finding the other names associated with that of Ethan in 1 Chron. ii. 6, as 'sons of Zerah,' *i. e.* of Ezra, the same as Ezrahites. The evidence of identity afforded by this collocation of names is too strong to be resisted; and we must therefore conclude that Ethan and the others, the tradition of whose wisdom had descended to the time of Solomon, are the same who, in 1 Chron. ii. 6, appear as sons of Zerah, who was himself the son of the patriarch Judah. With this agrees the Jewish chronology, which counts them as prophets during the sojourn in Egypt.

2. ETHAN, a Levite, the son of Kishi, and one of the masters of the Temple music (1 Chron. vi. 44; xv. 17), to whom the 89th Psalm is ascribed, and whom some interpreters suppose to be the Ethan of 1 Kings iv. 31, to whose wisdom that of Solomon is compared.

ETH'ANIM. [Tisri.]

ETHIO'PIA is the name by which the English and most other versions render the Hebrew CUSH. As used among the Greeks and Romans, the word was employed, in all the latitude of its etymological meaning, to denote any of the countries where the people are of a sable, sunburnt complexion. But we have shown in the article CUSH (to which we refer the reader) that its use in the language of Scripture is much more restricted, and that while it may sometimes include part of Southern Arabia, it for the most part exclusively designates the 'Ethiopia of Africa,' which is the subject of the present article.

By Ethiopia, or African Cush, in the widest acceptation of the name, the Hebrews understood the whole of the region lying south of Egypt above Syene, the modern Assouan (Ezek. xxix. 10; xxx. 6). Its limits on the west and south were undefined; but they probably regarded it as extending eastward as far as the Red Sea, if not as including some of the islands in that sea, such as the famous Topaz Isle (Job xxviii. 19). It thus corresponded, though only in a vague and general sense, to the countries known to us as Nubia and Abyssinia, so famous for the Nile and other great rivers.

But that part of the vast region of Cush which seems chiefly intended in these and most other passages of Scripture is the tract of country in Upper Nubia, which became famous in antiquity as the *kingdom of Ethiopia*, or the state of Meroë. The Ethiopian nations generally ranked low in the scale of civilization; nevertheless (to use the language of Heeren), there did exist a better cultivated, and, to a certain degree, a civilized Ethiopian people; who dwelt in cities; who erected temples and other edifices; who, though without letters, had hieroglyphics; who had government and laws; and the fame of whose progress in knowledge and the social arts spread in the earliest ages over a considerable part of the earth.' Meroë Proper lay between the river Astaboras (now the Atbara or Tacazzé) on the east, and the Nile on the west. Though not completely enclosed with rivers, it was called an island, because, as Pliny observes, the various streams which flowed around it were all considered as branches of the Nile. Its surface exceeded that of Sicily more than a half, and it corresponded pretty nearly to the present province of Atbara, between 13° and 18° N. lat. In modern times it formed a great part of the kingdom of Sennaar, and the southern portion belongs to Abyssinia. Upon the island of Meroë lay a city of the same name, the metropolis of the kingdom, the site of which has been discovered near a place called Assur, about twenty miles N. of the town of Shendy, under 17° N lat. The splendid ruins of temples, pyramids, and other edifices found here and throughout the district attest the high degree of civilization and art among the ancient Ethiopians.

According to Josephus, the ancient name of Meroë was Seba. Now in the Scriptures this country of African Seba is classed with the Arabian Sheba as a rich but far-distant land (Ps. lxxii. 10). In Isa. xliii. 3, God says to Israel, 'I have given Egypt for thy ransom; Cush and Seba in thy stead:' and in Isa. xlv. 14, 'The wealth of Egypt, and the merchandise of Cush and of the Sebaïm, men of stature, shall pass over to thee and shall be thine.'

In the age of Herodotus, the countries known to us as Nubia and Sennaar were occupied by two different races, one of whom he includes under the general appellation of Ethiopians, the other an immigratory Arabian race leading, for the most part, a nomadic life. This distinction has continued down to the present day. Among the aboriginal inhabitants the first place is due to the Nubians, who are well-formed, strong, and muscular, and with nothing whatever of the negro physiognomy. They go armed with spear, sword, and a shield of the skin of the hippopotamus. South of Dongola is the country of the Scheygias, whose warriors are horsemen, also

armed with a double-pointed spear, a sword, and a large shield (comp. Jer. xlvi. 9, the 'Cushites who handle the shield'). They were completely independent till subdued by Mehemet Ali, pacha of Egypt. It is in their country that the pyramidal monuments which adorned the ancient Meroë are first met with. Next comes the territory of the Berbers, strictly so called, who, though speaking Arabic, evidently belong to the Nubian race. Above these regions beyond the Tacazzé and along the Nile the great mass of the inhabitants, though sometimes with a mixture of other blood, may be regarded as of Arab origin. But between the valley of the Nile and the Red Sea there is still, as of old, a variety of scattered aboriginal tribes, among whom the Arabic is much less common. Some of them spread themselves over the plains of the Astaboras, or Tacazzé, being compelled to remove their encampments, sometimes by the inundations of the river, at other times by the attacks of the dreaded *zimb*, or gad-fly, described by Bruce, and which he supposes to be the 'fly which is in the utmost part of the rivers of Egypt' (Isa. vii. 18). Another remarkable Ethiopic race in ancient times was the *Macrobians*, so called from their supposed longevity. They were represented by the ambassadors of Cambyses as a very tall race, who elected the highest in stature as king: gold was so abundant that they bound their prisoners with golden fetters—circumstances which again remind us of Isaiah's description of Ethiopia and Seba in ch. xlv. 14.

With regard to the ancient civilization of Ethiopia Proper, or the kingdom of Meroë, it was closely connected with the religion of the country, which was the worship of Ammon and his kindred deities, and the 'Oracles of Ammon' were its main support. The government was in the hands of a race or caste of priests, who chose from among themselves a king; and this form continued down to the reign in Egypt of the second Ptolemy, when Ergamenes, at that time king, massacred the priests in their sanctuary, and became absolute monarch.

Of the history of Ethiopia, previous to that last revolution, only scanty information has been preserved, but it is enough to evince its high antiquity and its early aggrandizement. In the Persian period it was certainly an independent and important state, which Cambyses in vain endeavoured to subdue. But its most flourishing era was between the years B.C. 800 and 700, when arose three potent kings, Sabaco, Sevechus, and Tarhako, or Tirhakah, who extended their conquests over a great part of Egypt. Sevechus is supposed to have been the So or Sua king of Egypt, to whom an embassy was sent by Hoshea, king of Israel (2 Kings xvii. 4), whose reign ended B.C. 722. He was thus the contemporary of Salmanassar, king of Assyria, as was Tirhakah of the next Assyrian monarch, Sennacherib, who (about the year B.C. 714) was deterred from the invasion of Egypt merely by the rumour that Tirhakah was advancing against him (2 Kings xix. 9). There seems no reason to doubt that the remarkable prophecy in the 18th chapter of Isaiah was addressed to Tirhakah and his people, to announce to them the sudden overthrow of the Assyrian host before Jerusalem. In verse 7 almost *verbatim*, it is intimated that, struck at the mighty deeds of the God of Judah, this distant people should send gifts to his dwelling-place at Zion. They were, no doubt, among the 'many' who are described in 2 Chr. xxxii. 23, as having 'brought gifts unto Jehovah at Jeru-salem, and presents to king Hezekiah, so that he was magnified in the sight of all the nations.' But it is remarked by Gesenius that the expec-tation of the entire conversion of the Ethiopians is frequently expressed by the Hebrew prophets (Isa. xlv. 14; Zeph. iii. 10; Ps. lxviii. 32; lxxxvii. 4); and he adds, 'Those who take pleasure in tracing the fulfilment of such pre-dictions in subsequent history may find it in Acts viii. 27 (the conversion both to Judaism and Christianity of the treasurer of Queen Candace), and still more in the circumstance that Abyssinia is to this day the only great Christian state in the eastern world.'

If we go back about two centuries, to the reign of Asa, king of Judah (B.C. 950), we read of Zerah, or rather Zerach, an Ethiopian going out against him with a host of a thousand thousand men and three hundred chariots (2 Chron. xiv. 9). It is doubtful whether this was an Ethiopian monarch or commander, or only a mere Cushite adventurer; but that his army was mainly of African and not Arabian original is evident from the fact of its having included Libyans as well as Cushites (2 Chron. xvi. 8), and from the mention of war-chariots, which never were in use in Arabia. Farther back than this the records of history are silent.

The state of Meroë appears to have resembled the larger states in the interior of Africa at the present day, comprising a number of different races or tribes united together by no strong poli-tical bond, but by a common form of worship, which placed the rule in the hands of the priest-hood, the dominant caste of the country. There is every reason to conclude that the separate colonies of the priest-caste spread from Meroë into Egypt; and the primæval monuments in Ethiopia strongly confirm the native traditions reported by Diodorus Siculus, that the worship of Ammon and Osiris originated in Meroë, and thus render highly probable the opinion that commerce and civilization, science and art, de-scended into Egypt from Nubia and the upper regions of the Nile. One great cause of the early prosperity and grandeur of Ethiopia was the carrying-trade, of which it was the centre, between India and Arabia on the one hand, and the interior of Africa, and especially Egypt, on the other.

Queen Candace, who is mentioned in Acts viii. 27, was doubtless the reigning sovereign of Meroë [CANDACE], where it is likely a form of Judaism was at that period professed by a portion of the inhabitants, as seems to have been the case in the adjacent region of Abyssinia. The prophets (e. g. Isa. xi. 11) sometimes allude to the Jews who were scattered throughout Cush. Ebed-melech, the benevolent eunuch of King Zede-kiah, who showed such kindness to the prophet Jeremiah, was an Ethiopian (Jer. xxxviii. 7; comp. Acts viii. 27). Josephus calls the queen of Sheba, who visited Solomon, a queen of Egypt and Ethiopia, and with this agrees the tradition of the Abyssinians. But Sheba was undoubtedly in Arabia Felix, though it is possible that, in

remote antiquity, the sovereignty of its monarchs extended across the Red Sea to the coast of Ethiopia.

EVANGELISTS. This term is applied in the New Testament to a certain class of Chris-tian teachers who were not fixed to any parti-cular spot, but travelled either independently, or under the direction of one or other of the Apos-tles, for the purpose of propagating the Gospel. Philip, one of the seven deacons, is termed *the Evangelist* (Acts xxi. 8). St. Paul exhorts Timothy 'to do the work of an *Evangelist*' (2 Tim. iv. 5); and though this name is not given to Titus, the injunctions addressed to him, and the services he rendered, are so similar as to render the propriety of applying it to him un-questionable. In the Epistle to the Ephesians (iv. 11) the *Evangelists* are expressly distin-guished from the *pastors and teachers*. The chief points of difference appear to be that the former were itinerant, the latter stationary; the former were employed in introducing the Gospel where it was before unknown; the business of the latter was to confirm and instruct the con-verts statedly and permanently.

EVE (*living*), the name of the first woman. Her history is contained in that of ADAM, which see.

EVENING. [DAY.]

EVIL-MERO'DACH, son and successor of Nebuchadnezzar, king of Babylon, who, on his accession to the throne (B.C. 562), released the captive king of Judah, Jehoiachin, from prison, treated him with kindness and distinction, and set his throne above the thrones of the other con-quered kings who were detained at Babylon (2 Kings xxv. 27; Jer. lii. 31-34) [CHALDÆANS]. A Jewish tradition (noticed by Jerome on Isa. xiv. 29) ascribes this kindness to a personal friendship which Evil-merodach had contracted with the Jewish king, when he was himself con-signed to prison by Nebuchadnezzar, who, on recovering from his seven years' monomania, took offence at some part of the conduct of his son, by whom the government had in the mean-time been administered. But this story was pro-bably invented to account for the fact.

EUNI'CE, the mother of Timothy, a Jewess, although married to a Greek and bearing a Greek name, which signifies *good victory*. She was a believer in Christ, and even her mother Lois lived in the faith of the expected Messiah, if she did not live to know that he had come in the person of Jesus of Nazareth (2 Tim. i. 5; Acts xvi. 1).

EUNUCH. This word, which we have adopted from the Greek, has, in its literal sense, the harmless meaning of 'bed-keeper,' *i. e.* one who has the charge of beds and bed-chambers; but as only persons deprived of their virility have, from the most ancient times, been em-ployed in Oriental harems, and as such persons are employed almost exclusively in this kind of service, the word 'bed-keeper' became sy-nonymous with 'castratus.' In fact there are few eastern languages in which the condition of those persons is more directly expressed than by the name of some post or station in which they are usually found. The admission to the re-cesses of the harem, which is in fact the domestic establishment of the prince, gives the eunuchs such peculiar advantages of access to the royal ear and person, as often enables them to exercise an important influence, and to rise to stations of great trust and power in Eastern courts. Hence it would seem that, in Egypt, for instance, the word which indicated an eunuch was applied to any *court* officer, whether a castratus or not (Gen. xxxvii. 36; xxxix. 1).

Authority would be superfluous in proof of a matter of such common knowledge as the employment of eunuchs, and especially of black eunuchs, in the courts and harems of the ancient and modern East. A noble law, which, however, evinces the prevalence of the custom prior to Moses, made castration illegal among the Jews (Lev. xxi. 20; Deut. xxiii. 1). But the Hebrew princes did not choose to understand this law as interdicting the use of those who had been made eunuchs by others; for that they had them, and that they were sometimes, if not generally, blacks, and that the chief of them was regarded as holding an important and influential post, appears from 1 Kings xxii. 9; 2 Kings viii. 6; ix. 32, 33; xx. 18; xxiii. 11; Jer. xxxviii. 7; xxxix. 16; xli. 16. Samuel was aware that eunuchs would not fail to be employed in a regal court; for he thus forewarns the people, 'He (the king) will take the tenth of your seed and of your vineyard, and give to his eunuchs [A. V. 'officers'] and to his servants' (1 Sam. viii. 15).

Under these circumstances, the eunuchs were probably obtained from a great distance, and at an expense which must have limited their employment to the royal establishment; and this is very much the case even at present.

In Matt. xix. 12, the term 'eunuch' is applied figuratively to persons naturally impotent. In the same verse mention is also made of persons 'who have made themselves eunuchs for the kingdom of heaven's sake;' which is a manifestly hyperbolical description of such as lived in voluntary abstinence (comp. Matt. v. 29, 30); although painful examples have occurred (as in the case of Origen) of a disposition to interpret the phrase too literally.

EUO'DIAS, a female member of the church at Philippi, who seems to have been at variance with another female member named Syntyche. Paul describes them as women who had 'laboured much with him in the Gospel,' and implores them to be of one mind (Philip. iv. 2, 3).

EUPHRA'TES, termed in Deut. i. 7, 'the great river,' where it is mentioned as the eastern boundary of the land which (ver. 8) God gave to the descendants of Abraham. In Gen. ii. 14, the Euphrates is stated to be the fourth of the rivers which flowed from a common stream in the garden of Eden. Divines and geographers have taken much trouble in order to learn the position of Eden from the geographical particulars given in the Bible, without remembering that probably nothing more than a popular description was intended.

In consequence of its magnitude and importance, the Euphrates was designated and known as 'the river,' being by far the most considerable stream in Western Asia. Thus in Exod. xxiii. 31, we read, 'from the desert unto the river' (comp. Isa. viii. 7).

It has two sources and two arms—a western and an eastern—which rise in the mountains of Armenia. Of these streams the western is the shorter, and is called Kara Sou or Melas; the eastern is itself made up of several streams, the longest of which bears the name of Murad, or Phrat. The two arms unite about three days' journey from Erzeroom, near which rise two of the tributaries that concur in forming the Phrat. Thus uniting, they give rise to the Euphrates strictly so called, which, flowing to the south, divides Armenia from Cappadocia; but, being driven westward by the Anti-Taurus and Taurus mountains, it works its circuitous way through narrow passes and over cataracts, until, breaking through a defile formed by the eastern extremity of Mons Amanus (Alma Dagh), and the northwestern extremity of Mons Taurus, it reaches the plain country not far from Samosata (Schemisat), then winds south and south-east, passing the north of Syria, and the north-east of Arabia Deserta, and at length, after many windings, unites with the Tigris, and thus united finds its termination in the Persian Gulf. In conjunction with the Tigris, it forms the rich alluvial lands of Mesopotamia, over which it flows or is carried by canals, and thus diffuses abroad fertility and beauty. At Bagdad and Hillah (Babylon), the Euphrates and Tigris approach comparatively near to each other, but separate again, forming a kind of ample basin, till they finally become one at Koorma. Under the Cæsars the Euphrates was the eastern boundary of the Roman empire, as under David it was the natural limit of the Hebrew monarchy.

Although occasionally much more, the breadth of the Euphrates varies between 200 and 400 yards; but for a distance of 60 miles through the Lemlun marshes the main stream narrows to about 80 yards. The general depth of the Upper Euphrates exceeds 8 feet, but is shallow enough in some places for laden camels to pass in autumn, the water rising to their bellies, or about 4½ feet. In point of current it is for the most part a sluggish stream; for, except in the height of the flooded season, when it approaches 5 miles an hour, it varies from 2¼ to 3½, with a much larger portion of its course under 3 than above. The length of the navigable part of the river, reckoning from Bir to Bussora, is 143 miles; the length of the entire stream, 1400 miles. It is very abundant in fish. The water is somewhat turbid; but, when purified, is pleasant and salubrious.

The river begins to rise in March, and continues rising till the latter end of May. The consequent increase of its volume and rapidity is attributable to the early rains, which, falling in the Armenian mountains, swell its mountain tributaries; and also in the main to the melting of the winter snows in these lofty regions. About the middle of November the Euphrates has reached its lowest ebb, and ceasing to decrease, becomes tranquil and sluggish.

In ancient as well as in modern times the Euphrates was used for navigation. Herodotus states that boats—either coracles or rafts, floated by inflated skins—brought the produce of Armenia down to Babylon. The trade thus carried on was considerable. A great deal of navigation is still carried on from Bagdad to Hillah, the ancient Babylon; but the disturbed state of the country prevents any above the latter place.

The prophets made use of the Euphrates as a figurative description of the Assyrian power, as the Nile with them represented the power of Egypt; thus in Isa. viii. 7, 'The Lord bringeth up upon them the waters of the river, strong and many, even the king of Assyria' (Jer. ii. 18).

EUROC'LYDON. [WINDS.]

EU'TYCHUS, a young man of Troas, who sat in the open window of the third floor while St. Paul was preaching late in the night, and who, being overcome by sleep, fell out into the court below. He was 'taken up dead;' but the Apostle, going down, extended himself upon the body and embraced it, like the prophets of old (1 Kings xvii. 21; 2 Kings iv. 34); and when he felt the signs of returning life, restored him to his friends, with the assurance that 'his life was in him.' Before Paul departed in the morning the youth was brought to him alive and well. It is disputed whether Eutychus was really dead, or only in a swoon; and hence, whether a miracle was performed or not. It is admitted that the circumstances, and the words of Paul himself, sanction the notion that the young man was not actually dead; but, on the other hand, it is contended that the words of the narrator, 'taken up dead,' are too plain to justify us in receiving them in the modified sense of 'taken up for dead,' which that interpretation requires (Acts xx. 5-12).

EXECRATION. The Greek word so rendered occurs in Num. xxiii. 8; xxiv. 9; Josh. vi. 26; 1 Sam. xvii. 43. It is used also in profane authors to denote the imprecations which it was customary among ancient nations to pronounce upon their enemies for the purpose of calling down the divine wrath, branding them with infamy, and exciting against them the passions of the multitude. These imprecations were chiefly pronounced by priests, enchanters, or prophets [BALAAM]. The Athenians made use of them against Philip of Macedon. They convened an assembly, in which it was decreed that all statues, inscriptions, or festivals among them, in any way relating to him or his ancestors, should be destroyed, and every other possible reminiscence of him profaned; and that the priests, as often as they prayed for the success of the Athenian affairs, should pray for the ruin of Philip. It was also customary, both among the Greeks and Romans, after having destroyed cities in war, the revival of whose strength they dreaded, to pronounce execrations upon those who should rebuild them. The Romans published a decree full of execrations against those who should rebuild Carthage. An incident somewhat analogous is related (Josh. vi. 26) after the taking of Jericho. From the words 'and Joshua adjured them at that time,' it is likely that he acted under a divine intimation that Jericho should continue in ruins, as a monument of the divine displeasure and a warning to posterity. The words 'cursed be the *man* (the *individual*) before the Lord that riseth up and buildeth this city Jericho,' although transformed into an execration by the word *supplied* by the translators, amount to no more than a *prediction* that 'he shall lay the foundation thereof in his first-born, and in his youngest son shall he set up the gates of it,' that is, he shall meet with so many impediments to his undertaking that he shall *out-live* all his children, *dying in the course of nature* be-

fore he shall complete it. Execrations were also pronounced upon cities and their inhabitants before undertaking a siege, and before engaging with enemies in war. The execrations in the 83rd Psalm, probably written on the occasion of the confederacy against Jehoshaphat, and other instances of a like nature, partake of the execrations of the heathen in nothing but form, being the inspired predictions or denunciations of divine vengeance against the avowed enemies of the God of Israel, notwithstanding the proofs they had witnessed of his supremacy; and the object of these imprecations, as in many other instances, is charitable, namely, their conversion to the true religion (ver. 18; see also Ps. lix. 12).

EXO'DUS. The intention of Jehovah to deliver the Israelites from Egyptian bondage was made known to Moses from the burning bush at Mount Horeb, while he kept the flock of Jethro, his father-in-law. Under the divine direction Moses, in conjunction with Aaron, assembled the elders of the nation, and acquainted them with the gracious design of Heaven. After this they had an interview with Pharaoh, and requested permission for the people to go, in order to hold a feast unto God in the wilderness. The result was, not only refusal, but the doubling of all the burdens which the Israelites had previously had to bear. Moses hereupon, suffering reproach from his people, consults Jehovah, who assures him that he would compel Pharaoh 'to drive them out of his land.' 'I will rid you out of their bondage, and I will redeem you with a stretched-out arm and with great judgments' (Exod. iii.-vi. 6). Then ensue a series of miracles, commonly called the plagues of Egypt (Exod. vi.-xii.) [PLAGUE]. At last, overcome by the calamities sent upon him, Pharaoh yielded all that was demanded, saying, 'Rise up, and get you forth from among my people, both ye and the children of Israel; and go serve the Lord as ye have said; also take your flocks and your herds, and be gone.' Thus driven out, the Israelites, to the number of about 600,000 adults, besides children, left the land, attended by a mixed multitude, with their flocks and herds, even very much cattle (Exod. xii. 31, sq.). Being 'thrust out' of the country, they had not time to prepare for themselves suitable provisions, and therefore they baked unleavened cakes of the dough which they brought forth out of Egypt.

On the night of the self-same day which terminated a period of 430 years, during which they had been in Egypt, were they led forth from Rameses, or Goshen [GOSHEN]. They are not said to have crossed the river Nile, whence we may infer that Goshen lay on the eastern side of the river. Their first station was at Succoth (Exod xii. 37). The nearest way into the Land of Promise was through the land of the Philistines. This route would have required them to keep on in a north-east direction. It pleased their divine conductor, however, not to take this path, lest, being opposed by the Philistines, the Israelites should turn back at the sight of war into Egypt. If, then, Philistia was to be avoided, the course would lie nearly direct east, or south-east. Pursuing this route, 'the armies' come to Etham, their next station, 'in the edge of the wilderness' (Exod xiii. 17, sq.). Here they encamped. Dispatch, however, was desirable. They journey

x

day and night, not without divine guidance, for 'the Lord went before them by day in a pillar of a cloud, to lead them the way; and by night in a pillar of fire, to give them light; to go by day and night.' This special guidance could not well have been meant merely to show the way through the desert; for it can hardly be supposed that in so great a multitude no persons knew the road over a country lying near to that in which they and their ancestors had dwelt, and which did not extend more than some forty miles across. The divine guides were doubtless intended to conduct the Israelites in that way and to that spot where the hand of God would be most signally displayed in their rescue and in the destruction of Pharaoh. 'I will be honoured upon Pharaoh and upon all his host, that the Egyptians may know that I am the Lord.' For this purpose Moses is directed of God to 'speak unto the children of Israel that they *turn* and encamp before Pi-hahiroth, between Migdol and the sea, over against Baal-zephon; before it shall ye encamp by the sea. and they did so' (Exod. xiv. 2-4). We have already seen reason to think that the direction of the Israelites was to the east or south-east; this turning must have been in the latter direction, else they would have been carried down towards the land of the Philistines, which they were to avoid. Let the word 'turn' be marked; it is a strong term, and seems to imply that the line of the march was bent considerably towards the south, or the interior of the land. The children of Israel then are now encamped before Pi-hahiroth, between Migdol and the sea, also 'by the sea.' Their position was such that they were 'entangled in the land, the wilderness had shut them in.'

A new scene is now laid open. News is carried to Pharaoh which leads him to see that the reason assigned (namely, a sacrifice in the wilderness) is but a pretext; that the Israelites had really fled from his yoke; and also that, through some (to him) unaccountable error, they had gone towards the south-east, had reached the sea, and were hemmed in on all sides. He summons his troops and sets out in pursuit—'all the horses and chariots of Pharaoh, and his horsemen and his army;' and he 'overtook them encamping by the sea, beside Pi-hahiroth, before Baal-zephon' (Exod. xiv. 9). The Israelites see their pursuing enemy approach, and are alarmed. Moses assures them of divine aid. A promise was given as of God that the Israelites should go on dry ground through *the midst* of the sea; and that the Egyptians, attempting the same path, should be destroyed: 'and I will get me honour upon Pharaoh and all his host, upon his chariots and his horsemen' (ver. 17). Here a very extraordinary event takes place: 'The angel of God, which went before the camp of Israel, removed and went behind them; and the pillar of the cloud went from before their face and stood behind them; and it came between the camp of the Egyptians and the camp of Israel; and it was a cloud and darkness to them, but it gave light by night to these; so that the one came not near the other all the night' (ver. 19, 20). Then comes the division of the waters, which we give in the words of the sacred historian: 'And Moses stretched out his hand over the sea, and the Lord caused the sea to go back by a strong

east wind all that night, and made the sea dry land, and the waters were divided. And the children of Israel went into the midst of the sea upon the dry ground; and the waters were a wall unto them on their right hand and on their left. And the Egyptians pursued and went in after them to *the midst of the sea*, even all Pharaoh's horses, his chariots, and his horsemen.' Delays are now occasioned to the Egyptians; their chariot-wheels are supernaturally taken off, so that 'in the morning-watch they drave them heavily.' The Egyptians are troubled; they urge each other to fly from the face of Israel. 'Then Moses stretched forth his hand over the sea, and the sea returned to his strength when the morning appeared; and the Egyptians fled against it; and the Lord overthrew the Egyptians in *the midst of the sea*. And the waters returned and *covered the chariots and the horsemen and all the host of Pharaoh* that came into the sea after them; there remained not as much as one of them. But the children of Israel walked upon dry land in the midst of the sea, and the waters were a wall unto them on their right hand and on their left. And Israel saw the Egyptians dead upon the sea-shore; and the people feared the Lord, and believed the Lord and his servant Moses' (ver. 28-31).

Such is the bearing and import of the sacred narrative. If any intelligent reader, knowing nothing of the theories of learned men, were to peruse the account given in Exodus with a map before him, he would, we doubt not, be led to conclude that the route of the Israelites lay towards the south-east, up the Red Sea, and that the spot where they crossed was at a place encircled by mountains on the side of the desert, and fronted by deep and impassable waters; he would equally conclude that the writer in Exodus intended to represent the rescue as from first to last the work of God. Had the Israelites been at a place which was fordable under any natural influences, Pharaoh's undertaking was absurd. He knew that they were entangled,—mountains behind and on either hand, while the deep sea was before them. Therefore he felt sure of his prey, and set out in pursuit. Nothing but the divine interposition foiled and punished him, at the same time redeeming the Israelites. And this view, which the unlearned but intelligent reader would be led to take, involves, in fact, all that is important in the case. But a dislike of the miraculous has had an influence, and erudition has tried to fix the precise spot: whence have arisen views and theories which are more or less discordant with the Scripture, or are concerned with comparative trifles. So far as aversion to miracle has had an influence in the hypotheses which have been given, all we shall remark is, that in a case which is so evidently represented as the sphere of miracle, there is but one alternative,—they who do not admit the miracle must reject the narrative; and far better would it be to do so frankly than to construct hypotheses which are for the most part, if not altogether, purely arbitrary. A narrative obviously miraculous (in the intention of the writer) can be explained satisfactorily on no rationalistic principles: this is not to expound but to 'wrest' the Scriptures; a position which, in our opinion, has been fully established, in relation to the Gospels, against the whole of the rationalistic school of interpretation.

The account now given must, as being derived immediately from the Scripture, be in the main correct. If the authority is denied, this can be done effectually by no other means than by disproving in general the authority of the books whence it is derived; and it may with truth be affirmed, that no view opposed to that given can possess greater claims on our credit, while any mere sceptical opinion must rest on its own intrinsic probability, contested, so far as it opposes the Scripture, by scriptural authority.

When, however, we descend from generals to particulars, and attempt to ascertain precise localities and determine details, diversity of opinion may easily arise, and varying degrees of probability only are likely to attend the investigation. For instance, the immediate spot which Moses proposed to reach was, we know, on the Red Sea; but the precise line which he took depended of course on the place whence he set out. With difference of opinion as to the spot where the Hebrews had their rendezvous, there cannot be agreement as to the route they followed.

The position of Goshen, where the Israelites were settled, we shall endeavour to fix in another article. It is enough here to say, that it was on the eastern side of the Nile, probably in the province of Esh-Shurkiyeh. Rameses was the place of rendezvous. The direct route thence to the Red Sea was along the valley of the ancient canal. By this way the distance was about thirty-five miles. From the vicinity of Cairo, however, there runs a range of hills eastward to the Red Sea, the western extremity of which, not far from Cairo, is named Jebel-Mokattem; the eastern extremity is termed Jebel-Attaka, which, with its promontory Ras Attaka, runs into the Red Sea. Between the two extremes, somewhere about the middle of the range, is an opening which affords a road for caravans. Two routes offered themselves here. Supposing that the actual starting-point lay nearer Cairo, the Israelites might strike in from the north of the range of hills, at the opening just mentioned, and pursue the ordinary caravan road which leads from Cairo to Suez; or they might go southward from Mokattem, through the Wady el Tih, that is, the Valley of Wandering, through which also a road, though less used, runs to Suez. According to Niebuhr, they took the first; according to ancient tradition, they took the last. Sicard found traces of the Israelites in the valley. He held Rameses to be the starting-point, and Rameses he placed about six miles from ancient Cairo, where Bezatin is now found. Here is a capacious sandy plain, on which Sicard thinks the Israelites assembled on the morning when they began their journey. In this vicinity a plain is still found, which the Arabs call the Jews' Cemetery, and where, from an indefinite period, the Jews have buried their dead. In the Mokattem chain is a hill, a part of which is called Mejanat Musa, 'Moses' Station.' On another hill in the vicinity ruins are found, which the Arabs name Meravad Musa, 'Moses' Delight.' Thus several things seem to carry the mind back to the time of the Hebrew legislator. Through the valley which leads from Bezatin (the Valley of Wandering) to the Red Sea, Sicard travelled in three days. He reckons the length to be twenty-

six hours, which, if we give two miles to each hour, would make the distance fifty-two miles. The valley running pretty much in a plain surface would afford a convenient passage to the mixed bands of Israelites. About eighteen miles from Bezatin you meet with Gendelhy, a plain with a fountain. The name signifies a military station, and in this Sicard finds the Succoth (tents) of Exodus, the first station of Moses. The haste with which they left (were driven out) would enable them to reach this place at nightfall of their first day's march. Sicard places their second station, Etham, in the plain Ramliyeh, eighteen miles from Gendelhy and sixteen from the sea. From this plain is a pass, four miles in length, so narrow that not more than twenty men can go abreast. To avoid this, which would have caused dangerous delay, the order was given to turn (Exod. xiv. 2). Etham is said (Exod. xiii. 20) to be on the edge of the wilderness. Jablonski says the word means terminus maris, the termination or boundary of the sea. Now, in the plain where Sicard fixes Etham (not to be confounded with the Eastern Etham, through which afterwards the Israelites travelled three days (Num. xxxiii. 8), is the spot where the waters divide which run to the Nile and to the Gulf of Suez, and Etham is therefore truly the boundary of the sea. Here the Israelites received command to turn and encamp (Exod. xiv. 2) before Pi-hahiroth, between Migdol and the sea, over against Baal-zephon. Pi-hahiroth (the mouth of the hiding-places) Sicard identifies with Thuarek (small caves), which is the name still given to three or four salt springs of the plain Baideah, on the south side of mount Attaka, which last Sicard identifies with Baal-zephon, and which is the northern boundary of the plain Baideah, while Kuiabeh (Migdol) is its southern limit. The pass which leads to Suez, between Attaka and the sea, is very narrow, and could be easily stopped by the Egyptians. In this plain of Baideah, Pharaoh had the Israelites hemmed in on all sides. This then, according to all appearance, is the spot where the passage through the sea was effected. Such is the judgment of Sicard and of Raumer. It cannot be denied that this route satisfies all the conditions of the case. Equally does the spot correspond with the miraculous narrative furnished by holy writ.

It is no small corroboration of the view now given from Sicard and Raumer, that in substance it has the support of Josephus, of whose account we shall, from its importance, give an abridgment. The Hebrews, he says (*Antiq.* ii. 15), took their journey by Latopolis, where Babylon was built afterwards when Cambyses laid Egypt waste. As they went in haste, on the third day they came to a place called Baal-zephon, on the Red Sea. Moses led them this way in order that the Egyptians might be punished should they venture in pursuit, and also because the Hebrews had a quarrel with the Philistines. When the Egyptians had overtaken the Hebrews they prepared to fight them, and by their multitude drove them into a narrow place: for the number that went in pursuit was 600 chariots, 50,000 horsemen, and 200,000 infantry, all armed. They also seized the passages, shutting the Hebrews up between inaccessible precipices and the sea; for there was on each side a ridge of mountains that terminated

x 2

at the sea, which were impassable, and obstructed their flight. Moses, however, prayed to God, and smote the sea with his rod, when the waters parted, and gave the Israelites free passage. The Egyptians at first supposed them distracted; but when they saw the Israelites proceed in safety, they followed. As soon as the entire Egyptian army was in the channel the sea closed, and the pursuers perished amid torrents of rain and the most terrific thunder and lightning.

The opposition to the scriptural account has been of two kinds. Some writers (Wolfenb. *Fragm.* p. 64, sq.) have at once declared the whole fabulous; a course which appears to have been taken as early as the time of Josephus (*Antiq.* ii. 16. 5). Others have striven to explain the facts by the aid of mere natural causes, for which see Winer, *Handworterbuch*, in Meer Rothes. A third mode of explanation is pursued by those who do not deny miracles as such, and yet, with no small inconsistency, seek to reduce this particular miracle to the smallest dimensions. Writers who see in the deliverance of the Hebrews the hand of God and the fulfilment of the divine purposes, follow the account in Scripture implicitly, placing the passage at Ras Attaka, at the termination of the Valley of Wandering; others, who go on rationalistic principles, find the sea here too wide and too deep for their purpose, and endeavour to fix the passage a little to the south or the north of Suez. In answer to this opinion, we shall content ourselves with quoting the testimony of one or two travellers who have visited and carefully examined the spot.

The following are the remarks of Mr. Blumhardt, who passed through Suez (October, 1836), in his missionary visit to Abyssinia. ' The Red Sea at Suez is exceedingly narrow, and in my opinion it cannot be that the Israelites here experienced the power and love of God in their passage through the Red Sea. The breadth of the sea is at present scarcely a quarter of an hour by Suez. Now if this be the part which they crossed, how is it possible that all the army of Pharaoh, with his chariots, could have been drowned? I am rather inclined to believe that the Israelites experienced that wonderful deliverance about thirty miles lower down. This opinion is also strengthened by most of the Eastern churches, and the Arabs, who believe that the Israelites reached the opposite shore at a place called Gebel Pharaon, which on that account has received this name. If we accept this opinion, it agrees very well with the Scripture.' Still more important is the evidence of Dr. Olin (*Travels in the East*, New York, 1843). He agrees with Robinson in fixing Etham ' on the border of the wilderness which stretches along the eastern shore of the arm of the sea which runs up above Suez.' At this point he says the Hebrews were commanded to turn. They turned directly southward and marched to an exposed position, hemmed in completely by the sea, the desert, and Mount Attaka. A false confidence was thus excited in Pharaoh, and the deliverance was made the more signal and the more impressive alike to the Israelites and to Egypt. Admitting the possibility that the sea at Suez may have been wider and deeper than it is now, Olin remarks, ' it must still have been very difficult, if not impossible, for the army of Israel, encum-

bered with infants and aged people, as well as with flocks, to pass over (near Suez) in face of their enemies.' Besides, the peculiarities of the place must have had a tendency to disguise the character and impair the effect of the miracle. The passage made at the intervention of Moses was kept open all night The Egyptians followed the Hebrews to *the midst of the sea*, when the sea engulfed them. ' The entire night seems to have been consumed in the passage. It is hardly credible that so much time should have been consumed in crossing near Suez, to accomplish which one or two hours would have been sufficient.' ' Nor is it conceivable that the large army of the Egyptians should have been at once within the banks of so narrow a channel. The more advanced troops would have reached the opposite shore before the rear had entered the sea; and yet we know that all Pharaoh's chariots and horsemen followed to the *midst* of the sea, and, together with all the host that came in after them, were covered with the returning waves' (i. 348). Preferring the position at Ras Attaka, Olin states that the gulf is here ten or twelve miles wide. ' The valley expands into a considerable plain, bounded by lofty precipitous mountains on the right and left, and by the sea in front, and is sufficiently ample to accommodate the vast number of human beings who composed the two armies.' ' An east wind would act almost directly across the gulf. It would be unable to co-operate with an ebb tide in removing the waters—no objection certainly if we admit the exercise of God's miraculous agency;' but a very great impediment in the way of any rationalistic hypothesis. ' The channel is wide enough to allow of the movements described by Moses, and the time, which embraced an entire night, was sufficient for the convenient march of a large army over such a distance.' ' The opinion which fixes the point of transit in the valley or wady south of Mount Attaka derives confirmation from the names still attached to the principal objects in this locality. Jebel Attaka means in the language of the Arabs " The Mount of Deliverance." Baideah or Bedeah, the name of this part of the valley, means " the Miraculous," while Wady el Tih means " the Valley of Wanderings." Pi-hahiroth, where Moses was commanded to encamp, is rendered by scholars " the mouth of Hahiroth," which answers well to the deep gorge south of Attaka, but not at all to the broad plain about Suez.'

Other parts of the line of march pursued by the Israelites will be found treated of under the heads MANNA, SINAI, WANDERING.

EXODUS, the second book of Moses, so called from the principal event recorded in it, namely, *the departure* of the Israelites from Egypt. With this book begins the proper history of that people, continuing it until their arrival at Sinai, and the erection of the sanctuary there. It transports us in the first instance to Egypt, and the quarter in which the Israelites were domiciled in that country. We do not find in the Pentateuch a real history of the people of Israel during this period. Such a history, in the more strict acceptation of the term, has no place in an historical sketch of the kingdom of God, where the mere description of the situation and condition of the people is all that is requisite. From that description we learn satisfactorily how the people of the Lord were negatively prepared for the great object which God had decreed with regard to them. This is the important theme of the history of the Pentateuch during the whole long period of four hundred years. Exodus is very circumstantial in its account of the life of Moses, which, instead of partaking of the character of usual biography, manifests in all its details a decided aim of evincing how, by the miraculous dispensation of the Lord, Moses had been even from his earliest years prepared and reared to become the chosen instrument of God. In this book is developed, with particular clearness, the summons of Moses to his sacred office, which concludes the first important section of his life (Exod. i.-vi.). No human choice and no self-will, but an immediate call from Jehovah alone could decide in so important an affair. Jehovah reveals himself to him by his covenant-name, and vouchsafes him the power to work miracles such as no man before him had ever wrought. It was not the natural disposition and bent of his mind that induced Moses to accept the office, but solely his submission to the express will of God, his OBEDIENCE alone, that influenced him, the LAWGIVER, to undertake the mission. The external relation of Moses to his people is also clearly defined (comp. *ex. gr.* Exod. vi. 14, sq.). This furnishes the firm basis on which is founded his own as well as Aaron's personal authority, and the respect for his permanent regulations. A new section (vii.-xv.) then gives a very detailed account of the manner in which the Lord glorified himself in Israel, and released the people from the land of bondage. This section of the history then concludes with a triumphal song, celebrating the victory of Israel. In ch xvi.-xviii. we find the introduction to the second principal part of this book, in which is sketched the manifestation of God in the midst of Israel, as well as the promulgation of the law itself, in its original and fundamental features. This preparatory section thus furnishes us with additional proof of the special care of God for his people; how he provided their food and water, and how he protected them from the assaults of their foes. In ch. xv. 22, sq., not all, but only the remarkable resting-places are mentioned, where Jehovah took special care of his people. In the account (xviii.) of the civil regulations framed by the advice of Jethro, a strong line of demarcation is drawn between the changeable institutions of man and the divine legislation which began then to be established, and which thenceforth claims by far the greatest part of the work. At the commencement of the legislation is a brief summary of the laws, with the decalogue at their head (xix.-xxiii.). The decalogue is the true fundamental law, bearing within itself the germ of the entire legislation. The other legal definitions are only further developments of the decalogue. These definitions manifest the power and extent of the law itself, showing what an abundance of new regulations result from the simple and few words of the decalogue. Upon this basis the covenant is concluded with the Israelites, in which God reveals himself in agreement with the understanding and the exigencies of the people. Not until this covenant was completed did it become possible for the Israelites to enter into a communion with God, confirmed and consecrated by laws and offerings, and thereby to receive further revelations from him (ch. xxiv.). Whatsoever after this, in the twenty-fifth and in the following chapters, is communicated to the people, concerns the dwelling of God in the midst of Israel. By this dwelling of God among Israel it is intended to show, that the communion is permanent on the part of God, and that on the part of the people it is possible to persevere in communion with God. Consequently there follows the description of the sanctuary, the character of which is symbolical. The sacred symbols are, however, not so much expressed in formal declarations, as contained in the whole tenor of the descriptions. The symbolics begin with the central point, the holy of holies, which unites in itself the impeaching law and the redeeming symbol of divine mercy, and thus sets forth the reconciliation of God with the people. This is followed by the description of the sanctuary, representing those blessings which through the holy of holies were communicated to the subjects of the theocracy, and serving as a perpetual monument of Israel's exalted destiny, pointing at the same time to the means of attaining it. Last comes the description of the fore-court, symbolising the participation of the people in those blessings, and their sanctified approach to the Lord. The description then proceeds from the sanctuary to the persons officiating in it, the priests, characterized both by their various costumes (xxviii.), and the manner of their inauguration (xxix.). Then follows, as a matter of course, the description of the service in that sanctuary and by those priests, but merely in its fundamental features, confining itself simply to the burnt and incense offerings, indicating by the former the preparatory inferior service, and by the latter the complete and higher office of the sacerdotal function. But, by contributing to the means of establishing public worship, the whole nation shares in it; and therefore the description of the officiating persons very properly concludes with the people (xxx.). As a suitable sequel to the former follows the description of the use and nature of the implements requisite for the service of the priests, such as the brass laver for sacred ablutions, the preparation of the perfume and anointing oil (xxx. 17-38). These regulations being made, men endowed with the Spirit of God were also to be appointed for making the sacred tabernacle and all its furniture (xxxi. 1-2). The description of the sanctuary, priesthood, and mode of worship, is next followed by that of the sacred times and periods (xxxi. 12, sq.). Of the sacred times there is here only appointed the Sabbath, in which the other regulations are contained as in their germ. God having delivered to Moses the tables of the law, the construction and arrangement of the tabernacle might thus at once have been begun, had its further progress not been interrupted by an act of idolatry on the part of the people, and their punishment for that offence, which form the subject of the narrative in ch. xxxii.-xxxiv. Contrary and in opposition to all that had been done by Jehovah for and in the presence of Israel, the formidable apostacy of the latter manifests itself in a most melancholy manner, as an ominously significant prophetic fact, which is incessantly repeated in the history of subsequent generations. The narrative of it is therefore closely connected with the foregoing accounts—Jehovah's mercy and gracious faithfulness on the one hand, and Israel's barefaced ingratitude on the other, being intimately connected. This connection forms the leading idea of the whole history of the theocracy. It is not till after the narrative of this momentous event that the account of the construction and completion of the tabernacle can proceed (xxxv.-xl.), which account becomes more circumstantial in proportion as the subject itself is of greater importance. Above all, it is faithfully shown that all was done according to the commands of Jehovah.

This brief statement of the contents of the book of Exodus will show that in the descriptive history a fixed plan, in conformity with the principles above stated, is consistently and visibly carried through the whole of the book, thus giving us the surest guarantee for the unity of both the book and its author.

For neological criticism it was of the utmost importance to stamp this book as a later production, the miracles contained in its first part but too manifestly clashing with the principles in which that criticism takes its rise. Its votaries therefore have endeavoured to show that those miracles were but mythological fictions which had been gradually developed in process of time, so that the very composition of the book itself must necessarily have been of a later date. Neither do we wonder at such attempts and efforts, since the very essence and central point of the accounts of the miracles given in the book are altogether at variance with the principles and the criticism of the rationalist system, which can by no means admit the rise and formation of a people under such miraculous circumstances, such peculiar belief, and, in a religious point of view, such an independent existence. Indeed, the spiritual substance of the whole, the divine idea which pervades and combines all its details, is in itself such a miracle, such a peculiar and wondrous phenomenon, as to lend natural support and undeniable confirmation to the isolated and physical wonders themselves; so that it is impossible to deny the latter without creating a second and new wonder, entirely adverse to the whole course of the Jewish history. Nor is that part of the book which contains the miracles deficient in numerous historical proofs in verification of them. As the events of this history are laid in Egypt and Arabia, we have ample opportunity of testing the accuracy of the Mosaical accounts, and surely we find nowhere the least transgression against Egyptian institutions and customs; on the contrary, it is most evident that the author had a thorough knowledge of the Egyptian institutions and the spirit that pervaded them. Exodus contains a mass of incidents and detailed descriptions which have gained new force from the modern discoveries and researches in the field of Egyptian antiquities. The description of the passage of the Israelites through the desert also evinces such a thorough familiarity with the localities as to excite the utmost respect of scrupulous and scientific travellers of our own time for the authenticity of the Pentateuch. Nor is the passover-festival, its rise and nature, less confirmatory of the incidents connected with it. The arrangements of the tabernacle, described in the second part of Exodus, likewise throw a favourable light on the historical authenticity of the preceding events; and the least tenable of all the objections against it are, that the architectural arrangements of the tabernacle were too artificial, and the materials and richness too costly and precious, for the condition and position of the Jews at that early period, &c. But the critics seem to have overlooked the fact that the Israelites of that period were a people who had come out from Egypt, a people possessing wealth, Egyptian culture and arts, which we admire even now, in the works which have descended to us from ancient Egypt; so that it cannot seem strange to see the Hebrews in possession of the materials or artistical knowledge requisite for the construction of the tabernacle. Moreover, the establishment of a TENT as a sanctuary for the Hebrews can only be explained from their abode in the desert, being in perfect unison with their then roving and nomadic life. The extremely simple and sober style and views throughout the whole narrative afford a sure guarantee for its authenticity and originality. All the incidents related in it are described in plain and clear terms, without the least vestige of later embellishments and false extolling of former ages. The whole representation indicates the strictest impartiality and truth. On the literature of Exodus, see PENTATEUCH.

EXORCISM AND EXORCIST (Acts xix. 13). The belief in demoniacal possessions, which may be traced in almost every nation, has always been attended by the professed ability, on the part of some individuals, to release the unhappy victims from their calamity. The allusions to the practice of exorcism among the Jews, contained both in their own authors and in the New Testament are too well known to render quotations necessary. In some instances this power was considered as a divine gift; in others it was thought to be acquired by investigations into the nature of demons and the qualities of natural productions, as herbs, stones, &c., and of drugs compounded of them; by the use of certain forms of adjurations, invocations, ceremonies, and other observances. Among all the references to exorcism, as practised by the Jews, in the New Testament (Matt. xii. 27; Mark ix. 38; Luke ix. 49, 50), we find only one instance which affords any clue to the means employed (Acts xix. 13); from which passage it appears that certain professed exorcists took upon them to call over a demoniac the name of the Lord Jesus, saying, 'We adjure you by Jesus whom Paul preacheth.' Their proceeding seems to have been in conformity with the well-known opinions of the Jews in those days, that miracles might be wrought by invoking the names of the Deity, or angels, or patriarchs, &c. The epithet applied to these exorcists, 'vagabond Jews,' indicates that they were travelling mountebanks, who, beside skill in medicine, pretended to the knowledge of magic. The office of the exorcist is not mentioned by Paul in his enumeration of the miraculous gifts (1 Cor. xii. 9), though it was a power which he possessed himself, and which the Saviour had promised (Mark xvi. 17; Matt. x. 8).

EXPIATION. [ATONEMENT; SACRIFICE.]

EXPIATION, DAY OF. [ATONEMENT, DAY OF.]

EYE. In most languages this important organ is used by figurative application, as the symbol of a large number of objects and ideas. In the East such applications of the word ' eye ' have always been uncommonly numerous; and they were so among the Hebrews. It may be serviceable to distinguish the following uses of the word, few of which are common in this country, unless so far as they have become so through the translation of the Bible.

1. *A fountain.* This use of the word probably originated from the eye being regarded as the fountain of tears.

2. *Colour,* as in the phrase ' and the eye (colour) of the woman was as the eye (colour) of bdellium ' (Num. xi. 7). This originated perhaps in the eye being the part of the body which exhibits different colours in different persons.

3. *The surface,* as ' the surface (eye) of the land ' (Exod. x. 5, 15; Num. xxii. 5, 11).

4. In Cant. iv. 9, ' eye' seems to be used poetically for ' look,' as is usual in most languages; ' Thou hast stolen my heart with one of thy looks ' (eyes).

5. In Prov. xxiii. 31, the term ' eye ' is applied to the beads or bubbles of wine, when poured out, but our version preserves the sense of ' colour.'

To these some other phrases, requiring notice and explanation, may be added:

' Before the eyes ' of any one, meaning in his presence; or, as we should say, ' before his face' (Gen. xxiii. 11, 18; Exod. iv. 30).

' In the eyes ' of any one, means what appears to be so, or so in his individual judgment or opinion; and is equivalent to ' seeming ' or ' appearing ' (Gen. xix. 8; xxix. 20; margin 2 Sam. x. iii.).

To set the eyes' upon any one, is usually to regard him with favour (Gen. xliv. 21; Job xxiv. 23; Jer. xxxix. 12); but it occurs in a bad sense, as of looking with anger, in Amos ix. 8. But anger is more usually expressed by the contrary action of turning the eyes away.

As many of the passions, such as envy, pride, pity, desire, are expressed by the eye; so, in the Scriptural style, they are often ascribed to that organ. Hence such phrases as ' evil eye ' (Matt. xx. 15); ' bountiful eye' (Prov. xxii. 9); ' haughty eyes' (Prov. vi. 17); ' wanton eyes' (Isa. iii. 16); ' eyes full of adultery ' (2 Pet. ii. 14); ' the lust of the eyes' (1 John ii. 16). This last phrase is applied by some to lasciviousness, by others to covetousness; but it is best to take the expression in the most extensive sense, as denoting a craving for the gay vanities of this life (Comp. Ezek. xxiv. 25). In the same chapter of Ezekiel (ver. 16), ' the desire of thy eyes ' is put not for the prophet's wife directly, as often understood, but for whatever is one's greatest solace and delight; which in this case was the prophet's wife—but which in another case might have been something else.

In Zech. iv. 10, the angels of the Lord are called ' his eyes,' as being the executioners of his judgments, and watching and attending for his glory. From some such association of ideas, the favourite ministers of state in the Persian monarchy were called ' the king's eyes.' So, in Num. x. 31, ' to be instead of eyes ' is equivalent to being a prince, to rule and guide the people.

The expression in Psalm cxxiii. 2, ' As the eyes of servants look unto the hands of their masters,' has suggested a number of curious illustrations from Oriental history and customs, tending to show that masters, especially when in the presence of others, are in the habit of communicating to their servants orders and intimations by certain motions of their hands, which, although scarcely noticeable by other persons present, are clearly understood and promptly acted upon by the attendants. This custom keeps them with their attention bent upon the hand of their master, watching its slightest motions.

Respecting blinding the eyes as a punishment, or political disqualification, see PUNISHMENT.

' PAINTING THE EYES,' or rather the eyelids, with a kind of black powder, is more than once

169.

alluded to in Scripture, although this scarcely appears in the Authorized Version, as our translators, unaware of the custom, usually render ' eye' by ' face,' although 'eye ' is still preserved in the margin. So Jezebel ' painted her eyes,' literally, ' put her eyes in paint,' before she showed herself publicly (2 Kings ix. 30). This action is forcibly expressed by Jeremiah (iv. 30), ' though thou rentest thine eyes with painting.' Ezekiel (xxiii. 40) also represents this as a part of high dress—' For whom thou didst wash thyself, *paintedst thy eyes,* and deckedst thyself with ornaments.' The custom is also, very possibly, alluded to in Prov. vi. 25—' Lust not after her beauty in thine heart, neither let her take thee *with her eyelids.*' It certainly is the general impression in Western Asia that this embellishment adds much to the languishing expression and seducement of the eyes, although Europeans find some difficulty in appreciating the beauty which the Orientals find in this adornment.

EZE′KIEL (*God-strengthened*), one of the greater prophets, whose writings, both in the Hebrew and Alexandrian canons, are placed next to those of Jeremiah. He was the son of Busi the priest (ch. i. 3), and, according to tradition, was a native of Sarera. Of his early history we have no authentic information. We first find him in the country of Mesopotamia, ' by the river Chebar ' (ch. i. 1), now *Khabûr,* a stream of considerable length flowing into the Euphrates near Circesium, *Kirkesia.* On this river Nebuchadnezzar founded a Jewish colony from the captives whom he brought from Jerusalem when he besieged it in the eighth year of King Jehoiachim (2 Kings xxv. 14). This colony (or at least a part of it) was settled at a place called Tel-Abib, and it seems to have been here that the prophet fixed his residence. He received his commission as a prophet in the fifth year of his captivity (B.C. 594). Ezekiel is remarkably silent respecting his personal history; the only event which he records (and that merely in its connection with his prophetic office) is the death of his wife in the ninth year of the captivity (ch. xxiv. 18). He continued to exercise the prophetic office during a period of at least twenty-two years, that is, to the 27th year of the captivity (ch. xxix. 17); and it appears probable that he remained with the captives by the river Chebar during the whole of his life. That he exercised a very command-ing influence over the people is manifest from the numerous intimations we have of the elders coming to inquire of him what message God had sent through him (ch. viii. 1; xiv. 1; xx. 1; xxxiii. 31, 32, &c.). Carpzov relates several traditions respecting his death and sepulchre. It is said that he was killed at Babylon by the chief of the people, on account of his having reproved him for idolatry; that he was buried in the field of Maur in the tomb of Shem and Arphaxad, and that his sepulchre was still in existence. Such traditions are obviously of very little value.

Ezekiel was contemporary with Jeremiah and Daniel. The former had sustained the prophetic office during a period of thirty-four years before Ezekiel's first predictions, and continued to pro-phesy for six or seven years after. It appears probable that the call of Ezekiel to the prophetic office was connected with the communication of Jeremiah's predictions to Babylon (Jer. li. 59), which took place the year preceding the first revelation to Ezekiel. The greater part of Da-niel's predictions are of a later date than those of Ezekiel; but it appears that his piety and wisdom had become proverbial in the early part of Ezekiel's ministry (ch. xiv. 14, 16; xxviii. 3).

Most critics have remarked the vigour and sur-prising energy which are manifest in the charac-ter of Ezekiel. The whole of his writings show how admirably he was fitted, as well by natural disposition as by spiritual endowment, to oppose the 'rebellious house,' the 'people of stubborn front and hard heart,' to whom he was sent. The figurative representations which abound through-out his writings, whether drawn out into length-ened allegory, or expressing matters of fact by means of symbols, or clothing truths in the garb of enigma, all testify by their definiteness the vigour of his conceptions. Things seen in vision are described with all the minuteness of detail and *sharpness* of outline which belong to real existences. But this characteristic is shown most remarkably in the entire subordination of his whole life to the great work to which he was called. We never meet with him as an ordinary man; he always acts and thinks and feels as a prophet. This energy of mind developed in the one direction of the prophetic office is strikingly dis-played in the account he gives of the death of his wife (ch. xxiv. 15-18). It is the only memorable event of his personal history which he records, and it is mentioned merely in reference to his soul-absorbing work. There is something inexpres-sibly touching as well as characteristic in this brief narrative—the 'desire of his eyes' taken away with a stroke—the command not to mourn, and the simple statement, 'so I spake unto the people ih the morning, and at even my wife died; and I did in the morning as I was commanded.' That he possessed the common sympathies and affections of humanity is manifest from the beau-

tiful touch of tenderness with which the narrative is introduced. We may even judge that a mind so earnest as his would be more than usually alive to the feelings of affection when once they had obtained a place in his heart. He then, who could thus completely subordinate the strongest interests of his individual life to the great work of his prophetic office, may well command our admiration, and be looked upon as (to use Häver-nick's expression) 'a truly gigantic phenomenon.' It is interesting to contrast Ezekiel in this respect with his contemporary Jeremiah, whose personal history is continually presented to us in the course of his writings; and the contrast serves to show that the peculiarity we are noticing in Ezekiel belongs to his individual character, and was not necessarily connected with the gift of prophecy.

That Ezekiel was a poet of no mean order is acknowledged by almost all critics. Michaelis remarks that Ezekiel lived at a period when the Hebrew language was declining in purity, when the *silver* age was succeeding to the *golden* one. It is, indeed, to the matter rather than the language of Ezekiel that we are to look for evi-dence of poetic genius.

The genuineness of the writings of Ezekiel has been the subject of very little dispute. Its canonicity in general is satisfactorily established by Jewish and Christian authorities. There is, indeed, no explicit reference to it, or quotation from it, in the New Testament. Eichhorn (*Ein-leit.* p. 218) mentions the following passages as having apparently a reference to this book: Rom. ii. 24; comp. Ezek. xxxvi. 21: Rom. x. 5; Gal. iii. 12; comp. Ezek. xx. 11: 2 Pet. iii. 4; comp. Ezek. xii. 22; but none of these are quo-tations. The closing visions of Ezekiel are clearly referred to, though not quoted, in the last chapters of the Apocalypse.

The central point of Ezekiel's predictions is the destruction of Jerusalem. Previously to this catastrophe his chief object is to call to repentance those who were living in careless security; to warn them against indulging in blind confidence, that by the help of the Egyptians (Ezek. xvii. 15-17; comp. Jer. xxxvii. 7) the Babylonian yoke would be shaken off; and to assure them that the destruction of their city and temple was inevitable and fast approaching. After this event his principal care is to console the captives by promises of future deliverance and return to their own land, and to encourage them by as-surances of future blessings. His predictions against foreign nations stand between these two great divisions, and were for the most part ut-tered during the interval of suspense between the divine intimation that Nebuchadnezzar was be-sieging Jerusalem (ch. xxiv. 2), and the arrival of the news that he had taken it (ch. xxxiii. 21). The predictions are evidently arranged on a plan corresponding with these the chief subjects of them, and the time of their utterance is so fre-quently noted that there is little difficulty in ascertaining their chronological order. This order is followed throughout, except in the middle portion relating to foreign nations, where it is in some instances departed from to secure greater unity of subject (e g. ch. xxix. 17).

The whole book is divided by Hävernick into nine sections, as follows:—

1. Ezekiel's call to the prophetic office (ch. i.-iii. 15).

2. Series of symbolical representations and particular predictions foretelling the approaching destruction of Judah and Jerusalem (ch. iii. 16-vii.).

3. Series of visions presented to the prophet a year and two months later than the former, in which he is shown the temple polluted by the worship of Adonis—the consequent judgment on the inhabitants of Jerusalem and on the priests,—and closing with promises of happier times and a purer worship (ch. viii.-xi.).

4. A series of reproofs and warnings directed especially against the particular errors and prejudices then prevalent amongst his contemporaries (ch. xii.-xix.).

5. Another series of warnings delivered about a year later, announcing the coming judgments to be yet nearer (ch. xx.-xxiii.).

6. Predictions uttered two years and five months later, when Jerusalem was besieged, announcing to the captives that very day as the commencement of the siege (comp. 2 Kings xxv. 1), and assuring them of its complete overthrow (ch. xxiv.).

7. Predictions against foreign nations (ch. xxv.-xxxii.).

8. After the destruction of Jerusalem a prophetic representation of the triumph of Israel and of the kingdom of God on earth (ch. xxxiii.-xxxix.).

9. Symbolic representation of Messianic times, and of the establishment and prosperity of the kingdom of God (ch. xl.-xlviii.).

E'ZION-GE'BER, a very ancient city lying not far from Elath, on the eastern arm of the Red Sea. It is first mentioned in Num. xxxiii. 35, as one of the stations where the Hebrews halted in their journeyings through the desert (Deut. ii. 8). From its harbour it was that Solomon (1 Kings ix. 26) built the fleet which he had there built to the land of Ophir, whence they fetched four hundred and twenty talents of gold. Here, also, Jehoshaphat (1 Kings xxii. 47; 2 Chron. xx. 35) built a fleet 'to go to Ophir,' but because he had joined himself with Ahaziah, 'king of Israel, who did wickedly,' 'the ships were broken that they were not able to go to Tarshish.' Eziongeber is probably the same with the once populous city Assyan. Robinson says, 'no trace of Eziongeber seems now to remain, unless it be in the name of a small wady with brackish water, el-Ghudyan, opening into el-Arabah from the western mountain, some distance north of Akabah.

EZ'RA (help). Ezra was a Jewish scribe and priest, who, about the year B.C. 458, led the second expedition of Jews back from the Babylonian exile in Palestine. This Ezra ought to be distinguished from the Ezra who went up as one of the chiefs of the priests and Levites under Zerubbabel (Neh. xii. 1, 12, 33). Ezra was a lineal descendant from Phineas, the son of Aaron. He is stated in Scripture to be the son of Seraiah, the son of Azariah; which Seraiah was slain at Riblah by order of Nebuchadnezzar, having been brought thither a captive by Nebuzaradan. But, as 130 years elapsed between the death of Seraiah and the departure of Ezra from Babylon, and we read that a grandson of Seraiah was the high

priest who accompanied Zerubbabel on the first return to Jerusalem, seventy years before Ezra returned thither, we may suppose that by the term *son* here, as in some other places, the relationship of grandson, or of a still more remote direct descendant, is intended. In addition to the information given in the books of Ezra and Nehemiah, that Ezra was a 'scribe,' a 'ready scribe of the law of Moses,' 'a scribe of the words of the Commandments of the Lord and of his statutes to Israel,' 'a scribe of the law of the God of Heaven,' and 'a priest,' we are told by Josephus that he was high-priest of the Jews who were left in Babylon; that he was particularly conversant with the laws of Moses, and was held in universal esteem on account of his righteousness and virtue.

The rebuilding of the temple of Jerusalem, which had been decreed by Cyrus in the year B.C. 536, was, after much powerful and vexatious opposition, completed in the reign and by the permission of Darius Hystaspis, in the year B.C. 515.

In the year B.C. 457 Ezra was sent by 'Artaxerxes Longimanus and his counsellors to inquire concerning Judah and Jerusalem, according to the law of his God which was in his hand; and to carry the silver and gold which the king and his counsellors freely offered unto the God of Israel.' Permission was also granted to him to take with him all the silver and the gold which he could find in all the province of Babylon, together with the free-will offerings which the people and priests offered for the house of God at Jerusalem. Of this treasure he was directed to employ as much as was requisite in the purchase of offerings according to the law of Moses, and the surplus he was to lay out according to his discretion for the maintenance of the externals of religion. Ezra was also charged to convey vessels for the house of God in Jerusalem; and, lest these gifts should be insufficient, he was empowered to take from the king's treasure-house as much as should be wanted to supply everything needful for the house of the Lord. At the same time that this commission was given to Ezra, Artaxerxes Longimanus issued a decree to the keepers of the king's treasure beyond the river, to assist Ezra in everything in which he needed help, and to supply him liberally with money, corn, wine, oil, and salt. It was further enacted that it should not be lawful to impose tribute upon any priest, Levite, or other person concerned in the ministration in the house of God. Ezra was commissioned to appoint 'according to the wisdom of God which was in his hand,' magistrates and judges to judge all the people beyond the river, that knew the laws of his God; and was enjoined to teach them to those who knew them not. The reason of the interest for the worship of God at this time evinced by Artaxerxes, appears to have been a fear of the divine displeasure, for we read in the conclusion of the decree to the treasurers beyond the river, 'Whatsoever is commanded by the God of Heaven, let it be diligently done for the house of the God of Heaven; FOR WHY SHOULD THERE BE WRATH AGAINST THE REALM OF THE KING AND HIS SONS?' We are also told (Ezra vii. 6) that the king granted Ezra all his request; and Josephus informs us that Ezra, being desirous of going to Jerusalem, requested the king to grant him recommendatory letters to the governor of

Syria. We may therefore suppose that the dread which Artaxerxes entertained of the divine judgments was the consequence of the exposition to him by Ezra of the history of the Jewish people.

Ezra assembled the Jews who accompanied him on the banks of the river Ahava, where they halted three days in tents. Here Ezra proclaimed a fast, as an act of humiliation before God and a season of prayer for divine direction and safe conduct; for, on setting out, he 'was ashamed to require a band of soldiers and horsemen to help them against the enemy by the way,' because he had asserted to the king that the hand of his God is upon all them that seek him for good. Ezra next committed the care of the treasures which he carried with him to twelve of the chief priests, assisted by ten of their brethren, appointing these to take charge of the treasures by the way, and deliver them safely in the house of the Lord at Jerusalem. On the twelfth day from their first setting out, Ezra and his companions left the river Ahava, and arrived safely at Jerusalem in the fifth month, having been delivered from the hand of the enemy and of such as lay in wait by the way. Three days after their arrival the treasures were weighed and delivered into the custody of some Levites. The returning exiles offered burnt-offerings to the Lord. They delivered also the king's commissions to the viceroys and governors, and gave needful help to the people and the ministers of the Temple. When Ezra had discharged the various trusts committed to him, the princes of the Jews came to him and complained that the Jewish people generally who had returned from the captivity, and also the priests and Levites, but especially the rulers and princes, had not kept themselves separate from the people of the land, but had done according to the abominations of the remnant of the nations whom their forefathers had driven out, and married their daughters, and allowed their children to intermarry with them. On hearing this Ezra was deeply afflicted; and, according to the Jewish custom, he rent his mantle and tore the hair of his head and beard. There gathered round him all those who still feared God, and dreaded his wrath for the transgression of those whom he had brought back from captivity. Having waited till the time of the evening sacrifice, Ezra rose up, and, having again rent his hair and his garments, made public prayer and confession of sin. The assembled people wept bitterly, and Shecaniah, one of the sons of Elam, came forward to propose a general covenant to put away the foreign wives and their children. Ezra then arose and administered an oath to the people that they would do accordingly. Proclamation was also made that all those who had returned from captivity should within three days gather themselves together unto Jerusalem, under pain of excommunication and forfeiture of their goods. The people assembled at the time appointed, trembling on account of their sin and of the heavy rain that fell. Ezra addressed them, declaring to them their sin, and exhorting them to amend their lives by dissolving their illegal connections. The people acknowledged the justice of his rebukes, and promised obedience. They then requested that, as the rain fell heavily, and the number of transgressors was great, he would

appoint times at which they might severally come to be examined respecting this matter, accompanied by the judges and elders of every city. A commission was therefore formed, consisting of Ezra and some others, to investigate the extent of the evil. This investigation occupied three months.

In Neh. viii. we read that, on the occasion of the celebration of the feast of the seventh month, subsequently to Nehemiah's numbering the people, Ezra was requested to bring the book of the law of Moses; and that he read therein standing upon a pulpit of wood, which raised him above all the people.

Contradictory accounts are given by the Jewish writers as to the time and place of Ezra's death. The Talmudic statement is that he died at Zamzumu, a town on the Tigris, while on his road from Jerusalem to Susa, whither he was going to converse with Artaxerxes about the affairs of the Jews. A tomb said to be his, represented in the present engraving, is shown on the Tigris, about twenty miles above its junction with the Euphrates.

170. [Tomb of Ezra.

Ezra is commonly regarded as the author of the books of Chronicles. But as the reasons for ascribing the books of Chronicles to the authorship of Ezra have already been investigated in the Article CHRONICLES, we confine ourselves here to the book of Ezra. Some authors have ascribed the books of Nehemiah and Esther likewise to Ezra, although they differ in style. [ESTHER; NEHEMIAH.]

EZRA, BOOK OF.—The book of Ezra contains records of events occurring about the termination of the Babylonian exile. It comprises accounts of the favours bestowed upon the Jews by Persian kings; of the rebuilding of the temple; of the mission of Ezra to Jerusalem, and his regulations and reforms. Such records forming the subject of the book of Ezra, we must not be surprised that its parts are not so intimately connected with each other as we might have expected if the author had set forth his intention to furnish a complete history of his times.

The events narrated in the book of Ezra are spread over a period of about 79 years, under the reigns of Cyrus, Cambyses, Magus, or Pseudo-Smerdis, Darius Hystaspis, Xerxes, Artaxerxes (in the eighth year of whose reign the records of Ezra cease).

The beginning of the book of Ezra agrees verbatim with the conclusion of the second book of Chronicles, and terminates abruptly with the statement of the divorces effected by his authority, by which the marriages of Israelites with foreign women were dissolved.

Since the book of Ezra has no marked conclusion, it was, even in early times, considered to form part of the book of Nehemiah, the contents of which are of a similar description. As, however, the book of Ezra is a collection of detached records of remarkable events occurring at the conclusion of the exile and in the times immediately following it, attempting no display of the art of book-making, the mere want of an artificial conclusion cannot be considered a sufficient reason for regarding it as the first portion of Nehemiah. It is, however, likely that the similarity of the contents of the books of Ezra and Nehemiah was the cause of their being placed together in the Hebrew Bible.

The arrangement of the facts in the book of Ezra is chronological. The book may be divided into two portions. The *first* consists of chapters i.-vi., and contains the history of the returning exiles and of their rebuilding of the temple, and comprises the period from the first year of Cyrus, B C. 536, to the sixth year of Darius Hystaspis, B.C. 515.

The *second* portion contains the personal history of the migration of Ezra to Palestine, in the seventh year of Artaxerxes. This latter portion, embracing chapters vii.-x., is an autobiography of Ezra during about twelve or thirteen months, in the seventh and eighth years of the reign of Artaxerxes Longimanus.

We have spoken thus far of the canonical book of Ezra; there are, however, four books that have received this name, viz. the book noticed above, the only one which was received into the Hebrew canon under that name, the book of Nehemiah, and the two apocryphal books of Esdras, concerning which see ESDRAS.

F.

FACE, in Scripture, is often used to denote *presence* in the general sense, and, when applied to the Almighty, denotes such a complete manifestation of the divine presence, by sound or sight, as was equivalent, in the vividness of the impression, to the seeing of a fellow-creature 'face to face.' The 'face of God' therefore denotes in Scripture any thing or manner by which God is wont to manifest himself to man.

It was a very ancient and common opinion that our mortal frame could not survive the more sensible manifestations of the divine presence, or 'see God face to face and live' (Gen. xxxii. 30). Hence, in this passage, the gratitude and astonishment of Jacob, that he still lived after God had manifested himself to him more sensibly than by dreams and visions. This impression was confirmed to Moses, who was told, 'Thou canst not see my face: no man can see my face and live' (Exod. xxxiii. 20); which clearly signifies that no one can, in this present state of being, endure the view of that glory which belongs to Him (1 Cor. xiii. 12; 1 John iii. 2; Rev. xxii. 4).

It is to be borne in mind that God is usually represented to us in Scripture under a human form; and it is indeed difficult for even more spiritualized minds than those of the Hebrews to conceive of Him apart from the form and attributes of the highest nature actually known to us. The Scripture sanctions this concession to the weakness of our intellect, and hence arise the anthropomorphous phrases which speak of the face, the eyes, the arm of God. The appearances of the angels in the Old Testament times were generally in the human form (Judg. xiii. 6, &c.); and from this cause alone it would have been natural, in the imagination, to transfer the form of the messengers to Him by whom they were sent.

FAIR HAVENS, a harbour or roadstead of Crete, the unsafeness of which to winter in, occasioned that attempt to make for Phenice, on the other side of the island, which led to the eventual loss of the vessel in which Paul sailed for Rome (Acts xxvii. 8). As the name is still preserved, there is no difficulty in fixing the situation to a small bay a little to the north-east of Cape Leon, the present Cape Matala.

FALLOW-DEER. The original terms *Ajal* and *Ajalah* are rendered in our common version by the names hart and hind (Deut. xii. 15; Ps. xlii. 1; Isa. xxxv. 6; Gen. xlix. 21; 2 Sam. xxii. 34; Job xxxix. 1; Ps. xviii. 31; Prov. v. 19; Cant. ii. 7; Jer. xiv. 5; Habak. iii. 19).

171. [Cervus barbarus.]

Sir J. G. Wilkinson believes Ajal to be the Ethiopian oryx, with nearly straight horns. But an Ethiopian species could not well be meant where the clean animals fit for the food of Hebrews are pointed out, nor where allusion is made to suffering from thirst, and to high and rocky places as the refuge of females, or of both, since all the species of oryx inhabit the open plains, and are not remarkable for the desire of drinking; nor can either of these propensities be properly ascribed to the true antelopes, or gazellæ, of Arabia and Syria, all being residents of the plain and the desert; like the oryges, often seen at immense distances from water, and unwilling to venture into forests, where their velocity of flight and delicacy of structure impede and destroy them. Animals of the stag kind prefer the security of forests, are always most robust in rocky mountain covers, and seek water with considerable anxiety; for of all the lightfooted ruminants, they alone protrude the tongue when hard pressed in the chace. Now, comparing these qualities with several texts, we find them perfectly appropriate to the species of these genera alone.

The first species here referred to is now known by the name of Cervus Barbarus, or Barbary stag, in size between our red and fallow deer, distinguished by the want of a bisantler, or second branch on the horns, reckoning from below, and a spotted livery, which is effaced only in the third or fourth year. This species is figured on Egyptian monuments, is still occasionally seen about the Natron lakes west of the Nile, and, it seems, was observed by a reverend friend in the desert east of the Dead Sea on his route from Cairo towards Damascus. We take this to be the Igial or Ajal of the Arabs, the same which they accuse of eating fish—that is, the neps, lizards, and snakes, a propensity common to other species, and similarly ascribed to the Virginian and Mexican deer.

The other is the Persian stag, or Maral of the Tahtar nations, and Gewazen of Armenia, larger than the stag of Europe, clothed with a heavy mane, and likewise destitute of bisantlers. We believe this species to be the Soëgur of Asiatic Turkey, and many of the Arabs, therefore, residing on the borders of the mountain forests of Syria and Palestine. One or both of these species were dedicated to the local *bona dea* on Mount Libanus—a kind of proof that deer were found in the vicinity.

Of the hind it is unnecessary to say more than that she is the female of stag, or hart, and that in the manners of these animals the males always are the last to hurry into cover.

FASTS. The observance of religious fasts established itself in the world at a very early period, and is found to have prevailed in most of the nations of antiquity. In such a religion as Moses was commissioned by the creator of the world to offer to the chosen people, it was not likely that an observance which, such as fasts, seems to have had its origin in false and heathen conceptions, should hold a very prominent position, or be invested with much importance. There is but one fast enjoined by the great Hebrew lawgiver. And this injunction we are disposed to place among those things which Moses allowed rather than originated, bore with rather than approved, in consideration of the force of established custom, and from a wise fear of defeating his own good ends by attempting too much. The manner in which this observance is spoken of in Scripture (Lev. xvi. 29; xxiii. 27) seems to imply that it was no new institution that the lawgiver was establishing, but merely an old and well known practice, to which he gave a modified sanction. Had it been otherwise, had the law been a new one, details would have been both needed and given, as is customary with Moses in his injunctions. Instead of that, the children of Israel are required in general terms to 'afflict their souls.' But this language is not only vague, it is figurative, and could have no definite mean-

ing unless to persons with whom afflicting the soul was in general use. There seems, however, no reason to doubt that 'to afflict the soul,' bore with it the meaning of fasting. To a mere English reader the phrase seems to comprise all kinds of voluntary mortifications, but 'soul' in Hebrew not seldom denotes the 'appetite' (Prov. xxvii. 7). Accordingly the words regard immediately abstinence from food, and most probably (so far as they go) nothing more.

The sole fast required by Moses was on the great day of annual atonement. This observance seems always to have retained some prominence as 'the fast' (Acts xxvii. 9). But what the observance of the enjoined duty involved we are nowhere expressly informed. Other general fasts, however, were in course of ages introduced, which were celebrated at fixed times every successive year. In the reign of Zedekiah, Nebuchadnezzar besieged and captured Jerusalem, which calamity led to the establishment of a fast on the seventeenth day of the fourth month (Thammuz, July), (Jer. lii. 6, 7; Zech. viii. 19). In the last passage other fasts are enumerated, namely, 'the fast of the fifth, and the fast of the seventh, and the fast of the tenth.' That of the fifth month (Ab, August) was held on the ninth day, in mournful commemoration of the burning of the city by 'Nebuzar-adan, a servant of the king of Babylon,' who 'burnt the house of the Lord, and the king's house, and all the houses of Jerusalem, and every great man's house' (2 Kings xxv. 8, sq.; Jer. lii. 12; Zech. vii. 3-5; viii. 19). The fast of the seventh month (Tishri, October) was established to bewail the murder of Gedaliah at Mizpah (Jer. xli. 1, sq.; 2 Kings xxv. 25). That of the tenth month (Tebeth, January) was held on the tenth day to commemorate the commencement of the siege of Jerusalem on the part of Nebuchadnezzar (2 Kings xxv. 1; Zech. viii. 19).

On particular and signal occasions extraordinary fasts were appointed (Judges xx. 26; 1 Sam. xxxi. 11-13; Baruch i. 5; 1 Kings xxi. 9; comp. Jer. xxxvi. 9; 2 Chron. xx. 3). In Joel i. ii. a fast is enjoined with a view to turn away the wrath of God as displayed in the terrible consequences of the invasion of the land of Judæa by an army of devastating locusts. The notion also prevailed that a special fast might have the effect of averting the divine displeasure and securing the divine co-operation in any great undertaking (Jonah iii. 5; 1 Sam. vii. 5, 6, 8, 10, 12; 1 Macc. iii. 47; 2 Macc. xiii. 12; Judith iv. 11; vi. 19). Local fasts were at a later period sometimes held in order to avert calamity or procure a favour from heaven; and the Sanhedrim ordered general fasts when the nation was threatened with any great evil, such as drought or famine.

There were also private fasts, though the Mosaic law did not require them. They were held in connection with individual or family incidents, and agreed in aim and tendency with fasts of a general and public nature. Examples may be found in 1 Sam. i. 7; xx. 34; 1 Kings xxi. 9; Ez. x. 6; Neh. i. 4. After the exile private fasts became very frequent, awaiting the call of no special occasion, but entering as a regular part of the current religious worship. The parable of the Pharisee and Publican (Luke xviii. 9; comp. Matt. ix. 14) shows how much the Pharisees were given to voluntary and private fasts—'I fast twice in the week.' The first was on the fifth day of the week, on which Moses ascended to the top of Mount Sinai; the second was on the second day, on which he came down. The Essenes and the Therapeutæ also were much given to such observances. Fasts were considered as a useful exercise in preparing the mind for special religious impressions. Thus Dan. x. 2, sq., 'In those days I Daniel was mourning three full weeks. I ate no pleasant bread, neither came flesh nor wine in my mouth. Then I lifted up my eyes and looked, and behold a certain man,' &c. (see also Acts xiii. 3; xiv. 23). From Matt. xvii. 21, 'Howbeit this kind (of demons) goeth not out but by prayer and fasting,' it would appear that the practice under consideration was considered in the days of Christ to act in certain special cases as an exorcism. Fasting was accompanied by the ordinary signs of grief among the Israelites, as may be seen in 1 Macc. iii. 47, 'Then they fasted that day and put on sackcloth, and cast ashes upon their heads and rent their clothes.' The fast ordinarily lasted from evening to evening, but was not observed on the sabbath or on festival days. The abstinence was either partial or total. In the case of the latter food was entirely foregone, but this ordinarily took place only in fasts of short duration; and abstinence from food in eastern climes is more easy and less detrimental (if not in some cases positively useful) than keeping from food would be with us in these cold, damp, northern regions (Esther iv. 16). In the case of partial abstinence the time was longer, the denial in degree less. When Daniel (x. 2) was 'mourning three full weeks,' he ate no *pleasant* bread, neither came *flesh* nor *wine* in my mouth.' There does not appear to have been any fixed and recognized periods during which these fasts endured. From one day to forty days fasts were observed. The latter period appears to have been regarded with feelings of peculiar sanctity, owing doubtless to certain events in Jewish history. Thus Moses 'was with the Lord on Mount Sinai forty days and forty nights, he did neither eat bread nor drink water' (Exod. xxxiv. 28). So Elijah (1 Kings xix. 8) 'arose and did eat and drink, and went in the strength of that meat forty days and forty nights unto Horeb the mount of God.' The same was the number of days that our Lord fasted in the desert in connection with his temptation (Matt. iv. 1-11; Mark i. 12, 13; Luke iv. 1-13). We have already seen how qualified the sanction was which Moses gave to the observance of fasting as a religious duty. In the same spirit which actuated him, the prophets bore testimony against the lamentable abuses to which the practice was turned in the lapse of time and with the increase of social corruption (Isa. lviii. 4, sq.; Jer. xiv. 12; Zech. vii. 5). Continuing the same species of influence and perfecting that spirituality in religion which Moses began, our Lord rebuked the Pharisees sternly for their outward and hypocritical pretences in the fasts which they observed (Matt. vi. 16, sq.), and actually abstained from appointing any fast whatever as a part of his own religion (Matt. ix. 14). From the passage referred to this at least is clear, that Jesus ascribed to fasts no essential worth, nor required any such observance from his fol-

lowers. Whether and how far he *allowed* fasting as a means of religious improvement, is a question which our space does not permit us to discuss. That the early Christians observed the ordinary fasts which the public practice of their day sanctioned, is clear from more than one passage in the New Testament Scriptures (Acts xiii. 2; xiv. 23; 2 Cor. vi. 5); but in this they probably did nothing more than yield obedience, as in general they thought themselves bound to do, to the law of their fathers so long as the Mosaic institutions remained entire. And though the great body of the Christian Church held themselves free from all ritual and ceremonial observances when God in his providence had brought Judaism to a termination in the rasure of the holy city and the closing of the temple, yet the practice of fasting thus originated might have easily and unobservedly been transmitted from year to year and from age to age, and that the rather because so large a portion of the disciples being Jews (to say nothing of the influence of the Ebionites in the primitive church), thousands must have been accustomed to fasting from the earliest days of their existence, either in their own practice or the practice of their fathers, relatives, and associates.

FAT. In Lev. iii. there are minute details of the parts of victims which were to be specially appropriated to the altar. Among these all the internal *fat* is minutely specified, particularly the rat of the kidneys; and of external parts the tail of the sheep, which, in the common species of Western Asia, is a mass of fat (iii. 4, 9, 10, 15): and the whole concludes with 'All the fat is the Lord's; ye shall eat neither fat nor blood' (iii. 17). The reason assigned, namely, that the fat was consecrated to the altar, could only apply with respect to that of animals used in sacrifice, which were also usually employed for food. One point seems to have been very generally overlooked, which is, that not fat absolutely, but particular fat parts only are interdicted. They might eat the fat involved in the muscular tissue —in short, fat meat; and we know that animals were actually fattened for food (1 Kings iv. 23; Jer. xlvi. 21; Luke xv. 23). This was, however, not a usual practice; and even at this day in the East, domestic cattle seldom undergo any preparatory feeding or fattening before being killed. Hence there is little fat in the carcass, except that belonging to the parts specified in the prohibition, which is all more or less of the nature of suet. Various reasons have been assigned for this somewhat remarkable restriction. The secondary cause, that the fat was consecrated to the altar, and therefore was to be abstained from, is not all; for it is usually considered that it was thus consecrated to give a religious sanction to a prohibition expedient on other grounds. The true reason probably is, that this suet or suet-like fat is not particularly wholesome or digestible in warm climates, if anywhere, and is particularly unsuitable for persons subject to cutaneous diseases, as the Israelites appear to have been at the time of their leaving Egypt.

'Fatness,' in Scripture, expresses plumpness or exuberance, whether in men, animals, or vegetables; and is hence often applied metaphorically to any kind of abundance, as to large possessions, or to excessive fertility in the earth.

FATHER. This word, besides its obvious and primary sense, bears, in Scripture, a number of other applications, most of which have, through the use of the Bible, become more or less common in all Christian countries.

1. The term Father is very often applied to God himself (Exod. iv. 22; Deut. xxxii. 6; 2 Sam. vii. 14; Ps. lxxxix. 27, 28; Isa. lxiii. 16; lxiv. 8). In some of these passages he is set before us as the Father of all men, in the general sense of creator and preserver of all men, but more especially of believers, whether Jews or Christians.

Without doubt, however, God is in a more especial and intimate manner, even as by covenant, the Father of the Jews (Jer. xxxi. 9; Isa. lxiii. 16; lxiv. 8; John viii. 41; v. 45; 2 Cor. vi. 18); and also of Christians, or rather of all pious and believing persons, who are called 'sons of God' (John i. 12; Rom. viii. 16, etc.). Thus Jesus, in speaking to his disciples, calls God their Father (Matt. vi. 4, 8, 15, 18; x. 20, 29; xiii. 43, etc.). The Apostles, also, for themselves and other Christians, call him 'Father' (Rom. i. 7; 1 Cor. i. 3; 2 Cor. i. 2; Gal. i. 4; and many other places).

2. *Father* is applied to any ancestor near or remote, or to ancestors ('fathers') in general. The progenitor, or founder, or *patriarch* of a tribe or nation, was also pre-eminently its father, as Abraham of the Jews. Examples of this abound. See, for instance, Deut. i. 11; 1 Kings viii. 21; Matt. iii. 9; xxiii. 30; Mark xi. 10; Luke i. 32, 73; vi. 23, 26; John vii. 22, &c.

3. *Father* is also applied as a title of respect to any head, chief, ruler, or elder, and especially to kings, prophets, and priests (Judg. xvii. 10; xviii. 19; 1 Sam. x. 12; 2 Kings ii. 12; v. 13; vi. 21; xiii. 14; Prov. iv. 1; Matt. xxiii. 9; Acts vii, 2; xxii. 1; 1 Cor. iv. 15, etc.).

4. The author, source, or beginner of anything is also called the Father of the same, or of those who follow him. Thus Jabal is called 'the father of those who dwell in tents, and have cattle;' and Jubal, 'the father of all such as handle the harp and the organ' (Gen. iv. 20, 21; comp. Job xxxviii. 28; John viii. 44; Rom. iv. 12).

The authority of a father was very great in patriarchal times; and although the power of life and death was virtually taken from the parent by the law of Moses, which required him to bring his cause of complaint to the public tribunals (Deut. xxi. 18-21), all the more real powers of the paternal character were not only left unimpaired, but were made in a great degree the basis of the judicial polity which that law established. The children and even the grandchildren continued under the roof of the father and grandfather; they laboured on his account, and were the most submissive of his servants. The property of the soil, the power of judgment, the civil rights, belonged to him only, and his sons were merely his instruments and assistants.

Filial duty and obedience were, indeed, in the eyes of the Jewish legislator, of such high importance, that great care was taken that the paternal authority should not be weakened by the withdrawal of a power so liable to fatal and barbarous abuse as that of capital punishment. Any outrage against a parent—a blow, a curse, or

incorrigible profligacy—was made a capital crime (Exod. xxi. 15, 17; Lev. xx. 9). If the offence was public, it was taken up by the witnesses as a crime against Jehovah, and the culprit was brought before the magistrates whether the parent consented or not; and if the offence was hidden within the paternal walls, it devolved on the parents to denounce him and to require his punishment.

It is a beautiful circumstance in the law of Moses that this filial respect is exacted for the mother as well as for the father. The threats and promises of the legislator distinguish not the one from the other; and the fifth commandment associates the father and mother in a precisely equal claim to honour from their children. The development of this interesting feature of the Mosaical law belongs, however, to another head [WOMEN].

FEASTS. The root-idea of the word is to be found in what we should term the pleasures of the table, the exercise of hospitality.

To what an early date the practices of hospitality are referable may be seen in Gen. xix. 3. It was usual not only to receive persons with choice viands, but also to dismiss them in a similar manner; accordingly Laban, when he had overtaken the fleeing Jacob, complains (Gen. xxxi. 27), 'Wherefore didst thou steal away from me and didst not tell me, that I might have sent thee away with mirth, and with songs, and with tabret, and with harp?' See also 2 Sam. iii. 20; 2 Kings vi. 23; Job. viii. 20; 1 Macc. xvi. 15. This practice explains the reason why the prodigal, on his return, was welcomed by a feast (Luke xv. 23). Occasions of domestic joy were hailed with feasting; thus, in Gen. xxi. 8, Abraham 'made a great feast the same day that Isaac was weaned.' Birth-days were thus celebrated (Gen. xl. 20), 'Pharaoh, on his birth-day made a feast unto all his servants' (Job. i. 4; Matt. xiv. 6; comp. Herod. i. 133). Marriage-feasts were also common. Samson (Judg. xiv. 10) on such an occasion 'made a feast,' and it is added, 'for so used the young men to do.' So Laban, when he gave his daughter Leah to Jacob (Gen. xxix. 22), 'gathered together all the men of the place, and made a feast.' These festive occasions seem originally to have answered the important purpose of serving as evidence and attestation of the events which they celebrated, on which account relatives and neighbours were invited to be present (Ruth iv. 10; John ii. 1). Those processes in rural occupations by which the Divine bounties are gathered into the hands of man, have in all ages been made seasons of festivity; accordingly in 2 Sam. xiii. 23, Absalom invites all the king's sons, and even David himself, to a sheep-shearing feast, on which occasion the guests became 'merry with wine' (1 Sam. xxv. 2, sq.). The vintage was also celebrated with festive eating and drinking (Judg. ix. 27). Feasting at funerals existed among the Jews (2 Sam. iii. 33). In Jer. xvi. 7, among other funeral customs mention is made of 'the cup of consolation, to drink for their father or their mother,' which brings to mind the indulgence in spirituous liquors to which our ancestors were given, at interments, and which has not yet entirely disappeared. To what an extent expense was sometimes carried on these occasions, may be learned from Josephus, who, having remarked that Archelaus 'mourned for his father seven days, and had given a very expensive funeral feast to the multitude,' states, 'which custom is the occasion of poverty to many of the Jews,' adding, 'because they are forced to feast the multitude, for if any one omits it he is not esteemed a holy person.'

As among heathen nations, so also among the Hebrews, feasting made a part of the observances which took place on occasion of animal sacrifices (Deut. xii. 6, 7 ; 1 Sam. ix. 19 ; xvi. 3, 5 ; 2 Sam. vi. 19). These sacrificial meals were enjoyed in connection with peace-offerings, whether eucharistic or votive. To the feast at the second tithe of the produce of the land, which was to be made every year and eaten at the annual festivals before Jehovah, not only friends, but strangers, widows, orphans, and Levites, were to be invited, as well as the slaves. If the tabernacles were so distant as to make it inconvenient to carry thither the tithe, it was to be turned into money, which was to be spent at the place at which the festivals were held in providing feasts (Deut. xiv. 22-27; xii. 14; Tobit i. 6). Charitable entertainments were also provided, at the end of three years, from the tithe of the increase. The Levite, the stranger, the fatherless, and the widow, were to be present (Deut. xii. 17-19; xiv. 28, 29 ; xxvi. 12-15). At the feast of Pentecost the command is very express (Deut. xvi. 11), 'Thou shalt rejoice before the Lord thy God, thou, and thy son, and thy daughter, and thy man-servant, and thy maid-servant, and the Levite that is within thy gates, and the stranger, and the fatherless, and the widow, that are among you.' The Israelites were forbidden to partake of food offered in sacrifice to idols (Exod. xxxiv. 15), lest they should be thereby enticed into idolatry or appear to give a sanction to idolatrous observances (1 Cor. x. 28).

FE'LIX, a Roman procurator of Judæa, before whom Paul so 'reasoned of righteousness, temperance, and judgment to come,' that the judge trembled, saying, 'Go thy way for this time; when I have a convenient season I will call for thee' (Acts xxiv. 25). The context states that Felix had expected a bribe from Paul; and, in order to procure this bribe, he appears to have had several interviews with the Apostle. The depravity which such an expectation implies is in agreement with the idea which the historical fragments preserved respecting Felix would lead the student to form of the man.

The year in which Felix entered on his office cannot be strictly determined. From the words of Josephus it appears that his appointment took place before the twelfth year of the Emperor Claudius.

Felix was a remarkable instance of the elevation to distinguished station of persons born and bred in the lowest condition. Originally a slave, he rose to little less than kingly power. For some unknown, but probably not very creditable services, he was manumitted by Claudius Cæsar (Sueton. Claud. 28 ; Tacit. Hist. v. 9); on which account he is said to have taken the prænomen of Claudius.

The character which the ancients have left of Felix is of a very dark complexion. Suetonius speaks of the military honours which the emperor loaded him with, and specifies his appointment as governor of the province of Judæa; adding an inuendo, which loses nothing by its brevity, namely, that he was the husband of three queens or royal ladies. Tacitus, in his History (v. 9), declares that, during his governorship in Judæa, he indulged in all kinds of cruelty and lust, exercising regal power with the disposition of a slave; and, in his Annals (xii. 54) he represents Felix as considering himself licensed to commit any crime, relying on the influence which he possessed at court. The country was ready for rebellion, and the unsuitable remedies which Felix applied served only to inflame the passions and to incite to crime. Under his sway the affairs of the country grew worse and worse. The land was filled with robbers and impostors who deluded the multitude. Felix used his power to repress these disorders to little purpose, since his own example gave no sanction to justice. Having a grudge against Jonathan, the high-priest, who had expostulated with him on his misrule, he made use of Doras, an intimate friend of Jonathan, in order to get him assassinated by a gang of villains, who joined the crowds that were going up to the temple to worship,—a crime which led subsequently to countless evils, by the encouragement which it gave to the Sicarii, or leagued assassins of the day, to whose excesses Josephus ascribes, under Providence, the overthrow of the Jewish state. Among other crimes, some of these villains misled the people under the promise of performing miracles, and were punished by Felix. An Egyptian impostor, who escaped himself, was the occasion of the loss of life to four hundred followers, and of the loss of liberty to two hundred more, thus severely dealt with by Felix.

While in his office, being inflamed by a passion for the beautiful Drusilla, a daughter of King Herod Agrippa, who was married to Azizus, king of Emesa, he employed one Simon, a magician, to use his arts in order to persuade her to forsake her husband and marry him, promising that if she would comply with his suit he would make her a happy woman. Drusilla, partly impelled by a desire to avoid the envy of her sister, Berenice, was prevailed on to transgress the laws of her forefathers, and consented to a union with Felix. In this marriage a son was born, who was named Agrippa: both mother and son perished in an eruption of Mount Vesuvius, which took place in the days of Titus Cæsar. With this adulteress was Felix seated when Paul reasoned before the judge, as already stated (Acts xxiv. 24).

Paul, being apprehended in Jerusalem, was sent by a letter from Claudius Lysias to Felix at Cæsarea, where he was at first confined in Herod's judgment-hall till his accusers came. They arrived. Tertullus appeared as their spokesman, and had the audacity, in order to conciliate the good will of Felix, to express gratitude on the part of the Jews, 'seeing that by thee we enjoy great quietness, and that very worthy deeds are done unto this nation by thy providence' (Acts xxiii. xxiv.). Paul pleaded his cause in a worthy speech; and Felix, consigning the Apostle to the custody of a centurion, ordered that he should have such liberty as the circumstances admitted, with permission that his acquaintance might see him and minister to his wants. This imprisonment the Apostle suffered for a period of two years, being left bound when Felix gave place to Festus, as that unjust judge ' was willing,' not to do what was right, but ' to show the Jews a pleasure.'

FERRET. [Lizard.]

FESTIVALS. The Hebrew festivals were occasions of public religious observances, recurring at certain set and somewhat distant intervals. In general they may be divided into two kinds:—1. Those of divine institution; 2. Those of human origin. Those which owe their existence to the authority of God are, the seventh day of the week, or the Sabbath; the Passover; Pentecost; the Feast of Trumpets; the Day of Atonement; the Feast of Tabernacles; the New Moon. Festivals which arose under purely human influences are, the Feast of Lots or Purim; the death of Holofernes; the Dedication; the Sacred Fire; the death of Nicanor.

Reserving details for separate articles on such of these as shall seem to require and justify a distinct treatment, we confine ourselves here to a general outline, with some remarks on the origin and tendency of the chief festivals.

We have inserted the Sabbath for the sake of completeness, and, with the same view, we proceed to set down a few brief particulars respecting the daily service, so that we may at once present a general outline of the temple worship.

At the daily service two lambs of the first year were to be offered at the door of the tabernacle; one in the morning, the other in the evening, a continual burnt-offering. With each lamb was to be offered one-tenth of an ephah of flour, mingled with one-fourth of a hin of fresh oil, for a meat-offering, and one-fourth of a hin of wine for a drink-offering. Frankincense was to be placed on the meat-offering, a handful of which, with the frankincense, was to be burnt, and the remainder was to be eaten by the priest in the holy place, without leaven. The priests were to offer daily the tenth of an ephah of fine flour, half in the morning and half in the evening, for themselves. The high-priest was to dress the lamps in the tabernacle every morning, and light them every evening; and at the same time burn incense on the altar of incense. The people provided oil for the lamps which were to burn from evening to morning: the ashes were removed by a priest, dressed in his linen garment and his linen drawers, and then carried by him out of the camp, in his common dress. Great stress was laid on the regular observance of these requirements (Num. xxviii. 1-8; Exod. xxix. 38-42; Lev. vi. 8-23; Exod. xxx. 7-9; xxvii. 20; Lev. xxiv. 1-4; Num. viii. 2).

Labour was to last not longer than six days. The seventh was a Sabbath, a day of rest, of holy convocation, on which no one, not even strangers or cattle, was allowed to do any servile work. The offender was liable to stoning.

On the Sabbath two lambs of the first year, without blemish, were to be offered for a burnt-offering, morning and evening, with two-tenths of an ephah of flour, mingled with oil, for a meat-offering, and one-half of a hin of wine for a drink-offering, thus doubling the offering for ordinary days. Twelve cakes of fine flour were to be placed every Sabbath upon the table in the tabernacle, in two piles, and pure frankincense laid on the

uppermost of each pile. These were to be furnished by the people; two were offered to Jehovah, the rest were eaten by the priests in the holy place (Exod. xxxi. 12; Lev. xxiii. 1; xxvi. 2; Exod. xix. 3, 30; xx. 8-11; xxiii. 12; Deut. v. 12-15; Lev. xxiii. 3; xxiv. 5-9; Num. xv. 35; xxviii. 9).

At the *New Moon* festival, in the beginning of the month, in addition to the daily sacrifice, two heifers, one ram, and seven lambs of the first year, were to be offered as burnt-offerings, with three-tenths of an ephah of flour, mingled with oil, for each heifer; two-tenths of an ephah of flour, mingled with oil, for the ram; and one-tenth of an ephah of flour, mingled with oil, for every lamb; and a drink-offering of half a hin of wine for a heifer, one-third of a hin for the ram, and one-fourth of a hin for every lamb. One kid of the goats was also to be offered as a sin-offering.

The first day of the *seventh month* was to be a Sabbath, a holy convocation, accompanied by the *blowing of trumpets*. In addition to the daily and monthly sacrifices, one ram and seven lambs were to be offered as burnt-offerings, with their respective meat-offerings, as at the usual New Moon festival (Num. xxviii. 11-15; xxix. 1-6; Lev. xxiii. 23-25).

Three times in the year—at the Feast of Unleavened Bread, in the month Abib; at the Feast of Harvest, or of Weeks; and at the Feast of Ingathering, or of Tabernacles—all the males were to appear before Jehovah, at the place which he should choose. None were to come empty-handed, but every one was to give according as Jehovah had blessed him; and there before Jehovah was every one to rejoice with his family, the Levite, the stranger, the fatherless, and the widow (Exod. xxiii. 14-17; xxxiv. 22-24; Deut. xvi. 16, 17).

The first of these three great festivals, that of Unleavened Bread, called also the Passover, was kept in the Month Abib, in commemoration of the rescue of the Israelites by Jehovah out of Egypt, which took place in that month. The ceremonies that were also connected with it will be detailed under the head PASSOVER. In order to make the season more remarkable, it was ordained that henceforward the month in which it took place should be reckoned the first of the national religious year (Exod. xii. 2). From this time, accordingly, the year began in the month Abib, or Nisan (March—April), while the civil year continued to be reckoned from Tishri (September—October) (Exod. xii. 3, 14, 27, 43-49; Lev. xxiii. 5; Num. xxviii. 16; Deut. xvi. 1-7). The Passover lasted one week, including two Sabbaths. The first day and the last were holy, that is, devoted to the observances in the public temple, and to rest from all labour (Exod. xii. 16; Lev. xxiii. 6 Num. xxviii. 18; Deut. xvi. 8).

On the day after the Sabbath, on the Feast of Passover, a sheaf of the first-fruits of the barley-harvest was to be brought to the priest to be waved before Jehovah, accompanied by a burnt-offering. Till this sheaf was presented, neither bread nor parched corn, nor full ripe ears of the harvest, could be eaten (Exod. xii. 15-20; xiii. 6-10; Lev. xxiii. 6-8; Deut. xvi. 2-8; Num. xxviii. 17-25).

The Feast of Pentecost or of Weeks was kept

to Jehovah at the end of seven weeks from the day of the Festival of Unleavened Bread, on which the sheaf was presented. On the morrow after the seventh complete week, or on the fiftieth day, two wave loaves were presented as first fruits of the wheat harvest, together with a burnt-offering, a sin-offering, and a peace-offering, &c. The day was a holy convocation, in which no servile work was done. The festival lasted but one day. It is said to have been designed to commemorate the giving of the law on Mount Sinai (Deut. xvi. 9–11; Lev. xiii. 15–21; Num. xxviii. 26–31; xv. 17–21).

The Feast of In-gathering or of Tabernacles began on the fifteenth day of the seventh month, and continued eight days, the first and last being Sabbaths. During the feast all native Israelites dwelt in booths made of the shoots of beautiful trees, palm-branches, boughs of thick-leaved trees, and of the willows of the brook, when they rejoiced with their families, with the Levite, the stranger, the fatherless, and the widow, before Jehovah. Various offerings were made. At the end of every seven years, in the year of release, at the Feast of Tabernacles, the law was required to be read by the priests in the hearing of all the Israelites (Deut. xvi. 13–15; xxxi. 10–13; Lev. xxiii. 39–43; 33–36; Num. xxix. 12–38, 40).

The Feast of Tabernacles was appointed partly to be an occasion of annual thanksgiving after the in-gathering of the harvest (Exod. xxxiv. 22; Lev. xxiii. 39; Deut. xvi. 13), and partly to remind the Israelites that their fathers had lived in tents in the wilderness (Lev. xxiii. 40–43). This feast took place in the end of the year, September or October.

The tenth day of the seventh month was the Day of Atonement—a day of abstinence, a day of holy convocation, in which all were to afflict themselves. Special offerings were made [ATONE-MENT] (Lev. xxiii. 26–32; xvi. 1, 34; Num. xxix. 7–11; Exod. xxx. 10).

Brown, in his *Antiquities* (vol. i. p. 520), remarks that the time of the year in which the three great festivals were observed was during the dry season of Judæa. The latter rains fell before the Passover, the former rains after the Feast of Tabernacles; so that the country was in the best state for travelling at the time of these festivals.

On these solemn occasions food came partly from hospitality (a splendid instance of which may be found in 2 Chron. xxxv. 7-9), partly from the feasts which accompanied the sacrifices in the temple, and partly also from provision expressly made by the travellers themselves. Lodging, too, was afforded by friends, or found in tents erected for the purpose in and around Jerusalem.

The three great festivals have corresponding events (but of far greater importance) in the new dispensation. The Feast of Tabernacles was the time when our Saviour was born; he was crucified at the Passover; while at Pentecost the effusion of the Holy Spirit took place.

The rest and recreation enjoyed during these festivals would be the more pleasant, salutary, and beneficial, because of the joyous nature of the religious services in which they were, for the greater part, engaged. These solemn festivals were not only commemorations of great

national events, but they were occasions for the reunion of friends, for the enjoyment of hospitality, and for the interchange of kindness. The feasts which accompanied the sacrifices opened the heart of the entire family to joy, and gave a welcome which bore a religious sanction even to the stranger, the fatherless, and the widow.

How much, too, would these gatherings tend to foster and sustain a spirit of nationality! By intercourse the feelings of tribe and clan would be worn away; men from different parts became acquainted with and attached to each other; partial interests were found to be more imaginary than real; while the predominant idea of a common faith and a common rallying-place at Jerusalem could not fail to fuse into one strong and overpowering emotion of national and brotherly love, all the higher, nay, even the lower feelings, of each Hebrew heart.

Another effect of these festivals Michaelis has found in the furtherance of internal commerce. They would give rise to something resembling our modern fairs. Among the Mahometans similar festivals have had this effect.

These festivals, in their origin, had an obvious connection with agriculture. Passover saw the harvest upon the soil; at Pentecost it was ripe; and Tabernacles was the festival of gratitude for the fruitage and vintage (Michaelis, art. 197). The first was a natural pause after the labours of the field were completed; the second, after the first-fruits were gathered; and the third, a time of rejoicing in the feeling that the Divine bounty had crowned the year with its goodness. Spring, summer, and autumn, which have moved all nations of men with peculiar and characteristic emotions, had each its natural language and symbols in the great Israelitish festivals, a regard to which may well be supposed to have had an influence in the mind of the legislator, as well as in the consuetudinary practices of the people.

The Feast of Purim or of Lots originated in the gratitude of the Jews in escaping the plot of Haman, designed for their destruction. It took its name from the lots which were cast before Haman by the astrologers, who knew his hatred against Mordecai and his wish to destroy his family and nation (Esther iii. 7: ix. 2, 5). The feast was suggested by Esther and Mordecai, and was celebrated on the 13th, 14th, and 15th days of the twelfth month (Adar). The 13th was a fast, being the day on which the Jews were to have been destroyed; and the 14th and 15th were a feast held in commemoration of their deliverance. The fast is called the Fast of Esther, and the feast still holds the name of Purim.

The slaughter of Holofernes by the hand of Judith, the consequent defeat of the Assyrians, and the liberation of the Jews, were commemorated by the institution of a festival (Judith xiv. xv).

The Feast of Dedication was appointed by Judas Maccabæus, on occasion of the purification of the temple, and reconstruction of the altar, after they had been polluted by Antiochus Epiphanes.

The new dedication took place on the 25th day of the ninth month, called Chisleu, in the year before Christ 170. This would be in December. The day was chosen as being that on which Antiochus, three years before, had polluted the altar by heathen sacrifices.

Y

The joy of the Israelites must have been great on the occasion, and well may they have prolonged the observance of it for eight days. A general illumination formed a part of the festival, whence it obtained the name of the Feast of Lights.

In John x. 22 this festival is alluded to when our Lord is said to have been present at the Feast of Dedication. The historian marks the time by stating ' it was winter.'

The festival ' of the Fire ' was instituted by Nehemiah to commemorate the miraculous rekindling of the altar-fire. The circumstances are narrated in 2 Macc. i. 18.

The defeat by Judas Maccabæus of the Greeks, when the Jews ' smote off Nicanor's head and his right hand which he stretched out so proudly,' caused the people to ' rejoice greatly, and they kept that day a day of great gladness; moreover, they ordained to keep yearly this day, being the thirteenth day of Adar '—February or March (1 Macc. vii. 47).

FESTUS. Porcius Festus was the successor of Felix as the Roman governor of Judæa, to the duties of which office he was appointed by the Emperor Nero in the first year of his reign. One of his first official acts was hearing the case of the Apostle Paul, who had been left in prison by his predecessor. He was at least not a thoroughly corrupt judge; for when the Jewish hierarchy begged him to send for Paul to Jerusalem, and thus afford an opportunity for his being assassinated on the road, he gave a refusal, promising to investigate the facts at Cæsarea, where Paul was in custody, alleging to them, ' it is not the manner of the Romans to deliver any man to die before that he which is accused have the accusers face to face, and have licence to answer for himself concerning the crime laid against him ' (Acts xxv. 16). On reaching Cæsarea he sent for Paul, heard what he had to say, and, finding that the matters which ' his accusers had against him ' were ' questions of their own superstition, and of one Jesus which was dead, whom Paul affirmed to be alive,' he asked the Apostle whether he was willing to go to Jerusalem, and there be tried, since Festus did not feel himself skilled in such an affair. Paul, doubtless because he was unwilling to put himself into the hands of his implacable enemies, requested ' to be reserved unto the hearing of Augustus,' and was in consequence kept in custody till Festus had an opportunity to send him to Cæsar. Agrippa, however, with his wife Bernice, having come to salute Festus on his new appointment, expressed a desire to see and ' hear the man.' Accordingly Paul was brought before Festus, Agrippa, and Bernice, made a famous speech, and was declared innocent. But having appealed to Cæsar, he was sent to Rome.

Festus on coming into Judæa, found the country infested with robbers, who plundered the villages and set them on fire; the Sicarii also were numerous. Many of both classes were captured, and put to death by Festus. He also sent forces, both of horse and foot, to fall upon those that had been seduced by a certain impostor, who promised them deliverance and freedom from the miseries they were under if they would but follow him as far as the wilderness. These troops destroyed both the impostor and his dupes

King Agrippa had built himself a splendid dining-room, which was so placed, that, as he reclined at his meals, he commanded a view of what was done in the Temple. The priests, being displeased, erected a wall so as to exclude the monarch's eye. On which Festus took part with Agrippa against the priests, and ordered the wall to be pulled down. The priests appealed to Nero, who suffered the wall to remain, being influenced by his wife Poppæa, ' who was a religious woman.' Festus died shortly afterwards. The manner in which Josephus speaks is favourable to his character as a governor.

FIGS. [FRUITS.]

FIG-TREE. The fig-tree has from the earliest times been a highly esteemed fruit in the East, and its present, as well as ancient Arabic name, is *teen*. Though now successfully cultivated in a great part of Europe, even as far north as the southern parts of England, it is yet a native of the East, and probably of the Persian region, where it is most extensively cultivated. The climate there is such that the tree must necessarily be able to bear some degree of cold, and thus be fitted to travel northwards, and ripen its fruit where there is a sufficient amount and continuance of summer heat. The fig is still extensively cultivated in the East, and in a dried state, strung upon cords, it forms an extensive article of commerce from Persia to India.

The fig is mentioned in so many passages of Scripture, that our space will not allow us to enumerate them. The first notice of it, however, occurs in Gen. iii. 7, where Adam and Eve are described as sewing fig-leaves together to make themselves aprons. The common fig-leaf is not

172. [Ficus carica.]

so well suited, from its lobed nature, for this purpose; but the practice of sewing or pinning leaves together is very common in the East even in the present day, and baskets, dishes, and umbrellas, are made of leaves so pinned or sewn together. The fig-tree is enumerated (Deut. viii. 8) as one of the valuable products of Palestine, ' a land of wheat, and barley, and vines, and fig-trees, and pomegranates.' The spies, who were sent from the wilderness of Paran, brought back from the brook of Eshcol, clusters of grapes, pomegranates, and figs. The fig-tree is referred to as one of the signs of prosperity (1 Kings iv. 25), ' And Judah and Israel dwelt safely, every man under his vine and under his fig-tree.' And its failure is noted as a sign of affliction (Ps. cv. 33), ' He smote their fig-trees, and broke the trees of their coasts.' The very frequent references which are made in the Old Testament to the fig and other fruit trees, are in consequence of fruits forming a much more important article of diet in the warm and dry countries of the East, than they can ever do in the cold and moist regions of the north. Figs are also used medicinally, and we have a notice in 2 Kings xx. 7, of their employment as a poultice.

FIGURES. [TYPES.]

FIR occurs in several passages of Scripture, as in 2 Sam. vi. 5; 1 Kings v. 8; vi. 15 and 34; ix. 11; 2 Kings ix. 23; 2 Chron. ii. 8; iii. 5; Ps. civ. 17; Isa. xiv. 8; xxxvii. 24; xli. 19; lv. 13; lx. 13; Ezek. xxvii. 5; xxxi. 8; Hos. xiv. 8; Nah. ii. 3; Zech. xi. 2. There is great difference of opinion as to the precise tree referred to in these passages. Some suppose it to be the cedar of Lebanon, others the box, ash, juniper, &c. In Scripture the terms Eres and Berosh, the one rendered ' cedar' and the other ' fir,' are very frequently associated together, and it is probable that the former may indicate the cedar with the wild pine-tree, while the latter may comprehend the juniper and cypress tribe.

173. [Cypress. Cupressus sempervirens.]

The different species of juniper have by some botanists been ranked under Cedar. Of juniper there are several species in Syria. Of these the only species which could have been the Berosh of Scripture are the prickly or brown-berried juniper, an evergreen shrub from 10 to 12 feet high, and the Phœnician juniper, a native of the south of Europe, Russia, and Syria. Some are of opinion that the wood of the prickly juniper, rather than that of the so-called cedar of Lebanon, is the cedar-wood so famed in ancient times for its durability, and which was therefore em-

ployed in making statues. It is to the wood of certain species of juniper that the name of cedarwood is now specially applied.

The evergreen cypress of botanists is a tree well known as being tapering in form, in consequence of its branches growing upright and close to the stem. In its general appearance it resembles the Lombardy poplar, so that the one is often mistaken for the other when seen in Oriental drawings. In southern latitudes it usually grows to a height of 50 or 60 feet. Its branchlets are closely covered with very small imbricated leaves, which remain on the tree for five or six years. Du Hamel states that he has observed on the bark of young cypresses small particles of a substance resembling gum tragacanth, and that he has seen bees taking great pains to detach these particles. probably to supply some of the matter required for forming their combs. This cypress is a native of the Grecian Archipelago, particularly of Candia (the ancient Crete) and Cyprus, and also of Asia Minor, Syria, and Persia. It may be seen on the coast of Palestine as well as in the interior, as the Mahomedans plant it in their cemeteries. It is also found on the mountains of Syria. ' The wood of the cypress is hard, fragrant, and of a remarkably fine close grain, very durable, and of a beautiful reddish hue, which Pliny says it never loses.' As to the opinion respecting the durability of the cypress-wood entertained by the ancients, it may be sufficient to adduce the authority of Pliny, who says ' that the statue of Jupiter in the Capitol, which was formed of cypress, had existed above 600 years without showing the slightest symptom of decay, and that the doors of the Temple of Diana at Ephesus, which were also of cypress, and were 400 years old, had the appearance of being quite new.' This wood was used for a variety of purposes, as for wine-presses, poles, rafters, and joists. In all the passages of Scripture, therefore, the cypress will be found to answer completely to the descriptions and uses of the Berosh; for it is well adapted for building, is not subject to destruction, and was therefore very likely to be employed in the erection of the Temple, and also for its gates and flooring; for the decks of ships, and even for musical instruments and lances.

FIRE. Besides the ordinary senses of the word ' fire,' which need no explanation, there are other uses of it in Scripture which require to be discriminated. The destructive energies of this element and the torment which it inflicts, rendered it a fit symbol of—1. Whatever does damage and consumes (Prov. xvi. 27; Isa. ix. 18);—2. Of severe trials, vexations, and misfortunes (Zech. xii. 9; 1 Cor. iii. 13, 15; 1 Pet. i. 7); —3. Of the punishments beyond the grave (Matt. v. 22; Mark ix. 44; Rev. xiv. 10; xxi. 8) [HELL]. ' Fire from heaven,' ' fire of the Lord,' usually denotes lightning in the Old Testament; but, when connected with sacrifices, the ' fire of the Lord ' is often to be understood as the fire of the altar, and sometimes the holocaust itself (Exod. xxix. 18; Lev. i. 9; ii. 3; iii. 5, 9; Num. xxviii. 6; 1 Sam. ii. 28; Isa. xx. 16; Mal. i. 10). The uses of fire among the Hebrews were various:—

1. The domestic use, for cooking, roasting, and baking [BREAD; FOOD].

Y 2

2. In winter they warmed themselves and their apartments by ' a fire of coals ' (Jer. xxxvi. 22, 23 ; Luke xxii. 30).

3. The religious use of fire was for consuming the victims on the altar of burnt-offerings, and in burning the incense on the golden altar; hence the remarkable phrase in Isa. xxxi. 9, ' the Lord, whose fire is in Zion, and his furnace in Jerusalem.

4. In time of war torches were often carried by the soldiers, which explains the use of torches in the attack of Gideon upon the camp of the Midianites (Judg. vii. 6).

5. Burning criminals alive does not appear to have been known to the Hebrews; but as an additional disgrace the bodies were in particular cases burnt after death had been inflicted (Josh. vii. 25; compare verse 15); and it is in this sense that the allusions to burning as a punishment are to be understood, except when the reference is to a foreign usage, as in Dan. iii. 22, 24, sq.

6. In time of war towns were often destroyed by fire. This, as a war usage, belongs to all times and nations; but among the Hebrews there were some particular notions connected with it, as an act of strong abhorrence, or of devotement to abiding desolation. The principal instances historically commemorate are the destruction by fire of Jericho (Josh. vi. 24); Ai (Josh. viii. 19); Hazor (Josh. xi. 11); Laish (Judg. xviii. 27); the towns of the Benjamites (Judg. xx. 48); Ziklag, by the Amalekites (1 Sam. xxx. 1); Jazer, by Pharaoh (1 Kings ix. 16); and the temple and palaces of Jerusalem by Nebuchadnezzar (2 Kings xxv. 9). Even the war-chariots of the Canaanites were burnt by the Israelites, probably on the principle of precluding the possibility of recovery, by the enemy, of instruments of strength for which they had themselves no use. The frequency with which towns were fired in ancient warfare is shown by the very numerous threats by the prophets that the towns of Israel should be burned by their foreign enemies. Some great towns, not of Israel, are particularly named; and it would be an interesting task to trace, so far as the materials exist, the fulfilment of these prophecies in those more marked examples. Among the places thus threatened we find Damascus (Isa. xliii. 12, 13), Gaza, Tyre, Teman (Amos i. 7, 10, 11). The temples and idols of a conquered town or people were very often burned by the victors, and this was enjoined as a duty to the Israelites (Deut. vii. 5, 25 ; xii. 13 ; xiii. 6 ; Isa. liii. 12, 13).

There were some special regulations respecting the use of fire among the Israelites. The most remarkable of these was the prohibition to light a fire on the Sabbath (Exod. xxxiii. 3). As the primary design of this law appears to have been to prevent the proper privileges of the Sabbath-day from being lost to any one through the care and time required in cooking victuals (Exod. xvi. 23), it is doubted whether the use of fire for warmth on the Sabbath-day was included in this interdiction. In practice, it would appear that the fire was never lighted or kept up for cooking on the Sabbath-day, and that consequently there were no fires in the houses during the Sabbaths of the greater part of the year; but it may be collected that, in winter, fires for warming apartments were kept up from the previous day.

Another law required the damage done by a conflagration in the fields to be made good by the party through whose incaution it had been kindled (Exod. xxii. 6). This was a most useful and necessary law in a country where the warmth and drought of summer soon render the herbage and underwood highly combustible, so that a fire once kindled often spreads most extensively, and produces disastrous consequences (Judg. ix. 15 ; xv. 5).

In the sacerdotal services no fire but that of the altar of burnt-offerings could lawfully be used. That fire was originally kindled supernaturally, and was ever after kept up. From it the fire used in the censers for burning incense was always taken; and for neglecting this and using common fire, Nadab and Abihu were struck dead by ' fire from heaven ' (Lev. x. 8, sq.; Num. iii. 4, 26, 61).

Respecting ' passing through the fire,' see MoLOCH ; and for the ' pillar of fire,' see EXODUS.

FIRMAMENT (Gen. i. 6, 14, 15, 17), that which is distended, expanded—the expanse of heaven, i. e. the visible arch or vault of heaven resting on the earth.

With some old astronomers the *firmament* is the orb of the fixed stars, or the highest of all the heavens. But in Scripture and in common language it is used for the middle regions, the space or expanse appearing like an arch immediately above us in the heavens. Many of the ancients, and of the moderns also, account the firmament a fluid substance; but those who gave it the name of ' firmament' must have regarded it as solid, and so we would infer from Gen. i. 6, where it forms the division between water and water.

The Hebrews seem to have considered the *firmament* as transparent, like a crystal or sapphire (Ezek. i. 22 ; Dan. xii. 3 ; Exod. xxiv. 10 ; Rev. iv. 6).

FIRST-BORN. The privileges of the firstborn son, among the Hebrews, are indicated under BIRTHRIGHT.

FIRST-FRUITS. There are various regulations in the law of Moses respecting first-fruits, which would be of much interest to us, could we in every case discern the precise object in view. No doubt the leading object, as far as regards the offering of the first-fruits to God, was, that all the after-fruits and after-gatherings might be consecrated in and through them; and it was not less the dictate of a natural impulse that the first-fruits should be offered to God in testimony of thankfulness for his bounties. Hence we find some analogous custom among most nations in which material offerings were used. There are, however, some particulars in the Mosaical regulations which these considerations do not adequately explain.

1. FIRST-FRUITS OF FRUIT-TREES. It was directed that the first-fruits of every tree whose fruit was used for food, should, for the first three years of bearing. be counted ' uncircumcised,' and regarded as unclean (Lev. xix. 23, 24). It was unlawful to sell them, to eat them, or to make any benefit of them. It was only in the fourth year of bearing that they were accounted ' holy, and the fruit of that year was made an offering of first-fruits, and was either given to the priests (Num. xviii. 12, 13), or, as the Jews themselves understand, was eaten by the owners of it

before the Lord, at Jerusalem,' as was the case with second tithe. After the fourth year all fruits of trees were available for use by the owner. As the general principle of the law was, that only that which was perfect should be used in offerings, it is an obvious inference that the fruits of trees were considered imperfect until the fourth year; and if so, the law may have had the ulterior object of excluding from use crude, immature, and therefore unwholesome fruits. Michaelis (iii. 267-8), indeed, finds a benefit to the trees themselves in this regulation.

2. FIRST-FRUITS OF THE YEARLY INCREASE. Of these there were two kinds—1. *The first-fruits in the sheaf* (Lev. xxiii. 10). 2. *The first-fruits in the two wave-loaves* (Lev. xxiii. 17). These two bounded the harvest, that in the sheaf being offered at the beginning of the harvest, upon the 15th of the month Nisan; the other at the end of the harvest, on the Feast of Pentecost. 3. *The first of the dough,* being the twenty-fourth part thereof, which was given to the priests (Num. xv. 20); and this kind of offering was not neglected even after the return from Babylon (Neh. x. 37). 4. *The first-fruits of the threshing-floor.*

The oblation of the first-fruits of the threshing-floor was distinguished by the Jewish writers into two sorts. The *first* of these was the first-fruits of seven things only, namely, wheat, barley, grapes, figs, pomegranates, olives, and dates. The *second* sort consisted of corn, wine, oil, and whatever other produce was fit for the support of human life. Under this class of first-fruits was included the first of the fleece, by which the priests were provided with clothes, as by the other offerings with food. The hair of goats, which are shorn in the East, was included under this denomination.

FISH (Gen. ix. 2; Num. xi. 22; Jonah ii. 1, 10; Matt. vii. 10; xiv. 17; xv. 34; Luke v. 6; John xxi. 6, 8, 11). Fishes, strictly so called, that is, oviparous, vertebrated, cold-blooded animals, breathing water by means of gills or branchiæ, and generally provided with fins, are not unfrequently mentioned in the Bible, but never specifically. In the Mosaic law (Lev. xi. 9-12), the species proper for food are distinguished by having scales and fins, while those without scales are held to be unclean, and therefore rejected. The law may have given rise to some casuistry, as many fishes have scales, which, though imperceptible when first caught, are very apparent after the skin is in the least dried. The species which were known to the Hebrews, or at least to those who dwelt on the coast, may have been very numerous, because the usual current of the Mediterranean sets in, with a great depth of water, at the Straits of Gibraltar, and passes eastward on the African side until the shoals of the Delta of the Nile begin to turn it towards the north; it continues in that direction along the Syrian shores, and falls into a broken course only when turning westward on the Cyprian and Cretan coasts. Every spring, with the sun's return towards the north, innumerable troops of littoral species, having passed the winter in the offings of Western Africa, return northward for spawning, or are impelled in that direction by other unknown laws. A small part only ascends along the Atlantic coast of Spain and Portugal toward the British Channel, while the main bodies

pass chiefly into the Mediterranean, follow the general current, and do not break into more scattered families until they have swept round the shores of Palestine. The Pelagian, or truly deep sea fishes, in common with the indigenous species, remain the whole year, or come about midsummer, and follow an uncertain course more in the centre and towards the deepest waters. Off Nice alone Risso found and described 315 species; and there is every reason to believe that the coasts of Tyre and Sidon would produce at least as great a number. The name of the latter place, indeed, is derived from the Phœnician word fish, and it is the oldest fishing establishment for commercial purposes known in history. Industry and security alone are wanting to make the same locality again a flourishing place in this respect. The Hebrews had a more imperfect acquaintance with the species found in the Red Sea, whither, to a certain extent, the majority of fishes found in the Indian Ocean resort. Beside these, in Egypt they had anciently eaten those of the Nile; subsequently those of the lake of Tiberias and of the rivers falling into the Jordan; and they may have been acquainted with species of other lakes, of the Orontes, and even of the Euphrates. The supply, however, of this article of food, which the Jewish people appear to have consumed largely, came chiefly from the Mediterranean; and we have the authority of Neh. xiii. 16, for the fact, that Phœnicians of Tyre actually resided in Jerusalem as dealers in fish, which must have led to an exchange of that commodity for corn and cattle. Those which might be eaten, because they had scales and fins, were among the most nutritious and common, probably such as still abound on the coast. It is difficult to select the most interesting of these, and to point them out with other names than are absolutely scientific, because many are unknown on our coasts, and others have names indeed, but nearly all repetitions of such as occur in England, without being of the same species.

Though the Egyptian priesthood abstained from their use, all the other castes dwelling in the valley of the Nile chiefly subsisted on the fish of the river, while they capriciously abhorred those of the sea. There was a caste of fishermen; and allusion to the artificial reservoirs and fish-ponds of Egypt occurs in the Prophets (Isa. xix. 8-10).

But the Hebrews could draw only a small supply from the lake of Tiberias and the affluents of the Jordan. On the coast the great sea-fisheries were in the slack waters, within the dominion of the Phœnicians, who must have sent the supply into the interior in a cured or salted state; although the fact involves the question how far in that condition, coming out of pagan hands, consumption by a Hebrew was strictly lawful: perhaps it may be presumed that national wants had sufficient influence to modify the law. The art of curing fish was well understood in Egypt, and unquestionably in Phœnicia, since that industrious nation had early establishments for the purpose at the Golden Horn or Byzantium, at Portus Symbolorum in Tauric Chersonesus, and even at Calpe (Bisepharat?), in the present bay of Gibraltar. With regard to the controversy respecting the prophet Jonah having been swallowed by a huge sea-monster [WHALE], it may be observed that great cetaceans occur in the Mediterranean, as well as great sharks, and that, in a case where the miraculous intervention of Almighty power is manifest, learned trifling about the presence of a mysticete, or the dimensions of its gullet, is out of place.

FITCHES. This word occurs only in Isa. xxviii. 25, 27. It is no doubt from the difficulty of proving the precise meaning of the original term *ketzach*, that different plants have been assigned as its representative. But if we refer to the context, we learn some particulars which at least restrict it to a certain group, namely, to such as are cultivated. Thus, ver. 25, 'When he (the ploughman) hath made plain the face thereof, doth he not cast abroad the *fitches?*' And again, ver. 27, 'For the *fitches* are not threshed with a threshing instrument, neither is a cartwheel turned about upon the cummin; but *fitches* are beaten out with a staff, and the cummin with a rod.' From which we learn that this grain was easily separated from its capsule, and therefore beaten out with a stick.

Interpreters have had great difficulty in determining the particular kind of seed intended, some translating it *peas*, others, as Luther and the English Version, *vetches*, but without any proof. Meibomius considers it to be the *white poppy*, and others, a *black seed*. This last interpretation has the most numerous, as well as the oldest, authorities in its support. Of these a few are in favour of the black poppy-seed, but the majority, of a very black-coloured and aromatic seed, still cultivated and in daily employment as a condiment in the East. The plant is called Nigella by botanists, and continues in the present day, as in the most ancient times, to be used both as a condiment and as a medicine. The various species of nigella are herbaceous (several of them being indigenous in Europe, others cultivated in most parts of Asia), with their leaves deeply cut and linear, their flowers terminal, most of them having under the calyx leafy involucres which often half surround the flower. The fruit is composed of five or six capsules, which are compressed, oblong, pointed, sometimes said to be hornlike, united below, and divided into several cells, and enclosing numerous, angular, scabrous, black-coloured seeds. From the nature of the capsules, it is evident, that when they are ripe, the seeds might easily be shaken out by moderate blows of a stick, as is related to have been the case with the *ketzach* of the text.

FLAG. This word (in the original *achu*) occurs in Job viii. 11, where it is said, 'Can the rush grow up without mire? can the FLAG grow without water?' *Achu* occurs also twice in Gen. xli. 2, 18: 'And, behold, there came up out of the river seven well-favoured kine and fat-fleshed, and they fed in a *meadow:*' here it is rendered *meadow*, and must, therefore, have been considered by our translators as a general, and not a specific term.

From the context of the few passages in which *achu* occurs, it is evident that it indicates a plant or plants which grew in or in the neighbourhood of water, and also that it or they were suitable as pasturage for cattle. Now it is generally well known that most of the plants which grow in water, as well as many of those which grow in its vicinity, are not well suited as food for cattle; some

being very watery, others very coarse in texture, and some possessed of acrid and even poisonous properties. Some species of scirpus, or club-rush, however, serve as food for cattle: *S. cespitosus*, for instance, is the principal food of cattle and sheep in the highlands of Scotland, from the beginning of March till the end of May. Varieties of *S. maritimus*, found in different countries, and a few of the numerous kinds of Cyperaceæ common in Indian pastures, as *Cyperus dubius* and *hexastachyus*, are also eaten by cattle. Therefore, if any specific plant is intended, as seems implied in what goes before, it is perhaps one of the edible species of scirpus or cyperus, perhaps *C. esculentus*, which, however, has distinct Arabic names: or it may be a true grass; some species of panicum, for instance, which form excellent pasture in warm countries, and several of which grow luxuriantly in the neighbourhood of water.

174. [Cyperus esculentus.]

But it is well known to all acquainted with warm countries subject to excessive drought, that the only pasturage to which cattle can resort is a green strip of different grasses, with some sedges, which runs along the banks of rivers or of pieces of water, varying more or less in breadth according to the height of the bank, that is, the distance of water from the surface. Cattle emerging from rivers, which they may often be seen doing in hot countries, as has been well remarked in the 'Pictorial Bible' on Gen. xli. 2, would naturally go to such green herbage as intimated in this passage of Genesis, and which, as indicated in Job xviii. 2, could not grow without water in a warm dry country and climate.

FLAGON. The word thus rendered in the English Bibles (2 Sam. vi. 19; 1 Chron. xvi. 3; Hos. iii. 1; Cant. ii. 5) means rather a *cake*, especially of dried figs or raisins, pressed into a particular form [FRUITS].

FLAX. From the numerous references to flax and linen, there is no doubt that the plant was extensively cultivated, not only in Egypt, but also in Palestine. As to Egypt we have proof in the mummy cloth being made of linen, and also in the representations of the flax cultivation in the paintings of the Grotto of el Kab, which represent the whole process with the utmost clearness; and numerous testimonies might be adduced from ancient authors, of the esteem in which the linen of

Egypt was held. Flax continues to be extensively cultivated in the present day. That it was also much cultivated in Palestine, and well known to the Hebrews, we have proofs in the number of times it is mentioned; as in Josh. xi. 6, where Rahab is described as concealing the two Hebrew spies with the stalks of flax which she had laid in order upon the roof. In several passages, as Lev. xiii. 47, 48, 52, 59; Deut. xxii. 11; Jer. xiii. 1; Ezek. xl. 3; xliv. 17, 18, we find it mentioned as forming different articles of clothing, as girdles, cords, and bands. In Prov. xxxi. 13, the careful housewife 'seeketh wool and flax, and worketh it willingly with her hands.'

FLEA occurs only 1 Sam. xxiv. 14; xxvi. 20, where David thus addresses his persecutor Saul at the cave of Adullam: 'After whom is the king of Israel come out? after whom dost thou pursue?—after a flea;' 'The king of Israel is come out to seek a flea!' In both these passages the Hebrew means to pursue after, to seek *one* or a *single* flea. David's allusion to the flea displays great address. It is an appeal founded upon the immense disparity between Saul as the king of Israel, and himself as the poor contemptible object of the monarch's laborious pursuit. Hunting a flea is a comparison, in other ancient writings, for much labour expended to secure a worthless result.

Although this insect has been used as a *popular* emblem for insignificance, yet, when considered by itself, it has high claims upon the attention of the naturalist. Even to the naked eye there is something pleasing in its appearance, and elegant in its postures; but it is indebted to the *microscope* for our acquaintance with the flexible, highly polished, and ever clean suit of armour in which it is encased *cap-a-pie*, its finely-arched neck, large beautiful eye, antennæ, muscular jointed legs, its piercer and sucker—forming one most complicated instrument—the two long, hooked, sharp claws, in which its legs severally terminate. The agility of the flea places it at the head of all the leaping insects, when its strength is considered in relation to its size, it being able to leap, unaided by wings, 200 times its own length. Owing to the habits of the lower orders, fleas abound so profusely in Syria, especially during the spring, in the streets and dusty bazaars, that persons of condition always change their long dresses upon returning home. There is a popular saying in Palestine that 'the king of the fleas keeps his court at Tiberias;' though many other places in that region might dispute the distinction with that town (Kitto's *Physical History of Palestine*, p. 421).

FLESH. This word bears a variety of significations in Scripture:—

1. It is applied, generally, to the whole animated creation, whether man or beast; or, to all beings whose material substance is flesh (Gen. vi. 13, 17, 19; vii. 15, &c.).

2. But it is more particularly applied to 'mankind;' and is, in fact, the only Hebrew word which answers to that term (Gen. vi. 12; Ps. xlv. 3; cxlv. 21; Isa. xl. 5, 6). In this sense it is used somewhat figuratively to denote that evil principle which is opposed to the spirit, and to God, and which it is necessary to correct and subdue (Gen. vi. 5; Job x. 4; Isa. xxxi. 3; Matt. xvi. 17; Gal. i. 16, &c.).

3. The word 'flesh' is opposed to 'soul,' or 'spirit,' just as we oppose *body* and soul (Job xiv. 22; Prov. xiv. 30; Isa. x. 18).

4. The ordinary senses of the word, namely, the flesh of men or beasts (Gen. xli. 2, 19; Job xxxi. 23-25), and flesh as used for food (Exod. xvi. 12; Lev. viii. 19), are both sufficiently obvious; and with respect to the latter see FOOD.

5. The word 'flesh' is also used as a modest general term for the secret parts, in such passages as Gen. xvii. 11; Exod. xxviii. 42; Lev. xx. 2; Ezek. xxiii. 20; 2 Pet. ii. 7, 8, 10; Jude 7. In Prov. v. 11, the 'flesh of the intemperate' is described as being consumed by infamous diseases.

FLOCKS. [PASTURAGE.]

FLOOD. [DELUGE.]

FLOUR. [BREAD; MILL; OFFERINGS.]

FLUTE. [MUSIC.]

FLY. This word occurs Exod. viii. 21, 22, 24, 29, 31; Ps. lxxviii. 45, and cv. 21; all which passages relate to the plague of flies inflicted upon Pharaoh and his people. Some suppose that the dog-fly is meant. Philo, in his *Life of Moses*, expressly describes this insect as a biting insidious creature, which comes like a dart, with great noise, and rushing with great impetuosity on the skin, sticks to it most tenaciously. All the ancient translators understand by the original word a mixture of noxious creatures. More modern writers are of opinion that a single species only is intended, and have proposed several different insects. Thus, one of the meanings of the original word is 'to darken,' and Mouffet observes that the name agrees with no kind of flies better than with those *black*, large, compressed flies, which boldly beset cattle, and not only obtain ichor, as other flies, but also suck out blood from beneath, and occasion great pain. He observes that they have no proboscis, but, instead of it, have double sets of teeth, like wasps, which they infix deeply in the skin; and adds that they greatly infest *the ears of dogs*. Others have proposed the blatta Orientalis or Ægyptia of Linnæus, as answering considerably to the characteristics of voracity, intrusion into houses, &c. &c. The miracle involved in the plague of flies consisted, partly at least, in the creature being brought against the Egyptians in so great an abundance during *winter*. The particular species is, however, at present undetermined.

FOLD. [PASTURAGE.]

FOOD. The productions of a country, at an early period of the world, necessarily determined its food. Palestine abounded with grain and various kinds of vegetables, as well as with animals of different species. Such, accordingly, in general, was the sustenance which its inhabitants took.

The use of fire, and the state of the arts of life in a country, must also have important influence on its cookery; in other words, will go far to determine the state in which the natural productions of the earth will be eaten. If the grain is to become bread, a long and by no means easy process has to be gone through. Skill in preparing food is therefore held in high repute.

Bread formed 'the staff of life' to the ancient Hebrews even more than to ourselves; but the modes of preparing it have been noticed under other heads [BREAD; MILL].

On a remarkable occasion a calf, tender and

good, is taken, slain, dressed (roasted, most probably, Judg. vi. 19; Gen. xxvii. 7; 1 Sam. ii.
13; Exod. xii. 8, 9; boiling was not known till
long afterwards), and set before the guests, while
the entertainer (Abraham) respectfully stood at
their side, doubtless to render any desirable service   The sauce or accompaniments on this
occasion were butter and milk. From ch. xix.
3, it may be inferred that the bread was unleavened.

The cases, however, to which reference has
been made were of a special nature; and from
them, as well as from what is recorded touching
Isaac and Esau and Jacob, it appears that flesh
meat was reserved as food for guests, or as a
dainty for the sick; lentils, pulse, onions, grain,
honey, and milk being the ordinary fare.

The agreeable, and perhaps in part the salubrious qualities of salt, were very early known
and recognised: in Lev. ii. 13, it is expressly
enjoined, 'Every oblation of thy meat-offering
shalt thou season with salt; with all thine offerings shalt thou offer salt.'

Locusts were a permitted (Lev. xi. 22) and a
very common food. At the present day they are
gathered by the Bedouins at the beginning of
April, and being roasted on plates of iron, or
dried in the sun, are kept in large bags, and,
when needed, eaten strewed with salt by handfuls.

Of four-footed animals and birds, the favourite
food were sheep, goats, oxen, and doves. There
are few traces of the eating of fish, at least in
Palestine (Num. xi. 5; Lev. xi. 9-22). In the
last passage a distinction is made between certain
fish which might be eaten, and others which were
forbidden. 'These shall ye eat of all that are in
the waters: whatsoever hath fins and scales in
the waters, in the seas, and in the rivers, them
shall ye eat; and all that have not fins and scales,
they shall be an abomination unto you.'

The distinction of clean and unclean animals,
and of animals which might and those which
might not be eaten, is found to have existed to a
great extent in ancient Egypt. Among fish the
oxyrinchus, the phagrus, and the lepidotus, were
sacred, and might not even be touched. The inhabitants of Oxyrinchus objected to eat any fish
caught by a hook, lest it should have been defiled
by the blood of one they held so sacred. The
phagrus was the eel; and the reason of its sanctity,
like that of the oxyrinchus, was probably owing
to its unwholesome qualities; the most effectual
method of forbidding its use being to assign it
a place among the sacred animals of the country.

Neither the hippopotamus nor the crocodile
appears to have been eaten by the ancient Egyptians. Some of the Egyptians considered the
crocodile sacred, while others made war upon it
(Herod. ii. 69). In some places it was treated
with the most marked respect, fed, attended,
adorned, and after death embalmed. But the
people of Apollinopolis, Tentyris, Heracleopolis,
and other places, held the animal in abhorrence.

Cats as well as dogs were held in high esteem
by the ancient Egyptians. The former especially
were objects of superstitious regard. When a cat
died in a house a natural death, a general mourning throughout the family ensued; and to kill
one of these revered animals was a capital offence.

Though it appears that swine frequently formed
part of the stock of an Egyptian farm-yard, yet

was the animal unclean and an abomination in
the estimation of the Egyptians.

The Mosaic laws which regulated the use of
animal food may be found in Lev. xi. and Deut.
xiv. The grounds of many of these regulations
may be ascertained with a greater or less degree
of probability, provided the student is well acquainted with the mind and spirit of Hebrew
antiquity. Considerations drawn from idolatrous
usages, regard to health, the furtherance of agriculture, and established customs and tastes, had
in each case an influence in the promulgation of
these laws.

In the earliest times water was the common
drink. That wine of an intoxicating tendency
was drunk at a very early period appears from
what happened to Noah (Gen. ix. 20), who seems
to have made as well as drunk wine. Bread and
wine are spoken of in Gen. xiv. 18, as offered
for refreshment to Abraham by Melchizedek,
king of Salem. Water was sometimes put to the
wine; at others a strong drink was made by mixing with the wine aromatic herbs (Ps. lxxv. 9;
Isa. v. 22), or a decoction derived from them;
myrrh was used for this purpose. Date-wine
was in use, and probably the Egyptian or malt-
wine. 'The common people' (Mark xii. 37)
drank an acrid sort of wine, which is rendered
vinegar in our English version (Ruth ii. 14;
Matt. xxvii. 48). The Orientals frequently used
wine in excess, so as to occasion intoxication,
whence are drawn many striking figures in Holy
Writ (Isa. v. 11; xxviii. 1; xlix. 26; Jer. viii.
14; ix. 14; xvi. 48; Deut. xxxii. 42; Ps.
lxxviii. 65). That indulgence in wine was practised in very ancient days is manifest from there
being in the court of Pharaoh, at the time of Joseph, state-officers, who had charge of the wine,
and served the monarch with it when he drank
(Gen. xl. 1, 11; comp. Neh. i. 11; 1 Kings x. 5;
2 Chron. ix. 4).

For drinking-vessels there were used the cup
and the bowl (Jer. xxxv. 5; Amos vi. 6; Exod.
xxv. 33; Num. vii. 13, 84). The cup was generally of brass covered with tin, in form resembling a lily, sometimes circular. It is still used
by travellers, and may be seen in both shapes in
the ruins of Persepolis (1 Kings vii. 26). The
bowl (Exod. xxv. 33) assumed a variety of shapes,
and bears many names. Some of these 'chargers'
appear, from the presents made by the princes of
Israel (Num. vii.), to have been of large size and
great splendour; some were silver, some gold
(1 Kings x. 21).

In eastern climes the chief meal, or what we

175. [Egyptian Table with Dishes.]

term dinner, is, in consequence of the heat of the
middle period of the day, deferred till towards

evening, a slight repast being taken before noon. But from Gen. xliii. 16, 25, it appears to have been the custom to dine at noon in the days of the patriarchs. The same seems to have been the case in Palestine at a later period (1 Kings xx. 16; comp. Acts x. 10; Luke xi. 37). Convivialities, however, were postponed till evening, and sometimes protracted to the following morning (Isa. v. 11; Mark vi. 21; Luke xiv. 24). The meal was preceded by washing of hands (Luke xi. 38; Mark vii. 2), which the mode of eating rendered necessary; and by an invocation of the divine blessing (1 Sam. ix. 13; Luke ix. 16; John vi. 11).

176. [Modern Syrians at Meat.]

The Hebrews, like the Greeks and Romans in their earlier history, ate sitting (Gen. xxvii. 19; Judg. xix. 6; 1 Sam. xx. 25). A carpet was spread, on which the meal was partaken. At a later period, however, particularly when Palestine came under the influence of Roman manners, the Jews reclined on cushions or couches (Esth. i. 6; Amos vi. 4; Luke vii. 37; not 'sat,' as in the common translation, but ' reclined '). The custom of giving preference in point of seat or position to guests of high consideration appears from 1 Sam. ix. 22, to have been of ancient date (Amos iii. 12). In the time of Christ (Luke xiv. 8) the Pharisees, always eager for distinction, coveted the place of honour at meals and feasts. Women were not admitted to eat with the men, but had their meals supplied in their own private apartment (Esth. i. 6-9). In Babylon and Persia, however, females mingled with males on festive occasions (Dan. v. 2). In general the manner of eating was similar to what it is in the East at the present day. Special care was taken of favoured persons (Gen. xliii. 34; 1 Sam. i. 4; ix. 22; John xiii. 26). Neither knives, forks, nor spoons were employed for eating. The food was conveyed from the dish to the mouth by the right hand. The parties sat with their legs bent under them round a dish placed in the centre, and either took the flesh meat with their fingers from the dish, or dipped bits of their bread into the savoury mess, and conveyed them to their mouths. In Ruth ii. 14, Boaz says to Ruth, ' Dip thy morsel in the vinegar ;' which explains the language of our Lord, John xiii. 26, ' He it is to whom I shall give a sop when I have dipped it.' This presenting of food to a person is still customary, and was designed originally as a mark of distinction, the choice morsels being selected by the head of the family for the purpose. Drink was handed to each one of the guests in cups or goblets, and, at a very ancient period, in a separate cup to each person. Hence the word cup is used as equivalent to what we term a man's lot or destiny (Ps. xi. 6; lxxv. 8; Isa. li. 22; Matt. xxvi. 39).

FOOL. The fool of Scripture is not an idiot, but an absurd person; not one who does not reason at all, but one who reasons wrong; also any one whose conduct is not regulated by the dictates of reason and religion. Foolishness, therefore, is not a private condition, but a condition of wrong action in the intellectual or sentient being, or in both (2 Sam. xiii. 12, 13; Ps. xxxviii. 5). In the Proverbs, however, ' foolishness ' appears to be sometimes used for lack of understanding, although more generally for perverseness of will.

FOOT. Of the various senses in which the word 'foot' is used in Scripture, the following are the most remarkable. Such phrases as the ' slipping ' of the foot, the 'stumbling' of the foot, ' from head to foot ' (to express the entire body), and 'foot-steps' (to express tendencies, as when we say of one that he walks in another's footsteps), require no explanation, being common to most languages. The extreme modesty of the Hebrew language, which has perhaps seldom been sufficiently appreciated, dictated the use of the word 'feet,' to express the parts and the acts which it is not allowed to name. Hence such phrases as the ' hair of the feet,' the ' water of the feet,' ' between the feet,' ' to open the feet,' ' to cover the feet,' all of which are sufficiently intelligible, except perhaps the last, which certainly does not mean 'going to sleep' as some interpreters suggest, but ' to dismiss the refuse of nature.'

' To be under any one's feet ' denotes the subjection of a subject to his sovereign, or of a servant to his master (Ps. viii. 6; comp. Heb. ii. 8; 1 Cor. xv. 25); and was, doubtless, derived from the symbolical action of conquerors, who set their feet upon the neck or body of the chiefs whom they had vanquished, in token of their triumph. This custom is expressly mentioned in Scripture (Josh. x. 24), and is figured on the monuments of Egypt, Persia, and Rome.

In like manner, 'to be at any one's feet,' is used for being at the service of any one, following him, or willingly receiving his instructions (Judg. iv. 10). The passage (Acts xxii. 3) where Paul is described as being brought up 'at the feet of Gamaliel,' will appear still clearer, if we understand that, as the Jewish writers allege, pupils actually did sit on the floor before, and therefore at the feet of, the doctors of the law, who themselves were raised on an elevated seat.

' Lameness of feet ' generally denotes affliction or calamity, as in Ps. xxxv. 15; xxxviii. 18; Jer. xx. 10; Micah iv. 6, 7; Zech. iii. 9.

' To set one's foot ' in a place signifies to take possession of it, as in Deut. i. 36; xi. 34, and elsewhere.

' To water with the feet ' (Deut. xi. 10) implies that the soil was watered with as much ease as a garden, in which the small channels for irrigation may be turned, &c. with the foot [GARDEN].

An elegant phrase, borrowed from the feet, occurs in Gal. ii. 14, where St. Paul says, ' When I saw that they walked not uprightly '—literally, ' not with a straight foot,' or 'did not foot it straightly.'

Nakedness of feet expressed mourning (Ezek. xxiv. 17). This must mean appearing abroad with naked feet; for there is reason to think that the Jews never used their sandals or shoes within doors. The modern Orientals consider it disrespectful to enter a room without taking off the outer covering of their feet. It is with them equivalent to uncovering the head among Europeans. The practice of feet-washing implies a similar usage among the Hebrews [WASHING OF FEET]. Uncovering the feet was also a mark of adoration. Moses put off his sandals to approach the burning where the presence of God was manifested (Exod. iii. 5). Among the modern Orientals it would be regarded as the height of profanation to enter a place of worship with covered feet. The Egyptian priests officiated barefoot; and most commentators are of opinion that the Aaronite priests served with bare feet in the tabernacle, as, according to all the Jewish writers, they did afterwards in the temple, and as the frequent washings of their feet enjoined by the law seem to imply [SANDALS].

Respecting the 'washing of feet,' see ABLUTION and WASHING.

FOREHEAD. Marks upon the forehead, for the purpose of distinguishing the holy from the profane, are mentioned in Ezek. ix. 4, and again in Rev. vii. 3.

The classical idolaters used to consecrate themselves to particular deities on the same principle. The marks used on these occasions were various. Sometimes they contained the name of the god; sometimes his particular ensign, or else they marked themselves with some mystical number whereby the god was described.

If this analogy be admitted, the mark on the forehead may be taken to be derived from the analogous custom among the heathen of bearing on their forehead the mark of the gods whose votaries they were. Some, however, would rather understand the allusion to refer to the custom of marking cattle, and even slaves, with the sign of ownership [STIGMATA].

FORESKIN, the prepuce, which was taken off in circumcision [CIRCUMCISION].

FOREST. Tracts of wood-land are mentioned by travellers in Palestine, but rarely what we should call a forest. The word translated by ' forest' does not necessarily mean more than ' wood-land.' There are, however, abundant intimations in Scripture that the country was in ancient times much more wooded than at present, and in parts densely so. The localities more particularly mentioned as woods or forests are—

1. *The forest of cedars on Mount Lebanon* (1 Kings vii. 2; 2 Kings xix. 23; Hos. xiv. 5, 6), which must have been much more extensive formerly than at present.

The name of ' *House of the Forest of Lebanon*' is given in Scripture (1 Kings vii. 2; x. 27) to a palace which was built by Solomon in, or not far from, Jerusalem, and which is supposed to have been so called on account of the quantity of cedar-trees employed in its construction; or, perhaps, because the numerous pillars of cedar-wood suggested the idea of a forest of cedar-trees.

2. *The forest of oaks,* on the mountains of Bashan. The trees of this region have been already noticed under BASHAN.

3. *The forest or wood of Ephraim,* already noticed under EPHRAIM, 4.

4. *The forest of Hareth,* in the south of Judah, to which David withdrew to avoid the fury of Saul (1 Sam. xxii. 5). The precise situation is unknown.

FOREST is used symbolically to denote a city, kingdom, polity, or the like (Ezek. xiv. 26). Devoted kingdoms are also represented under the image of a forest, which God threatens to burn or cut down. See Isa. x. 17, 18, 19, 34, where the briers and thorns denote the common people; 'the glory of the forest' are the nobles and those of highest rank and importance. See also Isa. xxxii. 19; xxxvii. 24; Jer. xxi. 14; xxii. 7; xlvi. 23; Zech. xi. 2.

FORNICATION. In Scripture this word occurs more frequently in its symbolical than in its ordinary sense.

In the Prophets woman is often made the symbol of the church or nation of the Jews, which is regarded as affianced to Jehovah by the covenant on Mount Sinai. Therefore when the Israelites acted contrary to that covenant, by forsaking God and following idols, they were very properly represented by the symbol of a harlot or adulteress, offering herself to all comers (Isa. i. 21; Jer. ii. 20; Ezek. xvi.; Hos. i. 2; iii. 11). And thus fornication, or adultery (which is fornication in a married state), became, and is used as, the symbol of idolatry itself (Jer. iii. 8, 9; Ezek. xvi. 26, 29; xxiii. 37).

FORTIFICATIONS. 'FENCED CITIES.' Inventions for the defence of men in social life are older than history. The walls, towers, and gates represented on Egyptian monuments, though dating back to a period of fifteen centuries before the Christian era, bear evidence of an advanced state of fortifications—of walls built of squared stones, or of squared timber judiciously placed on the summit of scarped rocks, or within the circumference of one or two wet ditches, and furnished on the summit with regular battlements to protect the defenders. All these are of later invention than the accumulation of unhewn or rudely chipped uncemented stones, piled on each other in the form of walls, in the so-called Cyclopean, Pelasgian, Etruscan, and Celtic styles, where there are no ditches, or towers, or other gateways than mere openings occasionally left between the enormous blocks employed in the work. As the three first styles occur in Etruria they show the progressive advance of military architecture, and may be considered as more primitive, though perhaps posterior to the era when the progress of Israel, under the guidance of Joshua, expelled several Canaanitish tribes, whose system of civilization, in common with that of the rest of Western Asia, bore an Egyptian type, and whose towers and battlements were remarkably high, or rather were erected in very elevated situations. When, therefore, the Israelites entered Palestine, we may assume that the ' fenced cities' they had to attack were, according to their degree of antiquity, fortified with more or less of art, but all with huge stones in the lower walls, like the Etruscan. Indeed, Asia Minor, Armenia, Syria, and even Jerusalem, still bear marks of this most ancient system. Stones from six to fifty feet in length, with suitable proportions, can still be detected in many walls of the cities of those regions, wherever quarries existed, from

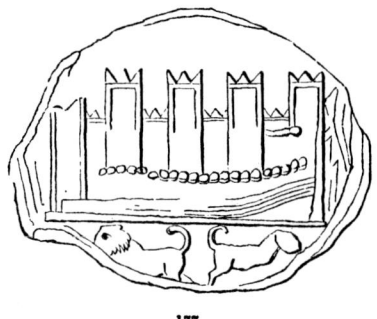

177.

Nineveh, where beneath the surface there still remain ruins and walls of huge stones, sculptured with bas-reliefs, originally painted, to Babylon, and Bassorah, where bricks, sun-dried or baked, and stamped with letters, are yet found, as well as in all the plains of the rivers where that material alone could be easily procured. The wall was sometimes double or triple (2 Chron. xxxii. 5), successively girding a rocky elevation; and 'building a city' originally meant the construction of the wall.

Before wall-towers were introduced, the gate of a city, originally single, formed a kind of citadel, and was the strongest part of all the defences: it was the armoury of the community, and the council-house of the authorities. 'Sitting in the gate' was, and still is, synonymous with the possession of power, and even now there is commonly in the fortified gate of a royal palace in the East, on the floor above the door-way, a council-room with a kind of balcony, whence the sovereign sometimes sees his people, and where he may sit in judgment. The tower was another fortification of the earliest date, being often the citadel or last retreat when a city was taken; or, standing alone in some naturally strong position, was intended to protect a frontier, command a pass, or to be a place of refuge and deposit of

178.

treasure in the mountains, when the plain should be no longer defensible. Watch-towers used by shepherds all over Asia, and even now built on eminences above some city in the plain, in order

to keep a look-out upon the distant country, were already in use and occasionally converted into places of defence (2 Chron. xxvi. 10; xxvii. 4). The gateways were closed by ponderous folding doors, the valves or folds being secured by wooden bars: both the doors and bars were in after times plated with metal. A ditch, where the nature of the locality required it, was dug in front of the rampart, and sometimes there was an inner wall, with a second ditch before it. As the experience of ages increased, huge 'counter forts,' double buttresses, or masses of solid stone and masonry were built in particular parts to sustain the outer wall, and afford space on the summit to place military engines (2 Chron. xxvi. 15).

In the cut, No. 179, taken from another Egyptian work, we have a series of towers, that in the middle being evidently the citadel or keep, and a gateway indicating that the wall is omitted, or is intended by the lines of the oval surrounding the whole. Here also we see a regular labarum, the most ancient example extant of this form of ensign, and the towers are manned with armed soldiers. No. 177 is taken from a seal, and is a symbol of Babylon, where the city, sustained by two lions, is shown standing on both sides of the Euphrates, having an outer wall; the inner rampart is flanked by numerous elevated and embattled towers. There is another, but less antique representation of Babylon, with its lions and towers, &c.; but the battlements are squared, not pointed, as in the first. The towers are here crowded with soldiers, some of whom, from the form of their shields, are obviously Egyptians.

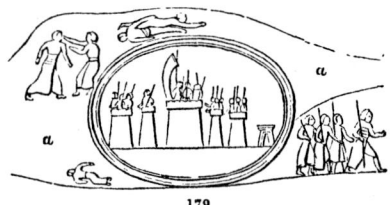

179.

These are sufficient to give a general idea of cities fenced entirely by art.

FORTUNA'TUS, a disciple of Corinth, of Roman birth or origin, as his name indicates, who visited Paul at Ephesus, and returned, along with Stephanus and Achaicus, in charge of that Apostle's first Epistle to the Corinthian church, B.C. 59 (1 Cor. xvi. 17).

FOUNTAIN, a stream of 'living' or constantly running water, in opposition to standing or stagnant pools, whether it issues immediately from the ground or from the bottom of a well.

From the value of such supplies of water in arid countries, fountains figure much in the poetry of the East as the natural images of perennial blessings of various kinds. In the Scriptures fountains are made the symbols of refreshment to the weary, and also denote the perpetuity and inexhaustible nature of the spiritual comforts which God imparts to his people, whether by the influences of the Spirit, or through the ordinances of public worship. There are also various texts in which children, or an extended posterity, are, by a beautifully apt image, described as a fountain, and the father or progenitor as the source or spring from which that fountain flows (Deut. xxxiii. 28; Ps. lxviii. 26; Prov. v. 16, 18; xiii. 14, &c).

FOWL. [BIRD; COCK.]

FOX. Two distinct terms are in our version rendered by the word ' fox,' although that denomination is not uniformly employed in different texts (Judg. xv. 4; Neh. iv. 3; xi. 27; Ps. lxiii. 10; Cant. ii. 15; Lam. v. 18; Ezek. xiii. 4). Fox is thus applied to two or more species, though only strictly applicable in a systematic view to *Taaleb*, which is the Arabic name of a wild canine, probably the Syrian fox, *Vulpes Thaleb* or *Taaleb* of modern zoologists, and the only genuine species indigenous in Palestine. There is in the language of the ancients, how-

180. [Syrian Fox.]

ever, a vague and often an indiscriminating use of zoological names: the name may therefore be employed as a general denomination; for, of vulpine animals, though the taaleb alone is considered indigenous, there is the so-called Turkish fox of Asia Minor, not unknown to the south as far as the Orontes, and therefore likely to be an occasional visitant at least of the woods of Libanus: There is, besides, one of a third group, namely, *Thous anthus*, or *deeb* of the Arabs, occasionally held to be the wolf of Scripture, because it resembles the species in general appearance, though so far inferior in weight, size, and powers, as not to be in the least dangerous, or likely to be the wolf of the Bible. The two first do not howl, and the third is solitary and howls seldom; but there is a fourth (*Canis Syriacus*) which howls, is lower and smaller than a fox, has a long ill-furnished tail, small ears, and a rufous-grey livery. This may be the jackal of Palestine. The German naturalists seem not to have considered it identical with the common jackal, which is sufficiently common along the coast, is eminently gregarious, offensive in smell; howls intolerably in complete concert with all others within hearing: burrows; is crepuscular and nocturnal, impudent, thievish; penetrates into outhouses; ravages poultry-yards more ruinously than the fox; feeds on game, lizards, locusts, insects, garbage, grapes; and leaves not even the graves of man himself undisturbed. It may ultimately turn out that *Canis Syriacus* is not a jackal, but a chryseus, or wild-dog, belonging to the group of Dholes, well known in India, and, though closely allied to, distinct from the jackal.

Vulpes Taaleb, or *Taleb*, the Syrian fox, is of the size of an English cur fox, and similarly formed; but the ears are wider and longer, the fur in general ochry-rufous above, and whitish beneath; there is a faint black ring towards the

tip of the tail, and the back of the ears are scoty, with bright fulvous edges. The species burrows, is silent and solitary, extends eastward into Southern Persia, and is said to be found in Natolia. It is reputed to be very destructive in the vineyards, or rather a plunderer of ripe grapes; but he is certainly less so than the jackal, whose ravages are carried on in troops and with less fear of man.

None of the explanations which we have seen of the controverted passage in Judg. xv. 4, 5, relative to the foxes, jackals, or other canines, which Samson employed to set fire to the corn of the Philistines, is altogether satisfactory to our mind.

Commentators, following the reading of the Sept., have with common consent adopted the interpretation, that two foxes were tied together by their tails with a firebrand between them. We consider this highly improbable, and therefore understand the text to mean that each fox had a separate brand; and most naturally so, for it may be questioned whether two united would run in the same direction. They would assuredly pull counter to each other, and ultimately fight most fiercely; whereas there can be no doubt that every canine would run, with fire attached to its tail, not from choice but necessity, through standing corn, if the field lay in the direction of the animal's burrow; for foxes and jackals, when chased, run direct to their holes, and sportsmen well know the necessity of stopping up those of the fox while the animal is abroad, or there is no chance of a chace. We therefore submit that by the words rendered ' tail to tail ' we should understand the end of the firebrand attached to the extremity of the tail. Finally, as the operation of tying 300 brands to as many fierce and irascible animals could not be effected in one day by a single man, nor produce the result intended if done in one place, it seems more probable that the name of Samson, as the chief director of the act, is employed to represent the whole party who effected his intentions in different places at the same time, and thereby insured that general conflagration of the harvest which was the signal of open resistance on the part of Israel to the long-endured oppression of the Philistine people.

FRANKINCENSE. The original word is *lebonah*, which first occurs here, and is afterwards constantly mentioned among the ingredients of the perfume to be consumed upon the incense altar (Lev. ii. 1, 2, 15, 16; v. 11; vi. 15; xxiv. 7; Num. v. 15; 1 Chron. ix. 29; Neh. xiii. 5). In some other passages it is used in a figurative sense (Sol. Song, iii. 6; iv. 6; Isa. xliii. 23; lxvi. 3). In other passages, as an article of distant commerce, it is described as being brought by caravans from Sheba, &c. (Isa. lx. 6; Jer. vi. 20). From all which texts we learn that it was an article of foreign and distant commerce, that it was known very early, and that it was probably of a resinous nature, and very fragrant. In the New Testament the same word is employed in the Greek form of *libanos*. also rendered by ' frankincense.' The original is supposed to be found in the Hebrew *laban*, ' white;' but it is equally similar to the Arabic *laban*, signifying ' milk;' and, in a secondary sense, a gummy or resinous exudation from a tree, especially *frank-*

incense. There are other words in the Arabic which have a similar meaning, and which it is most probable were all originally derived from the same root as the Hebrew *lebonah,* and the Arabic *laban,* applied in both languages to the same substance. This was called by the Greeks *libanos,* and by the Romans *thus,* and now commonly as olibanum, from the addition of the letter *o* to the original name. Several kinds of resinous substances have at different times been confounded together under the names of ' incense' and 'frankincense,' as well as under the Latin *thus,* which is derived from *thuo,* ' to sacrifice.'

The ancient writers seem to state that there were two sorts of frankincense, one from the coasts of Arabia, and the other from India, but they more generally speak of it as derived from the former quarter, specially indicating the region of Saba or Sheba, from whence the Scripture also describes it as being brought. The Periplus, however, refers it to Africa. There is, however, no direct evidence for the existence of the tree or shrub producing frankincense in the southern coasts of Arabia. Wellsted could not see it when travelling in the quarter where it should be sought; and although Niebuhr affirms that it is cultivated, he adds that it was introduced from Abyssinia, a fact which would not have passed out of memory had it been anciently produced in the country. That it might be described as coming from or produced in Arabia, even though grown in another country, is common to other products which the regions west and north of Arabia received through Arabian merchants. A number of circumstances render it probable that it was obtained by the Arabians from the coast of Africa, to which it was brought from the interior. Mr. Johnson, in his *Travels in Southern Abyssinia,* states that frankincense, called *attar,* is exported in large quantities from Berbera, on the Soumalee coast of Africa; that it is brought thither from the interior, and that a camel load of two hundred and fifty pounds is sold for three dollars. In conformity with this is the statement of Cosmo Indicopleuestes, who describes the land of frankincense as lying ' at the furthest end of Ethiopia, fifty days' journey from Axum, at no great distance from the ocean. The inhabitants of the neighbouring Barbaria, or the country of Sozee, fetch from thence frankincense and other costly spices, which they transport by water to Arabia Felix and India.' The substance thus indicated, called on the Continent African or Arabian olib, is rarely met with in this country. Dr. Pereira states it consists of smaller tears than that of the Indian variety, and is intermixed with crystals of carbonate of lime. Even the country which produces the olibanum being itself uncertain, the cautious naturalist will hesitate to indicate with decisiveness the species of tree by which it is afforded. More distinct information on the subject is still needed.

FROG (Exod. liii. 2). Although the common frog is so well known that no description is needed to satisfy the reader, it may be necessary to mention that the only species recorded as existing in Palestine is the green (*Rana esculenta*), and that of all the authorities we have been able to consult, Dr. Richardson alone refers the species of Egypt to the green speckled grey frog (*Rana punctata*). But considering the immense extent of the Nile from south to north, and the amazing abundance of these animals which it contains in the state of spawn, tadpole, and complete frog, it is likely that the speckled is not the only species found in its waters, and that different species, if they do not occur in the same locality, are at least to be met with in different latitudes. The speckled species is found westward even to the north of France, but is not common in Europe. It is lively, but no strong swimmer, the webs on the hinder toes extending only half their length; hence, perhaps, it is more a terrestrial animal than the common green frog, and, like the brown species, is given to roam on land in moist weather.

Although it is very hazardous, in transactions of an absolutely miraculous nature, to attempt to point out the instruments that may have served to work out the purposes of the Almighty, we may conjecture that, in the plague of frogs, a species, the one perhaps we have just mentioned, was selected for its agility on land, and that, although the fact is not expressly mentioned, the awful visitation was rendered still more ominous by the presence of dark and rainy weather—an atmospheric condition never of long duration on the coast of Egypt, and gradually more and more rare up the course of the river. We have ourselves witnessed, during a storm of rain, frogs crowding into our cabin, in the low lands of Guiana, till they were packed up in the corners of the apartment, and continually falling back in their attempts to ascend above their fellows; and the door could not be opened without others entering more rapidly than those within could be expelled. Now, as the temples, palaces, and cities of Egypt stood, in general, on the edge of the ever dry desert, and always above the level of the highest inundations, to be there visited by a continuation of immense number of frogs was assuredly a most distressing calamity; and as this phenomenon, in its ordinary occurrence within the tropics, is always accompanied by the storms of the monsoon or of the setting in of the rainy season, the dismay it must have caused may be judged of when we reflect that the plague occurred where rain seldom or never falls, where none of the houses are fitted to lead off the water, and that the animals appeared in localities where they had never before been found, and where, at all other times, the scorching sun would have destroyed them in a few minutes. Nor was the selection of the frog as an instrument of God's displeasure without portentous meaning in the minds of the idolatrous Egyptians, who considered that animal a type of their creative power, and also an indication of man in embryo. The magicians, indeed, appeared to make frogs come up out of the waters; but we must not understand that to them was given also the power of producing the animals. The effect which they claimed as their own was a simple result of the continuation of the prodigy effected by Moses and Aaron; for that they had no real power is evident, not only from their inability to stop the present plague, the control which even Pharaoh discovered to be solely in the hands of Moses, but also the utter failure of their enchantments in that of lice, where their artifices were incompetent to impose upon the king and his people.

FRONTLETS. [PHYLACTERIES.]

FRUITS. Under this head may perhaps be most appropriately noticed a classification of produce of great importance to a right understanding of the Bible. We propose to show that the Hebrews had three generic terms designating three great classes of the fruits of the land, closely corresponding to what may be expressed in English as, 1. *Corn-fruit*, or field produce; 2. *Vintage fruit*; 3. *Orchard-fruit*.

The term ' summer-fruits' appears to denote those less important species of fruit which were adapted only to immediate consumption, or could not be easily or conveniently conserved for winter use (Jer. xl. 10, 12). It would seem to indicate either the existence of some contrasted term, as ' winter-fruits,' or to imply that the products of the class under which it ranked as a species were generally distinguished by their capability of being preserved throughout the year. The three terms spoken of as being so frequently associated in the Scriptures, and expressive of a most comprehensive triad of blessings, are DAGAN, TIROSH, and YITZHAR.

1. *Dagan*, 'fruit of the field,' or agricultural produce. Under this term the Hebrews classed almost every object of *field* culture [AGRICULTURE]. Dr. Jahn says, 'the word is of general signification, and comprehends in itself different kinds of grain and pulse, such as wheat, millet, spelt, wall-barley, barley, beans, lentils, meadowcumin, pepper-wort, flax, cotton, various species of the cucumber, and perhaps rice.' There is now no doubt among scholars that *dagan* comprehends the largest and most valuable species of vegetable produce; and therefore it will be allowed that the rendering of the word in the common version by ' corn,' and sometimes by '*wheat*,' instead of ' *every species of corn*' or field produce, tends to limit our conceptions of the Divine bounty, as well as to impair the beauty of the passages where it occurs.

2. *Tirosh*, 'the fruit of the vine' in its natural or its solid state, comprehending grapes, moist or dried, and the fruit in general, whether in the early cluster or the mature and ripened condition (1 Sam. xxv. 18; 2 Sam. xvi. 1; 1 Chron. xii. 40; Hos. iii. 1; Isa. lxv. 8). In the Authorized Version it is usually rendered ' wine,' which is an improper restriction of its meaning.

It is also distinctly referred to as the *yielder* of wine, and therefore was not wine itself, but the raw material from which it was expressed or prepared. Dr. Conquest's amended translation of Micah vi. 15, is, ' Thou shalt sow, but thou shalt not reap.'

3. *Yitzhar*, 'orchard-fruits,' especially winter or keeping fruits, as dates, figs, olives, pomegranates, citrons, nuts, &c.

Thus the triad of terms we have been considering would comprehend every vegetable substance of necessity and luxury commonly consumed by the Hebrews, of which first-fruits were presented or tithes paid; and this view of their meaning will also explain why the injunctions concerning offerings and tithes were sufficiently expressed by these terms alone (Num. xviii. 12; Deut. xiv. 23). Had *dagan* in these texts been restricted to *wheat*, no obligation would thereby have been imposed to present the first-fruits or the tithes of barley and other grain · had *tirosh* signified grape-juice, then this law could have been easily evaded by drying the fruit as raisins, or preserving it in other ways; and had *yitzhar* signified *oil*, it would have been difficult at all, and from these texts impossible, to educe the obligation to pay tithes or present first-fruits of a large and most valuable class of products, as dates, citrons, pomegranates, &c. But these texts are the most definite we can find in relation to the subject, and are evidently designed to be very comprehensive; and, consequently, as tithes *were* paid of all those fruits, the practice must interpret these expressions as including, 1st. Fruits of the field or land; 2nd. Fruits of the vintage; and, 3rd. Fruits of the orchard, including both summer and preserving fruits.

FULLER. At the transfiguration our Saviour's robes are said to have been white, ' so as no fuller on earth could white them' (Mark ix. 3). Elsewhere we read of ' fullers' soap ' (Mal. iii. 2), and of ' the fullers' field ' (2 Kings xviii. 17). Of the processes followed in the art of cleaning cloth and the various kinds of stuff among the Jews we have no direct knowledge. In an early part of the operation they seem to have trod the cloths with their feet, as the Hebrew *Ain Rogel*, or En-rogel, literally Foot-fountain, has been rendered, on Rabbinical authority, ' Fullers' fountain,' on the ground that the fullers trod the cloths there with their feet. A subsequent operation was probably that of rubbing the cloth on an inclined plane, in a mode which is figured in the Egyptian paintings, and still preserved in the East.

FULLERS' FOUNTAIN. [EN-ROGEL.]

FULLERS' SOAP. The word thus rendered occurs in two passages of Scripture—first, in Jerem. ii. 22; and again in Malachi iii. 2. From neither of these passages does it distinctly appear whether the substance referred to was obtained from the mineral or from the vegetable kingdom. But it is evident that it was possessed of cleansing properties. It is probable that the ashes of plants may be alluded to, as there is no proof that soap is intended, though it may have been known to the same people at very early periods. Usually the ashes only of plants growing on the sea-shore have been thought to be intended. All these would yield barilla, or carbonate of soda. Many of them have been burnt, for the soda they yield, on the coasts of India, of the Red Sea, and of the Mediterranean.

FUNERALS. [BURIAL; MOURNING.]

G.

GA'AL (*miscarriage*), son of Ebed. He went to Shechem with his brothers when the inhabitants became discontented with Abimelech, and so engaged their confidence that they placed him at their head. At the festival at which the Shechemites offered the first-fruits of their vintage in the temple of Baal, Gaal, by apparently drunken bravadoes, roused the valour of the people, and strove yet more to kindle their wrath against the absent Abimelech. It would seem as if the natives had been in some way intimately connected with, or descended from, the original inhabitants; for Gaal endeavoured to awaken their attachment to the ancient family of Hamor, the father of Shechem, which ruled the place in the time of Abraham (Gen. xxxiv. 2, 6), and which seems to have been at this time represented by Gaal and his brothers. Although deprived of Shechem, the family appears to have maintained itself in some power in the neighbourhood; which induced the Shechemites to look to Gaal when they became tired of Abimelech. Whether he succeeded in awakening among them a kind feeling towards the descendants of the ancient masters of the place does not appear; but eventually they went out under his command, and assisted doubtless by his men, to intercept and give battle to Abimelech, when he appeared before the town. He, however, fled before Abimelech, and his retreat into Shechem being cut off by Zebul, the commandant of that place, he went to his home, and we hear of him no more. The account of this attempt is interesting, chiefly from the slight glimpse it affords of the position, at this period, of what had been one of the reigning families of the land before its invasion by the Israelites (Judg. ix. 26-48) B.C. 1026.

GAB'BATHA occurs John xix. 13, where the Evangelist states that Pontius Pilate, alarmed at last in his attempts to save Jesus, by the artful insinuation of the Jews, 'If thou let this man go thou art not Cæsar's friend,' went into the prætorium again, and brought Jesus out to them, and sat down once more upon the tribunal, in a place called in Greek Lithostratos, but in the Hebrew Gabbatha. The Greek word signifies literally stone-paved, and is frequently used to denote a pavement formed of ornamental stones of various colours, commonly called a tesselated or mosaic pavement. The partiality of the Romans for this kind of pavement is well known. From this fact it has been inferred by many eminent writers, that the place where Pilate's tribunal was set on this occasion, was covered by a tesselated pavement, which, as a piece of Roman magnificence, was appended to the prætorium at Jerusalem. The emphatic manner in which St. John speaks of it agrees with this conjecture. It further appears from his narrative that it was outside the prætorium; for Pilate is said to have 'come out' to the Jews, who, for ceremonial reasons, did not go into it, on this as well as on other occasions (John xviii. 28, 29, 38; xix. 4, 13). Besides which, the Roman governors, although they tried causes, and conferred with their council (Acts xxv. 12), within the prætorium, always pronounced sentence in the open air. May not then this tesselated pavement, on which the tribunal was now placed, have been inlaid on some part of the terrace, &c. running along one side of the prætorium, and overlooking the area where the Jews were assembled, or upon a landing-place of the stairs immediately before the grand entrance?

The word Gabbatha is probably synonymous with Lithostratos.

GA'BRIEL (the mighty one [or hero] of God), the heavenly messenger who was sent to Daniel to explain the vision of the ram and the he-goat (Dan. viii.), and to communicate the prediction of the Seventy Weeks (Dan. ix. 21-27). Under the new dispensation he was employed to announce the birth of John the Baptist to his father Zechariah (Luke i. 11), and that of the Messiah to the Virgin Mary (Luke i. 26). Both by Jewish and Christian writers, Gabriel has been denominated an archangel. The Scriptures, however, affirm nothing positively respecting his rank, though the importance of the commissions on which he was employed, and his own words ' I am Gabriel, that stand in the presence of God' (Luke i. 19), are rather in favour of the notion of his superior dignity. But the reserve of the Inspired Volume on such points strikingly distinguishes its angelology from that of the Jews and Mohammedans, and we may add, of the Fathers and some later Christian writers. In all the solemn glimpses of the other world which it gives, a great moral purpose is kept in view. Whatever is divulged tends to elevate and refine: nothing is said to gratify a prurient curiosity.

GAD (a troop, or fortunate). 1. A son of Jacob by his concubine Zilpah (Gen. xxx. 10, sq.), and who became the progenitor of one of the twelve tribes. The sons of Gad are enumerated in Gen. xlvi. 15, sq., and Num. xxvi. 15, sq. At the time of the conquest of Canaan, the tribe of Gad counted 45,650 warriors (Num. i. 24, 25): the position of their camp in the desert is given Num. ii. 14, and the names of their chiefs, i. 14; ii. 14; vii. 42, sq.

As a reward for their having formed the vanguard in war of the army of the tribes collectively, they were allowed to appropriate to their exclusive use some pastoral districts beyond the Jordan (Num. xxxii. 17, sq.).

The inheritance of this tribe, called the land of Gad (1 Sam. xiii. 7; Jer. xlix. 1), was situated beyond the Jordan in Gilead, north of Reuben, and separated on the east from Ammon by the river Jabbok. According to 1 Chron. v. 11, the Gadites had extended their possessions on the east as far as Salcah, though the latter had been allotted by Moses to Manasseh (Deut. iii. 10, 13): a proof how difficult it is to draw a strong line of demarcation between the possessions of pastoral tribes. The territory of Gad forms a part of the present Belka.

In Josh. xiii. 25, the land of Gad is called ' half the land of the children of Ammon;' not because the latter were then in possession of it, but probably because the part west of the Jabbok had formerly borne that name (comp. Judg. xi. 13).

The principal cities of Gad pass by the general appellation of the Cities of Gilead (Josh. xiii. 25).

The Gadites were a warlike people, and were compelled to be continually armed and on the alert against the inroads of the surrounding Arabian hordes (comp. Gen. xlix. 19; Deut. xxxiii. 20; 1 Chron. v. 19, sq.).

2. GAD, a prophet contemporary with David, and probably a pupil of Samuel, who early attached himself to the son of Jesse (1 Sam. xxii. 5). Instances of his prophetic intercourse with David occur in 2 Sam. xxiv. 11, sq.; 1 Chron. xxi. 9, sq.; xxix. 25. Gad wrote a history of the reign of David, to which the author of the 2nd book of Samuel seems to refer for further information respecting that reign (1 Chron. xxix. 29), B.C. 1062-1017.

GAD'ARA was the chief city or metropolis of Peræa, lying in the district termed Gadaritis some small distance from the southern extremity of the sea of Galilee, sixty stadia from Tiberias, to the south of the river Hieromax, and also of the Scheriat-al-Mandhur. It was fortified, and stood on a hill of limestone. Its inhabitants were mostly heathens. After the place had been destroyed in the domestic quarrels of the Jews, it was rebuilt by Pompey, in order to gratify Demetrius of Gadara, one of his freedmen. Augustus added Gadara, with other places, to the kingdom of Herod ; from which, on the death of that prince, it was sundered, and joined to the province of Syria (Joseph. *De Bell. Jud.* ii. 6. 3). At a later period it was the seat of an episcopal see.

Most modern authorities find Gadara in the present village of Om-keis. The hill on which it stood was full of caverns, which were used for tombs. The summit of the hill commands a very fine view.

The city formed nearly a square. The upper part of it stood on a level spot, and appears to have been walled all round, the acclivities of the hill being on all sides exceedingly steep. The eastern gate of entrance has its portals still remaining. Among the ruins Buckingham found a theatre, an Ionic temple, a second theatre, besides traces and remnants of streets and houses. The prevalent orders of architecture are the Ionic and the Corinthian.

Burckhardt also found near Gadara warm sulphurous springs. According to Epiphanius, a yearly festival was held at these baths.

Gadara is the scene of the miracle recorded in Matt. viii. 28 ; Mark v. 1 ; Luke viii. 26. Buckingham's remarks on this event are well worth quoting :—' The accounts given of the habitation of the demoniac from whom the legion of devils was cast out here struck us very forcibly, while we ourselves were wandering among rugged mountains, and surrounded by tombs still used as dwellings by individuals and whole families. A finer subject for a masterly expression of the passions of madness in all their violence, contrasted with the serenity of virtue and benevolence in him who went about doing good, could hardly be chosen for the pencil of an artist; and a faithful delineation of the rugged and wild majesty of the mountain scenery here on the one hand, with the still calm of the waters of the lake on the other, would give an additional charm to the picture.' One of the ancient tombs was, when our traveller saw it, used as a carpenter's shop, the occupier of it being employed in constructing a rude plough. A perfect sarcophagus remained within, which was used by the family as a provision-chest.

GALA'TIA, a province of Asia Minor, bounded on the north by Bithynia and Paphlagonia, on the south by Lycaonia, on the east by Pontus and Cappadocia, and on the west by Phrygia and Bithynia. It derived its name from the Gallic or Keltic tribes who, about 280 years B.C., made an irruption into Macedonia and Thrace. At the invitation of Nicomedes, king of Bithynia, they passed over the Hellespont to assist that prince against his brother Ziboeta. Having accomplished this object, they were unwilling to retrace their steps; and, strengthened by the accession of fresh hordes from Europe, they overran Bithynia and the neighbouring countries, and supported themselves by predatory excursions, or by imposts exacted from the native chiefs. After the lapse

of forty years, Attalus I., king of Pergamus, succeeded in checking their nomadic habits, and confined them to a fixed territory. Of the three principal tribes, the Trocmi settled in the eastern part of Galatia, near the banks of the Halys; the Tectosages in the country round Ancyra; and the Tolistobogii in the south-western parts, near Pessinus. They retained their independence till the year B.C. 189, when they were brought under the power of Rome by the consul Cn. Manlius, though still governed by their own princes. In the year B.C. 25 Galatia became a Roman province. Under the successors of Augustus the boundaries of Galatia were so much enlarged, that it reached from the shores of the Euxine to the Pisidian Taurus. In the time of Constantine a new division was made, which reduced it to its ancient limits; and by Theodosius I. or Valens it was separated into *Galatia Prima*, the northern part, occupied by the Trocmi and Tectosages, and *Galatia Secunda* or *Salutaris:* Ancyra was the capital of the former, and Pessinus of the latter.

From the intermixture of Gauls and Greeks, Galatia was also called Gallo-Græcia, and its inhabitants Gallo-Græci. But even in Jerome's time they had not lost their native language.

The Gospel was introduced into this province by the Apostle Paul. His first visit is recorded in Acts xvi. 6, and his second in Acts xviii. 23.

GALA'TIANS, EPISTLE TO THE. The Pauline origin of this epistle is attested not only by the superscription which it bears (i. 1), but also by frequent allusions in the course of it to the great Apostle of the Gentiles (comp. i. 13-23 ; ii. 1-14), and by the unanimous testimony of the ancient church. It is corroborated also by the style, tone, and contents of the epistle, which are perfectly in keeping with those of the Apostle's other writings.

The parties to whom this epistle was addressed are described in the epistle itself as ' the churches of Galatia' (i. 2 ; comp. iii. 1). Into this district the Gospel was first introduced by Paul himself (Acts xvi. 6 ; Gal. i. 8 ; iv. 13, 19). Churches were then also probably formed; for on revisiting this district some time after his first visit, it is mentioned that he ' strengthened the disciples' (Acts xviii. 23). These churches seem to have been composed principally of converts directly from heathenism, but partly, also, of Jewish converts, both pure Jews and proselytes. Unhappily, the latter, not thoroughly emancipated from early opinions and prepossessions, or probably influenced by Judaizing teachers who had visited these churches, had been seized with a zealous desire to incorporate the rites and ceremonies of Judaism with the spiritual truths and simple ordinances of Christianity. So active had this party been in disseminating their views on this head through the churches of Galatia, that the majority at least of the members had been seduced to adopt them (i. 6 ; iii. 1, &c.). From some passages in this epistle (*e. gr.* i. 11-24 ; ii. 1-21) it would appear also that insinuations had been disseminated among the Galatian churches to the effect that Paul was not a divinely-commissioned Apostle, but only a messenger of the church at Jerusalem; that Peter and he were at variance upon the subject of the relation of the Jewish rites to Christianity; and that Paul himself was not at all times so strenuously opposed to those rites as he had chosen to be among the Galatians. Of this state of things intelligence having been conveyed to the Apostle, he wrote this epistle for the purpose of vindicating his own pretensions and conduct, of counteracting the influence of these false views, and of recalling the Galatians to the simplicity of the Gospel which they had received. The importance of the case was probably the reason why the Apostle put himself to the great labour of writing this epistle with his own hand (vi. 11).

The epistle consists of *three* parts. In the *first* part (i.-ii.), after his usual salutations, Paul vindicates his own Apostolic authority and independence as a directly-commissioned ambassador of Christ to men, and especially to the Gentile portion of the race, asserting that the Gospel which he preached was the only Gospel of Christ,—expressing his surprise that the Galatians had allowed themselves to be so soon turned from him who had called them, to a different Gospel,— denouncing all who had thus seduced them as troublers of the church, perverters of the doctrine of Christ, and deserving, even had they been angels from heaven, to be placed under an anathema instead of being followed,—maintaining the divine origin of his Apostolic commission, which he illustrates by the history of his conversion and early conduct in the service of Christ,— and declaring that, so far from being inferior to the other Apostles, he had ever treated with them on equal terms, and been welcomed by them as an equal. Having in the close of this part of the epistle been led to refer to his zeal for the great doctrine of salvation by the grace of God through faith in Christ, he enters at large, in the *second* part (iii.-iv.), upon the illustration and defence of this cardinal truth of Christianity. He appeals to the former experience of the Galatians as to the way in which they had received the Spirit, to the case of Abraham, and to the testimony of Scripture in support of his position that it is by faith and not by the works of the law that men are accepted of God (iii. 1-9). He proceeds to remind them that the law has brought a curse upon men because of sin, a curse which it has no power to remove, and from which the sinner can be redeemed only through the substitutionary work of Christ, by whose means the blessing of Abraham comes upon the Gentiles. And lest any should object that the law being of more recent origin than the covenant must supersede it, he shows that this cannot be the case, but that the covenant must be perpetual, whilst the law is to be regarded only in the light of a temporary and intercalary arrangement, the design of which was to forward the fulfilment of the promise in Christ (10-29). The relation of the Jewish church to the Christian is then illustrated by the case of an heir under tutors and governors as contrasted with the case of the same person when he is of age and has become master of all; and the Galatians are exhorted not willingly to descend from the important and dignified position of sons to that of mere servants in God's house—an exhortation which is illustrated and enforced by an allegorical comparison of the Jewish church to Ishmael, the son of Hagar, and of the Christian to Isaac, the son of Sarah, and the Child of Promise **(iv. 1-31).** The *third* part of the Epistle

(v.-vi.) is chiefly hortatory and admonitory. It sets forth the necessity of steadfast adherence to the liberty of the Gospel in connection with obedience to the moral law as a rule of duty, the importance of mutual forbearance and love among Christians, and the desirableness of maintaining a firm adherence to the doctrine of Christ and Him crucified. The epistle concludes with benedictions and prayers.

Respecting the time when and the place where this epistle was written, great diversity of opinion prevails. But the majority of writers on this subject concur in the opinion that the Apostle wrote and despatched this epistle not long after he had left Galatia for the second time, and, perhaps, whilst he was residing at Ephesus (comp. Acts xviii. 23; xix. 1, sqq.).

GALBANUM is mentioned in Exod. xxx. 34, as one of the substances from which the incense for the sanctuary was to be prepared: 'Take unto thee sweet spices, stacte and onycha and galbanum.' The substance itself is well known, but the plant which yields it is yet to be ascertained.

Galbanum is in the present day imported into this country both from the Levant and from India. That from the latter country is exported from Bombay, having been first imported thither, probably from the Persian Gulf. It is therefore probable that it may be produced in the countries at the head of that gulf, that is, in the northern parts of Arabia or in Persia, (portions of which, as is well known, were included in the Syria of the ancients;) perhaps in Kurdistan, which nearly corresponds with ancient Assyria.

Galbanum, then, is either a natural exudation, or obtained by incisions from some umbelliferous plant. It occurs in commerce in the form either of tears or masses, commonly called *lump-galbanum*. The latter is of the consistence of wax, tenacious, of a brownish or brownish yellow colour, with white spots in the interior, which are the agglutinated tears. Its odour is strong and balsamic, but disagreeable, and its taste warm and bitter. It is composed of 66 per cent. of resin, and 6 of volatile oil, with gum, &c., and impurities. It was formerly held in high esteem as a stimulant and anti-spasmodic medicine, and is still employed as such, and for external application to discuss indolent tumours. It was the practice of the ancients to mix galbanum with the most fragrant substances with which they were acquainted. The effect of such mixture must depend upon the proportion in which it or any other strong-smelling substance is intermixed, more than upon what is its peculiar odour when in a concentrated state. We need not, therefore, inquire into the reasons which have been assigned to account for galbanum being intermixed with stacte and onycha as sweet spices. We see it was the custom so to do both in other ancient nations, as the Greeks and the Egyptians.

GAL'ILEE, the name given to one of the three principal divisions of Palestine, the other two being Judæa and Samaria. This name of the region was very ancient. It occurs in the Hebrew forms of *Galil* and *Galilah*, Josh. xx. 7; xxi. 3; 1 Kings ix. 11; 2 Kings xv. 29; and in Isa. viii. 23 we have 'Galilee of the nations;' 1 Macc. v. 15; Matt. iv. 15.

Galilee was the northernmost of the three divi
z

sions, and was divided into Upper and Lower. The former district had Mount Lebanon and the countries of Tyre and Sidon on the north; the Mediterranean Sea on the west; Abilene, Ituræa, and the country of Decapolis on the east; and Lower Galilee on the south. This was the portion of Galilee which was distinctively called ' Galilee of the nations,' or of the ' Gentiles,' from its having a more mixed population, *i. e.* less purely Jewish than the others. Cæsarea Philippi was its principal city. Lower Galilee had Upper Galilee on the north, the Mediterranean on the west, the Sea of Galilee or Lake of Gennesareth on the east, and Samaria on the south. Its principal towns were Tiberias, Chorazin, Bethsaida, Nazareth. Cana, Capernaum, Nain, Cæsarea of Palestine, and Ptolemais. This is the district which was of all others the most honoured with the presence of our Saviour. Here he lived entirely until he was thirty years of age; and although, after the commencement of his ministry, he frequently visited the other provinces, it was here that he chiefly resided. Here also he made his first appearance to the Apostles after his resurrection; for they were all of them natives of this region, and had returned hither after the sad events at Jerusalem (Matt. xxviii. 7).

Hence the disciples of Christ were called ' Galileans.' They were easily recognised as such; for the Galileans spoke a dialect of the vernacular Syriac different from that of Judæa, and which was of course accounted rude and impure, as all provincial dialects are considered to be, in comparison with that of the metropolis. It was this which occasioned the detection of St. Peter as one of Christ's disciples (Mark xiv. 70). The Galilean dialect was of a broad and rustic tone, which affected the pronunciation not only of letters but of words.

The Galileans are mentioned by Josephus as a turbulent and rebellious people, ready on all occasions to rise against the Roman authority. This character of them explains what is said in Luke xiii. 1, with regard to ' the Galileans whose blood Pilate had mingled with their sacrifices.' Josephus, indeed, does not mention any Galileans slain in the Temple by Pilate; but the character which he gives that people sufficiently corroborates the statement. The tumults to which he alludes were, as we know, chiefly raised at the great festivals, when sacrifices were slain in great abundance; and on all such occasions the Galileans were much more active than the men of Judæa and Jerusalem, as is proved by the history of Archelaus, which case, indeed, furnishes an answer to those who deny that the Galileans attended the feasts with the rest of the Jews.

This seditious character of the Galileans also explains why Pilate, when sitting in judgment upon Jesus, caught at the word Galilee when used by the chief priests, and asked if he were a Galilean (Luke xxiii. 6). To be known to belong to that country was of itself sufficient to prejudice Pilate against him, and to give some countenance to the charges, unsupported by impartial evidence, which were preferred against him, and which Pilate himself had, just before, virtually declared to be false.

GALILEE, SEA OF. [SEA.]

GALL occurs in its *primary* and *proper* meaning, as denoting the substance secreted in the gall-bladder of animals, commonly called bile, in the following passages; Job. xvi. 13, ' He poureth out my gall.' The metaphors in this verse are taken from the practice of huntsmen, who first surround the beast, then shoot it, and next take out the entrails. The meaning, as given by Bp. Heath, is, ' he entirely destroyeth me.' Job xx. 14 (describing the remorse of a wicked man), ' the gall of adders' (which according to the ancients is the seat of their poison). Job xx. 25, where, to describe the certainty of gall a wicked man's destruction, it is said, ' the glittering sword cometh out of his gall.' In the story of Tobit the *gall* of a fish is said to have been used to cure his father's blindness (Tobit vi. 8; xi. 10, 13). Pliny refers to the use of the same substance for diseases of the eye. Galen and other writers praise the use of the liver of the *silurus* in cases of dimness of sight.

GALL is also employed in the Authorized Version as the meaning of the word *Rosh*, which is generally considered to signify some plant. This we may infer from its being frequently mentioned along with ' wormwood,' as in Deut. xxix. 18, ' lest there should be among you a root that beareth *gall (rosh)* and *wormwood;* so also in Jer. ix. 15; xxiii. 15; and in Lament. iii. 19, ' Remembering mine affliction and my misery, the *wormwood* and the *gall*.' That it was a berry-bearing plant, has been inferred from Deut. xxxii. 32, ' For their vine is of the vine of Sodom, and their grapes are grapes of gall (*rosh*), their clusters are bitter.' In Jer. viii. 14, ' water of gall' (*rosh*), is mentioned; which may be either the expressed juice of the fruit or of the plant, or a bitter infusion made from it. That it was a plant is very evident from Hosea x. 4, where it is said ' their judgment springeth up as *hemlock* (*rosh*) in the furrows of the field.'

Though *ro.h* is generally acknowledged to indicate some plant, yet a variety of opinions have been entertained respecting its identification: some, as the Auth. Vers. in Hosea x. 4, and Amos vi. 12, consider *cicuta* or *hemlock* to be the plant intended, but there is little or no proof adduced that this is the case.

Some have concluded that it must be *darnel,* which is remarkable among grasses for its poisonous and intoxicating properties. It is, however, rather sweetish in taste, and its seeds being intermixed with corn, are sometimes made into bread. It is well known to grow in corn-fields, and would therefore suit the passage of Hosea; but it has not a berry-like fruit, nor would it yield any juice: the infusion in water, however, might be so understood, though it would not be very bitter or disagreeable in taste. Hiller adduces the *centaury* as a bitter plant, which corresponds with much of what is required. Two kinds of *centaury*, the larger and smaller, and both conspicuous for their bitterness, were known to the ancients. The latter is one of the family of gentians, and still continues to be employed as a medicine on account of its bitter and tonic properties. From the extreme bitterness of taste, from growing in fields, and being a native of warm countries, some plant like *centaury*, and of the tribe of gentians, might answer all the passages in which *rosh* is mentioned, with the exception of that (Deut. xxxii. 32) where it is supposed to have a berried fruit. Dr. Harris, quoting

Blaney on Jerem. viii. 14, says, ' In Ps. lxix. 21, which is justly considered as a prophecy of our Saviour's sufferings, it is said, "they gave me gall to eat." And accordingly it is recorded in the history, Matt. xxvii. 34, " They gave him vinegar to drink, mingled with gall." But in the parallel passage (Mark xv. 23) it is said to be " wine mingled with myrrh," a very bitter ingredient. From whence I am induced to think that perhaps *rosh* may be used as a general name for whatever is exceedingly bitter; and consequently, when the sense requires, it may be put specially for any bitter herb or plant.'

GAL'LIO. Junius Annæus Gallio, elder brother of Seneca the philosopher. His name was originally M. Ann. Novatus, but changed to Jun. Ann. Gallio in consequence of his adoption by Jun. Gallio the rhetorician. Seneca dedicated to him his treatise *De Vita Beata*, and in the preface to the fourth book of his *Naturales Quæstiones* describes him as a man universally beloved ; and who, while exempt from all other vices, especially abhorred flattery. According to Eusebius, he committed suicide before the death of Seneca ; but Tacitus speaks of him as alive after that event, and Dion Cassius states that he was put to death by order of Nero. He was *Proconsul of Achaia* (Acts xviii. 12) under the Emperor Claudius, when Paul first visited Corinth, and nobly refused to abet the persecution raised by the Jews against the Apostle. Dr. Lardner has noticed the strict accuracy of Luke in giving him this designation, which is obscured in the Auth. Vers. by the use of the term *deputy*.

GAMA'LIEL (*God is my rewarder*), a member of the Sanhedrim in the early times of Christianity, who, by his favourable interference, saved the Apostles from an ignominious death (Acts v. 34). He was the teacher of the Apostle Paul before the conversion of the latter (Acts xxii. 3). He bears in the Talmud the surname of ' the old man,' and is represented as the son of Rabbi Simeon, and grandson of the famous Hillel : he is said to have occupied a seat, if not the presidency, in the Sanhedrim during the reigns of Tiberius, Caligula, and Claudius, and to have died eighteen years after the destruction of Jerusalem.

There are idle traditions about his having been converted to Christianity by Peter and John ; but they are altogether irreconcilable with the esteem and respect in which he was held even in later times by the Jewish Rabbins, by whom his opinions are frequently quoted as an all-silencing authority on points of religious law. Neither does his interference in behalf of the Apostles at all prove—as some would have it—that he secretly approved their doctrines. He was a dispassionate judge, and reasoned in that affair with the tact of worldly wisdom and experience, urging that religious opinions usually gain strength by opposition and persecution (Acts v. 36, 37), while, if not noticed at all, they are sure not to leave any lasting impression on the minds of the people, if devoid of truth (ver. 38) ; and that it is vain to contend against them, if true (ver. 39). That he was more enlightened and tolerant than his colleagues and contemporaries, is evident from the very fact that he allowed his zealous pupil Saul to turn his mind to Greek literature, which, in a great measure, qualified him afterwards to become *the* Apostle of the Gentiles ; while by the Jewish

Palestine laws, after the Maccabæan wars, even the Greek *language* was prohibited to be taught to the Hebrew youth.

Another proof of the high respect in which Gamaliel stood with the Jews long after his death, is afforded by an anecdote told in the Talmud respecting his tomb, to the effect that Onkelos (the celebrated Chaldæan translator of the Old Testament) spent seventy pounds of incense at his grave in honour of his memory.

GAMES. If by the word are intended mere secular amusements, which are the natural expression of vigorous health and joyous feeling, fitted, if not designed, to promote health, hilarity, and friendly feeling, as well as to aid in the development of the corporeal frame, we must look to other quarters of the globe, rather than to Palestine, for their origin and encouragement. The Hebrew temperament was too deep, too earnest. too full of religious emotion, to give rise to games having a national and permanent character. Whatever of amusement, or rather of recreation, the descendants of Abraham possessed, partook of that religious complexion which was natural to them ; or rather the predominant religiousness of their souls gave its own hue, as to all their engagements, so to their recreations. The influence of religion pervaded their entire being ; so that whatever of recreation they needed or enjoyed is for the most part found blended with religious exercises. Hence their great national festivals served at once for the devout service of Almighty God, and the recreation and refreshment of their own minds and bodies.

Games, however, are so natural to man, especially in the period of childhood, that no nation has been or can be entirely without them. Accordingly a few traces are found in the early Hebrew history of at least private and childish diversions. The heat of the climate too in Syria would indispose the mature to more bodily exertion than the duties of life imposed, while the gravity which is characteristic of the Oriental character might seem compromised by anything so light as sports. Dignified ease therefore corresponds with the idea which we form of Oriental recreation. The father of the family sits at the door of his tent, or reclines on the housetop, or appears at the city gate, and there tranquilly enjoys repose, broken by conversation, under the light and amid the warmth of the bright and breezy heavens, in the cool of the retiring day, or before the sun has assumed his burning ardours (Deut. xvi. 14 ; Lam. v. 14). Even among the active Egyptians, whose games have been figured on their mural tablets, we find little which suggests a comparison with the vigorous contests of the Grecian games. One of the most remarkable is the following (No. 181), showing what appears to be play with the single-stick.

Zechariah (viii. 5) alludes to the sportiveness of children in the streets as a sign and consequence of that peace and prosperity which are so free from alarm that the young take their usual games, and are allowed entire liberty by their parents:—' and the streets of the city shall be full of boys and girls playing in the streets thereof' (comp. Jer. xxx. 19). An interesting passage illustrative of these street-amusements is found in Matt. xi. 16 :—' This generation is like unto children sitting in the markets and calling uuto their fellows, We have piped unto you and ye have not danced, we have mourned unto you, and ye have not lamented.'

181.

That the elegant amusement of playing with tamed and trained birds was not unusual may be learnt from Job xli. 5 :—' Wilt thou play with him (leviathan) as with a bird ?' Commenting on Zech. xii. 3, Jerome mentions an amusement of the young, which we have seen practised in more than one part of the north of England. ' It is customary,' he says, ' in the cities of Palestine, and has been so from ancient times, to place up and down large stones to serve for exercise for the young, who, according in each case to their degree of strength, lift these stones, some as high as their knees, others to their middle, others above their heads, the hands being kept horizontal and joined under the stone.'

Music, song, and dancing, were recreations reserved mostly for the young or for festive occasions. From Lam. v. 16, ' the crown is fallen from our head' (see the entire passage on the subject of games), it might be inferred that, as among the Greeks and Latins, chaplets of flowers were sometimes worn during festivity. To the amusements just mentioned frequent allusions are found in holy writ, among which may be given Ps. xxx. 11 ; Jer. xxxi. 13 ; Luke xv. 25. In Isaiah xxx. 29, a passage is found which serves to show how much of festivity and mirth was mingled with religious observances; the journey on festival occasions up to Jerusalem was enlivened by music, if not by dancing:—' Ye shall have a song as in the night when a holy solemnity is kept ; and gladness of heart, as when one goeth with a pipe to come into the mountain of the Lord, to the Mighty One of Israel.' A passage occurs in 2 Sam. ii. 14, which may indicate the practice among the ancient Israelites of games somewhat similar to the jousts and tournaments of the middle ages. No trace is found in Hebrew antiquity of any of the ordinary games of skill or hazard which are so numerous in the western world.

The Grecian influence which made itself felt after the Exile, led to a great change in the manners and customs of the Hebrew nation. They were soon an almost different people from what we find them in the days of their national independence and primitive simplicity. In Macc. i. 14, we find evidence that the Grecian games were introduced, and that a gymnasium was built under Antiochus Epiphanes :—' They built a place of exercise at Jerusalem, according to the custom of the heathen.' Compare 2 Macc. iv. 12,

13, 14, where special mention is made of the prevalence of ' Greek fashions,' and ' the game of discus ;' though, as appears clearly from the last passage (v. 17), these practices were considered contrary to the Mosaic institutions, and were hateful to pious Israelites. The Herodian princes had theatres and amphitheatres built in Jerusalem and other cities of Palestine, in which were held splendid games, sometimes in honour of their Roman masters. The drama does not appear to have been introduced, but Jews were in foreign countries actors of plays.

These facts make it the less surprising that allusions should be found in the New Testament writings to the Grecian games, on which we think it desirable to supply somewhat detailed information, in order to serve as illustrations of Scriptural language.

The fact that, as we have seen, the games of the amphitheatre were celebrated even in Jerusalem, serves to make it very likely that Paul, in 1 Cor. xv. 32 ; iv. 9, alludes to these detestable practices, though it is not probable that the Apostle was himself actually exposed to the fury of the raging animals. Contrary to the opinion of some writers, the reference to these combats appears to us very clear, though it was only metaphorically that Paul ' fought with beasts at Ephesus.'

The word which the Apostle (1 Cor. xv. 32) uses is emphatic and descriptive. The beast-fight constituted among the Romans a part of the amusements of the circus or amphitheatre. It consisted in the combat of human beings with animals. The persons destined to this barbarous kind of amusement were generally of two classes —1. Voluntary, that is, persons who fought either for amusement or for pay : these were clothed and provided with offensive and defensive weapons. 2. Condemned persons, who were

182.

mostly exposed to the fury of the animals unclothed, unarmed, and sometimes bound. As none but the vilest of men were in general devoted to these beast-fights, no punishment could be more condign and cruel than what was frequently inflicted on the primitive Christians, when they were hurried away ' to the lions' (as the phrase was), merely for their fidelity to conscience and to Christ, its Lord. Ephesus appears to have had some unenviable distinction in these brutal exhibitions, so that there is a peculiar propriety in the language of the Apostle.

The New Testament, in several places, contains references to the celebrated Grecian Games, though it may be allowed that some commentators have imagined allusions where none were designed. As might, from his heathen learning, be expected, it is Paul who chiefly supplies the passages in question (see Gal. ii. 2; v. 7; Phil. ii. 16; Heb. xii. 1, 4; Phil. iii. 14; 2 Tim. ii. 5). The most signal passage, however, is found in 1 Cor. ix. 24-27, ' Know ye not that they which run in a race run all, but one receiveth the prize? So run that ye may obtain. And every man that striveth for the mastery is temperate in all things. Now they do it to obtain a corruptible crown; but we an incorruptible. I therefore so run, not as uncertainly; so fight I, not as one that beateth the air; but I keep under my body, and bring it into subjection, lest that by any means, when I have preached to others, I myself should be a castaway.' In the Old Testament two passages contain a clear reference to games; Ps. xix. 5; Eccl. ix. 11.

Four of these games stood far above the rest, bearing the appellation of ' sacred,' and deriving their support from the great Hellenic family at large, though each one had special honour in its own locality : these four were the Olympic, Pythian, Nemean, and Isthmian. The first were held in the highest honour. The victors at the Olympic games were accounted the noblest and happiest of mortals, and every means was taken that could show the respect in which they were held. These games were celebrated every five years at Olympia, in Elis, on the west side of the Peloponnesus. Hence the epoch called the Olympiads.

The gymnastic exercises were laid down in a well-planned systematic series, beginning with the easier, and proceeding on to the more difficult.

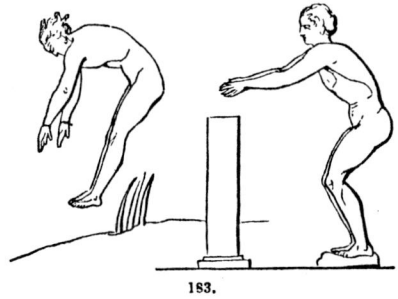

183.

Some of these were specially fitted to give strength, others agility; some educated the hands, others the feet. Among the lighter exercises was reckoned running, leaping, quoiting, hurling the javelin. When skill had been obtained in these, and the consequent strength, then followed a severer course of discipline. This was two-fold—1, simple; 2, compound. The simple consisted of wrestling, boxing; the compound

184

we find in the Pentathlon (the five contests), and the Pankration (or general trial of strength).

The Pentathlon was made up of the union of leaping, running, quoiting, wrestling, and hurling

185.

the spear; the Pankration consisted of wrestling and boxing.

Racing may be traced back to the earliest periods of Grecian antiquity, and may be regarded as the first friendly contest in which men engaged. Accordingly the Olympic and Pythian, probably also the other games, opened with foot-races. Foot-racing, perfected by systematic practice, was divided into different kinds. If you ran merely to the end of the course, it was called stadium; if you went thither and back, you ran the double course. The long course re-

186.

quired extraordinary speed and power of endurance. What it involved the ancients have left in no small uncertainty. It is sometimes given as seven times over the stadium; at others, twelve times; at others again, twenty; and even the number of four and twenty times is mentioned. These lengths will give some idea of the severity of the trial, and serve to illustrate the meaning of the Apostle when he speaks of running with patience (*sustained effort*) the race set before him (Heb. xii. 1). Indeed, one Ladas, a victor at the Olympic games, in the ' long race,' was so exhausted by his efforts, that, immediately on gaining the honour and being crowned, he yielded up his breath,—a fact which also serves to throw light on Scriptural language, as showing with what intense eagerness these aspirants strove for perishing chaplets. In the preparatory discipline everything was done which could conduce to swiftness and strength. The exercises were performed with the body naked and well oiled. Minute directions were established in order to prevent foul play of any kind, so that all the competitors might start and run on terms of entire equality, illustrating the words of Paul on the necessity of running lawfully (2 Tim. ii. 5). The contest was generally most severe; to reach the goal sooner by one foot was enough to decide the victory. How true and graphic then the descriptions given by Paul; it was, as the Apostle states, in the race-course that the contests took place: every one striving for the victory was temperate in all things; nay more, he kept under his body, and brought it into subjection. A passage is found in the *Enchiridion* of Epictetus, which shows with what propriety the terms which the Apostle employs were chosen by him: ' You wish to conquer at the Olympic games? so also do I; for it is honourable; but bethink yourself what this attempt implies, and then begin the undertaking. You must subject yourself to a determinate course; must submit to dietetic discipline; must pursue the established exercises at fixed hours in heat and cold; must abstain from all delicacies in meat and drink; yield yourself unreservedly to the control of the presiding physician, and even endure flogging.'

It may well be supposed that the competitors employed all their ability, and displayed the greatest eagerness to gain the prize. The nearer, too, they approached to the goal, the more did they increase their efforts. Sometimes the victory depended on a final spring; happy he that retained power enough to leap first to the goal. The spectators also used every encouragement in their power, these favouring one competitor, those another.

All these remarks go to show how wisely Paul acted in selecting the figure, and how carefully he has preserved the imagery which belongs to it. A word employed in the Common Version, 1 Cor. ix. 27, ' Lest when I have *preached* to others I myself should be a castaway '—namely, *preached*, mars the figure. The original means ' acted the part of herald,' whose business it was to call the competitors to the contest and proclaim their victory, functions which Paul spent his life in performing.

Paul speaks in the same connection of running not as uncertainly, of fighting not as one who beateth the air; alluding to the preludial exercises, trials of individual and of comparative strength, which took place in the course of training. These runnings and boxings had no immediate aim nor result, and implied no real competitor; hence the propriety of the terms which the sacred writer employs.

In writing to the Christians at Corinth there was a special propriety, on the part of the Apostle, in making allusions to the public games. Corinth was the place where one of the four Greek national games was celebrated, namely, the Isthmian. These games were so called from being held on the isthmus which joins northern with southern Greece, a spot of land most celebrated in Grecian history, alike in martial and commercial matters. The Corinthians appear to have been inordinately fond of these amusements. They were held every three years. They comprised three leading divisions—musical, gymnastical, and equestrian contests. In the first the tyrant Nero carried off a crown, by destroying his too highly-gifted antagonist. The gymnastic contests were the same as those of which we have already spoken. A few words, however, may here be introduced as to the horse-racing, which has not been hitherto described. Generally the same kinds prevailed as at the Olympic and Pythian games. Chariot-races seem to have been practised in the earliest heroic times, since chariots were as early as this used in battle, and the notices which have come down to us refer this kind of sport to the early period now indicated. It stood pre-eminently before other games. The skill and outlay which it required prevented any but persons of distinction—the wealthy, governors, princes, and kings—from engaging in its enjoyments. The number of chariots that

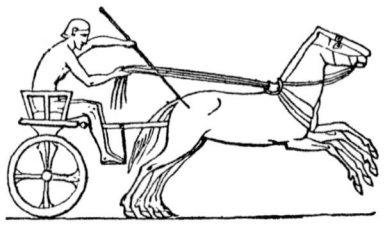

187.

might appear on the course at once cannot be accurately determined. Pindar praises Arkesilas of Cyrene for having calmly brought off his chariot uninjured, in a contest where no fewer than forty took part. The course had to be gone over twelve times. The urgency of the drivers, the speed and exhaustion of the horses, may easily be imagined. The greatest skill was needed in turning the pillar which marked the extremity of the course, especially when the contending chariots were numerous.

At the Olympic games the prize was simply a chaplet made of wild olive. The crowns were laid on a tripod, and placed in the middle of the course, so as to be seen of all. On the same table there were also exposed to view palm-branches, one of which was given into the hand of each conqueror at the same time with the chaplet. The victors, having been summoned by proclamation, were presented with the ensigns of victory, and conducted along the stadium, preceded by a herald, who proclaimed their honours, and announced their name, parentage, and country.

The real reward, however, was in the fame which ensued. A chaplet won in the chariot-races at Olympia was the highest of earthly honours. What congratulations from friends: how was the public eye directed to the fortunate conqueror; what honour had he conferred on his native city, and for what office was such an one unfit! What intense and deep delight must his bosom have been filled with when the full acclaim of assembled Greece fell upon his ear, coming in loud salutations and applauses from every part of the crowded course! Then came the more private attentions of individual friends. One brought a chaplet of flowers; another bound his head with ribbons. Afterwards came the triumphal sacrifice made to the twelve gods, accompanied by sumptuous feasting. The poet now began his office, gaining, in some cases, both for himself and the happy victor, an unexpected immortality. Music also lent her aid, and his name was sung wherever the noble accents of the Greek tongue asserted their supremacy. In order to perpetuate the memory of these great men, their names and achievements were entered into a public register, which was under the care of suitable officers. A no less privilege was that of having a statue of themselves placed either at tne expense of their country or their friends, in the sacred grove of Jupiter. A perhaps still greater honour awaited the victor on his return home. The conquerors at the Isthmian games were wont to be received in their chariots, superbly attired, amid thronging and jubilant multitudes.

One or two other privileges belonged to these victors, such as immunity from public offices, and a certain yearly stipend. If to all this be added the strict scrutiny which competitors were obliged to undergo (in the best ages), so that none could enter the lists but such as were of pure Greek blood, and incorrupt in life, none but such as had undergone the required disciplinary training, and (in the case of the chariot and horse-races) none but those who could afford to possess and train horses in a country in which, as in Greece, horses, particularly in the earlier ages, were very scarce and dear; it will be seen that the distinction of the prize was not over-rated, when it was compared with a Roman triumph.

At the Isthmian games the prize was parsley during the mythic periods. In later ages the victor was crowned with a chaplet of pine leaves. Parsley, however, appears to have been also employed. If the conqueror had come off victorious in the three great divisions—music, gymnastics, and racing—he was in the Pythian, as well as in the other sacred games, presented also with a palm-branch.

GARDEN. Several gardens are mentioned in the Scriptures, as the garden of Eden (Gen. ii. 8, 9, 10, 15), Ahab's garden of herbs (1 Kings xxi. 2), the royal garden near the fortress of Zion (2 Kings xxi. 18; xxv. 4), the royal garden of the Persian kings at Susa (Esther i. 5; vii. 7, 8), the garden of Joseph of Arimathea (John xix. 41), and the garden of Gethsemane (John xviii. 1). It is clear, from Josh. v. 2, and Lam. ii. 6, that gardens were generally hedged or walled, as indeed Josephus expressly states respecting the gardens near Jerusalem. In Neh. ii. 5, and John xx. 15, gardeners and keepers of gardens by occupation are indicated.

Gardens were planted not only with fragrant and beautiful plants, but with various fruit-bearing and other trees (Gen. ii. 9; Jer. xxix. 5; Amos ix. 14). Thus we find mention of nut-gardens (Cant. vi. 14), pomegranate - gardens (Cant. iv. 13), olive-gardens (Deut. viii. 8; 1 Chron. xxvii. 28), vine-gardens (Cant. iv. 2; viii. 8). Here, however, we are not to suppose that the gardens were exclusively occupied by these fruits, but that they were severally predominant in the gardens to which they gave name. The distinction, for instance, between a vine-garden and a vineyard would be, that, in the latter, the vine was cultivated solely for use, whereas in the former it was planted for solace and ornament, to cover walls, and to be trained in arbours and on trellises.

Gardens were, when possible, planted near streams, which afforded the means of easy irrigation. This explains such passages as Gen. ii. 9, sq., and Isa. i. 30. But streams were few in Palestine, at least such as afforded water in summer, when alone water was wanted for irrigation; hence rain-water, or water from the streams which dried up in summer, was in winter stored up in reservoirs, spacious enough to contain all the water likely to be needed during the dry season. In fact many of our own large nurseries are watered in the same manner from reservoirs of rain-water. The water was distributed through the garden in numerous small rills, which traversed it in all directions, and which were supplied either by a continued stream from the reservoir, or had water poured into them by the gardeners, in the manner shown in the Egyptian monuments. These rills being turned and directed by the foot, gave rise to the phrase 'watering by the foot,' as indicative of garden irrigation (Deut. xi. 10). The following representation (No. 188) very clearly shows the way in which water was raised, by a balanced lever, from the stream or reservoir, and poured into a trough, whence it flowed into the various canals for irrigation. This method is still in use.

188. [Watering Garden.]

Gardens were dedicated to various uses among the Hebrews, such as we still find prevailing in the East. One most essential difference between them and our own is that they are not attached to or in any way connected with the residence but are situated in the suburbs. We have known gardens from half a mile to a mile distant from the houses of the persons to whom they belonged It is manifest that all the gardens mentioned in Scripture were outside the several towns. This is, however, to be understood of regular gardens, for shrubs and flowers were often planted in the open courts of the dwelling-houses.

People repair to their suburban gardens to take the air, to walk, and to refresh and solace themselves in various ways. For their use there is mostly in each garden a kind of summer-house or pavilion, fitted up with much neatness, gaily painted, and furnished with seats, where the visitants may sit and enjoy themselves. Here sometimes banquets were and are still given, attended by singing and music (Isa. li. 3; lxv. 3). The custom of burying the dead in gardens is indicated in Gen. xxiii. 19, 20; 2 Kings xxi. 4; 1 Sam. xxv. 1; Mark xv. 46; and still occurs sometimes in the East, but is not very prevalent.

We find it also among the Greeks and the Romans.

189. [Garden-houses.]

It is evident that the gardens of the Hebrews were in a very considerable degree devoted to the culture of medicinal herbs, the preparation of which in various ways was a matter of much solicitude with them (Jer. viii. 22). This is still the case in the East, where vegetable simples are as much employed in medicine as they were in this country in the times of Gerarde and Culpepper.

It would seem that the Jews were much in the habit of performing their devotions in gardens (Gen. xxiv. 63; Matt. xvi. 30; John ii. 48; xviii. 1, 2). This interesting practice, however, was idolatrously abused; for the worship of idols in these shady seclusions was not of unfrequent occurrence, and is often mentioned in Scripture (1 Kings xiv. 23; 2 Kings xvi. 4; xvii. 10 2 Chron. xviii. 4; Isa. lxv. 3; lxvi. 17; Jer. ii. 20; iii. 6; Ezek. xx. 28).

Such are the principal points of information concerning gardens which may be collected from Scripture, or which may be connected with the Scriptural intimations.

There is no reason to suppose that the gardens of the ancient Jews differed in any material respect from those which are still found in Palestine. Such difference as did exist was doubtless occasioned chiefly by the minute rules which were founded upon the law forbidding the intermixture of diverse plants and seeds. The gardens of the Holy Land have been mentioned by travellers in terms too vague and general to afford the basis of a satisfactory description. Dr. Olin seems to have paid most attention to them. Of the gardens near Shechem he says, 'Upon turning an angle in the steep gorge we found ourselves, as if by enchantment, in the midst of fruitful gardens filled with vegetables, flowers, and fruit-trees, and all in the highest perfection of luxuriance and beauty. Olives, vines, acacias, pomegranates, figs, mulberries, and several species of trees which I did not recognise,

are crowded together in small enclosures, forming an impervious shade as well as an impenetrable thicket; and yet the capabilities of the soil seem not to be overburdened. Each separate tree and plant thrives to admiration, and seems rather to profit than suffer from the thick dark canopy of branches and foliage, which entirely excludes the sun's rays from the tangled huddle of trunks and roots. A beautiful mountain stream runs through the midst of this forest of gardens, in a channel mostly artificial and sometimes covered; but the water often rises into small fountains, and forms several cascades.' The orange and citron trees which abound in these gardens near Shechem were probably those not recognised by Dr. Olin, from their not being in fruit at the time of his visit.

GARLIC occurs only once in Scripture, and that in the passage (Num. xi. 5) in which the Israelites are described as murmuring, among other things, for the leeks, the onions, and the garlic (*shumim*) of Egypt. There can be no doubt of its being correctly so translated, as the corresponding Arabic word still signifies a species of garlic, which is cultivated and esteemed throughout Eastern countries. Ancient authors mention that garlic was cultivated in Egypt and highly esteemed there. Herodotus enumerates it as one of the substances upon which a large sum (1600 talents) was spent for feeding labourers employed in building the Pyramids. The species considered to have been thus cultivated in Egypt, is *Allium Ascalonicum*, which is the most common in Eastern countries, and obtains its specific name from having been brought into Europe from Ascalon. It is now usually known in the kitchen garden by the name of 'eschalot' or 'shallot,' and is too common to require a fuller notice.

GATE, DOOR, the entrance to enclosed grounds, buildings, dwelling-houses, towns, &c. Thus we find mentioned—1. *Gates of cities*, as of Jerusalem, its sheep-gate, fish-gate, &c. (Jer. xxxvii. 13; Neh. i. 3; ii. 3; vii. 3); of Sodom (Gen. xix. 1); of Gaza (Judg. xvi. 1). 2. *Gates of royal palaces* (Neh. ii. 8). 3. *Gates of the Temple*. The temple of Ezekiel had two gates, one towards the north, the other towards the east; the latter closed (Ezek. xliv. 1, 2), the other must have been open. 4. *Gates of tombs* (Matt. xxvii. 60). 5. *Gates of prisons*. In Acts xii. 10, mention is made of the iron-gate of Peter's prison (xvi. 27). Prudentius speaks of gatekeepers of prisons. 6. *Gates of caverns* (1 Kings xix. 13). 7. *Gates of camps* (Exod. xxxii. 26, 27; see Heb. xiii. 12). The camps of the Romans had generally four gates. The camp of the Trojans is also described as having had gates.

We do not know of what materials the enclosures and gates of the temporary camps of the Hebrews were formed. In Egyptian monuments such enclosures are indicated by lines of upright shields, with gates apparently of wicker, defended by a strong guard.

GATES OF TOWNS.—As the gates of towns served the ancients as places of security [FORTIFICATIONS], a durable material was required for them, and accordingly we find mentioned— 1. *Gates of iron and brass* (Ps. cvii. 16; Isa. xlv. 2; Acts xii. 10). It is probable that gates thus described were, in fact, only sheeted with plates of copper or iron; and it is probably in this sense we are to interpret the hundred brazen gates ascribed to the ancient Babylon. Thevenot describes the six gates of Jerusalem as covered with iron, which is probably still the case with the four gates now open. Other iron-covered gates are mentioned by travellers, such as some of the town gates of Algiers, and of the towers of the so-called iron-bridge at Antioch. The principal gates of the great mosque at Damascus are covered with brass. Gates of iron are also mentioned by Hesiod and by Ovid.

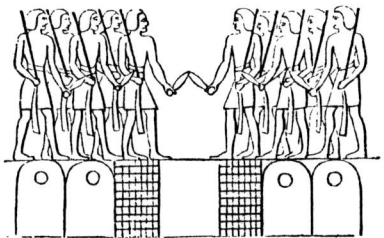

190. [Egyptian Camp-gate.]

2. *Gates of stone* and of pearls are mentioned in Isa. liv. 12, and Rev. xxi. 21, which, it has justly been supposed, refer to such doors, cut out of a single slab, as are occasionally discovered in ancient countries. At Essouan (Syene), in Upper Egypt, there is a granite gateway bearing the name of Alexander, the son of Alexander the Great (Wilkinson, iii. 403). The doors leading to the several chambers of the so-called ' Tombs of the Kings ' near Jerusalem, were each formed of a single stone seven inches thick, sculptured so as to resemble four panels: the styles, muntins, and other parts were cut with great art, and exactly resembled those of a door made by a carpenter at the present day, the whole being completely smooth and polished, and most accurate in their proportions. The doors turned on pivots, of the same stone of which the rest of them were composed, which were inserted in corresponding sockets above and below, the lower tenon being of course short. This is one of the modes in which heavy doors of wood are now hung in the East. One of these doors was still hanging in Maundrell's time, and ' did not touch its lintel by at least three inches.' But all these doors are now thrown down and broken. Similar doors are described by Dr. Clarke in the remarkable excavated sepulchres at Telmessus, on the southern coast of Asia Minor; and others were noticed by Irby and Mangles in the sepulchres near Beisân (Bethshan). There are stone doors to the houses in the Haouran beyond the Jordan; and the present writer has repeatedly seen in the north of Persia the street-doors of superior houses composed of a single slab of a kind of slate.

3. *Gates of wood.* Of this kind were probably the gates of Gaza (Judg. xvi. 3). They had generally two valves, which, according to Faber's description, had sometimes smaller doors, or wickets, to afford a passage when the principal gate was closed, a fact which he applies to the illustration of Matt. vii. 13.

Gates were generally protected by some works against the surprises of enemies (Jer. xxxix. 4). Sometimes two gates were constructed, one be-

hind another, an outer and inner one; or there were turrets on both sides (2 Sam. xviii. 24, 33) The gates of the ancients were generally secured with strong heavy bolts and locks of brass or iron (Deut. iii. 5; 1 Sam. xxiii. 7; 1 Kings iv. 13; 2 Chron. viii. 5; Jer. xiv. 2; xlix. 31; Ps. cxlvii. 13). This was probably done with a view to the safety of the town, and to prevent hostile inroads. The keys of gates, as well as of doors, were generally of wood; and Thevenot observes that gates might be opened even with the finger put into the key-hole, from which Harmer elucidates the passage in the Song of Solomon, v. 4.

The gates of towns were kept open or shut according to circumstances: in time of war they were closed against the inroads of the enemy (Josh. ii. 5), but they were opened when the enemy had been conquered. On festive occasions they were also thrown wide open, to which Ps. xxiv. 7 alludes. This opening of the gates, as well as closing them, was done by means of keys. That near the gates towers were often constructed, serving for defence against attacks of the enemy, may be inferred from Deut. iii. 5; 2 Sam. xviii. 24; Judg. ix. 35, comp. with 52. Enemies, therefore, in besieging towns were most anxious to obtain possession of the gates as quickly as possible (Deut. xxviii. 52; Judg. ix. 40; 2 Sam. x. 8; xi. 23; 1 Kings viii. 37; Job v. 4; Isa. xxii. 7; xxviii. 6); and generally the town was

191. [Gate of Konieh.]

conquered when its gates were occupied by the invading troops (Deut. xxviii. 57; Judg. v. 8). In or near the gates, therefore, they placed watchmen, and a sufficiently strong guard, to keep an eye on the movements of the enemy, and to defend the works in case of need (Judg. xviii. 16; 2 Kings vii. 3; Neh. xiii. 22).

We read that some portions of the law were to be written on the gates of towns, as well as on the doors of houses (Deut. vi. 9; xi. 20); and if this is to be literally understood, it receives illustration from the practice of the Moslems in painting passages of the Koran on their public and private gates. Various artificial figures and inscriptions were engraved on their gates by the Romans.

Criminals were punished without the gates (1 Kings xxi. 13; Acts vii. 59), which explains the passage in Heb. xiii. 12. The same custom existed among the Romans. As to the gate through which Christ was led, before his crucifixion, opinions differ; some taking it to have been the dung-gate; others understand it of the gate of judgment. But for all that concerns the gates of Jerusalem, we must refer to the article Jerusalem.

Gates are often mentioned in Scripture as places at which were holden courts of justice, to administer the law and determine points in dispute: hence *judges in the gate* are spoken of (Gen. xix. 1; xxiii. 10, 18; xxxiv. 20; Deut. xvi. 18; xvii. 8; xxi. 19; xxv. 6, 7; Josh. xx. 4; Ruth iv. 1; 1 Sam. iv. 18; 2 Sam. xviii. 24; xix. 8; 1 Kings xxii. 10; Job xxix. 7; Prov. xxii. 22; xxiv. 7; Lament. v. 14; Amos v. 12; Zech. viii. 16). The reason of this custom is apparent; for the gates being places of great concourse and resort, the courts held at them were of easy access to all the people; witnesses and auditors to all transactions were easily secured (a matter of much importance in the absence or scanty use of written documents); and confidence in the integrity of the magistrate was ensured by the publicity of the proceedings. There was within the gate a particular place, where the judges sat on chairs, and this custom must be understood as referred to when we read that courts were held *under the gates*, as may be proved from 1 Kings xxii. 10; 2 Chron. xviii. 9. Apart from the holding of courts of justice, the gate served for reading the law, and for proclaiming ordinances, &c. (2 Chron. xxxii. 6; Neh. viii. 1, 3). We see from Prov. xxxi. 23; Lam. v. 14, that the inferior magistrates held a court in the gates, as well as the superior judges (Jer. xxxvi. 10); and even kings, at least occasionally, did the same (1 Kings xxii. 10, comp. with Ps. cxxvii. 5). The gates at Jerusalem served the same purpose; but for the great number of its inhabitants, many places of justice were required. Thus we find that Nehemiah (iii. 32) calls a particular gate of this city the counsel-gate, or justice-gate; which seems to have had a preference, though not exclusive, since courts must have been holden in the other gates also. The same custom prevails to the present day among other Oriental nations, as in the kingdom of Marocco, where courts of justice were holden in the gate of the capital town. Respecting the Abyssinians and inhabitants of Hindostan, we are likewise assured that they employed their gates for courts of justice. Homer states of the Trojans that their elders assembled in the gates of the town to determine causes, and Virgil says the same. From Juvenal it appears that with the Romans the Porta Capena was used for this purpose.

In Palestine gates were, moreover, the places where, sometimes at least, the priests delivered their sacred addresses and discourses to the people; and we find that the prophets often proclaimed their warnings and prophecies in the gates (Prov. i. 21; viii. 3; Isa. xxix. 21 Jer. xvii. 19, 20; xxvi. 10; xxxvi. 10).

Among the heathen gates were connected with sacrifices, which were offered in their immediate vicinity; in which respect the hills near the gates are mentioned (2 Kings xxiii. 8). In Acts xiv 13, the gates of Lystra are referred to, near which sacrifice was offered.

The gate was, further, a public place of meeting and conversation, where the people assembled in large numbers to learn the news of the day, and by various talk to while away the too tedious hours (Ps. lxix. 12). It was probably with this view that Lot sat under the gate of Sodom (Gen. xix. 1); which is more probable than the Jewish notion that he sat there as one of the judges of the city.

Under the gates they used to sell various merchandises, provisions, victuals, *e. g.* at Samaria (2 Kings vii. 1); and for this purpose there were generally recesses in the space under them. The same is stated by Aristophanes of the gates of the Greeks. But with respect to the markets at gates, the present writer would note what has often occurred to his own notice in different parts of the East, which is, that the commodities sold at the gates are almost exclusively country produce, animal or vegetable, for the supply of the city, and not manufactured goods, which are invariably sold in the bazaars in the heart of the town. The gate-markets also are only held for a few hours early in the morning.

On an uproar having broken out at Jerusalem, the heads of the people met under the New-gate (Jer. xxix. 26), where they were sure to find insurgents. The town-gates were to the ancient Orientals what the coffee-houses, exchanges, markets, and courts of law, are in our large towns: and such is still the case in a great degree, although the introduction of coffee-houses has in this, and other respects, caused some alteration of Eastern manners.

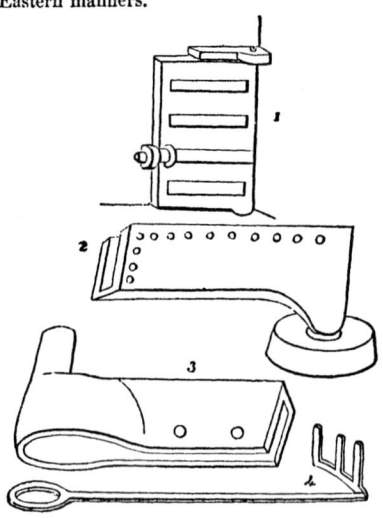

192.

Gates are put figuratively for public places of towns and palaces. The gates of a town are also put instead of the town itself (Gen. xii. 17; xxiv 60; Deut. xii. 12; Ps. lxxxvii. 2).

The *gates of death*, and of *hell*, occur in Job xxxviii. 17; Ps. ix. 14; Micah ii. 13. Doors and gates of hell are chiefly introduced, Prov. v. 5; Isa. xxxviii. 10; Matt. xvi. 19; and the Jews go so far in their writings as to ascribe real gates to hell. The origin of this metaphorical expression is not difficult to explain; for it was very common to use the word gates as an image of large empires (Ps. xxiv. 7); and in pagan authors the abode of departed souls is represented as the residence of Pluto. In the passage, then, Matt. xvi. 19, by 'gates of hell' must be understood all aggressions by the infernal empire upon the Christian church.

Among the ancient Egyptians, doors were frequently stained so as to imitate foreign wood. They were either of one or two valves, turning on pins of metal, and were secured within by bars and bolts. Some of the bronze pins have been discovered in the tombs of Thebes, and two of them, after Wilkinson, are figured in No. 192, figs. 2, 3. They were fastened to the wood with nails of the same metal. The stone lintels and floor behind the threshold of the tombs and temples still exhibit the holes in which the pins turned, as well as those of the bolts and bars, and the recess for receiving the opening valves. The folding-doors had bolts in the centre, sometimes above as well as below; a bar was placed across from one wall to the other; and in many cases they were secured by wooden locks passing over the centre (No. 193, fig. 4) at the junction of the

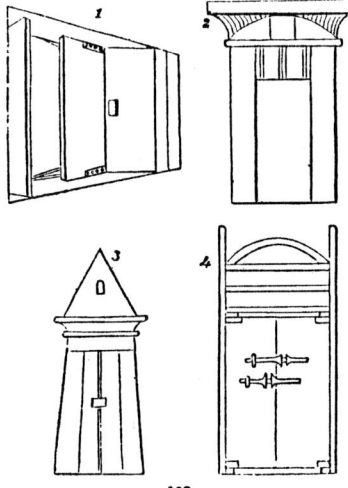

193.

two folds. For greater security they are also occasionally sealed with a mass of clay. This was also a custom of the ancient Egyptians, as appears from Herodotus (ii. 121); from tombs actually so closed at Thebes; and from the sculptures, as in No. 193, fig. 3, where the door is thus closed and sealed. To this custom there is an allusion in Job [CLAY]. At a later period, when iron came into general use, keys were made of that metal, of the shape shown in No. 192, fig. 4. Of the kind thus indicated were probably the lock and key which fastened the summer-parlour of King Eglon (Judg. iii. 23, 25). In this case Ehud locked the door and took away the key; but when the servants became alarmed, they easily opened it with another key; which suggests that the lock, as in ancient Egypt or the modern

East, was nothing more than a peculiarly constructed open bolt of wood, which the wooden or metal key was adapted to raise and thrust back. The forms of the Egyptian doors may be seen from the cuts. Fig. 1, No. 192, is from a curious ancient model in the British Museum, of a small ancient Egyptian house, and may serve to show very clearly how the doors of small houses were formed, hung, and secured. The elegant cornice of the door, fig. 2, No. 193, will not escape observation; fig. 1 is a remarkable instance of a folding-door.

194.

A comparison of the ancient Egyptian doors with those now used in the East will probably suggest no incorrect notion of the provision among the ancient Hebrews in this respect. A sort of intermediate idea arising from this comparison will be found to furnish very satisfactory illustrations of most of the passages of Scripture which relate to the subject. No. 194 is a very usual form of the street door of a private house. The inscription on the central compartment is usually painted in white or black. It means, 'He (i. e. God) is the Creator, the Everlasting,' and brings strongly to mind the Hebrew custom to which we have more than once alluded. Doors are generally unpainted throughout Western Asia and Egypt. The other doors shown in the cuts belong to the internal front of the houses, and not to the external frontage or screen. Fig. 2, No. 193, has an open lattice over the door, and the elegant proportion of the whole entrance claims attention. No. 195 shows different forms of

195.

common doors, and the whole piece affords an interesting illustration of the basement of an Eastern house, with the stone steps leading to the gallery, into which all the state rooms and family rooms open.

In the interior of houses it is not unusual to see curtains instead of doors, especially in summer. This helps to keep the apartment cool, and also

enables servants to enter without noise. This
custom originated in the use of tents. Accordingly we find that all the entrances of the tabernacle had curtains, although the framework was
of wood (Exod. xxvi. 31-33, 36, 37); and even in
the temple a curtain or 'vail' formed the separation between the Holy and the Most Holy place.

GATH, one of the five princely cities of the
Philistines, of which mention is made in Josh.
xiii. 3. It was one of the cities upon which the
ark is said to have brought calamity (1 Sam v.
8, 9), and which offered in connection therewith
a trespass-offering, each one a golden emerod (1
Sam. vi. 17). Goliath, of the family of giants
which Joshua spared (Josh. xi. 22), of which other
members may be found mentioned in Scripture (1
Chron. xxi. 5-8; 2 Sam. xxi. 19-22), has rendered
Gath a word familiar from our childhood; but it
is not certain whether Goliath was a native or
merely a resident of Gath (1 Sam. xvii. 4). To
Achish, king of Gath, David fled for fear of Saul
(1 Sam. xxi. 10; xxvii. 2-7; Ps. lvi.). At his
own entreaty David received from Achish the city
of Ziklag. David dwelt in the country of the
Philistines 'a full year and four months.' It was
conquered by David, and fortified both by him
and by Rehoboam (2 Sam. viii. 1; 1 Chron. xviii.
1; 2 Chron. xi. 8). From 2 Sam. xv. 18, it appears that David had a band (600 men) of Gittites
in his service at the time of the rebellion of Absalom. Their devotedness to him under Ittai their
leader forms a beautiful episode in the history of
David's varied fortune (2 Sam. xv. 19, sq.).
Shimei's visit to Gath and its fatal consequences
to himself may be read in 1 Kings ii. 39-46. In
the reign of Solomon mention is made of a king
of Gath (1 Kings iv. 24), who was doubtless a
tributary prince, but powerful enough to cause
apprehension to Solomon, as appears from the
punishment he inflicted on Shimei. Under Jehoash, Hazael, king of Syria, took Gath (2 Kings
xii. 17); from his successor, Benhadad, the place
was recovered (2 Kings xiii. 24). It must, however, have soon revolted; for Uzziah (2 Chron.
xxvi. 6), finding it necessary to war against the
Philistines, 'broke down the wall of Gath.' Probably the conquest was not of long duration.
This constant withstanding of the power of Jerusalem shows that Gath was a place of great resources and high eminence—a conclusion which
is confirmed by the language employed by the
prophets (Amos vi. 2; Micah i. 10). 'Gath,'
says Jerome, (on Micah i.), is one of the five
Philistine cities lying near the confines of Judah,
on the road from Eleutheropolis to Gaza; now it
is a very large village.' On Jerem. xxv. the same
authority declares that Gath was not far from
Azotus. Modern travellers give no description of
the place.

There was a Gath-hepher belonging to the children of Zebulun (Josh. xix. 10, sq.), the birth-
place of the prophet Jonah (2 Kings xiv. 25),
lying not far from Sepphoris on the road to Tiberias. Another Gath (Gath-rimmon, Josh. xix.
45) lay in the territory of Dan. It was a Levite
city (Josh. xxi. 24; 1 Chron. vi. 69). In the
time of Eusebius it was a very large village,
'twelve miles from Diospolis, as you go hence to
Eleutheropolis.'

GAULONITIS. [GOLAN.]

GA'ZA lies on the road leading from Akabah

to Hebron, which passes along nearly the whole
length of the great Wady-el-Arabah. It is on the
sea-coast, in lat. 31° 29', long. 34° 29' in the
country of the Philistines (Josh. xv. 47). It is a
very ancient place, as we find it mentioned in
Gen. x. 19, where it is given as one of the border-
cities of the Canaanites. In Deut. ii. 23, it is found
as the place unto which the Avim dwelt. Joshua

196.

smote the Canaanites as far as Gaza (Josh. x. 41),
but spared the Anakim (giants) that dwelt there
(Josh. xi. 21, 22). In the division of the land,
Gaza fell to the lot of Judah (Josh. xv. 47), and
was taken by him with the coast thereof (Judg.
i. 18), but its inhabitants were not exterminated
(Judg. iii. 3). Gaza was one of the five Philistine
cities which gave each a golden emerod as a trespass-offering to the Lord (1 Sam. vi. 17). Solomon's kingdom extended as far as Gaza (1 Kings
iv. 24). But the place appears always as a Philistine city in Scripture (Judg. iii. 3; xvi. 1; 1
Sam. vi. 17; 2 Kings xviii. 8). Hezekiah smote
the Philistines as far as Gaza (2 Kings xviii. 8).
Gaza fell into the hands of the Egyptians, probably Pharaoh-Necho (Jer. xlvii. 1; comp. Herod.
ii. 159). The prophets speak in severe terms
against it (Jer. xxv. 20; xlvii. 5; Amos i. 6, 7;
Zeph. ii. 4; Zech. ix. 5). After the destruction
of Tyre it sustained a siege of two months against
Alexander the Great. Jonathan Maccabæus destroyed its suburbs; Simon Maccabæus took the
city itself, though not without extraordinary
efforts. Alexander Jannæus spent a year in besieging it and punishing its inhabitants. The
place was rebuilt by Gabinius. It was among the
cities given by Augustus to Herod, after whose
death it was united to the province of Syria.

Gaza is celebrated for the exploit recorded of
Samson (Judg. xvi. 1-3), who 'took the doors of
the gate of the city, and the two posts, and went
away with them, bar and all, and put them on his
shoulders, and carried them up to the top of a hill
that is before Hebron.' The Philistines afterwards took Samson, and put out his eyes, and
brought him to Gaza, and bound him with fetters
of brass, and he did grind in the prison-house: he,
however, pulled down the temple of Dagon, god
of the Philistines, and slew, together with himself,
'all the lords of the Philistines,' besides men and
women (Judg. xvi. 21-30). It was near Gaza—

on the road from Jerusalem to that place—that Philip baptized the eunuch 'of great authority under Candace, queen of the Ethiopians' (Acts viii. 26, sq.).

Gaza lay some distance from the sea, though it had a port on the sea,' called 'Gaza on the sea,' called also Majuma, which Constantine called Constantia, from the name of his son, giving it, at the same time, municipal rights. Julian took away this name and ordered it to be called the port of Gaza. Subsequent emperors restored the name and the privileges of the place. It was afterwards called the sea-coast of Gaza.

GE'BA. It is often stated that Geba and Gibeah were names of the same place. The two names are indeed only masculine and feminine forms of the same word, signifying 'hill;' but that they were two different places is evident from Josh. xviii. 24; comp. 28; 1 Sam. xiii. 2, comp. 3; Isa. x. 29. Geba belonged to the tribe of Benjamin (Josh. xviii. 24), and was assigned to the priests (Josh. xxi. 17; 1 Chron. vii. 40). The Philistines were smitten from Geba unto Gazer by David (2 Sam. v. 25); Asa rebuilt Geba and Mizpeh with the stones of Ramah (1 Kings xv. 22; 2 Chron. xvi. 6). 'From Geba (in the north) to Beersheba' (in the south) (2 Kings xxiii. 8), expressed the whole extent of the separate kingdom of Judah, just as 'from Dan to Beersheba' expressed the whole length of Palestine. It would seem, from the manner in which Geba (Gaba) and Ramah are coupled in Neh. vii. 30, that they were very near each other; but the site of Geba is unknown.

1. GE'BAL, a district, or perhaps sovereignty, south of Judæa, in the land of Edom. Gebal signifies a mountain, and apparently belongs not to the most ancient times, as it does not occur when the Israelites were actually in this quarter, but is first found in Ps. lxxxiii. 8, which was probably written in the time of Jehoshaphat. The country south of the Dead Sea, and on the east of the Ghor, or great valley, bears the same name (Jebal or Djebal) at the present day, and is doubtless the same as the Gebal of Scripture. We may therefore take Gebal as the name of the northernmost portion of Idumæa, which was nearest to Palestine.

2. GEBAL. [GIBLITES.]

GEDALI'AH (God-greatened); son of Ahikam, and appointed by Nebuchadnezzar governor of Judæa after the destruction of Jerusalem. He was probably of the number of those who quitted the city at the instance of the prophet, justly despairing of the successful defence of a place which God had abandoned. Gedaliah had inherited his father's respect for Jeremiah (Jer. xl. 5, sq.), and was moreover enjoined by Nebuzaradan to look to his safety and welfare. Gedaliah was in every way worthy of the difficult post he had to fill; and he adopted as the principle of his conduct that submission to existing circumstances which was requisite in one who believed that Judah had, according to the declared will of God, been justly doomed and punished for her iniquities, and who yet believed that His loving kindness had not utterly departed from her. He established the seat of his melancholy government at Mizpeh in the tribe of Benjamin: and there the Jews, who had fled at the advance of the Chaldæan armies, or when the troops of Zedekiah were dispersed in the plains of Jericho, quitting their retreats, began to gather

around him. Gedaliah wisely counselled them to submission and quietness; and he promised on that condition to ensure them the undisturbed enjoyment of their possessions, and of the produce of the ground. In this hope the labours of the field were resumed, and the extraordinary returns of that season secured as if specially given to repair the recent injuries of war. But this calm was of short duration. Among those who returned was a member of the royal family, named Ishmael, who had taken refuge with Baalis, king of the Ammonites. He appears to have been irritated at seeing one who was not of the house of David seated upon even the shadow of David's throne; and some of the friends of Gedaliah believed him to be in a plot with Baalis to take away his life. But the noble-minded governor refused to entertain such a suspicion, and rejected with horror the proposal of an over-zealous friend, who offered to assassinate Ishmael. The suspicion which he thus generously repelled was, however, correct. He was murdered in the midst of a repast by this very Ishmael, whom he had received as a friend. This event happened about two months after the destruction of Jerusalem, and by it the present ruin of Judæa seemed to be consummated, B.C. 588 (2 Kings xxv. 22-26; Jer. xxxix. 14; xl. 5; xli. 18).

GE'DER. This word signifies a wall, enclosure, or fortified place, and must be understood in this sense in the ensuing names. Geder itself was the name of an ancient town of the Canaanites, in the plain country of Judah (Josh. xii. 13), and was perhaps the same as Gederah.

GEDE'RAH, a city in the plain of Judah (Josh. xv. 36), probably the same with the preceding Geder, and with Bethgader of 1 Chron. ii. 51. It seems to have belonged to the family of Caleb.

GEDE'ROTH, a city in the plain country of Judah (Josh. xv. 41), and one of those which the Philistines took from king Ahaz (2 Chron. xxviii. 18).

GE'DOR, an ancient city in the mountains of Judah (Josh. xv. 58), some of whose inhabitants joined David at Ziklag (1 Chron. xii. 7). It is doubtful whether this be the same Gedor in whose fertile valley the Simeonites found good pasture for their flocks (1 Chron. iv. 39). Dr. Robinson, travelling from Jerusalem to Gaza, came in sight of a place called Jedur, with ruins, on the brow of a mountain ridge, which he identifies with Gedor.

GE'HAZI (vision valley), a servant of Elisha, whose entire confidence he enjoyed. His history is involved in that of his master [ELISHA]. He personally appears in reminding his master of the best mode of rewarding the kindness of the Shunamite (2 Kings iv. 14). He was present at the interview in which the Shunamite made known to the prophet that her son was dead, and was sent forward to lay Elisha's staff on the child's face, which he did without effect (2 Kings iv. 31). The most remarkable incident in his career is that which caused his ruin. When Elisha, with a noble disinterestedness, declined the rich gifts pressed upon him by the illustrious leper whom he had healed, Gehazi felt distressed that so favourable an opportunity of profiting by the gratitude of Naaman had been so wilfully thrown away. He therefore ran after the retiring chariots, and requested, in his master's name, a portion of the gifts which had before been refused, on the ground that visitors had just arrived for whom he was unable to provide. He asked a talent of silver and two dresses; and the grateful Syrian made him take two talents instead of one. Having deposited this spoil in a place of safety, he again appeared before Elisha, whose honour he had so seriously compromised. His master asked him where he had been? and on his answering, 'Thy servant went no whither,' the prophet put on the severities of a judge, and having denounced his crime, passed upon him the terrible doom, that the leprosy of which Naaman had been cured, should cleave to him and his for ever. 'And he went forth from his presence a leper as white as snow' (2 Kings v. 20-27). B.C. 894.

We afterwards find Gehazi recounting to king Joram the great deeds of Elisha, and, in the providence of God, it so happened that when he was relating the restoration to life of the Shunamite's son, the very woman with her son appeared before the king to claim her house and lands, which had been usurped while she had been absent abroad during the recent famine. Struck by the coincidence, the king immediately granted her application (2 Kings viii. 1-6).

GEMARI'AH (*God-perfected*), the son of Shaphan, and a scribe of the temple in the time of Jehoiakim. Baruch read aloud the prophecies of Jeremiah to the people at the official chamber of Gemariah, which was attached to the new gate of the temple built by king Jotham (Jer. xxxvi. 10; comp. 2 Kings xv. 35). Gemariah's son Michaiah having reported this to his father, Baruch was invited to repeat the reading at the scribes' chamber in the palace, before Gemariah and other scribes and councillors, who gave an account of the matter to the king (Jer. xxxvi. 10-26). B.C. 607.

2. GEMARIAH, son of Hilkiah, who, with Elasah, son of Shaphan, was sent to Babylon by king Zedekiah with his tribute-money for Nebuchadnezzar. He also took charge of a letter from Jeremiah to the Jewish captives at Babylon, warning them against the false prophets who deluded them by promises of a speedy return to their own land (Jer. xxix. 3, 4). B.C. 599.

GEMS. [STONES, PRECIOUS.]

GENEALOGY signifies a list of ancestors set down both in their direct and collateral order.

We read of no nation which was more careful to frame and preserve its genealogical tables than Israel. Their sacred writings contain genealogies which extend through a period of more than 3500 years, from the creation of Adam to the captivity of Judah. Indeed, we find from the books of Ezra and Nehemiah that the same carefulness in this

matter was observed *after* the captivity; for in Ezra ii. 62 it is expressly stated that some who had come up from Babylon had sought their register among those that were reckoned by genealogy, but were not found; therefore were they, as polluted, removed from the priesthood. The division of the whole Hebrew nation into tribes, and the allotment to each tribe of a specified portion of the land of Canaan as an inalienable possession, rendered it indispensable that they should keep genealogical tables. God had, however, a still higher object than that of giving stability to property in Israel, in leading successive generations of His people thus to keep an accurate list of their ancestry. That they should do this was especially required from the moment that the voice of prophecy declared that the promised Messiah should be of the seed of Abraham, of the posterity of Isaac, of the sons of Jacob, of the tribe of Judah, and of the family of David.

The Rabbins affirm that after the Captivity the Jews were most careful in keeping their pedigrees (*Babyl. Gemar. Gloss.* fol. xiv. 2). Josephus (*De Vita sua*, p. 998, D) states that he traced his own descent from the tribe of Levi by *public registers*. And he informs us that, however dispersed and depressed his nation were, they never neglected to have exact genealogical tables prepared from the authentic documents which were kept at Jerusalem; and that in all their sufferings they were particularly careful to preserve those tables, and to have them renewed from time to time. Since, however, the period of their destruction as a nation by the Romans, all their tables of descent seem to be lost, and now they are utterly unable to trace the pedigree of any one Israelite who might lay claim to be their promised, and still expected, Messiah. Hence Christians assert, with a force that no reasonable and candid Jew can resist, that *Shiloh must have come*.

We find traces of the existence of the public tables of descent, to which Josephus refers, in the New Testament: the taxation spoken of by St. Luke (ii. 2, 3) would clearly indicate this; for how could each one be able to go to his own city, unless he knew the specific tribe to which he belonged? Hence it was, we think, that St. Paul was able with confidence to appeal to the Hebrews concerning the lineage of Christ; 'for it is evident,' says he, 'that our Lord sprung out of Judah' (Heb. vii. 14; 2 Tim. ii. 8). To evince this beyond reasonable doubt, it pleased God to give us by his inspired servants, St. Matthew and St. Luke, the following genealogies:—

MATTHEW i. 2.

1 Abraham.	1 Solomon.	1 Jechonias, *i. e.* Jehoiachin.
2 Isaac.	2 Roboam.	2 Salathiel.
3 Jacob.	3 Abia.	3 Zorobabel.
4 Judas.	4 Asa.	4 Abiud.
5 Phares.	5 Josaphat.	5 Eliakim.
6 Esrom.	6 Joram.	6 Azor.
7 Aram.	7 Ozias.	7 Sadoc.
8 Aminadab.	8 Joatham.	8 Achim.
9 Naasson.	9 Achaz.	9 Eliud.
10 Salmon.	10 Ezekias.	10 Eleazar.
11 Booz.	11 Manasses.	11 Matthan.
12 Obed.	12 Amon.	12 Jacob.
13 Jesse.	13 Josias.	13 Joseph.
14 David.	{ 14 Jechonias, *i. e.* Jehoiakim or Eliakim. }	14 Jesus.

GOD.   **LUKE iii. 23.**

1 Adam	1 Thara	1 Eliakim	1 Joanna.
2 Seth	2 Abraham.	2 Jonan	2 Juda.
3 Enos	3 Isaac	3 Joseph	3 Joseph.
4 Cainan	4 Jacob	4 Juda	4 Semei.
5 Maleleel	5 Juda	5 Simeon	5 Mattathias.
6 Jared	6 Phares	6 Levi	6 Maath.
7 Enoch	7 Esrom	7 Matthat	7 Nagge.
8 Mathusala	8 Aram.	8 Jorim	8 Esli.
9 Lamech	9 Aminadab	9 Eliezer	9 Naum.
10 Noe	10 Naasson	10 Jose	10 Amos.
11 Sem	11 Salmon	11 Er	11 Mattathias.
12 Arphaxad	12 Booz	12 Elmodan	12 Joseph.
13 Cainan	13 Obed	13 Cosam	13 Janna.
14 Sala	14 Jesse	14 Addi	14 Melchi.
15 Heber	15 David	15 Melchi	15 Levi.
16 Phalec	16 Nathan	16 Neri	16 Matthat.
17 Ragau	17 Mattatha	17 Salathiel	17 Heli.
18 Saruch	18 Menan	18 Zorobabel	18 Joseph.
19 Nachor	19 Melca	19 Rhesa	19 Jesus.

We do not find that there was any objection made to these genealogies, either by Jew or Gentile, during the first century. Had any difficulty on this head existed, we may reasonably suppose that the Jews, of all others, would have been but too ready to detect and expose it. We may therefore fairly conclude that, whatever difficulty meets us now in harmonizing our Lord's pedigree as given by the two Evangelists, it could have had no place in the first age of the Christian church. In subsequent ages, however, objections were and still are made to the genealogies of Matthew and Luke.

The chief ground of objection is the alleged inconsistency of the Evangelists with each other. The first solution of their apparent discrepancies is that of Africanus, which, he informs us, he received from the relatives of our Lord. It is to the effect that Matthan, the third in the list from Joseph, in Matthew's genealogy, and Melchi, the third in Luke's list, married successively the same woman, by whom the former begat Jacob, and the latter Heli. Heli dying without issue, his maternal brother took his widow to wife, by whom he had Joseph, who, according to law (Deut. xxv. 6), was registered by Luke as the son of Heli, though naturally the son of Jacob, as Matthew records him. This is the explanation which was generally admitted by Eusebius, Nazianzen, and others, *for ages*.

Grotius, however, availing himself of the tradition that Heli and Jacob were both sons of the same mother, but of different fathers (Matthan and Melchi), supposes that *Luke* traces the *natural* pedigree of Christ, and Matthew the *legal*. This he argues on two grounds. First, that Salathiel *could not* have been the natural son of *Jechonias*, who was *childless*—according to the declaration of God by Jeremiah (xxii.)—and was, therefore, as Luke states, the son, properly so called, of Neri, of Nathan's line; and, secondly, that the *Levirate* law imposed no necessity on Jacob to marry Heli's widow, they being only *uterine* brothers. But both the reasons assigned by Grotius for differing from the solution of Africanus would seem to be founded on a *petitio principii*. It does not appear an ascertained fact that Salathiel was not the natural son of Jechonias, nor yet that the law which obliged a man to marry the widow of his deceased brother might be departed from when they were only *maternal* brethren; for even in cases of distant relationship the law seemed obligatory, as we see in the case of Boaz marrying Ruth, the widow of his distant kinsman.

Dr. Barrett objects to the above theory as given by Africanus and altered by Grotius, on the ground principally, that it refers entirely to the descent of Joseph from David, without attempting to prove that the son of Mary was the son of David. Dr. Barrett then states his own hypothesis, viz., that Matthew relates the genealogy of Joseph, and Luke that of Mary. He supposes a sufficient reason, that after Matthew had given his genealogical table another should be added by St. Luke, fully to prove that Christ, according to the flesh, derived his descent from David, not only by his supposed father Joseph, but also by his real mother Mary.

In constructing their genealogical tables, it is well known that the Jews reckoned wholly by males, rejecting, where the blood of the grandfather passed to the grandson through a daughter, the name of the daughter herself, and counting that daughter's husband for the son of the maternal grandfather (Num. xxvi. 33; xxvii. 4-7). On this principle Joseph, begotten by Jacob, marries Mary, the daughter of Heli; and in the genealogical register of his wife's family, is counted for Heli's son. Salathiel, begotten by Jeconiah, marries the daughter of Neri, and, in like manner, is accounted his son: in Zorobabel, the offspring of Salathiel and Neri's daughter, the lines of Solomon and Nathan coalesce; Joseph and Mary are of the same tribe and family; they are both descendants of David in the line of Solomon; they have in them both the blood of Nathan, David's son. Joseph deduces his descent from Abiud (Matt. i. 13), Mary from Rhesa (Luke iii. 27), sons of Zorobabel. The genealogies of Matthew and Luke are parts of one perfect whole, and each of them is essential to the explanation of the other. By Matthew's table we prove the descent of Mary, as well as Joseph, from Solomon; by Luke's we see the descent of Joseph, as well as Mary, from Nathan.

GENERATION. Considerable obscurity attends the use of this word in the English Version, which arises from the translators having merged the various meanings of the same original word, and even of several different words, in one common term ‘generation.’ The following instances seem to require the original words to be understood in some or other of their *derivative* senses —Gen. ii. 4, 'These are the generations,' rather 'origin,' 'history,' &c. The same Greek words, Matt i. 1, are rendered 'genealogy,' &c., by recent translators: Campbell has 'lineage.' Gen. v. 1, 'The book of the generations' is properly *a family register*, a history of Adam. The same words, Gen. xxxvii. 2, mean a history of Jacob and his descendants; so also Gen. vi. 9, x. 1, and elsewhere. Gen. vii. 1, 'In this generation' is evidently 'in this age.' Gen. xv. 6, 'In the fourth generation' is an instance of the word in the sense of a *certain assigned period*. Ps. xlix. 19, 'The generation of his fathers' Gesenius renders 'the *dwelling* of his fathers,' *i. e.* the grave, and adduces Isa. xxxviii. 12. Ps. lxxiii. 15, 'The generation of thy children' is 'class,' 'order,' 'description;' as in Prov. xxx. 11, 12, 13, 14. Isa. liii. 8, 'Who shall declare his generation?' Lowth renders 'manner of life.' Michaelis renders it 'Where was the providence that cared for his life?' Gesenius and Rosenmüller, 'Who of his contemporaries reflected?' Seiler, 'Who can describe his length of life?' In the New Testament, Matt. i. 17, it is a series of persons, a succession from the same stock. Matt. iii. 7, is well rendered by Doddridge and others 'brood of vipers.' Matt. xxiv. 34, means the generation or persons *then* living *contemporary with Christ*. Luke xvi. 8, 'in their generations,' &c., wiser in regard to their dealings with the *men* of their generation. 1 Pet. ii. 8, is 'a chosen people.' The ancient Greeks, and, if we may credit Herodotus and Diodorus Siculus, the Egyptians also, assigned a *certain period* to a generation. The Greeks reckoned three generations for every hundred years, *i. e.* 33⅓ years to each. This is nearly the present computation. The ancient Hebrews also reckoned by the generation, and assigned different spaces of time to it at different periods of their history. In the time of Abraham it was one hundred years (comp. Gen. xv. 16, 'in the fourth generation they shall come hither'). This is explained in verse 13, and in Exod. xii. 40, to be four hundred years. Caleb was *fourth* in descent from Judah, and Moses and Aaron were *fourth* from Levi. In Deut. i. 35, ii. 14, Moses uses the term for thirty-eight years. In later times it clearly means ten years. In Matt. i. 17, it means a single descent from father to son [GENEALOGY].

GEN'ESIS, the first book of the Pentateuch. This venerable monument, with which the sacred literature of the Hebrews commences, and which forms its real basis, is divided into two main parts; one universal, and one special. The most ancient history of the whole human race is contained in chapters i.-xi., and the history of Israel's ancestors, the patriarchs, in chapters xii.-l. These two parts are, however, so intimately connected with each other, that it would be erroneous to ascribe to the first merely the aim of furnishing a universal history. The chief aim which pervades the whole is to show how the theocratic institution subsequently founded by Moses was rendered possible and necessary. The book, therefore, takes its starting-point from the original unity of the human race, and their original relation to God, and proceeds thence to the interruption of that relation by the appearance of sin,

which gradually and progressively wrought an external and internal division in the human race for want of the principles of divine life which originally dwelt in man in general, but which had subsequently been preserved only among a small and separate race—a race which in progress of time became more and more isolated from all the other tribes of the earth, and enjoyed for a series of generations the special care, blessing, and guidance of the Lord. The mosaical theocracy appears, therefore, by the general tenor of Genesis, partly as a restoration of the original relation to God, of the communion of man with God, and partly as an institution which had been preparing by God himself through a long series of manifestations of his power, justice, and love. Genesis thus furnishes us with the primary view and notion of the whole of the theocracy, and may therefore be considered as the historical foundation without which the subsequent history of the covenant people would be incomplete and unintelligible.

The *unity* and *composition* of the work, which is a point in dispute among the critics in regard to *all* the books of the Pentateuch, have been particularly questioned in the case of Genesis. Some suppose that Genesis is founded on two principal original documents, distinguished by the terms *Elohim* and *Jehovah*, the names which they respectively give to God. That of *Elohim* is closely connected in its parts, and forms a whole, while that of *Jehovah* is a mere complementary document, supplying details at those points where the former is abrupt and deficient, &c. These two documents are said to have been subsequently combined by the hand of an editor, so able as often to render their separation difficult, if not altogether impossible. Others maintain that Genesis is a book closely connected in all its parts, and composed by only one author, while the use of the two different names of God is not owing to two different sources on which Genesis is founded, but solely to the different significations of these two names. The use of each of the two names, Jehovah and Elohim, is everywhere in Genesis adapted to the sense of the passages in which the writer has purposely inserted the one name or the other. This point of view is the more to be considered, as it is the peculiar object of the author to point out in Genesis the gradual and progressive development of the divine revelations. The opponents have in vain attempted to discover in Genesis a few contradictions indicative of different documents in it; their very admission, that a fixed plan and able compilation visibly pervade the whole of the book, is in itself a refutation of such supposed contradictions, since it is hardly to be conceived, that an editor or compiler who has shown so much skill and anxiety to give unity to the book should have cared so little about the removal of those contradictions. The whole of Genesis is pervaded by such a freedom in the selection and treatment of the existing traditions, such an absence of all trace of any previous source or documents which might in some measure have confined the writer within certain limits of views and expressions, as to render it quite impracticable to separate and fix upon them specifically, even if there were portions in Genesis drawn from earlier written documents.

That first question concerning the unity of the book is closely connected with another question, respecting its authenticity, or whether Moses was the author of Genesis. We confine ourselves here to only a few remarks on the authenticity of Genesis in particular, and refer the reader for further information to the article PENTATEUCH. Some critics have attempted to ascertain the period when Genesis was composed, from a few passages in it, which they say must be *anachronisms*, if Moses was really the author of the book. Among such passages are, in particular, Gen. xii. 6; xiii. 7; 'And the Canaanite was then in the land.' This remark, they say, could only have been made by a writer who lived in Palestine after the extirpation of the Canaanites. But the sense of the passage is not that the Canaanites had not as yet been extirpated, but merely that Abraham, on his arrival in Canaan, had already found there the Canaanites. This notice was necessary, since the author subsequently describes the intercourse between Abraham and the Canaanites, the lords of the country. According to the explanation given to the passage by the opponents, such an observation would be quite a superfluous triviality. Also the name *Hebron* (Gen. xiii. 18; xxiii. 2), they say, was not introduced till after the time of Moses (Josh. xiv. 15; xv. 13). This, however, does not prove anything, since *Hebron* was the original Hebrew name for the place, which was subsequently changed into *Arba* (by a man of that name), but was restored by the Israelites on their entrance into Canaan. The opponents also maintain that the name of the place Dan (Gen. xiv. 14) was given only in the post-Mosaical period (Josh. xix. 47; Judg. xviii. 29). But the two last passages speak of quite a different place. There were two places called *Dan*; Dan-*Jaan* (2 Sam. xxiv. 6), and Dan-*Laish*, or *Leshem*. In Genesis, they further add. frequently occurs the name *Bethel* (xii. 8; xxviii. 19; xxxv. 15); while even in the time of Joshua the place was as yet called Luz (Josh. xviii. 13). But the name *Bethel* was not first given to the place by the Israelites in the time of Joshua, there being no occasion for it, since Bethel was the old patriarchal name, which the Israelites restored in the place of Luz, a name given by the Canaanites. Another passage in Genesis (xxxvi. 31), 'Before there reigned any king over the children of Israel,' is likewise supposed to have been written at a period when the Jews had already a king over them. But the broachers of these objections forget that this passage refers to those promises contained in the Pentateuch in general, and in Genesis in particular (comp. Gen. xxxv. 11), that there should hereafter be kings among the Israelites as an independent nation. In comparing Israel with Edom (Gen. xxxvi.), the sacred writer cannot refrain from observing that Edom, though left without divine promises of possessing kings, nevertheless possessed them, and obtained the glory of an independent kingdom, long before Israel could think of such an independence; and a little attention to the sense of the passage will show how admirably the observation suits a writer in the Mosaical period. The passage (Gen. xv. 18) where the land of Israel is described as extending from the river of Egypt (the Nile) to the great river (Euphrates), it is alleged, could only have

been penned during the splendid period of the Jews, the times of David and Solomon. *Literally* taken, however, the remark is inapplicable to any period, since the kingdom of the Jews at no period of their history extended so far. That promise, must, therefore, be taken in a rhetorical sense, describing the central point of the proper country as situated between the two rivers.

With regard to the historical character of the book, *Genesis* consists of two contrasting parts: the first part introduces us into the greatest problems of the human mind, such as the Creation and the fall of man; and the second, into the quiet solitude of a small defined circle of families. In the former, the most sublime and wonderful events are described with childlike simplicity; while, in the latter, on the contrary, the most simple and common occurrences are interwoven with the sublimest thoughts and reflections, rendering the small family circle a whole world in history, and the principal actors in it prototypes for a whole nation, and for all times. The contents in general are strictly religious. Not the least trace of mythology appears in it. It is true that the narrations are fraught with wonders. But primeval wonders, the marvellous deeds of God, are the very subject of Genesis. None of these wonders, however, bear a fantastical impress, and there is no useless prodigality of them. They are all penetrated and connected by one common leading idea, and are all related to the counsel of God for the salvation of man. This principle sheds its lustrous beams through the whole of Genesis; therefore the wonders therein related are as little to be ascribed to the invention and imagination of man as the whole plan of God for human salvation. The foundation of the divine theocratical institution throws a strong light upon the early patriarchal times; the reality of the one proves the reality of the other, as described in Genesis.

The separate accounts in Genesis also manifest great internal evidence of truth if we closely examine them. They bear on their front the most beautiful impress of truth. The *cosmogony* in Genesis stands unequalled among all others known in the ancient world. No mythology, no ancient philosophy, has ever come up to the idea of a *creation out of nothing*. All the ancient systems end in Pantheïsm, Materialism, emanation-theory, &c. But the Biblical cosmogony occupies a place of its own, and therefore must not be ranked among, or confounded with, any of the ancient systems of mythology or philosophy. The mythological and philosophical cosmogonies may have been derived from the Biblical, as being later depravations and misrepresentations of Biblical truth; but the contents of Genesis cannot, *vice versâ*, have been derived from mythology or philosophy. The historical delineation also of the Creation and of the fall of man does not bear the least national interest or colouring, but is of a truly universal nature, while every mythus bears the stamp of the national features of the nation and country where it originated and found development. All mythi are subject to continual development and variations, but among the Hebrews the accounts in Genesis stand firm and immutable for all times, without the least thing being added or altered in them for the purpose of further development,

2 A

even by the New Testament. What a solid guarantee must there be in this foundation of all subsequent revelations, since it has been admitted and maintained by all generations with such immovable firmness! The ancient heathen traditions coincide in many points with the Biblical accounts, and serve to illustrate and confirm them. This is especially the case in the ancient traditions concerning the Deluge (Gen. vi. 9), and in the list of nations in the tenth chapter ; for instance (Gen. x. 4), Tarshish is called the son of Javan. This indicates that the ancient inhabitants of Tarshish or Tartessus in Spain were erroneously considered to be a Phœnician colony like those of other towns in its neighbourhood, and that they sprang from Javan, that is, Greece. That they were of Greek origin is clear from the account of Herodotus. Also (ver. 8), Nimrod, the ruler of Babel, is called the son of *Cush*, which is in remarkable unison with the mythological tales concerning *Bel* and his Egyptian descent. *Sidon* alone is mentioned (ver. 15), but not *Tyrus* (comp. xlix. 13), which arose only in the time of Joshua (Josh. xix. 29) ; and that *Sidon* was an older town than *Tyrus*, by which it was afterwards eclipsed, is certified by a number of ancient reports.

With the patriarchal history (xii. sqq.) begins an historical sketch of a peculiar character. The circumstantial details in it allow us to examine more closely the historical character of these accounts. The numerous descriptions of the mode of life in those days furnish us with a very vivid picture. We meet everywhere a sublime simplicity quite worthy of patriarchal life, and never to be found again in later history. One cannot suppose that it would have been possible in a later period, estranged from ancient simplicity, to invent such a picture.

The fidelity of the author everywhere exhibits itself. Neither the blemishes in the history of Abraham, nor the gross sins of the sons of Jacob, among whom even Levi, the progenitor of the sacerdotal race, forms no exception, are concealed.

The same author, whose moral principles are so much blamed by the opponents of Genesis, on account of the description given of the life of Jacob, produces, in the history of Abraham, a picture of moral greatness which could have originated only in facts.

The faithfulness of the author manifests itself also especially in the description of the expedition of the kings from Upper to Western Asia; in his statements concerning the person of Melchizedek (Gen. xiv.); in the circumstantial details given of the incidents occurring at the purchase of the hereditary burial-place (ch. xxiii.); in the genealogies of Arabian tribes (ch. xxv.); in the genealogy of Edom (ch. xxxvi.); and in many remarkable details which are interwoven with the general accounts. In the history of Joseph the patriarchal history comes into contact with Egypt, and here the accounts given by ancient classical writers, as well as the monuments of Egypt, frequently furnish some splendid confirmations. For instance, the account given (xlvii. 13-26) of the manner in which the Pharaohs became proprietors of all the lands, with the exception of those belonging to the priests, is confirmed by Herodotus, and by Diodorus Siculus. The manner of embalming described in Gen. l. entirely agrees with the description of Herodotus, ii. 84, &c.

For the important commentaries and writings on Genesis, see the article PENTATEUCH.

GENNESARETH. [CINNERETH.]

GENNESARETH, LAKE OF. [SEA.]

GENTILES, a word which means literally, 'the nations.' It was applied by the Hebrews to all individuals or communities not under the law—that is, all the nations of the world excepting the Jews. But in later times some small states, and many individuals, embraced the law: and they were distinguished from the Gentiles, as well as from the Jews, by the name of PROSELYTES. In some places our authorized version has the word 'Gentiles' where the original should properly be rendered 'Greeks.'

GE'RAH, the smallest piece of money among the Hebrews. Twenty made a shekel; one of them would therefore be worth three halfpence, according to the present value of silver (Exod. xxx. 13).

GE'RAR, a town and district on the southernmost borders of Palestine, in the country of the Philistines, and not far from Gaza. It was visited by Abraham after the destruction of Sodom (Gen. xx. 1), and by Isaac when there was a dearth in the rest of Canaan (Gen. xxvi. 1). The incidents of their sojourn show that the district was very fertile. It was the seat of the first Philistine kingdom we read of, and gave name to it. The intercourse, differences, and alliances of the Hebrew fathers with the king and people of Gerar form a very curious and interesting portion of patriarchal history. It was still an important place in later times, as we may gather from 1 Chron. xiv. 13, 14. According to the ancient accounts Gerar lay in or near a valley, which appears to be no other than the great Wady Sheriah (or one of the branches of it), that comes down from Beersheba ; besides we know that it was in the land of the Philistines, and that it was not far from Beersheba when Isaac resided there (Gen. xxvi. 1, 20, 23; 26-33; comp. xx. 1). The name continued to exist (perhaps as a matter of tradition) for several centuries after the Christian era, but no traces of it can now be found.

GER'ASA, not JERASH (not named in the Bible), was in the Decapolis, and formed the eastern boundary of Peræa. It lay on elevated ground, according to Ptolemy, in 68° 15' = 31° 45'. Its inhabitants were mostly heathen. After the Roman conquests in the East, the country in which Gerasa lies became one of their favourite colonies, and ten principal cities were built on the east of the Jordan, giving the name of Decapolis to the land in which they stood. Gerasa was one, but not the greatest of these. The place was taken by storm by Alexander Jannæus, who was actuated by a desire of gaining a large treasure. Alexander died near it while besieging Regaba. Before the place had time to recover from this calamity, it was included among the number of those cities which were burnt by the enraged Jews in their vengeance on the Syrians, and on the Roman power generally, for the massacre of a number of their nation at Cæsarea. A terrible revenge was taken by other cities, but Gerasa is honourably excepted. Annius, general under Vespasian, took the city; 'after which he set fire to their houses,' 'and what was remaining was all burnt down.' Its ruins were first discovered by Seetzen and have often been subse-

197.

quently visited. They have been pronounced superior 'to those of Palmyra.

GERGESENES'. [GADARA.]

GER'IZIM, MOUNT. [EBAL AND GERIZIM.]

GE'RSHOM (*a stranger here*), one of the two sons (the other was Eliezer) who were born to Moses in the land of Midian by Zipporah (Exod. ii. 22; xviii. 3). These sons of the great lawgiver held no other rank than that of simple Levites, while the sons of their uncle Aaron enjoyed all the privileges of the priesthood (1 Chron. xxiii. 14). The glory of being the children of such a father doubtless availed them more than the highest dignities; but we must nevertheless admire the rare disinterestedness of Moses in making no public provision—as he might so easily have done—for his own children.

GER'SHON (*same as Gershom*), eldest son of the patriarch Levi, born in Canaan before the going down into Egypt. He is only known from his name having been given to one of the three great branches of the Levitical tribe. The office of the Gershonites, during the marches in the wilderness, was to carry the veils and curtains of the tabernacle, and their place in the camp was west of the tabernacle (Gen. xlvi. 11; Exod. vi. 16; Num. iii. 17).

GE'SHEM (*rain*), one of the enemies of the Jews under Nehemiah (Neh. vi. 6). He was probably a Samaritan, although on some account or other designated an Arabian (Neh. ii. 19), and seems to have been a subaltern officer at Jerusalem. He opposed the designs of the Jewish governor, talking of them as seditious, and turning them into ridicule. Eventually he took part in the plots of Tobiah against the life of Nehemiah (Neh. ii. 19; vi. 2-9), about B.C. 445.

GE'SHUR, a district of Syria (2 Sam. xv. 8; 1 Chron. ii. 23), which adjoined, on the east side of the Jordan, the northern border of the Hebrew territory, and lay between Mount Hermon, Maachah, and Bashan (Deut. iii. 13, 14; Josh. xii. 5). According to the boundaries of the Holy Land, as defined by Moses, Geshur would have formed part of it; but in Josh. xiii. 2, 13, it is stated that the Israelites had expelled neither the Geshurites nor

the Maachathites, but dwelt together with them. That the Hebrews did not afterwards permanently subdue Geshur appears from the circumstance that, in David's time, this district had a king of its own, called Talmai, whose daughter, Maacah, was one of the wives of David (2 Sam. iii. 3). She was the mother of Absalom, who took refuge with his grandfather after the murder of Amnon, and remained three years in Geshur (2 Sam. xiii. 37; xv. 8). The word *Geshur* signifies a bridge, and corresponds with the Arabic *Jisr;* and in the same region where, according to the above data, we must fix Geshur, between Mount Hermon and the lake of Tiberias, there still exists an ancient stone bridge over the upper Jordan, called Jisr-Beni-Jakub, or 'the bridge of the children of Jacob,' *i. e.* the Israelites.

GESH'URITES, GESHURI; 1. The inhabitants of the above region [GESHUR]. 2. A people in the south of Palestine, near the Philistines (Josh. xiii. 2; 1 Sam. xxvii. 8).

GETHSEM'ANE (seemingly from *oil-press*), the name of a small field, or garden, just out of Jerusalem, over the brook Kidron, and at the foot of the Mount of Olives. That which is now pointed out as the garden in which our Lord underwent his agony, occupies part of a level space between the brook and the foot of the Mount, and corresponds well enough in situation and distance with all the conditions which the narrative requires. It is about fifty paces square, and is enclosed by a wall of no great height, formed of rough loose stones. Eight very ancient olive-trees now occupy this enclosure, some of which are of very large size, and all exhibit symptoms of decay clearly denoting their great age. The garden belongs to one of the monastic establishments, and much care has been taken to preserve the old trees from destruction. Dr. Robinson admits the probability that this is the site which Eusebius and Jerome had in view; and, as no other site is suggested as preferable, we may be content to receive the traditional indication.

GE'ZER, formerly a royal city of the Canaanites, and situated in what became the western part of the tribe of Ephraim. The Canaanites were not expelled from it at the conquest (Josh. x. 33; xvi. 5, 10; Judg. i. 29). It was, nevertheless, assigned to the Levites (Josh. xxi. 21). In after times, having been, on some occasion, destroyed by the Egyptians, it was rebuilt by Solomon.

GIANTS. These beings of unusual height are found in the early history of all nations, sometimes of a purely human origin, but more frequently supposed to have partaken also, in some way, of the supernatural and the divine.

1. In Gen. vi. 4, we have the first mention of giants—'There were giants in the earth in those days; and also after that, when the sons of God came in unto the daughters of men, and they bare children to them, the same became mighty men which were of old, men of renown.' In our judgment the bearing of this passage obviously favours the common notion of giants, and that the rather because their origin is traced to some unexplained connection with 'the sons of God,' that is, with beings of high endowments, if not of a superior nature.

2. In Gen. xiv. 5, we meet with a race termed Rephaim, as settled on the other side of the Jordan, in Ashteroth-Karnaim, whom Chedorlaomer

2 A 2

defeated. Of this race was Og, king of Bashan, who alone remained, in the days of Moses (Deut. iii. 10), of the remnant of the Rephaim. This race gave their name to a valley near Jerusalem.

3. The Anakim. In Num. xiii., the spies sent by Moses before his army to survey the promised land, report among other things—' The people be strong that dwell in the land; and, moreover, we saw the children of Anak' (ver. 28). This indirect mention of the children of Anak shows that they were a well-known gigantic race. In the 32nd and 33rd verses the statement is enhanced, —' It is a land that eateth up the inhabitants; and all the people that we saw in it are men of great stature. And there we saw the giants, the sons of Anak which came of the giants; and we were in our own sight as grasshoppers, and so we were in their sight.' However much of exaggeration fear may have given to the description, the passage seems beyond a doubt to show the writer's belief in a race of giants (Deut. ix. 2). From Deut. ii. 10 it appears that the size of the Anakim became proverbial, and was used as a standard with which to compare others. In the time of Moses they dwelt in the environs of Hebron (Josh. xi. 22). They consisted of three branches or clans—' Ahiman, Sheshai, and Talmai—the children of Anak' (Num. xiii. 22). They were destroyed by Joshua (Josh. xi. 21; xiv. 12; Judg. i. 20).

4. From the remnant of the Anakim left in Gath of the Philistines (Judg. i. 20; Josh. xiv. 12) proceeded the famous Goliath (1 Sam. xvii. 4). This giant is said to have been in height six cubits and a span. Other giants of the Philistines are mentioned in the passage before cited, 2 Sam. xxi. 16, sq., namely :—1. ' Ishbi-benob, which was of the sons of the giant, the weight of whose spear weighed three hundred shekels of brass, he being girded with a new sword, thought to have slain David; but Abishai, the son of Zeruiah, succoured him, and smote the Philistine and killed him.' 2. Saph, which was of the sons of the giant who was slain by Sibbechai. 3. ' A man of great stature, that had on every hand six fingers and on every foot six toes, four and twenty in number, and he also was born to the giant; and when he defied Israel, Jonathan, the son of Shimeah, the brother of David, slew him.' These four were sons of the giant in Gath, that is, probably of the Goliath of Gath whom David slew (1 Kings xx. 8; 2 Sam. xx. 20; 1 Sam. xvii. 4).

5. Another race is mentioned in Deut. ii. 10, the Emim, who dwelt in the country of the Moabites. They are described as a people ' great and many, and tall as the Anakims, which were also accounted giants' (Gen. xiv. 5).

6. The Zamzummim also (Deut. xxi. 20), whose home was in the land of Ammon—' that also was accounted a land of giants : giants dwelt therein of old time, and the Ammonites called them Zamzummims, a people great and many, and tall as the Anakims; but the Lord destroyed them before them, and they (the Israelites) succeeded them, and dwelt in their stead.'

From this enumeration it is clear that the Scriptures tell of giants in the olden time, and of races of giants ; and that, though giants are mentioned as something singular, and consequently as comparatively rare, they appear to have been,

relatively to the numbers of the population, of frequent occurrence.

That the primitive races of men greatly surpassed others in stature is an opinion which finds ample support in ancient authors generally ; and at an early period and under favourable circumstances, individuals and even tribes may have reached an unusual height and been of extraordinary strength. But many things concur to show that the size of the race did not differ materially from what it is at present. This is seen in the remains of human beings found in tombs; especially among the mummies of Egypt. To the same effect is the size of ancient armour, as well as architectural dimensions, and the measures of length which have been received from antiquity. Ancient writers who are free from the influence of fable, are found to give a concurrent testimony.

That great diversity as to height and size prevails in the human family, is well known. What the precise limits may be within which nature has worked in the formation of man, it would be difficult to determine. But the inhabitants of northern latitudes are well known to be below the ordinary standard, many of them scarcely exceeding four feet; while in temperate climates the height of the human race averages from four feet and a half to six feet ; and instances are not wanting of persons who measured eight or nine feet.

The possibility of a race of giants cannot well be denied. There is a known tendency in the human frame to perpetuate peculiarities which have been once evolved. Why not extraordinary ' procerity' as well as any other? In fact, the propagation of stature, whether high or low, is a phenomenon which we all see presented daily before our own eyes. Tall parents give birth to tall children. The tallness is found to remain in families ; and, doubtless, did not circumstances intervene to reduce the stature by intermarriage with short persons, the unusual height would be perpetuated in any given line. The inhabitants of Potsdam, descended to a great extent from the famous regiment of tall grenadiers which Frederick of Prussia took so much pains to bring together, are said to be still remarkable for exceeding the average height. The family of Scaligers appears to have been unusually tall.

GIB'BETHON, a city of the Philistines, which was included in the territories of the tribe of Dan (Josh. xix. 44), and was assigned to the Levites (Josh. xxi. 23). It was still in the hands of the Philistines in the time of Nadab, king of Israel, who besieged it, and was slain under its walls by Baasha, one of his own officers (1 Kings xx. 27; xvi. 15). Nothing is known of its site.

GIB'EAH. There were several places of this name, which, as before remarked [GEBA], is the feminine form of the word Gibeah, and signifies a hill. Without doubt all the places so named were situated upon hills.

1. GIBEAH OF BENJAMIN is historically the most important of the places bearing this name. It is often mentioned in Scripture. It was the scene of that abominable transaction which involved in its consequences almost the entire extirpation of the tribe of Benjamin (Judg. xix. 14, sq.). It was the birth-place of Saul, and continued to be his residence after he became

king (1 Sam. x. 26; xi. 4; xv. 33; xxiii. 19; xxvi. 1); and here was the scene of Jonathan's romantic exploit against the Philistines (1 Sam. xiv.). It was doubtless on account of this its intimate connection with Saul, that the Gibeonites hanged up here his seven descendants (2 Sam. xxi. 6). Jerome speaks of Gibeah as, in his time, level with the ground, and since then it does not appear to have been visited by travellers till recently. Dr. Robinson, who made many valuable observations in this neighbourhood, detected Gibeah in the small and half-ruined village of Jeba, which lies upon a low, conical, or rather round eminence, on the broad ridge which shelves down towards the Jordan valley, and spreads out below the village in a fine sloping plain. The views of the Dead Sea and the Jordan, and of the Eastern mountains, are here very extensive. Among the ruins some large hewn stones, indicating antiquity, are occasionally seen. This place is about five miles north by east from Jerusalem.

2. GIBEAH in the mountains of Judah (Josh. xv. 57), which, under the name of Gabaatha, Eusebius and Jerome place twelve Roman miles from Eleutheropolis, and state that the grave of the prophet Habakkuk was there to be seen. Dr. Robinson identifies it with the village of Jebah, which stands upon an isolated hill, in the midst of Wady-el-Musurr, about ten miles south-west of Jerusalem.

3. GIBEAH in Mount Ephraim, called Gibeah of Phineas, where the high-priest Eleazar, son of Aaron, was buried by his son Phineas (Josh. xxiv. 33). Dr. Robinson finds it in a narrow valley called Wady-el-Jib, the Geeb of Maundrell, lying just midway on the road between Jerusalem and Shechem.

GIB'EON, a town celebrated in the Old Testament, but not mentioned in the New. It was 'a great city,' as one of the royal cities; and to its jurisdiction originally belonged Beeroth, Chephirah, and Kirjath-jearim (Josh. ix. 17; x. 2). It is first mentioned in connection with the deception practised by the inhabitants upon Joshua, by which, although Canaanites (Hivites), they induced the Jewish leader not only to make a league with them, and to spare their lives and cities, but also, in their defence, to make war upon the five kings by whom they were besieged. It was in the great battle which followed, that 'the sun stood still upon Gibeon' (Josh. x. 12, 1-14). The place afterwards fell to the lot of Benjamin, and became a Levitical city (Josh. xviii. 25; xxi. 17), where the tabernacle was set up for many years under David and Solomon (1 Chron. xvi. 39; xxi. 29; 2 Chron. i. 3), the ark being at the same time at Jerusalem (2 Chron. i. 4). It was here, as being the place of the altar, that the young Solomon offered a thousand burnt-offerings, and was rewarded by the vision which left him the wisest of men (1 Kings iii. 4-15; 2 Chron. i. 3-13). This was the place where Abner's challenge to Joab brought defeat upon himself, and death upon his brother Ashael (2 Sam. ii. 12-32), and where Amasa was afterwards slain by Joab (2 Sam. xx. 8-12). None of these passages mark the site of Gibeon; but there are indications of it in Josephus, who places it fifty stadia north-west from Jerusalem; and in Jerome: which leave little doubt that Gibeon is to be iden-

tified with the place which still bears the name of El-Jib.

El-Jib is a moderately sized village, seated on the summit of a hill, five miles north by west from Jerusalem. The houses stand very irregularly and unevenly, sometimes almost above one another. They seem to be chiefly rooms in old massive ruins, which have fallen down in every direction. One large building still remains, probably a former castle or tower of strength. Towards the east the ridge of the hill sinks a little, and here, a few rods from the village, just below the top of the ridge towards the north, is a fine fountain of water. It is in a cave, excavated in and under the high rock, so as to form a large subterranean reservoir. Not far below it, among olive-trees, are the remains of an open reservoir, about one hundred and twenty feet in length by one hundred in breadth. It was doubtless designed to receive the superfluous waters of the cavern, and there can be little question but that this was 'the Pool of Gibeon' mentioned in 2 Sam. ii. 13; and, in the whole, we find the 'Great [or many] waters of Gibeon' of Jer. xli. 12.

GIB'LITES, the inhabitants of the city and district of Gebal in Phœnicia, 34° 7' N. lat., 35° 42' E. long., on the shore of the Mediterranean, under Mount Lebanon. 'The land of the Giblites,' with 'all Lebanon,' was assigned to the Israelites by the original appointment (Josh. xiii. 5); but it does not seem that they ever possessed themselves of it. The Giblites are denoted by the word rendered 'stone-squarers' in 1 Kings v. 18; from which it would seem that they were then subject to, or in close connection with Tyre. It is doubtful whether this Gebal, or the one in Edom, is that mentioned in Ps. lxxxiii. 7. But in Ezek. xxvii. 9, the Phœnician Giblites are distinctly mentioned as such, and preferably employed upon the shipping which formed the glory and strength of Tyre.

Gebal was an important place, and celebrated for the birth and worship of Adonis, the Syrian Thammuz. The town still subsists under the name of Jebail. It is seated on a rising ground near the sea, at the foot of Lebanon, which here approaches close to the coast. It is walled on the three sides towards the land, and open on the west towards the sea, being perhaps about half a mile in circuit. Within the wall, which seems of the age of the Crusades, the chief building is an old castle, which has received modern repairs, and is now used as the abode of the agha or commandant. There are three or four open and lofty buildings belonging to the chief people of the place, a mosque with a low minaret, and an old Maronite church of good masonry; but the houses generally are of poor construction, and nearly half the space within the walls is occupied with the gardens of the inhabitants. The population is estimated at 2000.

GID'EON (destroyer), surnamed JERUBBAAL or JERUBBESHETH, fifth Judge in Israel, and the first of them whose history is circumstantially narrated. He was the son of Joash, of the tribe of Manasseh, and resided at Ophrah in Gilead beyond the Jordan.

The Midianites, in conjunction with the Amalekites and other nomade tribes, invaded the country every year, at the season of produce, in great numbers, with their flocks and herds. They plundered and trampled down the fields, the vineyards, and the gardens; they seized the cattle, and plundered man and house, rioting in the country, after the manner which the Bedouin Arabs practise at this day. After Israel had been humbled by seven years of this treatment, the Lord raised up a deliverer in the person of Gideon. He was threshing corn by stealth, for fear of its being taken away by the Midianites, when an angel of God appeared before him, and thus saluted him:—'the Lord is with thee, thou mighty man of valour.' Gideon expressed some doubt whether God was still with a people subject to such affliction, and was answered by the most unexpected commission—'Go in this thy might, and thou shalt save Israel from the hand of the Midianites: have not I sent thee?' Gideon still urged, 'Wherewith shall I save Israel? Behold my family is poor in Manasseh, and I am the least in my father's house.' The 'Wherewith' was answered by 'Surely I will be with thee.' He then demurred no more, but pressed his hospitality upon the heavenly stranger, who, however, ate not of what was set before him, but directing Gideon to lay it out upon the rock as upon an altar, it was consumed by a supernatural fire, and the angel disappeared. Assured by this of his commission, Gideon proceeded at once to cast down the local image and altar of Baal; and, when the people would have avenged this insult to their false god, their anger was averted through the address of his father, who, by dwelling on the inability of Baal to avenge himself, more than insinuated a doubt of his competency to protect his followers. This was a favourite argument among the Hebrews against idolatry. It occurs often in the prophets, and was seldom urged upon idolatrous Israelites without some effect upon their consciences.

Gideon soon found occasion to act upon his high commission. The allied invaders were encamped in the great plain of Jezreel or Esdraelon, when he blew the trumpet, and thus gathered round him a daily increasing host, the summons to arms which it implied having been transmitted through the northern tribes by special messengers. The inquietude connected with great enterprises is more sensibly felt some days before than at the moment of action; and hence the two miraculous signs which, on the two nights preceding the march, were required and given as tokens of victory. The first night a fleece was laid out in the middle of an open threshing-floor, and in the morning it was quite wet, while the soil was dry all around. The next night the wonder was reversed, the soil being wet and the fleece perfectly dry (Judg. vii.).

Encouraged by these divine testimonies, Gideon commenced his march, and advanced to the brook Harod, in the valley of Jezreel. He was here at the head of 32,000 men; but, lest so large a host should assume the glory of the coming deliverance, which of right belonged to God only, two operations, remarkable both in motive and procedure, reduced this large host to a mere handful of men. First, by divine direction, proclamation was made that all the faint-hearted might withdraw; and no fewer than 22,000 availed themselves of the indulgence. The remaining 10,000 were still declared too numerous: they were therefore all taken down to the brook, when only those who lapped the water from their hands, like active men in haste, were reserved for the enterprise, while all those who lay down leisurely to drink were excluded. The former numbered no more than 300, and these were the appointed vanquishers of the huge host which covered the great plain (Judg. vii. 1-8).

The overheard relation of a dream, by which Gideon was encouraged (Judg. vii. 9-14), and the remarkable stratagem, with pitchers and torches, by which he overcame (ver. 15-23), are well known.

The routed Midianites fled towards the Jordan, but were pursued with great slaughter, the country being now roused in pursuit of the flying oppressor. The Ephraimites rendered good service by seizing the lower fords of the Jordan, and cutting off all who attempted escape in that direction, while Gideon himself pursued beyond the river those who escaped by the upper fords. Gideon crossed the Jordan a little below where it leaves the lake of Gennesareth, in pursuit of the Midianitish princes Zeba and Zalmunna. On that side the river, however, his victory was not believed or understood, and the people still trembled at the very name of the Midianites. Hence he could obtain no succour from the places which he passed, and town after town refused to supply even victuals to his fatigued and hungry, but still stout-hearted troop. He denounced vengeance upon them, but postponed its execution till his return; and when he did return, with the two princes as his prisoners, he by no means spared those towns which, like Succoth and Penuel, had added insult to injury (Judg. viii. 4-17).

In his days captives of distinction taken in war were almost invariably slain. Zeba and Zalmunna had made up their minds to this fate; and yet it was Gideon's intention to have spared them, till he learned that they had put to death his own brothers under the same circumstances; upon which, as the avenger of their blood, he slew the captives with his own hand (Judg. viii. 18-21).

Among the fugitives taken by the Ephraimites were two distinguished emirs of Midian, named Oreb and Zeeb, whom they put to death. They took their heads over to Gideon, which amounted to an acknowledgment of his leadership; but still the always haughty and jealous Ephraimites were greatly annoyed that they had not in the first instance been summoned to the field; and serious consequences might have followed, but for the tact of Gideon in speaking in a lowly spirit of his own doings in comparison with theirs (Judg. vii. 14; viii. 1, sq.).

Gideon having thus delivered Israel from the most afflictive tyranny to which they had been subject since they quitted Egypt, the grateful people, and particularly the northern tribes, made him an offer of the crown for himself and his sons. But the hero was too well acquainted with his true position, and with the principles of the theocratical government, to accept this unguarded offer: 'I will not rule over you,' he said, 'neither shall my son rule over you: JEHOVAH, he shall rule over you.' He would only accept the golden ear-rings which the victors had taken from the ears of their slaughtered foes [EAR-RINGS]; and a cloth being spread out to receive them, the admiring Israelites threw in, not only the ear-rings, but other ornaments of gold, including the chains of the royal camels, and added the purple robes which the slain monarchs had worn, being the first indication of purple as a royal colour. The ear-rings alone weighed 1700 shekels, equal to 74 pounds 4 ounces, and worth, at the present value of gold, about 3300l. With this 'Gideon made an ephod, and put it in his city, even in Ophrah; and all Israel went thither a whoring after it; which thing became a snare unto Gideon and to his house.' An ephod, at least that of the high-priest, was an outer garment like a sleeveless tunic, to which was attached the oracular breast-plate, composed of twelve precious stones set in gold, and graven with the names of the twelve tribes. Another plainer description of ephod was worn by the common priests. The object of Gideon in making an ephod with his treasure is not very clear. Some suppose that it was merely designed as a trophy of Israel's deliverance: if so, it was a very strange one. It is more probable that as Gideon had, on his being first called to his high mission, been instructed to build an altar and offer sacrifice at this very place, he conceived himself authorized, if not required, to have there a sacerdotal establishment—for at least the tribes beyond the river—where sacrifices might be regularly offered. In this case the worship rendered there was doubtless in honour of Jehovah, but was still, however well intended, highly schismatical and irregular. Even in his lifetime it must have had the effect of withdrawing the attention of the people east of the Jordan from the Tabernacle at Shiloh, and thus so far tended to facilitate the step into actual idolatry, which was taken soon after Gideon's death. The probability of this explanation is strengthened when we recollect the schismatical sacerdotal establishments which were formed by Micah on Mount Ephraim, and by the Danites at Laish (Judg. xvii. 5-13; xviii. 29-31).

The remainder of Gideon's life was peaceable. He had seventy sons by many wives, and died at an advanced age, after he had 'ruled Israel' (principally the northern tribes and those beyond the river) for forty years: B.C. 1249 to 1209. He is mentioned in the discourse of Samuel (1 Sam. xii. 11), and his name occurs in Heb. xi. 32, among those of the heroes of the faith.

1. GI'HON, a fountain near Jerusalem. The place outside the city to which the young Solomon was taken to be anointed king, was called Gihon, but its direction is not indicated (1 Kings i. 33, 38). Subsequently king Hezekiah 'stopped the upper water-course [or upper out-flow of the waters] of Gihon, and brought it straight down to the west side of the city of David (2 Chron. xxxii. 30; xxxiii. 14). This was, perhaps, on occasion of the approach of the Assyrian army under Sennacherib, when, to prevent the besiegers from finding water, great numbers of the people laboured with much diligence in stopping the water of the fountains without the city, and in particular of 'the brook that ran through the midst of the land ' (2 Chron. xxxii. 3, 4). The author of the book of Sirach (xlviii. 17) also states, that 'Hezekiah brought water into the midst of the city ; he dug with iron into the rock, and built fountains for the waters.' The foun-

tain of Gihon is also mentioned by Josephus. From a comparison of these passages the editor of the Pictorial Bible (on 2 Chron. xxxii.) arrived at the conclusion, since confirmed by Dr. Robinson, that there existed anciently a fountain of Gihon, on the west side of the city, which was 'stopped' or covered over by Hezekiah, and its waters brought by subterraneous channels into the city. Before that time it would naturally have flowed down through the valley of Gihon, and probably formed the brook which was stopped at the same time. ' The fountain may have been stopped, and its waters thus secured very easily by digging deep and erecting over it one or more vaulted subterranean chambers.'

2. GIHON; the name of one of the rivers of Paradise. [PARADISE.]

GIL'BOA, a mountain memorable for the defeat of Saul by the Philistines, where his three sons were slain, and where he himself died by his own hand (1 Sam. xxviii. 4; xxxi. 1-8; 2 Sam. i. 6-21). The circumstances of the narrative would alone suffice to direct our attention to the mountains which bound the great plain of Esdraelon on the south-east, and are interposed between it and the Jordan valley. Here there are a number of ridges with a general direction from north-west to south-east, separated by valleys running in the same direction. The largest of these valleys is the southernmost: it is a broad deep plain about two miles and a half wide, and leading direct into the Jordan valley. This is supposed to be distinctively (for the plain of Esdraelon is sometimes so called) the Valley of Jezreel. The mountains which bound it on the north appear to be those of Little Hermon ; and the higher mountains which bound it on the south undoubtedly form Mount Gilboa. There is still, indeed, an inhabited village, in whose name of Jelbon that of Gilboa may be recognised.

GIL'EAD. 1. A group of mountains connected with Lebanon by means of Mount Hermon. It begins not far from the latter, and extends southward to the sources of the brooks Jabbok and Arnon, thus enclosing the whole eastern part of the land beyond the Jordan (Gen. xxxi. 21; Cant. iv. 1). According to Michaelis, this mountain, which gave its name to the country so called, must be situated beyond the region sketched in our maps, and somewhere about the Euphrates.

2. (a) The name of a large district beyond the Jordan, continually mentioned in the Scriptures in contradistinction to, or apart from, Bashan (Deut. iii. 13; Josh. xii. 5; xiii. 11; xvii. 1; 2 Kings x. 33; 1 Chron. v. 16; Mic. vii. 14); though, to judge from its geographical position (as given Num. xxxii. 26; Deut. iii. 12), it must have comprised the entire possessions of the two tribes of Gad and Reuben, and even the southern part of Manasseh (Deut. iii. 13; Num. xxxii. 40; Josh. xvii. 1-6). The cities Ramoth, Jabosh, and Jazer, are usually designated as lying in Gilead.

This region was distinguished for its rich pastures (Num. xxxii. 1) and aromatic simples; from which latter different sorts of balsam were prepared—facts confirmed by modern travellers, with the addition that the whole region is covered with groups of limestone mountains, intersected by fertile valleys.

(b) The name of the whole eastern part of the

Jordan (Deut. xxxiv. 1; comp. 2 Kings x. 33; Judg. xx. 1).

The name *Gilead* continued to be used, in a general and geographical sense, even after the exile.

1. GIL'GAL, the place where the Israelites formed their first encampment in Palestine, and which continued for some time to be their headquarters while engaged in the conquest of the land (Josh. iv. 19, 20; ix. 6: x. 6, 7, &c.). It was here that they set up the twelve stones which they took out of the bed of the Jordan (iv. 19), which another head will bring under consideration [STONES]. Samuel used to visit Gilgal in his annual circuit as a judge; and here there was a school of the prophets (1 Sam. vii. 16; 2 Kings iv. 38). There is no notice of the place after the Captivity. Indeed, it does not seem that the name belonged at first to a town, although Gilgal eventually became an inhabited place. It appears to have been early abandoned, and Josephus does not seem to mention it as existing in his time. This writer places it on the east border of Jericho, ten stadia from that city, and fifty from the Jordan. From this it would seem to have been in the vicinity of the present village of the pseudo-Jericho, Riha, which is about the assigned distance from the river. No trace of the name or site can now be discovered.

2. GILGAL, a place in the region of Dor, whose king was subdued by Joshua (Josh. xii. 23). The Gilgal of Neh. xii. 29, and 1 Macc. ix. 2, is probably the same as this; as well as the ancient Galgala, which Eusebius and Jerome place six Roman miles north of Antipatris. In this neighbourhood there is still a village called Jiljuleh, which probably represents the ancient site.

GIRDLE. The original word translated 'girdle'

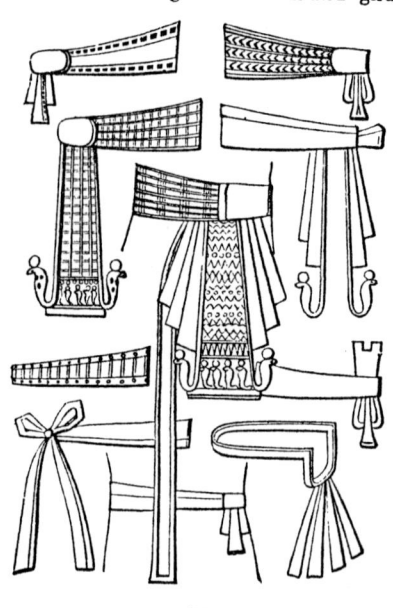

198.

literally means a *band* **or** *bandage,* **and from the**

places in which it occurs it appears to have been made of fine linen, variously wrought and used to bind as a girdle about the body of persons in authority, especially the Jewish priests (Exod. xxix. 9; xxviii. 39; xxxix. 29; Lev. viii. 13; Isa. xxii. 21). These girdles may be considered as fairly represented by those which we observe on such persons in the Egyptian paintings.

GIR'GASHITES, one of the families of Canaan, who are supposed to have been settled in that part of the country which lay to the east of the Lake of Gennesareth.

The Girgashites are conjectured to have been a part of the large family of the Hivites, as they are omitted in nine out of ten places in which the nations or families of Canaan are mentioned, while in the tenth they are mentioned, and the Hivites omitted. Josephus states that nothing but the name of the Girgashites remained in his time. In the Jewish commentaries of R. Nachman, and elsewhere, the Girgashites are described as having retired into Africa, fearing the power of God; and Procopius, in his *History of the Vandals,* mentions an ancient inscription in Mauritania Tingitana, stating that the inhabitants had fled thither from the face of Joshua the son of Nun. The fact of such a migration is not unlikely: but we have very serious doubts respecting the inscription.

GIT'TITES, inhabitants or natives of Gath (Josh. xiii. 3). Obed-edom, although a Levite, is called a Gittite (2 Sam. vi. 10), possibly because he had been with David when at Gath, but much more probably from his being a native of Gath-rimmon, which was a city of the Levites. There seems no reason for extending this interpretation to Ittai (2 Sam. xv. 19), seeing that David expressly calls him 'a stranger' (foreigner), and, what is more, 'an exile.' He was at the head of 600 men, who were also Gittites, for they are called (ver. 22) his 'brethren.' They appear to have formed a foreign troop of experienced warriors, chiefly from Gath, in the pay and service of David; which they had perhaps entered in the first instance for the sake of sharing in the booty obtainable in his wars. We can conceive that the presence of such a troop must have been useful to the king in giving to the Hebrew army that organization and discipline which it did not possess before his time.

GIT'TITH, a word which occurs in the title of Ps. viii., lxxxi., lxxxiv. [PSALMS.]

GLASS, according to Pliny, was discovered by what is termed accident. Some merchants kindled a fire on that part of the coast of Phœnicia which lies near Ptolemais, between the foot of Carmel and Tyre, at a spot where the river Belus casts the fine sand which it brings down; but, as they were without the usual means of suspending their cooking vessels, they employed for that purpose logs of nitre, their vessel being laden with that substance; the fire fusing the nitre and the sand produced glass. The Sidonians, in whose vicinity the discovery was made, took it up, and having in process of time carried the art to a high degree of excellence, gained thereby both wealth and fame. Other nations became their pupils; the Romans especially attained to very high skill in the art of fusing, blowing, and colouring glass. Even glass mirrors were invented by the Sidonians.

This account of Pliny is in substance corroborated by Strabo and by Josephus. Yet, notwithstanding this explicit statement, it was long denied that the ancients were acquainted with glass properly so called; nor did the denial entirely disappear even when Pompeii offered evidences of its want of foundation. Our knowledge of Egypt has, however, set the matter at rest—showing at the same time how careful men should be in setting up mere abstract reasonings in opposition to the direct testimony of history. Wilkinson, in his *Ancient Egyptians* (iii. 88, sq.), has adduced the fullest evidence that glass was known to and made by that ingenious people at a very early period of their national existence. Upward of 3500 years ago, in the reign of the first Osirtasen, they appear to have practised the art of blowing glass. The process is represented

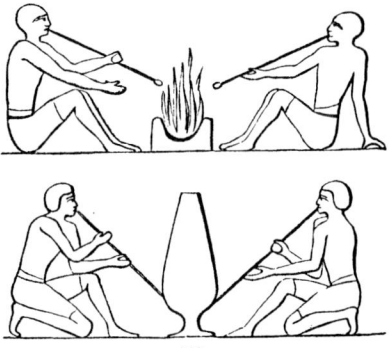

199.

in the paintings of Beni Hassan, executed in the reign of that monarch. In the same age images of *glazed* pottery were common. Ornaments of glass were made by them about 1500 years B.C.; for a bead of that date has been found, being of the same specific gravity as that of our crown glass. Many glass bottles, &c. have been met with in the tombs, some of very remote antiquity. Glass vases were used for holding wine as early as the Exodus. Such was the skill of the Egyptians in this manufacture, that they successfully counterfeited the amethyst, and other precious stones. It was sometimes used by the Egyptians even for coffins. They also employed it, not only for drinking utensils and ornaments of the person, but for mosaic-work, the figures of deities, and sacred emblems, attaining to exquisite workmanship, and a surprising brilliancy of colour. The art too of cutting glass was known to them at the most remote periods; for which purpose, as we learn from Pliny, the diamond was used. That the ancients had mirrors of glass is clear from the above-cited words of Pliny; but the mirrors found in Egypt are made of mixed metal, chiefly copper. So admirably did the skill of the Egyptians succeed in the composition of metals, that their mirrors were susceptible of a polish which has been but partially revived at the present day. The mirror was nearly round, having a handle of wood, stone, or metal. The form varied with the taste of the owner. The same kind of metal mirror was used by the Israelites, who, doubtless, brought it from Egypt. In Exod. xxxviii. 8, it

is expressly said that Moses 'made the laver of brass of the looking-glasses (brazen mirrors) of the women.'

It would be justifiable to suppose that the Hebrews brought glass, and a knowledge how to manufacture it, with them out of Egypt, were not the evidence of history so explicit that it was actually discovered and wrought at their own doors. Whether it was used by them for mirrors is another question. That glass, however, was known to the Hebrews appears beyond a doubt.

GLEDE (Deut. xiv. 13) is an obsolete name for the common kite. It is a species that rises to a towering height, hangs apparently motionless in the sky, and darts down with immense velocity; but the legs and claws being weak, it is cowardly, and feeds upon carrion, fish, insects, mice, and small birds. About Cairo kites are particularly abundant, mixing with the carrion vultures in their wheeling flight, and coming in numbers to the daily distribution of food awarded them. But the question whether the kite of Europe and that of Egypt are the same species, is not decided, though there is no want of scientific names for both species found in the valley of the Nile; one of which is certainly distinct from the European, and the other, if not so, is still a strongly marked variety. The bill of this species

200. [Milvus Ater.]

is dark; head and throat whitish, with brown streaks; body above dark grey brown, pale ferruginous below; tail but slightly forked; legs yellow. It is found in hieroglyphic paintings coloured with sufficient accuracy not to be mistaken. The other species, which we figure above as *Milvus ater*, is the black kite. It has the head, neck, and back dark rusty grey; scapulars bordered with rusty; wing-coverts and primaries black, the last mentioned tipped with white; tail rusty grey above, white beneath; bill dark; legs yellow. The manners of both species are much the same: it is likely that they are equally abundant at Cairo, and spread into Palestine [HAWK].

GNAT. Our Saviour's allusion to the gnat is a kind of proverb, either in use in his time, or invented by himself, 'Blind guides, who strain out a gnat, and swallow down [*bolt*, as we say] a camel.' He adopts the antithesis of the *smallest insect* to the *largest animal*, and applies it to those who are superstitiously anxious in avoiding small faults, yet do not scruple to commit the greatest sins. The typographical error, 'strain at a gnat,' first found its way into King James's translation, 1611. It is 'strain out' in the previous translations. The custom of filtering wine, among the Jews, for this purpose, was founded on the prohibition of 'all flying, creeping things' being used for food, excepting the *saltatorii* (Lev. xi. 23). According to the Talmud, eating a gnat incurred scourging or excommunication.

GOAT. The races of this animal either known to or kept by the Hebrew people were

201. [Syrian Goat.]

probably—1. The domestic Syrian long-eared breed, with horns rather small and variously bent; the ears longer than the head, and pendulous; hair long, often black;—2. The Angora, or rather Anadoli breed of Asia Minor, with long hair, more or less fine;—3. The Egyptian breed, with small spiral horns, long brown hair, very long ears;—4. A breed from Upper Egypt without horns, having the nasal bones singularly elevated, the nose contracted, with the lower jaw protruding the incisors, and the female with udder very low and purse-shaped. This race, the most degraded by climate and treatment of all the domestic varieties, is clad in long coarse hair, commonly of a rufous brown colour, and so early distinct, that the earlier monuments of Egypt represent it with obvious precision.

The natural history of the domestic goat requires no illustration in this place, and its economic uses demand only a few words. Notwithstanding the offensive lasciviousness which causes it to be significantly separated from sheep, the goat was employed by the people of Israel in many respects as their representative. It was a pure animal for sacrifice (Exod. xii. 5), and a kid might be substituted as equivalent to a lamb: it formed a principal part of the Hebrew flocks; and both the milk and the young kids were daily articles of food. Among the poorer and more sober shepherd families, the slaughter of a kid was a token of hospitality to strangers, or of unusual festivity; and the prohibition, thrice repeated in the Mosaic law, 'not to seethe a kid in its mother's milk' (Exod. xxiii. 19; xxxiv. 26; and Deut. xiv. 21), may have originated partly in a desire to recommend abstemiousness, which the legislators and moralists of the East have since invariably enforced with success, and partly with a view to discountenance a practice which was connected with idolatrous festivals, and the rites they involved. It is from goatskins that the leathern bottles to contain wine and other liquids are made in the Levant. For this purpose, after the head and feet are cut away, the

case or hide is drawn off the carcass over the neck, without opening the belly; and the extremities being secured, it is dried with the hair in or outside, according to the use it is intended for. The old worn-out skins are liable to burst: hence the obvious propriety of putting new wine into new bottles (Matt. ix. 17). Harmer appears to have rightly referred the allusion in Amos iii 12, to the long-eared race of goats: 'As the shepherd taketh out of the mouth of the lion two legs or a piece of ear, so shall the children of Israel be taken out that dwell in Samaria and Damascus.'

Beside the domestic goats, Western Asia is possessed of one or more wild species—all large and vigorous mountain animals, resembling the ibex or bouquetin of the Alps. Of these, Southern Syria, Arabia, Sinai, and the borders of the Red Sea, contain at least one species, known to the Arabs by the name of Beden or Beddan, and Taytal. We take this animal to be that noticed in 1 Sam. xxiv. 2; Job xxxix. 1; Ps. civ. 18; Prov. v. 19. The male is considerably taller and more robust than the larger he-goats, the horns forming regular curves backwards, and with from 15 to 24 transverse elevated cross ridges, being sometimes near three feet long, and exceedingly ponderous: there is a beard under the chin, and the fur is dark brown; but the limbs are white, with regular black marks down the front of the legs, with rings of the same colour above the knees and on the pasterns. The females are smaller than the males, more slenderly made, brighter rufous, and with the white

202. [Wild Goat of Sinai.]

and black markings on the legs not so distinctly visible. This species live in troops of 15 or 20, and plunge down precipices with the same fearless impetuosity which distinguishes the ibex. Their horns are sold by the Arabs for knife-handles, &c.; but the animals themselves are fast diminishing in number.

GOAT, SCAPE. The particulars respecting the two goats, one of which was to be offered in sacrifice and the other suffered to escape, are contained in Lev. xvi. 7–10. The two goats were to be brought to the door of the tabernacle and the high-priest was to cast lots upon them, 'one lot for the Lord, and the other *for the scapegoat*,' or rather ' for Azazel.' The goat on which the lot of the Lord fell was to be brought and offered up for a sin-offering, but the goat on which the lot of Azazel fell was to be presented alive before the Lord, to make an atonement with him, to let him go for a scape-goat (or 'for Azazel') into the wilderness. Of the former the blood was to be carried within the veil to be sprinkled upon the mercy-seat, and before the mercy-seat, in order that atonement might be made for the holy place because of the uncleanness of the children of Israel. When, on the other hand, the live goat was brought, the high-priest was to lay both his hands upon his head to confess over it all the iniquities of the children of Israel; after which he was to send it by the hand of 'a fit man' that it might bear upon it all their iniquities into a land not inhabited.

The only difficulty here, and that is a great one, is with respect to the meaning of the word Azazel, which our translators, in common with a large class of modern commentators, regard as applied to the goat itself, and render it by 'scape-goat.' Others produce reasons, not easily answered, for showing that the word must be taken as a proper name. Then arises the question, What is the name? Several of the Rabbinical writers regard it as the name of the place to which the scape-goat was conducted; but this notion has obtained little attention among Biblical scholars. Others, taking a hint from the Septuagint, which translates the difficult phrase by 'one lot for the Apopompeus,' or 'the sender away,' or 'the averter,' hold it to denote one of that class of demons or deities called by the Latins Dii Averrunci, or 'the deities who send away or avert evil from their votaries;' in which case the word would denote here a demon dwelling in the wilderness, and placated by victims. It is hard to suppose that a solemn ceremony was framed so as to give some sanction to the notion supposed to be involved in this statement. A step further, however, brings it more within the range of our recognition—this is, that Azazel is but a name for Satan, as was the opinion of most of the Jewish writers and of the early Christian church; and that the meaning of the ceremony is, that while the remission of sin is effected by the sacrificed goat (for without shedding of blood there was no remission, Heb. ix. 22), the other was laden with the sins already, through the other goat, pardoned, by way of symbolically notifying the fact to Satan, and of triumphing in his discomfiture. That, in any case, the liberated goat is understood to bear away the burden of pardoned sin, so that it shall be seen no more, and stands in the place which the victim goat would have occupied could it have been brought to life again after having been offered, seems to be shown by the somewhat parallel case of the two figures used in the purification of the leprous person (Lev. i. 4), one of which is slain, and the other dipped in its blood, and then suffered to fly away. There is another more common explanation, which, if correct, forms a very beautiful interpretation of the typical rite. This view recognises the substantial typical identity of the two goats, and in the victim goat sees Christ dying for our sins, and in the liberated goat views him as rising again for our justification. But it must be admitted that the whole subject forms one of the greatest difficulties of Scripture.

GOD. The two principal Hebrew names of the Supreme Being used in the Scriptures are Jehovah and Elohim. Dr. Hävernick proposes the reading Jahveh instead of Jehovah, meaning 'the Existing One.' Both names, he admirably proves, are used by Moses discriminately, in strict conformity with the theological idea he wished to express in the immediate context; and, pursuing the Pentateuch nearly line by line, it is astonishing to see that Moses never uses any of the names at mere random or arbitrarily, but is throughout consistent in the application of the respective terms. Elohim is the abstract expression for absolute Deity apart from the special notions of unity, holiness, substance, &c. It is more a philosophical than devotional term, and corresponds with our term Deity, in the same way as state or government is abstractedly expressive of a king or monarch. Jehovah, however, he considers to be the revealed Elohim, the Manifest, Only, Personal, and Holy Elohim : Elohim is the Creator, Jehovah the Redeemer, &c.

To Elohim, in the later writers, we usually find affixed the adjective ' the living' (Jer. x. 10; Dan. vi. 20, 26; Acts xiv. 15; 2 Cor. vi. 16), probably in contradistinction to idols, which might be confounded in some cases with the true God.

The attributes ascribed to God by Moses are systematically enumerated in Exod. xxxiv. 6, 7, though we find in isolated passages in the Pentateuch and elsewhere, additional properties specified, which bear more directly upon the dogmas and principles of religion, such as e. g. that he is not the author of sin (Gen. i. 31), although since the fall, man is born prone to sin (Gen. vi. 5; viii. 21, &c.). But as it was the avowed design of Moses to teach the Jews the Unity of God in opposition to the polytheism of the other nations with whom they were to come in contact, he dwelt particularly and most prominently on that point, which he hardly ever omitted when he had an opportunity of bringing forward the attributes of God (Deut. vi. 4; x. 17; iv. 39; ix. 16, &c.; Num. xvi. xxii.; xxxiii. 19, &c.; Exod. xv. 11; xxxiv. 6, 7, &c.).

In the Prophets and other sacred writers of the Old Testament, these attributes are still more fully developed and explained by the declarations that God is the first and the last (Isa. xliv. 6), that He changes not (Hab. iii. 6), that the earth and heaven shall perish, but He shall endure (Ps. cii. 26)—a distinct allusion to the last doomsday—and that He is Omnipresent (Prov. xv. 3; Job xxxiv. 22, &c.).

In the New Testament also we find the attributes of God systematically classified (Rev. v. 12, and vii. 12), while the peculiar tenets of Christianity embrace, if not a farther, still a more developed idea, as presented by the Apostles and the primitive teachers of the church.

The expression ' to see God' (Job xix. 26; xlii. 5; Isa. xxxviii. 11) sometimes signifies merely to experience his help; but in the Old Testament Scriptures it more usually denotes the approach of death (Gen. xxxii. 30; Judg. vi. 23; xiii. 22; Isa. vi. 5).

The term ' son of God' applies to kings (Ps. ii. 7; lxxxii. 6, 27). The usual notion of the ancients, that the royal dignity was derived from God, may here be traced to its source. This notion, entertained by the Oriental nations with regard to kings, made the latter style themselves gods (Ps. lxxxii. 6).

' Sons of God,' in the plural, implies inferior gods, angels (Gen. vi. 2; Job i. 6); as also faithful adherents, worshippers of God (Deut. xiv. 1; Ps. lxxiii. 15; Prov. xiv. 26).

' Man of God' is sometimes applied to an angel (Judg. xiii. 6, 8); as also to a prophet (1 Sam. ii. 27; ix. 6; 1 Kings xiii. 1).

GOG occurs Ezek. xxxviii. 3, 14, and xxxix. 11, as a proper name—that of a prince of *Magog*, a people that were to come from the North to invade the land of Israel, and be there defeated. In a different sense, but corresponding with the assertions of other Oriental authors, in whose traditions this people occupy an important place, *Gog* occurs in Rev. xx. 8, as the name of a country.

Interpreters have given very different explanations of the terms Gog and Magog; but they have generally understood them as symbolical expressions for the heathen nations of Asia, or more particularly for the Scythians, a vague knowledge of whom seems to have reached the Jews in Palestine about that period. As a collective name, *Magog* seems also to indicate in the Hebrew the tribes about the Caucasian mountains. According to Reinegge, some of the Caucasian people call their mountains *Gog*, and the highest northern point *Magog*.

GO'LAN or GAULON, a Levitical town of Bashan, in the tribe of Manasseh (Deut. iv. 43; Josh. xx. 8; xxi. 27; 1 Chron. vi. 71), from which the small province of Gaulonitis took its name. The word is recognised in the present Jolan or Djolan, mentioned by Burckhardt as giving name to a district lying east of the lake of Tiberias, and composed of the ancient Gaulonitis, with part of Bashan and Argob.

GOLD was known and valued in very early times. Abraham was rich in gold (Gen. xiii. 2; xxiv. 35); and female ornaments were made of gold (Gen. xxiv. 22).

To judge from 1 Chron. xxii. 14; xxix. 4, the Jews must have been, in their prosperous days, in possession of enormous quantities of this metal, considering the many tons of gold that were spent in the building of the temple alone, though the expression, *plenteous as stones* (2 Chron. i. 15), may be considered as hyperbolical. It is, however, confirmed by the history of the other Asiatic nations, and more especially of the Persians, that the period referred to really abounded in gold, which was imported in vast masses from Africa and the Indies. The queen of Sheba brought with her (from Arabia Felix), among other presents, 120 talents of gold (2 Chron. ix. 9).

GOL'GOTHA. The original word signifies ' a skull,' as does its Latin representative, *Calvaria, Calvary*. Different opinions have prevailed as to why the place was so termed. Many have held that Golgotha was the place of public execution, the Tyburn of Jerusalem; and that hence it was termed the ' place of a skull.' Another opinion is that the place took its name from its shape, being a hillock of a form like a human skull. The last is the opinion to which the writer of these remarks inclines. That the place was of some such shape seems to be generally agreed, and the traditional term *mount*, applied to Calvary, appears to confirm this idea. And such a shape, it must be allowed, is in entire agreement with the name—that is, ' skull.' To these considerations there are added certain difficulties which arise from the second explanation. So far as we know there is no historical evidence to

show that there was a place of public execution where Golgotha is commonly fixed, nor that any such place, in or near Jerusalem, bore the name Golgotha. In truth, the context seems to show that the Roman guard hurried Jesus away and put him to death at the first convenient spot; and that the rather because there was no small fear of a popular insurrection, especially as he was attended by a crowd of people. But where was the place? Not far, we may suppose from what has been said, from the judgment-hall, which was doubtless near the spot (Fort Antonia) where the Roman forces in Jerusalem were concentrated. From our plan of Jerusalem it will be seen that Fort Antonia lay on the north-west angle of the temple. Was it likely, then, that in the highly excited state of the public mind the soldiers should take Jesus southward, that is, through the whole breadth of the city? Somewhere in the north, it is clear, they would execute him, as thus they would most easily effect their object. But if they chose the north, then the road to Joppa or Damascus would be most convenient; and no spot in the vicinity would probably be so suitable as the slight rounded elevation which bore the name of Calvary. That some hillock would be preferred, it is easy to see, as thus the exposure of the criminal and the alleged cause of his crucifixion would be most effectually secured. But the particulars detailed by the sacred historians show that our Lord was not crucified on the spot, or very near the spot, where he was condemned, but was conducted some distance through the city. If so, this, as appears from our plan, must have been towards the west. Two points seem thus determined: the crucifixion was at the *north-west* of the city.

The account, as given in the Evangelists, touching the place of the crucifixion and burial of our Lord, is as follows:—Having been delivered by Pilate to be crucified, Jesus was led away, followed by a great company of people and women, who bewailed his fate. On the way the soldiers met one Simon, a Cyrenian, *coming out of the country*, who is compelled to bear Jesus' cross. When they were come to the place which is called Calvary, there they crucified him. This place was nigh to the city; and, sitting down, they watched him there. They that passed by reviled him, wagging their heads and scoffing. Likewise also the chief priests mocked him, with the scribes and elders; and the people stood beholding. The soldiers too mocked him. There stood by the cross of Jesus his mother, and his mother's sister, and Mary Magdalene. And all his acquaintance and the women that followed him from Galilee stood afar off, beholding these things. *In the place where he was crucified* there was a garden, and in the garden a new sepulchre, hewn out in the rock; *there* laid they Jesus, and rolled a great stone to the door of the sepulchre. The writer of the epistle to the Hebrews adds, that Jesus suffered *without the gate*, subjoining, ' let us, therefore, go forth to him without the camp (or the city) bearing his reproach' (Heb. xiii. 12, 13; Matt. xxvii.; Mark xv.; Luke xxiii.; John xix.).

We thus learn, as a positive fact, that the crucifixion and burial took place out of the city, and yet nigh to the city; and the statement of the writer to the Hebrews is confirmed by the incidental remark (Mark xv. 21), that the soldiers seized Simon, as he was ' coming out of the country.' It now appears, then, that Calvary lay at the north-west, and at the outside, of the city. The reader, on perusing the abstract just given of the evangelical narrators, combined with previous remarks, will find reason to think that Calvary was only just on the outer side of the second wall. It is also clear that the place was one around which many persons could assemble, near which wayfarers were passing, and the sufferers in which could be seen or addressed by persons who were both near and remote : all which concurs in showing that the spot was one of some elevation, and equally proves that ' this thing was not done in a corner,' but at a place and under circumstances likely to make Calvary well known and well remembered alike by the foes and the friends of our Lord. Other events which took place immediately after, in connection with the resurrection, would aid (if aid were needed) in fixing the recollection of the spot deep and ineffaceably in the minds of the primitive disciples.

Was it likely that this recollection would perish ? Surely of all spots Calvary would become the most sacred, the most endearing, in the primitive church. The spot where Jesus was crucified, died, was buried, and rose again, must have been bound to the heart of every disciple in the strongest and most grateful bonds. Perhaps no one spot on earth had ever so many to remember it and know its precise locality, as the place where Jesus died and rose again. First in Jerusalem, and soon in all parts of the earth, were there hearts that held the recollection among their most valued treasures.

The traditionary recollection of this remarkable spot must have been greatly strengthened by the erection of the Temple of Venus on the place, after the capture of Jerusalem by the Romans. The temple thus takes up the tradition and transmits it in stone and marble to coming ages. This continuation of the tradition is the more important, because it begins to operate at a time when the Christians were driven from Jerusalem. But the absence of the Christians from the holy city was not of long duration, and even early in the third century we find pilgrimages from distant places to the Holy Land had already begun, for the express purpose of viewing the spots which the presence and sufferings of the Saviour had rendered sacred and memorable. A century later, Eusebius (A.D. 315) informs us that Christians visited Jerusalem from all regions of the earth for the same object. So early and so decided a current towards the holy city presupposes a strong, wide-spread, and long pre-eminent feeling—an established tradition in the church touching the most remarkable spots ; a tradition of that nature which readily links itself with the actual record in Hebrews.

Early in the fourth century Eusebius and Jerome write down the tradition and fix the locality of Calvary in their writings. Pilgrims now streamed to Jerusalem from all parts of the world, and that site was fixed for Golgotha which has remained to the present hour. This was done not merely by the testimony of these two learned fathers, but by the acts of the Emperor Constantine and his mother Helena. This empress, when very far advanced in life, visited Jerusalem for

the express purpose of erecting a church on the spot where the Lord Jesus had been crucified. ' On her arrival at Jerusalem she inquired diligently of the inhabitants. Yet the search was uncertain and difficult, in consequence of the obstructions by which the heathen had sought to render the spot unknown. These being all removed, the sacred sepulchre was discovered, and by its side three crosses, with the tablet bearing the inscription written by Pilate.' On the site thus ascertained was erected, whether by Constantine or Helena, certainly by Roman influence and treasure, a splendid and extensive Christian temple. This church was completed and dedicated A.D. 335. It was a great occasion for the Christian world. In order to give it importance and add to its splendour, a council of bishops was convened, by order of the emperor, from all the provinces of the empire, which assembled first at Tyre, and then at Jerusalem. The church of the holy sepulchre was burnt by the Persians in A.D. 614. It was shortly after rebuilt by Modestus with resources supplied by John Eleemor, patriarch of Alexandria. The Basilica or Martyrion erected under Constantine remained as before. The Mohammedans next became masters of Jerusalem. At length Harun er Rashid made over to Charlemagne the jurisdiction of the holy sepulchre. Palestine again became the scene of battles and bloodshed. Muez, of the race of the Fatimites, transferred the seat of his empire to Cairo, when Jerusalem fell into the hands of new masters, and the holy sepulchre is said to have been again set on fire. It was fully destroyed at the command of the third of the Fatimite kalifs in Egypt, the building being razed to the foundations. In the reign of his successor it was rebuilt, being completed A.D. 1048 ; but instead of the former magnificent Basilica over the place of Golgotha, a small chapel only now graced the spot. The crusades soon began. The crusaders regarded the edifices connected with the sepulchre as too contracted, and erected a stately temple, the walls and general form of which are admitted to remain to the present day. So recently, however, as A.D. 1808 the church of the holy sepulchre was partly consumed by fire; but being rebuilt by the Greeks, it now offers no traces of its recent desolation.

We have thus traced down to the present day the history, traditional and recorded, of the buildings erected on Golgotha, and connected these edifices with the original events by which they are rendered memorable. To affirm that the evidence is irresistible may be going too far ; but few antiquarian questions rest on an equally solid basis, and few points of history would remain settled were they subject to the same sceptical, not to say unfair, scrutiny which Robinson has here applied.

The sole evidence of any weight in the opposite balance is that urged by Robinson, that the place of the crucifixion and the sepulchre are now found in the midst of the modern city. But to render this argument decisive it should be proved that the city occupies now the same ground that it occupied in the days of Christ. It is, at least, as likely that the city should have undergone changes as that the site of the crucifixion should have been mistaken. The identity of such a spot is more likely to be preserved than the site and relative proportions of a city which has undergone more violent changes than probably any other place on earth. The present walls of Jerusalem were erected so late as A.D. 1542; and Robinson himself remarks, *en passant*, that a part of Zion is now left out (p. 67). If, then, the city has been contracted on the south, and if, also, it was after the death of Christ expanded on the north, what should we expect but to find Golgotha in the midst of the modern city?

Two or three additional facts in confirmation of the identity of the present place may, finally, be adduced. Buckingham says, 'the present rock called Calvary, and enclosed within the church of the holy sepulchre, bears marks in every part that is naked, of its having been a round nodule of rock standing above the common level of the surface.' Scholz states that he traced the remains of a wall, which ran as the second wall on the plan runs, excluding Golgotha and taking in the pool of Hezekiah. At most, a very few hundred yards only can the original Golgotha have lain from the present site; and the evidence in favour of its identity, if not decisive, is far stronger than any that has been adduced against it.

GO'MER. 1. The eldest son of Japhet, son of Noah, whose descendants Bochart supposes to have settled in Phrygia (Gen. x. 3; comp. 1 Chron. i. 5). Most of the interpreters take him to be the ancestor of the Celtæ, and more especially of the *Cimmerii*, who were already known in the time of Homer. To judge from the ancient historians, they had in early times settled to the north of the Black Sea, and gave their name to the Crimea, the ancient *Chersonesus Taurica*. But the greater part of them were driven from their territories by the Scythians, when they took refuge in Asia Minor, B.C. 7.

In the Scriptures, however, the people named Gomer imply rather an obscure and but vaguely known nation of the barbarous north.

Josephus says expressly, that the ancestor of the Galatians, a Celtic colony, was called Gomer.

2. The name of the daughter of Diblaim, wife of the prophet Hosea (Hosea i. 3).

GOMORR'AH, one of 'the cities of the plain,' destroyed along with Sodom. An account of that catastrophe is given under SODOM.

GOPHER WOOD is mentioned only once in Scripture, as the material of which Noah was directed to build the ark (Gen. vi. 14), 'Make thee an ark of gopher wood; rooms shalt thou make in the ark, and shalt pitch it within and without with pitch' (probably 'bitumen'). In endeavouring to ascertain the particular kind of wood which is mentioned in the above passage, we can get assistance only from the name, the country where the wood was supposed to have been procured, or the traditional opinions respecting it. That nothing very satisfactory has been ascertained is evident from the various interpretations that have been given of this word, so that some have preferred, as in our Authorized Version, to retain the original Hebrew. The greatest number of writers have been of opinion that by the gopher wood we are to understand the cypress. Besides an argument attempted to be drawn from the similarity of the name, it is argued that the wood of the cypress, being almost incorruptible, was likely to be preferred; that it was frequently employed in later ages in the construction of temples, bridges, and even ships; and that it was very abundant in the countries

where, according to these authors, the ark is supposed to have been built, that is, in Assyria, where other woods are scarce. But wherever the ark was built, there would be no deficiency of timber if there was a certain degree of moisture with warmth of climate; and we know not what change of climate may have taken place at the Deluge. The pine tribe, including the cypress, appears as likely as any other to have been employed, usually growing as they do in extensive forests, and yielding straight and easily worked timber, calculated, from its resinous nature, effectually to resist moisture, especially if covered with pitch and tar, which might easily have been prepared from the refuse branches and timber, and used as well as the natural bitumen. But the whole of these suggestions amount only to conjectures, and there seems no possibility of arriving at a satisfactory conclusion.

GO'SHEN, a province or district of Egypt in which Jacob and his family were placed through the instrumentality of his son Joseph, and in which they and their descendants remained for a period of 430 years (Gen. xlv. 10; xlvi. 28; xlvii. 27; l. 8; Exod. viii. 22; ix. 26). The Bible does not present any definite information as to the precise locality of Goshen, and of course later authorities possess only an inferior value. There are, however, incidental expressions, allusions, and implications in the Scriptures, which afford aid in determining the spot. That Goshen lay on the eastern side of the Nile may be justifiably inferred from the fact that Jacob is not reported to have crossed that river; nor does it appear that the Israelites did so in their flight out of Egypt. With this inference all the language employed (see the passages as given above), to say the least, agrees, if it does not afford an indirect evidence in its favour. By comparing Exod. xiii. 17 and 1 Chron. vii. 21, it appears that Goshen bordered on Arabia as well as Palestine, and the passage of the Israelites out of Egypt shows that the land was not far removed from the Red Sea. It appears probable that we may fix the locality of Goshen in Lower Egypt, on the east side of the Pelusiac branch of the Nile, in the district around Heroopolis.

This district was suitable for a nomadic people, who would have been misplaced in the narrow limits of the valley of the Nile. Children of the desert, or at least used as they were to wander freely from one fertile plain to another with their flocks and herds, the sons of Jacob required a spot where the advantages of an advanced civilization could be united with unrestricted freedom, and abundance be secured without the forfeiture of early and cherished habits. The several opinions entertained on this point substantially agree in referring Goshen to the country intervening between the desert of Arabia and Palestine on the one side, and the Pelusiac arm of the Nile on the other, with the Mediterranean at the base. The district assigned to Jacob and his family was chosen for its superiority (Gen. xlvii. 6), 'In the best of the land make thy father and brethren to dwell, in the land of Goshen let them dwell;' and the subsequent increase of the Israelites themselves, as well as the multiplication of their cattle, shows that the territory was one of extraordinary fertility. Time and circumstances have doubtless had their effect on the fertility of a country in which the desert is ever ready to make encroachments as soon as the repelling hand of man is relaxed or withdrawn. But Laborde represents the vicinity of Heliopolis as still covered with palm-trees, and as having an enclosure, comprehending a considerable space of ground, which is covered every year by the inundation of the Nile to the height of five feet. We are not, however, to expect evidences of luxuriant fertility. The country was chosen for its pre-eminent fitness for shepherds. If a nomadic tribe had wide space and good pasture-grounds. they would have 'the best (for themselves) of the land,' and these advantages the district in which we have placed Goshen abundantly supplied in ancient times, when the waters of the Nile were more liberally dispensed than at present to the eastern side of the country. Nothing is needed but water to make the desert fertile. ' The water of the Nile soaks through the earth for some distance under the sandy tract (the neighbourhood of Heliopolis), and is everywhere found on digging wells eighteen or twenty feet deep. Such wells are very frequent in parts which the inundation does not reach. The water is raised from them by wheels turned by oxen and applied to the irrigation of the fields. Whenever this takes place the desert is turned into a fruitful field. In passing to Heliopolis we saw several such fields in the different stages of being reclaimed from the desert; some just laid out, others already fertile. In returning by another way more eastward, we passed a succession of beautiful plantations wholly dependent on this mode of irrigation' (Robinson's *Palestine*, vol. i. p. 36).

GOSPEL. The Greek word, which literally signifies *glad tidings*, is translated in the English Version by the word *Gospel*, viz., *God's spell*, or the *Word of God*. The central point of Christian preaching was the joyful intelligence that the Saviour had come into the world (Matt. iv. 23; Rom. x. 15); and the first Christian preachers, who characterized their account of the person and mission of Christ by the term Gospel. This name was also prefixed to the written accounts of Christ. We possess four such accounts; the first by Matthew, announcing the Redeemer as the promised King of the Kingdom of God; the second by Mark, declaring him 'a Prophet mighty in deed and word' (Luke xxiv. 19); the third by Luke, of whom it might be said that he represented Christ in the special character of the Saviour of sinners (Luke vii. 36, sq.; xv. 18-9, sq.); the fourth by John, who represents Christ as the son of God, in whom deity and humanity became one. The ancient church gave to Matthew the symbol of the lion, to Mark that of man, to Luke that of the ox, and to John that of the eagle; these were the four faces of the cherubim. The cloud in which the Lord revealed himself was borne by the cherubim, and the four Evangelists were also the bearers of that glory of God which appeared in the form of man.

Concerning the order which they occupy in the Scriptures, the oldest Latin and Gothic Versions place Matthew and John first, and after them Mark and Luke, while the other MSS. and the old versions follow the order given to them in our Bibles. As dogmatical reasons render a different order more natural, there is much in favour of

the opinion that their usual position arose from regard to the chronological dates of the respective composition of the four gospels: this is the opinion of Origen, Irenæus, and Eusebius. All ancient testimonies agree that Matthew was the earliest, and John the latest Evangelist. The relation of the Gospel of John to the other three Gospels, and the relation of the Gospels of Matthew, Mark, and Luke to each other, is very remarkable. With the exception of the history of the Baptist, and that of Christ's passion and resurrection, we find in John not only narratives of quite different events, but also different statements even in the above sections. On the other hand, the first three Evangelists not only tolerably harmonize in the substance and order of the events they relate, but correspond even sentence by sentence in their separate narratives (comp. *ex. gr.* Mark i. 21-28 with Luke iv. 31-37; Matt. viii. 31-34; Mark vi. 34; v. 17; Luke viii. 32-37, etc.). The thought that first suggests itself on considering this surprising harmony is, that they all had mutually drawn their information from one another. Some critics are of opinion that Matthew was the oldest source, and that Mark drew his information both from Matthew and Luke; again, according to others, Luke was the oldest, and Matthew made use of Luke and Mark; while most critics in Germany have adopted the view that Matthew was the oldest, and was made use of by Luke, and that Mark derived his information both from Matthew and Luke. Some of the most modern critics are, on the other hand, of opinion that Mark was the original evangelist, and that Matthew and Luke derived their information from him. The difference of these opinions leads to the suspicion that none of them are right, more especially when we consider that, notwithstanding the partial harmony of the three evangelists in the choice of their *sentences*, there is still a surprising difference in them as regards the *words* of those sentences; a fact which compelled the critics who suppose that the evangelists made use of each other's writings, to account everywhere for such deviations, and frequently to have recourse to the most trivial and pedantic arguments. To us these differences in word and phrase would appear inconceivable were we disposed to assume that the evangelists had copied one another.

As the three Evangelists mutually supply and explain each other, they were early joined to each other, by Tatian, about A.D. 170, and by Ammonius, about A.D. 230,[*] and the discrepancies among them early led to attempts to reconcile them.[†] And with this view various elaborate treatises have been composed, both in ancient and modern times. But when we consider that one and the same writer, namely, Luke, relates the conversion of Paul (Acts ix. 22, 26), with different incidental circumstances, after three various documents, though it would have been very easy for him to have annulled the discrepancies, we cannot help being convinced that the Evangelists attached but little weight to minute preciseness in the incidents, since, indeed, the historical truth of a narration consists less in them, in the relation of minute details, than in

---

[*] Such *putting together* is called *synopsis*.
[†] Harmonies.

the correct conception of the *character* and *spirit* of the event.

GOURD. The word thus rendered (*kikayon*) occurs only in Jonah iv., where it is several times mentioned, as in ver. 6, 7, 9, 10. In the margin of the English Bible, *Palm-Christ* is given. In the Vulgate it is translated 'ivy.' Neither the gourd nor ivy is considered by modern writers to indicate the plant intended; which is remarkable for having given rise to some fierce controversies in the early ages of the Church. The difficulties here, however, do not appear to be so great as in many other instances. But before considering these, it is desirable to ascertain what are the characteristics of the plant as required by the text. We are told, 'The Lord God prepared a *gourd* (*kikayon*), and made it to come over Jonah, that it might be a shadow over his head' (ver. 6). ' But God prepared a worm when the morning rose the next day, and it smote the gourd that it withered' (ver. 7). And in ver. 10 it is said of the gourd that it 'came up in a night, and perished in a night.' Hence it appears that the growth of the *kikayon* was miraculous, but that it was probably a plant of the country, being named specifically; also that it was capable of affording shade, and might be easily destroyed. There does not appear anything in this account to warrant us in considering it to be the ivy, which is a plant of slow growth, cannot support itself, and is, moreover, not likely to be found in the hot and arid country of ancient Nineveh, though we have ourselves found it in more southern latitudes, but only in the temperate climate of the Himalayan Mountains. ' The Christians and Jews of Mosul (Nineveh) say it was not the *keroa* whose shadow refreshed Jonah, but a sort of gourd, *el-kera*, which has very large leaves, very large fruit, and lasts but about four months'

203. [Ricinus communis.]

(Niebuhr, *Arabia*, as quoted by Dr. Harris). So Volney : ' Whoever has travelled to Cairo or

Rosetta knows that the species of gourd called *kerra* will, in twenty-four hours, send out shoots near four inches long' (*Trav.* i. 71).

The Hebrew name *kikayon* is so similar to the *kiki* of Dioscorides, that it was early thought to indicate the same plant. The *kiki* or *croton* corresponds with the castor-oil plant, of which the seeds have some resemblance to the insect commonly called *tick* in English, and which is found on dogs and other animals. It has also been called *Penta-dactylus* and *Palma Christi*, from the palmate division of its leaves. It was known at much earlier times, as Hippocrates employed it in medicine; and Herodotus mentions, when speaking of Egypt:—' The inhabitants of the marshy grounds make use of an oil which they term *kiki*, expressed from the Sillicyprian plant.' That it has been known there from the earliest times is evident from Cailliaud having found castor-oil seeds in some very ancient sarcophagi. This oil was not only employed by the Greeks, but also by the Jews, being the *kik*-oil of the Talmudists, prepared from the seeds of the *ricinus*. Lady Calcott states that the modern Jews of London use this oil, by the name of oil of *kik*, for their Sabbath lamps, it being one of the five kinds of oil which their traditions allow them to employ.

Having ascertained that the *kiki* of the Greeks is what is now called *Ricinus communis*, or castor-oil plant, we shall find that its characters correspond with everything which is required, except the rapidity of growth, which must be granted was miraculous. Dr. Harris indeed states that the passage means, ' Son of the night it was, and as a son of the night it died;' and that, therefore, we are not compelled to believe that it grew in a single night, but rather, by a strong Oriental figure, that it was of rapid growth. This, there is no doubt, it is highly susceptible of in warm countries where there is some moisture. It attains a considerable size in one season ; and though in Europe it is only known as a herb, in India it frequently may be seen, especially at the margins of fields, the size of a tree. So at Busra Niebuhr saw an *el-keroa* which had the form and appearance of a tree. The stems are erect, round, and hollow; the leaves broad, palmate, 5 to 8 or 10 lobed, peltate, supported on long foot-stalks. From the erect habit, and the breadth of its foliage, this plant throws an ample shade, especially when young. From the softness and little substance of its stem, it may easily be destroyed by insects, which Rumphius describes as sometimes being the case. It would then necessarily dry up rapidly. As it is well suited to the country, and to the purpose indicated in the text, and as its name *kiki* is so similar to *kikayon*, it is doubtless the plant which the sacred penman had in view.

GO'ZAN, a river of Media, to the country watered by which Tiglathpileser first, and afterwards Shalmaneser, transported the captive Israelites (1 Chron. v. 26; 2 Kings xvii. 6). It is now almost universally admitted that the Gozan is no other than the present Ozan, or, with the prefix, Kizzil-Ozan (Golden River), which is the principal river of that part of Persia that answers to the ancient Media. This river rises eight or nine miles south-west of Sennah, in Kurdistan. It runs along the north-west frontier of Irak, and passes under the Kafulan Koh, or

Mountain of Tigris, where it is met by the Karanku. These two rivers combined force a passage through the great range of Caucasan, and, during their course, form a junction with the Sharood. The collective waters, under the designation of Sifeed Rood or White River, so named from the foam occasioned by the rapidity of its current, flow in a meandering course through Ghilan to the Caspian Sea.

GRAPE. [VINE.]

GRASS. The original word which is thus translated in 1 Kings xviii. 5, 2 Kings xix. 26, Job xl. 15, Ps. xxxvii. 2, &c.; is rendered *herb* in Job. viii. 12; *hay*, in Prov. xxvii. 25, and Isa. xv. 6; and *court*, in Isa. xxxiv. 13: but in Num. xi. 5, it is translated *leeks*. Hebrew scholars state that the word signifies 'greens' or 'grass' in general; and it is no doubt clear, from the context of most of the above passages, that this must be its meaning. There is therefore no reason why it should not be so translated in all the passages where it occurs, except in the last. It is evidently incorrect to translate it *hay*, as in the above passages of Proverbs and Isaiah, because the people of Eastern countries, as it has been observed, do not make hay.

In Num. xi. 5, the word is rendered *leeks*, and the name is supposed to have been applied to them from the resemblance of their leaves to grass, and from their being conspicuous for their green colour. It is probable, however, as suggested by Hengstenberg, that the vegetable really meant is a kind of grass called the fenu-grec, an annual plant known in Egypt under the name of Helbeh. It very much resembles clover, except that it has more pointed leaves and whitish blossoms, and is eaten by the common people in Egypt with special relish. 'Although,' says Sonnini, 'horses, oxen, and the buffaloes eat this helbeh with equal relish, it appears not to be destined equally for the sustenance of animals. The Egyptians themselves eat the fenu-grec so much, that it can properly be called the food of *men*. In the month of November they cry 'Green helbeh for sale' in the streets of the towns. It is tied up in large bunches which the inhabitants eagerly purchase at a low price, and which they eat with incredible greediness, without any species of seasoning. They pretend that this singular diet is an excellent stomachic or specific against worms and dysentery; in fine, a preservative against a great number of maladies. After so many excellent properties, real or supposed, it is not astonishing that the Egyptians hold this 'grass' in so great estimation, that, according to one of their proverbs, 'Fortunate are the feet which tread the earth on which grows the helbeh.'

GRASSHOPPER. The creature denoted by this Hebrew word so evidently belongs to the class of '*flying* creeping things' (Lev. xi. 21, 22), that the *grasshopper*, according to the common acceptation of the word, can scarcely be the proper translation. Other reasons render it most probable that *a species of locust* is intended. It is, therefore, referred to the general English word [LOCUST].

GRAVE. [BURIAL.]

GREECE. The relations of the Hebrews with the Greeks were always of a distant kind, until the Macedonian conquest of the East: hence in the Old Testament the mention of the Greeks is naturally rare.

The few dealings of the Greeks with the Hebrews seem to have been rather unfriendly, to judge by the notice in Zech. ix. 13. In Joel iii. 6, the Tyrians are reproached for selling the children of Judah and Jerusalem to the Grecians: but at what time, and in what circumstances, must depend on the date assigned to the book of Joel [see JOEL]. With the Greeks of Cyprus or Chittim, the Hebrews were naturally better acquainted; and this name, it would seem, might easily have extended itself in their tongue to denote the whole Greek nation. Such at least is the most plausible explanation of its use in 1 Macc. i. 1, and viii. 1.

The Greeks were eminent for their appreciation of beauty in all its varieties: indeed their religious creed owed its shape mainly to this peculiarity of their mind; for their logical acuteness was not exercised on such subjects until quite a later period. The puerile or indecent fables of the old mythology may seem to a modern reader to have been the very soul of their religion; but to the Greek himself these were a mere accident, or a vehicle for some embodiment of beauty. He thought little whether a legend concerning Artemis or Apollo was true, but much whether the dance and music celebrating the divinity were solemn, beautiful, and touching. The worship of Apollo, the god of youth and beauty, has been regarded as characterizing the Hellenic in contrast with the older Pelasgian times; nor is the fact without significance, that the ancient temple and oracle of Jupiter at Dodona fell afterwards into the shade in comparison with that of Apollo at Delphi. Indeed the Dorian Spartans and the Ionian Athenians alike regarded Apollo as their tutelary god. Whatever the other varieties of Greek religious ceremonies, no violent or frenzied exhibitions arose out of the national mind; but all such *orgies* (as they were called) were imported from the East, and had much difficulty in establishing themselves on Greek soil. Quite at a late period the managers of orgies were evidently regarded as mere jugglers of not a very reputable kind; nor do the Greek States, as such, appear to have patronized them. On the contrary, the solemn religious processions, the sacred games and dances, formed a serious item in the public expenditure; and to be permanently exiled from such spectacles would have been a moral death to the Greeks. Wherever they settled they introduced their native institutions, and reared temples, gymnasia, baths, porticoes, sepulchres, of characteristic simple elegance. The morality and the religion of such a people naturally were alike superficial; nor did the two stand in any close union. Bloody and cruel rites could find no place in their creed, because faith was not earnest enough to endure much self-abandonment. Religion was with them a sentiment and a taste rather than a deep-seated conviction. On the loss of beloved relatives they felt a tender and natural sorrow, but unclouded with a shade of anxiety concerning a future life. Through the whole of their later history, during Christian times, it is evident that they had little power of remorse, and little natural firmness of conscientious principle: and, in fact, at an earlier and critical time, when the intellect of the nation was ripening, an atrocious civil war, that lasted for twenty-seven years, inflicted a political and social demoralization, from the effects of which they could never recover. Besides this, their very admiration of beauty, coupled with the degraded state of the female intellect, proved a frightful source of corruption, such as no philosophy could have adequately checked. From such a nation then, whatever its intellectual pretensions, no healthful influence over its neighbours could flow, until other and higher inspiration was infused into its sentiment.

Among the Greeks the arts of war and peace were carried to greater perfection than among any earlier people. In navigation they were little behind the Tyrians and Carthaginians ; in political foresight they equalled them ; in military science, both by sea and land, they were decidedly their superiors ; while in the power of reconciling subject-foreigners to the conquerors and to their institutions, they perhaps surpassed all nations of the world. Their copious, cultivated, and flexible tongue carried with it no small mental education to all who learned it thoroughly ; and so sagacious were the arrangements of the great Alexander throughout his rapidly acquired Asiatic empire, that in the twenty years of dreadful war between his generals which followed his death, no rising of the natives against Greek influence appears to have been thought of. Without any change of population adequate under other circumstances to effect it, the Greek tongue and Greek feeling spread far and sank deep through the Macedonian dominions. Half of Asia Minor became a new Greece ; and the cities of Syria, North Palestine, and Egypt, were deeply imbued with the same influence. Yet the purity of the Hellenic stream varied in various places ; and some account of the mixture it underwent will be given in the Article HELLENISTS.

When a beginning had been made of preaching Christianity to the Gentiles, Greece immediately became a principal sphere for missionary exertion. The vernacular tongue of the Hellenistic Christians was understood over so large an extent of country, as almost of itself to point out in what direction they should exert themselves. The Grecian cities, whether in Europe or Asia, were the peculiar field for the Apostle Paul ; for whose labours a superintending Providence had long before been providing, in the large number of devout Greeks who attended the Jewish synagogues. Greece Proper was divided by the Romans into two provinces, of which the northern was called Macedonia, and the southern Achaia (as in 2 Cor. ix. 2, &c.); and we learn incidentally from Acts xviii. that the proconsul of the latter resided at Corinth. To determine the exact division between the provinces is difficult ; nor is the question of any importance to a Biblical student. Achaia, however, had probably very nearly the same frontier as the kingdom of modern Greece, which is limited by a line reaching from the gulf of Volo to that of Arta, in great part along the chain of Mount Othrys. Of the cities celebrated in Greek history, none are prominent in the early Christian times except Corinth. Laconia, and its chief town Sparta, had ceased to be of any importance : Athens was never eminent as a Christian church. In Macedonia were the two great cities of Philippi and Thessalonica (formerly called Therme); yet of these the former was rather recent, being founded by Philip the Great ; the latter was not distinguished above the other Grecian cities on the same coast. Nicopolis, on the gulf of Ambracia (or Arta), had been built by Augustus, in memory of his victory at Actium, and was, perhaps, the limit of Achaia on the western coast. It had risen into some importance in St. Paul's days, and, as many suppose, it is to this Nicopolis that he alludes in his epistle to Titus. (See further under ACHAIA and NICOPOLIS.)

GRINDING. [MILL.]

GUEST. [HOSPITALITY.]

H.

HAB'AKKUK (*embrace*), one of the most distinguished Jewish prophets, who flourished about 610 B.C., the name denoting as well a 'favourite' as a 'struggler.' Of this prophet's birth-place, parentage, and life we have only apocryphal and conflicting accounts. The Pseudo-Epiphanius states that he was of the tribe of Simeon, and born in a place called Bedzoker ; that he fled to Ostrarine when Nebuchadnezzar attacked Jerusalem, but afterwards returned home, and died two years before the return of his countrymen. But rabbinical writers assert that he was of the tribe of Levi, and name different birth-places. Eusebius notices that in his time the tomb of Habakkuk was shown in the town of Ceila, in Palestine ; still there are other writers who name different places where, according to common opinion, he had been buried.

A full and trustworthy account of the life of Habakkuk would explain his imagery, and many of the events to which he alludes ; but since we have no information on which we can depend, nothing remains but to determine from the book itself its historical basis and its age. Now, we find that in chap. i. the prophet sets forth a vision, in which he discerned the injustice, violence, and oppression committed in his country by the rapacious and terrible Chaldæans, whose oppressions he announces as a divine retribution for sins committed ; consequently he wrote in the Chaldæan period, shortly before the invasion of Nebuchadnezzar which rendered Jehoiakim tributary to the king of Babylon (2 Kings xxiv. 1). When he wrote the first chapter of his prophecies, the Chaldæans could not yet have invaded Palestine, otherwise he would not have introduced Jehovah saying (i. 5), ' I *will work* a work in your days, which ye will not believe, though it be told you ;' (ver. 6) ' for I raise up the Chaldæans, that bitter and hasty nation, which *shall march* through the breadth of the land to possess the dwelling-places that are not theirs.' From ver. 12 it is also evident that the ruin of the Jews had not then been effected ; it says, ' the Lord ordained them for judgment, established them for correction.' Agreeably to the general style of the prophets, who to lamentations and announcements of divine punishment add consolations and cheering hopes for the future, Habakkuk then proceeds in the second chapter to foretell the future humiliation of the conquerors who plundered so many nations. He also there promulgates a vision of events shortly to be expected; (ver. 3) 'the vision is yet for an appointed time, but at the end *it shall speak*, and not lie; though it tarry, wait for it, because it *will surely come*; it will not tarry.' This is succeeded in the third chapter by an ode, in which the prophet celebrates the deliverances wrought by the Almighty for his people in times past, and prays for a similar interference now to mitigate the coming distresses of the nation; which he goes on to describe, representing the land as already waste and desolate, and yet giving encouragement to hope for a return of better times. Some interpreters are of opinion that ch. ii. was written in the reign of Jehoiachin, the son of Jehoiakim (2 Kings xxiv. 6), after Jerusalem had been besieged and conquered by Nebuchadnezzar, the king made a prisoner, and, with many thousands of his subjects, carried away to Babylon; none remaining in Jerusalem, save the poorest class of the people (2 Kings xxiv. 14). But of all this nothing is said in the book of Habakkuk, nor even so much as hinted at; and what is stated of the violence and injustice of the Chaldæans does not imply that the Jews had already experienced it. The prophet distinctly mentions that he sets forth what he had discerned in a vision, and he, therefore, speaks of events to be expected and coming. It is also a supposition equally gratuitous, according to which some interpreters refer ch. iii. to the period of the last siege of Jerusalem, when Zedekiah was taken, his sons slain, his eyes put out, the walls of the city broken down, and the temple burnt (2 Kings xxv. 1-10). There is not the slightest allusion to any of these incidents in the third chapter of Habakkuk; and from the 16th verse it appears, that the destroyer is only coming, and that the prophet expresses fears, not of the entire destruction of the city, much less of the downfall of the state, but only of the desolation of the country. It thus appears beyond dispute, that Habakkuk prophesied in the beginning of the reign of Jehoiakim, about the year stated above. Carpzov and Jahn refer our prophet to the reign of Manasseh, thus placing him thirty odd years earlier; but at that time the Chaldæans had not as yet given just ground for apprehension, and it would have been injudicious in Habakkuk prematurely to fill the minds of the people with fear of them. Some additional support to our statement of the age of this book is derived from the tradition, reported in the apocryphal appendix to Daniel and by the Pseudo-Epiphanius, that Habakkuk lived to see the Babylonian exile; for if he prophesied under Manasseh he could not have reached the exile at an age under 90 years; but if he held forth early in the reign of Jehoiakim he would have been only 50 odd years old at the time of the destruction of Jerusalem and of the exile. He was, then, a contemporary of Jeremiah, but much younger, as the latter made his first appearance in public as early as B.C. 629, in the thirteenth year of Josiah.

The style of this prophet has been always much admired. He equals the most eminent prophets of the Old Testament—Joel, Amos, Nahum, Isaiah; and the ode in ch. iii. may be placed in competition with Ps. xviii. and lxviii. for originality and sublimity. His figures are all great, happily chosen, and properly drawn out. His denunciations are terrible, his derision bitter, his

consolation cheering. Instances occur of borrowed ideas (ch. iii. 19, comp. Ps. xviii. 34; ch. ii. 6, comp. Isa. xiv. 7; ch. ii. 14, comp. Isa. xi. 9); but he makes them his own in drawing them out in his peculiar manner. With all the boldness and fervour of his imagination, his language is pure and his verse melodious. The ancient catalogues of canonical books of the Old Testament do not mention Habakkuk by name; but they must have counted him in the twelve minor prophets, whose number would otherwise not be full. In the New Testament some expressions of his are introduced, but his name is not added (Rom. i. 17; Gal. iii. 11; Heb. x. 38, comp. Hab. ii. 4; Acts xiii. 40, 41, comp. Hab. i. 5).

HABERGEON. [Arms; Armour.]

HA'BOR, or rather Chabor, a city or country of Media, to which portions of the ten tribes were transported, first by Tiglathpileser, and afterwards by Shalmaneser (2 Kings xvii. 6; xviii. 11). It is thought by some to be the same mountainous region between Media and Assyria which Ptolemy calls Chaboras. This notion has the name, and nothing but the name, in its favour Habor was by the river Gozan; and as we have accepted Major Rennell's conclusion, that Gozan was the present Kizzil-Ozan [Gozan], we are bound to follow him in fixing the position of Habor at the town of Abbar, which is situated on a branch of that river, and has the reputation of being very ancient. At this place Mr. Morier found ruins composed of large sun-dried bricks compacted with straw, like some of those found at Babylon. As this kind of construction is an infallible sign of remote antiquity, so far affords a most important corroboration of Major Rennell's conjecture.

HA'DAD (*sharp*) is equivalent to Adad, the name of the chief deity of the Syrians [Adad], and borne, with or without additions, as a proper name, or more probably as a title, like 'Pharaoh' in Egypt, by several of the kings of Southern Syria

1. Hadad, king of Edom, who defeated the Midianites in the intervening territory of Moab (Gen. xxxvi. 35; 1 Chron. i. 46). This is the only one of the ancient kings of Edom whose exploits are recorded by Moses. Another king of Edom of the same name is mentioned in 1 Chron. i. 51.

2. Hadad, king of Syria, who reigned in Damascus at the time that David attacked and defeated Hadadezer, king of Zobah, whom he marched to assist, and shared in his defeat. This fact is recorded in 2 Sam. viii. 5, but the name of the king is not given. It is supplied, however, by Josephus, who reports, after Nicolas of Damascus, that he carried succours to Hadadezer as far as the Euphrates, where David defeated them both.

3. Hadad, a young prince of the royal race of Edom, who, when his country was conquered by David, contrived, in the heat of the massacre committed by Joab, to escape with some of his father's servants, or rather was carried off by them into the land of Midian. Thence Hadad went into the desert of Paran, and eventually proceeded to Egypt. He was there most favourably received by the king, who assigned him an estate and establishment suited to his rank, and even gave him in marriage the sister of his own consort, by whom he had a son, who was brought up in the palace

with the sons of Pharaoh. Hadad remained in Egypt till after the death of David and Joab, when he returned to his own country in the hope of recovering his father's throne (1 Kings xi. 14-22). The Scripture does not record the result of this attempt further than by mentioning him as one of the troublers of Solomon's reign, which implies some measure of success.

HADADE'ZER (*Hadad-helped*), or HADAD-REZER, king of Zobah, a powerful monarch in the time of David, and the only one who seems to have been in a condition seriously to dispute with him the predominancy in south-western Asia. He was defeated by the Israelites in the first campaign (B.C. 1032) in the neighbourhood of the Euphrates, with a great loss of men, war-chariots, and horses, and was despoiled of many of his towns (2 Sam. viii. 3; 1 Chron. xviii. 3). This check not only impaired, but destroyed his power. A diversion highly serviceable to him was made by a king of Damascene-Syria (whom the Scripture does not name, but who is the same with Hadad 3), who, coming to his succour, compelled David to turn his arms against him, and abstain from reaping all the fruits of his victory (2 Sam. x. 6, sq.; 1 Chron. xix. 6, sq.). The breathing-time thus afforded Hadadezer was turned by him to such good account that he was able to accept the subsidies of Hanun, king of the Ammonites, and to take a leading part in the confederacy formed by that monarch against David. The first army brought into the field was beaten and put to flight by Abishai and Joab; but Hadadezer, not yet discouraged, went into the countries east of the Euphrates, and got together the forces of all his allies and tributaries, which he placed under the command of Shophach, his general. To confront so formidable an adversary, David took the field in person, and in one great victory so completely broke the power of Hadadezer, that all the small tributary princes seized the opportunity of throwing off his yoke, of abandoning the Ammonites to their fate, and of submitting quietly to David, whose power was thus extended to the Euphrates.

HADES, a Greek word, which occurs frequently in the New Testament, where it is usually rendered 'hell' in the English version. The word *hades* means literally *that which is in darkness*. In the classical writers it is used to denote *Orcus*, or the infernal regions. According to the notions of the Jews, *sheol* or *hades* was a vast receptacle where the souls of the dead existed in a separate state until the resurrection of their bodies. The region of the blessed during this interval, or the inferior paradise, they supposed to be in the upper part of this receptacle; while beneath was the abyss or *gehenna* (Tartarus), in which the souls of the wicked were subjected to punishment.

The question whether this is or is not the doctrine of the Scriptures is one of much importance, and has, first and last, excited no small amount of discussion. It is a doctrine received by a large portion of the nominal Christian church; and it forms the foundation of the Roman Catholic doctrine of Purgatory, for which there would be no ground but for this interpretation of the word *hades*.

The question therefore rests entirely upon the interpretation of this word, and as the Septuagint gives this as the meaning of the Hebrew word *sheol*, the real question is, what is the meaning which *sheol* bears in the Old Testament, and *hades* in the New? A careful examination of the passages in which these words occur will probably lead to the conclusion, that they afford no real sanction to the notion of an intermediate place of the kind indicated, but are used by the inspired writers to denote *the grave*—the resting-place of the bodies both of the righteous and the wicked; and that they are also used to signify *hell*, the abode of miserable spirits. But it would be difficult to produce any instance in which they can be shown to signify the abode of the spirits of just men made perfect, either before or after the resurrection.

In the great majority of instances *sheol* is in the Old Testament used to signify *the grave*, and in most of these cases is so translated in the Authorized Version. It can have no other meaning in such texts as Gen. xxxvii. 35; xlii. 38; 1 Sam. ii. 6; 1 Kings ii. 6; Job xiv. 13; xvii. 16; and in numerous other passages in the writings of David, Solomon, and the prophets. But as the grave is regarded by most persons, and was more especially so by the ancients, with awe and dread, as being the region of gloom and darkness, so the word denoting it soon came to be applied to that more dark and gloomy world which was to be the abiding place of the miserable. Where our translators supposed the word to have this sense, they rendered it by 'hell.' Some of the passages in which this has been done may be doubtful; but there are others of which a question can scarcely be entertained. Such are those (as Job xi. 8; Ps. cxxxix. 8; Amos ix. 2) in which the word denotes the opposite of heaven, which cannot be the grave, nor the general state or region of the dead, but hell. Still more decisive are such passages as Ps. ix. 17; Prov. xxiii. 14; in which *sheol* cannot mean any place, in this world or the next, to which the righteous as well as the wicked are sent, but the penal abode of the wicked as distinguished from and opposed to the righteous. The only case in which such passages could by any possibility be supposed to mean the grave, would be if the grave—that is, extinction—were the *final* doom of the unrighteous.

In the New Testament the word *hades* is used in much the same sense as *sheol* in the Old, except that in a less proportion of cases can it be construed to signify 'the grave.' There are still, however, instances in which it is used in this sense, as in Acts ii. 31; 1 Cor. xv. 55; but in general the *hades* of the New Testament appears to be no other than the world of future punishments (*e.g.* Matt. xi. 23; xvi. 18; Luke xvi. 23).

The principal arguments for the intermediate *hades*, as deduced from Scripture, are founded on those passages in which things 'under the earth' are described as rendering homage to God and the Saviour (Philip. ii. 10; Rev. v. 13, &c.). If such passages, however, be compared with others (as with Rom. xiv. 10, 11, &c.), it will appear that they must refer to the day of judgment, in which every creature will render some sort of homage to the Saviour; but *then* the bodies of the saints will have been already raised, and the intermediate region, if there be any, will have been deserted.

One of the seemingly strongest arguments **for**

the opinion under consideration is founded on 1 Pet. iii. 19, in which Christ is said to have gone and 'preached to the spirits in prison.' These spirits in prison are supposed to be the holy dead —perhaps the virtuous heathen—imprisoned in the intermediate place, into which the soul of the Saviour went at death, that he might preach to them the Gospel. This passage must be allowed to present great difficulties. The most intelligible meaning suggested by the context is, however, that Christ by his spirit preached to those who in the time of Noah, while the ark was preparing, were disobedient, and whose spirits are *now* in prison, abiding the general judgment. The prison is doubtless *hades*, but what *hades* is must be determined by other passages of Scripture; and, whether it is the grave or hell, it is still a prison for those who yet await the judgment-day. This interpretation is in unison with other passages of Scripture, whereas the other is conjecturally deduced from this single text.

Another argument is deduced from Rev. xx. 14, which describes 'death and *hades*' as 'cast into the lake of fire' at the close of the general judgment—meaning, according to the advocates of the doctrine in question, that *hades* should then cease as an intermediate place. But this is also true if understood of the grave, or of the general intermediate *condition* of the dead, or even of hell, as once more and for ever reclaiming what it had temporarily yielded up for judgment—just as we every day see criminals brought from prison to judgment, and after judgment returned to the prison from which they came.

It is further urged, in proof of Hades being an intermediate place other than the grave, that the Scriptures represent the happiness of the righteous as incomplete till after the resurrection. This must be admitted; but it does not thence follow that their souls are previously imprisoned in the earth, or in any other place or region corresponding to the Tartarus of the heathen. Although at the moment of death the disembodied spirits of the redeemed ascend to heaven, and continue there till the resurrection, it is very possible that their happiness shall be incomplete until they have received their glorified bodies from the tomb, and entered upon the full rewards of eternity.

A view supported by so little force of Scripture, seems unequal to resist the contrary evidence which may be produced from the same source, and which it remains briefly to indicate. The effect of this is to show that the souls of the redeemed are described as proceeding, after death, at once to heaven—*the place* of final happiness, and those of the unredeemed to *the place* of final wretchedness.

In Heb. vi. 12, the righteous dead are described as being in actual inheritance of the promises made to the fathers. Our Saviour represents the deceased saints as already, before the resurrection (for so the context requires), 'like unto the angels,' and 'equal to the angels' (Matt. xxii. 30; Luke xx. 36); which is not very compatible with their imprisonment even in the happier region of the supposed Hades. Our Lord's declaration to the dying thief—'This day shalt thou be with me in Paradise' (Luke xxiii. 43), has been urged on both sides of the argument; but the word is here not Hades, but Paradise, and

no instance can be produced in which the paradise beyond the grave means anything else than that 'third heaven,' that 'paradise' into which the Apostle was caught up, and where he heard 'unutterable things' (2 Cor. xii. 2, 4). In the midst of that paradise grows the mystic 'tree of life' (Rev. ii. 7), which the same writer represents as growing near the throne of God and the Lamb (xxii. 2). In Eph. iii. 15, the Apostle describes the whole church of God as being at present in heaven or on earth. But, according to the view under consideration, the great body of the church would be neither in heaven nor on earth, but in Hades—the intermediate place. In Heb. xii. 21-24, we are told that in the city of the living God dwell not only God himself, the judge of all, and Jesus, the mediator of the new covenant, and the innumerable company of angels, but also 'the spirits of just men made perfect'— all dwelling together in the same holy and happy place. To the same effect, but, if possible, still more conclusive, are the various passages in which the souls of the saints are described as being, when absent from the body, present with Christ in heaven (comp. 2 Cor. v. 1-8; Philip. i. 23; 1 Thess. v. 10). To this it is scarcely necessary to add the various passages in the Apocalyptic vision, in which St. John beheld, as inhabitants of the highest heaven, around the throne of God, myriads of redeemed souls, even before the resurrection (Rev. v. 9; vi. 9; vii. 9; xiv. 1, 3). Now the 'heaven' of these passages cannot be the place to which the term Hades is ever applied, for that word is never associated with any circumstances or images of enjoyment or happiness [HEAVEN].

As these arguments seem calculated to disprove the existence of the more favoured region of the alleged intermediate place, a similar course of evidence militates with equal force against the existence of the more penal region of the same place. It is admitted by the staunchest advocates for the doctrine of an intermediate place, that the souls of the wicked, when they leave the body, go immediately into punishment. Now the Scripture knows no place of punishment after death but that which was prepared for the devil and his angels. This place they *now* inhabit; and this is the place to which, after judgment, the souls of the condemned will be consigned (comp. 2 Pet. ii. 4; Matt. xxv. 41). This verse of Peter is the only one in Scripture in which any reference to the word Tartarus occurs: here then, if anywhere, we should find that intermediate place corresponding to the Tartarus of the heathen, from whom the word is borrowed. But from the other text we can be quite certain that the Tartarus of Peter is no other than the hell which is to be the final, as it is, in degree, the present doom of the wicked. That this hell is Hades is readily admitted, for the course of the argument has been to show that Hades is hell, whenever it is not the grave. Dr. Enoch Pond, whose interesting article on the subject, in the American *Biblical Repository*, we have chiefly followed, well remarks: 'Whether the righteous and the wicked, after the judgment, will go literally to the same places in which they were before situated, it is not material to inquire. But, both before and after the judgment, the righteous will be in the same place with their glorified Saviour and his holy angels; and this will be heaven: and before and after the judgment the wicked will be in the same place with the devil and his angels; and this will be hell.

HA'GAR (*a stranger*), a native of Egypt, and servant of Abraham; but how or when she became an inmate of his family we are not informed. Whatever were her origin and previous history, her servile condition in the family of Abraham must have prevented her from being ever known beyond the limits of her humble sphere, had not her name, by a spontaneous act of her mistress, become indissolubly linked with the patriarch's history. The long continued sterility of Sarah suggested to her the idea (not uncommon in the East) of becoming a mother by proxy through her handmaid, whom, with that view, she gave to Abraham as a secondary wife [ABRAHAM: ADOPTION; CONCUBINE].

The honour of such an alliance and elevation was too great and unexpected for the weak and ill-regulated mind of Hagar: and no sooner did she find herself in a delicate situation, which made her, in the prospect of becoming a mother, an object of increasing interest and importance to Abraham, than she openly indulged in triumph over her less favoured mistress, and showed by her altered behaviour a growing habit of disrespect and insolence. The feelings of Sarah were severely wounded, and she broke out to her husband in loud complaints of the servant's petulance; and Abraham, whose meek and prudent behaviour is strikingly contrasted with the violence of his wife, leaves her with unfettered power, as mistress of his household, to take what steps she pleases to obtain the required redress.

Hagar, though taken into the relation of concubine to Abraham, continued still, being a dotal maid-servant, under the absolute power of her mistress, who was neither reluctant nor sparing in making the minion reap the fruits of her insolence. Sarah, indeed, not content with the simple exertion of her authority, seems to have resorted even to corporal chastisement. Sensible, at length, of the hopelessness of getting the better of her mistress, Hagar determined on flight; and having seemingly formed the purpose of returning to her relations in Egypt, she took the direction of that country; which led her to what was afterwards called Shur, through a long tract of sandy uninhabited country, lying on the west of Arabia Petræa, to the extent of 150 miles between Palestine and Egypt. In that lonely region she was sitting by a fountain to replenish her skin-bottle or recruit her wearied limbs, when the angel of the Lord, whose language on this occasion bespeaks him to have been more than a created being, appeared, and in the kindliest manner remonstrated with her on the course she was pursuing, and encouraged her to return by the promise that she would ere long have a son, whom Providence destined to become a great man, and whose wild and irregular features of character would be indelibly impressed on the mighty nation that should spring from him. Obedient to the heavenly visitor, and having distinguished the place by the name of Beer-lahai-roi, ' the well of the visible God,' Hagar retraced her steps to the tent of Abraham, where in due time she had a son; and having probably narrated this remarkable interview to Abraham,

that patriarch, as directed by the angel, called the name of the child Ishmael, ' God hath heard.'

Fourteen years had elapsed after the birth of Ishmael when an event occurred in the family of Abraham, by the appearance of the long-promised heir, which entirely changed the prospects of that young man, though nothing materially affecting him took place till the weaning of Isaac, which, as is generally thought, was at the end of his third year. Ishmael was then a lad of seventeen years of age; and being fully capable of understanding his altered relations to the inheritance, as well as having felt perhaps a sensible diminution of Sarah's affection towards him, it is not wonderful that a disappointed youth should inconsiderately give vent to his feelings on a festive occasion, when the newly-weaned child, clad according to custom with the sacred symbolic robe, which was the badge of the birth-right, was formally installed heir of the tribe. The harmony of the weaning feast was disturbed by Ishmael being discovered mocking. This conduct gave mortal offence to Sarah, who from that moment would be satisfied with nothing short of his irrevocable expulsion from the family; and as his mother also was included in the same condemnation, there is ground to believe that she had been repeating her former insolence, as well as instigating her son to his improprieties of behaviour. So harsh a measure was extremely painful to the affectionate heart of Abraham; but his scruples were removed by the timely appearance of his divine counsellor, who said, ' Let it not be grievous in thy sight, because of the lad, and because of thy bondwoman: in all that Sarah hath said unto thee, hearken unto her voice.' The incident affords a very remarkable instance of an overruling Providence in making this family feud in the tent of a pastoral chief 4000 years ago the occasion of separating two mighty nations, who, according to the prophecy, have ever since occupied an important chapter in the history of man. Hagar and Ishmael departed early on the day fixed for their removal, Abraham furnishing them with the necessary supply of travelling provisions.

In spite of their instructions for threading the desert, the two exiles missed their way. Overcome by fatigue and thirst, increasing at every step under the unmitigated rays of a vertical sun, the strength of the young Ishmael, as was natural, first gave way, and his mother laid him down in complete exhaustion under one of the stunted shrubs of this arid region, in the hope of his obtaining some momentary relief from smelling the damp in the shade. The burning fever, however, continued unabated, and the poor woman, forgetting her own sorrow, destitute and alone in the midst of a wilderness, and absorbed in the fate of her son, withdrew to a little distance, unable to witness his lingering sufferings; and there 'she lifted up her voice and wept.' In this distressing situation the angel of the Lord appeared for the purpose of comforting her, and directed her to a fountain, which, concealed by the brushwood, had escaped her notice, and from which she drew a refreshing draught, that had the effect of reviving the almost lifeless Ishmael.

Of the subsequent history of Ishmael we have no account, further than that he established himself in the wilderness of Paran, in the neighbourhood of Sinai, was married by his mother to a countrywoman of her own, and maintained both himself and family by the produce of his bow.

HAGARENES'. [ARABIA.]

HAG'GAI, one of the twelve minor prophets, and the first of the three who, after the return of the Jews from the Babylonian exile, prophesied in Palestine. Of the place and year of his birth, his descent, and the leading incidents of his life, nothing is known which can be relied on. This much appears from his prophecies, that he flourished during the reign of the Persian monarch Darius Hystaspis, who ascended the throne B.C. 521. These prophecies are comprised in a book of two chapters, and consist of discourses remarkably brief and summary. Their object generally is to urge the rebuilding of the Temple, which had indeed been commenced as early as B.C. 535 (Ezra iii. 10), but was afterwards discontinued, the Samaritans having obtained an edict from the Persian king, which forbade further procedure, and influential Jews pretending that the time for rebuilding the Temple had not arrived, since the seventy years predicted by Jeremiah applied to the Temple also, from the time of the destruction of which it was then only the sixty-eighth year. As on the death of Pseudo-Smerdis, and the consequent termination of his interdict, the Jews still continued to wait for the end of the seventy years, and were only engaged in building splendid houses for themselves, Haggai began to prophesy in the second year of Darius, B.C. 520.

His first discourse (ch. i.), delivered on the first day of the sixth month of the year mentioned, foretells that a brighter era would begin as soon as Jehovah's house was rebuilt; and a notice is subjoined, stating that the address of the prophet had been effective, the people having resolved on resuming the restoration of the Temple. The second discourse (ch. ii. 1-9), delivered on the twenty-first day of the seventh month, predicts that the glory of the new Temple would be greater than that of Solomon's, and shows that no fear need be entertained of the Second Temple not equalling the first in splendour, since, in a remarkable political revolution, the gifts of the Gentiles would be brought thither. The third discourse (ch. ii. 10-19), delivered on the twenty-fourth day of the ninth month, refers to a period when building materials had been collected, and the workmen had begun to put them together; for which a commencement of the Divine blessing is promised. The fourth and last discourse (ch. ii. 20-23), delivered also on the twenty-fourth day of the ninth month, is exclusively addressed to Zerubbabel, the political chief of the new Jewish colony, who, it appears, had asked for an explanation regarding the great political revolutions which Haggai had predicted in his second discourse: it comforts the governor by assuring him they would not take place very soon, and not in his lifetime. The style of the discourses of Haggai is suitable to their contents: it is pathetic when he exhorts; it is vehement when he reproves; it is somewhat elevated when he treats of future events; and it is not altogether destitute of a poetical colouring, though a prophet of a higher order would have depicted the splendour of the Second Temple in brighter hues. The

language labours under a poverty of terms, as may be observed in the constant repetition of the same expressions. The prophetical discourses of Haggai are referred to in the Old and New Testament (Ezra v. 1; vi. 14; Heb. xii. 26; comp. Hag. ii. 7, 8, 22). In most of the ancient catalogues of the canonical books of the Old Testament, Haggai is not, indeed, mentioned by name; but as they specify the twelve minor prophets, he must have been included among them, as otherwise their number would not be full.

HAIR is frequently mentioned in Scripture, and in scarcely anything has the caprice of fashion been more strikingly displayed than in the various forms which the taste of different countries and ages has prescribed for disposing of this natural covering of the head. The Greeks let their hair grow to a great length. The early Egyptians, again, who were proverbial for their habits of cleanliness, removed the hair as an incumbrance, and the almost unavoidable occasion of sordid and offensive negligence. All classes amongst that people, not excepting the slaves imported from foreign countries, were required to submit to the tonsure (Gen. xli. 14); and yet, what was remarkable in the inhabitants of a hot climate, while they removed their natural hair, they were accustomed to wear wigs, which were so constructed that 'they far surpassed,' says Wilkinson, 'the comfort and coolness of the modern turban, the reticulated texture of the groundwork on which the hair was fastened allowing the heat of the head to escape, while the hair effectually protected it from the sun.' Different from the custom both of the Greeks and the Egyptians, that of the Hebrews was to wear their hair generally short, and to check its growth by the application of scissors only. The priests at their inauguration shaved off all their hair, and when on actual duty at the temple, were in the habit, it is said, of cutting it every fortnight. The only exceptions to this prevailing fashion are found in the case of the Nazarites, whose hair, from religious duty, was *not* to be cropped during the term of their vow; of young persons who, during their minority, allowed their hair to hang down in luxuriant ringlets on their shoulders; of such effeminate persons as Absalom (2 Sam. xiv. 26); and of Solomon's horse-guards, whose vanity affected a puerile extravagance, and who strewed their heads every day with particles of gold-dust. Although the Hebrews wore their hair short, they were great admirers of strong and thickset locks; and so high a value did they set on the possession of a good head of hair, that they deprecated nothing so much as baldness. To prevent or remedy this defect they seem, at an early period, to have availed themselves of the assistance of art, not only for beautifying the hair, but increasing its thickness; while the heads of the priests were anointed with an unguent of a peculiar kind, the ingredients of which, with their various proportions, were prescribed by divine authority, and the composition of which the people were prohibited, under severe penalties, from attempting to imitate (Exod. xxx. 32). This custom spread till anointing the hair of the head became a general mark of gentility and an essential part of the daily toilet; the usual cosmetics employed consisting of the best oil of olives mingled with spices, a decoction of parsley-

seed in wine, and more rarely of spikenard (Ps.
xxiii. 5; xlv. 7; Eccles. ix. 8; Mark xiv. 3).
The prevailing colour of hair among the Hebrews was dark; 'locks bushy and black as a
raven,' being mentioned in the description of the
bridegroom as the perfection of beauty in mature manhood (Sol. Song v. 11). Hence the appearance of an old man with a snow-white head
in a company of younger Jews, all whose heads,
like those of other Eastern people, were jet black
—a most conspicuous object—is beautifully compared to an almond-tree, which in the early part
of the year is in full blossom, while all the others
are dark and leafless (Eccles. xii. 5). Among
the Romans it was customary to employ artificial
means for changing or disguising the silver hue
of age. From Rome the fashion spread into
Greece and other provinces, and it appears that
the members of the church of Corinth were, to a
certain extent, captivated by the prevailing taste,
some Christians being evidently in the eye of
the Apostle, who had attracted attention by the
cherished and womanly decoration of their hair
(1 Cor. xi. 14-16). To them the letter of Paul
was intended to administer a timely reproof for
allowing themselves to fall in with a style of
manners which, by confounding the distinctions
of the sexes, threatened a baneful influence on
good morals: and that not only the Christian
converts in that city, but the primitive church
generally, were led by this admonition to adopt
simpler habits, is evident from the remarkable
fact that a criminal, who came to trial under the
assumed character of a Christian, was proved to
the satisfaction of the judge to be an impostor, by
the luxuriant and frizzled appearance of his hair.

With regard to women, the possession of long
and luxuriant hair is allowed by Paul to be an
essential attribute of the sex—a graceful and
modest covering provided by nature; and yet the
same Apostle elsewhere (1 Tim. ii. 9) concurs
with Peter (1 Pet. iii. 9) in launching severe in-
vectives against the ladies of his day for the
pride and passionate fondness they displayed in
the elaborate decorations of their head-dress. As
the hair was pre-eminently the 'instrument of
their pride' (Ezek. xvi. 39, margin), all the resources of ingenuity and art were exhausted to
set it off to advantage and load it with the most
dazzling finery; and many when they died caused
their longest locks to be cut off, and placed separately in an urn, to be deposited in their tomb as
the most precious and valued relics.

From the great value attached to a profuse
head of hair arose a variety of superstitious and
emblematic observances, such as shaving parts of
the head, or cropping it in a particular form;
parents dedicating the hair of infants to the gods;
young women theirs at their marriage; warriors
after a successful campaign; sailors after deliverance from a storm; hanging it up on consecrated trees, or depositing it in temples; burying
it in the tomb of friends, as Achilles did at the
funeral of Patroclus; besides shaving, cutting off,
or plucking it out, as some people did; or allowing it to grow in sordid negligence, as was the
practice with others, according as the calamity
that befel them was common or extraordinary,
and their grief was mild or violent.

Various metaphorical allusions are made to
hair by the sacred writers, especially the pro-

phets. 'Cutting off the hair' is a figure used to
denote the entire destruction of a people by the
righteous retributions of Providence (Isa. vii. 20)
'Gray hairs here and there on Ephraim' portended the decline and fall of the kingdom of
Israel (Hos. vii. 9). 'Hair like women's' forms
part of the description of the Apocalyptic locusts,
and historically points to the prevailing head-
dress of the Saracens, as well as the voluptuous
effeminacy of the Antichristian clergy (Rev ix.
8). And, finally, 'hair like fine wool' was a
prominent feature in the appearance of the deified
Redeemer, emblematic of the majesty and wisdom
that belong to him (Rev. i. 14).

HA'LAH, or rather CHALACH, a city or district of Media, upon the river Gozan, to which,
among other places, the captives of Israel were
transplanted by the Assyrian kings. Many have
conceived this Halah or Chalach to be the Cala-
chene which Ptolemy places in the north of
Assyria. But if the river Gozan be the Kizzil-
Ozan, Halah must needs be sought elsewhere,
and near that river. Accordingly Major Rennell indicates as lying along its banks a district
of some extent, and of great beauty and fertility,
named Chalchal, having within it a remarkably
strong position of the same name, situated on one
of the hills adjoining to the mountains which
separate it from the province of Ghilan.

HALLELU'JAH, or ALLELUIA, a word which
stands at the beginning of many of the Psalms.
From its frequent occurrence in this position it
grew into a formula of praise, and was chanted
as such on solemn days of rejoicing. This expression of joy and praise was transferred from
the synagogue to the church, and is still occasionally heard in devotional psalmody.

HAM. 1. The youngest son of Noah (Gen.
v. 32; comp. ix. 24). Having provoked the
wrath of his father by an act of indecency towards him, the latter cursed him and his descendants to be slaves to his brothers and their
descendants (ix. 25). To judge, however, from
the narrative, Noah directed his curse only
against Canaan (the fourth son of Ham) and his
race, thus excluding from it the descendants of
Ham's three other sons, Cush, Mizraim, and
Phut (Gen. x. 6). The general opinion is, that
all the Southern nations derive their origin from
Ham. Cush is supposed to have been the progenitor of the nations of East and South Asia,
more especially of South Arabia, and also of
Ethiopia; Mizraim, of the African nations, including the Philistines and some other tribes
which Greek fable and tradition connect with
Egypt; Phut, likewise of some African nations;
and Canaan, of the inhabitants of Palestine and
Phœnicia.

2. A poetical name for the land of Egypt (Ps.
lxxviii. 51; cv. 23, 27; cvi. 22).

In Gen. xiv. 5 occurs a country or place called
Ham, belonging to the Zuzim, but its geographical situation is unknown.

HA'MAN, a name of the planet Mercury; a
favourite of the king of Persia, whose history is
involved in that of Esther and Mordecai. He is
called an Agagite; and as Agag was a kind of
title of the kings of the Amalekites [AGAG], it is
supposed that Haman was descended from the
royal family of that nation. He or his parents
probably found their way to Persia as captives

or hostages; and that the foreign origin of Haman was no bar to his advancement at court, is a circumstance quite in union with the most ancient and still subsisting usages of the East. Joseph, Daniel, and Mordecai afford other examples of the same kind.

It is unnecessary to repeat the particulars of a story so well known as that of Haman. The circumstantial details of the height which he attained and of his sudden downfall, afford, like all the rest of the book of Esther, a most faithful picture of the customs of an Oriental court and government, and furnish invaluable materials for a comparison between the regal usages of ancient and modern times. The result of such a comparison will excite surprise by the closeness of the resemblance; for there is not a single fact in the history of Haman which might not occur at the present day, and which, indeed, is not of frequent occurrence in different combinations. The death of Haman appears to have taken place about the year B.C. 510.

HA'MATH, one of the smaller kingdoms of Syria, having Zobah on the east and Rehob on the south. This last kingdom, lying within the greater Mount Hermon, is expressly said to have been taken possession of by the Israelites, and, like Dan or Laisb, which is represented to have been in the valley of Bethrehob (Judg. xviii. 28), is used to denote the northern boundary of the Holy Land. The approach to it from the south is by an opening or mountain-pass, called 'the entrance of Hamath,' and 'the entering in of Hamath,' which, being the passage from the northern extremity of the land of Israel into Syria, is sometimes used to describe the boundary of the former in this direction, as 'from the entering in of Hamath to the river of Egypt' (1 Kings viii. 65).

The kingdom of Hamath, or, at least, the southern or central parts of it, appear to have nearly corresponded with what was afterwards denominated Cœle-Syria; but northwards, it stretched as far as the city Hamath on the Orontes, which seems to have been the capital of the whole country. Toi was king of Hamath at the time when David conquered the Syrians of Zobah; and it appears that he had reason to rejoice in the humiliation of a dangerous neighbour, as he sent his own son Joram to congratulate the victor (2 Sam. viii. 9, 10). In the time of Hezekiah the town along with its territory was conquered by the Assyrians (2 Kings xvii. 24; xviii. 34; xix. 13; Isa. x. 9; xi. 11); and afterwards by the Chaldæans (Jer. xxxix. 2, 5). Hamath is still a picturesque town, of considerable circumference, and with wide and convenient streets. In Burckhardt's time the attached district contained 120 inhabited villages, and 70 or 80 that lay waste. The western part of this district forms the granary of Northern Syria, though the harvest never yields more than a tenfold return, chiefly on account of the immense numbers of mice, which sometimes completely destroy the crops.

HANAM'EEL, a kinsman of Jeremiah, to whom, before the siege of Jerusalem, he sold a field which he possessed in Anathoth, a town of the Levites (Jer. xxxii. 6-12). If this field belonged to Hanameel as a Levite, the sale of it would imply that an ancient law had fallen into disuse (Lev. xxv. 34); but it is possible that it

may have been the property of Hanameel in right of his mother. The transaction was conducted with all the forms of legal transfer, and was intended to evince the certainty of restoration from the approaching exile, by showing that possessions which could be established by documents would yet be of future value to the possessor (B.C. 587).

1. HAN'ANI (*gracious*), a prophet under the reign of Asa, king of Judah, by whom he was seized and imprisoned for announcing that he had lost, from want of due trust in God, an advantage which he might have gained over the king of Syria (2 Chron. xvi. 7).

2. HANA'NI, a brother of Nehemiah, who went from Jerusalem to Shushan, being sent most probably by Ezra, and brought that information respecting the miserable condition of the returned Jews which led to the mission of Nehemiah. Hanani came back to Judæa, probably along with his brother, and, together with one Hananiah, was appointed to take charge of the gates of Jerusalem, and see that they were opened in the morning and closed in the evening at the appointed time. The circumstances of the time and place rendered this an important and responsible duty, not unattended with some danger (Neh. vii. 2, 3). B.C. 455.

1. HANANI'AH (*Jehovah's goodness*), a false prophet of Gibeon, who, by opposing his prophecies to those of Jeremiah, brought upon himself the terrible sentence, 'Thou shalt die *this year*, because thou hast taught rebellion against the Lord.' He died accordingly (Jer. xxviii. 1, sq.), B.C. 596.

2. HANANIAH. [SHADRACH.]

3. HANANIAH, the person who was associated with Nehemiah's brother Hanani in the charge of the gates of Jerusalem. The high eulogy is bestowed upon him, that 'he was a faithful man, and feared God above many' (Neh. vii. 2) [HANANI 2].

HAND, the organ of feeling, rightly denominated by Galen the instrument of instruments, since by its position at the end of the fore-arm, its structure and its connection with the mind, the hand admirably executes the behests of the human will, and acquires and imparts to man incomparable skill and power. By the peculiarities of its conformation—the inclination of the thumb to the palm, the comparative length of the thumb and of the fingers, 'the hollow of the hand,' and the fleshy protuberances by which that hollow is mainly formed—this member is wonderfully adapted to the purposes for which it was designed, and serves to illustrate the wisdom and providence of the great Creator. The hand itself serves to distinguish man from other terrestrial beings. No other animal has any member comparable with the human hand. Of the two hands the right has a preference derived from natural endowment. Its universal use, as the chief instrument in acting, serves to show that its superiority is something more than an accident. But the preference which it holds is only a part of the general advantage which the right side has over the left, not only in muscular strength, but also in its vital or constitutional properties.

From the properties already described, the student of Scripture is prepared to see the hand employed in holy writ as a symbol of skill, strength, and efficacy. As a part of that general anthropomorphism, without whose aid men in the early ages could probably have formed no conception of God, the Deity is frequently spoken of in the records of revelation as if possessed of hands.

The phrase 'sitting at the right hand of God,' as applied to the Saviour of the world, is derived from the fact that with earthly princes a position on the right hand of the throne was accounted the chief place of honour, dignity, and power: —'upon thy right-hand did stand the queen' (Ps. xlv. 9; compare 1 Kings ii. 19; Ps. lxxx. 17). The immediate passage out of which sprang the phraseology employed by Jesus may be found in Ps. cx. 1: 'Jehovah said unto my Lord, sit thou at my right hand until I make thine enemies thy footstool.' Accordingly the Saviour declares before Caiaphas (Matt. xxvi. 64; Mark xiv. 62), 'Ye shall see the Son of man sitting on the right hand of power, and coming in the clouds of heaven;' where the meaning obviously is that the Jews of that day should have manifest proofs that Jesus held the most eminent place in the divine favour, and that his present humiliation would be succeeded by glory, majesty, and power (Luke xxiv. 26; 1 Tim. iii. 16). So when it is said (Mark xvi. 19; Rom. viii. 34; Col. iii. 1; 1 Pet. iii. 22; Heb. i. 3; viii. 1) that Jesus 'sits at the right hand of God,' 'at the right hand of the Majesty on high,' we are obviously to understand the assertion to be that, as his Father, so he worketh always (John v. 17) for the advancement of the kingdom of heaven, and the salvation of the world.

As the hand is the great instrument of action, so is it eminently fitted for affording aid to the mind, by the signs and indications which it makes. Thus to lay the hand on any one was a means of pointing him out, and consequently an emblem of setting any one apart for a particular office or dignity. *Imposition of hands* accordingly formed, at an early period, a part of the ceremonial observed on the appointment and consecration of persons to high and holy undertakings. (See Num. xxvii. 19; Acts viii. 15-17; 1 Tim. iv. 14; 2 Tim. i. 6.) A corruption of this doctrine was, that the laying on of hands gave of itself divine powers; and on this account Simon, the magician (Acts viii. 18), offered money, saying, 'Give me also this power, that on whomsoever I lay hands he may receive the Holy Ghost,' intending probably to carry on a gainful trade by communicating the gift to others.

HANDICRAFT. In the early periods to which the Scriptural history refers we do not meet with those artificial feelings and unreasonable prejudices against hand-labour which prevail and are so banefully influential in modern society. The primitive history which the Bible presents is the history of hand-labourers. Adam dressed the garden in which God had placed him (Gen. ii. 15), Abel was a keeper of sheep, Cain a tiller of the ground (Gen. iv. 3), Tubal-cain a smith (Gen. iv. 22). The general nature of this article does not require any extensive or detailed inquiry into the hand-labours which the Israelites practised before their descent into Egypt; but the high and varied culture which they found there must have contributed greatly to increase their knowledge of the practical arts of life, though the herdsman-sort of life which the Hebrews continued to lead was not favourable to their advancement in either science or art.

Another source of knowledge to the Hebrews of handicrafts were the maritime and commercial Phœnicians. Commerce and navigation imply great skill in art and science; and the pursuits to which they lead largely increase the skill whence they emanate. It is not, therefore, surprising that the origin of so many arts has been referred to the north-eastern shore of the Mediterranean Sea; nor is there any difficulty in understanding how arts and letters should be propagated from the coast to the interior, conferring high advantages on the inhabitants of Syria in general, as well before as after the settlement of the Hebrew tribes in the land of promise.

The skill of the Hebrews during their wanderings in the desert does not appear to have been inconsiderable; but the pursuits of war and the entire absorption of the energies of the nation in the one great work of gaining the land which had been given to them, may have led to their falling off in the arts of peace; and from a passage in 1 Sam. (xiii. 20) it would appear that not long after they had taken possession of the country they were in a low condition as to the instruments of handicraft. A comparatively settled state of society, however, soon led to the revival of skill by the encouragement of industry. A more minute division of labour ensued. Trades, strictly so called, arose, carried on by persons exclusively devoted to one pursuit. Thus in Judg. xvii. 4 and Jer. x. 14, 'the founder' is mentioned, a trade which implies a practical knowledge of metallurgy; the smelting and working of metals were well known to the Hebrews (Job xxxvii. 18); brass was in use before iron; arms and instruments of husbandry were made of iron. In Exodus (xxxv. 30-35) a passage occurs which may serve to specify many arts that were practised among the Israelites, though it seems also to intimate that at the time to which it refers artificers of the description referred to were not numerous. From the ensuing chapter (ver. 34) it appears that gilding was known before the settlement in Canaan. The ark (Exod. xxxvii. 2) was overlaid with pure gold within and without. The cherubim were wrought ('beaten,' Exod. xxxvii. 7) in gold. The candlestick was of beaten gold (verses 17, 22). Wire-drawing was probably understood (Exod. xxxviii. 4; xxxix. 3). Covering with brass (Exod. xxxviii. 2) and with silver (Prov. xxvi. 23) was practised. Architecture and the kindred arts do not appear to have made much progress till the days of Solomon, who employed an incredible number of persons to procure timber (1 Kings v. 13, sq.); but the men of skill for building his temple he obtained from Hiram, king of Tyre (1 Kings v. sq.; 1 Chron. xiv. 1; 2 Chron. ii. 7). The intercourse which the Babylonish captivity gave the Jews seems to have greatly improved their knowledge and skill in both the practical and the fine arts, and to have led them to hold them in very high estimation. The arts were even carried on by persons of learning, who took a title of honour from their trade. It was held a sign of a bad education if a father did not teach his son some handicraft.

In the Apocrypha and New Testament there

are mentioned tanners (Acts ix. 43), tent-makers (Acts xviii. 3); in Josephus, cheese-makers, domestics; in the Talmud, with others we find tailors, shoe-makers, blood-letters, glaziers, goldsmiths, plasterers. Certain handicraftsmen could never rise to the rank of high-priest, such as weavers, barbers, fullers, perfumers, cuppers, tanners; which pursuits, especially the last, were held in disesteem. In large cities particular localities were set apart for particular trades, as is the case in the East to the present day. Thus in Jeremiah (xxxvii. 21) we read of 'the bakers' street.' So in the Talmud mention is made of a flesh-market; in Josephus, of a cheese-market; and in the New Testament (John v. 2) we read of a sheep-market.

HANDKERCHIEF, NAPKIN, occurs in Luke xix. 20; John xi. 44; xx. 7; Acts xix. 12. The word is employed in Scripture in a variety of meanings. In the first instance (Luke xix. 20) it means a wrapper, in which the 'wicked servant' had laid up the pound intrusted to him by his master. In the second instance (John xi. 44) it appears as a kerchief, or cloth attached to the head of a corpse. It was perhaps brought round the forehead and under the chin. In many Egyptian mummies it does not *cover the face.* In ancient times among the Greeks it *did.* The next instance is that of the 'napkin' which had been 'about the head' of our Lord, but which, after his resurrection, was found rolled up, as if deliberately, and put in a place separately from the linen clothes. The last instance of the Biblical use of the word occurs in the account of 'the special miracles' wrought by the hands of Paul (Acts xix. 11); 'so that handkerchiefs, napkins, wrappers, shawls, &c., were brought from his body to the sick; and the diseases departed from them, and the evil spirits went out of them.' The Ephesians had not unnaturally inferred that the apostle's miraculous power could be communicated by such a mode of contact; and certainly cures thus received by parties at a distance, among a people famed for their addictedness to 'curious arts,' *i. e.* magical skill, &c., would serve to convince them of the truth of the gospel, by a mode well suited to interest their minds.

HANGING. [Punishments.]

HAN'NAH, properly Channah (*graciousness*), wife of a Levite named Elkanah, and mother of Samuel. She was very dear to her husband, but being childless was much aggrieved by the insults of Elkanah's other wife Peninnah, who was blessed with children. The family lived at Ramathaim-zophim, and, as the law required, there was a yearly journey to offer sacrifices at the sole altar of Jehovah, which was then at Shiloh. Women were not bound to attend; but pious females free from the cares of a family often did so, especially when the husband was a Levite. Every time that Hannah went there childless she declined to take part in the festivities which followed the sacrifices, being then, as it seems, peculiarly exposed to the taunts of her rival. At length, on one of these visits to Shiloh, while she prayed before returning home, she vowed to devote to the Almighty the son which she so earnestly desired (Num. xxx. 1, sq.). It seems to have been the custom to pronounce all vows at the holy place in a loud voice, under the immediate notice of the priest (Deut. xxiii. 23; Ps.

xxvi. 14); but Hannah prayed in a low tone, so that her lips only were seen to move. This attracted the attention of the high-priest, Eli, who suspected that she had taken too much wine at the recent feast. From this suspicion Hannah easily vindicated herself, and returned home with a lightened heart. Before the end of that year Hannah became the rejoicing mother of a son, to whom the name of Samuel was given, and who was from his birth placed under the obligations of that condition of Nazariteship to which his mother had vowed him. B.C. 1171.

Hannah went no more to Shiloh till her child was old enough to dispense with her maternal services, when she took him up with her to leave him there, as it appears was the custom when one already a Levite was placed under the additional obligations of Nazariteship. When he was presented in due form to the high-priest, the mother took occasion to remind him of the former transaction: 'For this child,' she said, ' I prayed, and the Lord hath given me my petition which I asked of him' (1 Sam. i. 27). Hannah's gladness afterwards found vent in an exulting chant, which furnishes a remarkable specimen of the early lyric poetry of the Hebrews, and of which many of the ideas and images were in after times repeated by the Virgin Mary on a somewhat similar occasion (Luke i. 46. sq.).

After this Hannah failed not to visit Shiloh every year, bringing a new dress for her son, who remained under the eye and near the person of the high-priest [Samuel]. That great personage took kind notice of Hannah on these occasions, and bestowed his blessing upon her and her husband. The Lord repaid her abundantly for that which she had, to use her own expression, ' lent to him;' for she had three sons and two daughters after Samuel.

HANUN (*bestower*), son and successor of Nahash, king of the Ammonites. David, who had in his troubles been befriended by Nahash, sent, with the kindest intentions, an embassy to condole with him on the death of his father, and to congratulate him on his own accession. The rash young king, however, was led to misapprehend the motives of this embassy, and to treat with gross and inexpiable indignity the honourable personages whom David had charged with this mission. Their beards were *half* shaven, and their robes cut short by the middle, and they were dismissed in this shameful trim, which can be appreciated only by those who consider how reverently the beard has always been regarded by the Orientals [Beard] (B.C. 1038). When the news of this affront was brought to David, he sent word to the ambassadors to remain at Jericho till the growth of their beards enabled them to appear with decency in the metropolis. He vowed vengeance upon Hanun for the insult; and the vehemence with which the matter was taken up forms an instance, interesting from its antiquity, of the respect expected to be paid to the person and character of ambassadors. Hanun himself looked for nothing less than war as the consequence of his conduct; and he subsidized Hadarezer and other Syrian princes to assist him with their armies. The power of the Syrians was broken in two campaigns, and the Ammonites were left to their fate, which was severe even beyond the usual severities of war in that remote age [AMMONITES; DAVID] (2 Sam. x.; 1 Chron. xix.).

HARA (*mountain*). One of the places to which the tribes beyond the Jordan were carried away by Tiglath-pileser. The word occurs only in a single passage (1 Chron. v. 26). Bochart and Gesenius conjecture that it is a name for the northern part of Media.

HARADAH, a camp or station of the Israelites (Num. xxxiii. 24) [WANDERING].

HARAM. [HOUSE.]

1. HARAN, eldest son of Terah, brother of Abraham and Nahor, and father of Lot, Milcah, and Iscah. He died before his father Terah, which, from the manner in which it is mentioned, appears to have been a much rarer case in those days than at present (Gen. xi. 27, sq.).

HA'RAN, or rather CHARAN, called by the Greeks Charran, and by the Romans Charræ. It was situated in the north-western part of Mesopotamia, on a river of the same name running into the Euphrates. It is supposed to have been so called from Haran, the father of Lot and brother of Abraham; but there appears no ground for this conclusion except the identity of names. Abraham, after he had been called from Ur of the Chaldees, tarried here till his father Terah died, when he proceeded to the land of Canaan (Gen. xi. 31, 38; Acts vii. 4). The elder branch of the family still remained at Haran, which led to the interesting journeys thither described in the patriarchal history—first, that of Abraham's servant to obtain a wife for Isaac (Gen. xxiv.), and next, that of Jacob when he fled to evade the wrath of Esau (Gen. xxviii. 10). The plain bordering on this town is celebrated in history as the scene of a battle in which the Roman army was defeated by the Parthians, and the Triumvir Crassus killed.

Haran still retains its ancient name in the form of Harran, and is only peopled by a few families of wandering Arabs, who are led thither by a plentiful supply of water from several small streams. It is situated in a flat and sandy plain, in 36° 40' N. lat., 39° 2' 45" E. long.

HARE occurs in Lev. xi. 6, and Deut. xiv. 7, and in both instances it is prohibited from being used as food, because it chews the cud, although

204. [Syrian Hare.]

it has not the hoof divided. The hare however does not actually chew the cud, but has incisor teeth above and below, set like chisels, and calculated for gnawing, cutting, and nibbling, and when in a state of repose is engaged in working the incisor teeth upon each other. This practice is a necessary condition of existence, for the friction keeps them fit for the purpose of nibbling, and prevents their growing beyond a proper length. As hares do not subsist on hard substances, but

on tender shoots and grasses, they have more cause, and therefore a more constant craving, to abrade their teeth; and this they do in a manner which, combined with the slight trituration of the occasional contents of the cheeks, even modern writers, not zoologists, have mistaken for real rumination. It follows therefore we should understand the original in the above passages, rendered ' chewing the cud,' as merely implying a second mastication, more or less complete. The act of ' chewing the cud ' and ' re-chewing' being considered identical by the Hebrews, the sacred lawgiver, not being occupied with the doctrines of science, no doubt used the expression in the sense in which it was then understood. It may be added, that a similar opinion, and consequent rejection of the hare as food, pervaded many nations of antiquity.

There are two distinct species of hare in Syria: one, the Syrian hare, nearly equal in size to the common European, having the fur ochry buff; and the hare of the desert, smaller and brownish. They reside in the localities indicated by their names, and are distinguished from the common hare, by a greater length of ears, and a black tail with white fringe. There is found in Egypt, and higher up the Nile, a third species, represented in the outline paintings on ancient monuments, but not coloured with that delicacy of tint required for distinguishing it from the others, excepting that it appears to be marked with the black speckles which characterize the existing species.

HARETH, a forest in Judah, to which David fled from Saul (1 Sam. xxii. 5) [FOREST].

HAROD, a brook not far from Jezreel and Mount Gilboa. The name means ' palpitation,' and it has been suggested that it originated in consequence of the alarm and terror of most of the men who were here tested by Gideon (Judg. vii. 1-3); but this supposition seems very far-fetched, and the name more probably arose from some peculiarity in the outflow of the stream.

HAR'OSHETH OF THE GENTILES, a city supposed to have been situated near Hazor, in the northern parts of Canaan, called afterwards Upper Galilee, or Galilee of the Gentiles [GALILEE]. Harosheth is said to have been the residence of Sisera, the general of the armies of Jabin, king of Canaan, who reigned in Hazor. To this place Jabin himself was pursued and defeated by Deborah and Barak (Judg. iv. 2, 13, 16).

HARP. [MUSIC.]

HART. The word thus translated is AJAIL (it occurs in Deut. xii. 15; Ps. xlii. 1; Isa. xxxv. 6), and differs only by the feminine termination from that rendered ' hind' in many other passages of Scripture. There is, upon the whole, no reason to doubt that the male and female of a species of deer are really intended by these words. It is indeed true that the existence of animals of the deer kind in Asia has been denied, and Cuvier for some time doubted whether any could be found in Africa. Yet, although never abundant where water is scarce, the existence of deer from Morocco and the Nile has now been satisfactorily established, and there are traces of their presence in Syria, where they were probably more numerous formerly than at present. The Cervus Barbatus, or Barbary Stag, is the African species; and an individual of this species was obtained by a friend of the writer in the region east of the Jordan. This species is in size between our red and fallow deer, distinguished by the want of a bis-antler, or second branch in the horns reckoned from below, and for a spotted livery which is effaced only in the third or fourth year. There is also in Asia the Persian stag, or Maral of the Tartar natives, and Gewaze of the Armenians. This is larger than the stag of Europe, has a heavy mane, and is, like the former, destitute of bis-antlers. This species seems, under the name of Soëgur, to extend its habitat to the northern frontier of Syria and Palestine; but taking all circumstances into account, it seems less probable that this should be the 'hart' of Scripture than the *Cervus Barbatus.*

HAVI'LAH. 1. A district in Arabia Felix, deriving its name from the second son of Cush (Gen. x. 7), or, according to others, from the second son of Joktan (Gen. x. 29; comp. xxv. 18). There can be no doubt, however, of the existence of a double Havilah; one founded by the descendant of *Ham,* and the other by that of *Shem.* From Gen. xxv. 18, it would appear that the land of Havilah formed the eastern boundary of the Israelites, and so likewise from 1 Sam. xv. 7, where it seems, moreover, to have been a possession belonging to the Amalekites. 2. A land rich in gold, bdellium, and shoham, mentioned in Gen. ii. 11, in the geographical description of Paradise. Some identify this with the preceding; but others take it to be *Chwala* on the Caspian Sea; and others suppose it a general name for India, in which case the river *Pison,* mentioned as surrounding it, would be identified with the *Ganges.*

HA'VOTH-JA'IR. *Havoth* signifies 'cabins' or 'huts,' such as belong to the Arabians, and a collection of which is regarded as forming a hamlet or village. The district of Havoth-jair (*Jair's hamlets*), mentioned in Num. xxxii. 41, and Deut. iii. 14, was beyond the Jordan in the land of Gilead, and belonged to the half-tribe of Manasseh.

HAU'RAN, a tract or region of Syria, south of Damascus, which is twice mentioned under this name in Scripture (Ezek. xlvii. 16, 18). It was probably of small extent originally; but received extensive additions from the Romans under the name of Auranitis. At present it reaches from about twenty miles south of Damascus to a little below Bozra, including the rocky district of el-Ledja, the ancient Trachonitis, and the mountainous region of Jebel-Haouran. Within its limits are also included, besides Trachonitis, Ituræa or Ittur, now called Jedour, and part of Batanæa or Bashan. It is represented by Burckhardt as a volcanic region, composed of porous tufa, pumice, and basalt, with the remains of a crater on the Tel Shoba, which is on its eastern border. It produces, however, crops of corn, and has many patches of luxuriant herbage, which are frequented in summer by the Arab tribes for pasturage. It also abounds with interesting remains of cities, scattered over its surface, among which are found Greek inscriptions.

HAWK, an unclean bird (Lev. xi. 16; Deut. xiv. 15; Job xxxix. 26). The English name is an altered form of the old word 'fawk' or 'falk.' Western Asia and Lower Egypt, and consequently the intermediate territory of Syria and Palestine, are the habitation or transitory residence of a con-siderable number of species of the order *Raptores,* which, even including the shortest-winged, have great powers of flight, are remarkably enterprising, live to a great age, are migratory, or followers upon birds of passage, or remain in a region so abundantly stocked with pigeon and turtle-dove as Palestine, and affording such a variety of ground to hunt their particular prey—abounding as it does in mountain and forest, plain, desert, marsh, river and sea-coast. We shall here enumerate, so far as our information will permit, the *Falconidæ* of this region, exclusive of those mentioned in other articles [EAGLE; GLEDE; KITE; OSPREY].

205. [Peregrine Falcon.]

Falcons, or the 'noble' birds of prey used for hawking, have for many ages been objects of great interest, and still continue to be bought at high prices. They are consequently imported from distant countries, as central Asia, Iceland, Barbary, &c. Their love of liberty often renders them irreclaimable when once on the wing; and their powers and boldness, independent of circumstances, and the extent of range which the long-winged species in particular can take, are exemplified by their presence in every quarter of the globe. The Peregrine falcon is so generally diffused as to occur even in New Holland and South America.

Next we may place *Falco Aroeris* of Sir J. G. Wilkinson, the sacred hawk of Egypt. This, if it be not in reality the same as, or a mere variety of the Peregrine, should have retained the ancient epithet of *Hierax,* and the hawker's name of *Sacre.* Innumerable representations of it occur in Egyptian monuments.

The Hobby is no doubt a second or third species of sacred hawk, having similar gernonia. Both this bird and the tractable Merlin are used in the falconry of the inferior Moslem landowners of Asiatic Turkey.

Besides these the Kestril occurs in Syria, and the lesser Kestril in Egypt; and it is probable that both species visit these two territories according to the seasons.

To the 'noble' birds we may add the Gerfalcon, which is one-third larger than the Peregrine: it is imported from Tartary and sold at Constantinople, Aleppo, and Damascus. The great birds fly at antelopes, bustards, cranes, &c.; and of the genus *Astur,* with shorter wings than true falcons, the Goshawk, and the Falcon Gentil are either imported, or taken in their nests, and used to fly at lower and aquatic game. The smaller and less powerful hawks of the genus

Nisus are mostly in use on account of the sport they afford being less fatiguing, as they are employed to fly at pigeons, partridges, quails, &c.

HAZAEL (*vision of God*), an officer of Benhadad, king of Syria, whose eventual accession to the throne of that kingdom was made known to Elijah (1 Kings xix. 15); and who, when Elisha was at Damascus, was sent by his master, who was then ill, to consult the prophet respecting his recovery. He was followed by forty camels bearing presents from the king. When Hazael appeared before the prophet, he said, 'Thy son Benhadad, king of Syria, hath sent me to thee saying, Shall I recover of this disease?' The answer was, that he *might* certainly recover. 'Howbeit,' added the prophet, 'the Lord hath showed me that he shall surely die.' He then looked stedfastly at Hazael till he became confused: on which the man of God wept; and when Hazael respectfully inquired the cause of this outburst, Elisha replied by describing the vivid picture then present to his mind of all the evils which the man now before him would inflict upon Israel. Hazael exclaimed, 'But what! Is thy servant a dog that he should do this great thing?' The prophet exclaimed that it was as king of Syria he should do it. Hazael then returned, and delivered to his master that portion of the prophetic response which was intended for him. But the very next day this man, cool and calculating in his cruel ambition, took a thick cloth, and, having dipped it in water, spread it over the face of the king, who, in his feebleness, and probably in his sleep, was smothered by its weight, and died what seemed to his people a natural death (2 Kings viii. 8, &c.), B.C. 885. We are not to imagine that such a project as this was conceived and executed in a day, or that it was suggested by the words of Elisha. His discomposure at the earnest gaze of the prophet, and other circumstances, show that Hazael at that moment regarded Elisha as one to whom his secret purposes were known. In that case, his cry, 'Is thy servant a dog,' &c., was not, as some suppose, a cry of joy at the first view of a throne, but of horror at the idea of the public atrocities which the prophet described. This was likely to shock him more than it would do after he had committed his first crime, and obtained possession of a throne acquired at such a cost.

The further information respecting Hazael which the Scriptures afford is limited to brief notices of his wars with Ahaziah and Joash, kings of Judah, and with Jehoram, Jehu, and Jehoahaz, kings of Israel (2 Kings viii. 28; ix. 14; x. 32; xii. 17; xiii. 3; 2 Chron. xxii. 5). It is difficult to distinguish the several campaigns and victories involved in these allusions, and spread over a reign of forty years; but it is certain that Hazael always had the advantage over the Hebrew princes. He devastated their frontiers, rent from them all their territories beyond the Jordan, traversed the breadth of Palestine, and carried his arms into the states of the Philistines; he laid siege to Jerusalem, and only retired on receiving the treasures of the temple and the palace. The details of these conquests redeemed to the very letter the appalling predictions of Elisha. This able and successful, but unprincipled usurper left the throne at his death to his son Benhadad.

HA'ZAR-MA'VETH, the third son of Jokta, (Gen. x. 26), whose name is judged to have been preserved in the Arabian province of Hadramau [ARABIA].

HAZEL occurs only once in the Old Testament, namely, in Gen. xxx. 37, where it indicates one of the kinds of rod from which Jacob peeled the bark and which he placed in the watertroughs of the cattle. *Luz* is translated *hazel* in the Authorized Version, as well as in several others; in some it is rendered by words equivalent to 'walnut,' but 'almond' appears to be its true meaning; for the same word denotes that tree in the Arabic language [ALMOND].

HAZE'ROTH, the third station of the Israelites after leaving Sinai, and either four or five days' march from that mountain (Num. xi. 35; xxxiii. 17; comp. x. 33) [WANDERING].

HA'ZEZON-TA'MAR. [EN-GEDI.]

HA'ZOR, a city near the waters of lake Merom (Huleh), the seat of Jabin, a powerful Canaanitish king, as appears from the summon sent by him to all the neighbouring kings to assist him against the Israelites. He and his confederates were, however, defeated and slain by Joshua, and the city burnt to the ground (Josh. xi. 1, 10-13; Joseph. *Antiq.* v. 5. 1). But by the time of Deborah and Barak the Canaanites had recovered part of the territory then lost, had rebuilt Hazor, and were ruled by a king with the ancient royal name of Jabin, under whose power the Israelites were, in punishment for their sins, reduced. From this yoke they were delivered by Deborah and Barak, after which Hazor remained in quiet possession of the Israelites, and belonged to the tribe of Naphtali (Josh. xix. 36; Judg. iv. 2). Hazor was one of the towns rebuilt or much improved by Solomon (1 Kings ix. 15), and was one of the fortified places of Galilee which the Assyrians under Tiglath-pileser first took on invading Palestine from the north (2 Kings xv. 29). There is no modern notice of this town.

HEAD. As the head is the topmost part of the human body, it came derivatively to signify that which is highest, chief, the highest in position locally being regarded as highest in office, rank, or dignity: whence, as the head is the centre of the nervous system, holds the brain, and stands above all the other parts, Plato regarded it as the seat of the deathless soul; and it has generally been considered as the abode of the intellect or intelligence by which man is enlightened and his walk in life directed; while the heart, or the parts placed near it, have been accounted the place where the affections lie (Gen. iii. 15; Ps. iii. 3; Eccles. ii. 14). The head and the heart are sometimes taken for the entire person (Isa. i. 5). Even the head alone, as being the chief member, frequently stands for the man (Prov. x. 6). The head also denotes sovereignty (1 Cor. xi. 3). Covering the head, and cutting off the hair, were signs of mourning and tokens of distress, which were enhanced by throwing ashes on the head, together with sack cloth (Amos viii. 10; Job i. 20; Lev. xxi. 5, Deut. xiv. 1; 2 Sam. xiii. 10; Esther iv. 1); while anointing the head was practised on festive occasions, and considered an emblem of felicity (Eccles. ix. 8; Ps. xxiii. 5; Luke vii. 46). It was usual to swear by the head (Matt. v. 36).

The general character of the human head is such as to establish the identity of the human race, and to distinguish man from every other animal. At the same time different families of

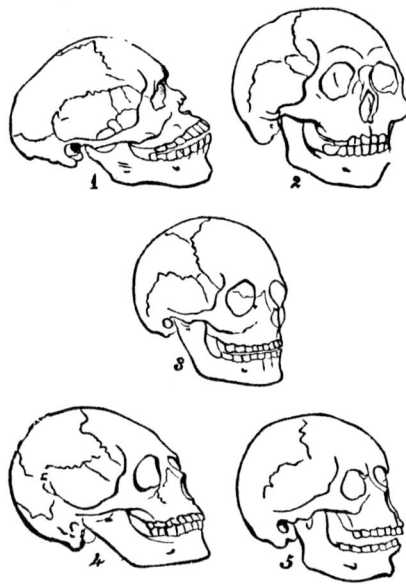

206. 1. Ethiopian; 2. Mongolian; 3. Caucasian; 4. Malay; 5. American.

mankind are marked by peculiarities of construction in the head, which, though in individual cases, and when extremes are compared together, they run one into the other to the entire loss of distinctive lines, yet are in the general broadly contrasted one with the other. These peculiarities in the structure of the skull give rise to and are connected with other peculiarities of feature and general contour of face. In the union of cranial peculiarities with those of the face certain clear marks are presented, by which physiologists have been able to range the individuals of our race into a few great classes, and in so doing to afford an unintentional corroboration of the information which the Scriptures afford regarding the origin and dispersion of mankind. Physiologists have established five classes of heads, corresponding with five great families. 1. The Caucasian family, comprising the nations of Europe, some of the Western Asiatics, &c., have the head of the most symmetrical shape, almost round, the forehead of moderate extent, the cheek bones rather narrow, without any projection, but a direction downwards from the molar process of the frontal bone; the alveolar edge well rounded; the front teeth of each jaw placed perpendicularly; the face of oval shape, straight, features moderately prominent; forehead arched: nose narrow, slightly arched; mouth small; chin full and round. 2. The second is the Mongolian variety. 3. Ethiopian. 4. Malay and South Sea Islanders. 5. American. The description of their peculiarities may be found in Prichard's *Researches into the Physical History of Man*, 2nd edition, vol. i. p. 167, sq.

HEART. All the phrases, more or less metaphorical, in which this word occurs, are rendered intelligible, without detailed examples, when we are told that the heart was, among the Hebrews, regarded poetically not only as the seat of the passions and emotions, as of love, pleasure, and grief, but also of the intellectual faculties—the mind, the understanding. In the original Scriptures, as well as in the English and other translations, the word 'heart' therefore, constantly occurs where 'mind' is to be understood, and would be used by a modern English writer. We say modern, because the ancient usage of the English word 'heart' was more conformable than the present to that of the Hebrews.

HEATH. *Oror*, the word thus rendered occurs in two or three places of Scripture, and has been variously translated, as *tamarisk; tamarin*, which is an Indian tree, the tamarind; *retama*, that is the broom; and also, as in the French and English versions, *heath*, which is perhaps the most incorrect of all, though Hasselquist mentions finding heath near Jericho, in Syria. As far as the context is concerned, some of these plants, as the *retam* and *tamarisk*, would answer very well; but the Arabic name *arar*, is applied to a totally different plant, a species of juniper.

Several species of juniper are no doubt found in Syria and Palestine. Robinson met with some in proceeding from Hebron to Wady Musa, near the romantic pass of Nemela: 'On the rocks above we found the juniper tree, Arabic *ar'ar;* its berries have the appearance and taste of the common juniper, except that there is more of the aroma of the pine. These trees were ten or fifteen feet in height, and hung upon the rocks even to the summits of the cliffs and needles.' In a note the author says: 'This is doubtless the Hebrew *aroer* (Jer. xlvii. 6); whence both the English version and Luther read incorrectly *heath'* (*Bibl. Researches*, ii. 506). In proceeding S.E. he states: 'Large trees of the juniper become quite common in the Wadys and on the rocks.' It is mentioned in the same situations by other travellers, and is no doubt common enough, particularly in wild, uncultivated, and often inaccessible situations, and is thus suitable to Jer. xlviii. 6: 'Flee, save your lives, and be like the *heath* (*oror*) in the wilderness.'

HEAVEN, the state and place of blessedness in the life to come.

As we can have no distinct conception of those joys which never have been and never will be experienced by us here in their full extent, we have of course no words in human language to express them, and cannot therefore expect any clear description of them even in the Holy Scriptures. Hence the Bible describes this happiness sometimes in general terms designating its greatness (as in Rom. viii. 18–22; 2 Cor. iv. 17, 18); and sometimes by various figurative images and modes of speech, borrowed from every thing which we know to be attractive and desirable.

The following are the principal terms, both literal and figurative, which are applied in Scripture to the condition of future happiness.

Among the *literal* appellations we find 'life,' 'eternal life,' and 'life everlasting,' literally 'a happy life,' or 'eternal well-being' (Matt. vii. 14; xix. 16, 29; xxv. 46); 'glory,' 'the glory of God' (Rom. ii. 7, 10; v. 2); and 'peace'

(Rom. ii. 10). Also 'an eternal weight of glory' (2 Cor. iv. 17); and 'salvation,' 'eternal salvation' (Heb. v. 9), &c.

Among the *figurative* representations, we may place the word 'heaven' itself. The abode of departed spirits, to us who live upon earth, and while we remain here, is invisible and inaccessible, beyond the bounds of the visible world, and entirely separated from it. There they live in the highest well-being, and in a nearer connection with God and Christ than here below. This place and state cannot be designated by any more fit and brief expression than that which is found in almost every language, namely, 'heaven,' —a word in its primary and material signification denoting the region of the skies, or the visible heavens. It is there that the highest sanctuary or temple of God is situated, *i. e.*, it is there that the omnipresent God most gloriously reveals himself. This, too, is the abode of God's highest spiritual creation. Thither Christ was transported: he calls it the house of his Father, and says that he has therein prepared an abode for his followers (John xiv. 2).

This place, this 'heaven,' was never conceived of in ancient times, as it has been by some modern writers, as a particular planet or world, but as the wide expanse of heaven, high above the atmosphere, or starry heavens; hence it is sometimes called the *third* heaven, as being neither the atmosphere nor the starry heavens.

Another figurative name is 'Paradise,' taken from the abode of our first parents in their state of innocence, and transferred to the abode of the blessed (Luke xxiii. 43; 2 Cor. xii. 4; Rev. ii. 7; xxii. 2).

Again, this place is called 'the heavenly Jerusalem' (Gal. iv. 26; Heb. xii. 22; Rev. iii. 12), because the earthly Jerusalem was the capital city of the Jews, the royal residence, and the seat of divine worship; 'the kingdom of heaven' (Matt. xxv. 1; Jas. ii. 5); the 'heavenly kingdom' (2 Tim. iv. 18); the 'eternal kingdom' (2 Pet. i. 11). It is also called an 'eternal inheritance' (1 Pet. i. 4; Heb. ix. 15), meaning the possession and full enjoyment of happiness, typified by the residence of the ancient Hebrews in Palestine. The blessed are said 'to sit down at table with Abraham, Isaac, and Jacob,' that is, to be a sharer with the saints of old in the joys of salvation; 'to be in Abraham's bosom' (Luke xvi. 22; Matt. viii. 11), that is, to sit near or next to Abraham [Bosom]; 'to reign with Christ' (2 Tim. ii. 11), *i. e.* to be distinguished, honoured, and happy as he is—to enjoy regal felicities: to enjoy 'a Sabbath,' or 'rest' (Heb. iv. 10, 11), indicating the happiness of pious Christians, *both* in this life and in the life to come.

All that we can with certainty know or infer from Scripture or reason respecting the blessedness of the life to come, may be arranged under the following particulars:—1. We shall hereafter be entirely freed from the sufferings and adversities of this life. 2. Our future blessedness will involve a continuance of the real happiness of this life.

I. The entire exemption from suffering and all that causes suffering here, is expressed in the Scripture by words which denote rest, repose, refreshment, after performing labour and enduring affliction. But all the terms which are employed to express this condition, define (in the original) the promised 'rest,' as rest after labour, and exemption from toil and grief; and not the absence of employment, not inactivity or indolence (2 Thess. i. 7: Heb. iv. 9, 11; Rev. xiv. 13; comp. vii. 17).

This deliverance from the evils of our present life includes—

1. Deliverance from this earthly body, the seat of the lower principles of our nature and of our sinful corruption, and the source of so many evils and sufferings (2 Cor. vi. 1, 2; 1 Cor. xviii. 15).

2. Entire separation from the society of wicked and evil-disposed persons, who, in various ways, injure the righteous man and embitter his life on earth (2 Tim. iv. 18).

3. Upon this earth everything is inconstant, and subject to perpetual change; and nothing is capable of completely satisfying our expectations and desires. But in the world to come it will be different. The bliss of the saints will continue without interruption or change, without fear of termination, and without satiety (Luke xx. 36; 2 Cor. iv. 16, 18; 1 Pet. i. 4; v. 10; 1 John iii. 2, sq.).

II. Besides being exempt from all earthly trials, and having a continuance of that happiness which we had begun to enjoy even here, we have good reason to expect hereafter other rewards and joys, which stand in no natural or necessary connection with the present life. For our entire felicity would be extremely defective and scanty, were it to be confined merely to that which we carry with us from the present world, or were we compelled to stop short with that meagre and elementary knowledge which we possess here. Besides the natural rewards of goodness, there must, therefore, be others, which are *positive*, and dependent on the will of the Supreme Legislator.

In the doctrine of the New Testament positive rewards are considered most obviously as belonging to our future felicity, and as constituting a principal part of it. For it always represents the joys of heaven as resulting strictly from *the favour of God*, and as being *undeserved* by those on whom they are bestowed. Hence there must be something more added to the natural good consequences of our actions, something which cannot be considered as the necessary and natural consequences of the good actions we may have here performed. But, on this subject, we know nothing more in general than this, that God will so appoint and order our circumstances, and make such arrangements, that the principal faculties of our souls— reason and affection, will be heightened and developed, so that we shall continually obtain more pure and distinct knowledge of the truth, and make continual advances in holiness.

Some theologians have supposed that the saints in heaven may be taught by *immediate divine revelations*, especially those who may enter the abodes of the blessed without knowledge, or with only a small measure of it; *e. g.* children and others who have died in ignorance, for which they themselves were not to blame. On this subject nothing is definitely taught in the Scriptures; but both Scripture and reason warrant us in believing that provision will be made for all such persons in the world to come. A principal part of our future happiness will consist, according to the Christian doctrine, in the enlarging and correcting of our knowledge respecting God, his nature, attributes, and works, and in the salutary application of this knowledge to our own moral benefit, to the increase of our faith, love, and obedience.

In the Scripture revelations respecting heaven Christ is always represented as one who will be *personally visible* to us, and whose personal, familiar intercourse and guidance we shall enjoy. Herein Christ himself places a chief part of the joy of the saints (John xiv. xvii., &c.); and the apostles often describe the blessedness of the pious by the phrase *being with Christ.* To his guidance has God intrusted the human race, in heaven and on earth. And Paul says (2 Cor. iv. 6), we see 'the brightness of the divine glory in the face of Christ,' he is 'the visible representative of the invisible God' (Col. i. 15). According to the representation contained in the Holy Scriptures, the saints will dwell together in the future world, and form, as it were, a kingdom or state of God (Luke xvi.; xx. 38; Rom. viii. 10; Rev. vii. 9; Heb. xii. 22). They will there partake of a common felicity. Their enjoyment will doubtless be very much heightened by friendship, and by their confiding intercourse with each other.

1. HE'BER (*one of the other side*), son of Salah, who became the father of Peleg at the age of 34 years, and died at the age of 464 (Gen. x. 24; xi. 14; 1 Chron. i. 25). His name occurs in the genealogy of Christ (Luke iii. 35). There is nothing to constitute Heber an historical personage; but there is a degree of interest connected with him from the notion, which the Jews themselves entertain, that the name of Hebrews, applied to them, was derived from this alleged ancestor of Abraham.

2. HEBER, a descendant of Hobab, son of Jethro, and brother of the wife of Moses. His wife was the Jael who slew Sisera, and he is called Heber the Kenite (Judg. iv. 11, 17; v. 24), which seems to have been a name for the whole family (Judg. i. 16). Heber appears to have lived separate from the rest of the Kenites, leading a patriarchal life, amid his tents and flocks. He must have been a person of some consequence, from its being stated that there was peace between the house of Heber and the powerful king Jabin. At the time the history brings him under our notice his camp was in the plain of Zaanaim, near Kedesh in Naphtali [JAEL; KENITES].

HEBREW OF THE HEBREWS, emphatically a Hebrew, one who was so by both parents, and that by a long series of ancestors, without admixture of Gentile or even proselyte blood.

HEBREWS, EPISTLE TO THE. In the received text this composition appears as part of the Canonical Scriptures of the New Testament, and also as the production of the apostle Paul. But on no subject, perhaps, in the department of the higher criticism of the New Testament, have opinions been more divided and more keenly discussed, than on this. Of those who have rejected the claims of the apostle Paul to the authorship of this epistle, some have advocated those of Barnabas, others those of Luke, others those of Clement of Rome, others those of Silas, others those of Apollos, others those of some unknown Christian of Alexandria, and others those of some 'apostolic man,' whose name is no less unknown. Of these hypotheses some are so purely conjectural

and destitute of any basis either historical or internal, that the bare mention of them as the vagaries of learned men is almost all the notice they deserve. Our limited space will not permit us to enter upon an examination of these theories; we must therefore content ourselves with presenting a condensed outline of the evidence that the epistle was written by the Apostle Paul; and we shall commence with the *internal* evidence.

1. A person familiar with the doctrines on which Paul is fond of insisting in his acknowledged epistles, will readily perceive that there is such a correspondence in this respect between these and the Epistle to the Hebrews, as supplies good ground for presuming that the latter proceeded also from his pen. That Christianity as a system is superior to Judaism in respect of clearness, simplicity, and moral efficiency; that the former is the substance and reality of what the latter had presented only the typical adumbration; and that the latter was to be abolished to make way for the former, are points which, if more fully handled in the Epistle to the Hebrews, are familiar to all readers of the Epistles of Paul (comp. 2 Cor. iii. 6-18; Gal. iii. 22; iv. 1-9, 21-31; Col. ii. 16, 17, &c.). The same view is given in this epistle as in those of Paul, of the divine glory of the Mediator, as the 'image of God,' the reflection or manifestation of Deity to man (comp. Col. i. 15-20; Phil. ii. 6; Heb. i. 3, &c.); His condescension is described as having consisted in an impoverishing, and lessening, and lowering of Himself for man's behalf (2 Cor. viii. 9; Phil. ii. 7, 8; Heb. ii. 9); and His exaltation is set forth as a condition of royal dignity, which shall be consummated by all His enemies being put under His footstool (1 Cor. xv. 25-27; Heb. ii. 8; x. 13; xii. 2). He is represented as discharging the office of a mediator, a word which is never used except by Paul and the writer of this epistle (Gal. iii. 19, 20; Heb. viii. 6); His death is represented as a sacrifice for the sins of man; and the peculiar idea is announced in connection with this, that He was prefigured by the sacrifices of the Mosaic dispensation (Rom. iii. 22-26; 1 Cor. v. 7; Eph. i. 7; v. 2; Heb. vii.-x.). Peculiar to Paul and the author of this epistle is the phrase 'the God of peace' (Rom. xv. 33, &c.; Heb. xiii. 20). It is worthy of remark also that the momentous question of a man's personal acceptance with God is answered in this epistle in the same peculiar way as in the acknowledged Epistles of Paul. All is made to depend upon the individual's exercising what both Paul and the author of this epistle call 'faith,' and which they both represent as a realizing apprehension of the facts, and truths, and promises of revelation. By both also the power of this 'faith' is frequently referred to and illustrated by the example of those who had distinguished themselves in the annals of the Jewish race (comp. Rom. iii. 4; v. 2; Heb. iii. 6; Gal. iii. 5-14; Heb. x. 38; xi. 40). On all these points the sentiments of this epistle are so obviously Pauline, that even the most decided opponents of its Pauline authorship in recent times have laid it down as undeniable that it must have been written by some companion and disciple of Paul. 2. Some of the figures and allusions employed in this epistle are strictly Pauline. Thus the word of God is compared to a *sword* (Eph. vi. 17; Heb. iv. 12); inexperienced Christians are

2 c

children who need *milk*, and must be instructed in the *elements*, whilst those of *maturer* attainments are *full-grown men* who require *strong meat* (1 Cor. iii. 1, 2; xiv. 20; Gal. iv. 9; Col. iii. 14; Heb. v. 12, 13; vi. 1); redemption through Christ is an *introduction* and an *entrance with confidence* unto God (Rom. v. 2; Eph ii. 18; iii. 12; Heb. x. 19); afflictions are a *contest* or *strife* (Phil. i. 30; Col. ii. 1; Heb. x. 32); the Christian life is a *race* (1 Cor. ix. 24; Phil. iii. 14; Heb. xii. 1); a person under the constraint of some unworthy feeling or principle is 'a subject of bondage' (Gal. v. 1; Heb ii. 15), &c. The fact that these and other such like figurative phrases occur only in this epistle and in the acknowledged Epistles of Paul, affords strong evidence that the former is his production, for in nothing does a writer more readily betray himself than by the use of peculiar and favourite figures. 3. Certain marked characteristics of Paul's style are found in this epistle. Paley, in enumerating these (*Horæ Paulinæ*), has laid stress chiefly on the following: A disposition to the frequent use of a word, which cleaves as it were to the memory of the writer, so as to become a sort of *cant* word in his writings; a propensity 'to go off at a word,' and enter upon a parenthetic series of remarks suggested by that word; and a fondness for the paronomasia, or play upon words. In the Epistle to the Hebrews these peculiarities of Paul's style are richly exemplified. 4. There is a striking analogy between Paul's use of the Old Testament and that made by the writer of this epistle. Both make frequent appeals to the Old Testament; both are in the habit of accumulating passages from different parts of the Old Testament, and making them bear on the point under discussion (comp. Rom. iii. 10-18; ix. 7-33, &c.; Heb. i. 5-14; iii.; x. 5-17); both are fond of linking quotations together by means of the expression 'and again' (comp. Rom. xv. 9-12; 1 Cor. iii. 19, 20; Heb. i. 5; ii. 12, 13; iv. 4; x. 30); both make use of the same passages, and that occasionally in a sense not naturally suggested by the context whence they are quoted (1 Cor. xv. 27; Eph. i. 22; Heb. ii. 8; Rom. i. 17; Gal. iii. 11; Heb. x. 38); and both, in one instance, quote the same passage in the same way, but in a form in which it does not agree with the Sept., and with an addition of the words 'saith the Lord,' not found in the Hebrew; thereby indicating that the passage is given in both instances as it was present to the memory of one and the same writer (comp. Rom. xii. 19; Heb. x. 30). *In fine*: The Epistle to the Hebrews contains some personal allusions on the part of the writer which strongly favour the supposition that he was Paul. These are the mention of his intention to pay those to whom he was writing a visit speedily, in company with Timothy, whom he affectionately styles 'our brother,' and whom he describes as having been set at liberty, and expected soon to join the writer (Heb. xiii. 23); the allusion to his being in a state of imprisonment at the time of writing, as well as of his having partaken of their sympathy while formerly in a state of bondage among them (Heb. xiii. 19; x. 34); and the transmission to them of a salutation from the believers in Italy (Heb. xiii. 24); all of which agree well with the supposition that Paul wrote this epistle while a prisoner at Rome.

It now remains that we should look at the ex-ternal evidence bearing on this question. Here we shall find the same conclusion still more decisively supported.

Passing by, as somewhat uncertain, the alleged testimony of Peter, who is supposed (2 Pet. iii. 15, 16) to refer to the Epistle to the Hebrews as the composition of Paul, and passing by, also, the testimonies of the apostolic fathers, which, though very decisive as to the antiquity and canonical authority of this epistle, yet say nothing to guide us to the author, we come to the testimony of the Eastern church upon this subject. Here we meet the important fact, that of the Greek fathers not one ascribes this epistle to any but Paul. Nor does it appear that in any part of the Eastern church the Pauline origin of this epistle was ever doubted or suspected.

In the Western church this epistle did not meet with the same early and universal reception. Notwithstanding the regard shown for it by Clement, the church at Rome seems to have placed it under a ban; and hence Tertullian ascribed it to Barnabas, and others to Luke and Clement, whilst no Latin writer is found during the first three centuries who ascribed it to Paul. In the middle of the fourth century, Hilary of Poictiers quotes it as Paul's; and from that time the opinion seems to have gained ground till the commencement of the fifth century, when it speedily became as general in the Western as it had been in the Eastern churches.

The result of the previous inquiry may be thus stated. 1. There is no substantial evidence external or internal in favour of any claimant to the authorship of this epistle except Paul. 2. There is nothing incompatible with the supposition that Paul was the author of it. 3. The preponderance of the internal, and all the direct external, evidence, go to show that it was written by Paul.

Assuming the Pauline authorship of the epistle, it is not difficult to determine *when* and *where* it was written. The allusions in ch. xiii. 19, 21, point to the closing period of the apostle's two years' imprisonment at Rome as the season during 'the serene hours' of which, as Hug describes them, he composed this noblest production of his pen. In this opinion almost all who receive the epistle as Paul's concur; and even by those who do not so receive it, nearly the same time is fixed upon, in consequence of the evidence furnished by the epistle itself of its having been written a good while after those to whom it is addressed had become Christians, but yet before the destruction of the Temple.

That the parties to whom this epistle was addressed were converted Jews, the epistle itself plainly shows. Ancient tradition points out the church at Jerusalem, or the Christians in Palestine generally, as the recipients. Stuart contends for the church at Cæsarea, not without some show of reason.

Some have doubted whether this composition be justly termed an epistle, and have proposed to regard it rather as a treatise. The salutations, however, at the close, seem rather to favour the common opinion; though it is of little moment which view we espouse.

The *design* of this epistle is to dissuade those to whom it is written from relapsing into Judaism, and to exhort them to hold fast the truths of

Christianity which they had received. For this purpose the apostle shows the superiority of the latter over the former, in that it was introduced by one far greater than angels, or than Moses, from whom the Jews received their economy (i. iii.), and in that it affords a more secure and complete salvation to the sinner than the former (iv.-x.). In demonstrating the latter position the apostle shows that in point of dignity, perpetuity, sufficiency, and suitableness, the Jewish priesthood and sacrifices were far inferior to those of Christ, who was the substance and reality, whilst these were but the type and shadow. He shows, also, that by the appearance of the anti-type the type is necessarily abolished; and adduces the important truth, that now, through Christ, the privilege of personal access to God is free to all. On all this he founds an exhortation to a life of faith and obedience, and shows that it has ever been only by a spiritual recognition and worship of God that good men have participated in his favour (xi.). The epistle concludes, as is usual with Paul, with a series of practical exhortations and pious wishes (xii.-xiii.).

HE'BRON, a town in the south of Palestine and in the tribe of Judah, 18 miles south from Jerusalem, in 31° 32' 30" N. lat., 35° 8' 20" E. long., at the height of 2664 Paris feet above the level of the sea. It is one of the most ancient cities existing, having, as the sacred writer informs us, been built 'seven years before Zoan in Egypt,' and being mentioned even prior to Damascus (Num. xiii. 22; Gen. xiii. 18; comp. xv. 2). Its most ancient name was Kirjath-arba, that is, ' the city of Arba,' from Arba, the father of Anak and of the Anakim who dwelt in and around Hebron (Gen. xxiii. 2; Josh. xiv. 15; xv. 3; xxi. 12; Judg. i. 10). It appears to have been also called Mamre, probably from the name of Abraham's Amoritish ally (Gen. xxiii. 19; xxxv. 27; comp. xiv. 13, 28). The ancient city lay in a valley; and the two remaining pools, one of which at least existed in the time of David, serve, with other circumstances, to identify the modern with the ancient site (Gen. xxxvii. 1; 2 Sam. iv. 12). Much of the life-time of Abraham, Isaac, and Jacob was spent in this neighbourhood, where they were all entombed; and it was from hence that the patriarchal family departed for Egypt by the way of Beersheba (Gen. xxxvii. 14; xlvi. 1). After the return of the Israelites, the city was taken by Joshua and given over to Caleb, who expelled the Anakim from its territories (Josh. x. 36, 37; xiv. 6-15; xv. 13, 14; Judg. i. 20). It was afterwards made one of the cities of refuge, and assigned to the priests and Levites (Josh. xx. 7; xxi. 11, 13). David, on becoming king of Judah, made Hebron his royal residence. Here he reigned seven years and a half; here most of his sons were born; and here he was anointed king over all Israel (1 Sam. ii. 1-4, 11; 1 Kings ii. 11; 2 Sam. v. 1, 3). On this extension of his kingdom Hebron ceased to be sufficiently central, and Jerusalem then became the metropolis. It is possible that this step excited a degree of discontent in Hebron which afterwards encouraged Absalom to raise in that city the standard of rebellion against his father (2 Kings xv. 9, 10). Hebron was one of the places fortified by Rehoboam (2 Chron. xi. 10); and after the exile the Jews who returned to Pales-

tine occupied Hebron and the surrounding villages (Neh. xi. 15).

Hebron is not named by the prophets, nor in the New Testament; but we learn from the first book of Maccabees, and from Josephus, that it came into the power of the Edomites who had taken possession of the south of Judah, and was recovered from them by Judas Maccabæus. During the great war, Hebron was seized by the rebel Simon Giorides, but was re-captured and burnt by Cerealis, an officer of Vespasian. Josephus describes the tombs of the patriarchs as existing in his day; and both Eusebius and Jerome, and all subsequent writers who mention Hebron down to the time of the Crusades, speak of the place chiefly as containing these sepulchres. Among the Moslems it is still called el-Khulil, from the name which they give to Abraham, meaning ' the friend ' (of God).

Since the capture of Jerusalem by Saladin in 1187, Hebron has always remained in the possession of the Moslems. In the modern history of Hebron the most remarkable circumstance is the part which the inhabitants of the town and district took in the rebellion of 1834, and the heavy retribution which it brought down upon them. They held out to the last, and gave battle to Ibrahim Pasha near Solomon's Pools. They were defeated; but retired and entrenched themselves in Hebron, which Ibrahim carried by storm, and gave over to sack and pillage. The town has not yet recovered from the blow it then sustained.

In the fourteenth century pilgrims passed from Sinai to Jerusalem direct through the desert by Beersheba and Hebron, and it continued to be occasionally visited by European travellers down to the latter part of the seventeenth century; but from that time till the present century it appears to have been little frequented by them.

The town of Hebron lies low down on the sloping sides of a narrow valley (of Mamre), chiefly on the eastern side, but in the southern part stretches across also to the western side. The houses are all of stone, high and well built, with windows and flat roofs, and on these roofs are small domes, sometimes two or three to each house. The shops are well furnished, better indeed than those of towns of the same class in Egypt, and the commodities are of a very similar description. The only display of local manufactures is the produce of the glass-works, for which the place has long been celebrated in these parts. Gates are placed not only at the entrance of the city, but in different parts of the interior, and are closed at night for the better preservation of order, as well as to prevent communication between the different quarters.

There are nine mosques in Hebron, none of which possess any architectural or other interest, with the exception of the massive structure which is built over the tombs of the patriarchs. This is esteemed by the Moslems one of their holiest places, and Christians are rigorously excluded from it. At the period, however, when the Holy Land was in the power of the Christians, access was not denied; and Benjamin of Tudela says that the sarcophagi above ground were shown to the generality of pilgrims as what they desired to see; but if a rich Jew offered an additional fee, ' an iron door is opened, which dates from the time of our forefathers who rest in peace, and with a burning taper in his hands the visitor descends into a first cave, which is empty, traverses a second in the same state, and at last reaches a third, which contains six sepulchres, those of Abraham, Isaac, and Jacob, and of Sarah, Rebekah, and Leah, one opposite the other. All these sepulchres bear inscriptions, the letters being engraved; thus upon that of Abraham: "This is the sepulchre of our father Abraham, upon whom be peace:" even so upon that of Isaac and all the other sepulchres.' The identity of this place with the cave of Machpelah has not been called in question.

The court in which the mosque stands is surrounded by an extensive and lofty wall, formed of large stones, and strengthened by square buttresses. This wall is the greatest antiquity in Hebron, and even Dr. Robinson supposes that it may be substantially the same which is mentioned by Josephus, and by Eusebius and Jerome as the sepulchre of Abraham. Besides this venerable wall, there is nothing at Hebron bearing the stamp of antiquity, save two reservoirs for rain water outside the town. As these pools are doubtless of high antiquity, one of them is in all likelihood the 'pool of Hebron' over which David hanged up the assassins of Ishbosheth (2 Sam. iv. 12).

The present population of Hebron has not been clearly ascertained, but it probably amounts to about 5000. Most of the inhabitants are Moslems, of fierce and intolerant character. There are no resident Christians. The Jews amount to about one hundred families, mostly natives of different countries of Europe, who have emigrated to this place for the purpose of having their bones laid near the sepulchres of their illustrious ancestors. They have two synagogues and several schools.

The environs of Hebron are very fertile. Vineyards and plantations of fruit-trees, chiefly olive-trees, cover the valleys and arable grounds; while the tops and sides of the hills, although stony, are covered with rich pastures, which support a great number of cattle, sheep, and goats, constituting an important branch of the industry and wealth of Hebron. The hill country of Judah, of which it is the capital, is indeed highly productive, and under a paternal government would be capable of sustaining a large population. That it did so once, is manifest from the great number and extent of ruined terraces and dilapidated towns. It is at present abandoned, and cultivation ceases at the distance of two miles north of the town. The hills then become covered with prickly and other stunted trees, which furnish Bethlehem and other villages with wood.

HEIFER, RED. [SACRIFICE.]

HEIR. [BIRTHRIGHT; INHERITANCE.]

HEL'BON, or CHELBON, a name which occurs only in Ezek. xxvii. 18, where 'the wine of Helbon' is named among the commodities brought to the great market of Tyre. Helbon is supposed to be identified with Chalybon, an old city of Syria, famous for wine.

Now, it is generally agreed that the ancient Chalybon is represented by the modern Aleppo. Aleppo, styled by the natives Haleb, is situated in N. lat. 36° 11' 25", E. long. 37° 9', and is seventy-six miles from the sea by way of Scanderoon, in a straight line, and ninety miles by way of Antioch. It is one of the few ancient cities of these parts which have retained their ancient importance; and this it owes to its happy position upon the line of the commercial intercourse of Asia Minor and Syria with Egypt, and of Europe and Westernmost Asia with the countries beyond the Euphrates. It has long ranked as the capital of Syria, and as the third, if not the second city of the Ottoman empire. It has suffered dreadfully from earthquakes at different times, and has never recovered the terrible visitation of this kind which it sustained in 1822: the population, which was formerly reckoned above 200,000, is not supposed to reach half that number at present.

HELL, the name given in our Authorized Version of the Scriptures to the place of final punishment for sinners. It is also distinctively indicated by such phrases as ' the place of torment' (Luke xvi. 28); 'everlasting fire' (Matt. xxv. 41); ' the hell of fire, where the worm dieth not, and the fire is not quenched' (Mark ix. 44). The dreadful nature of the abode of the wicked is implied in various figurative expressions, such as ' outer darkness,' ' I am tormented in this flame,' ' furnace of fire,' ' unquenchable fire,' ' where the worm dieth not,' ' the blackness of darkness,' 'torment in fire and brimstone,' ' the ascending smoke of their torment,' ' the lake of fire that burneth with brimstone' (Matt. viii. 12; xiii. 42; xxii. 13; xxv. 30; Luke xvi. 24; comp. Matt. xxv. 41; Mark ix. 43-48; Jude 13; comp. Rev. xiv. 10, 11; xix. 20; xx. 14; xxi. 8). The figure by which hell is represented as burning with fire and brimstone is probably derived from the fate of Sodom and Gomorrah, as well as that which describes the smoke as ascending from it (comp. Rev. xiv. 10, 11, with Gen. xix. 24, 28). To this coincidence of description Peter also most probably alludes in 2 Pet. ii. 6.

The names which in many of the other instances are given to the punishments of hell are doubtless in part figurative, and many of the terms which were commonly applied to the subject by the Jews are retained in the New Testament. The images, it will be seen, are generally taken from death, capital punishments, tortures, prisons, &c. And it is the obvious design of the sacred writers, in using such figures, to awaken the idea of something terrible and fearful. They mean to teach that the punishments beyond the grave will excite the same feelings of distress as are produced on earth by the objects employed to represent them. We are so little acquainted with the state in which we shall be hereafter, and with the nature of our future body, that no strictly literal representation of such punishments could be made intelligible to us. Many of the Jews, indeed, and many of the Christian fathers, took the terms employed in Scripture in an entirely literal sense, and supposed there would be actual fire, &c. in hell. But from the words of Christ and his apostles nothing more can with certainty be inferred than that they meant to denote great and unending miseries.

The punishments of sin may be distinguished into two classes—1. *Natural* punishments, or such as necessarily follow a life of servitude to sin: 2. *Positive* punishments, or such as God shall see fit, by his sovereign will, to inflict.

1. Among the natural punishments we may rank the privation of eternal happiness (Matt. vii. 21, 23 ; xxii. 13 ; xxv. 41 ; comp. 2 Thess. i. 9); the painful sensations which are the natural consequence of committing sin, and of an impenitent heart; the propensities to sin, the evil passions and desires which in this world fill the human heart, and which are doubtless carried into the world to come. The company of fellow-sinners and of evil spirits, as inevitably resulting from the other conditions, may be accounted among the natural punishments, and must prove not the least grievous of them.

2. The positive punishments have been already indicated. It is to these chiefly that the Scripture directs our attention. ' There are but few men in such a state that the merely natural punishments of sin will appear to them terrible enough to deter them from the commission of it. Experience also shows that to threaten positive punishment has far more effect, as well upon the cultivated as the uncultivated, in deterring them from crime, than to announce, and lead men to expect, the merely natural consequences of sin, be they ever so terrible. Hence we may see why it is that the New Testament says so little of natural punishments (although these beyond question await the wicked), and makes mention of them in particular far less frequently than of positive punishments ; and why, in those passages which treat of the punishments of hell, such ideas and images are constantly employed as suggest and confirm the idea of positive punishments.'

As the sins which shut out from heaven vary so greatly in quality and degree, we should expect from the justice of God a corresponding variety both in the natural and the positive punishments. This is accordingly the uniform doctrine of Christ and his apostles. ' The servant who knows his lord's will and does it not, deserves to be beaten with many stripes:' ' To whom much is given, of him much will be required ' (Matt. x. 15 ; xi. 22, 24 ; xxiii. 15 ; Luke xii. 48). Hence St. Paul says that the heathen who acted against the law of nature would indeed be punished; but that the Jews would be punished more than they, because they had more knowledge (Rom. ii. 9-29). In this conviction, that God will, even in hell, justly proportion punishment to sin, we must rest satisfied. We cannot now know more; the precise degrees as well as the precise nature of such punishments are things belonging to another state of being, which in the present we are unable to understand.

HELLENIST. In the New Testament this word seems to be appropriated as the name of those persons who, being of Jewish extraction, nevertheless talked Greek as their mother-tongue; which was the case generally with the Jews in Egypt, Syria, Asia Minor, and Greece ; and in fact through the influence of the Greek cities in northern Palestine (Decapolis), it would appear that the Galilæans from their childhood learned nearly as much Greek as Hebrew. The appellation *Hellenist* is opposed to that of *Hebrew* in Acts vi. 1 : in Acts ix. 29, the reading is not so certain, yet probably it should there also be ' Hellenists,' meaning unconverted Jews.

HELMET. [ARMS; ARMOUR.]

HELPS. In the New Testament it occurs once, viz. in the enumeration of the several orders or classes of persons possessing miraculous gifts among the primitive Christians (1 Cor. xii. 28), where it seems to be used by metonymy, the abstract for the concrete, and to mean *helpers ;* like the words ' miracles,' i. e. *workers* of miracles; ' governments,' that is, *governors,* &c., in the same enumeration. The Americans, it is well known, by a similar idiom, call their servants ' helps.' Great difficulty attends the attempt to ascertain the nature of the office so designated among the first Christians. Many conjectures have been hazarded regarding it; but after all it must be confessed, with Doddridge, that ' we can only guess at the meaning of the words in question, having no principles on which to proceed in fixing it absolutely.'

1. HE'MAN, a person of the tribe of Judah, named with others celebrated for their wisdom, to which that of Solomon is compared (1 Kings iv. 31 ; 1 Chron. ii. 6). The considerations stated under ETHAN will distinguish this Heman from the following, with whom he is sometimes confounded.

2. HEMAN, a Kohathite of the tribe of Levi, and one of the leaders of the temple music as organized by David (1 Chron. vi. 33 ; xvi. 41, 42). This, doubtless, is the Heman to whom the 88th Psalm is ascribed,

HERA'KLES is mentioned in 2 Macc. iv. 19, as the Tyrian god to whom the Jewish highpriest Jason sent a religious embassy, with the offering of 300 drachmæ of silver. There can be little doubt that this Tyrian Hercules is the same as the Tyrian Baal, whose worship prevailed in the reign of Ahab, and was introduced directly from Phœnicia by Ahab's marriage with the Sidonian princess Jezebel (1 Kings xvi. 31).

The power of nature, which was worshipped under the form of the Tyrian Hercules, Melkarth, Baal, Adonis, Moloch, and whatever his other names are, was that which originates, sustains, and destroys life. These functions of the Deity, according to the Phœnicians, were represented, although not exclusively, by the *sun,* the influence of which both animates vegetation by its genial warmth, and scorches it up by its fervour.

Almost all that we know of the worship of the Tyrian Hercules is preserved by the classical writers, and relates chiefly to the Phœnician colonies, and not to the mother-state. The eagle, the lion, and the thunny-fish, were sacred to him, and are often found on Phœnician coins. Pliny expressly testifies that human sacrifices were offered up every year to the Carthaginian Hercules; which coincides with what is stated of Baal in Jer. xix. 5, and with the acknowledged worship of Moloch.

HER'MAS, one of the Christians at Rome to whom Paul addressed special salutations in his Epistle (Rom. xvi. 14). Of his history and station in life nothing is known. By several writers, ancient and modern, he has been reputed to be the author of a work entitled *The Shepherd of Hermas,* which, from its high antiquity and the supposed connection of the writer with St. Paul, has been usually classed with the epistles of the so-called Apostolic Fathers. It was originally written in Greek, but we possess it only in a Latin version (as old as the time of Tertullian), a few fragments excepted, which are found as quotations in other ancient authors. It has been divided by modern editors (for in the manuscript copies there is no such division) into three books; the first consisting of four visions, the second of twelve commands, and the third of ten similitudes. It is called 'The Shepherd,' because the Angel of Repentance, at whose dictation Hermas professes that he wrote the second and third books, appeared in the garb of a shepherd. It is doubtful whether the author really believed that he saw the visions he describes, or merely adopted the fiction to render his work more attractive. Impartial judges will probably agree with Mosheim, that 'The Shepherd' contains such a mixture of folly and superstition with piety, of egregious nonsense with momentous truth, as to render it a matter of astonishment that men of learning should ever have thought of giving it a place among the inspired writings.

HER'MES, the Mercurius of the Romans, was the messenger of the gods, and was equally characterized by adroitness of action and readiness of speech. He was also the customary attendant of Jupiter when he appeared on earth. These circumstances explain why the inhabitants of Lystra (Acts xiv. 12), as soon as ever they were disposed to believe that the gods had visited them in the likeness of men, discovered Hermes in Paul, as the chief speaker, and as the attendant of Jupiter.

HERMOG'ENES and PHYGELLUS, disciples of Asia Minor, and probably companions in labour of St. Paul. They abandoned him during his second imprisonment at Rome, doubtless from alarm at the perils of the connection (2 Tim. i. 15).

HER'MON, a mountain which formed the northernmost boundary of the country beyond the Jordan which the Hebrews conquered from the Amorites (Deut. iii. 8), and which, therefore, must have belonged to Anti-Libanus. Since modern travellers have made us acquainted with the country beyond the Jordan, no doubt has been entertained that the Mount Hermon of those texts is no other than the present Jebel esh-sheikh, or the Sheikh's mountain, or, which is equivalent, Old Man's Mountain, a name it is said to have obtained from its fancied resemblance (being topped with snow, which sometimes lies in lengthened streaks upon its sloping ridges) to the hoary head and beard of a venerable sheikh. This Jebel esh-sheikh is a south-eastern, and in that direction culminating, branch of Anti-Libanus. It is probably the highest of all the Lebanon mountains, and is thought to rival Mont Blanc, though, as Elliot observes, the high ground on which it stands detracts considerably from its apparent altitude, and makes it a less imposing object than that king of European mountains as viewed from the Italian valley of Aösta. Its top is covered with snow throughout the summer, and must therefore rise above the point of perpetual congelation, which in this quarter is about 11,000 feet. It might, perhaps, be safe to add another 1000 feet for the height above that point, making in all 12,000 feet; but we must wait the result of more accurate observations than have yet been made.

HERODIAN FAMILY. Josephus introduces us to the knowledge of the Herodian family in the fourteenth book of his *Antiquities*. He there

tells us (c. i. § 3) that among the chief friends of Hyrcanus, the high-priest, was an Idumæan, named Antipater, distinguished for his riches, and no less for his turbulent and seditious temper. He also quotes an author who represented him as descended from one of the best of the Jewish families which returned from Babylon after the captivity, but adds that this statement was founded on no better grounds than a desire to flatter the pride and support the pretensions of Herod the Great. The times were favourable to men of Antipater's character; and, while he obtained sovereign authority over his native province of Idumæa, he contrived to subject Hyrcanus completely to his will, and to induce him to form an alliance with Aretas, from which he trusted to secure the best means for his own aggrandizement. Having so far accomplished his designs as to make himself the favourite ally of Rome, he obtained for his son Phasælus the governorship of Jerusalem, and for Herod, then only fifteen years old, the chief command in Galilee.

Herod soon distinguished himself by his talents and bravery. The country was at that time infested with numerous bands of robbers. These he assailed and vanquished, and his success was proclaimed, not only throughout Galilee, but in Judæa and the neighbouring countries. This increasing popularity of a member of the family of Antipater alarmed the ruling men at Jerusalem, and they willingly hearkened to the complaints made against Herod by some of the relatives of those whom he had slain. He was accordingly summoned to take his trial before the Sanhedrim: nor did he disobey the summons; but on the day of trial he appeared at the tribunal gorgeously clad in purple, and surrounded by a numerous band of armed attendants. His acquittal was speedily pronounced. One only of the judges ventured to speak of his guilt, and the venerable old man prophesied that, sooner or later, this same Herod would punish both them and Hyrcanus for their pusillanimity.

In the events which followed the death of Cæsar, Herod found fresh opportunities of accomplishing his ambitious designs. By collecting a considerable tribute for Cassius in Galilee, he obtained the friendship of that general, and was appointed to the command of the army in Syria. No less successful with Marc Antony, he overcame the powerful enemies who represented the dangerous nature of his ambitious views, and was exalted, with his brother Phasælus, to the dignity of tetrarch of Judæa. They had not, however, long enjoyed their office when the approach of Antigonus against Jerusalem compelled them to meditate immediate flight. Phasælus and Hyrcanus fell into the hands of the enemy; but Herod, making good his escape, hastened to Rome, where he pleaded his cause and his former merits with so much skill, that he was solemnly proclaimed king of the Jews, and endowed with the proper ensigns and rights of royalty. Augustus, three years afterwards, confirmed this act of the senate; and Herod himself scrupled not to perpetrate the most horrible crimes to give further stability to his throne. The murder of his wife Mariamne, a daughter of Hyrcanus, and of his two sons Alexander and Aristobulus, place him in the foremost rank of those tyrants whose names blacken the page of history. Of the massacre at Bethlehem the Jewish historian says nothing; but it has been well observed that such an event, in a reign marked by so many horrible deeds, and occurring as it did in a small, obscure town, was not likely to obtain a place in the national annals. The reign of Herod, prolonged through thirty-seven years, was in many respects prosperous; and the splendour of his designs restored to Jerusalem, as a city, much of its earlier magnificence.

According to the custom of the times, Herod made his sons the heirs to his kingdom by a formal testament, leaving its ratification to the will of the emperor. Augustus assenting to its main provisions, Archelaus became tetrarch of Judæa, Samaria, and Idumæa; Philip, of Trachonitis and Ituræa; and

Herod Antipas, of Galilee and Peræa. This Herod was first married to a daughter of King Aretas of Arabia; but forming an unholy attachment for Herodias, the wife of his brother Philip, he soon became involved in a course of guilt which ended in his utter ruin. Aretas, to avenge his daughter, sent a considerable army against Herod, whose generals in vain attempted to oppose its progress. The forces which they led were totally destroyed, and instant ruin seemed to threaten both Herod and his dominions. An appeal to the Romans afforded the only hope of safety. Aretas was haughtily ordered by the emperor to desist from the prosecution of the war; and Herod accordingly escaped the expected overthrow. But he was not allowed to enjoy his prosperity long. His nephew Agrippa having obtained the title of King, Herodias urged him to make a journey to Italy and demand the same honour. He weakly assented to his wife's ambitious representations; but the project proved fatal to them both. Agrippa anticipated their designs; and when they appeared before Caligula they were met by accusations of hostility to Rome, the truth of which they in vain attempted to disprove. Sentence of deposition was accordingly passed upon Herod, and both he and his wife were sent into banishment, and died at Lyons in Gaul.

Herod Agrippa, alluded to above, was the son of Aristobulus, so cruelly put to death by his father Herod the Great. The earlier part of his life was spent at Rome, where the magnificence and luxury in which he indulged reduced him to poverty. After a variety of adventures and sufferings he was thrown into bonds by Tiberius; but on the succession of Caligula was not only restored to liberty, but invested with royal dignity, and made tetrarch of Abilene, and of the districts formerly pertaining to the tetrarchy of Philip. His influence at the Roman court increasing, he subsequently obtained Galilee and Peræa, and at length Judæa and Samaria, his dominion being thus extended over the whole country of Palestine.

To secure the good-will of his subjects, he yielded to their worst passions and caprices. Memorable instances are afforded of this in the apostolic history, where we are told that 'He stretched forth his hands to vex certain of the church, and he killed James, the brother of John, with the sword; and because he saw it pleased the Jews, he proceeded further to take Peter also' (Acts xii. 1-3). His awful death, described in the same chapter, and by Josephus almost in the same words, occurred in the fifty-fourth year of his age.

Herod Agrippa, the son of the above-named, was in his seventeenth year when his father died. The emperor Claudius, at whose court the young Agrippa was then residing, purposed conferring upon him the dominions enjoyed by his father. From this he was deterred, says Josephus, by the advice of his ministers, who represented the danger of trusting an important province of the empire to so youthful a ruler. Herod was, therefore, for the time, obliged to content himself with the small principality of Chalcis, but was not long after created sovereign of the tetrarchies formerly belonging to Philip and Lysanias; a dominion increased at a subsequent period by the grant of a considerable portion of Peræa. The habits which he had formed at Rome, and his strong attachment to the people to whose rulers he was indebted for his prosperity, brought him into frequent disputes with his own nation. He died, at the age of seventy, in the early part of the reign of Trajan.

HERO'DIANS, a class of Jews that existed in the time of Jesus Christ, whether of a political or religious description it is not easy, for want of materials, to determine. The passages of the New Testament which refer to them are the following: Mark iii. 6; xii. 13; Matt. xxii. 16; Luke xx. 20. They were associated with the emissaries of the chief priests sent to our Lord with the express but covert design of ensnaring him in his speech, that thus they might compass his destruction. The question they put to him was one of the most difficult—'Is it lawful to pay tribute to Cæsar?' The way in which Jesus extricated himself from the difficulty and discomfited his enemies is well known.

Herod Antipas, Tetrarch of Galilee, was at that time specially the ruler of Jesus, whose home was in that province. The Herodians then may have been subjects of Herod, Galilæans, whose evidence the priests were wishful to procure, because theirs would be the evidence of fellow-countrymen, and of special force with Antipas as being that of his own immediate subjects (Luke xxiii. 7).

Herod's relations with Rome were in an unsafe condition. He was a weak prince, given to ease and luxury, and his wife's ambition conspired with his own desires to make him strive to obtain from the Emperor Caligula the title of king. For this purpose he took a journey to Rome, and was banished to Lyons in Gaul.

The Herodians may have been favourers of his pretensions: if so, they would be partial hearers, and eager witnesses against Jesus before the Roman tribunal. It would be a great service to the Romans to be the means of enabling them to get rid of one who aspired to be king of the Jews. It would equally gratify their own lord, should the Herodians give effectual aid in putting a period to the mysterious yet formidable claims of a rival claimant of the crown.

We do not see that the two characters here ascribed to the Herodians are incompatible; and if they were a Galilæan political party who were eager to procure from Rome the honour of royalty for Herod (Mark vi. 14, the name of king is merely as of courtesy), they were chosen as associates by the Sanhedrim with especial propriety. The deputation were to 'feign themselves just men,' that is, men whose sympathies were entirely

Jewish, and, as such, anti-heathen : they were to intimate their dislike of paying tribute, as being an acknowledgment of a foreign yoke ; and by flattering Jesus, as one who loved truth, feared no man, and would say what he thought, they meant to inveigle him into a condemnation of the practice. In order to carry these base and hypocritical designs into effect, the Herodians were appropriately associated with the Pharisees ; for as the latter were the recognised conservators of Judaism, so the former were friends of the aggrandisement of a native as against a foreign prince.

HERODIAS. [HERODIAN FAMILY.]

HERON (Lev. xi. 19 ; Deut. xiv. 18). The original word *anaphah* is a disputed name of an unclean bird, and which has also been translated kite, woodcock, parrot, and crane. For the first of these see GLEDE ; the second is rare and only a momentary visitor in Palestine ; the third, surely, required no prohibition where it was not a resident species, and probably not imported till the reign of Solomon ; and as the crane, we have already shown it to have been likewise exotic, making only a momentary appearance, and that rarely, in Syria. If the Hebrew name be derived from a word signifying ' to breathe short,' or ' to sniff through the nostrils with an irritated expression,' the most obvious application would be to the goose, a bird not, perhaps, otherwise noticed in the Hebrew Scriptures, though it was constantly eaten in Egypt, was not held unclean by the Jews, and, at some seasons, must have frequented the lakes of Palestine. The heron, though not constantly hissing, can utter a similar sound of displeasure with much more meaning, and the common species is found in Egypt, and is also abundant in the Hauran of Palestine, where it frequents the margins of lakes and pools, and the reedy watercourses in the deep ravines, striking and devouring an immense quantity of fish.

207. [Ardea cinerea.]

HESH'BON, a town in the southern district of the Hebrew territory beyond the Jordan, parallel with, and twenty-one miles east of, the point where the Jordan enters the Dead Sea, and nearly midway between the rivers Jabbock and Arnon. It originally belonged to the Moabites ; but when the Israelites arrived from Egypt, it was found to be in the possession of the Amorites, whose king, Sihon, is styled both king of the Amorites and king of Heshbon, and is expressly said to have ' reigned in Heshbon ' (Josh. iii. 10 ; comp. Num. xxi. 26 ; Deut. ii. 9). It was taken by Moses (Num. xxi. 23-26), and eventually became a Levitical city (Josh. xxi. 39 ; 1 Chron. vi. 81)

in the tribe of Reuben (Num. xxxii. 37 ; Josh. xiii. 17) ; but being on the confines of Gad, is sometimes assigned to the latter tribe (Josh. xxi. 39 ; 1 Chron. vi. 81). After the ten tribes were sent into exile, Heshbon was taken possession of by the Moabites, and hence is mentioned by the prophets in their declarations against Moab (Isa. xv. 4 ; Jer. xlviii. 2, 34, 45). Under King Alexander Jannæus we find it again reckoned as a Jewish city. At the present day it is known by its ancient name of Heshbon, in the slightly modified form of Hesban. The ruins of a considerable town still exist, covering the sides of an insulated hill, but not a single edifice is left entire. The view from the summit is very extensive, embracing the ruins of a vast number of cities, the names of some of which bear a strong resemblance to those mentioned in Scripture.

HEZEKI'AH, son of Ahaz, and thirteenth king of Judah, who reigned from B.C. 725 to B.C. 696. From the commencement of his reign the efforts of Hezekiah were directed to the reparation of the effects of the grievous errors of his predecessors ; and during his time the true religion and the theocratical policy flourished as they had not done since the days of David. The temple was cleared and purified ; the utensils and forms of service were restored to their ancient order ; all the changes introduced by Ahaz were abolished ; all the monuments of dolatry were destroyed, and their remains cast into the brook Kedron. Among the latter was the brazen serpent of Moses, which had been deposited first in the tabernacle, and then in the temple, as a memorial of the event in which it originated : and it is highly to the credit of Hezekiah, and shows more clearly than any other single circumstance the spirit of his operations, that even this interesting relic was not spared when it seemed in danger of being turned to idolatrous uses. Having succeeded by his acts and words in rekindling the zeal of the priests and of the people, the king appointed a high festival, when, attended by his court and people, he proceeded in high state to the temple, to present sacrifices of expiation for the past irregularities, and to commence the re-organised services. A vast number of sacrifices evinced to the people the zeal of their superiors, and Judah, long sunk in idolatry, was at length reconciled to God (2 Kings xviii. 1-8 ; 2 Chron. xxix.).

The revival of the great annual festivals was included in this reformation. The Passover, which was the most important of them all, had not for a long time been celebrated according to the rites of the law ; and the day on which it regularly fell, in the first year of Hezekiah, being already past, the king, nevertheless, justly conceiving the late observance a less evil than the entire omission of the feast, directed that it should be kept on the 14th day of the second month, being one month after its proper time. Couriers were sent from town to town, inviting the people to attend the solemnity ; and even the ten tribes which formed the neighbouring kingdom were invited to share with their brethren of Judah in a duty equally incumbent on all the children of Abraham. Of these some received the message gladly, and others with disdain ; but a considerable number of persons belonging to the *northernmost* tribes (which had more seldom than the others been brought into hostile contact with

Judah) came to Jerusalem, and by their presence imparted a new interest to the solemnity. A profound and salutary impression appears to have been made on this occasion; and so strong was the fervour and so great the number of the assembled people, that the festival was prolonged to twice its usual duration; and during this time the multitude was fed abundantly from the countless offerings presented by the king and his nobles. Never since the time of Solomon, when the whole of the twelve tribes were wont to assemble at the Holy City, had the Passover been observed with such magnificence (2 Chron. xxx.).

The good effect of this procedure was seen when the people carried back to their homes the zeal for the Lord which had thus been kindled, and proceeded to destroy and cast forth all the abominations by which their several towns had been defiled; thus performing again, on a smaller scale, the doings of the king in Jerusalem. Even the 'high places,' which the pious kings of former days had spared, were on this occasion abolished and overthrown; and even the men of Israel, who had attended the feast, were carried away by the same holy enthusiasm, and, on returning to their homes, broke all their idols in pieces (2 Chron. xxxi. 1).

The attention of this pious and able king was extended to whatever concerned the interests of religion in his dominions. He caused a new collection of Solomon's proverbs to be made, being the same which occupy chaps. xxv. to xxix. of the book which bears that name. The sectional divisions of the priests and Levites were re-established; the perpetual sacrifices were recommenced, and maintained from the royal treasure; the stores of the temple were once more filled by the offerings of the people, and the times of Solomon and Jehoshaphat seemed to have returned (2 Chron. xxxi.).

This great work having been accomplished and consolidated (2 Kings xvii. 7, &c.), Hezekiah applied himself to repair the calamities, as he had repaired the crimes, of his father's government. He took arms, and recovered the cities of Judah which the Philistines had seized. Encouraged by this success, he ventured to withhold the tribute which his father had paid to the Assyrian king; and this act, which the result shows to have been imprudent, drew upon the country the greatest calamities of his reign. Only a few years before, namely, in the fourth of his reign, the Assyrians had put an end to the kingdom of Israel and sent the ten tribes into exile; but had abstained from molesting Hezekiah, as he was already their tributary. Seeing his country invaded on all sides by the Assyrian forces under Sennacherib, and Lachish, a strong place which covered Jerusalem, on the point of falling into their hands, Hezekiah, not daring to meet them in the field, occupied himself in all necessary preparations for a protracted defence of Jerusalem, in hope of assistance from Egypt, with which country he had contracted an alliance (Isa. xxx 1-7). Such alliances were not favoured by the Divine sovereign of Israel and his prophets, and no good ever came of them. But this alliance did not render the good king unmindful of his true source of strength; for in quieting the alarms of the people he directed their attention to the consideration that they in fact had more of power and strength in the divine protection than the Assyrian king possessed in all his host. Nevertheless, Hezekiah was himself distrustful of the course he had taken, and at length, to avert the calamities of war, sent to the Assyrian king offers of submission. Sennacherib, who was anxious to proceed against Egypt, consented to withdraw his forces on the payment of three hundred talents of silver and thirty talents of gold; which the king was not able to raise without exhausting both his own treasury and that of the temple, and stripping off the gold with which the doors and pillars of the Lord's house were overlaid (2 Kings xviii. 7-16).

But after he had received the silver and gold, the Assyrian king broke faith with Hezekiah, and continued to prosecute his warlike operations. While he employed himself in taking the fortresses of Judæa, which it was important to secure before he marched against Egypt, he sent three of his generals, Rabshakeh, Tartan, and Rabsaris, with part of his forces, to threaten Jerusalem with a siege unless it were surrendered, and the inhabitants submitted to be sent into Assyria; and this summons was delivered in language highly insulting not only to the king and people, but to the God they worshipped. When the terms of the summons were made known to Hezekiah, he gathered courage from the conviction that God would not fail to vindicate the honour of his insulted name. In this conviction he was confirmed by the prophet Isaiah, who, in the Lord's name, promised the utter discomfiture and overthrow of the blasphemous Assyrian: 'Lo, I will send a blast upon him, and he shall hear a rumour, and shall return to his own land, and I will cause him to die by the sword in his own land' (2 Kings xix. 7). The rumour which Sennacherib heard was of the advance of Tirhakah the Ethiopian to the aid of the Egyptians, with a force which the Assyrians did not deem it prudent to meet; but, before withdrawing to his own country, Sennacherib sent a threatening letter to Hezekiah, designed to check the gladness which his retirement was likely to produce. But that very night the predicted blast—probably the hot pestilential south wind—smote 180,000 men in the camp of the Assyrians, and released the men of Judah from all their fears (2 Kings xviii. 17-37; xix. 1-34; 2 Chron. xxxii. 1-23; Isa. xxxvi. 37).

It was in the same year, and while Jerusalem was still threatened by the Assyrians, that Hezekiah fell sick of the plague; and the aspect which the plague-boil assumed assured him that he must die. In this he was confirmed by Isaiah, who warned him that his end approached. The love of life, the condition of the country—the Assyrians being present in it, and the throne of David without an heir—caused him to grieve at this doom, and to pray earnestly that he might be spared. And his prayer was heard in heaven. The prophet returned with the assurance that in three days he should recover, and that fifteen additional years of life should be given to him. This communication was altogether so extraordinary, that the king required some token by which his belief might be justified; and accordingly the 'sign' which he required was granted to him. The shadow of the sun went back upon the dial of Ahaz the ten degrees it had gone down [DIAL]. This was a marvel greater than that of the cure which the king distrusted; for there is no known principle of astronomy or natural philosophy by which such a result could be produced. A cataplasm of figs was then applied to the plague-boil, under the direction of the prophet, and on the third day, as foretold, the king recovered (2 Kings xx. 1-11; 2 Chron. xxxii. 24-26; Isa. xxxviii.). [PLAGUE.]

The destruction of the Assyrians drew the attention of foreign courts for a time towards Judæa, and caused the facts connected with Hezekiah's recovery, and the retrogression of the shadow on the dial, to be widely known. Among others, Merodach Baladan, king of Babylon, sent ambassadors with presents to make inquiries into those matters, and to congratulate the king on his recovery. Since the time of Solomon the appearance of such embassies from distant parts had been rare at Jerusalem; and the king, in the pride of his heart, made a somewhat ostentatious display to Baladan's ambassadors of all his treasures, which he had probably recovered from the Assyrians, and much increased with their spoil. Josephus (*Antiq.* x. 2. 2) says that one of the objects of the embassy was to form an alliance with Hezekiah against the Assyrian empire; and if so, his readiness to enter into an alliance adverse to the theocratical policy, and his desire to magnify his own importance in the eyes of the king of Babylon, probably furnished the ground of the divine disapprobation with which his conduct in this matter was regarded. He was reprimanded by the prophet Isaiah, who revealed to him the mysteries of the future, so far as to apprise him that all these treasures should hereafter be in the possession of the Babylonians, and his family and people exiles in the land from which these ambassadors came. This intimation was received by the king with his usual submission to the will of God; and he was content to know that these evils were not to be inflicted in his own days. He has sometimes been blamed for this seeming indifference to the fate of his successors; but it is to be borne in mind that at this time he had no children. This was in the fourteenth year of his reign, and Manasseh, his successor, was not born till three years afterwards (2 Kings xx. 12-19; 2 Chron. xxxii. 31; Isa. xxxix.). The rest of Hezekiah's life appears to have been peaceable and prosperous. No man before or since ever lived under the certain knowledge of the precise length of the span of life before him. When the fifteen years had expired, Hezekiah was gathered to his fathers, after a reign of twenty-nine years. He died sincerely lamented by all his people, and the public respect for his character and memory was testified by his corpse being placed in the highest niche of the royal sepulchre (2 Kings xx. 20, 21; 2 Chron. xxxii. 32, 33).

HI'EL (*God liveth*), a native of Beth-el, who rebuilt Jericho, above 500 years after its destruction by the Israelites, and who, in so doing, incurred the effects of the imprecation pronounced by Joshua (1 Kings xvi. 34):
Accursed the man in the sight of Jehovah,
Who shall arise and build this city, even Jericho;
With the loss of his first-born shall he found it,
And with the loss of his youngest shall he fix its
    gates (Josh. vi. 26).

HIERAP'OLIS, a city of Phrygia, not far from Colossæ and Laodicea, where there was a Christian church under the charge of Epaphros, as early as the time of St. Paul, who commends him for his fidelity and zeal (Colos. iv. 12, 13). The place is visible from the theatre at Laodicea, from which it is five miles distant northward.

The place now bears the name of Pamluck-kale (Cotton-castle), from the white appearance of the cliffs of the mountain on the lower summit, or rather an extended terrace, on which the ruins are situated. It owed its celebrity, and probably the sanctity indicated by its ancient name (Holy City), to its very remarkable springs of mineral water, the singular effects of which, in the formation of stalactites and incrustations by its deposits, are shown in the accounts of Pococke and Chandler, to have been accurately described by Strabo. A great number and variety of sepulchres are found in the different approaches to the site, which on one side is sufficiently defended by the precipices overlooking the valleys of the Lycus and Mæander, while on the other sides the town walls are still observable. The magnificent ruins clearly attest the ancient importance of the place.

HIGH PLACES AND GROVES. As high places and groves are almost constantly associated in Scripture, it seems undesirable to separate them in our consideration.

By 'high places' we are content to understand natural or artificial eminences, where worship by sacrifice or offering was made, usually upon an altar erected thereon.

By a 'grove' we understand a plantation of trees around a spot in the open air set apart for worship and other sacred services, and therefore around or upon the 'high places' which were set apart for the same purposes.

We find traces of the custom of worshipping in groves and upon high places so soon *after* the deluge, that it is probable they existed *prior* to that event. It appears that the first altar after the deluge was built by Noah upon the mountain on which the ark rested (Gen. viii. 20). Abraham, on entering the Promised Land, built an altar upon a mountain between Bethel and Hai (xii. 7, 8). At Beersheba he planted a grove, and called there upon the name of the everlasting God (Gen. xxi. 33). The same patriarch was required to travel to the mount Moriah, and there to offer up his son Isaac (xxii. 2, 4). It was upon a mountain in Gilead that Jacob and Laban offered sacrifices before they parted in peace (xxxi. 54). In fact, such seem to have been the general places of worship in those times; nor does any notice of a temple, or other covered or enclosed building for that purpose, occur. Thus far all seems clear and intelligible. There is no reason in the mere nature of things why a hill or a grove should be an objectionable, or, indeed, why it should not be a very suitable, place for worship. Yet by the time the Israelites returned from Egypt, some corrupting change had taken place, which caused them to be repeatedly and strictly enjoined to overthrow and destroy the high places and groves of the Cannanites wherever they found them (Exod. xxxiv. 13; Deut. vii. 5; xii. 2, 3). That they were not themselves to worship the Lord on high places or in groves is implied in the fact that they were to have but one altar for regular and constant sacrifice; and it was expressly enjoined that near this sole altar no trees should be planted (Deut. xvi. 21).

It is possible that the Canaanites had not yet fallen into rank idolatry in the time of Abraham —at least, not into such idolatries as defiled the very places in which they worshipped. We know, at all events, that their iniquity was not full in those earlier times, but that when the Israelites invaded the land their iniquity was full to over-flowing. As included in this, we may with toler-able certainty infer that their religion had become so grossly erroneous and impure, that it was need-ful to place under ban even their places of wor-ship, which might otherwise bring the Israelites into danger by the associations which had become connected with them.

The great object of the law was to attach the Israelites to the worship of the One Jehovah, the Creator of heaven and earth, and to preserve them from the polytheism into which the nations had fallen. Now it is certain that the Canaanites had become polytheistic, and, consequently, that their high places and groves were dedicated to different gods. By continuing or adopting the use of this custom, the Israelites would infallibly have fallen into the same notions.

The groves which ancient usage had esta-blished around the places of sacrifice for the sake of shade and seclusion, idolatry preserved not only for the same reasons, but because they were found convenient for the celebration of the rites and mysteries, often obscene and abominable, which were gradually superadded. Then the presence of a grove of a particular species of tree at the principal seat of the worship of a particular god, would occasion trees of the same kind to be planted at other seats of the same worship; whence that kind of tree came to be regarded as specially appropriate to the particular idol; and, in pro-cess of time, there was no important tree which had not become the property of some god or goddess, so that every stranger who passed by a sacred grove could determine by the species of tree of which it was composed to what God the high place, altar, or temple with which it was con-nected belonged.

This statement of the notions connected with religious worship in high places and in groves seems amply to support the view we have taken as to the nature of the dangers which the prohi-bition of it was designed to obviate. The expla-nation as to the special appropriation of trees to particular gods alone suffices to throw a flood of light upon the injunction to cut down the sacred groves of the Canaanites; seeing that while these groves remained, it would be impossible to dis-sociate the idea of the god to which the trees had been consecrated; and the disgraceful orgies which were celebrated under their obscure shade, would alone suffice to explain the same injunc-tion on the ground of the holy abhorrence with which the scene of such abominations must be re-garded by One who is of purer eyes than to behold iniquity.

The injunctions, however, respecting the high places and groves were very imperfectly obeyed by the Israelites; and their inveterate attachment to this mode of worship was such that even pious kings, who opposed idolatry by all the means in their power, dared not abolish the high places at which the Lord was worshipped. And it appears

to us likely, that this toleration of an acknow-ledged irregularity arose from the indisposition of the people living at a distance from the temple to be confined to the altar which existed there; to their determination to have places nearer home for the chief acts of their religion—sacrifice and offering; and to the apprehension of the kings that if they were prevented from having places for offerings to the Lord in their own neighbour-hood, they would make the offerings to idols. This view of the case seems to be strongly con-firmed by the fact that we hear no more of this proneness to worship in high places and in groves after synagogues and regular religious services had been established in the towns and gave suf-ficient operation to the disposition among men to create a local interest in religious observances.

HIGH-PRIEST. [PRIESTS.]

HILKI'AH. Several persons of this name occur in Scripture, of whom the following are the chief: 1. The father of Jeremiah (Jer. i. 1). 2. A high-priest in the reign of Josias (2 Kings xxii. 4, 8, 10). 3. The father of Eliakim (2 Kings xviii. 18, 26; Isa. xxii. 20).

HIN, a Hebrew liquid measure [WEIGHTS AND MEASURES].

HIND (Gen. xlix. 21; 2 Sam. xxii. 34; Job xxxix. 1; Ps. xviii. 33, &c.), the female of the hart or stag, doe being the female of the fallow-deer, and roe being sometimes used for that of the roebuck. All the females of the *Cervidæ*, with the exception of the reindeer, are hornless. It may be remarked that the emendation of Bochart on the version of Gen. xlix. 21, where for ' Naph-thali is a hind let loose, he giveth goodly words,' he, by a small change in the punctuation of the original, proposes to read ' Naphthali is a spread-ing tree, shooting forth beautiful branches,' re-stores the text to a consistent meaning, agreeing with the Sept., the Chaldee paraphrase, and the Arabic version. [HART.]

HIN'NOM, or rather Ben-Hinnom, an unknown person, whose name was given to the valley which bounds Jerusalem on the north, below Mount Zion, and which in Scripture is often mentioned in connection with the horrid rites of Moloch, which under idolatrous kings were there celebra-ted (Josh. xv. 8; xviii. 16; Neh. xi. 30; Jer. vii. 31; xix. 2). When Josiah overthrew this idolatry, he defiled the valley by casting into it the bones of the dead, the greatest of all pollu-tions among the Hebrews: and from that time it became the common jakes of Jerusalem, into which all refuse of the city was cast, and where the combustible portions of that refuse were con-sumed by fire. Hence it came to be regarded as a sort of type of hell, the Gehenna of the New Testament being no other than the name of this valley of Hinnom (Ge-Hinnom); see Matt. v. 22, sq.; Mark ix. 43; Luke vii. 5; John iii. 6.

1. HI'RAM, king of Tyre, at the commencement of David's reign. He sent an embassy to felicitate David on his accession, which led to an alliance, or strengthened a previous friendship between them. It seems that the dominion of this prince extended over the western slopes of Lebanon; and when David built himself a palace, Hiram materially assisted the work by sending cedar-wood from Lebanon, and able workmen to Jerusalem (2 Sam. v. 11; 1 Chron. xiv. 1), B.C. 1055.

2. HIRAM, king of Tyre, son of Abibaal, and grandson of the Hiram who was contemporary with David, in the last years of whose reign he ascended the throne of Tyre. Following his grandfather's example, he sent to Jerusalem an embassy of condolence and congratulation when David died and Solomon succeeded, and contracted with the new king a more intimate alliance than ever before or after existed between a Hebrew king and a foreign prince. The alliance seems to have been very substantially beneficial to both parties, and without it Solomon would scarcely have been able to realise all the great designs he had in view. In consideration of large quantities of corn, wine, and oil, furnished by Solomon, the king of Tyre agreed to supply from Lebanon the timber required for the temple, to float it along the coast, and deliver it at Joppa, which was the port of Jerusalem (1 Kings v. 1, sq.; ix. 10, sq.; 1 Chron. ii. 3, sq.). The vast commerce of Tyre made gold very plentiful there; and Hiram supplied no less than 500 talents to Solomon for the ornamental works of the temple, and received in return twenty towns in Galilee; which, when he came to inspect them, pleased him so little, that he applied to them a name of contempt, and restored them to the Jewish king (2 Chron. viii. 2) [CABUL]. It does not, however, appear that the good understanding between the two kings was broken by this unpleasant circumstance; for it was after this that Hiram suggested, or at least took part in, Solomon's traffic to the Eastern seas—which certainly could not have been undertaken by the Hebrew king without his assistance in providing ships and experienced mariners (1 Kings ix. 27; x. 11, &c.; 2 Chron. viii. 18; ix. 10, &c.), B.C. 1007 [OPHIR; SOLOMON; PHŒNICIANS].

3. HIRAM, or HURAM, son of a widow of the tribe of Dan, and of a Tyrian father. He was sent by the king of the same name to execute the principal works of the interior of the temple, and the various utensils required for the sacred services. It is probable that he was selected for this purpose by the king from among others equally gifted, in the notion that his half Hebrew blood would render him the more acceptable at Jerusalem.

HIT'TITES, or children of Heth, one of the tribes of Canaanites which occupied Palestine before the Israelites (Gen. xv. 20; Exod. iii. 8; xxiii. 23). They lived in and about Hebron; and Abraham, when he abode in that neighbourhood, was treated by them with respect and consideration (Gen. xxiii. 3-7, 11, 12). This intimacy led to Esau's marriage with two women of this nation, to the grief and annoyance of his parents (Gen. xxvi. 34, 35; xxxvi. 2). The Hittites are described in Num. xiii. 29, along with the Amorites, as 'dwelling in the mountains,' that is, in what were afterwards called 'the mountains of Judah,' of which Hebron was the chief town. Uriah, who had the high honour of being one of David's thirty 'worthies,' is called a Hittite (2 Sam. xi. 3, 6; 1 Kings ix. 20). He was, doubtless, a proselyte, and probably descended from several generations of proselytes; but the fact shows that Canaanitish blood was in itself no bar to advancement in the court and army of David. Solomon subjected the remaining Hittites to the same tribute of bond-service as the other remnants of the Canaanite nations (1 Kings ix. 20). Of all these the Hittites appear to have been the most important, and to have been under a king of their own: for 'the kings of the Hittites' are, in 1 Kings x. 29, coupled with the kings of Syria as purchasers of the chariots which Solomon imported from Egypt. The Hittites were still present in Palestine as a distinct people after the Exile, and are named among the alien tribes with whom the returned Israelites contracted those marriages which Ezra urged, and Nehemiah compelled, them to dissolve (Ezra ix. 1, &c.; comp. Neh. xiii. 23-28). After this we hear no more of the Hittites, who probably lost their national identity by intermixture with the neighbouring tribes or nations.

HI'VITES, one of the nations of Canaan which occupied Palestine before the Israelites (Gen. x. 17; Exod. iii. 8, 17; xxiii. 23; Josh. iii. 10). They occupied the northern and north-eastern part of the country. In Judg iii. 3, it is stated that 'the Hivites dwelt in Mount Hermon, from Mount Baal-hermon unto the entering in of Hamath;' and in Josh. xi. 3, the Hivites are described as living 'under Hermon in the land of Mizpeh.' The 'cities of the Hivites' are mentioned in 2 Sam. xxiv. 7, and, from being associated with Sidon and Tyre, must have been in the northwest. A remnant of the nation still existed in the time of Solomon, who subjected them to a tribute of personal labour, with the remnants of other Canaanitish nations which the Israelites had been unable to expel (1 Kings ix. 20). A colony of this tribe was also found in Northern Palestine, occupying the towns of Gideon, Chephirah, Beeroth, and Kirjath-jearim: and these obtained from Joshua a treaty of peace by stratagem (Josh. ix. 3-17; xi. 19).

HO'BAB, kinsman of Moses and priest or prince of Midian, a tract of country in Arabia Petræa, on the eastern border of the Red Sea, at no great distance from Mount Sinai. The family of this individual seems to have observed the worship of the true God in common with the Hebrews (Exod. xviii. 11, 12).

Considerable difficulty has been felt in determining who this person was, as well as his exact relation to Moses; for the word, which, in Exod. iii. 1, Num. x. 29, Judg. iv. 11, is translated father-in-law, and in Gen. xix. 14, son-in-law, is a term of indeterminate signification, denoting simply relationship by marriage; and besides, the transaction which in one place (Exod. xviii. 27) is related of Jethro, is in another related of Hobab. The probability is, that as forty years had elapsed since Moses' connection with this family was formed, his father-in-law (Exod. ii. 18) Reuel or Raguel (the same word in the original is used in both places) was dead, or confined to his tent by the infirmities of age, and that the person who visited Moses at the foot of Sinai was his brother-in-law, called Hobab in Num. x. 29, Judg. iv. 11; Jethro in Exod. iii. 1; and the Kenite in Judg. i. 16.

About a year after the Exodus he paid a visit to Moses, while the Hebrew camp was lying in the environs of Sinai, bringing with him Zipporah, Moses' wife, who, together with her two sons, had been left with her family while her husband was absent on his embassy to Pharaoh. The interview was on both sides affectionate, and was celebrated first by the solemn rites of religion, and afterwards by festivities, of which Aaron and the elders of Israel were invited to partake. On the following day, observing Moses incessantly occupied in deciding causes that were submitted to him for judgment, his experienced kinsman remonstrated with him on the speedy exhaustion which a perseverance in such arduous labours would superinduce; and in order to relieve himself, as well as secure a due attention to every case, he urged Moses to appoint a number of subordinate officers to divide with him the duty of the judicial tribunals, with power to decide in all common affairs, while the weightier and more serious matters were reserved to himself. This wise suggestion the Hebrew legislator adopted (Exod. xviii.).

When the Hebrews were preparing to decamp from Sinai, the kinsman of Moses announced his intention to return to his own territory; but if he did carry that purpose into execution, it was in opposition to the urgent solicitations of the Jewish leader, who entreated him, for his own advantage, to cast in his lot with the people of God; at all events to continue with them, and afford them the benefit of his thorough acquaintance with the wilderness. 'Leave us not, I pray thee,' said Moses, 'forasmuch as thou knowest how we are to encamp in the wilderness, and thou *mayest be to us instead of eyes;*' in other words, that Hobab might perform the office of a hybeer or guide [CARAVAN]—his influence as an Arab chief, his knowledge of the routes, the situation of the wells, the places for fuel, the prognostics of the weather, and the most eligible stations for encamping, rendering him peculiarly qualified to act in that important capacity. It is true that God was their leader, by the pillar of cloud by day and of fire by night, the advancement or the halting of which regulated their journeys and fixed their encampments. But beyond these general directions the tokens of their heavenly guide did not extend. And as smaller parties were frequently sallying forth from the main body in quest of forage and other necessaries, which human observation or enterprise was sufficient to provide, so Moses discovered his wisdom and good sense in enlisting the aid of a native sheik, who, from his family connection with himself, his powerful influence, and his long experience, promised to render the Israelites most important services.

HOG. [BOAR; SWINE.]

HONEY. In the Scripture there are three words denoting different sweet substances, all of which are rendered by 'honey' in the Authorized Version. These it is necessary to distinguish.

1. *Yaar*, which only occurs in 1 Sam. xiv. 25, 27, 29; Cant. v. 1; and denotes the honey of bees, and that only.

2. *Nopeth*, honey that drops, usually associated with the comb, and therefore bee-honey. This occurs in Ps. xix. 10; Prov. v. 3; xxiv. 13; xxvii. 7; Cant. iv. 11.

3. *Debesh*. This is the most frequent word. It sometimes denotes bee-honey, as in Judg. xiv. 8, but more commonly a vegetable honey distilled from trees, and called *manna* by chemists; also the syrup of dates, and even dates themselves. It appears also sometimes to stand as a general term for all kinds of honey.

We shall here confine our remarks to honey in general, and that of bees in particular, referring for the vegetable honey to MANNA, and for the date-honey to DRINK, STRONG.

It is very evident that the land of Canaan abounded in honey. It is indeed described as ' a land flowing with milk and honey' (Exod. iii. 8, &c.); which we apprehend to refer to *all* the sweet substances which the different Hebrew words indicate, as the phrase seems too large to be confined to the honey of bees alone. Yet the great number of bees in Palestine has been noticed by many travellers; and hey were doubtless still more common in ancient times when the soil was under more general cultivation [BEE; FOOD].

The ' wild honey' which, with locusts, formed the diet of John the Baptist, was probably the vegetable honey, which we refer to MANNA.

Honey was not permitted to be offered on the altar (Lev. ii. 11). As it is coupled with leaven in this prohibition, it would seem to amount to an interdiction of things sour and sweet. Aben Ezra and others allege that it was because honey partook of the fermenting nature of leaven, and when burnt yielded an unpleasant smell—qualities incompatible with offerings made by fire of a sweet savour unto the Lord. But Maimonides and others think it was for the purpose of making a difference between the religious customs of the Jews and the heathen, in whose offerings honey was much employed. The first-fruits of honey were, however, to be presented, as these were destined for the support of the priests, and not to be offered upon the altar.

Under the different heads to which we have referred, the passages of Scripture relating to honey are explained. The remarkable incident related in 1 Sam. xiv. 24-32, requires, however, to be here noticed. Jonathan and his party coming to the wood, find honey dropping from the trees to the ground, and the prince extends his rod to the honeycomb to taste the honey. On this the present writer is unable to add anything to what he has stated elsewhere (*Pictorial Bible*, in loc.), which is to the following effect:—First, we are told that the honey was on the ground, then that it dropped, and lastly, that Jonathan put his rod into the honeycomb. From all this it is clear that the honey was bee-honey, and that honeycombs were above in the trees, from which honey dropped upon the ground; but it is not clear whether Jonathan put his rod into a honeycomb that was in the trees or shrubs, or into one that had fallen to the ground, or that had been formed there.

Where wild bees are abundant they form their combs in any convenient place that offers, particularly in cavities, or even on the branches of trees. In India particularly, and in the Indian islands, the forests often swarm with bees. We have good reason to conclude, from many allusions in Scripture, that this was also, to a considerable extent, the case formerly in Palestine. The woods on the western coast of Africa, between Cape Blanco and Sierra Leone, and particularly near the Gambia, are full of bees, to which the negroes formerly, if they do not now, paid considerable attention for the sake of the wax. They had bee-hives, like baskets, made of reeds and sedge, and hung on the out-boughs of the trees, which the bees easily appropriated for the purpose of forming their combs in them. In some parts these hives were so thickly placed that at a distance they looked like fruit. There was also much wild honey in the cavities of the trees. As to the other supposition, that the honeycomb had been formed on the ground, we think the context rather bears against it; but the circumstance is not in itself unlikely, or incompatible with the habits of wild bees. For want of a better resource they sometimes form their honey in any tolerably convenient spot they can find in the ground, such as small hollows, or even holes formed by animals.

HOOK, HOOKS. Several Hebrew words are so rendered in the English Version.

1. (2 Kings xix. 28), 'I will put my hook in thy nose.' The parallel passage (Isa. xxxvii. 29) the Sept. reads 'I will put my *muzzle*, halter, or noose,' &c. Jehovah here intimates his absolute control over Sennacherib, by an allusion to the practice of leading buffaloes, camels, dromedaries, &c. by means of a cord, or of a cord attached to a *ring*, passed through the nostrils. Job xli. 1 [xl. 25] 'Canst thou draw out Leviathan with a hook? or his tongue with a cord which thou lettest down? Canst thou place a reed-cord in his nose, or bore through his cheek with a thorn?' (*clasp*, or possibly bracelet, &c.). 'Wilt thou draw out a dragon with a hook? Wilt thou bind a band about his nose? Wilt thou fasten a ring in his nose, or bore his lip with a bracelet?' This passage in Job has undergone the following speculations. It has been assumed, that Bochart has completely proved the Leviathan to mean the *crocodile*. Herodotus has then been quoted, where he relates that the Egyptians near Lake Mœris select a crocodile, render him tame, and suspend ornaments to his ears, and sometimes gems of great value; his fore-feet being adorned with *bracelets* (ii. 69); and the mummies of crocodiles, having their ears thus bored, have been discovered. Hence it is concluded that this passage in Job refers to the facts mentioned by Herodotus; and, doubtless, the terms employed, especially by the Sept. and Vulg., and the *third and following verses*, favour the supposition; for there the captive is represented as suppliant and obsequious, in a state of security and servitude, and the object of diversion, 'played with' as with a bird, and serving for the sport of maidens. Herodotus is further quoted to show that in his time the Egyptians captured the crocodile with a hook, and with which he was *drawn* ashore; and accounts are certainly given by modern travellers of the continuance of this practice. But does not the *entire description* go upon the supposition of the *impossibility* of so treating *Leviathan?* Supposing the allusions to be correctly interpreted, is it not as much as to say, 'Canst thou treat *him* as thou canst treat the crocodile and *other fierce* creatures?' Dr. Lee has, indeed, given reasons which render it *doubtful*, at least, whether the leviathan *does* mean the crocodile in this passage, or whether it does not mean some species of *whale*, as was formerly supposed; the common grampus, found in the Mediterranean, the Red Sea, and also in the Nile. [LEVIATHAN.] Ezek. xxix. 4, 'I will put my hooks in thy jaws,' &c.; 'and I will *cause thee to come up out of the midst of thy rivers*,' where the prophet foretells the destruction of Pharaoh, king of Egypt, by allusions

to the destruction, possibly, of a crocodile, the symbol of Egypt. Thus Pliny states, that the Tentyritæ (inhabitants of Egypt) followed the crocodile, swimming after it in the river, sprung upon its back, thrust a bar into its mouth, which, being held by its two extremities, serves as a bit, and enables them *to force it on shore* (comp. Ezek. xxix. 3 4).

2. (Exod. xxvi. 32, 37; xxxviii. 19), 'hooks,' where the Sept. and Jerome seem to have understood the *capitals of the pillars;* and it has been urged that this is more likely to be the meaning than *hooks*, especially as 1775 shekels of silver were used in making them for the pillars, overlaying the chapiters, and filleting them (ch. xxxviii. 28); and that the *hooks* are really the *taches* (Exod. xxvi. 6, 11, 33, 35; xxxix. 33). Yet the Sept. also renders the word 'rings' or 'clasps' (Exod. xxvii. 10, 11; Exod. xxxviii. 17, 19); and from a comparison of these two latter passages it would seem that these hooks, or rather *tenters*, rose out of the chapiters or heads of the pillars.

3. (1 Sam. ii. 13, 14), 'flesh-hook.' This was evidently a trident 'of three teeth,' a kind of fork, &c for turning the sacrifices on the fire, and for collecting fragments, &c. (2) (Is. ii. 4, and elsewhere) 'beat their spears into pruning-hooks.' In Mic. iv. 3, weeding-hooks, or shovels, spades, &c. Joel reverses the metaphor 'pruning-hooks into spears' (iii. 10). (3) Ezek. xl. 43, 'hooks,' which Gesenius explains *stalls* in the courts of the Temple, where the sacrificial victims were fastened: our translators give in the margin 'endirons, or the two hearth-stones.' Dr. Lightfoot, in his chapter 'on the altar, the rings, and the laver,' observes, 'On the north side of the altar were six orders of rings, each of which contained six, at which they killed the sacrifices. Near by were *low pillars* set up, upon which were laid overthwart beams of cedar; on these were fastened rows of *hooks*, on which the sacrifices were hung; and they were flayed on marble tables, which were between these pillars.'

HOPH'NI AND PHIN'EHAS, the sons of Eli, whose misconduct in the priesthood (as described in 1 Sam. ii. 12-17) brought down that doom of ruin and degradation upon the house of Eli which formed the first divine communication through the young Samuel (1 Sam. iii.). Hophni and Phinehas were slain in the battle in which the ark of God was taken by the Philistines, B.C. 1141 (1 Sam. iv. 11). [ELL.]

HOPH'RA (or PHARAOH-HOPHRA), king of Egypt in the time of Zedekiah king of Judah, and of Nebuchadnezzar king of Babylon. He formed alliance with the former against the latter, and his advance with an Egyptian army constrained the Chaldæans to raise the siege of Jerusalem (Jer. xxxvii. 5); but they soon returned and took and destroyed the city. This momentary aid, and the danger of placing reliance on the protection of Hophra, led Ezekiel to compare the Egyptians to a broken reed, which was to pierce the hand of him that leaned upon it (Ezek. xxix. 6, 7). This alliance was, however, disapproved by God; and Jeremiah was authorized to deliver the prophecy contained in his 44th chapter, which concludes with a prediction of Hophra's death and the subjugation of his country by the Chaldæans [comp. EGYPT].

This Pharaoh-hophra is identified with the Apries or Vaphres of ancient authors, and he may be the Psamatik III. of the monuments. Under this identification we may conclude that his wars with the Syrians and Cyrenæans prevented him from affording any great assistance to Zedekiah. Apries is described by Herodotus (ii. 169) as a monarch who, in the zenith of his glory, felt persuaded that it was not in the power even of a deity to dispossess him of his kingdom, or to shake the stability of his sway; and this account of his arrogance fully accords with that contained in the Bible. Ezekiel (xxix. 3) speaks of this king as 'the great dragon that lieth in the midst of the rivers, which hath said, my river is mine own, and I have made it for myself.' His overthrow and subsequent captivity and death are foretold with remarkable precision by Jeremiah xliv. 30); 'I will give Pharaoh-hophra, king of Egypt, into the hands of his enemies, and into the hands of them that seek his life.' This was brought about by a revolt of the troops, who placed Amasis at their head, and after various conflicts took Apries prisoner. He was for a time kept in easy captivity by Amasis, who wished to spare his life; but he was at length constrained to give him up to the vengeance of his enemies, by whom he was strangled.

HOR, a mountain of Arabia Petræa, on the confines of Idumæa, and forming part of the mountain of Seir or Edom. It is only mentioned in Scripture in connection with the circumstances recorded in Num. xx. 22-29. The Israelites were encamped before it, when Aaron was summoned to its top to die there, in the presence of his brother and son, who alone witnessed his final departure [AARON].

The mountain now identified with Mount Hor

208. [Mount Hor.]

is the most conspicuous in the whole range of Mount Seir, and at this day bears the name of Mount Aaron (Jebel Haroun). It is in N. lat. 30° 18', E. long. 35° 33', about mid-way between the Dead Sea and the Ælanitic Gulf. It may be open to question if this is really the Mount Hor on which Aaron died, seeing that the whole range of Seir was anciently called by that name; yet, from its height and the conspicuous manner in which it rises among the surrounding rocks, it seems not unlikely to have been the chosen scene of the high-priest's death. To this may be added that Josephus affirms Mount Hor to have been near Petra; and near *that* place there is certainly no mountain which can contest the distinction with the one now in view. The base of the highest pinnacle of this mountain is in fact but a little removed from the skirts of the city to the westward. The account of it given twenty years since by Captains Irby and Mangles, in their then unpublished volume of Travels, is the best we yet possess, and we therefore present the substance of their description slightly abridged.

'The ascent of the mountain is extremely steep and toilsome. Much juniper grows on it, almost to the very summit, and many flowering plants which we had not observed elsewhere; some of these are very beautiful; most of them are thorny. On the top there is an overhanging shelf in the rock which forms a sort of cavern. The tomb itself is enclosed in a small building, differing not at all in external form and appearance from those of Mahommedan saints common throughout every province of Turkey. It has probably been rebuilt at no remote period: some small columns are bedded in the walls, and some fragments of granite and slabs of white marble are lying about. The door is near the south-west angle, within which a constructed tomb, with a pall thrown over it, presents itself immediately upon entering: it is patched together out of fragments of stone and marble that have made part of other fabrics.

'Not far from the north-west angle is a passage, descending by steps to a vault or grotto beneath. The roof is covered, but the whole is rude, illfashioned, and quite dark. Towards the further end of this dark vault lie the two corresponding leaves of an iron grating, which formerly prevented all nearer approach to the tomb; they have, however, been thrown down, and we advanced so as to touch it; it was covered by a ragged pall.'

It is highly interesting to know what view it was which last greeted the eyes of the dying high-priest from this lofty eminence; and it is the more so from the fact that the region over which the view extends is that in which the Israelites wandered for forty years. Our travellers supply this information:—

'The view from the summit of the edifice is extremely extensive in every direction, and the eye rests on few objects which it can clearly distinguish to give a name to, although an excellent idea is obtained of the general face and features of the country. The chain of Idumæan mountains, which form the western shore of the Dead Sea, seem to run on to the southward, though losing considerably in their height. They appear in this point of view barren and desolate. Below them is spread out a white sandy plain, seamed with the beds of occasional torrents, and presenting much the same features as the most desert parts of the Ghor. Where this desert expanse approaches the foot of Mount Hor, there arise out of it, like islands, several lower peaks and ridges, of a purple colour, probably composed of the same kind of sandstone as that of Mount Hor itself, which, variegated as it is in its hues, presents in the distance one uniform mass of dark purple. Towards the Egyptian side there is an expanse of country without features or limit, and lost in the distance. The lofty district which we had quitted in our descent to Wady Mousa shuts up the prospect on the south-east side; but there is no part of the landscape which the eye wanders over with more curiosity and delight than the crags of Mount Hor itself, which stand up on every side in the most rugged and fantastic forms, sometimes strangely piled one on the other, and sometimes as strangely yawning in clifts of a frightful depth. ..... An artist who would study rock-scenery in all its wildest and most extravagant forms would find himself rewarded should he resort to Mount Hor for that sole purpose.'

HO'REB. [SINAI.]

HOR-HAGID'GAD, an encampment of the Israelites during their wandering (Num. xxxiii. 32, 33) [WANDERING].

HO'RITES, or HORIM, the people who inhabited Mount Seir before the Edomites [IDUMÆA].

HORN, from its primary use for defence in the case of horned animals, came to acquire several derivative meanings, some of which are connected with the illustration and right understanding of holy writ. As horns are hollow and easily polished, they have in ancient and modern times been used for drinking-vessels and for military purposes; and as they are the chief source of strength for attack and defence with the animals

to which God has given them, they serve in Scripture as emblems of power, dominion, glory, and fierceness (Dan. viii. 5, 9; 1 Sam. xvi. 1, 13; 1 Kings i. 39; Josh. vi. 4, 5; 1 Sam. ii. 1; Ps. lxxv. 5, 10; Jer. xlviii. 25; Ezek. xxix. 21; Amos vi. 13). Hence to defile the horn in the dust (Job xvi. 2), is to lower and degrade oneself, and, on the contrary, to lift up, to exalt the horn (Ps. lxxv. 4; lxxix. 17; cxlviii. 14), is poetically to raise oneself to eminent honour or prosperity, to bear oneself proudly. In the East, at present, horns are used as an ornament for the head, and as a token of eminent rank. The women among the Druses on Mount Lebanon wear on their heads silver horns of native make, 'which are the distinguishing badge of wifehood.'

209.

By an easy transition, horn came to denote an elevation or hill (Isa. v. 1); in Switzerland mountains still bear this name, thus, Schreckhorn, Buchhorn. The altar of burnt-offerings (Exod. xxvii. 2) and the altar of incense (Exod. xxx. 2), had each at the four corners four horns of shittim-wood, the first being overlaid with brass, the second with gold (Exod. xxxvii. 25; xxxviii. 2; Jer. xvii. 1; Amos iii. 14). Upon the horns of the altar of burnt-offerings was to be smeared with the finger the blood of the slain bullock (Exod. xxix. 12; Lev. iv. 7-18; viii. 15; ix. 9; xvi. 18; Ezek. xliii. 20). By laying hold of these horns of the altar of burnt-offering the criminal found an asylum and safety (1 Kings i. 50; ii. 28). These horns are said to have served as a means for binding the animal destined for sacrifice (Ps. cxviii. 27); but this use Winer denies, asserting that they did not and could not answer for such a purpose.

HORNET, WASP (Exod. xxiii. 28; Deut. vii. 20; Josh. xxiv. 12; Wisd. Sol. xii. 8, 'wasps'). The question has been raised whether in these passages of Scripture the word is to be taken as literally meaning this well-known and terrific insect, or whether it is to be understood in a metaphorical and figurative sense for diseases, supernatural terror, &c., by which Jehovah 'drove out the Hivites, Canaanites, and Hittites, from before Israel.' Among the moderns, Michaelis has defended the figurative sense. In addition to other reasons for it, he doubts whether the expulsion of the Canaanites could be effected by swarms of hornets, and proposes to derive the Hebrew from a root signifying 'scourges,' 'plagues;' but his reasons are ably refuted by Rosenmüller. In favour of the possibility of such an event, it is observed that Ælian relates that the Phaselitæ were actually driven from their locality by such means; and Bochart has shown that these Phaselitæ were a *Phœnician* people. Michaelis's doubt of the abstract possibility seems very unreasonable, when the irresistible power of bees and wasps, &c., attested by numerous modern occurrences, and the thin and partial clothing of the Canaanites, are considered. It is observable that the event is represented by the author of the book of Wisdom as a merciful dispensation, by which the Almighty, he says, 'spared as men' the old inhabitants of his holy land,' and 'gave them place for repentance.' If the hornet, considered as a *fly*, was in any way connected with their idolatry, the visitation would convey a practical refutation of their error [see Baalzebub, under BAAL]. It may be remarked that the hornet, no less than the whole species of wasps, renders an essential service in checking the multiplication of flies and other insects, which would otherwise become intolerable to man; and that in regard to their architecture, and especially their *instincts* and *habits*, they do not yield to their more popular congener, the bee, but even in several respects greatly excel it.

HORSE (Gen. xlvii. 17; xlix. 17; Exod. xiv. 9, 23, and in many other places; James iii. 3; Rev. vi. 2, &c.). It appears to be substantiated that the horse was derived from High Asia, and was not indigenous in Arabia, Syria, or Egypt. They are not mentioned among the presents which Pharaoh bestowed upon Abraham, and occur in Scripture for the first time when the patriarch Joseph receives them from the Egyptians in exchange for bread (Gen. xlvii. 17), evidently as valuable animals, disposed of singly, and not in droves or flocks, like cattle and asses. They were still sufficiently important to be expressly mentioned in the funeral procession which accompanied the body of Jacob to his sepulchre in Canaan (Gen. i. 9); and for centuries after it does not appear that, under the domestic management of the Egyptians, unless the murrain had greatly reduced them, horses had multiplied as they would have done in a land more congenial to their habits, since only six hundred chariots appear to have pursued Israel (Exod. xiv. 7); even admitting that there were other chariots and horsemen not included in that number. In the sculptured battle-scenes, which are believed to represent victories of Sesostris, or of Thothmes II. and III., over nations of Central Asia, it is evident that the enemy's armies, as well as the foreign allies of Egypt, are abundantly supplied with horses, both for chariots and for riders; and in triumphal processions they are shown as presents or tribute, proving that they were portions of the national wealth of conquered states sufficiently valuable to be prized in Egypt. At a later period the books of Deuteronomy (xvii. 16, for the future kings of Israel are forbidden to possess many) and Joshua (xi. 4) furnish similar evidence of abundance of horses in the plains of Syria; and in Job occurs a description of a perfect war-horse couched in the bold figurative language of inspiration, such as remains unequalled by any other poet, ancient or modern. Though the Israelites had chariots and horsemen

opposed to them in the plain country from their first entrance into the land of promise—as in Judg. iv. 15, where we find Sisera with his chariots of war defeated at the foot of Mount Tabor —yet not being intended to make military conquests beyond the mountain basin and the adjacent territory assigned them, they long remained without cavalry or chariots themselves (Deut. xvii. 16; 2 Sam. viii. 4): they obeyed the divine injunction to abstain from possessing horses, and, to the time of David, hamstrung such as they captured from their enemies. It appears, however, that a small cavalry force was raised by him; and as in all the military operations of Western Asia, there was a tendency to increase the mounted force and neglect the infantry, on the full establishment of royalty, when the Hebrew government acquired a more political structure, the reign of Solomon displayed a military system which embraced a regular body of horse and of chariots, evidently become the more necessary, since the limits of his sway were extended to the shores of the Arabian Gulf, and far into the Syrian desert (1 Kings x. 26). Solomon likewise acted with commercial views in the monopolizing spirit which Eastern sovereigns have been prone to exercise in all ages. He bought chariots and teams of horses in Egypt, and probably in Armenia, 'in all lands,' and had them brought into his dominions in strings, in the same manner as horses are still conducted to and from fairs: for this interpretation, as offered by Mr. Charles Taylor, appears to convey the natural and true meaning of the text, and not 'strings of linen yarn,' which here seem to be out of place (2 Chron. i. 16, 17; ix. 25, 28).

The Tyrians purchased these objects from Solomon; but in the time of Ezekiel they imported horses themselves from Togarmah or Armenia. On returning from the Babylonish captivity, the common possession of horses in Palestine was no longer opposed; for Nehemiah numbers seven hundred and thirty-six belonging to the liberated Hebrews (Neh. vii. 68).

All the great original varieties or races of horses were then known in Western Asia, and the Hebrew prophets themselves have not unfrequented distinguished the nations they had in view, by means of the predominant colours of their horses, and that more correctly than commentators have surmised. Taking Bochart's application of the Hebrew names, the bay race emphatically belonged to Egypt and Arabia Felix; the white to the regions above the Euxine Sea, Asia Minor, and northern High Asia; the dun, or cream-coloured, to the Medes; the spotted piebald, or skewbald, to the Macedonians, the Parthians, and later Tahtars; and the black to the Romans; but the chesnuts do not belong to any known historical race (Zech. i. 8; vi. 2).

Bay or red horses occur most frequently on Egyptian painted monuments, this being the primitive colour of the Arabian stock; but white horses are also common, and in a few instances black, the last probably only to relieve the paler colour of the one beside it in the picture. There is also, we understand, an instance of a spotted pair, tending to show that the valley of the Nile was originally supplied with horses from foreign sources and distinct regions, as indeed the tribute pictures further attest. The spotted, if not real,

2 D

but painted horses, indicate the antiquity of a practice still in vogue; for staining the hair of riding animals with spots of various colours, and dyeing their limbs and tails crimson, is a practice of common occurrence in the East [Ass].

On the natural history of the horse there is no occasion to enter in this place; but it may be proper to notice that the riding bridle was long a mere slip-knot, passed round the under jaw into the mouth, thus furnishing only one rein; and that a rod was commonly added to guide the animal with more facility. The bridle, however, and the reins of chariot-horses were, at a very early age, exceedingly perfect; as the monuments of Egypt, Etruria, and Greece, amply prove. Saddles were not used, the rider sitting on the bare back, or using a cloth or mat girded on the animal. The Romans, no doubt copying the Persian Cataphractæ, first used pad-saddles, and from the northern nations adopted stimuli or spurs. Stirrups were unknown. Avicenna first mentions the *rikiab*, or Arabian stirrup, perhaps the most ancient; although in the tumuli of Central Asia, Tahtar horse skeletons, bridles, and stirrup-saddles, have been found along with idols; which proves the tombs to be more ancient than the introduction of Islam. With regard to horseshoeing, Bishop Lowth and Bracy Clark were mistaken in believing that the Roman horse or mule shoe was fastened on without nails driven through the horny part of the hoof, as at present. A contrary conclusion may be inferred from several passages in the poets: and the figure of a horse in the Pompeii battle mosaic, shod in the same manner as is now the practice, leaves little doubt on the question.

HORSE-LEECH occurs only in Prov. xxx. 15. The horse-leech is properly a *species* of leech, discarded for medical purposes on account of the coarseness of its bite.

Although the Hebrew word is translated ' *leech* ' in all the versions, there has been much dispute whether that is its proper meaning. Against the received translation it has been urged that upon an examination of the context in which it occurs, the introduction of the leech seems strange; that it is impossible to understand what is meant by its 'two daughters;' and that instead of the incessant craving apparently attributed to it, the leech drops off when filled: hence it has been attempted to give a different sense to the Hebrew word, and to render it ' destiny.' But there seems no good reason for altering the received translation. In the preceding verse the writer speaks of ' a generation whose teeth are as swords, and their jaw-teeth as knives to *devour* the *poor* from off the earth, and the needy from among men;' and then, after the abrupt and picturesque style of the East, the leech is introduced as an illustration of the covetousness of such persons, and of the two distinguishing vices of which it is the parent, avarice and cruelty. May not also the ' two daughters' of the leech ' crying, Give, give be a figurative description of the two *lips* of the creature (for these it has, and perfectly formed) which are a part of its very complicated mouth?' It certainly is agreeable to the Hebrew style to call the offspring of inanimate things *daughters*, for so branches are called daughters of trees (Gen. xlix. 22, margin). A similar use of the word is given in Eccles. xii. 4,—' All the *daughters* of

musick shall be brought low,' meaning the lips, front teeth, and other parts of the mouth. It is well remarked by Professor Paxton that ' this figurative application of the entire genus is sufficient to justify the interpretation. The leech, as a symbol in use among rulers of every class and in all ages for avarice, rapine, plunder, rapacity, and even assiduity, is too well known to need illustration.

HOSAN'NA, a form of acclamatory blessing or wishing well, which signifies, Save now! Succour now! Be now propitious! It occurs in Matt. xxi. 9 (also Mark xi. 9, 10; John xii. 13) —' Hosanna to the Son of David; Blessed is he that cometh in the name of the Lord; Hosanna in the highest!' This was on the occasion of our Saviour's public entry into Jerusalem, and, fairly construed, would mean, ' Lord, preserve this Son of David; heap favours and blessings on him !' It is further to be observed that Hosanna was a customary form of acclamation at the Feast of Tabernacles. This feast was celebrated in September, just before the commencement of the civil year; on which occasion the people carried in their hands bundles of boughs of palms, myrtles, &c. They then repeated the 25th and 26th verses of Ps. cxviii., which commence with the word Hosanna; and from this circumstance they gave the boughs, and the prayers, and the feast itself, the name of Hosanna. They observed the same forms also at the Encænia (1 Macc. x. 6, 7; 2 Macc. xiii. 51; Rev. vii. 9) and the Passover. And as they celebrated the Feast of Tabernacles with great joy and gladness, in like manner, on this occasion, did they hail the coming of the Messiah, whose advent they believed to be represented in all the feasts.

HOSE'A (*deliverance*), the first in order of the minor prophets in the common editions of the Hebrew Scriptures, as well as of the Alexandrian and Vulgate translations. We are not, however, to suppose from this that he flourished earlier than all the other minor prophets: by the best computation he seems to have been preceded by Joel, Amos, and Jonah.

The figments of Jewish writers regarding Hosea's parentage need scarcely be mentioned. His father, Beeri, has been confounded with Beerah, a prince of the Reubenites, 1 Chron. v. 6. So, too, Beeri has been reckoned a prophet himself, according to the rabbinical notion that the mention of a prophet's father in the introduction to his prophecies, is a proof that sire as well as son was endowed with the oracular spirit.

Whether Hosea was a citizen of Israel or Judah has been disputed. Various arguments have been adduced to show that he belonged to the kingdom of Judah; but we accede to the opinion that he was an Israelite, a native of that kingdom with whose sins and fates his book is specially and primarily occupied.

The superscription of the book determines the length of time during which Hosea prophesied. That period was both long and eventful, commencing in the days of Jeroboam, the son of Joash, extending through the lives of Uzziah, Jotham, Ahaz, and concluding in the reign of Hezekiah. Uzziah and Jeroboam were contemporary sovereigns for a certain length of time. If we compute from the first year of Uzziah to the last of Hezekiah, we find a period of 113 years. Such a period appears evidently to be too long; and the most probable calculation is to reckon from the last years of Jeroboam to the first of Hezekiah.

We have then at least of Uzziah's reign 26 years.

„	„	Jotham	„ 16	„
„	„	Ahaz	„ 16	„
„	„	Hezekiah	„ 2	„
			60*	

This long duration of office is not improbable, and the book itself furnishes strong presumptive evidence in support of this chronology. The first prophecy of Hosea foretells the overthrow of Jehu's house; and the menace was fulfilled on the death of Jeroboam, his great-grandson. ' This was the word of the Lord which he spake unto Jehu, saying, Thy sons shall sit on the throne of Israel unto the fourth generation; and so it came to pass' (2 Kings xv. 12). A prediction of the ruin which was to overthrow Jehu's house at Jeroboam's death, must have been uttered during Jeroboam's life. This fact defines the period of Hosea's commencement of his labours, and verifies the inscription, which states that the word of the Lord came to him in the reign of Jeroboam, the son of Joash, king of Israel. Again, in ch. x. 14, allusion is made to an expedition of Shalmanezer against Israel; and if it was the first inroad against king Hoshea, who began to reign in the twelfth year of Ahaz, the event referred to by the prophet as past must have happened close upon the beginning of the government of Hezekiah (2 Kings xvii. 5). Data are thus in like manner afforded to corroborate the statement that Hezekiah had ascended the throne ere the long-lived servant of Jehovah was released from his toils The extended duration indicated in the superscription is thus borne out by the contents of the prophecy.

The years of Hosea's life were melancholy and tragic. The vials of the wrath of heaven were poured out on his apostate people. The nation suffered under the evils of that schism which was effected by the craft of him who has been branded with the indelible stigma—' Jeroboam, who made Israel to sin.' The obligations of law had been relaxed, and the claims of religion disregarded; Baal became the rival of Jehovah, and in the dark recesses of the groves were practised the impure and murderous rites of heathen deities; peace and prosperity fled the land, which was harassed by foreign invasion and domestic broils; might and murder became the twin sentinels of the throne ; alliances were formed with other nations, which brought with them seductions to paganism ; captivity and insult were heaped upon Israel by the uncircumcised ; the nation was thoroughly debased, and but a fraction of its population maintained its spiritual allegiance (2 Kings xix. 18). The death of Jeroboam II. was followed by an interregnum of ten years. At the expiry of this period, his son Zechariah assumed the sovereignty, and was slain by Shallum, after the short space of six months (2 Kings xv. 10). In four weeks Shallum was assassinated by Mena-

hem. The assassin, during a disturbed reign of ten years, became tributary to the Assyrian Pul. His successor, Pekahiah, wore the crown but two years, when he was murdered by Pekah. Pekah, after swaying his bloody sceptre for twenty years, met a similar fate in the conspiracy of Hoshea ; Hoshea, the last of the usurpers, after another interregnum of eight years, ascended the throne, and his administration of nine years ended in the overthrow of his kingdom and the expatriation of his people. ' The Lord was very angry with Israel, and removed them out of his sight. So was Israel carried out of their own land to Assyria unto this day' (2 Kings xvii. 18, 23).

The prophecies of Hosea were directed especially against the country whose sin had brought upon it such disasters—prolonged anarchy and final captivity. Israel, or Ephraim, is the people especially addressed. Their homicides and fornications, their perjury and theft, their idolatry and impiety, are censured and satirised with a faithful severity. Judah is sometimes, indeed, introduced, warned, and admonished; but the oracles having relation to Israel are primary, while the references to Judah are only incidental. The prophet's mind was intensely interested in the destinies of his own people. The nations around him are unheeded ; his prophetic eye beholds the crisis approaching his country, and sees its cantons ravaged, its tribes murdered or enslaved. No wonder that his rebukes were so terrible, his menaces so alarming, that his soul poured forth its strength in an ecstacy of grief and affection. Invitations, replete with tenderness and pathos, are interspersed with his warnings and expostulations. Now we are startled with a vision of the throne, at first shrouded in darkness, and sending forth lightnings, thunders, and voices : but while we gaze, it becomes encircled with a rainbow, which gradually expands till it is lost in that universal brilliancy which itself had originated (ch. xi. and xiv.).

The peculiar mode of instruction which the prophet details in the first and third chapters of his oracles has given risen to many disputed theories. We refer to the command expressed in ch. i. 2—' And the Lord said unto Hosea, Go, take unto thee a wife of whoredoms and children of whoredoms,' &c. ; ch. iii. 1, ' Then said the Lord unto me, Go yet, love a woman beloved of her friend, yet an adulteress,' &c. What was the precise nature of the transactions here recorded ? Were they real events, the result of divine injunctions literally understood, and as literally fulfilled ? or were these intimations to the prophet only intended to be pictorial illustrations of the apostacy and spiritual folly and unfaithfulness of Israel ? The former view, viz. that the prophet actually and literally entered into this impure connubial alliance, has found advocates both in ancient and modern times. Fanciful theories are also rife on this subject. Luther supposed the prophet to perform a kind of drama in view of the people, giving his lawful wife and children these mystical appellations. Newcome thinks that a wife of fornication means merely an Israelite, a woman of apostate and adulterous Israel. Hengstenberg supposes the prophet to relate actions which happened, indeed, actually, but not outwardly. Some, with Maimonides, imagine it to be a nocturnal vision ; while others make it

---

* Maurer, in the *Comment. Theol.* p. 284, and more lately in his *Comment. Gram. Hist. Crit. in Proph. Min.*, Lipsiæ, 1840.

wholly an allegory. The first opinion has been refuted by Hengstenberg at great length and with much force. Besides other arguments resting on the impurity and loathsomeness of the supposed nuptial contract, it may be argued against the external reality of the event, that it must have required several years for its completion, and that the impressiveness of the symbol would therefore be weakened and obliterated. Whichever way this question may be solved; whether these occurrences be regarded as a real and external transaction, or as a piece of spiritual scenery, or only, as is most probable, an allegorical description; it is agreed on all hands that the actions are typical.

Expositors are not at all agreed as to the meaning of the phrase rendered 'wife of whoredoms;' whether the phrase refers to harlotry before marriage, or to unfaithfulness after it. It may afford an easy solution of the difficulty, if we look at the antitype in its history and character. Adultery is the appellation of idolatrous apostacy. The Jewish nation were espoused to God. The contract was formed on Sinai; but the Jewish people had prior to this period gone a-whoring. Josh. xxiv. 2-14, 'Your fathers dwelt on the other side of the flood in old time, and they served other gods.' Comp. Lev. xvii. 7, in which it is implied that idolatrous propensities had also developed themselves during the abode in Egypt: so that the phrase may signify one devoted to lasciviousness prior to her marriage. The marriage must be supposed a real contract, or its significance would be lost. Jer. ii. 2, 'I remember thee, the kindness of thy youth, the love of thine espousals, when thou wentest after me in the wilderness, in a land that was not sown.' *Children of whoredoms* refers most naturally to the two sons and daughters afterwards to be born. They were not the prophet's own, as is intimated in the allegory, and they followed the pernicious example of the mother.

The names of the children being symbolical, the name of the mother has probably a similar signification, and may have the symbolic sense of 'one thoroughly abandoned to sensual delights.' The names of the children are Jezreel, Lo-ruhamah, and Lo-ammi. The prophet explains the meaning of the appellations. It is generally supposed that the names refer to three successive generations of the Israelitish people. Hengstenberg, on the other hand, argues that 'wife and children both are the people of Israel: the three names must not be considered separately, but taken together.' But as the marriage is first mentioned, and the births of the children are detailed in order, some time elapsing between the events, we rather adhere to the ordinary exposition. Nor is it without reason that the second child is described as a female.

The first child, Jezreel, may refer to the first dynasty of Jeroboam I. and his successors, which was terminated in the blood of Ahab's house which Jehu shed at Jezreel. The name suggests also the cruel and fraudulent possession of the vineyard of Naboth, 'which was in Jezreel,' where, too, the woman Jezebel was slain so ignominiously (1 Kings xvi. 1; 2 Kings ix. 21). But as Jehu and his family had become as corrupt as their predecessors, the scenes of Jezreel were again to be enacted, and Jehu's race must perish. Jezreel,

the spot referred to by the prophet, is also, according to Jerome, the place where the Assyrian army routed the Israelites. The name of this child associates the past and future, symbolizes past sins, intermediate punishments, and final overthrow. The name of the second child, Lo-ruhamah, 'not-pitied,' the appellation of a degraded *daughter*, may refer to the *feeble, effeminate* period which followed the overthrow of the first dynasty, when Israel became weak and helpless as well as sunk and abandoned. The favour of God was not exhibited to the nation: they were as abject as impious. But the reign of Jeroboam II. was prosperous; new energy was infused into the kingdom; gleams of its former prosperity shone upon it. This revival of strength in that generation may be typified by the birth of a third child, a *son*, Lo-ammi, 'not-my-people' (2 Kings xiv. 25). Yet prosperity did not bring with it a revival of piety; still, although their vigour was recruited, they were not God's people.

The peculiarities of Hosea's style have been often remarked. His style, says De Wette, 'is abrupt, unrounded, and ebullient; his rhythm hard, leaping, and violent. The language is peculiar and difficult.' Lowth speaks of him as the most difficult and perplexed of the prophets. Eichhorn's description of his style was probably at the same time meant as an imitation of it:—'His discourse is like a garland woven of a multiplicity of flowers: images are woven upon images, comparison wound upon comparison, metaphor strung upon metaphor. He plucks one flower, and throws it down that he may directly break off another. Like a bee, he flies from one flower-bed to another, that he may suck his honey from the most varied pieces. It is a natural consequence that his figures sometimes form strings of pearls. Often is he prone to approach to allegory—often he sinks down in obscurity' (comp. ch. v. 9; vi. 3; vii. 8; xiii. 3, 7, 8, 16).

Hosea, as a prophet, is expressly quoted by Matthew (ii. 15). The citation is from the first verse of ch. xi. Hosea vi. 6 is quoted twice by the same evangelist (ix. 13; xii. 7). Quotations from his prophecies are also to be found in Rom. ix. 25, 26. References to them occur in 1 Cor. xv. 55, and in 1 Pet. ii. 10. Messianic references are not clearly and prominently developed. This book, however, is not without them; but they lie more in the spirit of its allusions than in the letter. Hosea's Christology appears written not with ink, but with the spirit of the living God, on the fleshly tables of his heart. The future conversion of his people to the Lord their God, and David their king, their glorious privilege in becoming sons of the living God, the faithfulness of the original promise to Abraham, that the number of his spiritual seed should be as the sand of the sea, are among the oracles whose fulfilment will take place only under the new dispensation.

HOSEA, son of Elah, and last king of Israel. He conspired against and slew his predecessor Pekah, and seized his dominions. 'He did evil in the sight of the Lord,' but not in the same degree as his predecessors: and this, by the Jewish commentators, is understood to mean that he did not, like former kings of Israel (2 Kings xv. 30), restrain his subjects from going up to Jerusalem to worship. The intelligence that Hosea had entered into a confederacy with So, king of Egypt, with the view of shaking off the Assyrian yoke, caused Shalmaneser, the king of Assyria, to march an army into the land of Israel; and after a three years' siege Samaria was taken and destroyed, and the ten tribes were sent into the countries beyond the Euphrates, B.C. 720 (2 Kings xv. 30; xvii. 1-6; xviii. 9-12). The chronology of this reign is much perplexed [see CHRONOLOGY, ISRAEL].

HOSPITALITY. The practice of receiving strangers into one's house and giving them suitable entertainment, may be traced back to the early origin of human society. It is not, however, confined to any age or to any country, but has been observed in all parts of the globe wherever circumstances have been such as to render it desirable—thus affording one among many instances of the readiness with which human nature, in its moral as well as in its physical properties, adapts itself to every varying condition. Hospitality is therefore not a peculiarly Oriental virtue. It was practised, as it still is, among the least cultivated nations. It was not less observed, in the early periods of their history, among the Greeks and Romans. With the Greeks, hospitality was under the immediate protection of religion. Jupiter bore a name signifying that its rights were under his guardianship. In the *Odyssey* we are told expressly that all guests and poor people are special objects of care to the gods. There were both in Greece and Italy two kinds of hospitality, the one private, the other public. The first existed between individuals, the second was cultivated by one state towards another. Hence arose a new kind of social relation : between those who had exercised and partaken of the rites of hospitality an intimate friendship ensued,—a species of freemasonry, which was called into play wherever the individuals might afterwards chance to meet, and the right, duties, and advantages of which passed from father to son, and were deservedly held in the highest estimation.

But though not peculiarly Oriental, hospitality has nowhere been more early or more fully practised than in the East. It is still honourably observed among the Arabs, especially at the present day. An Arab, on arriving at a village, dismounts at the house of some one who is known to him, saying to the master, ' I am your guest.' On this the host receives the traveller, and performs his duties, that is, he sets before his guest his supper, consisting of bread, milk, and borgul, and, if he is rich and generous, he also takes the necessary care of his horse or beast of burden. Should the traveller be unacquainted with any person, he alights at any house, as it may happen, fastens his horse to the same, and proceeds to smoke his pipe until the master bids him welcome, and offers him his evening meal. In the morning the traveller pursues his journey, making no other return than ' God be with you ' (good bye).

We find hospitality practised and held in the highest estimation at the earliest periods in which the Bible speaks of human society (Gen. xviii. 3; xix. 2; xxiv. 25; Exod. ii. 20; Judg. xix. 16). Express provision for its exercise is made in the Mosaic law (Lev. xix. 33; Deut. xiv. 29). In the New Testament also its observance is enjoined, though in the period to which its books refer the nature and extent of hospitality would be changed with the change that society had undergone

(1 Pet. iv. 9; 1 Tim. iii. 2; Tit. i. 8; 1 Tim. v. 10; Rom. xii. 13, Heb. xiii. 2). The disposition which generally prevailed in favour of the practice was enhanced by the fear lest those who neglected its rites should, after the example of impious men, be subjected by the divine wrath to frightful punishments. Even the Jews, in ' the latter days,' laid very great stress on the obligation: the rewards of Paradise, their doctors declared, were his who spontaneously exercised hospitality.

The guest, whoever he might be, was on his appearing invited into the house or tent (Gen. xix. 2; Exod. ii. 20; Judg. xiii. 15; xix. 21). Courtesy dictated that no improper questions should be put to him, and some days elapsed before the name of the stranger was asked, or what object he had in view in his journey (Gen. xxiv. 33). As soon as he arrived he was furnished with water to wash his feet (Gen. xviii. 4; xix. 2; 1 Tim. v. 10); received a supply of needful food for himself and beast (Gen. xviii. 5; xix. 3; xxiv. 25; Exod. ii. 20; Judg. xix. 20); and enjoyed courtesy and protection from his host (Gen. xix. 5; Josh. ii. 2; Judg. xix. 23). The case of Sisera, decoyed and slain by Jael (Judg. iv. 18, sq.), was a gross infraction of the rights and duties of hospitality. On his departure the traveller was not allowed to go alone or empty-handed (Judg. xix. 5). As the free practice of hospitality was held right and honourable, so the neglect of it was considered discreditable (Job xxxi. 32; Odyss. xiv. 56); and any interference with the comfort and protection which the host afforded, was treated as a wicked outrage (Gen. xix. 4, sq.). Though the practice of hospitality was general, and its rites rarely violated, yet national or local enmities did not fail sometimes to interfere ; and accordingly travellers avoided those places in which they had reason to expect an unfriendly reception. So in Judg. xix. 12, the ' certain Levite' spoken of said, ' We will not turn aside hither into the city of a stranger, that is not of the children of Israel.' The quarrel which arose between the Jews and Samaritans after the Babylonish captivity destroyed the relations of hospitality between them. Regarding each other as heretics, they sacrificed every better feeling. It was only in the greatest extremity that the Jews would partake of Samaritan food, and they were accustomed, in consequence of their religious and political hatred, to avoid passing through Samaria in journeying from one extremity of the land to the other. The animosity of the Samaritans towards the Jews appears to have been somewhat less bitter; but they showed an adverse feeling towards those persons who, in going up to the annual feast at Jerusalem, had to pass through their country (Luke ix. 53). At the great national festivals hospitality was liberally practised so long as the state retained its identity. On these festive occasions no inhabitant of Jerusalem considered his house his own; every home swarmed with strangers; yet this unbounded hospitality could not find accommodation in the houses for all who stood in need of it, and a large proportion of visitors had to be content with such shelter as tents could afford.

HOURS. The ancient Hebrews, like the Greeks, were unacquainted with any other means of distinguishing the times of day than the natural divisions of morning, midday or noon, twilight, and night (Gen. xv. 12; xviii. 1; xix. 1, 15, 23). The earliest mention of hours occurs in Daniel (iii. 15; iv. 19; v. 5); and, as the Chaldæans claimed the honour of inventing this system of notation, it is most probable that it was during their residence in Babylon that the Jews became familiar with their artificial distribution of the day. At all events no trace of it occurs before the captivity of that people; while, subsequently to their return to their own land, we find the practice adopted, and, in the time of Christ, universally established, of dividing the day and night respectively into twelve equal portions (Matt. xx. 3-5; John xi. 9; Acts v. 7; xix. 34). The Jewish horology, however, in common with that of other Eastern nations, had this inherent defect, that the hours, though always equal to one another, were unequal in regard to the seasons, and that as their day was reckoned from sunrise to sunset, and not from the fixed period of noon, as with us, the twelve hours into which it was divided varied, of course, in duration according to the fluctuations of summer and winter. The mid-day, which with us is the twelfth hour, the Jews counted their sixth, while their twelfth hour did not arrive till sunset. At the equinoxes, their hours were exactly of the same length with ours, and the time from which they began to reckon their day at those seasons corresponded precisely with our six o'clock A.M.; their first hour being our seven o'clock, their third (Acts ii. 15), our nine, their ninth (Acts iii. 1), our three o'clock P.M., and their eleventh (Matt. xx. 6), our five. This equality, however, in the duration of their hours, as well as in their correspondence to ours, was disturbed as the season approached towards the summer or winter solstice. In midsummer, when sunrise in Judæa takes place at five o'clock A.M., and sunset at seven P.M., the Jewish hours were a little longer than ours; and the only one of their hours which answered exactly to ours was the sixth, or twelve o'clock, while in all the rest there was a considerable difference. Their third hour was shortly *before* our nine, and their ninth a little *after* our three. In like manner, in winter, when the sun rises at seven and sets at five, the Jewish hour was proportionally shorter than ours, their third hour not occurring till a little *after* our nine, and their ninth a little *before* our three. Hence it is evident that in order to determine exactly the duration of Daniel's silence, for instance ('he was astonied one hour,' Dan. iv. 19), or the exact time when the darkness at Christ's crucifixion ended, it is necessary to ascertain the particular seasons when these incidents occurred.

In ancient times the only way of reckoning the progress of the day was by the length of the shadow—a mode of reckoning which was both contingent on the sunshine, and served only for the guidance of individuals. By what means the Jews calculated the length of their hours— whether by dialling, by the clepsydra or water-clock, or by some horological contrivance, like what was used anciently in Persia by the Romans, and which is still used in India, a servant notifying the intervals, it is now impossible to discover.

Besides these smaller hours, there was another division of the day into larger hours, with reference to the stated periods of prayer, viz. the third, sixth, and ninth hours of the day (Ps. xlv. 17).

The night was divided into twelve equal portions or hours, in precisely the same manner as the day. The most ancient division, however, was into three watches; the first, or beginning of the watches, as it is called (Lament. ii. 19); the middle-watch (Judg. vii. 19); and the morning-watch (Exod. xiv. 24). When Judæa became a province of Rome, the Roman distribution of the night into four watches was introduced [see Cock-crowing and Day]; to which division frequent allusions occur in the New Testament (Luke xii. 38; Matt. xiv. 25; xiii. 35), as well as to that of hours (Matt. xxv. 13; xxvi. 40; Mark xiv. 37; Luke xvii. 59; Acts xxiii. 23; Rev. iii. 3).

It remains only to notice that the word *hour* is sometimes used in Scripture to denote some determinate season, as 'mine *hour* is not yet come,' 'this is your *hour*, and the power of darkness,' 'the *hour* is coming,' &c.

HOUSE. Houses are often mentioned in Scripture, several important passages of which cannot be well understood without a clearer notion of the houses in which the Hebrews dwelt, than can be realized by such comparisons as we naturally make with those in which we ourselves live. But things so different afford no grounds for instructive comparison. We must therefore bring together such facts as can be collected from the Scripture and from ancient writers, with such details from travellers and our own observations, as may tend to illustrate these statements; for there is every reason to conclude that little substantial difference exists between the ancient houses and those which are at this day found in south-western Asia.

210.

Our information respecting the abodes of men in the ages before the Deluge is, however, too scanty to afford much ground for notice.

We may, therefore, pass over this early period, and proceed at once to the later times in which the Hebrews flourished.

The observations offered under ARCHITECTURE will preclude the expectation of finding among this Eastern people an accomplished style of building. The reason of this is plain. Their ancestors had roved through the country as nomade shepherds, dwelling in tents; and if ever they built huts they were of so light a fabric as easily to be taken down when a change of station became necessary. In this mode of life solidity in the structure of any dwelling was by no means required; much less were regular arrangement and the other requisites of a well-ordered dwelling matters of consideration. Under such circumstances as these, no improvement in the habitation takes place. The tents in which the Arabs now dwell are in all probability the same as those in which the Hebrew patriarchs spent their lives.

On entering Palestine, the Israelites occupied the dwellings of the dispossessed inhabitants; and for a long time no new buildings would be needed. The generation which began to build new houses must have been born and bred in the country, and would naturally erect buildings like those which already existed in the land. Their mode of building was therefore that of the Canaanites whom they had dispossessed. Of *their* style of building we are not required to form any exalted notions. In all the history of the conquest of the country by the Israelites, there is no account of any large or conspicuous building being taken or destroyed by them. It would seem also as if there had been no temples; for we read not that any were destroyed by the conquerors; and the command that the monuments of idolatry should be overthrown, specifies only altars, groves, and high places—which seems to lead to the same conclusion; since, if there had been temples existing in the land of Canaan, they would doubtless have been included. It is also manifest from the history that the towns which the Hebrews found in Palestine were mostly small, and that the largest were distinguished rather by their number than by the size or magnificence of their buildings.

It is impossible to say to what extent Solomon's improvements in state architecture operated to the advancement of domestic architecture. He built different palaces, and it is reasonable to conclude that his nobles and great officers followed more or less the models which these palaces presented. In the East, however, the domestic architecture of the bulk of the people is little affected by the improvements in state buildings. Men go on building from age to age as their forefathers built; and in all probability the houses which we now see in Palestine are such as those in which the Jews, and the Canaanites before them, dwelt—the mosques, the Christian churches, and the monasteries being the only new features in the scene.

There is no reason to suppose that many houses in Palestine were constructed with wood. A great part of that country was always very poor in timber, and the middle part of it had scarcely any wood at all. But of stone there was no want; and it was consequently much used in the building of houses. Having premised this, the principal building materials mentioned in Scripture may be enumerated with reference to their place in the three kingdoms of nature.

I. VEGETABLE SUBSTANCES:—

1. *Shittim*, or the timber of the acacia tree, which grows abundantly in the valleys of Arabia Petræa, and was therefore employed in the construction of the tabernacle. Not being, however, a tree of Palestine, the wood was not subsequently used in building.

2. The wood of the *sycamore fig-tree*, mentioned in Isa. ix. 10, as a building timber in more common use than cedar, or perhaps than any other wood known in Palestine.

3. *Cedar*. As this was a wood imported from Lebanon, it would only be used in the higher class of buildings.

4. *Algum-wood*, which, being imported from the Eastern seas, must have been valued at a high price. It was used by Solomon for pillars for his own palace, and for the temple (1 Kings x. 11, 12).

5. *Cypress-wood*. Boards of this were used for the floor of the Temple, which may suggest the use to which it was ordinarily applied (1 Kings vi. 15; 2 Chron. iii. 5).

Particular accounts of all these woods, and of the trees which afforded them, may be seen under the respective words.

II. MINERAL SUBSTANCES:—

1. *Marble*. We find the court of the king of Persia's palace covered with marble of various colours (Esth. i. 6). David is recorded to have possessed abundance of marble (1 Chron. xxx. [xxix.] 2; comp. Cant. v. 13), and it was used by Solomon for his palace, as well as for the Temple.

2. *Porphyry and Granite* are supposed to be 'the glistering stones, and stones of divers colours' named in 1 Chron. xxix. 2. If so, the mountains of Arabia Petræa furnished the nearest source of supply, as these stones do not exist in Palestine or Lebanon.

3. *Bricks*. Bricks hardened by fire were employed in the construction of the tower of Babel (Gen. xi. 3), and the hard bondage of the Israelites in Egypt consisted in the manufacture of sun-dried bricks (Exod. v. 7, 10-13). This important building-material has been noticed under another head [BRICKS]; and it only remains to remark that no subsequent notice of bricks as being used by the Hebrews occurs after they had entered Palestine. Yet, judging from existing analogies, it is more than probable that bricks were to a considerable extent employed in their buildings.

3. *Chalk and Gypsum*. That the Hebrews were acquainted with these materials appears from Deut. xxvii. 2; and from Dan. v. 5; Acts xxiii. 3, it further appears that walls were covered with them.

4. *Mortar*, a cement made of lime, ashes, and chopped straw, or of gypsum and chopped straw. This is probably meant in Jer. xliii. 9; Ezek. xiii. 10, 11, 20.

5. *Asphaltum*, or *Bitumen*, which is mentioned as being used for a cement by the builders of Babel. This must have been in the want of lime-mortar, the country being a stoneless plain. But the Israelites, who had no lack of the usual cements, did not employ asphaltum [BITUMEN].

6. The metals also must be, to a certain extent, regarded as building materials: lead, iron, and copper are mentioned; and even silver and gold were used in combination with wood, for various kinds of solid, plated, and inlaid work (Exod. xxxvi. 34, 38).

III. ANIMAL SUBSTANCES:—

Such substances can be but in a small degree applicable to building. *Ivory* houses are mentioned in 1 Kings xxii. 39; Amos iii. 14; most likely from certain parts of the wood-work, probably about the doors and windows, being inlaid with this valuable substance. Solomon obtained ivory in great quantities from Tyre (1 Kings x. 22; 2 Chron. ix. 21). [IVORY.]

In describing the houses of ancient Palestine, there is no way of arriving at distinct notions but by taking the texts of Scripture and illustrating them by the existing houses of those parts of Western Asia which have been the least exposed to the changes of time, and in which the manners of ancient days have been the best preserved. Writers on the subject have seen this, and have brought together the descriptions of travellers bearing on the subject; but these descriptions have generally been applied with very little judgment, from the want of that distinct knowledge of the matter which actual observation can give. Travellers have seldom been students of Scripture, and students of Scripture have seldom been travellers. The present writer, having resided for a considerable time in Turkish Arabia, where the type of Scriptural usages has been better preserved than in Egypt, or even in Palestine itself, is enabled to speak on this matter with somewhat more precision. Of four houses in which he there resided, two were first-rate, and two were second-rate. One of the latter has always seemed to him to suggest a more satisfactory idea of a Scriptural house than any of the others, or than any that he ever saw in other Eastern countries. That one has therefore formed the basis of all his ideas on this subject; and where it seemed to fail, the others have usually supplied the illustration he required. This course he has found so beneficial that he will endeavour to impart a clear view of the subject to the reader by giving a general notion of the house referred to, explaining any points in which the others differed from it, and producing the passages of Scripture which seem to be illustrated in the process.

211.

We may premise that the houses present little more than a dead wall to the street. The privacy of Oriental domestic habits would render our plan of throwing the front of the houses towards the street most repulsive. On coming to a house, one finds a lofty wall, which would be blank but for the low door of entrance [GATE]; over which is usually the kiosk, or latticed window (sometimes projecting like the huge bay windows of Elizabethan houses), or screened balcony of the 'summer parlour.' Besides this, there may be a small latticed window or two high up the wall, giving light and air to upper chambers. This seems,

from the above engraving (No. 211), to have been the character of the fronts of ancient Egyptian houses.

The buildings which form the house fron towards an inner square or court. Small houses have one of these courts, but superior houses have two, and first-rate houses three, communicating with each other; for the Orientals dislike ascending stairs or steps, and prefer to gain room rather by the extent than height of their habitations. It is only when the building-ground is confined by nature or by fortifications, that they build high houses. Not one out of four houses we ourselves inhabited had more than one story; but, from the loftiness of the rooms, they were as high as houses of three stories among ourselves. If there are three or more courts, all except the outer one are much alike in size and appearance; but the outer one, being devoted to the more public life of the occupant, and to his intercourse with society, is materially different from all the others. If there are more than two, the second is devoted chiefly to the use of the master, who is there attended only by his eunuchs, children, and females, and sees only such persons as he calls from the third or interior court in which they reside. In the history of Esther, she incurs danger by going from her interior court to that of the king, to invite him to visit her part of the palace; but she would not on any account have gone to the outermost court, in which the king held his public audiences. When there are only two courts, the innermost is the harem, in which the women and children live, and which is the true domicile of the master, to which he withdraws when the claims of business, of society, and of friends have been satisfied, and where no man but himself ever enters, or could be induced to enter, even by strong persuasions.

Entering at the street-door, a passage, usually sloping downward, conducts to the outer court; the opening from the passage to this is not opposite the gate of entrance, but by a side turn, to preclude any view from the street into the court when the gate is opened. On entering the outer court through this passage, we find opposite to us the public room, in which the master receives and gives audience to his friends and clients. This is entirely open in front, and, being richly fitted up, has a splendid appearance when the first view of it is obtained. A refreshing coolness is sometimes given to this apartment by a fountain throwing up a jet of water in front of it. Some idea of the apartment may be formed from the annexed cut (No. 212). This is the 'guest-chamber' of Luke xxii. 11. A large portion of the other side of the court is occupied with a frontage of lattice-work filled with coloured glass, belonging to a room as large as the guest-chamber, and which in winter is used for the same purpose, or serves as the apartment of any visitor of distinction, who cannot of course be admitted into the interior parts of the house. The other apartments in this outer court are comparatively small, and are used for the accommodation of visitors, retainers, and servants. These various apartments are usually upon what we should call the first floor, or at least upon an elevated terrace. The ground-floor is in that case occupied by various store-rooms and servants' offices. In all cases the upper floor, containing the principal rooms, is fronted by a gallery or terrace, protected from the sun by a sort of pent-house roof supported by pillars of wood.

212.

In houses having but one court, the reception-room is on the ground-floor, and the domestic establishment in the upper part of the house. This arrangement is shown in the annexed engraving (No. 213), which is also interesting from its showing the use of the 'pillars' so often men-

213.

tioned in Scripture, particularly the pillars on which the house stood, and by which it was borne up' (Judg. xvi. 29).

The kiosk, which has been mentioned above as

fronting the street, over the gateway, is connected with one of the larger rooms already described, or forms a separate apartment, which is the summer parlour of Scripture. Here, in the heat of the afternoon, the master lounges or dozes listlessly, refreshed by the air which circulates between the openings of the lattice-work; and here he can, if he pleases, notice unobserved what passes in the street. In this we are to seek the summer parlour in which Ehud smote the king of Moab (Judg. iii. 20), and the 'chamber on the wall,' which the Shunamite prepared for the prophet (2 Kings iv. 10). The projecting construction over the reception chamber in No. 213 is, like the kiosk, towards the street as a summer parlour; but there it belongs to the women's apartments, and looks into the court, and not the street.

It is now time to proceed to the inner court, which we enter by a passage and door similar to those by which we entered from the street. This passage and door are usually at one of the innermost corners of the outer court. Here a much more extended prospect opens to us, the inner court being generally much larger than the former. The annexed cut (No. 214) will convey some notion of it; but being a Persian house, it somewhat differs from that which we have more particularly in view. It is lower, the principal apartments standing upon a terrace or bank of earth, and not upon a basement story of offices; and it also wants the veranda or covered gallery in front, which we find in Syro-Arabian houses. The court is for the most part paved, excepting a portion in the middle, which is planted with trees (usually two) and shrubs, with a basin of water in the midst. In our Arabian house the two trees were palm-trees, in which a number of wild doves built their nests. In the second cut (No. 347), showing an ancient Egyptian house, we see the same arrangement: two palm-trees growing in the court extend their tops above, and, as it were, out of the house—a curious effect frequently noticed in the towns of South-western Asia. That the Jews had the like arrangement of trees in the courts of their houses, and that the birds nested

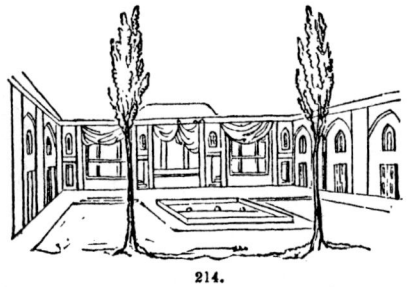

214.

in them, appears from Psa. lxxxiv. 2, 3. They had also the basin of water in the inner court, or haram; and among them it was used for bathing, as is shown by David's discovering Bathsheba bathing as he walked on the roof of his palace. This use of the reservoir has now been superseded by the establishment of public *warm* baths in every town, and in private mansions. Cold bathing has all but ceased in Western Asia.

The arrangement of the inner court is very similar to that of the outer; but the whole is more open and airy. The buildings usually occupy two sides of the square, of which the one opposite the entrance contains the principal apartments. They are upon what we should call the first floor, and open into a wide gallery or veranda, which in good houses is nine or ten feet deep, and covered by a wooden penthouse supported by a row of wooden columns. This terrace, or gallery, is furnished with a strong wooden balustrade, and is usually paved with squared stones, or else floored with boards. In the centre of the principal front is the usual open drawing-room, on which the best art of the Eastern decorator is expended. Much of one of the sides of the court front is usually occupied by the large sitting-room, with the latticed front covered with coloured glass, similar to that in the outer court. The other rooms, of smaller size, are the more private apartments of the mansion. There are usually no doors to the sitting or drawing-rooms of Eastern houses: they are closed by curtains, at least in summer, the opening and shutting of doors being odious to most Orientals. The same seems to have been the case among the Hebrews, as far as we may judge from the curtains which served instead of doors to the tabernacle, and which separated the inner and outer chambers of the temple. The curtained entrances to our Westminster courts of law supply a familiar example of the same practice.

These observations apply to the principal story. The basement is occupied by various offices, stores of corn and fuel, places for the water-jars to stand in, places for grinding corn, baths, kitchens, &c. The kitchens are always in this inner court, as the cooking is performed by women, and the ladies of the family superintend or actually assist in the process. The kitchen, open in front, is on the same side as the entrance from the outer court; and the top of it forms a terrace, which affords a communication between the first floor of both courts by a private door, seldom used but by the master of the house and attendant eunuchs.

The kitchen is surrounded by a bank of brickwork, on the top of which are the fireplaces formed in compartments, and separated by little walls of fire-brick or tile. In these different compartments the various dishes of an Eastern feast may be at once prepared at charcoal fires. This place being wholly open in front, the half-tame doves, which have their nests in the trees of the court, often visit it, in the absence of the servants, in search of crumbs, &c. As they sometimes blacken themselves, this perhaps explains the obscure passage in Ps. lxviii. 13, 'Though ye have lien among the pots, ye shall be as the wings of a dove covered with silver,' &c. In Turkish Arabia most of the houses have underground cellars or vaults, to which the inhabitants retreat during the mid-day heat of summer, and there enjoy a refreshing coolness. In the rest of the year these cellars, or *serdaubs*, as they are called, are abandoned to the bats, which swarm in them in scarcely credible numbers (Isa. ii. 20).

From the court a flight of stone steps, usually at the corner, conducts to the gallery, from which a plainer stair leads to the house-top. If the house be large, there are two or three sets of steps

to the different sides of the quadrangle, but seldom more than one flight from the terrace to the house-top of any one court. There is, however, a separate stair from the outer court to the roof, and it is usually near the entrance. This will bring to mind the case of the paralytic, whose friends, finding they could not get access to Jesus through the people who crowded the court of the house in which he was preaching, took him up to the roof, and let him down in his bed through the tiling, to the place where Jesus stood (Luke v. 17-26). If the house in which our Lord then was had more than one court, he and the auditors were certainly in the outer one; and it is reasonable to conclude that he stood in the veranda addressing the crowd below. The men bearing the paralytic therefore perhaps went up the steps near the door; and finding they could not even then get near the person of Jesus, the gallery being also crowded, continued their course to the roof of the house, and removing the boards over the covering of the gallery, at the place where Jesus stood, lowered the sick man to his feet. But if they could not get access to the steps near the door, as is likely, from the door being much crowded, their alternative was to take him to the roof of the next house, and there hoist him over the parapet to the roof of the house which they desired to enter.

The roof of the house is, of course, flat. It is formed by layers of branches, twigs, matting, and earth, laid over the rafters and trodden down; after which it is covered with a compost which acquire considerable hardness when dry. Such roofs would not, however, endure the heavy and continuous rains of our climate; and in those parts of Asia where the climate is more than usually moist, a stone roller is usually kept on every roof, and after a shower a great part of the population is engaged in drawing these rollers over the roofs. It is now very common, in countries where timber is scarce, to have domed roofs; but in that case the flat roof, which is indispensable to Eastern habits, is obtained by filling up the hollow intervals between the several domes, so as to form a flat surface at the top. These flat roofs are often alluded to in Scripture; and the allusions show that they were made to serve the same uses as at present. In fine weather the inhabitants resorted much to them to breathe the fresh air, to enjoy a fine prospect, or to witness any event that occurred in the neighbourhood (2 Sam. xi. 2; Isa. xxii. 1; Matt. xxiv. 17; Mark xiii. 15). The dryness of the summer atmosphere enabled them, without injury to health, to enjoy the bracing coolness of the night-air by sleeping on the house-tops; and in order to have the benefit of the air and prospect in the daytime, without inconvenience from the sun, sheds, booths, and tents, were sometimes erected on the house-tops (2 Sam. xvi. 22).

The roofs of the houses are well protected by walls and parapets. Towards the street and neighbouring houses is a high wall; and towards the interior court-yard usually a parapet or wooden rail. 'Battlements' of this kind, for the prevention of accidents, are strictly enjoined in the Law (Deut. xxii. 8); and the form of the battlements of the Egyptian houses, as shown in the annexed engravings, suggest some interesting analogies, when we consider how recently the

Israelites had quitted Egypt when that law was delivered.

215.

216.

Of the inferior kinds of Oriental dwellings, such as are met with in villages and very small towns, the subjoined is not an unfavourable specimen. In these there is no central court, but there is generally a yard attached, either on one side or at the rear. The shaded platform in front is such as is usually seen attached to coffee-houses, which is, in fact, the character of the house represented in No. 217. Here the customers sit and smoke their pipes, and sip their coffee. The village cabins and abodes of the peasantry are, of course, of a still inferior description; and, being the abodes of people who live much in the open air, will not bear comparison with the houses of the same class in Northern Europe, where the cottage is the *home* of the owner.

No ancient houses had chimneys. The word so translated in Hos. xiii. 3, means a hole through which the smoke escaped; and this existed only in the lower class of dwellings, where raw wood was employed for fuel or cooking, and where there was an opening immediately over the hearth to let out the smoke. In the better sort of houses the rooms were warmed in winter by charcoal in braziers, as is still the practice (Jer. xxxvi. 22; Mark xiv. 54; John xviii. 18).

The windows had no glass. They were only latticed, and thus gave free passage to the air and admitted light, while birds and bats were excluded. In winter the cold air was kept out by veils over the windows, or by shutters with holes in them sufficient to admit light (1 Kings vii 17; Cant. ii. 9).

In the East, where the climate allows the people to spend so much of their time out of doors, the articles of furniture and the domestic

217.

utensils have always been few and simple. They are in this work noticed under separate heads [BED; LAMPS; POTTERY; SEATS; TABLES]. The rooms, however, although comparatively vacant of moveables, are far from having a naked or unfurnished appearance. This is owing to the high ornament given to the walls and ceilings. The walls are broken up into various recesses, and the ceiling into compartments. The ceiling, if of wood and flat, is of curious and complicated joinery; or, if vaulted, is wrought into numerous coves, and enriched with fret-work in stucco; and the walls are adorned with arabesques, mosaics, mirrors, painting, and gold; which, as set off by the marble-like whiteness of the stucco, has a truly brilliant and rich effect. There is much in this to remind one of such descriptions of splendid interiors as that in Isa. liv. 11, 12.

HULDAH, or rather CHULDAH, wife of Shallum, a prophetess, who, in the reign of Josiah, abode in that part of Jerusalem called the Mishneh, where the book of the Law was discovered by the high-priest Hilkiah. This prophetess was consulted respecting the denunciations which it contained. She then delivered an oracular response of mingled judgment and mercy; declaring the not remote destruction of Jerusalem, but promising Josiah that he should be taken from the world before these evil days came; B.C. 623 (2 Kings xxii. 14-20; 2 Chron. xxxiv. 22-28). Huldah is only known for this circumstance. She was probably at this time the widow of Shallum, a name too common to suggest any information; but he is said to have been grandson of one Harhas, 'keeper of the wardrobe,' but whether the priestly or the royal wardrobe is uncertain. If the former, he must have been a Levite, if not a priest. As to her residence, it is said to have been 'in the Mishneh,' which the Auth. Vers. renders 'in the college.' But there is no ground to conclude that any school or college of the prophets is to be understood. The name means 'second' or 'double;' and many of the Jews themselves (as Jarchi states) understood it as the name of the suburb lying between the inner and outer wall of Jerusalem. It is safest to regard it as a proper name denoting some quarter of Jerusalem about which we are not certain, and, accordingly, to translate 'in the Mishneh.'

HUNTING. The pursuit and capture of beasts of the field was the first means of sustenance which the human race had recourse to, this mode of gaining a livelihood having naturally preceded the engagements of agriculture, as it presented food already provided, requiring only to be taken and slaughtered; whereas tillage must have been an afterthought, and a later resource, since it implies accumulated knowledge, skill, and such provision aforehand of subsistence as would enable a clan or a family to wait till the fruits of the earth were matured. Hunting was, therefore, a business long ere it was a sport. And originally, before man had established his empire on the earth, it must have been not only a serious but a dangerous pursuit. In process of time, however, when civilization had made some progress, when cities were built and lands cultivated, hunting was carried on not so much for the food which it brought as for the recreation it gave and its conduciveness to health.

The East—the cradle of civilization—presents us with hunting in both the characters now spoken of, originally as a means of support, then as a manly amusement. In the early records of history we find hunting held in high repute, partly, no doubt, from its costliness, its dangers, its similitude to war, its capability of combining the energies of many, and also from the relief which it afforded to the stagnant monotony of a court, in the high and bounding spirits that it called forth. Hunting has always borne somewhat of a regal character, and down to the present hour has worn an aristocratical air. In Babylon and Persia this attribute is presented in bold relief. Immense parks were enclosed for nurturing and preserving beasts of the chace. The monarch himself led the way to the sport, not only in these preserves, but also over the wide surface of the country, being attended by his nobles, especially by the younger aspirants to fame and warlike renown.

In the Bible we find hunting connected with royalty so early as in Gen. x. The great founder of Babel was in general repute as 'a mighty hunter before the Lord.' The patriarchs, however, are to be regarded rather as herdsmen than hunters, if respect is had to their habitual mode of life. The condition of the herdsman ensues next to that of the hunter in the early stages of civilization; and so we find that even Cain was a keeper of sheep. This, and the fact that Abel is designated 'a tiller of the ground,' would seem to indicate a very rapid progress in the arts and pursuits of social life. The same contrast and similar hostility we find somewhat later, in the case of Jacob and Esau; the first, 'a plain man dwelling in tents;' the second, 'a cunning hunter, a man of the field' (Gen. xxv. sq.). The account given of Esau in connection with his father seems to show that hunting was, conjointly with tillage, pursued at that time as a means of subsistence, and that hunting had not then passed into its secondary state, and become an amusement.

In Egypt the children of Israel would be spectators of hunting carried on extensively and pursued in different manners, but chiefly, as appears probable, with a view rather to recreation than subsistence. That the land of promise into which

the Hebrews were conducted on leaving Egypt was plentifully supplied with beasts of the chace appears clear from Exod. xxii. 29, 'I will not drive them out in one year, lest the land become desolate and the beast of the field multiply against thee' (comp. Deut. iii. 22). And from the regulation given in Lev. xvii. 15, it is manifest that hunting was practised after the settlement in Canaan, and was pursued with the view of obtaining food. Prov. xii. 27 proves that hunting animals for their flesh was an established custom among the Hebrews, though the turn of the passage may serve to show that, at the time it was penned, sport was the chief aim. If hunting was not forbidden in the 'year of rest,' special provision was made that not only the cattle, but 'the beast of the field' should be allowed to enjoy and flourish on the uncropped spontaneous produce of the land (Exod. xxiii. 11; Lev. xxv. 7). That the lion and other ravenous beasts of prey were not wanting in Palestine, many passages of the Bible make obvious (1 Sam. xvii. 34; 2 Sam. xxiii. 20; 1 Kings xiii. 24). The lion was even made use of to catch other animals (Ezek. xix. 3), and Harmer long ago remarked, that as in the vicinity of Gaza, so also in Judæa, leopards were trained and used for the same purpose (Harmer, iv. 358; Hab. i. 8). That lions were taken by pitfalls as well as by nets appears from Ezek. xix. 4, 8 (Shaw, p. 172). In the latter verse the words of the prophet, 'and spread their net over him,' allude to the custom of enclosing a wide extent of country with nets, into which the animals were driven by hunters. The spots thus enclosed were usually in a hilly country and in the vicinity of water-brooks; whence the propriety and force of the language of Ps. xlii. 1, 'As the (hunted) hart panteth after the water-brooks.' These places were selected because they were those to which the animals were in the habit of repairing in the morning and evening. Scenes like the one now supposed are found portrayed in the Egyptian paintings. Hounds were used for hunting in Egypt, and, if the passage in Josephus (Antiq. iv. 8, 9) may be considered decisive, in Palestine as well. From Gen. xxvii. 3, 'Now take thy weapons, thy quiver and thy bow,' we learn what arms were employed at least in capturing game. Bulls, after being taken, were kept at least for a time in a net (Is. li. 20). Various missiles, pitfalls, snares, and gins were made use of in hunting (Ps. xci. 3; Amos iii. 5; 2 Sam. xxiii. 20). That hunting continued to be followed till towards the end of the Jewish state appears from Josephus, who speaks of Herod as 'ever a most excellent hunter, for in one day he caught forty wild beasts.' The same passage makes it clear that horses were employed in the pursuits of the chace.

HUSKS. The word which is thus rendered in the Authorized Version (Luke xv. 10) is really the name of a tree called in English Carob-tree. It is extremely common in the south of Europe, in Syria, and in Egypt. Celsius states that no tree is more frequently mentioned in the Talmud, where its fruit is stated to be given as food to cattle and swine: it is now given to horses, asses, and mules. During the Peninsular war the horses of the British cavalry were often fed on the beans of the Carob-tree. Both Pliny and Columella mention that it was given as food to swine. By some it has been thought, but apparently without reason, that it was upon the husks of this tree that John the Baptist fed in the wilderness: from this idea, however, it is often called St. John's Bread and Locust-tree.

213. [Ceratonia Siliqua.]

The Carob-tree grows in the south of Europe and north of Africa, usually to a moderate size, but it sometimes becomes very large, with a trunk of great thickness, and affords an agreeable shade. The quantity of pods borne by each tree is very considerable, being often as much as 800 or 900 pounds weight: they are flat, brownish-coloured, from six to eight inches in length, of a sub-astringent taste when unripe, but when come to maturity they secrete, within the husks and round the seeds, a sweetish-tasted pulp. When on the tree, the pods have an unpleasant odour; but when dried upon hurdles they become eatable, and are valued by poor people, and during famine in the countries where the tree is grown, especially in Spain and Egypt, and by the Arabs. They are given as food to cattle in modern, as we read they were in ancient, times; but at the best can only be considered very poor fare.

HYÆNA (*Tzeboa*), (Ecclus. xiii. 18). Excepting in Ecclesiasticus just noted, the word does not occur in the English Bible, although there are several passages in the Hebrew canonical books, where Tzeboa, 'streaked' or 'variegated,' is assumed to designate the hyæna. The most noted of these is Jer. xii. 9, where the words which the Septuagint render 'the cave of the hyæna,' are rendered in our version 'a speckled bird.' But Bochart and the continuator of Calmet vindicate what we take to be the true reading, 'the striped rusher,' *i. e.* the hyæna, turning round upon his lair, introduced after an allusion in the previous verse to the lion calling to the beasts of the field (other hyænas and jackals) to come and devour. This allusion, followed up as it is by a natural association of ideas, with a de-

scription of the pastor, feeder, or rather consumer or devourer of the vineyard, treading down and destroying the vines, renders the natural and poetical picture complete; for the hyæna seeks burrows and caverns for a lair; like the dog it turns round to lie down; howls, and occasionally acts, in concert; is loathsome, savage, insatiable in appetite, offensive in smell; and will in the season, like canines, devour grapes, as the writer has himself ascertained by actual experiment.

Tzeboa, therefore, we consider proved to be, generically, the hyæna. The striped species is one of three or four—all, it seems, originally African; and, by following armies and caravans, gradually spread over Southern Asia to beyond the Ganges, though not as yet to the east of the Bramapootra. It is now not uncommon in Asia Minor, and has extended into Southern Tartary; but this progress is comparatively so recent, that no other than Semitic names are well known to belong to it. The head and jaws of all the species are broad and strong; the muzzle truncated; the tongue like a rasp; the teeth 34 instead of 42, as in the *canidæ*, but robust, large, and eminently formed for biting, lacerating, and reducing the very bone; the neck stiff; the body short and compact; the limbs tall, with only four toes on each foot; the fur coarse, forming a kind of semi-erectile mane along the back; the tail rather short, with an imperfect brush, and with a fetid pouch beneath it. In stature the species varies from that of a large wolf to much less. Hyænas are not bold in comparison with wolves, or in proportion to their powers. They do not in general act collectively; they prowl chiefly in the night; attack asses, dogs, and weaker animals; feed most willingly on corrupt animal offal, dead camels, &c.; and dig into human

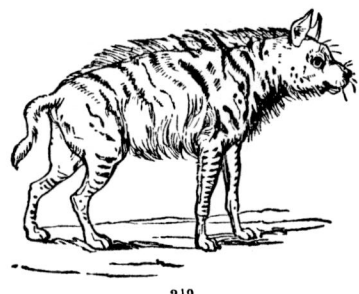

219.

graves that are not well protected with stakes and brambles. The striped species is of a dirty ashy buff, with some oblique black streaks across the shoulders and body, and numerous cross-bars on the legs; the muzzle and throat are black, and the tip of the tail white.

There is reason to believe that the *deeb*, or Scriptural wolf, when represented as carrying off a lamb, is no other than the hyæna, unless the real wolf has been extirpated; for zoologists have not found the wolf in Syria.

HYMENE'US, a professor of Christianity at Ephesus, who, with Alexander (1 Tim. i. 20) and Philetus (2 Tim. ii. 18), had departed from the truth both in principle and practice, and led others into apostacy. The chief doctrinal error of these persons consisted in maintaining that 'the resurrection was past already.' The precise meaning of this expression is by no means clearly ascertained: the most general and perhaps best founded opinion is, that they understood the resurrection in a figurative sense of the great change produced by the Gospel dispensation. Most critics suppose that the same person is referred to in both the Epistles to Timothy by the name of Hymeneus. Dr. Mosheim, however, contends that there were two. But his reasoning on the subject is far from satisfactory.

HYMN. In the only places of the New Testament where this word occurs, it is connected with two others of very similar import. 'Speaking to yourselves in *psalms*, and *hymns*, and spiritual songs, singing and making melody in your heart to the Lord' (Eph. v. 19; Col. iii. 16). It has been conjectured that by 'psalms and hymns' the poetical compositions of the Old Testament are chiefly to be understood, and that the epithet spiritual,' here applied to 'songs,' is intended to mark those devout effusions which resulted from the spiritual gifts granted to the primitive church; yet in 1 Cor. xiv. 26 a production of the latter class is called 'a psalm.' Josephus, it may be remarked, uses the terms 'hymns' and 'songs,' in reference to the Psalms of David (*Antiq.* vii. 12. 3). Our information respecting the hymnology of the first Christians is extremely scanty; the most distinct notice we possess of it is that contained in Pliny's celebrated Epistle (*Ep.* x. 97): 'They sing a hymn to Christ as God.' The hymn which our Lord sung with his disciples at the Last Supper is generally supposed to have been the latter part of the *Hallel*, or series of psalms which were sung by the Jews on the night of the Passover, comprehending Ps. cxiii.-cxviii.; Ps. cxiii. and cxiv. being sung before, and the rest after the Passover.

HYSSOP. A great variety of opinions have been entertained respecting the plant called *esobh*, translated 'hyssop' in the Authorized Version both of the Old and the New Testament; but it is difficult to fix with certainty on the plant intended. The first notice of it occurs in Exod. xii. 22, where a bunch of hyssop is directed to be dipped in blood and struck on the lintels and the two side-posts of the doors of the houses in which the Israelites resided. It is next mentioned in Lev. xiv. 4, 6, 52, in the ceremony for declaring lepers to be cleansed; and again, in Num xix. 6, 18, in preparing the water of separation. To these passages the apostle alludes in Heb. ix. 19: 'For when Moses had spoken every precept to all the people, according to the law, he took the blood of calves, and of goats, with water, and scarlet wool, and hyssop, and sprinkled both the book and all the people.' From these texts we find that the plant must have been leafy, and large enough to serve for the purposes of sprinkling, and that it must have been found in Lower Egypt, as well as in the country towards Mount Sinai, and onwards to Palestine. From the following passages we get some information respecting the habits and the supposed properties of the plant. Thus, in 1 Kings iv. 33, it is said, ' Solomon spoke of trees, from the cedar-tree that is in Lebanon, even unto the hyssop that springeth out of the wall;' and in the penitential psalm of David (li. 7), 'Purge me with hyssop, and I

shall be clean: wash me, and I shall be whiter than snow.' In this passage it is, no doubt, considered by some commentators that hyssop is used in a figurative sense; but still it is possible that the plant may have possessed some general cleansing properties, and thus come to be employed in preference to other plants in the ceremonies of purification. It ought, at all events, to be found growing upon walls, and in Palestine. In the account of the crucifixion of our Saviour, the Apostle John says (John xix. 29). 'Now there was set a vessel full of vinegar, and they filled a sponge with vinegar, and put it upon *hyssop*, and put it to his mouth.' In the parallel passages of Matthew (xxvii. 48) and Mark (xv. 36), it is stated that the sponge filled with vinegar was put upon a reed or stick. To reconcile these statements, some commentators have supposed that both the sponge and the hyssop were tied to a stick, and that one apostle mentions only the hyssop, because he considered it as the most important; while, for the same reason, the other two mention only the stick; but the simplest mode of explaining the apparent discrepancy is to consider the hyssop and the stick to be the same thing—in other words, that the sponge was affixed to a stick of hyssop.

A great variety of plants have been adduced by different authors as that alluded to in the above passages. Some contend for several plants belonging to the class of ferns, such as maiden-hair, wall-rue, pearlwort, and hair-moss: others for a species of wormwood, that it might be more distasteful to our Saviour. The majority, however, have selected different kinds of fragrant plants belonging to the natural family of *Labiatæ*, several of which are found in dry and barren situations in Palestine, and also in some parts of the Desert. Of these may be mentioned the rosemary, species of lavender, of mint, of marjoram, of thyme, of savory, of thymbra, and others of the same tribe, resembling each other much in characters as well as in properties: but it does not appear that any of them grow on walls, or are possessed of cleansing properties; and, with the exception of the rosemary, they are not capable of yielding a stick, nor are they found in all the required situations. Dr. Royle, who has recently investigated the subject, is of opinion that as the *caper plant* has an Arabic name, *asuf,* similar to the Hebrew *esob* or *esof*; as it is found in Lower Egypt, in the deserts of Sinai, and in New Jerusalem; as it grows upon rocks and walls, was always supposed to be possessed of cleansing qualities, is large enough to yield a stick; and as its different parts used to be preserved in vinegar, as its buds now are, he is warranted, from the union of all these properties in this plant, corresponding so closely to those of the original *esof*, in considering it as proved that the *caper plant* is the *hyssop* of Scripture.

I.

IBZAN (*illustrious*), the tenth 'judge of Israel.' He was of Bethlehem, probably the Bethlehem of Zebulun and not of Judah. He governed seven years. The prosperity of Ibzan is marked by the great number of his children (thirty sons and thirty daughters), and his wealth by their marriages—for they were all married.

ICH'ABOD (*where is the glory*), son of Phinehas and grandson of Eli. He is only known from the unhappy circumstances of his birth, which occasioned this name to be given to him. The pains of labour came upon his mother when she heard that the ark of God was taken, that her husband was slain in battle, and that these tidings had proved fatal to his father Eli. They were death-pains to her; and when those around sought to cheer her, saying, ' Fear not, for thou hast borne a son,' she only answered by giving him the name of Ichabod, saying, ' The glory is departed from Israel' (1 Sam. iv. 19-22); B.C. 1141. The name again occurs in 1 Sam. xiv. 3 [ELI].

ICO'NIUM, a town, formerly the capital of Lycaonia, as it is now, by the name of Konieh, of Karamania, in Asia Minor. It is situated in N. lat. 37° 51', E. long. 32° 40', about one hundred and twenty miles inland from the Mediterranean. It was visited by St. Paul in A.D. 45, when many Gentiles were converted; but some unbelieving Jews excited against him and Barnabas a persecution, which they escaped with difficulty (Acts xiii. 51; xiv. 1, &c.). He undertook a second journey to Iconium in A.D. 51. The church planted at this place by the apostle continued to flourish, until, by the persecutions of the Saracens, and afterwards of the Seljukians, who made it one of their sultanies, it was nearly extinguished. But some Christians of the Greek and Armenian churches, with a Greek metropolitan bishop, are still found in the suburbs of the city, not being permitted to reside within the walls.

Konieh is situated at the foot of Mount Taurus, upon the border of the lake Trogolis, in a fertile plain, rich in valuable productions, particularly apricots, wine, cotton, flax, and grain. The circumference of the town is between two and three miles, beyond which are suburbs not much less populous than the town itself. The town, suburbs, and gardens are plentifully supplied with water from streams which flow from some hills to the westward, and which, in the north-east, join the lake, which varies in size with the season of the year. In the town carpets are manufactured, and blue and yellow leathers are tanned and dried. Cotton, wool, hides, and a few of the other raw productions which enrich the superior industry and skill of the manufacturers of Europe, are sent to Smyrna by caravans.

The city, like all those renowned for superior sanctity, abounds with dervishes, who meet the passenger at every turning of the streets, and demand paras with the greatest clamour and insolence. The bazaars and houses have little to recommend them to notice.

1. ID'DO (*seasonable*), a prophet of Judah, who wrote the history of Rehoboam and Abijah; or rather perhaps who, in conjunction with Seraiah, kept the public rolls during their reigns. It seems by 2 Chron. xiii. 22, that he named his book *Midrash*, or ' Exposition.' Josephus states that this Iddo was the prophet who was sent to Jeroboam at Bethel, and consequently the same who was slain by a lion for disobedience to his instructions (1 Kings xiii.); and many commentators have followed this statement.

2. IDDO, grandfather of the prophet Zechariah Zech. i. 1; Ezra. v. 1; vi. 14).

3. IDDO, chief of the Jews of the Captivity established at Casiphia, a place of which it is difficult to determine the position. It was to him that Ezra sent a requisition for Levites and Nethinim, none of whom had yet joined his caravan. Thirty-eight Levites and two hundred and fifty Nethinim responded to his call (Ezra viii. 17-20), B.C. 457. It would seem from this that Iddo was a chief person of the Nethinim, descended from those Gibeonites who were charged with the servile labours of the tabernacle and temple. This is one of several circumstances which indicate that the Jews in their several colonies under the Exile were still ruled by the heads of their nation, and allowed the free exercise of their worship.

4. IDDO (*lovely*), a chief of the half tribe of Manasseh beyond the Jordan (1 Chron. xxvii. 21).

IDLE. The ordinary uses of this word require no illustration. But the very serious passage in Matt. xii. 36 may suitably be noticed in this place. In the Authorized Version it is translated, ' I say unto you, that *every idle word* that men shall speak, they shall give an account thereof in the day of judgment.' The whole question depends upon the meaning, or rather the force, of the term rendered ' idle word.' concerning which there has been no little difference of opinion. Many understand it to mean ' wicked and injurious words;' but this interpretation has been examined with much nicety by Dr. Tittmann, and shown to be untenable. He contends that we must necessarily understand by the phrase a certain kind of words or discourse, which, under the appearance of sincerity or candour, is often the worst possible, and ' condemns a man,' because it is uttered with an evil purpose. The meaning of the expression, then, seems to be *void of effect, without result, followed by no corresponding event*. Therefore ' idle words' are *empty or vain words* or *discourse, i. e.* void of truth, and to which the event does not correspond. In short, it is the empty, inconsiderate, insincere language of one who says one thing and means another. This Tittmann confirms by a number of citations; and then deduces from the whole that the sense of the passage under review is: ' Believe me, he who uses false and insincere language shall suffer grievous punishment: your words, if uttered with sincerity and ingenuousness, shall be approved; but if they are dissembled, although they bear the strongest appearance of sincerity, they shall be condemned.'

IDOLATRY. In giving a summary view of the forms of idolatry which are mentioned in the Bible, it is expedient to exclude all notice of those illegal images which were indeed designed to bear some symbolical reference to the worship of the true God, but which partook of the nature of idolatry; such, for example, as the golden calf of Aaron (cf. Neh. ix. 18); those of Jeroboam; the singular ephods of Gideon and Micah (Judg. viii. 27; xvii. 5); and the Teraphim.

Idolatry was the most heinous offence against the Mosaic law, which is most particular in defining the acts that constitute the crime, and severe in apportioning the punishment. Thus, it is forbidden to make any image of a strange god; to prostrate oneself before such an image, or before those natural objects which were also worshipped without images, as the sun and moon (Deut. iv. 19); to suffer the altars, images, or groves of idols to stand (Exod. xxxiv. 13); or to keep the gold and silver of which their images were made, and to suffer it to enter the house (Deut. vii. 25, 26); to sacrifice to idols, most especially to offer human sacrifices; to eat of the victims offered to idols by others; to prophesy in the name of a strange god; and to adopt any of the rites used in idolatrous worship, and to transfer them to the worship of the Lord (Deut. xii. 30, 31). As for punishment, the law orders that if an individual committed idolatry he should be stoned to death (Deut. xvii. 2-5); that if a town was guilty of this sin, its inhabitants and cattle should be slain, and its spoils burnt together with the town itself (Deut. xiii. 12-18). To what degree also the whole spirit of the Old Testament is abhorrent from idolatry. is evident (besides legal prohibitions, prophetic denunciations, and energetic appeals like that in Isa. xliv. 9-20) from the literal sense of the terms which are used as synonymes for idols and their worship. Thus idols are called *the inane* (Lev. xix. 4); *vanities* (Acts xiv. 15; Jer. ii. 5); *nothing* (Isa. lxvi. 3); *abominations* (1 Kings xi. 5); and their worship is called *whoredom.*

The early existence of idolatry is evinced by Josh. xxiv. 2, where it is stated that Abram and his immediate ancestors dwelling in Mesopotamia 'served other gods.' The terms in Gen. xxxi. 53, and particularly the plural form of the verb, seem to show that some members of Terah's family had each different gods. From Josh. xxiv. 14, and Ezek. xx. 8, we learn that the Israelites, during their sojourn in Egypt, were seduced to worship the idols of that country; although we possess no particular account of their transgression. In Amos v. 25, and Acts vii. 42, it is stated that they committed idolatry in their journey through the wilderness; and in Num. xxv. 1, sq., that they worshipped the Moabite idol Baal-peor at Shittim. After the Israelites had obtained possession of the promised land, we find that they were continually tempted to adopt the idolatries of the Canaanite nations with which they came in contact. The book of Judges enumerates several successive relapses into this sin. The gods which they served during this period were Baal and Ashtoreth, and their modifications; and Syria, Sidon, Moab, Ammon, and Philistia, are named in Judg. x. 6, as the sources from which they derived their idolatries. Then Samuel appears to have exercised a beneficial influence in weaning the people from this folly (1 Sam. vii.); and the worship of the Lord acquired a gradually increasing hold on the nation until the time of Solomon, who was induced in his old age to permit the establishment of idolatry at Jerusalem. On the division of the nation, the kingdom of Israel (besides adhering to the sin of Jeroboam to the last) was specially devoted to the worship of Baal, which Ahab had renewed and carried to an unprecedented height; and although the energetic measures adopted by Jehu, and afterwards by the priest Jehoiada, to suppress this idolatry, may have been the cause why there is no later express mention of Baal, yet it is evident from 2 Kings xiii. 6, and xvii. 10, that the worship of Asherah continued until the deportation of the ten tribes. This event

also introduced the peculiar idolatries of the Assyrian colonists into Samaria. In the kingdom of Judah, on the other hand, idolatry continued during the two succeeding reigns; was suppressed for a time by Asa (1 Kings xv. 12); was revived in consequence of Joram marrying into the family of Ahab; was continued by Ahaz; received a check from Hezekiah; broke out again more violently under Manasseh; until Josiah made the most vigorous attempt to suppress it. But even Josiah's efforts to restore the worship of the Lord were ineffectual; for the later prophets, Zephaniah, Jeremiah, and Ezekiel, still continue to utter reproofs against idolatry. Nor did the capture of Jerusalem under Jehoiachim awaken this peculiarly sensual people; for Ezekiel (viii.) shows that those who were left in Jerusalem under the government of Zedekiah had given themselves up to many kinds of idolatry; and Jeremiah (xliv. 8) charges those inhabitants of Judah who had found an asylum in Egypt, with having turned to serve the gods of that country. On the restoration of the Jews after the Babylonian captivity, they appear, for the first time in their history, to have been permanently impressed with a sense of the degree to which their former idolatries had been an insult to God, and a degradation of their own understanding—an advance in the culture of the nation which may in part be ascribed to the influence of the Persian abhorrence of images, as well as to the effects of the exile as a chastisement. In this state they continued until Antiochus Epiphanes made the last and fruitless attempt to establish the Greek idolatry in Palestine (1 Macc. i.).

The particular forms of idolatry into which the Israelites fell are described under the names of the different gods which they worshipped [ASHTORETH, BAAL, &c.]: the general features of their idolatry require a brief notice here. According to Movers, the religion of all the idolatrous Syro-Arabian nations was a deification of the powers and laws of nature, an adoration of those objects in which these powers are considered to abide, and by which they act. The deity is thus the invisible power in nature itself, that power which manifests itself as the generator, sustainer, and destroyer of its works. This view admits of two modifications: either the separate powers of nature are regarded as so many different gods, and the objects by which these powers are manifested—as the sun, moon, &c.— are regarded as their images and supporters; or the power of nature is considered to be one and indivisible, and only to differ as to the forms under which it manifests itself. Both views coexist in almost all religions. The most simple and ancient notion, however, is that which conceives the deity to be in a human form, as male and female, and which considers the male sex to be the type of its active, generative, and destructive power; while that passive power of nature whose function is to conceive and bring forth, is embodied under the female form. The human form and the diversity of sex lead naturally to the different ages of life—to the old man and the youth, the matron and the virgin—according to the modifications of the conception; and the myths which represent the influences, the changes, the laws, and the relations of these natural powers under the sacred histories of such gods, constitute a harmonious development of such a religious system.

Those who saw the deity manifested by, or conceived him as resident in, any natural objects, could not fail to regard the sun and moon as the potent rulers of day and night, and the sources of those influences on which all animated nature depends. Hence star-worship forms a prominent feature in all the false religions mentioned in the Bible. Of this character chiefly were the Egyptian, the Canaanite, the Chaldæan, and the Persian religions. The Persian form of astrolatry, however, deserves to be distinguished from the others; for it allowed no images nor temples of the god, but worshipped him in his purest symbol, fire. It is understood that this form is alluded to in most of those passages which mention the worship of the sun, moon, and heavenly host, by incense, on heights (2 Kings xxiii. 5, 12; Jer. xix. 13). The other form of astrolatry, in which the idea of the sun, moon, and planets is blended with the worship of the god in the form of an idol, and with the addition of a mythology (as may be seen in the relations of Baal and his cognates to the sun), easily degenerates into lasciviousness and cruel rites.

The images of the gods were, as to material, of stone, wood, silver, and gold. Those of metal had a trunk or stock of wood, and were covered with plates of silver or gold (Jer. x. 4); or were cast. The general rites of idolatrous worship consist in burning incense; in offering bloodless sacrifices, as the dough-cakes and libations in Jer. vii. 18, and the raisin-cakes in Hos. iii. 1; in sacrificing victims (1 Kings xviii. 26), and especially in human sacrifices [MOLOCH]. These offerings were made on high places, hills, and roofs of houses, or in shady groves and valleys. Some forms of idolatrous worship had libidinous orgies [ASHTORETH]. Divinations, oracles (2 Kings i. 2), and rabdomancy (Hos. iv. 12) form a part of many of these false religions. The priesthood was generally a numerous body; and where persons of both sexes were attached to the service of any god, that service was infamously immoral. It is remarkable that the Pentateuch makes no mention of any *temple* of idols; afterwards we read often of such.

IDUMÆ'A is the Greek form of the Hebrew name EDOM. It was derived from Isaac's son *Edom*, otherwise called Esau, the elder twin-brother of Jacob [ESAU]. It signifies *red*, and seems first to have been suggested by his appearance at his birth, when ' he came out all red' (*i.e.* covered with red hair, Gen. xxv. 25), and was afterwards more formally and permanently imposed on him on account of his unworthy disposal of his birthright for a mess of red lentiles (Gen. xxv. 30). The region which came to bear his name is the mountainous tract on the east side of the great valleys el-Ghor and el-Arabah, extending between the Dead Sea and the Elanitic Gulf of the Red Sea. Into this district Esau removed during his father's lifetime, and his posterity gradually obtained possession of it as the country which God had assigned for their inheritance in the prophetic blessing pronounced by his father Isaac (Gen. xxvii. 39, 40; xxxii. 3; Deut. ii. 5-12, 22). Previously to their occupation of the country, it was called *Mount Seir*, a designation indeed which it never entirely lost. The word

seir means *hairy* (being thus synonymous with Esau), and, when applied to a country, may signify *rugged, mountainous,* and so says Josephus (*Antiq.* i. 20. 3): ' Esau named the country " Roughness" from his own hairy roughness.' But in Gen. xxxvi. 20, we read of an individual of the name of Seir, who had before this inhabited the land, and from whom it may have received its first appellation.

The first mention made of Mount Seir in Scripture is in Gen. xiv. 6, where Chedorlaomer and his confederates are said to have smitten ' the Horim in their Mount Seir.' Among the earliest human habitations were caves, either formed by nature or easily excavated, and for the construction of these the mountains of Edom afforded peculiar facilities. Hence the designation given to the Aboriginal inhabitants—*Horim, i.e.* cave-dwellers, an epithet of similar import with the Greek *Troglodytes.* Even in the days of Jerome ' the whole of the southern part of Idumæa, from Eleutheropolis to Petra and Aila, was full of caverns used as dwellings on account of the sun's excessive heat;' and there is reason to believe that the possessors of the country in every age occupied similar habitations, many traces of which are yet seen in and near Petra, the renowned metropolis.

We are informed in Deut. ii. 12, that ' the children of Esau succeeded [*marg.* inherited] the Horim when they had destroyed them from before them, and dwelt in their stead, as Israel did unto the land of his possession, which Jehovah gave unto them.' From this it may be inferred, that the extirpation of the Horim by the Esauites was, like that of the Canaanites by Israel, very gradual and slow. From Genesis xxxvi. (compare 1 Chron. i.) we learn this much of the political constitution of the Seirite Aborigines, that, like the Esauites and Israelites, they were divided into tribes, and these tribes were subdivided into families—the very polity which still obtains among the Arabs by whom Idumæa is now peopled. Each tribe had its own *Alluf*—a term which is unhappily rendered in the English Version by ' Duke '—for though that has, no doubt, the radical meaning of the Latin *dux*, a ' leader,' it now only suggests the idea of a feudal title of nobility. Of these chiefs of the Horites *seven* are enumerated, viz., Lotan, Shobal, Zibeon, Anah, Dishon, Ezer, and Dishan. The only one of these who is spoken of as related to the other is *Anah*, the son of Zibeon. The primitive and pastoral character of the people is incidentally brought out by the circumstance that this Anah, though a chieftain's son, was in the habit of tending his father's asses. It was when thus employed that he found in the wilderness *eth-ha-yemim*, rendered in the English Version by ' the mules,' but meaning more probably ' the hot springs;' and thus interpreted, the passage seems to be an intimation that he was the first to discover the faculty with which asses and other animals are endowed, of snuffing the moisture of the air, and thus sometimes leading to the opportune discovery of hidden waters in the desert. There is in the country to the south-east of the Dead Sea (which formed part of the Seirite possessions), a place, *Kallirhoë,* celebrated among the Greeks and Romans for its warm baths, and which has been visited by modern travellers.

2 E

Esau first married into two Canaanitish families of the Hittite and Hivite tribes (Gen. xxvi. 34; xxxvi. 2; in one or other of which places, however, the text seems corrupt); but anxious to propitiate his offended parents, he next formed a matrimonial alliance with one of the race of Abraham, viz., Mahalath, otherwise called Bashemath, daughter of Ishmael, and sister of Nebaioth, whose descendants, the Nabathæans, by a singular coincidence, obtained in after-times possession of the land of Edom (Gen. xxviii. 9). Esau's first-born (by Adah or Bashemath, of the daughters of Heth) was Eliphaz, whose son *Teman* gave name to a district of the country (Gen. xxxvi. 11, 34; 1 Chron. i. 45; Ezek. xxv. 13; Obad. verse 9). The Temanites were renowned for their wisdom (Jer. xlix. 7, 20; Baruch iii. 22, 23). The chief speaker in the book of Job is another Eliphaz, a Temanite,—which is one of the circumstances that have led many to place the scene of that story in the land of Edom [JOB]. The name of Teman was preserved to the days of Eusebius in that of Thaiman, a small town five Roman miles from Petra. Another son of the first-mentioned Eliphaz was *Amalek*, who is not to be confounded, however, with the father of the Amalekites, one of the doomed nations of Canaan, of whom we hear so early as the age of Abraham (Gen. xiv. 7).

As a modern Arab *sheikh* is often found to exercise influence far beyond the sphere of his hereditary domain, so in the list of the Edomite *emirs* preserved by Moses we have perhaps only the names of the more distinguished individuals who acquired more or less authority over all the tribes. This oligarchy appears gradually to have changed into a monarchy, as happened too among the Israelites; for in addition to the above mentioned lists, both of Horite and Esauite leaders, we have, at Gen. xxxvi. 31, a catalogue of eight kings (Bela, Jobab, Husham, Hadad, Samlah, Saul, Baal-hanan, Hadar or Hadad) who 'reigned in the land of Edom before there reigned any king over the children of Israel.' It is not necessary to suppose that this was said by Moses *prophetically*: it is one of those passages which may have been inserted by Ezra when finally arranging the canon, inasmuch as it occurs also in the first book of Chronicles, of which he is the reputed compiler. The period when this change to regal government took place in Idumæa can only be matter of conjecture. In the Song of Moses (Exod. xv. 15) it is said that at the tidings of Israel's triumphant passage of the Red Sea the rulers or princes (*Alluf*) of Edom trembled with affright, but when, some forty years afterwards, application had to be made by the Israelites for leave to traverse the land of Edom, it was to the king (*Melek*) that the request was addressed (Num. xx. 14). The road by which it was sought to penetrate the country was termed 'the king's highway' (ver. 17), supposed by Robinson to be the Wady el-Ghuweir, for it is almost the only valley that affords a direct and easy passage through those mountains. From a comparison of these incidents it may be inferred that the change in the form of government took place during the wanderings of the Israelites in the desert, unless we suppose, with Rosenmuller, that it was only this north-eastern part of Edom which was now subject to a monarch, the rest of the country re-

maining under the sway of its former chieftains. But whether the regal power at this period embraced the whole territory or not, perhaps it did not supplant the ancient constitution, but was rather grafted on it, like the authority of the Judges in Israel, and of Saul, the first king, which did not materially interfere with the government that previously existed. It further appears, from the list of Idumæan kings, that the monarchy was not hereditary, but elective (for no one is spoken of as the son or relative of his predecessor); or probably that chieftain was acknowledged as sovereign who was best able to vindicate his claim by force of arms. Every successive king appears to have selected his own seat of government: the places mentioned as having enjoyed that distinction are Dinhabah, Avith, Pagu or Pai. Even foreigners were not excluded from the throne, for the successor of Samlah of Masrekah was Saul, or Shaul, ' of Rechoboth, on the river.' The word ' Rechoboth' means, literally, *streets*, and was a not uncommon name given to towns; but the emphatic addition of ' the river,' points evidently to the Euphrates, and between Rakkah and Anak, on that river, there are still the remains of a place called by the Arabs Rachabath-Malik-Ibn Tauk. In the age of Solomon we read of one Hadad, who ' was of the king's seed in Edom ' (1 Kings xi. 14); from which some have conjectured that by that period there was a royal dynasty of one particular family; but all that the expression may imply is, that he was a blood-relation of the last king of the country. Hadad was the name of one of the early sovereigns ' who smote Midian in the field of Moab' (Gen. xxxvi. 35).

The unbrotherly feud which arose between Esau and Jacob was prolonged for ages between their posterity. The Israelites, indeed, were commanded ' not to abhor an Edomite, for he was their brother' (Deut xxiii. 7); but a variety of circumstances occurred to provoke and perpetuate the hostility. The first time they were brought into direct collision was when the Edomites, though entreated by their ' brother Israel,' refused the latter a passage through their territories; and they had consequently to make a retrograde and toilsome march to the Gulf of Elath, whence they had to ' compass the land of Edom ' by the mountain desert on the east. We do not again hear of the Edomites till the days of Saul, who warred against them with partial success (1 Sam. xiv. 47); but their entire subjugation was reserved for David, who first signally vanquished them in the Valley of Salt (supposed to be in the Ghôr, beside *Usdum*, the Mountain of Salt); and finally placed garrisons in all their country (2 Sam. viii. 14; 1 Chron. xviii. 11-13; 1 Kings xi. 15. Comp. the inscription of Ps. lx. and v. 8, 9; cviii. 9, 10, where ' the strong city' may denote Selah or Petra). Then were fulfilled the prophecies in Gen. xxv. 23 and xxvii. 40, that the ' elder should serve the younger;' and also the prediction of Balaam (Num. xxiv. 18), that Edom and Seir should be for possessions to Israel. Solomon created a naval station at Ezion-geber, at the head of the Gulf of Elath, the modern Akaba (1 Kings ix. 26; 2 Chron. viii. 18). Towards the close of his reign an attempt was made to restore the independence of the country by one Hadad, an Idumæan prince, who, when a child, had been carried into Egypt at the time of David's invasion, and had there married the sister of Tahpanes the queen (1 Kings xi. 14-23) [HADAD]. If Edom then succeeded in shaking off the yoke, it was only for a season, since in the days of Jehoshaphat, the fourth Jewish monarch from Solomon, it is said, 'there was no king in Edom; a deputy was king;' *i.e.* he acted as viceroy for the king of Judah. For that the latter was still master of the country is evident from the fact of his having fitted out, like Solomon, a fleet at Ezion-geber (1 Kings xxii. 47, 48; 2 Chron. xx 36, 37). It was, no doubt, his deputy (called *king*) who joined the confederates of Judah and Israel in their attack upon Moab (2 Kings iii. 9, 12, 26). Yet there seems to have been a partial revolt of the Edomites, or at least of the mountaineers of Seir, even in the reign of Jehoshaphat (2 Chron. xx. 22): and under his successor, Jehoram, they wholly rebelled, and 'made a king over themselves' (2 Kings viii. 20, 22; 2 Chron. xxi. 8, 10). From its being added that, notwithstanding the temporary suppression of the rebellion, 'Edom revolted from under the hand of Judah unto this day,' it is probable that the Jewish dominion was never completely restored. Amaziah, indeed, invaded the country, and having taken the chief city, Selah or Petra, he, in memorial of the conquest, changed its name to Joktheel (*q. d.* subdued of God); and his successor, Uzziah, retained possession of Elath (2 Kings xiv. 7; 2 Chron. xxv. 11-14; xxvi. 3). But in the reign of Ahaz, hordes of Edomites made incursions into Judah and carried away captives (2 Chron. xxviii. 17). About the same period Rezin, king of Syria, expelled the Jews from Elath, which (according to the correct reading of 2 Kings xvi. 6) was thenceforth occupied by the Edomites. Now was fulfilled the other part of Isaac's prediction, viz. that, in course of time, Esau 'should take his brother's yoke from off his neck' (Gen. xxvii. 40). It appears from various incidental expressions in the later prophets, that the Edomites employed their recovered power in the enlargement of their territory in all directions. They spread as far south as Dedan in Arabia, and northward to Bozrah in the Hauran; though it is doubtful if the Bozrah of Scripture may not have been a place in Idumæa Proper (Isa. xxxiv. 6; lxiii. 1; Jer. xlix. 7, 8-20; Ezek. xxv. 13; Amos i. 12). When the Chaldæans invaded Judah, under Nebuchadnezzar, the Edomites became their willing auxiliaries, and triumphed with fiendish malignity over the ruin of their kinsmen the Jews, of whose desolated land they hoped to obtain a large portion to themselves (Obad. verses 10 16; Ezek. xxv. 12-14; xxxv. 3-10; xxxvi. 5; Lament. iv. 21). By this circumstance the hereditary hatred of the Jews was rekindled in greater fury than ever, and hence the many dire denunciations of the 'daughter of Edom,' to be met with in the Hebrew prophets (Ps. cxxxvii. 7-9; Obad. *passim*; Jer. xlix. 7; Ezek. xxv. and xxxv.). From the language of Malachi (i. 2, 3), and also from the accounts preserved by Josephus (*Antiq.* x. 9. 7), it would seem that the Edomites did not wholly escape the Chaldæan scourge; but instead of being carried captive, like the Jews, they not only retained possession of their own territory, but became masters of the south of Judah, as far as Hebron (1 Macc. v. 65, comp. with Ezek.

xxxv. 10; xxxvi. 5). Here, however, they were, in course of time, successfully attacked by the Maccabees, and about B.C. 125, were finally subdued by John Hyrcanus, who compelled them to submit to circumcision and other Jewish rites, with a view to incorporate them with the nation (1 Macc. v. 3, 65; 2 Macc. x. 16; xii. 32; Joseph. *Antiq.* xiii. 9. 1; 15, 4). The amalgamation, however, of the two races seems never to have been effected, for we afterwards hear of Antipater, an Idumæan by birth, being made by Cæsar procurator of all Judæa; and his son, commonly called Herod the Great, was, at the time of Christ's birth, king of Judæa, including Idumæa; and hence Roman writers often speak of all Palestine under that name. Not long before the siege of Jerusalem by Titus, 20,000 Idumæans were called in to the defence of the city by the Zealots; but both parties gave themselves up to rapine and murder. This is the last mention made of the Edomites in history. The author of a work on Job, once ascribed to Origen, says that their name and language had perished, and that, like the Ammonites and Moabites, they had all become Arabs. In the second century Ptolemy limits the name Idumæa to the country west of the Jordan.

But while, during the captivity of the Jews in Babylon, the Edomites had thus been extending their territory to the north-west, they were themselves supplanted in the southern part of their native region by the Nabathæans, the descendants of Ishmael's eldest son; and to the article NEBAIOTH we must refer the reader for the subsequent history of the land of Edom.

From the era of the Crusades down to the present century the land of Esau was, to Europeans, a *terra incognita*. Its situation was laid down on the best maps more than a hundred miles from the true position, and as if lying in a direction where it is now known there is nothing but a vast expanse of desert. Volney had his attention drawn towards it, when at Gaza, by the vague reports of the Arabs; and in 1807 the unfortunate Seetzen penetrated a certain way into the country and heard of the wonders of the Wady Mûsa; but the first modern traveller who 'passed through the land of Edom' was Burckhardt, in the year 1812. And it has been well remarked by Dr. Robinson that 'had he accomplished nothing but his researches in these regions, his journey would have been worth all the labour and cost expended on it, although his discoveries thus shed their strongest light upon subjects which were not comprehended in the plan or purpose either of himself or his employers.' Burckhardt entered Idumæa from the north, and in the year 1818 he was followed in the same direction by Messrs. Legh, Bankes, Irby and Mangles. In 1828 Laborde and Linant found access from the south; and since then it has been visited and described by so many that the names of its localities have become familiar as household words.

The limit of the wanderings of the Israelites in the desert was the brook Zered, after crossing which they found themselves in the territory of Moab (Deut ii. 13-18). This brook is supposed to be identical with the *Wady el-Ahsy*, which, rising near the Castle el-Ahsy, on the route to Mecca of the Syrian caravan upon the high eastern desert, penetrates through the whole chain of mountains to near the south-east corner of the Dead Sea. It was thus the southern border of Moab and the northern of Edom, whence the latter region extended southwards as far as to Elath on the Red Sea. The valley which runs between the two seas consists first of El-Ghor, which is comparatively low, but gradually rises into the more elevated plain of El-Arabah to the south. The country lying *east* of this great valley is the land of Idumæa. It is a mountain tract, consisting at the base of low hills of limestone or argillaceous rock, then lofty mountains of porphyry forming the body of the mountain; above these, sandstone broken up into irregular ridges and grotesque groups of cliffs; and again farther back, and higher than all, long elevated ridges of limestone without precipices. East of all these stretches off indefinitely the high *plateau* of the great eastern desert. The whole breadth of the mountainous tract between the Arabah and the eastern desert does not exceed fifteen or twenty geographical miles. Of these mountains the most remarkable is *Mount Hor*, near the Wady Mûsa [HOR, MOUNT]. While the mountains on the west of the Arabah, though less elevated, are wholly barren, those of Idumæa seem to enjoy a sufficiency of rain, and are covered with tufts of herbs and occasional trees. The wadys, too, are full of trees and shrubs and flowers, while the eastern and higher parts are extensively cultivated, and yield good crops. This mountainous region is at present divided into two districts. The northern bears the name of *Jebâl, i. e.* 'The Mountain,' the Gebal of the Hebrews (Ps. lxxxiii. 8), and the Gebalene of the Greeks and Romans. The southern district is *esh-Sherah*, extending as far as Akabah, and including Shôbak, Wady Mûsa, Maan, &c. Burckhardt mentions a *third* district, *Jebal Hesma;* but Robinson says that though there is a sandy tract, el-Hismah, with mountains around it, on the east of Akabah, it does not constitute a separate division.

The whole of this region is at present occupied by various tribes of Bedouin Arabs. The chief tribe in the *Jebal* is the Hejaya, with a branch of the Kaabineh, while in *esh-Sherah* they are all of the numerous and powerful tribe of the Haweitat, with a few independent allies. The Bedouins in Idumæa have of late years been partially subject to the Pasha of Egypt, paying an annual tribute, which, in the case of the Beni Sukhr, is one camel for two tents. The fellahin, or peasants, are half Bedouin, inhabiting the few villages, but dwelling also in tents; they, too, pay tribute to the Egyptian government, and furnish supplies of grain.

Among the localities connected with Edom which are mentioned in Scripture may be noticed Dinhabah, Bozrah, Theman, Maon (now Maan), Kadesh-barnea (which Robinson identifies with el-Weibeh in the Wady el-Jeib), Zephath (which he supposes to be the pass of Es-Sufah), Elath, and Ezion-geber, &c.; but the most celebrated place in all the region was the chief city, Selah or Petra, for a description of which the reader is referred to the latter head [PETRA].

Could the scene of the book of Job be with certainty fixed in Idumæa, we should then possess much curious and valuable information respecting both the country and people soon after it had been colonized by the descendants of Esau (See Mason Good, Wemyss, and others upon Job). But all that we learn directly of the ancient Edomites from the historical books of Scripture represents them as not, indeed, neglecting agriculture or trade (Num. xx. 17), yet, on the whole, a warlike and predatory race, who, according to the prediction of their progenitor Isaac, 'lived by their sword.' The situation of the country afforded peculiar facilities for commerce, which seems to have been prosecuted from a very early period. 'Bordering,' says Volney, 'upon Arabia on the east and south, and Egypt on the south-west, and forming, from north to south, the most commodious channel of communication between Jerusalem and her dependencies on the Red Sea, through the continuous valleys of el-Ghor and el-Arabah, Idumæa may be said to have long formed the emporium of the commerce of the East.' The era of its greatest prosperity was after the Nabathæans had become masters of the country and founded the kingdom of Arabia Petræa, of which the renowned metropolis was Petra. The *religion* of the early Edomites was, perhaps, comparatively pure; but in process of time they embraced idolatry: in 2 Chron. xxv. 20, we read of the 'gods of Edom,' one of whom, according to Josephus (*Antiq.* xv. 7. 9), was called *Kotzé.* With respect to the striking fulfilment of the prophetic denunciations upon Edom, we need only refer the reader to the well-known work of Keith, who frequently errs, however, in straining the sense of prophecy beyond its legitimate import, as well as in seeking out too literally minute an accomplishment.

ILLYRICUM, a country lying to the north-west of Macedonia, and answering nearly to that which is at present called Dalmatia; by which name indeed the southern part of Illyricum itself was known, and whither St. Paul informs Timothy that Titus had gone (2 Tim. iv. 10). Paul himself preached the Gospel in Illyricum, which was at that time a province of the Roman Empire (Rom. xv. 19).

IMMAN'UEL, or EMMANUEL. This word, meaning ' *God with us.*' occurs in the celebrated verse of Isaiah (vii. 14), ' Behold, a virgin shall conceive and bear a son, and shall call his name IMMANUEL.' In the name itself there is no difficulty; but the verse, as a whole, has been variously interpreted. From the manner in which the word God, and even Jehovah, is used in the composition of Hebrew names, there is no such peculiarity in that of Immanuel as in itself requires us to understand that he who bore it should be in fact God. Indeed, it is used as a proper name among the Jews at this day. This high sense has, however, been assigned to it in consequence of the application of the whole verse by the Evangelist Matthew (i. 23) to our Divine Saviour. Even if this reference did not exist, the history of the Nativity would irresistibly lead us to the conclusion that the verse—whatever may have been its intermediate signification —had an ultimate reference to Christ.

The state of opinion on this point has been thus neatly summed up by Dr. Henderson, in his note on the text:—' This verse has long been a subject of dispute between Jews and professedly Christian writers, and among the latter mutually. While the former reject its application to the

Messiah altogether,—the earlier rabbins explaining it of the queen of Ahaz and the birth of his son Hezekiah; and the later, as Kimchi and Abarbanel, of the prophet's own wife,—the great body of Christian interpreters have held it to be directly and exclusively in prophecy of our Saviour, and have considered themselves fully borne out by the inspired testimony of the Evangelist Matthew. Others, however, have departed from this construction of the passage, and have invented or adopted various hypotheses in support of such dissent. Grotius and others suppose either the then present or a future wife of Isaiah to be the 'virgin' referred to. A second class are of opinion that the prophet had nothing more in view than an ideal virgin, and that both she and her son are merely imaginary personages, introduced for the purpose of prophetic illustration. A third think that the prophet pointed to a young woman in the presence of the king and his courtiers. A fourth class admit the hypothesis of a double sense : one in which the words apply primarily to some female living in the time of the prophet, and her giving birth to a son according to the ordinary laws of nature ; or, as Dathe holds, to some virgin, who at that time should miraculously conceive ; and the other, in which they received a secondary and plenary fulfilment in the miraculous conception and birth of Jesus Christ.'

INCENSE, a perfume which gives forth its fragrance by burning, and, in particular, that perfume which was burnt upon the altar of incense [ALTAR; CENSER]. Indeed, the burning of incense seems to have been considered among the Hebrews so much of an act of worship or sacred offering, that we read not of any other use of incense than this among them. Nor among the Egyptians do we discover any trace of burnt perfume except in sacerdotal use; but in the Persian sculptures we see incense burnt before the king. The prohibition of the Hebrews to make any perfume for private use—' to smell to' —like that prepared for the altar, merely implies, we apprehend, that the sacred incense had a peculiarly rich fragrance for being burnt, which was forbidden to be imitated in common perfumes.

The ingredients of the sacred incense are enumerated with great precision in Exod. xxx. 34, 35 : ' Take unto thee sweet spices, stacte and galbanum; these sweet spices with pure frankincense ; of each shall there be a like weight. And thou shalt make of it a perfume, a confection after the art of the apothecary, tempered together, pure and holy.' For an explanation of these various ingredients, we must refer to their several names in the present work. The further directions are, that this precious compound should be made or broken up into minute particles, and that it should be deposited, as a very holy thing, in the tabernacle ' before the testimony' (or ark). As the ingredients are so minutely specified, there was nothing to prevent wealthy persons from having a similar perfume for private use : and this, therefore, was forbidden under pain of excommunication : ' Ye shall not make to yourselves according to the composition thereof : it shall be unto thee holy for the Lord. Whosoever shall make like unto that, to smell thereto, shall even be cut off from his people' (ver. 37, 38).

According to Maimonides, the reason for the use of incense was to prevent the stench which would otherwise have been occasioned by the number of beasts every day slaughtered in the sanctuary, and to render the odour of the sanctuary, and of the vestments of those that ministered, exceedingly grateful.

This is very well ; and no doubt the use of incense, which we always find in religions where worship is rendered by sacrifice, had its origin in some such considerations. But we are not to lose sight of the symbolical meaning of this grateful offering. It was a symbol of *prayer*. It was offered at the time when the people were in the posture and act of prayer ; and their orisons were supposed to be presented to God by the priest, and to ascend to Him in the smoke and odour of that fragrant offering. This beautiful idea of the incense frequently occurs in Scripture (comp. Ps. cxli. 2 ; Mal. i. 11 ; Zech. xiv. 16 ; Acts x. 4 ; Rev. v. 8 ; viii. 4).

INCHANTMENTS. [WITCHCRAFT.]

INDIA. This name occurs only in Esther i. 1 ; viii. 9, where the Persian king is described as reigning ' from India unto Ethiopia, over a hundred and seven and twenty provinces.' It is found again, however. in the Apocrypha, where India is mentioned among the countries which the Romans took from Antiochus and gave to Eumenes (1 Macc. viii. 8).

It is evident from all ancient history, that the country known as India in ancient times extended more to the west, and did not reach so far to the east—that is, was not known so far to the east— as the India of the moderns. When we read of ancient India, we must clearly not understand the whole of Hindostan, but chiefly the northern parts of it, or the countries between the Indus and the Ganges; although it is not necessary to assert that the rest of that peninsula, particularly its western coast, was then altogether unknown. It was from this quarter that the Persians and Greeks (to whom we are indebted for the earliest accounts of India) invaded the country ; and this was consequently the region which first became generally known. The countries bordering on the Ganges continued to be involved in obscurity, the great kingdom of the Prasians excepted, which, situated nearly above the modern Bengal, was dimly discernible. Besides, the western and northern boundaries were not the same as at present. To the west, India was not then bounded by the river Indus, but by a chain of mountains which, under the name of Koh (whence the Grecian appellation of the Indian Caucasus), extended from Bactria to Makran, or Gedrosia, enclosing the kingdoms of Candahar and Cabul, the modern kingdom of Eastern Persia or Afghanistan. These districts anciently formed part of India, as well as, further to the south, the less perfectly known countries of the Arabi and Haurs, bordering on Gedrosia. This western boundary continued at all times the same, and was removed to the Indus only in consequence of the victories of Nadir Shah.

Towards the north, ancient India overpassed not less its present limit. It comprehended the whole of the mountainous region above Cashmir, Badakshan, Belur Land, the western boundary mountains of Little Bucharia, or Little Thibet, and even the desert of Cobi, so far as it was known. The discovery of a passage by sea to the coasts of India has contributed to withdraw from these regions the attention of Europeans, and left them in an obscurity which hitherto has been little disturbed, although the current of events seems likely ere long to lead to our better knowledge.

From this it appears that the India of Scripture included no part of the present India, seeing that it was confined to the territories possessed by the Persians and the Syrian Greeks, that never extended beyond the Indus, which, since the time of Nadir Shah, has been regarded as the western boundary of India. Something of India beyond the Indus became known through the conquering march of Alexander, and still more through that of Seleucus Nicator, who penetrated to the banks of the Ganges; but the notions thus obtained are not embraced in the Scriptural notices, which, both in the canonical and the apocryphal text, are confined to Persian India.

INHERITANCE. The laws and observances which determine the acquisition and regulate the devolution of property, are among the influences which affect the vital interests of states; and it is therefore of high consequence to ascertain the nature and bearing of the laws and observances relating to this subject which come to us with the sanction of the Bible. We may also premise that, in a condition of society such as that in which we now live, wherein the two diverging tendencies which favour immense accumulations on the one hand, and lead to poverty and pauperism on the other, are daily becoming more and more decided, disturbing, and baneful, there seems to be required on the part of those who take Scripture as their guide, a careful study of the foundations of human society, and of the laws of property, as they are developed in the divine records which contain the revealed will of God.

That will, in truth, as it is the source of all created things, and specially of the earth and its intelligent denizen, man, so is it the original foundation of property, and of the laws by which its inheritance should be regulated. God, as the Creator of the earth, gave it to man to be held, cultivated, and enjoyed (Gen. i. 28, sq.; Ps. cxv. 16; Eccles. v. 9). The primitive records are too brief and fragmentary to supply us with any details respecting the earliest distribution or transmission of landed property; but from the passages to which reference has been made, the important fact appears to be established beyond a question, that the origin of property is to be found, not in the achievements of violence, the success of the sword, or any imaginary implied contract, but in the will and the gift of the common Creator and bountiful Father of the human race. It is equally clear that the gift was made, not to any favoured portion of our race, but to the race itself—to man as represented by our great primogenitor, to whom the use of the divine gift was first graciously vouchsafed.

The impression which the original gift of the earth was calculated to make on men, the Great Donor was pleased, in the case of Palestine, to render, for his own wise purposes, more decided and emphatic by an express re-donation to the patriarch Abraham (Gen xiii. 14, sq.). Many years, however, elapsed before the promise was fulfilled. Meanwhile the notices which we have regarding the state of property in the patriarchal ages, are few and not very definite. The products of the earth, however, were at an early period accumulated and held as property. Violence invaded the possession; opposing violence recovered the goods. War soon sprang out of the passions of the human heart. The necessity of civil government was felt. Consuetudinary laws accordingly developed themselves. The head of the family was supreme His will was law. The physical superiority which he possessed gave him this dominion. The same influence would secure its transmission in the male rather than the female line. Hence too the rise of the rights of primogeniture. In the early condition of society which is called patriarchal, landed property had its origin, indeed, but could not be held of first importance by those who led a wandering life, shifting continually, as convenience suggested, from one spot to another. Cattle were then the chief property (Gen. xxiv. 35). But land, if held, was held on a freehold tenure; nor could any other tenure have come into existence till more complex and artificial relations arose, resulting in all probability, from the increase of population and the relative insufficiency of food. When Joseph.went down into Egypt, he appears to have found the freehold tenure prevailing, which, however, he converted into a tenancy at will, or, at any rate, into a conditional tenancy. Other intimations are found in Genesis which confirm the general statements which have just been made. Daughters do not appear to have had any inheritance. If there are any exceptions to this rule, they only serve to prove it. Thus Job (the book so called is undoubtedly very old, so that there is no impropriety in citing it in this connection) is recorded (xlii. 15) to have given his daughters an inheritance conjointly with their brothers—a record which of itself proves the singularity of the proceeding, and establishes our position that inheritance generally followed the male line. How highly the privileges conferred by primogeniture were valued, may be learnt from the history of Jacob and Esau. In the patriarchal age doubtless these rights were very great. The eldest son, as being by nature the first fitted for command, assumed influence and control, under his father, over the family and its dependents; and when the father was removed by death, he readily, and as if by an act of Providence, took his father's place. Thus he succeeded to the property in succeeding to the headship of the family, the clan, or the tribe. At first the eldest son most probably took exclusive possession of his father's property and power; and when, subsequently, a division became customary, he would still retain the largest share—a double portion, if not more (Gen. xxvii 25, 29, 40). That in the days of Abraham other sons partook with the eldest, and that too though they were sons of concubines, is clear from the story of Hagar's expulsion:—'Cast out (said Sarah) this bondwoman and her son; for the son of this bondwoman shall not be heir with my son, even with Isaac' (Gen. xxi. 10). The few notices left us in Genesis of the transfer of property from hand to hand are interesting, and bear a remarkable similarity to what takes place in Eastern countries even at this day (Gen. xxi. 22, sq; xxiii. 9, sq.). The purchase of the Cave of

Machpelah as a family burying-place for Abraham, detailed in the last passage, serves to show the safety of property at that early period, and the facility with which an inheritance was transmitted even to sons' sons (comp. Gen. xlix. 29). That it was customary, during the father's lifetime, to make a disposition of property, is evident from Gen. xxiv. 35, where it is said that Abraham had given all he had to Isaac. This statement is further confirmed by ch. xxv. 5, 6, where it is added that Abraham gave to the sons of his concubines ' gifts, sending them away from Isaac his son, while he yet lived, eastward unto the east country.' Sometimes, however, so far were the children of unmarried females from being dismissed with a gift, that they shared with what we should term the legitimate children, in the father's property and rights. Thus Dan and Naphtali were sons of Bilhah, Rachel's maid, whom she gave to her husband, failing to bear children herself. So Gad and Asher were, under similar circumstances, sons of Zilpah, Leah's maid (Gen. xxx. 2–14). In the event of the eldest son's dying in the father's lifetime, the next son took his place; and if the eldest son left a widow, the next son made her his wife (Gen. xxxviii. 7, sq.), the offspring of which union was reckoned to the first-born and deceased son. Should the second likewise die, the third son took his place (Gen. xxxviii. 11). While the rights of the first-born were generally established and recognised, yet were they sometimes set aside in favour of a younger child. The blessing of the father or the grandsire seems to have been an act essential in the devolution of power and property—in its effects not unlike wills and testaments with us; and instances are not wanting in which this (so to term it) testamentary bequest set aside consuetudinary laws, and gave precedence to a younger son (Gen. xlviii. 15, sq.). Special claims on the parental regards were acknowledged and rewarded by special gifts, as in the case of Jacob's donation to Joseph (Gen. xlviii. 22). In a similar manner, bad conduct on the part of the eldest son (as well as of others) subjected him, if not to the loss of his rights of property, yet to the evil influence of his father's dying malediction (Gen. xlix. 3); while the good and favoured, though younger, son was led by the paternal blessing to anticipate, and probably also to reap, the richest inheritance of individual and social happiness (Gen. xlix. 8–22).

The original promise made to Abraham of the land of Palestine was solemnly repeated to Isaac (Gen. xxvi. 3), the reason assigned being, because ' Abraham obeyed my voice and kept my charge, my commandments, my statutes, and my laws;' while it is expressly declared that the earlier inhabitants of the country were dispossessed and destined to extermination for the greatness of their iniquity. The possession of the promised land was embraced by Isaac in his dying benediction to Jacob (Gen. xxviii. 3, 4), to whom God vouchsafed (Gen. xxviii. 15; see also xxxv. 10, 11) to give a renewed assurance of the destined inheritance. That this donation, however, was held to be dependent for the time and manner of its fulfilment on the divine will, appears from Gen. xxxiii. 18, where Jacob, on coming into the land of Canaan, bought for an hundred pieces of money ' a parcel of a field, at the hand of the children of Hamor.' Delayed though the execution of the promise was, confidence never deserted the family of Abraham, so that Joseph, dying in the land of Egypt, assured his brothers that they would be visited of God and placed in possession of Canaan, enjoining on them, in this conviction, that when conducted to their possession, they should carry his bones with them out of Egypt (Gen. l. 25).

A promise thus given, thus repeated, and thus believed, easily, and indeed unavoidably, became the fundamental principle of that settlement of property which Moses made when at length he had effected the divine will in the redemption of the children of Israel. The observances and practices, too, which we have noticed as prevailing among the patriarchs would, no doubt, have great influence on the laws which the Jewish legislator originated or sanctioned. The land of Canaan was divided among the twelve tribes descended through Isaac and Jacob from Abraham. The division was made by lot for an inheritance among the families of the sons of Israel, according to the tribes, and to the number and size of families in each tribe. The tribe of Levi, however, had no inheritance, but forty-eight cities with their suburbs were assigned to the Levites, each tribe giving according to the number of cities that fell to its share (Num. xxxiii. 50; xxxiv. 1; xxxv. 1). The inheritance thus acquired was never to leave the tribe to which it belonged; every tribe was to keep strictly to its own inheritance. An heiress, in consequence, was not allowed to marry out of her own tribe, lest property should pass by her marriage into another tribe (Num. xxxvi. 6-9). This restriction led to the marriage of heiresses with their near relations: thus the daughters of Zelophehad ' were married unto their father's brother's sons,' ' and their inheritance remained in the tribe of the family of their father ' (ver. 11, 12). In general cases the inheritance went to sons, the first-born receiving a double portion, ' for he is the beginning of his father's strength.' If a man had two wives, one beloved, the other hated, and if the first-born were the son of her who was hated, he nevertheless was to enjoy ' the right of the first-born ' (Deut. xxi. 15). If a man left no sons, the inheritance passed to his daughters; if there was no daughter, it went to his brothers; in case there were no brothers, it was given to his father's brothers; if his father had no brothers, it came into possession of the nearest kinsman (Num. xxvii. 8). The land was Jehovah's, and could not therefore be permanently alienated. Every fiftieth year, whatever land had been sold returned to its former owner. The value and price of land naturally rose or fell in proportion to the number of years there were to elapse prior to the ensuing fiftieth or jubilee-year. If he who sold the land, or a kinsman, could redeem the land before the year of jubilee, it was to be restored to him on his paying to the purchaser the value of the produce of the years remaining till the jubilee. Houses in villages or unwalled towns might not be sold for ever; they were restored at the jubilee, and might at any time be redeemed. If a man sold a dwelling-house situated in a walled city, he had the option of redeeming it within the space of a full year after it had been sold; but if it remained unredeemed, it belonged to the purchaser, and did not return to him who sold it even at the jubilee (Lev. xxv. 8, 23). The Levites were not allowed to sell the land in the suburbs of their cities, though they might dispose of the cities themselves, which, however, were redeemable at any time, and must return at the jubilee to their original possessors (Lev. xxvii. 16).

The regulations which the laws of Moses established rendered wills, or a testamentary disposition of (at least) landed property, almost, if not quite, unnecessary; we accordingly find no provision for anything of the kind. Some difficulty may have been now and then occasioned, when near relations failed; but this was met by the traditional law, which furnished minute directions on the point. Personal property would naturally follow the land, or might be bequeathed by word of mouth. At a later period of the Jewish polity the mention of wills is found, but the idea seems to have been taken from foreign nations. In princely families they appear to have been used, as we learn from Josephus; but such a practice can hardly suffice to establish the general use of wills among the people. In the New Testament, however, wills are expressly mentioned (Gal. iii. 15; Heb. ix. 17).

INK, INKHORN. [WRITING]

INN. In the days of the elder patriarchs there seem to have been no places specially devoted to the reception of travellers, at least in the pastoral districts frequented by those venerable nomades; for we find Abraham, like the Oriental shepherds of the present day, under a strong sense of the difficulties and privations with which journeying in those regions was attended, deeming it a sacred duty to keep on the outlook, and offer the wayfaring man the rites of hospitality in his own tent. Nor could the towns of Pales-

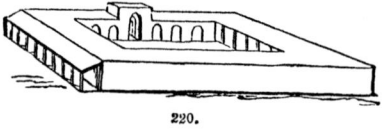

220.

tine, as it would seem, at that remote period, boast of any greater advance with respect to establishments of this sort (see Gen. xix. 2); from which it is evident that the custom, which is still frequently witnessed in the cities of the East, was then not uncommon, for travellers who were late in arriving, and who had no introductions to a private family, to bivouac in the streets, or wrapping themselves up in the ample folds of their hykes, to pass the night as they best could in the open air (see also Judges xix. 15). In the Arab towns and villages, however, when a traveller arrives in the daytime, the sheikh, or some principal person of the place, goes out to welcome him, and treats him with great civility in his own house; or else he conducts him to the menzil, which, though a place of rather a nondescript character, is understood to be the house occupied by those who entertain strangers, when there are no other lodgings, and to which the women in the sheikh's house, having surveyed the number of the guests, send provisions of every kind, according to the season, and provide every accommodation the place can afford.

The first mention of an inn, or house set apart for the accommodation of travellers, occurs in the account of the return of Jacob's sons from Egypt (Gen. xlii. 27); and as it was situated within the confines of that country, and at the first stage from the metropolis, it is probable that the erection of such places of entertainment originated with the Egyptians, who were far superior to all their contemporaries in the habits and the arts of civilized life. The Egyptian inn, where the sons of Israel halted to bait their asses, was probably, from the remote period to which it belonged, of a rude and humble description, in point both of appearance and accommodation; and such is the low state of art, or the tyrannical force of custom in the East, that establishments of this kind in the present day can, with few exceptions, boast of improvements, that render them superior to the mean and naked poverty of those which received the pilgrims of the patriarchal age.

Khan, or karavanserai, is the name which this kind of building bears; and though the terms are often applied indiscriminately, there is an acknowledged distinction, which seems to be, that khan is applied to those which are situated in or near towns, whereas caravanserais (a lodge for caravans, as the compound word imports) is the more appropriate designation of such as are erected in desert and sequestered places. Some of these buildings are provided at the public expense, or owe their existence to devoted Mussulmans, who bestow a portion of their wealth, as a meritorious act of charity, in promoting the comfort and refreshment of pilgrims; while others are erected by the contributions of private merchants for their own accommodation. The latter, of course, are the most spacious, the most elegant, and best appointed; but though varying in character and size, this class of establishments preserves so generally the same uniform plan of construction, that a description of one may serve to convey an idea of all. The caravanserai then is a large edifice presenting the form of a square, the sides of which, about 100 yards in length each, are surrounded by an external wall of fine brickwork, based on stone, rising generally to the height of twenty feet. In the middle of the front wall there is a wide and lofty archway, having on one or both sides a lodge for the porter and other attendants; while the upper part of it, being faced with carving or ornamental masonwork, and containing several rooms, surmounted by elegant domes, is considered the most honourable place of the building, and is therefore appropriated to the use of the better sort. This archway leads into a spacious rectangle, the area forming a courtyard for cattle, in the midst of which is a well or fountain. Along the sides of the rectangle are piazzas extending the whole length, and opening at every few steps into arched and open recesses, which are the entrances into the travellers' apartments. An inner door behind each of these conducts to a small oblong chamber, deriving all its light from the door, or from a small open window in the back wall entirely destitute of furniture, and affording no kind of accommodation in the way of presses or shelves, except some rude niches excavated in the thick walls. This cell is intended for the dormitory of the traveller, who generally prefers, however, the recess in front for sitting in under shade during the daytime, as well as for sleeping in during the night, when the season allows. There being no other door but the entrance arch, each occupant remains isolated in his own quarters, and is cut off from all communication with the other inmates of the caravanserai. But in the middle of one of the three sides, or in large caravanserais of each of the sides, there is a large hall, which serves as a travellers' room, where all may indiscriminately assemble : while at the end of each side there is a staircase leading to the flat roof of the house, where the cool breeze and a view of the surrounding country may be enjoyed. These chambers generally stand on the ground-floor, which is a few feet above the level of the court-yard; but in the few buildings of this sort which have two stories, the travellers are accommodated above, while the under flat is reserved for the use of their servants, or appropriated as warehouses for goods. And in such establishments there is found one other additional advantage in having a supply of servants and cooks, as well as a shop in the porter's house, where all commodities may be procured. Caravanserais of this superior class, however, are rarely to be met with. The most part are but wretched lodging-places—filled, it may be, with dirt and vermin—consisting only of bare walls, in which not an article of furniture is to be seen, nor a cooking utensil to be found, nor provisions of any sort to be obtained for love or money. The traveller must carry along with him, as well as provide with his own hands, whatever is necessary for his use and comfort. He must also subsist on the supply of food and articles of luxury he may have had the foresight to provide, as no addition to his stores can be made till he reaches the next town. In short, in many of the khans or caravanserais to which he may come, he can look for nothing from the keeper except to show him the way to his chamber, and give him the key if it is furnished with a door. One assistance only he may depend upon, and it is no inconsiderable one—that of receiving some attendance and aid if overtaken by sickness; for one of the requisite qualifications for the office is, that the functionary possess a knowledge of simples, and the most approved practice in case of fracture or common ailments. And hence the good Samaritan in the parable (Luke x. 30), although he was obliged, in the urgency of the case, himself to apply from his own store a few simple remedies for the relief of the distressed man, left him with full confidence to be treated and nursed by the keeper of the khan, whose assiduities in dressing the wounds and bruises of his patient might be quickened, perhaps, by the liberal remuneration he was promised, as well as by the example of the humane traveller.

Among the Egyptians, and indeed among the ancients generally, the keepers of houses of public entertainment were always women; and hence we can easily account for the ready admission which the spies obtained into the house of Rahab, ' on the wall of Jericho,' situated, as such houses were, for the reception of strangers, for the most part at the gate or entrance into the town (Josh. ii. 1). This woman is called a harlot in our translation, but the original Hebrew admits of being translated by another word, to which no degrading or infamous associations are attached.

Although it is probable that the state of Judæa in the time of Christ and the Apostles was, in respect to means of communication, much superior to that of any Oriental country in the present day, yet the warm commendations of hospitality so frequently met with in the works of contemporary classical writers, as well as the pressing exhortations of the inspired Apostle to the practice of that virtue, too plainly prove that travellers were then chiefly dependent on the kindness of private individuals. The strong probability is, that the ' inns ' mentioned in the New Testament find their true and correct representations in the Eastern khans and caravanserais of the present day; and that the Jews of that period had experience of nothing better than the bare walls and cell-like apartments of such edifices as we have described above.

This subject acquires additional interest from its connection with the birth of our Lord; and there has been a good deal of controversy both respecting the character of the building from which Mary was excluded by the influx of company, and also the nature of the place where she ' brought forth her first-born son.' No explanation, however, that we have met with, appears so satisfactory, and conveys such an intelligible picture to the eye, as that given by the editor of the *Pictorial Bible* (Luke ii. 7); with whose words we shall conclude this article. ' The most complete establishments have very excellent stables in covered avenues, which extend *behind* the ranges of apartments—that is, between the back wall of these ranges of building and the *external* wall of the khan; and the entrance to it is by a covered passage at one of the corners of the quadrangle. The stable is on a level with the court, and consequently below the level of the buildings, by the height of the platform on which they stand. Nevertheless, this platform is allowed to project behind into the stable, so as to form a bench, to which the horses' heads are turned, and on which they can, if they like, rest the nose-bag of hair-cloth, from which they eat, to enable them to reach the bottom when its contents get low. It also often happens that not only this bench exists in the stable, but also recesses corresponding to those in front of the apartments, and formed by the side walls which divide the rooms, being allowed to project behind into the stable, just as the projection of the same walls into the great area forms the recesses in front. These recesses in the stable, or the bench if there are no recesses, furnish accommodation to the servants and others who have charge of the beasts; and when persons find on their arrival that the apartments usually appropriated to travellers are already occupied, they are glad to find accommodation in the stable, particularly when the nights are cold or the season inclement. It is evident, then, from this description, that the part of the stable called ' the manger,' could not reasonably have been other than one of those recesses, or at least a portion of the bench which we have mentioned, as affording accommodation to travellers under certain circumstances.'

INSPIRATION. This word is sometimes used to denote the excitement and action of a fervent imagination in the poet or orator. But even in this case there is generally a reference to some supposed divine influence, to which the excited action is owing. It is once used in Scripture to denote that Divine agency by which man is endued with the faculties of an intelligent being, when it is said, ' the inspiration of the Almighty giveth him understanding.' But the inspiration now to be considered is that which belonged to those who wrote the Scriptures, and which is particularly spoken of in 2 Tim. iii. 16, and in 2 Pet. i. 21: 'All Scripture is given by inspiration of God ;' ' Holy men of God spake as they were moved by the Holy Ghost.' These passages relate specially to the Old Testament; but there is at least equal reason to predicate Divine inspiration of the New Testament.

The definition which Dr. Knapp gives of inspiration is the one we shall adopt. He says, ' It may be best defined, according to the representations of the Scriptures themselves, as *an extraordinary Divine agency upon teachers while giving instruction, whether oral or written, by which they were taught what and how they should write or speak.*' Or we may say more briefly that the sacred penmen were completely under the direction of the Holy Spirit, or that they wrote under a plenary inspiration. Dr Calamy's definition agrees substantially with that of Dr. Knapp.

To prove that the Scriptures are divinely inspired we might with propriety refer to the excellence of the doctrines, precepts, and promises, and other instructions. which they contain; to the simplicity and majesty of their style; to the agreement of the different parts, and the scope of the whole ; especially to the full discovery they make of man's fallen and ruined state, and the way of salvation through a Redeemer; together with their power to enlighten and sanctify the heart, and the accompanying witness of the Spirit in believers. These are circumstances of real importance, and the discerning advocates of inspiration have not overlooked them. But the more direct and conclusive evidence that the Scriptures were Divinely inspired is found in *the testimony of the writers themselves*. And as the writers did, by working miracles, and in other ways, sufficiently authenticate their Divine commission, and establish their authority and infallibility as teachers of Divine truth, their testimony, in regard to their own inspiration, is entitled to our full confidence. For who can doubt that they were as competent to judge of, and as much disposed to speak the truth on this subject as on any other? If then we admit their Divine commission and authority, why should we not rely upon the plain testimony which they give concerning the Divine assistance afforded them in their work? To reject their testimony in this case would be to impeach their veracity, and thus to take away the foundation of the Christian religion. And it is well known that those who deny the justice of the claim which they set up to Divine inspiration do in fact give up the infallible truth and authority of the Scriptures, and adopt the principles of deism.

It is, then. of the first importance to inquire what representations are made by the prophets, and by Christ and his Apostles, respecting the inspiration, and the consequent authority, of the sacred Scriptures.

The prophets generally professed to speak *the word of God*. What they taught was introduced and confirmed by a ' Thus saith the Lord ;' or ' The Lord spake to me, saying.' And, in one way or another, they gave clear proof that they were Divinely commissioned, and spoke in the name of God, or as it is expressed in the New Testament, *that God spake by them*.

But the strongest and most satisfactory proof of the inspiration and Divine authority of the Old Testament writings, is found in the testimony of Christ and the Apostles.

The Lord Jesus Christ possessed the spirit of wisdom without measure, and came to bear witness to the truth. His works proved that he was what he declared himself to be—the Messiah, the great Prophet, the infallible Teacher. The faith which rests on him rests on a rock. As soon then as we learn how *he* regarded the Scriptures, we have reached the end of our inquiries. His word is truth. Now every one who carefully attends to the four Gospels will find that Christ everywhere spoke of that collection of writings called the Scripture as the word of God; that he regarded the whole in this light; that he treated the Scripture, and every part of it, as infallibly true, and as clothed with divine authority, thus distinguishing it from every mere human production. Nothing written by man can be entitled to the respect which Christ showed to the Scriptures. This, to all Christians, is direct and incontrovertible evidence of the Divine origin of the Scriptures, and is by itself perfectly conclusive.

But there is clear concurrent evidence, and evidence still more specific, in the writings of the Apostles. In two texts in particular Divine inspiration is positively asserted. In the first (2 Tim. iii. 16), Paul lays it down as the characteristic of ' *all Scripture*,' that it ' *is given by inspiration of God*,' and from this results its profitableness.

The other text (2 Pet. i. 21) teaches that ' Prophecy came not by the will of man, but holy men of God spake as they were moved by the Holy Ghost.' This passage, which the Apostle Peter applied particularly to the subject of which he was speaking, may be considered as explanatory of what is intended by inspiration. For to say that all Scripture is Divinely inspired, and that men of God wrote it as they were moved by the Holy Ghost, is one and the same thing.

The various texts in which Christ and the Apostles speak of Scripture as *the word of God*, and as invested with authority to decide all questions of truth and duty, fully correspond with the texts above considered.

From this view of the subject it follows that the attempt which has been made by a certain class of writers to account for the production of the whole or any part of the Scriptures by the will or agency, the ingenuity, diligence, or fidelity of men, in the use of the means within their reach, without the supernatural influence of the Spirit, is utterly at variance with the teachings of Christ and the Apostles as to the origin of the Sacred Writings.

As the Christian dispensation surpasses the former in all spiritual privileges and gifts, it is reasonable to presume that the New Testament was written under at least an equal degree of Divine influence with the Old, and that it comes recommended to us by equal characteristics of infallible truth. But of this there is clear positive evidence from the New Testament itself.

In the first place, *Jesus Christ*, whose works proved him to be the great unerring Teacher, and to be possessed of all power in Heaven and earth, *gave commission to his Apostles to act in his stead, and to carry out the work of instruction which he had begun*, confirming their authority by investing them with power to perform miracles. But how could such a commission have answered the end proposed, had not the Divine Spirit so guided the Apostles as to render them infallible and perfect teachers of Divine truth?

But, secondly, in addition to this, *Jesus expressly promised to give them the Holy Spirit, to abide with them continually, and to guide them into all the truth*. He said to them, 'When they shall deliver you up, take no thought how or what ye shall speak for it shall be given you in the same hour what ye shall speak. For it is not ye that speak, but the Spirit of your Father that speaketh in you.' Storr and Flatt think this is the idea intended: 'The instructions which ye in general give are derived not so much from yourselves as from the Holy Spirit. Hence, when ye are called on to defend your doctrines, ye need feel no anxiety, but may confidently rely on the Holy Spirit to vindicate his own doctrines, by suggesting to you the very words of your defence.' If these promises were not fulfilled, then Jesus was not a true prophet. If they were fulfilled, as they certainly were, then the Apostles had the constant assistance of the Holy Spirit, and, whether engaged in speaking or writing, were under Divine guidance, and, of course, were liable to no mistakes either as to the matter or manner of their instructions.

In the third place, *the writers of the New Testament manifestly considered themselves to be under the guidance of the Holy Spirit, and their instructions, whether oral or written, to be clothed with Divine authority, as the word of God*. 'We speak,' they say, 'as of God.' Again, 'Which things we speak, not in the words which man's wisdom teacheth, but in words which the Holy Ghost teacheth.' They declared what they taught to be *the word of God*, and the things they wrote to be the *commandments of God*. Now the Apostles, being honest, unassuming, humble men, would never have spoken of themselves and their writings in such a manner, had they not known themselves to be under the unerring guidance of the Holy Spirit, and their instructions perfectly in accordance with the mind of God.

It is perfectly consistent with the plenary inspiration here maintained, that God operated on the minds of inspired men in a variety of ways, sometimes by audible words, sometimes by direct inward suggestions, sometimes by outward visible signs, sometimes by the Urim and Thummim, and sometimes by dreams and visions. This variety in the mode of Divine influence detracted nothing from its certainty. God made known his will equally in different ways; and, whatever the mode of his operation, he made it manifest to his servants that the things revealed were from him.

But inspiration was concerned not only in making known the will of God to prophets and Apostles, but also *in giving them direction in writing the Sacred Books*. They wrote *as they were moved by the Holy Ghost*. And in this, also, there was a diversity in the mode of Divine influence. Sometimes the Spirit of God moved and guided his servants to write things which they could not know by natural means, such as new doctrines or precepts, or predictions of future events. Sometimes he moved and guided them to write the history of events which were wholly or partly known to them by tradition, or by the testimony of their contemporaries, or by their own observation or experience. In all these cases the Divine Spirit effectually preserved them from all error, and influenced them to write just so much and in such a manner as God saw to be best. Sometimes he moved and guided them to write a summary record of larger histories, containing what his infinite wisdom saw to be adapted to the end in view, that is, the benefit of his people in all ages. Sometimes he influenced them to make a record of important maxims in common use, or to write new ones, derived either from their own reason or experience, or from special Divine teaching. Sometimes he influenced them to write parables or allegories, particularly suited to make a salutary impression of Divine things on the minds of men; and sometimes to record supernatural visions. In these and all other kinds of writing the sacred penmen manifestly needed special Divine guidance, as no man could of himself attain to infallibility, and no wisdom, except that of God, was sufficient to determine what things ought to be written for permanent use in the church, and what manner of writing would be best fitted to promote the great ends of revelation.

Some writers speak of different modes and different kinds, and even different degrees of inspiration. And if their meaning is that God influenced the minds of inspired men in different ways; that he adopted a variety of modes in revealing Divine things to their minds; that he guided them to give instruction in prose and in poetry, and in all the different forms of composition; that he moved and guided them to write history, prophecy, doctrines, commands, promises, reproofs, and exhortations, and that he adapted his mode of operation to each of these cases— against this no objection can be made. It is a fact, that the Scriptures exhibit specimens of all these different kinds of writing and these different modes of Divine instruction. Still each and every part of what was written was Divinely inspired, and equally so. It is all the word of God, and clothed with Divine authority, as much as if it had all been made known and written in one way.

Dr. Henderson, who labours perhaps with too much zeal against carrying inspiration to extreme lengths, still says that if those who hold to different modifications of inspiration intend that there are different modifications and degrees of *authority* given to Scripture, their opinion must meet with unqualified reprobation from every sincere believer. He insists that a diversity in the modes and degrees of Divine operation did exist in the work of inspiration, and that this diversity was the result of infinite wisdom adapting itself to different circumstances. He thinks that, unless we admit such a diversity, we cannot form correct ideas of the subject. But he is confident that the distinction which he endeavours to establish is not in the slightest degree hostile to the Divine authority of Scripture. He affirms that *no part of that holy book was written without miraculous influence; that all parts were equally inspired;* that in regard to the whole volume the great end was infallibly attained, namely, the commitment to writing of precisely such matters as God designed for the religious instruction of mankind; that the sacred penmen wrote what had for its object not merely the immediate benefit of individual persons or churches, but what would be useful to Christians in all future times; and that in regard to the most minute and inconsiderable things which the Scripture contains we are compelled to say, *This also cometh from the Lord.*

The controversy among orthodox divines respecting what is called *verbal inspiration,* appears to arise, in a great measure, from the different senses affixed to the phrase.

The real question, and the whole question at issue, may be stated thus: *did the work of the Divine Spirit in the sacred penmen relate to the language they used, or their manner of expressing their ideas; and if so, how far, and in what way?*

All those with whom we are concerned in the discussion of this question, hold that Divine inspiration had some respect to the language employed by the inspired writers, at least in the way of general *supervision.* And Dr. Henderson shows, in various passages of his excellent lectures, that there is no material difference between him and those who profess to maintain higher ground. He allows that, to a certain extent, what is called *verbal inspiration,* or the *inspiration of words,* took place. 'In recording what was immediately spoken with an audible voice by Jehovah, or by an angel interpreter; in giving expression to points of revelation which entirely surpassed the comprehension of the writers; in recording prophecies, the minute bearings of which they did not perceive; in short, in committing to writing any of the dictates of the Spirit, which they could not have otherwise accurately expressed, the writers,' he alleges, 'were supplied with the words as well as the matter.' He says, that even when Biblical writers made use of their own faculties, and wrote each one in his own manner, without having their mental constitution at all disturbed, they were yet 'always secured by celestial influence against the adoption of any forms of speech, or collocation of words, that would have injured the exhibition of Divine truth, or that did not adequately give it expression;' that the characteristic differences of style, so apparent among the sacred writers, were employed by the Holy Spirit for the purposes of inspiration, and 'were called forth in a rational way;' that the writers, 'being acted upon by the Divine Spirit, expressed themselves naturally; that while the Divine influence adapted itself to whatever was peculiar in the minds of inspired men, it constantly guided them in writing the Sacred Volume.' He declares his belief that the Scriptures were written not under a partial or imperfect, but under a plenary and infallible, inspiration; that they were entirely the result of Divine intervention, and are to be regarded as the oracles of Jehovah.

The doctrine of a plenary inspiration of all Scripture in regard to the language employed, as well as the thoughts communicated, ought not to be rejected without valid reasons. The doctrine is so obviously important, and so consonant to the feelings of sincere piety, that those evangelical Christians who are pressed with speculative objections against it, frequently, in the honesty of their hearts, advance opinions which fairly imply it. This is the case, as we have seen, with Dr. Henderson, who says that the Divine Spirit guided the sacred penmen in *writing* the Scriptures; that their *mode of expression* was such as they were instructed by the Spirit to employ; that Paul ascribes not only the doctrines which the Apostles taught, but *the entire character of their style,* to the influence of the Spirit. He indeed says that this does not always imply the *immediate communication of the words* of Scripture; and he says it with good reason. For *immediate* properly signifies *acting without a medium,* or *without the intervention of another cause or means, not acting by second causes.* Now those who hold the highest views of inspiration do not suppose that the Divine Spirit, except in a few instances, so influenced the writers of Scripture as to interfere with the use of their rational faculties or their peculiar mental habits and tastes, or in any way to supersede secondary causes as the medium through which his agency produced the desired effect.

In regard to this point, therefore, there appears to be little or no ground for controversy. For, if God so influenced the sacred writers that, either with or without the use of secondary causes, they wrote just *what* he intended, and in the *manner* he intended, the end is secured; and what they wrote is as truly *his word,* as though he had written it with his own hand on tables of stone, without any human instrumentality. The very words of the decalogue were all such as God chose. And they would have been equally so if Moses had been moved by the Divine Spirit to write them with *his* hand. The expression, that God *immediately imparted* or *communicated* to the writers the very words which they wrote, is evidently not well chosen. The exact truth is that *the writers themselves* were the subjects of the Divine influence. The Spirit employed them as active instruments, and directed them in writing, both as to matter and manner. They wrote 'as they were moved by the Holy Ghost.' The matter, in many cases, was what they before knew, and the manner was entirely conformed to their habits; it was *their own.* But what was written was none the less inspired on that account. God may have influenced and guided an Apostle as infallibly in writing what he had before known, and that guidance may have been as really necessary, as in writing a new revelation. And God may have influenced Paul or John to write a book in *his own peculiar style,* and that influence may have been as real and as necessary as if the style had been what some would call a *Divine style.* It *was* a Divine style, if the writer used it under Divine direction. It was a *Divine* style, and it was, at the same time, a *human* style, and the *writer's own* style, all in one. Just as the believer's exercises, faith and love, are his own acts, and at the same time are the effects of Divine influence. The mental exercises of Paul and of John had their own characteristic peculiarities, as much as their style. God was the author of John's mind and all that was peculiar to his mental faculties and habits, as really as of Paul's mind and what was peculiar to him. And in the work of inspiration he used and directed, for his own purposes, what was peculiar to each. When God inspired different men he did not make their minds and tastes all alike, nor did he make their language alike. Nor had he any occasion for this; for while they had different mental faculties and habits, they were as capable of being infallibly directed by the Divine Spirit, and infallibly speaking and writing Divine truth, as though their mental faculties and habits had been all exactly alike. And it is manifest that the Scriptures, written by such a variety of inspired men, and each part agreeably to the peculiar talents and style of the writer, are not only equally from God, but, taken together, are far better adapted to the purposes of general instruction, and all the objects to be accomplished by revelation, than if they had been written by one man, and in one and the same manner.

This view of plenary inspiration is fitted to relieve the difficulties and objections which have arisen in the minds of men from the variety of talent and taste which the writers exhibited, and the variety of style which they used. See, it is said, how each writer expresses himself naturally, in his own way, just as he was accustomed to do when not inspired. And see too, we might say in reply, how each Apostle, Peter, Paul, or John, when speaking before rulers, with the promised aid of the Holy Spirit, spoke naturally, *with his own voice*, and in his own way, as he had been accustomed to do on other occasions when not inspired. There is no more objection to plenary inspiration in the one case than in the other. The mental faculties and habits of the Apostles, their style, their voice, their mode of speech, all remained as they were. What, then, had the divine Spirit to do? What was the work which appertained to Him? We reply, His work was so to direct the Apostles in the use of their own talents and habits, their style, their voice, and all their peculiar endowments, that they should speak or write, each in his own way, just what God would have them speak or write, for the good of the Church in all ages.

The fact that the individual peculiarities of the sacred penmen are everywhere so plainly impressed on their writings, is often mentioned as an objection to the doctrine, that inspiration extended to their *language* as well as their thoughts. This is, indeed, one of the most common objections, and one which has obtained a very deep lodgment in the minds of some intelligent Christians. It may, therefore, be necessary to take some further pains completely to remove it. And in our additional remarks relative to this and other objections, it will come in our way to show that such a writer as Gaussen, who contends with great earnestness and ability for the highest views of inspiration, does still, on all important points, agree with those who advocate lower views of the subject.

Gaussen says, ' Although the title of each book should not indicate to us that we are passing from one author to another; yet we could quickly discover, by the change of their characters, that a new hand has taken the pen. It is perfectly easy to recognise each one of them, although they speak of the same master, teach the same doc-

trines, and relate the same incidents.' But how does this prove that Scripture is not, in all respects, inspired? ' So far are we,' says this author, ' from overlooking human individuality everywhere impressed on our Sacred Books, that, on the contrary, it is with profound gratitude, and with an ever-increasing admiration, that we regard this living, real, human character infused so charmingly into every part of the Word of God. We admit the fact, and we see in it clear proof of the Divine wisdom which dictated the Scriptures.'

Those who urge the objection above mentioned are plainly inconsistent with themselves. For while they deny the plenary inspiration of some parts of Scripture, *because they have these marks of individuality*, they acknowledge inspiration in the fullest sense in other parts, particularly in the prophecies, where this individuality of the writers is equally apparent.

In truth, what can be more consonant with our best views of the wisdom of God, or with the general analogy of his works, than that he should make use of the thoughts, the memories, the peculiar talents, tastes, and feelings of his servants in recording his Word for the instruction of men? Why should he not associate the peculiarities of their personal character with what they write under his personal guidance? But, independently of our reasoning, this matter is decided by the Bible itself. ' All Scripture is Divinely inspired,' and it is all the Word of God. And it is none the less the Word of God, and none the less inspired, because it comes to us in the language of Moses, and David, and Paul, and the other sacred writers. ' It is God who speaks to us, but it is also man; it is man, but it is also God.' The word of God, in order to be intelligible and profitable to us, ' must be uttered by mortal tongues, and be written by mortal hands, and must put on the features of human thoughts. This blending of humanity and Divinity in the Scriptures reminds us of the majesty and the condescension of God. Viewed in this light, the Word of God has unequalled beauties, and exerts an unequalled power over our hearts.'

There are some who maintain that all which was necessary to secure the desired results was an infallible guidance of the *thoughts* of the sacred writers; that with such a guidance they might be safely left to express their thoughts in their own way, without any special influence from above.

Now, if those who take this view of the subject mean that God not only gives the sacred penmen the very ideas which they are to write, but, in some way, secures an infallible connection between those ideas and a just expression of them in words; then, indeed, we have the desired result—an infallible revelation from God, made in the proper language of the writers. But if any one supposes that there is naturally such an infallible connection between right thoughts and a just expression of them in language, without an effective Divine superintendence, he contradicts the lessons of daily experience. But those to whom we refer evidently do not themselves believe in such an infallible connection. For when they assign their reason for denying that inspiration related to the language of the Scriptures, they speak of the different, and, as they regard them, the contradictory statements of facts by different writers. But it is easy to see that the difficulty presses with all its force upon those who assert the inspiration of the *thoughts*. For surely they will not say that the sacred writers had *true thoughts* in their minds, and yet uttered them in the language of falsehood. This would contradict their own idea of a sure connection between the conceptions of the mind and the utterance of them in suitable words, and would clearly show that they themselves feel it to be necessary that the Divine guidance should extend to the *words* of inspired men as well as their thoughts. But if the inspired writer through inadvertence committed a real mistake as to a matter of fact, it must have been a mistake in his *thoughts* as well as in his words. If, then, there was a mistake, it lay in his *thoughts* But if there was no mistake, then there is nothing to prove that inspiration did not extend to the language. If, however, there was a real mistake, then the question is not, what becomes of *verbal* inspiration, but what becomes of inspiration *in any sense*

It is sometimes said that the sacred writers were of themselves generally competent to express their ideas in *proper language*, and in this respect had *no need* of supernatural assistance. But there is just as much reason for saying that they were of themselves generally competent to form their own *conceptions*, and so had no need of supernatural aid in this respect. It is just as reasonable to say that Moses could recollect what took place at the Red Sea, and that Paul could recollect that he was once a persecutor, and Peter what took place on the mount of transfiguration, without supernatural aid, as to say that they could, without such aid, make a proper record of these recollections. We believe a real and infallible guidance of the Spirit in both respects, because this is taught in the Scriptures. And it is obvious that the Bible could not be what Christ and the Apostles considered it to be, unless they were Divinely inspired.

The diversity in the narratives of the Evangelists is sometimes urged as an objection against the position we maintain in regard to inspiration, but evidently without reason, and contrary to reason. For what is more reasonable than to expect that a work of Divine origin will have marks of consummate wisdom, and will be suited to accomplish the end in view. Now it will not be denied that God determined that there should be four narratives of the life and death of Jesus from four historians. If the narratives were all alike, three of them would be useless. Indeed such a circumstance would create suspicion, and would bring discredit upon the whole concern. The narratives must then be different. And if, besides this useful diversity, it is found that the seeming contradictions can be satisfactorily reconciled, and if each of the narratives is given in the peculiar style and manner of the writers, then all is natural and unexceptionable, and we have the highest evidence of the credibility and truth of the narratives.

We shall advert to one more objection. It is alleged that writers who were constantly under a plenary Divine inspiration would not descend to the unimportant details, the trifling incidents, which are found in the Scriptures. To this it may be replied that the details alluded to must be admitted to be according to truth, and that those things which, at first view, seem to be trifles may, when taken in their connections, prove to be of serious moment. And it is moreover manifest that, considering what human beings and human affairs really are, if all those things which are called trifling and unimportant were excluded, the Scriptures would fail of being conformed to fact; they would not be faithful histories of human life: so that the very circumstance which is demanded as proof of inspiration would become an argument against it. And herein we cannot but admire the perfect wisdom which guided the sacred writers, while we mark the weakness and shallowness of the objections which are urged against their inspiration.

On the whole, after carefully investigating the subject of inspiration, we are conducted to the important conclusion that 'all Scripture is Divinely inspired ;' that the sacred penmen wrote 'as they were moved by the Holy Ghost ;' and that these representations are to be understood as implying that the writers had, in all respects, the effectual guidance of the Divine Spirit. And we are still more confirmed in this conclusion because we find that it begets in those who seriously adopt it an acknowledgment of the Divine origin of Scripture, a reverence for its teachings, and a practical regard to its requirements, like what appeared in Christ and his Apostles. Being convinced that the Bible has, in all parts and in all respects, the seal of the Almighty, and that it is truly and entirely from God, we are led by reason, conscience, and piety to bow submissively to its high authority, implicitly to believe its doctrines, however incomprehensible, and cordially to obey its precepts, however contrary to our natural inclinations. We come to it from day to day, not as judges, but as learners, never questioning the propriety or utility of any of its contents. This precious Word of God is the perfect standard of our faith, and the rule of our life, our comfort in affliction, and our sure guide to heaven.

IRON. Tubal-Cain is the *first-mentioned* smith, ' a forger of every instrument of iron' (Gen. iv. 22). From that time we meet with manufactures in iron of the utmost variety (*some* articles of which seem to be anticipations of what are commonly supposed to be modern inventions); as iron weapons or instruments (Num. xxv. 7 ; Job xx. 24) ; barbed irons, used in hunting (Job xli. 7) ; *an iron bedstead* (Deut. iii. 11) ; chariots of iron (Josh. xvii. 16, and elsewhere) ; iron weights (shekels) (1 Sam. xvii. 7) ; harrows of iron (2 Sam. xii. 31) ; iron armour (2 Sam. xxiii. 7) : tools (1 Kings vi. 7 ; 2 Kings vi. 5) ; horns (1 Kings xxii. 11) ; nails, hinges (1 Chron. xxii. 3) ; fetters (Ps. cv. 18) ; bars (Ps. cvii 16) ; iron bars used in fortifying the gates of towns (Ps. cvii. 16 ; Isa. xlv. 2) ; a *pen of iron* (Job xix. 24 ; Jer. xvii. 1) ; a pillar (Jer. i. 18) ; yokes (Jer. xxviii. 13) ; pan (Ezek. iv. 3) ; trees bound with iron (Dan. iv. 15) ; gods of iron (Dan. v. 4) ; threshing-instruments (Amos i. 3) ; and in later times, an iron gate (Acts xii 10) ; the actual cautery (1 Tim. iv. 2) ; breastplates (Rev. ix. 9).

The mineral origin of iron seems clearly alluded to in Job xxviii. 2. It would seem that in ancient times it was a plentiful production of Palestine (Deut. viii. 9). There appear to have been furnaces for smelting at an early period in Egypt (Deut. iv. 20). The requirement that the altar should be made of ' whole stones over which no man had lift up any iron,' recorded in Josh. viii. 31, does not imply any objection to iron as such, but seems to be merely a mode of directing that, in order to prevent idolatry, the stones must not undergo any preparation by art. Iron was prepared in abundance by David for the building of the temple (1 Chron. xxii. 3), to the amount of one hundred thousand talents (1 Chron. xxix. 7), or rather 'without weight' (1 Chron. xxii. 14). Working in iron was considered a calling (2 Chron. ii. 7) [SMITH]. Iron seems to have been better from some countries, or to have undergone some hardening preparation by the inhabitants of them, such as were the people called Chalybes, living near the Euxine Sea (Jer. xv. 12); to have been imported from Tarshish to Tyre (Ezek. xxvii. 12), and ' bright iron' from Dan and Javan (ver. 19). The superior hardness of iron above all other substances is alluded to in Dan. ii. 40. It was found among the Midianites (Num. xxxi. 22), and was part of the wealth distributed among the tribes at their location in the land (Josh. xxii. 8).

Iron is *metaphorically* alluded to in the following instances :—affliction is signified by the furnace for smelting it (Deut. iv. 20); under the same figure, chastisement (Ezek. xxii. 18, 20, 22); reducing the earth to total barrenness by turning it into iron (Deut. xxviii. 23); slavery, by a yoke of iron (Deut. xxviii. 48); strength, by a bar of it (Job xl. 18); the extreme of hardness (Job xli. 27); severity of government, by a rod of iron (Ps. ii. 9); affliction, by iron fetters (Ps. cvii. 10); prosperity, by giving silver for iron (Isa. lx. 17); political strength (Dan. ii 33); obstinacy, by an iron sinew in the neck (Isa. xlviii. 4); giving supernatural fortitude to a prophet, making him an iron pillar (Jer. i. 18); destructive power of empires, by iron teeth (Dan. vii. 7); deterioration of character, by becoming iron (Jer. vi. 28; Ezek. xxii. 18), which resembles the idea of the iron age; a tiresome burden, by a mass of iron (Ecclus. xxii. 15); the greatest obstacles, by walls of iron (2 Macc. xi. 9); the certainty with which a real enemy will ever show his hatred, by the rust returning upon iron (Ecclus. xii. 10). Iron seems used, as by the Greek poets, metonymically for the sword (Isa. x 34). The following is selected as a *beautiful comparison* made to iron (Prov xxvii. 17): 'Iron (literally) uniteth iron ; so a man uniteth the countenance of his friend,' gives stability to his appearance by his presence. A most graphic *description of a smith at work* is found in Ecclus. xxxviii. 28.

I'SAAC, son of Abraham and Sarah, born in his parents' old age. The promise of a son had been made to them when Abraham was visited by the Lord in the plains of Mamre, and appeared so unlikely to be fulfilled, seeing that both Abraham and Sarah were ' well-stricken in years,' that its utterance caused the latter to laugh incredulously. Being reproved for her unbelief, she denied that she had laughed. The reason assigned for the special visitation thus promised was, in effect, that Abraham was pious, and would train his offspring in piety, so that he would become the founder of a great nation, and

all the nations of the earth should be blessed in him.

In due time Sarah gave birth to a son, who received the name of Isaac, in reference to the laughter occasioned by the announcement of the Divine intention (comp. Gen. xxi. 6 ; xviii. 12 ; xvii. 17).

The first fact that we read of in the history of Isaac, is the command given to his father to offer the youth—' thy son, thine only son Isaac, whom thou lovest '— for a burnt-offering on a mountain in the land of Moriah   Abraham proceeded to obey the Divine direction, and was on the point of slaying Isaac, when his hand was withheld by the interposition of God, a ram for sacrifice being provided instead.

This event has found no few detractors, and various attempts have been made to explain it away. But the only proper way is to consider it as it is represented in the sacred page. The command, then, was expressly designed to try Abraham's faith. Destined as the patriarch was to be the father of the faithful, was he worthy of his high and dignified position? If his own obedience was weak, he could not train others in faith, trust, and love : hence a trial was necessary. That he was not without holy dispositions was already known, and indeed recognised in the Divine favours of which he had been the object ; but was he prepared to do and to suffer all God's will? Religious perfection and his position alike demanded a perfect heart: hence the kind of trial. If he were willing to surrender even his only child, and act himself both as offerer and priest in the sacrifice of the required victim, if he could so far conquer his natural affections, so subdue the father in his heart, then there could be no doubt that his will was wholly reconciled to God's, and that he was worthy of every trust, confidence, and honour. The trial was made, the fact was ascertained, the victim was not slain. What is there in this to which either religion or morality can take exception? This view is both confirmed and justified by the words of God (Gen. xxii 16, sq.), '*because* thou hast not withheld thy only son, in blessing I will bless thee. and in multiplying I will multiply thy seed as the stars of the heaven, and in thy seed shall all the nations of the earth be blessed.'

Isaac passed his youthful days under the eye of his father, engaged in the care of flocks and herds up and down the plains of Canaan.   At length his father wished to see him married. Abraham therefore gave a commission to his oldest and most trustworthy servant to the effect that, in order to prevent Isaac from taking a wife from among the daughters of the Canaanites, he should proceed into Mesopotamia, and, under the divine direction, choose a partner among his own relatives for his beloved son. Rebekah, in consequence, becomes Isaac's wife, when he was now forty years of age.

Isaac having, in conjunction with his half-brother Ishmael, buried Abraham his father, ' in a good old age. in the cave of Machpelah,' took up a somewhat permanent residence ' by the well Lahai-roi,' where, being blessed of God, he lived in prosperity and at ease.   One source of regret, however, he deeply felt.   Rebekah was barren. In time, two sons, Jacob and Esau, are granted to his prayers.   As the boys grow, Isaac gave a preference to Esau, who seems to have possessed those robuster qualities of character in which his father was defective, and therefore gratified him by such dainties as the pursuits of the chace enabled the youth to offer; while Jacob, 'a plain man dwelling in tents,' was an object of special regard to Rebekah—a division of feeling and a kind of partiality which became the source of much domestic unhappiness, as well as of jealousy and hatred between the two sons.

A famine compels Isaac to seek food in some foreign land. Divinely warned not to go down to Egypt, the patriarch applies to a petty prince of Philistia, by name Abimelech, who permits him to dwell at Gerar. Here an event took place which has a parallel in the life of his father Abraham. Rebekah was his cousin : afraid lest she should be violently taken from him, and his own life sacrificed to the lust of Abimelech, he represented her as his sister, employing a latitude of meaning which the word 'sister' admits in Oriental usage. The subterfuge was discovered, and is justified by Isaac on the grounds which prompted him to resort to it.

Another parallel event in the lives of Abraham and Isaac may be found by comparing together Gen. xxvi. 26, sq., and xxi. 22, sq. If these parallels should excite a doubt in the mind of any one as to the credibility of the narratives, let him carefully peruse them, and we think that the simplicity and naturalness which pervade and characterize them will effectually substantiate the reality of the recorded events, and explode the notion that fiction has had anything to do in bringing the narrative into its present shape.

Isaac, in his old age, was, by the practices of Rebekah and the art of Jacob, so imposed upon as to give his blessing to the younger son Jacob, instead of to the first-born Esau, and with that blessing to convey, as was usual, the right of headship in the family, together with his chief possessions. In the blessing which the aged patriarch pronounced on Jacob, it deserves notice how entirely the wished-for good is of an earthly and temporal nature, while the imagery which is employed serves to show the extent to which the poetical element prevailed as a constituent part of the Hebrew character (Gen. xxvii. 27, sq). Most natural, too, is the extreme agitation of the poor blind old man, on discovering the cheat which had been put upon him:—' And Isaac trembled very exceedingly, and said (to Esau), Who ? where is he that hath taken venison and brought it me, and I have eaten, and have blessed him ? Yea, and he shall be blessed.' Equally natural is the reply of Esau. The entire passage is of itself enough to vindicate the historical character and entire credibility of those sketches of the lives of the patriarchs which Genesis presents.

The stealing, on the part of Jacob, of his father's blessing having angered Esau, who seems to have looked forward to Isaac's death as affording an opportunity for taking vengeance on his unjust brother, the aged patriarch is induced, at his wife's entreaty, to send Jacob into Mesopotamia, that, after his own example, his son might take a wife from amongst his kindred and people, ' of the daughters of Laban, thy mother's brother.'

This is the last important act recorded of Isaac. Jacob having, agreeably to his father's command, married into Laban's family, returned, after some time, and found the old man at Mamre, in the city of Arbah, which is Hebron, where Abraham and Isaac sojourned. Here, ' being old and full of days' (180), Isaac ' gave up the ghost, and died, and was gathered unto his people, and his sons Esau and Jacob buried him' (Gen. xxxv. 27, sq.).

ISAI'AH (*help of Jehovah*). The heading of this book places the prophet under the reigns of Uzziah, Jotham, Ahaz, and Hezekiah, kings of Judah ; and an examination of the prophecies themselves, independently of the heading, leads us to the same chronological results. Chapter vi., in which is related the call of Isaiah, not to his prophetic office, but to a higher degree of it, is thus headed: ' In the year in which king Uzziah died I saw the Lord,' &c. The collection of prophecies is chronologically arranged, and the utterances in the preceding chapters (i. to vi.) belong to an earlier period, preceding the last year of the reign of Uzziah. These two prophecies contain the sum and substance of what Isaiah taught during twenty years of his life.

The continuation of prophetic authorship, or the writing down of uttered prophecies, depended upon the commencement of new historical developments, such as took place under the reigns of Ahaz and Hezekiah. Several prophecies in the seventh and following chapters belong to the reign of Ahaz; and most of the subsequent prophecies to the reign of Hezekiah. The prophetic ministry of Isaiah under Hezekiah is also described in an historical section contained in chapters xxxvi.-xxxix. The data which are contained in this section come down to the fifteenth year of the reign of Hezekiah ; consequently we are in the possession of historical documents proving that the prophetic ministry of Isaiah was in operation during about forty-seven or fifty years, commencing in the year B C. 763 or 759, and extending to the year B.C. 713. Of this period, from one to four years belong to the reign of Uzziah, sixteen to the reign of Jotham, sixteen to the reign of Ahaz, and fourteen to the reign of Hezekiah.

Some writers have advanced the opinion that Isaiah lived to a much later period, and that his life extended to the reign of Manasseh, the successor of Hezekiah. But their arguments will not stand a strict scrutiny. While, on the other hand, the inscription of the book itself shows that all the prophecies of Isaiah in our collection are included within the period from Uzziah to Hezekiah. Not one of the prophecies which are headed by an inscription of their own is placed after the fifteenth year of Hezekiah; and the internal evidence leads us in none beyond this period. Hence we infer that the prophetic ministry of Isaiah terminated soon after its fullest development, to which it attained during the period of the Assyrian invasion, in the reign of Hezekiah.

According to these statements, Isaiah belongs to the cycle of the most ancient prophets whose predictions have been preserved in writing. He was a contemporary of Hosea, Amos, and Jonah, although younger than those prophets, who belonged to the kingdom of Israel. He was likewise a contemporary and co-worker of the prophet

Micah in the kingdom of Judah. We infer also from the circumstance that the prophecies of Joel are inserted among the books of the minor prophets before those of Micah, that Isaiah must have been a contemporary of Joel, since the minor prophets are chronologically arranged.

Little is known respecting the circumstances of Isaiah's life. His father's name was Amoz. The fathers of the church confound him with the prophet Amos, because they were unacquainted with Hebrew, and in Greek the two names are spelled alike. The opinion of the Rabbins, that Isaiah was a brother of King Amaziah, rests also on a mere etymological combination. Isaiah resided at Jerusalem, not far from the temple. We learn from chapters vii. and viii. that he was married. Two of his sons are mentioned, Shear-jashul and Maher-shalal-hash-baz [See the words]. Isaiah calls his wife a *prophetess*. This indicates that his marriage-life was not in opposition to his vocation, and also that it not only went along with his vocation, but that it was intimately interwoven with it. This name cannot mean the wife of a prophet, but indicates that the prophetess of Isaiah had a prophetic gift, like Miriam, Deborah, and Huldah. The appellation here given denotes the genuineness of their conjugal relation.

Even the dress of the prophet was subservient to his vocation. According to chap. xx. 2, he wore a garment of hair-cloth or sackcloth. This seems also to have been the costume of Elijah, according to 2 Kings i. 8; and it was the dress of John the Baptist. Hairy sackcloth is in the Bible the symbol of repentance (compare Isa. xxii. 12, and 1 Kings xxi. 27). This costume of the prophets was a prophetic preaching by fact. The prophetic preacher comes forward in the form of personified repentance. What he does exhibits to the people what they should do. Before he has opened his lips his external appearance proclaims, *Repent*.

Besides the collection of prophecies which has been preserved to us, Isaiah also wrote two historical works, which did not originate from prophets.

The first of these was a biography of King Uzziah (comp. 2 Chron. xxvi. 22): 'Now the rest of the acts of Uzziah, first and last, did Isaiah the prophet, the son of Amoz, write.' The second historical work of Isaiah, was a biography of King Hezekiah, which was subsequently inserted in the annals of Judah and Israel. These annals consisted of a series of prophetic monographies, which were received partly entire, partly in abstracts, and are the chief source from which the information contained in the Chronicles is derived. In this work of Isaiah, although its contents were chiefly historical, numerous prophecies were inserted. Hence it is called in 2 Chron. xxxii. 32, *The Vision of Isaiah*. In a similar manner the biography of Solomon by Ahijah is called, in 2 Chron. ix. 29, 'the prophecy of Ahijah.' The two historical works of Isaiah were lost, together with the annals of Judah and Israel, into which they were embodied. Whatever these annals contained that was of importance for all ages, has been preserved to us by being received into the historical books of the Old Testament, and the predictions of the most distinguished prophets have been

formed into separate collections. After this was effected, less care was taken to preserve the more diffuse annals, which also comprehended many statements, of value only for particular times and places.

The Jewish synagogue, and the Christian church during all ages, have considered it as an undoubted fact that the prophecies which bear the name of Isaiah really originated from that prophet. But in the last quarter of the eighteenth century this prevailing conviction appeared to some divines to be inconvenient. In the theology of the natural man it passed as certain, that nature was complete in itself, and that prophecies, as well as miracles, never had occurred, and were even impossible. The assumption of the impossibility of miracles necessarily demanded that the genuineness of the Pentateuch should be rejected; and, in a similar manner, the assumption of the impossibility of prophecy demanded that a great portion of the prophecies of Isaiah should be rejected likewise. Here also the wish was father to the thought, and interest led to the decision of critical questions, the arguments for which were subsequently discovered. All those who attack the integral authenticity of Isaiah agree in considering the book to be an anthology, or gleanings of prophecies, collected after the Babylonian exile, although they differ in their opinions respecting the origin of this collection. Koppe gave gentle hints of this view, which was first explicitly supported by Eichhorn in his *Introduction*. Eichhorn advances the hypothesis that a collection of Isaian prophecies (which might have been augmented, even before the Babylonian exile, by several not genuine additions) formed the basis of the present anthology, and that the collectors, after the Babylonian Exile, considering that the scroll on which they were written did not form a volume proportionate to the size of the three other prophetic scrolls, containing Ezekiel, Jeremiah, and the minor prophets, annexed to the Isaian collection all other oracles at hand whose authors were not known to the editors. Gesenius, on the contrary, maintained, in his introduction to Isaiah, that all the non-Isaian prophecies extant in that book originated from one author and were of the same date. Umbreit and Köster on the main point follow Gesenius, considering chapters xl. to lxvi. to be a continuous whole, written by a pseudo-Isaiah who lived about the termination of the Babylonian exile. In reference to other portions of the book of Isaiah, the authenticity of which has been questioned, Umbreit expresses himself doubtingly, and Köster assigns them to Isaiah. Gesenius declines to answer the question, how it happened that these portions were ascribed to Isaiah, but Hitzig felt that an answer to it might be expected. He accordingly attempts to explain why such additions were made to Isaiah and not to any of the other prophetical books, by the extraordinary veneration in which Isaiah was held. He says that the great authority of Isaiah occasioned important and distinguished prophecies to be placed in connection with his name. But he himself soon after destroys the force of this assertion by observing, that the great authority of Isaiah was especially owing to those prophecies which were falsely ascribed to him. A considerable degree of suspicion must, however, attach to the boasted certainty of such critical investigations, if we notice how widely these learned men differ in defining what is of Isaian origin and what is not, although they are all linked together by the same fundamental tendency and interest. There are very few portions in the whole collection whose authenticity has not been called in question by some one or other of the various impugners. The only portions left to Isaiah are chaps. i. 3-9, xvii., xx., xxviii., xxxi., and xxxiii. All the other chapters are defended by some and rejected by others; they are also referred to widely different dates. In the most modern criticism, however, we observe an inclination again to extend the sphere of Isaian authenticity as much as the dogmatic principle and system of the critics will allow. Modern criticism is inclined to admit the genuineness of chaps. i. to xxiii., with the only exception of the two prophecies against Babylon in chaps. xiii. and xiv., and in chap. xxi. 1-10. Chaps. xxviii.-xxxiii. are allowed to be Isaian by Ewald, Umbreit, and others.

After this survey of the present state of the inquiry, we proceed to furnish, first, the external arguments for the integral authenticity of Isaiah.

1. The most ancient testimony in favour of Isaiah's being the author of all the portions of the collection which bears his name, is contained in the heading of the whole (i. 1), 'The vision of Isaiah the son of Amoz, which he saw concerning Judah and Jerusalem, in the days of Uzziah, Jotham, Ahaz, Hezekiah, kings of Judah.' It is here clearly stated that Isaiah was the author of the following prophecies, uttered during the reign of four successive kings. This inscription is of great importance, even if it originated not from Isaiah, but from a later compiler. If we adopt the latest date at which this compilation could have been made, we must fix it at the time of its reception into the canon in the days of Ezra and Nehemiah. Consequently the compiler could not be separated by many years from the pseudo-Isaiah who is said to have prophesied just before Babylon was conquered, or who, according to most critics, wrote even after the fall of Babylon. It is not credible that a compiler living so near the times of the author, should have erroneously ascribed these prophecies to Isaiah, who lived so much earlier, especially if we bear in mind that this so-called pseudo-Isaiah must have been a very remarkable person in an age so devoid of the prophetic spirit as that in which he is said to have lived.

It is still less credible that a pseudo-Isaiah should himself have fraudulently ascribed his prophecies to Isaiah. None of the adversaries of the authenticity of the book make such an assertion.

If the compiler lived before the Exile, the inscription appears to be of still greater importance. That the collection was made so early is very likely, from the circumstance that Jeremiah and other prophets apparently made use of the prophecies of Isaiah. This fact indicates that the prophecies of Isaiah early excited a lively interest, and that the compiler must have lived at a period earlier than that which is ascribed to the pseudo-Isaiah himself. From all this we infer that the compiler lived before the Exile. The adversaries themselves felt the weight of this argument. They, therefore, attempted to remove it by various hypotheses, which received a semblance of probability from the circumstance that even the considerate Vitringa had called in question the authenticity of the heading. Vitringa conjectured that this heading belonged originally to the first chapter alone. He further conjectured that it originally contained only the words, *prophecy of Isaiah, the son of Amoz, which he saw concerning Judah and Jerusalem.* The following words, he says, were added by the compiler, who enlarged the particular inscription of the first chapter to a general one of the whole collection. According to Vitringa the inscription does not suit the whole book, the contents of which are not confined to Judah and Jerusalem alone. But Judah and Jerusalem are always the chief subject, and, in a certain sense, the only subject of these prophecies; and there is no prophecy concerning other nations without a bearing upon the covenant-people. No prophet against foreign nations prophesied concerning them with the view to spread his predictions among them, because the mission of all prophets was to Israel. The predictions against foreign nations are intended to preserve the covenant-people from despair, and to strengthen their faith in the omnipotence and justice of their God. It is their object to annihilate all reliance upon political combinations and human confederacies. They are intended to lead Israel to the question, ' If they do these things in the green tree, what shall be done in the dry?' But they are also designed to indicate the future conversion of the heathen, and to open to the view of the faithful the future glory of the kingdom of God, and its final victory over the kingdoms of this world; and thus to extirpate all narrow-minded nationality. God shall be revealed not only as Jehovah, but also as Elohim. His relation to Israel is misunderstood, if that relation is exclusively kept in view without any regard to the universe. Therefore the whole collection is justly entitled Prophecies concerning Judah and Jerusalem. No matter whether this inscription originated from Isaiah himself or from an ancient compiler.

The inscription in ch. i. has a general bearing upon the whole collection. Then follows the first portion, which contains, as it were, the general prophetic programme. Thereupon follows a series of prophecies directly bearing upon Judah and Jerusalem, commencing again with a particular heading (ii. 1). To this succeeds a series of prophecies indirectly bearing upon Judah and Jerusalem, but directly upon foreign nations. The first of this series has again its own heading (xiii. 1).

Gesenius, advancing in the direction to which Vitringa had pointed, although he grants the integral authenticity of ch. i. 1, nevertheless maintains that this heading belonged originally only to chs. i.-xii., in which were contained genuine prophecies of Isaiah. To this collection, he asserts, were afterwards subjoined the anthologies contained in the following chapters, and the heading was then misunderstood as applying to the whole volume. This opinion is more inconsistent than that of Vitringa, since there occur in the first twelve chapters two prophecies against foreign nations: one against the Assyrians, in ch. x., and another against Ephraim, in ch. ix.

Vitringa, Gesenius, and their followers, are also refuted by the parallel passage in the heading of Amos, ' The words of Amos, which he saw concerning Israel.' The prophecies of Amos in general are here said to be concerning Israel, although there are, as in Isaiah, several against foreign nations, a series of which stands even at the commencement of the book. To this we may add the similarity of the headings of other prophetical books. For instance, the commencement of Jeremiah, Hosea, Micah, and Zephaniah.

2. It cannot be proved that there ever existed any so-called prophetic anthology as has been supposed to exist in the book of Isaiah. We find nothing analogous in the whole range of prophetic literature. It is generally granted that the collections bearing the names of Jeremiah and Ezekiel contain only productions of those authors whose name they bear. In the book of the minor prophets, the property of each is strictly distinguished from the rest by headings. The authenticity of only the second portion of Zechariah has been attacked; and this with very feeble arguments, which have been refuted.

But even if it could be proved that the prophecies of Zechariah belonged to two different authors, namely, as Bertholdt and Gesenius suppose, to the two Zechariahs, each of whom happened to be the son of a Berechiah, this identity of names might be considered an inducement for uniting the productions of the two authors in one collection: still this case would not be analogous to what is asserted to be the fact in Isaiah. In Isaiah it is alleged not only that a series of chapters belonging to a different author were subjoined, commencing about chap. xxxiv.; but it is affirmed that, even in the first thirty-three chapters, the genuine and spurious portions are intermixed. Before we admit that the compilers proceeded here in a manner so unreasonable and so contrary to their usual custom, we must expect some cogent proof to be adduced, but instead of this, nothing but bald conjecture and feeble illustrations have been offered.

3 According to the opinion of several critics, all the spurious portions of Isaiah belong to one and the same author. But it so happens that the portion which is most emphatically declared to be spurious, namely, chaps. xiii. and xiv., bear an inscription which expressly ascribes them to Isaiah. Now, as the internal arguments against the authenticity of all the portions which are said to be spurious are nearly identical, if the opposition to chaps. xiii. and xiv. is given up, it cannot with consistency be maintained against the other portions. This argument serves also as an answer to those who ascribe the portions which they consider spurious to several authors. The contents of these portions are similar. They contain predictions of the fall of Babylon, and of the redemption of Israel from captivity. Whatever proves the genuineness of one of these portions, indirectly proves the others also to be genuine.

4. According to Josephus (*Antiq.* xi. c. 1. § 1, 2), Cyrus was induced by the prophecies of Isaiah respecting him to allow the return of the Jews, and to aid them in rebuilding the temple. The credibility of Josephus, who in regard to facts of ancient history is not always to be relied upon, is here supported by two circumstances. First, the favour shown by Cyrus to the Jews, which remains inexplicable except by the fact mentioned, in combination with the influence of Daniel. In modern times, the favour of Cyrus to the Jews has been called a prudential measure; but it does not appear what he could either hope or fear from a people so enfeebled as the Jews were at that period. It has been added that Cyrus was favourable to the Jews on account of the similarity between the Persian and the Jewish religion; but there is no historical proof that the Persians, on any other occasion, favoured the Jews on account of their religion. The favours shown to Nehemiah on behalf of Israel were only personal favours, owing to his position at the Persian court. We allow that all this would be insufficient to prove the correctness of the above statement in Josephus, but it must render us inclined to admit its truth.

The second argument is much stronger: it is, that the statement of Josephus is supported by the edict of Cyrus (Ezra i.). This edict presupposes the fact related by Josephus, so that Jahn calls the passage in Josephus a commentary on the first chapter of Ezra, in which we read that Cyrus announces in his edict that he was commanded by Jehovah to build him a temple in Jerusalem, and that he received all the conquered kingdoms of the earth as a gift from Jehovah. This cannot refer to any other predictions of the prophet, but only to what are called the spurious portions of Isaiah, in which the Lord grants to Cyrus all his future conquests, and appoints him to be the restorer of his temple (comp. xli. 2-4; xliv. 24-28; xlv. 1-13; xlvi 11; xlviii. 13-15). The edict adopts almost the words of these passages. In reply to this, our adversaries assert that Cyrus was deceived by pseudo-prophecies forged in the name of Isaiah; but if Cyrus could be deceived in so clumsy a manner, he was not the man that history represents him; and to have committed forgery is so contrary to what was to be expected from the author of chaps. xl -lxvi., that even the feelings of our opponents revolt at the supposition that the pseudo-Isaiah should have forged prophecies after the event in the name of the prophets.

5. Again, the most ancient production of Jewish literature after the completion of the canon, furnishes proof of the integral authenticity of Isaiah. The book of Jesus Sirach, commonly called Ecclesiasticus, was written as early as the third century before Christ, as Hug has clearly demonstrated, in opposition to those who place it in the second century before Christ. In Ecclesiasticus xlviii. 22-25, Isaiah is thus praised: ' For Hezekiah had done the thing that pleased the Lord, and was strong in the ways of David his father, as Isaiah the prophet, who was great and faithful in his vision, had commanded him. In his time the sun went backward, and he lengthened the king's life. He saw by an excellent spirit what should come to pass at the last, and he comforted them that mourned in Sion. He showed what should come to pass for ever, and secret things or ever they came.'

This commendation especially refers, as even Gesenius grants, to the disputed portions of the prophet, in which we find predictions of the most distant futurity. The comfort for Zion is found more particularly in the second part of Isaiah, which begins with the words ' Comfort ye, comfort ye my people.' The author of this second part himself says (xlviii. 3), ' I have declared the former things from the beginning; and they went forth out of my mouth, and I showed them.' Thus we perceive that Jesus Sirach, the learned scribe, confidently attributes the debated passages to Isaiah in such a manner as plainly indicates that there was no doubt in his days respecting the integral authenticity of that book, which has the testimony of historical tradition in its favour. Jesus Sirach declares his intention (Ecclus. xliv.-l.) to praise the most celebrated men of his nation. The whole tenor of these chapters shows that he does not confine himself to celebrated authors. We therefore say that the praise which he bestows upon Isaiah is not intended for the book personified, but for the person of the prophet. If Jesus Sirach had entertained doubts respecting the genuineness of those prophecies on which, in particular, he bases his praise, he could not have so lauded the prophet.

In the Jewish synagogue the integral authenticity of Isaiah has always been recognised. This general recognition cannot be accounted for except by the power of tradition based upon truth; and it is supported as well by the New Testament, in which Isaiah is quoted as the author of the whole collection which bears his name, as also by the express testimony of Josephus, especially in his *Antiquities* (x. 2. 2, and xi. 1. 1). After such confirmation it would be superfluous to mention the Talmudists.

Thus we have seen that we possess a series of external arguments in favour of the integral authenticity of Isaiah. Each of these arguments is of importance, and, in their combination, they have a weight which could only be counterbalanced by insurmountable difficulties in the contents of these prophecies; and it has been clearly shown that there are no such difficulties, and that the internal arguments unite with the external in demonstrating the authenticity of Isaiah as a whole.

No definite account respecting the method pursued in collecting into books the utterances of the Prophets has been handed down to us. Concerning Isaiah, as well as the rest, these accounts are wanting. We do not even know whether he collected his prophecies himself. But we have no decisive argument against this opinion. The argument of Kleinert, in his abovementioned work (p. 112), is of slight importance. He says, If Isaiah himself had collected his prophecies, there would not be wanting some which are not to be found in the existing book. To this we reply that it can by no means be proved, with any degree of probability, that a single prophecy of Isaiah has been lost. the preservation of which would have been of importance to posterity, and which Isaiah himself would have deemed it necessary to preserve. Kleinert appeals to the fact that there is no prophecy in our collection which can with certainty be ascribed to the days of Jotham; and he thinks it incredible that the prophet, soon after having been consecrated to his office, should have passed full sixteen years without any revelation from God This, certainly, is unlikely; but it is by no means unlikely that during this time he uttered no prophecy which he thought proper to pre-

serve. Nay, it appears very probable, if we compare the rather general character of chapters i.-v., the contents of which would apply to the days of Jotham also, since during his reign no considerable changes took place; consequently the prophetic utterances moved in the same sphere with those preserved to us from the reign of Uzziah. Hence it was natural that Isaiah should confine himself to the communication of some important prophetic addresses, which might as well represent the days of Jotham as those of the preceding reign. We must not too closely identify the utterances of the prophets with their writings. Many prophets have spoken much and written nothing. The minor prophets were generally content to write down the quintessence alone of their numerous utterances. Jeremiah likewise, of his numerous addresses under Josiah, gives us only what was most essential.

To us it seems impossible that Isaiah left it to others to collect his prophecies into a volume, because we know that he was the author of historical works; and it is not likely that a man accustomed to literary occupation would have left to others to do what he could do much better himself.

Hitzig has of late recognised Isaiah as the collector and arranger of his own prophecies. But he supposes that a number of pieces were inserted at a later period. The chronological arrangement of these prophecies is a strong argument in favour of the opinion that Isaiah himself formed them into a volume. There is no deviation from this arrangement, except in a few instances where prophecies of similar contents are placed together; but there is no interruption which might appear attributable to either accident or ignorance. There is not a single piece in this collection which can satisfactorily be shown to belong to another place. All the portions, the date of which can be ascertained either by external or internal reasons, stand in the right place. This is generally granted with respect to the first twelve chapters, although many persons erroneously maintain that ch. vi. should stand at the beginning.

Chaps. i.-v. belong to the later years of Uzziah; chap. vi. to the year of his death. What follows next, up to chap. x. 4, belongs to the reign of Ahaz. Chaps. x.-xii. is the first portion appertaining to the reign of Hezekiah. Then follows a series of prophecies against foreign nations, in which, according to the opinions of many, the chronological arrangement has been departed from, and, instead of it, an arrangement according to contents has been adopted. But this is not the case. The predictions against foreign nations are also in their right chronological place. They all belong to the reign of Hezekiah, and are placed together because, according to their dates, they belong to the same period. In the days of Hezekiah the nations of Western Asia, dwelling on the banks of the Euphrates and Tigris, more and more resembled a threatening tempest. That the prophecies against foreign nations belong to this period is indicated by the home-prophecy in ch. xxii., which stands among the foreign prophecies. The assertion that the first twelve chapters are a collection of home-prophecies is likewise refuted by the fact that there occur in these chapters two foreign prophecies. The prophetic gift of Isaiah was more fully unfolded in sight of the Assyrian invasion under the reign of Hezekiah. Isaiah, in a series of visions, describes what Assyria would do, as a chastising rod in the hand of the Lord, and what the successors of the Assyrians, the Chaldees, would perform, according to the decree of God, in order to realise divine justice on earth, as well among Israel as among the heathen. The prophet shows that mercy is hidden behind the clouds of wrath. There is no argument to prove that the great prophetic picture in chaps. xxiv.-xxvii. was not depicted under Hezekiah. Chaps. xxviii.-xxxiii. manifestly belong to the same reign, but somewhat later than the time in which chaps. x., xi., xii. were written. They were composed about the time when the result of the war against the Assyrians was decided. With the termination of this war terminated also the public life of Isaiah, who added an historical section in chaps. xxxvi.-xxxix., in order to facilitate the right understanding of the prophecies uttered by him during the most fertile period of his prophetic ministry. Then follows the conclusion of his work on earth. The second part, which contains his prophetic legacy, is addressed to the small congregation of the faithful, strictly so called. This part is analogous to the last speeches of Moses in the fields of Moab, and to the last speeches of Christ in the circle of his disciples, related by John. Thus we have everywhere order, and such an order as could scarcely have proceeded from any one but the author.

It was not the vocation of the prophets to change anything in the religious constitution of Moses, which had been introduced by divine authority; and they were not called upon to substitute anything new in its place. They had only to point out the new covenant to be introduced by the Redeemer, and to prepare the minds of men for the reception of it. They themselves in all their doings were subject to the law of Moses. They were destined to be extraordinary ambassadors of God, whose reign in Israel was not a mere name, not a mere shadow of earthly royalty, but rather its substance and essence. They were to maintain the government of God, by punishing all, both high and low, who manifested contempt of the Lawgiver by offending against his laws. It was especially their vocation to counteract the very ancient delusion, according to which an external observance of rites was deemed sufficient to satisfy God. This opinion is contrary to many passages of the law itself, which admonish men to circumcise the heart, and represent the sum of the entire law as consisting in loving God with the whole heart; which make salvation to depend upon being internally turned towards God, and which condemn not only the evil deed, but also the wicked desire. The law had, however, at the first assumed a form corresponding to the wants of the Israelites, and in accordance with the symbolical spirit of antiquity. But when this form, which was destined to be the living organ of the Spirit, was changed into a corpse by those who were themselves spiritually dead, it offered a point of coalescence for the error of those who contented themselves with external observances.

The prophets had also to oppose the delusion of those who looked upon the election of the people of God as a preservative against the divine judgments; who supposed that their descent from the

patriarchs, with whom God had made a covenant, was an equivalent for the sanctification which they wanted. Even Moses had strongly opposed this delusion; for instance, in Lev. xxvi. and Deut. xxxii. David also, in the Psalms, as in xv. and xxiv., endeavours to counteract this error, which again and again sprang up. It was the vocation of the prophets to insist upon genuine piety, and to show that a true attachment to the Lord necessarily manifests itself by obedience to his precepts; that this obedience would lead to happiness, and disobedience to misfortune and distress. The prophets were appointed to comfort the faint-hearted, by announcing to them the succour of God, and to bring glad tidings to the faithful, in order to strengthen their fidelity. They were commissioned to invite the rebellious to return, by pointing out to them future salvation, and by teaching them that without conversion they could not be partakers of salvation; and in order that their admonitions and rebukes, their consolations and awakenings, might gain more attention, it was granted to them to behold futurity, and to foresee the blessings and judgments which would ultimately find their full accomplishment in the days of Messiah. In Deut. xviii. 18, where the Lord says, ' I will raise them up a prophet from among their brethren like unto thee, and will put my words in his mouth; and he shall speak unto them all that I shall command him,' we have a description of the prophetical calling, and also a statement of the contents of the prophecies of Isaiah. He refers expressly in many places to the basis of the ancient covenant, that is, to the law of Moses; for instance, in viii. 16, 20, and xxx. 9, 10. In many other passages his utterance rests on the same basis, although he does not expressly state it. All his utterances are interwoven with references to the law. It is of importance to examine at least one chapter closely, in order to understand how prophecies are related to the law. Let us take as an example the first. The beginning, ' Hear, O heavens, and give ear, O earth,' is taken from Deut. xxxii. Thus the prophet points out that his prophecies are a commentary upon the Magna Charta of prophetism contained in the books of Moses. During the prosperous condition of the state under Uzziah and Jotham, luxury and immorality had sprung up. The impiety of Ahaz had exercised the worst influence upon the whole people. Great part of the nation had forsaken the religion of their fathers and embraced gross idolatry; and a great number of those who worshipped God externally had forsaken Him in their hearts. The divine judgments were approaching. The rising power of Assyria was appointed to be the instrument of divine justice. Among the people of God internal demoralisation was always the forerunner of outward calamity. This position of affairs demanded an energetic intervention of prophetism. Without prophetism the number of the elect would have been constantly decreasing, and even the judgments of the Lord, if prophetism had not furnished their interpretation, would have been mere facts, which would have missed their aim, and, in many instances, might have had an effect opposite to that which was intended, because punishment which is not recognised to be punishment, necessarily leads away from God.

The prophet attacks the distress of his nation, not at the surface, but at the root, by rebuking the prevailing corruption. Pride and arrogance appear to him to be the chief roots of all sins.

He inculcates again and again not to rely upon the creature, but upon the Creator, from whom all temporal and spiritual help proceeds; that in order to attain salvation, we should despair of our own and all human power, and rely upon God. He opposes those who expected help through foreign alliances with powerful neighbouring nations against foreign enemies of the state.

The people of God have only one enemy, and one ally, that is, God. It is foolish to seek for aid on earth against the power of heaven, and to fear man if God is our friend. The panacea against all distress and danger is true conversion. The politics of the prophets consist only in pointing out this remedy. The prophet connects with his rebuke and with his admonition, his threatenings of divine judgment upon the stiff-necked. These judgments are to be executed by the invasion of the Syrians, the oppression of the Assyrians, the Babylonian exile, and by the great final separation in the times of the Messiah. The idea which is the basis of all these threatenings, is pronounced even in the Pentateuch (Lev. x. 3), 'I will be sanctified in them that come nigh me, and before all the people I will be glorified;' and also in the words of Amos (iii. 2), 'You only have I known of all the families of the earth; therefore I will punish you for all your iniquities.' That is, if the people do not voluntarily glorify God, He glorifies Himself against them. Partly in order to recall the rebellious to obedience, partly to comfort the faithful, the prophet opens a prospect of those blessings which the faithful portion of the covenant people shall inherit. In almost all prophetic utterances, we find in regular succession three elements — rebuke, threatening, and promise. The prophecies concerning the destruction of powerful neighbouring states, partly belong, as we have shown, to the promises, because they are intended to prevent despair, which, as well as false security, is a most dangerous hindrance to conversion.

In the direct promises of deliverance the purpose to comfort is still more evident. This deliverance refers either to burdens which pressed upon the people in the days of the prophet, or to burdens to come, which were already announced by the prophet; such, for instance, as the oppressions of the Syrians, the Assyrians, and finally, of the Chaldæans

The proclamation of the Messiah is the inexhaustible source of consolation among the prophets. In Isaiah this consolation is so clear that some fathers of the church were inclined to style him rather *evangelist* than *prophet*.

Isaiah, however, was not the first who attained to a knowledge of the personality of Messiah. Isaiah's vocation was to render the knowledge of this personality clearer and more definite, and to render it more efficacious upon the souls of the elect by giving it a greater individuality. The person of the Redeemer is mentioned even in Gen. xlix. 10, 'The sceptre shall not depart from Judah, nor a lawgiver from between his feet, until Shiloh (*the tranquilliser*) come; and unto Him shall the gathering of the people be' (i. e. *Him shall the nations obey*). The personality of Messiah occurs also in several psalms which were written before the times of Isaiah; for instance, in the 2nd and 110th, by David; in the 45th, by the sons of Korah; in the 72nd, by Solomon. Isaiah has especially developed the perception of the prophetic and the priestly office of the Redeemer, while in the earlier annunciations of the Messiah the royal office is more prominent; although in Psalm cx. the priestly office also is pointed out. Of the two states of Christ, Isaiah has expressly described that of the examination of the suffering Christ, while, before him, his state of glory was made more prominent. In the Psalms the inseparable connection between justice and suffering, from which the doctrine of a suffering Messiah necessarily results, is not expressly applied to the Messiah. We must not say that Isaiah first perceived that the Messiah was to suffer, but we must grant that this knowledge was in him more vivid than in any earlier writer: and that this knowledge was first shown by Isaiah to be an integral portion of Old Testament doctrine.

The following are the outlines of Messianic prophecies in the book of Isaiah:—A scion of David, springing from his family, after it has fallen into a very low estate, but being also of divine nature, shall, at first in lowliness, but as a prophet filled with the Spirit of God, proclaim the divine doctrine, develope the law in truth, and render it the animating principle of national life: he shall, as high-priest, by his vicarious suffering and his death, remove the guilt of his nation, and that of other nations, and finally rule as a mighty king, not only over the covenant-people, but over all nations of the earth who will subject themselves to his peaceful sceptre, not by violent compulsion, but induced by love and gratitude. He will make both the moral and the physical consequences of sin to cease; the whole earth shall be filled with the knowledge of the Lord, and all enmity, hatred, and destruction shall be removed even from the brute creation. This is the survey of the Messianic preaching by Isaiah, of which he constantly renders prominent those portions which were most calculated to impress the people under the then existing circumstances. The first part of Isaiah is directed to the whole people, consequently the glory of the Messiah is here dwelt upon. The fear lest the kingdom of God should be overwhelmed by the power of heathen nations, is removed by pointing out the glorious king to come, who would elevate the now despised and apparently mean kingdom of God above all the kingdoms of this world. In the second part, which is more particularly addressed to *the elect*, than to the whole nation, the prophet exhibits the Messiah more as a divine teacher and high priest. The prophet here preaches righteousness through the blood of the servant of God, who will support the weakness of sinners and take upon Himself their sorrows.

We may show, by an example, in chap. xix. 18-25, that the views of futurity which were granted to Isaiah were great and comprehensive, and that the Spirit of God raised him above all narrow-minded nationality. It is there stated that a time should come when all the heathen, subdued by the judgments of the Lord, should be converted to him, and being placed on an equality with Israel, with equal laws, would equally partake of the kingdom of God, and form a brotherly alliance for his worship. Not the whole mass of Israel is destined, according to Isaiah, to future salvation, but only the small number of the converted. This truth he announces most definitely in the sketch of his prophecies contained in chapter vi.

Isaiah describes with equal vivacity the divine justice which punishes the sins of the nation with inexorable severity. Holy, holy, holy, is the Lord of Sabaoth, is the key-note of his prophecies. He describes also the divine mercy and covenant-fidelity, by which there is always preserved a remnant among the people: to them punishment itself is a means of salvation, so that life everywhere proceeds from death, and the congregation itself is led to full victory and glory

Isaiah saw the moral and religious degradation of his people, and also its external distress, both then present and to come (chap. vi.). But this did not break his courage; he confidently expected a better futurity, and raised himself in God above all that is visible. Isaiah is not afraid when the whole nation and its king tremble. Of this we see a remarkable instance in chapter vii., and another in the time of the Assyrian invasion under Hezekiah, during which the courage of his faith rendered him the saviour of the commonwealth, and the originator of that great religious revival which followed the preservation of the state. The faith of the king and of the people was roused by that of Isaiah.

Isaiah stands pre-eminent above all other prophets, as well in the contents and spirit of his predictions, as also in their form and style. Simplicity, clearness, sublimity, and freshness, are the never-failing characters of his prophecies. Even Eichhorn mentions, among the first merits of Isaiah, the concinnity of his expressions, the beautiful outline of his images, and the fine execution of his speeches. In reference to richness of imagery he stands between Jeremiah and Ezekiel. Symbolic actions, which frequently occur in Jeremiah and Ezekiel, seldom occur in Isaiah. The same is the case with visions, strictly so called, of which there is only one, namely, that in chapter vi.; and even it is distinguished by its simplicity and clearness above that of the later prophets. But one characteristic of Isaiah is, that he likes to give signs—that is, a fact then present, or near at hand—as a pledge for the more distant futurity; and that he thus supports the feebleness of man (comp. vii. 20; xxxvii. 30; xxxviii. 7. sqq.). The instances in chapters vii. and xxxviii. show how much he was convinced of his vocation, and in what intimacy he lived with the Lord, by whose assistance alone he could effect what he offers to do in the one passage, and what he grants in the other. The spiritual riches of the prophet are seen in the variety of his style, which always befits the subject. When he rebukes and threatens, it is like a storm, and when he comforts, his language is as tender and mild as (to use his own words) that of a mother comforting her son. With regard to style, Isaiah is comprehensive, and the other prophets divide his riches.

Isaiah enjoyed an authority proportionate to his gifts. We learn from history how great this authority was during his life, especially under the reign of Hezekiah. Several of his most definite prophecies were fulfilled while he was yet alive; for instance, the overthrow of the kingdoms of Syria and Israel; the invasion of the Assyrians, and the divine deliverance from it; the prolongation of life granted to Hezekiah; and several predictions against foreign nations. Isaiah is honourably mentioned in the historical books. The later prophets, especially Nahum, Habakkuk, Zephaniah, Jeremiah, Haggai, Zechariah, and Malachi, clearly prove that his book was diligently read, and that his prophecies were attentively studied.

The authority of the prophet greatly increased after the fulfilment of his prophecies by the Babylonian exile, the victories of Cyrus, and the deliverance of the covenant-people. Even Cyrus (according to the above-mentioned account in Josephus, *Antiq.* xi. 1. § 1, 2) was induced to set the Jews at liberty by the prophecies of Isaiah concerning himself. This prediction of Isaiah made so deep an impression upon him that he probably took from it the name by which he is generally known in history. Jesus Sirach (xlviii. 22-25) bestows splendid praise upon Isaiah, and both Philo and Josephus speak of him with great veneration. He attained the highest degree of authority after the times of the New Testament had proved the most important part of his prophecies, namely, the Messianic, to be divine. Christ and the Apostles quote no prophecies so frequently as those of Isaiah, in order to prove that He who had appeared was one and the same with Him who had been promised. The fathers of the church abound in praises of Isaiah.

ISH'BI, or ISHBI-BENOB. [GIANTS.]

ISH'-BOSHETH (*man of shame*), a son of king Saul, and the only one who survived him. In 1 Chron. viii. 33, and ix. 39, this name is given as *Eshbaal*. Baal was the name of an idol, accounted abominable by the Hebrews, and which scrupulous persons avoided pronouncing, using the word *bosheth*, 'shame' or 'vanity,' instead. This explains why the name Eshbaal is substituted for Ish-bosheth, Jerubbaal for Jerubbesheth (comp. Judg. viii. 35 with 2 Sam. xi. 21), and Merib-baal for Mephibosheth (comp. 2 Sam. iv. 4 with 1 Chron. viii. 34 and ix. 40). Ish-bosheth was not present in the disastrous battle at Gilboa, in which his father and brothers perished; and, too feeble of himself to seize the sceptre which had fallen from the hands of Saul, he owed the crown entirely to his uncle Abner, who conducted him to Mahanaim, beyond the Jordan, where he was recognised as king by ten of the twelve tribes. He reigned seven, or, as some will have it, two years—if a power so uncertain as his can be called a reign. Even the semblance of authority which he possessed he owed to the will and influence of Abner, who himself kept the real substance in his own hands. A sharp quarrel between them led at last to the ruin of Ish-bosheth. Although accustomed to tremble before Abner, even his meek temper was roused to resentment by the discovery that Abner had invaded the harem of his late father Saul, which was in a peculiar manner sacred under his care as a son and a king. By this act Abner exposed the king to public contempt; if it did not indeed leave himself open to the suspicion of intending to advance a claim to the crown on his own behalf. Abner highly resented the rebuke of Ish-bosheth, and from that time contemplated uniting all the tribes under the sceptre of David. Ish bosheth, however, reverted to his ordinary timidity of character. At the first demand of David, he restored to him his sister Michal, who had been given in marriage to the son of Jesse by Saul, and had afterwards been taken from him and bestowed upon another. It is, perhaps, right to attribute this act to his weakness; al though, as David allows that he was a righteous man, it may have been owing to his sense of justice. On the death of Abner Ish-bosheth lost all heart and hope, and perished miserably, being murdered in his own palace, while he took his mid-day sleep, by two of his officers, Baanah and Rechab. They sped with his head to David, expecting a great reward for their deed; but the monarch—as both right feeling and good policy required—testified the utmost horror and concern. He slew the murderers, and placed the head of Ish-bosheth with due respect in the sepulchre of Abner, B.C. 1048 (2 Sam. ii, 8-11; iii. 6-39; iv.).

1. ISH'MAEL (*heard of God*), Abraham's eldest son, born to him by Hagar; the circumstances of whose birth, early history, and final expulsion from his father's tents, are related in the articles ABRAHAM, HAGAR [see also ISAAC, INHERITANCE]. He afterwards made the desert into which he had been cast his abode, and by attaching himself to, and acquiring influence over, the native tribes, rose to great authority and influence. It would seem to have been the original intention of his mother to have returned to Egypt, to which country she belonged; but this being prevented, she was content to obtain for her son wives from thence. Although their lots were cast apart, it does not appear that any serious alienation existed between Ishmael and Isaac; for we read that they both joined in the sepulchral rites of their father Abraham (Gen. xxv. 9). This fact has not been noticed as it deserves. It is full of suggestive matter. As funerals in the East take place almost immediately after death, it is evident that Ishmael must have been called from the desert to the death-bed of his father; which implies that relations of kindness and respect had been kept up, although the brevity of the sacred narrative prevents any special notice of this circumstance. Ishmael had probably long before received an endowment from his father's property, similar to that which had been bestowed upon the sons of Keturah (Gen. xxv. 6). Nothing more is recorded of him than that he died at the age of 137 years, and was the father of twelve sons, who gave their names to as many tribes (Gen. xvii. 20; xxv. 13). He had also two daughters, one of whom became the wife of Esau.

It has been shown, in the article ARABIA, that Ishmael has no claim to the honour, which is usually assigned to him, of being the founder of the Arabian nation. That nation existed before he was born. He merely joined it, and adopted its habits of life and character; and the tribes which sprung from him formed eventually an important section of the tribes of which it was c mposed. The celebrated prophecy which describes the habits of life which he, and in him

his descendants, would follow, is therefore to be regarded not as describing habits which he would first establish, but such as he would adopt The description is contained in the address of the angel to Hagar, when, before the birth of Ishmael, she fled from the tents of Abraham :— ' Behold, thou art with child, and shalt bear a son, and shalt call his name Ishmael (*God hears*), because the Lord hath heard thine affliction. And he shall be a wild man: his hand shall be against every man, and every man's hand against him, and he shall dwell in the presence of all his brethren' (Gen. xvi. 11, 12). This means, in short, that he and his descendants should lead the life of the Bedouins of the Arabian deserts; and how graphically this description portrays their habits, may be seen in the article ARABIA, in the notes on these verses in the ' Pictorial Bible,' and in the works of Niebuhr, Burckhardt, Lane, &c.; and, more particularly, in the Arabian romance of Antar, which presents the most perfect picture of real Bedouin manners now in existence. The last clause, ' He shall dwell in the presence of all his brethren,' is pointedly alluded to in the brief notice of his death, which states that ' he died in the presence of all his brethren' (Gen. xxxv. 18). Of this expression various explanations have been given, but the plainest is the most probable: which is, that Ishmael and the tribes springing from him should always be located near the kindred tribes descended from Abraham.

2. ISHMAEL, a prince of the royal line of Judah, who found refuge among the Ammonites from the ruin which involved his family and nation. After the Chaldæans had departed he returned, and treacherously slew the too-confiding Gedaliah, who had been made governor of the miserable remnant left in the land [GEDALIAH]. Much more slaughter followed this, and Ishmael, with many people of consideration as captives, hastened to return to the Ammonites. But he was overtaken near the pool of Gibeon, by Johanan. a friend of Gedaliah, and was compelled to abandon his prey and escape for his life, with only eight attendants, to Baalis, king of the Ammonites, with whom he appears to have had a secret understanding in these transactions: B.C. 588 (Jer. xli.).

ISLE, ISLAND. These words occur in the Scriptures in the three following senses. First, that of dry land in opposition to water; as ' I will make the rivers islands' (Isa. xlii. 15). In Isa. xx. 6, the Isle of Ashdod means the country, and is so rendered in the margin. In Isa. xxiii. 2, 6, ' the isle' means the country of Tyre, and in Ezek. xxvii. 6, 7, that of Chittim and Elisha. (See also Job xxii. 30.) Secondly, it is used both in Hebrew and English, according to its geographical meaning, for a country surrounded by water, as in Jer. xlvii. 4, ' the isle (margin) of Caphtor, which is probably that of Cyprus. ' The isles of the sea' (Esth. x. 1) are evidently put in opposition to ' the land,' or continent. In Ps. xcvii. 1, ' the multitude of the isles' seem distinguished from the earth or continents, and are evidently added to complete the description of the whole world. Thirdly: the word is used by the Hebrews to designate all those countries divided from them by the sea. In Isa. xi. 11, after an enumeration of countries lying on their own continent, the words ' and the islands of the sea' are added in order to comprehend those situate beyond the ocean. The following are additional instances of this usage of the word, which is of very frequent occurrence (Isa xlii. 10; lix. 18; lxvi. 19, Jer. xxv 22; Ezek. xxvii. 3, 15, Zeph. ii. 11). It is observed by Sir I. Newton (*On Daniel*, p. 276), ' By the earth the Jews understood the great continent of all Asia and Africa, to which they had access by land; and by the isles of the sea they understood the places to which they sailed by sea, particularly all Europe.'

IS'RAEL is the sacred and divinely bestowed name of the patriarch Jacob, and is explained to mean, ' A prince with God.' Although, as applied to Jacob personally, it is an honourable or poetical appellation, it is the common prose name of his descendants; while, on the contrary, the title Jacob is given to them only in poetry.

The separation of the Hebrew nation into two parts, of which one was to embrace ten of the tribes, and be distinctively named Israel, had its origin in the early power and ambition of the tribe of Ephraim. The rivalry of Ephraim and Judah began almost from the first conquest of the land; nor is it unsignificant, that as Caleb belonged to the tribe of Judah, so did Joshua to that of Ephraim. From the very beginning Judah learned to act by itself; but the central position of Ephraim, with its fruitful and ample soil, and the long-continued authority of Joshua, must have taught most of the tribes west of the Jordan to look up to Ephraim as their head; and a still more important superiority was conferred on the same tribe by the fixed dwelling of the ark at Shiloh for so many generations (Josh. xviii. &c.). Judah could boast of Hebron, Machpelah, Bethlehem, names of traditional sanctity; yet so could Ephraim point to Shechem, the ancient abode of Jacob; and while Judah, being on the frontier, was more exposed to the attack of the powerful Philistines, Ephraim had to fear only those Canaanites from within who were not subdued or conciliated. The haughty behaviour of the Ephraimites towards Gideon, a man of Manasseh (Judg. viii. 1), 'sufficiently indicates the pretensions they made. Still fiercer language towards Jephthah the Gileadite (Jud. xii. 1) was retorted by less gentleness than Gideon had shown; and a bloody civil war was the result, in which their pride met with a severe punishment. This may in part explain their quiet submission, not only to the priestly rule of Eli and his sons, who had their centre of authority at Shiloh, but to Samuel, whose administration issued from three towns of Benjamin. Of course his prophetical character and personal excellence eminently contributed to this result; and it may seem that Ephraim, as well as all Israel besides, became habituated to the predominance of Benjamin, so that no serious resistance was made to the supremacy of Saul. At his death a new schism took place through their jealousy of Judah; yet in a few years' time, by the splendour of David's victories, and afterwards by Solomon's peaceful power, a permanent national union might seem to have been effected. But the laws of inheritance in Israel, excellent as they were for preventing permanent alienation of landed property, and the degrada-

tion of the Hebrew poor into prædial slaves, necessarily impeded the perfect fusion of the tribes, by discouraging intermarriage, and hindering the union of distant estates in the same hands. Hence, when the sway of Solomon began to be felt as a tyranny, the old jealousies of the tribes revived, and Jeroboam, an Ephraimite (1 Kings xi. 26), being suspected of treason, fled to Shishak, king of Egypt. The death of Solomon was followed by a defection of ten of the tribes, which established the separation of *Israel* from *Judah* (B.C. 975).

This was the most important event which had befallen the Hebrew nation since their conquest of Canaan. The chief territory and population were now with Jeroboam, but the religious sanction, the legitimate descent, lay with the rival monarch. From the political danger of allowing the ten tribes to go up to the sanctuary of Jerusalem, the princes of *Israel*, as it were in self-defence, set up a sanctuary of their own; and the intimacy of Jeroboam with the king of Egypt may have determined his preference for the form of idolatry (the calves) which he established at Dan and Bethel. In whatever else his successors differed, they one and all agreed in upholding this worship. which, once established, appeared essential to their national unity. Nevertheless it is generally understood to have been a worship of Jehovah, though under unlawful and degrading forms. Worse by far was the worship of Baal, which came in under one monarch only, Ahab, and was destroyed after his son was slain, by Jehu. A secondary result of the revolution was the ejection of the tribe of Levi from their lands and cities in Israel; at least, such as remained were spiritually degraded by the compliances required, and could no longer offer any resistance to the kingly power by aid of their sacred character. When the priestly tribe had thus lost independence, it lost also the power to assist the crown. The succession of Jeroboam's family was hallowed by no religious blessing; and when his son was murdered, no Jehoiada was found to rally his supporters and ultimately avenge his cause. The example of successful usurpation was so often followed by the captains of the armies, that the kings in Israel present to us an irregular series of dynasties, with several short and tumultuous reigns. This was one cause of disorder and weakness to Israel, and hindered it from swallowing up Judah: another was found in the relations of Israel towards foreign powers, which will presently be dwelt upon.

With regard to chronology, the following scheme agrees with Winer in its total range, but has minor changes by a single unit in some of the kings:—

	B.C.	
Rehoboam.	975	Jeroboam.
Abijah.	957	
Asa	955	
	954	Nadab
	952	Baasha.
	929	Elah.
	928	Zimri, Omri.
	917	Ahab.
Jehoshaphat	914	
	897	Ahaziah.
	896	Jehoram.
Jehoram	889	

	B.C.	
Ahaziah . . .	885	
Queen Athaliah .	884	Jehu
Jehoash . . .	878	
	855	Jehoahaz.
	840	Jehoash.
Amaziah . . .	838	
	824	Jeroboam II.
Uzziah. . . .	809	
	772	Zachariah.
	771	Shallum, Menahem.
	760	Pekahiah.
	758	Pekah.
Jotham . . .	757	
Ahaz	741	
	729	Hosea.
Hezekiah . . .	726	
	721	Samaria captured.

The dynasties in Israel are denoted by brackets.

Jeroboam originally fixed on *Shechem* as the centre of his monarchy, and fortified it; moved perhaps not only by its natural suitability, but by the remembrances of Jacob which clove to it, and by the auspicious fact that here first Israel had decided for him against Rehoboam. But the natural delightfulness of *Tirzah* (Cant. vi. 4) led him, perhaps late in his reign, to erect a palace there (1 Kings xiv. 17). After the murder of Jeroboam's son, Baasha seems to have intended to fix his capital at *Ramah*, as a convenient place for annoying the king of Judah, whom he looked on as his only dangerous enemy; but when forced to renounce this plan (xv. 17, 21), he acquiesced in Tirzah, which continued to be the chief city of Israel, until Omri, who, since the palace at Tirzah had been burned during the civil war (1 Kings xvi. 18), built Samaria, with the ambition not uncommon in the founder of a new dynasty (xvi. 24). Samaria continued to the end of the monarchy to be the centre of administration; and its strength appears to have justified Omri's choice. For details, see SAMARIA; also TIRZAH and SHECHEM.

There is reason to believe that Jeroboam carried back with him into Israel the good will, it not the substantial assistance, of Shishak; and this will account for his escaping the storm from Egypt which swept over Rehoboam in his fifth year. During that first period Israel far from quiet within. Although the ten tribes collectively had decided in favour of Jeroboam, great numbers of individuals remained attached to the family of David and to the worship at Jerusalem, and in the first three years of Rehoboam migrated into Judah (2 Chron. xi. 16, 17). Perhaps it was not until this process commenced, that Jeroboam was worked up to the desperate measure of erecting rival sanctuaries with visible idols (1 Kings xii. 27): a measure which met the usual ill-success of profane state-craft, and aggravated the evil which he feared. It set him at war with the whole order of priests and Levites, whose expulsion or subjugation, we may be certain, was not effected without convulsing his whole kingdom, and so occupying him as to free Rehoboam from any real danger, although no peace was made. The king of Judah improved the time by immense efforts in fortifying his territory (2 Chron. xi. 5-11);

and, although Shishak soon after carried off the most valuable spoil, no great or definite impression could be made by Jeroboam. Israel having so far taken the place of heathen nations, and being already perhaps even in alliance with Egypt, at an early period—we know not how soon—sought and obtained the friendship of the kings of Damascus. A sense of the great advantage derivable from such a union seems to have led Ahab afterwards to behave with mildness and conciliation towards Benhadad, at a time when it could have been least expected (1 Kings xx. 31-34). From that transaction we learn that Benhadad I. had made in Damascus 'streets for Omri,' and Omri for Benhadad in Samaria. This, no doubt, implied that 'a quarter' was assigned for Syrian merchants in Samaria, which was probably fortified like the 'camp of the Tyrians' in Memphis, or the English factory at Calcutta; and in it, of course, Syrian worship would be tolerated. Against such intercourse the prophets, as might be expected, entered their protest (ver. 35-43); but it was in many ways too profitable to be renounced. In the reign of Baasha, Asa king of Judah, sensible of the dangerous advantage gained by his rival through the friendship of the Syrians, determined to buy them off at any price [see also under JUDAH]; and by sacrificing 'the treasures of the house of the Lord and the treasures of the king's house' (xv. 18), induced Benhadad I. to break his league with Baasha and to ravage all the northern district of Israel. This drew off the Israelitish monarch, and enabled Asa to destroy the fortifications of Ramah, which would have stopped the course of his trade (xv. 17), perhaps that with the sea-coast and with Tyre. Such was the beginning of the war *between Israel and Syria*, on which the safety of Judah at that time depended. Cordial union was not again restored between the two northern states until the days of Rezin king of Syria, and Pekah the son of Remaliah, when Damascus must have already felt the rising power of Nineveh. The renewed alliance instantly proved so disastrous to Judah, which was reduced to extremest straits (Isa. vii. 2; 2 Kings xv. 37; 2 Chron. xxviii. 5, 6), as may seem to justify at least the *policy* of Asa's proceeding. Although it was impossible for a prophet to approve of it (2 Chron. xvi. 7), we may only so much the more infer that Judah was already brought into most pressing difficulties, and that the general course of the war, in spite of occasional reverses, was decidedly and increasingly favourable to Israel.

The wars of Syria and Israel were carried on chiefly under three reigns, those of Benhadad II., Hazael, and Benhadad III., the two first monarchs being generally prosperous, especially Hazael, the last being as decidedly unsuccessful. Although these results may have depended in part on personal qualities, there is high probability that the feebleness displayed by the Syrians against Jehoash and his son Jeroboam was occasioned by the pressure of the advancing empire of Nineveh.

Asa adhered, through the whole of his long reign, to the policy of encouraging hostility between the two northern kingdoms; and the first Benhadad had such a career of success that his son found himself in a condition to hope for an entire conquest of Israel. His formidable invasions wrought an entire change in the mind of Jehoshaphat (1 Kings xxii 44), who saw that if Israel was swallowed up by Syria, there would be no safety for Judah. We may conjecture that this consideration determined him to unite the two royal families. for no common cause would have induced so religious a king to select for his son s wife Athaliah the daughter of Jezebel. The age of Ahaziah. who was sprung from this marriage, forces us to place it as early as B.C. 912, which is the third year of Jehoshaphat and s xth of Ahab. Late in his reign Jehoshaphat threw himself most cordially (1 Kings xxii. 4) into the defence of Ahab, and by so doing probably saved Israel from a foreign yoke. Another mark of the low state into which both kingdoms were falling, is that after Ahab's death the Moabites refused their usual tribute to Israel, and (as far as can be made out from the ambiguous words of 2 Kings iii. 27), the united force of the two kingdoms failed of doing more than irritate them Soon after, in the reign of Jehoram son of Jehoshaphat, the Edomites followed the example, and established their independence. This event possibly engaged the whole force of Judah, and hindered it from succouring Samaria during the cruel siege which it sustained from Benhadad II., in the reign of Jehoram son of Ahab. The declining years and health of the king of Syria gave a short respite to Israel; but, in B.C. 885, Hazael, by defeating the united Hebrew armies, commenced the career of conquest and harassing invasion by which he 'made Israel like the dust by threshing.' Even under Jehu he subdued the trans-Jordanic triles (2 Kings x. 32). Afterwards, since he took the town of Gath (2 Kings xii. 17) and prepared to attack Jerusalem—an attack which Jehoash king of Judah averted only by strictly following Asa's precedent—it is manifest that all the passes and chief forts of the country west of the Jordan must have been in his hand. Indeed, as he is said ' to have left to Jehoahaz only fifty horsemen, ten chariots. and ten thousand footmen,' it would seem that Israel was strictly a conquered province, in which Hazael dictated (as the English to the native rajahs of India) what military force should be kept up. From this thraldom Israel was delivered by some unexplained agency. We are told merely that ' Jehovah gave to Israel *a saviour*, so that they went out from under the hand of the Syrians; and the children of Israel dwelt in their tents as beforetime.' 2 Kings xiii. 5. It is allowable to conjecture that the (apparently unknown) deliverer was the Assyrian monarchy. which, assaulting Hazael towards the end of the reign of Jehoahaz, entirely drew away the Syrian armies. That it was some urgent, powerful, and continued pressure, considering the great strength which the empire of Damascus had attained, seems clear from the sudden weakness of Syria through the reigns of Jehoash and Jeroboam II., the former of whom thrice defeated Benhadad III. and 'recovered the cities of Israel;' the latter not only regained the full territory of the ten tribes, but made himself master (for a time at least) of Damascus and Hamath How entirely the friendship of Israel and Judah had been caused and cemented by their common fear of Syria, is proved by the fact that no sooner is the power of Damascus broken than new war breaks out between the two kingdoms, which ended in the

plunder of Jerusalem by Jehoash, who also broke down its walls and carried off hostages, after which there is no more alliance between Judah and Israel. The *empire* of Damascus seems to have been entirely dissolved under the son of Hazael. and no mention is made of its kings for eighty years or more. When Pekah. son of Remaliah, reigned in Samaria, Rezin, as king of Damascus. made a last but ineffectual effort for its independence.

The same Assyrian power which had doubtless so seriously shaken, and perhaps temporarily overturned, the kingdom of Damascus, was soon to be felt by Israel. Menahem was invaded by Pul (the first sovereign of Nineveh whose name we know), and was made tributary. His successor, Tiglath-pileser, in the reign of Pekah, son of Remaliah, carried captive the eastern and northern tribes of Israel (*i. e.* perhaps all their chief men as hostages?), and soon after slew Rezin, the ally of Pekah, and subdued Damascus. The following emperor, Shalmanezer, besieged and captured Samaria, and terminated the kingdom of Israel, B.C. 721.

This branch of the Hebrew monarchy suffered far greater and more rapid reverses than the other. From the accession of Jeroboam to the middle of Baasha's reign it probably increased in power, it then waned with the growth of the Damascene empire; it struggled hard against it under Ahab and Jehoram, but sank lower and lower; it was dismembered under Jehu, and made subject under Jehoahaz. From B.C. 940 to B.C. 850 is, as nearly as can be ascertained, the period of depression; and from B.C. 914 to B.C. 830 that of friendship or alliance with Judah. But after (about) B.C. 850 Syria began to decline, and Israel soon shot out rapidly; so that Joash and his son Jeroboam appear, of all Hebrew monarchs, to come next to David and Solomon. How long this burst of prosperity lasted does not distinctly appear; but it would seem that entire dominion over the ten tribes was held until Pekah received the first blow from the Assyrian conqueror.

Besides that which was a source of weakness to Israel from the beginning, viz., the schism of the crown with the whole ecclesiastical body, other causes may be discerned which made the ten tribes less powerful, in comparison with the two, than might have been expected. The marriage of Ahab to Jezebel brought with it no political advantages at all commensurate with the direct moral mischief, to say nothing of the spiritual evil; and the reaction against the worship of Baal was a most ruinous atonement for the sin. To suppress the monstrous iniquity, Jehu not only put to death Ahab's wife, grandson, and seventy sons, but murdered first the king of Judah himself, and next forty-two youthful and innocent princes of his house; while, strange to tell, the daughter of Jezebel gained by his deed the throne of Judah, and perpetrated a new massacre. The horror of such crimes must have fallen heavily on Jehu, and have caused a widespread disaffection among his own subjects. Add to this, that the Phœnicians must have deeply resented his proceedings, so that we get a very sufficient clue to the prostration of Israel under the foot of Hazael during the reign of Jehu and his son.

Another and more abiding cause of political

debility in the ten tribes was found in the imperfect consolidation of the inhabitants into a single nation. Since those who lived east of the Jordan retained, to a great extent at least, their pastoral habits, their union with the rest could never have been very firm; and when a king was neither strong independently of them, nor had good hereditary pretensions, they were not likely to contribute much to his power. After their conquest of the Hagarenes and the depression of the Moabites and Ammonites by David, they had free room to spread eastward; and many of their chief men may have become wealthy in flocks and herds (like Machir the son of Ammiel, of Lodebar, and Barzillai the Gileadite, 2 Sam. xvii. 27), over whom the authority of the Israelitish crown would naturally be precarious; while west of the Jordan the agrarian law of Moses made it difficult or impossible for a landed nobility to form itself, which could be formidable to the royal authority. That the Arab spirit of freedom was rooted in the eastern tribes, may perhaps be inferred from the case of the Rechabites, who would neither live in houses nor plant vines; undoubtedly like some of the Nabathæans, lest, by becoming settled and agricultural, they should be enslaved. Yet the need of imposing this law on his descendants would not have been felt by Jonadab, had not an opposite tendency been rising,—that of agricultural settlement.

Although the priests and Levites nearly disappeared out of Israel, prophets were perhaps even more numerous and active there than in Judah; and Ahijah, whose prediction first endangered Jeroboam (1 Kings xi. 29-40), lived in honour at Shiloh to his dying day (xiv. 2). Obadiah alone saved one hundred prophets of Jehovah from the rage of Jezebel (xviii. 13). Possibly their extra-social character freed them from the restraint imposed on priests and Levites; and while they felt less bound to the formal rites of the Law, the kings of Israel were also less jealous of them.

1. IS'SACHAR (*price-bought*), a son of Jacob and Leah, born B C. 1749, who gave name to one of the tribes of Israel (Gen. xxx. 18; Num. xxvi. 25).

2. The tribe called after Issachar. Jacob, on his death-bed, speaking metaphorically of the character and destinies of his sons, or rather of the tribes which should spring from them, said, ' Issachar is a strong ass couching down between two burdens' (Gen. xlix. 14, 15). Remembering the character of the ass in Eastern countries, we may be sure that this comparison was not intended in disparagement. The ass is anything but stupid; and the proverbial obstinacy which it sometimes exhibits in our own country, is rather the result of ill-treatment than a natural characteristic of the animal. Its true attributes are patience, gentleness, great capability of endurance, laborious exertion, and a meek submission to authority. Issachar, therefore, the progenitor of a race singularly docile, and distinguished for their patient industry, is exhibited under the similitude of the meekest and most laborious of quadrupeds. The descriptive character goes on :—' And he saw that rest was good, and the land that it was pleasant, and he bowed his shoulder to bear, and became a servant unto tribute.' which probably

does not imply that reproach upon Issachar, as addicted to ignominious ease, which some commentators find in it. It seems simply to mean that finding itself in possession of a most fertile portion of Palestine, the tribe devoted itself to the labours of agriculture, taking little interest in the public affairs of the nation. Accordingly Josephus says that the heritage of the tribe ' was fruitful to admiration, abounding in pastures and nurseries of all kinds, so that it would make any man in love with husbandry' (*Antiq.* v. 1. 22). But although a decided preference of agricultural over commercial or military pursuits is here indicated, there seems no reason to conclude, as some gather from the last clause, that the tribe would be willing to purchase exemption from war by the payment of a heavy tribute. The words do not necessarily imply this; and there is no evidence that the tribe ever declined any military service to which it was called. On the contrary, it is specially commended by Deborah for the promptitude with which it presented itself in the war with Jabin (Judg. v. 15); and in the days of David honourable testimony is borne to its character (1 Chron. xii. 32). In this passage the ' children of Issachar ' are described as ' men that had understanding of the times, to know what Israel ought to do,' which probably means that they were men held in esteem for their prudence and wisdom, and who knew that the time was come when it was no longer safe to delay calling David to the throne of all Israel. On quitting Egypt the tribe of Issachar numbered 54,000 adult males, which gave it the fifth numerical rank among the twelve tribes, Judah, Simeon, Zebulun, and Dan, being alone above it. In the wilderness it increased nearly 10,000, and then ranked as the third of the tribes, Judah and Dan only being more numerous (Num. i. xxvi.). The territory of the tribe comprehended the whole of the plain of Esdraelon and the neighbouring districts—the granary of Palestine. It was bounded on the east by the Jordan, on the west and south by Manasseh, and on the north by Asher and Zebulun. It contained the towns of Megiddo, Taanach, Shunem, Jezreel, and Bethshan, with the villages of Endor, Aphek, and Ibleam, all historical names: the mountains of Tabor and Gilboa, and the valley of Jezreel, were in the territory of this tribe, and the course of the river Kishon lay through it.

ITH'AMAR (*palm-coast*), fourth son of Aaron. He was consecrated to the priesthood along with his brothers (Exod. vi. 23; Num. iii. 2, 3). Nothing is individually recorded of him, except that the property of the tabernacle was placed under his charge (Exod. xxxviii. 21), and that he superintended all matters connected with its removal by the Levitical sections of Gershon and Merari (Num. iv. 28). The sacred utensils and their removal were entrusted to his elder brother Eleazar. Ithamar, with his descendants, occupied the position of common priests till the highpriesthood passed into his family in the person of Eli, under circumstances of which we are ignorant. Abiathar, whom Solomon deposed, was the last high-priest of that line ; and the pontificate then reverted to the elder line of Eleazar in the person of Zadok (1 Kings ii. 27).

ITURÆ'A, a district in the north-east of Palestine, forming the tetrarchy of Philip. The name is supposed to have originated with *Itur*, or *Jetur*, one of Ishmael's sons (1 Chron. i. 31). In 1 Chron. v. 19 this name is given as that of a tribe or nation with which Reuben (beyond the Jordan) warred; and from its being joined with the names of other of Ishmael's sons it is evident that a tribe descended from his son Jetur is intimated.

During the Exile this and other border countries were taken possession of by various tribes, whom, although they are called after the original names, as occupants of the countries which had received those names, we are not bound to regard as descendants of the original possessors. These new Ituræans were eventually subdued by King Aristobulus (B.C. 100); by whom they were constrained to embrace the Jewish religion, and were at the same time incorporated with the state. Nevertheless the Ituræans were still recognisable as a distinct people in the time of Pliny. As already intimated, Herod the Great, in dividing his dominions among his sons, bequeathed Ituræa to Philip, as part of a tetrarchy composed, according to Luke, of Trachonitis and Ituræa. The name is so loosely applied by ancient writers, that it is difficult to fix its boundaries with precision. Perhaps it may suffice for general purposes to describe it as a district of indeterminate extent, traversed by a line drawn from the Lake of Tiberias to Damascus. The present Jedur probably comprehends the whole or greater part of the proper Ituræa. This is described by Burckhardt as 'lying south of Jebelkessoue, east of Jebel es-Sheik (Mount Hermon), and west of the Hadj road.' He adds, that it now contains only twenty inhabited villages. By the help of these lights we may discover that Ituræa was a plain country, about thirty miles long from north to south, and twenty-four from east to west, having on the north Abilene and the Damascene district; on the south Auranitis and part of Bashan; on the east the stony region of Trachonitis; and on the west the hill country of Bashan.

IVORY (1 Kings x. 22; 2 Chron. ix. 21; Rev. xviii. 12). 'Elephant's tooth,' or simply 'elephant,' is a common name for ivory, not only in the Oriental languages and in Greek, but also in the Western tongues; although in all of them teeth of other species may be included. Elephants' teeth were largely imported as merchandise, and also brought as tribute into Egypt. The processions of human figures bearing presents, &c., still extant on the walls of palaces and tombs, attest by the black crisp-haired bearers of huge teeth, that some of these came from Ethiopia or Central Africa; and by white men similarly laden, who also bring an Asiatic elephant and a white bear, that others came from the East. Phœnician traders had ivory in such abundance, that the chief seats of their galleys were inlaid with it. In the Scriptures, according to the Chaldee Paraphrase, Jacob's bed was made of this substance (Gen. xlix. 33); we find king Solomon importing it from Tarshish (1 Kings x. 22); and if Psalm xlv. 8 was written before his reign, ivory was extensively used in the furniture of royal residences at a still earlier period. The tusks of African elephants are generally much longer than those of the Asiatic; and it may be observed in this place, that the ancients, as well as the moderns, are mistaken when they assert

elephants' tusks to be a kind of horns. They are genuine teeth, combining in themselves, and occupying, in the upper jaw, the whole mass of secretions which in other animals form the upper incisor and laniary teeth. They are useful for defence and offence, and for holding down green branches, or rooting up water-plants; but still they are not absolutely necessary, since there is a variety of elephant in the Indian forests entirely destitute of tusks, and the females in most of the races are either without them or have them very small; not turned downwards, as Bochart states, but rather straight, as correctly described by Pliny.

IYAR is the late name of that month which was the second of the sacred, and the seventh of the civil year of the Jews, and which began with the new moon of May. The few memorable days in it are the 10th, as a fast for the death of Eli; the 14th, as the second or lesser Passover, for those whom uncleanness or absence prevented from celebrating the feast in Nisan (Num. ix. 11); the 23rd, as a feast instituted by Simon the Maccabee in memory of his taking the citadel Acra in Jerusalem (1 Macc. xiii. 51, 52); the 28th, as a fast for the death of Samuel.

The name Iyar does not occur in the Old Testament, this month being always described as the second month, except in four places in which it is called Ziv (1 Kings v. 1, 37; Dan. ii. 1; iv. 33); which is a curtailed form for 'zehív,' *bright*, an appropriate epithet of the month of flowers.

J.

JA'BAL (*a stream*), a descendant of Cain, son of Lamech and Adah, who is described in Gen. iv. 20, as 'the father of such as dwell in tents, and have cattle.' This obviously means that Jabal was the first who adopted that nomade life which is still followed by numerous Arabian and Tartar tribes in Asia. Abel had long before been a keeper of sheep; but Jabal invented such portable habitations (formed, doubtless, of skins) as enabled a pastoral people to remove their dwellings with them from one place to another, when they led their flocks to new pastures.

JAB'BOK, one of the streams which traverse the country east of the Jordan, and which, after a course nearly from east to west, falls into that river about thirty miles below the lake of Tiberias. It seems to rise in the Hauran mountains, and its whole course may be computed at sixty-five miles. It is mentioned in Scripture as the boundary which separated the kingdom of Sihon, king of the Amorites, from that of Og, king of Bashan (Josh. xii. 1-6); and it appears afterwards to have been the boundary between the tribe of Reuben and the half-tribe of Manasseh. The earliest notice of it occurs in Gen. xxxii. 22. The Jabbok now bears the name of Zerka. In its passage westward across the plains it more than once passes under ground; and in summer the upper portion of its channel becomes dry. But on entering the more hilly country immediately east of the Jordan, it receives tribute from several springs, which maintain it as a perennial stream, although very low in summer On approaching the Jordan it flows through a deep ravine, the steep banks being overgrown with the *Solanum furiosum*, which attains a considerable size. But the ravine is not so well wooded as the immediate neighbourhood. The water is pleasant, and the bed being rocky the stream runs clear.

JA'BESH, or JABESH GILEAD, a town beyond the Jordan, in the land of Gilead.

Jabesh belonged to the half tribe of Manasseh, and was sacked by the Israelites for refusing to join in the war against Benjamin (Judg. xxi. 8). It is chiefly memorable for the siege it sustained from Nahash, king of the Ammonites, the raising of which formed the first exploit of the newly-elected king, Saul, and procured his confirmation in the sovereignty. The inhabitants had agreed to surrender, and to have their right eyes put out (to incapacitate them from military service), but were allowed seven days to ratify the treaty. In the meantime Saul collected a large army, and came to their relief (1 Sam. xi.). This service was gratefully remembered by the Jabeshites; and, about forty years after, when the dead bodies of Saul and his sons were gibbeted on the walls of Bethshan, on the other side of the river, they made a forced march by night, took away the bodies, and gave them honourable burial (1 Sam. xxxi.).

Jabesh still existed as a town in the time of Eusebius, who places it six miles from Pella towards Gerasa; but the knowledge of the site is now lost, unless we accept the conclusion of Mr. Buckingham, who thinks it may be found in a place called Jehaz or Jejaz, marked by ruins upon a hill, in a spot not far from which, according to the above indications, Jabesh must have been situated.

1. JA'BIN (*discerner*), king of Hazor, and one of the most powerful of all the princes who reigned in Canaan when it was invaded by the Israelites. His dominion seems to have extended over all the north part of the country; and after the ruin of the league formed against the Hebrews in the south of Adonizedek, king of Jerusalem, he assembled his tributaries near the waters of Merom (the lake Huleh), and called all the people to arms. This coalition was destroyed, as the one in the south had been, and Jabin himself perished in the sack of Hazor, his capital, B.C. 1450. This prince was the last powerful enemy with whom Joshua combated, and his overthrow seems to have been regarded as the crowning act in the conquest of the Promised Land (Josh. xi. 1-14).

2. JABIN, king of Hazor, and probably descended from the preceding. It appears that during one of the servitudes of the Israelites, probably when they lay under the yoke of Cushan or Eglon, the kingdom of Hazor was reconstructed. The narrative gives to this second Jabin even the title of 'king of Canaan;' and this, with the possession of 900 iron-armed war-chariots, implies unusual power and extent of dominion. The iniquities of the Israelites having lost them the Divine protection, Jabin gained the mastery over them; and, stimulated by the remembrance of ancient wrongs, oppressed them heavily for twenty years. From this thraldom they were relieved by the great victory won by Barak in the plain of Esdraelon over the hosts

of Jabin, commanded by Sisera, one of the most renowned generals of those times, B C. 1285. The well-compacted power of the king of Hazor was not yet, however, entirely broken. The war was still prolonged for a time, but ended in the entire ruin of Jabin, and the subjugation of his territories by the Israelites (Judg. iv.).

This is the Jabin whose name occurs in Ps. lxxxiii. 10.

JA'CHIN and BO'AZ, the names of two brazen pillars in the porch of Solomon's temple [TEMPLE].

JACINTH. The stone which is called Jacinth in Rev. xxi. 20, is the same which is called in the Old Testament a LIGURE. [See the word.]

JA'COB was the second son of Isaac by his wife Rebekah. Her conceiving is stated to have been supernatural. Led by peculiar feelings she went to inquire of the Lord, and was informed that she was indeed with child; that her offspring should be the founders of two nations, and that the elder should serve the younger: circumstances which ought to be borne in mind when a judgment is pronounced on her conduct in aiding Jacob to secure the privileges of birth to the exclusion of his elder brother Esau.

As the boys grew, Jacob appeared to partake of the gentle, quiet, and retiring character of his father, and was accordingly led to prefer the tranquil safety and pleasing occupations of a shepherd's life to the bold and daring enterprises of the hunter, for which Esau had an irresistible predilection. Jacob, therefore, passed his days in or near the paternal tent, simple and unpretending in his manner of life, and finding in the flocks and herds which he kept images and emotions which both filled and satisfied his heart. That selfishness and a prudence which approached to cunning had a seat in the heart of the youth Jacob, appears but too plain in his dealing with Esau, when he exacted from a famishing brother so large a price for a mess of pottage as the surrender of his birthright.

The leaning which his mother had in favour of Jacob would naturally be augmented by the conduct of Esau in marrying, doubtless contrary to his parents' wishes, two Hittite women, who are recorded to have been a grief of mind unto Isaac and to Rebekah.

Circumstances thus prepared the way for procuring the transfer of the birthright, when Isaac, being now old, proceeded to take steps to pronounce the irrevocable blessing which acted with all the force of a modern testamentary bequest. This blessing, then, it was essential that Jacob should receive in preference to Esau. Here Rebekah appears the chief agent; Jacob is a mere instrument in her hands. Isaac directs Esau to procure him some venison. This Rebekah hears, and urges her reluctant favourite to personate his elder brother. Jacob suggests difficulties; they are met by Rebekah, who is ready to incur any personal danger so that her object be gained. Her voice is obeyed, the venison is brought, Jacob is equipped for the deceit; he helps out his fraud by direct falsehood, and the old man, whose senses are now failing, is at last with difficulty deceived. It cannot be denied that this is a most reprehensible transaction, and presents a truly painful picture; in which a mother conspires with one son in order to cheat her aged husband, with a view to deprive another son of his rightful inheritance. Justification is here impossible; but it should not be forgotten in the estimate we form that there was a promise in favour of Jacob, that Jacob's qualities had endeared him to his mother, and that the prospect to her was dark and threatening which arose when she saw the neglected Esau at the head of the house, and his hateful wives assuming command over herself.

Punishment in this world always follows close upon the heels of transgression. Fear seized the guilty Jacob, who is sent by his father, at the suggestion of Rebekah, to the original seat of the family, in order that he might find a wife among his cousins, the daughters of his mother's brother, Laban the Syrian. Before he is dismissed Jacob again receives his father's blessing, the object obviously being to keep alive in the young man's mind the great promise given to Abraham, and thus to transmit that influence which, under the aid of Divine Providence, was to end in placing the family in possession of the land of Palestine, and in so doing to make it 'a multitude of people.' On his journey eastward he tarried all night upon a certain plain, where he was favoured with a vision, and received a promise of divine protection in all the way on which he should go.

Jacob, on coming 'into the land of the people of the East,' providentially met with Rachel, Laban's daughter, to whom, with true Eastern simplicity and politeness, he showed such courtesy as the duties of pastoral life suggest and admit. And here his gentle and affectionate nature displays itself under the influence of the bonds of kindred and the fair form of youth:—'Jacob kissed Rachel, and lifted up his voice and wept.'

After he had been with his uncle the space of a month, Laban inquires of him what reward he expects for his services. He asks for the 'beautiful and well-favoured Rachel.' His request is granted on condition of a seven years' service—a long period truly, but to Jacob 'they seemed but a few days for the love he had to her.' When the time was expired, the crafty Laban availed himself of the customs of the country, in order to substitute his elder and 'tender-eyed' daughter Leah. In the morning Jacob found how he had been beguiled; but Laban excused himself, saying, 'It must not be done in our country, to give the younger before the first-born.' Another seven years' service gains for Jacob the beloved Rachel. Leah, however, has the compensatory privilege of being the mother of the first-born—Reuben; three other sons successively follow, namely, Simeon, Levi, and Judah, sons of Leah. This fruitfulness was a painful subject of reflection to the barren Rachel, who employed language on this occasion that called forth a reply from her husband which shows that, mild as was the character of Jacob, it was by no means wanting in force and energy (Gen. xxx. 2). An arrangement, however, took place, by which Rachel had children by means of her maid Bilhah, of whom Dan and Naphtali were born. Two other sons—Gad and Asher—were born to Jacob of Leah's maid, Zilpah. Leah herself bare two more sons, namely, Issachar and Zebulun; she also bare a daughter, Dinah. At length Rachel herself bare a son, and she called his name Joseph.

Most faithfully, and with great success, had Jacob served his uncle for fourteen years, when he became desirous of returning to his parents. At the urgent request of Laban, however, he is induced to remain. The language employed upon this occasion (Gen. xxx. 25, sq) shows that Jacob's character had gained considerably during his service both in strength and comprehensiveness: but the means which he employed in order to make his bargain with his uncle work so as to enrich himself, prove too clearly that his moral feelings had not undergone an equal improvement, and that the original taint of prudence, and the sad lessons of his mother in deceit, had produced some of their natural fruit in his bosom.

The prosperity of Jacob displeased and grieved Laban, so that a separation seemed desirable. His wives are ready to accompany him. Accordingly he set out, with his family and his property, 'to go to Isaac his father in the land of Canaan.' It was not till the third day that Laban learned that Jacob had fled, when he immediately set out in pursuit of his nephew, and after seven days' journey overtook him in Mount Gilead. Laban, however, is divinely warned not to hinder Jacob's return. Reproach and recrimination ensued. Even a charge of theft is put forward by Laban —'Wherefore hast thou stolen my gods?' In truth, Rachel had carried off certain images which were the objects of superstitious reverence. Ignorant of this misdeed, Jacob boldly called for a search, adding, 'With whomsoever thou findest thy gods, let him not live.' A crafty woman's cleverness eluded the keen eye of Laban. Rachel by an appeal which one of her sex alone could make, deceived her father.

Laban's conduct on this occasion called forth a reply from Jacob, from which it appears that his service had been most severe, and which also proves that however this severe service might have encouraged a certain servility, it had not prevented the development in Jacob's soul of a high and energetic spirit, which when roused could assert its rights and give utterance to sentiments both just, striking, and forcible.

Peace, however, being restored, Laban, on the ensuing morning, took a friendly, if not an affectionate farewell of his daughters and their sons, and returned home. Meanwhile Jacob, going on his way, had to pass near the land of Seir, in which Esau dwelt. Remembering his own conduct and his brother's threat, he was seized with fear, and sent messengers before in order to propitiate Esau, who, however, had no evil design against him; but, when he 'saw Jacob, ran to meet him and embraced him, and fell on his neck and kissed him, and they wept'—the one tears of joyful recognition, the other of gladness at unexpected escape.

It was immediately preceding this interview that Jacob passed the night in wrestling with 'a man,' who is afterwards recognised as God, and who at length overcame Jacob by touching the hollow of his thigh. His name also was on this event changed by the mysterious antagonist into Israel, 'for as a prince hast thou power with God and with men and hast prevailed' (Gen. xxxii. 28). It is added that on this account his descendants abstained from eating the thigh of slaughtered animals.

Having, by the misconduct of Hamor the

Hivite and the hardy valour of his sons, been involved in danger from the natives of Shechem in Canaan, Jacob is divinely directed, and under the divine protection proceeds to Bethel, where he is to 'make an altar unto God that appeared unto thee when thou fleddest from the face of Esau thy brother.' Obedient to the divine command, he first purifies his family from 'strange gods,' which he hid under 'the oak which is by Shechem;' after which God appeared to him again with the important declaration, 'I am God Almighty,' and renewed the Abrahamic covenant. While journeying from Beth-el to Ephrath his beloved Rachel lost her life in giving birth to her second son, Benjamin. At length Jacob came to his father Isaac at Mamre, the family residence, in time to pay the last attentions to the aged patriarch. Not long after this bereavement Jacob was robbed of his beloved son Joseph through the jealousy and bad faith of his brothers. This loss is the occasion of showing us how strong were Jacob's paternal feelings; for on seeing what appeared to be proofs that 'some evil beast had devoured Joseph,' the old man 'rent his clothes, and put sackcloth upon his loins, and mourned for his son many days, and refused to be comforted'—'I will go down into the grave unto my son mourning' (Gen. xxxvii. 33).

A widely extended famine induced Jacob to send his sons down into Egypt, where he had heard there was corn, without knowing by whose instrumentality. The patriarch, however, retained his youngest son Benjamin, 'lest mischief should befall him,' as it had befallen Joseph. The young men returned with the needed supplies of corn. They related, however, that they had been taken for spies, and that there was but one way in which they could disprove the charge, namely, by carrying down Benjamin to 'the lord of the land.' This Jacob vehemently refused:—'Me have ye bereaved; Joseph is not, and Simeon is not, and ye will take Benjamin; my son shall not go down with you; if mischief befall him, then shall ye bring down my grey hairs with sorrow to the grave' (Gen. xlii. 36). The pressure of the famine, however, at length forced Jacob to allow Benjamin to accompany his brothers on a second visit to Egypt; whence in due time they brought back to their father the pleasing intelligence, 'Joseph is yet alive, and he is governor over all the land of Egypt.' How naturally is the effect of this on Jacob told—'and Jacob's heart fainted, for he believed them not.' When, however, they had gone into particulars, he added, 'Enough, Joseph my son is yet alive; I will go and see him before I die.'

Encouraged 'in the visions of the night,' Jacob goes down to Egypt. 'And Joseph made ready his chariot, and went up to meet Israel his father, to Goshen, and presented himself unto him; and he fell on his neck, and wept on his neck a good while. And Israel said unto Joseph, Now let me die, since I have seen thy face, because thou art yet alive' (Gen. xlvi. 29). Joseph proceeded to conduct his father into the presence of the Egyptian monarch, when the man of God, with that self-consciousness and dignity which religion gives, instead of offering slavish adulation, 'blessed Pharaoh.' Struck with the patriarch's venerable air, the king asked, 'How old art thou?' What composure and elevation is there in the reply, 'The days of the years of my pilgrimage are an hundred and thirty years; few and evil have the days of the years of my life been, and have not attained unto the days of the years of the life of my fathers in the days of their pilgrimage: and Jacob blessed Pharaoh, and went out from before Pharaoh' (Gen. xlvi. 8-10).

Jacob, with his sons, now entered into possession of some of the best land of Egypt, where they carried on their pastoral occupations, and enjoyed a very large share of earthly prosperity. The aged patriarch, after being strangely tossed about on a very rough ocean, found at last a tranquil harbour, where all the best affections of his nature were gently exercised and largely unfolded. After a lapse of time Joseph, being informed that his father was sick, went to him, when 'Israel strengthened himself, and sat up in his bed.' He acquainted Joseph with the divine promise of the land of Canaan which yet remained to be fulfilled, and took Joseph's sons, Ephraim and Manasseh, in place of Reuben and Simeon, whom he had lost. Then having convened his sons, the venerable patriarch pronounced on them also a blessing, which is full of the loftiest thought, expressed in the most poetical diction, and adorned by the most vividly descriptive and engaging imagery, showing how deeply religious his character had become, how freshly it retained its fervour to the last, and how greatly it had increased in strength, elevation, and dignity:—'And when Jacob had made an end of commanding his sons, he gathered up his feet into the bed and yielded up the ghost, and was gathered unto his people' (Gen. xlix. 33).

JA'EL (*wild goat*), wife of Heber, the Kenite. When Sisera, the general of Jabin, had been defeated, he alighted from his chariot, hoping to escape best on foot from the hot pursuit of the victorious Israelites. On reaching the tents of the nomade chief, he remembered that there was peace between his sovereign and the house of Heber; and, therefore, applied for the hospitality and protection to which he was thus entitled. This request was very cordially granted by the wife of the absent chief, who received the vanquished warrior into the inner part of the tent, where he could not be discovered by strangers without such an intrusion as Eastern customs would not warrant. She also brought him milk to drink, when he asked only water; and then covered him from view, that he might enjoy repose the more securely. As he slept, a horrid thought occurred to Jael, which she hastened too promptly to execute. She took one of the tent nails, and with a mallet, at one fell blow, drove it through the temples of the sleeping Sisera. Soon after, Barak and his people arrived in pursuit, and were shown the lifeless body of the man they sought.

It does not seem difficult to understand the object of Jael in this painful transaction. Her motives seem to have been entirely prudential, and, on prudential grounds, the very circumstance which renders her act the more odious—the peace subsisting between the nomade chief and the king of Hazor—must, to her, have seemed to make it the more expedient. She saw that the Israelites had now the upper hand, and was aware that, as being in alliance with the oppressors of Israel, the camp might expect very rough treatment from the pursuing force; which would be greatly aggravated if Sisera were found sheltered within it. This calamity she sought to avert, and to place the house of Heber in a favourable position with the victorious party. She probably justified the act to herself, by the consideration that, as Sisera would certainly be taken and slain, she might as well make a benefit out of his inevitable doom, as incur utter ruin in the attempt to protect him. We have been grieved to see the act vindicated as authorized by the usages of ancient warfare, of rude times, and of ferocious manners. There was not warfare, but peace between the house of Heber and the prince of Hazor; and, for the rest, we will venture to affirm that there does not now, and never did exist, in any country, a set of usages under which the act of Jael would be deemed right.

1. JA'IR (*enlightener*), son of Segub, of the tribe of Manasseh by his mother, and of Judah by his father. He appears to have distinguished himself in an expedition against the kingdom of Bashan, the time of which is disputed, but may probably be referred to the last year of the life of Moses, B.C. 1451. It seems to have formed part of the operations connected with the conquest of the country east of the Jordan. He settled in the part of Argob bordering on Gilead, where we find twenty-three villages named collectively Havoth-jair, or 'Jair's villages' (Num. xxxii. 41; Deut. iii. 14; Josh. xiii. 30; 1 Chron. ii. 22).

2. JAIR, eighth judge of Israel, of Gilead, in Manasseh, beyond the Jordan; and, therefore, probably descended from the preceding, with whom, indeed, he is sometimes confounded. He ruled twenty-two years, and his opulence is indicated in a manner characteristic of the age in which he lived. ' He had thirty sons, that rode on thirty ass-colts, and they had thirty cities, which are called Havoth-jair, in the land of Gilead.' The twenty-three villages of the more ancient Jair were probably among the thirty which this Jair possessed (Judg. x. 3). B.C. 1210.

JA'IRUS, a ruler of the synagogue at Capernaum, whose daughter Jesus restored to life (Mark v. 22; Luke viii. 41).

JAMES. Two, if not three persons of this name are mentioned in the New Testament.

1. JAMES, the son of Zebedee, and brother of the Evangelist John. Their occupation was that of fishermen, probably at Bethsaida, in partnership with Simon Peter (Luke v. 10). On comparing the account given in Matt. iv. 21, Mark i. 19, with that in John i., it would appear that James and John had been acquainted with our Lord, and had received him as the Messiah some time before he called them to attend upon him statedly—a call with which they immediately complied. Their mother's name was Salome. We find James, John, and Peter associated on several interesting occasions in the Saviour's life. They alone were present at the Transfiguration (Matt. xvii. 1; Mark ix. 2; Luke ix. 28); at the restoration to life of Jairus's daughter (Mark v. 42; Luke viii. 51); and in the garden of Gethsemane during the agony (Mark xiv. 33; Matt. xxvi. 37; Luke xxi. 37). With Andrew they listened in private to our Lord's discourse on the fall of Jerusalem (Mark xiii. 3). James and his brother appear to have indulged in false notions of the

kingdom of the Messiah, and were led by ambitious views to join in the request made to Jesus by their mother (Matt. xx. 20-23; Mark x. 35). From Luke ix. 52, we may infer that their temperament was warm and impetuous. On account, probably, of their boldness and energy in discharging their Apostleship, they received from their Lord the appellation of Boanerges, or *Sons of Thunder*. James was the first martyr among the Apostles. Clement of Alexandria, in a fragment preserved by Eusebius, reports that the officer who conducted James to the tribunal was so influenced by the bold declaration of his faith as to embrace the Gospel and avow himself also a Christian; in consequence of which he was beheaded at the same time.

2. JAMES, the son of Alphæus, one of the twelve Apostles (Mark iii. 18: Matt. x. 3; Luke vi. 15; Acts i. 13). His mother's name was Mary (Matt. xxvii. 56; Mark xv. 40); in the latter passage he is called James *the Less*, either as being younger than James the son of Alphæus, or on account of his low stature (Mark xvi. 1; Luke xxiv. 10).

3. JAMES, 'the brother of the Lord' (Gal. i. 19). Whether this James is identical with the son of Alphæus, is a question which Dr. Neander pronounces to be the most difficult in the Apostolic history, and which cannot yet be considered as decided. It is probable, however, that he was a different person.

JAMES, EPISTLE OF. This is called by Eusebius the first of the Catholic Epistles. As the writer simply styles himself *James, a servant of God and of the Lord Jesus Christ*, doubts have existed, both in ancient and modern times, respecting the true

Author of this Epistle.—It has been ascribed to no less than four different persons, viz. James, the son of Zebedee; James, the son of Alphæus (who were both of the number of the twelve Apostles); James, our Lord's brother (Gal. i. 19), and to an anonymous author who assumed the name of James in order to procure authority to a supposititious writing.

It is highly improbable that James the son of Zebedee is the author of this epistle, for it is not credible that so great progress as the epistle implies had been made among the dispersed Jews before the martyrdom of James, which took place at Jerusalem about A.D. 32; and if the author, as has been commonly supposed, alludes to St. Paul's Epistles to the Romans (A.D. 58) and Galatians (A.D. 55), it would be a manifest anachronism to ascribe this epistle to the son of Zebedee.

The claim to the authorship of the epistle, therefore, rests between James 'the Lord's brother,' and James the son of Alphæus. In the preceding article the difficult question, whether these names do not, in fact, describe the same person, has been referred to: it suffices, in this place, to state that no writer who regards James 'the Lord's brother' as distinct from James the son of Alphæus, has held the latter to be the author of the epistle: and therefore, if no claim be advanced for the son of Zebedee, James 'the brother of the Lord' remains the only person whom the name at the head of this epistle could be intended to designate.

Hegesippus, cited by Eusebius, acquaints us that James, the brother of Jesus, who obtained the surname of the Just, governed the church of

Jerusalem along with, or after the apostles. Eusebius relates that he was the first who held the episcopate of Jerusalem (Jerome says for thirty years); and both he and Josephus give an account of his martyrdom. To him, therefore, is the authorship of an epistle addressed to the Jewish Christians with good reason ascribed.

The other opinion, which considers the epistle as written by an anonymous writer, we shall consider in treating of its author.

Eusebius observes that ' James, the brother of Jesus, who is called Christ,' is said to have written the first of the Catholic Epistles ; but it is to be observed that it is considered spurious. Not many of the ancients have mentioned it, nor that called the Epistle of Jude . . . . Nevertheless we know that these, with the rest, are publicly read in most of the churches.' It is, however, cited by Clemens Romanus in his first or genuine *Epistle to the Corinthians.* It seems to be alluded to in the Shepherd of Hermas, ' Resist the devil. and he will be confounded and flee from you.' It is also generally believed to be referred to by Irenæus, ' Abraham believed God, and it was,' &c. Origen cites it in his *Comment. on John,* i. xix. iv. 306, calling it, however, the *reputed* epistle of James. We have the authority of Cassiodorus for the fact that Clemens Alexandrinus commented on this epistle; and it is not only expressly cited by Ephrem Syrus (51, ' James the brother of our Lord says "weep and howl," ' together with other references), but it forms part of the ancient Syriac version, a work of the second century. But though ' not quoted expressly by any of the Latin fathers before the fourth century,' it was, soon after the time of the Council of Nice, received both in the Eastern and Western churches without any marks of doubt, and was admitted into the canon along with the other Scriptures by the Councils of Hippo and Carthage. Nor (with the above exceptions) does there appear to have been a voice raised against it since that period until the era of the Reformation, when the ancient doubts were revived by Erasmus. The latter objected to it principally on the ground that it ' directly opposes St. Paul and the other Scriptures in ascribing justification to works.' This opinion, however, has been successfully combated by Neander, who maintains that there is no discrepancy whatever between St. Paul and St. James; that it was not even the design of the latter to oppose any misapprehension respecting St. Paul's doctrine, but that they each addressed different classes of people from different standing points, using the same familiar examples. ' Paul,' he says, ' was obliged to point out to those who placed their dependence on the justifying power of the works of the law, the futility of such works in reference to justification, and to demonstrate that justification and sanctification could proceed only from the faith of the Gospel : James, on the other hand, found it necessary to declare to those who imagined that they could be justified in God's sight by faith in the Jewish sense . . . . that this was completely valueless if their course of life were not conformed to it.'

By those who consider James the Just, bishop of Jerusalem, to have been the author of this epistle, it is generally believed to have been

written shortly before his martyrdom, which took place A.D. 62, six years before the destruction of Jerusalem, whose impending fate is alluded to in chap. v. Neander fixes its date at a time preceding the separate formation of Gentile Christian churches, before the relation of Gentiles and Jews to one another in the Christian Church had been brought under discussion, in the period of the first spread of Christianity in Syria, Cilicia, and the adjacent regions. It is addressed to Jewish Christians, the descendants of the twelve tribes; but the fact of its being written in Greek exhibits the author's desire to make it generally available to Christians.

Contents and Character of the Epistle.—This epistle commences with consolations addressed to the faithful converts, with exhortations to patience, humility, and practical piety (ch. i. 1-27). Undue respect to persons is then condemned, and love enjoined (ch. ii.). Erroneous ideas on justification are corrected (ii. 13-26), the temerity of new teachers is repressed (iii. 12); an unbridled tongue is inveighed against, and heavenly wisdom contrasted with a spirit of covetousness (13-18). Swearing is prohibited (v. 12). The efficacy of prayer is proved by examples, and the unction of the sick by the Presbyters, together with prayer and mutual confession, are enjoined as instruments of recovery and of forgiveness of sins (v. 14-18). The approaching advent of the Lord is foretold (v. 7).

The style of this epistle is close and sententious. The general manner of the writer, says Jebb, ' combines the plainest and most practical good sense with the most vivid and poetical conception; the imagery various and luxuriant ; the sentiments chastened and sober; his images, in truth, are so many analogical arguments, and if, at the first view, we are disposed to recreate ourselves with the poet, we soon feel that we must exert our hardier powers to keep pace with the logician.' Seiler designates the style of this epistle as ' sometimes sublime and prophetical, nervous, and full of imagery.'

The eloquence and persuasiveness of St. James's Epistle, as an ethical composition, are such as must command universal admiration.

JAN'NES AND JAM'BRES, two of the Egyptian magicians who attempted by their enchantments to counteract the influence on Pharaoh's mind of the miracles wrought by Moses. Their names occur nowhere in the Hebrew Scriptures, and only once in the New Testament (2 Tim. iii. 8). The Apostle Paul became acquainted with them, most probably, from an ancient Jewish tradition, or, as Theodoret expresses it, ' from the unwritten teaching of the Jews.' They are found frequently in the Talmudical and Rabbinical writings, but with some variations.

JA'PHETH, a son of Noah. In Gen. v. 32 he is mentioned third in order ; but some think, from Gen. x. 21 (comp. ix. 24), that he was the eldest of Noah's sons, begotten one hundred years before the flood. In Gen. x. 2, sq he is called the progenitor of the extensive tribes in the west (of Europe) and north (of Asia), of the Armenians, Medes, Greeks, Thracians, &c. The Arabian traditions rank Japheth among the prophets, and enumerate eleven of his sons, the progenitors of as many Asiatic nations. In these traditions he is therefore simply called progenitor of the Turks and Barbarians.

JAR'HA, the Egyptian slave of a Hebrew named Sheshan, who married the daughter of his master, and was, of course, made free. As Sheshan had no sons, his posterity is traced through this connection (1 Chron. ii. 34-41), which is the only one of the kind mentioned in Scripture. Jarha was doubtless a proselyte, and the anecdote seems to belong to the period of the sojourn in Egypt, although it is not easy to see how an Egyptian could there be slave to an Israelite.

JA'SHER, BOOK OF, a work no longer extant, but cited in Josh. x. 13, and 2 Sam. i 18. In the former it is thus introduced : ' And the sun stood still, and the moon stayed, until the people had avenged themselves upon their enemies. Is not this written in the book of Jasher? So the sun stood still in the midst of heaven, and hasted not to go down about a whole day,' &c. And in the passage referred to in 2 Sam. i. it stands thus : ver. 17. ' And David lamented with this lamentation over Saul and over Jonathan his son :' ver. 18. '(Also he bade them teach the children of Judah [the use of] the bow : behold it is written in the book of Jasher.)' After which follows the lamentation of David. As the word Jasher signifies *just* or *upright*, by which word it is rendered in the margin of our Bibles, this book has been generally considered to have been so entitled as containing a history of *just men*. Bishop Lowth, however, conceives, from the poetical character of the two passages cited from it, that it was most probably a collection of national songs written at various times, and that it derived its name from *jashar*, ' he sang.' It is, at the same time, by no means an improbable conjecture, that the book was so called from the name of its author. Josephus speaks of the book of Jasher as one of the ' books laid up in the temple.'

The chief interest connected with the Scriptural book of Jasher arises from the circumstance that it is referred to as the authority for the standing still of the sun and moon. There are few passages in Biblical literature the explanation of which has more exercised the skill of commentators than this celebrated one. We shall here give a brief account of the most generally received interpretations.

The first is that which maintains that the account of the miracle is to be *literally* understood. According to this interpretation, which is the most ancient, the sun itself, which was then believed to have revolved round the earth, stayed his course for a day. Those who take this view argue that the theory of the *diurnal motion of the earth*, which has been the generally received one since the time of Galileo and Copernicus, is inconsistent with the Scripture narrative. Notwithstanding the general reception of the Copernican system of the universe, this view continued to be held by many divines, Protestant as well as Roman Catholic, and was strenuously maintained by Buddeus and others in the last century. But in more recent times the miracle has been explained so as to make it accord with the now received opinion respecting the earth's motion, and the Scripture narrative supposed to contain rather an optical and popular, than a literal account of what took place on this occasion. So that it was in reality the earth, and not the sun, which stood still at the command of Joshua.

Another opinion is that first suggested by Spinoza, and afterwards maintained by Le Clerc, that the miracle was produced by refraction only, causing the sun to appear above the horizon after its setting, or by some other atmospherical phenomena, which produced sufficient light to enable Joshua to pursue and discomfit his enemies.

The last opinion we shall mention is that of the learned Jew Maimonides, viz. that Joshua only asked of the Almighty to grant that he might defeat his enemies before the going down of the sun, and that God heard his prayer, inasmuch as before the close of day the five kings with their armies were cut in pieces. Grotius, while he admitted that there was no difficulty in the Almighty's arresting the course of the sun, or making it reappear by refraction, approved of the explanation of Maimonides, which has been since that period adopted by many divines.

JASHO'BEAM, son of Hachmoni, one of David's worthies, and the first named in the two lists which are given of them (2 Sam. xxxii. 8; 1 Chron. xi. 11).

The exploit of breaking through the host of the Philistines to procure David a draught of water from the well of Bethlehem, is ascribed to the three chief heroes, and therefore to Jashobeam, who was the first of the three (2 Sam. xxiii. 13-17; 1 Chron. xi. 15-19).

A Jashobeam is named among the Korhites who came to David at Ziklag (1 Chron. xii. 6); but this could scarcely have been the same with the preceding.

We also find a Jashobeam who commanded 24,000, and did duty in David's court in the month Nisan (1 Chron. xxvii. 2). He was the son of Zabdiel ; if, therefore, he was the same as the first Jashobeam, his patronymic of 'the Hachmonite' must be referred to his race rather than to his immediate father. This seems likely.

JA'SON, a kinsman of St. Paul, and his host at Thessalonica, where the Jews forced his house in order to seize the Apostle. Not finding the Apostle, they dragged Jason himself and some other converts before the magistrates, who released them with an admonition (A.D. 53). Jason appears to have accompanied the Apostle to Corinth (Acts xvii. 5-9 ; Rom. xvi. 21).

JASPER. Our word Jasper is plainly from the Greek *jaspis*, which comes from the Hebrew word *yashpheh*. Jasper is a species of the quartz family, and embraces a great many varieties. The brown Egyptian variety was perhaps the one selected for the breastplate of the high-priest (Exod. xxxviii. 19 ; xxxix. 1). The brown is of various shades, disposed in concentric stripes. It occurs loose in the sands of Egypt, and is cut into ornaments.

JA'VAN. the fourth son of Japhet. The interest connected with his name arises from his being the supposed progenitor of the original settlers in Greece and its isles [NATIONS, DISPERSION OF].

JAVELIN. [ARMS.]

2 G 2

JEB'USITES, one of the most powerful of the nations of Canaan, who settled about Mount Moriah, where they built Jerusalem, and called it Jebus, after the name of their founder (1 Chron. xi. 4). Although they were defeated with much slaughter, and Adonizedek, their king, slain by Joshua.(Josh. x.), they were not wholly subdued, were able to retain their city till after his death (Judg. i. 8), and were not entirely dispossessed of it till the time of David (2 Sam. v.). By that time the inveteracy of the enmity between the Hebrews and such of the original inhabitants as remained in the land had much abated, and the rights of private property were respected by the conquerors. This we discover from the fact that the site on which the Temple afterwards stood belonged to a Jebusite, named Araunah, from whom it was purchased by King David, who declined to accept it as a free gift from the owner (2 Sam. xxiv.). This is the last we hear of the Jebusites.

JED'UTHUN (*praise-giver*), a Levite of Merari's family, and one of the four great masters of the temple music (1 Chron. xvi. 41, 42). This name is also put for his descendants, who occur later as singers and players on instruments (2 Chron. xxxv. 15; Neh. xi. 17).

1. JEHO'AHAZ (*God-sustained*), son of Jehu, king of Israel, who succeeded his father in B.C. 856, and reigned seventeen years. As he followed the evil courses of the house of Jeroboam, the Syrians under Hazael and Benhadad were suffered to prevail over him; so that, at length, he had only left of all his forces fifty horsemen, ten chariots, and 10,000 foot. Overwhelmed by his calamities, Jehoahaz at length acknowledged the authority of Jehovah over Israel, and humbled himself before him; in consideration of which a deliverer was raised up for Israel in the person of Joash, this king's son, who was enabled to expel the Syrians and re-establish the affairs of the kingdom (2 Kings xiii. 1-9, 25).

2. JEHOAHAZ, otherwise called SHALLUM, seventeenth king of Judah, son of Josiah, whose reign began and ended in the year B.C. 608. After his father had been slain in resisting the progress of Pharaoh Necho, Jehoahaz, who was then twenty-three years of age, was raised to the throne by the people, and received at Jerusalem the regal anointing, which seems to have been usually omitted in times of order and of regular succession. He found the land full of trouble, but free from idolatry. Instead, however, of following the excellent example of his father, Jehoahaz fell into the accustomed crimes of his predecessors; and under the encouragements which his example or indifference offered, the idols soon re-appeared. It seems strange that in a time so short, and which must have been much occupied in arranging plans for resisting or pacifying the Egyptian king, he should have been able to deserve the stigma which the sacred record has left upon his name. But there is no limit except in the greatness of the divine power to the activity of evil dispositions. The sway of Jehoahaz was terminated in three months, when Pharaoh Necho, on his victorious return from the Euphrates, thinking it politic to reject a king not nominated by himself, removed him from the throne, and set thereon his brother Jehoiakim. This reign was the shortest in the kingdom of Judah, al-

though in that of Israel there were several shorter. The deposed king was at first taken as a prisoner to Riblah in Syria; but was eventually carried to Egypt, where he died (2 Kings xxiii. 30-35; 2 Chron. xxxvi. 1-4; 1 Chron. iii. 15; Jer. xxii. 10-12).

The anointing of this king has drawn attention to the defect of his title as the reason for the addition of that solemn ceremony. It appears from 1 Chron. iii. 15 that Josiah had four sons, of whom Johanan is expressly said to have been 'the first-born.' But he seems to have died before his father, as we nowhere find his name historically mentioned, while those of the other brothers are familiar to us. If, therefore, he died childless and Jehoahaz were the next son, his claim would have been good. But he was not the next son. His name, as Shallum, occurs last of the four in 1 Chron. iii. 15; and from the historical notices in 2 Kings xxiii. and 1 Chron. xxxvi. we ascertain that when Josiah died the ages of the three surviving sons were, Eliakim (Jehoiakim) twenty-five years, Jehoahaz (Shallum) twenty-three years, Mattaniah (Zedekiah) ten years; consequently Jehoahaz was preferred by the popular favour above his elder brother Jehoiakim, and the anointing, therefore, was doubtless intended to give to his imperfect claim the weight of that solemn ceremony. It was also probably suspected that, as actually took place, the Egyptian king would seek to annul a popular election unsanctioned by himself; but as the Egyptians anointed their own kings, and attached much importance to the ceremony, the possibility that he would hesitate more to remove an anointed than an unanointed king might afford a further reason for the anointing of Jehoahaz [ANOINTING].

Jehoahaz is supposed to be the person who is designated under the emblem of a young lion carried in chains to Egypt (Ezek. xix. 3, 4).

JEHO'ASH. [JOASH.]

JEHOI'ACHIN (*God-appointed*), by contraction JECONIAH and CONIAH, nineteenth king of Judah, and son of Jehoiakim. When his father was slain, B.C. 599, the king of Babylon allowed him, as the rightful heir, to succeed. He was then eighteen years of age, according to 2 Kings xxiv. 8; but only eight according to 2 Chron. xxxvi. 9. Many attempts have been made to reconcile these dates, the most usual solution being that he had reigned ten years in conjunction with his father, so that he was eight when he began his joint reign, but eighteen when he began to reign alone. There are, however, difficulties in this view, which, perhaps, leave it the safest course to conclude that 'eight' in 2 Chron. xxxvi. 9, is a corruption of the text, such as might easily occur from the relation of the numbers eight and eighteen.

Jehoiachin followed the evil courses which had already brought so much disaster upon the royal house of David, and upon the people under its sway. He seems to have very speedily indicated a political bias adverse to the interests of the Chaldæan empire; for in three months after his accession we find the generals of Nebuchadnezzar again laying siege to Jerusalem, according to the predictions of Jeremiah (xxii. 18; xxiv. 30). Convinced of the futility of resistance, Jehoiachin went out and surrendered as soon as Nebuchadnezzar arrived in person before the city. He was sent away as a captive to Babylon, with his mother, his generals, and his troops, together with the artificers and other inhabitants of Jerusalem, to the number of ten thousand. Thus ended an unhappy reign of three months and ten days. If the Chaldæan king had then put an end to the show of a monarchy, and annexed the country to his own dominions, the event would probably have been less unhappy for the nation. But still adhering to his former policy, he placed on the throne Mattaniah, the only surviving son of Josiah, whose name he changed to Zedekiah (2 Kings xxiv. 1-16; 2 Chron. xxxvi. 9, 10; Jer. xxix. 2; xxxvii. 1).

Jehoiachin remained in prison at Babylon during the lifetime of Nebuchadnezzar: but when that prince died, his son, Evil-merodach, not only released him, but gave him an honourable seat at his own table, with precedence over all the other dethroned kings who were kept at Babylon, and an allowance for the support of his rank (2 Kings xxv. 27-30; Jer. lii. 31-34). To what he owed this favour we are not told; but the Jewish commentators allege that Evil-merodach had himself been put into prison by his father during the last year of his reign, and had there contracted an intimate friendship with the deposed king of Judah.

The name of Jehoiachin re-appears to fix the epoch of several of the prophecies of Ezekiel (Ezek. i. 2), and of the deportation which terminated his reign (Esth. ii. vi.). In the genealogy of Christ (Matt. i. 11) he is named as the ' son of Josias' his uncle.

JEHOI'ADA (*God-known*), high-priest in the times of Ahaziah and Athaliah. He is only known from the part which he took in recovering the throne of Judah for the young Joash, who had been saved by his wife Jehoshebah from the massacre by which Athaliah sought to exterminate the royal line of David. The particulars of this transaction are related under other heads [ATHALIAH; JOASH]. Jehoiada manifested much decision and forecast on this occasion; and he used for good the great power which devolved upon him during the minority of the young king, and the influence which he continued to enjoy as long as he lived. The value of this influence is shown by the misconduct and the disorders of the kingdom after his death. He died in B.C. 834, at the age of 130, and his remains were honoured with a place in the sepulchre of the kings at Jerusalem (2 Kings xi. 12; 2 Chron. xxiii. xxiv.).

JEHOI'AKIM (*God-established*), originally ELIAKIM, second son of Josiah, and eighteenth king of Judah. On the death of his father the people raised to the throne his younger brother Jehoahaz; but three months after, when the Egyptian king returned from the Euphrates, he removed Jehoahaz, and gave the crown to the rightful heir, Eliakim, whose name he changed to Jehoiakim. This change of name often took place in similar circumstances; and the altered name was in fact the badge of a tributary prince. Jehoiakim began to reign in B.C. 608, and reigned eleven years. He, of course, occupied the position of a vassal of the Egyptian empire, but however heavy may have been the Egyptian yoke, Jehoiakim was destined to pass under one heavier still.

In the third year of his reign, being besieged in Jerusalem, he was forced to submit to Nebuchadnezzar, and was by his order laden with chains, with the intention of sending him captive to Babylon (2 Chron. xxxvi. 6); but eventually the conqueror changed his mind and restored the crown to him. Many persons, however, of high family, and some even of the royal blood, were sent away to Babylon. Among these was Daniel, then a mere youth. A large proportion of the treasures and sacred vessels of the temple were also taken away and deposited in the idol-temple at Babylon (Dan. i. 1, 2). The year following the Egyptians were defeated upon the Euphrates (Jer. xlvi. 2), and Jehoiakim, when he saw the remains of the defeated army pass by his territory, could not but perceive how vain had been that reliance upon Egypt against which he had been constantly cautioned by Jeremiah (Jer. xxxi. 1; xlv. 1). In the same year the prophet caused a collection of his prophecies to be written out by his faithful Baruch, and to be read publicly by him in the court of the temple. This coming to the knowledge of the king, he sent for it and had it read before him. But he heard not much of the bitter denunciations with which it was charged, before he took the roll from the reader, and after cutting it in pieces threw it into the brasier, which, it being winter, was burning before him in the hall. The counsel of God against him, however, stood sure; a fresh roll was written, with the addition of a further and most awful denunciation against the king, occasioned by this foolish and sacrilegious act: ' He shall have none to sit upon the throne of David: and his dead body shall be cast out in the day to the heat and in the night to the frost' (Jer. xxxvi.). All this, however, appears to have made little impression upon Jehoiakim, who still walked in his old paths.

After three years of subjection, Jehoiakim, finding the king of Babylon fully engaged elsewhere, and deluded by the Egyptian party in his court, ventured to withhold his tribute, and thereby to throw off the Chaldæan yoke. This step, taken contrary to the earnest remonstrances of Jeremiah, was the ruin of Jehoiakim. The land was ere long invaded by the armies of the Chaldæans, accompanied by a vast number of auxiliaries from the neighbouring countries, the Edomites, Moabites, and others, who were for the most part actuated by a fierce hatred against the Jewish name and nation. The events of the war are not related. Jerusalem was taken, or rather surrendered on terms, which Josephus alleges were little heeded by Nebuchadnezzar. It is certain that Jehoiakim was slain, but whether in one of the actions, or, as Josephus says, after the surrender, we cannot determine. His body remained exposed and unlamented without the city, under the circumstances foretold by the prophet—' He shall be buried with the burial of an ass, drawn and cast forth beyond the gates of Jerusalem' (Jer. xxii. 18, 19; 1 Chron. iii. 15; 2 Kings xxiii. 34-37; xxiv. 1-7; 2 Chron. xxxvi. 4-8).

It was not the object of Nebuchadnezzar to destroy altogether a power which, as tributary to him, formed a serviceable outpost towards Egypt, which seems to have been the great final object of all his designs in this quarter. He therefore still maintained the throne of Judah, and placed on it Jehoiachin, the son of the late king. He, however, sent away another body, a second corps of the nobles and chief persons of the nation, three thousand in number, among whom was Ezekiel, afterwards called to prophesy in the land of his exile.

JEHON'ADAB. [Jonadab.]

JEHO'RAM (*God-exalted*), eldest son and successor of Jehoshaphat, and fifth king of Judah, who began to reign (separately) in B.C. 889, at the age of thirty-five years, and reigned five years. Jehoram was associated with his father in the later years of his reign, but he profited little by this association. He had unhappily been married to Athaliah, the daughter of Ahab and Jezebel; and her influence seems to have neutralized all the good he might have derived from the example of his father. One of the first acts of his reign was to put his brothers to death and seize the valuable appanages which their father had in his lifetime bestowed upon them. After this we are not surprised to find him giving way to the gross idolatries of that new and strange kind—the Phœnician—which had been brought into Israel by Jezebel, and into Judah by her daughter Athaliah. For these atrocities the Lord let forth his anger against Jehoram and his kingdom. The Edomites revolted, and, according to old prophecies (Gen. xxvii. 40), shook off the yoke of Judah. The Philistines on one side, and the Arabians and Cushites on the other, also grew bold against a king forsaken of God, and in repeated invasions spoiled the land of all its substance; they even ravaged the royal palaces, and took away the wives and children of the king, leaving him only one son, Ahaziah. Nor was this all; Jehoram in his last days afflicted with a frightful disease in his bowels, which, from the terms employed in describing it, appears to have been malignant dysentery in its most shocking and tormenting form. After a disgraceful reign, and a most painful death, public opinion inflicted the posthumous dishonour of refusing him a place in the sepulchre of kings. Jehoram was by far the most impious and cruel tyrant that had as yet occupied the throne of Judah, though he was rivalled or surpassed by some of his successors (2 Kings viii. 16-24; 2 Chron. xxi.).

2. **JEHO'RAM**, King of Israel. [Joram.]

JEHOSH'APHAT (*God-judged*), the fourth king of Judah, and son of Asa, whom he succeeded in B.C. 914, at the age of thirty five, and reigned twenty-five years. He commenced his reign by fortifying his kingdom against Israel; and having thus secured himself against surprise from the quarter which gave most disturbance to him, he proceeded to purge the land from the idolatries and idolatrous monuments by which it was still tainted. Even the high places and groves, which former well-disposed kings had suffered to remain, were by the zeal of Jehoshaphat in a great measure destroyed. The chiefs, with priests and Levites, proceeded from town to town, with the book of the law in their hands, instructing the people, and calling back their wandering affections to the religion of their fathers. This was a beautiful and interesting circumstance in the operations of the young king.

Jehoshaphat was too well instructed in the great principles of the theocracy not to know that his faithful conduct had entitled him to expect the divine protection. Of that protection he soon had manifest proofs. At home he enjoyed peace and abundance, and abroad security and honour. His renown extended into the neighbouring nations, and the Philistines, as well as the adjoining Arabian tribes, paid him rich tributes in silver and in cattle. He was thus enabled to put all his towns in good condition, to erect fortresses, to organize a powerful army, and to raise his kingdom to a degree of importance and splendour which it had not enjoyed since the revolt of the ten tribes.

The weak and impious Ahab at that time occupied the throne of Israel; and Jehoshaphat, having nothing to fear from his power, sought, or at least did not repel, an alliance with him. This is alleged to have been the grand mistake of his reign; and that it was such is proved by the consequences.

A few years after we find Jehoshaphat on a visit to Ahab, in Samaria, being the first time any of the kings of Israel and Judah had met in peace. He here experienced a reception worthy of his greatness; but Ahab failed not to take advantage of the occasion, and so worked upon the weak points of his character as to prevail upon him to take arms with him against the Syrians, with whom hitherto the kingdom of Judah never had any war or occasion of quarrel. However, Jehoshaphat was not so far infatuated as to proceed to the war without consulting God. The false prophets of Ahab poured forth ample promises of success, and one of them, named Zedekiah, resorting to material symbols, made him horns of iron, saying, 'Thus saith the Lord, with these shalt thou smite the Syrians till they be consumed.' Still Jehoshaphat was not satisfied; and the answer to his further inquiries extorted from him a rebuke of the reluctance which Ahab manifested to call Micah, 'the prophet of the Lord.' The fearless words of this prophet did not make the impression upon the king of Judah which might have been expected; or probably he then felt himself too deeply bound in honour to recede. He went to the fatal battle of Ramoth-Gilead, and there nearly became the victim of a plan which Ahab had laid for his own safety at the expense of his too confiding ally. He persuaded Jehoshaphat to appear as king, while he himself went disguised to the battle. This brought the heat of the contest around him, as the Syrians took him for Ahab; and if they had not in time discovered their mistake, he would certainly have been slain. Ahab was killed, and the battle lost [Ahab]; but Jehoshaphat escaped, and returned to Jerusalem.

On his return from this imprudent expedition he was met by the just reproaches of the prophet Jehu. The best atonement he could make for this error was by the course he actually took. He resumed his labours in the further extirpation of idolatry, in the instruction of the people, and the improvement of his realm. He now made a tour of his kingdom in person, that he might see the ordinances of God duly established, and witness the due execution of his intentions respecting the instruction of the people in the divine law. This tour enabled him to discern many defects in the local administration of justice, which he then applied himself to remedy. He appointed magistrates in every city, for the determination of causes civil and ecclesiastical. Then he established a supreme council of justice at Jerusalem, composed of priests, Levites, and ' the chiefs of the fathers;' to which difficult cases were referred, and appeals brought from the provincial tribunals.

The activity of Jehoshaphat's mind was then turned towards the revival of that maritime commerce which had been established by Solomon. The land of Edom and the ports of the Elanitic Gulf were still under the power of Judah: and in them the king prepared a fleet for the voyage to Ophir. Unhappily, however, he yielded to the wish of the king of Israel, and allowed him to take part in the enterprise. For this the expedition was doomed of God, and the vessels were wrecked almost as soon as they quitted port. Instructed by Eliezer, the prophet, as to the cause of this disaster, Jehoshaphat equipped a new fleet, and having this time declined the co-operation of the king of Israel, the voyage prospered. The trade was not, however, prosecuted with any zeal, and was soon abandoned [COMMERCE].

In accounting for the disposition of Jehoshaphat to contract alliances with the king of Israel, we are to remember that there existed a powerful tie between the two courts in the marriage of Jehoshaphat's eldest son with Athaliah, the daughter of Ahab; and, when we advert to the part in public affairs which that princess afterwards took, it may well be conceived that even thus early she possessed an influence for evil in the court of Judah.

After the death of Ahaziah, king of Israel, Joram, his successor, persuaded Jehoshaphat to join him in an expedition against Moab. This alliance was, however, on political grounds, more excusable than the two former, as the Moabites, who were under tribute to Israel, might draw into their cause the Edomites, who were tributary to Judah. Besides, Moab could be invaded with most advantage from the south, round by the end of the Dead Sea; and the king of Israel could not gain access to them in that quarter but by marching through the territories of Jehoshaphat. The latter not only joined Joram with his own army, but required his tributary, the king of Edom, to bring his forces into the field. During seven days' march through the wilderness of Edom, the army suffered much from want of water; and by the time the allies came in sight of the army of Moab, they were ready to perish from thirst. In this emergency the pious Jehoshaphat thought, as usual, of consulting the Lord; and hearing that the prophet Elisha was in the camp, the three kings proceeded to his tent. For the sake of Jehoshaphat, and for his sake only, deliverance was promised, and it came during the ensuing night, in the shape of an abundant supply of water, which rolled down the exhausted wadys, and filled the pools and hollow grounds. Afterwards Jehoshaphat took his full part in the operations of the campaign, till the armies were induced to withdraw in horror, by witnessing the dreadful act of Mesha, king of Moab, in offering up his eldest son in sacrifice upon the wall of the town in which he was shut up.

This war kindled another much more dangerous to Jehoshaphat. The Moabites, being highly exasperated at the part he had taken against them, turned all their wrath upon him. They induced their kindred, the Ammonites, to join them, obtained auxiliaries from the Syrians, and even drew over the Edomites; so that the strength of all the neighbouring nations may be said to have been united for this great enterprise. The allied forces entered the land of Judah and encamped at Engedi, near the western border of the Dead Sea. In this extremity Jehoshaphat felt that all his defence lay with God A solemn fast was held, and the people repaired from the towns to Jerusalem to seek help of the Lord. In the presence of the assembled multitude the king, in the court of the temple, offered up a fervent prayer to God. He ceased; and in the midst of the silence which ensued, a voice was raised pronouncing deliverance in the name of the Lord, and telling them to go out on the morrow to the cliffs overlooking the camp of the enemy, and see them all overthrown without a blow from them. The voice was that of Jahaziel, one of the Levites. His words came to pass. The allies quarrelled among themselves, and destroyed each other; so that when the Judahites came the next day they found their dreaded enemies all dead, and nothing was left for them but to take the rich spoils of the slain. This done, they returned with triumphal songs to Jerusalem. This great event was recognised even by the neighbouring nations as the act of God; and so strong was the impression which it made upon them, that the remainder of the good king's reign was altogether undisturbed. His death, however, took place not very long after this, at the age of sixty, after having reigned twenty-five years, B.C. 896. He left the kingdom in a prosperous condition to his eldest son Jehoram, whom he had in the last years of his life associated with him in the government.

JEHOSHAPHAT, VALLEY OF, the name now given to the valley which bounds Jerusalem on the East, and separates it from the Mount of Olives [JERUSALEM].

In Joel iii. 2. 12, we read, 'the Lord will gather all nations in the valley of Jehoshaphat, and plead with them there.' Many interpreters, Jewish and Christian, conclude from this that the last judgment is to take place in the above-mentioned valley. But there is no reason to suppose that the valley then bore any such name; and more discreet interpreters understand the text to denote a valley in which some great victory was to be won, most probably by Nebuchadnezzar, which should utterly discomfit the ancient enemies of Israel, and resemble the victory which Jehoshaphat obtained over the Ammonites, Moabites, and Edomites (2 Chron. xx. 22-26). Others *translate* the name Jehoshaphat into *God's judgment*, and thus read, 'the valley of God's judgment,' which is doubtless symbolical, like 'the valley of decision,' *i. e.* of punishment, in the same chapter.

JEHOSH'EBA, daughter of Jehoram, sister of Ahaziah, and aunt of Joash, kings of Judah. The last of these owed his life to her, and his crown to her husband, the high-priest Jehoiada [JEHOIADA].

JEHO'VAH, or rather perhaps JAHVEH, the

name by which God was pleased to make himself known, under the covenant, to the ancient Hebrews (Exod. vi. 2, 3). The import of this name has been considered under the head GOD.

JE'HU (*God is*), tenth king of Israel, and founder of its fourth dynasty, who began to reign in B.C. 884, and reigned twenty-eight years.

Jehu held a command in the Israelite army posted at Ramoth-Gilead to hold in check the Syrians, who of late years had made strenuous efforts to extend their frontier to the Jordan, and had possessed themselves of much of the territory of the Israelites east of that river. Ahaziah, king of Judah, had taken part with Joram, king of Israel, in this war; and as the latter had been severely wounded in a recent action, and had gone to Jezreel to be healed of his wounds, Ahaziah had also gone thither on a visit of sympathy to him.

In this state of affairs a council of war was held among the military commanders in camp, when very unexpectedly one of the disciples of the prophets, known for such by his garb, appeared at the door of the tent, and called forth Jehu, declaring that he had a message to deliver to him. He had been sent by Elisha the prophet, in discharge of a duty which long before had been confided by the Lord to Elijah (1 Kings xix. 16), and from him had devolved on his successor. When they were alone the young man drew forth a horn of oil and poured it upon Jehu's head, with the words, 'Thus saith the Lord God of Israel, I have anointed thee king over the people of the Lord, even over Israel. And thou shalt smite the house of Ahab thy master, that I may avenge the blood of my servants the prophets, and the blood of all the servants of the Lord, at the hand of Jezebel' (2 Kings ix. 7, 8). Jehu returned to the council, probably with an altered air, for he was asked what had been the communication of the young prophet to him. He told them plainly; and they were obviously ripe for defection from the house of Ahab, for immediately, taking him in triumph to 'the top of the stairs,' they spread their mantles beneath his feet, and proclaimed him king by sound of trumpet in the presence of all the troops.

Jehu was not a man to lose any advantage through remissness. He immediately entered his chariot, in order that his presence at Jezreel should be the first announcement which Joram could receive of this revolution.

As soon as the advance of Jehu and his party was seen in the distance by the watchmen upon the palace-tower in Jezreel, two messengers were successively sent forth to meet him, and were commanded by Jehu to follow in his rear. But when the watchman reported that he could now recognise the furious driving of Jehu, Joram went forth himself to meet him, and was accompanied by the king of Judah. They met in the field of Naboth, so fatal to the house of Ahab. The king saluted him with ' Is it peace, Jehu?' and received the answer, 'What peace, so long as the whoredoms (idolatries) of thy mother Jezebel and her witchcrafts are so many?' This completely opened the eyes of Joram, who exclaimed to the king of Judah, 'There is treachery, O Ahaziah!' and turned to flee. But Jehu immediately drew a bow with his full strength and sent forth an arrow which passed through the

king's heart. He then caused the body to be thrown back into the field of Naboth, out of which he had passed in his attempt at flight. The king of Judah contrived to escape, but not without a wound, of which he afterwards died at Megiddo [AHAZIAH]. Jehu then entered the city, whither the news of this transaction had already preceded him. As he passed under the walls of the palace Jezebel herself, studiously arrayed for effect, appeared at one of the windows, and saluted him with a question such as might have shaken a man of weaker nerves, ' Had Zimri peace, who slew his master?' But Jehu was unmoved, and instead of answering her, called out, 'Who is on my side, who?' when several eunuchs made their appearance at the window, to whom he cried, ' Throw her down!' and immediately this proud and guilty woman lay a blood-stained corpse in the road, and was trodden under foot by the horses [JEZEBEL]. Jehu then went in and took possession of the palace.

He was now master of Jezreel, which was, next to Samaria, the chief town of the kingdom; but he could not feel secure while the capital itself was in the hands of the royal family, and of those who might be supposed to feel strong attachment to the house of Ahab. The force of the blow which he had struck was, however, felt even in Samaria. When therefore he wrote to the persons in authority there the somewhat ironical but designedly intimidating counsel, to set up one of the young princes in Samaria as king and fight out the matter which lay between them, they sent a very submissive answer, giving in their adhesion, and professing their readiness to obey in all things his commands. A second letter from Jehu tested this profession in a truly horrid and exceedingly Oriental manner, requiring them to appear before him on the morrow, bringing with them the heads of all the royal princes in Samaria. A fallen house meets with little pity in the East; and when the new king left his palace the next morning, he found seventy human heads piled up in two heaps at his gate. There, in the sight of these heaps, Jehu took occasion to explain his conduct, declaring that he must be regarded as the appointed minister of the divine decrees, pronounced long since against the house of Ahab by the prophets, not one of whose words should fall to the ground. He then continued his proscriptions by exterminating in Jezreel not only all in whose veins the blood of the condemned race flowed, but also—by a considerable stretch of his commission—those officers, ministers, and creatures of the late government, who, if suffered to live, would most likely be disturbers of his own reign. He then proceeded to Samaria. So rapid had been these proceedings that he met some of the nephews of the king of Judah, who were going to join their uncle at Jezreel, and had as yet heard nothing of the revolution which had taken place. These also perished under Jehu's now fully-awakened thirst for blood, to the number of forty-two persons.

On the way he took up into his chariot the pious Jehonadab the Rechabite, whose austere virtue and respected character would, as he felt, go far to hallow his proceedings in the eyes of the multitude. At Samaria he continued the extirpation of the persons more intimately connected with the late government. This, far from being in any way singular, is a common circumstance in Eastern revolutions. But the great object of Jehu was to exterminate the ministers and more devoted adherents of Baal, who had been much encouraged by Jezebel. There was even a temple to this idol in Samaria; and Jehu, never scrupulous about the means of reaching objects which he believed to be good, laid a snare by which he hoped to cut off the main body of Baal's ministers at one blow. He professed to be a more zealous servant of Baal than Ahab had been, and proclaimed a great festival in his honour, at which none but his true servants were to be present. The prophets, priests, and officers of Baal assembled from all parts for this great sacrifice, and sacerdotal vestments were given to them, that none of Jehovah's worshippers might be taken for them. When the temple was full, soldiers were posted so that none might escape; and so soon as the sacrifice had been offered, the word was given by the king, the soldiers entered the temple, and put all the worshippers to the sword. The temple itself was then demolished, the images overthrown, and the site turned into a common jakes.

Notwithstanding this zeal of Jehu in exterminating the grosser idolatries which had grown up under his immediate predecessors, he was not prepared to subvert the policy which had led Jeroboam and his successors to maintain the schismatic establishment of the golden calves in Dan and Beth-el. Here Jehu fell short: and this very policy, apparently so prudent and far-sighted, by which he hoped to secure the stability and independence of his kingdom, was that on account of which the term of rule granted to his dynasty was shorted. For this, it was foretold that his dynasty should extend only to four generations; and for this, the divine aid was withheld from him in his wars with the Syrians under Hazael on the eastern frontier. Hence the war was disastrous to him, and the Syrians were able to maintain themselves in the possession of a great part of his territories beyond the Jordan. He died in B.C. 856, and was buried in Samaria, leaving the throne to his son Jehoahaz.

2. JEHU, son of Hanani, a prophet, who was sent to pronounce upon Baasha, king of Israel, and his house, the same awful doom which had been already executed upon the house of Jeroboam (1 Kings xvi. 1-7). The same prophet was, many years after, commissioned to reprove Jehoshaphat for his dangerous connection with the house of Ahab (2 Chron. xix. 2).

JEPH'THAH (*opener*), ninth judge of Israel, of the tribe of Manasseh. He was the son of a person named Gilead by a concubine. After the death of his father he was expelled from his home by the envy of his brothers, who refused him any share of the heritage, and he withdrew to the land of Tob, beyond the frontier of the Hebrew territories. It is clear that he had before this distinguished himself by his daring character and skill in arms; for no sooner was his withdrawment known than a great number of men of desperate fortunes repaired to him, and he became their chief. His position was now very similar to that of David when he withdrew from the court of Saul. To maintain the people who had thus linked their fortunes with his, there was no other resource than that sort of brigandage which is accounted honourable in the East, so

long as it is exercised against public or private enemies, and is not marked by needless cruelty or outrage.

Jephthah led this kind of life for some years, during which his dashing exploits and successful enterprises procured him a higher military reputation than any other man of his time enjoyed.

After the death of Jair the Israelites gradually fell into their favourite idolatries, and were punished by subjection to the Philistines on the west of the Jordan, and to the Ammonites on the east of that river. The oppression which they sustained for eighteen years became at length so heavy that they recovered their senses and returned to the God of their fathers with humiliation and tears; and he was appeased, and promised them deliverance from their affliction (B.C. 1143).

The tribes beyond the Jordan having resolved to oppose the Ammonites, Jephthah seems to occur to every one as the most fitting leader. A deputation was accordingly sent to invite him to take the command. After some demur, on account of the treatment he had formerly received, he consented. The rude hero commenced his operations with a degree of diplomatic consideration and dignity for which we are not prepared. The Ammonites being assembled in force for one of those ravaging incursions by which they had repeatedly desolated the land, he sent to their camp a formal complaint of the invasion, and a demand of the ground of their proceeding. Their answer was, that the land of the Israelites beyond the Jordan was theirs. It had originally belonged to them, from whom it had been taken by the Amorites, who had been dispossessed by the Israelites. and on this ground they claimed the restitution of these lands. Jephthah's reply laid down the just principle which has been followed out in the practice of civilized nations, and is maintained by all the great writers on the law of nations. The land belonged to the Israelites by right of conquest from the *actual* possessors; and they could not be expected to recognise any antecedent claim of former possessors, for whom they had not acted, who had rendered them no assistance, and who had themselves displayed hostility against the Israelites. But the Ammonites re-asserted their former views, and on this issue they took the field.

When Jephthah set forth against the Ammonites he solemnly vowed to the Lord, 'If thou shalt without fail deliver the children of Ammon into my hands, then it shall be, that whatsoever cometh forth of the doors of my house to meet me, when I return in peace from the children of Ammon, shall surely be the Lord's, and I will offer it up for a burnt offering.' He *was* victorious. The Ammonites sustained a terrible overthrow. He *did* return in peace to his house in Mizpeh. As he drew nigh his house, the one that came forth to meet him was his own daughter, his only child, in whom his heart was bound up. She, with her fair companions, came to greet the triumphant hero 'with timbrels and with dances.' But he no sooner saw her than he rent his robes, and cried, 'Alas, my daughter! thou hast brought me very low; . . . for I have opened my mouth unto the Lord, and cannot go back.' Nor did she ask it. She replied, 'My father, if thou hast opened thy mouth unto the Lord, do to me according to that which has proceeded out of thy mouth; forasmuch as the Lord hath taken vengeance for thee of thine enemies, the children of Ammon.' But after a pause she added, 'Let this thing be done for me: let me alone two months, that I may go up and down upon the mountains, and bewail my virginity, I and my fellows.' Her father of course assented; and when the time expired she returned, and, we are told, 'he did with her according to his vow.' It is then added that it became 'a custom in Israel, that the daughters of Israel went yearly to lament the daughter of Jephthah the Gileadite three days in the year.'

The victory over the Ammonites was followed by a quarrel with the proud and powerful Ephraimites on the west of the Jordan. This tribe was displeased at having had no share in the glory of the recent victory, and a large body of men belonging to it, who had crossed the river to share in the action, used very high and threatening language when they found their services were not required. Jephthah, finding his remonstrances had no effect, re-assembled some of his disbanded troops and gave the Ephraimites battle, when they were defeated with much loss. The victors seized the fords of the Jordan, and when any one came to pass over, they made him pronounce the word *Shibboleth* [an ear of corn], but if he could not give the aspiration, and pronounced the word as *Sibboleth*, they knew him for an Ephraimite, and slew him on the spot.

Jephthah judged Israel six years, during which we have reason to conclude that the exercise of his authority was almost if not altogether confined to the country east of the Jordan.

Volumes have been written on the subject of 'Jephthah's rash vow;' the question being whether, in doing to his daughter 'according to his vow,' he really did offer her in sacrifice or not. The negative has been stoutly maintained by many able pens, from a natural anxiety to clear the character of one of the heroes in Israel from so dark a stain. But the more the plain rules of common sense have been exercised in our view of biblical transactions, and the better we have succeeded in realizing a distinct idea of the times in which Jephthah lived and of the position which he occupied, the less reluctance there has been to admit the interpretation which the first view of the passage suggests to every reader, which is, that he really did offer her in sacrifice. The explanation which denies this maintains that she was rather doomed to perpetual celibacy; but to *live* unmarried was required by no law, custom, or devotement among the Jews: no one had a right to impose so odious a condition on another, nor is any such condition implied or expressed in the vow which Jephthah uttered. The Jewish commentators themselves generally admit that Jephthah really sacrificed his daughter; and even go so far as to allege that the change in the pontifical dynasty from the house of Eleazar to that of Ithamar was caused by the high-priest of the time having suffered this transaction to take place.

It is very true that human sacrifices were forbidden by the law. But in the rude and unsettled age in which the judges lived, when the Israelites had adopted a vast number of erroneous notions and practices from their heathen neighbours, many things were done, even by good men, which the law forbade quite as positively as human sacrifice.

Again, Jephthah vows that whatsoever came forth from the door of his house to meet him 'shall surely be the Lord's, and I will offer it up for a burnt-offering,' which, in fact, was the regular way of making a thing wholly the Lord's. Afterwards we are told that 'he did with her according to his vow,' that is, according to the plain meaning of plain words, offered her for a burnt-offering. Then follows the intimation that the daughters of Israel lamented her four days every year. People lament the dead, not the living. The whole story is consistent and intelligible, while the sacrifice is understood to have actually taken place; but becomes perplexed and difficult as soon as we begin to turn aside from this obvious meaning in search of recondite explanations.

Professor Bush, in his elaborate note on the text, maintains with us that a human sacrifice was all along contemplated. But he suggests that during the two months Jephthah might have obtained better information respecting the nature of vows, by which he would have learned that his daughter could not be legally offered, but might be redeemed at a valuation (Lev. xxvii. 2-12). This is possible, and is much more likely than the popular alternative of perpetual celibacy; but we have serious doubts whether even this meets the conclusion that 'he did with her according to his vow.' Besides, in this case, where was the ground for the annual 'lamentations' of the daughters of Israel, or even for the 'celebrations' which some understand the word to mean?

JEREMI'AH (*raised up* or *appointed by God*), was the son of Hilkiah, a priest of Anathoth, in the land of Benjamin [ANATHOTH]. Jeremiah was very young when the word of the Lord first came to him (ch. i. 6). This event took place in the thirteenth year of Josiah (B.C. 629), whilst the youthful prophet still lived at Anathoth. It would seem that he remained in his native city several years, but at length, in order to escape the persecution of his fellow townsmen (ch. xi. 21), and even of his own family (ch. xii. 6), as well as to have a wider field for his exertions, he left Anathoth and took up his residence at Jerusalem. The finding of the book of the law five years after the commencement of his predictions, must have produced a powerful influence on the mind of Jeremiah, and king Josiah no doubt found him a powerful ally in carrying into effect the reformation of religious worship (2 Kings xxiii. 1-25). During the reign of this monarch we may readily believe that Jeremiah would be in no way molested in his work; and that from the time of his quitting Anathoth to the eighteenth year of his ministry, he probably uttered his warnings without interruption, though with little success (see ch. xi.). Indeed, the reformation itself was nothing more than the forcible repression of idolatrous and heathen rites, and the re-establishment of the external service of God, by the command of the king. No sooner, therefore, was the influence of the court on behalf of the true religion withdrawn, than it was evident that no real improvement had taken place in the minds of the people. Jeremiah, who hitherto was at least protected by the influence of the pious king Josiah, soon became the object of attack, as he must doubtless have long been the object of dislike to those whose interests were identified with the corruptions of religion. We hear nothing of the prophet during the three months which constituted the short reign of Jehoahaz; but ' in the beginning of the reign of Jehoiakim' the prophet was interrupted in his ministry by ' the priests and the prophets,' who with the populace brought him before the civil authorities, urging that capital punishment should be inflicted on him for his threatenings of evil on the city unless the people amended their ways (ch. xxvi.). The princes seem to have been in some degree aware of the results which the general corruption was bringing on the state, and if they did not themselves yield to the exhortations of the prophet, they acknowledged that he spoke in the name of the Lord, and were quite averse from so openly renouncing His authority as to put His messenger to death. It appears, however, that it was rather owing to the personal influence of one or two, especially Ahikam, than to any general feeling favourable to Jeremiah, that his life was preserved. In the fourth year of Jehoiakim (B.C. 606) he was commanded to write the predictions which had been given through him, and to read them to the people. As he was at that time ' shut up,' and could not himself go into the house of the Lord (ch. xxxvi. 5), he deputed Baruch to write the predictions after him, and to read them publicly on the fast-day. These threatenings being thus anew made public, Baruch was summoned before the princes to give an account of the manner in which the roll containing them had come into his possession. The princes, who, without strength of principle to oppose the wickedness of the king, had sufficient respect for religion, as well as sagacity enough to discern the importance of listening to the voice of God's prophet, advised both Baruch and Jeremiah to conceal themselves, whilst they endeavoured to influence the mind of the king by reading the roll to him. The result showed that their precautions were not needless. The bold self-will and reckless daring of the monarch refused to listen to any advice, even though coming with the professed sanction of the Most High. Having read three or four leaves, ' he cut the roll with the penknife and cast it into the fire that was on the hearth, until all the roll was consumed,' and gave immediate orders for the apprehension of Jeremiah and Baruch, who, however, were both preserved from the vindictive monarch. Of the history of Jeremiah during the eight or nine remaining years of the reign of Jehoiakim we have no certain account. At the command of God he procured another roll, in which he wrote all that was in the roll destroyed by the king, ' and added besides unto them many like words' (ch. xxxvi. 32). In the short reign of his successor Jehoiachin or Jeconiah, we find him still uttering his voice of warning (see ch. xiii. 18; comp. 2 Kings xxiv. 12, and ch. xxiii. 24-30), though without effect. It was probably either during this reign, or at the commencement of the reign of Zedekiah, that he was put in confinement by Pashur, the ' chief governor of the house of the Lord.' He seems, however, soon to have been liberated, as we find that ' they had not put him into prison' when the army of Nebuchadnezzar commenced the siege of Jerusalem. The Chaldæans drew off their army for a time, on the report of help coming from Egypt to the besieged city; and now feeling the danger to be imminent, and yet a ray of hope brightening their prospects, the king entreated Jeremiah to pray to the Lord for them. The hopes of the king were not responded to in the message which Jeremiah received from God. He was assured that the Egyptian army should return to their own land, that the Chaldæans should come again, and that they should take the city and burn it with fire (ch. xxxvi. 7, 8). The princes, apparently irritated by a message so contrary to their wishes, made the departure of Jeremiah from the city, during the short respite, the pretext for accusing him of deserting to the Chaldæans, and he was forthwith cast into prison. The king seems to have been throughout inclined to favour the prophet, and sought to know from him the word of the Lord; but he was wholly under the influence of the princes, and dared not communicate with him except in secret (ch. xxxviii. 14, 28); much less could he follow advice so obnoxious to their views as that which the prophet gave. Jeremiah, therefore, more from the hostility of the princes than the inclination of the king, was still in confinement when the city was taken. Nebuchadnezzar formed a more just estimate of his character and of the value of his counsels, and gave a special charge to his captain Nebuzar-adan, not only to provide for him but to follow his advice (ch. xxxix. 12). He was accordingly taken from the prison and allowed free choice either to go to Babylon, where doubtless he would have been held in honour in the royal court, or to remain with his own people. We need scarcely be told that he who had devoted more than forty years of unrequited service to the welfare of his falling country should choose to remain with the remnant of his people rather than seek the precarious fame which might await him at the court of the king of Babylon. Accordingly he went to Mizpah with Gedaliah, whom the Babylonian monarch had appointed governor of Judæa; and after his murder sought to persuade Johanan, who was then the recognised leader of the people, to remain in the land, assuring him and the people, by a message from God in answer to their inquiries, that if they did so the Lord would build them up, but if they went to Egypt the evils which they sought to escape should come upon them there (ch. xlii.). The people refused to attend to the divine message, and under the command of Johanan went into Egypt, taking Jeremiah and Baruch along with them (ch. xliii. 6). In Egypt the prophet still sought to turn the people to the Lord, from whom they had so long and so deeply revolted (ch. xliv.); but his writings give us no subsequent information respecting his personal history. Ancient traditions assert that he spent the remainder of his life in Egypt. According to the pseudo-Epiphanius he was stoned by the people at Taphnæ, the same as Tahpanhes, where the Jews were settled. It is said that his bones were removed by Alexander the Great to Alexandria.

Jeremiah was contemporary with Zephaniah, Habakkuk, Ezekiel, and Daniel. None of these, however, are in any remarkable way connected with him, except Ezekiel. The writings and character of these two eminent prophets furnish many very interesting points both of comparison and contrast. Both, during a long series of years, were labouring at the same time and for the same object. The representations of both, far separated as they were from each other, are in substance singularly accordant; yet there is at the same time a marked difference in their modes of statement, and a still more striking diversity in the character and natural disposition of the two. No one who compares them can fail to perceive that the mind of Jeremiah was of a softer and more delicate texture than that of his illustrious contemporary. His whole history convinces us that he was by nature mild and retiring, highly susceptible and sensitive, especially to sorrowful emotions, and rather inclined, as we should imagine, to shrink from danger than to brave it. Yet, with this acute perception of injury, and natural repugnance from being 'a man of strife,' he never in the least degree shrinks from publicity; nor is he at all intimidated by reproach or insult, or even by actual punishment and threatened death, when he has the message of God to deliver. He is, in truth, as remarkable an instance, though in a different way, of the overpowering influence of the divine energy, as Ezekiel. The one presents the spectacle of the power of divine inspiration acting on a mind naturally of the firmest texture, and at once subduing to itself every element of the soul; whilst the other furnishes an example, not less memorable, of moral courage sustained by the same divine inspiration against the constantly opposing influence of a love of retirement and strong susceptibility to impressions of outward evil.

The style of Jeremiah corresponds with this view of the character of his mind; though not deficient in power, it is peculiarly marked by pathos. He delights in the expression of the tender emotions, and employs all the resources of his imagination to excite corresponding feelings in his readers. He has an irresistible sympathy with the miserable, which finds utterance in the most touching descriptions of their condition. He seizes with wonderful tact those circumstances which point out the objects of his pity as the objects of sympathy, and founds his expostulations on the miseries which are thus exhibited. His book of Lamentations is an astonishing exhibition of his power to accumulate images of sorrow. The whole series of elegies has but one object—the expression of sorrow for the forlorn condition of his country; and yet he presents this to us in so many lights, alludes to it by so many figures, that not only are his mournful strains not felt to be tedious reiterations, but the reader is captivated by the plaintive melancholy which pervades the whole.

The genuineness and canonicity of the writings of Jeremiah in general are established both by the testimony of ancient writers, and by quotations and references which occur in the New Testament.

The principal predictions relating to the Messiah are found in ch. xxiii. 1-8; xxx. 31-40; xxxiii. 14-26.

JER′ICHO, a town in the plain of the same name, not far from the river Jordan, at the point where it enters the Dead Sea. It lay before the Israelites when they crossed the river, on first entering the Promised Land; and the account which the spies who were sent by them into the city received from their hostess Rahab, tended much to encourage their subsequent operations, as it showed that the inhabitants of the country were greatly alarmed at their advance, and the signal miracles which had marked their course from the Nile to the Jordan. The strange manner in which Jericho itself was taken must have strengthened this impression in the country, and appears, indeed, to have been designed for that effect. The town was utterly destroyed by the Israelites, who pronounced an awful curse upon whoever should rebuild it; and all the inhabitants were put to the sword, except Rahab and her family (Josh. ii. 6). In these accounts Jericho is repeatedly called 'the city of palm-trees;' which shows that the hot and dry plain, so similar to the land of Egypt, was noted beyond other parts of Palestine for the tree which abounds in that country, and which was and is less common in the land of Canaan than general readers and painters suppose. It has now almost disappeared even from the plain of Jericho, although specimens remain in the plain of the Mediterranean coast.

Notwithstanding the curse, Jericho was soon rebuilt [HIEL], and became a school of the prophets (Judg. iii. 13; 1 Kings xvi. 34; 2 Kings ii. 4, 5). Its inhabitants returned after the exile, and it was eventually fortified by the Syrian general Bacchides (Ezra ii. 34; Neh. iii. 2; 1 Macc. ix. 50). Pompey marched from Scythopolis, along the valley of the Jordan, to Jericho, and thence to Jerusalem; and Strabo speaks of the castles Thrax and Taurus, in or near Jericho, as having been destroyed by him. Herod the Great, in the beginning of his career, captured and sacked Jericho, but afterwards strengthened and adorned it, when he had redeemed its revenues from Cleopatra, on whom the plain had been bestowed by Antony. He appears to have often resided here, probably in winter: he built over the city a fortress called Cypros, between which and the former palace he erected other palaces, and called them by the names of his friends. Here also was a hippodrome or circus, in which the same tyrant, when lying at Jericho on his death-bed, caused the nobles of the land to be shut up, for massacre after his death. He died here; but his bloody intention was not executed. The palace at this place was afterwards rebuilt more magnificently by Archelaus. By this it will be seen that the Jericho which existed in the time of our Saviour was a great and important city—probably more so than it had ever been since its foundation. It was once visited by him, when he lodged with Zaccheus, and healed the blind man (Luke xviii. 35-43; xix. 1-7; Matt. xx. 29-34; Mark x. 46-52). Jericho was afterwards made the head of one of the toparchies, and was visited by Vespasian before he left the country, who stationed there the tenth legion in garrison. Eusebius and Jerome describe Jericho as having been destroyed during the siege of Jerusalem, on account of the perfidy of the inhabitants, but add that it was afterwards rebuilt. The town, however, appears to have been overthrown during the Mohammedan conquest; for Adamnanus, at the close of the seventh century, describes the site as without human habitations, and covered with corn and vines. The celebrated palm-groves still existed. In the next century a church is mentioned; and in the ninth century several monasteries appear. About the same time the plain of Jericho is again noticed for its fertility and peculiar products; and it appears to have been brought under cultivation by the Saracens, for the sake of the sugar and other products for which the soil and climate were more suitable than any other in Palestine. Ruins of extensive aqueducts, with pointed Saracenic arches, remain in evidence of the elaborate irrigation and culture of this fine plain—which is nothing without water, and everything with it—at a period long subsequent to the occupation of the country by the Jews. It is to this age that we may probably refer the origin of the castle and village, which have since been regarded as representing Jericho. The place has been mentioned by travellers and pilgrims down to the present time as a poor hamlet consisting of a few houses. In the fifteenth century the square castle or tower began to pass among pilgrims as the house of Zaccheus, a title which it bears to the present day.

The village now regarded as representing Jericho is supposed to date its origin from the ninth century, It bears the name of Rihah, and is situated about the middle of the plain, six miles west from the Jordan, in N. lat. 31° 57', and E. long. 35° 33'. Dr. Olin describes the present village as ' the meanest and foulest of Palestine.' It may perhaps contain forty dwellings, formed of small loose stones. The most important object is a square castle or tower, which Dr. Robinson supposes to have been constructed to protect the cultivation of the plain under the Saracens. It is thirty or forty feet square, and about the

221. [Jericho.]

same height, and is now in a dilapidated condition.

Rihah may contain about two hundred inhabitants, who have a sickly aspect, and are reckoned vicious and indolent. They keep a few cattle and sheep, and till a little land for grain as well as for gardens. A small degree of industry and skill bestowed on this prolific soil, favoured as it is with abundant water for irrigation, would amply reward the labour. But this is wanting; and everything bears the mark of abject, and, which is unusual in the East, of squalid poverty. There are some fine fig-trees near the village, and some vines in the gardens. But the most distinguishing feature of the whole plain is a noble grove of trees which borders the village on the west, and stretches away northward to the distance of two miles or more.

This grove owes its existence to the waters of one of the fountains, the careful distribution of which over the plain by canals and aqueducts did once, and might still, cover it with abundance. One of these fountains is called by the natives Ain es-Sultan, but by pilgrims the Fountain of Elias, being supposed to be the same whose bitter waters were cured by that prophet. Dr. Robinson thinks there is reason for this conclusion. It lies almost two miles N.W. from the village, and is a large and beautiful fountain of sweet and pleasant waters. Beyond the fountain rises up the bold perpendicular face of the mountain Quarantana (Kuruntul), from the foot of which a line of low hills runs out N.N.E. in front of the mountains, and forms the ascent to a narrow tract of table-land along their base. On this tract, at the foot of the mountains, about two and a half miles N.N.W. from the Ain es-Sultan, is the still larger fountain of Duk, the waters of which are brought along the base of Quarantana in a canal to the top of the declivity at the back of Ain es-Sultan, whence they were formerly distributed to several mills, and scattered over the upper part of the plain.

Under the mountains on the western confine of the plain, about two miles west of Rihah, and just where the road from Jerusalem comes down into the plain, are considerable ruins, extending both on the north and south side of the road. Mr. Buckingham was the first to suspect that these were the ruins of the ancient Jericho. He shows that the situation agrees better with the ancient intimations than does that of the modern village, near which no trace of ancient ruins can be found. Since this idea was started the matter has been examined by other travellers; and the conclusion seems to be that Rihah is certainly not the ancient Jericho, and that there is no site of ancient ruins on the plain which so well answers to the intimations as that now described; although even here some drawback to a satisfactory conclusion is felt, in the absence of any traces of those great buildings which belonged to the Jericho of king Herod.

JEROBO'AM, son of Nebat, and first king of Israel, who became king B.C. 975, and reigned 22 years.

He was of the tribe of Ephraim, the son of a widow named Zeruiah, when he was noticed by Solomon as a clever and active young man, and was appointed one of the superintendents of the works which that magnificent king was carrying on at Jerusalem. This appointment, the reward of his merits, might have satisfied his ambition had not the declaration of the prophet Ahijah given him higher hopes. When informed that, by the divine appointment, he was to become king over the ten tribes about to be rent from the house of David, he was not content to wait patiently for the death of Solomon, but began to form plots and conspiracies, the discovery of which constrained him to flee to Egypt to escape condign punishment. The king of that country was but too ready to encourage one whose success must necessarily weaken the kingdom which had become great and formidable under David and Solomon, and which had already pushed its frontier to the Red Sea (1 Kings xi. 26-40).

When Solomon died, the ten tribes sent to call Jeroboam from Egypt; and he appears to have headed the deputation which came before the son of Solomon with a demand of new securities for the rights which the measures of the late king had compromised. It may somewhat excuse the harsh answer of Rehoboam, that the demand was urged by a body of men headed by one whose pretensions were so well known and so odious to the house of David. The imprudent answer of Rehoboam rendered a revolution inevitable, and Jeroboam was then called to reign over the ten tribes, by the style of 'king of Israel' (1 Kings xii. 1-20).

The general course of his conduct on the throne has already been indicated in the article ISRAEL, and need not be repeated in this place. The leading object of his policy was to widen the breach between the two kingdoms, and to rend asunder those common interests among all the descendants of Jacob, which it was one great object of the law to combine and interlace. To this end he scrupled not to sacrifice the most sacred and inviolable interests and obligations of the covenant people, by forbidding his subjects to resort to the one temple and altar of Jehovah at Jerusalem, and by establishing shrines at Dan and Beth-el—the extremities of his kingdom—where 'golden calves' were set up as the symbols of Jehovah, to which the people were enjoined to resort and bring their offerings. The pontificate of the new establishment he united to his crown, in imitation of the Egyptian kings. He was officiating in that capacity at Beth-el, offering incense, when a prophet appeared, and in the name of the Lord announced a coming time, as yet far off, in which a king of the house of David, Josiah by name, should burn upon that unholy altar the bones of its ministers. He was then preparing to verify, by a commissioned prodigy, the truth of the oracle he had delivered, when the king attempted to arrest him, but was smitten with palsy in the arm he stretched forth. At the same moment the threatened prodigy took place, the altar was rent asunder, and the ashes strewed far around. This measure had, however, no abiding effect. The policy on which he acted lay too deep in what he deemed the vital interests of his separate kingdom, to be even thus abandoned : and the force of the considerations which determined his conduct may in part be appreciated from the fact that no subsequent king of Israel, however well disposed in other respects, ever ventured to lay a finger on this schismatical establishment. Hence 'the sin of Jeroboam the son of Nebat, wherewith he sinned and made Israel to sin,' became a standing phrase in describing that iniquity from which no king of Israel departed (1 Kings xii. 25-33; xiii.).

The contumacy of Jeroboam eventually brought upon him the doom which he probably dreaded beyond all others—the speedy extinction of the dynasty which he had taken so much pains and incurred so much guilt to establish on firm foundations. His son Abijah being sick, he sent his wife disguised to consult the prophet Ahijah, who had predicted that he should be king of Israel. The prophet, although he had become blind with age, knew the queen, and saluted her with—'Come in, thou wife of Jeroboam, for I am sent to thee with heavy tidings.' These were not merely that the son should die—for that was intended in mercy to one who alone, of all the house of Jeroboam, had remained faithful to his God, and was the only one who should obtain an honoured grave—but that his race should be violently and utterly extinguished: 'I will take away the remnant of the house of Jeroboam as a man taketh away dung, till it be all gone' (1 Kings xiv. 1-18).

The son died so soon as the mother crossed the threshold on her return; and as the death of Jeroboam himself is the next event recorded, it would seem that he did not long survive his son. He died in B.C. 954 (1 Kings xiv. 20).

Jeroboam was perhaps a less remarkable man than the circumstance of his being the founder of a new kingdom might lead us to expect. The tribes would have revolted without him; and he was chosen king merely because he had been pointed out by previous circumstances. His government exhibits but one idea—that of raising a barrier against the re-union of the tribes. Of this idea he was the slave and victim; and although the barrier which he raised was effectual for its purpose, it only served to show the weakness of the man who could deem needful the protection for his separate interests which such a barrier offered.

2. JEROBOAM, thirteenth king of Israel, son of Joash, whom, in B C. 824, he succeeded on the throne, and reigned forty-one years. He followed the example of the first Jeroboam in keeping up the idolatry of the golden calves. Nevertheless the Lord had pity upon Israel, the time of its ruin was not yet come, and this reign was long and flourishing. Jeroboam brought to a successful result the wars which his father had undertaken, and was always victorious over the Syrians. He even took their chief cities of Damascus and Hamath, which had formerly been subject to the sceptre of David, and restored to the realm of Israel the ancient eastern limits from Lebanon to the Dead Sea. He died in B.C. 783 (2 Kings xiii 13 . xiv. 16, 23-29).

The Scriptural account of this reign is too short to enable us to judge of the character of a prince under whom the kingdom of Israel seems to have reached a degree of prosperity which it had never before enjoyed, and was not able long to preserve.

JERUB'-BAAL. [GIDEON.]

JERU'SALEM (*habitation of peace*), the Jewish capital of Palestine. It is mentioned very early in Scripture, being usually supposed to be the Salem of which Melchizedek was king. The Psalmist says (lxxvi. 2): 'In Salem is his tabernacle, and his dwelling-place in Sion.'

The mountain of the land of Moriah, which Abraham (Gen. xxii. 2) reached on the third day from Beersheba, there to offer Isaac, is, according to Josephus, the mountain on which

222. [Jerusalem.]

Solomon afterwards built the temple (2 Chron. iii 1).

The name Jerusalem first occurs in Josh. x. 1, where Adoni-zedek, king of Jerusalem, is mentioned as having entered into an alliance with other kings against Joshua, by whom they were all overcome (comp. Josh. xii. 10).

In drawing the northern border of Judah, we find Jerusalem again mentioned (Josh. xv. 8; comp. Josh. xviii. 16). This border ran through the valley of Ben Hinnom; the country on the south of it, as Bethlehem, belonged to Judah; but the mountain of Zion, forming the northern wall of the valley, and occupied by the Jebusites, appertained to Benjamin, therefore, is also mentioned (Josh. xviii. 28) 'Jebus, which is Jerusalem' (comp. Judg. xix. 10; 1 Chron. xi. 4).

After the death of Joshua, when there remained for the children of Israel much to conquer in Canaan, the Lord directed Judah to fight against the Canaanites; and they took Jerusalem, smote it with the edge of the sword, and set it on fire (Judg i. 1-8). After that, the Judahites and the Benjamites dwelt with the Jebusites at Jerusalem; for it is recorded (Josh. xv. 63) that the children of Judah could not drive out the Jebusites inhabiting Jerusalem; and we are further informed (Judg. i. 21) that the children of Benjamin did not expel them from Jerusalem. Probably the Jebusites were removed by Judah only from the lower city, but kept possession of the mountain of Zion, which David conquered at a later period. Jerusalem is not again mentioned till the time of Saul, when it is stated (1 Sam. xvii. 54) that David took the head of Goliath and brought it to Jerusalem After David, who had previously reigned over Judah alone in Hebron, was called to rule over all Israel, he led his forces against the Jebusites, and conquered the castle of Zion, which Joab first scaled (2 Sam. v. 5-9; 1 Chron. xii. 4-8). He then fixed his abode on this mountain, and called it 'the city of David.' Thither he carried the ark of the covenant and there he built unto the Lord an altar in the threshing-floor of Araunah the Jebusite, on the place where the angel stood who threatened Jerusalem with pestilence (2 Sam. xxiv. 15-25).

The reasons which led David to fix upon Jerusalem as the metropolis of his kingdom have been alluded to elsewhere [ISRAEL; JUDAH]; being chiefly, that it was in his own tribe of Judah, in which his influence was the strongest, while it was the nearest to the other tribes of any site he could have chosen in Judah. The peculiar strength also of the situation, enclosed on three sides by a natural trench of valleys, could not be without weight.

The promise made to David received its accomplishment when Solomon built his temple upon Mount Moriah. By him and his father Jerusalem had been made the imperial residence of the king of all Israel: and the temple, often called 'the house of Jehovah,' constituted it at the same time the residence of the King of kings, the supreme head of the theocratical state, whose vicegerents the human kings were taught to regard themselves. It now belonged, even less than a town of the Levites, to a particular tribe: it was the centre of all civil and religious affairs, the very place of which Moses spoke, Deut. xii. 5: 'The place which the Lord your God shall choose out of all your tribes to put his name there. even unto his habitation shall ye seek, and thither thou shalt come' (comp. ix. 6; xiii. 14; xiv 23; xvi. 11-16; Ps. cxxii.).

The importance and splendour of Jerusalem were considerably lessened after the death of Solomon; under whose son, Rehoboam, ten of the tribes rebelled, Judah and Benjamin only remaining in their allegiance. Jerusalem was then only the capital of the very small state of Judah. And when Jeroboam instituted the worship of golden calves in Beth-el and Dan, the ten tribes went no longer up to Jerusalem to worship and sacrifice in the house of the Lord (1 Kings xii. 26-30).

After this time the history of Jerusalem is continued in the history of Judah, for which the second book of the Kings and of the Chronicles are the principal sources of information.

After the time of Solomon, the kingdom of Judah was almost alternately ruled by good kings, 'who did that which was right in the sight of the Lord,' and by such as were idolatrous and evil disposed; and the reign of the same king often varied, and was by turns good or evil. The condition of the kingdom, and of Jerusalem in particular as its metropolis, was very much affected by these mutations. Under good kings the city flourished, and under bad kings it suffered greatly. Under Rehoboam (B.C. 973) it was conquered by Shishak, king of Egypt, who pillaged the treasures of the temple (2 Chron. xii. 9). Under Amaziah it was taken by Jehoash, king of Israel, who broke down 400 cubits of the wall of the city, and took all the gold and silver,

and all the vessels that were found in the temple (2 Kings xiv. 13, 14). Uzziah, son of Amaziah, who at first reigned well, built towers in Jerusalem at the corner-gate, at the valley-gate, and at the turning of the wall, and fortified them (2 Chron. xxvi. 9). His son, Jotham, built the high gate of the temple, and reared up many other structures (2 Chron. xxvii. 3, 4). Hezekiah (B.C. 728) added to the other honours of his reign that of an improver of Jerusalem. His most eminent work in that character was the stopping of the upper course of Gihon, and bringing its waters by a subterraneous aqueduct to the west side of the city (2 Chron. xxxii. 30). This work is inferred, from 2 Kings xx., to have been of great importance to Jerusalem, as it cut off a supply of water from any besieging enemy, and bestowed it upon the inhabitants of the city. Hezekiah's son, Manasseh, in his later and best years, built a strong and very high wall on the west side of Jerusalem (2 Chron. xxxiii. 14). The works in the city connected with the names of the succeeding kings of Judah were, so far as recorded, confined to the defilement of the house of the Lord by bad kings, and its purgation by good kings, till about 100 years after Manasseh, when, for the abounding iniquities of the nation, the city and temple were abandoned to destruction. After a siege of three years, Jerusalem was taken by Nebuchadnezzar, who razed its walls, and destroyed its temple and palaces with fire (2 Kings xxv.; 2 Chron. xxxvi.; Jer. xxxix.). Thus was Jerusalem smitten with the calamity which Moses had prophesied would befal it, if the people would not keep the commandments of the Lord, but broke his covenant (Lev. xxvi. 14; Deut. xxviii.).

But God, before whom a thousand years are as one day, gave to the afflicted people a glimpse beyond the present calamity and retributive judgment, into a distant futurity. The same prophets who foretold the destruction of Jerusalem, also announced the consolations of a coming time.

Moses had long before predicted that if in the land of their captivity they repented of their evil, they should be brought back again to the land out of which they had been cast (Deut. xxx. 1-5; comp. 1 Kings viii. 46-53; Neh. i. 8, 9). The Lord also, through Isaiah, condescended to point out the agency through which the restoration of the holy city was to be accomplished, and even named long before his birth the very person, Cyrus, under whose orders this was to be effected (Isa. xliv. 28; comp. Jer. iii. 2, 7, 8; xxiii. 3; xxxi. 10; xxxii. 36, 37).

Among the remarkably precise indications should be mentioned that in which Jeremiah (xxv. 9, 12) limits the duration of Judah's captivity to 70 years.

These encouragements were continued through the prophets, who themselves shared the captivity. Of this number was Daniel (ix. 16, 19), who lived to see the reign of Cyrus, king of Persia (Dan. x. 1), and the fulfilment of his prayer. It was in the year B.C. 536, 'in the first year of Cyrus,' that in accomplishment of the prophecy of Jeremiah, the Lord stirred up the spirit of this prince, who made a proclamation throughout all his kingdom, expressed in these remarkable words: 'The Lord God of heaven hath given me all the kingdoms of the earth, and he has charged me to build him a house at Jerusalem, which is in Judah. Who is there among you of all his people? his God be with him, and let him go up to Jerusalem, and build the house of the Lord God of Israel' (Ezra i. 2, 3). This important call was answered by a considerable number of persons, particularly priests and Levites; and the many who declined to quit their houses and possessions in Babylonia, committed valuable gifts to the hands of their more zealous brethren. Cyrus also caused the sacred vessels of gold and silver which Nebuchadnezzar had taken from the temple to be restored to Sheshbazzar, the prince of Judah, who took them to Jerusalem, followed by 42,360 people, beside their servants, of whom there were 7337 (Ezra i. 5-11).

On their arrival at Jerusalem they contributed according to their ability to rebuild the temple; Jeshua, the priest, and Zerubbabel, reared up an altar to offer burnt-offerings thereon; and when in the following year the foundation was laid of the new house of God, 'the people shouted for joy, but many of the Levites who had seen the first temple wept with a loud voice' (Ezra iii 2, 12). When the Samaritans expressed a wish to share in the pious labour, Zerubbabel declined the offer; and in revenge the Samaritans sent a deputation to king Artaxerxes of Persia, carrying a presentment in which Jerusalem was described as a rebellious city of old time, which, if rebuilt, and its walls set up again, would not pay toll, tribute, and custom, and would thus endamage the public revenue. The deputation succeeded, and Artaxerxes ordered that the building of the temple should cease. The interruption thus caused lasted to the second year of the reign of Darius (Ezra iv. 24), when Zerubbabel and Jeshua, supported by the prophets Haggai and Zechariah, again resumed the work, and would not cease. though cautioned by the Persian governor of Judæa. On the matter coming before Darius Hystaspis, and the Jews reminding him of the permission given by Cyrus, he decided in their favour, and also ordered that the expenses of the work should be defrayed out of the public revenue (Ezra vi. 8). In the sixth year of the reign of Darius the temple was finished, when they kept the Feast of Dedication with great joy, and next celebrated the Passover (Ezra vi. 15, 16, 19). Afterwards, in the seventh year of the second Artaxerxes Ezra, a descendant of Aaron, came up to Jerusalem, accompanied by a large number of Jews who had remained in Babylon. He was highly patronised by the king, who not only made him a large present in gold and silver, but published a decree enjoining all treasurers of Judæa speedily to do whatever Ezra should require of them; allowing him to collect money throughout the whole province of Babylon for the wants of the temple at Jerusalem; and also giving him full power to appoint magistrates in his country to judge the people (Ezra vii. viii.). At a later period, in the twentieth year of king Artaxerxes, Nehemiah, who was his cupbearer, obtained permission to proceed to Jerusalem, and to complete the rebuilding of the city and its wall, which he happily accomplished, despite of all the opposition which he received from the enemies of Israel (Neh. i. ii. iv. vi.). The city

was then capacious and large, but the people in it were few, and many houses lay still in ruins (Neh. vii. 4). At Jerusalem dwelt the rulers of the people and ' certain of the children of Judah and of the children of Benjamin;' but it was now determined that the rest of the people should cast lots to bring one of ten to the capital (Neh. xi. 1-4). All strangers. Samaritans, Ammonites, Moabites, &c., were removed, to keep the chosen people from pollution; ministers were appointed to the temple, and the service was performed according to the law of Moses (Ezra x.; Neh. viii. x. xii. xiii.). Of the Jerusalem thus by such great and long-continued exertions restored, very splendid prophecies were uttered by those prophets who flourished after the exile: the general purport of which was to describe the temple and city as destined to be glorified far beyond the former, by the advent of the long and eagerly expected Messiah, 'the desire of all nations' (Zech. ix. 9; xii. 10; xiii. 3; Hagg. ii. 6, 7; Mal. iii. 11).

Thus far the Old Testament has been our guide in the notices of Jerusalem. For what follows, down to its destruction by the Romans, we must draw chiefly upon Josephus, and the books of the Maccabees. The difficulty here, as before, is to separate what properly belongs to Jerusalem from that which belongs to the country at large. For as Jerusalem was invariably affected by whatever movement took place in the country of which it was the capital, its history might be made, and often has been made, the history of Palestine.

It is said by Josephus, that, when the dominion of this part of the world passed from the Persians to the Greeks, Alexander the Great advanced against Jerusalem to punish it for the fidelity to the Persians which it had manifested while he was engaged in the siege of Tyre. His hostile purposes, however, were averted by the appearance of the high-priest Jaddua at the head of a train of priests in their sacred vestments Alexander recognised in him the figure which in a dream had encouraged him to undertake the conquest of Asia. He therefore treated him with respect and reverence, spared the city against which his wrath had been kindled, and granted to the Jews high and important privileges. The historian adds that the high-priest failed not to apprise the conqueror of those prophecies in Daniel by which his successes had been predicted. The whole of this story is, however, liable to suspicion, from the absence of any notice of the circumstance in the histories of this campaign which we possess.

After the death of Alexander at Babylon (B.C. 324), Ptolemy surprised Jerusalem on the Sabbath-day, when the Jews would not fight, plundered the city, and carried away a great number of the inhabitants to Egypt, where, however, from the estimation in which the Jews of this period were held as citizens, important privileges were bestowed upon them. In the contests which afterwards followed for the possession of Syria (including Palestine), Jerusalem does not appear to have been directly injured. and was even spared when Ptolemy gave up Samaria, Acco, Joppa, and Gaza to pillage. The contest was ended by the treaty in B.C. 302, which annexed the whole of Palestine, together

2 H

with Arabia Petræa and Cœle-Syria, to Egypt. Under easy subjection to the Ptolemies the Jews remained in much tranquillity for more than a hundred years, in which the principal incident, as regards Jerusalem itself, was the visit which was paid to it, in B.C 245, by Ptolemy Euergetes, on his return from his victories in the East. He offered many sacrifices, and made magnificent presents to the temple. In the wars between Antiochus the Great and the kings of Egypt, from B.C. 221 to 197, Judæa could not fail to suffer severely; but we are not acquainted with any incident in which Jerusalem was principally concerned till the alleged visit of Ptolemy Philopator in B.C. 211. He offered sacrifices, and gave rich gifts to the temple, but, venturing to enter the sanctuary, in spite of the remonstrances of the high-priest, he was seized with a supernatural dread, and fled in terror from the place. It is said that on his return to Egypt he vented his rage on the Jews of Alexandria in a very barbarous manner [ALEXANDRIA]. But the whole story of his visit and its results rests upon the sole authority of the third book of Maccabees (chaps. i. and ii.), and is therefore not entitled to implicit credit. Towards the end of this war the Jews seemed to favour the cause of Antiochus; and after he had subdued the neighbouring country, they voluntarily tendered their submission, and rendered their assistance in expelling the Egyptian garrison from Mount Zion. For this conduct they were rewarded by many important privileges by Antiochus.

Under their new masters the Jews enjoyed for a time nearly as much tranquillity as under the generally benign and liberal government of the Ptolemies. But in B C. 176, Seleucus Philopator, hearing that great treasures were hoarded up in the temple, and being distressed for money to carry on his wars, sent his treasurer, Heliodorus, to bring away these treasures. But this personage is reported to have been so frightened and stricken by an apparition that he relinquished the attempt; and Seleucus left the Jews in the undisturbed enjoyment of their rights. His brother and successor, Antiochus Epiphanes, however, was of another mind. He took up the design of reducing them to a conformity of manners and religion with other nations; or, in other words, of abolishing those distinctive features which made the Jews a peculiar people, socially separated from all others. This design was odious to the great body of the people, although there were many among the higher classes who regarded it with favour. Of this way of thinking was Menelaus, whom Antiochus had made a high-priest, and who was expelled by the orthodox Jews with ignominy, in B.C. 169, when they heard the joyful news that Antiochus had been slain in Egypt. The rumour proved untrue, and Antiochus on his return punished them by plundering and profaning the temple. Worse evils befel them two years after: for Antiochus, out of humour at being compelled by the Romans to abandon his designs upon Egypt, sent his chief collector of tribute, Apollonius, with a detachment of 22,000 men, to vent his rage on Jerusalem. This person plundered the city, and razed its walls, with the stones of which he built a citadel that commanded the temple mount. A statue of Jupiter was set up

in the temple; the peculiar observances of the Jewish law were abolished; and a persecution was commenced against all who adhered to these observances, and refused to sacrifice to idols. Jerusalem was deserted by priests and people, and the daily sacrifice at the altar was entirely discontinued.

This led to the celebrated revolt of the Maccabees, who, after an arduous and sanguinary struggle, obtained possession of Jerusalem (B C. 163), and repaired and purified the temple, which was then dilapidated and deserted. The sacrifices were then recommenced, exactly three years after the temple had been dedicated to Jupiter Olympius. The castle, however, remained in the hands of the Syrians, and long proved a sore annoyance to the Jews; but at length, in B.C. 142, it was taken by Simon Maccabæus, who demolished it altogether, that it might not again be used against the Jews by their enemies. Simon then strengthened the fortifications of the mountain on which the temple stood, and built there a palace for himself, which was strengthened and enlarged by Herod the Great, who called it the castle of Antonia, under which name it makes a conspicuous figure in the Jewish wars with the Romans.

Of Jerusalem itself we find nothing of consequence till it was taken by Pompey in the summer of B.C. 63, and on the very day observed by the Jews as one of lamentation and fasting, in commemoration of the conquest of Jerusalem by Nebuchadnezzar. Twelve thousand Jews were massacred in the temple courts, including many priests, who died at the very altar rather than suspend the sacred rites. On this occasion Pompey, attended by his generals, went into the temple and viewed the sanctuary; but he left untouched all its treasures and sacred things, while the walls of the city itself were demolished. From this time the Jews are to be considered as under the dominion of the Romans. The treasures which Pompey had spared were seized a few years after (B.C. 51) by Crassus. In the year B.C. 43, the walls of the city, which Pompey had demolished, were rebuilt by Antipater, the father of that Herod the Great under whom Jerusalem was destined to assume the new and more magnificent aspect which it bore in the time of Christ, and which constituted the Jerusalem which Josephus describes. The temple itself was taken down and rebuilt by Herod the Great, with a magnificence exceeding that of Solomon's (Mark xiii. 1; John ii. 20; see TEMPLE). It was in the courts of the temple as thus rebuilt, and in the streets of the city as thus improved, that the Saviour of men walked up and down. Here he taught, here he wrought miracles, here he suffered; and this was the temple whose 'goodly stones' the apostle admired (Mark xiii. 1), and of which he foretold that ere the existing generation had passed away not one stone should be left upon another.

Jerusalem seems to have been raised to this greatness, as if to enhance the misery of its overthrow. So soon as the Jews had set the seal to their formal rejection of Christ, by putting him to death, and invoking the responsibility of his blood upon the heads of themselves and of their children (Matt. xxvii. 25), its doom went forth. After having been the scene of horrors without example, it was, in A.D. 70, abandoned to the Romans, who razed the city and temple to the ground, leaving only three of the towers and a part of the western wall to show how strong a place the Roman arms had overthrown. Since then the holy city has lain at the mercy of the Gentiles, and will so remain 'until the times of the Gentiles are fulfilled.'

MODERN HISTORY.—The destruction of Jerusalem by the Romans did not cause the site to be utterly forsaken: but for a considerable period there is no mention of it in history. Up to A.D. 131 the Jews remained tolerably quiet. The then emperor, Aarian, among other measures of precaution, ordered Jerusalem to be rebuilt as a fortified place wherewith to keep in check the whole Jewish population. The works had made some progress, when the Jews, unable to endure the idea that their holy city should be occupied by foreigners, and that strange gods should be set up within it, broke out into open rebellion under the notorious Barchochebas, who claimed to be the Messiah. His success was at first very great; but he was crushed before the tremendous power of the Romans, so soon as it could be brought to bear upon him: and a war scarcely inferior in horror to that under Vespasian and Titus was, like it, brought to a close by the capture of Jerusalem, of which the Jews had obtained possession. This was in A.D. 135, from which period the final dispersion of the Jews has been often dated. The Romans then finished the city according to their first intention. It was made a Roman colony, inhabited wholly by foreigners, the Jews being forbidden to approach it on pain of death: a temple to Jupiter Capitolinus was erected on Mount Moriah, and the old name of Jerusalem was sought to be supplanted by that of Ælia Capitolina, conferred upon it in honour of the emperor, Ælius Adrianus, and Jupiter Capitolinus. This name was retained for some time by the Mohammedans; and it was not till after they recovered the city from the Crusaders that it became generally known among them by the name of El-Khuds—the holy—which it still bears.

From the rebuilding by Adrian the history of Jerusalem is almost a blank till the time of Constantine, when its history, as a place of extreme solicitude and interest to the Christian church, properly begins. Pilgrimages to the Holy City now became common and popular. Such a pilgrimage was undertaken in A.D. 326 by the emperor's mother Helena, then in the 80th year of her age, who built churches on the alleged site of the nativity at Bethlehem, and of the resurrection on the Mount of Olives. This example may probably have excited her son to the discovery of the site of the holy sepulchre, and to the erection of a church thereon. He removed the temple of Venus, with which, in studied insult, the site had been encumbered. The holy sepulchre was then purified, and a magnificent church was, by his order, built over and around the sacred spot. This temple was completed and dedicated with great solemnity in A.D. 335. There is no doubt that the spot thus singled out is the same which has ever since been regarded as the place in which Christ was entombed, but the correctness of the identification then made has been of late years much disputed.

By Constantine the edict, excluding the Jews from the city of their fathers' sepulchres, was so far repealed that they were allowed to enter it once a-year to wail over the desolation of 'the holy and beautiful house' in which their fathers worshipped God. When the nephew of Constantine, the Emperor Julian, abandoned Christianity for the old Paganism, he endeavoured, as a matter of policy, to conciliate the Jews. He allowed them free access to the city, and permitted them to rebuild their temple. They accordingly began to lay the foundations in A.D. 362; but the speedy death of the emperor probably occasioned that abandonment of the attempt which contemporary writers ascribe to supernatural hinderances. The edicts seem then to have been renewed which excluded the Jews from the city, except on the day of annual wailing.

In the following centuries the roads to Zion were thronged with pilgrims from all parts of Christendom. After much struggle of conflicting dignities, the 'holy city' was, in A.D. 451, declared a patriarchate by the council of Chalcedon. In the next century it found a second Constantine in Justinian, who ascended the throne A.D. 527. He repaired and enriched the former structures, and built upon Mount Moriah a magnificent church to the Virgin, as a memorial of the persecution of Jesus in the temple.

In A.D. 614 the Persians took it by storm, and slew thousands of the inhabitants, and inflicted much injury on the buildings.

Their inroad was speedily repaired. But in A.D. 636 it fell into the hands of a more formidable enemy, the Khalif Omar. By his orders the magnificent mosque which still bears his name was built upon Mount Moriah, upon the site of the Jewish temple.

Jerusalem remained in possession of the Arabians, and was occasionally visited by Christian pilgrims from Europe, till towards the year 1000, when a general belief that the second coming of the Saviour was near at hand drew pilgrims in unwonted crowds to the Holy Land. The sight, by such large numbers, of the holy place in the hands of infidels, the exaction of tribute by the Moslem government, and the insults to which the pilgrims, often of the highest rank, were exposed from the Moslem rabble, excited an extraordinary ferment in Europe, and led to those remarkable expeditions for recovering the Holy Sepulchre from the Mohammedans, which, under the name of the Crusades, will always fill a most important and curious chapter in the history of the world.

On the 17th of June, 1099, the Crusaders, under Godfrey of Bouillon, appeared before Jerusalem, which was at that time in possession of the Fatemite khalifs of Egypt.

After a siege of forty days the holy city was taken by storm on the 15th day of July; and a dreadful massacre of the Moslem inhabitants followed, without distinction of age or sex. As soon as order was restored, and the city cleared of the dead, a regular government was established by the election of Godfrey as king of Jerusalem. The Christians kept possession of Jerusalem eighty-eight years. During this long period they appear to have erected several churches and many convents. Of the latter few, if any, traces remain; and of the former, save one or two ruins, the church of the holy sepulchre, which they rebuilt, is the only memorial which attests the existence of the Christian kingdom of Jerusalem. In A.D. 1187 the holy city was wrested from the hands of the Christians by the Sultan Saladin. From that time to the present day Jerusalem has remained, with slight interruption, in the hands of the Moslems. On the threatened siege by Richard of England in 1192, Saladin took great pains in strengthening its defences. New walls and bulwarks were erected, and deep trenches cut, and in six months the town was stronger than it ever had been, and the works had the firmness and solidity of a rock. But in A.D. 1219 the Sultan Melek el-Moaddin of Damascus, who then had possession of Jerusalem, ordered all the walls and towers to be demolished, except the citadel and the enclosure of the mosque, lest the Franks should again become masters of the city and find it a place of strength. In this defenceless state Jerusalem continued till it was delivered over to the Christians in consequence of a treaty with the emperor Frederick II., in A.D. 1229, with the understanding that the walls should not be rebuilt. Yet ten years later (A.D. 1239) the barons and knights of Jerusalem began to build the walls anew, and to erect a strong fortress on the west of the city. But the works were interrupted by the emir David of Kerek, who seized the city, strangled the Christian inhabitants, and cast down the newly erected walls and fortress. Four years after, however (A.D. 1243), Jerusalem was again made over to the Christians without any restriction, and the works appear to have been restored and completed; for they are mentioned as existing when the city was stormed by the wild Kharismian hordes in the following year; shortly after which the city reverted for the last time into the hands of its Mohammedan masters, who have kept it to the present day.

From this time Jerusalem appears to have sunk very much in political and military importance; and it is scarcely named in the history of the Memluk sultans who reigned over Egypt and the greater part of Syria in the fourteenth and fifteenth centuries. At length, with the rest of Syria and Egypt, it passed under the sway of the Turkish sultan Selim I., who paid a hasty visit to the holy land from Damascus after his return from Egypt. From that time Jerusalem has formed a part of the Ottoman empire, and during this period has been subject to few vicissitudes; its history is accordingly barren of incident. The present walls of the city were erected by Suleiman the Magnificent, the successor of Selim, in A.D. 1542, as is attested by an inscription over the Jaffa gate. So lately as A.D. 1808, the church of the holy sepulchre was partially consumed by fire; but the damage was repaired with great labour and expense by September, 1810, and the traveller now finds in this imposing fabric no traces of the recent calamity.

In A.D. 1832 Jerusalem became subject to Mohammed Ali, the pasha of Egypt, the holy city opening its gates to him without a siege. During the great insurrection in the districts of Jerusalem and Nabulus, in 1834, the insurgents seized upon Jerusalem, and held possession of it for a time; but by the vigorous operations of the government, order was soon restored, and the city reverted quietly to its allegiance on the approach of Ibrahim Pasha with his troops. In 1841 Mohammed Ali was deprived of all his Syrian possessions by European interference, and Jerusalem was again subjected to the Turkish government, under which it now remains. It is not, perhaps, the happier for the change. The only subsequent event of interest has been the establishment of a Protestant bishopric at Jerusalem by the English and Prussian governments, and the erection upon Mount Zion of a church, calculated to hold 500 persons, for the celebration of divine worship according to the ritual of the English church.

GENERAL TOPOGRAPHY.—Jerusalem lies near the summit of a broad mountain-ridge, extending, without interruption, from the plain of Esdraelon to a line drawn between the south end of the Dead Sea and the south-east corner of the Mediterranean; or, more properly, perhaps, it may be regarded as extending as far south as to Jebel Aràif in the Desert, where it sinks down at once to the level of the great western plateau. This tract, which is everywhere not less than from 20 to 25 geographical miles in breadth, forms the precipitous western wall of the great valley of the Jordan and the Dead Sea, and is everywhere rocky, uneven, and mountainous; and is, moreover, cut up by deep valleys which run east or west on either side towards the Jordan or the Mediterranean. The line of division, or watershed, between the waters of these valleys, follows for the most part the height of land along the ridge; yet not so but that the heads of the valleys, which run off in different directions, often interlap for a considerable distance. Thus, for example, a valley which descends to the Jordan often has its head a mile or two westward of the commencement of other valleys which run to the western sea.

From the great plain of Esdraelon onwards toward the south, the mountainous country rises gradually, forming the tract anciently known as the mountains of Ephraim and Judah; until, in the vicinity of Hebron, it attains an elevation of nearly 3000 Paris feet above the level of the Mediterranean Sea. Further north, on a line drawn from the north end of the Dead Sea towards the true west, the ridge has an elevation of only about 2500 Paris feet; and here, close upon the watershed, lies the city of Jerusalem. Its mean geographical position is in lat. 31° 46′ 43″ N., and long. 35° 13′ E. from Greenwich.

The surface of the elevated promontory, on which the city stands, slopes somewhat steeply towards the east, terminating on the brink of the valley of Jehoshaphat. From the northern part, near the present Damascus gate, a depression or shallow wady runs in a southern direction, having on the west the ancient hills of Akra and Zion, and on the east the lower ones of Bezetha and Moriah. Between the hills of Akra and Zion another depression or shallow wady (still easy to be traced) comes down from near the Jaffa gate, and joins the former. It then continues obliquely down the slope, but with a deeper bed, in a southern direction, quite to the pool of Siloam and the valley of Jehoshaphat. This is the ancient Tyropœon. West of its lower part Zion rises loftily, lying mostly without the modern city; while on the east of the

Tyropœon and the valley first mentioned lie Bezetha, Moriah, and Ophel, the last a long and comparatively narrow ridge, also outside of the modern city, and terminating in a rocky point over the pool of Siloam. These three last hills may strictly be taken as only parts of one and the same ridge. The breadth of the whole site of Jerusalem, from the brow of the valley of Hinnom, near the Jaffa gate, to the brink of the valley of Jehoshaphat, is about 1020 yards, or nearly half a geographical mile.

The country around Jerusalem is all of limestone formation, and not particularly fertile. The rocks everywhere come out above the surface, which in many parts is also thickly strewed with loose stones; and the aspect of the whole region is barren and dreary; yet the olive thrives here abundantly, and fields of grain are seen in the valleys and level places, but they are less productive than in the region of Hebron and Nabulus. Neither vineyards nor fig-trees flourish on the high ground around the city, though the latter are found in the gardens below Siloam, and very frequently in the vicinity of Bethlehem.

ANCIENT JERUSALEM.—Every reader of Scripture feels a natural anxiety to form some notion of the appearance and condition of Jerusalem, as it existed in the time of Jesus, or rather as it stood before its destruction by the Romans. There are unusual difficulties in the way of satisfying this desire, although it need not be left altogether ungratified. The principal sources of these difficulties have been indicated by different travellers, and by none more forcibly than by Richardson (*Travels*, ii. 251). ' It is a tantalizing circumstance, however, for the traveller who wishes to recognise in his walks the site of particular buildings, or the scenes of memorable events, that the greater part of the objects mentioned in the description, both of the inspired and of the Jewish historian, are entirely razed from their foundation, without leaving a single trace or name behind to point out where they stood. Not an ancient tower, or gate, or wall, or hardly even a stone, remains. The foundations are not only broken up, but every fragment of which they were composed is swept away, and the spectator looks upon the bare rock with hardly a sprinkling of earth to point out her gardens of pleasure, or groves of idolatrous devotion.'

To the difficulties originating in these causes may be added those which arise from the many ambiguities in the description left by Josephus, the only one which we possess, and which must form the ground-work of most of our notices respecting the ancient city. There are indeed some manifest errors in his account, which the critical reader is able to detect without having the means to rectify.

In describing Jerusalem as it stood just before its destruction by the Romans, Josephus states that the city was built upon two hills, between which lay the valley Tyropœon (Cheesemonger's Valley), to which the buildings on both hills came down. This valley extended to the fountain of Siloam. The hill on which the upper town stood was much higher than the other, and straighter in its extent. On account of its fortifications, David called it the Fortress or Castle; but in the time of Josephus it was known by the name of the Upper Market. The other hill, on

which was situated the lower town, was called Akra. It was in the form of a horseshoe or crescent. Opposite to Akra was a third, and naturally lower hill (Moriah), on which the temple was built; and between this and Akra was originally a broad valley, which the inhabitants of Jerusalem filled up in the time of Simon Maccabæus for the purpose of connecting the town with the temple. At the same time they lowered the hill Akra, so as to make the temple rise above it. Both the hills on which the upper and lower towns stood were externally surrounded by deep valleys, and here there was no approach because of the precipices on every side.

The single wall which enclosed that part of the city skirted by precipitous valleys began at the tower of Hippicus. On the west it extended (southward) to a place called Bethso, and the gate of the Essenes; thence it kept along on the south to a point over against Siloam; and thence on the east was carried along by Solomon's Pool and Ophla (Ophel), till it terminated at the eastern portico of the temple. Of the triple walls, we are told that the first and oldest of these began at the tower of Hippicus, on the northern part, and, extending (along the northern brow of Zion) to the Xystus, afterwards terminated at the western portico of the temple. The second wall began at the gate of Gennath (apparently near Hippicus), and, encircling only the northern part of the city, extended to the castle of Antonia at the north-west corner of the area of the temple. The third wall was built by Agrippa at a later period : it also had its beginning at the tower of Hippicus, ran northward as far as the tower Psephinos; and thence sweeping round towards the north-east by east, it turned afterwards towards the south, and was joined to the ancient wall at or in the valley of the Kidron. This wall enclosed the hill Bezetha. From other passages we learn that the Xystus, named in the above descriptions, was an open place in the extreme part of the upper city, where the people sometimes assembled, and that a bridge connected it with the temple.

Dr. Robinson, in comparing the information derived from Josephus with his own more detailed account, declares that the main features depicted by the Jewish historian may still be recognised. ' True,' he says, ' the valley of the Tyropœon, and that between Akra and Moriah, have been greatly filled up with the rubbish accumulated from the repeated desolations of nearly eighteen centuries. Yet they are still distinctly to be traced · the hills of Zion, Akra, Moriah, and Bezetha, are not to be mistaken; while the deep valleys of the Kidron, and of Hinnom, and the Mount of Olives, are permanent natural features, too prominent and gigantic indeed to be forgotten, or to undergo any perceptible change.'

The details embraced in this general notice must be more particularly examined in connection with modern observations; for it is to be remembered that the chief or only value of these observations consists in the light which they throw on the ancient condition and history of the site.

The first or most ancient wall appears to have enclosed the whole of Mount Zion. The greater part of it, therefore, must have formed the exterior and sole wall on the south, overlooking the deep valleys below Mount Zion; and the northern part evidently passed from the tower of Hippicus on the west side, along the northern brow of Zion, and across the valley, to the western side of the temple area. It probably nearly coincided with the ancient wall which existed before the time of David. and which enabled the Jebusites to maintain themselves in possession of the upper city, long after the lower city had been in the hands of the Israelites. Mount Zion is now unwalled, and is excluded from the modern city. No trace of this wall can now be perceived, but by digging through the rubbish the foundations might perhaps be discovered.

The account given by Josephus, of the second wall, is very short and unsatisfactory. It seems to have enclosed the whole of the lower city, or Akra, excepting that part of the eastern side of it which fronted the Temple area on Mount Moriah, and the southern side, towards the valley which separated the lower from the upper city. In short, it was a continuation of the external wall, so far as necessary, on the west and north, and on so much of the east as was not already protected by the strong wall of the Temple area.

Although these were the only walls that existed in the time of our Saviour, we are not to infer that the habitable city was confined within their limits. On the contrary, it was because the city had extended northward far beyond the second wall that a third was built to cover the defenceless suburb: and there is no reason to doubt that this unprotected suburb, called Bezetha, existed in the time of Christ. This wall is described as having also begun at the tower of Hippicus: it ran northward as far as to the tower Psephinos, then passed down opposite the sepulchre of Helena (queen of Adiabene), and, being carried along through the royal sepulchres, turned at the corner tower by the Fullers' monument, and ended by making a junction with the ancient wall at the valley of the Kidron. It was begun ten or twelve years after our Lord's crucifixion by the elder Herod Agrippa, who desisted from completing it for fear of offending the Emperor Claudius. But the design was afterwards taken up and completed by the Jews themselves, although on a scale of less strength and magnificence. Dr. Robinson thinks that he discovered some traces of this wall, which are described in his great work.

The same writer thinks that the wall of the new city, the Ælia of Adrian, nearly coincided with that of the present Jerusalem.

We know from Josephus that the circumference of the ancient city was 33 stadia, equivalent to nearly three and a half geographical miles. The circumference of the present walls does not exceed two and a half geographical miles; but the extent of Mount Zion, now without the walls, and the tract on the north formerly enclosed, or partly so, by the third wall, sufficiently account for the difference.

The history of the modern walls has already been given in the sketch of the modern history of the city. The present walls have a solid and formidable appearance, especially when cursorily observed from without; and they are strength-

ened, or rather ornamented, with towers and battlements after the Saracenic style. They are built of limestone, the stones being not commonly more than a foot or 15 inches square. The height varies with the various elevations of the ground. The lower parts are probably about 25 feet high, while in more exposed localities, where the ravines contribute less to the security of the city, they have an elevation of 60 or 70 feet.

Much uncertainty exists respecting the ancient gates of Jerusalem. Many gates are named in Scripture; and it has been objected that they are more in number than a town of the size of Jerusalem could require—especially as they all occur within the extent embraced by the first and second walls, the third not then existing. It has, therefore, been suggested as more than probable that some of these gates were within the city, in the walls which separated the town from the temple, and the upper town from the lower, in which gates certainly existed. On the other hand, considering the circumstances under which the wall was rebuilt in the time of Nehemiah, it is difficult to suppose that more than the outer wall was then constructed, and certainly it was in the wall then built that the ten or twelve gates mentioned by Nehemiah occur. But these may be considerably reduced by supposing that two or more of the names mentioned were applied to the same gate. If this view of the matter be taken, no better distribution of these gates can be given than that suggested by Raumer.

A. On the north side.

1. The *Old Gate*, probably at the north-east corner (Neh. iii. 6; xii. 39).

2. The *Gate of Ephraim* or *Benjamin* (Jer. xxxviii. 7; xxxvii. 13; Neh. xii. 9; 2 Chron. xxv. 23). This gate doubtless derived its names from its leading to the territory of Ephraim and Benjamin; and Dr. Robinson supposes it may possibly be represented by some traces of ruins which he found on the site of the present gate of Damascus.

3. The *Corner-gate*, 300 cubits from the former, and apparently at the north-west corner (2 Chron. xxv. 9; 2 Kings xiv. 13; Zech. xiv. 10). Probably the *Gate of the Furnaces* is the same (Neh. iii. 2; xii. 38).

B. On the west side.

4. The *Valley-gate*, over against the Dragon-fountain of Gihon (Neh. ii. 13; iii. 13; 2 Chron. xxxvi. 9). It was probably about the north-west corner of Zion, where there appears to have been always a gate, and Dr. Robinson supposes it to be the same with the Gennath of Josephus.

c. On the south side.

5. The *Dung-gate*, perhaps the same as Josephus's Gate of the Essenes (Neh. ii. 13; xii. 31). It was 1000 cubits from the valley gate (Neh. iii. 14), and the dragon-well was between them (Neh. ii 13). This gate is probably also identical with 'the gate between two walls' (2 Kings xxv. 4; Jer. xxxix. 4; Lam. ii. 7).

6. The *Gate of the Fountain*, to the south-east (Neh. ii. 14; iii. 15); the gate of the fountain near the king's pool (Neh. ii. 14), the gate of the fountain near 'the pool of Siloah by the king's garden' (Neh. iii. 15). The same gate is probably denoted in all these instances, and the pools seem to have been also the same. It is also

possible that this fountain-gate was the same otherwise distinguished as the brick-gate (or potter's gate), leading to the valley of Hinnom (Jer. xix. 2, where the Auth. Ver. has 'east-gate').

D. On the east side.

7. The *Water-gate* (Neh. iii. 26).

8. The *Prison-gate*, otherwise the *Horse-gate*, near the temple (Neh. iii. 28 ; xii. 39, 40).

9. The *Sheep-gate*, probably near the sheep-pool (Neh. iii. 1-32 ; xii. 29).

10. The *Fish-gate* was quite at the north-east (Neh. iii. 3 ; xii. 39 ; Zeph. i. 10 ; 2 Chron. xxxiii. 14).

In the middle ages there appear to have been two gates on each side of the city, making eight in all; and this number, being only two short of those assigned in the above estimate to the ancient Jerusalem, seems to vindicate that estimate from the objections which have been urged against it.

On the west side were two gates, of which the principal was the Gate of David, often mentioned by the writers on the Crusades. It corresponds to the present Jaffa gate. The other was the gate of the Fullers' Field, so called from Isa. vii. 3. There is no trace of it in the present wall.

On the north there were also two gates; and all the middle-age writers speak of the principal of them as the gate of St. Stephen, from the notion that the death of the protomartyr took place near it. This was also called the gate of Ephraim, in reference to its probable ancient name. The present gate of St. Stephen is on the *east* of the city, and the scene of the martyrdom is now placed near it; but there is no account of the change. Farther east was the gate of Benjamin, corresponding apparently to what is now called the gate of Herod.

On the east there seem to have been at least two gates. The northernmost is described by Adamnanus as a small portal leading down to the valley of Jehoshaphat. It was called the gate of Jehoshaphat, from the valley to which it led. It seems to be represented by the present gate of St. Stephen. The present gate of St. Stephen has four lions sculptured over it on the outside, which, as well as the architecture, show that it existed before the present walls. The other gate is the famous Golden Gate in the eastern wall of the temple area. This gate is, from its architecture, obviously of Roman origin, and is conjectured to have belonged to the enclosure of the temple of Jupiter which was built by Adrian upon Mount Moriah. The exterior is now walled up; but being double, the interior forms within the area a recess, which is used for prayer by the Moslem worshipper.

On the south side were also two gates. The easternmost is now called by the Franks the Dung-gate. The earliest mention of this gate is by Brocard, about A.D. 1283, who regards it as the ancient Water-gate. Farther west, between the eastern brow of Zion and the gate of David, the Crusaders found a gate which they call the Gate of Zion, corresponding to one which now bears the same name.

Of the seven gates mentioned as still existing, three, the Dung Gate, the Golden Gate, and Herod's Gate, are closed. Thus there are only four gates now in use, one on each side of the town,

all of which have been enumerated. St. Stephen's, on the east, leads to the Mount of Olives, Bethany, and Jericho. Zion Gate, on the south side of the city, connects the populous quarter around the Armenian convent with that part of Mount Zion which is outside the walls, and which is much resorted to as being the great field of Christian burial, as well as for its traditionary sanctity as the site of David's tomb, the house of Caiaphas, house of Mary, &c. The Jaffa Gate, on the west, is the termination of the important routes from Jaffa, Bethlehem, and Hebron. The Damascus Gate, on the north, is also planted in a vale, which in every age of Jerusalem must have been a great public way, and the easiest approach from Samaria and Galilee.

The towers of Jerusalem are often mentioned in Scripture and in Josephus. Most of the towers mentioned by Josephus were erected by Herod the Great, and were, consequently, standing in the time of Christ. It was on these, therefore, that his eyes often rested when he approached Jerusalem, or viewed its walls and towers from the Mount of Olives. Of all these towers, the most important is that of Hippicus, which Josephus, as we have already seen, assumed as the starting-point in his description of all the walls of the city. Herod gave to it the name of a friend who was slain in battle. It was a quadrangular structure, 25 cubits on each side, and built up entirely solid to the height of 30 cubits. The altitude of the whole tower was 80 cubits. Dr. Robinson has shown that this tower should be sought at the north-west corner of the upper city, or Mount Zion. This part, a little to the south of the Jaffa Gate, is now occupied by the citadel. It is an irregular assemblage of square towers, surrounded on the inner side towards the city by a low wall, and having on the outer or west side a deep fosse. The towers which rise from the brink of the fosse are protected on that side by a low sloping bulwark or buttress, which rises from the bottom of the trench at an angle of forty-five degrees. This part bears evident marks of antiquity, and Dr. Robinson is inclined to ascribe these massive outworks to the time of the rebuilding and fortifying of the city by Adrian. The north-eastern tower bears among the Franks the name of the Tower of David, while they sometimes give to the whole fortress the name of the Castle of David. Taking all the circumstances into account, Dr. Robinson thinks that the antique lower portion of this tower is in all probability a remnant of the tower of Hippicus, which, as Josephus states, was left standing by Titus when he destroyed the city.

Josephus describes two other towers—those of Phasaelus and Mariamne, both built by Herod, one of them being named after a friend, and the other after his favourite wife. They stood not far from Hippicus, upon the first or most ancient wall, which ran from the latter tower eastward, along the northern brow of Zion. Connected with these towers and Hippicus was the royal castle or palace of the first Herod, which was enclosed by this wall on the north, and on the other sides by a wall 30 cubits high. These were the three mighty towers which Titus left standing as monuments of the strength of the place which had yielded to his arms. But nothing now remains save the above-mentioned supposed remnant of the tower of Hippicus.

A fourth tower, called Psephinos, is mentioned by Josephus. It stood at the north-west corner of the third or exterior wall of the city. It did not, consequently, exist in the time of Christ, seeing that the wall itself was built by Herod Agrippa, to whom also the tower may be ascribed

The above are the only towers which the historian particularly mentions. But in describing the outer or third wall of Agrippa, he states that it had battlements of two cubits, and turrets of three cubits more: and as the wall was 20 cubits high, this would make the turrets of the height of 25 cubits, or nearly 38 feet. Many loftier and more substantial towers than these were erected on each of the walls at regulated distances, and furnished with every requisite for convenience or defence. Of those on the third or outer wall are enumerated ninety; on the middle or second wall, forty; and on the inner or ancient wall, sixty.

The temple was in all ages the great glory and principal public building of Jerusalem, as the heathen temple, church, or mosque, successively occupying the same site, has been ever since the Jewish temple was destroyed. That temple is reserved for a separate article [TEMPLE], and there are few other public edifices which require a particular description. Those most connected with Scripture history are the palace of Herod and the tower of Antonia. The former has already been noticed. In the time of Christ it was the residence of the Roman procurators while in Jerusalem; and as such provincial residences were called by the Romans *Prætoria*, this was the prætorium or judgment-hall of Pilate (Matt. xxvii. 27; Mark xv. 16; John xviii. 28). In front of the palace was the tribunal or 'judgment-seat,' where the procurator sat to hear and determine the causes; and where Pilate was seated when our Lord was brought before him. It was a raised pavement of mosaic work, called in the Hebrew *Gabbatha*, or 'an elevated place' [JUDG-MENT-HALL].

The tower or castle of Antonia stood on a steep rock adjoining the north-west corner of the temple. It has already been mentioned that it originated under the Maccabees, who resided in it. As improved by Herod, who gave it the name of Antonia, after his patron Mark Antony, this fortress had all the extent and appearance of a palace, being divided into apartments of every kind, with galleries and baths, and also broad halls or barracks for soldiers; so that, as having everything necessary within itself, it seemed a city, while in its magnificence it was a palace. At each of the four corners was a tower, one of which was 70 cubits high, and overlooked the whole temple with its courts. The fortress communicated with the cloisters of the temple by secret passages, through which the soldiers could enter and quell any tumults, which were always apprehended at the time of the great festivals. It was to a guard of these soldiers that Pilate referred the Jews as a 'watch' for the sepulchre of Christ. This tower was also 'the castle' into which St. Paul was carried when the Jews rose against him in the temple, and were about to kill him; and where he gave his able and manly ac-

count of his conversion and conduct (Act xxi. 27-40; xxii.). This tower was, in fact, the citadel of Jerusalem.

In the narratives of all the sieges which Jerusalem has suffered, we never read of the besieged suffering from thirst, although driven to the most dreadful extremities and resources by hunger, while the besiegers are frequently described as suffering greatly from want of water, and as being obliged to fetch it from a great distance. This is a very singular circumstance, and is perhaps only in part explained by reference to the system of preserving water in cisterns, as at this day in Jerusalem. There is, however, good ground to conclude that from very ancient times there has been under the temple an unfailing source of water, derived by secret and subterraneous channels from springs to the west of the town, and communicating by other subterraneous passages with the pool of Siloam and the fountain of the Virgin in the east of the town, whether they were within or without the walls of the town. The ordinary means taken by the inhabitants to secure a supply of water have been described under the article CISTERN.

MODERN JERUSALEM.—In proceeding to furnish a description of the present Jerusalem, we shall, for the most part, place ourselves under the guidance of Dr. Olin, whose account is not only the most recent, but is by far the most complete and satisfactory which has of late years been produced.

The general view of the city from the Mount of Olives is mentioned more or less by all travellers as that from which they derive their most distinct and abiding impression of Jerusalem.

The summit of the Mount of Olives is about half a mile east from the city, which it completely overlooks, every considerable edifice and almost every house being visible. The city seen from this point appears to be a regular inclined plain, sloping gently and uniformly from west to east, or towards the observer, and indented by a slight depression or shallow vale, running nearly through the centre in the same direction. The south-east corner of the quadrangle—for that may be assumed as the figure formed by the rocks—that which is nearest to the observer, is occupied by the mosque of Omar and its extensive and beautiful grounds. This is Mount Moriah, the site of Solomon's temple; and the ground embraced in the sacred enclosure, which conforms to that of the ancient temple, occupies about an eighth of the whole modern city. It is covered with green sward and planted sparingly with olive, cypress, and other trees, and it is certainly the most lovely feature of the town, whether we have reference to the splendid structures or the beautiful lawn spread out around them.

The south-west quarter, embracing that part of Mount Zion which is within the modern town, is to a great extent occupied by the Armenian convent, an enormous edifice, which is the only conspicuous object in this neighbourhood. The north-west is largely occupied by the Latin convent, another very extensive establishment. About midway between these two convents is the castle or citadel, close to the Bethlehem gate, already mentioned. The north-east quarter of Jerusalem is but partially built up, and it has more the aspect of a rambling agricultural village than that of a crowded city. The vacant spots here are green with gardens and olive-trees. There is another large vacant tract along the southern wall, and west of the Haram, also covered with verdure. Near the centre of the city also appear two or three green spots, which are small gardens. The church of the Holy Sepulchre is the only conspicuous edifice in this vicinity, and its domes are striking objects. There are no buildings which, either from their size or beauty, are likely to engage the attention. Eight or ten minarets mark the position of so many mosques in different parts of the town, but they are only noticed because of their elevation above the surrounding edifices. Upon the same principle the eye rests for a moment upon a great number of low domes, which form the roofs of the principal dwellings, and relieve the heavy uniformity of the flat plastered roofs which cover the greater mass of more humble habitations.

From the same commanding point of view a few olive and fig trees are seen in the lower part of the valley of Jehoshaphat, and scattered over the side of Olivet from its base to the summit. They are sprinkled yet more sparingly on the southern side of the city on Mounts Zion and Ophel. North of Jerusalem the olive plantations appear more numerous as well as thriving, and thus offer a grateful contrast to the sun-burnt fields and bare rocks which predominate in this landscape. The region west of the city appears to be destitute of trees. Fields of stunted wheat, yellow with the drought rather than white for the harvest, are seen on all sides of the town.

Jerusalem, as seen from Mount Olivet, is a plain inclining gently and equably to the East. Once enter its gates, however, and it is found to be full of inequalities. The passenger is always ascending or descending. There are no level streets, and little skill or labour has been employed to remove or diminish the inequalities which nature or time has produced. Houses are built upon mountains of rubbish, which are probably twenty, thirty, or fifty feet above the natural level, and the streets are constructed with the same disregard to convenience, with this difference, that some slight attention is paid to the possibility of carrying off surplus water. The latter are, without exception, narrow, seldom exceeding eight or ten feet in breadth. The houses often meet, and in some instances a building occupies both sides of the street, which runs under a succession of arches barely high enough to permit an equestrian to pass under them. A canopy of old mats or of plank is suspended over the principal streets when not arched. This custom had its origin, no doubt, in the heat of the climate, which is very intense in summer, and it gives a gloomy aspect to all the most thronged and lively parts of the city. These covered ways are often pervaded by currents of air when a perfect calm prevails in the street. The principal streets of Jerusalem run nearly at right angles to each other. Very few, if any, of them bear names among the native population. They are badly paved, being merely laid irregularly with raised stones, with a deep square channel, for beasts of burden, in the middle; but the steepness of the ground contributes to keep them cleaner than in most Oriental cities.

The houses of Jerusalem are substantially built of the limestone of which the whole of this part of Palestine is composed: not usually hewn, but broken into regular forms, and making a solid wall of very respectable appearance. For the most part there are no windows next to the street, and the few which exist for the purposes of light or ventilation are completely masked by casements and lattice-work. The apartments receive their light from the open courts within. The ground plot is usually surrounded by a high enclosure, commonly forming the walls of the house only, but sometimes embracing a small garden and some vacant ground. The rain-water which falls upon the pavement is carefully conducted, by means of gutters, into cisterns, where it is preserved for domestic uses. The people of Jerusalem rely chiefly upon these reservoirs for their supply of this indispensable article. Stone is employed in building for all the purposes to which it can possibly be applied, and Jerusalem is hardly more exposed to accidents by fire than a quarry or subterranean cavern. The floors, stairs, &c., are of stone, and the ceiling is usually formed by a coat of plaster laid upon the stones, which at the same time form the roof and the vaulted top of the room. Doors, sashes, and a few other appurtenances, are all that can usually be afforded of a material so expensive as wood. A large number of houses in Jerusalem are in a dilapidated and ruinous state.

Nothing of this would be suspected from the general appearance of the city as seen from the various commanding points without the walls, nor from anything that meets the eye in the streets. Few towns in the East offer a more imposing spectacle to the view of the approaching stranger. He is struck with the height and massiveness of the walls, which are kept in perfect repair, and naturally produce a favourable opinion of the wealth and comfort which they are designed to protect. Upon entering the gates, he is apt, after all that has been published about the solitude that reigns in the streets, to be surprised at meeting large numbers of people in the chief thoroughfares, almost without exception decently clad. A longer and more intimate acquaintance with Jerusalem, however, does not fail to correct this too favourable impression, and demonstrate the existence and general prevalence of the poverty and even wretchedness which must result in every country from oppression, from the absence of trade, and the utter stagnation of all branches of industry. Considerable activity is displayed in the bazaars, which are supplied scantily, like those of other Eastern towns, with provisions, tobacco, coarse cottons, and other articles of prime necessity. A considerable business is still done in beads, crosses, and other sacred trinkets, which are purchased to a vast amount by the pilgrims who annually throng the holy city. The support and even the existence of the considerable population of Jerusalem depend upon this transient patronage—a circumstance to which a great part of the prevailing poverty and degradation is justly ascribed. With the exception of some establishments for soap-making, a tannery, and a very few weavers of coarse cottons, there do not appear to be any manufacturers properly belonging to the place. Agriculture is almost equally wretched, and can only give employment to a few hundred people. The masses really seem to be without any regular employment. A considerable number, especially of the Jews, professedly live on charity Many Christian pilgrims annually find their way hither on similar resources, and the approaches to the holy places are thronged with beggars, who in piteous tones demand alms in the name of Christ and the Blessed Virgin. The general condition of the population is that of abject poverty. A few Turkish officials, ecclesiastical, civil, and military ; some remains of the old Mohammedan aristocracy—once powerful and rich, but now much impoverished and nearly extinct : together with a few tradesmen in easy circumstances, form almost the only exceptions to the prevailing indigence. There is not a single broker among the whole population, and not the smallest sum can be obtained on the best bills of exchange short of Jaffa or Beirout.

The number of the inhabitants of Jerusalem has been variously estimated by different travellers. The estimate lately given by Dr. Schulz, the Prussian consul at Jerusalem, is as follows :—

I. Mohammedans			5,000
II. Christians :—			
a. Greeks	2,000		
b. Roman Catholics	900		
c. Armenians	350		
d. Copts	100		
e. Syrians	20		
f. Abyssinians	20		
			——3,390
III. Jews :—			
a. Turkish subjects (*Sephardim*)	6,000		
b. Foreign (*ashkenazim*), namely,			
Polish, Russian, and German	1,100		
c. Karaites	20		
			——7,120
			15,510

The language most generally spoken among them is the Arabic. Schools are rare, and consequently facility in reading is not often met with. The general condition of the inhabitants has already been indicated.

The Turkish governor of the town holds the rank of Pasha, but is responsible to the Pasha of Beirout. The government is somewhat milder than before the period of the Egyptian dominion ; but it is said that the Jewish and Christian inhabitants at least have ample cause to regret the change of masters, and the American missionaries lament that change without reserve. Formerly there were in Palestine monks of the Benedictine and Augustine orders, and of those of St. Basil and St. Anthony ; but since 1304 there have been none but Franciscans, who have charge of the Latin convent and the holy places. They resided on Mount Zion till A.D. 1561, when the Turks allowed them the monastery of St. Salvador, which they now occupy. They had formerly a handsome revenue out of all Roman Catholic countries, but these sources have fallen off since the French revolution, and the establishment is said to be poor and deeply in debt. The expenses arise from the duty imposed upon the convent of entertaining pilgrims ; and the cost of maintaining the twenty convents belonging to the establishment of the Terra Santa is estimated at 40,000 Spanish dollars a-year. The convent contains fifty monks, half Italians and half

Spaniards. In it resides the Intendant or the Principal of all the convents, with the rank of abbot, and the title of Guardian of Mount Zion and Custos of the Holy Land. There is also a president or vicar, who takes the place of the guardian in case of absence or death. The procurator, who manages their temporal affairs, is always a Spaniard. A council, called Discretorium, composed of these officials and three other monks, has the general management of both spiritual and temporal matters.

There is a Greek patriarch of Jerusalem, but he usually resides at Constantinople, and is represented in the holy city by one or more vicars, who are bishops residing in the great convent near the Church of the Holy Sepulchre. In addition to thirteen monasteries in Jerusalem, they possess the convent of the Holy Cross, near Jerusalem, that of St. Helena, between Jerusalem and Bethlehem, and that of St. John, between Jerusalem and the Dead Sea. All the monks of the convents are foreigners. The Christians of the Greek rite who are not monks are all native Arabs, with their native priests, who are allowed to perform the church services in their mother tongue—the Arabic.

The Armenians in Jerusalem have a patriarch, with three convents and 100 monks. They have also convents at Bethlehem, Ramleh, and Jaffa. Few of the Armenians are natives : they are mostly merchants, and among the wealthiest inhabitants of the place ; and their convent in Jerusalem is deemed the richest in the Levant. Their church of St. James upon Mount Zion is very showy in its decorations, but void of taste. The Coptic Christians at Jerusalem are only some monks residing in the convent of Es-Sultan, on the north side of the pool of Hezekiah. There is also a convent of the Abyssinians, and one belonging to the Jacobite Syrians.

The Jews inhabit a distinct quarter of the town between Mount Zion and Mount Moriah. This is the worst and dirtiest part of the holy city, and that in which the plague never fails to make its first appearance. Few of the Jerusalem Jews are natives ; and most of them come from foreign parts to die in the city of their fathers' sepulchres. They are for the most part wretchedly poor, and depend in a great degree for their subsistence upon the contributions of their brethren in different countries. The expectation of support from the annual European contributions leads many of them to live in idleness. Hence there are in Jerusalem 500 acknowledged paupers, and 500 more who receive charity in a quiet way. Many are so poor that, if not relieved, they would not stand out the winter season. A few are shopkeepers, and a few more hawkers, and a very few are operatives. None of them are agriculturists—not a single Jew cultivates the soil of his fathers.

JESH'UA, or JOSHUA, son of Jozedech, and high-priest of the Jews when they returned, under Zerubbabel, from the Babylonian exile (B.C. 536). He was, doubtless, born during the exile. His presence and exhortations greatly promoted the rebuilding of the city and temple. The altar of the latter being first erected, enabled him to sanctify their labour by the religious ceremonies and offerings which the law required. Jeshua joined with Zerubbabel in opposing the machinations of the Samaritans (Ezra iv. 3) ; and he was not found wanting in zeal when the works, after having been interrupted, were resumed in the second year of Darius Hystaspis (Ezra v. 2 ; Hagg. i. 12). Several of the prophet Haggai's utterances are addressed to Jeshua (Hagg. i. 1 ; ii. 2), and his name occurs in two of the symbolical prophecies of Zechariah (iii. 1-10 ; vi. 11-15). In the first of these passages Jeshua, as pontiff, represents the Jewish people covered at first with the garb of slaves, and afterwards with the new and glorious vestures of deliverance. In the second he wears for a moment crowns of silver and gold, as symbols of the sacerdotal and regal crowns of Israel, which were to be united on the head of the Messiah.

JESH'URUN, a name poetically applied to Israel in Deut. xxxii. 15 ; xxxiii. 5, 26 ; Isa. xliv. 2. It has been very variously understood, but it is generally agreed to be a poetical diminutive expressive of affection. It is derived from a word signifying *to be straight, right, upright, righteous.* In this character, as entirely upright (for the termination is intensive), Jehovah recognises his people in consideration of their covenant relation to him, whereby, while they observed the terms of that covenant, they stood legally righteous before him and clean in his sight. It is in this sense that the ancient kings are said to have done 'that which was right' in the eyes of Jehovah.

JES'SE (*firm*), a descendant of Obed, the son of Boaz and Ruth. He was the father of eight sons from the youngest of whom, David, is reflected all the distinction which belongs to the name. He seems to have been a person of some note and substance at Bethlehem, his property being chiefly in sheep. It would seem, from 1 Sam. xvi. 10, that he must have been aware of the high destinies which awaited his son ; but it is doubtful if he ever lived to see them realized. The last historical mention of Jesse is in relation to the asylum which David procured for him with the king of Moab (1 Sam. xxii. 3).

JE'SUS CHRIST, the ordinary designation of the incarnate Son of God, and Saviour of mankind. This double designation is not, like Simon Peter, John Mark, Joses Barnabas, composed of a name and a surname, but, like John the Baptist, Simon Magus, Par-Jesus Elymas, of a proper name, and an official title. JESUS was our Lord's proper name, just as Peter, James, and John were the proper names of three of his disciples. The name seems not to have been an uncommon one among the Jews (Acts xiii. 6 ; Col. iv. 11). To distinguish our Lord from others bearing the name, he was termed Jesus of Nazareth (John xviii. 7, &c.), and Jesus the son of Joseph (John vi. 42, &c.).

The conferring of this name on our Lord was not the result of accident, or of the ordinary course of things, there being ' none of his kindred,' so far as we can trace from the two genealogies, ' called by that name' (Luke i. 61). It was the consequence of a twofold miraculous interposition. The angel who announced to his virgin mother that she was to be ' the most honoured of women,' in giving birth to the Son of God and the Saviour of men, intimated also to her the name by which the holy child was to be called : ' Thou shalt call his name Jesus' (Luke

i. 31). And it was probably the same heavenly messenger who appeared to Joseph, and, to remove his suspicions and quiet his fears, said to him, ' That which is conceived in thy wife Mary is of the Holy Ghost, and she shall bring forth a son, and thou shalt call his name Jesus' (Matt. i. 20, 21). The pious pair were ' not disobedient to the heavenly vision.' ' When eight days were accomplished for the circumcising of the child, his name was called Jesus, which was so named of the angel before he was conceived in the womb' (Luke ii. 21).

The *precise* import of the name has been a subject of doubt and debate among interpreters. As to its *general* meaning there is all but an unanimous concurrence. It was intended to denote that he who bore it was to be a Deliverer or Saviour. But while some interpreters hold that it simply signifies ' he shall save,' others hold that it is a compound word equivalent to ' The Salvation of the Lord,' or ' The Lord the Saviour.' It is not a matter of vital importance. The ' name of Jesus' (Phil. ii. 10) is not the name Jesus, but ' the name above every name' (ver. 9), i. e. the supreme dignity and authority with which the Father has invested Jesus Christ, as the reward of his disinterested exertions in the cause of the divine glory and human happiness ; and the bowing ' at the name of Jesus' is obviously not an external mark of homage when the name Jesus is pronounced, but the inward sense of awe and submission to him who is raised to a station so exalted.

CHRIST. This is not, strictly speaking, a proper name, or an official title. Jesus Christ, or rather, as it generally ought to be rendered, Jesus *the* Christ, is a mode of expression of the same kind as John the Baptist, or Baptiser. In consequence of not adverting to this, the force and even the meaning of many passages of Scripture are misapprehended. When it is stated that Paul asserted, ' This Jesus whom I preach unto you is Christ' (Acts xvii. 3), that he ' testified to the Jews that Jesus was Christ' (Acts xviii. 5), the meaning is, that he proclaimed and proved that Jesus was the Christ, or Messiah — the rightful owner of a title descriptive of a high official station which had been the subject of ancient prediction. When Jesus himself says that ' it is life eternal to know the only true God, and Jesus Christ whom he has sent' (John xvii. 3), he represents the knowledge of himself as the Christ, the Messiah, as at once necessary and sufficient to make men truly and permanently happy. When he says, ' What think ye of Christ? whose son is he ?' (Matt. xxii. 42), he does not mean, What think ye of ME, or of my descent ? but, What think ye of the Christ—the Messiah—and especially of his paternity. There can be no doubt that the word, though originally an appellative, and intended to bring before the mind a particular official character possessed by him to whom it is applied, came at last, like many other terms of the same kind, to be often used very much as a proper name, to distinguish our Lord from other persons bearing the name Jesus. This is a sense, however, of comparatively rare occurrence in the New Testament.

Proceeding, then, on the principle that Christ is an appellative, let us inquire into its origin and signification as applied to our Lord. CHRIST is the English form of a Greek word, corresponding in meaning to the Hebrew word Messiah, and the English word Anointed. 'The Christ' is just equivalent to 'the Anointed One.' The important question, however, remains behind, What is meant when the Saviour is represented as the Anointed One? To reply to this question satisfactorily, it will be necessary to go somewhat into detail.

Unction, from a very early age, seems to have been the emblem of consecration, or setting apart to a particular, and especially to a religious, purpose. Under the Old Testament economy high-priests and kings were regularly set apart to their offices, both of which were, strictly speaking, sacred ones, by the ceremony of anointing, and the prophets were occasionally designated by the same rite. This rite seems to have been intended as a public intimation of a Divine appointment to office. Thus Saul is termed 'the Lord's anointed' (1 Sam. xxiv. 6); David, 'the anointed of the God of Israel' (2 Sam. xxiii. 1); and Zedekiah, 'the anointed of the Lord' (Lam. iv. 20). The high-priest is called 'the anointed priest' (Lev. iv. 3).

From the origin and design of the rite, it is not wonderful that the term should have, in a secondary and analogical sense, been applied to persons set apart by God for important purposes, though not actually anointed. Thus Cyrus, the King of Persia, is termed 'the Lord's anointed' (Isa. xlv. 1); the Hebrew patriarchs, when sojourning in Canaan, are termed 'God's anointed ones' (Ps. cv. 15; and the Israelitish people receive the same appellation from the prophet Habakkuk (Hab. iii. 13).

In the prophetic Scriptures we find this appellation given to an illustrious personage, who, under various designations, is so often spoken of as destined to appear in a distant age as a great deliverer. The royal prophet David seems to have been the first who spoke of the great deliverer under this appellation (Ps. ii. 2; xx. 1; xlv. 7). In all the passages in which the great deliverer is spoken of as 'the anointed one,' by David, he is plainly viewed as sustaining the character of a king.

The prophet Isaiah also uses the appellation, 'the anointed one,' with reference to the promised deliverer, but, when he does so, he speaks of him as a prophet or great teacher. He introduces him as saying, 'The Spirit of the Lord God is upon me, because the Lord God hath *anointed* me to preach good tidings unto the meek; he hath sent me to bind up the brokenhearted, to proclaim liberty to the captives, and the opening of the prison to them who are bound, to proclaim the acceptable year of the Lord, and the day of vengeance of our God, to comfort all that mourn,' &c. (Isa. lxi. 1, &c.).

Daniel is the only other of the prophets who uses the appellation 'the anointed one' in reference to the great deliverer, and he plainly represents him as not only a prince, but also a highpriest, an expiator of guilt (Dan. ix. 24-26).

During the period which elapsed from the close of the prophetic canon till the birth of Jesus, no appellation of the expected deliverer seems to have been so common as the Messiah or Anointed One; and this is still the name which the unbelieving Jews ordinarily employ when speaking of him whom they still look for to avenge their wrongs and restore them to more than their former honours.

Messiah, Christ, Anointed, is, then, a term equivalent to consecrated, sacred, set apart; and as the record of Divine revelation is called, by way of eminence, *The* Bible, or book, so is the Great Deliverer called *The* Messiah, or Anointed One, much in the same way as he is termed *The* Man, *The* Son of Man.

The import of this designation as given to Jesus of Nazareth may now readily be apprehended.— (1.) When he is termed the Christ it is plainly indicated that HE is the great deliverer promised under that appellation, and many others in the Old Testament Scriptures, and that all that is said of this deliverer under this or any other appellation is true of HIM. No attentive reader of the Old Testament can help noticing that in every part of the prophecies there is ever and anon presented to our view an illustrious personage destined to appear at some future distant period, and, however varied may be the figurative representations given of him, no reasonable doubt can be entertained as to the identity of the individual. It is quite obvious that the Messiah is the same person as the 'seed of the woman' who was to 'bruise the head of the serpent' (Gen. iii. 15); 'the seed of Abraham, in whom all the nations of the earth were to be blessed' (Gen. xxii. 18); the great 'prophet to be raised up like unto Moses,' whom all were to be required to hear and obey (Deut. xviii. 15); the 'priest after the order of Melchizedek;' 'the rod out of the stem of Jesse, which should stand for an ensign of the people to which the Gentiles should seek' (Isa. xi. 1, 10); the virgin's son whose name was to be Immanuel (Isa. vii. 14); 'the branch of Jehovah' (Isa. iv. 2); 'the Angel of the Covenant' (Mal. iii. 1); 'the Lord of the Temple,' &c. &c. (ib.). When we say, then, that Jesus is the Christ, we in effect say, 'This is HE of whom Moses, in the law, and the prophets did write' (John i. 45); and all that they say of HIM is true of Jesus.

Now what is the sum of the prophetic testimony respecting him? It is this—that he should belong to the very highest order of being, the incommunicable name Jehovah being represented as rightfully belonging to him; that 'his goings forth have been from old, from everlasting' (Mic. v. 2); that his appropriate appellations should be 'Wonderful, Counsellor, the Mighty God' (Isa. ix. 6); that he should assume human nature, and become 'a child born' of the Israelitish nation of the tribe of Judah (Gen. xlix. 10), of the family of David (Isa. xi. 1); that the object of his appearance should be the salvation of mankind, both Jews and Gentiles (Isa. xlix. 6); that he should be 'despised and rejected' of his countrymen; that he should be 'cut off, but not for himself;' that he should be 'wounded for men's transgressions, bruised for their iniquities, and undergo the chastisement of their peace;' that 'by his stripes men should be healed;' that 'the Lord should lay on him the iniquity' of men; that 'exaction should be made and he should answer it;' that he should 'make his soul an offering for sin;' that after these sufferings he should be 'exalted and extolled and made very high;' that he should 'see of the travail of his soul and be satisfied, and by his knowledge justify many' (Isa. liii. *passim*); that Jehovah should say to him, 'Sit at my right hand until I make thine enemies thy footstool' (Ps. cx. 1); that he should be brought near to the Ancient of Days, and that to him should be given 'dominion, and glory, and a kingdom, that all people, and nations, and languages should serve him—an everlasting dominion which shall not pass away,—a kingdom that shall not be destroyed' (Dan. vii. 13, 14). All this is implied in saying Jesus is the Christ. In the plainer language of the New Testament 'Jesus is the Christ' is equivalent to Jesus is 'God manifest in the flesh' (1 Tim. iii. 16),—the Son of God, who, in human nature, by his obedience, and sufferings, and death in the room of the guilty, has obtained salvation for them, and all power in heaven and earth for himself, that he may give eternal life to all coming to the Father through him.

(2.) While the statement 'Jesus is the Christ' is thus materially equivalent to the statement 'all that is said of the Great Deliverer in the Old Testament Scriptures is true of HIM,' it brings more directly before our mind those truths respecting him which the appellation 'the Anointed One' naturally suggests. He is a prophet, a priest, and a king. He is the great revealer of divine truth; the only expiator of human guilt, and reconciler of man to God; the supreme and sole legitimate ruler over the understandings, consciences, and affections of men. In his person, and work, and word, by his spirit and providence, he unfolds the truth with respect to the divine character and will, and so conveys it into the mind as to make it the effectual means of conforming man's will to God's will, man's character to God's character. He has by his spotless, all-perfect obedience, amid the severest sufferings, 'obedience unto death even the death of the cross,' so illustrated the excellence of the divine law and the wickedness and danger of violating it, as to make it a righteous thing in 'the just God' to 'justify the ungodly,' thus propitiating the offended majesty of heaven; while the manifestation of the divine love in appointing and accepting this atonement, when apprehended by the mind under the influence of the Holy Spirit, becomes the effectual means of reconciling man to God and to his law, 'transforming him by the renewing of his mind.' And now, possessed of 'all power in heaven and earth,' 'all power over all flesh,' 'He is Lord of All.' All external events and all spiritual influences are equally under his control, and as a king he exerts his authority in carrying into full effect the great purposes which his revelations as a prophet, and his great atoning sacrifice as a high-priest, were intended to accomplish.

(3) But the full import of the appellation the CHRIST is not yet brought out. It indicates that He to whom it belongs is the *anointed* prophet, priest, and king—not that he was anointed by material oil, but that he was divinely *appointed*, *qualified*, *commissioned*, and *accredited* to be the Saviour of men. These are the ideas which the term *anointed* seems specially intended to convey. Jesus was divinely *appointed* to the offices he filled. He did not ultroneously assume them, 'he was called of God as was Aaron' (Heb. v. 4; Isa. xi. 2-4). He was divinely *commissioned*:

'The Father sent him' (Isa. xlix. 6). He is divinely *accredited* (Acts ii. 22; John v. 37). Such is the import of the appellation *Christ*.

If these observations are clearly apprehended there will be little difficulty in giving a satisfactory answer to the question which has sometimes been proposed—when did Jesus become Christ? when was he *anointed* of God? We have seen that the expression is a figurative or analogical one, and therefore we need not wonder that its references are various. The *appointment* of the Saviour, like all the other divine purposes, was, of course, from eternity. 'He was set up from everlasting' (Prov. viii. 23); he 'was foreordained before the foundation of the world' (1 Pet. i. 20). His qualifications, such of them as were conferred, were bestowed in or during his incarnation, when 'God anointed him with the Holy Ghost and with power' (Acts x. 38). His commission may be considered as given him when called to enter on the functions of his office. He himself, after quoting, in the synagogue of Nazareth, in the commencement of his ministry, the passage from the prophecies of Isaiah in which his unction to the prophetical office is predicted, declared ' *This day* is this Scripture fulfilled in your ears.' And in his resurrection and ascension, God, as the reward of his loving righteousness and hating iniquity, 'anointed him with the oil of gladness above his fellows' (Ps. xlv. 7), *i. e.* conferred on him a regal power, fruitful in blessings to himself and others, far superior to that which any king had ever possessed, making him, as the Apostle Peter expresses it, 'both Lord and Christ' (Acts ii. 36). As to his being *accredited*, every miraculous event performed in reference to him or by him may be viewed as included in this species of anointing—especially the visible descent of the Spirit on him in his baptism.

These statements, with regard to the import of the appellation 'the Christ,' show us how we are to understand the statement of the Apostle John, 'Whosoever believeth that Jesus is the Christ is born of God' (1 John v. 1), *i. e.* is 'a child of God,' 'born again,' 'a new creature;' and the similar declaration of the Apostle Paul, 'No man can say that Jesus is the Lord,' *i. e.* the Christ, the Messiah, 'but by the Holy Ghost' (1 Cor. xii. 3). It is plain that the proposition, 'Jesus is the Christ,' when understood in the latitude of meaning which we have shown belongs to it, contains a complete summary of the truth respecting the divine method of salvation. To believe that principle rightly understood is to believe the Gospel—the saving truth, by the faith of which a man is, and by the faith of which only a man can be, brought into the relation or formed to the character of a child of God; and though a man may, without divine influence, be brought to acknowledge that 'Jesus is the Lord,' 'Messiah the Prince,' and even firmly to believe that these words embody a truth, yet no man can be brought really to believe and cordially to acknowledge the truth contained in these words, as we have attempted to unfold it, without a peculiar divine influence.

JESUS, surnamed JUSTUS. [JUSTUS.]

JETHRO. [HOBAB.]

JEW, a name formed from that of the patriarch Judah, and applied in its first use to one belonging to the tribe or country of Judah, or rather perhaps to a subject of the separate kingdom of Judah (2 Kings xvi. 6; xxv. 5). During the Captivity the term seems to have been extended to all the people of the Hebrew language and country, without distinction (Esth iii. 6, 9; Dan. iii. 8, 12); and this loose application of the name was preserved after the restoration to Palestine, when it came to denote not only every descendant of Abraham in the largest possible sense, but even proselytes who had no blood-relation to the Hebrews (Acts ii. 5; comp. 10). See the articles ISRAEL; JUDAH.

JEZ'EBEL (*not inhabited*, comp. *Isabella*), daughter of Ethbaal, king of Tyre and Sidon, and consort of Ahab, king of Israel (B.C. 918). This unsuitable alliance proved most disastrous to the kingdom of Israel; for Jezebel induced her weak husband not only to connive at her introducing the worship of her native idols, but eventually to become himself a worshipper of them, and to use all the means in his power to establish them in the room of the God of Israel. This was a great enormity. The worship of the golden calves which previously existed was, however mistakenly, intended in honour of Jehovah; but this was an open alienation from him, and a turning aside to foreign and strange gods, which, indeed, were no gods. Most of the particulars of this bad but apparently highly-gifted woman's conduct have been related in the notices of AHAB and ELIJAH. From the course of her proceedings it would appear that she grew to hate the Jewish system of law and religion, on account of what must have seemed to her its intolerance and its anti-social tendencies. She hence sought to put it down by all the means she could command; and the imbecility of her husband seems to have made all the powers of the state subservient to her designs. The manner in which she acquired and used her power over Ahab is strikingly shown in the matter of Naboth, which, perhaps, more than all the other affairs in which she was engaged, brings out her true character, and displays the nature of her influence. When she found him puling, like a spoiled child, on account of the refusal of Naboth to gratify him by selling him his patrimonial vineyard for a ' garden of herbs,' she teaches him to look to her, to rely upon her for the accomplishment of his wishes; and for the sake of this impression, more perhaps than from savageness of temper, she scrupled not at murder under the abused forms of law and religion. She had the reward of her unscrupulous decisiveness of character in the triumph of her policy in Israel, where, at last, there were but 7000 people who had not bowed the knee to Baal, nor kissed their hand to his image. Nor was her success confined to Israel, for through Athaliah—a daughter after her own heart—who was married to the son and successor of Jehoshaphat, the same policy prevailed for a time in Judah, after Jezebel herself had perished and the house of Ahab had met its doom. It seems that after the death of her husband Jezebel maintained considerable ascendancy over her son Joram; and her measures and misconduct formed the principal charge which Jehu cast in the teeth of that unhappy monarch before he sent forth the arrow which slew him. The last effort of Jezebel was to inti-

midate Jehu as he passed the palace, by warning him of the eventual rewards of even successful treason. It is eminently characteristic of the woman, that, even in this terrible moment, when she knew that her son was slain, and must have felt that her power had departed, she displayed herself not with rent veil and dishevelled hair, ' but tired her head and painted her eyes ' before she looked out at the window. The eunuchs, at a word from Jehu, having cast her down, she met her death beneath the wall [JEHU]; and when afterwards the new monarch bethought him that, as ' a king's daughter,' her corpse should not be treated with disrespect, nothing was found of her but the palms of her hands and the soles of her feet. The dogs had eaten all the rest. B.C. 884 (1 Kings xvi. 31; xviii. 4, 13, 19, xxi. 5-25; 2 Kings ix. 7, 22, 30-37).

JEZ'REEL, a town in the tribe of Issachar (Josh. xix. 18), where the kings of Israel had a palace, and where the court often resided, although Samaria was the metropolis of the kingdom. It is most frequently mentioned in the history of the house of Ahab. Here was the vineyard of Naboth, which Ahab coveted to enlarge the palace-grounds (1 Kings xviii. 45, 46; xxi.), and here Jehu executed his dreadful commission against the house of Ahab, when Jezebel, Joram, and all who were connected with that wretched dynasty, perished (2 Kings ix. 14-37; x. 1-11). These horrid scenes appear to have given the kings of Israel a distaste to this residence, as it is not again mentioned in their history. It is, however, named by Hosea (i. 4; comp. i. 11; ii. 22); and in Judith (i. 8; iv. 3; vii. 3) it occurs under the name of Esd·aelon. In the days of Eusebius and Jerome it was still a large village, called Esdraela. Nothing more is heard of it till the time of the crusades, when it was called by the Franks Parvum Gerinum, and by the Arabs Zerin; and it is described as commanding a wide prospect—on the east to the mountains of Gilead, and on the west to Mount Carmel. But this line of identification seems to have been afterwards lost sight of, and it is only of late that the identification of Zerin and Jezreel has been restored.

Zerin is seated on the brow of a rocky and very steep descent into the great and fertile valley of Jezreel, which runs down between the mountains of Gilboa and Hermon. Lying comparatively high, it commands a wide and noble view, extending down the broad valley on the east to Beisan (Bethshean), and on the west quite across the great plain to the mountains of Carmel. It is described by Dr. Robinson (*Researches*, iii. 163) as a most magnificent site for a city, which, being itself a conspicuous object in every part, would naturally give its name to the whole region. In the valley directly under Zerin is a considerable fountain, and another still larger somewhat farther to the east, under the northern side of Gilboa, called Ain Jalud. There can, therefore, be little question that, as in Zerin we have Jezreel, so in the valley and the fountain we have the ' valley of Jezreel,' and the fountain of Jezreel, of Scripture.

Zerin has at present little more than twenty humble dwellings, mostly in ruins, and with few inhabitants.

JO'AB (*God-fathered*), one of the three sons

of Zeruiah, the sister of David, and ' captain of the host' (generalissimo) of the army during nearly the whole of David's reign.

He first appears associated with his two brothers. Abishai and Asahel, in the command of David's troops against Abner, who had set up the claims of a son of Saul in opposition to those of David, who then reigned in Hebron. The armies having met at the pool of Gibeon, a general action was brought on, in which Abner was worsted. In his flight he had the misfortune to kill Joab's brother, the swift-footed Asahel, by whom he was pursued (2 Sam. ii. 13-32). The consequences of this deed have been explained elsewhere [ABNER; ASAHEL]. Joab smothered for a time his resentment against the shedder of his brother's blood; but being whetted by the natural rivalry of position between him and Abner, he afterwards made it the instrument of his policy by treacherously, in the act of friendly communication, slaying Abner, at the very time when the services of the latter to David, to whom he had then turned, had rendered him a most dangerous rival to him in power and influence (2 Sam. iii. 22-27). That Abner had at first suspected that Joab would take the position of blood-avenger [BLOOD-REVENGE] is clear, from the apprehension which he expressed (2 Sam. ii. 22); but that he thought that Joab had, under all the circumstances, abandoned this position, is shown by the unsuspecting readiness with which he went aside with him (2 Sam. iii. 26, 27); and that Joab placed his murderous act on the footing of vengeance for his brother's blood, is plainly stated in 2 Sam. iii. 30; by which it also appears that the other brother, Abishai, shared in some way in the deed and its responsibilities. At the same time, as Abner was perfectly justified in slaying Asahel to save his own life, it is very doubtful if Joab would ever have asserted his right of blood-revenge if Abner had not appeared likely to endanger his influence with David. The king, much as he reprobated the act, knew that it had a sort of excuse in the old customs of blood-revenge, and he stood habitually too much in awe of his impetuous and able nephew to bring him to punishment, or even to displace him from his command. ' I am this day weak,' he said, ' though anointed king, and these men, the sons of Zeruiah, be too hard for me' (2 Sam. iii. 39 ; 1 Chron. xi. 4-9).

Desirous probably of making some atonement before David and the public for this atrocity, in a way which at the same time was most likely to prove effectual—namely, by some daring exploit—he was the first to mount to the assault at the storming of the fortress on Mount Sion, which had remained so long in the hands of the Jebusites. By this service he acquired the chief command of the army of all Israel, of which David was by this time king (2 Sam. v. 6-10).

It is not necessary to trace the subsequent acts of Joab, seeing that they are in fact the public acts of the king he served. And he served him faithfully ; for although he knew his power over David, and often treated him with little ceremony, there can be no doubt that he was most truly devoted to his interests, and sometimes rendered him good service even against his own will, as in the affair at Mahanaim (2 Sam. xix. 5-8). But Joab had no principles apart from what he deemed his duty to the king and the people, and was quite as ready to serve his master's vices as his virtues, so long as they did not interfere with his own interests, or tended to promote them by enabling him to make himself useful to the king. His ready apprehension of the king's meaning in the matter of Uriah, and the facility with which he made himself the instrument of the murder, and of the hypocrisy by which it was covered, are proofs of this, and form as deep a stain upon his character as his own murders (2 Sam. xi. 14-25). As Joab was on good terms with Absalom, and had taken pains to bring about a reconciliation between him and his father, we may set the higher value upon his firm adhesion to David when Absalom revolted, and upon his stern sense of duty to the king—from whom he expected no thanks— displayed in putting an end to the war by the slaughter of his favourite son, when all others shrunk from the responsibility of doing the king a service against his own will (2 Sam. xviii. 1-14). In like manner, when David unhappily resolved to number the people, Joab discerned the evil, and remonstrated against it; and although he did not venture to disobey, he performed the duty tardily and reluctantly, to afford the king an opportunity of reconsidering the matter, and took no pains to conceal how odious the measure was to him (2 Sam. xxiv. 1-4). David was certainly ungrateful for the services of Joab, when, in order to conciliate the powerful party which had supported Absalom, he offered the command of the host to Amasa, who had commanded the army of Absalom (2 Sam. xix. 13). But the inefficiency of the new commander, in the emergency which the revolt of Bichri's son produced, arising perhaps from the reluctance of the troops to follow their new leader, gave Joab an opportunity of displaying his superior resources, and also of removing his rival by a murder very similar to, and in some respects less excusable and more foul than, that of Abner [AMASA]. Besides, Amasa was his own cousin, being the son of his mother's sister (2 Sam. xx. 1-13).

When David lay on his death-bed, and a demonstration was made in favour of the succession of the eldest surviving son, Adonijah, whose interests had been compromised by the preference of the young Solomon, Joab joined the party of the natural heir. It would be unjust to regard this as a defection from David. It was nothing more or less than a demonstration in favour of the natural heir, which, if not then made, could not be made at all. But an act which would have been justifiable, had the preference of Solomon been a mere caprice of the old king, became criminal as an act of contumacy to the Divine king, the real head of the government, who had called the house of David to the throne, and had the sole right of determining which of its members should reign. When the prompt measures taken under the direction of the king rendered this demonstration abortive (1 Kings i. 7), Joab withdrew into private life till some time after the death of David, when the fate of Adonijah, and of Abiathar—whose life was only spared in consequence of his sacerdotal character—warned Joab that he had little mercy to expect from the new king. He fled for refuge to the altar; but when Solomon heard this, he sent Benaiah to put him to death; and, as he refused to come forth, gave orders that he should be slain even at the altar. Thus died one of the most accomplished warriors and unscrupulous men that Israel ever produced. His corpse was removed to his domain in the wilderness of Judah, and buried there, B.C. 1015 (1 Kings ii. 5, 28-34).

JOAN'NA, wife of Chuza, the steward of Herod Antipas, the tetrarch of Galilee. She was one of those women who followed Christ, and ministered to the wants of him and his disciples out of their abundance. They had all been cured of grievous diseases by the Saviour, or had received material benefits from him; and the customs of the country allowed them to testify in this way their gratitude and devotedness without reproach. It is usually supposed that Joanna was at this time a widow (Luke viii. 3; xxiv. 10).

1. JO'ASH (*God-given*), a contraction of JEHOASH, son of Ahaziah and eighth king of Judah, who began to reign in B C. 878, at the age of seven, and reigned forty-one years.

Joash, when an infant, was secretly saved by his aunt Jehoshebah, who was married to the high-priest Jehoiada, from the general massacre of the family by Athaliah, who had usurped the throne [ATHALIAH; JEHOIADA]. By the high-priest and his wife the child was privily brought up in the chambers connected with the temple till he had attained his eighth year, when Jehoiada deemed that the state of affairs required him to produce the youthful heir of the throne to the people, and claim for him the crown which his grandmother had so unrighteously usurped. Finding the influential persons whom he consulted favourable to the design, everything was secretly, but admirably, arranged for producing Joash, and investing him with the regalia, in such a manner that Athaliah could have no suspicion of the event till it actually occurred. On the day appointed, the sole surviving scion of David's illustrious house appeared in the place of the kings, by a particular pillar in the temple-court, and was crowned and anointed with the usual ceremonies. The high-wrought enthusiasm of the spectators then found vent in clapping of hands and exulting shouts of 'Long live the king!' The joyful uproar was heard even in the palace, and brought Athaliah to the temple, from which, at a word from Jehoiada, she was led to her death.

Joash behaved well during his non-age, and so long after as he remained under the influence of the high-priest. But when he died the king seems to have felt himself relieved from a yoke; and, to manifest his freedom, began to take the contrary course to that which he had followed while under pupilage. Gradually the persons who had possessed influence formerly, when the house of David was contaminated by its alliance with the house of Ahab, insinuated themselves into his councils, and ere long the worship of Jehovah and the observances of the law were neglected, and the land was defiled with idolatries and idolatrous usages. The prophets then uttered their warnings, but were not heard; and the infatuated king had the atrocious ingratitude to put to death Zechariah, the son and successor of his benefactor Jehoiada. For these deeds Joash was made an example of the divine judgments. He saw his realm devastated by the Syrians under

Hazael; his armies were cut in pieces by an enemy of inferior numbers; and he was even besieged in Jerusalem, and only preserved his capital and his crown by giving up the treasures of the temple. Besides this, a painful malady embittered all his latter days, and at length he became so odious that his own servants conspired against him, and slew him on his bed. Joash was buried in the city of David; but a place in the sepulchre of the kings was denied to his remains (2 Kings xi.; xii.; 2 Chron. xxiv.).

2. JOASH, son and successor of Jehoahaz on the throne of Israel, of which he was the twelfth king. He began to reign in B.C. 840, and reigned sixteen incomplete years. He followed the example of his predecessors in the policy of keeping up the worship of the golden calves; but, apart from this, he bears a fair character, and had intervals, at least, of sincere piety and true devotion to the God of his fathers. He held the prophet Elisha in high honour, looking up to him as a father. When he heard of his last illness he repaired to the bed-side of the dying prophet, and was favoured with promises of victories over the Syrians, by whom his dominions were then harassed. These promises were accomplished after the prophet's death. In three signal and successive victories Joash overcame the Syrians, and retook from them the towns which Hazael had rent from Israel.

These advantages rendered the kingdom of Israel more potent than that of Judah. He, however, sought no quarrel with that kingdom; but when he received a defiance from Amaziah, king of Judah, he answered with becoming spirit in a parable, which by its images calls to mind that of Jotham [PARABLES]: the cool disdain of the answer must have been, and in fact was, exceedingly galling to Amaziah. In the war, or rather action, which followed, Joash was victorious. Having defeated Amaziah at Beth-shemesh, in Judah, he advanced to Jerusalem, broke down the wall to the extent of 400 cubits, and carried away the treasures both of the temple and the palace, together with hostages for the future good behaviour of the crest-fallen Amaziah. Joash himself did not long survive this victory; he died in peace, and was buried in Samaria (2 Kings xiii. 9-25; xiv. 1-17).

JOB, THE BOOK OF. We shall consider, first, the contents of this book; secondly, its object; thirdly, its composition; and, lastly, the country, descent, and age of its author.

I. CONTENTS. In the land of Uz, belonging to the northern part of Arabia Deserta, lived an honest, pious man, called Job. For his sincere and perfect devotedness, God had amply blessed him with worldly property and children; but on Satan obtaining leave *to tempt him*, he suddenly lost the fortune of his life. Ultimately he is smitten with a severe and painful disease; but though his wife *moves* him to forsake God, he still continues true and stanch to the Lord Three friends, Eliphaz, Bildad, and Zophar, hear of his calamities, and come to console him. His distressed state excites their heartfelt compassion; but the view which they take of its origin prevents them from at once assisting him, and they remain silent, though they are sensible that by so doing they further wound his feelings. Seven days thus pass, until Job, suspecting the cause of their conduct, becomes discomposed and breaks silence. His first observations are based on the assertion—not, indeed, broadly expressed—that God acts harshly and arbitrarily in inflicting calamity on men. This causes a discussion between him and his friends, which is divided into three main parts, each with subdivisions, and embraces the speeches of the three friends of Job, and his answers: the last part, however, consists of only two subdivisions, the third friend, Zophar, having nothing to rejoin. By this silence the author of the book generally designates the defeat of Job's friends, who are defending a common cause. Taking a general view of the argument which they urge against him, they may be considered as asserting the following positions:—

1. No man being free from sin, we need not wonder that we are liable to calamities, for which we must account by a reference, not to God, but to ourselves. From the misery of the distressed, others are enabled to infer their guilt; and they must take this view in order to vindicate divine justice.

2. The distress of a man proves not only *that he has sinned*, but shows also the degree and measure of his sin; and thus, from the extent of calamity sustained, may be inferred the extent of sins committed; and from this the measure of impending misfortune.

3. A distressed man may recover his former happiness, and even attain to greater fortune than he ever enjoyed before, if he takes a warning from his afflictions, repents of his sins, reforms his life, and raises himself to a higher degree of moral rectitude. Impatience and irreverent expostulation with God serve but to prolong and increase punishment; for, by accusing God of injustice. a fresh sin is added to former transgressions.

4. Though the wicked man is capable of prosperity, still it is never lasting. The most awful retribution soon overtakes him; and his transient felicity must itself be considered as punishment, since it renders him heedless, and makes him feel misfortune more keenly.

In opposition to them, Job maintains:

1. The most upright man may be highly unfortunate—more so than the inevitable faults and shortcomings of human nature would seem to imply. There is a savage cruelty, deserving the severities of the Divine resentment, in inferring the guilt of a man from his distresses. In distributing good and evil, God regards neither merit nor guilt, but acts according to His sovereign pleasure. His omnipotence is apparent in every part of the creation; but His justice cannot be seen in the government of the world, the afflictions of the righteous, as well as the prosperity of the wicked, are evidence against it. There are innumerable cases, and Job considers his own to be one of them, in which a sufferer has a right to justify himself before God, and to repine at His decrees. Of this supposed right Job freely avails himself, and maintains it against his friends.

2. In a state of composure and calmer reflection, Job retracts, chiefly in his concluding speech, all his former rather extravagant assertions, and says that, although God generally afflicts the wicked and blesses the righteous, still there are exceptions to this rule, single cases in which the pious undergo severe trials; the infe-

rence, therefore, of a man's guilt from his misfortunes is by no means warranted. For the exceptions established by experience prove that God does not always distribute prosperity and adversity after this rule; but that he sometimes acts on a different principle, or as an absolute lord, according to his mere will and pleasure.

3. Humbly to adore God is our duty, even when we are subject to calamities not at all deserved; but we should abstain from harshly judging of those who, when distressed, send forth complaints against God.

The interest of the narrative is kept up with considerable skill, by progressively rising and highly passionate language. At first, Job's friends charge him, and he defends himself, in mild terms; but gradually they are all betrayed into warmth of temper, which goes on increasing until the friends have nothing more to object, and Job remains in possession of the field. The discussion then seems to be at an end, when a fresh disputant, Elihu, appears. Trusting in his just cause, Job had proudly opposed God, with whom he expostulated, and whom he charged with injustice, when the sense of his calamities should have led him to acknowledge the sinfulness of human nature, and humbly to submit to the Divine dispensations. Making every allowance for his painful situation, and putting the mildest construction on his expressions, he is still substantially wrong, and could not therefore be suffered to remain the vanquisher in this high argument. He had silenced his friends, but the general issue remained to be settled. Elihu had waited till Job and his friends had spoken, because they were older than he; but when he saw that the three visitors ceased to answer, he offers himself to reason with Job, and shows that God is just in his ways. He does this,

1. *From the nature of inflictions.*—He begins by urging that Job was very wrong in boasting of his integrity, and making it appear that rewards were due to him from God. How righteous soever he was, he still had no claim to reward; on the contrary, all men are sinners in God's eyes; and nobody can complain that he suffers unjustly, for the very greatest sufferings equal not his immense guilt. Then Elihu explains a leading point on which he differs from the friends of Job: he asserts that from greater sufferings inflicted on a person it was not to be inferred that he had sinned more than others afflicted with a less amount of calamity. Calamities were, indeed, under all circumstances, punishments for sins committed, but at the same time they were correctives also; and therefore they might be inflicted on the comparatively most righteous in preference to others. If the object of afflictions was attained, and the distressed acknowledged his sinfulness, he would humble himself before God, who would bless him with greater happiness than he ever before enjoyed. But he who took not this view, and did not amend his ways, would be ruined, and the blame would rest wholly with himself. Consequently, if Job made the best of his misfortune, God would render him most happy; but if he continued refractory, punishment would follow his offences.

2. *From a clear conception of the nature of God.* —'The whole creation shows forth His majesty, and evinces His justice. For a man to stand up

against Him and to assert that he suffers innocently, is the greatest anthropomorphism, because it *goes* to deny the Divine majesty, evident in all the facts of the created world, and including God's justice. His nature being one and indivisible, it cannot on one side exhibit infinite perfection, and on the other imperfection: each example, then, of God's grandeur in the creation of the world is evidence against the rash accusers of God's justice. God *must* be just—this is certain from the outset; and *how* His justice is not impaired by calamities inflicted on the righteous and on thyself, I have already explained.'

Job had, in a stirring manner, several times, challenged God to decide the contest. Elihu suspects the approach of the Lord, when, towards the end of his speech, a violent thunder-storm arises, and God answers Job out of the whirlwind, showing how foolishly the latter had acted in offering to reason with Him, when His works proved His infinite majesty, and, consequently, His absolute justice. Job now submits to God, and humbly repents of his offence. Hereupon God addresses Eliphaz, Bildad, and Zophar, declaring unto them His displeasure at their unmerciful dealing with their friend, the consequences of which could only be avoided by Job offering a propitiatory sacrifice This is done, and the Lord grants unto Job ample compensation for his sufferings.

II. DESIGN OF THE BOOK. All agree that the object of the book is the solution of the question, how the afflictions of the righteous and the prosperity of the wicked can be consistent with God's justice. But it should be observed that the direct problem exclusively refers to the first point, the second being only incidentally discussed on occasion of the leading theme. If this is overlooked, the author would appear to have solved only one half of his problem; the case from which the whole discussion proceeds, has reference merely to the leading problem.

The solution of the problem regarding the sufferings of the righteous rests on two positions.

1. Calamity is the only way that leads to the kingdom of God.

2. Calamity, as the veiled grace of God, is with the pious never alone, but manifest proofs of Divine favour accompany or follow it. Though sunk in misery, they still are happier than the wicked, and when it has attained its object, it is terminated by the Lord.

It is this exclusively correct solution of the problem which occurs in the book of Job. It is not given in Job's speeches or in the speeches of his friends, neither is it exclusively given in the addresses of God which contain only the basis of the solution, not the solution itself. But all interpreters allow that it is set forth in Elihu's speeches which appear to contain the opinion of the author.

The leading principle in Elihu's statement is, that calamity in the shape of trial was inflicted even on the comparatively best men, but that God allowed a favourable turn to take place as soon as it had attained its object. Now this is the key to the events of Job's life. Though a pious and righteous man, he is tried by severe afflictions. He knows not for what purpose he is smitten, and his calamity continues; but when he learns it from the addresses of Elihu and God,

and humbles himself, he is relieved from the burden which oppresses him, and ample prosperity atones for the afflictions he has sustained. Add to this, that the remaining portion of Elihu's speeches, in which he points to God's infinite majesty as including his justice, is continued in the addresses of God; that Elihu foretells God's appearance; that he is not punished by God as are the friends of Job; in fine, that Job by his very silence acknowledges the problem to have been solved by Elihu; and his silence is the more significant because Elihu had urged him to defend himself (xxxiii. 32), and because Job had repeatedly declared he would 'hold his peace,' if it was shown to him wherein he had erred (vi. 24, 25; xix. 4).

In regard to the character of the composition of the book there are three different opinions:—1. Some contend that the book contains an entirely true history. 2. Others assert that it is founded on a true history, which has been recast, modified, and enlarged by the author. 3. The third opinion is, that the book contains a narrative entirely imaginary, and constructed by the author to teach a great moral truth.

The first view, taken by numerous ancient interpreters, is now abandoned by nearly all interpreters. It seems, however, to have been adopted by Josephus, for he places Job in the list of the historical books; and it was prevalent with all the fathers of the church. In its support it is said, 1. That Job is (Ezek. xiv. 14–20) mentioned as a public character, together with Noah and Daniel, and represented as an example of piety. 2. In the epistle of James (v. 11), patience in sufferings is recommended by a reference to Job.

We must confine ourselves to contending for an historical foundation of the book, but must not undertake to determine the exact nature of the groundwork. That its historical framework was poetically enlarged by the author, has been already observed by Luther. As for the rest, the subtility displayed in explaining opposite views, the carefully drawn characters of the persons introduced, and their animated discourses, lead us to suppose that the question at issue had *previously* been the subject of various discussions in presence of the author, who, perhaps, took part in them. Thus there would be an historical foundation, not only for the facts related in the book, but to a certain extent also for the speeches.

Opinions differed in ancient times as to *the nation* to which the author belonged; some considering him to have been an Arab, others an Israelite; but the latter supposition is undoubtedly preferable. For, 1st, we find in our book many ideas of genuine Israelite growth: the creation of the world is described, in accordance with the prevailing notions of the Israelites, as the immediate effect of Divine omnipotence; man is formed of clay; the spirit of man is God's breath; God employs the angels for the performance of his orders; Satan, the enemy of the chosen children of God, is his instrument for tempting them; men are weak and sinful; nobody is pure in the sight of God; moral corruption is propagated. There is promulgated to men the law of God, which they must not infringe, and the transgressions of which are visited on offenders with punishments. Moreover, the nether world is depicted in hues entirely Hebrew. To these particulars might, without much trouble, be added many more; but the deep-searching inquirer will particularly weigh, 2ndly, the fact, that the book displays a strength and fervour of religious faith, such as could only be expected within the domain of revelation.

Proceeding to the inquiry as to *the age* of the author of this book, we meet with three opinions:—1. That he lived before Moses, or was, at least, his contemporary. 2. That he lived in the time of Solomon, or in the centuries next following. 3. That he lived shortly before, or during, or even after the Babylonian exile. The view of those who assert the book to have been written long after the Babylonian exile, can be supported neither by the nature of its language nor by reasons derived from its historical groundwork, and is therefore now generally rejected. Against this view, militate, first, the references to it in the Old Testament, which prove that it was before this period a generally known writing. Thus, in Ezek. xiv. 14-20, are mentioned 'three men, Noah, Daniel, and Job,' as examples of righteousness. Further, in Jeremiah xx. 14, we find evidently imitated Job's cursing of the day of his birth (ch. iii.). Not only the sentiments but the words are often the same. There are also in the *Lamentations* of Jeremiah, many passages clearly alluding to our book, which must have eminently suited the taste of this prophet and interested him (comp. xvi. 13 with Lam. ii. 16; and xix. 8, with Lam. iii. 7, 9). Another example of words borrowed from Job occurs in Psalm cvii. 42, where the second part of the verse agrees literally with Job v. 16. 2. A most decisive reason against assigning the composition of Job to the period of the Exile is derived from the language, since it is free from *those* Chaldaisms which occur in the books written about that time. Eichhorn justly observes, ' Let him who is fit for such researches, only read, first, a writing, tainted with Aramaisms, and next the book of Job : they will be found diverging as east and west.' 3. Equally conclusive is the poetical character of the book. The Exile might produce a soft, moving poem, but could not give birth to such a rich, compact, animated, and warm composition as ours, breathing youthful freshness throughout. Ewald, in acknowledging this, says justly, 'The high skill displayed in this book cannot be well expected from later centuries, when poetry had by degrees generally declined, and particularly in the higher art required by large compositions; and language so concise and expressive as that of our author, is not found in writings of later times '

To the view which places the age of the book of Job in the time of the Babylonian exile, is most opposed that which assigns the composition of it to a period prior to Moses. In support of this latter view, two arguments have been adduced. It is said, 1. 'There is in the book of Job no direct reference to the Mosaic legislation; and its descriptions and other statements are suited to the period of the patriarchs; as, for instance, the great authority held by old men, the high age of Job, and fathers offering sacrifices for their families—which leads to the supposition that when our book was written no

sacerdotal order yet existed.' These points, however, are quite intelligible, if the design of the book, as stated above, is kept in view. The author intended not to rest the decision of the question at issue on particular passages of Scripture, but on religious consciousness and experience. This at once explains why he places the scene without Palestine, why he places it in the patriarchal age, and why he avoids the use of the name Jehovah ; of these three items *the first* sufficiently accounts for no reference being made to the Mosaic legislation. 2. 'The language of the book of Job seems strongly to support the opinion of its having been written before Moses' It has been often said, that no writing of the Old Testament may be more frequently illustrated from the Arabic than this book. In answer to this it has been said that this inference would be safe only if the book were written in prose, and that the selection of obsolete and rare words and forms, with the Hebrews, was a peculiar feature of the poetical style, and served to distinguish it from the usual, habitual way of writing; and that this peculiarity belongs to our book more than to any other.

With regard to the reasons in support of the opinion that the book of Job was written after the age of Moses, most of them are either not conclusive at all, or not quite cogent. Thus it is an arbitrary assumption, proved by modern researches to be erroneous, that the art of writing was unknown previous to the age of Moses. The assertion too, that the marks of cultivation and refinement observable in our book belonged to a later age, rests on no historical ground. The evident correspondence also between this book and the Proverbs and Psalms is not a point proving with resistless force that they were all written at the same time. It is, indeed, sometimes of such a kind, that the authors of the Proverbs and Psalms cannot be exactly said to have copied our book; but it may be accounted for by their all belonging to the same class of writings, by the very great uniformity and accordance of religious conceptions and sentiments expressed in the Old Testament, and by the stability of its religious character.

Summing up the whole of our investigations, we take it to be a settled point that the book of Job does not belong to the time of the Babylonian exile, and it cannot have been composed later than the era of Isaiah, who alludes to it. With this result we must rest satisfied. There remains uncertainty, but it does not concern an important point of religion. The significancy of our book for the church rests on the evidence of our Lord and his apostles in support of the inspiration of the whole collection of the Old Testament, and on the confirmation which this external evidence has at all times received, and continues to receive, from the internal testimony among the true believers of all ages.

JOB'S DISEASE. The opinion that the malady under which Job suffered was elephantiasis, or black leprosy, is very ancient, and, in modern times, it is entertained by the best scholars generally. The passages which are considered to indicate this disease are found in the description of his skin burning from head to foot, so that he took a potsherd to scrape himself (ii 7, 8); in its being covered with putrefaction and crusts of earth, and being at one time stiff and hard, while at another it cracked and discharged fluid (vii. 5); in the offensive breath which drove away the kindness of attendants (xix. 17); in the restless nights, which were either sleepless or scared with frightful dreams (vii. 13, 14; xxx. 17); in general emaciation (xvi. 8); and in so intense a loathing of the burden of life, that strangling and death were preferable to it (vii. 15).

In this, as in most other Biblical diseases, there is too little distinct description of symptoms to enable us to determine the precise malady intended. But the general character of the complaint under which Job suffered, bears a greater resemblance to elephantiasis than to any other disease [LEPROSY].

JOCH'EBED (*God-glorified*), wife of Amram and mother of Miriam, Moses and Aaron. In Exod. vi. 20, Jochebed is expressly declared to have been the sister of Amram's father, and consequently the aunt of her husband. As marriage between persons thus related was afterwards forbidden by the law (Lev. xviii. 12), various attempts have been made to show that the relationship was more distant than the text in its literal meaning indicates. We see no necessity for this. The mere mention of the relationship implies that there was something remarkable in the case; but if we show that nothing is remarkable, we do away the occasion for the relationship being at all noticed. The fact seems to be, that where this marriage was contracted, there was no law forbidding such alliances, but they must in any case have been unusual, although not forbidden; and this, with the writer's knowledge that they were subsequently interdicted, sufficiently accounts for this one being so pointedly mentioned. The candour of the historian in declaring himself to be sprung from a marriage, afterwards forbidden by the law, delivered through himself, deserves especial notice.

JO'EL (*worshipper of Jehovah*), one of the twelve minor prophets, the son of Pethuel. Of his birth-place nothing is known with certainty. From the local allusions in his prophecy, we may infer that he discharged his office in the kingdom of Judah. But the references to the temple, its priests and sacrifices, are rather slender grounds for conjecturing that he belonged to the sacerdotal order. Various opinions have been held respecting the period in which he lived. It appears most probable that he was contemporary with Amos and Isaiah, and delivered his predictions in the reign of Uzziah, between 800 and 780 B.C.

This prophet opens his commission by announcing an extraordinary plague of locusts, accompanied with extreme drought, which he depicts in a strain of animated and sublime poetry under the image of an invading army. The fidelity of his highly-wrought description is corroborated and illustrated by the testimonies of Shaw, Volney, Forbes, and other eminent travellers, who have been eye-witnesses of the ravages committed by this most terrible of the insect tribe. In the second chapter, the formidable aspect of the locusts—their rapid progress—their sweeping devastation—the awful murmur of their countless throngs—their instinctive marshalling—the irresistible perseverance with which they make their way over every obstacle and through every aperture—are delineated with the utmost

graphic force. There is considerable diversity of sentiment as to the point whether these descriptions are to be understood literally or figuratively. The figurative interpretation has, it must be allowed, the support of antiquity. It was adopted by the Chaldee paraphrast, Ephrem the Syrian (A.D. 350), and the Jews in the time of Jerome (A.D. 400). Ephrem supposes that by the four different denominations of the locusts were intended Tiglath-pileser, Shalmaneser, Sennacherib, and Nebuchadnezzar. The Jews, in the time of Jerome, understood by the first term the Assyrians and Chaldeans; by the second, the Medes and Persians; by the third, Alexander the Great and his successors; and by the fourth, the Romans. Grotius applies the description to the invasions by Pul and Shalmaneser. Holzhausen attempts to unite both modes of interpretation, and applies the language literally to the locusts, and metaphorically to the Assyrians. It is singular, however, that, if a hostile invasion be intended, not the least hint is given of personal injury sustained by the inhabitants; the immediate effects are confined entirely to the vegetable productions and the cattle.

The prophet, after describing the approaching judgments, calls on his countrymen to repent, assuring them of the divine placability and readiness to forgive (ii. 12-17). He foretels the restoration of the land to its former fertility, and declares that Jehovah would still be their God (ii. 18-26). He then announces the spiritual blessings which would be poured forth in the Messianic age (iii. 1-5, Heb. text; ii. 28-32, Auth. Vers.). This remarkable prediction is applied by the Apostle Peter to the events that transpired on the day of Pentecost (Acts ii. 16-21). In the last chapter the divine vengeance is denounced against the enemies and oppressors of the chosen people, of whom the Phœnicians, Egyptians, and Edomites are especially named.

The style of Joel, it has been remarked, unites the strength of Micah with the tenderness of Jeremiah. In vividness of description he rivals Nahum, and in sublimity and majesty is scarcely inferior to Isaiah and Habakkuk.

The canonicity of this book has never been called in question.

JOHA'NAN (*God-bestowed*); one of the officers who came and recognised Gedaliah as governor of Judæa after the destruction of Jerusalem, and who appears to have been the chief in authority and influence among them. He penetrated the designs of Ishmael against the governor, whom he endeavoured, without success, to put upon his guard. When Ishmael had accomplished his design by the murder of Gedaliah, and was carrying away the principal persons at the seat of government as captives to the Ammonites, Johanan pursued him, and released them. Being fearful, however, that the Chaldæans might misunderstand the affair, and make him and those who were with him responsible for it, he resolved to withdraw for safety into Egypt, with the principal persons of the remnant left in the land. Jeremiah remonstrated against this decision; but Johanan would not be moved, and even constrained the prophet himself to go with them. They proceeded to Taphanes, but nothing further is recorded of Johanan. B.C. 588 (2 Kings xxv. 23; Jer. xl. 8-16; xli.; xlii; xliii.).

JOHN THE BAPTIST. The name John denotes *grace* or *favour*. In the church John commonly bears the honourable title of 'fore-runner of the Lord.'

His parents were Zacharias and Elisabeth, the latter 'a cousin of Mary,' the mother of Jesus, whose senior John was by a period of six months (Luke i.). According to the account contained in the first chapter of Luke, his father, while engaged in burning incense, was visited by the angel Gabriel, who informed him that in compliance with his prayers his wife should bear a son, whose name he should call John—in allusion to the grace thus accorded. A description of the manner of his son's life is given, which in effect states that he was to be a Nazarite, abstaining from bodily indulgences, was to receive special favour and aid of God, was to prove a great religious and social reformer, and so prepare the way for the long-expected Messiah. Zacharias was slow to believe these tidings and sought some token in evidence of their truth. Accordingly a sign was given which acted also as a punishment of his want of faith—his tongue was sealed till the prediction should be fulfilled by the event. Six months after Elisabeth had conceived she received a visit from Mary, the future mother of Jesus. On being saluted by her relation, Elisabeth felt her babe leap in her womb, and, being filled with the holy spirit, she broke forth into a poetic congratulation to Mary, as the destined mother of her Lord. At length Elisabeth brought forth a son, whom the relatives were disposed to name Zacharias, after his father—but Elisabeth was in some way led to wish that he should be called John. The matter was referred to the father, who signified in writing that his name was to be John. This agreement with Elisabeth caused all to marvel. Zacharias now had his tongue loosed, and he first employed his restored power in praising God. These singular events caused universal surprise, and led people to expect that the child would prove a distinguished man.

The parents of John were not only of a priestly order, but righteous and devout. Their influence, in consequence, in the training of their son, would be not only benign but suitable to the holy office which he was designed to fill. More than this—the special aids of God's Spirit were with him (Luke i. 66). As a consequence of the lofty influences under which he was nurtured, the child waxed strong in spirit. The sacred writer adds that 'he was in the deserts till the day of his showing unto Israel' (Luke i. 80).

In the fifteenth year of the Emperor Tiberius, John made his public appearance, exhibiting the austerity, the costume, and the manner of life of the ancient Jewish prophets (Luke iii.; Matt. iii.). His raiment was camel's hair; he wore a plain leathern girdle about his loins; his food was what the desert spontaneously offered—locusts and wild honey from the rock. The burden of John's preaching bore no slight resemblance to the old prophetic exhortations, whose last echo had now died away for centuries. He called upon the Jewish people to repent, to change their minds, their dispositions and affections, and thus prepared the way for the great doctrine promulgated by his Lord, of the necessity of a spiritual regeneration. That the change which John had in view was by no means of so great or so elevated

a kind as that which Jesus required, is very probable; but the particulars into which he enters when he proceeds to address classes or individuals (Matt. iii. 7, sq.; Luke iii. 7, sq.), serve fully to show that the renovation at which he aimed was not merely of a material or organic, but chiefly of a moral nature. In a very emphatic manner did he warn the ecclesiastical and legal authorities of the land of the necessity under which they lay of an entire change of view, of aim, and of desire; declaring in explicit and awful terms that their pride of nationality would avail them nothing against the coming wrathful visitation, and that they were utterly mistaken in the notion that Divine Providence had any need of them for completing its own wise purposes (Luke iii. 8, 9). The first reason assigned by John for entering on his most weighty and perilous office was announced in these words—'the kingdom of heaven is at hand.' It was his great work to prepare the mind of the nation, so that when Jesus himself came they might be a people made ready for the Lord.

Had we space to develope the moral character of John, we could show that this fine, stern, high-minded teacher possessed many eminent qualities; but his personal and official modesty in keeping, in all circumstances, in the lower rank assigned him by God, must not pass without special mention. The doctrine and manner of life of John appear to have roused the entire of the south of Palestine, and people flocked from all parts to the spot where, on the banks of the Jordan, he baptized thousands unto repentance. Such, indeed, was the fame which he had gained, that 'people were in expectation, and all men mused in their hearts of John, whether he were the Christ or not' (Luke iii. 15). Had he chosen, John might without doubt have assumed to himself the higher office, and risen to great worldly power. But he was faithful to his trust, and never failed to declare, in the fullest and clearest manner, that he was not the Christ, but merely his harbinger, and that the sole work he had to do was to usher in the day-spring from on high.

The more than prophetic fame of the Baptist reached the ears of Jesus in his Nazarene dwelling, far distant from the locality of John (Matt. ii. 22, 23). The nature of the report—namely, that his Divinely-predicted forerunner had appeared in Judæa—showed our Lord that the time was now come for his being made manifest to Israel. Accordingly he comes to the place where John is to be baptized of him, in order that thus he might fulfil all that was required under the dispensation which was about to disappear (Matt. iii. 13). John's sense of inferiority inclines him to ask rather than to give baptism in the case of Jesus, who, however, wills to have it so, and is accordingly baptized of John. Immediately on the termination of this symbolical act, a Divine attestation is given from the opened vault of heaven, declaring Jesus to be in truth the long-looked-for Messiah—'This is my beloved Son, in whom I am well pleased' (Matt. iii. 17).

The relation which subsisted between John and Jesus, after the emphatic testimony above recorded had been borne, we have not the materials to describe with full certainty.

It seems but natural to think, when their hitherto relative position is taken into account, that John would forthwith lay down his office of harbinger, which, now that the Sun of Righteousness himself had appeared, was entirely fulfilled and terminated. Such a step he does not appear to have taken. On the contrary, the language of Scripture seems to imply that the Baptist church continued side by side with the Messianic (Matt. xi 3; Luke vii. 19; Matt. ix. 14; Luke xi. 1; John iii. 23), and remained long after John's execution (Acts xix. 3). Still, though it has been generally assumed that John did not lay down his office, we are not satisfied that the New Testament establishes this alleged fact. John may have ceased to execute his own peculiar work, as the forerunner, but may justifiably have continued to bear his most important testimony to the Messiahship of Christ; or he may even have altogether given up the duties of active life some time, at least, before his death; and yet his disciples, both before and after that event, may have maintained their individuality as a religious communion. Nor is it impossible that some misconception or some sinister motive may have had weight in preventing the Baptist church from dissolving and passing into that of Christ. It was, not improbably, with a view to remove some error of this kind that John sent the embassy of his disciples to Jesus which is recorded in Matt. xi. 3; Luke vii. 19. No intimation is found in the record that *John* required evidence to give him satisfaction; and all the language that is used is proper and pertinent if we suppose that the doubt lay only in the minds of his disciples. That the terms employed *admit* the interpretation that John was not without some misgivings (Luke vii. 23; Matt. xi. 6), we are free to allow. And if any doubt had grown up in the Baptist's mind, it was most probably owing to the defective spirituality of his views; for even of him Jesus has declared, 'he that is least in the kingdom of heaven is greater than he' (Matt. xi. 11). Were this the case, it would of itself account not only for the embassy sent by John to Jesus, but also for the continuance and perpetuation of John's separate influence as the founder of a sect.

The manner of John's death is too well known to require to be detailed here (Matt. iv. 12; xiv. 3; Luke iii. 19; Mark vi. 17; Joseph. *Antiq.* xviii. 5. 2). He reproved a tyrant for a heinous crime, and received his reward in decapitation.

JOHN THE EVANGELIST. This eminent Apostle was the son of Zebedee, a fisherman, and of Salome. It is probable that he was born at Bethsaida, on the lake of Galilee. His parents appear to have been in easy circumstances; at least, we find that Zebedee employed hired servants (Mark i. 20), and that Salome was among the number of those women who contributed to the maintenance of Jesus (Matt. xxvii. 56). We also find that John received Mary into his house after the death of Jesus. Since this house seems to have been situated at Jerusalem, it would appear that he was the owner of two houses. John's acquaintance, also, with the high-priest (xviii. 15) seems to indicate that he lived at Jerusalem, and belonged to the wealthier class. We may suppose that from a tender age he nourished religious feelings, since Salome, who evinced so much love for Jesus, probably fostered at an earlier period those hopes of a Messiah which

she expresses in Matt. xx. 20; and we find that he entered into communion with the Baptist from pure motives. On the banks of the Jordan the Baptist directed John to Jesus, and he immediately became the Lord's disciple, and accompanied him on his return to Galilee. Having arrived there, he at first resumed his trade, but was afterwards called to remain permanently with the Redeemer (Luke v. 5-10). Jesus was particularly attached to John (John xiii. 23; xix. 26; xx. 2; xxi. 7), who was one of the three who were distinguished above the other apostles (Matt. xvii. 1; xxvi. 37; Mark v. 37). After the ascension, John abode at Jerusalem, where Paul met him on his third journey, about the year 52 (Gal. ii. 3-9). Since he had undertaken the care of the mother of Jesus, we cannot well suppose that he left Jerusalem before Mary's death; and, indeed, we find that about the year 58, when Paul was at Ephesus, John was not yet living there. If we consider the great importance of Ephesus among the various churches of Asia Minor, and the dangers arising from false teachers, who were prevalent there as early as the days of Paul (Acts xx. 29), it will appear likely that John was sent to Ephesus after Paul had left that scene, about the year 65. During the time of his activity in Asia Minor he was exiled by the Roman emperor to Patmos, one of the Sporadic isles in the Ægean Sea, where, according to Revelations i. 9, he wrote the Apocalypse. Irenæus and, following him, Eusebius state that John beheld the visions of the Apocalypse about the close of the reign of Domitian. If this statement can be depended upon, the exile to Patmos also took place under Domitian, who died A.D. 96. Tertullian relates that in the reign of Domitian John was forcibly conveyed to Rome, where he was thrown into a cask of oil; that he was miraculously released, and then brought to Patmos. But since none of the ancient writers besides the rather undiscriminating Tertullian, relate this circumstance, and since this mode of capital punishment was unheard of at Rome, we ought not to lay much stress upon it. It is, however, likely that John was called to suffer for his faith, since Polycrates, bishop of Ephesus, writing about A.D. 200, calls him 'martyr.' According to Eusebius, he returned from exile during the reign of Nerva. The three epistles of John, as also the affecting account concerning his fidelity as a spiritual pastor, given by Clemens Alexandrinus, testify that he was the pastor of a large diocese. John's second Epistle, ver. 12, and third Epistle, ver. 14, indicate that he made journeys of pastoral visitation. John died at Ephesus past the age of ninety, in the reign of the Emperor Trajan. According to Jerome, he was a hundred years old, and according to Suidas, a hundred and twenty.*

---

* Jerome relates that when John had attained a great age he was so feeble that he could not walk to the assemblies of the church; he, therefore, caused himself to be carried in by young men. He was no longer able to say much, but he constantly repeated the words, 'Little children, love one another.' On being asked why he constantly repeated this one saying, he replied, 'Because it is the command of the Lord; and enough is done if this is done.'

JOHN, THE. GOSPEL OF. During the eighteenth century and the first ten years of the nineteenth, the Gospel of John was attacked, but with feeble arguments, by some English Deists, and by four German theologians. A similar attack has lately been made by Strauss, who, although in the third edition of *The Life of Jesus* he manifested an inclination to give up his doubts, yet resolutely returned to them in the fourth edition, principally, as he himself confesses, because ' without them one could not escape from believing the miracles of Christ.' It is unnecessary, however, to refute his arguments, as they are quite unimportant, and have met with little sympathy even in Germany. It may suffice to observe, that during the lapse of ages up to the conclusion of the eighteenth century, no one ever expressed a doubt respecting the genuineness of John's Gospel, except one small sect, whose scepticism, however, was not based upon historical, but merely upon dogmatical grounds.

John's Gospel differs very much in substance from the first three Gospels. But the most striking difference is that of the speeches; and even here the difference is, perhaps, still more apparent in the form than in the substance of them. The difference of the CONTENTS may be accounted for by supposing that John intended to relate and complete the history of the Lord according to his own view of it. We are led to this supposition from the following circumstances: that, with the exception of the history of his passion and his resurrection, there are only two sections in which John coincides with the synoptic gospels (vi. 1-21; xii. 1); that he altogether omits such important facts as the baptism of Jesus by John, the history of his temptation and transfiguration, the institution of the Lord's supper, and the internal conflict at Gethsemane; and that chapters i. 32, iii. 24, xi. 2, indicate that he presupposed his readers to be already acquainted with the Gospel history. He confined himself to such communications as were wanting in the others, especially with regard to the speeches of Jesus.

The peculiarities of John's Gospel more especially consist in the four following doctrines:—

1. That of the mystical relation of the Son to the Father.

2. That of the mystical relation of the Redeemer to believers.

3. The announcement of the Holy Ghost as the Comforter.

4. The peculiar importance ascribed to Love.

Although there can be shown in the writings of the other Evangelists some isolated dicta of the Lord, which seem to bear the impress of John, it can also be shown that they contain thoughts not originating with that disciple, but with the Lord himself. Matthew (xi. 27) speaks of the relation of the Son to the Father so entirely in the style of John, that persons not sufficiently versed in Holy Writ are apt to search for this passage in the Gospel of John. The mystical union of the Son with believers is expressed in Matt. xxviii. 20. The promise of the effusion of the Holy Ghost, in order to perfect the disciples, is found in Luke xxiv. 49. The doctrine of Paul with respect to love, in 1 Cor. xiii., entirely resembles what, according to John, Christ taught on the same subject. Paul here deserves our particular attention. In the writings of Paul are found Christian truths which have their points of coalescence only in John, viz., that Christ is *the image of the invisible God*, by whom all things are created (Col. i. 15, 16). Paul considers the Spirit of God in the church, *the spiritual Christ*, as Jesus himself does (John xiv. 16).

That the speeches of Christ have been faithfully reported may be seen by a comparison of the speeches of the Baptist in the Gospel of John. The Baptist's speeches bear an entirely Old Testament character: they are full of allusions to the Old Testament, and abound in sententious expressions (John iii. 27-30; i. 26-36).

We have already intimated our opinion as to the purport and plan of the Gospel of John. Most of the earlier critics considered the Gospel of John to have had a polemico-dogmatical purport. According to Irenæus, John wrote with the intention of combating the errors of Cerinthus the Gnostic. Others suppose that his writings were directed against the disciples of John the Baptist. It is not improbable that the Evangelist had in view, both in his Introduction and also in ch. xix. 34, 35, some heretical opinions of those times; but it cannot be maintained that this is the case throughout the whole of the Gospel. He himself states (xx. 31) that his work had a more general object.

One of the peculiarities of John is, that in speaking of the adversaries of Jesus, he always calls them the Jews. This observation has, in modern times, given rise to a peculiar opinion concerning the plan of John's Gospel, namely, that the Evangelist has, from the very beginning of the Gospel, the following theme before his eyes:—The eternal combat between Divine light and the corruption of mankind, exemplified by the mutual opposition subsisting between the hostile Jewish party and the manifestation of the Son of God, which combat terminates in the victory of light.

The Introduction of the Gospel of John expresses this theme in speaking of the opposition of the world to the incarnate Logos. This theme is here expressed in the same manner as the leading idea of a musical composition is expressed in the overture. As the leading idea of the whole Epistle to the Romans is contained in ch. i. 17, so the theme of the Gospel of John is contained in ch. i. 11-13. The Gospel is divided into two principal sections. The first extends to ch. xii. It comprehends the public functions of Jesus, and terminates with a brief summary (ver. 44-50). The second section contains the history of the Passion and of the Resurrection. The reader is prepared for this section by ch. xii. 23-32. The leading idea of this speech is, that Destruction is necessary, because without it there can be no Resurrection. With ch. xiii. begins the history of our Lord's Passion. In the third verse the Apostle directs attention to the fact that the suffering would finally lead to glory. In the first section is described how the opposition of the influential men among the Jews was gradually increased until the decisive fact of the resurrection of Lazarus led to a public outburst of their hatred. This description terminates with the official decree of Caiaphas (xi. 49, 50).

The Fathers supposed that the Gospel of John

was written at Ephesus, and there is some internal evidence in favour of the statement. One writer affirms that John wrote the Gospel which bears his name in Patmos, but that it was edited by the same Gaius whom Paul in the epistle to the Romans calls *mine host*. One might be inclined to explain by this circumstance the postscript contained in John xxi 24, 25.

JOHN, THE EPISTLES OF. For the authenticity of the first epistle very ancient testimony may be adduced. Papias, the disciple of John, quotes some passages from it. Polycarp, also, another disciple of John, quotes a passage from this epistle. So, also, Irenæus.

The author of the first epistle describes himself, at its commencement, as an eye-witness of the life of our Lord. The style and language manifestly harmonize with those of the author of the Gospel of John. The polemics, also, which in ch. ii. 18-26, are directed against the Docetic Gnostics, in ch. iv. 1-3, agree with the sphere of action in Asia Minor in which the Evangelist John was placed. We may, therefore, suppose that the epistle was written to Christian congregations in Asia Minor, which were placed under the spiritual care of the apostle. It is generally admitted that ch. i. 2 refers to the Gospel. If this is correct, the apostle wrote this epistle at a very advanced age, after he had written his gospel. The epistle breathes love and devotion, but also zeal for moral strictness (iii. 6-8 ; v. 16). There is a remarkable absence of logical connection in the form of separate expressions, and in the transitions from one thought to another. Some writers have been inclined to find a reason for this in the advanced age of the writer. Old age may, perhaps, have contributed to this characteristic, but it is chiefly attributable to the mental peculiarity of the apostle. There has been no subject connected with Biblical literature which has attracted more attention than this epistle, in consequence of the controversies which have existed since the commencement of the sixteenth century, respecting the celebrated passage in 1 John v. 7, 8. We cannot enter here into the history of that controversy, which has continued with more or less of asperity to our own day. We shall merely remark that the disputed passage is found in no Greek manuscript, save only in two, both belonging to the fifteenth century; and that it has not once been quoted by any of the Greek, Latin, or Oriental fathers. It is now, therefore, generally omitted in all critical editions of the New Testament.

The second and third epistles of John were originally wanting in the ancient Syriac translation. From their nature, it may easily be explained how it happened that they were less generally known in ancient Christian congregations, and that the fathers do not quote them so often as other parts of Scripture, since they are very short, and treat of private affairs. The private nature of their contents removes also the suspicion that they could have been forged, since it would be difficult to discover any purpose which could have led to such a forgery.

The second epistle is addressed to a lady, called Kuria, which name frequently occurs in ancient writers as that of a woman.

The third epistle is addressed to Gaius, a person otherwise unknown. It is remarkable that the writer of this epistle calls himself 'the presbyter' or 'elder.' Some writers have been inclined to ascribe these letters to the presbyter John, who is sometimes spoken of in the ancient church, and to whom even the Apocalypse has been attributed ; but if the presbyter John wrote these epistles, John's Gospel also must be ascribed to the same person, of whom otherwise so little is known. This, however, is inadmissible. We may suppose that the term 'presbyter' or 'elder' expressed in the epistles of John a degree of friendliness, and was chosen on account of the advanced age of the writer. The apostle Paul, also, in his friendly letter to Philemon, abstains from the title Apostle. The circumstances and events in the church, to which the second epistle alludes, coincide with those which are otherwise known to have happened in John's congregation. Here, also, are allusions to the dangers arising from the Gnostic heresy. The admonition, in verse 10, not to receive such heretics as Christian brethren, agrees with the ancient tradition, that John made haste to quit a public bath after Cerinthus the Gnostic entered it, declaring he was afraid the building would fall down.

JOHN MARK. [MARK.]

JOHN HYRCANUS. [MACCABEES.]

JOI'ADA (contraction of JEHOIADA, which see), a high-priest of the Jews, successor to Eliashib, or Joashib, who lived under Nehemiar., about B.C. 434 (Neh. xiii. 28).

JOK'SHAN (*fowler*), second son of Abraham and Keturah, whose sons Sheba and Dedan appear to have been the ancestors of the Sabæans and Dedanites, who peopled a part of Arabia Felix (Gen. xxv. 2, 3) [ARABIA].

JOK'TAN (*small*), one of the sons of Eber, a descendant from Shem (Gen. x. 25, 26), and the supposed progenitor of many tribes in Southern Arabia. The Arabians call him Kahtan, and recognise him as one of the principal founders of their nation.

JOK'THEEL (*God-subdued*). 1. A name given by King Azariah to the city Sela, or Petra, the capital of Arabia Petræa, when he took it from the Edomites (2 Kings xiv. 7) [PETRA]. 2. There was also a city of this name in the tribe of Judah (Josh. xv. 38).

JON'ADAB (*God-impelled*). 1. A nephew of David, a crafty person, whose counsel suggested to his cousin Ammon the means by which he accomplished his abominable design upon his half-sister Tamar (2 Sam. xiii. 4, 5).

2. A son or descendant of Rechab, the progenitor of those nomadic Rechabites, who held themselves bound by a vow to abstain from wine, and never to relinquish the nomadic life. The principle on which the tribe acted may be considered elsewhere [RECHABITES]. Jonadab was at the head of this tribe at the time when Jehu received his commission to exterminate the house of Ahab, and is supposed to have added to its ancient austerities the inhibition of wine. He was held in great respect among the Israelites generally : and Jehu, alive to the importance of obtaining the countenance and sanction of such a man to his proceedings, took him up in his chariot, when on his road to Samaria to complete the work he had begun at Jezreel. The terms of the colloquy which took place on this occasion are rather

remarkable. Perceiving Jonadab, he saluted him, and called out, ' Is thine heart right, as my heart is with thy heart?' Jonadab answered, ' It is.' Then said Jehu, ' If it be, give me thine hand.' And he gave him his hand, and was taken up into the chariot, Jehu inviting him to ' Come and see my zeal for the Lord ' (2 Kings x. 15-17; Jer. xxxv. 6-10) It would seem that the Rechabites were a branch of the Kenites, over another branch of whom Heber was chief in the time of Deborah and Barak (Judg. iv. 11, 17): and as it is expressly said that Jonadab went out to meet Jehu, it seems probable that the people of Samaria, alarmed at the menacing letter which they had received from Jehu, had induced Jonadab to go to meet and appease him on the road. His venerated character, his rank as the head of a tribe, and his neutral position, well qualified him for this mission; and it was quite as much the interest of Jonadab to conciliate the new dynasty, in whose founder he beheld the minister of the divine decrees, as it was that of Jehu to obtain his concurrence and support in proceedings which he could not but know were likely to render him odious to the people.

JO'NAH (*a dove*), the fifth in order of the minor prophets. No era is assigned to him in the book of his prophecy, yet there is little doubt of his being the same person who is spoken of in 2 Kings xiv. 25. His birthplace was Gath-hepher, in the tribe of Zebulon. Jonah flourished in or before the reign of Jeroboam II., and predicted the successful conquests, enlarged territory, and brief prosperity of the Israelitish kingdom under that monarch's sway.

The book of Jonah contains an account of the prophet's commission to denounce Nineveh, and of his refusal to undertake the embassy—of the method he employed to escape the unwelcome task [TARSHISH], and the miraculous means which God used to curb his self-willed spirit, and subdue his petulant and querulous disposition. The third and fourth chapters briefly detail Jonah's fulfilment of the divine command, and present us with another exemplification of his refractory temper. His attempt to flee from the presence of the Lord must have sprung from a partial insanity, produced by the excitement of distracting motives in an irascible and melancholy heart. The temerity and folly of the fugitive could scarcely be credited, if they had not been equalled by future outbreaks of a similar peevish and morbid infatuation. The mind of Jonah was dark and moody. not unlike a lake which mirrors in the waters the gloomy thunder-clouds which overshadow it, and flash over its sullen waves a momentary gleam.

The history of Jonah is certainly striking and extraordinary. Its characteristic prodigy does not resemble the other miraculous phenomena recorded in Scripture; yet we must believe in its literal occurrence, as the Bible affords no indication of its being a mythus, allegory, or parable. On the other hand, our Saviour's pointed and peculiar allusion to it is a presumption of its reality (Matt. xii. 40). The opinion of the earlier Jews is also in favour of the literality of the adventure. It requires less faith to credit this simple excerpt from Jonah's biography, than to believe the numerous hypotheses that have been invented to deprive it of its supernatural character, the great majority of them being clumsy and far-fetched, doing violence to the language, and despite to the spirit of revelation. In vindication of the reality of this striking narrative, it may be argued that the allusions of Christ to Old Testament events on similar occasions are to actual occurrences (John iii. 14; vi. 48); that the purpose which God had in view justified his miraculous interposition; that this miracle must have had a salutary effect both on the minds of the Ninevites and on the people of Israel. Neither is the character of Jonah improbable. Many reasons might induce him to avoid the discharge of his prophetic duty—fear of being thought a false prophet, scorn of a foreign and hostile race, desire for their utter destruction, a false dignity which might reckon it beneath his prerogative to officiate among uncircumcised idolaters. Some, who cannot altogether reject the reality of the narrative, suppose it to have had an historical basis, though its present form be fanciful or mythical. Grimm regards it as a dream produced in that sleep which fell upon Jonah as he lay on the sides of the ship, and others regard this book as an allegory.

Various other hypotheses have been proposed which are all vague and baseless, and do not merit a special refutation. Endeavouring to free us from one difficulty they plunge us into others yet more intricate and perplexing. Much profane wit has been expended on the miraculous means of Jonah's deliverance, very unnecessarily and very absurdly; it is simply said, ' The Lord had prepared a great fish to swallow up Jonah.' Now the species of marine animal is not defined, and the original word is often used to specify, not the genus whale, but any large fish or sea-monster. All objections to its being a whale which lodged Jonah in its stomach from its straitness of throat, or rareness of haunt in the Mediterranean, are thus removed. The Scripture speaks only of an enormous fish, which under God's direction swallowed the prophet, and does not point out the species to which the voracious prowler belonged. Since the days of Bochart it has been a common opinion that the fish was of the shark species or ' sea-dog.' Entire human bodies have been found in some fishes of this kind. The stomach, too, has no influence on any living substance admitted into it. Granting all these facts as proof of what is termed the economy of miracles, still must we say, in reference to the supernatural preservation of Jonah, Is anything too hard for the Lord?

On what portion of the coast Jonah was set down in safety we are not informed. The prophet proceeded, on receiving a second commission, to fulfil it. The fearful menace had the desired effect. The city humbled itself before God, and a respite was vouchsafed. The king (Pul, according to Usher) and his people fasted, and their penitence was accepted. The spirit of Jonah was chafed that the doom he had uttered was not executed. He retired to a station out of the city whence he might witness the threatened catastrophe. Under the shadow of a gourd prepared by God he reclined, while Jehovah taught him by the growth and speedy death of this plant, and his attachment to it, a sublime lesson of patient and forgiving generosity. The book of Jonah is a simple narrative, with the exception of the prayer or thanksgiving in chap. ii. Its style and mode of narration are uniform. There are no traces of compilation, as Nactigall supposed; neither is the prayer, as De Wette imagines, improperly borrowed from some other sources. That prayer contains, indeed, not only imagery peculiar to itself, but also such imagery as at once was suggested to the mind of a pious Hebrew preserved in circumstances of extreme jeopardy. On this principle we account for the similarity of some portions of its phraseology to Ps. lix., xlii., &c. The language in both places had been hallowed by frequent usage, and had become the consecrated idiom of a distressed and succoured Israelite. The hymn seems to have been composed after his deliverance, and the reason why his deliverance is noted after the hymn is recorded may be to show the occasion of its composition.

1. JONATHAN (*God-given*), a Levite descended from Gershom, the son of Moses, not Manasseh. as in our common copies, an interpolation made (Judg. xviii. 30) in order to save the character of the great lawgiver from the stain of having an idolater among his immediate descendants. The history of this Jonathan is involved in the narrative which occupies Judges xvii., xviii.; and the events themselves appear to have occurred soon after the death of Joshua, and of the elders who outlived him, when the government was in a most unsettled state.

Jonathan, who was resident at Bethlehem, lived at a time when the dues of the sanctuary did not afford a livelihood to the numerous Levites who had a claim upon them; and belonged to a tribe destitute of the landed possessions which gave to all others a sufficient maintenance. He, therefore, went forth to seek his fortune. In Mount Ephraim he came to 'a house of gods,' which had been established by one Micah, who wanted nothing but a priest to make his establishment complete [MICAH]. This person made Jonathan what was manifestly considered the handsome offer of engaging him as his priest for his victuals, a yearly suit of clothes, and ten shekels (twenty-five shillings) a year in money. Here he lived for some time, till the Danite spies, who were sent by their tribe to explore the north, passed this way and formed his acquaintance. When, not long after, the body of armed Danites passed the same way when going to settle near the sources of the Jordan, the spies mentioned Micah's establishment to them; on which they went and took away not only 'the ephod, the teraphim, and the graven image,' but the priest also, that they might set up the same worship in the place of which they were going to take possession. Micah vainly protested against this robbery; but Jonathan himself was glad at the improvement in his prospects, and from that time, even down to the captivity, he and his descendants continued to be priests of the Danites in the town of Laish, the name of which they changed to Dan.

There is not any reason to suppose that this establishment, whether in the hands of Micah or of the Danites, involved an apostacy from Jehovah. It appears rather to have been an attempt to localize or domesticate His presence, under those symbols and forms of service which were common among the neighbouring nations, but

were forbidden to the Hebrews. The offence here was twofold,—the establishment of a sacred ritual different from the only one which the law recognised, and the worship by symbols, naturally leading to idolatry, with the ministration of one who could not legally be a priest, but only a Levite, and under circumstances in which no Aaronic priest could legally have officiated. It is more than likely that this establishment was eventually merged in that of the golden calf, which Jeroboam set up in this place, his choice of which may very possibly have been determined by its being already in possession of 'a house of gods.'

2. JONATHAN, eldest son of Saul, king of Israel, and consequently heir apparent of the throne which David was destined to occupy (1 Sam. xiv. 9; 1 Chron. viii. 33; ix. 39). The war with the Philistines, which occupied the early part of his father's reign, afforded Jonathan more than one opportunity of displaying the chivalrous valour and the princely qualities with which he was endowed. His exploit in surprising the Philistine garrison at Michmash, attended only by his armour-bearer, is one of the most daring which history or even romance records (1 Sam. xiv. 1-14). His father came to follow up this victory, and in the ensuing pursuit of the confounded Philistines, Jonathan, spent with fatigue and hunger, refreshed himself with some wild honey which he found in a wood through which he passed. He knew not that his father had rashly vowed to put to death any one who touched a morsel of food before night. When the fact transpired, Saul felt himself bound to execute his vow even upon his gallant son; but the people, with whom the young prince was a great favourite, interposed and prevented the execution of his design (1 Sam. xiv. 16-52).

Jealousy and every mean or low feeling were strangers to the generous heart of Jonathan. Valiant and accomplished himself, none knew better how to acknowledge valour and accomplishment in others. The act of David in meeting the challenge of Goliath, and in overcoming that huge barbarian, entirely won his heart; and from that day forward the son of Jesse found no one who loved him so tenderly, who admired his high gifts with so much enthusiasm, or who risked so much to preserve him from harm, as the very prince whom he was destined to exclude from a throne. Jonathan knew well what was to happen, and he submitted cheerfully to the appointment which gave the throne of his father to the young shepherd of Bethlehem. In the intensity of his love and confidence he shrank not to think of David as his destined king and master; and his dreams of the future pictured nothing brighter than the day in which David should reign over Israel, and he be one with him in friendship, and next to him in place and council.

When Saul began to hate David as his intended successor, he was highly displeased at the friendship which had arisen between him and his son. This exposed Jonathan to much contumely, and even to danger of life; for, once at least, the king's passion against him on this account rose so high that he cast a javelin at him 'to smite him to the wall.'

This unequivocal act taught Jonathan that the court of Saul was no safe place for David. He

223. [Joppa.]

told him so, and they parted with many tears. David then set forth upon those wanderings among strangers and in solitary places, which lasted all the time of Saul. The friends met only once more. Saul was in pursuit of David when he was in the wilderness of Ziph; and Jonathan could not forbear coming to him secretly in the wood to give him comfort and encouragement (1 Sam. xxiii. 16-18). Nothing more is related of Jonathan till both he and his father lost their lives in the fatal battle of Gilboa, combating against the enemies of their country.

JOP'PA, a sea-port town and haven on the coast of Palestine, situated on an eminence, in a sandy soil, about forty miles N.W. of Jerusalem, and nine miles W.N.W. from Ramleh. It was a very ancient town. To say nothing respecting the fabulous accounts of its great antiquity, it existed when the Israelites invaded the land of Canaan. and is mentioned as lying on the border of the tribe of Dan (Josh. xix. 46). Joppa was the only port possessed by the Israelites till Herod formed the harbour at Cæsarea; and hence it was here that the timber from Lebanon destined for both the first and second temples was landed (1 Kings v. 9; 2 Chron. ii. 16; Ezra iii. 7). It was the place to which Jonah went, in expectation of finding a ship bound on some distant voyage, and where he found one going to Tarshish (Jonah i. 3). Joppa belonged to the powers which were successively dominant on this shore; and it does not again appear in Jewish history till the time of Judas Maccabæus, when the inhabitants having, contrary to the faith of treaties, thrown 200 Jews into the sea, the hero, to avenge them, surprised the haven by night, and set the shipping on fire (2 Macc. xii. 3-7). It is mentioned in the New Testament only in connection with the visit of the Apostle Peter, who here raised Tabitha from the dead, and lodged in the outskirts of the town with Simon, the tanner, when favoured with the vision which taught him to 'call no man common or unclean' (Acts ix. 36-39; x. 5, 18; xi. 5). From the first crusade down to our own day, Joppa has been the landing-place of pilgrims going to Jerusalem. There is still here an hospital for pilgrims, dependent on the convent of St. Salvador in Jerusalem, and occupied by Spanish monks. In 1797 the place was taken by storm by the French army under Napoleon, and was sacked without mercy; when the Turkish prisoners, to the number of 500 or 600, were carried to the neighbouring sand-hills and put to death by his order.

Joppa is naturally very unfit for a haven. The port is so dangerous, from exposure to the open sea, that the surf often rolls in with the utmost violence, and even so lately as 1842 a lieutenant and some sailors were lost in pulling to the shore from an English steamer that lay in the harbour. But however bad, it was the only port which existed within reach of the important district which lay behind it inland: and the miserable state of the ancient roads, or rather perhaps the absence of any roads, made a near harbour, however incommodious, of more immediate consequence than a good one at a greater distance.

The town is approached on the land side through rich and extensive gardens and orchards, and is very picturesquely situated upon an eminence or promontory, which is crowned by a castle. It chiefly faces the north; and the buildings appear, from the steepness of the site, as if standing upon one another. The aspect of the whole is mean and gloomy, and inside the place has all the appearance of a poor though large village. There are no public buildings to engage the eye, and the houses are mean and comfortless. No ancient ruins have been observed, nor are any to be expected in a place so often destroyed in war. There are three mosques in Joppa, and Latin, Greek, and Armenian convents. The former is that in which European pilgrims and travellers usually lodge. The town still enjoys a considerable trade with the neighbouring coasts. Its chief manufacture is soap, which is largely consumed in the baths of Cairo and Damascus ; and its excellent fruits are exported in large quantities, especially water-melons, which are very extensively cultivated here and in other parts of the plain of Sharon. The inhabitants are said not to exceed 4000, of whom one-fourth are reckoned to be Christians. A British consul is now resident in the place.

JO'RAM (*God-exalted*, a contraction of JEHORAM), ninth king of Israel, son of Ahab, and successor to his elder brother Ahaziah, who died childless. He began to reign B.C. 896, and reigned twelve years (2 Kings i. 17 ; iii. 1). Joram adhered to the sinful policy of Jeroboam in the matter of the golden calves ; but, although his mother Jezebel was still alive, he discontinued the dark idolatries of Baal which she had introduced and maintained at such high cost of guilt and blood to the nation.

The Moabites had been tributary to the crown of Israel since the separation of the two kingdoms. But king Mesha deemed the defeat and death of Ahab so heavy a blow to the power of Israel that he might safely assert his independence. He accordingly did so, by withholding his tribute of ' 100,000 lambs, and 100,000 rams, with the wool.' The short reign of Ahaziah had afforded no opportunity for any operations against the revolters ; but the new king hastened to reduce them again under the yoke they had cast off. The good king of Judah, Jehoshaphat, was too easily induced to take a part in the war. He perhaps feared that the example of Moab, if allowed to be successful, might seduce into a similar course his own tributary, the king of Edom, whom he now summoned to join in this expedition. The deliverance of the allies from perishing for lack of water, and the signal overthrow of the Moabites at the word of Elisha, have been already described under ELISHA and JEHOSHAPHAT.

After this a more redoubtable enemy, Benhadad, king of Syria, occupied for a long time the attention and strength of the king. In the sacred records the more striking events of this war seem to be recorded for the sake of showing forth the great acts of ELISHA, and they have therefore been related under his name. It suffices here to indicate that they consisted in the Syrian king being constrained to terminate one campaign in consequence of all his plans being made known by the prophet to the king of Israel (2 Kings vi. 1–23) ; and in the deliverance of Samaria, according to the prediction of the prophet, from a horrible famine, caused by the city being besieged by the Syrians (2 Kings vi. 24–33 ; vii.). An interval of the war also afforded occasion for the remarkable cure of Naaman, the Syrian leper, by the same prophet (2 Kings v.) [NAAMAN].

After the death of Benhadad, Joram found a new and active enemy in his murderer and successor, Hazael. During the illness of Benhadad, the king of Israel seems to have employed himself in strengthening his eastern frontier against the Syrians, and in fortifying Ramoth-Gilead, which had fallen into his hands, and which his father had perished in the attempt to recover from the Syrians. This strong fortress thenceforth became the head-quarters of the operations beyond the river. Hazael was scarcely settled on the throne before he took arms, and marched against Ramoth, in the environs of which the Israelites sustained a defeat, and the king was wounded. He returned to Jezreel to be healed of his wounds, leaving the army in the charge of Jehu, one of his ablest and most active generals. It was in this interval that Jehu was anointed king of Israel by the messenger of Elisha, and immediately proceeded to Jezreel to fulfil his commission to exterminate the house of Ahab. The king, who went forth from the city to meet him when the watchman on the tower of Jezreel announced his approach, was slain under the circumstances described in the article JEHU ; and Ahaziah, the king of Judah, who was at Jezreel on a visit to his sick cousin, shared his fate (B.C. 884). With Joram ended the dynasty of Ahab, which reigned forty-four years in Israel (2 Kings viii. 25–29 ; ix. 1–20).

JOR'DAN, the principal river of Palestine. [PALESTINE.]

JO'SEPH (*God-increased*), son of Jacob and Rachel, born under peculiar circumstances, as may be seen in Gen. xxx. 22 ; on which account, and because he was the son of his old age (xxxvii. 3), he was beloved by his father more than were the rest of his children, though Benjamin, as being also a son of Jacob's favourite wife, Rachel, was in a peculiar manner dear to the patriarch. The partiality evinced towards Joseph by his father excited jealousy on the part of his brethren, the rather that they were born of different mothers (xxxvii. 2). Joseph had reached his seventeenth year, when some conduct on the part of his brothers seems to have been such as in the opinion of Joseph to require the special attention of Jacob, to whom, accordingly, he communicated the facts. This greatly increased their dislike to him, and they henceforth ' hated him, and could not speak peaceably unto him ' (xxxvii. 4). Their aversion, however, was carried to the highest pitch when Joseph acquainted them with two dreams, which appeared to indicate that Joseph would acquire pre-eminence in the family, if not sovereignty ; and while even his father rebuked him, his brothers were filled with envy. Jacob, however, was not aware of the depth of their ill will ; so that on one occasion, having a desire to hear intelligence of his sons, who were pasturing their flocks at a distance, he did not hesitate to make Joseph his messenger for that purpose. His appearing in view of his brothers was the signal for their malice to gain head. They began to devise means for his immediate destruction, which they would unhesitatingly have effected, but for his half-brother, Reuben, who, as the eldest son, might well be the party to interfere on behalf of Joseph. A compromise was entered into, in virtue of which the youth was stripped of the distinguishing vestments which he owed to his father's affection, and cast into a pit. Having performed this evil deed, and while they were taking refreshment, the brothers beheld a caravan of Arabian merchants, who were bearing the spices and aromatic gums of India down to the well-known and much-frequented mart, Egypt. On the proposal of Judah they resolved that, instead of allowing Joseph to perish, they should sell him to the merchants. This was accordingly done. Joseph was sold for a slave, to be conveyed by his masters into Egypt. While on his way thither, Reuben returned to the pit, intending to rescue his brother, and convey him safely back to their father. Joseph was gone. On which Reuben went to the wicked young men, who, not content with selling a brother into slavery, determined to punish their father for his partiality towards the unoffending sufferer. With this view they dipped Joseph's party-coloured garment in the blood of a kid and sent it to Jacob, in order to make him believe that his favourite child had been torn to pieces by some wild beast. The trick succeeded, and Jacob was grieved beyond measure.

Meanwhile the merchants sold Joseph to Potiphar, an officer of Pharaoh's, and captain of the royal guard, who was a native of the country. In Potiphar's house Joseph enjoyed the highest confidence and the largest prosperity. A higher power watched over him; and whatever he undertook succeeded, till at length his master gave everything into his hands. But a second time he innocently brought on himself the vengeance of the ill-disposed. Charged by his master's wife with the very crime to which he had in vain been tempted, he was at once cast by his master into the state prison.

The narrative, which is obviously constructed in order to show the workings of divine Providence, states, however, that Joseph was not left without special aid, in consequence of which he gained favour with the keeper of the prison to such an extent that every thing was put under his direction. Two of the regal officers, ' the chief of the butlers' and ' the chief of the bakers,' having offended their royal master, were consigned to the same prison with Joseph. While there, each one had a dream, which Joseph interpreted correctly. The butler, whose fate was auspicious, promised the young Hebrew to employ his influence to procure his deliverance; but when again in the enjoyment of his ' butlership,' ' he forgat' Joseph (xl.). Pharaoh himself, however, had two dreams, which found in Joseph a successful expounder; for the butler then remembered the skill of his prison-companion, and advised his royal master to put it to the test in his own case. Pharaoh's dream, as interpreted by Joseph, foreboded the approach of a seven years' famine; to abate the evils of which Joseph recommended that some ' discreet and wise ' man should be chosen and set in full power over the land of Egypt. The monarch was alarmed, and called a council of his advisers. The wisdom of Joseph was recognised as of divine origin and supereminent value; and the king and his ministers (whence it appears that the Egyptian monarchy—at Memphis—was not despotic, but constitutional) resolved that Joseph should be made (to borrow a term from Rome) Dictator in the approaching time of need. The highest honours were conferred upon him. He was made ruler over all the land of Egypt, and the

daughter of Poti-pherah, priest of On, given him to wife.

Seven years of abundance afforded Joseph opportunity to carry into effect such plans as secured an ample provision against the seven years of need. The famine came, but it found a prepared people. The visitation did not depend on any mere local causes, for ' the famine was over all the face of the earth,' ' and all countries came into Egypt to Joseph to buy corn' (ver. 56, 57). Among these customers appeared ten brethren, sons of the Hebrew Jacob. They had of necessity to appear before Joseph, whose licence for the purchase of corn was indispensable. Joseph had probably expected to see them, and he seems to have formed a deliberate plan of action. His conduct has brought on him the always ready charges of those who would rather impeach than study the Bible, and even friends of that sacred book have hardly in this case done Joseph full justice. Joseph's main object appears to have been to make his brothers feel and recognise their guilt in their conduct towards him. For this purpose suffering, then as well as now, was indispensable. Accordingly Joseph feigned not to know his brothers, charged them with being spies, threatened them with imprisonment, and allowed them to return home to fetch their younger brother, as a proof of their veracity, only on condition that one of them should remain behind in chains, with a prospect of death before him should not their words be verified. Then it was, and not before, that ' they said one to another, We are verily guilty concerning our brother, in that we saw the anguish of his soul and would not hear; therefore is this distress come upon us' (xlii. 21). On which, after weeping bitterly, he by common agreement bound his brother Simeon, and left him in custody. At length Jacob consented to Benjamin's going in company with his brothers, and provided with a present consisting of balm, honey, spices and myrrh, nuts and almonds, and with double money in their hands (double, in order that they might repay the sum which Joseph had caused to be put into each man's sack at their departure, if, as Jacob supposed, ' it was an oversight'), they went again down to Egypt and stood before Joseph (xliii. 15); and there, too, stood Benjamin, Joseph's beloved brother. The required pledge of truthfulness was given. If it is asked why such a pledge was demanded, since the giving of it caused pain to Jacob, the answer may be thus: Joseph knew not how to demean himself towards his family until he ascertained its actual condition. That knowledge he could hardly be certain he had gained from the mere words of men who had spared his life only to sell him into slavery. How had these wicked men behaved towards his venerable father? His beloved brother Benjamin, was he safe? or had he suffered from their jealousy and malice the worse fate with which he himself had been threatened? Nothing but the sight of Benjamin could answer these questions, and resolve these doubts.

Benjamin had come, and immediately a natural change took place in Joseph's conduct: the brother began to claim his rights in Joseph's bosom. Jacob was safe, and Benjamin was safe. Joseph's heart melted at the sight of Benjamin: ' And he said to the ruler of his house, Bring these men home, and slay and make ready, for these men shall dine with me at noon' (xliii. 16). But guilt is always the ready parent of fear. Accordingly the brothers expected nothing but being reduced to slavery. When taken to their own brother's house, they imagined they were being entrapped. A colloquy ensued between them and Joseph's steward, whence it appeared that the money put into their sacks, to which they now attributed their peril, was in truth a present from Joseph, designed, after his own brotherly manner, to aid his family in their actual necessities. Noon came, and with it Joseph, whose first question regarded home : ' He asked them of their welfare, and said, Is your father well, the old man of whom ye spake ? is he yet alive ? And he lifted up his eyes and saw his brother Benjamin, his mother's son, and said, Is this your younger brother ? And he said, God be gracious unto thee, my son !' ' And Joseph made haste, for his bowels did yearn upon his brother, and he sought where to weep, and he entered into his chamber and wept there.' Does this look like harshness ?

The connection brings into view an Egyptian custom, which is of more than ordinary importance, in consequence of its being adopted in the Jewish polity; 'And they set on (food) for him by himself (Joseph), and for them by themselves (the brethren), and for the Egyptians which did eat with them, by themselves, because the Egyptians might not eat bread with the Hebrews; for that is an abomination with the Egyptians' (ver. 32). This passage is also interesting, as proving that Joseph had not, in his princely grandeur, become ashamed of his origin, nor consented to receive adoption into a strange nation: he was still a Hebrew, waiting, like Moses after him, for the proper season to use his power for the good of his own people.

Joseph, apparently with a view to ascertain how far his brethren were faithful to their father, hit upon a plan which would in its issue serve to show whether they would make any, and what, sacrifice, in order to fulfil their solemn promise of restoring Benjamin in safety to Jacob. Accordingly he ordered not only that every man's money (as before) should be put in his sack's mouth, but also that his 'silver cup in which my lord drinketh, and whereby he divineth,' should be put in the sack's mouth of the youngest. The brethren departed, but were soon overtaken by Joseph's steward, who charged them with having surreptitiously carried off this costly and highly-valued vessel. They on their part vehemently repelled the accusation, adding, 'with whomsoever of thy servants it be found, both let him die, and we also will be my lord's bondmen.' A search was made, and the cup was found in Benjamin's sack. Accordingly they returned to the city. And now came the hour of trial : Would they purchase their own liberation by surrendering Benjamin ? After a most touching interview, in which they proved themselves worthy and faithful, Joseph declared himself unable any longer to withstand the appeal of natural affection. On this occasion Judah, who was the spokesman, showed the deepest regard to his aged father's feelings, and entreated for the liberation of Benjamin even at the price of his own liberty. In the whole of literature we know of

nothing more simple, natural, true, and impressive.

Most natural and impressive is the scene also which ensues, in which Joseph, after informing his brethren who he was, and inquiring, first of all, ' Is my father alive ?' expresses feelings free from the slightest taint of revenge, and even shows how, under Divine Providence, the conduct of his brothers had issued in good—' God sent me before you to preserve a posterity in the earth, and to save your lives by a great deliverance.' Five years had yet to ensue in which ' there would be neither earing nor harvest,' and therefore the brethren were directed to return home and bring Jacob down to Egypt with all speed. ' And he fell upon his brother Benjamin's neck and wept; and Benjamin wept upon his neck. Moreover, he kissed all his brethren, and wept upon them; and after that his brethren talked with him' (xlv 14, 15).

The news of these striking events was carried to Pharaoh, who being pleased at Joseph's conduct, gave directions that Jacob and his family should come forthwith into Egypt. The brethren departed, being well provided for—' And to his father Joseph sent ten asses laden with the good things of Egypt, and ten she asses laden with corn and bread and meat for his father by the way.'

The intelligence which they bore to their father was of such a nature that ' Jacob's heart fainted, for he believed them not.' When, however, he had recovered from the thus naturally told effects of his surprise, the venerable patriarch said, ' Enough; Joseph my son is yet alive: I will go and see him before I die' (xlv. 26, 28).

Accordingly Jacob and his family, to the number of threescore and ten souls, went down to Egypt, and by the express efforts of Joseph, were allowed to settle in the district of Goshen, where Joseph met his father: ' And he fell on his neck, and wept on his neck a good while.' There Joseph ' nourished his father and his brethren, and all his father's household, with bread, according to their families' (xlvii. 12).

Meanwhile the predicted famine was pauperizing Egypt. The inhabitants found their money exhausted, and their cattle and substance all gone, being parted with in order to purchase food from the public granaries, until at length they had nothing to give in return for sustenance but themselves. ' Buy us'—they then imploringly said to Joseph—' and our land for bread, and we and our land will be slaves unto Pharaoh ' ' And Joseph bought all the land of Egypt for Pharaoh, so the land became Pharaoh's.' The people, too, ' Joseph removed to cities from one end of the borders of the land to the other end.' Religion, however, was too strong to submit to these political and social changes, and so the priests still retained their land, being supplied with provisions out of the common store gratuitously. The land, which was previously the people's own, was now let to them on a tenancy, at the rent of one-fifth of the produce : the land of the priests being exempted.

Joseph had now to pass through the mournful scenes which attend on the death and burial of a father. Having had Jacob embalmed, and seen the rites of mourning fully observed, the faithful and affectionate son proceeded into the land of Canaan, in order, agreeably to a promise which the patriarch had exacted, to lay the old man's bones with those of his fathers, in 'the field of Ephron the Hittite.' Having performed with long and bitter mourning Jacob's funeral rites, Joseph returned into Egypt. The last recorded act of his life forms a most becoming close. After the death of their father, his brethren, unable, like all guilty people, to forget their criminality, and characteristically finding it difficult to think that Joseph had really forgiven them, grew afraid, now they were in his power, that he would take an opportunity of inflicting some punishment on them. They accordingly go into his presence, and, in imploring terms and an abject manner, entreat his forgiveness. 'Fear not'—this is his noble reply—'I will nourish you and your little ones.'

Joseph lived an hundred and ten years, kind and gentle in his affections to the last; for we are told, 'The children of Machir, the son of Manasseh, were brought up upon Joseph's knees' (l. 23). And so having obtained a promise from his brethren, that when the time came, as he assured them it would come, that God should visit them, and 'bring them unto the land which he sware to Abraham, to Isaac, and to Jacob,' they would carry up his bones out of Egypt, Joseph at length 'died, and they embalmed him, and he was put in a coffin' (l. 26). This promise was religiously fulfilled. His descendants, after carrying the corpse about with them in their wanderings, at length put it in its final resting-place in Shechem, in a parcel of ground that Jacob bought of the sons of Hamor, which became the inheritance of the children of Joseph (Josh. xxiv. 32).

By his Egyptian wife, Asenath, daughter of the high priest of Heliopolis, Joseph had two sons, Manasseh and Ephraim (Gen. xli. 50, sq.), whom Jacob adopted (Gen. xlviii. 5), and who accordingly took their place among the heads of the twelve tribes of Israel.

JOSEPH, 'the husband of Mary, of whom was born Jesus, who is called Christ' (Matt. i. 16). By Matthew he is said to have been the son of Jacob, whose lineage is traced by the same writer through David up to Abraham. Luke represents him as being the son of Heli, and traces his origin up to Adam. How these accounts are to be reconciled, is shown under GENEALOGY. The statements of Holy Writ in regard to Joseph are few and simple. According to a custom among the Jews, traces of which are still found, Joseph had pledged his faith to Mary; but before the marriage was consummated she proved to be with child. Grieved at this, Joseph was disposed to break off the connection; but, not wishing to make a public example of one whom he loved, he contemplated a private disruption of their bond. From this step, however, he is deterred by a heavenly messenger, who assures him that Mary has conceived under a divine influence. 'And she shall bring forth a son, and thou shalt call his name Jesus; for he shall save his people from their sins' (Matt i. 18, sq.; Luke i. 27). To this account various objections have been taken; but most of them are drawn from the ground of a narrow, short-sighted, and half-informed rationalism, which

judges everything by its own small standard, and either denies miracles altogether, or admits only such miracles as find favour in its sight.

Joseph was by trade a carpenter, in which business he probably educated Jesus (Matt. xiii. 55; Mark vi. 3). The word rendered 'carpenter' is of a general character, and may be fitly rendered by the English word 'artificer' or 'artizan.' Schleusner asserts that the universal testimony of the ancient church represents our Lord as being a carpenter's son. Hilarius, on Matthew, asserts, in terms which cannot be mistaken, that Jesus was a smith. Of the same opinion was the venerable Bede; while others have held that our Lord was a mason, and Cardinal Cajetan, that he was a goldsmith. The last notion probably had its origin in those false associations of more modern times which disparage hand-labour. Among the ancient Jews all handicrafts were held in so much honour, that they were learned and pursued by the first men of the nation.

Christian tradition makes Joseph an old man when first espoused to Mary, being no less than eighty years of age, and father of four sons and two daughters. The painters of Christian antiquity conspire with the writers in representing Joseph as an old man at the period of the birth of our Lord—an evidence which is not to be lightly rejected, though the precise age mentioned may be but an approximation to fact.

It is not easy to determine when Joseph died, but it has been alleged, with great probability, that he must have been dead before the crucifixion of Jesus. There being no notice of Joseph in the public life of Christ, nor any reference to him in the discourses and history, while 'Mary' and 'His brethren' not unfrequently appear, these circumstances afford evidence not only of Joseph's death, but of the inferior part which, as legal father only of our Lord, Joseph might have been expected to sustain. So far as our scanty materials enable us to form an opinion, Joseph appears to have been a good, kind, simple-minded man, who, while he afforded aid in protecting and sustaining the family, would leave Mary unrestrained to use all the impressive and formative influence of her gentle, affectionate, pious, and thoughtful soul.

JOSEPH OF ARIMATHEA. The name Arimathea denotes probably the place where Joseph was born, not that where he resided. [ARIMATHEA.]

Joseph was a secret disciple of Jesus—'an honourable counsellor, who waited for the kingdom of God' (Mark xv. 43) and who, on learning the death of our Lord, 'came and went in boldly unto Pilate, and craved the body of Jesus.' Pilate having learned from the centurion, who commanded at the execution, that Jesus 'was actually dead,' gave the body to Joseph, who took it down and wrapped his deceased Lord in fine linen which he had purchased for the purpose; after which he laid the corpse in a sepulchre which was hewn out of a rock, and rolled a stone unto the door of the sepulchre (Mark xv. 43, sq.). From the parallel passages in Matthew (xxvii. 58, sq.), Luke (xxiii. 50, seq.) and John (xix. 38, seq.), it appears that the body was previously embalmed at the cost of another secret disciple, Nicodemus, and that the sepulchre was new, 'wherein never man before was laid;' also that it lay in a garden, and was the property of Joseph himself. This garden was 'in the place where Jesus was crucified.' Luke describes the character of Joseph as 'a good man and a just,' adding, that 'he had not consented to the counsel and deed of them,' *i. e.* of the Jewish authorities. From this remark it is clear that Joseph was a member of the Sanhedrim: a conclusion which is corroborated by the epithet 'counsellor,' applied to him by both Luke and Mark. Tradition represents Joseph as having been one of the Seventy, and as having first preached the Gospel in our own country.

JOSEPH called BARSABAS was one of the two persons whom the primitive church, immediately after the resurrection of Christ, nominated, praying that the Holy Spirit would show which of them should enter the apostolic band in place of the wretched Judas. On the lots being cast, it proved that not Joseph, but Matthias, was chosen.

Joseph bore the honourable surname of Justus, which was not improbably given him on account of his well-known probity. He was one of those who had 'companied with the Apostles all the time that the Lord Jesus went in and out amongst them, beginning from the baptism of John,' until the ascension (Acts i. 15, sq.). Tradition also accounted him one of the Seventy.

1. JO'SES, son of Mary and Cleopas, and brother of James the Less, of Simon and of Jude, and, consequently, one of those who are called the 'brethren' of our Lord (Matt. xiii. 55; xxvii. 56; Mark vi. 3; xv. 40, 47). [JAMES; JUDE.] He was the only one of these brethren who was not an apostle—a circumstance which has given occasion to some unsatisfactory conjecture. It is perhaps more remarkable that three of them were apostles than that the fourth was not.

2. JOSES [BARNABAS].

JOSH'UA. This is the name of four persons in the Old Testament, and means *whose salvation is Jehovah.* The most distinguished of the four persons so called, who occur in the Old Testament, is Joshua the son of Nun, of the tribe of Ephraim, the assistant and successor of Moses. His name was originally Oshea, *salvation* (Num. xiii. 8), and it seems that the subsequent alteration of it by Moses (Num. xiii. 16) was significant, and proceeded on the same principle as that of Abram into Abraham (Gen. xvii. 5), and of Sarai into Sarah (Gen. xvii. 15).

In the Bible Joshua is first mentioned as being the victorious commander of the Israelites in their battle against the Amalekites at Rephidim (Exod. xvii 8-16). He distinguished himself by his courage and intelligence during and after the exploration of the land of Canaan, on which occasion he represented his tribe, which was that of Ephraim (Num. xiii, xiv.). Moses, with the divine sanction, appointed him to command the Israelites, even during his own lifetime (Num. xxvii. 18-23; Deut. iii. 28; xxxi. 23). After the death of Moses he led the Israelites over the Jordan, fortified a camp at Gilgal (Josh. ix. 6; x. 6-43), conquered the southern and middle portions of Canaan (vi.-x.), and also some of the northern districts (ix). But the hostile nations, although subdued, were not entirely driven out and destroyed (xiii.; xxiii. 13, Judg. i. 27-35).

In the seventh year after entering the land, it was distributed among the various tribes, which then commenced individually to complete the conquest by separate warfare (xv. 13, sq.; xvi. 10; xvii. 12, sq.). Joshua died 110 years old (B.C. 1427), and was buried at Timnath-serah (Josh. xxiv.), on Mount Ephraim.

There occur some vestiges of the deeds of Joshua in other historians besides those of the Bible. Procopius mentions a Phœnician inscription near the city of Tingis in Mauritania, the sense of which was:—'We are those who fled before the face of Joshua the robber, the son of Nun.'

The book of Joshua is so called from the personage who occupies the principal place in the narration of events contained therein, and may be considered as a continuation of the Pentateuch. The Pentateuch, and especially Deuteronomy, are repeatedly referred to in the book of Joshua, the narration of which begins with the death of Moses and extends to the death of Joshua, embracing a chronological period of somewhat less than thirty years. The subject of the book is thus briefly stated in ch. i. 5, 6: 'There shall not any man be able to stand before thee all the days of thy life. As I was with Moses, so I will be with thee: I will not fail thee, nor forsake thee. Be strong and of a good courage; for unto this people shalt thou divide for an inheritance the land which I sware unto their fathers to give them.' In these two verses is also indicated the division of the book into two principal portions, with reference to the conquest and the distribution of the land of Canaan. The conquest is narrated in the first twelve, and the distribution in the following ten chapters. In the last two chapters are subjoined the events subsequent to the distribution up to the death of Joshua. The history of the conquest of Canaan is a series of miracles, than which none more remarkable are recorded in any part of sacred history. The passage into the Promised Land, as well as that out of Egypt, was through water. Jericho was taken not by might, but by the falling of the walls on the blast of the trumpets of seven priests; and in the war against Gibeon the day was prolonged to afford time for the completion of the victory.

It is generally granted that the first twelve chapters form a continuous whole: although the author, in ch. x. 13, refers to another work, he not merely transcribes but intimately combines the quotation with the tenor of his narration. It is certain that there sometimes occur episodes which seem to interrupt the chronological connection, as for instance the portion intervening between chs. i, ii., and iii. 1. But it belongs to the nature of detailed historical works to contain such episodes.

The whole tenor of the first twelve chapters bespeaks an eye-witness who bore some part in the transactions—a fact proved not merely by such expressions as 'WE passed over,' in ch. v. 1, but especially by the circumstantial vividness of the narrative, which clearly indicates that the writer was an eye-witness.

The statement that the monuments which he erected were extant *to this day*, indicates that Joshua did not promulgate the book immediately after the events narrated (comp. iv. 9; vii. 26; viii. 28, 29, x. 27). The book, however, could not have been written very long after the time of

Joshua, because we find that Rahab was still alive when it was composed (vi. 29). The section from chapter xiii. to xxii. inclusive, which contains an account of the distribution of the land, seems to be based upon written documents, in which the property was accurately described. That this was the case is likely not merely on account of the peculiar nature of the diplomatic contents by which this 'Doomsday Book' is distinguished from the preceding part of Joshua, but also on account of the statement in chapter xviii. 4, where Joshua says to the children of Israel, 'Give out from among you three men from each tribe: and I will send them, and they shall rise, and go through the land, and describe it according to the inheritance of them ; and they shall come again to me.' Compare ver. 6, 'Ye therefore shall describe the land into seven parts.' Compare also verses 8 and 9, 'And the men arose and went away ; and Joshua charged them that went to *describe* the land, saying, Go, and walk through the land, and *describe* it, and come again to me, that I may here cast lots for you before the Lord in Shiloh. And the men went and passed through the land, and *described* it by cities into seven parts in a *book*, and came again to Joshua to the host at Shiloh.'

The author of the book of Joshua frequently repeats the statements of the Pentateuch in a more detailed form, and mentions the changes which had taken place since the Pentateuch was written. Compare Num. xxxiv. 13 and 14, with Josh. xiii. 7, sq.; Num. xxxii. 37, with Josh. xiii. 17, sq.; Num. xxxv. with Josh. xxi.

There is also considerable similarity between the following passages in the books of Joshua and Judges:—Josh. xiii. 4, Judg. iii. 3 ; Josh. xv. 13, sq., Judg. i. 10, 20; Josh. xv. 15-19, Judg. i. 11-15; Josh. xv. 62, Judg. i. 21 ; Josh. xvi. 10, Judg. i. 29 ; Josh. xvii. 12, Judg. i. 27 ; Josh. xix. 47, Judg. xviii.

It seems to have been the intention of the author of chapters xiii.-xxii. to furnish authentic records concerning the arrangements made by Joshua after the conquest of Canaan. Since we do not find in the subsequent history that the tribes, after the death of Joshua, disagreed among themselves about the ownership of the land, it would appear that the object of the book of Joshua, as a 'Doomsday Book,' was fully attained. The circumstance that the book of Joshua contains many Canaanitish names of places to which the Hebrew names are added, seems also to indicate that the second part originated in an early age, when neither the Canaanitish name was entirely forgotten, nor the Hebrew name fully introduced ; so that it was expedient to mention both.

In the last two chapters occur two orations of Joshua, in which he bids farewell to the people whom he had commanded. In chapter xxiv. 26, we read, ' And Joshua WROTE these words in the book of the law of God.' The expression, *these words*, seems to refer only to his last address, and the subsequent resolution of the people to follow his example. We are here, however, expressly informed that Joshua did WRITE this much ; and consequently we deem it the more likely that he also committed to writing the other memorable events connected with his career, such as the conquest and the distribution of the land.

Viewing all the circumstances together, we consider it highly probable that the whole book of Joshua was composed by himself up to the twenty-eighth verse of the last chapter; to which a friendly hand subjoined some brief notices, contained in verses 29-33, concerning the death, age, and burial of Joshua ; the continuance of his influence upon the people ; the interment, in Shechem, of the bones of Joseph, which the children of Israel had brought from Egypt; and the death and burial of Eleazar, the son of Aaron, whom his son Phinehas interred in his allotment on Mount Ephraim.

The authority of the book of Joshua mainly rests upon the manner in which it is treated in other parts of the Bible.

Besides the allusions in the book of Judges, we find Joshua referred to in 1 Kings xvi. 34. (Comp. Josh. vi. 26). The second and third verses of Psalm xliv. contain a brief summary of the whole book of Joshua:—'Thou didst drive out the heathen with thy hand, and plantedst them : thou didst afflict the people, and cast them out. For they got not the land in possession by their own sword, neither did their own arm save them: but thy right hand and thine arm, and the light of thy countenance, because thou hadst a favour unto them.' (Compare Psalm lxviii. 12-14; lxxviii. 54, 55; cxiv. 3 and 5, which refer to the book of Joshua.) Also, Hab. iii. 11 : ' The sun and moon stood still in their habitation,' &c. Heb. xiii. 5 : ' For he hath said, I will never leave thee, nor forsake thee.' (Compare Josh. i. 5.) Heb. xi. 31 : 'By faith the harlot Rahab perished not with them that believed not, when she had received the spies with peace ;' and James ii. 25 : ' Likewise also was not Rahab the harlot justified by works, when she had received the messengers, and had sent them out another way ?' (Compare Josh. ii. and vi. 22-25.) Acts vii. 45 : ' Which (the tabernacle) also our fathers that came after brought in with Jesus into the possession of the Gentiles, whom God drave out before the face of our fathers.' (Compare Josh. iii. 14.) Heb. xi. 30 : 'By faith the walls of Jericho fell down, after they were compassed about seven days.' (Compare Josh. vi. 17-23.) Heb. iv. 8 : ' For if Jesus [JOSHUA] had given them rest, then would he not afterwards have spoken of another day.'

The other persons of this name in the Bible are:

JOSHUA, a Beth-shemite (1 Sam. vi. 14, 18), an Israelite, the owner of the field into which the cart came which bore the ark on its return from the land of the Philistines.

JOSHUA (2 Kings xxiii. 8), the governor of the city of Jerusalem at the commencement of the reign of Josiah.

JOSHUA, the son of Josedec (Hagg. i. 1, 12, 14 ; Zech. iii. 1, 3, 9 ; vi. 11), a high-priest in the time of Haggai and Zechariah [JESHUA].

JOSI'AH (*God-healed*), seventeenth king of Judah, and son of Amon, whom he succeeded on the throne in B.C. 698, at the early age of eight years, and reigned thirty-one years.

As Josiah thus early ascended the throne, we may the more admire the good qualities which he manifested. Avoiding the example of his immediate predecessors, he · did that which was right in the sight of the Lord, and walked in all the ways of David his father, and turned not

2 K

aside to the right hand or to the left' (2 Kings xxii. 1. 2; 2 Chron. xxxiv. 1. 2). So early as the sixteenth year of his age he began to manifest that enmity to idolatry in all its forms which distinguished his character and reign; and he was not quite twenty years old when he proclaimed open war against it, although more or less favoured by many men of rank and influence in the court and kingdom. He then commenced a thorough purification of the land from all taint of idolatry, by going about and superintending in person the operations of the men who were employed in breaking down idolatrous altars and images, and cutting down the groves which had been consecrated to idol-worship. His detestation of idolatry could not have been more strongly expressed than by ransacking the sepulchres of the idolatrous priests of former days, and consuming their bones upon the idol-altars before they were overturned. Yet this operation, although unexampled in Jewish history, was foretold 326 years before Josiah was born, by the prophet who was commissioned to denounce to Jeroboam the future punishment of his sin. He even named Josiah as the person by whom this act was to be performed; and said that it should be performed in Beth-el, which was then a part of the kingdom of Israel (1 Kings xiii. 2). All this seemed much beyond the range of human probabilities. But it was performed to the letter; for Josiah did not confine his proceedings to his own kingdom, but went over a considerable part of the neighbouring kingdom of Israel, which then lay comparatively desolate, with the same object in view; and at Beth-el in particular, executed all that the prophet h d foretold (2 Kings xxiii. 1–19; 2 Chron. xxxiv. 3–7, 32). In these proceedings Josiah seems to have been actuated by an absolute *hatred* of idolatry, such as no other king since David had manifested, and which David had scarcely occasion to manifest in the same degree.

In the eighteenth year of his reign and the twenty-sixth of his age, when the land had been thoroughly purified from idolatry and all that belonged to it, Josiah proceeded to repair and beautify the temple of the Lord. In the course of this pious labour, the high-priest Hilkiah discovered in the sanctuary a volume, which proved to contain the books of Moses, and which, from the terms employed, seems to have been considered the original of the law as written by Moses. On this point there has been much anxious discussion and some rash assertion. Some writers of the German school allege that there is no external evidence--that is, evidence beside the law itself—that the book of the law existed till it was thus produced by Hilkiah. This assertion it is the less necessary to answer here, as it is duly noticed in the art. PENTATEUCH. But it may be observed that it is founded very much on the fact that the king was greatly astonished when some parts of the law were read to him. It is indeed perfectly manifest that he had previously been entirely ignorant of much that he then heard; and he rent his clothes in consternation when he found that, with the best intentions to serve the Lord, he and all his people had been living in the neglect of duties which the law declared to be of vital importance. It is certainly difficult to account for this ignorance.

Some suppose that all the copies of the law had perished, and that the king had never seen one. But this is very unlikely; for however scarce complete copies may have been, the pious king was likely to have been the possessor of one. The probability seems to be that the passages read were those awful denunciations against disobedience with which the book of Deuteronomy concludes, and which from some cause or other the king had never before read, or which had never before produced on his mind the same strong conviction of the imminent dangers under which the nation lay, as now when read to him from a volume invested with a character so venerable, and brought with such interesting circumstances under his notice.

The king in his alarm sent to Huldah 'the prophetess,' for her counsel in this emergency [HULDAH]: her answer assured him that, although the dread penalties threatened by the law had been incurred and would be inflicted, he should be gathered in peace to his fathers before the days of punishment and sorrow came.

It was perhaps not without some hope of averting this doom that the king immediately called the people together at Jerusalem, and engaged them in a solemn renewal of the ancient covenant with God. When this had been done, the Passover was celebrated with careful attention to the directions given in the law, and on a scale of unexampled magnificence. But all was too late; the hour of mercy had passed; for 'the Lord turned not from the fierceness of his great wrath, wherewith his anger was kindled against Judah' (2 Kings xxii. 3–20; xxiii. 21–27; 2 Chron. xxxiv. 8–33; xxxv. 1–19).

That removal from the world which had been promised to Josiah as a blessing, was not long delayed, and was brought about in a way which he had probably not expected. His kingdom was tributary to the Chaldæan empire; and when Pharaoh-necho, king of Egypt, sought a passage through his territories, on an expedition against the Chaldæans, Josiah, with a very high sense of the obligations which his vassalage imposed, refused to allow the march of the Egyptian army through his dominions, and prepared to resist the attempt by force of arms. Necho was very unwilling to engage in hostilities with Josiah; the appearance of the Hebrew army at Megiddo, however, brought on a battle, in which the king of Judah was so desperately wounded by arrows that his attendants removed him from the warchariot, and placed him in another, in which he was taken to Jerusalem, where he died. No king that reigned in Israel was ever more deeply lamented by all his subjects than Josiah: and we are told that the prophet composed on the occasion an elegiac ode. which was long preserved among the people, but which is not now in existence (2 Kings xxiii. 29–37; 2 Chron. xxxv. 20–27).

JOT. properly IOTA. designates the smallest letter of the Greek alphabet (ι); derived from the Hebrew *jod* ($\cdot$) and employed metaphorically to express the minutest trifle. It is, in fact, one of several metaphors derived from the alphabet— as when *alpha*, the first letter, and *omega*, the last, are employed to express the beginning and the end.

1. JO'THAM (*God is upright*), the youngest of

Gideon's seventy legitimate sons; and the only one who escaped when the rest were massacred by the order of Abimelech. When the fratricide was made king by the people of Shechem, the young Jotham was so daring as to make his appearance on Mount Gerizim for the purpose of lifting up a protesting voice, and of giving vent to his feelings. This he did in a beautiful parable, wherein the trees are represented as making choice of a king, and bestowing on the bramble the honour which the cedar, the olive, and the vine would not accept. The obvious application, which indeed Jotham failed not himself to point out, must have been highly exasperating to Abimelech and his friends; but the speaker fled. as soon as he had delivered his parable, to the town of Beer, and remained there out of his brother's reach. We hear no more of him; but three years after, if then living, he saw the accomplishment of the malediction he had pronounced (Judg. ix. 5-21).

2. JOTHAM, tenth king of Judah, and son of Uzziah, whom he succeeded in B C. 758, at the age of twenty-five: he reigned sixteen years. His father having during his last years been excluded by leprosy from public life [UZZIAH], the government was administered by his son. Jotham profited by the experience which the reign of his father, and of the kings who preceded him, afforded, and he ruled in the fear of God, although he was unable to correct all the corrupt practices into which the people had fallen. His sincere intentions were rewarded with a prosperous reign. He was successful in his wars. The Ammonites, who had 'given gifts' as a sort of tribute to Uzziah, but had ceased to do so after his leprosy had incapacitated him from governing, were constrained by Jotham to pay for three years a heavy tribute in silver, wheat, and barley (2 Chron. xxvi. 8; xxvii. 5, 6). Many important public works were also undertaken and accomplished by Jotham. The principal gate of the temple was rebuilt by him on a more magnificent scale; the quarter of Ophel, in Jerusalem, was strengthened by new fortifications; various towns were built or rebuilt in the mountains of Judah; and castles and towers of defence were erected in the wilderness. Jotham died greatly lamented by his people, and was buried in the sepulchre of the kings (2 Kings xv. 38; 2 Chron. xvii. 3-9).

JU'BAL (*music*); one of Cain's descendants, son of Lamech and Adar. He is described as the inventor of the KINNOR, and the UGAB, rendered in our version 'the harp and the organ,' but perhaps more properly 'the lyre and mouth-organ.' or Pandean pipe (Gen. iv. 21) [MUSIC].

JU'BILEE, according to some a period of fifty years, according to others, though less probably, of forty-nine years, the termination of which led to certain great changes in the condition of the Hebrews, all of which seem to have been designed and fitted to bring about from time to time a restoration of the original social state instituted by Moses, and so to sustain in its unimpaired integrity the constitution of which he was the author.

Intimately connected with the Jubilee was another singular Mosaic institution, namely, the Sabbatical year. On this account we shall speak briefly of the latter, as preparatory to a right understanding of the former.

While yet wandering in the wilderness, and, therefore, before they had entered 'the land of promise,' the children of Israel received from the lips of their great legislator the following law— 'six years thou shalt sow thy land, and shalt gather in the fruits thereof: but the *seventh year* thou shalt let it rest; that thine ox and thine ass may rest, and the son of thy handmaid and the stranger may be refreshed' (Exod. xxiii. 10, sq.). This injunction is repeated in Lev. xxv. 1-7, where it stands as proceeding immediately from the Lord. The land is to keep 'a sabbath for the Lord.' Then in immediate sequence follows the law relating to the Jubilee (Lev. xx. 8). 'And thou shalt number seven sabbaths of years unto thee, seven times seven years, forty and nine years, then shalt thou cause the trumpet of the Jubilee to sound in the tenth day of the seventh month, in the day of atonement shall ye make the trumpet sound throughout all your land. And ye shall *hallow the fiftieth year,* and proclaim liberty throughout all the land unto all the inhabitants thereof; and ye shall return every man unto his possession and unto his family,' &c. &c. (Lev. xxv 8-24). Land might be redeemed by a kinsman or by the party who sold it; but in the Jubilee year it must return to its original proprietor. Dwelling-houses within a walled city might be redeemed within the first year; if not redeemed within the space of a full year they became the freehold of the purchaser. The houses of villages were to be counted as the fields of the country. The cities and houses of the Levites were redeemable at any time, and could never be held longer than the ensuing Jubilee: the field of the suburbs of their cities might not be sold (vers. 25-38). Israelites who were hired servants (Israelitish *bond*-servants were not allowed) might serve till the year of Jubilee, when they returned to their possessions. A Hebrew sold as a slave to a foreigner resident in Palestine was redeemable by himself or relatives at any time, by making payment according to the number of years to elapse before the next Jubilee; but at the Jubilee such bondsman was, under all circumstances, to be set at liberty (vers. 39-55). The only exception to this system of general restitution was in the case of property set apart and devoted to the Divine service—'Every devoted thing is most holy unto the Lord; none devoted shall be redeemed' (Lev. xxvii. 28-29).

With these scriptural details the account given by Josephus (*Antiq.* iii. 12. 3) substantially agrees; and it is worthy of notice that the Jewish historian speaks of the law as a reality, as a present reality, as something in actual operation.

The time required by the Sabbatical year and by the Jubilee to be rescued from the labours of the field, was very considerable. Strictly interpreted the language we have cited would take out of the ordinary course of things every sixth, seventh, and eighth year, during each successive septenary. till the circle of fifty years was in each period completed. Nay more, the old store, produced in the sixth year, was to last until the ninth year, for the sixth year was to bring forth fruits for three years.

The reader has now before him the whole of this extraordinary piece of legislation, which, viewed in all its bearings—in its effects on human labour, on character, on religious institutions and observances, as well as on the general condition

2 K 2

JUDÆA

of society, no less than on the productiveness of the land, and the means of sustenance to its inhabitants—is wholly unparalleled by any event in the history of the world. It is, however, in strict harmony with the Mosaic economy.

The recurring periods of seven years are in keeping with the institution of the seventh day as a Sabbath for man and beast. The aim in both is similar—needful repose. The leading idea involved in the Jubilee—namely, restitution—also harmonizes with the fundamental principles of the Mosaic system. The land was God's, and was entrusted for use to the chosen people in such a way that every individual had his portion. A power of perpetual alienation would have been a virtual denial of God's sovereign rights, while the law of Jubilee was one continued recognition of them. The conception is purely *theocratical* in its whole character and tendencies. The theocracy was of such a nature as to disallow all subordinate 'thrones, principalities, and powers;' and consequently, to demand entire equality on the part of the people. But the power of perpetual alienation in regard to land would have soon given rise to the greatest inequalities of social condition, presenting splendid affluence on one side and sordid pauperism on the other. A passage in Deuteronomy (xv. 4), when rightly understood, as in the marginal translation—'to the end that there be no poor among you'—seems expressly to declare that the aim in view, at least, of the Sabbatical release, was to prevent the rise of any great inequality of social condition, and thus to preserve unimpaired the essential character of the theocracy. Equally benevolent in its aim and tendency does this institution thus appear, showing how thoroughly the great Hebrew legislator cared and provided for individuals, instead of favouring classes. Beginning with a narrow cycle of seven days, he went on to a wider one of as many years, embracing at last seven times seven annual revolutions, seeking in all his arrangements rest for man and beast. and, by a happy personification, rest even for the brute earth; and in the rest which he required for human beings, providing for that more needful rest of mind which the sharp competitions and eager rivalries of modern society deny to ten thousand times ten thousand. As being of a benign character and tendency, the law of the Sabbatical and Jubilee year is in accordance with the general spirit of the Mosaic legislation, and appears not unworthy of its divine origin.

Warburton adduced this law in order to show that Moses was in truth sent and sustained by God, since nothing but a divine power could have given the necessary supplies of food in the sixth year; and no unprejudiced person can deny the force of the argument.

Now these laws either emanated from Moses, or they did not. If they did not, they arose after the settlement in Canaan, and are of such a nature as to convict their fabricator of imposture, if, indeed, any one could have been found so daring as to bring forth laws implying institutions which did not exist, and which under ordinary circumstances could not find permanence, even if they could ever be carried into operation at all. But if these laws emanated from Moses, is it credible that he would have given utterance to commands which convict themselves of impossibility? or caused the rise of institutions, which, if unsup-

ported of heaven, must come to a speedy termination, and in so doing act to his own discredit as a professed divine messenger?

But it may be asked, Could the land sustain the people? On this point we find the following important passage in Palfrey's *Lectures on the Jewish Scriptures*, Boston, 1841, vol. i. p. 303: 'I find no difficulty arising from any inadequacy of the produce of six years to afford sustenance to the people for seven. To say that this was intended would merely be to say that the design was that the consumption of each year should only amount on an average to six-sevenths of its produce. In such an arrangement it cannot be thought that there was anything impracticable. There are states of this Union which export yearly more than half their produce, and subsist substantially on the remainder, their imports consisting mostly of luxuries. Again, in England nearly three quarters of the families are engaged in commerce, manufactures, professions, and unproductive pursuits; but in Judæa every man was a producer of food, with the advantage of a fine climate and a rich soil.'

In spite of all these arguments, some rationalistic writers have hazarded the surprising assertion that these laws were not executed before the Babylonish exile. But in addition to the proofs already mentioned, we have the positive evidence of the Roman historian Tacitus (*Hist.* v. 4), of Josephus (*Antiq.* xiv. 10-6), of Ezekiel (xlvi. 17), and of Isaiah (lxi. 1-2), to the observance of the Sabbatical year at least. And since the essential element of this system of law, namely, the Sabbatical year, was an established institution in the days of Tacitus, Josephus, the Maccabees, Ezekiel, and Isaiah, we think the fair and legitimate inference is in favour of those laws having been long previously observed, probably from the early periods of the Hebrew republic. Their existence in a declining state of the commonwealth cannot be explained without seeking their origin nearer the fountain-head of those pure, living waters, which, with the force of all primitive enthusiasm, easily effected great social wonders, especially when divinely guided and divinely sustained.

JUDÆ'A, the southernmost of the three divisions of the Holy Land. It denoted the kingdom of Judah as distinguished from that of Israel. But after the captivity, as most of the exiles who returned belonged to the kingdom of Judah, the name Judæa (Judah) was applied generally to the whole of Palestine west of the Jordan (Hag. i. 1, 14; ii. 2). Under the Romans, in the time of Christ, Palestine was divided into Judæa, Galilee, and Samaria (John iv. 4, 5; Acts ix. 31), the last including the whole of the southern part west of the Jordan. But this division was only observed as a political and local distinction, for the sake of indicating the part of the country, just as we use the name of a county (Matt. ii. 1, 5; iii. 1; iv. 25 Luke i. 65); but when the whole of Palestine was to be indicated in a general way, the term Judæa was still employed.

It is only Judæa, in the provincial sense, that requires our present notice, the country at large being described in the article PALESTINE. In this sense, however, it was much more extensive than the domain of the tribe of Judah, even more so than the kingdom of the same name. There are no materials for describing its limits with precision; but it included the ancient territories of Judah, Benjamin, Dan, Simeon, and part of Ephraim.

Judæa is a country full of hills and valleys. The hills are generally separated from one another by valleys and torrents, and are, for the most part, of moderate height, uneven, and seldom of any regular figure. The rock of which they are composed is easily converted into soil, which being arrested by the terraces when washed down by the rains, renders the hills cultivable in a series of long, narrow gardens, formed by these terraces from the base upwards. In this manner the hills were in ancient times cultivated most industriously, and enriched and beautified with the fig-tree, the olive-tree, and the vine; and it is thus that the scanty cultivation which still subsists is now carried on. But when the inhabitants were rooted out, and the culture neglected, the terraces fell to decay, and the soil which had been collected in them was washed down into the valleys, leaving only the arid rock, naked and desolate. This is the general character of the scenery; but in some parts the hills are beautifully wooded, and in others the application of the ancient mode of cultivation still suggests to the traveller how rich the country once was and might be again, and how beautiful the prospects which it offered. As, however, much of this was the result of cultivation, the country was probably anciently, as at present, *naturally* less fertile than either Samaria or Galilee.

JU'DAH (*celebrated*), fourth son of Jacob and Leah (B.C. 1755). The narrative in Genesis brings this patriarch more before the reader, and makes known more of his history and character, than it does in the case of any other of the twelve sons of Jacob, with the single exception of Joseph. It is indeed chiefly in connection with Joseph that the facts respecting Judah transpire; and as they have already been given in the articles JACOB and JOSEPH, it is only necessary to indicate them shortly in this place. It was Judah's advice that the brethren followed when they sold Joseph to the Ishmaelites, instead of taking his life. By the light of his subsequent actions we can see that his conduct on this occasion arose from a generous impulse, although the form of the question he put to them has been sometimes held to suggest an interested motive:—'What profit is it if we slay our brother and conceal his blood? Come, let us sell him,' &c. (Gen. xxxvii. 26, 27).

Not long after this Judah withdrew from the paternal tents, and went to reside at Adullam, in the country which afterwards bore his name. Here he married a woman of Canaan, called Shuah, and had by her three sons, Er, Onan, and Shelah. When the eldest of these sons became of fit age, he was married to a woman named Tamar, but soon after died. As he died childless, the patriarchal law, afterwards adopted into the Mosaic code (Deut. xxv. 6), required him to bestow upon the widow his second son. This he did: but as Onan also soon died childless, Judah became reluctant to bestow his only surviving son upon this woman, and put her off with the excuse that he was not yet of sufficient age. Tamar accordingly remained in her father's house at Adullam. She had the usual passion of Eastern women for offspring, and could not endure the stigma of having been twice married without bearing children, while the law precluded her from contracting any alliance but that which Judah withheld her from completing.

Meanwhile Judah's wife died, and after the time of mourning had expired, he went, accompanied by his friend Hirah, to attend the shearing of his sheep at Timnath in the same neighbourhood. These circumstances suggested to Tamar the strange thought of connecting herself with Judah himself, under the guise of a loose woman. Having waylaid him on the road to Timnath, she succeeded in her object, and when the consequences began to be manifest in the person of Tamar, Judah was highly enraged at her crime, and, exercising the powers which belonged to him as the head of the family she had dishonoured, he commanded her to be brought forth and committed to the flames as an adulteress. But when she appeared, she produced the ring, the bracelet, and the staff, which he had left in pledge with her; and put him to confusion by declaring that they belonged to the father of her coming offspring. Judah acknowledged them to be his, and confessed that he had been wrong in withholding Shelah from her. The result of this painful affair was the birth of two sons, Zerah and Pharez, from whom, with Shelah, the tribe of Judah descended. Pharez was the ancestor of the line from which David, the kings of Judah, and Jesus came (Gen. xxxviii.; xlvi. 12; 1 Chron. ii. 3-5; Matt. i. 3; Luke iii. 33).

These circumstances seem to have disgusted Judah with his residence in towns; for we find him ever afterwards at his father's tents. His experience of life, and the strength of his character, appear to have given him much influence with Jacob; and it was chiefly from confidence in him that the aged father at length consented to allow Benjamin to go down to Egypt. That this confidence was not misplaced has already been shown [JOSEPH]; and there is not in the whole range of literature a finer piece of true natural eloquence than that in which Judah offers himself to remain as a bond-slave in the place of Benjamin, for whose safe return he had made himself responsible to his father. The strong emotions which it raised in Joseph disabled him from keeping up longer the disguise he had hitherto maintained, and there are few who have read it without being, like him, moved even to tears.

We hear nothing more of Judah till he received, along with his brothers, the final blessing of his father, which was conveyed in lofty language, glancing far into futurity, and strongly indicative of the high destinies which awaited the tribe that was to descend from him.

2. JUDAH, TRIBE OF. This tribe sprang from Judah, the son of Jacob. When the Israelites quitted Egypt, it already exhibited the elements of its future distinction in a larger population than any of the other tribes possessed. It numbered 74,000 adult males, being nearly 12,000 more than Dan, the next in point of numbers, and 34,100 more than Ephraim, which in the end contested with it the superiority among the tribes. During the sojourn in the wilderness, Judah neither gained, like some tribes, nor lost like others. Its numbers had increased to 76,500, being 12,100 more than Issachar, which had become next to it in population (Num. i. 25). In the first distribution of lands, the tribe of Judah

received the southernmost part of Palestine, to the extent of fully one-third of the whole country to be distributed among the nine and a half tribes for which provision was to be made. This oversight was discovered and rectified at the time of the second distribution, which was founded on an actual survey of the country, when Simeon and Dan received allotments out of the territory which had before been wholly assigned to Judah (Josh. xix. 9). That which remained was still very large, and more proportioned to the future greatness than the actual wants of the tribe. When Judah became a kingdom, the original extent of territory assigned to the tribe was more than restored or compensated, for it must have included the domains of Simeon, and we know that Benjamin was included in it.

The history of the Judges contains fewer facts respecting this important tribe than might be expected. It seems however to have been usually considered that the birthright which Reuben forfeited had passed to Judah under the blessing of Jacob; and a sanction was given to this impression when, after the death of Joshua, the divine oracle nominated Judah to take precedence of the other tribes in the war against the Canaanites (Judg. i. 2). It does not appear that any tribe was disposed to dispute the superior claim of Judah on its own account, except Ephraim, although in doing this Ephraim had the support of other tribes. Ephraim appears to have rested its claims to the leadership of the tribes upon the ground that the house of Joseph, whose interest it represented, had received the birthright, or double portion of the eldest, by the adoption of the two sons of Joseph, who became the founders of *two* tribes in Israel. The existence of the sacerdotal establishment at Shiloh, in Ephraim, was doubtless also alleged by the tribe as a ground of superiority over Judah. When, therefore, Judah assumed the sceptre in the person of David, and when the sacerdotal establishment was removed to Jerusalem, Ephraim could not brook the eclipse it had sustained, and took the first opportunity of erecting a separate throne, and of forming separate establishments for worship and sacrifice. Perhaps the separation of the kingdoms may thus be traced to the rivalry of the two tribes. After that separation the rivalry was between the two kingdoms; but it was still popularly considered as representing the ancient rivalry of these great tribes; for the prophet, in foretelling the repose of a coming time, describes it by saying, 'The envy also of Ephraim shall depart, and the adversaries of Judah shall be cut off: Ephraim shall not envy Judah, and Judah shall not vex Ephraim' (Isa. xiii. 12).

3 JUDAH, KINGDOM OF. When the territory of all the rest of Israel, except Judah and Benjamin, was lost to the kingdom of Rehoboam, a special single name was needed to denote that which remained to him; and almost of necessity the word *Judah* received an extended meaning, according to which it comprised not Benjamin only, but the priests and Levites, who were ejected in great numbers from Israel, and rallied round the house of David. At a still later time, when the nationality of the ten tribes had been dissolved, and every practical distinction between the ten and the two had vanished during the captivity, the scattered body had no visible head,

except in Jerusalem, which had been re-occupied by a portion of *Judah's* exiles. In consequence the name Judah (or *Jew*) attached itself to the entire nation from about the epoch of the restoration. But in this article Judah is understood of the people over which David's successors reigned, from Rehoboam to Zedekiah. Under the article ISRAEL the chronology of the two kingdoms has been discussed, which, however, was not carried below the capture of Samaria. In the lower part of the list we lose the check which the double line of kings afforded; but for the same reason the problem is simpler. The only difficulty encountered here rises out of the *ages* assigned to some of the kings of Judah. For this reason, in the following list, all their ages are inserted, so far as they are recorded. It has been thought sufficient to add Winer's chronology to the dates as given above in the article ISRAEL.

Accession of	Years of Reign.	Age.	B.C.	Father's Age at Son's Birth.
Rehoboam . . .	17	41	975	—
Abijah	3	—	957	*22
Asa	41	—	955	*22
Jehoshaphat . .	25	35	914	*22
[Jehoram installed]	8	32	—	—
Jehoram alone . .	—	(35)	889	25
Ahaziah	1	22	885	17
[Queen Athaliah] .	7	—	884	—
Jehoash . . .	39?	7	878	22
Amaziah . . .	29	25	838	22
Uzziah	53?	16	809	38
Jotham	16	25	757	43
Ahaz	16	20	741	22
Hezekiah . . .	29	25	726	10
Manasseh . . .	55	12	696	42
Amon	2	22	641	45
Josiah . . .	31	8	639	16
Jehoahaz . . .	¼	23	609	15
Jehoiakim, his brother	11	25?	609	13?
Jehoiachin . . .	¼	18	598	18
Zedekiah, his father's brother .	11	21	598	28
Zedekiah is deposed	—	—	588	—

The ages of Abijah and Asa at their accession not being given, the three first numbers in the last column are averages only, Rehoboam having been born 66 or 67 years before Jehoshaphat. A glance at the table is sufficient to show that various errors must have crept into the numbers, but it is now extremely difficult, if not impossible, to correct them.

When the kingdom of Solomon became rent with intestine war, it might have been foreseen that the Edomites, Moabites, and other surrounding nations would at once refuse their accustomed tribute, and become again practically independent; and some irregular invasion of these tribes might have been dreaded. It was a mark of conscious weakness, and not a result of strength, that Rehoboam formed 15 cities (2 Chron xi. 5-11), in which his people might find defence against the irregular armies of his roving neighbours. But a more formidable enemy came in, Shishak king of Egypt, against whom the fortresses were of no avail (xii. 4), and to whom Jerusalem was forced to open its gates; and, from the despoiling of his treasures. Rehoboam probably sustained a still greater shock in its moral effect on the Moabites and Edomites, than in the direct loss: nor is it easy to conceive that he any longer retained the commerce of the Red Sea, or any very lucrative trade.

After Jehoshaphat followed the calamitous affinity with the house of Ahab, and the massacres of both families. Under Jehoiada the priest, and Jehoash his pupil, no martial efforts were made; but Amaziah son of Jehoash, after hiring 100,000 Israelites to no purpose, made war on the Edomites. slew 10,000, and threw 10,000 more down from the top of their rock (xxv. 5, 6, 11, 12). His own force in Judah, from 20 years old and upwards, was numbered at 300,000 choice men, able to handle spear and shield. His son Uzziah had 2600 military officers, and 307,500 men of war (xxvi. 12, 13). Ahaz lost, in a single battle with Pekah, 120,000 valiant men (xxviii. 6), after the severe slaughter he had received from Rezin king of Syria; after which no further military strength is ascribed to the kings of Judah.

These figures have caused no small perplexity, and have suggested to some the need of conjectural emendation. It perhaps deserves remark, that in the book of Kings no numbers of such startling magnitude are found. The army ascribed to Rehoboam (1 Kings xii. 21) is, indeed, as in Chronicles, 180,000 men; but if we explain it of those able to fight, the number, though certainly large, may be dealt with historically.

As the most important external relations of Israel were with Damascus, so were those of Judah with Edom and Egypt. Some revolution in the state of Egypt appears to have followed the reign of Shishak. Apparently the country must have fallen under the power of an Ethiopian dynasty, for the name of the *Lubim*, who accompanied Zerah in his attack on Asa, is generally regarded as proving that Zerah was from Sennaar, the ancient Meroe. But as this invasion was signally repulsed, the attempt was not repeated; and Judah enjoyed entire tranquillity from that quarter until the invasion of Pharaoh Necho. In fact it may seem that this success assisted the reaction, favourable to the power of Judah, which was already begun, in consequence of a change in the policy of Damascus. Asa having bought, by a costly sacrifice, the serviceable aid of the Damascene king, Israel was soon distressed, and Judah became once more formidable to her southern neighbours. Jehoshaphat appears to have re-asserted the Jewish authority over the Edomites without war, and to have set his own viceroy over them (1 Kings xxii. 47). Intending to resume the distant commerce which had been so profitable to Solomon. he built ships suitable for long voyages ('ships *of* Tarshish' as they are rightly called in 1 Kings xxii. 48), but not having the advantage of Tyrian sailors, as Solomon had, he lost the vessels by violent weather before they had sailed. Upon this, Ahaziah, king of Israel, offered the service of his own mariners, probably from the tribe of Asher and others accustomed to the Mediterranean; but Jehoshaphat was too discouraged to accept his offer, and the experi-

ment was never renewed by any Hebrew king. The Edomites, who paid only a forced allegiance, soon after revolted from Jehoram, and elected their own king (2 Kings viii. 20, 22). At a later time they were severely defeated by Amaziah (2 Kings xiv. 7), whose son, Uzziah, fortified the town of Elath, intending, probably, to resume maritime enterprise; but it remained a barren possession, and was finally taken from them by Rezin, in the reign of Ahaz (2 Kings xvi. 6). The Philistines, in these times, seem to have fallen from their former greatness, their league having been so long dissolved. The most remarkable event in which they are concerned is the assault on Jerusalem, in the reign of Jehoram (2 Chron. xxi. 16, 17).

It is strikingly indicative of the stormy scenes through which the line of David passed, that the treasures of the king and of the Temple were so often plundered or bargained away. First, under Rehoboam, all the hoards of Solomon, consecrated and common alike, were carried off by Shishak (1 Kings xiv. 26). Two generations later, Asa emptied out to Benhadad all that had since accumulated ·in the house of Jehovah or in the king's house.' A third time, when Hazael had taken Gath, and was preparing to march on Jerusalem, Jehoash. king of Judah, turned him away by sending to him all 'that Jehoshaphat, Jehoram, Ahaziah and Jehoash himself had dedicated, and all the gold that was found in the treasures of the house of Jehovah and in the king's house' (2 Kings xii. 18). In the very next reign Jehoash, king of Israel, defeated and captured Amaziah, took Jerusalem, broke down the walls, carried off hostages, and plundered the gold and silver deposited in the temple and in the royal palace (2 Kings xiv. 11-14). A fifth sacrifice of the sacred and of the royal treasure was made by Ahaz to Tiglath-pileser (2 Kings xvi. 8). The act was repeated by his son Hezekiah to Sennacherib, who had demanded '300 talents of silver and 30 talents of gold.' It is extraordinary, therefore, to find expressions used when Nebuchadnezzar took the city, which at first sight imply that Solomon's far-famed stores were still untouched (2 Kings xxiv. 13).

The severest shock which the house of David received was the double massacre which it endured from Jehu and from Athaliah. After a long minority, a youthful king, the sole surviving male descendant of his great-grandfather, and reared under the paternal rule of the priest Jehoiada, to whom he was indebted not only for his throne but even for his recognition as a son of Ahaziah, was not in a situation to uphold the royal authority. That Jehoash conceived the priests to have abused the power which they had gained. sufficiently appears in 2 Kings xii., where he complains that they had for twenty-three years appropriated the money, which they ought to have spent on the repairs of the temple. Jehoiada gave way; but we see here the beginning of a feud (hitherto unknown in the house of David) between the crown and the priestly order, which, after Jehoiada's death, led to the murder of his son Zachariah. The massacre of the priests of Baal, and of Athaliah, granddaughter of a king of Sidon, must also have destroyed cordiality between the Phœnicians and the kingdom of Judah; and when the victorious

Hazael had subjugated all Israel and showed himself near Jerusalem, Jehoash could look for no help from without, and had neither the faith of Hezekiah nor a prophet like Isaiah to support him. The assassination of Jehoash in his bed by 'his own servants' is described in the Chronicles as a revenge taken upon him by the priestly party for his murder of 'the sons' of Jehoiada; and the same fate, from the same influence, fell upon his son Amaziah, if we may so interpret the words in 2 Chron. xxv. 27: 'From the time that Amaziah turned away from following Jehovah they made a conspiracy against him,' &c. Thus the house of David appeared to be committing itself, like that of Saul, to permanent enmity with the priests. The wisdom of Uzziah, during a long reign, averted this collision, though a symptom of it returned towards its close. No further mischief from this cause followed, until the reign of his grandson, the weak and unfortunate Ahaz: after which the power of the kingdom rapidly mouldered away.

The struggle of the crown against (what we might call) the constitutional check of the priests, was perhaps the most immediate cause of the ruin of Judah. Ahaz was probably less guided by policy than by superstition, or by architectural taste, in erecting his Damascene altar (2 Kings xvi. 10-18). But the far more outrageous proceedings of Manasseh seem to have been a systematic attempt to extirpate the national religion because of its supporting the priestly power; and the 'innocent blood very much,' which he is stigmatized for shedding (2 Kings xxi. 16), was undoubtedly a sanguinary attack on the party opposed to his impious and despotic innovations. The storm which he had raised did not burst in his lifetime; but, two years after, it fell on the head of his son Amon; and the disorganization of the kingdom which his madness had wrought is commemorated as the cause of the Babylonish captivity (2 Kings xxiii. 26; xxiv. 3, 4). It is also credible that the long-continued despotism had greatly lessened patriotic spirit; and that the Jewish people of the declining kingdom were less brave against foreign invaders than against kindred and neighbour tribes or civil opponents. Faction had become very fierce within Jerusalem itself (Ezek. xxii.), and civil bloodshed was common. Wealth, where it existed, was generally a source of corruption, by introducing foreign luxury, tastes, manners, superstitions, immorality, or idolatry; and when consecrated to pious purposes, as by Hezekiah and Josiah, produced little more than a formal and exterior religion.

The appointment of Hilkiah to the office of high priest seems to mark the era at which (by a reaction after the atrocities of Manasseh and Amon) the purer priestly sentiment obtained its triumph over the crown. But the victory came too late. Society was corrupt and convulsed within, and the two great powers of Egypt and Babylon menaced it from without. True lovers of their God and of their country, like Jeremiah, saw that it was a time rather for weeping than for action; and that the faithful must resign themselves to the bitter lot which the sins of their nation had earned.

JU'DAS is merely the Greek form of the Hebrew name JUDAH.

1. JUDAS MACCABÆUS. [MACCABEES.]

2. JUDAS ISCAR'IOT. The object of this article is not to elucidate all the circumstances recorded respecting this person, but simply to investigate his motives in delivering up Jesus to the chief-priests. The evangelists relate his proceedings, but give no opinion. The subject is consequently open to inquiry. Our conclusions must be guided by the facts of the case, and by the known feelings and principles of human nature. The only conceivable motives for the conduct of Judas are, a sense of duty in bringing his Master to justice, resentment, avarice, dissatisfaction with the procedure of Jesus, and a consequent scheme for the accomplishment of his own views. With regard to the first of these motives, if Judas had been actuated by a sense of duty in bringing his Master to justice for anything censurable in his intentions, words, or actions, he would certainly have alleged some charge against him in his first interview with the chief-priests, and they would have brought him forward as a witness against Jesus, especially when they were at so great a loss for evidence; or they would have reminded him of his accusations when he appealed to them after our Lord's condemnation, saying, 'I have sinned in that I have betrayed innocent blood'—a confession which amounts to an avowal that he had never seen anything to blame in his Master, but everything to approve. The second motive supposed, namely, that of resentment, is rather more plausible. Jesus had certainly rebuked him for blaming the woman who had anointed him in the house of Simon the leper, at Bethany (comp. Matt. xxvi. 8-17; John xii. 4, 5); and Matthew's narrative seems to connect his going to the chief-priests with that rebuke (ver. 14): 'Then one of the twelve, called Judas Iscariot, went unto the chief-priests;' but closer inspection will convince the reader that those words are more properly connected with ver. 3. Besides, the rebuke was general, 'Why trouble ye the woman?' Nor was it nearly so harsh as that received by Peter, 'Get thee behind me, Satan' (Matt. xvi. 23), and certainly not so public (Mark viii. 32, 33). Even if Judas had felt ever so much resentment, it could scarcely have been his sole motive; and as nearly two days elapsed between his contract with the chief-priests and its completion, it would have subsided during the interval, and have yielded to that covetousness which we have every reason to believe was his ruling passion. St. John expressly declares that Judas 'was a thief, and had the bag, and bare (that is, conveyed away from it, stole) what was put therein' (xii. 6; comp. xx. 15, in the original). This rebuke, or rather certain circumstances attending it, might have determined him to act as he did, but is insufficient, of itself, to account entirely for his conduct, by which he endangered all his expectations of worldly advancement from Jesus, at the very moment when they seemed upon the verge of being fulfilled. It is, indeed, a most important feature in the case, that the hopes entertained by Judas, and all the apostles, from their Master's expected elevation, as the Messiah, to the throne of Judæa, and, as they believed, to the empire of the whole world, were never more stedfast than at the time when he covenanted with the chief-priests to deliver him into their hands. Nor

does the theory of mere resentment agree with the terms of censure in which the conduct and character of Judas are spoken of by our Lord and the evangelists. Since, then, this supposition is insufficient, we may consider another motive to which his conduct is more commonly ascribed, namely, covetousness. But if by covetousness be meant the eager desire to obtain 'the thirty pieces of silver,' with which the chief-priests 'covenanted with him' (Matt. xxvi. 15), it presents scarcely a less inadequate motive. Can it be conceived that Judas would deliberately forego the prospect of immense wealth from his Master, by delivering him up for about four pounds ten shillings of our money, upon the highest computation, and not more than double in value, a sum which he might easily have purloined from the bag? Is it likely that he would have made such a sacrifice for any further sum, however large, which we may suppose 'they promised him' (Mark xiv. 11), and of which the thirty pieces of silver might have been the mere earnest (Luke xxii. 5)? Had covetousness been his motive, he would have ultimately applied to the chief-priests, not to bring again the thirty pieces of silver with the confession, 'I have sinned in that I have betrayed the innocent blood' (Matt. xxvii. 4), but to demand the completion of their agreement with him. We are now at liberty to consider the only remaining motive for the conduct of Judas, namely, dissatisfaction with the procedure of his Master, and a consequent scheme for the furtherance of his own views. It seems to us likely, that the impatience of Judas for the accomplishment of his worldly views, which we conceive to have ever actuated him in following Jesus, could no longer be restrained, and that our Lord's observations at Bethany served to mature a stratagem he had meditated long before. He had no doubt been greatly disappointed at seeing his Master avoid being made a king, after feeding the five thousand in Galilee. Many a favourable crisis had he seemed to lose, or had not dared to embrace, and now while at Bethany he talks of his burial (John xii. 7); and though none of his apostles, so firm were their worldly expectations from their Master, could clearly understand such 'sayings' (Luke xviii. 34); yet they had been made 'exceeding sorry' by them (Matt. xvii. 23). At the same time Judas had long been convinced by the miracles he had seen his Master perform that he was the Messiah (John vii 31). He had even heard him accept this title from his apostles in private (Matt. xvi. 16). He had promised them that when he should 'sit upon the throne of his glory, they should sit upon twelve thrones judging the twelve tribes of Israel' (Matt. xix. 28). Yet now, when everything seemed most favourable to the assumption of empire, he hesitates and desponds. Within a few days, the people, who had lately given him a triumphal entry into the city, having kept the passover, would be dispersed to their homes, and Judas and his fellow apostles be, perhaps, required to attend their Master on another tedious expedition through the country. Hence it seems most probable that Judas resolved upon the plan of delivering up his Master to the Jewish authorities, when he would be compelled, in self-defence, to prove his claims, by giving them the

sign from heaven they had so often demanded; they would, he believed, elect him in due form as the King Messiah, and thus enable him to reward his followers. He did, indeed, receive from Jesus many alarming admonitions against his design; but the plainest warnings are lost upon a mind totally absorbed by a purpose, and agitated by many violent passions. The worst he would permit himself to expect. was a temporary displeasure for placing his Master in this dilemma; but as he most likely believed, judging from himself, that Jesus anticipated worldly aggrandizement, he might calculate upon his forgiveness when the emergency should have been triumphantly surmounted. Judas could not doubt his master's ability to extricate himself from his enemies by miracle. He had known him do so more than once (Luke iv. 30; John viii. 59; x. 39). Hence his directions to the officers to 'hold him fast,' when he was apprehended (Matt. xxvi. 48). With other Jews he believed the Messiah would never die (John xii. 34); accordingly, we regard his pecuniary stipulation with the priests as a mere artful cover to his deeper and more comprehensive design; and so that he served their purpose in causing the apprehension of Jesus, they would little care to scrutinize his motive. All they felt was being 'glad' at his proposal (Mark xiv. 11), and the plan appeared to hold good up to the very moment of our Lord's condemnation; for after his apprehension his miraculous power seemed unabated, from his healing Malchus. Judas heard him declare that he could even then 'ask, and his father would give him twelve legions of angels' for his rescue. But when Judas, who awaited the issue of the trial with such different expectations, saw that though Jesus had avowed himself to be the Messiah, he had not convinced the Sanhedrim; and, instead of extricating himself from their power by miracle, had submitted to be 'condemned, buffeted, and spit upon,' by his judges and accusers; then it should seem he awoke to a full view of all the consequences of his conduct. The prophecies of the Old Testament, 'that Christ should suffer,' and of Jesus, concerning his own rejection and death, flashed on his mind in their true sense and full force, and he found himself the wretched instrument of their fulfilment. He made a last desperate effort to stay proceedings. He presented himself to the chief-priests, offered to return the money, confessed that he had sinned in that he had betrayed the innocent blood, and upon receiving their heartless answer was wrought into a phrenzy of despair, during which he committed suicide. There is much significancy in these words of Matt. xxvii. 3, 'Then Judas, *when he saw he was condemned,*' not expiring on the cross, 're-pented himself,' &c. If such be the true hypothesis of his conduct, then, however culpable it may have been, as originating in the most inordinate covetousness, impatience of the procedure of Prov'dence, crooked policy, or any other bad quality, he is certainly absolved from the direct *intention* of procuring his Master's death. 'The difference,' says Archbishop Whately, 'between Iscariot and his fellow apostles was, that though they all had the same expectations and conjectures, *he* dared to *act* on his conjectures, departing from the plain course of his known duty to follow the calculations of his worldly wisdom, and the schemes of his worldly ambition.'

3. JUDAS, or JUDE, surnamed BARSABAS, a Christian teacher sent from Jerusalem to Antioch along with Paul and Barnabas (Acts xv. 22, 27, 32). He is supposed to have been one of the seventy disciples, and brother of Joseph, also surnamed Barsabas (son of Sabas), who was proposed, with Matthias, to fill up the place of the traitor Judas (Acts i. 23). Judas and Silas (who was also of the party) are mentioned together as ' prophets ' and ' chief men among the brethren.'

4. JUDAS. [JUDE.]

5. JUDAS, a Jew of Damascus, with whom Paul lodged (Acts ix. 11).

6. JUDAS, surnamed the Galilæan (Acts v. 37), so called also by Josephus, and likewise ' the Gaulonite.' In company with one Sadoc he attempted to raise a sedition among the Jews, but was destroyed by Cyrenius (Quirinus), then proconsul of Syria and Judæa.

JUDE, OR JUDAS. There were two of this name among the twelve Apostles—Judas, called also Lebbæus and Thaddæus (Matt. x. 4 ; Mark iii. 18, which see), and Judas Iscariot. Judas is the name of one of our Lord's brethren, but it is not agreed whether our Lord's brother is the same with the Apostle of this name [JAMES]. We are not informed as to the time of the vocation of the Apostle Jude to that dignity. Indeed, the only circumstance relating to him which is recorded in the Gospels consists in the question put by him to our Lord (John xiv. 22). ' Judas saith unto him (not Iscariot, Lord, how is it that thou wilt manifest thyself to us, and not unto the world ?' Nor have we any account given of his proceedings after our Lord's resurrection, for the traditionary notices which have been preserved of him rest on no very certain foundation. It has been asserted that he was sent to Edessa, to Abgarus, king of Osroene, and that he preached in Syria, Arabia, Mesopotamia, and Persia; in which latter country he suffered martyrdom.

JUDE, EPISTLE OF. Doubts have been thrown upon the genuineness of this Epistle from the fact of the writer having been supposed to have cited two Apocryphal books—Enoch and the Assumption of Moses. But notwithstanding the difficulties connected with this point, it was treated by the ancients with the highest respect, and regarded as the genuine work of an inspired writer. Although Origen on one occasion speaks doubtfully, calling it the ' reputed Epistle of Jude,' yet on another occasion, and in the same work, he says, ' Jude wrote an Epistle, of few lines indeed, but full of the powerful words of heavenly grace, who at the beginning says, " Jude, the servant of Jesus Christ and brother of James." ' The same writer calls it the writing of Jude the *Apostle* The moderns are, however, divided in opinion between Jude the Apostle and Jude the Lord's brother, if indeed they be different persons. The author simply calls himself Jude, the brother of James, and a servant of Jesus Christ. This form of expression has given rise to various conjectures. Hug supposes that he intimates thereby a nearer degree of relationship than that of an Apostle. At the same time it must be acknowledged that the circumstance of his not naming himself an apostle is not of itself necessarily sufficient to militate against his being the Apostle of that name, inasmuch as St. Paul does not upon all occasions (as in Philippians, Thessalonians, and Philemon) use this title. From his calling himself the brother of James, rather than the brother of the Lord. Michaelis deduces that he was the son of Joseph by a former wife, and not a full brother of our Lord's, as Herder contends [JAMES, JUDE]. From the great coincidence both in sentiment and subject which exists between this Epistle and the second of St. Peter, it has been thought by many critics that one of these writers had seen the other's work ; but we shall reserve the discussion as to which was the earlier writing until we come to treat of St. Peter's Epistle. Dr. Lardner supposes that Jude's Epistle was written between the years 64 and 66, Beausobre and L'Enfant between 70 and 75 (from which Dodwell and Cave do not materially differ), and Dr. Mill fixes it to the year 90. If Jude has quoted the apocryphal book of Enoch, as seems to be agreed upon by most modern critics, and if this book was written, as Lücke thinks, after the destruction of Jerusalem, the age of our Epistle best accords with the date assigned to it by Mill.

It is difficult to decide who the persons were to whom this Epistle was addressed, some supposing that it was written to converted Jews, others to all Christians, without distinction. Many of the arguments seem best adapted to convince the Jewish Christians, as appeals are so strikingly made to their sacred books and traditions.

The design of this Epistle is to warn the Christians against the false teachers who had insinuated themselves among them and disseminated dangerous tenets of insubordination and licentiousness. The author reminds them, by the example of Sodom and Gomorrah, that God had punished the rebellious Jews ; and that even the disobedient angels had shared the same fate The false teachers to whom he alludes ' speak evil of dignities,' while the archangel Michael did not even revile Satan. He compares them to Balaam and Korah, to clouds without water, and to raging waves. Enoch, he says, foretold their wickedness ; at the same time he consoles believers, and exhorts them to persevere in faith and love. The Epistle is remarkable for the vehemence, fervour, and energy of its composition and style.

JUDGES. This name is applied to fifteen persons who at intervals presided over the affairs of the Israelites during the 450 years which elapsed from the death of Joshua to the accession of Saul. The station and office of these ' rulers of the people,' as the original literally signifies, are involved in great obscurity, partly from the want of clear intimations in the history in which their exploits and government are recorded, and partly from the absence of parallels in the history of other nations, by which our notions might be assisted. They may be briefly described as faithful men, who acted for the most part as agents of the Divine will, regents for the Invisible King of the chosen people ; and who, holding their commission directly from him, or with his sanction, would be more inclined to act as dependent vassals of Jehovah than kings, who, as members of royal dynasties, would come to reign with notions of independent rights and royal privileges, which would draw away their attention from their true place in the theocracy. In this greater dependence of the judges upon the Divine King we see the secret of their institution. The Israelites were disposed to rest upon their separate interests as tribes; and having thus allowed the standing general government to remain inoperative through disuse, they would in cases of emergency have been disposed to forget that Jehovah had taken upon himself the function of their Supreme Ruler, and 'to make themselves a king like the nations,' had their attention not been directed to the appointment of officers whose authority could rest on no tangible right apart from character and services, which, with the temporary nature of their power, rendered their functions more accordant with the principles of the theocracy than those of any other public officers could be. And it is probably in this adaptation to the peculiar circumstances of the Hebrew theocracy that we shall discover the reason of our inability to find any similar office among other nations.

With regard to the nature of the office held by these judges, it is usual to consider them as commencing their career with military exploits to deliver Israel from foreign oppression; but this is by no means invariably the case. Eli and Samuel were not military men; Deborah judged Israel before she planned the war against Jabin; and of Jair, Ibzan, Elon, and Abdon, it is at least uncertain whether they ever held any military command. The command of the army can therefore be scarcely considered the distinguishing characteristic of these men, or military exploits the necessary introduction to the office In many cases it is true that military achievements were the means by which they elevated themselves to the rank of judges; but in general the appointment may be said to have varied with the exigencies of the times, and with the particular circumstances which in times of trouble would draw the public attention to persons who appeared suited by their gifts or influence to advise in matters of general concernment, to decide in questions arising between tribe and tribe, to administer public affairs, and to appear as their recognised head in their intercourse with their neighbours and oppressors.

In nearly all the instances recorded the appointment seems to have been by the free unsolicited choice of the people. The only cases of direct Divine appointment are those of Gideon and Samson, and the last stood in the peculiar position of having been from before his birth ordained 'to begin to deliver Israel.' Deborah was called to deliver Israel, but was already a judge. Samuel was called by the Lord to be a prophet, but not a judge, which ensued from the high gifts which the people recognised as dwelling in him, and as to Eli, the office of judge seems to have devolved naturally, or rather ex-officio, upon him, and his case seems to be the only one in which the high-priest appears in the character which the theocratical institutions designed for him.

The following clear summary of their duties and privileges is given by Jahn:—'The office of judges or regents was held during life, but it was not hereditary, neither could they appoint their successors. Their authority was limited by the law alone; and in doubtful cases they were directed to consult the Divine King through the priest by Urim and Thummim (Num. xxvii. 21). They were not obliged in common cases to ask advice of the ordinary rulers, it was sufficient if these did not remonstrate against the measures of the judge. In important emergencies, however, they convoked a general assembly of the rulers, over which they presided and exerted a powerful influence. They could issue orders, but not enact laws, they could neither levy taxes nor appoint officers, except perhaps in the army. Their authority extended only over those tribes by whom they had been elected or acknowledged, for it is clear that several of the judges presided over separate tribes. There was no income attached to their office, nor was there any income appropriated to them, unless it might be a larger share in the spoils, and those presents which were made them as testimonials of respect (Judg viii. 24). They bore no external marks of dignity, and maintained no retinue of courtiers, though some of them were very opulent. They were not only simple in their manners, moderate in their desires, and free from avarice and ambition, but noble and magnanimous men, who felt that whatever they did for their country was above all reward, and could not be recompensed, who desired merely to promote the public good, and who chose rather to deserve well of their country than to be enriched by its wealth. This exalted patriotism, like everything else connected with politics in the theocratical state of the Hebrews, was partly of a religious character, and those regents always conducted themselves as the officers of God; in all their enterprises they relied upon Him, and their only care was, that their countrymen should acknowledge the authority of Jehovah, their invisible king (Judg. viii. 22, sq ; comp. Heb. xi.). Still they were not without faults, neither are they so represented by their historians; they relate, on the contrary, with the utmost frankness, the great sins of which some of them were guilty. They were not merely deliverers of the state from a foreign yoke, but destroyers of idolatry, foes of pagan vices, promoters of the knowledge of God, of religion, and of morality; restorers of theocracy in the minds of the Hebrews, and powerful instruments of Divine providence in the promotion of the great design of preserving the Hebrew constitution, and, by that means, of rescuing the true religion from destruction.'

The times of the judges would certainly not be considered so turbulent and barbarous, much less would they be taken, contrary to the clearest evidence and to the analogy of all history, for a heroic age, if they were viewed without the prejudices of a preconceived hypothesis. It must never be forgotten that the book of Judges is by no means a complete history. This no impartial inquirer can ever deny. It is, in a manner, a mere register of diseases, from which, however, we have no right to conclude that there were no healthy men, much less that there were no healthy seasons; since the book itself, for the most part, mentions only a few tribes in which the epidemic prevailed, and notices long periods during which it had universally ceased. Whatever may be the result of more accurate investigation, it remains undeniable that the condition of the Hebrews during this period perfectly corresponds throughout to the sanctions of the law; and they were always prosperous when they complied with the conditions on which prosperity was promised them; it remains undeniable that the government of God was clearly manifested, not only to the Hebrews, but to their heathen neighbours; that the fulfilling of the promises and threatenings of the law were so many sensible proofs of the universal dominion of the Divine King of the Hebrews; and, consequently, that all the various fortunes of that nation were so many means of preserving the knowledge of God on the earth. The Hebrews had no sufficient reason to desire a change in their constitution; all required was, that they should observe the conditions on which national prosperity was promised them.

The chronology of the period in which the judges ruled is beset with great and perhaps insuperable difficulties. There are intervals of time the extent of which is not specified; as, for instance, that from Joshua's death to the yoke of Chushan-rishathaim (ii. 8); that of the rule of Shamgar (iii. 31); that between Gideon's death and Abimelech's accession (viii. 31, 32); and that of Israel's renewal of idolatry previous to their oppression by the Ammonites (x. 6, 7). Sometimes round numbers seem to have been given, as forty years for the rule of Othniel, forty years for that of Gideon, and forty years also for the duration of the oppression by the Philistines. Twenty years are given for the subjection to Jabin, and twenty years for the government of Samson; yet the latter never completely conquered the Philistines, who, on the contrary, succeeded in capturing him. Some judges, who are commonly considered to have been successive, were in all probability contemporaneous, and ruled over different districts. Under these circumstances, it is impossible to fix the date of each particular event in the book of Judges; but attempts have been made to settle its general chronology, of which we must in this place mention the most successful.

The whole period of the judges, from Joshua to Eli, is usually estimated at 299 years, in order to meet the 480 years which (1 Kings vi. 1) are said to have elapsed from the departure of the Israelites from Egypt to the foundation of the temple by Solomon. But St. Paul says (Acts xiii. 20), 'God gave unto the people of Israel judges about the space of 450 years until Samuel the prophet.' Again, if the number of years specified by the author of our book, in stating facts, is summed up, we have 410 years, exclusive of those years not specified for certain intervals of time above mentioned. In order to reduce these 410 years and upwards to 299, events and reigns must, in computing their years of duration, either be entirely passed over, or, in a most arbitrary way, included in other periods preceding or subsequent. This has been done by Archbishop Usher, whose system, here peculiarly faulty, has been adopted in the Authorized Version of the Scriptures. He excludes the repeated intervals during which the Hebrews were in subjection to their enemies, and reckons only the years of peace and rest which were assigned to the successive judges. For example, he passes over the eight years of servitude inflicted upon the Hebrews by Chushan-

rishathaim, and, without any interruption, connects the peace obtained by the victories of Othniel with that which had been conferred on the land by the government of Joshua; and although the sacred historian relates in the plainest terms possible that the children of Israel served the king of Mesopotamia eight years, and were afterwards delivered by Othniel, who gave the land rest forty years, the archbishop maintains that the forty years now mentioned began, not after the successes of this judge, but immediately after the demise of Joshua. Nothing certainly can be more obvious than that in this case the years of tranquillity and the years of oppression ought to be reckoned separately. Again, we are informed by the sacred writer, that after the death of Ehud the children of Israel were under the oppression of Jabin king of Hazor for twenty years, and that afterwards, when their deliverance was effected by Deborah and Barak, the land had rest forty years. Nothing can be clearer than this; yet Usher's system leads him to include the twenty years of oppression in the forty of peace, making both but forty years. All this arises from the obligation which Usher unfortunately conceived himself under of following the scheme adopted by the Masoretic Jews, who, as Dr. Hales remarks, have by a curious invention included the four first servitudes in the years of the judges who put an end to them, contrary to the express declarations of Scripture, which represents the administrations of the judges, not as synchronising with the servitudes, but as succeeding them. The Rabbins were indeed forced to allow the fifth servitude to have been distinct from the administration of Jephthah, because it was too long to be included in that administration; but they deducted a year from the Scripture account of the servitude, making it only six instead of seven years. They sank entirely the sixth servitude of forty years under the Philistines, because it was too long to be contained in Samson's administration; and, to crown all, they reduced Saul's reign of forty years to two years only.

The necessity for all these tortuous operations has arisen from a desire to produce a conformity with the date in 1 Kings vi. 1, which, as already cited, gives a period of only 480 years from the Exode to the foundation of Solomon's temple. As this date is incompatible with the sum of the different numbers given in the book of Judges, and as it differs from the computation of Josephus and of all the ancient writers on the subject, whether Jewish or Christian, it is not unsatisfactory to find grounds which leave this text open to much doubt and suspicion. We cannot here enter into any lengthened proof; but that the text did not exist in the Hebrew and Greek copies of the Scripture till nearly three centuries after Christ, is evident from the absence of all reference to it in the works of the learned men who composed histories of the Jews from the materials supplied to them in the sacred books. This might be shown by reference to various authors, who, if the number specified in it had existed, could not fail to have adduced it.

It only remains to arrange the different systems of the chronology of this period so as to exhibit them in one view to the eye of the reader. It has been deemed right, for the better apprehension of the differences, to make the table embrace the whole period from the exode to the building of Solomon's temple. The *headings* are taken from Hales, simply because, from being the most copious, they can afford a framework within which all the explanations may be inserted.

The authorities for this table are: Josephus, *Antiquities*, v. 1-10; Theophilus, Bp. of Antioch (A.D. 330), *Epist. ad Autolycum*, iii.; Eusebius (A.D. 330), *Præparatio Evangelica*, x. 14; Usher (1650), *Chronologia Sacra*, p. 71; Jackson (1752), *Chronological Antiquities*, p. 145; Hales (1811), *Analysis of Chronology*, i. 101; Russell (1827), *Connection of Sacred and Profane History*, i. 147.

	Hales.		Jackson.		Russell.	Josephus.	Theophilus.	Eusebius.	Usher.	
	Yrs.	B.C.	Years.	B.C.	Yrs.	Yrs.	Yrs.	Years.	Years.	B.C.
Exode to death of Moses	40	1648	40	1593	40	40	40	40	40	1491
Joshua (and the) }	26	1608		..	25	25	27	27	..	1451
Elders }			} 27	1553					6 4 m	1444
First Division of Lands	..	1602								
Second Division of Lands	..	1596			..	..	..	..		
Anarchy or Interregnum	10	1582	..	..	2					
I. Servitude, Mesopotam.	8	1572	8	1526	8	18	8	8 }	40	1413
1. Othniel	40	1564	40	1518	40	40	40	40 }		1405
II. Servitude, Moabit.	18	1524	18	1478	..	..	18	18		1343
2. Ehud (and) }	80	1506	80	1460	80	{ 80 / 1	80 / 1	80 / omitted	} 80	1323
3. Shamgar }										
III. Servitude, Canaanit.	20	1426	20	1380	20	20	20	20 }	40	1285
4. Deborah and Barak	40	1406	40	1360	40	40	40	40 }		1265
IV. Servitude, Midian.	7	1368	7	1320	7	7	7	7 }	40	1252
5. Gideon	40	1359	40	1313	40	40	40	40 }		1245
6. Abimelech	3	1319	3	1273	3	3	3	3	9 2 m	1236
7. Tola	23	1316	22	1270	22	22	22	23 }	48	1232
8. Jair	22	1293	22	1248	22	22	22	22 }		1210
V. Servitude, Ammon.	18	1271	18	1226	18	18	18	18 }	6	1206
9. Jephthah	6	1253	6	1208	6	6	6	6 }		1188
10. Ibzan	7	1247	7	1202	7	7	7	7 }		1182
11. Elon	10	1240	10	1195	10 }	10	10	10 }	25	1175
12. Abdon	8	1230	8	1185	8 }		8	8 }		1165
VI. Servitude, Philist. 20 }	40	1222	40	1177	40	40 / 20	40 / 20	40 / 20 }		
13. Samson. .20 }									40	
Interregnum	..		..	..			40			
14. Eli .30 }	40	1182	20 ?	1137	20†	40	20	40 }		1157
Samuel called as a prophet 10 }										
VII. Servitude or Anarchy	20	1142	20	1117	20½				21	1116
15. Samuel	12	1122	20	1097	12	12	..	..		
Samuel and Saul .18 }	40	1110	{ .. / 20	1077	40	18 / 2	20	40	40	1095
Saul .22 }										
David	40	1070	40	1057	40	40	40	40 }	43	1055
Solomon to Found. of the Temple	3	1030	3	1017	3	3	3	3 }		1014
Exode to F. of Temple	621	1027	579	1014	591½	592	612	600	478¼	1012

JUDGES BOOK OF, the third in the list of the historical compositions of the Old Testament. It consists of two divisions, the first comprising chaps. i.-xvii.; the second, being an appendix, chaps. xvii.-xxi.

That the author, in composing this work, had a certain design in view, is evident from ch. ii. 11-23, where he states the leading features of his narrative. He introduces it by relating (ch. i.) the extent to which the wars against the Canaanites were continued after the death of Joshua, and what tribes had spared them in consideration of a tribute imposed; also by alluding (ch. ii. 1-10) to the benefits which Jehovah had conferred on them, and the distinguished protection with which he had honoured them. Next he states his leading object, namely, to prove that the calamities to which the Hebrews had been exposed since the death of Joshua were owing to their apostacy from Jehovah, and to their idolatry. 'They forsook the Lord, and served Baal and Ashtaroth' (ch. ii. 13); for which crimes they were deservedly punished and greatly distressed (ch. ii. 15). Nevertheless, when they repented and obeyed again the commandments of the Lord, he delivered them out of the hand of their enemies by the 'judges' whom he raised up, and made them prosper (ch. ii. 16-23). To illustrate this theme, the author

---

* Samson and Eli are supposed to have been judges simultaneously during 20 years of this period.

† Besides the 20 years under the sixth servitude.

collected several fragments of the Hebrew history during the period between Joshua and Eli. Some episodes occur; but in arguing his subject he never loses sight of his leading theme, to which, on the contrary, he frequently recurs while stating facts, and shows how it applied to them; the moral evidently being, that the only way to happiness was to shun idolatry and obey the commandments of the Lord. The design of the author was not to give a connected and complete history of the Hebrews in the period between Joshua and the kings; for if he had intended a plan of that kind, he would also have described the state of the domestic affairs and of the government in the several tribes, the relation in which they stood to each other, and the extent of power exercised by a judge; he would have further stated the number of tribes over whom a judge ruled, and the number of years during which the tribes were not oppressed by their heathen neighbours, but enjoyed rest and peace. The appendix, containing two narratives (that of Micah with his 'house of gods,' and the brutal outrage committed by the Benjamites of Gibeah), further illustrates the lawlessness and anarchy prevailing in Israel after Joshua's death.

If the first and second divisions had been by the same author, the chronological indications would also have been the same. Now the author of the second division always describes the period of which he speaks thus: 'In those days there was no king in Israel, but every man did that which was right in his own eyes' (ch. xvii. 6: xviii. 1; xix 1; xxi. 25); but this expression never once occurs in the first division. If one author had composed both divisions, instead of this chronological formula, we should rather have expected, 'In the days of the judges,' 'At a time when there was no judge,' &c., which would be consonant with the tenor of the first sixteen chapters. The style also in the two divisions is different, and it will be shown that the appendix was written much later than the first part. All modern critics, then, agree in this, that the author of the first sixteen chapters of our book is different from him who composed the appendix. The authorship of the first sixteen chapters has been ascribed to Joshua, Samuel, and Ezra. There is no evidence, however, in support of any of these opinions, and various conclusive reasons can be assigned to show that they are incorrect.

But though we cannot determine the authorship of the book of Judges, still its age may be determined from internal evidence. The first sixteen chapters must have been written under Saul, whom the Israelites made their king in the hope of improving their condition. Phrases used in the period of the Judges may be traced in them, and the author must consequently have lived near the time when they were yet current. He says that in his time 'the Jebusites dwelt with the children of Benjamin in Jerusalem' (ch. i. 21): now this was the case only before David, who conquered the town and drove out the Jebusites. Consequently, the author of the first division of the book of Judges must have lived and written before David, and under king Saul. If he had lived under David, he would have mentioned the capture of Jerusalem by that monarch, as the nature of his subject did not allow him to pass it over in silence. The omission, moreover, of the history, not only of Samuel but also of Eli, indicates an author who, living in an age very near that of Eli, considered his history as generally known, because so recent. The exact time when the appendix was added to the book of Judges cannot indeed be determined, but its author certainly lived in an age much later than that of the recorded events.

It was published at a time when the events related were generally known, and when the veracity of the author could be ascertained by a reference to the original documents. Several of its narratives are confirmed by the books of Samuel (comp. Judg. iv. 2; vi. 14; xi., with 1 Sam. xii. 9-12: Judg. ix. 53 with 2 Sam. xi. 21). The Psalms not only allude to the book of Judges (comp. Ps. lxxxiii. 11, with Judg. vii. 25), but copy from it entire verses (comp. Ps. lxviii 8, 9; xcvii 5; with Judg. v. 4, 5). Philo and Josephus knew the book, and made use of it in their own compositions. The New Testament alludes to it in several places (comp. Matt. ii 13 23 with Judg. xiii 5; xvi. 17; Acts xiii 20; Heb. xi. 32). This external evidence in support of the authority of the book of Judges is corroborated by many internal proofs of its authenticity. All its narratives are in character with the age to which they belong, and agree with the natural order of things. We find here that shortly after the death of Joshua the Hebrew nation had, by several victories, gained courage and become valorous (ch. i. and xix.); but that it afterwards turned to agriculture, preferred a quiet life, and allowed the Canaanites to reside in its territory in consideration of a tribute imposed on them, when the original plan was that they should be expelled. This changed their character entirely: they became effeminate and indolent—a result which we find in the case of all nations who, from a nomadic and warlike life, turn to agriculture. The intercourse with their heathen neighbours frequently led the uncultivated Hebrews to idolatry; and this, again, further prepared them for servitude. They were consequently overpowered and oppressed by their heathen neighbours. The first subjugation, indeed, by a king of Mesopotamia, they endured but eight years; but the second, more severe, by Eglon, lasted longer: it was the natural consequence of the public spirit having gradually more and more declined, and of Eglon having removed his residence to Jericho with a view of closely watching all their movements (Joseph. Antiq. v. 5). When Ehud sounded the trumpet of revolt, the whole nation no longer rose in arms, but only the inhabitants of Mount Ephraim (ch. iii. 27); and when Barak called to arms against Sisera, many tribes remained quietly with their herds (ch. v. 14, 15, 26, 28). Of the 30,000 men who offered to assist Gideon, he could make use of no more than 300, this small number only being, as it would seem, filled with true patriotism and courage. Thus the people had sunk gradually, and deserved for forty years to bear the yoke of the Philistines, to whom they had the meanness to deliver Samson, who, however, loosed the cords with which he was tied, and killed a large number of them (ch. xv.). It is impossible to consider such an historical work, which perfectly agrees with the natural course of things, as a fiction: at that early period of authorship, no writer could have, from fancy, depicted the character of the Hebrews so conformably with nature and established facts. All in this book breathes the spirit of the ancient world. Martial law we find in it, as could not but be expected, hard and wild. The conquered people are subjected to rough treatment, as is the case in the wars of all uncivilized people; the inhabitants of cities are destroyed wholesale (ch. viii. 16, 17; xx.) Hospitality and the protection of strangers received as guests is considered the highest virtue (ch. xix.; comp. Gen. xix.).

In the state of oppression in which the Hebrews often found themselves during the period from Joshua to Eli, it was to be expected that men, filled with heroism, should now and then rise up and call the people to arms in order to deliver them from their enemies. Such valiant men are introduced by our author, and he extols them, indeed, highly; but on the other hand he is not silent respecting their faults, which he discloses in a way proper to true history, but impossible to fiction which could have no other object than the aggrandisement of the national character and exploits. And this frank, impartial tone pervades the whole work. It begins with displaying the Israelites as a refractory and obstinate people, and the appendix ends with the statement of a crime committed by the Benjamites, which had the most disastrous consequences. At the same time due praise is bestowed on acts of generosity and justice, and valiant feats are carefully recorded.

Objections have been made to the authenticity of this book, in consequence of the remarkable exploits ascribed to its heroes. But it will be easy to show that, when properly understood, these exploits do not necessarily exceed the limits of human power. Extraordinary indeed they were; but they are not alleged by the Scripture itself to have been supernatural. Those, however, who do hold them to have been supernatural cannot reasonably take exception to them on the ground of their extraordinary character. Considering the very remote period at which our book was written—considering also the manner of viewing and describing events and persons which prevailed with the ancient Hebrews, and which very much differs from that of our age—taking, moreover, into account the brevity of the narratives, which consist of historical fragments, we may well wonder that there do not occur in it more difficulties, and that not more doubts have been raised as to its historical authority.

JUDGMENT-HALL occurs Matt. xxvii. 27; Mark xv. 16; John xviii. 28, 33; xix. 9; Acts xxiii. 35; Phil. i. 13. In all these passages except one (Mark xv. 16) the English version gives an explanation of the word rather than a translation: thus, Matt. xxvii. 27, 'the common-hall' margin, 'or governor's house:' John xviii. 28, 33, 'the judgment-hall;' margin, 'or Pilate's house:' Philipp. i. 13, 'the palace;' margin, 'or Cæsar's court.' Originally the word signified the general's tent in a camp, but it came at length to be applied to the residence of the civil governor in provinces and cities, and was used to signify whatever appertained to the prætor or governor; for instance, his residence, either the whole or any part of it, as his dwelling-house, or the place where he administered justice, or even the large enclosed court at the entrance to the prætorian residence.

Upon comparing the instances in which the evangelists mention the prætorium, it will be seen, first, that in John xviii. 28, it means the residence of Pilate, which seems to have been the magnificent palace built by Herod, situated in the north part of the upper city, west of the temple, and overlooking the temple. Secondly, the word is applied in the New Testament, by synecdoche, to a particular part of the prætorian residence. Thus, Matt. xxvii. 27 and Mark xv. 16, 'And the soldiers led Jesus away into the hall called Prætorium, and gathered unto them the whole band, and they clothed him with purple,' &c.; where the word rather refers to the court or area in front of the prætorium, or some other court where the procurator's guards were stationed. In John xix. 9, the word seems applied, when all the circumstances are considered, to Pilate's private examination room. In like manner, when Felix 'commanded Paul to be kept in Herod's prætorium' (Acts xxiii. 25), the words apply not only to the whole palace originally built at Cæsarea by Herod, and now most likely inhabited by the prætor, but also to the keep or donjon, a prison for confining offenders, such as existed in our ancient royal palaces and grand baronial castles. Thirdly, in the remaining instance of the word, Phil. i. 3, 'So that my bonds in Christ are manifest in all the prætorium,' 'palace,' it is, in the opinion of the best commentators, used to signify the prætorian camp at Rome, a select body of troops constituted by Augustus to guard his person and to have charge of the city, so that the words of the apostle really mean, 'My bonds in Christ are manifest to all the prætorians, and by their means to the public at large.'

JUDITH the name of one of the apocryphal or deutero-canonical books of the Old Testament, is placed in manuscripts of the Alexandrine version between the books of Tobit and Esther. In its external form this book bears the character of the record of an historical event, describing the complete defeat of the Assyrians by the Jews through the prowess of a woman.

The following is a sketch of the narrative:—Nebuchadnezzar, or, as he is called in the Greek, Nabuchodonosor, king of the Assyrians, having, in the twelfth year of his reign, conquered and taken Arphaxad, by whom his territory had been invaded, formed the design of subduing the people of Asia to the westward of Nineveh his capital, who had declined to aid him against Arphaxad. With this view he sent his general, Holofernes, at the head of a powerful army, and soon made himself master of Mesopotamia, Syria, Libya, Cilicia, and Idumæa. The inhabitants of the sea-coast made a voluntary submission; which however, did not prevent their territories from being laid waste, their sacred groves burned, and their idols destroyed, in order that divine honours should be paid only to Nebuchadnezzar. Holofernes, having finally encamped in the plain of Esdraelon (ch. i. 3), remained inactive for a whole month—or two, according to the Latin version. But the Jews, who had not long returned from captivity, and who had just restored their temple and its worship, prepared for war under the direction of their high-priest Joacim, or Eliakim, and the senate. The high-priest addressed letters to the inhabitants of Bethulia and Betomestham, near Esdraelon (ch. iv. 6), charging them to guard the passes of the mountains. The

Jews at the same time kept a fast, and called upon God for protection against their enemies. Holofernes, astonished at their audacity and preparations, inquired of the Moabites and Ammonites who these people were. Achior, the leader of the Ammonites, informed him of the history of the Jews, adding, that if they offended their God he would deliver them into the hands of their enemies, but that otherwise they would be invincible. Holofernes, however, prepares to lay siege to Bethulia, and commences operations by taking the mountain passes, and intercepting the water, in order to compel the inhabitants to surrender. Ozias, the governor of the city, holds out as long as possible; but at the end of thirty four days' siege, the inhabitants are reduced to that degree of distress from drought, that they are determined to surrender unless relieved within five days. Meantime Judith, a rich and beautiful woman, the widow of Manasseh, forms the patriotic design of delivering the city and the nation. With this view she entreats the governor and elders to give up all idea of surrender, and to permit the gates of the city to be opened for her. Arrayed in rich attire, she proceeds to the camp of Holofernes, attended only by her maid, bearing a bag of provisions. She is admitted into the presence of Holofernes, and informs him that the Jews could not be overcome so long as they remained faithful to God, but that they had now sinned against Him in converting to their own use the tithes, which were sacred to the priests alone; and that she had fled from the city to escape the impending and inevitable destruction which awaited it. She obtains leave to remain in the camp, with the liberty of retiring by night for the purpose of prayer, and promises that at the proper moment she will herself be the guide of Holofernes to the very walls of Jerusalem. Judith is favourably entertained; Holofernes is smitten with her charms, gives her a magnificent entertainment, at which, having drunk too freely, he is shut up with her alone in the tent. Taking advantage of her opportunity, while he is sunk in sleep, she seizes his falchion and strikes off his head. Giving it to her maid, who was outside the tent door, she leaves the camp as usual, under pretence of devotion, and returns to Bethulia, displaying the head of Holofernes. The Israelites, next morning, fall on the Assyrians, who, panic-struck at the loss of their general, are soon discomfited, leaving an immense spoil in the hands of their enemies. The whole concludes with the triumphal song of Judith, who accompanies all the people to Jerusalem to give thanks to the Lord. After this she returns to her native city Bethulia, gives freedom to her maid, and dies at the advanced age of 105 years. The Jews enjoying a profound and happy peace, a yearly festival (according to the Vulgate) is instituted in honour of the victory.

The difficulties, historical, chronological, and geographical, comprised in the narrative of Judith are so numerous and serious as to be held by many divines altogether insuperable. Events, times, and manners are said to be confounded, and the chronology of the times before and those after the exile, of the Persian and Assyrian, and even of the Maccabæan period, confusedly and unaccountably blended.

The authorship of the book is as uncertain as its date. It is not named either by Philo or Josephus; nor have we any indication whatever by which to form a conjecture respecting its author.

The original language is uncertain. Eichhorn and Jahn and Seiler, with whom is Bertholdt, conceive it to have been Greek. Calmet states, on the authority of Origen, that the Jews had the book of Judith in Hebrew in his time. Jerome states that it is written in Chaldee, from which he translated it, with the aid of an interpreter, giving rather the sense than the words.

Although the book of Judith never formed part of the Jewish canon, and finds no place in the ancient catalogues, its authority in the Christian church has been very great.

Along with the other deutero-canonical books. it has been at all times read in the church, and lessons are taken from it in the Church of England in course.

JU'LIA (a name common among the Romans). a Christian woman of Rome, to whom St. Paul sent his salutations (Rom. xvi. 15); she is named with Philologus, and is supposed to have been his wife or sister.

JU'LIUS, the centurion who had the charge of conducting Paul as a prisoner to Rome, and who treated him with much consideration and kindness on the way (Acts xxvii. 1, 3).

JU'NIAS, a person who is joined with Andronicus in Rom. xvi. 7: 'Salute Andronicus and Junias, my kinsmen and fellow-prisoners, who are of note among the apostles.' They were, doubtless, Jewish Christians.

1. JUS'TUS, surnamed Barsabas. [JOSEPH.]

2. JUSTUS, a Christian at Corinth, with whom Paul lodged (Acts xviii. 7).

3. JUSTUS, called also JESUS, a believing Jew, who was with Paul at Rome when he wrote to the Colossians (Col. iv. 11). The apostle names him and Marcus as being at that time his only fellow-labourers.

K.

KA'DESH, or KADESH-BARNEA, a site on the south-eastern border of the Promised Land towards Edom, of much interest as being the point at which the Israelites twice encamped with the intention of entering Palestine, and from which they were twice sent back; the first time in pursuance of their sentence to wander forty years in the wilderness, and the second time from the refusal of the king of Edom to permit a passage through his territories. It was from Kadesh that the spies entered Palestine by ascending the mountains; and the murmuring Israelites, afterwards attempting to do the same, were driven back by the Amalekites and Canaanites, and afterwards apparently by the king of Arad, as far as Hormah, then called Zephath (Num. xiii. 17; xiv. 40–45; xxi. 1–3; Deut. i. 41–44; comp. Judg. i. 7). There was also at Kadesh a fountain (En-mishpat) mentioned long before the exode of the Israelites (Gen. xiv. 7); and the miraculous supply of water took place only on the second visit, which implies that at the first there was no lack of this necessary article. After this, Moses sent messengers to the king of Edom, informing him that they were in Kadesh, a city in the uttermost part of his border, and asking leave to pass through his country, so as to continue their course round Moab, and approach Palestine from the east. This Edom refused, and the Israelites accordingly marched to Mount Hor, where Aaron died; and then along the Arabah (desert of Zin) to the Red Sea (Num. xx. 14-29). The name of Kadesh again occurs in describing the southern quarter of Judah, the line defining which is drawn ' from the shore of the Salt Sea, from the bay that looked southward; and it went out to the south side of Akrabim, and passed along to Zin, and ascended up in the south side to Kadesh-barnea' (Josh. xv. 1-3; comp. Num. xxxiv. 3, 4).

From these intimations the map-makers, who found it difficult to reconcile them with the place usually assigned to Kadesh (in the desert about midway between the Mediterranean and Dead Sea), were in the habit of placing a second Kadesh nearer the Dead Sea and the Wady Arabah. But it was shown by Dr. Kitto in the *Pictorial Bible* (Note on Num. xx. 1) that one Kadesh would sufficiently answer all the conditions required, by being placed more to the south, nearer to Mount Hor, on the west border of the Wady Arabah, than this second Kadesh.

According to this view Kadesh was laid down in his map in the same line, and not far from the place which has since been assigned to it from actual observation by Dr. Robinson. This concurrence of different lines of research in the same result is curious and valuable, and the position of Kadesh will be regarded as now scarcely open to dispute. It was clear that the discovery of the fountain in the northern part of the great valley would go far to fix the question. Robinson accordingly discovered a fountain called Ain el-Weibeh, which is even at this day the most frequented watering-place in all the Arabah, and he was struck by the entire adaptedness of the site to the Scriptural account of the proceedings of the Israelites on their second arrival at Kadesh. 'Over against us lay the land of Edom; we were in its uttermost border ; and the great Wady el-Ghuweir afforded a direct and easy passage through the mountains to the table-land above, which was directly before us; while further in the south Mount Hor formed a prominent and striking object, at the distance of two good days' journey for such a host' (*Bib. Researches*, ii. 538). Further on (p. 610) he adds: 'There the Israelites would have Mount Hor in the S S E. towering directly before them....in the N.W. rises the mountain by which they attempted to ascend to Palestine, with the pass still called Sufah (Zephath); while further north we find also Tell Arad, marking the site of the ancient Arad. To all this comes the vicinity of the southern bay of the Dead Sea, the line of cliffs or offset separating the Ghôr from the Arabah, answering to the ascent of Akrabbim; and the desert of Zin, with the place of the same name between Akrabbim and Kadesh, not improbably at the water of Hasb, in the Arabah. In this way all becomes easy and natural, and the Scriptural account is entirely accordant with the character of the country.'

KAD'MONITES, one of the nations of Canaan, which is supposed to have dwelt in the north-east part of Palestine, under Mount Hermon, at the time that Abraham sojourned in the land (Gen. xv. 19). It is supposed that the name denotes ' an eastern people,' and that they were situated to the east of the Jordan, or rather that it was a term applied collectively, like ' Easterns,' or ' Orientals,' to all the people living in the countries beyond that river.

KE'DAR (*black*), a son of Ishmael, and the name of the tribe of which he was the founder. The name is sometimes used in Scripture as that of the Bedouins generally, probably because this tribe was the nearest to them, and was best acquainted with them (Cant. i. 5 ; Isa. xxi. 16, 17 ; lx. 7). A great deal of speculation founded upon the meaning of the word, namely, ' black,' may be dismissed as wholly useless. The Kedarenes were so called from Kedar, and not because they lived in ' black' tents, or because they were ' blackened' by the hot sun of Southern Arabia; neither of which circumstances could, even if true, have been foreseen at the time that Kedar received his name.

KED'EMOTH, a city in the tribe of Reuben (Josh. xiii. 18), near the river Arnon, which gave its name to the wilderness of Kedemoth, on the borders of that river, from whence Moses sent messengers of peace to Sihon, king of Heshbon (Deut. ii. 26), the southern frontier of whose kingdom, and the boundary between the kingdom of the Ammonites and the Moabites, was the Arnon.

KE'DESH. There were two cities of this name; one in the tribe of Judah (Josh. xv. 23), and the other in the tribe of Naphtali (xix. 37). This last was the more considerable of the two; it was a Levitical city, and one of the six cities of refuge. As the Kedesh whose king was slain by Joshua is mentioned among the cities of the north (xii. 22), it was doubtless the Kedesh of Naphtali, of which also Barak was a native (Judg. iv. 6).

KED'RON. [KIDRON.]

KEI'LAH, a city of the tribe of Judah (Josh. xv. 44), about twenty miles south-west from Jerusalem. When this city was besieged by the Philistines, David was commissioned by God to relieve it; notwithstanding which, if he had not made his escape, the ungrateful inhabitants would have delivered him into the hands of Saul (1 Sam. xxiii. 1-13). Keilah was a considerable city in the time of Nehemiah (Neh. iii. 17, 18), and existed in the days of Eusebius and Jerome, who place it eight Roman miles from Eleutheropolis on the road to Hebron.

KEM'UEL (*assembly of God*), third son of Abraham's brother Nahor, and father of six sons, the first of whom is named Aram, and the last Bethuel (Gen. xxii. 21, 23). All these are unknown, except the last, who was the father of Laban and Rebekah (Gen. xxiv. 15).

KE'NAZ (*hunting*). 1. A descendant of Esau; also a place or tract of country in Arabia Petræa, named after him (Gen. xxxvi. 11, 15, 42).

2. The younger brother of Caleb, and father of Othniel, who married Caleb's daughter (Josh. xv. 17 ; Judg. i. 13 ; 1 Chron. iv. 13).

3. A grandson of Caleb (1 Chron. iv. 15).

KE'NITES, a tribe of Midianites dwelling among the Amalekites (1 Sam. xv. 6; comp. Num. xxiv. 20, 21), or occupying in semi-no-

2 L

madic life the same region with the latter people in Arabia Petræa. When Saul was sent to destroy the Amalekites, the Kenites, who had joined them, perhaps upon compulsion, were ordered to depart from them that they might not share their fate; and the reason assigned was, that they 'shewed kindness to the children of Israel when they came out of Egypt.' This kindness is supposed to have been that which Jethro and his family showed to Moses, as well as to the Israelites themselves, in consequence of which the whole tribe appears to have been treated with consideration, while the family of Jethro itself accompanied the Israelites into Palestine, where they continued to lead a nomade life, occupying there a position similar to that of the Tartar tribes in Persia at the present day. To this family belonged Heber, the husband of that Jael who slew Sisera, and who is hence called ' Heber the Kenite' (Judg. iv. 11). At a later age other families of Kenites are mentioned as resident in Palestine, among whom were the Rechabites (1 Chron. ii. 55 ; Jer. xxxv. 2); but it is not clear whether these were subdivisions of the increasing descendants of Jethro, as seems most likely, or families which availed themselves of the friendly dispositions of the Israelites towards the tribe to settle in the country. It appears that, whatever was the general condition of the Midianites, the tribe of the Kenites possessed a knowledge of the true God in the time of Jethro [HOBAB]; and that those families which settled in Palestine did not afterwards lose that knowledge, but increased it, is clear from the passages which have been cited [MIDIANITES; RECHABITES].

KEN'IZZITES, a Canaanitish tribe, mentioned in Gen. xv. 19, along with others, over which it was promised that the seed of Abraham should have dominion. The notion that they sprung from Kenaz, the grandson of Edom, and had their dwelling somewhere in Idumæa, cannot be entertained, seeing that the tribe is named long before Kenaz had existence. The Kenizzites of Num. xxxii. 12 ; Josh. xiv. 6, appear, however, to be a different race, the origin of which may without improbability be ascribed to Kenaz. The Kenizzites are not named among the nations whom the Israelites eventually subdued; whence it may be supposed that they had by that time merged into some of the other nations which Israel overcame.

KETU'RAH (incense), the second wife, or, as she is called in 1 Chron. i. 32, the concubine of Abraham, by whom he had six sons, Zimran, Jokshan, Medan, Midian, Ishbak, and Shuah, whom he lived to see grow to man's estate, and whom he established ' in the East country,' that they might not interfere with Isaac (Gen. xxv. 1-6). As Abraham was 100 years old when Isaac was born, who was given to him by the special bounty of Providence when ' he was as good as dead' (Heb. xi. 12), as he was 140 years old when Sarah died; and as he himself died at the age of 175 years, it has seemed improbable that these six sons should have been born to Abraham by one woman after he was 140 years old, and that he should have seen them all grow up to adult age, and have sent them forth to form independent settlements in that last and feeble period of his life. If Isaac was born to him out of the course of nature when he was 100 years old, how

could six sons be born to him in the course of nature after he was 140 ? It has therefore been suggested by good commentators, that as Keturah is called Abraham's ' concubine' in Chronicles, and as she and Hagar are probably indicated as his ' concubines' in Gen. xxv. 6, Keturah had in fact been taken by Abraham as his secondary or concubine-wife before the death of Sarah, although the historian relates the incident after that event, that his leading narrative might not be interrupted. According to the standard of morality then acknowledged, Abraham might quite as properly have taken Keturah before as after Sarah's death ; nor can any reason why he should not have done so. or why he should have waited till then, be conceived. This explanation obviates many difficulties, and does not itself contain any.

KIB'ROTH-HATTA'AVAH, an encampment of the Israelites in the wilderness [WANDERING].

KID'RON (the turbid), the brook or winter torrent which flows through the valley of Jehoshaphat (as it is now called), on the east side of Jerusalem. 'The brook Kidron' is the only name by which ' the valley' itself is known in Scripture ; for it is by no means certain, nor even probable, that the name 'valley of Jehoshaphat' in Joel (iii. 12) was intended to apply to this valley. The word rendered ' brook' (2 Sam. xv. 23; 1 Kings ii. 37, &c.), may be taken as equivalent to the Arabic Wady, meaning a stream and its bed or valley, or properly the valley of a stream, even when the stream is dry. The Septuagint, Josephus, and the Evangelists (John xviii. 1), designate it a storm brook, or winter torrent.

The brook Kidron derives all its importance from its vicinity to the holy city, being nothing more than the dry bed of a winter torrent, bearing marks of being occasionally swept over by a large volume of water. No stream flows through it, except during the heavy rains of winter, when the waters descend into it from the neighbouring hills. But even in winter there is no constant flow, and the resident missionaries assured Dr. Robinson that they had not during several years seen a stream running through the valley. The ravine in which the stream is collected takes its origin above a mile to the north-east of the city. This ravine deepens as it proceeds, and forms an angle opposite the temple. It then takes a southeast direction, and, passing between the village of Siloam and the city, runs off in the direction of the Dead Sea, through a singularly wild gorge, the course of which few travellers have traced. It is in this ravine that the celebrated monastery of Santa Saba is situated. Dr. Madden, who went through the valley to the Dead Sea, thus speaks of the character which it assumes as it approaches the monastery :—' After traversing for the last hour a wild ravine, formed by two rugged perpendicular mountains, the sides of which contained innumerable caverns, which once formed a sort of troglodyte city, in which the early Christians resided, the sight of the convent in this desolate place was like a glimpse of paradise.' On leaving the convent the next day he says that he ' marched through the bed of the Kidron, along the horrible ravine which he entered the day before;' but he gives no account of its outlet into the Dead Sea. This defect is supplied by Dr. Robinson, who, on passing along the western borders of the lake, came ' to the deep and almost impassable ravine of the Kidron, running down by Mar Saba, and thence called Wady-er-Rahib, " Monk's Valley ;" but here also bearing the name of Wady en-Nar, "Fire Valley." At this place it was running E.S.E., in a deep narrow channel, between perpendicular walls of rock, as if worn away by the rushing waters between these desolate chalky hills. There was, however, no water in it now; nor had there apparently been any for a long time.'

KING, a title applied in the Scriptures to men (Luke xxii. 25 ; 1 Tim. ii. 1, 2 ; 1 Pet. ii. 13-17), to God (1 Tim. i. 17 ; vi. 15, 16), and to Christ (Matt. xxvii. 11 ; Luke xix. 38 ; John i. 49 ; vi. 15 ; xviii. 32-37)—to men, as invested with regal authority by their fellows ; to God, as the sole proper sovereign and ruler of the universe ; and to Christ, as the Messiah, the Son of God, the King of the Jews, the sole Head and Governor of his church.

Regal authority was altogether alien to the institutions of Moses in their original and unadulterated form. Their fundamental idea was that Jehovah was the sole king of the nation (1 Sam. viii 7) . to use the emphatic words in Isa. xxxiii. 22, ' The Lord is our judge, the Lord is our lawgiver, the Lord is our king.' We consider it as a sign of that self-confidence and moral enterprise which are produced in great men by a consciousness of being what they profess, that Moses ventured, with his half-civilized hordes, on the bold experiment of founding a society without a king, and that in the solicitude which he must have felt for the success of his great undertaking, he forewent the advantages which a regal government would have afforded. Nor is such an attempt a little singular and novel at a period and in a part of the world in which royalty was not only general, but held in the greatest respect, and sometimes rose to the very height of pure despotism. Its novelty is an evidence of the divine original to which Moses referred all his polity. Equally honourable is the conduct of Moses in denying to his lower nature the gratifications which a crown might have imparted, and it is obvious that this self-denial on the part of Moses, this omission to create any human kingship, is in entire accordance with the import, aim, and spirit of the Mosaic institutions, as being divine in their origin, and designed to accomplish a special work of Providence for man : and, therefore, affords, by its consistency with the very essence of the system of which it forms a part, a very forcible argument in favour of the divine legation of Moses.

That great man, however, well knew what were the elements with which he had to deal in framing institutions for the rescued Israelites. Slaves they had been, and the spirit of slavery was not yet wholly eradicated from their souls. They had, too, witnessed in Egypt the more than ordinary pomp and splendour which environ a throne, dazzling the eyes and captivating the heart of the uncultured. Not improbably the prosperity and abundance which they had seen in Egypt, and in which they had been, in a measure, allowed to partake, might have been ascribed by them to the regal form of the Egyptian government. Moses may well, therefore, have apprehended a

not very remote departure from the fundamental type of his institutions. Accordingly he makes a special provision for this contingency (Deut. xvii. 14), and labours, by anticipation, to guard against the abuses of royal power. Should a king be demanded by the people, then he was to be a native Israelite ; he was not to be drawn away by the love of show, especially by a desire for that regal display in which horses have always borne so large a part, to send down to Egypt, still less to cause the people to return to that land ; he was to avoid the corrupting influence of a large harem, so common among Eastern monarchs ; he was to abstain from amassing silver and gold ; he was to have a copy of the law made expressly for his own study—a study which he was never to intermit till the end of his days ; so that his heart might not be lifted up above his brethren, that he might not be turned aside from the living God, but observing the divine statutes, and thus acknowledging himself to be no more than the vicegerent of heaven, he might enjoy happiness, and transmit his authority to his descendants.

The Jewish polity, then, was a sort of sacerdotal republic—we say sacerdotal, because of the great influence which, from the first, the priestly order enjoyed, having no human head, but being under the special supervision, protection, and guidance of the Almighty. The nature of the consequences, however, of that divine influence avowedly depended on the degree of obedience and the general faithfulness of the nation. The good, therefore, of such a superintendence in its immediate results was not necessary, but contingent. The removal of Moses and of Joshua by death soon left the people to the natural results of their own condition and character. Anarchy ensued. Noble minds, indeed, and stout spirits appeared in those who were termed Judges ; but the state of the country was not so satisfactory as to prevent an unenlightened people, having low and gross affections, from preferring the glare of a crown and the apparent protection of a sceptre, to the invisible and, therefore, mostly unrecognised arm of omnipotence. A king accordingly was requested. The misconduct of Samuel's sons, who had been made judges, was the immediate occasion of the demand being put forth. The request came with authority, for it emanated from all the elders of Israel, who, after holding a formal conference, proceeded to Samuel, in order to make him acquainted with their wish. Samuel was displeased ; but, having sought in prayer to learn the divine will, he is instructed to yield to the demand on a ground which we should not assuredly have found stated, had the book in which it appears been tampered with or fabricated for any courtly purposes or any personal ends, whether by Samuel himself, or by David, or any of his successors—' for they have not rejected thee (Samuel), but they have rejected me, that I should not reign over them' (ver. 7, see also ver. 8). Samuel was, moreover, directed to ' protest solemnly unto them, and show them the manner of the king that shall reign over them.' Faithfully did the prophet depict the evils which a monarchy would inflict on the people. In vain : they said, ' Nay, but we will have a king over us.' Accordingly, Saul the son of Kish, of the tribe of Benjamin, was, by divine direction, selected, and privately anointed by Samuel ' to be captain over God's inheritance.'

2 L 2

thus he was to hold only a delegated and subordinate authority. Under the guidance of Samuel, Saul was subsequently chosen by lot from among the assembled tribes; and though his personal appearance had no influence in the choice, yet when he was plainly pointed out to be the individual designed for the sceptre, Samuel called attention to those qualities which in less civilized nations have a preponderating influence, and are never without effect, at least, in supporting 'the divinity which doth hedge a king:' ' See ye him whom the Lord hath chosen, that there is none like him among all the people,' for he was higher than any of the people from his shoulders and upward; ' and all the people shouted, God save the king.'

Emanating as the royal power did from the demand of the people and the permission of a prophet, it was not likely to be unlimited in its extent or arbitrary in its exercise. The government of God, indeed, remained, being rather concealed and complicated than disowned, much less superseded. The king ruled not in his own right, nor in virtue of the choice of the people, but by concession from on high, and partly as the servant and partly as the representative of the theocracy. How insecure, indeed, was the tenure of the kingly power, how restricted it was in its authority, appears clear from the comparative facility with which the crown was transferred from Saul to David; and the part which the prophet Samuel took in effecting that transference points out the quarter where lay the power which limited, if it did not primarily, at least, control the royal authority. We must not, however, expect to find any definite and permanent distribution of power, any legal determination of the royal prerogatives as discriminated from the divine authority; circumstances, as they prompted certain deeds, restricted or enlarged the sphere of the monarch's action. Thus, in 1 Sam. xi. 4, sq., we find Saul, in an emergency, assuming, without consultation or deliberation, the power of demanding something like a levy *en masse,* and of proclaiming instant war. With the king lay the administration of justice in the last resort (2 Sam. xv. 2; 1 Kings iii. 16, sq.). He also possessed the power of life and death (2 Sam. xiv.). To provide for and superintend the public worship was at once his duty and his highest honour (1 Kings viii.; 2 Kings xii. 4; xviii. 4; xxiii. 1). One reason why the people requested a king was, that they might have a recognised leader in war (1 Sam. viii. 20). The Mosaic law offered a powerful hindrance to royal despotism (1 Sam. x. 25). The people also, by means of their elders, formed an express compact, by which they stipulated for their rights (1 Kings xii. 4), and were from time to time appealed to, generally in cases of 'great pith and moment' (1 Chron. xxix. 1; 2 Kings xi. 17.) Nor did the people fail to interpose their will, where they thought it necessary, in opposition to that of the monarch (1 Sam. xiv. 45). The part which Nathan took against David shows how effective, as well as bold, was the check exerted by the prophets; indeed, most of the prophetic history is the history of the noblest opposition ever made to the vices alike of royalty, priesthood, and people. When needful, the prophet hesitated not to demand an audience of the king, nor was he dazzled or deterred by royal power

and pomp (1 Kings xx. 22, 38; 2 Kings i. 15). As, however, the monarch held the sword, the instrument of death was sometimes made to prevail over every restraining influence (1 Sam. xxii. 17).

After the transfer of the crown from Saul to David, the royal power was annexed to the house of the latter, passing from father to son, with preference to the eldest born, though he might be a minor. Jehoash was seven years old when he began to reign (2 Kings xi. 21). This rule was not, however, rigidly observed, for instances are not wanting in which nomination of a younger son gave him a preferable title to the crown (1 Kings i. 17; 2 Chron. xi. 21): the people, too, and even foreign powers, at a later period, interrupted the regular transmission of loyal authority (2 Kings xxi. 24; xxiii. 24, 30; xxiv. 17). The ceremony of anointing, which was observed at least in the case of Saul, David, and Solomon (1 Sam. ix. 14; x. 1; xv. 1; xvi. 12; 2 Sam. ii. 4; v. 1; 1 Kings i. 34; xxxix. 5), and in which the prophet or high-priest who performed the rite acted as the representative of the theocracy and the expounder of the will of heaven, must have given to the spiritual power very considerable influence. Indeed, the ceremony seems to have been essential to constitute a legitimate monarch (2 Kings xi. 12; xxiii. 30); and thus the authorities of the Jewish church held in their hands, and had subject to their will, a most important power, which they could use either for their own purposes or the common good. We have seen in the case of Saul that personal and even external qualities had their influence in procuring ready obedience to a sovereign; and further evidence to the same effect may be found in Ps. xlv. 3; Ezek. xxviii. 12: such qualities would naturally excite the enthusiasm of the people, who appear to have manifested their approval by acclamations (1 Sam. x. 24; 1 Kings i. 25; 2 Kings ix. 13; xi. 13; 2 Chron. xi. 11). Jubilant music formed a part of the popular rejoicings (1 Kings i. 40); thank-offerings were made (1 Kings i. 25); the new sovereign rode in solemn procession on the royal mule of his predecessor (1 Kings i. 38), and took possession of the royal harem—an act which seems to have been scarcely less essential than other observances which appear to us to wear a higher character (1 Kings ii. 13, 22; 2 Sam. xvi. 22). A numerous harem, indeed, was among the most highly estimated of the royal luxuries (2 Sam. v. 13; 1 Kings xi. 1; xx. 3). It was under the supervision and control of eunuchs, and passed from one monarch to another as a part of the crown-property (2 Sam. xii. 8). The law (Deut. xvii. 17), foreseeing evils such as that by which Solomon, in his later years, was turned away from his fidelity to God, had strictly forbidden many wives; but Eastern passions and usages were too strong for a mere written prohibition, and a corrupted religion became a pander to royal lust, interpreting the divine command as sanctioning eighteen as the minimum of wives and concubines. In the original distribution of the land no share, of course, was reserved for a merely possible monarch; yet the kings were not without several sources of income. In the earlier periods of the monarchy the simple manners which prevailed would render copious revenues unnecessary; and a throne which was the result of a spontaneous demand on the part of the people, would easily find support in free-will offerings, especially in a part of the world where the great are never approached without a present. There seems also reason to conclude that the amount of the contributions made by the people for the sustenance of the monarch depended, in a measure, on the degree of popularity which, in any particular case, he enjoyed, or the degree of service which he obviously rendered to the state (1 Sam. x. 27; xvi. 20; 2 Sam. viii. 11; 1 Kings x. 11, 25, sq.). That presents of small value and humble nature were not despised or thought unfit for the acceptance of royalty, may be learnt from that which Jesse sent to Saul (1 Sam. xvi. 20), 'an ass, with bread and a bottle of wine, and a kid.' The indirect detail ' of the substance which was king David's,' found in 1 Chron. xxvii. 25, sq. (comp. 1 Sam. viii. 14; 2 Chron. xxvi. 10, sq.), shows at how early a period the Israelitish throne was in possession of very large property, both personal and real. The royal treasury was replenished by confiscation, as in the case of Naboth (1 Kings xxi. 16; comp. Ezek. xlvi. 16, sq.; 2 Sam. xvi. 4). Nor were taxes unknown. Samuel had predicted (1 Sam. viii. 15), 'He will take the tenth of your seed and of your vineyards,' &c. ; and so in other passages (1 Kings v. 13; ix. 21) we find that levies both of men and money were made for the monarch's purposes ; and, in cases of special need, these exactions were large and rigorously levied (2 Kings xxiii. 35), as when Jehoiakim ' taxed the land to give the money according to the commandment of Pharaoh; he exacted the silver and the gold of the people of the land, of every one according to his taxation.' So long, however, as the native vigour of a young monarchy made victory easy and frequent, large revenues came to the king from the spoils of war (2 Sam. viii. 2, sq.). Commerce also then supplied abundant resources (1 Kings x. 15).

According to Oriental custom, much ceremony and outward show of respect were observed. Those who were intended to be received with special honour were placed on the king's right hand (1 Kings ii. 19). The most profound homage was paid to the monarch, which was required not merely by common usage, but by the voice of religious wisdom (Prov. xxiv. 21)—a requirement which was not unnatural in regard to an office that was accounted of divine origin, and to have a sort of vice-divine authority. Those who presented themselves before the royal presence fell with their face towards the ground till their forehead touched it (1 Sam. xxv. 23 ; 2 Sam. ix. 6; xix. 18), thus worshipping or doing obeisance to the monarch, a ceremony from which even the royal spouse was not exempted (1 Kings i. 16). A kiss was among the established tokens of reverence (1 Sam. x. 1; Ps. ii. 12), as were also hyperbolical wishes of good (Dan. ii. 4; iii. 9). Serious offences against the king were punished with death (1 Kings xxi. 10).

Deriving their power originally from the wishes of the people, and being one of the same race, the Hebrew kings were naturally less despotic than other Oriental sovereigns, mingled more with their subjects, and were by no means difficult of access (2 Sam. xix. 8; 1 Kings xx. 39; Jer. xxxviii. 7; 1 Kings iii. 16; 2 Kings vi. 26; viii. 3). After

death the monarchs were interred in the royal cemetery in Jerusalem : ' So David slept with his fathers, and was buried in the city of David' (1 Kings ii. 10; xi. 43; xiv. 31). But bad kings were excluded ' from the sepulchres of the kings of Israel' (2 Chron. xxviii 27). In 1 Kings iv. will be found an enumeration of the high officers of state under the reign of Solomon (see also 1 Kings x. 5; xii. 18; xviii. 3; 2 Kings viii. 16; x. 22; xviii. 18; xix 2; 1 Chron. xxvii. 25; Isa. xxii. 15; Jer. lii. 25). The misdeeds of the Jewish crown, and the boldness with which they were reproved, may be seen exemplified in Jer. xxii.: ' Thus saith the Lord, Execute judgment and righteousness, and do no wrong; do no violence to the stranger, the fatherless, nor the widow; neither shed innocent blood. But if ye will not hear these words, this house shall become a desolation,' &c.

KINGS, BOOKS OF. The two books of Kings formed anciently but one book in the Jewish Scriptures. But great stress cannot always be laid on the Jewish forms of the sacred books, as they were arranged so as to correspond with the letters of the Hebrew alphabet.

The books of Kings contain the brief annals of a long period, from the accession of Solomon till the dissolution of the commonwealth. The first chapters describe the reign of Solomon over the united kingdom, and the revolt under Rehoboam. The history of the rival states is next narrated in parallel sections till the period of Israel's downfal on the invasion of Shalmanezer. Then the remaining years of the principality of Judah are recorded till the conquest of Nebuchadnezzar and the commencement of the Babylonish captivity. In the article ISRAEL, the period comprised has been exhibited under the name and reign of the kings who are mentioned in these books, and there also, and in the article JUDAH, the chronology of the books has been sufficiently considered.

There are some peculiarities in this succinct history worthy of attention. It is very brief, but very suggestive. It is not a biography of the sovereigns, nor a mere record of political occurrences, nor yet an ecclesiastical register. King, church, and state are all comprised in their sacred relations. It is a theocratic history, a retrospective survey of the kingdoms as existing under a theocratic government. The character of the sovereign is tested by his fidelity to the religious obligations of his office, and this decision in reference to his conduct is generally added to the notice of his accession. The new king's religious character is commonly portrayed by its similarity or opposition to the way of David, of his father, or of Jeroboam, son of Nebat, ' who made Israel to sin.' Ecclesiastical affairs are noticed with a similar purpose, and in contrast with past or prevalent apostacy, especially as manifested in the popular superstitions, whose shrines were on the ' high places.' Political or national incidents are introduced in general for the sake of illustrating the influence of religion on civic prosperity ; of showing how the theocracy maintained a vigilant and vengeful guardianship over its rights and privileges—adherence to its principles securing peace and plenty, disobedience to them bringing along with it sudden and severe retribution. The books of Kings are a verification of the Mosaic warnings, and the author of them has kept this steadily in view. He has given a brief history of his people, arranged under the various political chiefs in such a manner as to show that the government was essentially theocratic, that its spirit, as developed in the Mosaic writings, was never extinct, however modified or inactive it might sometimes appear.

Thus the books of Kings appear in a religious costume, quite different from the form they would have assumed either as a political or ecclesiastical narrative. In the one case legislative enactments, royal edicts, popular movements, would have occupied a prominent place; in the other, sacerdotal arrangements, Levitical service, music and pageantry, would have filled the leading sections of the treatise. In either view the points adduced would have had a restricted reference to the palace or the temple, the sovereign or the pontiff, the court or the priesthood, the throne or the altar, the tribute or tithes, the nation on its farms, or the tribes in the courts of the sacred edifice. But the theocracy conjoined both the political and religious elements, and the inspired annalist unites them as essential to his design. The agency of divinity is constantly recognised, the hand of Jehovah is continually acknowledged. The chief organ of theocratic influence enjoys peculiar prominence. We refer to the incessant agency of the prophets, their great power and peculiar modes of action as detailed by the composer of the books of Kings. They interfered with the succession, and their instrumentality was apparent in the schism. They roused the people, and they braved the sovereign. The balance of power was in their hands; the regal dignity seemed to be sometimes at their disposal. In times of emergency they dispensed with usual modes of procedure, and assumed an authority with which no subject in an ordinary state can safely be intrusted, executing the law with a summary promptness which rendered opposition impossible, or at least unavailing. They felt their divine commission, and that they were the custodiers of the rights of Jehovah, while at the same time they protected the interests of the nation. The divine prerogative was to them a vested right, guarded with a sacred jealousy from royal usurpation or popular invasion: and the interests of the people were as religiously protected against encroachments, too easily made under a form of government which had not the safeguard of popular representation or aristocratic privilege. The priesthood was in many instances, though there are some illustrious exceptions, merely the creature of the crown, and therefore it became the duty of the prophets to assert its dignity and stand forth in the majestic insignia of an embassy from heaven.

The truth of these sentiments as to the method, design, and composition of the books of Kings, is confirmed by ample evidence.

1. Large space is occupied with the building of the temple—the palace of the Divine Protector —his throne in it being above the mercy-seat and between the cherubim (ch. v.-viii.). Care is taken to record the miraculous phenomenon of the descent of the Shekinah (ch. viii. 10). The prayer of Solomon at the dedication of the house is full of theocratic views and aspirations.

2. Reference is often made to the Mosaic Law with its provisions; and allusions to the earlier history of the people frequently occur (1 Kings ii. 3; iii. 14; vi 11, 12; viii. 58, &c.; 2 Kings x. 31; xiv. 6; xvii. 13, 15, 37; xviii. 4-6; xxi. 1-8). Allusions to the Mosaic code are found more frequently toward the end of the second book, when the kingdom was drawing near its termination, as if to account for its decay and approaching fate.

3. Phrases expressive of Divine interference are frequently introduced (1 Kings xi. 31; xii. 15; xiii. 1, 2, 9; and xx. 13, &c.).

4. Prophetic interposition is a very prominent theme of record. It fills the vivid foreground of the historical picture. Nathan was occupied in the succession of Solomon (1 Kings i. 45); Ahijah was concerned in the revolt (xi. 29-40). Shemaiah disbanded the troops which Rehoboam had mustered (xii. 21). Ahijah predicted the ruin of Jeroboam, whose elevation he had promoted (xiv. 7). Jehu, the prophet, doomed the house of Baasha (xvi. 1). The reign of Ahab and Ahaziah is marked by the bold, rapid, mysterious movements of Elijah. Under Ahab occurs the prediction of Micaiah (xxii. 8). The actions and oracles of Elisha form the marvellous topics of narration under several reigns. The agency of Isaiah is also recognised (2 Kings xix. 20; xx. 16). Besides, 1 Kings xiii. presents another instance of prophetic operation; and in xx. 35 the oracle of an unknown prophet is also rehearsed. Huldah, the prophetess, was an important personage under the government of Josiah (2 Kings xxii. 14). Care is also taken to report the fulfilment of striking prophecies, in the usual phrase, 'according to the word of the Lord' (1 Kings xii. 15; xv. 29; xvi. 12; 2 Kings xxiii. 15-18; ix. 36; xxiv. 2). So, too, the Old Syriac version prefixes, 'Here follows the book of the kings who flourished among the ancient people; and in this is also exhibited the history of the prophets who flourished during their times.'

5. Theocratic influence is recognised both in the deposition and succession of kings (1 Kings xiii. 33; xv. 4, 5, 29, 30; 2 Kings xi. 17, &c.). It is thus apparent that the object of the author of the Books of Kings was to describe the history of the kingdoms, especially in connection with the theocratic element.

The authorship and age of this historical treatise may admit of several suppositions. Whatever were the original sources, the books are evidently the composition of one writer. The style is generally uniform throughout. The same forms of expression are used to denote the same thing, e. g. the male sex (1 Kings xiv. 10, &c.); the death of a king (1 Kings xi. 43, &c.); modes of allusion to the law (1 Kings xi. 13); fidelity to Jehovah (1 Kings viii. 63, &c.). Similar idioms are ever recurring, so as to produce a uniformity of style. The sources whence this historic information has been derived have been variously named. That annals contemporary with the events which they describe were written in the early period of the Jewish state, may be at once admitted. Eichhorn supposes that the sources of 'Kings' were private historical works. Bertholdt, Havernick, and Movers hold that the books are extracts from the public annals. The inspired historiographer refers his readers to these sources of evidence in such frequent phrases as 'the *rest* of the acts.' Such a reference is made especially to the sources, when other royal acts than those narrated in the books of Kings are glanced at. These sources are styled the book of the Chronicles of the kings of Judah or Israel. Similar phraseology is used in Esther x. 2; vi. 1, to denote the official annals of the Persian empire. Public documents are spoken of in the same way (Neh. xii. 23). There is little reason to suppose that the book referred to in this last passage is that styled Chronicles in our copy of the Scriptures. So we infer that the 'Book of the Chronicles of the Kings' so often alluded to, was an authentic document, public and official. Once indeed mention is made of a work entitled 'The Book of the Acts of Solomon.'

That the prophets themselves were employed in recording contemporaneous events is evident from 2 Chron. xx. 34; 1 Chron. xxix. 29. In the course of the narrative we meet with many instances of description, having the freshness and form of nature, and which are apparently direct quotations from some journal, written by one who testified what he had seen (1 Kings xx. 10; 2 Kings xii. 15; xiv. 8). Thus the credibility of the history contained in these books rests upon a sure foundation.

Now, the compiler from these old documents —he who shaped them into the form they have in our present books of Kings—must have lived in a late age. The Second Book of Kings concludes with an account of the liberation of Jehoiachin, king of Judah, from prison in Babylon —an event which, according to Jahn, happened in the twenty-sixth, or, according to Prideaux, in the twenty-eighth year after the destruction of Jerusalem. Jahn and Hävernick place the composition of 'Kings' in the reign of Evil-merodach; and De Wette, towards the end of the Captivity. Jewish tradition makes Jeremiah the author. Calmet ascribes the anthorship to Ezra. The former opinion, adopted by Grotius, and lately revindicated by Havernick, certainly appears the more probable. It explains the close similarity of the books of Kings and Jeremiah in spirit, style, and tendency, more easily and more satisfactorily than any other conjecture of like nature. The age of the book of Kings may be intermediate between the early work of Samuel and the later treatise of Chronicles.

KIR, a people and country subject to the Assyrian empire, to which the conquered Damascenes were transplanted (2 Kings xvi. 9; Isa. xxii. 6; Amos i. 5), and whither also the Aramæans in the east of Syria once wandered (Amos ix. 7). This is supposed by Major Rennel to be the same country which still bears the name of *K*urdistan or *K*ourdistan. There are, however, objections to this view, which do not apply so strongly to the notion of Rosenmuller and others, that it was a tract on the river Cyrus, or rather Kuros, in Zend Koro, which rises in the mountains between the Euxine and Caspian Seas, and runs into the latter after being joined by the Araxes. Gurjistan, or Grusia (Grusiana), commonly called Georgia, seems also to have derived its name from this river Kur, which flows through it.

KIR-HA'RESH; KIR-HARESETH; KIR-HERES. [KIR-MOAB.]

KIR'JATH. This word means *town* or *city*, and is much used in the formation of names of places, like our own *town*. The following are the principal places distinguished by this term:—

1. KI'R-JATHA'IM (*double town*), one of the most ancient towns in the country east of the Jordan, as it was possessed by the gigantic Emim (Gen. xiv. 5), who were expelled by the Moabites (Deut. ii. 9, 10), who in their turn were dispossessed by the Amorites, from whom it was taken by the Israelites. Kir-jathaim was then assigned to Reuben (Num. xxxii. 37; Josh. xiii. 19). But during the Assyrian exile the Moabites again took possession of this and other towns (Jer. xlviii. 1-23; Ezek. xxv. 9). Eusebius places it about half an hour west of the ruins of Medeba. There was another place of this name in the tribe of Naphtali (1 Chron. vi. 76).

2. KIR'JATH-AR'BA, the ancient name of Hebron, but still in use in the time of Nehemiah (vi. 26) [HEBRON].

3. KIR'JATH-BAAL (*city of Baal*). This city is more usually called KIRJATH-JEARIM.

4. KIR'JATH-HU'ZOTH (*city of streets*), a town in Moab (Num. xxii. 39).

5. KIR'JATH-JE'ARIM (*city of forests*), one of the towns of the Gibeonites (Josh. ix. 17). It was to this place that the ark was brought from Bethshemesh, after it had been removed from the land of the Philistines, and where it remained till removed to Jerusalem by David (1 Sam. vii.; 1 Chron. xiii.). This was one of the ancient sites which were again inhabited after the exile (Ezra ii. 25; Neh. vii. 29). Eusebius and Jerome speak of it as being in their day a village nine or ten miles from Diospolis (Lydda), on the road to Jerusalem. Dr. Robinson thinks it possible that the ancient Kirjath-jearim may be recognised in the present Kuryet-el-Enab. The close correspondence of name and position seems to warrant this conclusion. This place is that which ecclesiastical tradition has identified with the Anathoth of Jeremiah, which Dr. Robinson refers to Anata [ANATHOTH]. It is now a poor village, its principal buildings being an old convent of the Minorites, and a Latin church. The latter is now deserted, but not in ruins, and is said to be one of the largest and most solidly constructed churches in Palestine (Robinson, ii. 109; 334-337).

6. KIR'JATH-SAN'NAH (*city of palms*; Josh. xv. 49), otherwise KIRJATH-SEPHER (*city of the book*), a city of the tribe of Judah, called also DEBIR, which see (Josh. xv. 15, 16; Judg. i. 11, 12).

KIR'-MO'AB ('*the wall, stronghold, or citadel of Moab*'), Isa. xv. 1; called also KIR-HARESETH and KIR-HERES (*brick-fortress*; Isa. xvi. 7, 11; Jer xlviii. 31), a fortified city in the territory of Moab. Joram king of Israel took the city, and destroyed it, except the walls; but it appears from the passages here cited that it must have been rebuilt before the time of Isaiah. Abulfeda describes Karak as a small town, with a castle on a high hill, and remarks that it is so strong that one must deny himself even the wish to take it by force. In the time of the Crusades, and when in possession of the Franks, it was invested by Saladin; but after lying before it a month he was compelled to raise the siege. The first person who visited the place in modern times was Seetzen, who says, 'Karak, formerly a city and bishop's see, lies on the top of the hill near the end of a deep valley, and is surrounded on all sides with lofty mountains. The hill is very steep, and in many places the sides are quite perpendicular. The walls round the town are for the most part destroyed, and Karak can at present boast of little more than being a small country town. The castle, which is uninhabited, and in a state of great decay, was formerly one of the strongest in these countries. The inhabitants of the town consist of Mohammedans and Greek Christians. The present bishop of Karak resides at Jerusalem. From this place one enjoys, by looking down the Wady Karak, a fine view of part of the Dead Sea, and even Jerusalem may be distinctly seen in clear weather. The hill on which Karak lies is composed of limestone and brittle marl, with many beds of blue, black, and grey flints. In the neighbouring rocks there are a number of curious grottoes; in those which are under ground wheat is sometimes preserved for a period of ten years.' A fuller account of the place is given by Burckhardt, by whom it was next visited; and another description is furnished by Irby and Mangles. From their account it would seem that the caverns noticed by Seetzen were probably the sepulchres of the ancient town. We also learn that the Christians of Karak (which they and Burckhardt call Kerek) are nearly as numerous as the Turks, and boast of being stronger and braver. They were, however, on good terms with the Turks, and appeared to enjoy equal freedom with them.

KISH, son of Ner, and father of King Saul (1 Sam. ix. 1).

KI'SHON, a river which, after traversing the plain of Acre, enters the bay of the same name at its south-east corner. It is celebrated in Scripture for the overthrow of the host of Sisera in its overflowing stream (Judg. iv. 13; v. 21). It has been usual to trace the source of this river to Mount Tabor; but Dr. Shaw affirms that in travelling along the south-eastern brow of Mount Carmel, he had an opportunity of seeing the sources of the river Kishon, three or four of which lie within less than a furlong of each other, and are called Ras el-Kishon, or the head of the Kishon. These alone, without the lesser contributions near the sea, discharge water enough to form a river half as large as the Isis. During the rainy season all the waters which fall upon the eastern side of Carmel, or upon the rising grounds to the southward, empty themselves into it in a number of torrents, at which time it overflows its banks, acquires a wonderful rapidity, and carries all before it. It was doubtless in such a season that the host of Sisera was swept away, in attempting to ford it. But such inundations are only occasional, and of short duration, as is indeed implied in the destruction in its waters of the fugitives, who doubtless expected to pass it safely.

The course of the stream, as estimated from the sources thus indicated, is not more than seven miles. It runs very briskly till within half a league of the sea; but when not augmented by rains, it never falls into the sea in a full stream, but insensibly percolates through a bank of sand, which the north winds have thrown up at its mouth. It was in this state that Shaw himself found it in the month of April, 1722, when it was crossed by him.

Notwithstanding Shaw's contradiction, the assertion that the Kishon derives its source from Mount Tabor has been repeated by modern travellers as confidently as by their ancient predecessors. We have had opportunities of seeing much of streams similarly constituted; and it does not seem to us difficult to reconcile the seemingly conflicting statements with reference to the Kishon. On further inquiry, and more extensive comparison of observations made at different times of the year, it will probably be found that the remoter source of the river is really in Mount Tabor; but that the supply from this source is cut off in early summer, when it ceases to be maintained by rains or contributory torrents; whereas the copious supply from the nearer springs at Ras el-Kishon, with other springs lower down, keep it up from that point, as a perennial stream, even during the drought of summer. Thus during one part of the year the source of the river may appear to be in Mount Tabor, while during another part the source of the diminished stream is at Ras el-Kishon.

The Scriptural account of the overthrow of Sisera's host manifestly shows that the stream crossed the plain, and must have been of considerable size.

The transaction of the prophet Elijah, who, after his sacrifice on Carmel, commanded the priests of Baal to be slain at the river Kishon (1 Kings xviii. 40), requires no explanation, seeing that it took place at the perennial lower stream. This also explains, what has sometimes been asked, whence, in that time of drought, the water was obtained with which the prophet inundated his altar and sacrifice.

KISS. Originally the act of kissing had a symbolical character, and, though this import may now be lost sight of, yet it must be recognised the moment we attempt to understand or explain its signification. Acts speak no less, sometimes far more forcibly, than words. In the language of action, a kiss, inasmuch as it was a bringing into contact of parts of the body of two persons, was naturally the expression and the symbol of affection, regard, respect, and reverence; and if any deeper source of its origin were sought for, it would, doubtless, be found in the fondling and caresses with which the mother expresses her tenderness for her babe. That the custom is of very early date appears from Gen. xxix. 13, where we read—'When Laban heard the tidings of Jacob, his sister's son, he ran to meet him, and embraced him and kissed him, and brought him to his house:' the practice was even then established and recognised as a matter of course. In Gen. xxvii. 26, 27, a kiss is a sign of affection between a parent and child. It was also, as with some modern nations, a token of friendship and regard bestowed when friends or relations met or separated (Tobit vii. 6; x. 12; Luke vii. 45; xv. 20; Acts xx. 37; Matt. xxvi. 48; 2 Sam. xx. 9). The church of Ephesus wept sore at Paul's departure, and fell on his neck and kissed him. When Orpah quitted Naomi and Ruth (Ruth i. 14), after the three had lifted up their voice and wept, she 'kissed her mother-in-law, but Ruth clave unto her.' It was usual to kiss the mouth (Gen. xxxiii. 4; Exod. iv. 27; xviii. 7; 1 Sam. xx. 41; Prov. xxiv. 26) or the beard, which was then taken hold of by the hand (2 Sam. xx. 9). Kissing of the feet was an expression of lowly and tender regard (Luke vii. 38). Kissing of the hand of another appears to be a modern practice: the passage of Job xxxi. 27, 'Or my mouth hath kissed my hand,' is not in point, and refers to idolatrous usages, namely, the adoration of the heavenly bodies. It was the custom to throw kisses towards the images of the gods, and towards the sun and moon (1 Kings xix. 18; Hosea xiii. 2). The kissing of princes was a token of homage (Ps. ii. 12; 1 Sam. x. 1). Xenophon says that it was a national custom with the Persians to kiss whomsoever they honoured. Kissing the feet of princes was a token of subjection and obedience; which was sometimes carried so far that the print of the foot received the kiss, so as to give the impression that the very dust had become sacred by the royal tread, or that the subject was not worthy to salute even the prince's foot, but was content to kiss the earth itself near or on which he trod (Isa. xlix. 23; Micah vii. 17; Ps. lxxii. 9). The Rabbins, in the meddlesome, scrupulous, and falsely delicate spirit which animated much of what they wrote, did not permit more than three kinds of kisses, the kiss of reverence, of reception, and of dismissal.

The peculiar tendency of the Christian religion to encourage honour towards all men, as men, to foster and develop the softer affections, and, in the trying condition of the early church, to make its members intimately known one to another, and unite them in the closest bonds, led to the observance of kissing as an accompaniment of that social worship which took its origin in the very cradle of our religion. Hence the exhortation—'Salute each other with a holy kiss' (Rom. xvi. 16; see also 1 Cor. xvi. 20; 2 Cor. xiii. 12; 1 Thess. v. 26; in 1 Pet. v. 14, it is termed 'a kiss of charity'). The observance was continued in later days, and has not yet wholly disappeared, though the peculiar circumstances have vanished which gave propriety and emphasis to such an expression of brotherly love and Christian friendship.

KITE. [GLEDE.]

KNEADING-TROUGHS. [BREAD.]

KO'HATH (assembly), son of Levi, and father of Amram, Izhar, Hebron, and Uzziel (Gen. xlvi. 11). The descendants of Kohath formed one of the three great divisions of the Levitical tribe. This division contained the priestly family which was descended from Aaron, the son of Amram. In the service of the tabernacle, as settled in the wilderness, the Kohathites had the distinguished charge of bearing the ark and the sacred vessels (Exod. vi. 16; Num. iv. 4-6).

KO'PHER, or COPHER, occurs twice in the Song of Solomon (i. 14; iv. 13), and is in both places translated camphire in the Authorized Version. It has been supposed to indicate a bunch of grapes (Botrus kopher), also camphor. The word camphire is the old mode of spelling camphor, but this substance does not appear to have been known to ancient commerce, at least we cannot adduce any proof that it was so. The word Kopher closely resembles the Greek Kupros, usually written Cypros. Indeed, as has been observed, it is the same word, with the Greek pronunciation and termination. Mariti remarks, that 'the shrub known in the Hebrew language by the name of kopher is common in the island of Cyprus, and thence had its Latin name:' also, that 'the Botrus Cypri has been supposed to be a kind of rare and exquisite grapes, transplanted from Cyprus to Engaddi; but the Botrus is known to the natives of Cyprus as an odoriferous shrub called henna, or alkanna.' This identity is now universally acknowledged: the Kupros, therefore, must have been Lawsonia inermis, as the Hinna of the Arabs is well known to be. If we examine the works of Oriental travellers and naturalists, we shall find that this plant is universally esteemed in Eastern countries, and appears to have been so from the earliest times, both on account of the fragrance of its flowers and the colouring properties of its leaves.

224. [Lawsonia inermis.]

Thus Rauwolff, when at Tripoli, 'found there another tree, not unlike unto our privet, by the Arabians called Alcana, or Henna, and by the Grecians, in their vulgar tongue, Schenna, which they have from Egypt, where, but above all in Cayre, they grow in abundance. The Turks and Moors nurse these up with great care and diligence, because of their sweet-smelling flowers. They also, as I am informed, keep their leaves all winter, which leaves they powder and mix with the juice of citrons, and stain therewith against great holidays the hair and nails of their children of a red colour, which colour may perhaps be seen with us on the manes and tails of Turkish horses.' This custom of dyeing the nails and the palms of the hands and soles of the feet, of an iron-rust colour, with henna, exists throughout the East, from the Mediterranean to the Ganges, as well as in Northern Africa. In some parts the practice is not confined to women and children, but is also followed by men, especially in Persia. In dyeing the beard, the hair is turned to red by this application, which is then changed to black by a preparation of indigo. In dyeing the hair of children, and the tails and manes of horses and asses, the process is allowed to stop at the red colour which the *henna* produces. In reference to this universal practice of the East, Dr. Harris observes that ' the expression in Deut. xxi. 12, " pare her nails," may perhaps rather mean " adorn her nails," and imply the antiquity of this practice. This is a universal custom in Egypt, and not to conform to it would be considered indecent. It seems to have been practised by the ancient Egyptians, for the nails of the mummies are most commonly of a reddish hue.' Seeing, then, that the *henna* is so universally admired in the East, both on account of the fragrance of its flowers and the dye yielded by its leaves, and as there is no doubt that it is the Cypros of the Greeks, and as this word is so similar to the *kopher* of the Hebrews, there is every probability of this last being the *henna* of the Arabs, *Lawsonia alba* of botanists.

KO'RAH (*ice*), a Levite, son of Izhar, the brother of Amram, the father of Moses and Aaron, who were therefore cousins to Korah (Exod. vi. 21). From this near relationship we may, with tolerable certainty, conjecture, that the source of the discontent which led to the steps afterwards taken by this unhappy man, lay in his jealousy that the high honours and privileges of the priesthood, to which he, who remained a simple Levite, might, apart from the divine appointment, seem to have had as good a claim, should have been exclusively appropriated to the family of Aaron. When to this was added the civil authority of Moses, the whole power over the nation would seem to him to have been engrossed by his cousins, the sons of Amram. Under the influence of these feelings he organized a conspiracy, for the purpose of redressing what appeared to him the evil and injustice of this arrangement. Dathan, Abiram, and On, the chief persons who joined him, were of the tribe of Reuben ; but he was also supported by many more from other tribes, making up the number of 250, men of name, rank and influence, all who may be regarded as representing the families of which they were the heads. The private object of Korah was apparently his own aggrandizement, but his ostensible object was the general good of the people ; and it is perhaps from want of attention to this distinction that the transaction has not been well understood. The design seems to have been made acceptable to a large body of the nation, on the ground that the first-born of Israel had been deprived of their sacerdotal birthright in favour of the Levites, while the Levites themselves announced that the priesthood had been conferred by Moses (as they considered) on his own brother's family, in preference to those who had equal claims ; and it is easy to conceive that the Reubenites may have considered the opportunity a favourable one for the recovery of their birthright—the double portion and civil pre-eminence—which had been forfeited by them and given to Joseph.

The leading conspirators having organized their plans, repaired in a body to Moses and Aaron, boldly charged them with their usurpations, and required them to lay down their ill-gotten power. Moses no sooner heard this than he fell on his face, confounded at the enormity of so outrageous a revolt against a system framed so carefully for the benefit of the nation. He left the matter in the Lord's hands, and desired them

to come on the morrow, provided with censers for incense, that the Lord himself, by some manifest token, might make known his will in this great matter. As this order was particularly addressed to the rebellious Levites, the Reubenites left the place, and when afterwards called back by Moses, returned a very insolent refusal, charging him with having brought them out of the land of Egypt under false pretences, ' to kill them in the wilderness.'

The next day Korah and his company appeared before the tabernacle, attended by a multitude of people out of the general body of the tribes. Then the Shekinah, or symbol of the Divine presence, which abode between the cherubim, advanced to the entrance of the sacred fabric, and a voice therefrom commanded Moses and Aaron to stand apart, lest they should share in the destruction which awaited the whole congregation. On hearing these awful words the brothers fell on their faces, and, by strong intercession, moved the Lord to confine his wrath to the leaders in the rebellion, and spare their unhappy dupes. The latter were then ordered to separate themselves from their leaders and from the tents in which they dwelt. The terrible menace involved in this direction had its weight, and the command was obeyed ; and after Moses had appealed to what was to happen as a proof of the authority by which he acted, the earth opened, and received and closed over the tents of Korah, Dathan, and Abiram. The Reubenite conspirators were in their tents, and perished in them ; and at the same instant Korah and his 250, who were offering incense at the door of the tabernacle, were destroyed by a fire which ' came out from the Lord ;' that is, most probably, in this case, from out of the cloud in which his presence dwelt. The censers which they had used were afterwards made into plates, to form an outer covering to the altar, and thus became a standing monument of this awful transaction (Num. xvi.). On, although named in the first instance along with Dathan and Abiram, does not further appear either in the rebellion or its punishment. It is hence supposed that he repented in time : and Abendana and other Rabbinical writers allege that his wife prevailed upon him to abandon the cause.

It might be supposed from the Scripture narrative that the entire families of the conspirators perished in the destruction of their tents. Doubtless all who were in the tents perished ; but as the descendants of Korah afterwards became eminent in the Levitical service, it is clear that his sons were spared. They were probably living in separate tents, or were among those who sundered themselves from the conspirators at the command of Moses. There is no reason to suppose that the sons of Korah were children when their father perished. The Korahites were appointed by David to the office of guarding the doors of the temple, and of singing praises. They, in fact, occupied a distinguished place in the choral service of the temple, and several of the Psalms (xlii. xliv.-xlix. lxxxiv. lxxxv. lxxxvii. lxxxviii.) are inscribed to them. Heman, the master of song under David, was of this family, and his genealogy is traced through Korah up to **Levi** (1 Chron. vi. 31-38).

L.

LA'BAN, son of Bethuel, and grandson of Nahor, brother of Rebekah, and father of Jacob's two wives. Leah and Rachel [JACOB].

LA'CHISH, a city in the south of Judah, in the plain between Adoraim and Azekah (Josh x. 3, 5, 31; xv. 39). It was rebuilt and fortified by Rehoboam (2 Chron. xi. 9), and seems after that time to have been regarded as one of the strongest fortresses of the kingdom of Judah, having for a time braved the assaults of the Assyrian army under Sennacherib (2 Kings xviii. 17; xix. 8; 2 Chron. xxxii. 9). Eusebius and Jerome place it seven Roman miles from Eleutheropolis towards the south. There has not been any more recent notice of the place, and no modern vestige of the name or site has been discovered.

LA'ISH. [DAN.]

LAKES. [PALESTINE.]

LA'MECH, son of Methusael, and father of Jabal, Jubal, Tubal-cain, and Naamah (Gen. iv. 18, 24, &c.). He is recorded to have taken two wives, Adah and Zillah; and there appears no reason why the fact should have been mentioned, unless to point him out as the author of the evil practice of polygamy. The manner in which the sons of Lamech distinguished themselves as the inventors of useful arts, is mentioned under their several names. The most remarkable circumstance in connection with Lamech is the poetical address which he is very abruptly introduced as making to his wives. This is not only remarkable in itself, but is the first and most ancient piece of poetry in the Hebrew Scriptures; and, indeed, the only example of Antediluvian poetry extant:—

> ' Adah and Zillah, hear my voice!
>   Wives of Lamech, receive my speech!
> If I slew a man to my wounding,
>   And a young man—to my hurt:
> If Cain was avenged seven times,
>   Then Lamech—seventy times seven.'

This exhibits the parallelism and other characteristics of Hebrew poetry, the development of which belongs to another article [POETRY]. It has all the appearance of an extract from an old poem, which we may suppose to have been handed down by tradition to the time of Moses. It is very difficult to discover to what it refers, and the best explanation can be nothing more than a conjecture. So far as we can make it out, it would seem to be, as Bishop Lowth explains, an apology for committing homicide, in his own defence, upon some man who had violently assaulted him, and, as it would seem, struck and wounded him: and he opposes a homicide of this nature to the wilful and inexcusable fratricide of Cain. Under this view Lamech would appear to have intended to comfort his wives by the assurance that he was really exposed to no danger from this act, and that any attempt upon his life on the part of the friends of the deceased would not fail to bring down upon them the severest vengeance.

2. LAMECH, son of Methuselah, and father of Noah (Gen. v. 28-31).

LAMENTATIONS. This book is called by the Hebrews, ' how,' from the first word of the book; but sometimes they call it ' tears,' or ' lamentation,' in allusion to the mournful character of the work, of which one would conceive, says Bishop Lowth, ' that every letter was written with a tear, every word the sound of a broken heart.' From this, or rather from the translation of it in the Septuagint, comes our title of LAMENTATIONS.

The ascription of the Lamentations in the title is of no authority in itself, but its correctness has never been doubted. The style and manner of the book are those of Jeremiah, and the circumstances alluded to, those by which he is known to have been surrounded. This reference of the Lamentations to Jeremiah occurs in the introductory verse which is found in the Septuagint:—' And it came to pass, after Israel had been carried away captive, and Jerusalem was become desolate, that Jeremiah sat weeping, and lamented with this lamentation over Jerusalem, and said.'

It is disputed whether or not this verse existed in the Hebrew copies from which the translation of the Seventy was made. We are certainly not bound by its authority if disposed to question the conclusion which it supports. But it at least shows the opinion which prevailed as to the author, and the occasion of the book, at the time the translation was made. That opinion is now all but universally acquiesced in. It is adopted by nearly all commentators, who, as they proceed through the book, find that they cannot follow out the details on any other supposition. We may, under this view, regard the two first chapters as occupied chiefly with the circumstances of the siege, and those immediately following that event. In the third the prophet deplores the calamities and persecutions to which he had himself been exposed: the fourth refers to the ruin and desolation of the city, and the unhappy lot of Zedekiah; and the fifth and last seems to be a sort of prayer in the name, or on behalf of, the Jews in their dispersion and captivity. As Jeremiah himself was eventually compelled to withdraw into Egypt much against his will (Jer. xliii. 6), it has been suggested that the last chapter was possibly written there. Pareau refers chap. i. to Jer. xxxvii. 5, sqq.; chap. iii. to Jer. xxxviii. 2, sqq.; chap. iv. to Jer. xxxix. 1, sqq., and 2 Kings xxv. 1, sqq.; chap. ii. to the destruction of the city and temple; chap. v. is admitted to be the latest, and to refer to the time after that event. Ewald says that the situation is the same throughout, and only the time different. In chaps. i. and ii. we find sorrow without consolation; in chap. iii. consolation for the poet himself; in chap iv. the lamentation is renewed with greater violence; but soon the whole people, as if urged by their own spontaneous impulse, fall to weeping and hoping.

Dr. Blayney, regarding both the date and occasion of the Lamentations as established by the internal evidence, adds, ' Nor can we admire too much the flow of that full and graceful pathetic eloquence, in which the author pours out the effusions of a patriotic heart, and piously weeps over the ruins of his venerable country.' ' Never,' says an unquestionable judge of these matters, ' was there a more rich and elegant variety of beautiful images and adjuncts, arranged together within so small a compass, nor more happily chosen and applied.'

In the ancient copies this book is supposed to have occupied the place which is now assigned to it, after Jeremiah. Indeed, from the manner in which Josephus reckons up the books of the Old Testament, it has been supposed that Jeremiah and it originally formed but one book. In the Bible now used by the Jews, however, the book of Lamentations stands in the Hagiographa, and among the five Megilloth, or books of Ruth, Esther, Ecclesiastes, and Solomon's Song. They believe that it was not written by the gift of prophecy, but by the spirit of God (between which they make a distinction), and give this as a reason for not placing it among the prophets. It is read in their synagogues on the ninth of the month Ab, which is a fast for the destruction of the holy city.

LAMP. Lamps are very often mentioned in Scripture; but there is nothing to give any notion of their form. Almost the only fact we

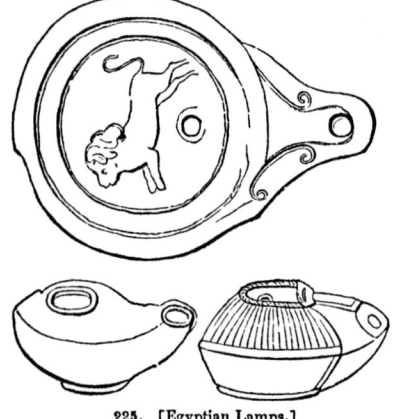

225. [Egyptian Lamps.]

can gather is, that vegetable oils were burnt in them, and especially, if not exclusively, olive-oil. This, of the finest quality, was the oil used in the seven lamps of the Tabernacle (Exod. xxvii. 20). It is somewhat remarkable, that while the golden candlestick, or rather candelabrum, is so minutely described, not a word is said of the shape, or even the material, of the lamps (Exod. xxv. 37). This was, perhaps, because they were to be of the common forms, already familiarly known to the Hebrews, and the same probably which were used in Egypt, which they had just quitted. They were in this instance doubtless of gold, although metal is scarcely the best substance for a lamp. The golden candlestick may also suggest that lamps in ordinary use were placed on stands, and where more than one was required, on stands with two or more branches. The modern Orientals, who are satisfied with very little light in their rooms, use stands of brass or wood, on which to raise the lamps to a sufficient height above the floor on which they sit. Such stands are shaped not unlike a tall candlestick, spreading out at the top. Sometimes the lamps are placed on brackets against the wall, made for the purpose, and often upon stools. Doubtless the same contrivances were employed by the Hebrews.

From the fact that lamps were carried in the pitchers of Gideon's soldiers, from which, at the end of the march, they were taken out, and borne in the hand (Judg. vii. 16, 20), we may with certainty infer that they were not. like many of the classical lamps, entirely open at top, but so shaped that the oil could not easily be spilled.

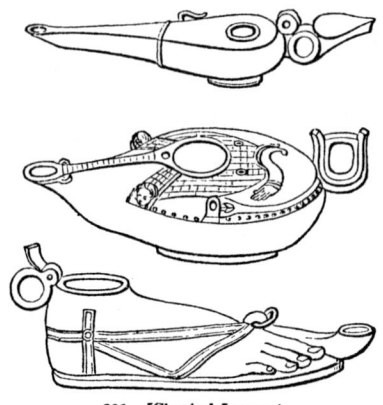

226. [Classical Lamps.]

This was remarkably the case in the Egyptian specimens, and is not rare in the classical. Gideon's lamps must also have had handles; but that the Hebrew lamps were always furnished with handles we are not bound to infer: in Egypt we find lamps both with and without handles.

Although the lamp-oils of the Hebrews were exclusively vegetable, it is probable that animal fat was used, as it is at present by the Western Asiatics, by being placed in a kind of lamp, and burnt by means of a wick inserted in it. This we have often witnessed in districts where oil-yielding plants are not common.

Cotton wicks are now used throughout Asia; but the Hebrews, like the Egyptians, probably employed the outer and coarser fibre of flax; and perhaps linen yarn, if the Rabbins are correct in alleging that the linen dresses of the priests were unravelled when old, to furnish wicks for the sacred lamps [CANDLESTICK].

It seems that the Hebrews, like the modern Orientals, were accustomed to burn lamps overnight in their chambers; and this practice may appear to give point to the expression of 'outer darkness,' which repeatedly occurs in the New Testament (Matt. viii. 12; xxii. 13): the force is greater, however, when the contrast implied in the term outer is viewed with reference to the effect produced by sudden expulsion into the darkness of night from a chamber highly illuminated for an entertainment. This custom of burning lamps at night, with the effect produced by their going out or being extinguished, supplies various figures to the sacred writers (2 Sam. xxi. 17; Prov. xiii. 9; xx. 20). And, on the other hand, the keeping up of a lamp's light is used as a symbol of enduring and unbroken succession (1 Kings xi. 36; xv. 4; Ps. cxxxii. 17).

It appears from Matt. xxv. 1, that the Jews used lamps and torches in their marriage ceremonies, or rather when the bridegroom came to conduct home the bride by night. This is still the custom in those parts of the East where, on account of the heat of the day, the bridal procession takes place in the night-time. The connection of lamps and torches with marriage ceremonies, it may be observed, is still preserved in Western Asia, even where it is no longer usual to bring home the bride by night. During two, or three, or more nights preceding the wedding, the street or quarter in which the bridegroom lives is illuminated with chandeliers and lanterns, or with lanterns and small lamps suspended from cords drawn across from the bridegroom's and several other houses on each side to the houses opposite; and several small silk flags, each of two colours, generally red and green, are attached to other cords. Lamps of this kind are sometimes hung over doors. There are some indications that the ancient Egyptians had lamps of glass; and, if so, there is no reason why the Jews also might not have had them, especially as this material is more proper for lamps intended to be hung up, and therefore to cast their light down from above. The Jews certainly used lamps in other festivals besides those of marriage. If this custom had not been so general in the ancient and modern East, it might have been supposed that the Jews adopted it from the Egyptians, who, according to Herodotus, had a 'Feast of Lamps,' which was celebrated at Sais, and, indeed, throughout the country at a certain season of the year. The description which the historian gives of the lamps employed on this occasion, strictly applies to those in modern use already described, and the concurrence of both these sources of illustration strengthens the probable analogy of Jewish usage. He speaks of them as 'small vases filled with salt and olive-oil, in which the wick floated, and burnt during the whole night.' It does not indeed appear of what materials these vases were made; but we may reasonably suppose them to have been of glass.

The later Jews had even something like this feast among themselves. A 'Feast of Lamps' was held every year on the twenty-fifth of the month Chisleu. It was founded by Judas Maccabæus in celebration of the restoration of the temple worship, and has ever since been observed by the lighting up of lamps or candles on that day in all the countries of their dispersion. Other Orientals have at this day a similar feast, of which the 'Feast of Lanterns' among the Chinese is, perhaps, the best known.

LANGUAGE. [TONGUES, CONFUSION OF.]

LANTERN. This word occurs only in John xviii. 3, where the party of men which went out of Jerusalem to apprehend Jesus in the garden of Gethsemane is described as being provided ' with *lanterns* and torches.' In the article LAMP it has been shown that the Jewish lantern, or, if we may so call it, lamp-frame, was similar to that now in use among the Orientals.

As the streets of Eastern towns are not lighted at night, and never were so, lanterns are used to an extent not known among us. Such, doubtless, was also formerly the case; and it is therefore remarkable that the only trace of a lantern which the Egyptian monuments offer, is that contained in the present engraving (No. 227). In this case it seems to be borne by the night-watch, or civic

guard, and is shaped like those in common use among ourselves. A similar lantern is at this

227.

day used in Persia, and perhaps does not materially differ from those mentioned in Scripture. More common at present in Western Asia is a large folding lantern of waxen cloth strained over rings of wire, with a top and bottom of tinned copper. It is usually about two feet long by nine inches in diameter, and is carried by servants before their masters, who often pay visits to their friends at or after supper-time. In many Eastern towns the municipal law forbids any one to be in the streets after nightfall without a lantern.

LAODICEA. There were four places of this name, which it may be well to distinguish, in order to prevent them from being confounded with one another. The first was in the western part of Phrygia, on the borders of Lydia; the second, in the eastern part of the same country, denominated Laodicea Combusta; the third, on the coast of Syria, called Laodicea ad Mare, and serving as the port of Aleppo; and the fourth, in the same country, called Laodicea ad Libanum, from its proximity to that mountain. The third of these, that on the coast of Syria, was destroyed by the great earthquake of Aleppo in August, 1822, and at the time of that event was supposed by many to be the Laodicea of Scripture, although in fact not less than four hundred miles from it. But the first named, lying on the confines of Phrygia and Lydia, about forty miles east of Ephesus, is the only Laodicea mentioned in Scripture, and is that one of the 'seven churches in Asia' to which St. John was commissioned to deliver the awful warning contained in Rev. iii. 14-19. The fulfilment of this warning is to be sought, as we take it, in the history of the Christian church which existed in that city, and not in the stone and mortar of the city itself; for, although it is true that the city is utterly ruined, it is not the city, but ' the church of the Laodiceans,' which is denounced.

Laodicea was the capital of Greater Phrygia, and a very considerable city at the time it was named in Scripture; but the frequency of earthquakes, to which this district has always been liable, demolished, some ages after, great part of the city, destroyed many of the inhabitants, and eventually obliged the remainder to abandon the spot altogether.

Laodicea is now a deserted place, called by the Turks Eski-hissar (*Old Castle*). From its ruins, Laodicea seems to have been situated upon six or seven hills, taking up a large extent of ground. To the north and north-east runs the river Lycus, about a mile and a half distant; but nearer it is watered by two small streams, the Asopus and Caprus, the one to the west, and the other to the south-east, both passing into the Lycus, which last flows into the Mæander.

Laodicea preserves great remains of its importance as the residence of the Roman governors of Asia under the emperors; namely, a stadium, in uncommon preservation, three theatres, one of which is 450 feet in diameter, and the ruins of several other buildings. Col. Leake says: 'There are few ancient sites more likely than Laodicea to preserve many curious remains of antiquity beneath the surface of the soil; its opulence, and the earthquakes to which it was subject, rendering it probable that valuable works of art were often there buried beneath the ruins of the public and private edifices.'

LAPWING. The original word thus rendered in our version has been surmised to mean 'double-crest;' and is supposed on good grounds to mean the hoopoe, rather than the lapwing.

228. [Hoopoe.]

The hoopoe is not uncommon in Palestine at this day, and was from remote ages a bird of mystery. The summit of the augural rod is said to have been carved in the form of a hoopoe's head; and one of the kind is still used by Indian gosseins, and even Armenian bishops, attention being no doubt drawn to the bird by its peculiarly arranged black and white bars upon a delicate vinous fawn-colour, and further embellished with a beautiful fan-shaped crest of the same colour, tipped with white and black. Its appellations in all languages appear to be either imitations of the bird's voice or indications of its filthy habits; which, however, modern ornithologists deny, or do not notice. In Egypt these birds are numerous; forming, probably, two species, the one permanently resident about human habitations, the other migratory, and the same that visits Europe. The latter wades in the mud when the Nile has subsided, and seeks for worms and insects; and the former is known to rear its young so much immersed in the shards and fragments of beetles, &c. as to cause a disagreeable smell about its nest, which is always in holes or in hollow trees. Though an unclean bird in the Hebrew law, the common migratory hoopoe is eaten in Egypt, and sometimes also in Italy; but the stationary species is considered inedible. It is unnecessary to give further description of a bird so well known as the hoopoe, which, though not common, is nevertheless an annual visitant of England, arriving soon after the cuckoo.

LAVER, a basin to contain the water used by the priests in their ablutions during their sacred ministrations. There was one of brass (fabricated out of the metal mirrors which the women brought from Egypt, Exod. xxxviii. 8). It had a 'foot' or base, which, from the manner in which 'the laver *and* its foot' are mentioned, must have been a conspicuous feature, and was perhaps separable from the basin itself for the purpose of removal. We are not informed of the size or shape of this laver, but it appears to have been large. It stood between the altar of burnt-offerings and the door of the tabernacle (Exod. xxx. 18-21; xl. 30-32). The water of this laver seems to have served the double purpose of washing the parts of the sacrifices, and the hands and feet of the priests. But in the temple of Solomon, when the number of both priests and victims had greatly increased, ten lavers were used for the sacrifices, and the molten sea for the personal ablutions of the priests (2 Chron. iv. 6). These lavers are more minutely described than that of the tabernacle. So far as can be made out from the description, they consisted of a square base or stand mounted upon rollers or wheels, and adorned with figures of palm-trees, cherubim, lions, and oxen. The stand doubtless formed a hollow basin for receiving the water which fell from the laver itself, and which appears to have been drawn from it by means of cocks (1 Kings vii. 27-39). Each of the lavers contained forty baths, or, according to the usual computation, about 300 English gallons.

In the second temple there appears to have been only one laver. Of its size or shape we have no information, but it was probably like those of Solomon's temple.

LAWYER. This word, in its general sense, denotes one skilled in the law, as in Tit. iii. 13. When, therefore, one is called a lawyer, this is understood with reference to the laws of the land in which he lived or to which he belonged. Hence among the Jews a lawyer was one versed in the laws of Moses, which he taught in the schools and synagogues (Matt. xxviii. 35; Luke x. 25). The same person who is called 'a lawyer' in these texts, is in the parallel passage (Mark xii. 28) called a scribe; whence it has been inferred that the functions of the lawyers and the scribes were identical. The individual may have been *both* a lawyer and a scribe; but it does not thence follow that all lawyers were scribes. Some suppose, however, that the 'scribes' were the public expounders of the law, while the 'lawyers' were the private expounders and teachers of it. But this is a mere conjecture; and nothing more is really known than that the 'lawyers' were expounders of the law, whether publicly or privately or both.

LAZARUS (an abridged form of the Hebrew name Eleazer), an inhabitant of Bethany, brother of Mary and Martha, who was honoured with the friendship of Jesus, by whom he was raised from the dead after he had been four days in the tomb. This great miracle is minutely described in John xi. The credit which Christ obtained among the people by this illustrious act, of which the life and presence of Lazarus afforded a standing evidence, induced the Sanhedrim, in plotting against Jesus, to contemplate the destruction of Lazarus also (John xii. 10). Whether they accomplished this object or not, we are not informed: but the probability seems to be that when they had satiated their malice on Christ, they left Lazarus unmolested.

LEAD, a well-known metal, the first Scriptural notice of which occurs in the triumphal song in which Moses celebrates the overthrow of Pharaoh, whose host is there said to have '*sunk like lead*' in the waters of the Red Sea (Exod. xv. 10).

Before the use of quicksilver was known, lead was used for the purpose of purifying silver, and separating it from other mineral substances   To this Jeremiah alludes where he figuratively describes the corrupt condition of the people: 'In their fire the lead is consumed (in the crucible); the smelting is in vain, for the evil is not separated' (Jer. vi. 29).

Job (xix. 23, 24) expresses a wish that his words were engraven 'with an iron pen and lead.' These words are commonly supposed to refer to engraving on a leaden tablet; and it is undeniable that such tablets were anciently used as a writing material. But our authorized translators, by rendering 'an iron pen and lead in the rock for ever,' seem to have entertained the same view with Rosenmuller, who supposes that molten lead was to be poured into letters sculptured on stone with an iron chisel, in order to raise the inscription.

Although the Hebrew weights were usually of stone, and are indeed called 'stones,' a leaden weight denominated *anach*, which is the Arabic word for lead, occurs in Amos vii. 7, 8.   In Acts xxvii. 28, a plummet for taking soundings at sea is mentioned, and this was of course of lead.

The ancient uses of lead in the East seem to have been very few; nor are they now numerous. One may travel far in Western Asia without discovering any trace of this metal in any of the numerous useful applications which it is made to serve in European countries.

We are not aware that any trace of lead has been yet found within the limits of Palestine. But ancient lead-mines, in some of which the ore has been exhausted by working, have been discovered by Mr. Burton in the mountains between the Red Sea and the Nile; and lead is also said to exist at a place called Sheff, near Mount Sinai.

LE'AH (*wearied*), one of the two daughters of Laban who became the wives of Jacob [JACOB].

LEAVEN AND FERMENT.   The organic chemists define the process of fermentation, and the substance which excites it, as follows:—
'*Fermentation* is nothing else but the putrefaction of a substance containing no nitrogen.   *Ferment*, or yeast, is a substance in a state of putrefaction, the atoms of which are in a continual motion.' This definition is in strict accordance with the views of the ancients, and gives point and force to many passages of Sacred Writ (Ps. lxxix. 21; Matt. xvi. 6, 11, 12; Mark viii. 15; Luke xii. 1; xiii. 21; 1 Cor. v. 5-8; Gal. v. 9). *Leaven*, and fermented or even some readily fermentible substances (as honey), were prohibited in many of the typical institutions both of the Jews and Gentiles.   Plutarch assigns as the rea-

son why the priest of Jupiter was not allowed to touch *leaven*, 'that it comes out of corruption, and corrupts that with which it is mingled.' All fermented substances were prohibited in the Paschal Feast of the Jews (Exod. xii. 8, 19, 20); also during the succeeding seven days, usually called 'The Feast of Unleavened *Bread*,' though *bread* is not in the original.   God forbade either *ferment* or *honey* to be offered to Him in his temple (*i. e.* in the symbolical rites), while they were permitted in offerings designed to be consumed as food (Num. xv. 20, 21). On the same principle of symbolism, God prescribes that *salt* shall always constitute a part of the oblations to Him (Lev. ii. 13). Salt prevents corruption or decay, and preserves flesh. Hence it is used as a symbol of incorruption and perpetuity. Thus St. Paul (comp. Col. iv. 6; Eph. iv. 29) uses 'salt' as preservative from corruption, on the same principle which leads him to employ that which is *unfermented* as an emblem of purity and uncorruptedness.

'The usual *leaven* in the East is dough kept till it becomes sour, and which is kept from one day to another for the purpose of preserving leaven in readiness. Thus, if there should be no leaven in all the country for any length of time, as much as might be required could easily be produced in twenty-four hours. *Sour dough*, however, is not exclusively used for leaven in the East, the *lees of wine* being in some parts employed as yeast.'

LEB'ANON, a long chain of mountains on the northern border of Palestine. The term Libanus is more convenient in use than the Hebrew form Lebanon, as enabling us to distinguish the parallel ranges of Libanus and Anti-Libanus, which have no such distinctive names in connection with the Hebrew designation. Lebanon seems to be applied in Scripture to either or both of these ranges; and we shall also use it in this general sense: but Libanus means distinctively the westernmost of those ranges, which faces the Mediterranean, and Anti-Libanus the eastern, facing the plain of Damascus; in which sense these names will be used in this article.   The present inhabitants of the country have found the convenience of distinguishing these parallel ranges; and give to Libanus the name of 'Western Mountain' (Jebel esh-Sharki), and to Anti-Libanus that of 'Eastern Mountain' (Jebel el-Gharbi); although Jebel Libnân (the same name in fact as Lebanon) occurs among the Arabs with special reference to the eastern range.

These two great ranges, which together form the Lebanon of Scripture, commence about the parallel of Tripoli (lat. 34° 28'), run in a general direction from N.E. to S.W., through about one degree of latitude, and form, at their southern termination, the natural frontier of Palestine. These parallel ranges enclose between them a fertile and well-watered valley, averaging about fifteen miles in width, which is the Cœle-Syria (Hollow Syria) of the ancients, but is called by the present inhabitants, by way of pre-eminence, el-Bekaa, or 'the Valley,' which is watered through the greater portion of its length by the river Litany, the ancient Leontes.

Nearly opposite Damascus the Anti-Libanus separates into two ridges, which diverge somewhat, and enclose the fertile Wady et-Teim. The easternmost of these two ridges, which has already been pointed out as the Hermon of Scripture [Hermon], Jebel esh-Sheikh, continues its S.W. course, and is the proper prolongation of Anti-Libanus. From the base of the higher part of this ridge, a low broad spur or mountainous tract runs off towards the south, forming the high land which shuts in the basin and Lake of el-Huleh on the east. This tract is called Jebel Heish, the higher portion of which terminates at Tel el-Faras, nearly three hours north of Fiek. The other ridge of Anti-Libanus takes a more westerly direction. It is long, low, and level; and continues to border the lower part of the great valley of Bekaa, until it seems to unite with the higher bluffs and spurs of Lebanon, and thus entirely to close that valley. In fact, only a narrow gorge is here left between precipices, in some places of great height, through which the Litany finds its way down to the sea, north of Tyre. The chain of Lebanon, or at least its higher ridges, may be said to terminate at the point where it is thus broken through by the Litany. But a broad and lower mountainous tract continues towards the south, bordering the basin of the Huleh on the west. It rises to its greatest elevation about Safed (Jebel Safed); and at length ends abruptly in the mountains of Nazareth, as the northern wall of the plain of Esdraelon. This high tract may very properly be regarded as a prolongation of Lebanon.

The mountains of Lebanon are of limestone rock, generally of a whitish hue, and from the aspect which the range thus bears in the distance, in its cliffs and naked parts, the name of Lebanon (which signifies 'white') has been supposed to be derived; but others seek its origin in the snows which rest long upon its summits, and perpetually upon the highest of them.

Of the two ranges, that of Libanus is by far the highest. Its uppermost ridge is marked by a line, drawn at the distance of about two hours' journey from the summit, above which all is barren; but the slopes and valleys below this line afford pasturage, and are capable of cultivation, by reason of the numerous springs which are met with in all directions. Cultivation is, however, chiefly found on the seaward slopes, where numerous villages flourish, and every inch of ground is turned to account by the industrious natives, who, in the absence of natural levels, construct artificial terraces in order to prevent the earth from being swept away by the winter rains, and at the same time to retain the water requisite for the irrigation of the crops. When one looks upward from below, the vegetation on these terraces is not visible; so that the whole mountain appears as if composed only of immense rugged masses of naked whitish rock, traversed by deep wild ravines, running down precipitously to the plain. No one would suspect among these rocks the existence of a vast multitude of thrifty villages, and a numerous population of mountaineers, hardy, industrious, and brave. Here, amidst the crags of the rocks, are to be seen the remains of the renowned cedars; but a much larger proportion of firs, oaks, brambles, mulberry-trees, fig-trees, and vines.

Although the general elevation of Anti-Libanus is inferior to that of Libanus, the easternmost of the branches into which it divides towards its termination (Jebel esh-Sheikh) rises loftily, and overtops all the other summits of heaven. Our information respecting Anti-Libanus is less distinct than that concerning the opposite range. It appears, however, that it has fewer inhabitants, and is scarcely in any part cultivated.

None of the summits of Libanus or Anti-Libanus have been measured. By comparing the accounts of different travellers, however, as to the continuance of snow upon the higher summits, and adjusting them with reference to the point of perpetual congelation in that latitude, a rough estimate may be formed, that the average height of the Libanus mountains, from the top of which the snow entirely disappears in summer, must be considerably below 11,000 feet, probably about 10,000 feet above the level of the sea. But the higher points, particularly the Sannin, which is the highest of all, must be above that limit, as the snow rests on them all the year. By the same rule the average height of the Anti-Libanus range is reckoned as not exceeding 9000 feet; but its highest point, in the Jebel es-Sheik, or Mount Hermon, is considered to be somewhat more lofty than the Sannin, the highest point of Libanus.

In Scripture Lebanon is very generally mentioned in connection with the cedar-trees in which it abounded; but its wines are also noticed (Hosea xiv. 8); and in Cant. iv. 11; Hosea xiv. 7, it is celebrated for various kinds of fragrant plants.

LEECH occurs only in Prov. xxx. 15. 'The *horse*-leech' is properly a *species* of leech discarded for medical purposes on account of the coarseness of its bite. The leech, as a symbol, in use among rulers of every class and in all ages, for avarice, rapine, plunder, rapacity, and even assiduity, is too well known to need illustration.

LEES. The original word (Shemarim) thus rendered is generally understood to denote the lees or dregs of wine. But this cannot be the meaning of the term in Isa. xxv. 6, where, we think, it must refer to some rich *preserves* appropriate to the feast of which that text speaks. The verse may be rendered thus:—'And Jehovah of hosts shall make to all peoples in this mountain a feast of fat things, a feast of preserves, of the richest fatness, of preserves well refined.' Considerable diversity of opinion has obtained among Biblical critics in regard to both the literal meaning and prophetic bearing of this text. The most usual interpretation supposes a reference to *wines on the lees;* but there are strong objections to this view, the most obvious of which is, that it is exceedingly inappropriate. There is no mention of wine in the original, but simply of dregs; and interpreters have been forced to suppose a reference to the former, from a conviction that the latter was altogether inapt. The mention of dregs does not naturally call up the idea of wine which has been drawn from them. We agree with the great majority of interpreters, that a signal blessing is here referred to; but we cannot agree with those who suppose that wine drawn off from dregs is made the emblem of that blessing. Such wine would evidently not answer the purpose. It was not the best wine. We regard it as indicating something excellent in its kind, and the best of its kind. It seems to refer to some rich *preserves* made from grapes or other fruits.

It is difficult to say how these *preserves* were prepared. ' In the East grapes enter very largely into the provisions at an entertainment. Thus Norden was treated by the Aga of Assaoun with coffee, and some bunches of grapes of an excellent taste.' It is probable, however, that some solid preparation of the dried grape is here intended. The very best grapes were anciently, and still are, employed to make such preparations in Palestine. The finest grapes in that country grow in the vineyards around Hebron. ' The produce of these vineyards,' says Professor Robinson, ' is celebrated throughout Palestine. No wine, however, nor 'Arak is made from them, except by the Jews, and this is not in great quantity. The wine is good. *The finest grapes are dried as raisins ;* and the rest, being trodden and pressed, the juice is boiled down to a syrup, which, under the name of Dibs, is much used by all classes, wherever vineyards are found, as a condiment with their food. It resembles thin molasses, but is more pleasant to the taste.' The fact here stated regarding the use made of the finest grapes, supplies us with an article worthy of the feast mentioned in the text. Buckingham mentions the following facts :—' By way of dessert, some walnuts and dried figs were afterwards served to us, besides a very curious article, probably resembling the dried wine of the ancients, which they are said to have preserved in cakes. They were of the size of a cucumber, and were made out of the fermented juice of the grape formed into a jelly, and in this state wound round a central thread of the kernel of walnuts; the pieces of the nuts thus forming a support for the outer coat of jelly, which became harder as it dried, and would keep, it is said, fresh and good for many months, forming a welcome treat at all times, and being particularly well adapted for sick or delicate persons, who might require some grateful provisions capable of being carried in a small compass, and without risk of injury on a journey.'

After a full consideration of the subject, we conclude that the *shemárim* of this text was a solid article, different from *grape-cake*, as not being pressed in any particular form, and different from *dried grapes*, as being refined and prepared for being served up at a sumptuous entertainment.

Neither of the other passages (Jer. xlviii. 11, Zeph. i. 12), where the word under discussion occurs, is invested with special interest. The wine was separated from the lees, sometimes at least, by being drawn off from one vessel to another, as appears from Jeremiah xlviii. 11, which Bishop Lowth renders thus :—

' Moab hath been at ease from his youth,
    And he hath settled upon his lees ;
Nor hath he been drawn off from vessel to
    vessel,
Neither hath he gone into captivity :
Therefore his taste remaineth in him,
    And his flavour is not changed.'

Moab is here represented as spending a life of quiet indifference, living undisturbed in sin. Such, too, was the situation of those of whom Jehovah says (Zeph. i. 12), 'I will punish the men that are settled on their lees;' that is, those who disregarded his admonitions, and prosecuted their sinful courses, unmoved by his threatenings.

LEGION, a division of the Roman army. It always comprised a large body of men ; but the number varied so much at different times, that there is considerable discrepancy in the statements with reference to it. The legion appears to have originally contained about 3000 men, and to have risen gradually to twice that number, or even more. In and about the time of Christ it seems to have consisted of 6000 men ; but this was exclusive of horsemen, who usually formed an additional body amounting to one-tenth of the infantry. As all the divisions of the Roman army are noticed in Scripture, we may add that each legion was divided into ten *cohorts* or regiments, each cohort into three *maniples* or bands, and each maniple into three *centuries* or companies of 100 each. This smaller division into centuries or hundreds, from the form in which it is exhibited as a constituent of the larger divisions, clearly shows that 6000 had become at least the formal number of a legion.

The word *legion* came to be used to express a great number or multitude. Thus, the unclean spirit (Mark v. 7), when asked his name, answers, ' My name is Legion, for *we* are many.'

LENTILES. Lentiles appear to have been chiefly used for making a kind of pottage. The *red* pottage for which Esau bartered his birthright was of lentiles (Gen. xxv. 29-34). The term *red* was, as with us, extended to *yellowish brown*, which must have been the true colour of the pottage, if derived from lentiles. The Greeks and Romans also called lentiles red. Lentiles were among the provisions brought to David when he fled from Absalom (2 Sam. xvii. 28), and a field of lentiles was the scene of an exploit of one of David's heroes (2 Sam. xxiii. 11). From Ezek. iv. 9, it would appear that lentiles were sometimes used as bread. This was, doubtless, in times of scarcity, or by the poor. Sonnini assures us that in southernmost Egypt, where corn is comparatively searce, lentiles mixed with a little barley form almost the only bread in use among the poorer classes. It is called *bettan*, is of a golden yellow colour, and is not bad, although rather heavy. In that country, indeed, probably even more than in Palestine, lentiles anciently, as now, formed a chief article of food among the labouring classes. Large quantities of lentiles were exported from Alexandria. Pliny, in mentioning two Egyptian varieties, incidentally lets us know that one of them was red, by remarking that they like a red soil, and by speculating whether the pulse may not have thence derived the reddish colour which it imparted to the pottage made with it. This illustrates Jacob's red pottage. Dr. Shaw also states that these lentiles easily dissolve in boiling, and form a red or chocolate coloured pottage, much esteemed in North Africa and Western Asia. Putting these facts together, it is likely that the reddish lentile, which is now so common in Egypt, is the sort to which all these statements refer.

The tomb-paintings actually exhibit the operation of preparing pottage of lentiles, or, as Wilkinson describes it, ' a man engaged in cooking lentiles for a soup or porridge ; his companion brings a bundle of faggots for the fire, and the lentiles themselves are seen standing near him in

2 M

wicker baskets.' The lentiles of Palestine have been little noticed by travellers.

229.

The lentile is an annual plant, and the smallest of all the leguminosæ which are cultivated. It rises with a weak stalk about eighteen inches high, having pinnate leaves at each joint composed of several pairs of narrow leaflets, and terminating in a tendril, which supports it by fastening about some other plant. The small

230. [Lentiles—Cicer lens.]

flowers, which come out of the sides of the branches on short peduncles, three or four together, are purple, and are succeeded by the short and flat legumes, which contain two or three flat round seeds slightly curved in the middle. The flower appears in May, and the seeds ripen in July. When ripe, the plants are rooted up, if they have been sown along with other plants, as is sometimes done; but they are cut down when grown by themselves. They are threshed, winnowed, and cleaned like corn.

LEOPARD (Cant. iv. 8. Isa. xi. 6; Jer. v. 6; xiii. 23; Hos. xiii. 7; Hab. i. 8; Dan. vii. 6;

231.

Rev. xiii. 2; Ecclus. xxviii. 23). Though zoologists differ in opinion respecting the identity of the leopard and the panther, and dispute, supposing them to be distinct, how these names should be respectively applied, and by what marks the animals should be distinguished, nevertheless there can be no doubt that the leopard of the Bible is that great spotted feline which anciently infested the Syrian mountains, and even now occurs in the wooded ranges of Libanus. The variety of leopard, or rather panther, of Syria, is considerably below the stature of a lioness, but very heavy in proportion to its bulk. Its general form is so well known as to require no description beyond stating, that the spots are rather more irregular, and the colour more mixed with whitish, than in the other pantherine felinæ, excepting the Felis Uncia, or Felis Irbis, of High Asia, which is shaggy and almost white. It is a nocturnal, cat-like animal in habits, dangerous to all domestic cattle, and sometimes even to man. In the Scriptures it is constantly placed in juxtaposition with the lion or the wolf; which last, if the hyæna be intended, forms a natural association. There is in Asia Minor a species or variety of panther, much larger than the Syrian, not unfrequent on the borders of the snowy tracts even of Mount Ida, above ancient Troy; and the group of these spotted animals is spread over the whole of Southern Asia to Africa. From several names of places, it appears that, in the earlier ages of Israelitish dominion, it was sufficiently numerous in Palestine. Leopard skins were worn as a part of ceremonial costume by the superiors of the Egyptian priesthood, and by other personages in Nubia; and the animal itself is represented in the processions of tributary nations.

LEPROSY. Leprosy is a name that was given by the Greek physicians to a scaly disease of the skin. During the dark ages it was indiscriminately applied to all chronic diseases of the skin, and more particularly to elephantiasis, to which latter, however, it does not bear the slightest resemblance. The disease, as it is known at the present day, commences by an eruption of small reddish spots slightly raised above the level of the skin, and grouped in a circle. These spots are soon covered by a very thin, semi-transparent scale or epidermis, of a whitish colour, and very smooth, which in a little time falls off, and leaves the skin beneath red and uneven. As the circles increase in diameter the skin recovers its healthy appearance towards the centre fresh scales are formed, which are now thicker, and superimposed one above the other, especially at the edges, so that the centre of the scale appears to be depressed. The scales are of a greyish white colour, and have something of a micaceous or pearly lustre. The circles are generally of the size of a shilling or half-crown, but they have been known to attain half a foot in diameter. The disease generally affects the knees and elbows, but sometimes it extends over the whole body; in which case the circles become confluent. It does not at all affect the general health, and the only inconvenience it causes the patient is a slight itching when the skin is heated; or, in inveterate cases, when the skin about the joints is much thickened, it may in some degree impede the free motion of the limbs. It is common to both sexes, to almost all ages, and all ranks of society. It is not in the least infectious, but it is always difficult to be cured, and in old persons, when it is of long standing, may be pronounced incurable. It is commonly met with in this country and in all parts of Europe. On turning to the Mosaic account, we find three species mentioned, which were all included under the generic term of *Bahéret*, or 'bright spot.' The first is called *Bóhaq*, which signifies 'brightness,' but in a subordinate degree. This species did not render a person unclean. The second was called *Bahéret lebanáh*, or a bright white *Bahéret*. The third was *Bahéret kéháh*, or dusky *Bahéret*, spreading in the skin. These two last were also called 'a stroke,' as if a chastisement, and rendered a person unclean. The characteristic marks of the *Bahéret lebanáh* mentioned by Moses, are a glossy white and spreading scale upon an elevated base, the elevation depressed in the middle, the hair on the patches participating in the whiteness, and the patches themselves perpetually increasing. There are some other slight affections mentioned by name in Leviticus, which the priest was required to distinguish from leprosy. If a person had any of the above diseases he was brought before the priest to be examined. If the priest found the distinctive signs of a contagious leprosy, the person was immediately declared unclean. If the priest had any doubt on the subject, the person was put under confinement for seven days, when he was examined a second time. If in the course of the preceding week the eruption had made no advance, he was shut up for another seven days; and if then the disease was still stationary, and had none of the distinctive signs above noticed, he was declared clean (Lev. xiii.).

It may be useful here to subjoin a description of elephantiasis, or the leprosy of the middle ages, as this is the disease from which most of the prevalent notions concerning leprosy have been derived, and to which the notices of lepers contained in modern books of travels exclusively refer.

Elephantiasis first of all makes its appearance by spots of a reddish, yellowish, or livid hue, irregularly disseminated over the skin and slightly raised above its surface. These spots are glossy, and appear oily, or as if they were covered with varnish. After they have remained in this way for a longer or shorter time, they are succeeded by an eruption of tubercles. These are soft, roundish tumours, varying in size from that of a pea to that of an olive, and are of a reddish or livid colour. They are principally developed on the face and ears, but in the course of years extend over the whole body. The face becomes frightfully deformed; the forehead is traversed by deep lines and covered with numerous tubercles; the eyebrows become bald, swelled, furrowed by oblique lines, and covered with nipple-like elevations; the eyelashes fall out, and the eyes assume a fixed and staring look; the lips are enormously thickened and shining; the beard falls out; the chin and ears are enlarged and beset with tubercles; the lobe and alæ of the nose are frightfully enlarged and deformed; the nostrils irregularly dilated, internally constricted, and excoriated, the voice is

hoarse and nasal, and the breath intolerably fetid. After some time, generally after some years, many of the tubercles ulcerate, and the matter which exudes from them dries to crusts of a brownish or blackish colour; but this process seldom terminates in cicatrization. The extremities are affected in the same way as the face. The hollow of the foot is swelled out, so that the sole becomes flat; the sensibility of the skin is greatly impaired, and, in the hands and feet, often entirely lost; the joints of the toes ulcerate and fall off one after the other; insupportable fœtor exhales from the whole body. The patient's general health is not affected for a considerable time, and his sufferings are not always of the same intensity as his external deformity. Often, however, his nights are sleepless or disturbed by frightful dreams; he becomes morose and melancholy; he shuns the sight of the healthy, because he feels what an object of disgust he is to them, and life becomes a loathsome burden to him; or he falls into a state of apathy, and after many years of such an existence he sinks either from exhaustion, or from the supervention of internal disease. The Greeks gave the name of elephantiasis to this disease, because the skin of the person affected with it was thought to resemble that of an elephant, in dark colour, ruggedness, and insensibility, or, as some have thought, because the foot, after the loss of the toes, when the hollow of the sole is filled up and the ankle enlarged, resembles the foot of an elephant. About the period of the Crusades elephantiasis spread itself like an epidemic over all Europe, even as far north as the Faroe Islands; and henceforth, owing to the above-named mistakes, every one became familiar with leprosy under the form of the terrible disease that has just been described. Leper or lazar-houses abounded everywhere; as many as 2000 are said to have existed in France alone. The disease was considered to be contagious possibly only on account of the belief that was entertained respecting its identity with Jewish leprosy, and the strictest regulations were enacted for secluding the diseased from society. Towards the commencement of the seventeenth century, the disease gradually disappeared from Europe, and is now confined to intertropical countries. It existed in Faroe as late as 1676, and in the Shetland Islands in 1736, long after it had ceased in the southern parts of Great Britain. The best authors of the present day who have had an opportunity of observing the disease do not consider it to be contagious. There seems, however, to be little doubt as to its being hereditary.

LE'VI (*a joining*), the third son of Jacob and Leah, born in Mesopotamia B.C. 1750 (Gen. xxix. 34). No circumstance is recorded of him save the part which he and his full brother Simeon took in the massacre of the Shechemites, to avenge the wrong done to their sister Dinah (Gen. xxxiv. 25, 26). This transaction was to his last hour regarded by Jacob with abhorrence, and he failed not to allude to it in his dying declaration. As Simeon and Levi were united in that act, so the patriarch couples them in his prophecy: 'Accursed be their anger, for it was fierce; and their wrath, for it was cruel! I will divide them in Jacob, and disperse them in Israel.' And, accordingly, their descendants were afterwards, in different ways, dispersed among the other tribes; although, in the case of Levi, this curse was eventually turned into a benefit and blessing.

LEVI'ATHAN (Job iii. 8; xli. 1; Ps. lxxiv. 14; civ. 26: Isa. xxvii. 1) [BEHEMOTH, CROCODILE, DRAGON]. Gesenius very justly remarks that this word, which denotes any twisted animal, is especially applicable to every great tenant of the waters, such as the great marine serpents and crocodiles, and, it may be added, the colossal serpents and great monitors of the desert. In general it points to the crocodile, and Job xli. is unequivocally descriptive of that Saurian. Probably the Egyptian crocodile is therein depicted in all its magnitude, ferocity, and indolence, such as it was in early days, when as yet unconscious of the power of man, and only individually tamed for the purposes of an imposture, which had sufficient authority to intimidate the public and protect the species, under the sanctified pretext that it was a type of pure water, and an emblem of the importance of irrigation; though the people in general seem ever to have been disposed to consider it a personification of the destructive principle. At a later period the Egyptians, probably of such places as Tentyris, where crocodiles were not held in veneration, not only hunted and slew them, but it appears from a statue that a sort of Bestiarii could tame them sufficiently to perform certain exhibitions mounted on their backs. The intense musky odour of its flesh must have rendered the crocodile, at all times, very unpalatable food, but breast-armour was made of the horny and ridged parts of its back. We have ourselves witnessed a periodical abstinence in the great Saurians, and have known negro women, while bathing, play with young alligators; which, they asserted, they could do without danger, unless they hurt them and thereby attracted the vengeance of the mother; but the impunity most likely resulted from the period of inactivity coinciding with the then state of the young animals, or from the negro women being many in the water at the same time. The occurrence took place at Old Harbour, Jamaica.

LE'VITES, the descendants of Levi, through his sons Gershon, Kohath and Merari, whose descendants formed so many sub-tribes or great families of the general body. In a narrower sense the term Levites designates the great body of the tribe employed in the subordinate offices of the hierarchy, to distinguish them from that one family of their body—the family of Aaron—in which the priestly functions were vested.

While the Israelites were encamped before Mount Sinai, the tribe of Levi, to which Moses and Aaron belonged, was, by special ordinance from the Lord, set specially apart for sacerdotal services, in the place of the first-born of the different tribes and families to whom such functions, according to ancient usage, belonged; and which indeed had already been set apart as holy, in commemoration of the first-born of the Israelites having been spared when the first-born of the Egyptians were destroyed (Num. iii. 12, 13, 40-51; Exod. xiii.). When it was determined to set apart a single tribe of Levi for this service, the numbers of the first-born in Israel and of the tribe selected were respectively taken, when it was found that the former amounted to 22,273,

and the latter to 22,000. Those of the first-born beyond the number of the Levites were then redeemed at the rate of five shekels, or 12s. 6d. each, and the money assigned to the priests. At the same time the cattle which the Levites then happened to possess were considered as equivalent to all the firstlings of the cattle which the Israelites had; and, accordingly, the firstlings were not required to be brought, as in subsequent years, to the altar and to the priesthood (Num. iii. 41-51).

In the wilderness the office of the Levites was to carry the Tabernacle and its utensils and furniture from place to place, after they had been packed up by the priests (Num. iv. 4-15). In this service each of the three Levitical families had its separate department; the Gershonites carried the hangings and cords of the Tabernacle, for which they were allowed two wains, each drawn by four oxen (Num. iii. 25, 26; iv. 24-28; vii. 7). The Kohathites carried the ark, the table of shew-bread, the candlestick, the two altars, and such of the hangings as belonged to the sanctuary; for this they had no wains or oxen, the whole being carried upon their shoulders (Num. iii. 31; iv. 4-15; vii. 9); the Merarites had charge of the substantial parts of the Tabernacle—the boards, pillars, bars, bases, &c., and also all the ordinary vessels of service, for which they were allowed four wains and eight oxen (Num. iii. 36, 37; iv. 31, 32; vii. 8). In this manner they proceeded in all their journeys; and when they settled in a place, and had erected the Tabernacle, the different families pitched their tents around it in the following manner: the Gershonites behind it on the west (Num. iii. 23), the Kohathites on the south (iii. 29), the Merarites on the north (iii. 35), and the priests on the east (iii. 38). They all assisted Aaron and his sons in taking care of, and attending on, the Tabernacle, when it was pitched; but they were allowed to take no part in the services of the altar (xviii. 2-7).

This was the nature of their service in the desert: but when they entered the land of Canaan, and the tabernacle ceased to be migratory, the range of their service was considerably altered. While part attended at the tabernacle, the rest were distributed through the country in the several cities which were allotted to them. These cities are commonly reckoned forty-eight; but thirteen of them were reserved for the priests, so that only thirty-five belonged to the Levites. The names of these cities, and the tribes in which they were situated, are given in Josh. xxi. 20-42; 1 Chron. vi. 64-81. Of the forty-eight cities six were cities of refuge for the unintentional homicide, of which one, Hebron, was a priestly city (Deut. iv. 41-43; Josh. xx. 2-9).

In the time of David, when the number of the priests and Levites had much increased, a third and very important alteration was effected, as much, or more, with reference to the Temple, for which he made every possible preparation, as for the existing service at the Tabernacle. While the priests were divided into twenty-four courses, that they might attend the Temple in rotation weekly, and only officiate about two weeks in the year, the Levites were also divided into twenty-four courses. In the book of Chronicles we have four times twenty-four courses of Levites mentioned, but all their employments are not distinctly stated (1 Chron. xxiii. 7-23, xxiv. 20-31; xxv. 1-31; xxvi. 1-12). The most conspicuous classification is that of twenty-four courses of porters and servitors, and twenty-four of musicians.

The office of the porters was to open and shut the doors and gates of the Temple-courts, at which they also attended throughout the day to prevent the entrance of any harmful or unclean person or thing (1 Chron. xxvi. 17, 18). They had also the charge of the treasure-chambers in their respective wards; for we find four of the chief porters holding this trust in 1 Chron. ix. 26, and their names and the articles in their charge are given in 1 Chron. xxvi. 20-29; 2 Chron. xxxi. 12-14.

Besides acting as porters and servants during the day, we learn that they were also the guards of the Temple. Without entering into specific details, it may be remarked that the whole number of guards to the Temple at night is stated to have been twenty-four, of whom three were priests. These are described as having been under an overseer called ' the man of the mountain of the house.' He went his rounds to see that the guards were at their posts: if he found any one seated who should have been standing, he said, ' Peace be unto thee;' but if he found any one asleep, he struck him, and sometimes set fire to his clothes.

We have thus seen that one division of the Levites was employed as porters during the day, and another as guards during the night: a third division served as musicians. A catalogue of these is given in 1 Chron. xxi. 1-9, according to their employments; and another, according to their courses, in 1 Chron. xxi. 9-31. We shall have to speak of MUSIC under that head, and need only here state that on grand occasions, when a full band was formed, the family of Heman sung in the middle (1 Chron. vi. 33-38), the family of Asaph on the right hand (vi. 39-43), and the family of Ethan on the left. The ordinary place for the musicians, vocal and instrumental, was at the east end of the court of the priests, between the court of Israel and the altar.

It seems that the singers could never be under twelve, because that number was particularly mentioned at their first appointment (1 Chron. xxv. 9); but there was no objection to any larger number. The young sons of the Levites were, on such occasions only, allowed to enter the court of the priests with their fathers, that their small voices might relieve the deep bass of the men; and for this authority was supposed to be found in Ezra iii. 9.

The Levites were not at liberty to exercise any properly sacerdotal functions. but on extraordinary occasions they were permitted to assist in preparing the sacrifices, without, however, in any way concerning themselves with the blood (2 Chron. xxix. 34; xxx. 16. 17; xxxv. 1).

In Num. iv. 3 the Levites are described as commencing their actual service at thirty years of age; but in Num. viii. 24, 25, twenty-five is the age mentioned; and in 1 Chron. xxiii. 24, 25, and Ezra iii. 8, twenty. The reason of these apparent discrepancies is, that from twenty-five to thirty they were in the state of probationers, doing some things, but excluded from others (Aben Ezra, on Num. viii.). At thirty they became qualified for every part of the Levitical service. This was under the Tabernacle; but when the Temple was built, and bodily strength was less required, the age was reduced to twenty. After fifty they were no longer called upon to serve as a matter of obligation: but they might attend if they thought proper, and perform any usual service which was not considered burthensome. Thus, in the wilderness, they ceased at that age to carry any part of the burdens when the ark and Tabernacle were removed (Num. viii. 25, 26).

When the Levitical body was first set apart for its sacred duties, the existing members were consecrated in the manner particularly described in Num. viii. 6, 22. They, and in them their descendants, were thus inducted into their particular office; and, in later times, when any one became of age, it was sufficient for his admission to prove that he belonged to a Levitical family, and, probably, to offer some trifling sacrifice. It does not appear that the Levites, when at home, had any particular dress to distinguish them from their countrymen; nor is there any positive evidence that they had any distinctive garb, even when on actual service at the tabernacle or temple. Josephus relates that only six years before the destruction of the Temple by the Romans, the Levites were allowed by Agrippa to wear a linen tunic, like the priests—an innovation with which the latter were highly displeased. This shows that the dress of the Levites, even when on duty, had not previously been in any respect similar to that of the priests.

The subsistence of the Levites was provided for in a peculiar manner. It consisted, first, of a compensation for the abandonment of their right to one-twelfth of the land of Canaan; and, secondly, of a remuneration for their services in their official capacity as devoted to the services of the sanctuary. The territorial compensation lay in the 48 cities which were granted to the whole tribe, including the priests. These cities were scattered among the different tribes, as centres of instruction, and had 1000 square cubits, equal to above 305 English acres, attached to each of them, to serve for gardens, vineyards, and pasturage. It is obvious, however, that this alone could not have been an adequate compensation for the loss of one-twelfth of the soil, seeing that the produce of 305 acres could not in any case have sufficed for the wants of the inhabitants of these cities. The further provision, therefore, which was made for them must be regarded as partly in compensation for their sacrifice of territory, although we are disposed to look upon it as primarily intended as a remuneration for the dedication of their services to the public. This provision consisted of the tithe, or tenth of the produce of the grounds allotted to the other tribes. The simplest view of this payment is to regard it, first, as the produce of about as much land as the Levites would have been entitled to if placed on the same footing with regard to territory as the other tribes; and also as the produce of so much more land, which the other tribes enjoyed in consequence of its not having been assigned to the tribe of Levi. In giving the produce of this land to the Levites the Israelites were therefore to be regarded as simply releasing them from the cares of agriculture, to enable them to devote themselves to the service of the sanctuary. The land which produced the tithe was just so much land held by the other tribes in their behalf; and the labour of cultivating this land was the salary paid to the Levites for their official services. The tenth was paid to the whole tribe of Levi; but as the Levites had to give out of this one-tenth to the priests, their own allowance was only nine-tenths of the tenth. A more particular account of tithes belongs to another head |TITHES|. The Levites had also a certain interest in the 'second tithe,' being the portion which, after the first tithe had been paid, the cultivator set apart for hospitable feasts, which were held at the place of the sanctuary in two out of three years, but in the third year at home. This interest, however, extended no further than that the offerer was particularly enjoined to invite the priests and Levites to such feasts.

The earliest notice we have of the numbers of the Levites occurs at their first separation in the desert, when there were 22,300, of a month old and upwards; of whom 8580 were fit for service, or between the ages of 30 and 50 (Num. iii. 22, 28, 34; iv. 2, 34-49). Thirty-eight years after, just before the Israelites entered Canaan, they had increased to 23,000, not one of whom had been born at the time of the former enumeration (Num. xxvi. 57, 62-65). About 460 years after the entry into Canaan (B.C. 1015) they were again numbered by David, a little before his death, and were found to have increased to 38,000 men fit for Levitical service—of whom 24,000 were 'set over the work of the Lord,' 6000 were officers and judges, 4000 were porters, and 4000 were musicians (1 Chron. xxiii. 3, 4, 5). If the same proportion then existed between those come of age and those a month old which existed when the tribe quitted Egypt, the entire number of the Levitical body, in the time of David, must have been 96,433.

After the revolt of the ten tribes, those of the Levites who resided in the territories of those tribes, having resisted the request of Jeroboam to transfer their services to his idolatrous establishments at Dan and Bethel, were obliged to abandon their possessions and join their brethren in Judah and Benjamin (2 Chron xi 12, 13, 14; xiii. 9); and this concentration of the Levitical body in the kingdom of Judah must have had an important influence upon its condition and history. That kingdom thus actually consisted of three tribes—Judah, Benjamin, and Levi—of which one was devoted to sacerdotal uses. This altered position of the Levites—after they had been deprived of most of their cities, and the tithes from ten of the tribes were cut off—presents a subject for much interesting investigation, into which we cannot enter. Their means must have been much reduced, for it cannot be supposed that Judah and Benjamin alone were able, even if willing, to undertake the support of the whole Levitical body on the same scale as when the dues of all Israel flowed into its treasuries. In the subsequent history of Judah the Levites appear less frequently than might have been expected. The chief public measure in which they were engaged was the restoration of the house of David in the person of young Joash (2 Chron xxiii 1-11): which may be regarded as mainly the work of the Levitical body, including the priests.

Under the edict of Cyrus, only 341 Levites, according to Ezra (ii. 40-42), or 350, according to Nehemiah (vii. 43-45), returned with Zerubbabel to Jerusalem. This is less surprising than might at first sight appear; for if, before the captivity, the great body of them had been in straitened circumstances and without fixed possessions in Judah, it was only consistent with human prudence that those who had, in all probability, comfortably settled themselves in Babylon, should not be anxious to return in such numbers to Palestine as were likely to produce similar effects. A few more are mentioned in Neh. xii. 24-26. Those who did return seem to have had no very correct notion of their obligations and duties; for there were many who formed matrimonial alliances with the idolaters of the land, and thereby corrupted both their morals and genealogies. But they were prevailed upon to reform this abuse; and, as a token of obedience, signed the national covenant with Nehemiah, and abode at Jerusalem to influence others by their authority and example (Neh. x. 9-13; xi. 15-19).

The Levites are not mentioned in the Apocryphal books, and very slightly in the New Testament (Luke x. 32; John i. 19; Acts iv. 36); but the 'scribes' and the 'lawyers,' so often named in the Gospels, are usually supposed to have belonged to them.

It would be taking a very narrow view of the duties of the Levitical body if we regarded them as limited to their services at the sanctuary. On the contrary, we see in their establishment a provision for the religious and moral instruction of the great body of the people, which no ancient lawgiver except Moses ever thought of attending to. But that this was one principal object for which a twelfth of the population—the tribe of Levi—was set apart, is clearly intimated in Deut. xxxii. 9, 10 : 'They shall teach Jacob thy judgments and Israel thy law; they shall put incense before thee, and whole burnt sacrifice upon thine altar.' They were to read the volume of the law publicly every seventh year at the Feast of Tabernacles (Deut. xxxi. 10-13). 'This public and solemn periodical instruction,' observes Dean Graves (*Lectures*, p. 170), 'though eminently useful, was certainly not the entire of their duty; they were bound from the spirit of this ordinance to take care that at all times the aged should be improved and the children instructed in the knowledge and fear of God, the adoration of his majesty, and the observance of his law; and for this purpose the peculiar situation and privileges of the tribe of Levi, as regulated by the divine appointment, admirably fitted them.'

LEVITICUS, the third book of Moses.

CONTENTS —Leviticus contains the further statement and development of the Sinaitic legislation, the beginnings of which are described in Exodus. It exhibits the HISTORICAL progress of this legislation; consequently we must not expect to find the laws detailed in it in a systematic form. There is, nevertheless, a certain order observed, which arose from the nature of the subject, and of which the plan may easily be perceived. The whole is intimately connected with the contents of Exodus, at the conclusion of which book that sanctuary is described with which all external worship was connected (Exod. xxxv.-xl.).

Some critics have strenuously endeavoured to prove that the laws contained in Leviticus originated in a period much later than is usually supposed. But the following observations sufficiently support their Mosaical origin, and show that the whole of Leviticus is historically genuine. The laws in ch. i.-vii. contain manifest vestiges of the Mosaical period. Here, as well as in Exodus, when the priests are mentioned, Aaron and his sons are named ; as, for instance, in ch. i. 4, 7, 8, 11, &c. The tabernacle is the sanctuary, and no other place of worship is mentioned anywhere. Expressions like the following constantly occur, *before the tabernacle of the congregation*, or *the door of the tabernacle of the congregation* (ch. i. 3 : iii. 8, 13, &c.). The Israelites are always described as a congregation (ch. iv. 13, sq.), under the command of the *elders of the congregation* (ch. iv 15), or of a *ruler* (ch. iv. 22). Every thing has a reference to life in a camp, and that camp commanded by Moses (ch. iv. 12, 21 ; vi. 11 ; xiv. 8 ; xvi. 26, 28). A later writer could scarcely have placed himself so entirely in the times, and so completely adopted the modes of thinking of the age, of Moses : especially if, as has been asserted, these laws gradually sprung from the usages of the people, and were written down at a later period with the object of sanctioning them by the authority of Moses. They so entirely befit the Mosaical age, that, in order to adapt them to the requirements of any later period, they must have undergone some modification, accommodation, and a peculiar mode of interpretation. This inconvenience would have been avoided by a person who intended to forge laws in favour of the later modes of Levitical worship. A forger would have endeavoured to identify the past as much as possible with the present.

In ch. xvii. occurs the law which forbids the slaughter of any beast except at the sanctuary. This law could not be strictly kept in Palestine, and had therefore to undergo some modification (Deut. xii.). Our opponents cannot show any rational inducement for contriving such a fiction. The law (ch. xvii. 6, 7) is adapted to the nation only while emigrating from Egypt. It was the object of this law to guard the Israelites from falling into the temptation to imitate the Egyptian rites and sacrifices offered to he-goats ; which word signifies also demons represented under the form of he goats, and which were supposed to inhabit the desert.

The laws concerning food and purifications appear especially important if we remember that the people emigrated from Egypt The fundamental principle of these laws is undoubtedly Mosaical, but in the individual application of them there is much which strongly reminds us of Egypt. This is also the case in Lev. xviii. sq , where the lawgiver has manifestly in view the two opposites, Canaan and Egypt That the lawgiver was intimately acquainted with Egypt, is proved by such remarks as those about the Egyptian marriages with sisters (ch. xviii. 3) ; a custom which stands as an exception among the prevailing habits of antiquity.

The book of Leviticus has a prophetical character. The lawgiver represents to himself the future history of his people. This prophetical character is especially manifest in chs. xxv.,

xxvi., where the law appears in a truly sublime and divine attitude, and when its predictions refer to the whole futurity of the nation. It is impossible to say that these were prophecies delivered after the event, unless we would assert that this book was written at the close of Israelitish history. We must rather grant that passages like this are the real basis on which the authority of later prophets is chiefly built. Such passages prove also, in a striking manner, that the lawgiver had not merely an external aim, but that his law had a deeper purpose, which was clearly understood by Moses himself That purpose was to regulate the national life in all its bearings, and to consecrate the whole nation to God. See especially ch. xxv. 18, sq.

But this ideal tendency of the law does not preclude its applicability to matters of fact. The law had not merely an *ideal*, but also a *real* character, evidenced by its relation to the faithlessness and disobedience of the nation. The whole future history of the covenant people was regulated by the law, which has manifested its eternal power and truth in the history of the people of Israel. Although this section has a general bearing, it is nevertheless manifest that it originated in the times of Moses. At a later period, for instance, it would have been impracticable to promulgate the law concerning the Sabbath and the year of Jubilee : for it was soon sufficiently proved how far the nation in reality remained behind the ideal Israel of the law. The sabbatical law bears the impress of a time when the whole legislation, in its fulness and glory, was directly communicated to the people, in such a manner as to attract, penetrate, and command.

LIBERTINES. 'Certain of the synagogue, which is called (the synagogue) of the *Libertines*, and Cyrenians, and Alexandrians,' &c, are mentioned in Acts vi. 9. There has been much diversity in the interpretation of this word. The most probable opinion, and that which is now generally entertained, is, that the Libertini were Jews, whom the Romans had taken in war and conveyed to Rome, but afterwards freed ; and that this synagogue had been built at their expense. Libertini is, therefore, to be regarded as a word of Roman origin, and to be explained with reference to Roman customs. Further, we know that there were in the time of Tiberius many *libertini*, or 'freed-men,' of the Jewish religion at Rome.

LIB'NAH, one of the royal cities of the Canaanites, taken by Joshua immediately after Makkedah (Josh. x. 20, 30). It lay within the territory assigned to Judah (Josh. xv. 42), and became one of the Levitical towns in that tribe (Josh. xxi. 13 ; 1 Chron. vi. 57). It was a strongly fortified place. The Assyrian king Sennacherib was detained some time before it when he invaded Judæa in the time of Hezekiah ; and it was before it that he sustained that dreadful stroke which constrained him to withdraw to his own country (2 Kings xix. 8 ; Isa. xxxvii. 8). In the reign of King Jehoram, Libnah is said to have revolted from him (2 Kings viii. 22 ; 2 Chron. xxi. 10). Libnah existed as a village in the time of Eusebius and Jerome, and is placed by them in the district of Eleutheropolis.

LIB'NATH, or, more fully, SHIHOR-LIBNATH, a stream near Carmel, on the borders of Asher (Josh. xix. 26). Michaelis conceives this to be the 'glass-river,' i. e. the Belus, from whose sands the first glass was made by the Phœnicians.

LIB'YA. This name, in its largest acceptation, was used by the Greeks to denote the whole of Africa. But Libya Proper, which is the Libya of the New Testament and the country of the Lubim in the Old, was a large tract, lying along the Mediterranean, to the west of Egypt.

Libya is supposed to have been first peopled by, and to have derived its name from, the Lehabim or Lubim [NATIONS, DISPERSION OF]. These, its earliest inhabitants, appear, in the time of the Old Testament, to have consisted of wandering tribes, who were sometimes in alliance with Egypt, and at others with the Ethiopians, as they are said to have assisted both Shishak, king of Egypt, and Zerah the Ethiopian in their expeditions against Judæa (2 Chron. xii. 4; xiv. 8; xvi 9). They were eventually subdued by the Carthaginians: and it was the policy of that people to bring the nomade tribes of Northern Africa which they mastered into the condition of cultivators, that by the produce of their industry they might be able to raise and maintain the numerous armies with which they made their foreign conquests. But Herodotus assures us that none of the Libyans beyond the Carthaginian territory were tillers of the ground. Since the time of the Carthaginian supremacy the country, with the rest of the East, has successively passed into the hands of the Greeks, Romans, Saracens, and Turks. The name of Libya occurs in Acts ii. 10, where 'the dwellers in the parts of Libya about Cyrene' are mentioned among the stranger Jews who came up to Jerusalem at the feast of Pentecost.

LICE occurs in Exod. viii. 16, 17, 18 (Heb. 12, 13, 14); Ps. cv. 31. The name of the creature employed in the third plague upon Egypt, miraculously produced from the dust of the land. Its exact nature has been much disputed. Those who suppose the name to be derived from a Hebrew word which means to fix, settle, or establish, infer lice to be meant, from their fixing themselves on mankind, animals, &c. Dr. A. Clarke has further inferred from the words 'in man and in beast,' that it was the 'tick.' It is probable, however, that not lice, but some species of gnats is the proper rendering. It is not a valid objection, that if this plague were gnats, &c., the plague of flies would be anticipated, since the latter most likely consisted of one particular species having a different destination [FLY]; whereas this may have consisted of not only mosquitoes or gnats, but of some other species which also attack domestic cattle, as the œstrus, or tabanus, or zimb; on which supposition these two plagues would be sufficiently distinct.

But since mosquitoes, gnats, &c., have ever been one of the evils of Egypt, there must have been some peculiarity attending them on this occasion, which proved the plague to be 'the finger of God.' From the next chapter, ver. 31, it appears that the flax and the barley were smitten by the hail; that the former was beginning to grow, and that the latter was in the ear —which, according to Shaw, takes place in

Egypt in March. Hence these gnats would be sent about February, i. e. before the increase of the Nile, which takes place at the end of May, or beginning of June. Since, then, the innumerable swarms of mosquitoes, gnats, &c., which every year affect the Egyptians come, according to Hasselquist, at the increase of the Nile, the appearance of them in February would be as much a variation of the course of nature as the appearance of the gadfly in January would be in England. They were also probably numerous and fierce beyond example on this occasion; and as the Egyptians would be utterly unprepared for them (for it seems that this plague was not announced), the effects would be signally distressing. For a description of the evils inflicted by these insects upon man, see Kirby and Spence, Introduction to Entomology, Lond. 1828, i. 115, &c.

LIGHT is represented in the Scriptures as the immediate result and offspring of a divine command (Gen. i. 3). The earth was void and dark, when God said, 'Let light be, and light was.' This is represented as having preceded the placing of 'lights in the firmament of heaven, the greater light to rule the day, and the lesser light to rule the night: he made the stars also' (Gen. i. 14, sq). Whatever opinion may be entertained as to the facility with which these two separate acts may be reconciled, it cannot be questioned that the origin of light, as of every other part of the universe, is thus referred to the exertion of the divine will: as little can it be denied that the narrative in the original is so simple, yet at the same time so majestic and impressive, both in thought and diction, as to fill the heart with a lofty and pleasurable sentiment of awe and wonder.

The divine origin of light made the subject one of special interest to the Biblical nations— the rather because light in the East has a clearness, a brilliancy, is accompanied by an intensity of heat, and is followed in its influence by a largeness of good, of which the inhabitants of less genial climes can have no conception. Light easily and naturally became, in consequence, with Orientals, a representative of the highest human good. All the more joyous emotions of the mind, all the pleasing sensations of the frame, all the happy hours of domestic intercourse, were described under imagery derived from light (i Kings xi. 36; Isa. lvii. 8; Esther viii. 16; Ps. xcvii. 11). The transition was natural from earthly to heavenly, from corporeal to spiritual things; and so light came to typify true religion and the felicity which it imparts. But as light not only came from God, but also makes man's way clear before him, so it was employed to signify moral truth, and pre-eminently that divine system of truth which is set forth in the Bible, from its earliest gleamings onward to the perfect day of the Great Sun of Righteousness. The application of the term to religious topics had the greater propriety because the light in the world, being accompanied by heat, purifies, quickens, enriches; which efforts it is the peculiar province of true religion to produce in the human soul (Isa. viii. 20; Matt. iv. 16; Ps. cxix. 105; 2 Pet. i. 19; Eph. v. 8; 2 Tim. i. 10; 2 Pet. ii. 9).

It is doubtless owing to the special providence

under which the divine lessons of the Bible were delivered, that the views which the Hebrews took on this subject, while they were high and worthy, did not pass into superstition, and so cease to be truly religious. Other Eastern nations beheld the sun when it shined, or the moon walking in brightness, and their hearts were secretly enticed, and their mouth kissed their hand in token of adoration (Job xxxi. 26, 27). This 'iniquity' the Hebrews not only avoided, but when they considered the heavens they recognised the work of God's fingers, and learnt a lesson of humility as well as of reverence (Ps. viii. 3, sq.).

Among the personifications on this point which Scripture presents we may specify, 1. God. The Apostle James (i. 17) declares that 'every good and perfect gift cometh down from the Father of lights, with whom is no variableness, neither shadow of turning;' obviously referring to the faithfulness of God, and the constancy of his goodness, which shine on undimmed and unshadowed. So Paul (1 Tim. vi. 16); 'God who dwelleth in the light which no man can approach unto.' Here the idea intended by the imagery is the incomprehensibleness of the self-existent and eternal God.

2. Light is also applied to Christ: 'The people who sat in darkness have seen a great light' (Matt. iv. 16; Luke ii. 32: John i. 4, sq.). 'He was the true light,' 'I am the light of the world' (John viii. 12; xii. 35, 36).

3. It is further used of angels, as in 2 Cor. xi. 14: 'Satan himself is transformed into an angel of light.' 4. Light is moreover employed of men: John the Baptist ' was a burning and a shining light' (John v. 35); 'Ye are the light of the world' (Matt. v. 14; see also Acts xiii. 47; Eph. v. 8).

LIGN ALOES. [ALOES.]

LIGURE. The Hebrew word Leshem is thus rendered in Exod. xxviii. 19; xxxix. 12; and in Rev. xxi. 20 it is put as equivalent to the Jacinth or Hyacinth; and it is certain that the ligure and the jacinth are regarded as the same stone. The prevailing colour of the jacinth is orange-yellow-red; which passes over sometimes into reddish-brown, sometimes into brownish and pale red, and sometimes into imperfect pistachio green. It is harder than the emerald, but the artists of antiquity frequently engraved upon it. It comes to us from the East Indies.

LILY. This plant is mentioned in the well-known and beautiful passage (Matt. vi. 26): 'Consider the lilies of the field, how they grow; they toil not, neither do they spin, and yet I say unto you, that even Solomon, in all his glory, was not arrayed like one of these;' so also in Luke xii. 27. Here it is evident that the plant alluded to must have been indigenous or grown wild, in the vicinity of the sea of Galilee, must have been of an ornamental character, and, from the Greek name given to it, of a liliaceous nature. Travellers in Palestine mention that in the month of January the fields and groves everywhere abound with various species of lily, tulip, and narcissus. Benard noticed, near Acre, on Jan. 18th, and about Jaffa, on the 23rd, tulips, white, red, blue, &c. Gumpenberg saw the meadows of Galilee covered with the same flowers on the 31st. Tulips figure conspicuously among the flowers of Palestine. So Pococke says, 'I

saw many tulips growing wild, in the fields (in March), and any one who considers how beautiful those flowers are to the eye, would be apt to conjecture that these are the lilies to which Solomon in all his glory was not to be compared.' This is much more likely to be the plant intended than some others which have been adduced, as, for instance, the scarlet *amaryllis*, having white flowers with bright purple streaks, found by Salt at Adowa. Others have preferred the *Crown imperial*, which is a native of Persia and Cashmere. Most authors have united in considering the white lily, *Lilium candidum*, to be the plant to which our Saviour referred; but it is doubtful whether it has ever been found in a wild state in Palestine. This opinion is confirmed by a correspondent at Aleppo, who has resided long in Syria, but is acquainted only with the botany of Aleppo and Antioch: 'I never saw the white lily in a wild state, nor have I heard of its being so in Syria. It is cultivated here on the roofs of the houses in pots as an exotic bulb, like the daffodil.' The following extract of a letter from Dr. Bowring throws a new light upon the subject: 'I cannot describe to you with botanical accuracy the lily of Palestine. I heard it called by the title of *Lilia syriaca*, and I imagine under this title its botanical characteristics may be hunted out. Its colour is a brilliant red; its size about half that of the common tiger lily. The white lily I do not remember to have seen in any part of Syria. It was in April and May that I observed my flower, and it was most abundant in the district of Galilee, where it and the *Rhododendron* (which grew in rich abundance round the paths) most strongly excited my attention.' On this Dr. Lindley observes, 'It is clear that neither the white lily, nor the *Oporanthus luteus*, nor *Ixiolirion*, will answer to Dr. Bowring's description, which seems to point to the Chalcedonian or scarlet *martagon* lily, formerly called the lily of Byzantium, found from the Adriatic to the Levant, and which, with its scarlet turban-like flowers, is indeed a most stately and striking object.' As this lily (the *Lilium chalcedonicum* of botanists) is in flower at the season of the year when the sermon on the Mount is supposed to have been spoken, is indigenous in the very locality, and is conspicuous, even in the garden, for its remarkable showy flowers, there can now be little doubt that it is the plant alluded to by our Saviour.

LINEN, FINE. The word SHESH, thus translated in the Authorized Version, occurs twenty-eight times in Exodus, once in Genesis, once in Proverbs, and three times in Ezekiel. Considerable doubts have, however, always been entertained respecting the true meaning of the word; but it appears to us to signify hemp, which is a plant that in the present day is extensively distributed, being cultivated in Europe, and extending through Persia to the southernmost parts of India. In the plains of that country it is cultivated on account of its intoxicating product, so well known as *bang*; in the Himalayas both on this account and for its yielding the ligneous fibre which is used for sack and rope-making. There is no doubt that it might easily have been cultivated in Egypt. Herodotus mentions it as being employed by the Thracians for making garments. ' These were so like linen, that none but a very experienced person could tell whether they were of hemp or flax; one who had never seen hemp would certainly suppose them to be linen.' Hemp is used in the present day for smockfrocks and tunics; and Russia sheeting and Russia duck are well known. Dioscorides describes it as being employed for making ropes, and it was a good deal cultivated by the Greeks for this purpose. Though we are unable at present to prove that it was cultivated in Egypt at an early period, and used for making garments, yet there is nothing improbable in its having been so. Indeed, as it was known to various Asiatic nations, it could hardly have been unknown to the Egyptians. Hemp might thus have been used at an early period, along with flax and wool, for making cloth for garments and for hangings, and would be much valued until cotton and the finer kinds of linen came to be known.

LI'NUS, one of the Christians at Rome whose salutations Paul sent to Timothy (2 Tim. iv. 21). He is said to have been the first bishop of Rome after the martyrdom of Peter and Paul.

LION, the most powerful, daring, and impressive of all carnivorous animals, the most magnificent in aspect and awful in voice. Being very common in Syria in early times, the lion naturally supplied many forcible images to the poetical language of Scripture, and not a few historical incidents in its narratives. This is shown by the great number of passages where this animal, in all the stages of existence—as the whelp, the young adult, the fully mature, the lioness— occurs under different names, exhibiting that multiplicity of denominations which always results when some great image is constantly present to the popular mind. Thus we have, 1. *Gor*, a lion's whelp, a very young lion (Gen. xlix. 9; Deut. xxxiii. 20; Jer. li. 38; Ezek. xix. 2; Nahum ii. 11, 12, &c.). 2. *Chephir*, a young lion, when first leaving the protection of the old pair to hunt independently (Ezek. xix. 2, 3; Ps. xci. 13; Prov. xix. 12, &c.). 3. *Ari*, an adult and vigorous lion, a lion having paired, vigilant and enterprising in search of prey (Nahum ii. 12; 2 Sam. xvii. 10; Num. xxiii. 24). This is the common name of the animal. 4. *Sachal*, a mature lion in full strength; a black lion? (Job iv. 10; x. 16; Ps. xci. 13; Prov. xxvi. 13; Hosea v. 14; xiii. 7). This denomination may very possibly refer to a distinct variety of lion, and not to a black species or race, because neither black nor white lions are recorded, excepting in Oppian; but the term may be safely referred to the colour of the skin, not of the fur;

for some lions have the former fair, and even rosy, while in other races it is perfectly black. An Asiatic lioness, formerly at Exeter Change, had the naked part of the nose, the roof of the mouth, and the bare soles of all the feet pure black, though the fur itself was very pale buff. 5. *Laish*, a fierce lion, one in a state of fury (Job iv. 11; Prov. xxx 30; Isa. xxx. 6). 6. *Labia*, a lioness (Job iv. 11, where the lion's whelps are denominated 'the sons of Labiah,' (or of the lioness).

The lion is the largest and most formidably armed of all carnassier animals, the Indian tiger alone claiming to be his equal. One full grown, of Asiatic race, weighs above 450 pounds, and those of Africa often above 500 pounds. The fall of a fore paw in striking has been estimated to be equal to twenty-five pounds' weight, and the grasp of the claws, cutting four inches in depth, is sufficiently powerful to break the vertebræ of an ox. The huge laniary teeth and jagged molars worked by powerful jaws, and the tongue entirely covered with horny papillæ, hard as a rasp, are all subservient to an immensely strong, muscular structure, capable of prodigious exertion, and minister to the self-confidence which these means of attack inspire. In Asia the lion rarely measures more than nine feet and a half from the nose to the end of the tail, though a tiger-skin of which we took the dimensions was but a trifle less than 13 feet. In Africa they are considerably larger, and supplied with a much greater quantity of mane. Both tiger and lion are furnished with a small horny apex to the tail—a fact noticed by the ancients, but only verified of late years, because this object lies concealed in the hair of the tip, and is very liable to drop off. All the varieties of the lion are spotted when whelps; but they become gradually buff or pale. One African variety, very large in size, perhaps a distinct species, has a peculiar and most ferocious physiognomy, a dense black mane extending half way down the back, and a black fringe along the abdomen and tip of the tail; while those of southern Persia and the Dekkan are nearly destitute of that defensive ornament. The roaring voice of the species is notorious to a proverb, but the warning cry of attack is short, snappish, and sharp. Like all the felinæ, they are more or less nocturnal, and seldom go abroad to pursue their prey till after sunset. When not pressed by hunger, they are naturally indolent, and, from their habits of uncontrolled superiority, perhaps capricious, but often less sanguinary and vindictive than is expected.

Lions are monogamous, the male living constantly with the lioness, both hunting together, or for each other when there is a litter of whelps; and the mutual affection and care for their offspring which they display are remarkable in animals by nature doomed to live by blood and slaughter. It is while seeking prey for their young that they are most dangerous; at other times they bear abstinence, and when pressed by hunger will sometimes feed on carcasses found dead. They live to more than fifty years; consequently, having annual litters of from three to five cubs, they multiply rapidly when not seriously opposed. In ancient times, when the devastations of Egyptian, Persian, Greek, and Roman armies passed over Palestine, there can

232.

be little doubt that these destroyers made their appearance in great numbers. The fact, indeed, is arrested by the impression which their increase made upon the mixed heathen population of Samaria, when Israel was carried away into captivity (2 Kings xvii. 25, 26).

The Scriptures present many striking pictures of lions, touched with wonderful force and fidelity : even where the animal is a direct instrument of the Almighty, while true to his mission, he still remains so to his nature. Thus nothing can be more graphic than the record of the man of God (1 Kings xiii. 28), disobedient to his charge, struck down from his ass, and lying dead, while the lion stands by him, without touching the lifeless body, or attacking the living animal, usually a favourite prey. See also Gen. xlix. 9 ; Job iv. 10, 11 ; Nahum ii. 11, 12. Samson's adventure also with the young lion (Judg. xiv. 5, 6), and the picture of the young lion coming up from the underwood cover on the banks of the Jordan, all attest a perfect knowledge of the animal and its habits. Finally, the lions in the den with Daniel, miraculously leaving him unmolested, still retain, in all other respects, the real characteristics of their nature.

The lion, as an emblem of power, was symbolical of the tribe of Judah (Gen. xlix. 9). The type recurs in the prophetical visions, and the figure of this animal was among the few which the Hebrews admitted in sculpture, or in cast metal, as exemplified in the throne of Solomon. Lions, in remote antiquity, appear to have been trained for the chace, and are, even now, occasionally domesticated with safety. Placability and attachment are displayed by them even to the degree of active defence of their friends, as was exemplified at Birr, in Ireland, in 1839, when ' a keeper of wild beasts, being within the den, had fallen accidentally upon a tiger, who immediately caught the man by the thigh, in the presence of numerous spectators; but a lion, being in the same compartment, rose up, and seizing the tiger by the neck, compelled it to let go, and the man was saved.' Numerous anecdotes of a similar character are recorded both by ancient and modern writers.

Zoologists consider Africa the primitive abode of lions, their progress towards the north and west having at one time extended to the forests of Macedonia and Greece; but in Asia, never to the south of the Nerbudda, nor east of the lower Ganges. Since the invention of gunpowder, and even since the havoc which the ostentatious barbarism of Roman grandees made among them, they have diminished in number exceedingly, although at the present day individuals are not unfrequently seen in Barbary, within a short distance of Ceuta.

LITTER. The word translated litter, in Isa. lxvi. 20, is the same which, in Num. vii. 3, denotes the wains or carts *drawn* by oxen, in which the materials of the tabernacle were removed from place to place. It was not, therefore, a litter, which is not drawn, but carried. This is the only place in which the word occurs in the Authorized translation. We are not, however, to infer from this that the Hebrews had no vehicles of the kind. Litters or palanquins were, as we know, in use among the ancient Egyptians. They were borne upon the shoulders of men (No.

233), and appear to have been used for carrying persons of consideration short distances on visits, like the sedan chairs of a former day in England. We doubt if the Hebrews had this kind of litter, as it scarcely agrees with their simple, unluxurious habits; but that they had litters borne by beasts, such as are still common in Western Asia, seems in the highest degree probable.

In Cant. iii. 9 we find a word which occurs nowhere else in Scripture, and is applied to a vehicle used by king Solomon. This word is rendered ' chariot' in our Authorized version, although unlike any other word so rendered in that version. It literally means a *moving couch*, and is usually conceived to denote a kind of

233.

sedan, litter, or rather palanquin, in which great personages and women were borne from place to place. The name, as well as the object, immediately suggests that it may have been nearly the same thing as the *moving throne* or *seat* of the Persians. It consists of a light frame fixed on

234.

two strong poles, like those of our sedan-chair. The frame is generally covered with cloth, and has a door, sometimes of lattice work, at each side. It is carried by two mules, one between the poles before, the other behind. These conveyances are used by great persons when disposed for retirement or ease during a journey, or when sick or feeble from age. But they are chiefly used by ladies of consideration in their journeys (No. 234).

The popular illustrators of Scripture do not appear to have been acquainted with this and the other litters of Western Asia; and have, therefore, resorted to India, and drawn their illustrations from the palanquins borne by men, and from the *howdahs* of elephants. This is unnecessary, as Western Asia still supplies conveyances of this description, more suitable and more likely to have been anciently in use, than any which the further east can produce. If the one already described should seem too humble, there are other takht-ravans of more imposing appearance. Some readers may remember the ' litter of red cloth, adorned with pearls and jewels,' together with ten mules (to bear it by turns), which the king Zahr Shah prepaied for the journey of his daughter. This was, doubtless, of the kind which is borne by four mules, two behind and two before. In Arabia, or in the countries where Arabian usages prevail, two camels are usually employed to bear the takht-ravan, and sometimes two horses. When borne by camels, the head of the hindmost of the animals is bent painfully down under the vehicle. This is the most comfortable kind of litter, and two light persons may travel in it.

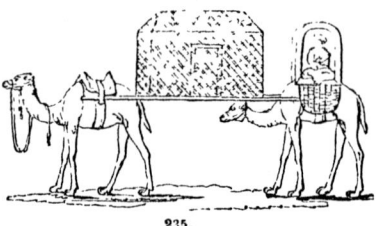

235.

The *shibreeyeh* is another kind of camel-litter, resembling the Indian *howdah*, by which name (or rather *hódaj*) it is sometimes called. It is composed of a small square platform with a canopy or arched covering. It accommodates

236.

but one person, and is placed upon the back of a camel, and rests upon two square camel-chests, one on each side of the animal. It is very evident, not only from the text in view, but from others, that the Hebrews had litters; and there is little reason to doubt that they were the same as those now employed in Palestine and the neighbouring countries, where there are still the same circumstances of climate, the same domestic animals, and essentially the same habits of life, as in the Biblical period.

LIVER occurs in Exod. xxix. 13, 22; Lev. iii. 4, 10, 15; iv. 9; vii. 4; viii. 16, 25; ix. 10, 19; Prov. vii. 23; Lam. ii. 11; Ezek. xxi. 21. In all the instances where the word occurs in the Pentateuch, it forms part of the phrase translated in the Authorized Version 'the caul that is above the liver,' but which Gesenius understands to be the great lobe of the liver itself, rather than the caul over it. Jahn thinks the smaller lobe to be meant. It appears from the same passages that it was burnt upon the altar, and not eaten as sacrificial food. The liver was supposed by the ancient Jews, Greeks, and Romans, to be the seat of the passions, pride, love, &c. Thus, Gen **xlix.** 6, 'with their assembly let not' literally 'my liver be united.' Wounds in the liver were supposed to be mortal; thus the expressions in Prov. vii 23, 'a dart through his liver,' and Lam. ii. 11, 'my liver is poured out upon the earth,' are each of them a periphrasis for death itself. The passage in Ezekiel (ch. xxi. 21) contains an interesting reference to the most ancient of all modes of divination, by the inspection of the viscera of animals and even of mankind sacrificially slaughtered for the purpose. It is there said that the king of Babylon, among other modes of divination, referred to in the same verse, 'looked upon the liver.' The liver was always considered the most important organ in the ancient art of divination by the entrails. Philostratus felicitously describes it as 'the prophesying tripod of all divination.' It is an interesting inquiry how this regard to it originated. Vitruvius suggests a plausible theory of the first rise of divination by the liver. He says the ancients inspected the livers of those animals which frequented the places where they wished to settle; and if they found the liver, to which they chiefly ascribed the process of sanguification, was injured, they concluded that the water and nourishment collected in such localities were unwholesome (i. 4). But divination is coeval and co-extensive with a belief in the divinity. We know that as early as the days of Cain and Abel there were certain means of communication between God and man, and that those means were connected with the sacrifice of animals; and we prefer to consider those means as the source of divination in later ages, conceiving that when the real tokens of the divine interest with which the primitive families of man were favoured ceased, in consequence of the multiplying of human transgressions, their descendants endeavoured to obtain counsel and information by the same external observances. We believe that thus only will the minute resemblances be accounted for, which we discover between the different methods of divination, utterly untraceable to reason, but which have prevailed from unknown antiquity among the most distant regions. It is further important to remark that the first recorded instance of divination is that of the teraphim of Laban, a native of Padan-aram, a district bordering on that country (1 Sam. xix. 13, 16), but by which teraphim both the Sept. and Josephus understood 'the *liver* of goats.'

LIZARD. Under this denomination the modern zoologist places all the cold-blooded animals that have the conformation of serpents with the addition of four feet. Thus viewed, as one great family, they constitute the Saurians, Lacertinæ, and Lacertidæ of authors; embracing numerous generical divisions, which commence with the largest, that is, the crocodile group, and pass through sundry others, a variety of species, formidable, disgusting, or pleasing in appearance —some equally frequenting the land and water, others absolutely confined to the earth and to the most arid deserts; and though in general harmless, there are a few with disputed properties, some being held to poison or corrode by means of the exudation of an ichor, and others extolled as of medical use in pharmacy; but these properties in most, if not in all, are undetermined

or illusory. Of some genera, such as the crocodile and chameleon, we have already made
mention [CHAMELEON: CROCODILE; DRAGON;
LEVIATHAN], and therefore we shall confine our
present remarks to the lizards that are inhabitants
of Western Asia and Egypt, and to those more
particularly noticed in the Bible. Of these commentators indicate six or seven species, whereof
some indeed may be misapprehended; but when
it is considered that the regions of Syria, Arabia,
and Egypt are overrun with animals of this
family, there is every reason to expect allusion
to more than one genus in the Scriptures, where
so many observations and similes are derived
from the natural objects which were familiar to
the various writers. In Lev. xi. 29 mention is
made of a species called *tzab*, which Bochart
refers to one of the group of Monitors or Varanus,
the Nilotic lizard. Like the other of this form,
it is possessed of a tail double the length of the
body, but is not so well known in Palestine,
where there is only one real river (Jordan),
which is not tenanted by this species. We have
already shown that the true crocodile frequented
the shores and marshes of the coast down to a
comparatively late period; and therefore it may
well have had a more specific name than Leviathan—a word apparently best suited to the dignified and lofty diction of the prophets, and clearly
of more general signification than the more collo-
quial designation. Jerome was of this opinion;
and it is thus likely that *tzab* was applied to both,
as *waran* is now considered only a variety of, or
a young, crocodile. There is a second of the
same group, *Lacerta Scincus* of Merrem (*Varanus
Arenarius*), Waran-el-hard, also reaching to six
feet in length; and a third, not as yet clearly
described, which appears to be larger than either,
growing to nine feet, and covered with bright
cupreous scales. This last prefers rocky and
stony situations. It is in this section of the
Saurians that most of the gigantic fossil species,
the real 'children of the giants,' are found to be
located; and of the existing species some are reported to possess great strength. One of the last-
mentioned pursues its prey on land with a rapid
bounding action, feeds on the larger insects, and
is said to attack game in a body, sometimes
destroying even sheep. The Arabs, in agreement
with the ancients, assert that this species will do
fierce and victorious battle with serpents.

237. [Lacerta Stellio.]

We come next to the group of lizards more
properly so called, which Hebrew commentators
take to be the *letaah*, a name having some allusion to poison and adhesiveness. The word
occurs only once (Lev. xi. 30), where Saurians
alone appear to be indicated. If the Hebrew root
were to guide the decision, *letaah* would be another

name for the *gecko* or *anakah*, for there is but one
species which can be deemed venomous; and with
regard to the quality of adhesiveness, though the
geckos possess it most, numerous common lizards
run up and down perpendicular walls with great
facility. We, therefore, take *chomet*, or the
sand lizard of Bochart, to be the true lizard,
several (probably many) species existing in myriads on the rocks in sandy places and in ruins in
every part of Palestine and the adjacent countries.
There is one species particularly abundant and
small, well known in Arabia by the name of Sara-
bandi. We now come to the *Stelliones*, which
have been confounded with the noxious *geckos*
and others from the time of Aldrovandus, and
thence have been a source of inextricable trouble
to commentators. They are best known by the
bundles of starlike spines on the body.

Next we place the *Geckotians*, among which
comes *anakah*, in our versions denominated *ferret*, but which is with more propriety transferred
to the noisy and venomous *abu-burs* of the Arabs.
The particular species most probably meant is
the *lacerta gecko* of Hasselquist, the *gecko lobatus*
of Geoffry, distinguished by having the soles of
the feet dilated and striated like open fans, from
whence a poisonous ichor is said to exude, in-
flaming the human skin, and infecting food that
may have been trod upon by the animal. Hence
the Arabic name of *abu-burs*, or 'father-leprosy,'
at Cairo.

To these we add the *Chameleons*, already
described [CHAMELEON]; and then follows the
Scincus.

Of the species of *Seps*, that is, viviparous
serpent-lizards, having the body of snakes, with
four weak limbs, a species, with only three toes
on each foot, appears to extend to Syria.

LOAN. The Mosaic laws which relate to the
subject of borrowing, lending, and repaying, are
in substance as follows:—If an Israelite became
poor, what he desired to borrow was to be freely
lent to him, and no interest, either of money or
produce, could be exacted from him; interest
might be taken of a foreigner, but not of an
Israelite by another Israelite (Exod. xxii. 25;
Deut. xxiii. 19, 20; Lev. xxv. 35, 38). At the
end of every seven years a remission of debts was
ordained; every creditor was to remit what he
had lent: of a foreigner the loan might be exacted,
but not of a brother. If an Israelite wished to
borrow, he was not to be refused because the year
of remission was at hand (Deut. xv. 1-11). Pledges
might be taken, but not as such the mill or the
upper millstone, for that would be to take a man's
life in pledge. If the pledge was raiment, it was
to be given back before sunset, as being needful
for a covering at night. The widow's garment
could not be taken in pledge (Exod. xxii. 26, 27;
Deut. xxiv. 6, 17).

These laws relating to loans may wear a strange
aspect to the mere modern reader, and cannot be
understood, either in their bearing or their sanctions, unless considered from the Biblical point of
view. The land of Canaan (as the entire world)
belonged to its Creator, but was given of God to
the descendants of Abraham under certain conditions, of which this liberality to the needy was
one. The power of getting loans therefore was a
part of the poor man's inheritance. It was a lien
on the land (the source of all property with agri-

cultural people), which was as valid as the tenure of any given portion by the tribe or family to whose lot it had fallen. This is the light in which the Mosaic polity represents the matter, and in this light. so long as that polity retained its force, would it, as a matter of course. be regarded by the owners of property. Thus the execution of this particular law was secured by the entire force with which the constitution itself was recommended and sustained. But as human selfishness might in time endanger this particular set of laws, so Moses applied special support to the possibly weak part. Hence the emphasis with which he enjoins the duty of lending to the needy. Of this emphasis the very essence is the sanction supplied by that special providence which lay at the very basis of the Mosaic commonwealth; so that lending to the destitute came to be enforced with all the power derivable from the express will of God.

That the system of law regarding loans was carried into effect there is no reason to doubt. It formed an essential part of the general constitution, and therefore came recommended with the entire sanction which that system had on its own behalf; nor were there any predominant antagonist principles at work which would prevent this from proceeding step by step, in its proper place and time. with the residue of the Mosaic legislation. Nor do the passages of Scripture (Job xxii. 6; xxiv. 3; Matt. xviii. 28; Prov. xxviii. 8; Ezek. xviii. 8; Ps xv. 5; cix. 11), which give us reason to think that usury was practised and the poor debtor oppressed, show anything but those breaches to which laws are always liable, especially in a period when morals grow corrupt and institutions in consequence decline.

While, however, the benign tendency of the laws in question is admitted, may it not be questioned whether they were strictly just? Such a doubt could arise only in a mind which viewed the subject from the position of our actual society. A modern might plead that he had a right to do what he pleased with his own; that his property of every kind—land, food, money—was his own; and that he was justified to turn all and each part to account for his own benefit. Apart from religious considerations this position is impregnable. But such a view of property finds no support in the Mosaic institutions. In them property has a divine origin, and its use is entrusted to man on certain conditions, which conditions are as valid as is the tenure of property itself. In one sense, indeed, the entire land—all property—was a great loan, a loan lent of God to the people of Israel, who might well therefore acquiesce in any arrangement which required a portion—a small portion—of this loan to be under certain circumstances accessible to the destitute. This view receives confirmation from the fact that interest might be taken of persons who were not Hebrews, and therefore lay beyond the sphere embraced by this special arrangement.

Had the Hebrews enjoyed a free intercourse with other nations. the permission to take usury of foreigners might have had the effect of impoverishing Palestine by affording a strong inducement for employing capital abroad; but, under the actual restrictions of the Mosaic law, this evil was impossible. Some not inconsiderable advantages must have ensued from the observance of these laws. The entire alienation and loss of the

lent property were prevented by that peculiar institution which restored to every man his property at the great year of release. In the interval between the jubilees the system under consideration would tend to prevent those inequalities of social condition which always arise rapidly, and which have not seldom brought disaster and ruin on states. The affluent were required to part with a portion of their affluence to supply the wants of the needy, without exacting that recompense which would only make the rich richer and the poor more needy; thus superinducing a state of things scarcely more injurious to the one than to the other of these two parties. There was also in this system a strongly conservative influence. Agriculture was the foundation of the constitution. Had money-lending been a trade, money-making would also have been eagerly pursued. Capital would be withdrawn from the land; the agriculturist would pass into the usurer; huge inequalities would arise; commerce would assume predominance, and the entire commonwealth be overturned—changes and evils which were prevented, or, if not so, certainly retarded and abated, by the code of laws regarding loans. As it was, the gradually increasing wealth of the country was in the main laid out on the soil, so as to augment its productiveness and distribute its bounties.

These views may prepare the reader for considering the doctrine of 'the Great Teacher' on the subject of loans. It is found forcibly expressed in Luke's Gospel (vi. 34, 35): 'If ye lend to them of whom ye hope to receive, what thank have ye? for sinners also lend to sinners, to receive as much again: but love ye your enemies, and do good, and lend, hoping for nothing again; and your reward shall be great, and ye shall be the children of the Highest; for he is kind unto the unthankful and to the evil.' The meaning of the passage is distinct and full, unmistakeable, and not to be evaded. He commands men to lend, not as Jews to Jews, but even to enemies, without asking or receiving any return, after the manner of the Great Benefactor of the Universe, who sends down his rains, and bids his sun to shine on the fields of the unjust as well as of the just. To attempt to view this command in the light of reason and experience would require space which cannot here be given; but we must add, that any attempt to explain the injunction away is most unworthy on the part of professed disciples of Christ; and that, not impossibly at least, fidelity to the behests of Him whom we call Lord and Master would of itself answer all doubts and remove all misgivings, by practically showing that this, as every other doctrine that fell from His lips, is indeed of God (John vii. 17).

LOAVES. [BREAD.]

LOCUST. There are ten Hebrew words which appear to signify 'locust' in the Old Testament. It has been supposed. however, that some of these words denote merely the different states through which the locust passes after leaving the egg, viz. the larva, the pupa, and the perfect insect—all which much resemble each other, except that the larva has no wings, and that the pupa possesses only the rudiments of those members, which are fully developed only in the adult locust (Michaelis, *Supplem. ad Lex. Hebr.* ii. 667, 1080). But this supposition is manifestly wrong with regard to four of the terms, because. in Lev. xi. 22, the word 'after his kind,' or species, is added after each of them (comp. ver. 14, 15, 16). It is most probable, therefore, that all the rest are also the names of species, but we know not how to distinguish the several species from each other.

Locusts, like many other of the general provisions of nature, may occasion incidental and partial evil; but upon the whole they are an immense benefit to those portions of the world which they inhabit; and so connected is the chain of being that we may safely believe that the advantage is not confined to those regions. 'They clear the way for the renovation of vegetable productions which are in danger of being destroyed by the exuberance of some particular species, and are thus fulfilling the law of the Creator, that of all which he has made should nothing be lost. A region which has been choked up by shrubs and perennial plants and hard half-withered impalatable grasses, after having been laid bare by these scourges, soon appears in a far more beautiful dress, with new herbs, superb lilies, fresh annual grasses, and young and juicy shrubs of perennial kinds, affording delicious herbage for the wild cattle and game.' Meanwhile their excessive multiplication is repressed by numerous causes. Contrary to the order of nature with all other insects, the males are far more numerous than the females. It is believed that if they were equal in number they would in ten years annihilate the vegetable system. Besides all the creatures that feed upon them, rains are very destructive to their eggs, to the larvæ, pupæ, and perfect insect. When perfect, they always fly with the wind, and are therefore constantly being carried out to sea, and often ignorantly descend upon it as if upon land. Myriads are thus lost in the ocean every year, and become the food of fishes. On land they afford in all their several states sustenance to countless tribes of birds, beasts, reptiles, &c.; and if their office as the scavengers of nature, commissioned to remove all superfluous productions from the face of the earth, sometimes *incidentally* and as the operation of a general law, interferes with the labours of man, as do storms, tempests, &c, they have. from all antiquity to the present hour, afforded him an excellent supply till the land acquires the benefit of their visitations, by yielding him in the meantime an agreeable, wholesome, and nutritious aliment. They are eaten as meat, are ground into flour, and made into bread. They are even an extensive article of commerce. Diodorus Siculus mentions a people of Ethiopia who were so fond of eating them that they were called Acridophagi, 'eaters of locusts.' Whole armies have been relieved by them when in danger of perishing. Their great flights occur only every fourth or fifth season. Those locusts which come in the first instance only fix on trees, and do not destroy grain: it is the young before they are able to fly which are chiefly injurious to the crops. Nor do all the species feed upon vegetables; one, comprehending many varieties, the truxalis, feeds upon insects Latreille says the house-cricket will do so. 'Locusts,' remarks a very sensible tourist, 'seem to devour not so much from a ravenous appetite as from a rage for destroying.' Destruction, therefore, and not

food, is the chief impulse of their devastations, and in this consists their utility: they are in fact omnivorous. The most poisonous plants are indifferent to them; they will prey even upon the crowfoot, whose causticity burns the very hides of beasts. They simply consume *everything* without predilection, vegetable matter, linen, woollen, silk, leather, &c.; and Pliny does not exaggerate when he says, 'and even the doors of houses,' for they have been known to consume the very varnish of furniture. They reduce everything indiscriminately to shreds, which become manure. It might serve to mitigate popular misapprehensions on the subject to consider what would have been the consequence if locusts had been carnivorous like wasps. All terrestrial beings, in such a case, not excluding man himself, would have become their victims. There are, no doubt, many things respecting them yet unknown to us which would still further justify the belief that this, like 'every' other 'work of God is good'—benevolent upon the whole.

LOG. [WEIGHTS AND MEASURES.]

LOIS, the grandmother of Timothy. not by the side of his father, who was a Greek, but by that of his mother. Hence the Syriac has 'thy mother's mother' She is commended by St. Paul for her faith (2 Tim. i. 5); for although she might not have known that the Christ was come, and that Jesus of Nazareth was he, she yet believed in the Messiah to come, and died in that faith.

LONGEVITY. The lengthened ages of some of the ante and post-diluvian fathers, as given by Moses in the Hebrew text, are as follows:—

				Years.
Adam	Gen. v.	5		930
Seth	„	8		912
Enos	„	11		905
Cainan.	„	14		910
Mahalaleel	„	17		895
Jared	„	20		962
Enoch	„	23		365
Methuselah	„	27		969
Lamech	„	31		777
Noah	„ ix.	29		950
Shem	„ xi.	10, 11		600
Arphaxad.	„	12, 13		438
Salah	„	14, 15		433
Eber	„	16, 17		464
Peleg	„	18, 19		239
Reu	„	20, 21		239
Serug	„	22, 23		230
Nahor.	„	24, 25		148
Terah	„	32		205
Abraham	„ xxv.	7		175

Infidelity has not failed, in various ages, to attack revelation on the score of the supposed absurdity of assigning to any class of men this lengthened term of existence. In reference to this Josephus remarks:—'Let no one upon comparing the lives of the ancients with our lives, and with the few years which we now live, think that what we say of them is false; or make the shortness of our lives at present an argument that neither did they attain to so long a duration of life.' When we consider the compensating process which is going on, the marvel is that the human frame should not last longer than it does. Some, however, have supposed that the years above named are *lunar*, consisting of about thirty days; but this supposition, with a view to reduce the lives of the ante-diluvians to our standard, is replete with difficulties. At this rate the whole time, from the creation of man to the Flood, would not be more than about 140 years; and Methuselah himself would not have attained to the age which many even now do, whilst many must have had children when mere infants! Besides, if we compute the age of the post diluvians by this mode of calculation—and why should we not?—we shall find that Abraham, who is said to have died in *a good old* age (Gen. xxv. 8) could not have been more than *fifteen years* old! Moses must therefore have meant *solar*, not *lunar* years —not, however, exactly so long as ours, for the ancients generally reckoned twelve months, of thirty days each, to the year.

But it is asked, if Moses meant solar years, how came it to pass that the patriarchs did not begin to beget children at an earlier period than they are reported to have done? Seth was 105 years old, on the lowest calculation, when he begat Enos; and Methuselah 187 when Lamech was born! St. Augustine (i. 15) explains this difficulty in a two-fold manner, by supposing

1. Either that the age of puberty was later in proportion as the lives of the ante-diluvians were longer than ours; or

2. That Moses does not record the first-born sons, but as the order of the genealogy required, his object being to trace the succession from Adam, through Seth, to Abraham.

As to the probable reasons why God so prolonged the life of man in the earlier ages of the world, and as to the subordinate means by which this might have been accomplished, Josephus says: ' For those ancients were beloved of God, and lately made by God himself; and because their food was then fitter for the prolongation of life, they might well live so great a number of years: and because God afforded them a longer time of life on account of their virtue and the good use they made of it in astronomical and geometrical discoveries, which would not have afforded the time for foretelling the periods of the stars unless they had lived 600 years; for the great year is completed in that interval.'

In the above passage Josephus enumerates *four* causes of the longevity of the earlier patriarchs. As to the first, viz., their being dearer to God than other men, it is plain that it cannot be maintained; for the profligate descendants of Cain were equally long-lived, as mentioned above, with others. Neither can we agree in the second reason he assigns; because we find that Noah and others, though born so long subsequently to the creation of Adam, yet lived to as great an age, some of them to a greater age than he did. If, again, it were right to attribute longevity to the superior quality of the food of the ante-diluvians, then the seasons, on which this depends, must, about Moses' time—for it was *then* that the term of human existence was reduced to its present standard—have assumed a fixed character. But no change at that time took place in the revolution of the heavenly bodies, by which the seasons of heat, cold, &c, are regulated: hence we must not assume that it was the nature of the fruits they ate which caused longevity. How far the ante-diluvians had advanced in scientific research generally, and in astronomical

discovery particularly, we are not informed; nor can we place any dependence upon what Josephus says about the two inscribed pillars which remained from the old world. We are not, therefore, able to determine, with any confidence, that God permitted the earlier generations of man to live so long, in order that they might arrive at a high degree of mental excellence. From the *brief* notices which the Scriptures afford of the character and habits of the ante-diluvians, we should rather infer that they had not advanced very far in discoveries in natural and experimental philosophy [see ANTE-DILUVIANS]. We must suppose that they did not reduce their language to alphabetical order; nor was it necessary to do so at a time when human life was so prolonged, that the tradition of the creation passed through only two hands to Noah. It would seem that the book ascribed to Enoch is a work of post-diluvian origin. Possibly a want of mental employment, together with the labour they endured ere they were able to extract from the earth the necessaries of life, might have been some of the proximate causes of that degeneracy which led God in judgment to destroy the old world. If the ante-diluvians began to bear children at the age on an average of 100, and if they ceased to do so at 600 years, the world might then have been far more densely populated than it is now. Supposing, moreover, that the earth was no more productive antecedently than it was subsequently to the flood; and that the ante-diluvian fathers were ignorant of those mechanical arts which so much abridge human labour now, we can easily understand how difficult they must have found it to secure for themselves the common necessaries of life, and this the more so if animal food was not allowed them. The prolonged life, then, of the generations before the flood, would seem to have been rather an *evil* than a blessing, leading as it did to the too rapid peopling of the earth. We can readily conceive how this might conduce to that awful state of things expressed in the words, ' And the whole earth was filled with violence.' In the absence of any well regulated system of government, we can imagine what evils must have arisen; the unprincipled would oppress the weak, the crafty would outwit the unsuspecting, and, not having the fear of God before their eyes, destruction and misery would be in their ways. Still we must admire the providence of God in the longevity of man immediately after the creation and the flood. After the creation, when the world was to be peopled by one man and one woman, the age of the greatest part of those on record was 900 and upwards. But after the flood, when there were three couples to re-people the earth, none of the patriarchs, except Shem, reached the age of 500; and only the three first of his line, viz., Arphaxad, Selah, and Eber, came near that age, which was in the first century after the flood. In the second century we do not find that any attained the age of 240; and in the third century (about the latter end of which Abraham was born) none, except Terah, arrived at 200; by which time the world was so well peopled, that they had built cities, and were formed into distinct nations under their respective kings. See Gen. xv.

That the common age of man has been the same in all times since the world was peopled, is manifest from profane as well as sacred history. Plato lived to the age of 81, and was accounted an old man; and those whom Pliny reckons up (vii. 48) as rare examples of long life, may, for the most part, be equalled in modern times. We cannot, then, but see the hand of God in the proportion that there is between births and deaths; for by this means the population of the world is kept up. If the fixed standard of human life were that of Methuselah's age, or even that of Abraham's, the world would soon be overstocked; or if the age of man were limited to that of divers other animals, to 10, 20, or 30 years only, the decay of mankind would then be too fast. But on the present scale the balance is nearly even, and life and death keep an equal pace. In thus maintaining throughout all ages and places these proportions of mankind, and all other creatures, God declares himself to be indeed the ruler of the world.

LOOKING-GLASSES. [MIRRORS.]

LORD, a Saxon word signifying ruler or governor. In the Authorized translation of the Scriptures it is used without much discrimination for all the names applied to God, which cannot be helped, as our language does not afford the same number of distinguishing titles as the Hebrew. When, however, the word represents the dread name of JEHOVAH, it is printed in small capitals, LORD, and is by this contrivance made a distinguishing term. As the Hebrew name JEHOVAH is one never used with reference to any but the Almighty, it is to be regretted that the Septuagint, imitated by our own and other versions, has represented it by a word which is also used for the Hebrew 'Adonai,' which is applied not only to God, but, like our 'Lord,' to creatures also, as to angels (Gen. xix. 2; Dan. x. 16, 17), to men in authority (Gen. xli. 30, 33), and to proprietors, owners, masters (Gen. xlv. 8). The leading idea of the Hebrew, the Greek, and the English words, is that of an owner or proprietor, whether God or man; and it occurs in the inferior application with great frequency in the New Testament. This application is either literal or complimentary; literal, when the party is really an owner or master, as in Matt. x. 24; xx. 8; xxi. 40; Acts xvi. 16, 19; Gal. iv. 1, &c.; or when he is so as having absolute authority over another (Matt. ix. 38; Luke x. 2), or as being a supreme lord or sovereign (Acts xxv. 26); and complimentary, when used as a title of address, especially to superiors, like the English Master, Sir, as in Matt. xiii. 27; xxi. 20; Mark vii. 8; Luke ix. 54.

It cannot but be deemed desirable that, instead of the extensive use of the word Lord which we have described, discriminating terms should be adopted in translations. Apart from the Jewish superstitions which influenced the Seventy in their translation, there can be no good reason why the name JEHOVAH should not be retained wherever it occurs in the Hebrew. Then LORD might represent Adonai; or perhaps Sir, or Master, might be used when that word is applied to creatures; and GOD would very properly represent Elohim.

LORD'S DAY. The expression so rendered in the Authorized English Version occurs only once in the New Testament, viz. in Rev. i. 10, and is there unaccompanied by any other words tending to explain its meaning. It is, however, well known that the same phrase was, in after ages of the Christian church, used to signify the first day of the week, on which the resurrection of Christ was commemorated. Hence it has been inferred that the same name was given to that day during the time of the Apostles, and was in the present instance used by St. John in this sense, as referring to an institution well known, and therefore requiring no explanation [see article SABBATH].

LOT (a covering); son of Haran and nephew of Abraham, who by the early death of his father had already come into possession of his property when Abraham went into the land of Canaan (Gen. xi. 31). Their united substance, consisting chiefly in cattle, was not then too large to prevent them from living together in one encampment. Eventually, however, their possessions were so greatly increased, that they were obliged to separate; and Abraham with rare generosity conceded the choice of pasture-grounds to his nephew. Lot availed himself of this liberality of his uncle, as he deemed most for his own advantage, by fixing his abode at Sodom, that his flocks might pasture in and around that fertile and well-watered neighbourhood (Gen. xiii. 5-13). He had soon very great reason to regret this choice; for although his flocks fed well, his soul was starved in that vile place, the inhabitants of which were sinners before the Lord exceedingly. There 'he vexed his righteous soul from day to day with the filthy conversation of the wicked' (2 Pet. ii. 7).

About eight years after his separation from Abraham (B C. 1913), Lot was carried away prisoner by Chedorlaomer, along with the other inhabitants of Sodom, and was rescued and brought back by Abraham (Gen. xiv.), as related under other heads [ABRAHAM; CHEDORLAOMER]. This exploit procured for Abraham much celebrity in Canaan; and it ought to have procured for Lot respect and gratitude from the people of Sodom, who had been delivered from hard slavery and restored to their homes on his account. But this does not appear to have been the result.

At length the guilt of 'the cities of the plain' brought down the signal judgments of Heaven. The avenging angels, after having been entertained by Abraham, repaired to Sodom, where they were received and entertained by Lot, who was sitting in the gate of the town when they arrived. While they were at supper the house was beset by a number of men, who demanded that the strangers should be given up to them, for the unnatural purposes which have given a name of infamy to Sodom in all generations. Lot resisted this demand, and was loaded with abuse by the vile fellows outside on that account. They had nearly forced the door, when the angels smote them with instant blindness, by which their attempts were rendered abortive, and they were constrained to disperse. Towards morning the angels apprised Lot of the doom which hung over the place, and urged him to hasten thence with his family. He was allowed to extend the benefit of this deliverance to the families of his daughters who had married in Sodom; but the warning was received by those families with incredulity and insult, and he therefore left Sodom accompanied only by his wife and two daughters. As they went, being hastened by the angels, the wife, anxious for those who had been left behind, or reluctant to remove from the place which had long been her home, and where much valuable property was necessarily left behind, lingered behind the rest, and was suddenly involved in the destruction, by which—smothered and stiffened as she stood by saline incrustations—she became 'a pillar of salt.'

Lot and his daughters then hastened on to Zoar, the smallest of the five cities of the plain, which had been spared on purpose to afford him a refuge: but, being fearful, after what had passed, to remain among a people so corrupted, he soon retired to a cavern in the neighbouring mountains, and there abode. After some stay in this place, the daughters of Lot became apprehensive lest the family of their father should be lost for want of descendants, than which no greater calamity was known or apprehended in those times· and in the belief that, after what had passed in Sodom, there was no hope of their obtaining suitable husbands, they, by a contrivance which has in it the taint of Sodom, where they had been brought up, made their father drunk with wine, and in that state seduced him into an act which, as they well knew, would in soberness have been most abhorrent to him. They thus became the mothers, and he the father, of two sons, named Moab and Ammon, from whom sprung the Moabites and Ammonites, so often mentioned in the Hebrew history (Gen. xix). This circumstance is the last which the Scripture records of the history of Lot; and the time and place of his death are unknown.

LOTS, FEAST OF. [Purim.]

LOVE FEAST, usually termed *Agape*, and signifying the social meal of the primitive Christians, which generally accompanied the Eucharist. If we reflect on the profound impression which the transactions of 'the night on which the Lord was betrayed' (1 Cor. xi. 23) must have made on the minds of the apostles, nothing can be conceived more natural, or in closer accordance with the genius of the new dispensation, than a wish to perpetuate the commemoration of his death in connection with their social meal. The primary celebration of the Eucharist had impressed a sacredness on the previous repast (comp. Matt. xxvi. 26, Mark xiv. 22, with Luke xxii. 20, 1 Cor. xi. 25); and when to this consideration we add the ardent faith and love of the new converts on the one hand, and the loss of property with the disruption of old connections and attachments on the other, which must have heightened the feeling of brotherhood, we need not look further to account for the institution of the Agapæ, at once a symbol of Christian love and a striking exemplification of its benevolent energy. However soon its purity was soiled, at first it was not undeserving of the eulogy pronounced by the great orator of the church—'A custom most beautiful and most beneficial; for it was a supporter of love, a solace of poverty, a moderator of wealth, and a discipline of humility!'

Thus the common meal and the Eucharist formed together one whole, and were conjointly denominated the *Lord's Supper* and *agape*. They were also signified (according to Mosheim, Neander, and other eminent critics) by the phrases *breaking of bread* (Acts ii. 42, 46, xx. 7). We find the term *agapæ* thus applied once, at least, in the New Testament (Jude 12), 'These are spots in your feasts of charity.'

The following is the description given by Tertullian of these feasts. 'The nature of our *Cœna*,' he says, 'may be gathered from its name, which is the Greek term for love. However much it may cost us, it is real gain to incur such expense in the cause of piety: for we aid the poor by this refreshment; we do not sit down to it till we have first tasted of prayer to God; we eat to satisfy our hunger; we drink no more than befits the temperate; we feast as those who recollect that they are to spend the night in devotion; we converse as those who know that the Lord is an ear-witness. After water for washing hands, and lights have been brought in, every one is required to sing something to the praise of God, either from the Scriptures or from his own thoughts; by this means, if any one has indulged in excess, he is detected. The feast is closed with prayer.' Contributions or oblations of provisions or money were made on these occasions, and the surplus placed in the hands of the presiding elder—compare 1 Tim. v. 17, by whom it was applied to the relief of orphans and widows, the sick and destitute, prisoners and strangers.

From the passages in the Epistles of Jude and Peter, already quoted, and more particularly from the language of Paul in 1 Cor. xi, it appears that at a very early period the Agapæ were perverted from their original design: the rich frequently practised a selfish indulgence, to the neglect of their poorer brethren : '*every one taketh before other his own supper*' (1 Cor. xi. 21); i.e. the rich feasted on the provisions they brought, without waiting for the poorer members, or granting them a portion of their abundance.

On account of these and similar irregularities, and probably in part to elude the notice of their persecutors, the Christians, about the middle of the second century, frequently celebrated the Eucharist by itself and before daybreak. From Pliny's Epistle it appears that the agapæ were suspected by the Roman authorities of belonging to the class of unions or secret societies which were often employed for political purposes, and as such denounced by the imperial edicts.

In modern times social meetings bearing a resemblance to the agapæ, and in allusion to them termed 'Love Feasts,' have been regularly held by the church of the United Brethren and the Wesleyan Methodists, also in Scotland by the followers of Mr. Robert Sandeman.

LU'BIM, the Libyans. [Libya.]

LU'CIFER, a word that occurs once in the English Version in the lines—

'How art thou fallen from heaven,
Lucifer, son of the morning!
How art thou felled to the ground,
That didst weaken the nations!'

(Isa. xiv. 12). The meaning of the Hebrew word seems to be 'brilliant,' 'splendid,' 'illustrious,' and it appears to have been the Hebrew name of the morning star. Tertullian and Gregory the Great understood this passage of

Isaiah in reference to the fall of Satan; in consequence of which the name Lucifer has since been applied to Satan; and this is now the usual acceptation of the word. But Dr. Henderson, who in his *Isaiah* renders the line, 'Illustrious son of the morning!' justly remarks in his annotation: 'The application of this passage to Satan, and to the fall of the apostate angels, is one of those gross perversions of Sacred Writ which so extensively obtain, and which are to be traced to a proneness to seek for more in any given passage than it really contains, a disposition to be influenced by sound rather than sense, and an implicit faith in received interpretations. The scope and connection show that none but the king of Babylon is meant. In the figurative language of the Hebrews *a star* signifies an illustrious king or prince (Num. xxiv. 17; comp. Rev. ii 28: xxii. 16). The monarch here referred to, having surpassed all other kings in royal splendour, is compared to the harbinger of day, whose brilliancy surpasses that of the surrounding stars. Falling from heaven denotes a sudden political overthrow—a removal from the position of high and conspicuous dignity formerly occupied (comp. Rev. vi. 13; viii. 10).

LU'CIUS of Cyrene, a person named along with Barnabas, Saul, and others, as 'prophets and teachers' in the church at Antioch (Acts xiii. 1). Lucius was probably one of 'the synagogue of the Cyrenians,' and was without doubt one of the men of Cyrene, who went abroad in consequence of the persecution raised on the death of Stephen (Acts vi. 9; xi. 20). Some suppose that he was one of the seventy disciples: and the tradition is, that he was eventually bishop of Cyrene. This is probably the same Lucius who is mentioned in Rom. xvi. 21 as Paul's kinsman; and he has been supposed by some the same with Luke the Evangelist.

LUD, fourth son of Shem (Gen. x. 22). For his descendants, see NATIONS, DISPERSION OF.

LU'DIM, the descendants of (Gen. x. 13), concerning whom see NATIONS, DISPERSION OF.

LUKE. This name is a contraction of *Lucanus*, and indicates that Luke was descended from heathen ancestors, and that he was either a slave or a freedman. According to ecclesiastical tradition, the author of the Gospel is the same Luke who is mentioned in Paul's Epistles (Philem. 24; 2 Tim. iv. 11; Coloss. iv. 14), and who is called, in the last-mentioned passage, 'the physician.' This tradition is confirmed by the Acts of the Apostles, according to which the author of that work accompanied the Apostle Paul in his journeys (Acts xvi. 10, sq.; xx. 5-13). Luke accompanied Paul also in his last journeys to Jerusalem and Rome (Acts xxi. 1-17; xxvii. 28). The profession of a physician harmonises also with the condition of a freedman, indicated by the form of the name. The higher ranks of the Romans were disinclined to practise medicine, which they left rather to their freedmen. It harmonises with this that Paul (Coloss. iv. 14) distinguishes Luke from the Christians of Jewish descent, whom, in verses 11 and 12, he styles, 'being of the Circumcision.' Eusebius states that Antioch in Syria was the native city of Luke. In this city there was at an early period a congregation of Christians converted from heathenism. Since Luke was a physician,

we must suppose that he was a man of education. To those sceptics who excuse their disbelief of the miracles recorded in the Gospels, by the assertion that their authors were ill-informed Jews, greedy of the marvellous, it must appear of some importance to meet in Luke a well-informed Greek, skilled even in the medical sciences. The higher degree of his education is further proved by the classical style in which the introduction to his Gospel, and the latter portion of the Acts, are written; and also by the explicit and learned details which he gives in the Acts on various antiquarian, historical, and geographical subjects.

It is important to notice what he himself says, in his introduction, of the relation borne by his writings to those of others. It is evident that even then 'many' had attempted to compose a history of our Lord from the statements of eye-witnesses and of the first ministers of the word of God. As these 'many' are distinguished from eye-witnesses, we must suppose that many Christians wrote brief accounts of the life of Jesus, although they had not been eye-witnesses. It is possible that Luke made use of such writings. He states that he had accurately investigated the truth of the accounts communicated, and that, following the example of the 'many,' he had made use of the statements of eye-witnesses, whom he must have had frequent opportunities of meeting with when he travelled with Paul.

The Gospel of St. Luke contains exceedingly valuable accounts, not extant in the books of the other evangelists; for instance, those concerning the childhood of Jesus, the admirable parables in chapters xv. and xvi., the narration respecting the disciples at Emmaus, the section from chap ix. 51 to xix. 27, which contains particulars mostly wanting in the other evangelists. It has been usual, since the days of Schleiermacher, to consider this portion as the report of a single journey to the feast at Jerusalem; but it is evident that it contains accounts belonging to several journeys, undertaken at different periods.

As to the statements of the ancients concerning the date or time when the Gospel of St. Luke was written, we find in Irenæus, that Mark and Luke wrote after Matthew. According to Eusebius, Origen stated that Luke wrote after Matthew and Mark; but Clemens Alexandrinus, according to the same writer, asserted, on the authority of the 'tradition of the earlier elders,' that the Gospels containing the genealogies were written before the others. According to this view, Mark was written after Luke. It is however likely that this statement arose from a desire to explain why the genealogies were omitted by Mark and John.

From the circumstance that the book of Acts leaves St. Paul a captive, without relating the result of his captivity, most critics have, with considerable probability, inferred that Luke accompanied St Paul to Rome, that he employed his leisure while there in composing the Acts, and that he left off writing before the fate of Paul was decided. Now, since the Gospel of St. Luke was written before the Acts, it seems to follow that it was written a considerable time before the destruction of Jerusalem.

It is likely that Luke, during Paul's captivity at Cæsarea, employed his leisure in collecting the accounts contained in his Gospel in the localities where the events to which they relate happened. The most ancient testimonies in behalf of Luke's Gospel are those of Marcion, at the beginning of the second century, and of Irenæus, in the latter half of that century.

Besides the Gospel which bears his name, Luke wrote the Acts of the Apostles. This work contains the history of the foundation of the Christian church in two great sections: the first embracing the spread of Christianity among the Jews, chiefly by the instrumentality of Peter (ch. i.-xii.); and the second, its spread among the heathen, chiefly by the instrumentality of Paul (ch. xiii.-xxviii.).

That the accounts of Luke are authentic may be perceived more especially from a close examination of the inserted discourses and letters The characteristic marks of authenticity in the oration of the Roman lawyer Tertullus, in ch. xxiv., and in the official letters in ch. xxiii. 26, sq.; xv. 23, sq.; can scarcely be overlooked. The address of Paul to the elders of the Ephesian church is characteristically Pauline, and even so full of definite allusions and of similarity to the Epistle to the Ephesians, that it furnishes a confirmation of the authenticity of that letter.

As for the testimonies in behalf of the authenticity of the Acts, they are the same as for Luke's Gospel. Clemens Alexandrinus, Irenæus, and Tertullian, expressly mention the Acts, and Eusebius reckons them among the Homologoumena. However, the book of Acts was not read and quoted so often in the early church as other parts of Scripture.

LUNATICS. [DEMONIACS.]

LUZ, the ancient name of Bethel (Gen. xxviii. 19) [BETHEL]. The spot to which the name of Bethel was given appears, however, to have been at a little distance in the environs of Luz, and they are accordingly distinguished in Josh. xvi. 2, although the name of Bethel was eventually extended to that town. A small place of the same name, founded by an inhabitant of this Luz, is mentioned in Judg. i. 26.

LYCAO'NIA, a province of Asia Minor, having Cappadocia on the east, Galatia on the north, Phrygia on the west, and Isauria and Cilicia on the south. It extends in length about twenty geographical miles from east to west, and about thirteen in breadth. It was an undulating plain, involved among mountains, which were noted for the concourse of wild-asses. The soil was so strongly impregnated with salt that few of the brooks supplied drinkable water, so that good water was sold for money. But sheep throve on the pasturage, and were reared with great advantage. It was a Roman province when visited by Paul (Acts xiv. 6), and its chief towns were Iconium, Lystra, and Derbe, of which the first was the capital. 'The speech of Lycaonia' (Acts xiv 11) is supposed by some to have been the ancient Assyrian language, also spoken by the Cappadocians; but it is more usually conceived to have been a corrupt Greek, intermingled with many Syriac words.

LYC'IA, a province in the south-west of Asia Minor, having Pamphylia on the east, Phrygia on the north, Caria on the west, and the Mediterranean on the south. Great part of the country, however, consists of a peninsula projecting south into the Mediterranean. It is mountainous, and is watered by numerous small rivers which flow from the mountains. Its inhabitants were believed to be descendants of Cretans, who came thither under Sarpedon, brother of Minos. One of their kings was Bellerophon, celebrated in mythology. The Lycians were a warlike people, powerful on the sea, and attached to their independence, which they successfully maintained against Crœsus, king of Lydia, and were afterwards allowed by the Persians to retain their own kings as satraps. Lycia is named in 1 Macc. xv. 23, as one of the countries to which the Roman senate sent its missive in favour of the Jews. The victory of the Romans over Antiochus (B.C. 189) gave Lycia rank as a free state, which it retained till the time of Claudius, when it was made a province of the Roman empire. Lycia contained many towns, two of which are mentioned in the New Testament; Patara (Acts xxi. 1, 2); Myra (Acts xxvii. 5); and one, Phaselis, in the Apocrypha (1 Macc. xv. 23).

LYD'DA, a town within the limits of the tribe of Ephraim, nine miles east of Joppa, on the road between that port and Jerusalem. It bore in Hebrew the name of Lod, and appears to have been first built by the Benjamites, although it lay beyond the limits of their territory; and we find it again inhabited by Benjamites after the Exile (1 Chron. viii. 12; Ezra ii. 33; Neh. xi. 35). It is mentioned in the Apocrypha (1 Macc. xi. 34), as having been taken from Samaria and annexed to Judæa by Demetrius Nicator; and at a later date its inhabitants are named among those who were sold into slavery by Cassius when he inflicted the calamity of his presence upon Palestine after the death of Julius Cæsar. In the New Testament the place is only noticed, under the name of Lydda, as the scene of Peter's miracle in healing Æneas (Acts ix. 32, 35). Some years later the town was reduced to ashes by Cestius Gallus, in his march against Jerusalem; but it must soon have revived, for not long after we find it at the head of one of the toparchies of the later Judæa, and as such it surrendered to Vespasian. At that time it is described by Josephus as a village equal to a city; and the Rabbins have much to say of it as a seat of Jewish learning, of which it was the most eminent in Judæa after Jabneh and Bethar. In the general change of names which took place under the Roman dominion, Lydda became Diospolis, and under this name it occurs in coins of Severus and Caracalla, and is often mentioned by Eusebius and Jerome. It was early the seat of a bishopric, and is known to have continued such until at least A.D. 518. Lydda early became connected with the homage paid to the celebrated saint and martyr St. George, who is said to have been a native of this place, and who was not less renowned in the east than afterwards in the west. A church was here erected in honour of him by the Emperor Justinian. This church, which stood outside the town, had just been levelled to the ground by the Moslems when the Crusaders arrived at Lydda; but it was soon rebuilt by them, and they established a bishopric of Lydda and Ramleh. The church was destroyed by Saladin in 1191: and there is no evidence that it was ever rebuilt, although there was in later centuries an unfounded impression that the church, the ruins of which were then seen, and which still exist, had been built by our king Richard. From that time there has been little notice of Lydda by travellers. It now exists, under its ancient name of Lud, as a considerable village of small houses, with nothing to distinguish it from ordinary Moslem villages, save the ruins of the celebrated church of St. George, which are situated in the eastern part of the town. The building must have been very large. The walls of the eastern end are standing only in the parts near the altar, including the arch over the latter; but the western end remains more perfect, and has been built into a large mosque, the lofty minaret of which forms the landmark of Lud.

LYD'IA, a province in the west of Asia Minor, supposed to have derived its name from Lud, the fourth son of Shem (Gen. x. 22; see NATIONS, DISPERSION OF). It was bounded on the east by Greater Phrygia, on the north by Æolis or Mysia, on the west by Ionia and the Ægean Sea, and on the south it was separated from Caria by the Mæander. The country is for the most part level. Among the mountains, that of Tmolus was celebrated for its saffron and red wine. In the palmy days of Lydia its kings ruled from the shores of the Ægean to the river Halys; and Crœsus, who was its king in the time of Solon and of Cyrus, was reputed the richest monarch in the world. He was able to bring into the field an army of 420,000 foot and 60,000 horse against Cyrus, by whom, however, he was defeated, and his kingdom annexed to the Persian empire (Herod. i. 6). Lydia afterwards formed part of the kingdom of the Seleucidæ; and it is related in 1 Macc. viii. 3, that Antiochus the Great was compelled by the Romans to cede Lydia to king Eumenes. In the time of the travels of the Apostles it was a province of the Roman empire. Its chief towns were Sardis (the capital), Thyatira, and Philadelphia, all of which are mentioned in the New Testament, although the name of the province itself does not occur. The manners of the Lydians were corrupt even to a proverb.

LYD'IA, a woman of Thyatira, 'a seller of purple,' who dwelt in the city of Philippi in Macedonia (Acts xvi. 14, 15). Lydia was not by birth a Jewess, but a proselyte, as the phrase 'who worshipped God' imports. She was converted by the preaching of Paul; and after she and her household had been baptised, she pressed the use of her house so earnestly upon him and his associates, that they were constrained to accept the invitation. The Lydians were famous for the art of dyeing purple vests, and Lydia, as 'a seller of purple,' is supposed to have been a dealer in vests so dyed, rather than in the dye itself.

LYSA'NIAS, tetrarch of Abilene, when John commenced his ministry as the harbinger of Christ (Luke iii. 1). He is supposed to have been son or grandson of another Lysanias, known in history, who was put to death by Mark Antony, and part of his territories given to Cleopatra [ABILENE].

LYS'IAS, or CLAUDIUS LYSIAS, chiliarch and commandant of the Roman troops who kept guard at the temple of Jerusalem, by whom Paul was secured from the fury of the Jews, and sent under guard to the procurator Felix at Cæsarea (Acts xxi. 27; xxiii. 31).

LYS'TRA, a city of Lycaonia in Asia Minor, to which Paul and Barnabas fled from the danger which threatened them at Iconium (Acts xiv. 6). Here, Paul having miraculously cured a cripple, they were both adored as gods; but afterwards, at the instigation of the Jews, Paul was stoned and left for dead (Acts xiv. 8-21). Timothy was a native of Lystra (Acts xvi. 1). This city was south of Iconium, but its precise site is uncertain, as well as that of Derbe, which is mentioned along with it.

M.

MA'ACAH, or MAACATH, a city and region at the foot of Mount Hermon, not far from Geshur, a district of Syria (Josh. xiii. 13; 2 Sam. x. 6, 8; 1 Chron. xix 7). Hence the adjacent portion of Syria is called Aram-Maachah or Syria of Maachah (1 Chron. xix. 7). The Israelites seem to have considered this territory as included in their grant, but were never able to get possession of it (Josh. xiii. 13). In the time of David the small state had a king of its own, who contributed 1000 men to the grand alliance of the Syrian nations against the Jewish monarch (2 Sam. x. 6, 8). The lot of the half-tribe of Manasseh beyond the Jordan extended to this country, as had previously the dominion of Og, king of Bashan (Deut. iii. 14; Josh. xii. 5). Near, or within the ancient limits of Maacah, was the town called for that reason Abel beth-Maacah [ABEL].

MAACAH, or MAACHAH, is also the name of several persons in the Old Testament, male and female, who may be mentioned to distinguish them from one another, namely—

1. MAACAH, the father of Achish, king of Gath (1 Kings ii. 39).

2. MAACAH, the father of Hanan, one of David's worthies (1 Chron. xi. 43).

3. MAACAH, the father of Shephatiah, the military chief of the Simeonites in the time of David (1 Chron. xxvii. 16).

4. MAACAH, a person whose sex does not appear, one of the offspring of Nahor's concubine Reumah (Gen. xxii. 24).

5. MAACAH, a concubine of Caleb (1 Chron. ii. 48).

6. MAACAH, grand-daughter of Benjamin, who was married to Machir, son of Manasseh (1 Chron. vii. 16).

7. MAACAH. daughter of Talmai, king of Geshur, wife of David and mother of Absalom (2 Sam. iii. 3). In 1 Sam. xxvii. 8, we read of David's invading the land of the Geshurites, and the Jewish commentators allege that he then took the daughter of the king captive, and, in consequence of her great beauty, married her, after she had been made a proselyte according to the law in Deut. xxi. But this is a gross mistake, for the Geshur invaded by David was to the south of Judah, whereas the Geshur over which Talmai ruled was to the north, and was regarded as part of Syria (2 Sam. xv 8). The fact appears to be that David, having married the daughter of this king, contracted an alliance with him, in order to strengthen his interest against Ishbosheth in those parts.

8. MAACAH, daughter of Abishalom, wife

of Rehoboam, and mother of Abijam (1 Kings xv. 1). In verse 10 we read that Asa's 'mother's name was Maacah, the daughter of Abishalom.' It is evident that here 'mother' is used in a loose sense, and means 'grandmother,' which the Maacah named in verse 1 must have been to the Asa of verse 10. The Abishalom who was the father of this Maacah is called Absalom in 2 Chron. xi. 20, 21, and is generally supposed by the Jews to have been Absalom the son of David; which seems not improbable, seeing that Rehoboam's other two wives were of his father's family (2 Chron. xi. 18). But Josephus says that she was the daughter of Tamar, the daughter of Absalom, and consequently his granddaughter. This seems not unlikely [ABIJAH]. It would appear that Asa's own mother was dead before he began to reign; for Maacah bore the rank and state of queen-mother (resembling that of the Sultaness Valide among the Turks), the powers of which she so much abused to the encouragement of idolatry, that Asa commenced his reforms by 'removing her from being queen, because she had made an idol in a grove' (1 Kings xv. 13; 2 Chron. xv. 16).

MAC'CABEES. The etymology of this word is too uncertain to reward the inquiries made respecting it. As a family, the Maccabees commenced their career of patriotic and religious heroism during the persecution of Antiochus Epiphanes, about the year B C. 167. At this time the aged Mattathias, a descendant of the Asmonæans, and his five sons, inhabited the town of Modin, to which place Antiochus sent certain of his officers with instructions to erect an altar for heathen sacrifices, and to engage the inhabitants in the celebration of the most idolatrous and superstitious rites. The venerable Mattathias openly declared his resolution to oppose the orders of the tyrant, and one of the recreant Jews approaching the altar which had been set up, he rushed upon him, and slew him with his own hand. His part thus boldly taken, he called his sons and his friends around him, and immediately fled to the mountains, inviting all to follow him who had any zeal for God and the law. A small band of resolute and devoted men was thus formed, and the governor of the district saw reason to fear that a general insurrection would be the consequence of their proceeding. By a sudden attack directed against them on the Sabbath, when he knew the strictness of their principles would not allow them to take measures for their defence, he threw them into disorder, and slew about a thousand of their number, consisting of men, women, and children.

Warned by this event, and yielding to the necessity of their present condition, Mattathias and his sons determined that for the future they would defend themselves on the Sabbath in the same manner as on other days. The mountain-hold of the little band was now guarded more cautiously than before. Fresh adherents to the holy cause were continually flocking in; and in a few months the party found itself sufficiently strong to make attacks upon the towns and villages of the neighbourhood, throwing down the heathen altars, and punishing the reprobates who had taken part with the enemies of God.

By the death of Mattathias, the leadership of the party devolved upon his son Judas Macca-

bæus, whose worth and heroic courage pointed him out as most capable of carrying on the enterprise thus nobly begun. Judas lost no time in attacking the enemy. He made himself master of several towns, which he fortified and garrisoned. Apollonius, general of the army in Samaria, hastened to stop the progress of the insurgents. Judas met him on the way, joined battle with him, slew him and routed his army. The same success attended him in his encounter with Seron, general of the Syrians; and it now became evident to Antiochus that the Jewish nation would soon be delivered from his yoke, unless he proceeded against them with a more formidable force. While, therefore, he himself went into Persia to recruit his treasures, Lysias, whom he left as regent at home, sent an army into Judæa, composed of forty thousand foot and seven thousand cavalry. This powerful array was further increased by auxiliaries from the provinces, and by bands of Jews, who dreaded nothing more than the triumph of those virtuous men of their own nation, who were struggling to save it from reprobation. So unequal did the forces of Judas appear to an encounter with such an army, that in addressing his followers he urged those among them who had any especial reason to love the present world to retire at once; while to those who remained he pointed out the promises of God as the best support of their courage and fidelity. By a forced march he reached a portion of the enemy encamped at Emmaus, while utterly unprepared for his approach. Complete success attended this bold proceeding. The several parts of the hostile army were successively put to flight, a splendid booty was secured, and Judas gained a position which made even the most powerful of his opponents tremble. Another and more numerous army was sent against him the following year, but with no better success. At the head of ten thousand determined followers, Judas defeated the army of Lysias, consisting of sixty thousand. A way was thereby opened for his progress to Jerusalem, whither he immediately hastened, with the devout purpose of purifying the temple and restoring it to its former glory. The solemn religious rites having been performed which were necessary to the cleansing of the sacred edifice, the Festival of the Purification was instituted, and added to the number of the other national festivals of more ancient date.

Judas had full occupation for his courage and ability in repelling the incursions of those numerous foes who dreaded the restoration of order and religion. But every day added to his successes. Having overthrown the Syrian commanders sent against him, he occupied Samaria, made himself master of the strong city of Hebron, of Azotus, and other important places, taking signal vengeance on the people of Joppa and Jamnia, who had treacherously plotted the destruction of numerous faithful Jews.

Antiochus Epiphanes was succeeded by Antiochus Eupator. At first this prince acted towards the Jews with moderation and tolerance. But he soon afterwards invaded Judæa with a powerful army, and was only induced to make peace with Maccabæus by the fears which he entertained of a rival aspirant to the throne. His caution did not save him. He was put to death by his own uncle, Demetrius, who, obtaining the throne of Syria, made peace with Judas, but took possession of the citadel of Jerusalem, which was occupied by his general, Nicanor, and a body of troops. This state of things was not allowed to last long. Demetrius listened to the reports of Nicanor's enemies, and threatened to deprive him of his command unless he could disprove the accusation that he had entered into a league with Judas, and was betraying the interests of his sovereign. Nicanor immediately took measures to satisfy Demetrius, and Judas saw it necessary to escape from Jerusalem, and put himself in a posture of defence. A battle took place in which he defeated his enemy. Another was soon after fought at Beth-horon, where he was again victorious. Nicanor himself fell in this battle, and his head and right hand were sent among the spoils to Jerusalem. But the forces of Demetrius were still numerous. Judas had retired to Laish with about three thousand followers. He was there attacked by overwhelming numbers. Only eight hundred of his people remained faithful to him on this occasion. Resolved not to flee, he bravely encountered the enemy, and was speedily slain, regarding his life as a fitting sacrifice to the cause in which he was engaged.

Simon and Jonathan, the brothers of Judas, rallied around them the bravest of their companions, and took up a strong position in the neighbourhood of Tekoa. Jonathan proved himself a worthy successor of his heroic brother, and skilfully evaded the first attack of Bacchides, the Syrian general. For two years after this, the brothers were left in tranquillity, and they established themselves in a little fortress called Bethtasi, situated among the rocks near Jericho. The skill and resolution with which they pursued their measures rendered them formidable to the enemy; and the state of affairs in Syria some time after obliged Demetrius to make Jonathan the general of his forces in Judæa, and to invest him with the authority of governor of Jerusalem. To this he was compelled by the rivalry of Alexander Balas; but his policy was too late to secure the attachment of his new ally. Jonathan received offers from Alexander to support his interests among the Jews, and the high-priesthood was the proffered reward. The invitation was accepted; and Jonathan became the first of the Asmonæan line through which the high-priesthood was so long transmitted. Alexander Balas left nothing undone which might tend to secure the fidelity of Jonathan. He gave him a high rank among the princes of his kingdom, and adorned him with a purple robe. Jonathan continued to enjoy his prosperity till the year B.C. 143, when he fell a victim to the treachery of Trypho, who aspired to the Syrian throne. He was succeeded by his brother Simon, who confirmed the Jews in their temporary independence; and in the year B.C. 141 they passed a decree whereby the dignity of the high-priesthood and of prince of the Jews was rendered hereditary in the family of Simon. He fell a victim to the treachery of his son-in-law, Ptolemy, governor of Jericho; but was succeeded by his son, the celebrated John Hyrcanus, who possessed the supreme authority above thirty years, and at his death left it to be enjoyed by his son Aristobulus, who, soon after his accession to power, assumed the title of king. This dignity

continued to be enjoyed by descendants of the Asmonæan family till the year B.C. 34, when it ceased with the downfall of Antigonus, who conquered by Herod and the Romans, was put to death by the common executioner.

MACCABEES, BOOKS OF [APOCRYPHA]. The books of Maccabees are the titles of certain Jewish histories containing principally the details of the heroic exploits referred to in the preceding article.

There were in all four books (to which some add a fifth) known to the ancients, of which three are still read in the eastern, and two in the western church. Of these the *third* is the first in order of time. We shall, however, to avoid confusion, speak of them in the order in which they are commonly enumerated.

THE FIRST BOOK OF MACCABEES contains a lucid and authentic history of the undertakings of Antiochus Epiphanes against the Jews, from the year B.C. 175 to the death of Simon Maccabæus, B.C. 135. This history is confessedly of great value. Although its brevity, observes De Wette, renders it in some instances unsatisfactory, defective, and uncritical, and occasionally extravagant, it is upon the whole entitled to credit, chronologically accurate, and advantageously distinguished above all other historical productions of this period. It is the second book in order of time. There is little question that this book was written in Hebrew, although the original is now lost. The Greek version abounds in Hebraisms and errors of translation.

Of the author nothing is known; but he must have been a Palestinian Jew, who wrote some considerable time after the death of Simon Maccabæus, and even of Hyrcanus, and made use of several written, although chiefly of traditionary, sources of information. At the same time it is not impossible that the author was present at several of the events which he so graphically describes.

THE SECOND BOOK OF MACCABEES (the third in order of time) is a work of very inferior character to the first. It is an abridgment of a more ancient work, written by a Jew named Jason, who lived at Cyrene in Africa, comprising the principal transactions of the Jews which occurred during the reigns of Seleucus IV., Antiochus Epiphanes, and Antiochus Eupator. It partly goes over the same ground with the first book, but commences ten or twelve years earlier, and embraces in all a period of fifteen years. It does not appear that the author of either saw the other's work. The second book of Maccabees is divided into two unconnected parts. It commences with a letter from the citizens of Jerusalem and Judæa to the Greek Jews in Egypt, written B.C. 123 (which refers to a former letter written to the same, B.C. 143, acquainting them of their sufferings), and informs them that their worship was now restored, and that they were celebrating the Feast of Dedication. The second part (ii. 18) contains a still more ancient letter, written B.C. 159, to the priest Aristobulus, the tutor of King Ptolemy, recounting, besides some curious matter, the death of Antiochus Epiphanes. The third part contains the preface, in which the author states that he is about to epitomise the five books of Jason. The work commences with the attack of Heliodorus on the temple, and closes with the death of Nicanor, a period of fifteen years. The history supplies some blanks in the first book; but the letters prefixed to it contradict some of the facts recorded in the body of the work, and are consequently supposed to have been added by another hand. Neither are the letters themselves considered genuine, and they were probably written long after the death of Nicanor, and even of John Hyrcanus. This book gives a different account of the place and manner of the death of Antiochus Epiphanes from that contained in the first book.

The narrative, as De Wette observes, abounds in miraculous adventures, historical and chronological errors, extraordinary and arbitrary embellishments, affected descriptions, and moralising reflections. We are not aware when either Jason himself or his epitomiser lived. Jahn refers the age of the epitomiser to some time previous to the middle of the last century before the birth of Christ, and De Wette maintains that Jason must have written a considerable time after the year B C. 161.

Jerome observes that the phraseology of this book evinces a Greek original. The elegance and purity of the style have misled some persons into the supposition that its author was Josephus.

THE THIRD BOOK OF MACCABEES, still read in the Greek church, is, as has been already observed, the first in order of time. It contains an account of the persecution of the Egyptian Jews by Ptolemy Philopator, who is said to have proceeded to Jerusalem after his victory at Raphia over Antiochus the Great, B.C. 217, and after sacrificing in the temple, to have attempted to force his way into the Holy of Holies, when he was prostrated and rendered motionless by an invisible hand. Upon his return to Egypt, he revenged himself by shutting up the Jews in the Hippodrome, and exposing them to be crushed beneath the feet of elephants. This book contains an account of their deliverance by divine interposition. It is anterior in point of date to the Maccabæan period, and has received its designation from a general resemblance to the two first books in the heroic character of the actions which it describes. Calmet (*Commentary*) observes that this book is rejected as apocryphal in the Latin Church; not, however, as not containing a true history, but as not being inspired, as he considers the first two books to be. It is nevertheless regarded by De Wette as a tasteless fable, and notwithstanding the relation which it contains of an annual festival, considered by him as most probably destitute of any historical foundation. Dr. Milman (*Hist. of the Jews*) describes it as a 'romantic story.'

The author is unknown.

THE FOURTH BOOK OF MACCABEES, which is also found in the Alexandrian and Vatican manuscripts, is generally supposed to be the same with the *Supremacy of Reason*, attributed to Josephus, with which it for the most part accords. It consists of an inflated amplification of the history of the martyrdom of Eleazar, and of the seven brothers, whose torments and death, with that of their mother, form the subject of 2 Macc. ch. vi. vii.

Calmet has pointed out several contradictions between this and the second book, as well as the

books of Moses, together with some opinions derived from the Stoics, such as the equality of crimes; which, he supposes, together with its tedious descriptions, have consigned it to the rank of an Apocryphal book.

What has been called the FIFTH BOOK OF MACCABEES is now extant only in the Arabic and Syriac languages.

It is impossible to ascertain the author, who could scarcely have been Josephus, as he disagrees in many things with that historian.

The work consists of a history of Jewish affairs, commencing with the attempt on the treasury at Jerusalem by Heliodorus, and ending with the tragic fate of the last of the Asmonæan princes, and with the inhuman execution by Herod of his noble and virtuous wife Mariamne, and of his two sons. This history thus fills up the chasm to the birth of Christ.

Dr. Cotton has pointed out among the 'remarkable peculiarities' found in this book the phrases, 'Peace be unto thee,' and 'God be merciful to them,' showing that the practice of prayer for the dead was at this time prevalent. But the most remarkable passage in reference to this subject is 2 Macc. xii. 40-45, where Judas forwards to Jerusalem 2000, or according to the Syriac 3000, and according to the Vulgate 12,000 drachmas of silver, to make a sin-offering for the Jews slain in action, on whose persons were found things consecrated to idols, which they had sacrilegiously plundered in violation of the law of Moses (Deut. vii. 25, 26). The author of the book remarks that it was a holy and good thought to pray for the dead, which, he observes, would have been superfluous had there been no resurrection. Calmet observes that, according to the notions of the Jews and some of the Christian Fathers, the pains of hell for those who died in mortal sin (as appears to have been the case of these Jews) were alleviated by the prayers and alms of the living, if not entirely removed; and cites a passage from a very ancient Christian Liturgy to the same effect. This learned commentator supposes that the ancient and Catholic practice of prayer for the dead had its origin in this usage of the Jews, although he admits it to be a distinct thing from the doctrine of purgatory as held in the Roman Church.

The first two books of Maccabees have been at all times treated with a very high degree of respect in the Christian Church. Origen, professing to give a catalogue of the twenty-two canonical books, of which, however, he actually enumerates only twenty-one, adds, 'besides, there are the Maccabees.' This has given rise to the notion that he intended to include these books in the canon, while others have observed that he has omitted the minor prophets from his catalogue. In his preface to the Psalms he excludes the two books of Maccabees from the books of Holy Scripture, but in his *Princip.* (ii. 1), and in his *Comment ad Rom* ch. v., he speaks of them as inspired, and as of equal authority with the other books. St. Jerome says that the *Church* does not acknowledge them as canonical, although he elsewhere cites them as *Holy Scripture*. Bellarmine acknowledges that these, with the other deuterocanonical books, are *rejected* by Jerome, as they had not been then determined by any general council. The first councils which included them in the canonical Scriptures were those of Hippo and Carthage. They were received with the other Apocryphal books by the Council of Trent. Basnage, cited by Lardner (*Credibility*), thinks that the word ' Canonical ' may be supposed to be used here [by the councils of Hippo and Carthage] loosely, so as to comprehend not only those books which are admitted as a rule of faith, but those which are esteemed useful, and may be publicly read for the edification of the people, in contradistinction to such books as were entirely rejected. This is also the opinion of the Roman Catholic Professor Jahn, who expresses himself in nearly the same words. Dr. Lardner conceives that Augustine also, unless he would contradict himself, must be understood to have used the word in the same sense.

MACEDO'NIA, a country lying to the north of Greece Proper, having on the east Thrace and the Ægean Sea, on the west the Adriatic and Illyria, on the north Dardania and Mæsia, and on the south Thessaly and Epirus. The country is supposed to have been first peopled by Chittim or Kittim, a son of Javan (Gen. x. 4) [NATIONS, DISPERSION OF]; and in that case it is probable that the Macedonians are sometimes intended when the word Chittim occurs in the Old Testament. Macedonia was the original kingdom of Philip and Alexander, by means of whose victories the name of the Macedonians became celebrated throughout the East, and is often used for the Greeks in Asia generally. The rise of the great empire formed by Alexander is described by the prophet Daniel under the emblem of a goat with one horn (Dan. viii. 3-8). As the horn was a general symbol of power, and as the oneness of the horn implies merely the unity of that power, we are not prepared to go the lengths of some overzealous illustrators of Scripture, who argue that if a one-horned goat were not a recognised symbol of Macedonia we should not be entitled to conclude that Macedonia was intended. We hold that there could be no mistake in the matter, whatever may have been the usual symbol of Macedonia. It is, however, curious and interesting to know that Daniel did describe Macedonia under its usual symbol, as coins still exist in which that country is represented under the figure of a one-horned goat. There has been much discussion on this subject—more curious than valuable—but the kernel of it lies in this fact.

When subdued by the Romans under Paulus Æmilius (B.C. 168), Macedonia was divided into four provinces; but afterwards (B.C. 142) the whole of Greece was divided into two great provinces, Macedonia and Achaia [GREECE, ACHAIA]. Macedonia therefore constituted a Roman province, governed by a proconsul, in the time of Christ and his Apostles.

The Apostle Paul being summoned in a vision, while at Troas, to preach the Gospel in Macedonia, proceeded thither, and founded the churches of Thessalonica and Philippi (Acts xvi. 9), A.D. 55. This occasions repeated mention of the name, either alone (Acts xviii. 5; xix. 21; Rom. xv. 26; 2 Cor. i. 16; xi. 9; Phil. iv. 15), or along with Achaia (2 Cor. ix. 2; 1 Thess. i. 8). The principal cities of Macedonia were Amphipolis, Thessalonica, and Pella (Liv. xlv. 29); the towns of the province named in the New Testament, and noticed in the present work, are Amphipolis, Thessalonica, Neapolis, Apollonia, and Berœa.

MACHPE'LAH (*twofold, double*), the name of the plot of ground containing the cave which Abraham bought of Ephron the Hittite for a family sepulchre (Gen. xxiii. 9, 17) [HEBRON].

MAD'AI, third son of Japhet (Gen. x 2), from whom the Medes, &c., are supposed to have descended (GOG; NATIONS, DISPERSION OF].

MADMAN'NAH, a city of Simeon (Josh. xv. 31), very far south towards Gaza (1 Chron. ii. 49), which in the first distribution of lands had been assigned to Judah. Eusebius and Jerome identify it with a town of their time, called Menois, near the city of Gaza.

MADME'NAH, a town only named in Isa. x. 31, where it is manifestly placed between Nob and Gibeah. It is generally confounded with the preceding, which is much too far southward to suit the context.

MAG'DALA, a town mentioned in Matt. xv. 39, and the probable birthplace of Mary Magdalene, *i. e.* Mary of Magdala. It must have taken its name from *a tower* or *castle*, as the name signifies. It was situated on the lake Gennesareth, but it has usually been placed on the *east* side of the lake, although a careful consideration of the route of Christ before he came to, and after he left, Magdala, would show that it must have been on its *western* shore. This is confirmed by the Jerusalem Talmud (compiled at Tiberias), which several times speaks of Magdala as being adjacent to Tiberias and Hamath, or the hot-springs. It was a seat of Jewish learning after the destruction of Jerusalem, and the Rabbins of Magdala are often mentioned in the Talmud. A small Moslem village, bearing the name of Mejdel, is now found on the shore of the lake about three miles north by west of Tiberias; and although there are no ancient ruins, the name and situation are very strongly in favour of the conclusion that it represents the Magdala of Scripture. This was probably also the Migdal-el, in the tribe of Naphtali, mentioned in Josh. xix. 38.

MAGI. The Magi were originally one of the six tribes into which the nation of the Medes was divided, who, like the Levites under the Mosaic institutions, were intrusted with the care of religion: an office which was held in the highest honour, gave the greatest influence, and which they probably acquired for themselves only after a long time, as well as many worthy efforts to serve their country, and when they had proved themselves superior to the rest of their brethren. As among other ancient nations, as the Egyptians, and Hebrews, for instance, so among the Medes, the priestly caste had not only religion, but the arts and all the higher culture, in their charge. Their name points immediately to their sacerdotal character (from *Mag* or *Mog*, which denotes ' priest '), either because religion was the chief object of their attention, or more probably because, at the first, religion and art were so allied as to be scarcely more than different expressions of the same idea.

Little in detail is known of the Magi during the independent existence of the Median government; they appear in their greatest glory after the Medes were united with the Persians. This doubtless is owing to the general imperfection of the historical materials which relate to the earlier periods. So great, however, was the influence which the Magi attained under the united empire, that the Medes were not ill compensated for their loss of national independence. Under the Medo-Persian sway the Magi formed a sacred caste or college, which was very famous in the ancient world for the practice of divination, astrology and magic. According to Strabo the Magi practised different sorts of divination—1. by evoking the dead; 2. by cups or dishes (Joseph's divining cup, Gen. xliv. 5); 3. by means of water. By the employment of these means the Magi affected to disclose the future, to influence the present, and to call the past to their aid. Even the visions of the night they were accustomed to interpret, not empirically, but according to such established and systematic rules as a learned priesthood might be expected to employ. The success, however, of their efforts over the invisible world, as well as the holy office which they exercised, demanded in themselves peculiar cleanliness of body, a due regard to which and to the general principles of their caste would naturally be followed by professional prosperity, which in its turn conspired with prevailing superstition to give the Magi great social consideration, and make them of high importance before kings and princes—an influence which they appear to have sometimes abused, when, descending from the peculiar duties of their high office, they took part in the strife and competitions of politics, and found themselves sufficiently powerful even to overturn thrones.

Abuses bring reform; and the Magian religion, which had lost much of its original character, and been debased by some of the lowest elements of earthly passions, loudly called for a renovation, when Zoroaster appeared to bring about the needful change. As to the time of his appearance, and in general the particulars of his history, differences of opinion prevail, after all the critical labour that has been expended on the subject. Winer says he lived in the second half of the seventh century before Christ. He was not the founder of a new system, but the renovator of an old and corrupt one, being, as he himself intimates, the restorer of the word which Ormuzd had formerly revealed, but which the influence of Dews had degraded into a false and deceptive magic. To destroy this, and restore the pure law of Ormuzd, was Zoroaster's mission. After much and long-continued opposition on the part of the adherents and defenders of existing corruptions, he succeeded in his virtuous purposes, and caused his system eventually to prevail. The Magi, as a caste, did not escape from his reforming hand. He appears to have remodelled their institute, dividing it into three great classes:—1. learners; 2. masters; 3. perfect scholars. The Magi alone he allowed to perform the religious rites; they possessed the forms of prayer and worship; they knew the ceremonies which availed to conciliate Ormuzd, and were obligatory in the public offerings. They accordingly became the sole medium of communication between the Deity and his creatures. and through them alone Ormuzd made his will known; none but they could see into the future, and they disclosed their knowledge to those only who were so fortunate as to conciliate their good will. Hence the power which the

Magian priesthood possessed. **The general belief** in the trustworthiness of their predictions, especially when founded on astrological calculations, the all but universal custom of consulting the will of the divinity before entering on any important undertaking, and the blind faith which was reposed in all that the Magi did, reported, or commanded, combined to create for that sacerdotal caste a power, both in public and in private concerns, which has probably never been exceeded. Neither the functions nor the influence of this sacred caste were reserved for peculiar, rare, and extraordinary occasions, but ran through the web of human life. At the break of day they had to chant the divine hymns. This office being performed, then came the daily sacrifice to be offered, not indiscriminately, but to the divinities whose day in each case it was—an office therefore which none but the initiated could fulfil. As an illustration of the high estimation in which the Magi were held, it may be mentioned that it was considered a necessary part of a princely education to have been instructed in the peculiar learning of their sacred order, which was an honour conceded to no other but royal personages, except in very rare and very peculiar instances. This Magian learning embraced everything which regarded the higher culture of the nation, being known in history under the designation of the law of the Medes and Persians. It comprised the knowledge of all the sacred rites, customs, usages, and observances, which related not merely to the worship of the gods, but to the whole private life of every worshipper of Ormuzd —the duties which, as such, he had to observe, and the punishments which followed the neglect of these obligations; whence may be learnt how necessary the act of the priest on all occasions was. Under the veil of religion the priest had bound himself up with the entire of public and domestic life. The judicial office, too, appears to have been, in the time of Cambyses, in the hands of the Magi, for from them was chosen the college or bench of royal judges, which makes its appearance in the history of that monarch. Men who held these offices, possessed this learning, and exerted this influence with the people, may have proved a check to Oriental despotism, no less powerful than constitutional, though they were sometimes unable to guarantee their own lives against the wrath of the monarch.

If we turn to the books of Scripture we find the import of what has been said confirmed, especially in the book of Daniel, where the great influence of the Magi is well illustrated.

The Magi were not confined to the Medes and Persians. Since they are mentioned by Herodotus as one of the original tribes of the Medes, they may have been primitively a Median priesthood. If so they extended themselves into other lands. Possibly Magi may have been at first not the name of a particular tribe or priestly caste, but a general designation for priests or learned men; as Pharaoh denoted not an individual, but generally king or ruler. However this may be, the Chaldæans also had an organized order of Magi, a caste of sacerdotal scholars, which bore the name of ' wise men ' (Jer. l. 35); ' the wise men of Babylon' (Dan. ii. 12), among whom Daniel is classed (ii. 18, 24). Among the Greeks and Romans they were known under the name of

Chaldæans, and also of Magi. They lived scattered over the land in different places (Dan. ii. 14), and had possessions of their own The temple of Belus was employed by them for astronomical observations, but their astronomy was connected with the worship of the heavenly bodies practised by the Babylonians, and was specially directed to vain attempts to foretell the future, predict the fate of individuals or of communities, and sway the present, in alliance with augury, incantation, and magic (Isa. xlvii. 9, 13; Dan. ii.)

It is easy to understand how the lofty science (so called) of these Magi—lofty while its scholars surpassed the rest of the world in knowledge, and were the associates, the advisers, the friends, and the monitors of great and flourishing monarchs, of indeed successively the rulers of the world—might, could indeed hardly fail, as resting on no basis of fact or reality, in process of time, to sink into its own native insignificance, and become either a mere bugbear to frighten the ignorant, or an instrument to aid the fraudulent: thus hastening on to the contempt into which all falsities are sure sooner or later to fall. The decline was indeed gradual; ages passed ere it was completed; but as soon as it ceased to have the support afforded by the mighty and splendid thrones of Asia, it began to lose its authority, which the progress of knowledge and the advent of Christ prevented it from ever regaining The estimation, however, in which Simon Magus was evidently held, as recorded in the Acts ('some great one,' &c.), gives reason to think that Magianism still retained a large share of its influence at the commencement of our era. It seems, indeed, to have held a sort of middle position, half way between its ancient splendour and its coming degradation: whence we may understand the propriety of the visit paid by the Magi to the new-born King of the Jews (Matt. ii., 'star in the East'). For if the system had been then sunk so low as to correspond in any degree with our conception of these pretended arts, it is difficult to assign, at least to the unbeliever, a sufficient reason why the visit was made, or at any rate why it was recorded; but its credibility is materially furthered if the circumstances of the case are such as to allow us to regard that visit as a homage paid by the representatives of the highest existing influences to the rising star of a new day, in the fuller light of which they were speedily to vanish.

MAGICIANS, the title which in our version is applied to the 'wise men' of Egypt (Gen. xli. 8, 22, Exod. vii. 11; viii. 7, 18, 19; ix. 11), and of Babylon (Dan. i. 20; ii. 2) The Hebrew word properly denotes 'wise men,' as they called themselves and were called by others; but, as we should call them, 'men eminent in learning and science,' their exclusive possession of which in their several countries enabled them occasionally to produce effects which were accounted supernatural by the people.

MA GOG, son of Japhet (Gen. x. 2). In Ezekiel (xxxviii. 2; xxxix. 6) it occurs as the name of a nation, coupled with Gog, and is supposed to represent certain Scythian or Tartar tribes descended from the son of Japhet [NATIONS, DISPERSION OF]

MAHALATH, the title of Psalms liii. and lxxxviii. [PSALMS.]

MAHANA'IM (*two hosts*), a place beyond the Jordan, north of the river Jabbok, which derived its name from Jacob's having been there met by the angels on his return from Padan-aram (Gen. xxxii. 2). The name was eventually extended to the town which then existed, or which afterwards arose in the neighbourhood. This town was in the territory of the tribe of Gad (Josh. xiii. 26, 30), and was a city of the Levites (Josh. xxi. 39). It was in this city that Ish bosheth, the son of Saul, reigned (2 Sam. ii. 8), probably because he found the influence of David's name less strong on the east than on the west of the Jordan. The choice, at least, seems to show that Mahanaim was then an important and strong place. Hence, many years after, David himself repaired to Mahanaim when he sought refuge beyond the Jordan from his son Absalom (2 Sam. xvii. 24, 27; 1 Kings ii. 8) We only read of Mahanaim again as the station of one of the twelve officers who had charge, in monthly rotation, of raising the provisions for the royal establishments under Solomon (1 Kings iv. 14). The site has not yet been identified.

MAHER-SHALAL-HASH-BAZ, words prognostic of the sudden attack of the Assyrian army ('he hasteth to the spoil'), which the prophet Isaiah was first commanded to write in large characters upon a tablet, and afterwards to give as a symbolical name to a son that was to be born to him (Isa. viii. 1, 3). It is, as Dr. Henderson remarks, the longest of any of the Scripture names, but has its parallels in this respect in other languages, especially in our own during the time of the Commonwealth.

MAH'LON, one of the two sons of Elimelech and Naomi, and first husband of Ruth the Moabitess (Ruth i. 2, sq.). [RUTH.]

MAKKE'DAH, a royal city of the ancient Canaanites (Josh. xii. 16), in the neighbourhood of which was the cave in which the five kings who confederated against Israel took refuge after their defeat (Josh. x. 10-29). It afterwards belonged to Judah (Josh. xv. 41). Makkedah is placed by Eusebius and Jerome 8 Roman miles to the east of Eleutheropolis.

MAL'ACHI, the last of the minor prophets, and consequently the latest writer in the canon of the Old Testament. Nothing is known of his person or history. It appears that he lived after Zechariah, since in his time the second temple was already built (ch. iii. 10); and it is probable that he was contemporary with Nehemiah (comp. ch. ii. 11, with Neh. xiii. 23-27, and ch. iii. 8, with Neh. xiii. 10).

The name Malachi means, as some understand it, *my angel*; but it seems more correct to regard it as a contracted form of *angel of Jehovah*. As the word translated 'angel' means also a 'messenger,' angels being, in fact, the messengers of God; and as the prophets are often styled angels or messengers of Jehovah, it is supposed that 'Malachi' is merely a general title descriptive of this character, and not a proper name. It has very generally been supposed that this prophet is the same with Ezra, but the weight of authority is decidedly in favour of his separate existence.

Although it is well agreed that Malachi was the last of the prophets, the date of his prophecy has been variously determined. Usher makes him contemporary with Nehemiah, in B.C. 416;

and the general opinion that this prophet was contemporary with, or immediately followed, Nehemiah, makes most of the proposed alternatives range within a few years of that date. He censures the same offences which excited the indignation of Nehemiah, and which that governor had not been able entirely to reform. Speaking of God's greater kindness to the Israelites than to the Edomites, he begins with declaiming against the priests for their profane and mercenary conduct, and against the people for their multiplied divorces and intermarriages with idolatrous nation; he threatens them with punishment and rejection, declaring that God would 'make his name great among the Gentiles' (ch. i. 11), for that he was wearied with the impiety of Israel (ch. i. ii). From this the prophet takes occasion solemnly to proclaim that the Lord whom they sought should suddenly come to his temple, preceded by that messenger who, like a harbinger, should prepare his way, that the Lord when he should appear would purify the sons of Levi from their unrighteousness, and refine them as metal from the dross (ch. iii. 1-3); that then 'the offering of Judah,' the spiritual sacrifice of the heart, 'should be pleasant to the Lord,' as was that of the patriarchs and their uncorrupted ancestors (ch. iii. 4); and that the Lord would quickly exterminate the corruptions and adulteries which prevailed. The prophet then proceeds with an earnest exhortation to repentance; promising high rewards and remembrance to the righteous in that last day when the Lord shall make up his peculiar treasures, and finally establish a distinction of doom and condition between the righteous and the wicked (ch. iii. 16-18). Malachi then concludes with an impressive assurance of approaching salvation to those who feared God's name from that 'sun of righteousness,' who should arise with healing in his wings, and render them triumphant; enjoining in the solemn close of his exhortation, when uttering as it were the last admonition of the Jewish prophets, an observance of the law of Moses, till the advent of Elijah the prophet (ch. iv. 5, or John the Baptist, who came in the spirit and power of Elias, Mark xi. 12; Luke i. 17), who before the coming of that 'great and dreadful day of the Lord, should turn the hearts of the fathers to the children, and the heart of the children to their fathers' (ch. iv.). Thus Malachi sealed up the volume of prophecy with the description of that personage at whose appearance the evangelists begin their gospel history.

The claim of the book of Malachi to its place in the canon of the Old Testament has never been disputed; and its authority is established by the references to it in the New Testament (Matt. xi. 10; xvii. 12; Mark i. 2; ix. 11, 12; Luke i. 17; Rom. ix. 13).

The manner of Malachi offers few, if any, distinguishing characteristics. The style, rhythm, and imagery of his writings are substantially those of the old prophets, but they possess no remarkable vigour or beauty. This is accounted for by his living during that decline of Hebrew poetry, which we trace more or less in all the sacred writings posterior to the Captivity.

MAL'CHUS, the servant of the high-priest Caiaphas, whose right ear was cut off by Peter in the garden of Gethsemane (John xviii. 10).

MALLOWS (Job xxx. 4). The proper meaning of the word (*malluach*), which is thus rendered in the Authorized Version, has given rise to considerable discussion. Mallows are still used as food in India, as they formerly were in Europe, and probably in Syria. 'We saw,' says Biddulph, 'many poor people collecting *mallows* and three-leaved grass, and asked them what they did with it; and they answered, that it was all their food, and that they boiled it, and did eat it.' Lady Calcott is of opinion that the plant mentioned by the patriarch is Jews' mallow, which still continues to be eaten in Egypt and Arabia, as well as in Palestine.

The learned Bochart, however, contends that the word *malluach* denotes a saltish plant, which is supposed to be the *Atriplex Halimus* of botanists, or tall shrubby *Orache*. There is no doubt that species of *Orache* were used as articles of diet in ancient times, and probably still are so in the countries where they are indigenous, but there are many other plants, similar in nature, that is, soft and succulent, and usually very saline, which, like the species of *Atriplex*, belong to the same natural family of *Chenopodeæ*, and which from their saline nature have received their respective names. Some of these are shrubby, but most of them are herbaceous, and extremely common in all the dry, desert, and saline soils which extend from the south of Europe to the north of India. Most of them are saline and bitter, but some are milder in taste and mucilaginous, and are therefore employed as articles of diet, as spinach is in Europe. *Salsola indica*, for instance, which is common on the coasts of the Peninsula of India, Dr. Roxburgh states, saved the lives of many thousands of the poor natives of India during the famine of 1791-2-3; for while the plant lasted, most of the poorer classes who lived near the sea had little else to eat; and indeed its green leaves ordinarily form an essential article of the food of those natives who inhabit the maritime districts.

MAM'MON, a Chaldee word signifying 'wealth' or 'riches,' and bearing that sense in Luke xvi. 9, 11; but also used by our Saviour (Matt. vi. 24; Luke xvi. 13) as a personification of the god of riches: 'Ye cannot serve God and Mammon.'

MAM'RE, the name of an Amoritish chief who, with his brothers Aner and Eshcol, was in alliance with Abraham (Gen. xiv. 13, 24). Hence, in the Authorized Version, 'the oaks of Mamre,' 'plain of Mamre' (Gen. xiii. 18; xviii. 1), or simply 'Mamre' (xxiii. 17, 19; xxxv. 27), a grove in the neighbourhood of Hebron.

MAN. The derivation of the word is probably from *dam*, *likeness*, because man was made *in the likeness of God*. Others have, however, sought to derive it from a term signifying to be 'red' or 'red-haired.' Adam is 1. the proper name of the first man, though Gesenius thinks that when so applied it has the force rather of an appellative, and that, accordingly, in a translation, it would be better to render it *the man*. It seems, however, to be used by St. Luke as a proper name in the genealogy (iii. 38); by St. Paul (Rom. v. 14; 1 Tim. ii. 13, 14); and by Jude (14). St. Paul's use of it in 1 Cor. xv. 45 is remarkably clear. This derivation is as old as Josephus, who says that 'the first man was called Adam, because he was formed from the red earth,' and adds, ' for the true virgin earth is of this colour' (*Antiq.* i. 1, § 2). But is this true? and when man is turned again to his earth, is *that* red? 2. It is the generic name of the human race as originally created, and afterwards, like the English word man, person, whether man or woman (Gen. i. 26, 27; v. 2; viii. 21; Deut. viii. 3; Matt. v. 13, 16; 1 Cor. vii. 7), and even without regard to age (John xvi. 21). It is applied to women only, 'the *human* persons of women' (Num. xxxi. 35). 3. It denotes man in opposition to woman (Gen. iii. 12; Matt. xix. 10), though, more properly, the husband in opposition to the wife (comp. 1 Cor. vii. 1). 4. It is used, though very rarely, for those who maintain the dignity of human nature, a *man*, as we say, meaning one that deserves the name: 'One man in a thousand have I found, but a woman,' &c. (Eccles. vii. 28). Perhaps the word here glances at the original uprightness of man. 5. It is frequently used to denote the more degenerate and wicked portion of mankind: an instance of which occurs very early, 'The sons, or worshippers, of God married the daughters of men, or the irreligious' (Gen. vi. 2). 6. The word is used to denote other men, in opposition to those already named, as, 'both man Israel and other men' (Jer. xxxii. 20), *i. e.* the Egyptians. 'Like other men' (Ps. lxxiii. 5), *i. e.* common men, in opposition to better men (Ps. lxxxii. 7); men of inferior rank, as opposed to men of higher rank (see Heb., Is. ii. 9; v. 15; Ps. xlix. 3; lxii. 10; Prov. viii. 4). The phrase 'son of man,' in the Old Testament, denotes man as frail and unworthy (Num. xxiii. 19; Job xxv. 6; Ezek. ii. 1, 3); as applied to the prophet, so often, it has the force of 'oh mortal!' There are three other Hebrew words thus translated in our version, and which in the original are used with much precision: one denoting a man as distinguished from a woman; another, ' mortals,' as transient, perishable, liable to sickness; and a third, man, in regard to the superior powers and faculties with which he is endowed above all earthly creatures.

MAN'AEN, a Christian teacher at Antioch, who had been foster-brother of Herod Antipas (Acts xiii. 1). He is supposed to have been one of the seventy disciples, but this is uncertain, as no particulars of his life are known.

MANAS'SEH, TRIBE OF. When the tribe of Manasseh quitted Egypt, it numbered 32,200 adult males (Num. i. 34, 35), being 8300 less than the tribe of Ephraim, the younger son of Joseph. This was the lowest number of adult males in any tribe at that period; but if we add the two together, the tribe of Joseph, composed of these two tribes, reached to 72,700, which was more than any other tribe contained, except Judah. During the sojourn in the wilderness, the tribe of Manasseh rose to 52,700 (Num. xxvi. 34), being an increase of 20,500. This gave it rank in point of population as the sixth of the tribes, Judah, Issachar, Zebulon, Dan, and Asher only being more numerous. In the same period Ephraim had declined to nearly the same position which Manasseh had previously occupied, its numbers being reduced to 32,500. Yet the prophecy of Jacob was fulfilled, and, when settled in Canaan, Ephraim became superior in wealth, power and population, not only to Manasseh, but to all the tribes except Judah. One circumstance

tending to weaken Manasseh may have been the division which took place in it on entering Palestine. The pastoral half of the tribe was allowed to establish itself with Reuben and Gad, on the east of the Jordan, where it occupied the northernmost portion, consisting of Argob and Bashan, from the Jabbok to Mount Hermon (Num. xxxii. 39; xxxiv. 14; Deut. iii. 3; Josh xii. 6; xiii. 7; 1 Chron. vi. 23), while the other half was provided for with the rest of the tribes in Canaan proper, west of the Jordan, where it had a fine tract of country extending from that river to the Mediterranean, with the kindred tribe of Ephraim on the south, and Issachar on the north (Josh. xvi. 9; xvii. 7-11). The half-tribe west of the river was not, however, for some time able to expel the former inhabitants of the territory, so as to obtain the exclusive possession of it (Josh. xvii. 12; Judg. i. 27). The tribe of Manasseh makes no figure in the history of the Hebrews.

1. MANASSEH (*who makes forget*, see Gen. xli. 51), the elder of the two sons of Joseph, born in Egypt (Gen. xli. 51; xlvi. 20), whom Jacob adopted as his own (xlviii. 1)—by which act each became the head of a tribe in Israel. The act of adoption was however accompanied by a clear intimation from Jacob, that the descendants of Manasseh, although the elder, would be far less numerous and powerful than those of the younger Ephraim. The result corresponded remarkably with this intimation [EPHRAIM].

2. MANASSEH, fourteenth king of Judah, son and successor of Hezekiah, who began to reign in B.C. 699, at the early age of twelve years, and reigned fifty-five years. It appears that the secret enemies of the vigorous reforms of Hezekiah re-appeared, and managed to gain much influence at court during the youth of Manasseh; and he was prevailed upon to re-establish all the idolatries and abominations which it had taken his excellent father so much pains to subvert. This bent having been unhappily given to the mind of one old enough to listen to evil counsels, but too young to see their danger, the king followed it with all the reckless ardour of youth, and without any of the prudent reservations which older sovereigns, more discreet in evincing the same inclinations, had maintained. Idolatry in its worst forms, and all the abominations connected with its observances, were practised without stint and without shame, not only in the face of the temple, but in its very courts, where altars to the heavenly bodies were set up, and rites of idolatrous worship performed. Under this altered state of things, the Judahites, with the sanction of the king's example, rushed into all the more odious observances of Syrian idolatry, with all the ardour which usually attends the outbreak of a restrained propensity, till they became far 'worse than the heathen, whom the Lord destroyed before the children of Israel.' In vain did the prophets raise their voice against these iniquities, and threaten Manasseh and his kingdom with awful tokens of Divine indignation. Instead of profiting by these warnings, the king vented his rage against those by whom they were uttered, and in this, and other ways, filled Jerusalem with innocent blood beyond any king who reigned before him (1 Kings xxi. 1-16; 2 Chron. xxxiii. 1-10).

At length the wrath of God burst over the guilty king and nation. At this time there was constant war between Assyria and Egypt, and it would seem that Manasseh adhered to the policy of his father in making common cause with the latter power. This or some other cause not stated by the sacred historian, brought into Judæa an Assyrian army, under the generals of Esarhaddon, which carried all before it. The miserable king attempted flight, but was discovered in a thorn-break in which he had hidden himself, was laden with chains, and sent away as a captive to Babylon, which was then subject to the Assyrians, where he was cast into prison (B.C. 677). Here, at last, Manasseh had ample opportunity and leisure for cool reflection; and the hard lessons of adversity were not lost upon him. He saw and deplored the evils of his reign, he became as a new man, he humbly besought pardon from God, and implored that he might be enabled to evince the sincerity of his contrition, by being restored to a position for undoing all that it had been the business of his life to effect. His prayer was heard. His captivity is supposed to have lasted a year, and he was then restored to his kingdom under certain obligations of tribute and allegiance to the king of Assyria, which, although not expressed in the account of this transaction, are alluded to in the history of his successors (2 Chron. xxxiii. 11-13).

On his return to Jerusalem, Manasseh exerted himself to the utmost in correcting the errors of his early reign, and in establishing the worship of Jehovah in its former purity and splendour. The good conduct of his latter reign was rewarded with such prosperity as enabled him to do much for the improvement and strengthening of his capital and kingdom. He thoroughly repaired the old walls of Jerusalem, and added a new wall on the side towards Gihon; he surrounded and fortified by a separate wall the hill or ridge on the east of Zion, which bore the name of Ophel, and he strengthened, garrisoned, and provisioned 'the fenced cities of Judah' (2 Chron. xxxiii. 13-17). He died in peace (B.C. 664), at the age of sixty-eight, after having reigned longer than any other king of Judah, and was buried in a sepulchre which he had prepared for himself in his own garden (xxxiii. 20).

MANAS'SES, PRAYER OF [APOCRYPHA]. This pseudepigraphal work has come down to us in the MSS. of the Latin Vulgate. and is found in the early printed editions of that version. Du Pin asserts that the Latin fathers have often cited this prayer; but the earliest reference to it which we know of is in the *Apostolical Constitutions* attributed to Clemens Romanus, but which are generally believed to be a work of the fourth century. In this work the prayer is cited as if it were an integral portion of the book of Chronicles, together with some traditionary accounts of the nature of his imprisonment in shackles of iron, and of his miraculous release: which are also alluded to in the Targum on Chronicles. It is entitled 'The Prayer of Manasses, king of Judah, when he was holden captive in Babylon,' and had doubtless its origin from 2 Chron. xxxiii. 12, 13. This prayer, however, not being found in the Hebrew, and not being cited by the more eminent fathers, nor contained in any of the catalogues of ancient councils, has not been received in the church as genuine or canonical. It is classed in the Sixth Article of the Church of England, among the 'other books read by the church for example of life and instruction of manners;' but the Church of Rome classes it with 3rd and 4th Esdras, removing it to the end of the Bible, and rejecting it from the deutero-canonical, as well as from the proto-canonical books.

The prayer of Manasses abounds in pious sentiments. Dr. Horne describes it as not unworthy of the occasion on which it is pretended to have been composed. Du Pin observes that, though not very eloquent, it is full of good thoughts.

MANDRAKE. This word only occurs in two places of Scripture; first in Genesis xxx. 14-16; and secondly, in Canticles vii. 13. From the notices given in these passages of their qualities it is evident that mandrakes were collected in the fields, that they were fit for gathering in the wheat harvest in Mesopotamia, where the first occurrence took place; that they were found in Palestine; that they or the plants which yielded them diffused a peculiar odour, and that they were supposed to be possessed of aphrodisiac powers, or of assisting in producing conception.

The plant referred to is probably *mandragora*.

238. [Atropa Mandragora]

'At the village of St. John in the mountains,' says Mariti, 'about six miles south-west from Jerusalem, this plant is found at present, as well as in Tuscany. It grows low, like lettuce, to which its leaves have a strong resemblance, except that they have a dark green colour. The flowers are purple, and the root is for the most part forked. The fruit, when ripe in the beginning of May, is of the size and colour of a small apple, exceedingly ruddy, and of a most agree-

able odour; our guide thought us fools for suspecting it to be unwholesome.' Maundrell was
informed by the chief priest of the Samaritans
that it was still noted for its genial virtue. Hasselquist also seems inclined to consider this the
plant referred to, for, when at Nazareth, he says,
' what I found most remarkable in their villages
was the great quantity of mandrakes that grew
in a vale below it. The fruit was now (May 16)
ripe. From the season in which this mandrake
blossoms and ripens its fruit, one might form
a conjecture that it is Rachel's *dudaim* (mandrakes). These were brought her in the wheat
harvest, which in Galilee is in the month of May,
about this time, and the mandrake was now in
fruit.'

MANNA, or MAN. The name given to the
miraculous food upon which the Israelites were
fed for forty years, during their wanderings in
the desert. The same name has in later ages
been applied to some natural productions, chiefly
found in warm dry countries, but which have
little or no resemblance to the original manna.
This is first mentioned in Exod. xvi. It is there
described as being first produced after the eighth
encampment in the desert of Sin, as white like
hoar frost (or of the colour of *bdellium*, Num. xi.
7), round, and of the bigness of coriander seed
(*gad*). It fell with the dew every morning, and
when the dew was exhaled by the heat of the
sun, the manna appeared alone, lying upon the
ground or the rocks round the encampment of the
Israelites. 'When the children of Israel saw it,
they said one to another, *What is it?* for they
knew not what it was' (Exod xvi. 15). In the
Authorized, and some other versions, this passage
is inaccurately translated—which indeed is apparent from the two parts of the sentence contradicting each other. Josephus (*Antiq.* iii. 1. § 10),
as quoted by Dr. Harris, says: ' The Hebrews
call this food *manna*, for the particle *man* in our
language is the asking of a question, *What is
this?* (*man-hu*). Moses answered this question
by telling them, ' This is the bread which the
Lord hath given you to eat.' We are further
informed that the manna fell every day, except
on the Sabbath. Every sixth day, that is on Friday, there fell a double quantity of it. Every
man was directed to gather an omer (about three
English quarts) for each member of his family:
and the whole seems afterwards to have been
measured out at the rate of an omer to each
person: ' He who gathered much had nothing
over, and he who gathered little had no lack.'
That which remained ungathered dissolved in the
heat of the sun, and was lost. The quantity collected was intended for the food of the current
day only; for if any were kept till next morning,
it corrupted and bred worms. Yet it was directed
that a double quantity should be gathered on the
sixth day for consumption on the Sabbath. And
it was found that the manna kept for the Sabbath
remained sweet and wholesome, notwithstanding
that it corrupted at other times, if kept for more
than one day. In the same manner as they would
have treated grain, they reduced it to meal,
kneaded it into dough, and baked it into cakes,
and the taste of it was like that of wafers made
with honey, or of fresh oil. In Num. xi. 6-9,
where the description of the manna is repeated,
an omer of it is directed to be preserved as a

memorial to future generations, 'that they may
see the bread wherewith I have fed you in the
wilderness;' and in Joshua v. 12 we learn that
after the Israelites had encamped at Gilgal, and
' did eat of the old corn of the land, the manna
ceased on the morrow after, neither had the children of Israel manna any more.'

239. [1. Alhagi maurorum. 2. Tamarix gallica]

This miracle is referred to in Deut. viii. 3;
Neh. ix. 20; Ps. lxxviii. 24; John vi. 31, 49,
58; Heb. ix. 4. Though the manna of Scripture
was so evidently miraculous, both in the mode and
in the quantities in which it was produced, and
though its properties were so different from any
thing with which we are acquainted, yet, because
its taste is in Exodus said to be like that of wafers
made with honey, many writers have thought
that they recognised the manna of Scripture in a
sweetish exudation which is found on several
plants in Arabia and Persia. The name *man*, or
manna, is applied to this substance by the Arab
writers, and was probably so applied even before
their time. But the term is now almost entirely
appropriated to the sweetish exudation of the ash
trees of Sicily and Italy. These, however, have
no relation to the supposed manna of Scripture.
Of this one kind is known to the Arabs by the
name of *guzunjbeen*, being the produce of a plant
called *guz*, and which is ascertained to be a species
of tamarisk. The same species seems also to be
called *toorfa*, and is common along different parts
of the coast of Arabia. It is also found in the
neighbourhood of Mount Sinai. In the month of
June it drops from the thorns of the tamarisk
upon the fallen twigs, leaves and thorns, which
always cover the ground beneath the tree in the
natural state. The Arabs use it as they do honey,
to pour over their unleavened bread, or to dip
their bread into; its taste is agreeable, somewhat
aromatic, and as sweet as honey. If eaten in any
quantity it is said to be highly purgative' When
Lieut. Wellsted visited this place in the month of
September, he found the extremities of the twigs
and branches retaining the peculiar sweetness and
flavour which characterize the manna. The Bedouins collect it early in the morning, and, after
straining it through a cloth, place it either in
skins or gourds, a considerable quantity is consumed by themselves, a portion is sent to Cairo;

and some is also disposed of to the monks at Mount Sinai. The latter retail it to the Russian pilgrims.' 'The Bedouins assured me that the whole quantity collected throughout the Peninsula, in the most fruitful season, did not exceed 150 wogas (about 700 pounds); and that it was usually disposed of at the rate of 60 dollars the woga.'

Another kind of manna, which has been supposed to be that of Scripture, is yielded by a thorny plant very common from the north of India to Syria, and which by the Arabs is called Al-haj; whence botanists have constructed the name Alhagi. The *Alhagi maurorum* is remarkable for the exudation of a sweetish juice, which concretes into small granular masses, and which is usually distinguished by the name of Persian manna. The climates of Persia and Bokhara seem also well suited to the secretion of this manna, which in the latter country is employed as a substitute for sugar, and is imported into India for medicinal use through Caubul and Khorassan. These two, from the localities in which they are produced, have alone been thought to be the manna of Scripture. But, besides these, there are several other kinds of manna. Indeed, a sweetish secretion is found on the leaves of many other plants, produced sometimes by the plant itself, at others by the punctures of insects. It has been supposed, also, that these sweetish exudations being evaporated during the heat of the day in still weather, may afterwards become deposited, with the dew, on the ground, and on the leaves of plants; and thus explain some of the phenomena which have been observed by travellers and others. But none of these mannas explain, nor can it be expected that they should explain, the miracle of Scripture, by which abundance is stated to have been produced for millions, where hundreds cannot now be subsisted.

MANOAH, father of Samson [SAMSON].

MANSLAYER. [BLOOD-REVENGE].

MA'ON, a town in the tribe of Judah (Josh. xv. 55), which gave name to a wilderness where David hid himself from Saul, and around which the churlish Nabal had great possessions (1 Sam. xxiii. 24, 25; xxv. 2). Jerome places it to the east of Daroma. The name does not occur in modern times, and Dr. Robinson regards it as one of the sites first identified by himself. He finds it in the present Main, which is about seven miles south by east from Hebron. Here there is a conical hill about 200 feet high, on the top of which are some ruins of no great extent, consisting of foundations of hewn stone, a square enclosure, the remains probably of a tower or castle, and several cisterns. The view from the summit is extensive. This is Main. The traveller found here a band of peasants keeping their flocks, and dwelling in caves amid the ruins (*Bibl. Researches*, ii. 190-196).

MA'RAH (*bitterness*). The Israelites, in departing from Egypt, made some stay on the shores of the Red Sea, at the place where it had been crossed by them. From this spot they proceeded southward for three days without finding any water, and then came to a well, the waters of which were so bitter, that, thirsty as they were, they could not drink them. The well was called *Marah* from the quality of its waters. This name, in the form of Amarah, is now borne by the barren bed of a winter torrent, a little beyond which is still found a well called Howara, the bitter waters of which answer to this description. Camels will drink it; but the thirsty Arabs never partake of it themselves; and it is said to be the only water on the shore of the Red Sea which they cannot drink. The water of this well, when first taken into the mouth, seems insipid rather than bitter, but when held in the mouth a few seconds it becomes exceedingly nauseous. The well rises within an elevated mound surrounded by sand-hills, and two small date-trees grow near it.

The Hebrews, unaccustomed as yet to the hardships of the desert, and having been in the habit of drinking their full of the best water in the world, were much distressed by its scarcity in the region wherein they now wandered; and in their disappointment of the relief expected from this well, they murmured greatly against Moses for having brought them into such a dry wilderness, and asked him, 'What shall we drink?' On this Moses cried to Jehovah, who indicated to him 'a certain tree,' on throwing the branches of which into the well, its waters became sweet and fit for use. The view which has been taken of this transaction by Dr. Kitto, in the *Pictorial Hist. of Palestine*, ii. 209, 210, is here introduced, as it has been judged satisfactory, and as no new information on the subject has since been obtained.

'The question connected with this operation is —whether the effect proceeded from the inherent virtue of the tree in sweetening bad water; or that it had no such virtue, and that the effect was purely miraculous. In support of the former alternative, it may be asked why the tree should have been pointed out and used at all, unless it had a curative virtue? And to this the answer may be found in the numerous instances in which God manifests a purpose of working even his miracles in accordance with the general laws by which he governs the world, and for that purpose disguising the naked exhibition of supernatural power, by the interposition of an *apparent* cause; while yet the true character of the event is left indisputable, by the utter inadequacy of the apparent cause to produce, by itself, the resulting effect. This tends to show that the tree, or portion of it, need not be supposed, from the mere fact of its being employed, to have had an inherent curative virtue. It had not *necessarily* any such virtue; and that it positively had not such virtue seems to follow, or, at least, to be rendered more than probable by the consideration that, in the scanty and little diversified vegetation of this district, any such very desirable virtues in a tree, or part of a tree, could scarcely have been undiscovered before the time of the history, and if they had been discovered, could not but have been known to Moses; and the Divine indication of the tree would not have been needful. And, again, if the corrective qualities were inherent, but were at this time first made known, it is incredible that so valuable a discovery would ever have been forgotten; and yet it is manifest that in after-times the Hebrews had not the knowledge of any tree which could render bad water drinkable; and the inhabitants of the desert have not only not preserved the knowledge of a fact which would have been so important to them, but have not discovered it in the thirty-five centuries which have since passed. This is shown by the inquiries of travellers, some of whom were actuated by the wish of finding a plant which might supersede the miracle. No such plant, however, can be found ; and whatever the tree was, it can have had no more inherent virtue in sweetening the bitter well of Marah, than the salt had, which produced the same effect, when thrown by Elisha into the well of Jericho.'

MARA'NA'THA. [ANATHEMA.]

MARCHESHVAN is the name of that month which was the eighth of the sacred and the second of the civil year of the Jews, which began with the new moon of our November. There was a fast on the 6th, in memory of Zedekiah's being blinded, after he had witnessed the slaughter of his sons (2 Kings xxv. 7).

This month is always spoken of in the Old Testament by its numerical designation, except once, when it is called Bul (1 Kings vi. 38), supposed to be a shortened form of the Hebrew word signifying ' rain;' and the signification of *rainmonth* is well suited to November in the climate of Palestine.

MARE'SHAH, a town in the tribe of Judah (Josh. xv. 14), rebuilt and fortified by Rehoboam (2 Chron. xi. 8). The Ethiopians under Zerah were defeated by Asa in the valley near Mareshah (2 Chron. xiv. 9-13). It was laid desolate by Judas Maccabæus, on his march from Hebron to Ashdod (1 Macc. v. 65-68 ; Joseph. *Antiq.* xii. 8. 6). Josephus mentions it among the towns possessed by Alexander Jannæus, which had been in the hands of the Syrians (*Ib.* xiii. 15. 4); but by Pompey it was restored to the former inhabitants, and attached to the province of Syria (*Ib.* xiv. 4. 4). Maresa was among the towns rebuilt by Gabinius (*Ib.* xiv. 5. 3), but was again destroyed by the Parthians in their irruption against Herod (*Ib.* xiv. 5. 3). A place so often mentioned in history must have been of considerable importance; but it does not appear that it was ever again rebuilt. The site, however, is set down by Eusebius and Jerome as within two miles of Eleutheropolis, but the direction is not stated. Dr. Robinson found, at a mile and a half *south* of the site of Eleutheropolis, a remarkable *tell*, or artificial hill, with foundations of some buildings. As there are no other ruins in the vicinity, and as the site is admirably suited for a fortress, this, he supposes, may have been Mareshah.

MARK. According to ecclesiastical testimonies, the evangelist Mark is the same person who in the Acts is called by the Jewish name John, whose Roman surname was Marcus (Acts xii. 12, 25). This person is sometimes called simply John (Acts xiii. 5, 13); and sometimes Mark (Acts xv. 39).

Mary, Mark's mother, had a house at Jerusalem, in which the Apostles were wont to assemble (Acts xii. 12). In the Epistle to the Colossians (iv. 10. 11) Mark is mentioned among the assistants of Paul, and as being one of the converts from Judaism. From this passage we learn also that Mark was a cousin of Barnabas, which circumstance confirms the opinion that he was of Jewish descent. It was probably Barnabas who first introduced him to Paul. He accompanied Paul and Barnabas on their travels as an assistant (Acts xii. 25 ; xiii. 5). When they had arrived in Pamphylia, Mark left them and returned to Jerusalem, from which city they had set out (Acts xiii. 13). On this account Paul refused to take Mark with him on his second apostolical journey, ' and so Barnabas took Mark, and sailed unto Cyprus' (Acts xv. 37-39). It seems, however, that Mark, at a later period, became reconciled to Paul, since, according to Col. iv. 10, and Philem. 24, he was with the Apostle during his first captivity at Rome ; and, according to 2 Tim. iv. 11, he was also with him during his second captivity. The passage in Colossians proves also that he was about to undertake for Paul a journey to Colosse.

There is a unanimous ecclesiastical tradition that Mark was the companion and ' interpreter ' of Peter, probably so called because he was the assistant of Peter, and either orally or in writing communicated and developed what Peter taught. This tradition is the more credible, as the New Testament does not contain any passage that could have led to its invention. The testimony in favour of the connection between Mark and Peter is so old and respectable, that it cannot be called in question. It first occurs at the commencement of the second century, and proceeds from the presbyter John ; it afterwards appears in Irenæus; in Tertullian ; in Clemens Alexandrinus, Jerome, and others.

Eusebius represents (*Hist. Eccles.* ii. 15) from the later life of Mark, that he was with Peter at Rome. Epiphanius and others inform us that he introduced the Gospel into Egypt, founded the church at Alexandria, and that he died in the eighth year of Nero's reign.

THE GOSPEL OF MARK.—The same ancient authors, who call Mark a disciple and secretary of Peter, state also that he wrote his Gospel according to the discourses of that Apostle. The most ancient statement of this fact is that of the presbyter John and of Papias, which we thus translate from Eusebius (*Hist. Eccles.* iii. 39):—Mark having become secretary to Peter, whatever he put into style he wrote with accuracy, but did not observe the chronological order of the discourses and actions of Christ, because he was neither a hearer nor a follower of the Lord ; but at a later period. as I have said, wrote for Peter to meet the requisites of instruction, but by no means with the view to furnish a connected digest of the discourses of our Lord. Consequently Mark was not in fault when he wrote down circumstances as he recollected them ; for he had only the intention to omit nothing of what he had heard, and not to misrepresent anything.

It has been noticed in the article LUKE that, according to Irenæus, the Gospels of Mark and Luke were written later than that of Matthew ; and according to a tradition preserved by Clemens Alexandrinus, the Gospels of Matthew and Luke preceded that of Mark. The chronological order of the Gospels is, according to Origen, the same in which they follow each other in the codices Irenæus states that Mark wrote after the death of Peter and Paul ; but, according to Clemens Alexandrinus and Eusebius, he wrote at Rome while Peter was yet living. These various data leave us in uncertainty.

In the article GOSPELS we have stated our opinion concerning the relative position in which

2 O

the evangelists stand to each other. We do not see any reason to contradict the unanimous tradition of antiquity concerning the dependence of Mark upon Peter. We deem it possible, and even probable, that Luke read Mark, and that he also alludes to him by reckoning him among the *many* who had written gospel history before him. This supposition, however, is by no means necessary or certain; and it is still possible that Mark wrote after Luke. Some of the ancient testimonies which we have quoted, namely, those of Irenæus, Clemens Alexandrinus, Jerome, and others, state that Mark's Gospel was written at Rome. Whether this was the case or not, it is certain that it was written for Gentile Christians. This appears from the explanation of Jewish customs (ch. vii. 2, 11; xii. 18; xiii. 3; xiv. 12; xv. 6, 42). The same view is confirmed by the scarcity of quotations from the Old Testament, perhaps also by the absence of the genealogy of Christ, and by the omission of the Sermon on the Mount, which explains the relation of Christ to the Old Testament dispensation, and which was, therefore, of the greatest importance to Matthew.

The characteristic peculiarity of Mark as an author is particularly manifest in two points: 1. He reports rather the works than the discourses of our Saviour; 2. He gives details more minutely and graphically than Matthew and Luke; for instance, he describes the cures effected by Jesus more exactly (iv. 31, 41; vi. 5, 13; vii. 33; viii. 23). He is also more particular in stating definite numbers (v. 13, 42; vi. 7, 14, 30), and furnishes more exact dates and times (i. 32, 35; ii. 1, 26; iv. 26, 35; vi. 2; xi. 11, 19, 20, &c.). It may be that these characteristics of Mark originated from his connection with Peter.

Most of the materials of Mark's narrative occur also in Matthew and Luke. He has, however, sections exclusively belonging to himself, viz. iii. 21, 31, sq.; vi. 17, sq.; xi. 11; xii. 28, sq.

We mention the conclusion of Mark's Gospel separately, since its genuineness may be called in question.

Among the *Codices Majusculi* the Codex B. omits ch. xvi. 9-20 altogether, and several of the *Codices Minusculi* mark this section with asterisks as doubtful. Several ancient Fathers and authors of *Scholia* state that it was wanting in some manuscripts. We cannot, however, suppose that it was arbitrarily added by a copyist, since at present all codices, except B. and all ancient versions contain it, and the Fathers in general quote it. We may also say that Mark could not have concluded his Gospel with ver. 8, unless he had been accidentally prevented from finishing it. Hence Michaelis and Hug have inferred that the addition was made by the evangelist at a later period, in a similar manner as John made an addition in ch. xxi. of his gospel. Perhaps also an intimate friend, or an amanuensis, supplied the defect. If either of these two hypotheses is well founded, it may be understood why several codices were formerly without this conclusion, and why, nevertheless, it was found in most of them.

MARRIAGE.—THE LEVIRATE LAW.—The divine origin of marriage, and the primitive state of the institution, are clearly recorded in the instance of the first human pair (Gen. ii. 18-25), whence it appears that woman was made after man to be 'a helper suited to him.' The narrative is calculated to convey exalted ideas of the institution. It is introduced by a declaration of the Lord God, that 'it is not good that the man should be alone' (ver. 18); of the truth of which Adam had become convinced by experience. In order still further to enliven his sense of his deficiency, the various species of creatures are made to pass in review before him, 'to see what he would call them;' on which occasion he could behold each species accompanied by its appropriate helper, and upon concluding his task would become still more affectingly aware, that amid all animated nature 'there was not found an help meet for himself.' It was at this juncture, when his heart was thus thoroughly prepared to appreciate the intended blessing, that a divine slumber, or trance, fell upon him—a state in which, as in after ages, the exercise of the external senses being suspended, the mental powers are peculiarly prepared to receive revelations from God (Gen. xv. 12; Acts x. 10; xxvii. 17; 2 Cor. xii. 2). His exclamation when Eve was brought to him shows that he had been fully conscious of the circumstances of her creation, and had been instructed by them as to the nature of the relation which would thenceforth subsist between them. 'The man said, *this time*, it is bone of my bone, and flesh of my flesh; *this* shall be called woman, for out of man was this taken.' The remaining words, 'for this cause shall a man leave his father and mother, and shall cleave unto his wife, and they (two) shall be one flesh,' which might otherwise seem a proleptical announcement by the historian of the social obligations of marriage, are by our Lord ascribed to the Divine agent concerned in the transaction, either uttered by him personally, or by the mouth of Adam while in a state of inspiration. 'Have ye not read that he that made them at the beginning, made them male and female, *and said*, for this cause,' &c. (Matt. xix. 4, 5). It is a highly important circumstance in this transaction, that God created only *one* female for *one* man, and united them—a circumstance which is the very basis of our Lord's reasoning in the passage against divorce and remarriage; but which basis is lost, and his reasoning consequently rendered inconclusive, by the inattention of our translators to the absence of the article, 'he made them *a* male and *a* female, and said, they shall become one flesh; so that they are no more two, but one flesh. What, therefore, God hath joined together, let no man put asunder.' 'The weight of our Lord's argument,' says Campbell, 'lay in this circumstance, that God at first created no more than a single pair, one of each sex, whom he united in the bond of marriage, and, in so doing, exhibited a standard of that union to all generations.' The apostacy introduced a new feature into the institution, namely, the subjection of the wife's will to that of her husband (Gen. iii. 16; comp. Num. xxx. 6-16). The primitive model was adhered to even by Cain, who seems to have had but one wife (Gen. iv. 17). Polygamy, one of the earliest developments of human degeneracy, was introduced by Lamech, who 'took unto him two wives' (Gen. iv. 19; circa 3874 B.C.). The intermarriage of 'the Sons of God,' *i. e.* the worshippers of the true God, with 'the daughters of men,' *i. e.* the irreligious (B.C. 2468), is the next incident in the history of marriage. They indulged in unrestrained polygamy

'they took them wives of all that they chose.'
From this event may be dated that headlong degeneracy of mankind at this period, which ultimately brought on them extirpation by a deluge
(Gen. vi. 3-7) At the time of that catastrophe
Noah had but one wife (Gen. vii. 7), and so each
of his sons (ver. 13). Pursuing the investigation
of the subject according to chronological arrangement, Job next appears (B.C. 2130) as the husband
of one wife (Job ii. 9; xix. 17). Reference is
made to the adulterer, who is represented as in
terror and accursed (xxiv. 15-18). The wicked
man is represented as leaving ' widows' behind
him; whence his polygamy may be inferred
(xxvii. 15). Job expresses his abhorrence of
fornication (xxxi. 1), and of adultery (ver. 9),
which appears in his time to have been punished
by the judges (ver. 11). Following the same arrangement, we find Abraham and Nahor introduced as having each one wife (Gen. xi. 29).
From the narrative of Abraham's first equivocation concerning Sarah, it may be gathered that
marriage was held sacred in Egypt. Abraham
fears that the Egyptians would sooner rid themselves of him by murder than infringe by adultery
the relation of his wife to an obscure stranger.
The reproof of Pharaoh, 'Why didst thou say,
She is my sister? so I might have taken her to
me to wife: now therefore behold thy *wife*, take
her, and go thy way' (Gen. xii. 11-19), affords
a most honourable testimony to the views of marriage entertained by Pharaoh at that period, and
most likely by his court and nation. It seems
that Sarah was Abraham's half-sister. Such marriages were permitted till the giving of the law
(Lev. xviii. 9). Thus Amram, the father of Moses
and Aaron, married his father's sister (Exod. vi.
20), a union forbidden in Lev. xviii. 12.

The first mention of concubinage, or the condition of a legal though subordinate wife, occurs
in the case of Hagar, Sarah's Egyptian handmaid,
whom Sarah, still childless, after a residence of
ten years in Canaan, prevailed on Abraham, apparently against his will, to receive into that relation (Gen. xvi. 1), which was however considered
inviolable (Gen. xlix. 4; Lev. xviii. 8; 2 Sam.
iii. 8, 16, 21, 22; 1 Chron. v. 1). The vehement
desire for offspring, common to women in the
East, as appears from the histories of Rebecca
(Gen. xxv. 21), of Rachel (xxx. 1), of Leah (ver.
5), and of Hannah (1 Sam. i. 6, 7), seems to have
been Sarah's motive for adopting a procedure
practised in such cases in that region in all ages.
The miseries naturally consequent upon it are
amply portrayed in the history of the Patriarchs
(Gen. xvi. 4-10; xxx. 1, 3, 15).

Lot does not appear to have exceeded one wife
(Gen. xix. 15). The second equivocation of the
same kind by Abraham respecting Sarah elicits
equally honourable sentiments concerning marriage, on the part of Abimelech, king of Gerar
(Gen. xx. 5, 6, 9, 10, &c), who, it appears, had
but one proper wife (ver. 17; see also ch. xxvi.
7-11). Perhaps Abraham relied on the ancient
custom, which will shortly be adverted to, of the
consent of the 'brother' being requisite to the
sister's marriage, and thus hoped to secure his
wife's safety and his own. In ancient times the
parents chose wives for their children (Gen. xxi.
21; xxxviii. 5; Deut. xxii. 16); or the man who
wished a particular female asked his father to
obtain her from *her* father, as in the case of
Shechem (B.C. 1732; Gen. xxxiv. 4-6; comp.
Judges xiv. 2. 3). The consent of her brothers
seems to have been necessary (ver. 5, 8, 11, 13,
14; comp. Gen. xxiv. 50; 2 Sam. xiii. 20-29).
A dowry was given by the suitor to the father
and brethren of the female (ver. 11, 12; comp.
1 Sam. xviii. 25; Hos. iii. 2). This, in a common case, amounted to from 30 to 50 shekels,
according to the law of Moses (comp. Exod. xxii.
16; Deut. xxii. 29). Pausanias considers it so
remarkable for a man to part with his daughter
without receiving a marriage-portion with her,
that he takes pains, in a case he mentions, to explain the reason. In later times we meet with
an exception (Tobit viii. 23). It is most likely
that from some time before the last-named period
the Abrahamidæ restricted their marriages to
circumcised persons (Gen. xxviii. 8; comp. Judg.
iii. 6; 1 Kings xi. 8, 11, 16; Joseph. *Antiq.* xi.
8. 2; xii. 4, 6: xviii. 9, 5). The marriage of
Isaac developes additional particulars; for beside
Abraham's unwillingness that his son should
marry a Cananitess (Gen. xxiv. 3; comp. xxvi.
34; xxvii. 46; Exod. xxxiv. 16; Josh. xxiii.
12; Ezra ix. 2; x. 3, 10, 11), costly jewels are
given to the bride at the betrothal (ver. 22), and
'precious things to her mother and brother'
(ver. 53); a customary period between espousals
and nuptials is referred to (ver. 55); and the
blessing of an abundant offspring invoked upon
the bride by her relatives (ver. 60)—which most
likely was the only marriage ceremony then and
for ages afterwards (comp. Ruth iv. 11-13; Ps.
xlv. 16, 17); but in Tobit vii. 3, the father places
his daughter's right hand in the hand of Tobias
before he invokes his blessing. It is remarkable
that no representation has been found of a marriage ceremony among the tombs of Egypt. The
Rabbins say that among the Jews it consisted of
a kiss (Cant. i. 2). It is probable that the marriage covenant was committed to writing (Prov.
ii. 17; Mal. ii. 14; Tobit vii. 13, 14); perhaps,
also, confirmed with an oath (Ezra xvi. 8). It
seems to have been the custom with the patriarchs
and ancient Jews to bury their wives in their
own graves, but not their concubines (Gen. xlix.
31). In Gen. xxv. 1, Abraham, after the death
of Sarah, marries a second wife. Esau's polygamy is mentioned Gen. xxviii. 9; xxxvi. 2-13
(B.C. 1760). Jacob serves seven years to obtain
Rachel in marriage (Gen. xxix. 18-20); and has
a marriage feast, to which the men of the place
are invited (ver. 22; comp. Cant. v. 1; viii. 33).
Samson's marriage feast lasts a week (Judg. xiv.
10-12; B.C. 1136; comp. John ii. 1, &c.); in
later times it lasted longer (Tobit viii. 19). The
persons invited to Samson's marriage are young
men (Judg xiv. 10); called 'sons of the bridechamber,' Matt. ix. 15. Females were invited to
marriages (Ps. xlv. 14), and attended the bride
and bridegroom to their abode (1 Macc. ix. 37);
and in the time of Christ, if it was evening, with
lamps and flambeaux (Matt. xxv. 1-10). In later
ages the guests were summoned when the banquet
was ready (Matt. xxii. 3), and furnished with a
marriage garment (ver. 11). The father of the
bride conducted her at night to her husband
(Gen. xxix. 23; Tobit viii. 1). The bride and
bridegroom were richly ornamented (Isa. lxi.
10). In Mesopotamia, and the East generally, it

was the custom to marry the eldest sister first (Gen. xxix. 26). By the deception practised upon Jacob in that country, he marries two wives, and, apparently, without any one objecting (ver. 31). Laban obtains a promise from Jacob not to marry any more wives than Rachel and Leah (Gen. xxxi. 50). The wives and concubines of Jacob and their children travel together (Gen. xxxii. 22, 23); but a distinction is made between them in the hour of danger (Gen. xxxiii. 1, 2; comp. Gen. xxv. 6). Following the arrangement we have adopted, we now meet with the first reference to *the Levirate Law*. Judah, Jacob's son by Leah, had married a Canaanitish woman (Gen. xxxviii. 2). His first-born son was Er (ver. 3). Judah took a wife for him (ver. 6). Er soon after died (ver. 7), and Judah said to Onan, 'Go in unto thy brother's wife, Tamar, and marry her, and raise up seed to thy brother.' 'Onan knew that the offspring would not be his.' All these circumstances bespeak a pre-established and well known law, and he evaded the purpose of it, and thereby, it is said, incurred the wrath of God (ver. 10). It seems, from the same account, to have been well understood, that upon his death the duty devolved upon the next surviving brother. No change is recorded in this law till just before the entrance of Israel into Canaan (B.C. 1451), at which time Moses modified it by new regulations to this effect:—'If brethren dwell together (*i. e.* in the same locality), and one of them die, and leave no child, the wife of the dead must not marry out of the family, but her husband's brother or his next kinsman must take her to wife, and perform the duty of a husband's brother, and the first-born of this union shall succeed in the name of his deceased father, that his name may be extant in Israel;' not literally bear his name, for Ruth allowed her son by Boaz to be called Obed, and not Mahlon, the name of her first husband (Ruth iv. 17, yet see Josephus, *Antiq.* iv. 8, 23). In case the man declined the office, the woman was to bring him before the elders, loose his shoe from off his foot, and spit in, or, as some render it, before his face, by way of contempt (Deut. xxv. 9, 10: Josephus understands *in* the face, *Antiq.* v. 9. 4), and shall say, 'So shall it be done unto the man that will not build up his brother's house; and his name shall be called in Israel, the house of him that hath his shoe loosed,' *quasi* Baresole! It does not appear that the original law was binding on the brother, if already married; and we may well believe that Moses, who wished to mitigate it, allowed of that exception. The instance of Ruth (B.C. 1245), who married Boaz, her husband's relation, exhibits the practice of the law under the Judges. Boaz was neither the father of, nor the nearest relation to, Elimelech, father-in-law to Ruth, the wife of Mahlon, and yet he married her after the refusal of him who was the nearest relation (Ruth ii. 20; iii., iv.).

It should seem, from the instance of Potiphar's wife, that monogamy was practised in Egypt (Gen. xxxix. 7) Pharaoh gave to Joseph one wife (Gen. xli. 45). The Israelites, while in Egypt, seem to have restricted themselves to one. One case is recorded of an Israelite who had married an Egyptian woman (Lev. xxiv. 10). The giving of the law (B.C. 1491) acquaints us

with many regulations concerning marriage, which were different from the practices of the Jews while in Egypt, and from those of the Canaanites, to whose land they were approaching (Lev. xviii. 3). There we find laws for regulating the marriages of bondmen (Exod. xxi. 3, 4), and of a bondmaid (ver. 7-12). The prohibition against marriages with the Canaanites is established by a positive law (Exod. xxiv. 16). Marriage is prohibited with any one near of kin, ' of the remainder of his flesh ' (Lev. xviii. 6-19). A priest is prohibited from marrying one that had been a harlot, or divorced (Lev. xxi. 7.) The high-priest was also excluded from marrying a widow, and restricted to one wife (ver. 13, 14). Daughters who, through want of brothers, were heiresses to an estate, were required to marry into their own tribe, and, if possible, a kinsman, to prevent the estate passing into another family (Num. xxvii. 1-11; xxxvi. 1-12). The husband had power to annul his wife's vow, if he heard it, and interfered at the time (Num. xxx. 6-16). If a man had betrothed a wife, he was exempt from the wars, &c. (Deut. xx. 7; xxiv. 5). It was allowed to marry a beautiful captive in war, whose husband probably had been killed (Deut. xxi. 10-14, &c.). Abundance of offspring was one of the blessings promised to obedience, during the miraculous providence which superintended the Theocracy (Lev. xxvi. 9; Deut. vii. 13, 14; xxviii. 11; Ps. cxxvii. 3; cxxviii. 3); and disappointment in marriage was one of the curses (Deut. xxviii. 18. 30: comp. Ps. xlvii. 9; Jer. viii. 10). A daughter of a distinguished person was offered in marriage as a reward for perilous services (Josh. xv. 16, 17; 1 Sam. xvii. 25). Concubinage appears in Israel (B.C. 1413), (Judg. xix. 1-4). The violation of a concubine is avenged (Judg. xx. 5-10). Polygamy (Judg. viii. 30). The state of marriage among the Philistines may be inferred, in the time of Samson, from the sudden divorce from him of his wife by her father, and her being given to his friend (Judg. xiv. 20), and from the father offering him a younger sister instead (Judg. xv. 2). David's numerous wives (2 Sam. iii. 3-5). In Ps. xlv., which is referred to this period by the best harmonists, there is a description of a royal marriage upon a most magnificent scale. The marriage of Solomon to Pharaoh's daughter is recorded in 1 Kings iii. 1; to which the Song of Solomon probably relates, and from which it appears that his mother ' crowned him with a crown on the day of his espousals' (ver. 3, 11). It would appear that in his time females were married young (Prov. ii. 17; comp. Joel i. 8); also males (Prov. v. 18). An admirable description of a good wife is given in Prov. xxxi. 10-31. The excessive multiplication of wives and concubines was the cause and effect of Solomon's apostacy in his old age (1 Kings xi 1-8). He confesses his error in Ecclesiastes, where he eulogizes monogamy (viii. 9; vii. 29). Rehoboam took a plurality of wives (2 Chron. xi. 18-21); and so Abijah (2 Chron. xiii 21), and Ahab (1 Kings xx. 3), and Belshazzar, king of Babylon (Dan. v. 2). It would seem that the outward manners of the Jews, about the time of our Lord's advent, had become improved, since there is no case recorded in the New Testament of polygamy or concubinage among them. Our Lord excludes all causes of divorce, except whoredom (Matt. v. 32), and ascribes the origin of the Mosaic law to the hardness of their hearts. The same doctrine concerning divorce had been taught by the prophets (Jer. iii. 1; Micah ii. 9; Mal. ii. 14-16). The apostles inculcate it likewise (Rom. vii. 3; 1 Cor. vii. 4, 10, 11, 39); yet St. Paul considers obstinate desertion by an unbelieving party as a release (1 Cor. vii. 15). Our Lord does not reprehend celibacy for the sake of religion, 'those who make themselves eunuchs for the kingdom of heaven's sake' (Matt. xix. 12; comp 1 Cor. vii. 32, 36). Second marriages not condemned in case of death (Rom. vii. 12). Mixed marriages disapproved (1 Cor. vii. 39; 2 Cor. vi. 14). Early marriage not recommended (1 Cor. vii. 36). Marriage affords the means of copious illustrations to the writers of Scripture. The prophets employ it to represent the relation of the Jewish church to Jehovah, and the apostles that of the Christian church to Christ. The applications they make of the idea constitute some of the boldest and most touching figures in the Scripture.

MARS' HILL. [AREOPAGUS.]

MAR'THA, sister of Lazarus and Mary, who resided in the same house with them at Bethany [LAZARUS]. From the house at Bethany being called 'her house,' in Luke x. 38, and from the leading part which Martha is always seen to take in domestic matters, it has seemed to some that she was a widow, to whom the house at Bethany belonged, and with whom her brother and sister lodged; but this is uncertain, and the common opinion, that the sisters managed the household of their brother, is more probable. Luke probably calls it her house because he had no occasion to mention, and does not mention, Lazarus; and when we speak of a house which is occupied by different persons, we avoid circumlocution by calling it the house of the individual who happens to be the subject of our discourse. Jesus was intimate with this family, and their house was often his home when at Jerusalem, being accustomed to retire thither in the evening, after having spent the day in the city. The point which the Evangelists bring out most distinctly with respect to Martha, lies in the contrariety of disposition between her and her sister Mary. The first notice of Christ's visiting this family occurs in Luke x. 38-42. He was received with great attention by the sisters; and Martha soon hastened to provide suitable entertainment for the Lord and his followers, while Mary remained in his presence, sitting at his feet, and drinking in the sacred words that fell from his lips. The active, bustling solicitude of Martha, anxious that the best things in the house should be made subservient to the Master's use and solace, and the quiet earnestness of Mary, more desirous to profit by the golden opportunity of hearing his instructions, than to minister to his personal wants, strongly mark the points of contrast in the characters of the two sisters.

The part taken by the sisters in the transactions connected with the death and resurrection of Lazarus, is entirely and beautifully in accordance with their previous history. Martha is still more engrossed with outward things, while Mary surrenders herself more to her feelings, and to inward meditation. When they heard that Jesus was approaching, Martha hastened beyond the village to meet him, 'but Mary sat still in the house' (John xi. 20, 22). When she saw Jesus actually appear, whose presence had been so anxiously desired, she exhibits a strong degree of faith, and hesitates not to express a confident hope that he, to whom all things were possible, would even yet afford relief. But, as is usual with persons of her lively character, when Christ answered, with what seemed to her the vague intimation, 'Thy brother shall rise again,' she was instantly cast down from her height of confidence, the reply being less direct than she expected: she referred this saying to the general resurrection at the last day, and thereon relapsed into despondency and grief. This feeling Jesus reproved, by directing her attention, before all other things, to that inward, eternal, and divine life, which consists in union with him, and which is raised far above the power even of the grave. This he did in the magnificent words, 'I am the resurrection, and the life: he that believeth in me, though he were dead, yet shall he live: and whosoever liveth and believeth in me shall never die. Believest thou this?' Sorrow and shame permitted the troubled Martha, in whose heart the feeling of an unconditional and entire surrender to his will was re-awakened, to make only the general confession that he was actually the promised Messiah; in which confession she, however, comprised an acknowledgment of his power and greatness. It is clear, however, that she found nothing in this discourse with Christ, to encourage her first expectation of relief; and with the usual rapid change in persons of lively susceptibilities, she had now as completely abandoned all hope of rescue for her brother, as she had before been sanguine of his restoration to life. Thus, when Jesus directed the stone to be rolled away from the sepulchre, she gathered from this no ground of hope; but rather objected to its being done, because the body, which had been four days in the tomb, must already have become disagreeable. The reproof of Christ, 'Said I not unto thee, that, if thou wouldest believe, thou shouldest see the glory of God?' suggests that more discourse had passed between them than the evangelist has recorded, seeing that no such assurance is contained in the previous narrative (John xi. 39, 40).

Nothing more is recorded of Martha, save that some time after, at a supper given to Christ and his disciples at Bethany, she, as usual, busied herself in the external service. Lazarus, so marvellously restored from the grave, sat with her guests at table. 'Martha served,' and Mary occupied her favourite station at the feet of Jesus, which she bathed with her tears, and anointed with costly ointment (John xii. 1, 2) [LAZARUS; MARY].

There are few characters in the New Testament, and certainly no female character, so strongly brought out in its natural points as that of Martha; and it is interesting to observe that Luke and John, although relating different transactions in which she was concerned, perfectly agree in the traits of character which they assign to her.

MARTYR. This word means properly *a witness*, and is applied in the New Testament—

1. To judicial witnesses (Matt. xviii. 16; xxvi. 65; Mark xiv. 63; Acts vi. 13; vii. 58; 2 Cor. xiii. 1; 1 Tim. v. 19; Heb. x. 28). 2. To one who has testified, or can testify to the truth of what he has seen, heard, or known. This is a frequent sense in the New Testament: as in Luke xxiv. 48; Acts i. 8, 22; Rom. i. 9; 2 Cor. i. 23; 1 Thes. ii. 5, 10; 1 Tim. vi. 12; 2 Tim. ii. 2; 1 Pet. v. 1; Rev. i. 5; iii. 14; xi. 3, and elsewhere. 3. The meaning of the word which has now become the most usual, is that in which it occurs most rarely in the Scripture, *i. e.*, one who by his death bears witness to the truth. In this sense we only find it in Acts xxii. 20; Rev. ii. 13; xvii. 6. This now exclusive sense of the word was brought into general use by the early ecclesiastical writers, who applied it to every one who suffered death in the Christian cause. Stephen was in this sense the first martyr [STEPHEN]; and the spiritual honours of his death tended in no small degree to raise to the most extravagant estimation, in the early church, the value of the testimony of blood. Eventually a martyr's death was supposed, on the alleged authority of the under-named texts, to cancel all the sins of the past life (Luke xii. 50; Mark x. 39); to supply the place of baptism (Matt. x. 39); and at once to secure admittance to the presence of the Lord in Paradise (Matt. v. 10-12). In imitation of the family custom of annually commemorating at the grave the death of deceased members, the churches celebrated the deaths of their martyrs by prayer at their graves, and by love-feasts. From this high estimation of the martyrs, Christians were sometimes led to deliver themselves up voluntarily to the public authorities—thus justifying the charge of fanaticism brought against them by the heathen. For the most part, however, this practice was discountenanced, the words of Christ himself being brought against it (Matt. x. 23; see *Gieseler, Eccles. Hist.* i. 109, 110).

1. MARY (*Miriam*), 'the Mother of Jesus' (Acts i. 14), and 'Mary his Mother' (Matt. ii. 11), are the appellations of one who has in later times been generally called the 'Virgin Mary,' but who is never so designated in Scripture.

Little is known of this 'highly favoured' individual, in whom was fulfilled the first prophecy made to man, that 'the seed of the *woman* should bruise the serpent's head' (Gen. iii. 15). As her history was of no consequence to Christianity, it is not given at large. Her genealogy is recorded by St. Luke (ch. iii.), in order to prove the truth of the predictions which had foretold the descent of the Messiah from Adam through Abraham and David, with the design evidently of showing that Christ was of that royal house and lineage.

Eusebius, the early ecclesiastical historian, although unusually lengthy upon 'the name Jesus,' and the genealogies in Matthew and Luke's Gospels, throws no new light upon Mary's birth and parentage. The legends respecting Anne, who is said to have been her mother, are pure fables without the slightest evidence.

The earliest event in her history, of which we have any notice, was the annunciation to her by the angel Gabriel that she was destined, whilst yet a pure virgin, to become the mother of the Messiah—an event which was a literal fulfilment of the prophecy given centuries before by Isaiah,

that ' a *virgin* should conceive, and bear a son, and should call his name Immanuel,' which being interpreted, is 'God with us' (Isa. vii. 14; Matt. i. 23). On this occasion she was explicitly informed that she should conceive by the miraculous power of God, and that her child should be 'Holy,' and be called 'the Son of God.' As a confirmation of her faith in this announcement she was also told by the angel that her cousin Elizabeth, who was the wife of one of the chief priests, and who was now far advanced in years, had conceived a son, and that the time was not far off when her reproach among women should cease (Luke i. 36).

Almost immediately on receiving this announcement Mary hastened from Nazareth, where she was when the angel visited her, to the house of her cousin, who was then residing in the hilly district in 'a city of Judah,' supposed to be Hebron. The meeting of these two pious females, on whom such unexpected privileges had been conferred, was one of mutual congratulations, and united thanksgiving to the author of their blessings. It was on this occasion that Mary uttered the *Magnificat* — that splendid burst of grateful adoration which Christians of all parties have from the earliest times delighted to adopt as expressive of the best feelings of the pious heart towards God (Luke i. 39-56). After spending three months with her relative, Mary returned to Nazareth, where a severe trial awaited her, arising out of the condition in which it had now become apparent she was. Betrothed (perhaps in early life) to a person of the name of Joseph, an artificer of some sort (Matt. xiii. 55, probably, as our translators suppose, a carpenter), the Jewish law held her exposed to the same penalties which awaited the married wife who should be found unfaithful to the spousal vow. Joseph, however, being a right-hearted man (one who feels and acts as a man ought to do in the circumstances in which he is placed), was unwilling to subject her to the evils of a public exposure of what he deemed her infidelity; and accordingly was turning in his mind how he might privately dissolve his connection with her, when an angel was sent to him also to inform him in a dream of the true state of the case, and enjoin upon him to complete his engagement with her by taking her as his wife. This injunction he obeyed, and hence came to be regarded by the Jews as the father of Jesus (Matt. i. 18-25).

Summoned by an edict of Augustus, which commanded that a census of the population of the whole Roman empire should be taken, and that each person should be enrolled in the chief city of his family or tribe, Mary and her husband went up to Bethlehem, the city of the Davidic family; and whilst there the child Jesus was born. After this event the only circumstances in her history mentioned by the sacred historians are her appearance and offerings in the temple according to the law of Moses (Luke i. 22, ff.); her return with her husband to Nazareth (Luke ii. 39); their habit of annually visiting Jerusalem at the Feast of the Passover (ver. 41); the appearance of the Magi, which seems to have occurred at one of these periodic visits (Matt. ii. 1-12); the flight of the holy family into Egypt, and their return, after the death of Herod, to

Nazareth (ver. 13-23); the scene which occurred in another of those periodic visits when, after having proceeded two days' journey on her way homeward, she discovered that her son was not in the company, and, on returning to Jerusalem, found him sitting in the temple with the doctors of the law, ' both hearing them and asking them questions' (Luke ii. 42-52); her appearance and conduct at the marriage-feast in Cana of Galilee (John ii. 1, ff.); her attempt in the synagogue at Capernaum to induce Jesus to desist from teaching (Matt. xii. 46, ff.); her accompanying of her son when he went up to Jerusalem immediately before his crucifixion; her following him to Calvary; her being consigned by him while hanging on the cross to the care of his beloved apostle John, who from that time took her to reside in his house (John xix. 25, ff.); and her associating with the disciples at Jerusalem after his ascension (Acts i. 14).

The traditions respecting the death of Mary differ materially from each other. There is a letter of the General Council of Ephesus in the fifth century, which states that she lived at Ephesus with St. John, and there died and was buried. Another epistle of the same age says she died at Jerusalem, and was buried in Gethsemane. The legend tells that three days after her interment, when the grave was opened (that Thomas the Apostle might pay reverence to her remains), her body was not to be found, ' but only an exceeding fragrance,' whereupon it was concluded that it had been taken up to heaven. The translations of Enoch and Elijah, and the ascension of the Lord Jesus Christ, took place while they were *alive*, and the facts are recorded by the inspiration of God; but when the *dead* body of Mary was conveyed through the earth, and removed thence, there were *no witnesses*, and no revelation was ever made of the extraordinary and novel incident, which certainly has no parallel in Scripture. This miraculous event is appropriately called ' the Assumption.'

It is said that Mary died in A.D. 63. The Canon of Scripture was closed in A D. 96, thirty-three years after her decease; which, however, is never alluded to by any of the Apostles in their writings, nor by St. John, to whose care she was entrusted.

In the Romish Church many facts are believed and doctrines asserted concerning the Virgin Mary, such as her immaculate conception—her perpetual virginity—her right to receive worship, and her mediation and intercession, which not only are without any authority from Scripture, but many of which are diametrically opposed to its declarations.

It does not appear that Mary ever saw Christ after the resurrection; for she was not one of the chosen witnesses' specified in Scripture, as Mary Magdalene was.

2 MARY MAGDALENE was probably so called from Magdala in Galilee, the town where she may have dwelt. According to the Talmudists, Magdalene signifies ' a plaiter of hair.'

Much wrong has been done to this individual from imagining that she was the person spoken of by St. Luke in ch. vii. 39; but there is no evidence to support this opinion. How Mary Magdalene came to be identified with the person here mentioned, it is difficult to say: but such is the

case: and accordingly she is generally regarded as having been a woman of depraved character. For such an inference, however, there appears to be no just ground whatever.

The earliest notice of Mary Magdalene is in St Luke's Gospel (viii. 2), where it is recorded that out of her ' had gone seven devils,' and that she was ' with Joanna, the wife of Herod's steward, and Susanna, and many others, which ministered unto Christ of their substance '

This is sufficient to prove that she had not been known as a person of bad character; and it also implies that she was not poor, or amongst the lower classes, when she was the companion of one whose husband held an important office in the king's household.

It is as unjust to say that she who had been so physically wretched as to be possessed by seven devils, was dissolute, as to affirm that an insane person is necessarily depraved.

In the Saviour's last hours, and at his death and resurrection, Mary Magdalene was a chief and important witness. She was one of the women who stood by the cross (Matt. xxvi. 55-56): who after his death beheld where the body was laid (Mark xv. 47), and who prepared spices and ointments to embalm it. She visited the sepulchre early on the first day of the week, while it was yet dark (John xx. 1); and when Peter and John returned to their own homes she remained at the sepulchre weeping, and had her patient waiting rewarded by the appearance of her risen Lord.

3. MARY, wife of Cleophas or Alphæus, and sister of the Lord's mother (Mat. xxvii. 56; Mark xv. 40; John xix. 25). This Mary was one of those holy women who followed Christ, and was present at the crucifixion; and she is that ' other Mary ' who, with Mary Magdalene, attended the body of Christ to the sepulchre when taken down from the cross (Matt. xxvii. 61 Mark xv. 47; Luke xxiii. 55). She was also among those who went on the morning of the first day of the week to the sepulchre to anoint the body, and who became the first witnesses of the resurrection (Matt. xxviii. 1; Mark xvi. 1; Luke xxiv. 1). James, Joses, Jude, and Simon, who are called the Lord's brethren [see the names; also ALPHÆUS; BROTHER], are very generally supposed to have been the sons of this Mary, and therefore *cousins* of Jesus, the term brother having been used with great latitude among the Hebrews.

4. MARY, sister of Lazarus and Martha. The friendship of our Lord for this family has been explained in other articles [LAZARUS, MARTHA].

The points of interest in connection with Mary individually arise from the contrast of character between her and her sister Martha, and from the incidents by which that contrast was evinced. Apart from this view, the most signal incident in the history of Mary is her conduct at the supper which was given to Jesus in Bethany, when he came thither after having raised Lazarus from the dead. The intense love which distinguished her character then glowed with the highest fervour, manifesting the depth of her emotion and gratitude for the deliverance from the cold terrors of the grave of that brother who now sat alive and cheerful with the guests at table. She took the station she best loved, at the feet of Jesus. Among the ancients it was usual to wash the feet of guests before an entertainment, and with this the anointing of the feet was frequently connected [ANOINTING]. Mary possessed a large quantity of very costly ointment; and in order to testify her gratitude she sacrificed it all by anointing with it the feet of Jesus. We are told that the disciples murmured at the extravagance of this act, deeming that it would have been much wiser, if she had sold the ointment and given the money to the poor. But Jesus, looking beyond the mere external act to the disposition which gave birth to it—a disposition which marked the intensity of her gratitude—vindicated her deed. Always meditating upon his departure, and more especially at that moment, when it was so near at hand, he attributed to this act a still higher sense —as having reference to his approaching death. The dead were embalmed: and so, he said, have I received, by anticipation, the consecration of death (John xii. 1-8; Matt. xxvi. 6-13; Mark xiv. 3-9).

MAS'CHIL, a title of some of the Psalms [PSALMS].

MAS'SA, an encampment of the Israelites [WANDERING].

MATTH'EW. According to Mark ii. 14, Matthew was a son of Alphæus. It is generally supposed that Jacobus, or James, the son of Alphæus, was a son of Mary, the wife of Cleophas, who was a sister of the mother of Jesus (John xix. 25). If this opinion is correct, Matthew was one of the relations of Jesus. Matthew was a *portitor*, or inferior collector of customs at Capernaum, on the Sea of Galilee. He was not a *publicanus*, or general farmer of customs. We may suppose either that he held his appointment at the port of Capernaum, or that he collected the customs on the high road to Damascus, which went through what is now called Khan Minyeh, which place, as Robinson has shown, is the ancient Capernaum. Thus we see that Matthew belonged to the lower class of people.

In Mark ii. 14, and Luke v. 27, he is called Levi. We hence conclude that he had two names. This circumstance is not mentioned in the list of the apostles (Matt. x. and Luke vi.); but the omission does not prove the contrary, as we may infer from the fact that Lebbæus is also called Judas in Luke vi. 16, in which verse the name Lebbæus is omitted. In Matt. ix. 9 is related how Matthew was called to be an apostle. We must, however, suppose that he was previously acquainted with Jesus, since we read in Luke vi. 13, that when Jesus, before delivering the Sermon on the Mount. selected twelve disciples, who were to form the circle of his more intimate associates, Matthew was one of them. After this Matthew returned to his usual occupation; from which Jesus, on leaving Capernaum, called him away. On this occasion Matthew gave a parting entertainment to his friends. After this event he is mentioned only in Acts i. 13.

According to a statement in Clemens Alexandrinus, Matthew abstained from animal food. Hence some writers have rather hastily concluded that he belonged to the sect of the Essenes. It is true that the Essenes practised abstinence in a high degree; but it is not true that they rejected animal food altogether. Admitting the

account in Clemens Alexandrinus to be correct, it proves only a certain ascetic strictness, of which there occur vestiges in the habits of other Jews.

According to another account, which is as old as the first century, Matthew, after the death of Jesus, remained about fifteen years in Jerusalem This agrees with the statement in Eusebius (*Hist. Eccles.* iii. 24), that Matthew preached to his own nation before he went to foreign countries. Rufinus (*Hist. Eccles.* x. 9) and Socrates (*Hist. Eccles.* i. 19) state that he afterwards went into Ethiopia; and other authors mention other countries. There also he probably preached specially to the Jews. According to Heracleon (about A.D. 150) and Clemens Alex. (*Strom.* iv. 9), Matthew was one of those apostles who did not suffer martyrdom.

THE GOSPEL OF ST. MATTHEW.—The genuineness of this Gospel has been more strongly attacked than that of any of the three others, as well by EXTERNAL as by INTERNAL arguments. With regard to the former, external testimonies are clearly in favour of the genuineness of this Gospel. Its authenticity, indeed, is as well supported as that of any work of classical antiquity. It can also be proved that it was early in use among Christians, and that the Apostolical Fathers at the end of the first century ascribed to it a canonical authority.

A good deal of discussion respecting the question—whether or not there was a Hebrew Gospel of St. Matthew, has arisen out of a statement made by Papias, that 'Matthew wrote the sayings in the Hebrew tongue.' Tholuck, who inclines to the opinion that the original Gospel of St. Matthew was written in Hebrew, thinks it by no means improbable that, after several inaccurate and imperfect translations of this original came into circulation, Matthew himself was prompted by this circumstance to publish a Greek translation, or to have his Gospel translated under his own supervision.

With regard to the internal arguments which have been brought against the authenticity of this Gospel, it has been objected, 1st, that the representations of Matthew have not that vivid clearness which characterizes the narration of an eyewitness, and which we find, for instance, in the Gospel of John. Even Mark and Luke surpass Matthew in this respect. Compare, for example, Matt. iv. 18 with Luke v. 1, sq.; Matt. viii. 5, sq. with Luke vii. 1, sq. This is most striking in the history of his own call, where we should expect a clearer representation.

2nd. He omits some facts which every apostle certainly knew. For instance, he mentions only one journey of Christ to the passover at Jerusalem. namely, the last; and seems to be acquainted only with one sphere of Christ's activity, namely, Galilee.

3rd. He relates unchronologically, and transposes events to times in which they did not happen; for instance, the event mentioned in Luke iv. 14-30 must have happened at the commencement of Christ's public career, but Matthew relates it as late as ch. xiii. 53, sq.

4th. He embodies in one discourse several sayings of Christ which, according to Luke, were pronounced at different times (comp. Matt. v. vii., and xxiii.).

To these objections we may reply as follows:—
1st. The gift of narrating luminously is a personal qualification of which even an apostle might be destitute, and which is rarely found among the lower orders of people : this argument therefore has recently been given up altogether. In the history of his call to be an apostle, Matthew has this advantage over Mark and Luke, that he relates the discourse of Christ (ix. 13) with greater completeness than these evangelists. Luke relates that Matthew prepared a great banquet in his house, while Matthew simply mentions that an entertainment took place, because the apostle could not well write that he himself prepared a great banquet.

2nd. An *argumentum a silentio* must not be urged against the evangelists. The raising of Lazarus is narrated only by John ; and the raising of the youth at Nain only by Luke ; the appearance to five hundred brethren after the resurrection, which, according to the testimony of Paul (1 Cor. xv. 6), was a fact generally known, is not recorded by any of the evangelists. The apparent restriction of Christ's sphere of activity to Galilee we find also in Mark and Luke. This peculiarity arose perhaps from the circumstance that the apostles first taught in Jerusalem, where it was unnecessary to relate what had happened there, but where the events which had taken place in Galilee were unknown, and required to be narrated : thus the sphere of narration may have gradually become fixed.

3rd. There is no reason to suppose that the Evangelists intended to write a chronological biography. On the contrary, we learn from Luke i. 4, and John xx. 31, that their object was of a more practical and apologetical tendency. With the exception of John, the Evangelists have grouped their communications more according to the subjects than according to chronological succession. This fact is now generally admitted. The principal groups of facts recorded by St. Matthew are : — 1. The preparation of Jesus, narrated in ch. i.-iv. 16. 2. The public ministry of Jesus, narrated in ch. iv. 17-xvi. 20. 3. The conclusion of the life of Jesus, narrated in ch. xvi. 21-xxviii.

But our opponents further assert that the Evangelist not only groups together events belonging to different times, but that some of his dates are incorrect : for instance, the date in Matt. xiii. 53 cannot be correct if Luke, ch. iv., has placed the event rightly. If, however, we carefully consider the matter, we shall find that Matthew has placed this fact more chronologically than Luke. It is true that the question in Matt. xiii. 54, and the annunciation in Luke iv. 18-21, seem to synchronize best with the first public appearance of Jesus. But even Schleiermacher, who, in his work on Luke, generally gives the preference to the arrangement of that evangelist, nevertheless observes (p. 63) that Luke iv. 23 leads us to suppose that Jesus abode for a longer period in Capernaum (comp. the words ' as his custom was ' in ver. 16).

4th. If the evangelist arranges his statements according to subjects, and not chronologically, we must not be surprised that he connects similar sayings of Christ, inserting them in the longer discourses after analogous topics had been mentioned. These discourses are not compiled by

the Evangelist, but always form the fundamental framework to which sometimes analogous subjects are attached. But even this is not the case in the Sermon on the Mount ; and in ch. xiii. it may be doubted whether the parables were spoken at different times. In the discourses recorded in ch. x. and xxiii., it can be proved that several sayings are more correctly placed by Matthew than by Luke (comp. especially Matt. xxiii. 37-39 with Luke xiii. 34, 35).

These arguments may be supported by adding the positive internal proofs which exist in favour of the apostolical origin of this Gospel. 1. The nature of the book agrees entirely with the statements of the Fathers of the church, from whom we learn that it was written for Jewish readers. None of the other Evangelists quote the Old Testament so often as Matthew, who, moreover, does not explain the Jewish rites and expressions, which are explained by Mark and John. 2. If there is a want of precision in the narration of facts, there is, on the other hand, a peculiar accuracy and richness in the reports given of the discourses of Jesus ; so that we may easily conceive why Papias styled the Gospel of Matthew, *the sayings of the Lord.*

Some of the most beautiful and most important sayings of our Lord, the historical credibility of which no sceptic can attack, have been preserved by Matthew alone (Matt. xi. 28-30 ; xvi. 16-19 ; xxviii. 20 ; comp. also xi. 2-21 ; xii. 3-6, 25-29 ; xvii. 12, 25, 26 ; xxvi. 13). Above all, the Sermon on the Mount must here be considered, which is given by Matthew, and which forms the most beautiful and the best arranged whole of all the evangelical discourses.

With regard to the DATE of this gospel, Clemens Alexandrinus and Origen state that it was written before the others. Irenæus agrees with them, but places its origin rather late—namely, at the time when Peter and Paul were at Rome. Even De Wette grants that it was written before the destruction of Jerusalem. In proof of this we may also quote ch. xxvii. 8.

MATTHI'AS (*Matthew*), one of the seventy disciples who was chosen by lot, in preference to Joseph Barsabas, into the number of the apostles, to supply the deficiency caused by the treachery and suicide of Judas (Acts i. 23-26). Nothing is known of his subsequent career.

MAZZA'ROTH (Job xxxviii. 32). [ASTRONOMY.]

MEASURES. [WEIGHTS AND MEASURES.]

ME'DAD and EL'DAD, two of the seventy elders who were nominated to assist Moses in the government of the people, but who remained in the camp, probably as modestly deeming themselves unfit for the office, when the others presented themselves at the Tabernacle. The Divine spirit, however, rested on them even there, ' and they prophesied in the camp ' (Num. xi. 24-29). The Targum of Jonathan alleges that these two men were brothers of Moses and Aaron by the mother's side.

ME'DAN or MADAN, son of Abraham, by Keturah (Gen. xxv. 2). He and his brother Midian are supposed to have peopled the country of Midian, east of the Dead Sea.

MED'EBA, a town east of the Jordan, in the tribe of Reuben (Josh. xiii. 9. 16), before which was fought the great battle in which Joab defeated the Ammonites and their allies (1 Chron. xix. 7). It originally belonged to the Moabites (Num. xxi. 30); and after the captivity of the tribes beyond the Jordan, they again took possession of it (Isa. xv. 2). The *Onomasticon* places it near Heshbon; and it was once the seat of one of the thirty-five bishoprics of Arabia (Reland, *Palæstina*, pp. 217, 223, 226) Medeba, now in ruins, still retains its ancient name, and is situated upon a round hill seven miles south of Heshbon. The ruins are about a mile and a half in circuit, but not a single edifice remains perfect.

MEDES, the inhabitants in ancient times of one of the most fruitful and populous countries of Asia, called Media, the precise boundaries of which it is not easy, if indeed it is now possible, to ascertain. Winer defines it as the country which lies westward and southward from the Caspian Sea, between 35° and 40° of N. lat. Nature has divided Media into three great divisions. On the north is a flat, moist, and insalubrious district, stretching along the Caspian Sea, which is made a separate portion by a chain of hills connected with Anti-Taurus. In this plain and on these mountains there live uncultivated and independent tribes. The country is now known under the names of Masanderan and Gilan. South of this mountain range lies the country which the ancients denominated Atropatene, being separated on the west from Armenia by Mount Caspius, which springs from Ararat; and on the south and south-east by the Orontes range of hills, which runs through Media. South and south-east of the Orontes is a third district, formerly termed Great Media, which Mount Zagros separates from Assyria on the west, and from Persia on the south: on the east it is bordered by deserts, and connected on the north-east with Parthia and Hyrcania by means of Mount Caspius, being now called Irak-Ajemi. This for the most part is a high hilly country, yet not without rich and fruitful valleys, and even plains. The sky is clear and bright, and the climate healthy. Media Atropatene, which corresponds pretty nearly with the modern Azerbijan, contains fruitful and well-peopled valleys and plains. The northern mountainous region is cold and unfruitful. In Great Media lay the metropolis of the country, Ecbatana, as well as the province of Rhagiana and the city Rhagæ, with the plain of Nisæum, celebrated in the time of the Persian empire for its horses and horse-races. This plain was near the city Nisæa, around which were fine pasture lands producing excellent clover. The horses were entirely white, and of extraordinary height and beauty, as well as speed. They constituted a part of the luxury of the great, and a tribute in kind was paid from them to the monarch, who, like all Eastern sovereigns, used to delight in equestrian display. Some idea of the opulence of the country may be had when it is known that, independently of imposts rendered in money, Media paid a yearly tribute of not less than 3000 horses, 4000 mules, and nearly 100,000 sheep. The races, once celebrated through the world, appear to exist no more; but Ker Porter saw the Shah ride on festival occasions a splendid horse of pure white. Cattle abounded, as did the richest fruits, as pines, citrons, oranges, all of peculiar excellence, growing as in their native land. Here also was found the Silphium (pro-

bably assafœtida), which formed a considerable article in the commerce of the ancients, and was accounted worth its weight in gold. The Median dress was proverbially splendid; the dress, that is, of the highest class, which seems to have gained a sort of classical authority, and to have been at a later period worn at the Persian court, probably in part from its antiquity. This dress the Persian monarchs used to present to those whom they wished to honour, and no others were permitted to wear it. It consisted of a long white loose robe, or gown, flowing down to the feet, and enclosing the entire body. The nature and the celebrity of this dress combine with the natural richness of the country to assure us that the ancient Medians had made no mean progress in the arts; indeed, the colours of the Persian textures are known to have been accounted second only to those of India. If these regal dresses were of silk, then was there an early commerce between Media and India; if not, weaving, as well as dyeing, must have been practised and carried to a high degree of perfection in the former country (Dan. iii. 21).

The religion of the Medes consisted in the worship of the heavenly bodies, more particularly the sun and moon, and the planets Jupiter, Venus, Saturn, Mercury, and Mars. The priestly caste were denominated magi; they were a separate tribe, and had the charge not only of religion, but of all the higher culture.

The language of the ancient Medes was not connected with the Shemitic, but the Indian; and divided itself into two chief branches, the Zend, spoken in North Media, and the Pehlvi, spoken in Lower Media and Parthia; which last was the dominant tongue among the Parthians.

The Medes originally consisted of six tribes, of which the Magi were one. Being overcome by Ninus, they formed a part of the great Assyrian empire, which, however, lost in course of time the primitive simplicity of manners to which its dominion was owing, and fell into luxury and consequent weakness; when Arbaces, who governed the country as a satrap for Sardanapalus, taking advantage of the effeminacy of that monarch, threw off his yoke, destroyed his capital, Nineveh, and became himself sovereign of the Medes, in the ninth century before the Christian era. According to Diodorus, this empire extended through nine monarchs, enduring 310 years, until Astyages, son of Cyaxares, was dethroned by Cyrus in the year of the world 3495, when Media became a part of the Persian empire, sinking from the same inevitable causes as those which enabled it to gain over the Assyrian power the dominion of Asia. The account given by Herodotus varies from that now set forth. We do not propose to subject the diversities to a critical investigation, believing that little, if any, good could result, at least within our narrow space. Dates, names, and dynasties may be more or less uncertain, but the facts we have given are unimpeached. The magnitude of the Median empire is another important fact equally well ascertained. Being in their time the most valorous, as well as the most powerful nation of Asia, the Medes extended their power towards the east and the west beyond any strictly definable limits, though, like dominion generally in Oriental countries, it was of a vague, variable, and unstable kind. That they regarded the Tigris as their western boundary appears from the fact that they erected on its banks strongholds, such as Mespila and Larissa; but that they carried their victorious arms still farther westward, appears from both Herodotus (i. 134) and Isaiah (xiii. 17, 18). The eastern limits of the empire seem to have been different at different periods. Heeren inclines to the opinion that it may have reached as far as the Oxus, and even the Indus. Many, however, were the nations and tribes which were under the sway of its sovereigns. The government was a succession of satrapies, over all of which the Medes were paramount; but the different nations exerted a secondary dominion over each other, diminishing with the increase of distance from the centre of royal power, to which ultimately the tribute paid by each dependent to his superior eventually and securely came. Not only were the Medes a powerful, but also a wealthy and cultivated people; indeed, before they sank, in consequence of their degeneracy, into the Persian empire, they were during their time the-foremost people of Asia, owing their celebrity not only to their valour, but also to the position of their country, which was the great commercial highway of Asia. The sovereigns exerted absolute and unlimited dominion, exacted a rigid court-ceremonial, and displayed a great love of pomp. Under the Persian monarchs Media formed a province, or satrapy, by itself, whose limits did not correspond with independent Media, but cannot be accurately defined. To Media belonged another country, namely, Aria, which, Heeren says, took its name from the river Arius (now Heri), but which appears to contain the elements of the name in the Zend language, which was common to the two, if not to other Eastern nations, who were denominated Indians by Alexander the Great, as dwellers in or near the Indus, which he also misnamed, but who were known in their own tongue as Arians. Subsequently, however, from whatever cause, the Arians were separated from the Medes, forming a distinct satrapy in the Persian empire. Thus the name of a clan, or gens, became the name of a nation, and then of an individual tribe. It may be added that Schlosser holds it as a fundamental fact, that the Medes and Persians formed in reality one kingdom, only that now one, now another, of the two elements gained predominance: whence he thinks himself enabled to explain the discrepancies which the ancients present as to the names and succession of monarchs.

The Medes are not mentioned in sacred Scripture till the days of Hoshea, king of Israel, about 740 B.C., when Shalmaneser, king of Assyria, brought that monarch under his yoke, and in the ninth year of his reign took Samaria, and carried Israel away into Assyria, placing them in Halah and in Habor, by the river of Gozan, and in the cities of the Medes. Here the Medes appear as a part of the Assyrian empire; but at a later period Scripture exhibits them as an independent and sovereign people (Isa. xiii. 17; Jer. xxv. 25; li. 11, 28). In the last passage their kings are expressly named: 'The Lord hath raised up the kings of the Medes; for his device is against Babylon to destroy it.' 'Prepare against her (Babylon) the kings of the Medes, the captains thereof, and all the rulers thereof.' It has been conjectured that soon after the time of Arbaces they

again fell under the dominion of the Assyrians; but availing themselves of the opportunity afforded by the distant expeditions which Sennacherio undertook, they gained their freedom, and founded a new line of kings under Dejoces. Indeed, so sudden and rapid are the changes of government, even to the present day, in Oriental monarchies, that we need not be surprised at any difficulties which may occur in arranging the dynasties or the succession of kings, scarcely in any ancient history, certainly least of all in the fragmentary notices preserved regarding the kings of Media and other neighbouring empires. According, however, to other historical testimony, we find the Medes and Persians united as one people in holy writ (Dan. v. 28; vi. 15; viii. 20; Esth. i. 3, 18; x. 2), in the days of Cyrus, who destroyed the separate sovereignty of the former. To the united kingdom Babylon was added as a province. After the lapse of about 200 years, Media, in junction with the entire Persian monarchy, fell under the yoke of Alexander the Great (B.C. 330); but after the death of Alexander it became, under Seleucus Nicator, the Macedonian governor of Media and Babylonia, a portion of the new Syrian kingdom (1 Macc. vi. 56), and, after many variations of warlike fortune, passed over to the Parthian monarchy (1 Macc. xiv. 2; Strabo, xvi. p. 745).

The ancient Medes were a warlike people, and much feared for their skill in archery. They appear armed with the bow in the army of the Persians, who borrowed the use of that weapon from them. Those who remained in the more mountainous districts did not lose their valour; but the inhabitants of the cities and towns which covered the plains, in becoming commercial lost their former hardy habits, together with their bravery, and, giving way to luxury, became in process of time an easy prey to new aspirants to martial fame and civil dominion.

MEDIATOR. 1. 'Mediator' is a word peculiar to the Scriptures, and is used, in an accommodated sense, by many of the ancient Fathers, to denote one who intervenes between two dispensations. Hence it is applied to John the Baptist, because he came, as it were, between the Mosaic and Christian dispensations.

2. Again, it signifies, in its more proper sense, an internuncius, or ambassador, one who stands as the channel of communication between two contracting parties. Some commentators think that the Apostle Paul, in Gal. iii. 19, calls Moses mediator, because he conveyed the expression of God's will to the people, and reported to God their wants, wishes, and determinations. Many ancient and modern divines, however, are of opinion that Christ himself, and not Moses, is here meant by the inspired Apostle, and this view would seem to be confirmed by comparing Deut. xxxiii. 2 with Acts vii. 38-52.

3. Christ is called Mediator by virtue of the reconciliation He has effected between a justly offended God and his rebellious creature man. In this sense of the term Moses was, on many occasions, an eminent type of Christ. The latter, however, was not Mediator, merely by reason of his coming between God and his creatures, as certain heretics would affirm; but because he appeased his wrath, and made reconciliation for iniquity.

MEGID'DO, in Zech. xii. 11, a town belonging to Manasseh, although within the boundaries of Issachar (Josh. xvii. 11). It had been originally one of the royal cities of the Canaanites (Josh. xii. 21), and was one of those of which the Israelites were unable for a long time to gain actual possession. Megiddo was rebuilt and fortified by Solomon (1 Kings ix. 15), and thither Ahaziah king of Judah fled when wounded by Jehu, and died there (2 Kings ix. 27). It was in the battle near this place that Josiah was slain by Pharaoh-Necho (2 Kings xxiii. 29, 30; 2 Chron. xxxv. 20-25). From the great mourning held for his loss, it became proverbial to compare any grievous mourning as being 'like the mourning of Hadadrimmon in the valley of Megiddon' (Zech. xii. 11). 'The waters of Megiddo' are mentioned in Judges v. 19; and are probably those formed by the river Kishon. Eusebius and Jerome do not attempt to mark the situation of the place, and it appears that the name Megiddo was in their time already lost. They often mentioned a town called Legio, which must in their day have been an important and well-known place, as they assume it as a central point from which to mark the position of several other places in this quarter. This has been identified with the village now called Lejjun, which is situated upon the western border of the great plain of Esdraelon, where it begins to rise gently towards the low range of wooded hills that connect Carmel with the mountains of Samaria. This place was visited by Maundrell, who speaks of it as an old village near a brook, with a khan then in good repair. This khan was for the accommodation of the caravan on the route between Egypt and Damascus, which passes here. Having already identified the present village of Taannuk with the ancient Taanach, the vicinity of this to Lejjun induced Dr. Robinson to conceive that the latter might be the ancient Megiddo, seeing that Taanach and Megiddo are constantly named together in Scripture; and to this a writer in a German review adds the further consideration that the name of Legio was latterly applied to the plain, or low valley along the Kishon, as that of Megiddo had been in more ancient times. If this explanation be accepted, and it is certainly probable, though not certain, it only remains to conclude that the ancient Legio was not founded by the Romans, but that this was a new name imposed upon a still older place, which, like the names Neapolis (now Nabulus) and Sebaste (now Sebûstieh), has maintained itself in the mouths of the native population, while the earlier name has perished.

MELCHIZ'EDEK (*king of righteousness*), 'priest of the most high God,' and king of Salem, who went forth to meet Abraham on his return from the pursuit of Chedorlaomer and his allies, who had carried Lot away captive. He brought refreshment, described in the general terms of 'bread and wine,' for the fatigued warriors, and bestowed his blessing upon their leader, who, in return, gave to the royal priest a tenth of all the spoil which had been acquired in his expedition (Gen. xiv. 18, 20).

This statement seems sufficiently plain, and to offer nothing very extraordinary; yet it has formed the basis of much speculation and controversy. In particular, the fact that Abraham gave a tithe to Melchizedek attracted much attention among the later Jews. In one of the Messianic Psalms (cx. 4), it is foretold that the Messiah should be 'a priest after the order of Melchizedek;' which the author of the Epistle to the Hebrews (vi. 20) cites as showing that Melchizedek was a type of Christ, and the Jews themselves, certainly on the authority of this passage of the Psalms, regarded Melchizedek as a type of the regal-priesthood, higher than that of Aaron, to which the Messiah should belong. The bread and wine which were set forth on the table of shew-bread, was also supposed to be represented by the bread and wine which the king of Salem brought forth to Abraham (Schottgen, *Hor. Heb.* ii. 645). A mysterious supremacy came also to be assigned to Melchizedek, by reason of his having received tithes from the Hebrew patriarch; and on this point the Epistle to the Hebrews (vii. 1-10) expatiates strongly, as showing the inferiority of the priesthood represented, to that of Melchizedek, to which the Messiah belonged. 'Consider how great this man was, unto whom even the patriarch Abraham gave a tenth of the spoils;' and he goes on to argue that the Aaronic priesthood, who themselves received tithes of the Jews, actually paid tithes to Melchizedek in the person of their great ancestor. This superiority is, as we take it, inherent in his typical rather than his personal character. But the Jews, in admitting this official or personal superiority of Melchizedek to Abraham, sought to account for it by alleging that the royal priest was no other than Shem, the most pious of Noah's sons, who, according to the shorter chronology, might have lived to the time of Abraham. Such conjectures require no refutation. The best founded opinion seems to be that of Carpzov and the most judicious moderns, who, after Josephus, allege that Melchizedek was a principal person among the Canaanites and posterity of Noah, and eminent for holiness and justice, and therefore discharged the priestly as well as regal functions among the people: and we may conclude that his twofold capacity of king and priest (characters very commonly united in the remote ages) afforded Abraham an opportunity of testifying his thankfulness to God in the manner usual in those times, by offering a tenth of all the spoil. This combination of characters happens for the first time in Scripture to be exhibited in his person, which, with the abrupt manner in which he is introduced, and the nature of the intercourse between him and Abraham, render him in various respects an appropriate and obvious type of the Messiah in his united regal and priestly character.

Salem, of which Melchizedek was king, is usually supposed to have been the original of *Jerusalem*.

MEL'ITA, an island in the Mediterranean, on which the ship which was conveying St. Paul as a prisoner to Rome was wrecked, and which was the scene of the interesting circumstances recorded in Acts xxvii. 28.

Melita was the ancient name of Malta, and also of a small island in the Adriatic, now called Meleda, and each of these has found warm advocates for its identification with the Melita of Scripture. The received and long-established opinion is undoubtedly in favour of Malta; and those who uphold the claims of Meleda are to be regarded as dissenting from the general conclusion. This dissent proceeds chiefly upon the ground that the ship of St. Paul was 'driven about in (the sea of) Adria,' when wrecked on Melita. But it has been shown from ancient writers, that the name Adria was not, in its ancient acceptation, limited to the present Adriatic Sea, but comprehended the seas of Greece and Sicily, and extended even to Africa. Consequently the only strong argument in favour of Meleda must be regarded as having been entirely overthrown.

The name of St. Paul's Bay has been given to the place where the shipwreck is supposed to have taken place. This, the sacred historian says, was at 'a certain creek with a shore,' i. e. a seemingly practicable shore, on which they purposed, if possible, to strand the vessel, as their only apparent chance to escape being broken on the rocks. In attempting this the ship seems to have struck and gone to pieces on the rocky headland at the entrance of the creek. This agrees very well with St. Paul's Bay, more so than with any other creek of the island. This bay is a deep inlet on the north side of the island, being the last indentation of the coast but one from the western extremity of the island. It is about two miles deep, by one mile broad. The harbour which it forms is very unsafe at some distance from the shore, although there is good anchorage in the middle for light vessels. The most dangerous part is the western headland at the entrance of the bay, particularly as there is close to it a small island (Salamone), and a still smaller islet (Salamonetta), the currents and shoals around which are particularly dangerous in stormy weather. It is usually supposed that the vessel struck at this point. From this place the ancient capital of Malta (now Citta Vecchia, Old City) is distinctly seen at the distance of about five miles; and on looking towards the bay from the top of the church on the summit of the hill whereon the city stands, it occurred to the present writer that the people of the town might easily from this spot have perceived in the morning that a wreck had taken place; and this is a circumstance which throws a fresh light on some of the circumstances of the deeply interesting transactions which ensued.

The sacred historian calls the inhabitants 'barbarians:'—' the barbarous people showed us no small kindness.' This is far from implying that they were savages or uncivilized men; it merely intimates that they were not of Greek or Roman origin. This description applies to the ancient inhabitants of Malta most accurately; and as it could not apply to the inhabitants of Melida, who were Greeks, this is another argument to show that not Melida but Malta is the Melita of Scripture.

The island of Malta lies in the Mediterranean, about sixty miles south from Cape Passaro in Sicily. It is sixty miles in circumference, twenty in length, and twelve in breadth. Near it, on the west, is a smaller island, called Gozo, about thirty miles in circumference. Malta has no mountains or high hills, and makes no figure from the sea. It is naturally a barren rock, but has been made in parts abundantly fertile by the

industry and toil of man. The island was first colonized by the Phœnicians, from whom it was taken by the Greek colonists in Sicily, about B.C. 736; but the Carthaginians began to dispute its possession about B.C. 528, and eventually became entire masters of it. From their hands it passed into those of the Romans B.C. 242, who treated the inhabitants well, making Melita a municipium, and allowing the people to be governed by their own laws. The government was administered by a proprætor, who depended upon the prætor of Sicily; and this office appears to have been held by Publius when Paul was on the island (Acts xxviii. 7). On the division of the Roman empire, Melita belonged to the western portion; but having, in A.D. 553, been recovered from the Vandals by Belisarius, it was afterwards attached to the empire of the East. About the end of the ninth century the island was taken from the Greeks by the Arabs, who made it a dependency upon Sicily, which was also in their possession. The Arabs have left the impress of their aspect, language, and many of their customs, upon the present inhabitants, whose dialect is to this day perfectly intelligible to the Arabians and to the Moors of Africa. Malta was taken from the Arabs by the Normans in A.D. 1090, and afterwards underwent other changes till A.D. 1530, when Charles V., who had annexed it to his empire, transferred it to the Knights of St. John of Jerusalem, whom the Turks had recently dispossessed of Rhodes. Under the knights it became a flourishing state, and was the scene of their greatest glory and most signal exploits. The institution having become unsuited to modern times, the Order of St. John of Jerusalem, commonly called Knights of Malta, gradually fell into decay, and the island was surrendered to the French under Buonaparte when on his way to Egypt in 1798. From them it was retaken by the English with the concurrence and assistance of the natives; and it was to have been restored to the Knights of Malta by the stipulations of the treaty of Amiens; but as no sufficient security for the independence of the Order (composed mostly of Frenchmen) could be obtained, the English retained it in their hands, which necessary infraction of the treaty was the ostensible ground of the war which only ended with the battle of Waterloo. The island is still in the hands of the English, who have lately remodelled the government to meet the wishes of the numerous inhabitants. It has recently become the actual seat of an Anglican bishopric, which however takes its title from Gibraltar out of deference to the existing Roman Catholic bishopric of Malta, a deference not paid to the Oriental churches in recently establishing the Anglican bishopric of Jerusalem.

MELON. The word thus rendered, and no doubt correctly, occurs only in Num. xi. 5. The gourd tribe are remarkable for their power of adapting themselves to the different situations where they can be grown. Neither extreme heat nor extreme moisture prove injurious to them. Mr. Moorcroft describes an extensive cultivation of melons and cucumbers on the beds of weeds which float on the lakes of Cashmere. They are similarly cultivated in Persia and in China. In India 'some of the species may be seen in the most arid places, others in the densest jungles.

Planted at the foot of a tree, they emulate the vine in ascending its branches; and near a hut they soon cover its thatch with a coating of green. They form a principal portion of the culture of Indian gardens; the farmer even rears them in the neighbourhood of his wells' (Royle, *Himalayan Botany*, p. 218).

These plants, though known to the Greeks, are not natives of Europe, but of Eastern countries, whence they must have been introduced into Greece. They probably may be traced to Syria or Egypt, whence other cultivated plants, as well as civilization, have travelled westwards. In Egypt they formed a portion of the food of the people at the very early period when the Israelites were led by Moses from its rich cultivation into the midst of the desert. The melon, the water-melon, and several others of the Cucurbitaceæ, are mentioned by Wilkinson (*Thebes*, p. 212; *Ancient Egyptians*, iv. 62), as still cultivated there, and are described as being sown in the middle of December, and cut, the melons in ninety and the cucumbers in sixty days.

The melon was known to the Romans, and cultivated by Columella, with the assistance of some precaution at cold times of the year. It is said to have been introduced into this country about the year 1520, and was called musk-melon to distinguish it from the pumpkin, which was usually called melon.

The melon, being thus a native of warm climates, is necessarily tender in those of Europe, but, being an annual, it is successfully cultivated by gardeners with the aid of glass and artificial heat of about 75° to 80°. The fruit of the melon may be seen in great variety, whether with respect to the colour of its rind or of its flesh, its taste or its odour, and also its external form and size. The flesh is soft and succulent, of a white, yellowish, or reddish hue, of a sweet and pleasant taste, of an agreeable, sometimes musk-like odour, and forms one of the most delicious of fruits, which, when taken in moderation, is wholesome, but, like all other fruits of a similar kind, is liable to cause indigestion and diarrhœa when eaten in excess, especially by those unaccustomed to its use.

With the melon it is necessary to notice the Water-Melon, which at present is cultivated in all parts of Asia, in the north of Africa, and in the south of Europe.

The water-melon is clearly distinguished by Alpinus as cultivated in Egypt. Though resembling the other kinds very considerably in its properties, it is very different from them in its deeply-cut leaves, from which it is compared to a very different plant of this tribe—that is, the colocynth. A few others have cut leaves, but the water-melon is so distinguished among the edible species. The plant is hairy, with trailing cirrhiferous stems. The pulp abounds so much in watery juice, that it will run out by a hole made through the rind; and it is from this peculiarity that it has obtained the names of water-melon, melon d'eau, wasser-melon. Hasselquist says that it is cultivated on the banks of the Nile, in the rich clayey earth which subsides during the inundation, and serves 'the Egyptians for meat, drink, and physic. It is eaten in abundance, during the season, even by the richer sort of people; but the common people, on whom Providence hath bestowed nothing but poverty and patience, scarcely eat anything but these, and account this the best time of the year, as they are obliged to put up with worse at other seasons of the year.'

MEM'PHIS, a very ancient city, the capital of Lower Egypt, standing at the apex of the Delta, ruins of which are still found not far from its successor and modern representative, Cairo. Its Egyptian name, in the hieroglyphics, is Menofri; in Coptic, Memfi, Manfi, Membe, Panoufi or Mefi, being probably corrupted from Man-nofri, 'the abode,' or, as Plutarch terms it, 'the haven of good men.' It was called also Pthah-ei, the abode of Pthah. In Hebrew the city bears the name of Moph (Hos. ix. 6), or Noph (Isa. xix. 13). These several names are obviously variations of one, of which Meph seems to contain the essential sounds. Whether we may hence derive support to the statement that the place was founded by Menes, the first human king of Egypt, or whether we have here a very early instance of the custom which prevailed so extensively among the Greeks and Romans, of inventing founders for cities, having names correspondent with the names of the places they were said to have built, it is impossible, with the materials we possess, to determine with any fair approach to certainty. Menes, however, is universally reputed to have founded not only Memphis but Thebes; the addition of the latter may seem to invalidate his claim to the former, making us suspect that here, too, we have a case of that custom of referring to some one distinguished name great events which happened, in truth, at different and far distant eras. If, as is probable, Thebes as well as Memphis was, at any early period, the seat of a distinct dynasty, the cradle and the throne of a line of independent sovereigns, they could scarcely have had one founder.

Memphis is said to have been founded by Menes, who, according to tradition, having diverted the course of the Nile, which had washed the foot of the sandy mountains of the Libyan chain, obliged it to run in the centre of the valley, and built the city Memphis in the bed of the ancient channel. This change was effected by constructing a dyke about a hundred stadia above the site of the projected city, whose lofty mounds and strong embankments turned the water to the East and confined the river to its new bed. The dyke was carefully kept in repair by succeeding kings, and even as late as the Persian invasion, a guard was always maintained there to overlook the necessary repairs; for, as Herodotus asserts, if the river were to break through the dyke, the whole of Memphis would be in danger of being overwhelmed with water, especially at the period of the inundation. Subsequently, however, when the increased deposit of the alluvial soil had raised the circumjacent plains, the precautions became unnecessary; and though the spot where the diversion of the Nile was made may still be traced, owing to the great bend it takes about fourteen miles above ancient Memphis, the lofty mounds once raised there are no longer visible. The site of Memphis was first accurately fixed by Pococke, at the village of Metrahenny. According to the reports of the French, the heaps which mark the site of the ancient buildings have three leagues of circumference; but this is less than its extent in early times, since Diodorus gives it 150 stadia, or six leagues and a quarter. Memphis declined after the foundation of Alexandria, and its materials were carried off to build Cairo.

The kingdom of which Memphis was the capital was most probably the Egypt of the patriarchs, in which Abraham, Jacob, and the Israelites resided. Psammetichus, in becoming sole monarch of all Egypt, raised Memphis to the dignity of the one metropolis of the entire land, after which Memphis grew in the degree in which Thebes declined. It became distinguished for a multitude of splendid edifices, among which may be mentioned a large and magnificent temple to Vulcan, who was called by the Egyptians Phthah, the demiurgos, or creative power. Under the dominion of the Persians, as well as of the Ptolemies, Memphis retained its pre-eminence as the capital, though even in the time of the former it began to part with its splendour; and when the latter bestowed their favour on Alexandria, it suffered a material change for the worse, from which the place never recovered. In the days of Strabo many of its fine buildings lay in ruins, though the city was still large and populous. The final blow was given to the prosperity of Memphis in the time of Abdollatif, by the erection of the Arabian city of Cairo.

That the arts were carried to a great degree of excellence at Memphis is proved by the most abundant evidence. Its manufactures of glass were famed for the superior quality of their workmanship, with which Rome continued to be supplied long after Egypt became a province of the empire. The environs of Memphis presented cultivated groves of the acacia tree, of whose wood were made the planks and masts of boats, the handles of offensive weapons of war, and various articles of furniture. Memphis was also distinguished as being the place where Apis was kept, and where his worship received special honour.

MEN'AHEM (*consoler*), sixteenth king of Israel, who began to reign B.C. 772, and reigned ten years. Menahem appears to have been one of the generals of king Zechariah. When he heard the news of the murder of that prince, and the usurpation of Shallum, he was at Tirzah, but immediately marched to Samaria, where Shallum had shut himself up, and slew him in that city. He then usurped the throne in his turn; and forthwith marched to Tiphsah, which refused to acknowledge his rule. Having taken this place after a siege, he treated the inhabitants with a degree of savage barbarity, which, as Josephus remarks (*Antiq.* ix. 11. 1), would not have been pardonable even to foreigners. He adhered to the sin of Jeroboam, like the other kings of Israel. In his time the Assyrians, under their king Pul, made their first appearance on the borders of Palestine; and Menahem was only able to save himself from this great invading power at the heavy price of 1000 talents of silver, which he raised by a tax of 50 shekels from every man of substance in Israel. This was probably the only choice left to him; and he is not therefore to be blamed, as he had not that resource in the treasures of the temple of which the kings of Judah availed themselves in similar emergencies. Menahem died in B.C. 761, leaving the throne to his son Pekahiah (2 Kings xv. 14-22).

ME'NE, ME'NE, TE'KEL, UPHAR'SIN, the inscription supernaturally written 'upon the plaster of the wall' in Belshazzar's palace at Babylon (Dan. v. 5-25), which 'the astrologers, the Chaldæans, and the soothsayers' could neither read nor interpret, but which Daniel first read, and then interpreted. Yet the words, as they are found in Daniel, are pure Chaldee, and if they appeared in the Chaldee character, could have been read, at least, by any person present on the occasion who understood the alphabet of his own language. To account for their inability to decipher this inscription, it has been supposed that it consisted of those Chaldee words written in another character. Dr. Hales thinks that it may have been written in the primitive Hebrew character, from which the Samaritan was formed, and that, in order to show on this occasion that the writer of the inscription was the offended God of Israel, whose authority was being at that moment peculiarly despised (ver. 2, 3, 4), he adopted his own sacred character, in which he had originally written the Decalogue, which Daniel could understand, though it would be unknown to the wise men of Babylon. This theory has the recommendation, that it involves as little as possible of miraculous agency. It has been supposed by some, that 'the wise men' were not so much at fault to read the inscription, as to explain its meaning; and certainly it is said throughout our narrative that 'the wise men could not read the writing, nor make known the interpretation of it,' phrases which would seem to mean one and the same thing; since, if they mean different things, the order of ideas would be that they could not interpret nor even read it, and Wintle accordingly translates, 'could not read so as to interpret it' (*Improved Version of Daniel*, Lond. 1807). At all events the meaning of the inscription by itself would be extremely enigmatical and obscure. To determine the application, and to give the full sense, of an isolated device which amounted to no more than 'he or it is numbered, he or it is numbered, he or it is weighed, they are divided,' must surely have required a supernatural endowment on the part of Daniel—a conclusion which is confirmed by the exact coincidence of the event with the prediction, which he propounded with so much fortitude (ver. 30, 31).

MENI is mentioned in Isa. lxv. 11, together with Gad, as receiving an offering of mixed wine. The word is either taken, by those namely who consider Gad in that passage to mean *troop*, to signify a *multitude*, a *number*; or, by those who suppose the whole verse to refer to idolatrous worship, to be the name of a god, and to mean *destiny*. Pocock has, moreover, pointed out the resemblance between Meni and Manât, an idol of the ancient Arabs. The fact of Meni being a Babylonian god renders it probable that some planet was worshipped under this name: but there is much diversity of opinion as to the particular planet to which the designation of *destiny* would be most applicable. It also deserves notice that there are some, who consider Gad and Meni to be names for one and the same god, and who chiefly differ as to whether the sun or the moon is the god intended.

MEPHIB'OSHETH (*extermination of idols*; also in 1 Chron. ix. 40, MERIB-BAAL), son of Jonathan and nephew of Saul (2 Sam. iv. 4). He was only five years of age when his father and grandfather were slain in Mount Gilboa: and on the news of this catastrophe, the woman who had charge of the child, apprehending that David would exterminate the whole house of Saul, fled away with him, but in her hasty flight she stumbled with the child, and lamed him for life (B.C. 1055). Under this calamity, which was very incapacitating in times when agility and strength were of prime importance, Mephibosheth was unable to take any part in the stirring political events of his early life. According to our notions, he should have been the heir of the house of Saul; but in those times a younger son of an actual king was considered to have at least as good a claim as the son of an heir apparent who had never reigned, and even a better claim if the latter were a minor. This, with his lameness, prevented Mephibosheth from ever appearing as the opponent or rival of his uncle Ishbosheth on the one hand, or of David on the other (2 Sam. ix). He thus grew up in quiet obscurity in the house of Machir, one of the great men of the country beyond the Jordan (2 Sam. ix. 4, xvii. 27); and his very existence was unknown to David till that monarch, when firmly settled in his kingdom, inquired whether any of the family of Jonathan survived, to whom he might show kindness for his father's sake. Hearing then of Mephibosheth from Ziba, who had been the royal steward under Saul, he invited him to Jerusalem, assigned him a place at his own table, and bestowed upon him lands, which were managed for him by Ziba, and which enabled him to support an establishment suited to his rank. He lived in this manner till the revolt of Absalom, and then David, in his flight, having noticed the absence of Mephibosheth, inquired for him of Ziba, and being informed that he had remained behind in the hope of being restored to his father's throne, instantly and very hastily revoked the grant of land, and bestowed it on Ziba (2 Sam. xvi. 1-4). Afterwards, on his return to Jerusalem, he was met with sincere congratulations by Mephibosheth, who explained that being lame he had been unable to follow the king on foot, and that Ziba had purposely prevented his beast from being made ready to carry him: and he declared that so far from having joined in heart, or even appearance, the enemies of the king, he had remained as a mourner, and, as his appearance declared, had not changed his clothes, or trimmed his beard, or even dressed his feet, from the day that the king departed to the day on which he returned. David could not but have been sensible that he had acted wrong, and ought to have been touched by the devotedness of his friend's son, and angry at the imposition of Ziba; but to cover one fault by another, or from indifference, or from reluctance to offend Ziba, who had adhered to him when so many old friends forsook him, he answered coldly, 'Why speakest thou any more of thy matters? I have said, thou and Ziba divide the land.' The reply of Mephibosheth was worthy of the son of the generous Jonathan:—'Yea, let him take all; forasmuch as my lord the king is come again in peace unto his own house' (2 Sam. xix. 24-30).

We hear no more of Mephibosheth, except that David was careful that he should not be included in the savage vengeance which the Gideonites were suffered to execute upon the house of Saul for the great wrong they had sustained during his reign (2 Sam. xxi. 7). Another Mephibosheth,

a son of Saul by his concubine Rizpah, was, however, among those who suffered on that occasion (ver. 8, 9).

ME'RAB (*increase*) eldest daughter of king Saul. who was promised in marriage to David; but when the time fixed for their union approached, she was, to the surprise of all Israel, bestowed in marriage upon an unknown personage named Adriel (1 Sam. xiv. 49; xviii. 17-19). By him she had six sons, who were among those of the house of Saul that were given up to the Gibeonites, who put them to death in expiation for the wrongs they had sustained from their grandfather.

MERA'RI (*bitter*), youngest son of Levi, born in Canaan (Gen. xlvi. 11; Exod. vi. 16; Num. iii. 17; 1 Chron. vi. 1). He is only known from his name having been given to one of the three great divisions of the Levitical tribe.

MERCURY. [HERMES.]

MERCY-SEAT. The Hebrew name literally denotes a *cover*, and, in fact, describes the lid of the ark with cherubim, over which appeared 'the glory of God' (Exod. xxvi. 17, sq.; xxx. 8; xxxi. 7, and elsewhere) [ARK]. The word used in the Septuagint and New Testament to translate this term, signifies the 'expiatory' or 'propitiatory,' in allusion to that application of the Hebrew word which we have noted: which application is in this instance justified and explained by reference to the custom of the high-priest once a-year entering the most holy place, and sprinkling the lid of the ark with the blood of an expiatory victim, whereby 'he made atonement for the sins of the people.' As this was the most solemn and significant act of the Hebrew ritual, it is natural that a reference to it should be involved in the name which the covering of the ark acquired. By a comparison of the texts in which the word occurs, it will be seen that there would, in fact, have been little occasion to name the cover of the ark separately from the ark itself, but for this important ceremonial.

MERI-BA'AL, or MERIB-BAAL, a name given to Mephibosheth, son of Jonathan, in 1 Chron. viii. 34; ix. 40 [MEPHIBOSHETH]. Of the two the latter seems the more correct form. It means 'contender against Baal.' Some think that the difference has arisen from some corruption of the text; but, from the analogy of Ishbosheth, whose original name was Esh-baal, it seems more like a designed alteration, arising probably from the reluctance of the Israelites to pronounce the name of Baal [ISHBOSHETH].

1. MER'IBAH (*quarrel, strife*), one of the names given by Moses to the fountain in the desert of Sin, on the western gulf of the Red Sea, that issued from the rock which he smote by the divine command (Exod. xvii. 1-17). He called the place, indeed, Massa (temptation) *and* Meribah, and the reason is assigned 'because of the *chiding* of the children of Israel, and because they did there *tempt* the Lord' [WANDERING].

2. MER'IBAH, another fountain produced in the same manner, and under similar circumstances, in the desert of Zin (Wady Arabah), near Kadesh; and to which the name was given with a similar reference to the previous misconduct of the Israelites (Num. xx. 13, 24; Deut. xxxiii. 8). In the last text, which is the only one where the two places are mentioned together, the former is

called Massah only, to prevent the confusion of the two Meribahs, 'Whom thou didst prove at Massah, and with whom thou didst strive at the waters of Meribah.' Indeed this latter Meribah is almost always indicated by the addition of 'waters,' i e 'waters of Meribah,' as if further to distinguish it from the other (Ps. lxxxi. 8; cvi. 32); and still more distinctly 'waters of Meribah in Kadesh' (Num. xxvii. 14; Deut. xxxii. 51; Ezek. xlvii. 19). Only once is this place called simply Meribah (Ps. xcv. 8).

MERO'DACH occurs in Jer. l. 2, in such connection with idols as to leave no doubt that it is the name of a Babylonian god. In conformity with the general character of Babylonian idolatry, Merodach is supposed to be the name of a planet; and, as the Tsabian and Arabic names for Mars are Nerig and Mirrich, 'arrow,' there is some presumption that it may be Mars. As for etymologies of the word, Gesenius has suggested that it is the Persian mardak, the diminutive of mard, 'man,' used as a term of endearment; or, rather, that it is from the Persian and Indo-Germanic mord, or mort (which means death, and is so far in harmony with the conception of Mars, as the lesser star of evil omen), and the affix och, which is found in many Assyrian names, as Nisroch, &c.

ME'ROM. 'The waters of Merom,' of Josh. ix. 5, are doubtless the lake Samechonitis, now called Huleh, the upper or highest lake of the Jordan [PALESTINE].

ME'ROZ, a place in the northern part of Palestine, the inhabitants of which are severely reprehended in Judg. v. 23, for not having taken the field with Barak against Sisera. It would seem as if they had had an opportunity of rendering some particular and important service to the public cause, which they neglected. The site is not known: Eusebius and Jerome fix it twelve Roman miles from Sebaste, on the road to Dothaim; but this position would place it south of the field of battle, and therefore scarcely agrees with the history.

ME'SECH; ME'SHECH. [NATIONS, DISPERSION OF.]

1. ME'SHA, a place mentioned in describing that part of Arabia inhabited by the descendants of Joktan (Gen. x. 30). [See NATIONS, DISPERSION OF.]

2. MESHA (deliverance), a king of Moab, who possessed an immense number of flocks and herds, and appears to have derived his chief wealth from them. In the time of Ahab, he being then under tribute, 'rendered unto the king of Israel 100,000 lambs, and 100,000 rams, with the wool (2 Kings iii. 4). These numbers may seem exaggerated, if understood as the amount of yearly tribute. It is, therefore, more probable that the greedy and implacable Ahab had at some one time levied this enormous impost upon the Moabites; and it is likely that it was in the apprehension of a recurrence of such ruinous exactions, that they seized the opportunity for revolt, which the death of Ahab seemed to offer (2 Kings i. 1; iii. 5). The short reign of Ahaziah afforded no opportunity for reducing them to obedience; but after his death his brother and successor, Jehoram, made preparations for war; and induced Jehoshaphat to join him in this expedition. The result, with the part taken by Elisha the prophet, has been

related under other heads [ELISHA; JEHORAM; JEHOSHAPHAT]. King Mesha was at length driven to shut himself up, with the remnant of his force, in Areopolis, his capital. He was there besieged so closely, that, having been foiled in an attempt to break through the camp of the Edomites (who were present as vassals of Judah), he was reduced to extremities, and, in the madness of his despair, sought to propitiate his angry gods by offering up his own son, the heir of his crown. as a sacrifice, upon the wall of the city. On beholding this fearful sight, the besiegers withdrew in horror, lest some portion of the monstrous crime might attach to their own souls. By this withdrawal they, however, afforded the king the relief he desired, and this was, no doubt, attributed by him to the efficacy of his offering, and to the satisfaction of his gods therewith. The invaders, however, ravaged the country as they withdrew, and returned with much spoil to their own land [MOABITES].

MESOPOTA'MIA. [ARAM.]

MESSI'AH (anointed, which is also the signification of CHRIST). In order to have an accurate idea of the Scriptural application of the term, we must consider the custom of anointing which obtained amongst the Jews. That which was specifically set apart for God's service was anointed, whether persons or things [ANOINTING]. Thus we read that Jacob poured oil upon the pillar (Gen. xxviii. 18, 22). The tabernacle also and its utensils were anointed (Lev. viii. 10), being thereby appropriated to God's service. But this ceremony had, moreover, relation to persons. Thus priests, as Aaron and his sons, were anointed, that they might minister unto God (Exod. xl. 13, 15). Kings were anointed. Hence it is that a king is designated the Lord's anointed Saul and David were, according to the divine appointment, anointed by Samuel (1 Sam. x. 1, xv. 1; xvi. 3, 13). Zadok anointed Solomon, that there might be no dispute who should succeed David (1 Kings i. 39). We cannot speak with confidence as to whether the prophets were actually anointed with the material oil. We have neither an express law nor practice to this effect on record. True it is that Elijah is commanded to anoint Elisha to be prophet in his room (1 Kings xix. 16); but no more may be meant by this expression than that he should constitute him his successor in the prophetic office; for all that he did, in executing his divine commission, was to cast his own garment upon Elisha (1 Kings xix. 19); upon which he arose and ministered unto him (ver. 21). For kings and priests the precept and practice are unquestionable.

But the name Messiah is, par excellence, applied to the Redeemer of man in the Old Testament (Dan. ix. 16; Ps. ii. 2). The words of Hannah, the mother of Samuel, at the close of her divine song, are very remarkable (1 Sam. ii. 10): 'The adversaries of the Lord shall be broken in pieces; out of heaven shall He thunder upon them: the Lord shall judge the ends of the earth; and he shall give strength unto his king, and exalt the horn of his Messiah.' The Hebrews as yet had no king; hence the passage may be taken as a striking prophecy of the promised deliverer. In various parts of the New Testament is this epithet applied to Jesus. St. Peter (Acts x. 36, 38) informs Cornelius the centurion that God had anointed Jesus of Nazareth to be the *Christ*, and our Lord himself acknowledges to the woman of Samaria that he is the expected Messiah (John iv. 25). This term, however, as applied to Jesus, is less a *name* than the expression of his office.

Thus the Jews had in *type*, under the Mosaic dispensation, what we have in *substance* under the Christian system. The prophets, priests, and kings of the former economy were types of Him who sustains these offices as the head of his mystical body, the Church. As the priests and kings of old were set apart for their offices and dignities by a certain form prescribed in the law of Moses, so was the blessed Saviour by a better anointing (of which the former was but a shadow), even by the Holy Ghost. Thus the apostle tells us that God anointed Jesus of Nazareth with the Holy Ghost, and with power (Acts x. 38). He was anointed :—

First, at his *conception*: the angel tells Mary, 'The Holy Ghost shall come upon thee, and the power of the Highest shall overshadow thee: therefore that holy thing which shall be born of thee shall be called the Son of God' (Luke i. 35).

Second, at his *baptism* at the river Jordan (Matt. iii. 13; Mark i. 9, 10, 11, 12). St. Luke, moreover, records (Luke iv. 17, 21) that our Lord being at Nazareth, he had given unto him the book of the prophet Isaiah; and on reading from ch. lxi. 1, 'The Spirit of the Lord is upon me,' &c., he said to his hearers, 'This day is this Scripture fulfilled in your ears.'

But as the Jews will not acknowledge the right of either Jesus or his apostles to apply the prophetic passages which point to the Messiah to himself, it now remains for us to show—

First, That the promised Messiah *has already come*.

Second, That Jesus of Nazareth *is unquestionably he*.

To prove the first assertion, we shall confine our remarks to *three* prophecies. The first occurs in Gen. xlix. 8, 10, where Jacob is giving his sons his parting benediction, &c. When he comes to Judah he says: 'The sceptre shall not depart from Judah, nor a lawgiver from between his feet, until Shiloh come; and unto him shall the gathering of the people be.' It is evident that by Judah is here meant, not the *person* but the *tribe*; for Judah died in Egypt, without any pre-eminence. By *sceptre* and *lawgiver* are obviously intended the legislative and ruling power, which did, in the course of time, commence in David, and which, for centuries afterwards, was continued in his descendants. Whatever variety the form of government—whether monarchical or aristocratical—might have assumed, the *law* and polity *were still the same*. This prediction all the ancient Jews referred to the Messiah. Now, that the sceptre has departed from Judah, and, consequently, that the Messiah has come, we argue from the acknowledgments of some most learned Jews themselves. The *precise* time when all authority departed from Judah is disputed. Some date its departure from the time when Herod, an Idumæan, set aside the Maccabees and Sanhedrim. Others think that it was when Vespasian and Titus destroyed Jerusalem and the temple, that the Jews lost the last vestige of authority. If, therefore, the sceptre *has* departed from Judah

—and who can question it who looks at the broken-up, scattered, and lost state of that tribe for ages?—the conclusion is clearly irresistible, that the Messiah *must have long since come!*

The next proof that the Messiah has long since come, may be adduced from Dan. ix. 25, 26, 27. It is evident that the true Messiah is here spoken of. He is twice designated by the very name. And if we consider what the work is which he is here said to accomplish, we shall have a full confirmation of this. Who but He could finish and take away transgression, make reconciliation for iniquity, bring in everlasting righteousness, seal up the vision and prophecy, confirm the covenants with many, and cause to cease the sacrifice and oblation? If then it be the *true* Messiah who is described in the above prophecy, it remains for us to see how the time predicted for his coming has long since transpired. This is expressly said to be seventy weeks from the going forth of the commandment to restore and build Jerusalem. That by seventy weeks are to be understood seventy sevens of years, a day being put for a year, and a week for seven years, making up 490 years, is allowed by Kimchi, Jarchi, Rabbi Saadias, and other learned Jews, as well as by many Christian commentators. This period of time then *must have long since* elapsed, whether we date its commencement from the first decree of Cyrus (Ezra i. 1, 2), the second of Darius Hystaspes (ch. vi. 15), or that of Artaxerxes (ch. viii. 11).

We can only barely allude to one remarkable prediction more, which fixes the time of the Messiah's advent, viz., Hag. ii. 7–9: 'I will shake all nations, and the desire of all nations shall come: and I will fill this house with glory, saith the Lord of Hosts. The silver is mine, and the gold is mine, saith the Lord of Hosts. The glory of this latter house shall be greater than of the former, saith the Lord of Hosts.' The glory here spoken of *must* be in reference to the Messiah, or on some other account. It could not have been said that the second Temple exceeded in glory the former one; for in many particulars, according to the acknowledgment of the Jews themselves, it was far inferior both as a building (Ezra iii. 3, 12), and in respect of the symbols and tokens of God's special favour being wanting. The promised glory, therefore, must refer to the coming and presence of him who was promised to the world before there was any nation of the Jews; and who is aptly called the '*Desire of all nations*.' This view is amply confirmed by the prophet Malachi (ch. iii. 1). Since then the very Temple into which the Saviour was to enter, has for ages been destroyed, *He must*, if the integrity of this prophecy be preserved, *have come*. That there was, at the time of our Lord's birth, a great expectation of the Messiah, both amongst Jews and Gentiles, may be seen from Tacitus, Suetonius, and Josephus, as well as from the sacred Scriptures. We may just add, that as there was a general expectation of the Messiah at this time, so there were many impostors who drew after them many followers (Joseph. *Antiq.* xx. 2. 6; *De Bell. Jud.* lvii. 31). Christ prophesies of such persons (Matt. xxiv. 24, 29).

The limits of this article will admit of our only touching upon the proofs that Jesus of Nazareth, and none other, is the very Messiah who was to come. What was predicted of the Messiah was fulfilled in Jesus. Was the Messiah to be of the seed of the woman (Gen. iii. 15), and this woman a virgin? (Isa. vii. 14). So we are told (Gal. iv. 4; Matt. i. 18, and 22, 23) that Jesus was made of a woman, and born of a virgin. Was it predicted that he (Messiah) should be of the tribe of Judah, of the family of Jesse, and of the house of David? (Mich. v. 2; Gen. xlix 10; Isa. xi. 10; Jer. xxiii. 5). This was fulfilled in Jesus (Luke i. 27, 69; Matt. i. 1) [GENEALOGY].

2. If the Messiah was to be a prophet like unto Moses, so was Jesus also (Isa. xviii.; John vi. 14) If the Messiah was to appear in the second Temple, so did Jesus (Hag. ii. 7, 9; John xviii. 20).

3. Was Messiah to work miracles? (Isa. xxxv. 5, 6; comp. Matt. xi. 4, 5).

4. If the Messiah was to suffer and die (Isa. liii.), we find that Jesus died in the same manner, at the very time, and under the identical circumstances, which were predicted of him. The very man who betrayed him, the price for which he was sold, the indignities he was to receive in his last moments, the parting of his garments, and his last words, &c., were all foretold of the Messiah, and accomplished in Jesus.

5. Was the Messiah to rise from the dead? So did Jesus. How stupendous and adorable is the Providence of God, who, through so many apparent contingencies, brought such things to pass!

METALS. The principal metals are in this work considered separately under their several names; and a few general observations alone are necessary in this place.

The mountains of Palestine contained metals, nor were the Hebrews ignorant of the fact (Deut. viii. 9); but they do not appear to have understood the art of mining. They therefore obtained from others the superior as well as the inferior metals, and worked them up. They received also metal utensils ready made, or metal in plates (Jer. x. 9), from neighbouring and distant countries of Asia and Europe. The metals named in the Old Testament are iron (steel, Jer. xv. 12); copper, or copper ore; silver; gold; lead; and tin. The trade in these metals was chiefly in the hands of the Phœnicians (Ezek. xxvii. 7), who obtained them from their colonies, principally those in Spain (Jer. x. 9; Ezek. xxvii. 12). Some also came from Arabia (Ezek. xxvii. 19), and some apparently from the countries of the Caucasus (Ezek. xxvii. 13). A composition of several metals is expressed by the Hebrew word *chasmil.* In general the ancients had a variety of metallic compositions, and that which the word *chasmil* describes appears to have been very valuable. Whether it was the same as that precious compound known among the ancients as Corinthian brass is uncertain, but it is likely that in later times the Jews possessed splendid vessels of the costly compound known by that name. Indeed this is distinctly affirmed by Josephus (*Vita,* 13).

The vast quantity of silver and gold used in the temple in the time of Solomon, and which was otherwise possessed by the Jews during the flourishing time of the nation, is very remarkable, under whatever interpretation we regard

such texts as 1 Chron. xxii. 14; xxix. 4. &c. In like manner, we find among other ancient Asiatic nations, and also among the Romans, extraordinary wealth in gold and silver vessels and ornaments of jewellery. As all the accounts, received from sources so various, cannot be founded on exaggeration, we may rest assured that the precious metals were in those ancient times obtained abundantly from mines—gold from Africa, India, and perhaps even then from Northern Asia; and silver principally from Spain.

The following are the metallic manufactures named in the Old Testament:—Of *iron,* axes (Deut. xix. 5; 2 Kings vi. 5); saws (2 Sam. xii. 31); stone-cutters' tools (Deut. xxvii. 5); saucepans (Ezek. iv. 3); bolts, chains, knives, &c., but especially weapons of war (1 Sam. xvii. 7; 1 Macc. vi. 35). Bedsteads were even sometimes made of iron (Deut. iii. 11); 'chariots of iron,' *i. e.* war-chariots, are noticed elsewhere [CHARIOTS]. Of *copper* we find vessels of all kinds (Lev. vi. 28; Num. xvi. 39; 2 Chron. iv. 16; Ezek. viii. 27); and also weapons of war, principally helmets, cuirasses, shields, spears (1 Sam. xvii. 5; vi. 38; 2 Sam. xxi. 16); also chains (Judg. xvi. 21); and even mirrors (Exod. xxxviii. 8) [COPPER]. *Gold* and *silver* furnished articles of ornament, also vessels, such as cups, goblets, &c. The holy vessels of the temple were mostly of gold (Ezra v. 14). Idolaters had idols and other sacred objects of silver (Exod. xx 20; Isa. ii. 20; Acts xvii. 29; xix 24). *Lead* is mentioned as being used for weights, and for plumb-lines in measuring (Amos vii. 7; Zech. v. 8). Some of the tools of workers in metal are also mentioned: anvil (Isa. xli. 7); hammer (Isa. xli. 7); pincers; and bellows (Jer. vi. 29); crucible (Prov. xvii. 3); melting-furnace (Ezek. xxii. 18).

There are also allusions to various operations connected with the preparation of metals. 1 The smelting of metal was not only for the purpose of rendering it fluid, but in order to separate and purify the richer metal when mixed with baser minerals, as silver from lead, &c. (Isa. i. 25; comp. Plin. *Hist. Nat.* xxxvii. 47; Ezek. xxii. 18–20). For the actual or chemical separation other materials were mixed in the smelting such as alkaline salts (Isa. i. 25); and lead (Jer. vi. 29; comp. Plin. *Hist. Nat.* xxxiii. 31). 2. The casting of images (Exod. xxv. 12; xxxi. 37; Isa. xl. 19); which are always of gold, silver, or copper. The casting of iron is not mentioned, and was perhaps unknown to the ancients. 3. The hammering of metal, and making it into broad sheets (Num. xvi. 38; Isa. xliv. 12; Jer. x.). 4. Soldering and welding parts of metal together (Isa. xli. 7). 5. Smoothing and polishing metals (1 Kings vii. 45). 6. Overlaying with plates of gold and silver and copper (Exod. xxv. 11–24; 1 Kings vi. 20; 2 Chron. iii. 5; comp. Isa. xl. 19). The execution of these different metallurgic operations appears to have formed three distinct branches of handicraft before the Exile; for we read of the blacksmith, by the name of the 'worker in iron' (Isa. xliv. 12); the brass-founder (1 Kings vii. 14); and the gold and silver smith (Judg. xvii. 4; Mal. iii. 2).

The invention of the metallurgic arts is in Scripture ascribed to Tubal-cain (Gen. iv. 22). In later times the manufacture of useful utensils and implements in metals seems to have been carried on to a considerable extent among the Israelites, if we may judge from the frequent allusions to them by the poets and prophets. But it does not appear that, in the finer and more elaborate branches of this great art, they made much, if any progress, during the flourishing times of their commonwealth; and it will be remembered that Solomon was obliged to obtain assistance from the Phœnicians in executing the metal work of the temple (1 Kings vii. 13).

The Hebrew workers in iron, and especially such as made arms, were frequently carried away by the different conquerors of the Israelites (1 Sam. xiii. 19; 2 Kings xxiv. 14, 15; Jer. xxiv. 1; xxix. 2); which is one circumstance among others to show the high estimation in which this branch of handicraft was anciently held.

METHU'SAEL (*man of God*), son of Mehujael, of the race of Cain (Gen. iv. 18).

METHU'SELAH (*man of the dust*), son of Enoch, and remarkable as being the oldest of those antediluvian patriarchs whose great ages are recorded (Gen. v. 21, 22). At the age of 187 years he begat Lamech (the father of Noah); after which he lived 782 years, making altogether 969 years [LONGEVITY].

MI'CAH, one of the twelve Minor Prophets, who, according to the inscription of the book, prophesied during the reigns of Jotham, Ahaz, and Hezekiah (B.C. 759-699), and was consequently contemporary with Isaiah. It is, however, doubtful whether any accurate separation of the particular prophecies of Micah can be ascertained. He was a native of Moresheth of Gath (i. 14, 15), so called to distinguish it from another town of the same name, in the tribe of Judah (Josh. xv. 44; 2 Chron. xiv. 9, 10). Micah is to be distinguished from a former prophet of the same name, called also Micaiah, mentioned in 1 Kings xxii. 8 (B C. 897).

The contents of Micah's prophecy may be briefly summed up. It consists of two parts, the first of which terminates with chapter v. He commences with a majestic exordium (i. 2-4), in which is introduced a sublime theophany, the Lord descending from his dwelling-place to judge the nations of the earth, who are approaching to receive judgment. There is then a sudden transition to the judgment of Israel, whose captivity is predicted (chaps. i. and ii.). That of Judah follows, when the complete destruction of Jerusalem is foretold, with the expatriation of the Jews to Babylon, their future return, the glories of Sion, and the celebrity of its temple (iv. 1, 8, 9, 12), with the chastisement prepared for the oppressors of the Jews (ver. 13). After this, glorious wars are seen in perspective, attended with great slaughter (ch. v.); after many calamities a ruler is seen to arise from Bethlehem. An invasion of the Assyrians is predicted, to oppose which there will be no want of able leaders (v. 4-8). A new monarchy is beheld, attended with wars and destruction.

The second part, from this to the end, consists of an elegant dialogue or contestation between the Lord and his people, in which the corruption of their morals is reproved, and their chastisement threatened; but they are consoled by the promise of a return from their captivity.

Jahn (*Introd.*) points out the following predictions as contained in the prophet Micah. 1. The destruction of the kingdom of Israel, which was impending when the prophecy was delivered, and which was fulfilled in the taking of Samaria by Shalmaneser, in the sixth year of Hezekiah (2 Kings xvii.), and then that of the kingdom of Judah, with the destruction of Jerusalem (iii. 12; vii. 13). 2. The Babylonian captivity (iv. 10, 11; vii. 7, 8, 13). These predictions were delivered 150 years before the event, when the Chaldæans, by whom they were accomplished, were scarcely known as a people. 3. The return from the exile, with its happy effects, and the tranquillity enjoyed by the Jews under the Persian and Grecian monarchies, which referred to events from 200 to 500 years distant (iv. 18; vii. 11; xiv. 12). 4. The heroic deeds of the Maccabees, and their victories over the Syrians or Syro-Macedonians, called Assyrians in Micah v., as well as Zechariah x. 11 (iv. 13). 5. The establishment of the royal residence in Sion (iv. 8). 6. The birth and reign of the Messiah (v. 2). The three last prophecies, observes this learned writer, are more obscure than the others, by reason of the remote distance, in point of time, of their accomplishment, from the period of their being delivered.

There is no prophecy in Micah so interesting to the Christian as that in which the native place of the Messiah is announced. 'But thou, Bethlehem Ephratah [though] thou be little among the thousands of Judah, [yet] out of thee shall he come forth unto me, [that is] to be ruler in Israel' (Eng. Authorized Version). The citation of this passage by the Evangelist differs both from the Hebrew and the Septuagint:—'And thou, Bethlehem, [in] the land of Judah, art not the least among the princes of Judah: for out of thee shall come a governor, that shall rule [Gr. feed] my people Israel' (Matt. ii. 6). The difference, however, is but verbal.

Of more importance is the application of the prophecy. It is evident that the Jews in the time of Jesus interpreted this passage of the birth-place of the Messiah (Matt. ii. 5; John vii. 41, 42). But some of the later Rabbinical writers have maintained that it had only an indirect reference to the birth-place of the Messiah, who was to be a descendant of David, a Bethlehemite, but not of necessity himself born in Bethlehem. Others, however, expressly mention Bethlehem as the birth-place of the Messiah. Jahn observes that it is evident that the Jews in the time of Christ expected the Messiah's birth to take place at Bethlehem; and he contends that it is not possible to apply the prophecy fully and literally to any but Him who was not only of the house and lineage of David, but was actually born at Bethlehem, according to the direct testimony of both St. Matthew's and St. Luke's Gospels.

The style of Micah is sublime and vehement, in which respects he exceeds Amos and Hosea. De Wette observes that he has more roundness, fulness, and clearness in his style and rhythm than the latter prophet. He abounds in rapid transitions and elegant tropes, and piquant plays upon words. He is successful in the use of the dialogue, and his prophecies are penetrated by the purest spirit of morality and piety (see especially ch. vi. 6-8; and vii. 1-10).

Micah is the third of the minor prophets according to the arrangement of the Septuagint, the sixth according to the Hebrew, and the fifth according to the date of his prophecies.

2. MICAH. An Ephraimite, apparently contemporary with the elders who outlived Joshua. He secretly appropriated 1100 shekels of silver which his mother had saved; but being alarmed at her imprecations on the author of her loss, he confessed the matter to her, and restored the money. She then forgave him, and returned him the silver, to be applied to the use for which it had been accumulated. Two hundred shekels of the amount were given to the founder, as the cost or material of two teraphim, the one molten and the other graven; and the rest of the money served to cover the other expenses of the semi-idolatrous establishment which was formed in the house of Micah, of which a wandering Levite became the priest, at a yearly stipend; till the Danite army, on their journey to settle northward in Laish, took away both the establishment and the priest, which they afterwards maintained in their new settlement (Judg. xvii. 18) [DAN; JONATHAN 2]. The establishments of this kind, of which there are other instances—as that of Gideon at Ophrah—were, although most mistakenly, formed in honour of Jehovah, whom they thus sought to serve by means of a local worship, in imitation of that at Shiloh. This was in direct contravention of the law, which allowed but one place of sacrifice and ceremonial service; and was something of the same kind, although different in extent and degree, as the service of the golden calves, which Jeroboam set up, and his successors maintained, in Dan and Bethel. The previous existence of Micah's establishment in the former city no doubt pointed it out to Jeroboam as a suitable place for one of his golden calves.

MICAI'AH (*who as Jehovah?*), a prophet of the time of Ahab. He was absent from the mob of false prophets who incited the kings of Israel and Judah to march against the Syrians in Ramoth-gilead; for Ahab, having been offended by his sincerity and boldness, had not called for him on this occasion. But he was sent for at the special desire of Jehoshaphat; and as he declared against the enterprise, which the other prophets encouraged, Ahab commanded him to be imprisoned, and allowed only 'bread and water of affliction' till he returned from the wars in peace. To which the prophet ominously answered, 'If thou return at all in peace, then the Lord hath not spoken by me' (1 Kings xxii. 8-28). The event corresponded with this intimation [AHAB]; but we have no further information concerning the prophet.

2. MICAIAH. One of the princes whom Jehoshaphat sent to 'teach in the cities of Judah' (2 Chron. xviii. 7).

3. MICHAIAH, son of Gemariah, who, after having heard Baruch read the terrible predictions of Jeremiah in his father's hall, went, apparently with good intentions, to report to the king's officers what he had heard (Jer. xxxvi. 11-13).

MI'CHAEL (*who as God?*), the name given to one of the chief angels, who, in Dan. x. 13-21, is described as having special charge of the Israelites as a nation; and in Jude 9, as disputing with Satan about the body of Moses, in which dispute, instead of bringing against the arch-enemy any railing accusation, he only said, 'The Lord rebuke thee. O Satan!' Again, in Rev. xii. 7-9, Michael and his angels are represented as warring with Satan and his angels in the upper regions, from which the latter are cast down upon the earth. This is all the reference to Michael which we find in the Bible.

The passages in Daniel and Revelations must be taken as symbolical, and in that view offer little difficulty. The allusion in Jude 9 is more difficult to understand, unless, with Vitringa, Lardner, Macknight, and others, we regard it also as symbolical; in which case the dispute referred to is that indicated in Zech. iii. 1; and 'the body of Moses' as a symbolical phrase for the Mosaical law and institutions [JUDE]. A comparison of Jude 9 with Zech iii. 1 gives much force and probability to this conjecture.

MI'CHAL (*who as God?*), youngest daughter of king Saul (1 Sam. xiv. 49). She became attached to David, and made no secret of her love; so that Saul, after he had disappointed David of the elder daughter [MERAB], deemed it prudent to bestow Michal in marriage upon him (1 Sam. xviii. 20-28). Saul had hoped to make her the instrument of his designs against David, but was foiled in his attempt through the devoted attachment of the wife to her husband. Of this a most memorable instance is given in 1 Sam. xix. 11-17. When David escaped the javelin of Saul he retired to his own house, upon which the king set a guard over-night, with the intention to slay him in the morning. This being discovered by Michal, she assisted him to make his escape by a window, and afterwards amused the intended assassins under various pretences, in order to retard the pursuit. When these were detected, Michal pretended to her father that David had threatened her with death if she did not assist his escape. Saul probably did not believe this; but he took advantage of it by cancelling the marriage, and bestowing her upon a person named Phalti (2 Sam. xxv. 44). David, however, as the divorce had been without his consent, felt that the law (Deut. xxiv. 4) against a husband taking back a divorced wife could not apply in this case: he therefore formally reclaimed her of Ish-bosheth, who employed no less a personage than Abner to take her from Phalti, and conduct her with all honour to David. It was under cover of this mission that Abner sounded the elders of Israel respecting their acceptance of David for king, and conferred with David himself on the same subject at Hebron (2 Sam. iii. 12-21).

The re-union was less happy than might have been hoped. On that great day when the ark was brought to Jerusalem, Michal viewed the procession from a window, and the royal notions she had imbibed were so shocked at the sight of the king not only taking part in, but leading, the holy transports of his people, that she met him on his return home with a keen sarcasm on his undignified and unkingly behaviour. This ill-timed sneer, and the unsympathising state of feeling which it manifested, drew from David a severe but not unmerited retort: and the Great King, in whose honour David incurred this contumely, seems to have punished the wrong done to him, for we are told that '*therefore* Michal, the daughter of Saul, had no child to the day of her death' (2 Sam. vi. 16-23). It was thus, perhaps, as

Abarbanel remarks, ordered by Providence that the race of Saul and David should not be mixed, and that no one deriving any apparent right from Saul should succeed to the throne.

MICH'MAS, or MICHMASH, a town of Benjamin (Ezra ii. 27; Neh. xi. 31; comp. vii. 31), east of Beth-aven (1 Sam. xiii. 5), and south from Migron, on the road to Jerusalem (Isa. x. 28). The words of 1 Sam. xiii. 2, xiv. 4, and Isa. x. 29, show that at Michmas was a pass where the progress of a military body might be impeded or opposed. It was perhaps for this reason that Jonathan Maccabæus fixed his abode at Michmas (1 Macc. ix. 73); and it is from the chivalrous exploit of another hero of the same name, the son of Saul, that the place is chiefly celebrated (1 Sam. xiii, xiv. 4-16). Eusebius describes Michmas as a large village nine Roman miles from Jerusalem, on the road to Ramah. Travellers have usually identified it with Bir or el-Bireh; but Dr. Robinson recognises it in a place still bearing the name of Mukhmas, at a distance and position which correspond well with these intimations. This is a village situated upon a slope to the north of a valley called Wady es-Suweinit. It is small, and almost desolate, but bears marks of having been once a place of strength and importance. There are many foundations of hewn stones, and some columns lie among them. The valley es-Suweinit, steep and precipitous, is probably the 'passage of Michmash' mentioned in Scripture. In it, says Dr. Robinson, 'just at the left of where we crossed, are two hills of a conical, or rather spherical, form, having steep rocky sides, with small wadys running up between each so as almost to isolate them. One of them is on the side towards Jeba (Gibeah), and the other towards Mukhmas. These would seem to be the two rocks mentioned in connection with Jonathan's adventure (1 Sam. xiv. 4, 5). They are not, indeed, so "sharp" as the language of Scripture would seem to imply; but they are the only rocks of the kind in this vicinity. The northern one is connected towards the west with an eminence still more distinctly isolated.'

MID'IAN, fourth son of Abraham, by Keturah, and progenitor of the Midianites (Gen. xxv. 2).

MID'IANITES, a tribe of people descended from Abraham's son Midian. His descendants must have settled in Arabia, and engaged in trade at an early period, if we identify them with those who in the time of Jacob appear, along with the Ishmaelites, as merchants travelling from Gilead to Egypt, and who, having in their way bought Joseph from his brethren, sold him in the latter country (Gen. xxxvii. 28, 36). It is, however, very difficult to conceive that the descendants of a son of Abraham, born so many years after Isaac, had become a tribe of people at the time when the descendants of Isaac himself were so few. One is therefore much inclined to suppose that these Midianites were different and distinct from those descended from Abraham's son; and there appears the more ground for this when at a later period we find two tribes of Midianites, different in locality and character, and different in their feelings towards the Israelites. If this distinction be admitted, then it would be necessary to seek the earlier Midianites in those dwelling about the eastern arm of the Red Sea, among whom Moses found refuge when 'he fled from Egypt,' and

whose priest or sheikh was Jethro, who became the father-in-law of the future lawgiver (Exod. iii. 1; xviii. 5; Num. x. 29). These, if not of Hebrew, would appear to have been of Cushite origin, and descended from Midian the son of Cush. We do not again meet with these Midianites in the Jewish history, but they appear to have remained for a long time settled in the same quarter, where indeed is the seat of the only Midianites known to Oriental authors.

The other Midianites, undoubtedly descended from Abraham and Keturah, occupied the country east and south-east of the Moabites, who were seated on the east of the Dead Sea; or rather, perhaps, we should say that, as they appear to have been a semi-nomade people, they pastured their flocks in the unsettled country beyond the Moabites, with whom, as a kindred, although more settled tribe, they seem to have been' on the most friendly terms, and on whose borders were situated those 'cities and goodly castles which they possessed' (Num. xxxi 10). These Midianites, like the other tribes and nations who had a common origin with them, were highly hostile to the Israelites. In conjunction with the Moabites, they designedly enticed them to idolatry as they approached Canaan (Num. xxxi. 2, 5; xxv. 6, 14-18); on which account Moses attacked them with a strong force, killed all their fighting men, including their five princes or emirs, and made the women and children captives (Num. xxxi.). The account of the spoil confirms the view which we have taken of the semi-nomade position of the Midianites—namely, 675,000 sheep, 72,000 beeves, 61,000 asses, 32,000 persons. This was only the 'prey,' or live stock; but besides this there was a great quantity of 'barbaric pearl and gold,' in the shape of 'jewels of gold, chains, and bracelets, rings, ear-rings, and tablets.'

Some time after the Israelites obtained possession of Canaan, the Midianites had become so numerous and powerful, that, for seven successive years, they made inroads into the Hebrew territory in the time of harvest, carrying off the fruits and cattle, and desolating the land. At length Gideon was raised up as the deliverer of his country, and his triumph was so complete that the Israelites were never more molested by them (Judg. vi. 1-7; vii; viii.). To this victory there are subsequent allusions in the sacred writings (Ps. lxxxiii. 10, 12; Isa. ix. 4; x. 6); but the Midianites do not again appear in sacred or profane history.

MIG'DOL, a place between which and the Red Sea the Israelites were commanded to encamp on leaving Egypt (Exod. xiv. 2; Num. xxxiii. 7) [EXODUS]. The name, which means a tower, appears to indicate a fortified place. In Jer. xliv. 1; xlvi. 14, it occurs as a city of Egypt, and it would seem to have been the last town on the Egyptian frontier, in the direction of the Red Sea; hence 'from Migdol to Syene,' in Ezek. xxix. 10; xxx. 6.

MIG'RON, a town which, from the historical indications, must have been south or south-west of Ai, and north of Michmas (Isa. x. 28). From Michmas northward a narrow valley extends out of and at right angles with that which has been identified as the pass of Michmas [MICHMAS]. The town of Migron seems to have been upon and to have commanded the pass through this valley, but its precise situation has not been determined. Saul was stationed at the further side of Gibeah, 'under a pomegranate-tree which is by Migron' (1 Sam. xiv. 2), when Jonathan performed his great exploit at Michmas; and this is to be explained on the supposition that Migron was on the border, towards Michmas, of the district to which Gibeah gave its name.

MIL'COM. [MOLOCH.]

MILE. This word is only mentioned in Matt. v. 41, where Christ says, 'If any one compel thee to go with him one mile, go with him two' The mile was originally (as its derivation from *mille*, 'a thousand,' implies) a Roman measure of 1000 geometrical paces (*passus*) of 5 feet each, and was therefore equal to 5000 Roman feet. Taking the Roman foot at 11·6496 English inches, the Roman mile would be 1618 English yards, or 142 yards less than the English statute mile. By another calculation, in which the foot is taken at 11·62 inches, the mile would be little more than 1614 yards. The number of Roman miles in a degree of a large circle of the earth is very little more than 75. The Roman mile contained 8 Greek stadia. The Greek stade hence bore the same relation to the Roman mile which the English furlong does to the English mile.

MILE'TUS, a city and sea-port of Ionia in Asia Minor, about thirty-six miles south of Ephesus. St. Paul touched at this port on his voyage from Greece to Syria, and delivered to the elders of Ephesus, who had come to meet him there, a remarkable and affecting address (Acts xx. 15-38). Miletus was a place of considerable note, and the ancient capital of Ionia and Caria. It was the birth-place of several men of renown—Thales, Timotheus, Anaximander, Anaximenes, Democritus. Ptolemy places Miletus in Caria by the sea, and it is stated to have had four havens, one of which was capable of holding a fleet. It was noted for a famous temple of Apollo, the oracle of which is known to have been consulted so late as the fourth century. There was, however, a Christian church in the place; and in the fifth, seventh, and eighth centuries we read of bishops of Miletus, who were present at several councils. The city fell to decay after its conquest by the Saracens, and is now in ruins, not far from the spot where the Meander falls into the sea. The site bears, among the Turks, the name of Melas.

MILK. Milk, and the preparations from it, butter and cheese, are often mentioned in Scripture. Milk, in its fresh state, appears to have been used very largely among the Hebrews, as is usual among people who have much cattle, and yet make but sparing use of their flesh for food. The proportion which fresh milk held in the dietary of the Hebrews, must not, however, be measured by the comparative frequency with which the word occurs; because, in the greater number of examples, it is employed figuratively, to denote great abundance, and in many instances it is used as a general term for all or any of the preparations from it.

In its figurative use, the word occurs sometimes simply as the sign of abundance (Gen. xlix. 12; Ezek. xxv. 4; Joel iii. 18, &c.); but more frequently in combination with honey—'milk and honey' being a phrase which occurs about twenty times in Scripture. Thus a rich and fertile soil is described as a 'land flowing with milk and honey:' which, although usually said of Palestine, is also applied to other fruitful countries, as Egypt (Num. xvi. 13). Hence its use to denote the food of children. Milk is also constantly employed as a symbol of the elementary parts or rudiments of doctrine (1 Cor. iii. 2; Heb. v. 12, 13); and from its purity and simplicity, it is also made to symbolize the unadulterated word of God (1 Pet. ii. 2; comp. Isa. lv. 1).

In reading of milk in Scripture, the milk of cows naturally presents itself to the mind of the European reader; but in Western Asia, and especially among the pastoral and semi-pastoral people, not only cows, but goats, sheep, and camels, are made to give their milk for the sustenance of man. That this was also the case among the Hebrews, may be clearly inferred even from the slight intimations which the Scriptures afford. Thus we read of 'butter of kine, and milk of sheep' (Deut. xxxii. 14); and in Prov. xxvii. 27, the emphatic intimation, 'Thou shalt have goats' milk for food,' seems to imply that this was considered the best for use in the simple state. 'Thirty milch camels' were among the cattle which Jacob presented to his brother Esau (Gen. xxxii. 15), implying the use of camels' milk.

The Hebrew word for curdled milk is always translated 'butter' in the Authorized Version. It seems to mean both butter and curdled milk, but most generally the latter; and the context will, in most cases, suggest the distinction, which has been neglected by our translators. It was this curdled milk, highly esteemed as a refreshment in the East, that Abraham set before the angels (Gen. xviii. 8), and which Jael gave to Sisera, instead of the water which he asked (Judg. v. 25). In this state milk acquires a slightly inebriating power, if kept long enough. Isaiah vii. 22, where it is rendered 'butter,' is the only text in which the word is coupled with 'honey,' and there it is a sign of scarcity, not of plenty, as when honey is coupled with fresh milk. It means that there being no fruit or grain, the remnant would have to live on milk and honey; and, perhaps, that milk itself would be so scarce, that it would be needful to use it with economy; and hence to curdle it, as fresh milk cannot be preserved for chary use. Although, however, this word properly denotes curdled milk, it seems also to be sometimes used for milk in general (Deut. xxxii. 14; Job xx. 15; Isa. vii. 15).

The most striking Scriptural allusion to milk is that which forbids a kid to be seethed in its mother's milk, and its importance is attested by its being thrice repeated (Exod. xxiii. 19; xxxiv. 26; Deut. xiv. 21). There is, perhaps, no precept of Scripture which has been more variously interpreted than this. It is probable that the prohibition refers not to a common act of cookery, but to an idolatrous or magical rite. Maimonides urges this opinion. He says, 'Flesh eaten with milk, or in milk, appears to me to have been prohibited, not only because it affords gross nourishment, but because it savoured of idolatry, some of the idolaters probably doing it in their worship, or at their festivals.' This is confirmed by an extract which Cudworth gives from an ancient Karaite commentary on the Pentateuch. 'It was a custom of the ancient heathen, when they had gathered in all their fruits, to take a kid, and boil it in the dam's milk, and then in a magical way to go about and besprinkle with it all their trees, and fields, and gardens, and orchards, thinking that by this means they should make them fructify, and bring forth more abundantly the following year.' Some such rite as this is supposed to be the one interdicted by the prohibition.

BUTTER is not often mentioned in Scripture, and even less frequently than our version would suggest. Indeed, it may be doubted whether it denotes butter in any place besides Deut. xxxii. 14, 'butter of kine,' and Prov. xxx. 33, 'the churning of milk bringeth forth butter,' as all the other texts will apply better to curdled milk than to butter. Butter was, however, doubtless much in use among the Hebrews, and we may be sure that it was prepared in the same manner as at this day among the Arabs and Syrians. The milk is put into a large copper pan over a slow fire, and a little *leben* or sour milk (the same as the curdled milk mentioned above), or a portion of the dried entrails of a lamb, is thrown into it. The milk then separates, and is put into a goatskin bag, which is tied to one of the tent poles, and constantly moved backwards and forwards for two hours. The buttery substance then coagulates, the water is pressed out, and the butter put into another skin. In two days the butter is again placed over the fire, with the addition of a quantity of *burgul* (wheat boiled with leaven, and dried in the sun), and allowed to boil for some time, during which it is carefully skimmed. It is then found that the burgul has precipitated all the foreign substances, and that the butter remains quite clear at the top. This is the process used by the Bedouins, and it is also the one employed by the settled people of Syria and Arabia. The chief difference is, that in making butter and cheese the townspeople employ the milk of cows and buffaloes, whereas the Bedouins, who do not keep these animals, use that of sheep and goats. The butter is generally white, of the colour and consistence of lard, and is not much relished by English travellers. It is eaten with bread in large quantities by those who can afford it, not spread out thinly over the surface, as with us, but taken in mass with the separate morsels of bread [CHEESE].

MILL. The mill for grinding corn had not wholly superseded the mortar for pounding it in the time of Moses. The mortar and the mill are named together in Num. xi. 8. But fine meal, that is, meal ground or pounded fine, is mentioned so early as the time of Abraham (Gen. xviii. 6): hence mills and mortars must have been previously known. The mill common among the Hebrews differed little from that which is in use to this day throughout Western Asia and Northern Africa. It consisted of two circular stones two feet in diameter, and half a foot thick. The lower is called the 'nether millstone,' Job xli. 16 (24), and the upper the 'rider' (Judg. ix. 53: 2 Sam. xi. 21). The former was usually fixed to the floor, and had a slight elevation in the centre, or, in other words, was slightly convex in the upper surface. The upper stone had a concavity in its under surface fitting to, or receiving, the convexity of the lower stone. There was a hole in the top, through which the corn was introduced by handfuls at a time. The upper stone

had an upright stick fixed in it as a handle, by which it was made to turn upon the lower stone, and by this action the corn was ground, and came out at the edges. As there were neither public mills nor bakers, except the king's (Gen. xl. 2; Hos. vii. 4-8), each family possessed a mill; and

G.F.SARGENT.   E.EVANS.

240.

as it was in daily use, it was made an infringement of the law for a person to take another's mill or millstone in pledge (Deut. xxiv. 6). The mill was, as now, commonly turned by two persons, usually women, and these, the work being laborious, the lowest maid-servants in the house. They sat opposite each other. One took hold of the mill-handle, and impelled it half way round; the other then seized it, and completed the revolution (Exod. xi. 5; Job xxxi. 10, 11; Isa. xlvii. 2; Matt. xxiv. 41). As the labour was severe and menial, enemies taken in war were often condemned to perform it (Judg. xvi. 21; Lam v. 13). It will be seen that this millstone does not materially differ from the Highland *quern;* and is, indeed, an obvious resource in those remote quarters, where a population is too thin or too scattered to afford remunerative employment to a miller by trade. In the East this trade is still unknown, the hand-mill being in general and exclusive use among the corn-consuming, and the mortar among the rice-consuming, nations [BREAD].

MILLET occurs in Ezek. iv. 9, where the Prophet is directed to take unto him wheat, and barley, and beans, and lentiles, and millet and fitches, and to put them into one vessel, and to make bread thereof for himself. All the grains enumerated in this verse continue to form the chief articles of diet in the East in the present day, as they appear to have done in ancient times. The common millet is cultivated from the middle of Europe to the most southern part of India, and is sometimes cultivated in England on account of the seeds being used for feeding birds and poultry. But the grain is usually imported into this country from the Mediterranean. In India it is cultivated in the cold weather, that is, in the same season with wheat and barley, and is an article of diet with the inhabitants. Having mentioned the extreme points where this grain is cultivated, it is hardly necessary to state that it is produced in the intermediate countries.

241. [Millet—Panicum miliaceum.]

Tournefort says that in the Isle of Samos the inhabitants, in preparing their bread, knead together one half wheat and the other half barley and millet mixed together. It is also an article of diet both in Persia and India, and is so universally cultivated in the East as one of their smaller corn-grasses, that it is most likely to be the kind alluded to in the passage of Ezekiel.

MIL'LO. This word denotes 'fulness,' and is applied to a mound or rampart, probably as being filled up with stones or earth. Hence it is the name given to

1. Part of the citadel of Jerusalem, probably the rampart (2 Sam. v. 9; 1 Kings ix. 15, 24; xi. 27; 1 Chron. xi. 8; 2 Chron. xxxii. 5).

2. The fortress in Shechem. 'All the men of Shechem, and all that dwelt in the house of Millo;' that is, in the castle or citadel (Judg. ix. 6, 20).

MINISTER, one who acts as the less or inferior agent, in obedience or subservience to another, or who serves, officiates, &c., as distinguished from the master or superior. In the Old Testament the term is applied to Joshua as the minister of Moses (Exod. xxiv. 13), and to Elisha as the minister to Elijah (2 Kings vi. 15). Persons thus designated sometimes succeeded to the office of their principal, as did Joshua and Elisha. The word is applied to the angels, Ps. ciii. 21; comp. Ps. civ. 4; Heb. i 7; and also to the Jews in their capacity as a sacred nation, 'Men shall call you the ministers of our God' (Isa. lxi. 6); and to the priests (Jer. xxxiii. 21; Ezek. xliv. 11; xlv. 4; Joel i. 9). In the New Testament the term is applied to Christian teachers, Acts xiii. 2; Rom. xv. 16, and to Christ, Heb. viii. 2; to the collectors of the Roman tribute, in consequence of the divine authority of political government, 'they are God's ministers.' The word diakonos, 'minister,' is applied to Christian teachers, 1 Cor. iii. 5; 2 Cor. iii. 6; vi. 4; xi 23; 1 Thess. iii. 2; to false teachers, 2 Cor. xi. 15; to Christ, Rom. xv. 8, 16; Gal. ii. 17; to heathen magistrates, Rom. xiii. 4; in all which passages it has the sense of a minister, assistant, or servant in general, as in Matt. xx. 26; but it means a particular sort of minister, 'a deacon,' in Philip. i. 1; 1 Tim. iii. 8, 12. Another word similarly rendered is applied to Christian ministers, Luke i. 2; Acts xxvi. 16; 2 Cor. iv. 1. The word denotes, in Luke iv. 20, the attendant in a synagogue who handed the volume to the reader, and returned it to its place. In Acts xiii. 5 it is applied to 'John whose surname was Mark,' in his capacity as an attendant or assistant on Barnabas and Saul. It primarily signifies an under-rower on board a galley, of the class who used the longest oars, and consequently performed the severest duty, as distinguished from the rower upon the upper bench of the three, and from the sailors or the marines: hence in general a hand, agent, minister, attendant, &c.

MIN'NI. [ARMENIA.]

MIN'NITH, a town in the country of the Ammonites (Judg. xi. 33), celebrated for the excellence of its wheat, which was exported to the markets of Tyre (Ezek. xxvii. 17). It still existed in the age of Eusebius, four R. miles from Heshbon, on the road to Philadelphia.

MINT is mentioned in Matt. xxiii. 23: 'Woe unto you, Scribes and Pharisees, hypocrites! for ye pay tithe of *mint* and anise (properly *dill*) and cummin, and have omitted the weightier matters of the law;' and, again, in Luke xi. 42: 'But woe unto you, Pharisees! for ye tithe *mint* and rue, and all manner of herbs, and pass over judgment and the love of God: these ought ye to have done, and not to leave the other undone.' All the plants mentioned in the above passages belong to the smaller ones cultivated in gardens in Europe, and which usually come under the denomination of sweet herbs. Lady Calcott inquires whether mint was one of the bitter herbs which the Israelites ate with the Paschal Lamb; and infers the probability of its being so from our own practice of eating lamb with mint sauce. Dr. Harris argues that mint, anise, and cummin were not tithed, and that the Pharisees only paid tithes of these plants from an overstrained interpretation of the law. But, in the article DILL, it may be seen that dill was tithed, and it is one of the herbs mentioned along with mint. The meaning, therefore, seems to be, that the Pharisees, while, in conformity with the law, they paid these minute tithes, neglected the most important moral duties,—truth, justice, and mercy; for it is added, 'these ought ye to have done, and not to leave the other undone.'

The species of mint most common in Syria is *Mentha sylvestris*, found by Russell at Aleppo, and mentioned by him as one of the herbs cultivated in the gardens there. It also occurs in Greece, Taurus, Caucasus, the Altai Range, and as far as Cashmere, whence we have obtained specimens. Mint is highly esteemed in Eastern countries, and apparently was so also by the Jews. It was much esteemed by the ancients, as Pliny testifies. Dioscorides also mentions it as useful to the stomach, and peculiarly grateful as a condiment. Mint was employed by the ancients in the preparation of many dishes.

It is difficult to determine the exact species or variety of mint employed by the ancients. There are numerous species very nearly allied to one another. They usually grow in moist situations, and are herbaceous, perennial, of powerful odour, especially when bruised, and have small reddish-coloured flowers, arranged in spikes or whorls. The taste of these plants is bitter, warm, and pungent, but leaving a sensation of coolness on the tongue: in their properties they are so similar to each other, that either in medicine, or as a condiment, one species may safely be substituted for another.

MIRACLES. God sees fit to carry on his common operations on established and uniform principles. These principles, whether relating to the physical or moral world, are called *the laws of nature.* And by the laws of nature the most enlightened philosophers and divines have understood *the uniform plan according to which,* or *the uniform manner in which,* God exercises his power *throughout the created universe.*

This uniform method of divine operation is evidently conducive to the most important ends. It manifests the immutable wisdom and goodness of God, and, in ways too many to be here specified, promotes the welfare of his creatures. Without the influence of this uniformity, rational beings would have no effectual motive to effort, and the affairs of the universe, intelligent and unintelligent, would be in a state of total confusion. And this general fact may be considered as a sufficient reason why God, in the common course of his providence, has adopted a uniform method of operation in preference to any other.

But if, in conducting the affairs of his great empire, God sees, in any particular case, as good a reason for a *deviation* from this uniform order, as there is generally for *uniformity,* that is, if the glory of his attributes and the good of his creatures require it—and no one can say that such a case may not occur—then, unquestionably, the unchangeable God will cause such a deviation; in other words, will work *miracles.*

It is admitted that no man, apart from the knowledge of facts, could ever, by mere reasoning, have arrived at a confident belief, that the conjuncture supposed would certainly occur. But to us, who know that mankind are so depraved and wretched, and that the efforts of human wisdom to obtain relief have been in vain, the importance of a special divine interposition is very apparent. And being informed what the plan is, which a merciful God has adopted for our recovery to holiness and happiness, and being satisfied that this plan, so perfectly suited to the end in view, could never have been discovered by man, and never executed, except by a divine dispensation involving miracles, we conclude, that the introduction of a new and miraculous dispensation was in the highest degree an honour to God and a blessing to the world. The mode which God has chosen to impart the knowledge of this dispensation to man, is that of making a revelation to a number of individuals, who are to write and publish it for the benefit of the world. This revelation to individuals is made in such a manner as renders it certain to their minds, that the revelation is from God. But how can that revelation be made available to others? It will not answer the purpose for those who receive it merely to declare that God has made such a revelation to them, and authorized them to proclaim it to their fellow-creatures. For how shall we know that they are not deceivers? Or, if their character is such as to repel any suspicion of this kind, how shall we know that they are not themselves deceived? Have we not a right, nay, are we not bound in duty, to ask for evidence of the divine authority of what they reveal? But what evidence will suffice? The reply is obvious. The revelation, in order to be of use to us, as it is to those who receive it directly from God, must not only be declared by them to us, but must have a divine attestation. In other words, those who declare it to us must show, by some incontestable proof, that *it is from God.* Such proof is found in a miracle. If an event takes place which we know to be contrary to the laws of nature, we at once recognise it as the special act of him who is the God of nature, and who alone can suspend its laws, and produce effects in another way. The evidence of a direct interposition of God given in this way is irresistible. No man, no infidel, could witness an obvious miracle, without being struck with awe, and recognising *the finger of God.*

It is clear that no event, which can be accounted for on natural principles, can prove a supernatural interposition, or contain a divine attestation to the truth of a prophet's claim. But when we look at an event which cannot be traced to the laws of nature, and is clearly above them, such as the burning of the wood upon the altar in the case of Elijah's controversy with the false prophets, or the resurrection of Lazarus, we cannot avoid the conviction, that the Lord of heaven and earth does, by such a miracle, give his testimony, that Elijah is his prophet, and that Jesus is the Messiah. The evidence arising from miracles is so striking and conclusive, that there is no way for an infidel to evade it, but to deny the existence of miracles, and to hold that all the events called miraculous may be accounted for according to the laws of nature.

Hume arrays *uniform experience* against the credibility of miracles. But the shallow sophistry of his argument has been fully exposed by Campbell, Paley, and many others. We inquire what and how much he means by *uniform experience.* Does he mean his own experience? But because *he* has never witnessed a miracle, does it follow that others have not? Does he mean the uniform experience of the greater part of mankind? But how does he know that the experience of a smaller part has not been different from that of the greater part? Does he mean, then, the uniform experience of all mankind in all ages? How then does his argument stand? He undertakes to prove that no man has ever witnessed or experienced a miracle, and his real argument is, that no one *has* ever witnessed or experienced it. In other words, to *prove* that there has never been a miracle, he *asserts* that there never has been a miracle. This is the nature of his argument— an example of begging the question, which a man of Hume's logical powers would never have resorted to, had it not been for his enmity to religion.

The miraculous events recorded in the Scriptures, particularly those which took place in the times of Moses and Christ, have all the marks which are necessary to prove them to have been matters of fact, and worthy of full credit, and to distinguish them from the feats of jugglers and impostors. This has been shown very satisfactorily by Leslie, Paley, Douglas, and many others. These miracles took place in the most public manner, and in the presence of many witnesses; so that there was opportunity to subject them to the most searching scrutiny. Good men and bad men were able and disposed to examine them thoroughly, and to prove them to have been impostures, if they had been so.

A large number of men, of unquestionable honesty and intelligence, constantly affirmed that the miracles took place before their eyes. And some of these original witnesses wrote and published histories of the facts, in the places where they were alleged to have occurred, and near the time of their occurrence. In these histories it was openly asserted that the miracles, as described, were publicly known and acknowledged to have taken place; and this no one took upon him to contradict, or to question. Moreover, many persons who stood forth as witnesses of these miracles passed their lives in labours, dangers, and sufferings, in attestation of the accounts they delivered, and solely in consequence of their belief of the truth of those accounts; and, from the same motive, they voluntarily submitted to new rules of conduct; while nothing like this is true respecting any other pretended miracles.

It has been a long agitated question, whether miracles have ever been wrought, or can be consistently supposed to be wrought, *by apostate spirits.*

It is sufficient to say here, that it would be evidently inconsistent with the character of God to empower or to suffer wicked beings to work miracles *in support of falsehood.* And if wicked spirits in the time of Christ had power to produce preternatural effects upon the minds or bodies of men, and if those effects are to be ranked among real miracles (which, however, we do not affirm), still the end of miracles is not contravened. For those very operations of evil spirits were under the control of divine providence, and were made in two ways to subserve the cause of Christ. First; they furnished an occasion, as doubtless they were designed to do, for Christ to show his power over evil spirits, and, by his superior miracles, to give a new proof of his Messiahship. Secondly; the evil spirits themselves were constrained to give their testimony, that Jesus was the Christ, the Holy One of Israel.

As to the time when the miraculous dispensation ceased, we can only remark, that the power of working miracles, which belonged pre-eminently to Christ and his apostles, and, in inferior degrees, to many other Christians in the apostolic age, subsided gradually. After the great object of supernatural works was accomplished in the establishment of the Christian religion, with all its sacred truths, and its divinely appointed institutions, during the life of Christ and his apostles, there appears to have been no further

occasion for miracles, and no satisfactory evidence that they actually occurred.

MIR'IAM (*bitterness*), sister of Moses and Aaron, and supposed to be the same that watched her infant brother when exposed on the Nile; in which case she was probably ten or twelve years old at the time (Exod. ii. 4, sq.). When the Israelites left Egypt, Miriam naturally became the leading woman among them. She is called 'a prophetess' (Exod. xv. 20). After the passage of the Red Sea, she led the music, dance, and song, with which the women celebrated their deliverance (Exod. xv. 20–22). The arrival of Moses' wife in the camp seems to have created in her an unseemly dread of losing her influence and position, and led her into complaints of and dangerous reflections upon Moses, in which Aaron joined. For this she was smitten with leprosy, and, although healed at the intercession of Moses, was excluded for seven days from the camp (Num. xii.; Deut. xxiv. 9). Her death took place in the first month of the fortieth year after the Exodus, at the encampment of Kadesh-barnea (Num. xx. 1), where her sepulchre was still to be seen in the time of Eusebius.

MIRROR (Exod. xxxviii. 8; Job xxxii. 8). In the first of these passages the mirrors in the possession of the women of the Israelites, when

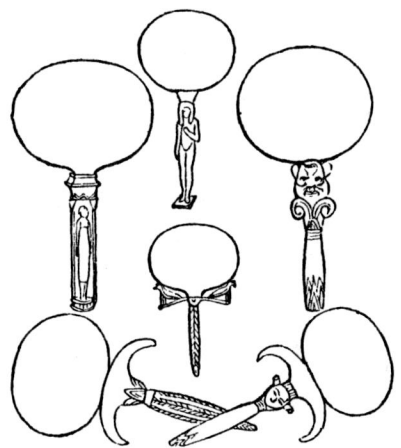

242. [Egyptian Metal Mirrors.]

they quitted Egypt, are described as being of brass; for 'the laver of brass, and the foot of it,' are made from them. In the second, the firmament is compared to 'a molten mirror.' In fact, all the mirrors used in ancient times were of metal; and as those of the Hebrew women in the wilderness were brought out of Egypt, they were doubtless of the same kind as those which have been found in the tombs of that country, and many of which now exist in our museums and collections of Egyptian antiquities. These are of mixed metals. chiefly copper, most carefully wrought and highly polished; and so admirably did the skill of the Egyptians succeed in the composition of metals, that this substitute for our modern looking-glass was susceptible of a lustre which has even been partially revived at the present day in some of those discovered at

Thebes, though buried in the earth for so many centuries. The mirror itself was nearly round, and was inserted in a handle of wood, stone, or metal, the form of which varied according to the taste of the owner.

MISH'AEL, one of the three companions of Daniel, who were cast into the burning furnace by Nebuchadnezzar, and were miraculously delivered from it (Dan. iii. 13-30). The Chaldæan name was Meshech (Dan. i. 7).

MISH'PAT, a fountain in Kadesh [see KADESH].

MIS'REPHOTH-MA'IM, a place or district near Sidon (Josh. xi. 8; xiii. 6). The name means 'burnings of water,' which Kimchi understands of warm baths; but more probably it means burnings *by* or *beside* the water—either lime-kilns or smelting furnaces situated near water.

MITE, a small piece of money, two of which made a quadrans—four of the latter being equal

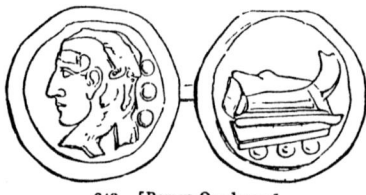

243. [Roman Quadrans]

to the Roman *as*. The *as* was of less weight and value in later than in early times. Its original value was 3·4 farthings, and afterwards 2¼ farthings. The latter was its value in the time of Christ, and the mite being one-eighth of that sum, was little more than one-fourth of an English farthing. It was the smallest coin known to the Hebrews (Luke xii. 59).

MITH'CAH, one of the encampments of the Israelites [WANDERING].

MITYLE'NE, the capital of the isle of Lesbos, in the Ægean Sea, about seven miles and a half from the opposite point on the coast of Asia Minor. It was a well-built town, but unwholesomely situated. It was the native place of Pittacus, Theophanes, Theophrastus, Sappho, Alcæus, and Diophanes. St. Paul touched at Mitylene in his voyage from Corinth to Judæa (Acts xx. 14). It does not appear that any Christian church was established at this place in the apostolic age. No mention is made of it in ecclesiastical history until a late period; and in the second century heathenism was so rife in Mitylene that a man was annually sacrificed to Dionysus. In the fifth, sixth, seventh, and eighth centuries, we, however, find bishops of Mitylene present at several councils. Mitylene still exists, and has given its name, in the form of Mytilni, to the whole island; but it is now a place of no importance.

MIZ'PAH. The word signifies *a watch-tower*, and is the name of several towns and places in lofty situations, whether furnished with a watch-tower or not.

1. MIZPAH, a town or city in Gilead (Judg. x. 17; xi. 11, 34; Hos. v. 1). The place originated in the heap of stones set up by Laban, and to which he gave his name (Gen. xxxi. 49). Some

confound this with the Mizpeh of Gilead in Judg. xi. 29; but it is better to distinguish them [MIZPEH 3].

2. MIZPAH, a city of Benjamin, where the people were wont to convene (Josh. xviii. 26; Judg. xx. 1, 3; xxi. 1; 1 Sam. vii. 5-16; x. 17, sq.). It was afterwards fortified by Asa, to protect the borders against the kingdom of Israel (1 Kings xv. 22; 2 Chron. xvi. 6). In later times it became the residence of the governor under the Chaldæans (Jer. xl. 6, sq.; comp Neh. iii. 7, 15, 19). Its position is nowhere mentioned in Scripture or by Josephus; but it could not have been far from Ramah, since king Asa fortified it with materials taken from that place; and that it was situated on an elevated spot is clear from its name. Neby Samwil, a poor village seated upon the summit of an elevated ridge about four and a half miles N.N.W. from Jerusalem, is supposed to correspond with the position of Mizpah.

MIZ'PEH. This name has the same meaning and application as Mizpah, and is borne by several places mentioned in Scripture.

1. MIZPEH, a town in the plains of Judah (Josh. xv. 38). Eusebius and Jerome identify it with a place which, in their time, bore the name of Mapha, on the borders of Eleutheropolis southward, on the road to Ælia or Jerusalem.

2. MIZPEH, the place more usually called Mizpah, in the tribe of Benjamin, is once called Mizpeh (Josh. xviii. 26) [MIZPAH 2].

3. MIZPEH OF GILEAD, through or by which Jephthah passed in his pursuit of the Ammonites (Judg. xi. 29). Some think it the same with Mizpah 1; and it is possibly the same with the Ramath-mizpeh of Josh. xiii. 26.

4. MIZPEH, a valley in the region of Lebanon (Josh. xi. 8; comp. xi. 3).

MIZ'RAIM, or LAND OF MIZRAIM, the name by which, in Scripture, Egypt is generally designated, apparently from its having been peopled by Mizraim, the son of Ham (Gen. x.). This ancient title is still preserved in Misr, the existing Arabic name of the country [EGYPT].

MNA'SON, an 'old disciple,' with whom St. Paul lodged when at Jerusalem in A.D. 58 (Acts xxi. 16). He seems to have been a native of Cyprus, but an inhabitant of Jerusalem, like Joses and Barnabas. Some think that he was converted by Paul and Barnabas while at Cyprus (Acts xiii. 9); but the designation 'an old disciple,' has more generally induced the conclusion that he was converted by Jesus himself, and was perhaps one of the seventy.

MOAB, son of Lot and his eldest daughter (Gen. xix. 30-38). He was born about the same time with Isaac, and became the founder of the Moabites.

MO'ABITES, a tribe descended from Moab the son of Lot, and consequently related to the Hebrews (Gen. xix. 37). Previous to the exodus of the latter from Egypt, the former, after expelling the original inhabitants, called Emims (Gen. xiv. 5; Deut. ii. 11), had possessed themselves of the region on the east of the Dead Sea and the Jordan, as far north as the river Jabbok. But the northern, and indeed the finest and best, portion of the territory, viz. that extending from the Jabbok to the Arnon, had passed into the hands of the Amorites, who founded there one of their kingdoms, with Heshbon for its capital (Num. xxi.

26). Og had established another at Bashan. Hence at the time of the exodus the valley and river Arnon constituted the northern boundary of Moab (Num. xxi. 13; Judg xi. 18). As the Hebrews advanced in order to take possession of Canaan, they did not enter the proper territory of the Moabites (Deut. ii. 9; Judg. xi. 18), but conquered the kingdom of the Amorites (a Canaanitish tribe), which had formerly belonged to Moab; whence the western part, lying along the Jordan, frequently occurs under the name of 'plains of Moab' (Deut. i. 5; xxix. 1). The Moabites, fearing the numbers that were marching around them, showed them at least no kindness (Deut. xxiii. 3); and their king (Balak) hired Balaam to utter prophetic curses, which, however, were converted into blessings in his mouth (Num. xii. sq.). The Gadites now took possession of the northern portion of this territory, which the Amorites had wrested from the Moabites, and established themselves there; while the Reubenites settled in the southern part (Num. xxxii. 34; comp. Josh. xiii., which, however, differs somewhat in the designation of particular towns).

We see the first hostilities breaking out in the beginning of the period of the Judges, when the Hebrews had been for a long time tributary to the Moabites, but threw off their yoke under Ehud (Judg. iii. 12-30). Towards the end of this period, however, peace and friendship were restored, mutual honours were reciprocated (as the history of Ruth shows), and Moab appears often to have afforded a place of refuge to outcasts and emigrant Hebrews (Ruth i. 1; comp. 1 Sam. xxii. 3, 4; Jer. xl. 11; Isa. xvi. 2). After Saul had waged successful war against them (1 Sam. xiv. 47), David made them tributary (2 Sam. viii. 2, 12; xxiii. 20). The right to levy this tribute seems to have been transferred to Israel after the division of the kingdom; for upon the death of Ahab (about B.C. 896), they refused to pay the customary tribute of 100,000 lambs and as many rams (2 Kings i. 1; iii. 4; comp. Isa. xvi. 1). Jehoram (B.C. 896), in alliance with Judah and Edom, sought indeed to bring them back to their subjection. The invading army, after having been preserved from perishing by thirst through the intervention of Elisha, defeated the Moabites and ravaged the country; but, through the strange conduct of the king, in offering up in sacrifice his son [MESHA], were induced to retire without completing the object of the expedition. The Moabites deeply resented the part which the king of Judah took in this invasion, and formed a powerful confederacy with the Ammonites, Edomites, and others, who marched in great force into Judæa, and formed their camp at Engedi, where they fell out among themselves and destroyed each other, through the special interposition of Providence in favour of Jehoshaphat and his people (2 Kings iii. 4, sq.; comp. 2 Chron. xx. 1-30) [ELISHA; JEHORAM; JEHOSHAPHAT]. Under Jehoash (B.C. 849) we see them undertake incursions into the kingdom of Israel, and carry on offensive war against it (2 Kings xiii. 20).

Though the subsequent history of Israel often mentions the Moabites, yet it is silent respecting a circumstance which, in relation to one passage, is of the greatest importance, namely, the re-conquest of the territory between the Arnon and the Jabbok, which was wrested from the Moabites by the Amorites, and afterwards of the territory possessed by the tribes of Reuben and Gad. This territory in general we see, according to Isa. xvi., in the possession of the Moabites again. Even Selah, the ancient capital of the Edomites, seems likewise, from Isa xvi. 1, to have belonged to them, at least for a time. The most natural supposition is, that, after the carrying away of those tribes into captivity, the Moabites occupied their territory; as it is expressly stated (Jer. xlix 1-5) that the Amorites intruded themselves into the territory of the captive Gadites, as the Edomites did in respect to the Jews at a later period.

Still later, under Nebuchadnezzar, we see the Moabites acting as the auxiliaries of the Chaldæans (2 Kings xxiv. 2), and beholding with malicious satisfaction the destruction of a kindred people (Ezek. xxv. 8-11); yet, according to an account in Josephus (Antiq. x. 9. 7), Nebuchadnezzar, when on his way to Egypt, made war upon them, and subdued them, together with the Ammonites, five years after the destruction of Jerusalem.

That continual wars and contentions must have created a feeling of national hostility between the Hebrews and the Moabites, may be readily conceived. This feeling manifested itself on the part of the Hebrews, sometimes in bitter proverbs, sometimes in the denunciations of the prophets; on the part of the Moabites in proud boastings and expressions of contempt (Isa. xvi. 6).

Among the prophecies, however, that of Balaam (Num. xxii.-xxiv.) is above all remarkable, in which this ancient prophet (who withal was not an Israelite), hired by Moab to curse, is impelled by the Divine Spirit to bless Israel, and to announce the future destruction of Moab by a mighty hero in Israel (Num. xxiv. 17). The destruction of the Moabites for their scorn and contempt of Israel is predicted by Jeremiah, Ezekiel, Amos, and Zephaniah.

After the exile an intimate connection between the two nations had found place by means of intermarriages (Ezra ix. 1, sq.; Neh. xiii. 1), which, however, were dissolved by the theocratic zeal of Ezra. The last (chronologically) notice of the Moabites which occurs in Scripture is in Dan. xi. 41, which contains an obscure intimation of the escape of the Moabites from the overthrow with which neighbouring countries would be visited (Antiq. xiii. 15). Thenceforth their name is lost under that of the Arabians, as was also the case with Ammon and Edom. Until of late the accounts of the territory of Moab are uncommonly meagre, but within these few years it has been explored by various travellers, who have shed a new light on the topography of this region.

From their researches we learn that in the land of Moab, which lay to the east and southeast of Judæa, and which bordered on the east, north-east, and partly on the south of the Dead Sea, the soil is rather more diversified than that of Ammon; and, where the desert and plains of salt have not encroached upon its borders, of equal fertility. There are manifest and abundant signs of its ancient importance. The whole of the plains are covered with the sites of towns on every eminence or spot convenient for the construction of one; and as the land is capable of rich cultivation, there can be no doubt that the country, now so deserted, once presented a continued picture of plenty and fertility. The form of fields is still visible, and there are remains of Roman highways which are in some places completely paved, 'and on which there are milestones of the times of Trajan, Marcus Aurelius, and Severus, with the numbers of the miles legible upon them. Wherever any spot is cultivated the corn is luxuriant; and the frequency and almost, in many instances, the close vicinity of the sites of ancient towns, prove that the population of the country was formerly proportioned to its fertility. It was in its state of highest prosperity that the prophets foretold that the cities of Moab should become desolate, without any to dwell in them; and accordingly we find, that although the sites, ruins, and names of many ancient cities of Moab can be traced, not one of them exists at the present day as tenanted by man. The argument for the inspiration of the sacred records deducible from this, among other facts of the same kind, is produced with considerable force by Dr. Keith in his work on Prophecy.

MOLE (*choled*, Lev. xi. 29, in our version 'weasel'). Although the similarity of sound in names is an unsafe ground to depend upon when it is applied to specific animals, still, the Hebrew and Syriac appearing likewise to imply creeping into, creeping underneath by burrowing—characteristics most obvious in moles—and the Arabic denomination being undoubted, *choled* may be assumed to indicate the above animal. This conclusion is the more to be relied on as the animal is rather common in Syria, and in some places abundant. Zoologists have considered the particular species to be the *Talpa Europæa*, which, under the name of the common mole, is so well known as not to require a more particular description. The ancients represented the mole to have no eyes: which assertion later scientific writers believed they had disproved by showing our species to be possessed of these organs, though exceedingly small. Nevertheless, recent observations have proved that a species, in other respects scarcely, if at all, to be distinguished from the common, is totally destitute of eyes. It is to be found in Italy, and probably extends to the East, instead of the *Europæa*. Moles must not, however, be considered as forming a part of the Rodent order, whereof all the families and genera are provided with strong incisor teeth, like rats and squirrels, and therefore intended for subsisting chiefly on grain and nuts: they are on the contrary supplied with a great number of small teeth, to the extent of twenty-two in each jaw—indicating a partial regimen; for they feed on worms, larvæ, and under-ground insects, as well as on roots, and thus belong to the insectivorous order: which brings the application of the name somewhat nearer to carnivora and its received interpretation 'weasel.'

MO'LOCH, or rather MOLECH, is chiefly found in the Old Testament as the national god of the Ammonites, to whom children were sacrificed by fire. There is some difficulty in ascertaining at what period the Israelites became acquainted with this idolatry; yet various reasons render it probable that it was before the time of Solomon, the date usually assigned for its introduction. Nevertheless, it is for the first time directly stated that Solomon erected a high-place for Molech on the Mount of Olives (1 Kings xi. 7); and from that period his worship continued uninterruptedly there, or in Tophet, in the valley of Hinnom, until Josiah defiled both places (2 Kings xxiii. 10, 13). Jehoahaz, however, the son and successor of Josiah, again 'did what was evil in the sight of Jehovah, according to all that his fathers had done' (2 Kings xxiii. 32). The same broad condemnation is made against the succeeding kings, Jehoiakim, Jehoiachin, and Zedekiah; and Ezekiel, writing during the captivity, says, 'Do you, by offering your gifts, and by making your sons pass through the fire, pollute yourselves with all your idols *until this day*, and shall I be enquired of by you?' (xx. 31). After the restoration, all traces of this idolatry disappear.

It has been attempted to explain the terms in which the act of sacrificing children is described in the Old Testament so as to make them mean a mere passing between two fires, without any risk of life, for the purpose of purification. This theory—which owes its origin to a desire in some Rabbins to lessen the mass of evidence which their own history offers of the perverse idolatries of the Jews—is effectually declared untenable by such passages as Ps. cvi. 38; Jer. vii. 31; Ezek. xvi. 20; xxiii. 37; the last two of which may also be adduced to show that the victims were slaughtered before they were burnt.

MONEY. This term is used to denote whatever commodity the inhabitants of any country may have agreed or are compelled to receive as an equivalent for their labour, and in exchange for other commodities.

Different commodities have been used as money in the primitive state of society in all countries, such as skins, cattle, corn, dried fish, sugar, and salt. A long period of time must have intervened between the first introduction of the precious metals into commerce, and their becoming generally used as money. The peculiar qualities which so eminently fit them for this purpose would only be gradually discovered. They would probably be first introduced in their gross and unpurified state. A sheep, an ox, a certain quantity of corn, or any other article, would afterwards be bartered or exchanged for pieces of gold or silver in bars or ingots, in the same way as they would formerly have been exchanged for iron, copper, cloth, or anything else. The merchants would soon begin to estimate their proper value, and, in effecting exchanges, would first agree upon the quality of the metal to be given, and then the quantity which its possessor had become bound to pay would be ascertained by weight. This, according to Aristotle and Pliny, was the manner in which the precious metals were originally exchanged in Greece and Italy. The same practice is still observed in different countries. In many parts of China and Abyssinia the value of gold and silver is always ascertained by weight. Iron was the first money of the Lacedæmonians, and copper of the Romans.

In the sacred writings there is frequent mention of gold, silver, and brass, sums of money, purchases made with money, current money, and money of a certain weight. Indeed, the money of Scripture is all estimated by weight. 'Abraham weighed to Ephron the silver which he had named in the audience of the sons of Heth, four hundred shekels of silver, current money with the merchant' (Gen. xxiii. 19). The brethren of Joseph carried back into Egypt the money 'in full weight' which they had found in their sacks (Gen xlii. 21). (See also Gen. xxiv. 22; Jer. xxxii. 9; Amos viii. 5; Deut. xxv. 13). It was customary for the Jews to have scales attached to their girdles for weighing the gold and silver they received; but the Canaanites carried them in their hands.

There is no direct allusion in the sacred writings to coined money as belonging to the Jewish nation. In Gen. xxxiii. 19, Jacob is said to have bought a part of a field 'for an hundred pieces of money;' and the friends of Job are said to have given him each 'a piece of money' (Job xlii. 11). The term in the original is *kesitoth*, and is by some thought to denote 'sheep' or 'lamb;' by others a kind of money having the impression of a sheep or lamb; and by others again a purse of money. The most correct translation may be presumed to be that which favours the idea of a piece of money bearing some stamp or mark indicating that it was of the value of a sheep or lamb. Maurice, in his *Antiquities of India* (vol. vii.), bears testimony to the fact that the earliest coins were stamped with the figure of an ox or sheep. In the British Museum there is a specimen of the original Roman As, the surface of which is nearly the size of a brick, with the figure of a bull impressed upon it. Other devices would suggest themselves to different nations as arising out of, or connected with, particular places or circumstances, as the Babylonish lion, Ægina's tortoise, Bœotia's shield, the lyre of Mitylene, the wheat of Metapontum. Religion would also at an early period claim to be distinguished, and accordingly the effigies of Juno, Diana, Ceres, Jove, Hercules, Apollo, Bacchus, Pluto, Neptune, and many other of the heathen deities are found impressed upon the early coins. The Jews, however, were the worshippers of the one only true God; idolatry was strictly forbidden in their law; and therefore their shekel never bore a head, but was impressed simply with the almond rod and the pot of manna.

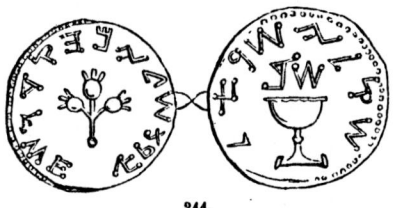

244.

The first Roman coinage took place, according to Pliny (*Hist. Nat.* xxxiii. 3), in the reign of Servius Tull.us, about 550 years before Christ; but it was not until Alexander of Macedon had subdued the Persian monarchy, and Julius Cæsar had consolidated the Roman empire, that the image of a living ruler was permitted to be stamped upon the coins. Previous to that period heroes and deities alone gave currency to the money of imperial Rome.

Antiochus Sidetes, king of Syria, is represented to have granted to Simon Maccabæus the privilege of coining money in Judæa (1 Macc. xv. 6). This is considered to be the first mention of Hebrew money, properly so called. It consisted of shekels and demi-shekels, the third part of a shekel, and the quarter of a shekel, of silver.

From the time of Julius Cæsar, who first struck a living portrait on his coins, the Roman coins run in a continued succession of so-called Cæsars, their queens and crown-princes, from about B.C. 48 down to Romulus Augustulus, emperor of the West, who was dethroned by Odoacer about A.D. 475.

After its subjugation by Rome much foreign money found its way into the land of Judæa. The piece of tribute money, or coin mentioned in Luke xx. 24, as presented to our Saviour, bore the image and superscription of the Roman emperor, and it is reasonable to suppose that a large quantity of Roman coins was at that time in circulation throughout Judæa.

MONEY CHANGERS. It is mentioned by Volney that in Syria, Egypt, and Turkey, when any considerable payments are to be made, an agent of exchange is sent for, who counts paras by thousands, rejects pieces of false money, and weighs all the sequins either separately or together. It has hence been suggested that the 'current money with the merchant,' mentioned in Scripture (Gen. xxiii. 16), might have been such as was approved of by competent judges whose business it was to detect fraudulent money if offered in payment. It appears that there were bankers or money-changers in Judæa, who made a trade of receiving money in deposit and paying interest for it (Matt. xxv. 27). Some of them had even established themselves within the precincts of the temple at Jerusalem (xxi. 12), where they were in the practice of exchanging one species of money for another. Persons who came from a distance to worship at Jerusalem would naturally bring with them the money current in their respective districts, and it might therefore be a matter of convenience for them to get this money exchanged at the door of the temple for that which was current in Jerusalem, and upon their departure to receive again that species of money which circulated in the districts to which they were journeying. These money-changers would, of course, charge a commission upon all their transactions, but from the observation of our Saviour, when he overthrew the tables of those in the temple, it may be inferred that they were not distinguished for honesty and fair dealing: 'It is written, my house shall be called the house of prayer, but ye have made it a den of thieves' (ver. 13).

MOON. The worship of the heavenly bodies was among the earliest corruptions of religion, which would naturally take its rise in the eastern parts of the world, where the atmosphere is pure and transparent, and the heavens as bright as they are glowing. In these countries the moon is of exceeding beauty. If the sun 'rules the day,' the moon has the throne of night, which, if less gorgeous than that of the sun, is more attractive, because of a less oppressively brilliant light, while her retinue of surrounding stars seems to give a sort of truth to her regal state, and certainly adds not inconsiderably to her beauty. The moon was therefore worshipped as a goddess in the East at a very early period; in India under the name of Maja; among the Assyrians at

Mylitta; with the Phœnicians she was termed Astarte or Ashteroth, who was also denominated the Syrian mother. The Greeks and Romans worshipped her as Artemis and Diana. Job (xxxi. 26) alludes to the power of the moon over the human soul : 'If I beheld the sun when it shined, or the moon walking in brightness, and my heart hath been secretly enticed, or my mouth hath kissed my hand : this also were an iniquity, for I should have denied the God that is above.' The moon, as being mistress of the night, may well have been considered as the lesser of the two great lights of heaven (Gen. i. 16). It was accordingly regarded in the old Syrian superstition as subject to the sun's influence, which was worshipped as the active and generative power of nature, while the moon was reverenced as the passive and producing power. The moon, accordingly, was looked upon as feminine. Herein Oriental usage agrees with our own. But this usage was by no means universal.

The epithet 'queen of heaven' appears to have been very common. Nor was it, any more than the worship of the moon, unknown to the Jews, as may be seen in a remarkable passage in Jeremiah (xliv. 17), where the Israelites (men and women, the latter exert most influence) appear given over to this species of idolatry : ' We will certainly burn incense to the *queen of heaven*, and pour out drink-offerings unto her, as we have done, we and our fathers ; for then had we plenty of victuals, and were well, and saw no evil. But since we left off to burn incense to the queen of heaven, we have wanted all things ' The last verse of the passage adds to the burnt-offerings and drink-offerings, 'cakes to worship her.' Vows were also made by the Jews to the moon, which superstition required to be fulfilled (ver. 25).

The baneful influence of the moon still finds credence in the East. Moonlight is held to be detrimental to the eyes. In Ps. cxxi. 6 we read, ' The sun shall not smite thee by day, nor the moon by night;' so that the impression that the moon may do injury to man is neither partial nor vague. Rosenmuller refers this to the cold of night, which, he says, is very great and sensible in the East, owing, partly, to the great heat of the day. If this extreme (comparative) cold is considered in connection with the Oriental custom of sleeping out of doors, on the flat roofs of houses, or even on the ground, without in all cases sufficient precautionary measures for protecting the frame, we see no difficulty in understanding whence arose the evil influence ascribed to the moon.

MOON, NEW. [FESTIVALS.]

MOR'DECAI (supposed to come from the Persian word signifying *little man, mannihin* : or, according to others, from the idol *Merodach*, thus signifying *a votary of Merodach*. The last supposition is not unlikely, seeing that Daniel had the Chaldæan name of Belshazzar), son of Jair, of the tribe of Benjamin, descended from one of the captives transported to Babylon with Jehoiachin (Esth. ii. 5). He was resident at Susa, then the metropolis of the Persian empire, and had under his care his niece Hadessa, otherwise Esther, at the time when the fairest damsels of the land were gathered together, that from among them a fitting successor to queen Vashti might be selected for king Ahasuerus. Among them was Esther, and on her the choice fell ; while, by what management we know not, her relationship to Mordecai, and her Jewish descent, remained unknown at the palace. The uncle lost none of his influence over the niece by her elevation, although the seclusion of the royal harem excluded him from direct intercourse with her. He seems to have held some office about the court ; for we find him in daily attendance there, and it appears to have been through this employment that he became privy to a plot of two of the chamberlains against the life of the king, which through Esther he made known to the monarch. This great service was however suffered to pass without reward at the time. On the rise of Haman to power at court, Mordecai alone, of all the nobles and officers who crowded the royal gates, refused to manifest the customary signs of homage to the royal favourite. It would be too much to attribute this to an independence of spirit, which, however usual in Europe, is unknown in Eastern courts. Haman was an Amalekite ; and Mordecai brooked not to bow himself down before one of a nation which from the earliest times had been the most devoted enemies of the Jewish people The Orientals are tenacious of the outward marks of respect, which they hold to be due to the position they occupy ; and the erect mien of Mordecai among the bending courtiers escaped not the keen eye of Haman. He noticed it, and brooded over it from day to day : he knew well the class of feelings in which it originated, and—remembering the eternal enmity vowed by the Israelites against his people, and how often their conquering sword had all but swept his nation from the face of the earth— he vowed by one great stroke to exterminate the Hebrew nation, the fate of which he believed to be in his hands. The temptation was great, and to his ill-regulated mind irresistible. He therefore procured the well-known and bloody decree from the king for the massacre of all the Israelites in the empire in one day. When this decree became known to Mordecai, he covered himself with sackcloth and ashes, and rent the air with his cries. This being made known to Esther through the servants of the harem, who now knew of their relationship, she sent Hatach, one of the royal eunuchs, to demand the cause of his grief : through that faithful servant he made the facts known to her, urged upon her the duty of delivering her people, and encouraged her to risk the consequences of the attempt. She was found equal to the occasion. She risked her life by entering the royal presence uncalled, and having by discreet management procured a favourable opportunity, accused Haman to the king of plotting to destroy *her* and her people. His doom was sealed on this occasion by the means which in his agitation he took to avert it; and when one of the eunuchs present intimated that this man had prepared a gallows fifty cubits high on which to hang Mordecai, the king at once said, ' Hang him thereon.' This was, in fact, a great aggravation of his offence, for the previous night, the king, being unable to sleep, had commanded the records of his reign to be read to him; and the reader had providentially turned to the part recording the conspiracy which had been frustrated through Mordecai. The king asked what had been the reward of this mighty service, and being answered 'Nothing,' he commanded that any one who happened to be in attendance without, should be called. Haman was there, having come for the very purpose of asking the king's leave to hang Mordecai upon the gallows he had prepared, and was asked what should be done to the man whom the king delighted to honour? Thinking that the king could delight to honour no one but himself, he named the highest and most public honours he could conceive, and received from the monarch the astounding answer, 'Make haste, and do even so to Mordecai that sitteth in the king's gate!' Then was Haman constrained, without a word, and with seeming cheerfulness, to repair to the man whom he hated beyond all the world, to invest him with the royal robes, and to conduct him in magnificent cavalcade through the city, proclaiming, 'Thus shall it be done to the man whom the king delighteth to honour.' After this it may seem that it was a strong sense of the fitness of the case for the literal application of the *lex talionis*, that induced the king, when he heard of the gallows prepared for Mordecai, to command that Haman himself should be hanged thereon.

Mordecai was invested with power greater than that which Haman had lost, and the first use he made of it was, as far as possible, to neutralize or counteract the decree obtained by him. It could not be recalled, as the kings of Persia had no power to rescind a decree once issued; but as the altered wish of the court was known, and as the Jews were permitted to stand on their defence, they were preserved from the intended destruction, although much blood was, on the appointed day, shed even in the royal city. The Feast of Purim was instituted in memory of this deliverance, and is celebrated to this day (Esth. ii. 5; x.) [PURIM].

A Mordecai, who returned from the exile with Zerubbabel, is mentioned in Ezra ii. 2, and Neh. vii. 7; but this cannot well have been the Mordecai of Esther, as some have supposed.

MORI'AH, one of the hills of Jerusalem, on which the temple was built by Solomon (2 Chron. iii. 1). The name seldom occurs, being usually included in that of Zion, to the north-east of which it lay, and from which it was separated by the valley of Tyropœon (Joseph. *Antiq.* viii. 3-9) [JERUSALEM]. THE LAND OF MORIAH, whither Abraham went to offer up Isaac (Gen. xxii. 2), is generally supposed to denote the same place, and may at least be conceived to describe the surrounding district. The Jews themselves believe that the altar of burnt-offerings in the temple stood upon the very site of the altar on which the patriarch purposed to sacrifice his son.

MOSE'RAH, MOSEROTH, a station of the Israelites near Mount Hor (Num. xxxiii. 30) [WANDERING].

MO'SES, the lawgiver of Israel, belonged to the tribe of Levi, and was a son of Amram and Jochebed (Exod. vi. 20). According to Exod. ii. 10, the name means *drawn out of water*, and is therefore a significant memorial of the marvellous preservation of Moses when an infant, in spite of those Pharaonic edicts which were promulgated in order to lessen the number of the Israelites. It was the intention of divine pro-

vidence that the great and wonderful destiny of the child should be from the first apparent: and what the Lord had done for Moses he intended also to accomplish for the whole nation of Israel.

It was an important event that the infant Moses, having been exposed near the banks of the Nile, was found there by an Egyptian princess; and that, having been adopted by her, he thus obtained an education at the royal court (Exod. ii. 1-10). Having been taught all the wisdom of the Egyptians (Acts vii. 22; comp. Joseph. *Antiq.* ii. 9. 7), the natural gifts of Moses were fully developed, and he thus became in many respects better prepared for his future vocation.

After Moses had grown up, he returned to his brethren, and, in spite of the degraded state of his people, manifested a sincere attachment to them. He felt deep compassion for their sufferings, and showed his indignation against their oppressors by slaying an Egyptian whom he saw ill treating an Israelite. This doubtful act became by Divine Providence a means of advancing him further in his preparation for his future vocation, by inducing him to escape into the Arabian desert, where he abode for a considerable period with the Midianitish prince, Jethro. whose daughter Zipporah he married (Exod. ii. 11, sq.). Here, in the solitude of pastoral life, he was appointed to ripen gradually for his high calling, before he was unexpectedly and suddenly sent back among his people, in order to achieve their deliverance from Egyptian bondage.

His entry upon this vocation was not in consequence of a mere natural resolution of Moses, whose constitutional timidity and want of courage rendered him disinclined for such an undertaking. An extraordinary divine operation was required to overcome his disinclination. On Mount Horeb he saw a burning thorn-bush, in the flame of which he recognised a sign of the immediate presence of Deity, and a divine admonition induced him to resolve upon the deliverance of his people. He returned into Egypt, where neither the dispirited state of the Israelites, nor the obstinate opposition and threatenings of Pharaoh, were now able to shake the man of God.

Supported by his brother Aaron, and commissioned by God as his chosen instrument, proving, by a series of marvellous deeds, in the midst of heathenism, the God of Israel to be the only true God, Moses at last overcame the opposition of the Egyptians. According to a divine decree, the people of the Lord were to quit Egypt, under the command of Moses, in a triumphant manner. The punishments of God were poured down upon the hostile people in an increasing ratio, terminating in the death of the firstborn, as a sign that all had deserved death. The formidable power of paganism, in its conflict with the theocracy, was obliged to bow before the apparently weak people of the Lord. The Egyptians paid tribute to the emigrating Israelites (Exod. xii. 35), who set out laden with the spoils of victory.

The enraged king vainly endeavoured to destroy the emigrants. Moses, firmly relying upon miraculous help from the Lord, led his people through the Red Sea into Arabia, while the host of Pharaoh perished in its waves (Exod. xii.-xv.).

2 Q

After this began the most important functions of Moses as the lawgiver of the Israelites, who were destined to enter into Canaan as the people of promise, upon whom rested the ancient blessings of the patriarchs. By the instrumentality of Moses they were appointed to enter into intimate communion with God through a sacred covenant, and to be firmly bound to him by a new legislation. Moses, having victoriously repulsed the attack of the Amalekites, marched to Mount Sinai, where he signally punished the defection of his people, and gave them the law as a testimony of divine justice and mercy. From Mount Sinai they proceeded northward to the desert of Paran, and sent spies to explore the Land of Canaan (Num. x.-xiii.). On this occasion broke out a violent rebellion against the lawgiver, which he, however, by divine assistance, energetically repressed (Num. xiv.-xvi.).

The Israelites frequently murmured, and were disobedient during about forty years. In a part of the desert of Kadesh, which was called Zin, near the boundaries of the Edomites, after the sister of Moses had died, and after even the new generation had, like their fathers, proved to be obstinate and desponding, Moses fell into sin, and was on that account deprived of the privilege of introducing the people into Canaan. He was appointed to lead them only to the boundary of their country, to prepare all that was requisite for their entry into the land of promise, to admonish them impressively, and to bless them.

It was according to God's appointment that the new generation also, to whom the occupation of the country had been promised, should arrive at their goal only after having vanquished many obstacles. Even before they had reached the real boundaries of Canaan they were to be subjected to a heavy and purifying trial. It was important that a man like Moses was at the head of Israel during all these providential dispensations. His authority was a powerful preservative against despondency under heavy trials.

Having in vain attempted to pass through the territory of the Edomites, the people marched round its boundaries by a circuitous and tedious route. Two powerful kings of the Amorites, Sihon and Og, were vanquished. Moses led the people into the fields of Moab over against Jericho, to the very threshold of Canaan (Num. xx., xxi.).

Moses happily averted the danger which threatened the Israelites on the part of Midian (Num. xxv.-xxxi.). Hence he was enabled to grant to some of the tribes permanent dwellings in a considerable tract of country situated to the east of the river Jordan (Num. xxxii.), and to give to his people a foretaste of that well-being which was in store for them.

Moses made excellent preparations for the conquest and distribution of the whole country, and took leave of his people with powerful admonitions and impressive benedictions, transferring his government to the hands of Joshua, who was not unworthy to become the successor of so great a man. With a longing but gratified look, he surveyed, from the elevated ground on the border of the Dead Sea, the beautiful country destined for his people.

Moses died in a retired spot at the age of one hundred and twenty years. He remained vigorous in mind and body to the last. His body was not buried in the promised land, and his grave remained unknown, lest it should become an object of superstitious and idolatrous worship.

The Pentateuch is the greatest monument of Moses as an author. The ninetieth psalm also seems to be correctly ascribed to him. Some learned men have endeavoured to prove that he was the author of the book of Job, but their arguments are inconclusive [JOB].

Numerous traditions, as might have been expected, have been current respecting so celebrated a personage. Some of these were known to the ancient Jews, but most of them occur in later rabbinical writers.

The name of Moses is celebrated among the Arabs also, and is the nucleus of a mass of legends. The Greek and Roman classics repeatedly mention Moses, but their accounts contain the authentic Biblical history in a greatly distorted form.

MOTH occurs in Job iv. 19; xiii. 28; xxvii. 18; Isa. l. 9; li. 8; Hosea v. 12; Matt. vi. 19, 20; Luke xii. 33; Ecclus. xix. 3; xlii. 13. There is no Biblical insect whose identity is better ascertained. The following allusions to the moth occur in Scripture:—to its being produced in clothes—' for from garments cometh a moth' (Ecclus. xlii. 13): to its well-known fragility— ' mortal men are crushed *before* the moth' (Job iv. 19), literally ' before the face of the moth.' The allusion to ' the house of the moth' (Job xxvii. 18) seems to refer plainly to the silky spindle-shaped case, covered with detached hairs and particles of wool, made and inhabited by the larva of the *Tinea sarcitella ;* or to the felted case or tunnel formed by the larva of the *Tinea pellionella ;* or to the arched gallery formed by eating through wool by the larva of the *Tinea tapetzella.* References occur to the destructiveness of the clothes-moth: ' as a garment that is moth-eaten' (Job xiii. 28); ' the moth shall eat them up' (Isa. l. 9); ' the moth shall eat them up like a garment' (li. 8); ' I will be to Ephraim as a moth,' *i. e.* will secretly consume him (Hos. v. 12); comp. Matt. vi. 19, 20; Luke xii. 33; James v. 2, metaphorically. Since the ' treasures' of the Orientals, in ancient times, consisted partly of ' garments, both new and old ' (Matt. xiii. 52; and comp. Josh. vii. 21; Judg. xiv. 12), the ravages of the clothes-moth afforded them a lively emblem of destruction. Moths, like fleas, &c., amid other more immediate purposes of their existence, incidentally serve as a stimulus to human industry and cleanliness; for, by a remarkable discrimination in her instinct, the parent moth never deposits her eggs in garments frequently overlooked or kept clean. Indeed, the most remarkable of all proofs of animal intelligence is to be found in the larvae of the water-moth, which get into straws, and adjust the weight of their case so that it can always float: when too heavy they add a piece of straw or wood, and when too light a bit of gravel.

MOTHER. The ordinary applications of the word require no illustration; but the following points of Hebrew usage may be noticed. When the father had more than one wife, the son seems to have confined the title of ' mother' to his real mother, by which he distinguished her from the other wives of his father. Hence the source of

Joseph's peculiar interest in Benjamin is indicated in Gen. xliii. 29, by his being ' his mother's son.' The other brethren were the sons of his father by other wives. Nevertheless, when this precision was not necessary, the step-mother was sometimes styled mother. Thus Jacob (Gen. xxxvii. 10) speaks of Leah as Joseph's mother, for his real mother had long been dead. The step-mother was however more properly distinguished from the womb-mother by the name of ' father's wife.' The word ' mother ' was also, like father, brother, sister, employed by the Hebrews in a somewhat wider sense than is usual with us. It is used of a grandmother (1 Kings xv. 10), and even of any female ancestor (Gen. iii. 20); of a benefactress (Judg. v. 7), and as expressing intimate relationship (Job xvii. 14). In Hebrew, as in English, a nation is considered as a mother, and individuals as her children (Isa. l. 1; Jer. l. 12; Ezek. xix. 2; Hos. ii. 4; iv. 5); so our ' mother-country,' which is quite as good as ' father-land,' which we seem beginning to copy from the Germans. Large and important cities are also called mothers, *i. e.* ' mother-cities,' with reference to the dependent towns and villages (2 Sam. xx. 19), or even to the inhabitants, who are called her children (Isa. iii. 12; xlix. 23) [WOMAN].

MOUNTAINS. The mountains mentioned in Scripture are noticed under their different names, and a general statement with reference to the mountains of Palestine is given under that head. We have therefore in this place only to notice more fully some remarkable symbolical or figurative uses of the word in the Bible.

In Scripture the governing part of the body politic appears under symbols of different kinds. If the allegory or figurative representation is taken from the heavens, the luminaries denote the governing body; if from an animal, the head or horns; if from the earth, a mountain or fortress; and in this case the capital city or residence of the governor is taken for the supreme power. These mutually illustrate each other. For a capital city is the head of the political body; the head of an ox is the fortress of the animal; mountains are the natural fortresses of the earth; and therefore a fortress or capital city, though seated in a plain, may be called a mountain. Thus the words head, mountain, hill, city, horn, and king, are used in a manner as synonymous terms to signify a kingdom, monarchy, or republic, united under *one* government, only with this difference, that it is to be understood in different respects: for the term head represents it in respect of the capital city; mountain or hill in respect of the strength of the metropolis, which gives law to, or is above, and commands the adjacent territory. When David says, ' Lord, by thy favour thou hast made my mountain to stand strong ' (Ps. xxx. 7), he means to express the stability of his kingdom.

It is according to these ideas that the kingdom of the Messiah is described under the figure of a mountain (Isa. ii. 2; xi. 9; Dan. ii. 35), and its universality by its being the resort of all nations, and by its filling the whole earth. The mystic mountains in the Apocalypse denote kingdoms and states subverted to make room for the Messiah's kingdom (Rev. vi. 14, xvi. 20).

The Chaldæan monarchy is described as a

mountain in Jer. li. 25; Zech. iv. 7. In this view, then, a mountain is the symbol of a kingdom, or of a capital city with its domains, or of a king, which is the same.

Mountains are frequently used to signify places of strength, of what kind soever, and to whatsoever use applied (Jer. iii. 23).

Eminences were very commonly chosen for the sites of pagan temples: these became places of asylum, and were looked upon as the fortresses and defenders of the worshippers, by reason of the presence of the false deities in them. On this account mountains were the strongholds of paganism, and therefore in several parts of Scripture they signify idolatrous temples and places of worship (Jer. ii. 23; Ezek. vi. 2-6; Mic. iv. 1; comp. Deut. xii. 2; Jer. ii. 20; iii. 16; Ezek. vi. 3).

MOURNING. This head embraces both the outward expressions of sorrow for the dead, referred to in the Scriptures, and those expressions which were intended to exhibit repentance, &c. These subjects may be noticed according to Townsend's chronological arrangement, and since they nearly approximate, will be pursued together. Under this arrangement, the earliest reference to any kind of mourning is that of Job (B C. 2130), who, being informed of the destruction of his children as the climax of his calamities, ' arose, rent his mantle, shaved his head, and fell down upon the ground and worshipped ' (Job i. 29), uttered sentiments of submission (ver. 21), and sat down among the ashes (ch. ii. 8). His friends came to him by an appointment among themselves to mourn with him and comfort him (ver. 11); they lift up their voices and wept upon a view of his altered appearance; they rent every man his mantle and sprinkled dust upon their heads towards heaven (ver. 12), and sat down with him on the ground seven days and seven nights, waiting till his grief should subside before they commenced their office as mourners. Job then bewails aloud his unhappy condition (ch. iii.). In ch. xvi. 15, 16, reference is made to the customs of sewing sackcloth upon the skin, defiling the head with dust, and suffering the face to be begrimed with weeping. Clamour in grief is referred to (xix. 7; xx. 28): it is considered a wicked man's portion that his widows shall not weep at his death (xxvii. 15). However it is to be accounted for, in the course of the book of Job nearly all the chief characteristics of eastern mourning are introduced. This will appear as we proceed. The next instance is that of Abraham, who came to mourn and weep for Sarah (B C. 1871), words which denote a formal mourning (Gen. xxiii. 2). Days of mourning are referred to in regard to the expected death of Isaac (Gen. xxvii. 41). These appear generally to have consisted of seven, as for Saul (1 Sam. xxxi. 13). Weeping appears (B.C. 1729), either as one chief expression of mourning, or as the general name for it. Hence when Deborah, Rebecca's nurse, was buried at Bethel under an oak, at this period, the tree was called Allon-bachuth, the oak of weeping (Gen. xxxv. 8). The children of Israel were heard to weep by Moses throughout their families, every man in the door of his tent (Num. xi 10; comp. xiv. 1; xxv. 6). So numerous are the references to tears in the Scriptures as to give the impression that the Orientals had them nearly at command (comp. Ps. vi. 6). Reuben rent his clothes upon finding Joseph gone (Gen. xxxvii. 29), and uttered lamentations (ver. 30). Jacob rends his clothes and puts sackcloth upon his loins, and mourns for his son many days; his sons and his daughters rise up to comfort him. and he gives utterance to his grief; 'thus his father wept for him' (Gen. xxxvii 34, 35). Joseph's brothers rend their clothes (Gen. xliv. 13); and this act, as expressive of grief or horror, occurs in multitudes of passages down to the last age of the Jewish empire (Acts xiv. 14). Scarcely less numerous are the references to sackcloth on the loins as an expression of mourning; we have even lying in sackcloth (1 Kings xxi. 27), and sackcloth upon both man and beast at Nineveh (Jonah iii. 8). Joseph's brethren fell to the ground before him in token of grief (Gen. xliv. 14); and this, or lying or sitting on the ground, was a common token of mourning (comp. Ps. xxxv. 14; 1 Sam. xxv. 24; Isa. iii. 26; xlvii. 1; Ezek. xxvi. 16, &c.). The next incident in the history of the subject is the mourning for Jacob by the Egyptians, which was conducted, no doubt, by professional mourners during threescore and ten days (Gen. l. 3), called the days of mourning (ver. 4), though most likely that computation includes the process of embalming. It seems to have amounted to a royal mourning, doubtless out of regard to Joseph. The mourning for Joseph's father was renewed by Joseph's command, with a very great and sore lamentation, upon the funeral cavalcade having arrived in Canaan, and continued seven days (ver. 10). When the children of Israel (B C. 1491) mourned under the threat of the divine displeasure, they did not put on their ornaments (Exod. xxxiii. 4; comp. Joel ii. 16; Ezek. xxiv. 17). At the giving of the law the modes of mourning were regulated by several enactments. It was forbidden the Jews to make cuttings in their flesh for the dead (Lev. xix. 28). The ancient Egyptians, according to Herodotus, did not cut themselves (ii. 61); it was a Syrian custom, as appears from the votaries of Baal (1 Kings xviii. 28); nor were the Jews allowed to make any baldness between their eyes for the dead (Deut. xiv. 1). The priests were forbidden to uncover the head in mourning (Lev. x. 6), or to rend their clothes, or to contract the ceremonial defilement involved in mourning except for their nearest kindred (Lev. xxi. 1, 4); but the high-priest was entirely forbidden to do so even for his father or his mother (ver. 11), and so was the Nazarite (Num. vi. 7). These prohibitions respecting the head and the beard (Lev. xix. 27) seem to have been restricted to funeral occasions, as the customs referred to were lawfully practised on other sorrowful events (comp. Ezra ix. 3; Job i. 20; Isa. xxii. 12; Jer. vii. 29; Micah i. 16). Even the food eaten by mourners was considered unclean (comp. Deut. xxvi. 14, with Hos. ix. 4; Ezek. xxiv. 17). The Jews were commanded to afflict their souls on the day of atonement (Lev. xxiii. 27), and at the Feast of Trumpets (Num. xxix. 7). All the house of Israel mourned for Aaron thirty days (Num. xx 29). The Israelites wept for Moses thirty days, called the days of weeping and mourning for Moses (Deut. xxxiv. 8; B C. 1451). Joshua and the elders of Israel put dust upon their heads at the defeat of Ai, and fasted (Josh. vii. 6), as did the eleven tribes

after the defeat at Gibeah, and wept (Judg. xx. 26), as did all the Israelites at the command of Joshua, on which occasion it is said 'they drew water and poured it out before the Lord' (1 Sam. vii 6; comp. Ps. xxii. 14). The prophet Joel commanded a fast as part of a national mourning. A fast is proclaimed to all the inhabitants or visitors at Jerusalem (Jer. xxxvi 9; comp. Zech. vii. 5). Fasting is practised at Nineveh as part of a public humiliation (Jonah iii. 5). In our Lord's language, 'to fast' and 'to mourn' are the same thing (Matt ix. 15). Public humiliations attended with religious assemblies and prayers (Joel ii. 16, 17); with fasts (Isa. lviii. 3); see all these united (1 Macc. iii. 44, 47, 48). The first complete description of mourning for the dead occurs in 2 Sam iii. 31, 35. Elegies were composed by the prophets on several disastrous occasions (Ezek. xxvi. 1-18; xxvii. 1-36; Amos v. 1, &c). In Ps. xxxv., which is ascribed to David, there is a description of the humiliations practised by the friends of the sick, in order to procure their recovery. Samuel is honoured with a public mourning by the Israelites (1 Sam. xxv. 1), B C. 1058. Upon the death of Saul, David wrote an elegy (2 Sam. i 17-27). This, like that upon the death of Abner, seems to be a poetical description of the character of the departed, like the dirge for an Egyptian king. Lifting up the hands seems to have been an expression of grief (Ps. cxli. 2; Lam. i. 17; Ezra ix. 5). Messengers were sent to condole with survivors; thus David sent such to Hanun, king of Ammon, upon the death of his father (2 Sam. x. 1, 2); 'Many of the Jews came to comfort Martha and Mary' (John xi. 19); 'A great company of women attended our Lord to the cross, bewailing and lamenting him' (Luke xxiii. 27); 'Much people' were with the widow of Nain (Luke vii. 12). Indeed, if persons met a funeral procession they were expected to join it—a custom which is thought to illustrate St. Paul's words, 'Weep with them that weep' (Rom. xii. 15). Ashes were often laid on the head in token of mourning; thus 'Tamar put ashes on her head, rent her garment, and laid her hand upon her head, and went on crying' (2 Sam. xiii. 19, 20; comp. Isa. lxi. 3; 2 Esdras ix. 38). They even wallowed in ashes (Ezek. xxvii. 30). Mourning apparel is first mentioned in 2 Sam. xiv. 2, where it appears that the wearer did not anoint himself with oil (comp Matt. vi. 17). The first reference to hired mourners occurs in Eccles. xii. 5, 'The mourners go about the streets.' They are certainly alluded to in Jer. ix. 17-20, 'the mourning women' (probably widows, comp. Ps. lxxvii. 64; Acts ix. 39). Another reference to them occurs in 2 Chron. xxxv. 25. The greater number of the mourners in ancient Egypt were women, as in the modern East. In the following cut (No. 245) mourners, all females, are shown casting dust upon their heads before the mummy of a man. Mourning for the dead was conducted in a tumultuous manner; they also wept and wailed greatly (Mark v. 38). Even devout men made great lamentations (Acts viii. 2).

Among other signs of mourning they shaved the head. and even tore off the hair (Amos viii. 10; Micah i. 16, Isa. xv. 2; xxii. 12; Jer. vii. 29). Ezra plucked off the hair of his head and of his beard (Ezra ix. 3; Joseph. Antiq. xvi. 7. 5).

The Jews went up to the house-tops to mourn (Isa. xv. 2, 3; xxii. 1); and so did the Moabites

245. [Egyptian Mourners—ashes on Head.]

(Jer. xlviii. 37, 38; Judith viii. 5). They also made cuttings in their hands (Jer. xlviii. 37, 38). they smote upon the thigh (Jer. xxxi. 19; Ezek. xxi. 12); on the breast (Nahum ii. 7; Luke xviii. 13; xxiii. 48); they smote both hands together (Num. xxiv. 10), stamped with the foot (Ezek. vi. 11), bowed down the head (Lam. ii. 10), covered the lips (Micah iii. 7), the face (2 Sam. xix. 4), and the head (2 Sam. xv. 30), and went barefoot (2 Sam. xv. 30). Neighbours and friends provided food for the mourners (2 Sam. iii. 35; Jer. xvi. 7; comp. Ezek. xxiv. 17); this was

246. [Wail with Tabrets, &c.]

called 'the bread of bitterness,' 'the cup of consolation.' In later times the Jews had a custom of giving bread to the poor, at funerals, and leaving it for their use at tombs and graves. Women went to tombs to indulge their grief (John xi. 31); anniversary mournings (1 Esdras i. 22).

MOUSE. The word occurs where, it seems, the nomenclature in modern zoology would point out two species of distinct genera (Lev. xi. 29, 1 Sam. vi. 4, 5, 11, 18; Isa. lxvi. 17). It is likely that the Hebrews extended the acceptation of the word achbar, in the same manner as was the familiar custom of the Greeks, and still more of the Romans, who included within their term mus several species, such as shrews, stoats, &c. In the above texts, all in 1 Sam. vi. apparently refer to the short-tailed field mouse, which is still the most destructive animal to the harvests of Syria, and is most likely the species noticed in antiquity and during the crusades; for, had they been jerbcas in shape and resembled miniature kangaroos, we would expect William of Tyre to have mentioned the peculiar form of the destroyers, which was then unknown to Western Europe; whereas, they being of species or ap-

pearance common to the Latin nations, no particulars were required. But in Leviticus and Isaiah, where the mouse is declared an unclean animal, the species most accessible and likely to invite the appetite of nations who, like the Arabs, were apt to covet all kinds of animals, even when expressly forbidden, were, no doubt, the hamster and the dormouse: and both are still eaten in common with the jerboa, by the Bedouins, who are but too often driven to extremity by actual want of food.

MOUTH. The ordinary applications of this word, common to all languages, require no explanation; but the following somewhat peculiar uses may be noted: 'Heavy-mouthed,' that is, slow of speech, and so translated in Exod. iv. 10; 'smooth mouth' (Ps. xxvi. 28), that is, a flattering mouth; so also 'a mouth of deceit' (Ps. cix. 2). The following are also remarkable phrases: 'To speak with one mouth to mouth, that is, in person, without the intervention of an interpreter (Num. xii. 8; comp. 1 Kings viii. 15; Jer. xxxii. 4). 'With one mouth,' that is, with one voice or consent (Josh. ix. 2; 1 Kings xxii. 13; 2 Chron. xviii. 12). 'With the whole mouth,' that is, with the utmost strength of voice (Job xix. 16; Ps. lxvi. 17). 'To put words into one's mouth,' that is, to suggest what one shall say (Exod. iv. 15; Num. xxii. 38; xxiii. 5, 12; 2 Sam. xiv. 19, &c.). 'To be in one's mouth,' is to be often spoken of, as a law, &c. (Exod. xiii. 9; comp. Ps. v. 10; xxxviii. 15). 'To lay the hand upon the mouth,' is to be silent (Judg. xviii. 19; Job xxi. 5; xl. 4; comp. Prov. xxx. 32), just as we lay the finger on the mouth to enjoin silence. 'To write from the mouth of any one' is to do so from his dictation (Jer. xxxvi. 4, 27, 32; xlv. 1).

The mouth, as the organ of speech, also signifies the words that proceed out of it, which in the sacred style are the same as commands and actions. Hence, for a person or thing to come out of the mouth of another is to be constituted or commanded to become an agent or minister under a superior power: this is frequent in the Revelations (Rev. xvi. 13, 14; i. 16; xi. 4, 5; xii. 15; ix. 19). The term *mouth* is not only applied to a speech or words, but to the speaker (Exod. iv. 16; Jer. xv. 19), in which sense it has a near equivalent in our expression 'mouthpiece.'

MUSIC. It seems probable that music is the oldest of all the fine arts. It is more than any other an immediate work of nature. Hence we find it among all nations, even those which are totally ignorant of every other art. Some instruments of music are in Scripture named even before the deluge, as being invented by Jubal, one of Cain's descendants (Gen iv. 21), and some will regard this as confirmed by the common opinion of the Orientals. Chardin relates that the Persians and Arabians call musicians and singers *Kayne*, or 'descendants from Cain.' The instruments invented by Jubal seem to have remained in use after the flood, or at least the names were still in use, and occur in the latest books of the Old Testament. Music, in practical use, is almost constantly mentioned in connection with the song and the dance (Gen xxxi. 27, Exod. xv. 20), and was doubtless employed to elevate the former and regulate the latter. Women especially are seen to have employed it in this connection from the earliest times (Exod. xv. 20; Judg. xi. 34; 1 Sam. xviii. 6). At a later period we trace the appearance of foreign girls in Palestine, as in Greece and Italy, who visited the towns like the Bayaderes of the present day (Isa. xxiii. 16). Music was also through all periods used in social meetings, and in public rejoicings (1 Kings i. 40; Isa. v. 12; xiv. 11; xxiv. 8; Amos vi. 5; Hag. v. 14; 1 Macc. ix. 39; Judith iii. 8). By David music was variously and conspicuously connected with the temple worship (1 Chron. xxv. 1); in particular, the Levites, in their several choirs, performed their music divided into different classes at the great sacrifices (2 Chron. xxix. 25; xxx. 21; xxxv. 15). The prophets also appear to have regarded music as necessary to their services (1 Sam. x. 5); and they used it sometimes for the purpose, apparently, of bringing their minds into the frame suited for prophetic inspirations (2 Kings iii. 15). In the case of David playing before Saul, we have marked and interesting evidence that the effect of music in soothing the perturbations of a disordered intellect was well known among the Hebrews (1 Sam. xvi. 16).

With respect to the nature of the Hebrew music, it was doubtless of the same essential character as that of other ancient nations, and of all the present Oriental nations; consisting not so much in harmony (in the modern sense of the term) as in unison or melody.

The old, the young, maidens, &c., appear to have sung one part. The instruments by which, in singing, this melody was accompanied, occupied the part of a sustained base; and, if we are disposed to apply in this case what Niebuhr has told us, the beauty of the concerts consisted in this—that other persons repeated the music which had just been sung, three, four, or five notes, lower or higher. Such, for instance, was the concert which Miriam held with her musical fellows, and to which the 'toph,' or tabret, furnished the continued base. To this mode of performance belongs the 24th Psalm, which rests altogether upon the varied representation; in like manner, also, the 20th and 21st Psalms. This was all the change it admitted; and although it is very possible that this monotonous, or rather unisonous music, might not be interesting to ears tuned to musical progressions, modulations, and cadences, there is something in it with which the Orientals are well pleased.

A music of this description could easily dispense with the compositions which mark the time by notes; and the Hebrews do not appear to have known anything of musical notation; for that the accents served that purpose is a position which yet remains to be proved. At the best the accent must have been a very imperfect instrument for this purpose, however high its antiquity.

The Hebrew music is judged to have been of a shrill character; for this would result from the nature of the instruments—harps, flutes, and cymbals—which were employed in the temple service.

The manner of singing single songs was, it seems, ruled by that of others in the same measure, and it is usually supposed that many of the titles of the Psalms are intended to indicate the names of other songs according to which these were to be sung [PSALMS].

The allusions to music in the Scriptures are so incidental and concise, that it will never be possible to form out of them a complete or connected view of the state of musical science among the ancient Hebrews. The little knowledge which has been realized on the subject has been obtained chiefly through the patient labours and minute investigations of Calmet, Forkel, Pfeiffer, Jahn, Winer, De Wette, and other authors.

It is less difficult to determine the general character of the Hebrew instruments of music, than to identify the particular instruments which are named in the Hebrew Scriptures. We see certain instruments different from our own in use among the modern Orientals, and we infer that the Hebrew instruments were probably not unlike these. When, however, we endeavour to identify with these a particular instrument named by the Hebrews, our difficulty begins; because the Hebrew names are seldom to be recognised in those which they now bear, and because the Scripture affords us little information respecting the form of the instruments which it mentions.

The matter naturally arranges itself under the following heads—

    I. Stringed Instruments.
    II. Wind Instruments.
    III. Instruments of Percussion.

I.—1. At the head of the STRINGED INSTRUMENTS we must place the *kinnor*, which is rendered 'harp' in the Authorized Version. The invention and first use of this instrument are ascribed to Jubal (Gen. iv. 21); and Laban names it among the instruments which should have celebrated the departure of his son-in-law (Gen. xxxi. 27). In the first ages the *kinnor* was consecrated to joy and exultation; hence the frequency of its use by David and others in praise of the Divine Majesty. It is thought probable that the instrument received some improvements from David (comp. Amos vi. 5). In bringing back the ark of the covenant (1 Chron. xvi. 5), as well as afterwards, at the consecration of the temple, the *kinnor* was assigned to players of known eminence, chiefly of the family of Jeduthun (1 Chron. xxv. 3). The sorrowing Jews of the captivity, far removed from their own land and the shadow of the sanctuary, hung their *kinnors* upon the willows by the waters of Babylon, and refused to sing the songs of Zion in a strange land (Ps. cxxxvii. 2). Many other passages of similar purport might be adduced in order to fix the uses of an instrument, the name of which occurs so often in the Hebrew Scriptures. They mostly indicate occasions of joy, such as jubilees and festivals. Of the instrument itself the Scripture affords us little further information than that it was composed of the sounding parts of good wood, and furnished with strings. David made it of the berosh wood [BEROSH]; Solomon of the more costly algum (2 Sam. vi. 5; 2 Kings x. 12); and Josephus mentions some composed of the mixed metal called electrum. He also asserts that it was furnished with ten strings, and played with a plectrum (*Antiq.* vii. 12. 3); which however is not understood to imply that it never had any other number of strings, or was always played with the plectrum. David certainly played it with the hand (1 Sam. xvi.

23; xviii. 10; xix. 9), and it was probably used in both ways, according to its size.

That this instrument was really a harp, is now very generally denied; some writers on the subject conclude that it was a kind of guitar, and there is little room to doubt that this instrument was known to the Hebrews, and probably in use among them. It has been suggested, however, by the editor of the *Pictorial Bible* (on Ps xliii. 4) that the *lyre*, in some of its various kinds, was denoted by the word *kinnor*; and subsequent inquiry has tended to establish this conclusion as firmly perhaps as the nature of the subject admits.

247 [Egyptian figures of lyres. 1, 2, played without, and 3, 4, with the plectrum; 4 is the supposed Hebrew lyre.]

2. The NEBEL is the next instrument which requires attention. The word is rendered 'psaltery' in the Authorized Version. As to when this instrument was invented, and when it came into use among the Hebrews, nothing can be determined with certainty. The first mention of it is in the reign of Saul (1 Sam. x. 5), and from that time forward we continue to meet with it in the Old Testament. The use of the instrument prevailed particularly in the public worship of God. It was played upon by several persons in the grand procession at the removal of the ark (1 Chron. xv. 16; xvi. 5); and in the final organization of the temple music it was entrusted to the families of Asaph, Heman, and Jeduthun (1 Chron. xxv. 1-7). Out of the worship of God, it was employed at festivals and for luxurious purposes (Amos vi. 5). In the manufacture of this instrument a constant increase of splendour was exhibited. The first we meet with were made simply of the wood of the *berosh* (2 Sam. vi. 5; 1 Chron. xiii. 8), others of the rarer *algum* tree (1 Kings x 12; 2 Chron. ix. 11); and some perhaps of metal (Joseph. *Antiq.* i 8. 3), unless the last is to be understood of particular parts of the instrument.

Conjectures respecting the probable form of this instrument have been exceedingly various. Passing by the eccentric notion that the *nebel* was a kind of bagpipe, we may assume from the evident tendency of the Scriptural intimations, and from the general bearing of other authorities, that it was composed of strings stretched over a wooden frame This being assumed or granted, we must proceed to seek some hint concerning its shape; and we find nothing more tangible than the concurrent testimony of Jerome, Isidorus, and Cassiodorus, that it was like the Greek letter Δ inverted (∇).

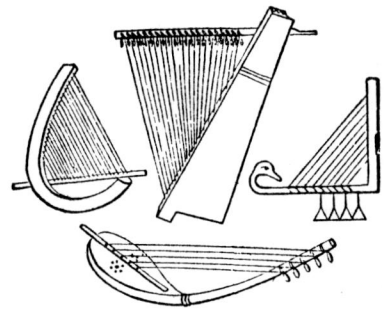

248. [Egyptian triangular instruments.]

We are, however, far from thinking that the *nebel* was always of this shape. It appears to us to be a general name for several of the larger stringed instruments of the harp kind, and also to denote, in a more special sense, one particular sort. In fact we have the names of several instruments which are generally conceived to be different varieties of the *nebel*. One of these kinds, if not the principal kind, or the one most frequently denoted by the word, was the ancient harp, agreeing more or less with that represented in the Egyptian monuments.

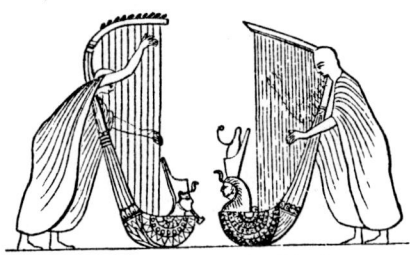

249. [Grand Egyptian harps.]

3. ASOR occurs as an instrument in only a few places, and never but in connection with the *nebel* This has given rise to the conjecture that the two instruments may have differed from each other only in the number of their strings, or the openings at the bottom. We see no reason to dissent from this conclusion.

4. GITTITH is a word which occurs in the titles to Ps. viii, lxxxi., lxxxiv., and is generally supposed to denote a musical instrument. From the name it has been supposed to be an instrument which David brought from Gath; and it has been inferred from Isa. xvi. 10, that it was in particular use at the vintage season. If an instrument of music, it is remarkable that it does not occur in the list of the instruments assigned by David to the temple musicians; nor even in that list which appears in verses 1 and 2 of Ps. lxxxi., in the title of which it is found. The

supposition of Gesenius, that it is a general name for a *stringed instrument*, obviates this difficulty.

5. The word MINNIM, which occurs in Ps xlv. 8, and cl. 4, is supposed by some to denote a stringed instrument. but it seems merely a poetical allusion to the *strings* of any instrument.

6. The SABECA is the instrument rendered 'sackbut,' in Dan. iii. 5. 7, 10, 15. It seems to have been a species of harp or lyre, and, as some think. was only a species of the *nebel*, distinguished by the number of its strings.

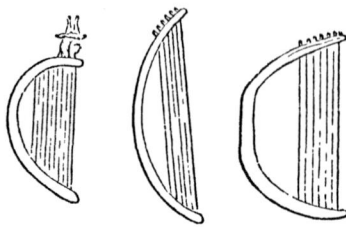

250. [Bow-shaped Egyptian instruments]

7. The PESANTERIN is the psaltery of the Greeks: it occurs only in Dan. iii. 7, 10, 15, where it is supposed to represent the Hebrew *nebel.*

8. The word MACHALATH, which occurs in the titles of Ps. liii. and lxxxviii., is supposed by Gesenius and others to denote a kind of lute or guitar, which instrument others find in the *minnim* above noticed. There can be little doubt that the Hebrews were in possession of instruments of this kind, although we cannot say with certainty that these are the precise words by which they are denoted.

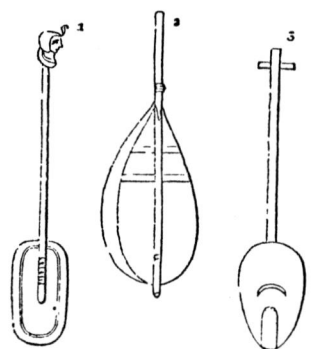

251. [Egyptian Instruments of the Lute kind]

II. WIND INSTRUMENTS.—There is, happily, less difficulty with respect to instruments of this class than with respect to stringed instruments The most ordinary division of these is into trumpets and pipes. of which the Hebrews had both, and of various kinds.

1. The word KEREN, 'horn,' sometimes, but not often, occurs as the name of a musical instrument (Josh. vi. 5; 1 Chron. xxv. 5; Dan. iii. 5, 7, 10, 15). Of natural horns, and of instruments in the shape of horns, the antiquity and general use are evinced by every extensive collection of antiquities. It is admitted that natural horns were at first used, and that they at length came to be

imitated in metal, but were still called horns. This use and application of the word are illustrated in our 'cornet.' It is generally conceived that rams' horns were the instruments used by the early Hebrews; and these are, indeed, expressly named in our own and many other versions, as the instruments used at the noted siege of Jericho (Josh. vi. 5); and the horns are those of the ram which Josephus assigns to the soldiers of Gideon (*Antiq.* v. 6. 5; comp. Judg. vii. 16).

2. The name SHOPHAR, which is a far more common word than *keren*, is rendered 'trumpet' in the Authorized Version. This name seems, first, to denote horns of the straighter kind. including, probably, those of neat cattle, and all the instruments which were eventually made in imitation of and in improvement upon such horns. It is, however, difficult to draw a distinction between it and the *keren*, seeing that the words are sometimes used synonymously. Upon the whole, we may take the *shophar*, however distinguished from the *keren*, to have been that kind of horn or horn-shaped trumpet which was best known to the Hebrews. The name *shophar* means *bright*

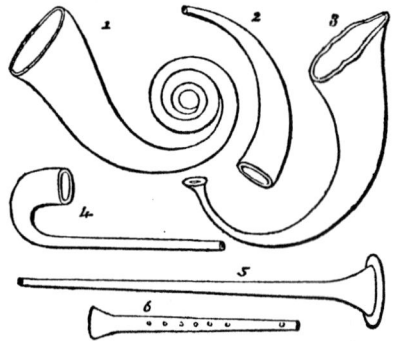

252. [1, 2, 3, 4, Ancient horns and curved trumpets ; 5, straight trumpet ; 6, pipe.]

or *clear*, and the instrument may be conceived to have been so called from its clear and shrill sound, just as we call an instrument a 'clarion,' and speak of a musical tone as 'brilliant' or 'clear.' In the service of God this *shophar* or trumpet was only employed in making announcements, and for calling the people together in the time of the holy solemnities, of war, of rebellion, or of any other great occasion (Exod. xix. 13; Num. x. 10; Judg. iii. 7; 1 Sam. xiii. 3; xv. 10; 2 Chron. xv. 14; Isa. xviii. 3).

3. The CHATZOZERAH was the straight trumpet, different from the *shophar*, which was more or less bent like a horn. There has been various speculation on the name; but we are disposed to assent to the conclusion of Gesenius, that it is an onomatopoetic word, imitating the broken pulse-like sound of the trumpet, like the Latin *taratantara*. Among the Israelites these trumpets were a divine regulation, Moses having been expressly directed how to make them (Num. x. 2). They were of pure beaten silver, but the particular form does not appear in Scripture. They are figured, however, on the arch of Titus, among the other spoils of the Jewish Temple (Fig. 5, No. 252), and they correspond with the description which Josephus, who, as a priest, could not in this matter

be mistaken, has given: 'Moses,' he says, 'invented a kind of trumpet of silver; in length it was little less than a cubit, and it was somewhat thicker than a pipe; its opening was oblong, so as to permit blowing on it with the mouth: at the lower end it had the form of a bell, like the horn.' The tone of this trumpet, or rather the noise made by blowing on it, was very variable, and is distinguished by different terms in Scripture.

4. JOBEL. There has been much speculation concerning the term, and it seems now to be agreed that the word does not denote a separate instrument, but is an epithet applied to the trumpets with which the jubilees were proclaimed, i.e the '*jubilee*-trumpet;' and as the same trumpets were used for signals and alarms, 'the alarm-trumpet, the alarm-horn.' This name for the sound of music is supposed to be derived from Jubal, the inventor of instruments of music.

Wind instruments of softer sound next require attention. The first and principal of these is the

5. CHALIL, the meaning of which is *bored through*, denotes a pipe, perforated and furnished with holes. There are but five places where it occurs in the Old Testament (1 Sam. x. 5; 1 Kings i. 40; Isa. v. 12; xxx. 29; Jer. xlviii. 36); but would seem to have come rather late into use among the Hebrews, and probably had a foreign origin. The passages to which we have referred will indicate the use of this instrument or class

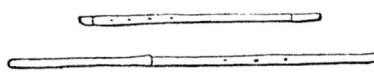

253. [Egyptian reed-pipes.]

of instruments; but of the form we can only guess by reference to those of the ancient Egyptians, which are very similar to those still in use in Western Asia. The pipe is, however, rarely introduced in the Egyptian sculptures, and does not seem to have been held in much estimation. The principal are the single and double pipes. The single pipe of the Greeks is allowed to have been introduced from Egypt, from which the Jews probably had theirs. It was a straight tube, without any increase at the mouth, and when played was held with both hands. It was usually of moderate length, about eighteen inches, but occasionally less, and sometimes so exceedingly long, and the holes so low that the player was obliged to extend his arms to the utmost. Some had three holes, others four, and actual specimens made of common reed have been found.

254. [1, 2, 3, Single pipes; 4, double pipe.]

The double pipe was formed with two of such tubes, of equal or unequal lengths, having a common mouth-piece, and each played with the corresponding hand. They were distinguished as the right and left pipes, and the latter, having but few holes and emitting a deep sound, served as a base; the other had more holes and gave a sharp sound: this pipe is still used in Palestine.

From the references which have been given it will be seen that the pipe was, among the Jews, chiefly consecrated to joy and pleasure. So much was this the case that in the time of Judas Maccabæus the Jews complained ' that joy was taken from Jacob, and the pipe with the harp ceased' (1 Macc. iii. 45). It was particularly used to enliven the periodical journeys to Jerusalem to attend the great festivals (Isa. xxx. 29); and this custom of enlivening with music the tedium of travelling is common in the East at this day. Athenæus tells us of a plaintive pipe which was in use among the Phœnicians. This serves to illustrate Matt. ix. 23, where our Saviour, finding the flute-players with the dead daughter of the ruler, orders them away, because the damsel was not dead; and in this we also recognise the regulation of the Jews, that every one, however poor he might be, should have at least two pipes at the death of his wife.

6. The word MISHROKITHA occurs four times in Daniel (ch. iii. 5, 7, 10, 15), but nowhere else, and appears to be the Chaldæan name for the flute with two reeds, of which we have already spoken.

7. UGAB is the word rendered 'organ' in our version. This and the *kinnor* are the instruments whose invention is ascribed to Jubal (Gen. iv. 21), and higher antiquity cannot therefore be claimed for any instrument. There are only three other places in which it is mentioned in the Old Testament; two in the book of Job (xxi. 12; xxx. 31), and one in the Psalms (cl. 4). The name is taken from the term *organon*, employed by the Septuagint, which simply denotes a double or manifold pipe; and hence in particular the Pandæan or shepherd's pipe, which is at this day called a 'mouth organ' among ourselves. Formerly it was called simply 'organ,' and 'mouth' has been added to distinguish it from the comparatively modern instrument which has usurped the more simple designation of 'organ.' The Pandæan pipe is an instrument of such antiquity that the profane writers do not know to whom to ascribe it. This antiquity corresponds with the Scriptural intimation concerning the *ugab*, and justifies us in seeking for the *syrinx* among the more ancient instruments of the Orientals, especially as it is still common in Western Asia. Niebuhr saw it in the hands of a peasant at Cairo; and Russell says that ' the *syrinx* or Pan's pipe is still a festival instrument in Syria; it is known also in the city, but very few performers can sound it tolerably well. The higher notes are clear and pleasing, but the longer reeds are apt, like the dervise flute, to make a hissing sound, though blown by a good player. The number of reeds of which the *syrinx* is composed varies in different instruments from five to twenty-three.' The classical *syrinx* is usually said to have had seven reeds, but we find some in the monuments with a greater number, and the shepherd of Theocritus had one of nine reeds.

III. INSTRUMENTS OF PERCUSSION,—or such

as give forth their sounds on being struck or shaken.

1. The word TOPH seems to have denoted primarily the tambourine, and generally all instruments of the drum kind which were in use among the Israelites. There is not the slightest doubt about this instrument. All the translations and lexicons agree in this one point; and we have, besides, the actual evidence of existing instruments of this kind among the Arabians, bearing the same name in the forms of *doff* and *adufe*. The *toph* was known to the Jews before they quitted Syria (Gen. xxxi. 27); it is also mentioned by Job (xxi. 12), and it is the first instrument named after the exode, being that with which Miriam led the dances with which the daughters of Israel celebrated the overthrow of Pharaoh (Exod. xv. 20). It was employed by David in all the festivities of religion (2 Sam. vi. 5). Isaiah adduces it as the instrument of voluptuaries, but left in silence amid wars and desolations (Isa. xxiv. 8). The occasions on which it was used were mostly joyful, and those who played upon it were generally females (Ps. lxviii. 25), as was the case among most ancient nations, and is so at the present day in the East. It is nowhere mentioned in connection with battles or warlike transactions.

255. [Tambourines. 1, angular; 2, circular.]

Whether the Israelites had drums or not does not clearly appear, and in the absence of evidence *pro* or *con* it is useless to speculate on the subject. If they had, they must be included under the general name of *toph*. The ancient Egyptians had a long drum, very similar to the tom-toms of

256. [Ancient Egyptian drums]

India (No. 256, figs. 1, 3). It was about two feet

or two feet and a half in length, and was beaten with the hand. The case was of wood or copper, covered at both ends with parchment or leather, and braced with cords extended diagonally over the exterior of the cylinder. It was used chiefly in war. There was another larger drum, less unlike our own; it was about two feet and a half long by about two feet broad, and was shaped much like a sugar-cask (No. 257, fig. 3). It was formed of copper, and covered at the ends with red leather, braced by catgut springs passing through small holes in its broad margin. This kind of drum was beaten with sticks (fig. 5) It does not appear on the monuments, but an actual specimen was found in the excavations made by D'Athanasi, in 1823, and is now in the museum at Paris.

Another species of drum is represented in the Egyptian paintings, and is of the same kind which is still in use in Egypt and Arabia, under the name of the *darabooka* drum. It is made of parchment stretched over the top of a funnel-shaped case of metal, wood, or pottery (No. 257, figs. 1, 2, 4). It is beaten with the hand, and when relaxed, the parchment is braced by exposing it for a few moments to the sun, or the warmth of a fire. This kind of drum claims

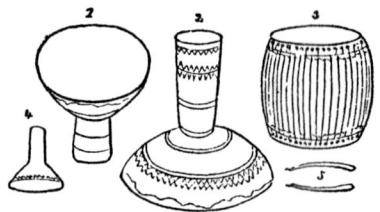

257. [Drums. 1, 2, 4, modern oriental; 3, ancient Egyptian; 5, sticks to 3.]

particular attention from its being supposed to be represented on one of the coins ascribed to Simon Maccabæus.

2. The word PHAAMON denotes the small golden appendages to the robe of the high-priest (Exod. xxviii. 33; xxxix. 25), which all versions agree in rendering ' bells,' or ' little bells.'

3. The words TZELTZELIM, METZILLOTH, and METZILTHAIM, are translated *cymbals* in most versions, except in Zech. xiv. 20, where they are rendered 'bells'—the ' bells of the horses.' If the words, however, denote cymbals in other

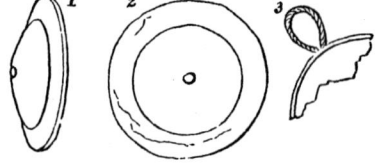

258. [Cymbals—Egyptian.]

places, they cannot well denote a different thing there. There is an important passage (Ps. cl. 5), ' Praise him with the clear cymbal, praise him with the resounding cymbal,' which clearly points to two instruments under the same name, and leaves us to conclude that the Hebrews had both hand-cymbals and finger-cymbals (or castagnets), although it may not in all cases be easy to say which of the two is intended in particular texts Cymbals figure in the grand procession at the removal of the ark (1 Chron. xiii. 8): other instances occur of their being used in the worship of God (Neh. xii. 27 ; Ps. cl. 5 ; 1 Chron. xv. 2); and the illustrious Asaph was himself a player on the cymbal (1 Chron. xvi 5). The sound of these instruments is very sharp and piercing, but it does not belong to fine, speaking, expressive music.

4. The name SHALISHIM occurs but once, viz. in 1 Sam. xviii. 6, and is there uncertainly rendered, in the Authorized Version, 'instruments of music,' and in the margin 'three-stringed instruments.' The word is plural, and means 'threes.' Most writers, proceeding upon this interpretation, identify it with the triangle, which Athenæus (iv. 23) alleges to have been a Syrian invention.

5. MENAANEIM is another word which occurs but once in Scripture (2 Sam. vi. 5), where our version translates it by 'cymbals,' although it has appropriated another word to that instrument. It is now more generally thought to denote the *sistrum*. The sistrum was generally from eight

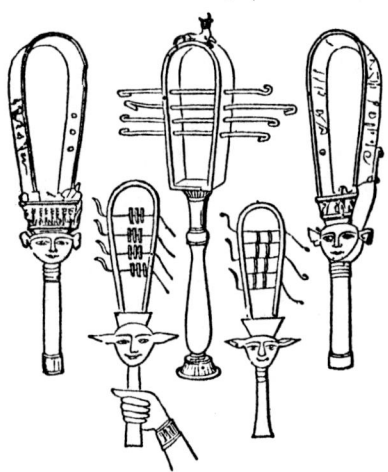

259. [Sistra—various Egyptian specimens.]

to sixteen or eighteen inches in length, and entirely of bronze or brass. It was sometimes inlaid with silver, gilt, or otherwise ornamented, and being held upright was shaken, the rings moving to and fro upon the bars. The last were frequently made to imitate snakes, or simply bent at each end to secure them from slipping through the holes. Several actual specimens of these instruments have been found, and are deposited in the British, Berlin, and other museums. They are mostly furnished with sacred symbols, and were chiefly used by the priests and priestesses in the ceremonies of religion, particularly in those connected with the worship of Isis.

MUSTARD TREE   The *Sinapi* of the Greek Testament, rendered 'mustard tree' in the Authorized Version, has engaged the attention of many commentators, great difficulty having been experienced in finding a plant with the requisite

characteristics, notwithstanding the several attempts which have been made. The subject was investigated by Dr. Royle in a paper read before

260. [Salvadora Persica]

the Royal Asiatic Society, on the 16th March, 1844. Having referred to the passages of the New Testament in which the word occurs (Matt. xiii. 31 ; xvii. 20 ; Mark iv. 31 ; Luke xiii. 19; xvii. 6), he first showed how unsuitable were the plants which had been adduced to the circumstances of the sacred narrative, and mentioned that his own attention had been turned to the subject in consequence of the present Bishop of Lichfield having informed him that Mr. Amueny, a Syrian student of King's College, was well acquainted with the tree. Mr. A. stated that this tree was found near Jerusalem, but most abundantly on the banks of the Jordan and round the sea of Tiberias ; that its seed was employed as a substitute for mustard, and that it was called *khardal*, which, indeed, is the common Arabic name for mustard. Dr. Royle knew a tree of N. W. India, which was there called *kharjal*, and which appeared possessed of the requisite properties, but he could not find it mentioned in any systematic work, or local Flora, as a native of Palestine. The plant is *Salvadora Persica*, a large shrub, or tree of moderate size, a native of the hot and dry parts of India, of Persia, and of Arabia. Dr. Roxburgh describes the berries as much smaller than a grain of black pepper, having a strong aromatic smell, and a taste much like that of garden cresses. Irby and Mangles, in their travels, mention a tree which they suppose to be the mustard tree of Scripture. They met with it while advancing towards Kerak, from the southern extremity of the Dead Sea. It bore its fruit in bunches resembling the currant; and the seeds had a pleasant, though strongly aromatic taste, nearly resembling mustard. They say, 'We think it possible that this is the tree our Saviour alluded to in the parable of the mustard seed, and not the mustard plant which we have in the north, and which, even when growing large, can never be called a tree, whereas the other is really such, and birds might easily, and actually do, take shelter under its shadow.' On further inquiry, Dr. Royle learned that a specimen of the tree had been brought home by Mr. W. Barker, and that it had been ascertained by Messrs. Don and

Lambert to be the *Salvadora Persica* of botanists.

The paper above referred to concludes by stating it as an important fact, that the writer had come to the same conclusion as Irby and Mangles, by an independent mode of investigation, even when he could not ascertain that the plant existed in Palestine; which is, at all events, interesting, as proving that the name *kharjal* is applied, even in so remote a country as the north-west of India, to the same plant which, in Syria, is called *khardal*, and which no doubt is the *ahardal* of the Talmudists, one of whom describes it as a tree of which the wood was sufficient to cover a potter's shed, and another says that he was wont to climb into it, as men climb into a fig-tree. Hence there can be little doubt but that *Salvadora Persica* is the mustard tree of Scripture. The plant has a small seed, which produces a large tree with numerous branches, in which the birds of the air may take shelter. The seed is possessed of the same properties, and is used for the same purposes, as mustard, and has a name, *khardal*, of which *sinapi* is the true translation, and which, moreover, grows abundantly on the very shores of the sea of Galilee, where our Saviour addressed to the multitude the parable of the mustard seed.

MY'RA, one of the chief towns of Lycia, in Asia Minor. It lay about a league from the sea (in N. lat. 36° 18'; E. long. 30°), upon a rising ground, at the foot of which flowed a navigable river with an excellent harbour at its mouth. The town now lies desolate. When Paul was on his voyage from Cæsarea to Rome, he and the other prisoners were landed here, and were re-embarked in a ship of Alexandria bound to Rome (Acts xxvii. 5).

MYRRH is the exudation of a little-known tree found in Arabia, but much more extensively in Abyssinia. It formed an article of the earliest commerce, was highly esteemed by the Egyptians and Jews, as well as by the Greeks and Romans, as it still is both in the East and in Europe. The earliest notice of it occurs in Exod. xxx. 23, 'Take thou also unto thee principal spices, of *pure myrrh (morderor)* 500 shekels.' It is afterwards mentioned in Esther ii. 12, as employed in the purification of women; in Ps. xlv. 8, as a perfume, 'All thy garments smell of myrrh, and aloes, and cassia;' also in several passages of the Song of Solomon (iv. 6; v. 5). We find it mentioned in Matt. ii. 11, among the gifts presented by the wise men of the East to the infant Jesus— 'gold, and frankincense, and myrrh.' It may be remarked as worthy of notice, that myrrh and frankincense are frequently mentioned together. In Mark xv. 23, we learn that the Roman soldiers 'gave him (Jesus) to drink wine mingled with *myrrh*; but he received it not' The Apostle John (xix. 39) says, 'Then came also Nicodemus, and brought a mixture of myrrh and aloes, about an hundred pound weight,' for the purpose of embalming the body of our Saviour.

Though myrrh seems to have been known from the earliest times, and must consequently have been one of the most ancient articles of commerce, the country producing it long remained unknown. Some is undoubtedly procured in Arabia, but the largest quantity has always been obtained from Africa. Mr. Johnson, in his re-

cently published *Travels in Abyssinia* (i. 249), mentions that 'Myrrh and mimosa trees abounded in this place' (Koranhedudah in Adal). The former he describes as being 'a low, thorny, ragged-looking tree, with bright-green trifoliate leaves; the gum exudes from cracks in the bark of the trunk near the root, and flows freely upon

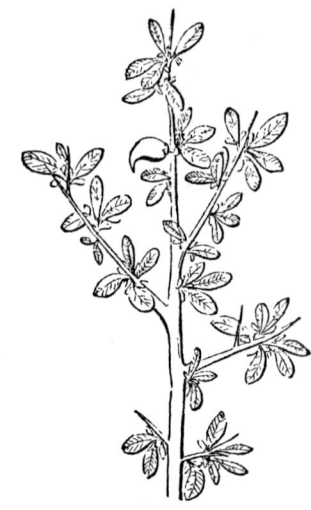

261. [Balsamodendron Myrrha.]

the stones immediately underneath. Artificially it is obtained by bruises made with stones. The natives collect it principally in the hot months of July and August, but it is to be found, though in very small quantities, at other times of the year.

Several kinds of myrrh were known to the ancients; and in modern commerce we have Turkish and East Indian myrrh, and different names used to be, and are still applied to it, as red and fatty myrrh, myrrh in tears, in sorts, and myrrh in grains. In the Bible also several kinds of myrrh are enumerated, respecting which various opinions have been entertained.

Myrrh, it is well known, was celebrated in the most ancient times as a perfume, and a fumigator, as well as for its uses in medicine. Myrrh was burned in the temples, and employed in embalming the bodies of the dead. It was offered in presents, as natural products commonly were in those days, because such as were procured from distant countries were very rare. The ancients prepared a *wine of myrrh*, and also an *oil of myrrh*, and it formed an ingredient in many of the most celebrated compound medicines, as the *Theriaca*, the *Mithridata*, *Manus Dei*, &c. Even in Europe it continued to recent times to enjoy the highest medicinal reputation, as it does in the East in the present day. From the sensible properties of this drug, and from the virtues which were ascribed to it, we may satisfactorily account for the mention of it in the several passages of Scripture which have been quoted.

MYRTLE occurs in several passages of the Old Testament, as in Isa. xli. 19; lv. 13; Neh. viii. 15, Zech i. 8, 10, 11.

The myrtle has from the earnest periods been

highly esteemed in all the countries of the south of Europe. By the Greeks and Romans it was dedicated to Venus, and employed in making wreaths to crown lovers, but among the Jews it was the emblem of justice. The note of the Chaldee Targum on the name Esther, according to Dr. Harris, is, ' they call her Hadassah because she was *just*, and those that are just are compared to *myrtles*.'

The repute which the myrtle enjoyed in ancient times it still retains, notwithstanding the great accession of ornamental shrubs and flowers which has been made to the gardens and greenhouses of Europe. This is justly due to the rich colouring of its dark green and shining leaves, contrasted with the white starlike clusters of its flowers, affording in hot countries a pleasant shade under its branches, and diffusing an agreeable odour from its flowers or bruised leaves. It is, however, most agreeable in appearance when in the state of a shrub, for when it grows into a tree, as it does in hot counties, the traveller looks under instead of over its leaves, and a multitude of small branches are seen deprived of their leaves by the crowding of the upper ones. This shrub is common in the southern provinces of Spain and France, as well as in Italy and Greece; and also on the northern coast of Africa, and in Syria. The poetical celebrity of this plant had, no doubt, some influence upon its employment in medicine, and numerous properties are ascribed to it by Dioscorides (i. 127). It is aromatic and astringent, and hence, like many other such plants, forms a stimulant tonic, and is useful in a variety of complaints connected with debility. Its berries were formerly employed in Italy, and still are so in Tuscany, as a substitute for spices, now imported so plentifully from the far East. A wine was also prepared from them, which was called myrtidanum, and their essential oil is possessed of excitant properties. In many parts of Greece and Italy the leaves are employed in tanning leather. The myrtle, possessing so many remarkable qualities, was not likely to have escaped the notice of the sacred writers, as it is a well-known inhabitant of Judæa.

MYS'IA, a province occupying the north-west angle of Asia Minor, and separated from Europe only by the Propontis and Hellespont: on the south it joined Æolis, and was separated on the east from Bithynia by the river Æsopus. Latterly Æolis was included in Mysia, which was then separated from Lydia and Ionia by the river Hermus, now Sarabad or Djedis. In ancient times the province of Mysia was celebrated for its fertility in corn and wine, and although now but poorly tilled, it is still one of the finest tracts in Asia Minor. Paul passed through this province and embarked at its chief port, Troas, on his first voyage to Europe (Acts xvi. 7, 8).

MYSTERY. A most unscriptural and dangerous sense is but too often put upon this word, as if it meant something absolutely unintelligible and incomprehensible; whereas, in every instance in which it occurs in the Sept. or New Testament, it is applied to something which is *revealed*, declared, explained, spoken, or which may be known or understood. This fact will appear from the following elucidation of the passages in which it is found. First, it is sometimes used to denote the meaning of a symbolical represent-ation, whether addressed to the mind by a parable, allegory, &c., or to the eye, by a vision, &c. (Matt. xiii. 10; Mark iv. 11). Again, the mystery or symbolical vision of the ' seven stars and of the seven golden candlesticks ' (Rev. i. 12. 16), is explained to mean ' the angels of the seven churches of Asia, and the seven churches themselves' (ver. 20). Again, ' the mystery ' or symbolical representation ' of the woman upon a scarlet-coloured beast' (Rev. xvii. 3-6) is also explained : ' I will tell thee the mystery of the woman,' &c. (xvii. 7). When St. Paul, speaking of marriage, says, ' this is a great mystery ' (Eph. v. 32), he evidently treats the original institution of marriage as affording a figurative representation of the union betwixt Christ and the church. The word is also used to denote anything whatever which is hidden or concealed, till it is explained. Thus it is employed in the New Testament to denote those doctrines of Christianity, general or particular. which the Jews and the world at large did not understand, till they were revealed by Christ and his apostles, ' Great is the mystery of godliness,' *i. e.* the Christian religion (1 Tim. iii. 16), the chief parts of which the apostle instantly proceeds to adduce,—' God was manifest in the flesh, justified by the Spirit, seen of angels,' &c.—facts which had not entered into the heart of man (1 Cor. ii. 9) until God visibly accomplished them, and revealed them to the apostles by inspiration (ver. 10). Thus also the Gospel in general is called ' the mystery of the faith' (1 Tim. iii. 9), and ' the mystery which from the beginning of the world had been hid with God, but which was now made known through means of the church' (Eph. iii. 9). The same word is used respecting certain particular doctrines of the Gospel, as, for instance, ' the partial and temporary blindness of Israel,' of which mystery ' the Apostle would not have Christians' ignorant (Rom. xi. 25), and which he explains (ver. 25-32). He styles the calling of the Gentiles ' a mystery which, in other ages, was not made known unto the sons of men as it is now revealed unto the holy apostles and prophets by the Spirit' (Eph. iii. 4-6; comp. i. 9, 10, &c.). To this class we refer the well-known phrase, ' Behold I show you a mystery (1 Cor. xv. 51), we shall all be changed;' and then follows an explanation of the change (ver. 51-55). And in the prophetic portion of his writings ' concerning the mystery of iniquity ' (2 Thess. ii. 7), he speaks of it as being ultimately ' revealed' (ver. 8); and to complete the proof that the word ' mystery ' is used in the sense of *knowable* secrets, we add the words ' Though *I understand all mysteries*' (1 Cor. xiii. 2).

N.

1. NA'AMAH (*pleasant*), daughter of Lamech and Zillah, and sister of Tubal-cain (Gen. iv. 22).

2. NAAMAH, an Ammonitess, one of the wives of Solomon, and mother of Rehoboam (1 Kings xiv. 21).

NA'AMAN (*pleasantness*), commander of the armies of Damascene Syria, in the time of Joram, king of Israel. Through his valour and abilities Naaman held a high place in the esteem of his king Benhadad: and although he was afflicted with leprosy, it would seem that this did not. as among the Hebrews, operate as a disqualification for public employment. Nevertheless, the condition of a leper could not but have been in his high place both afflicting and painful: and when it was heard that a little Hebrew slave-girl. who waited upon Naaman's wife, had spoken of a prophet in Samaria who could cure her master of his leprosy. the faint and uncertain hope thus offered was eagerly seized; and the general obtained permission to visit the place where this relief was to be sought. Benhadad even furnished him with a letter to his old enemy king Joram; but as this letter merely stated that Naaman had been sent for him to cure, the king of Israel rent his clothes in astonishment and anger, suspecting that a request so impossible to grant, involved a studied insult or an intention to fix a quarrel upon him with a view to future aggressions When tidings of this affair reached the prophet Elisha, he desired that the stranger might be sent to him. Naaman accordingly went, and his splendid train of chariots, horses, and laden camels filled the street before the prophet's house. As a leper, Naaman could not be admitted into the house; and Elisha did not come out to him as he expected, and as he thought civility required; but he sent out his servant to tell him to go and dip himself seven times in the Jordan, and that his leprosy would then pass from him. He was, however, by this time so much chafed and disgusted by the apparent neglect and incivility with which he had been treated, that if his attendants had not prevailed upon him to obey the directions of the prophet, he would have returned home still a leper. But he went to the Jordan, and having bent himself seven times beneath its waters, rose from them clear from all leprous stain. His gratitude was now proportioned to his previous wrath, and he drove back to vent the feelings of his full heart to the prophet of Israel. He avowed to him his conviction that the God of Israel, through whom this marvellous deed had been wrought, was great beyond all gods; and he declared that henceforth he would worship Him only, and to that end he proposed to take with him two mules' load of the soil of Israel wherewith to set up in Damascus an altar to Jehovah This shows he had heard that an altar of earth was necessary (Exod. xx. 24); and the imperfect notions which he entertained of the duties which his desire to serve Jehovah involved, were natural in an uninstructed foreigner. He had also heard that Jehovah was a very jealous God, and had forbidden any of his servants to bow themselves down before idols; and therefore he expressed to Elisha a hope that he should be forgiven if, when his public duty required him to attend his king to the temple of Rimmon, he bowed with his master The grateful Syrian would gladly have pressed upon Elisha gifts of high value. but the holy man resolutely refused to take anything, lest the glory redounding to God from this great act should in any degree be obscured. His servant, Gehazi, was less scrupulous, and hastened with a lie in his mouth to ask in his master's name for a portion of that which Elisha had refused. The illustrious Syrian no sooner saw the man running after his chariot, than he alighted to meet him, and happy to relieve himself in some degree under the

sense of overwhelming obligation, he sent him back with more than he had ventured to ask (2 Kings v.). Nothing more is known of Naaman; and what befal Gehazi is related under another head [GEHAZI].

NA'BAL (*stupid, foolish*), a descendant of Caleb, dwelling at Maon, and having large possessions near Carmel of Judah, in the same neighbourhood. He had abundant wealth, being the possessor of 3000 sheep and 1000 goats, but his churlish and harsh character had not been softened by the prosperity with which he had been favoured. He was holding a great sheep-shearing of his numerous flocks at Carmel—which was a season of great festivity among the sheep-masters of Israel—when David sent some of his young men to request a small supply of provisions, of which his troop was in great need. He was warranted in asking this, as, while Nabal's flocks were out in the desert, the presence of David and his men in the neighbourhood had effectually protected them from the depredations of the Arabs. But Nabal refused this application, with harsh words, reflecting coarsely upon David and his troop as a set of worthless runagates. On learning this, David was highly incensed, and set out with his band to avenge the insult. But his intention was anticipated and averted by Nabal's wife Abigail, who met him on the road with a most acceptable supply of provisions, and, by her consummate tact and good sense, mollified his anger, and, indeed, caused him in the end to feel thankful that he had been prevented from the bloodshed which would have ensued. When Nabal, after recovering from the drunkenness of the feast, was informed of these circumstances, he was struck with such intense terror at the danger to which he had been exposed, that 'his heart died within him, and he became as a stone;' which seems to have been the exciting cause of a malady that carried him off about ten days after. David. not long after, evinced the favourable impression which the good sense and comeliness of Abigail had made upon him, by making her his wife, B.C. 1061 (1 Sam. xxv.) [ABIGAIL].

NABATHÆ'ANS. [NEBAIOTH.]

NA'BOTH (*fruit, produce*), an inhabitant of Jezreel, who was the possessor of a patrimonial vineyard adjoining the garden of the palace which the kings of Israel had there. King Ahab had conceived a desire to add this vineyard to his ground, to make of it 'a garden of herbs,' but found that Naboth could not, on any consideration, be induced to alienate a property which he had derived from his fathers. This gave the king so much concern, that he took to his bed and refused his food; but when his wife, the notorious Jezebel, understood the cause of his trouble, she bade him be of good cheer, for *she* would procure him the vineyard. Some time after Naboth was, at a public feast, accused of blasphemy, by an order from her under the royal seal, and, being condemned through the testimony of false witnesses, was stoned to death, according to the law, outside the town (Lev. xxiv. 16; Num. xv. 30). His estate, by a usage which appears to have crept in, was forfeited to the crown.

When Ahab heard of the death of Naboth—and he must have known how that death had been accomplished, or he would not have supposed himself a gainer by the event—he hastened to take possession. But he was speedily taught that this horrid crime had not passed without notice by the all-seeing God, and would not remain unpunished. The only tribunal to which he remained accountable, pronounced his doom through the prophet Elijah, who met him on the spot, ' In the place where dogs licked the blood of Naboth, shall dogs lick thy blood, even thine' (1 Kings xxi.).

NA'CHON. The floor of Nachon is the name given to the threshing-floor near which Uzzah was slain, for laying his hand upon the ark (2 Sam. vi. 6).

NA'CHOR. [NAHOR.]

' 1. NA'DAB (liberal), eldest son of Aaron, who, with his brother Abihu, was slain for offering strange fire to the Lord [ABIHU].

2. NADAB, son of Jeroboam, and second king of Israel. He ascended the throne upon the death of his father (B.C. 954), whose deep-laid, but criminal and dangerous policy, he followed.

NAHA'LIEL, an encampment of the Israelites in the wilderness [WANDERING].

NAHAL'LAL, a town in the tribe of Zebulun (Josh. xix. 15), which was assigned to the Levites (Josh. xxi. 35), but of which Zebulun was slow in dispossessing the Canaanites (Judg. i. 30).

1. NA'HASH (a serpent), a person named only in 2 Sam. xvii. 25 ; and as he is there described as the father of Abigail and Zeruiah, who are elsewhere called the sisters of David, this must have been either another name for Jesse, or, as some suppose, of a former husband of David's mother.

2. NAHASH, king of the Ammonites, noted for the barbarous terms of capitulation which he offered to the town of Jabesh-Gilead, and for his subsequent defeat by Saul [JABESH].

1. NAHOR (snorting), or rather Nachor, as in Luke iii. 34, son of Serug, and father of Terah, the father of Abraham (Gen. xi 22-25).

2. NAHOR, grandson of the preceding, being one of the sons of Terah, and brother of Abraham. Nahor espoused Milcah his niece, daughter of his eldest brother Haran (Gen. xi. 27-29). Nahor did not quit his native place, ' Ur of the Chaldees,' when the rest of the family removed to Haran (Gen. xi. 30); but it would appear that he went thither afterwards, as we eventually find his son Bethuel, and his grandson Laban, established there (Gen. xxvii. 43 ; xxix. 5).

NAH'SHON (enchanter), from which he is called Naason in the genealogies of Christ in Matt. i. 4 ; Luke iii. 32, son of Aminadab, and prince or chief of the tribe of Judah, at the time of the exode (Num. i. 7 ; ii. 3).

NAHUM (consolation), the seventh of the minor prophets, according to the arrangement of both the Greek and Hebrew, but the sixth in point of date. was a native of Elkosh, a village of Galilee. He prophesied in Judah after the deportation of the ten tribes, and soon after the unsuccessful irruption of Sennacherib (ch. i. 11-13; ii. 1, 14), consequently towards the close of the reign of Hezekiah. Attempts have been made to fix the date with precision, from the allusion to the destruction of No-Ammon or Thebes in Egypt (ch. iii 8); but as it is uncertain when this event took place, Eichhorn and others have conjectured that it was near the beginning of the reign of Hezekiah, or about B.C. 720, as about this time Sargon, king of

Assyria, waged an unsuccessful war for three years against Egypt (Isa. xx.).

The contents of the prophecy of Nahum are as follows :— Chap. i. 2-7. The destruction of Nineveh and of the Assyrian monarchy is depicted in the liveliest colours, together with the relief of Judah from oppression. The destruction of Nineveh is detailed with still greater particularity in the third chapter; which has induced some to suppose that the prophet refers to two different events—the sack of Nineveh by the Medes, B C. 867, in the reign of Sardanapalus, and its second and final destruction. under Chyniladan, by Cyaxares the First and Nabopolassar, B C. 625. But this opinion has been satisfactorily refuted by Jahn and De Wette.

The beauty of the style of Nahum has been universally felt. It is classic, observes De Wette, in all respects. It is marked by clearness, by its finished elegance, as well as by fire, richness, and originality. The rhythm is regular and lively. The whole book remarkably coherent, and the author only holds his breath, as it were, in the last chapter. Jahn observes that the language is pure, with a single exception; that the style is ornate, and the tropes bold and elegant (rendering it, however, necessary for the reader to supply some omissions; see ii. 8; ix. 3, 16); and that the descriptions of the divine omnipotence, and of the destruction of Nineveh, are resplendent with all the perfection of oratory.

NAIL. There are two Hebrew words thus translated in the Auth. Vers., which it may be well to distinguish.

1. Yathed, which usually denotes a peg, pin, or nail, as driven into a wall (Ezek. xv. 3 ; Isa. xxii. 25); and more especially a tent-pin driven into the earth to fasten the tent (Exod. xxvii. 19 ; xxxv. 18; xxxviii. 31; Judg. iv. 21, 22; Isa. xxxiii. 20 ; liv. 2).

2. Mismeroth, which, with some variations of form, is applied to ordinary and ornamental nails. It always occurs in the plural, and is the word which we find in 1 Chron. xxii. 3. 2 Chron. iii. 9 ; Isa. xli. 7 ; Jer. x. 4 ; Eccles. xii. 11. The last of these texts involves a very significant proverbial application—' The words of the wise are as nails infixed,' &c.

NA'IN, a town of Palestine. where Jesus raised the widow's son to life (Luke vii. 11-17). Eusebius and Jerome describe it as near Endor.

NAI'OTH. a place in or near Ramah, where Samuel abode with his disciples (1 Sam. xix. 18, 19, 22, 23; xx. 1).

NAKED. The word arom, rendered 'naked' in our Bibles, does not in many places mean absolute nakedness. It has this meaning in such passages as Job i. 21 ; Eccles. v. 15 ; Mic. i. 8 ; Amos ii. 16. But in other places it means one who is ragged or poorly clad (1 John xxi. 7 ; Isa. lviii. 7); which does not indeed differ from a familiar application of the word 'naked' among ourselves. A more peculiar and Oriental sense of the word is that in which it is applied to one who has laid aside his loose outer garment, and goes about in his tunic, and it was thus that Isaiah went ' naked ' and barefoot (Isa. xx. 2; comp. John xxi. 7). Persons in their own houses freely laid aside their outer garment, and appeared in their tunic and girdle , but this is undress, and they would count it improper to appear abroad, or to see company in their own house without the outer robe.

NA'OMI, wife of Elimelech of Bethlehem, and mother-in-law of Ruth, in whose history hers is involved [RUTH].

NAPH'TALI (*my wrestling*), the sixth son of Jacob, and his second by Bilhah, Rachel's handmaid, born B.C. 1747, in Padan-Aram Nothing of his personal history is recorded. The description given of Naphtali in the testamentary blessing of Jacob (Gen. xlix. 21) has been variously rendered. In the Authorized Version it is translated ' a hind let loose, he giveth goodly words.' But, according to the reading in the Septuagint, the verse may be rendered, ' Naphtali is a goodly tree [terebinth or oak] that puts forth lovely branches.' We certainly incline to this view of the text; the metaphor which it involves being well adapted to the residence of the tribe of Naphtali, which was a beautiful woodland country, extending to Mount Lebanon, and producing fruits of every sort. With this interpretation, better than with the other, agrees the blessing of Moses upon the same tribe: ' O Naphtali, satisfied with favour, and full with the blessing of the Lord, possess thou the west and the south' (Deut. xxxiii. 23).

When the Israelites quitted Egypt, the tribe of Naphtali numbered 53,400 adult males (Num. i. 43), which made it the sixth in population among the tribes; but at the census taken in the plains of Moab it counted only 45,400 (Num. xxvi. 50), being a decrease of 8000 in one generation, whereby it became the seventh in point of numbers. The limits of the territory assigned to this tribe are stated in Josh. xix. 32–39, which show that it possessed one of the finest and most fertile districts of Upper Galilee, extending from the Lake Gennesareth and the border of Zebulun, on the south, to the sources of the Jordan and the spurs of Lebanon on the north, and from the Jordan, on the east, to the borders of Asher on the west. But it was somewhat slow in acquiring possession of the assigned territory (Judg. i. 33). The chief towns of the tribe were Kedesh, Hazor, Harosheth, and Chinnereth, which last was also the name of the great lake afterwards called Gennesareth. In the Hebrew history Naphtali is distinguished for the alacrity with which it obeyed the call to arms against the oppressors of Israel when many other tribes held back (Judg. iv. 10; v. 18; vi. 35; vii. 23). In the time of David the tribe had on its rolls 37,000 men fit for military service, armed with shields and spears, under a thousand officers (1 Chron. xii. 34).

NARCIS'SUS, a person of Rome, apparently of some consequence, to the believers of whose household St. Paul sent his greetings (Rom. xvi. 11). Many commentators have supposed this person the same Narcissus who was the freedman and favourite of the Emperor Claudius.

NA'THAN (*given*), a prophet of the time of David When that monarch conceived the idea of building a temple to Jehovah, the design and motives seemed to Nathan so good that he ventured to approve of it without the Divine authority, but the night following he received the Divine command, which prevented the king from executing this great work (2 Sam. vii. 2, sq.; 1 Chron. xvii.). Nathan does not again appear in the sacred history till he comes forward in the name of the Lord to reprove David, and to denounce dire punishment for his frightful crime in the matter of Uriah and Bathsheba. This he does by exciting the king's indignation, and leading him to condemn himself, by reciting to him the very striking parable of the traveller and the lamb. Then, changing the voice of a suppliant for that of a judge and a commissioned prophet, he exclaims, ' *Thou* art the man !' and proceeds to announce the evils which were to embitter the remainder of his reign (2 Sam. xii. 1, sq.; comp. Ps. li.). The lamentations of the repentant king drew forth some mitigation of punishment; but the troubled history of the remainder of his reign shows how completely God's righteous doom was fulfilled. The child conceived in adultery died; but when Bathsheba's second son was born, the prophet gave him the name of Jedidiah (*beloved of Jehovah*), although he is better known by that of Solomon (2 Sam. xii. 24, 25). He recognised in this young prince the successor of David; and it was in a great measure through his interposition that the design of Adonijah to seize the crown was unsuccessful (1 Kings i. 8, sq.). Nathan probably died soon after the accession of Solomon, for his name does not again historically occur. It is generally supposed that Solomon was brought up under his care. His sons occupied high places in this king's court (1 Kings iv. 5). He assisted David by his counsels when he re-organized the public worship (2 Chron. xxix 25); and he composed annals of the times in which he lived (1 Chron. xxix. 29; 2 Chron. ix. 29); but these have not been preserved to us. In Zechariah (xii. 12) the name of Nathan occurs as representing the great family of the prophets.

NATHAN'AEL (*given of God*), a person of Cana in Galilee, who, when informed by Philip that the Messiah had appeared in the person of Jesus of Nazareth, asked, ' Can any good thing come out of Nazareth?' But he nevertheless accepted Philip's laconic invitation, ' Come and see !' When Jesus saw him coming he said, ' Behold an Israelite indeed, in whom is no guile.' Astonished to hear this from a man to whom he supposed himself altogether unknown, he asked, ' Whence knowest thou me?' And the answer, ' Before that Philip called thee, when thou wast under the fig-tree, I saw thee,' wrought such conviction on his mind that he at once exclaimed, ' Rabbi, thou art the son of God; thou art the king of Israel !' (John i. 45-51). It is clear, from the effect, that Nathanael knew by this that Jesus was supernaturally acquainted with his disposition and character, as the answer had reference to the private acts of devotion, or to the meditations which filled his mind, when under the fig-tree in his garden. It is questioned whether Jesus had actually seen Nathanael or not with his bodily eyes. It matters not to the result; but the form of the words employed seems to suggest that he had actually noticed him when under the fig-tree, and had then cast a look through his inward being. It is believed that Nathanael is the same as the apostle Bartholomew. All the disciples of John the Baptist named in the first chapter of St. John became apostles; and St. John does not name Bartholomew, nor the other evangelists Nathanael in the lists of the apostles (Matt. x. 3; Mark iii 18, Luke vi. 14): besides, the name of Bartholomew always follows that of Philip; and it would appear that Bartholomew (son of Tholmai) is no more than a surname [BARTHOLOMEW].

NATIONS, DISPERSION OF. Under this or some similar designation, it has been the prevalent opinion that the *outspreading*, which is the entire subject of Genesis, ch. x., and the *scattering* narrated in ch. xi. 1-9, refer to the same event, the latter being included in the former description, and being a statement of the *manner* in which the separation was effected. From this opinion, however, we dissent. An unbiassed reading of the text appears most plainly to mark the distinctness, in time and character, of the two narratives. The first was universal, regulated, orderly, quiet, and progressive: the second, local, embracing only a part of mankind, sudden, turbulent, and attended with marks of the Divine displeasure.

The former is introduced and entitled in these words:—'Shem, and Ham, and Japheth;—these are the three sons of Noah; and from them was the whole earth overspread.' After the mention of the sons of Japheth, it is added, 'From these the isles of the nations were dispersed, in their lands, each to its language, to their families, in their nations.' A formula somewhat differing is annexed to the descendants of Ham: 'These are the sons of Ham, [according] to their families, to their tongues, in their lands, in their nations.' The same phrase follows the enumeration of the house of Shem: and the whole concludes with, 'These are the families of the sons of Noah, [according] to their generations, in their nations; and from these the nations were dispersed in the earth after the Flood' (Gen. ix. 19; x. 5, 20, 31, 32).

The second relation begins in the manner which often, in the Hebrew Scriptures, introduces a new subject. We shall present it in a literality even servile, that the reader may gain the most prompt apprehension of the meaning. 'And it was all the earth (but with perfect propriety it might be rendered *the whole land, country, region,* or *district*): lip one and words one [*i. e. the same, similar*]. And it was in their going forwards that they discovered a plain in the country Shinar; and they fixed [their abode] there.' Then comes the narrative of their resolving to build a lofty tower which should serve as a signal-point for their rallying and remaining united. The defeating of this purpose is expressed in the anthropomorphism which is characteristic of the earliest Scriptures, and was adapted to the infantile condition of mankind. 'And Jehovah scattered them from thence upon the face of the whole earth [or *land*], and they ceased to build the city' (ch. xi. 2-9).

NAVIGATION. [SHIP.]

NAZARENE', an epithet constituting a part of one of the names given to our Lord. From the number of times that the epithet is employed, it appears that it became at the very first an appellation of our Lord, and was hence applied to designate his followers. Considering that the name was derived from the place where Jesus resided during the greater part of his life, we see no reason to think that at first it bore with it, in its application to him or his followers, anything of an offensive nature. Such a designation was in this case natural and proper. In process of time, however, other influences came into operation. Nazareth was in Galilee, a part of Palestine which was held in disesteem for several

reasons:—its was a provincial dialect; lying remote from the capital, its inhabitants spoke a strange tongue, which was rough, harsh, and uncouth, having peculiar combinations of words, and words also peculiar to themselves; its population was impure, being made up not only of provincial Jews, but also of heathens of several sorts, Egyptians, Arabians, Phœnicians; its people were in an especial manner given to be seditious, which quality of character they not rarely displayed in the capital itself on occasion of the public festivals; whence may be seen the point of the accusation made against Paul, as 'ringleader of the sect of Nazarenes' (Acts xxiv. 5). As Galilee was a despised part of Palestine, so was Nazareth a despised part of Galilee, being a small, obscure, if not mean place. Accordingly its inhabitants were held in little consideration by other Galileans, and, of course, by those Jews who dwelt in Judæa. Hence the name Nazarene came to bear with it a bad odour, and was nearly synonymous with a low, ignorant, and uncultured, if not non-Jewish person (Kuinoel, in Matt. ii. 23). It became accordingly a contemptuous designation and a term of reproach, and as such, as well as a mere epithet of description, it is used in the New Testament.

NAZ'ARITE. This word is derived from a Hebrew word, which signifies to 'separate one's-self;' and as such separation from ordinary life to religious purposes must be by abstinence of some kind, so it denotes 'to refrain from anything.' Hence the import of the term Nazarite—one, that is, who, by certain acts of self-denial, consecrated himself in a peculiar manner to the service, worship, and honour of God.

We are here, it is clear, in the midst of a sphere of ideas totally dissimilar to the genius of the Christian system; a sphere of ideas in which the outward predominates, in which self-mortification is held pleasing to God, and in which man's highest service is not enjoyment with gratitude, but privation with pain.

It may be questioned, if at least so much of this set of notions as supposes the Deity to be gratified and conciliated by the privations of his creatures, is in harmony with the ideas of God which the books of Moses exhibit, or had their origin in the law he promulgated. The manner in which he speaks on the subject (Num. vi. 1-21) would seem to imply that he was not introducing a new law, but regulating an old custom; for his words take for granted, that the subject was generally and well known, and that all that was needed was such directions as should bring existing observances into accordance with the Mosaic ritual.

The law of the Nazarite, which may be found in Num. vi. is, in effect, as follows:—male and female might assume the vow; on doing so a person was understood to separate himself unto the Lord; this separation consisted in abstinence from wine and all intoxicating liquors, and from everything made therefrom: 'From vinegar of wine, and vinegar of strong drink; neither shall he drink any liquor of grapes, nor eat moist grapes or dried;' he was to 'eat nothing of the vine-tree, from the kernels even to the husks.' Nor was a razor to come upon his head all the time of his vow; he was to 'be holy, and let the locks of the hair of his head grow.' With special care was he to avoid touching any dead body whatever. Being holy unto the Lord, he was not to make himself unclean by touching the corpse even of a relative. Should he happen to do so, he was then to shave his head and offer a sin-offering and a burnt-offering; thus making an atonement for himself, 'for that he sinned by the dead.' A lamb also, of the first year, was to be offered as a trespass-offering. On the termination of the period of the vow the Nazarite himself was brought unto the door of the tabernacle of the congregation, there to offer a burnt-offering, a sin-offering, a peace-offering, and a meat and a drink-offering. The Nazarite also shaved his head at the door of the tabernacle, and put the hair grown during the time of separation into the fire which was under the sacrifice of the peace-offerings. 'And the priest shall take the sodden shoulder of the ram and one unleavened cake out of the basket, and one unleavened wafer, and shall put them in the hands of the Nazarite after the hair of his separation is shaven; and the priest shall wave them for a wave-offering.' 'After that the Nazarite may drink wine.'

There are not wanting individual instances which serve to illustrate this vow, and to show that the law in the case went into operation. Hannah, Samson's mother, became a Nazarite that she might have a son. Samson himself was a Nazarite from the time of his birth (Judg. xiii.).

From the language employed by Samson, as well as from the tenor of the law in this case, the retention of the hair seems to have been one essential feature in the vow. It is, therefore, somewhat singular that any case should have been considered as the Nazaritic vow in which the shaving of the head is put forth as the chief particular. St. Paul is supposed to have been under *this* vow, when (Acts xviii. 18) he is said to have 'shorn his head in Cenchrea, for he had a vow' (see also Acts xxi. 24). The head was not shaven till the vow was performed, when a person had *not* a vow.

NAZ'ARETH, a town in Galilee, in which the

262. [Nazareth.]

parents of Jesus were resident, and where in consequence he lived till the commencement of his ministry. It derives all its historical importance from this circumstance, for it is not even named in the Old Testament or by Josephus: which suffices to show that it could not have been a place of any consideration, and was probably no more than a village.

Nazareth is situated about six miles W.N.W. from Mount Tabor, on the western side of a narrow oblong basin, or depressed valley, about a mile long by a quarter of a mile broad. The buildings stand on the lower part of the slope of the western hill, which rises steep and high above them. It is now a small, but more than usually well-built place, containing about three thousand inhabitants, of whom two-thirds are Christians.

The flat-roofed houses are built of stone, and are mostly two stories high. The environs are planted with luxuriantly-growing fig-trees, olive-trees, and vines, and the crops of corn are scarcely equalled throughout the length and breadth of Canaan. All the spots which could be supposed to be in any way connected with the history of Christ are, of course, pointed out by the monks and local guides, but on authority too precarious to deserve any credit, and with circumstances too puerile for reverence. It is enough to know that the Lord dwelt here; that for thirty years he trod this spot of earth, and that his eyes were familiar with the objects spread around. In the south-west part of the town is a small Maronite church, under a precipice of the hill, which here breaks off in a perpendicular wall forty or fifty feet in height. Dr. Robinson noticed several such precipices in the western hill around the village, and with very good reason concludes that one of these, probably the one just indicated, may well have been the spot whither the Jews led Jesus, 'unto the brow of the hill whereon the city was built, that they might cast him down headlong' (Luke iv. 28-30); and not the precipice, two miles from the village, overlooking the plain of Esdraelon, which monkish tradition indicates to the traveller as the 'Mount of Precipitation.'

NEAP'OLIS, a maritime city of Macedonia, near the borders of Thrace, now called Napoli. Paul landed here on his first journey into Europe (Acts xvi. 11).

NEBAI'OTH, or NEBAJOTH, the first-born son of Ishmael (Gen. xxv. 13; 1 Chron. i. 29), and the prince or *sheikh* of one of the twelve Ishmaelitish tribes, which, as well as the territory they occupied, continued to bear his name in after times (Gen. xxv. 16; comp. ch. xvii. 20). One of Esau's wives, Mahalath, otherwise called Bashemath, is expressly designated as 'the sister of Nebaioth' (Gen. xxviii. 9; xxxvi. 3); and by a singular coincidence the land of Esau, or Edom, was ultimately possessed by the posterity of Nebaioth. In common with the other Ishmaelites, they first settled in the wilderness 'before' (*i. e.* to the east of) their brethren, the other descendants of Abraham; by which we are probably to understand the great desert lying to the east and south-east of Palestine (Gen. xxv. 18; xxi. 21; xvi. 12; and see the article ARABIA). From various references in Scripture it is evident that the tribe of Nebaioth for ages followed the nomadic life of shepherds.

The successful invasion of Western Asia, first by the Assyrians and afterwards by the Chaldæans, could not but affect the condition of the tribes in Northern Arabia, though we possess no record of the special results. The prophet Isaiah, after his obscure oracle regarding Dumah (ch. xxi. 11, 12), introduces a 'judgment upon Arabia,' *i. e.* Desert Arabia, which some suppose to have been fulfilled by Sennacherib, while others think it refers to the later events that are foretold by Jeremiah (ch. xlix. 28-33) as befalling 'Kedar and the kingdoms of Hazor,' in consequence of the ravages of Nebuchadnezzar. Be this as it may, we know that when the latter carried the Jews captive to Babylon, the Edomites made themselves masters of a great part of the south of Palestine [IDUMÆA], while either then or at a later period they themselves were supplanted in the southern part of their own territory by the Nabathæans, though doubtless this general designation included a variety of Arab races who took their common name from the progenitor of the largest or most influential tribe, Nebaioth, the first-born of Ishmael.

The territory occupied by the Nabathæans in its widest sense included the whole of Northern Arabia from the Euphrates to the Elanitic Gulf of the Red Sea; but more strictly taken it denoted (at least in later times) only a portion of the southern part of that vast region. We first hear of the Nabathæans in history in the reign of Antigonus, who succeeded Alexander the Great in Babylon, and died in the year B.C. 301. He sent two expeditions against them; but both were unsuccessful. The Nabathæans were as yet essentially a pastoral people, though they were likewise engaged in commerce, which they afterwards prosecuted to a great extent, and thereby acquired great riches and renown. It was in this way that they gradually became more fixed in their habits; and living in towns and villages they were at length united under a regular monarchical government, constituting the kingdom of Arabia, or more strictly Arabia Petræa, the name being derived not, as some suppose, from the rocky nature of the country, but from the chief city Petra.

The common name of the kings of Arabia Petræa was either Aretas or Obodas. Even in the time of Antiochus Epiphanes (about B.C. 166), we read in 2 Macc. v. 8, of an Aretas, king of the Arabians; and from that period downwards they came frequently into contact both with the Jews and Romans, as may be seen in the books of the Maccabees and the writings of Josephus. Long before the kingdom of Arabia was actually conquered by the Romans, its sovereigns were dependent on the Roman power. An expedition was sent thither by Augustus, under Ælius Gallus, governor of Egypt, and a personal friend of the geographer Strabo, who has left us an account of it. After various obstacles, he at last reached Albus Pagus, the emporium of the Nabathæans, and the port of Petra, which was probably at or near Elath. Another friend of Strabo, the Stoic philosopher Athenodorus, had spent some time in Petra, and related to him with admiration how the inhabitants lived in entire harmony and union under excellent laws. The kingdom was hereditary; or at least the king was always one of the royal family, and had a prime minister or vizier, who was styled *the king's brother*. Another Arabian king of the name of Aretas is the one mentioned by St. Paul (2 Cor. ii. 32; comp. Acts vii. 24, 25; Joseph. *Antiq.* xviii. 5. 1). We find that a former Aretas had been invited to assume the sovereignty by the inhabitants of Damascus: and now, during the weak reign of Caligula, the same city is seized by another Aretas, and governed through an *ethnarch*, as related by Paul. The kingdom of Arabia Petræa maintained its nominal independence till about A.D. 105, in the reign of the Emperor Trajan, when it was subdued by Cornelius Palma, governor of Syria, and annexed to the vast empire of Rome.

The Nabathæans had, as we have seen, early applied themselves to commerce, especially as carriers of the products of Arabia, India, and the far-distant East, which, as we learn from Strabo, were transported on camels from the above-mentioned Leuke Komé to Petra, and thence to Rhinocoloura (el-Arish) and elsewhere. 'But under the Roman dominion the trade of these regions appears to have widely extended itself, and to have flourished in still greater prosperity; probably from the circumstance that the lawless rapacity of the adjacent nomadic hordes was now kept in check by the Roman power, and particularly by the garrisons which were everywhere established for this specific purpose. The country, too, was now rendered more accessible, and the passage of merchants and caravans more practicable, by military ways. But as the power of Rome fell into decay, the Arabs of the desert would seem again to have acquired the ascendancy. They plundered the cities, but did not destroy them; and hence those regions are still full of uninhabited, yet stately and often splendid ruins, of ancient wealth, and taste, and greatness. Even Petra, the rich and impregnable metropolis, was subjected to the same fate; and now exists, in its almost inaccessible loneliness, only to excite the curiosity of the scholar, and the wonder of the traveller, by the singularity of its site, its ruins, and its fortunes.'

In the course of the fourth century this region came to be included under the general name of 'Palestine.' It became the diocese of a metropolitan, whose seat was at Petra, and who was afterwards placed under the patriarch of Jerusalem. With the Mohammedan conquest in the seventh century its commercial prosperity disappeared. Lying between the three rival empires of Arabia, Egypt, and Syria, it lost its ancient independence; the course of trade was diverted into new channels; its great routes were abandoned; and at length the entire country was quietly yielded up to the Bedawees of the surrounding wilderness, whose descendants still claim it as their domain. During the twelfth century it was partially occupied by the Crusaders, who gave it the name of *Arabia Tertia*, or *Syria Sobal*. From that period it remained unvisited by Europeans, and had almost disappeared from their maps, until it was partially explored, first by Seetzen in 1807, and more fully by Burckhardt in 1812; and now the wonders of the Wady Mûsa are familiarly known to all.

1. NE'BO, a Chaldæan idol mentioned in Isa. xlvi. 1, and supposed to have been the symbol of the planet Mercury, the celestial scribe and interpreter of the gods, answering to the Hermes and Anubis of the Egyptians. He was likewise worshipped by the Sabians in Arabia. The divine worship paid to this idol by the Chaldæans and Assyrians is attested by many compound proper names of which it forms part, as *Nebu*chadnezzar, *Nebuzaradan, Nebuhashban*; besides others mentioned in classical writers,— *Nabonedus, Nabonassar, Naburianus, Nabonabus, Nabopolassar*.

2. NEBO, the name of a mountain on the confines of Moab (Deut. xxxii. 49; xxxiv. 1), and of a town near it (Num. xxxii. 3, 38; Isa. xv. 2). Since the time of Seetzen and Burckhardt, Mount Nebo has been usually identified with Mount Attarus, east of the Dead Sea.

3. NEBO, a town in the tribe of Judah (Ezra ii. 29); or more fully, in order to distinguish it from the preceding, 'the other Nebo' (Neh. vii. 33).

NEBUCHADNEZ'ZAR (Kings, Chronicles, and Daniel; Jer. xxvii.; xxviii; xxxiv. 1; xxxix 1; Ezek. xxvi. 7; and Ezra v. 12; written also Nebuchadnezzar, generally in Jeremiah, and in Ezek. xxx. 18) was the name of the Chaldæan monarch of Babylon by whom Judah was conquered, and the Jews led into their seventy years' captivity. The name of this monarch has been commonly explained to signify *the treasure of Nebo*, but according to some it signifies *Nebo the prince of gods*.

The only notices which we have of this monarch in the canonical writings are found in the books of Kings, Chronicles, Daniel, and Ezra, and in the allusions of the prophets Jeremiah and Ezekiel.

From 2 Kings xxiii. 29, and 2 Chron. **xxxv.** 20, we gather that in the reign of Josiah (B.C. 610), Pharaoh-Necho, king of Egypt, having approached by sea the coast of Syria, made a friendly application to King Josiah to be allowed a passage through his territories to the dominions of the Assyrian monarch, with whom he was then at war (2 Chron xxxv. 20, 21). The design of Pharaoh-Necho was to seize upon Carchemish (Circesium or Cercus'um), a strong post on the Euphrates; but Josiah, who was tributary to the Babylonian monarch, opposed his progress at Megiddo, where he was defeated and mortally wounded [JOSIAH]. Necho marched upon Jerusalem, when the Jews became tributary to the king of Egypt. Upon this, Nebuchadnezzar, king of Babylon (2 Kings xxiv. 1; 2 Chron. xxxvi. 6, where this monarch's name is for the first time introduced), invaded Judah, retook Carchemish, with the territory which had been wrested from him by Necho, seized upon Jehoiakim, the vassal of Pharaoh-Necho, and reduced him to submission (B.C. 607). Jehoiachim was at first loaded with chains, in order to be led captive to Babylon, but was eventually restored by Nebuchadnezzar to his throne, on condition of paying an annual tribute. Nebuchadnezzar carried off part of the ornaments of the Temple, together with several hostages of distinguished rank, among whom were the youths Daniel and his three friends Hananiah, Azariah, and Mishael (Dan. i.). These were educated at court in the language and sciences of the Chaldæans, where they subsequently filled offices of distinction. The sacred vessels were transferred by Nebuchadnezzar to his temple at Babylon (Isa. **xxxix.**; 2 Chron. xxxvi. 6, 7) [BABYLON].

After the conquest of Judæa, Nebuchadnezzar turned his attention towards the Egyptians, whom he drove out of Syria, taking possession of all the land between the Euphrates and the *river* (2 Kings xxiv. 7): which some suppose to mean the Nile, but others a small river in the desert, which was reckoned the boundary between Palestine and Egypt.

The fate of Jerusalem was now rapidly approaching its consummation. After three years of fidelity, Jehoiachim renounced his allegiance to Babylon, and renewed his alliance with Necho, when Nebuchadnezzar sent incursions of Ammonites, Moabites, and Syrians, together with Chaldæans, to harass him. At length, in the eleventh year of his reign, he was made prisoner, and slain (Jer xxii.) [JEHOAKIM]. He was succeeded by his son Jehoiachin, who, after three months' reign, surrendered himself with his family to Nebuchadnezzar, who had come in person to besiege Jerusalem, in the eighth year of his reign (2 Kings xxiv. 10–12) [JEHOIACHIN]. Upon this occasion all the most distinguished inhabitants, including the artificers, were led captive [CAPTIVITIES]. Among the captives, who amounted to no less than 50,000, were Ezekiel (Ezek i. 1) and Mordecai [ESTHER]. The golden vessels of Solomon were now removed, with the royal treasures, and Mattaniah, the brother of Jehoiachin, placed on the throne by Nebuchadnezzar, who gave him the name of Zedekiah, and bound him by an oath not to enter into an alliance with Egypt. Zedekiah, however, in the ninth year of his reign, formed an alliance with Pharaoh-Hophra, the successor of Necho. Hophra, coming to the assistance of Zedekiah, was driven back into Egypt by Nebuchadnezzar, who finally captured Jerusalem in the eleventh year of Zedekiah's reign (B.C. 588) [ZEDEKIAH]. The Temple, and the whole city, with its towers and walls, were all razed to the ground by Nebuzaradan, Nebuchadnezzar's lieutenant, and the principal remaining inhabitants put to death by Nebuchadnezzar at Riblah. Jeremiah was, however, spared, and Gedaliah appointed governor. He was shortly after murdered by Ishmael, a member of the royal family, who was himself soon obliged to take refuge among the Ammonites. Many of the remaining Jews fled into Egypt, accompanied by Jeremiah; those who remained were soon after expatriated by Nebuchadnezzar, who depopulated the whole country.

He next undertook the siege of Tyre, and after its destruction proceeded to Egypt, now distracted by internal commotions, and devastated or made himself master of the whole country from Migdol to Syene (according to the reading of the Seventy, Ezek. xxix. 10; xxx. 6), transferring many of the inhabitants to the territory beyond the Euphrates.

We have referred to the captivity of the prophet Daniel, and have to turn to the book which bears his name for the history of this prophet, who, from an exile, was destined to become the great protector of his nation. In the second year of the reign of Nebuchadnezzar, Daniel, who was found superior in wisdom to the Chaldæan magi, was enabled not only to interpret, but to reveal a dream of Nebuchadnezzar's, the very subject of which that monarch had forgotten [DREAMS]. This was the dream of the statue consisting of four different metals, which Daniel interpreted of four successive monarchies, the last of which was to be the reign of the Messiah. Daniel was elevated to be first minister of state, and his three friends were made governors of provinces. The history of these events (Dan. ii. 4, 8, 9) is written in the Chaldee language, together with the narrative which immediately follows (ch. iii.), of the golden statue erected by Nebuchadnezzar in the plain of Dura, for refusing to worship which, Daniel's three friends were thrown into a furnace, but miraculously preserved. The fourth chapter, also written in Chaldee, contains the singular history of the judgment inflicted on Nebuchadnezzar as a punishment for his pride, and which is narrated in the form of a royal proclamation from the monarch himself, giving an account to his people of his affliction and recovery. This affliction had been, by the monarch's account, predicted by Daniel a year before, in the interpretation of his fearful dream of the tree in the midst of the earth. While walking in his palace, and admiring his magnificent works, he uttered, in the plenitude of his pride, the remarkable words recorded in ver. 30, 'Is not this great Babylon that I have built for the house of the kingdom, by the might of my power, and for the honour of my majesty?' He had scarce uttered the words, when a voice from heaven proclaimed to him that his kingdom was departed from him; that he should be for seven *times* (generally supposed to mean years, although some reduce the period to fourteen months) driven from the habitations of men to dwell among the beasts of the field, and made to eat grass as an ox, until he learned 'that the Most High ruleth in the kingdom of men, and giveth it to whomsoever he will.' The sentence was immediately fulfilled, and Nebuchadnezzar continued in this melancholy state during the predicted period, at the end of which he was restored to the use of his understanding (ver. 36). We have no account in Scripture of any of the actions of this monarch's life after the period of his recovery, but the first year of the reign of his successor Evil-merodach is represented as having taken place in the thirty-seventh year of Jehoiachin, answering to B.C. 562 (2 Kings xxv. 27).

The difficulties attending the nature of the disease and recovery of Nebuchadnezzar have not escaped the notice of commentators in ancient as well as modern times. Origen supposed that the account of Nebuchadnezzar's metamorphosis was merely a representation of the fall of Lucifer. Bodin maintains that Nebuchadnezzar underwent an actual metamorphosis of soul and body, a similar instance of which is given by Cluvier on the testimony of an eye-witness. Tertullian confines the transformation to the body only, but without loss of reason, of which kind of metamorphosis St. Augustine reports some instances said to have taken place in Italy, to which he himself attaches little credit; but Gaspard Peucer asserts that the transformation of men into wolves was very common in Livonia. Some Jewish Rabbins have asserted that the soul of Nebuchadnezzar, by a real transmigration, changed places with that of an ox; while others have supposed not a real, but an apparent or docetic change, of which there is a case recorded in the life of St. Macarius, the parents of a young woman having been persuaded that their daughter had been transformed into a mare. The most generally received opinion, however, is, that Nebuchadnezzar laboured under that species of hypochondriacal monomania which leads the patient to fancy himself changed into an animal or other substance, the habits of which he adopts. To this disease of the imagination physicians have given the name of Lycanthropy, Zoanthropy, or Insania Canina [DISEASES OF THE JEWS].

NEBUSHAS'BAN (Jer. xxxix. 13), a follower of Nebu; the name of one of the Babylonian officers sent by Nebuzar-adan to take Jeremiah out of prison.

NEBUZAR'-ADAN (1 Kings xxv. 8; Jer. xxxix. 9; xl. 1; lii. 12, &c.). '*Nebu is the Lord*,' according to the Hebrew; or, according to the Persian, ' Nebu is wise.' The name of the captain of Nebuchadnezzar's guard, by whom the ruin of Jerusalem was completed.

NE'CHO, an Egyptian king, son and successor (according to Herodotus, ii. 158) of Psammetichus, and contemporary of the Jewish king Josias (B.C. 610). The wars and success of Necho, in Syria, are recorded by sacred as well as profane writers. Studious of military renown, and the furtherance of commerce, Necho, on ascending the throne of Egypt, applied himself to reorganize the army, and to equip a powerful fleet. In order to promote his purposes, he courted the Greeks, to whose troops he gave a post next to his Egyptians. He fitted out a fleet in the Mediterranean, and another in the Red Sea. Having engaged some expert Phœnician sailors, he sent them on a voyage of discovery along the coast of

Africa. To him belongs the honour of being the first to equip an expedition for the purpose of circumnavigating Africa, and he thereby ascertained the peninsular form of that continent, twenty-one centuries before the Cape of Good Hope was seen by Diaz, or doubled by Vasco de Gama.

Before entering on this voyage of discovery, Necho had commenced re-opening the canal from the Nile to the Red Sea, which had been cut many years before by Sesostris or Rameses the Great. The work, however, if we may believe Herodotus, was abandoned, an oracle warning the Egyptian monarch that he was labouring for the barbarian (Herod. ii. 158).

Necho also turned his attention to the Egyptian conquests already made in Asia: and, fearing lest the growing power of the Babylonians should endanger the territories acquired by the arms of his victorious predecessors, he determined to check their progress, and to attack the enemy on his own frontier. With this view he collected a powerful army, and entering Palestine, followed the route along the sea-coast of Judæa, intending to besiege the town of Carchemish on the Euphrates. But Josiah, king of Judah, offended at the passage of the Egyptian army through his territories, resolved to impede, if unable to prevent, their march. Necho sent messengers to induce him to desist, assuring him that he had no hostile intentions against Judæa, 'but against the house wherewith I have war; for God commanded me to make haste.' This conciliatory message was of no avail. Josiah posted himself in the valley of Megiddo, and prepared to oppose the Egyptians. In this valley the feeble forces of the Jewish king, having attacked Necho, were routed with great slaughter. Josiah, being wounded in the neck with an arrow, ordered his attendants to take him from the field. Escaping from the heavy shower of arrows with which their broken ranks were overwhelmed, they removed him from the chariot in which he had been wounded, and placing him in a 'second one that he had,' they conveyed him to Jerusalem, where he died (2 Kings xxiii. 29, sq.; 2 Chron. xxxv. 20, sq).

Intent upon his original project, Necho did not stop to revenge himself upon the Jews, but continued his march to the Euphrates. Three months had scarcely elapsed, when, returning from the capture of Carchemish and the defeat of the Chaldæans, he learned that, though Josiah had left an elder son, Jehoahaz had caused himself to be proclaimed king on the death of his father, without soliciting Necho to sanction his taking the crown. Incensed at this, he ordered Jehoahaz to meet him 'at Riblah, in the land of Hamath;' and having deposed him, and condemned the land to pay a heavy tribute, he carried him a prisoner to Jerusalem. On arriving there, Necho made Eliakim, the eldest son, king, changing his name to Jehoiakim; and taking the silver and gold which had been levied upon the Jewish nation, he returned to Egypt with the captive Jehoahaz, who there terminated his short and unfortunate career. Herodotus says that Necho, after having routed the Syrians (the Jews) at Magdolus, took Cadytis, a large city of Syria, in Palestine, which, he adds, is very little less than Sardis (ii. 159; iii. 5). By Cadytis there is scarcely a doubt

he meant Jerusalem; the word is only a Greek form of the ancient, as well as the modern, name of that city.

Pleased with his success, the Egyptian monarch dedicated the dress he wore to the Deity who was supposed to have given him the victory. He did not long enjoy the advantages he had obtained. In the fourth year after his expedition, being alarmed at the increasing power of the Babylonians, he again marched into Syria, and advanced to the Euphrates. The Babylonians were prepared for his approach. Nebuchadnezzar completely routed his army, recovered the town of Carchemish, and, pushing his conquests through Palestine, took from Necho all the territory belonging to the Pharaohs, from the Euphrates to the southern extremity of Syria (2 Kings xxiv. 7; Jer. xlvi. 2; 2 Chron. xxxvi. 9; 2 Kings xxiv. 8). Nebuchadnezzar deposed Jehoiachin, who had succeeded his father, and carried the warriors and treasures away to Babylon; a short time previous to which Necho died, and was succeeded by Psammetichus II.

NEG'INIOTH, a word which occurs in the titles of several Psalms [PSALMS].

NEHEMI'AH (*comforted of Jehovah*). Three persons of this name occur in Scripture; one, the son of Azbuk (Neh. iii. 16), respecting whom no more is known than that he was ruler in Beth-zur, and took a prominent part in repairing the wall of Jerusalem [BETH-ZUR]. Another is mentioned (Ezra ii. 2; Neh. vii. 7) among those who accompanied Zerubbabel on the first return from captivity. Nothing further is known of this man, though some writers hold him, without valid reasons, to be the same with the well-known Jewish patriot.

NEHEMIAH, whose genealogy is unknown, except that he was the son of Hachaliah (Neh. i. 1), and brother of Hanani (Neh. vii. 2). Some think he was of priestly descent, because his name appears at the head of a list of priests in Neh. x. 1-8; but it is obvious, from Neh. ix. 38, that he stands there as a prince, and not as a priest—that he heads the list because he was head of the nation. Others with some probability infer, from his station at the Persian court and the high commission he received, that he was, like Zerubbabel, of the tribe of Judah and of the house of David.

While Nehemiah was cupbearer in the royal palace at Shushan, in the twentieth year of Artaxerxes Longimanus, or 444 years B C. [ARTAXERXES], he learned the mournful and desolate condition of the returned colony in Judæa. This filled him with such deep and prayerful concern for his country, that his sad countenance revealed to the king his 'sorrow of heart;' which induced the monarch to ascertain the cause, and also to vouchsafe the remedy, by sending him, with full powers, to rebuild the wall of Jerusalem, and 'to seek the welfare of the children of Israel.' Being furnished with this high commission, and enjoying the protection of a military escort (ch. ii. 9), Nehemiah reached Jerusalem in the year B C. 444, and remained there till B.C. 432, being actively engaged for twelve years in promoting the public good (ch. v. 14). The principal work which he then accomplished was the rebuilding, or rather the repairing, of the city wall, which was done 'in fifty and two days' (ch. vi. 15), notwithstanding many discouragements and difficulties, caused chiefly by Sanballat, a Moabite of Horonaim, and Tobiah, an Ammonite, who were leading men in the rival and unfriendly colony of Samaria (ch. iv. 1-3). These men, with their allies among the Arabians, Ammonites, and Ashdodites (ch. iv. 7), sought to hinder the re-fortifying of Jerusalem, first by scoffing at the attempt; then by threatening to attack the workmen—which Nehemiah averted by 'setting a watch against them day and night,' and arming the whole people, so that 'every one with one of his hands wrought in the work, and with the other hand held a weapon' (ch. iv. 7-18); and finally, when scoffs and threats had failed, by using various stratagems to weaken Nehemiah's authority, and even to take his life (ch. vi. 1-14). But in the midst of these dangers from without, our patriot encountered troubles and hinderances from his own people, arising out of the general distress, which was aggravated by the cruel exactions and oppression of their nobles and rulers (ch. v. 1-5). These popular grievances were promptly redressed on the earnest and solemn remonstrance of Nehemiah, who had himself set a striking example of retrenchment and generosity in his high office (ch. v. 6-19). It appears also (ch. vi. 17-19) that some of the chief men in Jerusalem were at that time in conspiracy with Tobiah against Nehemiah. The wall was thus built in 'troublous times' (Dan. ix. 25); and its completion was most joyously celebrated by a solemn dedication (ch. xii. 27-43).

Having succeeded in fortifying the city, Nehemiah turned his attention to other measures in order to secure its good government and prosperity. He appointed some necessary officers (ch. vii. 1-3; also ch. xii. 44-47), and excited among the people more interest and zeal in religion by the public reading and exposition of the law (ch. viii. 1-12), by the unequalled celebration of the Feast of Tabernacles (ch. viii. 13-18), and by the observance of a national fast, when the sins of the people and the iniquities of their fathers were publicly and most strikingly confessed (ch. ix.), and when also a solemn covenant was made by all ranks and classes 'to walk in God's law,' by avoiding intermarriages with the heathen, by strictly observing the Sabbath, and by contributing to the support of the temple service (ch. x). But the inhabitants of the city were as yet too few to defend it and to ensure its prosperity; and hence Nehemiah brought one out of every ten in the country to take up his abode in the ancient capital, which then presented so few inducements to the settler, that 'the people blessed all the men that willingly offered themselves to dwell at Jerusalem' (ch. vii. 4; also ch. xi. 1-19).

In these important public proceedings, which appear all to have happened in the first year of his government, Nehemiah enjoyed the assistance of Ezra, who is named on several occasions as taking a prominent part in conducting affairs (ch. viii. 1, 9, 13; xii. 36). Ezra had gone up to Jerusalem thirteen years before according to some, or thirty-three years according to others; but on either reckoning, without supposing unusual longevity, he might well have lived to be Nehemiah's fellow-labourer [EZRA].

Nehemiah, at the close of his successful administration, 'from the twentieth year even to the thirty-second year of Artaxerxes the king' (ch. v.

14), returned to Babylon in the year B.C. 432, and resumed, as some think, his duties as royal cupbearer.

He returned, however, after a while, to Jerusalem, where his services became again requisite, in consequence of abuses that had crept in during his absence. His stay at the court of Artaxerxes was not very long (certainly not above nine years); 'for after certain days he obtained leave of the king and came to Jerusalem' (ch. xiii. 6, 7).

After his return to the government of Judæa, Nehemiah enforced the separation of all the mixed multitude from Israel (ch. xiii. 1-3); and accordingly expelled Tobiah the Ammonite from the chamber which the high-priest, Eliashib, had prepared for him in the temple (ch. xiii. 4-9). Better arrangements were also made for the support of the temple service (ch. xiii. 10-14), and for the rigid observance of the Sabbath (ch. xiii. 15-22). One of the last acts of his government was an effort to put an end to mixed marriages, which led him to 'chase' away a son of Joiada the high-priest, because he was son-in-law to Sanballat the Horonite (ch. xiii. 23-29). His second administration probably lasted about ten years, and terminated about the year B.C. 405, towards the close of the reign of Darius Nothus, who is mentioned in ch. xii. 22 [DARIUS]. At this time Nehemiah would be between sixty and seventy years old, if we suppose him (as most do) to have been only between twenty and thirty when he first went to Jerusalem. Of the place and year of his death nothing is known.

THE BOOK OF NEHEMIAH, which bears the title *Nehemiah's Words*, was anciently connected with Ezra, as if it formed part of the same work. It arose, doubtless, from the fact that Nehemiah is a sort of continuation of Ezra [EZRA].

The canonical character of Nehemiah's work is established by very ancient testimony.

The contents of the book have been specified above in the biography of the author. The work can scarcely be called a history of Nehemiah and his times. It is rather a collection of notices of some important transactions that happened during the first year of his government, with a few scraps from his later history. The contents appear to be arranged in chronological order, with the exception perhaps of ch. xii. 27-43, where the account of the dedication of the wall seems out of its proper place : we might expect it rather after ch. vii. 1-4, where the completion of the wall is mentioned.

As to the date of the book, it is not likely that it came from Nehemiah's hand till near the close of his life. Certainly it could not have been all written before the expulsion of the priest, recorded in ch. xiii. 23-29, which took place about the year B.C. 413.

While the book as a whole is considered to have come from Nehemiah, it consists in part of compilation. He doubtless wrote the greater part himself, but some portions he evidently took from other works. It is allowed by all that he is, in the strictest sense, the author of the narrative from ch. i. to ch. vii. 5. The account in ch vii. 6-73 is avowedly compiled, for he says in ver. 5, 'I found a register,' &c. This register we actually find also in Ezra ii. 1-70: hence it might be thought that our author borrowed this part from Ezra;

but it is more likely that they both copied from public documents, such as ' the book of the chronicles,' mentioned in Neh. xii. 23.

Chapters viii.–x. were probably not written by Nehemiah, since the narrative respecting him is in the third person (ch. viii. 9; x. 1), and not in the first, as usual (ch. ii. 9–20). Hávernick, indeed, makes it appear, from the contents and style, that Ezra was the writer of this portion. The remaining chapters (xi.–xiii.) also exhibit some marks of compilation (ch. xii. 26, 47); but there are, on the contrary, clear proofs of Nehemiah's own authorship in ch. xii. 27–43, and in ch. xiii. 6–31; and hence Hávernick thinks he wrote the whole except ch. xii. 1–26, which he took from ' the book of the chronicles,' mentioned in ver. 23.

NEHILOTH, a word which occurs in the title of the fifth Psalm [PSALMS].

NEHUSH'TA (*brass*), the mother of king Jehoiachin (2 Kings xxiv. 8).

NER (*a light*), grandfather of king Saul (1 Sam. xiv. 50, 51; xxvi. 5; 1 Chron. viii. 33).

NERD or NARD is mentioned in three places in the Song of Solomon, and by Mark and John in the New Testament. It is translated in the Authorized Version by the word *spikenard*, which indicates a far-famed perfume of the East, that has often engaged the attention of critics, but the plant which yields it has only been ascertained in very recent times. That the *nerd* of Scripture was a perfume is evident from the fact that, in

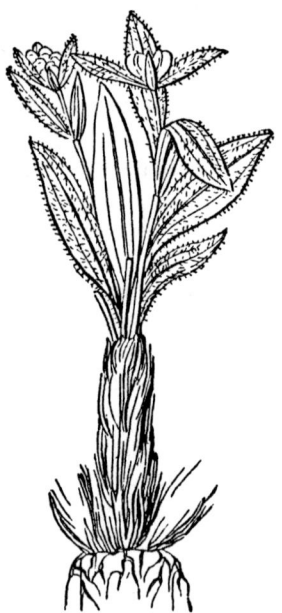

263. [Nardostachys Jatamansi.]

Cant. i. 12; iv. 14, it is mentioned along with many of the most valued aromatics which were known to the ancients. That the nard or nardus was of great value we learn from the New Testament (Mark xiv. 3; John xii. 3).

NER'GAL. Recent inquiries into the astro-

latry of the Assyrians and Chaldæans have led to the conclusion that Nergal is one of the names for the planet Mars. This name of the planet, both among the Zabians and Arabians, means *ill-luck, misfortune;* and it was by no means peculiar to the mythology of the West to make it the symbol of bloodshed and war. Among the people first named, the planet Mars was typified under the figure of a man holding in one hand a drawn sword, and in the other a human head just cut off; and his garments were also red, which, as well as the other ideas attached to this idol, were no doubt founded on the reddish hue which the body of the planet presents to the eye. Among the southern Arabs his temple was painted red; and they offered to him garments stained with blood, and also a warrior (probably a prisoner), who was cast into a pool.

NER'GAL - SHARE'ZER (*Nergal, prince of fire*). 1. A military chieftain under Nebuchadnezzar (Jer. xxxix. 3). 2. The chief of the magi (Rab-mag) under the same king, and present in the same expedition (Jer. xxxix. 3, 13).

NET. There are in Scripture several words denoting different kinds of nets, and this, with the frequency of images derived from them, shows that nets were much in use among the Hebrews for fishing, hunting, and fowling. Indeed, for the two latter purposes, nets were formerly used to an extent of which now, since the invention of fire-arms, a notion can scarcely be formed.

We have no positive information concerning the nets of the Hebrews, and can only suppose that they were not materially different from those of the ancient Egyptians, concerning which we now possess very good information. Indeed, the nets of Egypt, the fishers who used them, and the fish caught by them, are more than once mentioned in Scripture (Isa. xix. 8). The usual fishing net among this people was of a long form, like the common drag-net, with wooden floats on the upper, and leads on the lower side. It was sometimes let down from a boat, but those who pulled it usually stood on the shore, and landed the fish on a shelving bank. This mode, how-

264.

ever, was more adapted to river than to lake fishing; and hence, in all the detailed examples of fishing in the New Testament, the net is cast from and drawn into boats, excepting in one case where, the draft being too great to take into the boat, the fishers dragged the net after their boats to the shore (John xxi. 6, 8). Sometimes use was made of a smaller net for catching fish in shallow water, furnished with a pole on either side, to which it was attached; and the fisherman, holding one of the poles in either hand, thrust it below the surface of the water, and awaited the moment when a shoal of fish passed over it.

It is interesting to observe that the fishermen in the boat, excepting the master (No. 264), are

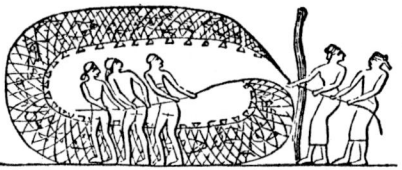

265.

almost naked, as are also those who have occasion to wade in the water in hauling the net to the shore (No. 265). Such seems also to have been the practice among the Hebrew fishermen; for Peter, when he left the boat to hasten on shore to his risen Lord, 'girt his fisher's coat unto him, for he was naked' (John xxi. 7); although, in this case, the word 'naked' must be understood with some latitude [NAKED].

Nets were also used in taking birds, to an extent of which we can scarcely form an adequate conception. A clap-net was usually employed. This was of different kinds. It consisted of two sides or frames, over which the net-work was spread: at one end was a short net, which they fastened to a bush, or a cluster of reeds, and at the other was one of considerable length, which, as soon as the birds were seen feeding in the area within, was pulled by the fowlers, causing the instantaneous collapse of the two sides (No. 266).

266.

In hunting, a space of considerable size was sometimes enclosed with nets, into which the animals were driven by beaters. The spots thus enclosed were usually in the vicinity of the water-brooks to which they were in the habit of repairing in the morning and evening; and having awaited the time when they went to drink, the hunters disposed their nets, occupied proper positions for observing them unseen, and gradually closed in upon them. These practices are obviously alluded to in such passages as Job xix. 6; Ps. cxl. 5; Isa. li. 20.

NETH'INIM. This name, which means 'the given' or 'the devoted,' was applied to the servants of the temple, or temple slaves, who were under the Levites in the ministry of the tabernacle and temple. The first servants whom the Levites obtained were the Gibeonites, on whom devolved the very laborious services of fetching water and collecting wood (Josh. ix. 3-27). The number of such servants appears to have been increased by David; and it seems to have been then, when these servants ceased to be wholly Gibeonites, that Nethinim came into use as a proper name for the whole class (Ezra viii. 20). From that time forward, they appear

to have been no longer regarded or treated as slaves, but as the lowest order of the servants of the sanctuary; who, although in their origin foreigners and heathen, had doubtless embraced the Jewish religion. These did not all forget their relationship to the sanctuary during the Captivity. Some of them returned to their duties under the decree of Cyrus, and were placed in cities with the Levites (Neh. xi. 3, Ezra ii. 70; 1 Chron. ix. 27). It was not to be expected that many of them would return to this humble station in Palestine, but 220 accompanied Ezra (Ezra viii. 20), and 392 Zerubbabel (ii. 5-8). The voluntary devotedness which was thus manifested by these persons considerably raised the station of the Nethinim, which was thenceforth regarded rather as honourable than degrading. Their number was, however, insufficient for the service of the temple: whence, as Josephus tells us, a festival, called Xylophoria, was established, in which the people, to supply the deficiency, were obliged to bring a certain quantity of wood to the temple for the use of the altar of burnt-offering.

NETO'PHAH, a place not far from Bethlehem in Judæa (Ezra ii. 22; Neh. vii. 26). Hence the Gentile name Netophite (2 Sam. xxiii. 28, 29; 2 Kings xxv. 23).

NETTLES. The word (charul) which is so rendered, occurs in three places in Scripture. Thus in Prov. xxiv. 30, 31, it is written, 'I went by the field of the slothful, &c., and, lo, it was all grown over with thorns, and nettles (charullim) had covered the face thereof.' So in Job xxx. 7 it is stated that he was insulted by the children of those whom he would formerly have disdained to employ, and who were so abject and destitute that 'among the bushes they brayed; under the nettles they were gathered together;' and in Zeph. ii. 9, 'Surely Moab shall be as Sodom, and the children of Ammon as Gomorrah, even the breeding of nettles, and salt-pits, and a perpetual desolation.' Considerable difficulty has been experienced in determining the plant which is alluded to in the above passages. The majority of translators and commentators have thought that some thorny or prickly plant, or a nettle, is intended. Hence brambles, the wild plum, and thistles, have been severally selected; but nettles have had the greatest number of supporters.

NETTLE. [THORN.]
NEW MOON. [FESTIVALS; MOON.]
NEW YEAR. [YEAR.]
NIB'HAZ, an idol of the Avites (2 Kings xvii. 31). In the Zabian books the corresponding name is that of an evil demon, who sits on a throne upon the earth, while his feet rest on the bottom of Tartarus; but it is doubtful whether this should be identified with the Avite Nibhaz.

NICODE'MUS, a Pharisee and member of the Sanhedrim, who was impressed by what he had heard concerning Jesus; but being unwilling, on account of his station, to commit himself without greater surety than he possessed, repaired by night to the house in which Christ dwelt, and held with him that important discourse which occupies the third chapter of John's Gospel. The effect which was then produced upon his mind may be collected from the fact that subsequently, at one of the sittings of the venerable body to which he belonged, he ventured to let fall a few words in favour of Jesus, whose proceedings were then in question (John vii. 50); and that he took part with his colleague, Joseph of Arimathea, in rendering the last honours to the body of the crucified Redeemer (John xix. 39). Nothing further is known of Nicodemus from Scripture. Tradition, however, adds that after he had thus openly declared himself a follower of Jesus, and had been baptized by Peter, he was displaced from his office, and expelled from Jerusalem (Phot. *Cod.* p. 171). It is added that he found refuge in a country house of his cousin Gamaliel, and remained there till his death. Too strong an appreciation of the world s good opinion seems to have been the failing of Nicodemus. We do not lay much stress upon what he ventured to say in the Sanhedrim; for he suffered himself to be easily put down, and did not come forward with any bold avowal of his belief. Winer calls attention to the fact, that although he took part in the sepulchral rites of Jesus, he did not join Joseph in his application to Pilate for the body of his crucified Lord; and justly remarks that such characters usually require a strong external impulse to bring them boldly forward, which impulse was probably in this case supplied by the resurrection of Jesus.

NICOLA'ITANS. This word occurs twice in the New Testament (Rev. ii. 6, 15). In the former passage the conduct of the Nicolaitans is condemned; in the latter, the angel of the church in Pergamus is censured because certain members of his church held their doctrine. Various traditionary accounts of the origin and practices of this sect have been given by the fathers, but none of them are entitled to any credit.

It is evident from the accounts which they give, that the Nicolaitans with whom they were acquainted were Gnostics; since they impute to them the distinctive tenets and practices of the Gnostics. But in the short allusion in Rev. ii. 6, 15, there is nothing to identify the tenets or conduct alluded to with Gnosticism, even supposing that Gnosticism, properly so called, existed in the Apostolic age, which, to say the least, has not been proved to be the case. So that the conjecture mentioned by Mosheim, and which Tertullian appears to favour, may be regarded as probable, that the Nicolaitans mentioned in Revelation had erroneously been confounded with a party of Gnostics formed at a later period by one Nicholas.

The ingenious conjecture of Michaelis is worthy of consideration, who supposes that by Nicolaitans (Rev. ii. 6, 15) the same class of persons is intended whom St. Peter (2 Ep. ii. 15) describes as *followers of the way of Balaam;* and that their name, Nicolaitans, is merely a Greek translation of their Hebrew designation. The only objection which occurs to us against this very ingenious and probable supposition, arises from the circumstance that, in the passage, Rev. ii. 14, 15, both 'they that hold the doctrine of Balaam,' and ' the Nicolaitans,' are specified, and are distinguished from each other: ' So hast thou also,' the Nicolaitans, as well as the Balaamites, mentioned in the previous verse. So that whatever general agreement there might be between those two classes of heretics—and their collocation in the passage before us seems to imply that

there was such agreement—it appears equally evident that some distinction also must have separated them the one from the other.

NIC'OLAS, a proselyte of Antioch, and one of the seven deacons (Acts vi. 5). Nothing further is known of him; but a large body of unsafe tradition has been connected with his name, under the supposition that he was the founder of the heresy of the Nicolaitans, stigmatised in Rev. ii. 6, 15. (See the preceding article.)

NICOP'OLIS, a city of Thrace, now Nicopi, on the river Nessus, now Karasou, which was here the boundary between Thrace and Macedonia; and hence the city is sometimes reckoned as belonging to the latter. In Titus iii. 15, Paul expresses an intention to winter at Nicopolis, and invites Titus, then in Crete, to join him there.

NI'GER. [SIMON.]

NIGHT. The general division of the night among the Hebrews has been described under DAY; and it only remains to indicate a few marked applications of the word. The term of human life is usually called a day in Scripture; but in one passage it is called *night*, to be followed soon by day, ' the day is at hand' (Rom. viii. 12). Being a time of darkness, the image and shadow of death, in which the beasts of prey go forth to devour, it was made a symbol of a season of adversity and trouble, in which men prey upon each other, and the strong tyrannize over the weak (Isa. xxi. 12; Zech. xiv. 6, 7; comp. Rev. xxi. 23; xxii. 5). Hence continued day, or the absence of night, implies a constant state of quiet and happiness, undisturbed by the vicissitudes of peace and war. Night is also put, as in our own language, for a time of ignorance and helplessness (Mic. iii. 6). In John ix. 4, night represents death, a necessary result of the correlative usage which makes life a day.

NIGHT-HAWK (Lev. xi. 16; Deut. xiv. 15) is mentioned as one of the unclean birds in the Pentateuch, but so little characterized that no decided opinion can be expressed as to what species is really intended. Commentators incline to the belief that the name imports voracity, and therefore indicates a species of owl, which, however, we take to be not this bird, but the *lilith;* and as the night-hawk of Europe, or a species very nearly allied to it, is an inhabitant of Syria, there is no reason for absolutely rejecting it in this place, since it belongs to a genus highly connected with superstitions in all countries; and though a voracious bird among moths, and other insects that are abroad during darkness, it is absolutely harmless to all other animals, and as wrongfully accused of sucking the udders of goats, as of being an indicator of misfortune and death to those who happen to see it fly past them after evening twilight; yet, beside the name of ' goat-sucker,' it is denominated 'night-hawk' and 'night-raven,' as if it were a bulky species, with similar powers of mischief as those day birds possess. The night-hawk is a migratory bird, inferior in size to a thrush, and has very weak talons and bill; but the gape or mouth is wide; it makes now and then a plaintive cry, and preys on the wing; it flies with the velocity and action of a swallow, the two genera being nearly allied. Like those of most night birds, the eyes are large and remarkable, and the plumage a mixture of colours and dots, with a pre-

vailing grey effect; it is finely webbed, and
entirely noiseless in its passage through the air.
Thus the bright eyes, wide mouth, sudden and
inaudible flight in the dusk, are the original
causes of the superstitious fear these birds have
excited; and as there are in southern climates
other species of this genus, much larger in size,
with peculiarly contrasted colours, strangely disposed feathers on the head, or paddle-shaped
single plumes, one at each shoulder, projecting
in the form of two additional wings, and with
plaintive loud voices often uttered in the night,
all the species contribute to the general awe
they have inspired in every country and in all
ages.

NILE. [EGYPT.]

NIM'RA. [BETH-NIMRA.]

NIM'ROD, a son of Cush, the eldest son of
Ham (Gen. x. 8-10). Five sons of Cush are
enumerated in ver. 7 in the more usual manner
of this chapter; but a change of phrase introduces Nimrod. This difference may indicate that
while, in relation to the other five, the names
have a national and geographical reference, this
appellation is exclusively personal. It denotes
intensively *the extremely impious rebel.* Hence
we conceive that it was not his original proper
name, but was affixed to him afterwards, perhaps
even after his death, as a characteristic appellative.

No other persons connected with this work
must be considered as answerable for the opinion
which the writer of this article thinks to rest
upon probable grounds, that the earlier part of
the book of Genesis consists of several independent and complete compositions, of the highest
antiquity and authority, marked by some differences of style, and having clear indications of
commencement in each instance. If this supposition be admitted, a reason presents itself for the
citation of a proverbial phrase in ch. x. 9. The
single instance of minute circumstantiality, in so
brief a relation, seems to imply that the writer
lived near the age of Nimrod, while his history
was still a matter of traditional notoriety, and
the comparison of any hero with him was a familiar form of speech. It is also supposed that
those, not fragments, but complete, though short
and separate compositions (of which eight or
more are hypothetically enumerated in J. Pye
Smith's *Scripture and Geology,* p. 202), were,
under Divine authority, prefixed by Moses to his
own history. Their series has a continuity generally, but not rigorously exact. If we place ourselves in such a point of time, suppose the age
succeeding Nimrod, which might be the third
century after the Deluge, we may see how naturally the origination of a common phrase would
rise in the writer's mind; and that a motive of
usefulness would be suggested with it. But both
these ideas involve that of nearness to the time;
a period in which the country traditions were yet
fresh, and an elucidation of them would be acceptable and consonant to general feeling. The
following is a close translation of the passage in
which mention is made of Nimrod:—' And Cush
begat Nimrod: he began to be a hero in the
earth [or in the land]: he was a hero at the chace
in the presence of Jehovah; on which account
the saying is, Like Nimrod, the hero of the chace,
in the presence of Jehovah. And the chief [city]

of his dominion was Babel; and [he founded]
Ezek and Akkad, and Kalneh, in the land of
Shinar.'

Interpreters, with scarcely an exception, from
the Septuagint and the Targums down to our
own times, understand the whole case thus: that
Nimrod was a man of vast bodily strength, and
eminent for courage and skill in the arts of hunting down and capturing or killing the dangerous
animals, which probably were both very numerous and frequently of enormous size; that, by
these recommendations, he made himself the
favourite of bold and enterprising young men,
who readily joined his hunting expeditions; that
hence he took encouragement to break the patriarchal union of venerable and peaceful subordination, to set himself up as a military chieftain,
assailing and subduing men, training his adherents into formidable troops, by their aid subduing the inhabitants of Shinar and its neighbouring districts; and that, for consolidating and
retaining his power, now become a despotism, he
employed his subjects in building forts, which
became towns and cities, that which was afterwards called Babel being the principal. Combining this with the contents of chapter xi., we
infer that Nimrod either was an original party
in the daring impiety of building the tower, or
subsequently joined himself to those who had
begun it. The former fact is positively affirmed
by Josephus; but it is not probable that he could
have any other evidence than that of the general
interpretation of his countrymen. The late Mr.
Rich, not thirty years ago, in the extensive plain
where lie buried the ruins of Babylon, discovered
the very remarkable mound with remains of
buildings on its summit (of which see the figure
in the article BABEL), which even now bears the
name of *Birs Nimrod;* and this may well be
regarded as some confirmation of the common
opinion.

As a great part of the ancient mythology and
idolatry arose from the histories of chiefs and
sages, decorated with allegorical fables, it is by
no means improbable that the life and actions of
Nimrod gave occasion to stories of this' kind.
Hence, some have supposed him to have been
signified by the Indian Bacchus, deriving that
name from *Bar-Chus,* 'son of Cush;' and, it is
probable, by the Persian giant *Gibber* (answering
to the Hebrew *Gibbor,* 'mighty man,' 'hero,' in
Gen. x. 8, 9); and by the Greek *Orion,* whose
fame as a 'mighty hunter' is celebrated by
Homer, in the *Odyssey,* xi. 571-4. The Persian
and the Grecian fables are both represented by
the well-known and magnificent constellation.

NIN'EVEH, meaning the dwelling of Ninus;
a famous city of the ancient world, capital of the
great Assyrian empire, which stood on the eastern
bank of the river Tigris, opposite to the present
Mosul; its actual site being most probably the
same with that of Nunia and the tomb of Jonah,
about three-fourths of a mile from the river, in
the midst of ruins, N. lat. 36° 20′ 17″; E. long. 43°
10′ 17″. The Bible makes the city a sort of
colony from Babylon or Babel, Shinar [see
BABEL], stating (Gen. x. 11), ' out of that land
(Babel, &c., in the land of Shinar) went forth
Asshur and builded Nineveh.' After this simple
statement the sacred record is for a long time
entirely silent respecting Nineveh, which, we

may therefore presume, remained inconsiderable for many generations. At length, some fifteen hundred years after the first mention of the place, in the days of Jeroboam II., king of Israel (B.C. 825), Nineveh again enters by name on the Biblical record, having meanwhile grown into a mighty power. This re-appearance of Nineveh is accidental, and shows that the Bible does not profess to give any orderly and systematic history of the world. Other countries come on the scene and disappear, just as the course of events in the kingdoms of Judah and Israel seems to require or may chance to occasion. Nineveh is described in the book of Jonah as ' that great city,' ' an exceeding great city of three days' journey,' probably in a straight line through the place, as the large cities of Asia stood on a great extent of country, having gardens, and even fields, in the midst of them; and Jonah is said to enter into the city a day's journey ' (ch. iii. 4)

before he began to foretell its overthrow; that is, as is most likely, he penetrated into the heart of the place, as being that which was most suitable for delivering his burden. The magnitude of the place may also be gathered from what is said in the last verse of the book: ' That great city, wherein are more than six score thousand persons that cannot discern between their right hand and their left hand, and also much cattle (grazing).' The population of a place must have been immense in which there were no fewer than 120,000 children—young children the language employed seems to denote. It also appears from the same book that the state of society was highly complex, organized in divers ranks from the king and the noble to the peasant; and, if we may argue from the exactness with which the number of children is given, we should be justified in asserting that the people were in an advanced stage of civilization, seeing that their social sta-

267. [Nineveh.]

tistics were well attended to and carefully preserved. Civilization, however, had brought luxury, and luxury corruption of morals, for ' their wickedness had gone up before God ' (ch. i. 2). Yet was not their iniquity of the lowest kind, for the Ninevites repented at the preaching of Jonah.

A few years later we find the prophet Nahum intrusted with ' the burden of Nineveh.' From this book it would appear that the repentance of the city, if sincere, was not durable. Therefore was the anger of Jehovah about to fall upon it and make it a perpetual waste. The impending destruction of this ' great city' was also foretold by Zephaniah (ii. 13), and by Isaiah (xiv. 24) in language which gives a striking view of its commercial greatness (it was the entrepôt for the trade of Eastern and Western Asia), its surpassing opulence, its high culture, its immense population, and deep criminality (see Nahum, chap. iii.,

and Ezek. chap. xxxi.). From Strabo we learn that the place was much greater than even Babylon; and from Diodorus Siculus, that it measured 480 stadia in circumference, having very high and broad walls, which, aided by the river, rendered it impregnable. This safety was, however, merely imaginary. Sardanapalus, who had a full share of the vices of his subjects, endured in the eighth century before Christ a siege of three years' duration at the hands of the Medes, under Arbaces, which led to the overthrow of the city (Diod. Sic. ii. 26). But so large and so powerful a capital was not easily destroyed. Nineveh was the seat of an Assyrian kingdom till the year B.C. 625, when it was taken by Nabopolassar of Babylon, and Cyaxares, king of the Medes, which led to the destruction of the Assyrian kingdom. Nineveh flourished no more. Strabo represents it as lying waste; though in the times of the Roman emperors some remains of it seem to have survived, as a Nineveh on the Tigris is mentioned in Tacitus, and is characterized as a fort, probably some small fortification raised out of the ruins of the city for predatory purposes.

The present remains comprise a rampart and foss, four miles in circuit, with a moss-covered wall about twenty feet in height. The ruins at first sight present a range of hills. From these hills large stones are constantly dug out, from which probably a bridge over the Tigris has been built.

Jonah's connection with the city is still preserved in a tomb which bears his name; but how far back in antiquity this building runs, it is now impossible to say. The tomb stands on a hill, and is covered by a mosque which is held in great veneration. Bricks, partly whole, partly in fragments, and pieces of gypsum with inscriptions in the arrow-head character, are found from time to time. Landseer, in his *Sabæan Researches*, gives an engraving of cylinders dug up at Nineveh, which he states to be numerous in the East, and supposes to have been employed as signets: they are of jasper, chalcedony, and jade, and bear astronomical emblems, the graving of which, especially considering the hardness of the materials, shows a high state of art.

Mosul, with which Nineveh is commonly identified, stands on the opposite, or western bank of the Tigris, and lies so near the river that its streets are often flooded. This place, like its great prototype, carries on a trade (though to a small extent) between the East and the West. The climate is stated to be very healthy; the average temperature of summer not exceeding 66° Fahr.; but in spring, during the floods, epidemics are common, though not fatal.

NI'SAN, the first month of the Hebrew civil year. Abib, by which name this month is called in the Pentateuch (Exod. xiii. 4; xxiii. 15; Deut. xvi. 1), means an ear of grain, a green ear; and hence 'the month Abib' is 'the month of green ears.' It thus denoted the condition of the barley in the climate of Egypt and Palestine in this month. Nisan, otherwise Abib, began with the new moon of April, or, according to the Rabbins, of March [MONTH].

NIS'ROCH, an idol of the Ninevites (2 Kings xix. 37; Isa. xxxvii. 38). The word is now usually supposed to mean 'great eagle.' This bird was held in peculiar veneration by the ancient Persians; and was likewise worshipped by the Arabs before the time of Mohammed.

NITRE occurs in Prov. xxv. 20; Jer. ii. 22; where the substance in question is described as effervescing with vinegar, and as being used in washing; neither of which particulars applies to what is now, by a misappropriation of this ancient name, called 'nitre,' and which in modern usage means the saltpetre of commerce, but they both apply to the *natron*, or true *nitrum* of the ancients. Natron, though found in many parts of the East, has ever been one of the distinguishing natural productions of Egypt. The principal natron lakes now found in that country, six in number, are situate in a barren valley about thirty miles westward of the Delta, where it both floats as a whitish scum upon the water, and is found deposited at the bottom in a thick incrustation, after the water is evaporated by the heat of summer. It is a natural mineral alkali, composed of the car-

bonate, sulphate, and muriate of soda, derived from the soil of that region. Forskal says that it is known by the name *atrun*, or *natrun*, that it effervesces with vinegar, and is used as soap in washing linen, and by the bakers as yeast, and in cookery to assist in boiling meat, &c. Combined with oil it makes a harder and firmer soap than the vegetable alkali.

NO, or NO-AMMON. [THEBES.]

NO'AH, the second father of the human race, was the son of the second Lamech, the grandson of Methuselah, and the tenth in descent from Adam.

The father of Noah must not be confounded with the Lamech who was the fourth in descent from Cain. The two Lamechs have one remarkable circumstance in common; to each of them a fragment of inartificial poetry is attached as his own composition. That of the Cainitic Lamech is in Gen. iv. 23, 24. That of the Sethite now comes before us in ch. v. 28, 29:—' Lamech lived 182 years, and then begat a son, and he called his name NOAH, saying

This shall comfort us
From our labour,
And from the sorrowful toils of our hands;
From the ground,
Which Jehovah hath cursed.'

The allusion is undoubtedly to the penal consequences of the fall in earthly toils and sufferings, and to the hope of a Deliverer excited by the promise made to Eve. That this expectation was grounded upon a divine communication we infer from the importance attached to it, and the confidence of its expression.

That the conduct of Noah corresponded to the faith and hope of his father we have no reason to doubt. The brevity of the history satisfies not human curiosity. He was born six hundred years before the Deluge. We may reasonably suppose that through that period he maintained the character given of him :—' Noah found favour in the eyes of the Lord. Noah was a just man, and perfect in his generations. Noah walked with God' (ch. vi. 8, 9). These words declare his piety, sincerity, and integrity, that he maintained habitual communion with the Father of Mercies, by the exercises of devotion, and that he was an inspired instrument of conveying the will of God to mankind. The wickedness of the human race had long called upon the wisdom and justice of God for some signal display of his displeasure, as a measure of righteous government and an example to future ages. For a long time, probably many centuries, the better part of men, the descendants of Seth, had kept themselves from society with the families of the Cainite race. The former class had become designated as 'the sons of God,' faithful and obedient: the latter were called by a term evidently designed to form an appellation of the contrary import, 'daughters of men,' of impious and licentious men. These women possessed beauty and blandishments, by which they won the affections of unwary men, and intermarriages upon a great scale took place. As is usual in such alliances the worse part gained the ascendancy. The offspring became more depraved than the parents, and a universal corruption of minds and morals took place. Many of them became 'giants, the mighty men of old, men of renown,' apostates (as the word implies), heroes, warriors, plunderers, 'filling the earth with violence.' God mercifully afforded a respite of one hundred and twenty years (ch. vi. 3; 1 Pet. iii. 20; 2 Pet. ii. 5), during which Noah sought to work salutary impressions upon their minds, and to bring them to repentance. Thus he was 'a preacher of righteousness,' exercising faith in the testimony of God, moved with holy reverence, obeying the divine commands, and, by the contrast of his conduct, condemning the world (Heb. xi. 7): and probably he had during a long previous period laboured in that benevolent and pious work.

At last the threatening was fulfilled. All human kind perished in the waters, except this eminently favoured and righteous man, with his three sons (born about a hundred years before) and the four wives [DELUGE].

At the appointed time this terrible state of the earth ceased, and a new surface was disclosed for the occupation and industry of the delivered family. In some places that surface would be washed bare to the naked rock, in others sand would be deposited, which would be long uncultivable; but by far the larger portion would be covered with rich soil. With agriculture and its allied arts the antediluvians must have been well acquainted [ADAM]. The four men, in the vigour of their mental faculties and bodily strength, according to the then existing scale of human life, would be at no loss for the profitable application of their powers. Immediately after the desolating judgment the merciful Jehovah gave intimations of his acceptance of the sacrifice and thanksgivings of Noah and his family, and of his gracious purposes revealed in the form of a solemn covenant for the continual benefit of them and their posterity. The beautiful phenomenon of the rainbow was put to a new and significant use. As infallibly certain as is the production of a rainbow under certain conditions of the atmosphere, so certain and sure of fulfilment are the promises of Jehovah.

As the flood affected equally the common ancestry of mankind, all nations that have not sunk into the lowest barbarism would be likely to preserve the memory of the chief person connected with it; and it would be a natural fallacy that every people should attach to itself a principal interest in that catastrophe, and regard that chief person as the founder of their own nation and belonging to their own locality. Hence we can well account for the traditions of so many peoples upon this capital fact of ancient history, and the chief person in it;—the Xisuthrus of the Chaldæans, with whom is associated a remarkable number of precise circumstances, corresponding to the Mosaic narrative; the Phrygian *Noe* of the celebrated Apamean medal, which, besides Noah and his wife with an ark, presents a raven, and a dove with an olive-branch in its mouth; the *Manes* of the Lydians: the Deucalion of the Syrians and the Greeks, of whose deluge the account given by Lucian is a copy almost exactly circumstantial of that in the book of Genesis; the many coincidences in the Greek mythology in respect of Saturn, Janus, and Bacchus; the traditions of the aboriginal Americans, as stated by Clavigero, in his *History of Mexico;* and many others.

NOB, a city of Benjamin, in the vicinity of Jerusalem, belonging to the priests, and where the tabernacle was stationed in the time of Saul (1 Sam. xxi. 2; xxii. 9, 11, 19; Neh. xi. 32; Isa. x. 32). From the last of these texts it would appear that Jerusalem was visible from Nob, which, therefore, must have been situated somewhere upon the ridge of the Mount of Olives, north-east of the city.

NOBLEMAN. The word so rendered in John iv. 46, probably signifies one belonging to the court. This person was. therefore, probably of the court of Herod Antipas, who reigned over Galilee and Peræa.

NOD, the land to which Cain withdrew, and in which he appears to have settled (Gen. iv. 16). While the site of paradise itself remains undetermined, it is useless to seek for that of the land of Nod. This land, wherever it was, could not have had a name till Cain went to it; and it was doubtless called Nod (which signifies *flight, wandering*), from the circumstance that Cain fled to it.

NOPH. [MEMPHIS.]

NORTH. The Shemite, in speaking of the quarters of the heavens and of the earth, supposes his face turned towards the east, so that the east is before him, the west behind, the south on the right hand, and the north on the left. Hence the words which signify east, west, north, and south, signify also that which is before, behind, on the right hand, and on the left. The Hebrew word, translated north, occurs in the five following senses:—1. It denotes a particular quarter of the heavens; thus, 'fair weather cometh out of the north' (Job xxxvii. 22; see also Eccles. i. 6, and Ezek. i. 4). 2. It means a quarter of the earth (Ps. cvii. 3; Isa. xliii. 6; Ezek. xx. 47; xxxii. 30; comp. Luke xiii. 29). 3. It occurs in the sense of a northern aspect or direction, &c.; thus, 'looking north' (1 Kings vii. 25; 1 Chron. ix. 24; Num. xxxiv. 7); on 'the north side' (Ps. xlviii. 2; Ezek. viii. 14; xl. 44; comp. Rev. xxi. 13). 4. It seems used as the conventional name for certain countries, irrespectively of their true geographical situation, namely, Babylonia, Chaldæa, Assyria, and Media, which are constantly represented as being to the north of Judæa, though some of them lay rather to the east of Palestine. Thus Assyria is called the north (Zeph. ii. 13), and Babylonia (Jer. i. 14; xlvi. 6, 10, 20, 24; Ezek. xxvi. 7; Judith xvi. 4). 5. The Hebrew word is applied to the north wind; see Prov. xxvii. 16, and Cant. iv. 6.

NOSE-JEWEL. [WOMEN.]

NOVICE, or NEOPHYTE, one newly converted (literally *newly planted*), not yet matured in Christian experience (1 Tim. iii. 6). The word continued to be in use in the early church; but it gradually acquired a meaning somewhat different from that which it bore under the Apostles, when 'newly converted' and 'newly baptized' described, in fact, the same condition, the converted being at once baptized. For when, in subsequent years, the church felt it prudent to put converts under a course of instruction before admitting them to baptism and the full privileges of Christian brotherhood, the term Novices was sometimes applied to them, although more usually distinguished by the general term of Catechumens.

NUMBERS is the appellation given to the fourth book of Moses.

This book embraces more especially the continuation of the Sinaitic legislation, the march through the wilderness, the rejection of a whole generation, and the commencement of the conquest of Canaan. Thus we see that it treats on very different subjects, and on this account it has frequently been attempted to resolve it into separate fragments and documents, and to represent it as being composed of the most heterogeneous materials. We will endeavour to refute this opinion, by furnishing an accurate survey of its contents, and by describing the internal connection of its component parts, so that the organization of the book may be clearly understood.

The sum and substance of the law having been stated in the preceding books, that of Numbers commences with the arrangements requisite for preserving good order in the camp of the Israelites. The people are numbered for the express purpose of separating the Levites from those Israelites who had to bear arms, and of thus introducing into practice the law concerning the first-born, for whom the tribe of Levi became a substitute. For this reason the people are not merely numbered, but also classed according to their descent; the order which each tribe should occupy in the camp is defined, and the Levites are introduced into their respective functions (ch. i.-iv.).

The camp, having been consecrated, was to be kept pure according to the law of Levitical cleansings; consequently all persons were excluded from it who were afflicted with leprosy, who had become unclean by a flux, and who had touched a corpse (ch. v. 1-4).

Thus, after civil and sacerdotal life had been brought into a definite form, other laws based upon this form came into force, especially those laws which regulated the authority of the priests in civil affairs (ch. v. 5; vi. 27). These regulations conclude with the beautiful form of benediction which indicates the blessing to be expected from the true observance of the preceding directions. The people are impressed with this fact; the hearts of the Israelites are willing to offer the required gifts, and to intrust them to the Levites.

Jehovah is faithful to his promise, and gloriously reveals himself to his people (ch. vii.). Before the Levites enter upon the discharge of their sacred functions, the law concerning the lamps to be lighted in the sanctuary is significantly repeated (ch. viii.). These lamps symbolize the communication of the Holy Spirit, and bring to the recollection of the nation the blessings of theocracy to be derived from setting apart the tribe of Levi, which had recently been separated from the rest of the people.

Then follows a description of the celebration of the Passover, preparatory to the departure of the people from Mount Sinai (ch. ix. 1-14). Some regulations are connected with the celebration of the Passover, and the whole miraculous guidance of the people is described (ch. ix. 15-x.).

Thus the entrance of Israel into the Holy Land seemed to be fully prepared; and it was of great importance to show how they were prevented from entering it. Accurate details are therefore given of the spirit which pervaded the nation; a spirit which, in spite of the forbearance of God,

manifested itself in daring rebellions against the divine authority (ch. xi., xii.).

Now comes the turning point of the history. Everything seems externally prepared for the conquest of the country, when it appears that the nation are not yet internally ripe for the performance of so important an act (ch. xiii, xiv.).

In immediate connection with this are some laws which were given in the desert; the intention of which was to recal to the recollection of the rejected race, which had been justly condemned to suffer severe punishment, that nevertheless they had not ceased to be the people of the covenant, and the depositary of divine revelation (comp. ch. xv. 2, 13-16, 22, 23, 37, sq.). In this respect the facts mentioned in ch. xv. 32-36, and ch. xvi. are also of great importance. They show, on the one hand, the continuance of an evil disposition in the people, and, on the other, the majesty of God watching over his holy law.

The contents of ch. xv.-xix. are of a similar character. The facts there recorded relate to a period of thirty-eight years. The conciseness with which they are stated significantly indicates the strictly legal and theocratical principles of the Mosaical legislation. The period of Israel's rejection is characterized by the circumstance, that the historian is almost silent respecting it, as being a period not strictly belonging to theocratical history. During this period the striking deeds of God, his miracles and signs, the more prominent operations of his grace, and his peculiar blessings, cease. The rejection of the nation consisted in this suspension of the divine operations. During this period God, as it were, ignored his people. Consequently, the historian also almost ignores the rebellious race. But the period in which the divine promises were to be fulfilled again forms a prominent portion of the history. The termination of the penal period is the commencement of the most important era in the Mosaical history. It brings the legislation to a splendid conclusion. The most glorious facts here follow each other in close succession; facts which were intended clearly to demonstrate that the chosen people entered into the land of promise, not by their own power and might, but that this land was given into their hands by the God of promise.

There have frequently been raised strong doubts against the historical credibility of the book of Numbers, although it is impressed with indubitable marks of the age to which it refers, and of perfect authenticity. The author proves himself to possess an intimate knowledge of Egypt and of Egyptian history, and manners and customs. Narratives like the history of Balaam furnish also numerous proofs of their high antiquity. Its geographical statements are found to be uncommonly accurate, and the nations particularly mentioned in that prophecy belong to the Mosaical period, and some of them at a later era disappeared entirely from history. The list of stations in chap. xxxiii. bears undeniable marks of antiquity; and the historical notices which the list contains demonstrate the accurate historical information of the author. Moreover the great fact which is the basis of the narrative of the whole book—the sojourn of the Israelites during forty years in the wilderness—can only be accounted for by assuming an extraordinary divine intervention.

NUN (*a fish*), the father of Joshua, who is hence constantly called Joshua ben-Nun, ' Joshua the son of Nun.' Nothing is known of the person who bore this name.

NUTS. This word occurs only in Gen. xliii. 11, where Jacob, wishing to conciliate the ruler of Egypt, desires his sons on their return to ' take of the best fruits in the land in their vessels and carry down the man a present,' and along with other articles mentions ' *nuts* and almonds.' There is little doubt that *pistachio-nuts* is the article here meant.

The pistachio-nut-tree is well known, extending as it does from Syria to Affghanistan. From the latter country the seeds are carried as an article of commerce to India, where they are eaten in their uncooked state, added to sweetmeats, or as a dessert fried with pepper and salt, being much relished by Europeans for the delicacy of their flavour. The pistacia-tree is most common in the northern, that is. the cooler parts of Syria, but it is also found wild in Palestine in some very remarkable positions, as Mount Tabor, and the summit of Mount Attarus (Nebo?). It delights in a dry soil, and rises to the height of 20, and sometimes 30 feet. As it belongs to the same genus as the terebinth-tree, so like it the male and female flowers grow on separate trees.

O.

OAK. In our version various words are rendered by ' oak,' particularly *Alah*, which more probably denotes the terebinth-tree. The oak is, in fact, less frequently mentioned in the original than in the A. V., where it occurs so often as to suggest that the oak is as conspicuous and as common in Palestine as in this country. But in Syria oaks are by no means common, except in hilly regions, where the elevation gives the effect of a more northern climate; and even in such circumstances it does not attain the grandeur in which it often appears in our latitudes. Indeed, Syria has not the species which forms the glory of our own forests. The ' oaks of Bashan ' are in Scripture mentioned with peculiar distinction (Isa. ii. 3; Ezek. xxvii. 6; Zech xi. 2), as if in the hills beyond the Jordan the oaks had been more abundant and of larger growth than elsewhere. This is the case even at the present day. In the hilly regions of Bashan and Gilead, Burckhardt repeatedly mentions forests of thick oaks—thicker than any forests which he had seen in Syria. Oaks of low stature are frequent on the hills and plains near the sources of the Jordan, and in the lower slopes of Lebanon. Lord Lindsay describes the hills of northern Judæa about Hebron as covered to the top with low shrubs of the prickly oak. Prickly and evergreen oaks occur between Samaria and Mount Carmel, and on the banks of the Kishon. The thick trees which cover Mount Tabor are composed chiefly of oaks and pistachio-trees.

The species of oak found in Palestine are, 1. The Evergreen Oak. This is a tall but not widespreading tree, and the timber being very hard, is much used for purposes in which compactness and durability are required. 2. The Holly-leaved Montpelier Oak, another evergreen. This tree also, as its name imports, is a native of Southern Europe, and is markedly distinguished from the former by its numerous straggling branches and the thick underdown of its leaves. 3. The Hairy-cupped Oak, so called from the bristly appearance of the calyx. It grows to a considerable size, and furnishes an excellent timber, much used by the Turks in the building of ships and houses. 4. The Great Prickly-cupped Oak, which takes its name from its large prickly calyx. This species is common in the Levant, where it is a handsome tree, which it is not in our ungenial climate, though it has long been cultivated. The wood of this species is of little worth; but its acorns form the valonia of commerce, of which 150,000 cwt. are yearly imported into this country for the use of tanners. 5. The Kermes Oak takes its name from an insect (*kermes*, of the genus *coccus*) which adheres to the branches of this bushy evergreen shrub, in the form of small reddish balls about the size of a pea. This affords a crimson dye, formerly celebrated, but now superseded by cochineal. This dye was used by the ancient Hebrews.

From the hints of travellers there appear to be some other species of oaks in Palestine, but their information is not sufficiently distinct to enable us to identify them.

OATH, an appeal to God in attestation of the truth of what you say, or in confirmation of what you promise or undertake. Cicero correctly terms an oath a religious affirmation; that is, an affirmation with a religious sanction. Hence it appears that there are two essential elements in an oath: first, the human, a declared intention of speaking the truth, or performing the action in a given case; secondly, the divine, an appeal to God, as a Being who knows all things and will punish guilt. According to usage, however, there is a third element in the idea which ' oath ' commonly conveys, namely, that the oath is taken only on solemn, or, more specifically, on juridical occasions.

The essence of an oath lies obviously in the appeal which is thereby made to God, or to divine knowledge and power. The customary form establishes this, ' So help me God.' The Latin words (known to have been used as early as the sixth century), whence our English form is taken, may be thus rendered: *so may God and these holy gospels help me*; that is, ' as I say the truth.' The present custom of kissing a book containing the Gospels has in England taken place of the latter clause in the Latin formula.

Oaths did not take their origin in any divine command. They were a part of that consuetudinary law which Moses found prevalent, and was bound to respect, since no small portion of the force of law lies in custom, and a legislator can neither abrogate nor institute a binding law of his own mere will. Accordingly, Moses made use of the sanction which an oath gave, but in that general manner, and apart from minute directions and express words of approval; which shows that he merely used, without intending to sanction, an instrument that he found in existence and could not safely dispense with. Examples are found in Exod. xxii. 11, where an oath is ordered to be applied in the case of lost property;

and here we first meet with what may strictly be called a judicial oath (Lev. vi. 3-5).

The forms of adjuration found in the Scriptures are numerous. Saul sware unto Jonathan, 'As the Lord liveth' (1 Sam. xix. 6). 'A heap and a pillar' were for a witness between Laban and Jacob, with the ensuing for a sanction, 'The God of Abraham and the God of Nahor, the God of their father, judge betwixt us. And Jacob sware *by the fear of his father Isaac'* (Gen. xxxi. 52, sq.). A common formula is, 'The Lord do so to me and more also' (Ruth i. 17; 1 Sam. iv. 44), which approaches nearly to our modern form, 'So help me God,' and is obviously elliptical. Reference appears to be had to the ancient custom of slaying some animal in confirmation of a treaty or agreement. The animal thus slain and offered in a burnt offering to God became an image or type, betokening the fate which would attend that one of the two contracting parties who failed in his engagement; subsequently the sacrifice was in ordinary cases omitted, and the form came in itself to have the force of a solemn asseveration.

An oath, making an appeal to the divine justice and power, is a recognition of the divinity of the being to whom the appeal is made. Hence to swear by an idol is to be convicted of idolatry. Such an act is accordingly given in Scripture as a proof of idolatry and a reason for condign punishment. 'How shall I pardon thee for this? Thy children have forsaken me, and sworn by them that are no gods' (Jer. v. 7; xii. 16; Amos viii. 14; Zeph. i. 5).

Other beings besides God are sometimes added in the form of an oath: Elijah said to Elisha, 'As the Lord liveth, and as thy soul liveth' (2 Kings ii. 2; 1 Sam. xx. 3). The party addressed is frequently sworn by, especially if a prince: 'As thy soul liveth, my lord, I am the woman,' &c. (1 Sam. i. 26; xvii. 55; xxv. 26; 2 Sam. xi. 11). The Hebrews as well as the Egyptians swore also by the head or the life of an absent as well as a present prince: 'By the life of Pharaoh' (Gen. xlii. 15). Hanway says that the most sacred oath among the Persians is 'by the king's head.'

The oath-taker swore sometimes by his own head (Matt. v. 36); or by some precious part of his body, as the eyes; sometimes, but only in the case of the later Jews, by the earth, the heaven, and the sun (Matt v. 34, 35); as well as by angels; by the temple (Matt. xxiii. 16), and even by parts of the temple (Matt. xxiii. 16). They also swore by Jerusalem, as the holy city (Matt. v. 35). The Rabbinical writers indulge in much prolixity on the subject of oaths, entering into nice distinctions, and showing themselves exquisite casuists.

We have already intimated that it was usual to put the hand under the thigh (Gen. xxiv. 2; xlvii. 29). The more usual employment of the hand was to raise it towards heaven; designed, probably, to excite attention, to point out the oath-taker, and to give solemnity to the act (Gen. xiv. 22, 23). In the strongly anthropomorphic language of parts of the Scripture, even God is introduced saying, 'I lift up my hand to heaven, and say, I live for ever' (Deut. xxxii. 40). It can only be by the employment of a similar licence that the Almighty is represented as in any

way coming under the obligation of an oath (Exod. vi. 8; Ezek. xx. 5). Instead of the head, the phylactery was sometimes touched by the Jews on taking an oath.

The levity of the Jewish nation in regard to oaths, though reproved by some of their doctors, was notorious; and their conduct in this respect was severely censured by Christ himself in language which seems to forbid the use of oaths altogether (Matt. v. 34-37; James v. 12).

OBADI'AH (*servant of Jehovah*), the name of several persons mentioned in Scripture.

1. OBADIAH, the fourth of the minor prophets according to the Hebrew, the fifth according to the Greek, and the eighth according to chronological arrangement, is supposed to have prophesied about the year B.C. 599. We have, however, but a small fragment of his prophecies, and it is impossible to determine anything with certainty respecting himself or his history. It is evident from ver. 20 that he prophesied while Jerusalem was subjected to the yoke of the Chaldæans, and after the expatriation of several of the citizens—which refers him to the period after the seventh year of the captivity, B.C. 599. From a comparison of Obad. ver. 1-4, with Jer. xlix. 14-16; Obad. ver. 6, with Jer. xlix. 9, 10; and Obad. ver. 8, with Jer. xlix. 7, it is evident that one of these prophets had read the other's work. It is not easy, observes Calmet, to decide which of the two copied from the other; but from the fact that Jeremiah had made use of the writings of other prophets also, it has been generally concluded that Obadiah was the original writer.

His prophecies are directed against the Edomites, and in this respect correspond with Amos i. 11, Jer. xlix. 22, Ezek. xxv. 12-14, and Ps. cxxxvii. 7. He menaces Edom with destruction for their hostile feeling towards Judah, and their insulting conduct towards the Hebrews when Jerusalem was taken (ver. 11, 12); but consoles the Jews with a promise of restoration from their captivity, when the Hebrews and the Ten Tribes shall repossess both their land and that of Edom and Philistia—a prophecy which was fulfilled in the time of the Maccabees, under John Hyrcanus, B.C. 125.

The language of Obadiah is pure; but Jahn and others have observed that he is inferior to the more ancient prophets in his too great addiction to the interrogatory form of expression (see ver. 8). His sentiments are noble, and his figures bold and striking.

2. OBADIAH, the governor of King Ahab's household, and high in the confidence of his master, notwithstanding his aversion to the idolatries which the court patronized. In the persecution raised by Jezebel, Obadiah hid one hundred of the Lord's prophets in caves, and supplied them secretly with nourishment during the famine. It was this person, when sent out to explore the country in the vain search of pasture unconsumed by the drought, whom Elijah encountered when about to show himself to Ahab, and who was reluctantly prevailed upon to conduct the prophet to his master (1 Kings xviii. 4-16), B.C. 906.

3. OBADIAH, one of the heroes of the tribe of Gad, who joined David at Ziklag (1 Chron. xii. 9).

4. OBADIAH, one of the nobles whom Je-

2 s

hoshaphat sent to teach in the cities of Judah (2 Chron. xvii. 7).

5. OBADIAH, one of the Levites who presided over the restoration of the temple under Josiah (2 Chron. xxxiv. 12).

6. OBADIAH, the head of a party, consisting of 218 males, with females and children in proportion, who returned with Ezra from Babylon (Ezra viii. 9).

7. OBADIAH, one of the priests who sealed the written covenant which Nehemiah caused the people to enter into (Neh. x. 5).

Other persons of this name occur in 1 Chron. iii. 21; vii. 3; viii. 38; ix. 16, 44; xxvii. 19.

O'BED (*serving*), son of Boaz and Ruth, and father of Jesse the father of David, according to the apparently incomplete genealogical list (Ruth iv. 17; 1 Chron. ii. 12). The name occurs in the genealogies of Matthew (i. 5) and Luke (iii. 32).

O'BED-E'DOM (*serving Edom*), a Levite in whose premises, and under whose care, the ark was deposited, when the death of Uzzah caused David to apprehend danger in taking it farther. It remained here three months, during which the family of Obed-edom so signally prospered, that the king was encouraged to resume his first intention, which he then happily carried into effect (2 Sam. vi. 10-12). We learn from 1 Chron. xvi. 38, that Obed-edom's connection with the ark did not then terminate, he and his brethren having charge of the doors of the sanctuary (1 Chron. xv. 18, 24).

O'BIL (*chief of the camels*), an Ishmaelite, or Arab, doubtless of the nomade tribes, who had charge of the royal camels in the time of David —an exceedingly fit employment for an Arab (1 Chron. xxvii. 30). As Obil means in Arabic ' a keeper of camels,' Jerome reasonably infers that the person had his name from his office, which has always been a very common circumstance in the East.

OBLATION. [OFFERING.]

O'BOTH, a station of the Israelites [WANDERING].

1. O'DED (*erecting*), the prophet who remonstrated against the detention as captives of the persons whom the army of King Pekah had brought prisoners from Judah, and at whose suggestion they were handsomely treated, and conducted back with all tenderness and care to their own country (2 Chron. xxviii. 9).

2. ODED, father of Azariah the prophet, who was commissioned to meet and encourage Asa on his return from defeating the Ethiopians (2 Chron. xv. 1-8).

OFFERING is anything presented to God as a means of conciliating his favour: which being in the Jewish, as well as in all other religions, considered as the one thing needful, offerings accordingly have always constituted an essential part of public worship and private piety.

Offerings have been divided into three kinds: those which are designed to procure some favour or benefit; those which are expressive of gratitude for bounties or mercies received; those which are meant to atone for sins and to propitiate the Deity. Among the Hebrews we find a complex and multiform system of offerings extending through the entire circle of divine worship, and prescribing the minutest details. A leading distinction separates their offerings into unbloody and bloody. Used in its widest sense the term offering. or oblation, indicates in the Hebrew ritual a very great number of things—as the firstlings of the flock, first-fruits, tithes, incense, the shew-bread, the wood for burning in the temple. The objects offered were salt, meal, baked and roasted grain, olive-oil, clean animals, such as oxen, goats, doves, but not fish. The animals were required to be spotless, and, with the exception of the doves, not under eight days old, younger animals being tasteless and innutritious. The smaller beasts, such as sheep, goats, and calves, were commonly one year old. Oxen were offered at three years of age; in Judges (vi. 25) one is offered which is seven years old. As to sex, an option was sometimes left to the offerer, as in peace and sin offerings; at other times males were required, as in burnt sacrifices, for, contrary to classical usage, the male was considered the more perfect. In burnt offerings and in thank offerings the kind of animal was left to the choice of the worshipper, but in trespass and sin offerings it was regulated by law. If the desire of the worshipper was to express his gratitude, he offered a peace or thank offering: if to obtain forgiveness, he offered a trespass or sin offering. Burnt-offerings were of a general kind. Hecatombs or large numbers of cattle were sacrificed on special occasions (see 1 Kings viii. 5, 63). Offerings were also either public or private, prescribed or free-will. Sometimes they were presented by an individual, sometimes by a family; once, or at regular and periodic intervals. Foreigners were permitted to make offerings on the national altar. Offerings were made by Jews for heathen princes. In the case of bloody offerings the possessor, after he had sanctified himself, brought the victim, in case of thank-offerings, with his horns gilded and with garlands, &c., to the altar, where, laying his hand on the head of the animal, he thus, in a clear and pointed way, devoted it to God. Having so done, he proceeded to slay the victim himself; which act might be, and in later times was, done by the priests, and probably by the Levites. The blood was taken, and, according to the kind of offering, sprinkled upon the altar, or brought into the temple and there shed upon the ark of the covenant and smeared upon the horns of the altar of incense, and then the remainder poured forth at the foot of the altar of burnt-offerings. Having slain the animal, the offerer struck off its head, which, when not burnt, belonged either to the priest or to the offerer. The victim was then cut into pieces, which were either all, or only the best and most tasty, set on fire on the altar by the priests or the offerer, or must be burnt without the precincts of the holy city. The treatment of doves may be seen in Lev. i. 14, sq.; v. 8. In some sacrifices heaving and waving were usual either before or after the slaying.

The place where offerings were exclusively to be presented was the outer court of the national sanctuary, at first the Tabernacle, afterwards the Temple. Every offering made elsewhere was forbidden under penalty of death. The precise spot is laid down in Lev. i. 3; iii. 2, 'at the door of the tabernacle of the congregation before the Lord.' The object of these regulations was to prevent any secret idolatrous rites from taking place under the mask of the national ritual; and a common place of worship must have tended considerably to preserve the unity of the people, whose constant disagreements required precautions of a special kind (1 Kings xii. 27). The oneness, however, of the place of sacrifice was not strictly preserved in the troubled period of the Judges, nor indeed till the time of David (1 Kings iii. 2, 3). Offerings were made in other places besides the door of the Tabernacle (1 Sam. vii. 17; Judg. ii. 5). High places, which had long been used by the Canaanites, retained a certain sanctity, and were honoured with offerings (Judg. vi. 26; xiii. 19). Even the loyal Samuel followed this practice (1 Sam.), and David endured it (1 Kings iii. 2). After Solomon these offerings on high places still continued. In the kingdom of Israel, cut off as its subjects were from the holy city, the national temple was neglected.

Under the load and the multiplicity of these outward oblations, however, the Hebrews forgot the substance, lost the thought in the symbol, the thing signified in the sign; and, failing in those devotional sentiments and that practical obedience which offerings were intended to prefigure and cultivate, sank into the practice of mere dead works. Hereupon began the prophets to utter their admonitory lessons, to which the world is indebted for so many graphic descriptions of the real nature of religion and the only true worship of Almighty God (Isa i. 11; Jer. vi. 20; vii. 21, sq.; Hos. vi. 6; Amos v. 22; Micah vi. 6, sq.; comp. Ps. xl. 6; li. 17, sq.; Prov. xxi 3).

OG (giant), an Amoritish king of Bashan (Num. xxi. 33; xxxii. 33; Deut. iv. 47; xxxi. 4). In form he was a giant, so that his bedstead was preserved as a memorial of his huge stature (Deut. iii. 11; Josh. xiii. 12) [BED]. He was defeated by the Israelites under Moses (Num. xxi. 33; Deut. i. 4; iii. 3); and his country, which contained many walled cities (Deut. iii. 4-10), was assigned to the tribe of Manasseh (Deut. iii. 13; Josh. xiii. 30).

OIL was far more extensively used among the ancient Hebrews than in our northern climate. The use of oil is equally general throughout Western Asia at the present time, as it was in primitive ages. Oil was much used instead of butter and animal fat, at meals and in various preparations of food (see FOOD, and comp. Ezek. xvi. 13). In such uses oil, when fresh and sweet, is more agreeable than animal fat. The Orientals think so; and Europeans soon acquire the same preference. Oil was also in many cases taken as a meat-offering; and it was then mixed with the meal of oblation [OFFERING]. The rite of sprinkling with oil, as a libation, does not occur in the law, but seems to be alluded to in Micah vi. 7.

The application of oil to the person has been described in the article ANOINTING. Whether for luxury or ceremony, the head and beard were the parts usually anointed, and this use of oil became at length proverbially common among the Israelites (Prov. xxi. 17).

The employment of oil for burning has been illustrated in the article LAMPS. It is only necessary to add, that for this, and indeed for most other purposes, olive-oil was considered the best,

and was therefore used in the lamps of the tabernacle.

OLIVE-TREE. It is more than probable that the olive was introduced from Asia into Europe; and though it continues to be much cultivated in Syria, it is yet much more extensively so in the south of Europe, whence the rest of the world is chiefly supplied with olive-oil.

The olive-tree is of slow growth, but remarkable for the great age it attains. It never, however, becomes a very large tree, though sometimes two or three stems rise from the same root, and reach from twenty to thirty feet high. The leaves are in pairs, lanceolate in shape, of a dull green on the upper, and hoary on the under surface. Hence in countries where the olive is extensively cultivated, the scenery is of a dull character from this colour of the foliage. The fruit is an elliptical drupe, with a hard stony kernel, and remarkable from the outer fleshy part being that in

268. [Olea Europea.]

which much oil is lodged, and not, as is usual, in the almond of the seed. It ripens from August to September.

Of the olive-tree two varieties are particularly distinguished; the long-leafed, which is cultivated in the south of France and in Italy, and the broad-leafed in Spain, which has also its fruit much larger than that of the former kind. That the olive grows to a great age, has long been known. Pliny mentions one which the Athenians of his time considered to be coeval with their city, and therefore 1600 years old. Near Terni, in the vale of the cascade of Marmora, there is a plantation of very old trees, supposed to consist of the same plants that were growing there in the time of Pliny. Chateaubriand says: 'Those in the garden of Olivet (or Gethsemane) are at least of the times of the Eastern empire, as is demonstrated by the following circumstance. In Turkey every olive-tree found standing by the Mussulmans, when they conquered Asia, pays one *medina* to the Treasury, while each of those planted since the conquest is taxed half its produce. The eight olives of which we are speaking are charged only eight *medinas*. By some, especially by Dr. Martin, it is supposed that these olive-trees may have been in existence even in the time of our Saviour.

The wood of the olive-tree, which is imported into this country from Leghorn, is described by M. Holtzapffel to be 'like that of the box, but softer, with darker grey-coloured veins. The roots have a very pretty knotted and curly character; they are much esteemed on the continent for making embossed boxes, pressed into engraved metallic moulds.' A resin-like exudation is obtained from it, which was known to the ancients, and is now sometimes called olive-gum; but the fruit, with its oil, is that which renders the tree especially valuable. The green unripe fruit is preserved in a solution of salt, and is well known at our desserts. The fruit when ripe is bruised in mills, and the oil pressed out of the paste.

The olive is one of the earliest of the plants specifically mentioned in the Bible, the fig being the first. Thus, in Gen. viii. 11, the dove is described as bringing the olive-branch to Noah. It is always enumerated among the valued trees of Palestine; which Moses describes (Deut. vi. 11; viii. 8) as 'a land of oil-olive and honey' (so in xxviii. 40, &c.); and (2 Chron. ii. 10) Solomon gave to the labourers sent him by Hiram, king of Tyre, 20,000 baths of oil. Besides this, immense quantities must have been required for home consumption, as it was extensively used as an article of diet, for burning in lamps, and for the ritual service. The olive still continues one of the most extensively cultivated of plants. The olive, being an evergreen, was adduced as an emblem of prosperity (Ps. lii. 8), and it has continued, from the earliest ages, to be an emblem of peace among all civilized nations.

OLIVES, MOUNT OF, a mountain or ridge now called by the Arabs Jebel et-Tur, lying to the east of Jerusalem, from which it is separated only by the narrow valley of Jehoshaphat. Towards the south it sinks down into a lower ridge, over against the so-called 'well of Nehemiah,' now called by Franks the Mount of Offence, in allusion to the idolatrous worship established by Solomon 'on the hill that is before,' that is, eastward of 'Jerusalem.' In this direction lies the usual road to Bethany, so often trodden by our Saviour. About a mile towards the north is another summit, nearly or quite as high as the middle one. The ridge between the two bends slightly eastward, leaving room for the valley below to expand somewhat in that part. The view of the Holy City and of the Dead Sea, from the southern summit, is described in the article JERUSALEM; that from the northern summit does not embrace the Dead Sea. The elevation of the central peak of the Mount of Olives is stated by Schubert at 2556 Paris feet, or 416 Paris feet above the valley of Jehoshaphat; and hence it appears to be 175 Paris feet above the highest part of Mount Zion. Beyond the northern summit the ridge sweeps round towards the west, and spreads out into the high level tract north of the city, which is skirted on the west and south by

the upper part of the valley of Jehoshaphat. This inconsiderable ridge derives all its importance from its connection with Jerusalem, and from the sacred associations which hence became connected with it. To the mount whose ascent David ' went up, weeping and barefoot,' to which our Saviour ofttimes withdrew with his disciples, over which he often passed, and from which he eventually ascended into heaven, belongs a higher degree of sacred and moral interest than is to be found in mere physical magnitude, or than the record connects even with Lebanon, Tabor, or Ararat.

OLYM'PAS, a Christian at Rome, whom Paul salutes in his Epistle to the Romans (Rom. xvi. 15).

OME'GA, the last letter of the Greek alphabet, proverbially applied to express the end, as Alpha, the first letter, the beginning of anything [ALPHA].

O'MER. [WEIGHTS AND MEASURES.]

OM'RI (*God-taught*), sixth king of Israel, who began to reign in B.C. 929, and reigned twelve years. He was raised to the throne by the army, while it was engaged in the siege of Gibbethon, a Levitical city in Dan, of which the Philistines had gained possession, when the news came to the camp of the death of Elah, and the usurpation of Zimri. On this, the army proclaimed their general, Omri, king of Israel. He then lost not a moment, but leaving Gibbethon in the power of the infidels, went and besieged his competitor in Tirzah. But he was no sooner delivered of this rival [ZIMRI], than another appeared in the person of Tibni, whom a part of the people had raised to the throne, probably from unwillingness to submit to military dictation. This occasioned a civil war, which lasted six years, and left Omri undisputed master of the throne, B.C. 925. His reign lasted six years more, and its chief event was the foundation of Samaria, which thenceforth became the capital city of the kingdom of Israel (1 Kings xvi. 15-28) [SAMARIA].

ON (*strength*), a chief of the tribe of Reuben, who was one of the accomplices of Korah in the revolt against the authority of Moses and Aaron. He is mentioned among the leaders of this conspiracy in the first instance (Num. xvi. 17). but does not appear in any of the subsequent transactions, and is not by name included in the final punishment. The Rabbinical tradition is, that the wife of On persuaded her husband to abandon the enterprise.

ON, one of the oldest cities in the world, situated in Lower Egypt, about two hours N N.E from Cairo. The Septuagint translates the name On by Heliopolis, which signifies 'city of the sun;' and in Jer. xliii. 13, it bears a name, Bethshemesh, of equivalent import. On is a Coptic and ancient Egyptian word, signifying light and the sun. The site is now marked by low mounds, enclosing a space about three-quarters of a mile in length by half a mile in breadth, which was once occupied by houses and by the celebrated Temple of the Sun. This area is at present a ploughed field, a garden of herbs; and the solitary obelisk which still rises in the midst of it is the sole remnant of the former splendours of the place. In the days of Edrisi and Abdallatif the place bore the name of Ain Shems; and in the neighbouring village, Matariyeh, is still shown an ancient well bearing the same name. Near by it is a very old sycamore, its trunk straggling and gnarled, under which legendary tradition relates that the holy family once rested. Heliopolis was the capital of a district or nomos bearing the same name.

The place is mentioned in Gen. xli. 45, where it is said that Pharaoh gave to Joseph a wife, Asenath, the daughter of Poti-pherah, priest of On (ver. 50). From the passage in Jeremiah it may be inferred that it was distinguished for idolatrous worship. The names, 'City of the Sun,' 'Temples of the Sun,' connected with the place, taken in conjunction with the passage just alluded to, seem to refer the mind to the purer form of worship which prevailed at a very early period in Egypt, namely, the worship of the heavenly bodies, and thence to carry the thoughts to the deteriorations which it afterwards underwent in sinking to the adoration of images and animals.

The traces of this city which are found in classic authors correspond with the little of it that we know from the brief intimations of Holy Writ. According to Herodotus, Heliopolis was one of the four great cities that were rendered famous in Egypt by being the centres of solemn religious festivals, which were attended by splendid processions and homage to the gods. In Heliopolis the observance was held in honour of the sun. It had its priesthood, a numerous and learned body, celebrated before other Egyptians for their historical and antiquarian lore; it long continued the university of the Egyptians, the chief seat of their science; the priests dwelt as a holy community in a spacious structure appropriated to their use. The city suffered heavily by the Persian invasion. At an early period remains of its famous temple were found. An obelisk which the Emperor Augustus caused to be carried to Rome, and placed in the Campus Martius, is held by Zoega to have been brought from Heliopolis, and to have owed its origin to Sesostris. This city furnished works of art to Augustus for adorning Rome, and to Constantine for adorning Constantinople. Ritter says that the sole remaining obelisk is from 60 to 70 feet high, of a block of red granite, bearing hieroglyphics which remind the beholder of what Strabo terms the Etruscan style. 'The figure of the cross which it bears has attracted the special notice of Christian antiquaries.'

O'NAN (*strong, stout*), second son of Judah, who, being constrained by the obligations of the ancient Levirate law to espouse Tamar, his elder brother's widow, took means to frustrate the intention of this usage, which was to provide heirs for a brother who had died childless. This crime, rendered without excuse by the allowance of polygamy, and the seriousness of which can scarcely be appreciated but in respect to the usages of the times in which it was committed, was punished by premature death (Gen. xxxviii. 4, sq.)

ONE'SIMUS (*profitable*), a slave belonging to Philemon of Colossæ, who fled from his master, and proceeded to Rome, where he was converted by St. Paul, who sent him back to his master, a friend and convert of the apostle, with an eloquent letter, the purport of which is described in the article PHILEMON. Onesimus, accompanied by Tychicus, left Rome with not only this epistle,

but with those to the Ephesians and Colossians (Col. iv. 9). It is believed that Onesimus, anxious to justify the confidence which Paul reposed in him, by appearing speedily before his master, left Tychicus to take the Epistle to the Ephesians; and hastened to Colossæ, where he doubtless received the forgiveness which Paul had so touchingly implored for him as 'a brother beloved.' An uncertain tradition makes Onesimus to have been bishop of Beræa, where he is said to have suffered martyrdom. The part which Paul took in this difficult and trying case is highly honourable to him; while for Onesimus himself, the highest praise is, that he obtained the friendship and confidence of the apostle.

ONESIPH'ORUS (*profit-bringer*), a believer of Ephesus, who came to Rome during the second captivity of St. Paul in that city; and having found out the apostle, who was in custody of a soldier, to whose arm his own was chained, was 'not ashamed of his chain,' but attended him frequently, and rendered him all the services in his power. This faithful attachment, at a time of calamity and desertion, was fully appreciated and well remembered by the apostle, who, in his Epistle to Timothy, carefully records the circumstance; and, after charging him to salute in his name 'the household of Onesiphorus,' expresses the most earnest and grateful wishes for his spiritual welfare (1 Tim. ii. 16-18). It would appear from this that Onesiphorus had then quitted Rome.

ONION. Onions are mentioned in Num. xi. 5, among the articles of food for which the Israelites murmured. The onion was early employed as an article of diet in Egypt. It is distinguished from other species of Allium by its fistular leaves and swelling stalks, and is well known to be cultivated in all parts of Europe and in most parts of Asia. Its native country is not known; but it is probable that some part of the Persian region may have first produced it in a wild state, as many species of Allium are found in the mountainous chain which extends from the Caspian to Cashmere, and likewise in the Himalayan Mountains. It is common in Persia, where it is called *piaz*, and has been long introduced into India, where it receives the same name. The onions of warm dry countries grow to a considerable size, and, instead of being acrid and pungent in taste, are comparatively bland, and mild and nutritious articles of diet. This is particularly conspicuous in the Portugal onions, which are largely imported into this country. Other celebrated varieties are those of Spain and Tripoli; but Egypt itself is famed for the production of fine onions, as stated by Hasselquist: 'Whoever has tasted onions in Egypt, must allow that none can be had better in any part of the universe. Here they are sweet; in other countries they are nauseous and strong. Here they are soft, whereas in the northern and other parts they are hard, and their coats are so compact, that they are difficult of digestion. Hence they cannot in any place be eaten with less prejudice and more satisfaction than in Egypt.'

O'NYX. The Hebrew word translated by 'onyx-stone' in Gen. ii. 12, is different from that so rendered in the descriptions of the breastplate of the high-priest (Exod. xxviii. 19; xxxix. 11), and it is doubtful if the onyx is really intended by either. This stone has a whitish ground, and is variegated with bands of white and brown which run parallel to each other. It is a semi-pellucid stone of a fine flinty texture, taking an excellent polish, and is strictly of the flint or siliceous class. '*Onyx*' is the Greek word for the human nail; and the stone takes its name from the resemblance of the ground-colour to that lunated spot at the base of the nail.

O'PHEL, a place or quarter of Jerusalem near the walls (2 Chron. xxvii. 3; xxxiii. 44), on the east side (Neh. iii. 26; xi. 21). From the intimations regarding it given by Josephus, Winer collects that Ophel was a high or ascending place, built over (in the ancient city) with houses. This view is confirmed by Dr. Robinson, who identifies it with the low ridge which extends southward from the temple mount to Mount Zion, between the exterior valley of Jehoshaphat and the interior valley of Tyropœon. This ridge is considerably below the level of Mount Moriah; its length is 1550 feet, and its breadth in the middle part, from brow to brow, 290 feet [Jerusalem].

O'PHIR occurs first, as the proper name of one of the thirteen sons of Joktan, the son of Eber, a great-grandson of Shem, in Gen. x. 26–29. Many Arabian countries are believed to have been peopled by these persons, and to have been called after their respective names, as Sheba, &c., and among others Ophir. Ophir occurs also as the name of a place, country, or region, famous for its gold, which Solomon's ships visited in company with the Phœnician. The difficulty is to ascertain where Ophir was situated. The first theory which appears to be attended with some degree of evidence not purely fanciful is that Ophir was situate in Arabia. In Gen. x. 29, Ophir stands in the midst of other Arabian countries. Still, as Gesenius observes, it is possibly mentioned in that connection only on account of its being an Arabian colony planted abroad. Though gold is not now found in Arabia, yet the ancients ascribe it to the inhabitants in great plenty (Judg. viii. 24, 26 ; 2 Chron. i.; 1 Kings x. 1, 2; Ps. lxxii. 15). This gold. Dr. Lee thinks, was no other than the gold of Havilah (Gen. ii. 11), which he supposes to have been situate somewhere in Arabia. Bu Diodorus Siculus ascribes gold-mines to Arabia. He also testifies to the abundance of 'precious stones' there (in. 54), especially among the inhabitants of Sabas (iii. 46; comp. Gen. ii. 12; 2 Chron. ix. 1; 1 Kings x. 1, 2). Others suppose that, though Ophir was situate somewhere on the coast of Arabia, it was rather an emporium, at which the Hebrews and Tyrians obtained gold, silver, ivory, apes, almug-trees, &c., brought thither from India and Africa by the Arabian merchants. and even from Ethiopia, to which Herodotus (iii. 114) ascribes gold in great quantities, elephants' teeth, and trees and shrubs of every kind. In behalf of the supposition that Ophir was the Arabian port Aphar, it may be remarked that the name has undergone similar changes to that of the Sept. of Ophir; for it is called by Arrian Aphar, by Pliny Saphar, by Ptolemy Sapphera, and by Stephanus Saphirini. Grotius thinks his to be Ophir. The very name El Ophir has been lately pointed out as a city of Oman, in former times the centre of a very active Arabian commerce. In favour of the theory which places Ophir in Africa, it has been suggested that we

have the very name in *afri*, Africa. Origen also says, on Job xxii. 24, that some of the interpreters understood Ophir to be Africa. Michaelis supposes that Solomon's fleet, coming down the Red Sea from Ezion-geber, coasted along the shore of Africa, doubling the Cape of Good Hope, and came to Tarshish, which he, with many others, supposes to have been Tartessus in Spain, and thence back again the same way; that this conjecture accounts for their three years' voyage out and home; and that Spain and the coasts of Africa furnished all the commodities which they brought back. Strabo indeed says that Spain abounded in gold, and immensely more so in silver (see 1 Macc. viii. 3). Others have not hesitated to carry Solomon's fleet round from Spain up the Mediterranean to Joppa. In behalf of the conjecture that Ophir was in India, the following arguments are alleged: that it is most natural to understand from the narrative that all the productions said to have been brought from Ophir came from one and the same country, and that they were all procurable only from India. The Sept. translators also appear to have understood it to be India. Josephus also gives to the sons of Joktan the locality from Cophen, an Indian river, and in part of Asia adjoining it (*Antiq.* i. 6. 4). He also expressly and unhesitatingly affirms that the land to which Solomon sent for gold was 'anciently called Ophir, but now the Aurea Chersonesus, which belongs to India' (*Antiq.* viii. 6. 4). There are several places comprised in that region which was actually known as India to the ancients [India], any of which would have supplied the cargo of Solomon's fleet: for instance, the coast of Malabar. Perhaps the most probable of all is Malacca, which is known to be the Aurea Chersonesus of the ancients. It is also worthy of remark that the natives of Malacca still call their gold-mines *ophirs*. On the other hand, some writers give a wider extent to the country in question. Heeren observes that 'Ophir, like the name of all other very distant places or regions of antiquity, like Thule, Tartessus, and others, denotes no particular spot, but only a certain region or part of the world, such as the East or West Indies in modern geography. Hence Ophir was the general name for the rich countries of the south lying on the African, Arabian, or Indian coasts, as far as at that time known.'

1. OPH'RAH, a town of Benjamin (Josh. xviii 23), seemingly in the north-east of that tribe's domain (1 Sam. xiii. 17). Accordingly it is placed by Eusebius and Jerome five Roman miles east of Bethel. This corresponds with the position of a place called et-Taiyibeh, which was visited by Dr. Robinson in his excursion to Bethel. It is now a small village, curiously situated upon a conical hill, on the summit of which is an old tower, whence is commanded a splendid view of the valley of the Jordan, the Dead Sea, and the eastern mountains.

2. OPHRAH, a town in the tribe of Manasseh, to which Gideon belonged, and where he continued to reside after he had delivered Israel from the Midianites, establishing there his ephod, which became a snare to Israel (Judg. vi. 11–24 ; viii. 27).

O'REB and ZE'EB, the remarkable names (*raven and wolf*) of two emirs of the Midianites, who were made prisoners by the Ephraimites in attempting to recross the Jordan after the victory of Gideon. They were put to death by the captors, and their heads carried as a trophy to the conqueror, who was then on the other side the Jordan (Judg. vii. 25; viii 3). The first of these princes met his death near a rock, which thenceforth bore his name (Isa. x. 26); the other seems to have at first sought refuge in one of those excavations in which wines were preserved, and which was thenceforth called the winepress of Zeeb (Judg. vii. 25).

ORI'ON. [ASTRONOMY.]

OR'PAH (*fawn*), daughter-in-law of Naomi, who remained behind among her kindred in Moab, when Ruth returned with Naomi to Bethlehem (Ruth i. 4-14) [RUTH].

OSPRAY, an unclean bird, which has been identified with the haliaëtus or sea-eagle. Species of this bird occur in Europe, *Asia*, Africa, America, and Australia.

Mr. Macgillivray describes ' its savage scream of anger when any one approaches the neighbourhood of its nest, its intimidating gestures, and even its attempts to molest individuals who have ventured among its native crags.'

Mr. Selby, respecting the ospray, observes, ' It is strictly piscivorous, and is found only in the vicinity of lakes, rivers, or such pools as abound with fish. It is a *powerful* bird, often weighing five pounds; the limbs are *very muscular* in proportion to its general dimensions; its feet are admirably adapted for retaining firm hold of *its slippery* prey.' Mr. Montagu remarks, ' Its principal food is fish, which it often catches with great dexterity, by *pouncing upon them* with *vast rapidity, and carrying them off in its talons*.

OSSIFRAGE, a bird of prey, which is supposed to be identical with the griffon of Cuvier, the *Gypaëtos barbatus* of nomenclators. The species in Europe is little if at all inferior in size to the *Condor* of South America, measuring from

269. [Gypaetos barbatus]

the point of the bill to the end of the tail four feet two or three inches, and sometimes ten feet in the expanse of wing; the head and neck are not, like those of vultures, naked, but covered with whitish narrow feathers; and there is a beard of bristly hair under the lower mandible: the rest of the plumage is nearly black and brown, with

some whitish streaks on the shoulders, and an abundance of pale rust-colour on the back of the neck, the thighs, vent, and legs; the toes are short and bluish, and the claws strong. In the young the head and neck are black, and the species or variety of Abyssinia appears to be rusty and yellowish on the neck and stomach.

OSTRICH. The ostrich is frequently mentioned in the Bible in terms of great beauty and precision; which commentators, perhaps more conversant with the exploded misstatements of the ancients than with the true physiological history of the bird in question, have not been happy in explaining, sometimes referring it to wrong species, such as the peacock, or mistaking

270.

it for the stork, the eagle, or the bustard (Lev. xi. 19; Deut. xiv 15; Job xxx. 29; xxxix. 13; Isa. xiii. 21; xxxiv. 13; xliii. 20; Jer. L 39; Lam. iv. 3; Micah i. 8). In several of these passages 'owls' has been used in our version for ostriches, which the original word there employed really means.

There are two varieties, if not two species, of the ostrich; one never attaining seven feet in height, and covered chiefly with grey and dingy feathers: the other sometimes growing to more than ten feet, and of a glossy black plumage; the males in both having the great feathers of the wings and tail white, but the females the tail only of that colour. Their dimensions render them both the largest animals of the feathered creation now existing. They appear promiscuously in Asia and Africa, but the troops or coveys of each are always separate; the grey is more common in the south, while the black, which grows largest in Caffraria, predominates to the north of the equator. The common-sized ostrich weighs about eighty pounds.

Ostriches are gregarious—from families consisting of a male with one or several female birds, and perhaps a brood or two of young, up to troops of near a hundred. They keep aloof from the presence of water in the wild and arid desert, mixing without hesitation among herds of gnu, wild asses, quaggas, and other striped Equidæ, and the larger species of Antilopidæ. From the nature of their food, which consists of seeds and vegetables, although seldom or never in want of drink, it is evident that they must often approach more productive regions, which, by means of the great rapidity of motion they possess, is easily accomplished; and they are consequently known to be very destructive to cultivated fields. As the organ of taste is very obtuse in these birds, they swallow with little or no discrimination all kinds of substances, and among others stones; it is also probable that, like poultry, they devour lizards, snakes, and the young of birds that fall in their way. It is not yet finally decided whether the two species are polygamous, though concurrent testimony seems to leave no doubt of the fact: there is, however, no uncertainty respecting the nest, which is merely a circular basin scraped out of the soil, with a slight elevation at the border, and sufficiently large to contain a great number of eggs; for from twelve to about sixty have been found in them, exclusive of a certain number, always observed to be outlying, or placed beyond the raised border of the nest, and amounting apparently to nearly one-third of the whole. These are supposed to feed the young brood when first hatched, either in their fresh state, or in a corrupted form, when the substance in them has produced worms. These eggs are of different periods of laying, like those within, and the birds hatched form only a part of the contents of a nest, until the breeding season closes. The eggs are of different sizes, some attaining to seven inches in their longer diameter, and others less, having a dirty white shell, finely speckled with rust-colour; and their weight borders on three pounds. Within the tropics they are kept sufficiently warm in the day-time not to require incubation, but beyond these one or more females sit constantly, and the male bird takes that duty himself after the sun is set. It is then that the short roar may be heard during darkness; and at other times different sounds are uttered, likened to the cooing of pigeons, the cry of a hoarse child, and the hissing of a goose; no doubt expressive of different emotions.

Although possessed of strength sufficient to carry with velocity two adult human beings, and although readily tamed, even when taken in a state of maturity, nay easily rendered familiar and docile, and although they are by no means the stupid creatures they have been believed, still their voracity, leading to the destruction of young poultry, and the impracticability of guiding their powers, will ever render them unsafe and unprofitable domestics. Though at first sight useless, we may be assured that Providence has not appointed their abode in the desert in vain; and they still continue to exist, not only in Africa, but in the region of Arabia, east and south of Palestine beyond the Euphrates; but it may be a question whether they extend so far to the eastward as Goa, although that limit is assigned them by late French ornithologists.

The flesh of a young ostrich is said to be not unpalatable; but its being declared unclean in the Mosaic legislation may be ascribed to a twofold cause. The first is sufficiently obvious from its indiscriminate voracity already mentioned, and the other may have been an intention to lay a restriction upon the Israelites in order to wean them from the love of a nomade life, which

hunting in the desert would have fostered; for ostriches must be sought on the barren plains, where they are not accessible on foot, except by stratagem. When pursued, they cast stones and gravel behind them with great force; and though it requires long endurance and skill, their natural mode of fleeing in a circular form enables well-mounted Arabs to overtake and slay them.

OTH'NIEL (*lion of God*), first judge of Israel, son of Kenaz, the younger brother of Caleb, whose daughter Achsah he obtained in marriage by his daring valour at the siege of Debir (Josh. xv. 17; Judg. i. 13; 1 Chron. iv. 13). Rendered famous among his countrymen by this exploit, and connected by a twofold tie with one of the only two Israelites of the former generation who had not died in the desert, we are prepared for the fact that on him devolved the mission to deliver Israel from the Mesopotamian oppression under which, in punishment for their sins, they fell after the death of Joshua and of the elders who outlived him (Judg. iii. 9). This victory secured to Israel a peace of forty years.

OWL. There are noticed in Egypt and Syria three well-known species of the genus *Strix*, or owl:—'the great-eared owl;' the common barn owl; and the little owl. In this list the long-eared owl, the short-eared owl, known nearly over the whole earth, and the Oriental owl of Hasselquist, are not included, and several other species of these wandering birds, both of Africa and Asiatic regions, occur in Palestine. The barn owl is still sacred in Northern Asia.

271.

The eagle-owl, or great-eared owl, we do not find in ornithological works as an inhabitant of Syria, though no doubt it is an occasional winter visitant; and the smaller species, which may be a rare but permanent resident, probably also visiting Egypt. It is not, however, we believe, that species, but the *Otus ascalaphus* of Cuvier, which is common in Egypt, and which in all probability is the type of the innumerable representations of an eared owl in hieroglyphical inscriptions.

Next we have the short-eared owl, likewise found in Egypt and Arabia, as well as to the north of Syria, a bold, pugnacious bird, residing in ruined buildings, mistaken by commentators for the screech-owl. The spectral species, again, confounded with the goat-sucker, is, we believe, *Strix coromanda* [NIGHT-HAWK], and the same as the Oriental owl of Hasselquist.

The little owl of Egypt is not likely to be the Passerine species of Europe, and probably does not occur under a distinct name in Biblical Hebrew; but that the owls which inhabited Palestine were numerous may be inferred with tolerable certainty from the abundance of mice, rats, and other vermin, occasioned by the offal and offerings at the numerous sacrifices, and consequently the number of nocturnal birds of prey that subsisted upon them, and were tolerated for that purpose.

OX. Having already noticed the domestic *beeves* under BULL and CALF (to which we refer), the few words added here will apply to the breeds of Western Asia and the manner of treating them. The earliest pastoral tribes appear to have had domesticated cattle in the herd; and judging from the manners of South Africa, where we find nations still retaining in many respects primeval usages, it is likely that the patriarchal families, or at least their moveables, were transported on the backs of oxen in the manner which the Caffres still practise, as also the Gwallahs and grain-merchants in India, who come down from the interior with whole droves bearing burthens.

The breeds of Egypt were various, differing in the length and flexures of the horns. There were some with long horns, others with short, and even none, while a hunched race of Nubia reveals an Indian origin, and indicates that at least one of the nations on the Upper Nile had come from the valleys of the Ganges; for it is to the east of the Indus alone that that species is to be found whose original stock appears to be the mountain yak.

The domestic buffalo was unknown to Western Asia and Egypt till after the Arabian conquest: it is now common in the last-mentioned region and far to the south, but not beyond the equator; and from structural differences it may be surmised that there was in early ages a domesticated distinct species of this animal in Africa. In Syria and Egypt the present races of domestic cattle are somewhat less than the large breeds of Europe, and those of Palestine appear to be of at least two forms, both with short horns and both used to the plough, one being tall and lanky, the other more compact; and we possess figures of the present Egyptian cattle with long horns bent down and forwards. From Egyptian pictures it is to be inferred that large droves of fine cattle were imported from Abyssinia, and that in the valley of the Nile they were in general stall-fed, used exclusively for the plough, and treated with humanity. In Palestine the Mosaic law provided with care for the kind treatment of cattle; for in treading out corn— the Oriental mode of separating the grain from the straw—it was enjoined that the ox should not be muzzled (Deut. xxv. 4), and old cattle that had long served in tillage were often suffered to wander at large till their death—a practice still in vogue, though from a different motive, in India. But the Hebrews and other nations of Syria grazed their domestic stock, particularly those tribes which, residing to the east of the Jordan, had fertile districts for that purpose. Here, of course, the droves became shy and wild; and though we are inclined to apply the passage in Ps. xxii. 12, to wild species, yet old bulls, roaming at large in a land where the lion still abounded, no doubt became fierce; and as they would obtain cows from the pastures, there must have been feral breeds in the woods, as fierce and resolute as real wild Uri.

P.

PA'DAN-A'RAM. [ARAM.]

PALACE, in Scripture, denotes what is contained within the outer enclosure of the royal residence, including all the buildings, courts, and gardens (2 Chron. xxxvi. 19; comp. Ps. xlviii. 4; cxxii. 7: Prov. ix. 3; xviii. 19; Isa. xxiii. 13 · xxv. 2; Jer. xxii. 14; Amos i. 7, 12, 14; Nah. ii. 6). In the New Testament the term palace is applied to the residence of a man of rank (Matt. xxvi. 3; Mark xiv. 66; Luke xi. 21; John xviii. 15). The specific allusions are to the palace built by Herod, which was afterwards occupied by the Roman governors, and was the prætorium, or hall, which formed the abode of Pilate when Christ was brought before him (Mark xv. 16): the other passages above cited, except Luke xi. 21, refer to the residence of the high-priest.

The particulars which have been given under the head HOUSE, require only to be aggrandized to convey a suitable idea of a palace; for the general arrangements and distribution of parts are the same in the palace as in the house, save that the courts are more numerous, and with more distinct appropriations, the buildings more extensive, and the materials more costly. The palace of the kings of Judah in Jerusalem was that built by Solomon, called 'the house of the forest of Lebanon,' of which some particulars are given in 1 Kings vii. 1-12; and if read along with the description which Josephus gives of the same pile (*Antiq.* v. 5), a faint idea may be formed of it, as a magnificent collection of buildings in adjoining courts, connected with and surrounded by galleries and colonnades.

PAL'ESTINE. This name, usually applied to the country formerly inhabited by the Israelites, does not occur in the Hebrew Bible. It is, however, derived from Philistia, or the country of the Philistines, which comprised the southern part of the coast plain of Canaan along the Mediterranean. The word *Philistia* occurs in Exod. xiii. 17; Ps. lx. 8; lxxxiii. 7; lxxxvii. 4; cvii. 9; Isa. xiv. 29, 31. From this arose the name Palestine, which was applied by most ancient writers, and even by Josephus, to the whole land of the Israelites.

NAMES.—The other names of the country may be given in the order of their occurrence in Scripture.

1. *Canaan*, from Canaan, the fourth son of Ham, from whom the first inhabitants were descended. It is the most ancient name of the country, and is first found as such in Gen. xi. 31. This denomination was confined to the country between the Mediterranean and the Jordan; but in later times it was understood to include Phœnicia (Isa. xxiii. 11; Matt. xv. 21, 22), and also the land of the Philistines.

2. *Land of Israel*. This name was given to the whole country as distributed among and occupied by the tribes of Israel.

3. *Land of Promise.* So called as the land which God promised to the patriarchal fathers to bestow on their descendants.

4. *Land of Jehovah.* So called as being in a special and peculiar sense the property of Jehovah, who, as the sovereign proprietor of the soil, granted it to the Hebrews (Lev. xxv. 23; Ps. lxxxv. 1; Isa. viii 8).

5. *The Holy Land.* This name only occurs in Zech. ii. 12. The land is here called 'Holy,' as being the Lord's property, and sanctified by his temple and worship.

5. *Judah, Judæa.* This name belonged at first to the territory of the tribe of Judah alone. After the separation of the two kingdoms, one of them took the name of Judah, which contained the territories both of that tribe and of Benjamin. After the Captivity, down to and after the time of Christ, Judæa was used in a loose way as a general name for the whole country of Palestine; but in more precise language, and with reference to internal distribution, it denoted nearly the territories of the ancient kingdom, as distinguished from Samaria and Galilee on the west of the Jordan, and Peræa on the east.

DIVISIONS.—The divisions of Palestine were different in different ages.

1. *In the time of the Patriarchs,* the country was divided among the tribes or nations descended from the sons of Canaan. The precise locality of each nation is not, in every case, distinctly known; but our map exhibits the most probable arrangement.

2. *After the Conquest* the land was distributed by lot among the tribes. The particulars of this distribution will be best seen by reference to the map.

3. *After the Captivity* we hear very little of the territories of the tribes, for ten of them never returned to occupy their ancient domains.

4. *In the time of Christ* the country on the west of the Jordan was divided into the provinces of Galilee, Samaria, and Judæa. Galilee is a name which was applied to that part of Palestine north of the plain of Esdraelon or Jezreel. This province was divided into Lower or Southern, and Upper or Northern Galilee. Samaria occupied nearly the middle of Palestine; but, although it extended across the country, it did not come down to the sea-shore. Judæa, as a province, corresponded to the northern and western parts of the ancient kingdom of that name; but the south-eastern portion formed the territory of Idumæa. On the other side of the Jordan the divisions were, at this time, more numerous and less distinct. The whole country generally was called Peræa, and was divided into eight districts or cantons, namely:—1. *Peræa,* in the more limited sense, which was the southernmost canton, extending from the river Arnon to the river Jabbok. 2. *Gilead,* north of the Jabbok, and highly populous. 3. *Decapolis,* or the district of ten cities, which were Scythopolis or Bethshan (on the west side of the Jordan), Hippos, Gadara, Pella, Philadelphia (formerly Rabbath), Dium, Canatha, Gerasa, Raphana, and perhaps Damascus. 4. *Gaulonitis,* extending to the north-east of the Upper Jordan and of the lake of Gennesareth. 5. *Batanæa,* the ancient Bashan, but less extensive, east of the lake of Gennesareth. 6. *Auranitis,* also called *Ituræa,* and known to this

day by the old name of Hauran (Ezek. xlvii. 16-18). to the north of Batanæa and the east of Gaulonitis. 7. *Trachonitis,* extending to the north of Gaulonitis, and east from Paneas (Cæsarea Philippi) and the sources of the Jordan, where it was separated from Galilee (Luke iii. 1). 8. *Abilene,* in the extreme north, among the mountains of Anti-Libanus, between Baalbec and Damascus. The more important of these names have been noticed under their several heads.

SITUATION AND BOUNDARIES.—Palestine is the south-western part of Syria, extending from the mountains of Lebanon to the borders of Egypt. It lies about midway between the equator and the polar circle, to which happy position it owes the fine medium climate which it possesses. Its length is embraced between 30° 40' and 33° 32' of N. latitude, and between 33° 45' of E longitude in the south-west, and 35° 48' in the north-east. The breadth may be taken at an average of sixty-five miles, the *extreme* breadth being about 100 miles. The length, from Mount Hermon in the north, to which the territory of Manasseh beyond the Jordan extended (Josh. xiii. 11), to Kadesh-barnea in the south, to which the territory of Judah reached, was 180 miles.

Palestine may be regarded as embracing an area of almost 11,000 square miles. But the real surface is much greater than this estimate would imply; for Palestine being essentially a hilly country, the sides of the mountains and the slopes of the hills enlarge the available surface to an extent which does not admit of calculation.

With regard to the lines of boundary, the clearest description of them is that contained in Num. xxxiv. From the statements there made it appears that the writer, after prolonging the *eastern* boundary-line from the end of the Dead Sea down the edge of the Arabah, to a point somewhere south of Kadesh-barnea, then turns off westward to form the southern line, which he extends to the Mediterranean, at a point where 'the river of Egypt' falls into the sea. This river of Egypt is usually, and on very adequate grounds, supposed to be the stream which falls into the sea near El-Arish.

The western border is stated as defined by the Mediterranean coast. But the Hebrews never possessed the whole of this territory. The northern part of the coast, from Sidon to Akko (Acre), was in the hands of the Phœnicians, and the southern part, from Azotus to Gaza, was retained by the Philistines, except at intervals; and a central portion, about one-third of the whole, from Mount Carmel to Jabneh (Jamnia) was alone permanently open to the Israelites.

The northern boundary-line commenced at the sea somewhere not far to the south of Sidon, whence it was extended to Lebanon, and crossing the narrow valley which leads into the great plain enclosed between Libanus and Anti-Libanus, terminated at Mount Hermon, in the latter range.

The eastern boundary, as respects Canaan Proper, was defined by the Jordan and its lakes; but as respects the whole country, including the portion beyond the Jordan, it extended to Salchah, a town on the eastern limits of Bashan. From this point it must have inclined somewhat sharply to the south-west, to the point where the Wady-ed-Deir enters the Zerka, and thence it probably extended almost due south to the Arnon, which was the southern limit of the eastern territory.

MINERALOGY.—The mountains on the west of the Jordan consist chiefly of chalk, on which basalt begins to occur beyond Cana (northward). The so-called white limestone, which is met with around Jerusalem and thence to Jericho, which covers the summit and forms the declivities of the Mount of Olives, and which is also found at Mount Tabor and around Nazareth, is a kind of chalk considerably indurated, and approaching to whitish compact limestone. ' Layers and detached masses of flint are very commonly seen in it. Besides this indurated chalk, a stone is found in the immediate vicinity of Jerusalem, chiefly towards the north, as well as towards Safet, and in other parts of the country, which, together with the dolomite formation occasionally met with, appears to be of what in Germany is called the Jura formation. Palestine may be most emphatically called the country of salt, which is produced in vast abundance, chiefly in the neighbourhood of the Dead Sea, which deserves to be regarded as one of the great natural salt-works of the world.'

Under this head it may be noted that the fine impalpable desert-sand, which proves so menacing to travellers, and even to inhabitants, is scarcely found in Palestine Proper; but it occurs beyond Lebanon, near Beirut, and in the neighbourhood of Damascus.

Palestine is eminently a country of caverns, to which there is frequent allusion in Scripture [CAVES], and which are hardly so numerous in any country of the same extent. Many of them were enlarged by the inhabitants, and even artificial grottoes were formed by manual labour. In these the inhabitants still like to reside: as in summer they afford protection from the heat, and in winter from cold and rain. Even now, in many places, houses are observed built so near to rocks, that their cavities may be used for rooms or sheds suited to the condition of the seasons. Though the country is not unfrequently visited by earthquakes, they leave behind no such frightful traces as those of Asia Minor; as the vaults of limestone offer more effectual resistance than the sandstone of the latter country.

We are glad to see so competent a witness as Schubert bear his testimony to the natural resources of the soil, which superficial observers, judging only from present appearance, have so often questioned. He says, 'no soil could be naturally more fruitful and fit for cultivation than that of Palestine, if man had not destroyed the source of fertility by annihilating the former green covering of the hills and slopes, and thereby destroying the regular circulation of sweet water, which ascends as vapour from the sea to be cooled in the higher regions, and then descends to form the springs and rivers, for it is well known that the vegetable kingdom performs in this circulation the function of capillary tubes. But although the natives, from exasperation against their foreign conquerors and rulers, and the invaders who have so often overruled this scene of ancient blessings, have greatly reduced its prosperity, still I cannot comprehend how not only scoffers like Voltaire, but early travellers, who doubtless intended to declare the truth, represent

Palestine as a natural desert, whose soil never could have been fit for profitable cultivation. Whoever saw the exhaustless abundance of plants on Carmel and the border of the desert, the grassy carpet of Esdraelon, the lawns adjoining the Jordan, and the rich foliage of the forests of Mount Tabor; whoever saw the borders of the lakes of Merom and Gennesareth, wanting only the cultivator to intrust to the soil his seed and plants, may state what other country on earth, devastated by two thousand years of warfare and spoliation, could be more fit for being again taken into cultivation. The bountiful hand of the Most High, which formerly showered abundance upon this renowned land, continues to be still open to those desirous of his blessings.'

The following table of levels in Palestine is copied from a recently published supplement to Raumer's *Palastina*' The measurements are in Paris feet, *above* and *below* the level of the Dead Sea.

	Above.
Great Hermon	10,000
Mount St. Catherine (in Sinai)	8063
Jebel Mousa (in Sinai). . .	7033
Jebel et Tyh (in Sinai). . .	4300
Jebel er-Ramah	3000
Kanneytra	2850
Hebron	2700
Mount of Olives.	2536
Sinjil	2520
Safet	2500
Mount Gerizim	2400
Semua	2225
Damascus	2186
Kidron (brook)	2140
Nabulus	1751
Mount Tabor	1748
Pass of Zephath.	1437
Desert of et-Tyh	1400
Nazareth.	821
Zerin	515
Plain of Esdraelon . . .	459
	Below.
Lake of Tiberias	329*
The Arabah at Kadesh. . .	91
Dead Sea	1312*

Some of these results are most extraordinary. First, here is the remarkable fact, that the Mount of Olives and the Kidron, and consequently Jerusalem, stand 700 feet higher than the top of Mount Tabor, and about 2500 feet above the level of the Mediterranean. More to the south, Hebron stands on still higher ground; and while it is 2700 feet above the sea on the one hand, the Asphaltic Lake lies 4000 feet below it on the other. This fact has no known parallel in any other region, and within so short a distance of the sea; and the extraordinary depression of the lake (1337 feet below the sea level) adequately accounts for the very peculiar climate which its remarkable basin exhibits. The points at Tiberias to the north, and Kadesh to the south of the Dead

---

* These measurements are in English feet, and give the results of the lines of altitude carried from the Mediterranean to the Dead Sea and the Lake of Tiberias, by the British engineers left in Syria to make a military survey of the country, when the fleet was withdrawn from the coast in 1841.

Sea, are both, and nearly equally, below the Mediterranean level, and taken, together, they show the great slope *both* from the north and from *the south* towards the Dead Sea, confirming the discovery of Dr. Robinson, that the water-shed to the south of the Asphaltic Lake is towards its basin, and that, therefore, the Jordan could not at any time, as the country is at present constituted, have flowed on southward to the Elanitic Gulf, as was formerly supposed.

MOUNTAINS.—As all the principal mountains of Palestine are noticed in this work under their respective names, it is unnecessary to offer any observations under this head.

The most important or the most distinguished of the plains and valleys of Palestine are those of Lebanon, of the Jordan, of Jericho, of Esdraelon, and of the Coast.

The Plain of Lebanon may be described as the valley which is enclosed between the parallel mountain ranges of Libanus and Anti-Libanus. This enclosed plain is the Cœle-Syria of the ancients, and now bears the name of el-Bekka (the Valley). It is about ninety miles in length, from north to south, by eleven miles in breadth, nearly equal throughout, except that it widens at the northern end and narrows at the southern. This plain is, perhaps, the most rich and beautiful part of Syria.

The Plain of the Jordan. By this name we understand the margin of the lakes, as well as the valley watered by the river. Here the heat is still greater than in the valley of Lebanon, and as water is usually wanting, the whole plain is barren and desolate.

The Plain of Jericho is but an opening or expansion in the plain of the Jordan, towards the Dead Sea. It is partly desert, but, from the abundance of water and the heat of the climate, it might be rendered highly productive; indeed, the fertility of this plain has been celebrated in every age. But of all the productions which once distinguished it, and the greater part of which it enjoyed in common with Egypt, very few now remain.

The Plain of Esdraelon is often mentioned in sacred history (Judg. iv. 13, 15, 16; v. 19; 2 Kings xxiii. 29; Zech. xii. 11; Judith i. 8), as the great battle-field of the Jewish and other nations, under the names of the *Valley of Megiddo* and the *Valley of Jezreel*; and by Josephus as the *Great Plain*. This extensive plain, exclusive of three great arms which stretch eastward towards the valley of the Jordan, may be said to be in the form of an acute triangle, having the measure of thirteen or fourteen miles on the north, about eighteen on the east, and above twenty on the south-west. In the western portion it seems perfectly level, with a general declivity towards the Mediterranean; but in the east it is somewhat undulated by slight spurs and swells from the roots of the mountains: from the eastern side three great valleys go off to the valley of the Jordan. These valleys are separated by the ridges of Gilboa and Little Hermon, and the space which lies between these two ridges is the *proper* valley of Jezreel, which name seems to be sometimes given to the whole plain of Esdraelon. The valley of Jezreel is a deep plain, and about three miles across. Before the verdure of spring and early summer has been parched up by the heat and drought of the late summer and autumn, the view of the Great Plain is, from its fertility and beauty, very delightful. The plain itself is almost without villages, but there are several on the slopes of the enclosing hills, especially on the side of Mount Carmel.

The Plain of the Coast is that tract of land which extends along the coast, between the sea and the mountains. In some places, where the mountains approach the sea, this tract is interrupted by promontories and rising grounds; but, taken generally, the whole coast of Palestine may be described as an extensive plain of various breadth. Sometimes it expands into broad plains, at others it is contracted into narrow valleys. With the exception of some sandy tracts the soil is throughout rich, and exceedingly productive. The climate is everywhere very warm, and is considered rather insalubrious as compared with the upland country. It is not mentioned by any one collective name in Scripture. The part fronting Samaria, and between Mount Carmel and Jaffa, near a rich pasture-ground, was called the *Valley of Sharon*; and the continuation southward, between Jaffa and Gaza, was called *The Plain*, as distinguished from the hill-country of Judah.

RIVERS.—The Jordan is the only river of any note in Palestine, and besides it there are only two or three perennial streams. The greater number of the streams which figure in the history, and find a place in the maps, are merely torrents or watercourses.

The Jordan. We should like to consider this river simply as the stream issuing from the reservoir of the lake Huleh, but custom requires its source to be traced to some one or more of the streams which form that reservoir. The two largest streams, which enter the lake on the north, are each formed by the junction of two others. It is usual to refer the origin of a river to its remotest sources; but in this case the largest and longest, being the most easterly of the two streams, does not appear to have been at any time identified with the Jordan—that honour having for ages been ascribed to the western stream; *this* river has distinct sources, at Banias and at Tel-el-Kâdi. It is the former of these where a stream issues from a spacious cavern under a wall of rock which Josephus describes as the main source of the Jordan.

The true Jordan—the stream that *quits* the lake Huleh—passes rapidly along the narrow valley, and between well-shaded banks, to the lake of Gennesareth: the distance is about nine miles. Nearly two miles below the lake is a bridge, called Jacob's bridge; and here the river is about eighty feet wide, and four feet deep.

On leaving the lake of Gennesareth the river enters a very broad valley, or *Ghor*, which varies in width from five to ten miles between the mountains on each side. Within this valley there is a lower one, and within that, in some parts, another still lower, through which the river flows; the inner valley is about half a mile wide, and is generally green and beautiful, covered with trees and bushes, whereas the upper or large valley is, for the most part, sandy or barren. The distance between the lake of Gennesareth and the Dead Sea, in a direct line, is about sixty miles. In the first part of its course the stream is clear, but it becomes turbid as it advances to the Dead Sea, probably from passing over beds of sandy clay. The water is very wholesome, always cool and nearly tasteless. The breadth and depth of the river vary much in different places and at different times of the year. Dr. Shaw calculates the average breadth at thirty yards, and the depth at nine feet. In the season of flood, in April and early in May, the river is full, and sometimes overflows its lower banks, to which fact there are several allusions in Scripture.

The *Kishon*, that 'ancient river,' by whose wide and rapid stream the hosts of Sisera were swept away (Judg. iv. 13; v. 21), has been noticed under the proper head [KISHON].

The *Belus*, now called *Nahr Kardanus*, enters the bay of Acre higher up than the Kishon. It is a small stream, fordable even at its mouth in summer. It is not mentioned in the Bible, and is chiefly celebrated for the tradition, that the accidental vitrefaction of its sands taught man the art of making glass.

The other streams of note enter the Jordan from the east; these are the Jarmuth, the Jabbok, and the Arnon, of which the last two have been noticed under their proper heads. *The Jarmuth,* called also *Sheriat-el-Mandhour,* anciently *Hieromax,* joins the Jordan five miles below the lake of Gennesareth. Its source is ascribed to a small lake, almost a mile in circumference, at Mezareib, which is thirty miles east of the Jordan. It is a beautiful stream, and yields a considerable body of water to the Jordan [ARNON; JABBOK].

LAKES.—The river Jordan in its course forms three remarkable lakes, in the last of which, called the Dead Sea, it is lost :—

The Lake Merom or *Samochonitis,* now called *Huleh,* the first of these, serves as a kind of reservoir to collect the waters which form the Jordan, and again to send them forth in a single stream. In the spring, when the waters are highest, the

272. [Ford of the Jordan.]

lake is seven miles long and three and a half broad; but in summer it becomes a mere marsh. In some parts it is sown with rice, and its reeds and rushes afford shelter to wild hogs.

The Lake of Gennesareth, called also the *Sea of Galilee,* and the *Lake of Tiberias.* After quitting the lake Merom, the river Jordan proceeds for about thirteen miles southward, and then enters the great lake of Gennesareth. This lake lies very deep, among fruitful hills and mountains, from which, in the rainy season, many rivulets descend; its shape will be seen from the map. Its extent has been greatly over-rated: Professor Robinson considers that its length, in a straight line, does not exceed eleven or twelve geographical miles, and that its breadth is from five to six miles. From numerous indications, it is judged that the bed of this lake was formed by some ancient volcanic eruption, which history has not recorded. Its waters are very clear and sweet, and contain various kinds of excellent fish in great abundance. It will be remembered that several of the apostles were fishermen of this lake, and that it was also the scene of several transactions in the life of Christ. The borders of the lake were in the time of Christ well peopled, being covered with numerous towns and villages; but now they are almost desolate, and the fish and water-fowl are but little disturbed.

The Dead Sea, called also the *Salt Sea,* the *Sea of Sodom,* and the *Asphaltic Lake* (*Lacus Asphaltites*), is from its size the most important, and from its history and qualities the most remarkable, of all the lakes of Palestine. It is now thought probable that before the destruction of the cities of the plain, a lake existed, which, as now, received the river Jordan, but that an encroachment of the waters, southward, took place when these cities were destroyed, overwhelming a beautiful and well-watered plain which lay on the southern border of the lake, and on which

Sodom, Gomorrah, Admah, Zeboim, and Zoar were situated.

The Dead Sea is about thirty-nine or forty geographical miles long from north to south, and nine or ten miles wide from east to west; and it lies embedded very deep between lofty cliffs on the western side, which are about 1500 feet high, and mountains on the eastern shore, the highest ridges of which are reckoned to be from 2000 to 2500 feet above the water. The water of the lake is much salter than that of the sea. From the quantity of salt which the water holds in solution it is thick and heavy, and no fish can live, or marine plants grow in it. Lying in its deep cauldron, surrounded by lofty cliffs of naked limestone rock, exposed for seven or eight months in the year to the unclouded beams of a burning sun, nothing but sterility and solitude can be looked for upon its shores; and nothing else is actually found, except in those parts where there are fountains or streams of fresh water; in all which places there is a fertile soil and abundant vegetation. Birds also abound, and they are observed to fly over and across the sea without being, as old stories tell, injured or killed by its exhalations.

On the borders of this lake is found much sulphur, in pieces as large as walnuts, and even larger. There is also a black shining stone, which will partly burn in the fire, and which then emits a bituminous smell: this is the 'stink-stone' of Burckhardt. At Jerusalem it is made into rosaries and toys, of which great quantities are sold to the pilgrims who visit the sacred places. Another remarkable production found here, from which, indeed, the lake takes one of its names, is *asphaltum*, or bitumen. Josephus says, that 'the sea in many places sends up black masses of asphaltum, which float upon the surface, having the size and shape of headless oxen.' From recent information it appears that large masses are rarely found, and then generally after earthquakes. The substance is doubtless produced from the bottom of the sea, in which it coagulates, and rises to the surface; or possibly the coagulation may have been ancient, and the substance adheres to the bottom until detached by earthquakes and other convulsions, when its buoyancy brings it to the surface. We know that 'the vale of Siddim' (Gen. xiv. 10) was anciently 'full of slime-pits' or sources of bitumen; and these, now under the water, probably supply the asphaltum which is found on such occasions.

CLIMATE AND SEASONS.—The variations of sunshine and rain which, with us, extend throughout the year, are in Palestine confined chiefly to the latter part of autumn and the winter. During all the rest of the year the sky is almost uninterruptedly cloudless, and rain very rarely falls.

The autumnal rains usually commence at the latter end of October, or beginning of November, not suddenly, but by degrees; which gives opportunity to the husbandman to sow his wheat and barley. During the months of November and December the rains continue to fall heavily; afterwards they return at longer intervals, and are not so heavy; but at no period during the winter do they entirely cease to occur. Rain continues to fall more or less during the month of March, but is afterwards very rare. Morning mists occur as late as May, but rain almost never. Rain in the time of harvest was as incomprehensible to an ancient Jew as snow in summer (Prov. xxvi. 1; 1 Sam. xii. 17; Amos iv. 7). The 'early' and the 'latter' rains, for which the Jewish husbandmen awaited with longing (Prov. xvi. 15; James v. 7), seem to have been the first showers of autumn, which revived the parched and thirsty soil, and prepared it for the seed; and the later showers of spring, which continued to refresh and forward the ripening crops and the vernal products of the fields.

The cold of winter is not severe, and the ground is never frozen. Snow falls more or less, but even in the higher lands it does not lie long on the ground. Thunder and lightning are frequent in the winter.

In the plains and valleys the heat of summer is oppressive, but not in the more elevated tracts, as at Jerusalem, except when the south wind (*Sirocco*) blows (Luke xii. 55). In such high grounds the nights are cool, often with heavy dew. The total absence of rain in summer soon destroys the verdure of the fields, and gives to the general landscape, even in the high country, an aspect of drought and barrenness. No green thing remains but the foliage of the scattered fruit-trees, and occasional vineyards and fields of millet. In autumn the whole land becomes dry and parched; the cisterns are nearly empty, and all nature, animate and inanimate, looks forward with longing for the return of the rainy season.

In the hill-country the season of harvest is later than in the plains of the Jordan and of the sea-coast. The barley-harvest is about a fortnight earlier than that of wheat. In the plain of the Jordan the wheat-harvest is early in May; in the plains of the Coast and of Esdraelon it is towards the latter end of that month; and in the hills, not until June. The general vintage is in September, but the first grapes ripen in July, and from that time the towns are well supplied with this fruit.

The climate of Palestine has always been considered healthy, and the inhabitants have for the most part lived to a good old age (Tacit. *Hist.* v. 6). Jerusalem, in particular, from its great elevation, clear sky and invigorating atmosphere, should be a healthy place, and so it is generally esteemed; but the plague frequently appears among its ill-fed and uncleanly population; and bilious fevers, the result of great and sudden vicissitudes of temperature, are more common than might be expected in such a situation.

INHABITANTS.—Under this head we present the reader with the following observations of Dr. Olin (*Travels*, ii. 438, 439):—'The inhabitants of Palestine are Arabs; that is, they speak the Arabic, though, with slight exceptions, they are probably all descendants of the old inhabitants of Syria. They are a fine, spirited race of men, and gave Mohammed Ali much trouble in subduing them, and still more in retaining them in subjection. They are said to be industrious for Orientals, and to have the right elements for becoming, under better auspices, a civilized intellectual nation. . . . . . The mercantile class is said to be little respected, and generally to lack integrity. Veracity is held very lightly by all classes. The people are commonly temperate and frugal, which may be denominated Oriental virtues. Their situation, with regard to the physical means of comfort and subsistence, is, in many respects, favourable, and under a tolerable government would be almost unequalled. As it is, the Syrian peasant and his family fare much better than the labouring classes of Europe. The people almost always appear well clothed. Their houses, too, though often of a slight construction and mean appearance, must be pronounced commodious when compared with the dark, crowded apartments usually occupied by the corresponding classes in Europe. Agricultural wages vary a good deal in different parts of the country, but I had reason to conclude that the average was not less than three or four piasters per day.' With all these advantages population is on the decline, arising from polygamy, military conscription, unequal and oppressive taxation, forced labour, general insecurity of property, the discouragement of industry, and the plague.

NATURAL HISTORY.—As all the objects of natural history, mentioned in Scripture, are in the present work examined under the proper heads with unexampled care and completeness, by writers eminent in their several departments, it is unnecessary in this place to go over the ground which has been so advantageously preoccupied. It may suffice to mention the following facts in respect to the *actual* natural history of the country.—The olive certainly was, and still continues to be, the chief of all the trees of Palestine, which seems to be its natural home. Excellent oil is still obtained from the fruit. But although the pre-eminence among the trees of Palestine must be assigned to the olive, *fig-trees* also occur in great numbers, and the plantations sometimes cover large tracts which the eye can scarcely embrace. The fruit has a peculiarly pleasant flavour, and an aromatic sweetness, but is generally smaller than that of Smyrna. The *vine*, which is now only found in some districts of Palestine, is not surpassed by any on earth for the strength of its juice, and—at least in the southern mountains—for the size and abundance of the grapes.

The first tree whose blossoms appear prior to the period of the latter rains, and open in the very deep valleys before the cold days of February set in, is the *Luz* or *almond-tree*. In March, the fruit-trees are in blossom, among which are the apricot, the apple, and the pear; in April the purple of the pomegranate flowers combines with the white of the myrtle blossoms; and at the same period the roses of the country, and the variegated ladanes (Cistus); the zukkim-tree (Elæagnus angustifolius), the storax-tree, whose flowers resemble those of the German jasmine (Philadelphus coronarius), emit their fragrant odours. The palm-tree is not now seen in the interior of the country; but it thrives well in the low lands near the coast. The tall cypress only exists in Palestine, as cultivated by man, in gardens, and in cemeteries, and other open places of towns. But as the spontaneous growth of the country, we find upon the heights and swelling hills the azarole (Cratægus azarolus), the walnut-tree, the strawberry-tree, the laurel-tree, the laurestinus, species of the pistachio and terebinth trees, of evergreen oaks, and of the rhamnus of the size of trees and shrubs, the cedrine juniper-tree, and some sorts of thymelæus; while on the

formerly wooded heights various kinds of pine-trees, large and small, still maintain their ground. The sycamore, the carob trees, and the opuntia fig-trees, are only found as objects of cultivation in or near towns; and orchards of orange and lemon trees occur chiefly in the neighbourhood of Nabulus (Shechem).

The various kinds of corn grow spontaneously in great plenty in many districts, chiefly in the plains of Jezreel and the heights of Galilee, being the wild progeny of formerly cultivated fields, and bearing testimony by their presence to the fitness of the soil for the production of grain. In addition to wheat and barley, among this wild growth, the common rye was often seen. The present course of agriculture, which is but carelessly practised, comprises nearly the same kinds of grain which are grown in Egypt. Fields are seen covered with the dhurah, or Holchus sorghum. Maize, spelt, and barley thrive everywhere; and rice is produced on the Upper Jordan and the marshy borders of the lake Merom. Upon the Jordan, near Jacob's bridge, may be seen fine tall specimens of the papyrus reed. Of pulse the inhabitants grow the chick pea, the blue chickling vetch, the Egyptian bean, the kidney bean, the *gilban* (Lathyrus sativus), together with the lentil, and the grey or field pea. Of esculent vegetables, the produce of the various species of hibiscus are much liked and cultivated. In some places the Christian inhabitants or Franks are endeavouring to introduce the potato. In the garden of the monasteries the artichoke is very common: in most districts, as about Nabulus (Shechem), the water-melon and cucumber are very common. Hemp is more generally grown in Palestine than flax; and in favourable localities cotton is cultivated, and also madder for dyeing.

Herds of black cattle are now but rarely seen in Palestine. The ox in the neighbourhood of Jerusalem is small and unsightly, and beef or veal is but rarely eaten. But in the northern parts of the country the ox thrives better and is more frequently seen. The buffalo thrives upon the coast, and is there equal in size and strength to the buffalo of Egypt. Sheep and goats are still seen in great numbers in all parts of the country: their flesh and milk serve for daily food, and their wool and hair for clothing. The common sort of sheep in Palestine manifest the tendency to form a fat and large tail. The long-eared Syrian goat is furnished with hair of considerable fineness, but seemingly not so fine as that of the same species of goat in Asia Minor. Of animals of the deer kind, Schubert saw only the female of the fallow-deer; but several species of antelopes are met with in the country.

Camels are not reared to any extent worth mentioning. Palestine cannot boast of its native breed of horses, although fine animals of beautiful shape, and apparently of high Arabian race, are not unfrequently seen. The ass of the country scarcely takes higher relative rank than the horse; asses and mules are still, however, much used for riding, as they afford a means of locomotion well suited to the difficult mountain paths of the country. Bears are very often observed upon Mount Tabor and the Lesser Hermon, as well as on the woody slopes of Mount Carmel. Among indigenous animals of the genus *felis*, we may name the common panther, which is found among the mountains of central Palestine; and in the genus *canis* there is the small *Abul Hhosseyn*, or Canis famelicus, and a kind of large fox (Canis Syriacus). In addition to these is the jackal, which is very injurious to the flocks. The hyæna is found chiefly in the valley of the Jordan, and in the mountains around the lake of Tiberias, but is also occasionally seen in other districts of Palestine. Bears are said to be found in the Anti-Libanus, not far from Damascus. A hedgehog, procured near Bethlehem, was found to resemble the common European animal. and not to be the long-eared Egyptian species. The hare is the same as the Arabian. The porcupine is frequently found in the clefts of the rocks.

Among the larger birds of prey the common vulture and the kite are oftenest seen. The native wild dove differs not perceptibly from our own species, which is also the case with the shrikes, crows, rollers, and other species found in Palestine.

Tortoises are not uncommon. Serpents are rare, and none of those which have been observed are poisonous. The Janthina fragilis, which yields the common purple dye, has been noticed near the coast. Among the insects the bee is the most conspicuous. Mosquitoes are somewhat troublesome. Beetles are abundant, and of various species.

PALM. [WEIGHTS AND MEASURES.]

PALM-TREE. The family of palms is characteristic of tropical countries, and but few of them extend into northern latitudes. In the old world, the species *P. dactylifera*, genus *Phœnix*, is that found farthest north. It spreads along the course of the Euphrates and Tigris across to Palmyra and the Syrian coast of the Mediterranean. It has been introduced into the south of Spain, and thrives well at Malaga; and is also cultivated at Bordaghière in the south of France, chiefly on account of its leaves, which are sold at two periods of the year, in Spring for Palm Sunday, and again at the Jewish Passover.

The peculiarities of the palm-tree are such that they could not fail to attract the attention of the writers of any country where it is indigenous, and especially from its being an indication of the vicinity of water even in the midst of the most desert country. Its roots, though not penetrating very deep, or spreading very wide, yet support a stem of considerable height, which is remarkable for its uniformity of thickness throughout. The centre of this lofty stem, instead of being the hardest part, as in other trees, is soft and spongy, and the bundles of woody fibres successively produced in the interior are regularly pushed outwards, until the outer part becomes the most dense and hard, and is hence most fitted to answer the purposes of wood. The outside, though devoid of branches, is marked with a number of protuberances, which are the points of insertion of former leaves. These are from four to six and eight feet in length, ranged in a bunch round the top of the stem, the younger and softer being in the centre, and the older and outer series hanging down. They are employed for covering the roofs or sides of houses, for fences, frame-work, mats, and baskets. The male and female flowers being on different trees, the latter require to be fecundated by the pollen of the former before the fruit can ripen. The

tender part of the spatha of the flowers being pierced, a bland and sweet juice exudes, which being evaporated, yield sugar, and is no doubt what is alluded to in some passages of Scripture: if it be fermented and distilled a strong spirit or *arak* is yielded. The fruit, however, which is yearly produced in numerous clusters and in the utmost abundance, is its chief value; for whole tribes of Arabs and Africans find their chief sustenance in the date, of which even the stony seeds, being ground down, yield nourishment to the camel of the desert.

273. [1. Cluster of dates; 2. flower; 3. a date; 4. section of the same.]

The palm-tree is first mentioned in Exod. xv. 27, when the Israelites encamped at Elim, where there were twelve wells and threescore and ten palm-trees. In the present day Wady Ghorendel is found the largest of the torrent beds on the west side of the Sinai peninsula, and is a valley full of date-trees, tamarisks, &c. Jericho was called the City of Palm-Trees, no doubt from the locality being favourable to their growth. Mariti and Shaw describe them as still existing there, though in diminished numbers. The palm-tree was considered characteristic of Judæa, not so much probably because it was more abundant there than in other countries, but because that was the first country where the Greeks and Romans would meet with it in proceeding southward. Hence the coins of the Roman conquerors of Judæa have inscribed on them a weeping female sitting under a palm-tree, with the inscription 'Judæa capta.'

PALSY. [DISEASES.]

PAMPHYL'IA, a province in the southern part of Asia Minor, having the Mediterranean on the south, Cilicia on the east, Pisidia on the north, and Lycia on the west. It was nearly opposite the island of Cyprus; and the sea between the coast and the island is called in Acts the sea of Pamphylia. The chief cities of this province were Perga and Attalia. Christianity was probably first preached in this country by some of the Jewish proselytes who were converted on the day of Pentecost (Acts ii. 10, 15, 38). It was afterwards visited by Paul and Barnabas (Acts xiii 13).

PAN'NAG occurs only once in Scripture, but so much uncertainty exists respecting the meaning of the word, that in many translations, as, for instance, in the Authorized English Version, the original is retained. Thus in the account of the commerce of Tyre, it is stated in Ezek. xxvii. 17, 'Judah and the land of Israel, they were thy merchants; they traded in thy markets wheat of Minnith, and *Pannaq*, and oil, and honey, and *balm*' (*tzeri*, translated also *rosin* in the margin of the English Bible). From the context it is evident that wheat, oil, and honey, were conveyed by Judah and Israel, that is, the products of their country as an agricultural people, as articles of traffic to the merchants and manufacturers of Tyre, who, it is certain, must, from their insular position, have obtained their chief articles of diet from the neighbouring land of Syria. It is probable, therefore, that *pannaq* and *tzeri*, whatever they may have been, were the produce of Palestine, or at least of Syria Some have considered *pannaq* to indicate *balsam*, others *cassia*, and some again *sweetmeats*. The Syrian version renders it by a word which signifies millet. The variety and conflicting character of these interpretations are a sufficient proof that *pannag* must still be considered undetermined.

PAPER, PAPYRUS. [WRITING.]

PA'PHOS, a city of Cyprus, at the western extremity of the island, and the seat of the Roman governor. That officer, when Paul visited the place, was named Sergius Paulus, who was converted through the preaching of the apostle and the miracle performed on Elymas (Acts xiii. 6-11). Paphos was celebrated for a temple of Venus, whose infamous rites were still practised here 400 years afterwards, notwithstanding the success of Paul, Barnabas, and others, in preaching the Gospel. Paphos is now a poor and inconsiderable place, but gives its name to a Greek bishopric.

PARABLE. The word parable denotes 1. an obscure or enigmatical saying, *e. g.* Ps. xlix. 4; lxxviii. 2.

2. It denotes a fictitious narrative, invented for the purpose of conveying truth in a less offensive or more engaging form than that of direct assertion. Of this sort is the parable by which Nathan reproved David (2 Sam. xii. 2, 3). To this class also belong the parables of Christ. 3. Any discourse expressed in figurative, poetical, or highly ornamented diction is called a *parable*. Thus it is said. 'Balaam took up his *parable*' (Num. xxiii. 7); and, 'Job continued his parable' (Job xxvii. 1).

In the New Testament the word seems to have a more restricted signification, being generally employed in the second sense mentioned above, viz., to denote a fictitious narrative, under which is veiled some important truth. Another meaning which the word occasionally bears in the New Testament is that of a *type* or *emblem*, as in Heb. ix. 9, where the original word is rendered in our version *figure*.

The excellence of a parable depends on the propriety and force of the comparison on which it is founded; on the general fitness and harmony of its parts; on the obviousness of its main scope or design; on the beauty and conciseness of the style in which it is expressed; and on its adaptation to the circumstances and capacities of the hearers. If the illustration is drawn from an object obscure or little known, it will throw no light on the point to be illustrated. If the resemblance is forced and inobvious, the mind is per-

plexed and disappointed in seeking for it. We must be careful, however, not to insist on too minute a correspondence of the objects compared. It is not to be expected that the resemblance will hold good in every particular; but it is sufficient if the agreement exists in those points on which the main scope of the parable depends.

If we test the parables of the Old Testament by the rules above laid down, we shall not find them wanting in any excellence belonging to this species of composition. What can be more forcible, more persuasive, and more beautiful than the parables of Jotham (Judg. ix. 7-15), of Nathan (2 Sam. xii. 1-14), of Isaiah (v. 1-5), and of Ezekiel (xix 1-9)?

But the parables uttered by our Saviour claim pre-eminence over all others on account of their number, variety, appositeness, and beauty. Indeed it is impossible to conceive of a mode of instruction better fitted to engage the attention, interest the feelings, and impress the conscience, than that which our Lord adopted. Among its advantages may be mentioned the following:—.

1. It secured the attention of multitudes who would not have listened to truth conveyed in the form of abstract propositions.

2. This mode of teaching was one with which the Jews were familiar and for which they entertained a preference.

3. Some truths which, if openly stated, would have been opposed by a barrier of prejudice, were in this way insinuated, as it were, into men's minds, and secured their assent unawares.

4. The parabolic style was well adapted to conceal Christ's meaning from those who, through obstinacy and perverseness, were indisposed to receive it. This is the meaning of Isaiah in the passage quoted in Matt. xiii. 13. Not that the truth was ever hidden from those who sincerely sought to know it; but it was wrapped in just enough of obscurity to veil it from those who 'had pleasure in unrighteousness,' and who would 'not come to the light lest their deeds should be reproved.' In accordance with strict justice, such were 'given up to strong delusions, that they might believe a lie.' '*With the upright man thou wilt show thyself upright; with the froward thou wilt show thyself froward.*'

The *scope* or *design* of Christ's parables is sometimes to be gathered from his own express declaration, as in Luke xii. 16-20; xiv. 11; xvi. 9. In other cases it must be sought by considering the context, the circumstances in which it was spoken, and the features of the narrative itself, *i. e.* the *literal* sense. For the right understanding of this, an acquaintance with the customs of the people, with the productions of their country, and with the events of their history, is often desirable. Most of our Lord's parables, however, admit of no doubt as to their main scope, and are so simple and perspicuous that 'he who runs may read,' 'if there be first a willing mind.' To those more difficult of comprehension, more thought and study should be given, agreeably to the admonition prefixed to some of them by our Lord himself, 'Whoso heareth, let him understand.'

PAR'ADISE, the term which by long and extensive use has been employed to designate the GARDEN *of* Eden, the first dwelling-place of human beings. The word was used by Xenophon

                                          2 T

and Plutarch to signify an extensive plot of ground, enclosed with a strong fence or wall, abounding in trees, shrubs, plants, and garden culture, and in which choice animals were kept in different ways of restraint or freedom, according as they were ferocious or peaceable; thus answering very closely to our English word *park*, with the addition of *gardens*, a *menagerie*, and an *aviary*.

From its original meaning the term came by degrees to be employed as a metaphor for the abstract idea of exquisite delight, and then was transferred still higher to denote the happiness of the righteous in the future state. The origin of this application must be assigned to the Jews of the middle period between the Old and the New Testament. The Talmudical writings contain frequent references to *Paradise* as the immortal heaven, to which the spirits of the just are admitted immediately upon the liberation from the body.

Hence we see that it was in the acceptation of the current Jewish phraseology that the expression was used by our Lord and the apostles: 'To-day thou shalt be with me in Paradise,' 'He was caught up into Paradise;' 'The tree of life, which is in the Paradise of my God' (Luke xxiii. 43; 2 Cor. xii. 4; Rev. ii. 7).

EDEN is the most ancient and venerable name in geography, the name of the first district of the earth's surface of which human beings could have any knowledge.

All that we know of it goes to show that *Eden* was a tract of country; and that in the most eligible part of it was the *Paradise*, the garden of all delights, in which the Creator was pleased to place his new and pre-eminent creature, with the inferior beings for his sustenance and solace.

Upon the question of the exact geographical position of Eden, dissertations innumerable have been written. Many authors have given descriptive lists of them, with arguments for and against each. But we more than doubt the possibility of finding any locality that will answer to all the conditions of the problem. That *Phrat* is the Euphrates, and *Hiddekel* the Tigris, is agreed, with scarcely an exception; but in determining the two other rivers, great diversity of opinion exists; and, to our apprehension, satisfaction is and must remain unattainable, from the impossibility of making the evidence to cohere in all its parts. It has been remarked that this difficulty might have been expected, and is obviously probable, from the geological changes that may have taken place, and especially in connection with the deluge. This remark would not be applicable, to the extent that is necessary for the argument, except upon the supposition before mentioned, that the earlier parts of the book of Genesis consist of primeval documents, even antediluvian, and that this is one of them. There is reason to think that *since the deluge* the face of the country cannot have undergone any change approaching to what the hypothesis of a postdiluvian composition would require. But we think it highly probable that the principal of the immediate causes of the deluge, the 'breaking up of the fountains of the great deep,' was a subsidence of 'a large part or parts of the land between the inhabited tract (which we humbly venture to place in E. long. from Greenwich, 30° to 90°, and N. lat. 25°

to 40°) and the sea which lay to the south; or an elevation of the bed of that sea. Either of these occurrences, produced by volcanic causes, or both of them conjointly or successively, would be adequate to the production of the awful deluge, and the return of the waters would be effected by an elevation of some part of the district which had been submerged; and that part could scarcely fail to be charged with animal remains. Now the recent geological researches of Dr. Falconer and Capt. Cautley have brought to light bones, more or less mineralized, of the giraffe in the Sewalik range of hills, which seems to be a branch of the Himalaya, westward of the river Jumna. But the giraffe is not an animal that can live in a mountainous region, or even on the skirts of such a region; its subsistence and its safety require 'an open country and broad plains to roam over.' The present position, therefore, of these fossil remains, lodged in ravines and vales among the peaks, at vast elevations, leads to the supposition of a late elevation of extensive plains.

Thus we seem to have a middle course pointed out between the two extremes; the one, that by the deluge, the ocean and the land were made to exchange places for permanency; the other, that very little alteration was produced in the configuration of the earth's surface. Indeed, such alteration might not be considerable in places very distant from the focus of elevation; but near that central district it could not but be very great. An alteration of level, five hundred times less than that effected by the upthrow of the Himalayas, would change the beds of many rivers, and quite obliterate others.

From all we can learn, then, of the Garden of Eden, it appears to have been a tract of country, the finest imaginable, lying probably between the 33rd and the 37th degree of N. latitude, of such moderate elevation, and so adjusted, with respect to mountain ranges and water-sheds and forests, as to preserve the most agreeable and salubrious conditions of temperature and all atmospheric changes. Its surface must therefore have been constantly diversified by hill and plain. From its hill-sides, between the croppings out of their strata, springs trickled out, whose streamlets, joining in their courses, formed at the bottom small rivers, which again receiving other streams (which had in the same way flowed down from the higher grounds), became, in the bottom of every valley, a more considerable river. These valleys inosculated, as must consequently their contained streams; wider valleys or larger plains appeared; the river of each united itself with that of its next neighbour; others contributed their waters as the augmenting stream proceeded; and finally it quitted the land of Eden, to continue its course to some sea, or to lose its waters by the evaporation of the atmosphere or the absorption of the sandy desert. In the finest part of this land of Eden, the Creator had formed an enclosure, probably by rocks and forests and rivers, and had filled it with every product of nature conducive to use and happiness. Due moisture, of both the ground and the air, was preserved by the streamlets from the nearest hills, and the rivulets from the more distant; and such streamlets and rivulets, collected according to the levels of the surrounding country ('it proceeded from Eden') flowed off afterwards in four larger streams, each of which thus became the source of a great river.

With regard to its locality. after the explication we have given it may seem the most suitable to look for the site of Paradise on the south of Armenia. From this opinion few, we think, will dissent.

PA'RAN, a name which seems to be applied in Scripture to the whole of the desert region extending from the frontiers of Judah to the borders of Sinai. The name is still preserved in that of Wady *Feiran*, a valley of the lower Sinai, through which lay the road which appears to have been taken by the Israelites in their march to the upper region. In this valley there are ruins of a town, and indeed of more than one, with towers, aqueducts, and sepulchral excavations; and here Rüppell found the remains of a church, which he assigns to the fifth century. This was the Pharan or Faran which had a Christian population, and was the seat of a bishopric so early as A.D. 400.

PARCHMENT. [WRITING.]

PARLOUR. [HOUSE.]

PAR'MENAS, one of the seven first deacons of the church formed at Jerusalem (Acts vi. 5). Nothing more is known of him; but the Roman martyrologies allege that he suffered martyrdom under Trajan.

PAR'THIA, the country of the Parthians, mentioned in Acts ii. 9, as being, with their neighbours the Medes and Elamites, present at Jerusalem on the day of Pentecost. The persons referred to were Jews from Parthia, and the passage is a strong evidence showing how widely spread were members of the Hebrew family in the first century of our era. The term originally referred to a small mountainous district lying to the northeast of Media. Afterwards it came to be applied to the great Parthian kingdom, into which this province expanded. Parthia Proper, or Ancient Parthia, lying between Aria and Hyrcania, the residence of a rude and poor tribe, and traversed by bare mountains, woods, and sandy steppes, formed a part of the great Persian monarchy, being a dependency on the satrapy of Hyrcania. Its inhabitants were of Scythian origin. They formed a part of the army of Xerxes, and were found in that of the last Darius. In the breaking up of the kingdom of Alexander the Parthians took sides with Eumenes, and became subject to Antigonus and the Seleucidæ. About 256 years before Christ Arsaces rose against the Syro-Macedonian power, and commenced a new dynasty in his own person, designated by the title of Arsacidæ. This was the beginning of the great Parthian empire, which extended itself in the early days of Christianity over all the provinces of what had been the Persian kingdom, having the Euphrates for its western boundary, by which it was separated from the dominions of Rome. It was divided into eighteen provinces. Now at peace, now in bitter hostilities with Rome, now the victor and now the vanquished, the Parthians were never subjugated by the Romans. At length Artaxerxes founded a new dynasty. Representing himself as a descendant of the ancient Persian kings, and calling upon the Persians to recover their independence, he raised a large army, defeated the Parthians in a great battle, succeeded to all the dominions of the Parthian kings, and founded the new Persian empire, to the rulers of which is commonly given the name of the Sassanidæ. The government of Parthia was monarchical; but as there was no settled and recognised line of succession, rival aspirants were constantly presenting themselves, which weakened the country with internal broils, especially as the Romans saw it to be their interest to foster dissensions and encourage rivalries, and led eventually to the overthrow of the dynasty in the case of the successful aspirant Artaxerxes. During the Syro-Macedonian period the Parthian and Jewish history kept apart in separate spheres, but under the Romans the Parthians defended the party of Antigonus against Hyrcanus, and even took and plundered Jerusalem.

PARTRIDGE (1 Sam. xxvi. 20; Jer. xvii. 11; Ecclus. xi. 31). Late commentators state that there are four species of the *tetrao* (grouse) of Linnæus abundant in Palestine; the francolin (*T. francolinus*), the katta (*T. alchata*), the red-legged or Barbary partridge (*T. petrosus*), and the Greek partridge (*T. saxatilis*). In this now obsolete classification there are included not less than three genera, according to the more correct systems of recent writers, and not one strictly a grouse occurs in the number, though the real *T. Urogallus*, or cock of the woods, is reported to frequent Asia Minor in winter, and in that case is probably no stranger in Libanus. There is, however, the genus *Pterocles*, of which the *P. alchata* is the katta, ganga, cata, and pin-tailed grouse of authors, a species very common in Palestine, and innumerable in Arabia; but it is not the only one, for the sand-grouse of Latham (*P. arenarius*) occurs in France, Spain, Barbary, Arabia, Persia, and on the north side of the Mediterranean, or all round Palestine. *P. Arabicus*, and probably *P. exustus*, or the Arabian and singed gangas, occur equally in the open districts of the south, peopling the desert along with the ostrich. All are distinguished from other genera of *Tetraonidæ* by their long and powerful wings, enabling them to reach water, which they delight to drink in abundance; and by this propensity they often indicate to the thirsty caravan in what direction to find relief. They feed more on insects, larvæ, and worms than on seeds, and none of the species having a perfect hind toe that reaches the ground, they run fast: these characteristics are of some importance in determining whether they were held to be really clean birds, and consequently could be the *selav* of the Israelites, which our versions have rendered 'quail' [QUAIL; UNCLEAN BIRDS].

The Francolin forms a second genus, whereof the common tree-partridge is the Syrian species best known, though most likely not the only one of that country. It is larger than the ganga; the male is always provided with one pair of spurs (though others of the genus have two), and has the tail longer than true partridges. This species is valued for the table, is of handsome plumage, and common from Spain and France, on both sides of the Mediterranean, eastward to Bengal.

The partridge is a third genus, reckoning in Syria the two species before named, both red-legged and furnished with orange and black crescents on the sides; but the other markings differ, and the Barbary species is smaller than the Greek. They are inferior in delicacy to the common partridge, and it is probable that *Perdix rufa*, and the Caspian partridge, both resembling

the former in many particulars, are no strangers in Syria.

The expostulation of David with Saul, where he says, 'The king of Israel is come out to seek a flea, as when one doth hunt a partridge on the mountains,' is perfectly natural, for the red-legged partridges are partial to upland brush-wood, which is not an uncommon character of

the hills and mountains of Palestine; and the koria sitting on her eggs and not hatching them Jer. xvii. 11), we take to allude to the liability of the nest being trodden under foot, or robbed by carnivorous animals, notwithstanding all the care and interesting manœuvres of the parent birds to save it or the brood; for this genus is monogamous, nestles on the ground, and both male and female sit and anxiously watch over the safety of their young.

PARVA'IM, a region producing the finest gold (2 Chron. iii. 6). There is very strong reason to conclude, with Bochart, that it is the same with Ophir.

1. PASH'UR, son of Immer, a priest, and chief overseer of the Temple, who smote Jeremiah and put him in the stocks for his prophecies of captivity and ruin; on which the prophet was commissioned to declare that he should be one of those to go into exile, and that he and all his friends should die in Babylon, and be buried there (Jer. xx. 1-6).

2. PASHUR, son of Melchiah, a high officer of

king Zedekiah, and one of those at whose instance Jeremiah was cast into prison (Jer. xxi. 1; xxxviii. 1-6). A descendant of his is mentioned among the new colonists of Jerusalem after the captivity (Neh. xi. 12).

PASS'OVER. The Passover, like the sabbath and other institutions, had a two-fold reference—historical and typical. As a commemorative institution it was designed to preserve amongst the Hebrews a grateful sense of their redemption from Egyptian bondage, and of the protection granted to their first-born on the night when all the first-born of the Egyptians were destroyed (Exod. xii. 27); as a typical institute its object was to shadow forth the great facts and consequences of the Christian Sacrifice (1 Cor. v. 7).

The word PASSOVER has three general acceptations in Scripture. 1st. It denotes the yearly solemnity celebrated on the 14th day of Nisan or Abib, which was strictly the *Passover of the Lamb*, for on that day the Israelites were commanded to roast the lamb and eat it in their own houses; 2nd. It signifies that yearly festivity, celebrated on the 15th of Nisan, which may be called the *Feast of the Passover* (Deut. xvi. 2; Num. xxviii. 16, 17); 3rd. It denotes the whole solemnity, commencing on the 14th, and ending on the 21st day of Nisan (Luke xxii. 1). The paschal lamb, in the age following the first institution of the Passover in Egypt, and after the settlement of the Hebrews in Palestine, could only be killed by the priests in the court of the temple (Deut. xvi. 5-7; 2 Chron. xxxv. 1-11, Lev. xvii. 3-6), whence the owner of the lamb received it from the priests, and 'brought it to his house *in Jerusalem*, and roasted it, and ate it in the evening,' and it was thus that Christ kept the Passover, eating it in a chamber within Jerusalem (Luke xxii. 7-11); but the feast of *unfermented things* (Exod. xii. 15) the Jews thought themselves bound to keep in every place in which they might dwell, if they could not visit Jerusalem. As, however, from the evening of the 14th to the 21st day of Abib or Nisan (April), all ferment was banished from the habitations of the Hebrews, both institutions thus received a common name (1 Cor. v. 5, 7, 8, 13).

On the 10th of the month Abib, the master of a family separated a ram or a goat of a year old, without blemish (Exod. xii. 1-6; 1 Pet. i. 19), which was slain on the 14th day, *between the two evenings*, before the altar (Deut. xvi. 2, 5, 6).*

---

* The Jewish day had twelve hours (John xi. 9), counting from sunrise, about six of the clock of our time. The ninth hour (or three in the afternoon) was the hour of prayer, when they went into the temple, at the daily evening sacrifice (Acts iii. 1). This was the ordinary time for the Passover, as appears from the Babylonian Talmud. ' The daily evening sacrifice was killed at the eighth hour and a-half, and it was offered up at the ninth hour and a-half. In the evening of the Passover it was killed at the seventh hour and a half, and offered at the eighth hour and a-half.' Thus in the evening of times (Heb. i. 2; 1 Pet. i. 19, 20), or *last days*, about the same hour of the day when the paschal lamb was offered in the temple, did Christ die on Calvary, so that the substance and the shadow corresponded (Mark xv. 25-33).

Originally the blood was sprinkled on the posts of the door (Exod. xii. 7), but afterwards the priests sprinkled the blood upon the bottom of the altar (comp. Deut. vi. 9; 1 Pet. i. 2; Heb. viii. 10; ix. 13, 14). The ram or kid was roasted in an oven whole, with two spits made of pomegranate wood thrust through it, the one lengthwise, the other transversely (crossing the longitudinal one near the fore-legs), thus forming a cross. Thus roasted with fire, as an emblem of purification, it was served up with a bitter salad unpickled, indicative of the bitterness of their bondage in Egypt, with the flesh of the other sacrifices (Deut. xvi. 2-6). What of the flesh remained uneaten was to be consumed with fire, lest it should see corruption (comp. Exod. xii. 10; Ps. xvi. 10; Acts ii. 27). Not fewer than ten, nor more than twenty persons, were admitted to this sacred solemnity. At its first observance the Hebrews ate the Passover with loins girt about, sandals on their feet, staves in their hands, and in haste, like travellers equipped and prepared for immediate departure (Exod. xii. 11); but subsequently the usual mode of reclining was adopted in token of rest and security (John xiii. 23).

PASTURAGE. In the first period of their history the Hebrews led an unsettled pastoral life, such as we still find among many Oriental tribes. One great object of the Mosaical polity was to turn them from this condition into that of fixed cultivators of the soil. Pasturage was, however, only discouraged as a *condition of life* unfriendly to settled habits and institutions, and not as a pursuit connected with agriculture. Hence, although in later times the principal attention of the Hebrews was given to agriculture, the tending of sheep and cattle was not at any time neglected.

The shepherds who move about with their flocks from one pasture-ground to another, according to the demands of the season, the state of the herbage, and the supply of water, are called *nomades*—that is, not merely *shepherds*, but *wandering shepherds*. They feed their flocks on the ' commons,' or the deserts and wildernesses, which no settled or cultivating people have appropriated. At first, no pastoral tribe can have any particular property in such tracts of ground in preference to another tribe; but, in the end, a particular tract becomes appropriated to some one tribe, or section of a tribe, either from long occupation, or from digging wells therein. According to the ideas of the East, the digging of a well is so meritorious an act, that he who performs it acquires a property in the waste-lands around. In the time of the patriarchs, Palestine was but thinly peopled by the Canaanites, and offered many such tracts of unappropriated grounds fit for pasturage. In these they fed their flocks, without establishing any exclusive claims to the soil, until they proceeded to dig wells, which, being considered as an act of appropriation, was opposed by some of the inhabitants (Gen. xxi. 25, 26). After the conquest of Canaan, those Israelites who possessed large flocks and herds sent them out, under the care of shepherds, into the ' wildernesses,' or commons, of the east and south, where there are rich and juicy pasturages during the moist seasons of the year. 1 Sam. xvii. 28; xxv. 4-15; 1 Chron. xxvii. 29-31; Isa. lxv. 10; Jer. l. 39.

PAT'ARA, a port of Lycia in Asia Minor, where Paul, on his voyage to Jerusalem, changed his ship for one bound to Phœnicia (Acts xxi. 1, 2). Patara was at the mouth of the river Xanthus, and had a famous temple and oracle of Apollo.

PATH'ROS, a name given to Egypt, particularly Upper Egypt, by the prophet Ezekiel (ch. xxix. 14; xxx. 14) [EGYPT].

PAT'MOS, a rocky and bare island of the Ægean Sea, about fifteen miles in circumference, and reckoned as one of the Sporades. On account of its stern and desolate character, the island was used, under the Roman empire, as a place of banishment, which accounts for the exile of John thither ' for the testimony of Jesus' (Rev. i. 9) [JOHN]. He was here favoured with those visions which are contained in the Apocalypse, and to which the place owes its Scriptural interest.

On approaching the island the coast is found to be high, and to consist of a succession of capes, which form so many ports, some of which are excellent. The only one in use is, however, a deep bay, sheltered by high mountains on every side but one, where it is protected by a projecting cape. The town attached to this port is situated upon a high rocky mountain, rising immediately from the sea; and this, with the Scala below upon the shore, consisting of some shops and houses, forms the only inhabited site of the island.

Patmos is deficient of trees, but abounds in flowering plants and shrubs, Walnuts and other fruit trees are grown in the orchards; and the wine of Patmos is the strongest and best flavoured of any in the Greek islands. Maize and barley are cultivated, but not in a quantity sufficient for the use of the inhabitants, and for the supply of their own vessels and others which often put in at the great harbour for provisions. The island now bears the names of Patino and Palmosa, and the inhabitants do not exceed 4000 or 5000, many of whom are emigrants from the neighbouring continent.

PAVEMENT. [GABBATHA.]

PAVILION. [TENT.]

PAUL, originally *Saul*, was a native of Tarsus, a city of Cilicia (Acts xxii. 3, &c.), and was of Jewish descent, of the tribe of Benjamin (Phil. iii. 5). From his father he inherited the rights of Roman citizenship, which had probably been earned by some of his ancestry through services rendered to the Roman state. The supposition that he enjoyed them in virtue of being a native of Tarsus is not well founded.

At that time Tarsus was the rival of Athens and Alexandria as a place of learning and philosophical research; but to what extent the future ' Apostle of the Gentiles' enjoyed the advantage of its schools we have no means of accurately determining. It must be allowed, however, that the mere circumstance of having spent his early years in such a city as Tarsus could not but exert a very powerful influence on the mind of such a man as Paul, in the way of sharpening his faculties, refining his tastes, and enlarging the circle of his sympathies and affections.

But whatever uncertainty may hang over the early studies of the Apostle in the department of Greek learning, there can be no doubt that, being

the son of a Pharisee, and destined, in all probability, from his infancy to the pursuits of a doctor
of Jewish law, he would be carefully instructed
from his earliest years in the elements of Rabbinical lore. It is probable also that at this time
he acquired his skill in that handicraft trade by
which in later years he frequently supported
himself (Acts xvii. 3; 1 Cor. iv. 12, &c.); for
it was a maxim among the Jews, that 'he who
does not teach his son a trade, teaches him to
steal.'

At the proper age (supposed to be after he was
fourteen years old), the Apostle proceeded to
Jerusalem, to prosecute his studies in the learning
of the Jews. Here he became a student under
Gamaliel, a distinguished teacher of the law, and
who is supposed to be the person of that name who
is celebrated in the writings of the Talmudists as
one of the seven teachers to whom the title 'Rabban' was given. Besides acquaintance with the
Jewish law, and a sincere conviction of the
supreme excellence of Judaism, Gamaliel appears
to have possessed a singularly calm and judicious
mind, and to have exercised a freedom of thought
as well as pursued a range of study very unlike
what was common among the party to which he
belonged (Acts v. 34-39). It cannot be doubted
that the instructions and example of such a
teacher must have exercised a powerful influence
on the mind of the future Apostle.

We now approach the period in Paul's history
when he becomes a prominent figure on the page
of the sacred historian, and when, consequently,
the facts of his life can be more confidently narrated. He is introduced to our notice by the
sacred historian for the first time in connection
with the martyrdom of Stephen, in which transaction he was, if not an assistant, something more
than a mere spectator. Immediately after this
event he is represented as sharing the counsels of
the chief priests, and as intrusted by them with
the entire responsibility of executing their designs
against the followers of Jesus (Acts xxvi. 10, 12).
For such a task he showed a painful aptitude, and
discharged it with a zeal which spared neither
age nor sex (Acts viii. 1-3; xxvi. 10, 11). But
whilst thus, in his ignorance and unbelief, he was
seeking to be 'injurious' to the cause of Christ,
the great Author of Christianity was about to
make him a distinguished trophy of its power, and
one of the most devoted and successful of its advocates. Whilst journeying to Damascus, with
a commission from the high priest, to arrest and
bring back as prisoners to Jerusalem the Christians who had escaped thither from the fury of
their persecutors, and when he had almost completed his journey, he was suddenly arrested by a
miraculous vision of Christ, who addressing him
from heaven, demanded the reason of his furious
zeal, in the remarkable words, 'Saul, Saul, why
persecutest thou me?' Struck to the ground by
the suddenness and overwhelming splendour of
the vision, and only able to ask by whom it was
he was thus addressed, he received for answer,
'I am Jesus of Nazareth whom thou persecutest;
but arise, and go into the city, and it shall be told
thee what to do.' This command the confounded
and now humble zealot immediately rose to obey,
but as the brilliancy of the light which had shone
around him had dazzled him to blindness, he had
to be led into the city by his attendants. Here

he remained for three days and nights in a state
of deep mental conflict and dejection, tasting
neither meat nor drink, until a person of the
name of Ananias appeared at the command of
Christ to relieve his distress, and to admit him
into the Christian fraternity by baptizing him
into the name of the Lord (Acts ix. 1-18).

Immediately on his conversion to Christianity
Saul seems to have gone into Arabia, where he
remained three years (Gal. i. 11-17); and where
he, in all probability, was chiefly occupied by
meditation and study, in preparing himself for
the great work to which he had been called.
Here also we may venture to suppose he received
that Gospel which afterwards he preached 'by
revelation' from Christ (Gal. i. 12).

Returning from Arabia to Damascus the Apostle
commenced his public efforts in the service of
Christ, by boldly advocating in the synagogues
of the Jews the claims of Jesus to be venerated as
the Son of God. At first astonished, the Jews
were afterwards furiously incensed at this change
in the opinions and conduct of Saul, and in consequence of their attempts upon his liberty and
life, he was obliged to make his escape from
Damascus This he effected with difficulty by
the aid of the Christians, some of whom let him
down in a basket from the window of a dwelling
erected upon the outer wall of the city (Acts ix.
21, &c.; 2 Cor. xi. 32). After this he went up
to Jerusalem (for the *first* time after his conversion), where, on the testimony of Barnabas,
he was acknowledged as a Christian brother, and
admitted by the Apostles to that place in their
fraternity which had been assigned to him by
Christ. From Jerusalem he was soon driven by
the hostility of the Jews; when, after visiting
Cæsarea, he went to his native town Tarsus,
where his abode several years (Acts ix. 26-30).
From this retreat he was summoned by Barnabas, who, having been appointed by the
Apostles at Jerusalem to visit the church at
Antioch, where accessions had been made to the
number of the followers of Jesus from among
the Gentiles as well as the Jews, and finding the
need of counsel and co-operation in his work,
went to Tarsus to procure the assistance of Saul
(Acts xi. 22-25). After residing and labouring
for a year in Antioch, these two distinguished
servants of Christ were sent up to Jerusalem
with certain contributions which had been made
among the Christians at Antioch, on behalf of
their brethren in Judea, who were suffering from
the effects of a dearth (Acts xi. 27-30). This, as
commonly received, was the Apostle's *second* visit
to Jerusalem after his conversion.

Having discharged this commission, they returned to Antioch, accompanied by John Mark,
the nephew of Barnabas, and were shortly afterwards despatched by that church, in obedience
to an injunction from heaven, on a general missionary tour. In the course of this tour, during
the earlier part only of which they were accompanied by Mark, in consequence of his shrinking
from the toils and dangers of the journey and
returning to Jerusalem, they visited Seleucia,
Cyprus, Perga in Pamphylia, Antioch in Pisidia,
Iconium, Lystra and Derbe, cities of Lycaonia
(in the former of which the fickle populace,
though at first they had with difficulty been prevented from offering them Divine honours, were

almost immediately afterwards, at the instigation of the Jews, led to stone the Apostle until he was left for dead) ; and then they returned by way of Attalia, a city of Pamphylia, by sea to Antioch, where they rehearsed to the church all that God had done by them (Acts xiii.-xiv.). This formed the Apostle's *first* great missionary tour.

In the narrative of this journey, given by Luke, the historian, without assigning any reason for so doing, drops the name Saul, and adopts that of Paul, in designating the Apostle. It is probable from this, that it was during this journey that the Apostle s change of name actually took place. What led to that change we can only conjecture ; and of conjectures on this point there has been no lack. The most probable opinion is, that as the Romans and Greeks were in the habit of softening the Hebrew names in pronunciation, and accommodating their form to that of the Latin or Greek, they substituted Paul for Saul, and the Apostle henceforward adopted the substituted name as his usual designation.

Not long after Paul and Barnabas had returned to Antioch, they were deputed by the church there again to visit Jerusalem, to consult the Apostles and elders upon the question, which certain members of the church at Jerusalem had raised in that at Antioch, whether converts from heathenism required to be circumcised, and so become Jews before they could be saved ? The Apostle on this occasion visited Jerusalem for the *third* time after his conversion ; and after the question had been settled by the parties in that city with whom the power to do so lay, he and his companion returned to Antioch. After restoring peace to the church there, Paul proposed to Barnabas to undertake another missionary tour, to which the latter cordially assented ; but, unhappily, on the very eve of their departure a contention arose between them, in consequence of Barnabas being determined to take with them his nephew John Mark ; and Paul being equally determined that one, who had on a former occasion ingloriously deserted them, should not again be employed in the work. Unable to come to an agreement on this point, they separated ; and Paul, accompanied by Silas, commenced his second missionary journey, in the course of which, after passing through Syria and Cilicia, he revisited Lystra and Derbe. At the former of these places he found Timothy, whom he associated with Silas, as the companion of his further travels, after he had been ordained by the Apostle and the presbytery of the church of which he was a member (1 Tim. iv. 14). Paul then passed through the regions of Phrygia and Galatia, and avoiding Asia, strictly so called, and Bithynia, he came with his companions by way of Mysia to Troas, on the borders of the Hellespont. Hence they crossed to Samothracia, and thence to Neapolis, and so to Philippi, whither he had been summoned in a vision by a man of Macedonia saying, 'Come over and help us.' After some time spent in this city, they passed through Amphipolis and Apollonia, cities of Macedonia, and came to Thessalonica, where, though they abode only a short time, they preached the Gospel with no small success. Driven from that city by the malice of the Jews, they came by night to Berea, another city of Macedonia, where at first they were favourably received by the Jews, until a party from Thessalonica, which had followed them. incited the Bereans against them. Paul, as especially obnoxious to the Jews, deemed it prudent to leave the place, and accordingly retired to Athens. where he determined to await the arrival of Silas and Timothy. Whilst residing in this city, and observing the manners and religious customs of its inhabitants, his spirit was stirred within him, when he saw how entirely they were immersed in idolatry ; and, unable to refrain, he commenced in the synagogues of the Jews and in the market-place to hold discussions with all whom he encountered. This led to his being taken to the Areopagus, where, surrounded by perhaps the shrewdest, most polished, most acute, most witty, and most scornful assemblage that ever surrounded a preacher of Christianity, he, with exquisite tact and ability, exposed the folly of their superstitions, and unfolded the character and claims of the living and true God. For the purpose of more effectually arresting the attention of his audience, he commenced by referring to an altar in their city, on which he had read the inscription, *to an unknown God ;* and, applying this to Jehovah, he proposed to declare to them that Deity whom thus, without knowing him, they were worshipping.

On being rejoined by Timothy (1 Thess. iii. 1), and perhaps also by Silas, the Apostle sent them both back to Macedonia, and went alone to visit Corinth, whither they soon after followed him (Acts xviii. 5). Here he abode for a year and a half preaching the Gospel, and supporting himself by his trade as a tent-maker, in which he was joined by a converted Jew of the name of Aquila, who, with his wife Priscilla, had been expelled from Rome by an edict of the emperor, forbidding Jews to remain in that city. Driven from Corinth by the enmity of the Jews, he, along with Aquila and Priscilla, betook himself to Ephesus, whence, after a residence of only a few days, he went up to Jerusalem, being commanded by God to visit that city, at the time of the approaching passover. His visit on this occasion—the *fourth* since his conversion—was very brief; and at the close of it he went down to Antioch, thereby completing his *second* great apostolic tour.

At Antioch he abode for some time, and then, accompanied, as is supposed, by Titus, he commenced another extensive tour, in the course of which, after passing through Phrygia and Galatia, he visited Ephesus. The importance of this city, in relation to the region of Hither Asia, determined him to remain in it for a considerable time; and he accordingly continued preaching the Gospel there for three years, with occasional brief periods of absence, for the purpose of visiting places in the vicinity. With such success were his efforts crowned, that the gains of those who were interested in supporting the worship of Diana, the tutelar goddess of the city, began to be seriously affected ; and at the instigation of one of these, by name Demetrius, a silversmith, who had enjoyed a lucrative traffic by the manufacture of what appear to have been miniature representations of the famous temple of Diana, a popular tumult was excited against the Apostle, from the fury of which he was with difficulty rescued by the sagacity and tact of the town-clerk, aided by others of the chief men of the place, who appear to have been friendly towards Paul. By this occurrence the Apostle's removal from Ephesus, on which, however, he had already determined (Acts xix. 21), was in all probability expedited; and, accordingly, he very soon after the tumult went by way of Troas to Philippi, where he appears to have resided some time, and from which, as his head-quarters, he made extensive excursions into the surrounding districts, penetrating even to Illyricum, on the eastern shore of the Adriatic (Rom. xv. 19). From Philippi he went to Corinth, where he resided three months, and then returned to Philippi, having been frustrated in his design of proceeding through Syria to Jerusalem by the malice of the Jews. Sailing from Philippi, he came to Troas, where he abode seven days; thence he journeyed on foot to Assos; thence he proceeded by sea to Miletus, where he had an affecting interview with the elders of the church at Ephesus (Acts xx. 17, sq.); thence he sailed for Syria, and, after visiting several intermediate ports, landed at Tyre; and thence, after a residence of seven days, he travelled by way of Ptolemais and Cæsarea to Jerusalem. This constituted his *fifth* visit to that city after his conversion.

On his arrival at Jerusalem he had the mortification to find that, whilst the malice of his enemies the Jews was unabated, the minds of many of his brother Christians were alienated from him on account of what they deemed his too lax and liberal notions of the obligations of the Mosaic ritual. To obviate these feelings on their part, he, at the suggestion of the Apostle James, joined himself to four persons who had taken on them the vows of a Nazarite, and engaged to pay the cost of the sacrifices by which the Mosaic ritual required that such should be absolved from their vows. But this somewhat questionable act of the Apostle had no effect whatever in securing for him any mitigation of the hatred with which he was regarded by the unconverted Jews; on the contrary, his appearance in the temple so much exasperated them, that, before his vow was accomplished, they seized him, and would have put him to death had not Lysias, the commander of the Roman cohort in the adjoining citadel, brought soldiers to his rescue. Under the protection of Lysias, the Apostle addressed the angry mob, setting forth the main circumstances of his life, and especially his conversion to Christianity, and his appointment to preach the Gospel to the Gentiles. Up to this point they heard him patiently; but no sooner had he insinuated that the Gentiles were viewed by him as placed on a par with the Jews, than all their feelings of national bigotry burst forth in a tempest of execration and fury against the Apostle. Lysias, ignorant of what Paul had been saying, from his having addressed the people in Hebrew, and suspecting from these vehement demonstrations of the detestation in which he was held by the Jews that something flagrantly vicious must have been committed by him, gave orders that he should be examined, and forced by scourging to confess his crime. From this indignity Paul delivered himself by asserting his privileges as a Roman citizen, whom it was not lawful to bind or scourge. Next day, in the presence of the Sanhedrim, he entered into a defence of his conduct, in the course of which, having avowed himself a believer in the doctrine of a bodily resurrection, he awakened so fierce a

controversy on this point between the Pharisees and the Sadducees in the council, that Lysias, fearing he might be torn to pieces among them, gave orders to remove him into the fort. From a conspiracy into which above forty of the Jews had entered to assassinate him he was delivered by the timely interposition of his nephew, who, having acquired intelligence of the plot, intimated it first to Paul, and then to Lysias. Alarmed at the serious appearance which the matter was assuming, Lysias determined to send Paul to Cæsarea, where Felix the procurator was residing, and to leave the affair to his decision. At Cæsarea Paul and his accusers were heard by Felix; but though the Apostle's defence was unanswerable, the procurator, fearful of giving the Jews offence, declined pronouncing any decision, and still retained Paul in bonds. Some time after he was again summoned to appear before Felix, who, along with his wife Drusilla, expressed a desire to hear him 'concerning the faith in Christ;' and on this occasion the faithful and fearless Apostle discoursed so pointedly on certain branches of good morals, in which the parties he was addressing were notoriously deficient, that Felix trembled, and hastily sent him from his presence. Shortly after this Felix was succeeded in his government by Porcius Festus, before whom the Jews again brought their charges against Paul; and who, when the cause came to be heard, showed so much of a disposition to favour the Jews, that the Apostle felt himself constrained to appeal to Cæsar. To gratify King Agrippa and his wife Bernice, who had come to Cæsarea to visit Festus, and whose curiosity was excited by what they had heard of Paul, he was again called before the governor, and 'permitted to speak for himself.' On this occasion he recapitulated the leading points of his history, and gave such an account of his views and designs, that a deep impression was made on the mind of Agrippa favourable to Christianity and to the Apostle; so much so that, but for his having appealed to Cæsar, it is probable he would have been set at liberty. His cause, however, having by that appeal been placed in the hands of the emperor, it was necessary that he should go to Rome, and thither accordingly Festus sent him. His voyage was long and disastrous. Leaving Cæsarea when the season was already considerably advanced, they coasted along Syria as far as Sidon, and then crossed to Myra, a port of Lycia; thence they sailed slowly to Cnidus; and thence, in consequence of unfavourable winds, they struck across to Crete, and with difficulty reached a port on the southern part of that island called 'The Fair Haven,' near the town of Lasea. There Paul urged the centurion, under whose charge he and his fellow-prisoners had been placed, to winter; but the place not being very suitable for this purpose, and the weather promising favourably, this advice was not followed, and they again set sail, intending to reach Phœnice, a port in the same island, and there to winter. Scarcely had they set sail, however, when a tempest arose, at the mercy of which they were driven for fourteen days in a westerly direction, until they were cast upon the coast of Malta, where they suffered shipwreck, but without any loss of life. Hospitably received by the natives, they abode there three months, during which time Paul had a favourable opportunity of preaching the Gospel, and of showing the power with which he was endued for the authentication of his message by performing many miracles for the advantage of the people. On the approach of spring they availed themselves of a ship of Alexandria which had wintered in the island, and set sail for Syracuse, where they remained three days; thence they crossed to Rhegium, in Italy; and thence to Puteoli, from which place Paul and his companions journeyed to Rome. Here he was delivered by the centurion to the captain of the guard, who permitted him to dwell in his own hired house under the surveillance of a soldier. And thus he continued for two years, 'receiving all that came to him, preaching the kingdom of God, and teaching those things which concern the Lord Jesus Christ, with all confidence, no man forbidding him' (Acts xxi. 17; xxviii. 31).

At this point the evangelist abruptly closes his narrative, leaving us to glean our information regarding the subsequent history of the Apostle from less certain sources. Tradition stedfastly affirms that he suffered martyrdom at Rome, and that the manner of his death was by beheading; but whether this took place at the close of the imprisonment mentioned by Luke, or after a second imprisonment incurred subsequent to an intervening period of freedom and active exertion in the cause of Christianity, has been much discussed by modern writers.

If, on the evidence furnished by the allusions in the Second Epistle to Timothy, we adopt the latter hypothesis, it will follow that Paul, during the interval between his first and second imprisonments, undertook an extensive apostolic tour, in the course of which he visited his former scenes of labour in Asia and Greece, and perhaps also fulfilled his purpose of going into Spain (Rom. xv. 24-28). He probably also visited Crete and Dalmatia.

PEACOCK. A good deal of discussion has taken place respecting the precise meaning of the word which is thus rendered in the Authorized Version (1 Kings x. 22; 2 Chron. ix. 21). Some have supposed that a crested parrot is meant, others that the pheasant is the bird intended, but the weight of evidence is in favour of the usual rendering.

There are only two species of true peacocks, viz., that under consideration, which is the *Pavo cristatus* of Linn.; and another, *Pavo muticus*, more recently discovered, which differs in some particulars, and originally belongs to Japan and China. Peacocks bear the cold of the Himalayas: they run with great swiftness, and where they are, serpents do not abound, as they devour the young with great avidity, and, it is said, attack with spirit even the cobra de capello when grown to considerable size, arresting its progress and confusing it by the rapidity and variety of their evolutions around it, till exhausted with fatigue it is struck on the head and despatched.

A detailed description of a species so well known, we deem superfluous.

PEARLS. It is doubtful that pearls are mentioned in the Old Testament. The word *gabish*, rendered 'pearl' in Job xxviii. 18, appears to mean crystal; and the word *peninim*, which our version translates by 'rubies,' is now supposed to

mean coral [CORAL]. But in the New Testament the pearls are repeatedly mentioned. In Matt. xiii. 45, 46, a merchant (travelling jeweller) seeking goodly *pearls*, finds one pearl of great price, and to be able to purchase it, sells all that he has— all the jewels he had previously secured. In 1 Tim. ii. 9, and Rev. xvii. 4, pearls are mentioned as the ornaments of females; in Rev xviii. 12-16, among costly merchandize; and Rev. xxi. 12, the twelve gates of the heavenly Jerusalem are 'twelve pearls.' These intimations seem to indicate that pearls were in more common use among the Jews after than before the captivity, while they evince the estimation in which they were in later times held. The island of Tylos (Bahrein) was especially renowned for its fishery of pearls; the Indian ocean was also known to produce pearls. ' Pearls have at all times been esteemed one of the most valuable commodities of the East. Their modest splendour and their beauty appear to have captivated the Orientals, even more than the dazzling brilliancy of the diamond, and have made them at all times the favourite ornament of despotic princes. In the West, the passion for this elegant luxury was at its height about the period of the extinction of Roman freedom, and they were valued in Rome and Alexandria as highly as precious stones. In Asia this taste was of more ancient date, and may be traced to a period anterior to the Persian dynasty; nor has it ever declined. A string of pearls of the largest size is an indispensable part of the decorations of an Eastern monarch. It was thus that Tippoo was adorned when he fell before the gates of his capital; and it is thus that the present ruler of the Persians is usually decorated.

PE'KAH (*open-eyed*), the officer who slew Pekahiah and mounted the throne in his stead (B.C. 758), becoming the eighteenth king of Israel. He reigned twenty years. Towards the close of his life (but not before the seventeenth year of his reign) he entered into a league with Rezin, king of Damascene-Syria, against Judah; and the success which attended their operations induced Ahaz to tender to Tiglath-pileser, king of Assyria, his homage and tribute, as the price of his aid and protection. The result was that the kings of Syria and Israel were soon obliged to abandon their designs against Judah in order to attend to their own dominions, of which considerable parts were seized and retained by the Assyrians. Israel lost all the territory east of the Jordan, and the two and a half tribes which inhabited it were sent into exile. These disasters seem to have created such popular discontent as to give the sanction of public opinion to the conspiracy headed by Hoshea, in which the king lost his life (2 Kings xv. 25, sq.; xvi. 5, sq.; Isa. vii.; viii. 1-9; xvii. 1-11).

PEKAHI'AH (*Jehovah has opened his eyes*), son and successor of Menahem, king of Israel, who began to reign in B.C. 760. He patronized and supported the idolatry of the golden calves; and after an undistinguished reign of two years, Pekah, one of his generals, conspired against him, and, with the aid of Argob and Arish, and fifty Gileadites, slew him in the haram of his own palace (2 Kings xv. 22-25).

PE'LEG, son of Eber, and fourth in descent from Shem. His name means *division*, and is

.aid to have been given him 'because in his days the earth was divided' (Gen. x. 25; xi. 16).

PELICAN (Lev. xi. 18; Deut. xiv. 17; Ps. cii. 6; Isa. xxxiv. 11; Zeph. ii. 14).

The name *kaath* thus rendered, is supposed to be derived from the action of throwing up food, which the bird really effects when discharging the contents of the bag beneath its bill. But it may be suggested, as not unlikely, that the name is imitative of the voice of the pelican, which, although seldom heard in captivity, is uttered frequently at the periods of migration, and is compared to the braying of an ass.

Pelicans are chiefly tropical birds, equal or superior in bulk to the common swan: they have powerful wings: fly at a great elevation; are partially gregarious; and though some always remain in their favourite subsolar regions, most of them migrate in our hemisphere with the northern spring, occupy Syria, the lakes and

276.

rivers of temperate Asia, and extend westward into Europe up the Danube into Hungary, and northward to some rivers of southern Russia. They likewise frequent salt-water marshes, and the shallows of harbours, but seldom alight on the open sea, though they are said to dart down upon fish from a considerable height.

PE'LITHITES. [Cherethites and Pelithites.]

PEN [Writing.]

PENI'EL (*face of God*), or Penuel, a place beyond the Jordan, where Jacob wrestled with the angel, and 'called the name of the place Peniel; for I have seen God face to face, and my life is preserved' (Gen. xxxii. 30). There was in after-times a fortified town in this place, the inhabitants of which exposed themselves to the resentment of Gideon, for refusing succour to his troops when pursuing the Midianites (Judg. viii. 8). The site is not known; but it must have been at some point on or not far from the north bank of the Jabbok. Men of this name occur in 1 Chron. iv. 4; viii. 25.

PENIN'NAH (*coral*), one of the two wives of Elkanah, the father of Samuel (1 Sam. i. 2).

PENNY. [Drachma; Denarius.]

PEN'TATEUCH is the title given to the five books of Moses. The Jews usually call the Pentateuch *the law*.

In considering the Pentateuch, the first question which arises is—Who was its author? It is of great importance to hear, first, what the book itself says on this subject. The Pentateuch does not present itself as an anonymous production. It is manifestly intended and destined to be a public muniment for the whole people, and it does not veil its origin in a mysterious obscurity; on the contrary, the book speaks most clearly on this subject.

According to Exod. xvii. 14, Moses was commanded by God to write the victory over the Amalekites *in the book*. This passage shows that the account to be inserted was intended to form a portion of a more extensive work, with which the reader is supposed to be acquainted. It also proves that Moses, at an early period of his public career, was filled with the idea of leaving to his people a written memorial of the Divine guidance, and that he fully understood the close and necessary connection of an authoritative law with a written code. It is, therefore, by no means surprising that the observation repeatedly occurs, that Moses wrote down the account of certain events (Exod. xxiv. 4, 7; xxxiv. 27, 28; Num. xxxiii. 2). Especially important are the statements in Deut. i. 5; xxviii. 58. In Deut. xxxi. 9, 24 (30) the whole work is expressly ascribed to Moses as the author, including the poem in Deut. xxxii. It may be made a question whether the hand of a later writer, who finished the Pentateuch, is perceptible from ch. xxxi. 24 (comp. xxxiii. 1, and xxxiv.), or whether the words in xxxi. 24-30 are still the words of Moses. In the former case we have two witnesses, viz. Moses himself, and the continuator of the Pentateuch; in the latter case, which seems to us the more likely, we have the testimony of Moses alone.

Modern criticism has raised many objections against these statements of the Pentateuch relative to its own origin. Many critics suppose that they can discover in the Pentateuch indications that the author intended to make himself known as a person different from Moses. The most important objection is the following: that the Pentateuch, speaking of Moses, always uses the third person, bestows praise upon him, and uses concerning him expressions of respect. The Pentateuch even exhibits Moses quite objectively in the blessing recorded in Deut. xxxiii. 4, 5.

To this objection we reply, that the use of the third person proves nothing. The later Hebrew writers also speak of themselves in the third person. We might adduce similar instances from the classical authors, as Cæsar, Xenophon, and others. The use of the third person, instead of the first, prevails also among Oriental authors. In addition to this we should observe, that the nature of the book itself demands the use of the third person, in reference to Moses, throughout the Pentateuch. This usage entirely corresponds with the character both of the history and of the law contained in the Pentateuch. If we consider that the Pentateuch was destined to be a book of divine revelation, in which God exhibited to his people the exemplification of his providential guidance, we cannot expect that Moses, by whom the Lord had communicated his latest revelations, should be spoken of otherwise than in the third person. In the poetry contained in Deut. xxxiii.

4, Moses speaks in the name of the people, which he personifies and introduces as speaking. The expressions in Exod. xi. 3, and Num. xii. 3 and 7, belong entirely to the context of history, and to its faithful and complete relation ; consequently it is by no means vain boasting that is there expressed, but admiration of the divine mercy glorified in the people of God. In considering these passages we must also bear in mind the far greater number of other passages which speak of the feebleness and the sins of Moses.

It is certain that the author of the Pentateuch asserts himself to be Moses. The question then arises, whether it is POSSIBLE to consider this assertion to be true—whether Moses CAN be admitted to be the author ? In this question is contained another, viz. whether the Pentateuch forms such a continuous whole that it is possible to ascribe it to one author ? This question has been principally discussed in modern criticism. In various manners it has been tried to destroy the unity of the Pentateuch, and to resolve its constituent parts into a number of documents and fragments. Eichhorn and his followers assert that GENESIS only is composed of several ancient documents. This assertion is still reconcilable with the Mosaical origin of the Pentateuch. But Vater and others allege that the whole Pentateuch is composed of fragments ; from which it necessarily follows that Moses was not the author of the whole. Modern critics are, however, by no means unanimous in their opinions. The latest writer on this subject, Ewald, in his history of the people of Israel, asserts that there were seven different authors concerned in the Pentateuch. On the other hand, the internal unity of the Pentateuch has been demonstrated in many able essays. The attempts at division are especially supported by an appeal to the prevailing use of the different names of God in various portions of the work ; but the arguments derived from this circumstance have been found insufficient to prove that the Pentateuch was written by different authors.

The inquiry concerning the unity of the Pentateuch is intimately connected with its HISTORICAL CHARACTER. If there are in the Pentateuch decided contradictions, or different contradictory statements of one and the same fact, not only its unity but also its historical truth would be negatived. On the other hand, if the work is to be considered as written by Moses, the whole style and internal veracity of the Pentateuch must correspond with the character of Moses. Considerate critics, who are not under the sway of dogmatic prejudices, find that the passages which are produced in order to prove that the Pentateuch was written after the time of Moses, by no means support such a conclusion, and that a more accurate examination of the contents of the separate portions discovers many vestiges demonstrating that the work originated in the age of Moses.

In the remote times of Jewish and Christian antiquity, we find no vestiges of doubt as to the genuineness of the Mosaical books. The Gnostics, indeed, opposed the Pentateuch, but attacked it merely on account of their dogmatical opinions concerning the Law, and Judaism in general ; consequently they did not impugn the authenticity, but merely the divine authority of the Law.

Heathen authors alone, as Celsus and Julian, represented the contents of the Pentateuch as being mythological, and paralleled them with Pagan mythology.

In the middle ages, but not earlier, we find some very concealed critical doubts in the works of some Jews—as Isaac Ben Jasos, who lived in the eleventh century, and Aben Ezra. After the Reformation, it was sometimes attempted to demonstrate the later origin of the Pentateuch. Such attempts were made by Spinoza, Richard Simon, Le Clerc, and Van Dale ; but these critics were not unanimous in their results.

In the period of English, French, and German deism, the Pentateuch was attacked rather by jests than by arguments. Attacks of a more scientific nature were made about the end of the eighteenth century. But these were met by such critics as John David Michaelis and Eichhorn, who energetically and effectually defended the genuineness of the Pentateuch. These critics, however, on account of their own false position, did as much harm as good to the cause.

A new epoch of criticism commences about the year 1805. This was produced by Vater's *Commentary* and de Wette's *Beiträge zur Einleitung in das alte Testament*. Vater embodied all the arguments which had been adduced against the authenticity of the Pentateuch, and applied to the criticism of the sacred books the principles which Wolf had employed with reference to the Homeric poems. He divided the Pentateuch into fragments, to each of which he assigned its own period, but referred the whole generally to the age of the Assyrian or Babylonian exile. Since the days of Vater a series of the most different hypotheses has been produced by German critics about the age of the Pentateuch, and that of its constituent sections. No one critic seems fully to agree with any other : and frequently it is quite evident that the opinions advanced are quite arbitrary, and destitute of any sure foundation.

PEN'TECOST, the name (signifying fiftieth) given in the New Testament to the Feast of Weeks, or of Ingathering, which was celebrated on the *fiftieth* day from the festival of unleavened bread, or the Passover ; or seven weeks from the 16th day of Nisan. It was a festival of thanks for the harvest, and commenced immediately after the Passover [FESTIVALS]. It was one of the three great yearly festivals, in which all the males were required to appear before God at the place of his sanctuary. Josephus states that in his time great numbers of Jews resorted from every quarter to Jerusalem to keep this festival. This testimony affords interesting corroboration of Acts ii. 1, 9-11 ; xx. 16 ; 1 Cor. xvi. 8, in which the same fact appears. The commencement of the Christian church on the day of Pentecost, preceded as it was by our Lord's ascension, attached a peculiar interest to this season, and eventually led to its being set apart for the commemoration of these great events. It was not, however, established as one of the great festivals until the fourth century. The combination of two events (the Ascension and the descent of the Holy Ghost) in one festival has a parallel in the original Jewish feast, which is held to have included the feast of first-fruits, and of the delivering of the law (Exod. xxiii. 16 ; Lev. xxiii. 14-21 ;

Num. xxviii. 26). Indeed, this festival in some respects bears a close analogy to the Jewish one; and is evidently little more than a modification of it. The converts of that day, on which the Holy Ghost descended, were the *first fruits* of the Spirit. This festival became one of the three baptismal seasons, and it derives its name of Whitsunday, or white-Sunday, from so many being clad in white on this the day of their baptism.

1. PE'OR, a mountain in the land of Moab (Num. xxiii. 28). Eusebius places it between Livias and Esbus, over against Jericho; which shows that it was not supposed to be east of the Dead Sea, as usually stated. It has not in modern times been recognised.

2. PEOR, an idol. [BAAL-PEOR.]

PE'REZ-UZ'ZAH, a place in the neighbourhood of Jerusalem, which obtained this name (meaning 'breach of Uzzah') from the judgment inflicted upon Uzzah for rashly handling the ark (2 Sam. vi. 8; 1 Chron. xiii. 11).

PERFUMES. In the article ANOINTING we have noticed the use of perfumes in Eastern countries; and in the botanical articles all the aromatic substances mentioned in Scripture are carefully examined. Here, therefore, we have only to add a few remarks, which the scope of those articles does not embrace.

The ointments and oils used by the Israelites were rarely simple, but were compound of various ingredients (Job xli. 22). Olive oil, the valued product of Palestine (Deut. xxviii. 40; Mic. vi. 15), was combined with sundry aromatics, chiefly foreign (1 Kings x. 10; Ezek. xxvii. 22), particularly bosem, myrrh, and nard [see these words]. Such ointments were for the most part costly (Amos vi. 6), and formed a much-coveted luxury. The ingredients, and often the prepared oils and resins in a state fit for use, were obtained chiefly in traffic from the Phœnicians, who imported them in small alabaster boxes [ALABASTER], in which the delicious aroma was best preserved. The preparation of the more costly unguents required peculiar skill and therefore formed a particular profession. The *rokechim* of Exod. xxx. 25, 35; Neh. iii. 8; Eccles. x. 1, called 'Apothecary' in the Auth. Vers., was no other than a maker of perfumes. So strong were the better kinds of ointments, and so perfectly were the different component substances amalgamated, that they have been known to retain their scent several hundred years. One of the alabaster vases in the museum at Alnwick Castle contains some of the ancient Egyptian ointment, between two and three thousand years old, and yet its odour remains.

The 'holy anointing oil,' employed in the sacerdotal unction, was composed of two parts 'myrrh,' two parts 'cassia,' one part 'cinnamon,' one part 'sweet calamus,' compounded 'according to the art of the perfumer,' with a sufficient quantity of the purest olive oil to give it the proper consistence (Exod. xxx. 23, 25). It was strictly forbidden that any perfume like this, that is, composed of the same ingredients, should be used for common purposes, or indeed made at all (xxx. 32, 33).

The prodigious quantity of this holy ointment made on the occasion which the text describes, being no less than 750 ounces of solids compounded with five quarts of oil, may give some idea of the profuse use of perfumes among the Hebrews. We are, indeed, told by the Psalmist (cxxxiii. 2), that when the holy anointing oil was poured upon the head of Aaron, it flowed down over his beard and dress, even to the skirts of his garments.

PER'GA, a town of Pamphylia, in Asia Minor, situated upon the river Cestrus, sixty stades from its estuary. On a hill near the town stood a celebrated temple of Artemis, at which the inhabitants of the surrounding country held a yearly festival in honour of the goddess. Perga was originally the capital of Pamphylia; but when that province was divided into two, Side became the chief town of the first, and Perga of the second Pamphylia. The apostle Paul was twice at this place (Acts xiii. 13; xiv. 25). In the first instance he seems to have *landed* at Perga, and the Cestrus was then, in fact, navigable to the town, although the entrance to the river is now impassable, having long been closed by a bar. The site has been established by Col. Leake, as that where extensive remains of vaulted and ruined buildings were observed by General Kohler on the Cestrus, west of Stavros. It is called by the Turks Eski-kalesi.

PER'GAMOS, or PERGAMUM, a town of the Great Mysia, the capital of a kingdom of the same name, and afterwards of the Roman province of Asia Propria. The river Caicus, which is formed by the union of two branches meeting thirty or forty miles above its mouth, waters an extensive valley not exceeded in natural beauty and fertility by any in the world. In this valley, in N. lat. 39° 4', E. long. 27° 12', stood Pergamos, at the distance of about twenty miles from the sea. It lay on the north bank of the Caicus, at the base and on the declivity of two high and steep mountains, on one of which now stands a dilapidated castle. About two centuries before the Christian era, Pergamos became the residence of the celebrated kings of the family of Attalus, and a seat of literature and the arts. King Eumenes, the second of the name, greatly beautified the town, and increased the library of Pergamos so considerably that the number of volumes amounted to 200,000. As the papyrus shrub had not yet begun to be exported from Egypt, sheep and goat skins, cleaned and prepared for the purpose, were used for manuscripts; and as the art of preparing them was brought to perfection at Pergamos, they, from that circumstance, obtained the name of pergamena, or parchment. The library remained at Pergamos after the kingdom of the Attali had lost its independence, until Antony removed it to Egypt, and presented it to Queen Cleopatra. The valuable tapestries, called in Latin aulæa, from having adorned the hall of King Attalus, were also wrought in this town. The last king of Pergamos bequeathed his treasures to the Romans, who took possession of the kingdom also, and erected it into a province under the name of Asia Propria. Pergamos retained under the Romans that authority over the cities of Asia, which it had acquired under the successors of Attalus, and it still preserves many vestiges of its ancient magnificence. Remains of the Asclepium and of some other temples, of the theatre, stadium, amphitheatre, and several other buildings, are still to been seen. Even now, Pergamos, under the name of Bergamo, is a place of considerable importance, containing a population estimated at 14,000, of whom about 3000 are Greeks, 300 Armenians, and the rest Turks. The town consists for the most part of small and mean wooden houses, among which appear the remains of early Christian churches, showing 'like vast fortresses amid vast barracks of wood.'

In Pergamos was one of 'the seven churches of Asia,' to which the Apocalypse is addressed. This church is commended for its fidelity and firmness in the midst of persecutions, and in a city so eminently addicted to idolatry. 'I know,' it is said, 'thy works, and *where thou dwellest, even where Satan's seat is*' (Rev. ii. 13). Now there was at Pergamos a celebrated and much frequented temple of Æsculapius, who probably there, as in other places, was worshipped in the form of a living serpent, fed in the temple, and considered as its divinity. Hence Æsculapius was called the god of Pergamos, and on the coins struck by the town Æsculapius appears with a rod encircled by a serpent. As the sacred writer mentions (Rev. xii. 9) the great dragon and the old serpent, there is reason to conclude that when he says in the above passage. that the church of Pergamos dwelt ' where Satan's seat is,' he alludes to the worship of the serpent, which was there practised.

PER'IZZITE, a Canaanitish tribe inhabiting the mountainous region which they eventually yielded to Ephraim and Judah (Josh. xi. 3; xvii. 15; Judg. i. 4, 5). They were kindred to the Canaanites strictly so called (Exod. xxiii. 23; Judg. i. 45): sometimes Canaanites and Perizzites are put for all the other tribes of Canaan (Gen. xiii. 7; xxxiv. 30); while in other places the Perizzites are enumerated with various other tribes of the same stock (Gen. xv. 20; Exod. iii. 8, 17; Deut. vii. 1, &c.). A residue of the Perizzites still remained in the time of Solomon, and were by him subjected to bond-service (1 Kings ix. 20).

PERSIANS, the name of people and nation which occurs only in the later periods of the biblical history, and then for the most part in conjunction with the Medes [MEDES]—a conjunction which tends to confirm the truth of the sacred records, since the most respectable historical authorities have found reason to conclude that the Medes and Persians were in truth but one nation, only that at an earlier period the Medes, at a later period the Persians, gained the upper hand and bore sway. This ascendancy, in the case of the Persians, as generally in the ancient Asiatic governments, was owing to the corrupting and enervating influence of supreme and despotic power on the one side, and on the other to the retention on the part of mountaineers, or of tribes seated remotely from the centre of the empire, of primitive simplicity,—in laborious lives, hard fare, and constant exposure, which create patient endurance, athletic strength, manly courage, independence: qualities which in their turn refuse or throw off a yoke, and convert a subject into a conquering and ruling nation. At what precise time this great change was brought about in regard to the Medes and Persians, we are not in a condition to determine historically. With Cyrus the elder, however, begins (B.C 558) the domination of the Persian dynasty which held rule over

Media as well as Persia. Whether Cyrus came to the throne by inheritance, as the son-in-law of Cambyses II., according to Xenophon, or whether he won the throne by vanquishing Astyages, the last Median king, agreeably to the statements of Herodotus, is one of those many points connected with early Eastern history, which, for want of documents, and in the midst of historical discrepancies, must remain probably for ever uncertain.

The most interesting event to the theologian in the history of Cyrus is the permission which he gave (B.C. 536) to the captive Jews to return to their native land. After a prosperous reign of the unusual length in Asiatic monarchies of thirty years, Cyrus was gathered to his fathers (B C 529). He was succeeded by Cambyses (B.C. 529), who, according to Herodotus, reigned seven years and five months. Then came (B.C. 522) Smerdis, nominally brother of Cambyses, but in reality a Magian; and as the Magi were of Median blood, this circumstance shows that, though the Medes had lost the sovereignty, they were not without great power. Smerdis being assassinated (B C 521), Darius Hystaspis was elected king. He favoured the Jews, and permitted them to resume and complete the building of their temple, which had been broken off by reason of jealousy on the part of the heterogeneous populations of Samaria (Ezra iv. 2 : 2 Kings xvii. 24), and the influence which they exerted at the Persian court (Ezra iv. 11). The last monarch had for successor Xerxes (B.C. 485), who is probably the Ahasuerus of Esther and Mordecai. After a reign of twenty years, Xerxes was murdered by Artabanus, who, however, enjoyed his booty only for the short period of seven months. The next in order was Artaxerxes (I.) Longimanus (B.C. 465), who enjoyed his power for the surprisingly long period of forty years, and then quietly handed the sceptre over to his son Xerxes II. (B.C. 424), who reigned but two months. He was followed by his stepbrother Sogdianus (B C. 424), whose rule came to an end in seven months; thus making way for Darius Nothus, whose reign lasted nineteen years. Artaxerxes (II.) Mnemon next took the throne (B.C. 404), and is reported to have reigned forty or forty-three years (Diod. xiii. 108 ; xv. 93). His successor was Artaxerxes Ochus (B.C. 364), who occupied the throne for twenty-six years. Then came Arses (B.C. 338), reigning three years. At last Darius Codomannus (B C. 335) ascended the throne But the valour, hardihood, and discipline which had gained the dominion, and which, as the length of several reigns in the succession shows, had sustained it with a firm ard effectual hand, were almost at an end, having been succeeded by the effeminacy, the luxuriousness, and the vices which had caused the dissolution of earlier Asiatic dynasties, and among them that of the Medes, which the Persians had set aside When this relaxation of morals has once taken place, a dynasty or a nation only waits for a conqueror. In this case one soon appeared in the person of Alexander, misnamed the Great, who assailing Darius on several occasions, finally overcame him at Arbela (B.C. 330), and so put a period to the Persian monarchy after it had existed for 219 years. On this the country shared the fate that befell the other parts of the world which the Macedonian madman had overrun; but, more fortunate than that of other eastern nations, the name of Persia and of Persians has been preserved even to the present day, as the representative of a people and a government.

The events which transpired during this succession of Persian kings, so far as they are connected with the biblical history, may be thus briefly narrated:—Cyrus, having conquered Babylon, permitted the Jews to quit their captivity and return into Palestine, affording them aid for the reconstruction of their national house of worship. Under Cambyses, who invaded Egypt and became master of the land, adversaries of the Jews tried to render them objects of suspicion at the court; which intrigues, however, had full effect only in the reign of his successor, Smerdis, who issued a decree expressly commanding the building of the temple to cease (Ezra iv. 21); in which prohibition Smerdis, as he was of the Magian tribe and therefore of the priestly caste, may have been influenced by religious considerations. A milder and more liberal policy ensued. Darius, having by search in the national records ascertained what Cyrus had done towards the Jews, took off the prohibition, and promoted the rebuilding of the temple. Darius Hystaspis was distinguished for great enterprises, as well as liberal ideas. He carried the renown of the Persian arms to India, Libya, and Europe, and began the Persian attempt to subjugate Greece. What Xerxes undertook, and what success he had in his warlike undertakings against Greece, is known to all. His conduct towards the Jews, as well as his own despotism and luxuriousness, are exhibited in the book of Esther with great force as well as truth. Artaxerxes Longimanus led an army into Egypt, which had rebelled against its Persian masters. He was compelled to make peace with the Greeks. Palestine must have suffered much by the passage of troops through its borders on their way from Persia to Egypt; the new colony at Jerusalem began to sink, when the monarch permitted Nehemiah to proceed with

277. [Ancient Persian king on throne.]

full powers to the Jewish capital, in order to strengthen the hands of his brethren. Darius Nothus had to fight on all sides of his kingdom, and made Phœnicia the scene of a war against the combined forces of Egypt and Arabia. Even Artaxerxes Mnemon, though long busied with his arms in other parts, did not lose sight of Egypt, which had thrown off his yoke, and sent new Persian armies into the vicinity of Palestine. In consequence, the Jews had much to endure from the insolence of a Persian general, namely, Bagoses, who polluted the temple, and 'punished the Jews seven years.' Ochus followed the plan

of his father, subdued the revolted Phœnicians, and again fell upon Egypt. The remaining period of the Persian dominion over the Jews passed away peaceably.

The biblical books, Daniel, Esther, Nehemiah, and Ezra, combine to present a true as well as high idea of the Persian court and government. The extent of the government as represented in the book of Esther, was from India to Ethiopia, including 127 provinces. The empire was under the control of vassal princes and nobles, 'the power of Persia and Media,' under whom were governors of various ranks, and officers for every species of duty. It was specially the duty of seven ministers of state ('chamberlains') to serve in the immediate presence of the monarch. Other officers, however high in rank, were admitted to the royal person only through the barriers of a strictly-observed ceremonial. Even the prime minister himself, and the favoured concubine who was honoured with the title of queen, durst come no nearer than the outer court, unless, on making

278. [Ancient Persian guards.]

their appearance, the king extended towards them his sceptre of gold. The gorgeousness of the court dazzles the mind, and surpasses imagination. Though the monarch was despotic, he was not strictly arbitrary. Aided by a council, controlled by a priesthood, guided by the past as well as influenced by the present, the king, much as he may have been given up to his personal pleasures, must yet have had a difficult office to fill, and heavy duties to discharge. Rulers are generally insecure in proportion to the degree of their despotism; and so we find, from the plot against the life of Ahasuerus (Xerxes, B.C. 485-465), which Mordecai discovered and made known, that even the recesses of a palace did not protect the kings of Persia from the attempts of the assassin. In the punishment, however, which fell upon the wicked Haman, we see the summary means which the Persian monarchs employed for avenging or defending themselves, as well as the unshared and unqualified power which they held over the life of their subjects even in the highest grades. Indeed it is not possible to read the book of Esther without fancying more than once that you are in the midst of the court of the Grand Seignior. Not least among the causes of this illusion is what is narrated in regard to the haram of Xerxes. The women, it seems, had a palace of their own, and dwelt there apart from the king, who paid them visits of ceremony.

The greatness of the power of the chief viziers of the Persian monarchy is illustrated in the recorded acts of Haman and Mordecai. The mode of delegating power was by presenting to the intrusted person the royal signet, which appears to have licensed him to do what he would, by such means as he pleased.

On the religion of the ancient Persians we refer to the articles MEDES and MAGI, from whom the Persians received their religion, as well as the constitution of their social state. If, indeed, the Persians, as a separate tribe in the general government of the Medes, succeeded in getting the upper hand of their effeminate masters, and wresting the sceptre from their enfeebled hands, the Medes were not without a recompense in that they perpetuated, even by the instrumentality of their conquerors, most of the higher appliances and effects of civilization to which in the course of ages they had given birth, and which have in all ages constituted the true honour of men and the best treasure of states. The oldest Persians were, however, fire-worshippers—a species of idolatry which is least removed from monotheism, and also least unpardonable in such a clime as that of Persia. That such a worship is not incompatible with the esoteric recognition of one intelligent Creator is obvious, for the fire may have been regarded, and doubtless by the wise and philosophic was regarded, as merely symbolical of the Great Power which, as imaged in the sun, quickens, vivifies, and blesses all things. But even this simple form of symbolical worship tended to corruption; and though we are unable to trace the steps of the progress, yet we know that it did gradually, in the case of the Persians, lead first to dualism, and then to gross idolatry.

The name 'Persia' is not found in the older records of the Bible, but after the Babylonish period it occurs frequently (2 Chron. xxxvi. 20, 22; Ezra iv. 5, sq.; vi. 14, sq.; Esth. i. 3; viii. 10; 1 Macc. i. 1), meaning the great Persian kingdom founded by Cyrus, which in the period of its highest glory comprised all Asiatic countries from the Mediterranean to the Indus, from the Black and Caspian Sea to Arabia and the Indian Ocean.

The Persian language was diverse from the Shemitic, and connected with the Indo-Germanic tongues, of which the Sanscrit may be considered as the eldest branch.

PESTILENCE. The terms pestilence and plague are used with much laxity in our Auth. Version. The latter, however, is by far the wider term, as we read of 'plagues of leprosy,' 'of hail,' and of many other visitations. Pestilence is employed to denote a deadly epidemic. In our time, however, both these terms are nearly synonymous; but *plague* is, by medical writers at least, restricted to mean the glandular plague of the East. There is indeed no description of any pestilence in the Bible, which would enable us to form an adequate idea of its specific character. Severe epidemics are the common accompaniments of dense crowding in cities, and of famine; and we accordingly often find them mentioned in connection (Lev. xxvi. 25; Jer. xiv. 12; xxix. 18; Matt. xxiv. 7; Luke xxi. 11). But there is no better argument for believing that 'pestilence' in these instances means the glandular plague, than the fact of its being at present a prevalent epidemic of the East. It is also remarkable that

the Mosaic law, which contains such strict rules for the seclusion of lepers, should have allowed a disease to pass unnoticed, which is above all others the most deadly, and, at the same time, the most easily checked by sanatory regulations of the same kind.

PE'TER (originally SIMEON or SIMON, *heard*) was a native of Bethsaida, in Galilee, and was the son of a certain Jonas, or John; whence he is named on one occasion in the Gospel history Simon Barjona, that is, son of Jona (Matt. xvi. 17). Along with his brother Andrew, he followed the occupation of a fisherman on the sea of Galilee. It is probable that, before they became known to Christ, they were both disciples of John the Baptist. Their becoming known to Christ was owing to John's pointing him out on the day after his baptism to Andrew and another disciple (probably the evangelist John), as 'the Lamb of God;' on which they immediately followed Christ, and spent some time in receiving his instructions. Shortly after this, Andrew finding Simon, carried him to Christ, who, on receiving him as his disciple, bestowed upon him that surname by which he has since that time been most commonly designated: 'When Jesus beheld him he said, Thou art Simon the son of Jona; thou shalt be called Cephas, which is by interpretation a stone.' After this interview the two brothers seem to have returned to their usual occupation for a season, as we have an account in Matthew (iv. 18-20) of their being summoned from that occupation by Christ on a subsequent occasion, posterior to his temptation in the wilderness, and to the commencement of his public ministry as a religious teacher. From this time forward they were his devoted and admiring followers. In the course of the evangelical history several anecdotes of Peter are incidentally recorded, for the purpose, doubtless, principally of illustrating the character and teaching of our Lord, but which tend also to throw light upon the history and character of his attached disciple. Such are the accounts furnished by the evangelists of his walking upon the agitated waters of the sea of Galilee to meet his master (Matt. xiv. 22-31; Mark vi. 45-50); of his bold and intelligent avowals of the undoubted Messiahship of Jesus, notwithstanding the difficulties which he, along with the rest of the disciples, felt in reconciling what they saw in him with what they had fondly expected the Christ to be (Matt. xvi. 13-20); of his rash but affectionate rebuke of his Lord for speaking of suffering and death as in prospect for him, and as forming a necessary part of his mediatorial work (Matt. xvi. 21-23); of his conduct in first rejecting, with an earnestness bordering on horror, the offer of Christ to wash his feet, and then, when the symbolical nature of that act had been explained to him, his over-ardent zeal that not his feet only, but also his hands and his head, might be washed (John xiii. 4-10); of his bold and somewhat vaunting avowal of attachment to his Master, and his determination never to forsake him, followed by his disgraceful denial of Jesus in the hour of trial (John xiii. 36, 37; Mark xiv. 29, &c.); of his deep and poignant contrition for this sin (Matt. xxvi. 75); and of his Lord's ample forgiveness of his offence, after he had received from him a profession of attachment as strong and as frequently repeated as his former denial of him

(John xxi. 15-18). From these notices it is easy to gather a tolerably correct conception of the predominating features of the apostle's character up to this period. He seems to have been a man of undoubted piety, of ardent attachment to his Master, and of great zeal for what he deemed his Master's honour; but, at the same time, with a mind rather quick than accurate in its apprehensions, and with feelings rather hasty in their impulse than determined and continuous in their exercise. Hence his readiness in avowing his opinions, and his rashness in forming them; and hence also the tendency which beset his honest openness to degenerate into bravado, and his determinations of valour to evaporate into cowardice at appalling forms of danger. His fall, however, and his subsequent restoration. connected as these were with the mysterious events of his Master's crucifixion and resurrection, and with the new light which had by them been cast around his character and work, produced a powerful change for the better upon the apostle's mind. From this time forward he comes before us under a new aspect. A sober dignity and firmness of purpose have displaced his former hasty zeal; sagacity and prudence characterize his conduct; and whilst his love to his Master shows no symptom of abatement, it displays itself rather in active labour and much-enduring patience in his service, than in loud protestations or extravagant exhibitions of attachment. In the subsequent Scripture history he is presented to us as the courageous herald of the kingdom of Christ, by whose mouth the first public declaration of salvation through the crucified Jesus was made to the people; by whose advice and counsel the early churches were planted and governed; and by whom the prejudices of Judaism were first fairly surmounted, and the Gospel preached in all its universal freeness to the Gentile world. The Acts of the Apostles contain recitals of many interesting incidents which befell him whilst engaged in those efforts. Of these, the chief are his imprisonment and trial before the Sanhedrim for preaching Christ, and his bold avowal of his determination to persist in that work (Acts iv. 1-22); his miraculously inflicting the punishment of death on the infatuated couple who had dared to try an experiment upon the omniscience of the Holy Ghost (v. 1-11); his visit to Samaria, and rebuke of Simon Magus, who deemed that the miracles of the apostle were the result of some deep magic spell of which he had not yet become possessed, and which, consequently, he was desirous of purchasing from Peter (viii. 14-24); the vision by which he was taught that the ancient ritual distinctions between clean and unclean had been abolished, and thereby prepared to attend on the summons of Cornelius, to whom he preached the Gospel (x. 1-48); his apprehension by Herod Agrippa, and his deliverance by the interposition of an angel, who opened for him the doors of his prison, and set him free (xii. 3-19); and his address to the council at Jerusalem, on the occasion of a request for advice and direction being sent to the church there by the church in Antioch, in which he advocated the exemption of Gentile converts from the ceremonial institutes of the law of Moses (xv. 6-11). In all these incidents we trace the evidences of his mind having undergone an entire change, both as to its views of truth and impressions of duty, from

what is displayed by the earlier events of his history. On one occasion only do we detect something of his former weakness, and that, strangely enough, in regard to a matter in which he had been the first of the apostles to perceive, and the first to recommend and follow, a correct course of procedure. The occasion referred to was his withdrawing, through dread of the censures of his Jewish brethren, from the Gentiles at Antioch, after having lived in free and friendly intercourse with them, and his timidly dissembling his convictions as to the religious equality of Jew and Gentile. For this Paul withstood him to the face, and rebuked him sharply, because of the injury which his conduct was calculated to produce to the cause of Christianity With this single exception, however, his conduct seems to have been in full accordance with the name which his Master had prophetically bestowed on him when he called him Simon the Rock, and with the position which Paul himself assigns to him, at the very time that he recounts his temporary dereliction, as one of 'the Pillars of the Church' (Gal. ii. 9, 14).

Thus far we are enabled, from the inspired documents, to trace the history of this apostle; but for what remains we must be indebted to evidence of a less explicit and certain character. Ecclesiastical tradition asserts that he performed an extensive missionary tour throughout those districts, to the converts in which his epistles are addressed. This tradition, however, though deriving some countenance from 1 Pet. v. 13, is very uncertain. Another tradition reports the apostle as having towards the close of his life visited Rome, become bishop of the church in that city, and suffered martyrdom in the persecution raised against the Christians by Nero. The importance of these points in connection with the claims urged by the Catholics on behalf of the supremacy of the pope, has led to a careful and sifting examination of the accuracy of this tradition; the result of which seems to be, that whilst it is admitted as *certain* that Peter suffered martyrdom, in all probability by crucifixion, and as *probable* that this took place at Rome, it has, nevertheless, been made pretty clear that he never was for any length of time resident in that city, and morally certain that he never was bishop of the church there.

The assertion that Peter was bishop of Rome is connected with another, by which the claims of the papacy are sought to be established, namely, that to him was conceded a right of supremacy over the other apostles. In support of this, an appeal is made to those passages in the Gospels, where declarations supposed to imply the bestowal of peculiar honour and distinction on Peter are recorded as having been addressed to him by our Lord. The most important of these are: 'Thou art Peter, and on this rock will I build my church' (Matt. xvi. 18); and, 'Unto thee will I give the keys of the kingdom of heaven,' &c. (Matt. xvi. 19). At first sight these passages would seem to bear out the assumption founded on them; but, upon a more careful investigation, it will be seen that this is rather in appearance than in reality. The force of both is greatly impaired for the purpose for which Catholics produce them, by the circumstance, that whatever of power or authority they may be supposed to confer upon Peter, must be regarded as shared by him with the other apostles, inasmuch as to them also are ascribed in other passages the same qualities and powers which are promised to Peter in those under consideration. If by the former of these passages we are to understand that the church is built upon Peter, the apostle Paul informs us that it is not on him *alone* that it is built, but upon *all* the apostles (Ephes. ii. 20); and in the book of Revelation we are told, that on the twelve foundations of the New Jerusalem (the Christian church) are inscribed ' the names of *the twelve apostles of the Lamb* ' (xxi. 14). As for the declaration in the latter of these passages, it was in all its essential parts repeated by our Lord to the other disciples immediately before his passion, as announcing a privilege which, as his apostles, they were to possess in common (Matt. xviii. 18; John xx. 23). It is, moreover, uncertain in what sense our Lord used the language in question. In both cases his words are metaphorical; and nothing can be more unsafe than to build a theological dogma upon language of which the meaning is not clear, and to which, from the earliest ages, different interpretations have been affixed. And, finally, even granting the correctness of that interpretation which Catholics put upon these verses, it will not bear out the conclusion they would deduce from them, inasmuch as the judicial supremacy of Peter over the other apostles does not necessarily follow from his possessing authority over the church. On the other side, it is certain that there is no instance on record of the apostle's having ever claimed or exercised this supposed power; but, on the contrary, he is oftener than once represented as submitting to an exercise of power upon the part of others, as when, for instance, he went forth as a messenger from the apostles assembled in Jerusalem to the Christians in Samaria (Acts viii. 14), and when he received a rebuke from Paul, as already noticed. This circumstance is so fatal, indeed, to the pretensions which have been urged in favour of his supremacy over the other apostles, that from a very early age attempts have been made to set aside its force, by the hypothesis that it is not of Peter the apostle, but of another person of the same name, that Paul speaks in the passage referred to. This hypothesis, however, is so plainly contradicted by the words of Paul, who explicitly ascribes apostleship to the Peter of whom he writes, that it is astonishing how it could have been admitted even by the most blinded zealot (vers. 8, 9). Whilst, however, it is pretty well established that Peter enjoyed no judicial supremacy over the other apostles, it would, perhaps, be going too far to affirm that no dignity or primacy whatsoever was conceded to him on the part of his brethren. His superiority in point of age, his distinguished personal excellence, his reputation and success as a teacher of Christianity, and the prominent part which he had ever taken in his Master's affairs, both before his death and after his ascension, furnished sufficient grounds for his being raised to a position of respect and of moral influence in the church and amongst his brother apostles. These circumstances, taken in connection with the prevalent voice of Christian antiquity, would seem to authorize the opinion that Peter occupied some such position as that of president in the apostolical college, but without

any power or authority of a judicial kind over his brother apostles.

PETER, EPISTLES OF. Of the seven Catholic Epistles, there are two ascribed to St. Peter. The first of these is one of those universally received in the early church. The second ranks among the controverted.

THE FIRST EPISTLE OF ST. PETER.—The external evidence in favour of the genuineness of this Epistle is complete. ' One Epistle of Peter,' says Eusebius, ' called the first, is universally received.' ' In fact,' says De Wette, ' if we except its omission in the ancient catalogue in Muratori, and its rejection by the Paulicians, it has been never called in question.'

The internal evidence is equally complete. The author calls himself the apostle Peter (ch. i. 1), and the whole character of the Epistle shows that it proceeds from a writer who possessed great authority among those whom he addresses, who were most probably composed chiefly of Jewish Christians. The writer describes himself as ' an elder,' and ' a witness of Christ's sufferings ' (v. 1). The vehemence and energy of the style are altogether appropriate to the warmth and zeal of Peter's character; and every succeeding critic, who has entered into its spirit, has felt impressed with the truth of the observation of Erasmus, ' that this epistle is full of apostolical dignity and authority, and worthy of the prince of the apostles.'

The only indication as to the place from whence this letter was addressed to the five provinces, is contained in ch. v. ver. 13: ' She in Babylon, elected with you, saluteth you.' For whether ' she in Babylon ' refers to the church or to an individual (in which latter case Peter's wife is the person generally believed to be referred to), the letter must have been written in, or at least in the neighbourhood of Babylon.

The Epistle must have been written before A.D. 67–68, the year of St. Peter's martyrdom. Lardner places the date in A.D. 63 or 64, chiefly from the fact that an earlier date than A D. 63 cannot be assigned for his arrival at Rome. Hug fixes the date in the eleventh year of Nero's reign, or A.D. 65, a year after the conflagration of the city, and five before the destruction of Jerusalem.

To afford consolation to the persecuted appears to have been the main object of this Epistle. To this the moral instructions are subsidiary. The exhortations to a pure conscience, to rebut the calumnies of the time by their innocence, to abstain from violent disputes, to pay respect to the existing authorities, to exercise increasing love and fidelity, were exhortations all given with a view to alleviate their fate, or enable them to bear it. The repeated references to the example of Jesus in his death and sufferings are designed to strengthen them for the endurance of calamities. The exhortation to the slaves, too, has reference to the unhappy days, in which, for real or imaginary wrongs and hardships, they frequently became the accusers and betrayers of their masters.

The following is a summary of the contents:—

The salutation and introduction, in which the inhabitants of the five provinces who were purchased by the sufferings of Christ, are exhorted to prepare themselves for a reward higher than the enjoyments of this fleeting life (i 1–13). They are, therefore, recommended to lay aside anything

2 U.

which could render them unworthy of Christ, the centre of their hopes, their pattern and their Saviour, and so to regulate their conduct to their superiors that none should be able to reproach them as 'evildoers.' These precepts were to extend to slaves, to whom the meek and suffering Jesus should be an example. Women, too, were to render their submissive noiseless virtue their chiefest ornament, and men should cherish and honour them. All should be full of sympathy and love, and mutual indulgence. Their innocence should be so marked as to shame the calumniator, and they should make preparation for the approaching catastrophe, when they should have an opportunity of imitating Jesus in their sufferings: hoping for them all to have no other reproach than that of being his disciples. The presbyters are enjoined to watch over their flocks, and the subordinate to pay them respect, and all should be on the watch, and lay aside their worldly cares. All these exhortations are enforced by the example of Christ, and by the punishment of the disobedient in the days of Noah, those spirits in prison to whom Christ went and preached (iii. 19, 20).

THE SECOND EPISTLE OF ST. PETER has been the subject of more discussion than any other book in the New Testament, and its genuineness has been contested by not a few of the ablest critics. We are informed both by Origen and Eusebius that though it was generally received in their time, doubts were entertained respecting its right to a place among the Catholic Epistles. Before the close of the fourth century, however, these doubts had subsided, and this epistle was received as genuine by Athanasius, Jerome, Augustine, and other eminent fathers.

It is enumerated in the canon of Laodicea (A.D. 360?), and in the 85th apostolical canon, and was finally adopted by the councils of Hippo and Carthage, which included among the canonical books all those which are now commonly received.

Although before this period certain books were rejected from the defect of historical evidence, or from internal grounds of suspicion, an undeviating uniformity now took place, and no controversy was raised respecting any of the books of the New Testament until the inquiring age which ushered in the Reformation. The genuineness of this epistle was then called in question by Erasmus and Calvin. It was, however, received by all the Reformed Confessions, as well as by the Council of Trent. It has been since that period rejected by Grotius, Scaliger, Salmasius, Semler, Eichhorn, Schmidt, Walker, Schott, Guericke, Credner, De Wette, Ullman, to some extent, and Neander. Among its numerous defenders it will be sufficient to mention the names of Michaelis, Lardner, Pott, Augusti, Flatt, Dahl, Bertholdt, who, however, rejects the second chapter; Nietzche and Olshausen, with the learned Roman Catholics Hug and Feilmoser: the latter, however, fluctuates in his opinion.

Before proceeding to consider the grounds for and against the rejection of this epistle, it may be useful to inquire into its internal structure and contents.

The writer designates himself here as the apostle Peter (2 Pet. i. 1) more clearly than in the first epistle, as personally known to Jesus (i. 14); as a beloved brother of Paul (iii. 15); and as the author of the first epistle (iii. 1). It is addressed to the same persons with the first, whom he presupposes to be acquainted with the writings of St. Paul (iii. 15; comp. Rom. ii. 4). He refers to his approaching death (i. 14). The main object is the refutation of erroneous teachers. He, therefore, as an eyewitness of the acting and teaching of Jesus, is enabled to give them more accurate instruction than those who would mislead them. He exhorts them to advance in the knowledge and doctrine of Jesus, by adding to their faith fortitude, and every other excellent quality. He denounces (ch. ii.) punishment against false teachers, by examples drawn from the disobedient angels, the world before the flood, and Sodom and Gomorrah. He inveighs against those teachers for resigning themselves to impurity, and speaking evil of God and angels, whereas angels have not ventured to do this even of Satan. He compares them to the false prophet Balaam, and to clouds filled with wind. He rebukes those mockers who doubted of the coming of Christ, which was only delayed in mercy, but predicts the dissolution of the world by fire, and warns them to keep themselves in readiness for the new heavens and the new earth.

The main reasons which induced many of the ancients to reject this epistle arose from the difference in style and structure between the first and second epistle. But in compensation for these alleged differences the resemblances are remarkably striking, and there are several words used in a peculiar sense in both epistles.

Some critics have, indeed, vindicated the genuineness of the epistle principally on the ground of resemblance in both sentiment and diction. Of these it will be sufficient for our purpose to refer to Hug and Michaelis. The former of these observes that the resemblance between the two is 'so thorough as to denote an identity of authorship;' and Michaelis had before this asserted that the agreement between them appeared to him to be such, 'that if the second was not written by St Peter, the person who forged it not only possessed the power of imitation in a very unusual degree, but understood likewise the design of the first epistle, with which the ancients do not appear to have been acquainted.' The principal difference of style, however, is found in the second chapter, the character of which is totally unlike anything contained in the first epistle. The resemblance, indeed, between this chapter and the short epistle of St. Jude is so striking, that it has been at all times perceived that one must have at least read, if not copied from the other.

All those theologians who have disputed the genuineness of Peter's second epistle, have maintained that its writer adopted the sentiments and language of Jude, and this opinion is favoured even by many of the modern advocates of its genuineness, including Olshausen and Hug. But which of the two wrote first is, notwithstanding, a question impossible to decide. 'St. Jude's Epistle is so like the second chapter of St. Peter's Second Epistle,' says Bishop Sherlock, 'the figures and images in both are so much the same,....that it has been commonly thought that St. Jude copied after St. Peter's Epistle.' This was the more generally received opinion, and was held among the ancients by Œcumenius, and maintained at the time of the Reformation by Luther. One set of critics have supposed that one of the writers of these epistles had intended to illustrate at large what the other had briefly stated; others, that one sought to abridge what the other had stated diffusely. The former of these views is maintained by Hug and Olshausen. The latter writer founds his view on the fact that Peter does not give the minute statements found in Jude, especially in regard to the history of angels; in which passages Jude alone goes into details, while Peter advances a general historical fact,—which he conceives to be characteristic of a later composition.

Dr. Sherlock, bishop of London, adopted a middle course, and endeavoured to account for the remarkable resemblance between the two writers by supposing that each quotes from a common Hebrew document. But this ingenious conjecture has been found untenable. Attempts have been made to support these arguments against the genuineness of this epistle by other alleged internal marks of spuriousness, such as the anachronisms which it is said to contain. But these arguments have been successfully combated by Nietzche, Olshausen, and other writers.

It is fully conceded that there is no other book in the New Testament against whose authority so many arguments can be adduced as against this epistle. One of the most impartial as well as ablest critics of modern times, after weighing them all, comes to the conclusion that neither its genuineness nor its spuriousness can be demonstrated by undoubted arguments; but, while he admits that unfriendly critics will see occasion for doubt, yet, relying on subjective grounds, he is persuaded of the authenticity of the epistle, and that the arguments which go to disprove its genuineness are not of sufficient weight to establish its spuriousness, or cause it to be 'stricken from the number of inspired books.'

By those who acknowledge its genuineness its date is generally fixed about the year A.D. 65. or not long before Peter's death, which they deduce from 2 Pet. i. 14. Wetstein concludes from 2 Pet. iii. that it must have been written before the destruction of Jerusalem, in which case none will allege that any but Peter could have been its author. If it were proved that Peter had Jude's epistle before him, this must have been written not long before the same period, which agrees with the time assigned by Dr. Lardner, between 64 and 66 [JUDE]. But if Jude certainly quoted the book of Enoch, and if the result of the investigation of Lucke, who concludes that this book was written in the first century, at the time of the Jewish war, and probably after the destruction of Jerusalem, be correct, this circumstance would of itself, cæteris paribus, settle the question in favour of the priority of St. Peter's second epistle [JUDE]. Bishop Sherlock maintains that there are no less than five years intervening between the date of the two epistles of Peter.

PETRA was the capital of the Nabathæan Arabs in the land of Edom, and seems to have given name to the kingdom and region of *Arabia Petræa*. As there is mention in the Old Testament of a stronghold which successively belonged to the Amorites (Judg. i. 36), the Edomites (2 Kings xiv. 7) and the Moabites (Isa. xvi. 1, comp. in Heb. ch. xlii. 11), and bore in Hebrew the name of *Selah*, which has the same meaning

as *Petra* in Greek, viz., 'a rock,' that circumstance has led to the conjecture that the Petra of the Nabathæans had been the Selah of Edom. But the consideration of that point in a work of this nature falls more naturally under the Bible head of SELAH, to which article accordingly the reader is referred; and there likewise the question will be disposed of as to whether (on the supposition of Petra being the Selah of Scripture) its site is to be identified with that of the modern *Kerek*, or with the locality of the far famed *Wady Músa* [ARABIA; IDUMÆA; NEBAIOTH].

PHA'RAOH, the general title of the kings of Egypt in the Old Testament, and found only there and in the writers who have drawn from that source. It often stands simply like a proper name (Gen. xii. 15; xxxvii. 36; xl. 2, sq.; xliv. 1, sq.; and so generally throughout the Pentateuch, and also in Cant. i. 9; Isa. xix. 11; xxx. 2). 'King of Egypt' is sometimes subjoined to it (1 Kings iii. 1; 2 Kings xvii. 7; xviii. 21); and sometimes also the more specific designation or real proper name of the monarch is indicated, as Pharaoh Necho (2 Kings xxiii. 33), Pharaoh Hophra (Jer. xliv. 30). Josephus intimates that the word signifies 'the king' in the Egyptian language (*Antiq.* viii. 6. 2). The idea has, however, been more recently started that Pharaoh corresponds to the Egyptian *phra*, 'the sun,' which is written as an hieroglyphic symbol over the titles of kings. It seems to us that this explanation might be admitted without contradicting the other, seeing that it is not only possible, but highly probable, that the Egyptians should make the name of the sun a royal title, and that at length custom rendered it equivalent to 'king.' The practice of ancient, and, indeed, modern Oriental kings, of associating the idea of their own dignity with the glory of the sun, is well known.

PHA'RAOH-HOPH'RA. [HOPHRA.]

PHA'RAOH-NE'CHO. [NECHO.]

PHAR'ISEES. The name denotes those who are separated, *i. e.* from ordinary persons, of course, by the correctness of their opinions and the holiness of their lives. They were a Jewish sect who had the dominant influence in the time of our Lord, to whose faults the overthrow of the state may be attributed, and who have to bear the awful burden of having crucified the Lord and giver of life.

The precise period when the Pharisees appeared as a sect, history does not supply us with the means of determining. That they, however, as well as their natural opponents, the Sadducees, existed in the priesthood of Jonathan—in the interval, that is, between 159 and 144 before Christ—is known from Josephus, who makes mention of them as well as of the sect of the Essenes. The terms he employs warrant the conviction that they were then no novelties, but well known, well defined, and two established religious parties. But from the time of Jonathan to that of Ezra (about 400 B.C.), there had taken place no great formative event such as could of itself cause so great a change in the Hebrew system as was the rise of these sects; whereas the influences to which the Israelites had been subject in the Medo-Persian dominions, and the necessarily somewhat new direction which things took on the rebuilding of the Temple and the restoration of the civil and religious polity, could hardly fail, considering the distance from Moses at which these changes happened, and the great extent to which the people had lost even the knowledge of the institutions and language of their forefathers, to lead to diversities of views, interests, and aims, whence sects would spring as a natural if not inevitable result. There is. therefore, good reason to refer the origin of the Pharisees to the time of the return from the Babylonish captivity, a period which constitutes a marked epoch, as dividing the Hebraism of the older and purer age from the Judaism of the later and more corrupt times. Nor, did our space allow, should we find it difficult to trace the leading features of the Pharisaic character back to those peculiar opinions and usages with which the old Israelitish type of mind had been made familiar, and at the same time corrupt, in the Persian empire.

But as we think it more for the reader's instruction to lay before him the very words in which this sect is described, than to give a philosophical account of the rise and connection of their principles, to which of necessity our own views would impart a colouring, we shall proceed to transcribe a nearly literal translation of the most important passages in the writings of Josephus referring to the opinions and practices of this powerful sect.

'The Pharisees have delivered to the people a great many observances by succession from their fathers, which are not written in the law of Moses, and for that reason it is that the Sadducees reject them, and say that we are to esteem those observances to be obligatory which are in the written word, but are not to observe what are derived from the tradition of our forefathers. Hence great disputes. The Sadducees are able to persuade none but the rich, and have not the populace obsequious to them, but the Pharisees have the multitude on their side.' 'The Pharisees are not apt to be severe in punishments' (Joseph. *Antiq.* xiii. 10. 5 and 6; Epiphan. *Hær.* 15).

'The Pharisees live meanly and despise delicacies in diet; and they follow the conduct of reason, and what that prescribes to them as good they do. They also pay respect to such as are in years; nor are they so bold as to contradict them in anything which they have introduced; and when they determine that all things are done by fate, they do not take away from men the freedom of acting as they think fit, since their notion is that it hath pleased God to make a constitution of things whereby what he wills is done, but so that the will of man can act virtuously or viciously. They also believe that souls have an immortal vigour in them, and that under the earth there will be rewards or punishments, according as men have lived virtuously or viciously in this life. The latter are to be detained in an everlasting prison; but the former shall have power to revive and live again: on account of which doctrine they are able greatly to persuade the body of the people; and whatsoever is done about divine worship, prayers, and sacrifices, is performed according to their directions, insomuch that the cities gave great attestations to them on account of their entire virtuous conduct' (Joseph. *Antiq.* xviii. 1. 3).

'The Pharisees are those who are esteemed most skilful in the exact interpretation of the laws. They ascribe all to Fate (or Providence) and to God, and yet allow that to act what is right, or the contrary, is for the most part in the power of man. They say that all souls are incorruptible, but that the souls of good men only are removed into other bodies, and that the souls of bad men are subject to eternal punishment. Moreover, the Pharisees are friendly to one another, and are for the exercise of concord and regard for the public' (Joseph. *De Bell. Jud.* ii. 8. 14).

'The Pharisees are a sect of Jews which appear to be more pious than others, and to expound the laws more accurately. These Pharisees artfully insinuated themselves into her (Queen Alexandra's) favour by little and little, and became the real administrators of public affairs; they banished and restored whom they pleased; they bound and loosed at their pleasure; they had the enjoyment of the royal authority, whilst the expenses and the difficulties of it belonged to Alexandra. She was a sagacious woman in the management of great affairs, and became not only very powerful at home, but terrible also to foreign potentates; while she governed other people, the Pharisees governed her. She was so superstitious as to comply with their desires, and accordingly they slew whom they pleased' (Joseph. *De Bell. Jud.* i. 5. 2. 3).

'There was a certain sect that were Jews, who valued themselves highly upon the exact skill they had in the law of their fathers, and made men believe they were highly favoured by God, by whom this sect of women were inveigled. These are those that are called the sect of the Pharisees, who were able to make great opposition to kings; a cunning sect they were, and soon elevated to a pitch of open fighting and doing mischief. Accordingly, when all the people of the Jews gave assurance of their good will to Cæsar and to the king's government, these men did not swear, being about 6000; and when the king imposed a fine upon them, Phreroras' wife paid it. In order to requite this kindness, since they were believed to have a foreknowledge of things to come by divine inspiration, they foretold how God had decreed that Herod's government should cease, and that the kingdom should come to her and Phreroras. and to their children; so the king Herod slew such of the Pharisees as were principally accused, and all who had consented to what the Pharisees had foretold' (Joseph. *Antiq.* xvii. 2. 4).

'The Pharisees say that some actions, but not all, are the work of fate; that some of them are in our own power, and that they are liable to fate, but are not caused by fate' (Joseph. *Antiq.* xiii. 5. 9).

'The sect of the Pharisees are supposed to excel others in the accurate knowledge of the laws of their country' (Joseph. *Vita*, § 39).

'The Pharisees have so great a power over the multitude that when they say anything against the king or against the high-priest, they are generally believed' (Joseph. *Antiq.* xiii. 10. 5).

'The bodies of all men are mortal, and are created out of corruptible matter, but the soul is ever immortal, and is a portion of the divinity that inhabits our bodies' (*De Bell. Jud.* iii. 8. 5).

'Being now nineteen years old, I began to conduct myself according to the rule of the sect of the Pharisees, which is of kin to the sect of Stoics, as the Greeks call them' (Joseph. *Vita* § 2).

There is another source of our knowledge of the Pharisees—the books of the New Testament. The light in which they here appear varies, of course, with the circumstances to which its origin is due. The reader has just had before him the account of a friend and an adherent, an account which, therefore, we may believe, is conceived and set forth in the most favourable manner. The Gospels present the character of the Pharisees in a darker hue, inasmuch as here a higher standard is brought into use. a loftier morality is the judge. To pass on to the views given in the New Testament. The high repute in which the Pharisees were held, as expositors of the national laws, whether civil or religious, may be seen in John vii. 48; Acts xxii. 3; the casuistry which they employed in expounding the Scriptures, in Matt. ix. 34; xv. 5; xxiii 16; Mark vii. 7, sq; their excessive zeal in proselytism, Matt. xxiii. 15; yet their concealment of light and hindrance of progress, Matt. xxiii. 13; their inordinate regard for externals, and oppressive but self-sparing rule, Matt. xxiii. 3, sq, 25; their affectation of grandeur and distinction, Matt. xxiii. 5, sq.; their shocking hypocrisy, Matt. xxiii. 14, 27, sq.; their standing on inconsiderable points, while they neglected such as were of consequence. preferring ceremonial rites to justice and charity, Matt. xxiii. 24; xii. 2–7; Luke vi. 7; John ix. 16, sq.; Mark vii. 1; the display which they affected even in works of religion, Matt vi. 1, sq.; xxiii. 5; their pride and self-gratulation as assuredly, and before others, religious men, Luke xviii. 9, sq.; their regard to tradition, Matt xv. 2; Mark vii. 3; they formed schools which had masters and disciples, Matt. xxii. 16; Luke v. 33; agreeably with their general doctrines, they regarded the act rather than the motive, Luke xi. 39; xviii. 11, sq.; and were given to fasts, prayers, washing, paying of tithes, alms, &c., Matt. ix. 14; xxiii. 15, 23; Luke xi. 39, sq.; xviii. 12; exhibiting themselves to the people, in order to gain their favour, as self-denying, holy men, zealous for God and the law, a kind of Jewish stoics, Matt ix. 11; Luke v. 30; vi. 2; Matt. xxiii. 5, 15, 29; while in reality they were fond of the pleasures of sense, and were men of lax morals, Matt. v. 20; xv. 4, 8, xxiii. 3, 14, 23, 25; John viii. 7. At an early period they determined in the Sanhedrim to withstand and destroy Jesus, instigated doubtless by the boldness with which he taught the necessity of personal righteousness and pure worship (Matt. xii. 14).

In regard to the opinions of the Pharisees, the New Testament affords only fragments of information, which are, however, in accordance with the fuller particulars furnished by Josephus. From Acts xxiii. 6, 8, we learn that they believed in the existence of higher created beings than man, doubtless the good and bad spirits of the Chaldee philosophy. The same places also instruct us that they held a resurrection of the dead (comp. Matt. xxii. 24, sq).

It thus appears that the Pharisees were in general a powerful religious party, or rather the predominant influence, in the Jewish state, who aspired to the control of the civil and religious institutions, affected popularity among the people, exerted influence in the councils of kings, queens, and people of rank; were the recognised teachers and guides of the national mind, proud of their orthodoxy. pluming themselves on their superior sanctity, practising austerities outwardly, but inwardly indulging their passions, and descending to unworthy and shameful acts; and withal of narrow spirit, contracted views, seeking rather their own aggrandisement than the public good, of which they used the name merely as a pretext and a cover.

We are not to suppose, however, that there were no individuals in the body free from its prevailing vices. There did not fail to be upright and pure-minded men, who united inward piety to outward correctness of conduct; and were indeed superior to the principles of their sect, such was Nicodemus (John iii. 1); such also Gamaliel may have been (Acts v. 34). Of men of this kind many were led to embrace the Gospel (Acts xv. 5).

In general, however, their power was all directed against Jesus and his work With what force they must have acted appears obvious from the preceding remarks. Nor is the reader to imagine that they were merely a few learned men, congregated together in the capital, engaged in learned pursuits or religious practices, and in consequence leaving our Lord at liberty to pursue his ordinary duties up and down the land. The capital was doubtless their head-quarters, but they pervaded the entire country in considerable numbers, and were therefore present in all parts to withstand the publication of the Gospel of that kingdom every feature of which they hated (Luke v. 17); and as they constituted a large portion of the Sanhedrim (Acts v. 34; xxiii. 6, sq.), and had an almost unlimited influence with the people, great indeed was the power which they wielded in their conflict with the infant church. Perhaps there never was an instance in any social condition in which the elements of power supplied by religion, politics, high life, and humble condition were more thoroughly or more densely combined in order to oppose and destroy the young power of new ideas and lofty aims. The victory, however, was for man, because it was also of God. Darkness, indeed, prevailed for three days, covering the land, and casting a thick shadow over the world. But the sun of righteousness arose, and still shines.

Pharisaism, how compact soever might be its appearance outwardly, and as against a common enemy, had its own internal dissensions. The question of more or less of moderate or extreme views, of what on one side would be called temporising and on the other consistency, agitated this school as it has agitated most others. In the age of our Lord there were two leading parties, that of Hillel and that of Schammai, the former representing a moderate Pharisaism. the latter 'the straitest sect,' to which Paul had probably belonged.

PHAR'PAR, one of the rivers of Damascus [ABANA and PHARPAR].

PHE'BE. [PHŒBE.]

PHENI'CE, a city on the south-east of Crete, with a harbour, in the attempt to reach which the ship in which Paul voyaged as a prisoner to Rome, was driven out of its course, and eventually wrecked (Acts xxvii. 12).

PHI'COL (*mouth of all*, i. e. *all commanding*), the proper or more probably the titular name of the commander of the troops of Abimelech, the

Philistine king of Gerar. If the Abimelech of the time of Isaac was the son of the Abimelech of the time of Abraham, we may conclude that the Phicol who attended on the second Abimelech was the successor of the one who was present with the first at the interview with Abraham (Gen. xxi. 22; xxvi. 26). But the whole subject of these interviews is beset with difficulties [ABIMELECH; ABRAHAM; ISAAC].

PHILADEL'PHIA, a city of Lesser Asia, and one of the seven containing the Christian churches to which the Apocalyptic admonitions were addressed. The town stood about twenty-five miles south-east from Sardis, in N. lat. 32° 28', E long. 28° 30', in the plain of Hermus, about midway between the river of that name and the termination of Mount Tmolus. It was the second in Lydia, and was built by King Attalus Philadelphus, from whom it took its name. In B.C. 133 the place passed, with the dominion in which it lay, to the Romans. The site is reputed by Strabo to have been very liable to earthquakes; but it continued a place of importance and of strength down to the Byzantine age, and of all the towns in Asia Minor it withstood the Turks the longest. It was taken by Bajazet I. in A.D. 1392.

Philadelphia still exists as a Turkish town, under the name of Allah Shehr, ' city of God,' i. e. High-town. It covers a considerable extent of ground, running up the slopes of four hills, or rather of one hill with four flat summits. The country, as viewed from these hills, is extremely magnificent—gardens and vineyards lying at the back and sides of the town, and before it one of the most extensive and beautiful plains of Asia. The town itself, although spacious, is miserably built and kept, the dwellings being remarkably mean, and the streets exceedingly filthy. Across the summits of the hill behind the town and the small valleys between them runs the town wall, strengthened by circular and square towers, and forming also an extensive and long quadrangle in the plain below. The missionaries Fisk and Parsons, in 1822, were informed by the Greek bishop that the town contained 3000 houses, of which he assigned 250 to the Greeks, and the rest to the Turks. On the same authority it is stated that there are five churches in the town, besides twenty others which were too old or too small for use. Six minarets, indicating as many mosques, are seen in the town; and one of these mosques is believed by the native Christians to have been the church in which assembled the primitive Christians addressed in the Apocalypse. There are few ruins; but in one part there are still found four strong marble pillars, which supported the dome of a church. The dome itself has fallen down, but its remains may be observed, and it is seen that the arch was of brick. On the sides of the pillars are inscriptions, and some architectural ornaments in the form of the figures of saints. One solitary pillar of high antiquity has been often noticed, as reminding beholders of the remarkable words in the Apocalyptic message to the Philadelphian church:—' Him that overcometh will I make a pillar in the temple of my God; and he shall go no more out' (Rev. iii. 12).

PHILE'MON, EPISTLE TO. That this epistle was written by the apostle Paul is the constant tradition of the ancient church. It is ex-

pressly cited as such by Origen; it is referred to as such by Tertullian; and both Eusebius and Jerome attest its universal reception as such in the Christian world.

This epistle was evidently written during the apostle's imprisonment (ver. 9, 10), and. as we have already endeavoured to show [COLOSSIANS, EPISTLE TO THE], during his two years' imprisonment at Rome. It was occasioned by his sending back to Philemon his runaway slave Onesimus, who, having found his way to Rome, was there, through the instrumentality of the apostle, converted to Christianity; and, after serving Paul for a season, was by him restored to his former master, without whose consent the apostle did not feel at liberty to retain him. The epistle commences with the apostle's usual salutation to those to whom he wrote; after which he affectionately alludes to the good reputation which Philemon, as a Christian, enjoyed, and to the joy which the knowledge of this afforded him (ver. 1–7). He then gently and gracefully introduces the main subject of his epistle by a reference to the spiritual obligations under which Philemon lay to him, and on the ground of which he might utter as a command what he preferred urging as a request. Onesimus is then introduced; the change of mind and character he had experienced is stated; his offence in deserting his master is not palliated; his increased worth and usefulness are dwelt upon, and his former master is intreated to receive him back, not only without severity, but with the feeling due from one Christian to another (ver. 8–16). The apostle then delicately refers to the matter of compensation for any loss which Philemon might have sustained either through the dishonesty of Onesimus, or simply through the want of his service; and though he reminds his friend that he might justly hold the latter his debtor for a much larger amount (seeing he owed to the apostle his own self), he pledges himself, under his own hand, to make good that loss (ver. 17-19). The epistle concludes with some additional expressions of friendly solicitude; a request that Philemon would prepare the apostle a lodging, as he trusted soon to visit him; and the salutations of the apostle and some of the Christians by whom he was surrounded at the time (ver. 20–25).

This epistle has been universally admired as a model of graceful, delicate, and manly writing. ' It is a voucher,' says Eichhorn, ' for the apostle's urbanity, politeness, and knowledge of the world. His advocacy of Onesimus is of the most insinuating and persuasive character, and yet without the slightest perversion or concealment of any fact. The errors of Onesimus are admitted, as was necessary, lest the just indignation of his master against him should be roused anew; but they are alluded to in the most admirable manner: the good side of Onesimus is brought to view, but in such a way as to facilitate the friendly reception of him by his master, as a consequence of Christianity, to which he had, during his absence, been converted; and his future fidelity is vouched for by the noble principles of Christianity which he had embraced. The apostle addresses Philemon on the softest side: who would wilfully refuse to an aged, a suffering, and an unjustly imprisoned friend a request? And such was he who thus pleaded for Onesimus. The person recommended is a Christian, a dear friend of the apostle's, and one who had personally served him: it Philemon will receive him kindly, it will afford the apostle a proof of his love, and yield him joy. What need, then, for long urgency? The apostle is certain that Philemon will, of his own accord, do even more than he is asked. More cogently and more courteously no man could plead.'

PHILE'TUS, an apostate Christian, mentioned by Paul in connection with Hymenæus, 2 Tim. ii. 17 [HYMENÆUS].

1. PHILIP, one of the twelve apostles. He was of Bethsaida, ' the city of Andrew and Peter' (John i. 44). He became one of the disciples of John the Baptist, and was in the neighbourhood where John was baptizing, at the time of our Lord's baptism. Andrew and John, who were also disciples of the Baptist, heard the testimony concerning Jesus which the latter gave, and thenceforth attached themselves to him as the promised Messiah. Through Andrew his brother, Simon (Peter) was brought to Christ; and as on the next day Philip unhesitatingly accompanied Jesus when called to follow him, it is probable that his townsmen had previously spoken to him of Jesus as the long-expected Saviour (John i. 35-44). Philip was thus the fourth of the apostles who attached themselves to the person of Jesus—of those ' who left all and followed him.' The first act of Philip was to bring to the Lord Nathanael, who is supposed to have also become an apostle under the name of Bartholomew (John i. 45-51). Little more is recorded of Philip in the Scriptures; but it is remarkable that when Christ beheld the five thousand people whom he afterwards fed with five loaves and two fishes, he singled out Philip for the question, ' Whence shall we buy bread that these may eat?' It is added, ' This he said to prove him, for he himself knew what he would do.' Bengel and others suppose that this was because the charge of providing food had been committed to Philip, while Chrysostom and Theodore of Mopsuestia rather suppose it was because this apostle was weak in faith. The answer of Philip agrees well enough with either supposition, ' Two hundred pennyworth of bread is not sufficient for them, that every one of them may take a little' (John vi. 1-7). But it is well to compare this with John xiv. 8, where the inappropriate remark of Philip, ' Lord, show us the Father, and it sufficeth us,' evinces that he experienced in a degree beyond his brother apostles the difficulty which they generally felt in raising themselves above the things of sense.

Intermediately, we find recorded the application to Philip of certain ' Greeks' (proselytes of the gate) at Jerusalem, who wished to be introduced to Jesus, of whom they had heard so much. Knowing that his Master was not forward to gratify mere curiosity, Philip was uncertain whether to comply with their wish or not, but first consulted Andrew, who went with him to mention the circumstance to Jesus (John xii. 21, 22). This incident, although slight, is indicative of character, as we feel sure that some of the other apostles, Peter for instance, would at once have complied with or declined this application on their own responsibility. The sacred history only adds to these facts, that Philip was present with the other apostles at the religious assembly following the Lord's resurrection (Acts i. 13).

The later traditions concerning this apostle are vague and uncertain; but there is nothing improbable in the statement that he preached the Gospel in Phrygia, and that he met his death at Hierapolis in Syria.

2. PHILIP, one of the seven first deacons (Acts vi. 5); also called an ' Evangelist' (xxi. 8), which denotes one of those ministers of the primitive church, who, without being attached to any particular congregation, preached the Gospel from place to place (Eph. iv. 11; 2 Tim. iv. 5). Being compelled to leave Jerusalem by the persecution which ensued on Stephen's death, Philip was induced to take refuge in Samaria. He there came to a city where Simon Magus was held in high reverence through the wonders which he wrought But the substantial and beneficent miracles which were performed by Philip in the name of Jesus, drew away their attention from the impostor, and prepared their minds for the reception of the Gospel. Simon himself seems to have regarded him as in league with some superhuman being, and looking upon baptism as the initiatory rite of a compact through which he might obtain the same powers, he solicited and obtained baptism from the Evangelist [SIMON MAGUS]. After Peter and John had come to Samaria to complete and carry on the work which Philip had been the means of commencing, the Evangelist himself was directed by a divine impulse to proceed towards Gaza, where he met the treasurer of Candace, queen of Ethiopia [CANDACE; ETHIOPIA], by whose conversion and baptism he became the instrument of planting the first seeds of the Gospel in Ethiopia (Acts viii. 1-39). Philip then retraced his steps, and after pausing at Azotus, preached the Gospel from town to town till he came to Cæsarea (ver. 40). At this place he seems to have settled; for when Paul was on his last journey to Jerusalem, he and his party were entertained in the house of Philip, on which occasion it is mentioned that he had ' four daughters, virgins, who did prophesy' (Acts xxi. 9), or who were endued with the faculty of speaking under divine inspiration and of predicting future events, together with other supernatural gifts vouchsafed to the primitive Christians in accordance with the prophecy in Acts ii. 18. With this fact the Scriptural history of Philip closes, and the traditions which refer to his subsequent proceedings are uncertain and conflicting.

3. PHILIP, son of Herod the Great, and tetrarch of Batanæa, Trachonitis, and Auranitis (Luke iii. 1) [HERODIAN FAMILY].

4 PHILIP, called by Josephus Herod, son of Herod the Great, and first husband of Herodias [HERODIAN FAMILY].

PHILIP'PI, a city of the proconsular Macedonia, situated eastward of Amphipolis, within the limits of ancient Thrace (Acts xvi. 12; xx. 6; Phil. i. 1). It was anciently called Krenides (*fountains*) from its many fountains; but having been taken and fortified by Philip of Macedon, he named it, after himself, Philippi. In the vicinity were mines of gold and silver; and the spot eventually became celebrated for the battle in which Brutus and Cassius were defeated. Paul made some stay in this place on his first arrival in Greece, and here founded the church to which he afterwards addressed one of his epistles. It was here that the interesting circumstances related in Acts xvi. occurred; and the city was again visited by the Apostle on his departure from Greece (Acts. xx. 6). In the former passage (xvi. 12) Philippi is called a colony, and this character it had in fact acquired through many of the followers of Antony having been colonized thither by Augustus (Dion. Cass. xlvii. 432). The fact that Philippi was a colony was formerly disputed; but its complete verification has strongly attested the minute accuracy of the sacred narrative. The plain in which the ruins of Philippi stand is embraced by the parallel arms of mountains extended from the Necrokop, which pour into the plain many small streams, by which it is abundantly watered and fertilized. The acropolis is upon a mount standing out into the plain from the north-east, and the city seems to have extended from the base of it to the south and south-west. The remains of the fortress upon the top consist of three ruined towers and considerable portions of walls of stone, brick, and very hard mortar. The plain below does not now exhibit anything but ruins—heaps of stone and rubbish, overgrown with thorns and briars; but nothing of the innumerable busts and statues, thousands of columns, and vast masses of classic ruins, of which the elder travellers speak. Ruins of private dwellings are still visible; also something of a semicircular shape, probably a forum or market-place, 'perhaps the one where Paul and Silas received their undeserved stripes.' The most prominent of the existing remains is the remainder of a palatial edifice, the architecture of which is grand, and the materials costly. The pilasters, chapiters, &c., are of the finest white marble, and the walls were formerly encased with the same stone. These marble blocks are gradually knocked down by the Turks, and 'wrought into their silly gravestones.' The travellers were informed that many of the ruins are now covered by stagnant water, at the bottom of which they may be seen; but they did not visit this spot.

PHILIPPIANS, EPISTLE TO THE. Of this part of the Apostle Paul's writings the authenticity has never been questioned. Professing to be written by that distinguished servant of Christ, it bears on every part of it the impress of his peculiar style, manner of thought, and form of doctrine; and the internal evidence of authenticity arising from the incidental allusions in it to persons and circumstances is very strong.

From allusions in the epistle itself, it is evident that it was written at Rome during the period of the apostle's two years' imprisonment in that city, and in all probability towards the close of that period (i. 13, 14, 23, 26; ii. 18, 25). It seems to have been composed on the occasion of the return to Philippi of Epaphroditus, a member of the church in that place, who had been deputed to Rome with a pecuniary contribution from the church in aid of the apostle. Full of gratitude for this work of friendly remembrance and regard, Paul addressed to the church in Philippi this epistle, in which, besides expressing his thanks for their kindness, he pours out a flood of eloquence and pathetic exhortation, suggested partly by his own circumstances, and partly by what he had learned of their state as a church. That state appears to have been on the whole very **prosperous, as there is much commendation of**

the Philippians in the epistle, and no censure is expressed in any part of it either of the church as a whole, or of any individuals connected with it. At the same time the apostle deemed it necessary to put them on their guard against the evil influences to which they were exposed from Judaizing teachers and false professors of Christianity. These cautions he interposes between the exhortations suggested by his own state and by the news he had received concerning the Philippians, with which his epistle commences and with which it closes. We may thus divide the epistle into *three* parts. In the *first* of these (i, ii.), after the usual salutation and an outpouring of warm-hearted affection towards the Philippian church (i. 1-11), the apostle refers to his own condition as a prisoner at Rome; and lest they should be cast down at the thought of the unmerited indignities he had been called upon to suffer, he assures them that these had turned out rather to the furtherance of that great cause on which his heart was set, and for which he was willing to live and labour, though, as respected his personal feelings, he would rather depart and be with Christ, which he deemed to be 'far better' (12-24). He then passes by an easy transition to a hortatory address to the Philippians, calling upon them to maintain steadfastly their profession, to cultivate humanity and brotherly love, to work out their own salvation with fear and trembling, and concluding by an appeal to their regard for his reputation as an apostle, which could not but be affected by their conduct, and a reference to his reason for sending to them Epaphroditus instead of Timothy, as he had originally designed (i. 25; ii. 30). In part *second* he strenuously cautions them, as already observed, against Judaizing teachers, whom he stigmatizes as 'dogs' (in reference probably to their impudent, snarling, and quarrelsome habits), 'evil-workers,' and 'the concision;' by which latter term he means to intimate, as Theophylact remarks (*in loc.*), that the circumcision in which the Jews so much gloried had now ceased to possess any spiritual significance, and was therefore no better than a useless mutilation of the person. On this theme he enlarges, making reference to his own standing as a Jew, and intimating, that if under the Christian dispensation Jewish descent and Jewish privileges were to go for anything, no one could have stronger claims on this ground than he; but at the same time declaring, that however he had once valued these, he now counted them 'all but lost for the excellency of the knowledge of Christ' (iii. 1-12). A reference to his own sanctified ambition to advance in the service of Christ leads him to exhort the Philippians to a similar spirit; from this he passes to caution them against unnecessary contention, and against those who walk disorderly, concluding by reminding them of the glorious hopes which, as Christians, they entertained (ver. 13-21). In the *third* part we have a series of admonitions to individual members of the church at Philippi (iv. 1-3), followed by some general exhortations to cheerfulness, moderation, prayer, and good conduct (ver. 4-9); after which come a series of allusions to the apostle's circumstances and feelings, his thanks to the Philippians for their seasonable aid, and his concluding benedictions and salutations (ver. 10-23).

This epistle is written throughout in a very animated and elevated style. It is full of the most sublime thoughts and the most affectionate exhortations. It resembles more the production of a father addressing his children, than that of an apostle laying down authoritatively what is to be received and followed. The whole of it shows, as Theophylact observes, how very much he loved and estimated those to whom it was addressed.

PHILISTINES, a tribe which gave its name to the country known as Palestine, though it occupied only a portion of the southern coast, namely, that which was bounded on the west by the hill country of Ephraim and Judah, and on the south extended from Joppa to the borders of Egypt, thus touching on the Israelite tribes Dan, Simeon, and Judah. Indeed the portions of Simeon and Dan covered a large part of Philistia, but its possession by the Israelites was disputed, and was never entirely achieved. This country was originally held by the Avims, who were destroyed and their land seized by the Caphtorims, coming forth out of Caphtor (Deut. ii. 23). In Jer. xlvii. 4 the Philistines are denominated 'the remnant of the country (or isle) of Caphtor.' In Amos ix. 7, the Divine Being asks, 'Have I not brought the Philistines from Caphtor?' The Caphtorim and the Philistim are also associated together as kindred tribes in the genealogical list of nations given in Gen. x. 14, both being descendants of Mizraim. Some imagine that Caphtor is Cappadocia : others with more reason affirm that it is Crete, and that the Philistines, being a part of the great Shemitic family, went westward under pressure from the wave of population which came down from the higher country to the sea-coast, but afterwards returned eastward from Crete to Palestine. Another opinion, which is supported by very plausible arguments, is, that the Philistines are to be identified with the Hycksos or Shepherd-kings, who were expelled from Egypt, and taking possession of Canaan gave to it the name of *Palisthan*, *i. e.*, Shepherd-land. This view appears to be countenanced by Gen. x. 13, 14, where the Philistines are derived from Mizraim, that is from Egypt.

If now we follow the Biblical accounts, we find the history of the Philistines to be in brief as follows. They had established themselves in their land as early as the time of Abraham, when they had founded a kingdom at Gerar (Gen. xxi. 32; xxvi. 1). When the Israelites left Egypt, they were deterred by fear of the power of the Philistines from returning by the shortest road—that which the caravans still take—because it lay through the country of the Philistines (Exod. xiii. 17). In the time of Joshua (xiii. 3) the Philistines appear in a league of five princes, governors of so many tribes or petty states—'all the borders of the Philistines from Sihor which is before Egypt even unto the borders of Ekron northward counted to the Canaanites.' Joshua appears to have thought it prudent to attempt nothing for the dispossession of the Philistines, and he therefore had no hostile relations with them; for the division of Philistia among the tribes was nothing more than a prospective but unfulfilled arrangement (Josh. xv. 45; xix. 43). The days of the Judges, however, brought conflicts between the Israelites and the Philistines, who dwelt wide over the land, and even exercised dominion over their Hebrew neighbours (Judg. iii. 31; x. 7; xiii. 1; xiv. 2, 4, 5; xv. 11).

In the time of Eli the Philistines succeeded in getting the ark into their possession (1 Sam. iv.); but a defeat which they suffered under Samuel put an end to their dominion, after it had lasted forty years (1 Sam. vii). This subjection of the Israelites began after the death of Jair, and continued to the termination of the period embraced in the book of Judges. Within this space of time fall the life and the heroic actions of Samson. Notwithstanding the total defeat which the Philistines had undergone, and the actual termination of their political supremacy, they continued to be troublesome neighbours. 'There was sore war against the Philistines all the days of Saul' (1 Sam. xiv. 52); a conflict which was carried on with various success, and in which the king found great support in the prudent bravery of his son Jonathan and the high courage of David (1 Sam. xiii. 4; xiv.; xvii. 18; xix. 8; xxiii. 28). Even after his separation from Saul David inflicted many blows on the Philistines (1 Sam. xxiii.); but soon saw himself obliged to seek refuge in Gath (1 Sam. xxvii.), and was in consequence near making common cause with them against Saul (1 Sam. xxix.), who met with his death at their hands while engaged in battle (1 Sam. xxxi.). They also raised their arms against David, when he had become king of all Israel, but were several times beaten by that brave monarch (2 Sam. v. 17, sq.; viii. 1). 'Mighty men,' performing valorous deeds in imitation of David's rencontre with Goliath, gave the king their support against this brave and persevering enemy (2 Sam. xxiii. 8, sq.). Solomon appears to have been undisturbed by the Philistines, but they had settlements in the land of Israel under the early Ephraimitic kings (1 Kings xv. 27; xvi. 15). To Jehoshaphat they became tributary (2 Chron. xvii. 11). Under Jehoram, however, they, in union with the Arabians, fell on Jerusalem, and carried off the king's substance, as well as his wives and children (2 Chron. xxi. 16). On the other hand, in the reign of king Jehoash, their city Gath was taken by Hazael, king of Syria, who also threatened Jerusalem (2 Kings xii. 17). But in the time of Ahaz they revolted, and carried with them a part of western Judah, having 'invaded the cities of the low country and of the south of Judah, and taken Bethshemesh and Ajalon,' &c. (2 Chron. xxviii. 18; comp. Isa. xiv. 29). Hezekiah in the first years of his reign obtained some advantages over them (2 Kings xviii. 8). Soon, however, Assyrian armies went against Philistia, and, with a view to an invasion of Egypt, got into their power the strong frontier-fortress of Ashdod (Isa. xx. 1), which at a later time Psammetichus took from them, after a siege of twenty-nine years (Herod. ii. 157). In consequence of the hostile relations between Assyria and Egypt, Philistia suffered for a long period, as the troops of the former power took their way through that land, and Pharaoh-Necho captured the stronghold Gaza (Isa. xlvii. 1). The same was done by Alexander the Great in his expedition to Egypt. On the destruction of the Jewish state, the Philistines, like other neighbouring peoples, acted ill towards the Jews, having 'taken vengeance with a despiteful heart' (Ezek. xxv. 15). Many of those who returned from the captivity ' had married wives of Ashdod, and their speech spoke half in the speech of Ashdod ' (Neh. xiii. 23, sq.). In the Maccabæan period the Philistines were Syrian subjects, and had at times to suffer at the hands of the Jews (1 Macc. x. 86; xi. 60, sq). King Alexander (Balus) gave Jonathan a part of their territory, Accaron, with the borders thereof in possession (1 Macc. x. 89). The Jewish monarch Alexander Jannæus overcame and destroyed Gaza. By Pompey Azotus, Jamnia, and Gaza were united to the Roman province of Syria ; but Gaza was given by Augustus to King Herod.

The Philistine cities were greatly distinguished. Along the whole coast from north to south there ran a line of towns—in the north the Phœnician, in the south the Philistine—which were powerful, rich, and well-peopled. The chief cities of the Philistines were five—Gaza, Ashdod, Askalon, Gath, and Ekron (Josh. xiii. 3; Judg. iii. 3). Several of these Palestinian cities flourished at the same time ; and though now these now those cities gained at different periods pre-eminence in power, wealth, and population, and though some did not rise till others had declined or perished, yet is it true that from the earliest times till the century after Christ a number of important towns existed on the narrow strip of land which borders the Mediterranean sea, such as was never seen in any other part of the world, the Ionian coast of Asia Minor not excepted.

The greatness of these cities was mainly owing to commerce, for the coast of Palestine was in the earliest ages exclusively in possession of the trade which was carried on between Europe and Asia. Besides a great transit trade, they had internal sources of wealth, being given to agriculture (Judg. xv. 5). In the time of Saul they were evidently superior in the arts of life to the Israelites ; for we read (1 Sam. xiii. 20) that the latter were indebted to the former for the utensils of ordinary life. Their religion was not essentially different from that of the Phœnicians. The idol which they most reverenced was Astarte, the Assyrian Semiramis, or Derketo, who was also honoured as Dagon, in a very ancient temple at Askalon and at Gaza, also at Ashdod (Judg. xvi. 23; 1 Sam. v. 1, sq.; 1 Macc. x. 83). This was a species of fish-worship, a remnant of which may still be found in the special care taken of certain holy fish in some parts of Syria. In Ekron Baalzebub had his chief seat. Priests and soothsayers were numerous (1 Sam. vi. 2). Their magicians were in repute (Isa. ii. 6), and the oracle of Baalzebub was consulted by foreigners (2 Kings i. 2). They had the custom of carrying with them in war the images of their gods (2 Sam. v. 21). Tradition makes the Philistines the inventors of the bow and arrow.

PHILOL'OGUS, one of the Christians at Rome to whom Paul sent his salutations (Rom. xvi. 15). Dorotheus makes him one of the seventy disciples, and alleges that he was placed by the apostle Andrew as bishop of Sinope, in Pontus. But this seems altogether improbable.

PHIN'EHAS (*mouth of brass*), son of Eleazar and grandson of Aaron the high-priest. An incident which illustrates the zealous and somewhat passionate character of Phinehas, occurred before the Israelites entered the Promised Land. The Israelites were encamped in the plains of Moab,

and were lamenting the sin into which they had been seduced by the Midianites, when a prince of Judah named Zimri was beheld conducting a woman of Midian named Cozbi to his tent. The licentious effrontery of this act kindled the wrath of Phinehas, who hastened after them into the tent, and transfixed them both with his javelin (Num. xxv. 7, sq.). This bold act pointed out Phinehas to Moses as a proper person to accompany as priest the expedition which was immediately after sent forth, under the command of Joshua, against the Midianites, and by which the cause of the deluded Israelites was abundantly avenged (Num. xxxi. 6, sq.). After the conquest of the Promised Land, when the warriors of the two and half tribes beyond the Jordan were permitted to return to their homes, Phinehas was at the head of the deputation sent after them to inquire and remonstrate concerning the altar which, on their way, they had set up on the bank of the Jordan ; and it was he doubtless who pronounced the forcible address to the supposed offenders. He was certainly the first to express his satisfaction and joy at the explanation which was given, and which, with a lightened heart, he bore back to the tribes assembled at Shiloh (Josh xxii. 5, sq.).

It appears that while his father lived Phinehas filled the post of superintendent or chief of the Levites, probably after Eleazar became highpriest (Num. iii. 32; 1 Chron. ix. 20). At the death of his father he succeeded to the pontificate (Josh. xxiv. 33); but the only case in which he appears officially in the Bible is in connection with the unhappy circumstances recorded at the end of the book of Judges, in which he comes forward as high-priest to consult Jehovah. This mention of his name enables us to conclude that the chronological place of these occurrences would be rather towards the beginning than at the latter end of the book in which they are found [JUDGES; PRIEST].

2. PHINEHAS, son of Eli the high-priest, and brother of Hophni [ELI; HOPHNI; SAMUEL].

PHLEG'ON, one of the Christians of Rome to whom Paul sent his salutations (Rom. xvi. 14). The legend (*ap.* Dorotheus) makes him to have been one of the seventy disciples, and bishop of Marathon

PHŒ'BE. a deaconess of the church at Cenchreæ, recommended to the kind attention of the church of Rome by St. Paul, who had received hospitable treatment from her (Rom. xvi 1). It is probable that she was the bearer of the Epistle to the Romans.

PHŒNI'CIA, and the PHŒNICIANS. This name was used by the ancients sometimes in a wider, sometimes in a narrower sense. Phœnicia, in its widest signification, embraces the whole coast of the Mediterranean situated between the river Orontes and Pelusium. In a more restricted sense it was regarded as the territory between the river Eleutheros on the north, and Dora on the south.

Phœnicia is situated between about lat. 33° and 35° N., and under long. 33° E. The whole of Phœnicia is situated at the western declivity of Mount Lebanon. Compare the article LIBANUS

Phœnicia was distinguished by the variety of its vegetable productions. This variety was occasioned by the great diversity of climate produced by the diversity in the elevation of the soil. The Lebanon is said to bear winter on its head, spring on its shoulders, autumn in its lap, and to have summer at its feet. The fertility of Phœnicia is increased by the numerous streams whose springs are in Mount Lebanon. Even in the Song of Solomon we read the praises of the spring of living waters which flows down from Lebanon. The dense population assembled in the great mercantile towns greatly contributed to augment by artificial means the natural fertility of the soil. The population of the country is at present very much reduced, but there are still found aqueducts and artificial vineyards formed of mould carried up to the terraces of the naked rock. Even now Phœnicia is among the most fertile in Western Asia. It produces wheat, rye. and barley, and, besides the more ordinary fruits, also apricots, peaches, pomegranates almonds, citrons, oranges, figs, dates, sugar-cane, and grapes, which furnish an excellent wine. In addition to these products, it yields cotton, silk, and tobacco. The country is also adorned by the variegated flowers of oleander and cactus. The higher regions are distinguished from the bare mountains of Palestine by being covered with oaks, pines, cypress-trees, acicias, and tamarisks; and above all by majestic cedars, of which there are still a few very old trees, whose stems measure from thirty to forty feet in circumference. The inhabitants of Sur still carry on a profitable traffic with the produce of Mount Lebanon, namely, wood and charcoal. Phœnicia produces also flocks of sheep and goats; and innumerable swarms of bees supply excellent honey. In the forests there are bears, wolves, panthers, and jackals. The sea furnishes great quantities of fish, so that Sidon, the most ancient among the Phœnician towns, derived its name from fishing.

The inhabitants of Phœnicia might at the first view appear to have derived their origin from the same source (pre Abrahamite) as the Hebrews; for they spoke the same language.

In the Old Testament the Phœnicians and Canaanites are, however, described as descending, not from Shem, but from Ham. Herodotus, also, on the authority of some Persian historians, states that the Phœnicians came as colonists to the Syrian coasts from the Erythræan Sea.

The first Phœnician colony was Sidon, which is therefore called in Genesis (x. 15) the firstborn of Canaan. But soon other colonies arose, like Arka (Gen. x. 17), Aradus, and Smyrna (Gen. x. 18), &c, whose power extended beyond the Jordan, and who drove out before them the earlier inhabitants of Palestine. Hence it arose that the appellation, 'the land of Canaan' (the netherlands or lowlands). was transferred to the whole of Palestine, although it is by no means a country of a low level, but is full of high elevations However, the Canaanites, in a stricter sense, were the people who resided in the lower regions along the coast, and on the banks of the Jordan.

When the Israelites conquered the country, the Canaanites on the Phœnician coast, who resided in powerful maritime towns, preserved their independence, and were called Canaanites in particular. Thus we read, in Isa. xxiii. 11, Canaan, in the signification of Phœnicia.

The Carthaginians, as Phœnician colonists,

maintained, even in the days of St. Augustine, that they were Canaanites.

During the period of the conquest of Canaan by the Israelites, the Phœnicians possessed the following towns, which we will enumerate successively, in the direction from south to north:— Dora (Josh. xi. 2; xvii. 11, sq.): Ptolemais (Judg. i. 33); Ecdippa (Josh. xix. 29); Tyre (Josh. xix. 29); Sarepta (1 Kings xvii 9, sq.; Luke iv. 26); Sidon (Gen. x. 15); Berytus (Ezek. xlvii. 16; 2 Sam. viii. 8); Byblus (Josh. xiii. 5); Tripolis, Simyra (Gen. x. 18); Arka (Gen. x. 17); Simna (Gen. x. 16); Aradus (Gen. x. 18).

Heeren, in his work, *On the Commerce and Politics of the Ancients*, vol. i. part ii. p. 9, Gottingen, 1824, justly observes that the numerous towns which were crowded together in the narrow space of Phœnicia covered almost the entire coast, and, together with their harbours and fleets. must have presented an aspect which has scarcely ever been equalled, and which was calculated to impress every stranger on his arrival with the ideas of wealth, power, and enterprise.

As the annals and public documents of the Phœnicians have all been lost, our knowledge of their history is consequently confined to occasional notices in the Hebrew and classical authors of antiquity. This deficiency of historical information arises also from the circumstance that the facts of Phœnician history were less connected than the events in the history of other nations. The Phœnicians never formed one compact body politic, and consequently did not always gradually advance in their political constitution and in the extent of their power. Every town endeavoured to advance its commerce in its own way. Thus there constantly entered into the life of the Phœnicians new elements, which disturbed a gradual historical progress. Phœnicia was a country favourable to the growth of maritime towns, but did not afford room for great political events. The history of the Phœnicians is that of their external commerce.

A mercantile nation cannot bear despotic government, because the greatest external liberty is requisite in order constantly to discover new sources of gain, and to enlarge the roads of commerce. The whole of Phœnicia consisted of the territories belonging to the various towns. Each of these territories had its own constitution, and in most of them a king exercised supreme power. We hear of kings of Sidon, Tyre, Aradus, and Byblus. It seems that after Nebuchadnezzar had besieged Tyre in vain, the royal dignity ceased for some time, and that there existed a kind of republican administration, under *suffetes* or judges. The regal power was always limited by the magistracy and the priesthood. The independent Phœnician states seem to have formed a confederation, at the head of which stood for some time Sidon, and at a later period Tyre. Tripolis was built conjointly by the various states in order to form the seat of their congress. The smaller states were sometimes so much oppressed by Tyre, that they preferred rather to submit to external enemies.

The position of Phœnicia was most favourable for the exchange of the produce of the East and West. The Libanus furnished excellent timber for ships. Corn was imported from Palestine. Persians, Lydians and Lycians frequently served as mercenaries in the Phœnician armies (Ezek. xxvii. 10, 11). Phœnicia exported wine to Egypt. Purple garments were best manufactured in Tyre. Glass was made in Sidon and Sarepta. In Phœnicia was exchanged the produce of all known countries. After David had vanquished the Edomites and conquered the coasts of the Red Sea, King Hiram of Tyre entered into a confederacy with Solomon, by which he ensured for his people the right of navigation to India. The combined fleet of the Israelites and Phœnicians sailed from the seaports of Ezion-geber and Elath. These ports were situated on the eastern branch of the Red Sea, the Sinus Ælaniticus, or Gulf of Akaba. Israelitish-Phœnician mercantile expeditions proceeded to Ophir, perhaps Abhira, situated at the mouth of the Indus. It seems, however, that the Indian coasts in general were also called Ophir. Three years were required in order to accomplish a mercantile expedition to Ophir and to return with cargoes of gold, algumwood, ivory, silver, monkeys, peacocks, and other Indian produce.

It seems, however, that these mercantile expeditions to India were soon given up, probably on account of the great difficulty of navigating the Red Sea. King Jehoshaphat endeavoured to recommence these expeditions, but his fleet was wrecked at Ezion-geber (1 Kings xxii. 49). About B.C. 616 or 601, Phœnician seamen undertook, at the command of Pharaoh-Necho, a voyage of discovery, proceeding from the Red Sea round Africa, and returning after two years through the columns of Hercules to Egypt (Herod. iv. 42). The 27th chapter of Ezekiel mentions the commerce by land between India and Phœnicia. The names of mercantile establishments on the coasts of Arabia along the Persian Gulf have partly been preserved to the present day. In these places the Phœnicians exchanged the produce of the west for that of India, Arabia, and Ethiopia. Arabia especially furnished incense, gold, and precious stones. The Midianites (Gen. xxxvii. 28) and the Edomites (Ezek. xxvii. 16) effected the transit by their caravans. The fortified Idumæan town Petra contained probably the storehouses in which the produce of southern countries was collected. From Egypt the Phœnicians exported especially byssus (Ezek. xxvii. 7) for wine. According to an ancient tradition, the tyrant of Thebes, Busiris, having soiled his hands with the blood of all foreigners, was killed by the Tyrian Hercules. This indicates that Phœnician colonists established themselves and their civilization successfully in Upper Egypt, where all strangers usually had been persecuted.

At a later period Memphis was the place where most of the Phœnicians in Egypt were established. Phœnician inscriptions found in Egypt prove that even under the Ptolemies the intimate connection between Phœnicia and Egypt still existed.

From Palestine the Phœnicians imported, besides wheat, especially from Judæa, ivory, oil, and balm; also wool, principally from the neighbouring nomadic Arabs. Damascus furnished wine (Ezek. xxvii. 5, 6, 17, 18, 21,) and the mountains of Syria wood. The tribes about the shores of the Caspian Sea furnished slaves and iron. Horsemen, horses, and mules, came from the Armenians.

The treasures of the East were exported from Phœnicia by ships which sailed first to Cyprus, the mountains of which are visible from the Phœnician coast. Cyprus was subject to Tyre up to the time of Alexander the Great. There are still found Phœnician inscriptions which prove the connection of Cyprus with Tyre. At Rhodes also are found vestiges of Phœnician influence. From Rhodes the mountains of Crete are visible. This was of great importance for the direction of navigators before the discovery of the compass. In Crete, and also in the Cycladic and Sporadic Isles, are vestiges of Phœnician settlements. On the Isle of Thasos, on the southern coast of Thrace, the Phœnicians had gold mines; and even on the southern shores of the Black Sea they had factories. However, when the Greeks became more powerful, the Phœnicians sailed more in other directions. They occupied also Sicily and the neighbouring islands, but were, after the Greek colonization, confined to a few towns, Motya, Soloes, Panormus. The Phœnician mercantile establishments in Sardinia and the Balearic Isles could scarcely be called colonies.

Carthage was a Phœnician colony, which probably soon became important by commerce with the interior of Africa, and remained connected with Tyre by means of a common sanctuary. After Phœnicia had been vanquished by the Assyrians, Babylonians, and Persians, the settlements in Sicily, Sardinia, and Spain came into the power of Carthage. The Phœnicians had for a long period exported from Spain gold, silver, tin, iron, lead (Ezek. xxxviii. 13), fruit, wine, oil, wax, fish, and wool. Their chief settlement was Tarshish.

There are other names of towns in Spain which have a Phœnician derivation, such as Gades, Malaga, and Belon.

The voyage to Tarshish was the most important of those undertaken by the Phœnicians. Hence it was that their largest vessels were all called *ships of Tarshish,* although they sailed in other directions (1 Kings x. 22).

It appears, also, that the Phœnicians exported tin from the British Isles, and amber from the coasts of Prussia. Their voyages on the western coasts of Africa seem to have been merely voyages of discovery, without permanent results. The Spanish colonies were probably the principal sources of Phœnician wealth, and were founded at a very remote period. The migration of the Phœnician, Cadmus, into Bœotia, likewise belongs to the earlier period of Phœnician colonization.

Phœnicia flourished most in the period from David to Cyrus, B.C. 1050-550. In this period were founded the African colonies, Carthage, Utica, and Leptis. These colonies kept up a frequent intercourse with the mother country, but were not politically dependent. This preserved Phœnicia from the usual stagnation of Oriental states. The civilization of the Phœnicians had a great influence upon other nations. Their voyages are described in Greek mythology as the expeditions of the Tyrian Hercules. The course of the Tyrian Hercules was not marked like that of other conquerors—viz., Medes and Assyrians—

by ruined cities and devastated countries, but by flourishing colonies, by agriculture, and the arts of peace.

According to the Phœnician religion, the special object of worship was the vital power in nature, which is either producing or destroying. The productive power of nature, again, is either procreative, *masculine*, or receptive, *feminine* These fundamental ideas are represented by the Phœnician gods, who appear under a great variety of names, because these leading ideas may be represented in many different ways.

We need not here enter into details concerning the Phœnician gods, as the principal of them have been noticed under their names [BAAL, ASHTORETH]. It suffices to state generally, that the procreative principle was worshipped as Baal, *lord*, and as the sun. The rays of the sun are, however, not only procreative, but destructive; and this destructive power is especially represented in the Ammonitish fire-god Moloch. Thus Baal represented both the generative and destructive principles of nature; in which latter capacity the Hebrews worshipped him by human sacrifice (1 Kings xviii. 28; Jer. xix. 5). He was the tutelary god of Tyre, and hence had the name of Melkar, equivalent to Melech-kereth, 'king of the city,' whom the Greeks called the Tyrian Hercules.

Of Baaltis, or Astarte, which are usually identified, although they seem to have been originally different, we shall here add nothing to what has been already stated under ASHTORETH.

Besides these principal deities, the Phœnicians worshipped seven *kabirim, mighty ones*, whose numbers corresponded with the seven planets. These kabirim were considered as protectors of men in using the powers of nature, especially navigation. With these seven kabirim was associated Esmun (*the eighth*), representing the sky full of fixed stars, surrounding the seven planets, the refreshing air and the warmth of life. Many Phœnician names are compounded with Esmun. Hence we infer that he was frequently worshipped.

PHRY'GIA, an inland province of Asia Minor, bounded on the north by Bithynia and Galatia, on the east by Cappadocia and Lycaonia, on the south by Lycia, Pisidia, and Isauria, and on the west by Caria, Lydia, and Mysia. In early times Phrygia seems to have comprehended the greater part of the peninsula of Asia Minor. It was subsequently divided into Phrygia Major on the south, and Phrygia Minor or Epictetus (*acquired*) on the north-west. The Romans divided the province into three districts: Phrygia Salutaris on the east, Phrygia Pacatiana on the west, and Phrygia Katakekaumene (*the burnt*) in the middle. The country, as defined by the specified limits, is for the most part level, and very abundant in corn, fruit, and wine. It had a peculiar and celebrated breed of cattle, and the fine raven-black wool of the sheep around Laodicea on the Lycus was in high repute. The Mæander and the Hermus were its chief rivers. The Phrygians were a very ancient people, and are supposed to have formed, along with the Pelasgi, the aborigines of Asia Minor. Jews from Phrygia were present in Jerusalem at the Feast of Pentecost (Acts ii. 10), and the province was afterwards twice traversed by St. Paul in his missionary journeys (Acts xvi. 6; xviii. 23). The cities of Laodicea, Hierapolis, and Colossæ, mentioned in the New Testament, belonged to Phrygia, and Antioch in Pisidia was also within its limits.

PHUL. [PUL.]

PHUT, a son of Ham (Gen. x. 6), progenitor of an African people of the same name, sometimes rendered 'Libya' (Jer. xlvi. 9; Ezek. xxvii. 10; xxx. 5; xxxviii. 5; Nah. iii. 9).

PHYLAC'TERY, strips of parchment inscribed with particular passages of Scripture (Deut. vi. 4-9; xi. 13-21; Exod. xiii. 1-10, 11-16). They were folded up and enclosed in a small leather box, and worn upon the forehead nearly between the eyes, or upon the left arm near to the heart, being attached by straps of leather. They were considered as thus reminding the wearers to fulfil the law with the head and heart; and they were also regarded as amulets, protecting the wearer from the powers of evil, especially demons. These

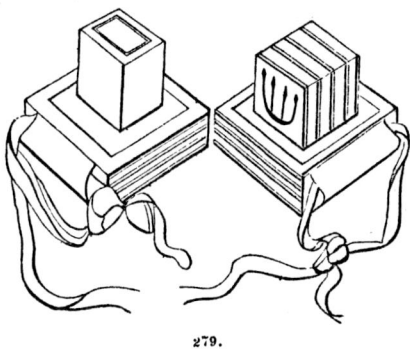

279.

appendages were used during the stated prayers, and only by men. The whole observance is founded on the authority of the texts which are written on the strips of parchment, as Exod. xiii. 16: 'It shall be for a token upon thine hand, and for frontlets (bands, fillets) between thine eyes;' which, although in all probability only figurative expressions, have been literally understood, and acted upon by the Jews since the Exile. In existing usage the skin employed in making the phylacteries is prepared with much care, and the writing traced with minute accuracy and neatness. The Hebrew ritualists give very exact and numerous directions on this subject, which are required to be closely observed. The case itself is composed of several layers of parchment or of black calf-skin. The phylacteries for the head have four cavities, in each of which is put one of the four texts to which we have referred; but the phylacteries for the arm have only one cavity, containing the same texts all written on one slip of parchment. Lightfoot thinks it not unlikely that our Saviour himself wore the Jewish phylacteries, as well as the fringes, according to the custom of his nation; and that in Matt. xxiii. 5, our Lord condemns not the wearing of them, but the pride and hypocrisy of the Pharisees in making them broad and visible, to obtain respect and reputation for wisdom and piety.

PHYSIC; PHYSICIANS. There can be no question that the Israelites brought some knowledge of medicine with them from Egypt, whose physicians were celebrated in all antiquity. To the state of medical knowledge in that country there are indeed some allusions in Scripture, as contained in the notice of the corps of physicians in the service of Joseph (Gen. l. 2); of the use of artificial help and practised midwives in child-birth (Exod. i 16); and of the 'many medicines' which their medical practice had brought into use (Jer. lxvi. 11).

In the early stage of medical practice attention was confined among all nations to surgical aid and external applications: even down to a compara-tively late period outward maladies appear to have been the chief subjects of medical treatment among the Hebrews (Isa. i. 6; Ezek. xxx. 21; 2 Kings viii. 29; ix. 15); and although they were not altogether without remedies for internal or even mental disorders (2 Chron. xvi. 12; 1 Sam. xvi. 16), they seem to have made but little progress in this branch of the healing art. The employ-ment of the physician was, however, very general both before and after the Exile (2 Chron .xvi. 12; Jer. viii. 22; Sirach xxxviii. 1; Mark v. 26; comp. Luke iv. 23; v. 31; viii. 43).

The medicines most in use were salves, par-ticularly balms (Jer. viii. 21; xlvi. 11), plasters or poultices (2 Kings xx. 7), oil-baths, mineral baths, river bathing (2 Kings v. 10). The re-medies for internal complaints were mostly very simple, such as our old herbalists would have been disposed to recommend.

Amulets were also much in use among the Jews. Strict persons, however, discountenanced such practices as belonging to 'the ways of the Amorites.' Enchantments were also employed by those who professed the healing art, especially in diseases of the mind; and they were much in the habit of laying their hands upon the patient (2 Kings v. 11; Joseph. *Antiq* ii. 5).

The part taken by the priest in the judgment on leprosy, &c., has led to an impression, that the medical art was in the hands of the Levitical body. This may in some degree be true; not be-cause they were Levites, but because they, more than any other Hebrews, had leisure, and some-times inclination for learned pursuits. The acts prescribed for the priest by the law do not, how-ever, of themselves, prove anything on this point, as the inspection of leprosy belonged rather to sanitary police than to medicine—although it was certainly necessary that the inspecting priest should be able to discriminate, according to the rules laid down in the law, the diagnosis of the disease placed under his control (Lev. xii. 13; xiv. 15). The priests themselves were apt to take colds, &c., from being obliged to minister at all times of the year with naked feet; whence there was in latter times a medical inspector at-tached to the temple to attend to their com-plaints.

Of anatomical knowledge some faint traces may be discerned in such passages as Job ix. 8, sq. It does not appear that the Hebrews were in the habit of opening dead bodies to ascertain the causes of death. We know that the Egyptians were so, and their practice of embalmment must have given them much anatomical knowledge. But to the acquisition of such knowledge there were great obstacles among a people to whom simple contact with a corpse conveyed pollution.

PI-BESETH, a city of Egypt, named with several others in Ezek. xxx. 17. The name was derived from the goddess Bubastis, whom the Greeks identified with their Artemis. A great festive pilgrimage was yearly made to her temple in this place by great numbers of people. Bu-bastus was taken by the Persians, who destroyed the walls; but it was still a place of some con-sideration under the Romans. It was near Bu-bastus that the canal leading to Arsinoe (Suez) opened to the Nile; and although the mouth was afterwards often changed and taken more south-ward, it has now returned to its first locality, as the present canal of Tel-el-Wadee commences in the vicinity of Tel Basta. This Tel Basta, which undoubtedly represents Bubastus, is in N. lat. 30° 30′; E. long. 31° 33′. The site is occupied by mounds of great extent, which consist of the crude brick houses of the town, with the usual heaps of broken pottery. The temple, of which Herodotus states that, although others in Egypt were larger and more magnificent, none were more beautiful, is entirely destroyed; but the re-maining stones, being of the finest red granite, confirm the historian's testimony.

PIGEON. [Dove; Turtle-Dove.]

PI-HAHI′ROTH, a place near the northern end of the Gulf of Suez, east of Baal-zephon (Exod. xiv. 2, 9; Num. xxxiii. 7). The Hebrew signification of the words would be equivalent to 'mouth of the caverns;' but it is doubtless an Egyptian name, and as such would signify a 'place where grass or sedge grows.'

PI′LATE, PON′TIUS, was the sixth Roman Procurator of Judæa (Matt. xxvii. 2; Mark xv. 1; Luke iii. 1; John xviii.-xix.), under whom our Lord taught, suffered, and died (Acts iii. 13; iv. 27; xiii. 28; 1 Tim. vi. 13; Tacit. *Annal.* xv. 44). The testimony of Tacitus on this point is no less clear than it is important; for it fixes beyond a doubt the time when the foundations of our religion were laid. The words of the great historian are: 'The author of that name (Chris-tian) or sect was Christ, who was capitally punished in the reign of Tiberius by Pontius Pilate.'

Pilate was the successor of Valerius Gratus, and governed Judæa, as we have seen, in the reign of Tiberius. He held his office for a period of ten years. The agreement on this point between the accounts in the New Testa-ment and those supplied by Josephus, is entire and satisfactory.

Pilate's conduct in his office was in many re-spects highly culpable. Josephus has recorded two instances in which Pilate acted very tyran-nically (*Antiq* xviii 3. 1; comp. *De Bell Jud.* ii. 9. 2, sq.) in regard to the Jews. He conducted himself with equal injustice and cruelty to the Samaritans also. His own misconduct led the Samaritans to take a step which in itself does not appear seditious or revolutionary, when Pilate seized the opportunity to slay many of the people, not only in the fight which ensued, but also in cold blood after they had given themselves up. 'But when this tumult was appeased, the Samari-tan Senate sent an embassy to Vitellius, now President of Syria, and accused Pilate of the murder of those who had been slain. So Vitel-lus sent Marcellus, a friend of his, to take care of the affairs of Judæa, and ordered Pilate to go to Rome to answer before the emperor to the accusation of the Jews. Pilate, when he had tarried ten years in Judæa, made haste to Rome, and this in obedience to the orders of Vitellius, which he durst not contradict; but before he could get to Rome, Tiberius was dead ' (Joseph. *Antiq.* xviii. 4. 2). This removal took place before the Passover, in A D. 36, probably about September or October, A.D. 35; Pilate must, therefore, as he spent ten years in Judæa, have entered on his government about October, A.D. 25, or at least before the Passover, A.D. 26, in the twelfth year of Tiberius's sole empire.

To be put out of his government by Vitellius, on the complaints of the people of his province, must have been a very grievous mortification to Pilate: and though the emperor was dead before he reached Rome, he did not long enjoy such impunity as guilt permits; for, as Eusebius states, he shortly afterwards made away with himself out of vexation for his many misfortunes.

Owing to the atrocity of the deed in which Pilate took a principal part, and to the wounded feelings of piety with which that deed has been naturally regarded by Christians, a very dark idea has been formed of the character of this Roman governor. That character was undoubtedly bad; but moral depravity has its degrees, and the cause of religion is too sacred to admit any spurious aid from exaggeration. It is therefore desirable to form a just conception of the character of Pilate, and to learn specifically what were the vices under which he laboured. For this purpose a brief outline of the evangelical account seems necessary. The narratives on which the following statement is founded may be found in John xviii., xix.; Matt. xxvii.; Mark xv.; Luke xxiii.

Jesus having been betrayed. apprehended. and found guilty of blasphemy by the Jewish Sanhedrim, is delivered to Pilate in order to undergo the punishment of death, according to the law in that case provided. This delivery of Jesus to Pilate was rendered necessary by the fact, that the Jews, though they retained for the most part their laws and customs, both civil and religious, did not possess the power of life and death which was in the hands of the Roman governor. Pilate could not have been igno ant of Jesus and his pretensions. He might, had he chosen, have immediately ordered Jesus to be executed, for he had been tried and condemned to death by the laws of the land; but he had an alternative. As the execution of the laws, in the case at least of capital punishments, was in the hands of the Roman Procurator, so without any violent straining might his tribunal be converted into a court of appeal in the last instance. At any rate, remonstrance against an unjust verdict was easy and proper on the part of a high officer, who. as having to inflict the punishment, was in a measure responsible for its character. And remonstrance might easily lead to a revision of the grounds on which the verdict had been given, and thus a cause might virtually be brought, *de novo*, before the Procurator: this took place in the case of our Lord. Pilate gave him the benefit of a new trial, and pronounced him innocent.

This review of the case was the alternative that lay before Pilate, the adoption of which speaks undoubtedly in his favour. and may justify us in declaring that his guilt was not of the deepest dye.

That the conduct of Pilate was, however, highly criminal cannot be denied. But his guilt was light in comparison of the criminal depravity of the Jews, especially the priests. His was the guilt of weakness and fear, theirs the guilt of settled and deliberate malice. His state of mind prompted him to attempt the release of an accused person in opposition to the clamours of a misguided mob; theirs urged them to compass the ruin of an acquitted person by instigating the populace, calumniating the prisoner, and terrifying the judge. If Pilate yielded against his judgment under the fear of personal danger, and so took part in an act of unparalleled injustice, the priests and their ready tools originated the false accusation, sustained it by subornation of perjury, and when it was declared invalid, enforced their own unfounded sentence by appealing to the lowest passions. Pilate, it is clear, was utterly destitute of principle. He was willing, indeed, to do right, if he could do right without personal disadvantage. Of gratuitous wickedness he was perhaps incapable, certainly in the condemnation of Jesus he has the merit of being for a time on the side of innocence. But he yielded to violence, and so committed an awful crime. In his hands was the life of the prisoner. Convinced of his innocence he ought to have set him at liberty, thus doing right regardless of consequences. But this is an act of high virtue which we hardly look for at the hands of a Roman governor of Judæa; and though Pilate must bear the reproach of acting contrary to his own declared convictions, yet he may equally claim some credit for the apparently sincere efforts which he made in order to defeat the malice of the Jews and procure the liberation of Jesus.

If now we wish to form a judgment of Pilate's character, we easily see that he was one of that large class of men who aspire to public offices, not from a pure and lofty desire of benefiting the public and advancing the good of the world, but from selfish and personal considerations, from a love of distinction, of power, of self-indulgence; being destitute of any fixed principles, and having no aim but office and influence, they act right only by chance and when convenient, and are wholly incapable of pursuing a consistent course, or of acting with firmness and self-denial in cases in which the preservation of integrity requires the exercise of these qualities. Pilate was obviously a man of weak, and therefore, with his temptations, of corrupt character. This went of strength will readily account for his failing to rescue Jesus from the rage of his enemies, and also for the acts of injustice and cruelty which he practised in his government—acts which, considered in themselves, wear a deeper dye than does the conduct which he observed in surrendering Jesus to the malice of the Jews. And this same weakness may serve to explain to the reader how much influence would be exerted on this unjust judge, not only by the stern bigotry and persecuting wrath of the Jewish priesthood, but specially by the not concealed intimations which they threw out against Pilate. that, if he liberated Jesus, he was no friend of Tiberius and must expect to have to give an account of his conduct at Rome. And that this was no idle threat, Pilate's subsequent deposition by Vitellius shows very plainly; nor could the procurator have been ignorant either of the stern determination of the Jewish character, or of the offence he had by his acts given to the heads of the nation, or of the insecurity, at that very hour, when the contest between him and the priests was proceeding regarding the innocent victim whom they lusted to destroy, of his own position in the office which he held, and which, of course, he desired to retain. On the whole, then, viewing the entire conduct of Pilate, his previous iniquities as well as his bearing on the condemnation of Jesus—viewing his own actual position and the malignity of the Jews, we cannot, we confess, give our vote with those who have passed the severest condemnation on this weak and guilty governor.

That Pilate made an official report to Tiberius of the condemnation and punishment of Jesus Christ, is likely in itself, and is confirmed by the voice of antiquity. Lardner, who has fully discussed the subject, decides that 'it must be allowed by all that Pontius Pilate composed some memoirs concerning our Saviour, and sent them to the emperor.' These documents have in some way been lost, and what we now have under the title of the *Acts* of Pontius Pilate and his letter to Tiberius, are manifestly spurious, though they have probably been fabricated in some keeping with the genuine pieces, the loss of which the composers of the existing documents sought as well as they could to repair.

PINE-TREE. The Hebrew name, *Oren*, occurs only once in Scripture, and is variously translated; but from the manner in which it is introduced, it is impossible to determine whether any of the translations are correct. The *oren* is mentioned with other trees, of whose timber idols were made, in Isa. xliv. 14: 'He heweth him down *cedars* (*eres*) and taketh the *cypress* (*tirzah*), and the *oak* (*allon*), which he strengtheneth for himself among the trees of the forest; he planteth an *ash* (*oren*), and the rain doth nourish it.' Though the English version renders it *ash*, others consider *pine-tree* to be the correct translation; but for neither does there appear to be any decisive proof, nor for the rubus or bramble, adopted for *oren* in the fable of the Cedar and Rubus.

PINNACLE. In the account of our Lord's temptation (Matt. iv. 5), it is stated that the devil took him to Jerusalem, 'and set him on a pinnacle of the temple.' The part of the temple denoted by this term has been much questioned by different commentators, and the only certain conclusion seems to be that it cannot be understood in the sense usually attached to the word, *i. e.* the point of a spiral ornament. Grotius, Hammond, Doddridge, and others, take it in the sense of balustrade or pinnated battlement. But it is now more generally supposed to denote what was called the king's portico, which is mentioned by Josephus (*Antiq.* xv. 11. 5), and is the same which is called in Scripture 'Solomon's porch.'

PIPE [MUSICAL INSTRUMENTS.]

PI'RATHON, a town in the land of Ephraim, to which Abdon, judge of Israel, belonged, and in which he was buried (Judg xii. 13. 15).

PIS'GAH, a mountain ridge in the land of Moab, on the southern border of the kingdom of Sihon (Num. xxi. 20; xxiii. 14; Deut. iii. 27; Josh. xii. 3). In it was Mount Nebo, from which Moses viewed the Promised Land before he died (Deut. xxxiv. 1) [NEBO].

PISID'IA, a district of Asia Minor, lying mostly on Mount Taurus, between Pamphylia, Phrygia, and Lycaonia. Its chief city was Antioch, usually called Antioch in Pisidia, to distinguish it from the metropolitan city of the same name [ANTIOCH, 2].

PITCH. [ASPHALTUM.]

PI'THOM, one of the 'treasure-cities' which the Israelites built in the land of Goshen 'for Pharaoh' (Exod. i. 11) [EGYPT; GOSHEN]. The site is by general consent identified with that of the Patumos of Herodotus (ii 158). Speaking of the canal which connected the Nile with the Red Sea, this author says, 'The water was admitted into it from the Nile. It began a little above the city Bubastus [PI-BESETH], near the Arabian city Patumos, but it discharged itself into the Red Sea.' According to this, Patumos was situated on the east side of the Pelusiac arm of the Nile, not far from the canal which unites the Nile with the Red Sea, in the Arabian part of Egypt. We gather from the *Itinerarium* of Antoninus that this city was twelve Roman miles distant from Heroopolis, the ruins of which are found in the region of the present Abu-Keisheid. All these designations are appropriate if, with the scholars who accompanied the French expedition, we place Pithom on the site of the present Abbaseh, at the entrance of the Wady Fumilat, where there was at all times a strong military post.

PLANE-TREE. The tree called in Hebrew Armon is named thrice in the Scriptures. It occurs among the 'speckled rods' which Jacob placed in the watering-troughs before the sheep (Gen. xxx. 37): its grandeur is indicated in Ezek. xxxi. 8, as well as in Ecclus. xxiv. 19: it is noted for its magnificence, shooting its high boughs aloft. This description agrees well with the plane-tree which is adopted by all the ancient

280. [Platanus Orientalis—Plane-tree.]

translators, to which the balance of critical opinion inclines, and which actually grows in Palestine. The beech, the maple, and the chesnut have been adopted, in different modern versions, as representing the Hebrew Armon; but scarcely any one now doubts that it means the plane-tree. It may be remarked that this tree is in Genesis associated with others—the willow and the poplar—whose habits agree with it; they are all trees of the low grounds, and love to grow where the soil is rich and humid.

PLAGUE. [Pestilence.]
PLEDGE. [Loan.]
PLOUGH. [Agriculture.]
POL'LUX. [Castor and Pollux.]
POLYGAMY. [Marriage.]
POMEGRANATE. The pomegranate is a native of Asia; and we may trace it from Syria, through Persia, even to the mountains of Northern India. It is common in Northern Africa, and was early cultivated in Egypt: hence the Israelites in the desert complain (Num. xx. 5), 'It is no place of seed, or of figs, or of vines, or of *pomegranates.*' Being common in Syria and Persia, it must have early attracted the attention of Eastern nations. In the present day it is highly valued, and travellers describe the pomegranate as being delicious throughout Persia. The late Sir A. Burnes states that the famous pomegranates without seeds are grown in gardens under the snowy hills, near the river Cabul. The bright and dark-green foliage of the pomegranate, and its flowers conspicuous for the crimson colour both of the calyx and petals, must have made it an object of desire in gardens; while its large reddish-coloured fruit, filled with numerous seeds, each surrounded with juicy pleasant-tasted pulp, would make it still more valuable as a fruit in warm countries. The pulpy grains of this fruit are sometimes eaten by themselves, sometimes sprinkled with sugar; at other times the juice is pressed out and made into wine, or one of the esteemed sherbets of the East. This seems also to have been the custom in ancient times, for it is said in Canticles, viii. 2, 'I would cause thee to drink of spiced wine of the juice of my pomegranate.'

The pomegranate was well known to the Greeks. It was employed as a medicine by Hippocrates, and is mentioned by Homer. Various parts of the plant were employed medicinally, as, for instance, the root, or rather its bark, the flowers, and the double flowers; also the rind of the pericarp. Some of the properties which these plants possess, make them useful both as drugs and as medicines. We have hence a combination of useful and ornamental properties, which would make the pomegranate an object sure to command attention: and these, in addition to the showy nature of the flowers, and the roundish form of the fruit, crowned by the protuberant remains of the calyx, would induce its selection as an ornament to be imitated in carved work. Hence we find frequent mention of it as an ornament on the robes of the priests (Exod. xxviii 33; xxxix. 24); and also in the temple (1 Kings vii. 18, 20, 42; 2 Kings xxv. 17; 2 Chron. iii. 16; iv. 13). It might, therefore, well be adduced by Moses among the desirable objects of the land of promise (Deut. viii. 8): 'a land of wheat, and barley, and vines, and fig-trees, and pomegranates; a land of oil-olive and honey.'

PONTIUS PILATE [Pilate.]
PONTUS, the north-eastern province of Asia Minor, which took its name from the sea [Pontus Euxinus] that formed its northern frontier. On the east it was bounded by Colchis, on the south by Cappadocia and part of Armenia, and on the west by Paphlagonia and Galatia. Ptolemy and Pliny regard Pontus and Cappadocia as one province; but Strabo rightly distinguishes them, seeing that each formed a distinct government with its own ruler or prince. The family of Mithridates reigned in Pontus, and that of Ariarathes in Cappadocia. The two countries were also separated naturally from each other by the Lithrus and Ophlimus mountains. The kingdom of Pontus became celebrated under Mithridates the Great, who waged a long war with the Romans, in which he was at length defeated, and his kingdom annexed to the Roman empire by Pompey. That Jews had settled in Pontus, previous to the time of Christ, is evident from the fact, that strangers from Pontus were among those assembled at Jerusalem at the Feast of Pentecost (Acts ii. 9). Christianity also became early known in this country, as the strangers 'in Pontus' are among those to whom Peter addressed his first epistle (1 Pet. i. 1). Of this province Paul's friend, Aquila, was a native (Acts xviii. 2). The principal towns of Pontus were Amasia, the ancient metropolis, and the birth-place of the geographer Strabo, Themiscyra, Cerasus, and Trapezus; which last is still an important town under the name of Trebizond.

POPLAR. (The word thus rendered (*Libneh*) occurs in two places of Scripture, viz. Gen. xxx. 37; Hos. iv. 13, and is supposed to indicate either the *white poplar* or the *storax tree.* The arguments in support of the respective claims of these are nearly equally balanced, although those in favour of the storax appear to us to preponderate. The white poplar is said to be called *white*, not on account of the whiteness of its bark, but of that of the under surface of its leaves. It may perhaps be so designated from the whiteness of its hairy seeds, which have a remarkable appearance when the seed-covering first bursts. The poplar is certainly common in the countries where the scenes are laid of the transactions related in the above passages of Scripture. *Lubne*, both in Arabic and in Persian, is the name of a tree, and of the fragrant resin employed for fumigating, which exudes from it, and which is commonly known by the name of Storax. This resin was well known to the ancients, and is mentioned by Hippocrates and Theophrastus. Dioscorides describes several kinds, all of which were obtained from Asia Minor; and all that is now imported is believed to be the produce of that country. But the tree is cultivated in the south of Europe, though it does not there yield any storax. It is found in Greece, and is supposed to be a native of Asia Minor, whence it extends into Syria, and probably farther south. It is therefore a native of the country which was the scene of the transaction related in the above passage of Genesis.

From the description of Dioscorides, and his comparing the leaves of the styrax to those of the quince, there is no doubt of the same tree being intended: especially as in early times, as at the present day, it yielded a highly fragrant balsamic substance which was esteemed as a medicine, and employed in fumigation. From the similarity of the Hebrew name *libneh* to the Arabic *lubne*, and from the Septuagint having in Genesis translated the former by *styrax*, it

2 x

seems most probable that this was the tree intended. It is capable of yielding white wands as well as the poplar; and it is also well qualified to afford complete shade under its ample foliage, as in the passage of Hos. iv. 13. We may also suppose it to have been more particularly alluded to, from its being a tree yielding incense. 'They sacrifice upon the tops of the mountains, and burn incense upon the hills, under the terebinth and the storax trees, because the shadow thereof is good.'

POR'CIUS FEST'US. [FESTUS.]

POSSESSION. [DEMONIACS.]

POT'IPHAR (contract. of Potipherah), an officer of Pharaoh, probably the chief of his body-guard (Gen. xxxix. 1). Of the Midianitish merchants he purchased Joseph, whose treatment by him is described under that head. The keeper of the prison into which the son of Jacob was eventually cast treated him with kindness, and confided to him the management of the prison; and this confidence was afterwards sanctioned by the 'captain of the guard' himself, as the officer responsible for the safe custody of prisoners of state. It is sometimes denied, but more usually maintained, that this 'captain of the guard' was the same with the Potiphar who is before designated by the same title. We believe that this 'captain of the guard' and Joseph's master were the same person. It would be in accordance with Oriental usage that offenders against the court, and the officers of the court, should be in custody of the captain of the guard; and that Potiphar should have treated Joseph well after having cast him into prison, is not irreconcilable with the facts of the case. After having imprisoned Joseph in the first transport of his choler, he might possibly discover circumstances which led him to doubt his guilt, if not to be convinced of his innocence. The mantle left in the hands of his mistress, and so triumphantly produced against him, would, when calmly considered, seem a stronger proof of guilt against her than against him: yet still, to avoid bringing dishonour upon his wife, and exposing her to new temptation, he may have deemed it more prudent to bestow upon his slave the command of the state prison, than to restore him to his former employment.

POTIPH'ERAH, the priest of On, or Heliopolis, whose daughter Azenath became the wife of Joseph [AZENATH]. The name is Egyptian, and means 'who belongs to the sun.'

POTSHERD. Potsherd is figuratively used in Scripture to denote a thing worthless and insignificant (Ps. xxii. 15; Prov. xxvi. 23; Isa. xlv. 9). It may illustrate some of these allusions to remind the reader of the fact, that the sites of ancient towns are often covered at the surface with great quantities of broken pottery. The present writer has usually found this pottery to be of coarse texture, but coated and protected with a strong and bright-coloured glaze, mostly bluish-green, and sometimes yellow. These fragments give to some of the most venerable sites in the world the appearance of a deserted pottery rather than of a town. The fact is, however, that they occur only upon the sites of towns which were built with crude brick; and this suggests that the heaps of ruin into which these had fallen being disintegrated, and worn at the surface by the action of the weather, bring to view and leave ex-

posed the broken pottery, which is not liable to be thus dissolved and washed away. This explanation was suggested by the actual survey of such ruins; and we know not that a better has yet been offered in any other quarter. It is certainly remarkable that of the more mighty cities of old time, nothing but potsherds now remain visible at the surface of the ground.

Towns built with stone, or kiln-burnt bricks, do not exhibit this form of ruin, which is, therefore, not usually met with in Palestine.

POTTER. The potter, and the produce of his labours, are often alluded to in the Scriptures. The fragility of his wares, and the ease with which they are destroyed, supply apt emblems of the facility with which human life and power may be broken and destroyed. It is in this figurative use that the potter's vessels are most frequently noticed in Scripture (Ps. ii. 9; Isa. xxx. 14; Jer. xix. 11; Rev. ii. 27). In one place, the power of the potter to form with his clay, by

281. [Modern Egyptian Potter.]

the impulse of his will and hand, vessels either for honourable or for mean uses, is employed with great force by the apostle to illustrate the absolute power of God in moulding the destinies of men according to his pleasure (Rom. ix. 21). The first distinct mention of earthenware vessels is in the case of the pitchers in which Gideon's men concealed their lamps, and which they broke in pieces when they withdrew their lamps from them (Judg. vii. 16, 19). Pitchers and bottles are indeed mentioned earlier; but the 'bottle' which contained Hagar's water (Gen. xxi. 14, 15) was undoubtedly of skin; and although Rebekah's pitcher was possibly of earthenware (Gen. xxiv. 14, 15), we cannot be certain that it was so.

POTTER'S-FIELD. [ACELDAMA.]

PRÆTO'RIUM. This word denotes the general's tent in the field, and also the house or palace of the governor of a province, whether a prætor or not. In the Gospels it is applied to the palace built by Herod the Great, at Jerusalem, and which eventually became the residence of the Roman governors in that city (Matt. xxvii. 27; Mark xv. 16; John xviii. 28, 38: xix. 9). In the two first of these texts it may, however, denote the court in front of the palace, where the procurator's guards were stationed [JERUSALEM]. Herod built another palace at Cæsarea, and this also is called the Prætorium in Acts xxiii. 35, probably because it had, in like manner, become the residence of the Roman governor, whose head-quarters were at Cæsarea. In Philipp. i. 13, the word denotes the Prætorian camp at Rome, *i. e.* the camp or quarters of the Prætorian cohort at Rome.

PRIEST, HIGH-PRIEST, &c. A priest may be defined as one who officiates or transacts with God on behalf of others statedly, or for the occasion (Heb. v. 1).

The designation and call of Aaron and his sons to the priesthood are commanded in Exod. xxviii. 1; and holy garments to be made for Aaron, 'for glory and for beauty' (ver. 2), and for his sons (ver. 40), by persons originally skilful, and now also inspired for the purpose (ver. 3), the chief of whom were Bezaleel and Aholiab (xxxi. 2-6). As there were some garments common both to the priests and the high-priest, we shall begin with those of the former, taking them in the order in which they would be put on. 1. The first was 'linen-breeches,' or drawers (xxviii. 42). These were to be of fine twined linen, and to reach from the loins to the middle of the thighs. Such drawers were worn universally in Egypt. No

282. [Drawers and girdle.]

mention occurs of the use of drawers by any other class of persons in Israel except the priests, on whom it was enjoined for the sake of decency. 2. The coat of fine linen or cotton (Exod xxxix. 27). This was worn by men in general (Gen. xxxvii. 3); also by women (2 Sam. xiii. 18; Cant. v. 3), next to the skin. It was to be of woven work. Josephus states that it reached down to the feet, and sat close to the body; and had sleeves, which were tied fast to the arms; and was girded to the breast a little above the elbows by a girdle. It had a narrow aperture about the neck, and was tied with certain strings hanging down from the edge over the breast and back, and was fastened above each shoulder. But this garment, in the case of the priests and high-priest, was to be broidered (xxviii. 4), 'a broidered coat,' by which Gesenius understands a coat of cloth worked in checkers or cells. 3. The girdle (xxviii. 40). This was also worn by magistrates (Isa. xxii. 21). The girdle for the priests was to be made of fine twined linen, and blue, and

purple, and scarlet, of needlework (xxxix. 29). Josephus describes it as often going round, four fingers broad, but so loosely woven that it might be taken for the skin of a serpent; and that it was

283. [Girdle and tunic.]

embroidered with flowers of scarlet, and purple, and blue, but that the warp was nothing but linen. The mode of its hanging down is illustrated by the cut No. 285, where the girdle is also richly embroidered; while the imbricated appearance of the girdle may be seen very plainly in No. 282. The next cut, No. 283, of a priestly scribe of ancient Egypt, offers an interesting specimen of both tunic and girdle. 4. The bonnet, cap, or turban, (xxviii. 40). The bonnet was to be of fine linen (xxxix. 28). In the time of Josephus it was circular, covering about half the head, something like a crown, made of thick linen swathes doubled round many times, and sewed together, surrounded by a linen cover to hide the seams of the swathes, and sat so close that it would not fall off when the body was bent down (*Antiq.* iii. 7. 3). The dress of the high-priest was precisely the same with that of the common priests in all the foregoing particulars; in addition to which he had (1) a robe (xxviii. 4). This was

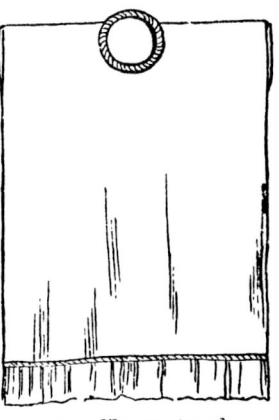

284. [Egyptian tunic.]

not a mantle, but a second and larger coat without sleeves; a kind of surtout worn by the laity, especially persons of distinction (Job. i. 20; ii. 12: by kings, 1 Sam. xv. 27; xviii. 4; xxiv. 5, 12). This garment, when intended for the high-priest, and then called 'the robe of the ephod,' was to be of one entire piece of woven work, all of blue, with an aperture for the neck in the middle of the upper part, having its rim strengthened and adorned with a border. The hem had a kind of fringe, composed of tassels, made of blue, purple, and scarlet, in the form of pomegranates; and between every two promegranates there was a small golden bell, so that there was a bell and a pomegranate alternately all round (xxviii. 31-35). The use of these bells may have partly been, that by the high-priest shaking his garment at the time of his offering incense on the great day of expiation, &c., the people without might be apprised of it, and unite their prayers with it (comp. Ecclus. xlv. 9; Luke i. 10; Acts x. 4; Rev. viii. 3, 4). Josephus describes this robe of the ephod as reaching to the feet, and consisting of one entire piece of woven-work, and parted where the hands came out (John xix. 23). He also states that it was tied round with a girdle, embroidered with the same colours as the former, with a mixture of gold interwoven (*Antiq.* iii. 7. 4). The fringe of bells and pomegranates seems to have been the priestly substitute for the fringe bound with a blue riband, which all the Israelites were commanded to wear. Many traces of this fringe occur in the Egyptian remains. (2.) The ephod (Exod. xxviii. 4). This was a short cloak covering the shoulders and breast. It is said to have been worn by Samuel while a youth minis-

285.   [Ephod and girdle.]

tering before the Lord (1 Sam. ii. 18); by David, while engaged in religious service (2 Sam. vi. 14); and by inferior priests (1 Sam. xxii. 18). But in all these instances it is distinguished as a linen ephod, and was not a sacred but honorary vestment; but the ephod of the high-priest was to be made of gold, of blue, of purple, of scarlet, and fine twined linen, with cunning work. Though it probably consisted of one piece, woven through-out, it had a back part and a front part, united by

shoulder-pieces. It had also a girdle; or rather strings went out from each side and tied it to the body. On the top of each shoulder was to be an onyx stone, set in sockets of gold, each having engraven upon it six of the names of the children of Israel, according to the precedence of birth, to memorialize the Lord of the promises made to them (Exod. xxviii. 6-12, 29). Josephus gives sleeves to the ephod (*Antiq.* iii. 7. 5). It may be considered as a substitute for the leopard-skin worn by the Egyptian high-priests in their most sacred duties, as in No. 285, where the ephod appears no less plainly. Then came (3) the breast-plate, a gorget, ten inches square, made of the same sort of cloth as the ephod, and doubled so as to form a kind of pouch or bag (Exod. xxxix. 9), in which was to be put the URIM and THUM-MIM, which are also mentioned as if already known (xxviii. 30). The external part of this gorget was set with four rows of precious stones; the first row, a sardius, a topaz, and a carbuncle; the second, an emerald, a sapphire, and a diamond; the third, a ligure, an agate, and an amethyst; and the fourth, a beryl, an onyx, and a jasper,—set in a golden socket. Upon each of these stones was to be engraven the name of one of the sons of Jacob. In the ephod, in which there was a space left open sufficiently large for the admission of this pectoral, were four rings of gold, to which four others at the four corners of the breastplate corresponded; the two lower rings of the latter being fixed inside. It was confined to the ephod by means of dark blue ribands, which passed through these rings; and it was also suspended from the onyx stones on the shoulder by chains of gold, or rather cords of twisted gold threads, which were fastened at one end to two other *larger* rings fixed in the upper corners of the pectoral, and by the other end going round the onyx stones on the shoulders, and returning and being fixed in the larger ring. The breastplate was further kept in its place by a girdle, made of the same stuff, which Josephus says was sewed to the breastplate, and which, when it had gone once round, was tied again upon the seam and hung down. It appears in No. 287. 4. The remaining portion of dress peculiar to the high-priest was the mitre (xxviii 4). The Bible says nothing of the difference between this and the turban of the common priests. It is, however, called by a different name. It was to be of fine linen (ver. 39). Josephus says it was the same in construction and figure with that of the common priest, but that above it there was another, with swathes of blue, embroidered, and round it was a golden crown, polished, of three rows, one above another, out of which rose a cup of gold, which resembled the calyx of the herb called by Greek botanists hyoscyamus. He ends a most laboured description by comparing the shape of it to a poppy (iii. 7. 6). Upon comparing his account of the bonnet of the priests with the mitre of the high-priests, it would appear that the latter was conical. The cut, No. 286, presents the principal forms of the mitres worn by the ancient priests of Egypt, and affords a substantial resemblance of that prescribed to the Jews, divested of idolatrous symbols, but which were displaced to make way for a simple plate of gold, bearing the inscription, 'Holiness to Jehovah.' This plate extended from one ear to the other, being bound to the forehead by strings tied behind, and further secured in its position by a blue riband attached to the mitre (Exod. **xxviii.** 36-39; **xxxix.** 30; Lev. viii. 9). The

286. [Egyptian mitres.]

magnificent dress of the high-priest was not always worn by him. It was exchanged for one wholly of linen, and therefore white, though of similar construction, when on the day of expiation he entered into the Holy of Holies (Lev. xvi. 4, 23); and neither he nor the common priests wore their appropriate dress, except when officiating. The garments of the inferior priests appear to have been kept in the sacred treasury (Ezra ii. 69; Neh. vii. 70).

The next incident in the *history* is, that Moses receives *a command to consecrate* Aaron and his sons to the priests' office (Exod. xxviii. 41), with the following ceremonies. They were to be washed at the door of the tabernacle of the congregation (xxix. 4), where the altar of burnt offering stood (xl. 6, 29). Aaron was then robed in his pontifical garments (vers. 4-6), and anointed with a profusion of oil (ver. 7); whence he was called ' the priest that is anointed ' (Lev. iv. 3, &c.; Ps. cxxxiii. 2). This last act was the peculiar and only distinguishing part of Aaron's consecration; for the anointing of his sons (xxx. 30) relates only to the unction (xxix. 31), by a mixture made of the blood of the sacrifice and of the anointing oil, which was sprinkled upon both Aaron and his sons, and upon their garments, as part of their consecration. Hence then Aaron received two unctions. In after-times the high-priest took an oath (Heb. vii. 23) to bind him, as the Jews say, to a strict adherence to established customs. The other details of this ceremony of consecration are all contained in one chapter (Exod. xxix.), to which we must be content to refer the reader. The entire ceremony lasted seven days, on each of which all the sacrifices were repeated (Lev. viii. 33), to which a promise was added, that God would sanctify Aaron and his sons, that is, declare them to be sanctified, which he did, by the appearance of his glory at their first sacrifice, and by the fire which descended and consumed their burnt-offerings (Lev. ix. 23, 24). Thus were Aaron and his sons and their descendants separated for ever, to the office of the priesthood, from all other Israelites. There was consequently no need of any further consecration for them or their descendants. The first-born son of Aaron succeeded him in the office, and the elder son among all his descendants: a rule which, though deviated from in after-times, was ultimately resumed. The next successor was to be anointed and consecrated in his father's holy garments (ver. 29), which he must wear seven days when he went into the tabernacle of the congregation to minister (ver. 30; comp. Num. xx. 26-28; xxxv. 25), and make an atonement for all things and persons (Lev. xvi. 32-34), and for himself (comp. ver. 11), besides the offering (vi. 20-22). The common priests were required to prove their descent from Aaron. No age was prescribed for their entrance on their ministry, or retirement from it.

We shall now give a summary of the *duties and emoluments* of the high-priest and common priests respectively. Besides his lineal descent from Aaron, the high-priest was required to be free from every bodily blemish or defect (Lev. xxi. 16-23); but though thus incapacitated, yet, his other qualifications being sufficient, he might eat of the food appropriated to the priests (ver. 22). He must not marry a widow, nor a divorced woman, or profane, or that had been a harlot, but a virgin Israelitess (ver. 14). In Ezekiel's vision a general permission is given to the priests to marry a priest's widow (xliv. 22). The high-

287. [High-priest.]

priest might not observe the external signs of mourning for any person, or leave the sanctuary upon receiving intelligence of the death of even father or mother (ver. 10-12; comp. x. 7). Public calamities seem to have been an exception, for Joacim the high-priest, and the priests, in such circumstances ministered in sackcloth with ashes on their mitres (Judith iv. 14, 15; comp. Joel i. 13). He must not eat anything that died of itself, or was torn of beasts (Lev. xxii. 8); must wash his hands and feet when he went into the tabernacle of the congregation, and when he came near to the altar to minister (Exod. xxx. 19-21). At first Aaron was to burn incense on the golden altar every morning when he dressed the lamps, and every evening when he lighted them, but in later times the common priest performed this duty (Luke i. 8, 9); to offer, as the Jews understand it, daily, morning and evening, the peculiar meat-offering he offered on the day of his consecration (Exod. xxix); to perform the ceremonies of the great day of expiation (Lev. xvi.); to arrange the shew-bread every Sabbath, and to eat it in the holy place (xxiv. 9); must abstain from the holy things during his uncleanness (xxii. 1-3); also if he became leprous, or contracted uncleanness (ver. 4-7). If he committed a sin of ignorance he must offer a sin-offering for it (iv. 3-13); and so for the people (ver. 12-22); was to eat the remainder of the people's meat-offerings with the inferior priests in the holy place (vi. 16); to judge of the leprosy in the human body or garments (xiii. 2-59); to adjudicate legal questions (Deut. xvii. 12). Indeed, when there was no divinely inspired judge, the high-priest was the supreme ruler till the time of David, and again after the captivity. He must be present at the appointment of a new ruler or leader (Num. xxvii. 19), and ask counsel of the Lord for the ruler (ver. 21). Eleazar with others distributes the spoils taken from the Midianites (Num. xxxi. 21, 26). To the high-priest also belonged the appointment of a maintenance from the funds of the sanctuary to an incapacitated priest (1 Sam. ii. 36, margin). Besides these duties, peculiar to himself, he had others in common with the inferior priests. Thus, when the camp set forward, 'Aaron and his sons' were to take the tabernacle to pieces, to cover the various portions of it in cloths of various colours (iv. 5-15), and to appoint the Levites to their services in carrying them; to bless the people in the form prescribed (vi. 23-27), to be responsible for all official errors and negligences (xviii. 1), and to have the general charge of the sanctuary (ver. 5).

Emoluments of the High-Priest.—Neither the high-priest nor common priests received ' any inheritance' at the distribution of Canaan among the several tribes (Num. xviii. 20; Deut. xviii. 1, 2), but were maintained, with their families, upon certain fees, dues, perquisites, &c., arising from the public services, which they enjoyed as a common fund. Perhaps the only distinct prerogative of the high-priest was a tenth part of the tithes assigned to the Levites (Num. xviii. 28; comp. Neh. x. 38); but Josephus represents this also as a common fund (*Antiq.* iv. 4. 4).

Duties of the Priests.—Besides those duties already mentioned as common to them and the high-priests, they were required to prove their descent from Aaron, to be free from all bodily defect or blemish (Lev. xxi. 16-23); must not observe mourning, except for near relatives (xxi. 1-5); must not marry a woman that had been a harlot, or divorced, or profane. The priest's daughter who committed whoredom was to be burnt, as profaning her father (xxi. 9). The priests were to have the charge of the sanctuary and altar (Num. xviii. 5). The fire upon the altar, being once kindled (Lev. i. 7), the priests were always to keep it burning (vi. 13). In later times, and upon extraordinary occasions, at least, they flayed the burnt-offerings (2 Chron. xxix. 34), and killed the Passover (Ezra vi. 20). They were to receive the blood of the burnt-offerings in basins (Exod. xxiv. 6), and sprinkle it round about the altar, arrange the wood and the fire,

and to burn the parts of the sacrifices (Lev. i. 5. 10). If the burnt-sacrifice were of doves, the priest was to nip off the head with his finger-nail, squeeze out the blood on the edge of the altar, pluck off the feathers, and throw them with the crop into the ash-pit, divide it down the wings, and then completely burn it (ver. 15-17). He was to offer a lamb every morning and evening (Num. xxviii. 3), and a double number on the Sabbath (ver. 9), the burnt-offerings ordered at the beginning of months (ver. 11), and the same on the Feast of Unleavened Bread (ver. 19), and on the day of the First Fruits (ver. 26); to receive the meat-offering of the offerer, bring it to the altar, take of it a memorial, and burn it upon the altar (Lev. ii.); to sprinkle the blood of the peace-offerings upon the altar round about, and then to offer of it a burnt-offering (iii.); to offer the sin-offering for a sin of ignorance in a ruler or any of the common people (iv. 22-25); to eat the sin-offering in the holy-place (vi. 26; comp. x. 16-18); to offer the trespass-offering (ver. 6-19; vi. 6, 7), to sprinkle its blood round about the altar (vii. 2), to eat of it, &c. (ver. 6); to eat of the shew-bread in the holy place (xxiv. 9); to offer for the purification of women after child-birth (xii. 6, 7); to judge of the leprosy in the human body or garments; to decide when the leper was cleansed, and to order a sacrifice for him (xiv. 3, 4); to administer the rites used at pronouncing him clean (ver. 6, 7); to present him and his offering before the Lord, and to make an atonement for him (ver. 10-32); to judge of the leprosy in a house (xiv. 33-47), to decide when it was clean (ver. 48), and to make an atonement for it (ver. 49-53); to make an atonement for men cleansed from an issue of uncleanness (xv. 14, 15), and for women (ver. 29, 30); to offer the sheaf of First Fruits (xxiii. 10, 11); to estimate the commutation in money for persons in cases of a singular or extraordinary vow (xxvii. 8), or for any devoted unclean beast (ver. 11, 12), or for a house (ver. 14), or field (xviii. 23); to conduct the ordeal of the bitter water (Num. v. 12-31); to make an atonement for a Nazarite who had accidentally contracted uncleanness (vi. 13); to offer his offering when the days of his separation were fulfilled (ver. 14, 16); to blow with the silver trumpets on all occasions appointed (vi. 13-17), and ultimately at morning and evening service (1 Chron. xvi. 6); to make an atonement for the people and individuals in case of erroneous worship (Num. xv. 15, 24, 25, 27); to make the ointment of spices (1 Chron. ix. 30); to prepare the water of separation (Num. xix. 1-11); to act as assessors in judicial proceedings (Deut. xvii. 9; xix. 7); to encourage the army when going to battle, and probably to furnish the officers with the speech (ver. 5-9); to superintend the expiation of an uncertain murder (xxi. 5), and to have charge of the law (xxxi. 9).

Christians are figuratively called priests (Rev. i. 6; xx. 6). The student will observe the important distinction, that the term 'priest,' with which term the idea of a sacrifice was always connected in ancient times, is never applied to the pastor of the Christian church.

PRIS'CA. [PRISCILLA.]

PRISCIL'LA, or PRISCA, wife of Aquila, and probably, like Phœbe, a deaconess. She shared the travels, labours, and dangers of her husband,

and is always named along with him (Rom. xvi. 3; 1 Cor. xvi. 19; 2 Tim. iv. 19) [AQUILA].

PRISON. [PUNISHMENT.]

PRIZE. [GAMES.]

PROCH'ORUS, one of the seven first deacons of the Christian church (Acts vi. 5). Nothing is known of him.

PROCONSUL, a Roman officer appointed to the government of a province with consular authority. He was chosen out of the body of the senate; and it was customary, when any one's consulate expired, to send him as a proconsul into some province. He enjoyed the same honour with the consuls, but was allowed only six lictors with the fasces before him.

The proconsuls decided cases of equity and justice, either privately in their palaces, where they received petitions, heard complaints, and granted writs under their seals; or publicly in the common hall, with the formalities generally observed in the courts at Rome. These duties were, however, more frequently delegated to their assessors, or other judges of their own appointment. As the proconsuls had also the direction of justice, of war, and of the revenues, these departments were administered by their lieutenants, or *legati*, who were usually nominated by the senate. The office of the proconsuls lasted generally for one year only, and the expense of their journeys to and from their provinces was defrayed by the public. After the partition of the provinces between Augustus and the people, those who presided over the provinces of the latter were especially designated proconsuls, from whom it appears to have been customary to decree temples. Livy (viii. and xxvi.) mentions two other classes of proconsuls: those who, being consuls, had their office continued beyond the time appointed by law; and those who, being previously in a private station, were invested with this honour, either for the government of provinces, or to command in war. Some were created proconsuls by the senate without being appointed to any province, merely to command in the army, and to take charge of the military discipline; others were allowed to enter upon their proconsular office before being admitted to the consulship, but having that honour in reserve.

When the Apostle Paul was at Corinth, he was brought before Gallio, the proconsul of Achaia, one of the provinces of Greece, of which Corinth was the chief city, and arraigned by the Jews as one who 'persuadeth men to worship God contrary to the law' (Acts xviii. 13); but Gallio refused to act as a judge of such matters, and 'drave them from the judgment-seat' (ver. 16).

PROGNOSTICATORS. The phrase 'monthly prognosticators' occurs in the Authorized Version of Isa. xlvii. 13, where the prophet is enumerating the astrological superstitions of the Chaldæans. The original might perhaps be more exactly rendered, as by Dr. Henderson, 'prognosticators at the new moons.' It is known that the Chaldæan astrologers professed to divine future events by the positions, aspects, and appearances of the stars, which they regarded as having great influence on the affairs of men and kingdoms; and it would seem, from the present text, that they put forth accounts of the events which might be expected to occur from month to month, like our old almanac-makers. Some carry the analogy further, and suppose that they also gave monthly tables of the weather; but *such* prognostications are only cared for in climates where the weather is uncertain and variable; while in Chaldæa, where (as we know from actual experience) the seasons are remarkably regular in their duration and recurrence, and where variations of the usual course of the weather are all but unknown, no prognosticator would gain much honour by foretelling what every peasant knows.

PROPHECY. The principal considerations involved in this important subject may be arranged under the following heads:—

I. *The nature of Prophecy, and its position in the economy of the Old Testament.*—Divine inspiration is only the general basis of the prophetic office, to which two more elements must be added:—

1. Inspiration was imparted to the prophets in *a peculiar form.* This appears decisively from Num. xii. 6, &c., which states it as characteristic of the prophet, that he obtained divine inspiration in *visions* and *dreams*, consequently in a state different from that in which inspirations were conveyed to Moses and the apostles.

2. Generally speaking, every one was a prophet to whom God communicated his mind in this peculiar manner. When the Mosaic economy had been established, a new element was added; the prophetic gift was after that time regularly connected with the prophetic office, so that the latter came to form part of the idea of a prophet. Speaking of office, we do not of course mean one conferred by men, but by God; the mission to Israel, with which the certainty of a continued, not temporary, grant of the *donum propheticum* was connected.

That the Lord would send such prophets was promised to the people by Moses, who by a special law (Deut. xviii. 1) secured them authority and safety. As his ordinary servants and teachers, God appointed the Priests: the characteristic mark which distinguished the prophets from them was inspiration; and this explains the circumstance that, in times of great moral and religious corruption, when the ordinary means no longer sufficed to reclaim the people, the number of prophets increased. The regular religious instruction of the people was no part of the business of the prophets; their proper duty was only to rouse and excite. In this point, however, there was a difference between the kingdom of Israel and the kingdom of Judah. In the latter the agency of the prophets was only subsidiary to that of the regular servants of God, the priests and the Levites. But in the former the prophets were the regular servants of God, for the priesthood there had no divine sanction, and was corrupt in its very source. With the office of the prophets therefore all stood or fell, and hence they were required to do many things besides what the original conception of the office of a prophet implied.

In their labours, as respected their own times, the prophets were strictly bound to the Mosaic law, and not allowed to add to it or to diminish ought from it; what was said in this respect to the whole people (Deut. iv. 2; xiii. 1) applied also to them. We find, therefore, prophecy always takes its ground on the Mosaic law, to which it refers, from which it derives its sanction, and with which it is fully impressed and saturated. They were indeed commissioned to foretell days when a new covenant will be made with the house of Israel and with the house of Judah (Jer. xxxi. 31). But for their own times they never once dreamt of altering any, even the minutest and least essential precept, even as to its form; how much less as to its spirit, which even the Lord himself declares (Matt. v. 18) to be immutable and eternal.

As to prophecy in its circumscribed sense, or the foretelling of future events by the prophets, some expositors would explain all predictions of special events; while others assert that no prediction contains anything but general promises or threatenings, and that the prophets knew nothing of the particular manner in which their predictions might be realized. Both these classes deviate from the correct view of prophecy; the former resort often to the most arbitrary interpretations, and the latter are opposed by a mass of facts against which they are unable successfully to contend.

Some interpreters, misunderstanding passages like Jer. xviii. 8; xxvi. 13, have asserted that all prophecies were conditional; and have even maintained that their revocability distinguished the true predictions from soothsaying. But beyond all doubt, when the prophet denounces the divine judgments, he proceeds on the assumption that the people will not repent, an assumption which he knows from God to be true. Were the people to repent, the prediction would fail; but because they will not, it is uttered *absolutely*. It does not follow, however, that the prophet's warnings and exhortations are useless. These serve 'for a witness against them;' and besides, amid the ruin of the mass, individuals might be saved. Viewing prophecies as conditional predictions nullifies them.

The sphere of action of the prophets was limited to Israel. Many predictions of the Old Testament concern, indeed, the events of foreign nations, but they are always uttered and written with reference to Israel, and the prophets thought not of publishing them among the heathens themselves.

II. *Duration of the Prophetic office.*—Although we meet with cases of prophesying as early as the age of the patriarchs, still the roots of prophetism among Israel are properly fixed in the Mosaic economy. The main business of Moses was not that of a prophet, but he was occasionally commissioned to foretell what was to befall Israel in the latter days, and he instilled into the congregation of Israel those truths which form the foundation of prophecy, and thus prepared the ground from which it could spring up. In the age of the Judges, prophecy, though existing only in scattered instances, exerted a powerful influence. From this time to the Babylonian exile, there happened hardly any important event in which the prophets did not appear as performing the leading part. About a hundred years after the return from the Babylonian exile, the prophetic profession ceased. The Jewish tradition uniformly states that Haggai, Zechariah, and Malachi were the last prophets.

III. *Manner of Life of the Prophets.*—The prophets went about poorly and coarsely dressed (2 Kings i 8), not as a mere piece of asceticism,

but that their very apparel might teach what the people ought to do. Generally the prophets were not anxious of attracting notice by ostentatious display; nor did they seek worldly wealth, most of them living in poverty and even want (1 Kings xiv. 3; 2 Kings iv. 1). Insult, persecution, imprisonment, and death, were often the reward of their godly life. Repudiated by the world in which they were aliens, they typified the life of Him whose appearance they announced, and whose spirit dwelt in them. The prophets addressed the people of both kingdoms: they were not confined to particular places, but prophesied where it was required. For this reason they were most numerous in capital towns, especially in Jerusalem, where they generally spoke in the temple. Sometimes their advice was asked, and then their prophecies take the form of answers to questions submitted to them (Isa. xxxvii., Ez. xx., Zech. vii.). But much more frequently they felt themselves inwardly moved to address the people without their advice having been asked, and they were not afraid to stand forward in places where their appearance, perhaps, produced indignation and terror. Whatever lay within or around the sphere of religion and morals, formed the object of their care. Priests, princes, kings, all must hear them —must, however reluctantly, allow them to perform their calling as long as they spoke in the name of the true God, and as long as the result did not disprove their pretensions to be the servants of the invisible King of Israel (Jer. xxxvii. 15-21). There were institutions for training prophets; the senior members instructed a number of pupils and directed them. These schools had been first established by Samuel (1 Sam. x. 8; xix. 19); and at a later time there were such institutions in different places, as Bethel and Gilgal (2 Kings ii. 3; iv. 38; vi. 1). The pupils of the prophets lived in fellowship united, and were called 'sons of the prophets;' whilst the senior or experienced prophets were considered as their spiritual parents, and were styled fathers (comp. 2 Kings ii. 12; vi. 21). Samuel, Elijah, and Elisha, are mentioned as principals of such institutions. From them the Lord generally chose his instruments. Amos relates of himself (vii. 14, 15), as a thing uncommon, that he had been trained in no school of prophets, but was a herdsman, when the Lord took him to prophesy unto the people of Israel. At the same time, this example shows that the bestowal of prophetic gifts was not limited to the schools of the prophets. Women also might come forward as prophetesses, as instanced in Miriam, Deborah, and Huldah, though such cases are of comparatively rare occurrence. We should also observe, that only as regards the kingdom of Israel we have express accounts of the continuance of the schools of prophets. What is recorded of them is not directly applicable to the kingdom of Judah, especially since, as stated above, prophecy had in it an essentially different position. We cannot assume that the organization and regulations of the schools of the prophets in the kingdom of Judah should have been as settled and established as in the kingdom of Israel. The prophets of the kingdom of Israel stood in a hostile position to the priests. These points of difference in the situation of the prophets of the two kingdoms must not be lost sight of; and we further add, that prophecy in the kingdom of Israel was much more connected with extraordinary events than in the kingdom of Judah: the history of the latter offers no prophetical deeds equalling those of Elijah and Elisha.

IV. *Symbolic Actions of the Prophets.*—In the midst of the prophetic declarations symbolic actions are often mentioned, which the prophets had to perform. The opinions of interpreters on these are divided. Some assert that they always, at least generally, were really done; others assert that they had existence only in the mind of the prophets, and formed part of their visions. The latter view, which was espoused by Calvin, is probably the correct one. Some of the symbolic actions prescribed to the prophets could not have been performed by them (Ezek. ii. 9; iii. 2, 3; iv. 4–8); others are inconsistent with decorum (Hos. i. 2-11; Ezek. iv. 12-15). These are therefore to be regarded as internal, not external facts.

V. *Criteria by which True and False Prophets were distinguished.*—As Moses had foretold, a host of false prophets arose in later times among the people, who promised prosperity without repentance, and preached the Gospel without the law. But how were the people to distinguish true and false prophets? In the law concerning prophets (Deut. xviii. 20; comp. xiii. 7-9), the following enactments are contained.

1. The prophet *who speaks in the name of other Gods* is to be considered as false, and to be punished capitally.

2. The same punishment is to be inflicted on him who speaks in the name of the true God, but *whose predictions are not accomplished.*

3. From the above two criteria of a true prophet, flows the third, that *his addresses must be in strict accordance with the law.*

4. In the above is also founded the fourth criterion, that *a true prophet must not promise prosperity without repentance;* and that he is a false prophet, 'of the deceit of his own heart,' who does not reprove the sins of the people, and who does not inculcate on them the doctrines of divine justice and retribution.

In addition to these negative criteria, there were positive ones to procure authority to true prophets. First of all, it must be assumed that the prophets themselves received, along with the divine revelations, assurance that these were really divine. Now, when the prophets themselves were convinced of their divine mission, they could in various ways prove it to others, whom they were called on to enlighten.

(*a.*) To those who had any sense of truth, the Spirit of God gave evidence that the prophecies were divinely inspired.

(*b.*) The prophets themselves utter their firm conviction that they act and speak by divine authority, not of their own accord. Their pious life bore testimony to their being worthy of a nearer communion with God, and defended them from the suspicion of intentional deception; their sobriety of mind distinguished them from all fanatics, and defended them from the suspicion of self-delusion; their fortitude in suffering for truth proved that they had their commission from no human authority.

(*c.*) Part of the predictions of the prophets referred to proximate events, and their accomplishment was divine evidence of their divine origin.

(See 1 Sam. iii. 19; Isa. xxxvii. 21, sq ; Jer. xxii. 11, 12; Ezek. xii. 12, 13; xxiv.) Whoever had been once favoured with such a testimonial, his authority was established for his whole life.

(*d.*) Sometimes the divine mission of the prophets was also proved by miracles, but this occurred only at important crises, when the existence of the kingdom of Israel was in jeopardy, as in the age of Elijah and Elisha.

VI. *Promulgation of the Prophetic Declarations.*—Usually the prophets promulgated their visions in public places before the congregated people. Still some portions of the prophetic books, as the entire second part of Isaiah and the description of the new temple (Ezek. xl.-xlviii), probably were never communicated orally. In other cases the prophetic addresses, first delivered orally, were next, when committed to writing, revised and improved. Especially the books of the lesser prophets consist, for the greater part, not of separate predictions, independent of each other, but form, as they now are, a whole, that is, give the quintessence of the prophetic labours of their authors. There is evidence to prove that the later prophets sedulously read the writings of the earlier, and that a prophetic canon existed before the present was formed. Zechariah explicitly alludes to writings of former prophets; 'to the words which the Lord has spoken to earlier prophets, when Jerusalem was inhabited and in prosperity' (Zech. i. 4; vii. 7, 12). In consequence of the prophets being considered as organs of God, much care was bestowed on the preservation of their publications. Ewald himself, though he thinks that a great number of prophetic compositions has been lost, cannot refrain from observing (p. 56), 'We have in Jer. xxvi. 1-19 a clear proof of the exact knowledge which the better classes of the people had of all that had, a hundred years before, happened to a prophet, of his words, misfortunes, and accidents.'

The collectors of the Canon arranged the prophets chronologically, but considered the whole of the twelve lesser prophets as one work, which they placed after Jeremiah and Ezekiel, inasmuch as the three last lesser prophets lived later than they. The collection of the lesser prophets themselves was again chronologically disposed; still Hosea is, on account of the extent of his work, allowed precedence before those lesser prophets, who, generally, were his contemporaries, and also before those who flourished at a somewhat earlier period.

PROSELYTE, the name applied in the New Testament and the Septuagint to converts from heathenism to Judaism. In the Old Testament such persons are called *strangers* and *settlers*. For the reception and treatment of these, provision was made in the law of Moses (Exod. xii. 48; Lev. xvii. 8; Num. xv. 15, &c.); and the whole Jewish state was considered as composed of the two classes, Jews, and strangers within their gates, or proselytes. In later years this distinction was observed even to the second generation.

It has been customary to make a distinction between two classes of Jewish proselytes, the one denominated proselytes of the gate, and the other proselytes of the covenant, or of righteousness. Under the former have been included those converts from heathenism who had so far renounced idolatry as to become worshippers of the one God, and to observe, generally, what have been called the seven Noachic precepts, viz.. against idolatry, profanity, incest, murder, dishonesty, eating blood, or things strangled, and allowing a murderer to live, but had not formally enrolled themselves in the Jewish state. The latter is composed of those who had submitted to circumcision. and in all respects become converts to Judaism. The accuracy of this distinction, however, has been called in question by several, especially by Lardner, whose arguments appear decisive of the question (*Works*, vol. vi. pp. 522-533 ; vol. xi. pp. 313-324, 8vo. edit. 1788). That there were, in later times especially, many among the Jews who had renounced the grosser parts of heathenism without having come over entirely to Judaism, is beyond all doubt ; but that these were ever counted *proselytes* admits of question. Certain it is that the proselytes mentioned in the New Testament were all persons who had received circumcision, and entered the pale of the Jewish community.

The rites by which a proselyte was initiated are declared by the Rabbins to have been, in the case of a man, *three*, viz., *circumcision. baptism*, and a *free-will sacrifice*. In the case of a woman the first was of necessity omitted. As to the first and last of these, their claim to be regarded as accordant with the ancient practice of the Jews has been on all hands admitted without scruple ; but it has been matter of keen question whether the second can be admitted to have been practised before the Christian era. The substance of much learned discussion on this head we shall attempt summarily to state.

There is no *direct* evidence that this rite was practised by the Jews before the second or third century of the Christian era ; but the fact that it was practised by them then necessitates the inquiry : when and how did such a custom arise among them? That they borrowed it from the Christians is an opinion which cannot be for a moment admitted by any who reflect on the implacable hatred with which the Jews for many centuries regarded Christianity, its ordinances, and its professors. Some learned men have adopted the notion that the custom of baptizing proselytes arose gradually out of the habit which the Jews had of purifying by ablution whatever they deemed unclean, and that it was not formally adopted as an initiatory rite till after the destruction of the temple service, and when in consequence of imperial edicts it became difficult to circumcise converts. But as the Rabbins prescribed *both* baptism and circumcision as initiatory rites for proselytes, it is manifestly absurd to say that the former was instituted in consequence of the difficulty of performing the latter. And this hypothesis still leaves unremoved the master difficulty of that side of the question which it is designed to support, viz.. the great improbability of the Jews adopting for the first time subsequently to the death of Christ, a religious rite which was well known to be the initiatory rite of Christianity. On the other hand we have, in favour of the hypothesis that proselyte baptism was practised anterior to the time of our Lord, some strongly corroborative evidence. We have, in the first place, the unanimous tradition of the Jewish Rabbins, who impute to the practice an antiquity commensurate almost with that of their nation. 2dly. We have the fact that the Baptism

of John the Baptist was not regarded by the people as aught of a novelty, nor was it represented by him as resting for its authority upon any special divine relation. 3dly. We have the fact that the Pharisees looked upon the baptism both of John and Jesus as a mode of proselyting men to their religious views (John iv. 1-3), and that the dispute between the Jews and some of John's disciples about purifying was apparently a dispute as to the competing claims of John and Jesus to make proselytes (John iii. 25, sq.). 4thly. We have the fact, that on the day of Pentecost Peter addressed to a multitude of persons collected from several different and distant countries, Jews and proselytes, an exhortation to ' Repent and be baptized ' (Acts ii. 38), from which it may be fairly inferred that they all knew what baptism meant, and also its connection with repentance or a change of religious views. 5thly. We have the fact that, according to Josephus, the Essenes were in the habit, before admitting a new convert into their society, solemnly and ritually to purify him with waters of cleansing, a statement which cannot be understood of their ordinary ablutions before meals, for Josephus expressly adds, that even after this lustration two years had to elapse before the neophyte enjoyed the privilege of living with the proficients. And, 6thly. We have the mode in which Josephus speaks of the baptism of John, when, after referring to John's having exhorted the people to virtue, righteousness, and godliness, as preparatory to baptism, he adds, ' For it appeared to him that baptism was admissible not when they used it for obtaining forgiveness of some sins, but for the purification of the body when the soul had been already cleansed by righteousness ' (*Antiq.* xviii. 5. 2) ; which seems to indicate the conviction of the historian that John did not *introduce* this rite, but only gave to it a peculiar meaning.

On these grounds we adhere to the opinion that proselyte baptism was known as a Jewish rite anterior to the birth of Christ.

From the time of the Maccabees the desire to make proselytes prevailed among the Jews to a very great extent, especially on the part of the Pharisees, whose intemperate zeal for this object our Lord pointedly rebuked (Matt. xxiii. 15). The greater part of their converts were females, which has been ascribed to the dislike of the males to submit to circumcision. Josephus tells us that the Jews at Antioch were continually converting great numbers of the Greeks, and that nearly all the women at Damascus were attached to Judaism.

PROSEUCHA, a word signifying ' prayer,' and always so translated in the Auth. Version. It is, however, applied, *per meton.*, to a place of prayer,—a place where assemblies for prayer were held, whether a building or not. In this sense it seems also to be mentioned in Luke vi. 12, where the words rendered by our translators. ' in prayer to God,' might rather signify, ' in an oratory of God,' or a place that was devoted to his service, especially for prayer. In the same sense the phrase must, still more certainly, be understood in Acts xvi. 13, where the Syriac has, ' because there was perceived to be *a house of prayer;*' and the Arabic, ' a certain place which was supposed to be *a place of prayer.*'

That there really were such places of devotion

among the Jews is unquestionable. They were mostly outside those towns in which there were no synagogues, because the laws or their administrators would not admit any. They appear to have been usually situated near a river, or the sea-shore, for the convenience of ablution (Joseph. *Antiq.* xiv. 10, 23). Sometimes the proseucha was a large building, as that at Tiberias (*l. c.* § 54), so that the name was sometimes applied even to synagogues. But, for the most part, the proseuchæ appear to have been places in the open air, in a grove, or in shrubberies, or even under a tree, although always, as we may presume, near water, for the convenience of those ablutions which with the Jews always preceded prayer.

PROVERBS, THE BOOK OF. That Solomon was the author of the Book of Proverbs has never been questioned. Some have indeed thought that he composed a part only of the Proverbs included in that book, and collected the others from various sources. It is probable, indeed, that he availed himself of any sayings already current which he regarded as useful and important. Whether he ever made any *collection* of his proverbs in writing is, however, doubtful. From the twenty-fifth chapter to the end, we are expressly informed, was written out and added to the previous portion, by order of King Hezekiah The divine authority of the book is sufficiently proved by the quotations made from it in the New Testament (Rom. xii. 16; Heb. xii. 5, 6; 1 Pet. iv. 8; 1 Thess. v. 15).

The characteristics of the proverbial style (in the more restricted sense of the word) are, according to Bishop Lowth, 1. Brevity; 2. Obscurity; 3. Elegance. The first of these is, however, the only one that can be considered at all universal. Many of the Proverbs of Solomon can hardly lay claim to elegance, according to the most liberal application of the term, and comparatively few of them are at all obscure as to meaning. The same remark applies with even greater force to the proverbs of every-day life, *e. g. Time and tide tarry for no man. Haste makes waste. Make hay while the sun shines. A fool and his money are soon parted.* We should be rather inclined to name, as a characteristic of the proverb, a *pointed* and sometimes *antithetical* form of expression; and this, in addition to *brevity* or *sententiousness*, constitutes perhaps the only universal distinction of this species of composition. Conciseness indeed enters into the very essence of the proverb.

We were about to adduce examples from the book of Proverbs, of these two excellencies—sententiousness and point—but it is impossible to select, where almost every verse is an illustration. Nor should it be forgotten that the structure of the Hebrew language admits of a much higher degree of excellence in this particular than is possible in the English tongue. We give two examples taken at random. ' *A man's heart deviseth his way: but the Lord directeth his steps.*' Here are twelve words; in the original seven only are employed. ' *When a man's ways please the Lord, he maketh even his enemies to be at peace with him.*' Eighteen words; in the Hebrew eight.

From its brevity, its appositeness, and its epigrammatic point, a proverb once heard remains fixed in the memory. Like an outline sketch which pleases more than a finished drawing, because it leaves more to the imagination, a proverb is peculiarly fitted to impress the mind, because it suggests more than it expresses. The same effect is produced by the obscurity observable in some proverbs; an obscurity consequent in part on their sententiousness, and in part on their figurative dress.

But Solomon must have had other reasons for selecting it, peculiar to the age and country in which he lived. The Hebrews have been called a nation of children. The mode of teaching by aphorisms is especially adapted to men in an early stage of culture, who have not yet learned to arrange and connect their various *knowledges* into a system. Accordingly we find this mode of writing employed in the most remote ages; and *wise sayings*, maxims, apophthegms, constitute a large part of the early literature of most nations. Especially is this true of the Oriental nations. The fondness of the people of the East for parables, enigmas, allegories, and pithy sayings, has itself become a proverb.

As an example of the former we may refer to Prov. ii. 1-5, and of the latter to Prov. x. 27-29.

The first nine chapters of the book of Proverbs are remarkably distinguished from the remainder, and form a continuous discourse, written in the highest style of poetry, adorned with apt and beautiful illustrations, and with various and striking figures.

At the tenth chapter a different style commences. From ch. x. to ch. xxii. 17, is a series of pithy disconnected maxims, on various subjects, and applicable to the most diverse situation. From ch. xxii. 17 to ch. xxv. a style resembling that of the exordium, though inferior in elegance and sublimity, prevails; and at the twenty-fifth chapter the separate maxims recommence. These compose the remainder of the book, with the exception of the thirtieth chapter, which is ascribed to Agur, and the thirty-first, which is said to be the advice given to king Lemuel by his mother. Who these persons are is not known. The supposition that Lemuel is another name of Solomon does not appear to be supported by proof.

The thirtieth chapter affords an example of another species of writing, closely allied to the proverb, and equally in favour among the Orientals. It is that of riddles or enigmas, designed to exercise the wit and ingenuity of the hearer, and to impart instruction through the medium of amusement.

The concluding chapter, containing the counsels addressed to King Lemuel by his mother, needs no elucidation. It presents a beautiful picture of female excellence in an age and country where modesty, industry, submission, and the domestic and matronly virtues, were esteemed the only appropriate ornaments of woman.

If we turn our attention to the maxims which compose the greater part of the book of Proverbs, we shall find enough to excite our wonder and admiration. Here are not only the results of the profoundest human sagacity, the counsels and admonitions of the man who excelled in wisdom all who went before, and all who came after him, but of such a man writing under divine inspiration And how numerous, how various, how profound, how important are his instructions!

These directions are adapted to the wants of

every class and rank of men, and to every relation of life. The rich and the poor, the learned and the ignorant, the master and the servant, the monarch and the subject, may here find the counsels they need. ' Apples of gold in baskets of silver' are fit emblems of such prudent and wholesome counsels, clothed in such an attractive garb.

PROVIDENCE. The word Providence originally meant *foresight*. By a well-known figure of speech, called metonymy, we use a word denoting the means by which we accomplish anything to denote the end accomplished; we exercise care over anything by means of foresight, and indicate that care by the word foresight. On the same principle the word Providence is used to signify the *care* God takes of the universe. As to its inherent nature, *it is the power which God exerts, without intermission, in and upon all the works of his hands.* But defined as to its visible manifestations, it is God's preservation and government of all things. As a thing is known by its opposites, the meaning of Providence is elucidated by considering that it is opposed to fortune and fortuitous accidents.

Providence, considered in reference to all things existing, is termed by Knapp *universal;* in reference to moral beings, *special;* and in reference to holy or converted beings, *particular*.

Providence is usually divided into three divine acts: preservation, co-operation, and government. 1. By preservation is signified the causing of *existence* to continue. 2. Co-operation is the act of God which causes the *powers* of created things to remain in being. 3. Government, as a branch of Providence, is God's controlling all created things so as to promote the highest good of the whole.

Among the *proofs* of divine *Providence* may be reckoned the following:—One argument in proof of Providence is analogous to one mode of proving a *creation*. If we cannot account for the existence of the world without supposing its coming into existence, or beginning to be; no more can we account for the world *continuing* to exist, without supposing it to be *preserved;* for it is as evidently absurd to suppose any creature *prolonging* as *producing* its own being.

A *second* proof of Providence results from the admitted fact of *creation*. Whoever has made any piece of mechanism, therefore takes pains to preserve it. Parental affection moves those who have given birth to children to provide for their sustentation and education. It is both reasonable and Scriptural to contemplate God as sustaining the universe because he made it.

A *third* proof of Providence is found in the *divine perfections*. Since, among the divine perfections, are all power and all knowledge, the non-existence of Providence, if there be none, must result from a want of will in God. But no want of will to exercise a Providence can exist, for God wills whatever is for the good of the universe, and for his own glory; to either of which a Providence is clearly indispensable. God therefore has resolved to exercise his power and knowledge so as to subserve the best ends with his creation.

A *fourth* proof of God's Providence appears in the *order* which *prevails* in the universe. That summer and winter, seed-time and harvest, cold and heat, day and night, are fixed by a law, was obvious even to men who never heard of God's covenant with Noah. But our sense of order is keenest where we discern it in apparent confusion. The motions of the heavenly bodies are eccentric and intervolved, yet are most regular when they seem most lawless. They were therefore compared by the earliest astronomers to the discords which blend in a harmony, and to the wild starts which often heighten the graces of a dance. Modern astronomy has revealed to us so much miraculous symmetry in celestial phenomena, that it shows us far more decisive proofs of a Ruler seated on the circle of the heavens, than were vouchsafed to the ancients.

A *fifth* proof of a Providence is furnished by the fact that so many men are here rewarded and punished according to a righteous law. The wicked often feel compunctious visitings in the midst of their sins, or smart under the rod of civil justice, or are tortured with natural evils. With the righteous all things are in general reversed. The miser and envious are punished as soon as they begin to commit their respective sins; and some virtues are their own present reward. But we would not dissemble that we are here met with important objections, although infinitely less, even though they were unanswerable, than beset such as would reject the doctrine of Providence. It is said, and we grant, that the righteous are trodden under foot, and the vilest men exalted; that the race is not to the swift, nor the battle to the strong: that virtue starves while vice is fed; and that schemes for doing good are frustrated, while evil plots succeed. But we may reply, 1. The prosperity of the wicked is often apparent, and well styled *a shining misery*. 2. We are often mistaken in calling such or such an afflicted man good, and such or such a prosperous man bad. 3. The miseries of good men are generally occasioned by their own fault, since they have been so foolhardy as to run counter to the laws by which God acts, or have aimed at certain ends while neglecting the appropriate means. 4. Many virtues are proved and augmented by trials, and not only proved, but produced, so that they would have had no existence without them. 5. The unequal distribution of good and evil, so far as it exists, carries our thoughts forward to the last judgment, and a retribution according to the deeds done in the body, and can hardly fail of throwing round the idea of eternity a stronger air of reality than it might otherwise wear. All perplexity vanishes as we reflect that, ' He cometh to judge the earth.' 6. Even if we limit our views to this world, but extend them to all our acquaintance, we cannot doubt that the *tendencies*, though not always the effects, of vice are to misery, and those of virtue to happiness. These tendencies are especially clear if our view embraces a whole lifetime, and the clearer the longer the period we embrace. Indeed, as soon as we leave what is immediately before our eyes, and glance at the annals of the world, we behold so many manifestations of God, that we may adduce as

A *sixth* proof of Providence the *facts of history*. The giving and transmission of a revelation, it has been justly said,—the founding of religious institutions, as the Mosaic and the Christian,—the raising up of prophets, apostles, and defenders of the faith,—the ordering of particular events, such as the Reformation,—the more remarkable deliverances noticed in the lives of those devoted to the good of the world, &c.—all indicate the wise and benevolent care of God over the human family. But the historical proof of a Providence is perhaps strongest where the wrath of man has been made to praise God, or where efforts to dishonour God have been constrained to do him honour.

As a *seventh* ground for believing in Providence, it may be said that Providence is the necessary basis of all religion. For what is religion? One of the best definitions calls it the belief in a superhuman Power, which has great influence in human affairs, and ought therefore to be worshipped. But take away this *influence in human affairs*, and you cut off all motive to worship. To the same purpose is the text in Hebrews : ' He that cometh to God must believe that he is, and that he is a rewarder of such as diligently seek him.' If then the religious sentiments thrill us not in vain,—if all attempts of all men to commune with God have not always and everywhere been idle,—there must be a Providence.

In the *eighth* place, we may advert to the proof of Providence from the common consent of mankind, with the single exception of atheists.

In the *last* place, the doctrine of Providence is abundantly proved by the Scriptures.

PRUNING-HOOK. [VINE.]

PSALMS, BOOK OF. This collection of sacred poetry received its name in consequence of the *lyrical* character of the pieces of which it consists, as intended to be sung to stringed and other instruments of music.

In Ps. lxxii. 20 we find all the preceding compositions (Ps. i.-lxxii.) styled *Prayers of David*, because many of them are strictly prayers, and all are pervaded by the spirit and tone of supplication.

All the Psalms, except thirty-four, bear superscriptions. The *authority* of the titles is a matter of doubt. By most of the ancient critics they were considered genuine, and of equal authority with the Psalms themselves, while most of the moderns reject them wholly or in part. It deserves to be noticed, however, that they are received by Tholuck and Hengstenberg in their works on the Psalms. Of the *antiquity* of the inscriptions there can be no question, for they are found in the Septuagint. They are supposed to be even much older than this version, since they were no longer intelligible to the translator, who often makes no sense of them.

A good deal may be plausibly said both for and against the authority of these titles, but on the whole it seems the part of sober criticism to receive the titles as historically valid, except when we find strong internal evidence against them.

The *design* of these inscriptions is to specify either the author, or the chief singer, or the historical subject or occasion, or the use, or the style of poetry, or the instrument and style of music. Some titles simply designate the author, as in Ps. xxv., while others specify several of the above particulars, as in Ps. li. The longest and fullest title of all is prefixed to Ps. lx., where we have the author, the chief musician (not by name), the historical occasion (comp. 2 Sam. viii.), the use or design, the style of poetry, and the instrument or style of music. It is confessedly very difficult,

if not impossible, to explain all the terms employed in the inscriptions , and hence critics have differed exceedingly in their conjectures. The difficulty, arising no doubt from ignorance of the Temple music, was felt, it would seem, as early as the age of the Sept.; and it was felt so much by the translators of our Authorized Version, that they generally retained the Hebrew words, even though Luther had set the example of translating them to the best of his ability.

Of the terms left *untranslated* or *obscure* in our Bible, it may be well to offer some explanation in this place, taking them in alphabetical order for the sake of convenience.

Aijeleth shahar, ' hind of the morning,' *i e.* the sun, or the dawn of day. This occurs only in Ps. xxii., where we may best take it to designate a song, perhaps commencing with these words, or bearing this name, to the melody of which the psalm was to be sung.

Alamoth, Ps. xlvi., probably signifies ' virgins,' and hence denotes music for female voices, or the *treble.*

Al-taschith, ' destroy thou not,' is found over Ps. lvii., lviii., lix., lxxv., and signifies, by general consent, some well-known ode beginning with the expression, to the tune of which these compositions were to be sung.

Degrees appears over fifteen Psalms (cxx - cxxxiv.), called *Songs of Degrees,* and has been explained in various ways, of which the following are the chief. 1. The ancients understood by it *stairs* or *steps;* and in accordance with this, Jewish writers relate that these Psalms were *sung on fifteen steps,* leading from the court of Israel to the court of the women. This explanation is now exploded. 2. Luther, whom Tholuck is inclined to follow, renders the title *a song in the higher choir,* supposing the Psalms to have been sung from an elevated place or ascent, or with elevated voice. 3. Gesenius and De Wette think the name refers to a peculiar rhythm in these songs, by which the sense advances by *degrees,* and so *ascends* from clause to clause. 4. According to the most prevalent and probable opinion, the title signifies *song of the ascents,* or *pilgrim song,* meaning a song composed for, or sung during the journeyings of the people up to Jerusalem, whether as they returned from Babylon, or as they stately repaired to the national solemnities. Journeys to Jerusalem are generally spoken of as *ascents,* on account of the elevated situation of the city and temple (see Ezra vii. 9, and especially Ps. cxxii. 4). This explanation of the name is favoured by the brevity and the contents of these songs.

Gittith appears over Ps. viii., lxxxi., lxxxiv., and is of very uncertain meaning, though not improbably it signifies an instrument or tune brought from the city of *Gath.* In the opinion of not a few the word denotes either an instrument or a melody used in the vintage.

Higgaion is found over Ps. ix. 16, and probably means either *musical sound,* according to the opinion of most, or *meditation,* according to Tholuck and Hengstenberg.

Jeduthun is found over Ps. xxxix., lxii., lxxvii., and is generally taken for the name of choristers descended from Jeduthun, of whom we read in 1 Chron. xxv. 1, 3, as one of David's three chief musicians or leaders of the Temple music.

Jonath-elem-rechokim, 'the mute dove among strangers,' found only over Ps. lvi., may well denote the subject of the song, viz., David himself, 'when the Philistines took him in Gath,' or it is the name or commencement of an ode to the air of which this psalm was sung.

Leannoth, in the title of Ps lxxxviii., means *to sing,* denoting that it was to be sung in the way described.

Mahalath occurs in Ps. liii. and lxxxviii., and denotes, according to some, a sort of *flute;* according to Gesenius, in his last edition of his *Thesaurus,* a *lute;* but in the opinion of Fürst, a *tune,* named from the first word of some popular song. *Upon Mahalath, Leannoth,* Ps. lxxxviii., is accordingly a direction to chant it to the instrument or tune called *mahalath.*

Maschil is found in the title of thirteen psalms. According to Gesenius, De Wette, and others, it means a *poem,* so called either for its *skilful* composition or for its *wise and pious* strain. The common interpretation, which Tholuck and Hengstenberg follow, makes it a *didactic poem.*

Michtam is prefixed to Ps. xvi., lvi., lx., and is subject to many conjectures. But the true explanation is most likely that offered by Gesenius, De Wette, Rosenmüller, and Tholuck, who hold it to signify a 'writing' or 'poem.'

Muth-labben (Ps. ix.) presents a perfect riddle, owing to the various readings of MSS., and the contradictory conjectures of the learned. Some explain it as the *subject* or *occasion* of the song, but most refer it to the music. Gesenius, in his last edition, renders it—*with virgins' voice for the boys, i. e.* to be sung by a choir of boys in the *treble.*

Neginoth, Ps. iv. and four others. This name clearly denotes 'stringed instruments' in general.

Nehiloth (Ps. v.) denotes 'pipes' or 'flutes.'

Selah is found seventy-three times in the Psalms, generally at the end of a sentence or paragraph; but in Ps. lv. 19 and lvii. 3 it stands in the middle of the verse. While most authors have agreed in considering this word as somehow relating to the *music,* their conjectures about its precise meaning have varied greatly. But at present these two opinions chiefly obtain: first, that it signifies a *raising* of the voice or music; or, second, a *pause* in the singing. Probably *selah* was used to direct the singer to be silent, or to pause a little, while the instruments played an interlude or symphony. In Ps. ix. 16 it occurs in the expression *higgaion selah,* which Gesenius, with much probability, renders *instrumental music, pause, i. e.* let the instruments strike up a symphony, and let the singer pause. By Tholuck and Hengstenberg, however, the two words are rendered *meditation, pause, i. e.* let the singer meditate or reflect while the music stops.

Sheminith (Ps. vi. and xii.) means properly *eighth,* and denotes either, as some think, an instrument with *eight* chords. or, more likely, music in the lower notes, or *bass.*

Shiggaion (Ps. vii.) denotes, according to Gesenius and Fürst, a *song* or *hymn;* but Ewald and Hengstenberg understand by it 'error or wandering,' supposing that the *aberrations* of the wicked are the subject of the Psalm. According to Rosenmüller, De Wette, and Tholuck, it means a 'plaintive song or elegy.'

Shushan (Ps. lx.), and in plural *shoshannim* (Ps. xlv., xlix., lxxx.). This word commonly signifies *lily,* and probably denotes either an instrument bearing some resemblance to a lily (perhaps *cymbal*), or a melody named lily for its pleasantness.

Respecting the *authors* of the Psalms, many of the ancients, both Jews and Christians, maintained that they were all written by David: which is one of the most striking proofs of their uncritical judgment. The titles and the contents of the Psalms most clearly show that they were composed at different and remote periods, by several poets, of whom David was only the largest and most eminent contributor. According to the inscriptions we have the following list of authors:—

1. *David,* 'the sweet Psalmist of Israel' (2 Sam. xxiii. 1). To him are ascribed seventy-three Psalms in the Hebrew text; and at least eleven others in the Sept., namely, xxxiii., xliii., xci., xciv.-xcix., civ., cxxxvii.; to which may be added Ps. x., as it forms part of Ps. ix. in that version. From what has been advanced above respecting the authority of the titles, it is obviously injudicious to maintain that David composed all that have his name prefixed in the Hebrew, or to suppose that he did not compose some of the eleven ascribed to him in the Sept., and of the others which stand without any author's name at all. We cannot feel sure that Ps. cxxxix. is David's, for its Chaldaisms (ver. 2, 8, 16, 17) betray a later age; and Ps. cxxii. can scarcely be his, for its style resembles the later Hebrew, and its description of Jerusalem can hardly apply to David's time. Besides, it is worthy of notice that the Sept. gives this and the other Songs of Degrees without specifying the author. Of those which the Sept. ascribes to David, it is not improbable that Ps. xcix. and civ. are really his; and of those which bear no name in either text, at least Ps. ii. appears to be David's.

David's compositions are generally distinguished by sweetness, softness, and grace; but sometimes, as in Ps. xviii., they exhibit the sublime. His prevailing strain is plaintive, owing to his multiplied and sore trials, both before and after his occupation of the throne. The celebrated singers who were contemporaries of David were men, like himself, moved by the divine afflatus not only to excel in music, but also to indite hallowed poetry. Of these Psalmists the names of several are preserved in the titles.

2. *Asaph* is named as the author of twelve Psalms, viz., l., lxxiii.-lxxxiii. He was one of David's chief musicians [ASAPH]. All the poems bearing his name cannot be his; for in Ps. lxxiv., lxxix., and lxxx., there are manifest allusions to very late events in the history of Israel. Asaph appears from Ps. l., lxxiii., and lxxviii., to have been the greatest master of didactic poetry, excelling alike in sentiment and in diction.

3. *The sons of Korah* was another family of choristers (see KORAH, at the end), to whom eleven of the most beautiful Psalms are ascribed.

4. *Heman* was another of David's chief singers (1 Chron. xv. 19): he is called the Ezrahite, as being descended from some Ezrah, who appears to have been a descendant of Korah: at least Heman is reckoned a Kohathite (1 Chron. vi. 33-38), and was therefore probably a Korahite; for the Kohathites were continued and counted in

the line of Korah; see 1 Chron. vi. 22. 37. 38 [HEMAN]. Thus Heman was both an Ezrahite and of the sons of Korah. That Ps. lxxxviii. was written by him is not unlikely, though many question it.

5. *Ethan* is reputed the author of Ps. lxxxix. He is doubtless the Levite of Merari's family whom David made chief musician along with Asaph and Heman (1 Chron. vi. 44 ; xxv. 1, 6). The Psalm could not, however, be composed by him, for it plainly alludes (ver. 38-44) to the downfall of the kingdom.

6. *Solomon* is given as the author of Ps. lxxii. and cxxvii, and there is no decided internal evidence to the contrary, though most consider him to be the subject and not the author of Ps. lxxii.

7. *Moses* is reputed the writer of Ps. xc., and there is no strong reason to doubt the tradition.

Jeduthun is sometimes, without just ground, held to be named as the author of Ps. xxxix. Many conjectures have been formed respecting other writers, especially of the anonymous psalms. The Sept. seemingly gives, as authors, Jeremiah, (Ps. cxxxvii.), and Haggai and Zechariah (Ps. cxxxviii.). But these conjectures are too uncertain to call for further notice in this place.

The *dates* of the Psalms, as must be obvious from what has been stated respecting the authors, are very various, ranging from the time of Moses to that of the Captivity—a period of nearly 1000 years.

The Psalter is divided in the Hebrew into five books, and also in the Sept. version, which proves the division to be older than B C. 200.

The *first book* (i.-xli.) consists wholly of David's songs, his name being prefixed to all except i., ii., x., and xxxiii.; and it is evidently the first collection, having been possibly made in the time of Hezekiah, who is known to have ordered a collection of Solomon's proverbs (Prov. xxv. 1), and to have commanded the Levites to sing the words of David (2 Chron. xxix. 30).

The *second book* (xlii.-lxxii.) consists mainly of pieces by the sons of Korah (xlii.-xlix.), and by David (li.-lxv.), which may have been separate minor collections. It is not likely that this collection was made till the period of the Captivity, if interpreters are right in referring Ps. xliv. to the days of Jeremiah.

The *third book* (lxxiii.-lxxxix.) consists chiefly of Asaph's psalms, but comprises apparently two smaller collections, the one Asaphitic (lxxiii.-lxxxiii.), the other mostly Korahitic (lxxxiv.-lxxxix.). The collector of this book had no intention to bring together songs written by David, and therefore he put the above notice at the end of the second book. The date of this collection must be as late as the return from Babylon, for Ps. lxxxv. implies as much.

The *fourth book* (xc.-cvi.) and the *fifth* (cvii.-cl.) are made up chiefly of anonymous liturgic pieces, many of which were composed for the service of the second temple. In the last book we have the Songs of Degrees (cxx.-cxxxiv.), which seem to have been originally a separate collection.

The *inspiration* and *canonical authority* of the Psalms are established by the most abundant and convincing evidence. They never were. and never can be, rejected, except by impious impugners of all divine revelation. Not to mention other

ancient testimonies, we find complete evidence in the New Testament, where the book is quoted or referred to as divine by Christ and his apostles *at least seventy times*. No other writing is so frequently cited ; Isaiah, the next in the scale of quotation, being cited only about fifty-five times.

PSALTERY. [MUSICAL INSTRUMENTS.]

PTOLEMA'IS. [ACCHO.]

PTOL'EMY. This common name of the Greek kings of Egypt does not occur in the canonical Scripture, but is frequent in the books of Maccabees and in Josephus (see the article EGYPT).

PUBLICAN, a person who farmed the taxes and public revenues. This office was usually held by Roman knights, an order instituted as early as the time of Romulus, and composed of men of great consideration with the government, 'the principal men of dignity in their several countries,' who occupied a kind of middle rank between the senators and the people. Although these officers were, according to Cicero, the ornament of the city and the strength of the commonwealth, they did not attain to great offices, nor enter the senate, so long as they continued in the order of knights. They were thus more capable of devoting their attention to the collection of the public revenue.

The publicans were distributed into three classes: the farmers of the revenue, their partners, and their securities, corresponding to the Mancipes, Socii, and Prædes. They were all under the Quæstores Ærarii, who presided over the finances at Rome. Strictly speaking, there were only two sorts of publicans, the Mancipes and the Socii. The former, who were generally of the equestrian order, and much superior to the latter in rank and character, are mentioned by Cicero with great honour and respect; but the common publicans, the collectors or receivers of the tribute, as many of the Socii were, are covered both by heathens and Jews with opprobrium and contempt.

The name and profession of a publican were, indeed, extremely odious among the Jews, who submitted with much reluctance to the taxes levied by the Romans. The Galileans or Herodians, the disciples of Judas the Gaulonite, were the most turbulent and rebellious (Acts v. 37). They thought it unlawful to pay tribute, and founded their refusal to do so on their being the people of the Lord, because a true Israelite was not permitted to acknowledge any other sovereign than God (Joseph. *Antiq.* xviii. 2). The publicans were hated as the instruments by which the subjection of the Jews to the Roman emperor was perpetuated; and the paying of tribute was regarded as a virtual acknowledgment of his sovereignty. They were also noted for their imposition, rapine, and extortion, to which they were, perhaps, more especially prompted by having a share in the farm of the tribute. as they were thus tempted to oppress the people with illegal exactions, that they might the more speedily enrich themselves. Those Jews who accepted the office of publican were execrated by their own nation equally with heathens: 'Let him be unto thee as an heathen man and a publican' (Matt. xviii. 17). It is said they were not allowed to enter the temple or synagogues, to engage in the public prayers, fill offices of judicature, or even give testimony in courts of justice.

According to the Rabbins, it was a maxim that a religious man who became a publican was to be driven out of the religious society. They would not receive their presents at the temple any more than the price of prostitution, of blood, or of anything wicked and offensive.

PUB'LIUS, governor of Melita at the time of Paul's shipwreck on that island (Acts xxviii. 7, 8) Paul having healed his father, probably enjoyed his hospitality during the three months of his stay in the island [MELITA].

PU'DENS, one of the persons whose salutations Paul, writing from Rome, sends to Timothy (2 Tim. iv. 21). Nothing is really known of him; but the martyrologies make him to have been a person of figure at Rome, of the senatorial order, and father of two pious virgins, Praxis and Pudentia.

PUL, king of Assyria. [ASSYRIA.]

PULSE. [BEANS.]

PUNISHMENTS. This subject is properly restricted to the penalty imposed on the commission of some crime or offence against law. It is thus distinguished from private retaliation or revenge, cruelty, torture, popular violence, certain customs of war, &c. Human punishments are such as are inflicted immediately on the person of the offender, or indirectly upon his goods, &c. For the leading points in the literature of the question concerning future and divine punishment see SOUL. *Capital punishment* is usually supposed to have been instituted at the deluge (Gen. ix. 5, 6). Arnheim, however, thus explains the precept: if one stranger slay another, the kinsmen of the murdered man are the avengers of blood; but if he be slain by one of his own kindred, the other kinsmen must not spare the murderer, for if they do, then divine providence will require the blood —that is, will avenge it. This interpretation would account for the custom of blood-revenge among all the ancient and Asiatic nations. The extensive prescription of capital punishment by the Mosaic law, which we cannot consider as a dead letter, may be accounted for by the peculiar circumstances of the people. They were a nation of newly-emancipated slaves, and were by nature perhaps more than commonly intractable; and if we may judge by the laws enjoined on them, which Mr. Hume well remarks are a safe index to the manners and disposition of any people, we must infer that they had imbibed all the degenerating influences of slavery among heathens. The *mode of capital punishment*, which constitutes a material element in the character of any law, was probably as humane as the circumstances of Moses admitted. It was probably restricted to lapidation or stoning, which, by skilful management, might produce instantaneous death. It was an Egyptian custom (Exod. viii. 26). The public effusion of blood by decapitation cannot be proved to have been a Mosaic punishment. The appearance of decapitation, 'slaying by the sword,' in later times (2 Sam. iv. 8, 20, 21, 22; 2 Kings x. 6-8), has no more relation to the Mosaic law than the decapitation of John the Baptist by Herod (Matt. xiv. 8-12); or than the hewing to pieces of Agag before the Lord by Samuel, as a punishment *in kind* (1 Sam. xv. 33). Execution was ordered by Moses, probably adopting an ancient custom, to be begun first by the witnesses, a regulation which constituted a tremendous appeal to their moral feelings, and afterwards to be completed by the people (Deut. xiii. 10; xvii. 7; Josh vii. 25; John viii. 7). It was a later innovation that immediate execution should be done by some personal attendant, by whom the office was probably considered as an honour (2 Sam. i. 15; iv. 12). Stoning therefore was, probably, the only capital punishment ordered by Moses. It is observable that neither this nor any other punishment was, according to his law, attended with insult or torture (comp. 2 Macc. vii.). Nor did his laws admit of those horrible mutilations practised by other nations. Mutilation of such a nature amounts to a perpetual condemnation to infamy and crime. It will shortly be seen that the *lex talionis*, 'an eye for an eye,' &c., was adopted by Moses as the *principle*, but not the mode of punishment. He seems also to have understood the true end of punishment, which is not to gratify the antipathy of society against crime, nor moral vengeance, which belongs to God alone, but prevention. 'All the people shall hear and fear, and do no more so presumptuously' (Deut. xvii. 13; xxix. 20). His laws are equally free from the characteristic of savage legislation, that of involving the family of the offender in his punishment. He did not allow parents to be put to death for their children, nor children for their parents (Deut. xxiv. 16), as did the Chaldæans (Dan. vi. 24), and the kings of Israel (comp. 1 Kings xxi.; 2 Kings ix. 26). Various punishments were introduced among the Jews, or became known to them by their intercourse with other nations,—viz., *precipitation*, or throwing, or causing to leap, from the top of a rock: to which ten thousand Idumæans were condemned by Amaziah, king of Judah (2 Chron. xxv. 12). The inhabitants of Nazareth intended a similar fate for our Lord (Luke iv. 29). This punishment resembles that of the Tarpeian rock among the Romans. *Cutting asunder* appears to have been a Babylonian custom (Dan. ii. 5; iii. 29; Luke xii. 46; Matt. xxiv. 51); but the passages in the Gospels admit of the milder interpretation of scourging with severity, discarding from office, &c. *Beating to death* was a Greek punishment for slaves. It was inflicted on a wooden frame, on which the criminal was bound and beaten to death (2 Macc. vi. 19, 28; comp. v. 30). *Fighting with wild beasts* was a Roman punishment, to which criminals and captives in war were sometimes condemned (Adam, *Roman Antiq.*, p. 344; 2 Tim. iv. 17; comp. 1 Cor. xv. 32). *Drowning* with a heavy weight around the neck, was a Syrian, Greek, and Roman punishment. For Crucifixion, see the Article.

Posthumous insults offered to the dead bodies of criminals, though common in other nations, were very sparingly allowed by Moses. He *permitted* only hanging on a tree or gibbet; but the exposure was limited to a day, and burial of the body at night was commanded (Deut. xxi. 22). Such persons were esteemed 'cursed of God' (comp. Josh. viii. 29; x. 26; 2 Sam. iv. 12)—a law which the later Jews extended to crucifixion (John xix. 31, &c.; Gal. iii. 13). *Hanging alive* may have been a Canaanitish punishment, since it was practised by the *Gibeonites* on the sons of Saul (2 Sam. xxi. 9). Another posthumous insult in later times consisted in heaping stones on the body or grave of the executed criminal (Josh. vii 25, 26). To 'make heaps' of houses or cities is a phrase denoting complete and ignominious destruction (Isa. xxv. 2; Jer. ix. 11). *Burning the dead body* seems to have been a very ancient posthumous insult: it was denounced by Judah against his daughter-in-law, Tamar, when informed that she was with child (Gen. xxxviii. 24). Selden thinks that this means merely branding on the forehead. Moses retained this ancient ignominy for two offences only, which from the nature of things must have been comparatively rare, viz., for *bigamy* with a mother and her daughter (Lev. xx. 4), and for the case of a priest's daughter who committed whoredom (xxi. 9). Though 'burning' only be specified in these cases, it may be safely inferred that the previous death of the criminals, probably by lapidation, is to be understood (comp. Josh vii. 25). Among the heathens this merciful preliminary was not always observed, as for instance in the case of Shadrach, Meshach, and Abednego (Dan. iii.).

Among the *minor corporal punishments* ordered by Moses, was scourging; or the infliction of blows on the back of an offender with a rod. It was limited by him to forty stripes, a number which the Jews in later times were so careful not to exceed, that they inflicted but thirty-nine (2 Cor. xi. 24). It was to be inflicted on the offender lying on the ground, in the presence of a judge (Lev. xix. 20; Deut xxii. 18; xxv. 2, 3). We have abundant evidence that it was an ancient Egyptian punishment. Corporal punishment of this kind was allowed by Moses, by masters to servants or slaves of both sexes (Exod. xxi. 20). Scourging was common in after times among the Jews, who associated with it no disgrace or inconvenience beyond the physical pain it occasioned, and from which no station was exempt (Prov. xvii. 26; comp. x. 13; Jer. xxxvii. 15-20). Hence it became the symbol for correction in general (Ps. lxxxix. 32). Solomon is a zealous advocate for its use in education (Prov. xiii. 24; xxiii. 13, 14; comp. Eccles. xxx. 1). It was inflicted for ecclesiastical offences in the synagogue (Matt. x. 17; Acts xxvi. 11). The Mosaic law, however, respecting it, affords a pleasing contrast to the extreme and unlimited scourging known among the Romans, but which, according to the Porcian law, could not be inflicted upon a Roman citizen (Acts xvi. 22-37; xxii. 25). Reference to the scourge with scorpions, *i.e.* a whip or scourge armed with knots or thorns, occurs in 1 Kings xii. 11.

Retaliation is doubtless the most natural of all kinds of punishment, and would be the most just of all, if it could be instantaneously and universally inflicted. But when delayed it is apt to degenerate into revenge. Hence the desirableness that it should be regulated and modified by law. Moses accordingly adopted the principle, but lodged the application of it in the judge. 'If a man blemish his neighbour, as he hath done, so shall it be done to him. Life for life, eye for eye, tooth for tooth, wound for wound, stripe for stripe, breach for breach' (Exod. xxi. 23-25; Lev. xxiv. 19-22). His system of compensations, &c., occurs in Exod. xxi. He, however, makes wilful murder, even of a slave, always capital, as did the Egyptians. The Egyptians doomed the false accuser to the same punishment which he endeavoured to bring on his victim, as did Moses (Deut. xix. 19). Im-

prisonment, not as a punishment, but custody, till the royal pleasure was known, appears among the Egyptians (Gen. xxxix. 20, 21). Moses adopted it for like purposes (Lev. xxvi. 12). In later times, it appears as a punishment inflicted by the kings of Judah and Israel (2 Chron. xvi. 10; 1 Kings xxii. 27; Jer. xxxvii. 21); and during the Christian era, as in the instance of John (Matt. iv. 12), and Peter (Acts xii. 4). Murderers and debtors were also committed to prison; and the latter 'tormented' till they paid (Matt. xviii. 30; Luke xxiii. 19) A common prison is mentioned (Acts v. 18); and also an inner prison or dungeon, which was sometimes a pit (Jer. xxxviii. 6), in which were 'stocks' (Jer. xx. 2; xxix. 26; Acts xvi. 24). Prisoners are alluded to (Job iii. 18), and stocks (xiii. 27). Banishment was impracticable among the Jews. It was inflicted by the Romans on John (Rev. i. 9). *Cutting or plucking off the hair* is alluded to (Isa. l. 6; Nehem. xiii. 25). *Excision*, or 'cutting off from his people.' is denounced against the uncircumcised as early as the covenant with Abraham (Gen. xvii. 14). This punishment is expressed in the Mosaic law by the formulæ— 'that soul shall be destroyed from its people' (Lev. xvii. 20, 21); 'from Israel' (Exod. xii. 15); 'from the midst of the congregation' (Num. xix. 20); 'it shall be destroyed' (Lev. xvii. 14; xx. 17); which terms sometimes denote capital punishment (Exod. xxxi. 14; comp xxxv. 2; Num. xv. 32, &c.) [ANATHEMA].

Ecclesiastical punishments are prescribed, as might be expected under a theocracy, but these were moderate. Involuntary transgressions of the Levitical law, whether of omission or commission, were atoned for by a sin-offering (Lev. iv. 2, &c.; v. 1, 4-7). This head embraced a rash or neglected oath, keeping back evidence in court (Lev. iv. 2, &c.; v. 1; iv. 7), breach of trust, concealment of property when found, or theft, even when the offender had already cleared himself by oath, but was now moved by conscience to make restitution. By these means, and by the payment of twenty per cent. beyond the amount of his trespass, the offender might cancel the crime as far as the church was concerned (Lev. vi. 1-7; Num. v. 6-10). Adultery with a slave was commuted from death to stripes and a trespass-offering (Lev. xix. 20-22). All these cases involved public confession, and the expenses of the offering.

Future punishment.—Though the doctrine of a future state was known to the ancient Hebrews, yet temporal punishment and reward were the immediate motives held out to obedience. Hence the references in the Old Testament to punishment in a future state are obscure and scanty. See HADES; HEAVEN: HELL.

PU'NON, one of the stations of the Israelites in the desert. [WANDERING.]

PURIFICATIONS. [ABLUTION.]

PU'RIM (Esther iii. 7; ix. 24, sq.), a celebrated Jewish festival instituted by Mordecai, at the suggestion of Esther, in the reign of Ahasuerus, king of Persia. to commemorate the deliverance of the Jews from the designs of Haman [ESTHER; HAMAN; MORDECAI]. It derived its name from the *lots* cast every day for twelve months in presence of Haman, with the view of discovering an auspicious day for the destruction

2 Y

of all the Jews in the Persian dominions; when the lot fell on the 13th day of Adar (February and part of March) [FESTIVALS].

The particulars of the mode in which the Jews observe this festival will be found detailed by Buxtorf. We shall select a few of the most striking. The book of Esther is read from beginning to end; and even the reading of the law is on this day postponed to it. It may be also read in any language which the reader understands. When Mordecai's name occurs, the whole congregation exclaim, *Blessèd be Mordecai!* and, on mention of that of Haman, they say, *May his name perish!* and it is usual for the children to hiss, spring rattles, strike the walls with hammers, and make all sorts of noises. These noisy portions of the ceremony have, however, been long discontinued in England, except in the synagogues of some foreign Jews. The remainder of the day is spent in festivity, in commemoration of Esther's feast: upon which occasion the Jews send presents to each other, the men to the men, and the women to the women. They also bestow alms on the poor, from- the benefit of which Christians and other Gentiles are not excluded. Plays and masquerades follow: nor is it considered a breach of the law of Moses on this occasion, for men and women to assume the garb of the other sex. Purim is the last festival in the Jewish ecclesiastical year, being succeeded by the next Passover.

PURPLE, BLUE, CRIMSON, SCARLET. There is no reason to doubt that this colour was obtained, like the far-famed Tyrian purple, from the juice of certain species of shell-fish. The dye called purple by the ancients, and its various shades, were obtained from many kinds of shell-fish, all of which are, however, ranged by Pliny under two classes: one called 'buccinum,' because shaped like a horn, found, he says, in cliffs and rocks, and yielding a sullen blue dye; the other called 'purpura,' or 'pelagia,' the proper purple shell, taken by fishing in the sea, and

288. [Murex trunculus.]

yielding the deep red colour which was chiefly valued. Both sorts were supposed to be as many years old as they had spirals round. The juice of the whole shell-fish was not used, but only a little thin liquor called the flower, contained in a white vein or vessel in the neck. The larger purples were broken at the top to get at this vein without injuring it, but the smaller were pressed in mills. The *Murex trunculus* was the species used by the ancient Tyrians. It is of common occurrence now on the same coasts, and through-

out the whole of the Mediterranean, and even of the Atlantic. The ancients applied the word translated 'purple,' not to one colour only, but to the whole class of dyes manufactured from the juices of shell-fish, as distinguished from the vegetable dyes, and comprehending not only what is commonly called purple, but also light and dark purple, and almost every shade between.

Purple was employed in religious worship both among Jews and Gentiles. It was one of the colours of the curtains of the tabernacle; of the vail; of the curtain over the grand entrance; of the ephod of the high priest, and of its girdle; of the breast-plate; of the hem of the robe of the ephod, &c. The Babylonians arrayed their idols in it. It was at an early period worn by kings (Judg. viii. 26). Homer speaks as if it were almost peculiar to them. In Acts x. 14, reference is found to Lydia, of the city of Thyatira, a seller of purple cloth. The manufacture seems to have decayed with its native city. A colony of Jews, which was established at Thebes in Greece in the twelfth century, carried on an extensive manufactory for dyeing purple. It ultimately became superseded by the use of indigo, cochineal, &c., whence a cheaper and finer purple was obtained, and free from the disagreeable odour which attended that derived from shell-fish.

2. *Blue*, a colour almost constantly associated with purple, is supposed to have been obtained

289. [Helix ianthina.]

from another purple shell-fish of the Mediterranean, the *conchylium* of the ancients, the *Helix ianthina* of Linnæus. The Scriptures afford no clue to this colour: some suppose it to be dark-coloured and deep purple, but Josephus evidently takes the Hebrew word to mean 'sky-colour.' These statements may be reconciled by the fact, that in proportion as the sky is clear and serene, it assumes a dark appearance, which is still more observable in an eastern climate. The chief references to this colour in Scripture are as follows:—The robe of the high-priest's *ephod* was to be all of blue (Exod. xxviii. 31); so the loops of the curtains to the tabernacle; the riband for the breast-plate, and for the plate for the mitre; the people were commanded to wear a riband of blue above the fringe of their garments (Num. xv. 38).

3. *Crimson* occurs in 2 Chron. ii. 7-14; iii. 14. This word is by some supposed to signify another kind of shell-fish, yielding a crimson dye, so called because found on the shore near Mount Carmel.

4. *Scarlet*, often associated with purple and blue. It is supposed to have been derived from the *coccus*, from which the ancients procured a blood-red crimson dye. It was the female of this remarkable insect that was employed; and though

supplanted by the cochineal, it is still used for the purpose in India and Persia. It attains the size and form of a pea, is of a violet black colour, covered with a whitish powder adhering to plants, chiefly various species of oak, and so closely resembling grains, that its insect nature was not generally known for many centuries. The word 'scarlet' *signified crimson in the time of our translators*, rather than the colour now called by that name, and which *was unknown in the time of James I.* This insect is widely distributed over many of the south-eastern countries of the ancient world. It occurs abundantly in Spain, and is found on the *Quercus coccifera*, or *kermes* oak in Palestine.

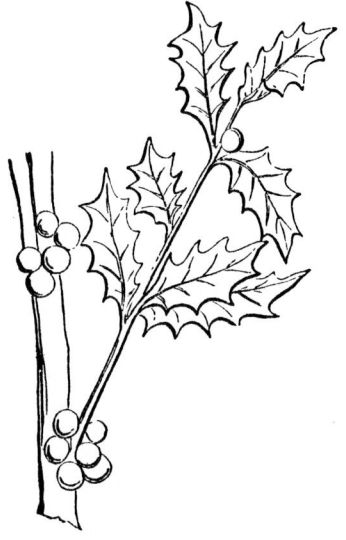

290. [Coccus ilicis, on a branch.]

PUTE'OLI, a maritime town of Campania, in Italy, on the north shore of the bay of Naples, and about eight miles north-west from the city of that name, where it still exists under the name of Pozzuoli. It derived its name from its tepid baths, whence the district in which it exists is now called Terra di Lavoro. It was a favourite watering-place of the Romans, as its numerous hot-springs were judged efficacious for the cure of various diseases. It was also the port where ships usually discharged their passengers and cargoes, partly to avoid doubling the promontory of Circeium, and partly because there was no commodious harbour nearer to Rome. Hence the ship in which Paul was conveyed from Melita, landed the prisoners at this place, where the apostle staid for a week (Acts xxviii. 13). The harbour was protected by a celebrated mole, the remains of which are still to be seen.

Q.

QUAIL occurs in Exod. xvi. 13; Num. xi. 31, 32; Ps. cv. 40. Quails form a subdivision of the *Tetraonidæ*, or grouse family, being distin-

guished from partridges by their smaller size, finer bill, shorter tail, and the want of a red naked eyebrow and of spurs on the legs. There are several species, whereof the common, now distinguished by the name of *Coturnix dactylisonans*, is abundant in all the temperate regions of Europe and Western Asia, migrating to and from Africa in the proper season.

Of a bird so well known no figure or further particular description appears to be necessary, beyond mentioning the enormous flights which, after crossing an immense surface of sea, are annually observed at the spring and fall to take a brief repose in the islands of Malta, Sicily, Sardinia, Crete, in the kingdom of Naples, and about Constantinople, where on those occasions there is a general shooting-match, which lasts two or three days. The providential nature of their arrival within and around the camp of the Israelites, in order that they might furnish meat to a murmuring people, appears from the fact of its taking place where it was not to be expected: the localities, we presume, being out of the direction of the ordinary passage; for, had this not been the case, the dwellers in that region, and the Israelites themselves, accustomed to tend their flocks at no great distance from the spot, would have regarded the phenomenon as a well-known periodical occurrence.

QUAR'TUS, a Christian resident at Corinth, and, from his name, apparently a Roman, whose salutations Paul communicated to the Church of Rome in his epistle thereto (Rom. xvi. 23).

QUATER'NION. A 'quaternion of soldiers' (Acts xii. 4) was a detachment of four men, which was the usual number of a Roman nightwatch. Peter, therefore, was guarded by four soldiers, two within the prison, and two outside the doors; and as the watch was usually changed every three hours, it was necessary that the 'four quaternions' mentioned in the text should be appointed for the purpose.

QUEEN. The Hebrews had no word properly answering to our term 'queen,' which is the feminine of 'king;' neither had they the dignity which that word denotes. Among them there was neither a 'queen regnant' nor a 'queen consort.' The Jewish kings however had, like other eastern monarchs, a chief wife in their harem, and this is no doubt the rank indicated in the Bible by the words which we render 'queen.'

Very different was, and is to this day, in Western Asia, the position of the king's mother, whose state is much the nearest to that of an European queen of any with which the East is acquainted. It is founded on that essential principle of Oriental manners which in all cases considers the mother of the husband as a far superior person to his wife, and as entitled to more respect and attention. This principle should be clearly understood, for it extends throughout the Bible, and is yet entirely different from our own social arrangements, under which the mother, as soon as she becomes widowed, abandons her place as head of the family to the daughter-in-law. Examples of the great influence possessed by the king's mother occur frequently in Scripture.

In how marked a manner does the mother of Solomon come forward at the end of her husband's and the beginning of her son's reign! She takes an active part in securing her son's succession;

it is in the conviction of her commanding influence that Adonijah engages her to promote his suit, alleging 'he will not say thee nay;' and then, when Bathsheba appears before her son, the monarch rises from his place, advances to meet her, bows himself before her, and seats her on the right hand of his throne (1 Kings i., ii.). That the king's mother possessed high dignity is further evinced by the fact that Asa found it necessary to remove his mother Maachah 'from being queen,' on account of her abuse of the power which that character conferred (1 Kings xv. 13). Jezebel was, as already stated, very powerful in the lifetime of her husband; but it is only under her son that she is called 'the queen,' and the whole history of his reign evinces the important part which she took in public affairs (2 Kings ix. 22, 30, 37; x. 13). Still more marked was the influence which her daughter Athaliah exercised in Judah during the reign of her son Ahaziah, which was indeed such as enabled her at his death to set the crown on her own head, and to present the anomaly in Jewish history of a regnant queen (2 Kings xi.).

QUEEN OF HEAVEN. [Ashtoreth.]
QUEEN OF SHEBA. [Sheba.]
QUIVER. [Armour, Arms.]

R.

RA'AMAH, a city of the Cushites, or of Cushite origin (Gen. x. 7; 1 Chron. i. 9; Ezek. xxvii. 22). Its situation is not clearly known.

RAAM'SES. [Rameses.]

RAB'BAH. This name, which properly denotes a great city or metropolis, is given in Scripture to the capital of the Ammonites (Josh. xiii. 25; 2 Sam. xi. 1; xii. 27; 1 Chron. xx. 1; Jer. xlix. 3); the full name of which, however, as given in Deut. iii. 11, appears to have been Rabbath-beni-Ammon. It was in this place that the great iron bedstead of Og king of Bashan was preserved (Deut. iii. 11). It was besieged by Joab, and when on the point of yielding to that general, was surrendered to David in person (2 Sam. xi. 12). After this Rabbah was included in the tribe of Gad. After the separation of the ten tribes, Rabbah, with the whole territory beyond the Jordan, adhered to the kingdom of Israel, till it was ravaged by the Assyrians under Tiglathpileser. and the inhabitants expatriated to Media. The Ammonites then recovered possession of Rabbah and the other cities and territories which had in former times been taken from them by the Israelites. Some centuries later, when these parts were subject to Egypt, Rabbah was restored or rebuilt by Ptolemy Philadelphus, and called by him Philadelphia, and under this name it is often mentioned by Greek and Roman writers.

Rabbah appears to have consisted, like Aroer, of two parts; the city itself, and 'the city of waters,' or royal city, which was probably a detached portion of the city itself, insulated by the stream on which it was situated. The 'city of waters' was taken by Joab; but against the city itself he was obliged to call for the assistance of David with a reinforcement (2 Sam xii. 29).

The ruins of Rabbah stand about 19 miles south-east of Szalt, in a long valley traversed by a stream. the Moiet Amman, which at this place is arched over, the bed as well as the banks being paved. The prophet Ezekiel foretold that Rabbah should become 'a stable for camels,' and the country 'a couching place for flocks' (Ezek. xxv. 5). This has been literally fulfilled, and Burckhardt actually found that a party of Arabs had stabled their camels among the ruins of Rabbah.

The Rabbah of Josh. xv. 60 was in the tribe of Judah.

RAB'BATH-AM'MON. [Rabbah.]

RAB'BATH-MOAB. [Ar.]

RABBI, a title of honour given to the teachers of the law in the time of Christ, and for which there is no exact equivalent in our language, though perhaps in purport and usage it comes near to 'doctor' or 'master:' a word combining both these significations would fairly represent it.

RABBONI, the title of highest honour applied by the Jews to the teachers of the law [Rabbi].

RAB'SARIS, one of the three Assyrian generals in command of the army which appeared before Jerusalem (2 Kings xviii. 17) [Rab-shakeh]. The word means 'chief of the eunuchs,' who is always an officer of high rank and dignity in the Oriental courts; and his cares are not confined to the harem, but many high public functions devolve upon him.

RAB'-SHAKEH (chief-cup-bearer). Notwithstanding its seemingly official significance, it appears to have been used as a proper name, as Butler with us; for the person who bore it was a military chief in high command, under Sennacherib king of Assyria. Yet it is not impossible, according to Oriental usages, that a royal cup-bearer should hold a military command; and the office itself was one of high distinction. He is the last named of three Assyrian generals who appeared before Jerusalem; and was the utterer of the insulting speeches addressed to the besieged. 2 Kings xviii. 17, 19, 26, 28, 37; xix. 4, 8; Isa. xxxvi. 2, 4, 12, 13, 22; xxxvii. 4, 8.

RA'CHEL (an ewe), one and the most beloved of the two daughters of Laban, whom Jacob married (Gen. xxix. 16, seq.), and who became the mother of Joseph and Benjamin, in giving birth to the latter of whom she died near Bethlehem, where her sepulchre is shown to this day (Gen. xxx. 22; xxxv. 16). For more minute particulars see Jacob, with whose history Rachel's is closely involved.

RAGU'EL, or Reuel (friend of God). 1. A son of Esau (Gen. xxxvi. 4, 10). 2. The father of Jethro (Exod. ii. 18; Num. x. 29). Some confound him with Jethro; but in the text last cited, he is called the father of Hobab, who seems to have been the same as Jethro. In the same passage, indeed, the daughters of the 'priest of Midian' relate to 'Reuel their father' their adventure with Moses: which might seem to support his identity with Jethro; but it is quite a Scriptural usage to call a grandfather 'father,' and a granddaughter, 'daughter' [Hobab]. 3. Another person of this name occurs in 1 Chron. ix. 8.

1. RA'HAB, a name signifying 'sea-monster,' which is applied as an appellation to Egypt in Ps. lxxiv. 13, 14; lxxxvii. 4; lxxxix. 10; Isa. li. 9 (and sometimes to its king, Ezek. xxix. 3; xxxiii. 3, comp. Ps. lxviii. 31); which meta-

phorical designation probably involves an allusion to the crocodiles, hippopotami, and other aquatic creatures of the Nile.

2. RA'HAB, properly RACHAB (*large*), a woman of Jericho who received into her house the two spies who were sent by Joshua into that city; concealed them under the flax laid out upon the house-top, when they were sought after; and, having given them important information, which showed that the inhabitants were much disheartened at the miracles which had attended the march of the Israelites, enabled them to escape over the wall of the town, upon which her dwelling was situated. For this important service Rahab and her kindred were saved by the Hebrews from the general massacre which followed the taking of Jericho (Josh. ii. 1-21; vi. 17; comp. Heb. xi. 31).

In the narrative of these transactions Rahab is called *zonah*, which our own, after the ancient versions, renders 'harlot.' The Jewish writers, however, being unwilling to entertain the idea of their ancestors being involved in a disreputable association at the commencement of their great undertaking, chose to interpret the word 'hostess,' one who keeps a public house. But the word signifies harlot in every other text where it occurs, the idea of 'hostess' not being represented by this or any other word in Hebrew, as the function represented by it did not exist. There were no inns; and when certain substitutes for inns eventually came into use, they were never, in any Eastern country, kept by women. On the other hand, strangers from beyond the river might have repaired to the house of a harlot without suspicion or remark. The house of such a woman was also the only one to which they, as perfect strangers, could have had access, and certainly the only one in which they could calculate on obtaining the information they required without danger from male inmates. If we are concerned for the morality of Rahab, the best proof of her reformation is found in the fact of her subsequent marriage to Salmon: this implies her previous conversion to Judaism, for which indeed her discourse with the spies evinces that she was prepared.

RAIN. [PALESTINE.]

RAM. [SHEEP.]

RA'MAH (*a high place, height*), the name of several towns and villages in Palestine, which it is not in all cases easy to distinguish from one another.

1. RAMAH, a town of Benjamin (Josh. xviii. 25), in the vicinity of Gibeah and Geba; on the way from Jerusalem to Bethel (Judg. iv. 5), and not far from the confines of the two kingdoms. Jerome places it six Roman miles north of Jerusalem, and Josephus places it forty stadia from Jerusalem. In accordance with all these intimations, at the distance of two hours' journey north of Jerusalem, upon a hill a little to the east of the great northern road, a village still exists under the name of er-Ram, in which we cannot hesitate to recognise the representative of the ancient Ramah.

2. RAMAH, of Samuel, so called, where the prophet lived and was buried (1 Sam. i. 19; ii. 11; vii. 17; viii. 4; xv. 34; xvi. 13, 19; xviii. 19, 22, 23; xxv. 1; xxviii. 3). It is probably the same with the Ramathaim-Zophim to which

his father Elkanah belonged (1 Sam. i. 1, 19). The position of this Ramah was early lost sight of by tradition, and the variety of conflicting opinions regarding it shows that nothing is known with certainty on the subject.

3. RAMAH, a city of Naphtali (Josh. xix. 36).

4. RAMAH, a town of Gilead (2 Kings viii. 29), the name of which is given more fully in Josh. xiii. 26, as Ramoth-Mizpeh.

RAME'SES, an Egyptian city in the land of Goshen, built, or at least fortified, by the labour of the Israelites (Gen. xlvii. 11; Exod. i. 11; xii. 37; Num. xxxiii. 3-5). The name of the city seems to have been sometimes given to the whole province (Gen. xlvii. 11), by which it would appear to have been the chief city of the district. It was probably situated on the water-shed between the Bitter Lakes and the Valley of the Seven Wells. not far from Heroopolis, but not identical with that city. The name means 'son of the sun,' and was borne by several of the ancient kings of Egypt, one of whom was probably the founder of the city.

RAMOTH (*heights*, pl. of Ramah). There were several places of this name, usually with some addition to distinguish them from one another.

1. RAMOTH-GILEAD, called also RAMOTH-MIZPEH, or simply RAMOTH, a town in Gilead, within the borders of Gad (Josh. xiii. 26), which belonged to the Levites (Josh. xxi. 38; 1 Chron. vi. 65, 80). It was one of the cities of refuge (Deut. iv. 43; Josh. xx. 8), and one of the towns in which an intendant was stationed by Solomon (1 Kings iv. 13). It was the last of their conquests which the Syrians held; and Ahab was killed (1 Kings xxii. 1-37; 2 Chron. xviii.), and fourteen years after his son Joram was wounded (2 Kings viii. 28), in the attempt to recover it. The strength of the place is attested by the length of time the Syrians were enabled to hold it, and by Ahab and Joram having both been solicitous to obtain the aid of the kings of Judah when about to attack it; these being two of the only three expeditions in which the kings of Judah and Israel ever co-operated. It was here also that Jehu was proclaimed and anointed king (2 Kings ix. 1-6); but it is not very clear whether the army was then still before the town, or in actual possession of it. Eusebius places Ramoth-Gilead on the river Jabbok, fifteen Roman miles west of Philadelphia (Rabbah), where the ruins of a town are still to be seen. Buckingham is, however, more disposed to seek the site of Ramoth-Gilead in a place now called Ramtha, or Rameza, which is about twenty-three miles N.W.N. from Philadelphia, and about four miles north of the Jabbok, where he noticed some ruins which he could not examine.

RA'MATH-LE'HI. This name, which means *height of the jawbone*, belonged to a place on the borders of Philistia, and is referred by the sacred writer to the jaw-bone with which Samson slaughtered the Philistines (Judg. xv. 17).

RA'MOTH-NE'GEB (*Ramoth of the south*), a city in the tribe of Simeon (Josh. xix. 8; 1 Sam. xxx. 27).

RAMS' HORNS. [MUSICAL INSTRUMENTS.]

RAMS' SKINS, RED, occurs in Exod. xxv. 5, and xxxv. 7. There is little doubt that the red rams' skins here noticed are to be understood as the produce of the African Aoudad, the *Ovis tragelaphus* of naturalists, whereof the bearded sheep are a domesticated race. We agree with Dr. Mason Harris, that the skins in question were most likely tanned and coloured crimson.

RAVEN. The raven is very generally confounded with the carrion crow, but though very similar is quite distinct from it. Its size is larger, its black colour more iridescent; it is gifted with greater sagacity; is naturally observant and solitary, while the crow is gregarious in its habits; lives in pairs; has a most acute scent; and flies to a great height.

Whether the raven of Palestine is the common species, or the *Corvus Montanus* of Temminck, is not quite determined; for there is of the ravens, or greater form of crows, a smaller group including two or three others, all similar in manners, and unlike the carrion crows, which are gregarious, and seemingly identical in both hemispheres. Sometimes a pair of ravens will descend without fear among a flight of crows, take possession of the carrion that may have attracted them, and keep the crows at a distance till they themselves are gorged. The habits of the whole genus render it unclean in the Hebrew law; and the malignant, ominous expression of the raven, together with the colour of its plumage, powers of voice, and solitary habits, are the causes of that universal and often superstitious attention with which mankind have ever regarded it. This bird is the first mentioned in the Bible, as being sent forth by Noah out of the ark on the subsiding of the waters; and in 1 Kings xvii. 4, ravens bring flesh and bread at morning and eve to the prophet Elijah.

REBEK'AH (*a noosed cord*); daughter of Bethuel, and sister of Laban, who became the wife of Isaac, and the mother of Jacob and Esau. The particulars of her history and conduct, as given in Scripture, chiefly illustrate her preference of Jacob over Esau, and have been related in the article JACOB: see also ISAAC.

RE'CHAB (*rider*), son of Hemath the Kenite, and probably a descendant of Jethro [KENITES]: he is only known as the father of Jonadab, the founder of the sect of Rechabites, which took from him its name (2 Kings x. 15; 1 Chron. ii. 55; Jer. xxxv. 6).

RE'CHABITES. The tribe or family of Kenites, whom Jonadab, the son of Rechab, subjected to a new rule of life; or rather bound to the continued observance of ancient usages which were essential to their separate existence, but which the progress of their intercourse with towns seemed likely soon to extinguish. By thus maintaining their independent existence as a pastoral people, they would keep themselves from being involved in the distractions and internal wars of the country, would be in no danger of becoming objects of jealousy and suspicion to the Israelites, and would be able at all times to remove from a country in which they were strangers. The Rechabites found so much advantage in these rules, that they observed them with great strictness for about 300 years, when we first become aware of their existence. Jeremiah put to the proof their adherence to their founder's rules, and they stood the test (Jer. xxxv. 6, 7).

What eventually became of the Rechabites is not known. The probability is that, when they found themselves no longer safe among the Hebrews, they withdrew into the desert from which they at first came, and which was peopled by men of similar habits of life, among whom, in the course of time, they lost their separate existence.

RECORDER, the title of a high officer in the court of the kings of Judah (2 Sam. viii. 16; 1 Kings iv. 3; 2 Kings xviii. 18). 'Remembrancer' would perhaps be a more exact translation of the title. The officer thus designated seems to have been not only the grand custodier of the public records, but to have kept the responsible registry of the current transactions of the government. This was an employment of the very first rank and dignity in the courts of the ancient East.

REED. The word thus translated in the Old Testament is *Kaneh*, which occurs in 1 Kings xiv. 15; 2 Kings xviii. 21; Job xl. 21; Isa. xix. 6; xxxv. 7; xxxvi. 6; xlii. 3; Ezek. xxix. 6. It is the probable source of our word *cane*, a term which seems to have been used at the time our translation was made in a more general sense than at present, when the term cane has been applied more particularly to the stems of the *Calamus rotang*, and other species of rattan canes, which we have good grounds for believing were unknown to the ancients. In most of the passages of the Old Testament the word *Kaneh* seems to be applied strictly to reeds of different kinds growing in water, that is, to the hollow stems or culms of grasses, which are usually weak, easily shaken about by wind or by water, fragile, and breaking into sharp-pointed splinters.

RED SEA. [SEA.]

RED SEA, PASSAGE OF. [EXODUS.]

REFINER. [METALS.]

REFUGE, CITIES OF. [CITIES OF REFUGE.]

RE'HOB, called also BETH-REHOB, a town on the northern border of Palestine (Num. xiii. 21), not far from Dan (Judg. xviii. 27-29). It was assigned to the tribe of Asher (Josh. xix. 28), and was a Levitical city (Josh. xxi. 31; 1 Chron. vi. 73). It does not, however, appear that the Israelites ever had it in actual possession (comp. Judg. i. 31; 2 Sam. x. 6, 8).

REHOB, the father of Hadadezer, king of Zobah, in Syria (2 Sam. viii. 3).

REHOBO'AM (*he enlarges the people*), only son of Solomon, born of an Ammonitess, called Naamah (1 Kings xiv. 21, 31). His reign commenced B.C. 975, when he was at the age of forty-one, and lasted seventeen years. This reign was chiefly remarkable for the political crisis which gave rise to it, and which resulted in the separation of the previously single monarchy into two kingdoms, of which the smaller, which took the name of Judah, adhered to the house of David. All the points involved in this important event, and its immediate results, have been considered in the articles ISRAEL, JEROBOAM, JUDAH.

REHO'BOTH, a name meaning 'wide places,' or 'ample room,' as is indicated by Isaac in giving it to some of the wells which he dug in the south of Palestine (Gen. xxvi. 22).

REHOBOTH-IR (*Rehoboth-city*), a town of ancient Assyria (Gen. x. 11), the site of which has not been ascertained.

REHOBOTH-HAN'NAHAR, or *Rehoboth of the river*, the birth-place of one of the Edomitish kings, named Saul (Gen. xxxvi. 37). The river is, doubtless, the Euphrates, and the place is probably represented by the modern er-Rahabeh, upon the west bank of that river, between Rakkah and Anah.

REM'PHAN, or REPHAN, a name quoted in Acts vii. 43, from Amos v. 26. But according to the received pointing, the passage would better read, ' Ye bore the tabernacle of your king (idol), and *the statue* (or statues) of your idols, the star of your god, which ye make to yourselves.' According to this reading, the name of the idol so worshipped by the Israelites is in fact not given, although the mention of a star still suggests that some planet is intended. The reference is probably to Saturn, who was worshipped by the Semitic nations along with Mars as an evil demon to be propitiated with sacrifices.

REPH'AIM, an ancient people of unusual stature, who, in the time of Abraham, dwelt in the country beyond the Jordan, in and about Ashtoreth-Karnaim (Gen. xiv. 5). There seems reason to think that the Rephaim were the most ancient or aboriginal inhabitants of Palestine prior to the Canaanites, by whom they were gradually dispossessed of the regions west of the Jordan, and driven beyond that river. Only a remnant of the race remained at the time of the ingress of the Israelites under Joshua.

REPHAIM, VALLEY OF, a valley beginning adjacent to the valley of Hinnom, southwest of Jerusalem, and stretching away southwest on the right of the road to Bethlehem (Josh. xv. 8; xvii. 5; xviii. 6; 2 Sam. v. 18, 22). This name corroborates the presumption that the Rephaim were originally west of the Jordan.

REPH'IDIM, a station of the Israelites in proceeding to Sinai. [SINAI.]

RE'SEN, an ancient town of Assyria, described as a great city lying between Nineveh and Calah (Gen. x. 12). Its site is unknown.

RESURRECTION OF CHRIST. After our Lord had completed the work of redemption by his death upon the cross, he rose victorious from the grave, and to those who through faith in him should become members of his body, he became ' the prince of life.' Since this event, however, independently of its importance in respect to the internal connection of the Christian doctrine, was manifestly a miraculous occurrence, the credibility of the narrative has been denied by some, while others who have admitted the facts as recorded to be beyond dispute, yet have attempted to show that Christ was not really dead; but that, being stunned and palsied, he wore for a time the appearance of death, and was afterwards restored to consciousness by the cool grave and the spices. Objections of this nature do not require notice here; but a few words upon the apparent discrepancies of the Gospel narratives will not be misplaced. These discrepancies were early perceived; and various writers have commented on them with the view of throwing uncertainty and doubt over the whole of this portion of Gospel history. A numerous host of theologians, however, rose to combat and refute these objections; among others Griesbach, who remarks that all the discrepancies are trifling, and not of such moment as to render the narrative uncertain and

suspected, or to destroy or even diminish the credibility of the Evangelists; but rather serve to show how extremely studious they were of truth, ' and how closely and even scrupulously they followed their documents.'

RESURRECTION OF THE BODY. This expression is used to denote the revivification of the human body after it has been forsaken by the soul, or the re-union of the soul hereafter to the body which it had occupied in the present world. Considerable diversity of opinion has prevailed respecting the extent to which the doctrine of the resurrection was known to the ancient Jews. In the time of Christ, however, the belief of this doctrine in connection with a state of future retribution, was held by the Pharisees and the great body of the Jewish people, and was only disputed by the Sadducees.

But although the doctrine of the resurrection was thus prevalent among the Jews in the time of Christ, it might still have been doubtful and obscure to us, had not Christ given to it the sanction of his authority, and declared it a constituent part of his religion (*e. g.*, Matt. xxii.; John v., viii. xi.).

The principal points which can be collected from the New Testament on this subject are the following:—1. The raising of the dead is everywhere ascribed to Christ, and is represented as the last work to be undertaken by him for the salvation of man (John v. 21; xi. 25; 1 Cor. xv. 22, sq.; 1 Thess. iv. 15; Rev. i. 18). 2. All the dead will be raised, without respect to age, rank, or character in this world (John v. 28, 29; Acts xxiv. 15; 1 Cor. xv. 22). 3. This event is to take place not before the end of the world, or the general judgment (John v. 21; vi. 39, 40; xi. 24; 1 Cor. xv. 22-28; 1 Thess. iv. 15; Rev. xx. 11). 4. The manner in which this marvellous change shall be accomplished is necessarily beyond our present comprehension; and, therefore, the Scripture is content to illustrate it by figurative representations, or by proving the possibility and intelligibility of the leading facts. Some of the figurative descriptions occur in John v.; Matt. xxiv.; 1 Cor. xv. 52; 1 Thess. iv. 16; Phil. iii. 21. 5. The possibility of a resurrection is powerfully argued by Paul in 1 Cor. xv. 32, sq., by comparing it with events of common occurrence in the natural world. (See also ver. 12-14, and compare Acts iv. 2.) But although this body shall be so raised as to preserve its identity, it must yet undergo certain purifying changes to fit it for the kingdom of heaven, and to render it capable of immortality (1 Cor. xv. 35, sq.), so that it shall become a glorified body like that of Christ (ver. 49; Rom. vi. 9; Phil. iii. 21); and the bodies of those whom the last day finds alive, will undergo a similar change without tasting death (1 Cor. xv. 51, 53; 2 Cor. v. 4; 1 Thess. iv. 15, sq.; Phil. iii. 21).

REU'BEN (*behold a son*), eldest son of Jacob by Leah (Gen. xxix. 32; xxxv. 23; xlvi. 8). His improper intercourse with Bilhah, his father's concubine wife, was an enormity too great for Jacob ever to forget, and he spoke of it with abhorrence even on his dying bed (Gen. xxxii. 22; xlix. 4). For his conduct in this matter, Jacob, in his last blessing, deprived him of the pre-eminence and double portion which belonged to his birth-right, assigning the former to Judah, and the latter to Joseph (Gen. xlix. 3, 4; comp. ver. 8-10; xlviii. 5). The doom, 'Thou shalt not excel,' was exactly fulfilled in the destinies of the tribe descended from Reuben, which makes no figure in the Hebrew history, and never produced any eminent person. At the time of the Exodus, this tribe numbered 46,500 adult males, which ranked it as the seventh in population; but at the later census before entering Canaan, its numbers had decreased to 43,730, which rendered it the ninth in population (Num. i. 21; xxvi. 5). The Reubenites received for their inheritance the fine pasture-land (the present Belka) on the east of the Jordan, which to a cattle-breeding people, as they were, must have been very desirable (Num. xxxii. 1 sq.; xxxiv 14; Josh. i. 14; xv. 17). This lay south of the territories of Gad (Deut iii. 12, 16), and north of the river Arnon. Although thus settled earlier than the other tribes, excepting Gad and half Manasseh, who shared with them the territory beyond the Jordan, the Reubenites willingly assisted their brethren in the wars of Canaan (Num xxxii. 27, 29; Josh. iv. 12); after which they returned to their own lands (Josh. xxii. 15); and we hear little more of them till the time of Hazael, king of Syria, who ravaged and for a time held possession of their country (2 Kings x. 33). The Reubenites, and the other tribes beyond the river, were naturally the first to give way before the invaders from the East, and were the first of all the Israelites sent into exile by Tiglath-pileser, king of Assyria, B C. 773 (1 Chron. v. 26).

REVELATION, BOOK OF. In respect to the authorship of this book, it is to be observed that the writer styles himself John, but does not call himself an apostle (i. 4, 9; xxii. 8). Hence some have attributed the book to another John, usually designated the presbyter. But there is no direct evidence that this was the case; while on the other hand Justin Martyr, Tertullian, Clement of Alexandria, and Origen, all ascribe it to the Apostle. We are disposed, therefore, to abide by the ancient opinion that the book was written by the beloved disciple. Ecclesiastical tradition clearly favours this view, while the objections from alleged internal evidence, so earnestly urged by recent German critics, do not appear sufficiently strong to overturn it.

But the entire question of authorship is more curious than profitable. The book may not have been written by an apostle, and yet be equal in authority to any acknowledged production of an apostle. Luke was only an evangelist; and yet his writings are infallibly true and correct in every particular, because they proceeded from the Holy Spirit. The question whether the Apocalypse was written by an apostle or not, is of trifling importance as long as its inspiration is maintained. If any imagine that, in attempting to destroy the *directly apostolic* authorship, they lessen the value or disturb the canonical credit of the book, they are mistaken.

The canonical authority of the book has been called in question, both in ancient and modern times. But the external evidence in favour of its authenticity and genuineness is overwhelming, while internal circumstances amply confirm it.

The style, language, and manner of the book cannot be mistaken. In dignity and sublimity it is equal to any of the New Testament writings, if not superior to them all. The variety and force of the images impress the mind of every reader with conceptions of a divine origin. Surely no uninspired man could have written in such a strain.

There is considerable difficulty in ascertaining the time and place at which it was written. The prevalent opinion is, that the book was written A.D. 96 or 97, at Patmos or Ephesus, after Domitian's death, *i. e.* under Nerva. There is no definite external evidence on this point, and, judging from internal circumstances, some writers assign it to the time of Nero, and the locality of Patmos, A.D. 67 or 68. Sir Isaac Newton fixed upon this date.

The books of the New Testament, like those of the Old, were designed to promote the instruction of God's people in all ages. They were adapted to teach, exhort, and reprove all mankind. They do not belong to the class of ephemeral writings that have long since fulfilled the purpose for which they were originally composed. Their object was not merely a local or partial one. So of the Apocalypse. It is suited to all. 'Blessed is he that readeth, and they that hear the words of this prophecy.' But this general characteristic is perfectly consistent with the fact that it arose out of specific circumstances, and was primarily meant to subserve a definite end. When first written, it was destined to suit the peculiar circumstances of the early Christians. The times were troublous. Persecution had appeared in various forms. The followers of Christ were exposed to severe sufferings for conscience sake. Their enemies were fierce against them. Comparatively few and feeble, the humble disciples of the Lamb seemed doomed to extinction. But the writer of the Apocalypse was prompted to present to them such views as were adapted to encourage them to steadfastness in the faith—to comfort them in the midst of calamity—and to arm them with resolution to endure all the assaults of their foes. Exalted honours, glorious rewards, are set before the Christian soldier who should endure to the end. A crown of victory—the approbation of the Redeemer—everlasting felicity;—these are prepared for the patient believer. In connection with such representations the final triumph of Christianity and the Messiah's peaceful reign with his saints, form topics on which the writer dwells with emphatic earnestness (See chap. i. 1-3; ii. 1; iii. 22; xxii. 6, 7, 10-17). The suffering Christians of primitive times may have sorrowfully thought that they should never be able to stand the shock of their bitter and bloody assailants, the power and policy of the world being leagued against them—but the statements of the writer all tend to the conclusion that truth should make progress in the earth, and the church, emerging out of all struggles, wax stronger and stronger. If such be the primary and principal aim of the book, it follows that we should not look in it for a history of the kingdoms of the world. To compose a civil history did not comport with the writer's object. The genius of Christ's kingdom is totally different from that of the kingdoms of the world. It advances steadily and silently, independently of, and frequently in opposition to them. Hence the Apocalypse cannot contain a history of the world. It exhibits *a history of the church.*

specially of its early struggles with the powers of darkness and the malice of superstition. Trials impending over the church, and judgments over her enemies,—these form the burden of the prophecy. The body of the work is contained in chaps. iv.-xxii. 6, and is almost entirely a series of symbolic representations. To this is prefixed a prologue (i.-iv). A brief epilogue is subjoined (xxii. 6-21). The prologue is of considerable length, embracing separate epistles to the seven churches in Asia Minor, peculiarly fitted to admonish and console amid the sufferings which were impending. After the prologue or introduction, we come to the body of the work itself, commencing with the *fourth* chapter. With regard to the symbolical predictions of which this part of the work consists, the mere statement of the various conflicting theories which have been propounded would occupy a large volume. We cannot therefore enter upon a subject so extensive, but must content ourselves with referring the reader to the works in which the interpretation of these prophecies is discussed in all its bearings.

RE'ZEPH, a city which occurs among those subdued by the Assyrians (2 Kings xix. 12; Isa. xxxvii. 12). It is possibly the same with the Rasapha which Abulfeda places at nearly a day's journey west of the Euphrates.

RE'ZIN, the last king of Damascene-Syria, slain by Tiglath-pileser (2 Kings xv. 37; xvi. 5-10; Isa. vii. 1; viii. 4-7) [DAMASCUS].

RE'ZON (*prince*); an officer of Hadadezer, king of Zobah, who established the independence of Damascus, and made it the seat of the kingdom of Damascene-Syria, so often mentioned in the history of the Hebrew kingdoms (1 Kings xi. 23, 24) [DAMASCUS].

RHE'GIUM, a city on the coast of Italy, near its south-western extremity, opposite Messina in Sicily (Acts xxviii. 13). It is now called Reggio, and is the capital of Calabria.

RHO'DA (*Rose*), a servant maid mentioned in Acts xii. 13.

RHO'DES, an island in the Mediterranean, near the coast of Asia Minor, celebrated from the remotest antiquity as the seat of commerce, navigation, literature, and the arts, but now reduced to a state of abject poverty by the devastations of war and the tyranny and rapacity of its Turkish rulers. It is of a triangular form, about forty-four leagues in circumference, twenty leagues long from north to south, and about six broad. It was famed in ancient times, and is still celebrated, for its delightful climate and the fertility of its soil. It contains two cities—Rhodes, the capital, inhabited chiefly by Turks, and a small number of Jews; and the ancient Lindus, now reduced to a hamlet, peopled by Greeks, who are almost all engaged in commerce. Besides these there are five villages occupied by Turks and a small number of Jews; and five towns and forty-one villages inhabited by Greeks. The whole population is estimated at 20,000. The city of Rhodes is famous for its huge brazen statue of Apollo, called Colossus, which stood at the mouth of the harbour, and was so high that ships passed in full sail between its legs. There is not a single vestige of this celebrated work of art now remaining. St. Paul appears to have visited

Rhodes while on his journey to Jerusalem, A.D. 58 (Acts xxi. 1).

The antiquities of Rhodes reach no farther back than the residence of the knights of St. John of Jerusalem. The remains of their fine old fortress, of great size and strength, are still to be seen. In modern times Rhodes has been chiefly celebrated as one of the last retreats of this military order, under whom it obtained great celebrity by its heroic resistance to the Turks; but in the time of Solyman the Great a capitulation was agreed upon, and the island was finally surrendered to the Turks, under whom it has since continued.

RIB'LAH, a town on the northern border of Palestine, in the district of Hamath, through which the Babylonians, both in their irruptions and departures, were accustomed to pass (Num. xxxiv. 11; 2 Kings xxiii. 33; xxv. 26; Jer. xxxix. 5; lii. 10). This place is nowhere mentioned but in the Bible.

RIDDLE, literally, 'something intricate or complicated.' An example of a riddle occurs in Judg. xiv. 12-19, where Samson proposes to the thirty young Philistines who attended his nuptials, an enigma, derived from the circumstance of his having lately found a swarm of bees and honey in the skeleton of the lion, which he had killed some months before, when he had come to espouse his wife. This riddle or enigma, though unfair in regard to those who accepted the pledge to unravel it, because they were ignorant of the particular fact by the knowledge of which alone it could be explained by them, nevertheless answers to the approved definition of an enigma, as consisting of an artful and abstruse proposition, put in obscure, ambiguous, and even contrary terms, in order to exercise the ingenuity of others in finding out its meaning.

RIM'MON, the name of several places in Palestine, probably distinguished by the presence of pomegranate-trees.

1. A city of the tribe of Simeon, in the south of Palestine (Josh. xv. 32; xix. 7; 1 Chron. iv. 32 : Zech. xiv. 10).

2. A town on a high conical chalky rock or peak, north-east of Gibeah and Michmash, near the desert (Judg. xx. 45, 47; xxi. 13). The *Onomasticon* places it fifteen miles north of Jerusalem, which corresponds to the situation of this rock, which is still crowned by a village bearing the name of Rummon.

3. A city of Zebulon (Josh. xix. 3; 1 Chron. vi. 62).

4. A station of the Israelites after leaving Sinai (Num. xxxiii. 19).

RIM'MON, an idol worshipped by the Syrians (2 Kings v. 18). As this name is found nowhere but in the Bible, and there only in the present text, nothing positive can be affirmed concerning the power it symbolized.

RI'PHATH, a northern people descended from Gomer (Gen. x. 3).

RIZ'PAH (*a coal*); a concubine of Saul, memorable for the touching example of maternal affection which she afforded, in watching the dead bodies of her sons, and driving the birds away from them, when they had been gibbeted by the Gibeonites (2 Sam. iii. 7; xxi. 8, 10, 11).

ROSE. The Hebrew word rendered 'rose' in Sol. Song xi. 1, and Isa. xxxv. 1, is not now generally understood to denote a rose, but probably a species of narcissus. But by the Greek word rendered 'rose' in the Apocryphal books (Ecclus. xxiv. 14; xxxix 13; l. 8; Wisd. xi. 8), that flower is generally allowed to be designated.

The rose was as highly esteemed among ancient, as it is among modern nations, if we may judge by the frequent references to it in the poets of antiquity. As we know that it continues to be the favourite flower of the Persians, and is much cultivated in Egypt, we might expect more frequent mention of some of its numerous species and varieties in the Jewish writings. This, however, is not the case, and probably arises from its being less common in a wild state in a comparatively dry and warm climate like that of Syria. It is, however, indigenous in some parts. Monro, as quoted in Kitto's *Physical History of Palestine*, 'found in the valley of Baalbek, a creeping rose of a bright yellow colour in full bloom, about the end of May. About the same time, on advancing towards Rama and Joppa from Jerusalem, the hills are found to be to a considerable extent covered with white and pink roses.' Mariti found the greatest quantity of roses in the hamlet of St. John, in the desert of the same name. 'In this place the rose-plants form small forests in the gardens. The greatest part of the roses reared there are brought to Jerusalem, where rose-water is prepared from them, of which the scent is so very exquisite, that in every part of Lycia, and also in Cyprus, it is in request above all other rose-waters.' Burckhardt was struck with the number of rose-trees which he found among the ruins of Bozra beyond the Jordan. That the rose was cultivated in Damascus is well known. Indeed one species is named *Rosa Damascena* from being supposed to be indigenous there. 'In the gardens of the city roses are still much cultivated. Monro says that in size they are inferior to our damask rose, and less perfect in form; but that their odour and colour are far more rich. The only variety that exists in Damascus is a white rose, which appears to belong to the same species, differing only in colour.'

ROE. The Arabian gazelle is probably denoted by the Hebrew word translated 'roe' in the Authorized Version.

ROLL. [WRITING.]

ROMANS, THE EPISTLE TO THE. This epistle claims our interest more than the other didactic epistles of the Apostle Paul, because it is more systematic, and because it explains especially that truth which became subsequently the principle of the reformation, viz., righteousness through faith.

At the period when the apostle wrote the Epistle to the Romans, he was between fifty and sixty years old. After having spent two years and a half at Ephesus, he planned a journey to Macedonia, Achaia, Jerusalem, and Rome (Acts xix. 21). Having spent about three months in travelling, he arrived at Corinth, where he remained three months (Acts xx. 2); and during this second abode at Corinth he wrote the Epistle to the Romans (comp. 1 Cor. xvi. 1-3, and 2 Cor. ix. with Rom xv. 25). Paul dispatched this letter by a Corinthian woman, who was just then travelling to Rome (xvi. 1), and sent greetings from an inhabitant of Corinth (xvi. 23; comp. 1 Cor. i. 14).

It is probable that the epistle was written about the year 58 or 59. The congregation of Christians at Rome was formed at a very early period, but its founder is unknown. Paul himself mentions two distinguished teachers at Rome, who were converted earlier than himself. According to Rom. i. 8, the Roman congregation had then attained considerable celebrity, as their faith was spoken of throughout the whole world. It is probable that the Jews at Rome were first converted to Christianity. But at the time when this epistle was written it appears that the Gentile Christians in the Roman church were then more numerous than the converted Jews.

In the introduction the apostle states that he had long entertained the wish of visiting the metropolis, in order to confirm the faith of the church, and to be himself comforted by that faith. But having hitherto been hindered from carrying his intention into effect, he avails himself of the opportunity afforded by the journey of Phœbe to Rome, to send in writing the sum and substance of the Christian doctrine which he had been prevented from preaching in that city.

The apostle commences his epistle by describing the two great divisions of the human race, viz., those who underwent the preparatory spiritual education of the Jews, and those who did not undergo such a preparatory education. The chief aim of all nations, according to him, should be the *righteousness before the face of God*, or absolute realization of the moral law. According to the apostle, the heathen also have their *law*, as well religious as moral internal revelation (Rom. i. 19, 32; ii. 15). The heathen have, however, not fulfilled that law which they knew, and are in this respect like the Jews, who also disregarded their own law (ii.). Both Jews and Gentiles are transgressors, or by the law separated from the grace and sonship of God (Rom. ii. 12; iii. 20); consequently if blessedness could only be obtained by fulfilling the demands of God, no man could be blessed. God, however, has gratuitously given righteousness and blessedness to all who believe in Christ (iii. 21-31); the Old Testament also recognises the value of religious faith (iv.): thus we freely attain to peace and sonship of God presently, and have before us still greater things, viz., the future development of the kingdom of God (v. 1-11). The human race has gained in Christ much more than it lost in Adam (v. 12, 21). This doctrine by no means encourages sin (vi.): on the contrary, men who are conscious of divine grace fulfil the law much more energetically than they were able to do before having attained to this knowledge, because the law alone is even apt to sharpen the appetite for sin, and leads finally to despair (vii.); but now we fulfil the law by means of that new spirit which is given unto us, and the full development of our salvation is still before us (viii. 1-27). The sufferings of the present time cannot prevent this development, and must rather work for good to them whom God from eternity has viewed as faithful believers; and nothing can separate such believers from the eternal love of God (viii. 28-39). It causes pain to behold the Israelites themselves shut out from salvation; but they themselves are the cause of this seclusion, because they wanted to attain salvation by their own resources and exertions, by their descent from Abraham, and by their fulfilment of the law: thus, however, the Jews have not obtained that salvation which God has freely offered under the sole condition of faith in Christ (ix.); the Jews have not entered upon the way of faith, therefore the Gentiles were preferred, which was predicted by the prophets. However, the Jewish race, as such, has not been rejected; some of them obtain salvation by a selection made not according to their works, but according to the grace of God. If some of the Jews are left to their own obduracy, even their temporary fall serves the plans of God, viz., the vocation of the Gentiles. After the mass of the Gentiles shall have entered in, the people of Israel also, in their collective capacity, shall be received into the church (xi).

The authenticity of this epistle has never been questioned.

ROME, the famous capital of the Western World, and the present residence of the Pope, stands on the river Tiber, about fifteen miles from its mouth, in the plain of what is now called the Campagna, in lat. 41° 54′ N., long. 12° 28′ E. The country around the city is not a plain, but a sort of undulating table-land, crossed by hills, while it sinks towards the south-west to the marshes of Maremma, which coast the Mediterranean. In ancient geography the country, in the midst of which Rome lay, was termed Latium, which, in the earliest times, comprised within a space of about four geographical square miles the country lying between the Tiber and the Numicius, extending from the Alban Hills to the sea, having for its chief city Laurentum. Here, on the Palatine Hill, was the city of Rome founded, but it was extended, by degrees, so as to take in six other hills, at the foot of which ran deep valleys that, in early times, were in part overflowed with water, while the hill sides were covered with trees. The site occupied by modern Rome is not precisely the same as that which was at any period covered by the ancient city: the change of locality being towards the north-west, the city has partially retired from the celebrated hills. About two-thirds of the area within the walls (traced by Aurelian) are now desolate, consisting of ruins, gardens, and fields, with some churches, convents, and other scattered habitations. Originally the city was a square mile in circumference. The ground on which the modern city is built covers about one thousand acres, or one mile and a half square; its walls form a circuit of fifteen miles, and embrace an area of three thousand acres. Three of the seven hills are covered with buildings, but are only thinly inhabited. The greatest part of the population is now comprised within the limits of the Campus Martius. The ancient city, however, was more than treble the size of the modern, for it had very extensive suburbs beyond the walls. The population in 1836 consisted of 153,678, exclusive of Jews, who amount to 3700.

The connection of the Romans with Palestine caused Jews to settle at Rome in considerable numbers. On one occasion, in the reign of Tiberius, when the Jews were banished from the city by the emperor, for the misconduct of some members of their body, not fewer than four thousand enlisted in the Roman army which was then stationed in Sardinia. From Philo also it appears that the Jews in Rome were allowed the free use of their national worship, and generally the observance of their ancestral customs. Then, as now, the Jews lived in a part of the city appropriated to themselves, where with a zeal for which the nation had been some time distinguished, they applied themselves with success to proselytising. They appear, however, to have been a restless colony; for when, after their expulsion under Tiberius, numbers had returned to Rome, they were again expelled from the city by Claudius. It is probable that the Christians, as well as the Jews, properly so called, were included in this expulsion.

The question, Who founded the church at Rome? is one of some interest as between Catholic and Protestant. The former assigns the honour to Peter, and on this grounds an argument in favour of the claims of the papacy. There is, however, no sufficient reason for believing that Peter was ever even so much as within the walls of Rome.

ROOF. [HOUSE.]

ROOM. [HOUSE.]

RUBY. The word rendered 'ruby' in the Authorized Version (Job xxviii. 18; Prov. iii. 15; viii. 11; xx. 15; xxxi. 10; Lam. iv. 7) appears rather to indicate 'pearls.' The ruby is, however, generally supposed to be represented by the word rendered 'agate' in Ezek. xxvii. 6, and Isa. liv. 12. The Oriental ruby is distinguished for its vivid red colour, and was regarded as the most valuable of precious stones next after the diamond.

RUE. The word rue occurs only in Luke xi. 42. 'But woe unto you, Pharisees! for ye tithe mint and rue and all manner of herbs, and pass over judgment,' &c. In the parallel passage, Matt. xxiii. 23, dill, translated anise in the English Version, is mentioned instead of rue. Both dill and rue were cultivated in the gardens of Eastern countries in ancient times as they are at the present day. Rue was highly esteemed as a medicine, even as early as the time of Hippocrates. Pliny says, ' Rue is an herbe as medicinable as the best. That of the garden hath a broader leafe, and brauncheth more than the wild, which is more hotte, vehement, and rigorous in all operations; also that is it sowed usually in Februarie, when the western wind, Favonius, bloweth.' That it was employed as an ingredient in diet, and as a condiment, is abundantly evident from Apicius, as noticed by Celsius, and is not more extraordinary than the fondness of some Eastern nations for assafœtida as a seasoning to food. That one kind was cultivated by the Israelites is evident from its being mentioned as one of the articles of which the Pharisees paid their tithes, though they neglected the weightier matters of the law. Rosenmüller states that in the Talmud the rue is indeed mentioned amongst kitchen herbs; but, at the same time, it is there expressly stated, that it is tithe free, it being one of those herbs which are not cultivated in gardens, according to the general rule established in the Talmud.

RUFUS. A person of this name was one of the sons of Simon the Cyrenian, who was compelled to bear the cross of Christ (Mark xv. 21): he is supposed to be the same with the Rufus to whom Paul, in writing to the Romans, sends his greeting in the remarkable words, ' Salute Rufus, chosen in the Lord, and his mother and mine'

(Rom. xvi. 13). He is said to have been one of the seventy disciples, and eventually to have had charge of the church at Thebes.

RUSH. The Hebrew word *gome*, translated 'rush' and 'bulrush' in our Authorized Version (Job viii. 11; Isa. xxxv. 7; Exod. ii. 3; Isa. xviii. 2) should be rendered *papyrus*.

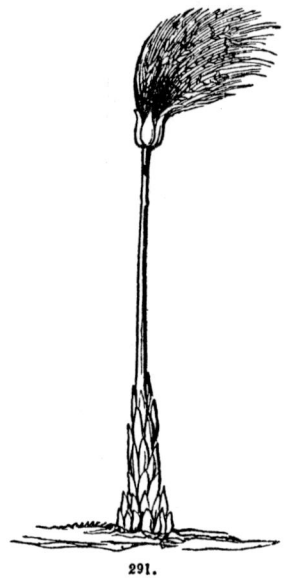

291.

This plant is now well known: it belongs to the tribe of *sedges*, and is not a rush or bulrush, as in the Authorized Version. It may be seen growing to the height of six or eight feet, even in tubs, in the hothouses of this country, and is described by the ancients as growing in the shallow parts of the Nile. The root is fleshy, thick, and spreading; the stems triangular, eight or ten feet in height, of which two or so are usually under water, thick below but tapering towards the apex, and destitute of leaves; those of the base broad, straight, and sword-shaped, but much shorter than the stem. Cassiodorus, as quoted by Carpenter, graphically described it as it appears on the banks of the Nile, 'There rises to the view this forest without branches, this thicket without leaves, this harvest of the waters, this ornament of the marshes.'

The *papyrus* was well known to the ancients as a plant of the waters of Egypt. It was found in almost every part of Egypt inundated by the Nile, in the Delta, especially in the Sebennytic nome, and in the neighbourhood of Memphis, &c. By some it was thought peculiar to Egypt; by others it was thought to be a native also of India, of the Euphrates near Babylon, of Syria, and of Sicily; and there is no reason why it should not grow in the waters of hot countries, as, for instance, near Babylon or in India.

A brief description of the uses of this plant, as given in the works of the ancients, is thus summed up by Parkinson in his *Herbal*, p. 1207: 'The plant, say the ancients, is sweete, and used by the Egyptians, before that bread of corne was known

unto them, for their food, and in their time was chawed, and the sweetnesse sucked forth, the rest being spit out; the roote serveth them not only for fewell to burne, but to make many sorts of vessels to use, for it yielded much matter for the purpose. The stalke is profitable to many uses, as to make ships, and of the barke to weave, and make sailes, mats, carpets, some kinds of garments, and ropes also.' The construction of *papyrus* boats is mentioned by Theophrastus; and Plutarch says, 'Isis circumnavigated the marshes in a *papyrus* wherry for the purpose of collecting the pieces of Osiris's body.' From Heliodorus's account it appears that the Ethiopians made use of similar boats; for he relates that the Ethiopians passed in reed wherries over the Astaboras; and he adds that these reed wherries were swift sailing, being made of a light material, and not capable of carrying more than two or three men. Bruce relates that a similar kind of boat was made in Abyssinia even in his time, having a keel of acacia wood, to which the *papyrus* plants, first sewed together, are fastened, being gathered up before and behind, and the ends of the plants thus tied together. Representations of some Egyptian boats are given in the *Pictorial Bible* (ii. p. 135); where the editor remarks that when a boat is described as being of reeds or rushes or *papyrus* (as in Egypt), a covering of skin or bitumen is to be understood. That the *papyrus* was employed for making paper is also well known, and Wilkinson mentions that from ancient paper being found at Thebes and elsewhere, it is evident that this application of it was much anterior to the time of Alexander the Great.

RUTH, a Moabitish woman, brought, under peculiar circumstances, into intimate relation with the stock of Israel, and whose history is given in one of the books of the sacred canon which bears her name. The narrative that brings her into the range of inspired story is constructed with idyllic simplicity and pathos, and forms a pleasant relief to the sombre and repulsive shades of the picture which the reader has just been contemplating in the later annals of the Judges. It is the domestic history of a family compelled, by the urgency of a famine, to abandon the land of Canaan, and seek an asylum in the territories of Moab. Elimelech, the head of the emigrating household, dies in the land of his sojourn, where his two surviving sons 'took them wives of the women of Moab; the name of the one was Orpah, and the name of the other Ruth.' On the death of the sons, the widowed parent resolving to return to her country and kindred, the filial affection of the daughters-in-law is put to a severe test, and Ruth determines at all hazards to accompany Naomi. She accordingly arrives at Bethlehem with her mother, where, in the extremity of want, she goes to glean after the reapers in the harvest-field of Boaz, a wealthy kinsman of her deceased father-in-law, Elimelech. Attracted by her appearance, and informed of her exemplary conduct towards her mother-in-law, Boaz bade her return from day to day, and directed his servants to give her a courteous welcome. An omen so propitious could not but be regarded as a special encouragement to both, and Naomi therefore counselled Ruth to seek an opportunity for intimating to Boaz the claim she had upon him as the nearest kinsman of her deceased husband. Boaz received this intimation favourably, yet he replied that there was another person more nearly related to the family than himself, whose title must first be disposed of. Without delay he applied himself to ascertain whether the kinsman in question was inclined to assert his right—a right which extended to a purchase of the ransom (at the Jubilee) of Elimelech's estate. Finding him indisposed to the measure, he obtained from him a release, ratified according to the legal forms of the time, and then proceeded himself to redeem the patrimony of Elimelech, and espoused the widow of his son, in order ' to raise up the name of the dead upon his inheritance.' From this union sprang David, the illustrious king of Israel, whose line the writer traces up, in conclusion, through Boaz, to Pharez, son of Judah.

THE BOOK OF RUTH is inserted in the Canon, according to the English arrangement, between the book of Judges and the books of Samuel, as a sequel to the former and an introduction to the latter. The true date and authorship of the book are alike unknown, though the current of opinion is in favour of Samuel as the writer. Its canonical authority has never been questioned.

RYE. The word thus rendered (*Kussemeth*) in Exod. ix. 32; Isa. xxviii. 25, is translated *fitches* in Ezek. iv. 9; but its true meaning still remains uncertain. It was one of the cultivated grains both of Egypt and of Syria, and one of those employed as an article of diet. It was also sown along with wheat, or, at least, its crop was in the same state of forwardness; for we learn from Exod. ix. 32, that in the seventh plague the hail-storm smote the barley which was in the ear, and the flax which was bolled; but that the wheat and the *kussemeth* were not smitten, for they were not grown up. That *kussemeth* was cultivated in Palestine we learn from Isa. xxviii. 25, where it is mentioned along with ketzah and cumin, wheat and barley; and sown, according to some translators, ' on the extreme border of the fields,' as a kind ' of fence for other kinds of corn. This is quite an Oriental practice, and may be seen in the case of flax and other grains in India, at the present day. The rye is a grain of cold climates, and is not cultivated even in the south of Europe. Korte declares that no rye grows in Egypt; and Shaw states that rye is little known in Barbary and Egypt. That the *kussemeth* was employed for making bread by the Hebrews we know from Ezek. iv. 9, where the prophet is directed to ' take wheat, and barley, and beans, and lentiles, and millet, and *kussemeth*, and put them in a vessel, and make bread thereof.'

Though it is very unlikely that *kussemeth* can mean rye, it is not easy to say what cultivated grain it denotes. The principal kinds of grain, it is to be observed, are mentioned in the same passages with the *kussemeth*. Celsius has, as usual, with great labour and learning, collected together the different translations which have been given of this difficult word. In the Arabic translation of Exod. ix. 32, it is rendered *julban*, a species of pulse. By other Arabian writers it is considered to mean peas, and also beans. Many translate it vetches, as in the Authorized Version of Exod. ix. 32. The majority, however, instead of a legume, consider *kussemeth* to indicate one of the cereal grains, as the rye or the oat, neither of which is it likely to have been. Several eminent

authors consider that ' spelt ' is the grain referred to, and it seems very probable that this is the true meaning. There are two kinds of spelt, both of which were cultivated and esteemed as food in Egypt and Syria. That it was highly esteemed by the ancients is evident from Dioscorides describing it as more nourishing than barley, and grateful in taste. The goodness of this grain is also implied from the name of semen having been especially applied to it.

Triticum Spelta, or *Spelt*, is in many respects so closely allied to the common wheats as to have been thought by some old authors to have been the original stock of the cultivated kinds; but for this there is no foundation, as the kind cultivated for ages in Europe does not differ from specimens collected in a wild state. These were found by a French botanist, Michaux, in Persia, on a mountain four days' journey to the north of Hamadan. It is cultivated in many parts of Germany, in Switzerland, in the south of France, and in Italy. It is commonly sown in spring, and collected in July and August. Though some circumstances seem to point to this species as the *kussemeth* of Scripture, the subject is still susceptible of further investigation, and can only be finally determined by first ascertaining the modern agriculture of eastern countries, and comparing it with the ancient accounts of the agriculture of Syria and Egypt.

S.

SABBATH. The original word signifies simply rest, cessation from labour or employment.

The term, however, became appropriated in a specific religious sense, to signify the dedication of a precise portion of time to cessation from worldly labour, and a peculiar consecration by virtue of which a sanctity was ascribed to the portion of time so set apart.

Was there any Sabbath before the Law? This is a question of great importance; for Paley distinctly admits that, ' if the divine command was actually delivered at the creation, it was addressed, no doubt, to the whole human species alike, and continues, unless repealed by some subsequent revelation, binding upon all who come to the knowledge of it.' The mention made of the Sabbath in Gen. ii. 3, would seem to decide this question in the affirmative. The meaning of the passage admits of no dispute. To sanctify the seventh day clearly means, to set it apart for a sacred use. An attempt has been made to evade the force of this passage by assuming it to be an anticipation of an event which took place upwards of 2000 years afterwards. That God did not *then* bless and sanctify the Sabbath, but that when he did so, it was for the reason mentioned in the text. But this argument proceeds on the assumption that the book of Genesis was not written till after the giving of the law from Sinai. Of this there is not the slightest evidence, and it is in itself exceedingly improbable; besides this interpretation does evident violence to the context.

The division of time into periods of seven days of which mention is made in the account of the deluge, and which is found among all ancient nations, Egyptians, Arabians, Greeks, Romans, and even among the American Indians, furnishes a strong confirmation of the opinion that the Sabbath is coeval with the creation. Besides, there is evidence that the Sabbath was known and observed by the Israelites before the law was delivered on Mount Sinai. This did not occur until the third month after the departure out of Egypt, whereas we are informed that in the second month the people of their own accord gathered a double portion of manna on the sixth day, because the seventh day was the Sabbath (Exod. xvi. 22). This is corroborated by the language of the fourth commandment, ' *Remember* the Sabbath day to keep it holy '—a mode of expression which is not used in reference to the Passover or any other festival which Moses had instituted. It is unnecessary to dwell on the fact that its position in the midst of the moral law distinctly points to its perpetual and universal obligation, while the circumstance that it had a peculiar relation to the Israelites did not alter its relation to other nations, or take it out of the class of laws to which it originally belonged.

That the Sabbath was binding under the Mosaic law, all are agreed, but some affirm that it is conclusively proved by Col. ii. 16 that the obligation ceased when the Jewish economy was abolished. ' The truth, however,' saith Bishop Horsley, ' is, that in the apostolical age, the first day of the week, though it was observed with great reverence, was not called the Sabbath-day, but the Lord's day; that the separation of the Christian church from the Jewish communion might be marked by the name as well as by the day of their weekly festival ; and the name of the sabbath-days was appropriated to the Saturdays and certain days in the Jewish church which were likewise called Sabbaths in the law, because they were observed with no less sanctity. The sabbath-days, therefore, of which St. Paul in this passage speaks, were not the Sundays of the Christians, but the Saturday and other sabbaths of the Jewish calendar. The Judaizing heretics, with whom St. Paul was all his life engaged, were strenuous advocates for the observance of these Jewish festivals in the Christian church ; and his (St. Paul's) admonition to the Colossians is, that they should not be disturbed by the censures of those who reproached them for neglecting to observe these sabbaths with Jewish ceremonies.'

The transfer of the day on which the Sabbath is observed from the seventh to the first day of the week, is justified on the ground that the change was made under the authority of the Apostles. Some divines of great authority are of opinion that the day itself was *not* an essential part of the original enactment, which ordains not necessarily every seventh day, but one day in seven, as holy time. In the primitive ages of man, the creation of the world was the benefaction by which God was principally known, and for which he was chiefly to be worshipped. The Jews, in their religious assemblies, had to commemorate other blessings—the political creation of their nation out of Abraham's family, and their deliverance from Egyptian bondage. Christians have to commemorate, besides the common benefit of the creation, the transcendant blessing of our redemption,—our new creation to the hope of everlasting life, of which our Lord's resurrec-

tion on the first day of the week was a sure pledge and evidence. Thus in the progress of ages, the Sabbath acquired new ends, by new manifestations of the divine mercy; and these new ends justify corresponding alterations of the original institution. Horsley, and those who agree with him, allege, that upon our Lord's resurrection, the Sabbath was transferred in memory of that event, the great foundation of the Christian's hope, from the last to the first day of the week. ' The alteration seems to have been made by the authority of the Apostles, and to have taken place the very day in which our Lord arose ; for on that day the Apostles were assembled; and on that day sevennight they were assembled again. The celebration of these two first Sundays was honoured by our Lord's presence. It was, perhaps, to set a mark of distinction upon this day in particular, that the intervening week passed off, as it would seem, without any repetition of his first visit to the eleven Apostles. From that time, the Sunday was the constant Sabbath of the primitive church. The Christian, therefore, who devoutly sanctifies one day in seven, although it be on the first day of the week, not the last, as was originally ordained, may rest assured, that he fully satisfies the spirit of the ordinance' (Horsley, i. 334, 335; compare Holden's *Christian Sabbath*, pp. 286, 287).

In justification of the change, it has also been well remarked, that the same portion of time which constituted the seventh day from the creation could not be simultaneously observed in all parts of the earth, and that it is not therefore probable that the original institution expressed more than one day in seven—a seventh day of rest after six days of toil, from whatever point the enumeration might set out or the weekly cycle begin. If more had been intended, it would have been necessary to establish a rule for the reckoning of days themselves, which has been different in different nations; some reckoning from evening to evening, as the Jews do now ; others from midnight to midnight, &c. Even if this point were determined, the difference of time produced by difference of latitude and longitude would again throw the whole into disorder; and it is not probable that a law intended to be universal would be fettered with that circumstantial exactness which would render difficult and sometimes doubtful astronomical calculations necessary in order to its being obeyed according to the intentions of the lawgiver.

SABBATH-DAY'S JOURNEY (Acts i. 12), the distance which the Jews were permitted to journey from and return to their places of residence upon the Sabbath-day (Exod. xvi. 29). There is some diversity of sentiment with respect to the precise distance indicated. But taking all circumstances into account, it seems likely that the ordinary Sabbath-day's journey was a somewhat loosely determined distance, seldom more than the whole and seldom less than three-quarters of a geographical mile.

SABBATIC YEAR. [Jubilee.]

SABÆANS. [Sheba.]

SACKCLOTH. The sackcloth mentioned in Scripture was, as it is still in the East, a coarse black cloth, commonly made of hair (Rev. vi. 12), and was used for straining liquids, for sacks, and for mourning garments. In the latter case it was worn instead of the ordinary raiment, or bound upon the loins, or spread under the mourner on the ground (Gen. xxxvii. 34; 1 Kings xxiii. 2; Isa. lviii. 5; Joel i. 8; Jon. iii. 5) [MOURNING]. Such garments were also worn by prophets, and by ascetics generally (Isa. xx. 2; Zech. iii. 4; comp. 2 Kings i. 8; Matt. v. 4).

SACRIFICES. The sacrifices and other offerings required by the Hebrew ritual have been enumerated under OFFERING; and in this place it is only requisite to offer a few remarks upon the great and much controverted questions—Whether sacrifice was in its origin a human invention, or a divine institution; and whether any of the sacrifices before the law, or under the law, were sacrifices or expiation.

From the universality of sacrifice, it is obvious that the rite arose either from a common source, or from a common sentiment among nations widely dispersed, and very differently constituted. Remembering that Noah, the common ancestor of the post-diluvian nations, offered sacrifice, we are enabled to trace back the custom through all nations to him; and he doubtless derived it through the antediluvian fathers, from the sacrifices which the first men celebrated, of which we have an example in that of Abel. The question concerning the divine or human origin of sacrifices, therefore, centres upon the conclusions which we may be able to draw from the circumstances and preliminaries of that transaction. Abel brought for sacrifice one of the lambs of his flock, for he was a shepherd; and with his offering God was well pleased: Cain brought of the fruits of the ground, for he was a husbandman; and with his offering God was not well pleased. We are told by the Apostle (Heb. xi. 4) that it was 'by faith that Abel offered a more acceptable sacrifice than Cain,' which presupposes a divine revelation: otherwise we cannot see how faith could have been exercised, or to what object it could be directed.

That this was not the first sacrifice is held by many to be proved by the fact, that 'unto Adam and his wife the Lord made coats of skin, and clothed them' (Gen. iii. 21); for, it is urged, that as animal food does not appear to have been used before the deluge, it is not easy to understand whence these skins came, probably before any animal had died naturally, unless from beasts offered in sacrifice. And if the first sacrifices had been offered by Adam, the arguments for the divine institution of the rite are of the greater force, seeing that it was less likely to occur spontaneously to Adam than to Abel, who was a keeper of sheep. Further, if the command was given to Adam, and his sons had been trained in observance of the rite, we can the better understand the merit of Abel, and the demerit of Cain, without further explanation. Apart from any considerations arising out of the skin-vestures of Adam and his wife, it would seem that if sacrifice was a divine institution, and, especially, if the rite bore a piacular significance, it would have been at once prescribed to Adam, after sin had entered the world, and death by sin, and not have been postponed till his sons had reached manhood.

Among the considerations urged in support of the opinion, that sacrifice must have originated in a divine command, it has been suggested as exceedingly doubtful, whether, independently of such a command, and as distinguished from vegetable oblations, animal sacrifice, which involves the practice of slaughtering and burning an innocent victim, could ever, under any aspect, have been adopted as a rite likely to gain the favour of God. Our own course of scriptural education prevents us, perhaps, from being competent judges on this point: but we have means of judging how so singular a rite must strike the minds of thinking men, not in the same degree prepossessed by early associations. The ancient Greek masters of thought not unfrequently expressed their astonishment how, and upon what rational principles, so strange an institution as that of animal sacrifice could ever have originated; for as to the notion of its being *pleasing* to the Deity, such a thing struck them as a manifest impossibility.

A strong moral argument in favour of the divine institution of sacrifice, somewhat feebly put by Hallet (*Comment on Heb.* xi. 4, cited by Magee, *On the Atonement*), has been reproduced with increased force by Faber (*Prim. Sacrifice*, p. 183). It amounts to this:—

Sacrifice, when uncommanded by God, is a mere act of gratuitous superstition. Whence, on the principle of St Paul's reprobation of what he denominates will-worship, it is neither acceptable nor pleasing to God.

But sacrifice, during the patriarchal ages, was accepted by God, and was plainly honoured with his approbation.

Therefore sacrifice, during the patriarchal age, could not have been an act of superstition uncommanded by God.

If, then, such was the character of primitive sacrifice: that is to say, if primitive sacrifice was *not* a mere act of gratuitous superstition uncommanded by God,—it must, in that case, indubitably have been a divine, and not a human institution.

If it be held that any of the ancient sacrifices were expiatory or piacular, the argument for their divine origin is strengthened; as it is hard to conceive the combination of ideas under which the notion of expiatory sacrifice could be worked out by the human mind. The doctrine of an atonement by animal sacrifice cannot be deduced from the light of nature, or from the principles of reason. If, therefore, the idea existed, it must either have arisen in the fertile soil of a guessing superstition, or have been divinely appointed. Now we know that God cannot approve of unwarranted and presumptuous superstition: if therefore he can be shown to have received with approbation a species of sacrifice undiscoverable by the light of nature, or from the principles of reason, it follows that it must have been of his own institution.

That piacular sacrifices existed under the law of Moses can scarcely admit of denial. But the question, of the existence of expiatory sacrifice before the law, is more difficult, and is denied by many, who believe that it was revealed under the law. The arguments already stated in favour of the divine institution of primitive sacrifice, go equally to support the existence of piacular sacrifice; the idea of which seems more urgently to have required a divine intimation. Besides, expiatory sacrifice is found to have existed among all nations, in conjunction with eucharistic and impetratory sacrifices; and it lies at the root of the principle on which human sacrifices were offered among the ancient nations. This being the case, it is difficult to believe but that the idea was derived, along with animal sacrifice itself, from the practice of Noah, and preserved among his various descendants. This argument, if valid, would show the primitive origin of piacular sacrifice. Now there can be no doubt that the idea of sacrifice which Noah transmitted to the postdiluvian world, was the same that he had derived from his pious ancestors, and the same that was evinced by the sacrifice of Abel, to which we are, by the course of the argument, again brought back. Now if that sacrifice was expiatory, we have reason to conclude that it was divinely commanded : and the supposition that it was both expiatory and divinely commanded, makes the whole history far more clear and consistent than any other which has been or can be offered. It amounts then to this—that Cain, by bringing an eucharistic offering, when his brother brought one which was expiatory, denied virtually that his sins deserved death, or that he needed the blood of atonement.

These are the principal considerations which seem suitable to this place, on a subject to the complete investigation of which many large volumes have been devoted.

SACRIFICE, HUMAN. The offering of human life, as the most precious thing on earth, came in process of time to be practised in most countries of the world. All histories and traditions darken our idea of the earlier ages with human sacrifices. But the period when such prevailed was not the earliest in time, though probably the earliest in civilization. The practice was both a result and a token of barbarism more or less gross. In this, too, the dearest object was primitively selected. Human life is the most precious thing on earth, and of this most precious possession the most precious portion is the life of one's child. Children therefore were offered in fire to the false divinities, and in no part of the world with less regard to the claims of natural affection than in the land where, at a later period, the only true God had his peculiar worship and highest honours.

It is under these circumstances a striking fact that the Hebrew religion, even in its most rudimental condition, should be free from the contamination of human sacrifices. The case of Isaac and that of Jephthah's daughter cannot impair the general truth, that the offering of human beings is neither enjoined, allowed, nor practised in the Biblical records. On the contrary, such an offering is strictly prohibited by Moses, as adverse to the will of God, and an abomination of the heathen. 'Thou shalt not let any of thy seed pass through the fire to Moloch : defile not yourselves with any of these things' (Lev. xviii. 21 ; see also ch. xx. 2 ; Deut. xii. 31 ; Ps. cvi. 37 ; Isa. lxvi. 3 ; Jer. xxiii. 37). We do not hesitate to urge this fact as not least considerable among many proofs not only of the superior character, but of the divine origin of the Hebrew worship.

SAD'DUCEES: one of the three sects of Jewish philosophers, of which the Pharisees and the Essenes were the others, who had reached their highest state of prosperity about the commencement of the Christian era.

The peculiar doctrines of the Sadducees natu-

rally sprung out of Pharisaic errors ; but the time when this sect came into existence history does not define. There can be no doubt, however, that they were posterior to the Pharisees. And although so soon as the Pharisaic elements began to become excessive, there existed in Judaism itself a sufficient source for Sadduceeism, yet, as a fact, we have no doubt that Grecian philosophy lent its aid to the development of Sadduceeism. Whence we are referred for the rise of the latter to the period when the conquests and the kingdoms which ensued from the expedition of Alexander had diffused a very large portion of Grecian civilization over the soil of the East, and especially over Western Asia.

As may be inferred from what has been advanced, the Sadducees stood in direct opposition to the Pharisees. So they are described by Josephus, and so they appear in the New Testament. Hostile, however, as these two sects were, they united for the common purpose of opposing our Lord (Matt. iii. 7 ; xvi. 1, 6, 11, sq. ; xxii. 23, 34 ; Acts iv. 1 ; v. 17). In opposing the Pharisees the Sadducees were led to impeach the principal doctrines, and so to deny all the 'traditions of the elders,' holding that the law alone was the written source of religious truth. By more than one consideration, however, it might be shown that they are in error who so understand the fact now stated, as if the Sadducees received no other parts of the Jewish canon than the Pentateuch ; for in truth they appear to have held the common opinion regarding the sacred books. The Sadducees taught that the soul of man perished together with his body, and that of course there was neither reward nor punishment after death (Joseph. *De Bell. Jud.* ii. 8. 14 ; comp. Matt. xxii. 23). Indeed they appear to have disowned the moral philosophy which obtrudes the idea of recompense.

They held that the Scriptures did not contain the doctrine of a future life. They were thus naturally led also to deny the existence of angels and spirits (Acts xxiii. 8). They taught the absolute freedom of the human mind, and according to Josephus, while 'the Pharisees ascribe all to fate and to God, the Sadducees take away fate entirely, and suppose that God is not concerned in our doing or not doing evil ; and they say that to act what is good or what is evil is in man's own choice ; and that all things depend on our own selves.' An inference injurious to them has been deduced from this position, as if they denied divine providence altogether ; but their reception of the canonical books, and their known observance of the usages for divine worship therein prescribed, are incompatible with such a denial.

As might be expected from the nature of their system, their doctrines held sway over but comparatively few persons, and those mostly men distinguished by wealth or station. What Josephus says of the repulsiveness of their manners is in keeping with their general principles. A sceptical materialism is generally accompanied by an undue share of self-confidence and self-esteem, which are among the least sociable of human qualities.

The Sadducees, equally with the Pharisees, were not only a religious but a political party Indeed as long as the Mosaic polity retained an influence, social policy could not be sundered from religion; for religion was everything. Accordingly the Sadducees formed a part of the Jewish parliament, the Sanhedrim (Acts xxiii. 6), and sometimes enjoyed the dignity of supreme power in the high-priesthood. Their possession of power, however, seems to have been owing mainly to their individual personal influence, as men of superior minds or eminent position, since the general current of favour ran adversely to them, and their enemies, the Pharisees, spared no means to keep them and their opinions in the background.

SAFFRON occurs only once in the Old Testament, viz in Cant. iv. 14, where it is mentioned along with several fragrant and stimulant substances, such as spikenard, calamus, and cinnamon, trees of frankincense, myrrh, and aloes; we may, therefore, suppose that it was some substance possessed of similar properties. Saffron has from the earliest times been cultivated in Asiatic countries, as it still is in Persia and Cashmere. Dioscorides describes the different kinds of it, and Pliny states that the benches of the public theatres were strewed with saffron: indeed 'the ancients frequently made use of this flower in perfumes. Not only saloons, theatres, and places which were to be filled with a pleasant fragrance were strewed with this substance, but all sorts of vinous tinctures retaining the scent were made of it, and this costly perfume was poured into small fountains, which diffused the odour that was so highly esteemed. Even fruit and comfitures placed before guests and the ornaments of the rooms were spread over with it. It was used for the same purpose as the modern pot-pourri.' In the present day a very high price is given in India for saffron imported from Cashmere; native dishes are often coloured and flavoured with it, and it is in high esteem as a stimulant medicine.

The name *saffron*, as usually applied, does not denote the whole plant, nor even the whole flower of *crocus sativus*, but only the stigmas, with part of the style, which, being plucked out, are carefully dried. These, when prepared, are dry, narrow, thread-like, and twisted together, of an orange-yellow colour, having a peculiar aromatic and penetrating odour, with a bitterish and somewhat aromatic taste, tinging the mouth and saliva of a yellow colour. Sometimes the stigmas are prepared by being submitted to pressure, and thus made into what is called *cake* saffron, a form in which it is still imported from Persia into India. Hay saffron is obtained in this country chiefly from France and Spain, though it is also sometimes prepared from the native crocus cultivated for this purpose. Saffron was formerly highly esteemed as a stimulant medicine, and still enjoys high repute in Eastern countries, both as a medicine and as a condiment.

SA'LAH (*a shoot*), a son or grandson of Arphaxad (Gen. x. 24; xi. 13; Luke iii. 35).

SAL'AMIS, one of the chief cities of Cyprus, on the south-east coast of the island (Acts xiii. 5). It was afterwards called Constantia, and in still later times Famagusta [CYPRUS].

SALA'THIEL. [SHEALTIEL.]

SA'LEM (*peace*), the original name of Jerusalem (Gen. xiv. 18; Heb. vii. 1, 2), and which continued to be used poetically in later times (Ps. lxxvi. 2) [JERUSALEM].

SA'LIM, a place near Ænon, where John baptized (John iii. 23). Nothing is known of this site.

SAL'MON (*clothed*), the father of Boaz (Ruth iv. 21; Matt. i. 4, 5; Luke iii. 32).

SALMO'NE, a promontory forming the eastern extremity of the island of Crete (Acts xxvii. 7).

SALO'ME, a woman of Galilee, who accompanied Jesus in some of his journeys, and ministered unto him; and was one of those who witnessed his crucifixion and resurrection (Mark xv. 40; xvi. 1). It is gathered by comparing these texts with Matt. xxvii. 56, that she was the wife of Zebedee, and mother of the apostles James and John.

SALOME was also the name (though not given in Scripture) of that daughter of Herodias, whose dancing before her uncle and father-in-law, Herod Antipas, was instrumental in procuring the decapitation of John the Baptist [HERODIAN FAMILY; JOHN THE BAPTIST].

SALT was procured by the Hebrews from two sources: first, from rock-salt, obtained from hills of salt which lie about the southern extremity of the Dead Sea; and secondly, from the waters of that sea, which, overflowing the banks yearly, and being exhaled by the sun and the heat, left behind a deposit of salt both abundant and good.

From Job vi. 6 it is clear that salt was used as a condiment with food. Salt was also mixed with fodder for cattle (Isa. xxx. 24). As offerings, viewed on their earthly side, were a presentation to God of what man found good and pleasant for food, so all meat-offerings were required to be seasoned with salt (Lev. ii. 13). Salt, therefore, became of great importance to Hebrew worshippers; it was sold accordingly in the temple market, and a large quantity was kept in the Temple itself, in a chamber appropriated to the purpose. The incense, 'perfume,' was also to have salt as an ingredient (Exod. xxx. 35; marginal reading 'salted'), where it appears to have been symbolical, as well of the divine goodness as of man's gratitude, on the principle that of every bounty vouchsafed of God, it became man to make an acknowledgment in kind.

As salt thus entered into man's food, so, to eat salt with any one, was to partake of his fare, to share his hospitality; and hence, by implication, to enjoy his favour, or to be in his confidence. Hence, also, salt became an emblem of fidelity and of intimate friendship. At the present hour the Arabs regard as their friend him who has eaten salt with them, that is, has partaken of their hospitality. The domestic sanctity which thus attached itself to salt was much enhanced in influence by its religious applications, so that it became symbolical of the most sacred and binding of obligations. Accordingly 'a covenant of salt' was accounted a very solemn bond (Num. xviii. 19; 2 Chron. xiii. 5; Lev. ii. 13): a signification to which force would be given by the preservative quality of salt.

But salt, if used too abundantly, is destructive of vegetation and causes a desert. Hence arose another class of figurative applications. Destroyed cities were sown with salt to intimate that they were devoted to perpetual desolation (Judg. ix. 45); salt became a symbol of barrenness (Deut. xxix. 23; Zeph. ii. 9); and 'a salt land' (Jer. xvii. 6) signifies a sterile and unproductive district (Job xxxix. 6).

We have reserved to the end reference to a singular usage among the Israelites, namely, washing new-born infants in salt water; which was regarded as so essential that those could have hardly any other fate who were deprived of the rite (Ezek. xvi. 4). The practice obviously arose from a regard to the preserving, the domestic, the moral, and the religious uses to which salt was applied, and of which it became the emblem.

SALUTATION. The forms of salutation that prevailed among the Hebrews, so far as can be collected from Scripture, are the following:—

1. '*Blessed be thou of the Lord,*' or equivalent phrases.

2. '*The Lord be with thee.*'

3. '*Peace be unto thee,*' or '*upon thee,*' or '*with thee.*' In countries often ravaged, and among people often ruined by war, 'peace' implied every blessing of life; and this phrase had therefore the force of 'Prosperous be thou.' This was the commonest of all salutations (Judg. xix. 20; Ruth ii. 4; 1 Sam. xxv. 6; 2 Sam. xx. 9; Ps. cxxix. 8).

4. '*Live, my lord,*' was a common salutation among the Phœnicians, and was also in use among the Hebrews, but was by them only addressed to their kings in the extended form of 'Let the king live for ever!' (1 Kings i. 31); which was also employed in the Babylonian and Persian courts (Dan. ii. 4; iii. 9; v. 10; vi. 7, 22; Neh. ii. 3).

5. '*Joy to thee! joy to you!*' rendered by *Hail!* an equivalent of the Latin *Ave! Salve!* (Matt. xxvii. 29; xxviii. 9; Mark xv. 18; Luke i. 28; John xix. 3).

The gestures and inflections used in salutation varied with the dignity and station of the person saluted; as is the case with the Orientals at this day. It is usual for the person who gives or returns the salutation, to place at the same time his right hand upon his breast, or to touch his lips, and then his forehead or turban, with the same hand. In some cases the body is gently inclined,

superior, does not always give the salam, but shows his respect to high rank by bending down his hand to the ground, and then putting it to his lips and forehead. It is a common custom for a man to kiss the hand of his superior instead of his own (generally on the back only, but sometimes on both back and front), and then to put it to his forehead in order to pay more particular respect. Servants thus evince their respect towards their masters. The son also thus kisses the hand of his father, and the wife that of her husband. Very often, however, the superior does

293.

not allow this, but only touches the hand extended to take his; whereupon the other puts the hand that has been touched to his own lips and forehead. The custom of kissing the beard is still preserved, and follows the first and preliminary gesture; it usually takes place on meeting after an absence of some duration, and not as an every-day compliment. In this case, the person who gives the kiss lays the right hand under the beard, and raises it slightly to his lips, or rather supports it while it receives his kiss. This custom strikingly illustrates 2 Sam. xx. 9. In Arabia Petræa, and some other parts, it is more usual for persons to lay the right sides of their cheeks together.

292.

while the right hand is laid upon the left breast. A person of the lower orders, in addressing a

294.

Among the Persians, persons in saluting under the same circumstances, often kiss each other on the lips; but if one of the individuals is of high rank, the kiss is given on the cheek instead of the

lips. This seems to illustrate 2 Sam. **xx. 9**;
Gen. **xxix.** 11, 13; **xxxiii.** 4; **xlviii.** 10–12;
Exod. **iv.** 27; **xviii.** 7.

SAMA'RIA (*watch-height*), a city, situated
near the middle of Palestine, built by Omri, king
of Israel, on a mountain or hill of the same name,
about **B.C.** 925. It was the metropolis of the
kingdom of Israel, or of the ten tribes. The hill
was purchased from the owner, Shemer, from
whom the city took its name (1 Kings xvi. 23,
24). Samaria continued to be the capital of
Israel for two centuries, till the carrying away of
the ten tribes by Shalmaneser, about **B.C.** 720
(2 Kings xvii. 3, 5). During all this time it was
the seat of idolatry, and is often as such denounced by the prophets, sometimes in connection with Jerusalem. It was the seat of a temple
of Baal, built by Ahab, and destroyed by Jehu
(1 Kings xvi. 32, 33; 2 Kings x. 18–28). It was
the scene of many of the acts of the prophets
Elijah and Elisha, connected with the various
famines of the land, the unexpected plenty of
Samaria, and the several deliverances of the city
from the Syrians. After the exile of the ten
tribes, Samaria appears to have continued, for a
time at least, the chief city of the foreigners
brought to occupy their place; although Shechem
soon became the capital of the Samaritans as a
religious sect. John Hyrcanus took the city
after a year's siege, and razed it to the ground.
Yet it must soon have revived, as it is not long
after mentioned as an inhabited place in the possession of the Jews. Pompey restored it to its
former possessors; and it was afterwards rebuilt
by Gabinius. Augustus bestowed Samaria on
Herod; who eventually rebuilt the city with great
magnificence, and gave it the name of Sebaste.
Here Herod planted a colony of 6000 persons,
composed partly of veteran soldiers, and partly of
people from the environs; enlarged the circumference of the city; and surrounded it with a
strong wall twenty stades in circuit In the
midst of the city—that is to say, upon the summit
of the hill—he left a sacred place of a stade and
a half, splendidly decorated, and here he erected
a temple to Augustus, celebrated for its magnitude and beauty. The whole city was greatly
ornamented, and became a strong fortress. Such
was the Samaria of the time of the New Testament, where the Gospel was preached by Philip,
and a church was gathered by the apostles (Acts
viii. 5, 9, sq.). At what time the city of Herod
became desolate, no existing accounts state; but
all the notices of the fourth century and later
lead to the inference that its destruction had
already taken place. A few scanty notices of
Samaria are found scattered through the works
of ancient travellers, but it was not till the present
century that it was fully explored and described.

The hill of Samaria is an oblong mountain of
considerable elevation, and very regular in form,
situated in the midst of a broad deep valley. Beyond this valley, which completely isolates the
hill, the mountains rise again on every side,
forming a complete wall around the city. They
are terraced to the tops, sown in grain, and
planted with olives and figs, in the midst of
which a number of handsome villages appear to
great advantage, their white stone cottages contrasting strikingly with the verdure of the trees.
' The hill of Samaria' itself is cultivated from

its base, the terraced sides and summits being
covered with corn and with olive-trees. The
most conspicuous ruin of the place, is the church
dedicated to John the Baptist, erected on the spot
which an old tradition fixed as the place of his
burial, if not of his martyrdom. It is said to

295. [Samaria: Church of St. John.]

have been built by the Empress Helena; but the
architecture limits its antiquity to the period of
the crusades, although a portion of the eastern
end seems to have been of earlier date. On the
summit of the hill is an area, once surrounded by
limestone columns, of which fifteen are still
standing, and two prostrate. There is no trace
of the order of their architecture, nor any indications of the nature of the edifice to which they
belong. On the W.S.W. descent of the hill there
is a very remarkable colonnade, of which eighty-
two columns are still standing, and the number of
those fallen and broken must be much greater.
They may without much hesitation be referred to
the time of Herod the Great, and must be regarded as belonging to some one of the splendid
edifices with which he adorned the city.

SAMAR'ITANS. In the books of Kings there
are brief notices of the origin of the people called
Samaritans. The ten tribes which revolted from
Rehoboam, son of Solomon, chose Jeroboam for
their king. After his elevation to the throne he
set up golden calves at Dan and Bethel, lest repeated visits of his subjects to Jerusalem, for the
purpose of worshipping the true God, should
withdraw their allegiance from himself. After
wards Samaria, built by Omri, became the metropolis of Israel, and thus the separation between
Judah and Israel was rendered complete. The
people took the name *Samaritans* from the capital
city. In the ninth year of Hosea, Samaria was
taken by the Assyrians under Shalmaneser, who
carried away the inhabitants into captivity, and
introduced colonies into their place from Babylon,
Cuthah, Ava, Hamath, and Sepharvaim. These
new inhabitants carried along with them their
own idolatrous worship; and on being infested
with lions, sent to Esarhaddon, king of Assyria.

2 z 2

A priest of the tribe of Levi was accordingly dispatched to them, who came and dwelt in Bethel, teaching the people how they should fear the Lord. Thus it appears that the people were a mixed race. The greater part of the Israelites had been carried away captive by the Assyrians, including the rich, the strong, and such as were able to bear arms. But the poor and the feeble had been left. With them, therefore, the heathen colonists became incorporated. As the people were a *mixed* race, their religion also assumed a *mixed* character. In it the worship of idols was associated with that of the true God. But apostacy from Jehovah was not universal. On the return of the Jews from the Babylonish captivity, the Samaritans wished to join them in rebuilding the temple (Ezra iv. 2). But the Jews declined the proffered assistance; and from this time the Samaritans threw every obstacle in their way. Hence arose that inveterate enmity between the two nations which afterwards increased to such a height as to become proverbial. In the reign of Darius Nothus, Manasses, son of the Jewish high-priest, married the daughter of Sanballat the Samaritan governor; and to avoid the necessity of repudiating her, as the law of Moses required, went over to the Samaritans, and became high-priest in the temple which his father-in-law built for him on Mount Gerizim. From this time Samaria became a refuge for all malcontent Jews; and the very name of each people became odious to the other. About the year B.C. 109, John Hyrcanus, high-priest of the Jews, destroyed the city and temple of the Samaritans; but B.C. 25, Herod rebuilt them at great expense. In their new temple, however, the Samaritans could not be induced to offer sacrifices, but still continued to worship on Gerizim. At the present day they have dwindled down to a few families. Shechem, now called Nabulus, is their place of abode. They still possess a copy of the Mosaic law, which, it is well known, forms the only portion of Scripture the Samaritans have ever received or acknowledged. The opinion that copies of the Pentateuch must have been in the hands of *Israel* from the time of Rehoboam, as well as among *Judah*, has been held by many distinguished critics, and appears to be correct. The prophets, who frequently inveigh against the Israelites for their idolatry and their crimes, never accuse them of being destitute of the law, or ignorant of its contents. It is wholly improbable, too, that the people, when carried captive into Assyria, took with them *all* the copies of the law. Thus we are brought to the conclusion, that the Samaritan, as well as the Jewish copy, originally flowed from the autograph of Moses. The two constitute, in fact, *different recensions of the same work*, and coalesce in point of antiquity.

SA'MOS, an island in the Ægean Sea, near the coast of Lydia, in Asia Minor, and separated only by a narrow strait from the promontory which terminates in Cape Trogyllium. The apostle Paul touched at the island in his voyage from Greece to Syria (Acts xx. 15). Samos contained, some years ago, about 60,000 people, inhabiting eighteen large villages, and about twenty small ones.

SAMOTHRA'CE, an island in the north-east part of the Ægean Sea, above the Hellespont, with a lofty mountain, and a city of the same name. The island was celebrated for the mysteries of Ceres and Proserpine, and was a sacred asylum. Paul touched at this island on his first voyage to Europe (Acts xvi. 11). The island is now called Samandrachi. It is but thinly peopled, and contains only a single village.

SAM'SON. This celebrated champion and judge of Israel, was the son of Manoah, of the tribe of Dan, and born A.M. 2848, of a mother whose name is nowhere given in the Scriptures. His birth was announced by a heavenly messenger, who declared to his mother that the child with which she was pregnant was to be a son, who should be a Nazarite from his birth, upon whose head no razor was to come, and who was to prove a signal deliverer to his people. She was directed, accordingly, to conform her own regimen to the tenor of the Nazarite law, and strictly abstain from wine and all intoxicating liquor, and from every species of impure food [NAZARITE]. According to the 'prophecy going before upon him,' Samson was born in the following year, and his destination to great achievements began to evince itself at a very early age by the illapses of superhuman strength which came from time to time upon him. Those specimens of extraordinary prowess, of which the slaying of the lion at Timnath without weapons was one, were doubtless the result of that special influence of the Most High which is referred to in Judg. xiii. 25.

As the position of the tribe of Dan, bordering upon the territory of the Philistines, exposed them especially to the predatory incursions of this people, it was plainly the design of heaven to raise up a deliverer in that region where he was most needed. The Philistines, therefore, became very naturally the objects of that retributive course of proceedings in which Samson was to be the principal actor, and upon which he could only enter by seeking some occasion of exciting hostilities that would bring the two peoples into direct collision. Such an occasion was afforded by his meeting with one of the daughters of the Philistines at Timnath, whom he besought his parents to procure for him in marriage.

At his wedding-feast, the attendance of a large company of friends of the bridegroom, convened ostensibly for the purpose of honouring his nuptials, but in reality to keep an insidious watch upon his movements, furnished the occasion of a common Oriental device for enlivening entertainments of this nature. He propounded a riddle, the solution of which referred to his obtaining a quantity of honey from the carcase of a slain lion, and the clandestine manner in which his guests got possession of the clue to the enigma cost thirty Philistines their lives. The next instance of his vindictive policy was prompted by the ill-treatment which he had received at the hands of his father-in-law, who, upon a frivolous pretext, had given away his daughter in marriage to another man, and was executed by securing a multitude of foxes, or rather *jackals*, and, by tying firebrands to their tails, setting fire to the cornfields of his enemies. The indignation of the Philistines, on discovering the author of the outrage, vented itself upon the family of his father-in-law, who had been the remote occasion of it, in the burning of their house, in which both father and daughter perished. This was a fresh provocation, for which Samson threatened to be revenged; and thereupon falling upon them without ceremony he smote them, as it is said, 'hip and thigh with a great slaughter.'

Having subsequently taken up his residence in the rock Etam, he was thence dislodged by consenting to a pusillanimous arrangement on the part of his own countrymen, by which he agreed to surrender himself in bonds provided *they* would not themselves fall upon him and kill him. Being brought in this apparently helpless condition to a place called from the event Lehi, *a jaw*, his preternatural potency suddenly put itself forth, and he snapping the cords asunder, and snatching up the jaw-bone of an ass, he dealt so effectually about him, that a thousand men were slain on the spot. That this was altogether the work, not of man, but of God, was soon demonstrated. Wearied with his exertions, the illustrious Danite became faint from thirst, and as there was no water in the place, he prayed that a fountain might be opened. His prayer was heard; God caused a stream to gush from a hollow rock hard by, and Samson in gratitude gave it the name of *En-hakkore*, a word that signifies 'the well of him that prayed,' and which continued to be the designation of the fountain ever after.

The Philistines were from this time held in such contempt by their victor, that he went openly into the city of Gaza, where he seems to have suffered himself weakly to be drawn into the company of a woman of loose character, the yielding to whose enticements exposed him to the most imminent peril. His presence being soon noised abroad, an attempt was made during the night forcibly to detain him, by closing the gates of the city and making them fast; but Samson, apprised of it, rose at midnight, and breaking away bolts, bars, and hinges, departed, carrying the gates upon his shoulders, to the top of a neighbouring hill that *looks towards Hebron* (not 'before Hebron,' as the words are rendered in the Authorized Version). After this his enemies strove to entrap him by guile rather than by violence; and they were too successful in the end. Falling in love with a woman of Sorek, named Delilah, he became so infatuated by his passion, that nothing but his bodily strength could equal his mental weakness. The princes of the Philistines, aware of Samson's infirmity, determined by means of it to get possession, if possible, of his person. For this purpose they propose a tempting bribe to Delilah, and she enters at once into the treacherous compact. She employs all her art and blandishments to worm from him the secret of his prodigious strength. Having for some time amused her with fictions, he at last, in a moment of weakness, disclosed to her the fact that it lay in his hair, which if it were shaved would leave him a mere common man. Not that his strength really lay in his hair, for this in fact had no natural influence upon it one way or the other. His strength arose from his *relation* to God as a Nazarite, and the preservation of his hair unshorn was the *mark* or *sign* of his Nazariteship, and a *pledge* on the part of God of the continuance of his miraculous physical powers. If he lost this sign, the badge of his consecration, he broke his vow, and consequently forfeited the thing signified. God abandoned him, and he was thenceforward no more, in this respect, than an ordinary man. His treacherous paramour

seized the first opportunity of putting his declaration to the test. She shaved his head while he lay sleeping in her lap, and at a concerted signal he was instantly arrested by his enemies lying in wait. Having so long presumptuously played with his ruin, Heaven leaves him to himself, as a punishment for his former guilty indulgence. He is made to reap as he had sown, and is consigned to the hands of his relentless foes. His punishment was indeed severe, though he amply revenged it, as well as redeemed in a measure his own honour, by the manner in which he met his death. The Philistines having deprived him of sight, at first immured him in a prison, and made him grind at the mill like a slave, thus reducing him to the lowest state of degradation and shame.

In process of time, while remaining in this confinement, his hair recovered its growth, and with it such a profound repentance seems to have wrought in his heart as virtually re-invested him with the character and the powers he had so culpably lost. Of this fact his enemies were not aware. Still exulting in their possession of the great scourge of their nation, they kept him, like a wild beast, for mockery and insult. On one of these occasions, when an immense multitude, including the princes and nobles of the Philistines, were convened in a large amphitheatre, to celebrate a feast in honour of their god Dagon, who had delivered their adversary into their hands, Samson was ordered to be brought out to be made a laughing-stock to his enemies, a butt for their scoffs, insults, mockeries, and merriment. Secretly determined to use his recovered strength to tremendous effect, he persuaded the boy who guided his steps to conduct him to a spot where he could reach the two pillars upon which the roof of the building chiefly rested. Here, after pausing for a short time, while he prefers a brief prayer to Heaven, he grasps the massy pillars, and bowing with resistless force, the whole building rocks and totters, and the roof, encumbered with the weight of the spectators, rushes down, and the whole assembly, including Samson himself, are crushed to pieces in the ruin.

Thus terminated the career of one of the most remarkable personages of all history, whether sacred or profane. The enrolment of his name by an apostolic pen (Heb. xi. 32) in the list of the ancient worthies, 'who had by faith obtained an excellent repute,' warrants us undoubtedly to entertain a favourable estimate of his character on the whole, while at the same time the fidelity of the inspired narrative has perpetuated the record of infirmities which must for ever mar the lustre of his noble deeds.

SAM'UEL, the last of those extraordinary regents that presided over the Hebrew commonwealth under the title of Judges. The circumstances of his birth are detailed at length in the first chapter of the book of Samuel. His mother vowed that if Jehovah should give her a man-child, she would devote him to the Lord all the days of her life. Her prayer was heard, and when the birth of a son fulfilled her hopes, this child of prayer was named SAMUEL (*heard of God*). In consequence of his mother's vow, the boy was from his early years set apart to the service of Jehovah, under the immediate tutelage of Eli.

The degeneracy of the people at this time was extreme. The tribes seem to have administered their affairs as independent republics, the national confederacy was weak and disunited, and the spirit of public patriotic enterprise had been worn out by constant turmoil and invasion. The theocratic influence was also scarcely felt, its peculiar ministers being withdrawn, and its ordinary manifestations, except in the routine of the Levitical ritual, having ceased; 'the word of the Lord was precious in those days, there was no open vision' (iii. 1). The young devotee, 'the child Samuel,' was selected by Jehovah to renew the deliverance of his oracles. As he lay in his chamber adjoining the sacred edifice, the Lord, by means adapted to his juvenile capacity, made known to him his first and fearful communication—the doom of Eli's apostate house. Other revelations speedily followed this; the frequency of God's messages to the young prophet established his fame; and the exact fulfilment of them secured his reputation. The fearful fate pronounced on the head and family of the pontificate was soon executed. Hophni and Phinehas, Eli's sons, both fell in one day; the Israelites were defeated with a great slaughter, and the ark of God was taken. Their father sat by the wayside to gather the earliest news of the battle, for his 'heart trembled for the ark of God;' and as a fugitive from the scene of conflict reported to him the sad disaster—Israel routed and fleeing in panic, Hophni and Phinehas both slain, and the ark of God taken—this last and overpowering intelligence so shocked him, that he fainted and fell from his seat, and in his fall 'brake his neck and died' (iv. 18). When the feeble administration of Eli, who had judged Israel forty years, was concluded by his death, Samuel was too young to succeed to the regency, and the actions of this earlier portion of his life are left unrecorded. The ark, which had been captured by the Philistines, soon vindicated its majesty, and after being detained among them seven months, was sent back to Israel. It did not, however, reach Shiloh, in consequence of the fearful judgment of Bethshemesh (vi. 19), but rested in Kirjath-jearim for no fewer than twenty years (vii. 2). It is not till the expiration of this period that Samuel appears again in the history. This long season of national humiliation was to some extent improved. 'All the house of Israel lamented after the Lord,' and Samuel, seizing upon the crisis, issued a public manifesto, exposing the sin of idolatry, urging on the people religious amendment, and promising political deliverance on their reformation. The people obeyed, the oracular mandate was effectual, and the principles of the theocracy again triumphed (vii. 4). The tribes were summoned by the prophet to assemble in Mizpeh, and at this assembly of the Hebrew comitia, Samuel seems to have been elected regent (vii. 6).

This mustering of the Hebrews at Mizpeh on the inauguration of Samuel alarmed the Philistines, and their 'lords went up against Israel.' Samuel assumed the functions of the theocratic viceroy, offered a solemn oblation, and implored the immediate protection of Jehovah. He was answered with propitious thunder. A fearful storm burst upon the Philistines they were signally defeated, and did not recruit their strength again during the administration of the prophet-

judge. The grateful victor erected a stone of remembrance, and named it Ebenezer (*the stone of help*). From an incidental allusion (vii. 14) we learn, too, that about this time the Amorites, the Eastern foes of Israel, were also at peace with them. The presidency of Samuel appears to have been eminently successful. From the very brief sketch given us of his public life, we infer that the administration of justice occupied no little share of his time and attention. He went from year to year in circuit to Bethel, Gilgal, and Mizpeh, places not very far distant from each other, but chosen perhaps because they were the old scenes of worship.

The dwelling of the prophet was at Ramah, where religious worship was established after the patriarchal model, and where Samuel, like Abraham, built an altar to the Lord.

In Samuel's old age two of his sons were appointed by him deputy-judges in Beersheba. These young men possessed not their father's integrity of spirit, but 'turned aside after lucre, took bribes, and perverted judgment' (1 Sam. viii. 3). The advanced years of the venerable ruler himself, and his approaching dissolution, the certainty that none of his family could fill his office with advantage to the country, the horror of a period of anarchy which his death might occasion, the necessity of having some one to put an end to tribal jealousies and concentrate the energies of the nation, especially as there appeared to be symptoms of renewed warlike preparations on the part of the Ammonites (xii. 12)—these considerations seem to have led the elders of Israel to adopt the bold step of assembling at Ramah and soliciting Samuel 'to make a king to judge them.' The proposed change from a republican to a regal form of government displeased Samuel for various reasons. Besides its being a departure from the first political institute, and so far an infringement on the rights of the divine head of the theocracy, it was regarded by the regent as a virtual charge against himself, and might appear to him as one of those examples of popular fickleness and ingratitude which the history of every realm exhibits in profusion. Jehovah comforts Samuel in this respect by saying, 'They have not rejected thee, but they have rejected me.' Being warned of God to accede to their request for a king, and yet to remonstrate with the people, and set before the nation the perils and tyranny of a monarchical government (viii. 10), Samuel proceeded to the election of a sovereign. Saul, son of Kish, 'a choice young man and a goodly,' whom he had met unexpectedly, was pointed out to him by Jehovah as the king of Israel. and by the prophet was anointed and saluted as monarch Samuel again convened the nation at Mizpeh, again with honest zeal condemned their project, but caused the sacred lot to be taken. The lot fell on Saul. The prophet now formally introduced him to the people, who shouted in joyous acclamation 'God save the king.'

Not content with oral explanations, this last of the republican chiefs not only told the people the manner of the kingdom, 'but wrote it in a book and laid it up before the Lord.' What is here asserted of Samuel may mean, that he extracted from the Pentateuch the recorded provision of Moses for a future monarchy, and added to it such warnings, and counsels, and safeguards as his inspired sagacity might suggest. Saul's first battle being so successful, and the preparations for it displaying no ordinary energy and promptitude of character, his popularity was suddenly advanced, and his throne secured. Taking advantage of the general sensation in favour of Saul, Samuel cited the people to meet again in Gilgal, to renew the kingdom, to ratify the new constitution, and solemnly instal the sovereign (xi. 14). Here the upright judge made a powerful appeal to the assembly in vindication of his government, and the whole multitude responded in unanimous approval of his honesty and intrepidity (xii. 3, 4). Then he, still jealous of God's prerogative and the civil rights of his people, briefly narrated their history, showed them how they never wanted chieftains to defend them when they served God, and declared that it was distrust of God's raising up a new leader in a dreaded emergency that excited the outcry for a king. In proof of this charge he appealed to Jehovah, who answered in a fearful hurricane of thunder and rain. The terrified tribes confessed their guilt, and besought Samuel to intercede for them in his disinterested patriotism.

It is said (vii. 15) that Samuel judged Israel all the days of his life. The assertion may mean that even after Saul's coronation Samuel's power, though formally abdicated, was yet actually felt and exercised in the direction of state affairs. No enterprise could be undertaken without Samuel's concurrence. His was an authority higher than the king's. We find Saul, having mustered his forces, about to march against the Philistines, yet delaying to do so till Samuel consecrated the undertaking. He came not at the time appointed, as Saul thought, and the impatient monarch proceeded to offer sacrifice—a fearful violation of the national law. The prophet arrived as the religious service was concluded, and rebuking Saul for his presumption, distinctly hinted at the short continuance of his kingdom. Again we find Samuel charging Saul with the extirpation of the Amalekites. The royal warrior proceeded on the expedition, but obeyed not the mandate of Jehovah. His apologies, somewhat craftily framed, for his inconsistencies, availed him not with the prophet, and he was by the indignant seer virtually dethroned. He had forfeited his crown by disobedience to God. Yet Samuel mourned for him. But now the Lord directed him to make provision for the future government of the country (xvi. 1). To prevent strife and confusion it was necessary, in the circumstances, that the second king should be appointed ere the first sovereign's demise. Samuel went to Bethlehem and set apart the youngest of the sons of Jesse, 'and came to see Saul no more till the day of his death.' At length Samuel died (xxv. 1) and all Israel mourned for him, and buried him in his house at Ramah.

SAMUEL, BOOKS OF. The two books of Samuel were anciently reckoned as but one among the Jews, and that they form only one treatise is apparent from their structure.

The contents of these books belong to an interesting period of Jewish history. The preceding book of Judges refers to the affairs of the republic as they were administered after the Conquest, when the nation was a congeries of independent cantons, sometimes partially united for a season under an extraordinary dictator. As, however, the mode of government was changed, and remained monarchical till the overthrow of the kingdom, it was of national importance to note the time, method, and means of the alteration. This change happening under the regency of the wisest and best of their sages, his life became a topic of interest. The first book of Samuel gives an account of his birth and early call to the duties of a seer, under Eli's pontificate; describes the low and degraded condition of the people, oppressed by foreign enemies; proceeds to narrate the election of Samuel as judge; his prosperous regency; the degeneracy of his sons, the clamour for a change in the civil constitution; the installation of Saul; his rash and reckless character; his neglect of, or opposition to, the theocratic elements of the government. Then the historian goes on to relate God's choice of David as king; his endurance of long and harassing persecution from the reigning sovereign; the melancholy defeat and death of Saul on the field of Gilboa; the gradual elevation of the man 'according to God's own heart' to universal dominion; his earnest efforts to obey and follow out the principles of the theocracy; his formal establishment of religious worship at Jerusalem, now the capital of the nation; and his series of victories over all the enemies of Judæa that were wont to molest its frontiers. The annalist records David's aberrations from the path of duty; the unnatural rebellion of his son Absalom, and its suppression; his carrying into effect a census of his dominions, and the Divine punishment which this act incurred; and concludes with a few characteristic sketches of his military staff. The second book of Samuel, while it relates the last words of David, yet stops short of his death. As David was the real founder of the monarchy and arranger of the religious economy; the great hero, legislator, and poet of his country; as his dynasty maintained itself on the throne of Judah till the Babylonian invasion; it is not a matter of wonder that the description of his life and government occupies so large a portion of early Jewish history. The books of Samuel thus consist of three interlaced biographies—those of Samuel, Saul, and David.

The attempt to ascertain the authorship of this early history is attended with difficulty. Ancient opinion is in favour of the usual theory, that the first twenty-four chapters were written by Samuel, and the rest by Nathan and Gad. Various arguments have of late been brought against this opinion, but they are more ingenious than solid. The striking circumstance that these books do not record David's death, though they give his last words—his last inspired effusion—afford, to say the least of it, a strong presumption that they must have been composed before that monarch 'slept with his fathers.'

The design of these books is not very different from that of the other historical treatises of the Old Testament. The books of Kings are a history of the nation as a theocracy; those of Chronicles have special reference to the form and ministry of the religious worship, as bearing upon its re-establishment after the return from Babylon. Samuel is more biographical, yet the theocratic element of the government is not overlooked. It is distinctly brought to view in the early chapters concerning Eli and his house, and the fortunes of the ark; in the passages which describe the change of the constitution; in the blessing which rested on the house of Obed-Edom; in the curse which fell on the Bethshemites, and Uzzah and Saul, for intrusive interference with holy things. The book shows clearly that God was a jealous God; that obedience to him secured felicity; that the nation sinned in seeking another king; that Saul's special iniquity was his impious oblivion of his station as only Jehovah's vicegerent, for he contemned the prophets and slew the priesthood; and that David owed his prosperity to his careful culture of the sacred principle of the Hebrew administration. This early production contained lessons both for the people and for succeeding monarchs, bearing on it the motto, 'Whatsoever things were written aforetime were written for our learning.'

SANBAL'LAT, a native of Horonaim, beyond the Jordan (Neh. ii. 10), and probably also a Moabitish chief, whom (perhaps from old national hatred) we find united in council with the Samaritans, and active in attempting to deter the returned exiles from fortifying Jerusalem (Neh. iv. 1, sq.; vi 1, sq.). Subsequently, during the absence of Nehemiah in Persia, a son of Joiada, the high priest, was married to his daughter (Neh. xiii. 28).

SANDAL, a covering for the feet, usually denoted by the word translated 'shoe' in the Authorized Version. It was usually a sole of hide, leather, or wood, bound on to the foot by thongs; but it may sometimes denote such shoes and buskins as eventually came into use.

Ladies of rank appear to have paid great attention to the beauty of their sandals (Cant. vii. 1); though, if the bride in that book was an Egyptian princess, as some suppose, the exclamation, 'How beautiful are thy feet with sandals, O prince's daughter!' may imply admiration of a luxury properly Egyptian, as the ladies of that country were noted for their sumptuous sandals. But this taste was probably general; for, at the present day, the dress slippers of ladies of rank are among the richest articles of their attire, being elaborately embroidered with flowers and other figures wrought in silk, silver, and gold.

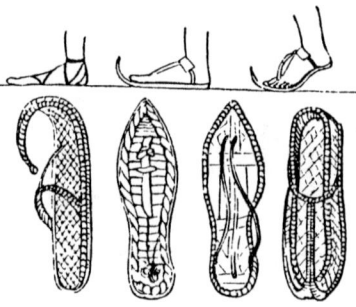

296. [Ancient Egyptian Sandals]

It does not seem probable that the sandals of the Hebrews differed much from those used in Egypt, excepting, perhaps, that from the greater roughness of their country, they were usually of more substantial make and materials. The Egyptian sandals varied slightly in form: those worn by the upper classes, and by women, were usually pointed and turned up at the end, like our skates and many of the Eastern slippers at the present day. They were made of a sort of woven or interlaced work of palm-leaves and papyrus-stalks or other similar materials, and sometimes of leather; and were frequently lined with cloth, on which the figure of a captive was painted; that humiliating position being considered suited to the enemies of their country, whom they hated and despised. It is not likely that the Jews adopted this practice: but the idea which it expressed, of treading their enemies under their feet, was familiar to them (Josh. x. 24). Those of the middle classes who were in the habit of wearing sandals, often preferred walking barefooted.

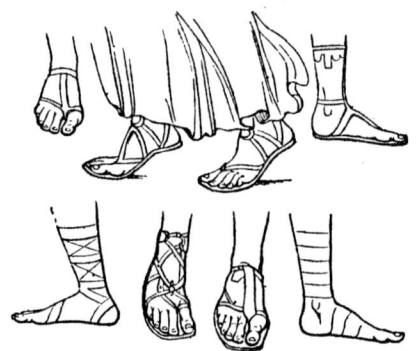

297. [Greek and Roman Sandals.]

In transferring a possession or domain it was customary to deliver a sandal (Ruth iv. 7), as in our middle ages, a glove. Hence the action of throwing down a shoe upon a region or territory, was a symbol of occupancy. So Ps. lx. 10. In Ruth, as above, the delivering of a sandal signified that the next of kin transferred to another a sacred obligation; and he was hence called 'sandal-loosed.'

It was undoubtedly the custom to take off the sandals on holy ground, in the act of worship, and in the presence of a superior. Hence the command to take the sandals from the feet under such circumstances (Exod. iii. 5; Josh. v. 15). This is still the well-known custom of the East—an Oriental taking off his shoe in cases in which a European would remove his hat. The shoes of the modern Orientals are, however, made to slip off easily, which was not the case with sandals, that required to be unbound with some trouble. This operation was usually performed by servants; and hence the act of unloosing the sandals of another became a familiar symbol of servitude (Mark i. 7; Luke iii. 16; John i. 27; Acts xiii 25).

SANHE'DRIM, more properly SANHEDRIN, the supreme judicial council of the Jews, especially for religious affairs. This council consisted of seventy members. To this number the high priest was added, 'provided he was a man endowed with wisdom.' According to Dr. Jost, the members of the council 'consisted of the most eminent priests, and of the scribes of the people, who were chosen for life, but each of whom had to look to his own industry for his support.' In the New Testament they are frequently termed *Priests, Elders,* and *Scribes.* By the first are to be understood, not such as had sustained the office of high-priest, but the chief men among the priests; probably the presidents of the twenty-four classes into which the priesthood was divided. By the second, we are probably to understand the select men of the people—persons whose rank or standing led to their being raised to this distinction. And by the last are designated those, whether of the Levitical family or not, who gave themselves to the pursuit of learning, especially to the interpretation of Scripture, and of the traditions of the fathers.

In the council the office of president belonged to the high-priest, if he was a member of it. Next in rank to him was the vice-president, who bore the title of *Father of the House of Judgment;* whose duty it was to supply the place of the president in case he should be prevented by any accidental cause from discharging his duties himself. The third grade of rank was that of the *sage,* whose business was to give counsel to the assembly. The assembly, when convened, sat in the form of a semicircle, or half-moon, the president occupying the centre. At each extremity stood a scribe, whose duty it was to record the sentence pronounced by the council. The meetings of this council were usually held in the morning. Their place of meeting was a hall, close by the great gate of the temple, and leading from the outer court of the women to the holy place. In cases of urgency the Sanhedrim might be convened in the house of the high-priest (Matt. xxvi. 3).

The functions of the Sanhedrim were, according to the Jewish writers, co-extensive with the civil and religious relations of the people. But in the notices of this body, contained in the New Testament, we find nothing which would lead us to infer that their powers extended beyond matters of a religious kind. Questions of blasphemy, of sabbath-breaking, of heresy, are those alone which we find referred to their judicature (comp. Matt. xxvi. 57-65; John v. 11, 18; Matt. xii. 14, sq.; Acts v. 17, sq., &c.). On those guilty of these crimes they could pronounce sentence of death: but under the Roman government, it was not competent for them to execute this sentence.

At what period in the history of the Jews the Sanhedrim arose, is involved in much uncertainty. The Jews trace this council to the times of Moses, and find the origin of it in the appointment of a body of elders as the assistants of Moses in the discharge of his judicial functions (Num. xi. 16, 17). There is no evidence, however, that this was any other than a temporary arrangement for the benefit of Moses; nor do we, in the historical books of the Old Testament, detect any traces whatever of the existence of this council in the times preceding the Babylonish captivity, nor in those immediately succeeding the return of the Jews to their own land The earliest mention of the existence of this council by Josephus, is in connection with the reign of Hyrcanus II., B.C. 69. It is probable, however, that it existed before this time—that it arose gradually after the cessation of the prophetic office in Judah, in conse-

quence of the felt want of some supreme direction and judicial authority—that the number of its members was fixed so as to correspond with that of the council of elders appointed to assist Moses—and that it first assumed a formal and influential existence in the later years of the Macedo-Grecian dynasty.

SAPPHI'RA, the wife of Ananias, and his accomplice in the sin for which he died (Acts v. 1-10). Unaware of the judgment which had befallen her husband, she entered the place about three hours after, probably to look for him; and being there interrogated by Peter, repeated and persisted in the 'lie unto the Holy Ghost,' which had destroyed her husband; on which the grieved apostle made known to her his doom, and pronounced her own—' Behold, the feet of those who have buried thy husband are at the door, and shall carry thee out.' On hearing these awful words, she fell dead at his feet [ANANIAS].

SAP'PHIRE, a precious stone, mentioned in Exod. xxiv. 10; xxviii. 18; Job xxviii. 16; Ezek. xxviii. 13; Rev. xxi. 19. It is next in hardness and value to the diamond, and is mostly of a blue colour of various shades. It is often found in collections of ancient gems.

SA'RAH (*a princess, a noble lady*), the wife of Abraham, and mother of Isaac. She was at first called Sarai, which Ewald explains to mean *contentious, quarrelsome.* As Sarah never appears but in connection with some circumstance in which her husband was principally concerned, all the facts of her history have already been given in the article ABRAHAM, and her conduct to Hagar is considered in the article which bears her name.

SAR'DIS, the capital of the ancient kingdom of Lydia, situated at the foot of Mount Tmolus, in a fine plain watered by the river Pactolus, is in N. lat. 38° 30'; E. long. 27° 57'. Sardis was a great and ancient city, and from its wealth and importance was the object of much cupidity and of many sieges. When taken by Cyrus, under Crœsus, its last king, who has become proverbial for his riches, Sardis was one of the most splendid and opulent cities of the East. After their victory over Antiochus it passed to the Romans, under whom it rapidly declined in rank and importance. In the time of Tiberius it was destroyed by an earthquake, but was rebuilt by order of the emperor. The inhabitants of Sardis bore an ill repute among the ancients for their voluptuous habits of life. The place that Sardis holds in the Apocalypse, as one of the 'Seven Churches of Asia,' is the source of the peculiar interest with which the Christian reader regards it. From what is said it appears that it had already declined much in real religion, although it still maintained the name and external aspect of a Christian church, 'having a name to live, while it was dead' (Rev. iii. 1).

Successive earthquakes, and the ravages of the Saracens and Turks, have reduced this once flourishing city to a heap of ruins, presenting many remains of its former splendour. The habitations of the living are confined to a few miserable cottages, forming a village called Sart.

SAR'DIUS, one of the precious stones in the breastplate of the high-priest (Exod. xxviii 17; xxxix. 10), and also mentioned in Ezek. xxviii. 13. The sardius is the stone now called the carnelian, from its colour, which resembles that of raw flesh. The Hebrew name is derived from a root which signifies being red. The sardius or carnelian is of the flint family, and is a kind of chalcedony. The more vivid the red in this stone, the higher is the estimation in which it is held. It was anciently, as now, more frequently engraved on than any other stone. The ancients called it sardius, because Sardis in Lydia was the place where they first became acquainted with it; but the sardius of Babylon was considered of greater value. The Hebrews probably obtained the carnelian from Arabia. In Yemen there is found a very fine dark-red carnelian, which is called *el-Akik*. The Arabs wear it on the finger, on the arm above the elbow, and in the belt before the abdomen. It is supposed to stop hemorrhage when laid on a fresh wound.

SARDO'NYX, a precious stone exhibiting a milk-white variety of the onyx or chalcedony, intermixed with shades or stripes of the sardian (or carnelian); hence the compound name of sardonyx. It is mentioned in Rev. xxi. 20.

SAREP'TA (Luke iv. 26), Hebrew *Zarephath*, a Phœnician town between Tyre and Sidon, mentioned in 1 Kings xvii. 9, 10; Obad. 20. It is the place where Elijah went to dwell, and where he performed the miracle of multiplying the barrel of meal and cruse of oil, and where he raised the widow's son to life. It still subsists as a large village, under the name of Sarafend.

SAR'GON, king of Assyria. [ASSYRIA.]

SA'TAN (*the adversary or opposer*). The doctrine of Satan and of Satanic agency is to be made out from revelation, and from reflection in agreement with revelation.

Besides Satan, he is called the Devil, the Dragon, the Evil One, the Angel of the Bottomless Pit, the Prince of this World, the Prince of the Power of the Air, the God of this World, Apollyon, Abaddon, Belial, Beelzebub. Satan and Devil are the names by which he is oftener distinguished than by any other, the former being applied to him about forty times, and the latter about fifty times.

The word Satan occurs in its *specific* sense as a proper name in Zech. iii. 1, 2, and in the 1st and 2nd chapters of Job. See also 1 Chron. xxi. 1. When we pass from the Old to the New Testament, this doctrine of an invisible evil agent becomes more clear. With the advent of Christ and the opening of the Christian dispensation, the great opposer of that kingdom, the particular adversary and antagonist of the Saviour, would naturally become more active and more known. The antagonism of Satan and his kingdom to Christ and his kingdom runs through the whole of the New Testament.

Devil is the more frequent term of designation given to Satan in the New Testament. With one or two exceptions, which go to confirm the rule, the *usus loquendi* of the New Testament shows this term to be a proper name, applied to an extraordinary being, whose influence upon the human race is great and mischievous (Matt. iv. 1-11; Luke viii. 12; John viii. 44; Acts xiii. 10; Ephes. vi. 11; 1 Pet. v. 8; 1 John iii. 8; Rev. xii. 9). In the original this name is given exclusively to the prince of evil spirits, never to these spirits themselves, who, in connection with demoniacal possessions, are almost always termed 'demons'—a distinction which the Authorized Version has failed to observe.

We determine the personality of Satan by the same criteria that we use in determining whether Cæsar and Napoleon were real, personal beings, or the personifications of abstract ideas, viz., by the tenor of history concerning them, and the ascription of personal attributes to them. All the forms of personal agency are made use of by the sacred writers in setting forth the character and conduct of Satan. They describe him as having power and dominion, messengers and followers. He tempts and resists; he is held accountable, charged with guilt; is to be judged, and to receive final punishment. On the supposition that it was the object of the sacred writers to teach the proper personality of Satan, they could have found no more express terms than those which they have actually used. And on the supposition that they did not intend to teach such a doctrine, their use of language, incapable of communicating any other idea, is wholly inexplicable.

The class of beings to which Satan originally belonged, and which constituted a celestial hierarchy, is very numerous: 'Ten thousand times ten thousand stood before him' (Dan. vii. 10). They were created and dependent (John i. 3). Analogy leads to the conclusion that there are different grades among the angels as among other races of beings. The Scriptures warrant the same. Michael is described as one of the chief princes (Dan. x. 13); as chief captain of the host of Jehovah (Josh. v. 14). Similar distinctions exist among the fallen angels (Col. ii. 15; Eph. vi. 12). It is also reasonable to suppose that they were created susceptible of improvement in all respects, except moral purity, as they certainly were capable of apostacy. As to the time when they were brought into being, the Bible is silent; and where it is silent, we should be silent, or speak with modesty. It is probable, that as they were the highest in rank among the creatures of God, so they were the first in the order of time; and that they may have continued for ages in obedience to their Maker, before the creation of man, or the fall of the apostate angels.

The Scriptures are explicit as to the apostacy of some, of whom Satan was the chief and leader (Jude, ver. 6; 2 Pet. ii. 4). Those who followed him in his apostacy are described as belonging to him. The company is called the devil and his angels (Matt. xxv. 41). The relation marked here denotes the instrumentality which the devil may have exerted in inducing those called his angels to rebel against Jehovah and join themselves to his interests. As to what constituted the first sin of Satan and his followers, there has been a diversity of opinions. Some have supposed that it was the beguiling of our first parents. Others have believed that the first sin of the angels is mentioned in Gen. vi. 2. The sacred writers intimate very plainly that the first transgression was pride, and that from this sprang open rebellion. Of a bishop, the apostle says (1 Tim. iii 6), 'He must not be a novice, lest, being puffed up with *pride*, he fall into the condemnation of the devil.' From which it appears that pride was the sin of Satan, and that for this he was condemned. This, however, marks the *quality* of the sin, and not the act.

The agency of Satan extends to all that he does

or causes to be done. To this agency the following restrictions have been generally supposed to exist: it is limited, first, by the direct power of God; he cannot transcend the power on which he is dependent for existence;—secondly, by the finiteness of his own created faculties;—thirdly, by the established connection of cause and effect, or the laws of nature. The miracles, which he has been supposed to have the power of working, are denominated lying signs and wonders (2 Thess. ii. 9). With these restrictions, the devil goes about like a roaring lion.

His agency is moral and physical. First, moral. He beguiled our first parents, and thus brought sin and death upon them and their posterity (Gen. iii.). He moved David to number the people (1 Chron. xxi. 1). He resisted Joshua the high-priest (Zech. iii. 1). He tempted Jesus (Matt. iv.); entered into Judas, to induce him to betray his master (Luke xxii. 3); instigated Ananias and Sapphira to lie to the Holy Ghost (Acts v. 3); hindered Paul and Barnabas on their way to the Thessalonians (1 Thess. ii. 18). He is the spirit that now worketh in the children of disobedience (Eph. ii. 2); and he deceiveth the whole world (Rev. xii. 9).

But his efforts are directed against the bodies of men, as well as against their souls. That the agency of Satan was concerned in producing physical diseases the Scriptures plainly teach (Job ii. 7; Luke xiii. 16). Peter says of Christ, that he went about doing good and healing all that were oppressed of the devil (Acts x. 38).

It is, no doubt, true that there are difficulties connected with the agency ascribed to Satan. But objections are of little weight when brought against well-authenticated facts. Any objections raised against the agency of Satan are equally valid against his existence. If he exists, he must act; and if he is evil, his agency must be evil. The influence exerted by wicked spirits no more militates against the benevolence of God, than does the agency of wicked men, or the existence of moral evil in any form. Evil agents are as really under the divine control as are good agents. And out of evil, God will cause good to come. He will make the wrath of devils as well as of men to praise him, and the remainder He will restrain.

SATYR. There is much to suggest the probability that the 'satyr' of Isa. xiii. 21, and xxxiv. 14, if not also the 'hairy ones' (rendered 'devils') of Lev. xvii. 7, were no other than a species of ape or baboon. The only species of ape of the baboon form known in Arabia is the Macacus Arabicus, remarkable for stature and aspect, having the doglike nose and approximating eyes of baboons; the skin of the face of a reddish colour; the snout, lips, and chin black; the forehead low, and the sides of the head furnished with bushy, long, white hair; the breast, arms and shoulders similarly covered, but the loins and lower extremities of a fine chestnut; the tail of the same colour, of no great length, tufted at the end, and all the hands black. It is found from the straits of Bab-el-Mandeb, through Southern Arabia to the Euphrates, and even beyond the junction of that river with the Tigris. Like other large and formidable Simiadæ, it is less solicitous about the vicinity of trees, because it is armed with powerful canines; holds its enemy firmly

grasped, and fights, not singly, but assisted by the whole troop: it frequents scrubby underwood near water, but becomes more rare eastward of Yemen. Comparing the characters of this species, we find it by configuration, colours, and manners peculiarly adapted to the purposes of idolatry in its grossest and most debasing aspect. The Hebrew people, already familiar with a similar worship in Egypt, may have copied the

298. [Macacus Arabicus.]

native tribes in the wilderness, and thus drawn upon themselves the remonstrance in Lev. xvii. 7, where the allusion to these animals is very descriptive, as is that in Isa. xiii. 21; and again, xxxiv. 14, where the image is perfect, when we picture to ourselves the 'hairy ones' lurking about the river in the juniper and liquorice jungle, as described by Mr. Rich in his *Memoir on the Ruins of Babylon.*

SAUL, son of Kish, of the tribe of Benjamin, was the first king of the Israelites. The corrupt administration of justice by Samuel's sons furnished an occasion to the Hebrews for rejecting that theocracy, of which they neither appreciated the value, nor, through their unfaithfulness to it, enjoyed the full advantages (1 Sam. viii.). An invasion by the Ammonites seems also to have conspired with the cause just mentioned, and with a love of novelty, in prompting the demand for a king (1 Sam. xii. 12)—an officer evidently alien to the genius of the theocracy, though contemplated as an historical certainty, and provided for by the Jewish lawgiver (1 Sam. xii. 17-20; Deut. xvii. 14-20). An explanation of the nature of this request, as not only an instance of ingratitude to Samuel, but of rebellion against Jehovah, and the delineation of the manner in which their kings—notwithstanding the restrictions prescribed in the law—might be expected to conduct themselves (1 Sam. viii. 11; x. 25), having failed to move the people from their resolution, the Lord sent Saul, who had left home in quest of his father's asses, which had strayed, to Samuel, who having informed Saul of the divine purpose regarding him, and having at a feast shown him a preference, which, no doubt, the other guests understood, privately anointed him king, and gave him various tokens, by which he might be assured that his designation was from Jehovah (1 Sam. ix. x.). Moved by the authority of Samuel, and by the fulfilment of these signs, Saul's reluctance to assume the office to which he was called was overcome. On his way home, meeting a company of prophets, he was seized with the prophetic afflatus, and so gave occasion to a proverb afterwards in use among the Jews. Immediately after, Saul was elected at Mizpah in a solemn assembly by the determination of the miraculous lot—and both previously to that election (x. 16), and subsequently, when insulted by the worthless portion of the Israelites, he showed that modesty, humility, and forbearance which seem to have characterised him till corrupted by the possession of power. The person thus set apart to discharge the royal function, possessed at least those corporeal advantages which most ancient nations desiderated in their sovereigns. His person was tall and commanding, and he soon showed that his courage was not inferior to his strength (1 Sam. ix. 1; x. 23). His belonging to Benjamin also, the smallest of the tribes, though of distinguished bravery, prevented the mutual jealousy with which either of the two great tribes, Judah and Ephraim, would have regarded a king chosen from the other; so that his election was received with general rejoicing, and a number of men, moved by the authority of Samuel (x. 20), even attached themselves to him as a body-guard, or as counsellors and assistants. In the mean time the Ammonites, whose invasion had hastened the appointment of a king, having besieged Jabesh in Gilead, and Nahash their king having proposed insulting conditions to them, the elders of that town, apparently not aware of Saul's election (1 Sam. xi. 3), sent messengers through the land imploring help. Saul acted with wisdom and promptitude; summoning the people, *en masse*, to meet him at Bezek, at the head of a vast multitude he totally routed the Ammonites. He and the people then betook themselves, under the direction of Samuel, to Gilgal, there with solemn sacrifices to reinstal the victorious leader in his kingdom (1 Sam. xi.). At Gilgal Saul was publicly anointed, and solemnly installed in the kingdom by Samuel, who took occasion to vindicate the purity of his own administration—which he virtually transferred to Saul—to censure the people for their ingratitude and impiety, and to warn both them and Saul of the danger of disobedience to the commands of Jehovah (1 Sam. xii.). [SAMUEL.]

The restrictions on which he held the sovereignty had (1 Sam. x. 25) been fully explained as well to Saul as to the people, so that he was not ignorant of his true position as merely the lieutenant of Jehovah, king of Israel, who not only gave all the laws, but whose will, in the execution of them, was constantly to be consulted and complied with. The first occasion on which his obedience to this constitution was put to the test brought out those defects in his character which showed his unfitness for his high office, and incurred a threat of that rejection which his subsequent conduct confirmed (1 Sam. xiii. 13).

Having organized a small standing army, part of which, under Jonathan, had taken a fort of the Philistines, Saul summoned the people to withstand the forces which their oppressors, now alarmed for their dominion, would naturally assemble. But so numerous a host came against Saul, that the people, panic-stricken, fled to rocks and caverns for safety—years of servitude having extinguished their courage, which the want of arms, of which the policy of the Philistines had deprived them, still further diminished. Appa-

rently reduced to extremity, and the seventh day being come, but not being ended, the expiration of which Samuel had enjoined him to wait, Saul 'offered a burnt offering,' thus intruding into the priest's office. Samuel having denounced the displeasure of Jehovah and its consequences, left him, and Saul returned to Gibeah. Left to himself, Saul's errors multiplied apace. Jonathan, having assaulted a garrison of the Philistines (apparently at Michmash, 1 Sam. xiv. 31, which, therefore, must have been situated near Migron in Gibeah, ver. 1, and within sight of it, ver. 15), Saul, aided by a panic of the enemy, an earthquake, and the co-operation of his fugitive soldiers, effected a great slaughter; but by a rash and foolish denunciation, he (1) impeded his success (ver. 30), (2) involved the people in a violation of the law (ver. 33), and (3), unless prevented by the more enlightened conscience of the people, would have ended with putting Jonathan to death for an act which, being done in ignorance, could involve no guilt.

Another trial was afforded Saul before his final rejection, the command to extirpate the Amalekites, whose hostility to the people of God was inveterate (Deut. xxv. 18; Exod. xvii. 8-16; Num. xiv. 42-45; Judg. iii. 13; vi. 3), and who had not by repentance averted that doom which had been delayed 550 years (1 Sam. xiv. 48). A second time Saul wilfully violated the divine commission with which he had been intrusted. This stubbornness in persisting to rebel against the directions of Jehovah was now visited by that final rejection of his family from succeeding him on the throne, which had before been threatened (ver. 23; xiii. 13, 14). After this second and flagrant disobedience, Saul received no more public countenance from the venerable prophet, who now left him to his sins and his punishment; 'nevertheless, he mourned for Saul,' and the Lord repented that he had made Saul king (xv. 35).

The denunciations of Samuel sunk into the heart of Saul, and produced a deep melancholy, which either really was, or which his physicians (1 Sam. xvi. 14, 15; comp. Gen. i. 2) told him, was occasioned by an evil spirit from the Lord. By the advice of his servants, music was employed for the purpose of removing the deep melancholy into which he had fallen, and David was recommended to his notice as one 'cunning in playing.' Some critics have supposed, however, and apparently with good reason, that this event occurred subsequently to the transactions recorded in chap. xviii.

Though not acquainted with the unction of David, yet having received intimation that the kingdom should be given to another, Saul soon suspected from his accomplishments, heroism, wisdom, and popularity, that David was his destined successor; and, instead of concluding that his resistance to the divine purpose would only accelerate his own ruin, Saul, in the spirit of jealousy and rage, commenced a series of murderous attempts on the life of his rival (xviii. 10, 11; xix. 10), that must have lost him the respect and sympathy of his people, which they secured for the object of his malice and envy, whose noble qualities also they both exercised and rendered more conspicuous. The slaughter of Ahimelech the priest (1 Sam. xxii.), under pretence of his being a partisan of David, and of eighty-five other priests of the house of Eli, to whom nothing could be imputed, as well as the whole inhabitants of Nob, was an atrocity perhaps never exceeded.

Having compelled David to assume the position of an outlaw, around whom gathered a number of turbulent and desperate characters, Saul might persuade himself that he was justified in bestowing on another the hand of his younger daughter whom he had given David to wife, and in making expeditions to apprehend and destroy him. A portion of the people were base enough to minister to the evil passions of Saul (1 Sam. xxii. 19; xxvi. 1), and others, perhaps, might colour their fear by the pretence of conscience (xxii. 12). But his sparing Saul's life twice, when he was completely in his power, must have destroyed all colour of right in Saul's conduct in the minds of the people, as it also did in his own conscience (xxiv. 3-7; xxvi.). Though thus degraded and paralysed by the indulgence of malevolent passions, Saul still acted with vigour in repelling the enemies of his country, and in other affairs wherein his jealousy of David was not concerned (xxiii. 27, 28).

The measure of Saul's iniquity, now almost full, was completed by an act of direct treason against Jehovah the God of Israel (Exod. xxii. 18; Lev. xix. 31; xx. 27; Deut. xviii. 10, 11), in consulting a woman that had a familiar spirit. [The question as to the character of the apparition evoked by the Witch of Endor, falls more properly to be considered under the article WITCHCRAFT.] Assured by this woman of his own death the next day, and that of his sons; of the ruin of his army, and the triumph of his most formidable enemies, whose invasion had tempted him to try this unhallowed expedient; Saul, in a state of dejection which could not promise success to his followers, met the enemy next day in Gilboa, on the extremity of the great plain of Esdraelon; and having seen the total rout of his army, and the slaughter of his three sons, of whom the magnanimous Jonathan was one; and, having in vain solicited death from the hand of his armourbearer, Saul perished at last by his own hand (1 Sam. xxxi. 1–7; 1 Chron. x. 13, 14).

When the Philistines came on the morrow to plunder the slain, they found Saul's body and the bodies of his sons, which, having beheaded them, they fastened to the wall of Bethshan; but the men of Jabesh-gilead, mindful of their former obligation to Saul (1 Sam. xi.), when they heard of the indignity, gratefully and heroically went by night and carried them off, and buried them under a tree in Jabesh, and fasted seven days. From Jabesh the bones of Saul and of his sons were removed by David, and buried in Zelah, in the sepulchre of Kish his father.

SCAPE-GOAT. [GOAT, SCAPE.]

SCARLET. [PURPLE.]

SCEPTRE. The Hebrew word thus rendered in its primary signification denotes a staff of wood (Ezek. xix. 11), about the height of a man, which the ancient kings and chiefs bore as an insigne of honour (Amos i. 5; Zech. x. 11; Ezek. xix. 11; Wisd. x. 14; comp. Gen. xlix. 10; Num. xxiv. 17; Isa. xiv. 5). As such it appears to have originated in the shepherd's staff, since the first kings were mostly nomade princes (Strabo, xvi. 783; comp. Ps. xxix.).

A golden sceptre, that is, one washed or plated with gold, is mentioned in Ezek. iv. 11. Inclining the sceptre was a mark of kingly favour (Esth. iv. 11), and the kissing it a token of submission (Esth. v. 2). Saul appears to have carried his javelin as a mark of superiority (1 Sam. xv. 10; xxii. 6).

SCRIBES, a learned body of men, otherwise denominated lawyers, whose influence with the Jewish nation was very great at the time when our Saviour appeared.

There is every probability that they must have taken their rise contemporaneously with the commencement of the Mosaic polity. They were both a learned and a sacred caste. They had the care of the law; it was their duty to make transcripts of it; they also expounded its difficulties, and taught its doctrines, and so performed several functions which are now distributed among different professions, being keepers of the records, consulting lawyers, authorized expounders of holy writ, and, finally, schoolmasters—thus blending together in one character the several elements of intellectual, moral, social, and religious influence.

In the New Testament the scribes are found as a body of high state functionaries, who, in conjunction with the Pharisees and the high-priests, constituted the Sanhedrim, and united all the resources of their power and learning in order to entrap and destroy the Saviour of mankind. The array of influence thus brought against 'the carpenter's son' was very great. That influence comprised, besides the supreme power of the state, the first legal functionaries, who watched Jesus closely in order to detect him in some breach of the law; the recognised expositors of duty, who lost no opportunity to take exception to his utterances, to blame his conduct, and misrepresent his morals; also the acutest intellects of the nation, who eagerly sought to entangle him in the web of their sophistries, or to confound him by their artful questions. Yet even all these malign influences failed. Jesus was triumphant in argument; he failed only when force interposed its revengeful arm.

SCRIPTURE (HOLY), or SCRIPTURES (HOLY), the term generally applied in the Christian Church since the second century, to denote the collective writings of the Old and New Testaments.

SCYTH'IAN, a name which occurs only in Col. iii. 11. It was anciently applied sometimes

299. [1. A Scythian. 2. A Scythian General.]

to a particular people, and sometimes to all the nomade tribes which had their seat to the north of the Black and Caspian seas, stretching indefinitely eastward into the unknown regions of Asia It had thus much the same latitude as 'Tartars,' and was in like manner synonymous with Barbarian.

The Scythians were, in fact, the ancient representatives of the modern Tartars, and like them moved from place to place in carts drawn by oxen.

SEA. The term 'sea' was much more in use among the Hebrews than with us, being applied by them generally to all large collections of water, as they had not a set of terms such as we employ to discriminate the different kinds.

1. THE MEDITERRANEAN, being on the west, and therefore behind a person facing the east, is called in Scripture the *Hinder Sea* (Deut. xi. 24; Joel ii. 20), that is, *Western Sea ;* and also, 'the *Sea of the Philistines'* (Exod. xxiii. 31), as that people possessed the largest proportion of its shore in Palestine. Being also the largest sea with which the Hebrews were acquainted, they called it by pre-eminence, '*the Great Sea'* (Num. xxxiv. 6, 7; Josh. i. 4; ix. 1; Ezek. xlvii. 10, 15, 20); or simply 'the sea' (Josh. xv. 47).

2. THE RED SEA.—How this gulf of the Indian Ocean came by the name of Red Sea is not agreed. Prideaux assumes (*Connection,* i. 14, 15) that the ancient inhabitants of the bordering countries called it *Yam Edom,* or, 'the sea of Edom' (it is *never* so called in Scripture), as its north-eastern part washed the country possessed by the Edomites. Now Edom means *red* (Gen. xxv. 30), and the Greeks, who borrowed the name from the Phœnicians, mistook it for an appellative instead of a proper name, and rendered by 'the Red Sea.' Others have conjectured that the Arabian Gulf derived its name from the coral rocks and reefs in which it abounds; but the coral of the Red Sea is white, not red. It is now in question whether the name originated from the singularly red appearance presented by some of the mountains along the western coast; or from the redness which the surface of the water sometimes assumes from its being covered to a great extent with a numberless multitude of very small mollusca.

The ancients applied the name of Erythræan Sea not only to the Arabian Gulf, but to that part of the Indian Ocean which is enclosed between the peninsulas of India and Arabia; but in modern usage the name of Red Sea is restricted to the Arabian Gulf, which enters into the land from the Indian Ocean in a westerly direction, and then, at the straits of Bab-el-Mandeb, turns N.N.W., maintaining that direction till it makes a near approach to the Mediterranean, from which its western arm is only separated by the isthmus of Suez. It thus separates the western coast of Arabia from the Eastern coast of the north-eastern part of Africa. It is about 1400 miles in length from Suez to the straits, and on an average 150 miles in breadth. On approaching its northern termination the gulf divides into two branches, which enclose between them the peninsula of Sinai. The western arm, which terminates a little above Suez, is far more extensive than the other, and is that which was crossed by the Israelites in their escape from Egypt. This arm, anciently called Heroopoliticus Sinus, and now the Gulf of Suez, is 190 miles long by an average

breadth of 21 miles; but at one part (Birket el-Faroun) it is as wide as 32 miles. The eastern arm, which terminates at Akabah, and bears the name of the Gulf of Akabah, was anciently called Ælaniticus Sinus, from the port of Ælana, the Scriptural Elath, and is about 112 miles long by an average breadth of 15 miles. Towards its extremity were the ports of Elath and Eziongeber, celebrated in the history of the attempts made by the Hebrew kings to establish a maritime traffic with the East [see the several words].

3. THE SEA OF CHINNERETH (Num. xxxiv. 11), called in the New Testament 'the Sea of Galilee' (Matt. iv. 18), the 'Sea of Tiberias' (John xxi 1), and 'the sea' or 'lake of Gennesareth' (Matt. xiv. 34; Mark vi. 53; Luke v. 17); which last is but a variation of the Hebrew name.

This lake lies very deep, among fruitful hills and mountains, from which, in the rainy season, many rivulets descend: its shape will be seen from the map. The Jordan enters it on the north, and quits it on the south; and it is said that the river passes through it without the waters mingling. Its extent has been greatly over-rated. Dr. Robinson considers that its length, in a straight line, does not exceed eleven or twelve geographical miles, and that its breadth is from five to six miles. From numerous indications it is inferred that the bed of this lake was formed by some ancient volcanic eruption, which history has not recorded: the waters are very clear and sweet, and contain various kinds of excellent fish in great abundance. It will be remembered that several of the apostles were fishermen of this lake, and that it was also the scene of several transactions in the life of Christ: it is thus frequently mentioned in the New Testament, but very rarely in the Old. The borders of the lake were in the time of Christ well peopled, being covered with numerous towns and villages; but now they are almost desolate, and the fish and water-fowl are but little disturbed.

4. THE DEAD SEA, called in Scripture the *Salt Sea* (Gen. xiv. 3), the *Sea of the Plain,* or the *Arabah* (Deut. iv. 40), and the *Eastern Sea* (Joel ii. 20; Ezek. xlvii. 18; Zech. xiv. 8) It is not named or alluded to in the New Testament. From its history and qualities, it is the most remarkable of all the lakes of Palestine; and is supposed either to have originated in, or at least to have been greatly enlarged by, the awful event which overwhelmed the cities of the plain.

It is about thirty-nine or forty geographical miles long from north to south, and nine or ten miles wide from east to west: it lies embedded very deep between lofty cliffs on the western side, which are about 1500 feet high, and mountains on the eastern shore, the highest ridges of which are reckoned to be from 2000 to 2500 feet above the water. The water of the lake is much salter than that of the sea. From the quantity of salt which it holds in solution it is thick and heavy, and no fish can live or marine plants grow in it. The old stories about the pestiferous qualities of the Dead Sea and its waters are mere fables or delusions; the actual appearances being the natural and obvious effects of the confined and deep situation. the intense heat, and the uncommon saltness of the waters.

On the borders of this lake is found much sulphur, in pieces as large as walnuts, and even larger. There is also a black shining stone, which will partly burn in the fire, and which then emits a bituminous smell: this is the 'stink-stone' of Burckhardt. At Jerusalem it is made into rosaries and toys, of which great quantities are sold to the pilgrims who visit the sacred places. Another remarkable production, from which, indeed, the lake takes one of its names, is the *asphaltum*, or bitumen. Josephus says, that 'the sea in many places sends up black masses of asphaltum, which float upon the surface, having the size and shape of headless oxen.' From recent information it appears that large masses are rarely found, and then generally only after earthquakes. The substance is doubtless produced from the bottom of the sea, in which it coagulates, and rises to the surface; or possibly the coagulation may have been ancient, and the substance adheres to the bottom until detached by earthquakes and other convulsions, when its buoyancy brings it to the surface. We know that 'the vale of Siddim' (Gen. xiv. 10) was anciently 'full of slime-pits,' or sources of bitumen; and these, now under the water, probably supply the asphaltum which is found on such occasions.

5. THE LAKE MEROM is named once only in Scripture, where it is called *waters of Merom* (Josh. xi. 5, 7). By Josephus it is called Semechonitis, and at present bears the name of Huleh: this is the uppermost and smallest of the three lakes on the Jordan. It serves as a kind of reservoir to collect the waters which form that river, and again to send them forth in a single stream. In the spring, when the waters are highest, the lake is seven miles long and three and a half broad; but in summer it becomes a mere marsh. In some parts it is sown with rice, and its reeds and rushes afford shelter to wild hogs.

SEA, MOLTEN. The immense brazen reservoir which, with smaller lavers [LAVER], stood in the court of Solomon's temple, was thus, by hyperbole, denominated. It was of a hemispherical figure, ten cubits in width, five deep, and thirty in circumference. In 1 Kings vii. 23, it is stated to have contained 2000 baths, equal to 16,000 gallons; but in 2 Chron. iv. 5, it is said to have contained 3000 baths, and the latter estimate is followed by Josephus. It was probably capable of holding the larger quantity, but did not usually contain more that the smaller. It was decorated on the upper edge with figures resembling lilies in bloom, and was enriched with various ornamental objects; and it rested, or seemed to rest, upon the backs of twelve oxen, three looking to the north, three to the east, three to the south, and three to the west (1 Kings vi. 26; vii. 40-47; 2 Chron. iv. 3-5. The conception, and still more the successful execution of this great work, gives a very favourable idea of the state of the metallurgical arts in the time of Solomon.

SEAL. There seem to have been two kinds of seals in use among the Hebrews. A notion appears to exist that all ancient seals, being signets, were rings, intended to be worn on the hand. But this was by no means the case; nor is it so now in the East, where signet rings are still, probably, as common as they ever were in ancient times. Their general use of seals was very different from ours, as they were employed not for the purpose of impressing a device on wax, but in the place

of a sign manual, to stamp the name of the owner upon any document to which he desired to affix it. The name thus impressed had the same legal validity as the actual signature, as is still the case in the East. This custom was ancient, and, no doubt, existed among the Hebrews (Gen. xxxviii. 18; Cant. viii. 6, Haggai ii. 23). These seals are often entirely of metal—brass, silver, or gold; but sometimes of stone set in metal.

If a door or box was to be sealed, it was first fastened with some ligament, over which was placed some well-compacted clay to receive the impression of the seal. Clay was used because it hardens in the heat, which would dissolve wax; and this is the reason that wax is not used in the East. There are distinct allusions to this custom in Job xxxviii. 14; Cant. iv. 12.

Signet rings were very common, especially among persons of rank. They were sometimes wholly of metal, but often the inscription was borne by a stone set in silver or gold. The impression from the signet ring of a monarch gave the force of a royal decree to any instrument to which it was affixed. Hence the delivery or transfer of it to any one gave the power of using the royal name, and created the highest office in the state (Gen. xli. 42; Esth. iii. 10, 12; viii. 2; Jer. xxii. 24; Dan. vi. 10, 13, 17: comp. 1 Kings xxi. 8).

SEBA was the eldest son of Cush (Gen. x. 7; 1 Chron. i. 9), and gave name to the country of Seba or Saba, and to one of the tribes called Sabæans, not, however, the *Shebaiim*, but the *Sebaiim*. There seems no reason to doubt that their ultimate settlement was in that region of Africa which was known to the Hebrews as the land of Cush, and to the Greeks and Romans as Ethiopia; and the Scriptural notices respecting them and their country have been already anticipated in the articles CUSH and ETHIOPIA.

SECUN'DUS, a disciple of Thessalonica, who accompanied Paul in some of his voyages (Acts xx. 4).

SEER. [PROPHECY.]

SE'IR (*hairy*). 1. A phylarch or chief of the Horim, who were the former inhabitants of the country afterwards possessed by the Edomites.

2. SEIR, MOUNT. The mountainous country of the Edomites, extending from the Dead Sea to the Elanitic Gulf. The name is usually derived from the Seir above mentioned, and as he was a great chief of the original inhabitants, it is difficult to reject such a conclusion. These mountains were first inhabited by the Horim (Gen. xiv. 6; Deut. ii. 12); then by Esau (Gen. xxxii. 3; xxxiii. 14, 16) and his posterity (Deut. ii. 4, 19; 2 Chron. xx. 10). The northern part of them now bears the designation of Jebal, and the southern that of esh-Sherah, which seems no other than a modification of the ancient name. The whole breadth of the mountainous tract between the Arabah (the great valley between the Dead Sea and Elanitic Gulf) and the eastern desert above is about 15 or 20 geog. miles. These mountains are quite different in character from those which front them on the other (west) side of the Arabah. The latter seem to be not more than two-thirds as high as the former, and are wholly desert and sterile; while those on the east appear to enjoy a sufficiency of rain, and are covered with tufts of herbs and occasional trees.

The valleys are also full of trees and shrubs and flowers, the eastern and higher parts being extensively cultivated, and yielding good crops. It is indeed the region of which Isaac said to his son Esau. 'Behold, thy dwelling shall be of the fatness of the earth, and of the dew of heaven from above' (Gen. xxvii. 39).

3. A mountain in the territory of Judah (Josh. xv. 10).

SE'LAH. [PSALMS.]

SE'LAH, or rather SELA (*rock*); Gr. Petra, which has the same signification as Selah, the metropolis of the Edomites in Mount Seir. In the Jewish history it is recorded that Amaziah, king of Judah, 'slew of Edom in the valley of Salt ten thousand, and took Selah by war, and called the name of it Joktheel unto this day' (2 Kings xiv. 7). This name seems however to have passed away with the Hebrew rule over Edom, for no further trace of it is to be found; and it is still called Selah by Isaiah (xvi. 1). These are all the certain notices of the place in Scripture. Mention is made of it by Strabo, Pliny, and other ancient writers; but from A.D. 536, down to the present century, not the slightest notice of the city is to be found in any quarter; and as no trace of it as an inhabited site is to be met with in the Arabian writers, the probability seems to be that it was destroyed in some unrecorded incursion of the desert hordes, and was afterwards left unpeopled. It was identified by Burckhardt in 1812 as the ancient capital of Arabia Petræa; and since that time has been visited by various travellers, who have given a minute description of its present condition.

300. [Petra, from above the Amphitheatre.]

The ruined city lies in a narrow valley, surrounded by lofty, and, for the most part, perfectly precipitous mountains. Those which form its southern limit are not so steep as to be impassable; and it is over these, or rather through them, along an abrupt and difficult ravine, that travellers from Sinai or Egypt usually wind their laborious way into the scene of magnificent desolation. The ancient and more interesting entrance is on the eastern side, through the deep narrow gorge of Wady Syke. The boundaries of the city are marked with perfect distinctness by the precipitous mountains by which the site is encompassed; and they give an extent of more than a mile in length, nearly from north to south, by a variable breadth of about half a mile. The sides of the valley are walled up by perpendicular rocks,

from four hundred to six or seven hundred feet high. The northern and southern barriers are neither so lofty nor so steep, and they both admit of the passage of camels.

The chief public buildings occupied the banks of the river and the high ground farther south, as their ruins sufficiently show. One sumptuous edifice, which seems to have been a palace, remains standing, though in an imperfect and dilapidated state. It is an imposing ruin, though not of the purest style of architecture, and is the only constructed edifice now standing in Petra.

In various other parts of the valley are piles of ruins—columns and hewn stones—parts no doubt of important public buildings, which indicate the great wealth and magnificence of this ancient capital, as well as its unparalleled calamities. A large surface on the north side of the river is covered with substructions, which probably belonged to private habitations.

The mountain torrents which, at times, sweep over the lower parts of the ancient site, have undermined many foundations, and carried away many a chiselled stone, and worn many a finished specimen of sculpture into unshapely masses. The soft texture of the rock seconds the destructive agencies of the elements. Even the accumulations of rubbish, which mark the site of all other decayed cities, have mostly disappeared; and the extent which was covered with human habitations can only be determined by the broken pottery scattered over the surface, or mingled with the sand—the universal, and, it would seem, an imperishable memorial of popular cities that exist no longer.

The attention of travellers has however been chiefly engaged by the excavations which, having more successfully resisted the ravages of time, constitute at present the great and peculiar attraction of the place. These excavations, whether formed for temples, tombs, or the dwellings of living men, surprise the visitor by their incredible number and extent. They not only occupy the front of the entire mountain by which the valley is encompassed, but of the numerous ravines and recesses which radiate on all sides from this enclosed area. Were these excavations, instead of following all the sinuosities of the mountain and its numerous gorges, ranged in regular order, they probably would form a street not less than five or six miles in length. By far the largest number were manifestly designed as places for the interment of the dead; and thus exhibit a variety in form and size, of interior arrangement and external decorations, adapted to the different fortunes of their occupants. Some of them are plain and unadorned, but there is a vast number of excavations enriched with various architectural ornaments. The interior of these unique and sumptuous monuments is quite plain and destitute of all decoration, but the exteriors exhibit some of the most beautiful and imposing results of ancient taste and skill which have remained to our times. The front of the mountain is wrought into façades of splendid temples, rivalling in their aspect and symmetry the most celebrated monuments of Grecian art. Columns of various orders, graceful pediments, broad rich entablatures, and sometimes statuary, all hewn out of the solid rock, and still forming part of the native mass, transform the base of the mountain into a vast splendid pile of architecture, while the overhanging cliffs, towering above in shapes as rugged and wild as any on which the eye ever rested, form the most striking and curious of contrasts.

301. [Interior of a tomb.]

But nothing contributes so much to the almost magical effect of some of these monuments, as the rich and various colours of the rock out of which, or more properly in which, they are formed. Red, purple, yellow, azure or sky blue, black and white, are seen in the same mass distinctly in successive layers, or blended so as to form every shade and hue of which they are capable—as brilliant and as soft as they ever appear in flowers, or in the plumage of birds, or in the sky when illuminated by the most glorious sunset. It is more easy to imagine than describe the effect of tall, graceful columns, exhibiting these exquisite colours in their succession of regular horizontal strata.

SELEU'CIA, a city of Syria, situated west of Antioch, on the sea-coast, near the mouth of the Orontes; sometimes called Seleucia Pieria, from the neighbouring Mount Pierus: and also Seleucia ad Mare, in order to distinguish it from several other cities of the same name, all of them denominated from Seleucus Nicanor. Paul and Barnabas on their first journey embarked at this port for Cyprus (Acts xiii. 4).

SE'NIR. [HERMON.]

SENNACHE'RIB, king of Assyria, who, in the fourteenth year of King Hezekiah (B C. 713), came up against all the fenced cities of Judah, and took them; on which Hezekiah agreed to pay the Assyrian monarch a tribute of three hundred talents of silver and thirty talents of gold. This, however, did not satisfy Sennacherib, who sent an embassy with hostile intentions, charging Hezekiah with trusting on ' this bruised reed Egypt.' The king of Judah in his perplexity had recourse to Isaiah, who counselled confidence and hope, giving a divine promise of miraculous aid. Meanwhile ' Tirhakah, king of Ethiopia,' and of Thebes in Egypt, had come out to fight against the Assyrians, who had threatened Lower Egypt with an invasion. On learning this, Sennacherib sent another deputation to Hezekiah, who thereon applied for aid to Jehovah, who promised to defend the capital. ' And it came to pass that night that the angel of the Lord went out and smote in the camp of the Assyrians an hundred fourscore and five thousand; and when they arose early in the morning, behold they were all dead corpses' (2

Kings xviii. 13, sq.). On this, Sennacherib returned to Nineveh, and was shortly after murdered by two of his sons as he was praying in the house of Nisroch his god (2 Kings xix. 36, sq.; 2 Chron. xxxii.; Isa. xxxvii.).

SE'PHAR, ' a mountain of the east,' a line drawn from which to Mesha formed the boundary of the Joktanite tribes (Gen. x. 30).

SEPH'ARAD, a region to which the exiles from Jerusalem were taken (Obad 20). It appears to have been a district of Asia Minor, or at least near to it.

SEPHARVA'IM, a city of the Assyrian empire, whence colonists were brought into the territory of Israel, afterwards called Samaria (2 Kings xvii. 24; xviii. 34; xix. 13; Isa xxxvi. 19; xxxvii. 13). The place is probably represented by Sipphara in Mesopotamia, situated upon the east bank of the Euphrates above Babylon.

SEPULCHRE. [BURIAL.]

SERAI'AH (warrior of Jehovah). There are several persons of this name in Scripture.

1. SERAIAH, the scribe or secretary of David (2 Sam. viii. 17).

2 SERAIAH, the father of Ezra (Ez. vii. 1).

3. SERAIAH, the high priest at the time that Jerusalem was taken by the Chaldæans. He was sent prisoner to Nebuchadnezzar at Riblah, who put him to death (2 Kings xxv. 18; 1 Chron. vi. 14; Jer. lii. 24; Ez. vii. 1).

4. SERAIAH, son of Azriel, one of the persons charged with the apprehension of Jeremiah and Baruch (Jer. xxxvi. 26).

5. SERAIAH, son of Neriah, who held a high office in the court of King Zedekiah, the nature of which is somewhat uncertain. In the Auth. Vers. we have, ' This Seraiah was a quiet prince,' which should be rendered, according to Gesenius, ' chief of the quarters' for the king and his army, that is quartermaster-general. This Seraiah was sent by Zedekiah on an embassy to Babylon, probably to render his submission to that monarch, about seven years before the fall of Jerusalem. He was charged by Jeremiah to communicate to the Jews already in exile a book, in which the prophet had written out his prediction of all the evil that should come upon Babylon. It is not stated how Seraiah acquitted himself of his task; but that he accepted it at all, shows such respect for the prophet as may allow us to conclude that he would not neglect the duty which it imposed.

6. SERAIAH, son of Tanhumeth, an accomplice of Ishmael in the conspiracy against Gedaliah (2 Kings xxv. 23; Jer. xl. 8).

SE'RAH (abundance), daughter of Asher, named among those who went down into Egypt (Gen. xlvi. 17; Num. xxvi. 46; 1 Chron. vii. 30).

SER'APHIM, or SERAPHS, the plural of the word saraph, ' burning,' or ' fiery:' celestial beings described in Isa. vi. 2–6, as an order of angels or ministers of God, who stand around his throne, having each six wings, and also hands and feet, and praising God with their voices. They were therefore of human form, and, like the Cherubim, furnished with wings as the swift messengers of God.

There is much symbolical force and propriety in the attitude in which the Seraphim are described as standing; while two of their wings were kept ready for instant flight in the service

3 A

of God, with two others they hid their face, to express their unworthiness to look upon the divine Majesty (comp. Exod. iii. 6), and with two others they covered their feet, or the whole of the lower part of their bodies—a practice which still prevails in the East, when persons appear in a monarch's presence.

SER'GIUS PAULUS, a Roman proconsul in command at Cyprus, who was converted by the preaching of Paul and Barnabas (Acts xiii. 7). The title given to this functionary exhibits one of those minute accuracies which, apart from its inspiration, would substantiate the sacred book as a genuine and contemporary record. Cyprus was originally a *prætorian* province, and not *proconsular*; but it was left by Augustus under the Senate, and hence was governed by a proconsul, as stated by the Evangelist (Acts xiii. 6, 8, 12). Sergius is described by the Evangelist as a 'discreet' or 'intelligent' man; by which we are probably to understand that he was a man of large and liberal views, and of an inquiring turn of mind. Hence he had entertained Elymas, and hence also he became curious to hear the new doctrine which the apostle brought to the island. Nothing of his history subsequent to his conversion is known from Scripture.

SERPENT. Serpents may be divided generally into two very distinct sections,—the first embracing all those that are provided with moveable tubular fangs and poison-bags in the upper jaw; all regarded as ovoviviparous, and called by contraction *vipers:* they constitute not quite one fifth of the species hitherto noticed by naturalists. The second section, much more numerous, is the *colubrine*, not so armed, but not therefore always entirely innocuous, since there may

302. [1. Shephiphon · Cerastes. 2. Peten Coluber Lebetina. 3. Python tigris Albicans; probably Thaïbanne.]

be in some cases venomous secretions capable of penetrating into the wounds made by their fixed teeth, which in all serpents are single points, and in some species increase in size as they stand back in the jaws. The greater part, if not all, the innocuous species are oviparous, including the largest or giant snakes, and the *pelamis* and *hydrophis*, or water-serpents, among which several are venomous.

Scriptural evidence attests the serpent's influence on the early destinies of mankind; and this fact may be traced in the history, the legends, and creeds of most ancient nations. It is far from being obliterated at this day among the pagan, barbarian, and savage tribes of both continents, where the most virulent and dangerous animals of the viviparous class are not uncommonly adored, but more generally respected, from motives originating in fear; and others of the oviparous race are suffered to abide in human dwellings, and are often supplied with food, from causes not easily determined, excepting that the serpent is ever considered to be possessed of some mysterious superhuman knowledge or power.

The supposed winged serpent, which appears to be alluded to in 'the fiery flying serpent' of Isaiah (xiv. 29; xxx. 6), seems, as well as the 'adder,' to have been a species of Haye, and probably one of the more eastern species or varieties, which have the faculty of actually distending the hood, as if they had wings at the side of the head, and are the same as, or nearly allied to, the well known spectacle-snake of India.

The serpent named Ephoeh (Job xx. 16, and Isaiah xxx. 6), and which seems to be the same as the 'viper' of the New Testament (Matt. iii. 7; xii. 34; xxiii. 33; Luke iii. 7; Acts xxviii. 3), was probably a species allied to the Effah, a serpent which, although not above a foot in length, is regarded as the most formidable of Northern Africa.

The serpent which in Deut. xxxii. 33; Job xx. 14, 16; Ps. lviii. 4; xci. 13; Isa. xi. 8, occurs under the Hebrew name of Pethen, is probably the Bætan of Forskal; the *Coluber (vipera) Lebetina* of Linn., and by him characterized as one foot in length, the body spotted with black and white, and oviparous (?), though excessively poisonous. This is usually regarded as the 'asp' of the ancients, and the 'deaf adder' of Ps. lviii. 5, 6. This is uncertain; and it may be remarked that the so-called 'deaf adder' is not without hearing, but is only not obedient to the musical notes of the serpent-charmers.

The serpent called in the Hebrew of Deut. viii. 15, by the name of *tzimmaon*, appears to be the 'Drought' of some versions, so called because of the intolerable thirst occasioned by its bite. It would therefore seemingly form in modern nomenclature one of the genus Hurria, and sub-genus Dipsas or Bongarus; but no species of this division of snakes has yet been found in Western Asia. Another serpent mentioned in Scripture is the *tzepha*, or *tziphoni*, translated 'cockatrice' in Prov. xxiii. 32, and Isa. xi. 8. This is an indefinite English name, which belongs to no identified serpent, and now appears only in the works of ancient compilers and heralds, where it is figured with a crest, though there is no really crested or frilled species known to exist in the whole Ophidian order. There are, however, two very distinct species of horned serpents in Egypt and Northern Africa, probably extending to Syria and Arabia. They are of different genera; for the Cerastes, supposed to be the *shephiphon* of the Bible, is a viper with two scales on the head, one above each eye, standing erect somewhat in the form of horns. This is a dangerous species, usually burrowing in sand near the holes of jerboas, and occasionally in the cattle-paths; for there are now few or no ruts of cart-wheels, where it is pretended they used to conceal themselves to assault unwary passers. It is still common in Egypt and Arabia.

SERVANT. [SLAVE]

SE'RUG (*shoot, tendril*), son of Reu, and father of Nahor the grandfather of Abraham (Gen. xi. 20, 1 Chron. i. 6). He was 130 years old at the birth of Nahor, and died at the age of 330. The name occurs in the genealogy of Christ (Luke iii. 35). The Jewish traditions affirm that Serug was the first of his line who fell into idolatry; and this seems to be sanctioned by, and is probably built upon, the charge of idolatry brought against Terah and the fathers beyond the Euphrates in Josh. xxiv. 2.

SETH (*compensation*), the third son of Adam, to whom Eve gave this name in consequence of regarding him as sent to replace Abel, whom Cain had slain (Gen. iv. 25, 26; v. 3, sq).

SEVEN. This word is used to express the number 6 + 1. The Lexicons generally, both ancient and modern, also assign to the word and its derivatives the further office of a round or indefinite number, to express a small number, in the sense of several (as we use *ten* or a *dozen*). It appears to us possible to resolve the passages quoted in support of this view into the idea of sufficiency, satisfaction, fulness, completeness, perfection, abundance, &c., intimated in the Hebrew root, from which the numeral in question is derived. For instance, 1 Sam. ii. 5, 'The barren hath born seven,' that is, hath been blessed with an ample family; Ruth iv. 15, 'Better to thee than seven sons,' *i. e.* an abundance of them; Prov. xxvi. 25, 'There are seven abominations in his heart,' *i. e.* completeness of depravity. Thus also the phrase, 'To flee seven ways' (Deut. xxviii. 7). denotes a total overthrow; to 'punish seven times' (Lev. xxvi. 24), to punish completely; 'Six and seven troubles,' a very great and entire calamity (Job v. 19); 'Give a portion to seven, also to eight,' be not only duly liberal, but abundant; 'Silver purified seven times,' perfectly purified (Ps. xii. 6). The word is used in the New Testament to express the same idea of abundance or completeness. Thus 'the seven spirits before the throne' would seem to be a periphrasis of perfection, denoting the Holy Spirit (Rev. i. 4). It is most likely that the idea of sufficiency and completeness became originally associated with the number seven, from the Creator having finished, completed, or made sufficient, all his work on the seventh day; and that hence also it was adopted as a sacred number, or a number chiefly employed in religious concerns, in order to remind mankind of the creation and its true author. Thus there were seven offerings in making a covenant (Gen. xxi 28); seven lamps in the golden candlestick (Exod. xxxvii. 23); the blood was sprinkled seven times (Lev. iv. 16, 17); every seventh year was sabbatical, seven sabbaths of years in the jubilee (xxv. 8); seven trumpets, seven priests that sounded them seven days round Jericho, seven lamps, seven seals, &c. &c. Seven was considered a fortunate number among the Persians (Esth. i. 10-14; ii. 9). Cicero calls it the knot and cement of all things, as being that by which the natural and spiritual world are comprehended in one idea. Nor is this subject devoid of practical utility. The references which occur in the patriarchal history to the number seven, as denoting a week or period of seven days,

sufficiency, &c., and a sacred number, afford a minute, indirect, but not an inconsiderable argument, that the institution of the Sabbath was both established and observed from the commencement; and not, as Paley thinks, during the wandering in the wilderness: an argument abundantly confirmed by the regard to the seventh day, which has prevailed too far and wide among various nations, to be attributed to their comparatively late intercourse with the Jews.

SHAAL'BIM (*city of foxes*), called also SHAALBIN, a city of the tribe of Dan (Josh. xix. 42), but of which it could not for a long while dispossess the Amorites (Judg. i. 35). In the time of Solomon it was the station of one of the twelve officers or intendants appointed to regulate the collection of provisions for the court (1 Kings iv. 9). One of David's worthies belonged to this place (2 Sam. xxiii. 32; 1 Chron. xi. 32).

SHAALIM (*foxes' region*), a district named in 1 Sam. ix. 4, probably that in which Shaalbim was situated.

SHAASH'GAZ, the appropriate name (meaning in Persian, *servant of the beautiful*) of a Persian eunuch, the keeper of the women in the court of Ahasuerus (Esth. ii. 14).

SHAD'DAI, an epithet or name applied to JEHOVAH. In Gen. xvii. 1 it is given as EL-SHADDAI in the Authorized Version; but is everywhere else rendered by 'Almighty,' which is its true signification.

SHA'DRACH, one of the three friends of Daniel, who were delivered from the burning, fiery furnace [ABEDNEGO].

SHAL'ISHA, a district in the vicinity of the mountains of Ephraim (1 Sam. ix. 4), in which appears to have been situated the city of Baal-Shalisha (2 Kings iv. 22). This city is called by Eusebius Beth-Shalisha, and is placed by him 15 miles from Diospolis (Lydda), towards the north.

SHALLOT. The original word (*shumim*) occurs only once in Scripture, and that in the passage (Num. xi. 5) where the Israelites are described as murmuring, among other things, for the leeks, the onions, and the garlic (*shumim*) of Egypt. There can be no doubt of its being correctly so translated. Ancient authors mention that garlic was cultivated in Egypt. Herodotus enumerates it as one of the substances upon which a large sum (1600 talents) was spent for feeding labourers employed in building the Pyramids. The species considered to have been thus cultivated in Egypt is *Allium Ascalonicum*, which is the most common in Eastern countries, and obtains its specific name from having been brought into Europe from Ascalon. It is now usually known in the kitchen garden by the name of ' eschalot' or ' shallot,' and is too common to require a fuller notice.

SHAL'LUM (*retribution*), the fifteenth king of Israel. In the troubled times which followed the death of Jeroboam II, B C. 772, his son Zechariah was slain in the presence of the people by Shallum, who by this act extinguished the dynasty of Jehu. Shallum then mounted the throne (B.C. 771), but occupied it only one month, being opposed and slain by Menahem, who mounted the throne thus vacated (2 Kings xv. 10-15).

2. A king of Judah, son of Josiah (Jer. xxii. 11), better known by the name of Jehoahaz [JEHOAHAZ II.].

3. The husband of Huldah the prophetess (2 Kings xxii. 14). Several other persons of this name occur in Ezra ii. 42; vii. 2; x. 24, 42; Neh. iii. 12; vii. 45; 1 Chron. ii. 40.

SHALMANE'SER, king of Assyria [Assyria].

SHAM'GAR, son of Anath, and third judge of Israel. It is not known whether the only exploit recorded of him was that by which his authority was acquired. It is said that he 'slew of the Philistines 600 men with an ox-goad' (Judg. iii. 31). It is supposed that he was labouring in the field, without any other weapon than the long staff armed with a strong point, used in urging and guiding the cattle yoked to the plough, when he perceived a party of the Philistines, whom, with the aid of the husbandmen and neighbours, he repulsed with much slaughter. The date and duration of his government are unknown, but may be probably assigned to the end of that long period of repose which followed the deliverance under Ehud. In Shamgar's time, as the song of Deborah informs us (Judg. v. 6), the condition of the people was so deplorably insecure, that the highways were forsaken, and travellers went through by-ways, and, for the same reason, the villages were abandoned for the walled towns.

1. SHA'MIR, a city of Judah (Josh. xv. 48).

2. SHAMIR, a city in the mountains of Ephraim, where Tola lived and was buried (Judg. x. 1, 2).

SHAM'MAH (*astonishment*), one of the three chief of the thirty champions of David. The exploit by which he obtained this high distinction, as described in 2 Sam. xxiii. 11, 12, is manifestly the same as that which in 1 Chron. xi. 12-14, is ascribed to David himself, assisted by Eleazar the son of Dodo. The inference, therefore, is, that Shammah's exploit lay in the assistance which he thus rendered to David and Eleazar. It consisted in the stand which the others enabled David to make, in a field of lentiles, against the Philistines. Shammah also shared in the dangers which Eleazar and Jashobeam incurred in the chivalric exploit of forcing a way through the Philistine host to gratify David's thirst for the waters of Bethlehem (2 Sam. xxiii. 16).

Other persons of this name occur. 2. A son of Reuel (Gen. xxxvi. 13, 17). 3. A brother of David (1 Sam. xvi. 9; xvii. 3), who is elsewhere called Shimeah (2 Sam. xiii. 3, 32) and Shimma (1 Chron. ii. 13). 4. One of David's thirty champions, seemingly distinct from the chief of the same name (2 Sam. xxiii. 33). 5. Another of the champions distinguished as Shammah the Harodite; he is called Shammoth in 1 Chron. xi. 27, and Shamhuth in 1 Chron. xxvii. 8. That three of the thirty champions should bear the same name is somewhat remarkable.

SHA'PHAN, the scribe or secretary of King Josiah (2 Kings xxii. 3, 12; Jer. xxxvi. 10; comp. Ezra viii. 11). Contemporary with him was a state officer named Ahikam, constantly mentioned as 'the son of Shaphan' (2 Kings xxii. 12; xxv. 22; Jer. xxvi. 24; xxxix. 14; and perhaps xxxix. 3); but this Shaphan, the father of Ahikam, can hardly be the same with Shaphan the scribe, although the heedless reader may be apt to confound them.

SHARE'ZER (Persic, *prince of fire*), a son of Sennacherib, one of those who slew his father

(2 Kings xix. 37; Isa. xxxvii. 38). Another person of this name occurs in Zech. vii. 2.

SHA'RON, a level tract along the Mediterranean, between Mount Carmel and Cæsarea, celebrated for its rich fields and pastures (Josh. xii. 18; Cant. ii. 1; Isa. xxxiii. 9; xxxv. 2; lxv. 10; 1 Chron. xxvii. 9). See the head 'Plains,' in the art. PALESTINE.

SHA'VEH, a valley on the north of Jerusalem called also the King's Dale (Gen. xiv. 17; comp. 2 Sam. xviii. 18).

SHA'VEH-KIR'JATHAIM (Gen. xiv. 5), a plain near the city of Kirjathaim, beyond Jordan, which eventually belonged to Reuben (Num. xxxii. 37; Josh. xiii. 19).

SHEAL'TIEL (*asked of God*), the father of Zerubbabel (Ezra iii. 2; Neh. xii. 1; Hag. i. 12, 14; ii 2); called also *Salathiel* (1 Chron. iii. 7).

SHE'AR-JA'SHUB (*the remnant shall return*), son of the prophet Isaiah, who accompanied his father when he proceeded to deliver to king Ahaz the celebrated prophecy contained in Isa. vii. (see verse 3). As the sons of Isaiah sometimes stood for signs in Israel (Isa. viii. 18), and the name of Maher-shalal-hash-baz was given to one of them by way of prophetic intimation, it has been conjectured that the somewhat remarkable name of Shear-jashub intimated that the people who had then retired within the walls of Jerusalem should return in peace to their fields and villages. But we cannot build on this, as it is not distinctly stated that the name of Shear-jashub was chosen. like that of his brother, with any prophetic intention.

SHE'BA, SABÆANS. As much confusion has been introduced by the variety of meanings which the name *Sabæans* has been made to bear, it may be proper to specify in this place their distinctive derivations and use. In our Authorized Version of Scripture the term seems to be applied to *three* different tribes. 1st. To the *Sebaim*, the descendants of Seba or Saba, son of Cush, who ultimately settled in Ethiopia. 2nd. To the *Shebaim*, the descendants of Sheba, son of Joktan, the *Sabæi* of the Greeks and Romans, who settled in Arabia Felix. They are the 'Sabæans' of Joel iii. 8, to whom the Jews were to sell the captives of Tyre. 3rd. To another tribe of *Shebans*, a horde of Bedawee marauders in the days of Job (ch. i. 15); for whether we place the land of Uz in Idumæa or in Ausitis, it is by no means likely that the Arabs of the south would extend their excursions so very far. We must, therefore, look for this tribe in Desert Arabia; and it is singular enough, that besides the Seba of Cush. and the Shaba of Joktan, there is another Sheba, son of Jokshan, and grandson of Abraham, by Keturah (Gen. xxv. 33); and his posterity appear to have been 'men of the wilderness,' as were their kinsmen of Midian, Ephah, and Dedan.

Yet, as if to increase the confusion in the use of this name of 'Sabæans,' it has also been applied—4th. To the ancient star-worshippers of Western Asia, though they ought properly to be styled *Tsabians*, and their religion not Sabaism but *Tsabaism*. 5th. The name of Sabæans, or Sabians, has also been given to a modern sect in the East, *the Mandaites*, or, as they are commonly but incorrectly called, the 'Christians' of St. John; for they deny the Messiahship of Christ, and pay superior honour to John the Baptist.

SHE'BAT, the eleventh month of the Hebrew year, from the new moon of February to the new moon of March. The name only occurs once in Scripture (Zech. i. 7), and is the same which is given in the Arabic and Syriac languages to the same month.

SHEB'NA (*a youth*), the prefect of the palace to king Hezekiah (Isa. xxii. 15); afterwards promoted to be scribe or secretary to the same monarch, when his former office was given to Eliakim (Isa. xxii. 15; xxxvi. 3; 2 Kings xviii. 26, 27; xix. 2).

SHE'CHEM, a town of central Palestine, in Samaria, among the mountains of Ephraim (Josh. xx. 7; 1 Kings xii. 25), in the narrow valley between the mountains of Ebal and Gerizim (comp. Judg. ix. 7), and consequently within the tribe of Ephraim (Josh. xxi. 20). It is in N. lat. 32° 17', E. long. 35° 20', being thirty-four miles north of Jerusalem and seven miles south of Samaria. It was a very ancient place, and appears to have arisen as a town in the interval between the arrival of Abraham in Palestine and the return of Jacob from Padan-aram, for it is mentioned only as a place, described by reference to the oaks in the neighbourhood, when Abraham came there on first entering the land of Canaan (Gen. xii. 6). But, in the history of Jacob it repeatedly occurs as a town having walls and gates: it could not, however, have been very large or important, if we may judge from the consequence which the inhabitants attached to an alliance with Jacob, and from the facility with which the sons of the patriarch were able to surprise and destroy them (Gen. xxxiii. 18, 19; xxxiv. 1, 2, 20, 24, 26). After the conquest of the country, Shechem was made a city of refuge (Josh. xx. 7), and one of the Levitical towns (Josh. xxi. 21), and during the lifetime of Joshua it was a centre of union to the tribes (Josh. xxiv. 1, 25), probably because it was the nearest considerable town to the residence of that chief in Timnath-serah. In the time of the judges, Shechem became the capital of the kingdom set up by Abimelech (Judg ix. 1. sq.), but was at length conquered and destroyed by him (Judg. ix. 34). It must, however, have been ere long rebuilt, for it had again become of so much importance by the time of Rehoboam's accession, that he there gave the meeting to the delegates of the tribes, which ended in the separation of the kingdom (1 Kings xii. 10). It was Shechem which the first monarch of the new kingdom made the capital of his dominions (1 Kings xii. 25; comp. xiv. 17), although later in his reign the pleasantness of Tirzah induced him to build a palace there, and to make it the summer residence of his court; which gave it such importance, that it at length came to be regarded as the capital of the kingdom, till Samaria eventually deprived it of that honour (1 Kings xiv. 7; xvi. 24) [ISRAEL]. Shechem, however, still throve. It subsisted during the exile (Jer. xli. 5), and continued, for many ages after, the chief seat of the Samaritans and of their worship, their sole temple being upon the mountain (Gerizim), at whose foot the city stood [SAMARITANS]. The city was taken, and the temple destroyed, by John Hyrcanus, B.C. 129. In the New Testament it occurs under the name of Sychar (John iv. 5), which seems to have been a sort of nick name, such as the Jews were fond of imposing upon places they disliked. Stephen,

however, in his historical retrospect, still uses the proper and ancient name (Acts vii. 16). Not long after the times of the New Testament the place received the name of Neapolis, which it still retains in the Arabic form of Nabulus, being one of the very few names imposed by the Romans in Palestine which have survived to the present day. It had probably suffered much, if it was not completely destroyed, in the war with the Romans, and would seem to have been restored or rebuilt by Vespasian, and then to have taken this new name. It has remained in the hands of the Mahometans since A.D. 1242.

There is no reason to question that the present town occupies the site of the ancient Shechem, although its dimensions are probably more contracted. The fertility and beauty of the deep and narrow valley in which the town stands, especially in its immediate neighbourhood, have been much admired by travellers, as far exceeding what they had seen in any other part of Palestine. The town itself is long and narrow, extending along the N.E. base of Mount Gerizim, and partly resting upon its declivity. The population of the place is rated by Dr. Olin at 8000 or 10,000, of whom 500 or 600 are Christians of the Greek communion, and the rest Moslems, with the exception of about 130 Samaritans, and one-third that number of Jews. The inhabitants bear the character of being an unusually valiant as well as a turbulent race, and some years since maintained a desperate struggle against the Egyptian government in some bloody rebellions.

2. SHECHEM, son of Hamor, prince of the country or district of Shechem, in which Jacob formed his camp on his return from Mesopotamia. This young man having seen Jacob's daughter Dinah, was smitten with her beauty, and deflowered her. This wrong was terribly and cruelly avenged by the damsel's uterine brothers, Simeon and Levi, as described in the article DINAH (Gen. xxxv.). It seems likely that the town of Shechem, even if of recent origin, must have existed before the birth of a man so young as Hamor's son appears to have been; and we may therefore suppose it a name preserved in the family, and which both the town and the princes inherited. Shechem's name is always connected with that of his father Hamor (Gen. xxxiii. 19; xxxv.; Acts vii. 16).

SHEEP. The normal animal, from which all or the greater part of the western domestic races of sheep are assumed to be descended, is still

303. [Syrian Sheep.]

found wild in the high mountain regions of Persia, and is readily distinguished from two other wild species bordering on the same region. What breeds the earliest shepherd tribes reared in and about Palestine can now be only inferred from negative characters; yet they are sufficient to show that they were the same, or nearly so, as the common horned variety of Egypt and continental Europe: in general white, and occasionally black, although there was on the upper Nile a speckled race; and so early as the time of Aristotle the Arabians possessed a rufous breed, another with a very long tail, and above all a broad-tailed sheep, which at present is commonly denominated the Syrian. Flocks of the ancient breed, derived from the Bedouins, are now extant in Syria, with little or no change in external characters, chiefly the broad-tailed and the common horned white, often with black and white about the face and feet, the tail somewhat thicker and longer than the European. The others are chiefly valued for the fat of their broad tails, which tastes not unlike marrow; for the flesh of neither race is remarkably delicate, nor are the fleeces of superior quality. Sheep in the various conditions of existence wherein they would occur among a pastoral and agricultural people, are noticed in numerous places of the Bible, and furnish many beautiful allegorical images, where purity, innocence, mildness, and submission are portrayed, —the Saviour himself being denominated 'the Lamb of God,' in twofold allusion to his patient meekness, and to his being the true paschal lamb, 'slain from the foundation of the world' (Rev. xiii. 8). Some commentators affirm that the Hebrew word *kesitah*, which occurs only in Gen. xxxiii. 19, and Job xlii. 11, and is in the Authorized Version rendered money, literally means *sheep* or *lambs*, and should be so translated. Others, with greater probability, suppose that it refers to a piece of coined money bearing the figure of a sheep; and it is certain that Phœnicia had sheep actually impressed on a silver coin.

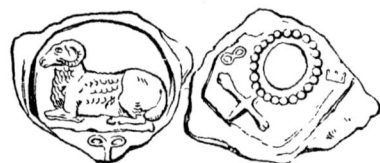

304. [Supposed Kesitah.]

SHEKEL. [WEIGHTS AND MEASURES.]

SHEKINAH or SHECHINAH, a term applied by the ancient Jews, especially in the Chaldee Targums, to that visible symbol of the divine glory which dwelt in the tabernacle and temple. It is evident from many passages of Scripture that the Most High, whose essence no man hath seen, or can see, was pleased anciently to manifest himself to the eyes of men by an external visible symbol. As to the *precise nature* of the phenomenon thus exhibited, we can only say, that it appears to have been a concentrated glowing brightness, a preternatural splendour, an effulgent something, which was appropriately expressed by the term 'Glory;' but whether in philosophical strictness it was material or immaterial, it is probably impossible to determine. A luminous object of this description seems intrinsically the most appropriate symbol of that Being of whom, perhaps in allusion to this very mode of manifesta-

tion, it is said that 'he is light,' and that 'he dwelleth in light unapproachable, and full of glory.' The presence of such a sensible representation of Jehovah seems to be absolutely necessary in order to harmonize what is frequently said of 'seeing God' with the truth of his nature as an incorporeal and essentially invisible spirit. While we are told in one place that 'no man hath seen God at any time,' we are elsewhere informed that Moses and Aaron, and the seventy elders, 'saw the God of Israel,' when called up to the summit of the Holy Mount. So also Isaiah says of himself (Isa. vi. 1, 5) that 'in the year that king Uzziah died he *saw* the Lord sitting upon his throne,' and that, in consequence, he cried out, 'I am undone; for mine eyes have *seen* the Lord of hosts.' In these cases it is obvious that the object seen was not God in his essence, but some external visible symbol, which, because it stood for God, is called by his name.

Of all the divine appearances granted in the earlier ages of the world, the most signal and illustrious was undoubtedly that which was vouchsafed in the pillar of cloud that guided the march of the children of Israel through the wilderness on their way to Canaan. There can be little doubt that the columnar cloud was the seat of the *shekinah*. Within the towering aerial mass, we suppose, was enfolded the inner effulgent brightness, to which the appellation 'Glory of the Lord' more properly belonged, and which was only *occasionally* disclosed. In several instances in which God would indicate his anger to his people, it is said that they looked to the cloud and beheld the 'Glory of the Lord' (Num. xiv. 10; xvi. 19, 42). So when he would inspire a trembling awe of his Majesty at the giving of the Law, it is said, the 'Glory of the Lord appeared as a devouring fire' on the summit of the mount. Nor must the fact be forgotten in this connection, that when Nadab and Abihu, the two sons of Aaron, offended by strange fire in their offerings, a fatal flash from the cloudy pillar instantaneously extinguished their lives. The evidence would seem then to be conclusive, that this wondrous pillar-cloud was the seat or throne of the *shekinah*, the visible representative of Jehovah dwelling in the midst of his people.

SHEM (*name*), one of the three sons of Noah (Gen. v. 32), from whom descended the nations enumerated in Gen. x. 22, sq., and who was the progenitor of that great branch of the Noachic family (called from him Shemitic or Semitic) to which the Hebrews belong. The name of Shem is placed first wherever the sons of Noah are mentioned together; whence he would seem to have been the eldest brother. But against this conclusion is brought the text Gen. x. 21, which, according to the Authorized, and many other versions, has 'Shem the brother of Japheth the elder;' whence it has been conceived very generally that Japheth was really the eldest, and that Shem is put first by way of excellency, seeing that from him the holy line descended. But this conclusion is not built upon a critical knowledge of the Hebrew, which would show that 'the elder' must in this text be referred not to Japheth but to Shem, so that it should be read 'Shem . . . . . the elder brother of Japheth.'

1. SHEMAI'AH (*whom Jehovah hears*), a prophet of the time of Rehoboam, who was commis-

sioned to enjoin that monarch to forego his design of reducing the ten tribes to obedience (1 Kings xii. 22-24). In 1 Chron. xii. 15, this Shemaiah is stated to have written the Chronicles of the reign in which he flourished.

2. SHEMAIAH, a person who, without authority, assumed the functions of a prophet among the Israelites in exile. He was so much annoyed by the prophecies which Jeremiah sent to Babylon, the tendency of which was contrary to his own, that he wrote to Jerusalem, denouncing the prophet as an impostor, and urging the authorities to enforce his silence. In return he received new prophecies, announcing that he should never behold that close of the bondage which he fancied to be at hand, and that none of his race should witness the re-establishment of the nation (Jer. xxix. 24-32).

SHEME'BER (*lofty flight*), king of Zeboim, one of the five 'cities of the plain' (Gen. xiv. 2).

SHE'MER (*lees*), the owner of the hill of Samaria, which derived its name from him. Omri bought the hill for two talents of silver, and built thereon the city, also called Samaria, which he made the capital of his kingdom (1 Kings xvi. 24) [SAMARIA]. As the Israelites were prevented by the law (Lev. xxv. 23) from thus alienating their inheritances, and as his name occurs without the usual genealogical marks, it is more than probable that Shemer was descended from those Canaanites whom the Hebrews had not dispossessed of their lands.

1. SHEPHATI'AH (*whom Jehovah defends*), a son of David by Abital (2 Sam. iii. 4).

2. SHEPHATIAH, one of the nobles who urged Zedekiah to put Jeremiah to death (Jer. xxxviii. 1).

3. SHEPHATIAH, one of the heads of families who settled in Jerusalem after the exile (Neh. xi. 6).

4. SHEPHATIAH, the head of one of the families, numbering three hundred and seventy-two persons, of the returned exiles (Ezra ii. 4, 57).

5. SHEPHATIAH, a son of king Jehoshaphat (2 Chron. xxi. 2).

6. SHEPHATIAH, one of the chief of those valiant men who went to David when at Ziklag (1 Chron. xii. 5).

7. SHEPHATIAH, the governor of the tribe of Simeon in the time of David (1 Chron. xxvii. 16).

SHEPHERD. [PASTURAGE.]

SHE'SHACH, a name twice given by Jeremiah to Babylon (Jer. xxv. 26; li. 41). Its etymology and proper signification are doubtful.

SHE'SHAN (*lily*), a Hebrew, who during the sojourn in Egypt gave his daughter in marriage to his freed Egyptian slave (1 Chron. ii. 34) [JARHAH].

SHESHBAZ'ZAR. [ZERUBBABEL.]

SHE'THAR (Pers., *a star*), one of the seven princes of Persia and Media, 'who saw the king's face, and sat the first in the kingdom' (Est i. 14).

SHE'THAR-BOZ'NAI (Pers., *shining star*), one of the Persian governors in Syria, who visited Jerusalem in company with Tatnai, to investigate the charges made against the Jews (Ezra v. 3; vi. 6) [TATNAI].

SHE'VA. [SERAIAH.]

SHEW-BREAD. In the outer apartment of the tabernacle, on the right hand, or north side, stood a table, made of acacia (shittim) wood, two cubits long, one broad, and one and a half high, and covered with laminæ of gold. The top of the leaf of this table was encircled by a border or rim of gold. The frame of the table, immediately below the leaf, was encircled with a piece of wood of about four inches in breadth, around the edge of which was a rim or border, similar to that around the leaf. A little lower down, but at equal distances from the top of the table, there were four rings of gold fastened to the legs, through which staves covered with gold were inserted for the purpose of carrying it (Exod. xxv. 23-28; xxxvii. 10-16). These rings were not found in the table which was afterwards made for the temple, nor indeed in any of the sacred furniture, where they had previously been, except in the ark of the covenant. Twelve unleavened loaves were placed upon this table, which were sprinkled with frankincense (the Sept. adds salt; Lev. xxiv. 7). The number twelve represented the twelve tribes, and was not diminished after the defection of ten of the tribes from the worship of God in his sanctuary, because the covenant with the sons of Abraham was not formally abrogated, and because there were still many true Israelites among the apostatizing tribes. The twelve loaves were also a constant record against them, and served as a standing testimonial that their proper place was before the forsaken altar of Jehovah.

The loaves were placed in two piles, one above another, and were changed every Sabbath day by the priests. The frankincense that had stood on the bread during the week was then burnt as an oblation, and the removed bread became the property of the priests, who, as God's servants, had a right to eat of the bread that came from his table; but they were obliged to eat it in the holy place, and nowhere else. No others might lawfully eat of it; but in a case of extreme emergency the priest incurred no blame if he imparted it to persons who were in a state of ceremonial purity, as in the instance of David and his men (1 Sam. xxi. 4-6; Matt. xii. 4). The bread was called 'the bread of the face,' or, 'of the presence,' because it was set forth before the face or in the presence of Jehovah in his holy place. This is translated 'shew-bread.' It is also called 'the bread arranged in order,' and 'the perpetual bread,' because it was never absent from the table (Lev. xxiv. 6, 7; 1 Chron. xxiii. 29).

Wine also was placed upon the table of 'shew-bread,' in bowls, some larger, and some smaller, also in vessels that were covered, and in cups, which were probably employed in pouring in and taking out the wine from the other vessels, or in making libations. They appear in the Authorized Version as 'spoons' (see generally Exod. xxv. 29, 30; xxxvii. 10-16; xl. 4, 24; Lev. xxiv. 5-9; Num. iv. 7).

SHIB'BOLETH. The word means a stream or flood, and was hence naturally suggested to the followers of Jephthah, when, having seized the fords of the Jordan to prevent the retreat of the defeated Ephraimites, they sought to distinguish them through their known inability to utter the aspirated sound *sh*. The fugitives gave instead the unaspirated *s*, *sibboleth*, on which they were slain without mercy (Judg. xii. 6). The certainty which was felt that the Ephraimites could not pronounce *sh*, is very remarkable, and strongly illustrates the varieties of dialect which had already arisen in Israel, and which perhaps even served to distinguish different tribes, as similar peculiarities distinguish men of different counties with us. If what is here mentioned as the characteristic of a particular tribe had been shared by other tribes, it would not have been sufficiently discriminating as a test.

SHIELD. [ARMS.]

SHI'LOH, the epithet applied, in the prophetic benediction of Jacob on his death-bed (Gen. xlix. 10), to the personage to whom 'the gathering of the nations should be,' and which has ever been regarded by Christians and by the ancient Jews as a denomination of the Messiah. The oracle occurs in the blessing of Judah, and is thus worded—'The sceptre shall not depart from Judah, nor a lawgiver from between his feet, until Shiloh come: and unto him the gathering of the people shall be.' The term itself, as well as the whole passage to which it belongs, has ever been a fruitful theme of controversy between Jews and Christians, the former, although they admit for the most part the Messianic reference of the text, being still fertile in expedients to evade the Christian argument founded upon it. Neither our limits nor our object will permit us to enter largely into the theological bearings of this prediction; but it is perhaps scarcely possible to do justice to the discussion as a question of pure philology, without at the same time displaying the strength of the Christian interpretation, and trenching upon the province occupied by the proofs of Jesus of Nazareth being the Messiah of the Old Testament prophecies.

Various etymologies have been assigned to the term. Some very eminent commentators trace it to the root *to rest, to be at peace*, and make it equivalent to Pacificator, Tranquillizer, or Great Author of Peace. This is a sense accordant with the anticipated and realized character of the Messiah, one of whose crowning denominations is ' Prince of Peace.' Another opinion is, that it is derived from a word which signifies *to ask, seek, require*, and that its import is *the asked, the desired*, a designation which is, equally with the former, in accordance with the character of the predicted Messiah, and is free from some philological objections to which the other derivation is liable.

2. SHILOH. a city in the tribe of Ephraim, situated among the hills to the north of Bethel, eastward of the great northern road, where the tabernacle and ark remained for a long time, from the days of Joshua, during the ministry of all the judges, down to the end of Eli's life (Josh. xviii. 1; 1 Sam. iv. 3). To this circumstance Shiloh owed all its importance; for after the loss of the ark—which never returned thither after it had been restored to Israel by the Philistines—it sunk into insignificance. It was, indeed, the residence of Ahijah the prophet (1 Kings xi. 29; xii. 15; xiv. 2), but it is more than once mentioned as accursed and forsaken (Ps. lxxviii. 60; Jer. vii. 12, 14; xxvi. 6). The last mention of it in Scripture is in Jer. xli. 5, which only shows that it survived the exile. Dr. Robinson identifies it with a place named Seilun, a city surrounded by hills, with an opening by a narrow valley into a plain on the south. The ruins consist chiefly of an old tower with walls four feet thick, and of large stones and fragments of columns indicative of an ancient site (Robinson's *Palestine*, iii. 85-89).

SHIM'EI (*renowned*), a member of the family of Saul, residing at Bahurim, who grievously insulted king David when he fled from Absalom (2 Sam. xvi. 5-13). The king not only saved him from the immediate resentment of his followers, but on his triumphant return by the same road after the overthrow of his rebellious son, he bestowed on Shimei the pardon which he implored (2 Sam. xix. 16). It seems, however, that it was policy which chiefly dictated this course, for it was by the advice of David himself (1 Kings ii. 8, 9) that Solomon, after his father's death, made Shimei a prisoner at large in Jerusalem (1 Kings ii. 36, 37). Three years after he broke his parole by leaving Jerusalem in pursuit of some runaway slaves, and was, on his return, put to death by order of the king (1 Kings ii. 39-46).

SHI'NAR, the proper name of Babylonia, particularly of the country around Babylon (Gen. x. 10; xiv. 1; Isa. xi. 11; Dan. i. 2; Zech. v. 11): [BABYLONIA].

SHIP. In few things is there greater danger of modern associations misleading the reader of the Scriptures than in regard to the subject of the present article. Both the ships and the navigation of the ancients, even of the most maritime states, were as dissimilar as things of the same kind can well be to the realities which the terms now represent. Navigation confined itself to coasting, or if necessity, foul weather, or chance drove a vessel from the land, a regard to safety urged the commander to a speedy return, for he had no guide but such as the stars might afford under skies with which he was but imperfectly acquainted. And ships, whether designed for commercial or warlike purposes, were small in size and frail in structure.

The Jews cannot be said to have been a seafaring people; yet their position on the map of the world is such as to lead us to feel that they could not have been ignorant of ships and the business which relates thereunto. Phœnicia, the north-western part of Palestine, was unquestionably among, if not at the head of, the earliest cultivators of maritime affairs. Then the Holy Land itself lay with one side coasting a sea which was anciently the great highway of navigation, and the centre of social and commercial enterprise. Within its own borders it had a navigable lake. And the Red Sea itself, which conducted towards the remote east, was at no great distance even from the capital of the land. Then at different points in its long line of sea-coast there were harbours of no mean repute. Yet the decidedly agricultural bearing of the Israelitish constitution checked such a development of power, activity, and wealth, as these favourable opportunities might have called forth on behalf of seafaring pursuits. And it is evident that the Israelites must have only partially improved their local advantages, since we find Hiram, king of Tyre, acting as carrier by sea for Solomon, engaging to convey in floats to Joppa the timber cut in Lebanon for the temple, and leaving to the Hebrew prince the duty of transporting the wood from the coast to Jerusalem. And when, after having conquered Elath and Ezion-geber on the further arm of the Red Sea, Solomon proceeded to convert them into naval stations for his own purposes, he was still, whatever he did himself, indebted to Hiram for 'shipmen that had knowledge of the sea' (1 Kings ix. 26; x. 22).

The reader of the New Testament is well aware how frequently he finds himself with the Saviour on the romantic shores of the sea of

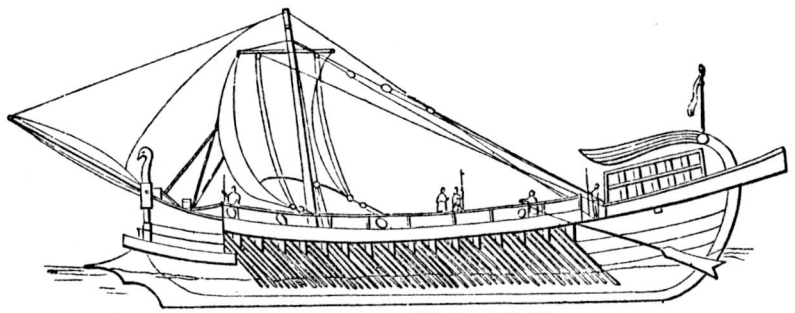

305. [Ancient Ship of the largest kind.]

Gennesareth. There Jesus is seen, now addressing the people from on board a vessel (Matt. xiii. 2; Luke v. 3); now sailing up and down the lake (Matt. viii. 23; ix. 1; xiv. 13; John vi. 17). Some of his earliest disciples were proprietors of barks which sailed on this inland sea (Matt. iv. 21; John xxi. 3; Luke v. 3). But it is evident that these 'ships' must have been small, though they were more than mere boats.

306. [Ancient Light-vessel, Pompeii.]

The vessels connected with Biblical history were for the most part ships of burden, almost indeed exclusively so, at least within the period of known historical facts. In a ship of this kind was Paul conveyed to Italy. They were, for the purposes to which they were destined, rounder and deeper than ships of war, and sometimes of great capacity. In consequence of their bulk, and when laden, of their weight, they were impelled by sails rather than by oars. On the prow stood the insignia from which the ship was named, and by which it was known. These in Acts (xxxviii. 11) are called 'sign,' which it appears consisted in this case of figures of Castor and Pollux, brilliant constellations, auspicious to navigators. Each ship was provided with a boat, intended in the case of peril to facilitate escape (Acts xxvii. 16; xxx. 32). and several anchors (Acts xxvii. 29, 40); also a plumb-line for sounding (Acts xxvii. 28). Mention is made (Acts xxvii. 40) of a 'mainsail,' which, however, should probably be rather termed the 'topsail.' In great danger it was customary to gird the vessel with cables, in order to prevent her from falling to pieces under the force of wind and sea (Acts xxvii. 17). The captain was denominated steersman, though he was a different person from him who had the actual charge of the helm.

The dangers of the ocean to sailors on board such ships as these were, and in the then ignorance of navigation, caused sailing to be restricted to the months of spring, summer, and autumn; winter was avoided. To the Romans the sea was opened in March and closed in November (Acts xxvii. 9); and ships which towards the end of the year were still at sea earnestly sought a harbour in which to pass the winter (Acts xxvii. 12).

SHI'SHAK, a king of Egypt contemporary with Jeroboam, to whom he gave an asylum when he fled from Solomon (1 Kings xi. 40). This was indicative of his politic disposition to encourage the weakening of the neighbouring kingdom, the growth of which under David and Solomon was probably regarded by the kings of Egypt with some alarm. After Jeroboam had become king of Israel, and probably at his suggestion, Shishak invaded the kingdom of Judah, B.C. 971, at the head of an immense army; and after having taken the fortified places, advanced against Jerusalem. Satisfied with the submission of Rehoboam, and with the immense spoils of the Temple, the king of Egypt withdrew without imposing any onerous conditions upon the humbled grandson of David (1 Kings xiv. 25, 26; 2 Chron xii. 2-9). Shishak has been identified as the first king of the 22nd or Diospolitan dynasty, the Sesonchis of profane history. His name has been found on the Egyptian monuments. He is said to have been of Ethiopian origin, and it is supposed that, with the support of the military caste, he dethroned the Pharaoh who gave his daughter to Solomon (1 Kings iii. 1). In the palace-temple of Karnak there still exists a large bas-relief representing Sesonchis, who bears to the feet of three great Theban gods the chiefs of vanquished nations. To each figure is attached an oval, indicating the town or district which he represents. One of the figures, with a pointed beard and a physiognomy decidedly Jewish, bears on his oval, characters which M. Champollion interprets YOODA MELCHI, or 'kingdom of Judah.' It is well to observe that this figure has not, as some have hastily conceived, been alleged to represent the king, but to personify the kingdom of Judah.

SHITTAH and SHITTIM occur in several passages of Exodus, and indicate the kind of wood which was employed in making various parts of the tabernacle while the Israelites were wandering in the wilderness. It is mentioned also as forming part of the offerings, as in Exod. xxv. 5, 'rams' skins dyed red, and badgers' skins, and shittim wood;' and in xxxv. 7, 24. In Isa. xli. 19, it is mentioned as a tree worthy of planting: 'I will plant in the wilderness the cedar, the shittah tree, and the myrtle, and the oil tree,' etc. It is exceedingly probable that the tree referred to belongs to the Acacia, found both in Egypt and in the deserts of Arabia. 'The acacia tree,' says Dr. Shaw, 'being by much the largest and most common tree in these deserts (Arabia Petræa), we have some reason to conjecture that the shittim wood was the wood of the acacia, especially as its flowers are of an excellent smell, for the shittah tree is, in Isa. xli. 19, joined with the myrtle and other fragrant shrubs.' Dr. Kitto says: 'The required species is found in either the Acacia gummifera, or in the A. Seyel, or rather in both. They both grow abundantly in the val-

307. [Acacia Seyel.]

leys of that region in which the Israelites wandered for forty years, and both supply products which must have rendered them of much value to the Israelites. We think the probability is, that the A. Seyel supplied the shittim wood, if, indeed, the name did not denote acacia wood in general. This tree grows from fifteen to twenty feet in height.' Robinson and Smith frequently mention the Seyel as occurring in the same situations. It is very probable therefore that it yielded the shittim wood of Scripture.

SHITTIM, a spot in the plain of Moab, east of the Dead Sea, where the Israelites formed their last encampment before passing the Jordan (Num. xxv. 1; comp. Micah vi. 5) [WANDERING].

SHITTIM, VALLEY OF, mentioned in Joel iii. 18. It must certainly have been west of the Jordan, and probably in the neighbourhood of Jerusalem, although the particular vale cannot now be distinguished. The name is probably to be regarded as an appellative—'acacia vale' denoting, perhaps, as that tree delights in a dry soil, an arid, unfruitful vale.

SHOE. [SANDAL.]

SHU'NEM, a town of the tribe of Issachar (Josh. xix. 18), where the Philistines encamped before Saul's last battle (1 Sam. xxviii. 4), and to which belonged Abishag, the last wife of David (1 Kings i. 3), and 'the Shunamite woman,' with whom Elisha lodged (2 Kings iv. 8-37; viii. 1-6). Eusebius and Jerome describe it as, in their day, a village, lying five Roman miles from Mount Tabor towards the south. They call it Sulem. It has of late years been recognised in a village called Solam, three miles and a half north of Zerin (Jezreel), which is a small place on the slope of a hill, where nothing occurs to denote an ancient site.

SHUR, a city on the confines of Egypt and Palestine (Gen. xvi. 7; xx. 1; xxv. 18; 1 Sam. xv. 7; xxvii. 8). Josephus makes it the same as Pelusium (Antiq. vi. 7. 3; comp. 1 Sam. xv. 7); but this city bore among the Hebrews the name of Sin. More probably Shur was somewhere in the vicinity of the modern Suez. The desert extending from the borders of Palestine to Shur, is called in Exod. xv. 22, the 'desert of Shur,' but in Num. xxxiii. 8, the 'desert of Etham.'

SHU'SHAN, or Susa, the chief town of Susiana, and capital of Persia, in which the kings of Persia had their winter residence (Dan. viii. 2; Neh. i. 1; Esther i. 2, 5). It was situated upon the Eulæus or Choaspes, probably on the spot now occupied by the village Shus. At that place there are extensive ruins, stretching perhaps twelve miles from one extremity to the other, and consisting, like the other ruins of this region, of hillocks of earth and rubbish covered with broken pieces of brick and coloured tile. At the foot of these mounds is the so-called tomb of Daniel, a small building erected on the spot where the remains of that prophet are locally believed to rest. It is apparently modern; but nothing but the belief that this was the site of the prophet's sepulchre could have led to its being built in the place where it stands; and it may be added that such identifications are of far more value in these parts, where occasion for them is rare, than among the crowded 'holy places' of Palestine. The city of Shus is now a gloomy wilderness, infested by lions, hyænas, and other beasts of prey. It is in N. lat. 31° 56' and E. long. 48° 26'.

SI'DON. [ZIDON.]

SI'HON (sweeping away; i. e. a warrior sweeping all before him), the king of the Amorites, reigning at Heshbon, who was destroyed, and his kingdom subjugated, in the attempt to resist the progress of the Israelites through his dominions (Num. xxi. 21, 23, sq.) [AMORITES].

SI'HOR, more properly SHICHOR, the Hebrew proper name for the Nile (Isa. xxiii. 3; Jer. ii. 18). The word means 'black;' and a corresponding name or epithet was by the Greeks applied to the same river on account of the black slime left after the subsidence of the inundation.

SI'HOR-LIB'NATH, a small stream or river emptying itself into the sea in the territory of Asher (Josh. xix. 26). Michaelis translates it 'glass-river,' and identifies it with the Belus, which joins the sea near Acre, and from whose sands the first glass was made by the Phœnicians.

SI'LAS, a contraction of SILVANUS, a distinguished Christian teacher in the church at Jerusalem, who, with Barnabas, was associated by that church with Paul (Acts xv. 22, 32), and accompanied him in his second journey through Asia Minor to Macedonia (Acts xv. 40; xvi. 19, 25; xvii. 4). He remained behind at Berea for a short time, when Paul was obliged to flee from that place (Acts xvii. 10, 14). They met again at Corinth (Acts xviii. 5; comp. Thess. i. 1), where Silas was active in the work of an evangelist (2 Cor. i. 19). He is invariably called Silvanus in the Epistles, but the contraction Silas is always used in the Acts. Whether this Silvanus is the same person who was the bearer of St. Peter's epistle to the churches in Asia Minor (1 Pet. v. 12), cannot be ascertained. The traditions regard Silas and Silvanus as different persons, making the former bishop of Corinth, and the latter bishop of Thessalonica.

SIL'OAH. [SILOAM.]

SIL'OAM or SHILOAH (Neh. ii. 15; John ix. 7-11). Neither of these passages affords any clue to the situation of Siloam; but this silence is supplied by Josephus, who makes frequent mention of it as a fountain (*De Bell. Jud.* v. 4, § 1, 2), and indicates its situation at the mouth of the valley of Tyropœon, where the fountain, now and long since indicated as that of Siloam, is still found. The pool of Siloam is within and at the mouth of the valley of Tyropœon, and about eighty paces above its termination is that of Jehoshaphat. The water flows out of a small artificial basin under the cliff, the entrance to which is excavated in the form of an arch, and is immediately received into a larger reservoir, fifty-three feet in length by eighteen feet in width. The water passes out of this reservoir through a channel cut in the rock, which is covered for a short distance; but subsequently it opens and discloses a lively copious stream, which is conducted into an enclosed garden planted with fig-trees. The small upper basin or fountain excavated in the rock is merely the entrance, or rather the termination of a long and narrow subterranean passage beyond, by which the water comes from the Fountain of the Virgin. This has been established beyond dispute by Dr. Robinson, who, with his companion, had the hardihood to crawl through the passage. It is thus proved that the water of both these fountains is the same, though some travellers have pronounced the water of Siloam to be bad, and that of the other fountain good. It has a peculiar taste, sweetish and very slightly brackish, but not at all disagreeable. The most remarkable circumstance is the ebb and flow of the waters, which, although often mentioned as a characteristic of Siloam, must belong equally to both fountains. Dr. Robinson himself witnessed this phenomenon in the fountain of the Virgin, where the water rose in five minutes one foot in the reservoir, and in another five minutes sunk to its former level. The intervals and the extent of the flow and ebb in this and the fountain of Siloam, vary with the season; but the fact, though

it has not yet been accounted for, is beyond dispute.

SILVA'NUS. [SILAS.]

SILVER. There is no mention of this metal in Scripture until the time of Abraham. Before that time brass and iron appear to have been the only metals in use (Gen. iv. 22). Abraham was rich in gold and silver, as well as in flocks and herds, and silver in his day was in general circulation as money. It was uncoined, and estimated always by weight. Coined money was not in use among the Israelites until an advanced period of their history. The Romans are said to have had only copper money until within five years of the first Punic war, when they began to coin silver. Their coins were extensively introduced into Judæa after it became a Roman province.

Silver, as well as gold, is frequently mentioned in Scripture. They were both largely used by the Jews in the manufacture of articles of ornament, and of various vessels for domestic purposes, and also for the service of the temple. Many of the idols, and other objects belonging to the idolatrous nations, are stated to have been of silver. This metal was so abundant as to be little thought of in the days of Solomon, although it was at that time, and both before and long afterwards, the principal medium of exchange among the Jews—the only recognised standard or measure of value.

SIM'EON (*favourable hearing*), the second son of Jacob, born of Leah (Gen. xxix. 33), and progenitor of the tribe of the same name. He was the full brother of Levi (Gen. xxxiv. 25; xxxv. 23), with whom he took part in cruelly avenging upon the men of Shechem the injury which their sister Dinah had received from the son of Hamor (Gen. xxxiv. 25-30) [DINAH]. The ferocity of character thus indicated probably furnishes the reason why Joseph singled Simeon out to remain behind in Egypt, when his other brethren were the first time dismissed (Gen. xlii. 24); but when they returned he was restored safely to them (Gen. xliii. 23). Nothing more of his personal history is known. The tribe descended from Simeon contained 59,300 able-bodied men at the time of the Exode (Num. i. 23), but was reduced to 22,000 before entering Palestine (Num. xxvi. 14). This immense decrease in the course of one generation was greater than that sustained by all the other tribes together, and reduced Simeon from the third rank to the lowest of all in point of numbers. It cannot well be accounted for but by supposing that the tribe erred most conspicuously, and was punished most severely in those transactions which drew down judgments from God. As it appeared that Judah had received too large a territory in the first distribution of lands, a portion of it was afterwards assigned to Simeon. This portion lay in the south-west, towards the borders of Philistia and the southern desert, and contained seventeen towns (Josh. xix. 1-9). However, the Judahites must afterwards have re-appropriated some of these towns; at least Beersheba (1 Kings ix. 3) and Ziklag (1 Sam. xxvii. 6) appear at a subsequent period as belonging to the kingdom of Judah. The remarkable passage in 1 Chron. iv. 41-43 points to an emigration of or from this tribe, perhaps more extensive than the words would seem to indicate, and suggests that when they ceased to have common interests, this small tribe was obliged to give way before the greater power of Judah and the pressure of its population (comp. Gen. xlix. 7). Nothing more of this tribe is recorded, although its name occurs in unhistorical intimations (Ezek. xlviii. 24; Rev. vii. 8).

2. SIMEON, the aged person who, when Jesus was presented by his mother at the temple, recognised the infant as the expected Messiah, and took him in his arms and blessed him, glorifying God (Luke ii 25-35). The circumstance is interesting, as evincing the expectations which were then entertained of the speedy advent of the Messiah; and important from the attestation which it conveyed in favour of Jesus, from one who was known to have received the divine promise that he should 'not taste of death till he had seen the Lord's Christ.' It has been often supposed that this Simeon was the same with Rabban Simeon, the son of the famous Hillel, and father of Gamaliel: but this is merely a conjecture, founded on circumstances too weak to establish such a conclusion.

SI'MON, the same name, in origin and signification, as SIMEON.

1. SIMON MACCABÆUS. [MACCABÆAN FAMILY]

2. SIMON, the apostle, to whom Christ gave the name of Peter, after which he was rarely called by his former name alone, but usually by that of Peter, or else Simon Peter [PETER].

3. SIMON, surnamed ZELOTES, one of the twelve apostles (Luke vi. 15; Acts i. 13), and probably so named from having been one of the Zealots. He is also called 'The Canaanite' in Matt. x. 4; Mark iii. 18. This, however, is not, as is usually the case, to be taken for a Gentile name, but is merely an Aramaic word signifying 'zeal,' and therefore of the same signification as Zelotes. Simon is the least known of all the apostles, not a single circumstance, beyond the fact of his apostleship, being recorded in the Scriptures. He is probably to be identified with Simon the son of Cleophas; and if so, the traditions concerning that person, given by those who make them distinct, must be assigned to him. These traditions, however, assign a different destiny to this Simon, alleging that he preached the Gospel throughout North Africa, from Egypt to Mauritania, and that he even proceeded to the remote isles of Britain.

4. SIMON, son of Cleophas and Mary, brother of the apostles James and Jude, and a kinsman of Jesus (Matt. xiii. 55; Mark vi. 3). He is probably the same with the Simon Zelotes above mentioned, and in that case we must regard the separate traditions respecting him as apocryphal, and take those assigned to the present Simon as proper to both. They amount to this, that after St. James had been slain by the Jews in A.D 62, his brother Simon was appointed to succeed him in the government of the church at Jerusalem, and that forty-three years after, when Trajan caused search to be made for all those who claimed to be of the race of David, he was accused before Atticus, the governor of Palestine, and after enduring great torture was crucified, being then 120 years of age.

5. SIMON, father of Judas Iscariot (John vi. 71; xii. 4; xiii. 2, 26).

6. SIMON, a Pharisee who invited Jesus to his house (Luke vii. 40, 43, 44).

7. SIMON THE LEPER, so called from having formerly been afflicted with leprosy (Matt. xxvi. 6; Mark xiv. 3). He was of Bethany, and after the raising of Lazarus, gave a feast, probably in celebration of that event, at which both Jesus and Lazarus were present (comp. John xii. 2). He was, therefore, probably a near friend or relation of Lazarus: some suppose that he was his brother; others that he was the husband of Mary, the sister of Lazarus, who at this feast anointed the Lord's feet, and that Lazarus abode with them. But all this is pure conjecture.

8. SIMON THE CYRENIAN, who was compelled to aid in bearing the cross of Jesus (Matt. xxvii. 32; Mark xv. 21; Luke xxiii. 26). Whether this surname indicated that Simon was one of the many Jews from Cyrene, who came to Jerusalem at the Passover, or that he was originally from Cyrene, although then settled at Jerusalem, is uncertain. The latter seems the more likely opinion, as Simon's two sons, Alexander and Rufus, were certainly disciples of Christ; and it was perhaps the knowledge of this fact which led the Jews to incite the soldiers to lay on him the burden of the cross. The family of Simon seems to have resided afterwards at Rome; for St. Paul, in his epistle to the church there, salutes the wife of Simon with tenderness and respect, calling her his 'mother,' though he does not expressly name her: 'Salute Rufus, and his mother and mine' (Rom. xvi. 13).

9. SIMON THE TANNER, with whom St. Peter lodged at Joppa (Acts ix. 43; x. 6; xvii. 32). He was doubtless a disciple. His house was by the seaside, beyond the wall, as the trade of a tanner was one which the Jews did not allow to be carried on inside their towns.

10. SIMON MAGUS. In the eighth chapter of the Acts we read that Philip the Evangelist, whilst preaching the Gospel in a city of Samaria, came in contact with a person of the name of Simon, who had formerly exercised immense power over the minds of the people by his skill in the resources of magic. So high were the pretensions of this impostor, and so profound the impression he had made on the minds of the multitude, that they not only received with readiness all that he taught, but admitted his claim to be regarded as an incarnation of the demiurgic power of God. The doctrines of Philip, however, concerning Christ as the true and only incarnation of Deity, supported by the unparalleled and beneficent miracles which he performed, had the effect of dispelling this delusion, and inducing the people to renounce their allegiance to Simon and receive baptism as the disciples of Christ. On the mind of Simon himself so deep an impression was produced, that he professed himself a disciple of Jesus, and as such was baptized by Philip.

On the news of Philip's success reaching Jerusalem, Peter and John went down to Samaria to confer upon the new converts the spiritual gifts which were vouchsafed to the primitive churches. During their visit Simon discovered that by means of prayer and the imposition of hands the Apostles were able to dispense the power of the Holy Ghost; and supposing probably that in this lay the much-prized secret of their superior power, he attempted to induce them to impart to him this power by offering them money. This, which for such a man was a very natural act, intimated to the Apostles at once his true character (or rather, to express more accurately our conviction, it enabled them to manifest to the people and publicly to act upon what their own power of discerning spirits must have already taught them of his true character); and accordingly Peter indignantly repudiated his offer, proclaimed his utter want of all true knowledge of Christian doctrine, and exhorted him to repentance and to prayer for forgiveness. The words of Peter on this occasion, it is justly remarked by Neander, ' present the doctrine of the Gospel, which so expressly intimates the absolute necessity of a right state of mind for the reception of all that Christianity conveys, in direct opposition to the Magianism, which denies all necessary connection between the state of mind and that which is divine and supernatural, brings down the divine and supernatural within the sphere of ordinary nature, and imagines that divine power may be appropriated by means of something else than that which is allied to it in man's nature, and which supplies the only point of union between the two.' The solemn and threatening words of the Apostle struck dread into the bosom of the impostor, who besought the Apostle to pray for him that none of the things he had threatened might come upon him—an entreaty which shows that his mind still laboured under what Neander above describes as the chief error of the Magian doctrine.

After this we read no more of Simon Magus in the New Testament.

Simon's doctrines were substantially those of the Gnostics, and he is not without reason regarded as the first who attempted to engraft the theurgy and egotism of the Magian philosophy upon Christianity. He represented himself, according to Jerome, as the Word of God, the Perfection, the Paraclete, the Almighty, the All of Deity; and Irenæus (i. 20) tells us he carried with him a beautiful female named Helena, whom he set forth as the first idea of Deity. If this be not exaggerated fable on the part of his enemies, we must suppose that such modes of speech and representation were adopted by him as suited to the highly allegorical character of Orientalism in his day; for were we to suppose him to have meant such utterances to be taken literally, we should be constrained to look upon him in the light of a madman.

SIN, a city of Egypt, which is mentioned in Ezek. xxx. 15, 16, in connection with Thebes and Memphis, and is described as ' the strength of Egypt,' showing it to have been a fortified place. The Sept. makes it to have been Sais, but Jerome regards it as Pelusium. This latter identification has been generally adopted, and is scarcely open to dispute. Pelusium was anciently a place of great consequence. It was strongly fortified, being the bulwark of the Egyptian frontier on the eastern side, and was considered the ' key,' or, as the prophet terms it, ' the strength' of Egypt. It was near this place that Pompey met his death, being murdered by order of Ptolemy, whose protection he had claimed. It lay among swamps and morasses on the most easterly estuary of the Nile (which received from it the name of Ostium Pelusiacum), and stood twenty stades from the Mediterranean. The site is now only approachable by boats during a high Nile, or by land when the summer sun has dried the mud left by the inundation : the remains consist merely of mounds and a few fallen columns. The climate is very unwholesome.

SIN, the desert which the Israelites entered on turning off from the Red Sea (Exod. xvi. 1; xvii. 1; Num. xxxiii. 12) [SINAI].

SI'NAI. The Hebrew name, denoting a district of broken or cleft rocks, is descriptive of the region to which it is applied. That region, according to Exod. xix. 1; Lev. vii. 38; Num. i. 1, 3, 4, is a wild mountainous country in Arabia Petræa, whither the Israelites went from Rephidim, after they had been out of Egypt for the space of three months. Here the law was given to Moses, which fact renders this spot one of special and lasting interest. From the magnitude and prominence of the Sinaitic group of mountains, the entire district of which it forms a part has received the name of the peninsula of Sinai. This peninsula may be roughly described as formed by a line running from Suez to Ailah, all that lies on the south of this line falling within the peninsula. In the present day the name Sinai is given by Christians to the cluster of mountains to which we have referred; but the Arabs have no other name for this group than Jebel et-Tur, sometimes adding the distinctive epithet Sina. In a stricter sense the name Sinai is applied to a very lofty ridge which lies between the two parallel valleys of Shu'eib and el-Leja. Of this ridge the northern end is termed Horeb, the southern Sinai, now called Jebel Mûsa, or Moses' Mount. The entire district is a heap of lofty granite rocks, with steep gorges and deep valleys. The Sinai ridge, including Horeb, is at least three miles in length. It rises boldly and majestically from the southern end of the plain Rahah, which is two geographical miles long, and ranges in breadth from one-third to two-thirds of a mile, making at least one square mile. This space is nearly doubled by extensions of the valley on the west and east. ' The examination convinced us,' says Robinson (Biblical Researches, i. 141), ' that here was space enough to satisfy all the requisitions of the Scriptural narrative, so far as it relates to the assembling of the congregation to receive the law.' Water is abundant in this mountainous region, to which the Bedouins betake themselves when oppressed by drought in the lower lands. As there is water, so also is there in the valleys great fruitfulness and sometimes luxuriance of vegetation, as well as beauty. What was the exact locality from which the law was given, it may not be easy to ascertain. The book of Deuteronomy (i. 6; iv. 18, &c.) makes it to be Horeb, which seems most probable; for this, the north end of the range, rises immediately from the plain of which we have just spoken as the head-quarters of the Israelites. Sinai is, indeed, generally reputed to be the spot, and, as we have seen, the southern extremity of the range is denominated Moses' Mount; but this may have arisen from confounding together two meanings of Sinai, inasmuch as it denotes. 1, a district; 2, a particular part of that district. It was no doubt on Horeb, in the region of Sinai, that the law was promulgated. Robinson imputes the common error to tradition, and declares that ' there is not the slightest reason for supposing that Moses had anything to do with the summit which now bears his name. It is three miles distant from the plain on which the Israelites must have stood, and hidden from it by the intervening peaks of modern Horeb. No part of the plain is visible from the summit, nor are the bottoms of the adjacent valleys, nor is any spot to be seen around it where the people could have been assembled.' Robinson also ascended the northern extremity of the ridge, and had there a prospect which he thus describes: —' The whole plain, er-Râhah, lay spread out beneath our feet with the adjacent Wadys and mountains. Our conviction was strengthened that here, nor are one of the adjacent cliffs, was the spot where the Lord " descended in fire," and proclaimed the law. Here lay the plain where the whole congregation might be assembled; here was the mount that could be approached and touched, if not forbidden; and here the mountain brow where alone the lightnings and the thick cloud would be visible, and the thunders and the voice of the trump be heard when " the Lord came down in the sight of all the people upon Mount Sinai." We gave ourselves up to the impressions of the awful scene, and read, with a feeling that will never be forgotten, the sublime account of the transaction and the commandment there promulgated.'

Having thus given a general view of Sinai, we shall now briefly trace the Israelites in their journey to the mountain. Another article [WANDERING] will follow their course into the Land of Promise. When safe on the eastern shore, the Israelites, had they taken the shortest route into Palestine, would have struck at once across the desert in a south-easterly direction to el-Arish or Gaza. But this route would have brought them into direct collision with the Philistines, with whom they were as yet quite unable to cope. Or they might have traversed the desert of Paran, following the pilgrim road of the present day to Elath, and, turning to the north, have made for Palestine. In order to accomplish this, however, hostile hordes and nations would have to be encountered, whose superior skill and experience in war might have proved fatal to the newly liberated tribes of Israel. They were, therefore, wisely directed to take a course which necessitated the lapse of time, and gave promise of affording intellectual and moral discipline of the highest value.

Moses did not begin his arduous journey till, with a piety and a warmth of gratitude which well befitted the signal deliverance that his people had just been favoured with, he celebrated the power, majesty, and goodness of God in a triumphal ode, full of the most appropriate, striking, and splendid images; in which commemorative festivity he was assisted by ' Miriam the prophetess, the sister of Aaron,' and her associated female band, with poetry, music, and dancing. The spot where these rejoicings were held, could not have been far from that which still bears the name of Ayûn Mûsa, ' the fountains of Moses,' the situation of which is even now marked by a few palm-trees. This was a suitable place for the encampment, because well supplied with water. Here Robinson counted seven fountains, near which he saw a patch of barley, and a few cab-

bage plants. Hence the Israelites proceeded along the coast, three days' journey, into what is termed the wilderness of Shur. During this march they found no water. The district is hilly and sandy, with a few watercourses running into the Red Sea, which, failing rain, are dry. At the end of three days the Israelites reached the fountain Marah, but the waters were bitter, and could not be drunk. The stock which they had brought with them being now exhausted, they began to utter murmurings on finding themselves disappointed at Marah. Moses appealed to God, who directed him to a tree, which, being thrown into the waters, sweetened them. The people were satisfied and admonished. About this station authorities are agreed. It is identified with the fountain Hawârah. The basin is six or eight feet in diameter, and the water Robinson found about two feet deep. Its taste is unpleasant, saltish, and somewhat bitter.

The next station mentioned in Scripture is Elim, where were twelve wells of water, and three score and ten palm-trees. As is customary with travellers in these regions, ' they encamped there by the waters' (Exod. xvi. 1). This place is generally admitted to be Wady Ghurundel, lying about half a day's journey south-east from Marah. The way from Egypt to Sinai lies through this valley; and, on account of its water and verdure, it is a chief caravan station at the present day. From Elim the Israelites marched, encamping on the shore of the Red Sea, for which purpose they must have kept the high ground for some time, since the precipices of Jebel Hûmmâm —a lofty and precipitous mountain of chalky limestone—run down to the brink of the sea. They, therefore, went on the land side of this mountain to the head of Wady Taiyikeh, which passes down south-west through the mountains to the shore. On the plain at the mouth of this valley was the encampment ' by the Red Sea ' (Num. xxxiii. 10).

According to Num. xxxiii. 11, the Israelites removed from the Red Sea, and encamped next in the wilderness of Sin. This Robinson identifies with ' the great plain which, beginning near el-Mûrkhâh, extends with greater or less breadth almost to the extremity of the peninsula. In its broadest part it is called el-Kâa' (i. 106). Thus they kept along the shore, and did not yet ascend any of the fruitful valleys which run up towards the centre of the district. They arrived in the wilderness of Sin on the fifteenth day of the second month after their departure out of the land of Egypt; and being now wearied with their journey, and tired of their scanty fare, they began again to murmur. The contrast between the scant supply of the desert and the abundance of Egypt, furnished the immediate occasion of the outbreak of dissatisfaction. Bread and flesh were the chief demand; bread and flesh were miraculously supplied; the former by manna, the latter by quails.

The next station mentioned in Exodus is Rephidim; but in Num. xxxiii. Dophkah and Alush are added. The two latter were reached after the people had taken ' their journey out of the wilderness of Sin.' Dophkah is probably to be found near the spot where Wady Feirân runs into the gulf of Suez. Alush may have lain on the shore near Ras Jehan. From this point a range of calcareous rocks, termed Jebal Hemam, stretches along the shore, near the southern end of which the Hebrews took a sudden turn to the north-east, and, going up Wady Hibrân, reached the central Sinaitic district.

This was the last station before Sinai itself was reached. Naturally enough is it recorded, that ' there was no water for the people to drink.' The road was an arid gravelly plain ; on either side were barren rocks. A natural supply was impossible. A miracle was wrought, and water was given. The Scripture makes it clear that it was from the Sinaitic group that the water was produced (Exod. xvii. 6). The plain received two descriptive names—Massah, ' Temptation;' and Meribah, ' Strife.' It appears that the congregation was not allowed to pursue their way to Sinai unmolested. The Arabs thought the Israelites suitable for plunder, and fell upon them. These hordes are termed Amalekites. It appears that the conflict was a severe and doubtful one, which, by some extraordinary aid, ended in favour of the children of Israel. This aggression on the part of Amalek gave occasion to a permanent national hatred, which ended only in the extermination of the tribe (Num. xxiv. 20 ; Exod. xvii. 14-16). In commemoration of this victory Moses was commanded to write an account of it in a book : he also erected there an altar to Jehovah, and called the name of it ' Jehovah, my banner.'

SI'NIM, a people whose country, ' land of Sinim,' is mentioned only in Isa. xlix. 12, where the context implies a remote region, situated in the eastern or southern extremity of the earth. Many Biblical geographers think this may possibly denote the Sinese or Chinese, whose country is Sina, China. This view is not void of probability, but objections to it are obvious and considerable. Some, therefore, think that by the Sinim the inhabitants of Pelusium (Sin) are, by synecdoche, denoted for the Egyptians. But as the text seems to point to a region more distant, others have upheld the claims of the people of Syene, taken to represent the Ethiopians [SYENE].

SIN'ITES, a people probably near Mount Lenon (Gen. x. 17 ; 1 Chron. i. 15).

SISERA (*battle-array*), the general in command of the mighty army of the Canaanitish king Jabin. As this is the only instance in those early times of armies being commanded by other than kings in person, the circumstance, taken in connection with others, intimates that Sisera was a general eminent for his abilities and success. He was, however, defeated by Barak, and slain (Judg. iv. 2-22), under the circumstances which have been described in the article JAEL.

SI'VAN, the third month of the Hebrew year, from the new moon of June to the new moon of July.

SLAVE (Auth. Eng. Version, *servant* and *bondman*). It is difficult to trace the origin of slavery. It may have existed before the deluge, when violence filled the earth, and drew upon it the vengeance of God. But the first direct reference to slavery, or rather slave-trading, in the Bible, is found in the history of Joseph, who was sold by his brethren to the Ishmaelites (Gen. xxxvii. 27, 28). In Ezek. xxvii. 12, 13, we find a reference to the slave-trade carried on with Tyre by Javan, Tubal, and Meshech. And in the Apocalypse we find enumerated in the merchandise of the mystic Babylon, *slaves* and the souls of men (Rev. xviii. 13).

The sacred historians refer to various kinds of bondage :—

1. *Patriarchal Servitude.*—The exact nature of this service cannot be defined : there can be no doubt, however, that it was regulated by principles of justice, equity, and kindness. The servants of the patriarchs were of two kinds, those ' born in the house,' and those ' bought with money ' (Gen. xvii. 13). The servants born in the house were perhaps entitled to greater privileges than the others. Eliezer of Damascus, a home-born servant, was Abraham's steward, and, in default of issue, would have been his heir (Gen. xv. 2-4). This class of servants was honoured with the most intimate confidence of their masters, and was employed in the most important services. An instance of this kind will be found in Gen. xxiv. 1-9, where the eldest or chief servant of Abraham's house, who ruled over all that he had, was sent to Mesopotamia to select a wife for Isaac, who was then forty years of age. The servants of Abraham were admitted into the same religious privileges with their master, and received the seal of the covenant (Gen. xvii. 9, 14, 24, 27).

There is a clear distinction made between the ' servants ' of Abraham and the things which constituted his property or wealth. Abraham was very rich in cattle, in silver, and in gold (Gen. xiii. 2, 5). But when the patriarch's power or greatness is spoken of, then servants are spoken of as well as the objects which constituted his riches (Gen. xxiv. 34, 35). A similar distinction is made in the case of Isaac and of Jacob. In no single instance do we find that the patriarchs either gave away or sold their servants, or purchased them of *third* persons. Abraham had servants ' bought with money.' It has been assumed that they were bought of third parties, whereas there is no proof that this was the case. The probability is that they sold themselves to the patriarch for an equivalent; that is to say, they entered into voluntary engagements to serve him for a longer or shorter period of time, in return for the money advanced them. Probably Job had more servants than either of the patriarchs to whom reference has been made (Job i. 2, 3). In what light he regarded, and how he treated, his servants. may be gathered from Job xxxi. 13-23. And that Abraham acted in the same spirit, we have the Divine testimony. in Jer. xxii. 15, 16, 17, where his conduct is placed in direct contrast with that of some of his descendants, who used their neighbour's service without wages, and gave him not for his work (ver. 13).

2. *Egyptian Bondage.*—The Israelites were frequently reminded, after their exode from Egypt, of the oppressions they endured in that ' house of bondage,' from which they had been delivered by the direct interposition of God. The design of these admonitions was to teach them justice and kindness towards their servants when they should become settled in Canaan, as well as to impress them with gratitude towards their great deliverer. The Egyptians had domestic servants, who may have been slaves (Exod. ix. 14, 20, 21 ; xi. 5). But the Israelites were not dispersed among the families of Egypt; they formed a special community. They had exclusive possession of the land of Goshen, ' the best'

part of the land of Egypt.' They lived in permanent dwellings, their own houses, and not in tents. Each family seems to have had its own house; and judging from the regulations about eating the Passover, they could scarcely have been small ones. They appear to have been well clothed. They owned ' flocks and herds, and very much cattle' They had their own form of government, and, although occupying a province of Egypt, and *tributary* to it, they preserved their tribes and family divisions, and their internal organization throughout. They had to a considerable degree the disposal of their own time. They were not unacquainted with the fine arts. They were all armed. The women seem to have known something of domestic refinement. They were familiar with instruments of music, and skilled in the working of fine fabrics; and both males and females were able to read and write. Their food was abundant and of great variety. The service required from the Israelites by their task-masters seems to have been exacted from males only, and probably a portion only of the people were compelled to labour at any one time. As tributaries, they probably supplied levies of men, from which the wealthy appear to have been exempted. The poor were the oppressed; ' and all the service wherewith they made them serve was with rigour.' But Jehovah saw their ' afflictions and heard their groanings,' and delivered them, after having inflicted the most terrible plagues on their oppressors.

3. *Jewish Servitude.*—Whatever difficulties may be found in indicating the precise nature of patriarchal servitude, none exists in reference to that which was sanctioned and regulated by the Mosaic institutes.

The moral law is a revelation of great principles. It requires supreme love to God and universal love among men; and whatever is incompatible with the exercise of that love, is strictly forbidden and condemned. Hence, immediately after the giving of the law at Sinai, as if to guard against all slavery and slave-trading on the part of the Israelites, God promulgated this ordinance: ' He that stealeth a man and selleth him, or if he be found in his hands, he shall surely be put to death' (Exod. xxi. 16; Deut. xxiv. 7). The crime is stated in its threefold form, man-*stealing*, *selling*, and *holding;* the penalty for either of which was DEATH. The law punished the stealing of mere property by enforcing restitution, in some cases twofold, in others fivefold (Exod. xxii. 14). When property was stolen, the legal penalty was compensation to the person injured; but when a man was stolen, no property compensation was allowed; death was inflicted, and the guilty offender paid the forfeit of his life for his transgression. Such was the operation of this law, and the obedience paid to it, that we have not the remotest hint that the sale and purchase of slaves ever occurred among the Israelites. The cities of Judæa were not, like the cities of Greece and Rome, slave-markets; nor were there found throughout all its coasts either helots or slaves. With the Israelites, service was either voluntary, or judicially imposed by the law of God (Lev. xxv. 39, 47; Exod. xxi. 7; xxii. 3, 4; Deut. xx. 14). Strangers only, or the descendants of strangers, became their possession by purchase (Lev. xxv. 44-46); but, however acquired, the

law gave the Jewish servants many rights and privileges; they were admitted into covenant with God; they were guests at all the national and family festivals. they were statedly instructed in morals and religion; and they were released from their regular labour nearly one-half of their term of servitude. The servants of the Israelites were protected by the law equally with their masters, and their civil and religious rights were the same. Finally, these servants had the power of changing their masters, and of seeking protection where they pleased (Deut. xxiii. 15, 16); and should their masters, by any act of violence, injure their persons, they were released from their engagements (Exod. xxi. 26, 27). The term of Hebrew servitude was six years, beyond which they could not be held unless they entered into new engagements (Exod. xxi. 1-11 : Deut. xv. 12); while that of strangers, over whom the rights of the master were comparatively absolute (Lev. xxv. 44-46), terminated in every case on the return of the jubilee, when liberty was proclaimed to all (Lev. xxv. 8, 10, 54).

4 *Gibeonitish Servitude.*—The condition of the inhabitants of Gibeon, Chephirah, Beeroth, and Kirjath-jearim, under the Hebrew commonwealth, was not that of slavery. It was voluntary (Josh ix. 8-11). They were not employed in the families of the Israelites, but resided in their own cities, tended their own flocks and herds, and exercised the functions of a distinct though not independent community (Josh. x. 6-18). The injuries inflicted on them by Saul were avenged by the Almighty on his descendants (2 Sam. xxi. 1-9). They appear to have been devoted exclusively to the service of the ' house of God' or the Tabernacles, and only a few of them comparatively could have been engaged at any one time. The rest dwelt in their cities, one of which was a great city, as one of the royal cities. The service they rendered may be regarded as a natural tribute for the privilege of protection. No service seems to have been required of their wives and daughters.

The laws which the great Deliverer and Redeemer of mankind gave for the government of his kingdom, were those of universal justice and benevolence, and as such were subversive of every system of tyranny and oppression. To suppose, therefore, as has been rashly asserted, that Jesus or his Apostles gave their sanction to the existing systems of slavery among the Greeks and Romans, is to dishonour them. That the reciprocal duties of masters and servants were inculcated, admits, indeed, of no doubt (Col. iii. 22; iv. 1; Tit. ii. 9; 1 Pet. ii. 18: Eph. vi. 5-9). But the performance of these duties on the part of the masters, supposing them to have been slave-masters, would have been tantamount to the utter subversion of the relation. There can be no doubt either that ' servants under the yoke,' or the slaves of heathens, are exhorted to yield obedience to their masters (1 Tim. vi. 1). But this argues no approval of the relation; for, 1. Jesus, in an analogous case, appeals to the paramount law of nature as superseding such temporary regulations as the ' hardness of men's hearts' had rendered necessary, and, 2. St. Paul, while counselling the duties of contentment and submission under inevitable bondage, inculcates at the same time on the slave the duty of adopting all legitimate means of obtaining his freedom (1 Cor. vii. 18-20).

5. *Roman Slavery.*—Our limits will not allow us to enter into detail on the only kind of slavery referred to in the New Testament, for there is no indication that the Jews possessed any slaves in the time of Christ. Suffice it therefore to say, that, in addition to the fact that Roman slavery was perpetual and hereditary, the slave had no protection whatever against the avarice, rage, or lust of his master. The bondsman was viewed less as a human being, subject to arbitrary dominion, than as an inferior animal, dependent wholly on the will of his owner. The master possessed the uncontrolled power of life and death over his slave,—a power which continued at least to the time of the emperor Hadrian. He might, and frequently did, kill, mutilate, and torture his slaves, for any or for no offence; so that slaves were sometimes crucified from mere caprice. He might force them to become prostitutes or gladiators; and, instead of the perpetual obligation of the marriage tie, their temporary unions were formed and dissolved at his command, families and friends were separated, and no obligation existed to provide for their wants in sickness or in health. But, notwithstanding all the barbarous cruelties of Roman slavery, it had one decided advantage over that which was introduced in modern times into European colonies, both law and custom being decidedly favourable to the freedom of the slave. The Mahommedan law also, in this respect, contrasts favourably with those of the European settlements.

Although the condition of the Roman slaves was no doubt improved under the emperors, the early effects of Christian principles were manifest in mitigating the horrors, and bringing about the gradual abolition of slavery. 'It is not,' says Robertson, 'the authority of any single detached precept in the Gospel, but the spirit and genius of the Christian religion, more powerful than any particular command, which has abolished the practice of slavery throughout the world.' Although, even in the most corrupt times of the church, the operation of Christian principles tended to this benevolent object, they unfortunately did not prevent the revival of slavery in the European settlements in the sixteenth and seventeenth centuries, together with that nefarious traffic, the suppression of which has rendered the name of Wilberforce for ever illustrious. Modern servitude had all the characteristic evils of the Roman, except, perhaps, the uncontrolled power of life and death, while it was destitute of that redeeming quality to which we have referred, its tendency being to perpetuate the condition of slavery. It has also been supposed to have introduced the unfortunate prejudice of colour, which was unknown to the ancients. It was the benevolent wish of the philosophic Herder that the time might come 'when we shall look back with as much compassion on our inhuman traffic in negroes, as on the ancient Roman slavery or Spartan helots.' This is now no longer a hope, so far as England is concerned, as she not only set the example of abolishing the traffic, but evinced the soundness of her Christian principles by the greatest national act of justice which history has yet recorded in the total abolition of slavery throughout all her dependencies.

SLIME. [ASPHALTUM.]

SMITH. The word so rendered literally signifies *a workman* in stone, wood, or metal, but is sometimes more accurately defined by what follows. The first smith mentioned in Scripture is Tubal-Cain. whom some writers, arguing from the similarity of the names, identify with Vulcan. He is said to have been 'an instructor of every artificer in brass and iron' (Gen. iv. 22), or perhaps more properly, a whetter or sharpener of every instrument of copper or iron. As the art of the smith is one of the first essentials to civilization, the mention of its founder was worthy of a place among the other fathers of inventions. So requisite was the trade of a smith in ancient warfare, that conquerors removed these artizans from a vanquished nation, in order the more effectually to disable it. Thus the Philistines deprived the Hebrews of their smiths (1 Sam. xiii. 19; comp. Judg. v. 8). So Nebuchadnezzar, king of Babylon, treated them in later times (2 Kings xxiv. 14; Jer. xxiv. 1; xxix. 2). In the New Testament we meet with Demetrius, 'the silversmith,' at Ephesus; but the commentators are not agreed whether he was a manufacturer of small silver models of the Temple of Diana, or at least of the chapel which contained the famous statue of the goddess, to be sold to foreigners, or used in private devotion, or taken with them by travellers as a safeguard; or whether he made large *coins* representing the temple and image. A *coppersmith* named Alexander is mentioned as an opponent of St. Paul (2 Tim. iv. 14) [COAL; IRON; METALS].

SMYR'NA, a celebrated commercial city of Ionia, situated near the bottom of that gulf of the Ægean Sea which received its name from it, at the mouth of the small river Meles, and 320 stades north of Ephesus. It is in N. lat. 38° 26', E. long. 27° 7'. Smyrna was a very ancient city, but having been destroyed by the Lydians it lay waste 400 years, to the time of Alexander the Great. It was rebuilt at the distance of twenty stades from the ancient city, and we soon find it flourishing greatly; and in the time of the first Roman emperors it was one of the finest cities of Asia. It was at this period that it became the seat of a Christian church, which is noticed in the Apocalypse, as one of' the seven churches of Asia' (Rev. i. 11; ii. 8-11). It was destroyed by an earthquake in A.D. 177; but the emperor Marcus Aurelius caused it to be rebuilt with even more than its former splendour. It afterwards, however, suffered greatly from earthquakes and conflagrations, and must be regarded as having declined much from its ancient importance, although from the convenience of its situation it has still maintained its rank as a great city and the central emporium of the Levantine trade. The Turks call it Izmir. It is a better built town than Constantinople, and in proportion to its size there are few places in the Turkish dominions which have so large a population. It is computed at 130,000 of which the Franks compose a far greater proportion than in any other town of Turkey; and they are generally in good circumstances. Next to the Turks the Greeks form the most numerous class of inhabitants, and they have a bishop and two churches. The unusually large proportion

3 B

of Christians in the town renders it peculiarly unclean in the eyes of strict Moslems, whence it has acquired among them the name of Giaour Izmir, or Infidel Smyrna. There are in it 20,000 Greeks, 8000 Armenians, 1000 Europeans, and 9000 Jews: the rest are Moslems.

The prosperity of Smyrna is now rather on the increase than the decline.

It stands at the foot of a range of mountains, which enclose it on three sides. The only ancient ruins are upon the mountains behind the town, and to the south. But nearly the whole of the relics of antiquity have been carried away. The stadium, of which the ground-plot only remains, is supposed to be the place where Polycarp, the disciple of St. John, and probably 'the angel of the church of Smyrna' (John ii. 8), to whom the Apocalyptic message was addressed, suffered martyrdom. The Christians of Smyrna hold the memory of this venerable person in high honour, and go annually in procession to his supposed tomb, which is at a short distance from the place of martyrdom.

SNAIL. Snails and slugs are not very common in countries so dry in summer as Palestine. Hence, perhaps, the fact, that there is only one allusion to them in Scripture. This occurs in Psalm lviii. 8, where the figure seems to be more significant, if understood of snails without shells, i. e. slugs, rather than shell-snails, though true of both.

SO, a king of Egypt, whom Hoshea, the last king of Israel, called to his help against the Assyrians under Shalmaneser (2 Kings xvii. 4). It has been questioned whether this So was the same with Sabaco, the first king of the Ethiopian dynasty in Upper Egypt, or his son and successor Sevechus, the second king of the same dynasty, and the immediate predecessor of Tirhakah.

SOAP. The word thus translated in the Auth. Version is in Hebrew *borith*. It occurs in two passages of Scripture—first, in Jerem. ii. 22, 'For though thou wash thee with nitre, and take thee much sope (*borith*), yet thine iniquity is marked before me, saith the Lord God;' and again, in Malachi iii. 2, 'But who may abide the day of his coming? and who shall stand when he appeareth? for he is like a refiner's fire, and like fuller's sope (*borith*).' From neither of these passages does it distinctly appear whether the substance referred to by the name of *borith* was obtained from the mineral or from the vegetable kingdom. But it is evident that it was possessed of cleansing properties.

In the above passage of Jeremiah we have *neter* (nitre) and *borith* (soap) indicated as being both employed for washing, or possessed of some cleansing properties; and yet, from occurring in the same passage, they must have differed in some respects. The nitre is, without doubt, the natural carbonate of soda; and as this is alluded to in one member of the sentence, it becomes probable that the artificial carbonates may be alluded to in the other, as both were in early times employed by Asiatic nations for the purposes of washing.

Hence it is probable that the ashes of plants, called *boruk* and *boreh* by Asiatic nations, may be alluded to under the name of *borith*, as there is no proof that soap is intended, though it may have been known to the same people at very early periods. Still less is it probable that borax is

meant, as has been supposed by some authors, apparently from the mere similarity of name.

SODOM, a city in the vale of Siddim, where Lot settled after his separation from Abraham (Gen. xiii. 12; xiv. 12: xix. 1). It had its own chief or 'king,' as had the other four cities of the plain (Gen. xiv. 2, 8, 10), and was along with them, Zoar only excepted, destroyed by fire from heaven, on account of the gross wickedness of the inhabitants; the memory of which event has been perpetuated in a name of infamy to all generations (Gen. xix.). The destruction of Sodom claims attention from the solemnity with which it is introduced (Gen. xviii. 20-22); from the circumstances which preceded and followed—the intercession of Abraham, the preservation of Lot, and the judgment which overtook his lingering wife (Gen. xviii. 25-33; xix.); and from the nature of the physical agencies through which the overthrow was effected. It has usually been assumed that the vale of Siddim occupied the basin of what is now the Dead Sea, which did not previously exist, but was one of the results of this catastrophe. It has now, however, been established by Dr. Robinson, that a lake to receive the Jordan and other waters must have occupied this basin long before the catastrophe of Sodom, but of much less extent than the present Dead Sea. It is extremely probable that its southern extremity covers the once fertile vale of Siddim, and the site of Sodom and the other cities which the Lord destroyed; and that, in the words of Dr. Robinson—'by some convulsion or catastrophe of nature, connected with the miraculous destruction of the cities, either the surface of this plain was scooped out, or the bottom of the sea was heaved up, so as to cause the waters to overflow, and cover permanently a larger tract than formerly. The country is, as we know, subject to earthquakes, and exhibits also frequent traces of volcanic action. It would have been no uncommon effect of either of these causes to heave up the bottom of the ancient lake, and thus produce the phenomenon in question. But the historical account of the destruction of the cities implies also the agency of fire. Perhaps both causes were therefore at work; for volcanic action and earthquakes go hand in hand; and the accompanying electric discharges usually cause lightnings to play and thunders to roll. In this way we have all the phenomena which the most literal interpretation of the sacred records can demand.'

SOLOMON (*pacific*). The reign of Solomon over all Israel, although second in importance only to that of David, has so little variety of incident as to occupy a far less space in the Bible narrative. In the declining age of David, his eldest surviving son, Adonijah, endeavoured to place himself on the throne, by the aid of Joab the chief captain, and Abiathar one of the chief priests, both of whom had been associated with David's early sufferings under the persecution of Saul. The aged monarch did not for a moment give way to the formidable usurpation, but at the remonstrance of his favourite, Bathsheba, resolved forthwith to raise her son Solomon to the throne. To Joab he was able to oppose the celebrated name of Benaiah; to Abiathar his colleague Zadok and the aged prophet Nathan. The plot of Adonijah was at once defeated by this decisive measure; and Solomon, being anointed by Nathan, was solemnly acknowledged as king. The date of this event is, as nearly as can be ascertained, B.C. 1015. The death of David would seem to have followed very quick upon these transactions. At least, no public measures in the interval are recorded, except Solomon's verbal forgiveness of Adonijah. But after the removal of David, the first events of which we hear are the destruction of Adonijah, Joab, and Shimei son of Gera, with the degradation of Abiathar.

After this the history enters upon a general narrative of the reign of Solomon; but we have very few notices of time, and cannot attempt to fix the order of any of the events. All the information, however, which we have concerning him may be consolidated under the following heads : (1) his traffic and wealth ; (2) his buildings; (3) his ecclesiastical arrangements ; (4) his general administration ; (5) his seraglio; (6) his enemies.

(1.) The overflowing wealth in which he is so vividly depicted is not easy to reduce to a modern financial estimate ; partly because the numbers are so often treacherous, and partly because it is uncertain what items of expenditure fell on the general funds of the government. But abandoning all attempt at numerical estimates, it cannot be doubted that the wealth of Solomon was very great.

The profound peace which the nation enjoyed as a fruit of David's victories stimulated the industry of all Israel. The tribes beyond the Jordan had become rich by the plunder of the Hagarenes, and had a wide district where their cattle might multiply to an indefinite extent. The agricultural tribes enjoyed a soil and climate in some parts eminently fruitful, and in all richly rewarding the toil of irrigation; so that, in the security of peace, nothing more was wanted to develope the resources of the nation than markets for its various produce. In food for men and cattle, in timber and fruit trees, in stone, and probably in the useful metals, the land supplied of itself all the first wants of its people in abundance. For exportation, it is distinctly stated that wheat, barley, oil, and wine, were in chief demand ; to which we may conjecturally add, wool, hides, and other raw materials. The king undoubtedly had large districts and extensive herds of his own ; but besides this, he received presents *in kind* from his own people and from the subject nations. He was himself at once monarch and merchant. By his intimate commercial union with the Tyrians he was put into the most favourable of all positions for disposing of his goods ; and by the aid of their enterprise and experience carried on a lucrative trade with various countries.

The visit of the Queen of Sheba to Solomon, although not strictly commercial, rose out of commercial intercourse, and may perhaps be here noticed. The territory of Sheba, according to Strabo, reached so far north as to meet that of the Nabathæans, although its proper seat was at the southernmost angle of Arabia. The very rich presents made by the queen show the extreme value of her commerce with the Hebrew monarch ; and this early interchange of hospitality derives a peculiar interest from the fact, that in much later ages—those of the Maccabees and downwards—the intercourse of the Jews with Sheba became so intimate, and their influence,

and even power, so great. Jewish circumcision took root there, and princes held sway who were called Jewish.

(2.) Besides the great work which has rendered the name of Solomon so famous—the Temple at Jerusalem—we are informed of the palaces which he built, viz., his own palace, the queen's palace, and the house of the forest of Lebanon, his porch (or piazza) for no specified object, and his porch of judgment, or law court. He also added to the walls of Jerusalem, and fortified Millo ('in the city of David,' 2 Chron. xxxii. 5), and many other strongholds. In all these works he had the aid of the Tyrians, whose skill in hewing timber and in carving stone, and in the application of machines for conveying heavy masses, was of the first importance.

(3.) The ecclesiastical arrangements of Solomon were of the most magnificent description, and for a time he zealously worshipped and faithfully served the God of his fathers. But after the death of Nathan and Zadok, those faithful friends of David, 'his wives turned away his heart after other gods, and his heart was not perfect with the Lord as was the heart of David his father' (1 Kings xi. 1-8). Side by side with the worship of Jehovah foreign idolatries were established ; and the disgust which this inspired in the prophets of Jehovah is clearly seen in the address of Ahijah the Shilonite to Jeroboam, so manifestly exciting him to rebel against the son of David (1 Kings xi. 29-39).

(4.) Concerning his general administration little is recorded beyond the names of various high officers. But it is probable that Solomon's peculiar talents and taste led him to perform one function which is always looked for in Oriental royalty, viz., to act personally as *Judge* in cases of oppression. His award between the two contending mothers cannot be regarded as an isolated fact : and 'the porch of judgment' which he built for himself may imply that he devoted fixed portions of time to the judicial duties (see 2 Kings xv. 5, of Jotham). The celebrity which Solomon gained for wisdom, although founded mainly perhaps on his political and commercial sagacity, must have received great popular impetus from his administration of law, and from his readiness in seeing through the entanglements of affairs which arise in commercial transactions.

(5.) For the harem of Solomon—consisting of 700 wives and 300 concubines—no other apology can be made, than the fact, that in countries where polygamy is not disreputable, an unlimited indulgence as to the number of wives is looked upon as the chief luxury of wealth, and the most appropriate appendage to royalty.

The commercial union of Tyre with Egypt, in spite of the vast diversity of genius between the two nations, was in those days very close; and it appears highly probable that the affinity to Pharaoh was sought by Solomon as a means of aiding his commercial projects. Although his possession of the Edomite ports on the gulf of Akabah made him to a certain extent independent of Egypt, the friendship of that power must have been of extreme importance to him in the dangerous navigation of the Red Sea ; and was perhaps a chief cause of his brilliant success in so new an enterprise. That Pharaoh continued for some time on good terms with him, appears from a singular present which the Egyptian king made him (1 Kings ix. 16): 'Pharaoh had gone up and taken Gezer, and burnt it with fire, and slain the Canaanites that dwelt in the city, and given it for a present unto his daughter, Solomon's wife;' in consequence of which Solomon rebuilt and fortified the town. In his declining years a very different spirit is manifested towards him by Shishak, the new Egyptian king; whether after the death of the princess who had been the link between the two kingdoms, or from a different view of policy in the new king, is unknown.

(6.) The enemies especially named as rising against him in his later years, are Jeroboam, Hadad the Edomite, and Rezon of Damascus. The first is described as having had no treasonable intentions, until Solomon sought to kill him, on learning the prophecy made to him by Ahijah. Jeroboam was received and fostered by Shishak, king of Egypt, and ultimately became the providential instrument of punishing Solomon's iniquity, though not without heavy guilt of his own. As for Hadad, his enmity to Israel began from the times of David, and is ascribed to the savage butchery perpetrated by Joab on his people. He also, when a mere child, was warmly received in Egypt, apparently by the father-in-law of Solomon; but this does not seem to have been prompted by hostility to David. Having married the sister of Pharaoh's queen, he must have been in very high station in Egypt; still, upon the death of David, he begged leave to depart into Edom, and during the earlier part of Solomon's reign was probably forming his party in secret, and preparing for that dangerous border warfare which he carried on somewhat later. Rezon, on the contrary, seems to have had no personal cause against the Hebrew monarchy; but having become powerful at Damascus and on its frontier, sought, not in vain, to aggrandize himself at its expense. The revenues which would have maintained it were spent on a thousand royal wives: the king himself was unwarlike; and a petty foe, if energetic, was very formidable. Such were the vexations which darkened the setting splendours of the greatest Israelitish king. But from within also his prosperity was unsound. Deep discontent pervaded his own people, when the dazzle of his grandeur had become familiar; when it had become clear, that the royal wealth, instead of denoting national well being, was really sucked out of the nation's vitals. Having no constitutional organ to express their discontent, they waited sullenly, until the recognition of a successor to the crown should give them the opportunity of extorting a removal of burdens which could not permanently be endured.

SOLOMON'S SONG. [CANTICLES.]

SONG. [POETRY.]

SOOTHSAYER. [DIVINATION.]

SOP'ATER, a Christian at Berœa, and one of the party of brethren who accompanied Paul into Asia Minor from Greece (Acts xx. 4). He is supposed to be the same with the Sosipater named in Rom. xvi. 21; and, if so, was a kinsman of St. Paul.

SORCERER. [DIVINATION.]

SO'REK, a valley, probably so called from its vineyards (Judg. xvi. 4). Eusebius and Jerome place it north of Eleutheropolis, and near to Zorah.

SOSIP'ATER. [SOPATER.]

SOS'THENES, the chief of the synagogue at Corinth, when Paul was in that city on his second journey into Greece (Acts xviii. 17). He was seized and beaten by the people, before the judgment-seat of Gallio, on account of the tumult raised by the Jews against Paul, of which he seems to have been one of the leaders. He is supposed to have been afterwards converted to Christianity, as a Sosthenes is mentioned by Paul as 'a brother,' and coupled with himself in 1 Cor. i. 1. This identity is, however, a pure conjecture, and not remarkably probable; but apart from it, we know nothing of this second Sosthenes. Eusebius makes him one of the seventy disciples, and later tradition describes him as bishop of Kolophon.

SOUL. The present article is a sequel to that on PUNISHMENT, in which the *literature* only of the question concerning *future punishment* will be briefly stated. The literature of the question concerning the nature and duration of future punishment consists of the following particulars. First, its duration was believed by the heathens to be eternal. Secondly, there is a still more striking similarity between the descriptions both of the nature and duration of future punishment given in the Apocryphal books and those of the New Testament. Thus Judith xvi. 17: 'Woe to the nations which rise up against my kindred! the Lord Almighty will take vengeance on them in the day of judgment, in putting fire and worms in their flesh; and they shall feel them, and weep for ever' (comp. Ecclus. vii. 17; Mark ix. 44). These terms seem *borrowed* from Isaiah's description of a different subject (ch. lxvi. 24). Thirdly, Josephus describes the doctrine of everlasting punishment as being held by the Pharisees and Essenes: 'that the souls of the wicked should be punished with perpetual punishment, and that there was appointed for them a perpetual prison' (*De Bell. Jud.* ii. 8. 11, 14; *Antiq.* xviii. 1. 3). In the New Testament the *nature* of future punishment is almost always described by figures. The most abstract description occurs in Rom. ii. 9-16: 'Tribulation and anguish upon every soul of man that doeth evil, in the day when God shall judge the secrets of men.' Our Lord generally describes it under figures suggested by some comparison he had just before made, and in unison with it. Thus, having described future happiness under the figure of a midnight banquet, lighted up with lamps, then the state of the rejected is described under that of 'outer darkness' outside the mansion, and 'gnashing' or chattering 'of teeth,' from the extreme cold of an Oriental night (Matt. viii. 12: Luke xiii. 28). If 'the end of the world' be described by him under the figure of a harvest, then the wicked, who are represented by the tares, are accordingly gathered and burned. Our Lord also frequently represents future punishment under the idea of fire, which Calvin, on Isa. lxvi. 24, remarks, must be understood metaphorically of spiritual punishment. Indeed both the *nature* and *variety* of the figures employed by our Saviour in regard to the subject fully justify Paley's observation, 'that our Lord's discourses exhibit no particular description of the invisible world. The future happiness of the good and the future misery of the bad, which is all we want to be assured of, is directly and positively affirmed, and is represented by metaphors and comparisons which were plainly intended as metaphors and comparisons, and nothing more. As to the rest a solemn reserve is maintained ' (*Evidences of Christianity*, part ii. ch. ii.). The question of the *duration* of future punishment chiefly turns on the force of the words translated 'ever,' 'everlasting,' 'never,' which our Lord and his apostles apply to it, and which it is well known have sometimes a limited signification, and are very variously translated in the English version. Hence, therefore, it is urged on the one side, that we can never settle the precise import of these words, as applied in the New Testament to the duration of future punishment, until we shall be able also to answer the following questions; namely, Was it part of the commission of Christ and his apostles to determine this matter? and if so, In what sense were the terms they used in regard to it meant by themselves, and understood by their hearers—whether as denoting a punishment of *unknown* duration, or one literally co-existent with the duration of the Eternal God? On the other side it is objected, that the same word is applied both to the happiness of the righteous and the misery of the wicked, though varied in our translation of Matt. xxv. 46: 'These shall go away into everlasting punishment, but the righteous into life eternal.' Upon this truly important subject we cordially acquiesce in the remark of Doddridge: ' Miserable are they who venture their souls upon the possibility that the words in question, when applied to future punishment, may have a limited meaning.'

SOUTH. The country, or quarter of the heavens, which the Shemite, standing with his face to the east, supposes to be on his right hand. An important use of the word is as the name or designation of the desert regions lying at the south of Judæa, consisting of the deserts of Shur, Zin, and Paran, the mountainous country of Edom or Idumæa, and part of Arabia Petræa (Gen. xii. 9; xiii. 1). In this region the Amalekites are said to have dwelt, 'in the land of the south,' when Moses sent the spies to view the land of Canaan (Num. xiii. 29), viz., the locality between Idumæa and Egypt, and to the east of the Dead Sea and Mount Seir [AMALEKITES]. The inhabitants of this region were included in the conquests of Joshua (x. 40). To the same region belongs the passage, 'Turn our captivity as the streams in the south' (Ps. cxxvi. 4); which suddenly fill the wadys or valleys during the season of rain (comp. Ezek. vi. 3; xxxiv. 13; xxxv. 8; xxxvi. 4, 6). These are dry in summer (Job vi. 15-18). Through part of this sterile region the Israelites must repass in their vain application to Egypt. It is called the Wilderness of Judæa (Matt. iii. 1; Josh. xv. 61). Through part of this region lay the road from Jerusalem to Gaza, 'which is desert' (Acts viii. 26).

SOWER, SOWING. [AGRICULTURE.]

SPAIN (Rom. xv. 24, 28). This name was anciently applied to the whole Peninsula which now comprises Spain and Portugal. In the time of Paul Spain was a Roman province, and many Jews appear to have settled there. It seems clear from Rom. xv. 24, 28, that Paul formed the design of proceeding to preach the Gospel in Spain: that he ever executed this intention is necessarily denied by those who hold that the apostle sustained but one imprisonment at Rome,

namely, that in which the Acts of the Apostles leave him; and even those who hold that he was released from this imprisonment can only conjecture that, in the interval between it and the second, he fulfilled his intention. There is, in fact, during the three first centuries, no evidence on the subject, beyond a vague intimation by Clement, which is open to different explanations [PAUL]; and later traditions are of small value.

SPARROW occurs in Gen. vii. 14; Lev. xiv. 4; Ps. lxxxiv. 3; cii. 7; Matt. x. 29; Luke xii. 6, 7. The Hebrew word includes not only the sparrow, but also the whole family of small birds not exclusively feeding on grain, but denominated clean, or those that might be eaten according to the law. It includes many insectivorous and frugivorous species, all the thrushes we have in Europe, and the rose-coloured ousel or locust-bird, rare with us, but numerous and cherished in the East, solely for the havoc it makes among locusts. It also includes perhaps the starlings, the nightingale, all the European larks, the wagtails, and all the tribe of finches; but not fly-catchers, nor indeed swallows, which, there is reason to believe, were reckoned, along with night-hawks or goatsuckers, and crows, among the unclean and prohibited species. In Syria the sparrow is the same vivacious familiar bird we find it in Europe, and equally frequents the residence of man.

SPEAR. [ARMS.]

SPICES. This word, which occurs very frequently in our translation of the Scriptures, has usually been considered to indicate several of the aromatic substances to which the same general name is applied in the present day. And we have as much assurance as is possible in such cases that the majority of the substances referred to have been identified, and that among the spices of early times were included many of those which now form articles of commerce from India to Europe.

SPIDER occurs in Job viii. 14; Isa. lix. 5. In the first of these passages, the reference seems clear to the spider's web, or literally, house, whose fragility is alluded to as a fit representation of the hope of a *profane, ungodly*, or *profligate* person; for so the original word really means, and not hypocrite,' as in our version. The object of such a person's trust or confidence, who is always really in imminent danger of ruin, may be compared for its uncertainty to the spider's web. 'He shall lean upon *his* house (*i. e.* to keep it steady when it is shaken); he shall hold it fast (*i. e.* when it is about to be destroyed); nevertheless it shall not endure (ver. 15). In the second passage (Isa. lix. 5) it is said, ' The wicked weave the spider's web' (literally, ' thin threads'); but it is added, 'their thin threads shall not become garments, neither shall they cover themselves with their works;' that is, their artifices shall neither succeed, nor conceal themselves, as does the spider's web. This allusion intimates no *antipathy* to the spider itself, or to its habits when directed towards its own purposes; but simply to the adoption of those habits by man towards his fellow-creatures. There has long been a popular prejudice against spiders, and the poet Thomson has stigmatized them as

  ' Cunning and fierce—

   Mixture abhorred ;'

but these epithets are in reality as unjustly applied to them (at least with reference to the mode by which they procure necessary subsistence), as to the patient sportsman, who lays snares for the birds that are to serve for the dinner of his family: while it can be further pleaded in behalf of spiders, that they are actively serviceable to the human race, in checking the superfecundity of other insects, and afford in their various procedures the most astonishing displays of that Supreme Intelligence by which they are directed.

SPIKENARD. [NERD.]

SPIRIT and HOLY SPIRIT. The leading significations of the original words thus rendered may be classed under the following heads:—

1. The primary sense of the term is *wind.* He that formeth the mountains and createth the wind' (Amos iv. 13; Isa. xxvii. 8). 'The wind bloweth where it listeth' (John iii. 8). This is the ground idea of the term 'spirit'—air—ether —air refined, sublimated, or vitalized: hence it denotes—

2. *Breath,* as of the mouth. 'At the blast of the breath of his nostrils are they consumed' (Job iv. 9). 'The Lord shall consume that wicked one with the breath of his mouth' (2 Thess. ii. 8).

3. The *vital* principle which resides in and animates the body (Eccles. viii. 8; Gen. vi. 17; vii. 15).

In close connection with this use of the word is another—

4. In which it has the sense of *apparition— spectre* (Luke xxiv. 37, 39; Matt. xiv. 26).

5. The *soul*—the rational immortal principle, by which man is distinguished from the brute creation (Luke xxiii. 46; Acts vii. 59; 1 Cor. v. 5; vi. 20; vii. 34; Heb. xii. 9).

6. The race of superhuman created intelligences.

7. The term is applied to the Deity, as the sole, absolute, and uncreated Spirit. 'God is a Spirit.' This, as a predicate, belongs to the divine nature, irrespective of the distinction of persons in that nature. But its characteristic application is to the third person in the Divinity, who is called the Holy Spirit, because of his essential holiness, and because in the Christian scheme it is his peculiar work to sanctify the people of God. He is denominated *The* Spirit, by way of eminence, as the immediate author of spiritual life in the hearts of Christians.

The words Spirit, and Holy Spirit, frequently occur in the New Testament, by metonymy, for the influence or effects of His agency.

a. As a procreative power—'the power of the Highest' (Luke i. 35).

b. As an influence, with which Jesus was endued (Luke iv. 4).

c. As a divine inspiration or *afflatus,* by which the prophets and holy men wrote and spoke. Holy men of God spake as they were moved by the Holy Ghost' (2 Pet. i. 21; Num. xi. 26; Neh. ix. 30; Ezek. iii. 12, 14; Rev. i. 10; iv. 2; xvii. 3).

d. As miraculous gifts and powers, with which the Apostles were endowed, to qualify them for the work to which they were called (John xx. 22, Acts ii. 4).

But the phrase, Holy Spirit, is specially used to denote a *divine personal agent.* The Holy Spirit is associated, as a distinct person, with the Father and the Son, in the baptismal formula and the apostolical benediction. The Father and Son are real persons. It is reasonable to think that the spirit who is joined with them in this solemn form of induction into the Christian church, is also a personal agent, and not an abstraction—a mere power or influence. The subject is baptized into the belief of three personal agents. To suppose that, in this solemn profession of faith, he avows his belief in the Father and the Son, and the *power* or *influence* of God, is forced and frigid.

He is baptized into the *name* of each of the three (Matt. xxviii. 19). We are not baptized into the name of an influence or a power, but into the name of a person—of three real and distinct subjects, the Father, the Son, and the Holy Ghost.

In the apostolical benedictions, the Spirit, as a person, is associated in the same way with the Father and Son (2 Cor. xiii. 13). In this uniting of the three there is the recognition of the distinct personality of each, in the separate gift which is appropriated to each.

Distinct personal acts and attributes are ascribed to the Holy Spirit too frequently and fully to admit of explanation by the prosopopœia.

The Holy Ghost *speaks,* by Esaias the prophet (Acts xxviii. 25), expressly (1 Tim. iv. 1). He *teaches* (Luke xii. 12). He *reproves* the world of sin (John xvi. 8). The spirit helpeth our infirmities, and maketh intercession for the saints (Rom. viii. 26, 27). He is *grieved* (Eph. iv. 30).

Apostles are set apart to him in the work of the ministry, and he appoints them to that work (Acts xiii. 2; xv. 28).

These are all acts which imply a personal agent. And these acts and attributes distinguish the Spirit from the person of the Father on the one hand, and from the personal subjects upon which he acts on the other.

The Spirit, as a personal agent, comes from the Father, is sent by the Father, and of course cannot be the Father. As sent by the Father, he maketh intercession for the saints, *according to the will of God,* i. e. the Father from whom he came. The Spirit searcheth all things, yea, the deep things of God (1 Cor. ii. 10). If there be no distinct personality of the Spirit separate from that of the Father, the real import of these passages must be, that the Father comes from himself, is sent by himself, makes intercession to himself, according to the will of himself, and that he searches the deep things of himself,— which is a style of writing not to be ascribed to any rational man, and certainly not to inspired apostles.

The Spirit of God (1 Cor. ii. 11) is not a created spirit; and if uncreated, it must be divine in the highest sense; but this Spirit is the Holy Spirit, and a proper person; hence he is God.

As the author of regeneration, or of the new spiritual and incorruptible life in the heart of the believer, he must be divine. This change, the Scriptures abundantly declare, is wrought by the Spirit and power of God

Blasphemy against the Holy Ghost is the only sin for which there is no remission (Matt. xii. 31). This sin against the Holy Spirit, in whatever it may consist, is distinguished from all other sins by a degree of guilt which renders it unpardonable. If he be not in his nature truly God, there is nothing in him to give to sin against him such a peculiar aggravation. Although it is not simply because the Spirit is God that blasphemy against him is unpardonable—for then would blasphemy against the Father and the Son also be unpardonable—yet it is a sin against God, and, as being against the third person of the Godhead, it is aggravated to a degree of enormity which it could not receive if committed against any other being than God.

The divine and incommunicable attributes of the Deity are ascribed to the Spirit. These attributes belong exclusively to the divine nature; he who possesses them must have the divine nature and honour as God.

Works truly divine are attributable to the Holy Spirit, as creation and preservation, and especially the work of sanctification.

Of the office of the Holy Spirit, it is only necessary to say, that it is not ministerial, like that of the angels and apostles, but it is the peculiar work in the salvation of man which he performs, as sent by the Father and the Son.

SPOUSE. [MARRIAGE.]

SPRING. [PALESTINE.]

STA'CHYS, an unknown person, from his name apparently a Greek, a disciple at Rome, and a friend of Paul (Rom. xvi. 9).

STAC'TE occurs only once in Scripture (Exod. xxx. 34). 'And the Lord said unto Moses, Take unto thee sweet spices, stacte (*nataf*), and onycha, and galbanum; these sweet spices with pure frankincense.' 'Thou shalt make it a perfume after the art of the apothecary' (ver. 35). *Nataf* has, however, been variously translated. Celsius is of opinion that it means the purest kind of myrrh, called *stacte* by the Greeks. But it is difficult if not impossible to arrive at certainty on the subject.

STANDARDS. Standards and ensigns are to be regarded as efficient instruments for maintaining the ranks and files of bodies of troops; and in Num. ii. 2 they are particularly noticed, the Israelites being not only enjoined to encamp 'each by the standard of his tribe and the ensign of his father's house,' but, as the sense evidently implies, in orders or lines. It is clear, when this verse is considered in connection with the religious, military, and battle pictures on Egyptian monuments, that the Hebrews had ensigns of at least three kinds, namely; 1. The great standards of the tribes, serving as rallying signals for marching, forming in battle array, and for encamping; 2. The divisional standards of clans; and, 3. Those of houses or families; which after the occupation of the Promised Land may gradually have been applied more immediately to corps and companies, when the tribes, as such, no longer regularly took the field.

It is very difficult to determine what were the form, colours, materials, and symbols of the Hebrew ensigns; but we may be certain that they could not have resembled modern banners, as has been generally supposed. We know that as early as the days of the exode of Israel the Egyptians had ensigns of different kinds, and it is very likely that the standards in use among that people were, under proper modifications, adopted by the Israelites when they were about to become wanderers over desert regions where order and discipline,

directing signals, telegraphs, and indications of water would be most useful.

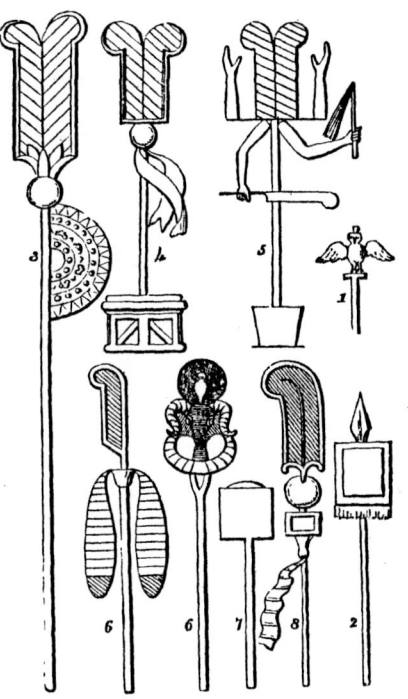

308.   1. Bactrian eagle; 2. Persian vexillum; 3 Standard of Sesostris; 4. Egyptian ensign set in a frame, signal of castrametation and of direction; 5. Telegraphic ensign, varying with each Pharaoh; 6. Subordinate Egyptian ensigns; 7. Tribal tablet; 8. Plume ensign used in temples.

STAR IN THE EAST. Matthew (ch. ii. 1, sq.) relates that at the time of the birth of our Lord there came wise men (magi) from the East to Jerusalem, to inquire after the newly-born king of the Jews, in order that they might offer him presents and worship him. A star, which they had seen in the East, guided them to the house where the infant Messiah was. Having come into his presence, they presented unto him gifts—gold, and frankincense, and myrrh.

Our space will not allow us to enter upon the consideration of the various theories which have been framed to explain this portion of the sacred narrative. We must content ourselves with a brief statement of the theory of the distinguished astronomer Kepler, which appears to us the right view of the case.

These wise men were Chaldæan magi. A conviction had long been spread throughout the East, that about the commencement of our era a great and victorious prince, or the Messiah, was to be born. His birth was, in consequence of words of Sacred Scripture (Num. xxiv. 17), connected with the appearance of a star. Calculations seem to have led the astrological astronomers of Mesopotamia to fix the time for the advent of this king in the latter days of Herod, and the place in the land of Judæa. Accordingly, at the appointed time two planets, Jupiter and Saturn, were in conjunction under such circumstances as to appear one resplendent heavenly body, and to marshal the way for the magi from their own homes to Jerusalem, Bethlehem, and the inn.

Kepler found by the calculations which he made that Jupiter and Saturn were in conjunction in the constellation of the Fishes (a fish is the astrological symbol of Judæa) in the latter half of the year of Rome 747, and were joined by Mars in 748. The two planets went past each other three times, came very near together, and showed themselves all night long for months in conjunction with each other, as if they would never separate again. Their first union in the East awoke the attention of the magi. told them the expected time had come, and bade them set off without delay towards Judæa (the fish land). When they reached Jerusalem the two planets were once more blended together. Then, in the evening, they stood in the southern part of the sky, pointing with their united rays to Bethlehem, where prophecy declared the Messiah was to be born. The magi followed the finger of heavenly light, and were brought to the child Jesus. The conclusion, in regard to the time of the advent, is, that our Lord was born in the latter part of the year of Rome 747, or six years before the common era.

STEPH'ANAS, a disciple at Corinth, whose household Paul baptized (1 Cor. i. 16), being the first converted to Christianity in Achaia (1 Cor. xvi. 15).

STE'PHEN, one of the seven first deacons, and the proto-martyr, of the Christian church. There have been various conjectures respecting his early history, but the first authentic notice we find of him is in Acts vi. 5. In the distribution of the common fund that was intrusted to the Apostles (Acts iv. 35–37) for the support of the poorer brethren, the Hellenistic Jews complained that a partiality was shown to the natives of Palestine, and that the poor and sick among their widows were neglected. The complaint of the Hellenists having reached the ears of the apostles, immediate directions were given by them with a view to remove the cause of it. Unwilling themselves to be called away from their proper employment of extending the bounds of the Christian community, they told the assembled multitude of believers to select seven men of their own number, in whose faith and integrity they might repose entire confidence, for the superintendence of everything connected with the relief of the poor. The proposal of the apostles met with the approbation of the brethren, who proceeded at once with the choice of the prescribed number of individuals, among whom Stephen is first mentioned. He is distinguished in Scripture as a man 'full of faith and of the Holy Ghost' (Acts vi. 5). The newly elected individuals were brought to the apostles, who ordained them to their office, and they entered upon their duties with extraordinary zeal and success. The number of the disciples was greatly increased, and many priests were among the converts. In this work Stephen greatly distinguished himself by the miracles he performed before the people, and by the arguments he advanced in support of the Christian cause. From his foreign descent and education he was naturally led to address himself to the Hellenists, and in his dis-

putations with Jews of the Synagogue of the Libertines and Cyrenians, &c. [Synagogue and Libertine], he brought forward views of the Christian scheme that could not be relished by the bigots of the ancient faith. As they were unable to withstand his powers of reasoning, their malice was excited; they suborned false witnesses against him, and dragged him before the Sanhedrim as a blasphemer. The speech which Stephen made in defending himself against this accusation is well deserving of the most careful study. He first enters upon a historical statement, involving a refutation of the charges which had been made against him of hostility to the Old Testament institutions; but at the same time showing that acceptance with God does not depend upon outward relations. Under the same form he illustrates the providential care exercised by the Almighty in regard to the Jewish people, along with the opposition exhibited by the Jews towards those sent to them by God. And he points the application of his whole discourse by charging his carnal-minded hearers with resisting, like their fathers, the Holy Ghost. The effect upon his auditors was terrible. Conscience-smitten, they united in wreaking their vengeance on the faithful denouncer of their guilt. They drowned his voice with their clamorous outcries, they stopped their ears against him, they rushed on him with one accord in a tumultuary manner, they carried him forth, and without waiting for the authority of law, they stoned him to death as a blasphemer. The frantic violence of his persecutors did not disturb the tranquillity of the martyr, and he died praying that his murderers might be forgiven (vii. 60).

The only other particular connected with Stephen, mentioned in Scripture, is, that 'devout men carried him to his burial, and made great lamentation over him' (viii. 2).

STOICS AND EPICUREANS. Reference is made in Acts xvii. 18 to certain philosophers belonging to these celebrated sects as having 'encountered' Paul at Athens.

The Stoics derive their name from stoa, 'a porch;' because their founder Zeno (who was born from 360 to 350 years B.C.) was accustomed to teach in a certain porch at Athens.

The Epicureans were named after their founder Epicurus, who is said to have been born at Athens B.C. 344, and to have opened a school (or rather a garden) where he propagated his tenets, at a time when the doctrines of Zeno had already obtained credit and currency.

STONING. [Punishments.]

STORAX. This tree is a native of Greece, Asia Minor, Syria, and Palestine, and is about twenty feet high, with leaves like those of the quince, and flowers somewhat resembling those of the orange. Storax was, and is still, much esteemed, both as an incense and for its medical properties. It consists chiefly of resin, a volatile oil, and some benzoic acid. It has a grateful balsamic odour, which no doubt made it valued in ancient times.

STORK. The Hebrew name of this bird implied affection, from the belief general throughout all ancient Asia in the attachment of these birds to each other, and some have supposed that their English name has a similar derivation. The strength of the affection of the parent birds towards their young has been verified by the moderns, in cases where the mother bird has perished while endeavouring to save her progeny.

309.

Storks are about a foot less in height than the crane, measuring only three feet six inches from the tip of the bill to the end of the toes, and nearly the same to the end of the tail. They have a stout, pointed, and rather long bill, which, together with their long legs, is of a bright scarlet colour; the toes are partially webbed, the nails at the extremities flat, and but little pointed beyond the tips of the joints. The orbits are blackish, but the whole bird is white, with the exception of a few scapulars, the greater wing covers, and all the quills, which are deep black: they are doubly scalloped out, with those nearest the body almost as long as the very foremost in the wing. This is a provision of nature, enabling the bird more effectually to sustain its after weight in the air: a faculty exceedingly important to its mode of flight with its long neck, and longer legs equally stretched out, and very necessary to a migrating species believed to fly without alighting from the lower Rhine, or even from the vicinity of Strasburg, to Africa, and to the Delta of the Nile. The passage is performed in October, and, like that of cranes, in single or in double columns, uniting in a point to cleave the air; but their departure is seldom seen, because they start generally in the night: they rise always with clapping wings, ascending with surprising rapidity out of human sight, and arriving at their southern destination as if by enchantment. Here they reside until the last days of March, when they again depart for the north, but more leisurely and less congregated. A feeling of attachment, not without superstition, procures them an unmolested life in all Moslem countries, and a notion of their utility still protects them in Switzerland, Western Germany, and Holland. Storks build their nests in pine, fir, cedar, and other coniferous trees, but seem to prefer lofty old buildings, towers, and ruins. With regard to the snake-eating habits of the species, the chief resort of storks, for above half the year, is in climates where serpents do not abound: and they seem at all times to prefer eels, frogs, toads, newts, and lizards; which sufficiently accounts for their being regarded as unclean. Storks feed also on field mice; but they do not appear to relish rats, though they break their bones by repeated blows of their bills.

STREETS. [TOWNS.]

STRIPES. [PUNISHMENTS.]

1. SUC'COTH (booths), the first encampment of the Israelites on the Egyptian side of the Red Sea (Exod. xii. 37; xiii. 20; Num. xxxiii. 5 [EXODUS].

2. SUC'COTH, a town in the tribe of Gad (Josh. xiii. 27), on the east of the Jordan (Judg. viii. 5; 1 Kings vii. 6). The spot in which the town stood is called 'the valley of Succoth,' and must have been part of the valley of the Jordan. The place derived its name from Jacob having tarried some time there on his return from Padanaram, and made booths for his cattle (Gen. xxxiii. 17).

SUMMER. [PALESTINE.]

SUPPER OF THE LORD, so called by St. Paul in his historical reference to the Passover Supper as observed by Jesus on the night in which he was betrayed (1 Cor. xi. 20; Matt. xxvi. 20-31). As regards the day on which our Lord observed the Passover, it seems more proper to say, that the Pharisees, the dominant party among the Jews, *deferred* its observance a day in accordance with their traditions, than that Jesus *anticipated* it. What one party considered the fourteenth Nisan, would to the other be the thirteenth. This supposition seems best to harmonize any apparent discrepancy in the accounts of the evangelists.

Several controverted points may perhaps be best adjusted by a connected harmony of the last Passover of the Lord, constructed from the evangelic narratives alluding to it, but filling up the various omitted circumstances from the known Passover rites [PASSOVER].

'Now, when it was evening, Jesus sat down with the twelve (Matt.) Apostles' (Mark). The first customary washing and purifications being performed, the blessing over *the first cup* of wine, which began the feast, would be pronounced, probably in the usual form—'We thank thee, O God, our Heavenly Father, who hast created the fruit of the vine.'

Then probably *the second cup* of wine was mingled, and with the flesh of the paschal lamb, feast offerings, and other viands, placed before the Lord. 'And he said unto them, With desire have I desired to eat this Pascha with you before I suffer; for I say unto you, I shall no more eat thereof until it be fulfilled in the kingdom of God And he took the [second] cup, and gave thanks, and said, Take this, and divide among you, for I say unto you, I will not henceforth drink of the fruit of the vine until the kingdom of God shall come' (Luke).

When the wine distributed to each would be drunk off, one of the unleavened cakes would next be broken, the blessing said over it, and a piece distributed to each disciple, probably with the usual formula:—'This is the bread of affliction which your fathers did eat in the land of Egypt' —*i. e.*, not the identical bread, transubstantiated, but a memorial or sign of it. The company would then proceed with the proper supper, eating of the feast-offering, and, after a benediction, of the paschal lamb.

'And as they were at supper, the Devil having now put it into the heart of Judas to betray him; Jesus, knowing that the Father had given all things into his hands, and that he was come from

God, and was going to God, riseth from supper; and ' after due preparations ' began to wash the disciples' feet' (John). After this striking symbolic exhortation to humility and mutual service (John xiii. 6–20), ' Jesus was troubled in spirit, and bare witness, and said, Verily, verily, I say unto you, that one of you will betray me. Then the disciples looked on one another, doubting of whom he spake' (John). ' And they were very sorry, and began each of them to say unto him, Lord, is it I?' (Matt.) ' One of the disciples, leaning back on Jesus's breast, saith unto him, Lord, is it I? Jesus answered, He it is to whom I shall give a sop, when I have dipped it. And after dipping the sop he giveth it to Judas Iscariot. Then Satan entered into him. Jesus saith unto him, What thou doest, do quickly. He then, on taking the sop, went immediately out; and it was night' (John).

The supper would then proceed, until each had eaten sufficient of the paschal lamb and feast-offering.

' And as they were eating, Jesus took the bread,' the other unleavened cake left unbroken, ' and blessed ' God ' and brake it, and gave it to the ' eleven ' disciples, and said, Take eat; this is my body (Matt., Mark), which is broken for you: this do in remembrance of me ' (Luke, Paul, 1 Cor. xi. 24).

The supper being concluded, the hands were usually washed the second time, and *the third cup* or ' cup of blessing ' (1 Cor. x. 16) prepared, over which the master usually gave thanks for the Covenant of Circumcision, and for the law given to Moses. Jesus, therefore, at this juncture, announced, with peculiar appropriateness, his New Covenant.

' After the same manner, also, Jesus took the cup after supper, and, having given thanks, gave it to them, saying, Drink all of you out of it; for this is my blood of the new covenant, which is shed for many for forgiveness of sins (Matt.): this do, as oft as ye drink, in remembrance of me' (1 Cor. xi. 24). ' But I say unto you, I shall not drink henceforth of this fruit of the vine, until that day when I drink it new with you in my Father's kingdom ' (Matt.).

' And when they had sung a hymn' (Matt.), probably the Hallel, our Lord discoursed long with his disciples about his approaching death and departure (John xiii. 31; xiv. 31), and when he had finished he said, ' Arise, let us go hence.' ' And they went out on to the Mount of Olives' (Matt.).

SU'SA. [SHUSHAN.]

SWALLOW. The species of this bird in Syria and Palestine, so far as they are known, appear all to be the same as those of Europe: they are, 1. The chimney swallow, with a forked tail, marked with a row of white spots.

2. The martin or common window swallow.

3. Sand-martin or shore-bird, not uncommon in northern Egypt, near the mouths of the Delta, and in southern Palestine, about Gaza, where it nestles in holes. even on the sea-shore.

4. The swift or black martin, distinguished by its larger size, short legs, very long wings, forked tail, and by all the toes of the feet turning forward: these, armed with small, crooked, and very sharp claws, enable the bird to hang against the sides of walls, but it cannot rise from the ground on account of the length of its wings.

310. [The Swift—Dururi.]

SWEARING. [OATH.]

SWEET CANE, or CALAMUS, is mentioned in various passages of Scripture (Exod. xxx. 23; Jer. vi. 20, &c.), from which we learn that it was fragrant and reed-like, and that it was brought from a far country (Jer. vi. 20; Ezek. xxvii. 19): Dan also and Javan going to and fro carried bright iron, cassia, and calamus to the markets of Tyre.

If we recur to the method which we have adopted in other cases, of examining the writings of ancient heathen authors, to ascertain if they describe anything like the substances noticed in the sacred writings, we shall experience no difficulty in identifying the ' sweet cane, or reed, from a far country.' It is stated to be a produce of India, of a tawny colour, much jointed, breaking into splinters, and having the hollow stem filled with pith, like the web of a spider; also that it is mixed with ointments and fumigations on account of its odour. Theophrastus describes both the calamus and schœnus as natives of Syria, or more precisely, of a valley between Mount Lebanon and a small mountain, where there is a plain and a lake, in parts of which there is a marsh, where they are produced, the smell being perceived by any one entering the place. This account is virtually followed by Pliny, though he also mentions the sweet calamus as a produce of Arabia. A writer in the *Gardener's Chronicle* (ii. 756) has adduced a passage from Polybius (v. 46), as elucidating the foregoing statement of Theophrastus : ' From Laodicea Antiochus marched with all his army, and having passed the desert, entered a close and narrow valley, which lies between the Libanus and Anti-Libanus, and is called the Vale of Marsyas. The narrowest part of the valley is covered by a lake with marshy ground, *from whence are gathered aromatic reeds.*'

That there may be some moderately sweet-scented grass, or rush-like plant, such as the *Acorus Calamus* of botanists (long used as a substitute for the true calamus), in the flat country between Libanus and Anti-Libanus, is quite possible; but we have no proof of the fact. Burckhardt, in that situation, could find only ordinary rushes and reeds. Though Theophrastus, Polybius, and Strabo mention this locality as that producing the calamus, yet others give Arabia, or the country of the Sabæans, as that which produced the aromatic reed; while Dioscorides, the only author who writes expressly of the drugs known to the ancients, mentions it as being the produce of India.

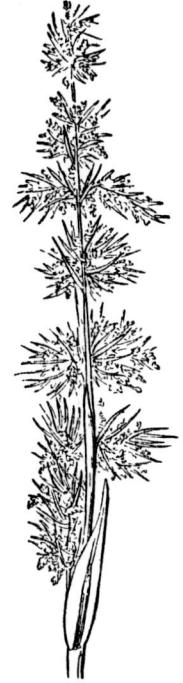

311. [Andropogon calamus aromaticus.]

As this plant is a true grass, it has necessarily reed-like stems. They are remarkable for their agreeable odour: so are the leaves when bruised, and also the delightfully fragrant oil distilled from them. Hence it appears more fully entitled to the commendations which the *calamus aromaticus* or sweet-cane has received, than any other plant that has been described, even the attar of roses hardly excepted. That a grass similar to the fragrant *andropogon*, or at least one growing in the same kind of soil and climate, was employed by the ancients, we have evidence in the fact of the Phœnicians who accompanied Alexander in his march across the arid country of Gedrosia having recognised and loaded their cattle with it, as one of the perfumes of commerce. It is in a similar country, that is, the arid plains of Central India, that the above *andropogon calamus aromaticus* is found, and where the fragrant essential oil is distilled from its leaves, culms, and roots.

If we compare the foregoing statement with the different passages of Scripture, we shall find that this fragrant grass answers to all that is required. Thus in Exod. xxx. 23, the fragrant reed, along with the principal spices, such as myrrh, sweet cinnamon, and cassia, is directed to be made into an oil of holy ointment. So the *calamus aromaticus* may be found mentioned as an ingredient in numerous fragrant oils and ointments, from the time of Theophrastus to that of the Arabs. Its essential oil is now sold in the shops, but under the erroneous name of oil of spikenard, which is a very different substance [SPIKENARD]. In Cant. iv. 14 it is mentioned along with spikenard, saffron, cinnamon, trees of frankincense, myrrh, and aloes. Again, its value is indicated in Isa (xliii. 24), 'thou hast bought me no sweet cane with money;' and that it was obtained from a distant land is indicated in Jer. vi. 20, 'to what purpose cometh there to me incense from Sheba, and the sweet cane from a far country?'—while the route of the commerce is pointed out in Ezek. xxvii 19, 'Dan also and Javan going to and fro occupied in thy fairs: bright iron, cassia, and calamus were in thy market.' To the Scripture notices, then, as well as to the description of Dioscorides, the tall grass which yields the fragrant grass-oil of Central India answers in every respect.

SWINE. Egyptian pictures, the parable of the Prodigal Son, and Christ's miraculous cure of the demoniac, when he permitted swine to be possessed and destroyed by rushing over a precipice into the sea of Galilee, furnish ample proofs that during the dominion of the Romans the domesticated breeds of these animals were reared in great numbers among the Jews, notwithstanding the strong prohibition in the law of Moses. Commentators ascribe this abundance of swine to the numerous Pagan sacrifices of these animals in the temples: but we do not deem this to be a sufficiently correct view of the case, since hogs of every denomination were less used for that purpose than oxen, goats, and sheep. May it not be conjectured that in those days of a greatly condensed population the poor found in swine's flesh, and still more in the fat and lard, melted for culinary purposes, as it still is in every part of Pagan Africa, a most desirable aliment, still more acceptable than the salt fish imported from Sidon, to season their usual vegetable diet?

SWORD. [ARMS.]

SYCAMINE TREE is mentioned only once in the New Testament, in Luke xvii. 6, 'And the Lord said, If ye had faith as a grain of mustard-seed, ye might say unto this *sycamine*-tree,' &c. From a slight similarity in name, this tree has often been confounded with the *sycamore*, both by ancient and modern writers. Both trees are, however, mentioned by the apostle, who must have had the technical knowledge necessary for distinguishing such things. Though the English version avoids translating the word, there can be little doubt of the mulberry-tree being intended; and it is frequently so rendered. The mulberry is a tree which we might expect to find mentioned in Scripture, since it is so common in Palestine. It is constantly alluded to by old travellers, and indeed is much cultivated in the present day, in consequence of its affording food for the silk-worm; and it must have been common also in early times, or the silk-worms would not have obtained suitable food when first introduced. As the mulberry-tree is common, as it is lofty and affords shade, it is well calculated for the illustration of the above passage of Luke.

SYCAMORE. This word occurs in several passages of the Old Testament. From the context it is evident that it must have been a tree of some size, common in the plains, unable to bear great cold, with wood of inferior quality, but still cultivated and valued on account of its fruit. It was not what is called sycamore in this country, which is a kind of maple, and in some of its characters the reverse of what is required, but rather the mulberry tree, the *Ficus Sycomorus* of botanists, which is a genuine species of *Ficus*. The fruit in its general characters resembles that of the fig, while the leaves resemble those of the mulberry tree.

312. [Sycamore-Fig. Ficus Sycomorus.]

The ancients were well acquainted with it; and it is common in Egypt as well as in Syria. In Egypt, being one of the few trees indigenous in that country, its wood was proportionally much employed, as in making mummy-cases, though it is coarse grained, and would not be valued where other trees are more common. Though the wood of this sycamore is coarse grained, it is yet very durable in a dry climate like that of Egypt; hence the mummy-cases even in the present day seem as if made with fresh wood. This may, no doubt, be partly ascribed to the preservative effects of the resinous coats, paints, &c. with which they are impregnated. That the sycamore was cultivated and esteemed in Palestine we learn from 1 Chron. xxvii. 28, 'And over the olive trees and the *sycamore* trees that were in the low plains was Baal-hanan the Gederite.' This was on account of its fruit, which it bears on its stem and branches, like the common fig, and continues to produce in succession for months. The fruit is palatable, sweetish in taste, and still used as food in the East. As the sycamore is a lofty, shady tree, it is well suited for climbing up into, as described in Luke xix. 4, where Zacchæus ascends one to see Jesus pass by.

SY'CHAR, a name of reproach applied by the Jews to Shechem [SHECHEM].

SY'CHEM, the name for Shechem in Acts vii. 16, being that also used in the Septuagint version of the Old Testament [SHECHEM].

SYE'NE, a city of Egypt, situated in the Thebais, on the southern extremity of the land towards Ethiopia. Ezekiel, describing the deso-lation to be brought upon Egypt through its whole extent, says, ' Thus saith the Lord, I will make the Land of Egypt utterly desolate, from the tower of Syene even to the border of Cush (Arabia),' or, as some read, 'from Migdol to Syene,' implying, according to either version of the passage, the whole length of the country from north to south. Syene is represented by the present Assouan, which exhibits few remains of the ancient city, except some granite columns of a comparatively late date, and the sekos of a small temple.

SYN'AGOGUE, a Jewish place of worship. The Greek, from which the word is immediately derived, denotes 'an assembly;' but afterwards, by a natural deflection of meaning, came to designate the building in which such assembly met.

The precise age of the introduction of synagogues among the Israelites it does not appear easy to determine. In all probability, however, they had their origin about the period of the exile; and there were then peculiar circumstances which called for their establishment. Deprived of the solemnities of their national worship, yet still retaining their religious convictions, and keenly feeling the loss they had endured, earnestly, too, longing and praying for a restoration of their forfeited privileges, the captive Israelites could not help meeting together for the purposes of mutual sympathy, counsel, and aid, or of prayer and other devout exercises. But prayer makes every spot holy ground. Some degree of secrecy, too, may have been needful in the midst of scoffing and scornful enemies. Thus houses of prayer would arise; and the peculiar form of the synagogue worship—namely, devotion apart from external oblations—would come into being.

The authority of the Talmudists (such as it is) would go to show that a synagogue existed wherever there were ten families. What, however, is certain is, that in the times of Jesus Christ synagogues were found in all the chief cities and lesser towns of Palestine. From Acts vi. 9, it appears that every separate tribe and colony had a synagogue in Jerusalem. Synagogues were built sometimes on the outside of cities, but more frequently within, and preferably on elevated spots. At a later period they were fixed near burial-places. A peculiar sanctity was attached to these spots, even after the building had fallen to ruin. In the Synagogue pious Israelites assembled every Sabbath and festival day, the women sitting apart from the men; and at a later period, on every second and fifth day of each week, for the purposes of common prayer, and to hear portions of the sacred books read: which was performed sometimes by any one of the company (Luke ii. 16), or, according to Philo, by any one of the priests or elders, who expounded each particular as he proceeded. The writings thus read aloud and expounded were the Law, the Prophets, and other Old Testament books (Acts xiii. 15; xv. 21).

The expositor was not always the same person as the reader. A memorable instance in which the reader and the expositor was the same person, and yet one distinct from the stated functionary, may be found in Luke iv. 16, sq., in which our Lord read and applied to himself the beautiful passage found in the prophecy of Isaiah (lxi. 4). After the reading and exposition were concluded, a blessing was pronounced, commonly by a priest. The people gave a response by uttering the word *Amen;* when the assembly broke up (1 Cor. xiv. 16).

At the head of the officers stood the ' ruler of the synagogue.' who had the chief direction of all the affairs connected with the purposes for which the synagogue existed (Luke viii. 49; xiii. 14; Mark v. 35, seq.; Acts xviii. 8). Next in rank were the elders (Luke vii. 3), called also 'heads of the synagogue' (Mark v. 22; Acts xiii. 15), as well as 'shepherds' and ' presidents,' who formed a sort of college or governing body under the presidency of the chief ruler. There was in the third place ' the angel of the church,' who in the synagogue meetings acted commonly as the speaker, or as the Protestant minister, conducting the worship of the congregation, as well as performed on other occasions the duties of secretary and messenger. Then came, fourthly, ' the minister ' (Luke iv. 20), the attendant who handed the books to the reader, was responsible for the cleanliness of the room, and for its order and decency, and opened and closed the synagogue, of which he had the general care. In addition, there probably were almoners or deacons (Matt. vi. 2), who collected, held, and distributed the alms of the charitable.

In regard to the furniture of the synagogue, seats merely are mentioned in the New Testament (Matt. xxiii. 6; James ii. 3). The 'chief seats,' or rather ' front seats,' were occupied by the Scribes and Pharisees. The outfit may have been more simple in the days of Christ; still there was probably then, as well as at a later period, a sort of pulpit, and a desk or shelf, for holding the sacred books. Some sort of summary judicature seems to have been held in the synagogues, and punishments of flogging and beating inflicted on the spot (Matt. x. 17; xxiii. 34; Mark xiii. 9; Luke xii. 11; xxi. 12; Acts xxii. 19; xxvi. 11; 1 Cor. xi. 22). The causes of which cognizance was here taken were perhaps exclusively of a religious kind. It certainly appears from the New Testament that heresy and apostacy were punished before these tribunals by the application of stripes.

SYN'TYCHE, a female Christian named in Phil. iv. 2.

SYR'ACUSE, a celebrated city on the southeast coast of the island of Sicily. It was a strong, wealthy, and populous place. The great wealth and power of Syracuse arose from its trade, which was carried on extensively while it remained an independent state under its own kings; but about 200 B.C. it was taken by the Romans, after a siege rendered famous by the mechanical contrivances whereby Archimedes protracted the defence. Syracuse still exists as a considerable town under its original name, and some ruins of the ancient city yet remain. St. Paul spent three days at Syracuse, after leaving Melita, when being conveyed as a prisoner to Rome (Acts xxviii. 12).

SYR'IA. It is difficult to define the limits of ancient Syria, as the name seems to have been very loosely applied by the old geographers. In general, however, we may perceive that they made it include the tract of country lying between the Euphrates and the Mediterranean, from the mountains of Taurus and Amanus in the north, to the desert of Suez and the borders of Egypt on the south; which coincides pretty well with the modern application of the name. It may be described as composed of three tracts of land, of very different descriptions. That which adjoins the Mediterranean is a hot, damp, and rather unwholesome, but very fruitful valley. The part next to this consists of a double chain of mountains, running parallel from south-west to northeast, with craggy precipitous rocks, devious valleys, and hollow defiles. The air is here dry and healthy; and on the western declivities of the mountains are seen beautiful and highly cultivated terraces, alternating with well-watered valleys, which have a rich and fertile soil, and are densely peopled. The eastern declivities, on the contrary, are dreary mountain deserts, connected with the third region, which may be described as a spacious plain of sand and rock, presenting an extensive and almost unbroken level.

Spring and autumn are very agreeable in Syria, and the heat of summer in the mountain districts is supportable. But in the plains, as soon as the sun reaches the equator, it becomes of a sudden oppressively hot, and this heat continues till the end of October. On the other hand, the winter is so mild, that orange-trees, fig-trees, palms, and many tender shrubs and plants flourish in the open air, while the heights of Lebanon are glittering with snow and hoar-frost. In the districts, however, which lie north and east of the mountains, the severity of winter is greater, though the heat of the summer is not less. At Antioch, Aleppo, and Damascus, there are ice and snow for several weeks every winter. Yet, upon the whole, the climate and soil combine to render this country one of the most agreeable residences throughout the East.

The principal Syrian towns mentioned in Scripture are the following, all of which are noticed under their respective names in the present work:—Antioch, Seleucia, Helbon, Rezeph, Tiphsah, Rehoboth, Hamath, Riblah, Tadmor, Baal-Gad, Damascus, Hobah, Beth-Eden.

Syria, when we first become acquainted with its history, was divided into a number of small kingdoms, of which the most important of those mentioned in Scripture was that of which Damascus was the metropolis. A sketch of its history is given under DAMASCUS. These kingdoms were broken up, or rather consolidated by conquerors, of whom the first appears to have been Tiglath-pileser, King of Assyria, about 750 B.C. After the fall of the Assyrian monarchy, Syria came under the Chaldæan yoke. It shared the fate of Babylonia when that country was conquered by the Persians; and was again subdued by Alexander the Great. At his death in B.C. 323 it was erected into a separate monarchy under the Seleucidæ, and continued to be governed by its own sovereigns until, weakened and devastated by civil wars between competitors for the throne, it was finally, about B.C. 65, reduced by Pompey to the condition of a Roman province, after the monarchy had subsisted 257 years. On the decline of the Roman empire, the Saracens became the next possessors of Syria, about A.D. 622; and when the crusading armies poured into Asia, this country became the chief theatre of the great contest between the armies of the Crescent and the Cross, and its plains were deluged with Christian and Moslem blood. For nearly a century the Crusaders remained masters of the chief places in Syria; but at length the power of the Moslems predominated, and in 1186 Saladin, Sultan of Egypt, found himself in possession of Syria. It remained subject to the sultans of Egypt till, in A.D. 1517, the Turkish sultan, Selim I., overcame the Memlook dynasty, and Syria and Egypt became absorbed in the Ottoman empire. In 1832, a series of successes over the Turkish arms gave Syria to Mehemet Ali, the Pasha of Egypt; from whom, however, after nine years, it again passed to the Turks, in consequence of the operations undertaken for that purpose by the fleet under the command of Admiral Stopford, the chief of which was the bombardment of Acre in November, 1840. The treaty restoring Syria to the Turks was ratified early in the ensuing year.

SYRO-PHŒNICIA, or PHŒNICIA PROPER, called Syro or Syrian Phœnicia, from being included in the Roman province of Syria. It includes that part of the coast of Canaan, on the borders of the Mediterranean, in which the cities of Tyre and Sidon were situated; and the same country, which is called Syro-Phœnicia in the Acts, is in the Gospels called the coasts of Tyre and Sidon. The woman also described as Syro-Phœnician in Mark vii. 2-6, is in Matt. xv. 22 called a Canaanitish woman, because that country was still occupied by the descendants of Canaan, of whom Sidon was the eldest son.

T.

TA'ANACH, a royal city of the Canaanites (Josh. xii. 21), in the territory of Issachar, but assigned to Manasseh (Judg. i. 27; v. 19; Josh. xvii. 11-21; 1 Kings iv. 12). Schubert, followed by Robinson, finds it in the modern Taannuk, now a mean hamlet on the south side of a small hill, with a summit of table-land. It lies on the southwestern border of the plain of Esdraelon, four miles south of Megiddo, in connection with which it is mentioned in the triumphal song of Deborah and Barak (Judg. v. 19).

TA'BEAL (God is good), father of the unnamed person on whom Rezin, king of Syria, and Pekah, king of Israel, proposed to bestow the crown of Judah in case they succeeded in dethroning Ahaz (Isa. vii. 6). Who 'Tabeal's son' was is unknown, but it is conjectured that he was some factious and powerful Ephraimite (perhaps Zichri, 2 Chron. xxviii. 7), who promoted the war in the hope of this result.

TAB'ERAH, one of the stations of the Israelites in the desert [WANDERING].

TABERNACLE (tent of assembly). We may distinguish in the Old Testament three sacred tabernacles: I. The ANTE-SINAITIC, which was probably the dwelling of Moses, and was placed by the camp of the Israelites in the desert, for the transaction of public business (Exod. xxxiii. 7).

II. The Ante-Sinaitic tabernacle, which had served for the transaction of public business probably from the beginning of the exodus, was superseded by the Sinaitic; this was constructed by Bezaleel and Aholiab as a portable mansion-house, guildhall, and cathedral, and set up on the first day of the first month in the second year

after leaving Egypt. Of this alone we have accurate descriptions.

III. The DAVIDIC tabernacle was erected by David in Jerusalem for the reception of the ark (2 Sam. vi. 12), while the old tabernacle remained to the days of Solomon at Gibeon, together with the brazen altar, as the place where sacrifices were offered (1 Chron. xvi. 39, and 2 Chron. i. 3).

The second of these sacred tents is, as the most important, called the tabernacle *par excellence*. Moses was commanded by Jehovah to have it erected in the Arabian desert, by the voluntary contributions of the Israelites, who carried it about with them in their migrations until after the conquest of Canaan, when it remained stationary for longer periods in various towns of Palestine.

The materials of which this tent was composed were so costly, that sceptics have questioned whether they could be furnished by a nomadic race. The tabernacle exceeded in costliness and splendour, in proportion to the slender means of a nomadic people, the magnificence of any cathedral of the present day, compared with the wealth of the surrounding population. The mode of collecting the voluntary offerings for this great work, and the design of the structure, are fully described in Exod. xxv. to xxvii., and in xxxv. to xxxvii.

TABERNACLES, FEAST OF, one of the three great festivals of the Jews, being that of the closing year, as the Passover was of the spring. In Lev. xxiii. 34-43, directions for observing the feast are given in very clear terms (comp. Num. xxix. 13-34). It was held in commemoration of the divine goodness as exercised towards the Jews when they were wandering in the desert, as well as expressive of gratitude for the supply of the rich fruits of the earth; and so was fitted to awaken the most lively feelings of piety in the minds of the Hebrews in each successive generation. From the writings of the Rabbins we learn, 1. That those who took part in the festival bore in their left hand a branch of citron, and in their right a palm branch, entwined with willows and myrtle. 2. A libation of water took place on each of the seven days (Isa. xii. 3; John vii. 37); at the time of the morning oblation a priest drew from the fount of Siloam water in a jar holding three logs, and poured it out, together with wine, into two channels or conduits, made on the west side of the altar, the water into the one, the wine into the other. 3. In the outer court of the women there began, on the evening of the first day, an illumination on great golden candlesticks, which threw its light over the whole of Jerusalem; and a dance by torch-light, attended by song and music, was performed before the candelabra. From these details, it appears that the Feast of Tabernacles was a season of universal joy. Jerusalem bore the appearance of a camp. The entire population again dwelt in tents, but not with the accompaniments of travel, fatigue, and solicitude; all was hilarity, all wore a holiday appearance; the varied green of the ten thousand branches of different trees; the picturesque ceremony of the water-libation, the general illumination, the sacred solemnities in and before the temple; the feast, the dance, the sacred song; the full harmony of the choral music; the bright joy that lighted up every face, and the gratitude at 'harvest home,' which swelled every bosom,

—all conspired to make these days a season of pure, deep, and lively joy, which, in all its elements, finds no parallel among the observances of men.

TABI'THA (*antelope*), the Aramæan name of a Christian female, called in Greek Dorcas, resident at Joppa, whose benevolent and liberal conduct, especially in providing the poor with clothing, so endeared her to the Church in that place, that on her death they sent for Peter, then six miles off at Lydda, imploring him to come to them. The apostle complied with their urgent request, and after fervent prayer to God, bade the dead arise ; on which Tabitha 'opened her eyes, and when she saw Peter, she sat up.' This great miracle was not only an act of benevolence, but tended to give authority to the teaching of the Apostles, and to secure attention to the doctrines which they promulgated (see Acts ix. 36-42).

1. TA'BOR. a mountain on the confines of Zebulun and Naphtali, standing out in the northeast border of the plain of Esdraelon, the name of which appears among Greek and Roman writers in the forms of Itabyrion and Atabyrion, and which is now known by the name of *Jebel Tur*. Mount Tabor stands out alone and eminent above the plain, with all its fine proportions from base to summit displayed at one view. It lies at the distance of two hours and a quarter south of Nazareth. According to the barometrical measurements of Schubert, the height of Tabor above the level of the sea is 1748 Paris feet, and 1310 Paris feet above the level of the plain at its base. Seen from the south-west, it presents a semi-globular appearance ; but from the north-west, it more resembles a truncated cone. By an ancient path, which winds considerably, one may *ride* to the summit, where is a small oblong plain, with the foundations of ancient buildings. The view of the country from this place is very beautiful and extensive. The mountain is of limestone, which is the general rock of Palestine. The sides of the mountain are mostly covered with bushes, and woods of oak trees (ilex and ægilops), with occasionally pistachio trees, presenting a beautiful appearance, and affording a fine shade.

This mountain is several times mentioned in the Old Testament (Josh. xix. 12, 22 ; Judg. iv. 6, 12, 14) ; but not in the New. Its summit has, however, been usually regarded as the 'high mountain apart,' where our Lord was transfigured before Peter, James, and John. But the probability of this is opposed by circumstances which cannot be gainsaid. It is manifest that the Transfiguration took place in a solitary place, not only from the word 'apart.' but from the circumstance that Peter in his bewilderment proposed to build 'three tabernacles ' on the spot (Matt. xvii. 1-8 : Luke ix. 28-36). But we know that a fortified town occupied the top of Tabor for at least 220 years before and 60 years after the birth of Christ, and probably much before and long after ; and the tradition itself cannot be traced back earlier than towards the end of the fourth century.

2. TABOR is also the name of a grove of oaks in the vicinity of Benjamin, in 1 Sam. x. 3, the topography of which chapter is usually much embarrassed by the groundless notion that Mount Tabor is meant.

3. TABOR, a Levitical city in Zebulun, situated upon Mount Tabor (1 Chron. vi. 62).

TABRET. [MUSICAL INSTRUMENTS.]

TABRET [WEIGHTS AND MEASURES.]

TAD'MOR or TAMAR, a town built by king Solomon (1 Kings ix. 18 : 2 Chron. viii. 4). The name Tamar signifies a palm-tree, and hence the Greek and Roman designation of PALMYRA, ' city of palms ;' but this name never superseded the other among the natives, who even to this day give it the name of Thadmor. Palm trees are still found in the gardens around the town, but not in such numbers as would warrant, as they once did, the imposition of the name. Tadmor was situated between the Euphrates and Hamath, to the south-east of that city, in a fertile tract or oasis of the desert. It was built by Solomon, probably with the view of securing an interest in and command over the great caravan traffic from the east, similar to that which he had established in respect of the trade between Syria and Egypt.

Tadmor was for a long period under the sway of the Romans. But in the third century it attained independence under Odenatus and his celebrated consort Zenobia. It returned again, however, under the dominion of the Romans, and after various vicissitudes of fortune, it ultimately fell into the hands of the successors of Mohammed. From about the middle of the eighth century it seems gradually to have fallen into decay, but its magnificent ruins were scarcely known in Europe till towards the close of the seventeenth century.

The ruins cover a sandy plain stretching along the bases of a range of mountains called Jebel Belaes, running nearly north and south, dividing the great desert from the desert plains extending westward towards Damascus, and the north of Syria. The general aspect which these relics of ancient art and magnificence present, is well described by Volney :—' In the space covered by these ruins we sometimes find a palace, of which nothing remains but the court and walls ; sometimes a temple whose peristyle is half thrown down ; and now a portico, a gallery, or triumphal arch. Here stand groups of columns, whose symmetry is destroyed by the fall of many of them ; there, we see them ranged in rows of such length that, similar to rows of trees, they deceive the sight and assume the appearance of continued walls. If from this striking scene we cast our eyes upon the ground, another, almost as varied, presents itself : on all sides we behold nothing but subverted shafts, some whole, others shattered to pieces, or dislocated in their joints ; and on which side soever we look, the earth is strewed with vast stones, half buried ; with broken entablatures, mutilated friezes, disfigured reliefs, effaced sculptures, violated tombs, and altars defiled by dust.'

The present Tadmor consists of numbers of peasants' mud huts, clustered together around the great Temple of the Sun. This temple is the most remarkable and magnificent ruin of Palmyra. The court by which it was enclosed was 179 feet square, within which a double row of columns was continued all round. They were 390 in number. of which about sixty still remain standing. In the middle of the court stood the temple, an oblong quadrangular building, surrounded with columns, of which about twenty still exist, though without capitals, of which they have been plundered, probably because they were composed of metal. In the interior, at the south end, is now the humble mosque of the village.

TAHP'ANHES, or TEHAPHNEHES, a city of Egypt. The former name is used by Jeremiah (ii. 16; xliii. 7-9; xliv. 1; xlvi. 14), and the latter by Ezekiel (xxx. 18). This was doubtless *Daphne*, a strong boundary city on the Pelusiac arm of the Nile. A mound called Tel Defenneh, nearly in a direct line between the modern Zan and Pelusium, is supposed from its name and position to mark the site of Daphne. Isaiah (xxx. 4) names it in the abbreviated form Hanes. It was to this place that Johanan and his party repaired, taking Jeremiah with them, after the murder of Gedaliah.

TAH'PENES (*head of the age*), a queen of Egypt, consort of the Pharaoh contemporary with David. Her sister was given in marriage to Hadad, the fugitive prince of Edom (1 Kings xi. 19) [HADAD].

TAL'MAI (*full of furrows*), king of Geshur, and father of David's wife Maacah, the mother of Absalom (2 Sam. iii. 3; xiii. 37; 1 Chron. iii. 1, 2) [GESHUR].

1. TA'MAR (*palm-tree*), a Canaanitish woman, espoused successively to the two sons of Judah, Er and Onan; but as they both died childless, Judah hesitated to give her his third son Shelah, as patriarchal usage required. This set her upon the contrivance described in Gen. xxxviii.; and two sons, Pharez and Zarah, thus became the fruit of her criminal intercourse with Judah himself [JUDAH].

2. TAMAR, daughter of David by Maacah, who was also the mother of Absalom. The unhappy consequences of the criminal passion entertained for this beautiful damsel by her half-brother Amnon, brutally gratified by him, and terribly avenged by Absalom, formed the groundwork of the family distractions which embittered the latter years of David's reign (2 Sam. xiii.) [ABSALOM; AMNON; DAVID].

TAMARISK. This is supposed to be the meaning of the word *eshel*, which occurs in three places of Scripture, in one of which, in our Authorized Version, it is rendered *grove*, and in the other two *tree*. The first notice of this tree is in Gen. xxi. 33, 'And Abraham planted a grove (*eshel*) in Beersheba, and called there on the name of the Lord.' The second notice is in 1 Sam. xxii. 6: 'Now Saul abode in Gibeah under a tree (*eshel*) in Ramah, having his spear in his hand, and all his servants were standing about him.' Under such a tree also he and his sons were buried, for it is said (1 Sam. xxxi. 13), 'And they took their bones, and buried them under a tree (*eshel*) at Jabesh, and fasted seven days.'

From the characteristics of the tamarisk-tree of the East, it certainly appears as likely as any to have been planted in Beersheba by Abraham, because it is one of the few trees which will flourish and grow to a great size even in the arid desert. It has also a name in Arabic, *asul*, very similar to the Hebrew *eshel*. Besides the advantage of affording shade in a hot country, it is also esteemed on account of the excellence of its wood, which is converted into charcoal. It is no less valuable on account of the galls with which its branches are often loaded, and which are nearly as astringent as oak-galls. It is also one of those trees which were esteemed by the ancients.

It is very remarkable that the only tree which is found growing among the ruins of Babylon is a tamarisk. Thus, on the north side of the Kasr, where Ker Porter thought he saw traces of the hanging gardens, there stands upon an artificial

313. [Tamarisk. Tamarix orientalis.]

eminence a tree to which the Arabs give the name of *athela*. It is a species of tree altogether foreign to the country. Two of the attendants of Ker Porter, who were natives of Bender Bushire, assured him that there are trees of that kind in their country, which attain a very great age, and are called *gaz*. 'The one in question is in appearance like the weeping-willow, but the trunk is hollow through age, and partly shattered. The Arabs venerate it as sacred, in consequence of the Calif Ali having reposed under its shade after the battle of Hillah.'

TAM'MUZ, a Syrian deity, for whom the Hebrew idolatresses were accustomed to hold an annual lamentation (Ezek. viii. 14). This idol was the same with the Phœnician Adon or Adonis, and the feast itself such as they celebrated. The feast held in honour of Tammuz was solstitial, and commenced with the new moon of July, in the month also called Tammuz; it consisted of two parts, the one consecrated to lamentation, and the other to joy; in the days of grief they mourned the disappearance of the god, and in the days of gladness celebrated his discovery and return. Tammuz appears to have been a sort of incarnation of the sun, regarded principally as in a state of passion and sufferance, in connection with the apparent vicissitudes in its celestial position, and with respect to the terrestrial metamorphoses produced, under its influence, upon vegetation in advancing to maturity.

TAP'PUAH, or BETH-TAPPUAH, a city in the tribe of Judah, not far from Hebron (Josh. xv. 53). Robinson identifies it with an old village, called Teffuh, which he found upon the hills north-west of Hebron. 2. Another Tappuah lay in the plain of Judah, apparently in the vicinity of Zanoah, Jarmuth, Socoh, etc. (Josh. xv. 34): which of these was the place conquered by Joshua is not very clear (Josh. xii. 17; comp. x. 6). 3. Another place of the same name occurs on the

confines of Ephraim and Manasseh (Josh xvi. 8).
4. And in 1 Chron. ii. 43, a man of this name
appears.

TARES. The word (*zizanion*) thus rendered
occurs in Matt. xiii. 25, and several of the following verses. It is evident from the narrative that
the wheat and the *zizanion* must have had considerable resemblance to each other in the herbaceous parts, which could hardly be the case, unless
they were both of the family of the grasses. That
such, however, is the case, is evident from what
Volney says, that the peasants of Palestine and
Syria do not cleanse away the seeds of weeds
from their corn, but even leave that called *Siwan*
by the Arabs, which stuns people and makes them
giddy, as he himself experienced. The *Ziwan* of
the Arabs is concluded to be our Darnel, the *Lo-
lium temulentum* of botanists, and is well suited to
the palate. It is a grass often found in corn-fields,
resembling the wheat until both are in ear, and
remarkable as one of the very few of the numerous
family of grasses possessed of deleterious properties.

TAR'SHISH, a celebrated part of the ancient
world, about the exact position of which opinions
are much divided. From a careful examination
of the various Scriptural accounts and allusions it
appears that Tarshish was an old, celebrated,
opulent, cultivated, commercial city, which carried on trade in the Mediterranean and with the
sea-ports of Syria, especially Tyre and Joppa,
and that in all probability it is to be identified
with Tartessus in Spain, which appears to have
lain not far from the Straits of Gibraltar and near
the mouth of the Guadalquivir, consequently at
no great distance from the famous Granada of
later days. It is not improbable, however, that
the name may have been employed in a wider
sense, and may have denoted the district of south-
western Spain, comprising the several colonies
which Tyre planted in that country.

TARSHISH, a precious stone, so called as
brought from Tarshish, as Ophir is also put for
the gold brought from thence (Exod. xxviii. 20;
xxxix. 13; Ezek. i. 16; x. 9; xxviii 13; Cant.
v. 14; Dan. x. 6). The Septuagint, followed by
Josephus, makes it the ' chrysolite,' *i. e.* the topaz
of the moderns, which is still found in Spain.
Others suppose it to be 'amber:' but this does
not agree with the passages in Exodus, which
make the Tarshish to have been one of the engraved stones of the high-priest's breast-plate.
The word is translated ' beryl ' in the Authorized
Version.

TAR'SUS, a celebrated city, the metropolis of
Cilicia, in Asia Minor, on the banks of the river
Cydnus, which flowed through it, and divided it
into two parts. Tarsus was a distinguished seat
of Greek philosophy and literature, and, from the
number of its schools and learned men, was ranked
by the side of Athens and Alexandria. Augustus
made Tarsus free. This seems to have implied
the privilege of being governed by its own laws
and magistrates, with freedom from tribute; but
did not confer the *jus coloniarum*, nor the *jus civi-
tatis:* and it was not therefore, as usually supposed, on this account, that Paul enjoyed the privilege of Roman citizenship. Tarsus, indeed,
eventually did become a Roman colony, which
gave to the inhabitants this privilege; but this
was not till long after the time of Paul. We thus

find that the Roman tribune at Jerusalem ordered
Paul to be scourged, though he knew that he was
a native of Tarsus, but desisted on learning that
he was a Roman citizen (Acts ix. 11; xxi. 39;
xxii. 24, 27). In the time of Abulfeda, that is,
towards the end of the thirteenth and beginning
of the fourteenth century, Tarsus was still large,
and surrounded by a double wall, and in the occupation of Armenian Christians It is now a
poor and decayed town, inhabited by Turks; but
it is not so much fallen as many other anciently
great towns of the same quarter, the population
being estimated at 30,000. There are some considerable remains of the ancient city.

TAR'TAK, an idol of the Avites, introduced
by them into Samaria (2 Kings xvii. 31).

TAR'TAN, an Assyrian general whom Sennacherib sent, accompanied by Rabsaris and Rabshakeh, to Jerusalem (2 Kings xviii. 17). It is
not known whether this is the same officer who in
a preceding reign besieged and took Ashdod for
his master (Isa. xx. 1).

TAT'NAI (Pers., perhaps *gift*), a Persian
governor, who succeeded Rehum in the rule of
Samaria, and probably of other provinces north
of Judæa. He appears to have been a more just
person, and more friendly to the Jews, than his
predecessor. An adverse report of their proceedings at Jerusalem reached him; but he resolved
to suspend his judgment till he had examined into
the matter on the spot. He accordingly repaired
thither, accompanied by another great officer,
named Shethar-boznai, and their colleagues, and
finding that the Jews alleged the authority of a
royal decree for their proceedings, he sent to the
supreme government a temperate and fair report,
founded on the information he had obtained, suggesting that the statement made by the Jews as to
the decree of Cyrus and other matters should be
verified by reference to the archives at Babylon.
Then, without one word to influence the decision
or to prejudice the claim advanced, Tatnai concludes with intimating that he awaits the royal
orders. This official letter of the Persian governor
is quite a model of exactness, moderation, and
truth, and gives a very favourable idea of the ad-
ministrative part of the Persian government. This
took place in the second year of Darius, B.C. 519.
The rescript being favourable to the claim of the
Jews, whose statement had been verified by the
discovery of the original decree of Cyrus, Tatnai
and his colleagues applied themselves with vigour
to the execution of the royal commands (Ezra v.
and vi.).

TAVERNS, THE THREE. The name of a
small place on the Appian way, mentioned in
Acts xxviii. 15. It probably derived its name
from three large inns, or eating-houses, for the
refreshment of travellers passing to and from
Rome. The place still remains, and is called Tre
Taverne: it is about thirty-three miles from
Rome.

TE'BETH, the tenth month (Esth. ii. 16) of
the sacred year of the Hebrews, commenced with
the new moon in December, and terminated at
the new moon in January.

TEIL-TREE (Isa. vi. 13) is the linden-tree, or
Tilia Europæus of botanists.

TE'KEL. [MENE, &c.]

TEKO'A, a city south of Bethlehem, on the
borders of the desert to which it gave name, and

3 c

noted as the residence of 'the wise woman' who interceded for Absalom; as one of the towns fortified by Rehoboam; and as the birthplace of the prophet Amos (2 Sam. xiv. 2; 1 Chron. ii. 24; 2 Chron. xx. 20; Jer. vi. 1; Amos i. 1). The site has long been known; it lies six miles south of Bethlehem, on an elevated hill, not steep, but broad at the top, and covered with ruins to the extent of four or five acres. The site commands extensive prospects, and towards the east is bounded only by the level mountains of Moab. Before and during the Crusades Tekoa was well inhabited by Christians; but in A.D. 1138 it was sacked by a party of Turks from beyond the Jordan, and nothing further is known of it till the seventeenth century, when it lay desolate, as it has ever since done.

TE'LEM, a city in Judah (Josh. xv. 24).

TE'MA, a tract and people in the northern part of the Arabian desert, adjacent to the Syrian desert, so called from Tema, the son of Ishmael (Gen. xxv. 15; Job vi. 19; Isa. xxi. 14; Jer. xxv. 23). This tract is still called Tema by the Arabs [ARABIA].

TE'MAN, a grandson of Esau (Gen. xxxvi. 11, 15); also a city, region, and people on the east of Idumæa sprung from him (Gen. xxxvi 42; Jer. xlix. 7; Ezek. xxv. 13; Amos i. 11, 12; Obad. 9). Like other Arabs (1 Kings v. 12), the Temanites were celebrated for wisdom (Jer. xlix. 7; Bar. iii. 22, 23; comp. Job ii. 11; xxi. 1).

TE'MANITE, one belonging to the tribe or country of Tema (Job ii. 11; xxi. 1).

TEMPLE. After the Israelites had exchanged their nomadic life for a life in permanent habitations, it was becoming that they should exchange also their movable sanctuary or tabernacle for a temple. There elapsed, however, after the conquest of Palestine, several centuries during which the sanctuary continued movable, although the nation became more and more stationary. It appears that the first who planned the erection of a stone-built sanctuary was David, who, when he was inhabiting his house of cedar, and God had given him rest from all his enemies, meditated the design of building a temple in which the ark of God might be placed, instead of being deposited 'within curtains,' or in a tent, as hitherto. This design was at first encouraged by the prophet Nathan; but he was afterwards instructed to tell David that such a work was less appropriate for him, who had been a warrior from his youth, and had shed much blood, than for his son, who should enjoy in prosperity and peace the rewards of his father's victories Nevertheless, the design itself was highly approved as a token of proper feelings towards the Divine King (2 Sam. vii. 1-12; 1 Chron. xvii. 1-14; xxviii.). We learn, moreover, from 1 Kings v., and 1 Chron. xxii, that David had collected materials which were afterwards employed in the erection of the temple, which was commenced four years after his death, about B C. 1012, four hundred and eighty years after the Exodus from Egypt, and was about seven years in building. We thus learn that the Israelitish sanctuary had remained movable more than four centuries subsequent to the conquest of Canaan.

The site of the temple was on Mount Moriah, which was at first insufficient for the temple and altar, and therefore walls and buttresses were built in order to gain more ground by filling up the interval with earth. The hill was also fortified by a threefold wall, the lowest tier of which was in some places more than 300 cubits high; and the depth of the foundation was not visible, because it had been necessary in some parts to dig deep into the ground in order to obtain sufficient support. The dimensions of the stones of which the walls were composed were enormous; Josephus mentions a length of 40 cubits.

The workmen and the materials employed in the erection of the temple were chiefly procured by Solomon from Hiram, king of Tyre, who was rewarded by a liberal importation of wheat. Josephus states that the foundation was sunk to an astonishing depth, and composed of stones of singular magnitude, and very durable. Being closely mortised into the rock with great ingenuity, they formed a basis adequate to the support of the intended structure.

The temple itself and its utensils are described in 1 Kings vi. and vii., and 2 Chron. iii. and iv.

Divines and architects have repeatedly endeavoured to represent the architectural proportions of the temple, which was 60 cubits long, 20 wide, and 30 high. The internal dimension of the 'holy' was 40 cubits long, 20 cubits wide, and 30 cubits high. The holy was separated from the 'holy of holies' by a partition, a large opening in which was closed by a suspended curtain. The holy of holies was on the western extremity of the entire building, and its internal dimensions formed a cube of 20 cubits. On the eastern extremity of the building was the porch, at the entrance of which stood the two columns called Jachin and Boaz, which were 23 cubits high.

The temple was also surrounded by three stories of chambers, each of which stories was five cubits high, so that there remained above, ample space for introducing the windows, which served chiefly for ventilation, as the light within the temple was obtained from the sacred candlesticks. The windows which are mentioned in 1 Kings vi. 4, consisted probably of lattice-work.

It seems from the descriptions of the temple to be certain that the holy of holies was an adytum without windows. To this fact Solomon seems to refer when he spake, 'The Lord said that he would dwell in the thick darkness' (1 Kings viii. 12).

From 1 Kings vii. 10, we learn that the private dwellings of Solomon were built of massive stone. We hence infer, that the framework of the temple also consisted of the same material. The temple was, however, wainscoted with cedar wood, which was covered with gold. The boards within the temple were ornamented by beautiful carvings representing cherubim, palms, and flowers. The ceiling of the temple was supported by beams of cedar wood. The wall which separated the holy from the holy of holies probably consisted not of stone, but of beams of cedar. The partitions were probably in part reticulated, so that the incense could spread from the holy to the most holy.

The floor of the temple was throughout of cedar, but boarded over with planks of fir (1 Kings vi. 15). The doors of the oracle were composed of olive-tree; but the doors of the outer temple had posts of olive-tree and leaves of fir (1 Kings vi. 31, sq.). Both doors, as well that which led into the temple as that which led from the holy to the holy of holies, had folding leaves, which, however, seem to have been usually kept open, the aperture being closed by a suspended curtain

Within the holy of holies stood only the ark of the covenant; but within the holy were ten golden candlesticks, and the altar of incense (comp. the separate articles).

The temple was surrounded by an inner court, which in Chronicles is called the Court of the Priests, and in Jeremiah the Upper Court. This again was surrounded by a wall consisting of cedar beams placed on a stone foundation (1 Kings vi. 36). Besides this inner court there is mentioned a Great Court (2 Chron. iv. 9). This court was also more especially called the court of the Lord's house (Jer. xix. 12; xxvi. 2). These courts were surrounded by spacious buildings, which, however, according to Josephus, seem to have been partly added at a period later than that of Solomon. From these descriptions we learn that the temple of Solomon was not distinguished by magnitude, but by good architectural proportions, beauty of workmanship, and costliness of materials. Many English churches have an external form not unlike that of the temple of Solomon.

There was a treasury in the temple, in which much precious metal was collected for the maintenance of public worship. The gold and silver of the temple was, however, frequently applied to political purposes, and the treasury was repeatedly plundered by foreign invaders. The sacred edifice was burned down by Nebuchadnezzar, B C. 588, having stood since its commencement 417 or 418 years. Thus terminated what the later Jews called *the first house.*

THE SECOND TEMPLE.—In the year B.C. 536 the Jews obtained permission from Cyrus to colonise their native land. Cyrus commanded also that the sacred utensils which had been pillaged from the first temple should be restored, and that for the restoration of the temple assistance should be granted (Ezra i. and vi.; 2 Chron. xxxvi. 22, sq.). The first colony, which returned under Zerubbabel and Joshua, having collected the necessary means, and having also obtained the assistance of Phœnician workmen, commenced in the second year after their return, B.C. 534, the rebuilding of the temple. The Sidonians brought rafts of cedar trees from Lebanon to Joppa. The Jews refused the co-operation of the Samaritans, who, being thereby offended, induced the king Artaxashta (probably Smerdis) to prohibit the building. And it was only in the second year of Darius Hystaspis, B.C. 520, that the building was resumed. It was completed in the sixth year of this king, B C. 516.

This second temple was erected on the site of the former, and probably after the same plan. The old men who had seen the first temple were moved to tears on beholding the second, which appeared insignificant in comparison with the first (Ezra iii. 12; Haggai ii. 3, sq.). It seems, however, that it was not so much in dimensions that the second temple was inferior to the first, as in splendour, and in being deprived of the ark of the covenant, which had been burned with the temple of Solomon.

TEMPLE OF HEROD.—Herod, wishing to ingratiate himself with the people, and being fond of architectural display, undertook not merely to repair the second temple, but to raise a perfectly new structure. As, however, the temple of Zerubbabel was not actually destroyed, but only removed after the preparations for the new temple were completed, there has arisen some debate whether the temple of Herod could properly be called the third temple.

The work was commenced in the eighteenth year of the reign of Herod; that is, about the year 734-735 from the building of Rome, or about twenty or twenty-one years before the Christian era. Priests and Levites finished the temple itself in one year and a half. The outbuildings and courts required eight years. However, some building operations were constantly in progress under the successors of Herod, and it is in reference to this we are informed that the temple was finished only under Albinus, the last procurator but one, not long before the commencement of the Jewish war in which the temple was again destroyed. It is in reference also to these protracted building operations that the Jews said to Jesus, 'Forty and six years was this temple in building' (John ii. 20).

The whole of the structures belonging to the temple were a stadium square, and consequently four stadia (or half a Roman mile) in circumference. The temple was situated on the highest point, not quite in the centre, but rather to the north-western corner of this square, and was surrounded by various courts, the innermost of which was higher than the next outward, which descended in terraces. The temple, consequently, was visible from the town, notwithstanding its various high enclosures. The outer court was called *the mountain of the house,* and had five principal gates. Annexed to the outer wall were halls which surrounded the temple. The Levites resided in these halls, and they seem likewise to have been used by religious teachers for the purpose of addressing their hearers. Thus we find that Jesus had there various opportunities for addressing the people and refuting cavillers. Here also the first Christians could daily assemble with one accord (Acts ii. 46). Within this outer court money-changers and cattle-dealers transacted a profitable business, especially during the time of Passover. The profaneness to which this money-changing and cattle-dealing gave rise caused the indignation of our Lord, who suddenly expelled all these traffickers from their stronghold of business (Matt. xxi. 12, sq.; Mark xi. 15-17; Luke xix. 45, 46; John ii. 13-17).

The holy of holies was entirely empty, but there was a stone in the place of the ark of the covenant, on which the high-priest placed the censer. Before the entrance of the holy of holies was suspended a curtain, which was rent by the earthquake that followed after the crucifixion.

The temple was situated upon the south-eastern corner of Mount Moriah, which is separated to the east by a precipitous ravine and the Kidron from the Mount of Olives, which is much higher than Moriah. On the south the temple was bounded by the ravine which separates Moriah from Zion, or the lower city from the upper city. Opposite to the temple, at the foot of Zion, were formerly the king's gardens, and higher up, in a south-westerly direction, the stronghold of Zion, or the city of David, on a higher level than the temple. The temple was in ancient warfare almost impregnable, from the ravines at the precipitous edge of which it stood; but it required more artificial fortifications on its western and northern sides, which were surrounded by the city of Jerusalem; for this reason there was erected at its north-western corner the tower of Antonia, which, although standing on a lower level than the temple itself, was so high as to overlook the sacred buildings, with which it was connected partly by a large staircase, partly by a subterraneous communication. This tower protected the temple from sudden incursions from the city of Jerusalem, and from dangerous commotions among the thousands who were frequently assembled within the precincts of the courts, which also were sometimes used for popular meetings. Under the sons of Herod, the temple remained apparently in good order, and Herod Agrippa, who was appointed by the Emperor Claudius its guardian, even planned the repair of the eastern part, which had probably been destroyed during one of the conflicts between the Jews and Romans of which the temple was repeatedly the scene (*Antiq.* xvii. 10). Many writers on the subject have adopted a style as if they possessed much information about the archives of the temple; there are a few indications from which we learn that important documents were deposited in the tabernacle and temple. Even in Deut. xxxi. 26, we find that the book of the law was deposited in the ark of the covenant. 2 Kings xxii. 8, Hilkiah rediscovered the book of the law in the house of Jehovah. In 2 Macc. ii. 13, we find a bibliotheca or library mentioned, apparently consisting chiefly of the canonical books, and probably deposited in the temple. In Josephus it is mentioned that a book of the law was found in the temple. It appears that the sacred writings were kept in the temple. Copies of political documents seem to have been deposited in the treasury of the temple.

During the final struggle of the Jews against the Romans, A.D. 70, the temple was the last scene of the tug of war. The Romans rushed from the tower Antonia into the sacred precincts, the halls of which were set on fire by the Jews themselves. It was against the will of Titus that a Roman soldier threw a firebrand into the northern outbuildings of the temple, which caused the conflagration of the whole structure, although Titus himself endeavoured to extinguish the fire.

The sacred utensils, the golden table of the shew-bread, the book of the law, and the golden candlestick, were displayed in the triumph at Rome. Representations of them are still to be seen sculptured in relief on the triumphal arch of Titus. The place where the temple had stood seemed to be a dangerous centre for the rebellious population, until, in A.D. 136, the Emperor Hadrian founded a Roman colony, under the name Ælia Capitolina, on the ruins of Jerusalem, and dedicated a temple to Jupiter Capitolinus on the ruins of the temple of Jehovah. Henceforth no Jew was permitted to approach the site of the ancient temple.

The Emperor Julian undertook, A.D. 363, to rebuild the temple; but after considerable preparations and much expense, he was compelled to desist by flames which burst forth from the foundations. A splendid mosque now stands on the site of the temple. This mosque was erected by the caliph Omar after the conquest of Jerusalem by the Saracens, A.D. 636.

TEMPTATION OF OUR LORD (Matt. iv. 1-11; Mark i. 12, 13; Luke iv. 1-12). The popular view of this undoubted portion of our Saviour's history, is, that it is a narrative of outward transactions; that our Saviour immediately after his baptism was conducted by the Spirit into the wilderness—either the desolate and mountainous region now called Quarantania by the people of Palestine, or the great desert of Arabia, mentioned in Deut. xxxii. 10; viii. 15; Hos. xiii. 5; Jer. ii. 6, &c.—where the devil tempted him in person, appeared to him in a visible form, spoke to him in an audible voice, removed him to the summit ' of an exceeding high mountain,' and to the top of 'a pinnacle of the temple at Jerusalem;' whereas the view taken by many learned commentators, ancient and modern, is, that it is the narrative of a *vision*, which was designed to ' supply that ideal experience of temptation or trial, which it was provided in the divine counsels for our Lord to receive, previously to entering upon the actual trials and difficulties of his ministry.'

TENT. The patriarchal fathers of the Israelites were dwellers in tents, and their descendants proceeded at once from tents to houses. We therefore read but little of *huts* among them; and never as the fixed habitations of any people with whom they were conversant. Tents were invented before the Deluge, and appear from the first to have been associated with the pastoral life, to which a movable habitation was necessary (Gen. iv. 20). The practice of the pastoral fathers was to pitch their tents near wells of water, and, if possible, under some shady tree (Gen. xviii. 4; Judg. iv. 5). The first tents were undoubtedly covered with skins, of which there are traces in the Pentateuch (Exod. xxvi

314. [Arabian Tent.]

14); but nearly all the tents mentioned in Scripture were, doubtless, of goats' hair, spun and woven by the women (Exod. xxxv. 26; xxxvi. 14); such as are now, in Western Asia, used by all who dwell in tents; hence their black colour (Sol. Song, i. 5). Tents of linen were, and still are, only used occasionally, for holiday or travelling purposes, by those who do not habitually live in them. The patriarchal tents were probably such as we now see in Arabia, of an oblong shape, and eight or ten feet high in the middle. They vary in size, and have, accordingly, a greater or less number of poles to support them—from three to nine. An encampment is generally arranged circularly, forming an enclosure, within which the cattle are driven at night, and the centre of which is occupied by the tent or tents of the Emir or Sheikh. If he is a person of much consequence, he may have three or four tents, for himself, his wives, his servants, and strangers respectively. The two first are of the most importance, and we know that Abraham's wife had a separate tent (Gen. xxiv. 27). It is more usual, however, for one very large tent to be divided into two or more apartments by curtains. The Holy Tabernacle was on this model (Exod. xxvi. 31-37).

TE′RAH, son of Nahor and father of Abraham, who, with his family, quitted Ur of the Chaldees to go to the land which God should show him, ' but tarried at Haran in Mesopotamia, and there died at the age of 205 years' (Gen. xi 24-32; Acts vii. 2-4). From the latter text, it appears that the first call which prompted them to leave Ur was addressed to Abraham, not to Terah, as well as the second, which, after the death of his father, induced him to proceed from Haran to Canaan [ABRAHAM]. The order to Abraham to proceed to Canaan immediately after Terah's death seems to indicate that the pause at Haran was on his account. Whether he declined to proceed any further, or his advanced age rendered him unequal to the fatigues of the journey, can only be conjectured.

TER′APHIM were tutelar household gods, by whom families expected, for worship bestowed, to be rewarded with domestic prosperity, such as plenty of food, health, and various necessaries of domestic life.

We have most remarkable proofs that the worship of teraphim co-existed with the worship of Jehovah even in pious families; and we have more than one instance of the wives of worshippers of Jehovah not finding full contentment and satisfaction in the stern moral truth of spiritual worship, and therefore carrying on some private symbolism by fondling the teraphim.

We find in Gen. xxxi. 19, that Rachel stole the images (teraphim) belonging to her father without the knowledge of her husband, who, being accused by his father-in-law of having stolen his gods, answered, 'With whomsoever thou findest thy gods, let him not live.' Laban searched, but found not the images (teraphim).

Among the ancient Israelites the worship of Jehovah was frequently blended with that of a graven image or teraphim, but on every revival of the knowledge of the written revelation of God the teraphim were swept away together with the worse forms of idolatry (2 Kings xxiii. 24).

The teraphim were consulted by persons on whom true religion had no firm hold, in order to elicit some supernatural omens similar to the auguries of the Romans (Zech. x. 2; Ezek. xxi. 21-26).

TEREBINTH. This is the proper rendering of the word (ALAH) which has been variously translated as *oak*, *teil tree*, *elm*, and even *plane*. In Palestine and the neighbouring countries, the terebinth seems to be regarded with much the same distinction as the oak is in our northern latitudes. The tree is long lived. About the time of Christ, there was at Mamre near Hebron a venerable terebinth, which a tradition, old in the time of Josephus, alleged to be that under which Abraham pitched his tent (Gen. xiii. 18).

Dr. Robinson states, that at the point where the roads from Gaza to Jerusalem, and from Hebron to Ramleh, cross each other, he observed an immense terebinth tree, the largest he saw anywhere in Palestine ; 'This species (*Pistacia Terebinthus*) is without doubt,' he adds, ' the terebinth of the Old Testament, and under the shade of such a tree Abraham may well have pitched his tent at Mamre.' The terebinth is not an evergreen, as has often been represented, but its small feathered lancet-shaped leaves fall in the autumn, and are renewed in the spring. The flowers are small, and are followed by small oval berries, hanging in clusters from two to five inches in length, resembling much the clusters of the vine when the grapes are just set. From incisions in the trunk, there is said to flow a sort of transparent balsam, constituting a very pure and fine species of turpentine, with an agreeable odour, and hardening gradually into a transparent gum [OAK].

315. [Terebinth tree]

TER′TIUS. We learn from Rom. xvi. 22 (' I Tertius, who wrote this epistle, salute you in the Lord '), that the Apostle Paul dictated that epistle to Tertius. Some writers say that Tertius was bishop of Iconium.

TERTUL′LUS, the Roman orator or advocate employed by the Sanhedrim, to sustain their accusation against Paul before the Roman governor (Acts xxiv. 1-8). The Jews, as well as the other peoples subject to the Romans, in their accusations and processes before the Roman magistrates, were obliged to follow the forms of the Roman law, of which they knew little. The different provinces, and particularly the principal cities, consequently abounded with persons who, at the same time advocates and orators, were equally ready to plead in civil actions or to harangue on public affairs. This they did, either in Greek or Latin, as the place or occasion required.

TESTAMENT. [BIBLE.]

TET′RARCH, a prince or sovereign who holds or governs a fourth part of a kingdom, without wearing the diadem or bearing the title of king. Such was the original import of the word, but it was afterwards applied to any petty king or sovereign, and became synonymous with ethnarch.

In the reign of Tiberius Cæsar Herod's kingdom of Judæa was divided into three parts, which were called tetrarchies, and the sovereigns tetrarchs. His sons were made the heirs to his kingdom. Archelaus became tetrarch of Judæa, Samaria, and Idumæa: Philip of Trachonitis and Ituræa; and Herod Antipas of Galilee and Peræa (Luke iii. 1). Herod Agrippa, the nephew of Herod Antipas, who afterwards obtained the title of king (Acts xxv. 13), was in the reign of Caligula invested with royalty, and appointed tetrarch of Abilene; to which was afterwards added Galilee and Peræa, Judæa and Samaria; until at length his dominion extended over the whole land of Palestine [HERODIAN FAMILY]. The title of tetrarch was frequently conferred upon the descendants of Herod the Great by the Roman emperors.

THADDE'US. a surname of the Apostle Jude, who was also called Lebbæus (Matt. x. 3; Mark iii. 18; comp. Luke vi. 16) [JUDE].

THAM'MUZ. [TAMMUZ.]

THEBES is a name borne by two of the most celebrated cities in the ancient world, Thebes in Bœotia, and Thebes in Egypt. Of the latter it is that we have here to speak in brief, referring those who wish for detailed information to the works of Wilkinson, especially his *Modern Egypt and Thebes.*

The name Thebes is corrupted from the Tápé of the ancient Egyptian language, the meaning of which appears to be ' the head,' Thebes being the capital of the Thebais in Upper Egypt. It is termed in Scripture No and No-Ammon (Jerem. xlvi. 25; Ezek. xxx. 14; Nahum iii. 8). Thebes was situate on both sides of the river Nile, and had canals cutting the land in all directions. It was probably the most ancient city of Egypt, and the residence in very early ages of Egyptian kings who ruled the land during several dynasties. The plain was adorned not only by large and handsome dwellings for man, but by temples and palaces, of whose grandeur words can give but a faint conception. Of these edifices there are still in existence ruins that astound and delight the traveller. The most ancient remains now existing are in the immense temple, or rather cluster of temples, of Karnak, the largest and most splendid ruin of which either ancient or modern times can boast, being the work of a number of successive monarchs, each anxious to surpass his predecessor by increasing the dimensions of the part he added. Osirtasen I., the contemporary of Joseph. is the earliest monarch whose name appears on the monuments of Thebes. On the western shore the chief points of interest are the palace and temple of Rameses II, erroneously called the Memnonium; the temples of Medinet Habu, the statue of Memnon, and the tombs of the kings. On the eastern shore are the temple of Luksor, and the temple of Karnak, already mentioned. 'It is impossible,' says Robinson (*Bib. Researches*, i. 29), ' to wander among these scenes and behold these hoary yet magnificent ruins without emotions of astonishment and deep solemnity. Everything around testifies of vastness and of utter desolation. Here

lay once that mighty city whose power and splendour were proverbial throughout the ancient world.' Yet, like all earthly things, Thebes had her period of death. She sprang up, flourished, declined, and sank. Memphis rose to be her rival when Thebes began to part with her glory. She was plundered by Cambyses, and destroyed by Ptolemy Lathyrus. In Strabo's time the city was already fallen; yet its remains then covered eighty stadia, and the inhabited part was divided into many separate villages, as the ruins now are portioned out between nine hamlets. The period in which Thebes enjoyed the highest prosperity Robinson considers to have been coeval with the reigns of David and Solomon. This, however, appears too late a date. From the passage in Nahum (iii. 8, sq.), it would seem that in his day (according to Josephus, cir. 750 B.C.) the city had suffered a terrible overthrow—how long previously is not recorded, for we do not know what conquest or what conqueror was here intended by the prophet. The walls of all the temples at Thebes are covered with sculptures and hieroglyphics, representing in general the deeds of the kings who founded or enlarged these structures. Many of these afford happy illustrations of Egyptian history.

THE'BEZ, a place near Shechem, where Abimelech met his death (Judg. ix. 50; 2 Sam. xi. 21). It seems to be the same with the place now called Tubas.

THEOPH'ILUS (*lover of God*), a person of distinction, to whom St Luke inscribed his Gospel and the Acts of the Apostles (Luke i. 3; Acts i. 1). The title given him, translated ' most excellent,' is the same which is given to governors of provinces, as Felix and Festus (Acts xxiii. 26; xxvi. 25); whence he is conceived by some to have been a civil magistrate in some high office.

THESSALONIANS, EPISTLES TO THE. —FIRST EPISTLE.—The authenticity and canonical authority of this epistle have been from the earliest ages admitted, nor have these points ever been called in question, either in ancient or modern times, by those who have received any of Paul's Epistles.

This epistle has generally been regarded as the first written by Paul of those now extant. In the Acts of the Apostles (xvii. 5, sq.) we are told that Paul, after preaching the Gospel with success at Thessalonica, had to flee from that city in consequence of the malice of the Jews; that he thence betook himself to Berea, in company with Silas; that, driven by the same influence from Berea, he journeyed to Athens, leaving Silas and Timothy (the latter of whom had probably preceded him to Berea) behind him; and that after remaining in that city for some time, he went to Corinth, where he was joined by Timothy and Silas. It appears also from this epistle (iii. 1, 2, 5), that whilst at Athens he had commissioned Timothy to visit the infant church at Thessalonica; and from Acts xvii. 15, 16, we learn that he expected to be joined by Timothy and Silas in that city. Whether this expected meeting ever took place there, is a matter involved in much uncertainty.

But whatever view we adopt on this point, it seems indisputable that this epistle was not written until Paul met Timothy and Silas at Corinth. The ancient subscription, indeed, testifies that it was written at Athens; but that this could not be the case is clear from the epistle itself. It must, however, have been written very soon after his arrival at Corinth; for, at the time of his writing, Timothy had just arrived from Thessalonica, and Paul had not been long in Corinth before Timothy and Silas joined him there (Acts xvii. 1-5).

The design of this epistle is to comfort the Thessalonians under trial, and to encourage them to the patient and consistent profession of Christianity. The epistle may be conveniently divided into two parts. The former of these, which comprises the first three chapters, is occupied with statements chiefly of a retrospective character: it details the apostle's experience among the Thessalonians, his confidence in them, his deep regard for them, and his efforts and prayers on their behalf. The latter part of the epistle (iv. 5) is, for the most part, of a hortatory character: it contains the apostle's admonitions to the Thessalonians to walk according to their profession; to avoid sensuality, dishonesty, and pride; to cultivate brotherly love, to attend diligently to the duties of life, to take the comfort which the prospect of Christ's second coming was calculated to convey, but not to allow that to seduce them into indolence or idle speculations; to render due respect to their spiritual superiors; and, by attention to a number of duties which the apostle specifies, to prove themselves worthy of the good opinion he entertained of them. He concludes the epistle by offering fervent supplication on their behalf, and the usual apostolic benediction.

SECOND EPISTLE.—The apostle's allusion in his former epistle to the second coming of Christ, and especially his statement in ch. iv. 15-18, appear to have been misunderstood by the Thessalonians or wilfully perverted by some among them, so as to favour the notion that that event was near at hand. This notion some inculcated as a truth specially confirmed to them by the Spirit; others advocated it as part of the apostolic doctrine; and some claimed for it the specific support of Paul in a letter (ii. 2). Whether the letter here referred to is the apostle's former epistle to the Thessalonians, or one forged in his name by some keen and unscrupulous advocates of the notion above referred to, is uncertain.

On receiving intelligence of the trouble into which the Thessalonians had been plunged, in consequence of the prevalence among them of the notion (from whatever source derived) that the second coming of Christ was nigh at hand, Paul wrote to them this second epistle, in which he beseechingly adjures them by the very fact that Christ is to come a second time, not to be shaken in mind or troubled, as if that event were near at hand. He informs them that much was to happen before that should take place, and especially predicts a great apostasy from the purity and simplicity of the Christian faith (ii. 5-12). He then exhorts them to hold fast by the traditions they had received, whether by word or epistle, and commends them to the consoling and sustaining grace of God (ver. 15-17). The rest of the epistle consists of expressions of affection to the Thessalonians, and of confidence in them: of prayers on their behalf, and of exhortations and directions suited to the circumstances in which they were placed.

There is the strongest reason for believing that this second epistle was written very soon after the first, and at the same place, viz. Corinth. The internal evidence in favour of the genuineness of this epistle is equally strong with that which attests the first.

THESSALONI'CA, now called Salonichi, is still a city of about sixty or seventy thousand inhabitants, situated on the present gulf of Salonichi, which was formerly called Sinus Thermaicus, at the mouth of the river Echedorus. It was the residence of a *præses*, the principal city of the second part of Macedonia, and was by later writers even styled *metropolis*. Under the Romans it became great, populous, and wealthy. It had its name from Thessalonice, wife of Cassander, who built the city on the site of the ancient Thermæ, after which town the *Sinus Thermaicus* was called. Thessalonica was 267 Roman miles east of Apollonia and Dyrrachium, 66 miles from Amphipolis, 89 from Philippi, 433 west from Byzantium, and 150 south of Sophia. A great number of Jews were living at Thessalonica in the time of the apostle Paul, and also many Christian converts, most of whom seem to have been either Jews by birth or proselytes before they embraced Christianity by the preaching of Paul. Jews are still very numerous in this town, and possess much influence there. They are unusually exclusive, keeping aloof from strangers. The apostolical history of the place is given in the preceding article. The present town stands on the acclivity of a steep hill, rising at the northeastern extremity of the bay. It presents an imposing appearance from the sea, with which the interior by no means corresponds. The principal antiquities are the propylæa of the hippodrome, the rotunda, and the triumphal arches of Augustus and Constantine.

THEU'DAS, a Jewish insurgent, who was slain, while a band of followers that he had induced to join him were scattered and brought to nought. This statement was made by Gamaliel at the meeting of the Sanhedrim held about A.D. 33, to consider what measures should be taken for the suppression of the Gospel now preached and recommended by the virgin zeal of Peter and the apostles (Acts v. 29, 34, sq.). Josephus (*Antiq.* xx. 5. 1) tells us of a Theudas who, under the procurator Phadus (A.D. 44), set up for a prophet, and brought ruin on himself and many whom he deluded, and attempts have been made, though not very successfully, to identify the Theudas of Gamaliel with the insurgent spoken of by Josephus, who appeared eleven years later.

These remarks have been made to meet the ordinary view of the case. But the name Theudas is an Aramaic form of the Greek *Theodotos*, which is a literal translation of the Hebrew Matthias or Matthew. It is, then, of a Matthew that Luke speaks; and in Josephus (*Antiq.* xvii. 6. 2-4) we find a detailed account of one Matthew, a distinguished teacher among the Jews, who, in the latter days of Herod the Great, raised a band of his scholars to effect a social reform in the spirit of the old Hebrew constitution, by 'destroying the heathen works which the king had erected contrary to the law of their fathers.' A large golden eagle, which the king had caused to be erected over the great gate of the Temple, in defiance of the law that forbids images or representations of any living creatures, was an object of their special dislike, which, on hearing a false report that Herod was dead, Matthias and his companions proceeded to demolish; when the king's captain, supposing the undertaking to have a higher aim than was the fact, came upon the riotous reformers with a band of soldiers, and arrested the proceedings of the multitude. Dispersing the mob, he apprehended forty of the bolder spirits, together with Matthias and his fellow-leader Judas. Matthias was burnt.

THIEF, PENITENT, ON THE CROSS (Luke xxiii. 39-43). It has been assumed that this man had been very wicked; that he continued so till he was nailed to the cross; that he joined the other malefactor in insulting the Saviour; and that then, by a miracle of grace, he was transformed into a penitent Christian. Some eminent writers, however, are of opinion, that he was, in all probability, not a thief who robbed for profit, but one of the insurgents who had taken up arms on a principle of resistance to the Roman oppression, and to what they thought an unlawful burden, the tribute-money. They are of opinion, also, that it is far from certain that either his faith or repentance was the fruit of this particular season. He must have known something of the Saviour, otherwise he could not have said 'he hath done nothing amiss.' He was convinced of our Lord's Messiahship: 'Lord, remember me when thou comest into thy kingdom.' Koecher tells us that it is a very ancient tradition that the thief was not converted at the cross, but was previously imbued with a knowledge of the Gospel.

THIGH, the part of the body from the legs to the trunk, of men, quadrupeds, &c. *Putting the hand under the thigh* appears to have been a very ancient custom, upon occasion of taking an oath to any one. Abraham required this of the oldest servant of his house, when he made him swear that he would not take a wife for Isaac of the daughters of the Canaanites (Gen. xxiv. 2-9). Jacob required it of his son Joseph, when he bound him by oath not to bury him in Egypt, but with his fathers in the land of Canaan (xlvii. 29-31). The origin, form, and import of this ceremony in taking an oath, are very doubtful. *Smiting on the thigh* denotes penitence (Jer. xxxi. 19), grief, and mourning (Ezek. xxi. 12).

THISTLE. [THORNS.]

THOMAS. The word is equivalent to the Greek *Didymus, twin.*

The Apostle Thomas (Matt. x. 3; Mark iii. 18; Luke vi. 15; Acts i. 13) has been considered a native of Galilee, like most of the other apostles (John xxi. 2); but according to tradition he was a native of Antiochia, and had a twin-sister called Lysia.

In the character of Thomas was combined great readiness to act upon his convictions, to be faithful to his faith even unto death, so that he even exhorted his fellow-disciples, on his last journey to Jerusalem, 'Let us also go, that we may die with him' (John xi. 16), together with that careful examination of evidence which will be found in all persons who are resolved really to obey the dictates of their faith. Whosoever is minded, like most religionists who complain of the scepticism of Thomas, to follow in the common transactions of life the dictates of vulgar

prudence, may easily abstain from putting his hands into the marks of the nails and into the side of the Lord (John xx. 25); but whosoever is ready to die with the Lord will be inclined to avail himself of extraordinary evidence for extraordinary facts, since nobody likes to suffer martyrdom by mistake. These remarks are directed against Winer and others, who find in the character of Thomas what they consider contradictory traits, viz., inconsiderate faith, and a turn for exacting the most rigorous evidence. We find that a resolute and lively faith is always necessarily combined with a sense of its importance, and with a desire to keep its objects unalloyed and free from error and superstition. Christ himself did not blame Thomas for availing himself of all possible evidence, but only pronounced those blessed who would be open to conviction even if some external form of evidence should not be within their reach.

Thomas preached the Gospel in Parthia (Origen), and, according to Jerome, in Persia; and was buried at Edessa. According to a later tradition Thomas went to India, and suffered martyrdom there.

THORNS AND THISTLES. There are a considerable number of words in Scripture which have been considered to indicate brambles, briers, thorns, thistles. Rabbinical writers state that there are no less than twenty-two words in the Bible signifying thorny and prickly plants; but some of these are probably so interpreted only because they are unknown, and may merely denote insignificant shrubs.

316. [Zizyphus Spina Christi.]

The cut given above represents the *Zizyphus Spina Christi,* of which Hasselquist says, 'In all probability this is the tree which afforded the crown of thorns put upon the head of Christ. It is very common in the East. This plant is very fit for the purpose, for it has many small and sharp spines, which are well adapted to give pain: the crown might easily be made of these soft, round, and pliant branches; and what in my opinion seems to be the greater proof is, that the leaves very much resemble those of ivy, as they are of a very deep glossy green. Perhaps the enemies of Christ would have a plant somewhat resembling that with which emperors and generals were crowned, that there might be a calumny even in the punishment.'

THRESHING. [Agriculture.]

THRONE, the ornamented seat on which royal personages gave audience on state occasions among the Hebrews (1 Kings ii. 19; xxii. 10; comp Esth. v. 1). It was originally a decorated arm-chair, higher than an ordinary seat, so as to require a foot-stool to support the feet. Sometimes the throne was placed on a platform ascended by steps (Isa. vi. 1). Solomon made a throne of ivory overlaid with gold, which had six steps, with six lions on each side (1 Kings x. 18). Archelaus addressed the multitude from ' an elevated seat and a throne of gold.' A throne became the emblem of regal power (Gen. xli. 40); whence the phrases, 'to sit on the throne of his kingdom' (Deut. xvii. 18), that is, to rule as a monarch; and ' to sit on the throne of a person' (1 Kings i. 13; 2 Kings x. 30), which signifies, to be his successor.

THUM'MIM. [Urim and Thummim]

THYATI'RA, a city on the northern border of Lydia, about twenty-seven miles from Sardis, the seat of one of the seven Apocalyptic churches (Rev. i. 11; ii. 18). Its modern name is Ak-hissar, or *the white castle*. According to Pliny, it was known in earlier times by the names Pelopia and Euhippa (*Hist. Nat.* v. 29). Strabo asserts that it was a Macedonian colony (xiii. p. 928). The Roman road from Pergamus to Sardis passed through it. It was noted for the art of dyeing, as appears from Acts xvi. 14. It still maintains its reputation for this manufacture, and large quantities of scarlet cloth are sent weekly to Smyrna. The town consists of about two thousand houses, for which taxes are paid to the government, besides two or three hundred small huts; of the former 300 are inhabited by Greeks, 30 by Armenians, and the rest by Turks. The common language of all classes is the Turkish; but in writing it, the Greeks use the Greek, and the Armenians the Armenian characters. There are nine mosques and one Greek church.

THYINE WOOD is mentioned as one of the articles of merchandise which would cease to be purchased in consequence of the fall of Babylon (Rev. xviii. 12). This wood was in considerable demand by the Romans, being much employed by them in the ornamental wood-work of their villas, and also for tables, bowls, and vessels of different kinds. It is noticed by most ancient authors, from the time of Theophrastus. It was the citron-wood of the Romans, and was produced only in Africa, in the neighbourhood of Mount Atlas, and in Granada. It grew to a great size.

This cedar or citron-wood was most likely produced by *Callitris quadrivalvis*, the *Thuja articulata* of Linnæus, which is a native of Mount Atlas, and of other uncultivated hills on the coast of Africa.

317.   [Callitris quadrivalvis.]

TIBE'RIAS is a small town situated about the middle of the western bank of the lake of Gennesareth; according to Joliffe, about twenty English miles from Nazareth and ninety from Jerusalem. Tiberias was chiefly built by the tetrarch Herodes Antipas, and called by him after the emperor Tiberius.

From the time of Herodes Antipas to the commencement of the reign of Herodes Agrippa II., Tiberias was the principal city of the province. It was one of the four cities which Nero added to the kingdom of Agrippa. Sepphoris and Tiberias were the largest cities of Galilee. In the last Jewish war the fortifications of Tiberias were an important military station.

According to Josephus, the inhabitants of Tiberias derived their maintenance chiefly from the navigation of the lake of Gennesareth, and from its fisheries. After the destruction of Jerusalem Tiberias was celebrated during several centuries for its famous Rabbinical academy.

Not far from Tiberias, in the immediate neighbourhood of the town of Emmaus, were warm mineral springs, whose celebrated baths are sometimes spoken of as belonging to Tiberias itself. These springs contain sulphur, salt, and iron; and were employed for medicinal purposes.

According to Joliffe (*Travels*, pp. 48, 49, sq.), the modern Tabaria has about four thousand inhabitants, a considerable part of whom are Jews.

TIBE'RIUS, the third Emperor of Rome. He is mentioned by name only by St. Luke, who fixes in the fifth year of his reign the commencement of the ministry of John the Baptist, and of Christ (Luke iii. 1). The other passages in which he is mentioned under the title of Cæsar, offer no points of personal allusion, and refer to him simply as the emperor (Matt. xxii. 17, sq.;

Mark xii. 14, sq.; Luke xx. 22, sq; xxiii. 2, sq; John xix. 12, sq.).

TIB'NI (*building of God*), one of those factious men who took a prominent part in the troubles which followed the violent death of Elah. He disputed the throne of Israel with Omri, and the civil war which was thus kindled between the two factions lasted for about three years with varying success, till the death of Tibni left his adversary master of the crown, B.C. 929 (1 Kings xvi. 21-23).

TI'DAL (*veneration*), one of the allies who with Chedorlaomer invaded Palestine in the time of Abraham (Gen. xiv. 1). Tidal bears the somewhat singular title of 'king of nations' or 'Gentiles' (*goyim*). We cannot tell who these Goyim were over whom Tidal ruled; but it seems probable that he was a chief of several confederated tribes, whose military force he contributed to the expedition of Chedorlaomer.

TIG'LATH-PILE'SER, the Assyrian king who subjected the kingdom of Israel in B.C. 747 [ASSYRIA, ISRAEL].

TIGRIS, one of the four rivers of Paradise, twice mentioned in Scripture under the name of HIDDEKEL (Gen. ii. 14; Dan. x. 4), which signifies 'the rapid Tigris.'

The Tigris rises in the mountains of Armenia, about fifteen miles south of the sources of the Euphrates, and pursues nearly a regular course south-east till its junction with that river at Korna, fifty miles above Basrah (Bassorah). The Tigris is navigable for boats of twenty or thirty tons' burden as far as the mouth of the Odorneh, but no further; and the commerce of Mosul is consequently carried on by rafts supported on inflated sheep or goats' skins. The Tigris, between Bagdad and Korna, is, on an average, about two hundred yards wide; at Mosul its breadth does not exceed three hundred feet. The banks are steep, and overgrown for the most part with brushwood, the resort of lions and other wild animals. The middle part of the river's course, from Mosul to Korna, once the seat of high culture and the residence of mighty kings, is now desolate, covered with the relics of ancient greatness in the shape of fortresses, mounds, and dams, which had been erected for the defence and irrigation of the country. At the ruins of Nimrod, eight leagues below Mosul, is a stone dam quite across the river, which, when the stream is low, stands considerably above the surface, and forms a small cataract; but when the stream is swollen, no part of it is visible, the water rushing over it like a rapid. and boiling up with great impetuosity. It is a work of great skill and labour, and now venerable for its antiquity. At some short distance below there is another Zikr (dyke), but not so high, and more ruined than the former. The river rises twice in the year: the first and great rise is in April, and is caused by the melting of the snows in the mountains of Armenia; the other is in November, and is produced by the periodical rains.

TIMBRELS. [MUSICAL INSTRUMENTS.]

TIM'NA (*restraint*), a concubine of Eliphaz, the son of Esau (Gen. xxxvi. 12-22; 1 Chron. i. 36) From her the name passed over to an Edomitish tribe (Gen. xxxvi. 40; 1 Chron. i. 51).

TIM'NAH or **TIMNATH**, an ancient city of the Canaanites (Gen. xxxviii. 12), first assigned to the tribe of Judah (Josh. xv. 10-57), and afterwards to Dan (Josh. xix. 43); but it long remained in the possession of the Philistines (Judg. xiv. 1; 2 Chron. xxviii. 18; comp. Joseph. *Antiq.* v. 8. 5). It is chiefly noted as the abode of Samson's bride, and the place where he held his marriage feast. It is probably represented by a deserted site now called Tibneh, which is about one hour's journey south-west of Zerah, the residence of Samson. Another Timnah lay in the mountains of Judah (Josh. xxv. 57; Gen. xxviii. 12-14).

TIM'NATH-HE'RES. [TIMNATH-SERAH.]

TIM'NATH-SE'RAH (*portion of abundance*, i. e. *remaining portion*), a town in the mountains of Ephraim, which was assigned to Joshua, and became the place of his residence and burial (Josh. xix. 50; xxiv. 30). In Judg. ii. 9, it is called Timnath-heres (*portion of the sun*); but the former is probably the correct reading, since a possession thus given to Joshua after the rest of the land was distributed (Josh. xix. 49), would strictly be a portion remaining. This was probably the same with the Timnah of Josephus, the head of a toparchy lying between those of Gophna and Lydda; which seems to be recognised in a place called Tibneh, lying north-west of Gophna on the Roman road to Antipatris.

TIMOTHY, a young Christian of Derbe, grandson of Lois, and son of Eunice, a Jewess, by a Greek father, who was probably a proselyte (Acts xvi. 1; xx. 4). He seems to have been brought up with great care in his family, and to have profited well by the example of the 'unfeigned faith' which dwelt in the excellent women named in 2 Tim. i. 5; iii. 15. The testimonials which Paul received in Lycaonia in favour of this young disciple, induced the apostle to make him the companion of his journeys and labours in preaching the Gospel (Acts xvi. 2, 3; 1 Tim. iv. 12). He became his most faithful and attached colleague; and is frequently named by Paul with truly paternal tenderness and regard. Timothy appears to have been with the apostle at Rome, and to have been, like him, a prisoner there, though liberated before him (Heb. xiii 23). His subsequent history is, however, unknown. It appears from 1 Tim. i. 3, that when Paul went into Macedonia he left Timothy in charge of the church at Ephesus, and there are indications that he was still at Ephesus when the apostle was (as usually understood) a second time captive at Rome, and without hope of deliverance (1 Tim. iii. 14). The tradition is, that Timothy retained the charge of the church at Ephesus till his death, and eventually suffered martyrdom in that city.

TIMOTHY, EPISTLES TO. The authenticity of these epistles is proved by the testimony of the earliest ecclesiastical writers, Barnabas, Clement of Rome, Polycarp, Ignatius, and many others; and though modern German critics have attempted to set aside this weighty mass of external evidence by minute and carping critical objections, they have completely failed. With regard to the time when they were composed, it is clear to that the first epistle was written not long after Paul had left Ephesus for Macedonia (ch. i. 3), and in all probability after the departure from Ephesus mentioned Acts xx. 1. With respect to the second epistle, it is certain that it was written at Rome, and while Paul was a prisoner there (i. 8-16; ii. 9; i. 17; iv. 21). Whether this was during his first or second imprisonment has been matter of dispute, and, though not without difficulties, the opinion that this epistle was written during his second imprisonment seems upon the whole the preferable.

The *design* of the first epistle is partly to instruct Timothy in the duties of that office with which he had been intrusted, partly to supply him with credentials to the churches which he might visit, and partly to furnish through him guidance to the churches themselves. It may be divided into *three* parts, exclusive of the introduction (i. 1, 2), and the conclusion (vi. 20, 21). In the *first* of these parts (i 3-20) the apostle reminds Timothy generally of his functions, and especially of the duties he had to discharge in reference to certain false teachers, who were anxious to bring the believers under the yoke of the law. In the *second* (ii -vi. 2) he gives Timothy particular instructions concerning the orderly conducting of divine worship, the qualifications of bishops and deacons, and the proper mode of behaving himself in a church. In the *third* (vi. 3-19) the apostle discourses against some vices to which the Christians at Ephesus seem to have been prone.

The design of the second epistle is partly to inform Timothy of the apostle's trying circumstances at Rome, and partly to utter a last warning voice against the errors and delusions which were corrupting and disturbing the churches. It consists of an inscription (i. 1-5); of a series of exhortations to Timothy, to be faithful in his zeal for sound doctrine, patient under affliction and persecution, careful to maintain a deportment becoming his office, and diligent in his endeavours to counteract the unhallowed efforts of the false teachers (i. 6; iv. 8); and a conclusion in which Paul requests Timothy to visit him, and sends the salutations of certain Christians at Rome to Timothy, and those of the apostle himself to some believers in Asia Minor.

TIN. If this substance be really intended by the Hebrew word, which seems somewhat doubtful, it is first mentioned among the metals which were to be purified by fire found among the prey taken from the Midianites (Num. xxxi. 22). It is also named among the articles of commerce which the Tyrians received from Tarshish (Ezek. xxvii. 12); and a levelling instrument of this metal used by builders is noticed in Zech iv. 10. The Hebrew word also denotes the *alloy* of lead, tin, and other inferior metals, combined with silver in the ore and separated from it by smelting (Isa. i. 25).

TINSHEMETH (Swan, Lev. xi. 18; Deut. xiv. 16). There is good reason to believe that this is not the true meaning of the word thus rendered in our common version, for the swan is not a bird which, in migrating to the south, even during the coldest seasons, appears to proceed further than France or Spain, though no doubt individuals may be blown onwards in hard gales to the African shore. In all probability the bird referred to is the porphyrion or purple gallinula. The porphyrion is superior in bulk to our water-hen or gallinula, has a hard crimson shield on the forehead, and flesh-coloured legs; the head, neck, and sides are of a beautiful

turquoise blue, the upper and back parts of a dark but brilliant indigo.

The porphyrion is a remarkable bird, abounding in the southern and eastern parts of Europe and Western Asia, feeding itself standing on one leg, and holding its food in the claws of the other. It was anciently kept tame in the precincts of pagan temples, and therefore perhaps was marked unclean, as most, if not all, the sacred animals of the heathens were.

318. [The Porphyrion.]

TIPH'SAH, a large and opulent city on the western bank of the Euphrates. It is doubtless the same as the Thapsacus of the Greeks and Romans. The name means 'ford;' and the town was, in fact, situated at the lowest fording-place of the Euphrates; whence it became the point of trading-communication between the natives east and west of the river. On this account, and as commanding the ford, the possession of the place was deemed of great importance by the ruling powers of the day. This circumstance explains the contentions of the kings of Syria and Egypt respecting Carchemish, which was a strong place a little lower down the river, at the junction of the Chaboras. Solomon obtained possession of Tiphsáh (1 Kings iv. 24), probably in connection with the series of operations (of which the building or fortification of Tadmor was one) adopted by him for the purpose of drawing the Eastern trade into his own dominions [Solomon; Tadmor]. Nothing remains of Tiphsah at the present day except the name; but the site is supposed to be marked by the village of Ed-Deyr.

TIRHA'KAH, king of Cush (Ethiopia in the Common Version), who in the days of Hezekiah came out against Sennacherib when he was making war on Judah (2 Kings xix. 9; Isa. xxxvii. 9). He is the Tarakos of Manetho, the third king of the twenty-fifth dynasty, and the Tearkon of Strabo (xv. 687), with whom the twenty-fifth Ethiopic dynasty came to an end. His successful opposition to the power of Assyria is recorded on the walls of a Theban temple, for at Medinet Abu are the figure and the name of this king and the captives he took. That Tirhakah ruled at Napata, now Gebel Berkel, and in the Thebaid at the same period, is proved by the additions he made to the temples of Thebes, and by the monuments he built in Ethiopia. That he was a very potent monarch is evident from his defeat of Sennacherib, as well as from the monuments he has left both in Egypt and

Ethiopia, and his maintenance of the Egyptian possessions in Asia.

TIR'SHATA, a title borne by Zerubbabel and Nehemiah as Persian governors of Judæa (Ezra ii. 63; Neh. vii. 65, 70; viii. 9; x. 2). It seems to come from the Persic *torsh*, 'severe,' and, in that case, would be equivalent to 'your severity:' comp. '*dread* sovereign.'

TIR'ZAH, an ancient Canaanitish city (Josh. xii. 24), pleasantly situated (Cant. vi. 4), which Jeroboam made the capital of his kingdom, and which retained that rank till Samaria was built by Omri (1 Kings x.; xv. 21; xvi. 24; 2 Kings xv. 4). The site is entirely unknown.

TISH'BITE, the Gentile name of Elijah— 'Elijah the Tishbite' (1 Kings xvii. 1, 2; xxi. 17)—derived from a town called Tishbi in the tribe of Naphtali, the name of which occurs only in the apocryphal book of Tobit, i. 2.

TIS'RI was the first month of the civil, and the seventh month of the ecclesiastical year, in which fell the Festival of Atonement and that of Tabernacles. In 1 Kings viii. 2, it is termed the month of Ethanim, that is, the month of streaming rivers, which are filled during this month by the autumnal rains. It corresponds with our September— October.

TITHE, &c. (Lev. xxvii. 30, 31, 32), derived from the word signifying ' ten,' which also means 'to be rich;' hence ten is the *rich* number, because *including* all the units under it. This number seems significant of completeness or abundance in many passages of Scripture. Jacob said unto Laban, ' Thou hast changed my wages these ten times' (Gen. xxxi. 41); 'Am not I better to thee than ten sons?' (1 Sam. i. 8); 'These ten times have ye reproached me' (Job xix. 3); 'Thy pound hath gained ten pounds' (Luke xix. 16), &c. This number, as the end of less numbers and beginning of greater, and as thus signifying perfection, sufficiency, &c., may have been selected for its suitableness to those Eucharistic donations to religion, &c., which mankind were required to make probably in primeval times. Abraham gave to Melchizedec, 'a priest of the most high God,' a tenth of all the spoils he had taken from Chedorlaomer (Gen. xiv. 20; Heb. vii. 4). The incidental way in which this fact is stated, seems to indicate an established custom. Jacob's vow (Gen. xxviii. 22) seems simply to relate to *compliance* with an established custom; his words are, literally, ' And all that thou shalt give me, I will assuredly tithe it unto thee.' The Mosaic law, therefore, in this respect, as well as in others, was simply a reconstitution of the patriarchal religion. Thus, the tenth of military spoils is commanded (Num. xxxi. 31). For the law concerning tithes generally, see Lev. xxvii. 30, &c., where they are first spoken of as things already known. These tithes consisted of a tenth of all that remained after payment of the first-fruits of seeds and fruits, and of calves, lambs, and kids. This was called the first tithe, and belonged to God as the sovereign and proprietor of the soil (Lev. xxvii. 30-32; 2 Chron. xxxi. 5, 6). The proceeds of this rent, God, as king, appropriated to the maintenance and remuneration of his servants the Levites, to be paid to them in their several cities (Num. xviii. 21-24). A person might redeem or commute in money his tithes of seeds and fruits, by adding the value

of a fifth part to them (Lev. xxvii. 31). Out of this tithe the Levites paid a tenth to the priests, called the tithe of tithes, or tithe of holy things (Num. xviii. 26-28); and another tithe of the produce of the fields belonging to their cities (ver. 29). The first tithe being paid, the proprietor had to set apart out of the remainder a second tithe, to be expended by him in the courts of the tabernacle, in entertaining the Levites and his own family, &c. (Deut. xii. 18). If the trouble and expense of transporting this second tithe in kind to the tabernacle were too great, he might turn it into money, but this he must take in person, and expend there for the appointed purpose (ver. 24-28). It seems that the people were left to their own consciences in regard to the just payment of their tithes, subject, however, to the solemn declaration ' before the Lord,' which they were required to make concerning it every third year (Deut. xxvi. 12-16). Possibly the Levites were not prohibited from taking due care that they received their rights, inasmuch as in later times, at least, they paid their own tithes to the priests under sacerdotal supervision (Neh x. 38).

Upon examination it will be found that the payments required by Moses of the Jewish people were exceedingly moderate, and were no doubt easily borne till they chose to incur the additional expenses of a regal establishment. It pleased God, while sustaining the relation to them of sovereign and proprietor of the land, to require the same quit-rent of one-tenth which was usually paid to the kings in other nations (1 Sam. viii. 14, 15, 17; comp. 1 Macc. ii. 35). Aristotle speaks of it as ' an ancient law' at Babylon. In Egypt one-fifth was paid to the king, which was more than the first-fruits and first and second tithes put together. This quit-rent God appointed to be paid to the Levites for their subsistence, since their festive share in the second tithes can hardly be accounted part of their income. They had, as a tribe of Israel, an original right to one-twelfth of the land, for which they received no other compensation than the tithes, subject to the sacerdotal decimation, their houses, and glebes. In return for these, they consecrated their time and talents to the service of the public [LEVITES]. The payment of tithes, &c., was re-established at the restoration of religion by Hezekiah (2 Chron. xxxi. 5, 6, 12), and upon the return from the captivity by Nehemiah (x. 37; xii. 44; xiii. 5). The prophet Malachi reproves the people for their detention of the tithes, &c., for which they had brought a divine chastisement by famine upon themselves, and promises a restoration of plenty upon their amendment (iii. 8-12; comp. iii. 9; Ecclus. xxxv. 9). In our Saviour's time the Pharisees scrupulously paid their tithes, but neglected the weightier matters of the law. His comment on their conduct conveys no censure on their punctiliousness on this point, but on their neglect of more important duties: ' These *ought ye to have done*, and not to leave the other undone' (Matt. xxiii. 23; Luke xviii. 12).

TI'TUS, a Christian teacher, and companion and fellow-labourer of St. Paul. He was of Greek origin, but was converted by the apostle, who therefore calls him his own son in the faith (Gal. ii. 3; Tit. i. 4). He was one of the persons sent by the church of Antioch to Jerusalem to consult the apostles, and it was not judged necessary that he should receive circumcision (Acts xv. 2; Gal. ii. 1). After a time we find him in company with Paul at Ephesus, whence he was sent to Corinth (2 Cor. xii. 18), where he was well received, discharged with discretion the task confided to him, and declined to suffer the church to defray his expenses (2 Cor. viii. 13, sq; xii. 18). He then proceeded to Macedonia, and at Philippi rejoined his master, who had vainly been expecting him at Troas (2 Cor. vii. 6; ii. 12, 13). He was then employed by Paul in preparing the collection for the poor saints in Judæa, and, as an incident of this mission, became the bearer of the second epistle to the Corinthians (2 Cor. viii. 16, 17, 23). On a subsequent journey, Titus was left by the apostle in Crete, to establish and regulate the churches in that island (Tit. i. 5), and he was still there when he received the epistle from St. Paul which bears his name (Tit. iii. 12). He is therein desired to join the apostle at Nicopolis; and it is presumed that he did so, and afterwards accompanied him in his last journey to Rome, whence he was sent into Dalmatia (2 Tim. iv. 10). Tradition states that Titus eventually returned to Crete, and died there at an advanced age.

TITUS, EPISTLE TO. The genuineness of this Epistle is attested by a large body of evidence, and seems never to have been questioned, except by the heretic Marcion, and that upon the most frivolous grounds, until, in recent times, it was attacked by Eichhorn and De Wette. But their objections are of such a nature that it is unnecessary to enter upon any examination of them here.

It has been supposed, on apparently good grounds, that the apostle wrote this epistle at Ephesus shortly after he had visited Crete (ch. i. 5), and when he was about to spend the winter in Nicopolis (iii. 12). From the close resemblance between this epistle and the first epistle to Timothy, we are naturally led to conclude that both must have been written while the same leading ideas and forms of expression were occupying the apostle's mind.

The task which Paul had committed to Titus, when he left him in Crete, was one of no small difficulty. The character of the people was unsteady, insincere, and quarrelsome; they were given to greediness, licentiousness, falsehood, and drunkenness, in no ordinary degree; and the Jews who had settled among them appear to have even gone beyond the natives in immorality. Among such a people it was no easy office which Titus had to sustain when commissioned to carry forward the work Paul had begun, and to set in order the affairs of the churches which had arisen there, especially as heretical teachers had already crept in among them. Hence Paul addressed to him this Epistle, the main design of which is to direct him how to discharge with success the duties to which he had been appointed. For this purpose the apostle dilates upon the qualifications of elders, and points out the vices from which such should be free (ch. i.).

He then describes the virtues most becoming in aged persons, in the female sex, in the young, in servants, and in Christians generally (ch. ii.). From this he proceeds to enjoin obedience to civil rulers, moderation, gentleness, and the avoidance of all idle and unprofitable speculations (iii. 1-11). He then invites Titus to join him at Nicopolis, commends to him certain brethren who were about to visit Crete, and concludes with the apostolic benediction (ver. 12-15).

TOB, a region or district beyond the Jordan, into which Jephthah withdrew when expelled from Gilead (Judg. xi. 5). As the name occurs nowhere else, it is impossible to determine with certainty its position.

TOBI'AH, a base Samaritan, who, having raised himself from a state of slavery to be a trusted favourite of Sanballat, did his utmost to gratify his master by resisting the proceedings of Nehemiah in rebuilding the walls of Jerusalem. His dishonest practices and threats proved alike unsuccessful; but during the temporary absence of Nehemiah, Tobiah succeeded, with the aid of his relative Eliashib, the priest, in getting himself comfortably and splendidly established in 'a great chamber in the house of God' (ch. xiii. 4). But his glory was short-lived. Nehemiah returned, and caused him and his household-stuff to be ignominiously cast out of the temple. This is the last that we know of this member of that vile class who are ready and unscrupulous tools in the hands of their superiors for any dishonourable undertaking.

TO'BIT, BOOK OF [APOCRYPHA], one of the deutero-canonical books, containing the private history of a venerable and pious old man of this name, who was carried captive into Assyria by Shalmaneser.

Nothing is known with certainty respecting either the author or the age of the book. Professor Stewart ascribes it to an early period of the exile. All ancient writers looked upon the narrative as historical and authentic. But the question has been raised in modern times, whether the book is to be regarded as a true history or a moral fiction. Luther was the first who adopted the latter view; others have maintained that the book is partly historical, partly mythical. Gutmann, a modern Jewish Rabbi, adopts the opinion that it is a fiction founded on facts.

Its authority in the early Christian church is beyond question.

TOGAR'MAH is the Hebrew name of Armenia. The Armenians consider themselves to be descended from Gomer, through Torgom, and therefore they call themselves the *house of Torgom*. The sons of Gomer were Ashkenaz, Riphath, and Togarmah (Gen. x. 3; 1 Chron. i. 6).

Armenia was, according to Strabo, distinguished by the production of good horses. This account harmonizes with the statement that the house of Togarmah traded in the fairs of Tyre in horses, and horsemen, and mules (Ezek. xxvii. 14). The situation of Togarmah was north of Palestine: 'Gomer and all his bands; the house of Togarmah of the north quarters' (Ezek. xxxviii. 6).

TOMB. [BURIAL.]

TONGUE is used, 1. *literally*, for the human tongue. 'Every one that lappeth the water with his tongue, as a dog lappeth' (Judg. vii. 5). Various explanations have been offered, why Gideon's three hundred followers should have been selected because they lapped water out of their hands, standing or perhaps moving onward, while they who stayed and 'bowed down to drink' were rejected. Josephus says, that the former thereby showed their timorousness and fear of being overtaken by the enemy, and that these poor-spirited men were chosen on purpose to illustrate the power of God in the victory (*Antiq.* v. 6. 3) 2. It is *personified.* 'Unto me every tongue shall swear,' that is, every man (Isa. xlv. 23 ; comp. Rom. xiv. 11 ; Phil. ii. 11 , Isa. liv. 17). 3. It is used by *metonymy* for speech generally. 'Let us not love in tongue only' (1 John iii. 18). 4. For a *particular language* or dialect, spoken by any particular people. 'Every one after his tongue' (Gen x. 5, 20, 31). 5. For the *people* speaking a language (Isa. lxvi. 18 ; Dan. iii. 4, 7, &c. ; Rev. v. 9). 6. It is used *figuratively* for anything resembling a tongue in shape. Thus, 'a wedge of gold,' literally a 'tongue' (Josh. vii. 21, 24). The miraculous *gift of tongues*, as well as its corresponding gift of interpretation, has been the subject of two opinions. It was promised by Christ to believers (Mark xvi. 17) ; and fulfilled at Pentecost (Acts ii. 4, 11). In 1 Cor. xiv. 2, 39, we have 'to pray in a tongue' (ver. 14), 'to speak words in a tongue' (ver. 19). The obvious explanation of most of these passages is, to speak in *other living languages*, the supernatural acquisition of which demonstrated the truth of the Gospel, and was a means of diffusing it. Some verses however in 1 Cor. xiv. have given rise to the notion of a *strange*, ecstatic, inspired, unearthly language; but these all admit of a different solution. In ver. 2, 'he who speaketh in a tongue' evidently means, he who speaks some foreign living language; the supplied word 'unknown' in the Auth. Vers. is needless, and misleads the English reader. It is further said that 'he edifieth himself' (which, as Macknight justly pleads, required that he should understand himself), and edifieth the church also if an interpreter were present (ver. 28). The key to the difficulties of this subject is the supposed absence of an inspired interpreter (ver. 28), in which case the gift would not be *profitable* to the hearers. The gift of tongues was to cease (1 Cor. xiii. 8).

TONGUES, CONFUSION OF. The part of the primeval history which relates this fact, so remarkable and influential upon the subsequent fortunes of mankind, is contained in Gen. xi. 1–10. This narrative, which is given in the style best adapted to the comprehension of mankind in the infantile state of our race, may, we conceive, be resolved into a statement to this effect :—

An orderly and peaceful distribution and migration of the families descended from Noah had been directed by divine authority, and carried into general effect. But there was a part of mankind who would not conform themselves to this wise and benevolent arrangement This rebellious party, having discovered a region to **their** taste, determined to remain in it. They proceeded to erect a lofty edifice, which was to be a *signal house*, a rallying point, and probably to erect around it groups of habitations, not mere tents, but houses with brick walls, so that the adventurers had both a city and a tower. This was an act of rebellion against the divine government. The omniscient and righteous God therefore frustrated it, by inflicting upon them a remarkable affection of the organs of speech, which produced discord and separation.

II. The date of this event we cannot satisfac-

torily place so early as at 100 years after the flood, as it is in the commonly received chronology. Every view that we can take of the previous history inclines us to one of the larger systems, that of the Septuagint, which gives 530 years, or that of Josephus, adopted with a little emendation by Dr. Hales, which gives 600 years; and thus we have at least five centuries for the intervening period.

III. Upon the question, Whether all of mankind were engaged in this act of concerted disobedience, or only a part? we confess ourselves unable to adduce irrefragable evidence on either side, but we think that there is a great preponderance of argument on the part of the latter supposition.

IV. Admitting, however, our inability to determine, with absolute certainty, on which side of this alternative the truth lies, no difference accrues to the subject of this article, What were the phenomena of the case? In WHAT did the Confusion of Tongues *actually consist?* For the answer a considerable variety of opinions has been promulgated.

But the hypothesis of a change in the pronunciation, leading to diversified results, some of which might be of permanent influence, appears to us to have the most of probability and reason on its side.

TOPAZ, a precious stone ; one of those which were in the breastplate of the high-priest (Exod. xxviii. 17), and the origin of which is referred to Cush (Job xxviii. 19). It has been identified with the gem to which the moderns have applied that name. This is a precious stone, having a strong glass lustre. Its prevailing colour is wine-yellow of every degree of shade. The dark shade of this colour passes over into carnation red, and sometimes, although rarely, into lilac ; the pale shade of the wine-yellow passes into greyish ; and from yellowish-white into greenish-white and pale green, tincal and celadon-green. It may thus be difficult to determine whether the stone in question was the yellow topaz ; but that it was a topaz there is little reason to doubt.

It is clear that the stone was highly prized by the Hebrews. Job declares that wisdom was more precious than the topaz of Cush (Job xxviii. 19) ; and as the name Cush includes Southern Arabia and the Arabian Gulf, the intimation coincides with the statement of Pliny and others, that the topazes known to them came from the Topaz Island in the Red Sea, whence they was probably brought by the Phœnicians. In Ezek. xxviii. 13, the topaz is named among the precious stones with which the king of Tyre was decked.

TO'PHET, a place very near to Jerusalem, on the south-east, in the valley of the children of Hinnom, where the ancient Canaanites, and afterwards the apostate Israelites, made their children to pass through the fire to Moloch (comp. Ps. cvi. 38 ; Jer. vii. 31). After the return from the captivity, the Jews resumed the ancient name for the whole valley, viz., the valley of Hinnom ; and in order to perpetuate the disgrace of idolatry, they made it the common receptacle of the filth, &c. of the city, in which 'fires' were *continually* kept burning, to consume the carcasses of animals, executed criminals, &c., the unconsumed portions of which, as well as the off-scourings in general, became the nidus of insects, whose larvæ, or 'worms,' revelled in the corruption. These circumstances furnished the most *apt* representation to the Jewish mind of future punishment.

TOWNS. We use the term in its general signification, so as to embrace any assemblage of inhabited human dwellings of larger size than a hamlet or a village.

The formation of towns was obviously a work of time, and they were, no doubt, originally built around a stronghold or fort, to which the inhabitants looked for protection against the incursions of enemies. In the time of the Patriarchs we find towns existing in Palestine which were originally surrounded with fortifications, so as to make them 'fenced cities.' In these dwelt the agricultural population, who by means of these places of strength defended themselves and their property from the nomad tribes of the neighbouring desert, who then, as they do now, lived by plunder. Nor were works of any great strength necessary. In Palestine at the present day, while walls are in most parts an indispensable protection, and agriculture can be advantageously prosecuted only so far as sheltered by a fortified town, erections of a very slight nature are found sufficient for the purpose, the rather because the most favourable localities offer themselves on all sides, owing to the natural inequality of the ground.

Of the ancient method of building in towns and cities we have no accurate knowledge. But the law of sameness which prevails so rigidly in Eastern countries, gives us an assurance that a modern town in Palestine may be roughly taken as a type of its ancient predecessors.

At the gates of the town, which were frequented as the court of justice, the town's market, the rendezvous for loungers, newsmongers, pleasure-seekers, there were wide open places of greater or less dimensions, where on important occasions the entire population assembled for consultation or for action (Neh. viii. 1, 16; 2 Chron. xxxii. 6; 2 Sam. xxi. 12; Job xxix. 7; 2 Kings vii. 1). The streets were not so narrow as streets generally are in modern Oriental towns. Their names were sometimes taken from the wares or goods that were sold in them: thus in Jer. xxxvii. 21, we read of 'the bakers' street.' The present bazaars seem to be a continuation of this ancient custom. The streets of Jerusalem at least were paved; but the streets of most cities of Palestine would not need paving, in consequence of the rocky nature of the foundations on which they lay. Herod the Great laid an open road in Antioch with polished stone. In regard to the earlier periods, we find only a notice to the effect that Solomon caused the fore-court of the temple to be laid with flags. Besides paved streets, Jerusalem before the exile had an extensive system of watercourses or aqueducts, which seems to have been rendered necessary by the natural supply having been limited to one or two spots in the immediate vicinity. The population of towns cannot now be ascertained with any degree of accuracy, for the materials are not only scanty and disconnected, but in a measure uncertain. Respecting the government of towns, we have no detailed information relating to the ante-exilian periods, though it was probably in the hands of the elders; and in Deut. xvi. 18, Moses commands, 'Judges and officers shalt thou make thee in all thy gates, and they shall judge the people with just judgment.' In the post-exilian era magistrates occur under the name of Council, at whose head was a president or mayor.

TRACHONI'TIS was, in the days of the Herodian dynasty, the name of the country situated between the Antilibanus and the Arabian mountains south of Damascus and west of the provinces of Batanœa, Gaulonitis, Iturœa, and Auranitis, under about the thirty-third degree of northern latitude. It is at present called *Ledja*. The eastern range of mountains is now called *Jebel Manai*, and contains great caverns in chalk rocks. The southern portions of the ancient Trachonitis, or the present Ledja, consist chiefly of basalt rocks.

TRANCE (Gen. ii. 21, &c.), a supernatural state of body and mind, the nature of which has been well conjectured by Doddridge, who defines it—'Such a rapture of mind as gives the person who falls into it a look of astonishment, and renders him insensible of the external objects around him, while in the meantime his imagination is agitated in an extraordinary manner with some striking scenes which pass before it and take up all the attention.'

TRANSFIGURATION. One of the most wonderful incidents in the life of our Saviour upon earth, and one so instructive that we can never exhaust its lessons, is the Transfiguration. The apostle Peter, towards the close of his life, in running his mind over the proofs of Christ's majesty, found none so conclusive and irrefragable as the scenes when he and others were with him in the holy mount, as eye-witnesses that he received from God the Father honour and glory, when there came such a voice to him from the excellent glory, 'This is my beloved Son, in whom I am well pleased.' If we divide Christ's public life into three periods—the first of miracles to prove his divine mission, the second of parables to inculcate virtue, and the third of suffering, first clearly revealed and then endured, to atone for sin—the transfiguration may be viewed as his baptism or initiation into the third and last. He went up the mount of transfiguration on the eighth day after he had bidden every one who would come after him take up his cross, declaring that his kingdom was not of this world, that he must suffer many things, and be killed, &c.

The mount of transfiguration was long thought to have been Mount Tabor; but as this height is fifty miles from Cæsarea Philippi, where Jesus last taught, it is now supposed to have been a mountain much less distant, namely, Mount Hermon.

The final causes of the transfiguration, although in part wrapped up in mystery, appear to be in part plain. Among its intended lessons may be the following:—First, to teach that, in spite of the calumnies which the Pharisees had heaped on Jesus, the old and new dispensations are in harmony with each other. To this end the author and the restorer of the old dispensation talk with the founder of the new, as if his scheme, even the most repulsive feature of it, was contemplated by theirs, as the reality of which they had promulgated only types and shadows.

Secondly, to teach that the new dispensation was superior to the old. Moses and Elias appear as inferior to Jesus, not merely since their faces did not, so far as we know, shine like the sun, but chiefly because the voice from the excellent glory commanded to hear *him*, in preference to them. Thirdly, to gird up the energies of Jesus for the great agony which was so soon to excruciate him. Fourthly, to comfort the hearts of the disciples, who, being destined to see their master, whom they had left all to follow, nailed to a cross, to be themselves persecuted, and to suffer the want of all things, were in danger of despair. But by being eye-witnesses of his majesty they became convinced that his humiliation, even though he descended into the place of the dead, was voluntary, and could not continue long.

TRIAL. [PUNISHMENT]

TRIBES,—the name of the great groups of families into which the Israelitish nation, like other Oriental races, was divided. The modern Arabs, the Bedouins, and the Berbers, and also the Moors on the northern shores of Africa, are still divided into tribes. The clans in Scotland are also analogous to the tribes of the ancient Israelites. In Gen. xlix. the tribes are enumerated according to their progenitors; viz., 1, REUBEN, the first-born; 2, SIMEON, and 3, LEVI, instruments of cruelty; 4, JUDAH, whom his brethren shall praise; 5, ZABULON, dwelling at the haven of the sea; 6, ISSACHAR, the strong; 7, DAN, the judge; 8, GAD, whom a troop shall overcome, but who shall vanquish at last; 9, ASHER, whose bread shall be fat; 10, NAPHTALI, giving goodly words; 11, JOSEPH, the fruitful bough; 12, BENJAMIN, the wolf: all these were originally the twelve tribes of Israel. In this enumeration it is remarkable that the subsequent division of the tribe of Joseph into the two branches of Ephraim and Manasseh, is not yet alluded to. After this later division of the very numerous tribe of Joseph into the two branches of Ephraim and Manasseh had taken place, there were, strictly speaking, thirteen tribes. It was, however, usual to view them as comprehended under the number twelve, which was the more natural, since one of them, namely, the caste of the Levites, did not live within such exclusive geographical limits as were assigned to the others after they exchanged their nomadic migrations for settled habitations, but dwelt in towns scattered through all the other twelve tribes. Concerning the arrangement of these tribes on their march through the wilderness, in their encampments around the ark, and in their occupation of the land of Canaan, see the cognate articles, such as EXODUS, ENCAMPMENT, GENEALOGIES, LEVITES, WANDERING, and the names of the several tribes.

TRIBUTE, a tax which one prince or state agrees, or is compelled, to pay to another, as the purchase of peace, or in token of dependence.

The Israelites were at various times subjected to heavy taxes and tributes by their foreign conquerors. After Judæa was reduced to a Roman province, a new poll of the people and an estimate of their substance were taken by command of Augustus, in order that he might more correctly regulate the tribute to be exacted. This was a capitation-tax levied at so much a head, and imposed upon all males from 14, and all females from 12, up to 65 years of age.

To oppose the levying of this tribute Judas the Gaulonite raised an insurrection of the Jews, asserting that it was not lawful to pay tribute to a foreigner, that it was a token of servitude, and that the Jews were not allowed to acknowledge any for their master who did not worship the Lord. They boasted of being a free nation, and of never having been in bondage to any man (John viii. 33). These sentiments were extensively promulgated, but all their efforts were of no avail in restraining or mitigating the exactions of their conquerors.

The Pharisees who sought to entangle Jesus in his talk, sent unto him demanding whether it was lawful to give tribute unto Cæsar or not; but knowing their wicked designs, he replied, 'Why tempt ye me, ye hypocrites?' 'Render unto Cæsar the things which are Cæsar's, and unto God the things that are God's.'

The apostles Peter and Paul severally recommended submission to the ruling powers, and inculcated the duty of paying tribute: 'tribute to whom tribute is due' (Rom. xiii. 1-8; 1 Peter ii. 13).

TRIBUTE-MONEY. The money collected by the Romans in payment of the taxes imposed upon the Jews. The phrase may apply to money of any description, coined or uncoined. The piece shown to our Saviour at his own request was a Roman coin, bearing the image of one of the Cæsars, and must have been at that time current in Judæa, and received in payment of the tribute in common with other descriptions of money. There is no reason to suppose that the tribute was collected exclusively in Roman coins, or that the tribute-money was a description of coin different from that which was in general circulation [MONEY].

TRO'AS, more fully Alexandria-Troas, a city of northern or Lesser Mysia, in Asia Minor, situated on the coast at some distance southward from the site of Troy, upon an eminence opposite the island of Tenedos. Paul was twice at this place (Acts xvi. 8, 9; xx. 6; 2 Cor. ii. 12; 2 Tim. iv. 13). The name Troas, or Troad, strictly belonged to the whole district around Troy. Alexandria-Troas is represented by the present Eski-Stamboul, and its ruins are now concealed in the heart of a thick wood of oaks, with which the country abounds.

TROGYL'LIUM, a town and promontory on the western coast of Asia Minor, opposite Samos, at the foot of Mount Mycale (Strabo, xiv. p. 636). It is mentioned in Acts xx. 15.

TROPH'IMUS, a disciple of Ephesus, who accompanied St. Paul into Judæa, and was the innocent cause of the dangers which the apostle there encountered; for having been recognised by some Jews of Asia Minor, and seen in company with Paul, they took occasion to accuse Paul of having brought Greeks into the temple (Acts xx. 4; xxi. 29). His name does not again occur till after, seemingly, the first imprisonment of Paul. In one of the ensuing journeys he remained behind at Miletus sick (2 Tim. iv. 20). This circumstance is regarded as furnishing a strong fact to show that Paul was twice imprisoned at Rome; for Trophimus, in the first passage to Miletus (Acts xx. 15). was not left behind, but proceeded to Judæa; after which we do not lose sight of Paul for one day, and know that he was not again at Miletus *before* his first imprisonment at Rome.

TRUMPET. [Musical Instruments.]

TRUMPETS, FEAST OF. [Festivals.]

TRYPHE'NA and TRYPHO'SA, female disciples at Rome, who laboured to extend the Gospel and to succour the faithful (Rom. xvi. 12). Their history is unknown; but, from their names, they were probably sisters.

TU'BAL, a son of Japhet, and a people descended from him (Gen. x. 2; Isa. lxvi. 19; Ezek. xxvii. 13; xxxii. 26; xxxviii. 2, 3; xxxix. 1), supposed to have been settled in Asia Minor near the Euxine [Nations, Dispersion of].

TU'BAL-CA'IN, son of Lamech and Zillah, to whom the invention of the art of forging metals is ascribed in Gen. iv. 22 [Smith].

TURTLE-DOVE occurs in Gen. xv. 9; Lev. i. 14; v. 7, 11, &c.; Luke ii. 24.

319.

The birds of this subgenus are invariably smaller than pigeons properly so called; they are mostly marked with a patch of peculiarly coloured scutellated feathers on the neck, or with a collar of black, and have often other markings on the smaller wing-covers. The species *Columba Turtur*, with several varieties merely of colour, extends from the north of Europe through the north of Africa, to the islands south of China. The turtle-dove of Palestine is specifically the same; but there is also a second, we believe local: both migrate farther south in winter, but return very early; when their cooing voice in the woods announces the spring. In the rites of the Hebrew law, full-grown or old turtle-doves might be offered in pairs, but only the young of pigeons not full grown. They were the usual offering of the poor, a circumstance, Bochart remarks, indicating the humble station of the Virgin Mary, since at her purification she offered a pair of turtle-doves instead of a lamb.

TYCH'ICUS is the name of an assistant and companion of the Apostle Paul. He accompanied Paul on his third missionary journey (Acts xx. 4), and was, at a later period, the bearer of Paul's letter from Rome to the Colossians. Paul styled him a beloved brother, faithful minister, and fellow-servant in the Lord, who should declare all his state unto the Colossians, to whom he was sent that he might know their estate and comfort their hearts (Col. iv. 7, 8). For a similar purpose Tychicus was sent to the Ephesians also (Eph. vi. 21, 22; 1 Tim. iv. 12). According to tradition, Tychicus was made bishop of Chalcedon.

TYPE. The best definition of this word, in its theological sense, is that which Heb. x. 1 supplies:

a type is a shadow of good things to come, or as the apostle elsewhere expresses it (Col. ii. 17), 'a shadow of things to come; but the body is of Christ.' Adopting this definition as the correct one, we proceed briefly to point out the different *types* by which God was pleased in various ways to adumbrate the *person* and *work* of the Redeemer. 1. Before the law, Adam, Enoch, Noah, Melchizedec, Abraham, Isaac, and Joseph were eminently typical of Christ. Again, under the law, Moses, Joshua, Samson, David, Solomon, Elijah, Elisha, Jonah, Zerubbabel, and Joshua the high priest, were, *in many points*, singularly types of Christ.

2. The first-born, the Nazarites, prophets, priests, and kings, were *typical orders of persons.*

3. Under the head of *things typical* may be noticed: Jacob's ladder, the burning bush, the pillar of cloud and fire, the manna, the rock, and the brazen serpent.

4. *Actions typical* were: the deliverance out of Egypt, passage of the Red sea, sojourn in the wilderness, passage over the Jordan, entrance into Canaan, and restoration from Babylon.

5. *Rites typical* were: circumcision, various sacrifices, and sundry purifications.

6. *Places typical* were: the land of Canaan, the cities of refuge, the tabernacle, and the temple.

The above types were designed to shadow forth Christ and the blessings of his salvation; but there were others also which pointed at our miseries without him. There were ceremonial uncleannesses; the *leprosy*, for instance, was a type of our natural pollution; and Hagar and Ishmael a type of the covenant of works.

As there must be a similarity or analogy between the type and the antitype, so there is also a disparity or dissimilitude between them.

It is not in the nature of type and antitype that they should agree *in all things*; else, instead of similitude, there would be *identity*. Hence the apostle, whilst making Adam a type of Christ, yet shows how infinitely the latter excelled the former (1 Cor. xv. 47). So the priests of old were types of Christ, though he infinitely excelled them both as to his own person and as to the character of his priesthood (see Heb. vii., viii., ix., and x.).

TYRAN'NUS, a sophist or rhetorician of Ephesus, who kept one of those schools of philosophy and eloquence so common at that period. St. Paul preached for two years daily in his school after quitting the synagogue (Acts xix. 9). This proves that the school was Greek, not Jewish. It does not appear whether Tyrannus was himself a convert or not; for it may be that he let to the apostle the house or hall which he used: but it is more pleasant to suppose that he was a convert, and that the apostle was hospitably entertained by him and obtained the use of the hall in which he himself taught.

TYRE. The original position of this famous city was on the eastern coast of the Mediterranean, about midway between Egypt and Asia Minor, near the north-western frontier of Palestine. It was a colony of Zidon, and was founded before the records of history.

As early as the eleventh century before the advent of Christ, the Tyrians had become famous for skill in the arts. About 1142 B.C. (2 Sam. v. 11), their king Hiram sent cedar-trees to Jerusalem, and workmen who built David a house. A

3 D

generation later, when Solomon, preparing to build the temple, sent to the same monarch for similar assistance, he said to him (1 Kings v. 6). 'Thou knowest that there is not among us any that can skill to hew timber like unto the Sidonians.' He also (1 Kings vii. 13) sent and fetched Hiram out of Tyre, a widow's son, filled with cunning to work all works in brass. In subsequent ages, every king coveted a robe of Tyrian purple, and Ezekiel (xxvii. 16) speaks of 'the multitude of wares of its making,'—emeralds, purple, and broidered work, and fine linen, and coral, and agate.

The commerce of Tyre was commensurate with its manufactures. Situate at the entry of the sea, it became a merchant of the people for many isles. It was inhabited by seafaring men, and was styled by way of eminence 'the merchant-city,' whose merchants were princes, whose traffickers were the honourable of the earth' (Isa. xxiii. 8). Among their other colonies, whither their own feet carried them afar off to sojourn,' were Cyprus, Utica, and Carthage. In the 27th chapter of Ezekiel, Syria, and Persia, and Egypt, Spain, Greece, and every quarter of the ancient world, are portrayed hastening to lay their most precious things at the feet of Tyre, who sat enthroned on ivory, covered with blue and purple from the isles of Elishah; while the Gammadims were in her towers, hanged their shields upon her walls round about, and made her beauty perfect.

Near the close of the eighth century before the Christian era, Shalmaneser, the king of Assyria who captured Samaria, was led by cupidity to ay siege to Tyre. He cut off its supplies of water which aqueducts had furnished, but wells within the walls supplied their place; and at the .nd of five years he gave up his blockade as nopeless.

It was against a city such as this, so confident, and to all appearance so justifiably confident, of sitting a queen for ever, that several prophets, particularly Isaiah and Ezekiel, fulminated the denunciations which Jehovah dictated. They prophesied that it should be overthrown by Nebuchadnezzar, that it should revive, but at length be destroyed and never rebuilt.

Before a generation had passed away, according to Josephus, Philostratus, and the Seder Olam, Nebuchadnezzar came up, as had been predicted (Ezek. xxvi. 7-13), making a fort, casting a mount, and lifting up the buckler. At the end of thirteen years (about A.M. 3422) he took the city, and Tyre was forgotten seventy years, as had been foretold by Isaiah (xxiii. 15). In the year B C. 332 Tyre, which had been rebuilt on an island half a mile from the shore, and had again become a flourishing emporium for all the kingdoms of the world upon the face of the earth, ' and heaped up silver as the dust, and fine gold as the mire of the streets,' was assailed by Alexander the Great in the midst of his Oriental career of conquest. It sustained a siege of seven months, and was at length taken only by means of a mole, by which the island was turned into a peninsula, and rendered accessible by land forces. In constructing this mole Alexander made use of the ruins of the old city, and thereby fulfilled two prophecies (Ezek. xxvi. 12, and ver. 21). So utterly were the ruins of old Tyre thrown into the sea, that its exact site is confessedly undeter minable.

The mole of Alexander has prevented Tyre from becoming insulated again. The revival of the city was long retarded by the rivalship of the newly-founded Alexandria, and by other causes, but it was at length partially restored, and was often the subject of contest during the crusades. It was in the hands of the Europeans till 1291, when it was finally yielded to the Moslems. Its fortifications, which were almost impregnable, were demolished, and it has never since been a place of consequence. Travellers of every succeeding century describe it as a heap of ruins, broken arches and vaults, tottering walls and towers, with a few starveling wretches housing amid the rubbish. It was half ruined by an earthquake in 1837. One of the best accounts of its present appearance is given by Dr. Robinson, who spent a sabbath there in 1838 (*Biblical Researches*, iii. 395): 'I continued my walk,' says he, 'along the shore of the peninsula, part of which is now unoccupied, except as "a place to spread nets upon," musing upon the pride and fall of ancient Tyre. Here was the little isle, once covered by her palaces and surrounded by her fleets: but alas! thy riches and thy fame, thy merchandise, thy mariners and thy pilots, thy caulkers, and the occupiers of thy merchandise that were in thee,—where are they? Tyre has indeed become like the "the top of a rock." The sole tokens of her more ancient splendour—columns of red and grey granite, sometimes forty or fifty heaped together, or marble pillars—lie broken and strewed beneath the waves in the midst of the sea; and the hovels that now nestle upon a portion of her site present no contradiction of the dread decree, "Thou shalt be built no more." '

U.

U'LAI, a river which flowed by Susa [SHUSHAN] into the united stream of the Tigris and Euphrates. It is mentioned in Dan. viii. 2. It is called by Pliny Eulæus, but is described by Greek writers under the name of Choaspes, and is now known by the name of Kerah, called by the Turks Karasu. This river is formed by the junction of many streams in the province of Ardelan, in Kurdistan. It runs through the plain of Kermanshah, and being greatly increased in magnitude by the junction of two small rivers, proceeds with a furious course towards Khuzistan, receiving numerous tributaries in its passage. It passes on the west of the ruins of Shus [Susa: see SHUSHAN], and enters the Shat-ul-Arab about twenty miles below Korna.

UNCLEAN BIRDS. The species which the law forbade the Israelites to use for food (Levit. xi. and Deut. xiv.) include bats, because in the most ancient classifications of animals, all flying animals were considered to belong more to birds than quadrupeds; in other respects the list is confined nearly to the same genera and species as are at the present day rejected in all Christian countries. There are only twenty named; but in the text the additional words 'of the like kind' clearly imply sometimes even more than genera, and the explanations of the law superadded by human authority indicate several which do not occur in either list. Every ornithologist who reviews this question with care will feel that, with certain exceptions, the proposed identifications cannot be regarded as claiming entire confidence.

UNICORN. The radical meaning of the Hebrew word (*reem*) thus rendered furnishes no evidence that an animal such as is now understood by 'unicorn' was known to exist, or that a rhinoceros is thereby absolutely indicated; and here is no authority whatever for the inference hat either was at any time resident in Western Asia.

320. [Bibos cavifrons.]

The Indian rhinocerotes are essentially tropical animals, and there is no indication extant that in a wild state they ever extended to the west of the Indus. Early colonies and caravans from the East most probably brought rumours of the power and obstinacy of these animals to Western Asia, and it might have been remarked that under excitement the rhinoceros raises its head and horn on high, as it were in exultation, though it is

321. [Horn of the unknown species of Rhinoceros.]

most likely because the sense of smelling is more potent in it than that of sight, which is only lateral, and confined by the thickness of the folds of skin projecting beyond the eye-balls. The rhinoceros is not absolutely untamiable—a fact implied even in Job. Thus we take this species as the original type of the unicorn; but the active invention of Arabic minds, accidentally, perhaps, in the first instance, discovered a species of *Oryx* (generically bold and pugnacious ruminants), with the loss of one of its long, slender, and destructive horns. In this animal the *reem* of the Hebrews and the far East became personified, being most probably an *Oryx Leucoryx*, since individuals of that species have been repeatedly exhibited in subsequent ages as unicorns, when accident or artifice had deprived them of one of their frontal weapons. In Africa, however, among three or four known species of rhinoceros, and vague rumours of a *Bisulcate* species of unicorn, probably only the repetition of Arabian reports, there appears to exist between Congo, Abyssinia, and the Cape, precisely the *terra incognita* of Africa, a real pachydermous animal, which seems to possess the characteristics of the poetical unicorn. In the narratives of the natives of the different regions in question there is certainly both exaggeration and error; but they all incline to a description which would make the animal indicated a pachyderm of the rhinoceros group, with a long and slender horn proceeding from the forehead, perhaps with another incipient behind it, and in general structure much lighter than other rhinocerotes.

U'PHAZ, a country from which gold was obtained (Jer. x. 9; Dan. x. 5). It is generally supposed to be a corruption of Ophir.

UPPER-ROOM. [HOUSE.]

UR, of the Chaldees, was the native place of the family of Abraham, whence he migrated first to Haran and then to Canaan (Gen. xi. 28, 31; xv. 7; Neh. ix. 7; Acts vii. 4). It is supposed to be a district identical with the modern pashalic of Urfa, to which there belong several districts, among others Rouha, which is the ancient Edessa.

UR'BAN, a disciple at Rome, and one of Paul's companions in labour (Rom. xvi. 9). Nothing is known of him; but his name shows him to have been a Roman.

URI'AH (*flame of Jehovah*), a Hittite, and therefore a descendant of the ancient inhabitants of Palestine, whose name occurs in the list of the 'worthies' or champions of king David, in whose army he was an officer. He was the husband of Bathsheba; and while he was absent with the army before Rabbah, David conceived and gratified a criminal passion for his wife. The king then directed Joab to send him to Jerusalem, but failing to make his presence instrumental in securing Bathsheba from the legal consequences of her misconduct, he sent him back with a letter directing Joab to expose him to the enemy in such a manner as to ensure his destruction. This the unscrupulous Joab accomplished; and David then took the widow into his own harem (2 Sam. xi.; xxiii. 39) [DAVID; BATHSHEBA].

1. URI'JAH (*flame of Jehovah*), high priest of the Jews in the time of King Ahaz. He received from this young prince, who was then at Damascus, the model of an altar which had there engaged his attention, with orders to make one like it at Jerusalem. It was his duty to refuse compliance with this dangerous order; but he made such haste in his obedience that the altar was completed by the time Ahaz returned; and he afterwards went so far in his subservience as to offer upon this new and unauthorized altar the sacrifices prescribed by the law of Moses (2 Kings xvi. 10-12). He was probably not so fully aware as he ought to have been of the crime and danger involved in this concession to a royal caprice, being a transgression of the law which fixed the form of the Mosaical altar (Exod. xxvii. 1-8; xxxviii. 1-7); for he appears to have been in intention a good man, as he is one of the 'faithful witnesses' chosen by Isaiah (viii. 2) to attest one of his prophecies.

2 URIJAH, a prophet, son of Shemaiah of Kirjath-jearim in Judah, who, in the time of Jehoiakim, uttered prophecies against Judæa and Jerusalem, of the same tenour as those which Jeremiah was commissioned to deliver. Menaced with death by the king, Urijah sought refuge in Egypt, but Judæa was at that time subject to

3 D 2

Pharaoh-Necho, who had no interest in protecting a proscribed fugitive who foretold the conquests of the Babylonians. He was therefore delivered up on the demand of Jehoiakim, who put him to death, and ordered him to be buried dishonourably in one of the graves of the meanest of the people (Jer. xxvi. 20, 21).

U′RIM and THUM′MIM. There are two principal opinions respecting the Urim and Thummim. One is, that these words simply denote the four rows of precious stones in the breastplate of the high priest, and are so called from their brilliancy and perfection; which stones, in answer to an appeal to God in difficult cases, indicated his mind and will by some supernatural appearance. Thus, as we know that upon each of the stones was to be engraven the name of one of the sons of Jacob, it has been conjectured that the letters forming the divine response became some way or other distinguished from the other letters. It has been conjectured by others that the response was given by an audible voice to the high-priest arrayed in full pontificals, and standing in the holy place with his face turned towards the ark. The other principal opinion is, that the Urim and Thummim were two small oracular images, similar to the Teraphim, personifying *revelation* and *truth*, which were placed in the cavity or pouch formed by the folds of the breastplate, and which uttered oracles by a voice. The latter is corroborated by the authority of Philo, and seems to be best supported by external evidence.

USURY, an unlawful contract for the loan of money, to be returned again with exorbitant increase. By the laws of Moses the Israelites were forbidden to take usury from their brethren upon the loan of money, victuals, or anything else, not, it has been observed by Michaelis, as if he absolutely and in all cases condemned the practice, for he expressly permitted interest to be taken from strangers, and from the Canaanites, but only out of favour to the poorer classes. After the return of the Jews from captivity, they were required by Nehemiah to ' leave off this usury,' and to restore to their brethren what they had exacted from them—' their lands, their vineyards, their olive-yards, and their houses; also the hundredth part of the money, and of the corn, the wine, and the oil ' (Neh. v. 10, 11). Our Saviour denounced all extortion, and promulgated a new law of love and forbearance :—' Give to every man that asketh of thee, and of him that taketh away thy goods, ask them not again.' ' Love ye your enemies, and do good, and lend, hoping for nothing again ' (Luke vi. 30, 35).

UZ, a region and tribe named in Job i. 1; Jer. xxv. 20; Lam. iv. 21; now generally supposed to have been situated in the south of Arabia Deserta, between Idumæa, Palestine, and the Euphrates.

U′ZAL, a descendant of Joktan, founder of one of the numerous tribes of Joktanidæ in Yemen (Gen. x. 27).

UZ′ZAH (*strength*), son of Abinadab, a Levite, who, with his brother Ahio, conducted the new cart on which the ark was taken from Kirjath-jearim to Jerusalem. When the procession reached the threshing-floor of Nachon, the oxen drawing the cart became unruly, and Uzzah hastily put forth his hand to stay the ark, which was shaken by their movements. For this the anger of the Lord smote him, and he died on the spot. This judgment appeared to David so severe, or even harsh, that he was much distressed by it, and becoming afraid to take the ark any farther, left it there, in charge of Obed-edom, till three months after, when he finally took it to Jerusalem (2 Sam. vi. 1-11). The whole proceeding was very irregular, and contrary to the distinct and far from unmeaning regulations of the law, which prescribed that the ark should be carried on the shoulders of the Levites (Exod. xxv. 14), whereas here it was conveyed in a cart drawn by oxen. The ark ought to have been enveloped in its coverings, and thus wholly concealed before the Levites approached it; but it does not appear that any priest took part in the matter, and it would seem as if the ark was brought forth, exposed to the common gaze, in the same manner in which it had been brought back by the Philistines (1 Sam. vi. 13-19). It was then the duty of Uzzah, as a Levite, to have been acquainted with the proper course of proceeding: he was therefore the person justly accountable for the neglect; and the judgment upon him seems to have been the most effectual course of ensuring attention to the proper course of proceeding, and of checking the growing disposition to treat the holy mysteries with undue familiarity. That it had this effect is expressly stated in 1 Chron. xv. 2, 13.

UZ′ZEN-SHE′RAH, a small city, founded by Sherah, the daughter of Ephraim (1 Chron. vii. 24).

UZZI′AH (*might of Jehovah*), otherwise called AZARIAH, a king of Judah, who began to reign B.C. 809, at the age of sixteen, and reigned fifty-three years, being, with the sole exception of Manasseh's, the longest reign in the Hebrew annals. Uzziah was but five years old when his father was slain. He was sixteen before he was formally called to the throne: and it is disputed by chronologers, whether to count the fifty-two years of his reign from the beginning or from the end of the eleven intervening years. In the first half of his reign, Uzziah behaved well, and was mindful of his true place as viceroy of the Divine King. He accordingly prospered in all his undertakings. His arms were successful against the Philistines, the Arabians, and the Ammonites. He restored and fortified the walls of Jerusalem, and planted on them engines for discharging arrows and great stones; he organized the military force of the nation into a kind of militia, composed of 307,500 men, under the command of 2600 chiefs, and divided into bands liable to be called out in rotation; for these he provided vast stores of all kinds of weapons and armour,—spears, shields, helmets, breastplates, bows, and slings.

Nor were the arts of peace neglected by him: he sowed and fostered agriculture; and he also dug wells, and constructed towers in the desert, for the use of the flocks. At length, when he had consolidated and extended his power, and developed the internal resources of his country, Uzziah fell. His prosperity engendered the pride which became his ruin. In the twenty-fourth year of his reign, incited probably by the example of the neighbouring kings, who united the regal and pontifical functions, Uzziah, unmindful of the fate of Dathan and Abiram, dared to attempt the exercise of one of the principal functions of the priests, by entering the holy place to burn incense at the golden altar. But, in the very act, he was smitten with leprosy, and was thrust forth by the priests. He continued a leper all the rest of his life. and lived apart as such, the public functions of the government being administered by his son Jotham, as soon as he became of sufficient age (2 Kings xv. 27, 28; 2 Chron. xxvi.).

V.

VASH'TI (*beauty*). the wife of Ahasuerus, king of Persia, whose refusal to present herself unveiled before the compotators of the king led to her degradation, and eventually to the advancement of Esther (Esth. i. 9-12) [AHASUERUS; ESTHER].

VAT, the receptacle in which grapes and olives were trodden with the feet. Vats were either formed with stones and covered with insoluble cement, or were, in favourable localities, hewn out of the rock, forming raised reservoirs, into which the picked grapes were cast and trodden upon by men to press out the *must*, or new wine, which flowed out through gratings or spouts into large vessels placed outside. In the Egyptian paintings these vats are represented as having a temporary beam extended over them, with short ropes hanging down, by which the treaders held fast, and which greatly helped them in their labour, inasmuch as the beam acted as a lever in its rebound, lifting them up from the mass of grapes into which they sank.

322.　[Wine-press.]

This work. although laborious, was performed with great animation, accompanied by vintage-songs, and with a peculiar shout or cry, and sometimes by instrumental music (Isa. xvi. 9, 10; Jer. xxv. 30; xlviii. 32, 33).

VEIL. In ancient as in modern times there were different kinds of this essential article of an Eastern female's attire. These are essentially of two descriptions. The first, and which alone offer any resemblance to the veils used among us, are those which the Eastern women wear in-doors, and which are usually of muslin or other light texture, attached to the head-dress and falling down over the back. They are of different kinds and names, some descending only to the waist, while others reach nearly to the ground. These are not used to conceal the face.

323.　[Dress Veils, &c. In-door.]

The veils mentioned in Scripture were, no doubt, mostly analogous to the wrappers of different kinds in which the Eastern women envelop

324.　[Out-door Veils.]

themselves when they quit their houses. These are of great amplitude, and, among the common people, of strong and coarse texture, like that in which Ruth carried home her corn (Ruth iii. 15).

VEIL OF THE TABERNACLE AND TEMPLE. [TABERNACLE; TEMPLE.]

VERMILION. [PURPLE.]

VINE, THE, with its fruit, the grape, as well as wine, is very frequently mentioned in Scripture, as might be expected from its being a native of the East, well known to ancient nations, and highly esteemed for its various natural and artificial products. The vine is a native of the hilly region on the southern shores of the Caspian, and in the Persian province of Ghilan. Every part of it was and still continues to be highly valued. The sap was at one time used in medicine. Verjuice expressed from wild grapes is well known for its acidity. The late Sir A. Burnes mentions that in Caubul they use grape powder, obtained by drying and powdering the unripe fruit, as a pleasant acid. When ripe, the fruit is everywhere highly esteemed, both fresh and in its dried state as raisins. The juice of the ripe fruit, called *must*, is valued as a pleasant beverage. By fermentation, wine, alcohol, and vinegar are obtained ; the lees yield tartar ; an oil is sometimes expressed from the seeds ; and the ashes of the twigs were formerly valued in consequence of yielding a salt, which we now know to be carbonate of potash.

It is not surprising, therefore, that the vine is so frequently mentioned both in the Old and in the New Testament, for it was one of the most valuable products of Palestine, and of particularly fine quality in some of the districts. Those of Eshcol, Sorek, Jibmah, Jazer, and Abel, were particularly distinguished.

VINE, WILD. It is related in 2 Kings iv. 38–40, that Elisha having come again to Gilgal, when there was a famine in the land, and many sons of the prophets were assembled there, he ordered his servant to prepare for them a dish of vegetables : ' One went out into the field to gather *herbs* (*oroth*), and found a *wild vine*, and gathered thereof *wild gourds* (*pakyoth sadeh*) his lap-full, and came and shred them into the pot of pottage, for they knew them not.' ' So they poured out for the men to eat : but as they were eating of the pottage, they cried out, ' O thou man of God, there is death in the pot ; and they could not eat thereof.' From this it appears that the servant mistook the fruit of one plant (*pakyoth*) for something else, called *oroth*, and that the former was vine like, that is, with long weak slender stems, and that the fruit had some remarkable taste, by which the mistake was discovered whenever the pottage was tasted. Though a few other plants have been indicated, the *pakyoth* has almost universally been supposed to be one of the family of the gourd or cucumber-like plants, several of which are conspicuous for their bitterness, and a few poisonous, while others, it is well known, are edible. Therefore one of the former may have been mistaken for one of the latter, or the *oroth* may have been some similarly shaped fruit, as for instance the egg-plant, used as a vegetable.

The plant referred to has usually been supposed to be the *colocynth*, which is essentially a desert plant. Dr. Kitto says, ' In the desert parts of Syria, Egypt, and Arabia, and on the banks of the rivers Tigris and Euphrates, its tendrils run over vast tracts of ground, offering a prodigious number of gourds, which are crushed under foot by camels, horses, and men. In winter we have seen the extent of many miles covered with the connecting tendrils and dry gourds 'of the preceding season, the latter exhibiting precisely the same appearance as in our shops, and when crushed, with a crackling noise, beneath the feet, discharging, in the form of a light powder, the valuable drug which it contains.' The Globe Cucumber, Dr. Kitto continues, ' derives its specific name (*Cucumis prophetarum*) from the notion that it afforded the gourd which "the sons of the prophets" shred by mistake into their pottage, and which made them declare, when they came to taste it, that there was "death in the pot."

This plant is smaller in every part than the common melon, and has a nauseous odour, while its fruit is to the full as bitter as the *Coloquintida*. The fruit has a rather singular appearance from the manner in which its surface is armed with prickles, which are, however, soft and harmless' (*Pictorial Palestine*; *Physical Geog.* p. cclxxxix.). But this plant, though it is nauseous and bitter as the *Colocynth*, yet the fruit, not being bigger than a cherry, does not appear likely to have been that which was *shred* into the pot. Celsius, however, was of opinion that the *Cucumis agrestis* of the ancients, and which was found by Belon in descending from Mount Sinai, was the plant. This plant is now called squirting cucumber, and is a well known drastic purgative, violent enough in its action to be considered even a poison. Its fruit is ovate, obtuse, and scabrous. But it is not easy to say whether this or the *Colocynth* is most likely to have been the plant mistaken for *oroth* ; but the fruit of this species might certainly be mistaken for young gherkins. Both are bitter and poisonous.

A fruitful vine is often adduced as an emblem of the Hebrew nation, and also the vine that was brought out of Egypt. A period of security and repose is figured by every one sitting under his own vine and fig-tree ; and prosperity by ' Judah, a lion's whelp, binding his foal to the vine, and his ass's colt to the choice vine ;' both indications of Eastern manners, where sitting in the shade is most pleasant, and tying cattle in similar situations a common practice.

The vine must have been cultivated in very early times, as we are informed in Gen. ix. 20, that Noah planted the vine immediately after the deluge ; and bread and wine are mentioned in Gen. xiv. 18. In Egypt also we have early notice of it (Gen. xl. 9, 10), as Pharaoh's chief butler saw in a dream a vine with three branches ; and the Israelites complain (Num. xx. 5) that Moses and Aaron had brought them out of Egypt into that dry and barren land, where there were neither figs nor vines. The wines of Syria were in early times also highly esteemed ; and though the growth of the vine has much decreased, from the diminished population and the Mohammedan rule, yet travellers still speak with enthusiasm of some of the wines, as of the vino d'oro of Lebanon.

VINEGAR. [WINE.]

VIOL. [MUSICAL INSTRUMENTS.]

VIPER. [SERPENT.]

VOW may be defined as a religious undertaking, either, 1. Positive, to do or perform ; 2. or Negative, to abstain from doing or performing a certain thing. The morality of vows we shall not here discuss, but merely remark that vows were quite in place in a system of religion which so largely consisted of doing or not doing certain outward acts, with a view of pleasing Jehovah and gaining his favour. The Israelite, who had been taught by performances of daily recurrence to consider particular ceremonies as essential to his possessing the divine favour, may easily have been led to the conviction which existed probably in the primitive ages of the world, that voluntary oblations and self-imposed sacrifices had a special value in the sight of God. And when once this conviction had led to corresponding practice, it could not be otherwise than of the highest consequence that these sacred promises, which in sanctity differed little from oaths, should be religiously and scrupulously observed.

Vows, which rest on a human view of religious obligations, assuming as they do that a kind of recompense is to be made to God for good enjoyed, or consideration offered for good desiderated, or a gratuity presented to buy off an impending or threatened ill, are found in existence in the antiquities of all nations, and present themselves in the earliest Biblical periods (Gen. xxviii. 20; Judg. xi. 30; 1 Sam. i. 11; 2 Sam. xv. 8). With great propriety the performance of these voluntary undertakings was accounted a highly religious duty (Judg. xi. 35; Eccles. v. 4, 5). The words of the last vow are too emphatic, and in the present day too important, not to be cited: ' Better is it that thou shouldest not vow, than that thou shouldest vow and not pay ' (comp. Ps. lxvi. 13, sq.; lxxvi. 11; cxvi. 18). The views which guided the Mosaic legislation were not dissimilar to those just expounded Like a wise lawgiver, Moses, in this and in other particulars, did not attempt to sunder the line of continuity between the past and the present. He found vows in practice; he aimed to regulate what it would have been folly to try to root out (Deut. xxiii. 21, sq.). The words in the 22nd verse are clearly in agreement with our remarks: ' If thou shalt forbear to vow, it shall be no sin in thee.'

VULTURE. An unclean bird (Lev. xi. 14). The species of vulture, properly so called, have the head naked or downy, the crop external, and very long wings; they have all an offensive smell, and we know of none that even the scavenger-ants will eat. When dead they lie on the ground untouched till the sun has dried them into mummies. Those found in and about the Egyptian territory are *Vultur fulvus, V. gyps* (Savigny), *V Ægyptius* (Savigny), *V. monachus* (Arabian vulture), *V. cinereus, V. Nubicus,* and a black species, which is often figured on Egyptian monuments as the bird of victory, hovering over the head of a national hero in battle, and sometimes with a banner in each talon. It is perhaps the *gypaetus barbatus (peres),* or *lammer geyer;* for though neither a vulture nor an eagle, it is the largest bird of prey of the old continent, and is armed like the eagle with formidable claws. The head is wholly feathered; its courage is equal to its powers, and it has a strength of wing probably superior to all raptorians, excepting the condor. It is found with little or no difference from Norway to the Cape of Good Hope, and' from the Pyrenees to Japan. Most of the above-named species are occasionally seen in the north of Europe. The voice varies in different species, but those of Egypt, frequenting the Pyramids, are known to bark in the night like dogs. Excepting the carrion vultures, all the other species are of large size; some superior in bulk to the swan, and others a little less.

There can be no doubt that the White Carrion Vulture (*Vultur percnopterus*) is the bird called in Hebrew (as it still is in Arabic) *Racham,* rendered Gier-eagle in Lev. xi. 18; Deut. xiv. 17. It forms a small group of Vulturidæ, subgenerically distinguished by the name of *Percnopterus* and *Neophron,* differing from the other vultures in the bill being longer, straight, more attenuated, and then uncinated, and in the back of the head

and neck being furnished with longish, narrow, suberectile feathers. In size the species is little bulkier than a raven, but it stands high on the legs. Always soiled with blood and garbage, offensive to the eye and nose, it yet is protected in Egypt both by law and public opinion for the services it renders in clearing the soil of dead carcasses putrefying in the sun, and the cultivated fields of innumerable rats, mice, and other vermin. It extends to Palestine in the summer season, but becomes scarce towards the north, where it is not specially protected; and it accompanies caravans, feasting on their leavings and on dead camels, &c.

325. [Vultur percnopterus.]

W.

WAGES. The word rendered in the English Version by this term, signifies primarily ' to purchase,' to obtain by some consideration on the part of the purchaser; thence to obtain on the part of the seller some consideration for something given or done, and hence to hire, to pay, or receive wages. Wages, then, according to the earliest usages of mankind, are a return made by a purchaser for something of value—specifically for work performed. And thus labour is recognised as property, and wages as the price paid or obtained in exchange for such property. In this relation there is obviously nothing improper or humiliating on the side either of the buyer or the seller. They have each a certain thing which the other wants, and in the exchange which they in consequence make, both parties are alike served. In these few words lies the theory and also the justification of all service. The entire commerce of life is barter. In hire, then, there is nothing improper or discreditable. It is only a hireling, that is, a mercenary, a mean sordid spirit, that is wrong. So long as a human being has anything to give which another human being wants, so long has he something of value in the great market of life; and whatever that something may be, provided it does not contribute to evil passions or evil deeds, he is a truly respectable capitalist, and a useful member of the social community. The Scriptural usage in applying the term translated ' wages ' to sacred subjects— thus the Almighty himself says to Abraham (Gen. xv. 1), ' I am thy exceeding great reward ' — tends to confirm these views, and to suggest the observance of caution in the employment of the words ' hire' and ' hireling,' which have acquired an offensive meaning by no means originally inherent in themselves, or in the Hebrew words for which they stand (Gen. xxx. 18, 32, 33).

WAGGON. [CART.]

WAIL. [MOURNING.]

WALLS. [FORTIFICATIONS; TOWNS.]

WALNUT. Walnuts are probably intended in the Song of Solomon, vi. 11, ' I went into the garden of *nuts*.' The Hebrew name (*egoz*) is evidently the same as the Persian *gowz*, which has been converted by the Arabs into *jowz*, by a process common in the case of many other words beginning with the interchangeable letters *gaf* and *jim*. In both languages these words, when they stand alone, signify the walnut, *gouz-bin* being the walnut-tree : when used in composition they may signify the nut of any other tree ; thus *jouz-i-boa* is the nutmeg, *jouz-i-hindi* is the Indian or cocoa-nut, &c. So the Greeks employed κάρυον, and the Romans *nux*, to denote the walnut, which last remains in modern languages, as Ital. *noce*, Fr. *noix*, Span. *nuez*, and Ger. *nusz*. The walnut was also called royal nut, and also Persian, from having been so highly esteemed, and from having been introduced into Greece from Persia. That the walnut was highly esteemed in the East we learn from Abulpharagius, and that it is found in Syria has been recorded by several travellers. That it was planted at an early period is well known, and might be easily proved from a variety of sources.

The walnut-tree is well known as a lofty, widespreading tree, affording a grateful shade, and of which the leaves have an agreeable odour when bruised. The flowers begin to open in April, and the fruit is ripe in September and October. The tree is much esteemed for the excellence of its wood ; and the kernel of the nut is valued not only as an article of diet, but for the oil which it yields. Being thus known to, and highly valued by, the Greeks in early times, it is more than probable that, if not indigenous in Syria, it was introduced there at a still earlier period, and that therefore it may be alluded to in the above passage, more especially as Solomon has said, ' I made me gardens and orchards, and planted trees in them of all kind of fruits' (Eccles. ii. 5).

WANDERING. In our office of tracing the steps of the Israelites from Goshen to Palestine, we have conducted them across the Red Sea to their first great station on its eastern bank, and thence onward along the shore and over the cliffs of that sea, till, following them up Wady Hebron, we placed and left them before Mount Horeb, in the capacious plain Rahah, which, having its widest part in the immediate front of that immense mass of rock, extends as it with two arms, one towards the north-west, the other towards the north-east. A belief prevailed that there was no

spot in the Sinaitic district on which the people of Israel could assemble. But Dr. Robinson has shown that this opinion is incorrect, and that in all probability the plain er-Râhah, over which Mount Horeb impends, is the spot where the congregation of Israel assembled. ' We were surprised,' says he, ' as well as gratified to find here, in the inmost recesses of these dark granite cliffs, this fine plain spread out before the mountain, and I know not where I have felt a thrill of stronger emotion than when, in first crossing the plain, the dark precipices of Horeb rising in solemn grandeur before us, we became aware of the entire adaptedness of the scene to the purposes for which it was chosen by the Great Hebrew legislator.'

After having been about a year in the midst of this mountainous region, the Israelites broke up their encampment, and began their journey in the order of their tribes, Judah leading the way with the ark of the covenant, under the guidance of the directing cloud (Num. ix. 15, sq. ; x. 11, sq.). They proceeded down Wady Seikh, having the wilderness of Paran before them, in a north-westerly direction ; but having come to a gorge in the mountains, they struck in a north-north-easterly direction across a sandy plain, and then over the Jebel et-Tih, and came down Wady Zulakah, to the station Taberah. It took the army three days to reach this station. Whatever name the place bore before, it now received that of Taberah (fire), from a supernatural fire with which murmurers, in the extreme parts of the camp, were destroyed as a punishment for their guilt. Here, too, the mixed multitude that was among the Israelites not only fell a-lusting themselves, but also excited the Hebrews to remember Egyptian fish and vegetables with strong desire, and to complain of the divinely supplied manna. The discontent was intense and widely spread. Moses became aware of it, and forthwith felt his spirit misgive him. He brings the matter before Jehovah, and receives Divine aid by the appointment of seventy elders to assist him in the important and perilous office of governing the gross, sensuous, and self-willed myriads whom he had to lead to Canaan. Moreover, an abundance of flesh meat was given in a most profuse supply of quails. It appears that there were now 600,000 footmen in the congregation.

The next station was Kibroth-hattaavah, near which there are fine springs and excellent pasturage. This spot, the name of which signifies ' graves of lust,' was so denominated from a plague inflicted on the people in punishment of their rebellious disposition (Num. xi. 33 ; 1 Cor. x. 6). Thence they journeyed to Hazeroth, which Robinson, after Burckhardt, finds in el-Hudhera, where is a fountain, together with palm-trees. At Hazeroth, where the people seem to have remained a short time, there arose a family dissension to increase the difficulties of Moses. Aaron, apparently led on by his sister Miriam, who may have been actuated by some feminine pique or jealousy, complained of Moses on the ground that he had married a Cushite, that is, an Arab wife, and the malcontents went so far as to set up their own claims to authority as not less valid than those of Moses. An appeal is made to Jehovah, who vindicates Moses, rebukes Aaron, and punishes Miriam (Num. xii.).

'And afterward the people removed from Hazeroth, and pitched in the wilderness of Paran,' at Kadesh (Num. xii. 16; xiii. 26). Here it was that twelve men (spies) were sent into Canaan to survey the country, who went up from the wilderness of Zin (Num. xiii. 21) to Hebron; and returning after forty days. brought back a very alarming account of what they had seen. It is evident that at this point there is a great blank in the Scripture narrative of the wanderings of the Israelites. They were ordered to turn back into the desert 'by the way of the Red Sea.' In this wilderness they wandered eight-and-thirty years, but little can be set forth respecting the course of their march. The next notice of the Israelites is, that in the first month they came into the desert of Zin and abode again at Kadesh; here Miriam dies; Moses and Aaron bring water from the rock; a passage is demanded through the land of Edom, and refused; and they then journeyed from Kadesh to Mount Hor, where Aaron dies in the fortieth year of the departure from Egypt, in the first day of the fifth month, corresponding to a part of August and September. Here, then, between August of the *second* year and August of the *fortieth* year, we have an interval of thirty-eight years of wandering in the desert.

In this way the Scriptural account of the journeyings of the Israelites becomes perfectly harmonious and intelligible. The eighteen stations mentioned only in the general list in the book of Numbers as preceding the arrival at Kadesh, are then apparently to be referred to this eight and thirty years of wandering, during which the people at last approached Ezion-geber, and afterwards returned northwards a second time to Kadesh, in the hope of passing directly through the land of Edom. Their wanderings extended, doubtless, over the western desert; although the stations named are probably only those head-quarters where the tabernacle was pitched, and where Moses and the elders and priests encamped; while the main body of the people was scattered in various directions.

Where, then, was Kadesh? Clearly, on the borders of Palestine. We agree with Robinson and Raumer in placing it nearly at the top of the Wady Arabah, where, indeed, it is fixed by Scripture, for in Numbers xii. 16 we read, 'Kadesh, a city in the uttermost of thy (Edom) border.' The precise spot it may be difficult to ascertain, but here, in the wilderness of Zin, which lay in the more comprehensive district of Paran, is Kadesh to be placed.

When we begin to take up the thread of the story at the second visit to Kadesh, we find time had, in the interval, been busy at its destructive work, and we thus gain confirmation of the view which has been taken of such second visit. No sooner has the sacred historian told us of the return of the Israelites to Kadesh, than he records the death and burial of Miriam, and has, at no great distance of time, to narrate that of Aaron and Moses. While still at Kadesh a rising against these leaders takes place, on the alleged ground of a want of water. Water is produced from the rock at a spot called hence Meribah (strife). But Moses and Aaron displeased God in this proceeding, probably because they distrusted God's general providence and applied for extraordinary resources. On account of this displeasure it was

announced to them that they should not enter Canaan. A similar transaction has been already spoken of as taking place in Rephidim (Exod. xvii. 1). The same name, Meribah, was occasioned in that as in this matter. Hence it has been thought that we have here two versions of the same story. But there is nothing surprising, under the circumstances, in the outbreak of discontent for want of water, which may well have happened even more than twice. The places are different, very wide apart; the time is different; and there is also the great variation arising out of the conduct and punishment of Moses and Aaron. On the whole, therefore, we judge the two records to speak of different transactions.

Relying on the ties of blood (Gen. xxxii. 8) Moses sent to ask of the Edomites a passage through their territory into Canaan. The answer was a refusal, accompanied by a display of force. The Israelites, therefore, were compelled to turn their face southward, and making a turn round the end of the Elanitic gulf reached Mount Hor, near Petra, on the top of which Aaron died. Finding the country bad for travelling, and their food unpleasant, Israel again broke out into rebellious discontent, and was punished by fiery serpents which bit the people, and much people died, when a remedy was provided in a serpent of brass set on a pole (Num. xxi. 4, sq.). Still going northward, and probably pursuing the caravan route from Damascus, they at length reached the valley of Zared (the brook), which may be the present Wady Kerak, that runs from the east into the Dead Sea. Hence they 'removed and pitched on the other side of Arnon, which is in the border of Moab, between Moab and the Amorites' (Num. xxi. 13). Beer (the well) was the next station, where, finding a plentiful supply of water. and being rejoiced at the prospect of the speedy termination of their journey, the people indulged in music and song, singing 'the song of the well' (Num. xxi. 17, 18). The Amorites being requested, refused to give Israel a passage through their borders, and so the nation was again compelled to proceed still in a northerly course. At length having beaten the Amorites, and Og, king of Bashan, they reached the Jordan, and pitched their tents at a spot which lay opposite Jericho. Here Balak, king of the Moabites, alarmed at their numbers and their successful prowess, invited Balaam to curse Israel, in the hope of being thus aided to overcome them and drive them out. The intended curse proved a blessing in the prophet's mouth. While here the people gave way to the idolatrous practices of the Moabites, when a terrible punishment was inflicted, partly by a plague which took off 24,000, and partly by the avenging sword. Moses, being commanded to take the sum of the children of Israel, from twenty years upwards, found they amounted to 600,730, among whom there was not a man of them whom Moses and Aaron numbered in the wilderness of Sinai (Num. xxvi. 47, 64). Moses is now directed to ascend Abarim, to Mount Nebo, in the land of Moab, over against Jericho, in order that he might survey the land which he was not to enter on account of his having rebelled against God's commandment in the desert of Zin (Num. xxvii. 12; Deut. xxxii. 49). Conformably with the divine command, Moses went up from the plains of Moab unto the mountain of Nebo, to the top of

Pisgah, and there he died, at the age of 120 years: 'His eye was not dim, nor his natural force abated' (Deut. xxxiv.). Under his successor, Joshua, the Hebrews were forthwith led across the Jordan, and established in the Land of Promise.

Thus a journey, which they might have performed in a few months, they spent forty years in accomplishing, bringing on themselves unspeakable toil and trouble, and in the end, death, as a punishment for their gross and sensual appetites, and their unbending indocility to the divine will (Num. xiv. 23; xxvi. 65). Joshua, however, gained thereby a great advantage; inasmuch as it was with an entirely new generation that he laid the foundations of the civil and religious institutions of the Mosaic polity in Palestine. This advantage assigns the reason why so long a period of years was spent in the wilderness.

WAR. Under this head we may notice some of the usages of Hebrew warfare which have not been considered under other heads, referred to at the end of this article.

The army of Israel was chiefly composed of infantry, formed into a trained body of spearmen, and, in greater numbers, of slingers and archers, with horses and chariots in small proportion, excepting during the periods when the kingdom extended over the desert to the Red Sea. The irregulars were drawn from the families and tribes, particularly Ephraim and Benjamin, but the heavy armed derived their chief strength from Judah, and were, it appears, collected by a kind of conscription, by tribes, like the earlier Roman armies; not through the instrumentality of selected officers, but by genealogists of each tribe, under the superintendence of the princes. Of those returned on the rolls, a proportion greater or less was selected, according to the exigency of the time; and the whole male population might be called out on extraordinary occasions. When kings had rendered the system of government better organised, there was a sort of muster-master, who had returns of the effective force, or number of soldiers ready for service, but who was a kind of secretary of state. These officers, or the *shoterim*, struck out, or excused from service:—1st, those who had built a house without having yet inhabited it; 2nd, those who had planted an olive or vineyard, and had not tasted the fruit—which gave leave of absence for five years; 3rd, those who were betrothed, or had been married less than one year; 4th, the *faint-hearted*, which may mean the constitutionally delicate, rather than the cowardly.

The levies were drilled to march in ranks (1 Chron. xii. 38), and in column by fives abreast (Exod. xiii. 18); hence it may be inferred that they borrowed from the Egyptian system a decimal formation, two fifties in each division making a solid square, equal in rank and file: for twice ten in rank and five in file being told off by right hand and left hand files, a command to the left hand files to face about and march six or eight paces to the rear, then to front and take one step to the right would make the hundred a solid square, with only the additional distance between the right hand or unmoved files necessary to use the shield and spear without hindrance; while the depth being again reduced to five files, they could face to the right or left, and march firmly in column, passing every kind of ground without breaking or lengthening their order.

With centuries thus arranged in masses, both movable and solid, a front of battle could be formed in simple decimal progression to a thousand, ten thousand, and to an army at all times formidable by its depth, and by the facility it afforded for the light troops, chariots of war, and cavalry, to rally behind and to issue from thence to the front. Archers and slingers could ply their missiles from the rear, which would be more certain to reach an enemy in close conflict, than was to be found the case with the Greek phalanx, because from the great depth of that body missiles from behind were liable to fall among its own front ranks. These divisions were commanded, it seems, by *ketsinim*, officers in charge of one thousand, who, in the first ages, may have been the heads of houses, but in the time of the kings were appointed by the crown, and had a seat in the councils of war; but the commander of the host, such as Joab, Abner, Benaiah, &c., was either the judge, or under the judge or king, the supreme head of the army, and one of the highest officers in the state. He, as well as the king, had an armour-bearer, whose duty was not only to bear his shield, spear, or bow, and to carry orders, but, above all, to be at the chief's side in the hour of battle (Judg. ix. 54; 1 Sam. xiv. 6; xxxi. 4, 5). Beside the royal guards, there was, as early at least as the time of David, a select troop of heroes, who appear to have had an institution very similar in principle to our modern orders of knighthood.

In military operations, such as marches in quest of, or in the presence of, an enemy, and in order of battle, the forces were formed into three divisions, each commanded by a chief captain or commander of a corps, or third part, as was also the case with other armies of the east; these constituted the centre, and right and left wing, and during a march formed the van, centre, and rear.

The war-cry of the Hebrews was not intonated by the ensign-bearers, as in the West, but by a Levite; for priests had likewise charge of the trumpets, and the sounding of signals; and one of them, called 'the anointed for war,' who is said to have had the charge of animating the army to action by an oration, may have been appointed to utter the cry of battle (Deut. xx. 2). It was a mere shout (1 Sam. xvii. 20), or, as in later ages, *Hallelujah!* while the so-called mottoes of the central banners of the four great sides of the square, of Judah, Reuben, Ephraim, and Dan, were more likely the battle-songs which each of the fronts of the mighty army had sung on commencing the march or advancing to do battle (Num. x. 34, 35, 36; Deut. vi. 4).

Before an engagement the Hebrew soldiers were spared fatigue as much as possible, and food was distributed to them; their arms were enjoined to be in the best order, and they formed a line, as before described, of solid squares of hundreds, each square being ten deep, and as many in breadth, with sufficient intervals between the files to allow of facility in the movements, the management of the arms, and the passage to the front or rear of slingers and archers. These lasts occupied posts according to circumstances, on the flanks, or in advance, but in the heat of battle were sheltered behind the squares of spearmen; the slingers were always stationed in the rear, until they were ordered forward to cover the front, impede an hostile approach, or commence an engagement. Meantime, the king, or his representative, appeared clad in holy ornaments, and proceeded to make the final dispositions for battle, in the middle of his chosen braves, and attended by priests, who, by their exhortations, animated the ranks within hearing, while the trumpets waited to sound the signal. It was now, with the enemy at hand, we may suppose, that the slingers would be ordered to pass forward between the intervals of the line, and, opening their order, would let fly their stone or leaden missiles, until, by the gradual approach of the opposing fronts, they would be hemmed in and recalled to the rear, or ordered to take an appropriate position. Then was the time when the trumpet-bearing priests received command to sound the charge, and when the shout of battle burst forth from the ranks. The signal being given, the heavy infantry would press forward under cover of their shields, the rear ranks might then, when so armed, cast their darts, and the archers, behind them all, shoot high, so as to pitch their arrows over the lines before them, into the dense masses of the enemy beyond. If the opposing forces broke through the line, we may imagine a body of charioteers reserve, rushing from their post, and charging in among the disjointed ranks of the enemy, before they could reconstruct their order; or wheeling round a flank, fall upon the rear; or being encountered by a similar manœuvre, and perhaps repulsed, or rescued by Hebrew cavalry. The king, meanwhile, surrounded by his princes, posted close to the rear of his line of battle, and in the middle of showered missiles, would watch the enemy and strive to remedy every disorder. Thus it was that several of the sovereigns of Judah were slain (2 Chron. xviii. 33; xxxv. 23), and that such an enormous waste of human life took place; for two hostile lines of masses, at least ten in depth, advancing under the confidence of breast-plate and shield, when once engaged hand to hand, had difficulties of no ordinary nature to retreat; because the hindermost ranks not being exposed personally to the first slaughter, would not, and the foremost could not, fall back; neither could the commanders disengage the line without a certainty of being routed. The fate of the day was therefore no longer within the control of the chief, and nothing but obstinate valour was left to decide the victory. Sometimes a part of the army was posted in ambush, but this manœuvre was most commonly practised against the garrisons of cities (Josh. viii. 12; Judg. xx. 38). In the case of Abraham (Gen. xiv. 15), when he led a small body of his own people, suddenly collected, and falling upon the guard of the captives, released them, and recovered the booty, it was a surprise, not an ambush; nor is it necessary to suppose that he fell in with the main army of the enemy. At a later period there is no doubt the Hebrews formed their armies, in imitation of the Romans, into more than one line of masses, and modelled their military institutions as near as possible upon the same system. [ARMS; ARMOUR; ENCAMPMENT; ENGINES; FORTIFICATIONS; STANDARDS.]

WASHING. [ABLUTION.]

WASHING OF FEET. The custom of washing the feet held, in ancient times, a place among the duties of hospitality, being regarded as a mark of respect to the guest, and a token of humble and affectionate attention on the part of the entertainer. It had its origin in circumstances for the most part peculiar to the East.

In general, in warm Oriental climes, cleanliness is of the highest consequence, particularly as a safeguard against the leprosy. The East knows nothing of the factitious distinctions which prevail in these countries between sanitary regulations and religious duties; but the one, as much as the other, is considered a part of that great system of obligations under which man lies towards God. What, therefore, the health demands, religion is at hand to sanction. Cleanliness is in consequence not next to godliness, but a part of godliness itself.

As in this Oriental view may be found the origin and reason of much of what the Mosaic law lays down touching clean and unclean, so the practice of feet-washing in particular, which considerations of purity and personal propriety recommended, hospitality adopted and religion sanctioned.

In temperate climes bathing is far too much neglected; but in the East the heat of the atmosphere and the dryness of the soil would render the ablution of the body peculiarly desirable, and make feet-washing no less grateful than salutary to the weary traveller. The foot, too, was less protected than with us. In the earliest ages it probably had no covering; and the sandal worn in later times was little else than the sole of our shoe bound under the foot. Even this defence, however, was ordinarily laid aside on entering a house, in which the inmates were either barefoot or wore nothing but slippers.

The washing of the feet is among the most ancient, as well as the most obligatory, of the rites of Eastern hospitality. From Gen. xviii. 4, xix. 2, it appears to have existed as early as the days of the patriarch Abraham. In Gen. xxiv. 32, also, 'Abraham's servant' is provided with water to wash his feet, and the men's feet that were with him. The same custom is mentioned in Judg. xix. 21. From 1 Sam. xxv. 41, it appears that the rite was sometimes performed by servants and sons, as their appropriate duty, regarded as of an humble character. Hence, in addition to its being a token of affectionate regard, it was a sign of humility.

The most remarkable instance is found in the 13th chapter of John's Gospel, where our Saviour is represented as washing the feet of his disciples, with whom he had taken supper. Minute particulars are given in the sacred narrative, which should be carefully studied, as presenting a true Oriental picture. From ver. 12, sq., it is clear that the act was of a symbolical nature, designed to teach brotherly humility and goodwill.

It was specially customary in the days of our Lord to wash before eating (Matt. xv. 2; Luke xi. 38). But Jesus did not pay a scrupulous regard to the practice, and hence drew blame upon himself from the Pharisees (Luke xi. 38). In this our Lord was probably influenced by the superstitious abuses and foolish misinterpretations connected with washing *before* meat. For the same reason he may purposely have postponed the act of washing his disciples' feet till *after* supper, lest, while he was teaching a new lesson of humility, he might add a sanction to current and baneful errors [ABLUTION].

The union of affectionate attention and lowly service is found indicated by feet-washing in 1 Tim. v. 10, where, among the signs of the widows that were to be honoured—supported, that is, at the expense of the church—this is given, if any one ' have washed the saints' feet.'

Feet-washing became, as might be expected, a part of the observances practised in the early Christian church. The real signification, however, was soon forgotten, or overloaded by superstitious feelings and mere outward practices. Traces of the practice abound in ecclesiastical history, and remnants of the abuse are still to be found, at least in the Romish church.

WATCH. Watching must have been coeval with danger, and danger arose as soon as man became the enemy of man, or had to guard against the attacks of wild animals. Accordingly we find traces of the practice of watching in early portions of the Hebrew annals. Watching must have been carried to some degree of completeness in Egypt, for we learn from Exod. xiv. 24, that the practice had, at the time of the Exodus, caused the night to be divided into different watches or portions, mention being made of the 'morning watch.' Compare 1 Sam. xi. 11. In the days of the Judges (vii. 19) we find 'the middle watch' mentioned. See Luke xii. 38. At a later period Isaiah plainly intimates (xxi. 5, 6), that there was a watch-tower in Jerusalem, and that it was customary on extraordinary occasions to set a watchman. Watchmen were, however, even at an earlier day, customarily employed in the metropolis, and their post was at the gates (2 Sam. xviii. 24, sq.; 2 Kings ix. 17, sq ; Ps. cxxvii. 1; Prov. viii. 34), where they gave signals and information, either by their voice or with the aid of a trumpet (Jer. vi. 17; Ezek. xxxiii. 6). At night watchmen were accustomed to perambulate the city (Cant. iii. 3; v. 7). In the New Testament we find mention made of the second, the third, and the fourth watch (Luke xii. 38 ; Matt. xiv. 25). The space of the natural night, from the setting to the rising of the sun, the ancient Jews divided into three equal parts of four hours each. But the Romans, imitating the Greeks, divided the night into four watches, and the Jews, from the time they came under subjection to the Romans, following this Roman custom, also divided the night into four watches, each of which consisted of three hours (Mark xiii. 35). The terms by which the old Hebrew division of the night was characterized are, 1. the first watch, beginning of the watches (Lam. ii. 19); 2. 'the middle-watch' (Judg. vii. 19); 3. 'the morning-watch' (Deut. xiv. 24 ; 1 Sam. xi. 11). The first extended from sun-set to our ten o'clock, the second from ten at night till two in the morning, and the third from that hour till sun-rise.

WATER. No one can read far in the sacred Scriptures without being reminded of the vast importance of water to the Hebrews in Palestine, and indeed in every country to which their history introduces us; and more particularly in the deserts in which they wandered on leaving Egypt, as well as those into which they before or afterwards sent their flocks for pasture. The natural

waters have already been disposed of in the articles PALESTINE and RIVER; and in CISTERN and JERUSALEM notice has been taken of some artificial collections. It now remains to complete the subject, under the present head, by the addition of such details as may not have been comprehended under the articles referred to.

It has been shown that the absence of small rivers, through the want of rain in summer, renders the people of the settled country, as well as of the deserts, entirely dependent upon the water derived from wells, and that preserved in cisterns and reservoirs, during the summer and autumn; and gives an importance unknown in our humid climate to the limited supply thus secured.

With respect to reservoirs, the articles to which reference has been made, will supply all the information necessary, except that we may avail ourselves of this opportunity of noticing the so-called Pools of Solomon, near Bethlehem. ' They consist of three enormous tanks,' says Dr. Wilde, ' sunk in the side of a sloping ground, and which from time immemorial have been considered to be the workmanship of Solomon ; and certainly they are well worthy the man to whom tradition has assigned their construction. These reservoirs are each upon a distinct level, one above the other, and are capable of holding an immense body of water. They are so constructed, both by conduits leading directly from one another, and by what may be termed anastamosing branches, that when the water in the upper one has reached to a certain height, the surplus flows off into the one below it, and so on into the third. These passages were obstructed and the whole of the cisterns were out of repair when we visited them, so that there was hardly any water in the lowest, while the upper one was nearly full of good pure water. Small aqueducts lead from each of these cisterns to a main one that conducts the water to Jerusalem. They are all lined with a thick layer of hard whitish cement, and a flight of steps leads to the bottom of each, similar to some of those in the holy city. Where the lowest cistern joins the valley of Etham it is formed by an embankment of earth, and has a sluice to draw off the water occasionally. A short distance from the upper pool I descended into a narrow stone chamber, through which the water passes from the neighbouring spring on its course to the cisterns.

'On our return to the city we followed the track of the aqueduct as far as Bethlehem, and afterwards crossed it in several places on the road. It is very small, but the water runs in it with considerable rapidity, as we could perceive by the open places left in it here and there. From the very tortuous course that this conduit takes in following the different sinuosities of the ground, being sometimes above and sometimes beneath the surface, it is difficult to persuade oneself that it does not run up hill, as many have supposed. Finally, it crosses over the valley of Rephaim, on a series of arches, to the north of the lower pool of Gihon, and winding round the southern horn of Zion, is lost to view in the ruins of the city. It very probably supplied the pool of Bethesda, after having traversed a course of certainly not less than from thirteen to fifteen miles.'

With respect to wells, their importance is very great, especially in the desert, where the means of forming them are deficient, as well as the supply of labour necessary for such undertakings, which, after all, are not always rewarded by the discovery of a supply of water. Hence in such situations, and indeed in the settled countries also, the wells are of the utmost value, and the water in most cases is very frugally used (Num. xx 17–19; Deut ii. 6, 28; Job xxii. 7). We are not, however, to seek an explanation of the contests about wells which we find in the histories of Abraham and Isaac (Gen. xxi. 25–31; xxvi. 15–22) merely in the value of the well itself, but in the apprehension entertained by the Philistines that by the formation of such wells the patriarchs would be understood to create a lien on the lands in which they lay, and would acquire an indefeasible right of occupation, or rather of possession; and it might seem to them inconvenient that so powerful a clan should acquire such a right in the soil of so small a territory as that which belonged to them. Hence their care, when Abraham afterwards left their part of the country, to fill up the wells which he had digged; and hence, also, the renewed and more bitter strife with Isaac when he, on arriving there, proceeded to clear out those wells and to dig new ones himself.

326.   [Well and Bucket at Jaffa.]

It appears in Scripture that the wells were sometimes owned by a number of persons in common, and that flocks were brought to them for watering on appointed days, in an order previously arranged. A well was often covered with a great stone, which being removed, the person descended some steps to the surface of the water, and on his return poured into a trough that which he had brought up (Gen. xxiv. 11–15; xxix. 3–10; Exod. ii. 16; Judg. v. 11). There is, in fact, no intimation of any other way of drawing water from wells in Scripture. But as this could only be applicable in cases where the well was not deep, we must assume that they had the use of those contrivances which are still employed in the East, and some of which are known from the Egyptian monuments to have been very ancient. This conclusion is the more probable as the wells in Palestine are mostly deep (Prov. xx. 5; John iv. 11). Jacob's well near Shechem is said to be 120 feet deep, with only fifteen feet of water in it; and the labour of drawing from so deep a well probably originated the first reluctance of the woman of Samaria to draw water for Jesus: 'Sir, thou hast nothing to draw with, and the well is deep.' From this deeper kind of well the water is drawn by hand in a leathern bucket not too heavy, sometimes by a windlass, but oftener, when the water is only of moderate depth, by the *shadoof,* which is the most common and simple of all the machines used in the East for raising

water, whether from wells, reservoirs, or rivers. This consists of a tapering lever unequally balanced upon an upright body variously constructed, and from the smaller end of which is suspended the bucket by a rope. This, when lowered into the well, is raised full of water by the weight of the heavier end. By this contrivance the manual power is applied in lowering the bucket into the well, for it rises easily, and it is only necessary to regulate the ascent. This machine is in use under slight modifications from the Baltic to the Yellow Sea, and was so from the most remote ages to the present day. The specimen in the annexed woodcut occurs in the neighbourhood of Jaffa. The water of wells, as well as of fountains, was by the Hebrews called 'living water,' translated 'running water,' and was highly esteemed (Lev. xiv. 5; Num. xix. 17). It was thus distinguished from water preserved in cisterns and reservoirs.

WEAPONS. [Arms.]

WEASEL. The *Viverridæ* and *Mustellidæ* appear, both anciently and among ourselves, collected into a kind of group, under an impression that they belong to the feline family; hence we, like the ancients, still use the words civet-cat, tree-cat, pole-cat, &c.; and, in reality, a considerable number of the species have partially retractile claws, the pupils of the eyes being contractile like those of cats, of which they even bear tho spotted and streaked liveries. All such naturally have arboreal habits, and from their low lengthy forms are no less disposed to burrow; but many of them, chiefly in other hemispheres, are excellent swimmers. One of these species, allied to if not the same as *genetta barbara,* is the *Thela Ælan,* by Bochart described as having 'various colours, and as being spotted like a pard.' There are besides, in the same region, the *nimse* ferret or polecat, for these two are not specifically distinct. the weasel differing from ours chiefly in its superior size and darker colours. A *paradoxurus,* identical with or nearly allied to *P. typus,* occurs in Arabia;

327.   [Paradoxurus Typus—the Palm-Martin.]

for it seems these animals are found wherever there are *palmiferæ,* the date-palm in particular being a favourite residence of the species. Two or three varieties, or perhaps species, of *nems* occur in Egypt solely. Arabia Proper has several other animals not clearly distinguished, though belonging to the families here noticed.

WEAVING is too necessary an art not to have existed in the early periods of the world. It appears, indeed, to have in all nations come into existence with the first dawnings of civilization. The Egyptians had, as might be expected, already made considerable progress therein when the Israelites tarried amongst them; and in this as well as in many other of the arts of life, they became the instructors of that people. Textures of cotton and of flax were woven by them; whence we read of the 'vestures of fine linen' with which Pharaoh arrayed Joseph (Gen. xli. 42); terms which show that the art of fabricating cloth had been successfully cultivated. Indeed Egypt was celebrated among the Hebrews for its manufacturing skill. Thus Isaiah (xix. 9) speaks of 'them that work in fine flax, and them that weave net-works.' That these fabrics displayed taste as well as skill may be inferred from Ezekiel xxvii. 7, 'Fine linen with broidered work from Egypt.' So in Prov. vii. 16, 'I have decked my couch with coverings of tapestry. with fine linen of Egypt.' If, however, the Hebrews learnt the art of weaving in Egypt, they appear to have made progress therein from their own resources. even before they entered Palestine; for having before them the prospect of a national establishment in that land, they would naturally turn their attention to the arts of life, and had leisure as well as occasion, during their sojourn of forty years in the wilderness, for practising those arts; and certainly we cannot but understand the words of Moses to imply that the skill spoken of in Exod. xxxv. 30, sq., came from a Hebrew and not a foreign impulse. Among the Israelites weaving, together with spinning, was for the most part in the hands of females (Prov. xxxi. 13, 19); nor did persons of rank and distinction consider the occupation mean (Exod. xxxv. 25; 2 Kings xxiii. 7). But as in Egypt males exclusively, so in Palestine men conjointly with women, wove (Exod. xxxv. 35). From 1 Chron. iv. 21 it may be inferred that there were in Israel a class of master-manufacturers. The loom, as was generally the case in the ancient world, was high, requiring the weaver to stand at his employment.

Connected with the loom are, 1. the shuttle (Job vii. 6); 2. the weaver's beam (1 Sam. xvii. 7; 2 Sam. xxi. 19); 3. a weaver's pin (Judg. xvi. 14). The degree of skill to which the Hebrews attained it is difficult to measure. The stuffs which they wove were of linen, flax, and wool. Among the latter must be reckoned those of camels' and goats' hair, which were used by the poor for clothing and for mourning (Exod. xxvi. 7; xxxv. 6; Matt. iii. 4). Garments woven in one piece throughout, so as to need no making, were held in high repute; whence the Jews have a tradition that no needle was employed on the clothing of the high priest, each piece of which was of one continued texture. This notion throws light on the language used by John xix. 23—'the coat was without seam,'—words that are explained by those which follow, and which Wetstein regards as a gloss—'woven from the top throughout.' This seamless coat, which has lately given occasion to the great religious reformatory movement begun by the priest Ronge, would seem to indicate that our Lord. knowing that his time was now come, had arrayed himself in vestments suitable to the dignity of his Messianic office.

WEDDING. [MARRIAGE.]

WEEK. [SABBATH.]

WEEKS, FEAST OF. [PENTECOST.]

WEIGHTS AND MEASURES. This is a subject on which our knowledge is by no means complete and satisfactory, as the notices respecting it which the Bible supplies are fragmentary and scattered.

With respect to the coins in use among the Hebrews, it is evident that there prevailed among the Hebrews at an early period a very considerable and much employed metallic medium. Mention is made of talents, shekels, half-shekels, and gerahs. It is impossible to determine with absolute certainty the relative value of these coins, but the following table has been constructed from an examination of the coins of Simon Maccabæus, and is probably very nearly correct:—

Gerah	=	13·7	Paris grains.
Bekah, or common shekel	,,	137	,,
Sacred shekel	,,	274	,,
Maneh	,,	13,700	,,
Talent	,,	822,000	,,

These conclusions find corroboration by being compared with the weights of other Eastern nations, and the whole inquiry authorizes the inference that one general system prevailed in the more civilized nations, being propagated from the East, from an early period of history.

In the New Testament (Matt. xvii. 24) the Temple-tax is a didrachm; from other sources we know that this 'tribute' was half a shekel; and in verse 27 the stater is payment of this tax for two persons. Now the stater—a very common silver Attic coin, the tetradrachm—weighed 328·8 Paris grains; thus not considerably surpassing the sacred shekel (274 Paris grains). And there is reason in the passage of Matthew and in early writers for regarding the stater of the New Testament as the same with the Attic tetradrachm.

Names of measures of length are for the most part taken from members of the human body, which offered themselves, so to say, naturally for the purpose, and have generally been used in all times and places in instances where minute accuracy was not demanded.

At the basis of the Hebrew system of measures of length lies the cubit, the fore-arm, or the distance from the point of the elbow to the tip of the third finger.

A longer measure, applied in measuring buildings, was the reed, or more properly 'rod' (Ezek. xli. 8; Apoc. xxi. 15). Smaller measures of length were, 1. a span, from a root meaning to expand (the hand). 2. The breadth of the hand (1 Kings vii. 26; Exod. xxv. 25). 3. The finger (Jerem. lii. 21), the denomination of the smallest measure of length. Thus we have the breadth of the finger, of the hand, of the span—the length from the tip of the little finger to the point of the thumb,—and the cubit.

As we have no unit of measure given us in the Scriptures, nor preserved to us in the remains of any Hebrew building, and as neither the Rabbins nor Josephus afford the information we want, we have no resource but to apply for information to the measures of length used in other countries. We go to the Egyptians. The longer Egyptian cubit contained about 234·333 **Paris lines**, the shorter about 204 8. According to this the Hebrew measures of length were these:—

Sacred cubit	.	234 333	Paris lines.
The span	. .	117·166	,,
The palm	. .	39·055	,,
The finger	. .	9·7637	,,
Common cubit	.	204·8	,,
The span	. .	102·4	,,
The palm	. .	34·133	,,
The finger	· .	8·533	,,

The two sets of measures, one for dry, another for liquid things, rest on the same system, as appears from the equality of the standard for dry goods, namely the ephah, with that for liquids, namely bath. Mention is made of the homer, cab, bath and ephah—which are the same, hin, and log. The relations of these measures to the homer, the greatest of them, is exhibited in the following table:—

Homer . . .	1					
Bath and Ephah	10	1				
Seah . . .	30	3	1			
Hin	60	6	2	1		
Gomer . .	100	10	3½	1⅔	1	
Cab . . .	180	18	6	3	1¼	1
Log . . .	720	72	24	12	7½	4 1

The actual size of these measures, as stated by Josephus, is as follows:—

	SIZE. Par cub in.	WEIGHT IN WATER. Par. gr.
Homer	19857·7	7398000
Ephah	1985·77	739800
Seah	661·92	246600
Hin	330·96	123300
Gomer	198·577	73980
Cab	110·32	41100
Log	27·58	10275

Böckh has proved that it is in Babylon we are to look for the foundations of the metrological systems of the ancient world; for the entire system of measures, both eastern and western, must be referred to the Babylonish foot as to its basis. On Babylon also the ancient world was dependent for its astronomy. Hence Babylon appears as the land which was the teacher of the east and the west in astronomical and mathematical knowledge, standing as it were in the middle of the ancient world, and sending forth rays of light from her two extended hands. Palestine could not be closed against these illuminations, which in their progress westward must have enlightened its inhabitants, who appear to have owed their highest earthly culture to the Babylonians and the Egyptians.

WELL. [WATER.]

WEST. The Shemite, in speaking of the quarters of the heavens, &c., supposes his face turned towards the east; so that the east is before him; the south on his right hand; the north on his left hand, and the west behind him; and the various words employed to designate the quarters of the heavens have literally the signification mentioned (*Voyage en Syrie*, tom. i. p. 297; Shaw's *Travels*, p. 329).

WHALE occurs in several places of the Old Testament, and once in the New Testament. In the passages where scales and feet are mentioned as belonging to the animals so designated, com-

mentators have shown that the crocodile is intended, which then is synonymous with the leviathan; and they have endeavoured also to demonstrate, where they draw the dugs to suckle their young, that seals are meant, although cetacea nourish theirs in a similar manner. It may be doubted whether, in most of the cases, the poetical diction points absolutely to any specific animal, particularly as there is more force and grandeur in a generalized and collective image of the huge monsters of the deep, not inappropriately so called, than in the restriction to any one species, since all are in Gen. i. 26 made collectively subservient to the supremacy of man. But criticism is still more inappropriate when, not contented with pointing to some assumed species, it attempts to rationalise miraculous events by such arguments; as in the case of Jonah, where the fact of whales having a small gullet, and not being found in the Mediterranean, is adduced to prove that the huge fish was not a cetacean, but a shark! It may be observed, besides, of cetaceous animals, that though less frequent in the Mediterranean than in the ocean, they are far from being unknown there.

WHEAT occurs in various passages of Scripture, and there can be no doubt that the word so rendered has this signification.

Wheat having been one of the earliest cultivated grains, is most probably of Asiatic origin, as no doubt Asia was the earliest civilized, as well as the first peopled country. As both wheat and barley are cultivated in the plains of India in the winter months, where none of the species of these

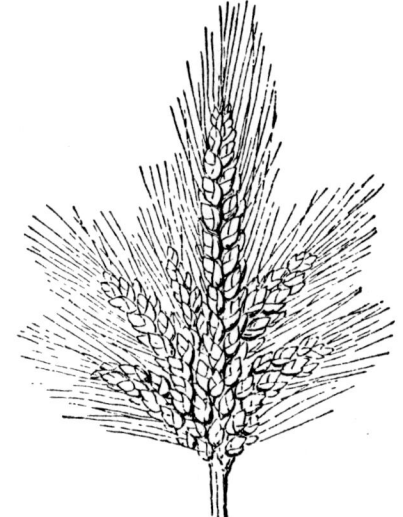

328. [Triticum compositum—Egyptian Wheat.]

genera are indigenous, it is probable that both have been introduced into India from the north, that is, from the Persian, and perhaps from the Tartarian region, where these and other species of barley are most successfully and abundantly cultivated. Different species of wheat were no doubt cultivated by the ancients; but both barley and wheat are too well known to require further illustration in this place.

WHIRLWIND. [WINDS.]
WILDERNESS. [DESERTS.]
WILLOW-TREE (Ezek. xvii. 5). The spe-
cies of willow here referred to is supposed to be a
peculiar sort called *safsaf*, the *Salix Ægyptiaca*

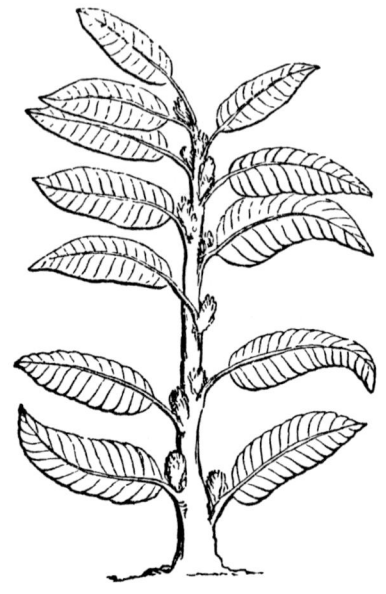

329. [Salix Ægyptiaca.]

of botanists. The stems and twigs are long, thin,
weak, and of a pale yellow-colour; on their twigs
here and there are shoots of a span long, like unto
the Cypriotish wild fig-trees, which put forth in
the spring tender and woolly flowers, like unto
the blossoms of the poplar-tree, only they are of a
more drying quality. of a pale colour, and a fragrant smell. The inhabitants pull of these great
quantities, and distil a very precious and sweet
water out of them.

WIMPLE. [VEIL.]

WIND. The Hebrew word signifies *air in motion* generally, as breath, wind, &c. It is used, 1.
for the wind as *a natural phenomenon* (Gen. iii. 8;
Job xxi. 18; xxx. 15, 22; xxxvii. 21; Ps i. 4;
cui. 16; Prov. xxx. 4; Eccles i. 6; xi. 4; Isa.
vii. 2; xvii. 13; xl. 7; Jer. x. 13; li. 16; Amos
xiv. 13). It is poetically ascribed to the immediate agency of God (Ps. cxxxv. 7; cxlvii. 18).
2. The wind occurs as the *medium of the divine
interposition*, or *agency* (Gen. i. 2; viii. 1; Ex.
xv. 10; Num. xi. 31; 1 Kings xviii. 45; xix. 11;
Job i. 19; Isa. xi. 5; Jonah i. 4). In the New
Testament, the wind was supernaturally employed
at the day of Pentecost, like the 'sound' and
'fire' (Acts ii. 3). [SPIRIT.] To this class of
instances we refer Gen. i. 2, 'and the Spirit of
God moved upon the face of the waters.' Along
with Patrick and Rosenmuller, we construe the
phrase, 'a wind of God,' a wind employed as the
medium of divine agency. 3. The wind is used
metaphorically in the following instances: The
wings of the wind' denote the most rapid motion
(2 Sam. xxii. 11). Anything light or trifling is

called wind (Job vii. 7; Isa. xli. 29; Ps. lxxviii.
39: comp. Eph. iv. 14; Ecclus. v. 9). Violent yet
empty speech is called 'a strong wind,' or a mere
tempest of words (Job viii. 2). 'Vain knowledge'
is called knowledge of wind (Job xv. 2); 'vain
words,' words of wind (xvi. 3). Many expressive
phrases are formed with this word 'To inherit
the wind,' denotes extreme disappointment (Prov.
xi. 29); 'to hide the wind,' impossibility (xxvii.
16); to 'labour for the wind,' to labour in vain
(Ecc. v. 16); 'to bring forth wind 'great patience
and pains for no purpose (Isa. xxvi. 18; comp.
Hos. viii 7; xii. 1); 'to become wind,' to result
in nothingness (Jer. v. 13). 'The four winds'
denote the four quarters of the globe (Ezek.
xxxvii 9); 'to scatter to all winds,' to disperse
completely (Ezek. v. 10; xii. 41; xvii. 21); 'to
cause to come from all winds,' to restore completely (xxxvii. 9). 'The wind hath bound her
upon her wings,' means deportation into a far
country (Hos. iv. 19): 'to sow the wind and reap
the whirlwind,' unwise labour and a fruitless
result (viii. 7); 'to feed on the wind,' to pursue
delusory schemes (xii 1); 'to walk in wind,' to
live and act in vain (Micah ii. 11); 'to observe
the wind,' to be over cautious (Eccles. xi. 4); to
'winnow with every wind,' to be credulous, apt to
receive impressions (v. 9). 4. The east wind.
Dr. Shaw remarks, that every wind is called by
the Orientals an east wind which blows from
any point of the compass between the east and
north, and between the east and south (*Travels*,
p. 285). If the east wind happens to blow a few
days in Palestine during the months of May,
June, July, and August, it occasions great destruction to the vines and harvests on the land, and also
to the vessels at sea on the Mediterranean. It is
accordingly often used to denote *any* pernicious
wind, as in Ps. xlviii. 7. It is used *metaphorically*
for pernicious speech, a storm of words (Job xv.
2); calamities, especially by war (Isa. xxvii. 8;
Jer. xviii. 17; Ezek. xvii. 10; xix. 12; xxvii. 26;
Hos. xiii. 15). The east wind denotes divine
judgment (Job xxvii. 21). *Phrases* —'To follow
the east wind,' is to pursue a delusory and fatal
course (Hos. xii. 1). 5. West wind. 6. North
wind (Prov. xxv. 23). 7. South wind (Job
xxxvii. 17; Ps. lxxviii. 26; Luke xii. 55); Sirocco (Acts xxvii. 13). 8. The *four winds*. This
phrase is equivalent to the four quarters of the
world (Ezek. xxxvii. 9; 2 Esdras xiii. 5), the
several points of the compass, as we should say
(Dan. viii. 8) *Phrases*.—'Striving of the four
winds,' is great political commotions (Dan. vii 2;
comp. Jer. iv. 11, 12; li. 1); to 'hold the four
winds,' is by contrary to secure peace (Rev. vii.
1); 'to be divided to the four winds,' implies
utter dispersion (Dan. xi. 4; Jer. xlix. 32; Ezek.
v. 10, 12; xvii. 2). The Hebrews, like other
ancient nations, had but few *names of winds* One
Greek name of a wind occurs in Acts xxvii. 14,
Euroclydon, a tempestuous wind in the Mediterranean, now called a *Levanter*. Εὖρος, *Eurus*,
'east wind,' and κλύδων, 'a wave,' quasi an eastern tempest. Other MSS. read Εὐρυκλύδων, *Eu-
ryclydon*, from εὐρύς, 'broad,' and κλύδων, 'a
wave,' or rough wavy sea; and then the word
would mean the wind which peculiarly excites
the waves. Shaw defends the common reading,
and describes the wind as blowing in all directions from the N.E. round by the N. to the S.E.

(*Travels*, p. 330, &c. 4to.; see Bowyer's conjectures, and Doddridge, *in loc.*). The Hebrews had no single terms indicating the relative velocity of the air in motion, like our words breeze, gale, &c. Such gradations they expressed by some additional word, as 'great,' רוח־גדולה, 'a great wind' (Jonah i. 4), 'rough,' קשה, &c. Nor have we any single word indicating the destructive effects of the wind, like their verbs סער and שער, as ואסערם (Zech. vii. 14, &c.), and answering to the Greek word ἀνεμόφθορος (see Sept. of Gen. xli. 6, 23). Our *metaphorical* use of the word *storm* comes nearest. The phrase רוח סערה, 'stormy wind,' πνεῦμα καταιγίδος, *spiritus procellæ*, occurs in Ps. cvii. 25; cxlviii. 8. It is metaphorically used for the divine judgments (Ezek. xiii. 11, 13). The word usually translated 'whirlwind' means more properly a storm (2 Kings ii 1, 11; Job xxxviii. 1; xl. 6; Zech. ix. 14). The Hebrew word is used metaphorically for the divine judgments (Isa. xl. 24; xli. 16); and to describe them as sudden and irresistible (Jer. xxiii. 19; xxv. 32; xxx. 23). Total defeat is often compared to 'chaff scattered by a whirlwind' (Isa. xvii. 13). It denotes the rapidity and irresistibleness of the divine judgments (Isa. lxvi. 5). The *phrase* 'to reap the whirlwind' denotes useless labour (Hos. viii. 7); 'the day of the whirlwind,' destruction by war (Amos i. 14). A beautiful comparison occurs in Prov. x. 25: 'As the whirlwind passeth, so is the wicked no more: but the righteous is an everlasting foundation.'

WINDOW. [HOUSE.]

WINE. No fewer than thirteen distinct Hebrew and Greek terms are rendered in our common version by the word 'wine.' Besides the pure juice of the grape, frequent mention is made in Scripture of a kind of boiled wine or syrup, the thickness of which rendered it necessary to mingle water with it previously to drinking (Prov. ix. 2, 5), and also of a mixed wine, made strong and inebriating by the addition of drugs, such as myrrh, mandragora, and opiates (Prov. xxiii. 30; Isa. v. 22). This custom has prevailed from the earliest ages, and is still extant in the East. We are not, however, to conclude that all mixed wine was pernicious or improper. There were two very opposite purposes sought by the mixture of drinks. While the wicked sought out a drugged mixture, and was 'mighty to mingle strong drink,' Wisdom, on the contrary, mingled her wine with water or with milk (Prov. ix. 2, 5) merely to dilute it and make it properly drinkable. Of the latter mixture Wisdom invites the people to drink freely, but on the use of the former an emphatic woe is pronounced. In Isa. xxv. 6, mention is made of 'wines on the lees.' The original signifies 'preserves' or 'jellies,' and is supposed to refer to the *wine cakes* which are esteemed a great delicacy in the East.

WINNOWING. [AGRICULTURE.]

WINTER. [PALESTINE.]

WISDOM OF SOLOMON [APOCRYPHA] is the name of one of the deuterocanonical books. The anonymous author personates King Solomon, whom he introduces as speaking; but from the citations of the prophets Isaiah and Jeremiah, it may be inferred that the writer had no intention of giving it to be understood that it was written by Solomon; but that he only followed a common custom of Greek and other writers, in employing the name of this distinguished royal penman. It is divided into two, or, according to some, into three parts. The first six chapters contain encomiums on Wisdom, which all, and especially kings, are admonished to acquire, as the true security against present evils, and as leading to future glory and immortality, while a contrary course tends to misery here, and still greater misery hereafter. In chaps. vii. and viii. Solomon is introduced, teaching how wisdom is to be acquired; and in chap. x. is given his prayer for this inestimable gift. Chaps. x.-xix. contain his torical examples, drawn from the Old Testament showing the happiness which had resulted from the pursuit of wisdom, and the fatal consequences of sin, especially the sin of idolatry. The book concludes with divers pious and philosophical observations.

The Book of Wisdom has been always 'admired for the sublime ideas which it contains of the perfections of God, and for the excellent moral tendency of its precepts' (Horne's *Introd.*). Its style, observes Bishop Lowth, after Calmet, 'is unequal, often pompous and turgid, as well as tedious and diffuse, and abounds in epithets directly contrary to the practice of the Hebrews: it is, however, sometimes temperate, poetical, and sublime.' Calmet supposes that the author had read the works of the Greek poets and philosophers.

Although there have not been wanting individuals who have contended for a Hebrew, Syriac, or Chaldee original, there can be little doubt that it was written in Greek.

Nothing is known with certainty respecting the author. All that can be concluded with any degree of probability is, that he was an Alexandrian Jew, who lived after the transplanting of the Greek philosophy into Egypt, and who seems to refer to the oppressions of the later Ptolemies. Jahn conceives that the book was written at the close of the first or beginning of the second century before the Christian era.

WISDOM OF JESUS, SON OF SIRACH, one of the books of the Apocrypha, consists of a collection of moral sentences after the manner of the Proverbs of Solomon (i.-ix. xxiv. comp. with Prov. i.-ix.). The work is arranged upon no systematic plan, but abounds in directions relating to religion and human conduct. Wisdom is represented here, as in Proverbs, as the source of human happiness, and the same views of human life, founded on the belief of a recompense, pervade the instructions of this book also, wherein, however, a more matured reflection is perceptible. It is in fact the composition of a philosopher who had deeply studied the fortunes and manners of mankind, and did not hesitate to avail himself of the philosophy of older moralists. It abounds in grace, wisdom, and spirit, although sometimes more particular in inculcating principles of politeness than those of virtue. It is not unfrequently marked by considerable beauty and elegance of expression, occasionally rising to the sublimest heights of human eloquence. It has been observed of it by Addison (see Horne's *Introd.*, vol. iv.) that 'it would be regarded by our modern wits as one of the most shining tracts of morality that are extant, if it appeared under the name

3 E

of a Confucius or of any celebrated Grecian philosopher.'

The author calls himself Jesus, son of Sirach, of Jerusalem, but we know nothing further of him. The original of the book was Hebrew. Its age is not easily determined; but according to the most probable hypothesis the author lived B.C. 180, and the translator, who was his grandson, B.C. 130.

WITCH. The fem., a sorceress, is found in Exod. xxii. 18; the mas., a sorcerer or magician, in Exod. vii. 11; Deut. xviii. 10; Dan. ii. 2; Mal. iii. 5. In the New Testament 'sorcerer' occurs in Rev. xxi. 8; xxii. 15.

WITCHCRAFTS occurs in 2 Kings ix. 22; Isa. xlvii. 9, 12; Mic. v. 12; Nah. iii. 4; and in the New Testament, Gal. v. 20; Rev. ix. 21; xviii. 23. The precise idea, if any, now associated with the word 'witch,' but, however, devoutly entertained by nearly the whole nation in the time of our translators, is that of a female, who, by the agency of Satan, or rather, of a familiar spirit or gnome appointed by Satan to attend on her, performs operations beyond the powers of humanity, in consequence of her compact with Satan, written in her own blood, by which she resigns herself to him for ever. Among other advantages resulting to her from this engagement is the power of transforming herself into any shape she pleases; which was, however, generally that of a hare; transporting herself through the air on a broomstick, sailing 'on the sea in a sieve,' gliding through a keyhole, inflicting diseases, &c. upon mankind or cattle. The belief in the existence of such persons cannot be traced higher than the middle ages, and was probably derived from the wild and gloomy mythology of the northern nations, amongst whom the Fatal Sisters, and other impersonations of destructive agency in a female form, were prominent articles of the popular creed. A very different idea was conveyed by the Hebrew word, which probably denotes a sorceress or magician, who pretended to discover, and even to direct the effects ascribed to the operation of the elements, conjunctions of the stars, the influence of lucky and unlucky days, the power of invisible spirits, and of the inferior deities. Sir Walter Scott well observes, that 'the sorcery or witchcraft of the Old Testament resolves itself into a trafficking with idols and asking counsel of false deities, or, in other words, into idolatry.' Accordingly, sorcery is in Scripture uniformly associated with idolatry (Deut. xviii. 9-14; 2 Kings ix. 22; 2 Chron. xxxiii. 5, 6, &c.; Gal. v. 20; Rev. xxi. 8). The modern idea of witchcraft, as involving the assistance of Satan, is inconsistent with Scripture, where, as in the instance of Job, Satan is represented as powerless till God gave him a limited commission; and when 'Satan desired to sift Peter as wheat,' no reference is made to the intervention of a witch. Nor do the actual references to magic in Scripture involve its reality. The mischiefs resulting from the *pretension*, under the theocracy, to an art which involved idolatry, justified the statute which denounced it with death; though instead of the unexampled phrase, 'thou shalt not suffer to live,' Michaelis conjectures, 'shall not be' (Exod xxii. 18), which also better suits the parallel, 'There shall not be found among you, &c., a witch' (Deut. xviii. 10). Indeed, as 'we know that an idol is nothing in the world, and that there is

none other gods but one' (1 Cor. viii. 4), we must believe all pretensions to traffic with the one, or ask counsel of the other, to be equally vain. Upon the same principle of suppressing idolatry, however, the prophets of Baal also were destroyed, and not because Baal had any real existence, or because they could avail anything by their invocations. 'The witch of Endor,' as she is commonly but improperly called, belongs to another class of pretenders to supernatural powers [DIVINATION]. She was a necromancer, or one of those persons who pretended to call up the spirits of the dead to converse with the living (see Isa. viii. 19; xxix. 4; lxv. 3). It is related as the last and crowning act of Saul's rebellion against God, that he consulted 'a woman who had a familiar spirit' (1 Sam. xxviii. 7), literally 'a mistress of the *Ob*,' —an act forbidden by the divine law (Lev. xx. 6), which sentenced the pretenders to such a power to death (ver. 27), and which law Saul himself had recently enforced (1 Sam. xxviii. 3, 9), because, it is supposed, they had freely predicted his approaching ruin; although after the well-known prophecies of Samuel to that effect, the disasters Saul had already encountered, and the growing influence of David, there 'needed no ghost to come from the grave to tell them this.' Various explanations of this story have been offered. It has been attempted to resolve the whole into *imposture and collusion*. Saul, who was naturally a weak and excitable man, had become, through a long series of vexations and anxieties, absolutely 'delirious,' as Patrick observes: 'he was afraid and his heart greatly trembled,' says the sacred writer. In this state of mind, and upon the very eve of his last battle, he commissions his *own servants* to seek him a woman that had a familiar spirit, and, attended by two of them, he comes to her 'by night,' the most favourable time for imposition. He converses with her alone, his two attendants, whether his secret enemies or real friends, being absent, *somewhere*, yet, however, close at hand. Might not one of these, or some one else, have agreed with the woman to personate Samuel in another room?—for it appears that Saul, though he spoke with, did not *see* the ghost (ver. 13, 14): who, it should be observed, told him nothing but what his own attendants could have told him, with the exception of those words, 'to-morrow shalt thou and thy sons be with me' (ver. 19); to which, however, it is replied, that Saul's death did not occur upon the morrow, and that the word so translated is sufficiently ambiguous, for though it means 'to-morrow' in some passages, it means the future, indefinitely, in others. It is further urged, that her 'crying with a loud voice,' and her telling Saul, at the same time, that she knew him, were the well-timed arts of the sorceress, intended to magnify her pretended skill. Others are of opinion that the story may be accounted for by the theory of ventriloquism. But it is objected against this, or any other hypothesis of collusion, that the sacred writer not only represents the Pythoness as affirming, but also himself affirms, that she saw Samuel, and that Samuel spoke to Saul, nor does he drop the least hint that it was not the real Samuel of whom he was speaking. Others have given a *literal interpretation* of the story, and have maintained that Samuel actually appeared to Saul. Such also is the view Josephus takes

(*Antiq* vi. 14. 3, 4), where he bestows a laboured eulogium upon the woman. It is, however, objected, that the actual appearance of Samuel is inconsistent with all we are taught by revelation concerning the state of the dead ; involves the possibility of a spirit or soul assuming a corporeal shape, conversing audibly, &c. ; and further, that it is incredible that God would submit the departed souls of his servants to be summoned back to earth, by rites either utterly futile, or else deriving their efficacy from the co-operation of Satan. Others have supposed that the woman induced Satan or some evil spirit to personate Samuel. But this theory, beside other difficulties, attributes nothing less than miraculous power to the devil ; for it supposes the apparition of a spiritual and incorporeal being, and that Satan can assume the appearance of any one he pleases. Others have maintained another interpretation, that the whole account is the narrative of a miracle, *a divine representation or impression*, partly upon the senses of Saul, and partly upon those of the woman, and intended for the rebuke and punishment of Saul. It is urged that God interposed with a miracle previously to the use of any magical formulæ, as he did when the king of Moab had recourse to sorceries to overrule the mind of Balaam, so that he was compelled to bless those whom Balak wanted him to curse (Num. xxiii.).

WITNESS. It occurs, 1st, in the sense of *a person* who deposes to the occurrence of any fact, a witness of any event. It means *a judicial witness* in Exod. xxiii. 1 ; Lev. v. 1 ; Num. v. 13 ; xxxv. 30 (comp. Deut. xvii. 6 ; xix. 15 ; Matt. xviii. 16 ; 2 Cor. xiii. 1) ; Prov. xiv. 5 ; xxiv. 28 ; Matt. xxvi. 65 ; Acts vi. 13 ; 1 Tim. v. 19 ; Heb. x. 28. It is applied, *generally*, to a person who certifies, or is able to certify, to any fact which has come under his cognizance (Josh. xxiv. 22 ; Isa. viii. 2 ; Luke xxiv. 48 ; Acts i. 8, 22 ; 1 Thess. ii. 10 ; 1 Tim. vi. 12 ; 2 Tim. ii. 2 ; 1 Pet. i. 5). So in allusion to those who witness the public games (Heb. xii. 1). It is also applied to any one who testifies to the world what God reveals through him (Rev. xi. 3). In the latter sense the Greek word is applied to our Lord (Rev. i. 5 ; iii. 14). It is further used in the ecclesiastical sense of *martyr*.

WIZARD. [DIVINATION.]

WOLF (Gen xlix. 27 ; Isa. xi. 6 ; lxv. 25 ; Jer. v. 6, &c. ; Matt. vii. 15 ; x. 16 ; Luke x. 3 ; John. x. 12 ; Acts xx. 29 ; Ecclus. viii 17), a fierce carnivorous animal, very nearly allied to the dog, and so well known in Europe as to require no particular description ; but the identity of the species in Palestine, though often asserted, is by no means established ; for no professed zoologist has obtained the animal in Syria, while other travellers only pretend to have seen it. Unquestionably a true wolf, or a wild canine with very similar manners, was not infrequent in that country during the earlier ages of the world, and even down to the commencement of our era. The prophets, as well as the Messiah, allude to it in explicit language. At this day the true wolf is still abundant in Asia Minor, as well as in the gorges of Cilicia, and from the travelling disposition of the species, wolves may be expected to reside in the forests of Libanus ; but there is no satisfactory evidence that this is at present the case. It may be, as there are no forests to the south of Lebanon, that these ravenous beasts, who never willingly range at a distance from cover, have forsaken the more open country.

330. [Egyptian Wolf.]

WOMAN. Like our own term Woman, the Hebrew word now so translated is used of married and unmarried females. The derivation of the word shows that according to the conception of the ancient Israelites woman was man in a modified form—one of the same race, the same genus, as man ; a kind of female man. How slightly modified that form is, how little in original structure woman differs from man, physiology has made abundantly clear. Different in make as man and woman are, they differ still more in character ; and yet the great features of their hearts and minds so closely resemble each other, that it requires no depth of vision to see that these twain are one. This most important fact is characteristically set forth in the Bible in the account given of the formation of woman out of one of Adam's ribs (Gen. ii. 21-24). Those who have been pleased to make free with this simple narrative may well be required to show how a rude age could more effectually have been taught the essential unity of man and woman—a unity of nature which demands, and is perfected only in, a unity of soul. The conception of the Biblical writer goes beyond even this, but does not extend farther than science and experience unite to justify. There was solid reason why it was not good for Adam ' to be alone.' Without an help meet he would have been an imperfect being. The genus homo consists of man and woman. Both are necessary to the idea of man. The one supplements the qualities of the other. They are not two, but one flesh, and as one body so one soul.

It will at once be seen that under the influence of a religion, at the bottom of which lay those ideas concerning the relations of the sexes one to another, slavery on the part of the woman was impossible. This fact is the more noticeable, and it speaks the more loudly in favour of the divine origin of the religion of the Bible, because the East has in all times, down to the present day, kept woman everywhere, save in those places in which Judaism and Christianity have prevailed, in a state of low, even if in some cases gilded, bondage, making her the mere toy, plaything, and instrument of man.

The singular beauty of the Hebrew women, and the natural warmth of their affections, have conspired to throw gems of domestic loveliness over the pages of the Bible. In no history can there be found an equal number of charming female portraits. From Hagar down to Mary

331. [Syro-Arabian costume. In-door dress.]

and Martha, the Bible presents pictures of womanly beauty that are unsurpassed and rarely paralleled. But we should very imperfectly represent in these general remarks the formative influence of the female character as seen in the Bible, did not we refer these amiable traits of character to the pure and lofty religious ideas which the Biblical books present. If woman there appears as the companion and friend of man, she owes her elevation in the main to the religion of Moses and to that of Jesus. The first system—as a preparatory one—did not and could not complete the emancipation of woman. There was

332. [Young lady in full dress.]

needed the finishing touch which the Great Teacher put to the Mosaic view of the relations between the sexes. Recognising the fundamental truths which were as old as the creation of man, Jesus proceeded to restrain the much-abused facility of divorce, leaving only one cause why the marriage-bond should be broken, and at the same time teaching that as the origin of wedlock was divine, so its severance ought not to be the work of man. Still further—bringing to bear on the domestic ties his own doctrine of immortality, he

made the bond co-existent with the undying soul, only teaching that the connection would be refined with the refinement of our affections and our liberation from these tenements of clay in which we now dwell (Matt. v. 32; xix. 3, sq.: xxii. 23, sq.). With views so elevated as these, and with affections of the tenderest benignity, the Saviour may well have won the warm and gentle hearts of Jewish women. Accordingly, the purest and richest human light that lies on the pages of the New Testament, comes from the band of high-minded, faithful, and affectionate women, who are found in connection with Christ from his cradle to his cross, his tomb and his resurrection. These ennobling influences have operated on society with equal benefit and power. Woman, in the better portions of society, is now a new being. And yet her angelic career is only just begun. She sees what she may, and what under the Gospel she ought to be; and ere very long, we trust, a way will be found to employ in purposes of good, energies of the finest nature which now waste away, from want of scope, in the ease and refinements of affluence, if not in the degradations of luxury—a most precious offering made to the Moloch of fashion, but which ought to be consecrated to the service of that God who gave these endowments, and of that Saviour who has brought to light the rich capabilities, and exhibited the high and holy vocation of the female sex.

WOMEN appear to have enjoyed considerably more freedom among the Jews than is now allowed them in western Asia, although in other respects their condition and employments seem to have been not dissimilar.

The employments of the women were very various, and sufficiently engrossing. In the earlier or patriarchal state of society, the daughters of men of substance tended their fathers' flocks (Gen. xxix. 9; Exod. ii. 16). In ordinary circumstances the first labour of the day was to grind corn and bake bread, as already noticed. The other cares of the family occupied the rest of the day. The women of the peasantry and of the poor consumed much time in collecting fuel, and in going to the wells for water. The wells were usually outside the towns, and the labour of drawing water from them was by no means confined to poor women. This was usually, but not always, the labour of the evening; and the water was carried in earthen vessels borne upon the shoulder (Gen. xxiv. 15-20; John iv. 7, 28). Working with the needle also occupied much of their time, as it would seem that not only their own clothes but those of the men were made by the women. Some of the needlework was very fine, and much valued (Exod. xxvi. 36; xxviii. 39; Judg. v. 30; Ps. xlv. 14). The women appear to have spun the yarn for all the cloth that was in use (Exod. xxxv. 25; Prov. xxxi. 19); and much of the weaving seems also to have been executed by them (Judg. xvi. 13, 14; Prov. xxxi. 22). The tapestries for bed-coverings, mentioned in the last-cited text, were probably produced in the loom, and appear to have been much valued (Prov. vii. 16).

We have no certain information regarding the dress of the women among the poorer classes; but it was probably coarse and simple, and not materially different from that which we now see among the Bedouin women, and the female peasantry of Syria. This consists of drawers, and a long and loose gown of coarse blue linen, with some ornamental bordering wrought with the needle, in another colour, about the neck and bosom. The head is covered with a kind of tur-

333. [Matron in full dress.]

ban, connected with which, behind, is a veil, which covers the neck, back, and bosom [VEIL]. We may presume, with still greater certainty, that women of superior condition wore over their inner dress a frock or tunic like that of the men, but more closely fitting the person, with a girdle formed by an unfolded kerchief. Their head-dress was a kind of turban, with different sorts of

334. [Nose-jewel.]

veils and wrappers used under various circumstances. The hair was worn long, and, as now, was braided into numerous tresses, with trinkets and ribands (1 Cor. xi. 15; 1 Tim. ii. 9; 1 Pet.

iii 3). With the head-dress the principal ornaments appear to have been connected, such as a jewel for the forehead, and rows of pearls (Sol. Song, i. 10; Ezek. xvi. 12). Ear-rings were also worn (Isa. iii. 20; Ezek. xvi. 12), as well as a nose-jewel, consisting, no doubt, as now, either of a ring inserted in the cartilage of the nose, or an ornament like a button attached to it. The nose-jewel was of gold or silver, and sometimes set with jewels (Gen. xxiv. 47; Isa. iii. 21). Bracelets were also generally worn (Isa. iii. 19; Ezek. xvi. 11), and anxiets, which, as now, were probably more like fetters than ornaments (Isa. iii. 16, 20). The Jewish women possessed the art of staining their eye-lids black, for effect and expression (2 Kings ix. 30; Jer. iv. 30; Ezek. xxiii. 40); and it is more than probable that they had the present practice of staining the nails, and the palms of their hands and soles of their feet, of an iron-rust colour, by means of a paste made from the plant called *henna*. This plant appears to be mentioned in Sol. Song, i. 14, and its present use is probably referred to in Deut. xxi. 12; 2 Sam. xix. 24.

The customs concerning marriage, and the circumstances which the relation of wife and mother involved, have been described in the article MARRIAGE.

The Israelites eagerly desired children, and especially sons. Hence the messenger who first brought to the father the news that a son was born, was well rewarded (Job iii. 3; Jer. xx. 15). The event was celebrated with music; and the father, when the child was presented to him, pressed it to his bosom, by which act he was understood to acknowledge it as his own (Gen. l. 23; Job iii. 12; Ps. xxii. 10). On the eighth day from the birth the child was circumcised (Gen. xvii. 10); at which time also a name was given to it (Luke i. 59). The first-born son was highly esteemed, and had many distinguishing privileges. He had a double portion of the estate (Deut. xxi. 17); he exercised a sort of parental authority over his younger brothers (Gen. xxv. 23, &c.; xxvii. 29; Exod. xii. 29; 2 Chron. xxi. 3); and before the institution of the Levitical priesthood he acted as the priest of the family (Num. iii. 12, 13; viii. 18). The patriarchs exercised the power of taking these privileges from the firstborn, and giving them to any other son, or of distributing them among different sons; but this practice was overruled by the Mosaical law (Deut xxi. 15-17).

The child continued about three years at the breast of the mother, and a great festival was given at the weaning (Gen. xxi. 8; 1 Sam. i. 22-24; 2 Chron. xxxi. 6; Matt. xxi. 16). He remained two years longer in charge of the women; after which he was taken under the especial care of the father, with a view to his proper training (Deut. vi. 20-25; xi. 19). It appears that those who wished for their sons better instruction than they were themselves able or willing to give, employed a private teacher, or else sent them to a priest or Levite, who had perhaps several others under his care. The principal object was, that they should be well acquainted with the law of Moses; and reading and writing were taught in subservience to this leading object.

The authority of a father was very great among the Israelites, and extended not only to his sons, but to his grandsons—indeed to all who were descended from him. His power had no recognised limit, and even if he put his son or grandson to death, there was, at first, no law by which he could be brought to account (Gen. xxi. 14; xxxviii. 24). But Moses circumscribed this power, by ordering that when a father judged his son worthy of death, he should bring him before the public tribunals. If, however, he had struck or cursed his father or mother, or was refractory or disobedient, he was still liable to capital punishment (Exod. xxi. 15, 17; Lev. xx. 9; Deut. xxi. 18-21).—Ed.

WOOL. [Sheep.]

WORMWOOD, STAR OF (Rev. viii. 10, 11), the Apocalyptic appellation for the national demon of Egypt, set forth in the vision of Patmos as a luminous *idol* presiding over 'the third part of the waters.' The vocation of this star was to destroy by *poison*, not by fire, sword, or famine.

St. John seems to employ this symbol of Egyptian poison and bitterness, as the prototype of a great Anti-Christian Power, which would poison and embitter the pure waters of Christian life and doctrine, converting them into 'wormwood.'

WORMWOOD. This proverbially bitter plant is used in the Hebrew, as in most other languages, metaphorically, to denote the moral bitterness of distress and trouble (Deut. xxix. 17; Prov. v. 4; Jer. ix. 15; xxiii. 15; Lam. iii 15, 19; Amos v. 7; vi. 12). Thence also the name given to the fatal star in Rev. viii. 10, 11. *Artemisia* is the botanical name of the genus of plants in which the different species of wormwoods are found. The plants of this genus are easily recognised by the multitude of fine divisions into which the leaves are usually separated, and the numerous clusters of small, round, drooping, greenish-yellow or brownish flower-heads with which the branches are laden.

335　[Artemisia Judaica.]

It must be understood that our common wormwood does not appear to exist in Palestine, and cannot therefore be that specially denoted by the Scriptural term. Indeed it is more than probable that the word is intended to apply to *all* the plants of this class that grew in Palestine, rather than to any one of them in particular. The examples of this genus that have been found in that country are:—1. *Artemisia Judaica*, which, if a particular species be intended, is probably the Absinthium of Scripture. Rauwolff found it about Bethlehem, and Shaw in Arabia and the deserts of Numidia plentifully. This plant is erect and shrubby, with stem about eighteen inches high. Its taste is very bitter; and both the leaves and seeds are much used in Eastern medicine, and are reputed to be tonic, stomachic, and anthelmintic. 2. *Artemisia Romana*, which was found by Hasselquist on Mount Tabor. This species is herbaceous, erect, with stem one or two feet high (higher when cultivated in gardens), and nearly upright branches. The plant has a pleasantly aromatic scent, and the bitterness of its taste is so tempered by the aromatic flavour as scarcely to be disagreeable. 3. *Artemisia abrotanum*, found in the south of Europe, as well as in Syria and Palestine, and eastward even to China. This is a hoary plant, becoming a shrub in warm countries; and its branches bear loose panicles of nodding yellow flower-heads. It is bitter and aromatic, with a very strong scent. It is not much used in medicine; but the branches are employed in imparting a yellow dye to wool.

WRESTLING. [Games.]

WRITING is an art by which facts or ideas are communicated from one person to another by means of given signs such as symbols or letters. It has been a generally received and popular opinion that writing was first used and imparted to mankind when God wrote the Ten Commandments on the tables of stone; but the silence of Scripture upon the subject would rather suggest that so necessary an art had been known long before that time, or otherwise the sacred historian would probably have added this extraordinary and divine revelation to the other parts of his information respecting the transactions on Mount Sinai.

After the gift of language (which was indispensable to rational creatures), it would seem that *writing* was the most highly beneficial and important boon which could be conferred on men possessed of intellect and understanding, who from their circumstances must divide and spread over the whole earth, and yet be forced from various necessities to maintain intercourse with each other. Even in the first ages of the world writing was requisite to transmit and receive accurately intelligence from the scattered communities, to convey to posterity events which were destined to act upon all time, and especially to preserve unimpaired the knowledge of God. Is it then too much to believe that God by revelation immediately imparted to mankind the power of writing? For it does not appear that any person ever invented an alphabet who had not previously heard of or seen one; and every nation which possessed the art always professed to have derived its knowledge from a God.

It was a matter of the utmost consequence that the most exact accounts should have been preserved of the creation, the fall of man, and many prophecies of deepest interest to unborn generations. The ages and genealogies of the patriarchs; the measures of the ark; the first kingly government in Assyria; the history of Abraham and his descendants for 430 years, including minute circumstances, changes, and conversations, in many different countries; could scarcely have been perfectly preserved by oral descent for twenty centuries, unless the antediluvians and their immediate posterity did not partake of the failings of Christians in the defects of forgetfulness and exaggeration; but allowing the art of *writing* to have been *given with language*, there is no difficulty, and it becomes obvious that each transaction would be recorded and kept exactly as it was either revealed or happened.

It is evident from the allusions made to the subject in the sacred Scriptures, that the knowledge of writing was possessed by the human family at a very early period. In the fifth chapter of Genesis it is said, ' This is the *book* of the generations.' If there had been merely a traditionary recollection of ' the generations of Adam,' preserved only by transmission from one memory to another for more than a thousand years, the term *book* would have been most inapplicable, and could not have been used.

In the book of Job, which is considered to be the most ancient written document extant, it is said (chap. xix. 23, 24), ' Oh, that my words were now written! Oh, that they were printed in a *book!* that they were graven with an iron *pen!*' Also Job xxxi. 35, ' mine adversary had *written* a book.' Such expressions could not have been used, and would have had no meaning, if the art of writing had been unknown; nor could there have been such terms as *book* and *pen*, if the things themselves had not existed.

If, then, it be granted that the book of Job was *written*, and such expressions were current before the Exode, it becomes evident from sacred history that writing was not only in use before the law was given on Mount Sinai, but that it was also known amongst other patriarchal tribes than the children of Israel.

Before the law was given by God to Moses, he had been commanded to write the important transactions which occurred during the progress of the Israelites from Egypt to Canaan; for in Exod. xvii. 14 it is recorded, ' And the Lord said unto Moses, Write this for a memorial in a book.' An account of the discomfiture of the Amalekites is the first thing said to have been written by Moses. This battle was fought ere the people left Rephidim (Exod. xvii. 13), from whence they departed into the wilderness of Sinai (Exod. xix. 2), and therefore that writing was drawn up before the events on the mount took place. The law was ' written by the finger of God' (Exod. xxxi. 18) B.C. 1491, and since that time there is no question as to the existence of the art of writing.

336. [Ancient Writing materials.]

Books and writing must have been familiar to Moses, ' who was learned in all the wisdom of the Egyptians' (Acts vii. 22), for at the time of his birth that people had arrived at a high pitch of civilization; and now that the mysterious hieroglyphics have been deciphered, it has been found that from the earliest era Egypt possessed a knowledge of writing, and that many of the inscriptions were written before the Exodus of the Hebrews.

Letters are generally allowed to have been introduced into Europe from Phœnicia, and to have been brought from thence by Cadmus into Greece, about fifteen centuries before Christ, which time coincides with the eighteenth Egyptian dynasty; but whilst none may deny such to have been the origin of European alphabetical characters, it does not prove the Phœnicians to have been the inventors of writing. That people occupied Phœnicia in very early times after the Deluge; and if the patriarch and his sons possessed the knowledge of letters, their posterity would doubtless preserve the remembrance and practice of such an invaluable bequest, which would be conveyed by their colonists into Greece and Africa. In the New World it was found that the Peruvians had no system of writing, whilst the Mexicans had made great advances in hieroglyphical paintings. The Aztecs, who preceded the Mexicans, had attained much proficiency in the art, such as was adequate to the wants of a people in an imperfect state of civilization.

Various have been the materials and implements used for writing. Paper made from the papyrus is now in existence which was fabricated 2000 years B C. Moses hewed out of the rock two tables of *stone* on which the Commandments were written (Exod. xxxiv. 1). After that time the Jews used rolls of *skins* for their sacred writings. They also engraved writing upon gems or gold plates (Exod. xxxix. 30).

Before the discovery of paper the Chinese wrote upon thin boards with a sharp tool. Reeds and canes are still used as writing implements amongst the Tartars; and the Persians and other Orientals write for temporary purposes on leaves, or smooth sand, or the bark of trees. The Arabs in ancient times wrote their poetry upon the shoulder-blades of sheep.

The Greeks occasionally engraved their laws on tables of brass. Even before the days of Homer table-books were used, made of wood, cut in thin slices, which were painted and polished, and the pen was an iron instrument called a style. In later times these surfaces were waxed over, that the writing might be obliterated for further use. Table-books were not discontinued till the fourteenth century of the Christian era.

At length the superior preparations of paper, parchment, and vellum, became general, and superseded other materials in many, and all entirely civilized, nations.

Y.

YEAR. The Hebrew year consisted of twelve unequal months, which, previously to the exile, were lunar. The twelve solar months made up only 354 days, constituting a year too short by no fewer than eleven days. This deficiency would have soon inverted the year, and could not have existed even for a short period of time without occasioning derangements and serious inconvenience to the Hebrews, whose year was so full of festivals. At an early day, then, we may well believe a remedy was provided for this evil. The course which the ancients pursued is unknown, but Ideler (*Chronol.* i. 490) may be consulted for an ingenious conjecture on the subject. The later Jews intercalated a month every two or every three years, taking care, however, to avoid making the seventh an intercalated year. The supplementary month was added at the termination of the sacred year, the twelfth month (February and March), and as this bore the name of Adar, so the interposed month was called Veadar, or Adar the Second. The year, as appears from the ordinary reckoning of the months (Lev. xxiii. 34; xxv. 9; Num. ix. 11; 2 Kings xxv. 8; Jer. xxxix. 2; comp. 1 Macc. iv. 52; x. 21), began with the month Nisan (Esth. iii. 7), agreeably to an express direction given by Moses (Exod. xii. 2; Num. ix. 1). This commencement is generally thought to be that of merely the ecclesiastical year; and most Jewish, and many Christian authorities, hold that the civil year originally began, as now, with the month Tisri. The ancient Hebrews possessed no such thing as a formal and recognised era. Their year and their months were determined and regulated, not by any systematic rules of astronomy, but by the first view or appearance of the moon. In a similar manner they dated from great national events, as the departure from Egypt (Exod. xix. 1; Num. xxxiii. 38; 1 Kings vi. 1); from the ascension of monarchs, as in the books of Kings and Chronicles; or from the erection of Solomon's temple (1 Kings viii. 1; ix. 10); and at a later period, from the commencement of the Babylonish captivity (Ezek. xxxiii. 21; xl. 1). When they became subjects of the Græco-Syrian empire they adopted the Seleucid era, which began with the year B.C. 312, when Seleucus conquered Babylon.

Z.

1. ZA'BAD (*God given*), a person of the tribe of Judah, mentioned in 1 Chron. ii. 36, among the descendants of Sheshan, by the marriage of his daughter with an Egyptian servant [JARHA; SHESHAN].

2. ZABAD, a grandson of Ephraim, who, with others of the family, was killed during the lifetime of Ephraim, by the men of Gath, in an attempt which the Hebrews seem to have made to drive off their cattle (1 Chron. vii. 21). [See EPHRAIM.]

3. ZABAD, son of an Ammonitess named Shimeath, who, in conjunction with Jehozabad, the son of a Moabitess, slew King Joash, to whom they were both household officers, in his bed (2 Kings xii. 21; 2 Chron. xxiv. 25, 26). In the first of these texts he is called Jozachar. The sacred historian does not appear to record the mongrel parentage of these men as suggesting a reason for their being more easily led to this act, but as indicating the sense which was entertained of the enormity of Joash's conduct, that even they, though servants to the king, and though only half Jews by birth, were led to conspire against him 'for the blood of the sons of Jehoiada the priest.' It would seem that their murderous act was not abhorred by the people; for Amaziah, the son of Joash, did not venture to call them to account till he felt himself well established on

the throne, when they were both put to death (2 Kings xiv. 5, 6; 2 Chron. xxv. 3, 4).

4. ZABAD, one of the persons who, at the instance of Ezra, put away the foreign wives they had taken after the return from captivity (Ezra x. 27).

ZAB'UD (*bestowed*), a son of Nathan the prophet, who held under Solomon the important place of 'king's friend,' or favourite (1 Kings iv. 5), which Hushai had held under David (1 Chron. xxvii. 33), and which a person named Elkanah held under Ahaz (2 Chron. xxviii. 7). Azariah, another son of Nathan, was 'over all the (household) officers' of king Solomon; and their advancement may doubtless be ascribed not only to the young king's respect for the venerable prophet, who had been his instructor, but to the friendship he had contracted with his sons during the course of education. The office, or rather honour, of 'friend of the king,' we find in all the despotic governments of the East. It gives high power, without the public responsibility which the holding of a regular office in the state necessarily imposes. It implies the possession of the utmost confidence of, and familiar intercourse with, the monarch, to whose person 'the friend' at all times has access, and whose influence is therefore often far greater, even in matters of state, than that of the recognised ministers of government.

ZABULUN. [ZEBULUN.]

ZACCHE'US, a superintendent of taxes at Jericho. Having heard of the Redeemer, he felt a great desire to see him as he drew near that place; for which purpose he climbed up into a sycamore-tree, because he was little of stature. Jesus, pleased with this manifestation of his eagerness, and knowing that it proceeded from a heart not far from the kingdom of God, saw fit to honour Zaccheus by becoming his guest. This offended the self-righteous Jews, who objected that 'he was gone to be a guest with a man that is a sinner.' This offensive imputation was met by Zaccheus in the spirit of the Mosaic conception of goodness—'The half of my goods I give to the poor; and if I have taken anything from any man by false accusation, I restore him fourfold.' He that knew the heart of man knew not only the truth of this statement, but that the good works of Zaccheus emanated from right motives, and therefore terminated the conversation with the words, 'This day is salvation come to this house, forsomuch as he also is a son of Abraham' —a declaration which, whether Zaccheus was by birth a Jew or not, signifies that he had the same principle of faith which was imputed to Abraham, the father of the faithful, for righteousness (Luke xix. 2, sq.).

Tradition represents Zaccheus as the first Christian bishop of Cæsarea.

ZACHARI'AH. [ZECHARIAH.]

ZACHARIAS. [ZECHARIAH.]

ZA'DOK (*just*). There are several men of this name mentioned in the Old Testament.

1. In the reign of David, ZADOK (the son of Ahitub and father of Ahimaaz) (1 Chron. vi. 8) and Ahimelech were the priests (2 Sam. viii. 17). Zadok and the Levites were with David, when, after the middle of the eleventh century B.C., he fled from Absalom; but the king ordered Zadok to carry back the ark of God into the city (2 Sam.

xv. 24, 25, 27, 29, 35, 36; xviii. 19, 22, 27). The king also, considering Zadok a seer, commanded him to return to the city, stating that he would wait in the plain of the wilderness until he should receive such information from him and his son Ahimaaz, and also from the son of Abiathar, as might induce him to remove farther away. On hearing that Ahithophel had joined Absalom, David requested Hushai, his friend, to feign himself to be also one of the conspirators, and to inform Zadok and Abiathar of the counsels adopted by Absalom and his rebellious confederates. The request of David was complied with, and the plans of the rebels made known to David by the instrumentality of Zadok and the others.

After Absalom was vanquished, David sent to Zadok and Abiathar, the priests, saying, ' Speak unto the elders of Judah, Why are ye the last to bring the king back to his house ?' &c. (2 Sam. xix. 11; xx. 25). When Adonijah attempted to succeed to the throne, Abiathar countenanced him, but Zadok was not called to the feast at which the conspirators assembled. King David sent for Zadok and Nathan the prophet to anoint Solomon king (1 Kings i. 32-45).

2. In 1 Chron. vi. 12, and Neh. xi. 11, another ZADOK is mentioned, the father of whom was also called Ahitub, and who begat Shallum. This Zadok descended from Zadok the priest in the days of David and Solomon, and was the ancestor of Ezra the scribe (Ezra vii. 2). We learn from Ezek. xl. 46; xliii. 19; xliv. 15; xlviii. 11, that the sons of Zadok were a pre-eminent sacerdotal family.

3. ZADOK was also the name of the father-in-law of Uzziah and the grandfather of king Jotham, who reigned about the middle of the eighth century before Christ (2 Kings xv. 33; 2 Chron. xxvii. 1).

4 and 5. Two priests of the name of Zadok are mentioned in Neh. iii. 4-29, as having assisted in rebuilding the wall of Jerusalem about B.C. 445.

The Zadok mentioned in Neh. x. 22 as having sealed the covenant, and Zadok the scribe named in Neh. xiii. 13, are probably the same who helped to build the wall.

ZAL'MON, a mountain in Samaria near to Shechem (Judg. ix. 48). Many suppose this to be the same with the Zalmon of Ps. lxviii. 15 : ' where the Almighty scattered kings in it (the land). there was snow as in Zalmon ;' *i. e.* the fields were whitened with the bones of the slain.

ZALMUN'NA. [ZEBAH AND ZALMUNNA.]

ZAMZUM'MIMS, a race of giants dwelling anciently in the territory afterwards occupied by the Ammonites, but extinct before the time of Moses (Deut. ii. 20).

ZANO'AH (*marsh, bog*), one of the towns of Judah ' in the valley' (Josh. xv. 34); which Jerome identifies with a village called in his time Zanua, on the borders of Eleutheropolis, on the road to Jerusalem. The name of Zanua is still connected with a site on the slope of a low hill not far east of Ain Shems (Beth-shemesh).

ZAPHNATH-PAANEAH, an Egyptian name given by Pharaoh to Joseph in reference to his public office. Rosellini interprets it to mean ' the salvation' or 'saviour of the age.' But Gesenius and others incline rather to regard it as signifying 'sustainer of the age.'

ZAR'EPHATH. [SAREPTA.]

ZEALOTS, the followers of Judas the Gaulonite or Galilean [JUDAS]. Josephus speaks of them as forming the 'fourth sect of Jewish philosophy,' and as distinguished from the Pharisees chiefly by a quenchless love of liberty and a contempt of death. Their leading tenet was the unlawfulness of paying tribute to the Romans, as being a violation of the theocratic constitution. This principle, which they maintained by force of arms against the Roman government, was soon converted into a pretext for deeds of violence against their own countrymen; and during the last days of the Jewish polity, the Zealots were lawless brigands or guerillas, the pest and terror of the land. After the death of Judas, and of his two sons, Jacob and Simon (who suffered crucifixion), they were headed by Eleazar, one of his descendants, and were often denominated *Sicarii*, from the use of a weapon resembling the Roman Sica.

ZE'BAH AND ZALMUN'NA, chiefs of the Midianites, whom Gideon defeated and slew [GIDEON].

ZEB'EDEE (*Jehovah's gift*), husband of Salome, and father of the apostles James and John (Matt. x. 2; xx. 20; xxvi. 37; xxvii. 56; Mark iii. 17; x. 35; John xxi. 2). He was the owner of a fishing boat on the lake of Gennesaret, and, with his sons, followed the business of a fisherman. He was present, mending the nets with them, when Jesus called James and John to follow him (Matt. iv. 21; Mark i. 19; Luke v. 10); and as he offered no obstacle to their obedience, but remained alone without murmuring in the vessel, it is supposed that he had been previously a disciple of John the Baptist, and, as such, knew Jesus to be the Messiah. At any rate, he must have known this from his sons, who were certainly disciples of the Baptist. It is very doubtful whether Zebedee and his sons were of that very abject condition of life which is usually ascribed to them. They seem to have been in good circumstances, and were certainly not poor. Zebedee was the owner of a ' ship,' or fishing smack, as we should call it—and, perhaps, of more than one; he had labourers under him (Mark i. 20); his wife was one of those pious women whom the Lord allowed ' to minister unto him of their substance;' and the fact that Jesus recommended his mother to the care of John, implies that he had the means of providing for her; whilst a still further proof that Zebedee's family was not altogether mean, may be found, perhaps, in the fact, that John was personally known to the high-priest (John xviii. 16).

1. ZEBO'IM, a valley and town in the tribe of Benjamin (1 Sam. xiii. 18; Neh. xi. 34).

2. ZEBOIM, a city in the vale of Siddim, destroyed along with Sodom and Gomorrah (Gen. x. 19; xiv. 2; Hos. xi. 8). [SODOM.]

ZE'BUL (*a dwelling*), an officer whom Abimelech left in command at Shechem in his own absence; and who discharged with fidelity and discretion the difficult trust confided to him (Judg. ix. 29-41). See the particulars in ABIMELECH.

ZEB'ULUN (*habitation*), the sixth and last son of Jacob by Leah (Gen. xxx. 19, seq.; xxxv. 23), who, in the order of birth, followed his brother Issachar, with whom, in history, as in the promised land, he was closely connected (Deut. xxxiii. 18). Zebulun was the founder of the tribe which bore his name (Gen. xlvi. 14), and which, while yet in the wilderness, was respectable for numbers (Num. i. 30; xxvi. 26). Zebulun obtained its lot in north Palestine between Naphtali on the north and Issachar on the south, while Asher stretched along both it and Naphtali on the west (Josh. xix. 10, seq.). The country of the Zebulonites bordered towards the east on the south-western side of the lake of Tiberias, and was connected with the Mediterranean by means of Carmel (Gen. xlix. 13). Its inhabitants in consequence took part in seafaring concerns. They failed to expel all the native race, but made those of them that remained tributaries (Judg. i. 30). One of the judges of Israel, Elon, was a Zebulonite (Judg. xii. 11). A city lying on the borders of Asher also bore the name of Zebulun (Josh xix. 27).

ZECHARI'AH (*whom Jehovah remembers*), a very common name among the Jews, borne by the following persons mentioned in Scripture.

1. ZECHARIAH, son of Jeroboam II., and fourteenth king of Israel. He ascended the throne in B.C. 772, and reigned six months. The few months of Zechariah's reign just sufficed to evince his inclination to follow the bad course of his predecessors; and he was then slain by Shallum, who usurped the crown. With his life ended the dynasty of Jehu (2 Kings xiv. 29; xv. 8-12).

2. ZECHARIAH, high priest in the time of Joash, king of Judah. He was son, or perhaps grandson, of Jehoiada and Jehosheba; the latter was the aunt of the king, who owed to her his crown, as he did his education and throne to her husband [JOASH]. Zechariah could not bear to see the evil courses into which the monarch eventually fell, and by which the return of the people to their old idolatries was facilitated, if not encouraged. Therefore, when the people were assembled at one of the solemn festivals, he took the opportunity of lifting up his voice against the growing corruptions. This was in the presence of the king, in the court of the temple. The people were enraged at his honest boldness, and with the connivance of the king, if not by a direct intimation from him, they seized the pontiff, and stoned him to death, even in that holy spot, 'between the temple and the altar.' His dying cry was not that of the first Christian martyr, 'Lord, lay not this sin to their charge' (Acts vii. 60), but 'The Lord look upon it, and require it' (2 Chron. xxiv. 20-22). It is to this dreadful affair that our Lord is supposed to allude in Matt. xxiii. 35; Luke xi. 51.

3. ZECHARIAH, described as one 'who had understanding in the visions of God' (2 Chron. xxvi. 7). It is doubtful whether this eulogium indicates a prophet, or simply describes one eminent for his piety and faith. During his lifetime Uzziah, king of Judah, was guided by his counsels, and prospered: but went wrong when death had deprived him of his wise guidance. Nothing is known of this Zechariah's history. It is possible that he may be the same whose daughter became the wife of Ahaz, and mother of Hezekiah (2 Kings xvi. 1, 2; 2 Chron. xxix. 1).

4. ZECHARIAH, son of Jeberechiah, a person whom, together with Urijah the high priest, Isaiah took as a legal witness of his marriage with 'the prophetess' (Isa. viii. 2). This was in the reign of Ahaz, and the choice of the prophet shows that Zechariah was a person of consequence.

5. ZECHARIAH, the eleventh in order of the minor prophets, was 'the son of Berechiah, the son of Iddo, the prophet' He seems to have entered upon his office in early youth (Zech. ii. 4). The period of his introduction to it is specified as the eighth month of the second year of Darius, a very short time later than the prophet Haggai. The mission of Zechariah had especial reference to the affairs of the nation that had been restored to its territory. The second edict, granting permission to rebuild the temple, had been issued, and the office of Zechariah was to incite the flagging zeal of the people, in order that the auspicious period might be a season of religious revival as well as of ecclesiastical reorganization; and that the theocratic spirit might resume its former tone and energy in the breasts of all who were engaged in the work of restoring the 'holy and beautiful house,' where their fathers had praised Jehovah. The prophet assures them of success in the work of re-erecting the sacred edifice, despite of every combination against them; for Zerubbabel 'should bring forth the head stone with shouting, Grace, grace unto it'— comforts them with a solemn pledge that, amidst fearful revolutions and conquests by which other nations were to be swept away, they should remain uninjured; for, says Jehovah, 'He that toucheth you toucheth the apple of mine eye'— sketches in a few vivid touches the blessings and glory of the advent of Messiah—imparts consolation to those who were mourning over their unworthiness, and pronounces a heavy doom on the selfish and disobedient, and on such as in a remote age, imbibing their spirit, 'should fall after the same example of unbelief.' The pseudo-Epiphanius records some prodigies wrought by Zechariah in the land of Chaldæa, and some wondrous oracles which he delivered; and he and Dorotheus both agree in declaring that the prophet died in Judæa in a good old age, and was buried beside his colleague Haggai.

The book of Zechariah consists of four general divisions.

I. The introduction or inaugural discourse (ch. i. 1-16).

II. A series of nine visions, extending onwards to ch. vii., communicated to the prophet in the third month after his installation. These visions were,—

1. A rider on a roan horse among the myrtle-trees, with his equestrian attendants, who report to him the peace of the world, symbolizing the fitness of the time for the fulfilment of the promises of God, his people's protector.

2. Four horns, symbols of the oppressive enemies by which Judah had been on all sides surrounded, and four carpenters, by whom these horns are broken, emblems of the destruction of these anti-theocratic powers.

3. A man with a measuring-line describing a wider circumference for the site of Jerusalem, as its population was to receive a vast increase, foreshowing that many more Jews would return from Babylon and join their countrymen, and indicating the conversion of heathen nations under the Messiah, when out of Zion should go forth the law and the word of the Lord from Jerusalem.

4. The high-priest Joshua before the angel of the Lord, with Satan at his right hand to oppose him. The sacerdotal representative of the people, clad in the filthy garments in which he had returned from captivity, seems to be a type of the guilt and degradation of his country; while forgiveness and restoration are the blessings which the pontiff symbolically receives from Jehovah, when he is reclad in holy apparel and crowned with a spotless turban, the vision at the same time stretching into far futurity, and including the advent of Jehovah's servant the BRANCH.

5. A golden lamp-stand fed from two olive-trees, one growing on each side, an image of the value and divine glory of the theocracy as now seen in the restored Jewish church, supported, not ' by might nor by power, but by the Spirit of Jehovah,' and of the spiritual development of the old theocracy in the Christian church, which enlightens the world through the continuous influence of the Holy Ghost.

6. A flying roll, the breadth of the temple-porch, containing on its one side curses against the ungodly, and on its other anathemas against the immoral, denoting that the head of the theocracy, the Lord of the temple, would from his place punish those who violated either the first or the second table of his law.

7. A woman in an ephah (at length pressed down into it by a sheet of lead laid over its mouth), borne along in the air by two female figures with storks' wings, representing the sin and punishment of the nation. The fury, whose name is WICKEDNESS, is repressed, and transported to the land of Shinar; i. e. idolatry, in the persons of the captive Jews, was for ever removed at that period from the Holy Land, and, as it were, taken to Babylon, the home of image-worship.

8. Four chariots issuing from two copper mountains, and drawn respectively by red, black, white, and spotted horses, the vehicles of the four winds of heaven, a hieroglyph of the swiftness and extent of divine judgments against the former oppressors of the covenant people. Judgments seem issuing from God's holy habitation in the midst of the ' mountains which are round about Jerusalem,' or from between those two hills, the ravine dividing which forms the valley of Jehoshaphat, directly under the temple mountain, where dwelt the head of the theocracy.

9. The last scene is not properly a vision, but an oracle in connection with the preceding visions, and in reference to a future symbolical act to be performed by the prophet. In presence of a deportation of Jews from Babylon, the prophet was charged to place a crown on the head of Joshua the high-priest, a symbol which, whatever was its immediate signification, was designed to prefigure the royal and sacerdotal dignity of the man whose name is BRANCH, who should sit as ' a priest upon his throne '
The meaning of all the preceding varied images and scenes is explained to the prophet by an attendant angelic interpreter.

III. A collection of four oracles delivered at various times in the fourth year of Darius, and partly occasioned by a request of the nation to be divinely informed, whether, now on their happy return to their fatherland, the month of Jerusalem's overthrow should be registered in their sacred calendar as a season of fasting and humiliation. The prophet declares that these times should in future ages be observed as festive solemnities.

IV. The 8th, 9th, 10th, and 11th chapters contain a variety of prophecies unfolding the fortunes of the people, their safety in the midst of Alexander's expedition, and their victories under the Maccabæan chieftains, including the fate of many of the surrounding nations, Hadrach (Persia), Damascus, Tyre, and Philistia.

V. The remaining three chapters graphically portray the future condition of the people, especially in Messianic times, and contain allusions to the siege of the city, the means of escape by the cleaving of the Mount of Olives, with a symbol of twilight breaking into day, and living water issuing from Jerusalem, concluding with a blissful vision of the enlarged prosperity and holiness of the theocratic metropolis, when upon the bells of the horses shall be inscribed ' holiness unto the Lord.'
The language of Zechariah has not the purity and freshness of a former age. A slight tinge of Chaldaism pervades the composition. The symbols with which he abounds are obscure, and their prosaic structure is diffuse and unvaried. The rhythm of his poetry is unequal, and its parallelisms are inharmonious and disjointed. His language has in many phrases a close alliance with that of the other prophets, and occasional imitations of them, especially of Ezekiel, characterize his oracles. He is also peculiar in his introduction of spiritual beings into his prophetic scenes.

6. ZECHARIAH, the father of John the Baptist [JOHN THE BAPTIST].

ZEDEKI'AH, son of Josiah, the twentieth and last king of Judah, was, in place of his brother Jehoiakim, set on the throne by Nebuchadnezzar, who changed his name from Mattaniah to that by which he is ordinarily spoken of. As the vassal of the Babylonian monarch, he was compelled to take an oath of allegiance to him, which, however, he observed only till an opportunity offered for throwing off his yoke. Success in such an undertaking was not likely to attend his efforts. His heart was not right before God, and therefore was he left without divine succour. Corrupt and weak, he gave himself up into the hands of his nobles, and lent an ear to false prophets; while the faithful lessons of Jeremiah were unwelcome, and repaid by incarceration. Like all of his class, he was unable to follow good, and became the slave of wicked men, afraid alike of his own nobility and of his foreign enemies. By his folly and wickedness he brought the state to the brink of ruin. Yet the danger did not open his eyes. Instead of looking to Jehovah, he threw himself for support on Egypt, when the Chaldæan came into the land and laid siege to his capital. The siege was begun on the tenth day of the tenth month in the ninth year of his reign. For a year and a half did Jerusalem effectually withstand Nebuchadnezzar. At the end of that time, however, the city was stormed and taken (B.C. 588), when Zedekiah, who had fled, was captured on the road to Jericho. Judgment was speedily executed: his sons were slain before his eyes, and he himself was deprived of sight and sent in chains to Babylon, where he died in prison (2 Kings

xxiv. 17, seq.; xxv. 1, seq.; 2 Chron. xxxvi. 10, seq.; Jer. xxviii.; xxxiv.; xxxvii.; xxxviii.; xxxix.; lii.; Ezek. xvii. 15).

ZELO'PHEHAD, son of Hepher, a descendant of Joseph, who had no sons, but five daughters. These came to Moses and Eleazar when now at the edge of the promised land, to lay their case before them for adjudication. Their father had died in the wilderness, leaving no male child. The daughters thought themselves entitled to take their father's share of the land. Moses on this brought their cause before Jehovah, who ordered that they should receive their father's inheritance, taking occasion to establish the general rule: 'If a man die, and have no son, then ye shall cause his inheritance to pass unto his daughter,' and failing daughters, to his next of kin (Num. xxvi. 33; xxvii. 1, sq. Compare Josh. xvii. 3, sq.).

ZE'NAS, a disciple who visited Crete with Apollos, bearing seemingly the epistle to Titus, in which Paul recommends the two to his attentions (Tit. iii. 13). He is called 'the lawyer;' and as his name is Greek, it seems doubtful whether he is so called as being, or having been, a doctor of the Jewish law, or as being a pleader at the Roman tribunals. The most probable opinion is, perhaps, that which makes him an Hellenistic Jew, and a doctor of the Mosaical law.

ZEPHANI'AH, the ninth in order of the minor prophets. The name seems to have been a common one among the Jews. Contrary to usual custom, the pedigree of the prophet is traced back for four generations—' the son of Cushi, the son of Gedaliah, the son of Amariah, the son of Hizkiah.' As there was at least another Zephaniah, a conspicuous personage at the time of the captivity, the parentage of the prophet may have been recounted so minutely to prevent any reader from confounding the two individuals. The so-called Epiphanius asserts that Zephaniah was of the tribe of Simeon, of the hill Sarabatha. The existence of the prophet is known only from his oracles, and these have no biographical sketches; so that our knowledge of this man of God comprises only the fact and the results of his inspiration. It may be safely inferred, however, that he laboured with Josiah in the pious work of re-establishing the worship of Jehovah in the land.

It is recorded (ch. i.) that the word of the Lord came to him 'in the days of Josiah, the son of Amon, king of Judah.' We have reason for supposing that he flourished during the earlier portion of Josiah's reign. In the second chapter (vers. 13-15) he foretells the doom of Nineveh, and the fall of that ancient city happened about the eighteenth year of Josiah. In the commencement of his oracles also, he denounces various forms of idolatry, and specially the remnant of Baal. The reformation of Josiah began in the twelfth, and was completed in the eighteenth year of his reign. So thorough was his extirpation of the idolatrous rites and hierarchy which defiled his kingdom, that he burnt down the groves, dismissed the priesthood, threw down the altars, and made dust of the images of Baalim. Zephaniah must have prophesied prior to this religious revolution, while some remains of Baal were yet secreted in the land, or between the twelfth and eighteenth years of the royal reformer. So Hitzig and Movers place him; while Eichhorn, Bertholdt, and Jaeger incline to give him a somewhat later date. At all events, he flourished between the years B.C. 642 and B.C. 611; and the portion of his prophecy which refers to the destruction of the Assyrian empire must have been delivered prior to the year B.C. 625, the year in which Nineveh fell. The publication of these oracles was, therefore, contemporary with a portion of those of Jeremiah, for the word of the Lord came to him in the thirteenth year of the reign of Josiah. Indeed, the Jewish tradition is, that Zephaniah had for his colleagues Jeremiah and the prophetess Huldah, the former fixing his sphere of labour in the thoroughfares and market-places, the latter exercising her honourable vocation in the college in Jerusalem.

The book consists of only three chapters. In the first, the sins of the nation are severely reprimanded, and a day of fearful retribution is menaced. The circuit of reference is wider in the second chapter, and the ungodly and persecuting states in the neighbourhood of Judæa are also doomed; but in the third section, while the prophet inveighs bitterly against Jerusalem and her magnates, he concludes with the cheering prospect of her ultimate settlement and blissful theocratic enjoyment.

The style of this prophet has not the sustained majesty of Isaiah, or the sublime and original energy of Joel: it has no prominent feature of distinction; yet its delineations are graphic, and many of its touches are bold and striking. For example, in the first chapter the prophet groups together in his descriptions of the national idolatry several characteristic exhibitions of its forms and worship. The verses are not tame and prosaic portraiture, but form a series of vivid sketches. The poet seizes on the more strange peculiarities of the heathen worship—uttering denunciations on the remnant of Baal, the worshippers of Chemarim—the star-adorers, the devotees of Malcham, the fanatics who clad themselves in strange apparel, and those who in some superstitious mummery leapt upon the threshold. Not a few verses occur in the course of the prophecy which, in tone and dignity, are not unworthy to be associated with the more distinguished effusions of the Hebrew bards. The language is pure: it has not the classic ease and elegance of the earlier compositions, but it wants the degenerate feebleness and Aramaic corruption of the succeeding era. Zephaniah is not expressly quoted in the New Testament; but clauses and expressions occur which seem to have been formed from his prophecy (Zeph. iii. 9; Rom. xv. 6, &c.). He was, in fine, as Cyril of Alexandria terms him, 'a true prophet, and filled with the Holy Ghost, and bringing his oracles from the mouth of God.'

ZE'PHATH, a Canaanitish city, afterwards called Hormah (Judg. i. 17). The ancient designation is perhaps retained in the modern Sufah, the name of a difficult pass leading up from the Arabah to the south of Judah.

ZEPH'ATHAH, a valley at Mareshah, in the tribe of Judah (2 Chron. xiv. 10), where Asa defeated Zerah the Cushite. Mareshah was near Eleutheropolis, and Robinson thinks the valley may have been the broad wady which comes down from Beit Jibrin (Eleutheropolis) towards Tell es-Saifeh; in which last name a trace of Zephathah may perhaps be recognised.

1. ZE'RAH (a rising), son of Judah and Tamar, and younger but twin brother of Pharez (Gen. xxxviii. 30; Matt i. 3).

2. ZERAH, son of Reuel and grandson of Esau (Gen. xxxvi. 13, 17).

3. ZERAH, son of Simeon and founder of a family in Israel (Num. xxvi. 13). He is called Zohar in Gen. xlvi. 10: his descendants are called Zarhites in Num. xxvi. 13, 20.

4. ZERAH, the Cushite king or leader who invaded Judah in the tenth year of king Asa (B.C. 941), with an army of 'a thousand thousands' (i. e. very many thousands) of men, and three hundred chariots. Asa defeated them in the valley of Zephathah at Mareshah, utterly routed them, pursued them to Gerar, and carried back much plunder from that neighbourhood. We are left uncertain as to the country from which Zerah came, and no conjecture has yet been made which is without serious difficulties.

ZE'RED, the name of a valley (Num. xxi. 12) and of the stream flowing through it, east of the Dead Sea [RIVER].

ZER'EDA, a city of Manasseh, near Beth-shan (1 Kings xi. 26; 2 Chron. iv. 17).

ZE'RESH (Pers. gold), the wife of Haman (Esth. v. 10; vi. 13), and well worthy of him, if we may judge from the advice she gave him to prepare a gibbet and ask the king's leave to hang Mordecai thereon [HAMAN; MORDECAI].

ZERU'AH (leprous), the widowed mother of Jeroboam (1 Kings xi. 26).

ZERUB'BABEL (sown in Babylon), called also 'Sheshbazzar, prince of Judah' (Ezra i. 8), son (comp. 1 Chron. iii. 17) of Shealtiel, of the royal house of David (1 Chron. iii.), was the leader of the first colony of Jews that returned from captivity to their native land under the permission of Cyrus, carrying with them the precious vessels belonging to the service of God. With the aid of Joshua and his body of priests, Zerubbabel proceeded, on his arrival in Palestine, to rebuild the fallen city, beginning with the altar of burnt-offerings, in order that the daily services might be restored. The Samaritans, however, having been offended at being expressly excluded from a share in the land, did all they could to hinder the work, and even procured from the Persian court an order that it should be stopped. Accordingly, everything remained suspended till the second year of Darius Hystaspis (B.C. 521), when the restoration was resumed and carried to completion, according to Josephus, owing to the influence of Zerubbabel with the Persian monarch (Antiq. xi. 3; Ezra; Haggai i. 1.14; ii. 1).

ZERUI'AH (wounded), daughter of Jesse, sister of David (1 Chron. ii. 16), and mother of Joab, Abishai, and Asahel (2 Sam. ii. 18; iii. 39; viii. 16; xvi. 9).

ZI'BA (statue), a servant of the house of Saul, of whom David inquired if there was any one left of the house of Saul to whom the monarch might show favour. Mephibosheth was in consequence found, and having been certified of David's friendship, Ziba, who was at the head of a large family, having fifteen sons and twenty slaves, was appointed to till the land for the prince, and generally to constitute his household and do him service (2 Sam. ix. 2-10). This position Ziba employed for his master's harm. When David had to fly from Jerusalem in consequence of the

rebellion of Absalom, Ziba met the king with a large and acceptable present:—'But where is Mephibosheth?' asked the fugitive monarch; 'in Jerusalem,' was the answer; 'for he said, To-day shall the house of Israel restore me the kingdom of my father.' Enraged at this, which looked like ingratitude as well as treachery, David thereupon gave to the faithless Ziba all the property of Mephibosheth (2 Sam. xvi. 1, sq.). On David's return to his metropolis an explanation took place, when Mephibosheth accused Ziba of having slandered him; and David, apparently not being perfectly satisfied with the defence, gave his final award, that the land should be divided between the master and his servant (2 Sam. xix. 24, sq.).

ZIB'EON (dyed), a son of Seir, phylarch or head of the Hivites (Gen. xxxvi. 2, 20, 24, 29).

ZICH'RI (renowned), an Ephraimite, probably one of the chiefs of the tribe, and one of the generals of Pekah king of Israel. It has been supposed that he took advantage of the victory of this monarch over the army of Judah to penetrate into Jerusalem, where he slew one of the sons of Ahaz, the governor of the palace, and the king's chief minister or favourite. It is difficult without this supposition to explain 2 Chron. xxviii. 17. There is some probability in the conjecture, that he was the 'Tabeal's son whom Pekah and Rezin designed to set upon the throne of Judah [TABAEL].

ZI'DON. 1. The eldest son of Canaan (Gen. x. 15). 2. One of the most ancient cities in Phœnicia. Justin derives the name from the Phœnician word for fish; but Josephus, from the son of Canaan. It had a very commodious harbour, which is now nearly choked up with sand: it was distant one day's journey from the fountains of the Jordan, 400 stadia from Berytus, and 200 stadia from Tyre (Strabo, xvi. pp. 756, 757). It was situated in the allotment of the tribe of Asher, but never conquered (Judg. i. 31); on the contrary, it was sometimes a formidable enemy (Judg. x. 12). Even in Joshua's time it was called Tsidon-Rabba, or Great Zidon (Josh. xix. 28). It was noted in very early times for its extensive traffic (Isa. xxiii. 2; Ezek. xxvii. 8) and manufactures, particularly glass. Frequent reference to it occurs in Homer. The best vessels in the fleet of Xerxes were Sidonian. Its modern name is Saide. In Hasselquist's time (1750) its exports to France were considerable; but at present its traffic is chiefly confined to the neighbouring towns; the population is about 15,000.

ZIF (bloom-month), an ante-Exilian name of the second Hebrew month (1 Kings vi. 1-37), corresponding with our April and May. This, the second month of the sacred, was the eighth of the civil year. The second month bore also the name Iyar.

ZIK'LAG, a city belonging to the tribe of Simeon (Josh. xv. 31; xix. 5), but at times subject to the Philistines of Gath, whose king, Achish, bestowed it upon David for a residence; after which it pertained to Judah (1 Sam. xxvii. 6; xxx. 1, 14, 26; 2 Sam. i. 1; 1 Chron. iv. 30; Neh. xi. 28).

While David was absent with his men to join Achish, Ziklag was burned and plundered by the Amalekites; and on his return, after receiving the spoil from them, he remained here till called to assume the crown after the death of Saul. It was during his stay in this place that he was joined by many considerable and valiant persons, whose adhesion to his cause was of much importance to him, and who were ever after held in high esteem in his court and army.

ZIL'LAH (*shade*), one of the wives of Lamech, and mother of Tubal-cain (Gen. iv. 19) [LAMECH].

ZIL'PAH (*a dropping*), a female servant of Laban, whom he gave to Leah on her marriage with Jacob (Gen. xxix. 24), and whom Leah eventually induced him to take as a concubine-wife; in which capacity she became the mother of Gad and Asher (Gen. xxx. 9-13; xxxv. 26; xxxvii 2; xlvi. 18).

ZIM'RAN (*sung, i. e. celebrated in song*), a son of Abraham by Keturah, and the name of an Arabian tribe descended from him (Gen. xxv. 2; 1 Chron. i. 32). This name may perhaps be connected with the Zabram mentioned by Ptolemy as a city with a king, situated between Mecca and Medina.

ZIM'RI. There are four persons of this name mentioned in the Old Testament:—

1. A son of Zerah, who was a son of Judah by Tamar (1 Chron. ii. 6).

2. The name of the Israelite slain, together with the Midianitish woman, in Shittim, by Phinehas, was ZIMRI, the son of Salu, a prince of a chief house among the Simeonites (Num. xxv. 14).

3. King Saul begat Jonathan, who begat Meribbaal, who begat Micah, who begat Ahaz, who begat Jehoadah, whose sons were Alemeth, Azmaveth, and ZIMRI. Zimri begat Moza, &c. (1 Chron. viii. 36; ix. 42).

4. In the twenty-sixth year of Asa, king of Judah, Elah, the son of Baasha, began to reign over Israel in Tirzah. After he had reigned two years, ZIMRI, the captain of half his chariots, conspired against him when he was in Tirzah, drunk in the house of his steward. Zimri went in and smote and killed him, and reigned in his stead, about B.C. 928; and he slew all the house of Baasha, so that no male was left. Zimri reigned only seven days at Tirzah. The people who were encamped at Gibbethon, which belonged to the Philistines, heard that Zimri had slain the king. They made Omri, the captain of the host, king over Israel in the camp. Omri besieged Tirzah and took it. Zimri, seeing that the city was taken, went into the king's palace, set it on fire, and perished in it for his sins in walking in the way of Jeroboam, and for making Israel to sin (1 Kings xvi. 1-20; 2 Kings ix. 31).

5. The kings of Zimri, mentioned in Jer. xxv. 25, seem to have been the kings of the Zimranites, the descendants of Zimran, son of Abraham by Keturah (Gen. xxv. 2; 1 Chron. i. 32).

ZIN, a desert on the south of Palestine, and westward from Idumæa, in which was situated the city of Kadesh-barnea (Num. xiii. 22; xx. 1; xxvii. 14). Its locality is therefore fixed by the considerations which determine the site of Kadesh to the western part of the Arabah south of the Dead Sea.

ZI'ON. [JERUSALEM.]

ZIPH, the name of a city in the tribe of Judah (Josh. xv. 55; 2 Chron. xi. 8), and of a desert in its vicinity (1 Sam. xxiii. 14, 15). It is mentioned by Jerome (*Onomast. s. v.*), but had not been since noticed till Dr. Robinson found the name in the Tell Zif (Hill of Zif), which occurs about four miles and a half S. by E. from Hebron, and is a round eminence about a hundred feet high, situated in a plain. A site also called Zif, lies about ten minutes east of this, upon a low hill or ridge between two small wadys, which commence here and run towards the Dead Sea. There is now little to be seen besides broken walls and foundations, mostly of unhewn stones, but indicative of solidity.

ZIPPOR'AH (*little bird*), one of the seven daughters of Reuel (comp Exod. xviii.), priest of Midian, who, in consequence of aid rendered to the young women when, on their going to procure water for their father's flocks, they were set on by a party of Bedouins, was given to Moses in marriage (Exod. ii. 16, sq.). A son, the fruit of this union, remained for some time after his birth uncircumcised, but an illness into which Moses fell in a khan when on his way to Pharaoh, being accounted a token of the divine displeasure, led to the circumcision of the child, when Zipporah, having it appears reluctantly yielded to the ceremony, exclaimed, 'Surely a bloody husband thou art to me' (Exod. iv. 26). This event seems to have caused some alienation of feeling, for Moses sent his wife back to her father, by whom she is again brought to her husband while in the desert, when a reconciliation took place, which was ratified by religious rites (Gen. xviii. 1, sq.).

ZIPPORIS, or SEPPHORIS, was, about the beginning of the Christian era, a principal and strongly fortified city of Galilee, under latitude 32° 44'. It was surrounded by many villages, and situated near Mount Asamon in the centre of Galilee, in a very strong and secure situation. It is also called Diocæsarea, Sepphoris, and Sephorum, and described as contiguous to Mount Carmel and Cana, six miles west of Nazareth, and twenty from Tiberias. Zipporis is celebrated in the works of Josephus as a military station, and in the Talmud on account of its famed rabbinical academy. Rabbi Judah Hakkadosh, or *the Saint*, resided seventeen years in Zipporis, and he used frequently to say that Jacob sojourned in Egypt seventeen years, and Judah in Zipporis seventeen years. He resided also in Beth-shaarim, but died in Zipporis. Josephus mentions Sepphoris frequently as the greatest town of Galilee, and built in a well-fortified situation. It was one of the five cities in which the assemblies of the Synedrium were held. It was destroyed A.D. 339, in consequence of the rebellion of its citizens.

ZIZ, a cliff or pass leading up from the Dead Sea towards Jerusalem, by which the bands of the Moabites and Ammonites advanced against Jehoshaphat (2 Chron. xx. 16). They seem to have come round the south end of the Dead Sea, and along the western shore as far as Engedi, where there is a pass which leads out northward towards Tekoa. This is the route which is taken by the Arabs in their marauding expeditions at the present day.

ZO'AN, an ancient city of Lower Egypt, situated on the eastern side of the Tanitic branch of the Nile. Zoan is of considerable Scriptural interest. It was one of the oldest cities in Egypt, having been built seven years after Hebron, which already existed in the time of Abraham (Num. xiii. 22; comp. Gen. xxii. 2). It seems also to have been one of the principal capitals, or royal abodes, of the Pharaohs (Isa. xix. 11, 13; xxx. 4); and accordingly 'the field of Zoan,' or the fine alluvial plain around the city, is described as the scene of the marvellous works which God wrought in the time of Moses (Ps. lxxviii. 12, 33). The destruction predicted in Ezek. xxx. 14, has long since befallen Zoan. The field' is now a barren waste; a canal passes through it without being able to fertilize the soil; 'fire has been set in Zoan,' and the royal city is now the habitation of fishermen, the resort of wild beasts, and infested by reptiles and malignant fevers. The locality is covered with mounds of unusual height and extent, full of the fragments of pottery which such sites usually exhibit. These extend for about a mile from north to south, by about three-quarters of a mile. The area in which the sacred enclosure of the temple stood, is about 1500 feet by 1250, surrounded by the mounds of fallen houses, whose increased elevation above the site of the temple is doubtless attributable to the frequent change in the level of the houses to protect them from the inundation, and the unaltered position of the sacred buildings. There is a gateway of granite and fine gritstone to the enclosure of this temple, bearing the name of Rameses the Great. Though in a very ruinous condition, the fragments of walls, columns, and fallen obelisks sufficiently attest the former splendour of the building to which they belonged. The obelisks are all of the time of Rameses the Great (B.C. 1355). The name of this king most frequently occurs; but the ovals of his successor Pthamen, of Osirtasen III., and of Tirhakah, have also been found. The time of Osirtasen III. ascends nearly to that of Joseph, and his name, therefore, corroborates the Scriptural account of the antiquity of the town. Two black statues, and a granite sphinx, with blocks of hewn and occasionally sculptured granite, are among the objects which engage the attention of the few travellers who visit this desolate place. The modern village of San consists of mere huts, with the exception of a ruined kasr of modern date.

ZO'AR, a town originally called Bala, and one of the five cities of the plain of Siddim. It was doomed with the rest to destruction, but spared at the intercession of Lot as a place to which he might escape. He alleged the smallness of the city as a ground for asking this favour; and hence the place acquired the name of Zoar, or 'SMALLNESS' (Gen. xiii. 10; xiv. 2, 8; xix. 20, 22, 30) It is only again mentioned in Deut. xxxiv. 3, Isa. xv. 5; Jer. xlviii. 34; which passages indicate that it belonged to the Moabites, and was a place of some consequence. Eusebius and Jerome describe it as having in their day many inhabitants, and a Roman garrison. Stephen of Byzantium calls it a large village and fortress. In the Ecclesiastical Notitia it is mentioned as the seat of a bishop of the Third Palestine, down to the centuries preceding the Crusades. The Crusaders seem to have found it under the name of Segor, and they describe the place as pleasantly situated, with many palm-trees. Dr. Robinson supposes that it must have lain on the *east* of the Dead Sea, and he thinks that Irby and Mangles

have rightly fixed its position at the mouth of the Wady Kerak, at the point where the latter opens upon the isthmus of the long peninsula which stands out from the eastern shore of the lake towards its southern end. At this point Irby and Mangles discovered the remains of an ancient town. Here 'stones that have been used in building, though for the most part unknown, are strewed over a great surface of uneven ground, and mixed with bricks and pottery. This appearance continues without interruption, during the space of at least half a mile, quite down to the plain, so that it would seem to have been a place of considerable extent. We noticed one column, and we found a pretty specimen of antique variegated glass. It may possibly be the site of the ancient Zoar' (*Travels*, p. 448).

ZO'BAH, a Syrian kingdom, whose king made war with Saul (1 Sam. xiv. 47), with David (2 Sam. viii. 3; x. 6), and with Solomon (2 Chron. viii. 3).

1. ZO'HAR (*whiteness*), a son of Simeon [ZE-RAH].

2. ZOHAR, the father of Ephron the Hittite (Gen. xxiii. 8; xxv. 9).

3. ZOHAR (in Keri; in Chetib, Jezoar), a descendant of Judah (1 Chron. iv. 7).

ZO'PHAR (*sparrow?*), one of Job's three friends and opponents in argument (Job ii. 11; xi. 1; xx. 1; xlii. 9). He is called a Naamathite, or inhabitant of Naamah, a place whose situation is unknown, as it could not be the Naamah mentioned in Josh. xv. 41. Wemyss, in his *Job and his Times* (p. 111), well characterizes this interlocutor:—'Zophar exceeds the other two, if possible, in severity of censure; he is the most inveterate of the accusers, and speaks without feeling or pity. He does little more than repeat and exaggerate the arguments of Bildad. He unfeelingly alludes (ch. xi. 15) to the effects of Job's disease as appearing in his countenance. This is cruel and invidious. Yet in the same discourse how nobly does he treat of the divine attributes, showing that any inquiry into them is far beyond the grasp of the human mind! And though the hortatory part of the first discourse bears some resemblance to that of Eliphaz, yet it is diversified by the fine imagery which he employs. He seems to have had a full conviction of the providence of God, as regulating and controlling the actions of men; but he limits all his reasonings to a present life, and makes no reference to a future world. This circumstance alone accounts for the weakness and fallacy of these men's judgments. In his second discourse there is much poetical beauty in the selection of images, and the general doctrine is founded in truth; its fallacy lies in its application to Job's peculiar case. The whole indicates great warmth of temper, inflamed by misapprehension of its object and by mistaken zeal.'

It is to be observed that Zophar has but two speeches, whereas the others have three each. When Job had replied (ch. xxvi.-xxxi.) to the short address of Bildad (ch. xxv.), a rejoinder might have been expected from Zophar; but he said nothing, the three friends, by common consent, then giving up the contest in despair (ch. xxxii. 1) [JOB].

ZO'RAH (*hornets' town*), a town reckoned as in the plain of Judah (Josh. xv. 33), but inhabited by Danites (xix. 41), not far from Eshtaol, and chiefly celebrated as the birthplace of Samson (Judg. xiii. 2, 25; xviii. 2, 8, 11; comp. 2 Chron. xi. 12; Neh. xi. 29). The site may still be recognised under the name of Surah, situated upon a spur of the mountains running into the plain north of Beth-shemesh.

ZU'RIEL (*God is my rock*), son of Abihail, and family chief or genesarch of the Merarites at the organization of the Levitical establishment (Num. iii. 35). It does not appear to which of the two great divisions of the Merarites he belonged.

ZU'ZIMS, one of the ancient tribes or nations conquered by Chedorlaomer and his allies (Gen. xiv. 5). The Zuzims were settled beyond the Jordan, and are perhaps the same as the Zamzummims of Deut. ii. 20. The Syriac and Onkelos, like the Septuagint, take the word for an appellative, signifying 'strong' or 'valiant.'

Printed in the United Kingdom
by Lightning Source UK Ltd.
107514UKS00002B/1